Conference of the North American Chapter of the Association for Computational Linguistics: Human Language Technologies 2016 (NAACL HLT 2016)

San Diego, California, USA
12 - 17 June 2016

Volume 1 of 2

ISBN: 978-1-5108-2512-3

The 2016 Conference of the North American Chapter of the Association for Computational Linguistics: Human Language Technologies

Proceedings of the Conference

June 12-17, 2016
San Diego, California, USA

This page intentionally left blank.

Message from the General Chair

Greetings,

Welcome to NAACL HLT 2016! This year's conference is held in San Diego, California, where we have assembled an exciting program of computational linguistics research.

The main program features a wide array of topics, and it includes excellent invited talks by Prof. Regina Barzilay and Prof. Ehud Reiter. In addition, we have six tutorials on the day before the main program, plus fifteen workshops on the following two days. Some of these workshops are back for their 10th or 11th incarnation, while others are brand-new. In parallel, we have a live demonstration track, and a Student Research Workshop that showcases work by the junior members of our research community.

This NAACL HLT meeting takes place only through the hard work of many people who deserve our gratitude.

Thanks to Priscilla Rasmussen for making local arrangements, handling registration, setting up social events, writing visa invitation letters, and solving a myriad of issues. Priscilla, your experience is a great asset to any conference!

The NAACL HLT organizing committee took all the steps to bring you a great conference. Many thanks to Ani Nenkova and Owen Rambow (Program Co-chairs), Mohit Bansal and Alexander M. Rush (Tutorial Co-chairs), Radu Soricut and Adrià de Gispert (Workshop Co-chairs), Jacob Andreas, Eunsol Choi, and Angeliki Lazaridou (Student Research Workshop Co-Chairs) and their faculty advisors Jacob Eisenstein and Nianwen Xue, Aliya Deri (Student Volunteer Coordinator), Julie Medero (Local Sponsorship Chair), Mark Finlayson, Sravana Reddy, and John DeNero (Demonstration Co-chairs), Adam Lopez and Margaret Mitchell (Publications Co-chairs), Jason Riesa (Website Chair), Wei Xu (Publicity Chair), and Jonathan May (Social Media Chair).

Thanks also to the NAACL Board for providing excellent advice, and thanks to previous chairs for their suggestions and timelines.

Sponsors of NAACL HLT 2016 include Baidu and Google (Platinum Sponsors), Amazon, Bloomberg, eBay, Microsoft Research, and UnitedHealth Group (Gold Sponsors), Huawei (Silver Sponsors), Civis Analytics, Facebook, @newsela, and Nuance (Bronze Sponsors), and the University of Washington (Supporter). Thanks for your extremely valuable contributions!

Finally, thanks to the scientists, engineers, authors, and attendees who come to share and learn at this leading venue for computational linguistics research!

Kevin Knight
Information Sciences Institute, University of Southern California
NAACL HLT 2016 General Chair

Message from the Program Co-Chairs

Welcome to San Diego for the 15th Annual Conference of the North American Chapter of the Association for Computational Linguistics: Human Language Technologies!

The conference has grown remarkably in the past five years: we had 698 submissions this year, despite our deadline right after the end-of-the-year holidays. As we worked on organizing the conference program, we made many changes to reflect the growth of the NAACL community, the increasing diversity of topics covered by the field, and the acceleration of the pace of the publication cycle.

We had a record short time between paper submission and author notification—less than two months. We settled on such compressed timeline in order to avoid spreading the reviewing period over the winter holidays, to ensure that papers spend only a short time under submission, and to coordinate submission deadlines with ACL. Our incredible team of area chairs and reviewers ensured that the planned schedule went smoothly.

As the computational linguistics field has expanded, it has become increasingly difficult to recruit a sufficient number of knowledgeable reviewers. We decided to reach out to the largest possible pool of computational linguists and provide convenient ways for the area chairs to control which reviewers they end up working with: we invited all researchers actively working in the area of computational linguistics/language processing to review for the conference. We defined "active researchers" to be those who have published at least five papers in the last ten years in the ACL, NAACL, EMNLP, EACL or COLING conferences. In order to be inclusive of the amazing young researchers who became active in the field only more recently, we also included everyone who had published at least three papers in the same venues for the last five years. This yielded a list of over 1,400 researchers that we invited to serve as reviewers for the conference. Of these, 685 agreed and participated in the review process. This is another record for NAACL HLT 2016, no previous NAACL has had such a large program committee. Among these, the area chairs recognized 120 as best reviewers.

Working with the reviewers were the 42 area chairs. We asked the area chairs to work in pairs, so they can have a back-up in case other obligations need their attention during the review period and to ensure that all decisions about reviewer assignment and paper recommendation are discussed in detail. All area chairs and reviewers submitted a list of keywords that describe their area of expertise (the full list appears in the conference call for papers). The area chairs were paired based on the keyword overlap.

To match reviewers to area chairs, we used a bidding system. For bidding, each area received a list of the 140 reviewers with best matching keyword profiles. If the area chairs did not know the work of a potential reviewer on their bidding list, they looked him or her up on DBLP or Google Scholar before making their final bid. Areas were assigned only reviewers for which the area chairs bid positively. Area chairs were free as usual to recruit additional reviewers they wished to work with.

Submissions were assigned to areas by taking into account the match between the paper keywords and the area chair keywords. Areas were capped at 40 submissions maximum (long and short combined). As in the past, reviewers bid on papers they wanted to review. 69% of the reviews were written by reviewers who had bid indicating that they want to review the paper; 29% of the reviews were written by reviewers who had bid indicating they are ok with reviewing the paper. The remaining 2% of reviews were written by reviewers who did not bid on the paper but were asked by an area chair to review it. Three reviewers were assigned a paper that they did not want to review according to their bid. The average reviewer load was 3 papers, which included a mix of long and short submissions. Only 43 reviewers had more than four papers to review.

Area chairs wrote meta-reviews, for use only by us, justifying their accept/reject recommendation. In making difficult decisions, we drew on these meta-reviews, the reviews themselves, the discussion among the reviewers, and the author response to the initial reviews.

We are happy with our changes to the review process: area chairs had control over the reviewers they worked with, reviewers were assigned papers they wanted to review and the overall reviewing load was low. Needless to say, there is room for further improvements. The reviewing process is crucial to the quality of this conference; only if the community has confidence in the quality of the reviewing process will this conference continue to be a leading conference in our field. Our goal has been to make sure that every single submission receives a complete and fair review and decision, and to make sure that the authors of every single submission understand why their paper was accepted or declined for the conference. We would like to thank our 685 reviewers, and we would especially like to thank our 42 area chairs, who were patient in allowing us to pursue some of the innovative aspects of this year's reviewing cycle.

Eighteen of the 698 initial submissions were withdrawn by the authors or rejected without review because of formatting violations. A total of 396 long and 284 short papers underwent review; 100 long and 82 short papers were accepted, for an acceptance rate of 25% and 29% respectively. In addition, ten TACL papers will be presented at the conference.

This year we decided to have shorter slots for oral presentations, in order to have more of the accepted papers presented as talks. In the program, long papers are allotted 20-minute slots (15 min presentation + 5 min questions). Short papers are allotted 10-minute slots (6 min presentation + 4 min questions).

The best paper award committee consisted of NAACL general and program chairs from the last three years. Not all past chairs could participate in the selection. The final best paper committee included Joyce Chai, Katrin Kirchhoff, Rada Mihalcea, Kristina Toutanova, Lucy Vanderwende and Hua Wu. They selected two best long papers and one best short paper, along with two runner-ups in each category.

Best Short Paper
Improving sentence compression by learning to predict gaze
Sigrid Klerke, Yoav Goldberg and Anders Søgaard

Short Paper, Runners Up
Patterns of Wisdom: Discourse-Level Style in Multi-Sentence Quotations
Kyle Booten and Marti A. Hearst

A Joint Model of Orthography and Morphological Segmentation
Ryan Cotterell, Tim Vieira and Hinrich Schütze

Best Long Papers
Feuding Families and Former Friends: Unsupervised Learning for Dynamic Fictional Relationships
Mohit Iyyer, Anupam Guha, Snigdha Chaturvedi, Jordan Boyd-Graber and Hal Daumé III

Learning to Compose Neural Networks for Question Answering
Jacob Andreas, Marcus Rohrbach, Trevor Darrell and Dan Klein

Long Paper, Runners Up
Multi-way, Multilingual Neural Machine Translation with a Shared Attention Mechanism
Orhan Firat, Kyunghyun Cho and Yoshua Bengio

Black Holes and White Rabbits: Metaphor Identification with Visual Features
Ekaterina Shutova, Douwe Kiela and Jean Maillard

The conference program includes two inspiring invited talks by Regina Barzilay and Ehud Reiter. Both push the boundaries of the field, discussing the potential for real-world impact of language technologies.

Finally we would like to thank all other people who supported us in the past year in our work for NAACL HLT 2016. Last year's program chairs, Anoop Sarkar and Joyce Chai shared their valuable advice and promptly answered the many questions we had throughout the process. The NAACL board chair for 2015 (Hal Daumé III) and 2016 (Emily Bender) were our effective link with the NAACL board. The conference general chair, Kevin Knight, was always available to us when we needed to consult about decisions we were making. The conference business manager, Priscilla Rasmussen, gave us details about the venue and coordinated with us at the final stages of making the conference schedule. The ACL treasurer, Greame Hirst, answered questions about the venue. The conference webmaster, Jason Riesa, put content on the conference webpage as soon as we made it available to him. The publication chairs, Meg Mitchell and Adam Lopez, answered all lingering author questions about formatting for submission and final versions. Many talks to all of them!

We look forward to an exciting conference!

NAACL HLT 2016 Program Co-Chairs
Ani Nenkova, University of Pennsylvania
Owen Rambow, Columbia University

Organizing Committee

General Chair
Kevin Knight, USC Information Sciences Institute

Program Co-chairs
Ani Nenkova, University of Pennsylvania
Owen Rambow, Columbia University

Workshop Co-chairs
Radu Soricut, Google
Adrià de Gispert, SDL

Local Sponsorship Chair
Julie Medero, Harvey Mudd College

Tutorial Co-chairs
Mohit Bansal, TTI Chicago
Alexander M. Rush, Harvard University

Demonstration Co-chairs
Mark Finlayson, Florida International University
Sravana Reddy, Wellesley College
John DeNero, University of California, Berkeley

Publication Co-chairs
Adam Lopez, University of Edinburgh
Margaret Mitchell, Microsoft Research

Local Arrangements Chair
Priscilla Rasmussen, ACL Business Manager

Student Research Workshop Co-chairs
Student Co-chairs
    Jacob Andreas, University of California, Berkeley
    Eunsol Choi, University of Washington
    Angeliki Lazaridou, University of Trento
Faculty Advisors
    Jacob Eisenstein, Georgia Tech
    Nianwen Xue, Brandeis University

Publicity Chair
Wei Xu, University of Pennsylvania

Social Media Chair
Jonathan May, USC Information Sciences Institute

Website Chair
Jason Riesa, Google

Student Volunteer Coordinator
Aliya Deri, USC Information Sciences Institute

Program Committee

Program Co-chairs
Ani Nenkova, University of Pennsylvania
Owen Rambow, Columbia University

Area Chairs
Mohit Bansal, TTI-Chicago
Regina Barzilay, MIT
Eduardo Blanco, University of North Texas
Asli Celikyilmaz, Microsoft
Cristian Danescu-Niculescu-Mizil, Cornell University
Markus Dreyer, Amazon
Chris Dyer, Carnegie Mellon University
Jacob Eisenstein, Georgia Institute of Technology
Micha Elsner, The Ohio State University
Eric Fosler-Lussier, The Ohio State University
Alexander Fraser, University of Munich
Michel Galley, Microsoft Research
Kevin Gimpel, Toyota Technological Institute at Chicago
Dilek Hakkani-Tür, Microsoft Research
Helen Hastie, Heriot-Watt University
Yulan He, Aston University
Dirk Hovy, University of Copenhagen
Heng Ji, Rensselaer Polytechnic Institute
Jing Jiang, Singapore Management University
Annie Louis, University of Essex
Chin-Yew Lin, Microsoft Research
Daniel Marcu, Information Sciences Institute, University of Southern California
Margaret Mitchell, Microsoft Research
Alessandro Moschitti, Qatar Computing Research Institute, HBKU
Hwee Tou Ng, National University of Singapore
Viet-An Nguyen, Facebook
Mari Ostendorf, University of Washington
Marius Pasca, Google
Slav Petrov, Google
Dan Roth, University of Illinois
Alexander Rush, Harvard University
Kenji Sagae, KITT.AI
Giorgio Satta, University of Padua
Hinrich Schuetze, LMU Munich
William Schuler, the Ohio State University
Mihai Surdeanu, University of Arizona
Kristina Toutanova, Microsoft Research
Byron Wallace, University of Texas at Austin

Xiaojun Wan, Peking University
Furu Wei, Microsoft Research
Dekai Wu, Hong Kong University of Science and Technology
Fei Xia, University of Washington

Reviewers

Omri Abend, Amjad Abu-Jbara, Apoorv Agarwal, Eneko Agirre, Željko Agić, Ahmet Aker, Yaser Al-Onaizan, Nikolaos Aletras, Enrique Alfonseca, Alexandre Allauzen, Silvio Amir, Waleed Ammar, Sophia Ananiadou, Daniel Andrade, Jacob Andreas, Nicholas Andrews, Ion Androutsopoulos, Gabor Angeli, Emilia Apostolova, Yoav Artzi, Masayuki Asahara, Nicholas Asher, Necip Fazil Ayan.

Tyler Baldwin, Miguel Ballesteros, David Bamman, Rafael E. Banchs, Ritwik Banerjee, Srinivas Bangalore, Denilson Barbosa, Marco Baroni, Alberto Barrón-Cedeño, Roberto Basili, Daniel Bauer, Beata Beigman Klebanov, Charley Beller, Emily M. Bender, Taylor Berg-Kirkpatrick, Raffaella Bernardi, Steven Bethard, Klinton Bicknell, Chris Biemann, Ann Bies, Or Biran, Alexandra Birch, Arianna Bisazza, Yonatan Bisk, Prakhar Biyani, Graeme Blackwood, Eduardo Blanco, Bernd Bohnet, Ondřej Bojar, Gemma Boleda, Danushka Bollegala, Kalina Bontcheva, Johan Bos, Florian Boudin, Fethi Bougares, David Bracewell, Fabienne Braune, Ted Briscoe, Chris Brockett, Julian Brooke, Paul Buitelaar, David Burkett, Jill Burstein, Benjamin Börschinger.

Aoife Cahill, Chris Callison-Burch, José Camacho-Collados, Marie Candito, Yunbo Cao, Ziqiang Cao, Fabienne Cap, Cornelia Caragea, John Carroll, Francisco Casacuberta, Taylor Cassidy, Vittorio Castelli, Daniel Cer, Joyce Chai, Yllias Chali, Nathanael Chambers, Kai-Wei Chang, Ming-Wei Chang, Angel Chang, Wanxiang Che, Chen Chen, Bin Chen, Boxing Chen, Yun-Nung Chen, Hsin-Hsi Chen, Xinchi Chen, Zhiyuan Chen, Qingcai Chen, Yubo Chen, Wenliang Chen, Colin Cherry, Jackie Chi Kit Cheung, David Chiang, Hai Leong Chieu, Laura Chiticariu, Do Kook Choe, Yejin Choi, Jinho D. Choi, Sumit Chopra, Christos Christodoulopoulos, Grzegorz Chrupała, Jason Chuang, Tagyoung Chung, Ken Church, Philipp Cimiano, Alina Maria Ciobanu, Jonathan Clark, Martin Cmejrek, Shay B. Cohen, Trevor Cohn, Nigel Collier, Matthieu Constant, Paul Cook, Marta R. Costa-jussà, Ryan Cotterell, Benoit Crabbé, Danilo Croce, Heriberto Cuayahuitl.

Jennifer D'Souza, Giovanni Da San Martino, Daniel Dahlmeier, Cristian Danescu-Niculescu-Mizil, Falavigna Daniele, Kareem Darwish, Dipanjan Das, Pradeep Dasigi, Hal Daumé III, Johannes Daxenberger, Adrià de Gispert, Eric De La Clergerie, Marie-Catherine de Marneffe, Gerard de Melo, Luciano Del Corro, Vera Demberg, John DeNero, Lingjia Deng, Li Deng, Pascal Denis, Tejaswini Deoskar, José G. C. de Souza, Nina Dethlefs, Jacob Devlin, Barbara Di Eugenio, Mona Diab, Liviu P. Dinu, Georgiana Dinu, Jesse Dodge, Li Dong, Daxiang Dong, Doug Downey, Gabriel Doyle, Mark Dras, Lan Du, Nan Duan, Kevin Duh, Long Duong, Nadir Durrani, Greg Durrett, Marc Dymetman.

Judith Eckle-Kohler, Steffen Eger, Vladimir Eidelman, Jason Eisner, Michael Elhadad, Desmond Elliott, Ramy Eskander.

James Fan, Hao Fang, Stefano Faralli, Richárd Farkas, Manaal Faruqui, Marcello Federico, Minwei Feng, Yansong Feng, Francis Ferraro, Olivier Ferret, Simone Filice, Katja Filippova, Radu Florian, Mikel Forcada, George Foster, James Foulds, Lea Frermann, Annemarie Friedrich, Akinori Fujino, Fumiyo Fukumoto.

Robert Gaizauskas, Kuzman Ganchev, Debasis Ganguly, Jianfeng Gao, Claire Gardent, Matt Gardner, Dan Garrette, Guillermo Garrido, Milica Gasic, Tao Ge, Dmitriy Genzel, Ulrich Germann, Daniel Gildea, Lee Giles, Alfio Gliozzo, Yoav Goldberg, Dan Goldwasser, Isao Goto, Pawan Goyal, Yvette Graham, Edouard Grave, Weiwei Guo, Yufan Guo, Jiang Guo, Hongyu Guo, Iryna Gurevych, Francisco

Guzmàn, Carlos Gómez-Rodríguez.

Barry Haddow, Matthias Hagen, Udo Hahn, John Hale, David Hall, Keith Hall, Xianpei Han, Sanda Harabagiu, Christian Hardmeier, Kazi Saidul Hasan, Sadid A. Hasan, Mohammed Hasanuzzaman, Hany Hassan, Hua He, He He, Yifan He, Zhongjun He, Kenneth Heafield, Michael Heilman, Karl Moritz Hermann, Ulf Hermjakob, Felix Hieber, Ryuichiro Higashinaka, Erhard Hinrichs, Tsutomu Hirao, Kai Hong, Yu Hong, Mark Hopkins, Yufang Hou, Yuening Hu, Ruihong Huang, Hen-Hsen Huang, Songfang Huang, Minlie Huang, Xuanjing Huang, Shujian Huang, Fei Huang, Hongzhao Huang, Mans Hulden, Rebecca Hwa, Seung-won Hwang.

Ryu Iida, Kenji Imamura, Abe Ittycheriah, Mohit Iyyer.

Minwoo Jeong, Rahul Jha, Yangfeng Ji, Donghong Ji, Wenbin Jiang, Hui Jiang, Anders Johannsen, Richard Johansson, Gareth Jones, Mahesh Joshi, Shafiq Joty, Dan Jurafsky, David Jurgens.

Nobuhiro Kaji, Min-Yen Kan, Dimitri Kartsaklis, David Kauchak, Daisuke Kawahara, Anna Kazantseva, Simon Keizer, Frank Keller, Casey Kennington, Mitesh M. Khapra, Douwe Kiela, Seokhwan Kim, Young-Bum Kim, Katrin Kirchhoff, Svetlana Kiritchenko, Dietrich Klakow, Alexandre Klementiev, Julien Kloetzer, Kevin Knight, Hayato Kobayashi, Philipp Koehn, Varada Kolhatkar, Mamoru Komachi, Grzegorz Kondrak, Lingpeng Kong, Fang Kong, Ioannis Konstas, Valia Kordoni, Anna Korhonen, Yannis Korkontzelos, Zornitsa Kozareva, Mikhail Kozhevnikov, Emiel Krahmer, Jayant Krishnamurthy, Marco Kuhlmann, Roland Kuhn, Shankar Kumar, Jonathan K. Kummerfeld, Sadao Kurohashi.

Siwei Lai, Wai Lam, Vasileios Lampos, Phillippe Langlais, Ni Lao, Mirella Lapata, Jey Han Lau, Angeliki Lazaridou, Joseph Le Roux, Kenton Lee, John Lee, Young-Suk Lee, Tao Lei, Johannes Leveling, Tomer Levinboim, Rivka Levitan, Omer Levy, Mike Lewis, Peifeng Li, Xiaoli Li, Junhui Li, Hang Li, Sheng Li, Yanran Li, Binyang Li, Chen Li, Fangtao Li, Junyi Jessy Li, Jiwei Li, Peng Li, Chin-Yew Lin, Chu-Cheng Lin, Wang Ling, Diane Litman, Marina Litvak, Bing Liu, Yang Liu, Shujie Liu, Kang Liu, Ting Liu, Qun Liu, Chi-kiu Lo, Adam Lopez, Wei Lu, Michal Lukasik, Xiaoqiang Luo, Minh-Thang Luong.

Yanjun Ma, Xuezhe Ma, Ji Ma, Wolfgang Macherey, Klaus Macherey, Nitin Madnani, Wolfgang Maier, Andreas Maletti, Suresh Manandhar, Christopher D. Manning, David Mareček, Benjamin Marie, Katja Markert, André F. T. Martins, Yuval Marton, Shigeki Matsubara, Mausam, Jonathan May, Diana McCarthy, David McClosky, Ryan McDonald, Kathy McKeown, Yashar Mehdad, Oren Melamud, Arul Menezes, Fandong Meng, Haitao Mi, Rada Mihalcea, Timothy Miller, Bonan Min, Einat Minkov, Margaret Mitchell, Prasenjit Mitra, Makoto Miwa, Daichi Mochihashi, Behrang Mohit, Christof Monz, Raymond Mooney, Shinsuke Mori, Véronique Moriceau, Emmanuel Morin, Hajime Morita, Lili Mou, Arjun Mukherjee, Philippe Muller, Dragos Munteanu, Yugo Murawaki, Brian Murphy.

Masaaki Nagata, Ajay Nagesh, Iftekhar Naim, Ndapandula Nakashole, Preslav Nakov, Karthik Narasimhan, Shashi Narayan, Alexis Nasr, Roberto Navigli, Mark-Jan Nederhof, Arvind Neelakantan, Matteo Negri, Graham Neubig, Vincent Ng, Raymond W. M. Ng, Jun-Ping Ng, Dominick Ng, Dong Nguyen, Thien Huu Nguyen, Garrett Nicolai, Massimo Nicosia, Vlad Niculae, Jian-Yun Nie, Hitoshi Nishikawa, Joakim Nivre, Hiroshi Noji, Joel Nothman.

Timothy O'Donnell, Stephan Oepen, Kemal Oflazer, Jong-Hoon Oh, Kiyonori Ohtake, Naoaki Okazaki, Manabu Okumura, Noam Ordan, Vicente Ordonez, Miles Osborne, Myle Ott, Cecilia Ovesdotter Alm.

Martha Palmer, Siddharth Patwardhan, Michael J. Paul, Adam Pauls, Ellie Pavlick, Gerald Penn, Marco Pennacchiotti, Nghia The Pham, Daniele Pighin, Mohammad Taher Pilehvar, Barbara Plank, Tamara Polajnar, Simone Paolo Ponzetto, Andrei Popescu-Belis, Matt Post, Christopher Potts, Vinodkumar Prabhakaran, Daniel Preoţiuc-Pietro, Emily Prud'hommeaux, Matthew Purver.

Ashequl Qadir, Behrang QasemiZadeh, Longhua Qian, Xian Qian, Lu Qin, Chris Quirk.

Will Radford, Preethi Raghavan, Altaf Rahman, Rohan Ramanath, Vivek Kumar Rangarajan Sridhar, Ari Rappoport, Mohammad Sadegh Rasooli, Marta Recasens, Sravana Reddy, Roi Reichart, Sebastian Riedel, Martin Riedl, Jason Riesa, Verena Rieser, Stefan Riezler, German Rigau, Michael Riley, Ellen Riloff, Eric Ringger, Alan Ritter, Brian Roark, Stephen Roller, Sophie Rosset, Paolo Rosso, Michael Roth, Benjamin Roth, Johann Roturier, Alla Rozovskaya, Josef Ruppenhofer.

Kugatsu Sadamitsu, Markus Saers, Kenji Sagae, Horacio Saggion, Benoît Sagot, Hassan Sajjad, Bahar Salehi, Avneesh Saluja, Ruhi Sarikaya, Anoop Sarkar, Ryohei Sasano, Asad Sayeed, Christian Scheible, Helmut Schmid, Sabine Schulte im Walde, Roy Schwartz, Wolfgang Seeker, Nina Seemann, Satoshi Sekine, Rico Sennrich, Hendra Setiawan, Izhak Shafran, Shuming Shi, Hiroyuki Shindo, Eyal Shnarch, Ekaterina Shutova, Maryam Siahbani, Carina Silberer, Khe Chai Sim, Yanchuan Sim, Khalil Sima'an, Sameer Singh, Noam Slonim, Jan Šnajder Thamar Solorio, Hyun-Je Song, Xuan Song, Radu Soricut, Aitor Soroa, Lucia Specia, Caroline Sporleder, Richard Sproat, Vivek Srikumar, Asher Stern, Mark Stevenson, Veselin Stoyanov, Carlo Strapparava, Karl Stratos, Tomek Strzalkowski, Jinsong Su, Keh-Yih Su, Amarnag Subramanya, Xu Sun, Yoshimi Suzuki, Jun Suzuki, Hisami Suzuki, Stan Szpakowicz, Anders Søgaard.

Hiroya Takamura, David Talbot, Partha Talukdar, Akihiro Tamura, Chenhao Tan, Xavier Tannier, Joel Tetreault, Kapil Thadani, Stefan Thater, Sam Thomson, Jörg Tiedemann, Ivan Titov, Tomoki Toda, Marc Tomlinson, Sara Tonelli, Kentaro Torisawa, Isabel Trancoso, Reut Tsarfaty, Yoshimasa Tsuruoka, Yulia Tsvetkov, Zhaopeng Tu, Marco Turchi, Ferhan Ture, Oscar Täckström.

Kiyotaka Uchimoto, Raghavendra Udupa, Lyle Ungar, Masao Utiyama.

Tim Van de Cruys, Lonneke van der Plas, Benjamin Van Durme, Marten van Schijndel, Lucy Vanderwende, Ashish Vaswani, Sriram Venkatapathy, David Vilar, Martin Villalba, Veronika Vincze, Andreas Vlachos, Svitlana Volkova, Clare Voss, Ivan Vulić.

Henning Wachsmuth, Marilyn Walker, Tong Wang, Xiaolin Wang, Baoxun Wang, Yiou Wang, Zhiguo Wang, Zhongqing Wang, William Yang Wang, Chang Wang, Hongning Wang, Leo Wanner, Taro Watanabe, Andy Way, Wouter Weerkamp, Zhongyu Wei, Gerhard Weikum, David Weir, Michael White, Michael Wiegand, Theresa Wilson, Shuly Wintner, Guillaume Wisniewski, Travis Wolfe, Kam-Fai Wong, Jian Wu, Hua Wu, Joern Wuebker.

Rui Xia, Bing Xiang, Min Xiao, Xinyan Xiao, Tong Xiao, Shasha Xie, Deyi Xiong, Ruifeng Xu, Wenduan Xu.

Ichiro Yamada, Elif Yamangil, Bishan Yang, Diyi Yang, Yaqin Yang, Min Yang, Wen-tau Yih, Wenpeng Yin, Dani Yogatama, Naoki Yoshinaga, Dianhai Yu, Liang-Chih Yu, Dian Yu, Mo Yu, François Yvon.

Roberto Zamparelli, Fabio Massimo Zanzotto, Klaus Zechner, Daojian Zeng, Xiaodong Zeng, Richard Zens, Torsten Zesch, Luke Zettlemoyer, Feifei Zhai, Jiajun Zhang, Wei Zhang, Min Zhang, Dongdong

Zhang, Jianwen Zhang, Congle Zhang, Yongfeng Zhang, Dongyan Zhao, Bing Zhao, Yaqian Zhou, Muhua Zhu, Imed Zitouni, Chengqing Zong, Bowei Zou, Diarmuid Ó Séaghdha, Gözde Özbal.

Best Reviewers

Yaser Al-Onaizan, Enrique Alfonseca, Daniel Andrade, Jacob Andreas, Ion Androutsopoulos, Gabor Angeli.

David Bamman, Ritmiek Banerjee, Emily Bender, Taylor Berg-Kirkpatrick, Chris Biemann, Arianna Bisazza, Graeme Blackwood, Gemma Boleda, Florian Boudin.

Jose Camacho-Collados, Marie Candito, Taylor Cassidy, Colin Cherry, Christos Christodopoulos, Alina Maria Ciobanu, Jon Clark, Trevor Cohn, Danilo Croce.

Hal Daumé III, Marie-Catherine de Marneffe, Jose G. C. de Souza, John DeNero, Jacob Devlin, Doug Downey, Gabe Doyle, Mark Dras, Greg Durrett.

Steffen Eger, Jason Eisner, Michael Elhadad.

Francis Ferraro, Mikel Forcada, James Foulds.

Matt Gardner, Dan Garrette, Yvette Graham, Dmitriy Genzel.

Barry Haddow, Matthias Hagen, David Hall, Mohammed Hasanuzzaman, Kai Hong.

Mohit Iyyer.

Yangfeng Ji, Anders Johannsen, Mahesh Joshi, Dan Jurafsky.

Dimitri Karsaklis, Daisuke Kawahara, Alexandre Klementiev, Grzegorz Kondrak, Ioannis Konstas, Yannis Korkontzelos, Roland Kuhn, Shankar Kumar, Jonathan K. Kummerfeld.

Tomer Levinboim, Rivka Levitan, Omer Levy, Junyi Jessy Li.

Klaus Macherey, Wolfgang Macherey, Wolfgang Maier, Andreas Maletti, Christopher D. Manning, Diana McCarthy, David McClosky, Lili Mou, Philippe Muller, Dragos Munteanu, Yugo Murawaki.

Masaki Nagaata, Ajay Nagesh, Mark-Jan Nederhof, Dominick Ng, Vincent Ng, Vlad Niculae, Jian-Yin Nie, Joel Nothman.

Stephan Oepen, Myle Ott.

Adam Pauls, Daniele Pighin, Andrei Popescu Belis, Matt Post, Vinod Prabhakaran, Matt Purver.

Ashequl Qadir.

Rohan Ramanath, Jason Riesa, Verena Rieser, Eric Ringger, Brian Roark, Stephen Roller, Sophie Rosset.

Wolfgang Seeker, Thamar Solorio, Vivek Kumar Rangarajan Sridhar, Vivek Srikumar, Jun Suzuki.

Akihiro Tamura, Joel Tetreault, Kapil Thadani, Ivan Titov, Marco Turchi.

Raghavendra Udupa.

Clare Voss, Ivan Vulic.

Henning Wachsmuth, Marilyn Walker, Taro Watanabe, Wouter Weerkamp, Michael Wiegand.

Min Yang.

Invited Talk: How can NLP help cure cancer?

Regina Barzilay

Massachusetts Institute of Technology

Abstract

Cancer inflicts a heavy toll on our society. One out of seven women will be diagnosed with breast cancer during their lifetime, a fraction of them contributing to about 450,000 deaths annually worldwide. Despite billions of dollars invested in cancer research, our understanding of the disease, treatment, and prevention is still limited.

Majority of cancer research today takes place in biology and medicine. Computer science plays a minor supporting role in this process if at all. In this talk, I hope to convince you that NLP as a field has a chance to play a significant role in this battle. Indeed, free-form text remains the primary means by which physicians record their observations and clinical findings. Unfortunately, this rich source of textual information is severely underutilized by predictive models in oncology. Current models rely primarily only on structured data.

In the first part of my talk, I will describe a number of tasks where NLP-based models can make a difference in clinical practice. For example, these include improving models of disease progression, preventing over-treatment, and narrowing down to the cure. This part of the talk draws on active collaborations with oncologists from Massachusetts General Hospital (MGH).

In the second part of the talk, I will push beyond standard tools, introducing new functionalities and avoiding annotation-hungry training paradigms ill-suited for clinical practice. In particular, I will focus on interpretable neural models that provide rationales underlying their predictions, and semi-supervised methods for information extraction.

Biography

Regina Barzilay is a professor in the Department of Electrical Engineering and Computer Science and a member of the Computer Science and Artificial Intelligence Laboratory at the Massachusetts Institute of Technology. Her research interests are in natural language processing. She is a recipient of various awards including of the NSF Career Award, the MIT Technology Review TR-35 Award, Microsoft Faculty Fellowship and several Best Paper Awards at NAACL and ACL. She received her Ph.D. in Computer Science from Columbia University, and spent a year as a postdoc at Cornell University.

Invited Talk: Evaluating Natural Language Generation Systems

Ehud Reitter

University of Aberdeen and Arria NLG

Abstract

Natural Language Generation (NLG) systems have different characteristics than other NLP systems, which effects how they are evaluated. In particular, it can be difficult to meaningfully evaluate NLG texts by comparing them against gold- standard reference texts, because (A) there are usually many possible texts which are acceptable to users and (B) some NLG systems produce texts which are better (as judged by human users) than human-written corpus texts. Partially because of these reasons, the NLG community places much more emphasis on human-based evaluations than most areas of NLP.

I will discuss the various ways in which NLG systems are evaluated, focusing on human-based evaluations. These typically either measure the success of generated texts at achieving a goal (eg, measuring how many people change their behaviour after reading behaviour-change texts produced by an NLG system); or ask human subjects to rate various aspects of generated texts (such as readability, accuracy, and appropriateness), often on Likert scales. I will use examples from evaluations I have carried out, and highlight some of the lessons I have learnt, including the importance of reporting negative results, the difference between laboratory and real-world evaluations, and the need to look at worse-case as well as average-case performance. I hope my talk will be interesting and relevant to anyone who is interested in the evaluation of NLP systems.

Biography

Ehud Reiter is a Professor of Computing Science at the University of Aberdeen and also Chief Scientist of Arria NLG. He has worked on natural language generation for the past 30 years, on methodology (including evaluation) and resources as well as algorithms, and is one of the most cited authors in NLG. His 2000 book Building Natural Language Generation Systems is widely used as an NLG textbook. Dr Reiter currently spends most of his time trying to commercialise NLG at Arria (one of the largest specialist NLG companies), which grew out of a startup he cofounded in 2009.

Table of Contents

Conference Program

Sunday, June 12, 2016

18:00–21:00 *Welcome reception, Pavilion*

Monday, June 13, 2016

7:30–8:45 *Breakfast, Pavilion*

9:00–9:15 *Welcome, Grande Ballroom*
Kevin Knight, Ani Nenkova, Owen Rambow

9:15–10:30 *Invited talk: "How can NLP help cure cancer?"*
Regina Barzilay

10:30–11:00 *Coffee break, Pavilion*

11:00–12:30 *Session 1*

1A. Machine translation

11:00–11:20 *Achieving Accurate Conclusions in Evaluation of Automatic Machine Translation Metrics*
Yvette Graham and Qun Liu

11:20–11:40 *Flexible Non-Terminals for Dependency Tree-to-Tree Reordering*
John Richardson, Fabien Cromierès, Toshiaki Nakazawa and Sadao Kurohashi

11:40–12:00 *Selecting Syntactic, Non-redundant Segments in Active Learning for Machine Translation*
Akiva Miura, Graham Neubig, Michael Paul and Satoshi Nakamura

12:00–12:10 *Multi-Source Neural Translation*
Barret Zoph and Kevin Knight

12:10–12:20 *Controlling Politeness in Neural Machine Translation via Side Constraints*
Rico Sennrich, Barry Haddow and Alexandra Birch

12:20–12:30   *An Empirical Evaluation of Noise Contrastive Estimation for the Neural Network Joint Model of Translation*
Colin Cherry

1B. Summarization

11:00–11:20   *Neural Network-Based Abstract Generation for Opinions and Arguments*
Lu Wang and Wang Ling

11:20–11:40   *A Low-Rank Approximation Approach to Learning Joint Embeddings of News Stories and Images for Timeline Summarization*
William Yang Wang, Yashar Mehdad, Dragomir R. Radev and Amanda Stent

11:40–12:00   *Entity-balanced Gaussian pLSA for Automated Comparison*
Danish Contractor, Parag Singla and Mausam

12:00–12:10   *Automatic Summarization of Student Course Feedback*
Wencan Luo, Fei Liu, Zitao Liu and Diane Litman

12:10–12:20   *Knowledge-Guided Linguistic Rewrites for Inference Rule Verification*
Prachi Jain and Mausam

12:20–12:30   *Abstractive Sentence Summarization with Attentive Recurrent Neural Networks*
Sumit Chopra, Michael Auli and Alexander M. Rush

1C. Dialog

11:00–11:20   *Integer Linear Programming for Discourse Parsing*
Jérémy Perret, Stergos Afantenos, Nicholas Asher and Mathieu Morey

11:20–11:40   *A Diversity-Promoting Objective Function for Neural Conversation Models*
Jiwei Li, Michel Galley, Chris Brockett, Jianfeng Gao and Bill Dolan

11:40–12:00   *Multi-domain Neural Network Language Generation for Spoken Dialogue Systems*
Tsung-Hsien Wen, Milica Gašić, Nikola Mrkšić, Lina M. Rojas-Barahona, Pei-Hao Su, David Vandyke and Steve Young

12:00–12:10   *A Long Short-Term Memory Framework for Predicting Humor in Dialogues*
Dario Bertero and Pascale Fung

12:10–12:20   *Conversational Flow in Oxford-style Debates*
Justine Zhang, Ravi Kumar, Sujith Ravi and Cristian Danescu-Niculescu-Mizil

12:20–12:30   *Counter-fitting Word Vectors to Linguistic Constraints*
Nikola Mrkšić, Diarmuid Ó Séaghdha, Blaise Thomson, Milica Gašić, Lina M. Rojas-Barahona, Pei-Hao Su, David Vandyke, Tsung-Hsien Wen and Steve Young

12:30–2:00   Lunch break

2:00–3:30   Session 2

2A. Language and Vision

2:00–2:20   *Grounded Semantic Role Labeling*
Shaohua Yang, Qiaozi Gao, Changsong Liu, Caiming Xiong, Song-Chun Zhu and Joyce Y. Chai

2:20–2:40   *Black Holes and White Rabbits: Metaphor Identification with Visual Features*
Ekaterina Shutova, Douwe Kiela and Jean Maillard

2:40–3:00   *Bridge Correlational Neural Networks for Multilingual Multimodal Representation Learning*
Janarthanan Rajendran, Mitesh M. Khapra, Sarath Chandar and Balaraman Ravindran

3:00–3:20   *Unsupervised Visual Sense Disambiguation for Verbs using Multimodal Embeddings*
Spandana Gella, Mirella Lapata and Frank Keller

3:20–3:30   *Stating the Obvious: Extracting Visual Common Sense Knowledge*
Mark Yatskar, Vicente Ordonez and Ali Farhadi

2B. Parsing

2:00–2:20   *Efficient Structured Inference for Transition-Based Parsing with Neural Networks and Error States [TACL]*
Ashish Vaswani and Kenji Sagae

2:20–2:40   *Recurrent Neural Network Grammars*
Chris Dyer, Adhiguna Kuncoro, Miguel Ballesteros and Noah A. Smith

2:40–3:00   *Expected F-Measure Training for Shift-Reduce Parsing with Recurrent Neural Networks*
Wenduan Xu, Michael Auli and Stephen Clark

3:00–3:20   *LSTM CCG Parsing*
Mike Lewis, Kenton Lee and Luke Zettlemoyer

3:20–3:30   *Supertagging With LSTMs*
Ashish Vaswani, Yonatan Bisk, Kenji Sagae and Ryan Musa

2C. Named Entity Recognition

2:00–2:20   *An Empirical Study of Automatic Chinese Word Segmentation for Spoken Language Understanding and Named Entity Recognition*
Wencan Luo and Fan Yang

2:20–2:40   *Name Tagging for Low-resource Incident Languages based on Expectation-driven Learning*
Boliang Zhang, Xiaoman Pan, Tianlu Wang, Ashish Vaswani, Heng Ji, Kevin Knight and Daniel Marcu

2:40–3:00   *Neural Architectures for Named Entity Recognition*
Guillaume Lample, Miguel Ballesteros, Sandeep Subramanian, Kazuya Kawakami and Chris Dyer

3:00–3:20   *Dynamic Feature Induction: The Last Gist to the State-of-the-Art*
Jinho D. Choi

3:20–3:30   *Drop-out Conditional Random Fields for Twitter with Huge Mined Gazetteer*
Eunsuk Yang, Young-Bum Kim, Ruhi Sarikaya and Yu-Seop Kim

3:30–4:00   ***Coffee break, Pavilion***

4:00–5:00   *Session 3*

3A. Event detection

4:00–4:20   *Joint Extraction of Events and Entities within a Document Context*
Bishan Yang and Tom M. Mitchell

4:20–4:40   *A Hierarchical Distance-dependent Bayesian Model for Event Coreference Resolution [TACL]*
Bishan Yang, Claire Cardie, and Peter Frazier

4:40–5:00   *Joint Event Extraction via Recurrent Neural Networks*
Thien Huu Nguyen, Kyunghyun Cho and Ralph Grishman

3B. Language Models

4:00–4:20   *Top-down Tree Long Short-Term Memory Networks*
Xingxing Zhang, Liang Lu and Mirella Lapata

4:20–4:40   *Recurrent Memory Networks for Language Modeling*
Ke Tran, Arianna Bisazza and Christof Monz

4:40–5:00   *A Latent Variable Recurrent Neural Network for Discourse-Driven Language Models*
Yangfeng Ji, Gholamreza Haffari and Jacob Eisenstein

3C. Non Literal Language

4:00–4:20   *Questioning Arbitrariness in Language: a Data-Driven Study of Conventional Iconicity*
Ekaterina Abramova and Raquel Fernández

4:20–4:40   *Distinguishing Literal and Non-Literal Usage of German Particle Verbs*
Maximilian Köper and Sabine Schulte im Walde

4:40–5:00   *Phrasal Substitution of Idiomatic Expressions*
Changsheng Liu and Rebecca Hwa

5:00–5:15   ***Break***

5:15–6:00   ***One Minute Madness***

6:00–8:00   ***Posters and Dinner***

Posters

Leverage Financial News to Predict Stock Price Movements Using Word Embeddings and Deep Neural Networks
Yangtuo Peng and Hui Jiang

Grammatical error correction using neural machine translation
Zheng Yuan and Ted Briscoe

Multimodal Semantic Learning from Child-Directed Input
Angeliki Lazaridou, Grzegorz Chrupała, Raquel Fernández and Marco Baroni

Recurrent Support Vector Machines For Slot Tagging In Spoken Language Understanding
Yangyang Shi, Kaisheng Yao, Hu Chen, Dong Yu, Yi-Cheng Pan and Mei-Yuh Hwang

Expectation-Regulated Neural Model for Event Mention Extraction
Ching-Yun Chang, Zhiyang Teng and Yue Zhang

Cross-lingual Wikification Using Multilingual Embeddings
Chen-Tse Tsai and Dan Roth

Deconstructing Complex Search Tasks: a Bayesian Nonparametric Approach for Extracting Sub-tasks
Rishabh Mehrotra, Prasanta Bhattacharya and Emine Yilmaz

6:00–8:00   ***System Demonstrations***

rstWeb - A Browser-based Annotation Interface for Rhetorical Structure Theory and Discourse Relations
Amir Zeldes

Instant Feedback for Increasing the Presence of Solutions in Peer Reviews
Huy Nguyen, Wenting Xiong and Diane Litman

Farasa: A Fast and Furious Segmenter for Arabic
Ahmed Abdelali, Kareem Darwish, Nadir Durrani and Hamdy Mubarak

iAppraise: A Manual Machine Translation Evaluation Environment Supporting Eye-tracking
Ahmed Abdelali, Nadir Durrani and Francisco Guzmán

Linguistica 5: Unsupervised Learning of Linguistic Structure
Jackson Lee and John Goldsmith

TransRead: Designing a Bilingual Reading Experience with Machine Translation Technologies
François Yvon, Yong Xu, Marianna Apidianaki, Clément Pillias and Pierre Cubaud

New Dimensions in Testimony Demonstration
Ron Artstein, Alesia Gainer, Kallirroi Georgila, Anton Leuski, Ari Shapiro and David Traum

ArgRewrite: A Web-based Revision Assistant for Argumentative Writings
Fan Zhang, Rebecca Hwa, Diane Litman and Homa B. Hashemi

Scaling Up Word Clustering
Jon Dehdari, Liling Tan and Josef van Genabith

Task Completion Platform
A self-serve multi-domain goal oriented dialogue platform: Paul Crook, Alex Marin, Vipul Agarwal, Khushboo Aggarwal, Tasos Anastasakos, Ravi Bikkula, Daniel Boies, Asli Celikyilmaz, Senthilkumar Chandramohan, Zhaleh Feizollahi, Roman Holenstein, Minwoo Jeong, Omar Khan, Young-Bum Kim, Elizabeth Krawczyk, Xiaohu Liu, Danko Panic, Vasiliy Radostev, Nikhil Ramesh, Jean-Phillipe Robichaud, Alexandre Rochette, Logan Stromberg and Ruhi Sarikaya

Student Workshop Posters

An End-to-end Approach to Learning Semantic Frames with Feedforward Neural Network
Yukun Feng, Yipei Xu and Dong Yu

Analogy-based detection of morphological and semantic relations with word embeddings
what works and what doesn't: Anna Gladkova, Aleksandr Drozd and Satoshi Matsuoka

Argument Identification in Chinese Editorials
Marisa Chow

Automatic tagging and retrieval of E-Commerce products based on visual features
Vasu Sharma and Harish Karnick

Combining syntactic patterns and Wikipedia's hierarchy of hyperlinks to extract relations: The case of meronymy extraction
Debela Tesfaye Gemechu, Michael Zock and Solomon Teferra

Cross-Lingual Question Answering Using Profile HMM & Unified Semantic Space
Amir Pouran Ben Veyseh

Data-driven Paraphrasing and Stylistic Harmonization
Gerold Hintz

Detecting "Smart" Spammers on Social Network
A Topic Model Approach: Linqing Liu, Yao Lu, Ye Luo, Renxian Zhang, Laurent Itti and Jianwei Lu

Developing language technology tools and resources for a resource-poor language: Sindhi
Raveesh Motlani

Tuesday, June 14, 2016

7:30–8:45 *Breakfast, Pavilion*

9:00–10:30 *Session 4*

4A. Semantic Parsing

9:00–9:20 *Transforming Dependency Structures to Logical Forms for Semantic Parsing [TACL]*
Siva Reddy, Oscar Täckström, Michael Collins, Tom Kwiatkowski, Dipanjan Das, Mark Steedman, and Mirella Lapata

9:20–9:40 *Imitation Learning of Agenda-based Semantic Parsers [TACL]*
Jonathan Berant and Percy Liang

9:40–10:00 *Probabilistic Models for Learning a Semantic Parser Lexicon*
Jayant Krishnamurthy

10:00–10:20 *Semantic Parsing of Ambiguous Input through Paraphrasing and Verification [TACL]*
Philip Arthur, Graham Neubig, Sakriani Sakti, Tomoki Toda, and Satoshi Nakamura

10:20–10:30 *Unsupervised Compound Splitting With Distributional Semantics Rivals Supervised Methods*
Martin Riedl and Chris Biemann

4B. Morphology and Phonology

9:00–9:20 *Weighting Finite-State Transductions With Neural Context*
Pushpendre Rastogi, Ryan Cotterell and Jason Eisner

9:20–9:40 *Morphological Inflection Generation Using Character Sequence to Sequence Learning*
Manaal Faruqui, Yulia Tsvetkov, Graham Neubig and Chris Dyer

9:40–10:00 *Towards Unsupervised and Language-independent Compound Splitting using Inflectional Morphological Transformations*
Patrick Ziering and Lonneke van der Plas

10:00–10:20 *Phonological Pun-derstanding*
Aaron Jaech, Rik Koncel-Kedziorski and Mari Ostendorf

10:20–10:30   *A Joint Model of Orthography and Morphological Segmentation*
Ryan Cotterell, Tim Vieira and Hinrich Schütze

4C. Various

9:00–9:20   *Syntactic Parsing of Web Queries with Question Intent*
Yuval Pinter, Roi Reichart and Idan Szpektor

9:20–9:40   *Visualizing and Understanding Neural Models in NLP*
Jiwei Li, Xinlei Chen, Eduard Hovy and Dan Jurafsky

9:40–10:00   *Bilingual Word Embeddings from Parallel and Non-parallel Corpora for Cross-Language Text Classification*
Aditya Mogadala and Achim Rettinger

10:00–10:20   *Joint Learning with Global Inference for Comment Classification in Community Question Answering*
Shafiq Joty, Lluís Màrquez and Preslav Nakov

10:20–10:30   *Weak Semi-Markov CRFs for Noun Phrase Chunking in Informal Text*
Aldrian Obaja Muis and Wei Lu

10:30–11:00   *Coffee break, Pavilion*

11:00–12:30   *Session 5*

5A. Generation

11:00–11:20   *What to talk about and how? Selective Generation using LSTMs with Coarse-to-Fine Alignment*
Hongyuan Mei, Mohit Bansal and Matthew R. Walter

11:20–11:40   *Generation from Abstract Meaning Representation using Tree Transducers*
Jeffrey Flanigan, Chris Dyer, Noah A. Smith and Jaime Carbonell

11:40–12:00   *A Corpus and Semantic Parser for Multilingual Natural Language Querying of OpenStreetMap*
Carolin Haas and Stefan Riezler

12:00–12:20   *Natural Language Communication with Robots*
Yonatan Bisk, Deniz Yuret and Daniel Marcu

12:20–12:30   *Inter-document Contextual Language model*
Quan Hung Tran, Ingrid Zukerman and Gholamreza Haffari

5B. Sentiment

11:00–11:20   *Ultradense Word Embeddings by Orthogonal Transformation*
Sascha Rothe, Sebastian Ebert and Hinrich Schütze

11:20–11:40   *Separating Actor-View from Speaker-View Opinion Expressions using Linguistic Features*
Michael Wiegand, Marc Schulder and Josef Ruppenhofer

11:40–12:00   *Clustering for Simultaneous Extraction of Aspects and Features from Reviews*
Lu Chen, Justin Martineau, Doreen Cheng and Amit Sheth

12:00–12:20   *Opinion Holder and Target Extraction on Opinion Compounds – A Linguistic Approach*
Michael Wiegand, Christine Bocionek and Josef Ruppenhofer

12:20–12:30   *Capturing Reliable Fine-Grained Sentiment Associations by Crowdsourcing and Best–Worst Scaling*
Svetlana Kiritchenko and Saif M. Mohammad

5C. Knowledge Acquisition

11:00–11:20   *Concept Grounding to Multiple Knowledge Bases via Indirect Supervision [TACL]*
Chen-Tse Tsai and Dan Roth

11:20–11:40   *Mapping Verbs in Different Languages to Knowledge Base Relations using Web Text as Interlingua*
Derry Tanti Wijaya and Tom M. Mitchell

11:40–12:00   *Comparing Convolutional Neural Networks to Traditional Models for Slot Filling*
Heike Adel, Benjamin Roth and Hinrich Schütze

12:00–12:20   *A Corpus and Cloze Evaluation for Deeper Understanding of Commonsense Stories*
Nasrin Mostafazadeh, Nathanael Chambers, Xiaodong He, Devi Parikh, Dhruv Batra, Lucy Vanderwende, Pushmeet Kohli and James Allen

12:20–12:30   *Dynamic Entity Representation with Max-pooling Improves Machine Reading*
Sosuke Kobayashi, Ran Tian, Naoaki Okazaki and Kentaro Inui

12:30–1:15   *Lunch*

1:15–2:15   ***Panel Discussion: How Will Deep Learning Change Computational Linguistics?***

2:30–3:30   *Session 6*

6A. Machine Translation II

2:30–2:50 *Speed-Constrained Tuning for Statistical Machine Translation Using Bayesian Optimization*
Daniel Beck, Adrià de Gispert, Gonzalo Iglesias, Aurelien Waite and Bill Byrne

2:50–3:10 *Multi-Way, Multilingual Neural Machine Translation with a Shared Attention Mechanism*
Orhan Firat, Kyunghyun Cho and Yoshua Bengio

3:10–3:30 *Incorporating Structural Alignment Biases into an Attentional Neural Translation Model*
Trevor Cohn, Cong Duy Vu Hoang, Ekaterina Vymolova, Kaisheng Yao, Chris Dyer and Gholamreza Haffari

6B. Relation Extraction

2:30–2:50 *Multilingual Relation Extraction using Compositional Universal Schema*
Patrick Verga, David Belanger, Emma Strubell, Benjamin Roth and Andrew McCallum

2:50–3:10 *Effective Crowd Annotation for Relation Extraction*
Angli Liu, Stephen Soderland, Jonathan Bragg, Christopher H. Lin, Xiao Ling and Daniel S. Weld

3:10–3:30 *A Translation-Based Knowledge Graph Embedding Preserving Logical Property of Relations*
Hee-Geun Yoon, Hyun-Je Song, Seong-Bae Park and Se-Young Park

6C. Semantic Similarity

2:30–2:50 *DAG-Structured Long Short-Term Memory for Semantic Compositionality*
Xiaodan Zhu, Parinaz Sobhani and Hongyu Guo

2:50–3:10 *Bayesian Supervised Domain Adaptation for Short Text Similarity*
Md Arafat Sultan, Jordan Boyd-Graber and Tamara Sumner

3:10–3:30 *Pairwise Word Interaction Modeling with Deep Neural Networks for Semantic Similarity Measurement*
Hua He and Jimmy Lin

3:30–4:00 ***Break***

4:00–5:00   *Session 7*

7A. Machine Translation III

4:00–4:20   *An Attentional Model for Speech Translation Without Transcription*
Long Duong, Antonios Anastasopoulos, David Chiang, Steven Bird and Trevor Cohn

4:20–4:40   *Information Density and Quality Estimation Features as Translationese Indicators for Human Translation Classification*
Raphael Rubino, Ekaterina Lapshinova-Koltunski and Josef van Genabith

4:40–4:50   *Interpretese vs. Translationese: The Uniqueness of Human Strategies in Simultaneous Interpretation*
He He, Jordan Boyd-Graber and Hal Daumé III

4:50–5:00   *LSTM Neural Reordering Feature for Statistical Machine Translation*
Yiming Cui, Shijin Wang and Jianfeng Li

7B. Anaphora Resolution

4:00–4:20   *A Novel Approach to Dropped Pronoun Translation*
Longyue Wang, Zhaopeng Tu, Xiaojun Zhang, Hang Li, Andy Way and Qun Liu

4:20–4:40   *Learning Global Features for Coreference Resolution*
Sam Wiseman, Alexander M. Rush and Stuart M. Shieber

4:40–4:50   *Search Space Pruning: A Simple Solution for Better Coreference Resolvers*
Nafise Sadat Moosavi and Michael Strube

4:50–5:00   *Unsupervised Ranking Model for Entity Coreference Resolution*
Xuezhe Ma, Zhengzhong Liu and Eduard Hovy

7C. Word Embeddings I

4:00–4:20   *Embedding Lexical Features via Low-Rank Tensors*
Mo Yu, Mark Dredze, Raman Arora and Matthew R. Gormley

4:20–4:40   *The Role of Context Types and Dimensionality in Learning Word Embeddings*
Oren Melamud, David McClosky, Siddharth Patwardhan and Mohit Bansal

4:40–5:00   *Improve Chinese Word Embeddings by Exploiting Internal Structure*
Jian Xu, Jiawei Liu, Liangang Zhang, Zhengyu Li and Huanhuan Chen

5:00–5:15   ***Break***

5:15–6:00   ***One-Minute Madness***

6:00–8:00   ***Posters, Demos, and Snacks***

Posters

Assessing Relative Sentence Complexity using an Incremental CCG Parser
Bharat Ram Ambati, Siva Reddy and Mark Steedman

Frustratingly Easy Cross-Lingual Transfer for Transition-Based Dependency Parsing
Ophélie Lacroix, Lauriane Aufrant, Guillaume Wisniewski and François Yvon

Geolocation for Twitter: Timing Matters
Mark Dredze, Miles Osborne and Prabhanjan Kambadur

Fast and Easy Short Answer Grading with High Accuracy
Md Arafat Sultan, Cristobal Salazar and Tamara Sumner

Interlocking Phrases in Phrase-based Statistical Machine Translation
Ye Kyaw Thu, Andrew Finch and Eiichiro Sumita

K-Embeddings: Learning Conceptual Embeddings for Words using Context
Thuy Vu and D. Stott Parker

Learning Composition Models for Phrase Embeddings [TACL]
Mo Yu and Mark Dredze

System Demonstrations

Illinois Math Solver: Math Reasoning on the Web
Subhro Roy and Dan Roth

LingoTurk: managing crowdsourced tasks for psycholinguistics
Florian Pusse, Asad Sayeed and Vera Demberg

Sentential Paraphrasing as Black-Box Machine Translation
Courtney Napoles, Chris Callison-Burch and Matt Post

A Tag-based English Math Word Problem Solver with Understanding, Reasoning and Explanation
Chao-Chun Liang, Kuang-Yi Hsu, Chien-Tsung Huang, Chung-Min Li, Shen-Yu Miao and Keh-Yih Su

Cross-media Event Extraction and Recommendation
Di Lu, Clare Voss, Fangbo Tao, Xiang Ren, Rachel Guan, Rostyslav Korolov, Tongtao Zhang, Dongang Wang, Hongzhi Li, Taylor Cassidy, Heng Ji, Shih-fu Chang, Jiawei Han, William Wallace, James Hendler, Mei Si and Lance Kaplan

SODA: Service Oriented Domain Adaptation Architecture for Microblog Categorization
Himanshu Sharad Bhatt, Sandipan Dandapat, Peddamuthu Balaji, Shourya Roy, Sharmistha Jat and Deepali Semwal

Lecture Translator - Speech translation framework for simultaneous lecture translation
Markus Müller, Thai Son Nguyen, Jan Niehues, Eunah Cho, Bastian Krüger, Thanh-Le Ha, Kevin Kilgour, Matthias Sperber, Mohammed Mediani, Sebastian Stüker and Alex Waibel

Zara The Supergirl: An Empathetic Personality Recognition System
Pascale Fung, Anik Dey, Farhad Bin Siddique, Ruixi Lin, Yang Yang, Yan Wan and Ho Yin Ricky Chan

Kathaa: A Visual Programming Framework for NLP Applications
Sharada Prasanna Mohanty, Nehal J Wani, Manish Srivastava and Dipti Misra Sharma

Why Should I Trust You?": Explaining the Predictions of Any Classifier
Marco Ribeiro, Sameer Singh and Carlos Guestrin

Student Workshop Posters

Effects of Communicative Pressures on Novice L2 Learners' Use of Optional Formal Devices
Yoav Binoun

Explicit Argument Identification for Discourse Parsing In Hindi: A Hybrid Pipeline
Rohit Jain and Dipti Sharma

Exploring Fine-Grained Emotion Detection in Tweets
Jasy Suet Yan Liew and Howard Turtle

Extraction of Bilingual Technical Terms for Chinese-Japanese Patent Translation
Wei Yang, Jinghui Yan and Yves Lepage

Hateful Symbols or Hateful People? Predictive Features for Hate Speech Detection on Twitter
Zeerak Waseem and Dirk Hovy

Non-decreasing Sub-modular Function for Comprehensible Summarization
Litton JKurisinkel, Pruthwik Mishra, Vigneshwaran Muralidaran, Vasudeva Varma and Dipti Misra Sharma

Phylogenetic simulations over constraint-based grammar formalisms
Andrew Lamont and Jonathan Washington

Question Answering over Knowledge Base using Weakly Supervised Memory Networks
Sarthak Jain

Using Related Languages to Enhance Statistical Language Models
Anna Currey, Alina Karakanta and Jon Dehdari

8:00–10:00   *Bayview Lawn Beach Social*

Wednesday, June 15, 2016

7:30–8:45	*Breakfast, Pavilion*

9:00–10:15   *Invited talk: "Human-based evaluations of language generation systems"*
Ehud Reiter

10:15–10:45   *Coffee break, Pavilion*

10:45–12:15   *Session 8*

8A. Question Answering

10:45–11:05   *A Joint Model for Answer Sentence Ranking and Answer Extraction [TACL]*
Md Arafat Sultan, Vittorio Castelli, and Radu Florian

11:05–11:25   *Convolutional Neural Networks vs. Convolution Kernels: Feature Engineering for Answer Sentence Reranking*
Kateryna Tymoshenko, Daniele Bonadiman and Alessandro Moschitti

11:25–11:45   *Semi-supervised Question Retrieval with Gated Convolutions*
Tao Lei, Hrishikesh Joshi, Regina Barzilay, Tommi Jaakkola, Kateryna Tymoshenko, Alessandro Moschitti and Lluís Màrquez

11:45–12:05   *Parsing Algebraic Word Problems into Equations [TACL]*
Rik Koncel-Kedziorski, Hannaneh Hajishirzi, Ashish Sabharwal, Oren Etzioni, and Siena Dumas Ang

12:05–12:15   *This is how we do it: Answer Reranking for Open-domain How Questions with Paragraph Vectors and Minimal Feature Engineering*
Dasha Bogdanova and Jennifer Foster

8B. Multilingual Processing

10:45–11:05   *Multilingual Language Processing From Bytes*
Dan Gillick, Cliff Brunk, Oriol Vinyals and Amarnag Subramanya

11:05–11:25   *Ten Pairs to Tag – Multilingual POS Tagging via Coarse Mapping between Embeddings*
Yuan Zhang, David Gaddy, Regina Barzilay and Tommi Jaakkola

11:25–11:45   *Part-of-Speech Tagging for Historical English*
Yi Yang and Jacob Eisenstein

11:45–12:05   *Statistical Modeling of Creole Genesis*
Yugo Murawaki

12:05–12:15   *Shallow Parsing Pipeline - Hindi-English Code-Mixed Social Media Text*
Arnav Sharma, Sakshi Gupta, Raveesh Motlani, Piyush Bansal, Manish Shrivastava, Radhika Mamidi and Dipti M. Sharma

8C. Word Embeddings II

10:45–11:05   *Bilingual Learning of Multi-sense Embeddings with Discrete Autoencoders*
Simon Šuster, Ivan Titov and Gertjan van Noord

11:05–11:25   *Polyglot Neural Language Models: A Case Study in Cross-Lingual Phonetic Representation Learning*
Yulia Tsvetkov, Sunayana Sitaram, Manaal Faruqui, Guillaume Lample, Patrick Littell, David Mortensen, Alan W Black, Lori Levin and Chris Dyer

11:25–11:45   *Learning Distributed Representations of Sentences from Unlabelled Data*
Felix Hill, Kyunghyun Cho and Anna Korhonen

11:45–12:05   *Learning to Understand Phrases by Embedding the Dictionary [TACL]*
Felix Hill, KyungHyun Cho, Anna Korhonen, and Yoshua Bengio

12:05–12:15   *Retrofitting Sense-Specific Word Vectors Using Parallel Text*
Allyson Ettinger, Philip Resnik and Marine Carpuat

12:15–1:00   ***Lunch***

1:00–2:00	*NAACL business meeting, Grande Ballroom A*

2:15–3:45 *Session 9*

9A. Argumentation and Discourse

2:15–2:35 *End-to-End Argumentation Mining in Student Essays*
Isaac Persing and Vincent Ng

2:35–2:55 *Cross-Domain Mining of Argumentative Text through Distant Supervision*
Khalid Al-Khatib, Henning Wachsmuth, Matthias Hagen, Jonas Köhler and Benno
Stein

2:55–3:15 *A Study of the Impact of Persuasive Argumentation in Political Debates*
Amparo Elizabeth Cano-Basave and Yulan He

3:15–3:35 *Lexical Coherence Graph Modeling Using Word Embeddings*
Mohsen Mesgar and Michael Strube

3:35–3:45 *Using Context to Predict the Purpose of Argumentative Writing Revisions*
Fan Zhang and Diane Litman

9B. Misc Semantics

2:15–2:35 *Automatic Generation and Scoring of Positive Interpretations from Negated Statements*
Eduardo Blanco and Zahra Sarabi

2:35–2:55 *Learning Natural Language Inference with LSTM*
Shuohang Wang and Jing Jiang

2:55–3:15 *Activity Modeling in Email*
Ashequl Qadir, Michael Gamon, Patrick Pantel and Ahmed Hassan Awadallah

3:15–3:35 *Clustering Paraphrases by Word Sense*
Anne Cocos and Chris Callison-Burch

3:35–3:45   *Unsupervised Learning of Prototypical Fillers for Implicit Semantic Role Labeling*
Niko Schenk and Christian Chiarcos

9C. Text Categorization

2:15–2:35   *Hierarchical Attention Networks for Document Classification*
Zichao Yang, Diyi Yang, Chris Dyer, Xiaodong He, Alex Smola and Eduard Hovy

2:35–2:55   *Dependency Based Embeddings for Sentence Classification Tasks*
Alexandros Komninos and Suresh Manandhar

2:55–3:15   *Deep LSTM based Feature Mapping for Query Classification*
Yangyang Shi, Kaisheng Yao, Le Tian and Daxin Jiang

3:15–3:35   *Dependency Sensitive Convolutional Neural Networks for Modeling Sentences and Documents*
Rui Zhang, Honglak Lee and Dragomir R. Radev

3:35–3:45   *MGNC-CNN: A Simple Approach to Exploiting Multiple Word Embeddings for Sentence Classification*
Ye Zhang, Stephen Roller and Byron C. Wallace

3:45–4:15   Coffee break, Pavilion

4:15–5:45   Best paper awards

4:15–4:35   *Improving sentence compression by learning to predict gaze*
Sigrid Klerke, Yoav Goldberg and Anders Søgaard

4:35–5:05   *Feuding Families and Former Friends: Unsupervised Learning for Dynamic Fictional Relationships*
Mohit Iyyer, Anupam Guha, Snigdha Chaturvedi, Jordan Boyd-Graber and Hal Daumé III

5:05–5:35   *Learning to Compose Neural Networks for Question Answering*
Jacob Andreas, Marcus Rohrbach, Trevor Darrell and Dan Klein

5:35–5:45   Closing remarks

Achieving Accurate Conclusions in Evaluation of Automatic Machine Translation Metrics

Yvette Graham
School of Computing
Dublin City University
graham.yvette@gmail.com

Qun Liu
ADAPT Research Centre
Dublin City University
qliu@computing.dcu.ie

Abstract

Automatic Machine Translation metrics, such as BLEU, are widely used in empirical evaluation as a substitute for human assessment. Subsequently, the performance of a given metric is measured by its strength of correlation with human judgment. When a newly proposed metric achieves a stronger correlation over that of a baseline, it is important to take into account the uncertainty inherent in correlation point estimates prior to concluding improvements in metric performance. Confidence intervals for correlations with human judgment are rarely reported in metric evaluations, however, and when they have been reported, the most suitable methods have unfortunately not been applied. For example, incorrect assumptions about correlation sampling distributions made in past evaluations risk over-estimation of significant differences in metric performance. In this paper, we provide analysis of each of the issues that may lead to inaccuracies before providing detail of a method that overcomes previous challenges. Additionally, we propose a new method of translation sampling that in contrast achieves genuine high conclusivity in evaluation of the relative performance of metrics.

1 Introduction

In empirical evaluation of Machine Translation (MT), automatic metrics are widely used as a substitute for human assessment for the purpose of measuring differences in MT system performance. The performance of a newly proposed metric is itself measured by the degree to which its automatic scores for a sample of MT systems correlate with human assessment of that same set of systems. A main venue for evaluation of MT metrics is the annual Workshop for Statistical Machine Translation (WMT) (Bojar et al., 2015) where large-scale human evaluation takes place, primarily for the purpose of ranking systems competing in the translation shared task, but additionally to use the resulting system rankings for evaluation of automatic metrics. Since 2014, WMT has used the Pearson correlation as the official measure for evaluation of metrics (Macháček and Bojar, 2014; Stanojević et al., 2015). Comparison of the performance of any two metrics involves the comparison of two Pearson correlation point estimates computed over a sample of MT systems, therefore. Table 1 shows correlations with human assessment of each of the metrics participating in the Czech-to-English component of WMT-14 metrics shared task, and, for example, if we wish to compare the performance of the top-performing metric, REDSYSSENT (Wu et al., 2014), with the popular metric BLEU (Papineni et al., 2001), this involves comparison of the correlation point estimate of REDSYSSENT, $r = 0.993$, with the weaker correlation point estimate of BLEU, $r = 0.909$, with both computed with reference to human assessment of a sample of 5 MT systems.

When a new metric achieves a stronger correlation with human assessment over a baseline metric, such as the increase achieved by REDSYSSENT over BLEU, it is important to consider the uncertainty surrounding the difference in correlation. Confidence intervals are very rarely reported in metric evaluations, however, and when attempts have been made,

Proceedings of NAACL-HLT 2016, pages 1–10,
San Diego, California, June 12-17, 2016. ©2016 Association for Computational Linguistics

Metric	r	CI	UCL
REDSYSSENT	0.993	± 0.018	1.011
REDSYS	0.989	± 0.021	1.010
NIST	0.983	± 0.025	1.008
DISCOTK-PARTY	0.983	± 0.025	1.008
APAC	0.982	± 0.026	1.008
METEOR	0.980	± 0.029	1.009
TER	0.976	± 0.031	1.007
DISCOTK-PARTY-TUNED	0.975	± 0.031	1.006
WER	0.974	± 0.033	1.007
CDER	0.965	± 0.035	1.000
TBLEU	0.957	± 0.040	0.997
DISCOTK-LIGHT	0.954	± 0.038	0.992
UPC-STOUT	0.948	± 0.040	0.988
BLEU-NRC	0.946	± 0.044	0.990
ELEXR	0.945	± 0.044	0.989
LAYERED	0.941	± 0.045	0.986
VERTA-EQ	0.938	± 0.048	0.986
VERTA-W	0.934	± 0.050	0.984
BLEU	0.909	± 0.054	0.963
PER	0.883	± 0.063	0.946
UPC-IPA	0.824	± 0.073	0.897
AMBER	0.744	± 0.095	0.839

Table 1: WMT-14 Czech-to-English metrics shared task Pearson correlation (r) point estimates for metrics with human assessment (5 MT systems), reported confidence intervals (CI), and corresponding upper confidence limits (UCL).

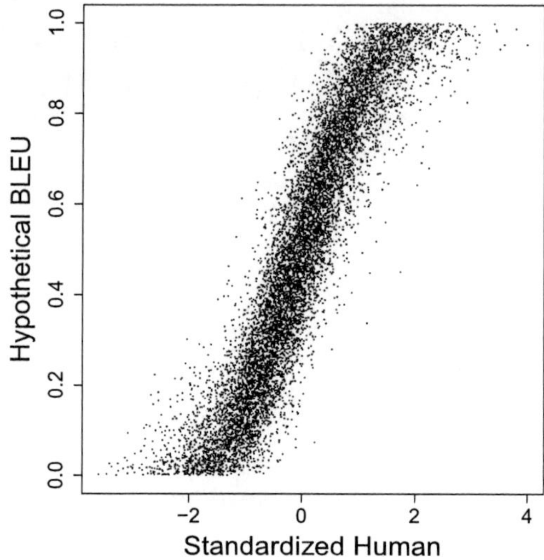

Figure 1: 10k simulated BLEU scores correlating with human assessment at $r = 0.91$ as in BLEU evaluation of Czech-to-English in WMT-14.

the most appropriate method has unfortunately not been applied. For example, although WMT constitutes a main authority on MT evaluation, and have made the best attempt to provide confidence intervals for metric correlations we could find, when we closely examine results of WMT-14 Czech-to-English metrics shared task, reproduced here in Table 1, a discrepancy can be identified. For the nine top-performing metrics participating in the shared task, upper confidence interval limits are reported to exceed 1.0.

Confidence intervals reported in the metrics shared task unfortunately also risk inaccurate conclusions about the relative performance of metrics for other less obvious reasons and risk conclusions that over-estimate the presence of significant differences. False-positives are problematic in metric evaluations because, if a given metric is mistakenly concluded to significantly outperform a competing metric, it is possible that had a larger sample of MT systems been employed in the evaluation, that the reverse conclusion should in fact be made. We demonstrate how this can occur for metrics, showing that in reality in current metric evaluation settings, it is only possible to identify a very small number of signifi-

cant differences in performance. A main cause is the small number of MT systems employed in evaluations, and we propose a new sampling technique, hybrid super-sampling, that overcomes previous challenges and facilities the evaluation of metrics with reference to a practically unlimited number of MT systems.

2 WMT-style Evaluation

Alongside the correlation sample point estimates achieved by metrics, WMT reports confidence intervals for correlations that unfortunately risk over-estimation of significant differences in metric performance, reasons for which we outline below (Macháček and Bojar, 2013; Macháček and Bojar, 2014; Stanojević et al., 2015).

2.1 Sampling Distribution Assumptions

As shown in Table 1, confidence intervals are reported for metric correlations using ± notation. The use of the ± notation implies that the sampling distribution is symmetrical. Since the sampling distribution of the Pearson correlation, r, is skewed, however, this means that, for a non-zero correlation, it is not possible for the portion of the confidence interval that lies above the correlation sample point estimate and the portion that lies below it to be equal. Ad-

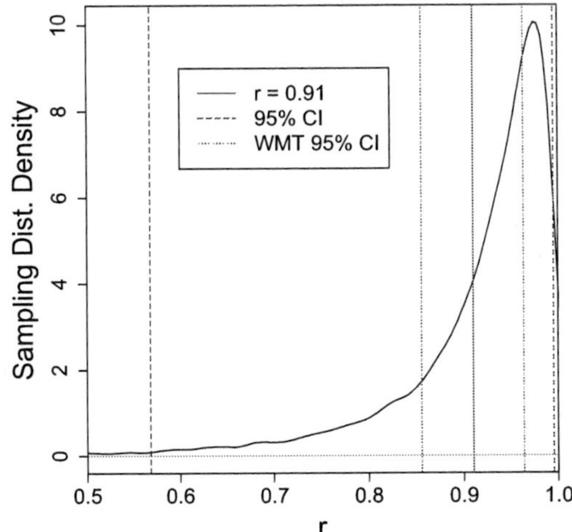

Figure 2: Sampling distribution of $r = 0.91$ and N = 5 for correlation of BLEU with human assessment for hypothetical "population" of MT systems in Figure 1.

ditionally, since the correlation sample statistic, r, cannot take on values greater than 1.0, the closer r is to 1.0 the more extreme the skew of its sampling distribution becomes.[1]

To demonstrate how the skew of the sampling distribution of r impacts on upper and lower confidence interval limits for metrics, in Figures 1 and 2, we simulate a possible population and sampling distribution for BLEU's correlation with human assessment, $r = 0.91$, achieved in WMT-14 Czech-to-English shared task, where the sample size, n, was 5 MT systems. Figure 1 depicts a hypothetical "population" of 10,000 MT systems and BLEU scores, where hypothetical BLEU scores for systems correspond with human assessment scores in such a way that a correlation of 0.91 is achieved. Figure 2 depicts the sampling distribution for r yielded by repeatedly drawing sets of 5 systems at random from the larger "population" of 10,000 systems, where the negative skew can be clearly observed. Figure 2 also depicts the 95% confidence interval (CI), within which 95% of sampled correlations lie, where the width of the lower portion of confidence interval is substantially wider than the upper portion, and the

overly conservative confidence interval reported for BLEU in WMT-14, where upper and lower portions of the confidence interval are incorrectly assumed to be equal in size.

2.2 Application of Bootstrap Resampling

A conventional approach to bootstrap resampling for the purpose of computing confidence intervals for a correlation sample point estimate is to create a correlation coefficient pseudo-distribution by sampling (at random with replacement) human and automatic scores for n MT systems from the set of n systems for which we have genuine metric and human scores. Instead, however, reported confidence intervals are the result of creating pseudo-distributions of human assessment scores for systems. The method unfortunately does not produce accurate confidence intervals for correlation sample point estimates, as confidence intervals produced in this way can unfortunately only inform us about the certainty surrounding human assessment scores for systems rather than the more relevant question of the certainty surrounding the correlation point estimates achieved by metrics. Confidence intervals computed in this way are substantially narrower than confidence intervals computed using the standard Fisher r-to-z transformation, that can also be directly applied to correlations of metrics with human assessment without application of randomized methods.

Table 2[2] includes reported confidence intervals of metric correlations for English-to-Czech in WMT-15, and those computed using the standard Fisher r-to-z transformation, where confidence intervals of the latter are substantially wider. An extreme example occurs for metric DREEM, where the difference between its original reported lower confidence interval limit and the correlation point estimate is 0.006, more than 34 times narrower than that computed with the Fisher r-to-z transformation, 0.206.

2.3 Difference in Dependent Correlations

When reporting the outcome of an empirical evaluation, along with sample point estimates, such as the mean or, in the case of metrics, correlation, we only

---

[1]It should be noted that the assumption of symmetry of the sampling distribution of r is not explicitly made in any WMT report.

[2]WMT confidence intervals have been recomputed from the published data set to remove the previously described error with respect to the symmetry of r's sampling distribution.

Metric	r	Method	Low. CI (-)	Upper CI (+)
CHRF3	0.977	WMT	0.003	0.002
		Fisher	0.046	0.015
CHRF	0.971	WMT	0.003	0.003
		Fisher	0.059	0.020
RATATOUILLE	0.965	WMT	0.003	0.003
		Fisher	0.071	0.024
BEER	0.962	WMT	0.004	0.003
		Fisher	0.076	0.026
METEORWSD	0.953	WMT	0.004	0.003
		Fisher	0.093	0.032
LEBLEU-DEF.	0.953	WMT	0.004	0.003
		Fisher	0.091	0.031
BS	0.953	WMT	0.004	0.003
		Fisher	0.032	0.092
BLEU	0.936	WMT	0.005	0.004
		Fisher	0.123	0.043
PER	0.908	WMT	0.005	0.004
		Fisher	0.168	0.062
DREEM	0.883	WMT	0.006	0.006
		Fisher	0.206	0.078

Table 2: WMT and Fisher r-to-z (Fisher) confidence intervals (CI) for Pearson correlation, ρ, in WMT-15 sample of English-to-Czech metrics (15 MT systems).

ever have access to a *sample* of the actual data that would be needed to compute the corresponding true value for the *population*. Confidence intervals provide a way of estimating the range of values within which we believe with a specified degree of certainty that the corresponding true value lies. Generally speaking, they can also provide a mechanism for drawing conclusions about significant differences in sample statistics. If, for example, mean scores are used to measure system performance, and the confidence intervals of a pair of systems do not overlap, a significant difference in sample means and subsequently system performance can be concluded.

Although confidence intervals for individual correlations do provide an indication of the degree of certainty with which we should interpret reported correlation sample point estimates, they unfortunately cannot be used in the above described way to conclude significant differences in the performance of metrics, however. All we can gain from confidence intervals for *individual* correlations with respect to significance differences is the following: if the confidence interval of a correlation sample point estimate does not include zero, then it can be concluded (with a specified degree of certainty) that this *individual* correlation is significantly different from *zero*. Confidence intervals for individual metric correlations with human assessment do not inform us about the certainty surrounding a *difference* in correlation with human assessment, the relevant question for comparing performance of competing MT metrics.

When computing confidence intervals for a difference in correlation, it is important to consider the nature of the data. For MT metric evaluation, data used to compute correlation point estimates for a given pair of metrics is *dependent*, as it includes three variables (Human, Metric_a, Metric_b), and, for each MT system that is a member of the sample, there is a value corresponding to each of these three variables. Besides the two correlations we are interested in comparing, $r(\text{Human}, \text{Metric}_a)$ and $r(\text{Human}, \text{Metric}_b)$, there is a third correlation to consider, therefore, the correlation that exists directly between the metric scores themselves, $r(\text{Metric}_a, \text{Metric}_b)$. Graham and Baldwin (2014) provide detail of Williams test, a test of significance of a difference in *dependent* correlations, suitable for evaluation of MT metrics. Confidence intervals are more informative than the binary conclusions that can be inferred from p-values produced by significance tests, however, and Zou (2007) presents a method of constructing confidence intervals for differences in *dependent* correlations also suitable for evaluation of MT metrics. We provide an implementation of Zou (2007) tailored to metric evaluation at `https://github.com/ygraham/MT-metric-confidence-intervals`.

Table 3 includes confidence intervals for differences in dependent correlations (Zou, 2007) for the seven top-performing German-to-English metrics in WMT-15. Besides providing an indication of the degree of certainty surrounding a given difference in correlation for a pair of metrics, confidence intervals that do not include *zero* can now be used to infer a significant difference in performance for a pair of metrics. For example, the 95% confidence interval for the difference in correlation between the top-performing metric, UPFCOBALT ($r = 0.981$) and METEORWSD ($r = 0.953$), [0.005, 0.123], in Table 3, does not include zero and subsequently implies a significant difference in performance.

Figure 3 depicts the contrast in conclusions for

	DPMFCOMB ($r = 0.973$)	DPMF ($r = 0.960$)	UOWLSTM ($r = 0.960$)	RATATOUILLE ($r = 0.958$)	CHRF3 ($r = 0.956$)	METEORWSD ($r = 0.953$)
($r = 0.981$) UPFCOBALT	$[-0.023, 0.061]$	$[-0.004, 0.101]$	$[-0.013, 0.106]$	$[-0.010, 0.109]$	$[-0.001, 0.114]$	**$[\ 0.005, 0.123]$**
DPMFCOMB	-	$[-0.025, 0.087]$	$[-0.032, 0.092]$	$[-0.026, 0.093]$	$[-0.024, 0.101]$	$[-0.017, 0.109]$
DPMF	-	-	$[-0.070, 0.073]$	$[-0.067, 0.075]$	$[-0.061, 0.079]$	$[-0.054, 0.087]$
UOWLSTM	-	-	-	$[-0.071, 0.077]$	$[-0.069, 0.084]$	$[-0.066, 0.094]$
RATATOUILLE	-	-	-	-	$[-0.072, 0.082]$	$[-0.064, 0.088]$
CHRF3	-	-	-	-	-	$[-0.067, 0.081]$

Table 3: Pairwise 95% confidence intervals for differences in correlation for seven top-performing metrics for German-to-English in WMT-15 (13 MT systems), confidence intervals not including zero imply a significant difference and are highlighted in bold.

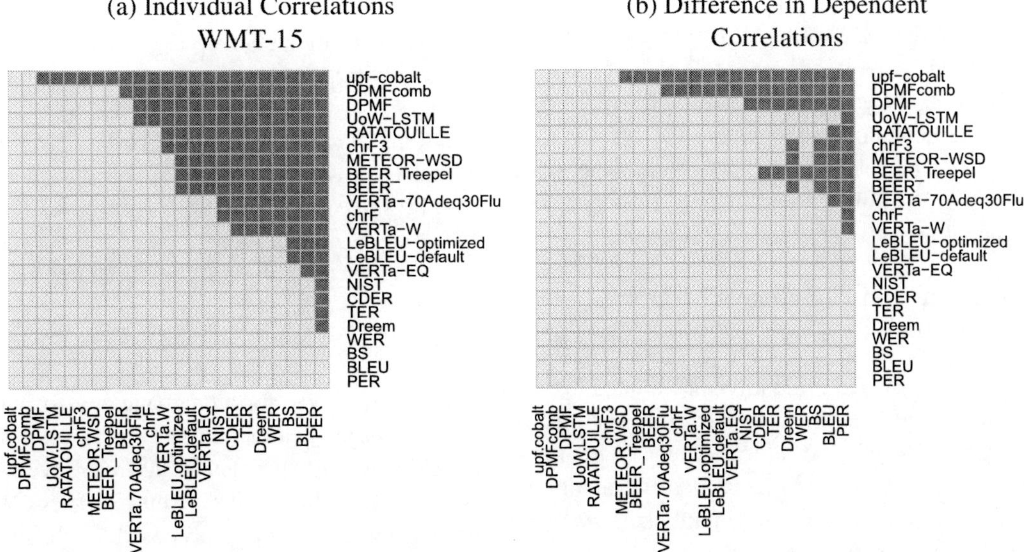

Figure 3: Conclusions of significant differences in correlation for WMT-15 German-to-English metrics (13 MT systems) drawn from the (a) non-overlap of individual correlation confidence intervals originally reported in WMT and from (b) confidence intervals of a difference in dependent correlations not including zero, green cells imply a significant win for the metric in that row over the metric in that column.

WMT-15 German-to-English metrics drawn from (a) a likely interpretation of confidence intervals originally reported in WMT, where the non-overlap of individual correlation confidence intervals of a pair of metrics is used to infer a significant difference, and (b) those drawn from the non-overlap of confidence intervals for differences in dependent correlations with zero (Zou, 2007), highlighting the over-estimation of significant differences in metric performance risked by current WMT confidence intervals. For example, for German-to-English with interpretation (a) a total of 91 significant differences are implied that are not identified according to our corresponding approach. For instance, the non-overlap of confidence intervals of the top-performing metric, UPFCOBALT, with those of all but one other metrics in the original report risks the interpretation of a significant increase in performance for that metric with all but one other competing metrics, but with the more appropriate method of Zou (2007), however, confidence intervals of this metric's difference in correlation with four of those competing metrics in fact include zero, with no significant difference identified. It is worth noting that original WMT reports *do not* state that the confidence intervals they provide *should* be interpreted in the way we have done here, where the non-overlap of individual correlation confidence intervals of a pair of metrics implies a significant difference, but this is nonetheless a very likely interpretation.

3 Accurate and Conclusive Metric Evaluations

Results of past metric evaluations have been highly inconclusive with relatively few significant differences in performance possible to identify for metrics.[3] The lack of conclusivity in metric evaluations is mainly caused by the small number of systems used to evaluate metrics. For example, in the original experiments used to justify the use of automatic metric BLEU, reported correlations with human as-

sessment were for a sample size of as small as 5, comprising three automatic systems and two human translators (Papineni et al., 2001). WMT have improved on this for some language pairs at least, as in the past four evaluations sample sizes have ranged from 5 (Czech-to-English WMT-14) to 22 systems (German-to-English WMT-12/WMT-13). Even at the maximum sample size of 22 systems, however, correlation point estimates are computed with a high degree of uncertainty.

3.1 Hybrid Super-Sampling

In an ideal world, MT metric evaluations would employ a much larger sample of systems than those relied upon in past evaluations, subsequently yielding correlation sample point estimates that can be relied on with more certainty. Although not immediately obvious, data sets currently used to evaluate MT metrics potentially contain data for a very large number of systems. If we consider the fact that, given the output of as little as two MT systems, there exists a very large number of possible ways of combining their translated segments to form a hybrid system, this opens up the evaluation of metrics to a vastly larger pool of systems. For example, even if we restrict the creation of hybrid systems to combinations of *pairs* of the n MT systems competing in a translation shared task (as opposed to hybrids created by sampling translations from *several* different MT systems at once), the number of potential hybrid systems is exponential in size of the test set, m:

$$n(n-1)/2 \cdot 2^m \tag{1}$$

For instance, even for a language pair for which human scores are available for as few as 5 MT systems, by *super-sampling* translations from every pair of competing systems, this results in 10 x $2^{3,000}$ hybrid systems. Including all possible hybrid systems is of course not necessary, and to make the approach feasible, we sample a large but manageable subset of 10,000 MT systems.

Obtaining automatic metric scores for this larger number of MT systems is feasible for any metric that is expected to be useful in practice, since automatic metrics must already be highly efficient to be used for optimizing systems. Obtaining human assessment of this large set of hybrid systems may seem

---

[3]Due to space limitations, it was only possible to include confidence intervals for differences in correlation for a subset of German-to-English WMT-15 metrics (Figure 3). Confidence intervals for the the remaining metrics and language pairs are available at `https://github.com/ygraham/MT-metric-confidence-intervals` for which very few significant differences in performance are identified.

	Metric	r	CI of Difference in r with next best metric	r	CI of Difference in r with next best metric
	TERRORCAT	0.971	[−0.019 , 0.155]	0.960	[**0.028 , 0.030**]
	SAGANSTS	0.942	[−0.120 , 0.136]	0.932	[**0.006 , 0.011**]
	METEOR	0.938	[−0.086 , 0.172]	0.923	[**0.028 , 0.032**]
	POSF	0.919	[−0.134 , 0.184]	0.893	[**0.004 , 0.008**]
	SPEDE07FP	0.907	[−0.138 , 0.162]	0.887	[−0.001 , 0.003]
•	SPEDE08FP	0.897	[−0.142 , 0.202]	0.886	[**0.004 , 0.007**]
•	SPEDE07F	0.902	[−0.156 , 0.176]	0.880	[**0.003 , 0.006**]
•	SPEDE07PP	0.879	[−0.161 , 0.202]	0.876	[**0.007 , 0.007**]
•	SPEDE07P	0.870	[−0.188 , 0.196]	0.869	[**0.006 , 0.009**]
•	XENERRCATS	0.884	[−0.174 , 0.193]	0.862	[**0.011 , 0.015**]
•	AMBER	0.859	[−0.084 , 0.398]	0.849	[**0.008 , 0.011**]
•	WORDBLOCKERRCATS	0.868	[−0.183 , 0.220]	0.839	[**0.057 , 0.065**]
•	SIMPBLEU	0.770	[−0.210 , 0.318]	0.778	[**0.033 , 0.036**]
•	BLEU	0.741	-	0.744	[**0.008 , 0.016**]
•	BLOCKERRCATS	0.779	[−0.257 , 0.293]	0.731	-
			12 Systems		10k Systems

Table 4: Correlations and confidence intervals of pseudo document-level metrics (averaged segment-level metrics) with human assessment evaluated on original 12 MT systems and 10k hybrid super-sample (WMT-12 Spanish-to-English). Metrics with a different rank order in the original sample and hybrid super-sample evaluations are marked with • and confidence intervals that do not include zero are in bold.

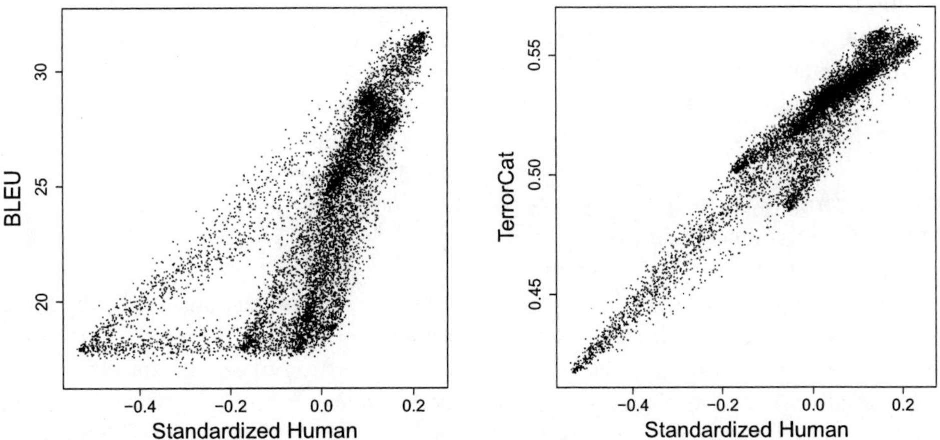

Figure 4: Human, TERRORCAT and BLEU scores for 10k super-sampled hybrid MT systems for WMT-12 Spanish-to-English.

more challenging, but the method of human evaluation we employ facilitates the straight-forward computation of human scores for vast numbers of systems directly from the original human evaluation of only n systems. Graham et al. (2013) provide a human evaluation of MT that elicits adequacy assessments of translations, independent of other translations on a fine-grained 100-point rating scale. After score standardization to iron-out differences in individual human assessor scoring strategies, the overall human score for a MT system is simply computed as the mean of the ratings attributed to its translations, and this facilitates the straight-forward computation of a human score for any hybrid system from the original human evaluation of n systems.

To demonstrate, we replicate a previous year's WMT metrics shared task, constructing a hybrid super-sample of 10,000 MT systems each with a corresponding metric and human score. Since we do not have access to all document-level metrics that participated in the original shared task, we use segment-level metric scores as *pseudo document-level metrics* by taking the average of segment-level scores of the segments that comprise the test set document. This allows retrospective computation of automatic metric scores for the large set of 10k hybrid MT systems. For the purpose of comparison, in addition to averaged segment-level metrics, we also include document-level BLEU and an analysis of the correlation it achieves in the context of hybrid super-sampling. Human evaluation scores were computed using the mean of a minimum of 1,500 crowd-sourced human ratings per system, where strict quality-controlling of crowd-sourced workers was applied.

Table 4 shows correlations achieved by metrics when evaluated on the original 12 and 10k systems, as well as confidence intervals of the difference in correlation achieved by each metric with that of the next best performing metric in each case.[4] As expected, confidence intervals for differences in correlation are substantially reduced for the larger sample of metrics. Importantly, the change in rank order of metrics when evaluated with reference to a sample

of 10k MT systems, as opposed to 12, highlights the risk of concluding an increase in performance from evaluations that include only a small sample of systems.

Figure 4 plots super-sampled human and automatic metric scores for BLEU providing insight into how BLEU scores correspond with human assessment. Worryingly for the range of systems with scores below 20 BLEU points, the plot shows an almost horizontal band of systems spread across a wide range of quality according to human assessors despite extremely similar BLEU scores. The top-performing automatic metric, TERRORCAT, on the other hand, impressively sustains its high correlation with human assessment when evaluated on as many as 10k MT systems, evidence that this metric is indeed highly consistent with human assessment of Spanish-to-English.

Due to space limitations, it is not possible to include pairwise confidence intervals for all pairs of metrics, and instead we include in Figure 5 a heatmap of significant differences in performance, where a significant win is inferred for the metric in a given row over the metric in a given column if the confidence interval of the difference in correlation for that pair did not include zero. Results show the super-sampled evaluation facilitates not only the identification of an outright best-performing metric, TERRORCAT, it also yields an almost total-order ranking of metrics, as significant differences are possible to identify for all but one pairs of competing metrics. Finally, we repeated the metric evaluation with ten distinct super-samples of 10k MT systems with all replications resulting in precisely the same ranking of metrics as shown in Table 4.

4   Conclusion

Analysis of evaluation methodologies applied to automatic MT metrics was provided and the risk of over-estimation of significant differences in metric performance identified. Confidence intervals for differences in dependent correlations were recommended as appropriate for evaluation of MT metrics. Hybrid super-sampling was proposed, evaluating metrics with reference to a substantially larger sample of MT systems, achieving genuinely highly conclusive metric rankings.

---

[4]It should be noted, since participating teams did not intend segment-level metric scores to be averaged as we have done here, correlations are for demonstrative purposes and do not reflect performance of participating teams.

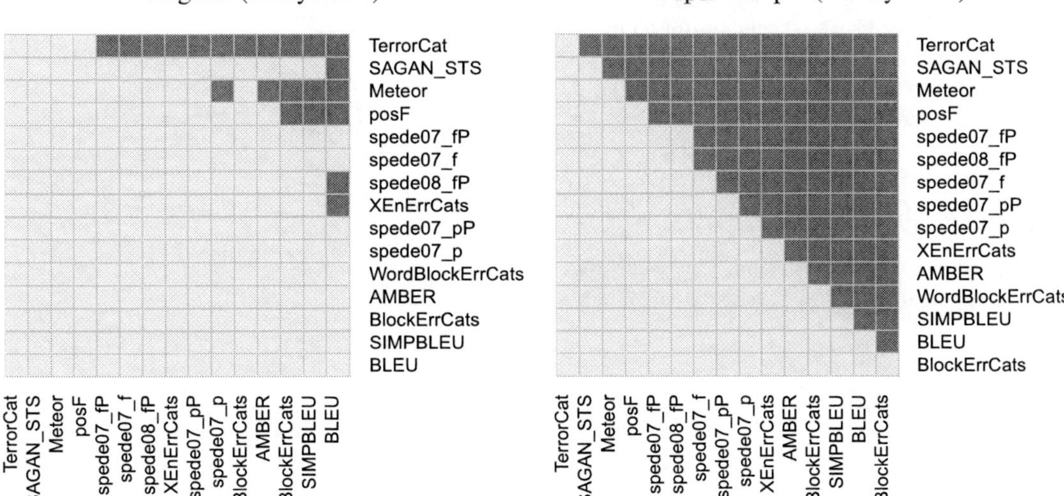

Figure 5: Pairwise conclusions for pseudo document-level metrics (averaged segment-level metrics) from WMT-12 Spanish-to-English metrics shared task, where a green cell indicates a significant win for the metric in a given row over the metric in the corresponding column.

Acknowledgments

We wish to thank the anonymous reviewers and Ondřej Bojar for valued feedback and WMT organisers for provision of data sets. This project has received funding from the European Union Horizon 2020 research and innovation programme under grant agreement 645452 (QT21) and the ADAPT Centre for Digital Content Technology (www.adaptcentre.ie) at Dublin City University funded under the SFI Research Centres Programme (Grant 13/RC/2106) co-funded under the European Regional Development Fund.

References

Ondřej Bojar, Rajen Chatterjee, Christian Federmann, Barry Haddow, Matthias Huck, Chris Hokamp, Philipp Koehn, Varvara Logacheva, Christof Monz, Matteo Negri, Matt Post, Carolina Scarton, Lucia Specia, and Marco Turchi. 2015. Findings of the 2015 Workshop on Statistical Machine Translation. In *Proceedings of the Tenth Workshop on Statistical Machine Translation*, pages 1–46, Lisbon, Portugal, September. Association for Computational Linguistics.

Yvette Graham and Timothy Baldwin. 2014. Testing for significance of increased correlation with human judgment. In *Proceedings of the Conference on Empirical Methods in Natural Language Processing*, pages 172–176, Doha, Qatar. Association for Computational Linguistics.

Yvette Graham, Timothy Baldwin, Alistair Moffat, and Justin Zobel. 2013. Continuous measurement scales in human evaluation of machine translation. In *Proceedings of the 7th Linguistic Annotation Workshop & Interoperability with Discourse*, pages 33–41, Sofia, Bulgaria. Association for Computational Linguistics.

Matouš Macháček and Ondřej Bojar. 2013. Results of the WMT13 metrics shared task. In *Proceedings of the Eighth Workshop on Statistical Machine Translation*, pages 45–51, Sofia, Bulgaria, August. Association for Computational Linguistics.

Matouš Macháček and Ondřej Bojar. 2014. Results of the WMT14 metrics shared task. In *Proceedings of the Ninth Workshop on Statistical Machine Translation*, pages 293–301, Baltimore, Maryland, USA, June. Association for Computational Linguistics.

Kishore Papineni, Salim Roukos, Todd Ward, and Wei-Jing Zhu. 2001. BLEU: A method for automatic evaluation of machine translation. Technical Report RC22176 (W0109-022), IBM Research, Thomas J. Watson Research Center.

Miloš Stanojević, Amir Kamran, Philipp Koehn, and Ondřej Bojar. 2015. Results of the WMT15 metrics shared task. In *Proceedings of the Tenth Workshop on*

Statistical Machine Translation, pages 256–273, Lisbon, Portugal, September. Association for Computational Linguistics.

Xiaofeng Wu, Hui Yu, and Qun Liu. 2014. RED, the DCU-CASICT submission of metrics tasks. In *Proceedings of the Ninth Workshop on Statistical Machine Translation*, pages 420–425, Baltimore, Maryland, USA, June. Association for Computational Linguistics.

Guang Yong Zou. 2007. Toward using confidence intervals to compare correlations. *Psychological Methods*, 12(4):399 – 413.

Flexible Non-Terminals for Dependency Tree-to-Tree Reordering

John Richardson[†], **Fabien Cromières**[‡], **Toshiaki Nakazawa**[‡] and **Sadao Kurohashi**[†]

[†]Graduate School of Informatics, Kyoto University, Kyoto 606-8501
[‡]Japan Science and Technology Agency, Kawaguchi-shi, Saitama 332-0012
`john@nlp.ist.i.kyoto-u.ac.jp`, `{fabien, nakazawa}@pa.jst.jp`,
`kuro@i.kyoto-u.ac.jp`

Abstract

A major benefit of tree-to-tree over tree-to-string translation is that we can use target-side syntax to improve reordering. While this is relatively simple for binarized constituency parses, the reordering problem is considerably harder for dependency parses, in which words can have arbitrarily many children. Previous approaches have tackled this problem by restricting grammar rules, reducing the expressive power of the translation model.

In this paper we propose a general model for dependency tree-to-tree reordering based on flexible non-terminals that can compactly encode multiple insertion positions. We explore how insertion positions can be selected even in cases where rules do not entirely cover the children of input sentence words. The proposed method greatly improves the flexibility of translation rules at the cost of only a 30% increase in decoding time, and we demonstrate a 1.2–1.9 BLEU improvement over a strong tree-to-tree baseline.

1 Introduction

Translation is most commonly performed by splitting an input sentence into manageable parts, translating these segments, then arranging them in an appropriate order. The first two steps have roughly the same difficulty for close and distant language pairs, however the reordering step is considerably more challenging for language pairs with dissimilar syntax. We need to be able to make linguistic generalizations, such as learning to translate between SVO and SOV clauses and converting post-modifying prepositional and pre-modifying postpositional phrases (Quirk et al., 2005). Such generalizations often require syntactically motivated long-distance reordering.

The first approaches to reordering were based on linear distortion (Koehn et al., 2003), which models the probability of swapping pairs of phrases over some given distance. The linear distance is the only parameter, ignoring any contextual information, however this model has been shown to work well for string-to-string translation. Linear reordering was improved with lexical distortion (Tillmann, 2004), which characterizes reordering in terms of type (monotone, swap, or discontinuous) as opposed to distance. This approach however is prone to sparsity problems, in particular for distant language pairs.

In order to improve upon linear string-based approaches, syntax-based approaches have also been proposed. Tree-to-string translation has been the most popular syntax-based paradigm in recent years, which is reflected by a number of reordering approaches considering source-only syntax (Liu et al., 2006; Neubig, 2013). One particularly interesting approach is to project source dependency parses to the target side and then learn a probability model for reordering children using features such as source and target head words (Quirk et al., 2005).

While tree-to-tree translation (Graehl and

Proceedings of NAACL-HLT 2016, pages 11–19,

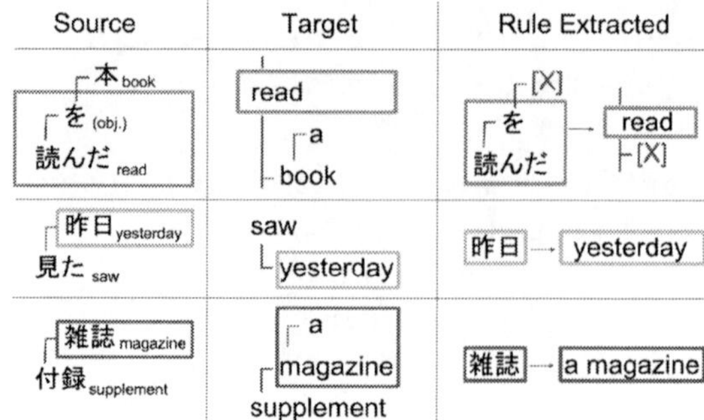

Figure 1: Examples of tree-to-tree translation rules extracted from an aligned and parsed bitext. Colored boxes represent aligned phrases and [X] is a non-terminal.

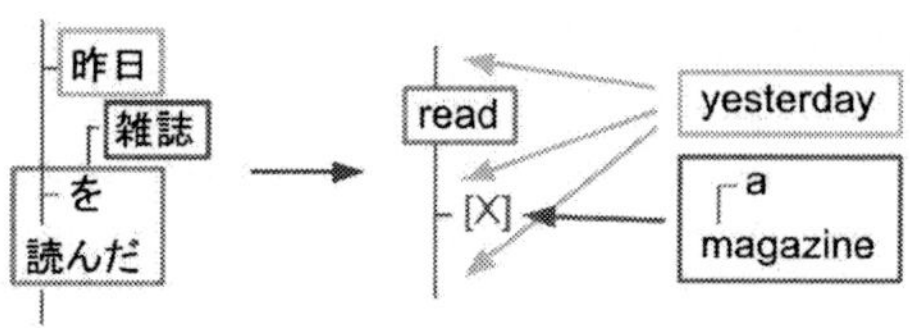

Figure 2: Combination of translation rules, demonstrating non-terminal substitution and multiple possible insertion positions for a non-matching input phrase ('昨日').

Knight, 2004; Cowan and Collins, 2006; Chiang, 2010) has been somewhat less popular than tree-to-string translation, we believe there are many benefits of considering target-side syntax. In particular, reordering can be defined naturally with non-terminals in the target-side grammar. This is relatively simple when the target structure of rules is restricted to 'well-formed' dependencies (Shen et al., 2008), however in this paper we consider more general rules with flexible non-terminal insertion positions.

2 Dependency Tree-To-Tree Translation

Dependency tree-to-tree translation begins with the extraction of translation rules from a bilingual corpus that has been parsed and word aligned. Figure 1 shows an example of three rules that can be extracted from aligned and parsed sentence pairs. In this paper we consider rules similar to previous work on tree-to-tree de-

pendency MT (Richardson et al., 2014).

The simplest type of rule, containing only terminal symbols, can be extracted trivially from aligned subtrees (see rules 2 and 3 in Figure 1). Non-terminals can be added to rules (see rule 1 in Figure 1) by omitting aligned subtrees and replacing on each side with non-terminal symbols. We can naturally express phrase reordering as the source/target-side non-terminals are aligned.

Decoding is performed by combining these rules to form a complete translation, as shown in Figure 2. We are able to translate part of the sentence with non-ambiguous reordering ('read a magazine'), as we can insert '雑誌 → a magazine' into the rule '[X] を 読んだ → read [X]'.

We cannot however decide clearly where to insert the rule '昨日 → yesterday' as there is no matching non-terminal in the rule containing its parent in the input sentence ('読んだ'). We use the term *floating* to describe words such as 'yesterday' in this example, i.e. for an input subtree matched to the source side of a rule, children of the input root that are not contained in the source side of the rule as terminals and cannot be inserted using fixed-position non-terminals in the rule.

Previous work deals with this problem by either using simple glue rules (Chiang, 2005) or limiting rules in a way to avoid isolated floating children (Shen et al., 2008). For example, it is possible to disallow the first rule in Figure 1 when translating a sentence such as that in Figure 2 with uncovered children (in this case the word 'yesterday'). This method greatly reduces the expressiveness and flexibility of translation rules.

In our generalized model, we allow any number of terminals and non-terminals and permit arbitrarily many floating children in each rule. To our knowledge this is the first study to take this more comprehensive approach.

Note that in the case of constituency-based tree-to-tree translation it is possible to binarize the input tree and therefore gluing floating children becomes simpler, as we only have to choose between pre-insertion and post-insertion. In the dependency case it is in general much more dif-

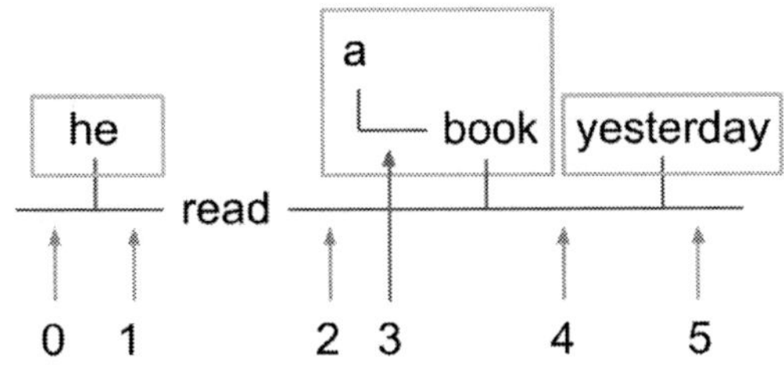

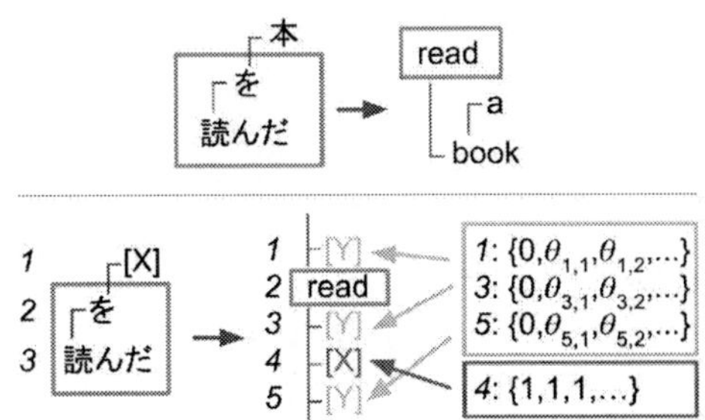

Figure 3: Possible insertion positions for flexible non-terminals with target-side head 'read'. Allowed positions are shown in green and disallowed positions are shown in red. We do not allow insertion position 3 because it could allow a non-projective dependency structure.

ficult because we must order an arbitrarily large group of children sharing a common head.

3 Flexible Non-Terminals

In this paper we propose flexible non-terminals in order to create generalized tree-to-tree translation rules that can overcome the problems described in the previous section. Rather than fixed insertion positions for child nodes, we instead consider multiple possible insertion positions and give features to each position. These are stored in a compact representation allowing for efficient decoding.

We define *flexible non-terminals* as non-terminals with multiple possible insertion positions and associated features. During decoding we select the most promising insertion position for each non-terminal.

3.1 Rule Augmentation

As is standard practice in phrase-based SMT, before translation we filter translation rules to those relevant to the input sentence. At this time, for each accepted rule we check the input sentence for floating children, and flexible non-terminals are added for each floating child.

We allow all insertion positions between the children (along with their descendants) of the target-side head for each floating child, including insertion before the first child and after the last child. We do not allow insertion positions between deeper descendants of the head to avoid

Figure 4: Example of translation rule with flexible non-terminals generated from the first parallel sentence in Figure 1. [X] has a fixed position (4) but [Y] can have multiple positions (1, 3, 5). Each position has an associated set of features shown in curly brackets, where $\theta_{i,j}$ is the jth feature for insertion position i. The first feature (0 or 1) shows whether the insertion position is unambiguous.

non-projective dependencies. See Figure 3 for an example of allowed/disallowed positions.

Features are then set for each insertion position and these are used to determine the best insertion position during decoding (see Section 3.2). Figure 4 shows an example of the proposed rule augmentation.

3.2 Features

In previous work reordering is mostly decided by the combination of a standard distortion model and language model to score possible insertion positions. We instead consider the following four features and combine them during decoding to find the most appropriate insertion positions for floating children. All features are real numbers between 0 and 1.

3.2.1 Insertion Position Features

We first define a set of features to estimate the likelihood of each insertion position for some given non-terminal. The features for inserting the translation f of a source phrase into the target-side e of a rule at insertion position i are defined as follows, for surface forms (S) and POS tags (P):

- Reordering probability:
  $P_S(i \mid f, e)$, $P_P(i \mid f, e)$

- Marginalized over target-side:
  $P_S(i \mid f)$, $P_P(i \mid f)$

- Marginalized over source-side:
  $P_S(i \mid e)$, $P_P(i \mid e)$

The probabilities $P(i \mid X)$ are calculated by counting insertions of X in each position i across the whole training corpus (aligned and parsed bitext). The exact formula is given below, for position i (X is one of $\{f\}$, $\{e\}$ or $\{f, e\}$):

$$P(i \mid X) = \frac{count(i, X)}{\sum_j count(j, X)} \qquad (1)$$

Instead of applying smoothing, in order to reduce sparsity issues we use both the full probability $P(i \mid f, e)$ and also probabilities marginalized over the source/target phrases. We also consider both probabilities trained on surface forms (S) and POS tags (P).

While traditional models use linear distance for i, this is impractical for long-distance reordering. Instead we restrict insertion types i to one of the following 6 types: first-pre-child, mid-pre-child, final-pre-child, first-post-child, mid-post-child, and final-post-child. These correspond to the first (first), last (final) or central (mid) children on the left (pre) or right (post) side of the parent word. We found this was more effective than using either linear distance or a binary (pre/post) position type.

3.2.2 Relative Position Feature

We also consider a relative position, or 'swapping' feature, inspired by the swap operation of classic lexical distortion (Tillmann, 2004).

Let T be the children of the root word of the target-side of a rule. We also include in T a pseudo-token M splitting the left and right children of the target-side root to differentiate between pre-insertion and post-insertion.

We first learn a model describing the probability of the translation of input phrase I appearing to the left ($P_L(I, t)$) or right ($P_R(I, t)$) of word t in the target-side of a translation rule. The probabilities are calculated by counting occurrences of I being translated to the left/right sides of t over the aligned and parsed training bitext.

The relative position feature is calculated by considering the relative position of the translation of I with all the target-side root children T. For each insertion position i, let $T_{i,L}$ be the $t \in T$ to the left of position i and $T_{i,R}$ the $t \in T$ to the right of position i. Then we have:

$$P(i \mid I, T) = \prod_{t \in T_{i,R}} P_L(I, t) \prod_{t \in T_{i,L}} P_R(I, t) \qquad (2)$$

3.2.3 Left/Right Attachment Preference

We also set an attachment direction preference feature for each rule, specifying whether we prefer to insert the rule as a left child or right child of the root of a parent rule.

The attachment preference is determined by the position of the target-side of the rule in the target-side of the parallel sentence from which it was extracted. For example, in Figure 1 the rule '昨日 → yesterday' was extracted from a parallel sentence in which 'yesterday' was a right-side child of its head ('saw'), so we set the attachment preference to 'right'. In cases when we cannot determine the attachment preference (for example 'read' in the first rule in Figure 1), because it is the sentence root), we arbitrarily choose 'right'.

3.2.4 Unambiguous Insertion Preference

In cases where we have a single unambiguous insertion position for a non-terminal (e.g. [X] in Figure 4), we set an additional binary feature to the value 1 (otherwise 0) to specify that this position is unambiguous. We found that a large positive weight is almost always given to this feature, which is to be expected as we would prefer to use fixed non-terminals if possible. We set all features related to insertion position choice to the maximum value (1).

3.3 Decoding

The flexible non-terminals that we are proposing can lead to some interesting challenges when it comes to decoding. A naive approach is to expand each translation rule containing flexible non-terminals into a set of 'simple' rules with fixed non-terminals, and then apply classic decoding with cube-pruning.

However, this can be quite inefficient in practice. Due to the combinatorial aspect, a single rule can expand into a very large number of simple rules. It is common for our translation rules to have more than four flexible non-terminals, each with more than four possible insertion positions. Such rules will already generate hundreds of simple rules. In the most extreme cases, we may encounter rules having more than ten flexible non-terminals, leading to the generation of many millions of simple rules. This explosion of rules can lead to impractical decoding time and memory usage.

It is therefore important to make use of the compact encoding of many simple rules provided by the concept of flexible non-terminals in the decoding process itself. We use the decoding approach of right-hand lattices (Cromières and Kurohashi, 2014), an efficient way of encoding many simple rules. The idea is to encode the translation rules into a lattice form, then use this lattice to decode efficiently without the need to expand the flexible non-terminals explicitly.

Figure 5 shows how the concept of flexible non-terminals can be efficiently encoded into lattice form. The top half shows a target-side tree translation rule with flexible non-terminals X1, X2, X3 and X4 allowed to be inserted at any position that is a child of the word 'a', with the constraint that X1 comes before X2 and that X2 comes before X3. X5 is another flexible non-terminal that will be a child of the word 'f'. The lower half shows a lattice compactly encoding all the possible combinations of non-terminal positions. Each path from the top-left to the bottom right in this lattice represents a choice for the insertion positions of the non-terminals. For example, the path marked with a dotted line represents the flattened sequence 'b c X1 X2 a X3 X4 d e f X5 g'. The lattice form has only 48 edges, while an explicit enumeration of all combinations of insertion positions for the flexible non-terminals would force the decoder to consider $^{8}C_{4} \times 3 \times 12 = 2520$ edges.

The insertion position features described above are added to the edges of the lattice. They are combined alongside the standard set of features, such as word penalty and language model

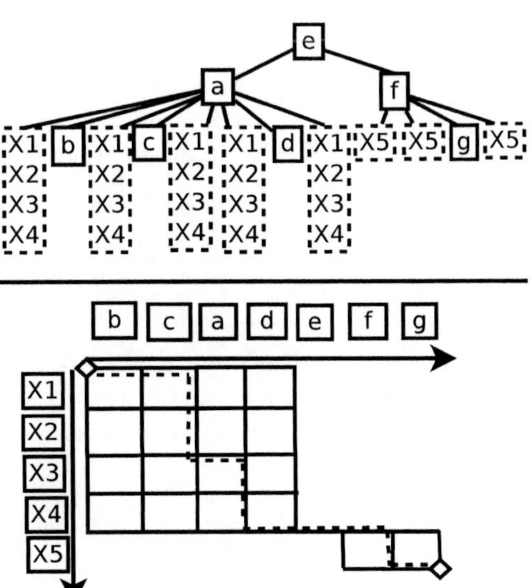

Figure 5: Example showing how a rule containing many flexible non-terminals is encoded into lattice form for decoding.

	JA–EN	EN–JA	JA–ZH	ZH–JA
Train	3M	3M	676K	676K
Dev	1790	1790	2123	2123
Test	1812	1812	2171	2171

Table 1: Translation experiment data (number of sentences).

score, using a standard log-linear model. The weights for the reordering features are tuned together with the standard features.

4   Experiments

4.1   Data and Settings

We performed translation experiments on four distant language pairs, Japanese–English (JA–EN), English–Japanese (EN–JA), Japanese–Chinese (JA–ZH) and Chinese–Japanese (ZH–JA), from the Asian Scientific Paper Excerpt Corpus (ASPEC)[1]. The data was split into training, development and test folds as shown in Table 1.

Our experiments were conducted using a state-of-the-art dependency tree-to-tree framework KyotoEBMT (Richardson et al., 2014).

---

[1] http://lotus.kuee.kyoto-u.ac.jp/ASPEC/

	JA–EN		EN–JA		JA–ZH		ZH–JA	
	BLEU	RIBES	BLEU	RIBES	BLEU	RIBES	BLEU	RIBES
Moses	18.09	63.97	27.48	68.37	27.96	79.03	34.65	77.25
Baseline	19.97	65.10	28.41	74.78	28.13	78.00	33.51	77.86
Flexible	21.23†	69.94†	**30.11†**	**77.11†**	29.42†	80.44†	35.37†	81.33†
+Pref	**21.66‡**	70.73‡	29.90†	76.85†	29.48†	80.43†	35.57‡	81.79‡
+Pref+Ins	21.47‡	**70.85‡**	30.03†	77.01†	29.64†	**80.65†**	35.71‡	**82.05‡**
+Pref+Ins+Rel	21.34†	70.69‡	29.99†	76.93†	**29.78‡**	80.51†	**35.81‡**	81.95‡

Table 2: Automatic evaluation of translation quality (BLEU and RIBES). Results marked with † are significantly higher than the baseline system and those marked with ‡ are significantly higher than the proposed system with no insertion position features ('Flexible'). Significance was calculated with bootstrapping for $p < 0.05$.

Experiments were performed with the default settings by adding the proposed non-terminal reordering features to the rules extracted with the baseline system. We used lattice-based decoding (Cromières and Kurohashi, 2014) to support multiple non-terminal insertion positions and default tuning using, k-best MIRA (Cherry and Foster, 2012). Dependency parsing was performed with: KNP (Kawahara and Kurohashi, 2006) (Japanese), SKP (Shen et al., 2012) (Chinese), NLParser (Charniak and Johnson, 2005) (English, converted to dependencies with hand-written rules). Alignment was performed with Nile (Riesa et al., 2011) and we used a 5-gram language model with modified Kneser-Ney smoothing built with KenLM (Heafield, 2011).

4.2 Evaluation

As our baseline ('Baseline'), we used the default tree-to-tree settings and features of KyotoEBMT, allowing only fixed-position non-terminals. We dealt with floating children not covered by any other rules by adding glue rules similar to those in hierarchical SMT (Chiang, 2005), joining floating children to the rightmost slots in the target-side parent. For reference, we also show results using Moses (Koehn et al., 2007) with default settings and distortion limit set to 20 ('Moses').

The proposed system ('Flexible') adds flexible non-terminals with multiple insertion positions, however we do not yet add the insertion choice features. This means that the insertion positions are in practice chosen by the language model. Note that we do not get a substantial hit in performance by adding the flexible non-terminals because of their compact lattice representation. The systems '+Pref', '+Pref+Ins' and '+Pref+Ins+Rel' show the results of adding insertion choice position features (left/right preference, insertion position choice, relative position choice).

We give translation scores measured in BLEU (Papineni et al., 2002) and RIBES (Isozaki et al., 2010), which is designed to reflect quality of translation word order more effectively than BLEU. The translation evaluation is shown in Table 2.

5 Discussion and Error Analysis

The experimental results showed a significantly positive improvement in terms of both BLEU and RIBES over the baseline tree-to-tree system. The baseline system uses fixed non-terminals and is competitive with the most popular string-to-string system (Moses).

The extensions of the proposed model (adding a variety of features) also all showed significant improvement over the baseline, and approximately half of the extended settings performed significantly better than the core proposed model. It is unclear however which of the extended settings is the most effective for all language pairs. There are a number of factors such as parse quality, corpus size and out-of-vocabulary occurrence that could affect the potential value of these features. Furthermore, Japanese is strongly left-branching (head-final), so the left/right preference distinction is likely to be less useful than for English and Chinese, which contain both left-branching and right-branching structures.

Compared to the baseline, the flexible non-terminals gave around a 1.2–1.9 BLEU improvement at the cost of only a 30% increase in decoding time (approximately 2.04 vs. 2.66 seconds per sentence). This is made possible by the compact non-terminal representation combined with lattice decoding.

5.1 Non-Terminal Matching Analysis

We found that roughly half of all our translation rules were augmented with flexible non-terminals, with one flexible non-terminal added per rule on average. This led to roughly half of non-terminals having flexible insertion positions. The decoder chose to use ambiguous insertion positions between 30%–60% of the time (depending on language pair), allowing for many more new translation hypotheses than the baseline system. For detailed results, see Table 3.

5.2 Translation Examples

The following translation is an example of an improvement achieved by using the proposed flexible non-terminals. There were multiple word order errors in the baseline translation that impeded understanding, and these have all been corrected.

- **Input:** 磁場入口と出口の温度差により生ずる磁性流体の圧力差と流速を測定した。

- **Reference:** The pressure difference and the flow velocity of the magnetized fluid caused by the temperature difference between the inlet and outlet of the magnetic field were measured.

- **Baseline:** We have measured the pressure difference and flow rate of a magnetic fluid generated by an entrance of a magnet and an exit temperature, and the difference between.

- **Proposed:** The pressure difference and the flow rate of a magnetic fluid generated by the temperature difference between the magnetic field inlet and exit were measured.

There are also cases where the proposed model decreases translation quality. In the example below, the proposed system output was selected by the decoder since it had a higher language model score than the baseline output, despite having incorrect word order. The incorrect translation was made available by the increased flexibility of the proposed model, and selected because the LM feature had a higher impact than the insertion position features.

- **Input:** このソフトウエアのR5バージョンの特徴，利用マニュアルと設計文書をまとめた。

- **Reference:** The characteristics of R5 version of this software, instruction manual, and design document were summarized.

- **Baseline:** The R5 version of this software features, the manual for the utilization and design documents are summarized.

- **Proposed:** This software design documents of R5 version features, the manual for the utilization and summarized.

6 Conclusion and Future Work

In this paper we have proposed flexible non-terminals for dependency tree-to-tree translation. We plan to continue working on feature design for insertion position choice, and in the future would like to consider using neural networks for learning these features. We believe that it is important to continue to explore approaches that exploit more general target-side syntax, faithful to the tree-to-tree translation paradigm.

Flexible non-terminals allow multiple insertion positions to be expressed compactly and selected with features based on both source and target syntax. We have shown that a significant improvement in BLEU and RIBES scores can be gained by using the proposed model to increase the generality of dependency tree-to-tree translation rules.

Acknowledgments

We would like to thank the anonymous reviewers for their feedback.

	JA–EN	EN–JA	JA–ZH	ZH–JA
% rules with flexible NTs	53.2	70.4	55.7	61.2
Average flexible NTs per rule	0.973	1.11	0.977	1.05
% all NTs that are flexible	48.0	48.6	54.5	56.1
% selected NTs that are flexible	32.2	35.1	40.5	58.4

Table 3: Results of non-terminal (NT) matching analysis.

References

Eugene Charniak and Mark Johnson. 2005. Coarse-to-fine n-best parsing and maxent discriminative reranking. In *Proceedings of the 43rd Annual Meeting on Association for Computational Linguistics*, ACL '05, pages 173–180. Association for Computational Linguistics.

Colin Cherry and George Foster. 2012. Batch tuning strategies for statistical machine translation. In *Proceedings of the 2012 Conference of the North American Chapter of the Association for Computational Linguistics: Human Language Technologies*, pages 427–436, Montréal, Canada, June. Association for Computational Linguistics.

David Chiang. 2005. A hierarchical phrase-based model for statistical machine translation. In *Proceedings of the 43rd Annual Meeting of the Association for Computational Linguistics (ACL'05)*, pages 263–270.

David Chiang. 2010. Learning to translate with source and target syntax. In *Proceedings of the 48th Annual Meeting of the Association for Computational Linguistics*, pages 1443–1452, Uppsala, Sweden, July. Association for Computational Linguistics.

Brooke Cowan and Michael Collins. 2006. A discriminative model for tree-to-tree translation. In *EMNLP*, pages 232–241.

Fabien Cromières and Sadao Kurohashi. 2014. Translation rules with right-hand side lattices. In *Proceedings of the 2014 Conference on Empirical Methods in Natural Language Processing (EMNLP)*, pages 577–588, Doha, Qatar, October. Association for Computational Linguistics.

Jonathan Graehl and Kevin Knight. 2004. Training tree transducers. In *HLT-NAACL 2004: Main Proceedings*, pages 105–112, Boston, Massachusetts, USA, May 2 - May 7. Association for Computational Linguistics.

Kenneth Heafield. 2011. KenLM: Faster and smaller language model queries. In *Proceedings of the Sixth Workshop on Statistical Machine Translation*.

Hideki Isozaki, Tsutomu Hirao, Kevin Duh, Katsuhito Sudoh, and Hajime Tsukada. 2010. Automatic evaluation of translation quality for distant language pairs. In *Proceedings of the 2010 Conference on Empirical Methods in Natural Language Processing*, pages 944–952, Cambridge, MA, October. Association for Computational Linguistics.

Daisuke Kawahara and Sadao Kurohashi. 2006. A fully-lexicalized probabilistic model for Japanese syntactic and case structure analysis. In *Proceedings of the Main Conference on Human Language Technology Conference of the North American Chapter of the Association of Computational Linguistics*, HLT-NAACL '06, pages 176–183. Association for Computational Linguistics.

P. Koehn, F.J. Och, and D. Marcu. 2003. Statistical Phrase-Based Translation. In *NAACL '03: Proceedings of the 2003 Conference of the North American Chapter of the Association for Computational Linguistics on Human Language Technology*, pages 48–54, Morristown, NJ. Association for Computational Linguistics, Association for Computational Linguistics.

Philipp Koehn, Hieu Hoang, Alexandra Birch, Chris Callison-Burch, Marcello Federico, Nicola Bertoldi, Brooke Cowan, Wade Shen, Christine Moran, Richard Zens, Chris Dyer, Ondřej Bojar, Alexandra Constantin, and Evan Herbst. 2007. Moses: Open source toolkit for statistical machine translation. In *Proceedings of the 45th Annual Meeting of the ACL on Interactive Poster and Demonstration Sessions*, ACL '07, pages 177–180, Stroudsburg, PA, USA. Association for Computational Linguistics.

Yang Liu, Qun Liu, and Shouxun Lin. 2006. Tree-to-string alignment template for statistical machine translation. In *Proceedings of the 21st International Conference on Computational Linguistics and 44th Annual Meeting of the Association for Computational Linguistics*, pages 609–616, Sydney, Australia, July. Association for Computational Linguistics.

Graham Neubig. 2013. Travatar: A forest-to-string machine translation engine based on tree transducers. In *ACL (Conference System Demonstra-*

tions), pages 91–96. The Association for Computational Linguistics.

Kishore Papineni, Salim Roukos, Todd Ward, and Wei-Jing Zhu. 2002. BLEU: A method for automatic evaluation of machine translation. In *Proceedings of the 40th Annual Meeting on Association for Computational Linguistics*, pages 311–318. Association for Computational Linguistics.

Chris Quirk, Arul Menezes, and Colin Cherry. 2005. Dependency treelet translation: Syntactically informed phrasal SMT. In *Proceedings of the 43rd Annual Meeting of the Association for Computational Linguistics (ACL'05)*, pages 271–279.

John Richardson, Fabien Cromières, Toshiaki Nakazawa, and Sadao Kurohashi. 2014. KyotoEBMT: An example-based dependency-to-dependency translation framework. In *Proceedings of 52nd Annual Meeting of the Association for Computational Linguistics: System Demonstrations*, pages 79–84, Baltimore, Maryland, June. Association for Computational Linguistics.

Jason Riesa, Ann Irvine, and Daniel Marcu. 2011. Feature-rich language-independent syntax-based alignment for statistical machine translation. In *Proceedings of the Conference on Empirical Methods in Natural Language Processing*, EMNLP '11, pages 497–507. Association for Computational Linguistics.

Libin Shen, Jinxi Xu, and Ralph M Weischedel. 2008. A new string-to-dependency machine translation algorithm with a target dependency language model. In *Association for Computational Linguistics*.

Mo Shen, Daisuke Kawahara, and Sadao Kurohashi. 2012. A reranking approach for dependency parsing with variable-sized subtree features. In *Proceedings of the 26th Pacific Asia Conference on Language, Information, and Computation*, pages 308–317, Bali, Indonesia, November. Faculty of Computer Science, Universitas Indonesia.

Christoph Tillmann. 2004. A unigram orientation model for statistical machine translation. In *Proceedings of HLT-NAACL 2004: Short Papers*, pages 101–104, Stroudsburg, PA, USA. Association for Computational Linguistics.

Selecting Syntactic, Non-redundant Segments
in Active Learning for Machine Translation

Akiva Miura[†], Graham Neubig[†], Michael Paul[‡], Satoshi Nakamura[†]
[†] Nara Institute of Science and Technology, Japan
[‡] ATR-Trek Co. Ltd., Japan
`miura.akiba.lr9@is.naist.jp` `neubig@is.naist.jp`
`michael.paul@atr-trek.co.jp` `s-nakamura@is.naist.jp`

Abstract

Active learning is a framework that makes it possible to efficiently train statistical models by selecting informative examples from a pool of unlabeled data. Previous work has found this framework effective for machine translation (MT), making it possible to train better translation models with less effort, particularly when annotators translate short phrases instead of full sentences. However, previous methods for phrase-based active learning in MT fail to consider whether the selected units are coherent and easy for human translators to translate, and also have problems with selecting redundant phrases with similar content. In this paper, we tackle these problems by proposing two new methods for selecting more syntactically coherent and less redundant segments in active learning for MT. Experiments using both simulation and extensive manual translation by professional translators find the proposed method effective, achieving both greater gain of BLEU score for the same number of translated words, and allowing translators to be more confident in their translations[1].

1 Introduction

In statistical machine translation (SMT) (Brown et al., 1993), large quantities of high-quality bilingual data are essential to achieve high translation accuracy. While in many cases large corpora can be collected, for example by crawling the web (Resnik and

---

[1]Code to replicate the experiments can be found at https://github.com/akivajp/naacl2016

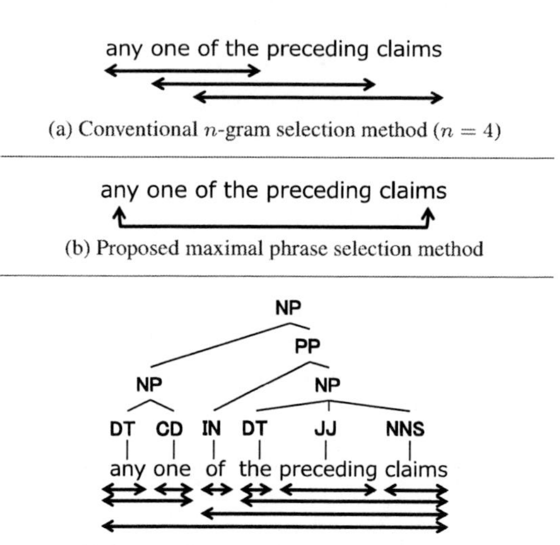

(a) Conventional n-gram selection method ($n = 4$)

(b) Proposed maximal phrase selection method

(c) Proposed parse subtree selection method

Figure 1: Conventional and proposed data selection methods

Smith, 2003), in many domains or language pairs it is still necessarily to create data by hand, either by hiring professionals or crowdsourcing (Zaidan and Callison-Burch, 2011). In these cases, *active learning* (§2), which selects which data to annotate based on their potential benefit to the translation system, has been shown to be effective for improving SMT systems while keeping the required amount of annotation to a minimum (Eck et al., 2005; Turchi et al., 2008; Haffari et al., 2009; Haffari and Sarkar, 2009; Ananthakrishnan et al., 2010; Bloodgood and Callison-Burch, 2010; González-Rubio et al., 2012; Green et al., 2014).

Most work on active learning for SMT, and natural language tasks in general, has focused on choosing which *sentences* to give to annotators. These

Proceedings of NAACL-HLT 2016, pages 20–29,
San Diego, California, June 12-17, 2016. ©2016 Association for Computational Linguistics

methods generally assign priority to sentences that contain data that is potentially useful to the MT system according to a number of criteria. For example, there are methods to select sentences that contain phrases that are frequent in monolingual data but not in bilingual data (Eck et al., 2005), have low confidence according to the MT system (Haffari et al., 2009), or are predicted to be poor translations by an MT quality estimation system (Ananthakrishnan et al., 2010). However, while the selected sentences may contain useful phrases, they will also generally contain many already covered phrases that nonetheless cost time and money to translate.

To solve the problem of wastefulness in full-sentence annotation for active learning, there have been a number of methods proposed to perform *sub-sentential annotation of short phrases* for natural language tasks (Settles and Craven, 2008; Bloodgood and Callison-Burch, 2010; Tomanek and Hahn, 2009; Sperber et al., 2014). For MT in particular, Bloodgood and Callison-Burch (2010) have proposed a method that selects poorly covered n-grams to show to translators, allowing them to focus directly on poorly covered parts without including unnecessary words (§3). Nevertheless, our experiments identified two major practical problems with this method. First, as shown in Figure 1 (a), many of the selected phrases overlap with each other, causing translation of *redundant* phrases, damaging efficiency. Second, it is common to see *fragments* of complex phrases such as "one of the preceding," which may be difficult for workers to translate into a contiguous phrase in the target language.

In this work, we propose two methods that aim to solve these two problems and improve the efficiency and reliability of segment-based active learning for SMT (§4). For the problem of overlapping phrases, we note that by merging overlapping phrases, as shown in Figure 1 (b), we can reduce the number of redundant words annotated and improve training efficiency. We adopt the idea of *maximal substrings* (Okanohara and Tsujii, 2009) which both encode this idea of redundancy, and can be calculated to arbitrary length in linear time using enhanced suffix arrays. For the problem of phrase structure fragmentation, we propose a simple heuristic to count only *well-formed syntactic constituents* in a parse tree, as shown in Figure 1 (c).

To investigate the effect of our proposed methods on learning efficiency, we perform experiments on English-French and English-Japanese translation tasks in which we incrementally add new parallel data, update models and evaluate translation accuracy. Results from both simulation experiments (§5) and 120 hours of work by professional translators (§6) demonstrate improved efficiency with respect to the number of words annotated. We also found that human translators took more time, but were more confident in their results on segments selected by the proposed method.

2 Active Learning for Machine Translation

In this section, we first provide an outline of the active learning procedure to select phrases for SMT data. In this paper, we regard a "phrase" as a word sequence with arbitrary length, which indicates that full sentences and single words both qualify as phrases. In Algorithm 1, we show the general procedure of incrementally selecting the next candidate for translation from the source language corpus, requesting and collecting the translation in the target language, and retraining the models.

Algorithm 1 Active learning for MT

1: **Init:**
2:    $SrcPool \leftarrow$ source language data including candidates for translation
3:    $Translated \leftarrow$ translated parallel data
4:    $Oracle \leftarrow$ oracle giving the correct translation for an input phrase
5: **Loop Until** $StopCondition$:
6:    $TM \leftarrow TrainTranslationModel(Translated)$
7:    $NewSrc \leftarrow SelectNextPhrase(SrcPool, Translated, TM)$
8:    $NewTrg \leftarrow GetTranslation(Oracle, NewSrc)$
9:    $Translated \leftarrow Translated \bigcup \{\langle NewSrc, NewTrg \rangle\}$

In lines 1-4, we define the datasets and initialize them. $SrcPool$ is a set with each sentence in source language corpus as an element. $Translated$ indicates a set with source and target language phrase pairs. $Translated$ may be empty, but in most cases will consist of a seed corpus upon which we would like to improve. $Oracle$ is an oracle (e.g. a human translator), that we can query for a correct translation for an arbitrary input phrase.

In lines 5-9, we train models incrementally. $StopCondition$ in line 5 is an arbitrary timing when to stop the loop, such as when we reach an accuracy goal or when we expend our translation budget. In line 6, we train the translation model using $Translated$, the available parallel data at this point. We evaluate the accuracy after training the translation model for each step in the experiments. In line 7, we select the next candidate for translation using features of $SrcPool$, $Translated$ and TM to make the decision.

In the following sections, we discuss existing methods (§3), and our proposed methods (§4) to implement the selection criterion in line 7.

3 Selection based on n-Gram Frequency

3.1 Sentence Selection using n-Gram Frequency

The first traditional method that we cover is a sentence selection method. Specifically, it selects the sentence including the most frequent uncovered phrase with a length of up to n words in the source language data. This method enables us to effectively cover the most frequent n-gram phrases and improve accuracy with fewer sentences than random selection. Bloodgood and Callison-Burch (2010) demonstrate results of a simulation showing that this method required less than 80% of the data required by randomly selected sentences to obtain the same accuracy.

However, as mentioned in the introduction, the selected full sentences include many phrases already covered in the parallel data. This may cause an additional cost for words in redundant segments, a problem resolved by the phrase selection approach detailed in the following section.

3.2 Phrase Selection using n-Gram Frequency

In the second baseline approach, we directly select and translate n-gram phrases that are the most frequent in the source language data but not yet covered in the translated data (Bloodgood and Callison-Burch, 2010). This method allows for improvement of coverage with fewer additional words than sentence selection, achieving higher efficiency by reducing the amount of data unnecessarily annotated. Bloodgood and Callison-Burch (2010) showed that by translating the phrases selected by this method using a crowdsourcing website, it was possible to achieve a large improvement of BLEU score, outperforming similar sentence-based methods.

However, as mentioned in the introduction, this method has several issues. First, because it uses short phrases, it often selects phrases that are not linguistically well-formed, potentially making them difficult to translate concisely. Second, it also has problems with redundancy, with no device to prevent multiple overlapping phrases being selected and translated. Finally, the previous work limits the maximum phrase length to $n = 4$, precluding the use of longer phrases. However, using a larger limit such as $n = 5$ is not likely to be a fundamental solution, as it increases the number of potentially overlapping phrases, and also computational burden. In the next section we cover our proposed solutions to these problems in detail.

4 Phrase Selection based on Maximal Phrases and Parse Trees

4.1 Phrase Selection based on Maximal Phrases

To solve both the problem of overlapping phrases and the problem of requiring limits on phrase length for computational reasons, we propose a method using the idea of *maximal substrings* (Okanohara and Tsujii, 2009). Maximal substrings are formally defined as "a substring that is *not* always included in a particular longer substring." For example, if we define p_i as a phrase and $occ(p_i)$ as its occurrence count in a corpus, and have the following data

$$p_1 = \text{"one of the preceding"}, \qquad occ(p_1) = 200,000$$
$$p_2 = \text{"one of the preceding claims"}, \qquad occ(p_2) = 200,000$$
$$p_3 = \text{"any one of the preceding claims"}, \quad occ(p_3) = 190,000$$

$p_1 = $ "one of the preceding" always co-occurs with the longer $p_2 = $ "one of the preceding claims" and thus is not a maximal substring. On the other hand, p_2 does not always co-occur with p_3, and thus p_2 will be maximal. This relationship can be defined formally with the following semi-order relation:

$$p_1 \preceq p_2 \Leftrightarrow \exists \alpha, \beta : p_1 = \alpha p_2 \beta \wedge occ(p_1) = occ(p_2). \quad (1)$$

Demonstrating this by the previous example, $p_1 = \alpha p_2 \beta$, $\alpha = $ "", $\beta = $ "claims" hold, meaning p_1 is a sub-sequence of p_2, and p_2 is a sub-sequence of p_3 in a similar manner. Since p_1 is a sub-sequence of p_2 and $occ(p_1) = occ(p_2) = 200,000$, $p_1 \preceq p_2$ holds. However, although p_2 is a sub sequence of p_3, because $occ(p_2) = 200,000 \neq 190,000 = occ(p_3)$, the relation $p_2 \preceq p_3$ does not hold. Here, we say p has *maximality* if there does not exist any q other than p itself that meets $p \preceq q$, and we call such a phrase a *maximal phrase*.

To apply this concept to active learning, our proposed method limits translation data selection to only maximal phrases. This has two advantages. First, it reduces overlapping phrases to only the maximal string, allowing translators to cover multiple high-frequency phrases in the translation of a single segment. Second, maximal phrases and their occurrence counts can be enumerated efficiently by using enhanced suffix arrays (Kasai et al., 2001) in linear time with respect to document length, removing the need to set arbitrary limits on the length of strings such as $n = 4$ used in previous work.

However, it can be easily noticed that while in the previous example p_2 is included in p_3, their occurrence counts are close but not equivalent, and thus both are maximal phrases. In such a case, the naïve implementation of this method can not remove these redundant phrases, despite the fact that it is intuitively preferable that the selection method combines phrases if they have almost the same occurrence count. Thus, we also propose to use the following semi-order relation generalized with parameter λ:

$$p_1 \stackrel{*}{\preceq} p_2 \Leftrightarrow \exists \alpha, \beta :$$
$$p_1 = \alpha p_2 \beta \wedge \lambda \cdot occ(p_1) < occ(p_2). \quad (2)$$

where λ takes a real numbered value from 0 to 1, which we set to $\lambda = 0.5$ in this research.

This removes the restriction that the two phrases under comparison be of exactly equal counts, allowing them to have only approximately the same occurrence count. We redefine maximality using this semi-order $\stackrel{*}{\preceq}$ as *semi-maximality*, and call maximal phrases defined with $\stackrel{*}{\preceq}$ *semi-maximal phrases* in contrast to normal maximal phrases. By using semi-maximal phrases instead of maximal phrases, we can remove a large number of phrases that are included in a particular longer phrase more than half the time, indicating that it might be preferable to translate the longer phrase instead.

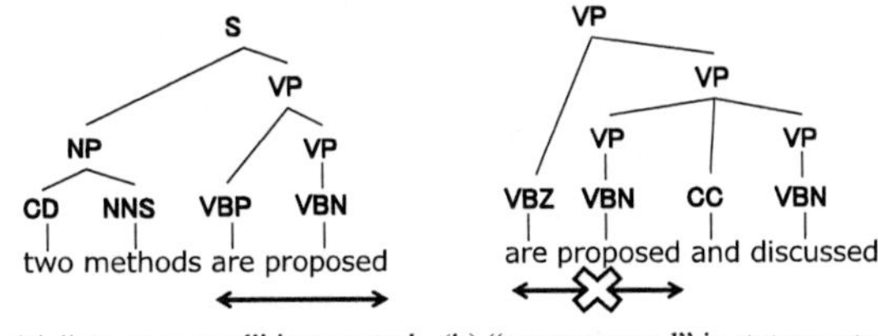

(a) "are proposed" is counted   (b) "are proposed" is not counted

Figure 2: Phrase counting based on parse trees

4.2 Phrase Selection based on Parse Trees

In this section, we propose a second phrase selection method based on the results from the syntactic analysis of source language data. This method first processes all the source language data with a phrase structure parser, traverses and counts up all the subtrees of parse trees as shown in Figure 2, and finally selects phrases corresponding to a subtree in frequency order.[2] We propose this method because we expect the selected phrases to have syntactically coherent meaning, potentially making human translation easier than other methods that do not use syntactic information.

It should be noted that because this method counts all subtrees, it is capable of selecting overlapping phrases like the methods based on n-grams. Therefore we also experiment with a method using together both subtrees and the semi-maximal phrases proposed in Section 4.1 to select both syntactic and non-redundant segments.

5 Simulation Experiment

5.1 Experimental Set-Up

To investigate the effects of the phrase selection methods proposed in Section 4, we first performed a simulation experiment in which we incrementally retrain translation models and evaluate the accuracy after each step of data selection. In this experiment, we chose English as a source language and French and Japanese as target languages. To simulate a realistic active learning scenario, we started from given parallel data in the general domain and sequentially added additional source language data in a specific target domain. For the English-French translation task, we adopted the Europarl corpus

---

[2]The method does not distinguish between equivalent word sequences even if they have different tree structures

Lang Pair	Domain	Dataset	Amount
En-Fr	General (Base)	Train	1.89M Sent. En: 47.6M Words Fr: 49.4M Words
	Medical	Train	15.5M Sent. En: 393M Words Fr: 418M Words
	(Target)	Test	1000 Sent.
		Dev	500 Sent.
En-Ja	General (Base)	Train	414k Sent. En: 6.72M Words Ja: 9.69M Words
	Scientific	Train	1.87M Sent. En: 46.4M Words Ja: 57.6M Words
	(Target)	Test	1790 Sent.
		Dev	1790 Sent.

Table 1: Details of parallel data

from WMT2014[3] as a base parallel data source and EMEA (Tiedemann, 2009), PatTR (Wäschle and Riezler, 2012), and Wikipedia titles, used in the medical translation task, as the target domain data. For the English-Japanese translation task, we adopted the broad-coverage example sentence corpus provided with the Eijiro dictionary[4] as general domain data, and the ASPEC[5] scientific paper abstract corpus as the target domain data. For pre-processing, we tokenized Japanese corpora using the KyTea word segmenter (Neubig et al., 2011) and filtered out the lines of length over 60 from all the training parallel data to ensure accuracy of parsing and alignment. We show the details of the parallel dataset after pre-processing in Table 1.

For the machine translation framework, we used phrase-based SMT (Koehn et al., 2003) with the Moses toolkit (Koehn et al., 2007) as a decoder. To efficiently re-train the models with new data, we adopted inc-giza-pp,[6] a specialized version of GIZA++ word aligner (Och and Ney, 2003) supporting incremental training, and the memory-mapped dynamic suffix array phrase tables (MMSAPT) feature of Moses (Germann, 2014) for on-memory construction of phrase tables. We train 5-gram models over the target side of all the general domain and target domain data using KenLM (Heafield, 2011).

For the tuning of decoding parameters, since it is not realistic to run MERT (Och, 2003) at each retraining step, we tuned the parameters to maximize the BLEU score (Papineni et al., 2002) for the baseline system, and re-used the parameters thereafter. We compare the following 8 segment selection methods, including 2 random selection methods, 2 conventional methods and 4 proposed methods:

sent-rand: Select sentences randomly.

4gram-rand: Select n-gram strings of length of up to 4 in random order.

sent-by-4gram-freq: Select the sentence including the most frequent uncovered phrase with length of up to 4 words (baseline 1, §3.1).

4gram-freq: Select the most frequent uncovered phrase with length of up to 4 words (baseline 2, §3.2).

maxsubst-freq: Select the most frequent uncovered maximal phrase (proposed, §4.1)

reduced-maxsubst-freq: Select the most frequent uncovered semi-maximal phrase (proposed, §4.1)

struct-freq: Select the most frequent uncovered phrase extracted from the subtrees (proposed, §4.2).

reduced-struct-freq: Select the most frequent uncovered semi-maximal phrase extracted from the subtrees (proposed, §4.1 and §4.2).

To generate oracle translations, we used an SMT system trained on all of the data in both the general and target-domain corpora. To generate parse trees, we used the Ckylark parser (Oda et al., 2015).

5.2 Results and Discussion

Comparison of efficiency: In Figure 3, we show the evaluation score results by the number of additional source words up to 100k and 1M words. We can see that in English-French translation, the accuracy of the selection methods using parse trees grows more rapidly than other methods and was significantly better even at the point of 1M additional words. In the case of English-Japanese translation, the gains over 4-gram frequency are much smaller, but the proposed methods still consistently perform as well or better than the other methods. Besides, in all the graphs we can see the improvement of reduced-maxsubst-freq and reduced-struct-freq over maxsubst-freq and struct-freq respectively, demonstrating that avoiding selecting redundant segments is helpful in improving efficiency.

---

[3] http://statmt.org/wmt14/

[4] http://eijiro.jp

[5] http://lotus.kuee.kyoto-u.ac.jp/ASPEC/

[6] https://github.com/akivajp/inc-giza-pp

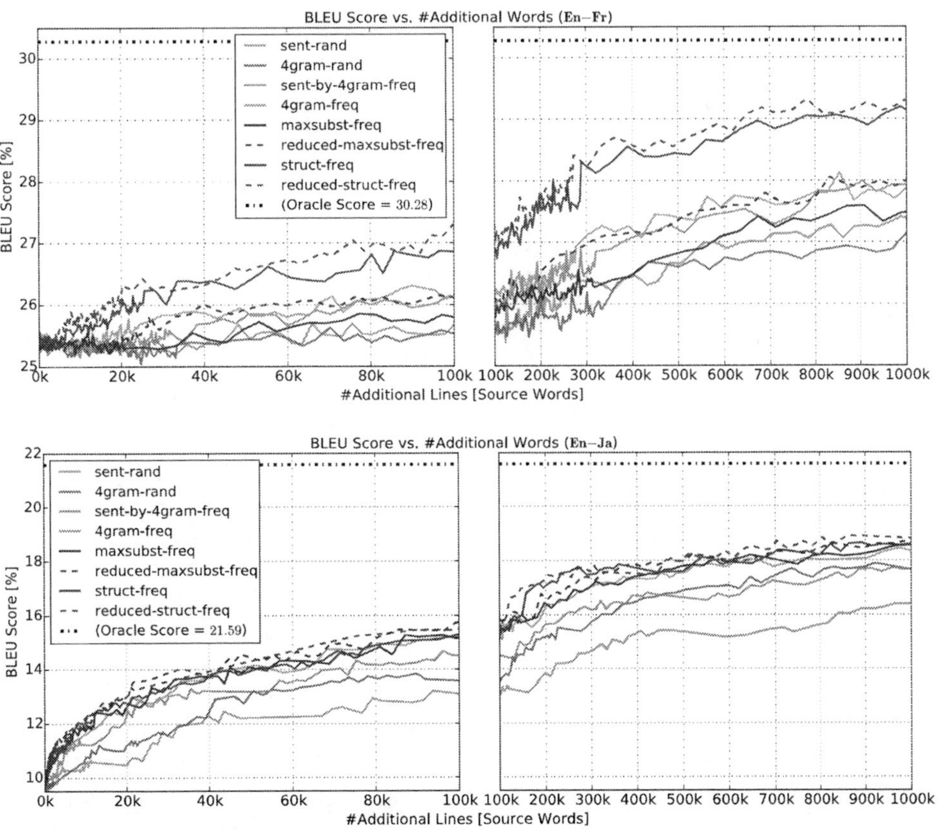

Figure 3: BLEU score vs. number of additional source words in each method

Length of selected phrases: Due to the different criteria used by each method, there are also significant differences in the features of the selected phrases. In Table 2, we show the details of the number of all selected phrases, words and average phrase length until the stop condition, and at the point of 10k additional source words. Here we see the tendency that the selection methods based on parse trees select shorter phrases than other methods. This is caused by the fact that longer phrases are only counted if they cover a syntactically defined phrases, and thus longer substrings that do not form syntactic phrases are removed from consideration.

Phrase coverage: This difference in the features of the selected phrases also affects how well they can cover new incoming test data. To demonstrate this, in Table 3 we show the 1-gram and 4-gram coverage of the test dataset after 10k, 100k and 1M words have been selected. From the results, we can see that

the reduced-struct-freq method attains the highest 1-gram coverage, efficiently covering unknown words. On the other hand, it is clear that methods selecting longer phrases have an advantage for 4-gram coverage, and we see the highest 4-gram coverage in the sent-by-4gram-freq method.

6 Manual Translation Experiment

6.1 Experimental Set-Up

To confirm that the results from the simulation in the previous section carry over to actual translators, we further performed experiments in which professional translators translated the selected segments. This also allowed us to examine the actual amount of time required to perform translation, and how confident the translators were in their translations.

We designed a web user interface as shown in Figure 4, and outsourced to an external organization

Lang Pair	Selection Method	All Selected Phrases			First 10k Words	
		#Phrases	#Words	Average Phrase Length	#Phrases	Average Phrase Length
En-Fr	sent-by-4gram-freq	10.6M	269M	25.4	310	32.1
	4gram-freq	40.1M	134M	3.34	3.62k	2.76
	maxsubst-freq	62.4M	331M	5.30	2.39k	4.17
	reduced-maxsubst-freq	45.9M	246M	5.36	2.95k	3.39
	struct-freq	14.1M	94.2M	6.68	4.01k	2.49
	reduced-struct-freq	7.33M	41.3M	5.63	4.55k	2.20
En-Ja	sent-by-4gram-freq	1.28M	33.6M	26.3	560	17.8
	4gram-freq	8.48M	26.0M	3.07	4.70k	2.13
	maxsubst-freq	7.29M	25.8M	3.54	4.51k	2.22
	reduced-maxsubst-freq	6.06M	21.7M	3.58	4.76k	2.10
	struct-freq	1.45M	4.85M	3.34	6.64k	1.51
	reduced-struct-freq	1.10M	3.33M	3.03	6.73k	1.49

Table 2: Number of phrases and average words/phrase in each method

Lang Pair	Selection Method	1-gram / 4-gram Coverage [%]			
		No Addition	10k Words	100k Words	1M Words
En-Fr	sent-rand		92.93 / 10.60	93.73 / 10.71	95.94 / 11.30
	4gram-rand		92.95 / 10.60	93.99 / 10.60	96.42 / 10.64
	sent-by-4gram-freq		92.95 / 10.60	93.96 / **10.72**	96.25 / **11.55**
	4gram-freq	92.72 / 10.60	92.92 / 10.60	94.46 / 10.66	96.60 / 11.16
	maxsubst-freq		92.79 / 10.60	93.61 / 10.62	95.99 / 10.92
	reduced-maxsubst-freq		92.92 / 10.60	94.38 / 10.66	96.55 / 11.13
	struct-freq		93.63 / 10.60	96.15 / 10.65	97.84 / 11.28
	reduced-struct-freq		**94.02** / 10.60	**96.38** / 10.69	**98.00** / 11.38
En-Ja	sent-rand		94.81 / 5.63	95.99 / 6.59	97.54 / 10.06
	4gram-rand		94.80 / 5.38	96.10 / 5.46	97.67 / 5.98
	sent-by-4gram-freq		95.10 / 5.84	96.28 / **7.23**	97.64 / **11.39**
	4gram-freq	94.36 / 5.38	95.64 / 5.97	96.87 / 7.14	97.97 / 10.43
	maxsubst-freq		95.59 / 5.96	96.83 / 7.07	97.91 / 10.20
	reduced-maxsubst-freq		95.73 / **6.00**	96.97 / 7.19	98.00/10.57
	struct-freq		96.60 / 5.44	97.80 / 5.79	98.58 / 7.02
	reduced-struct-freq		**96.64** / 5.44	**97.84** / 5.80	**98.61** / 7.14

Table 3: Effect on coverage in each selection method (rounded off to the second decimal place). Bold face indicates the highest coverage for each number of additional words.

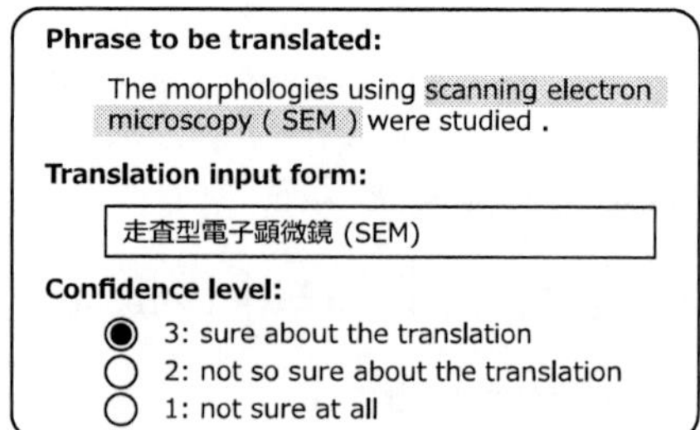

Figure 4: Example of the human translation interface

that had three professional translators translate the shown phrases. As is standard when hiring translators, we paid a fixed price per word translated for all of the methods. Because showing only the candidate phrase out of context could cause difficulty in translation, we follow Bloodgood and Callison-Burch (2010) in showing a sentence including the selected phrase,[7] highlighting the phrase, and requesting that the translator translate the highlighted part. We also requested that every worker select from 3 levels indicating how confident they were of their translation. In the background, the time required to complete the translation is measured from when the new phrase is shown until when the translation is submitted.

The methods selected for comparative evaluation are sentence selection based on 4-gram frequency (sent-by-4gram-freq) and phrase selection based on 4-gram frequency (4gram-freq) as baseline methods, and the phrase selection based on both parse trees and semi-maximality (reduced-struct-freq) as

---

[7]Specifically, we selected the shortest sentence including the phrase in the source corpus.

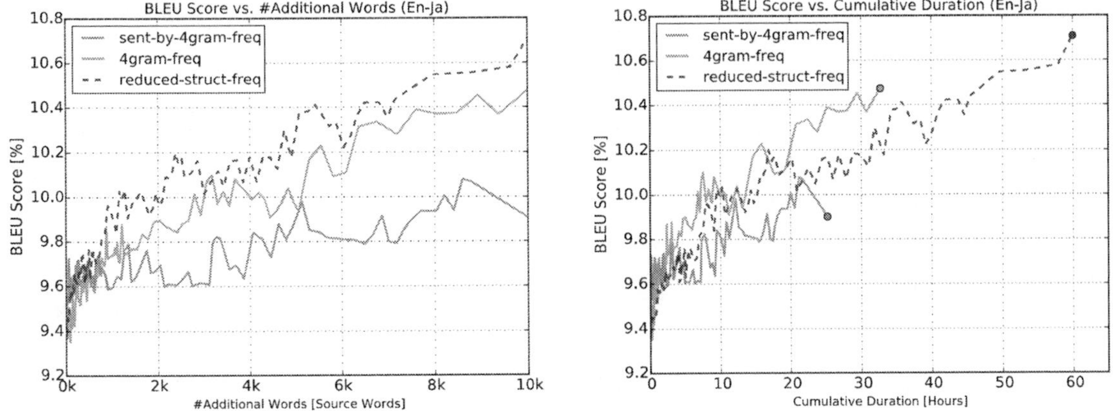

Figure 5: Transition of BLEU score vs. additional source words (left) and vs. cumulative working duration (right)

the proposed method. For each method we collected translations of 10k source words, alternating between segments selected by each method to prevent bias.

We used the same dataset as the English-Japanese translation task and the same tools in the simulation experiment (Section 5). However, for training target language models, we interpolated one trained with the base data and a second trained with collected data by using SRILM (Stolcke, 2002) because the hand-made data set was too small to train a full language model using only this data. We tuned the interpolation coefficient such that it maximizes the perplexity for the tuning dataset.

6.2 Results and Discussion

Efficiency results: Figure 5 shows the evaluation scores of SMT systems trained using varying amounts of collected phrases. In the left graph, we see the proposed method based on parse trees and phrase semi-maximality rapidly improves BLEU score, and requires fewer additional words than the conventional methods. Because the cost paid for translation often is decided by the number of words, this indicates that the proposed method has better cost performance in these situations. The right graph shows improvement by the amount of translation time. These results here are different, showing the 4-gram-freq baseline slightly superior. As discussed in Table 3, the methods based on parse trees select more uncovered 1-grams, namely unknown words, and specifically the proposed method selected more

Selection Methods	Total Working Time [Hours]	Average Confidence Level (3 Levels)
sent-by-4gram-freq	25.22	2.689
4gram-freq	32.70	2.601
reduced-struct-freq	59.97	**2.771**

Table 4: Total working time and average confidence level

technical terms that took a longer time to translate.

Working time and confidence: We show the total time to collect the translations of 10k source words and average confidence level for each method in Table 4. The total working time for the proposed method is nearly double that of other methods, as seen in the right graph of Figure 5. On the other hand, the segments selected by the proposed method were given the highest confidence level, receiving the maximum value of 3 for about 79% of phrase pairs, indicating that the generated parallel data is of high quality. To some extent, this corroborates our hypothesis that the more syntactic phrases selected by the proposed method are easier to translate.

We can also examine the tendency of working time for segments of different lengths in Table 5. Interestingly, single words consistently have a longer average translation time than phrases of length 2-4, likely because they tend to be technical terms that require looking up in a dictionary. We show the average confidence levels corresponding to phrase length in Table 6. The confidence level of single words in the proposed method is lower than in the baseline method, likely because the baseline selected a smaller amount of single words, and those se-

Selection Method	Average Working Time [Seconds]				
	1 Word	2 Word Phrase	3 Word Phrase	4 Word Phrase	5+ Word Phrase
sent-by-4gram-freq	-	-	-	-	160.64
4gram-freq	30.14	24.76	21.77	21.12	-
reduced-struct-freq	35.61	25.23	21.72	28.13	22.82

Table 5: Average working time of manual translation corresponding to phrase length

Selection Method	Average Confidence Level (3 Levels)				
	1 Word	2 Word Phrase	3 Word Phrase	4 Word Phrase	5+ Word Phrase
sent-by-4gram-freq	-	-	-	-	2.689
4gram-freq	2.885	2.585	2.422	2.300	-
reduced-struct-freq	2.802	2.796	2.778	2.708	2.737

Table 6: Average confidence level of manual translation corresponding to phrase length

lected were less likely to be technical terms. On the other hand, we can confirm that the confidence level for longer phrases in the baseline method decreases drastically, while it is stably high in our method, confirming the effectiveness of selecting syntactically coherent phrases.

Translation accuracy by confidence level: Finally, we show the accuracy of the SMT system trained by all the collected data in each method in Table 7. To utilize the confidence level annotation, we tested SMT systems trained by phrase pairs with confidence levels higher than 2 or 3. From the results, the accuracy of every method is improved when phrases pairs with confidence level 1 were filtered out. In contrast, the accuracy is conversely degraded if we use only phrase pairs with confidence level 3. The translation accuracy of 9.37% BLEU with the base SMT system without additional data became 10.72% after adding phrase pairs having confidence level 2 or higher, allowing for a relatively large gain of 1.35 BLEU points.

7 Conclusion and Future Work

In this paper, we proposed a new method for active learning in machine translation that selects syntactic, non-redundant phrases using parse trees and semi-maximal phrases. We first performed simulation experiments and obtained improvements in translation accuracy with fewer additional words. Further man-

Selection Methods	BLEU Score [%]		
	Confidence 1+ (All)	Confidence 2+	Confidence 3
sent-by-4gram-freq	9.88	9.92	9.85
4gram-freq	10.48	10.54	10.36
reduced-struct-freq	10.70	**10.72**	10.67

Table 7: BLEU score when training on phrases with a certain confidence level

ual translation experiments also demonstrated that our method allows for greater improvements in accuracy and translator confidence.

However, there are still a number of avenues for improvement. Particularly, as the proposed method selected segments that took more time to translate due to technical terms, the combination with methods to harvest unknown words (Daumé III and Jagarlamudi, 2011) or optimize the selected segments based on the time required (Sperber et al., 2014) is potentially useful. In addition, softer syntactic constraints that allow annotation of phrases with variables (Chiang, 2007) such as "one of the preceding X" are another interesting avenue of future work.

Acknowledgments

The authors thank anonymous reviewers for helpful suggestions. This research was supported by ATR-Trek Co. Ltd. The manual translation work was supported by BAOBAB Inc.

References

Sankaranarayanan Ananthakrishnan, Rohit Prasad, David Stallard, and Prem Natarajan. 2010. A Semi-Supervised Batch-Mode Active Learning Strategy for Improved Statistical Machine Translation. In *Proc. CoNLL*, pages 126–134, July.

Michael Bloodgood and Chris Callison-Burch. 2010. Bucking the Trend: Large-Scale Cost-Focused Active Learning for Statistical Machine Translation. In *Proc. ACL*, pages 854–864, July.

Peter F. Brown, Vincent J.Della Pietra, Stephen A. Della Pietra, and Robert L. Mercer. 1993. The Mathematics of Statistical Machine Translation: Parameter Estimation. *Computational Linguistics*, 19:263–312.

David Chiang. 2007. Hierarchical phrase-based translation. 33(2):201–228.

Hal Daumé III and Jagadeesh Jagarlamudi. 2011. Domain adaptation for machine translation by mining unseen words. In *Proc. ACL*, pages 407–412.

Matthias Eck, Stephan Vogel, and Alex Waibel. 2005. Low Cost Portability for Statistical Machine Translation based in N-gram Frequency and TF-IDF. In *Proc. IWSLT*, pages 61–67.

Ulrich Germann. 2014. Dynamic phrase tables for machine translation in an interactive post-editing scenario. In *Proc. AMTA 2014 Workshop on Interactive and Adaptive Machine Translation*, pages 20–31.

Jesús González-Rubio, Daniel Ortiz-Martínez, and Francisco Casacuberta. 2012. Active learning for interactive machine translation. In *Proc. EACL*, pages 245–254, April.

Spence Green, Sida I. Wang, Jason Chuang, Jeffrey Heer, Sebastian Schuster, and Christopher D. Manning. 2014. Human Effort and Machine Learnability in Computer Aided Translation. In *Proc. EMNLP*, pages 1225–1236, October.

Gholamreza Haffari and Anoop Sarkar. 2009. Active Learning for Multilingual Statistical Machine Translation. In *Proc. ACL*, pages 181–189, August.

Gholamreza Haffari, Maxim Roy, and Anoop Sarkar. 2009. Active Learning for Statistical Phrase-based Machine Translation. In *Proc. ACL*, pages 415–423, June.

Kenneth Heafield. 2011. KenLM: Faster and Smaller Language Model Queries. In *Proc. WMT*, July.

Toru Kasai, Gunho Lee, Hiroki Arimura, Setsuo Arikawa, and Kunsoo Park. 2001. Linear-Time Longest-Common-Prefix Computation in Suffix Arrays and Its Applications. In *Proc. CPM*, pages 181–192.

Phillip Koehn, Franz Josef Och, and Daniel Marcu. 2003. Statistical Phrase-Based Translation. In *Proc. NAACL*, pages 48–54.

Philipp Koehn, Hieu Hoang, Alexandra Birch, Chris Callison-Burch, Marcello Federico, Nicola Bertoldi, Brooke Cowan, Wade Shen, Christine Moran, Richard Zens, Chris Dyer, Ondrej Bojar, Alexandra Constantin, and Evan Herbst. 2007. Moses: Open Source Toolkit for Statistical Machine Translation. pages 177–180.

Graham Neubig, Yosuke Nakata, and Shinsuke Mori. 2011. Pointwise Prediction for Robust, Adaptable Japanese Morphological Analysis. In *Proc. ACL*, pages 529–533.

Franz Josef Och and Hermann Ney. 2003. A Systematic Comparison of Various Statistical Alignment Models. *Computational Linguistics*, 29(1):19–51.

Franz Josef Och. 2003. Minimum Error Rate Training in Statistical Machine Translation. In *Proc. ACL*, pages 160–167.

Yusuke Oda, Graham Neubig, Sakriani Sakti, Tomoki Toda, and Satoshi Nakamura. 2015. Ckylark: A More Robust PCFG-LA Parser. In *Proc. NAACL*, pages 41–45, June.

Daisuke Okanohara and Jun'ichi Tsujii. 2009. Text Categorization with All Substring Features. In *Proc. SDM*, pages 838–846.

Kishore Papineni, Salim Roukos, Todd Ward, and Wei-Jing Zhu. 2002. Bleu: a Method for Automatic Evaluation of Machine Translation. In *Proc. ACL*, pages 311–318, July.

Philip Resnik and Noah A Smith. 2003. The web as a parallel corpus. *Computational Linguistics*, 29(3):349–380.

Burr Settles and Mark Craven. 2008. An Analysis of Active Learning Strategies for Sequence Labeling Tasks. In *Proc. EMNLP*, pages 1070–1079, October.

Matthias Sperber, Mirjam Simantzik, Graham Neubig, Satoshi Nakamura, and Alex Waibel. 2014. Segmentation for Efficient Supervised Language Annotation with an Explicit Cost-Utility Tradeoff. *TACL*, 2:169–180.

Andreas Stolcke. 2002. SRILM - an extensible language modeling toolkit. In *Proc. ICSLP*, pages 901–904.

Jörg Tiedemann. 2009. News from OPUS-A collection of multilingual parallel corpora with tools and interfaces. In *Proc. RANLP*, volume 5, pages 237–248.

Katrin Tomanek and Udo Hahn. 2009. Semi-Supervised Active Learning for Sequence Labeling. In *Proc. ACL*, pages 1039–1047, August.

Marco Turchi, Tijl De Bie, and Nello Cristianini. 2008. Learning performance of a machine translation system: a statistical and computational analysis. In *Proc. WMT*, pages 35–43, June.

Katharina Wäschle and Stefan Riezler. 2012. Analyzing Parallelism and Domain Similarities in the MAREC Patent Corpus. *Multidisciplinary Information Retrieval*, pages 12–27.

Omar F Zaidan and Chris Callison-Burch. 2011. Crowdsourcing translation: Professional quality from non-professionals. In *Proc. ACL*, pages 1220–1229.

Multi-Source Neural Translation

Barret Zoph and Kevin Knight
Information Sciences Institute
Department of Computer Science
University of Southern California
{zoph,knight}@isi.edu

Abstract

We build a multi-source machine translation model and train it to maximize the probability of a target English string given French and German sources. Using the neural encoder-decoder framework, we explore several combination methods and report up to +4.8 Bleu increases on top of a very strong attention-based neural translation model.

1 Introduction

Kay (2000) points out that if a document is translated once, it is likely to be translated again and again into other languages. This gives rise to an interesting idea: a human does the first translation by hand, then turns the rest over to machine translation (MT). The translation system now has two strings as input, which can reduce ambiguity via "triangulation" (Kay's term). For example, the normally ambiguous English word "bank" may be more easily translated into French in the presence of a second, German input string containing the word "Flussufer" (river bank).

Och and Ney (2001) describe such a *multi-source* MT system. They first train separate bilingual MT systems $F \to E$, $G \to E$, etc. At runtime, they separately translate input strings f and g into candidate target strings e_1 and e_2, then select the best one of the two. A typical selection factor is the product of the system scores. Schwartz (2008) revisits such factors in the context of log-linear models and Bleu score, while Max et al. (2010) re-rank $F \to E$ n-best lists using n-gram precision with respect to $G \to E$ translations. Callison-Burch (2002) exploits

hypothesis selection in multi-source MT to expand available corpora, via co-training.

Others use system combination techniques to merge hypotheses at the word level, creating the ability to synthesize new translations outside those proposed by the single-source translators. These methods include confusion networks (Matusov et al., 2006; Schroeder et al., 2009), source-side string combination (Schroeder et al., 2009), and median strings (González-Rubio and Casacuberta, 2010).

The above work all relies on base MT systems trained on *bilingual data*, using traditional methods. This follows early work in sentence alignment (Gale and Church, 1993) and word alignment (Simard, 1999), which exploited trilingual text, but did not build trilingual models. Previous authors possibly considered a three-dimensional translation table $t(e|f, g)$ to be prohibitive.

In this paper, by contrast, we train a $P(e|f, g)$ model directly on *trilingual data*, and we use that model to decode an (f, g) pair simultaneously. We view this as a kind of multi-tape transduction (Elgot and Mezei, 1965; Kaplan and Kay, 1994; Deri and Knight, 2015) with two input tapes and one output tape. Our contributions are as follows:

- We train a $P(e|f, g)$ model directly on trilingual data, and we use it to decode a new source string pair (f, g) into target string e.
- We show positive Bleu improvements over strong single-source baselines.
- We show that improvements are best when the two source languages are more distant from each other.

We are able to achieve these results using

Proceedings of NAACL-HLT 2016, pages 30–34,
San Diego, California, June 12-17, 2016. ©2016 Association for Computational Linguistics

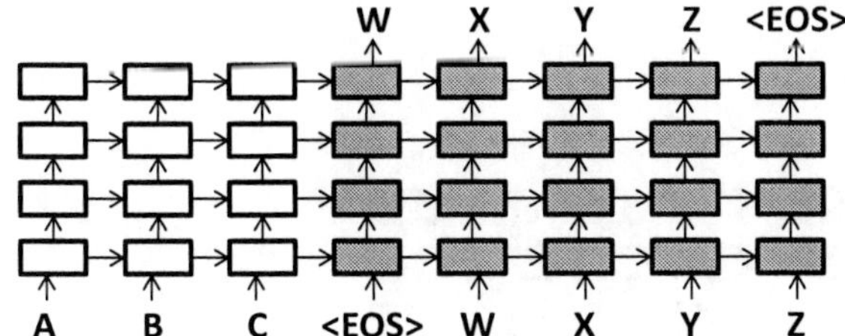

Figure 1: The encoder-decoder framework for neural machine translation (NMT) (Sutskever et al., 2014). Here, a source sentence C B A (presented in reverse order as A B C) is translated into a target sentence W X Y Z. At each step, an evolving real-valued vector summarizes the state of the encoder (white) and decoder (gray).

the framework of neural encoder-decoder models, where multi-target MT (Dong et al., 2015) and multi-source, cross-modal mappings have been explored (Luong et al., 2015a).

2 Multi-Source Neural MT

In the neural encoder-decoder framework for MT (Neco and Forcada, 1997; Castaño and Casacuberta, 1997; Sutskever et al., 2014; Bahdanau et al., 2014; Luong et al., 2015b), we use a recurrent neural network (*encoder*) to convert a source sentence into a dense, fixed-length vector. We then use another recurrent network (*decoder*) to convert that vector in a target sentence.[1]

In this paper, we use a four-layer encoder-decoder system (Figure 1) with long short-term memory (LSTM) units (Hochreiter and Schmidhuber, 1997) trained for maximum likelihood (via a softmax layer) with back-propagation through time (Werbos, 1990). For our baseline single-source MT system we use two different models, one of which implements the local attention plus feed-input model from Luong et al. (2015b).

Figure 2 shows our approach to multi-source MT. Each source language has its own encoder. The question is how to combine the hidden states and cell states from each encoder, to pass on to the decoder. Black *combiner* blocks implement a function whose input is two hidden states (h_1 and h_2) and two cell states (c_1 and c_2), and whose output is a single hid-

den state h and cell state c. We propose two combination methods.

2.1 Basic Combination Method

The Basic method works by concatenating the two hidden states from the source encoders, applying a linear transformation W_c (size 2000 x 1000), then sending its output through a tanh non-linearity. This operation is represented by the equation:

$$ h = \tanh\Big(W_c[h_1; h_2]\Big) \tag{1} $$

W_c and all other weights in the network are learned from example string triples drawn from a trilingual training corpus.

The new cell state is simply the sum of the two cell states from the encoders.

$$ c = c_1 + c_2 \tag{2} $$

We also attempted to concatenate cell states and apply a linear transformation, but training diverges due to large cell values.

2.2 Child-Sum Method

Our second combination method is inspired by the Child-Sum Tree-LSTMs of Tai et al. (2015). Here, we use an LSTM variant to combine the two hidden states and cells. The standard LSTM input, output, and new cell value are all calculated. Then cell states from each encoder get their own forget gates. The final cell state and hidden state are calculated as in a normal LSTM. More precisely:

$$ i = \text{sigmoid}\Big(W_1^i h_1 + W_2^i h_2\Big) \tag{3} $$

$$ f = \text{sigmoid}\Big(W_i^f h_i\Big) \tag{4} $$

$$ o = \text{sigmoid}\Big(W_1^o h_1 + W_2^o h_2\Big) \tag{5} $$

$$ u = \tanh\Big(W_1^u h_1 + W_2^u h_2\Big) \tag{6} $$

$$ c = i_f \odot u_f + f_1 \odot c_1 + f_2 \odot c_2 \tag{7} $$

$$ h = o_f \odot \tanh(c_f) \tag{8} $$

This method employs eight new matrices (the W's in the above equations), each of size 1000 x 1000. The $\odot$ symbol represents an elementwise multiplication. In equation 3, i represents the input gate of a typical LSTM cell. In equation 4,

---

[1] We follow previous authors in presenting the source sentence to the encoder in reverse order.

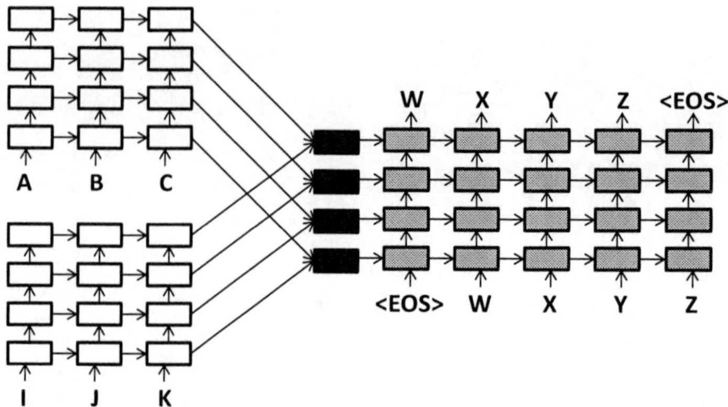

Figure 2: Multi-source encoder-decoder model for MT. We have two source sentences (C B A and K J I) in different languages. Each language has its own encoder; it passes its final hidden and cell state to a set of *combiners* (in black). The output of a combiner is a hidden state and cell state of the same dimension.

there are two forget gates indexed by the subscript i that serve as the forget gates for each of the incoming cells for each of the encoders. In equation 5, o represents the output gate of a normal LSTM. i, f, o, and u are all size-1000 vectors.

2.3 Multi-Source Attention

Our single-source attention model is modeled off the local-p attention model with feed input from Luong et al. (2015b), where hidden states from the top decoder layer can look back at the top hidden states from the encoder. The top decoder hidden state is combined with a weighted sum of the encoder hidden states, to make a better hidden state vector ($\tilde{h}_t$), which is passed to the softmax output layer. With input-feeding, the hidden state from the attention model is sent down to the bottom decoder layer at the next time step.

The local-p attention model from Luong et al. (2015b) works as follows. First, a position to look at in the source encoder is predicted by equation 9:

$$p_t = S \cdot \mathrm{sigmoid}(v_p^T \tanh(W_p h_t)) \qquad (9)$$

S is the source sentence length, and v_p and W_p are learned parameters, with v_p being a vector of dimension 1000, and W_p being a matrix of dimension 1000 x 1000.

After p_t is computed, a window of size $2D + 1$ is looked at in the top layer of the source encoder centered around p_t ($D = 10$). For each hidden state in this window, we compute an alignment score $a_t(s)$,

between 0 and 1. This alignment score is computed by equations 10, 11 and 12:

$$a_t(s) = \mathrm{align}(h_t, h_s)\exp\left(\frac{-(s - p_t)^2}{2\sigma^2}\right) \qquad (10)$$

$$\mathrm{align}(h_t, h_s) = \frac{\exp(\mathrm{score}(h_t, h_s))}{\sum_{s'} \exp(\mathrm{score}(h_t, h_{s'}))} \qquad (11)$$

$$\mathrm{score}(h_t, h_s) = h_t^T W_a h_s \qquad (12)$$

In equation 10, σ is set to be $D/2$ and s is the source index for that hidden state. W_a is a learnable parameter of dimension 1000 x 1000.

Once all of the alignments are calculated, c_t is created by taking a weighted sum of all source hidden states multiplied by their alignment weight.

The final hidden state sent to the softmax layer is given by:

$$\tilde{h}_t = tanh\left(W_c[h_t; c_t]\right) \qquad (13)$$

We modify this attention model to look at both source encoders simultaneously. We create a context vector from each source encoder named c_t^1 and c_t^2 instead of the just c_t in the single-source attention model:

$$\tilde{h}_t = tanh\left(W_c[h_t; c_t^1; c_t^2]\right) \qquad (14)$$

In our multi-source attention model we now have two p_t variables, one for each source encoder. We

	French	English	German
Word tokens	66.2m	59.4m	57.0m
Word types	424,832	381,062	865,806
Segment pairs	2,378,112		
Ave. segment length (tokens)	27.8	25.0	24.0

Figure 3: Trilingual corpus statistics.

also have two separate sets of alignments and therefore now have two c_t values denoted by c_t^1 and c_t^2 as mentioned above. We also have distinct W_a, v_p, and W_p parameters for each encoder.

3 Experiments

We use English, French, and German data from a subset of the WMT 2014 dataset (Bojar et al., 2014). Figure 3 shows statistics for our training set. For development, we use the 3000 sentences supplied by WMT. For testing, we use a 1503-line trilingual subset of the WMT test set.

For the single-source models, we follow the training procedure used in Luong et al. (2015b), but with 15 epochs and halving the learning rate every full epoch after the 10th epoch. We also re-scale the normalized gradient when norm > 5. For training, we use a minibatch size of 128, a hidden state size of 1000, and dropout as in Zaremba et al. (2014). The dropout rate is 0.2, the initial parameter range is [-0.1, +0.1], and the learning rate is 1.0. For the normal and multi-source attention models, we adjust these parameters to 0.3, [-0.08, +0.08], and 0.7, respectively, to adjust for overfitting.

Figure 4 shows our results for target English, with source languages French and German. We see that the Basic combination method yields a +4.8 Bleu improvement over the strongest single-source, attention-based system. It also improves Bleu by +2.2 over the non-attention baseline. The Child-Sum method gives improvements of +4.4 and +1.4. We confirm that two copies of the same French input yields no BLEU improvement. Figure 5 shows the action of the multi-attention model during decoding.

When our source languages are English and French (Figure 6), we observe smaller BLEU gains (up to +1.1). This is evidence that the more distinct the source languages, the better they disambiguate each other.

Target = English			
Source	**Method**	**Ppl**	**BLEU**
French	—	10.3	21.0
German	—	15.9	17.3
French+German	Basic	8.7	23.2
French+German	Child-Sum	9.0	22.5
French+French	Child-Sum	10.9	20.7
French	Attention	8.1	25.2
French+German	B-Attent.	5.7	30.0
French+German	CS-Attent.	6.0	29.6

Figure 4: Multi-source MT for target English, with source languages French and German. Ppl reports test-set perplexity as the system predicts English tokens. BLEU is scored using the multi-bleu.perl script from Moses. For our evaluation we use a single reference and they are case sensitive.

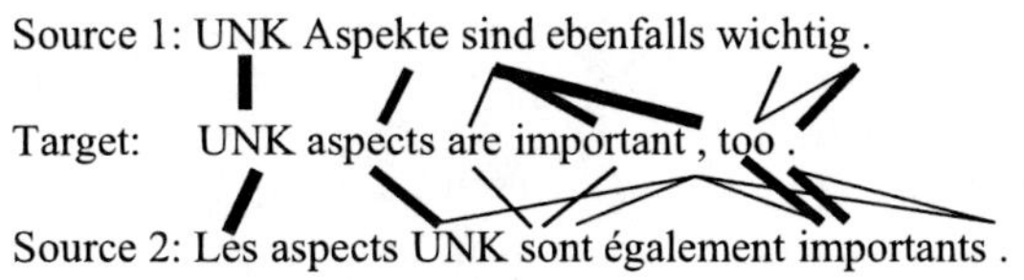

Figure 5: Action of the multi-attention model as the neural decoder generates target English from French/German sources (test set). Lines show strengths of $a_t(s)$.

4 Conclusion

We describe a multi-source neural MT system that gets up to +4.8 Bleu gains over a very strong attention-based, single-source baseline. We obtain this result through a novel encoder-vector combination method and a novel multi-attention system. We release the code for these experiments at www.github.com/isi-nlp/Zoph_RNN.

Target = German			
Source	**Method**	**Ppl**	**BLEU**
French	—	12.3	10.6
English	—	9.6	13.4
French+English	Basic	9.1	14.5
French+English	Child-Sum	9.5	14.4
English	Attention	7.3	17.6
French+English	B-Attent.	6.9	18.6
French+English	CS-Attent.	7.1	18.2

Figure 6: Multi-source MT results for target German, with source languages French and English.

5   Acknowledgments

This work was carried out with funding from DARPA (HR0011-15-C-0115) and ARL/ARO (W911NF-10-1-0533).

References

D. Bahdanau, K. Cho, and Y. Bengio. 2014. Neural machine translation by jointly learning to align and translate. In *Proc. ICLR*.

O. Bojar, C. Buck, C. Federmann, B. Haddow, P. Koehn, C. Monz, M. Post, and L. Specia, editors. 2014. *Proc. of the Ninth Workshop on Statistical Machine Translation*. Association for Computational Linguistics.

C. Callison-Burch. 2002. Co-training for statistical machine translation. Master's thesis, School of Informatics, University of Edinburgh.

M. A. Castaño and F. Casacuberta. 1997. A connectionist approach to machine translation. In *EUROSPEECH*.

A. Deri and K. Knight. 2015. How to make a Frenemy: Multitape FSTs for portmanteau generation. In *Proc. NAACL*.

D. Dong, H. Wu, W. he, D. Yu, and H. Wang. 2015. Multi-task learning for multiple language translation. In *Proc. ACL*.

C. Elgot and J. Mezei. 1965. On relations defined by generalized finite automata. *IBM Journal of Research and Development*, 9(1):47–68.

W. A Gale and K. W Church. 1993. A program for aligning sentences in bilingual corpora. *Computational linguistics*, 19(1):75–102.

J. González-Rubio and F. Casacuberta. 2010. On the use of median string for multi-source translation. In *Proc. ICPR*.

S. Hochreiter and J. Schmidhuber. 1997. Long short-term memory. *Neural Computation*, 9(8).

R. Kaplan and M. Kay. 1994. Regular models of phonological rule systems. *Computational Linguistics*, 20(3):331–378.

M. Kay. 2000. Triangulation in translation. Keynote at MT 2000 Conference, University of Exeter.

M. Luong, Q. V. Le, I. Sutskever, O. Vinyals, and L. Kaiser. 2015a. Multi-task sequence to sequence learning. In *arXiv*. http://arxiv.org/abs/1511.06114.

M. Luong, H. Pham, and C. Manning. 2015b. Effective approaches to attention-based neural machine translation. In *Proc. EMNLP*.

E. Matusov, N. Ueffing, and H. Ney. 2006. Computing consensus translation from multiple machine translation systems using enhanced hypotheses alignment. In *Proc. EACL*.

A. Max, J. Crego, and F. Yvon. 2010. Contrastive lexical evaluation of machine translation. In *Proc. LREC*.

R. Neco and M. Forcada. 1997. Asynchronous translations with recurrent neural nets. In *International Conf. on Neural Networks*, volume 4, pages 2535–2540.

F. J. Och and H. Ney. 2001. Statistical multi-source translation. In *Proc. MT Summit*.

J. Schroeder, T. Cohn, and P. Koehn. 2009. Word lattices for multi-source translation. In *Proc. EACL*.

L. Schwartz. 2008. Multi-source translation methods. *Proc. AMTA*.

M. Simard. 1999. Text-translation alignment: Three languages are better than two. In *Proc. EMNLP/VLC*.

I. Sutskever, O. Vinyals, and Q. V. Le. 2014. Sequence to sequence learning with neural networks. In *Proc. NIPS*.

K. S. Tai, R. Socher, and C. Manning. 2015. Improved semantic representations from tree-structured long short-term memory networks. In *Proc. ACL*.

P. J. Werbos. 1990. Backpropagation through time: what it does and how to do it. *Proc. IEEE*, 78(10):1550–1560.

W. Zaremba, I. Sutskever, and O. Vinyals. 2014. Recurrent neural network regularization. *CoRR*, abs/1409.2329.

Controlling Politeness in Neural Machine Translation via Side Constraints

Rico Sennrich and **Barry Haddow** and **Alexandra Birch**
School of Informatics, University of Edinburgh
`{rico.sennrich,a.birch}@ed.ac.uk, bhaddow@inf.ed.ac.uk`

Abstract

Many languages use honorifics to express politeness, social distance, or the relative social status between the speaker and their addressee(s). In machine translation from a language without honorifics such as English, it is difficult to predict the appropriate honorific, but users may want to control the level of politeness in the output. In this paper, we perform a pilot study to control honorifics in neural machine translation (NMT) via *side constraints*, focusing on English→German. We show that by marking up the (English) source side of the training data with a feature that encodes the use of honorifics on the (German) target side, we can control the honorifics produced at test time. Experiments show that the choice of honorifics has a big impact on translation quality as measured by BLEU, and oracle experiments show that substantial improvements are possible by constraining the translation to the desired level of politeness.

1 Introduction

Many languages use honorifics to express politeness, social distance, or the relative social status between the speaker and their addressee(s). A widespread instance is the grammatical T-V distinction (Brown and Gilman, 1960), distinguishing between the familiar (Latin *Tu*) and the polite (Latin *Vos*) second person pronoun. In machine translation from a language without honorifics such as English, it is difficult to predict the appropriate honorific, but users may want to control the level of politeness in the output.

We propose a simple and effective method for including target-side T-V annotation in the training of a neural machine translation (NMT) system, which allows us to control the level of politeness at test time through what we call *side constraints*. It can be applied for translation between languages where the T-V distinction is missing from the source, or where the distribution differs. For instance, both Swedish and French make the T-V distinction, but reciprocal use of T pronouns is more widespread in Swedish than in French (Schüpbach et al., 2006). Hence, the Swedish form is not a reliable signal for the appropriate form in the French translation (or vice-versa).

Our basic approach of using side constraints to control target-side features that may be missing from the source, or are unreliable because of a category mismatch, is not limited to the T-V distinction, but could be applied to various linguistic features. This includes grammatical features such as tense and the number/gender of discourse participants, and more generally, features such as dialect and register choice.

This paper has the following contributions:

- we describe rules to automatically annotate the T-V distinction in German text.

- we describe how to use target-side T-V annotation in NMT training to control the level of politeness at test time via side constraints.

- we perform oracle experiments to demonstrate the impact of controlling politeness in NMT.

2 Background: Neural Machine Translation

Attentional neural machine translation (Bahdanau et al., 2015) is the current state of the art for

The research presented in this publication was conducted in cooperation with Samsung Electronics Polska sp. z o.o. - Samsung R&D Institute Poland.

English→German (Jean et al., 2015b; Luong and Manning, 2015). We follow the neural machine translation architecture by Bahdanau et al. (2015), which we will briefly summarize here. However, our approach is not specific to this architecture.

The neural machine translation system is implemented as an attentional encoder-decoder network. The encoder is a bidirectional neural network with gated recurrent units (Cho et al., 2014) that reads an input sequence $x = (x_1, ..., x_m)$ and calculates a forward sequence of hidden states $(\overrightarrow{h_1}, ..., \overrightarrow{h_m})$, and a backward sequence $(\overleftarrow{h_1}, ..., \overleftarrow{h_m})$. The hidden states $\overrightarrow{h_j}$ and $\overleftarrow{h_j}$ are concatenated to obtain the annotation vector h_j.

The decoder is a recurrent neural network that predicts a target sequence $y = (y_1, ..., y_n)$. Each word y_i is predicted based on a recurrent hidden state s_i, the previously predicted word y_{i-1}, and a context vector c_i. c_i is computed as a weighted sum of the annotations h_j. The weight of each annotation h_j is computed through an *alignment model* α_{ij}, which models the probability that y_i is aligned to x_j. The alignment model is a single-layer feedforward neural network that is learned jointly with the rest of the network through backpropagation.

A detailed description can be found in (Bahdanau et al., 2015). Training is performed on a parallel corpus with stochastic gradient descent. For translation, a beam search with small beam size is employed.

3 NMT with Side Constraints

We are interested in machine translation for language pairs where politeness is not grammatically marked in the source text, but should be predicted in the target text. The basic idea is to provide the neural network with additional input features that mark *side constraints* such as politeness.

At training time, the correct feature is extracted from the sentence pair as described in the following section. At test time, we assume that the side constraint is provided by a user who selects the desired level of politeness of the translation.

We add side constraints as special tokens at the end of the source text, for instance <T> or <V>. The attentional encoder-decoder framework is then able to learn to pay attention to the side constraints. One could envision alternative architectures to in-

corporate side constraints, e.g. directly connecting them to all decoder hidden states, bypassing the attention model, or connecting them to the output layer (Mikolov and Zweig, 2012). Our approach is simple and applicable to a wide range of NMT architectures and our experiments suggest that the incorporation of the side constraint as an extra source token is very effective.

4 Automatic Training Set Annotation

Our approach relies on annotating politeness in the training set to obtain the politeness feature which we discussed previously. We choose a sentence-level annotation because a target-side honorific may have no word-level correspondence in the source. We will discuss the annotation of German as an example, but our method could be applied to other languages, such as Japanese (Nariyama et al., 2005).

German has distinct pronoun forms for informal and polite address, as shown in Table 1. A further difference between informal and polite speech are imperative verbs, and the original imperative forms are considered informal. The polite alternative is to use 3rd person plural forms with subject in position 2:

- *Ruf mich zurück.* (informal)
  (Call me back.)

- *Rufen Sie mich zurück.* (polite)
  (Call you me back.)

We automatically annotate politeness on a sentence level with rules based on a morphosyntactic annotation by ParZu (Sennrich et al., 2013). Sentences containing imperative verbs are labelled informal. Sentences containing an informal or polite pronoun from Table 1 are labelled with the corresponding class.

Some pronouns are ambiguous. Polite pronouns are distinguished from (neutral) 3rd person plural forms by their capitalization, and are ambiguous in sentence-initial position. In sentence-initial position, we consider them polite pronouns if the English source side contains the pronoun *you(r)*. For *Ihr* and *ihr*, we use the morphological annotation by ParZu to distinguish between the informal 2nd person plural nominative, the (neutral) 3rd person singular dative, and the possessive; for possessive pronouns, we

category	informal		polite
	sg.	pl.	sg./pl.
nominative	du	ihr	Sie
genitive	deiner	euer	Ihrer
dative	dir	euch	Ihnen
accusative	dich	euch	Sie
possessive (base form)	dein	euer	Ihr

Table 1: German address pronouns.

distinguish between polite forms and (neutral) 3rd person forms by their capitalization.

If a sentence matches rules for both classes, we label it as informal – we found that our lowest-precision rule is the annotation of sentence-initial *Sie*. All sentences without a match are considered neutral.

5   Evaluation

Our empirical research questions are as follows:

- can we control the production of honorifics in neural machine translation via side constraints?

- how important is the T-V distinction for translation quality (as measured by BLEU)?

5.1   Data and Methods

We perform English→German experiments on OpenSubtitles (Tiedemann, 2012)[1], a parallel corpus of movie subtitles. Machine translation is commonly used in the professional translation of movie subtitles in a post-editing workflow, and politeness is considered an open problem for subtitle translation (Etchegoyhen et al., 2014). We use OpenSubtitles2012 as training corpus, and random samples from OpenSubtitles2013 for testing. The training corpus consists of of 5.58 million sentence pairs, out of which we label 0.48 million sentence pairs as polite, and 1.09 million as informal.

We train an attentional encoder-decoder NMT system using Groundhog[2] (Bahdanau et al., 2015; Jean et al., 2015a). We follow the settings and training procedure described by Sennrich et al. (2015), using BPE to represent the texts with a fixed vocabulary of subword units (vocabulary size 90000).

<hr>

[1] http://www.opensubtitles.org
[2] github.com/sebastien-j/LV_groundhog

The training set is annotated as described in section 4, and the source side is marked with the politeness feature as described in section 3. Note that there are only two values for the politeness feature, and neutral sentences are left unmarked. This is to allow users to select a politeness level for the whole document, without having to predict which translations should contain an address pronoun. Instead, we want the NMT model to ignore side constraints when they are irrelevant.

To ensure that the NMT model does not overly rely on the side constraints, and that performance does not degrade when no side constraint is provided at test time, only a subset of the labelled training instances are marked with a politeness feature at training time. We set the probability that a labelled training instance is marked, α, to 0.5 in our experiments. To ensure that the NMT model learns to ignore side constraints when they are irrelevant, and does not overproduce address pronouns when side constraints are active, we also mark neutral sentences with a random politeness feature with probability α. Keeping the mark-up probability α constant for all sentences in the training set prevents the introduction of unwanted biases. We re-mark the training set for each epoch of training. In preliminary experiments, we found no degradation in baseline performance when politeness features were included in this way during training.

The model is trained for approximately 9 epochs (7 days). At test time, all results are obtained with the same model, and the only variable is the side constraint used to control the production of honorifics. We test translation without side constraint, and translations that are constrained to be polite or informal. In an oracle experiment, we use the politeness label of the reference to determine the side constraint. This simulates a setting in which a user controls the desired politeness.

5.2   Results

Our first test set is a random sample of 2000 sentences from OpenSubtitles2013 where the English source contains a 2nd person pronoun. Results are shown in Table 2. Side constraints very effectively control whether the NMT system produces polite or informal output. Translations constrained to be polite are overwhelmingly labelled polite or neutral

side constraint	output label			BLEU
	neutral	polite	informal	
(reference)	429	524	1047	-
none	178	351	1471	20.7
polite	208	1728	64	17.9
informal	141	28	1831	20.2
oracle	161	567	1272	23.9

Table 2: Politeness and translation quality on test set of 2000 sentences from OpenSubtitles2013 that contain second person pronoun *you(r(s(elf)))* in English source text.

	source	Give me the telephone!
	reference	Gib mir das Telefon! [T]
	none	Gib mir das Telefon! [T]
	polite	Geben Sie mir das Telefon! [V]
	informal	Gib mir das Telefon! [T]
	source	Are you kidding?
	reference	Das ist doch ein Witz! [N] (this is a joke!)
	none	Machst du Witze? [T]
	polite	Machen Sie Witze? [V]
	informal	Machst du Witze? [T]
	source	You foolish boy.
	reference	Du dummer Junge. [T]
	none	Du dummer Junge. [T]
	polite	Du dummer Junge. [T]
	informal	Du dummer Junge. [T]

Table 3: Translation examples with different side constraints. Translations marked as neutral [N], informal [T] or polite [V].

by our automatic target-side annotation (96%), and analogously, translations constrained to be informal are almost exclusively informal or neutral (98%).

We also see that BLEU is strongly affected by the choice. An oracle experiment in which the side constraint of every sentence is informed by the reference obtains an improvement of 3.2 BLEU over the baseline (20.7→23.9).

We note that the reference has a higher proportion of German sentences labelled neutral than the NMT systems. A close inspection shows that this is due to sentence alignment errors in OpenSubtitles, free translations as shown in Table 3, and sentences where *you* is generic and translated by the impersonal pronoun *man* in the reference.

The side constraints are only soft constraints, and are occasionally overridden by the NMT system. These cases tend to be sentences where the source text provides strong politeness clues, like the sen-

side constraint	output label			BLEU
	neutral	polite	informal	
(reference)	1406	189	405	-
none	1385	125	490	22.6
polite	1386	576	38	21.7
informal	1365	11	624	22.5
oracle	1374	185	441	24.0

Table 4: Politeness and translation quality on test set of 2000 random sentences from OpenSubtitles2013.

tence *You foolish boy.* Neither the address *boy* nor the attribute *foolish* are likely in polite speech, and the sentence is translated with a T pronoun, regardless of the side constraint.

While Table 2 only contains sentences with an address pronoun in the source text, Table 4 represents a random sample. There are fewer address pronouns in the random sample, and thus more neutral sentences, but side constraints remain effective. This experiment also shows that we do not overproduce address pronouns when side constraints are provided, which validates our strategy of including side constraints with a constant probability α at training time.

The automatic evaluation with BLEU indicates that the T-V distinction is relevant for translation. We expect that the actual relevance for humans depends on the task. For gisting, we expect the T-V distinction to have little effect on comprehensibility. For professional translation that uses MT with post-editing, producing the desired honorifics is likely to improve post-editing speed and satisfaction. In an evaluation of MT for subtitle translation, Etchegoyhen et al. (2014) highlight the production of the appropriate T-V form as "a limitation of MT technology" that was "often frustrat[ing]" to post-editors.

6 Related Work

Faruqui and Pado (2012) have used a bilingual English–German corpus to automatically annotate the T-V distinction, and train a classifier to predict the address from monolingual English text. Applying a source-side classifier is potential future work, although we note that the baseline encoder–decoder NMT system already has some disambiguating power. Our T-V classification is more comprehensive, including more pronoun forms and imperative verbs.

Previous research on neural language models has proposed including various types of extra information, such as topic, genre or document context (Mikolov and Zweig, 2012; Aransa et al., 2015; Ji et al., 2015; Wang and Cho, 2015). Our method is somewhat similar, with the main novel idea being that we can target specific phenomena, such as honorifics, via an automatic annotation of the target side of a parallel corpus. On the modelling side, our method is slightly different in that we pass the extra information to the encoder of an encoder–decoder network, rather than the (decoder) hidden layer or output layer. We found this to be very effective, but trying different architectures is potential future work.

In rule-based machine translation, user options to control the level of politeness have been proposed in the 90s (Mima et al., 1997), and were adopted by commercial systems (SYSTRAN, 2004, 26). To our knowledge, controlling the level of politeness has not been explicitly addressed in statistical machine translation. While one could use data selection or weighting to control the honorifics produced by SMT, NMT allows us to very elegantly support multiple levels of politeness with a single model.

7 Conclusion

Machine translation should not only produce semantically accurate translations, but should also consider pragmatic aspects, such as producing socially appropriate forms of address. We show that by annotating the T-V distinction in the target text, and integrating the annotation as an additional input during training of a neural translation model, we can apply side constraints at test time to control the production of honorifics in NMT.

We currently assume that the desired level of politeness is specified by the user. Future work could aim to automatically predict it from the English source text based on textual features such as titles and names, or meta-textual information about the discourse participants.

While this paper focuses on controlling politeness, side constraints could be applied to a wide range of phenomena. It is a general problem in translation that, depending on the language pair, the translator needs to specify features in the target text that cannot be predicted from the source text. Apart from from the T-V distinction, this includes grammatical features such as clusivity, tense, and gender and number of the discourse participants, and more generally, features such as the desired dialect (e.g. when translating into Arabic) and text register. Side constraints can be applied to control these features. All that is required is that the feature can be annotated reliably, either using target-side information or metatextual information, at training time.

Acknowledgments

The research presented in this publication was conducted in cooperation with Samsung Electronics Polska sp. z o.o. - Samsung R&D Institute Poland. This project has received funding from the European Union's Horizon 2020 research and innovation programme under grant agreement 644402 (HimL).

References

Walid Aransa, Holger Schwenk, and Loïc Barrault. 2015. Improving Continuous Space Language Models using Auxiliary Features. In *Proceedings of the 12th International Workshop on Spoken Language Translation*, pages 151–158, Da Nang, Vietnam.

Dzmitry Bahdanau, Kyunghyun Cho, and Yoshua Bengio. 2015. Neural Machine Translation by Jointly Learning to Align and Translate. In *Proceedings of the International Conference on Learning Representations (ICLR)*.

Roger Brown and A. Gilman. 1960. The pronouns of power and solidarity. In T. Sebeok, editor, *Style in Language*. The M.I.T. Press, Cambridge, MA.

Kyunghyun Cho, Bart van Merrienboer, Caglar Gulcehre, Dzmitry Bahdanau, Fethi Bougares, Holger Schwenk, and Yoshua Bengio. 2014. Learning Phrase Representations using RNN Encoder–Decoder for Statistical Machine Translation. In *Proceedings of the 2014 Conference on Empirical Methods in Natural Language Processing (EMNLP)*, pages 1724–1734, Doha, Qatar. Association for Computational Linguistics.

Thierry Etchegoyhen, Lindsay Bywood, Mark Fishel, Panayota Georgakopoulou, Jie Jiang, Gerard Van Loenhout, Arantza Del Pozo, Mirjam Sepesy Maucec, Anja Turner, and Martin Volk. 2014. Machine Translation for Subtitling: A Large-Scale Evaluation. In *Proceedings of the Ninth International Conference on Language Resources and Evaluation (LREC'14)*, Reykjavik, Iceland. European Language Resources Association (ELRA).

Manaal Faruqui and Sebastian Pado. 2012. Towards a model of formal and informal address in English. In *Proceedings of the 13th Conference of the European Chapter of the Association for Computational Linguistics*, pages 623–633, Avignon, France. Association for Computational Linguistics.

Sébastien Jean, Kyunghyun Cho, Roland Memisevic, and Yoshua Bengio. 2015a. On Using Very Large Target Vocabulary for Neural Machine Translation. In *Proceedings of the 53rd Annual Meeting of the Association for Computational Linguistics and the 7th International Joint Conference on Natural Language Processing (Volume 1: Long Papers)*, pages 1–10, Beijing, China. Association for Computational Linguistics.

Sébastien Jean, Orhan Firat, Kyunghyun Cho, Roland Memisevic, and Yoshua Bengio. 2015b. Montreal Neural Machine Translation Systems for WMT'15. In *Proceedings of the Tenth Workshop on Statistical Machine Translation*, pages 134–140, Lisbon, Portugal. Association for Computational Linguistics.

Yangfeng Ji, Trevor Cohn, Lingpeng Kong, Chris Dyer, and Jacob Eisenstein. 2015. Document Context Language Models. *ArXiv e-prints*, November.

Minh-Thang Luong and Christopher D. Manning. 2015. Stanford Neural Machine Translation Systems for Spoken Language Domains. In *Proceedings of the International Workshop on Spoken Language Translation 2015*, Da Nang, Vietnam.

Tomas Mikolov and Geoffrey Zweig. 2012. Context dependent recurrent neural network language model. In *2012 IEEE Spoken Language Technology Workshop (SLT)*, pages 234–239, Miami, FL, USA.

Hideki Mima, Osamu Furuse, and Hitoshi Iida. 1997. Improving Performance of Transfer-driven Machine Translation with Extra-linguistic Information from Context, Situation and Environment. In *Proceedings of the Fifteenth International Joint Conference on Artifical Intelligence - Volume 2*, IJCAI'97, pages 983–988, San Francisco, CA, USA. Morgan Kaufmann Publishers Inc.

Shigeko Nariyama, Hiromi Nakaiwa, and Melanie Siegel. 2005. Annotating Honorifics Denoting Social Ranking of Referents. In *Proceedings of the 6th International Workshop on Linguistically Interpreted Corpora (LINC-2005)*.

Doris Schüpbach, John Hajek, Jane Warren, Michael Clyne, Heinz-L. Kretzenbacher, and Catrin Norrby. 2006. A cross-linguistic comparison of address pronoun use in four European languages: Intralingual and interlingual dimensions . In *Annual Meeting of the Australian Linguistic Society*, Brisbane, Australia.

Rico Sennrich, Martin Volk, and Gerold Schneider. 2013. Exploiting Synergies Between Open Resources for German Dependency Parsing, POS-tagging, and Morphological Analysis. In *Proceedings of the International Conference Recent Advances in Natural Language Processing 2013*, pages 601–609, Hissar, Bulgaria.

Rico Sennrich, Barry Haddow, and Alexandra Birch. 2015. Neural Machine Translation of Rare Words with Subword Units. *CoRR*, abs/1508.07909.

SYSTRAN, 2004. *SYSTRAN 5.0 User Guide*.

Jörg Tiedemann. 2012. Parallel Data, Tools and Interfaces in OPUS. In *Proceedings of the Eight International Conference on Language Resources and Evaluation (LREC'12)*, Istanbul, Turkey.

Tian Wang and Kyunghyun Cho. 2015. Larger-Context Language Modelling. *ArXiv e-prints*, November.

An Empirical Evaluation of Noise Contrastive Estimation
for the Neural Network Joint Model of Translation

Colin Cherry
National Research Council Canada
`Colin.Cherry@nrc-cnrc.gc.ca`

Abstract

The neural network joint model of translation or NNJM (Devlin et al., 2014) combines source and target context to produce a powerful translation feature. However, its softmax layer necessitates a sum over the entire output vocabulary, which results in very slow maximum likelihood (MLE) training. This has led some groups to train using Noise Contrastive Estimation (NCE), which side-steps this sum. We carry out the first direct comparison of MLE and NCE training objectives for the NNJM, showing that NCE is significantly outperformed by MLE on large-scale Arabic-English and Chinese-English translation tasks. We also show that this drop can be avoided by using a recently proposed translation noise distribution.

1 Introduction

The Neural Network Joint Model of Translation, or NNJM (Devlin et al., 2014), is a strong feature for statistical machine translation. The NNJM uses both target and source tokens as context for a feed-forward neural network language model (LM). Unfortunately, its softmax layer requires a sum over the entire output vocabulary, which slows the calculation of LM probabilities and the maximum likelihood estimation (MLE) of model parameters.

Devlin et al. (2014) address this problem at run-time only with a self-normalized MLE objective. Others advocate the use of Noise Contrastive Estimation (NCE) to train NNJMs and similar monolingual LMs (Mnih and Teh, 2012; Vaswani et al., 2013; Baltescu and Blunsom, 2015; Zhang et al.,

2015). NCE avoids the sum over the output vocabulary at both train- and run-time by wrapping the NNJM inside a classifier that attempts to separate real data from sampled noise, greatly improving training speed. The training efficiency of NCE is well-documented, and will not be evaluated here. However, the experimental evidence that NCE matches MLE in terms of resulting model quality is all on monolingual language modeling tasks (Mnih and Teh, 2012). Since cross-lingual contexts provide substantially stronger signals than monolingual ones, there is reason to suspect these results may not carry over to NNJMs.

To our knowledge there is no published work that directly compares MLE and NCE in the context of an NNJM; this paper fills that gap as its primary contribution. We measure model likelihood and translation quality in large-scale Arabic-to-English and Chinese-to-English translation tasks. We also test a recently-proposed translation noise distribution for NCE (Zhang et al., 2015), along with a mixture of noise distributions. Finally, we test a widely known, but apparently undocumented, technique for domain adaptation of NNJMs, demonstrating its utility, as well as its impact on the MLE-NCE comparison.

2 Methods

The NNJM adds a bilingual context window to the machinery of feed-forward neural network language models, or NNLMs (Bengio et al., 2003). An NNLM calculates the probability $p(e_i|e_{i-n+1}^{i-1})$ of a word e_i given its $n - 1$ preceding words, while an NNJM assumes access to a source sentence F and an aligned source index a_i that points to the most influ-

Proceedings of NAACL-HLT 2016, pages 41–46,
San Diego, California, June 12-17, 2016. ©2016 Association for Computational Linguistics

ential source word for the next translation choice. It calculates $p(e_i|e_{i-n+1}^{i-1}, f_{a_i-m}^{a_i+m})$, which accounts for $2m + 1$ words of source context, centered around f_{a_i}. The two models differ only in their definition of the conditioning context, which we will generalize with the variable $c_i = e_{i-n+1}^{i-1}, f_{a_i-m}^{a_i+m}$. When unambiguous, we drop the subscript i from e and c.

The feed-forward neural network that powers both models takes a context sequence c as input to its network, which includes an embedding layer, one or more hidden layers, and a top-level softmax layer that assigns probabilities to each word in the vocabulary V. Let $s_c(e)$ represent the unnormalized neural network score for the word e. The softmax layer first calculates $Z_c = \sum_{e' \in V} \exp s_c(e')$, which allows it to then normalize the score into a log probability $\log p(e|c) = s_c(e) - \log Z_c$. Given a training set of word-context pairs, MLE training of NNJMs minimizes the negative log likelihood $\sum_{e,c} - \log p(e|c)$.

The problem with this objective is that calculating Z_c requires a sum over the entire vocabulary, which is very expensive. This problem has received much recent study, but Devlin et al. (2014) proposed a novel solution for their NNJM, which we refer to as *self-normalization*. Assume we are willing to incur the cost of calculating Z_c during training, which might be mitigated by special-purpose hardware such as graphical processing units (GPUs). One can modify the MLE objective to encourage $\log Z_c$ to be small, so that the term can be safely dropped at run-time:

$$\sum_{e,c} \left[- \log p(e|c) + \alpha \left(\log Z_c \right)^2 \right]$$

where α trades self-normalization against model likelihood. Devlin et al. (2014) have shown that self-normalization has minimal impact on model quality and a tremendous impact on run-time efficiency.

2.1 Noise Contrastive Estimation

Introduced by Gutmann and Hyvärinen (2010) and first applied to language modeling by Mnih and Teh (2012), NCE allows one to train self-normalized models without calculating Z. It does so by defining a noise distribution q over words in V, which is typically a **unigram noise** distribution q_u. It samples k noise words $\hat{e}_1^k$ for each training word e, and wraps the NNJM inside a binary classifier that attempts to separate true data from noise. Let D be a binary variable that is 1 for true data and 0 for noise. We know the joint noise probability $p(D = 0, e|c) = \frac{k}{k+1} q(e)$, and we can approximate the joint data probability using our neural network $p(D = 1, e|c) \approx \frac{1}{k+1} p(e|c) \approx \frac{1}{k+1} \exp s_c(e)$. Note that the final approximation drops Z_c from the calculation, improving efficiency and forcing the model to self-normalize. With these two terms in place, and a few manipulations of conditional probability, the NCE training objective can be given as:

$$- \sum_{e,c} \left[\log p(D = 1|e, c) + \sum_{j=1}^{k} \log p(D = 0|\hat{e}_j, c) \right]$$

which measures the probability that data is recognized as data, and noise is recognized as noise.

Note that q ignores the context c. Previous work on monolingual language modeling indicates that a unigram proposal distribution is sufficient for NCE training (Mnih and Teh, 2012). But for bilingual NNJMs, Zhang et al. (2015) have shown that it is beneficial to have q condition on *source* context. Recall that $c_i = e_{i-n+1}^{i-1}, f_{a_i-m}^{a_i+m}$. We experiment with a **translation noise** distribution $q_t(\hat{e}|f_{a_i})$. We estimate q_t by relative frequency from our training corpus, which implicitly provides us with one e_i, f_{a_i} pair for each training point e_i, c_i. Conditioning on f_{a_i} drastically reduces the entropy of the noise distribution, focusing training on the task of differentiating between likely translation candidates.

As our experiments will show, under NCE with translation noise, the NNJM no longer provides meaningful scores for the entire vocabulary. Therefore, we also experiment with a novel **mixture noise** distribution: $q_m(\hat{e}|f_{a_i}) = 0.5 q_u(\hat{e}) + 0.5 q_t(\hat{e}|f_{a_i})$.

3 Implementation details

We implement our NNJM and all candidate training objectives described above in a shared codebase in Theano (Bergstra et al., 2010). To ensure a fair comparison between MLE and NCE, the various systems share code for model structures and algorithms, differing only in their training objectives. A GeForce GTX TITAN GPU enables efficient MLE training. Following Devlin et al. (2014), all NNJMs use 3 tokens for target context, a source context window with $m = 5$, and a 192-node embedding layer.

We deviate from their configuration by using a single 512-node hidden layer, motivated by our internal development experiments. All NCE variants use $k = 100$ noise samples.

NNJM training data is pre-processed to limit vocabularies to 16K types for source or target inputs, and 32K types for target outputs. We build 400 deterministic word clusters for each corpus using `mkcls` (Och, 1999). Any word not among the 16K / 32K most frequent words is replaced with its cluster.

We train our models with mini-batch stochastic gradient descent, with a batch size of 128 words, and an initial learning rate of 0.3. We check our training objective on the development set every 20K batches, and if it fails to improve for two consecutive checks, the learning rate is halved. Training stops after 5 consecutive failed checks or after 60 checks. As NCE may take longer to converge than MLE, we occasionally let NCE models train to 90 checks, but this never resulted in improved performance. Finally, after training finishes on the complete training data, we use that model to initialize a second training run, on a smaller in-domain training set known to better match the test conditions.[1] This in-domain pass uses a lower initial learning rate of 0.03.

Our translation system is a multi-stack phrase-based decoder that is quite similar to Moses (Koehn et al., 2007). Its features include standard phrase table probabilities, KN-smoothed language models including a 6-gram model trained on the English Gigaword and a 4-gram model trained on the target side of the parallel training data, domain-adapted phrase tables and language models (Foster and Kuhn, 2007), a hierarchical lexicalized reordering model (Galley and Manning, 2008), and sparse features drawn from Hopkins and May (2011) and Cherry (2013). It is tuned with a batch-lattice variant of hope-fear MIRA (Chiang et al., 2008; Cherry and Foster, 2012).

4 Experiments

We test two translation scenarios drawn from the recent BOLT evaluations: Arabic-to-English and Chinese-to-English. The vital statistics for our corpora are given in Table 1. The training set mixes

Lang.	Train	In-dom	Dev	Test1	Test2
Arabic	38.6M	1.8M	72K	38K	40K
Chinese	29.2M	1.9M	77K	38K	36K

Table 1: Corpus sizes in terms of number of target tokens. Dev and Test sets have 3 references for Arabic and 5 for Chinese.

NIST data with BOLT-specific informal genres. The development and test sets are focused specifically on the web-forum genre, as is the in-domain subset of the training data (*In-dom*). The Arabic was segmented with MADA-ARZ (Habash et al., 2013), while the Chinese was segmented with a lexicon-based approach. All data was word-aligned with IBM-4 in GIZA++ (Och and Ney, 2003), with grow-diag-final-and symmetrization (Koehn et al., 2003).

4.1 Comparing Training Objectives

Our main experiment is designed to answer two questions: (1) does training NNJMs with NCE impact translation quality? and (2) can any reduction be mitigated through alternate noise distributions? To this end, we train four NNJMs.

- **MLE**: Maximum likelihood training with self-normalization $\alpha = 0.1$
- **NCE-U**: NCE with unigram noise
- **NCE-T**: NCE with translation noise
- **NCE-M**: NCE with mixture noise

and compare their performance to that of a system with no NNJM. Each NNJM was trained as described in Section 3, varying only the learning objective.[2] To measure intrinsic NNJM quality, we report average negative log likelihoods (NLL) and average $|\log Z|$, both calculated on Dev. Lower NLL scores indicate better prediction accuracy, while lower $|\log Z|$ values indicate more effective self-normalization. We also provide average BLEU scores and standard deviations for Test1 and Test2, each calculated over 5 random tuning replications. Statistical significance is calculated with MultEval (Clark et al., 2011).

Our results are shown in Table 2. By comparing MLE to no NNJM, we can confirm that the NNJM is a very effective translation feature, showing large

---

[1] Recommended by Jacob Devlin, personal communication.

[2] The only exception was the Arabic NCE-M system, which showed some instability during optimization, leading us to reduce its initial learning rate to 0.2.

Method	Arabic-English						Chinese-English					
	NLL	$|\log Z|$	test1	std	test2	std	NLL	$|\log Z|$	test1	std	test2	std
No NNJM	–	–	39.2	0.1	39.9	0.1	–	–	31.6	0.2	27.8	0.1
MLE	1.76	0.50	41.7	0.1	42.0	0.1	2.35	0.49	32.9	0.0	29.1	0.0
NCE-U	1.85	0.42	40.9	0.2	41.5	0.1	2.54	0.42	32.2	0.1	28.3	0.1
NCE-T	3.87	2.36	**41.6**	0.1	**42.4**	0.2	3.93	1.70	**32.7**	0.1	28.7	0.2
NCE-M	1.85	0.30	41.4	0.1	**42.1**	0.1	2.40	0.30	32.6	0.1	28.8	0.1

Table 2: Comparing various NNJM training objectives on two translation scenarios. BLEU results that are statistically better than NCE-U are underlined ($p \leq 0.05$). Those statistically equivalent to or better than MLE are in **bold** ($p \leq 0.05$).

BLEU improvements on all tests. By comparing MLE to NCE-U, we can see that NCE training does reduce translation quality. NCE-U outperforms having no NNJM, but lags behind MLE considerably, resulting in significantly worse performance on all tests. This is mitigated with translation noise: NCE-T and NCE-M both perform significantly better than NCE-U. Furthermore, in 3 out of 4 tests, NCE-T matches or exceeds the performance of MLE. The one Arabic-to-English case where NCE-T exceeds the performance of MLE is particularly intriguing, and warrants further study.

Though NCE-T performs very well as a translation feature, it is relatively lousy as a language model, with abnormally large values for both NLL and $|\log Z|$. This indicates that NCE-T is only good at predicting the next word from a pool of reasonable translation candidates. Scores for words drawn from the larger vocabulary are less accurate. However, the BLEU results for NCE-T show that this does not matter for translation performance. If model likelihoods over the complete vocabulary are needed, one can repair these estimates by mixing in unigram noise, as shown by NCE-M, which achieves the same or better likelihoods than NCE-U, with comparable BLEU scores to those of NCE-T.

Devlin et al. (2014) suggest that one drawback of NCE with respect to self-normalized MLE is NCE's lack of an α hyper-parameter to control the objective's emphasis on self-normalization. However, the $|\log Z|$ values for NCE-U are only slightly lower than those of MLE, and are larger than those of the superior NCE-M. This suggests that we could not have improved NCE-U's performance by adjusting its emphasis on self-normalization.

Method	General		Adapted	
	BLEU	Δ	BLEU	Δ
No NNJM	39.6	-1.4	39.6	-2.2
MLE	41.0	—	41.8	—
NCE-U	40.7	-0.3	41.2	-0.6
NCE-T	41.0	0.0	42.0	+0.2
NCE-M	40.9	-0.1	41.7	-0.1

Table 3: Comparing NNJM training objectives with and without a domain adaptation step for Arabic-to-English task.

4.2 Impact of the Domain Adaptation Pass

We began this project with the hypothesis that NCE may harm NNJM performance. But NCE-U performed worse than we expected. In particular, the differences between NCE-U and NCE-T are larger than those reported by Zhang et al. (2015). This led us to investigate the domain adaptation pass, which was used in our experiments but not those of Zhang et al. This step refines the model with a second training pass on an in-domain subset of the training data. We repeated our comparison for Arabic without domain adaptation, reporting BLEU averaged over two test sets and across 5 tuning replications. We also report each system's BLEU differential Δ with respect to MLE. The results are shown under *General* in Table 3, while *Adapted* summarizes our results from Table 2 in the same format.

The domain adaptation step magnifies the differences between training objectives, perhaps because it increases performance over-all. The spread between the worst and best NNJM is only 0.3 BLEU under *General*, while it is 0.8 BLEU under *Adapted*. Therefore, groups training unadapted models may not see as large drops from NCE-U as we have reported above. Note that we experimented with several configurations that account specifically for this domain-adaptation pass (noise distributions based on general versus in-domain corpora, alternate stopping criteria), so that NCE-U would be presented in the most positive possible light. Perhaps most importantly, Table 3 shows that the domain adaptation pass is quite effective, producing large improvements for all NNJMs.

4.3 Impact on Speed

MLE and NCE both produce self-normalized models, so they both have the same impact on decoding speed. With the optimizations described by Devlin et al. (2014), the impact of any single-hidden-layer NNJM is negligible.

For training, the main benefit of NCE is that it reduces the cost of the network's output layer, replacing a term that was linear in the vocabulary size with one that is linear in the sample size. In our experiments, this is a reduction from 32K to 100. The actual benefit from this reduction is highly implementation- and architecture-dependent. It is difficult to get a substantial speedup from NCE using Theano on GPU hardware, as both reward dense matrix operations, and NCE demands sparse vector operations (Jean et al., 2015). Therefore, our decision to implement all methods in a shared codebase, which ensured a fair comparison of model quality, also prevented us from providing a meaningful evaluation of training speed, as the code and architecture were implicitly optimized to favour the most demanding method (MLE). Fortunately, there is ample evidence that NCE can provide large improvements to per-batch training speeds for NNLMs, ranging from a $2\times$ speed-up for 20K-word vocabularies on a GPU (Chen et al., 2015) to more than $10\times$ for 70K-word vocabularies on a CPU (Vaswani et al., 2013). Meanwhile, our experiments show that 1.2M batches are sufficient for MLE, NCE-T and NCE-M to achieve very high quality; that is, none of these methods made use of early stopping during their main training pass. This indicates that per-batch speed is the most important factor when comparing the training times of these NNJMs.

5 Conclusions

We have shown that NCE training with a unigram noise distribution does reduce NNJM performance with respect to MLE training, both in terms of model likelihoods and downstream translation quality. This performance drop can be avoided if NCE uses a translation-aware noise distribution. We have emphasized the importance of a domain-specific training pass, and we have shown that this pass magnifies the differences between the various NNJM training objectives. In a few cases, NCE with translation noise actually outperformed MLE. This suggests that there is value in only considering plausible translation candidates during training. It would be interesting to explore methods to improve MLE with this intuition.

Acknowledgments

Thanks to George Foster, Eric Joanis, Roland Kuhn and the anonymous reviewers for their valuable comments on an earlier draft.

References

Paul Baltescu and Phil Blunsom. 2015. Pragmatic neural language modelling in machine translation. In *Proceedings of the Human Language Technology Conference of the NAACL (HLT-NAACL)*, pages 820–829, Denver, Colorado, May–June.

Yoshua Bengio, Réjean Ducharme, Pascal Vincent, and Christian Jauvin. 2003. A neural probabilistic language model. *Journal of Machine Learning Research*, 3:1137–1155.

James Bergstra, Olivier Breuleux, Frédéric Bastien, Pascal Lamblin, Razvan Pascanu, Guillaume Desjardins, Joseph Turian, David Warde-Farley, and Yoshua Bengio. 2010. Theano: a CPU and GPU math expression compiler. In *Proceedings of the Python for Scientific Computing Conference (SciPy)*, June.

X Chen, X Liu, MJF Gales, and PC Woodland. 2015. Recurrent neural network language model training with noise contrastive estimation for speech recognition. In *ICASSP*.

Colin Cherry and George Foster. 2012. Batch tuning strategies for statistical machine translation. In *Proceedings of the Human Language Technology Conference of the NAACL (HLT-NAACL)*, pages 427–436, Montréal, Canada, June.

Colin Cherry. 2013. Improved reordering for phrase-based translation using sparse features. In *Proceedings of the Human Language Technology Conference of the NAACL (HLT-NAACL)*, pages 22–31, Atlanta, Georgia, June.

David Chiang, Yuval Marton, and Philip Resnik. 2008. Online large-margin training of syntactic and structural translation features. In *Proceedings of the Conference on Empirical Methods in Natural Language Processing (EMNLP)*, pages 224–233.

Jonathan H. Clark, Chris Dyer, Alon Lavie, and Noah A. Smith. 2011. Better hypothesis testing for statistical machine translation: Controlling for optimizer instability. In *Proceedings of the Annual Meeting of the Association for Computational Linguistics (ACL)*, pages 176–181.

Jacob Devlin, Rabih Zbib, Zhongqiang Huang, Thomas Lamar, Richard Schwartz, and John Makhoul. 2014. Fast and robust neural network joint models for statistical machine translation. In *Proceedings of the Annual Meeting of the Association for Computational Linguistics (ACL)*, pages 1370–1380, Baltimore, Maryland, June.

George Foster and Roland Kuhn. 2007. Mixture-model adaptation for SMT. In *Proceedings of the Workshop on Statistical Machine Translation*, pages 128–135.

Michel Galley and Christopher D. Manning. 2008. A simple and effective hierarchical phrase reordering model. In *Proceedings of the Conference on Empirical Methods in Natural Language Processing (EMNLP)*, pages 848–856, Honolulu, Hawaii.

Michael Gutmann and Aapo Hyvärinen. 2010. Noise-contrastive estimation: A new estimation principle for unnormalized statistical models. In *International Conference on Artificial Intelligence and Statistics*, pages 297–304.

Nizar Habash, Ryan Roth, Owen Rambow, Ramy Eskander, and Nadi Tomeh. 2013. Morphological analysis and disambiguation for dialectal arabic. In *Proceedings of the Human Language Technology Conference of the NAACL (HLT-NAACL)*, pages 426–432, Atlanta, Georgia, June.

Mark Hopkins and Jonathan May. 2011. Tuning as ranking. In *Proceedings of the Conference on Empirical Methods in Natural Language Processing (EMNLP)*, pages 1352–1362.

Sébastien Jean, Kyunghyun Cho, Roland Memisevic, and Yoshua Bengio. 2015. On using very large target vocabulary for neural machine translation. In *Proceedings of the 53rd Annual Meeting of the Association for Computational Linguistics and the 7th International Joint Conference on Natural Language Processing (Volume 1: Long Papers)*, pages 1–10, Beijing, China, July.

Philipp Koehn, Franz Joesef Och, and Daniel Marcu. 2003. Statistical phrase-based translation. In *Proceedings of the Human Language Technology Conference of the NAACL (HLT-NAACL)*, pages 127–133.

Philipp Koehn, Hieu Hoang, Alexandra Birch, Chris Callison-Burch, Marcello Federico, Nicola Bertoldi, Brooke Cowan, Wade Shen, Christine Moran, Richard Zens, Chris Dyer, Ondrej Bojar, Alexandra Constantin, and Evan Herbst. 2007. Moses: Open source toolkit for statistical machine translation. In *Proceedings of the Annual Meeting of the Association for Computational Linguistics (ACL)*, pages 177–180, Prague, Czech Republic, June.

Andriy Mnih and Yee Whye Teh. 2012. A fast and simple algorithm for training neural probabilistic language models. In *Proceedings of the 29th International Conference on Machine Learning*, pages 1751–1758.

Franz Joesef Och and Hermann Ney. 2003. A systematic comparison of various statistical alignment models. *Computational Linguistics*, 29(1):19–52.

Franz Josef Och. 1999. An efficient method for determining bilingual word classes. In *Proceedings of the Conference of the European Chapter of the Association for Computational Linguistics (EACL)*.

Ashish Vaswani, Yinggong Zhao, Victoria Fossum, and David Chiang. 2013. Decoding with large-scale neural language models improves translation. In *Proceedings of the Conference on Empirical Methods in Natural Language Processing (EMNLP)*, pages 1387–1392, Seattle, Washington, USA, October.

Jingyi Zhang, Masao Utiyama, Eiichiro Sumita, Graham Neubig, and Satoshi Nakamura. 2015. A binarized neural network joint model for machine translation. In *Proceedings of the Conference on Empirical Methods in Natural Language Processing (EMNLP)*, pages 2094–2099, Lisbon, Portugal, September.

Neural Network-Based Abstract Generation for Opinions and Arguments

Lu Wang
College of Computer and Information Science
Northeastern University
Boston, MA 02115
luwang@ccs.neu.edu

Wang Ling
Google DeepMind
London, N1 0AE
lingwang@google.com

Abstract

We study the problem of generating abstractive summaries for opinionated text. We propose an attention-based neural network model that is able to absorb information from multiple text units to construct informative, concise, and fluent summaries. An importance-based sampling method is designed to allow the encoder to integrate information from an important subset of input. Automatic evaluation indicates that our system outperforms state-of-the-art abstractive and extractive summarization systems on two newly collected datasets of movie reviews and arguments. Our system summaries are also rated as more informative and grammatical in human evaluation.

1 Introduction

Collecting opinions from others is an integral part of our daily activities. Discovering what other people think can help us navigate through different aspects of life, ranging from making decisions on regular tasks to judging fundamental societal issues and forming personal ideology. To efficiently absorb the massive amount of opinionated information, there is a pressing need for automated systems that can generate concise and fluent opinion summary about an entity or a topic. In spite of substantial researches in opinion summarization, the most prominent approaches mainly rely on *extractive summarization* methods, where phrases or sentences from the original documents are selected for inclusion in the summary (Hu and Liu, 2004; Lerman et al., 2009). One of the problems that extractive methods suffer from

> **Movie**: *The Martian*
> **Reviews**:
> - One the **smartest**, sweetest, and most satisfyingly suspenseful sci-fi films in years.
> - ...an intimate sci-fi epic that is **smart**, spectacular and stirring.
> - The Martian is a **thrilling**, human and moving sci-fi picture that is easily the most emotionally engaging film Ridley Scott has made...
> - It's pretty sunny and often **funny**, a space oddity for a director not known for pictures with **a sense of humor**.
> - The Martian **highlights the book's best qualities**, tones down its worst, and adds its own style...
> **Opinion Consensus (Summary)**: **Smart**, **thrilling**, and surprisingly **funny**, The Martian offers **a faithful adaptation of the bestselling book** that brings out the best in leading man Matt Damon and director Ridley Scott.
>
> **Topic**: *This House supports the death penalty.*
> **Arguments**:
> - The state has a responsibility to protect the lives of innocent citizens, and enacting the death penalty may save lives by reducing the rate of violent crime.
> - While the prospect of life in prison may be frightening, surely death is a more daunting prospect.
> - A 1985 study by Stephen K. Layson at the University of North Carolina showed that a single execution deters 18 murders.
> - Reducing the wait time on death row prior to execution can dramatically increase its deterrent effect in the United States.
> **Claim (Summary)**: The death penalty deters crime.

Figure 1: Examples for an opinion consensus of professional reviews (critics) about movie *"The Martian"* from www.rottentomatoes.com, and a claim about "death penalty" supported by arguments from idebate.org. Content with similar meaning is highlighted in the same color.

is that they unavoidably include secondary or redundant information. On the contrary, *abstractive summarization* methods, which are able to generate text beyond the original input, can produce more coherent and concise summaries.

In this paper, we present *an attention-based neural network model for generating abstractive summaries of opinionated text*. Our system takes as input a set of text units containing opinions about the same topic (e.g. reviews for a movie, or arguments

Proceedings of NAACL-HLT 2016, pages 47–57,
San Diego, California, June 12-17, 2016. ©2016 Association for Computational Linguistics

for a controversial social issue), and then outputs a one-sentence abstractive summary that describes the opinion consensus of the input.

Specifically, we investigate our abstract generation model on two types of opinionated text: *movie reviews* and *arguments on controversial topics*. Examples are displayed in Figure 1. The first example contains a set of professional reviews (or critics) about movie "The Martian" and an opinion consensus written by an editor. It would be more useful to automatically generate fluent opinion consensus rather than simply extracting features (e.g. plot, music, etc) and opinion phrases as done in previous summarization work (Zhuang et al., 2006; Li et al., 2010). The second example lists a set of arguments on "death penalty", where each argument supports the central claim "death penalty deters crime". Arguments, as a special type of opinionated text, contain reasons to persuade or inform people on certain issues. Given a set of arguments on the same topic, we aim at investigating the capability of our abstract generation system for the novel task of *claim generation*.

Existing abstract generation systems for opinionated text mostly take an approach that first identifies salient phrases, and then merges them into sentences (Bing et al., 2015; Ganesan et al., 2010). Those systems are not capable of generating new words, and the output summary may suffer from ungrammatical structure. Another line of work requires a large amount of human input to enforce summary quality. For example, Gerani et al. (2014) utilize a set of templates constructed by human, which are filled by extracted phrases to generate grammatical sentences that serve different discourse functions.

To address the challenges above, we propose to use an attention-based abstract generation model — a data-driven approach trained to generate informative, concise, and fluent opinion summaries. Our method is based on the recently proposed framework of neural encoder-decoder models (Kalchbrenner and Blunsom, 2013; Sutskever et al., 2014a), which translates a sentence in a source language into a target language. Different from previous work, our summarization system is designed to support multiple input text units. An attention-based model (Bahdanau et al., 2014) is deployed to al-

low the encoder to automatically search for salient information within context. Furthermore, we propose an importance-based sampling method so that the encoder can integrate information from an important subset of input text. The importance score of a text unit is estimated from a novel regression model with pairwise preference-based regularizer. With importance-based sampling, our model can be trained within manageable time, and is still able to learn from diversified input.

We demonstrate the effectiveness of our model on two newly collected datasets for movie reviews and arguments. Automatic evaluation by BLEU (Papineni et al., 2002) indicates that our system outperforms the state-of-the-art extract-based and abstract-based methods on both tasks. For example, we achieved a BLEU score of 24.88 on Rotten Tomatoes movie reviews, compared to 19.72 by an abstractive opinion summarization system from Ganesan et al. (2010). ROUGE evaluation (Lin and Hovy, 2003) also indicates that our system summaries have reasonable information coverage. Human judges further rated our summaries to be more informative and grammatical than compared systems.

2 Data Collection

We collected two datasets for movie reviews and arguments on controversial topics with gold-standard abstracts.[1] Rotten Tomatoes (`www.rottentomatoes.com`) is a movie review website that aggregates both professional critics and user-generated reviews (henceforth *RottenTomatoes*). For each movie, a one-sentence critic consensus is constructed by an editor to summarize the opinions in professional critics. We crawled 246,164 critics and their opinion consensus for 3,731 movies (i.e. around 66 reviews per movie on average). We select 2,458 movies for training, 536 movies for validation and 737 movies for testing. The opinion consensus is treated as the gold-standard summary.

We also collect an argumentation dataset from `idebate.org` (henceforth *Idebate*), which is a Wikipedia-style website for gathering pro and con arguments on controversial issues. The arguments under each debate (or topic) are organized into dif-

---

[1]The datasets can be downloaded from `http://www.ccs.neu.edu/home/luwang/`.

ferent "for" and "against" points. Each point contains a one-sentence central claim constructed by the editors to summarize the corresponding arguments, and is treated as the gold-standard. For instance, on a debate about "death penalty", one claim is "the death penalty deters crime" with an argument "enacting the death penalty may save lives by reducing the rate of violent crime" (Figure 1). We crawled 676 debates with 2,259 claims. We treat each sentence as an argument, which results in 17,359 arguments in total. 450 debates are used for training, 67 debates for validation, and 150 debates for testing.

3 The Neural Network-Based Abstract Generation Model

In this section, we first define our problem in Section 3.1, followed by model description. In general, we utilize a Long Short-Term Memory network for generating abstracts (Section 3.2) from a latent representation computed by an attention-based encoder (Section 3.3). The encoder is designed to search for relevant information from input to better inform the abstract generation process. We also discuss an importance-based sampling method to allow encoder to integrate information from an important subset of input (Sections 3.4 and 3.5). Post-processing (Section 3.6) is conducted to re-rank the generations and pick the best one as the final summary.

3.1 Problem Formulation

In summarization, the goal is to generate a summary y, composed by the sequence of words $y_1, ..., |y|$. Unlike previous neural encoder-decoder approaches which decode from only one input, our input consists of an arbitrary number of reviews or arguments (henceforth *text units* wherever there is no ambiguity), denoted as $x = \{x^1, ..., x^M\}$. Each text unit x^k is composed by a sequence of words $x_1^k, ..., x_{|x^k|}^k$. Each word takes the form of a representation vector, which is initialized randomly or by pre-trained embeddings (Mikolov et al., 2013), and updated during training. The summarization task is defined as finding $\hat{y}$, which is the most likely sequence of words $\hat{y}_1, ..., \hat{y}_N$ such that:

$$\hat{y} = argmax_y \log P(y|x) \qquad (1)$$

where $\log P(y|x)$ denotes the conditional log-likelihood of the output sequence y, given the input text units x. In the next sections, we describe the attention model used to model $\log P(y|x)$.

3.2 Decoder

Similar as previous work (Sutskever et al., 2014b; Bahdanau et al., 2014), we decompose $\log P(y|x)$ into a sequence of word-level predictions:

$$\log P(y|x) = \sum_{j=1,...,|y|} \log P(y_j|y_1, ..., y_{j-1}, x) \qquad (2)$$

where each word y_j is predicted conditional on the previously generated $y_1, ..., y_{j-1}$ and input x. The probability is estimated by standard word softmax:

$$p(y_j|y_1, ..., y_{j-1}, x) = softmax(\mathbf{h}_j) \qquad (3)$$

$\mathbf{h}_j$ is the Recurrent Neural Networks (RNNs) state variable at timestamp j, which is modeled as:

$$\mathbf{h}_j = g(\mathbf{y}_{j-1}, \mathbf{h}_{j-1}, \mathbf{s}) \qquad (4)$$

Here g is a recurrent update function for generating the new state $\mathbf{h}_j$ from the representation of previously generated word $\mathbf{y}_{j-1}$ (obtained from a word lookup table), the previous state $\mathbf{h}_{j-1}$, and the input text representation $\mathbf{s}$ (see Section 3.3).

In this work, we implement g using a Long Short-Term Memory (LSTM) network (Hochreiter and Schmidhuber, 1997), which has been shown to be effective at capturing long range dependencies. Here we summarize the update rules for LSTM cells, and refer readers to the original work (Hochreiter and Schmidhuber, 1997) for more details. Given an arbitrary input vector $\mathbf{u}_j$ at timestamp $j - 1$ and the previous state $\mathbf{h}_{j-1}$, a typical LSTM defines the following update rules:

$$\begin{aligned}
\mathbf{i}_j &= \sigma(\mathbf{W}_{iu}\mathbf{u}_j + \mathbf{W}_{ih}\mathbf{h}_{j-1} + \mathbf{W}_{ic}\mathbf{c}_{j-1} + \mathbf{b}_i) \\
\mathbf{f}_j &= \sigma(\mathbf{W}_{fu}\mathbf{u}_j + \mathbf{W}_{fh}\mathbf{h}_{j-1} + \mathbf{W}_{fc}\mathbf{c}_{j-1} + \mathbf{b}_f) \\
\mathbf{c}_j &= \mathbf{f}_j \odot \mathbf{c}_{j-1} + \mathbf{i}_j \odot \tanh(\mathbf{W}_{cu}\mathbf{u}_j + \mathbf{W}_{ch}\mathbf{h}_{j-1} + \mathbf{b}_c) \\
\mathbf{o}_j &= \sigma(\mathbf{W}_{ou}\mathbf{u}_j + \mathbf{W}_{oh}\mathbf{h}_{j-1} + \mathbf{W}_{oc}\mathbf{c}_j + \mathbf{b}_o) \\
\mathbf{h}_j &= \mathbf{o}_j \odot \tanh(\mathbf{c}_j)
\end{aligned}$$
$$(5)$$

σ is component-wise logistic sigmoid function, and $\odot$ denotes Hadamard product. Projection matrices

$\mathbf{W}_{**}$ and biases $\mathbf{b}_*$ are parameters to be learned during training.

Long range dependencies are captured by the cell memory $\mathbf{c}_j$, which is updated linearly to avoid the vanishing gradient problem. It is accomplished by predicting two vectors $\mathbf{i}_j$ and $\mathbf{f}_j$, which determine what to keep and what to forget from the current timestamp. Vector $\mathbf{o}_j$ then decides on what information from the new cell memory $\mathbf{c}_j$ can be passed to the new state $\mathbf{h}_j$. Finally, the model concatenates the representation of previous output word $\mathbf{y}_{j-1}$ and the input representation $\mathbf{s}$ (see Section 3.3) as $\mathbf{u}_j$, which serves as the input at each timestamp.

3.3 Encoder

The representation of input text units $\mathbf{s}$ is computed using an attention model (Bahdanau et al., 2014). Given a single text unit $x_1, ..., x_{|x|}$ and the previous state $\mathbf{h_j}$, the model generates $\mathbf{s}$ as a weighted sum:

$$\sum_{i=1,...,|x|} a_i \mathbf{b}_i \qquad (6)$$

where a_i is the attention coefficient obtained for word x_i, and $\mathbf{b}_i$ is the context dependent representation of x_i. In our work, we construct $\mathbf{b}_i$ by building a bidirectional LSTM over the whole input sequence $x_1, ..., x_{|x|}$ and then combining the forward and backward states. Formally, we use the LSTM formulation from Eq. 5 to generate the forward states $\mathbf{h}_1^f, ..., \mathbf{h}_{|x|}^f$ by setting $\mathbf{u}_j = \mathbf{x}_j$ (the projection word x_j using a word lookup table). Likewise, the backward states $\mathbf{h}_{|x|}^b, ..., \mathbf{h}_1^b$ are generated using a backward LSTM by feeding the input in the reverse order, that is, $\mathbf{u}_j = \mathbf{x}_{|x|-j+1}$. The coefficients a_i are computed with a softmax over all input:

$$a_i = softmax(v(\mathbf{b}_i, \mathbf{h}_{j-1})) \qquad (7)$$

where function v computes the affinity of each word x_i and the current output context $\mathbf{h}_{j-1}$ — how likely the input word is to be used to generate the next word in summary. We set $v(\mathbf{b}_i, \mathbf{h}_{j-1}) = \mathbf{W}_s \cdot \tanh(\mathbf{W}_{cg}\mathbf{b}_i + \mathbf{W}_{hg}\mathbf{h}_{j-1})$, where $\mathbf{W}_*$ and $\mathbf{W}_{**}$ are parameters to be learned.

3.4 Attention Over Multiple Inputs

A key distinction between our model and existing sequence-to-sequence models (Sutskever et al., 2014b; Bahdanau et al., 2014) is that our input consists of multiple separate text units. Given an input of N text units, i.e. $\{x_1^k, ..., x_{|x^k|}^k\}_{k=1}^N$, a simple extension would be to concatenate them into one sequence as $z = x_1^1, ..., x_{|x^1|}^1, \text{SEG}, x_1^2, ..., x_{|x^2|}^2, \text{SEG}, x_1^N, ..., x_{|x^N|}^N$, where SEG is a special token that delimits inputs.

However, there are two problems with this approach. Firstly, the model is sensitive to the order of text units. Moreover, z may contain thousands of words. This will become a bottleneck for our model with a training time of $O(N|z|)$, since attention coefficients must be computed for all input words to generate each output word.

We address these two problems by sub-sampling from the input. The intuition is that even though the number of input text units is large, many of them are redundant or contain secondary information. As our task is to emphasize the main points made in the input, some of them can be removed without losing too much information. Therefore, we define an importance score $f(x^k) \in [0, 1]$ for each document x^k (see Section 3.5). During training, K candidates are sampled from a multinomial distribution which is constructed by normalizing $f(x^k)$ for input text units. Notice that the training process goes over the training set multiple times, and our model is still able to learn from more than K text units. For testing, top-K candidates with the highest importance scores are collapsed in descending order into z.

3.5 Importance Estimation

We now describe the importance estimation model, which outputs importance scores for text units. In general, we start with a ridge regression model, and add a regularizer to enforce the separation of summary-worthy text units from others.

Given a cluster of text units $\{x^1, ..., x^M\}$ and their summary y, we compute the number of overlapping content words between each text unit and summary y as its gold-standard importance score. The scores are uniformly normalized to $[0, 1]$. Each text unit x^k is represented as an $d-$dimensional feature vector $\mathbf{r_k} \in \mathbb{R}^d$, with label l_k. Text units in the training data are thus denoted with a feature matrix $\tilde{\mathbf{R}}$ and a label vector $\tilde{\mathbf{L}}$. We aim at learning $f(x^k) = \mathbf{r_k} \cdot \mathbf{w}$ by minimizing $||\tilde{\mathbf{R}}\mathbf{w} - \tilde{\mathbf{L}}||_2^2 + \beta \cdot ||\mathbf{w}||_2^2$. This is a standard formulation for ridge regression, and we use features in Table 1. Furthermore, pairwise preference constraints have been utilized for learning ranking models (Joachims, 2002). We then consider adding a *pairwise preference-based regularizing constraint* to incorporate a bias towards summary-worthy text units: $\lambda \cdot \sum_{\mathcal{T}} \sum_{x^p, x^q \in \mathcal{T}, l_p > 0, l_q = 0} ||(\mathbf{r_p} - \mathbf{r_q}) \cdot \mathbf{w} - 1||_2^2$, where $\mathcal{T}$ is a cluster of text units to be summarized. Term $(\mathbf{r_p} - \mathbf{r_q}) \cdot \mathbf{w}$ enforces the separation of summary-worthy text from the others. We further construct $\tilde{\mathbf{R}}'$ to contain all the pairwise differences $(\mathbf{r_p} - \mathbf{r_q})$. $\tilde{\mathbf{L}}'$ is a vector of the same size as $\tilde{\mathbf{R}}'$ with each element as 1. The objective function becomes:

$$J(\mathbf{w}) = ||\tilde{\mathbf{R}}\mathbf{w} - \tilde{\mathbf{L}}||_2^2 + \lambda \cdot ||\tilde{\mathbf{R}}'\mathbf{w} - \tilde{\mathbf{L}}'||_2^2 + \beta \cdot ||\mathbf{w}||_2^2 \quad (8)$$

λ, β are tuned on development set. With $\tilde{\beta} = \beta \cdot \mathbf{I_d}$ and $\tilde{\lambda} = \lambda \cdot \mathbf{I_{|R'|}}$, **closed-form** solution for $\hat{w}$ is:

$$\hat{\mathbf{w}} = (\tilde{\mathbf{R}}^{\mathbf{T}}\tilde{\mathbf{R}} + \tilde{\mathbf{R}}'^{\mathbf{T}}\tilde{\lambda}\tilde{\mathbf{R}}' + \tilde{\beta})^{-1}(\tilde{\mathbf{R}}^{\mathbf{T}}\tilde{\mathbf{L}} + \tilde{\mathbf{R}}'^{\mathbf{T}}\tilde{\lambda}\tilde{\mathbf{L}}') \quad (9)$$

- num of words	- category in General Inquirer
- unigram	(Stone et al., 1966)
- num of POS tags	- num of positive/negative/neutral
- num of named entities	words (General Inquirer,
- centroidness (Radev, 2001)	MPQA (Wilson et al., 2005))
- avg/max TF-IDF scores	

Table 1: Features used for text unit importance estimation.

3.6 Post-processing

For testing phase, we re-rank the n-best summaries according to their cosine similarity with the input text units. The one with the highest similarity is included in the final summary. Uses of more sophisticated re-ranking methods (Charniak and Johnson, 2005; Konstas and Lapata, 2012) will be investigated in future work.

4 Experimental Setup

Data Pre-processing. We pre-process the datasets with Stanford CoreNLP (Manning et al., 2014) for tokenization and extracting POS tags and dependency relations. For RottenTomatoes dataset, we replace movie titles with a generic label in training, and substitute it with the movie name if there is any generic label generated in testing.

Pre-trained Embeddings and Features. The size of word representation is set to 300, both for input and output words. These can be initialized randomly or using pre-trained embeddings learned from Google news (Mikolov et al., 2013). We also extend our model with additional features described in Table 2. Discrete features, such as POS tags, are mapped into word representation via lookup tables. For continuous features (e.g TF-IDF scores), they are attached to word vectors as additional values.

- part of a named entity?	- category in General Inquirer
- capitalized?	- sentiment polarity
- POS tag	(General Inquirer, MPQA)
- dependency relation	- TF-IDF score

Table 2: Token-level features used for abstract generation.

Hyper-parameters and Stop Criterion. The LSTMs (Equation 5) for the decoder and encoders are defined with states and cells of 150 dimensions. The attention of each input word and state pair is computed by being projected into a vector of 100 dimensions (Equation 6).

Training is performed via Adagrad (Duchi et al., 2011). It terminates when performance does not improve on the development set. We use BLEU (up to 4-grams) (Papineni et al., 2002) as evaluation metric, which computes the precision of n-grams in generated summaries with gold-standard abstracts as the reference. Finally, the importance-based sampling rate (K) is set to 5 for experiments in Sections 5.2 and 5.3.

Decoding is performed by beam search with a beam size of 20, i.e. we keep 20 most probable output sequences in stack at each step. Outputs with `end of sentence` token are also considered for re-ranking. Decoding stops when every beam in stack generates the `end of sentence` token.

5 Results

5.1 Importance Estimation Evaluation

We first evaluate the importance estimation component described in Section 3.5. We compare with Support Vector Regression (SVR) (Smola and Vapnik, 1997) and two baselines: (1) a *length baseline* that ranks text units based on their length, and (2) a *centroid baseline* that ranks text units according to their centroidness, which is computed as the cosine similarity between a text unit and centroid of the cluster to be summarized (Erkan and Radev, 2004).

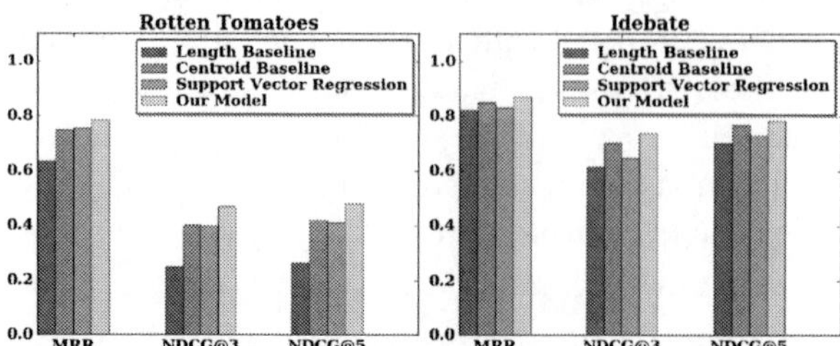

Figure 2: Evaluation of importance estimation by mean reciprocal rank (MRR), and normalized discounted cumulative gain at top 3 and 5 returned results (NDCG@3 and NDCG@5). Our regression model with pairwise preference-based regularizer uniformly outperforms baseline systems on both datasets.

We evaluate using mean reciprocal rank (MRR), and normalized discounted cumulative gain at top 3 and 5 returned results (NDCG@3). Text units are considered relevant if they have at least one overlapping content word with the gold-standard summary. From Figure 2, we can see that our importance estimation model produces uniformly better ranking performance on both datasets.

5.2 Automatic Summary Evaluation

For automatic summary evaluation, we consider three popular metrics. ROUGE (Lin and Hovy, 2003) is employed to evaluate n-grams recall of the summaries with gold-standard abstracts as reference. ROUGE-SU4 (measures unigram and skip-bigrams separated by up to four words) is reported. We also utilize BLEU, a precision-based metric, which has been used to evaluate various language generation systems (Chiang, 2005; Angeli et al., 2010; Karpathy and Fei-Fei, 2014). We further consider METEOR (Denkowski and Lavie, 2014). As a recall-oriented metric, it calculates similarity between generations and references by considering synonyms and paraphrases.

For comparisons, we first compare with an abstractive summarization method presented in Ganesan et al. (2010) on the RottenTomatoes dataset. Ganesan et al. (2010) utilize a graph-based algorithm to remove repetitive information, and merge opinionated expressions based on syntactic structures of product reviews.[2] For both datasets, we consider two extractive summarization approaches: (1) LEXRANK (Erkan and Radev, 2004) is an unsupervised method that computes text centrality based on PageRank algorithm; (2) Sipos et al. (2012) propose a supervised SUBMODULAR summarization model which is trained with Support Vector Machines. In addition, LONGEST sentence is picked up as a baseline.

Four variations of our system are tested. One uses randomly initialized word embeddings. The rest of them use pre-trained word embeddings, additional features in Table 2, and their combination. For all systems, we generate a one-sentence summary.

Results are displayed in Table 3. Our system with pre-trained word embeddings and additional features achieves the best BLEU scores on both datasets (in **boldface**) with statistical significance (two-tailed Wilcoxon signed rank test, $p < 0.05$). Notice that our system summaries are conciser (i.e. shorter on average), which lead to higher scores on precision based-metrics, e.g. BLEU, and lower scores on recall-based metrics, e.g. METEOR and ROUGE. On RottenTomatoes dataset, where summaries generated by different systems are similar in length, our system still outperforms other methods in METEOR and ROUGE in addition to their significantly better BLEU scores. This is not true on Idebate, since the length of summaries by extract-based systems is significantly longer. But the BLEU scores of our system are considerably higher. Among our four systems, models with pre-trained word embeddings in general achieve better scores. Though additional features do not always improve the performance, we find that they help our systems converge faster.

5.3 Human Evaluation on Summary Quality

For human evaluation, we consider three aspects: *informativeness* that indicates how much salient information is contained in the summary, *grammaticality* that measures whether a summary is grammatical, and *compactness* that denotes whether a summary contains unnecessary information. Each aspect is rated on a 1 to 5 scale (5 is the best). The judges are

---

[2] We do not run this model on Idebate because it relies on high redundancy to detect repetitive expressions, which is not observed on Idebate.

	RottenTomatoes				Idebate			
	Length	BLEU	METEOR	ROUGE	Length	BLEU	METEOR	ROUGE
Extract-Based Systems								
Longest	47.9	8.25	**8.43**	**6.43**	44.0	6.36	10.22	12.65
LexRank	16.7	19.93	5.59	3.98	26.5	13.39	9.33	10.58
Submodular	16.8	17.22	4.89	3.01	23.2	15.09	**10.76**	**13.67**
Abstract-Based Systems								
Opinosis	22.0	19.72	6.07	4.90	–	–	–	–
Our Systems								
words	15.7	19.88	6.07	5.05	14.4	22.55*	7.38	8.37
words (pre-trained)	15.8	23.22*	*6.51*	*5.70*	13.9	23.93*	7.42	9.09
words + features	17.5	19.73	6.43	5.53	13.5	23.65*	7.33	7.79
words (pre-trained) + features	14.2	**24.88***	6.00	4.96	13.0	**25.84***	7.56	8.81

Table 3: Automatic evaluation results by BLEU, METEOR, and ROUGE SU-4 scores (multiplied by 100) for abstract generation systems. The average lengths for human written summaries are 11.5 and 24.6 for RottenTomatoes and Idebate. The best performing system for each column is highlighted in **boldface**, where our system with pre-trained word embeddings and additional features achieves the best BLEU scores on both datasets. Our systems that are statistically significantly better than the comparisons are highlighted with * (two-tailed Wilcoxon signed rank test, $p < 0.05$). Our system also has the best METEOR and ROUGE scores (in *italics*) on RottenTomatoes dataset among learning-based systems.

	Info	Gram	Comp	Avg Rank	Best%
LexRank	3.4	4.5	4.3	2.7	11.5%
Opinosis	2.8	3.1	3.3	3.5	5.0%
Our System	**3.6**	**4.8**	4.2	**2.3**	**18.0%**
Human Abstract	4.2	4.8	4.5	1.5	65.5%

Table 4: Human evaluation results for abstract generation systems. Inter-rater agreement for overall ranking is 0.71 by Krippendorff's α. Informativeness (**Info**), grammaticality (**Gram**), and Compactness (**Comp**) are rated on a 1 to 5 scale, with 5 as the best. Our system achieves the best informativeness and grammaticality scores among the three learning-based systems. Our summaries are ranked as the best in 18% of the evaluations, and are also ranked higher than compared systems on average.

also asked to give a ranking on all summary variations according to their overall quality.

We randomly sampled 40 movies from Rotten-Tomatoes test set, each of which was evaluated by 5 distinct human judges. We hired 10 proficient English speakers for evaluation. Three system summaries (LexRank, Opinosis, and our system) and human-written abstract along with 20 representative reviews were displayed for each movie. Reviews with the highest gold-standard importance scores were selected.

Results are reported in Table 4. As it can be seen, our system outperforms the abstract-based system Opinosis in all aspects, and also achieves better informativeness and grammaticality scores than LexRank, which extracts sentences in their original form. Our system summaries are ranked as the best in 18% of the evaluations, and has an average ranking of 2.3, which is higher than both Opinosis and LexRank on average. An inter-rater agreement of Krippendorff's α of 0.71 is achieved for

overall ranking. This implies that our attention-based abstract generation model can produce summaries of better quality than existing summarization systems. We also find that our system summaries are constructed in a style closer to human abstracts than others. Sample summaries are displayed in Figure 3.

5.4 Sampling Effect

We further investigate whether taking inputs sampled from distributions estimated by importance scores trains models with better performance than the ones learned from fixed input or uniformly-sampled input. Recall that we sample K text units based on their importance scores (*Importance-Based Sampling*). Here we consider two other setups: one is sampling K text units uniformly from the input (*Uniform Sampling*), another is picking K text units with the highest scores (*Top K*). We try various K values. Results in Figure 4 demonstrates that Importance-Based Sampling can produce comparable BLEU scores to Top K methods, while both of them outperform Uniform Sampling. For METEOR score, Importance-Based Sampling uniformly outperforms the other two methods[3].

5.5 Further Discussion

Finally, we discuss some other observations and potential improvements. First, applying the re-ranking component after the model generates n-best abstracts leads to better performance. Preliminary experiments show that simply picking the top-1 gener-

---

[3]We observe similar results on the Idebate dataset

Movie: *The Neverending Story*
Reviews: (1) Here is a little adventure that fed on our uncultivated need to think, and wonder... (2) Magical storytelling targeted at children still fascinates. (3)...the art direction involved a lot of imagination.
Human: A magical journey about the power of a young boy's imagination to save a dying fantasy land, The Neverending Story remains a much-loved kids adventure.
LexRank: It pokes along at times and lapses occasionally into dark moments of preachy philosophy, but this is still a charming, amusing and harmless film for kids.
Opinosis: The Neverending Story is a silly fantasy movie that often shows its age .
Our System: The Neverending Story is an entertaining children's adventure, with heart and imagination to spare.

Movie: *Joe Strummer: The Future is Unwritten*
Reviews: (1) The late punk rock legend Joe Strummer is rendered fully human in Julian Temple's engrossing and all-encompassing portrait. (2) The movie fascinates not so much because of Strummer... but because of the way Temple organized and edited the film. (3) One of the most compelling documentary portraits of a musician yet made.
Human: Displaying Joe Strummer warts and all, The Future is Unwritten succeeds as both an engrossing documentary and a comprehensive examination of one of music's most legendary figures.
LexRank: Joe Strummer: The Future Is Unwritten is a film for fans – really big fans .
Opinosis: Joe Strummer: The Future Is Unwritten is for fans – really big fans .
Our System: Fascinating and insightful, Joe Strummer: The Future Is Unwritten is a thoroughly engrossing documentary.

Topic: *This House would detain terror suspects without trial.*
Arguments: (1) Governments must have powers to protect their citizens against threats to the life of the nation.(2) Everyone would recognise that rules that are applied in peacetime may not be appropriate during wartime.
Human: Governments must have powers to protect citizens from harm.
LexRank: This is not merely to directly protect citizens from political violence, but also because political violence handicaps the process of reconstruction in nation-building efforts.
Our System: Governments have the obligation to protect citizens from harmful substances.

Topic: *This House would replace Christmas with a festival for everyone.*
Arguments: (1) Christmas celebrations in the Western world... do not respect the rights of those who are not religious. (2) States should instead be sponsoring and celebrating events that everyone can join in equally, regardless of religion, race or class.
Human: States should respect the freedom from religion, as well as the freedom of religion.
LexRank: For school children who do not share the majority-Christian faith, Christmas celebrations require either their participation when they do not want to, through coercion, or their non-participation and therefore isolation whilst everyone else celebrations their inclusiveness.
Our System: People have a right to freedom of religion.

Figure 3: Sample summaries generated by different systems on movie reviews and arguments. We only show a subset of reviews and arguments due to limited space.

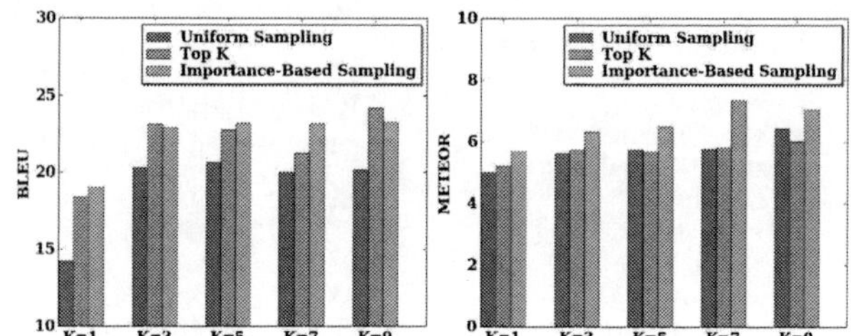

Figure 4: Sampling effect on RottenTomatoes.

ations produces inferior results than re-ranking them with simple heuristics. This suggests that the current models are oblivious to some task specific issues, such as informativeness. Post-processing is needed to make better use of the summary candidates. For example, future work can study other sophisticated re-ranking algorithms (Charniak and Johnson, 2005; Konstas and Lapata, 2012).

Furthermore, we also look at the difficult cases where our summaries are evaluated to have lower informativeness. They are often much shorter than the gold-standard human abstracts, thus the information coverage is limited. In other cases, some generations contain incorrect information on domain-dependent facts, e.g. named entities, numbers, etc. For instance, a summary "a poignant coming-of-age tale marked by a breakout lead performance from Cate Shortland" is generated for movie "Lore". This summary contains "Cate Shortland" which is the director of the movie instead of actor. It would require semantic features to handle this issue, which has yet to be attempted.

6 Related Work

Our work belongs to the area of opinion summarization. Constructing fluent natural language opinion summaries has mainly considered product reviews (Hu and Liu, 2004; Lerman et al., 2009), community question answering (Wang et al., 2014), and editorials (Paul et al., 2010). Extractive summarization approaches are employed to identify summary-worthy sentences. For example, Hu and Liu (2004) first identify the frequent product features and then attach extracted opinion sentences to the corresponding feature. Our model instead utilizes abstract generation techniques to construct natural language summaries. As far as we know, we are also the first to study claim generation for arguments.

Recently, there has been a growing interest in generating abstractive summaries for news articles (Bing et al., 2015), spoken meetings (Wang and Cardie, 2013), and product reviews (Ganesan et al., 2010; Di Fabbrizio et al., 2014; Gerani et al., 2014). Most approaches are based on phrase extraction, from which an algorithm concatenates them into sentences (Bing et al., 2015; Ganesan et al., 2010). Nevertheless, the output summaries are not guaranteed to be grammatical. Gerani et al. (2014) then design a set of manually-constructed realization templates for producing grammatical sentences that serve different discourse functions. Our approach does not require any human-annotated rules, and can be applied in various domains.

Our task is closely related to recent advances in neural machine translation (Kalchbrenner and Blunsom, 2013; Sutskever et al., 2014a). Based on the sequence-to-sequence paradigm, RNNs-based models have been investigated for compression (Filippova et al., 2015) and summarization (Filippova et al., 2015; Rush et al., 2015; Hermann et al., 2015) at sentence-level. Built on the attention-based translation model in Bahdanau et al. (2014), Rush et al. (2015) study the problem of constructing abstract for a single sentence. Our task differs from the models presented above in that our model carries out abstractive decoding from multiple sentences instead of a single sentence.

7 Conclusion

In this work, we presented a neural approach to generate abstractive summaries for opinionated text. We employed an attention-based method that finds salient information from different input text units to generate an informative and concise summary. To cope with the large number of input text, we deploy an importance-based sampling mechanism for model training. Experiments showed that our system obtained state-of-the-art results using both automatic evaluation and human evaluation.

References

Gabor Angeli, Percy Liang, and Dan Klein. 2010. A simple domain-independent probabilistic approach to generation. In *Proceedings of the 2010 Conference on Empirical Methods in Natural Language Processing*, pages 502–512. Association for Computational Linguistics.

Dzmitry Bahdanau, Kyunghyun Cho, and Yoshua Bengio. 2014. Neural machine translation by jointly learning to align and translate. *CoRR*, abs/1409.0473.

Lidong Bing, Piji Li, Yi Liao, Wai Lam, Weiwei Guo, and Rebecca Passonneau. 2015. Abstractive multi-document summarization via phrase selection and merging. In *Proceedings of the 53rd Annual Meeting of the Association for Computational Linguistics and the 7th International Joint Conference on Natural Language Processing (Volume 1: Long Papers)*, pages 1587–1597, Beijing, China, July. Association for Computational Linguistics.

Eugene Charniak and Mark Johnson. 2005. Coarse-to-fine n-best parsing and maxent discriminative reranking. In *Proceedings of the 43rd Annual Meeting on Association for Computational Linguistics*, ACL '05, pages 173–180, Stroudsburg, PA, USA. Association for Computational Linguistics.

David Chiang. 2005. A hierarchical phrase-based model for statistical machine translation. In *Proceedings of the 43rd Annual Meeting on Association for Computational Linguistics*, pages 263–270. Association for Computational Linguistics.

Michael Denkowski and Alon Lavie. 2014. Meteor universal: Language specific translation evaluation for any target language. In *Proceedings of the EACL 2014 Workshop on Statistical Machine Translation*.

Giuseppe Di Fabbrizio, Amanda J Stent, and Robert Gaizauskas. 2014. A hybrid approach to multi-document summarization of opinions in reviews. *INLG 2014*, page 54.

John Duchi, Elad Hazan, and Yoram Singer. 2011. Adaptive subgradient methods for online learning and stochastic optimization. *J. Mach. Learn. Res.*, 12:2121–2159, July.

Günes Erkan and Dragomir R. Radev. 2004. Lexrank: Graph-based lexical centrality as salience in text summarization. *J. Artif. Int. Res.*, 22(1):457–479, December.

Katja Filippova, Enrique Alfonseca, Carlos A. Colmenares, Lukasz Kaiser, and Oriol Vinyals. 2015. Sentence compression by deletion with lstms. In *Proceedings of the 2015 Conference on Empirical Methods in Natural Language Processing*, pages 360–368, Lisbon, Portugal, September. Association for Computational Linguistics.

Kavita Ganesan, ChengXiang Zhai, and Jiawei Han. 2010. Opinosis: a graph-based approach to abstractive summarization of highly redundant opinions. In *Proceedings of the 23rd international conference on com-*

putational linguistics, pages 340–348. Association for Computational Linguistics.

Shima Gerani, Yashar Mehdad, Giuseppe Carenini, Raymond T. Ng, and Bita Nejat. 2014. Abstractive summarization of product reviews using discourse structure. In *Proceedings of the 2014 Conference on Empirical Methods in Natural Language Processing (EMNLP)*, pages 1602–1613, Doha, Qatar, October. Association for Computational Linguistics.

Karl Moritz Hermann, Tomás Kociský, Edward Grefenstette, Lasse Espeholt, Will Kay, Mustafa Suleyman, and Phil Blunsom. 2015. Teaching machines to read and comprehend. *CoRR*, abs/1506.03340.

Sepp Hochreiter and Jürgen Schmidhuber. 1997. Long short-term memory. *Neural Comput.*, 9(8):1735–1780, November.

Minqing Hu and Bing Liu. 2004. Mining and summarizing customer reviews. In *Proceedings of the Tenth ACM SIGKDD International Conference on Knowledge Discovery and Data Mining*, KDD '04, pages 168–177, New York, NY, USA. ACM.

Thorsten Joachims. 2002. Optimizing search engines using clickthrough data. In *Proceedings of the Eighth ACM SIGKDD International Conference on Knowledge Discovery and Data Mining*, KDD '02, pages 133–142, New York, NY, USA. ACM.

Nal Kalchbrenner and Phil Blunsom. 2013. Recurrent continuous translation models. In *EMNLP*, pages 1700–1709. ACL.

Andrej Karpathy and Li Fei-Fei. 2014. Deep visual-semantic alignments for generating image descriptions. *arXiv preprint arXiv:1412.2306*.

Ioannis Konstas and Mirella Lapata. 2012. Concept-to-text generation via discriminative reranking. In *Proceedings of the 50th Annual Meeting of the Association for Computational Linguistics (Volume 1: Long Papers)*, pages 369–378, Jeju Island, Korea, July. Association for Computational Linguistics.

Kevin Lerman, Sasha Blair-Goldensohn, and Ryan McDonald. 2009. Sentiment summarization: Evaluating and learning user preferences. In *Proceedings of the 12th Conference of the European Chapter of the Association for Computational Linguistics*, EACL '09, pages 514–522, Stroudsburg, PA, USA. Association for Computational Linguistics.

Fangtao Li, Chao Han, Minlie Huang, Xiaoyan Zhu, Ying-Ju Xia, Shu Zhang, and Hao Yu. 2010. Structure-aware review mining and summarization. In *Proceedings of the 23rd International Conference on Computational Linguistics*, COLING '10, pages 653–661, Stroudsburg, PA, USA. Association for Computational Linguistics.

Chin-Yew Lin and Eduard Hovy. 2003. Automatic evaluation of summaries using n-gram co-occurrence statistics. In *Proceedings of the 2003 Conference of the North American Chapter of the Association for Computational Linguistics on Human Language Technology - Volume 1*, pages 71–78.

Christopher Manning, Mihai Surdeanu, John Bauer, Jenny Finkel, Steven Bethard, and David McClosky. 2014. The stanford corenlp natural language processing toolkit. In *Proceedings of 52nd Annual Meeting of the Association for Computational Linguistics: System Demonstrations*, pages 55–60, Baltimore, Maryland. Association for Computational Linguistics.

Tomas Mikolov, Kai Chen, Greg Corrado, and Jeffrey Dean. 2013. Efficient estimation of word representations in vector space. *CoRR*, abs/1301.3781.

Kishore Papineni, Salim Roukos, Todd Ward, and Wei-Jing Zhu. 2002. Bleu: a method for automatic evaluation of machine translation. In *Proceedings of the 40th annual meeting on association for computational linguistics*, pages 311–318. Association for Computational Linguistics.

Michael J. Paul, ChengXiang Zhai, and Roxana Girju. 2010. Summarizing contrastive viewpoints in opinionated text. In *Proceedings of the 2010 Conference on Empirical Methods in Natural Language Processing*, EMNLP '10, pages 66–76, Stroudsburg, PA, USA. Association for Computational Linguistics.

Dragomir R. Radev. 2001. Experiments in single and multidocument summarization using mead. In *In First Document Understanding Conference*.

Alexander M. Rush, Sumit Chopra, and Jason Weston. 2015. A neural attention model for abstractive sentence summarization. In *Proceedings of the 2015 Conference on Empirical Methods in Natural Language Processing*, pages 379–389, Lisbon, Portugal, September. Association for Computational Linguistics.

Ruben Sipos, Pannaga Shivaswamy, and Thorsten Joachims. 2012. Large-margin learning of submodular summarization models. In *Proceedings of the 13th Conference of the European Chapter of the Association for Computational Linguistics*, EACL '12, pages 224–233, Stroudsburg, PA, USA. Association for Computational Linguistics.

Alex Smola and Vladimir Vapnik. 1997. Support vector regression machines. *Advances in neural information processing systems*, 9:155–161.

Philip J. Stone, Dexter C. Dunphy, Marshall S. Smith, and Daniel M. Ogilvie. 1966. *The General Inquirer: A Computer Approach to Content Analysis*. MIT Press, Cambridge, MA.

Ilya Sutskever, Oriol Vinyals, and Quoc V. Le. 2014a. Sequence to sequence learning with neural networks.

In *Advances in Neural Information Processing Systems 27: Annual Conference on Neural Information Processing Systems 2014, December 8-13 2014, Montreal, Quebec, Canada*, pages 3104–3112.

Ilya Sutskever, Oriol Vinyals, and Quoc V. Le. 2014b. Sequence to sequence learning with neural networks. *CoRR*, abs/1409.3215.

Lu Wang and Claire Cardie. 2013. Domain-independent abstract generation for focused meeting summarization. In *Proceedings of the 51st Annual Meeting of the Association for Computational Linguistics (Volume 1: Long Papers)*, pages 1395–1405, Sofia, Bulgaria, August. Association for Computational Linguistics.

Lu Wang, Hema Raghavan, Claire Cardie, and Vittorio Castelli. 2014. Query-focused opinion summarization for user-generated content. In *Proceedings of COLING 2014, the 25th International Conference on Computational Linguistics: Technical Papers*, pages 1660–1669, Dublin, Ireland, August. Dublin City University and Association for Computational Linguistics.

Theresa Wilson, Janyce Wiebe, and Paul Hoffmann. 2005. Recognizing contextual polarity in phrase-level sentiment analysis. In *Proceedings of the Conference on Human Language Technology and Empirical Methods in Natural Language Processing*, HLT '05, pages 347–354, Stroudsburg, PA, USA. Association for Computational Linguistics.

Li Zhuang, Feng Jing, and Xiao-Yan Zhu. 2006. Movie review mining and summarization. In *Proceedings of the 15th ACM International Conference on Information and Knowledge Management*, CIKM '06, pages 43–50, New York, NY, USA. ACM.

A Low-Rank Approximation Approach to Learning
Joint Embeddings of News Stories and Images for Timeline Summarization

William Yang Wang[1]*, **Yashar Mehdad**[3], **Dragomir R. Radev**[2], **Amanda Stent**[4]

[1]School of Computer Science, Carnegie Mellon University, Pittsburgh, PA 15213, USA
[2]Department of EECS, University of Michigan, Ann Arbor, MI 48109, USA
[3]Yahoo, Sunnyvale, CA 94089, USA and [4]New York, NY 10036, USA
`yww@cs.cmu.edu,` `{ymehdad,stent}@yahoo-inc.com,` `radev@umich.edu`

Abstract

A key challenge for timeline summarization is to generate a concise, yet complete storyline from large collections of news stories. Previous studies in extractive timeline generation are limited in two ways: first, most prior work focuses on fully-observable ranking models or clustering models with hand-designed features that may not generalize well. Second, most summarization corpora are text-only, which means that text is the sole source of information considered in timeline summarization, and thus, the rich visual content from news images is ignored. To solve these issues, we leverage the success of matrix factorization techniques from recommender systems, and cast the problem as a sentence recommendation task, using a representation learning approach. To augment text-only corpora, for each candidate sentence in a news article, we take advantage of top-ranked relevant images from the Web and model the image using a convolutional neural network architecture. Finally, we propose a scalable low-rank approximation approach for learning joint embeddings of news stories and images. In experiments, we compare our model to various competitive baselines, and demonstrate the state-of-the-art performance of the proposed text-based and multimodal approaches.

1 Introduction

Timeline summarization is the task of organizing crucial milestones of a news story in a temporal order, e.g. (Kedzie et al., 2014; Lin et al., 2012). A

---

*This work was performed when William Wang and Dragomir Radev were visiting Yahoo NYC.

timeline example for the *2010 British Oil spill* generated by our system is shown in Figure 1. The task is challenging, because the input often includes a large number of news articles as the story is developing each day, but only a small portion of the key information is needed for timeline generation. In addition to the conciseness requirement, timeline summarization also has to be complete—all key information, in whatever form, must be presented in the final summary.

To distill key insights from news reports, prior work in summarization often relies on feature engineering, and uses clustering techniques (Radev et al., 2004b) to select important events to be included in the final summary. While this approach is unsupervised, the process of feature engineering is always expensive, and the number of clusters is not easy to estimate. To present a complete summary, researchers from the natural language processing (NLP) community often solely rely on the textual information, while studies in the computer vision (CV) community rely solely on the image and video information. However, even though news images are abundantly available together with news stories, approaches that jointly learn textual and visual representations for summarization are not common.

In this paper, we take a more radical approach to timeline summarization. We formulate the problem as a sentence recommendation task—instead of recommending items to users as in a recommender system, we recommend important sentences to a timeline. Our approach does not require feature engineering: by using a matrix factorization framework, we are essentially performing representation learn-

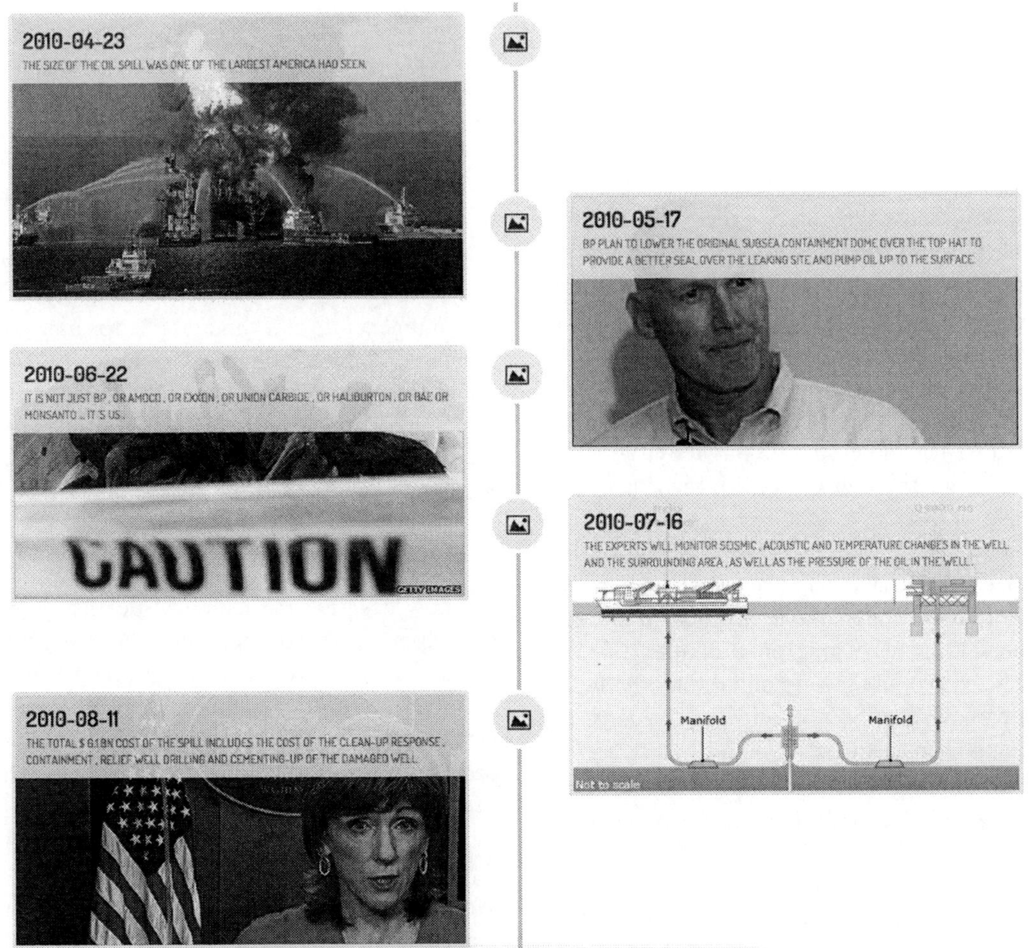

Figure 1: A timeline example for the BP oil spill generated by our proposed method. *Note that we use Yahoo! Image Search to obtain the top-ranked image for each candidate sentence.*

ing to model the continuous representation of sentences and words. Since most previous timeline summarization work (and therefore, corpora) only focuses on textual information, we also provide a novel web-based approach for harvesting news images: we query Yahoo! image search with sentences from news articles, and extract visual cues using a 15-layer convolutional neural network architecture. By unifying text and images in the low-rank approximation framework, our approach learns a joint embedding of news story texts and images in a principled manner. In empirical evaluations, we conduct experiments on two publicly available datasets, and demonstrate the efficiency and effectiveness of our approach. By comparing to various baselines, we show that our approach is highly scalable and achieves state-of-the-art performance. Our main contributions are three-fold:

- We propose a novel matrix factorization approach for extractive summarization, leveraging the success of collaborative filtering;

- We are among the first to consider representation learning of a joint embedding for text and images in timeline summarization;

- Our model significantly outperforms various competitive baselines on two publicly available datasets.

2 Related Work

Supervised learning is widely used in summarization. For example, the seminal study by Kupiec et al. (1995) used a Naive Bayes classifier for selecting sentences. Recently, Wang et al. (2015) proposed a regression method that uses a joint loss function, combining news articles and comments. Additionally, unsupervised techniques such as language modeling (Allan et al., 2001) have been used for temporal summarization. In recent years, ranking and graph-based methods (Radev et al., 2004b; Erkan and Radev, 2004; Mihalcea and Tarau, 2004; Fader et al., 2007; Hassan et al., 2008; Mei et al., 2010; Yan et al., 2011b; Yan et al., 2011a; Zhao et al., 2013; Ng et al., 2014; Zhou et al., 2014; Glavaš and Šnajder, 2014; Tran et al., 2015; Dehghani and Asadpour, 2015) have also proved popular for extractive timeline summarization, often in an unsupervised setting. Dynamic programming (Kiernan and Terzi, 2009) and greedy algorithms (Althoff et al., 2015) have also been considered for constructing summaries over time.

Our work aligns with recent studies on latent variable models for multi-document summarization and storyline clustering. Conroy et al. (2001) were among the first to consider latent variable models, even though it is difficult to incorporate features and high-dimensional latent states in a HMM-based model. Ahmed et al. (2011) proposed a hierarchical nonparametric model that integrates a Recurrent Chinese Restaurant Process with Latent Dirichlet Allocation to cluster words over time. The main issues with this approach are that it does not generate human-readable sentences, and that scaling nonparametric Bayesian models is often challenging. Similarly, Huang and Huang (2013) introduced a joint mixture-event-aspect model using a generative method. Navarro-Colorado and Saquete (2015) combined temporal information with topic modeling, and obtained the best performance in the cross-document event ordering task of SemEval 2015.

There has been prior work (Wang et al., 2008; Lee et al., 2009) using matrix factorization to perform sentence clustering. A key distinction between our work and this previous work is that our method requires no additional sentence selection steps after sentence clustering, so we avoid error cascades.

Zhu and Chen (2007) were among the first to consider multimodal timeline summarization, but they focus on visualization, and do not make use of images. Wang et al. (2012) investigated multimodal timeline summarization by considering cosine similarity among various feature vectors, and then using a graph based algorithm to select salient topics. In the computer vision community, Kim and Xing (2014) made use of community web photos, and generate storyline graphs for image recommendation. Interestingly, Kim et al. (2014) combined images and videos for storyline reconstruction. However, none of the above studies combine textual and visual information for timeline summarization.

3 Our Approach

We now describe the technical details of our low-rank approximation approach. First, we motivate our approach. Next, we explain how we formulate the timeline summarization task as a matrix factorization problem. Then, we introduce a scalable approach for learning low-dimensional embeddings of news stories and images.

3.1 Motivation

We formulate timeline summarization as a low-rank matrix completion task because of the following considerations:

- **Simplicity** In the past decade, a significant amount of work on summarization has focused on designing various lexical, syntactic and semantic features. In contrast to prior work, we make use of low-rank approximation techniques to learn representations directly from data. This way, our model does not require strong domain knowledge or lots of feature engineering, and it is easy for developers to deploy the system in real-world applications.

- **Scalability** A major reason that recommender systems and collaborative filtering techniques have been very successful in industrial applications is that matrix completion techniques are relatively sophisticated, and are known to scale up to large recommendation datasets with more than 100 million ratings (Bennett and Lanning,

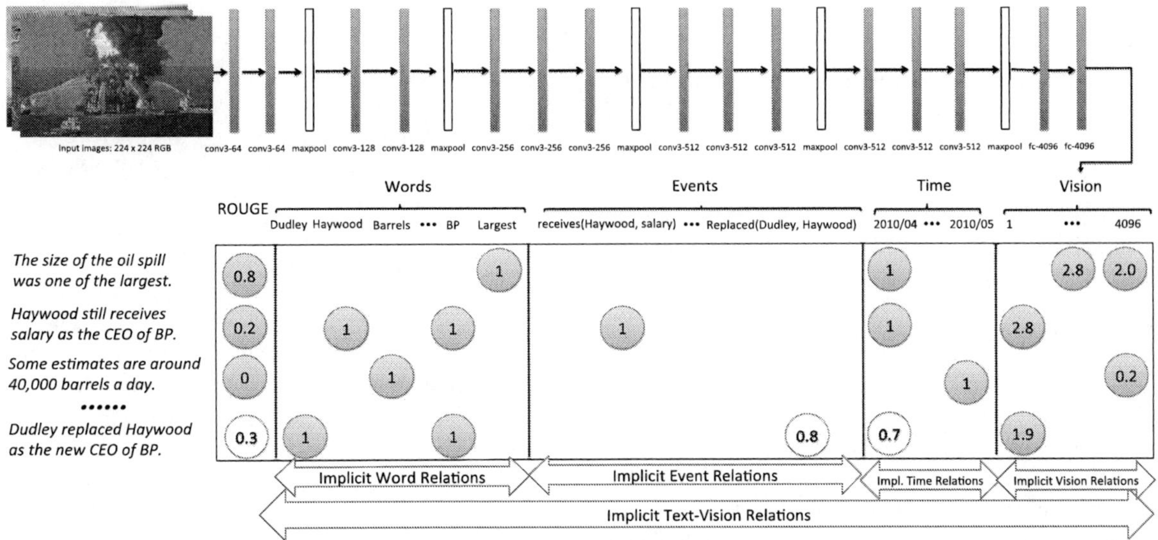

Figure 2: Our low-rank approximation framework for learning joint embedding of news stories and images for timeline summarization.

2007). Therefore, we believe that our approach is practical for processing large datasets in this summarization task.

- **Joint Multimodal Modeling** A key challenge of supervised learning approaches for summarization is to select informative sentences. In this work, we make use of multimodality to select important sentences.

3.2 Problem Formulation

Since the Netflix competition (Bell and Koren, 2007), collaborative filtering techniques with latent factor models have had huge success in recommender systems. These latent factors, often in the form of low-rank embeddings, capture not only explicit information but also implicit context from the input data. In this work, we propose a novel matrix factorization framework to "recommend" key sentences to a timeline. Figure 2 shows an overview of the framework.

More specifically, we formulate this task as a matrix completion problem. Given a news corpus, we assume that there are m total sentences, which are the rows in the matrix. The first column is the *metric* section, where we use ROUGE (Lin, 2004) as the metric to pre-compute a *sentence importance*

score between a candidate sentence and a human-generated summary. During training, we use these scores to tune model parameters, and during testing, we predict the sentence importance scores given the features in other columns. That is, we learn the embedding of important sentences.

The second set of columns is the *text feature* section. In our experiments, this includes word observations, subject-verb-object (SVO) events, and the publication date of the document from which the candidate sentence is extracted. In our preprocessing step, we run the Stanford part-of-speech tagger (Toutanova et al., 2003) and MaltParser (Nivre et al., 2006) to generate SVO events based on dependency parses. Additional features can easily be incorporated into this framework; we leave the consideration of additional features for future work.

Finally, for each sentence, we use an image search engine to retrieve a top-ranked relevant image, and then we use a convolutional neural network (CNN) architecture to extract visual features in an unsupervised fashion. We use a CNN model from Simonyan and Zisserman (2015), which is trained on the ImageNet Challenge 2014 dataset (Russakovsky et al., 2014). In our work, we keep the 16 convolutional layers and max-pool operations. To extract neural network features, we remove the final fully-connected-1000 layer and the softmax function, resulting in 4096 features for each image.

The total number of columns in the input matrix is n. Our matrix M now encodes preferences for a sentence, together with its lexical, event, and temporal attributes, and visual features for an image highly relevant to the sentence. Here we use i to index the i-th sentence and j to index the j-th column. We scale the columns by the standard deviation.

3.3 Low-Rank Approximation

Following prior work (Koren et al., 2009), we are interested in learning two low-rank matrices $P \in \mathbf{R}^{k \times m}$ and $Q \in \mathbf{R}^{k \times n}$. The intuitition is that P is the embedding of all candidate sentences, and Q is the embedding of textual and visual features, as well as the sentence importance score, event, and temporal features. Here k is the number of latent dimensions, and we would like to approximate $M_{(i,j)} \simeq \vec{p_i}^T \vec{q_j}$, where $\vec{p_i}$ is the latent embedding vector for the i-th sentence and $\vec{q_j}$ is the latent embedding vector for the j-th column. We seek to approximate the matrix M by these two low-rank matrices P and Q. We can then formulate the optimization problem for this task:

$$\min_{P,Q} \sum_{(i,j) \in M} (M_{(i,j)} - \vec{p_i}^T \vec{q_j})^2 + \lambda_P ||\vec{p_i}||^2 + \lambda_Q ||\vec{q_j}||^2$$

here, λ_P and λ_Q are regularization coefficients to prevent the model from overfitting. To solve this optimization problem efficiently, a popular approach is stochastic gradient descent (SGD) (Koren et al., 2009). In contrast to traditional methods that require time-consuming gradient computation, SGD takes only a small number of random samples to compute the gradient. SGD is also natural to online algorithms in real-time streaming applications, where instead of retraining the model with all the data, parameters might be updated incrementally when new data comes in. Once we have selected a random sample $M_{(i,j)}$, we can simplify the objective function:

$$(M_{(i,j)} - \vec{p_i}^T \vec{q_j})^2 + \lambda_P (\vec{p_i}^T \vec{p_i}) + \lambda_Q (\vec{q_j}^T \vec{q_j})$$

Now, we can calculate the sub-gradients of the two latent vectors $\vec{p_i}$ and $\vec{q_j}$ to derive the following vari-

able update rules:

$$\vec{p_i} \leftarrow \vec{p_i} + \delta(\ell_{(i,j)} q_j - \lambda_P \vec{p_i}) \qquad (1)$$
$$\vec{q_j} \leftarrow \vec{q_j} + \delta(\ell_{(i,j)} p_i - \lambda_Q \vec{q_j}) \qquad (2)$$

Here, δ is the learning rate, whereas $\ell_{(i,j)}$ is the loss function that estimates how well the model approximates the ground truth:

$$\ell(i, j) = M_{(i,j)} - \vec{p_i}^T \vec{q_j}$$

The low-rank approximation here is accomplished by reconstructing the M matrix with the two low-rank matrices P and Q, and we use the row and column regularizers to prevent the model from overfitting to the training data.

SGD-based optimization for matrix factorization can also be easily parallelized. For example, HOG-WILD! (Recht et al., 2011) is a lock-free parallelization approach for SGD. In contrast to synchronous approaches where idle threads have to wait for busy threads to sync up parameters, HOGWILD! is an asynchronous method: it assumes that because text features are sparse, there is no need to perform synchronization of the threads. In reality, although this approach might not work for speech or image related tasks, it performs well in various text based tasks. In this work, we follow a recently proposed approach called fast parallel stochastic gradient descent (FPSG) (Chin et al., 2015), which is partly inspired by HOGWILD!.

3.4 Joint Modeling of Mixed Effects

Matrix factorization is a relatively complex method for modeling latent factors. So, an important question to ask is: in the context of timeline summarization, what is this matrix factorization framework modeling?

From equation (1), we can see that the latent sentence vector $\vec{p_i}$ will be updated whenever we encounter a $M_{(i,\cdot)}$ sample (e.g., all the word, event, time, and visual features for this particular sentence) in a full pass over the training data. An interesting aspect about matrix factorization is that, in addition to using the previous row embedding $\vec{p_i}$ to update the variables in equation (1), the column embedding $\vec{q_j}$ will also be used. Similarly, when updating the latent column embedding $\vec{q_j}$ in equation (2), the pass will visit all samples that have non-zero items in that column, while making use of the $\vec{p_i}$ vector. Essentially, in timeline summarization, this approach is modeling the mixed effects of sentence importance, lexical features, events, temporal information, and visual factors. For example, if we are predicting the ROUGE score of a new sentence at testing, the model will take the explicit sentence-level features into account, together with the learned latent embedding of ROUGE, which is recursively influenced by other metrics and features during training.

Our approach shares similarities with some recent advances in word embedding techniques. For example, word2vec uses the continuous bag-of-words (CBOW) and SkipGram algorithms (Mikolov et al., 2013) to learn continuous representations of words from large collections of text and relational data. A recent study (Levy and Goldberg, 2014) shows that the technique behind word2vec is very similar to implicit matrix factorization. In our work, we consider multiple sources of information to learn the joint embedding in a unified matrix factorization framework. In addition to word information, we also consider event and temporal cues.

3.5 The Matrix Factorization Based Timeline Summarization

We outline our matrix factorization based timeline summarization method in Algorithm 1. Since this is a supervised learning approach, we assume the corpus includes a collection of news documents S, as well as human-written summaries H for each day of the story. We also assume the publication date of each news document is known (or computable).

During training, we traverse each sentence in this corpus, and compute a *sentence importance score* (I_i) by comparing the sentence to the human generated summary for that day using ROUGE (Lin, 2004). If a human summary is not given for that day, I_i will be zero. We also extract subject-verb-object event representations, using the Stanford part-of-speech tagger (Toutanova et al., 2003) and MaltParser (Nivre et al., 2006). We use the publication date of the news document as the publication date of the sentence. Visual features are extracted using a very deep CNN (Simonyan and Zisserman, 2015). Finally, we merge these vectors into a joint vector to represent a row in our matrix factorization framework. Then, we perform stochastic gradient descent

---

Algorithm 1 A Matrix Factorization Based Timeline Summarization Algorithm

---

1: Input: news documents S, human summaries H for each day t.
2: **procedure** TRAINING(S^{tr}, H)
3:     **for each** training sentence S_i^{tr} in S^{tr} **do**
4:         $I_i \leftarrow$ ComputeImportanceScores(S_i^{tr}, H_t)
5:         $\vec{E_i} \leftarrow$ ExtractSVOEvents(S_i^{tr})
6:         $\vec{D_i} \leftarrow$ ExtractPublicationDate(S_i^{tr})
7:         $\vec{V_i} \leftarrow$ ExtractVisualFeatures(V_i^{tr})
8:         $\vec{M_i} \leftarrow$ MergeVectors(I_i, $\vec{E_i}$, $\vec{D_i}$, $\vec{V_i}$)
9:     **end for**
10:     **for each** epoch e **do**
11:         **for each** cell i, j in M **do**
12:           $\vec{p_i}^{(e)} \leftarrow \vec{p_i}^{(e)} + \delta(\ell_{(i,j)}\vec{q_j}^{(e)} - \lambda_P \vec{p_i}^{(e)})$
13:           $\vec{q_j}^{(e)} \leftarrow \vec{q_j}^{(e)} + \delta(\ell_{(i,j)}\vec{p_i}^{(e)} - \lambda_Q \vec{q_j}^{(e)})$
14:         **end for**
15:     **end for**
16: **end procedure**
17: **procedure** TESTING(S^{te})
18:     **for each** test sentence S_i^{te} in S^{te} **do**
19:         $\vec{E_i} \leftarrow$ ExtractSVOEvents(S_i^{te})
20:         $\vec{D_i} \leftarrow$ ExtractPublicationDate(S_i^{te})
21:         $\vec{V_i} \leftarrow$ ExtractVisualFeatures(S_i^{te})
22:         $\vec{M_i} \leftarrow$ MergeVectors($\vec{E_i}$, $\vec{D_i}$, $\vec{V_i}$)
23:         $I_i \leftarrow$ PredictROUGE($\vec{M_i}$, P, Q)
24:     **end for**
25:     **for each** day t in S^{te} **do**
26:         $H^{te} \leftarrow$ SelectTopSentences(S_t^{te}, $\vec{I_t}$)
27:     **end for**
28: **end procedure**

---

training to learn the hidden low-rank embeddings of sentences and features P and Q using the update rules outlined earlier.

During testing, we still extract events and publication dates, and the PredictROUGE function estimates the sentence importance score I_i, using the trained latent low-rank matrices P and Q. To be more specific, we extract the text, vision, event, and publication date features for a candidate sentence i. Then, given these features, we update the embeddings for this sentence, and make the prediction by taking the dot product of this i-th column of P (i.e., $\vec{p_i}$) and the ROUGE column of Q (i.e., $\vec{q_1}$). This predicted scalar value I_i indicates the likelihood of the sentence being included in the final timeline summary. Finally, we go through the predicted results of each sentence in the timeline in temporal order, and include the top-ranked sentences with the highest sentence importance scores. It is natural to scale this method from daily summaries to weekly or monthly summaries.

4   Experiments

In this section, we investigate the empirical performance of the proposed method, comparing to various baselines. We first discuss our experimental settings, including our primary dataset and baselines. Then, we discuss our evaluation results. We demonstrate the robustness of our approach by varying the latent dimensions of the low-rank matrices. Next, we show additional experiments on a headline-based timeline summarization dataset. Finally, we provide a qualitative analysis of the output of our system.

4.1   Comparative Evaluation on the 17 Timelines Dataset

We use the 17 timelines dataset which has been used in several prior studies (Tran et al., 2013b; Tran et al., 2013a). It includes 17 timelines from 9 topics[1] from major news agencies such as CNN, BBC, and NBC News. Only English documents are included. The dataset contains 4,650 news documents. We use Yahoo! Image Search to retrieve the top-ranked image for each sentence.[2] We follow exactly the same topic-based cross-validation setup that was used in prior work (Tran et al., 2013b): we train on eight topics, test on the remaining topic, and repeat the process eight times. The number of training iterations was set to 20; the k was set to 200 for the text only model, and 300 for the joint text/image model; and the vocabulary is 10K words for all systems. The common summarization metrics ROUGE-1, ROUGE-2, and ROUGE-S are used to evaluate the quality of the machine-generated timelines. We consider the following baselines:

---

[1] The nine topics are the BP oil spill, Egyptian protests, Financial crisis, H1N1, Haiti earthquake, Iraq War, Libya War, Michael Jackson death, and Syrian crisis.

[2] We are not aware of any publicly available dataset for timeline summarization that includes both text and images. Most of these datasets are text-only, not including the original article file or links to accompanying images. We adopted this Web-based corpus enhancement technique as a proximity for news images. Our low-rank approximation technique can be applied to the original news images in the same way.

(a) ROUGE:0   (b) ROUGE:.009.

Figure 3: Examples of retrieved Web images. The left image was retrieved by using a non-informative sentence: *"The latest five minute news bulletin from BBC World Service"*. The right image was retrieved using a crucial sentence with a non-zero ROUGE score vs. a human summary, *"Case study : Gulf of Mexico oil spill and BP On 20 April 2010 a deepwater oil well exploded in the Gulf of Mexico"*.

- **Random**: summary sentences are randomly selected from the corpus.

- **MEAD**: a feature-rich, classic multi-document summarization system (Radev et al., 2004a) that uses centroid-based summarization techniques.

- **Chieu et al.** (Chieu and Lee, 2004): a multi-document summarization system that uses TFIDF scores to indicate the "popularity" of a sentence compared to other sentences.

- **ETS** (Yan et al., 2011b): a state-of-the-art unsupervised timeline summarization system.

- **Tran et al.** (Tran et al., 2013b): another state-of-the-art timeline summarization system based on learning to rank techniques, and for which results on the 17 Timelines dataset have been previously reported.

- **Regression**: a part of a state-of-the-art extractive summarization method (Wang et al., 2015) that formulates the sentence extraction task as a supervised regression problem. We use a state-of-the-art regression implementation in Vowpal Wabbit[3].

We report results for our system and the baselines on the 17 timelines dataset in Table 1. We see that the random baseline clearly performs worse than the other methods. Even though Chieu et al. (2004)

---

[3] https://github.com/JohnLangford/vowpal_wabbit

Methods	ROUGE-1	ROUGE-2	ROUGE-S
Random	0.128	0.021	0.026
Chieu et al.	0.202	0.037	0.041
MEAD	0.208	0.049	0.039
ETS	0.207	0.047	0.042
Tran et al.	0.230	0.053	0.050
Regression	0.303	0.078	0.081
Our approach			
Text	0.312	0.089	0.112
Text+Vision	**0.331**	**0.091**	**0.115**

Table 1: Comparing the timeline summarization performance to various baselines on the 17 Timelines dataset. The best-performing results are highlighted in **bold**.

and MEAD (Radev et al., 2004a) are not specifically designed for the timeline summarization task, they perform relatively well against the ETS system for timeline summarization (Yan et al., 2011b). Tran et al. (2013b) was previously the state-of-the-art method on the 17 timelines dataset. The ROUGE regression method is shown as a strong supervised baseline. Our matrix factorization approach outperforms all of these methods, achieving the best results in all three ROUGE metrics. We also see that there is an extra boost in the performance when considering visual features for timeline summarization. Figure 3 shows an example of the retrieved images we used. In general, images retrieved by using more important sentences (measured by ROUGE) include objects, as well a more vivid and detailed scene.

4.2 Comparative Evaluation Results for Headline Based Timeline Summarization

To evaluate the robustness of our approach, we show the performance of our method on the recently released *crisis* dataset (Tran et al., 2015). The main difference between the crisis dataset and the 17 timelines dataset is that here we focus on a headline based timeline summarization task, rather than using sentences from the news documents. The crisis dataset includes four topics: Egypt revolution, Libya war, Syria war, and Yemen crisis. There are a total of 15,534 news documents in the dataset, and each topic has around 4K documents. There are 25 manually created timelines for these topics, collected from major news agencies such as BBC, CNN, and Reuters. We perform standard cross-validation on

Methods	ROUGE-1	ROUGE-2	ROUGE-S
Regression	0.207	0.045	0.039
Our approach			
Text	0.211	0.046	0.040
Text+Vision	**0.232**	**0.052**	**0.044**

Table 3: Comparing the timeline summarization performance to the state-of-the-art supervised sentence regression approach on the crisis dataset. The best-performing results are highlighted in **bold**.

this dataset: we train on three topics, and test on the other. Here k is set to 300, and the vocabulary is 10K words for all systems. Table 3 shows the performance of our system. Our system is significantly better than the strong supervised regression baseline. When considering joint learning of text and vision, we see that there is a further improvement.

4.3 Headline Based Timeline Summarization: A Qualitative Analysis

In this section, we perform a qualitative analysis of the output of our system for the headline based timeline summarization task. We train the system on three topics, and show a sample of the output on the Syria war. Table 2 shows a subset of the timeline for the Syria war generated by our system. We see that most of the daily summaries are relevant to the topic, except the one generated on 2011-11-24. When evaluating the quality, we notice that most of them are of high quality: after the initial hypothesis of the Syria war on 2011-11-18, the following daily summaries concern the world's response to the crisis. We show that most of the relevant summaries are also providing specific information, with an exception on 2011-12-02. We suspect that this is because this headline contains three keywords "syria", "civil", "war", and also the key date information: the model was trained partly on the Libya war timeline, and therefore many features and parameters were activated in the matrix factorization framework to give a high recommendation in this testing scenario. In contrast, when evaluating the output of the joint text and vision system, we see that this error is eliminated: the selected sentence on 2011-12-02 is *"Eleven killed after weekly prayers in Syria on eve of Arab League deadline"*.

Date	Summary	Relevant?	Good?
2011-11-18	Syria is heading inexorably for a civil war and an appalling bloodbath	✓	✓
2011-11-19	David Ignatius Sorting out the rebel forces in Syria	✓	✓
2011-11-20	Syria committed crimes against humanity, U.N. panel finds	✓	✓
2011-11-21	Iraq joins Syria civil war warnings	✓	✓
2011-11-22	The Path to a Civil War in Syria	✓	✓
2011-11-23	Report Iran, Hezbollah setting up militias to prepare for post-Assad Syria	✓	✓
2011-11-24	Q&A Syria's daring actress Features Al Jazeera English	×	×
2011-11-25	Syria conflict How residents of Aleppo struggle for survival	✓	✓
2011-11-27	Syrian jets bomb rebel areas near Damascus as troops battle	✓	✓
2011-11-28	Is the Regional Showdown in Syria Rekindling Iraqs Civil War?	✓	✓
2011-11-29	Syria Crisis Army Drops Leaflets Over Damascus	✓	✓
2011-11-30	Russia says West's Syria push "path to civil war"	✓	✓
2011-12-01	UN extends Syria war crimes investigation despite opposition from China	✓	✓
2011-12-02	Un syria civil war 12 2 2011	✓	×
2011-12-03	Israel says fires into Syria after Golan attack on troops	✓	✓

Table 2: A timeline example for Syria war generated by our text-only system.

5 Conclusions

In this paper, we introduce a low-rank approximation based approach for learning joint embeddings of news stories and images for timeline summarization. We leverage the success of matrix factorization techniques in recommender systems, and cast the multi-document extractive summarization task as a sentence recommendation problem. For each sentence in the corpus, we compute its similarity to a human-generated abstract, and extract lexical, event, and temporal features. We use a convolutional neural architecture to extract vision features. We demonstrate the effectiveness of this joint learning method by comparison with several strong baselines on the 17 timelines dataset and a headline based timeline summarization dataset. We show that image features improve the performance of our model significantly. This further motivates investment in joint multimodal learning for NLP tasks.

Acknowledgments

The authors would like to thank Kapil Thadani and the anonymous reviewers for their thoughtful comments.

References

Amr Ahmed, Qirong Ho, Choon H Teo, Jacob Eisenstein, Eric Xing, and Alex Smola. 2011. Online inference for the infinite topic-cluster model: Storylines from streaming text. In *Proceedings of AISTATS*.

James Allan, Rahul Gupta, and Vikas Khandelwal. 2001. Temporal summaries of new topics. In *Proceedings of SIGIR*.

Tim Althoff, Xin Luna Dong, Kevin Murphy, Safa Alai, Van Dang, and Wei Zhang. 2015. TimeMachine: Timeline generation for knowledge-base entities. In *Proceedings of KDD*.

Robert Bell and Yehuda Koren. 2007. Lessons from the Netflix prize challenge. *ACM SIGKDD Explorations Newsletter*, 9(2).

James Bennett and Stan Lanning. 2007. The Netflix prize. In *Proceedings of the KDD Cup and Workshop*.

Hai Leong Chieu and Yoong Keok Lee. 2004. Query based event extraction along a timeline. In *Proceedings of SIGIR*.

Wei-Sheng Chin, Yong Zhuang, Yu-Chin Juan, and Chih-Jen Lin. 2015. A fast parallel stochastic gradient method for matrix factorization in shared memory systems. *ACM Transactions on Intelligent Systems and Technology*, 6(1).

James Conroy, Judith Schlesinger, Diane O'Leary, and Mary Okurowski. 2001. Using HMM and logistic regression to generate extract summaries for DUC. In *Proceedings of DUC*.

Nazanin Dehghani and Masoud Asadpour. 2015. Graph-based method for summarized storyline generation in Twitter. *arXiv preprint arXiv:1504.07361*.

Günes Erkan and Dragomir Radev. 2004. Lexrank: Graph-based lexical centrality as salience in text summarization. *Journal of Artificial Intelligence Research*, 22(1).

Anthony Fader, Dragomir Radev, Michael Crespin, Burt Monroe, Kevin Quinn, and Michael Colaresi. 2007. Mavenrank: Identifying influential members of the

US senate using lexical centrality. In *Proceedings of EMNLP-CoNLL*.

Goran Glavaš and Jan Šnajder. 2014. Event graphs for information retrieval and multi-document summarization. *Expert Systems with Applications*, 41(15).

Ahmed Hassan, Anthony Fader, Michael Crespin, Kevin Quinn, Burt Monroe, Michael Colaresi, and Dragomir Radev. 2008. Tracking the dynamic evolution of participant salience in a discussion. In *Proceedings of COLING*.

Lifu Huang and Lian'en Huang. 2013. Optimized event storyline generation based on mixture-event-aspect model. In *Proceedings of EMNLP*.

Chris Kedzie, Kathleen McKeown, and Fernando Diaz. 2014. Summarizing disasters over time. In *Proceedings of the Bloomberg Workshop on Social Good at KDD*.

Jerry Kiernan and Evimaria Terzi. 2009. Constructing comprehensive summaries of large event sequences. *ACM Transactions on Knowledge Discovery from Data*, 3(4).

Gunhee Kim and Eric Xing. 2014. Reconstructing storyline graphs for image recommendation from web community photos. In *Proceedings of CVPR*.

Gunhee Kim, Leonid Sigal, and Eric P Xing. 2014. Joint summarization of large-scale collections of web images and videos for storyline reconstruction. In *Proceedings of CVPR*.

Yehuda Koren, Robert Bell, and Chris Volinsky. 2009. Matrix factorization techniques for recommender systems. *Computer*, 8.

Julian Kupiec, Jan Pedersen, and Francine Chen. 1995. A trainable document summarizer. In *Proceedings of SIGIR*.

Ju-Hong Lee, Sun Park, Chan-Min Ahn, and Daeho Kim. 2009. Automatic generic document summarization based on non-negative matrix factorization. *Information Processing & Management*, 45(1).

Omer Levy and Yoav Goldberg. 2014. Neural word embedding as implicit matrix factorization. In *Proceedings of NIPS*.

Chen Lin, Chun Lin, Jingxuan Li, Dingding Wang, Yang Chen, and Tao Li. 2012. Generating event storylines from microblogs. In *Proceedings of CIKM*.

Chin-Yew Lin. 2004. Rouge: A package for automatic evaluation of summaries. In *Proceedings of the ACL workshop "Text summarization branches out"*.

Qiaozhu Mei, Jian Guo, and Dragomir Radev. 2010. Divrank: the interplay of prestige and diversity in information networks. In *Proceedings of KDD*.

Rada Mihalcea and Paul Tarau. 2004. TextRank: Bringing order into texts. In *Proceedings of EMNLP*.

Tomas Mikolov, Kai Chen, Greg Corrado, and Jeffrey Dean. 2013. Efficient estimation of word representations in vector space. *arXiv preprint arXiv:1301.3781*.

Borja Navarro-Colorado and Estela Saquete. 2015. GPLSIUA: Combining temporal information and topic modeling for cross-document event ordering. In *Proceedings of SemEval*.

Jun-Ping Ng, Yan Chen, Min-Yen Kan, and Zhoujun Li. 2014. Exploiting timelines to enhance multi-document summarization. In *Proceedings of the ACL*.

Joakim Nivre, Johan Hall, and Jens Nilsson. 2006. Malt-Parser: A data-driven parser-generator for dependency parsing. In *Proceedings of LREC*.

Dragomir Radev, Timothy Allison, Sasha Blair-Goldensohn, John Blitzer, Arda Celebi, Stanko Dimitrov, Elliott Drabek, Ali Hakim, Wai Lam, Danyu Liu, Jahna Otterbacher, Hong Qi, Horacio Saggion, Simone Teufel, Michael Topper, Adam Winkel, and Zhu Zhang. 2004a. MEAD – a platform for multidocument multilingual text summarization. In *Proceedings of LREC*.

Dragomir R Radev, Hongyan Jing, Małgorzata Styś, and Daniel Tam. 2004b. Centroid-based summarization of multiple documents. *Information Processing & Management*.

Benjamin Recht, Christopher Re, Stephen Wright, and Feng Niu. 2011. Hogwild: A lock-free approach to parallelizing stochastic gradient descent. In *Proceedings of NIPS*.

Olga Russakovsky, Jia Deng, Hao Su, Jonathan Krause, Sanjeev Satheesh, Sean Ma, Zhiheng Huang, Andrej Karpathy, Aditya Khosla, Michael Bernstein, Alexander C. Berg, and Li Fei-Fei. 2014. Imagenet large scale visual recognition challenge. *International Journal of Computer Vision*, 115(3).

Karen Simonyan and Andrew Zisserman. 2015. Very deep convolutional networks for large-scale image recognition. In *Proceedings of ICLR*.

Kristina Toutanova, Dan Klein, Christopher D Manning, and Yoram Singer. 2003. Feature-rich part-of-speech tagging with a cyclic dependency network. In *Proceedings of NAACL-HLT*.

Giang Binh Tran, Mohammad Alrifai, and Dat Quoc Nguyen. 2013a. Predicting relevant news events for timeline summaries. In *Proceedings of WWW*.

Giang Binh Tran, Tuan A Tran, Nam-Khanh Tran, Mohammad Alrifai, and Nattiya Kanhabua. 2013b. Leveraging learning to rank in an optimization framework for timeline summarization. In *Proceedings of the SIGIR Workshop on Time-Aware Information Access*.

Giang Tran, Mohammad Alrifai, and Eelco Herder. 2015. Timeline summarization from relevant headlines. In *Proceedings of ECIR*.

Dingding Wang, Tao Li, Shenghuo Zhu, and Chris Ding. 2008. Multi-document summarization via sentence-level semantic analysis and symmetric matrix factorization. In *Proceedings of SIGIR*.

Dingding Wang, Tao Li, and Mitsunori Ogihara. 2012. Generating pictorial storylines via minimum-weight connected dominating set approximation in multi-view graphs. In *Proceedings of AAAI*.

Lu Wang, Claire Cardie, and Galen Marchetti. 2015. Socially-informed timeline generation for complex events. In *Proceedings of NAACL-HLT*.

Rui Yan, Liang Kong, Congrui Huang, Xiaojun Wan, Xiaoming Li, and Yan Zhang. 2011a. Timeline generation through evolutionary trans-temporal summarization. In *Proceedings of EMNLP*.

Rui Yan, Xiaojun Wan, Jahna Otterbacher, Liang Kong, Xiaoming Li, and Yan Zhang. 2011b. Evolutionary timeline summarization: a balanced optimization framework via iterative substitution. In *Proceedings of SIGIR*.

Xin Wayne Zhao, Yanwei Guo, Rui Yan, Yulan He, and Xiaoming Li. 2013. Timeline generation with social attention. In *Proceedings of SIGIR*.

Wubai Zhou, Chao Shen, Tao Li, Shu-Ching Chen, and Ning Xie. 2014. Generating textual storyline to improve situation awareness in disaster management. In *Proceedings of the IEEE International Conference on Information Reuse and Integration*.

Weizhong Zhu and Chaomei Chen. 2007. Storylines: Visual exploration and analysis in latent semantic spaces. *Computers & Graphics*, 31(3).

Entity-balanced Gaussian pLSA for Automated Comparison

Danish Contractor[*]
IIT Delhi & IBM Research
New Delhi, India
dcontrac@in.ibm.com

Mausam and **Parag Singla**
IIT Delhi
New Delhi, India
{mausam,parags}@cse.iitd.ac.in

Abstract

Community created content (e.g., product descriptions, reviews) typically discusses one entity at a time and it can be hard as well as time consuming for a user to compare two or more entities. In response, we define a novel task of automatically generating *entity comparisons* from text. Our output is a table that semantically clusters descriptive phrases about entities. Our clustering algorithm is a Gaussian extension of probabilistic latent semantic analysis (pLSA), in which each phrase is represented in word vector embedding space. In addition, our algorithm attempts to balance information about entities in each cluster to generate meaningful comparison tables, where possible. We test our system's effectiveness on two domains, travel articles and movie reviews, and find that entity-balanced clusters are strongly preferred by users.

1   Introduction

The proliferation of Web 2.0 has enabled ready access to large amounts of community created content, such as status messages, blogs, wikis, and reviews. These form an important source of knowledge in our day to day decision making, such as deciding which restaurant to try, or which movie to watch, or which city to visit etc. Unfortunately, such content typically focuses on one real world entity at a time, whereas, a user deciding between alternatives is most interested in a *comparative* analysis of strengths and weaknesses of each.

There have been some recent attempts to create comparisons using expert knowledge, but generating such comparisons manually does not scale – even pairwise comparisons are quadratic in the number of entities. Few automated comparisons for specific products with pre-defined attributes (e.g., laptops, cameras) exist; they are typically powered by existing structured knowledge bases. To the best of our knowledge, prior work on automatically generating comparisons for arbitrary domains from unstructured text, does not exist.

We define a novel task of generating *entity comparisons* from textual corpora in which each document describes one entity at a time. For broad applicability, we do not restrict ourselves to a pre-defined ontology; instead, we use textual phrases that describe entities as our unit of information. We call these *descriptive phrases* – they encompass general attribute-value phrases, opinion phrases, and other descriptions of the facets of an entity. We generate entity comparisons in a tabular form where the phrases are organized semantically, thus, allowing for direct comparisons. Figure 1 shows a sample city comparison generated by our system for tourism.

Our comparison generation algorithm extracts descriptive phrases per entity and clusters them into semantic groups. We perform clustering via a topic model, where phrases from an entity are combined into one document. The topics identify prominent facets of the entities. Unfortunately, since the number of entities being compared is usually small, just statistical co-occurrence of words and phrases is not sufficient to identify good topics. In response, we use vector embeddings of descriptive phrases and

---

[*] This work was carried out as part of PhD research at IIT Delhi. The author is also a regular employee at IBM Research.

Proceedings of NAACL-HLT 2016, pages 69–79,
San Diego, California, June 12-17, 2016. ©2016 Association for Computational Linguistics

employ a *Gaussian extension* of probabilistic latent semantic analysis (pLSA) over these vectors.

We also modify Gaussian pLSA to additionally incorporate an *entity-balance* term, preferring topics in which phrases from the entities are represented in a proportionate measure. The balance term trades off the discovery of unique facets for each entity with that of common facets. This enables direct comparison between entities leading to an overall improved comparison table. Since the balance term is only a preference (not a constraint), it still allows the algorithm to exhibit clusters which may be sparsely represented (or not represented at all) in one of the entities.

We demonstrate the usefulness of our ideas on two domains – tourism and movies. Based on user experiments, we find that the entity-balanced model outputs much better comparisons as compared to an entity-oblivious model such as GMM. In summary, our paper makes the following contributions:

- We define a novel task of generating entity comparisons from a corpus that describes entities individually.

- We present the first system to output such a comparison. Our system runs Gaussian pLSA over the vector embeddings of extracted phrases, and preferentially tries to balance the entities in each topic.

- Human subject evaluations using Amazon Mechanical Turk (AMT) demonstrate that AMT workers overwhelmingly prefer comparisons generated using entity-balanced Gaussian pLSA compared to entity-oblivious clustering.

2 Related Work

Recently, the internet has seen a growth in websites offering comparisons for different entities. Product websites such as eBay maintain comparisons for products. Google also outputs pre-built comparisons between common entities when queried with the word "vs." between them. Both of these output purely structured attribute-value information and are unable to compare along more qualitative and descriptive dimensions such as ease of living or quality of nightlife when comparing cities, for example. Other websites such as WikiVS[1] contain user-

---

[1]http://www.wikivs.com/wiki/Main_Page

Cluster Labels	Granada (Spain)	New York City (U.S.)
art, arch.	moorish architecture religious art fine art beautiful architecture	contemporary art modern american art medieval art egyptian art
palace, courtyard	brick-walled courtyard lovely courtyard area nasrid royal palace alhambra palace	
museum, finest	alhambra museum archaeological museum world heritage site splendid arabic shops	fine art museums guggenheim museum islamic art collection metropolitan museum
gardens, park	partal gardens palace gardens pleasant gardens moorish style gardens	flushing meadows park central park renowned gardens natl. recreational area

Figure 1: Sample comparison (abridged) between Granada and New York generated by our system. A quick look reveals that that both cities have a nice set of museums and gardens to visit, while palaces and courtyards are only in Granada. Granada's art and architecture are more ornamental, whereas New York's might be more contemporary.

contributed comparisons that have been categorized based on the nature of the entities being compared. These are manually curated and therefore do not scale to the quadratic number of entity pairs.

Perhaps the most closely related work to ours is the field of contrastive opinion mining and summarization (Kim et al., 2011; Liu and Zhang, 2012). Examples include extraction of contrastive sentiments on a product (Lerman and McDonald, 2009) and summarization of opinionated political articles (Paul et al., 2010). Contrastive opinion mining extracts contrasting view points about a *single* entity or event instead of comparing multiple ones. A recent preliminary study extends this for comparing reviews of two products (Sipos and Joachims, 2013). It uses a supervised method for learning sentence alignments per product-type, and does not organize various opinions for an entity via clustering.

Other related work includes comparative text mining tasks where document collections are analyzed to extract shared topics or themes (Zhai et al., 2004). Since such methods only identify latent topics for the full document collection, they can't be directly used for a specific comparison task.

Since our system is a combination of IE and clustering, we briefly describe related approaches for these subtasks.

Information Extraction: Our work is related to

the vast literature in information extraction, in particular Open IE (Banko et al., 2007). Our use of POS patterns for extracting domain-specific descriptive phrases is similar in spirit to ReVerb's patterns for relation extraction (Etzioni et al., 2011) and adjective-noun bigrams for fine grained attribute extraction (Huang et al., 2012; Yatani et al., 2011). Adapting the literature on entity set expansion (Pantel et al., 2009; Voorhees, 1994; Natsev et al., 2007), our system expands seed nouns for broader coverage. We use Wordnet and distributional similarity-based approaches for this (Curran, 2003; Voorhees, 1994).

Clustering: Our entity-balanced clustering algorithm is related but different from previous work on *balanced* clustering. Prior work (Banerjee and Ghosh, 2006; Yuepeng et al., 2011) has focused on generating different clusters to be equi-sized. Other work (Zhu et al., 2010; Ganganath et al., 2014) enforces size constraints on clusters. Our idea of balance, on the other hand, is targeted towards a better comparison and prefers that entities are well represented (balanced) in each cluster.

3   Task & System Description

Our motivation is to concisely compare two or more entities to aid a user's decision making. We make several choices in our task definition to help with this goal. First, we decide to output comparisons using a succinct tabular representation (see Figure 1). It has higher information density compared to, say, writing a natural language comparison summary.

Second, our unit of information is a *descriptive phrase*. We define it as any short phrase that describes an entity – these include attribute-value pairs (e.g., "Greek art"), opinion phrases (e.g., "spectacular views"), as well as other descriptions (e.g., "oldest church of Europe").

Third, for better readability, our table must organize the information coherently along various aspects relevant for a comparison. We achieve this by grouping related descriptive phrases. The choice of aspects should be dependent on the specific entities being compared, e.g., the facet of "beaches" may split into "water activities" and "beach types" for Jamaica v.s. Hawaii, but not for San Francisco v.s. Bombay.

Moreover, comparisons are meant to highlight both the similarities and the differences between entities. We therefore need to trade-off the discovery of unique facets of an entity with those which are common to the entities being compared. Thus, while clusters that balance the entities are preferable, it is also acceptable to have clusters where one of the entities is sparsely represented (or not represented at all). This would happen in situations where that entity does not express a particular aspect and other entities do. Comparisons must trade off semantic coherence of facets with entity-balance in each facet.

Last, but not the least, since the comparisons are targeted to aiding user's decision making, understanding her intent is important. As an example, the user may be interested in city-comparison for the purpose of tourism, or for choosing a city to live in. Descriptive phrases for the former could be related to sightseeing, shopping, etc., but for the latter they may cover aspects such as living expenses, transportation, and pollution. We accommodate this necessity by allowing minimal human supervision for specifying user intent. This supervision can come in forms such as an intent-relevant seed noun list, or topic-level annotation following unsupervised topic modeling, etc. This supervision further guides descriptive phrase extraction.

System Architecture: Our system consists of a pipeline of information extraction, clustering, cluster labeling and phrase ordering. IE extracts descriptive phrases relevant to user-intent and we develop a new clustering algorithm that produces better comparisons by balancing the entities in each cluster. We identify cluster labels based on the most frequent words in a cluster. We order phrases within a cluster based on the distance from the centroid. We now describe our IE and clustering techniques in detail.

3.1   Information Extraction

Our IE pipeline works in two steps. We first extract descriptive phrases via POS patterns and then filter out the non-topical phrases. For filtering, first we create a seed list of relevant nouns via minimal human supervision, which are then expanded by itemset expansion. Descriptive phrases with a noun in the expanded list are retained, and rest are filtered.

Preliminary analysis on a devset revealed that

a large fraction of descriptive phrases are noun phrases (NPs). We first extract all NP chunks from the collection and, additionally, using POS tags, extract any adjective-noun bigrams that are part of a bigger NP chunk, or missed due to chunking errors. This forms the initial set of descriptive phrases.

Filtering for User Intent:

These descriptive phrases include those that are not relevant for user intent such as "excellent schools" for tourism. We filter these phrases by matching them to a list of intent-specific nouns. This list is created by first curating a seed list and then expanding it using item-set expansion. We employ two methods to obtain a seed list for specifying user intent: (1) a list of user-specified seed nouns, and (2) a labeling of LDA topics based on top words in each topic.

In the first approach we get the seed nouns directly from the domain expert. Our system supports the process by identifying frequent nouns and showing those to the annotator to annotate. For our tourism system, an author spent about three hours to produce a list of 100 seed nouns.

Since this process requires significant effort per user intent, we also investigate a semi-automatic approach in which we run Latent Dirichlet Allocation (LDA) (Blei et al., 2003) on the whole phrase list. We then show the top 20 words in each topic and ask the annotator to provide only topic-level annotations. We treat the top 15 words from each positively labeled topic to be in the seed set. Since the number of topics is usually not that large, this significantly reduces the time required for annotation. E.g., we ran LDA with 20 topics and it took about 10 mins. for an author to annotate them. However, the seed nouns are noisier due to noise in LDA.

Seed List Expansion: Finally, we use ideas from item-set expansion to expand the seed list for improved coverage. We implement two approaches for this step. In the first method (WN) we use Wordnet (Miller, 1995) to include words that are a direct hop away from the seed nouns. In the second approach (WV), we use word-vector embeddings (Collobert et al., 2011) and include top 10 neighbors of each seed in our expanded list. The expansions capture near-synonyms and topically related words.

IE Experiments: We now present comparisons of

Method	Prec.	Recall	F1
All nouns	0.53	**0.67**	**0.59**
Seed Nouns only (Manual)	**0.77**	0.32	0.44
Seed (Manual) + WN	0.71	0.35	0.46
Seed (Manual) + WV	0.70	0.40	0.49
Seed Nouns only (LDA)	0.74	0.19	0.30
Seed (LDA) + WN	0.74	0.20	0.31
Seed (LDA) + WV	0.74	0.26	0.38

Table 1: Quality of extracted descriptive phrases on a devset

various IE methods on a small development set. We selected seven WikiTravel[2] articles (each article is on one city) and manually annotated an exhaustive set of descriptive phrases. This forms our devset for IE comparisons.

We chose various parameters in our IE systems so that our precision never drops below 0.70. For example, we used K=15 for choosing the top words from LDA into seed list. We use this target precision, because we believe that for any human-facing system the precision needs to be high for it to be considered acceptable by people.

Table 1 compares the performance of the various IE methods. Not surprisingly, we find that manual seed lists obtain a much higher recall as compared to LDA seeds, at approximately the same level of precision. Both Wordnet and word-vector improve the recall substantially, though vectors are more effective. The recall of all nouns is only 0.67 because a large number of descriptive phrases were larger n-grams (not just adjective-noun bigrams) and were missed due to chunking errors.

3.2 Building Clusters for Comparison

Our next task is to construct meaningful comparisons using these phrases. A useful comparison of entities should organize the available information in a way that is easy to comprehend by the user. Towards this goal, we group the related descriptive phrases across a number of clusters. But simply having a good clustering of descriptive phrases may not be enough. We would like to have a clustering that explicitly captures the individual characteristics of each of the entities as well as makes the relative strengths and weaknesses of each entity apparent. For example, Figure 2 (Right) shows three different clusterings of phrases from two cities; phrases from each city are in a different color. Here, the third clus-

---

[2]www.wikitravel.com

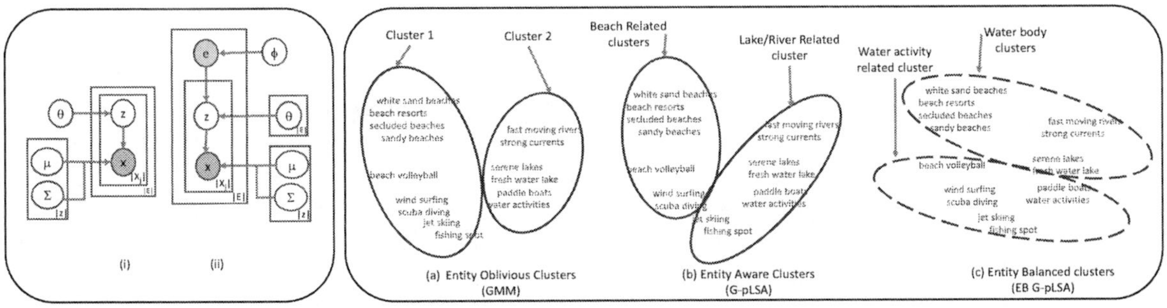

Figure 2: **Left**: Plate Notation of (i) Standard Gaussian Mixture Model (ii) Gaussian pLSA (and entity balanced Gaussian pLSA) **Right**: Three alternative clusterings (a), (b), (c) for descriptive phrases from two cities – each color is a different city. We prefer clusters shown in (c) as they balance information from both entities

tering is most appropriate for comparison, because not only is it a good clustering of descriptive phrases from each city considered separately, but the clusters produced also have *entity-balance*, i.e., the clusters produced have a good *balance* of both cities; both of these are key elements of comparison.

We first observe that a topic model such as Probabilistic Latent Semantic Analysis (pLSA) is a good fit to our clustering problem. In pLSA documents are characterized as mixtures of topics and topics as distributions over words. For our problem, we could combine all phrases for an entity into one document, and run pLSA to identify a coherent set of topics, which can then be used as clusters. Such a model will allow different entities to express topics in different proportions.

We note that LDA, which is a strict generalization of pLSA[3], is, in general, not a good fit for our task. LDA typically uses a *sparse* Dirichlet prior on document-topic distribution, which would not be appropriate since for comparison we would like to represent each entity in as many topics as possible.

Unfortunately, a direct application of pLSA may not yield good results. This is because typically the number of entities being compared (i.e., the number of documents in pLSA) is very small (often 2), therefore, there isn't enough statistical regularity to find good coherent topics. The alternative proposition of learning topics on the whole corpus isn't very appealing either, since that will learn global topics and not the topics particularly meaningful for the current comparison at hand.

In response, we exploit the availability of pre-trained word vectors as a source of background semantic knowledge for every phrase, and generalize the pLSA model to *Gaussian pLSA* (G-pLSA). We construct a vector representation for each descriptive phrase by averaging the word-vectors of individual words in a phrase (Mikolov et al., 2013)[4]. Thus, this model is pLSA with each topic-word distribution represented as a Gaussian distribution over descriptive phrases in the embedding space. This model is also similar to the recently introduced Gaussian LDA model (Das et al., 2015), but without LDA's Dirichlet priors as discussed above.

Gaussian pLSA has several advantages for our task. First, it can meaningfully learn topics only for the entities being compared, instead of needing to learn a global topic model over the whole corpus. Second, due to additional context from word vectors, the topics are expected to be much more coherent compared to traditional topic models for cases when the underlying corpus is small, as in our case. Finally, in our model the vectors are generated from a Gaussian distribution and that helps capture the *theme* of the cluster directly by enabling a centroid computation in the embedding space. This is especially useful for identifying and ranking important descriptive phrases per cluster while generating the comparison table.

Let $x_j^{(i)}, z_j^{(i)}$ denote the values of the ith phrase and the corresponding cluster (topic) id, respectively, for the jth entity e_j. Then, the log-likelihood

---

[3]LDA with uniform Dirichlet prior is equivalent to pLSA

[4]We use the pre-trained 300 dimension vectors available at http://code.google.com/p/word2vec/

$L(\Theta)$ of the observed data can be written as:

$$\sum_{j=1}^{|E|}\sum_{i=1}^{|X_j|} \log\left[\sum_{z_j^{(i)}=1}^{|Z|} P(x_j^{(i)}|z_j^{(i)};\Theta)\cdot P(z_j^{(i)}|e_j;\Theta)\cdot P(e_j;\Theta)\right]$$

$$(1)$$

Here, $|X_j|$ and $|Z|$ are the total number of phrases and clusters[5] respectively, for a given entity e_j and, $|E|$ is the total number of entities being considered for comparison. Θ denotes the vector of all the parameters. We optimize the expression $L(\Theta)$ using EM and estimate the parameters of the model. As can be seen, the clusters are shared across entities, and the phrases generated are independent of the entity given, a cluster and the entities themselves are free to exhibit clusters in different proportions.

We also note just as pLSA can be seen as a natural extension of mixture of unigrams (Blei et al., 2003), Gaussian pLSA is an extension from the Gaussian Mixture Model (GMM) which is entity-oblivious. GMM generates each phrase independent of the entity it came from and hence, distributes entity phrases arbitrarily across clusters. We use GMM as a baseline for our experiments. Figure 2 (left) illustrates the two models in plate notation.

Entity-Balanced Gaussian pLSA: Vanilla Gaussian pLSA may not always lead to a good clustering for comparison since the expression above does not involve any term to balance the entity-information in clusters, as motivated earlier. Thus, we incorporate a regularizer term to have a good balance (proportion) of entities in each cluster (see Figure 2 (right) (c)) resulting in our final model for comparison called *Entity-Balanced Gaussian pLSA (EB G-pLSA)*. The plate notation for EB G-pLSA is identical to G-pLSA.

Our regularizer is a function of the KL-divergence between multinomial distributions for every pair of entities. KL-divergence $KL(P||Q)$ between two discrete distributions $P(x)$ and $Q(x)$ is defined as $\sum_l P(x_l)log\left(\frac{P(x_l)}{Q(x_l)}\right)$. Its an asymmetric measure of similarity and is equal to 0 when the two distributions are identical (and greater than 0 otherwise). Symmetric KL-divergence is defined as $Sym\text{-}KL(P,Q) = KL(P||Q) + KL(Q||P)$.

Let $P_{\theta_j}(z|e_j)$ and $P_{\theta_k}(z|e_k)$ denote the multi-

nomial distributions for generating the cluster id z given the entities e_j and e_k, respectively. Here, θ_j and θ_k denote the respective multinomial parameters. We add a regularizer term to the log-likelihood minimizing the sum of symmetric KL-divergence between the distributions $P_{\theta_j}(z|e_j)$ and $P_{\theta_k}(z|e_k)$ for every pair of entities e_j and e_k. Adding this regularizer requires the multinomial distributions to be similar to each other, thereby preferring balanced clusters over unbalanced ones. Our regularized average log-likelihood can be written as:

$$L_{reg}^{avg}(\Theta) = \frac{1}{|M|}L(\Theta) - \alpha\cdot\left[\sum_{j,k=1|j<k}^{|E|} Sym\text{-}KL(P_{\theta_j}, P_{\theta_k})\right]$$

$$(2)$$

$L(\Theta)$ is the total log-likelihood as defined in the previous equation. $M = \sum_{j=1}^{|E|} |X_j|$ and $|E|$ is the total number of entities being compared. α is a constant controlling the weight of the regularizer. Note that we add the regularizer term to the *average* log-likelihood (instead of the total log-likelihood) in order to have the same regularizer value for comparisons having varying number of data points (descriptive phrases). This is important to obtain a single value of α which would work well across different entity comparisons. In our experiments, α was tuned using held-out data and was found to be robust to small perturbations.

We use standard EM to optimize the regularized log-likelihood. Since the regularizer does not have any hidden variables, E-step is identical to the one for the unregularized case. During M-step, the values maximizing the mean parameters μ_z and the ϕ parameter can be obtained analytically. There is no closed form solution for the parameters θ_j, θ_k. We perform gradient descent to optimize these parameters during the M-step. In our experiments, we did not estimate the co-variance matrices Σ_z and kept them fixed as a diagonal matrix with the diagonal entry (variance) being 0.1. We did not learn the co-variance matrices as that would have increased the number of parameters substantially, and thus, had the danger of over fitting. The small value of the variance chosen was to ensure less overlap between different clusters.

Clustering Experiments We conducted preliminary experiments to compare the performance of GMM (vanilla Gaussian mixture modeling using word vec-

---

[5]Note that number of clusters for all entities will be the same i.e $|Z_j| = Z$ for all j

	GMM	G-pLSA	EB G-pLSA
f-measure	0.42	0.43	0.44
pairwise accuracy	0.66	0.65	0.76

Table 2: Comparing clustering methods on development set

tors) with G-pLSA and EB G-pLSA on a development set consisting of 5 random city pairs. The descriptive phrases were constructed using the automated seed list as described in IE Section. We manually created the gold standard clusterings. The number of clusters was set to the number in the gold set for each of the city pairs.

We used f-measure and pairwise accuracy to evaluate the deviation from the gold standard for the clusterings produced by each of the algorithms. Table 2 shows the results. EB G-pLSA performs better than the other two algorithms on both the metrics, and especially on pairwise accuracy. Performance of G-pLSA is very similar to GMM.

4   Human Subject Evaluations

In order to evaluate the usefulness of our system we conducted extensive experiments on Amazon Mechanical Turk (AMT). Our experiments answer the following questions. (1) Are comparisons generated using our clustering methods G-pLSA and EB G-pLSA preferred by users against the entity oblivious baseline of GMM? (2) Are our system-generated comparison tables helpful to people for the task of entity comparison?

Datasets & System Settings: We experiment[6] on two datasets – tourism and movies. For tourism, we downloaded a collection of 16,785 travel articles from WikiTravel. The website contains articles that have been collaboratively written by Web users. Each article describes a city or a larger geographic area that is of interest to tourists. In addition, all articles contain sections[7] describing different aspects of a city from a tourism point of view (e.g., places to see, transportation, shopping and eating). For our proof of concept, we performed IE only on the 'places to see' sections.

For Movies dataset, we used the Amazon review data set (Leskovec and Krevl, 2014). It has over 7.9 million reviews for 250,000 movies. We combined all the reviews for a movie, thus, generating a large review document per movie. This dataset is much noisier compared to WikiTravel due to presence of slang, incorrect grammar, sarcasm, etc. In addition, users also tend to compare and contrast while reviewing movies so there are even references to other movies. As a result, the descriptive phrases extracted were much more noisy.

For the time consuming manual seed list setting of our IE system, we only use the tourism dataset. For movies, we generate seeds using annotation over LDA topics only. For all systems we use word-vectors to expand the seed list.

For each table, we generated k clusters where k was determined using a heuristic[8] (Mardia et al., 1980), and we displayed at most 30 phrases per cluster. We did not display any cluster that had less than 4 phrases.

4.1   Evaluation of Clustering Algorithms

In order to examine whether clustering using EB G-pLSA indeed produces best comparison tables, we conducted a human evaluation task on Amazon Mechanical Turk (AMT) where users of our system were asked to indicate their preference between two comparison tables. Since we have three systems we performed this pairwise study thrice. In each study, two comparison tables were generated from different systems. For each entity-pair we asked four workers each to select which comparison table they preferred. The order of the tables was randomized to remove any biasing effect. We paid $0.3 for each table comparison. Table 3 reports the results for both domains where descriptive phrases were generated using LDA+WV.

On 30 city-pairs in the Tourism domain, workers preferred the comparison tables generated using EB G-pLSA 53% of the time and GMM was preferred only 13% (the rest were ties). It is worthwhile to note that whereas in 20% of the comparisons, EB G-pLSA had a clear 4-0 margin, there was no such comparison where all the workers preferred the GMM model. We also requested users to provide the reasons for their preferences. While most users specified a non-informative reason such as "like it better", some users gave specific reasons such as "subdivides the parts I find useful into more specific

---

[6] Code and data available on request

[7] http://wikitravel.org/en/Wikitravel:Article_templates/Sections

[8] No. of clusters = square root of half the number of phrases

Domain	Total pairs	EB G-pLSA Win		GMM Win		EB G-pLSA Win		G-pLSA Win		G-pLSA Win		GMM Win	
		4-0	3-1	1-3	0-4	4-0	3-1	1-3	0-4	4-0	3-1	1-3	0-4
Tourism	30	20%	33%	13%	0%	13%	30%	30%	0%	17%	27%	13%	3%
Movies	20	20%	35%	10%	0%	5%	35%	15%	5%	5%	45%	15%	5%

Table 3: User preference win-loss statistics for different clustering methods on both city and movie comparison task using the same IE system. Both EB G-pLSA and G-pLSA significantly outperform the baseline GMM model. EB G-pLSA has some edge over the G-pLSA model. Note: Ties have not been shown in the table.

categories" and "easy to understand and more specific points of comparison". Our results also show that G-pLSA is a distinct improvement over GMM (44% vs. 16%). EB G-pLSA had a marginal edge over G-pLSA (43% vs. 30%).

On movies domain, we report results on 20 movie-pairs and we again found an overwhelming preference for the system using EB G-pLSA for clustering. 55% of the time, the output of EB G-pLSA was preferred over GMM's 10%. Other comparisons between G-pLSA and GMM, and between our G-pLSA and EB G-pLSA systems also follow trends similar to tourism domain. The performance of EB G-pLSA is statistically significantly better than GMM for both the tourism and the movie datasets, with p values being less than 0.00004 and 0.002, respectively, using a one-sided students t-test. This strong preference suggests that the clustering induced by incorporating entity balance in the clusters produces much better comparison tables.

4.2 Value of Comparison Tables

The goal of our experiments in this section was to assess whether our comparison tables add value to some realistic task and to understand the overall usefulness of our system. To our knowledge there are no other automated systems comparing cities for tourism (or movies), hence we could not evaluate our system against existing approaches. Therefore, we decided to evaluate the benefit of the output generated by our system (i.e., comparison tables) against reading the original WikiTravel articles. For fairness we only use the 'places to see' sections from WikiTravel, since that was the raw text used in generating comparison tables in the first place.

Since the comparisons are generated automatically, people may not find them understandable, or there may be missing valuable information. We test this in a human subject evaluation. We adapt the evaluation methodology developed recently for contrasting multiple ways of presenting information and testing the overall learning of the subjects (Shahaf et al., 2012; Christensen et al., 2014). The evaluation is divided into two parts. In the first part the workers are given a limited time to read the information provided (articles or comparison tables) for an entity-pair. They are then asked to write a short 150-300 word summary contrasting different aspects of the two entities. Each user writes two summaries, one based on articles and the other based on our table. Our study pairs two users such that if user1 read the articles for city pair 1 and the table for city pair 2, their partner user will see the reverse. The workers were additionally asked which knowledge source they preferred and why.

Making a worker create summaries using both information sources helps reduce the effect of worker comprehension and skill in the evaluation of our task, as each worker contributes to summaries created using our system as well as the baseline. In order to reduce the effects of any sequence bias, half the mechanical turk workers were first shown the output of our system followed by the articles and the other half (partners) were shown content the other way around.

In the second part of this experiment we directly compare the knowledge acquisition of these workers. In particular, we ask a different set of workers to evaluate the summaries created by the partnered workers. In each task, a worker has to compare two summaries for the same entity-pair, one created using tables by one worker and other created using articles by their partner. Each summary pair was shown to four different users and each of them was asked to select the summary they preferred for comparing and contrasting the entities. Since we perform this experiment on Tourism data, the MTurk task descriptions explained that the intent of the comparison is tourism and their summaries or preferences must be from that perspective.

4.2.1 Results

We performed this evaluation on twenty city pairs using both our information extraction methods i.e. Manual+WV expansion (referred as TABLE-M) and LDA+WV expansion (referred as TABLE-LDA) along with the EB G-pLSA method for clustering. The city pairs were chosen such that the cities are related but not too similar, and the workers would likely not have thought of the specific comparisons before.

We found that in the first part where workers were given 10 minutes to create the summaries, they on average asked for 30% more time to create the summaries when information was presented as article. This supports our belief that our system-generated tables successfully reduce information overload. It also suggests that the structure added by the system (clusters) was useful for the comparison task and reduced workers' cognitive load.

We now present the results for the second part of the study in which workers evaluated the comparison summaries written by the workers in the first part. Within 20 city-pairs, summaries for 5 city pairs (25%) generated based on TABLE-M were preferred and 5 (25%) generated based on original articles were chosen. The workers were indifferent in 10 of the city pairs (both summaries got two votes each). This shows that despite having a very high compression ratio, workers still managed to create summaries that were comparable in quality to those created by reading original documents. We repeated the same study using TABLE-LDA and found that summaries for 8 city pairs (40%) generated based on TABLE-LDA were preferred and 5 (25%) generated based on original articles were chosen. The workers were indifferent in 6 of the city pairs (both summaries got two votes each).

We did not repeat this experiment using the Movies data set as the source articles were concatenated reviews with no structure and it would not be surprising that users prefer our system. In summary, we find that both our systems convey adequate and useful information in the comparisons and the summaries generated by users using our systems were found to be as good as the ones created by users reading the full articles.

5 Conclusions

We define a novel task of automatically generating tabular entity comparisons from unstructured text. We also implement the first system for this task that first extracts descriptive phrases from text and then clusters them to generate comparison tables. Our clustering algorithm is a Gaussian extension of p-LSA, where the descriptive phrases are represented using embeddings in the word vector space. In order to have a better comparison between entities, we incorporate a balance term which prefers clusters where entities are proportionately represented.

We perform extensive human-subject evaluations for our systems over Amazon Mechanical Turk (AMT) on two datasets – tourism and movies. We find that AMT workers overwhelmingly prefer EB G-pLSA based comparisons over GMM-based. We also assess the value of our generated comparisons over reading the original articles. We find that while both sets of workers learned as much, the workers viewing tables asked for less additional time to narrate a comparison in words. Overall, we believe that comparison tables add value for users deciding between multiple entities. In the future we wish to perform joint extraction and clustering instead of our current pipelined approach.

Acknowledgments

We would like to thank the users of our system: Bhadra Mani, Dinesh Khandelwal, Eshita Sharma, Kuntal Dey, Leela Muthana, Noira Khan, Samuel Kumar, Seher Contractor and Prachi Jain, and the anonymous Amazon mechnical turk workers for their evaluation and insights. We would also like to thank Ankit Anand, Happy Mittal and anonymous reviewers for their suggestions on improving the paper. The work was supported by IBM Research, Google language understanding and knowledge discovery focused research grants to Mausam, a KISTI grant and a Bloomberg grant also to Mausam. We would also like to acknowledge the IBM Research India PhD program that enables the first author to pursue the PhD at IIT Delhi.

References

Arindam Banerjee and Joydeep Ghosh. 2006. Scalable clustering algorithms with balancing constraints. *Data Min. Knowl. Discov.*, 13(3):365–395, November.

Michele Banko, Michael J Cafarella, Stephen Soderland, Matt Broadhead, and Oren Etzioni. 2007. Open information extraction from the web. In *IN IJCAI*, pages 2670–2676.

David M. Blei, Andrew Y. Ng, Michael I. Jordan, and John Lafferty. 2003. Latent dirichlet allocation. *Journal of Machine Learning Research*, 3:2003.

Janara Christensen, Stephen Soderland, Gagan Bansal, and Mausam. 2014. Hierarchical summarization: Scaling up multi-document summarization. In *Proceedings of the 52nd Annual Meeting of the Association for Computational Linguistics, ACL 2014, June 22-27, 2014, Baltimore, MD, USA, Volume 1: Long Papers*, pages 902–912.

R. Collobert, J. Weston, L. Bottou, M. Karlen, K. Kavukcuoglu, and P. Kuksa. 2011. Natural language processing (almost) from scratch. *Journal of Machine Learning Research*, 12:2493–2537.

James Richard Curran. 2003. *From Distributional to Semantic Similarity*. Ph.D. thesis, Institute for Communicating and Collaborative Systems School of Informatics University of Edinburgh.

Rajarshi Das, Manzil Zaheer, and Chris Dyer. 2015. Gaussian lda for topic models with word embeddings. In *Proceedings of the 53rd Annual Meeting of the Association for Computational Linguistics and the 7th International Joint Conference on Natural Language Processing (Volume 1: Long Papers)*, pages 795–804, Beijing, China, July. Association for Computational Linguistics.

Oren Etzioni, Anthony Fader, Janara Christensen, Stephen Soderland, and Mausam. 2011. Open Information Extraction: the Second Generation. In *International Joint Conference on Artificial Intelligence (IJCAI)*, Barcelona, Spain, July.

N. Ganganath, Chi-Tsun Cheng, and C.K. Tse. 2014. Data clustering with cluster size constraints using a modified k-means algorithm. In *Cyber-Enabled Distributed Computing and Knowledge Discovery (CyberC), 2014 International Conference on*, pages 158–161, Oct.

Jeff Huang, Oren Etzioni, Luke Zettlemoyer, Kevin Clark, and Christian Lee. 2012. Revminer: An extractive interface for navigating reviews on a smartphone. In *Proceedings of the 25th Annual ACM Symposium on User Interface Software and Technology*, UIST '12, pages 3–12, New York, NY, USA. ACM.

Hyun Duk Kim, Kavita Ganesan, Parikshit Sondhi, and ChengXiang Zhai. 2011. Comprehensive review of opinion summarization.

Kevin Lerman and Ryan McDonald. 2009. Contrastive summarization: An experiment with consumer reviews. In *Proceedings of Human Language Technologies: The 2009 Annual Conference of the North American Chapter of the Association for Computational Linguistics, Companion Volume: Short Papers*, NAACL-Short '09, pages 113–116, Stroudsburg, PA, USA. Association for Computational Linguistics.

Jure Leskovec and Andrej Krevl. 2014. SNAP Datasets: Stanford large network dataset collection. http://snap.stanford.edu/data, June.

Bing Liu and Lei Zhang. 2012. A survey of opinion mining and sentiment analysis. pages 415–463.

K. V. Mardia, J. T. Kent, and J. M. Bibby. 1980. *Multivariate Analysis (Probability and Mathematical Statistics)*. Academic Press, 1 edition.

Tomas Mikolov, Ilya Sutskever, Kai Chen, Greg Corrado, and Jeffrey Dean. 2013. Distributed representations of words and phrases and their compositionality. *CoRR*, abs/1310.4546.

George A. Miller. 1995. Wordnet: A lexical database for english. *Commun. ACM*, 38(11):39–41, November.

Apostol (Paul) Natsev, Alexander Haubold, Jelena Tešić, Lexing Xie, and Rong Yan. 2007. Semantic concept-based query expansion and re-ranking for multimedia retrieval. In *Proceedings of the 15th International Conference on Multimedia*, MULTIMEDIA '07, pages 991–1000, New York, NY, USA. ACM.

Patrick Pantel, Eric Crestan, Arkady Borkovsky, Ana-Maria Popescu, and Vishnu Vyas. 2009. Web-scale distributional similarity and entity set expansion. In *Proceedings of the 2009 Conference on Empirical Methods in Natural Language Processing: Volume 2 - Volume 2*, EMNLP '09, pages 938–947, Stroudsburg, PA, USA. Association for Computational Linguistics.

Michael J. Paul, ChengXiang Zhai, and Roxana Girju. 2010. Summarizing contrastive viewpoints in opinionated text. In *Proceedings of the 2010 Conference on Empirical Methods in Natural Language Processing*, EMNLP '10, pages 66–76, Stroudsburg, PA, USA. Association for Computational Linguistics.

Dafna Shahaf, Carlos Guestrin, and Eric Horvitz. 2012. Trains of thought: Generating information maps. In *International World Wide Web Conference (WWW)*.

Ruben Sipos and Thorsten Joachims. 2013. Generating comparative summaries from reviews. In *22nd ACM International Conference on Information and Knowledge Management, CIKM'13, San Francisco, CA, USA, October 27 - November 1, 2013*, pages 1853–1856.

EllenM. Voorhees. 1994. Query expansion using lexical-semantic relations. In BruceW. Croft and C.J. Rijsbergen, editors, *SIGIR ?94*, pages 61–69. Springer London.

Koji Yatani, Michael Novati, Andrew Trusty, and Khai N. Truong. 2011. Review spotlight: A user interface for summarizing user-generated reviews using adjective-noun word pairs. In *Proceedings of the SIGCHI Conference on Human Factors in Computing Systems*, CHI '11, pages 1541–1550, New York, NY, USA. ACM.

Sun Yuepeng, Liu Min, and Wu Cheng. 2011. A modified k-means algorithm for clustering problem with balancing constraints. In *Proceedings of the 2011 Third International Conference on Measuring Technology and Mechatronics Automation - Volume 01*, ICMTMA '11, pages 127–130, Washington, DC, USA. IEEE Computer Society.

ChengXiang Zhai, Atulya Velivelli, and Bei Yu. 2004. A cross-collection mixture model for comparative text mining. In *Proceedings of the Tenth ACM SIGKDD International Conference on Knowledge Discovery and Data Mining*, KDD '04, pages 743–748, New York, NY, USA. ACM.

Shunzhi Zhu, Dingding Wang, and Tao Li. 2010. Data clustering with size constraints. *Knowledge-Based Systems*, 23(8):883 – 889.

Automatic Summarization of Student Course Feedback

Wencan Luo[†]   **Fei Liu**[‡]   **Zitao Liu**[†]   **Diane Litman**[†]
[†]University of Pittsburgh, Pittsburgh, PA 15260
[‡]University of Central Florida, Orlando, FL 32716
{wencan, ztliu, litman}@cs.pitt.edu   feiliu@cs.ucf.edu

Abstract

Student course feedback is generated daily in both classrooms and online course discussion forums. Traditionally, instructors manually analyze these responses in a costly manner. In this work, we propose a new approach to summarizing student course feedback based on the integer linear programming (ILP) framework. Our approach allows different student responses to share co-occurrence statistics and alleviates sparsity issues. Experimental results on a student feedback corpus show that our approach outperforms a range of baselines in terms of both ROUGE scores and human evaluation.

1 Introduction

Instructors love to solicit feedback from students. Rich information from student responses can reveal complex teaching problems, help teachers adjust their teaching strategies, and create more effective teaching and learning experiences. Text-based student feedback is often manually analyzed by teaching evaluation centers in a costly manner. Albeit useful, the approach does not scale well. It is therefore desirable to automatically summarize the student feedback produced in online and offline environments. In this work, student responses are collected from an introductory materials science and engineering course, taught in a classroom setting. Students are presented with prompts after each lecture and asked to provide feedback. These prompts solicit *"reflective feedback"* (Boud et al., 2013) from the students. An example is presented in Table 1.

Prompt
Describe what you found most interesting in today's class

Student Responses
S1: The main topics of this course seem interesting and correspond with my major (Chemical engineering)
S2: I found the group activity most interesting
S3: Process that make materials
S4: I found the properties of bike elements to be most interesting
S5: How materials are manufactured
S6: Finding out what we will learn in this class was interesting to me
S7: The activity with the bicycle parts
S8: "part of a bike" activity
... (rest omitted, 53 responses in total.)

Reference Summary
- group activity of analyzing bicycle's parts
- materials processing
- the main topic of this course

Table 1: Example student responses and a reference summary created by the teaching assistant. 'S1'–'S8' are student IDs.

In this work, we aim to summarize the student responses. This is formulated as an extractive summarization task, where a set of representative sentences are extracted from student responses to form a textual summary. One of the challenges of summarizing student feedback is its lexical variety. For example, in Table 1, "bike elements" (S4) and "bicycle parts" (S7), "the main topics of this course" (S1) and "what we will learn in this class" (S6) are different expressions that communicate the same or similar meanings. In fact, we observe 97% of the bigrams appear only once or twice in the student feedback corpus (§4), whereas in a typical news dataset (DUC 2004), it is about 80%. To tackle this challenge, we propose a new approach to summarizing

Proceedings of NAACL-HLT 2016, pages 80–85,
San Diego, California, June 12-17, 2016. ©2016 Association for Computational Linguistics

student feedback, which extends the standard ILP framework by approximating the co-occurrence matrix using a low-rank alternative. The resulting system allows sentences authored by different students to share co-occurrence statistics. For example, "The activity with the bicycle parts" (S7) will be allowed to partially contain "bike elements" (S4) although the latter did not appear in the sentence. Experiments show that our approach produces better results on the student feedback summarization task in terms of both ROUGE scores and human evaluation.

2 ILP Formulation

Let $\mathcal{D}$ be a set of student responses that consist of M sentences in total. Let $y_j \in \{0,1\}, j = \{1,\cdots,M\}$ indicate if a sentence j is selected ($y_j = 1$) or not ($y_j = 0$) in the summary. Similarly, let N be the number of unique concepts in $\mathcal{D}$. $z_i \in \{0,1\}$, $i = \{1,\cdots,N\}$ indicate the appearance of concepts in the summary. Each concept i is assigned a weight of w_i, often measured by the number of sentences or documents that contain the concept. The ILP-based summarization approach (Gillick and Favre, 2009) searches for an optimal assignment to the sentence and concept variables so that the selected summary sentences maximize coverage of important concepts. The relationship between concepts and sentences is captured by a co-occurrence matrix $A \in \mathbb{R}^{N \times M}$, where $A_{ij} = 1$ indicates the i-th concept appears in the j-th sentence, and $A_{ij} = 0$ otherwise. In the literature, bigrams are frequently used as a surrogate for concepts (Gillick et al., 2008; Berg-Kirkpatrick et al., 2011). We follow the convention and use 'concept' and 'bigram' interchangeably in the paper.

$$\max_{\boldsymbol{y},\boldsymbol{z}} \quad \sum_{i=1}^{N} w_i z_i \qquad (1)$$

$$s.t. \quad \sum_{j=1}^{M} A_{ij}\, y_j \geq z_i \qquad (2)$$

$$A_{ij}\, y_j \leq z_i \qquad (3)$$

$$\sum_{j=1}^{M} l_j y_j \leq L \qquad (4)$$

$$y_j \in \{0,1\}, z_i \in \{0,1\} \qquad (5)$$

Two sets of linear constraints are specified to ensure the ILP validity: (1) a concept is selected if and only if at least one sentence carrying it has been selected (Eq. 2), and (2) all concepts in a sentence will be selected if that sentence is selected (Eq. 3). Finally, the selected summary sentences are allowed to contain a total of L words or less (Eq. 4).

3 Our Approach

Because of the lexical diversity in student responses, we suspect the co-occurrence matrix A may not establish a faithful correspondence between sentences and concepts. A concept may be conveyed using multiple bigram expressions; however, the current co-occurrence matrix only captures a binary relationship between sentences and bigrams. For example, we ought to give partial credit to "bicycle parts" (S7) given that a similar expression "bike elements" (S4) appears in the sentence. Domain-specific synonyms may be captured as well. For example, the sentence "I tried to follow along but I couldn't *grasp the* concepts" is expected to partially contain the concept "understand the", although the latter did not appear in the sentence.

The existing matrix A is highly sparse. Only 2.7% of the entries are non-zero in our dataset (§4). We therefore propose to *impute* the co-occurrence matrix by filling in missing values. This is accomplished by approximating the original co-occurrence matrix using a low-rank matrix. The low-rankness encourages similar concepts to be shared across sentences. The data imputation process makes two notable changes to the existing ILP framework. First, it extends the domain of A_{ij} from binary to a continuous scale $[0,1]$ (Eq. 2), which offers a better sentence-level semantic representation. The binary concept variables (z_i) are also relaxed to continuous domain $[0,1]$ (Eq. 5), which allows the concepts to be "partially" included in the summary.

Concretely, given the co-occurrence matrix $A \in \mathbb{R}^{N \times M}$, we aim to find a low-rank matrix $B \in \mathbb{R}^{N \times M}$ whose values are close to A at the observed positions. Our objective function is

$$\min_{B \in \mathbb{R}^{N \times M}} \frac{1}{2} \sum_{(i,j)\in\Omega} (A_{ij} - B_{ij})^2 + \lambda \|B\|_* , \qquad (6)$$

where Ω represents the set of observed value positions. $\|B\|_*$ denotes the trace norm of B, i.e., $\|B\|_* = \sum_{i=1}^{r} \sigma_i$, where r is the rank of B and σ_i are the singular values. By defining the following projection operator P_Ω,

$$[P_\Omega(B)]_{ij} = \begin{cases} B_{ij} & (i,j) \in \Omega \\ 0 & (i,j) \notin \Omega \end{cases} \quad (7)$$

our objective function (Eq. 6) can be succinctly represented as

$$\min_{B \in \mathbb{R}^{N \times M}} \frac{1}{2}\|P_\Omega(A) - P_\Omega(B)\|_F^2 + \lambda\|B\|_*, \quad (8)$$

where $\|\cdot\|_F$ denotes the Frobenius norm.

Following (Mazumder et al., 2010), we optimize Eq. 8 using the proximal gradient descent algorithm. The update rule is

$$B^{(k+1)} = \text{prox}_{\lambda\rho_k}\left(B^{(k)} + \rho_k\left(P_\Omega(A) - P_\Omega(B)\right)\right), \quad (9)$$

where ρ_k is the step size at iteration k and the proximal function $\text{prox}_t(B)$ is defined as the singular value soft-thresholding operator, $\text{prox}_t(B) = U \cdot \text{diag}((\sigma_i - t)_+) \cdot V^\top$, where $B = U\text{diag}(\sigma_1, \cdots, \sigma_r)V^\top$ is the singular value decomposition (SVD) of B and $(x)_+ = \max(x, 0)$.

Since the gradient of $\frac{1}{2}\|P_\Omega(A) - P_\Omega(B)\|_F^2$ is Lipschitz continuous with $L = 1$ (L is the Lipschitz continuous constant), we follow (Mazumder et al., 2010) to choose fixed step size $\rho_k = 1$, which has a provable convergence rate of $O(1/k)$, where k is the number of iterations.

4   Dataset

Our dataset is collected from an introductory materials science and engineering class taught in a major U.S. university. The class has 25 lectures and enrolled 53 undergrad students. The students are asked to provide feedback after each lecture based on three prompts: 1) "describe what you found most interesting in today's class," 2) "describe what was confusing or needed more detail," and 3) "describe what you learned about how you learn." These open-ended prompts are carefully designed to encourage students to self-reflect, allowing them to "recapture experience, think about it and evaluate it" (Boud et al., 2013). The average response length is 10±8.3 words. If we concatenate all the responses to each lecture and prompt into a "pseudo-document", the document contains 378 words on average.

The reference summaries are created by a teaching assistant. She is allowed to create abstract summaries using her own words in addition to selecting phrases directly from the responses. Because summary annotation is costly and recruiting annotators with proper background is nontrivial, 12 out of the 25 lectures are annotated with reference summaries. There is one gold-standard summary per lecture and question prompt, yielding 36 document-summary pairs[1]. On average, a reference summary contains 30 words, corresponding to 7.9% of the total words in student responses. 43.5% of the bigrams in human summaries appear in the responses.

5   Experiments

Our proposed approach is compared against a range of baselines. They are 1) MEAD (Radev et al., 2004), a centroid-based summarization system that scores sentences based on length, centroid, and position; 2) LEXRANK (Erkan and Radev, 2004), a graph-based summarization approach based on eigenvector centrality; 3) SUMBASIC (Vanderwende et al., 2007), an approach that assumes words occurring frequently in a document cluster have a higher chance of being included in the summary; 4) BASELINE-ILP (Berg-Kirkpatrick et al., 2011), a baseline ILP framework without data imputation.

For the ILP based approaches, we use bigrams as concepts (bigrams consisting of only stopwords are removed[2]) and sentence frequency as concept weights. We use all the sentences in 25 lectures to construct the concept-sentence co-occurrence matrix and perform data imputation. It allows us to leverage the co-occurrence statistics both within and across lectures. For the soft-impute algorithm, we perform grid search (on a scale of [0, 5] with step-size 0.5) to tune the hyper-parameter λ. To make the most use of annotated lectures, we split them into three folds. In each one, we tune λ on two folds and test it on the other fold. Finally, we report the averaged results. In all experiments, summary length is set to be 30 words or less, corresponding to the

---

[1]This data set is publicly available at http://www.coursemirror.com/download/dataset.

[2]Bigrams with one stopword are not removed because 1) they are informative ("a bike", "the activity", "how materials'); 2) such bigrams appear in multiple sentences and are thus helpful for matrix imputation.

System	ROUGE-1			ROUGE-2			ROUGE-SU4			Human Preference
	R (%)	P (%)	F (%)	R (%)	P (%)	F (%)	R (%)	P (%)	F (%)	
MEAD	26.4	23.3	21.8	6.7	7.6	6.3	8.8	8.0	5.4	24.8%
LEXRANK	30.0	27.6	25.7	8.1	8.3	7.6	9.6	9.6	6.6	—
SUMBASIC	36.6	31.4	30.4	8.2	8.1	7.5	13.9	11.0	8.7	—
ILP BASELINE	35.5	31.8	29.8	11.1	10.7	9.9	12.9	11.5	8.2	69.6%
OUR APPROACH	**38.0**	**34.6**	**32.2**	**12.7**	**12.9**	**11.4**	**15.5**	**14.4**	**10.1**	**89.6%**

Table 2: Summarization results evaluated by ROUGE (%) and human judges. Shaded area indicates that the performance difference with OUR APPROACH is statistically significant ($p < 0.05$) using a two-tailed paired t-test on the 36 document-summary pairs.

average number of words in human summaries.

In Table 2, we present summarization results evaluated by ROUGE (Lin, 2004) and human judges. ROUGE is a standard evaluation metric that compares system and reference summaries based on n-gram overlaps. Our proposed approach outperforms all the baselines based on three standard ROUGE metrics.[3] When examining the imputed sentence-concept co-occurrence matrix, we notice some interesting examples that indicate the effectiveness of the proposed approach, shown in Table 3.

Because ROUGE cannot thoroughly capture the semantic similarity between system and reference summaries, we further perform human evaluation. For each lecture and prompt, we present the prompt, a pair of system outputs in a random order, and the human summary to five Amazon turkers. The turkers are asked to indicate their preference for system A or B based on the semantic resemblance to the human summary on a 5-Likert scale ('Strongly preferred A', 'Slightly preferred A', 'No preference', 'Slightly preferred B', 'Strongly preferred B'). They are rewarded \$0.08 per task. We use two strategies to control the quality of the human evaluation. First, we require the turkers to have a Human Intelligence Task (HIT) approval rate of 90% or above. Second, we insert some quality checkpoints by asking the turkers to compare two summaries of same text content but different sentence orders. Turkers who did not pass these tests are filtered out. Due to budget constraints, we conduct pairwise comparisons for three systems. The total number of comparisons

Sentence	Assoc. Bigrams
the printing needs to better so it can be easier to read	*the graph*
graphs make it *easier to* understand concepts	*hard to*
the naming system for the 2 *phase regions*	*phase diagram*
I tried to follow along but I couldn't *grasp the* concepts	*understand the*
no problems except for the specific equations used to determine properties from the stress - *strain graph*	*strain curves*

Table 3: Associated bigrams do not appear in the sentence, but after Matrix Imputation, they yield a decent correlation (cell value greater than 0.9) with the corresponding sentence.

is 3 system-system pairs $\times$ 12 lectures $\times$ 3 prompts $\times$ 5 turkers = 540 total pairs. We calculate the percentage of "wins" (strong or slight preference) for each system among all comparisons with its counterparts. Results are reported in the last column of Table 2. OUR APPROACH is preferred significantly more often than the other two systems[4]. Regarding the inter-annotator agreement, we find 74.3% of the individual judgements agree with the majority votes when using a 3-point Likert scale ('preferred A', 'no preference', 'preferred B').

Table 4 presents example system outputs. This offers intuitive understanding to our proposed approach.

---

[3]F-scores are slightly lower than P/R because of the averaging effect and can be illustrated in one example. Suppose we have P1=0.1, R1=0.4, F1=0.16 and P2=0.4, R2=0.1, F2=0.16. Then the macro-averaged P/R/F-scores are: P=0.25, R=0.25, F=0.16. In this case, the F-score is lower than both P and R.

[4]For the significance test, we convert a preference to a score ranging from -2 to 2 ('2' means 'Strongly preferred' to a system and '-2' means 'Strongly preferred' to the counterpart system), and use a two-tailed paired t-test with $p < 0.05$ to compare the scores.

Prompt
Describe what you found most interesting in today's class
Reference Summary
- unit cell direction drawing and indexing
- real world examples
- importance of cell direction on materials properties
System Summary (ILP BASELINE)
- drawing and indexing unit cell direction
- it was interesting to understand how to find apf and fd from last weeks class
- south pole explorers died due to properties of tin
System Summary (OUR APPROACH)
- crystal structure directions
- surprisingly i found nothing interesting today .
- unit cell indexing
- vectors in unit cells
- unit cell drawing and indexing
- the importance of cell direction on material properties

Table 4: Example reference and system summaries.

6 Related Work

Our previous work (Luo and Litman, 2015) proposes to summarize student responses by extracting phrases rather than sentences in order to meet the need of aggregating and displaying student responses in a mobile application (Luo et al., 2015; Fan et al., 2015). It adopts a clustering paradigm to address the lexical variety issue. In this work, we leverage matrix imputation to solve this problem and summarize student response at a sentence level.

The integer linear programming framework has demonstrated substantial success on summarizing news documents (Gillick et al., 2008; Gillick et al., 2009; Woodsend and Lapata, 2012; Li et al., 2013). Previous studies try to improve this line of work by generating better estimates of concept weights. Galanis et al. (2012) proposed a support vector regression model to estimate bigram frequency in the summary. Berg-Kirkpatrick et al. (2011) explored a supervised approach to learn parameters using a cost-augmentative SVM. Different from the above approaches, we focus on the co-occurrence matrix instead of concept weights, which is another important component of the ILP framework.

Most summarization work focuses on summarizing news documents, as driven by the DUC/TAC conferences. Notable systems include maximal marginal relevance (Carbonell and Goldstein, 1998),

submodular functions (Lin and Bilmes, 2010), jointly extract and compress sentences (Zajic et al., 2007), optimize content selection and surface realization (Woodsend and Lapata, 2012), minimize reconstruction error (He et al., 2012), and dual decomposition (Almeida and Martins, 2013). Albeit the encouraging performance of our proposed approach on summarizing student responses, when applied to the DUC 2004 dataset (Hong et al., 2014) and evaluated using ROUGE we observe only comparable or marginal improvement over the ILP baseline. However, this is not surprising since the lexical variety is low (20% of bigrams appear more than twice compared to 3% of bigrams appear more than twice in student responses) and thus less data sparsity, so the DUC data cannot benefit much from imputation.

7 Conclusion

We make the first effort to summarize student feedback using an integer linear programming framework with data imputation. Our approach allows sentences to share co-occurrence statistics and alleviates sparsity issue. Our experiments show that the proposed approach performs competitively against a range of baselines and shows promise for future automation of student feedback analysis.

In the future, we may take advantage of the high quality student responses (Luo and Litman, 2016) and explore helpfulness-guided summarization (Xiong and Litman, 2014) to improve the summarization performance. We will also investigate whether the proposed approach benefits other informal text such as product reviews, social media discussions or spontaneous speech conversations, in which we expect the same sparsity issue occurs and the language expression is diverse.

Acknowledgments

This research is supported by an internal grant from the Learning Research and Development Center at the University of Pittsburgh. We thank Muhsin Menekse for providing the data set. We thank Jingtao Wang, Fan Zhang, Huy Nguyen and Zahra Rahimi for valuable suggestions about the proposed summarization algorithm. We also thank anonymous reviewers for insightful comments and suggestions.

References

Miguel B. Almeida and Andre F. T. Martins. 2013. Fast and robust compressive summarization with dual decomposition and multi-task learning. In *Proceedings of ACL*.

Taylor Berg-Kirkpatrick, Dan Gillick, and Dan Klein. 2011. Jointly learning to extract and compress. In *Proceedings of ACL*.

David Boud, Rosemary Keogh, David Walker, et al. 2013. *Reflection: Turning experience into learning*. Routledge.

Jaime Carbonell and Jade Goldstein. 1998. The use of mmr, diversity-based reranking for reordering documents and producing summaries. In *Proceedings of the 21st Annual International ACM SIGIR Conference on Research and Development in Information Retrieval*, SIGIR '98, pages 335–336.

Günes Erkan and Dragomir R. Radev. 2004. LexRank: Graph-based lexical centrality as salience in text summarization. *Journal Artificial Intelligence Research*, 22(1).

Xiangmin Fan, Wencan Luo, Muhsin Menekse, Diane Litman, and Jingtao Wang. 2015. CourseMIRROR: Enhancing large classroom instructor-student interactions via mobile interfaces and natural language processing. In *Works-In-Progress of ACM Conference on Human Factors in Computing Systems*. ACM.

Dimitrios Galanis, Gerasimos Lampouras, and Ion Androutsopoulos. 2012. Extractive multi-document summarization with integer linear programming and support vector regression. In *Proceedings of COLING*.

Dan Gillick and Benoit Favre. 2009. A scalable global model for summarization. In *Proceedings of NAACL*.

Dan Gillick, Benoit Favre, and Dilek Hakkani-Tur. 2008. The icsi summarization system at tac 2008. In *Proceedings of TAC*.

Dan Gillick, Benoit Favre, Dilek Hakkani-Tur, Berndt Bohnet, Yang Liu, and Shasha Xie. 2009. The ICSI/UTD summarization system at TAC 2009. In *Proceedings of TAC*.

Zhanying He, Chun Chen, Jiajun Bu, Can Wang, Lijun Zhang, Deng Cai, and Xiaofei He. 2012. Document summarization based on data reconstruction. In *Proceedings of AAAI*.

Kai Hong, John Conroy, Benoit Favre, Alex Kulesza, Hui Lin, and Ani Nenkova. 2014. A repository of state of the art and competitive baseline summaries for generic news summarization. In Nicoletta Calzolari, Khalid Choukri, Thierry Declerck, Hrafn Loftsson, Bente Maegaard, Joseph Mariani, Asuncion Moreno, Jan Odijk, and Stelios Piperidis, editors, *Proceedings of the Ninth International Conference on Language Resources and Evaluation (LREC'14)*, pages 1608–1616, Reykjavik, Iceland, May. European Language Resources Association (ELRA). ACL Anthology Identifier: L14-1070.

Chen Li, Xian Qian, and Yang Liu. 2013. Using supervised bigram-based ILP for extractive summarization. In *Proceedings of ACL*.

Hui Lin and Jeff Bilmes. 2010. Multi-document summarization via budgeted maximization of submodular functions. In *Proceedings of NAACL*.

Chin-Yew Lin. 2004. ROUGE: a package for automatic evaluation of summaries. In *Proceedings of the Workshop on Text Summarization Branches Out*.

Wencan Luo and Diane Litman. 2015. Summarizing student responses to reflection prompts. In *Proceedings of the 2015 Conference on Empirical Methods in Natural Language Processing*, pages 1955–1960, Lisbon, Portugal, September. Association for Computational Linguistics.

Wencan Luo and Diane Litman. 2016. Determining the quality of a student reflective response. In *Proceedings 29th International FLAIRS Conference*, Key Largo, FL, May.

Wencan Luo, Xiangmin Fan, Muhsin Menekse, Jingtao Wang, , and Diane Litman. 2015. Enhancing instructor-student and student-student interactions with mobile interfaces and summarization. In *Proceedings of NAACL (Demo)*.

Rahul Mazumder, Trevor Hastie, and Robert Tibshirani. 2010. Spectral regularization algorithms for learning large incomplete matrices. *Journal of Machine Learning Research*.

Dragomir R. Radev, Hongyan Jing, Małgorzata Styś, and Daniel Tam. 2004. Centroid-based summarization of multiple documents. *Information Processing and Management*, 40(6):919–938.

Lucy Vanderwende, Hisami Suzuki, Chris Brockett, and Ani Nenkova. 2007. Beyond SumBasic: Task-focused summarization with sentence simplification and lexical expansion. *Information Processing and Management*, 43(6):1606–1618.

Kristian Woodsend and Mirella Lapata. 2012. Multiple aspect summarization using integer linear programming. In *Proceedings of EMNLP*.

Wenting Xiong and Diane Litman. 2014. Empirical analysis of exploiting review helpfulness for extractive summarization of online reviews. In *Proceedings of COLING 2014, the 25th International Conference on Computational Linguistics: Technical Papers*, pages 1985–1995, Dublin, Ireland, August. Dublin City University and Association for Computational Linguistics.

David Zajic, Bonnie J. Dorr, Jimmy Lin, and Richard Schwartz. 2007. Multi-candidate reduction: Sentence compression as a tool for document summarization tasks. *Information Processing and Management*.

Knowledge-Guided Linguistic Rewrites for Inference Rule Verification

Prachi Jain and **Mausam**
Indian Institute of Technology, Delhi
New Delhi, India
{csz148211,mausam}@cse.iitd.ac.in

Abstract

A corpus of inference rules between a pair of relation phrases is typically generated using the statistical overlap of argument-pairs associated with the relations (e.g., PATTY, CLEAN). We investigate *knowledge-guided linguistic rewrites* as a secondary source of evidence and find that they can vastly improve the quality of inference rule corpora, obtaining 27 to 33 point precision improvement while retaining substantial recall. The facts inferred using cleaned inference rules are 29-32 points more accurate.

1 Introduction

The visions of machine reading (Etzioni, 2007) and deep language understanding (Dorr, 2012) emphasize the ability to draw inferences from text to discover implicit information that may not be explicitly stated (Schubert, 2002). This has natural applications to textual entailment (Dagan et al., 2013), KB completion (Socher et al., 2013), and effective querying over Knowledge Bases (KBs).

One popular approach for fact inference is to use a set of *inference rules* along with probabilistic models such as Markov Logic Networks (Schoenmackers et al., 2008) or Bayesian Logic Programs (Raghavan et al., 2012) to produce human-interpretable proof chains. While scalable (Niu et al., 2011; Domingos and Webb, 2012), this is bound by the coverage and quality of the background knowledge – the set of inference rules that enable the inference (Clark et al., 2014).

Antecedent	Consequent	Y/N?
(X, make a note of, Y)	(X, write down, Y)	Y
(X, offer wide range of, Y)	(X, offer variety of, Y)	Y
(X, make full use of, Y)	(Y, be used by, X)	Y
(X, be wounded in, Y)	(X, be killed in, Y)	N
(X, be director of, Y)	(X, be vice president of, Y)	N
(X, be a student at, Y)	(X, be enrolled at, Y)	N

Figure 1: Sample rules verified (Y) and filtered (N) by our method. Rules #4, #5 were correctly and #6 wrongly filtered.

The paper focuses on generating a *high precision* subset of inference rules over Open Information Extraction (OpenIE) (Etzioni et al., 2011) relation phrases (see Fig 1). OpenIE systems generate a schema-free KB where entities and relations are represented via normalized but not disambiguated textual strings. Such OpenIE KBs scale to the Web.

Most existing large-scale corpora of inference rules are generated using distributional similarity, like argument-pair overlap (Schoenmackers et al., 2010; Berant et al., 2012), but often eschew any linguistic or compositional insights. Our early analysis revealed that such inference rules have very low precision, not enough to be useful for many real tasks. For human-facing applications (such as IE-based demos), high precision is critical. Inference rules have a multiplicative impact, since one poor rule could potentially generate many bad KB facts.

Contributions: We investigate the hypothesis that *"knowledge-guided linguistic rewrites can provide independent verification for statistically-generated Open IE inference rules."* Our system KGLR's rewrites exploit the compositional structure of Open IE relation phrases alongside knowledge in resources like Wordnet and thesaurus. KGLR independently verifies rules from existing inference rule

Proceedings of NAACL-HLT 2016, pages 86–92,
San Diego, California, June 12-17, 2016. ©2016 Association for Computational Linguistics

corpora (Berant et al., 2012; Pavlick et al., 2015) and can be seen as additional annotation on existing inference rules. The verified rules are 27 to 33 points more accurate than the original corpora and still retain a substantial recall. The precision of inferred knowledge also has a precision boost of over 29 points. We release our KGLR implementation, its annotations on two popular rule corpora along with gold set used for evaluation and the annotation guidelines for further use (available at *https://github.com/dair-iitd/kglr.git*).

2   Related work

Methods for inference over text include random walks over knowledge graphs (Lao et al., 2011), matrix completion (Riedel et al., 2013), deep neural networks (Socher et al., 2013; Rocktäschel et al., 2015a), natural logic inference (MacCartney and Manning, 2007) and graphical models (Schoenmackers et al., 2008; Raghavan et al., 2012). Most of these need (or benefit from) a background knowledge of inference rules, including matrix completion (Rocktäschel et al., 2015b).

Inference rules are predominantly generated via extended distributional similarity – two phrases having a high degree of argument overlap are similar, and thus candidates for a unidirectional or a bidirectional inference rule. Methods vary on the base representation, e.g., KB relations (Galárraga et al., 2013; Grycner et al., 2015), Open IE relation phrases (Schoenmackers et al., 2010), syntactic-ontological-lexical (SOL) patterns (Nakashole et al., 2012), and dependency paths (Lin and Pantel, 2001). An enhancement is global transitivity (TNCF algorithm) for improving recall (Berant et al., 2012). The highest precision setting of TNCF ($\lambda = 0.1$) was released as a corpus (informally called CLEAN) of Open IE inference rules.[1]

Distributional similarity approaches have two fundamental limitations. First, they miss obvious commonsense facts, e.g., $\langle$(X, married, Y) $\rightarrow$ (X, knows, Y)$\rangle$ – text will rarely say that a couple know each other. Second, they are consistently affected by statistical noise and end up generating a wide variety of inaccurate rules (see rules #4, and #5 in Figure 1).

---

[1] *http://u.cs.biu.ac.il/~nlp/resources/downloads/predicative-entailment-rules-learned-using-local-and-global-algorithms*

Our early experiments with CLEAN revealed its precision to be about 0.49, not enough to be useful in practice, especially for human-facing applications.

Similar to our paper, some past works have used alternative sources of knowledge. Weisman *et al.* (2012) study inference between verbs (e.g., $\langle$startle $\rightarrow$ surprise$\rangle$), but they get low (0.4) precision. Wordnet corpus to generate inference rules for natural logic (Angeli and Manning, 2014) improved noun-based inference. But, they recognize relation entailments as a key missing piece. Recently, natural logic semantics is added to a paraphrase corpus (PPDB2.0). Many of their features, e.g., lexical/orthographic, multilingual translation based, are complimentary to our method.

We test our KGLR algorithm on CLEAN and entailment/paraphrase subset of PPDB2.0 (which we call PPDB_e).

3   Knowledge-Guided Linguistic Rewrites (KGLR)

Given a rule $\langle$(X, r_1, Y) $\rightarrow$ (X, r_2, Y)$\rangle$ or $\langle$(X, r_1, Y) $\rightarrow$ (Y, r_2, X)$\rangle$ we present KGLR, a series of rewrites of relation phrase r_1 to prove r_2 (examples in Fig 1). The last two rewrites deal with reversal of argument order in r_2; others are for the first case.

Thesaurus Synonyms: Thesauri typically provide an expansive set of potential synonyms, encompassing near-synonyms and contextually synonymous words. Thesaurus synonyms are not that helpful for *generating* inference rules (or else we will generate rules like $\langle$produce $\rightarrow$ percolate$\rangle$). However, they are excellent in rule verification as they provide evidence independent from statistical overlap metrics.

We allow any word/phrase w_1 in r_1 to be replaced by any word/phrase w_2 from its thesaurus synsets as long as (1) w_2 has same part-of-speech as w_1 and (2) w_2 is seen in r_2 at the same distance from left of the phrase as w_1 in phrase r_1, but ignoring words dropped due to other rules whose details follows next. To define a thesaurus synset, we tag w_1 with its POS and look for all thesaurus synsets of that POS containing w_1. We allow this rewrite if $\text{PMI}(w_1, w_2) > \lambda$ (=-2.5 based on a devset). We calculate PMI as
$$log \frac{(\#w_1 \text{ occurs in synsets of } w_2 + \#w_2 \text{ occurs in synsets of } w_1)}{(\# \text{ of synsets of } w_1 \times \# \text{ of synsets of } w_2)}.$$
Some words can be both synonyms and antonyms in different situations. For example, thesaurus lists

'bad' as both a synonym and antonym of 'good'. We don't allow such antonyms in these rewrites.

Thesarus synonyms can verify ⟨offer a vast range of → provide a wide range of⟩, since offer-provide, and vast-wide are thesaurus synonyms. We use Roget's 21st Century Thesaurus in KGLR implementation.

Negating rules: We reject rules where r_2 explicitly negates r_1 or vice versa. We reject a rule if r_2 is same as r_1 if we drop 'not' from one of them. For example, the rule ⟨be the president of → be not the president of⟩, will be rejected.

Wordnet Hypernyms: We replace word/phrase w in r_1 by its Wordnet hypernym if it is in r_2. We prove ⟨be highlight of → be component of⟩, as Wordnet lists 'component' as a hypernym of 'highlight'.

Dropping Modifiers: We drop any adjective, adverb, superlatives or comparatives (e.g., 'more', 'most') from r_1. This lets us verify ⟨be most important part of → be part of⟩.

Gerund-Infinitive Equivalence: We convert infinitive constructions into gerunds and vice versa. For example, ⟨starts to drink ↔ starts drinking⟩.

Deverbal Nouns: We use Wordnet's derivationally related forms to compute a verb-noun pair list. We allow back and forth conversions from "be noun of" to related verb. So, we verify ⟨be cause of → cause⟩.

Light Verbs and Serial Verbs: If a light verb precede a word with derivationally related noun sense, we delete it. Similarly, if a serial verb precede a word with derivationally related verb sense, we delete it. We identify light verbs via the verbs that frequently precede a ⟨(a|an) (verb|deverbal noun)⟩ pair in Wikipedia. Serial verbs are identified as the verbs that frequently precede another verb in Wikipedia. Thus we can convert ⟨take a look at → look at⟩.

Preposition Synonyms: We manually create a list of preposition near-synonyms such as into-to, in-at, at-near. We replace a preposition by its near-synonym. This proves ⟨translated into → translated to⟩.

Be-Words & Determiners: We drop be-words ('is', 'was', 'be', etc.) and determiners from r_1 and r_2.

Active-Passive: We allow (X, *verb*, Y) to be rewritten as (Y, *be verb by*, X).

Redundant Prepositions: We find that often prepositions other than 'by' can be alternatively used

with passive forms of some verbs. Moreover, some prepositions can be redundantly used in active forms too. For example, ⟨(X, absorb, Y) ↔ (Y, be absorbed *in*, X)⟩, or similarly, ⟨(X, attack, Y) ↔ (X, attack *on*, Y)⟩. To create such a list of verb-preposition pairs, we simply trust the argument-overlap statistics. Statistics here does not make that many errors since the base verb in both relations is the same.

3.1 Implementation

KGLR allows repeated application of these rewrites to modify r_1 and r_2. If it achieves $r_1 = r_2$ it verifies the inference rule. For tractable implementation KGLR uses a depth first search approach where a search node maintains both r_1 and r_2. Search does not allow rewrites that introduce any new lexical (lemmatized) entries not in original words(r_1) ∪ words(r_2). If it can't apply any rewrite to get a new node, it returns failure.

Many rules are proved by a sequence of rewrites. E.g., to prove ⟨(X, be a major cause of, Y) → (Y, be caused by, X)⟩, the proof proceeds as: (X, be a major cause of, Y) → (X, be major cause of, Y) → (X, be cause of, Y) → (X, cause, Y) → (Y, be caused by, X) by dropping determiner, dropping adjective, deverbal noun, and active-passive transformation respectively. Similarly, ⟨(X, helps to protect, Y) → (X, look after, Y)⟩ follows from gerund-infinitive conversion (helps protect), dropping support from serial verbs (protect), and thesaurus synonym (look after).

4 Experiments

KGLR verifies a subset of rules from CLEAN and PPDB$_e$ to produce, VCLEAN and VPPDB$_e$. Our experiments answer these research questions: (1) What is the precision and size of the verified subsets compared to original corpora?, (2) How does additional knowledge generated after performing inference using these rules compare with each other? and (3) Which rewrites are critical to KGLR performance?

Comparison of CLEAN and VCLEAN: The original CLEAN corpus has about 102K rules. KGLR verifies about 36K rules and filter 66K rules out. To estimate the precisions of CLEAN and VCLEAN we independently sampled a random subset of 200 inference rules from each and asked two annotators (graduate level NLP students) to label the rules as correct or incorrect. Rules were mixed together and the annotators were blind to the system that generated a rule. Our initial annotation guideline was similar to that of textual entailment – label a rule as correct if the consequent can usually be inferred given the antecedent, for most naturally occurring argument-pairs for the antecedent.

Our annotators faced one issue with the guideline – some inference rules were valid if (X,Y) were bound to specific types, but not for others. For example, $\langle$(X, be born in, Y) → (Y, be birthplace of, X)$\rangle$ is valid if Y is a location, not if Y is a year. Even seemingly correct inference rules, e.g., $\langle$(X, is the father of, Y) → (Y, is the child of, X)$\rangle$, can make unusual incorrect inferences: (Gandhi, is the father of, India) does not imply (India, is the child of, Gandhi). Unfortunately, these corpora don't associate argument-type information with their inference rules.

To mitigate this we refined the annotation guidelines to accept inference rules as correct as long as they are valid for *some* type-pair. The inter-annotator agreement with this modification was 94% ($\kappa = 0.88$). On the subset of the tags where the two annotators agreed we find the precision of CLEAN to be 48.9%, whereas VCLEAN was evaluated to be 82.5% precise – much more useful for real-world applications. Multiplying the precision with their sizes, we find the effective yield[2] of CLEAN to be 50K compared to 30K for VCLEAN. Overall, we find that VCLEAN obtains a 33 point precision improvement with an effective yield of about 60%.

Error Analysis: Most of VCLEAN errors are due to erroneous (or unusual) thesaurus synonyms. For missed recall, we analyzed CLEAN's sample missed by VCLEAN. We find that only about 13% of those are world knowledge rules (e.g., rule #6 in Figure 1). Other missed recall is because of some missing rewrites, missing thesaurus synonyms, spelling mistakes. These can potentially be captured by using other resources and adding rewrite rules.

Comparison of PPDB$_e$ and VPPDB$_e$: Unlike CLEAN, PPDB2.0 associates a confidence value for each rule, which can be varied to obtain different levels of precision and yield. We control for yield so that we can compare precisions directly.

We operate on PPDB$_e$ subset that has an Open IE-like relation phrase on both sides; this was identified by matching to ReVerb syntactic patterns (Etzioni et al., 2011). This subset is of size 402K. KGLR on this produces 85K verified rules (VPPDB$_e$). We find the threshold for confidence values in PPDB$_e$ that achieves the same yield (confidence > 0.342).

We perform annotation on PPDB$_e$(0.342) and VPPDB$_e$ using same annotation guidelines as before. The inter-annotator agreement was 91% ($\kappa = 0.82$). On the subset of the tags where the two annotators agreed we find the precision of PPDB$_e$ to be low – 44.2%, whereas VPPDB$_e$ was evaluated to be 71.4% precise. We notice that about 4 in 5 PPDB relation phrases are of length 1 or 2 (whereas 50% of CLEAN relation phrases are of length ≥ 3). This contributes to a slightly lower precision of VPPDB$_e$, as most rules are proved by *thesaurus synonymy* and the power of KGLR to handle compositionality of longer relation phrases does not get exploited.

Comparison of Inferred Facts: A typical use case of inference rules is in generating new facts by applying inference rules to a KB. We independently apply VCLEAN's, CLEAN's, PPDB$_e$'s and VPPDB$_e$'s inference rules on a public corpus of 4.2 million ReVerb triples.[3] Since ReVerb itself has significant extraction errors (our estimate is 20% errors) and our goal is to evaluate the quality of inference, we restrict this evaluation to only the subset of accurate ReVerb extractions.

VCLEAN *and* CLEAN *facts:* We sampled about 200 facts inferred by VCLEAN rules and CLEAN rules each (applied over accurate ReVerb extractions) and gave the original sentence as well as inferred facts to two annotators. We obtained a high inter-annotator agreement of 96.3%($\kappa = 0.92$) and we discarded disagreements from final analysis. Overall, facts inferred by CLEAN achieved a precision of about 49.1% and those inferred by VCLEAN obtained a 81.6% precision. The estimated yields of fact corpora (precision×size) are 7 and 4.5 million for CLEAN and VCLEAN respectively. This yield estimate does not include the initial 4.2 million facts.

PPDB$_e$ *and* VPPDB$_e$ *facts:* As done previously, we sampled 200 facts inferred by PPDB$_e$ and VPPDB$_e$ rules, which were annotated by two annotators. We obtained a good inter annotator agree-

---

[2]Yield is proportional to recall

[3]Available at *http://reverb.cs.washington.edu*

System	CLEAN	VCLEAN
Size	102,565	36,229
Rule Precision	48.9%	82.5%
Rule Yield	50,154	29,889
Fact Precision	49.1%	81.6%
Fact Yield	7 million	4.5 million

System	PPDB_e(0.342)	VPPDB_e
Size	85,272	85,261
Rule Precision	44.2%	71.4%
Fact Precision	22.16%	51.30%
Fact Yield	41 million	35 million

Figure 2: The precision and yield of inference rules after KGLR validation, and that of KB generated by inference using these rule-sets. Comparison with PPDB_e is yield-controlled.

System	Precision	Recall
KGLR (all rules)	85.4%	62.0%
w/o Negating Rules	85.4%	62.0%
w/o Antonyms	84.2%	62.0%
w/o Wordnet Hypernyms	86.1%	59.3%
w/o Dropping Modifiers	84.9%	59.6%
w/o Gerund-Infinitive Equivalence	85.2%	61.0%
w/o Light and Serial Verbs	85.0%	59.9%
w/o Deverbal Nouns	85.4%	62.0%
w/o Preposition Synonyms	86.9%	56.9%
w/o Active-Passive	85.0%	54.5%
w/o Redundant Prepositions	86.1%	61.6%

Figure 3: Ablation study of rule verification using KGLR rewrites on our devset of 600 CLEAN rules

ment of 90.0%($\kappa = 0.8$) and we discarded disagreements from final analysis. Overall, facts inferred by PPDB_e achieved a really poor precision - 22.2% and those inferred by VPPDB_e obtained an improvement of about 29 points (51.3% precision). Short relation phrases (mostly of length 1 or 2, which forms 80% of PPDB_e) contribute to low precision of VPPDB_e. Example low precision VPPDB_e rules include $\langle$ (X, be, Y) $\rightarrow$ (X, obtain, Y)$\rangle$, $\langle$ (X, include, Y) $\rightarrow$ (X, come, Y)$\rangle$, which were inaccurately verified due to thesaurus errors. The estimated yields of fact corpora are 41 million and 35 million for PPDB_e and VPPDB_e respectively.

Ablation Study of KGLR rewrites: We evaluate the efficacy of different rewrites in KGLR by performing an ablation study (see Table 3). We ran KGLR by turning off one rewrite on a sample of 600 CLEAN rules (our development set) and calculating its precision and recall. The ablation study highlights that most rewrites add some value to the performance of KGLR, however *Antonyms* and *Dropping modifiers* are particularly important for precision and *Active-Passive* and *Redundant Preposition* add substantial recall.

5 Discussion

KGLR's value is in precision-sensitive tasks such as a human-facing demo, or downstream NLP application (like question answering) where error multiplication is highly undesirable. Along with high precision, it still obtains acceptably good yield.

Our annotators observe the importance of type-restriction of arguments for inference rules (similar to rules in (Schoenmackers et al., 2010)). Type annotation of existing inference rule corpora is an important step for obtaining high precision and clarity.

Inference rules are typically of two types – linguistic/synonym rewrites, which are captured by our work, and world knowledge rules (see rule #6 in Fig 1), which are not. We were surprised to estimate that about 87% of CLEAN, which is a statistically-generated corpus, is just linguistic rewrites! Obtaining world knowledge or common-sense rules at high precision and scale continues to be the key NLP challenge in this area.

6 Conclusions

We present Knowledge-guided Linguistic Rewrites (KGLR) which exploits the compositionality of relation phrases, guided by existing knowledge sources, such as Wordnet and thesaurus to identify a high precision subset of an inference rule corpus. Validated CLEAN has a high precision of 83% (vs 49%) at a yield of 60%. Validated PPDB_e has a precision of 71% (vs 44%) at same yield. The precision of inferred facts has about 29-32 pt precision gain. We expect KGLR to be effective for precision-sensitive applications of inference. The complete code and data has been released for the research community.

Acknowledgments: We thank Ashwini Vaidya and the anonymous reviewers for their helpful suggestions and feedback. We thank Abhishek, Aditya, Ankit, Jatin, Kabir, and Shikhar for helping with the data annotation. This work was supported by Google language understanding and knowledge discovery focused research grants to Mausam, a KISTI grant and a Bloomberg grant also to Mausam. Prachi was supported by a TCS fellowship.

References

Gabor Angeli and Christopher D Manning. 2014. Naturalli: Natural logic inference for common sense reasoning. In *Empirical Methods in Natural Language Processing (EMNLP)*.

Jonathan Berant, Ido Dagan, Meni Adler, and Jacob Goldberger. 2012. Efficient tree-based approximation for entailment graph learning. In *The 50th Annual Meeting of the Association for Computational Linguistics, Proceedings of the System Demonstrations, July 10, 2012, Jeju Island, Korea*.

Peter Clark, Niranjan Balasubramanian, Sumithra Bhakthavatsalam, Kevin Humphreys, Jesse Kinkead, Ashish Sabharwal, and Oyvind Tafjord. 2014. Automatic construction of inference-supporting knowledge bases.

Ido Dagan, Dan Roth, Mark Sammons, and Fabio Massimo Zanzotto. 2013. *Recognizing Textual Entailment: Models and Applications*. Synthesis Lectures on Human Language Technologies. Morgan & Claypool Publishers.

Pedro M. Domingos and William Austin Webb. 2012. A tractable first-order probabilistic logic. In *Proceedings of the Twenty-Sixth AAAI Conference on Artificial Intelligence, July 22-26, 2012, Toronto, Ontario, Canada*.

Bonnie Dorr. 2012. Language programs at Darpa. AKBC-WEKEX 2012 Invited Talk.

Oren Etzioni, Anthony Fader, Janara Christensen, Stephen Soderland, and Mausam. 2011. Open information extraction: The second generation. In *IJCAI*, volume 11, pages 3–10.

Oren Etzioni. 2007. Machine reading of web text. In *Proceedings of the 4th International Conference on Knowledge Capture (K-CAP 2007), October 28-31, 2007, Whistler, BC, Canada*, pages 1–4.

Luis Antonio Galárraga, Christina Teflioudi, Katja Hose, and Fabian Suchanek. 2013. Amie: association rule mining under incomplete evidence in ontological knowledge bases. In *Proceedings of the 22nd international conference on World Wide Web*, pages 413–422. International World Wide Web Conferences Steering Committee.

Adam Grycner, Gerhard Weikum, Jay Pujara, James Foulds, and Lise Getoor. 2015. Relly: Inferring hypernym relationships between relational phrases. In *Proceedings of the 2015 Conference on Empirical Methods in Natural Language Processing*, pages 971–981, Lisbon, Portugal, September. Association for Computational Linguistics.

Ni Lao, Tom Mitchell, and William W Cohen. 2011. Random walk inference and learning in a large scale knowledge base. In *Proceedings of the Conference on Empirical Methods in Natural Language Processing*, pages 529–539. Association for Computational Linguistics.

Dekang Lin and Patrick Pantel. 2001. Dirt@ sbt@ discovery of inference rules from text. In *Proceedings of the seventh ACM SIGKDD international conference on Knowledge discovery and data mining*, pages 323–328. ACM.

Bill MacCartney and Christopher D Manning. 2007. Natural logic for textual inference. In *Proceedings of the ACL-PASCAL Workshop on Textual Entailment and Paraphrasing*, pages 193–200. Association for Computational Linguistics.

Ndapandula Nakashole, Gerhard Weikum, and Fabian Suchanek. 2012. Patty: a taxonomy of relational patterns with semantic types. In *Proceedings of the 2012 Joint Conference on Empirical Methods in Natural Language Processing and Computational Natural Language Learning*, pages 1135–1145. Association for Computational Linguistics.

Feng Niu, Christopher Ré, AnHai Doan, and Jude W. Shavlik. 2011. Tuffy: Scaling up statistical inference in markov logic networks using an RDBMS. *PVLDB*, 4(6):373–384.

Ellie Pavlick, Johan Bos, Malvina Nissim, Charley Beller, Benjamin Van Durme, and Chris Callison-Burch. 2015. Adding semantics to data-driven paraphrasing. In *Proceedings of the 53rd Annual Meeting of the Association for Computational Linguistics (ACL 2015)*.

Sindhu Raghavan, Raymond J. Mooney, and Hyeonseo Ku. 2012. Learning to "read between the lines" using bayesian logic programs. pages 349–358, July.

Sebastian Riedel, Limin Yao, Andrew McCallum, and Benjamin M. Marlin. 2013. Relation extraction with matrix factorization and universal schemas. In *Human Language Technologies: Conference of the North American Chapter of the Association of Computational Linguistics, Proceedings, June 9-14, 2013, Westin Peachtree Plaza Hotel, Atlanta, Georgia, USA*, pages 74–84.

Tim Rocktäschel, Edward Grefenstette, Karl Moritz Hermann, Tomás Kociský, and Phil Blunsom. 2015a. Reasoning about entailment with neural attention. *CoRR*, abs/1509.06664.

Tim Rocktäschel, Sameer Singh, and Sebastian Riedel. 2015b. Injecting Logical Background Knowledge into Embeddings for Relation Extraction. In *Annual Conference of the North American Chapter of the Association for Computational Linguistics (NAACL)*.

Stefan Schoenmackers, Oren Etzioni, and Daniel S Weld. 2008. Scaling textual inference to the web. In *Proceedings of the Conference on Empirical Methods in*

Natural Language Processing, pages 79–88. Association for Computational Linguistics.

Stefan Schoenmackers, Oren Etzioni, Daniel S Weld, and Jesse Davis. 2010. Learning first-order horn clauses from web text. In *Proceedings of the 2010 Conference on Empirical Methods in Natural Language Processing*, pages 1088–1098. AssociaFrition for Computational Linguistics.

Lenhart Schubert. 2002. Can we derive general world knowledge from texts? In *Proceedings of the second international conference on Human Language Technology Research*, pages 94–97. Morgan Kaufmann Publishers Inc.

Richard Socher, Danqi Chen, Christopher D Manning, and Andrew Ng. 2013. Reasoning with neural tensor networks for knowledge base completion. In *Advances in Neural Information Processing Systems*, pages 926–934.

Hila Weisman, Jonathan Berant, Idan Szpektor, and Ido Dagan. 2012. Learning verb inference rules from linguistically-motivated evidence. In *Proceedings of the 2012 Joint Conference on Empirical Methods in Natural Language Processing and Computational Natural Language Learning, EMNLP-CoNLL 2012*, pages 194–204.

Abstractive Sentence Summarization
with Attentive Recurrent Neural Networks

Sumit Chopra
Facebook AI Research
spchopra@fb.com

Michael Auli
Facebook AI Research
michaelauli@fb.com

Alexander M. Rush
Harvard SEAS
srush@seas.harvard.edu

Abstract

Abstractive Sentence Summarization generates a shorter version of a given sentence while attempting to preserve its meaning. We introduce a conditional recurrent neural network (RNN) which generates a summary of an input sentence. The conditioning is provided by a novel convolutional attention-based encoder which ensures that the decoder focuses on the appropriate input words at each step of generation. Our model relies only on learned features and is easy to train in an end-to-end fashion on large data sets. Our experiments show that the model significantly outperforms the recently proposed state-of-the-art method on the Gigaword corpus while performing competitively on the DUC-2004 shared task.

1 Introduction

Generating a condensed version of a passage while preserving its meaning is known as text summarization. Tackling this task is an important step towards natural language understanding. Summarization systems can be broadly classified into two categories. *Extractive models* generate summaries by cropping important segments from the original text and putting them together to form a coherent summary. *Abstractive models* generate summaries from scratch without being constrained to reuse phrases from the original text.

In this paper we propose a novel recurrent neural network for the problem of *abstractive sentence summarization*. Inspired by the recently proposed architectures for machine translation (Bahdanau et al., 2014), our model consists of a conditional recurrent neural network, which acts as a decoder to generate the summary of an input sentence, much like a standard recurrent language model. In addition, at every time step the decoder also takes a conditioning input which is the output of an encoder module. Depending on the current state of the RNN, the encoder computes scores over the words in the input sentence. These scores can be interpreted as a soft alignment over the input text, informing the decoder which part of the input sentence it should focus on to generate the next word. Both the decoder and encoder are jointly trained on a data set consisting of sentence-summary pairs. Our model can be seen as an extension of the recently proposed model for the same problem by Rush et al. (2015). While they use a feed-forward neural language model for generation, we use a recurrent neural network. Furthermore, our encoder is more sophisticated, in that it explicitly encodes the position information of the input words. Lastly, our encoder uses a convolutional network to encode input words. These extensions result in improved performance.

The main contribution of this paper is a novel convolutional attention-based conditional recurrent neural network model for the problem of abstractive sentence summarization. Empirically we show that our model beats the state-of-the-art systems of Rush et al. (2015) on multiple data sets. Particularly notable is the fact that even with a simple generation module, which does not use any extractive feature tuning, our model manages to significantly outperform their ABS+ system on the Gigaword data set and is comparable on the DUC-2004 task.

Proceedings of NAACL-HLT 2016, pages 93–98,
San Diego, California, June 12-17, 2016. ©2016 Association for Computational Linguistics

2 Previous Work

While there is a large body of work for generating extractive summaries of sentences (Jing, 2000; Knight and Marcu, 2002; McDonald, 2006; Clarke and Lapata, 2008; Filippova and Altun, 2013; Filippova et al., 2015), there has been much less research on abstractive summarization. A count-based noisy-channel machine translation model was proposed for the problem in Banko et al. (2000). The task of abstractive sentence summarization was later formalized around the DUC-2003 and DUC-2004 competitions (Over et al., 2007), where the TOP-IARY system (Zajic et al., 2004) was the state-of-the-art. More recently Cohn and Lapata (2008) and later Woodsend et al. (2010) proposed systems which made heavy use of the syntactic features of the sentence-summary pairs. Later, along the lines of Banko et al. (2000), MOSES was used directly as a method for text simplification by Wubben et al. (2012). Other works which have recently been proposed for the problem of sentence summarization include (Galanis and Androutsopoulos, 2010; Napoles et al., 2011; Cohn and Lapata, 2013). Very recently Rush et al. (2015) proposed a neural attention model for this problem using a new data set for training and showing state-of-the-art performance on the DUC tasks. Our model can be seen as an extension of their model.

3 Attentive Recurrent Architecture

Let $\mathbf{x}$ denote the input sentence consisting of a sequence of M words $\mathbf{x} = [x_1, \ldots, x_M]$, where each word x_i is part of vocabulary $\mathcal{V}$, of size $|\mathcal{V}| = V$. Our task is to generate a target sequence $\mathbf{y} = [y_1, \ldots, y_N]$, of N words, where $N < M$, such that the meaning of $\mathbf{x}$ is preserved: $\mathbf{y} = \text{argmax}_y P(y|\mathbf{x})$, where y is a random variable denoting a sequence of N words.

Typically the conditional probability is modeled by a parametric function with parameters θ: $P(y|\mathbf{x}) = P(y|\mathbf{x}; \theta)$. Training involves finding the θ which maximizes the conditional probability of sentence-summary pairs in the training corpus. If the model is trained to generate the next word of the summary, given the previous words, then the above conditional can be factorized into a product of indi-

vidual conditional probabilities:

$$P(\mathbf{y}|\mathbf{x}; \theta) = \prod_{t=1}^{N} p(y_t|\{y_1, \ldots, y_{t-1}\}, \mathbf{x}; \theta). \quad (1)$$

In this work we model this conditional probability using an RNN Encoder-Decoder architecture, inspired by Cho et al. (2014) and subsequently extended in Bahdanau et al. (2014). We call our model RAS (Recurrent Attentive Summarizer).

3.1 Recurrent Decoder

The above conditional is modeled using an RNN:

$$P(y_t|\{y_1, \ldots, y_{t-1}\}, \mathbf{x}; \theta) = P_t = g_{\theta_1}(h_t, c_t),$$

where h_t is the hidden state of the RNN:

$$h_t = g_{\theta_1}(y_{t-1}, h_{t-1}, c_t).$$

Here c_t is the output of the encoder module (detailed in §3.2). It can be seen as a context vector which is computed as a function of the current state h_{t-1} and the input sequence $\mathbf{x}$.

Our Elman RNN takes the following form (Elman, 1990):

$$\begin{aligned}
h_t &= \sigma(W_1 y_{t-1} + W_2 h_{t-1} + W_3 c_t) \\
P_t &= \rho(W_4 h_t + W_5 c_t),
\end{aligned}$$

where σ is the sigmoid function and ρ is the softmax, defined as: $\rho(o_t) = e^{o_t}/\sum_j e^{o_j}$ and W_i $(i = 1, \ldots, 5)$ are matrices of learnable parameters of sizes $W_{\{1,2,3\}} \in \mathcal{R}^{d \times d}$ and $W_{\{4,5\}} \in \mathcal{R}^{d \times V}$.

The LSTM decoder is defined as (Hochreiter and Schmidhuber, 1997):

$$\begin{aligned}
i_t &= \sigma(W_1 y_{t-1} + W_2 h_{t-1} + W_3 c_t) \\
i'_t &= \tanh(W_4 y_{t-1} + W_5 h_{t-1} + W_6 c_t) \\
f_t &= \sigma(W_7 y_{t-1} + W_8 h_{t-1} + W_9 c_t) \\
o_t &= \sigma(W_{10} y_{t-1} + W_{11} h_{t-1} + W_{12} c_t) \\
m_t &= m_{t-1} \odot f_t + i_t \odot i'_t \\
h_t &= m_t \odot o_t \\
P_t &= \rho(W_{13} h_t + W_{14} c_t).
\end{aligned}$$

Operator $\odot$ refers to component-wise multiplication, and W_i $(i = 1, \ldots, 14)$ are matrices of learnable parameters of sizes $W_{\{1,\ldots,12\}} \in \mathcal{R}^{d \times d}$, and $W_{\{13,14\}} \in \mathcal{R}^{d \times V}$.

3.2 Attentive Encoder

We now give the details of the encoder which computes the context vector c_t for every time step t of the decoder above. With a slight overload of notation, for an input sentence $\mathbf{x}$ we denote by x_i the d dimensional learnable embedding of the i-th word ($x_i \in \mathcal{R}^d$). In addition the position i of the word x_i is also associated with a learnable embedding l_i of size d ($l_i \in \mathcal{R}^d$). Then the full embedding for i-th word in $\mathbf{x}$ is given by $a_i = x_i + l_i$. Let us denote by $B^k \in \mathcal{R}^{q \times d}$ a learnable weight matrix which is used to convolve over the full embeddings of consecutive words. Let there be d such matrices ($k \in \{1, \ldots, d\}$). The output of convolution is given by:

$$z_{ik} = \sum_{h=-q/2}^{q/2} a_{i+h} \cdot b_{q/2+h}^k, \tag{2}$$

where b_j^k is the j-th column of the matrix B^k. Thus the d dimensional aggregate embedding vector z_i is defined as $z_i = [z_{i1}, \ldots, z_{id}]$. Note that each word x_i in the input sequence is associated with one aggregate embedding vector z_i. The vectors z_i can be seen as a representation of the word which captures the position in which it occurs in the sentence and also the context in which it appears in the sentence. In our experiments the width q of the convolution matrix B^k was set to 5. To account for words at the boundaries of $\mathbf{x}$ we first pad the sequence on both sides with dummy words before computing the aggregate vectors z_i's.

Given these aggregate vectors of words, we compute the context vector c_t (the encoder output) as:

$$c_t = \sum_{j=1}^{M} \alpha_{j,t-1} x_j, \tag{3}$$

where the weights $\alpha_{j,t-1}$ are computed as

$$\alpha_{j,t-1} = \frac{\exp(z_j \cdot h_{t-1})}{\sum_{i=1}^{M} \exp(z_i \cdot h_{t-1})}. \tag{4}$$

3.3 Training and Generation

Given a training corpus $\mathcal{S} = \{(\mathbf{x}^i, \mathbf{y}^i)\}_{i=1}^{S}$ of S sentence-summary pairs, the above model can be trained end-to-end using stochastic gradient descent by minimizing the negative conditional log likelihood of the training data with respect to θ:

$$\mathcal{L} = -\sum_{i=1}^{S} \sum_{t=1}^{N} \log P(y_t^i | \{y_1^i, \ldots, y_{t-1}^i\}, \mathbf{x}^i; \theta), \tag{5}$$

where the parameters θ constitute the parameters of the decoder and the encoder.

Once the parametric model is trained we generate a summary for a new sentence $\mathbf{x}$ through a word-based beam search such that $P(y|\mathbf{x})$ is maximized, $\operatorname{argmax} P(y_t | \{y_1, \ldots, y_{t-1}\}, \mathbf{x})$. The search is parameterized by the number of paths k that are pursued at each time step.

4 Experimental Setup

4.1 Datasets and Evaluation

Our models are trained on the annotated version of the Gigaword corpus (Graff et al., 2003; Napoles et al., 2012) and we use only the annotations for tokenization and sentence separation while discarding other annotations such as tags and parses. We pair the first sentence of each article with its headline to form sentence-summary pairs. The data is pre-processed in the same way as Rush et al. (2015) and we use the same splits for training, validation, and testing. For Gigaword we report results on the same randomly held-out test set of 2000 sentence-summary pairs as (Rush et al., 2015).[1] We also evaluate our models on the DUC-2004 evaluation data set comprising 500 pairs (Over et al., 2007). Our evaluation is based on three variants of ROUGE (Lin, 2004), namely, ROUGE-1 (unigrams), ROUGE-2 (bigrams), and ROUGE-L (longest-common substring).

4.2 Architectural Choices

We implemented our models in the Torch library (http://torch.ch/)[2]. To optimize our loss (Equation 5) we used stochastic gradient descent with mini-batches of size 32. During training we measure the perplexity of the summaries in the validation set and adjust our hyper-parameters, such as the learning rate, based on this number.

---

[1] We remove pairs with empty titles resulting in slightly different accuracy compared to Rush et al. (2015) for their systems.

[2] Our code can found at www://github.com/facebook/namas

Model	Perplexity
Bag-of-Words	43.6
Convolutional (TDNN)	35.9
Attention-based (ABS)	27.1
RAS-Elman	**18.9**
RAS-LSTM	20.3

Table 1: Perplexity on the Gigaword validation set. Bag-of-words, Convolutional (TDNN) and ABS are the different encoders of Rush et. al., 2015.

For the decoder we experimented with both the Elman RNN and the Long-Short Term Memory (LSTM) architecture (as discussed in § 3.1). We chose hyper-parameters based on a grid search and picked the one which gave the best perplexity on the validation set. In particular we searched over the number of hidden units H of the recurrent layer, the learning rate η, the learning rate annealing schedule γ (the factor by which to decrease η if the validation perplexity increases), and the gradient clipping threshold κ. Our final Elman architecture (RAS-Elman) uses a single layer with $H = 512$, $\eta = 0.5$, $\gamma = 2$, and $\kappa = 10$. The LSTM model (RAS-LSTM) also has a single layer with $H = 512$, $\eta = 0.1$, $\gamma = 2$, and $\kappa = 10$.

5   Results

On the Gigaword corpus we evaluate our models in terms of perplexity on a held-out set. We then pick the model with best perplexity on the held-out set and use it to compute the F1-score of ROUGE-1, ROUGE-2, and ROUGE-L on the test sets, all of which we report. For the DUC corpus however, inline with the standard, we report the recall-only ROUGE. As baseline we use the state-of-the-art attention-based system (ABS) of Rush et al. (2015) which relies on a feed-forward network decoder. Additionally, we compare to an enhanced version of their system (ABS+), which relies on a range of separate extractive summarization features that are added as log-linear features in a secondary learning step with minimum error rate training (Och, 2003).

Table 1 shows that both our RAS-Elman and RAS-LSTM models achieve lower perplexity than

	RG-1	RG-2	RG-L
ABS	29.55	11.32	26.42
ABS+	29.76	11.88	26.96
RAS-Elman ($k = 1$)	33.10	14.45	30.25
RAS-Elman ($k = 10$)	**33.78**	**15.97**	**31.15**
RAS-LSTM ($k = 1$)	31.71	13.63	29.31
RAS-LSTM ($k = 10$)	32.55	14.70	30.03
Luong-NMT	33.10	14.45	30.71

Table 2: F1 ROUGE scores on the Gigaword test set. ABS and ABS+ are the systems of Rush et al. 2015. k refers to the size of the beam for generation; $k = 1$ implies greedy generation. RG refers to ROUGE. Rush et al. (2015) previously reported ROUGE recall, while as we use the more balanced F-measure.

	RG-1	RG-2	RG-L
ABS	26.55	7.06	22.05
ABS+	28.18	8.49	23.81
RAS-Elman ($k = 1$)	29.13	7.62	23.92
RAS-Elman ($k = 10$)	**28.97**	**8.26**	**24.06**
RAS-LSTM ($k = 1$)	26.90	6.57	22.12
RAS-LSTM ($k = 10$)	27.41	7.69	23.06
Luong-NMT	28.55	8.79	24.43

Table 3: ROUGE results (recall-only) on the DUC-2004 test sets. ABS and ABS+ are the systems of Rush et al. 2015. k refers to the size of the beam for generation; $k = 1$ implies greedy generation. RG refers to ROUGE.

ABS as well as other models reported in Rush et al. (2015). The RAS-LSTM performs slightly worse than RAS-Elman, most likely due to over-fitting. We attribute this to the relatively simple nature of this task which can be framed as English-to-English translation with few long-term dependencies. The ROUGE results (Table 2) show that our models comfortably outperform both ABS and ABS+ by a wide margin on all metrics. This is even the case when we rely only on very fast greedy search ($k = 1$), while as ABS uses a much wider beam of size $k = 50$; the stronger ABS+ system also uses additional extractive features which our model does not. These features cause ABS+ to copy 92% of words from the input into the summary, whereas our model copies only 74% of the words leading to more abstractive summaries. On DUC-2004 we report recall ROUGE as is customary on this dataset. The results (Table 3) show that our models are better than ABS+. However the improvements are smaller than for Gigaword which is likely due to two reasons: First, tokenization of DUC-2004 differs slightly from our training corpus. Second, headlines in Gigaword are much shorter than in DUC-2004.

For the sake of completeness we also compare our models to the recently proposed standard Neural Machine Translation (NMT) systems. In particular, we compare to a smaller re-implementation of the attentive stacked LSTM encoder-decoder of Luong et al. (2015). Our implementation uses two-layer LSTMs for the encoder-decoder with 500 hidden units in each layer. Tables 2 and 3 report ROUGE scores on the two data sets. From the tables we observe that the proposed RAS-Elman model is able to match the performance of the NMT model of Luong at al. (2015). This is noteworthy because RAS-Elman is significantly simpler than the NMT model at multiple levels. First, the encoder used by RAS-Elman is extremely light-weight (attention over the convolutional representation of the input words), compared to Luong's (a 2 hidden layer LSTM). Second, the decoder used by RAS-Elman is a single layer standard (Elman) RNN as opposed to a multi-layer LSTM. In an independent work, Nallapati et. al (2016) also trained a collection of standard NMT models and report numbers in the same ballpark as RAS-Elman on both datasets.

In order to better understand which component of the proposed architecture is responsible for the improvements, we trained the recurrent model with Rush et. al., (2015)'s ABS encoder on a subset of the Gigaword dataset. The ABS encoder, which does not have the position features, achieves a final validation perplexity of 38 compared to 29 for the proposed encoder, which uses position features as well as context information. This clearly shows the benefits of using the position feature in the proposed encoder.

Finally in Figure 1 we highlight anecdotal examples of summaries produced by the RAS-Elman system on the Gigaword dataset. The first two examples highlight typical improvements in the RAS model over ABS+. Generally the model produces more fluent summaries and is better able to capture the main actors of the input. For instance in Sentence 1, RAS-Elman correctly distinguishes the actions of "pepe" from "ferreira", and in Sentence 2 it identifies the correct role of the "think tank". The final two ex-

I(1): brazilian defender pepe is out for the rest of the season with a knee injury , his porto coach jesualdo ferreira said saturday .
G: football : pepe out for season
A+: ferreira out for rest of season with knee injury
R: brazilian defender pepe out for rest of season with knee injury

I(2): economic growth in toronto will suffer this year because of sars , a think tank said friday as health authorities insisted the illness was under control in canada 's largest city .
G: sars toll on toronto economy estimated at c$ # billion
A+: think tank under control in canada 's largest city
R: think tank says economic growth in toronto will suffer this year

I(3): colin l. powell said nothing – a silence that spoke volumes to many in the white house on thursday morning .
G: in meeting with former officials bush defends iraq policy
A+: colin powell speaks volumes about silence in white house
R: powell speaks volumes on the white house

I(4): an international terror suspect who had been under a controversial loose form of house arrest is on the run , british home secretary john reid said tuesday .
G: international terror suspect slips net in britain
A+: reid under house arrest terror suspect on the run
R: international terror suspect under house arrest

Figure 1: Example sentence summaries produced on Gigaword. **I** is the input, **G** is the true headline, **A** is ABS+, and **R** is RAS-ELMAN.

amples highlight typical mistakes of the models. In Sentence 3 both models take literally the figurative use of the idiom "a silence that spoke volumes," and produce fluent but nonsensical summaries. In Sentence 4 the RAS model mistakes the content of a relative clause for the main verb, leading to a summary with the opposite meaning of the input. These difficult cases are somewhat rare in the Gigaword, but they highlight future challenges for obtaining human-level sentence summary.

6 Conclusion

We extend the state-of-the-art model for abstractive sentence summarization (Rush et al., 2015) to a recurrent neural network architecture. Our model is a simplified version of the encoder-decoder framework for machine translation (Bahdanau et al., 2014). The model is trained on the Gigaword corpus to generate headlines based on the first line of each news article. We comfortably outperform the previous state-of-the-art on both Gigaword data and the DUC-2004 challenge even though our model does not rely on additional extractive features.

References

Dzmitry Bahdanau, Kyunghyun Cho, and Yoshua Bengio. 2014. Neural machine translation by jointly learning to align and translate. *CoRR*, abs/1409.0473.

Michele Banko, Vibhu O Mittal, and Michael J Witbrock. 2000. Headline generation based on statistical translation. In *Proceedings of the 38th Annual Meeting on Association for Computational Linguistics*, pages 318–325. Association for Computational Linguistics.

Kyunghyun Cho, Bart van Merrienboer, Çaglar Gülçehre, Dzmitry Bahdanau, Fethi Bougares, Holger Schwenk, and Yoshua Bengio. 2014. Learning phrase representations using RNN encoder-decoder for statistical machine translation. In *Proceedings of EMNLP 2014*, pages 1724–1734.

James Clarke and Mirella Lapata. 2008. Global inference for sentence compression: An integer linear programming approach. *Journal of Artificial Intelligence Research*, pages 399–429.

Trevor Cohn and Mirella Lapata. 2008. Sentence compression beyond word deletion. In *Proceedings of the 22nd International Conference on Computational Linguistics-Volume 1*, pages 137–144. Association for Computational Linguistics.

Trevor Cohn and Mirella Lapata. 2013. An abstractive approach to sentence compression. *ACM Transactions on Intelligent Systems and Technology (TIST'13)*, 4,3(41).

Jeffrey L. Elman. 1990. Finding structure in time. *Cognitive Science*, 14(2):179–211.

Katja Filippova and Yasemin Altun. 2013. Overcoming the lack of parallel data in sentence compression. In *EMNLP*, pages 1481–1491.

Katja Filippova, Enrique Alfonseca, Carlos A Colmenares, Lukasz Kaiser, and Oriol Vinyals. 2015. Sentence compression by deletion with lstms. In *EMNLP*.

Dimitrios Galanis and Ion Androutsopoulos. 2010. An extractive supervised two-stage method for sentence compression. In *Proceedings of NAACL-HLT 2010*.

David Graff, Junbo Kong, Ke Chen, and Kazuaki Maeda. 2003. English gigaword. *Linguistic Data Consortium, Philadelphia*.

S. Hochreiter and J. Schmidhuber. 1997. Long short-term memory. *Neural Computation*, 9(8):1735–1780.

H Jing. 2000. Sentence reduction for automatic text summarization. In *ANLP-00*, pages 703–711.

Kevin Knight and Daniel Marcu. 2002. Summarization beyond sentence extraction: A probabilistic approach to sentence compression. *Artificial Intelligence*, 139(1):91–107.

Chin-Yew Lin. 2004. Rouge: A package for automatic evaluation of summaries. In *Text Summarization Branches Out: Proceedings of the ACL-04 Workshop*, pages 74–81.

Minh-Thang Luong, Hieu Pham, and Christopher D. Manning. 2015. Effective approaches to attention-based neural machine translation. In *Proceedings of the 2015 Conference on Empirical Methods in Natural Language Processing*, pages 1412–1421, Lisbon, Portugal, September. Association for Computational Linguistics.

R McDonald. 2006. Discriminative sentence compression with soft syntactic evidence. In *EACL-06*, pages 297–304.

Ramesh Nallapati, Bing Xiang, and Zhou Bowen. 2016. Sequence-to-sequence rnns for text summarization. In *http://arxiv.org/abs/1602.06023*.

Courtney Napoles, Chris Callison-Burch, Juri Ganitkevitch, and Benjamin Van Durme. 2011. Paraphrastic sentence compression with a character-based metric: Tightening without deletion. In *Proceedings of the Workshop on Monolingual Text-To-Text Generation (MTTG'11)*.

Courtney Napoles, Matthew Gormley, and Benjamin Van Durme. 2012. Annotated gigaword. In *Proceedings of the Joint Workshop on Automatic Knowledge Base Construction and Web-scale Knowledge Extraction*, pages 95–100. Association for Computational Linguistics.

Franz Josef Och. 2003. Minimum error rate training in statistical machine translation. In *Proceedings of the 41st Annual Meeting on Association for Computational Linguistics-Volume 1*, pages 160–167. Association for Computational Linguistics.

Paul Over, Hoa Dang, and Donna Harman. 2007. Duc in context. *Information Processing & Management*, 43(6):1506–1520.

Alexander M Rush, Sumit Chopra, and Jason Weston. 2015. A neural attention model for abstractive sentence summarization. In *EMNLP*.

Kristian Woodsend, Yansong Feng, and Mirella Lapata. 2010. Generation with quasi-synchronous grammar. In *Proceedings of the 2010 conference on empirical methods in natural language processing*, pages 513–523. Association for Computational Linguistics.

Sander Wubben, Antal Van Den Bosch, and Emiel Krahmer. 2012. Sentence simplification by monolingual machine translation. In *Proceedings of the 50th Annual Meeting of the Association for Computational Linguistics: Long Papers-Volume 1*, pages 1015–1024. Association for Computational Linguistics.

David Zajic, Bonnie Dorr, and Richard Schwartz. 2004. Bbn/umd at duc-2004: Topiary. In *Proceedings of the HLT-NAACL 2004 Document Understanding Workshop, Boston*, pages 112–119.

Integer Linear Programming for Discourse Parsing

Jérémy Perret   **Stergos Afantenos**   **Nicholas Asher**   **Mathieu Morey**
IRIT, Université de Toulouse & CNRS
118 Route de Narbonne, 31062 Toulouse, France
{firstname.lastname@irit.fr}

Abstract

In this paper we present the first, to the best of our knowledge, discourse parser that is able to predict non-tree DAG structures. We use Integer Linear Programming (ILP) to encode both the objective function and the constraints as global decoding over local scores. Our underlying data come from multi-party chat dialogues, which require the prediction of DAGs. We use the dependency parsing paradigm, as has been done in the past (Muller et al., 2012; Li et al., 2014; Afantenos et al., 2015), but we use the underlying formal framework of SDRT and exploit SDRT's notions of *left* and *right distributive* relations. We achieve an F-measure of 0.531 for fully labeled structures which beats the previous state of the art.

1 Introduction

Multi-party dialogue parsing, in which complete discourse structures for multi-party dialogue or its close cousin, multi-party chat, are automatically constructed, is still in its infancy. Nevertheless, these are now very common forms of communication on the Web. Dialogue appears also importantly different from monologue. Afantenos et al. (2015) point out that forcing discourse structures to be trees will perforce miss 9% of the links in their corpus, because a significant number of discourse structures in the corpus are not trees. Although Afantenos et al. (2015) is the only prior paper we know of that studies dialogue parsing on multi-party dialogue, and that work relied on methods adapted to treelike structures, we think the area of multi-party dialogue

and non-treelike discourse structures is ripe for investigation and potentially important for other genres like the discourse analysis of fora (Wang et al., 2011, for example). This paper proposes a method based on constraints using Integer Linear Programming decoding over local probability distributions to investigate both treelike and non-treelike, full discourse structures for multi-party dialogue. We show that our method outperforms that of Afantenos et al. (2015) on the corpus they developed.

Discourse parsing involves at least three main steps: the segmentation of a text into *elementary discourse units* (EDUs), the basic building blocks for discourse structures, the attachment of EDUs together into connected structures for texts, and finally the labelling of the links between discourse units with discourse relations. Much current work in discourse parsing focuses on the labelling of discourse relations, using data from the Penn Discourse Treebank (PDTB) (Prasad et al., 2008). This work has availed itself of increasingly sophisticated features of the semantics of the units to be related (Braud and Denis, 2015); but as the PDTB does not provide full discourse structures for texts, it is not relevant to our concerns here. *Rhetorical Structure Theory* (RST) (Mann and Thompson, 1987; Mann and Thompson, 1988; Taboada and Mann, 2006) does take into account the global structure of the document, and the RST Discourse Tree Bank Carlson et al. (2003) has texts annotated according to RST with full discourse structures. This has guided most work in recent discourse parsing of multi-sentence text (Subba and Di Eugenio, 2009; Hernault et al., 2010; duVerle and Prendinger, 2009; Joty et al., 2013; Joty et al., 2015).

Proceedings of NAACL-HLT 2016, pages 99–109,
San Diego, California, June 12-17, 2016. ©2016 Association for Computational Linguistics

But RST requires that discourse structures be projective trees.

While projective trees are arguably a contender for representing the discourse structure of monologue text, multi-party chat dialogues exhibit crossing dependencies. This rules out using a theory like RST as a basis either for an annotation model or as a guide to learning discourse structure (Afantenos et al., 2015). Several subgroups of interlocutors can momentarily form and carry on a discussion amongst themselves, forming thus multiple concurrent discussion threads. Furthermore, participants of one thread may reply or comment to something said to another thread. One might conclude from the presence of multiple threads in dialogue that we should use non-projective trees to guide discourse parsing. But non-projective trees cannot always reflect the structure of a discourse either, as Asher and Lascarides (2003) argue on theoretical grounds. Afantenos et al. (2015) provide examples in which a question or a comment by speaker S that is addressed to all the engaged parties in the conversation receives an answer from all the other participants, all of which are then acknowledged by S with a simple *OK* or *No worries*, thus creating an intuitive, "lozenge" like structure, in which the acknowledgment has several incoming links representing discourse dependencies.

A final, important organizing element of the discourse structure for text and dialogue is the presence of clusters of EDUs that can act together as an argument to other discourse relations. This means that subgraphs of the entire discourse graph act as elements or nodes in the full discourse structure. These subgraphs are *complex discourse units* or CDUs.[1] Here is an example from the *Settlers* corpus:

(1)   gotwoodforsheep: [Do you have a sheep?]$_a$
       Thomas: [I do,]$_b$ [if you give me clay]$_c$
       Thomas: [or wood.]$_d$

Thomas's response to gotwoodforsheep spans two turns in the corpus. More interestingly, the response is a conditional "yes" in which EDUs (c) and (d) jointly specify the antecedent of the discourse relation that links both to the EDU *I do*.

CDUs have been claimed to be an important organizing principle of discourse structure and important for the analysis of anaphora and ellipsis for over 20 years (Asher, 1993). Yet the computational community has ignored them; when they are present in annotated corpora, they have been eliminated. This attitude is understandable, because CDUs, as they stand, are not representable as trees in any straightforward way. But given that our method can produce non-treelike graphs, we take a first step towards the prediction of CDUs as part of discourse structure by encoding them in a hypergraph-like framework. In particular, we will transform our corpus by distributing relations on CDUs over all their constituents as we describe in section 3.

Our paper is organized as follows. The data that we have used are described in more detail in the following section, while the underlying linguistic theory that we are using is described in section 3. In section 4 we present in detail the model that we have used, in particular the ILP decoder and the constraints and objective function it exploits. We report our results in section 5. Section 6 provides the related work while section 7 concludes this paper.

2   Input data

For our experiments we used a corpus collected from chats involving an online version of the game *The Settlers of Catan* described in (Afantenos et al., 2012; Afantenos et al., 2015). *Settlers* is a multiparty, win-lose game in which players use resources such as wood and sheep to build roads and settlements. Players take turns directing the bargaining. This is the only discourse annotated corpus of multi-agent dialogue of which we are aware, and it was one in which apparently non-treelike structures were already noted and also contains CDUs. Such a chat corpus is also useful to study because it approximates spoken dialogue in several ways—sentence fragments, non-standard orthography and occasional lack of syntax—without the inconvenience of transcribing speech. The corpus consists of 39 games annotated for discourse structure in the style of SDRT. Each game consists of several dialogues, and each dialogue represents a single bargaining session directed by a particular player or perhaps several connected sessions. Each dialogue is treated as hav-

---

[1]CDUs are a feature of SDRT as we explain below. They are also a feature of RST on some interpretations of the Satellite-Nucleus feature.

	Total	Training	Testing
Dialogues	1091	968	123
Turns	9160	8166	994
EDUs	10677	9545	1132
CDUs	1284	1132	152
Relation instances			
No distribution	10191	9127	1064
Partial dist.	11734	10507	1227
Full dist.	13675	12210	1465

Table 1: Dataset overview

ing its own discourse structure. About 10% of the corpus was held out for evaluation purposes while the rest was used for training. The dialogues in the corpus are mostly short with each speaker's turn containing typically only one, two or three EDUs, though the longest has 156 EDUs and 119 turns. Most of the discourse connections or relation instances in the corpus thus occur between speaker turns. Statistics on the number of dialogues, EDUs and relations contained in each sub-corpus can be found in table 1. Note that the number of relation instances in the corpus depends on how CDUs are translated, which we'll explain in the next section. The corpus has approximately the same number of EDUs and relations as the RST corpus (Carlson et al., 2003).

3   Linguistic Foundations

Segmented Discourse Representation Theory. We give a few details here on one discourse theory in which non-treelike discourse structures are countenanced and that underlies the annotations of the corpus we used. That theory is SDRT. In SDRT, a discourse structure, or *SDRS*, consists of a set of Discourse Units (DUs) and as Discourse Relations linking those units. DUs are distinguished into EDUs and CDUs. We identify EDUs here with phrases or sentences describing a state or an event; CDUs are SDRSs. Formally an SDRS for a given text segmented in EDUs $D = \{e_1, \ldots, e_n\}$, where e_i are the EDUs of D, is a tuple (V, E_1, E_2, ℓ) where V is a set of nodes or discourse units including $\{e_1, \ldots, e_n\}$, $E_1 \subseteq V \times V$ a set of edges representing discourse relations, $E_2 \subseteq V \times V$ a set of edges that rep-

resents parthood in the sense that if $(x, y) \in E_2$, then the unit x is an element of the CDU y; finally $\ell \colon E_1 \to Relations$ is a labelling function that assigns an edge in E_1 its discourse relation type.

From SDRT Structures to Dependency Structures. Predicting full SDRSs (V, E_1, E_2, ℓ) with $E_2 \neq \varnothing$ has been to date impossible, because no reliable method has been identified in the literature for calculating edges in E_2. Instead, most approaches (Muller et al., 2012; Afantenos et al., 2015, for example) simplify the underlying structures by a *head replacement strategy (HR)* that removes nodes representing CDUs from the original hypergraphs and replacing any incoming or outgoing edges on these nodes on the *heads* of those CDUs, forming thus dependency structures and not hypergraphs. A similar approach has also been followed by Hirao et al. (2013) and Li et al. (2014) in the context of RST to deal with multi-nuclear relations.

Transforming SDRSs using HR does not come without its problems. The decision to attach all incoming and outgoing links to a CDU to its head is one with little theoretical or semantic justification. The semantic effects of attaching an EDU to a CDU are not at all the same as attaching an EDU to the head of the CDU. For example, suppose we have a simple discourse with the following EDUs marked by brackets and discourse connectors in bold :

(2)   [The French economy continues to suffer]$_a$
         because [high labor costs remain high]$_b$ **and**
         [investor confidence remains low]$_c$.

The correct SDRS for (2) is one in which both b and c *together* explain why the French economy continues to suffer. That is, b and c form a CDU and give rise to the following graph:

$$a \xrightarrow{\text{EXPLANATION}} \boxed{b \xrightarrow{\text{CONTINUATION}} c}$$

HR on (2) produces a graph whose strictly compositional interpretation would be false—b alone explains why the French economy continues to suffer. Alternatively an interpretation of the proposed translation an SDRS with CDUs would introduce spurious ambiguities: either b alone or b and c together provide the explanation. To make matters worse, given the semantics of discourse relations in SDRT (Asher and Lascarides, 2003), some relations have a semantics that implies that a relation between a CDU and some other discourse unit can be distributed over the discourse units that make up the CDU. But not all relations are distributive in this sense. For example, we could complicate (2) slightly:

(3)   [The French economy continues to suffer]$_a$ **and** [the Italian economy remains in the doldrums]$_b$ **because of** [persistent high labor costs]$_c$ **and** [lack of investor confidence in both countries]$_d$.

In (3), the SDRS graph would be:

However, this SDRS entails that a is explained by $[c, d]$ *and* that b is explained by $[c, d]$. That is, EXPLANATION "distributes" to the left but not to the right. Once again, the HR translation from SDRSs into dependency structures described above would get the intuitive meaning of this example wrong or introduce spurious ambiguities.

Given the above observations, we decided to take into account the formal semantics of the discourse relations before replacing CDUs. More precisely, we distinguish between *left distributive* and *right distributive* relations. In a nutshell, we examined the temporal and modal semantics of relations and classified them as to whether they were distributive with respect to their left or to their right argument; left distributive relations are those for which the source CDU node should be distributed while right distributive relations are those for which the target CDU node should be distributed. A relation can be both left and right distributive. Left distributive relations include ACKNOWLEDGEMENT, EXPLANATION, COMMENT, CONTINUATION, NARRATION, CONTRAST, PARALLEL, BACKGROUND, while right distributive relations include RESULT, CONTINUATION, NARRATION, COMMENT, CONTRAST, PARALLEL, BACKGROUND, ELABORATION. In Figure 1 we show an example of how relations distribute between EDU/CDU, CDU/EDU and CDU/CDU.

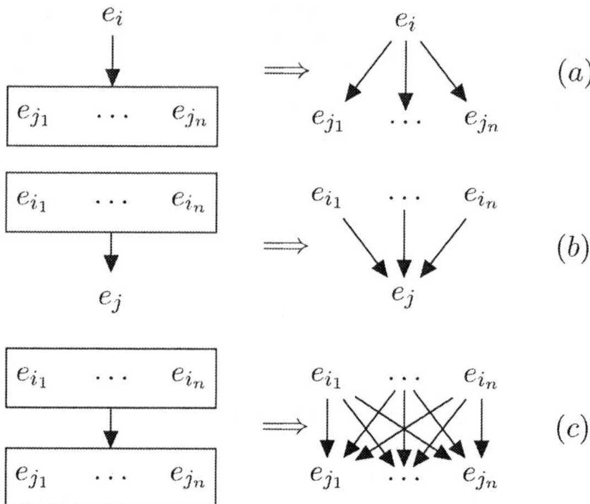

Figure 1: Distributing relations: (a) *right* distribution from an EDU to a CDU, (b) *left* distribution from a CDU to an EDU, (c) from a CDU to a CDU. We assume that all relations are both *right* and *left* distributive.

4 Underlying Model

Decoding over local scores. When we apply either a full or partial distributional (partial distribution takes into account which relations distribute in which direction) translation to the SDRSs in our corpus, we get dependency graphs that are not trees as input to our algorithms. We now approximate full SDRS graphs (V, E_1, E_2, ℓ) with graphs that distribute out E_2—that is, graphs of the form (V, E_1, ℓ) or more simply (V, E, ℓ). It is important to note that those graphs are not in general trees but rather Directed Acyclic Graphs (DAGs). We now proceed to detail how we learn such structures.

Ideally, what one wants is to learn a function $h : \mathcal{X}_{E^n} \mapsto \mathcal{Y}_{\mathcal{G}}$ where $\mathcal{X}_{E^n}$ is the domain of instances representing a collection of EDUs for each dialogue and $\mathcal{Y}_{\mathcal{G}}$ is the set of all possible SDRT graphs. However, given the complexity of this task and the fact that it would require an amount of training data that we currently lack in the community, we aim at the more modest goal of learning a function $h : \mathcal{X}_{E^2} \mapsto \mathcal{Y}_R$ where the domain of instances $\mathcal{X}_{E^2}$ represents parameters for a pair of EDUs and $\mathcal{Y}_R$ represents the set of SDRT relations.

An important drawback of this approach is that there are no formal guarantees that the predicted structures will be well-formed. They could for example contain cycles although they should be DAGs. Most approaches have circumvented this problem by using global decoding over local scores and by imposing specific constraints upon decoding. But, those constraints were mostly limited to the production of maximum spanning trees, and not full DAGs. We perform global decoding as well but use Integer Linear Programming (ILP) with an objective function and constraints that allow non-tree DAGs. We use a regularized maximum entropy (shortened MaxEnt) model (Berger et al., 1996) to get the local scores, both for attachment and labelling.

ILP for Global Decoding. ILP essentially involves an objective function that needs to be maximized under specific constraints. Our goal is to build the directed graph $G = \langle V, E, R \rangle$ with R being a function that provides labels for the edges in E. Vertices (EDUs) are referred by their position in textual order, indexed from 1. The m labels are referred by their index in alphabetical order, starting from 1. Let $n = |V|$.

The local model provides us with two real-valued functions:

$$s_a : \{1, \ldots, n\}^2 \mapsto [0, 1]$$
$$s_r : \{1, \ldots, n\}^2 \times \{1, \ldots, m\} \mapsto [0, 1]$$

$s_a(i, j)$ gives the score of attachment for a pair of EDUs (i, j); $s_r(i, j, k)$ gives the score for the attached pair of EDUs (i, j) linked with the relation type k. We define the n^2 binary variables a_{ij} and mn^2 binary variables r_{ijk}:

$$a_{ij} = 1 \ \equiv \ (i, j) \in V$$
$$r_{ijk} = 1 \ \equiv \ R(i, j) = k$$

The objective function that we want to maximize is

$$\sum_{i=1}^{n} \sum_{j=1}^{n} \left(a_{ij} s_a(i, j) + \sum_{k=1}^{m} r_{ijk} s_r(i, j, k) \right)$$

which gives us a score and a ranking for all candidate structures.

Our objective function is subject to several constraints. Because we have left the domain of trees well-explored by syntactic analysis and their computational implementations, we must design new constraints on discourse graphs, which we have developed from looking at our corpus while also being guided by theoretical principles. Some of these constraints come from SDRT, the underlying theory of

the annotations. In SDRT discourse graphs should be DAGs with a unique root or source vertex, i.e. one that has no incoming edges. They should also be weakly connected; i.e. every discourse unit in it is connected to some other discourse unit. We implemented connectedness and the unique root property as constraints in ILP by using the following equations.

$$\sum_{i=1}^{n} h_i = 1$$
$$\forall j \quad 1 \leq nh_j + \sum_{i=1}^{n} a_{ij} \leq n$$

where h_i is a set of auxiliary variables indexed on $\{1, \ldots, n\}$. The above constraint presupposes that our graphs are acyclic.

Implementing acyclicity is facilitated by another constraint that we call the *turn constraint*. This constraint is also theoretically motivated. The graphs in our training corpus are *reactive* in the sense that speakers' contributions are reactions and attach anaphorically to prior contributions of other speakers. This means that edges between the contributions of different speakers are always oriented in one direction. A turn by one speaker can't be anaphorically and rhetorically dependent on a turn by another speaker that comes after it. Once made explicit, this constraint has an obvious rationale: people do not know what another speaker will subsequently say and thus they cannot create an anaphoric or rhetorical dependency on this unknown future act. This is not the case within a single speaker turn though; people can know what they will say several EDUs ahead so they can make such kinds of future directed dependencies. ILP allows us to encode this constraint as follows. We indexed turns from different speakers in textual order from 1 to n_t, while consecutive turns from the same speaker were assigned the same index. Let $t(i)$ be the turn index of EDU i, and $T(k)$ the set of all EDUs belonging to turn k. The following constraint forbids backward links between EDUs from distinct turns:

$$\forall i, j \quad (i > j) \wedge (t(i) \neq t(j)) \implies a_{ij} = 0$$

The observation concerning the turn constraint is also useful for the model that provides local scores. We used it for attachment and relation labelling during training and testing.

Given the turn constraint we only need to ensure acyclicity of the same speaker turn subgraphs. We introduce an auxiliary set of integer variables, (c_{ki}), indexed on $\{1, \dots, n_t\} \times \{1, \dots, n\}$ in order to express this constraint:

$$\forall k, i \quad 1 \leq c_{ki} \leq |T(k)|$$
$$\forall k, i, j \text{ such that } t(i) = t(j) = k$$
$$c_{kj} \leq c_{ki} - 1 + n(1 - a_{ij})$$

Another interesting observation concerns the density of the graph. The objective function being additive on positive terms, every extra edge improves the global score of the graph, which leads to an almost-complete graph unless the edge count is constrained. So we imposed an upper limit $\delta \in [1, n]$ representing the density of the graphs:

$$\sum_{i=1}^{n} \sum_{j=1}^{n} a_{ij} \leq \delta(n - 1)$$

$\delta \in [1, n]$ since we need to have at least $n - 1$ edges for the graph to be connected and at maximum we can have $n(n - 1)$ edges if the graph is complete without loops. δ being a hyper-parameter, we estimated it on a development corpus representing 20% of our total corpus.[2]

The development corpus also shows that graph density decreases as the number of vertices grow. A high δ entails a too large number of edges in longer dialogues. We compensate for this effect by using an additive cap $\eta \geq 0$ on the edge count, also estimated on the development corpus:[3]

$$\sum_{i=1}^{n} \sum_{j=1}^{n} a_{ij} \leq n - 1 + \eta$$

Another empirical observation concerning the corpus was that the number of outgoing edges from any EDU had an upper bound $e_o \ll n$. We set that as an ILP constraint:[4]

$$\forall i \quad \sum_{j=1}^{n} a_{ij} \leq e_o$$

These observations don't have a semantic explanation, but they suggest a pragmatic one linked at least to the type of conversation present in our corpus. Short dialogues typically involve a opening question broadcast to all the players in search of a bargain, and typically all the other players reply. The replies are then taken up and either a bargain is reached or it isn't. The players then move on. Thus, the density of the graph in such short dialogues will be determined by the number of players (in our case, four). In a longer dialogue, we have more directed discourse moves and threads involving subgroups of the participants appear, but once again in these dialogues it never happens that our participants return again and again to the same contribution; if the thread of commenting on a contribution ϕ continues, future comments attach to prior comments, not to ϕ. Our ILP constraints on density and edge counts thus suggest a novel way of capturing different dialogue types and linguistic constraints.

Finally, we included various minor constraints, such as the fact that EDUs cannot be attached to themselves,[5] if EDUs i and j are not attached the pair is not assigned any discourse relation label,[6] EDUs within a sequence of contributions by the same speaker in our corpus are linked at least to the previous EDU (Afantenos et al., 2015)[7] and edges with zero score are not included in the graph.[8]

For purposes of comparison with the ILP decoder, we tested the Chu-Liu-Edmonds version of the classic Maximum Spanning Tree (MST) algorithm McDonald et al. (2005) used for discourse parsing by Muller et al. (2012) and Li et al. (2014) and by Afantenos et al. (2015) on the *Settlers* corpus. This algorithm requires a specific node to be the root, i.e. a node without any incoming edges, of the initial complete graph. For each dialogue, we made an artificial node as the root with special dummy features. At the end of the procedure, this node points to the real root of the discourse graph. As baseline measures, we included what we call a LOCAL decoder which creates a simple classifier out of the raw local probability distribution. Since we use MaxEnt, this

---

[2] δ takes the values 1.0, 1.2 and 1.4 for the head, partial and full distribution of the relations, respectively.

[3] η takes the value of 4 for the full distribution while it has no upper bound for the head and partial distributions.

[4] e_o is estimated on the development corpus to the value of 6 for the head, partial and full distributions.

[5] $\forall i \; a_{ii} = 0$

[6] $\forall i, j \; \sum_{k=1}^{m} r_{ijk} = a_{ij}$

[7] $\forall i \quad t(i) = t(i + 1) \implies a_{i,i+1} = 1$

[8] $\forall i, j \; s_a(i, j) = 0 \implies a_{ij} = 0$ and $\forall i, j, k \; s_r(i, j, k) = 0 \implies x_{ijk} = 0$

decoder selects

$$\hat{r} = \underset{r}{\operatorname{argmax}} \left(\frac{1}{Z(c)} \exp \left(\sum_{i=1}^{m} w_i f_i(p, r) \right) \right)$$

with r representing a relation type or a binary attachment value. A final baseline was LAST, where each EDU is attached to the immediately preceding EDU in the linear, textual order.

5   Experiments and Results

Features for training the local model and getting scores for the decoders were extracted for every pair of EDUs. Features concerned each EDU individually as well as the pair itself. We used obvious, surface features such as: the position of EDUs in the dialogue, who their speakers are, whether two EDUs have the same speaker, the distance between EDUs, the presence of mood indicators ('?', '!') in the EDU, lexical features of the EDU (e.g., does a verb signifying an exchange occur in the EDU), and first and last words of the EDU. We also used the structures and Subject lemmas given by syntactic dependency parsing, provided by the Stanford CoreNLP pipeline (Manning et al., 2014). Finally we used Cadilhac et al. (2013)'s method for classifying EDUs with respect to whether they involved an offer, a counteroffer, or were other.

As mentioned earlier, in addition to the ILP and MST decoders we used two baseline decoders, LAST and LOCAL. The LAST decoder simply selects the previous EDU for attachment no matter what the underlying probability distribution is. This has proved a very hard baseline to beat in discourse. The LOCAL decoder is a naive decoder which in the case of attachment returns "attached" if the probability of attachment between EDUs i and j is higher than .5 and "non-attached" in the opposite case.

Each of the three distribution methods described in Section 3 (Head, Partial and Full Distribution) yielded different dependency graphs for our input documents, which formed three distinct corpora on which we trained and tested separately. For each of them, our training set represented 90% of the dependency graphs from the initial corpus, chosen at random; the test set representing the remaining 10%. Table 2 shows our evaluation results, comparing decoders and baselines for each of the distribution strategies. As can be seen, our ILP de-

coder consistently performs significantly better than the baselines as well as the MST decoder, which was the previous state of the art (Afantenos et al., 2015) even when restricted to tree structures and HR (setting the hyper-parameter $\delta = 1$). This prompted us to investigate how our objective function compared to MST's. We eliminated all constraints in ILP except acyclicity, connectedness, turn constraint and eliminating any constraint on outgoing edges (setting $\delta = \infty$); in this case, ILP's objective function performed better on the full structure prediction (.531 F1) than MST with attachment and labelling jointly maximized (.516 F1). This means that our objective function, although it maximizes scores and not probabilities, produces an ordering over outputs that outperforms classic MST. Our analysis showed further that the constraints on outgoing edges (the tuning of the hyperparameter $e_o = 6$) were very important for our corpus and our (admittedly flawed) local model; in other words, an ILP constrained tree for this corpus was a better predictor of the data with our local model than an unrestrained MST tree decoding.

We also note that our scores dropped in distributive settings but that ILP performed considerably better than the alternatives and better than the previous state of the art on dependency trees using HR on the gold and MST decoding. We need to investigate further constraints, and to refine and improve our features to get a better local model. Our local model will eventually need to be replaced by one that takes into account more of the surrounding structure when it assigns scores to attachments and labels. We also plan to investigate the use of recurrent neural networks in order to improve our local model.

6   Related Work

ILP has been used for various computational linguistics tasks: syntactic parsing (Martins et al., 2010; Fernández-González and Martins, 2015), semantic parsing (Das et al., 2014), coreference resolution (Denis and Baldridge, 2007) and temporal analysis (Denis and Muller, 2011). As far as we know, we are the first to use ILP to predict discourse structures.

Our use of dependency structures for discourse also has antecedents in the literature. The first we know of is Muller et al. (2012). Their prediction

Decoder	Model	Unlabelled Attachment			Labelled Attachment		
		Precision	Recall	F1	Precision	Recall	F1
		Head (no distribution)					
LAST	–	0.602	0.566	0.584	0.403	0.379	0.391
LOCAL	local	0.664	0.379	0.483	0.591	0.337	0.429
MST	local	0.688	0.655	0.671	0.529	0.503	0.516
ILP	local	0.707	0.672	**0.689**	0.544	0.518	**0.531**
		Partial distribution					
LAST	–	0.651	0.545	0.593	0.467	0.391	0.426
LOCAL	local	0.647	0.370	0.471	0.544	0.311	0.396
MST	local	0.710	0.594	0.647	0.535	0.448	0.488
ILP	local	0.680	0.657	**0.668**	0.528	0.510	**0.519**
		Full distribution					
LAST	–	0.701	0.498	0.582	0.505	0.360	0.420
LOCAL	local	0.681	0.448	0.541	0.558	0.367	0.443
MST	local	0.737	0.524	0.613	0.561	0.399	0.466
ILP	local	0.703	0.649	**0.675**	0.549	0.507	**0.527**

Table 2: Evaluation results.

model uses local probability distributions and global decoding, and they transform their data using HR, and so ignore the semantics of discourse relations. Hirao et al. (2013) and Li et al. (2014) also exploit dependency structures by transforming RST trees. Li et al. (2014) used both the Eisner algorithm (Eisner, 1996) as well as the MST algorithm as decoders. We plan to apply ILP techniques to the RST Tree Bank to compare our method with theirs.

Most work on discourse parsing focuses on the task of discourse relation labeling between pairs of discourse units—e.g., Marcu and Echihabi (2002) Sporleder and Lascarides (2005) and Lin et al. (2009)—without worrying about global structure. In essence the problem that they treat corresponds only to our local model. As we have argued above, this setting makes an unwarranted assumption, as it assumes independence of local attachment decisions. There is also work on discourse structure within a single sentence; e.g., Soricut and Marcu (2003), Sagae (2009). Such approaches do not apply to our data, as most of the structure in our dialogues lies beyond the sentence level.

As for other document-level discourse parsers, Subba and Di Eugenio (2009) use a transition-based approach, following the paradigm of Sagae (2009). duVerle and Prendinger (2009) and Hernault et al. (2010) both rely on locally greedy methods. They treat attachment prediction and relation label prediction as independent problems. Feng and Hirst (2012) extend this approach by additional feature engineering but is restricted to sentence-level parsing. Joty et al. (2013) and Joty et al. (2015) present a text-level discourse parser that uses Conditional Random Fields to capture label inter-dependencies and chart parsing for decoding and have the best results on non-dependency based discourse parsing, with an F1 of 0.689 on unlabelled structures and 0.5587 on labelled structures.

The afore-cited work concerns only monologue. Baldridge and Lascarides (2005) predicted tree discourse structures for 2 party "directed" dialogues from the Verbmobil corpus by training a PCFG that exploited the structure of the underlying task. Elsner and Charniak (2010), Elsner and Charniak (2011) present a combination of local coherence models initially provided for monologues showing that those models can satisfactorily model local coherence in chat dialogues. However, they do not present a full discourse parsing model. Our data required a more open domain approach and a more sophisticated approach to structure. Afantenos et al. (2015) worked on multi-party chat dialogues with the same corpus, but they too did not consider the semantics of discourse relations and replaced CDUs with their heads using HR. While this allowed them to use MST decoding over local probability distributions, this meant that their implementation had inherent limitations because it is limited to producing tree structures. They also used the turn constraint, but imposed exogenously to decoding; ILP allows us to integrate it into the structural decoding. We achieve better results than they on treelike graphs and we can explore the full range of non-treelike discourse graphs within the ILP framework. Our parser has thus much more room to improve than those restricted to MST decoding.

7   Conclusions and future work

We have presented a novel method for discourse parsing of multiparty dialogue using ILP with linguistically and empirically motivated constraints and an objective function that integrates both attachment and labelling tasks. We have shown also that our method performs better than the competition on multiparty dialogue data and that it can capture non-treelike structures found in the data.

We also have a better treatment of the hierarchical structure of discourse than the competition. Our treatment of CDUs in discourse annotations proposes a new distributional translation of those annotations into dependency graphs, which we think is promising for future work. After distribution, our training corpus has a very different qualitative look. There are treelike subgraphs and then densely connected clusters of EDUs, indicating the presence of CDUs. This gives us good reason to believe that in subsequent work, we will be able to predict CDUs and attack the problem of hierarchical discourse structure seriously.

References

Stergos Afantenos, Nicholas Asher, Farah Benamara, Anas Cadilhac, Cdric Degremont, Pascal Denis, Markus Guhe, Simon Keizer, Alex Lascarides, Oliver Lemon, Philippe Muller, Soumya Paul, Verena Rieser, and Laure Vieu. 2012. Developing a corpus of strategic conversation in the settlers of catan. In Noriko Tomuro and Jose Zagal, editors, *Workshop on Games and NLP (GAMNLP-12)*, Kanazawa, Japan.

Stergos Afantenos, Eric Kow, Nicholas Asher, and Jérémy Perret. 2015. Discourse parsing for multiparty chat dialogues. In *Proceedings of the 2015 Conference on Empirical Methods in Natural Language Processing*, pages 928–937, Lisbon, Portugal, September. Association for Computational Linguistics.

Nicholas Asher and Alex Lascarides. 2003. *Logics of Conversation*. Studies in Natural Language Processing. Cambridge University Press, Cambridge, UK.

Nicholas Asher. 1993. *Reference to Abstract Objects in Discourse*. Kluwer Academic Publishers.

Jason Baldridge and Alex Lascarides. 2005. Probabilistic head-driven parsing for discourse structure. In *Proceedings of the Ninth Conference on Computational Natural Language Learning (CoNLL)*.

A. Berger, S. Della Pietra, and V. Della Pietra. 1996. A maximum entropy approach to natural language processing. *Computational Linguistics*, 22(1):39–71.

Chloé Braud and Pascal Denis. 2015. Comparing word representations for implicit discourse relation classification. In *Proceedings of the 2015 Conference on Empirical Methods in Natural Language Processing*, pages 2201–2211, Lisbon, Portugal, September. Association for Computational Linguistics.

Anais Cadilhac, Nicholas Asher, Farah Benamara, and Alex Lascarides. 2013. Grounding strategic conversation: Using negotiation dialogues to predict trades in a win-lose game. In *Proceedings of the 2013 Conference on Empirical Methods in Natural Language Processing*, pages 357–368, Seattle, Washington, USA, October. Association for Computational Linguistics.

Lynn Carlson, Daniel Marcu, and Mary Ellen Okurowski. 2003. Building a discourse-tagged corpus in the framework of rhetorical structure theory. In Jan van Kuppevelt and Ronnie Smith, editors, *Current Directions in Discourse and Dialogue*, pages 85–112. Kluwer Academic Publishers.

Dipanjan Das, Desai Chen, André F. T. Martins, Nathan Schneider, and Noah A. Smith. 2014. Frame-semantic parsing. *Computational Linguistics*, 40(1):9–56, March.

Pascal Denis and Jason Baldridge. 2007. Joint determination of anaphoricity and coreference resolution using integer programming. In *Human Language Technologies 2007: The Conference of the North American Chapter of the Association for Computational Linguistics; Proceedings of the Main Conference*, pages 236–243, Rochester, New York, April. Association for Computational Linguistics.

Pascal Denis and Philippe Muller. 2011. Predicting globally-coherent temporal structures from texts via endpoint inference and graph decomposition. In *Proc. of the International Joint Conference on Artificial Intelligence (IJCAI)*.

David duVerle and Helmut Prendinger. 2009. A novel discourse parser based on support vector machine classification. In *Proceedings of the Joint Conference of* the 47th Annual Meeting of the ACL and the 4th International Joint Conference on Natural Language Processing of the AFNLP*, pages 665–673, Suntec, Singapore, August. Association for Computational Linguistics.

Jason M. Eisner. 1996. Three new probabilistic models for dependency parsing: An exploration. In *Proceedings of the 16th International Conference on Computational Linguistics (COLING-96)*, volume 1, pages 340–345, Copenhagen, Denmark.

Micha Elsner and Eugene Charniak. 2010. Disentangling chat. *Computational Linguistics*, 36(3):389–409.

Micha Elsner and Eugene Charniak. 2011. Disentangling chat with local coherence models. In *Proceedings of the 49th Annual Meeting of the Association for Computational Linguistics: Human Language Technologies*, pages 1179–1189, Portland, Oregon, USA, June. Association for Computational Linguistics.

Vanessa Wei Feng and Graeme Hirst. 2012. Text-level discourse parsing with rich linguistic features. In *Proceedings of the 50th Annual Meeting of the Association for Computational Linguistics (Volume 1: Long Papers)*, pages 60–68, Jeju Island, Korea, July. Association for Computational Linguistics.

Daniel Fernández-González and André F. T. Martins. 2015. Parsing as reduction. In *Proceedings of the 53rd Annual Meeting of the Association for Computational Linguistics and the 7th International Joint Conference on Natural Language Processing (Volume 1: Long Papers)*, pages 1523–1533, Beijing, China, July. Association for Computational Linguistics.

Hugo Hernault, Helmut Prendinger, David A. duVerle, and Mitsuru Ishizuka. 2010. HILDA: A Discourse Parser Using Support Vector Machine Classification. *Dialogue and Discourse*, 1(3):1–33.

Tsutomu Hirao, Yasuhisa Yoshida, Masaaki Nishino, Norihito Yasuda, and Masaaki Nagata. 2013. Single-document summarization as a tree knapsack problem. In *Proceedings of the 2013 Conference on Empirical Methods in Natural Language Processing*, pages 1515–1520, Seattle, Washington, USA, October. Association for Computational Linguistics.

Shafiq Joty, Giuseppe Carenini, Raymond Ng, and Yashar Mehdad. 2013. Combining intra- and multi-sentential rhetorical parsing for document-level discourse analysis. In *Proceedings of the 51st Annual Meeting of the Association for Computational Linguistics (Volume 1: Long Papers)*, pages 486–496, Sofia, Bulgaria, August. Association for Computational Linguistics.

Shafiq Joty, Giuseppe Carenini, and Raymond Ng. 2015. Codra: A novel discriminative framework for rhetorical analysis. *Computational Linguistics*.

Sujian Li, Liang Wang, Ziqiang Cao, and Wenjie Li. 2014. Text-level discourse dependency parsing. In *Proceedings of the 52nd Annual Meeting of the Association for Computational Linguistics (Volume 1: Long Papers)*, pages 25–35, Baltimore, Maryland, June. Association for Computational Linguistics.

Ziheng Lin, Min-Yen Kan, and Hwee Tou Ng. 2009. Recognizing implicit discourse relations in the Penn Discourse Treebank. In *Proceedings of the 2009 Conference on Empirical Methods in Natural Language Processing*, pages 343–351, Singapore, August. Association for Computational Linguistics.

William C. Mann and Sandra A. Thompson. 1987. Rhetorical Structure Theory: A Framework for the Analysis of Texts. Technical Report ISI/RS-87-185, Information Sciences Institute, Marina del Rey, California.

William C. Mann and Sandra A. Thompson. 1988. Rhetorical Structure Theory: Towards a Functional Theory of Text Organization. *Text*, 8(3):243–281.

Christopher D. Manning, Mihai Surdeanu, John Bauer, Jenny Finkel, Steven J. Bethard, and David McClosky. 2014. The Stanford CoreNLP natural language processing toolkit. In *Proceedings of 52nd Annual Meeting of the Association for Computational Linguistics: System Demonstrations*, pages 55–60.

Daniel Marcu and Abdessamad Echihabi. 2002. An unsupervised approach to recognizing discourse relations. In *Proceedings of ACL*, pages 368–375.

Andre Martins, Noah Smith, Eric Xing, Pedro Aguiar, and Mario Figueiredo. 2010. Turbo parsers: Dependency parsing by approximate variational inference. In *Proceedings of the 2010 Conference on Empirical Methods in Natural Language Processing*, pages 34–44, Cambridge, MA, October. Association for Computational Linguistics.

Ryan T. McDonald, Fernando Pereira, Kiril Ribarov, and Jan Hajic. 2005. Non-projective dependency parsing using spanning tree algorithms. In *HLT/EMNLP*.

Philippe Muller, Stergos Afantenos, Pascal Denis, and Nicholas Asher. 2012. Constrained decoding for text-level discourse parsing. In *Proceedings of COLING 2012*, pages 1883–1900, Mumbai, India, December. The COLING 2012 Organizing Committee.

Rashmi Prasad, Nikhil Dinesh, Alan Lee, Eleni Miltsakaki, Livio Robaldo, Aravind Joshi, and Bonnie L. Webber. 2008. The Penn Discourse TreeBank 2.0. In *Proceedings of LREC 2008*.

Kenji Sagae. 2009. Analysis of discourse structure with syntactic dependencies and data-driven shift-reduce parsing. In *Proceedings of the 11th International Conference on Parsing Technologies*, IWPT '09, pages 81–84, Stroudsburg, PA, USA. Association for Computational Linguistics.

R. Soricut and D. Marcu. 2003. Sentence level discourse parsing using syntactic and lexical information. In *Proceedings of the 2003 Conference of the North American Chapter of the Association for Computational Linguistics on Human Language Technology-Volume 1*, pages 149–156. Association for Computational Linguistics.

Caroline Sporleder and Alex Lascarides. 2005. Exploiting linguistic cues to classify rhetorical relations. In *Proceedings of Recent Advances in Natural Langauge Processing (RANLP)*, Bulgaria.

Rajen Subba and Barbara Di Eugenio. 2009. An effective discourse parser that uses rich linguistic information. In *Proceedings of Human Language Technologies: The 2009 Annual Conference of the North American Chapter of the Association for Computational Linguistics*, pages 566–574, Boulder, Colorado, June. Association for Computational Linguistics.

Maite Taboada and William C. Mann. 2006. Rhetorical Structure Theory: Looking Back and Moving Ahead. *Discourse Studies*, 8(3):423–459, June.

Li Wang, Marco Lui, Su Nam Kim, Joakim Nivre, and Timothy Baldwin. 2011. Predicting thread discourse structure over technical web forums. In *Proceedings of the 2011 Conference on Empirical Methods in Natural Language Processing*, pages 13–25, Edinburgh, Scotland, UK., July. Association for Computational Linguistics.

A Diversity-Promoting Objective Function for Neural Conversation Models

Jiwei Li[1*]   Michel Galley[2]   Chris Brockett[2]   Jianfeng Gao[2]   Bill Dolan[2]

[1]Stanford University, Stanford, CA, USA
`jiweil@stanford.edu`
[2]Microsoft Research, Redmond, WA, USA
`{mgalley,chrisbkt,jfgao,billdol}@microsoft.com`

Abstract

Sequence-to-sequence neural network models for generation of conversational responses tend to generate safe, commonplace responses (e.g., *I don't know*) regardless of the input. We suggest that the traditional objective function, i.e., the likelihood of output (response) given input (message) is unsuited to response generation tasks. Instead we propose using Maximum Mutual Information (MMI) as the objective function in neural models. Experimental results demonstrate that the proposed MMI models produce more diverse, interesting, and appropriate responses, yielding substantive gains in BLEU scores on two conversational datasets and in human evaluations.

1 Introduction

Conversational agents are of growing importance in facilitating smooth interaction between humans and their electronic devices, yet conventional dialog systems continue to face major challenges in the form of robustness, scalability and domain adaptation. Attention has thus turned to learning conversational patterns from data: researchers have begun to explore data-driven generation of conversational responses within the framework of statistical machine translation (SMT), either phrase-based (Ritter et al., 2011), or using neural networks to rerank, or directly in the form of sequence-to-sequence (SEQ2SEQ) models (Sordoni et al., 2015; Vinyals and Le, 2015; Shang et al., 2015; Serban et al., 2015; Wen et al., 2015). SEQ2SEQ models offer the promise of scalability and language-independence, together with the capacity

to implicitly learn semantic and syntactic relations between pairs, and to capture contextual dependencies (Sordoni et al., 2015) in a way not possible with conventional SMT approaches (Ritter et al., 2011).

An engaging response generation system should be able to output grammatical, coherent responses that are diverse and interesting. In practice, however, neural conversation models tend to generate trivial or non-committal responses, often involving high-frequency phrases along the lines of *I don't know* or *I'm OK* (Sordoni et al., 2015; Serban et al., 2015; Vinyals and Le, 2015). Table 1 illustrates this phenomenon, showing top outputs from SEQ2SEQ models. All the top-ranked responses are generic. Responses that seem more meaningful or specific can also be found in the N-best lists, but rank much lower. In part at least, this behavior can be ascribed to the relative frequency of generic responses like *I don't know* in conversational datasets, in contrast with the relative sparsity of more contentful alternative responses.[1] It appears that by optimizing for the likelihood of outputs given inputs, neural models assign high probability to "safe" responses. This objective function, common in related tasks such as machine translation, may be unsuited to generation tasks involving intrinsically diverse outputs. Intuitively, it seems desirable to take into account not only the dependency of responses on messages, but also the inverse, the likelihood that a message will be provided to a given response.

We propose to capture this intuition by using Maximum Mutual Information (MMI), first introduced in

---

[1]In our training dataset from the OpenSubtitles database (OSDb), 0.45% sentences contain the sequence *I don't know*, a high rate considering huge diversity of this dataset.

** The entirety of this work was conducted at Microsoft.*

Proceedings of NAACL-HLT 2016, pages 110–119,
San Diego, California, June 12-17, 2016. ©2016 Association for Computational Linguistics

Input: What are you doing?	
−0.86 I don't know.	−1.09 Get out of here.
−1.03 I don't know!	−1.09 I'm going home.
−1.06 Nothing.	−1.09 Oh my god!
−1.09 Get out of the way.	−1.10 I'm talking to you.
Input: what is your name?	
−0.91 I don't know.	...
−0.92 I don't know!	−1.55 My name is Robert.
−0.92 I don't know, sir.	−1.58 My name is John.
−0.97 Oh, my god!	−1.59 My name's John.
Input: How old are you?	
−0.79 I don't know.	...
−1.06 I'm fine.	−1.64 Twenty-five.
−1.17 I'm all right.	−1.66 Five.
−1.17 I'm not sure.	−1.71 Eight.

Table 1: Responses generated by a 4-layer SEQ2SEQ neural model trained on 20 million conversation pairs take from the OpenSubtitles dataset. Decoding is implemented with beam size set to 200. The top examples are the responses with the highest average probability log-likelihoods in the N-best list. Lower-ranked, less-generic responses were manually chosen.

speech recognition (Bahl et al., 1986; Brown, 1987), as an optimization objective that measures the mutual dependence between inputs and outputs. Below, we present practical strategies for neural generation models that use MMI as an objective function. We show that use of MMI results in a clear decrease in the proportion of generic response sequences, generating correspondingly more varied and interesting outputs.

2 Related work

The approach we take here is data-driven and end-to-end. This stands in contrast to conventional dialog systems, which typically are template- or heuristic-driven even where there is a statistical component (Levin et al., 2000; Oh and Rudnicky, 2000; Ratnaparkhi, 2002; Walker et al., 2003; Pieraccini et al., 2009; Young et al., 2010; Wang et al., 2011; Banchs and Li, 2012; Chen et al., 2013; Ameixa et al., 2014; Nio et al., 2014).

We follow a newer line of investigation, originally introduced by Ritter et al. (2011), which frames response generation as a statistical machine translation (SMT) problem. Recent progress in SMT stemming from the use of neural language models (Sutskever et al., 2014; Gao et al., 2014; Bahdanau et

al., 2015; Luong et al., 2015) has inspired attempts to extend these neural techniques to response generation. Sordoni et al. (2015) improved upon Ritter et al. (2011) by rescoring the output of a phrasal SMT-based conversation system with a SEQ2SEQ model that incorporates prior context. (Serban et al., 2015; Shang et al., 2015; Vinyals and Le, 2015; Wen et al., 2015) apply direct end-to-end SEQ2SEQ models These SEQ2SEQ models are Long Short-Term Memory (LSTM) neural networks (Hochreiter and Schmidhuber, 1997) that can implicitly capture compositionality and long-span dependencies. (Wen et al., 2015) attempt to learn response templates from crowd-sourced data, whereas we seek to develop methods that can learn conversational patterns from naturally-occurring data.

Prior work in generation has sought to increase diversity, but with different goals and techniques. Carbonell and Goldstein (1998) and Gimpel (2013) produce *multiple* outputs that are mutually diverse, either non-redundant summary sentences or N-best lists. Our goal, however, is to produce a *single* non-trivial output, and our method does not require identifying lexical overlap to foster diversity.[2]

On a somewhat different task, Mao et al. (2015, Section 6) utilize a mutual information objective in the retrieval component of image caption retrieval. Below, we focus on the challenge of using MMI in response generation, comparing the performance of MMI models against maximum likelihood.

3 Sequence-to-Sequence Models

Given a sequence of inputs $X = \{x_1, x_2, ..., x_{N_x}\}$, an LSTM associates each time step with an input gate, a memory gate and an output gate, respectively denoted as i_k, f_k and o_k. We distinguish e and h where e_k denotes the vector for an individual text unit (for example, a word or sentence) at time step k while h_k denotes the vector computed by LSTM model at time k by combining e_k and h_{k-1}. c_k is the cell state vector at time k, and σ denotes the sigmoid function. Then, the vector representation h_k for each time step

---

[2]Augmenting our technique with MMR-based (Carbonell and Goldstein, 1998) diversity helped increase lexical but not semantic diversity (e.g., *I don't know* vs. *I haven't a clue*), and with no gain in performance.

k is given by:

$$i_k = \sigma(W_i \cdot [h_{k-1}, e_k]) \tag{1}$$

$$f_k = \sigma(W_f \cdot [h_{k-1}, e_k]) \tag{2}$$

$$o_k = \sigma(W_o \cdot [h_{k-1}, e_k]) \tag{3}$$

$$l_k = \tanh(W_l \cdot [h_{k-1}, e_k]) \tag{4}$$

$$c_k = f_k \cdot c_{k-1} + i_k \cdot l_k \tag{5}$$

$$h_k^s = o_k \cdot \tanh(c_k) \tag{6}$$

where $W_i, W_f, W_o, W_l \in \mathbb{R}^{D \times 2D}$. In SEQ2SEQ generation tasks, each input X is paired with a sequence of outputs to predict: $Y = \{y_1, y_2, ..., y_{N_y}\}$. The LSTM defines a distribution over outputs and sequentially predicts tokens using a softmax function:

$$p(Y|X) = \prod_{k=1}^{N_y} p(y_k|x_1, x_2, ..., x_t, y_1, y_2, ..., y_{k-1})$$

$$= \prod_{k=1}^{N_y} \frac{\exp(f(h_{k-1}, e_{y_k}))}{\sum_{y'} \exp(f(h_{k-1}, e_{y'}))}$$

where $f(h_{k-1}, e_{y_k})$ denotes the activation function between h_{k-1} and e_{y_k}, where h_{k-1} is the representation output from the LSTM at time $k - 1$. Each sentence concludes with a special end-of-sentence symbol *EOS*. Commonly, input and output use different LSTMs with separate compositional parameters to capture different compositional patterns.

During decoding, the algorithm terminates when an *EOS* token is predicted. At each time step, either a greedy approach or beam search can be adopted for word prediction. Greedy search selects the token with the largest conditional probability, the embedding of which is then combined with preceding output to predict the token at the next step.

4 MMI Models

4.1 Notation

In the response generation task, let S denote an input message sequence (source) $S = \{s_1, s_2, ..., s_{N_s}\}$ where N_s denotes the number of words in S. Let T (target) denote a sequence in response to source sequence S, where $T = \{t_1, t_2, ..., t_{N_t}, EOS\}$, N_t is the length of the response (terminated by an *EOS* token) and t denotes a word token that is associated with a D dimensional distinct word embedding e_t. V denotes vocabulary size.

4.2 MMI Criterion

The standard objective function for sequence-to-sequence models is the log-likelihood of target T given source S, which at test time yields the statistical decision problem:

$$\hat{T} = \arg\max_T \left\{ \log p(T|S) \right\} \tag{7}$$

As discussed in the introduction, we surmise that this formulation leads to generic responses being generated, since it only selects for targets given sources, not the converse. To remedy this, we replace it with Maximum Mutual Information (MMI) as the objective function. In MMI, parameters are chosen to maximize (pairwise) mutual information between the source S and the target T:

$$\log \frac{p(S, T)}{p(S)p(T)} \tag{8}$$

This avoids favoring responses that unconditionally enjoy high probability, and instead biases towards those responses that are specific to the given input. The MMI objective can written as follows:[3]

$$\hat{T} = \arg\max_T \left\{ \log p(T|S) - \log p(T) \right\}$$

We use a generalization of the MMI objective which introduces a hyperparameter λ that controls how much to penalize generic responses:

$$\hat{T} = \arg\max_T \left\{ \log p(T|S) - \lambda \log p(T) \right\} \tag{9}$$

An alternate formulation of the MMI objective uses Bayes' theorem:

$$\log p(T) = \log p(T|S) + \log p(S) - \log p(S|T)$$

which lets us rewrite Equation 9 as follows:

$$\hat{T} = \arg\max_T \left\{ (1 - \lambda) \log p(T|S) \right.$$
$$\left. + \lambda \log p(S|T) - \lambda \log p(S) \right\}$$
$$= \arg\max_T \left\{ (1 - \lambda) \log p(T|S) + \lambda \log p(S|T) \right\} \tag{10}$$

This weighted MMI objective function can thus be viewed as representing a tradeoff between sources

---

[3]Note: $\log \frac{p(S,T)}{p(S)p(T)} = \log \frac{p(T|S)}{p(T)} = \log p(T|S) - \log p(T)$

given targets (i.e., $p(S|T)$) and targets given sources (i.e., $p(T|S)$).

Although the MMI optimization criterion has been comprehensively studied for other tasks, such as acoustic modeling in speech recognition (Huang et al., 2001), adapting MMI to SEQ2SEQ training is empirically nontrivial. Moreover, we would like to be able to adjust the value λ in Equation 9 without repeatedly training neural network models from scratch, which would otherwise be extremely time-consuming. Accordingly, we did not train a joint model ($\log p(T|S) - \lambda \log p(T)$), but instead trained maximum likelihood models, and used the MMI criterion only during testing.

4.3 Practical Considerations

Responses can be generated either from Equation 9, i.e., $\log p(T|S) - \lambda \log p(T)$ or Equation 10, i.e., $(1 - \lambda) \log p(T|S) + \lambda \log p(S|T)$. We will refer to these formulations as MMI-antiLM and MMI-bidi, respectively. However, these strategies are difficult to apply directly to decoding since they can lead to ungrammatical responses (with MMI-antiLM) or make decoding intractable (with MMI-bidi). In the rest of this section, we will discuss these issues and explain how we resolve them in practice.

4.3.1 MMI-antiLM

The second term of $\log p(T|S) - \lambda \log p(T)$ functions as an anti-language model. It penalizes not only high-frequency, generic responses, but also fluent ones and thus can lead to ungrammatical outputs. In theory, this issue should not arise when λ is less than 1, since ungrammatical sentences should always be more severely penalized by the first term of the equation, i.e., $\log p(T|S)$. In practice, however, we found that the model tends to select ungrammatical outputs that escaped being penalized by $p(T|S)$.

Solution Again, let N_t be the length of target T. $p(T)$ in Equation 9 can be written as:

$$p(T) = \prod_{k=1}^{N_t} p(t_k|t_1, t_2, ..., t_{k-1}) \qquad (11)$$

We replace the language model $p(T)$ with $U(T)$, which adapts the standard language model by multiplying by a weight $g(k)$ that is decremented mono-

tonically as the index of the current token k increases:

$$U(T) = \prod_{i=1}^{N_t} p(t_k|t_1, t_2, ..., t_{k-1}) \cdot g(k) \qquad (12)$$

The underlying intuition here is as follows. First, neural decoding combines the previously built representation with the word predicted at the current step. As decoding proceeds, the influence of the initial input on decoding (i.e., the source sentence representation) diminishes as additional previously-predicted words are encoded in the vector representations.[4] In other words, the first words to be predicted significantly determine the remainder of the sentence. Penalizing words predicted early on by the language model contributes more to the diversity of the sentence than it does to words predicted later. Second, as the influence of the input on decoding declines, the influence of the language model comes to dominate. We have observed that ungrammatical segments tend to appear in the later parts of the sentences, especially in long sentences.

We adopt the most straightforward form of $g(k)$ by setting up a threshold (γ) by penalizing the first γ words where[5]

$$g(k) = \begin{cases} 1 & \text{if } k \le \gamma \\ 0 & \text{if } k > \gamma \end{cases} \qquad (13)$$

The objective in Equation 9 can thus be rewritten as:

$$\log p(T|S) - \lambda \log U(T) \qquad (14)$$

where direct decoding is tractable.

4.3.2 MMI-bidi

Direct decoding from $(1 - \lambda) \log p(T|S) + \lambda \log p(S|T)$ is intractable, as the second part (i.e., $p(S|T)$) requires completion of target generation *before* $p(S|T)$ can be effectively computed. Due to the enormous search space for target T, exploring all possibilities is infeasible.

For practical reasons, then, we turn to an approximation approach that involves first generating N-best lists given the first part of objective function, i.e.,

---

[4] Attention models (Xu et al., 2015) may offer some promise of addressing this issue.

[5] We experimented with a smooth decay in $g(k)$ rather than a stepwise function, but this did not yield better performance.

standard SEQ2SEQ model $p(T|S)$. Then we rerank the N-best lists using the second term of the objective function. Since N-best lists produced by SEQ2SEQ models are generally grammatical, the final selected options are likely to be well-formed. Model reranking has obvious drawbacks. It results in non-globally-optimal solutions by first emphasizing standard SEQ2SEQ objectives. Moreover, it relies heavily on the system's success in generating a sufficiently diverse N-best set, requiring that a long list of N-best lists be generated for each message.

Nonetheless, these two variants of the MMI criterion work well in practice, significantly improving both interestingness and diversity.

4.4 Training

Recent research has shown that deep LSTMs work better than single-layer LSTMs for SEQ2SEQ tasks (Vinyals et al., 2015; Sutskever et al., 2014). We adopt a deep structure with four LSTM layers for encoding and four LSTM layers for decoding, each of which consists of a different set of parameters. Each LSTM layer consists of 1,000 hidden neurons, and the dimensionality of word embeddings is set to 1,000. Other training details are given below, broadly aligned with Sutskever et al. (2014).

- LSTM parameters and embeddings are initialized from a uniform distribution in $[-0.08, 0.08]$.
- Stochastic gradient decent is implemented using a fixed learning rate of 0.1.
- Batch size is set to 256.
- Gradient clipping is adopted by scaling gradients when the norm exceeded a threshold of 1.

Our implementation on a single GPU processes at a speed of approximately 600-1200 tokens per second on a Tesla K40.

The $p(S|T)$ model described in Section 4.3.1 was trained using the same model as that of $p(T|S)$, with messages (S) and responses (T) interchanged.

4.5 Decoding

4.5.1 MMI-antiLM

As described in Section 4.3.1, decoding using $\log p(T|S) - \lambda U(T)$ can be readily implemented by predicting tokens at each time-step. In addition, we found in our experiments that it is also important to take into account the length of responses in decod-

ing. We thus linearly combine the loss function with length penalization, leading to an ultimate score for a given target T as follows:

$$Score(T) = p(T|S) - \lambda U(T) + \gamma N_t \qquad (15)$$

where N_t denotes the length of the target and γ denotes associated weight. We optimize γ and λ using MERT (Och, 2003) on N-best lists of response candidates. The N-best lists are generated using the decoder with beam size $B = 200$. We set a maximum length of 20 for generated candidates. At each time step of decoding, we are presented with $B \times B$ candidates. We first add all hypotheses with an *EOS* token being generated at current time step to the N-best list. Next we preserve the top B unfinished hypotheses and move to next time step. We therefore maintain beam size of 200 constant when some hypotheses are completed and taken down by adding in more unfinished hypotheses. This will lead the size of final N-best list for each input much larger than the beam size.

4.5.2 MMI-bidi

We generate N-best lists based on $P(T|S)$ and then rerank the list by linearly combining $p(T|S)$, $\lambda p(S|T)$, and γN_t. We use MERT to tune the weights λ and γ on the development set.[6]

5 Experiments

5.1 Datasets

Twitter Conversation Triple Dataset We used an extension of the dataset described in Sordoni et al. (2015), which consists of 23 million conversational snippets randomly selected from a collection of 129M context-message-response triples extracted from the Twitter Firehose over the 3-month period from June through August 2012. For the purposes of our experiments, we limited context to the turn in the conversation immediately preceding the message. In our LSTM models, we used a simple input model in which contexts and messages are concatenated to form the source input.

---

[6]As with MMI-antiLM, we could have used grid search instead of MERT, since there are only 3 features and 2 free parameters. In either case, the search attempts to find the best tradeoff between $p(T|S)$ and $p(S|T)$ according to BLEU (which tends to weight the two models relatively equally) and ensures that generated responses are of reasonable length.

Model	# of training instances	BLEU	distinct-1	distinct-2
SEQ2SEQ (baseline)	23M	4.31	.023	.107
SEQ2SEQ (greedy)	23M	4.51	.032	.148
MMI-antiLM: $\log p(T\|S) - \lambda U(T)$	23M	4.86	.033	.175
MMI-bidi: $(1-\lambda)\log p(T\|S) + \lambda \log p(S\|T)$	23M	**5.22**	.051	.270
SMT (Ritter et al., 2011)	50M	3.60	.098	.351
SMT+neural reranking (Sordoni et al., 2015)	50M	4.44	**.101**	**.358**

Table 2: Performance on the Twitter dataset of 4-layer SEQ2SEQ models and MMI models. *distinct-1* and *distinct-2* are respectively the number of distinct unigrams and bigrams divided by total number of generated words.

For tuning and evaluation, we used the development dataset (2118 conversations) and the test dataset (2114 examples), augmented using information retrieval methods to create a multi-reference set, as described by Sordoni et al. (2015). The selection criteria for these two datasets included a component of relevance/interestingness, with the result that dull responses will tend to be penalized in evaluation.

OpenSubtitles dataset In addition to unscripted Twitter conversations, we also used the OpenSubtitles (OSDb) dataset (Tiedemann, 2009), a large, noisy, open-domain dataset containing roughly 60M-70M scripted lines spoken by movie characters. This dataset does not specify which character speaks each subtitle line, which prevents us from inferring speaker turns. Following Vinyals et al. (2015), we make the simplifying assumption that each line of subtitle constitutes a full speaker turn. Our models are trained to predict the current turn given the preceding ones based on the assumption that consecutive turns belong to the same conversation. This introduces a degree of noise, since consecutive lines may not appear in the same conversation or scene, and may not even be spoken by the same character.

This limitation potentially renders the OSDb dataset unreliable for evaluation purposes. For evaluation purposes, we therefore used data from the Internet Movie Script Database (IMSDB),[7] which explicitly identifies which character speaks each line of the script. This allowed us to identify consecutive message-response pairs spoken by different characters. We randomly selected two subsets as development and test datasets, each containing 2k pairs, with source and target length restricted to the range of [6,18].

---

[7]IMSDB (http://www.imsdb.com/) is a relatively small database of around 0.4 million sentences and thus not suitable for open domain dialogue training.

Model	BLEU	distinct-1	distinct-2
SEQ2SEQ	1.28	0.0056	0.0136
MMI-antiLM	1.74 (+35.9%)	0.0184 (+228%)	0.066 (407%)
MMI-bidi	1.44 (+28.2%)	0.0103 (+83.9%)	0.0303 (+122%)

Table 3: Performance of the SEQ2SEQ baseline and two MMI models on the OpenSubtitles dataset.

5.2 Evaluation

For parameter tuning and final evaluation, we used BLEU (Papineni et al., 2002), which was shown to correlate reasonably well with human judgment on the response generation task (Galley et al., 2015). In the case of the Twitter models, we used multi-reference BLEU. As the IMSDB data is too limited to support extraction of multiple references, only single reference BLEU was used in training and evaluating the OSDb models.

We did not follow Vinyals et al. (2015) in using perplexity as evaluation metric. Perplexity is unlikely to be a useful metric in our scenario, since our proposed model is designed to steer away from the standard SEQ2SEQ model in order to diversify the outputs. We report degree of diversity by calculating the number of distinct unigrams and bigrams in generated responses. The value is scaled by total number of generated tokens to avoid favoring long sentences (shown as *distinct-1* and *distinct-2* in Tables 2 and 3).

5.3 Results

Twitter Dataset We first report performance on Twitter datasets in Table 2, along with results for different models (i.e., *Machine Translation* and *MT+neural reranking*) reprinted from Sordoni et al. (2015) on the same dataset. The baseline is the SEQ2SEQ model with its standard likelihood objective and a beam size of 200. We compare this baseline against greedy-search SEQ2SEQ (Vinyals and Le, 2015), which can help achieve higher diversity by increasing search errors.[8]

Machine Translation is the phrase-based MT system described in (Ritter et al., 2011). MT features include commonly used ones in Moses (Koehn et al., 2007), e.g., forward and backward maximum likelihood "translation" probabilities, word and phrase penalties, linear distortion, etc. For more details, refer to Sordoni et al. (2015).

MT+neural reranking is the phrase-based MT system, reranked using neural models. N-best lists are first generated from the MT system. Recurrent neural models generate scores for N-best list candidates given the input messages. These generated scores are re-incorporated to rerank all the candidates. Additional features to score [1-4]-gram matches between context and response and between message and context (context and message match CMM features) are also employed, as in Sordoni et al. (2015).

MT+neural reranking achieves a BLEU score of 4.44, which to the best of our knowledge represents the previous state-of-the-art performance on this Twitter dataset. Note that *Machine Translation* and *MT+neural reranking* are trained on a much larger dataset of roughly 50 million examples. A significant performance boost is observed from MMI-bidi over baseline SEQ2SEQ, both in terms of BLEU score and diversity.

The beam size of 200 used in our main experiments is quite conservative, and BLEU scores only slightly degrade when reducing beam size to 20. For MMI-bidi, BLEU scores for beam sizes of 200, 50, 20 are respectively 5.90, 5.86, 5.76. A beam size of 20 still produces relatively large N-best lists (173 elements on average) with responses of varying lengths, which offer enough diversity for the $p(S|T)$ model to have a significant effect.

OpenSubtitles Dataset All models achieve significantly lower BLEU scores on this dataset than on the Twitter dataset, primarily because the IMSDB data provides only single references for evaluation. We note, however, that baseline SEQ2SEQ models

Comparator	Gain	95% CI
SMT (Ritter et al., 2011)	0.29	[0.25, 0.32]
SMT+neural reranking	0.28	[0.25, 0.32]
SEQ2SEQ (baseline)	0.11	[0.07, 0.14]
SEQ2SEQ (greedy)	0.08	[0.04, 0.11]

Table 6: MMI-bidi gains over comparator systems, based on pairwise human judgments.

yield lower levels of unigram diversity (*distinct-1*) on the OpenSubtitles dataset than on the Twitter data (0.0056 vs 0.017), which suggests that other factors may be in play. It is likely that movie dialogs are much more concise and information-rich than typical conversations on Twitter, making it harder to match gold-standard responses and causing the learned models to strongly favor safe, conservative responses.

Table 3 shows that the MMI-antiLM model yields a significant performance boost, with a BLEU score increase of up to 36% and a more than 200% jump in unigram diversity. Our interpretation of this huge performance improvement is that the diversity and complexity of input messages lead standard SEQ2SEQ models to generate very conservative responses,[9] which fail to match the more interesting reference strings typical of this dataset. This interpretation is also supported by the fact that the MMI-bidi model does not produce as significant a performance boost as MMI-antiLM. In the case of MMI-bidi, N-best lists generated using standard SEQ2SEQ models remain conservative and uninteresting, attenuating the impact of later reranking. An important potential limitation of MMI-bidi model is thus that its performance hinges on the initial generation of a highly diverse, informative N-best list.

Qualitative Evaluation We employed crowd-sourced judges to provide evaluations for a random sample of 1000 items in the Twitter test dataset. Table 6 shows the results of human evaluations between paired systems. Each output pair was ranked by 5 judges, who were asked to decide which of the two outputs was better. They were instructed to prefer outputs that were more specific (relevant) to the message and preceding context, as opposed to those that

---

[8]Another method would have been to sample from the $p(T|S)$ distribution to increase diversity. While these methods have merits, we think we ought to find a proper objective and optimize it exactly, rather than cope with an inadequate one and add noise to it.

[9]The strings *I don't know*, *I don't know what you are talking about*, *I don't think that is a good idea*, and *Oh my god* constitute 32% percent of all generated responses.

message	SEQ2SEQ	MMI $P(T\mid S) - \lambda P(T)$
I did not get the report from an mi-6 agent.	I don't think that's a good idea.	You did the right thing, did you?
You haven't been given an assignment in this case.	I don't know what you are talking about.	I've been looking all over for you.
I'm losing my grip.	I don't know what you are talking about.	I'm the only one in the world.
I am ready to help.	Come on, come on	I have something we need to talk about.
You programmed me to gather intelligence. That's all I've ever done.	You know that, don't you?	You do have fun, don't you?
I mean, we'd have to talk to him.	I mean, I don't know.	I mean, he's a good guy.
This has nothing to do with him.	You don't know anything about him, do you?	I know him as much.
How come you never say it?	I don't know	Because I don't want to hurt you
He is the one behind this scheme to crash x-net.	I don't know what you are talking about	Yes, he is, isn't he?
How much time do you have here?	I don't know.	Not long enough. Sorry, sir.

Table 4: Responses from the SEQ2SEQ baseline and MMI-antiLM models on the OpenSubtitles dataset.

message	SEQ2SEQ	MMI-bidi
Ohh I've never seen that! How long does it take you guys to learn the drill?	I don't even know.	Like 2 weeks ago!!
You'll know when we sign Heskey in 2 weeks	I'll see what I can do	I sure hope so..
I'm waiting!! I have even got biscuits waiting for you??	I have no idea what you're talking about	I'll send you a pic when I get home xx
My parents actually had touch too much played at their wedding.	I have no idea what you're talking about	How old are they??
Say anything you want... I know you love me and I love you.	I love you so much.	I love you too, baby.
I am off all week next week	What time you going?	What time you going?
How are you doing?	I'm good, thanks.	I'm good, you?

Table 5: Responses from the SEQ2SEQ baseline and MMI-bidi models on the Twitter dataset.

Input: What are you doing?	
1. I've been looking for you.	4. I told you to shut up.
2. I want to talk to you.	5. Get out of here.
3. Just making sure you're OK.	6. I'm looking for a doctor.
Input: What is your name?	
1. Blue!	4. Daniel.
2. Peter.	5. My name is John.
3. Tyler.	6. My name is Robert.
Input: How old are you?	
1. Twenty-eight.	4. Five.
2. Twenty-four.	5. 15.
3. Long.	6. Eight.

Table 7: Examples generated by the MMI-antiLM model on the OpenSubtitles dataset.

systems, as well as the weaker SMT and SMT+RNN baselines. MMI-bidi outperforms SMT in human evaluations *despite* the greater lexical diversity of MT output.

Separately, judges were also asked to rate overall quality of MMI-bidi output over the same 1000-item sample in isolation, each output being evaluated by 7 judges in context using a 5-point scale. The mean rating was 3.84 (median: 3.85, 1st Qu: 3.57, 3rd Qu: 4.14), suggesting that overall MMI-bidi output does appear reasonably acceptable to human judges.[10]

Table 7 presents the N-best candidates generated using the MMI-bidi model for the inputs of Table 1.

were more generic. Ties were permitted. Identical strings were algorithmically assigned the same score. The mean of differences between outputs is shown as the gain for MMI-bidi over the competing system. At a significance level of $\alpha = 0.05$, we find that MMI-bidi outperforms both baseline and greedy SEQ2SEQ

---

[10] In the human evaluations, we asked the annotators to prefer responses that were more specific to the context only when doing the pairwise evaluations of systems. The absolute evaluation was conducted separately (on different days) on the best system, and annotators were asked to evaluate the overall quality of the response, specifically *Provide your impression of overall quality of the response in this particular conversation.*

We see that MMI generates significantly more interesting outputs than SEQ2SEQ.

In Tables 4 and 5, we present responses generated by different models. All examples were randomly sampled (without cherry picking). We see that the baseline SEQ2SEQ model tends to generate reasonable responses to simple messages such as *How are you doing?* or *I love you*. As the complexity of the message increases, however, the outputs switch to more conservative, duller forms, such as *I don't know* or *I don't know what you are talking about*. An occasional answer of this kind might go unnoticed in a natural conversation, but a dialog agent that *always* produces such responses risks being perceived as uncooperative. MMI-bidi models, on the other hand, produce far more diverse and interesting responses.

6 Conclusions

We investigated an issue encountered when applying SEQ2SEQ models to conversational response generation. These models tend to generate safe, commonplace responses (e.g., *I don't know*) regardless of the input. Our analysis suggests that the issue is at least in part attributable to the use of unidirectional likelihood of output (responses) given input (messages). To remedy this, we have proposed using Maximum Mutual Information (MMI) as the objective function. Our results demonstrate that the proposed MMI models produce more diverse and interesting responses, while improving quality as measured by BLEU and human evaluation.

To the best of our knowledge, this paper represents the first work to address the issue of output diversity in the neural generation framework. We have focused on the algorithmic dimensions of the problem. Unquestionably numerous other factors such as grounding, persona (of both user and agent), and intent also play a role in generating diverse, conversationally interesting outputs. These must be left for future investigation. Since the challenge of producing interesting outputs also arises in other neural generation tasks, including image-description generation, question answering, and potentially any task where mutual correspondences must be modeled, the implications of this work extend well beyond conversational response generation.

Acknowledgments

We thank the anonymous reviewers, as well as Dan Jurafsky, Alan Ritter, Stephanie Lukin, George Spithourakis, Alessandro Sordoni, Chris Quirk, Meg Mitchell, Jacob Devlin, Oriol Vinyals, and Dhruv Batra for their comments and suggestions.

References

David Ameixa, Luisa Coheur, Pedro Fialho, and Paulo Quaresma. 2014. Luke, I am your father: dealing with out-of-domain requests by using movies subtitles. In *Intelligent Virtual Agents*, pages 13–21. Springer.

Dzmitry Bahdanau, Kyunghyun Cho, and Yoshua Bengio. 2015. Neural machine translation by jointly learning to align and translate. In *Proc. of the International Conference on Learning Representations (ICLR)*.

L. Bahl, P. Brown, P. de Souza, and R. Mercer. 1986. Maximum mutual information estimation of hidden Markov model parameters for speech recognition. *Acoustics, Speech, and Signal Processing, IEEE International Conference on ICASSP '86.*, pages 49–52.

Rafael E Banchs and Haizhou Li. 2012. IRIS: a chat-oriented dialogue system based on the vector space model. In *Proc. of the ACL 2012 System Demonstrations*, pages 37–42.

Peter F. Brown. 1987. *The Acoustic-modeling Problem in Automatic Speech Recognition*. Ph.D. thesis, Carnegie Mellon University.

Jaime Carbonell and Jade Goldstein. 1998. The use of mmr, diversity-based reranking for reordering documents and producing summaries. In *In Research and Development in Information Retrieval*, pages 335–336.

Yun-Nung Chen, Wei Yu Wang, and Alexander Rudnicky. 2013. An empirical investigation of sparse log-linear models for improved dialogue act classification. In *Proc. of ICASSP*, pages 8317–8321.

Michel Galley, Chris Brockett, Alessandro Sordoni, Yangfeng Ji, Michael Auli, Chris Quirk, Margaret Mitchell, Jianfeng Gao, and Bill Dolan. 2015. ΔBLEU: A discriminative metric for generation tasks with intrinsically diverse targets. In *Proc. of ACL-IJCNLP*, pages 445–450, Beijing, China, July.

Jianfeng Gao, Xiaodong He, Wen-tau Yih, and Li Deng. 2014. Learning continuous phrase representations for translation modeling. In *Proc. of ACL*, pages 699–709.

Kevin Gimpel, Dhruv Batra, Chris Dyer, and Gregory Shakhnarovich. 2013. A systematic exploration of diversity in machine translation. In *Proceedings of the 2013 Conference on Empirical Methods in Natural Language Processing*, pages 1100–1111.

Sepp Hochreiter and Jürgen Schmidhuber. 1997. Long short-term memory. *Neural computation*, 9(8):1735–1780.

Xuedong Huang, Alex Acero, Hsiao-Wuen Hon, and Raj Foreword By-Reddy. 2001. *Spoken language processing: A guide to theory, algorithm, and system development*. Prentice Hall.

Philipp Koehn, Hieu Hoang, Alexandra Birch, Chris Callison-Burch, Marcello Federico, Nicola Bertoldi, Brooke Cowan, Wade Shen, Christine Moran, Richard Zens, Chris Dyer, Ondrej Bojar, Alexandra Constantin, and Evan Herbst. 2007. Moses: Open source toolkit for statistical machine translation. In *Proc. of the 45th Annual Meeting of the Association for Computational Linguistics*, pages 177–180, Prague, Czech Republic, June. Association for Computational Linguistics.

Esther Levin, Roberto Pieraccini, and Wieland Eckert. 2000. A stochastic model of human-machine interaction for learning dialog strategies. *IEEE Transactions on Speech and Audio Processing*, 8(1):11–23.

Thang Luong, Ilya Sutskever, Quoc Le, Oriol Vinyals, and Wojciech Zaremba. 2015. Addressing the rare word problem in neural machine translation. In *Proc. of ACL-IJCNLP*, pages 11–19, Beijing, China.

Junhua Mao, Wei Xu, Yi Yang, Jiang Wang, Zhiheng Huang, and Alan Yuille. 2015. Deep captioning with multimodal recurrent neural networks (m-RNN). *ICLR*.

Lasguido Nio, Sakriani Sakti, Graham Neubig, Tomoki Toda, Mirna Adriani, and Satoshi Nakamura. 2014. Developing non-goal dialog system based on examples of drama television. In *Natural Interaction with Robots, Knowbots and Smartphones*, pages 355–361. Springer.

Franz Josef Och. 2003. Minimum error rate training in statistical machine translation. In *Proceedings of the 41st Annual Meeting of the Association for Computational Linguistics*, pages 160–167, Sapporo, Japan, July. Association for Computational Linguistics.

Alice H Oh and Alexander I Rudnicky. 2000. Stochastic language generation for spoken dialogue systems. In *Proc. of the 2000 ANLP/NAACL Workshop on Conversational systems-Volume 3*, pages 27–32. Association for Computational Linguistics.

Kishore Papineni, Salim Roukos, Todd Ward, and Wei-Jing Zhu. 2002. BLEU: a method for automatic evaluation of machine translation. In *Proc. of ACL*.

Roberto Pieraccini, David Suendermann, Krishna Dayanidhi, and Jackson Liscombe. 2009. Are we there yet? research in commercial spoken dialog systems. In *Text, Speech and Dialogue*, pages 3–13. Springer.

Adwait Ratnaparkhi. 2002. Trainable approaches to surface natural language generation and their application to conversational dialog systems. *Computer Speech & Language*, 16(3):435–455.

Alan Ritter, Colin Cherry, and William Dolan. 2011. Data-driven response generation in social media. In *Proc. of EMNLP*, pages 583–593.

Iulian V Serban, Alessandro Sordoni, Yoshua Bengio, Aaron Courville, and Joelle Pineau. 2015. Hierarchical neural network generative models for movie dialogues. *arXiv preprint arXiv:1507.04808*.

Lifeng Shang, Zhengdong Lu, and Hang Li. 2015. Neural responding machine for short-text conversation. In *ACL-IJCNLP*, pages 1577–1586.

Alessandro Sordoni, Michel Galley, Michael Auli, Chris Brockett, Yangfeng Ji, Meg Mitchell, Jian-Yun Nie, Jianfeng Gao, and Bill Dolan. 2015. A neural network approach to context-sensitive generation of conversational responses. In *Proc. of NAACL-HLT*.

Ilya Sutskever, Oriol Vinyals, and Quoc Le. 2014. Sequence to sequence learning with neural networks. In *Advances in neural information processing systems*, pages 3104–3112.

Jörg Tiedemann. 2009. News from OPUS – a collection of multilingual parallel corpora with tools and interfaces. In *Recent advances in natural language processing*, volume 5, pages 237–248.

Oriol Vinyals and Quoc Le. 2015. A neural conversational model. In *Proc. of ICML Deep Learning Workshop*.

Oriol Vinyals, Lukasz Kaiser, Terry Koo, Slav Petrov, Ilya Sutskever, and Geoffrey Hinton. 2015. Grammar as a foreign language. In *Proc. of NIPS*.

Marilyn A Walker, Rashmi Prasad, and Amanda Stent. 2003. A trainable generator for recommendations in multimodal dialog. In *INTERSPEECH*.

William Yang Wang, Ron Artstein, Anton Leuski, and David Traum. 2011. Improving spoken dialogue understanding using phonetic mixture models. In *FLAIRS*.

Tsung-Hsien Wen, Milica Gasic, Nikola Mrkšić, Pei-Hao Su, David Vandyke, and Steve Young. 2015. Semantically conditioned LSTM-based natural language generation for spoken dialogue systems. In *Proc. of EMNLP*, pages 1711–1721, Lisbon, Portugal, September.

Kelvin Xu, Jimmy Ba, Ryan Kiros, Kyunghyun Cho, Aaron Courville, Ruslan Salakhudinov, Rich Zemel, and Yoshua Bengio. 2015. Show, attend and tell: Neural image caption generation with visual attention. In David Blei and Francis Bach, editors, *Proc. of the 32nd International Conference on Machine Learning (ICML-15)*, pages 2048–2057. JMLR Workshop and Conference Proceedings.

Steve Young, Milica Gašić, Simon Keizer, François Mairesse, Jost Schatzmann, Blaise Thomson, and Kai Yu. 2010. The hidden information state model: A practical framework for POMDP-based spoken dialogue management. *Computer Speech & Language*, 24(2):150–174.

Multi-domain Neural Network Language Generation for Spoken Dialogue Systems

Tsung-Hsien Wen, Milica Gašić, Nikola Mrkšić, Lina M. Rojas-Barahona,
Pei-Hao Su, David Vandyke, Steve Young
Cambridge University Engineering Department,
Trumpington Street, Cambridge, CB2 1PZ, UK
{thw28,mg436,nm480,lmr46,phs26,djv27,sjy}@cam.ac.uk

Abstract

Moving from limited-domain natural language generation (NLG) to open domain is difficult because the number of semantic input combinations grows exponentially with the number of domains. Therefore, it is important to leverage existing resources and exploit similarities between domains to facilitate domain adaptation. In this paper, we propose a procedure to train multi-domain, Recurrent Neural Network-based (RNN) language generators via multiple adaptation steps. In this procedure, a model is first trained on counterfeited data synthesised from an out-of-domain dataset, and then fine tuned on a small set of in-domain utterances with a discriminative objective function. Corpus-based evaluation results show that the proposed procedure can achieve competitive performance in terms of BLEU score and slot error rate while significantly reducing the data needed to train generators in new, unseen domains. In subjective testing, human judges confirm that the procedure greatly improves generator performance when only a small amount of data is available in the domain.

1 Introduction

Modern Spoken Dialogue Systems (SDS) are typically developed according to a well-defined *ontology*, which provides a structured representation of the *domain* data that the dialogue system can talk about, such as searching for a restaurant or shopping for a laptop. Unlike conventional approaches employing a substantial amount of handcrafting for each individual processing component (Ward and Issar, 1994; Bohus and Rudnicky, 2009), statistical approaches to SDS promise a domain-scalable framework which requires a minimal amount of human intervention (Young et al., 2013). Mrkšić et al. (2015) showed improved performance in belief tracking by training a general model and adapting it to specific domains. Similar benefit can be observed in Gašić et al. (2015), in which a Bayesian committee machine (Tresp, 2000) was used to model policy learning in a multi-domain SDS regime.

In past decades, adaptive NLG has been studied from linguistic perspectives, such as systems that learn to tailor user preferences (Walker et al., 2007), convey a specific personality trait (Mairesse and Walker, 2008; Mairesse and Walker, 2011), or align with their conversational partner (Isard et al., 2006). Domain adaptation was first addressed by Hogan et al. (2008) using a generator based on the Lexical Functional Grammar (LFG) f-structures (Kaplan and Bresnan, 1982). Although these approaches can model rich linguistic phenomenon, they are not readily adaptable to data since they still require many handcrafted rules to define the search space. Recently, RNN-based language generation has been introduced (Wen et al., 2015a; Wen et al., 2015b). This class of statistical generators can learn generation decisions directly from dialogue act (DA)-utterance pairs without any semantic annotations (Mairesse and Young, 2014) or hand-coded grammars (Langkilde and Knight, 1998; Walker et al., 2002). Many existing adaptation approaches (Wen et al., 2013; Shi et al., 2015; Chen et al., 2015) can be directly applied due to the

Proceedings of NAACL-HLT 2016, pages 120–129,
San Diego, California, June 12-17, 2016. ©2016 Association for Computational Linguistics

flexibility of the underlying RNN language model (RNNLM) architecture (Mikolov et al., 2010).

Discriminative training (DT) has been successfully used to train RNNs for various tasks. By optimising directly against the desired objective function such as BLEU score (Auli and Gao, 2014) or Word Error Rate (Kuo et al., 2002), the model can explore its output space and learn to discriminate between good and bad hypotheses. In this paper we show that DT can enable a generator to learn more efficiently when in-domain data is scarce.

The paper presents an incremental recipe for training multi-domain language generators based on a purely data-driven, RNN-based generation model. Following a review of related work in section 2, section 3 describes the detailed RNN generator architecture. The data counterfeiting approach for synthesising an in-domain dataset is introduced in section 4, where it is compared to the simple model fine-tuning approach. In section 5, we describe our proposed DT procedure for training natural language generators. Following a brief review of the data sets used in section 6, corpus-based evaluation results are presented in section 7. In order to assess the subjective performance of our system, a quality test and a pairwise preference test are presented in section 8. The results show that the proposed adaptation recipe improves not only the objective scores but also the user's perceived quality of the system. We conclude with a brief summary in section 9.

2 Related Work

Domain adaptation problems arise when we have a sufficient amount of labeled data in one domain (the *source* domain), but have little or no labeled data in another related domain (the *target* domain). Domain adaptability for real world speech and language applications is especially important because both language usage and the topics of interest are constantly evolving. Historically, domain adaptation has been less well studied in the NLG community. The most relevant work was done by Hogan et al. (2008). They showed that an LFG f-structure based generator could yield better performance when trained on in-domain sentences paired with pseudo parse tree inputs generated from a state-of-the-art, but out-of-domain parser. The SPoT-based generator proposed

by Walker et al. (2002) has the potential to address domain adaptation problems. However, their published work has focused on tailoring user preferences (Walker et al., 2007) and mimicking personality traits (Mairesse and Walker, 2011). Lemon (2008) proposed a Reinforcement Learning (RL) framework in which policy and NLG components can be jointly optimised and adapted based on online user feedback. In contrast, Mairesse et al. (2010) has proposed using active learning to mitigate the data sparsity problem when training data-driven NLG systems. Furthermore, Cuayhuitl et al. (2014) trained statistical surface realisers from unlabelled data by an automatic slot labelling technique.

In general, feature-based adaptation is perhaps the most widely used technique (Blitzer et al., 2007; Pan and Yang, 2010; Duan et al., 2012). By exploiting correlations and similarities between data points, it has been successfully applied to problems like speaker adaptation (Gauvain and Lee, 1994; Leggetter and Woodland, 1995) and various tasks in natural language processing (Daumé III, 2009). In contrast, model-based adaptation is particularly useful for language modeling (LM) (Bellegarda, 2004). Mixture-based topic LMs (Gildea and Hofmann, 1999) are widely used in N-gram LMs for domain adaptation. Similar ideas have been applied to applications that require adapting LMs, such as machine translation (MT) (Koehn and Schroeder, 2007) and personalised speech recognition (Wen et al., 2012).

Domain adaptation for Neural Network (NN)-based LMs has also been studied in the past. A feature augmented RNNLM was first proposed by Mikolov and Zweig (2012), but later applied to multi-genre broadcast speech recognition (Chen et al., 2015) and personalised language modeling (Wen et al., 2013). These methods are based on fine-tuning existing network parameters on adaptation data. However, careful regularisation is often necessary (Yu et al., 2013). In a slightly different area, Shi et al. (2015) applied curriculum learning to RNNLM adaptation.

Discriminative training (DT) (Collins, 2002) is an alternative to the maximum likelihood (ML) criterion. For classification, DT can be split into two phases: (1) decoding training examples using the current model and scoring them, and (2) adjusting the model parameters to maximise the separation between the correct target annotation and the competing incorrect annotations. It has been successfully applied to many research problems, such as speech recognition (Kuo et al., 2002; Voigtlaender et al., 2015) and MT (He and Deng, 2012; Auli et al., 2014). Recently, Auli and Gao (2014) trained an RNNLM with a DT objective and showed improved performance on an MT task. However, their RNN probabilities only served as input features to a phrase-based MT system.

3   The Neural Language Generator

The neural language generation model (Wen et al., 2015a; Wen et al., 2015b) is a RNNLM (Mikolov et al., 2010) augmented with semantic input features such as a dialogue act[1] (DA) denoting the required semantics of the generated output. At every time step t, the model consumes the 1-hot representation of both the DA $\mathbf{d}_t$ and a token $\mathbf{w}_t$[2] to update its internal state $\mathbf{h}_t$. Based on this new state, the output distribution over the next output token is calculated. The model can thus generate a sequence of tokens by repeatedly sampling the current output distribution to obtain the next input token until an end-of-sentence sign is generated. Finally, the generated sequence is lexicalised[3] to form the target utterance.

The Semantically Conditioned Long Short-term Memory Network (SC-LSTM) (Wen et al., 2015b) is a specialised extension of the LSTM network (Hochreiter and Schmidhuber, 1997) for language generation which has previously been shown capable of learning generation decisions from paired DA-utterances end-to-end without a modular pipeline (Walker et al., 2002; Stent et al., 2004). Like LSTM, SC-LSTM relies on a vector of memory cells $\mathbf{c}_t \in \mathbb{R}^n$ and a set of elementwise multiplication gates to control how information is stored, forgotten, and exploited inside the network. The SC-LSTM architecture used in this paper is defined by

the following equations,

$$\begin{pmatrix} \mathbf{i}_t \\ \mathbf{f}_t \\ \mathbf{o}_t \\ \mathbf{r}_t \\ \hat{\mathbf{c}}_t \end{pmatrix} = \begin{pmatrix} \text{sigmoid} \\ \text{sigmoid} \\ \text{sigmoid} \\ \text{sigmoid} \\ \text{tanh} \end{pmatrix} \mathbf{W}_{5n,2n} \begin{pmatrix} \mathbf{w}_t \\ \mathbf{h}_{t-1} \end{pmatrix}$$

$$\mathbf{d}_t = \mathbf{r}_t \odot \mathbf{d}_{t-1}$$

$$\mathbf{c}_t = \mathbf{f}_t \odot \mathbf{c}_{t-1} + \mathbf{i}_t \odot \hat{\mathbf{c}}_t + tanh(\mathbf{W}_{dc}\mathbf{d}_t)$$

$$\mathbf{h}_t = \mathbf{o}_t \odot \tanh(\mathbf{c}_t)$$

where n is the hidden layer size, $\mathbf{i}_t, \mathbf{f}_t, \mathbf{o}_t, \mathbf{r}_t \in [0,1]^n$ are input, forget, output, and reading gates respectively, $\hat{\mathbf{c}}_t$ and $\mathbf{c}_t$ are proposed cell value and true cell value at time t, $\mathbf{W}_{5n,2n}$ and $\mathbf{W}_{dc}$ are the model parameters to be learned. The major difference of the SC-LSTM compared to the vanilla LSTM is the introduction of the reading gates for controlling the semantic input features presented to the network. It was shown in Wen et al. (2015b) that these reading gates act like keyword and key phrase detectors that learn the alignments between individual semantic input features and their corresponding realisations without additional supervision.

After the hidden layer state is obtained, the computation of the next word distribution and sampling from it is straightforward,

$$p(w_{t+1}|w_t, w_{t-1}, ...w_0, \mathbf{d}_t) = softmax(\mathbf{W}_{ho}\mathbf{h}_t)$$

$$w_{t+1} \sim p(w_{t+1}|w_t, w_{t-1}, ...w_0, \mathbf{d}_t).$$

where $\mathbf{W}_{ho}$ is another weight matrix to learn. The entire network is trained end-to-end using a cross entropy cost function, between the predicted word distribution $\mathbf{p}_t$ and the actual word distribution $\mathbf{y}_t$, with regularisations on DA transition dynamics,

$$F(\theta) = \sum_t \mathbf{p}_t^\mathsf{T} log(\mathbf{y}_t) + \|\mathbf{d}_\mathsf{T}\| + \sum_{t=0}^{\mathsf{T}-1} \eta \xi^{\|\mathbf{d}_{t+1} - \mathbf{d}_t\|} \quad (1)$$

where $\theta = \{\mathbf{W}_{5n,2n}, \mathbf{W}_{dc}, \mathbf{W}_{ho}\}$, $\mathbf{d}_\mathsf{T}$ is the DA vector at the last index T, and η and ξ are constants set to 10^{-4} and 100, respectively.

4   Training Multi-domain Models

Given training instances (represented by DA and sentence tuples $\{d_i, \Omega_i\}$) from the source domain $\mathbb{S}$ (rich) and the target domain $\mathbb{T}$ (limited), the goal is to find a set of SC-LSTM parameters $\theta_\mathbb{T}$ that can perform acceptably well in the target domain.

---

[1] A combination of an action type and a set of slot-value pairs. e.g. *inform(name="Seven days",food="chinese")*

[2] We use *token* instead of *word* because our model operates on text for which slot values are replaced by their corresponding slot tokens. We call this procedure delexicalisation.

[3] The process of replacing slot token by its value.

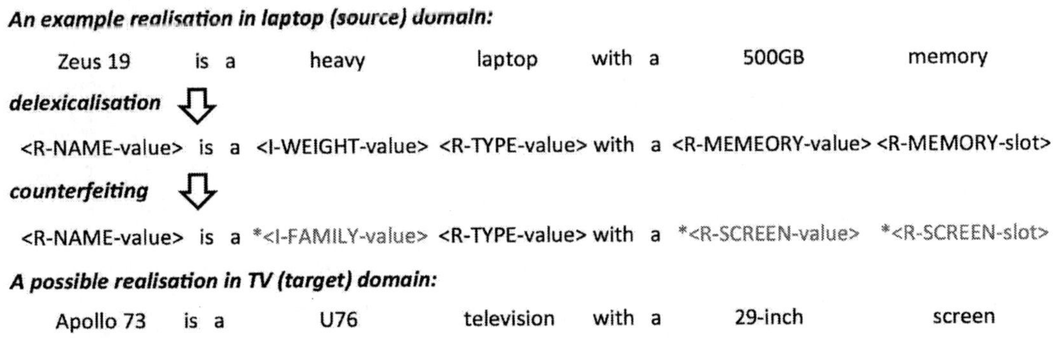

Figure 1: An example of data counterfeiting algorithm. Both slots and values are delexicalised. Slots and values that are not in the target domain are replaced during data counterfeiting (shown in *red* with * sign). The prefix inside bracket <> indicates the slot's functional class (I for *informable* and R for *requestable*).

4.1 Model Fine-Tuning

A straightforward way to adapt NN-based models to a target domain is to continue training or fine-tuning a well-trained generator on whatever new target domain data is available. This training procedure is as follows:

1. Train a source domain generator $\theta_{\mathbb{S}}$ on source domain data $\{d_i, \Omega_i\} \in \mathbb{S}$ with all values delexicalised[4].

2. Divide the adaptation data into training and validation sets. Refine parameters by training on adaptation data $\{d_i, \Omega_i\} \in \mathbb{T}$ with early stopping and a smaller starting learning rate. This yields the target domain generator $\theta_{\mathbb{T}}$.

Although this method can benefit from parameter sharing of the LM part of the network, the parameters of similar input slot-value pairs are not shared[4]. In other words, realisation of any unseen slot-value pair in the target domain can only be learned from scratch. Adaptation offers no benefit in this case.

4.2 Data Counterfeiting

In order to maximise the effect of domain adaptation, the model should be able to (1) generate acceptable realisations for unseen slot-value pairs based on similar slot-value pairs seen in the training data,

and (2) continue to distinguish slot-value pairs that are similar but nevertheless distinct. Instead of exploring weight tying strategies in different training stages (which is complex to implement and typically relies on ad hoc tying rules), we propose instead a data counterfeiting approach to *synthesise* target domain data from source domain data. The procedure is shown in Figure 1 and described as following:

1. Categorise slots in both source and target domain into classes, according to some similarity measure. In our case, we categorise them based on their functional type to yield three classes: *informable*, *requestable*, and *binary*[5].

2. Delexicalise all slots and values.

3. For each slot s in a source instance $(d_i, \Omega_i) \in \mathbb{S}$, randomly select a new slot s' that belongs to both the target ontology and the class of s to replace s. Repeat this process for every slot in the instance and yield a new pseudo instance $(\hat{d}_i, \hat{\Omega}_i) \in \mathbb{T}$ in the target domain.

4. Train a generator $\hat{\theta}_{\mathbb{T}}$ on the counterfeited dataset $\{\hat{d}_i, \hat{\Omega}_i\} \in \mathbb{T}$.

5. Refine parameters on real in-domain data. This yields final model parameters $\theta_{\mathbb{T}}$.

This approach allows the generator to share realisations among slot-value pairs that have similar functionalities, therefore facilitates the transfer learning

---

[4]We have tried training with both slots and values delexicalised and then using the weights to initialise unseen slot-value pairs in the target domain. However, this yielded even worse results since the learned semantic alignment stuck at local minima. Pre-training only the LM parameters did not produce better results either.

[5]*Informable* class include all non-binary informable slots while *binary* class includes all binary informable slots.

	Laptop	Television
informable slots	family, *pricerange, batteryrating, driverange, weightrange, **isforbusinesscomputing**	family, *pricerange, screensizerange, ecorating, hdmiport, **hasusbport**
requestable slots	*name, *type, *price, warranty, battery, design, dimension, utility, weight, platform, memory, drive, processor	*name, *type, *price, resolution, powerconsumption, accessories, color, screensize, audio
act type	*inform, *inform_only_match, *inform_on_match, inform_all, *inform_count, inform_no_info, *recommend, compare, *select, suggest, *confirm, *request, *request_more, *goodbye	

bold=binary slots, *=overlap with SF Restaurant and Hotel domains, all *informable slots* can take "dontcare" value

Table 1: Ontologies for Laptop and TV domains

of rare slot-value pairs in the target domain. Furthermore, the approach also preserves the co-occurrence statistics of slot-value pairs and their realisations. This allows the model to learn the gating mechanism even before adaptation data is introduced.

5 Discriminative Training

In contrast to the traditional ML criteria (Equation 1) whose goal is to maximise the log-likelihood of correct examples, DT aims at separating correct examples from competing incorrect examples. Given a training instance (d_i, Ω_i), the training process starts by generating a set of candidate sentences $Gen(d_i)$ using the current model parameter θ and DA d_i. The discriminative cost function can therefore be written as

$$F(\theta) = -\mathbb{E}[L(\theta)]$$

$$= -\sum_{\Omega \in Gen(d_i)} p_\theta(\Omega|d_i) L(\Omega, \Omega_i) \quad (2)$$

where $L(\Omega, \Omega_i)$ is the scoring function evaluating candidate Ω by taking ground truth Ω_i as reference. $p_\theta(\Omega|d_i)$ is the normalised probability of the candidate and is calculated by

$$p_\theta(\Omega|d_i) = \frac{\exp[\gamma \log p(\Omega|d_i,\theta)]}{\sum_{\Omega' \in Gen(d_i)} \exp[\gamma \log p(\Omega'|d_i,\theta)]} \quad (3)$$

$\gamma \in [0, \infty]$ is a tuned scaling factor that flattens the distribution for $\gamma < 1$ and sharpens it for $\gamma > 1$. The unnormalised candidate likelihood $\log p(\Omega|d_i, \theta)$ is produced by summing token likelihoods from the RNN generator output,

$$\log p(\Omega|d_i, \theta) = \sum_{w_t \in \Omega} \log p(w_t|d_i, \theta) \quad (4)$$

The scoring function $L(\Omega, \Omega_i)$ can be further generalised to take several scoring functions into account

$$L(\Omega, \Omega_i) = \sum_j L_j(\Omega, \Omega_i)\beta_j \quad (5)$$

where β_j is the weight for j-th scoring function. Since the cost function presented here (Equation 2) is differentiable everywhere, back propagation can be applied to calculate the gradients and update parameters directly.

6 Datasets

In order to test our proposed recipe for training multi-domain language generators, we conducted experiments using four different domains: finding a restaurant, finding a hotel, buying a laptop, and buying a television. Datasets for the restaurant and hotel domains have been previously released by Wen et al. (2015b). These were created by workers recruited by Amazon Mechanical Turk (AMT) by asking them to propose an appropriate natural language realisation corresponding to each system dialogue act actually generated by a dialogue system. However, the number of actually occurring DA combinations in the restaurant and hotel domains were rather limited (~200) and since multiple references were collected for each DA, the resulting datasets are not sufficiently diverse to enable the assessment of the generalisation capability of the different training methods over unseen semantic inputs.

In order to create more diverse datasets for the laptop and TV domains, we enumerated all possible combinations of dialogue act types and slots based on the ontology shown in Table 1. This yielded

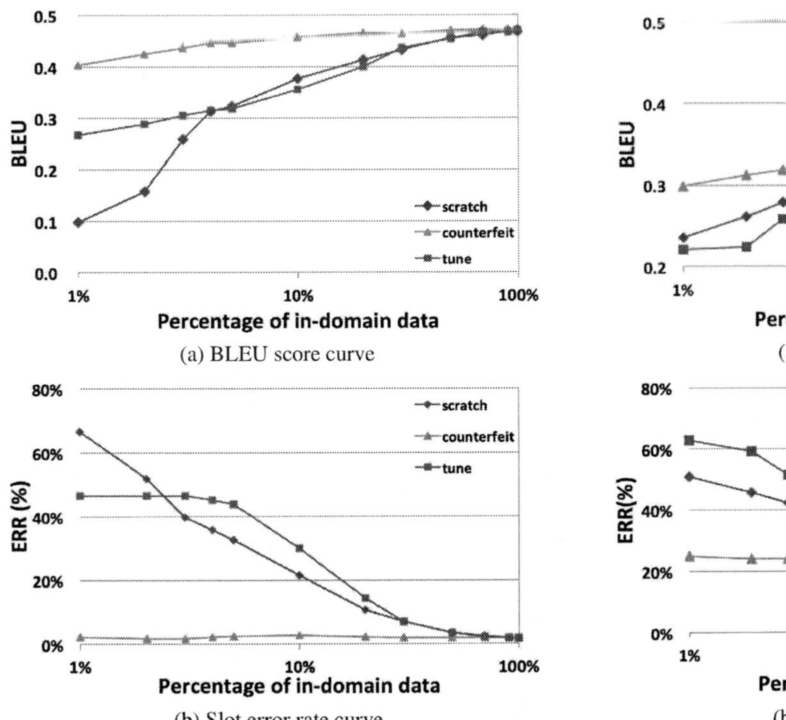

(a) BLEU score curve

(b) Slot error rate curve

Figure 2: Results evaluated on TV domain by adapting models from laptop domain. Comparing train-from-scratch model (*scratch*) with model fine-tuning approach (*tune*) and data counterfeiting method (*counterfeit*). $10\% \approx 700$ examples.

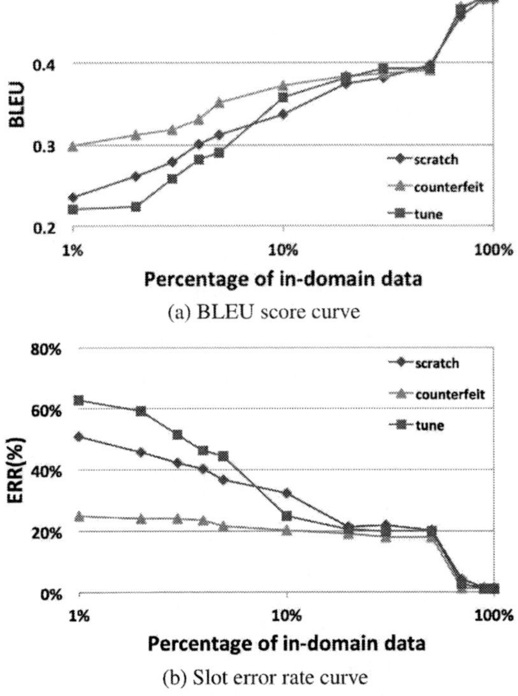

(a) BLEU score curve

(b) Slot error rate curve

Figure 3: The same set of comparison as in Figure 2, but the results were evaluated by adapting from SF restaurant and hotel joint dataset to laptop and TV joint dataset. $10\% \approx 2K$ examples.

about 13K distinct DAs in the laptop domain and 7K distinct DAs in the TV domain. We then used AMT workers to collect just one realisation for each DA. Since the resulting datasets have a much larger input space but only one training example for each DA, the system must learn partial realisations of concepts and be able to recombine and apply them to unseen DAs. Also note that the number of act types and slots of the new ontology is larger, which makes NLG in both laptop and TV domains much harder.

7 Corpus-based Evaluation

We first assess generator performance using two objective evaluation metrics, the BLEU-4 score (Papineni et al., 2002) and slot error rate ERR (Wen et al., 2015b). Slot error rates were calculated by averaging slot errors over each of the top 5 realisations in the entire corpus. We used multiple references to compute the BLEU scores when available (i.e. for the restaurant and hotel domains). In order to better compare results across different methods, we plotted the BLEU and slot error rate curves against different amounts of adaptation data. Note that in the graphs the x-axis is presented on a log-scale.

7.1 Experimental Setup

The generators were implemented using the Theano library (Bergstra et al., 2010; Bastien et al., 2012), and trained by partitioning each of the collected corpora into a training, validation, and testing set in the ratio 3:1:1. All the generators were trained by treating each sentence as a mini-batch. An l_2 regularisation term was added to the objective function for every 10 training examples. The hidden layer size was set to be 100 for all cases. Stochastic gradient descent and back propagation through time (Werbos, 1990) were used to optimise the parameters. In order to prevent overfitting, early stopping was implemented using the validation set.

During decoding, we over-generated 20 utterances and selected the top 5 realisations for each DA according to the following reranking criteria,

$$R = -(F(\theta) + \lambda \text{ERR}) \qquad (6)$$

where λ is a tradeoff constant, $F(\theta)$ is the cost generated by network parameters θ, and the slot error rate ERR is computed by exact matching of the slot tokens in the candidate utterances. λ is set to a large value (10) in order to severely penalise nonsensical outputs. Since our generator works stochastically and the trained networks can differ depending on the initialisation, all the results shown below were averaged over 5 randomly initialised networks.

7.2 Data Counterfeiting

We first compared the data counterfeiting (*counterfeit*) approach with the model fine-tuning (*tune*) method and models trained from scratch (*scratch*). Figure 2 shows the result of adapting models between similar domains, from laptop to TV. Because of the parameter sharing in the LM part of the network, model fine-tuning (*tune*) achieves a better BLEU score than training from scratch (*scratch*) when target domain data is limited. However, if we apply the data counterfeiting (*counterfeit*) method, we obtain an even greater BLEU score gain. This is mainly due to the better realisation of unseen slot-value pairs. On the other hand, data counterfeiting (*counterfeit*) also brings a substantial reduction in slot error rate. This is because it preserves the co-occurrence statistics between slot-value pairs and realisations, which allows the model to learn good semantic alignments even before adaptation data is introduced. Similar results can be seen in Figure 3, in which adaptation was performed on more disjoint domains: restaurant and hotel joint domain to laptop and TV joint domain. The data counterfeiting (*counterfeit*) method is still superior to the other methods.

7.3 Discriminative Training

The generator parameters obtained from data counterfeiting and ML adaptation were further tuned by applying DT. In each case, the models were optimised using two objective functions: BLEU-4 score and slot error rate. However, we used a soft version of BLEU called sentence BLEU as described in Auli and Gao (2014), to mitigate the sparse n-gram match problem of BLEU at the sentence level. In our experiments, we set γ to 5.0 and β_j to 1.0 and -1.0 for

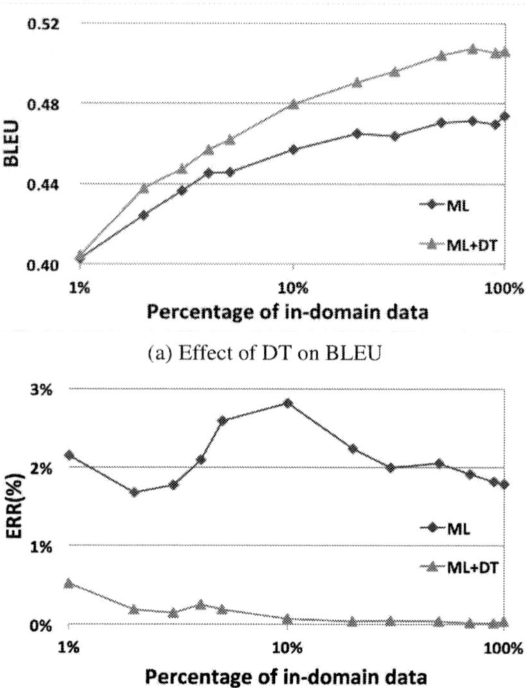

(a) Effect of DT on BLEU

(b) Effect of DT on slot error rate

Figure 4: Effect of applying DT training after ML adaptation. The results were evaluated on laptop to TV adaptation. $10\% \approx 700$ examples.

BLEU and ERR, respectively. For each DA, we applied our generator 50 times to generate candidate sentences. Repeated candidates were removed. We treated the remaining candidates as a single batch and updated the model parameters by the procedure described in section 5. We evaluated performance of the algorithm on the laptop to TV adaptation scenario, and compared models with and without discriminative training (*ML+DT* & *ML*). The results are shown in Figure 4 where it can be seen that DT consistently improves generator performance on both metrics. Another interesting point to note is that slot error rate is easier to optimise compared to BLEU (ERR$\rightarrow 0$ after DT). This is probably because the sentence BLEU optimisation criterion is only an approximation of the corpus BLEU score used for evaluation.

8 Human Evaluation

Since automatic metrics may not consistently agree with human perception (Stent et al., 2005), human testing is needed to assess subjective quality. To do

Method	TV to Laptop		laptop to TV	
	Info.	Nat.	Info.	Nat.
scrALL	2.64	2.37	2.54	2.36
DT-10%	**2.52**[**]	**2.25**[**]	**2.51**	2.19[**]
ML-10%	2.51[**]	2.22[**]	2.45[**]	**2.22**[**]
scr-10%	2.24[**]	2.03[**]	2.00[**]	1.92[**]

* $p < 0.05$, ** $p < 0.005$

Table 2: Human evaluation for utterance quality in two domains. Results are shown in two metrics (rating out of 3). Statistical significance was computed using a two-tailed Student's t-test, between the model trained with full data (*scrALL*) and all others.

Pref.%	scr-10%	ML-10%	DT-10%	scrALL
scr-10%	-	34.5[**]	33.9[**]	22.4[**]
ML-10%	65.5[**]	-	44.9	36.8[**]
DT-10%	66.1[**]	55.1	-	35.9[**]
scrALL	77.6[**]	63.2[**]	64.1[**]	-

* $p < 0.05$, ** $p < 0.005$

(a) Preference test on TV to laptop adaptation scenario

Pref.%	scr-10%	ML-10%	DT-10%	scrALL
scr-10%	-	17.4[**]	14.2[**]	14.8[**]
ML-10%	82.6[**]	-	48.1	37.1[**]
DT-10%	85.8[**]	51.9	-	41.6[*]
scrALL	85.2[**]	62.9[**]	58.4[*]	-

* $p < 0.05$, ** $p < 0.005$

(b) Preference test on laptop to TV adaptation scenario

Table 3: Pairwise preference test among four approaches in two domains. Statistical significance was computed using two-tailed binomial test.

this, a set of judges were recruited using AMT. We tested our models on two adaptation scenarios: laptop to TV and TV to laptop. For each task, two systems among the four were compared: training from scratch using full dataset (*scrALL*), adapting with DT training but only 10% of target domain data (*DT-10%*), adapting with ML training but only 10% of target domain data (*ML-10%*), and training from scratch using only 10% of target domain data (*scr-10%*). In order to evaluate system performance in the presence of language variation, each system generated 5 different surface realisations for each input DA and the human judges were asked to score each of them in terms of informativeness and naturalness (rating out of 3), and also asked to state a preference between the two. Here *informativeness* is defined as whether the utterance contains all the information specified in the DA, and *naturalness* is defined as whether the utterance could plausibly have been produced by a human. In order to decrease the amount of information presented to the judges, utterances that appeared identically in both systems were filtered out. We tested about 2000 DAs for each scenario distributed uniformly between contrasts except that allowed 50% more comparisons between *ML-10%* and *DT-10%* because they were close.

Table 2 shows the subjective quality assessments which exhibit the same general trend as the objective results. If a large amount of target domain data is available, training everything from scratch (*scrALL*) achieves a very good performance and adaptation is not necessary. However, if only a limited amount of in-domain data is available, efficient adaptation is critical (*DT-10% & ML-10% > scr-10%*). More-over, judges also preferred the DT trained generator (*DT-10%*) compared to the ML trained generator (*ML-10%*), especially for *informativeness*. In the laptop to TV scenario, the *informativeness* score of DT method (*DT-10%*) was considered indistinguishable when comparing to the method trained with full training set (*scrALL*). The preference test results are shown in Table 3. Again, adaptation methods (*DT-10% & ML-10%*) are crucial to bridge the gap between domains when the target domain data is scarce (*DT-10% & ML-10% > scr-10%*). The results also suggest that the DT training approach (*DT-10%*) was preferred compared to ML training (*ML-10%*), even though the preference in this case was not statistically significant.

9   Conclusion and Future Work

In this paper we have proposed a procedure for training multi-domain, RNN-based language generators, by data counterfeiting and discriminative training. The procedure is general and applicable to any data-driven language generator. Both corpus-based evaluation and human assessment were performed. Objective measures on corpus data have demonstrated that by applying this procedure to adapt models between four different dialogue domains, good performance can be achieved with much less training data. Subjective assessment by human judges confirm the effectiveness of the approach.

The proposed domain adaptation method requires a small amount of annotated data to be collected offline. In our future work, we intend to focus on training the generator on the fly with real user feedback during conversation.

Acknowledgments

Tsung-Hsien Wen and David Vandyke are supported by Toshiba Research Europe Ltd, Cambridge Research Laboratory.

References

Michael Auli and Jianfeng Gao. 2014. Decoder integration and expected bleu training for recurrent neural network language models. In *Proceedings of ACL*. Association for Computational Linguistics.

Michael Auli, Michel Galley, and Jianfeng Gao. 2014. Large-scale expected bleu training of phrase-based reordering models. In *Proceedings of EMNLP*. Association for Computational Linguistics.

Frédéric Bastien, Pascal Lamblin, Razvan Pascanu, James Bergstra, Ian J. Goodfellow, Arnaud Bergeron, Nicolas Bouchard, and Yoshua Bengio. 2012. Theano: new features and speed improvements. Deep Learning and Unsupervised Feature Learning NIPS 2012 Workshop.

Jerome R. Bellegarda. 2004. Statistical language model adaptation: review and perspectives. *Speech Communication*.

James Bergstra, Olivier Breuleux, Frédéric Bastien, Pascal Lamblin, Razvan Pascanu, Guillaume Desjardins, Joseph Turian, David Warde-Farley, and Yoshua Bengio. 2010. Theano: a CPU and GPU math expression compiler. In *Proceedings of the Python for Scientific Computing Conference*.

John Blitzer, Mark Dredze, and Fernando Pereira. 2007. Biographies, bollywood, boom-boxes and blenders: Domain adaptation for sentiment classification. In *Proceedings of ACL*. Association for Computational Linguistics.

Dan Bohus and Alexander I. Rudnicky. 2009. The ravenclaw dialog management framework: Architecture and systems. *Computer Speech and Language*.

Xie Chen, Tan Tian, Liu Xunying, Lanchantin Pierre, Wan Moquan, Mark Gales, and Woodland Phil. 2015. Recurrent neural network language model adaptation for multi-genre broadcast speech recognition. In *Proceedings of InterSpeech*.

Michael Collins. 2002. Discriminative training methods for hidden markov models: Theory and experiments with perceptron algorithms. In *Proceedings of EMNLP*. Association for Computational Linguistics.

Heriberto Cuayhuitl, Nina Dethlefs, Helen Hastie, and Xingkun Liu. 2014. Training a statistical surface realiser from automatic slot labelling. In *Spoken Language Technology Workshop (SLT), 2014 IEEE*.

Hal Daumé III. 2009. Frustratingly easy domain adaptation. *CoRR*, abs/0907.1815.

Lixin Duan, Dong Xu, and Ivor W. Tsang. 2012. Learning with augmented features for heterogeneous domain adaptation. *CoRR*, abs/1206.4660.

Milica Gašić, Nikola Mrkšić, Pei-hao Su, David Vandyke, Tsung-Hsien Wen, and Steve J. Young. 2015. Policy committee for adaptation in multi-domain spoken dialogue systems. In *Proceedings of ASRU*.

Jean-Luc Gauvain and Chin-Hui Lee. 1994. Maximum a posteriori estimation for multivariate gaussian mixture observations of markov chains. *Speech and Audio Processing, IEEE Transactions on*.

Daniel Gildea and Thomas Hofmann. 1999. Topic-based language models using em. In *Proceedings of EuroSpeech*.

Xiaodong He and Li Deng. 2012. Maximum expected bleu training of phrase and lexicon translation models. In *Proceedings of ACL*. Association for Computational Linguistics.

Sepp Hochreiter and Jürgen Schmidhuber. 1997. Long short-term memory. *Neural Computation*.

Deirdre Hogan, Jennifer Foster, Joachim Wagner, and Josef van Genabith. 2008. Parser-based retraining for domain adaptation of probabilistic generators. In *Proceedings of INLG*. Association for Computational Linguistics.

Amy Isard, Carsten Brockmann, and Jon Oberlander. 2006. Individuality and alignment in generated dialogues. In *Proceedings of INLG*. Association for Computational Linguistics.

Ronald M. Kaplan and Joan Bresnan. 1982. Lexical-Functional Grammar: a formal system for grammatical representation. In Joan Bresnan, editor, *The mental representation of grammatical relations*. MIT Press.

Philipp Koehn and Josh Schroeder. 2007. Experiments in domain adaptation for statistical machine translation. In *Proceedings of StatMT*. Association for Computational Linguistics.

Hong-kwang Kuo, Eric Fosler-lussier, Hui Jiang, and Chin-hui Lee. 2002. Discriminative training of language models for speech recognition. In *Proceedings of ICASSP*.

Irene Langkilde and Kevin Knight. 1998. Generation that exploits corpus-based statistical knowledge. In *Proceedings of ACL*. Association for Computational Linguistics.

Chris Leggetter and Philip Woodland. 1995. Maximum likelihood linear regression for speaker adaptation of continuous density hidden Markov models. *Computer Speech and Language*.

Oliver Lemon. 2008. Adaptive natural language generation in dialogue using reinforcement learning. In *Proceedings of SemDial*.

Franois Mairesse and Marilyn Walker. 2008. Trainable generation of big-five personality styles through data-driven parameter estimation. In *Proceedings of ACL*. Association for Computational Linguistics.

François Mairesse and Marilyn A. Walker. 2011. Controlling user perceptions of linguistic style: Trainable generation of personality traits. *Computer Linguistics*.

François Mairesse and Steve Young. 2014. Stochastic language generation in dialogue using factored language models. *Computer Linguistics*.

François Mairesse, Milica Gašić, Filip Jurčíček, Simon Keizer, Blaise Thomson, Kai Yu, and Steve Young. 2010. Phrase-based statistical language generation using graphical models and active learning. In *Proceedings of ACL*. Association for Computational Linguistics.

Tomáš Mikolov and Geoffrey Zweig. 2012. Context dependent recurrent neural network language model. In *Proceedings of SLT*.

Tomáš Mikolov, Martin Karafit, Lukáš Burget, Jan Černocký, and Sanjeev Khudanpur. 2010. Recurrent neural network based language model. In *Proceedings of InterSpeech*.

Nikola Mrkšić, Diarmuid Ó Séaghdha, Blaise Thomson, Milica Gašić, Pei-Hao Su, David Vandyke, Tsung-Hsien Wen, and Steve Young. 2015. Multi-domain Dialog State Tracking using Recurrent Neural Networks. In *Proceedings of ACL*.

Sinno Jialin Pan and Qiang Yang. 2010. A survey on transfer learning. *IEEE Trans. on Knowledge and Data Engineering*.

Kishore Papineni, Salim Roukos, Todd Ward, and Wei-Jing Zhu. 2002. Bleu: a method for automatic evaluation of machine translation. In *Proceedings of ACL*. Association for Computational Linguistics.

Yangyang Shi, Martha Larson, and Catholijn M. Jonker. 2015. Recurrent neural network language model adaptation with curriculum learning. *Computer, Speech and Language*.

Amanda Stent, Rashmi Prasad, and Marilyn Walker. 2004. Trainable sentence planning for complex information presentation in spoken dialog systems. In *Proceedings of ACL*. Association for Computational Linguistics.

Amanda Stent, Matthew Marge, and Mohit Singhai. 2005. Evaluating evaluation methods for generation in the presence of variation. In *Proceedings of CICLing 2005*.

Volker Tresp. 2000. A bayesian committee machine. *Neural Computation*.

Paul Voigtlaender, Patrick Doetsch, Simon Wiesler, Ralf Schluter, and Hermann Ney. 2015. Sequence-discriminative training of recurrent neural networks. In *Proceedings of ICASSP*.

Marilyn A Walker, Owen C Rambow, and Monica Rogati. 2002. Training a sentence planner for spoken dialogue using boosting. *Computer Speech and Language*.

Marilyn Walker, Amanda Stent, Franois Mairesse, and Rashmi Prasad. 2007. Individual and domain adaptation in sentence planning for dialogue. *Journal of Artificial Intelligence Research (JAIR)*.

Wayne Ward and Sunil Issar. 1994. Recent improvements in the cmu spoken language understanding system. In *Proceedings of Workshop on HLT*. Association for Computational Linguistics.

Tsung-Hsien Wen, Hung-Yi Lee, Tai-Yuan Chen, and Lin-Shan Lee. 2012. Personalized language modeling by crowd sourcing with social network data for voice access of cloud applications. In *Proceedings of SLT*.

Tsung-Hsien Wen, Aaron Heidel, Hung yi Lee, Yu Tsao, and Lin-Shan Lee. 2013. Recurrent neural network based language model personalization by social network crowdsourcing. In *Proceedings of InterSpeech*.

Tsung-Hsien Wen, Milica Gašić, Dongho Kim, Nikola Mrkšić, Pei-Hao Su, David Vandyke, and Steve Young. 2015a. Stochastic language generation in dialogue using recurrent neural networks with convolutional sentence reranking. In *Proceedings of SIGdial*. Association for Computational Linguistics.

Tsung-Hsien Wen, Milica Gašić, Nikola Mrkšić, Pei-Hao Su, David Vandyke, and Steve Young. 2015b. Semantically conditioned lstm-based natural language generation for spoken dialogue systems. In *Proceedings of EMNLP*. Association for Computational Linguistics.

Paul J Werbos. 1990. Backpropagation through time: what it does and how to do it. *Proceedings of the IEEE*.

Steve Young, Milica Gašić, Blaise Thomson, and Jason D. Williams. 2013. Pomdp-based statistical spoken dialog systems: A review. *Proceedings of the IEEE*.

Dong Yu, Kaisheng Yao, Hang Su, Gang Li, and Frank Seide. 2013. Kl-divergence regularized deep neural network adaptation for improved large vocabulary speech recognition. In *Proceedings of ICASSP*.

A Long Short-Term Memory Framework for Predicting Humor in Dialogues

Dario Bertero and **Pascale Fung**
Human Language Technology Center
Department of Electronic and Computer Engineering
The Hong Kong University of Science and Technology
Clear Water Bay, Hong Kong
dbertero@connect.ust.hk, pascale@ece.ust.hk

Abstract

We propose a first-ever attempt to employ a Long Short-Term memory based framework to predict humor in dialogues. We analyze data from a popular TV-sitcom, whose canned laughters give an indication of when the audience would react. We model the setup-punchline relation of conversational humor with a Long Short-Term Memory, with utterance encodings obtained from a Convolutional Neural Network. Out neural network framework is able to improve the F-score of 8% over a Conditional Random Field baseline. We show how the LSTM effectively models the setup-punchline relation reducing the number of false positives and increasing the recall. We aim to employ our humor prediction model to build effective empathetic machine able to understand jokes.

1 Introduction

There has been many recent attempts to detect and understand humor, irony and sarcasm from sentences, usually taken from Twitter (Reyes et al., 2013; Barbieri and Saggion, 2014; Riloff et al., 2013; Joshi et al., 2015), customer reviews (Reyes and Rosso, 2012) or generic canned jokes (Yang et al., 2015). Bamman and Smith (2015) and Karoui et al. (2015) included the surrounding context.

Our work has a different focus from the above. We analyze transcripts of funny dialogues, a genre somehow neglected but important for human-robot interaction. Laughter is the natural reaction of people to a verbal or textual humorous stimulus. We want to predict when the audience would laugh.

Compared to a typical canned joke or a sarcastic Tweet, a dialog utterance is perceived as funny only in relation to the dialog context and the past history. In a spontaneous setting a funny dialog is usually built through a setup which prepares the audience to receive the humorous discourse stimuli, followed by a punchline which releases the tension and triggers the laughter reaction (Attardo, 1997; Taylor and Mazlack, 2005). Automatic understanding of a humorous dialog is a first step to build an effective empathetic machine fully able to react to the user's humor and to other discourse stimuli. We are ultimately interested in developing robots that can bond with humans better (Devillers et al., 2015).

As a source of situational humor we study a popular TV sitcom: "The Big Bang Theory". The domain of sitcoms is of interest as it provides a full dialog setting, together with an indication of when the audience is expected to laugh, given by the background canned laughters. An example of dialog from this sitcom, as well as of the setup-punchline schema, is shown below (punchlines in bold):

PENNY: *Okay, Sheldon, what can I get you?*
SHELDON: *Alcohol.*
PENNY: *Could you be a little more specific?*
SHELDON: ***Ethyl alcohol.*** **LAUGH** ***Forty milliliters.*** **LAUGH**
PENNY: *I'm sorry, honey, I don't know milliliters.*
SHELDON: ***Ah. Blame President James Jimmy Carter.*** **LAUGH** ***He started America on a path to the metric system***

Proceedings of NAACL-HLT 2016, pages 130–135,
San Diego, California, June 12-17, 2016. ©2016 Association for Computational Linguistics

but then just gave up. **LAUGH**

The utterances before the punchline are the setup. Without them, the punchlines may not be perceived as humorous (the last utterance, out of context, may be a political complaint), only with proper setup a laughter would be triggered. The humorous intent is also strengthen by the fact the dialog takes place in a bar (evident from the previous and following utterances), where a request of 40 ml of "Ethyl Alcohol" is unusual and weird.

Our previous attempts on the same corpus (Bertero and Fung, 2016b; Bertero and Fung, 2016a) showed that using a bag-of-ngram representation over a sliding window or a simple RNN to capture the contextual information of the setup was not ideal. For this reason we propose a method based on a Long Short-Term Memory network (Hochreiter and Schmidhuber, 1997), where we encode each sentence through a Convolutional Neural Network (Collobert et al., 2011). LSTM is successfully used in context-dependent sequential classification tasks such as speech recognition (Graves et al., 2013), dependency parsing (Dyer et al., 2015) and conversation modelling (Shang et al., 2015). This is also to our knowledge the first-ever attempt that a LSTM is applied to humor response prediction or general humor detection tasks.

2 Methodology

We employ a supervised classification method to detect when punchlines occur. The bulk of our classifier is made of a concatenation of a Convolutional Neural Network (Collobert et al., 2011) to encode each utterance, followed by a Long Short-Term Memory (Hochreiter and Schmidhuber, 1997) to model the sequential context of the dialog. Before the output softmax layer we add a vector of higher level syntactic, structural and sentiment features. A framework diagram is shown in Figure 1.

2.1 Convolutional Neural Network for each utterance

The first stage of our classifier is represented by a Convolutional Neural Network (Collobert et al., 2011). Low-level, high-dimensional input feature vectors are fed into a first embedding layer to obtain a low dimensional dense vector. A sliding window is

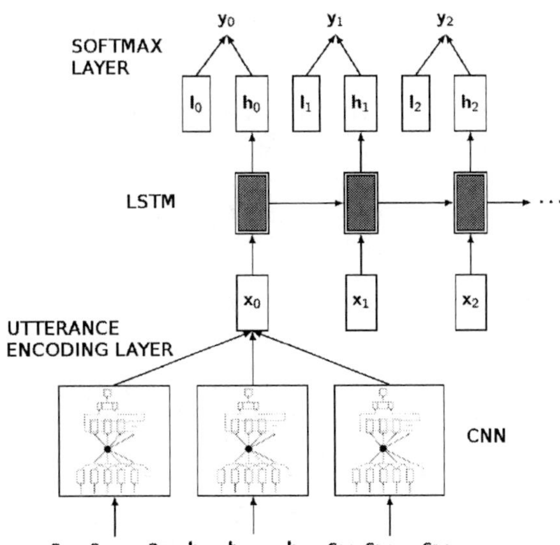

Figure 1: Framework diagram. $\mathbf{a}_t$, $\mathbf{b}_t$ and $\mathbf{c}_t$ are the CNN three input features (words, word2vec and character trigrams). $\mathbf{l}_t$ are the high level feature vectors, and $\mathbf{y}_t$ the outputs for each utterance.

then moved on these vectors and another layer is applied to each group of token vectors, in order to capture the local context of each token. A max-pooling operation is then applied to extract the most salient features of all the tokens into a single vector for the whole utterance. An additional layer is used to generalize and distribute each feature to its full range before obtaining the final utterance vector.

In our task we use three input features:

1. Word tokens: each utterance token is represented as a one-hot vector. This feature models how much each word is likely to trigger humor in the specific corpus.

2. Character trigrams: each token is represented as a bag-of-character-trigrams vector. The feature models the role of the word signifier and removes the influence of the word stems.

3. Word2Vec: we extract for each token a word vector from word2vec (Mikolov et al., 2013), trained on the text9 Wikipedia corpus[1]. This representation models the general semantic

---

[1]Extension of the text8 corpus, obtained from http://mattmahoney.net/dc/textdata

meanings, and matches words that do not appear to others similar in meaning.

The convolution and max-pooling operation is applied individually to each feature, and the three vectors obtained are then concatenated together and fed to the final sentence encoding layer, which combines all the contributions.

2.2 Long/Short Term Memory for the utterance sequence

The LSTM is an improvement over the Recurrent Neural Network aimed to improve its memory capabilities. In a standard RNN the hidden memory layer is updated through a function of the input and the hidden layer at the previous time instant:

$$\mathbf{h}_t = \tanh(\mathbf{W}_x \mathbf{x}_t + \mathbf{W}_h \mathbf{h}_{t-1} + \mathbf{b}) \qquad (1)$$

where $\mathbf{x}$ is the network input and $\mathbf{b}$ the bias term. This kind of connection is not very effective to maintain the information stored for long time instants, as well as it does not allow to forget unneeded information between two time steps. The LSTM enhances the RNN with a series of three multiplicative gates. The structure is the following:

$$\mathbf{i}_t = \sigma(\mathbf{W}_{i_x}\mathbf{x}_t + \mathbf{W}_{i_h}\mathbf{h}_{t-1} + \mathbf{b}_i) \qquad (2)$$
$$\mathbf{f}_t = \sigma(\mathbf{W}_{f_x}\mathbf{x}_t + \mathbf{W}_{f_h}\mathbf{h}_{t-1} + \mathbf{b}_f) \qquad (3)$$
$$\mathbf{o}_t = \sigma(\mathbf{W}_{o_x}\mathbf{x}_t + \mathbf{W}_{o_h}\mathbf{h}_{t-1} + \mathbf{b}_o) \qquad (4)$$
$$\mathbf{s}_t = \tanh(\mathbf{W}_{s_x}\mathbf{x}_t + \mathbf{W}_{s_h}\mathbf{h}_{t-1} + \mathbf{b}_h) \qquad (5)$$
$$\mathbf{c}_t = \mathbf{f}_t \odot \mathbf{c}_{t-1} + \mathbf{i}_t \odot \mathbf{s}_t \qquad (6)$$
$$\mathbf{h}_t = \tanh(\mathbf{c}_t) \odot \mathbf{o}_t \qquad (7)$$

where $\odot$ is the element-wise product. Each gate factor is able to let through or suppress a specific update contribution, thus allowing a selective information retaining. The input gate $\mathbf{i}$ is applied to the cell input $\mathbf{s}$, the forget gate $\mathbf{f}$ to the cell value at the previous time step $\mathbf{c}_{t-1}$, and the output gate $\mathbf{o}$ to the cell output for the current time instant $\mathbf{h}_t$. In this way a cell value can be retained for multiple time steps when $\mathbf{i} = 0$, ignored in the output when $\mathbf{o} = 0$, and forgotten when $\mathbf{f} = 0$.

As dialog utterances are sequential, we feed all utterance vectors of a sitcom scene in sequence into a Long Short-Term Memory block to incorporate contextual information. The memory unit of the LSTM keeps track of the context in each scene, and mimics human memory to accumulate the setup that may trigger a punchline.

Before the output we incorporate a set of high level features from our previous work (Bertero and Fung, 2016b) and past literature (Reyes et al., 2013; Barbieri and Saggion, 2014). They include:

- Structural features: average word length, sentence length, difference in sentence length with the five previous utterances.

- Part of speech proportion: noun, verbs, adjectives and adverbs.

- Antonyms: proportion of antonym words with the previous utterance (from WordNet (Miller, 1995)).

- Sentiment: positive, negative and average sentiment score among all words (from SentiWordNet (Esuli and Sebastiani, 2006)).

- Speaker and turn: speaker character identity and utterance position in the turn (beginning, middle, end, isolated).

- Speaking rate: time duration of the utterance from the subtitle files, divided by the sentence length.

All these features are concatenated to the LSTM output, and a softmax layer is applied to get the final output probabilities.

3 Experiments

3.1 Corpus

We built a corpus from the popular TV-sitcom "The Big Bang Theory", seasons 1 to 6. We downloaded the subtitle files (annotated with the timestamps of each utterance) and the scripts[2], used to segment all the episodes into scenes and get the speaker identity of each utterance. We extracted the audio track of each episode in order to retrieve the canned laughters timestamps, with a vocal removal tool followed by a silence/sound detector. We then annotated each utterance as a punchline in case it was followed by a laughter within $1s$, assuming that utterances not

---

[2]From bigbangtrans.wordpress.com

Classifier and features	Accuracy	Precision	Recall	F-score
CRF n-grams	61.8	56.8	45.1	50.2
CRF language features	67.8	**67.5**	47.8	56.0
CRF n-grams + language features	65.9	61.2	55.3	58.1
LSTM	63.1	56.7	58.7	57.6
LSTM + high level features	**70.0**	66.7	**59.4**	**62.9**

Table 1: Results, percentage.

Encoding stage	A	P	R	F1
CNN	70.0	66.7	59.4	**62.9**
LSTM	68.4	66.2	53.4	59.1

Table 2: Comparison between a CNN and a LSTM sentence encoding input.

followed by a laughter would be the setup for the punchline.

We obtained a total of 135 episodes, 1589 overall scenes, 42.8% of punchlines, and an average interval between two punchlines of 2.2 utterances. We built a training set of 80% of the overall episodes, and a development and test set of 10% each. The episodes were drawn from all the seasons with the same proportion. The total number of utterances is 35865 for the training set, 3904 for the development set and 3903 for the test set.

3.2 Experimental setup and baseline

In the neural network we set the size to 100 for all the hidden layers of the CNN and the LSTM, and 5 to the convolutional window. We applied a dropout regularization layer (Srivastava et al., 2014) after the output of the LSTM, and L2 regularization on the softmax output layer. The network was trained with standard backpropagation, using each scene as a training unit. The development set was used to tune the hyperparameters, and to determine the early stopping condition. When the error on the development set began to increase for the first time we kept training only the final softmax layer, this improved the overall results. The neural network was implemented with THEANO toolkit (Bergstra et al., 2010). We ran experiments with and without the extra high-level feature vector.

As a baseline for comparison we used an implementation of the Conditional Random Field (Lafferty et al., 2001) from CRFSuite (Okazaki, 2007), with L2 regularization. We ran experiments using

the same high level feature vector added at the end of the neural network, 1-2-3gram features of a window made by the utterance and the four previous, and the two feature sets combined. We also compared the overall system where we replace the CNN with an LSTM sentence encoder (Li et al., 2015), where we kept the same input features.

3.3 Results and discussion

Results of our system and our baselines are shown in table 1. The LSTM with the aid of the high level feature vector generally outperformed all the CRF baselines with the highest accuracy of 70.0% and the highest F-score of 62.9%. The biggest improvement of the LSTM is the improvement of the recall without affecting too much the precision. Lexical features given by n-gram from a context window are very useful to recognize more punchlines in our baseline experiment, but they also yield many false positives, when the same n-gram is used in different contexts. A CNN-LSTM network seems to overcome this issue as the CNN stage is better in modeling the lexical and semantic content of the utterance, as the LSTM allows to put each utterance in relation with the past context, filtering out many false positives from wrong contexts.

The choice of the CNN is further justified by the results obtained from the comparison between the CNN and the LSTM sentence encoding input, shown in table 2. The CNN is more effective, obtaining a recall of 10% higher and 6% more in F-score. The CNN is a simpler model that might benefit more of a small-size corpus. It also required a much shorter training time compared to the LSTM. We may consider in the future to use more data, and try other sentence input encoders, including deeper or bi-directional LSTMs, to find the most effective one.

Predicting humor response from the canned

laughters is a particularly challenging task. In some cases canned laughters are inserted by the show producers with the purpose of solicit response to weak jokes, where otherwise people would not laugh. The audience must also be kept constantly amused, extra canned laughters may help in scenes where fewer jokes are used.

4 Conclusion and future work

We proposed a Long Short-Term Memory based framework to predict punchlines in a humorous dialog. We showed that our neural network is particularly effective in increasing the F-score to 62.9% over a Conditional Random Field baseline of 58.1%. We furthermore showed that the LSTM is more effective in obtaining an higher recall with fewer false positives compared to simple n-gram shifting context window features.

As future work we plan to use a virtual agent system to collect a set of human-robot humorous interactions, and adapt our model to predict humor from them.

Acknowledgments

This work was partially funded by the Hong Kong Phd Fellowship Scheme, and partially by grant #16214415 of the Hong Kong Research Grants Council.

References

Salvatore Attardo. 1997. The semantic foundations of cognitive theories of humor. *Humor-International Journal of Humor Research*, (10):395–420.

David Bamman and Noah A Smith. 2015. Contextualized sarcasm detection on twitter. In *Ninth International AAAI Conference on Web and Social Media*.

Francesco Barbieri and Horacio Saggion. 2014. Modelling irony in twitter. In *Proceedings of the Student Research Workshop at the 14th Conference of the European Chapter of the Association for Computational Linguistics*, pages 56–64.

James Bergstra, Olivier Breuleux, Frédéric Bastien, Pascal Lamblin, Razvan Pascanu, Guillaume Desjardins, Joseph Turian, David Warde-Farley, and Yoshua Bengio. 2010. Theano: a CPU and GPU math expression compiler. In *Proceedings of the Python for Scientific Computing Conference (SciPy)*, June. Oral Presentation.

Dario Bertero and Pascale Fung. 2016a. Deep learning of audio and language features for humor prediction. *International Conference on Language Resources and Evaluation (LREC) 2016*.

Dario Bertero and Pascale Fung. 2016b. Predicting humor response in dialogues from TV sitcoms. In *Acoustics, Speech and Signal Processing (ICASSP), 2016 IEEE International Conference on*.

Ronan Collobert, Jason Weston, Léon Bottou, Michael Karlen, Koray Kavukcuoglu, and Pavel Kuksa. 2011. Natural language processing (almost) from scratch. *The Journal of Machine Learning Research*, 12:2493–2537.

Laurence Devillers, Sophie Rosset, Guillaume Dubuisson Duplessis, Mohamed A Sehili, Lucile Béchade, Agnes Delaborde, Clément Gossart, Vincent Letard, Fan Yang, Yucel Yemez, et al. 2015. Multimodal data collection of human-robot humorous interactions in the joker project. In *Affective Computing and Intelligent Interaction (ACII), 2015 International Conference on*, pages 348–354. IEEE.

Chris Dyer, Miguel Ballesteros, Wang Ling, Austin Matthews, and Noah A. Smith. 2015. Transition-based dependency parsing with stack long short-term memory. In *Proceedings of the 53rd Annual Meeting of the Association for Computational Linguistics and the 7th International Joint Conference on Natural Language Processing (Volume 1: Long Papers)*, pages 334–343, Beijing, China, July. Association for Computational Linguistics.

Andrea Esuli and Fabrizio Sebastiani. 2006. Sentiwordnet: A publicly available lexical resource for opinion mining. In *Proceedings of LREC*, volume 6, pages 417–422.

Alan Graves, Abdel-rahman Mohamed, and Geoffrey Hinton. 2013. Speech recognition with deep recurrent neural networks. In *Acoustics, Speech and Signal Processing (ICASSP), 2013 IEEE International Conference on*, pages 6645–6649. IEEE.

Sepp Hochreiter and Jürgen Schmidhuber. 1997. Long short-term memory. *Neural computation*, 9(8):1735–1780.

Aditya Joshi, Vinita Sharma, and Pushpak Bhattacharyya. 2015. Harnessing context incongruity for sarcasm detection. In *Proceedings of the 53rd Annual Meeting of the Association for Computational Linguistics and the 7th International Joint Conference on Natural Language Processing*, volume 2, pages 757–762.

Jihen Karoui, Benamara Farah, Véronique Moriceau, Nathalie Aussenac-Gilles, and Lamia Hadrich-Belguith. 2015. Towards a contextual pragmatic model to detect irony in tweets. In *Proceedings of the 53rd Annual Meeting of the Association for Computational Linguistics and the 7th International Joint*

Conference on Natural Language Processing (Volume 2: Short Papers), pages 644–650, Beijing, China, July. Association for Computational Linguistics.

John D. Lafferty, Andrew McCallum, and Fernando C. N. Pereira. 2001. Conditional random fields: Probabilistic models for segmenting and labeling sequence data. In *Proceedings of the Eighteenth International Conference on Machine Learning*, ICML '01, pages 282–289, San Francisco, CA, USA. Morgan Kaufmann Publishers Inc.

Jiwei Li, Minh-Thang Luong, and Dan Jurafsky. 2015. A hierarchical neural autoencoder for paragraphs and documents. *arXiv preprint arXiv:1506.01057*.

Tomas Mikolov, Kai Chen, Greg Corrado, and Jeffrey Dean. 2013. Efficient estimation of word representations in vector space. *CoRR*, abs/1301.3781.

George A Miller. 1995. Wordnet: a lexical database for english. *Communications of the ACM*, 38(11):39–41.

Naoaki Okazaki. 2007. Crfsuite: a fast implementation of conditional random fields (crfs). *URL http://www.chokkan.org/software/crfsuite*.

Antonio Reyes and Paolo Rosso. 2012. Making objective decisions from subjective data: Detecting irony in customer reviews. *Decision Support Systems*, 53(4):754–760.

Antonio Reyes, Paolo Rosso, and Tony Veale. 2013. A multidimensional approach for detecting irony in twitter. *Language Resources and Evaluation*, 47(1):239–268.

Ellen Riloff, Ashequl Qadir, Prafulla Surve, Lalindra De Silva, Nathan Gilbert, and Ruihong Huang. 2013. Sarcasm as contrast between a positive sentiment and negative situation. In *EMNLP*, pages 704–714.

Lifeng Shang, Zhengdong Lu, and Hang Li. 2015. Neural responding machine for short-text conversation. *arXiv preprint arXiv:1503.02364*.

Nitish Srivastava, Geoffrey Hinton, Alex Krizhevsky, Ilya Sutskever, and Ruslan Salakhutdinov. 2014. Dropout: A simple way to prevent neural networks from overfitting. *The Journal of Machine Learning Research*, 15(1):1929–1958.

Julia Taylor and Lawrence Mazlack. 2005. Toward computational recognition of humorous intent. In *Proceedings of Cognitive Science Conference*, pages 2166–2171.

Diyi Yang, Alon Lavie, Chris Dyer, and Eduard Hovy. 2015. Humor recognition and humor anchor extraction. In *Proceedings of the 2015 Conference on Empirical Methods in Natural Language Processing*, pages 2367–2376, Lisbon, Portugal, September. Association for Computational Linguistics.

Conversational Flow in Oxford-style Debates

Justine Zhang,[1] **Ravi Kumar,**[2] **Sujith Ravi,**[2] **Cristian Danescu-Niculescu-Mizil**[1]
[1]Cornell University, [2]Google

jz727@cornell.edu, ravi.k53@gmail.com,
ravi.sujith@gmail.com, cristian@cs.cornell.edu

Abstract

Public debates are a common platform for presenting and juxtaposing diverging views on important issues. In this work we propose a methodology for tracking how ideas flow between participants throughout a debate. We use this approach in a case study of Oxford-style debates—a competitive format where the winner is determined by audience votes—and show how the outcome of a debate depends on aspects of conversational flow. In particular, we find that winners tend to make better use of a debate's interactive component than losers, by actively pursuing their opponents' points rather than promoting their own ideas over the course of the conversation.

1   Introduction

Public debates are a common platform for presenting and juxtaposing diverging viewpoints. As opposed to monologues where speakers are limited to expressing their own beliefs, debates allow for participants to interactively attack their opponents' points while defending their own. The resulting flow of ideas is a key feature of this conversation genre.

In this work we introduce a computational framework for characterizing debates in terms of conversational flow. This framework captures two main debating strategies—promoting one's own points and attacking the opponents' points—and tracks their relative usage throughout the debate. By applying this methodology to a setting where debate winners are known, we show that conversational flow patterns are predictive of which debater is more likely to persuade an audience.

Case study: Oxford-style debates. Oxford-style debates provide a setting that is particularly convenient for studying the effects of conversational flow. In this competitive debate format, two teams argue for or against a preset motion in order to persuade a live audience to take their position. The audience votes before and after the debate, and the winning team is the one that sways more of the audience towards its view. This setup allows us to focus on the effects of conversational flow since it disentangles them from the audience's prior leaning.[1]

The debate format involves an opening statement from the two sides, which presents an overview of their arguments before the discussion begins. This allows us to easily identify talking points held by the participants prior to the interaction, and consider them separately from points introduced spontaneously to serve the discussion.

This work is taking steps towards better modeling of conversational dynamics, by: (i) introducing a debate dataset with rich metadata (Section 2), (ii) proposing a framework for tracking the flow of ideas (Section 3), and (iii) showing its effectiveness in a predictive setting (Section 4).

2   Debate Dataset: Intelligence Squared

In this study we use transcripts and results of Oxford-style debates from the public debate series "Intelligence Squared Debates" (IQ2 for short).[2] These debates are recorded live, and contain motions covering a diversity of topics ranging from for-

---

[1]Other potential confounding factors are mitigated by the tight format and topic enforced by the debate's moderator.

[2]http://www.intelligencesquaredus.org

Proceedings of NAACL-HLT 2016, pages 136–141,
San Diego, California, June 12-17, 2016. ©2016 Association for Computational Linguistics

eign policy issues to the benefits of organic food. Each debate consists of two opposing teams—one for the motion and one against— of two or three experts in the topic of the particular motion, along with a moderator. Each debate follows the Oxford-style format and consists of three rounds. In the *introduction*, each debater is given 7 minutes to lay out their main points. During the *discussion*, debaters take questions from the moderator and audience, and respond to attacks from the other team. This round lasts around 30 minutes and is highly interactive; teams frequently engage in direct conversation with each other. Finally, in the *conclusion*, each debater is given 2 minutes to make final remarks.

Our dataset consists of the transcripts of all debates held by IQ2 in the US from September 2006 up to September 2015; in total, there are 108 debates.[3] Each debate is quite extensive: on average, 12801 words are uttered in 117 turns by members of either side per debate.[4]

Winning side labels. We follow IQ2's criteria for deciding who wins a debate, as follows. Before the debate, the live audience votes on whether they are for, against, or undecided on the motion. A second round of voting occurs after the debate. A side wins the debate if the difference between the percentage of votes they receive post- and pre-debate (the "delta") is greater than that of the other side's. Often the debates are quite tight: for 30% of the debates, the difference between the winning and losing sides' deltas is less than 10%.

Audience feedback. We check that the voting results are meaningful by verifying that audience reactions to the debaters are related to debate outcome. Using laughter and applause received by each side in each round[5] as markers of positive reactions, we note that differences in audience reception of the two sides emerge over the course of the debate. While both sides get similar levels of reaction during the introduction, winning teams tend to receive more laughter during the discussion ($p < 0.001$)[6] and more applause during the conclusion ($p = 0.05$).

Example debate. We will use a debate over the motion "Millennials don't stand a chance" (henceforth *Millennials*) as a running example.[7] The For side won the debate with a delta of 20% of the votes, compared to the Against side which only gained 5%.

3 Modeling Idea Flow

Promoting one's own points and addressing the opponent's points are two primary debating strategies. Here we introduce a methodology to identify these strategies, and use it to investigate their usage and effect on a debate's outcome.[8]

Identifying talking points. We first focus on ideas which form the basis of a side's stance on the motion. We identify such *talking points* by considering words whose frequency of usage differs significantly between the two teams during the introduction, before any interaction takes place. To find these words, we use the method introduced by Monroe et al. (2008) in the context of U.S. Senate speeches. In particular, we estimate the divergence between the two sides' word-usage in the introduction, where word-usage is modeled as multinomial distributions smoothed with a uniform Dirichlet prior, and divergence is given by log-odds ratio. The most discriminating words are those with the highest and lowest z-scores of divergence estimates. For a side X, we define the set of talking points $\mathcal{W}_X$ to be the k words with the highest or lowest z-scores.[9] We distinguish between X's *own* talking points $\mathcal{W}_X$, and the *opposing* talking points $\mathcal{W}_Y$ belonging to its opponent Y. These are examples of talking points for the "Millennials" debate:

Side	Talking points
For	debt, boomer, college, reality
Against	economy, volunteer, home, engage

The flow of talking points. A side can either promote its own talking points, address its opponent's points, or steer away from these initially salient

---

[3]We omitted one debate due to pdf parsing errors.

[4]The processed data is available at `http://www.cs.cornell.edu/~cristian/debates/`.

[5]Laughter and applause are indicated in the transcripts.

[6]Unless otherwise indicated, all reported p-values are calculated using the Wilcoxon signed-rank test.

[7]`http://www.intelligencesquaredus.org/debates/past-debates/item/1019-millennials-dont-stand-a-chance`

[8]In the subsequent discussion, we treat all utterances of a particular side as coming from a single speaker and defer modeling interactions within teams to future work.

[9]In order to focus on concepts central to the sides' arguments, we discard stopwords, perform stemming on the text, and take $k = 20$. We set these parameters by examining one subsequently discarded debate.

Talking point	volunteer	boomer
Introduction	AGAINST: [millennials] **volunteer** more than any generation. 73 percent of millennials **volunteered** for a nonprofit in 2012. And the percentage of [students] believing that it's [...] important to help people in need is [at the highest level] in 40 years.	FOR: [*referring to college completion rate*] the **boomer** generation is now [at] 32 percent. [Millennials] are currently at [...] 33 percent. So this notion that [millennials] have more education at this point in time than anybody else is not actually true.
Discussion	FOR: I'd make the argument [that] **volunteering** [is done] for exntrinsic [sic] reasons. So, it's done for college applications, or it's done because it's a requirement in high school.	FOR: It stinks to be young, having gone through what your generation [*referring to millennials*] has gone through. But keep in mind that [...] the **boomers** [...] have gone through the same.

Table 1: Example talking points used throughout the "Millennials" debate. Each talking point belongs to the side uttering the first excerpt, taken from the introduction; the second excerpt is from the discussion section. In the first example, the For side addresses the opposing talking point **volunteer** during the discussion; in the second example the For side refers to their own talking point **boomer** and recalls it later in the discussion.

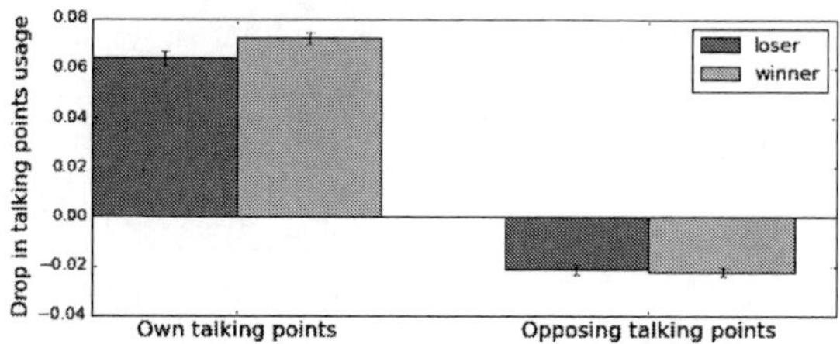

Figure 1: The start of the debate's interactive stage triggers a drop in self-coverage (> 0, indicated by leftmost two bars) and a rise in opponent-coverage (< 0, indicated by rightmost bars), with eventual winners showing a more pronounced drop in self-coverage (comparing the two bars on the left).

ideas altogether. We quantify the use of these strategies by comparing the airtime debaters devote to talking points. For a side X, let the *self-coverage* $f_r(X, X)$ be the fraction of content words uttered by X in round r that are among their own talking points $\mathcal{W}_X$; and the *opponent-coverage* $f_r(X, Y)$ be the fraction of its content words covering opposing talking points $\mathcal{W}_Y$.

Not surprisingly, we find that self-coverage dominates during the discussion ($f_{\text{Disc}}(X, X) > f_{\text{Disc}}(X, Y)$, $p < 0.001$). However, this does not mean debaters are simply giving monologues and ignoring each other: the effect of the interaction is reflected in a sharp drop in self-coverage and a rise in opponent-coverage once the discussion round begins. Respectively, $f_{\text{Disc}}(X, X) < f_{\text{Intro}}(X, X)$ and $f_{\text{Disc}}(X, Y) > f_{\text{Intro}}(X, Y)$, both $p < 0.001$. Examples of self- and opponent-coverage of two talking points in the "Millennials" debate from the introduction and discussion are given in Table 1.

Does the change in focus translate to any strategic advantages? Figure 1 suggests this is the case: the drop in self-coverage is slightly larger for the side that eventually wins the debate ($p = 0.08$). The drop in the sum of self- and opponent-coverage is also larger for winning teams, suggesting that they are more likely to steer away from discussing *any* talking points from either side ($p = 0.05$).

Identifying discussion points. Having seen that debaters can benefit by shifting away from talking points that were salient during the introduction, we now examine the ideas that spontaneously arise to serve the discussion. We model such *discussion points* as words introduced to the debate during the discussion by a debater and adopted by his opponents at least twice.[10] This allows us to focus on words that become relevant to the conversation; only 3% of all newly introduced words qualify, amounting to about 10 discussion points per debate.

The flow of discussion points. The adoption of discussion points plays an important role in persuading the audience: during the discussion, eventual winners adopt more discussion points introduced by their opponents than eventual losers ($p < 0.01$). Two possible strategic interpretations emerge. From a topic control angle (Nguyen et al., 2014), perhaps losers are more successful at imposing their discussion points to gain control of the discussion. This view appears counterintuitive given work linking topic control to influence in other settings (Planalp and Tracy, 1980; Rienks et al., 2006).

---

[10]Ignoring single repetitions discards simple echoing of words used by the previous speaker.

AGAINST: I would say [millennials] are effectively moving towards goals [...] it might seem like immaturity if you don't actually talk to millennials and look at the **statistics**.

FOR: –actually, the numbers are showing [...] that it's worsening [...] Same **statistics**, dreadful **statistics**.

AGAINST: [...] there's a incredible [sic] advantage that millennials have when it comes to social media [...] because we have an understanding of that landscape as **digital** natives [...]

FOR: Generation X [...] is also known as the **digital** generation. The companies [...] that make you **digital** natives were all founded by [...] people in generation X. It's simply inaccurate every time somebody says that the millennial generation is the only generation [...]

Table 2: Example discussion points introduced by the Against side in the "Millennials" debate. For each point, the first excerpt is the context in which the point was first mentioned by the Against side in the discussion, and the second excerpt shows the For side challenging the point later on.

An alternative interpretation could be that winners are more active than losers in contesting their opponents' points, a strategy that might play out favorably to the audience. A post-hoc manual examination supports this interpretation: 78% of the valid discussion points are picked up by the opposing side in order to be challenged;[11] this strategy is exemplified in Table 2. Overall, these observations tying the flow of discussion points to the debate's outcome suggest that winners are more successful at using the interaction to engage with their opponents' ideas.

4 Predictive Power

We evaluate the predictive power of our flow features in a binary classification setting: predict whether the For or Against side wins the debate.[12] This is a challenging task even for humans, thus the dramatic reveal at the end of each IQ2 debate that partly explains the popularity of the show. Our goal

---

[11]Three annotators (including one author) informally annotated a random sample of 50 discussion points in the context of all dialogue excerpts where the point was used. According to a majority vote, in 26 cases the opponents challenged the point, in 7 cases the point was supported, 4 cases were unclear, and in 13 cases the annotators deemed the discussion point invalid. We discuss the last category in Section 6.

[12]The task is balanced: after removing three debates ending in a tie, we have 52 debates won by For and 53 by Against.

here is limited to understanding which of the flow features that we developed carry predictive power.

Conversation flow features. We use all conversational features discussed above. For each side X we include $f_{\text{Disc}}(X, X)$, $f_{\text{Disc}}(X, Y)$, and their sum. We also use the drop in self-coverage given by subtracting corresponding values for $f_{\text{Intro}}(\cdot, \cdot)$, and the number of discussion points adopted by each side. We call these the *Flow* features.

Baseline features. To discard the possibility that our results are simply explained by debater verbosity, we use the number of words uttered and number of turns taken by each side (*length*) as baselines. We also compare to a unigram baseline (*BOW*).

Audience features. We use the counts of applause and laughter received by each side (described in Section 2) as rough indicators of how well the audience can foresee a debate's outcome.

Prediction accuracy is evaluated using a leave-one-out (LOO) approach. We use logistic regression; model parameters for each LOO train-test split are selected via 3-fold cross-validation on the training set. To find particularly predictive flow features, we also try using univariate feature selection on the flow features before the model is fitted in each split; we refer to this setting as *Flow**.[13]

We find that conversation flow features obtain the best accuracy among all listed feature types (Flow: 63%; Flow*: 65%), performing significantly higher than a 50% random baseline (binomial test $p < 0.05$), and comparable to audience features (60%). In contrast, the length and BOW baselines do not perform better than chance. We note that *Flow* features perform competitively despite being the only ones that do not factor in the concluding round.

The features selected most often in the Flow* task are: the number of discussion points adopted (with positive regression coefficients), the recall of talking points during the discussion round (negative coefficients), and the drop in usage of own talking points from introduction to discussion (positive coefficients). The relative importance of these features, which focus on the interaction between teams, suggests that audiences tend to favor debating strategies which emphasize the discussion.

---

[13]We optimize the regularizer (ℓ_1 or ℓ_2), and the value of the regularization parameter C (between 10^{-5} and 10^5). For Flow* we also optimize the number of features selected.

5 Further Related Work

Previous work on conversational structure has proposed approaches to model dialogue acts (Samuel et al., 1998; Ritter et al., 2010; Ferschke et al., 2012) or disentangle interleaved conversations (Elsner and Charniak, 2010; Elsner and Charniak, 2011). Other research has considered the problem of detecting conversation-level traits such as the presence of disagreements (Allen et al., 2014; Wang and Cardie, 2014) or the likelihood of relation dissolution (Niculae et al., 2015). At the participant level, several studies present approaches to identify ideological stances (Somasundaran and Wiebe, 2010; Rosenthal and McKeown, 2015), using features based on participant interactions (Thomas et al., 2006; Sridhar et al., 2015), or extracting words and reasons characterizing a stance (Monroe et al., 2008; Nguyen et al., 2010; Hasan and Ng, 2014). In our setting, both the stances and the turn structure of a debate are known, allowing us to instead focus on the debate's outcome.

Existing research on argumentation strategies has largely focused on exploiting the structure of monologic arguments (Mochales and Moens, 2011), like those of persuasive essays (Feng and Hirst, 2011; Stab and Gurevych, 2014). In addition, Tan et al. (2016) has examined the effectiveness of arguments in the context of a forum where people invite others to challenge their opinions. We complement this line of work by looking at the relative persuasiveness of participants in extended conversations as they exchange arguments over multiple turns.

Previous studies of influence in extended conversations have largely dealt with the political domain, examining moderated but relatively unstructured settings such as talk shows or presidential debates, and suggesting features like topic control (Nguyen et al., 2014), linguistic style matching (Romero et al., 2015) and turn-taking (Prabhakaran et al., 2013). With persuasion in mind, our work extends these studies to explore a new dynamic, the flow of ideas between speakers, in a highly structured setting that controls for confounding factors.

6 Limitations and Future Work

This study opens several avenues for future research. One could explore more complex representations of talking points and discussion points, for instance using topic models or word embeddings. Furthermore, augmenting the flow of content in a conversation with the speakers' linguistic choices could better capture their intentions. In addition, it would be interesting to study the interplay between our conversational flow features and relatively monologic features that consider the argumentative and rhetorical traits of each side separately. More explicitly comparing and contrasting monologic and interactive dynamics could lead to better models of conversations. Such approaches could also help clarify some of the intuitions about conversations explored in this work, particularly that engaging in dialogue carries different strategic implications from self-promotion.

Our focus in this paper is on capturing and understanding conversational flow. We hence make some simplifying assumptions that could be refined in future work. For instance, by using a basic unigram-based definition of discussion points, we do not account for the context or semantic sense in which these points occur. In particular, our annotators found that a significant proportion of the discussion points under our definition actually referred to differing ideas in the various contexts in which they appeared. We expect that improving our retrieval model will also improve the robustness of our idea flow analysis. A better model of discussion points could also provide more insight into the role of these points in persuading the audience.

While Oxford-style debates are a particularly convenient setting for studying the effects of conversational flow, our dataset is limited in terms of size. It would be worthwhile to examine the flow features we developed in the context of settings with richer incentives beyond persuading an audience, such as in the semi-cooperative environment of Wikipedia talk pages. Finally, our methodology could point to applications in areas such as education and cooperative work, where it is key to establish the link between conversation features and an interlocutor's ability to convey their point (Niculae and Danescu-Niculescu-Mizil, 2016).

Acknowledgements. We thank the reviewers and V. Niculae for their helpful comments, and I. Arawjo and D. Sedra for annotations. This work was supported in part by a Google Faculty Research Award.

References

Kelsey Allen, Giuseppe Carenini, and Raymond T Ng. 2014. Detecting disagreement in conversations using pseudo-monologic rhetorical structure. In *Proceedings of EMNLP*.

Micha Elsner and Eugene Charniak. 2010. Disentangling chat. *Computational Linguistics*, 36(3):389–409.

Micha Elsner and Eugene Charniak. 2011. Disentangling chat with local coherence models. In *Proceedings of ACL*.

Vanessa Wei Feng and Graeme Hirst. 2011. Classifying arguments by scheme. In *Proceedings of ACL*.

Oliver Ferschke, Iryna Gurevych, and Yevgen Chebotar. 2012. Behind the article: Recognizing dialog acts in Wikipedia talk pages. In *Proceedings of EACL*.

Kazi Saidul Hasan and Vincent Ng. 2014. Why are you taking this stance? Identifying and classifying reasons in ideological debates. In *Proceedings of EMNLP*.

Raquel Mochales and Marie-Francine Moens. 2011. Argumentation mining. *Artificial Intelligence and Law*, 19(1):1–22.

Burt L. Monroe, Michael P. Colaresi, and Kevin M. Quinn. 2008. Fightin'words: Lexical feature selection and evaluation for identifying the content of political conflict. *Political Analysis*, 16(4):372–403.

Dong Nguyen, Elijah Mayfield, and Carolyn P Rosé. 2010. An analysis of perspectives in interactive settings. In *Proceedings of the KDD 2010 Workshop on Social Media Analytics*.

Viet-An Nguyen, Jordan Boyd-Graber, Philip Resnik, Deborah A Cai, Jennifer E Midberry, and Yuanxin Wang. 2014. Modeling topic control to detect influence in conversations using nonparametric topic models. *Machine Learning*, 95(3):381–421.

Vlad Niculae and Cristian Danescu-Niculescu-Mizil. 2016. Conversational markers of constructive discussions. In *Proceedings of NAACL*.

Vlad Niculae, Srijan Kumar, Jordan Boyd-Graber, and Cristian Danescu-Niculescu-Mizil. 2015. Linguistic harbingers of betrayal: A case study on an online strategy game. In *Proceedings of ACL*.

Sally Planalp and Karen Tracy. 1980. Not to change the subject but: A cognitive approach to the management of conversation. *Communication Yearbook*, 4:680–690.

Vinodkumar Prabhakaran, Ajita John, and Dorée D. Seligmann. 2013. Who had the upper hand? Ranking participants of interactions based on their relative power. In *Proceedings of IJCNLP*.

Rutger Rienks, Dong Zhang, Daniel Gatica-Perez, and Wilfried Post. 2006. Detection and application of influence rankings in small group meetings. In *Proceedings of ICMI*.

Alan Ritter, Colin Cherry, and Bill Dolan. 2010. Unsupervised modeling of twitter conversations. In *Proceedings of NAACL*.

Daniel M Romero, Roderick I Swaab, Brian Uzzi, and Adam D Galinsky. 2015. Mimicry is presidential: Linguistic style matching in presidential debates and improved polling numbers. *Personality and Social Psychology Bulletin*, 41(10):1311–1319.

Sara Rosenthal and Kathleen McKeown. 2015. I couldn't agree more: The role of conversational structure in agreement and disagreement detection in online discussions. In *Proceedings of SIGDIAL*.

Ken Samuel, Sandra Carberry, and K. Vijay-Shanker. 1998. Dialogue act tagging with transformation-based learning. In *Proceedings of ACL*.

Swapna Somasundaran and Janyce Wiebe. 2010. Recognizing stances in ideological on-line debates. In *Proceedings of the NAACL HLT 2010 Workshop on Computational Approaches to Analysis and Generation of Emotion in Text*.

Dhanya Sridhar, James Foulds, Bert Huang, Lise Getoor, and Marilyn Walker. 2015. Joint models of disagreement and stance in online debate. In *Proceedings of ACL*.

Christian Stab and Iryna Gurevych. 2014. Identifying argumentative discourse structures in persuasive essays. In *Proceedings of EMNLP*.

Chenhao Tan, Vlad Niculae, Cristian Danescu-Niculescu-Mizil, and Lillian Lee. 2016. Winning arguments: Interaction dynamics and persuasion strategies in good-faith online discussions. In *Proceedings of WWW*.

Matt Thomas, Bo Pang, and Lillian Lee. 2006. Get out the vote: Determining support or opposition from congressional floor-debate transcripts. In *Proceedings of EMNLP*.

Lu Wang and Claire Cardie. 2014. A piece of my mind: A sentiment analysis approach for online dispute detection. In *Proceedings of ACL*.

Counter-fitting Word Vectors to Linguistic Constraints

Nikola Mrkšić[1], Diarmuid Ó Séaghdha[2], Blaise Thomson[2], Milica Gašić[1]
Lina Rojas-Barahona[1], Pei-Hao Su[1], David Vandyke[1], Tsung-Hsien Wen[1], Steve Young[1]
[1] Department of Engineering, University of Cambridge, UK
[2] Apple Inc.
{nm480,mg436,phs26,djv27,thw28,sjy}@cam.ac.uk
{doseaghdha, blaisethom}@apple.com

Abstract

In this work, we present a novel *counter-fitting* method which injects antonymy and synonymy constraints into vector space representations in order to improve the vectors' capability for judging semantic similarity. Applying this method to publicly available pre-trained word vectors leads to a new state of the art performance on the SimLex-999 dataset. We also show how the method can be used to tailor the word vector space for the downstream task of dialogue state tracking, resulting in robust improvements across different dialogue domains.

	east	expensive	British
	west	pricey	American
	north	cheaper	Australian
Before	south	costly	Britain
	southeast	overpriced	European
	northeast	inexpensive	England
	eastward	costly	Brits
	eastern	pricy	London
After	easterly	overpriced	BBC
	-	pricey	UK
	-	afford	Britain

Table 1: Nearest neighbours for target words using GloVe vectors before and after counter-fitting

1 Introduction

Many popular methods that induce representations for words rely on the *distributional hypothesis* – the assumption that semantically similar or related words appear in similar contexts. This hypothesis supports unsupervised learning of meaningful word representations from large corpora (Curran, 2003; Ó Séaghdha and Korhonen, 2014; Mikolov et al., 2013; Pennington et al., 2014). Word vectors trained using these methods have proven useful for many downstream tasks including machine translation (Zou et al., 2013) and dependency parsing (Bansal et al., 2014).

One drawback of learning word embeddings from co-occurrence information in corpora is that it tends to coalesce the notions of *semantic similarity* and *conceptual association* (Hill et al., 2014b). Furthermore, even methods that can distinguish similarity from association (e.g., based on syntactic co-occurrences) will generally fail to tell synonyms from antonyms (Mohammad et al., 2008). For example, words such

as *east* and *west* or *expensive* and *inexpensive* appear in near-identical contexts, which means that distributional models produce very similar word vectors for such words. Examples of such anomalies in GloVe vectors can be seen in Table 1, where words such as *cheaper* and *inexpensive* are deemed similar to (their antonym) *expensive*.

A second drawback is that similarity and antonymy can be application- or domain-specific. In our case, we are interested in exploiting distributional knowledge for the *dialogue state tracking* task (DST). The DST component of a dialogue system is responsible for interpreting users' utterances and updating the system's *belief state* – a probability distribution over all possible states of the dialogue. For example, a DST for the restaurant domain needs to detect whether the user wants a *cheap* or *expensive* restaurant. Being able to generalise using distributional information while still distinguishing between semantically different yet conceptually related words

Proceedings of NAACL-HLT 2016, pages 142–148,
San Diego, California, June 12-17, 2016. ©2016 Association for Computational Linguistics

(e.g. *cheaper* and *pricey*) is critical for the performance of dialogue systems. In particular, a dialogue system can be led seriously astray by false synonyms.

We propose a method that addresses these two drawbacks by using synonymy and antonymy relations drawn from either a general lexical resource or an application-specific ontology to fine-tune distributional word vectors. Our method, which we term *counter-fitting*, is a lightweight post-processing procedure in the spirit of *retrofitting* (Faruqui et al., 2015). The second row of Table 1 illustrates the results of counter-fitting: the nearest neighbours capture true similarity much more intuitively than the original GloVe vectors. The procedure improves word vector quality regardless of the initial word vectors provided as input.[1] By applying counter-fitting to the Paragram-SL999 word vectors provided by Wieting et al. (2015), we achieve new state-of-the-art performance on SimLex-999, a dataset designed to measure how well different models judge semantic similarity between words (Hill et al., 2014b). We also show that the counter-fitting method can inject knowledge of dialogue domain ontologies into word vector space representations to facilitate the construction of semantic dictionaries which improve DST performance across two different dialogue domains. Our tool and word vectors are available at `github.com/nmrksic/counter-fitting`.

2 Related Work

Most work on improving word vector representations using lexical resources has focused on bringing words which are known to be semantically related closer together in the vector space. Some methods modify the prior or the regularization of the original training procedure (Yu and Dredze, 2014; Bian et al., 2014; Kiela et al., 2015). Wieting et al. (2015) use the Paraphrase Database (Ganitkevitch et al., 2013) to train word vectors which emphasise word similarity over word relatedness. These word vectors achieve the current state-of-the-art performance on the SimLex-999 dataset and are used as input for counter-fitting in our experiments.

---

[1]When we write "improve", we refer to improving the vector space for a specific purpose. We do not expect that a vector space fine-tuned for semantic similarity will give better results on semantic relatedness. As Mohammad et al. (2008) observe, antonymous concepts are related but not similar.

Recently, there has been interest in lightweight post-processing procedures that use lexical knowledge to refine off-the-shelf word vectors without requiring large corpora for (re-)training as the aforementioned "heavyweight" procedures do. Faruqui et al.'s (2015) *retrofitting* approach uses similarity constraints from WordNet and other resources to pull similar words closer together.

The complications caused by antonymy for distributional methods are well-known in the semantics community. Most prior work focuses on extracting antonym pairs from text rather than exploiting them (Lin et al., 2003; Mohammad et al., 2008; Turney, 2008; Hashimoto et al., 2012; Mohammad et al., 2013). The most common use of antonymy information is to provide features for systems that detect contradictions or logical entailment (Marcu and Echihabi, 2002; de Marneffe et al., 2008; Zanzotto et al., 2009). As far as we are aware, there is no previous work on exploiting antonymy in dialogue systems. The modelling work closest to ours are Liu et al. (2015), who use antonymy and WordNet hierarchy information to modify the heavyweight Word2Vec training objective; Yih et al. (2012), who use a Siamese neural network to improve the quality of Latent Semantic Analysis vectors; Schwartz et al. (2015), who build a standard distributional model from co-occurrences based on *symmetric patterns*, with specified antonymy patterns counted as negative co-occurrences; and Ono et al. (2015), who use thesauri and distributional data to train word embeddings specialised for capturing antonymy.

3 Counter-fitting Word Vectors to Linguistic Constraints

Our starting point is an indexed set of word vectors $V = \{\mathbf{v}_1, \mathbf{v}_2, \ldots, \mathbf{v}_N\}$ with one vector for each word in the vocabulary. We will inject semantic relations into this vector space to produce new word vectors $V' = \{\mathbf{v}'_1, \mathbf{v}'_2, \ldots, \mathbf{v}'_N\}$. For antonymy and synonymy we have a set of constraints A and S, respectively. The elements of each set are pairs of word indices; for example, each pair (i, j) in S is such that the i-th and j-th words in the vocabulary are synonyms. The objective function used to counter-fit the pre-trained word vectors V to the sets of linguistic constraints A and S contains three different terms:

1. Antonym Repel (AR): This term serves to *push* antonymous words' vectors away from each other in the transformed vector space V':

$$\text{AR}(V') = \sum_{(u,w)\in A} \tau\left(\delta - d(\mathbf{v}'_u, \mathbf{v}'_w)\right)$$

where $d(v_i, v_j) = 1 - \cos(v_i, v_j)$ is a distance derived from cosine similarity and $\tau(x) \triangleq max(0, x)$ imposes a margin on the cost. Intuitively, δ is the "ideal" minimum distance between antonymous words; in our experiments we set $\delta = 1.0$ as it corresponds to vector orthogonality.

2. Synonym Attract (SA): The counter-fitting procedure should seek to bring the word vectors of known synonymous word pairs closer together:

$$\text{SA}(V') = \sum_{(u,w)\in S} \tau\left(d(\mathbf{v}'_u, \mathbf{v}'_w) - \gamma\right)$$

where γ is the "ideal" maximum distance between synonymous words; we use $\gamma = 0$.

3. Vector Space Preservation (VSP): the topology of the original vector space describes relationships between words in the vocabulary captured using distributional information from very large textual corpora. The VSP term bends the transformed vector space towards the original one as much as possible in order to preserve the semantic information contained in the original vectors:

$$\text{VSP}(V, V') = \sum_{i=1}^{N} \sum_{j\in N(i)} \tau\left(d(\mathbf{v}'_i, \mathbf{v}'_j) - d(\mathbf{v}_i, \mathbf{v}_j)\right)$$

For computational efficiency, we do not calculate distances for every pair of words in the vocabulary. Instead, we focus on the (pre-computed) neighbourhood $N(i)$, which denotes the set of words within a certain radius ρ around the i-th word's vector in the original vector space V. Our experiments indicate that counter-fitting is relatively insensitive to the choice of ρ, with values between 0.2 and 0.4 showing little difference in quality; here we use $\rho = 0.2$.

The objective function for the training procedure is given by a weighted sum of the three terms:

$$C(V, V') = k_1\text{AR}(V') + k_2\text{SA}(V') + k_3\text{VSP}(V, V')$$

where $k_1, k_2, k_3 \geq 0$ are hyperparameters that control the relative importance of each term. In our experiments we set them to be equal: $k_1 = k_2 = k_3$. To minimise the cost function for a set of starting vectors V and produce counter-fitted vectors V', we run stochastic gradient descent (SGD) for 20 epochs. An end-to-end run of counter-fitting takes less than two minutes on a laptop with four CPUs.

3.1 Injecting Dialogue Domain Ontologies into Vector Space Representations

Dialogue state tracking (DST) models capture users' goals given their utterances. Goals are represented as sets of constraints expressed by *slot-value* pairs such as [food: *Indian*] or [parking: *allowed*]. The set of slots S and the set of values V_s for each slot make up the *ontology* of a dialogue domain.

In this paper we adopt the recurrent neural network (RNN) framework for tracking suggested in (Henderson et al., 2014d; Henderson et al., 2014c; Mrkšić et al., 2015). Rather than using a spoken language understanding (SLU) decoder to convert user utterances into meaning representations, this model operates directly on the n-gram features extracted from the automated speech recognition (ASR) hypotheses. A drawback of this approach is that the RNN model can only perform exact string matching to detect the slot names and values mentioned by the user. It cannot recognise synonymous words such as *pricey* and *expensive*, or even subtle morphological variations such as *moderate* and *moderately*. A simple way to mitigate this problem is to use *semantic dictionaries*: lists of rephrasings for the values in the ontology. Manual construction of dictionaries is highly labour-intensive; however, if one could automatically detect high-quality rephrasings, then this capability would come at no extra cost to the system designer.

To obtain a set of word vectors which can be used for creating a semantic dictionary, we need to *inject* the domain ontology into the vector space. This can be achieved by introducing antonymy constraints between all the possible values of each slot (i.e. *Chinese* and *Indian*, *expensive* and *cheap*, etc.). The remaining linguistic constraints can come from semantic lexicons: the richer the sets of injected synonyms and antonyms are, the better the resulting word representations will become.

Model / Word Vectors	ρ
Neural MT Model (Hill et al., 2014a)	0.52
Symmetric Patterns (Schwartz et al., 2015)	0.56
Non-distributional Vectors (Faruqui and Dyer, 2015)	0.58
GloVe vectors (Pennington et al., 2014)	0.41
GloVe vectors + Retrofitting	0.53
GloVe + Counter-fitting	0.58
Paragram-SL999 (Wieting et al., 2015)	0.69
Paragram-SL999 + Retrofitting	0.68
Paragram-SL999 + Counter-fitting	**0.74**
Inter-annotator agreement	0.67
Annotator/gold standard agreement	0.78

Table 2: Performance on SimLex-999. Retrofitting uses the code and (PPDB) data provided by the authors

4 Experiments

4.1 Word Vectors and Semantic Lexicons

Two different collections of pre-trained word vectors were used as input to the counter-fitting procedure:

1. **Glove Common Crawl** 300-dimensional vectors made available by Pennington et al. (2014).

2. **Paragram-SL999** 300-dimensional vectors made available by Wieting et al. (2015).

The synonymy and antonymy constraints were obtained from two semantic lexicons:

1. **PPDB 2.0 (Pavlick et al., 2015):** the latest release of the Paraphrase Database. A new feature of this version is that it assigns relation types to its word pairs. We identify the *Equivalence* relation with synonymy and *Exclusion* with antonymy. We used the largest available (XXXL) version of the database and only considered single-token terms.

2. **WordNet (Miller, 1995):** a well known semantic lexicon which contains vast amounts of high quality human-annotated synonym and antonym pairs. Any two words in our vocabulary which had antonymous word senses were considered antonyms; WordNet synonyms were not used.

In total, the lexicons yielded 12,802 antonymy and 31,828 synonymy pairs for our vocabulary, which consisted of 76,427 most frequent words in Open-Subtitles, obtained from `invokeit.wordpress.com/frequency-word-lists/`.

Semantic Resource	Glove	Paragram
Baseline (no linguistic constraints)	0.41	0.69
PPDB− (PPDB antonyms)	0.43	0.69
PPDB+ (PPDB synonyms)	0.46	0.68
WordNet− (WordNet antonyms)	0.52	0.74
PPDB− and PPDB+	0.50	0.69
WordNet− and PPDB−	0.53	0.74
WordNet− and PPDB+	0.58	0.74
WordNet− and PPDB− and PPDB+	0.58	0.74

Table 3: SimLex-999 performance when different sets of linguistic constraints are used for counter-fitting

4.2 Improving Lexical Similarity Predictions

In this section, we show that counter-fitting pre-trained word vectors with linguistic constraints improves their usefulness for judging semantic similarity. We use Spearman's rank correlation coefficient with the SimLex-999 dataset, which contains word pairs ranked by a large number of annotators instructed to consider only semantic similarity.

Table 2 contains a summary of recently reported competitive scores for SimLex-999, as well as the performance of the unaltered, retrofitted and counter-fitted GloVe and Paragram-SL999 word vectors. To the best of our knowledge, the 0.685 figure reported for the latter represents the current high score. This figure is above the average inter-annotator agreement of 0.67, which has been referred to as the ceiling performance in most work up to now.

In our opinion, the average inter-annotator agreement is not the only meaningful measure of ceiling performance. We believe it also makes sense to compare: **a)** the model ranking's correlation with the gold standard ranking to: **b)** the average rank correlation that individual human annotators' rankings achieved with the gold standard ranking. The SimLex-999 authors have informed us that the average annotator agreement with the gold standard is 0.78.[2] As shown in Table 2, the reported performance of all the models and word vectors falls well below this figure.

Retrofitting pre-trained word vectors improves GloVe vectors, but not the already semantically specialised Paragram-SL999 vectors. Counter-fitting substantially improves both sets of vectors, showing that injecting antonymy relations goes a long way

---

[2]This figure is now reported as a potentially fairer ceiling performance on the SimLex-999 website: `http://www.cl.cam.ac.uk/~fh295/simlex.html`.

False Synonyms	Fixed	False Antonyms	Fixed
sunset, sunrise	✓	dumb, dense	
forget, ignore		adult, guardian	
girl, maid		polite, proper	✓✓
happiness, luck	✓✓	strength, might	
south, north	✓	water, ice	
go, come	✓	violent, angry	✓✓
groom, bride		cat, lion	✓✓
dinner, breakfast		laden, heavy	✓✓
-	-	engage, marry	

Table 4: Highest-error SimLex-999 word pairs using Paragram vectors (before counter-fitting)

Dataset	Train	Dev	Test	#Slots
Restaurants	1612	506	1117	4
Tourist Information	1600	439	225	9

Table 5: Number of dialogues in the dataset splits used for the Dialogue State Tracking experiments

Word Vector Space	Restaurants	Tourist Info
Baseline (no dictionary)	68.6	60.5
GloVe	72.5	60.9
GloVe + Counter-fitting	73.4	**62.8**
Paragram-SL999	73.2	61.5
Paragram-SL999 + Counter-fitting	**73.5**	61.9

Table 6: Performance of RNN belief trackers (ensembles of four models) with different semantic dictionaries

towards improving word vectors for the purpose of making semantic similarity judgements.

Table 3 shows the effect of injecting different categories of linguistic constraints. GloVe vectors benefit from all three sets of constraints, whereas the quality of Paragram vectors, already exposed to PPDB, only improves with the injection of WordNet antonyms. Table 4 illustrates how incorrect similarity predictions based on the original (Paragram) vectors can be fixed through counter-fitting. The table presents eight false synonyms and nine false antonyms: word pairs with predicted rank in the top (bottom) 200 word pairs and gold standard rank 500 or more positions lower (higher). Eight of these errors are fixed by counter-fitting: the difference between predicted and gold-standard ranks is now 100 or less. Interestingly, five of the eight corrected word pairs do not appear in the sets of linguistic constraints; these are indicated by double ticks in the table. This shows that secondary (i.e. *indirect*) interactions through the three terms of the cost function do contribute to the semantic content of the transformed vector space.

4.3 Improving Dialogue State Tracking

Table 5 shows the dialogue state tracking datasets used for evaluation. These datasets come from the Dialogue State Tracking Challenges 2 and 3 (Henderson et al., 2014a; Henderson et al., 2014b).

We used four different sets of word vectors to construct semantic dictionaries: the original GloVe and Paragram-SL999 vectors, as well as versions counter-fitted to each domain ontology. The constraints used for counter-fitting were all those from the previous section as well as antonymy constraints among the set of values for each slot. We treated all vocabulary words within some radius t of a slot value as rephrasings of that value. The optimal value of t was determined using a grid search: we generated a dictionary and trained a model for each potential t, then evaluated on the development set. Table 6 shows the performance of RNN models which used the constructed dictionaries. The dictionaries induced from the pre-trained vectors substantially improved tracking performance over the baselines (which used no semantic dictionaries). The dictionaries created using the counter-fitted vectors improved performance even further. Contrary to the SimLex-999 experiments, starting from the Paragram vectors did not lead to superior performance, which shows that injecting the application-specific ontology is at least as important as the quality of the initial word vectors.

5 Conclusion

We have presented a novel *counter-fitting* method for injecting linguistic constraints into word vector space representations. The method efficiently post-processes word vectors to improve their usefulness for tasks which involve making semantic similarity judgements. Its focus on separating vector representations of antonymous word pairs lead to substantial improvements on genuine similarity estimation tasks. We have also shown that counter-fitting can tailor word vectors for downstream tasks by using it to inject domain ontologies into word vectors used to construct semantic dictionaries for dialogue systems.

Acknowledgements

We would like to thank Felix Hill for help with the SimLex-999 evaluation. We also thank the anonymous reviewers for their helpful suggestions.

References

Mohit Bansal, Kevin Gimpel, and Karen Livescu. 2014. Tailoring continuous word representations for dependency parsing. In *Proceedings of ACL*.

Jiang Bian, Bin Gao, and Tie-Yan Liu. 2014. Knowledge-powered deep learning for word embedding. In *Machine Learning and Knowledge Discovery in Databases*.

James Curran. 2003. *From Distributional to Semantic Similarity*. Ph.D. thesis, School of Informatics, University of Edinburgh.

Marie-Catherine de Marneffe, Anna N. Rafferty, and Christopher D. Manning. 2008. Finding contradictions in text. In *Proceedings of ACL*.

Manaal Faruqui and Chris Dyer. 2015. Non-distributional word vector representations. In *Proceedings of ACL*.

Manaal Faruqui, Jesse Dodge, Sujay K. Jauhar, Chris Dyer, Eduard Hovy, and Noah A. Smith. 2015. Retrofitting Word Vectors to Semantic Lexicons. In *Proceedings of NAACL HLT*.

Juri Ganitkevitch, Benjamin Van Durme, and Chris Callison-burch. 2013. PPDB: The Paraphrase Database. In *Proceedings of NAACL HLT*.

Chikara Hashimoto, Kentaro Torisawa, Stijn De Saeger, Jong-Hoon Oh, and Junichi Kazama. 2012. Excitatory or inhibitory: A new semantic orientation extracts contradiction and causality from the Web. In *Proceedings of EMNLP-CoNLL*.

Matthew Henderson, Blaise Thomson, and Jason D. Wiliams. 2014a. The Second Dialog State Tracking Challenge. In *Proceedings of SIGDIAL*.

Matthew Henderson, Blaise Thomson, and Jason D. Wiliams. 2014b. The Third Dialog State Tracking Challenge. In *Proceedings of IEEE SLT*.

Matthew Henderson, Blaise Thomson, and Steve Young. 2014c. Robust Dialog State Tracking using Delexicalised Recurrent Neural Networks and Unsupervised Adaptation. In *Proceedings of IEEE SLT*.

Matthew Henderson, Blaise Thomson, and Steve Young. 2014d. Word-Based Dialog State Tracking with Recurrent Neural Networks. In *Proceedings of SIGDIAL*.

Felix Hill, Kyunghyun Cho, Sbastien Jean, Coline Devin, and Yoshua Bengio. 2014a. Embedding word similarity with neural machine translation. *Computing Research Repository*.

Felix Hill, Roi Reichart, and Anna Korhonen. 2014b. SimLex-999: Evaluating Semantic Models with (Genuine) Similarity Estimation. *Computing Research Repository*.

Douwe Kiela, Felix Hill, and Stephen Clark. 2015. Specializing word embeddings for similarity or relatedness. In *Proceedings of EMNLP*.

Dekang Lin, Shaojun Zhao, Lijuan Qin, and Ming Zhou. 2003. Identifying synonyms among distributionally similar words. In *Proceedings of IJCAI*.

Quan Liu, Hui Jiang, Si Wei, Zhen-Hua Ling, and Yu Hu. 2015. Learning semantic word embeddings based on ordinal knowledge constraints. In *Proceedings of ACL*.

Daniel Marcu and Abdsemmad Echihabi. 2002. An unsupervised approach to recognizing discourse relations. In *Proceedings of ACL*.

Tomas Mikolov, Ilya Sutskever, Kai Chen, Greg S Corrado, and Jeff Dean. 2013. Distributed Representations of Words and Phrases and their Compositionality. In *Proceedings of NIPS*.

George A. Miller. 1995. WordNet: A Lexical Database for English. *Communications of the ACM*.

Saif Mohammad, Bonnie Dorr, and Graeme Hirst. 2008. Computing word-pair antonymy. In *Proceedings of EMNLP*.

Saif M. Mohammad, Bonnie J. Dorr, Graeme Hirst, and Peter D. Turney. 2013. Computing lexical contrast. *Computational Linguistics*, 39(3):555–590.

Nikola Mrkšić, Diarmuid Ó Séaghdha, Blaise Thomson, Milica Gašić, Pei-Hao Su, David Vandyke, Tsung-Hsien Wen, and Steve Young. 2015. Multi-domain Dialog State Tracking using Recurrent Neural Networks. In *Proceedings of ACL*.

Masataka Ono, Makoto Miwa, and Yutaka Sasaki. 2015. Word Embedding-based Antonym Detection using Thesauri and Distributional Information. In *Proceedings of NAACL HLT*.

Diarmuid Ó Séaghdha and Anna Korhonen. 2014. Probabilistic distributional semantics. *Computational Linguistics*, 40(3):587–631.

Ellie Pavlick, Pushpendre Rastogi, Juri Ganitkevich, Benjamin Van Durme, and Chris Callison-Burch. 2015. PPDB 2.0: Better paraphrase ranking, fine-grained entailment relations, word embeddings, and style classification. In *Proceedings of ACL*.

Jeffrey Pennington, Richard Socher, and Christopher Manning. 2014. Glove: Global Vectors for Word Representation. In *Proceedings of EMNLP*.

Roy Schwartz, Roi Reichart, and Ari Rappoport. 2015. Symmetric pattern based word embeddings for improved word similarity prediction. In *Proceedings of CoNLL*.

Peter D. Turney. 2008. A uniform approach to analogies, synonyms, antonyms, and associations. In *Proceedings of COLING*.

John Wieting, Mohit Bansal, Kevin Gimpel, and Karen Livescu. 2015. From paraphrase database to compositional paraphrase model and back. *Transactions of the Association for Computational Linguistics*.

Wen-Tau Yih, Geoffrey Zweig, and John C. Platt. 2012. Polarity inducing Latent Semantic Analysis. In *Proceedings of ACL*.

Mo Yu and Mark Dredze. 2014. Improving lexical embeddings with semantic knowledge. In *Proceedings of ACL*.

Fabio Massimo Zanzotto, Marco Pennachiotti, and Alessandro Moschitti. 2009. A machine learning approach to textual entailment recognition. *Journal of Natural Language Engineering*, 15(4):551–582.

Will Y. Zou, Richard Socher, Daniel M. Cer, and Christopher D. Manning. 2013. Bilingual word embeddings for phrase-based machine translation. In *Proceedings of EMNLP*.

Grounded Semantic Role Labeling

Shaohua Yang[1], **Qiaozi Gao**[1], **Changsong Liu**[1], **Caiming Xiong**[2],
Song-Chun Zhu[3], and **Joyce Y. Chai**[1]

[1]Department of Computer Science and Engineering, Michigan State University, East Lansing, MI 48824

[2]Metamind, Palo Alto, CA 94301

[3]Center for Vision, Cognition, Learning, and Autonomy, University of California, Los Angeles, CA 90095

{yangshao,gaoqiaoz,cliu,jchai}@cse.msu.edu

cmxiong@metamind.io, sczhu@stat.ucla.edu

Abstract

Semantic Role Labeling (SRL) captures semantic roles (or participants) such as `agent`, `patient`, and `theme` associated with verbs from the text. While it provides important intermediate semantic representations for many traditional NLP tasks (such as information extraction and question answering), it does not capture grounded semantics so that an artificial agent can reason, learn, and perform the actions with respect to the physical environment. To address this problem, this paper extends traditional SRL to grounded SRL where arguments of verbs are grounded to participants of actions in the physical world. By integrating language and vision processing through joint inference, our approach not only grounds explicit roles, but also grounds implicit roles that are not explicitly mentioned in language descriptions. This paper describes our empirical results and discusses challenges and future directions.

1 Introduction

Linguistic studies capture semantics of verbs by their frames of thematic roles (also referred to as semantic roles or verb arguments) (Levin, 1993). For example, a verb can be characterized by `agent` (i.e., the animator of the action) and `patient` (i.e., the object on which the action is acted upon), and other roles such as `instrument`, `source`, `destination`, etc. Given a verb frame, the goal of Semantic Role Labeling (SRL) is to identify linguistic entities from the text that serve different thematic roles (Palmer et al., 2005; Gildea and Jurafsky,

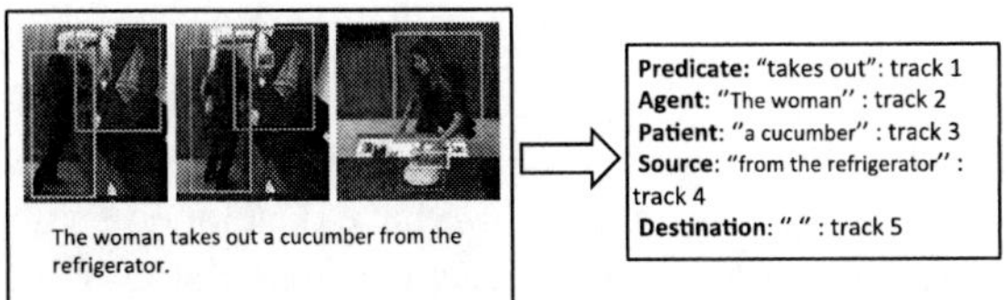

Figure 1: An example of grounded semantic role labeling for the sentence *the woman takes out a cucumber from the refrigerator*. The left hand side shows three frames of a video clip with the corresponding language description. The objects in the bounding boxes are tracked and each track has a unique identifier. The right hand side shows the grounding results where each role including the implicit role (`destination`) is grounded to a track id.

2002; Collobert et al., 2011; Zhou and Xu, 2015). For example, given the sentence *the woman takes out a cucumber from the refrigerator.*, *takes out* is the main verb (also called `predicate`); the noun phrase *the woman* is the `agent` of this action; *a cucumber* is the `patient`; and *the refrigerator* is the `source`.

SRL captures important semantic representations for actions associated with verbs, which have shown beneficial for a variety of applications such as information extraction (Emanuele et al., 2013) and question answering (Shen and Lapata, 2007). However, the traditional SRL is not targeted to represent verb semantics that are grounded to the physical world so that artificial agents can truly understand the ongoing activities and (learn to) perform the specified actions. To address this issue, we propose a new task on grounded semantic role labeling.

Figure 1 shows an example of grounded SRL.

The sentence *the woman takes out a cucumber from the refrigerator* describes an activity in a visual scene. The semantic role representation from linguistic processing (including implicit roles such as `destination`) is first extracted and then grounded to tracks of visual entities as shown in the video. For example, the verb phrase *take out* is grounded to a trajectory of the right hand. The role `agent` is grounded to the person who actually does the *take-out* action in the visual scene (*track 1*) ; the `patient` is grounded to the cucumber taken out (*track 3*); and the `source` is grounded to the refrigerator (*track 4*). The implicit role of `destination` (which is not explicitly mentioned in the language description) is grounded to the cutting board (*track 5*).

To tackle this problem, we have developed an approach to jointly process language and vision by incorporating semantic role information. In particular, we use a benchmark dataset (TACoS) which consists of parallel video and language descriptions in a complex cooking domain (Regneri et al., 2013) in our investigation. We have further annotated several layers of information for developing and evaluating grounded semantic role labeling algorithms. Compared to previous works on language grounding (Tellex et al., 2011; Yu and Siskind, 2013; Krishnamurthy and Kollar, 2013), our work presents several contributions. First, beyond arguments explicitly mentioned in language descriptions, our work simultaneously grounds explicit and implicit roles with an attempt to better connect verb semantics with actions from the underlying physical world. By incorporating semantic role information, our approach has led to better grounding performance. Second, most previous works only focused on a small number of verbs with limited activities. We base our investigation on a wider range of verbs and in a much more complex domain where object recognition and tracking are notably more difficult. Third, our work results in additional layers of annotation to part of the TACoS dataset. This annotation captures the structure of actions informed by semantic roles from the video. The annotated data is available for download [1]. It will provide a benchmark for future work on grounded SRL.

---

[1] `http://lair.cse.msu.edu/gsrl.html`

2   Related Work

Recent years have witnessed an increasing amount of work in integrating language and vision, from earlier image annotation (Ramanathan et al., 2013; Kazemzadeh et al., 2014) to recent image/video caption generation (Kuznetsova et al., 2013; Venugopalan et al., 2015; Ortiz et al., ; Elliott and de Vries, 2015; Devlin et al., 2015), video sentence alignment (Naim et al., 2015; Malmaud et al., 2015), scene generation (Chang et al., 2015), and multimodel embedding incorporating language and vision (Bruni et al., 2014; Lazaridou et al., 2015).

What is more relevant to our work here is recent progress on grounded language understanding, which involves learning meanings of words through connections to machine perception (Roy, 2005) and grounding language expressions to the shared visual world, for example, to visual objects (Liu et al., 2012; Liu and Chai, 2015), to physical landmarks (Tellex et al., 2011; Tellex et al., 2014), and to perceived actions or activities (Tellex et al., 2014; Artzi and Zettlemoyer, 2013).

Different approaches and emphases have been explored. For example, linear programming has been applied to mediate perceptual differences between humans and robots for referential grounding (Liu and Chai, 2015). Approaches to semantic parsing have been applied to ground language to internal world representations (Chen and Mooney, 2008; Artzi and Zettlemoyer, 2013). Logical Semantics with Perception (LSP) (Krishnamurthy and Kollar, 2013) was applied to ground natural language queries to visual referents through jointly parsing natural language (combinatory categorical grammar (CCG)) and visual attribute classification. Graphical models have been applied to word grounding. For example, a generative model was applied to integrate And-Or-Graph representations of language and vision for joint parsing (Tu et al., 2014). A Factorial Hidden Markov Model (FHMM) was applied to learn the meaning of nouns, verbs, prepositions, adjectives and adverbs from short video clips paired with sentences (Yu and Siskind, 2013). Discriminative models have also been applied to ground human commands or instructions to perceived visual entities, mostly for robotic applications (Tellex et al., 2011; Tellex et al., 2014). More recently, deep learning has been applied to ground phrases to image regions (Karpathy and Fei-Fei, 2015).

3 Method

We first describe our problem formulation and then provide details on the learning and inference algorithms.

3.1 Problem Formulation

Given a sentence S and its corresponding video clip V, our goal is to ground explicit/implicit roles associated with a verb in S to video tracks in V. In this paper, we focus on the following set of semantic roles: {predicate, patient, location, source, destination, tool}. In the cooking domain, as actions always involve hands, the predicate is grounded to the hand pose represented by a trajectory of relevant hand(s). Normally agent would be grounded to the person who does the action. As there is only one person in the scene, we thus ignore the grounding of the agent in this work.

Video tracks capture tracks of objects (including hands) and locations. For example, in Figure 1, there are 5 tracks: human, hand, cucumber, refrigerator and cutting board. Regarding the representation of locations, instead of discretization of a whole image to many small regions(large search space), we create locations corresponding to five spatial relations (center, up, down, left, right) with respect to each object track, which means we have 5 times number of locations compared with number of objects. For instance, in Figure 1, the source is grounded to

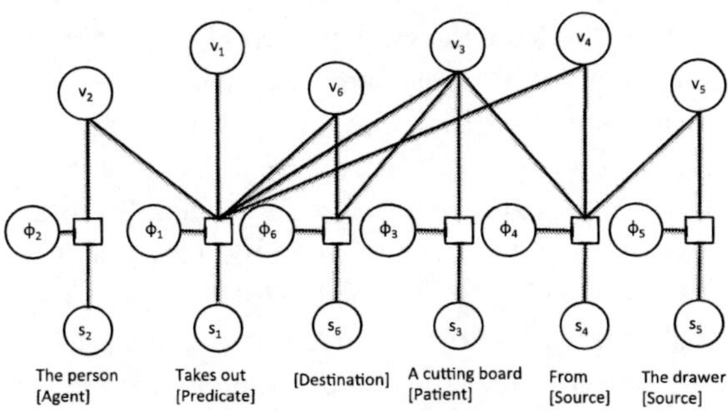

Figure 2: The CRF structure of sentence *"the person takes out a cutting board from the drawer"*. The text in the square bracket indicates the corresponding semantic role.

the center of the bounding boxes of the refrigerator track; and the destination is grounded to the center of the cutting board track.

We use Conditional Random Field(CRF) to model this problem. An example CRF factor graph is shown in Figure 2. The CRF structure is created based on information extracted from language. More Specifically, $s_1, ..., s_6$ refers to the observed text and its semantic role. Notice that s_6 is an implicit role as there is no text from the sentence describing destination. Also note that the whole prepositional phrase "from the drawer" is identified as the source rather than "the drawer" alone. This is because the prepositions play an important role in specifying location information. For example, "near the cutting boarding" is describing a location that is near to, but not exactly at the location of the cutting board. Here $v_1, ..., v_6$ are grounding random variables which take values from object tracks and locations in the video clip, and $\phi_1, ..., \phi_6$ are binary random variables which take values {0,1}. When ϕ_i equals to 1, it means v_i is the correct grounding of corresponding linguistic semantic role, otherwise it is not. The introduction of random variables ϕ_i follows previous work from Tellex and colleagues (Tellex et al., 2011), which makes CRF learning more tractable.

3.2 Learning and Inference

In the CRF model, we do not directly model the objective function as:

$$p(v_1, ..., v_k | S, V)$$

where S refers to the sentence, V refers to the corresponding video clip and v_i refers to the grounding variable. Because the gradient based learning method needs the expectation of $v_1, ..., v_k$, which is infeasible, we instead use the following objective function:

$$P(\phi | s_1, s_2, ..., s_k, v_1, v_2, ..., v_k, V)$$

where ϕ is a binary random vector $[\phi_1, ..., \phi_k]$, indicating whether the grounding is correct. In this way, the objective function factorizes according to the structure of language with local normalization at each factor.

Gradient ascent with L2 regularization was used for parameter learning to maximize the objective function:

$$\frac{\partial L}{\partial w} = \sum_i F(\phi_i, s_i, v_i, V) - \sum_i \mathbb{E}_{P(\phi_i|s_i,v_i,V)} F(\phi_i, s_i, v_i, V)$$

where F refers to the feature function. During the training, we also use random grounding as negative samples for discriminative training.

During inference, the search space can be very large when the number of objects in the world increases. To address this problem we apply beam search to first ground roles including `patient`, `tool`, and then other roles including `location`, `source`, `destination` and `predicate`.

4 Evaluation

4.1 Dataset

We conducted our investigation based on a subset of the TACoS corpus (Regneri et al., 2013). This dataset contains a set of video clips paired with natural language descriptions related to several cooking tasks. The natural language descriptions were collected through crowd-sourcing on top of the "MPII Cooking Composite Activities" video corpus (Rohrbach et al., 2012). In this paper, we selected two tasks "cutting cucumber" and "cutting bread" as our experimental data. Each task has 5 videos showing how different people perform the same task. Each video is segmented to a sequence of video clips where each video clip comes with one or more language descriptions. The original TACoS dataset does not contain annotation for grounded semantic roles.

To support our investigation and evaluation, we had made a significant effort adding the following annotations. For each video clip, we annotated the objects' bounding boxes, their tracks, and their labels (cucumber, cutting_board, etc.) using VATIC (Vondrick et al., 2013). On average, each video clip is annotated with 15 tracks of objects. For each sentence, we annotated the ground truth parsing structure and the semantic frame for each verb. The ground truth parsing structure is the representation of dependency parsing results. The semantic frame of a verb includes slots, fillers, and their groundings. For each semantic role (including both explicit roles and implicit roles) of a given verb, we also annotated the ground truth grounding in terms of the object tracks and locations. In total, our annotated dataset includes 976 pairs of video clips and corresponding sentences, 1094 verbs occurrences, and 3593 groundings of semantic roles. To check annotation agreement, 10% of the data was annotated by two annotators. The kappa statistics is 0.83 (Cohen and others, 1960).

From this dataset, we selected 11 most frequent verbs (i.e., *get, take, wash, cut, rinse, slice, place, peel, put, remove, open*) in our current investigation for the following reasons. First, they are used more frequently so that we can have sufficient samples of each verb to learn the model. Second, they cover different types of actions: some are more related to the change of the state such as *take*, and some are more related to the process such as *wash*. As it turns out, these verbs also have different semantic role patterns as shown in Table 1. The `patient` roles of all these verbs are explicitly specified. This is not surprising as all these verbs are transitive verbs. There is a large variation for other roles. For example, for the verb *take*, the `destination` is rarely specified by lin-

Table 1: Statistics for a set of verbs and their semantic roles in our annotated dataset. The entry indicates the number of explicit/implicit roles for each category. "–" denotes no such role is observed in the data.[1]

Verb	Patient	Source	Destn	Location	Tool
take	251 / 0	102 / 149	2 / 248	–	–
put	94 / 0	–	75 / 19	–	–
get	247 / 0	62 / 190	0 / 239	–	–
cut	134 / 1	64 / 64	–	3 / 131	5 / 130
open	23 / 0	–	–	0 / 23	2 / 21
wash	93 / 0	–	–	26 / 58	2 / 82
slice	69 / 1	–	–	2 / 68	2 / 66
rinse	76 / 0	0 / 74	–	8 / 64	–
place	104 / 1	–	105 / 7	–	–
peel	29 / 0	–	–	1 / 27	2 / 27
remove	40 / 0	34 / 6	–	–	–

---

[1]For some verbs (e.g., *get*), there is a slight discrepancy between the sum of implicit/explicit roles across different categories. This is partly due to the fact that some verb occurrences take more than one objects as grounding to a role. It is also possibly due to missed/duplicated annotation for some categories.

guistic expressions (i.e., only 2 instances), however it can be inferred from the video. For the verb *cut*, the `location` and the `tool` are also rarely specified by linguistic expressions. Nevertheless, these implicit roles contribute to the overall understanding of actions and should also be grounded too.

4.2 Automated Processing

To build the structure of the CRF as shown in Figure 2 and extract features for learning and inference, we have applied the following approaches to process language and vision.

Language Processing. Language processing consists of three steps to build a structure containing syntactic and semantic information. First, the Stanford Parser (Manning et al., 2014) is applied to create a dependency parsing tree for each sentence. Second, Senna (Collobert et al., 2011) is applied to identify semantic role labels for the key verb in the sentence. The linguistic entities with semantic roles are matched against the dependency nodes in the tree and the corresponding semantic role labels are added to the tree. Third, for each verb, the Propbank (Palmer et al., 2005) entries are searched to extract all relevant semantic roles. The implicit roles (i.e., not specified linguistically) are added as direct children of verb nodes in the tree. Through these three steps, the resulting tree from language processing has both explicit and implicit semantic roles. These trees are further transformed to the CRF structures based on a set of rules.

Vision Processing. A set of visual detectors are first trained for each type of objects. Here a random forest classifier is adopted. More specifically, we use 100 trees with HoG features (Dalal and Triggs, 2005) and color descriptors (Van De Weijer and Schmid, 2006). Both HoG and Color descriptors are used, because some objects are more structural, such as knives, human; some are more textured such as towels. With the learned object detectors, given a candidate video clip, we run the detectors at each 10th frame (less than 0.5 second), and find the candidate windows for which the detector score corresponding to the object is larger than a threshold (set as 0.5). Then using the detected window as a starting point, we adopt tracking-by-detection (Danelljan et al., 2014) to go forward and backward to track this object and obtain the candidate track with this object label.

Feature Extraction. Features in the CRF model can be divided into the following three categories:

1. *Linguistic features* include word occurrence and semantic role information. They are extracted by language processing.

2. *Track label features* are the label information for tracks in the video. The labels come from human annotation or automated visual processing depending on different experimental settings (described in Section 4.3).

3. *Visual features* are a set of features involving geometric relations between tracks in the video. One important feature is the histogram comparison score. It measures the similarity between distance histograms. Specifically, histograms of distance values between the tracks of the `predicate` and other roles for each verb are first extracted from the training video clips. For an incoming distance histogram, we calculate its Chi-Square distances (Zhang et al., 2007) from the pre-extracted training histograms with the same verb and the same role. its histogram comparison score is set to be the average of top 5 smallest Chi-Square distances. Other visual features include geometric information for single tracks and geometric relations between two tracks. For example, size, average speed, and moving direction are extracted for a single track. Average distance, size-ratio, and relative direction are extracted between two tracks. For features that are continuous, we discretized them into uniform bins.

To ground language into tracks from the video, instead of using track label features or visual features alone, we use a Cartesian product of these features with linguistic features. To learn the behavior of different semantic roles of different verbs, visual features are combined with the presence of both verbs and semantic roles through Cartesian product. To learn the correspondence between track labels and words, track label features are combined with the presence of words also through Cartesian product.

To train the model, we randomly selected 75% of annotated 976 pairs of video clips and corresponding sentences as training set. The remaining 25% were used as the testing set.

4.3 Experimental Setup

Comparison. To evaluate the performance of our approach, we compare it with two approaches.

- **Baseline**: To identify the grounding for each semantic role, the first baseline chooses the most possible track based on the object type conditional distribution given the verb and semantic role. If an object type corresponds to multiple tracks in the video, e.g., multiple drawers or knives, we then randomly select one of the tracks as grounding. We ran this baseline method five times and reported the average performance.

- **Tellex (2011)**: The second approach we compared with is based on an implementation (Tellex et al., 2011). The difference is that they don't explicitly model fine-grained semantic role information. For a better comparison, we map the grounding results from this approach to different explicit semantic roles according to the SRL annotation of the sentence. Note that this approach is not able to ground implicit roles.

More specifically, we compare these two approaches with two variations of our system:

- **GSRL$_{wo_v}$**: The CRF model using linguistic features and track label features (described in Section 4.2).

- **GSRL**: The full CRF model using linguistic features, track label features, and visual features(described in Section 4.2).

Configurations. Both automated language processing and vision processing are error-prone. To further understand the limitations of grounded SRL, we compare performance under different configurations along the two dimensions: (1) the CRF structure is built upon annotated ground-truth language parsing versus automated language parsing; (2) object tracking and labeling is based on annotation versus automated processing. These lead to four different experimental configurations.

Evaluation Metrics. For experiments that are based on annotated object tracks, we can simply use the traditional *accuracy* that directly measures the percentage of grounded tracks that are correct. However, for experiments using automated tracking, evaluation can be difficult as tracking itself poses significant challenges. The grounding results (to tracks) cannot be directly compared with the annotated ground-truth tracks. To address this problem, we have defined a new metric called *approximate accuracy*. This metric is motivated by previous computer vision work that evaluates tracking performance (Bashir and Porikli, 2006). Suppose the ground truth grounding for a role is track gt and the predicted grounding is track pt. The two tracks gt and pt are often not the same (although may have some overlaps). Suppose the number of frames in the video clip is k. For each frame, we calculate the distance between the centroids of these two tracks. If their distance is below a predefined threshold, we consider the two tracks overlap in this frame. We consider the grounding is correct if the ratio of the overlapping frames between gt and pt exceeds 50%. As can be seen, this is a lenient and an approximate measure of accuracy.

4.4 Results

The results based on the ground-truth language parsing are shown in Table 2, and the results based on automated language parsing are shown in Table 3. For results based on annotated object tracking, the performance is reported in *accuracy* and for results based on automated object tracking, the performance is reported in *approximate accuracy*. When the number of testing samples is less than 15, we do not show the result as it tends to be unreliable (shown as *NA*). Tellex (2011) does not address implicit roles (shown as "–"). The best performance score is shown in bold. We also conducted a two-tailed bootstrap significance testing (Efron and Tibshirani, 1994). The score with a "*" indicates it is statistically significant ($p < 0.05$) compared to the baseline approach. The score with a "+" indicates

Table 2: Evaluation results based on annotated language parsing.

| Accuracy On the Gold Recognition/Tracking Setting | | | | | | | | | | | | | | |
| Methods | Predicate | Patient | | Source | | Destination | | Location | | Tool | | Explicit All | Implicit All | All |
		explicit	implicit	explicit	implicit	explicit	implicit	explicit	implicit	explicit	implicit			
Baseline	0.856	0.372	NA	0.225	0.314	0.311	0.569	NA	0.910	NA	0.853	0.556	0.620	0.583
Tellex(2011)	0.865	0.745	–	0.306	–	0.763	–	NA	–	NA	–	0.722	–	–
GSRL$_{wo_v}$	0.854	0.794^{*}_{+}	NA	0.375^{*}	0.392^{*}_{+}	0.658^{*}	0.615^{*}_{+}	NA	0.920_{+}	NA	0.793_{+}	0.768^{*}_{+}	0.648^{*}_{+}	0.717^{*}
GSRL	$\mathbf{0.878^{*}_{+}}$	$\mathbf{0.839^{*}_{+}}$	NA	$\mathbf{0.556^{*}_{+}}$	$\mathbf{0.684^{*}_{+}}$	$\mathbf{0.789^{*}}$	$\mathbf{0.641^{*}_{+}}$	NA	$\mathbf{0.930_{+}}$	NA	$\mathbf{0.897^{*}_{+}}$	$\mathbf{0.825^{*}_{+}}$	$\mathbf{0.768^{*}_{+}}$	$\mathbf{0.8^{*}}$
Approximated Accuracy On the Automated Recognition/Tracking Setting														
Methods	Predicate	Patient		Source		Destination		Location		Tool		Explicit All	Implicit All	All
		explicit	implicit	explicit	implicit	explicit	implicit	explicit	implicit	explicit	implicit			
Baseline	0.529	0.206	NA	0.169	0.119	0.236	0.566	NA	**0.476**	NA	0.6	0.352	0.393	0.369
Tellex(2011)	**0.607**	0.233	–	0.154	–	0.333	–	NA	–	NA	–	0.359	–	–
GSRL$_{wo_v}$	0.582^{*}	0.244^{*}	NA	$\mathbf{0.262^{*}_{+}}$	0.126_{+}	$\mathbf{0.485^{*}_{+}}$	$\mathbf{0.613^{*}_{+}}$	NA	0.467_{+}	NA	$\mathbf{0.714^{*}_{+}}$	$\mathbf{0.410^{*}_{+}}$	$\mathbf{0.425^{*}_{+}}$	$\mathbf{0.417^{*}}$
GSRL	0.548	$\mathbf{0.263^{*}}$	NA	$\mathbf{0.262^{*}_{+}}$	0.086_{+}	0.394^{*}	0.514_{+}	NA	0.456_{+}	NA	0.688^{*}_{+}	0.399^{*}_{+}	0.381_{+}	0.391^{*}
Upper_Bound	0.920	0.309	NA	0.277	0.252	0.636	0.829	NA	0.511	NA	0.818	0.577	0.573	0.575

Table 3: Evaluation results based on automated language parsing.

| Accuracy On the Gold Recognition/Tracking Setting | | | | | | | | | | | | | | |
| Methods | Predicate | Patient | | Source | | Destination | | Location | | Tool | | Explicit All | Implicit All | All |
		explicit	implicit	explicit	implicit	explicit	implicit	explicit	implicit	explicit	implicit			
Baseline	0.881	0.318	NA	0.203	0.316	0.235	0.607	NA	0.877	NA	**0.895**	0.539	0.595	0.563
Tellex(2011)	**0.903**	0.746	–	0.156	–	0.353	–	NA	–	NA	–	0.680	–	–
GSRL$_{wo_v}$	0.873	0.813^{*}_{+}	NA	0.328^{*}_{+}	0.360_{+}	$\mathbf{0.412^{*}}$	0.648^{*}_{+}	NA	0.877_{+}	NA	0.818_{+}	0.769^{*}_{+}	0.611_{+}	0.7^{*}
GSRL	0.873	$\mathbf{0.875^{*}_{+}}$	NA	$\mathbf{0.453^{*}_{+}}$	$\mathbf{0.667^{*}_{+}}$	$\mathbf{0.412^{*}}$	$\mathbf{0.667^{*}_{+}}$	NA	$\mathbf{0.891_{+}}$	NA	0.891_{+}	$\mathbf{0.823^{*}_{+}}$	$\mathbf{0.741^{*}_{+}}$	$\mathbf{0.787^{*}}$
Approximated Accuracy On the Automated Recognition/Tracking Setting														
Methods	Predicate	Patient		Source		Destination		Location		Tool		Explicit All	Implicit All	All
		explicit	implicit	explicit	implicit	explicit	implicit	explicit	implicit	explicit	implicit			
Baseline	0.543	0.174	NA	0.121	0.113	0.093	0.594	NA	**0.612**	NA	0.567	0.327	0.405	0.362
Tellex(2011)	0.598	0.218	–	0.086	–	0.00	–	NA	–	NA	–	0.322	–	–
GSRL$_{wo_v}$	$\mathbf{0.618^{*}}$	$\mathbf{0.243^{*}}$	NA	$\mathbf{0.190^{*}_{+}}$	0.120_{+}	$\mathbf{0.133_{+}}$	0.641^{*}_{+}	NA	0.585_{+}	NA	$\mathbf{0.723^{*}_{+}}$	$\mathbf{0.401^{*}_{+}}$	$\mathbf{0.434^{*}_{+}}$	$\mathbf{0.415^{*}}$
GSRL	0.493	$\mathbf{0.243^{*}}$	NA	$\mathbf{0.190^{*}_{+}}$	0.063_{+}	$\mathbf{0.133_{+}}$	0.612_{+}	NA	0.554_{+}	NA	0.617_{+}	0.367^{*}_{+}	0.386_{+}	0.375
Upper_Bound	0.908	0.277	NA	0.259	0.254	0.4	0.854	NA	0.631	NA	0.830	0.543	0.585	0.561

it is statistically significant ($p < 0.05$) compared to the approach (Tellex et al., 2011).

For experiments based on automated object tracking, we also calculated an *upper_bound* to assess the best possible performance which can be achieved by a perfect grounding algorithm given the current vision processing results. This *upper_bound* is calculated based on grounding each role to the track which is closest to the ground-truth annotated track. For the experiments based on annotated tracking, the *upper_bound* would be 100%. This measure provides some understandings about how good the grounding approach is given the limitation of vision processing. Notice that the grounding results in the gold/automatic language processing setting are not directly comparable as the automatic SRL can misidentify frame elements.

4.5 Discussion

As shown in Table 2 and Table 3, our approach consistently outperforms the baseline (for both explicit and implicit roles) and the Tellex (2011) approach. Under the configuration of gold recognition/tracking, the incorporation of visual features further improves the performance. However, this performance gain is not observed when automated object tracking and labeling is used. One possible explanation is that as we only had limited data, we did not use separate data to train models for

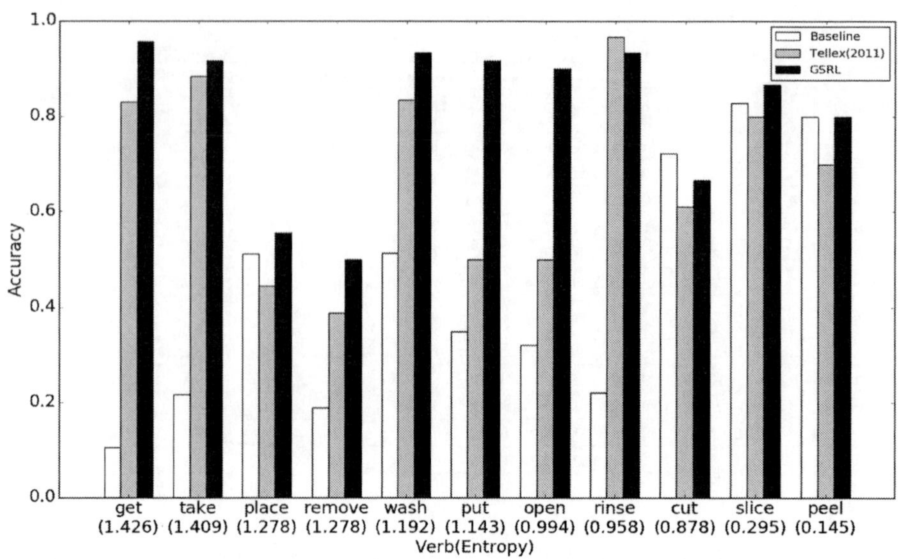

Figure 3: The relation between the accuracy and the entropy of each verb's patient from the gold language, gold visual recognition/tracking setting. The entropy for the patient role of each verb is shown below the verb.

object recognition/tracking. So the GSRL model was trained with gold recognition/tracking data and tested with automated recognition/tracking data.

By comparing our method with Tellex (2011), we can see that by incorporating fine grained semantic role information, our approach achieves better performance on almost all the explicit role (except for the `patient` role under the automated tracking condition).

The results have also shown that some roles are easier to ground than others in this domain. For example, the `predicate` role is grounded to the hand tracks (either left hand or right hand), there are not many variations such that the simple baseline can achieve pretty high performance, especially when annotated tracking is used. The same situation happens to the `location` role as most of the locations happen near the *sink* when the verb is *wash*, and near the *cutting board* for verbs like *cut*, etc. However, for the `patient` role, there is a large difference between our approach and baseline approaches as there is a larger variation of different types of objects that can participate in the role for a given verb.

For experiments with automated tracking, the *up-per_bound* for each role also varies. Some roles (e.g., `patient`) have a pretty low upper bound.

The accuracy from our full GSRL model is already quite close to the upper bound. For other roles such as `predicate` and `destination`, there is a larger gap between the current performance and the upper bound. This difference reflects the model's capability in grounding different roles.

Figure 3 shows a close-up look at the grounding performance to the `patient` role for each verb under the gold parsing and gold tracking configuration. The reason we only show the results of `patient` role here is every verb has this role to be grounded. For each verb, we also calculated its entropy based on the distribution of different types of objects that can serve as the `patient` role in the training data. The entropy is shown at the bottom of the figure. For verbs such as *take* and *put*, our full GSRL model leads to much better performance compared to the baseline. As the baseline approach relies on the entropy of the potential grounding for a role, we further measured the improvement of the performance and calculated the correlation between the improvement and the entropy of each verb. The result shows that Pearson coefficient between the entropy and the improvement of GSRL over the baseline is 0.614. This indicates the improvement from GSRL is positively correlated with the entropy value associated with a role, implying the GSRL model can deal with more uncertain situations. For the verb *cut*, The GSRL model performs slightly worse than the baseline. One explanation is that the possible objects that can participate as a patient for *cut* are relatively constrained where simple features might be sufficient. A large number of features may introduce noise, and thus jeopardizing the performance.

We further compare the performance of our full GRSL model with Tellex (2011) (also shown in Figure 3) on the `patient` role of different verbs. Our approach outperforms Tellex (2011) on most of the verbs, especially *put* and *open*. A close look at the results have shown that in those cases, the `patient` roles are often specified by pronouns. Therefore, the track label features and linguistic features are not very helpful, and the correct grounding mainly depends on visual features. Our full GSRL model can better capture the geometry relations between different semantic roles by incorporating fine-grained role information.

5   Conclusion and Future Work

This paper investigates a new problem on grounded semantic role labeling. Besides semantic roles explicitly mentioned in language descriptions, our approach also grounds implicit roles which are not explicitly specified. As implicit roles also capture important participants related to an action (e.g., tools used in the action), our approach provides a more complete representation of action semantics which can be used by artificial agents for further reasoning and planning towards the physical world. Our empirical results on a complex cooking domain have shown that, by incorporating semantic role information with visual features, our approach can achieve better performance compared to baseline approaches. Our results have also shown that grounded semantic role labeling is a challenging problem which often depends on the quality of automated visual processing (e.g., object tracking and recognition).

There are several directions for future improvement. First, the current alignment between a video clip and a sentence is generated by some heuristics which are error-prone. One way to address this is to treat alignment and grounding as a joint problem. Second, our current visual features have not shown effective especially when they are extracted based on automatic visual processing. This is partly due to the complexity of the scene from the TACoS dataset and the lack of depth information. Recent advances in object tracking algorithms (Yang et al., 2013; Milan et al., 2014) together with 3D sensing can be explored in the future to improve visual processing. Moreover, linguistic studies have shown that action verbs such as *cut* and *slice* often denote some change of state as a result of the action (Hovav and Levin, 2010; Hovav and Levin, 2008). The change of state can be perceived from the physical world. Thus another direction is to systematically study causality of verbs. Causality models for verbs can potentially provide top-down information to guide intermediate representations for visual processing and improve grounded language understanding.

The capability of grounding semantic roles to the physical world has many important implications. It will support the development of intelligent agents which can reason and act upon the shared physical world. For example, unlike traditional action recognition in computer vision (Wang et al., 2011), grounded SRL will provide deeper understanding of the activities which involve participants in the actions guided by linguistic knowledge. For agents that can act upon the physical world such as robots, grounded SRL will allow the agents to acquire the grounded structure of human commands and thus perform the requested actions through planning (e.g., to follow the command "put the cup on the table"). Grounded SRL will also contribute to robot action learning where humans can teach the robot new actions (e.g., simple cooking tasks) through both task demonstration and language instruction.

6   Acknowledgement

The authors are grateful to Austin Littley and Zach Richardson for their help on data annotation, and to anonymous reviewers for their valuable comments and suggestions. This work was supported in part by IIS-1208390 from the National Science Foundation and by N66001-15-C-4035 from the DARPA SIMPLEX program.

References

Yoav Artzi and Luke Zettlemoyer. 2013. Weakly supervised learning of semantic parsers for mapping instructions to actions. *TACL*, 1:49–62.

Faisal Bashir and Fatih Porikli. 2006. Performance evaluation of object detection and tracking systems. In *Proceedings 9th IEEE International Workshop on PETS*, pages 7–14.

Elia Bruni, Nam-Khanh Tran, and Marco Baroni. 2014. Multimodal distributional semantics. *J. Artif. Intell. Res.(JAIR)*, 49:1–47.

Angel Chang, Will Monroe, Manolis Savva, Christopher Potts, and Christopher D Manning. 2015. Text to 3d scene generation with rich lexical grounding. *arXiv preprint arXiv:1505.06289*.

David L Chen and Raymond J Mooney. 2008. Learning to sportscast: a test of grounded language acquisition. In *Proceedings of the 25th international conference on Machine learning*, pages 128–135. ACM.

Jacob Cohen et al. 1960. A coefficient of agreement for nominal scales. *Educational and psychological measurement*, 20(1):37–46.

Ronan Collobert, Jason Weston, Léon Bottou, Michael Karlen, Koray Kavukcuoglu, and Pavel Kuksa. 2011. Natural language processing (almost) from scratch. *The Journal of Machine Learning Research*, 12:2493–2537.

Navneet Dalal and Bill Triggs. 2005. Histograms of oriented gradients for human detection. In *Computer Vision and Pattern Recognition, 2005. CVPR 2005. IEEE Computer Society Conference on*, volume 1, pages 886–893. IEEE.

Martin Danelljan, Fahad Shahbaz Khan, Michael Felsberg, and Joost van de Weijer. 2014. Adaptive color attributes for real-time visual tracking. In *Computer Vision and Pattern Recognition (CVPR), 2014 IEEE Conference on*, pages 1090–1097. IEEE.

Jacob Devlin, Hao Cheng, Hao Fang, Saurabh Gupta, Li Deng, Xiaodong He, Geoffrey Zweig, and Margaret Mitchell. 2015. Language models for image captioning: The quirks and what works. *arXiv preprint arXiv:1505.01809*.

Bradley Efron and Robert J Tibshirani. 1994. *An introduction to the bootstrap*. CRC press.

Desmond Elliott and Arjen de Vries. 2015. Describing images using inferred visual dependency representations. In *Proceedings of the 53rd Annual Meeting of the Association for Computational Linguistics and the 7th International Joint Conference on Natural Language Processing (Volume 1: Long Papers)*, pages 42–52, Beijing, China, July. Association for Computational Linguistics.

Bastianelli Emanuele, Giuseppe Castellucci, Danilo Croce, and Roberto Basili. 2013. Textual inference and meaning representation in human robot interaction. In *Joint Symposium on Semantic Processing.*, page 65.

Daniel Gildea and Daniel Jurafsky. 2002. Automatic labeling of semantic roles. *Computational linguistics*, 28(3):245–288.

Malka Rappaport Hovav and Beth Levin. 2008. Reflections on manner/result complementarity. *Lecture notes*.

Malka Rappaport Hovav and Beth Levin. 2010. Reflections on Manner / Result Complementarity. *Lexical Semantics, Syntax, and Event Structure*, pages 21–38.

Andrej Karpathy and Li Fei-Fei. 2015. Deep visual-semantic alignments for generating image descriptions. June.

Sahar Kazemzadeh, Vicente Ordonez, Mark Matten, and Tamara Berg. 2014. Referitgame: Referring to objects in photographs of natural scenes. In *Proceedings of the 2014 Conference on Empirical Methods in Natural Language Processing (EMNLP)*, pages 787–798, Doha, Qatar, October. Association for Computational Linguistics.

Jayant Krishnamurthy and Thomas Kollar. 2013. Jointly learning to parse and perceive: Connecting natural language to the physical world. *Transactions of the Association for Computational Linguistics*, 1:193–206.

Polina Kuznetsova, Vicente Ordonez, Alexander C Berg, Tamara L Berg, and Yejin Choi. 2013. Generalizing image captions for image-text parallel corpus. In *ACL (2)*, pages 790–796. Citeseer.

Angeliki Lazaridou, Nghia The Pham, and Marco Baroni. 2015. Combining language and vision with a multimodal skip-gram model. *arXiv preprint arXiv:1501.02598*.

Beth Levin. 1993. *English verb classes and alternations: A preliminary investigation*. University of Chicago press.

Changsong Liu and Joyce Y. Chai. 2015. Learning to mediate perceptual differences in situated human-robot dialogue. In *The Twenty-Ninth Conference on Artificial Intelligence (AAAI-15)*. to appear.

Changsong Liu, Rui Fang, and Joyce Chai. 2012. Towards mediating shared perceptual basis in situated dialogue. In *Proceedings of the 13th Annual Meeting of the Special Interest Group on Discourse and Dialogue*, pages 140–149, Seoul, South Korea.

Jonathan Malmaud, Jonathan Huang, Vivek Rathod, Nick Johnston, Andrew Rabinovich, and Kevin Murphy. 2015. What's cookin'? interpreting cooking videos using text, speech and vision. *arXiv preprint arXiv:1503.01558*.

Christopher D. Manning, Mihai Surdeanu, John Bauer, Jenny Finkel, Steven J. Bethard, and David McClosky. 2014. The Stanford CoreNLP natural language processing toolkit. In *Proceedings of 52nd Annual Meeting of the Association for Computational Linguistics: System Demonstrations*, pages 55–60.

Anton Milan, Stefan Roth, and Kaspar Schindler. 2014. Continuous energy minimization for multitarget tracking. *Pattern Analysis and Machine Intelligence, IEEE Transactions on*, 36(1):58–72.

Iftekhar Naim, Young C. Song, Qiguang Liu, Liang Huang, Henry Kautz, Jiebo Luo, and Daniel Gildea. 2015. Discriminative unsupervised alignment of natural language instructions with corresponding video segments. In *Proceedings of the 2015 Conference of the North American Chapter of the Association for Computational Linguistics: Human Language Technologies*, pages 164–174, Denver, Colorado, May–June. Association for Computational Linguistics.

Luis Gilberto Mateos Ortiz, Clemens Wolff, and Mirella Lapata. Learning to interpret and describe abstract scenes. In *Proceedings of the 2015 Conference of the North American Chapter of the Association for Computational Linguistics: Human Language Technologies*, pages 1505–1515.

Martha Palmer, Daniel Gildea, and Paul Kingsbury. 2005. The proposition bank: An annotated corpus of semantic roles. *Computational linguistics*, 31(1):71–106.

Vignesh Ramanathan, Percy Liang, and Li Fei-Fei. 2013. Video event understanding using natural language descriptions. In *Computer Vision (ICCV), 2013 IEEE International Conference on*, pages 905–912. IEEE.

Michaela Regneri, Marcus Rohrbach, Dominikus Wetzel, Stefan Thater, Bernt Schiele, and Manfred Pinkal. 2013. Grounding action descriptions in videos. *Transactions of the Association for Computational Linguistics (TACL)*, 1:25–36.

Marcus Rohrbach, Michaela Regneri, Mykhaylo Andriluka, Sikandar Amin, Manfred Pinkal, and Bernt Schiele. 2012. Script data for attribute-based recognition of composite activities. In *Computer Vision–ECCV 2012*, pages 144–157. Springer.

Deb Roy. 2005. Grounding words in perception and action: computational insights. *TRENDS in Cognitive Sciences*, 9(8):389–396.

Dan Shen and Mirella Lapata. 2007. Using semantic roles to improve question answering. In *EMNLP-CoNLL*, pages 12–21.

Stefanie Tellex, Thomas Kollar, Steven Dickerson, Matthew R Walter, Ashis Gopal Banerjee, Seth J Teller, and Nicholas Roy. 2011. Understanding natural language commands for robotic navigation and mobile manipulation. In *AAAI*.

Stefanie Tellex, Pratiksha Thaker, Joshua Joseph, and Nicholas Roy. 2014. Learning perceptually grounded word meanings from unaligned parallel data. *Machine Learning*, 94(2):151–167.

Kewei Tu, Meng Meng, Mun Wai Lee, Tae Eun Choe, and Song-Chun Zhu. 2014. Joint video and text parsing for understanding events and answering queries. *MultiMedia, IEEE*, 21(2):42–70.

Joost Van De Weijer and Cordelia Schmid. 2006. Coloring local feature extraction. In *Computer Vision–ECCV 2006*, pages 334–348. Springer.

Subhashini Venugopalan, Huijuan Xu, Jeff Donahue, Marcus Rohrbach, Raymond Mooney, and Kate Saenko. 2015. Translating videos to natural language using deep recurrent neural networks. In *Proceedings of the 2015 Conference of the North American Chapter of the Association for Computational Linguistics: Human Language Technologies*, pages 1494–1504, Denver, Colorado, May–June. Association for Computational Linguistics.

Carl Vondrick, Donald Patterson, and Deva Ramanan. 2013. Efficiently scaling up crowdsourced video annotation. *International Journal of Computer Vision*, 101(1):184–204.

Heng Wang, Alexander Kläser, Cordelia Schmid, and Cheng-Lin Liu. 2011. Action recognition by dense trajectories. In *Computer Vision and Pattern Recognition (CVPR), 2011 IEEE Conference on*, pages 3169–3176. IEEE.

Yezhou Yang, Cornelia Fermuller, and Yiannis Aloimonos. 2013. Detection of manipulation action consequences (mac). In *Proceedings of the IEEE Conference on Computer Vision and Pattern Recognition*, pages 2563–2570.

Haonan Yu and Jeffrey Mark Siskind. 2013. Grounded language learning from video described with sentences. In *ACL (1)*, pages 53–63.

Jianguo Zhang, Marcin Marszałek, Svetlana Lazebnik, and Cordelia Schmid. 2007. Local features and kernels for classification of texture and object categories: A comprehensive study. *International journal of computer vision*, 73(2):213–238.

Jie Zhou and Wei Xu. 2015. End-to-end learning of semantic role labeling using recurrent neural networks. In *Proceedings of the 53rd Annual Meeting of the Association for Computational Linguistics and the 7th International Joint Conference on Natural Language Processing (Volume 1: Long Papers)*, pages 1127–1137, Beijing, China, July. Association for Computational Linguistics.

Black Holes and White Rabbits:
Metaphor Identification with Visual Features

Ekaterina Shutova
Computer Laboratory
University of Cambridge
es407@cam.ac.uk

Douwe Kiela
Computer Laboratory
University of Cambridge
dk427@cam.ac.uk

Jean Maillard
Computer Laboratory
University of Cambridge
jean@maillard.it

Abstract

Metaphor is pervasive in our communication, which makes it an important problem for natural language processing (NLP). Numerous approaches to metaphor processing have thus been proposed, all of which relied on linguistic features and textual data to construct their models. Human metaphor comprehension is, however, known to rely on both our linguistic and perceptual experience, and vision can play a particularly important role when metaphorically projecting imagery across domains. In this paper, we present the first metaphor identification method that simultaneously draws knowledge from linguistic and visual data. Our results demonstrate that it outperforms linguistic and visual models in isolation, as well as being competitive with the best-performing metaphor identification methods, that rely on hand-crafted knowledge about domains and perception.

1 Introduction

Metaphor lends vividness, sophistication and clarity to our thought and communication. At the same time, it plays a fundamental structural role in our cognition, helping us to organise and project knowledge (Lakoff and Johnson, 1980; Feldman, 2006). Metaphors arise due to systematic associations between distinct, and seemingly unrelated, concepts. For instance, when we talk about "the *turning wheels* of a political regime", "*rebuilding* the campaign *machinery*" or "*mending* foreign policy", we view *politics* and *political systems* in terms of *mechanisms*, they can *function, break, be mended* etc. The existence of this association allows us to transfer knowledge and imagery from the domain of *mechanisms* (the source domain) to that of *political systems* (the target domain). According to Lakoff and Johnson (1980), such metaphorical mappings, or *conceptual metaphors*, form the basis of metaphorical language.

Metaphor is pervasive in our communication, which makes it important for NLP applications dealing with real-world text. A number of approaches to metaphor processing have thus been proposed, using supervised classification (Gedigian et al., 2006; Mohler et al., 2013; Tsvetkov et al., 2013; Hovy et al., 2013; Dunn, 2013a), clustering (Shutova et al., 2010; Shutova and Sun, 2013), vector space models (Shutova et al., 2012; Mohler et al., 2014), lexical resources (Krishnakumaran and Zhu, 2007; Wilks et al., 2013) and web search with lexico-syntactic patterns (Veale and Hao, 2008; Li et al., 2013; Bollegala and Shutova, 2013). So far, these and other metaphor processing works relied on textual data to construct their models. Yet, several experiments indicated that perceptual properties of concepts, such as concreteness and imageability, are important features for metaphor identification (Turney et al., 2011; Neuman et al., 2013; Gandy et al., 2013; Strzalkowski et al., 2013; Tsvetkov et al., 2014). However, all of these methods used manually-annotated linguistic resources to determine these properties (such as the MRC concreteness database (Wilson, 1988)). To the best of our knowledge, there has not yet been a metaphor processing method that employed information learned from both linguistic and visual data. Ample re-

Proceedings of NAACL-HLT 2016, pages 160–170,
San Diego, California, June 12-17, 2016. ©2016 Association for Computational Linguistics

scarch in cognitive science suggests that human meaning representations are not merely a product of our linguistic exposure, but are also grounded in our perceptual system and sensori-motor experience (Barsalou, 2008; Louwerse, 2011). Semantic models integrating information from multiple modalities have been shown successful in tasks such as modeling semantic similarity and relatedness (Silberer and Lapata, 2012; Bruni et al., 2014), lexical entailment (Kiela et al., 2015a), compositionality (Roller and Schulte im Walde, 2013) and bilingual lexicon induction (Kiela et al., 2015b). Using visual information is particularly relevant to modelling metaphor, where imagery is ported across domains.

In this paper, we present the first metaphor identification method integrating meaning representations learned from linguistic and visual data. We construct our representations using a skip-gram model of Mikolov et al. (2013a) trained on textual data to obtain linguistic embeddings and a deep convolutional neural network (Kiela and Bottou, 2014) trained on image data to obtain visual embeddings. Linguistic word embeddings have been previously successfully used to answer analogy questions (Mikolov et al., 2013b; Levy and Goldberg, 2014). These works have shown that such representations capture the nuances of word meaning needed to recognise relational similarity (e.g. between pairs *"king : queen"* and *"man : woman"*), quantified by the respective vector offsets ($king - queen \approx man - woman$). In our experiments, we investigate how well these representations can capture information about source and target domains and their interaction in a metaphor. We then enrich these representations with visual information. We first acquire linguistic and visual embeddings for individual words and then extend the methods to learn embeddings for longer phrases. The focus of our experiments is on metaphorical expressions in verb–subject, verb–direct object and adjectival modifier–noun constructions. We thus learn embeddings for verbs, adjectives, nouns, as well as verb–noun and adjective–noun phrases. We then use a set of arithmetic operations on word and phrase embedding vectors to classify phrases as literal or metaphorical. To the best of our knowledge, our approach is also the first one to apply word or phrase embeddings to the task of metaphor identification.

Our results demonstrate that the joint model incorporating linguistic and visual representations outperforms the linguistic model in isolation, as well as being competitive with the best-performing metaphor identification methods that rely on hand-crafted information about domains, concreteness and imageability.

2 Related work

A strand of metaphor processing research cast the problem as a classification of linguistic expressions as metaphorical or literal. They experimented with a number of features, including lexical and syntactic information and higher-level features such as semantic roles and domain types. Gedigian et al. (2006) classified verbs related to MOTION and CURE within the domain of financial discourse. They used the maximum entropy classifier and the verbs' nominal arguments and their semantic roles as features, reporting encouraging results. Dunn (2013a) used a logistic regression classifier and high-level properties of concepts extracted from SUMO ontology, including domain types (ABSTRACT, PHYSICAL, SOCIAL, MENTAL) and event status (PROCESS, STATE, OBJECT). Tsvetkov et al. (2013) also used logistic regression and coarse semantic features, such as concreteness, animateness, named entity types and WordNet supersenses. They have shown that the model learned with such coarse semantic features is portable across languages. The work of Hovy et al. (2013) is notable as they focused on compositional rather than categorical features. They trained an SVM with dependency-tree kernels to capture compositional information, using lexical, part-of-speech tag and WordNet supersense representations of sentence trees. Mohler et al. (2013) aimed at modelling conceptual information. They derived semantic signatures of texts as sets of highly-related and interlinked WordNet synsets. The semantic signatures served as features to train a set of classifiers (maximum entropy, decision trees, SVM, random forest) that map new metaphors to the semantic signatures of the known ones.

Turney et al. (2011) hypothesized that metaphor is commonly used to describe abstract concepts in terms of more concrete or physical experiences. Thus, Turney and colleagues expected that there would be some discrepancy in the level of concreteness of source and target terms in the metaphor. They developed a method to automatically measure concreteness of words and applied it to identify verbal and adjectival metaphors. Neuman et al. (2013) and Gandy et al. (2013) followed in Turney's steps, extending the models by incorporating information about selectional preferences.

Heintz et al. (2013) and Strzalkowski et al. (2013) focused on modeling topical structure of text to identify metaphor. Their main hypothesis was that metaphorical language (coming from a different domain) would represent atypical vocabulary within the topical structure of the text. Strzalkowski et al. (2013) acquired a set of topic chains by linking semantically related words in a given text. They then looked for vocabulary outside the topic chain and yet connected to topic chain words via syntactic dependencies and exhibiting high imageability. Heintz et al. (2013) used LDA topic modelling to identify sets of source and target domain vocabulary. In their system, the acquired topics represented source and target domains, and sentences containing vocabulary from both were tagged as metaphorical.

Other approaches addressed automatic identification of conceptual metaphor. Mason (2004) automatically acquired domain-specific selectional preferences of verbs, and then, by mapping their common nominal arguments in different domains, arrived at the corresponding metaphorical mappings. For example, the verb *pour* has a strong preference for *liquids* in the LAB domain and for *money* in the FINANCE domain, suggesting the mapping MONEY is LIQUID. Shutova et al. (2010) pointed out that the metaphorical uses of words constitute a large portion of the dependency features extracted for abstract concepts from corpora. For example, the feature vector for *politics* would contain GAME or MECHANISM terms among the frequent features. As a result, distributional clustering of abstract nouns with such features identifies groups of diverse concepts metaphorically associated with the same source domain (or sets of source domains). Shutova et al. (2010) exploit this property of co-occurrence vectors to identify new metaphorical mappings starting from a set of examples. Shutova and Sun (2013) used hierarchical clustering to derive a network of concepts in which metaphorical associations are learned in an unsupervised way.

3 Method

3.1 Learning linguistic representations

We obtained our linguistic representations using the log-linear skip-gram model of Mikolov et al. (2013a). Given a corpus of words w and their contexts c, the model learns a set of parameters θ that maximize the overall corpus probability

$$\arg\max_{\theta} \prod_{w} [\prod_{c \in C(w)} p(c|w;\theta)], \qquad (1)$$

where $C(w)$ is a set of contexts of word w and $p(c|w;\theta)$ is a softmax function:

$$p(c|w;\theta) = \frac{e^{v_c \cdot v_w}}{\sum_{c' \in C} e^{v_{c'} \cdot v_w}}, \qquad (2)$$

where v_c and v_w are vector representations of c and w. The parameters we need to set are thus v_{c_i} and v_{w_i} for all words in our word vocabulary V and context vocabulary C, and the set of dimensions $i \in 1, \ldots, d$. Given a set D of word-context pairs, embeddings are learned by optimizing the following objective:

$$\arg\max_{\theta} \sum_{(w,c) \in D} \log p(c|w) =$$
$$\sum_{(w,c) \in D} (\log e^{v_c \cdot v_w} - \log \sum_{c' \in C} e^{v_{c'} \cdot v_w}) \qquad (3)$$

We used a recent dump of Wikipedia[1] as our corpus. The text was lemmatized, tagged, and parsed with Stanford CoreNLP (Manning et al., 2014). Words that appeared less than 100 times in their lemmatized form were ignored. The 100-dimensional word and phrase embeddings were learned in two stages: in a first pass, we obtained word-level embeddings (e.g. for *white* and *rabbit*) using the standard skip-gram with negative sampling of Eq. (3); we then obtained phrase embeddings (e.g. for *white rabbit*) through a second pass over the same corpus. In the second pass, the vectors v_c and $v_{c'}$ of Eq. (3) were set to their values from the first pass, and kept fixed. Verb-noun phrases were extracted by finding `nsubj` and `dobj` arcs with VB head and NN dependent; analogously, adjective-noun phrases were extracted by finding `amod` arcs with NN head and JJ dependent. No frequency cutoff was applied for

---

[1] https://dumps.wikimedia.org/enwiki/20150805/

phrases. All embeddings were trained on the corpus for 3 epochs, using a symmetric window of 5, and 10 negative samples per word-context pair.

3.2 Learning visual representations

Visual embeddings were obtained in a manner similar to Kiela and Bottou (2014). Using the deep learning framework Caffe (Jia et al., 2014), we extracted image embeddings from a deep convolutional neural network that was trained on the ImageNet classification task (Russakovsky et al., 2015). The network (Krizhevsky et al., 2012) consists of 5 convolutional layers, followed by two fully connected rectified linear unit (ReLU) layers that feed into a softmax for classification. The network learns through a multinomial logistic regression objective:

$$
J(\theta) = -\sum_{i=1}^{D}\sum_{k=1}^{K} \mathbf{1}\{y^{(i)} = k\}
$$
$$
\log \frac{\exp(\theta^{(k)\top}x^{(i)})}{\sum_{j=1}^{K}\exp(\theta^{(j)\top}x^{(i)})} \tag{4}
$$

where $\mathbf{1}\{\cdot\}$ is the indicator function and we train on D examples with K classes. We obtain image embeddings by doing a forward pass with a given image and taking the 4096-dimensional fully connected layer that precedes the softmax (typically called FC7) as the representation of that image.

To construct our embeddings, we used up to 10 images for a given word or phrase, which were obtained through Google Images. It has been shown that images from Google yield higher quality representations than comparable resources such as Flickr and are competitive with hand-crafted datasets (Fergus et al., 2005; Bergsma and Goebel, 2011). We created our final visual representations for words and phrases by taking the average of the extracted image embeddings for a given word or phrase.

3.3 Multimodal fusion strategies

While it is desirable to jointly learn representations from different modalities at the same time, this is often not feasible (or may lead to poor performance) due to data sparsity. Instead, we learn uni-modal representations independently, as described above, and then combine them into multi-modal ones. Previous work in multi-modal semantics (Bruni et al., 2014) investigated different ways of combining, or *fusing*, linguistic and perceptual cues. When calculating similarity, for instance, one can either combine the representations first and subsequently compute similarity scores; or compute similarity scores independently per modality and afterwards combine the scores. In contrast with joint learning (which has also been called *early fusion*), these two possibilities represent *middle* and *late* fusion, respectively (Kiela and Clark, 2015).

We experiment with middle and late fusion strategies. In middle fusion, we L-2 normalise and concatenate the vectors for linguistic and visual representations and then compute a metaphoricity score for a phrase based on this joint representation. In late fusion, we first compute the metaphoricity scores based on linguistic and visual representations independently, and then combine the metaphoricity scores by taking their average.

3.4 Measuring metaphoricity

We investigate a set of arithmetic operations on the linguistic, visual and multimodal embedding vectors to determine whether the two words in the phrase belong to the same domain or rather a word from one domain is metaphorically used to describe another.

3.4.1 Word-level embeddings

In our first set of experiments, we compare embeddings learned for individual words in order to determine whether they come from the same domain. This is done by determining similarity between the representations of the two words in a phrase:

$$
\mathrm{sim}(word_1, word_2), \tag{5}
$$

where $word_1$ is either a verb or an adjective, $word_2$ is a noun, and similarity is defined as cosine similarity:

$$
\cos(x, y) = \frac{x \cdot y}{||x||\,||y||} \tag{6}
$$

We expect the similarity of word representations to be lower for metaphorical expressions (where one word comes from the source domain and one from the target), than for the literal ones (where both words come from the target domain). We will further refer to this method as WORDCOS.

3.4.2 Phrase-level embeddings

In our second set of experiments, we investigate compositional properties of metaphorical phrases by comparing the embeddings learned for the whole phrase with those of the individual words in the phrase. This allows us to determine which properties the phrase shares with each of the words, providing another criterion for metaphor identification. We expect that the embeddings of literal phrases will be more similar to the embeddings of individual words in the phrase (or a combination thereof) than those of metaphorical phrases. We use the following measures to test this hypothesis:

$$\text{PHRASCOS1}: \cos(phrase - word_1, word_2) \quad (7)$$

$$\text{PHRASCOS2}: \cos(phrase - word_2, word_1) \quad (8)$$

$$\text{PHRASCOS3}: \cos(phrase, word_1 + word_2), \quad (9)$$

where $phrase$ is the phrase embedding vector, and $word_1$ and $word_2$ are defined as above.

3.4.3 Classification

We use a small development set (a collection of phrases annotated as metaphorical or literal) to determine an optimal classification threshold for each of the above scoring methods. We have optimized the threshold by maximizing classification accuracy on the development set.[2] All instances with values above the threshold were considered literal and those with values below the threshold metaphorical. The thresholds were then applied to classify the test instances as literal or metaphorical.

4 Experiments

4.1 Annotated datasets

We evaluate our method using two datasets manually annotated for metaphoricity:

Mohammad et al. dataset (MOH) Mohammad et al. (2016) annotated different senses of WordNet (Fellbaum, 1998) verbs for metaphoricity. They extracted verbs that had between three and ten senses in WordNet and the sentences exemplifying them in the corresponding glosses. The verb uses in the

---

[2]We have also experimented with optimizing F-score on the development set and the results exhibited similar trends across methods.

Verb noun	Class	Relation
blister foot	literal	SV
blister administration	metaphorical	VO
blur haze	literal	SV
blur vision	literal	VO
blur distinction	metaphorical	SV
boost economy	metaphorical	VO
boost voltage	literal	VO
bounce ball	literal	SV
bounce people	metaphorical	VO
bow person	literal	SV
bow government	metaphorical	SV
breathe person	literal	SV
breathe life	metaphorical	VO
breathe fabric	metaphorical	SV
breathe wine	metaphorical	SV

Figure 1: Annotated verb–direct object and verb–subject pairs from MOH

sentences (1639 in total) were then annotated for metaphoricity by 10 annotators each via the crowdsourcing platform CrowdFlower[3]. Mohammad et al. selected the verbs that were tagged by at least 70% of the annotators as metaphorical or literal to create their dataset. We extracted verb–direct object and verb–subject relations of the annotated verbs from this dataset, discarding the instances with pronominal or clausal subject or object. This resulted in a dataset of 647 verb–noun pairs, 316 of which were metaphorical and 331 literal. Figure 1 shows some examples of annotated verbs from Mohammad et al.'s dataset.

Tsvetkov et al. dataset (TSV) Tsvetkov et al. (2014) created a large dataset of adjective–noun pairs that they annotated for metaphoricity. Starting with a 1000 frequent adjectives, they extracted nouns they co-occur with in TenTen Web Corpus[4] using SketchEngine and in collections of metaphor on the Web. Tsvetkov et al. divided the data into a training set (containing 884 literal and 884 metaphorical pairs) and test set (111 literal and 111 metaphorical pairs). We will refer to their training set as TSV-TRAIN and to the test set as TSV-TEST. The test set was annotated for metaphoricity by 5 annotators with an inter-annotator agreement of $\kappa = 0.76$. Figure 2 shows a portion of the anno-

---

[3]www.crowdflower.com

[4]https://www.sketchengine.co.uk/xdocumentation/wiki/Corpora/enTenTen

Metaphorical:	Literal:
bald assertion	cold beer
blind alley	cold weather
breezy disregard	huge number
dry wit	dead animal
dumb luck	deep sea
foggy brain	gold coin
healthy balance	dry skin
hollow mockery	honest opinion
honest meal	empty can
juicy scandal	good idea
spicy language	foggy night
stale cliché	frosty morning
steep discount	firm mattress

Figure 2: Annotated adjective–noun pairs from TSV-TEST

tated test set. Metaphorical phrases that depend on wider context for their interpretation (e.g. *drowning students*) were removed. The training set was annotated by one annotator only, and it is thus likely that the annotations are less reliable than those in the test set. We thus evaluate our methods on Tsvetkov et al.'s test set (TSV-TEST). However, we will also report results on TSV-TRAIN to confirm whether the observed trends hold in a larger, though likely noisier, dataset.

We selected the above two datasets since they include examples for different senses (both metaphorical and literal) of the same verbs or adjectives. This allows us to test the extent to which our model is able to discriminate between different word senses, as opposed to merely selecting the most frequent class for a given word.

4.2 Experimental setup

We divided the verb- and adjective-noun datasets into development and test sets. The verb–noun development set contained 80 instances from MOH (40 literal and 40 metaphorical), leaving us with the test set of 567 verb-noun pairs from MOH. We created the adjective–noun development set using 80 adjective-noun pairs (40 literal and 40 metaphorical) from TSV-TRAIN, leaving all of the 222 adjective–noun pairs in TSV-TEST for evaluation. In a separate experiment, we also applied our methods to the remainder of TSV-TRAIN (1688 adjective–noun pairs) to evaluate our system on a larger adjective dataset.

We used the development sets to determine an op-

Features	Method	P	R	$F1$
Linguistic	WORDCOS	0.67	0.76	**0.71**
	PHRASCOS1	0.38	0.94	0.54
Visual	WORDCOS	0.49	0.97	0.65
	PHRASCOS1	0.56	0.79	0.66
Multimodal	WORDMID	0.56	0.86	0.68
	PHRASMID	0.44	0.93	0.59
	WORDLATE	0.49	0.96	0.65
	PHRASLATE	0.41	0.92	0.57
	MIXLATE	0.65	0.87	**0.75**

Table 1: System performance on Mohammad et al. dataset (MOH) in terms of precision (P), recall (R) and F-score ($F1$)

timal threshold value for each of our scoring methods. The thresholds for verb-noun and adjective-noun phrases were optimized independently using the corresponding development sets. We experimented with the three phrase-level scoring methods on the development sets, and found that PHRASCOS1 consistently outperformed PHRASCOS2 and PHRASCOS3 for both verb–noun and adjective–noun phrases. We thus report results for PHRASCOS1 on our test sets.

We first evaluated the performance of WORDCOS and PHRASCOS1 using linguistic and visual representations in isolation, and then evaluated the multimodal models using middle and late fusion strategies. In middle fusion, we concatenated the linguistic and visual vectors, and then applied WORDCOS and PHRASCOS1 methods to the resulting multimodal vectors. We will refer to these methods as WORDMID and PHRASMID respectively. In late fusion, we used an average of linguistic and visual scores to determine metaphoricity. We experimented with three different scoring methods: (1) WORDLATE, where linguistic and visual WORD-COS scores were combined; (2) PHRASLATE, where linguistic and visual PHRASCOS1 scores were combined; and (3) MIXLATE, where linguistic WORDCOS and visual PHRASCOS1 scores were combined.

4.3 Results and discussion

We evaluated the performance of our methods on the MOH and TSV-TEST test sets in terms of precision, recall and F-score and the results are presented in Tables 1 and 2 respectively. When using linguistic embeddings alone, WORDCOS outperforms

Features	Method	P	R	$F1$
Linguistic	WordCos	0.73	0.80	**0.76**
	PhrasCos1	0.43	0.96	0.57
Visual	WordCos	0.50	0.95	0.66
	PhrasCos1	0.60	0.91	**0.73**
Multimodal	WordMid	0.59	0.85	0.70
	PhrasMid	0.54	0.93	0.68
	WordLate	0.69	0.72	0.70
	PhrasLate	0.50	1.00	0.67
	MixLate	0.67	0.96	**0.79**

Table 2: System performance on Tsvetkov et al. test set (TSV-TEST) in terms of precision (P), recall (R) and F-score ($F1$)

PhraseCos1 for both verbs and adjectives by 17-19%. This suggests that linguistic word embeddings already successfully capture domain and compositional information necessary for metaphor identification. In contrast, the visual PhraseCos1 model, when applied in isolation, tends to outperform the visual WordCos model. PhrasCos1 measures to what extent the meaning of the phrase can be composed by simple combination of the representations of individual words. In metaphorical language, however, a meaning transfer takes place and this is no longer the case. Particularly in visual data, where no linguistic conventionality and stylistic effects take place, PhrasCos1 captures this property. For adjectives this trend was more evident than for verbs. The visual PhraseCos1 model, even when applied on its own, attains a high F-score of 0.73 on TSV-TEST, suggesting that concreteness and other visual features are highly informative in identification of adjectival metaphors. This effect was present, though not as pronounced, for verbal metaphors, where the vision-only PhraseCos1 attains an F-score of 0.66.

The multimodal model, integrating linguistic and visual embeddings, outperforms the linguistic models for both verbs and adjectives, clearly demonstrating the utility of visual features across word classes. The late fusion method MixLate, which combines the linguistic WordCos score and the visual PhraseCos1, attains an F-score of 0.75 for verbs and 0.79 for adjectives, which makes it best-performing among our fusion strategies. When the same type of scoring (i.e. either WordCos or PhrasCos1) is used with both linguistic and visual

embeddings, middle and late fusion techniques attain comparable levels of performance, with WordCos being the leading measure. The reason behind the higher performance of MixLate is likely to be the combination of different scoring methods, one of which is more suitable for the linguistic model and the other for the visual one.

The differences between verbs and adjectives with respect to the utility of visual information can be explained by the following two factors. Firstly, previous psycholinguistic research on abstractness and concreteness (Hill et al., 2014) suggests that humans find it easier to judge the level of concreteness of adjectives and nouns than that of verbs. It is thus possible that visual representations capture the concreteness of adjectives and nouns more accurately than that of verbs. Besides concreteness, it is also likely that perceptual properties in general are more important for the semantics of nouns (e.g. objects) and adjectives (their attributes), than for the semantics of verbs (actions), since the latter are grounded in our motor activity and not merely perception. Secondly, following the majority of multimodal semantic models, we used images as our visual data rather than videos. However, some verbs, e.g. stative verbs and verbs for continuous actions, may be better captured in video than images. We thus expect that using video data along with the images as input to the acquisition of visual embeddings is likely to improve metaphor identification performance for verbal metaphors. However, we leave the investigation of this issue for future work.

In an additional experiment, we evaluated our methods on the larger TSV-TRAIN dataset (specifically using its portion that was not employed for development purposes) and the trends observed were the same. MixLate attained an F-score of 0.71, outperforming language-only and vision-only models. The performance of all scoring methods on TSV-TRAIN was lower than that on the TSV-TEST. This may be the result of the fact that the labelling of TSV-TRAIN was less consistent than that of TSV-TEST. As TSV-TEST is a set of metaphors annotated by 5 annotators with a high agreement, the evaluation on TSV-TEST is likely to be more reliable (Tsvetkov et al., 2014).

It is important to note that, unlike other supervised approaches to metaphor, our methods do not require large training sets to learn the respective thresholds. The results reported here were obtained using only 80 annotated examples for training. This is sufficient since the necessary lexical knowledge and the knowledge about domain, concreteness and visual properties of concepts is already captured in the linguistic and visual embeddings. However, we additionally investigated how stable the thresholds learned by the model are using the TSV-TRAIN dataset. For this purpose, we divided the dataset into 10 portions of approximately 170 examples (balanced for metaphoricity). We then trained the thresholds first on a small set of 170 examples and then increasing the dataset by 170 examples at each round. The thesholds appear to be relatively stable, with a standard deviation of 0.03 for MIXLATE; 0.02 for WORDCOS (linguistic); and 0.05 for PHRASECOS1 (visual). This suggests that our methods do not require a large annotated dataset and training on a small number of examples is sufficient.

Despite the limited need in training data and no reliance on hand-coded lexical resources, the performance of our method favourably compares to that of existing metaphor identification systems (Turney et al., 2011; Neuman et al., 2013; Gandy et al., 2013; Dunn, 2013b; Tsvetkov et al., 2013; Hovy et al., 2013; Hovy et al., 2013; Shutova and Sun, 2013; Strzalkowski et al., 2013; Beigman Klebanov et al., 2015), that typically use such resources. For instance, Turney et al. (2011) used hand-annotated abstractness scores for words to develop their system, and reported an F-score of 0.68 for verb–noun metaphors and an accuracy of 0.79 for adjective–noun metaphors (though the latter was only evaluated on a small dataset of 10 adjectives and Turney and colleagues did not report results in terms of F-score, which is likely to be lower). Our use of visual features is in line with Turney's hypothesis concerning the relevance of concreteness features to metaphor processing. However, our results indicate that extracting this information from image data directly is a more suitable way to capture the concreteness itself, as well as capturing other relevant perceptual properties of concepts. The method of Tsvetkov et al. (2014) used both concreteness features (which they extracted from the MRC concreteness database) and hand-coded domain information for words (which they extracted from WordNet). They report a high F-score of 0.85 for adjective–noun classification on TSV-TEST. The performance of our method on the same dataset is a little lower than that of Tsvetkov et al. However, we do not use any hand-annotated resources and acquire linguistic, domain and perceptual information in the data-driven way. It is thus encouraging that, even though resource-lean, our methods approach the performance level of the methods using hand-annotated features (as in case of Tsvetkov et al. (2014)) or outperform them (as in case of Turney et al. (2011), Neuman et al. (2013), Dunn (2013b), Mohler et al. (2013), Gandy et al. (2013), Strzalkowski et al. (2013), Beigman Klebanov et al. (2015) and many others). For further comparison with these approaches and their results see a recent review by Shutova (2015).

5 Conclusion

We presented the first method that uses visual features for metaphor identification. Our results demonstrate that the multi-modal model combining both linguistic and visual knowledge outperforms language-only models, suggesting the importance of visual information for metaphor processing. Unlike previous metaphor processing approaches, that employed hand-crafted resources to model perceptual properties of concepts, our method learns visual knowledge from images directly, thus reducing the risk of human annotation noise and having a wider coverage and applicability. Since the method relies on automatically acquired lexical knowledge, in the form of linguistic and visual embeddings, and is otherwise resource-independent, it can be applied to unrestricted text in any domain and easily tailored to other metaphor processing tasks.

In the future, it would be interesting to apply multimodal word and phrase embeddings to automatically interpret metaphorical language, e.g. by deriving literal or conventional paraphrases for metaphorical expressions (similarly to the task of Shutova (2010)). Multimodal embeddings are also likely to provide useful information for the models of metaphor translation, as they have already proved successful in bilingual lexicon induction more generally (Kiela et al., 2015b). Finally, it would be interesting to further investigate compositional properties of metaphorical language using multimodal phrase embeddings and to apply the embeddings to automatically generalise metaphorical associations between distinct concepts or domains.

Acknowledgment

We are grateful to the NAACL reviewers for their helpful feedback. Ekaterina Shutova's research is supported by the Leverhulme Trust Early Career Fellowship. Douwe Kiela is supported by EPSRC grant EP/I037512/1.

References

Lawrence W. Barsalou. 2008. Grounded cognition. *Annual Review of Psychology*, 59(1):617–645.

Beata Beigman Klebanov, Chee Wee Leong, and Michael Flor. 2015. Supervised word-level metaphor detection: Experiments with concreteness and reweighting of examples. In *Proceedings of the Third Workshop on Metaphor in NLP*, pages 11–20, Denver, Colorado, June. Association for Computational Linguistics.

Shane Bergsma and Randy Goebel. 2011. Using visual information to predict lexical preference. In *RANLP*, pages 399–405.

Danushka Bollegala and Ekaterina Shutova. 2013. Metaphor interpretation using paraphrases extracted from the web. *PLoS ONE*, 8(9):e74304.

Elia Bruni, Nam-Khanh Tran, and Marco Baroni. 2014. Multimodal distributional semantics. *J. Artif. Intell. Res.(JAIR)*, 49:1–47.

Jonathan Dunn. 2013a. Evaluating the premises and results of four metaphor identification systems. In *Proceedings of CICLing'13*, pages 471–486, Samos, Greece.

Jonathan Dunn. 2013b. What metaphor identification systems can tell us about metaphor-in-language. In *Proceedings of the First Workshop on Metaphor in NLP*, pages 1–10, Atlanta, Georgia.

Jerome Feldman. 2006. *From Molecule to Metaphor: A Neural Theory of Language*. The MIT Press.

Christiane Fellbaum, editor. 1998. *WordNet: An Electronic Lexical Database (ISBN: 0-262-06197-X)*. MIT Press, first edition.

Robert Fergus, Li Fei-Fei, Pietro Perona, and Andrew Zisserman. 2005. Learning object categories from google's image search. In *Computer Vision, 2005. ICCV 2005. Tenth IEEE International Conference on*, volume 2, pages 1816–1823. IEEE.

Lisa Gandy, Nadji Allan, Mark Atallah, Ophir Frieder, Newton Howard, Sergey Kanareykin, Moshe Koppel, Mark Last, Yair Neuman, and Shlomo Argamon. 2013. Automatic identification of conceptual metaphors with limited knowledge. In *Proceedings of AAAI 2013*.

Matt Gedigian, John Bryant, Srini Narayanan, and Branimir Ciric. 2006. Catching metaphors. In *In Proceedings of the 3rd Workshop on Scalable Natural Language Understanding*, pages 41–48, New York.

Ilana Heintz, Ryan Gabbard, Mahesh Srivastava, Dave Barner, Donald Black, Majorie Friedman, and Ralph Weischedel. 2013. Automatic extraction of linguistic metaphors with lda topic modeling. In *Proceedings of the First Workshop on Metaphor in NLP*, pages 58–66, Atlanta, Georgia.

Felix Hill, Anna Korhonen, and Christian Bentz. 2014. A quantitative empirical analysis of the abstract/concrete distinction. *Cognitive Science*, 38(1):162–177.

Dirk Hovy, Shashank Shrivastava, Sujay Kumar Jauhar, Mrinmaya Sachan, Kartik Goyal, Huying Li, Whitney Sanders, and Eduard Hovy. 2013. Identifying metaphorical word use with tree kernels. In *Proceedings of the First Workshop on Metaphor in NLP*, pages 52–57, Atlanta, Georgia.

Yangqing Jia, Evan Shelhamer, Jeff Donahue, Sergey Karayev, Jonathan Long, Ross Girshick, Sergio Guadarrama, and Trevor Darrell. 2014. Caffe: Convolutional architecture for fast feature embedding. *arXiv preprint arXiv:1408.5093*.

Douwe Kiela and Léon Bottou. 2014. Learning Image Embeddings using Convolutional Neural Networks for Improved Multi-Modal Semantics. In *Proceedings of the Conference on Empirical Methods in Natural Language Processing (EMNLP-14)*.

Douwe Kiela and Stephen Clark. 2015. Multi- and cross-modal semantics beyond vision: Grounding in auditory perception. In *Proceedings of the 2015 Conference on Empirical Methods in Natural Language Processing*, pages 2461–2470, Lisbon, Portugal, September. Association for Computational Linguistics.

Douwe Kiela, Laura Rimell, Ivan Vulić, and Stephen Clark. 2015a. Exploiting image generality for lexical entailment detection. In *Proceedings of the 53rd Annual Meeting of the Association for Computational Linguistics and the 7th International Joint Conference on Natural Language Processing (Volume 2: Short Papers)*, Beijing, China.

Douwe Kiela, Ivan Vulić, and Stephen Clark. 2015b. Visual bilingual lexicon induction with transferred convnet features. In *Proceedings of the 2015 Conference on Empirical Methods in Natural Language Processing*, Lisbon, Portugal.

Saisuresh Krishnakumaran and Xiaojin Zhu. 2007. Hunting elusive metaphors using lexical resources. In *Proceedings of the Workshop on Computational Approaches to Figurative Language*, pages 13–20, Rochester, NY.

Alex Krizhevsky, Ilya Sutskever, and Geoffrey E Hinton. 2012. Imagenet classification with deep convolutional neural networks. In *Advances in neural information processing systems*, pages 1097–1105.

George Lakoff and Mark Johnson. 1980. *Metaphors We Live By*. University of Chicago Press, Chicago.

Omer Levy and Yoav Goldberg. 2014. Linguistic regularities in sparse and explicit word representations. In *Proceedings of the Eighteenth Conference on Computational Natural Language Learning*, pages 171–180, Ann Arbor, Michigan, June.

Hongsong Li, Kenny Q. Zhu, and Haixun Wang. 2013. Data-driven metaphor recognition and explanation. *Transactions of the Association for Computational Linguistics*, 1:379–390.

Max M Louwerse. 2011. Symbol interdependency in symbolic and embodied cognition. *Topics in Cognitive Science*, 3(2):273–302.

Christopher D. Manning, Mihai Surdeanu, John Bauer, Jenny Finkel, Steven J. Bethard, and David McClosky. 2014. The Stanford CoreNLP natural language processing toolkit. In *Proceedings of 52nd Annual Meeting of the Association for Computational Linguistics: System Demonstrations*, pages 55–60.

Zachary Mason. 2004. Cormet: a computational, corpus-based conventional metaphor extraction system. *Computational Linguistics*, 30(1):23–44.

Tomas Mikolov, Kai Chen, Greg Corrado, and Jeffrey Dean. 2013a. Efficient estimation of word representations in vector space. In *Proceedings of ICLR*, Scottsdale, AZ.

Tomas Mikolov, Wen-tau Yih, and Geoffrey Zweig. 2013b. Linguistic regularities in continuous space word representations. In *Proceedings of NAACL-HLT*, pages 746–751.

Saif Mohammad, Ekaterina Shutova, and Peter Turney. 2016. Metaphor as a medium for emotion: An empirical study. *Language Resources and Evaluation*, forthcoming.

Michael Mohler, David Bracewell, Marc Tomlinson, and David Hinote. 2013. Semantic signatures for example-based linguistic metaphor detection. In *Proceedings of the First Workshop on Metaphor in NLP*, pages 27–35, Atlanta, Georgia.

Michael Mohler, Bryan Rink, David Bracewell, and Marc Tomlinson. 2014. A novel distributional approach to multilingual conceptual metaphor recognition. In *Proceedings of COLING 2014, the 25th International Conference on Computational Linguistics: Technical Papers*, Dublin, Ireland.

Yair Neuman, Dan Assaf, Yohai Cohen, Mark Last, Shlomo Argamon, Newton Howard, and Ophir Frieder. 2013. Metaphor identification in large texts corpora. *PLoS ONE*, 8(4):e62343.

Stephen Roller and Sabine Schulte im Walde. 2013. A multimodal lda model integrating textual, cognitive and visual modalities. In *Proceedings of the 2013 Conference on Empirical Methods in Natural Language Processing*, pages 1146–1157.

Olga Russakovsky, Jia Deng, Hao Su, Jonathan Krause, Sanjeev Satheesh, Sean Ma, Zhiheng Huang, Andrej Karpathy, Aditya Khosla, Michael Bernstein, Alexander C. Berg, and Li Fei-Fei. 2015. ImageNet Large Scale Visual Recognition Challenge. *International Journal of Computer Vision (IJCV)*, 115(3):211–252.

Ekaterina Shutova and Lin Sun. 2013. Unsupervised metaphor identification using hierarchical graph factorization clustering. In *Proceedings of NAACL 2013*, Atlanta, GA, USA.

Ekaterina Shutova, Lin Sun, and Anna Korhonen. 2010. Metaphor identification using verb and noun clustering. In *Proceedings of Coling 2010*, pages 1002–1010, Beijing, China.

Ekaterina Shutova, Tim Van de Cruys, and Anna Korhonen. 2012. Unsupervised metaphor paraphrasing using a vector space model. In *Proceedings of COLING 2012*, Mumbai, India.

Ekaterina Shutova. 2010. Automatic metaphor interpretation as a paraphrasing task. In *Proceedings of NAACL 2010*, pages 1029–1037, Los Angeles, USA.

Ekaterina Shutova. 2015. Design and Evaluation of Metaphor Processing Systems. *Computational Linguistics*, 41(4).

Carina Silberer and Mirella Lapata. 2012. Grounded models of semantic representation. In *Proceedings of the 2012 Joint Conference on Empirical Methods in Natural Language Processing and Computational Natural Language Learning*, pages 1423–1433. Association for Computational Linguistics.

Tomek Strzalkowski, George Aaron Broadwell, Sarah Taylor, Laurie Feldman, Samira Shaikh, Ting Liu, Boris Yamrom, Kit Cho, Umit Boz, Ignacio Cases, and Kyle Elliot. 2013. Robust extraction of metaphor from novel data. In *Proceedings of the First Workshop on Metaphor in NLP*, pages 67–76, Atlanta, Georgia.

Yulia Tsvetkov, Elena Mukomel, and Anatole Gershman. 2013. Cross-lingual metaphor detection using common semantic features. In *Proceedings of the First Workshop on Metaphor in NLP*, pages 45–51, Atlanta, Georgia.

Yulia Tsvetkov, Leonid Boytsov, Anatole Gershman, Eric Nyberg, and Chris Dyer. 2014. Metaphor detection with cross-lingual model transfer. In *Proceedings of the 52nd Annual Meeting of the Association for Computational Linguistics (Volume 1: Long Papers)*, pages 248–258, Baltimore, Maryland, June. Association for Computational Linguistics.

Peter D. Turney, Yair Neuman, Dan Assaf, and Yohai Cohen. 2011. Literal and metaphorical sense identification through concrete and abstract context. In *Proceedings of the Conference on Empirical Methods in Natural Language Processing*, EMNLP '11, pages 680–690, Stroudsburg, PA, USA. Association for Computational Linguistics.

Tony Veale and Yanfen Hao. 2008. A fluid knowledge representation for understanding and generating creative metaphors. In *Proceedings of COLING 2008*, pages 945–952, Manchester, UK.

Yorick Wilks, Adam Dalton, James Allen, and Lucian Galescu. 2013. Automatic metaphor detection using large-scale lexical resources and conventional metaphor extraction. In *Proceedings of the First Workshop on Metaphor in NLP*, pages 36–44, Atlanta, Georgia.

M.D. Wilson. 1988. The MRC Psycholinguistic Database: Machine Readable Dictionary, Version 2. *Behavioural Research Methods, Instruments and Computers*, 20:6–11.

Bridge Correlational Neural Networks for Multilingual Multimodal Representation Learning

Janarthanan Rajendran
IIT Madras, India.
rsdjjana@gmail.com

Mitesh M. Khapra
IBM Research India.
mikhapra@in.ibm.com

Sarath Chandar
University of Montreal.
apsarathchandar@gmail.com

Balaraman Ravindran
IIT Madras, India.
ravi@cse.iitm.ac.in

Abstract

Recently there has been a lot of interest in learning common representations for multiple views of data. Typically, such common representations are learned using a parallel corpus between the two views (say, 1M images and their English captions). In this work, we address a real-world scenario where no direct parallel data is available between two views of interest (say, V_1 and V_2) but parallel data is available between each of these views and a pivot view (V_3). We propose a model for learning a common representation for V_1, V_2 and V_3 using only the parallel data available between $V_1 V_3$ and $V_2 V_3$. The proposed model is generic and even works when there are n views of interest and only one pivot view which acts as a bridge between them. There are two specific downstream applications that we focus on (i) transfer learning between languages $L_1, L_2, ..., L_n$ using a pivot language L and (ii) cross modal access between images and a language L_1 using a pivot language L_2. Our model achieves state-of-the-art performance in multilingual document classification on the publicly available multilingual TED corpus and promising results in multilingual multimodal retrieval on a new dataset created and released as a part of this work.

1 Introduction

The proliferation of multilingual and multimodal content online has ensured that multiple views of the same data exist. For example, it is common to find the same article published in multiple languages online in multilingual news articles, multilingual wikipedia articles, *etc*. Such multiple views can even belong to different modalities. For example, images and their textual descriptions are two views of the same entity. Similarly, audio, video and subtitles of a movie are multiple views of the same entity.

Learning common representations for such multiple views of data will help in several downstream applications. For example, learning a common representation for images and their textual descriptions could help in finding images which match a given textual description. Further, such common representations can also facilitate transfer learning between views. For example, a document classifier trained on one language (view) can be used to classify documents in another language by representing documents of both languages in a common subspace.

Existing approaches to common representation learning (Ngiam et al., 2011; Klementiev et al., 2012; Chandar et al., 2013; Chandar et al., 2014; Andrew et al., 2013; Wang et al., 2015) except (Hermann and Blunsom, 2014b) typically require parallel data between all views. However, in many real-world scenarios such parallel data may not be available. For example, while there are many publicly available datasets containing images and their corresponding English captions, it is very hard to find datasets containing images and their corresponding captions in Russian, Dutch, Hindi, Urdu, *etc*. In this work, we are interested in addressing such scenarios. More specifically, we consider scenarios where we have n different views but parallel data is only available between each of these views, and a pivot view. In particular, there is no parallel data available between the non-pivot views.

To this end, we propose Bridge Correlational

Proceedings of NAACL-HLT 2016, pages 171–181,
San Diego, California, June 12-17, 2016. ©2016 Association for Computational Linguistics

Neural Networks (Bridge CorrNets) which learn aligned representations across multiple views using a pivot view. We build on the work of (Chandar et al., 2016) but unlike their model, which only addresses scenarios where direct parallel data is available between two views, our model can work for $n(\geq 2)$ views even when no parallel data is available between all of them. Our model only requires parallel data between each of these n views and a pivot view. During training, our model maximizes the correlation between the representations of the pivot view and each of the n views. Intuitively, the pivot view ensures that similar entities across different views get mapped close to each other since the model would learn to map each of them close to the corresponding entity in the pivot view.

We evaluate our approach using two downstream applications. First, we employ our model to facilitate transfer learning between multiple languages using English as the pivot language. For this, we do an extensive evaluation using 110 source-target language pairs and clearly show that we outperform the current state-of-the art approach (Hermann and Blunsom, 2014b). Second, we employ our model to enable cross modal access between images and French/German captions using English as the pivot view. For this, we created a test dataset consisting of images and their captions in French and German in addition to the English captions which were publicly available. To the best of our knowledge, this task of retrieving images given French/German captions (and vice versa) without direct parallel training data between them has not been addressed in the past. Even on this task we report promising results. Code and data used in this paper can be downloaded from `http://sarathchandar.in/bridge-corrnet`.

2 Related Work

Canonical Correlation Analysis (CCA) and its variants (Hotelling, 1936; Vinod, 1976; Nielsen et al., 1998; Cruz-Cano and Lee, 2014; Akaho, 2001) are the most commonly used methods for learning a common representation for two views. However, most of these models generally work with two views only. Even though there are multi-view generalizations of CCA (Tenenhaus and Tenenhaus, 2011; Luo

et al., 2015), their computational complexity makes them unsuitable for larger data sizes.

Another class of algorithms for multiview learning is based on Neural Networks. One of the earliest neural network based model for learning common representations was proposed in (Hsieh, 2000). Recently, there has been a renewed interest in this field and several neural network based models have been proposed. For example, Multimodal Autoencoder (Ngiam et al., 2011), Deep Canonically Correlated Autoencoder (Wang et al., 2015), Deep CCA (Andrew et al., 2013) and Correlational Neural Networks (CorrNet) (Chandar et al., 2016). CorrNet performs better than most of the above mentioned methods and we build on their work as discussed in the next section.

One of the tasks that we address in this work is multilingual representation learning where the aim is to learn aligned representations for words across languages. Some notable neural network based approaches here include the works of (Klementiev et al., 2012; Zou et al., 2013; Mikolov et al., 2013; Hermann and Blunsom, 2014b; Hermann and Blunsom, 2014a; Chandar et al., 2014; Soyer et al., 2015; Gouws et al., 2015). However, except for (Hermann and Blunsom, 2014a; Hermann and Blunsom, 2014b), none of these other works handle the case when parallel data is not available between all languages. Our model addresses this issue and outperforms the model of Hermann and Blunsom (2014b).

The task of cross modal access between images and text addressed in this work comes under MultiModal Representation Learning where each view belongs to a different modality. Ngiam et al. (2011) proposed an autoencoder based solution to learning common representation for audio and video. Srivastava and Salakhutdinov (2014) extended this idea to RBMs and learned common representations for image and text. Other solutions for image/text representation learning include (Zheng et al., 2014a; Zheng et al., 2014b; Socher et al., 2014). All these approaches require parallel data between the two views and do not address multimodal, multilingual learning in situations where parallel data is available only between different views and a pivot view.

In the past, pivot/bridge languages have been used to facilitate MT (for example, (Wu and Wang, 2007; Cohn and Lapata, 2007; Utiyama and Isahara, 2007;

Nakov and Ng, 2009)), transitive CLIR (Ballesteros, 2000; Lehtokangas et al., 2008), transliteration and transliteration mining (Khapra et al., 2010a; Kumaran et al., 2010; Khapra et al., 2010b; Zhang et al., 2011). None of these works use neural networks but it is important to mention them here because they use the concept of a pivot language (view) which is central to our work.

3 Bridge Correlational Neural Network

In this section, we describe Bridge CorrNet which is an extension of the CorrNet model proposed by (Chandar et al., 2016). They address the problem of learning common representations between two views when parallel data is available between them. We propose an extension to their model which simultaneously learns a common representation for M views when parallel data is available only between one pivot view and the remaining $M - 1$ views.

Let these views be denoted by $V_1, V_2, ..., V_M$ and let $d_1, d_2, ..., d_M$ be their respective dimensionalities. Let the training data be $\mathcal{Z} = \{z^i\}_{i=1}^N$ where each training instance contains only two views, *i.e.*, $z^i = (v_j^i, v_M^i)$ where $j \in \{1, 2, .., M-1\}$ and M is a pivot view. To be more clear, the training data contains N_1 instances for which (v_1^i, v_M^i) are available, N_2 instances for which (v_2^i, v_M^i) are available and so on till N_{M-1} instances for which (v_{M-1}^i, v_M^i) are available (such that $N_1 + N_2 + ... + N_{M-1} = N$). We denote each of these disjoint pairwise training sets by $\mathcal{Z}_1, \mathcal{Z}_2$ to $\mathcal{Z}_{M-1}$ such that $\mathcal{Z}$ is the union of all these sets.

As an illustration consider the case when English, French and German texts are the three views of interest with English as the pivot view. As training data, we have N_1 instances containing English and their corresponding French texts and N_2 instances containing English and their corresponding German texts. We are then interested in learning a common representation for English, French and German even though we do not have any training instance containing French and their corresponding German texts.

Bridge CorrNet uses an encoder-decoder architecture with a correlation based regularizer to achieve this. It contains one encoder-decoder pair for each of the M views. For each view V_j, we have,

$$h_{V_j}(v_j) = f(W_j v_j + b) \tag{1}$$

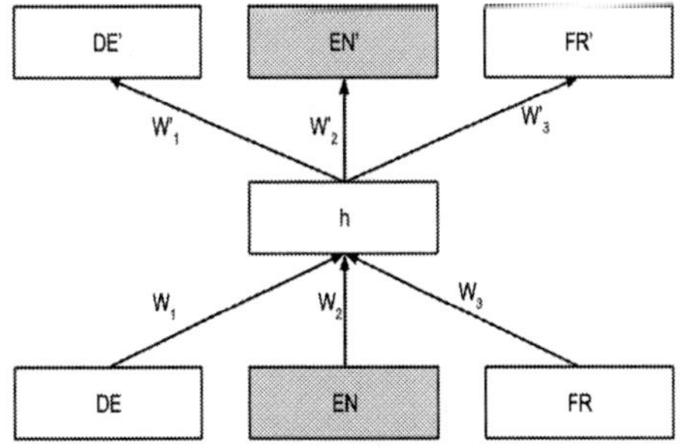

Figure 1: Bridge Correlational Neural Network. The views are English, French and German with English being the pivot view.

where f is any non-linear function such as sigmoid or tanh, $W_j \in \mathbb{R}^{k \times d_j}$ is the encoder matrix for view V_j, $b \in \mathbb{R}^k$ is the common bias shared by all the encoders. We also compute a hidden representation for the concatenated training instance $z = (v_j, v_M)$ using the following encoder function:

$$h_Z(z) = f(W_j v_j + W_M v_M + b) \tag{2}$$

In the remainder of this paper, whenever we drop the subscript for the encoder, then the encoder is determined by its argument. For example $h(v_j)$ means $h_{V_j}(v_j)$, $h(z)$ means $h_Z(z)$ and so on.

Our model also has a decoder corresponding to each view as follows:

$$g_{V_j}(h) = p(W_j' h + c_j) \tag{3}$$

where p can be any activation function, $W_j' \in \mathbb{R}^{d_j \times k}$ is the decoder matrix for view V_j, $c_j \in \mathbb{R}^{d_j}$ is the decoder bias for view V_j. We also define $g(h)$ as simply the concatenation of $[g_{V_j}(h), g_{V_M}(h)]$.

In effect, $h_{V_j}(.)$ encodes the input v_j into a hidden representation h and then $g_{V_j}(.)$ tries to decode/reconstruct v_j from this hidden representation h. Note that h can be computed using $h(v_j)$ or $h(v_M)$. The decoder can then be trained to decode/reconstruct both v_j and v_M given a hidden representation computed using any one of them. More formally, we train Bridge CorrNet by minimizing the following objective function:

$$\mathcal{J}_\mathcal{Z}(\theta) = \sum_{i=1}^N L(z^i, g(h(z^i))) + \sum_{i=1}^N L(z^i, g(h(v_{l(i)}^i)))$$
$$+ \sum_{i=1}^N L(z^i, g(h(v_M^i))) - \lambda \operatorname{corr}(h(V_{l(i)}), h(V_M)) \tag{4}$$

where $l(i) = j$ if $z^i \in \mathcal{Z}_j$ and the correlation term corr is defined as follows:

$$\text{corr} = \frac{\sum_{i=1}^{N}(h(x^i) - \overline{h(X)})(h(y^i) - \overline{h(Y)})}{\sqrt{\sum_{i=1}^{N}(h(x^i) - \overline{h(X)})^2 \sum_{i=1}^{N}(h(y^i) - \overline{h(Y)})^2}} \tag{5}$$

Note that $g(h(z^i))$ is the reconstruction of the input z^i after passing through the encoder and decoder. L is a loss function which captures the error in this reconstruction, λ is the scaling parameter to scale the last term with respect to the remaining terms, $\overline{h(X)}$ is the mean vector for the hidden representations of the first view and $\overline{h(Y)}$ is the mean vector for the hidden representations of the second view.

We now explain the intuition behind each term in the objective function. The first term captures the error in reconstructing the concatenated input z^i from itself. The second term captures the error in reconstructing both views given the non-pivot view, $v^i_{l(i)}$. The third term captures the error in reconstructing both views given the pivot view, v^i_M. Minimizing the second and third terms ensures that both the views can be predicted from any one view. Finally, the correlation term ensures that the network learns correlated common representations for all views.

Our model can be viewed as a generalization of the two-view CorrNet model proposed in (Chandar et al., 2016). By learning joint representations for multiple views using disjoint training sets $\mathcal{Z}_1$, $\mathcal{Z}_2$ to $\mathcal{Z}_{M-1}$ it eliminates the need for $^nC_2$ pair-wise parallel datasets between all views of interest. The pivot view acts as a bridge and ensures that similar entities across different views get mapped close to each other since all of them would be close to the corresponding entity in the pivot view.

Note that unlike the objective function of CorrNet (Chandar et al., 2016), the objective function of Equation 4, is a dynamic objective function which changes with each training instance. In other words, $l(i) \in \{1, 2, .., M-1\}$ varies for each $i \in \{1, 2, .., N\}$. For efficient implementation, we construct mini-batches where each mini-batch will come from only one of the sets $\mathcal{Z}_1$ to $\mathcal{Z}_{M-1}$. We randomly shuffle these mini-batches and use corresponding objective function for each mini-batch.

As a side note, we would like to mention that in addition to $\mathcal{Z}_1$, $\mathcal{Z}_2$ to $\mathcal{Z}_{M-1}$ as defined earlier, if additional parallel data is available between some of the non-pivot views then the objective function can be suitably modified to use this parallel data to further improve the learning. However, this is not the focus of this work and we leave this as a possible future work.

4 Datasets

In this section, we describe the two datasets that we used for our experiments.

4.1 Multlingual TED corpus

Hermann and Blunsom (2014b) provide a multilingual corpus based on the TED corpus for IWSLT 2013 (Cettolo et al., 2012). It contains English transcriptions of several talks from the TED conference and their translations in multiple languages. We use the parallel data between English and other languages for training Bridge Corrnet (English, thus, acts as the pivot langauge). Hermann and Blunsom (2014b) also propose a multlingual document classification task using this corpus. The idea is to use the keywords associated with each talk (document) as class labels and then train a classifier to predict these classes. There are one or more such keywords associated with each talk but only the 15 most frequent keywords across all documents are considered as class labels. We used the same pre-processed splits[1] as provided by (Hermann and Blunsom, 2014b). The training corpus consists of a total of 12,078 parallel documents distributed across 12 language pairs.

4.2 Multilingual Image Caption dataset

The MSCOCO dataset[2] contains images and their English captions. On an average there are 5 captions per image. The standard train/valid/test splits for this dataset are also available online. However, the reference captions for the images in the test split are not provided. Since we need such reference captions for evaluations, we create a new train/valid/test of this dataset. Specifically, we take 80K images from the standard train split and 40K images from the standard valid split. We then randomly split the merged 120K images into train(118K), validation (1K) and test set (1K).

---

[1] http://www.clg.ox.ac.uk/tedcorpus
[2] http://mscoco.org/dataset/

We then create a multilingual version of the test data by collecting French and German translations for all the 5 captions for each image in the test set. We use crowdsourcing to do this. We used the CrowdFlower platform and solicited one French and one German translation for each of the 5000 captions using native speakers. We got each translation verified by 3 annotators. We restricted the geographical location of annotators based on the target language. We found that roughly 70% of the French translations and 60% of the German translations were marked as correct by a majority of the verifiers. On further inspection with the help of in-house annotators, we found that the errors were mainly syntactic and the content words are translated correctly in most of the cases. Since none of the approaches described in this work rely on syntax, we decided to use all the 5000 translations as test data. This multilingual image caption test data (MIC test data) will be made publicly available[3] and will hopefully assist further research in this area.

5 Experiment 1: Transfer learning using a pivot language

From the TED corpus described earlier, we consider English transcriptions and their translations in 11 languages, *viz.*, Arabic, German, Spanish, French, Italian, Dutch, Polish, Portuguese (Brazilian), Roman, Russian and Turkish. Following the setup of Hermann and Blunsom (2014b), we consider the task of cross language learning between each of the $^{11}C_2$ non-English language pairs. The task is to classify documents in a language when no labeled training data is available in this language but training data is available in another language. This involves the following steps:

1. Train classifier: Consider one language as the source language and the remaining 10 languages as target languages. Train a document classifier using the labeled data of the source language, where each training document is represented using the hidden representation computed using a trained Bridge Corrnet model. As in (Hermann and Blunsom, 2014b) we used an averaged perceptron trained for 10 epochs as the classifier for all our experiments. The train split provided by (Hermann and Blunsom,

[3]http://sarathchandar.in/bridge-corrnet

2014b) is used for training.

2. Cross language classification: For every target language, compute a hidden representation for every document in its test set using Bridge CorrNet. Now use the classifier trained in the previous step to classify this document. The test split provided by (Hermann and Blunsom, 2014b) is used for testing.

5.1 Training and tuning Bridge Cornnet

For the above process to work, we first need to train Bridge Cornnet so that it can then be used for computing a common hidden representation for documents in different languages. For training Bridge CorrNet, we treat English as the pivot language (view) and construct parallel training sets $\mathcal{Z}_1$ to $\mathcal{Z}_{11}$. Every instance in $\mathcal{Z}_1$ contains the English and Arabic view of the same talk (document). Similarly, every instance in $\mathcal{Z}_2$ contains the English and German view of the same talk (document) and so on. For every language, we first construct a vocabulary containing all words appearing more than 5 times in the corpus (all talks) of that language. We then use this vocabulary to construct a bag-of-words representation for each document. The size of the vocabulary ($|V|$) for different languages varied from 31213 to 60326 words. To be more clear, $v_1 = v_{arabic} \in \mathbb{R}^{|V|_{arabic}}$, $v_2 = v_{german} \in \mathbb{R}^{|V|_{german}}$ and so on.

We train our model for 10 epochs using the above training data $\mathcal{Z} = \{\mathcal{Z}_1, \mathcal{Z}_2, ..., \mathcal{Z}_{11}\}$. We use hidden representations of size $D = 128$, as in (Hermann and Blunsom, 2014b). Further, we used stochastic gradient descent with mini-batches of size 20. Each mini-batch contains data from only one of the $\mathcal{Z}_i s$. We get a stochastic estimate for the correlation term in the objective function using this mini-batch. The hyperparameter λ was tuned to each task using a training/validation split for the source language and using the performance on the validation set of an averaged perceptron trained on the training set (notice that this corresponds to a monolingual classification experiment, since the general assumption is that no labeled data is available in the target language).

5.2 Results

We now present the results of our cross language classification task in Table 1. Each row corresponds to a source language and each column corresponds to a target language. We report the average F1-

Training	Test Language										
Language	Arabic	German	Spanish	French	Italian	Dutch	Polish	Pt-Br	Rom'n	Russian	Turkish
Arabic		0.662	0.654	0.645	0.663	0.654	0.626	0.628	0.630	0.607	0.644
German	0.920		0.544	0.505	0.654	0.672	0.631	0.507	0.583	0.537	0.597
Spanish	0.666	0.465		0.547	0.512	0.501	0.537	0.518	0.573	0.463	0.434
French	0.761	0.585	0.679		0.681	0.646	0.671	0.650	0.675	0.613	0.578
Italian	0.701	0.421	0.456	0.457		0.530	0.442	0.491	0.390	0.402	0.499
Dutch	0.847	0.370	0.511	0.472	0.600		0.536	0.489	0.458	0.470	0.516
Polish	0.533	0.387	0.556	0.535	0.536	0.454		0.446	0.521	0.473	0.413
Pt-Br	0.609	0.502	0.572	0.553	0.548	0.535	0.545		0.557	0.451	0.463
Rom'n	0.573	0.460	0.559	0.530	0.521	0.484	0.475	0.485		0.486	0.458
Russian	0.755	0.460	0.537	0.437	0.567	0.499	0.550	0.478	0.475		0.484
Turkish	0.950	0.373	0.480	0.452	0.542	0.544	0.585	0.297	0.512	0.412	

Table 1: F1-scores for TED corpus document classification results when training and testing on two languages that do not share any parallel data. We train a Bridge CorrNet model on all en-L2 language pairs together, and then use the resulting embeddings to train document classifiers in each language. These classifiers are subsequently used to classify data from all other languages.

Training	Test Language										
Language	Arabic	German	Spanish	French	Italian	Dutch	Polish	Pt-Br	Rom'n	Russian	Turkish
Arabic		0.378	0.436	0.432	0.444	0.438	0.389	0.425	0.42	0.446	0.397
German	0.368		0.474	0.46	0.464	0.44	0.375	0.417	0.447	0.458	0.443
Spanish	0.353	0.355		0.42	0.439	0.435	0.415	0.39	0.424	0.427	0.382
French	0.383	0.366	0.487		0.474	0.429	0.403	0.418	0.458	0.415	0.398
Italian	0.398	0.405	**0.461**	**0.466**		0.393	0.339	0.347	0.376	0.382	0.352
Dutch	0.377	0.354	0.463	0.464	0.46		0.405	0.386	0.415	0.407	0.395
Polish	0.359	0.386	0.449	0.444	0.43	0.441		0.401	0.434	0.398	0.408
Pt-Br	0.391	0.392	0.476	0.447	0.486	0.458	0.403		0.457	0.431	0.431
Rom'n	0.416	0.32	0.473	0.476	0.46	0.434	0.416	0.433		0.444	0.402
Russian	0.372	0.352	0.492	0.427	0.438	0.452	0.43	0.419	0.441		0.447
Turkish	0.376	0.352	0.479	0.433	0.427	0.423	0.439	**0.367**	0.434	0.411	

Table 2: F1-scores for TED corpus document classification results when training and testing on two languages that do not share any parallel data. Same procedure as Table 1, but with DOC/ADD model in (Hermann and Blunsom, 2014b).

Setting	Languages										
	Arabic	German	Spanish	French	Italian	Dutch	Polish	Pt-Br	Rom'n	Russian	Turkish
Raw Data NB	**0.469**	**0.471**	0.526	**0.532**	0.524	0.522	0.415	0.465	**0.509**	0.465	**0.513**
DOC/ADD (Single)	0.422	0.429	0.394	0.481	0.458	0.252	0.385	0.363	0.431	**0.471**	0.435
DOC/BI (Single)	0.432	0.362	0.336	0.444	0.469	0.197	0.414	0.395	0.445	0.436	0.428
DOC/ADD (Joint)	0.371	0.386	0.472	0.451	0.398	0.439	0.304	0.394	0.453	0.402	0.441
DOC/BI (Joint)	0.329	0.358	0.472	0.454	0.399	0.409	0.340	0.431	0.379	0.395	0.435
Bridge CorrNet	0.266	0.456	**0.535**	0.529	**0.551**	**0.565**	**0.478**	**0.535**	0.490	0.447	0.477

Table 3: : F1-scores on the TED corpus document classification task when training and evaluating on the same language. Results other than Bridge CorrNet are taken from (Hermann and Blunsom, 2014b).

scores over all the 15 classes. We compare our results with the best results reported in (Hermann and Blunsom, 2014b) (see Table 2). Out of the 110 experiments, our model outperforms the model of (Hermann and Blunsom, 2014b) in 107 experiments. This suggests that our model efficiently exploits the pivot language to facilitate cross language learning between other languages.

Finally, we present the results for a monolingual classification task in Table 3. The idea here is to see if learning common representations for multiple views can also help in improving the performance of a task involving only one view. Hermann and Blunsom (2014b) argue that a Naive Bayes (NB) classifier trained using a bag-of-words representation of the documents is a very strong baseline. In fact, a classifier trained on document representations learned using their model does not beat a NB classifier for the task of monolingual classification. Rows 2 to 5 in Table 3 show the different settings tried by them (we refer the reader to (Hermann and Blunsom, 2014b) for a detailed description of these settings). On the other hand our model is able to beat NB for 5/11 languages. Further, for 4 other languages (German, French, Romanian, Russian) its performance is only marginally poor than that of NB.

6   Experiment 2: Cross modal access using a pivot language

In this experiment, we are interested in retrieving images given their captions in French (or German) and vice versa. However, for training we do not have any parallel data containing images and their French (or German) captions. Instead, we have the following datasets: (i) a dataset $\mathcal{Z}_1$ containing images and their English captions and (ii) a dataset $\mathcal{Z}_2$ containing English and their parallel French (or German) documents. For $\mathcal{Z}_1$, we use the training split of MSCOCO dataset which contains 118K images and their English captions (see Section 4.2). For $\mathcal{Z}_2$, we use the English-French (or German) parallel documents from the train split of the TED corpus (see Section 4.1). We use English as the pivot language and train Bridge Corrnet using $\mathcal{Z} = \{\mathcal{Z}_1, \mathcal{Z}_2\}$ to learn common representations for images, English text and French (or German) text. For text, we use bag-of-words representation and for image, we use the 4096 (fc6) representation got from a pre-trained ConvNet (BVLC Reference CaffeNet (Jia et al., 2014)). We learn hidden representations of size $D = 200$ by training Bridge Corrnet for 20 epochs using stochastic gradient descent with mini-batches of size 20. Each mini-batch contains data from only one of the $\mathcal{Z}_i s$.

For the task of retrieving captions given an image, we consider the 1000 images in our test set (see section 4.2) as queries. The 5000 French (or German) captions corresponding to these images (5 per image) are considered as documents. The task is then to retrieve the relevant captions for each image. We represent all the captions and images in the common space as computed using Bridge Corrnet. For a given query, we rank all the captions based on the Euclidean distance between the representation of the image and the caption. For the task of retrieving images given a caption, we simply reverse the role of the captions and images. In other words, each of the 5000 captions is treated as a query and the 1000 images are treated as documents. λ was tuned to each task using a training/validation split. For the task of retrieving French/German captions given an image, λ was tuned using the performance on the validation set for retrieving French (or German) sentences for a given English sentence. For the other task, λ was tuned using the performance on the validation set for retrieving images, given English captions. We do not use any image-French/German parallel data for tuning the hyperparameters.

We use recall@k as the performance metric and compare the following methods in Table 4:

1. En-Image CorrNet: This is the CorrNet model trained using only $\mathcal{Z}_1$ as defined earlier in this section. The task is to retrieve English captions for a given image (or vice versa). This gives us an idea about the performance we could expect if direct parallel data is available between images and their captions in some language. We used the publicly available implementation of CorrNet provided by (Chandar et al., 2016).

2. Bridge CorrNet: This is the Bridge CorrNet model trained using $\mathcal{Z}_1$ and $\mathcal{Z}_2$ as defined earlier in this section. The task is to retrieve French (or German) captions for a given image (or vice versa).

3.   Bridge MAE: The Multimodal Autoencoder (MAE) proposed by (Ngiam et al., 2011) was the only competing model which was easily extendable to the bridge case. We train their model using $\mathcal{Z}_1$ and $\mathcal{Z}_2$ to minimize a suitably modified objective function. We then use the representations learned to retrieve French (or German) captions for a given image (or vice versa).

4. 2-CorrNet: Here, we train two individual CorrNets using $\mathcal{Z}_1$ and $\mathcal{Z}_2$ respectively. For the task of retrieving images given a French (or German) caption we first find its nearest English caption using the Fr-En (or De-En) CorrNet. We then use this English caption to retrieve images using the En-Image CorrNet. Similarly, for retrieving captions given an image we use the En-Image CorrNet followed by the En-Fr (or En-De) CorrNet.

5. CorrNet + MT: Here, we train an En-Image CorrNet using $\mathcal{Z}_1$ and an Fr/De-En MT system[4] using $\mathcal{Z}_2$. For the task of retrieving images given a French (or German) caption we translate the caption to English using the MT system. We then use this English caption to retrieve images using the En-Image CorrNet. For retrieving captions given images, we first translate all the 5000 French (or Germam) captions to English. We then embed these English translations (documents) and images (queries) in the com-

---

[4] http://www.statmt.org/moses/

Model	Captions	I To C			C To I		
		Recall@5	Recall@10	Recall@50	Recall@5	Recall@10	Recall@50
En-Image CorrNet	English	0.118	0.190	0.456	0.091	0.168	0.532
Bridge MAE	French	0.008	0.017	0.069	0.007	0.013	0.063
2-CorrNet	French	0.018	0.024	0.085	0.027	0.055	0.205
Bridge CorrNet	French	0.072	0.135	0.335	0.032	0.060	0.235
CorrNet+MT	French	0.101	0.163	0.414	0.069	0.127	0.416
Bridge MAE	German	0.005	0.009	0.053	0.006	0.013	0.058
2-CorrNet	German	0.009	0.013	0.071	0.012	0.023	0.098
Bridge CorrNet	German	0.063	0.105	0.298	0.027	0.049	0.183
CorrNet+MT	German	0.084	0.163	0.420	0.061	0.107	0.343
Random		0.006	0.009	0.044	0.005	0.009	0.050

Table 4: Performance of different models for image to caption (I to C) and caption to image (C to I) retrieval

mon space computed using Image-En CorrNet and do a retrieval as explained earlier.

6. Random: A random image is returned for the given caption (and vice versa).

From Table 4, we observe that `CorrNet + MT` is a very strong competitor and gives the best results. The main reason for this is that over the years MT has matured enough for language pairs such as Fr-En and De-En and it can generate almost perfect translations for short sentences (such as captions). In fact, the results for this method are almost comparable to what we could have hoped for if we had direct parallel data between Fr-Images and De-Images (as approximated by the first row in the table which reports cross-modal retrieval results between En-Images using direct parallel data between them for training). However, we would like to argue that learning a joint embedding for multiple views instead of having multiple pairwise systems is a more elegant solution and definitely merits further attention. Further, a "translation system" may not be available when we are dealing with modalities other than text (for example, there are no audio-to-video translation systems). In such cases, BridgeCorrNet could still be employed. In this context, the performance of BridgeCorrNet is definitely promising and shows that a model which jointly learns representations for multiple views can perform better than methods which learn pair-wise common representations (2-CorrNet).

6.1 Qualitative Analysis

To get a qualitative feel for our model's performance, we refer the reader to Table 5 and 6. The first row in Table 5 shows an image and its top-5 nearest German captions (based on Euclidean distance between their common representations). As per our parallel image caption test set, only the second and fourth caption actually correspond to this image. However, we observe that the first and fifth caption are also semantically very related to the image. Both these captions talk about horses, grass or water body (ocean), *etc*. Similarly the last row in Table 5 shows an image and its top-5 nearest French captions. None of these captions actually correspond to the image as per our parallel image caption test set. However, clearly the first, third and fourth caption are semantically very relevant to this image as all of them talk about baseball. Even the remaining two captions capture the concept of a *sport* and *raquet*. We can make a similar observation from Table 6 where most of the top-5 retrieved images do not correspond to the French/German caption but they are semantically very similar. It is indeed impressive that the model is able to capture such cross modal semantics between images and French/German even without any direct parallel data between them.

7 Conclusion

In this paper, we propose Bridge Correlational Neural Networks which can learn common representations for multiple views even when parallel data is available only between these views and a pivot view. Our method performs better than the existing state of the art approaches on the cross language classification task and gives very promising results on the cross modal access task. We also release a new multilingual image caption benchmark (MIC benchmark) which will help in further research in this field[5].

---

[5]Details about the MIC benchmark and performance of various state-of-the-art models will be maintained at `http://sarathchandar.in/bridge-corrnet`

1. Zwei Pferde stehen auf einem sandigen Strand nahe dem Ocean. (Two horses standing on a sandy beach near the ocean.)
2. grasende Pferde auf einer trockenen Weide bei einem Flughafen. (Horses grazing in a dry pasture by an airport.)
3. ein Elefant , Wasser aufseinen Rückend sprühend , in einem staubigen Bereich neben einem Baum.
(A elephant spraying water on its back in a dirt area next to tree .)
4. ein braunes pferd ißt hohes gras neben einem behälter mit wasser. (Brown horses eating tall grass beside a body of water .)
5. vier Pferde grasen auf ein Feld mit braunem gras. (Four horses are grazing through a field of brown grass.)

1. Ein Teller mit Essen wie Sandwich , Chips , Suppe und einer Gurke.
(Plate of food including a sandwich , chips , soup and a pickle.)
2. Teller , gefüllt mit sortierten Früchten und Gemüse und einigem Fleisch.
(Plates filled with assorted fruits and veggies and some meat.)
3. Ein Tisch mit einer Schüssel Salat und einem Teller Pizza. (a Table with a bowl of salad and plate with a cooked pizza .)
4. Ein Teller mit Essen besteht aus Brokkoli und Rindfleisch. (A plate of food consists of broccoli and beef.)
5. Eine Platte mit Fleisch und grünem Gemüse gemixt mit Sauce. (A plate with meat and green veggies mixed with sauce.)

1. un bus de la conduite en ville dans une rue entourée par de grands immeubles.
(A city bus driving down a street surrounded by tall buildings.)
2. un bus de conduire dans une rue dans une ville avec des bâtiments de grande hauteur.
(A bus driving down a street in a city with very tall buildings.)
3. bus de conduire dans une rue de ville surpeuplée. (Double - decker bus driving down a crowded city street.)
4. le bus conduit à travers la ville sur une rue animée. (The bus drives through the city on a busy street.)
5. un grand bus coloré est arrêté dans une rue de la ville. (A big , colorful bus is stopped on a city street.)

1. Un homme portant une batte de baseball à deux mains lors d'un jeu de balle professionnel.
(A man holding a baseball bat with two hands at a professional ball game.)
2. un joueur de tennis balance une raquette à une balle. (A tennis player swinging a racket t a ball.)
3. un garçon qui est de frapper une balle avec une batte de baseball. (A boy that is hitting a ball with a baseball bat.)
4. une équipe de joueurs de baseball jouant un jeu de base-ball. (A team of baseball players playing a game of baseball.)
5. un garçon se prépare à frapper une balle de tennis avec une raquette. (A boy prepares to hit a tennis ball with a racquet.)

Table 5: Images and their top-5 nearest captions based on representations learned using Bridge CorrNet. First two examples show German captions and the last two examples show French captions. English translations are given in parenthesis.

Speisen und Getränke auf einem
Tisch mit einer Frau essen im Hintergrund.
(Food and beverages set on a table with
a woman eating in the background .)

ein Foto von einem Laptop auf einem
Bett mit einem Fernseher im Hintergrund.
(A photo of a laptop on a bed with a tv
in the background .)

un homme debout à côté de aa groupe de vaches.
(A man standing next to a group of cows.)

personnes portant du matériel
de ski en se tenant debout dans la neige.
(People wearing ski equipment while
standing in snow.)

Table 6: French and German queries and their top-5 nearest images based on representations learned using Bridge CorrNet. First two queries are in German and the last two queries are French. English translations are given in parenthesis.

Acknowledgments

We thank the reviewers for their useful feedback. We also thank the workers from CrowdFlower for helping us in creating the MIC benchmark. Finally, we thank Amrita Saha (IBM Research India) for helping us in running some of the experiments.

References

S. Akaho. 2001. A kernel method for canonical correlation analysis. *In Proc. Int'l Meeting on Psychometric Society.*

Galen Andrew, Raman Arora, Jeff Bilmes, and Karen Livescu. 2013. Deep canonical correlation analysis. *ICML.*

L.A. Ballesteros. 2000. Cross language retrieval via transitive translation. In *W.B. Croft (Ed.), Advances in information retrieval: Recent research from the CIIR*, pages 203–234, Boston: Kluwer Academic Publishers.

Mauro Cettolo, Christian Girardi, and Marcello Federico. 2012. Wit^3: Web inventory of transcribed and translated talks. In *Proceedings of the 16th Conference of the European Association for Machine Translation (EAMT)*, pages 261–268, Trento, Italy, May.

Sarath Chandar, Mitesh M. Khapra, Balaraman Ravindran, Vikas C. Raykar, and Amrita Saha. 2013. Multilingual deep learning. *NIPS Deep Learning Workshop.*

Sarath Chandar, Stanislas Lauly, Hugo Larochelle, Mitesh M. Khapra, Balaraman Ravindran, Vikas C. Raykar, and Amrita Saha. 2014. An autoencoder approach to learning bilingual word representations. In *Advances in Neural Information Processing Systems 27: Annual Conference on Neural Information Processing Systems 2014, December 8-13 2014, Montreal, Quebec, Canada*, pages 1853–1861.

Sarath Chandar, Mitesh M. Khapra, Hugo Larochelle, and Balaraman Ravindran. 2016. Correlational neural networks. *Neural Computation*, 28(2):257 – 285.

Trevor Cohn and Mirella Lapata. 2007. Machine translation by triangulation: Making effective use of multiparallel corpora. In *Proceedings of the 45th Annual Meeting of the Association of Computational Linguistics*, pages 728–735, Prague, Czech Republic, June.

Raul Cruz-Cano and Mei-Ling Ting Lee. 2014. Fast regularized canonical correlation analysis. *Computational Statistics & Data Analysis*, 70:88 – 100.

Stephan Gouws, Yoshua Bengio, and Greg Corrado. 2015. Bilbowa: Fast bilingual distributed representations without word alignments. In *Proceedings of the 32nd International Conference on Machine Learning, ICML 2015, Lille, France, 6-11 July 2015*, pages 748–756.

Karl Moritz Hermann and Phil Blunsom. 2014a. Multilingual Distributed Representations without Word Alignment. In *Proceedings of International Conference on Learning Representations (ICLR)*.

Karl Moritz Hermann and Phil Blunsom. 2014b. Multilingual models for compositional distributed semantics. In *Proceedings of the 52nd Annual Meeting of the Association for Computational Linguistics, ACL 2014, June 22-27, 2014, Baltimore, MD, USA, Volume 1: Long Papers*, pages 58–68.

H. Hotelling. 1936. Relations between two sets of variates. *Biometrika*, 28:321 – 377.

W.W. Hsieh. 2000. Nonlinear canonical correlation analysis by neural networks. *Neural Networks*, 13(10):1095 – 1105.

Yangqing Jia, Evan Shelhamer, Jeff Donahue, Sergey Karayev, Jonathan Long, Ross Girshick, Sergio Guadarrama, and Trevor Darrell. 2014. Caffe: Convolutional architecture for fast feature embedding. *arXiv preprint arXiv:1408.5093.*

Mitesh M. Khapra, A. Kumaran, and Pushpak Bhattacharyya. 2010a. Everybody loves a rich cousin: An empirical study of transliteration through bridge languages. In *Human Language Technologies: Conference of the North American Chapter of the Association of Computational Linguistics, Proceedings, June 2-4, 2010, Los Angeles, California, USA*, pages 420–428.

Mitesh M. Khapra, Raghavendra Udupa, A. Kumaran, and Pushpak Bhattacharyya. 2010b. PR + RQ ALMOST EQUAL TO PQ: transliteration mining using bridge language. In *Proceedings of the Twenty-Fourth AAAI Conference on Artificial Intelligence, AAAI 2010, Atlanta, Georgia, USA, July 11-15, 2010.*

Alexandre Klementiev, Ivan Titov, and Binod Bhattarai. 2012. Inducing Crosslingual Distributed Representations of Words. In *Proceedings of the International Conference on Computational Linguistics (COLING)*.

A. Kumaran, Mitesh M. Khapra, and Pushpak Bhattacharyya. 2010. Compositional machine transliteration. *ACM Trans. Asian Lang. Inf. Process.*, 9(4):13.

Raija Lehtokangas, Heikki Keskustalo, and Kalervo Järvelin. 2008. Experiments with transitive dictionary translation and pseudo-relevance feedback using graded relevance assessments. *Journal of the American Society for Information Science and Technology*, 59(3):476–488.

Yong Luo, Dacheng Tao, Yonggang Wen, Kotagiri Ramamohanarao, and Chao Xu. 2015. Tensor canonical correlation analysis for multi-view dimension reduction. *In Arxiv.*

Tomas Mikolov, Quoc Le, and Ilya Sutskever. 2013. Exploiting Similarities among Languages for Machine Translation. Technical report, arXiv.

Preslav Nakov and Hwee Tou Ng. 2009. Improved statistical machine translation for resource-poor languages using related resource-rich languages. In *Proceedings of the 2009 Conference on Empirical Methods in Natural Language Processing*, pages 1358–1367, Singapore, August.

J. Ngiam, A. Khosla, M. Kim, J. Nam, H. Lee, and Ng. Andrew. 2011. Multimodal deep learning. *ICML.*

F. Å. Nielsen, L. K. Hansen, and S. C. Strother. 1998. Canonical ridge analysis with ridge parameter optimization, may.

Richard Socher, Andrej Karpathy, Quoc V. Le, Christopher D. Manning, and Andrew Y. Ng. 2014. Grounded compositional semantics for finding and describing images with sentences. *TACL*, 2:207–218.

Hubert Soyer, Pontus Stenetorp, and Akiko Aizawa. 2015. Leveraging monolingual data for crosslingual compositional word representations. In *Proceedings of the 3rd International Conference on Learning Representations*, San Diego, California, USA, May.

Nitish Srivastava and Ruslan Salakhutdinov. 2014. Multimodal learning with deep boltzmann machines. *Journal of Machine Learning Research*, 15:2949–2980.

Arthur Tenenhaus and Michel Tenenhaus. 2011. Regularized generalized canonical correlation analysis. *Psychometrika*, 76(2):257–284.

Masao Utiyama and Hitoshi Isahara. 2007. A comparison of pivot methods for phrase-based statistical machine translation. In *Proceedings of the Conference of the North American Chapter of the Association for Computational Linguistics*, pages 484–491, Rochester, New York, April.

H.D. Vinod. 1976. Canonical ridge and econometrics of joint production. *Journal of Econometrics*, 4(2):147 – 166.

Weiran Wang, Raman Arora, Karen Livescu, and Jeff Bilmes. 2015. On deep multi-view representation learning. In *ICML*.

Hua Wu and Haifeng Wang. 2007. Pivot language approach for phrase-based statistical machine translation. *Machine Translation*, 21(3):165–181.

Min Zhang, Xiangyu Duan, Ming Liu, Yunqing Xia, and Haizhou Li. 2011. Joint alignment and artificial data generation: An empirical study of pivot-based machine transliteration. In *Fifth International Joint Conference on Natural Language Processing, IJCNLP 2011, Chiang Mai, Thailand, November 8-13, 2011*, pages 1207–1215.

Yin Zheng, Yu-Jin Zhang, and Hugo Larochelle. 2014a. A deep and autoregressive approach for topic modeling of multimodal data. *CoRR*, abs/1409.3970.

Yin Zheng, Yu-Jin Zhang, and Hugo Larochelle. 2014b. Topic modeling of multimodal data: An autoregressive approach. In *2014 IEEE Conference on Computer Vision and Pattern Recognition, CVPR 2014, Columbus, OH, USA, June 23-28, 2014*, pages 1370–1377.

Will Y. Zou, Richard Socher, Daniel Cer, and Christopher D. Manning. 2013. Bilingual Word Embeddings for Phrase-Based Machine Translation. In *Conference on Empirical Methods in Natural Language Processing (EMNLP 2013)*.

Unsupervised Visual Sense Disambiguation for Verbs using Multimodal Embeddings

Spandana Gella, Mirella Lapata and Frank Keller
Institute for Language, Cognition and Computation
School of Informatics, University of Edinburgh
10 Crichton Street, Edinburgh EH8 9AB
S.Gella@sms.ed.ac.uk, mlap@inf.ed.ac.uk, keller@inf.ed.ac.uk

Abstract

We introduce a new task, visual sense disambiguation for verbs: given an image and a verb, assign the correct sense of the verb, i.e., the one that describes the action depicted in the image. Just as textual word sense disambiguation is useful for a wide range of NLP tasks, visual sense disambiguation can be useful for multimodal tasks such as image retrieval, image description, and text illustration. We introduce VerSe, a new dataset that augments existing multimodal datasets (COCO and TUHOI) with sense labels. We propose an unsupervised algorithm based on Lesk which performs visual sense disambiguation using textual, visual, or multimodal embeddings. We find that textual embeddings perform well when gold-standard textual annotations (object labels and image descriptions) are available, while multimodal embeddings perform well on unannotated images. We also verify our findings by using the textual and multimodal embeddings as features in a supervised setting and analyse the performance of visual sense disambiguation task. VerSe is made publicly available and can be downloaded at: https://github.com/spandanagella/verse.

1 Introduction

Word sense disambiguation (WSD) is a widely studied task in natural language processing: given a word and its context, assign the correct sense of the word based on a pre-defined sense inventory (Kilgarrif, 1998). WSD is useful for a range of NLP tasks, including information retrieval, information extraction, machine translation, content analysis, and lexicography (see Navigli (2009) for an overview).

Figure 1: Visual sense ambiguity: three of the senses of the verb *play*.

Standard WSD disambiguates words based on their *textual context*; however, in a multimodal setting (e.g., newspaper articles with photographs), *visual context* is also available and can be used for disambiguation. Based on this observation, we introduce a new task, *visual sense disambiguation* (VSD) for verbs: given an image and a verb, assign the correct sense of the verb, i.e., the one depicted in the image. While VSD approaches for nouns exist, VSD for verbs is a novel, more challenging task, and related in interesting ways to *action recognition* in computer vision. As an example consider the verb *play*, which can have the senses *participate in sport*, *play on an instrument*, and *be engaged in playful activity*, depending on its visual context, see Figure 1.

We expect visual sense disambiguation to be useful for multimodal tasks such as image retrieval. As an example consider the output of Google Image Search for the query *sit*: it recognizes that the verb has multiple senses and tries to cluster relevant images. However, the result does not capture the polysemy of the verb well, and would clearly benefit from VSD (see Figure 2).

Visual sense disambiguation has previously been attempted for nouns (e.g., *apple* can mean *fruit* or *computer*), which is a substantially easier task that can be solved with the help of an object detector

Proceedings of NAACL-HLT 2016, pages 182–192,
San Diego, California, June 12-17, 2016. ©2016 Association for Computational Linguistics

Figure 2: Google Image Search trying to disambiguate *sit*. All clusters pertain to the *sit down* sense, other senses (*baby sit*, *convene*) are not included.

Dataset	Verbs	Acts	Images	Sen	Des
PPMI (Yao and Fei-Fei, 2010)	2	24	4800	N	N
Stanford 40 Actions (Yao et al., 2011)	33	40	9532	N	N
PASCAL 2012 (Everingham et al., 2015)	9	11	4588	N	N
89 Actions (Le et al., 2013)	36	89	2038	N	N
TUHOI (Le et al., 2014)	–	2974	10805	N	N
COCO-a (Ronchi and Perona, 2015)	140	162	10000	N	Y
HICO (Chao et al., 2015)	111	600	47774	Y	N
VerSe (our dataset)	90	163	3518	Y	Y

Table 1: Comparison of VerSe with existing action recognition datasets. Acts (actions) are verb-object pairs; Sen indicates whether sense ambiguity is explicitly handled; Des indicates whether image descriptions are included.

(Barnard et al., 2003; Loeff et al., 2006; Saenko and Darrell, 2008; Chen et al., 2015). VSD for nouns is helped by resources such as ImageNet (Deng et al., 2009), a large image database containing 1.4 million images for 21,841 noun synsets and organized according to the WordNet hierarchy. However, we are not aware of any previous work on VSD for verbs, and no ImageNet for verbs exists. Not only image retrieval would benefit from VSD for verbs, but also other multimodal tasks that have recently received a lot of interest, such as automatic image description and visual question answering (Karpathy and Li, 2015; Fang et al., 2015; Antol et al., 2015).

In this work, we explore the new task of visual sense disambiguation for verbs: given an image and a verb, assign the correct sense of the verb, i.e., the one that describes the action depicted in the image. We present VerSe, a new dataset that augments existing multimodal datasets (COCO and TUHOI) with sense labels. VerSe contains 3518 images, each annotated with one of 90 verbs, and the OntoNotes sense realized in the image. We propose an algorithm based on the Lesk WSD algorithm in order to perform unsupervised visual sense disambiguation on our dataset. We focus in particular on how to best represent word senses for visual disambiguation, and explore the use of textual, visual, and multimodal embeddings. Textual embeddings for a given image can be constructed over object labels or image descriptions, which are available as gold-standard in the COCO and TUHOI datasets, or can be computed automatically using object detectors and image description models.

Our results show that textual embeddings perform best when gold-standard textual annotations are available, while multimodal embeddings perform best when automatically generated object labels are used. Interestingly, we find that automatically generated image descriptions result in inferior performance.

2 Related Work

There is an extensive literature on word sense disambiguation for nouns, verbs, adjectives and adverbs. Most of these approaches rely on lexical databases or sense inventories such as WordNet (Miller et al., 1990) or OntoNotes (Hovy et al., 2006). Unsupervised WSD approaches often rely on distributional representations, computed over the target word and its context (Lin, 1997; McCarthy et al., 2004; Brody and Lapata, 2008). Most supervised approaches use sense annotated corpora to extract linguistic features of the target word (context words, POS tags, collocation features), which are then fed into a classifier to disambiguate test data (Zhong and Ng, 2010). Recently, features based on sense-specific semantic vectors learned using large corpora and a sense inventory such as WordNet have been shown to achieve state-of-the-art results for supervised WSD (Rothe and Schutze, 2015; Jauhar et al., 2015).

As mentioned in the introduction, all existing work on visual sense disambiguation has used nouns, starting with Barnard et al. (2003). Sense discrimination for web images was introduced by Loeff et al. (2006), who used spectral clustering over multimodal features from the images and web text. Saenko and Darrell (2008) used sense definitions in a dictionary to learn a latent LDA space overs senses, which they then used to construct sense-specific classifiers by exploiting the text surrounding an image.

2.1 Related Datasets

Most of the datasets relevant for verb sense disambiguation were created by the computer vision community for the task of human action recognition (see

Table 1 for an overview). These datasets are annotated with a limited number of actions, where an
action is conceptualized as verb-object pair: *ride
horse, ride bicycle, play tennis, play guitar,* etc.
Verb sense ambiguity is ignored in almost all action
recognition datasets, which misses important generalizations: for instance, the actions *ride horse* and
ride bicycle represent the same sense of *ride* and
thus share visual, textual, and conceptual features,
while this is not the case for *play tennis* and *play
guitar*. This is the issue we address by creating a
dataset with explicit sense labels.

VerSe is built on top of two existing datasets,
TUHOI and COCO. The Trento Universal Human-
Object Interaction (TUHOI) dataset contains 10,805
images covering 2974 actions. Action (human-
object interaction) categories were annotated using
crowdsourcing: each image was labeled by multiple
annotators with a description in the form of a verb
or a verb-object pair. The main drawback of TUHOI
is that 1576 out of 2974 action categories occur only
once, limiting its usefulness for VSD. The Microsoft
Common Objects in Context (COCO) dataset is very
popular in the language/vision community, as it consists of over 120k images with extensive annotation,
including labels for 91 object categories and five descriptions per image. COCO contains no explicit action annotation, but verbs and verb phrases can be
extracted from the descriptions. (But note that not
all the COCO images depict actions.)

The recently created Humans Interacting with
Common Objects (HICO) dataset is conceptually
similar to VerSe. It consists of 47774 images annotated with 111 verbs and 600 human-object interaction categories. Unlike other existing datasets, HICO
uses sense-based distinctions: actions are denoted by
sense-object pairs, rather than by verb-object pairs.
HICO doesn't aim for complete coverage, but restricts itself to the top three WordNet senses of a
verb. The dataset would be suitable for performing
visual sense disambiguation, but has so far not been
used in this way.

3 VerSe Dataset and Annotation

We want to build an unsupervised visual sense disambiguation system, i.e., a system that takes an image and a verb and returns the correct sense of
the verb. As discussed in Section 2.1, most exist-

Verb: touch

- ☐ make physical contact with, possibly with the effect of physically manipulating. They touched their fingertips together and smiled
- ☐ affect someone emotionally The president's speech touched a chord with voters.
- ☐ be or come in contact without control They sat so close that their arms touched.
- ☐ make reference to, involve oneself with They had wide-ranging discussions that touched on the situation in the Balkans.
- ☐ Achieve a value or quality Nothing can touch cotton for durability.
- ☐ Tinge; repair or improve the appearance of He touched on the paintings, trying to get the colors right.

Figure 3: Example item for depictability and sense
annotation: synset definitions and examples (in blue)
for the verb *touch*.

ing datasets are not suitable for this task, as they do
not include word sense annotation. We therefore develop our own dataset with gold-standard sense annotation. The Verb Sense (VerSe) dataset is based on
COCO and TUHOI and covers 90 verbs and around
3500 images. VerSe serves two main purposes: (1) to
show the feasibility of annotating images with verb
senses (rather than verbs or actions); (2) to function
as test bed for evaluating automatic visual sense disambiguation methods.

Verb Selection Action recognition datasets often
use a limited number of verbs (see Table 1). We addressed this issue by using images that come with
descriptions, which in the case of action images typically contain verbs. The COCO dataset includes images in the form of sentences, the TUHOI dataset is
annotated with verbs or prepositional verb phrases
for a given object (e.g., *sit on* chair), which we use in
lieu of descriptions. We extracted all verbs from all
the descriptions in the two datasets and then selected
those verbs that have more than one sense in the
OntoNotes dictionary, which resulted in 148 verbs
in total (94 from COCO and 133 from TUHOI).

Depictability Annotation A verb can have multiple senses, but not all of them may be depictable,
e.g., senses describing cognitive and perception processes. Consider two senses of *touch*: *make physical
contact* is depictable, whereas *affect emotionally* describes a cognitive process and is not depictable. We
therefore need to annotate the synsets of a verb as
depictable or non-depictable. Amazon Mechanical
Turk (AMT) workers were presented with the definitions of all the synsets of a verb, along with ex-

Verb type	Examples	Verbs	Images	Senses	Depct	ITA
Motion	run, walk, jump, etc.	39	1812	10.76	5.79	0.680
Non-motion	sit, stand, lay, etc.	51	1698	8.27	4.86	0.636

Table 2: Overview of VerSe dataset divided into motion and non-motion verbs; Depct: depictable senses; ITA: inter-annotator agreement.

amples, as given by OntoNotes. An example for this annotation is shown in Figure 3. We used OntoNotes instead of WordNet, as WordNet senses are very fine-grained and potentially make depictability and sense annotation (see below) harder. Granularity issues with WordNet for text-based WSD are well documented (Navigli, 2009).

OntoNotes lists a total of 921 senses for our 148 target verbs. For each synset, three AMT workers selected all depictable senses. The majority label was used as the gold standard for subsequent experiments. This resulted in a 504 depictable senses. Inter-annotator agreement (ITA) as measured by Fleiss' Kappa was 0.645.

Sense Annotation We then annotated a subset of the images in COCO and TUHOI with verb senses. For every image we assigned the verb that occurs most frequently in the descriptions for that image (for TUHOI, the descriptions are verb-object pairs, see above). However, many verbs are represented by only a few images, while a few verbs are represented by a large number of images. The datasets therefore show a Zipfian distribution of linguistic units, which is expected and has been observed previously for COCO (Ronchi and Perona, 2015). For sense annotation, we selected only verbs for which either COCO or TUHOI contained five or more images, resulting in a set of 90 verbs (out of the total 148). All images for these verbs were included, giving us a dataset of 3518 images: 2340 images for 82 verbs from COCO and 1188 images for 61 verbs from TUHOI (some verbs occur in both datasets).

These image-verb pairs formed the basis for sense annotation. AMT workers were presented with the image and all the depictable OntoNotes senses of the associated verb. The workers had to chose the sense of the verb that was instantiated in the image (or "none of the above", in the case of irrelevant images). Annotators were given sense definitions and examples, as for the depictability annotation (see Figure 3). For every image-verb pair, five annotators

performed the sense annotation task. A total of 157 annotators participated, reaching an inter-annotator agreement of 0.659 (Fleiss' Kappa). Out of 3528 images, we discarded 18 images annotated with "none of the above", resulting in a set of 3510 images covering 90 verbs and 163 senses. We present statistics of our dataset in Table 2; we group the verbs into motion verbs and non-motion verb using Levin (1993) classes.

4 Visual Sense Disambiguation

For our disambiguation task, we assume we have a set of images I, and a set of polysemous verbs V and each image $i \in I$ is paired with a verb $v \in V$. For example, Figure 1 shows different images paired with the verb *play*. Every verb $v \in V$, has a set of senses $S(v)$, described in a dictionary $\mathcal{D}$. Now given an image i paired with a verb v, our task is to predict the correct sense $\hat{s} \in S(v)$, i.e., the sense that is depicted by the associated image. Formulated as a scoring task, disambiguation consists of finding the maximum over a suitable scoring function Φ:

$$\hat{s} = \arg\max_{s \in S(v)} \Phi(s, i, v, \mathcal{D}) \tag{1}$$

For example, in Figure 1, the correct sense for the first image is *participate in sport*, for the second one it is *play on an instrument*, etc.

The Lesk (1986) algorithm is a well known knowledge-based approach to WSD which relies on the calculation of the word overlap between the sense definition and the context in which a word occurs. It is therefore an unsupervised approach, i.e., it does not require sense-annotated training data, but instead exploits resources such as dictionaries or ontologies to infer the sense of a word in context. Lesk uses the following scoring function to disambiguate the sense of a verb v:

$$\Phi(s, v, \mathcal{D}) = |context(v) \cap definition(s, \mathcal{D})| \tag{2}$$

Here, $context(v)$ the set of words that occur close the target word v and $definition(s, \mathcal{D})$ is the set of words in the definition of sense s in the dictionary $\mathcal{D}$. Lesk's approach is very sensitive to the exact wording of definitions and results are known to change dramatically for different sets of definitions (Navigli, 2009). Also, sense definitions are often very

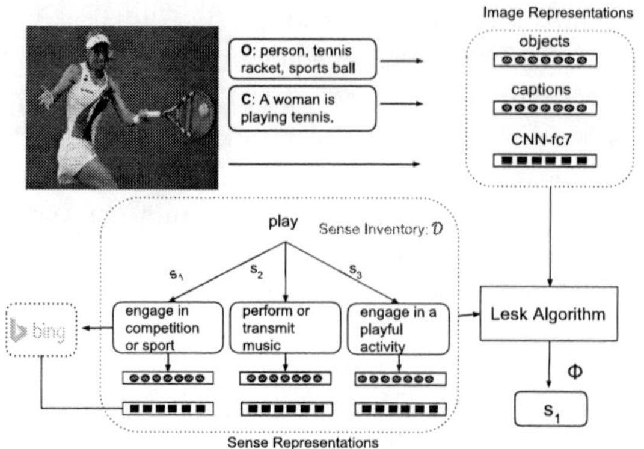

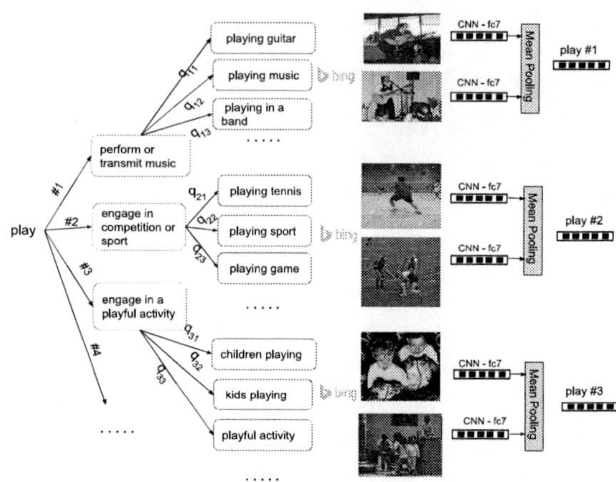

Figure 4: Schematic overview of the visual sense disambiguation model.

Figure 5: Extracting visual sense representation for the verb *play*.

short and do not provide sufficient vocabulary or context.

We propose a new variant of the Lesk algorithm to disambiguate the verb sense that is depicted in an image. In particular, we explore the effectiveness of textual, visual and multimodal representations in conjunction with Lesk. An overview of our methodology is given in Figure 4. For a given image i labeled with verb v (here *play*), we create a representation (the vector $\mathbf{i}$), which can be text-based (using the object labels and descriptions for i), visual, or multimodal. Similarly, we create text-based, visual, and multimodal representations (the vector $\mathbf{s}$) for every sense s of a verb. Based on the representations $\mathbf{i}$ and $\mathbf{s}$ (detailed below), we can then score senses as:[1]

$$\Phi(s, v, i, \mathcal{D}) = \mathbf{i} \cdot \mathbf{s} \qquad (3)$$

Note that this approach is unsupervised: it requires no sense annotated training data; we will use the sense annotations in our VerSe dataset only for evaluation.

4.1 Sense Representations

For each candidate verb sense, we create a text-based sense representation $\mathbf{s^t}$ and a visual sense representation $\mathbf{s^c}$.

Text-based Sense Representation   We create a vector $\mathbf{s^t}$ for every sense $s \in \mathcal{S}(v)$ of a verb v from its definition and the example usages provided in

the OntoNotes dictionary $\mathcal{D}$. We apply word2vec (Mikolov et al., 2013), a widely used model of word embeddings, to obtain a vector for every content word in the definition and examples of the sense. We then take the average of these vectors to compute an overall representation of the verb sense. For our experiments we used the pre-trained 300 dimensional vectors available with the word2vec package (trained on part of Google News dataset, about 100 billion words).

Visual Sense Representation   Sense dictionaries typically provide sense definitions and example sentences, but no visual examples or images. For nouns, this is remedied by ImageNet (Deng et al., 2009), which provides a large number of example images for a subset of the senses in the WordNet noun hierarchy. However, no comparable resource is available for verbs (see Section 2.1).

In order to obtain visual sense representation $\mathbf{s^c}$, we therefore collected sense-specific images for the verbs in our dataset. For each verb sense s, three trained annotators were presented with the definition and examples from OntoNotes, and had to formulate a query $Q(s)$ that would retrieve images depicting the verb sense when submitted to a search engine. For every query q we retrieved images $I(q)$ using Bing image search (for examples, see Figure 5). We used the top 50 images returned by Bing for every query.

Once we have images for every sense, we can turn these images into feature representations us-

---

[1]Taking the dot product of two normalized vectors is equivalent to using cosine as similarity measure. We experimented with other similarity measures, but cosine performed best.

ing a convolutional neural network (CNN). Specifically, we used the VGG 16-layer architecture (VGGNet) trained on 1.2M images of the 1000 class ILSVRC 2012 object classification dataset, a subset of ImageNet (Simonyan and Zisserman, 2014). This CNN model has a top-5 classification error of 7.4% on ILSVRC 2012. We use the publicly available reference model implemented using CAFFE (Jia et al., 2014) to extract the output of the fc7 layer, i.e., a 4096 dimensional vector c_i, for every image i. We perform mean pooling over all the images extracted using all the queries of a sense to generate a single visual sense representation s^c (shown in Equation 4):

$$s^c = \frac{1}{n} \sum_{q_j \in Q(s)} \sum_{i \in I(q_j)} c_i \qquad (4)$$

where n is the total number of images retrieved per sense s.

4.2 Image Representations

We first explore the possibility of representing the image indirectly, viz., through text associated with it in the form of object labels or image descriptions (as shown in Figure 4). We experiment with two different forms of textual annotation: GOLD annotation, where object labels and descriptions are provided by human annotators, and predicted (PRED) annotation, where state-of-the-art object recognition and image description generation systems are applied to the image.

Object Labels (O)   GOLD object annotations are provided with the two datasets we use. Each image sampled from COCO is annotated with one or more of 91 object categories. Each image from TUHOI is annotated with one more of 189 object categories. PRED object annotations were generated using the same VGG-16-layer CNN object recognition model that was used to compute visual sense representations. Only object labels with object detection threshold of $t > 0.2$ were used.

Descriptions (C)   To obtain GOLD image descriptions, we used the used human-generated descriptions that come with COCO. For TUHOI images, we generated descriptions of the form subject-verb-object, where the subject is always *person*, and the verb-object pairs are the action labels that come with TUHOI. To obtain PRED descriptions, we generated

three descriptions for every image using the state-of-the-art image description system of Vinyals et al. (2015).[2]

We can now create a textual representation i^t of the image i. Again, we used word2vec to obtain word embeddings, but applied these to the object labels and to the words in the image descriptions. An overall representation of the image is then computed by averaging these vectors over all labels, all content words in the description, or both.

Creating a visual representation i^c of an image i is straightforward: we extract the fc7 layer of the VGG-16 network when applied to the image and use the resulting vector as our image representation (same setup as in Section 4.1).

Apart from experimenting with separate textual and visual representations of images, it also makes sense to combine the two modalities into a multimodal representation. The simplest approach is a concatenation model which appends textual and visual features. More complex multimodal vectors can be created using methods such as Canonical Correlation Analysis (CCA) and Deep Canonical Correlation Analysis (DCCA) (Hardoon et al., 2004; Andrew et al., 2013; Wang et al., 2015). CCA allows us to find a latent space in which the linear projections of text and image vectors are maximally correlated (Gong et al., 2014; Hodosh et al., 2015). DCCA can be seen as non-linear version of CCA and has been successfully applied to image description task (Yan and Mikolajczyk, 2015), outperforming previous approaches, including kernel-based CCA.

We use both CCA and DCCA to map the vectors i^t and i^c (which have different dimensions) into a joint latent space of n dimensions. We represent the projected vectors of textual and visual features for image i as $i^{t'}$ and $i^{c'}$ and combine them to obtain multimodal representation i^m as follows:

$$i^m = \lambda_t i^{t'} + \lambda_c i^{c'} \qquad (5)$$

We experimented with a number of parameter settings for λ_t and λ_c for textual and visual models respectively. We use the same model to combine the multimodal representation for sense s as follows:

$$s^m = \lambda_t s^{t'} + \lambda_c s^{c'} \qquad (6)$$

---

[2]We used Karpathy's implementation, publicly available at
`https://github.com/karpathy/neuraltalk`.

We use these vectors $(\mathbf{i^t}, \mathbf{s^t})$, $(\mathbf{i^c}, \mathbf{s^c})$ and $(\mathbf{i^m}, \mathbf{s^m})$ as described in Equation 3 to perform sense disambiguation.

5 Experiments

5.1 Unsupervised Setup

To train the CCA and DCCA models, we use the text representations learned from image descriptions of COCO and Flickr30k dataset as one view and the VGG-16 features from the respective images as the second view. We divide the data into train, test and development samples (using a 80/10/10 split). We observed that the correlation scores for DCCA model were better than for the CCA model. We use the trained models to generate the projected representations of text and visual features for the images in VerSe. Once the textual and visual features are projected, we then merge them to get the multimodal representation. We experimented with different ways of combining visual and textual features projected using CCA or DCCA: (1) weighted interpolation of textual and visual features (see Equations 5 and 6), and (2) concatenating the vectors of textual and visual features.

To evaluate our proposed method, we compare against the first sense heuristic, which defaults to the sense listed first in the dictionary (where senses are typically ordered by frequency). This is a strong baseline which is known to outperform more complex models in traditional text-based WSD. In VerSe we observe skewness in the distribution of the senses and the first sense heuristic is as strong as over text. Also the most frequent sense heuristic, which assigns the most frequently annotated sense for a given verb in VerSe, shows very strong performance. It is supervised (as it requires sense annotated data to obtain the frequencies), so it should be regarded as an upper limit on the performance of the unsupervised methods we propose (also, in text-based WSD, the most frequent sense heuristic is considered an upper limit, Navigli (2009)).

5.1.1 Results

In Table 3, we summarize the results of the gold-standard (GOLD) and predicted (PRED) settings for motion and non-motion verbs across representations. In the GOLD setting we find that for both types of verbs, textual representations based on im-

age descriptions (C) outperform visual representations (CNN features). The text-based results compare favorably to the original Lesk (as described in Equation 2), which performs at 30.7 for motion verbs and 36.2 for non-motion verbs in the GOLD setting. This improvement is clearly due to the use of word2vec embeddings.[3] Note that CNN-based visual features alone performed better than gold-standard object labels alone in the case of motion verbs.

We also observed that adding visual features to textual features improves performance in some cases: multimodal features perform better than textual features alone both for object labels (CNN+O) and for image descriptions (CNN+C). However, adding CNN features to textual features based on object labels and descriptions together (CNN+O+C) resulted in a small decrease in performance. Furthermore, we note that CCA models outperform simple vector concatenation in case of GOLD setting for motion verbs, and overall DCCA performed considerably worse than concatenation. Note that for CCA and DCCA we report the best performing scores achieved using weighted interpolation of textual and visual features with weights $\lambda_t = 0.5$ and $\lambda_c = 0.5$.

When comparing to our baseline and upper limit, we find that the all the GOLD models which use descriptions-based representations (except DCCA) outperform to the first sense heuristic for motion-verbs (accuracy 70.8), whereas they performed below the first sense heuristic in case of non-motion verbs (accuracy 80.6). As expected, both motion and non-motion verbs performed significantly below the most frequent sense heuristic (accuracy 86.2 and 90.7 respectively), which we argued provides an upper limit for unsupervised approaches.

We now turn the PRED configuration, i.e., to results obtained using object labels and image descriptions predicted by state-of-the-art automatic systems. This is arguably the more realistic scenario, as it only requires images as input, rather than assuming human-generated object labels and image descriptions (though object detection and image description systems are required instead). In the PRED setting, we find that textual features based on ob-

---

[3]We also experimented with Glove vectors (Pennington et al., 2014) but observed that word2vec representations consistently achieved better results that Glove vectors.

(a) Motion verbs (39), FS: 70.8, MFS: 86.2

Annotation	Textual			Vis	Concat (CNN+)			CCA (CNN+)			DCCA (CNN+)		
	O	C	O+C	CNN	O	C	O+C	O	C	O+C	O	C	O+C
GOLD	54.6	**73.3**	**75.6**	58.3	66.6	**74.7**	**73.8**	50.5	**75.4**	**74.0**	52.4	66.3	68.3
PRED	65.1	54.9	61.6	58.3	**72.6**	63.6	66.5	54.0	56.6	56.2	57.1	56.5	56.2

(b) Non-motion verbs (51), FS: 80.6, MFS: 90.7

Annotation	Textual			Vis	Concat (CNN+)			CCA (CNN+)			DCCA (CNN+)		
	O	C	O+C	CNN	O	C	O+C	O	C	O+C	O	C	O+C
GOLD	57.0	72.7	72.6	56.1	66.0	72.2	71.3	53.6	71.6	70.2	57.3	59.8	55.1
PRED	59.0	64.3	64.0	56.1	63.8	66.3	66.1	50.7	55.3	54.8	49.5	50.0	50.0

Table 3: Accuracy scores for motion and non-motion verbs using for different types of sense and image representations (O: object labels, C: image descriptions, CNN: image features, FS: first sense heuristic, MFS: most frequent sense heuristic). Configurations that performed better than FS in **bold**.

Motion verbs (19), FS: 60.0, MFS: 76.1

Features	GOLD		PRED	
	Sup	Unsup	Sup	Unsup
O	82.3	35.3	80.0	43.8
C	78.4	53.8	69.2	41.5
O+C	80.0	55.3	70.7	45.3
CNN	82.3	58.4	82.3	58.4
CNN+O	83.0	48.4	83.0	60.0
CNN+C	82.3	66.9	82.3	53.0
CNN+O+C	83.0	58.4	83.0	55.3

Table 4: Accuracy scores for motion verbs for both supervised and unsupervised approaches using different types of sense and image representation features.

Non-Motion verbs (19), FS: 71.3, MFS: 80.0

Features	GOLD		PRED	
	Sup	Unsup	Sup	Unsup
O	79.1	48.6	78.2	46.0
C	79.1	53.9	77.3	61.7
O+C	79.1	66.0	77.3	55.6
CNN	80.0	55.6	80.0	55.6
CNN+O	80.0	56.5	80.0	52.1
CNN+C	80.0	56.5	80.3	60.0
CNN+O+C	80.0	59.1	80.0	55.6

Table 5: Accuracy scores for non-motion verbs for both supervised and unsupervised approaches using different types of sense and image representation features.

ject labels (O) outperform both first sense heuristic and textual features based on image descriptions (C) in the case of motion verbs. Combining textual and visual features via concatenation improves performance for both motion and non-motion verbs. The overall best performance of 72.6 for predicted features is obtained by combining CNN features and embeddings based on object labels and outperforms first sense heuristic in case of motion verbs (accuracy 70.8). In the PRED setting for both classes of verbs the simpler concatenation model performed better than the more complex CCA and DCCA models. Note that for CCA and DCCA we report the best performing scores achieved using weighted interpolation of textual and visual features with weights $\lambda_t = 0.3$ and $\lambda_c = 0.7$. Overall, our findings are consistent with the intuition that motion verbs are easier to disambiguate than non-motion verbs, as they are more depictable and more likely to involve objects. Note that this is also reflected in the higher inter-annotator agreement for motion verbs (see Table 2).

5.2 Supervised Experiments and Results

Along with the unsupervised experiments we investigated the performance of textual and visual representations of images in a simplest supervised setting. We trained logistic regression classifiers for sense prediction by dividing the images in VerSe dataset into train and test splits. To train the classifiers we selected all the verbs which has atleast 20 images annotated and has at least two senses in VerSe. This resulted in 19 motion verbs and 19 non-motion verbs. Similar to our unsupervised experiments we explore multimodal features by using both textual and visual features for classification (similar to concatenation in unsupervised experiments).

Verb	Image	Predicted Descriptions	Pred. Obj.
play		A man holding a nintendo wii game controller. A man and a woman playing a video game. A man and a woman are playing a video game.	person, bassoon, violin fiddle, oboe, hautboy
swing		A woman standing next to a fire hydrant. A woman walking down a street holding an umbrella. A woman standing on a sidewalk holding an umbrella.	person, horizontal bar, high bar, pole
feed		A couple of cows standing next to each other. A cow that is standing in the dirt. A close up of a horse in a stable	arabian camel, dromedary, person

Table 6: Images that were assigned an incorrect sense in the PRED setting.

In Table 4 we report accuracy scores for 19 motion verbs using a supervised logistic regression classifier and for comparison we also report the scores of our proposed unsupervised algorithm for both GOLD and PRED setting. Similarly in Table 5 we report the accuracy scores for 19 non-motion verbs. We observe that all supervised classifiers for both motion and non-motion verbs performing better than first sense baseline. Similar to our findings using an unsupervised approach we find that in most cases multimodal features obtained using concatenating textual and visual features has outperformed textual or visual features alone especially in the PRED setting which is arguably the more realistic scenario. We observe that the features from PRED image descriptions showed better results for non-motion verbs for both supervised and unsupervised approaches whereas PRED object features showed better results for motion verbs. We also observe that supervised classifiers outperform most frequent sense for motion verbs and for non-motion verbs our scores match with most frequent sense heuristic.

5.3 Error Analysis

In order to understand the cases where the proposed unsupervised algorithm failed, we analyzed the images that were disambiguated incorrectly. For the PRED setting, we observed that using predicted image descriptions yielded lower scores compared to predicted object labels. The main reason for this is that the image description system often generates irrelevant descriptions or descriptions not related to the action depicted, whereas the object labels predicted by the CNN model tend to be relevant. This highlights that current image description systems still have clear limitations, despite the high evaluation scores reported in the literature (Vinyals et al., 2015; Fang et al., 2015). Examples are shown in Table 6: in all cases human generated descriptions and object labels that are relevant for disambiguation, which explains the higher scores in the GOLD setting.

6 Conclusion

We have introduced the new task of visual verb sense disambiguation: given an image and a verb, identify the verb sense depicted in the image. We developed the new VerSe dataset for this task, based on the existing COCO and TUHOI datasets. We proposed an unsupervised visual sense disambiguation model based on the Lesk algorithm and demonstrated that both textual and visual information associated with an image can contribute to sense disambiguation. In an in-depth analysis of various image representations we showed that object labels and visual features extracted using state-of-the-art convolutional neural networks result in good disambiguation performance, while automatically generated image descriptions are less useful.

References

Galen Andrew, Raman Arora, Jeff A. Bilmes, and Karen Livescu. 2013. Deep canonical correlation analysis. In *Proceedings of the 30th International Conference on Machine Learning, ICML 2013, Atlanta, GA, USA, 16-21 June 2013*, pages 1247–1255.

Stanislaw Antol, Aishwarya Agrawal, Jiasen Lu, Margaret Mitchell, Dhruv Batra, C. Lawrence Zitnick, and Devi Parikh. 2015. VQA: visual question answering. In *2015 IEEE International Conference on Computer Vision, ICCV 2015, Santiago, Chile, December 7-13, 2015*, pages 2425–2433.

Kobus Barnard, Matthew Johnson, and David Forsyth. 2003. Word sense disambiguation with pictures. In *Proceedings of the HLT-NAACL 2003 workshop on Learning word meaning from non-linguistic data-Volume 6*, pages 1–5. Association for Computational Linguistics.

Samuel Brody and Mirella Lapata. 2008. Good neighbors make good senses: Exploiting distributional similarity for unsupervised wsd. In *Proceedings of the 22nd International Conference on Computational Linguistics-Volume 1*, pages 65–72. Association for Computational Linguistics.

Yu-Wei Chao, Zhan Wang, Yugeng He, Jiaxuan Wang, and Jia Deng. 2015. HICO: A benchmark for recognizing human-object interactions in images. In *2015 IEEE International Conference on Computer Vision, ICCV 2015, Santiago, Chile, December 7-13, 2015*, pages 1017–1025.

Xinlei Chen, Alan Ritter, Abhinav Gupta, and Tom M. Mitchell. 2015. Sense discovery via co-clustering on images and text. In *IEEE Conference on Computer Vision and Pattern Recognition, CVPR 2015, Boston, MA, USA, June 7-12, 2015*, pages 5298–5306.

Jia Deng, Wei Dong, Richard Socher, Li-Jia Li, Kai Li, and Fei-Fei Li. 2009. ImageNet: A large-scale hierarchical image database. In *2009 IEEE Computer Society Conference on Computer Vision and Pattern Recognition (CVPR 2009), 20-25 June 2009, Miami, Florida, USA*, pages 248–255.

Mark Everingham, S. M. Ali Eslami, Luc Van Gool, Christopher K. I. Williams, John M. Winn, and Andrew Zisserman. 2015. The Pascal visual object classes challenge: A retrospective. *International Journal of Computer Vision*, 111(1):98–136.

Hao Fang, Saurabh Gupta, Forrest N. Iandola, Rupesh K. Srivastava, Li Deng, Piotr Dollár, Jianfeng Gao, Xiaodong He, Margaret Mitchell, John C. Platt, C. Lawrence Zitnick, and Geoffrey Zweig. 2015. From captions to visual concepts and back. In *IEEE Conference on Computer Vision and Pattern Recognition, CVPR 2015, Boston, MA, USA, June 7-12, 2015*, pages 1473–1482.

Yunchao Gong, Liwei Wang, Micah Hodosh, Julia Hockenmaier, and Svetlana Lazebnik. 2014. Improving image-sentence embeddings using large weakly annotated photo collections. In *Computer Vision - ECCV 2014 - 13th European Conference, Zurich, Switzerland, September 6-12, 2014, Proceedings, Part IV*, pages 529–545.

David R. Hardoon, Sándor Szedmák, and John Shawe-Taylor. 2004. Canonical correlation analysis: An overview with application to learning methods. *Neural Computation*, 16(12):2639–2664.

Micah Hodosh, Peter Young, and Julia Hockenmaier. 2015. Framing image description as a ranking task: Data, models and evaluation metrics (extended abstract). In *Proceedings of the Twenty-Fourth International Joint Conference on Artificial Intelligence, IJCAI 2015, Buenos Aires, Argentina, July 25-31, 2015*, pages 4188–4192.

Eduard H. Hovy, Mitchell P. Marcus, Martha Palmer, Lance A. Ramshaw, and Ralph M. Weischedel. 2006. Ontonotes: The 90% solution. In *Human Language Technology Conference of the North American Chapter of the Association of Computational Linguistics, Proceedings, June 4-9, 2006, New York, New York, USA*, pages 57–60.

Sujay Kumar Jauhar, Chris Dyer, and Eduard H. Hovy. 2015. Ontologically grounded multi-sense representation learning for semantic vector space models. In *NAACL HLT 2015, The 2015 Conference of the North American Chapter of the Association for Computational Linguistics: Human Language Technologies, Denver, Colorado, USA, May 31 - June 5, 2015*, pages 683–693.

Yangqing Jia, Evan Shelhamer, Jeff Donahue, Sergey Karayev, Jonathan Long, Ross B. Girshick, Sergio Guadarrama, and Trevor Darrell. 2014. Caffe: Convolutional architecture for fast feature embedding. In *Proceedings of the ACM International Conference on Multimedia, MM '14, Orlando, FL, USA, November 03 - 07, 2014*, pages 675–678.

Andrej Karpathy and Fei-Fei Li. 2015. Deep visual-semantic alignments for generating image descriptions. In *IEEE Conference on Computer Vision and Pattern Recognition, CVPR 2015, Boston, MA, USA, June 7-12, 2015*, pages 3128–3137.

Adam Kilgarrif. 1998. Senseval: An exercise in evaluating word sense disambiguation programs. In *Proc. of the first international conference on language resources and evaluation*, pages 581–588.

Dieu Thu Le, Raffaella Bernardi, and Jasper Uijlings. 2013. Exploiting language models to recognize unseen actions. In *Proceedings of the 3rd ACM conference on International conference on multimedia retrieval*, pages 231–238. ACM.

Dieu-Thu Le, Jasper Uijlings, and Raffaella Bernardi, 2014. *Proceedings of the Third Workshop on Vision and Language*, chapter TUHOI: Trento Universal Human Object Interaction Dataset, pages 17–24. Dublin City University and the Association for Computational Linguistics.

Michael Lesk. 1986. Automatic sense disambiguation using machine readable dictionaries: how to tell a pine cone from an ice cream cone. In *Proceedings of the 5th Annual International Conference on Systems Documentation, SIGDOC 1986, Toronto, Ontario, Canada, 1986*, pages 24–26.

Beth Levin. 1993. *English verb classes and alternations: A preliminary investigation*. University of Chicago Press.

Dekang Lin. 1997. Using syntactic dependency as local context to resolve word sense ambiguity. In *Proceedings of the 35th Annual Meeting of the Association for Computational Linguistics and Eighth Conference of the European Chapter of the Association for Computational Linguistics*, pages 64–71. Association for Computational Linguistics.

Nicolas Loeff, Cecilia Ovesdotter Alm, and David A. Forsyth. 2006. Discriminating image senses by clustering with multimodal features. In *ACL 2006, 21st International Conference on Computational Linguistics and 44th Annual Meeting of the Association for Computational Linguistics, Proceedings of the Conference, Sydney, Australia, 17-21 July 2006*, pages 547–554. Association for Computational Linguistics.

Diana McCarthy, Rob Koeling, Julie Weeds, and John Carroll. 2004. Finding predominant word senses in untagged text. In *Proceedings of the 42nd Annual Meeting on Association for Computational Linguistics*, pages 279–286. Association for Computational Linguistics.

Tomas Mikolov, Kai Chen, Greg Corrado, and Jeffrey Dean. 2013. Efficient estimation of word representations in vector space. *CoRR*, abs/1301.3781.

George A Miller, Richard Beckwith, Christiane Fellbaum, Derek Gross, and Katherine J Miller. 1990. Introduction to wordnet: An on-line lexical database. *International Journal of Lexicography*, 3(4):235–244.

Roberto Navigli. 2009. Word sense disambiguation: A survey. *ACM Computing Surveys (CSUR)*, 41(2):10.

Jeffrey Pennington, Richard Socher, and Christopher D. Manning. 2014. Glove: Global vectors for word representation. In *Proceedings of the 2014 Conference on Empirical Methods in Natural Language Processing, EMNLP 2014, October 25-29, 2014, Doha, Qatar, A meeting of SIGDAT, a Special Interest Group of the ACL*, pages 1532–1543.

Matteo Ruggero Ronchi and Pietro Perona. 2015. Describing common human visual actions in images. In *Proceedings of the British Machine Vision Conference (BMVC 2015)*, pages 52.1–52.12. BMVA Press, September.

Sascha Rothe and Hinrich Schutze. 2015. Autoextend: Extending word embeddings to embeddings for synsets and lexemes. In *Proceedings of the 53rd Annual Meeting of the Association for Computational Linguistics and the 7th International Joint Conference on Natural Language Processing of the Asian Federation of Natural Language Processing, ACL 2015, July 26-31, 2015, Beijing, China, Volume 1: Long Papers*, pages 1793–1803.

Kate Saenko and Trevor Darrell. 2008. Unsupervised learning of visual sense models for polysemous words. In *Advances in Neural Information Processing Systems 21, Proceedings of the Twenty-Second Annual Conference on Neural Information Processing Systems, Vancouver, British Columbia, Canada, December 8-11, 2008*, pages 1393–1400.

Karen Simonyan and Andrew Zisserman. 2014. Very deep convolutional networks for large-scale image recognition. *CoRR*, abs/1409.1556.

Oriol Vinyals, Alexander Toshev, Samy Bengio, and Dumitru Erhan. 2015. Show and tell: A neural image caption generator. In *IEEE Conference on Computer Vision and Pattern Recognition, CVPR 2015, Boston, MA, USA, June 7-12, 2015*, pages 3156–3164.

Weiran Wang, Raman Arora, Karen Livescu, and Jeff A. Bilmes. 2015. On deep multi-view representation learning. In *Proceedings of the 32nd International Conference on Machine Learning, ICML 2015, Lille, France, 6-11 July 2015*, pages 1083–1092.

Fei Yan and Krystian Mikolajczyk. 2015. Deep correlation for matching images and text. In *IEEE Conference on Computer Vision and Pattern Recognition, CVPR 2015, Boston, MA, USA, June 7-12, 2015*, pages 3441–3450.

Bangpeng Yao and Li Fei-Fei. 2010. Grouplet: A structured image representation for recognizing human and object interactions. In *Computer Vision and Pattern Recognition (CVPR), 2010 IEEE Conference on*, pages 9–16. IEEE.

Bangpeng Yao, Xiaoye Jiang, Aditya Khosla, Andy Lai Lin, Leonidas Guibas, and Li Fei-Fei. 2011. Human action recognition by learning bases of action attributes and parts. In *Computer Vision (ICCV), 2011 IEEE International Conference on*, pages 1331–1338. IEEE.

Zhi Zhong and Hwee Tou Ng. 2010. It makes sense: A wide-coverage word sense disambiguation system for free text. In *ACL 2010, Proceedings of the 48th Annual Meeting of the Association for Computational Linguistics, July 11-16, 2010, Uppsala, Sweden, System Demonstrations*, pages 78–83.

Stating the Obvious:
Extracting Visual Common Sense Knowledge

Mark Yatskar[1], Vicente Ordonez[2], Ali Farhadi[1,2]
[1]Computer Science & Engineering, University of Washington, Seattle, WA
[2]Allen Institute for Artificial Intelligence (AI2), Seattle, WA
`[my89, ali]@cs.washington.edu, vicenteor@allenai.org`

Abstract

Obtaining common sense knowledge using current information extraction techniques is extremely challenging. In this work, we instead propose to derive simple common sense statements from fully annotated object detection corpora such as the Microsoft Common Objects in Context dataset. We show that many thousands of common sense facts can be extracted from such corpora at high quality. Furthermore, using WordNet and a novel submodular k-coverage formulation, we are able to generalize our initial set of common sense assertions to unseen objects and uncover over 400k potentially useful facts.

1 Introduction

How can we discover that bowls can hold broccoli, that if a knife touches a cake then a person is probably cutting cake, or that cutlery can be on dining tables? We propose to leverage the effort of computer vision researchers in creating large scale datasets for object detection and use these resources instead to extract symbolic representations of visual common sense. The knowledge we compile is physical, not commonly covered in text and more exhaustive than what people can usually produce.

Our focus is particularly on visual common sense, defined as the information about spatial and functional properties of entities in the world. We propose to extract three types of knowledge from the Microsoft Common Objects in Context dataset (Lin et al., 2014) (MS-COCO), consisting of 300,000 images, covering 80 objects, with object segments and natural language captions. First, we find spatial relations, e.g. *holds*(bed, dog), from outlines of co-occurring objects. Next, we construct entailment rules like *holds*(bed, dog) $\Rightarrow$ *laying-on*(dog, bed) by associating spatial relations with text in captions. Finally, we uncover general facts such as *holds*(furniture, domestic animal), applicable to object types not present in MS-COCO by using WordNet (Miller, 1995) and a novel submodular k-coverage formulation.

Evaluations using crowdsourcing show our methods can discover many thousands of high quality explicit statements of visual common sense. While some of this knowledge can be potentially extracted from text (Vanderwende, 2005), we found that from our top 100 extracted spatial relations, e.g. *holds*(bed, dog), only 4 are present in some form in the *AtLocation* relations in the popular ConceptNet (Speer and Havasi, 2013) knowledge base. This shows that the knowledge we derive provides complimentary information for other more general knowledge bases. Such common sense facts have proved useful for query expansion (Kotov and Zhai, 2012; Bouchoucha et al., 2013) and could benefit entailment (Dagan et al., 2010), grounded entailment (Bowman et al., 2015), or visual recognition tasks (Zhu et al., 2014).

2 Related Work

Common sense knowledge has been predominately created directly from human input or extracted from text (Lenat et al., 1990; Liu and Singh, 2004; Carlson et al., 2010). In contrast, our work is focused on visual common sense extracted from images anno-

Proceedings of NAACL-HLT 2016, pages 193–198,
San Diego, California, June 12-17, 2016. ©2016 Association for Computational Linguistics

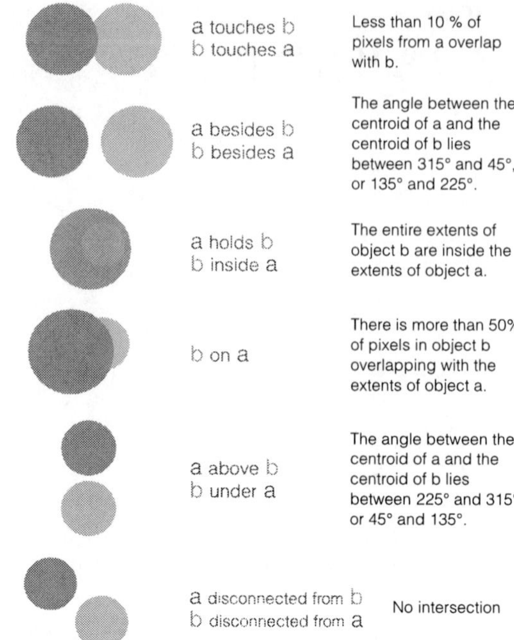

Figure 1: We define 6 types of unique relationships: {touches, above, besides, holds, on, disconnected}.

tated with regions and descriptions.

There has also been recent interest in the vision community to build databases of visual common sense knowledge. Efforts have focused on a small set of relations, such as *similar to* or *part of* (Chen et al., 2013). Webly supervised techniques (Divvala et al., 2014; Chen et al., 2013) have also been used to test whether a particular object-relation-object triplet occurs in images (Sadeghi et al., 2015). In contrast, we use seven spatial relations and allow natural language relations that represent a larger array of higher level semantics. We also leverage existing efforts on annotating large scale image datasets instead of relying on the noisy outputs of a computer vision system.

On a technical level, our methods for extracting common sense facts from images rely on Pointwise-Mutual Information (PMI), analogous to other rule extraction systems based on text (Lin and Pantel, 2001; Schoenmackers et al., 2010). We view objects as an analogy for words, images as documents, and object-object configurations as typed bigrams. Our methods for generalizing relations are inspired

by work that tries to predict a class label for an image given a hierarchy of concepts (Deng et al., 2012; Ordonez et al., 2013; Ordonez et al., 2015). Yet our work is the first to deal with visual relations between pairs of concepts in the hierarchy by using a sub-modular formulation that maximizes the amount of coverage of subordinate categories while avoiding contradictions with an initial set of discovered common-sense assertions.

3   Methods

We assume the availability of an object-level annotated image dataset D containing a set of images with textual descriptions. Each object in an image must be annotated with: (1) a mask or polygon outlining the extents of the object, and (2) the category of the object from a set of categories V and (3) an overall description of the image.

We produce three types of common sense facts, each with an associated scoring function: (1) Object-object relationships implicitly encoded in the relative configurations between objects in the annotated image data, i.e. *on*(bed, dog) (sec 3.1) , (2) Entailment relations encoded in the relationships between object-object configurations and textual descriptions i.e. *on*(bed, dog) $\Rightarrow$ *laying-on*(bed, dog) (sec 3.2), and (3) Generalized relations induced by using the semantic hierarchy of concepts in WordNet, i.e. *on*(furniture , domestic-animal) (sec 3.3).

3.1   Mining Object-Object Relations

Our objective in this section is to score and rank a set of relations $S_1 = \{r(o_1, o_2)\}$, where r is a object-object relation and $o_1, o_2 \in V$, using a function $\gamma_1 : S_1 \rightarrow \mathbb{R}$. First, we define a vocabulary R of object-object relations between pairs of annotated objects. Our relations are inspired by Region Connection Calculus (Randell et al., 1992), and the Visual Dependency Grammar of (Elliott et al., 2014; Elliott and de Vries, 2015), details in Figure 1.

For every image, we record the instances of each of these object-object relations $r(o_1, o_2)$ between all co-occurring objects in D^1. We use Point-wise Mutual Information (PMI) to estimate the evidence for

---

[1]For symmetric relations like *above*(o_1, o_2), and *under*(o_1, o_2) we only record one of the relations.

$r(o_1, o_2)$	holds(person, o_2)	holds(o_1, person)	$r(o_1, \text{frisbee})$
holds(pizza, broccoli)	holds(person, tie)	holds(bus, person)	touches(dog, frisbee)
holds(person, tie)	holds(person, toothbrush)	holds(train, person)	touches(person, frisbee)
holds(dining table, sandwich)	holds(person, cellphone)	holds(airplane, person)	holds(dog, frisbee)
holds(dining table, broccoli)	holds(person, baseball glove)	holds(boat, person)	holds(person, frisbee)
holds(dining table, pizza)	holds(person, remote)	holds(tv, person)	besides(umbrella, frisbee)
...	...	...	...
holds(cell_phone, person)	holds(person, bench)	holds(dining table, person)	besides(person, frisbee)
above(person, bus)	holds(person, dining table)	holds(cell phone, person)	above(car, frisbee)
above(bicycle, car)	holds(person, car)	holds(chair, person)	above(person, frisbee)

Figure 2: Example of our extracted object-object relations. The first column contains the overall 3 best and worst relations ranked by PMI, the following columns show similar results for the queries: what does a person hold? what holds a person?, and what interacts with a frisbee?

each relationship triplet:

$$\gamma_1(r(o_1, o_2)) = log\frac{p[r(o_1, o_2)]}{p[r]p[(o_1, o_2)]}, \qquad (1)$$

We estimate these probabilities by counting object-object-relation co-ocurrences using existential quantifiers for every image. This means every image can at most contribute one to the count of $r(o_1, o_2)$ so that we do not exacerbate the results by images with many identical object types taken from unusual viewpoints. In Figure 2, we provide examples of our extracted object-object relations.

3.2 Mining Entailment Relations

In this section we combine our relation-based tuples mined from visual annotations (section 2) with more than 400k textual descriptions included in MS-COCO. We generate a set of entailments $S_2 = \{r(o_1, o_2) \Rightarrow z\}$, where $r(o_1, o_2)$ is an element from S_1 and z is a consequent obtained from textual descriptions. Similarly as in the previous section, we rank the relations in S_2 using a function $\gamma_2 : S_2 \to \mathbb{R}$.

We start by generating an exhaustive list of candidate consequents z. We first pre-process the image captions with the part-of-speech tagger and lemmatizer from the Stanford Core NLP toolkit (Manning et al., 2014), and remove stop words. Then we generate a list of n-length skipgrams in each caption. The set of n-skipgrams are filtered based on predefined lexical patterns[2], and redundancies

are removed[3]. Skipgrams, z, are then paired with co-occurring relations, $r(o_1, o_2)$, removing pairs with the disconnected-from spatial relation (see Figure 1). Pairs are scored with the conditional probability:

$$\gamma_2(r(o_1, o_2) \Rightarrow z) = \frac{P[z, r(o_1, o_2)]}{P[r(o_1, o_2)]} \qquad (2)$$

The consequent z can take the form q, $q(o_1)$, $q(o_2)$, or $q(o_1, o_2)$, by performing a simple alignment with the arguments in the antecedent. We perform this alignment by mapping the object categories in the antecedent $r(o_1, o_2)$ to WordNet synsets, and matching any word in z to any word in the gloss set of the predicate arguments o_1 and o_2. The unmatched words in z form the relation, whereas matched words form arguments. We produce the form q if there are no matches, $q(o_1)$, or $q(o_2)$ when one argument word matches, and $q(o_1, o_2)$ when both match. Examples of discovered entailments are in Figure 3.

3.3 Generalizing Relations using WordNet

In this section we present an approach to generalize an initial set of relations, S, to objects not found in the original vocabulary V. Using WordNet we construct a superset G containing all possible parent relations for the relations in S by replacing their arguments o_1, o_2 by all their possible hypernyms. Our objective is to select a subset T from G that contains high quality and diverse generalized relations.

---

[2] $\langle$noun, verb$\rangle$, $\langle$noun,*, verb,*, noun$\rangle$, $\langle$noun,*, preposition, *, noun$\rangle$, $\langle$noun,*, verb, preposition,*,noun$\rangle$

[3] $\langle$noun,*, verb, *, noun$\rangle$ are collapsed to $\langle$noun,*, verb, preposition,*,noun$\rangle$.

Figure 3: Left: correctly identified entailment relations and right: failure cases.

Note that elements in G can be too general and contradict statements in S while others could be correct but add little new knowledge. To balance these concerns, we formulate the selection as an optimization problem by maximizing a fitness function $\mathcal{L}$:

$$\max_{T} \mathcal{L}(T), \text{ such that } |T| = k, \text{ and } T \subseteq G, \quad (3)$$

$$\mathcal{L}(T) = \lambda \log(1+\psi(T)) + \sum_{t \in T} \log(1+\phi(t, S)), \quad (4)$$

where ψ is a *coverage* term that computes the total number of facts implied through hyponym relationships by the elements in T. The second term ϕ is a *consistency* term that measures the compatibility of a generalized relation t with the relations in S. We assume that if a relation is missing from S, then it is false (this corresponds to a closed world assumption over the domain of S). Thus, ϕ is the ratio of the scores of relations in S consistent with relation t (i.e. evidence for t based on S), and a value that is proportional to the number of missing relations from S (i.e. the amount of counter-evidence). More concretely:

$$\phi(t, S) = \frac{\sum_{s:t\Rightarrow s \land s \in S} \gamma(s)}{\mu \cdot (1 + \sum_{s:t\Rightarrow s \land s \notin S} 1) \cdot d(t, S)}, \quad (5)$$

where μ is a constant and d is the product of the WordNet distances of the synsets involved in t to their nearest synset in S. This penalizes relations that are far away from categories in S. The optimization defined in Equation 3 is an instance of the submodular k-coverage problem. We use a greedy algorithm that adds elements to T that maximize $\mathcal{L}$, which due to the submodular nature of the problem approximates the solution up to a constant factor.

4 Experimental Setup

Object-Object Relations: We filter out from the initial set of candidate relations the ones that occur less than 20 times. We extract more than 3.1k unique statements (6k including symmetric spatial relations). *Entailment Relations*: We use skipgrams of length 2-6 allowing at most 6 skips, filter candidates such that they occur at least 5 times, and return the top 10 most likely entailments per spatial relation. Overall, 6.3k unique statements are extracted (10k including symmetric relations). *Generalized Relations*: We optimize Equation 4 only for object-object relations because the closed world assumption makes counts for implications sparse. The parameter μ is set to the average of the scores, $\lambda = 0.05$ and $k = 200$.

5 Evaluation

We evaluated the quality of the common sense we derive on Amazon Mechanical Turk. Annotators are presented with possible facts and asked to grade statements on a five point scale. Each fact was evaluated by 10 workers and we normalize their average responses to a scale from 0 to 1. Figure 4 shows plots of quality vs. coverage, where coverage means the top percent of relations sorted by our predicted quality scores.

Object-Object Relations As a baseline, 1000 randomly sampled relations have a quality of 0.225. Figure 4a shows our PMI measure ranks many high quality facts at the top, with the top quintile of the ranking being rated above 0.63 in quality. Facts about persons are higher quality, likely because this category is in over 50% of the images in MS-COCO.

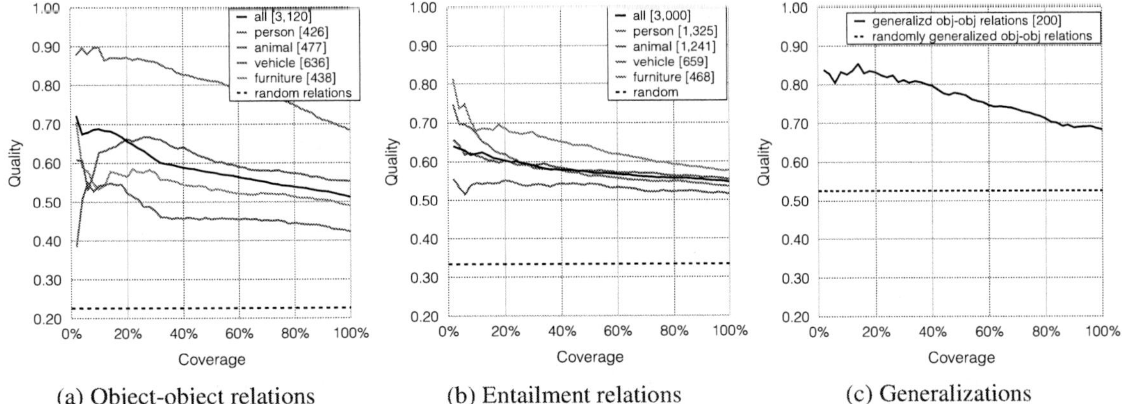

(a) Object-object relations   (b) Entailment relations   (c) Generalizations

Figure 4: Quality of extracted common sense, as judged by people. Legends show total relations covered at 100% for a few high level types in MS-COCO.

Entailment Relations   Turkers were instructed to assign the lowest score when they could not understand the consequent of the entailment relation. As a baseline, 1000 randomly sampled implications that meet our patterns have a quality of 0.33. Figure 4b shows that extracting high quality entailment is harder than object-object relations likely because supposition and consequent need to coordinate. Relations involving furniture are rated higher and manual inspection revealed that many relations about furniture imply stative verbs or spatial terms.

Generalized Relations   To evaluate generalizations, Figure 4c, we also present users with definitions[4]. As a baseline, 200 randomly sampled generalizations from our 3k object-object relations have a quality of 0.53. Generalizations we find are high quality and cover over 400k objects facts not present in MS-COCO. Examples from the 200 we derive include: *holds*(dining-table, cutlery), *holds*(bowl, edible fruit) or *on*(domestic animal, bed).

6   Conclusion

In this work, we use an existing object detection dataset to extract 16k common sense statements about annotated categories. We also show how to generalize using WordNet and induced hundreds of thousands of facts about *unseen* objects. The information we extracted is visual, large scale and good quality. It has the potential to be useful for both visual recognition and entailment applications.

---

[4]sometimes rules involve abstract concepts, for example *vessel*, any object that can be used as a container

7   Acknowledgments

The authors would like to thank Hannaneh Hajishirzi, Yejin Choi, and Luke Zettlemoyer for helpful comments on the draft and the reviewers for useful feedback. We also thank Ani Kembhavi, and Roozbeh Mottaghi for helping to formalize visual common sense and Mechanical Turkers who helped evaluate output.

References

Arbi Bouchoucha, Jing He, and Jian-Yun Nie. 2013. Diversified query expansion using conceptnet. In *Proceedings of the 22nd ACM international conference on Conference on information & knowledge management*, CIKM '13, pages 1861–1864, New York, NY, USA. ACM.

Samuel R Bowman, Gabor Angeli, Christopher Potts, and Christopher D Manning. 2015. A large annotated corpus for learning natural language inference. *arXiv preprint arXiv:1508.05326*.

Andrew Carlson, Justin Betteridge, Bryan Kisiel, Burr Settles, Estevam R Hruschka Jr, and Tom M Mitchell. 2010. Toward an architecture for never-ending language learning. In *AAAI Conference on Artificial Intelligence*, volume 5, page 3.

Xinlei Chen, Ashish Shrivastava, and Arpan Gupta. 2013. Neil: Extracting visual knowledge from web data. In *International Conference on Computer Vision (ICCV)*, pages 1409–1416. IEEE.

Ido Dagan, Bill Dolan, Bernardo Magnini, and Dan Roth. 2010. Recognizing textual entailment: Rational, evaluation and approaches–erratum. *Natural Language Engineering*, 16(01):105–105.

Jia Deng, Jonathan Krause, Alexander C Berg, and Li Fei-Fei. 2012. Hedging your bets: Optimizing accuracy-specificity trade-offs in large scale visual recognition. In *Conference on Computer Vision and Pattern Recognition (CVPR)*, pages 3450–3457. IEEE.

Santosh Divvala, Ali Farhadi, and Carlos Guestrin. 2014. Learning everything about anything: Webly-supervised visual concept learning. In *Proceedings of the IEEE Conference on Computer Vision and Pattern Recognition*, pages 3270–3277.

Desmond Elliott and Arjen P de Vries. 2015. Describing images using inferred visual dependency representations. *Association for Computational Linguistics (ACL)*.

Desmond Elliott, Victor Lavrenko, and Frank Keller. 2014. Query-by-example image retrieval using visual dependency representations. In *International Conference on Computational Linguistics (COLING)*, pages 109–120, August.

Alexander Kotov and ChengXiang Zhai. 2012. Tapping into knowledge base for concept feedback: Leveraging conceptnet to improve search results for difficult queries. In *Proceedings of the Fifth ACM International Conference on Web Search and Data Mining*, WSDM '12, pages 403–412, New York, NY, USA. ACM.

Douglas B Lenat, Ramanathan V. Guha, Karen Pittman, Dexter Pratt, and Mary Shepherd. 1990. Cyc: toward programs with common sense. *Communications of the ACM*, 33(8):30–49.

Dekang Lin and Patrick Pantel. 2001. Dirt@ sbt@ discovery of inference rules from text. In *Proceedings of the seventh ACM SIGKDD international conference on Knowledge discovery and data mining*, pages 323–328. ACM.

Tsung-Yi Lin, Michael Maire, Serge Belongie, James Hays, Pietro Perona, Deva Ramanan, Piotr Dollár, and C Lawrence Zitnick. 2014. Microsoft coco: Common objects in context. In *Computer Vision–ECCV 2014*, pages 740–755. Springer.

Hugo Liu and Push Singh. 2004. Conceptnet: A practical commonsense reasoning tool-kit. *BT technology journal*, 22(4):211–226.

Christopher D. Manning, Mihai Surdeanu, John Bauer, Jenny Finkel, Steven J. Bethard, and David McClosky. 2014. The Stanford CoreNLP natural language processing toolkit. In *Annual Meeting of the Association for Computational Linguistics (ACL): System Demonstrations*, pages 55–60.

George A Miller. 1995. Wordnet: a lexical database for english. *Communications of the ACM*, 38(11):39–41.

Vicente Ordonez, Jia Deng, Yejin Choi, Alexander C Berg, and Tamara Berg. 2013. From large scale image categorization to entry-level categories. In *International Conference on Computer Vision (ICCV)*, pages 2768–2775. IEEE.

Vicente Ordonez, Wei Liu, Jia Deng, Yejin Choi, Alexander C. Berg, and Tamara L. Berg. 2015. Predicting entry-level categories. *International Journal of Computer Vision*, pages 1–15.

David A Randell, Zhan Cui, and Anthony G Cohn. 1992. A spatial logic based on regions and connection. In *International Conference on Knowledge Representation and Reasoning*.

Fereshteh Sadeghi, Santosh K Divvala, and Ali Farhadi. 2015. Viske: Visual knowledge extraction and question answering by visual verification of relation phrases. In *Conference on Computer Vision and Pattern Recognition (CVPR)*, pages 1456–1464.

Stefan Schoenmackers, Oren Etzioni, Daniel S Weld, and Jesse Davis. 2010. Learning first-order horn clauses from web text. In *Empirical Methods in Natural Language Processing (EMNLP)*, pages 1088–1098.

Robert Speer and Catherine Havasi. 2013. Conceptnet 5: A large semantic network for relational knowledge. In *The Peoples Web Meets NLP*, pages 161–176. Springer.

Lucy Vanderwende. 2005. Volunteers created the web. In *Proceedings of the 2005 AAAI Spring Symposium, Knowledge Collection from Volunteer Contributors*. American Association for Artificial Intelligence, March.

Yuke Zhu, Alireza Fathi, and Li Fei-Fei. 2014. Reasoning about Object Affordances in a Knowledge Base Representation. In *European Conference on Computer Vision*.

Recurrent Neural Network Grammars

Chris Dyer[♠] **Adhiguna Kuncoro**[♠] **Miguel Ballesteros**[◇♠] **Noah A. Smith**[♡]
[♠]School of Computer Science, Carnegie Mellon University, Pittsburgh, PA, USA
[◇]NLP Group, Pompeu Fabra University, Barcelona, Spain
[♡]Computer Science & Engineering, University of Washington, Seattle, WA, USA
{cdyer,akuncoro}@cs.cmu.edu, miguel.ballesteros@upf.edu, nasmith@cs.washington.edu

Abstract

We introduce recurrent neural network grammars, probabilistic models of sentences with explicit phrase structure. We explain efficient inference procedures that allow application to both parsing and language modeling. Experiments show that they provide better parsing in English than any single previously published supervised generative model and better language modeling than state-of-the-art sequential RNNs in English and Chinese.

1 Introduction

Sequential recurrent neural networks (RNNs) are remarkably effective models of natural language. In the last few years, language model results that substantially improve over long-established state-of-the-art baselines have been obtained using RNNs (Zaremba et al., 2015; Mikolov et al., 2010) as well as in various conditional language modeling tasks such as machine translation (Bahdanau et al., 2015), image caption generation (Xu et al., 2015), and dialogue generation (Wen et al., 2015). Despite these impressive results, sequential models are *a priori* inappropriate models of natural language, since relationships among words are largely organized in terms of latent nested structures rather than sequential surface order (Chomsky, 1957).

In this paper, we introduce **recurrent neural network grammars** (RNNGs; §2), a new generative probabilistic model of sentences that explicitly models nested, hierarchical relationships among words and phrases. RNNGs operate via a recursive syntactic process reminiscent of probabilistic context-free grammar generation, but decisions are parameterized using RNNs that condition on the entire syntactic derivation history, greatly relaxing context-free independence assumptions.

The foundation of this work is a top-down variant of transition-based parsing (§3). We give two variants of the algorithm, one for parsing (given an observed sentence, transform it into a tree), and one for generation. While several transition-based neural models of syntactic generation exist (Henderson, 2003, 2004; Emami and Jelinek, 2005; Titov and Henderson, 2007; Buys and Blunsom, 2015b), these have relied on structure building operations based on parsing actions in shift-reduce and left-corner parsers which operate in a largely bottom-up fashion. While this construction is appealing because inference is relatively straightforward, it limits the use of top-down grammar information, which is helpful for generation (Roark, 2001).[1] RNNGs maintain the algorithmic convenience of transition-based parsing but incorporate top-down (i.e., root-to-terminal) syntactic information (§4).

The top-down transition set that RNNGs are based on lends itself to discriminative modeling as well, where sequences of transitions are modeled conditional on the full input sentence along with the incrementally constructed syntactic structures. Similar to previously published discriminative bottom-up transition-based parsers (Henderson, 2004; Sagae and Lavie, 2005; Zhang and Clark, 2011, *inter alia*), greedy prediction with our model yields a linear-time deterministic parser (provided an upper bound on the number of actions taken between processing subsequent terminal symbols is imposed); however, our algorithm generates arbitrary tree structures directly, without the binarization required by shift-reduce parsers. The discriminative model also lets us use ancestor sampling to obtain samples of parse trees for sentences, and this is used to solve

---

[1]The left-corner parsers used by Henderson (2003, 2004) incorporate limited top-down information, but a complete path from the root of the tree to a terminal is not generally present when a terminal is generated. Refer to Henderson (2003, Fig. 1) for an example.

Proceedings of NAACL-HLT 2016, pages 199–209,
San Diego, California, June 12-17, 2016. ©2016 Association for Computational Linguistics

a second practical challenge with RNNGs: approximating the marginal likelihood and MAP tree of a sentence under the generative model. We present a simple importance sampling algorithm which uses samples from the discriminative parser to solve inference problems in the generative model (§5).

Experiments show that RNNGs are effective for both language modeling and parsing (§6). Our generative model obtains (i) the best-known parsing results using a single supervised generative model and (ii) better perplexities in language modeling than state-of-the-art sequential LSTM language models. Surprisingly—although in line with previous parsing results showing the effectiveness of generative models (Henderson, 2004; Johnson, 2001)—parsing with the generative model obtains significantly better results than parsing with the discriminative model.

2   RNN Grammars

Formally, an RNNG is a triple (N, Σ, Θ) consisting of a finite set of nonterminal symbols (N), a finite set of terminal symbols (Σ) such that $N \cap \Sigma = \emptyset$, and a collection of neural network parameters Θ. It does not explicitly define rules since these are implicitly characterized by Θ. The algorithm that the grammar uses to generate trees and strings in the language is characterized in terms of a transition-based algorithm, which is outlined in the next section. In the section after that, the semantics of the parameters that are used to turn this into a stochastic algorithm that generates pairs of trees and strings are discussed.

3   Top-down Parsing and Generation

RNNGs are based on a top-down generation algorithm that relies on a stack data structure of partially completed syntactic constituents. To emphasize the similarity of our algorithm to more familiar bottom-up shift-reduce recognition algorithms, we first present the parsing (rather than generation) version of our algorithm (§3.1) and then present modifications to turn it into a generator (§3.2).

3.1   Parser Transitions

The parsing algorithm transforms a sequence of words x into a parse tree y using two data structures (a stack and an input buffer). As with the bottom-up algorithm of Sagae and Lavie (2005), our algorithm begins with the stack (S) empty and the complete sequence of words in the input buffer (B). The buffer contains unprocessed terminal symbols, and the stack contains terminal symbols, "open" nonterminal symbols, and completed constituents. At each timestep, one of the following three classes of operations (Fig. 1) is selected by a classifier, based on the current contents on the stack and buffer:

- NT(X) introduces an "open nonterminal" X onto the top of the stack. Open nonterminals are written as a nonterminal symbol preceded by an open parenthesis, e.g., "(VP", and they represent a nonterminal whose child nodes have not yet been fully constructed. Open nonterminals are "closed" to form complete constituents by subsequent REDUCE operations.

- SHIFT removes the terminal symbol x from the front of the input buffer, and pushes it onto the top of the stack.

- REDUCE repeatedly pops completed subtrees or terminal symbols from the stack until an open nonterminal is encountered, and then this open NT is popped and used as the label of a new constituent that has the popped subtrees as its children. This new completed constituent is pushed onto the stack as a single composite item. A single REDUCE operation can thus create constituents with an unbounded number of children.

The parsing algorithm terminates when there is a single completed constituent on the stack and the buffer is empty. Fig. 2 shows an example parse using our transition set. Note that in this paper we do not model preterminal symbols (i.e., part-of-speech tags) and our examples therefore do not include them.[2]

Our transition set is closely related to the operations used in Earley's algorithm which likewise introduces nonterminals symbols with its PREDICT

---

[2] Preterminal symbols are, from the parsing algorithm's point of view, just another kind of nonterminal symbol that requires no special handling. However, leaving them out reduces the number of transitions by $O(n)$ and also reduces the number of action types, both of which reduce the runtime. Furthermore, standard parsing evaluation scores do not depend on preterminal prediction accuracy.

operation and later COMPLETEs them after consuming terminal symbols one at a time using SCAN (Earley, 1970). It is likewise closely related to the "linearized" parse trees proposed by Vinyals et al. (2015) and to the top-down, left-to-right decompositions of trees used in previous generative parsing and language modeling work (Roark, 2001, 2004; Charniak, 2010).

A further connection is to $LL(*)$ parsing which uses an unbounded lookahead (compactly represented by a DFA) to distinguish between parse alternatives in a top-down parser (Parr and Fisher, 2011); however, our parser uses an RNN encoding of the lookahead rather than a DFA.

Constraints on parser transitions. To guarantee that only well-formed phrase-structure trees are produced by the parser, we impose the following constraints on the transitions that can be applied at each step which are a function of the parser state (B, S, n) where n is the number of open nonterminals on the stack:

- The NT(X) operation can only be applied if B is not empty and $n < 100$.[3]
- The SHIFT operation can only be applied if B is not empty and $n \geq 1$.
- The REDUCE operation can only be applied if the top of the stack is not an open nonterminal symbol.
- The REDUCE operation can only be applied if $n \geq 2$ or if the buffer is empty.

To designate the set of valid parser transitions, we write $\mathcal{A}_D(B, S, n)$.

3.2 Generator Transitions

The parsing algorithm that maps from sequences of words to parse trees can be adapted with minor changes to produce an algorithm that stochastically generates trees and terminal symbols. Two changes are required: (i) there is no input buffer of

---

[3]Since our parser allows unary nonterminal productions, there are an infinite number of valid trees for finite-length sentences. The $n < 100$ constraint prevents the classifier from misbehaving and generating excessively large numbers of nonterminals. Similar constraints have been proposed to deal with the analogous problem in bottom-up shift-reduce parsers (Sagae and Lavie, 2005).

unprocessed words, rather there is an output buffer (T), and (ii) instead of a SHIFT operation there are GEN(x) operations which generate terminal symbol $x \in \Sigma$ and add it to the top of the stack and the output buffer. At each timestep an action is stochastically selected according to a conditional distribution that depends on the current contents of B and T. The algorithm terminates when a single completed constituent remains on the stack. Fig. 4 shows an example generation sequence.

Constraints on generator transitions. The generation algorithm also requires slightly modified constraints. These are:

- The GEN(x) operation can only be applied if $n \geq 1$.
- The REDUCE operation can only be applied if the top of the stack is not an open nonterminal symbol and $n \geq 1$.

To designate the set of valid generator transitions, we write $\mathcal{A}_G(T, S, n)$.

This transition set generates trees using nearly the same structure building actions and stack configurations as the "top-down PDA" construction proposed by Abney et al. (1999), albeit without the restriction that the trees be in Chomsky normal form.

3.3 Transition Sequences from Trees

Any parse tree can be converted to a sequence of transitions via a depth-first, left-to-right traversal of a parse tree. Since there is a unique depth-first, left-ro-right traversal of a tree, there is exactly one transition sequence of each tree. For a tree y and a sequence of symbols x, we write $a(x, y)$ to indicate the corresponding sequence of generation transitions, and $b(x, y)$ to indicate the parser transitions.

3.4 Runtime Analysis

A detailed analysis of the algorithmic properties of our top-down parser is beyond the scope of this paper; however, we briefly state several facts. Assuming the availability of constant time push and pop operations, the runtime is linear in the number of the nodes in the parse tree that is generated by the parser/generator (intuitively, this is true since although an individual REDUCE operation may require

Stack$_t$	Buffer$_t$	Open NTs$_t$	Action	Stack$_{t+1}$	Buffer$_{t+1}$	Open NTs$_{t+1}$
S	B	n	NT(X)	$S \mid (\mathrm{X}$	B	$n+1$
S	$x \mid B$	n	SHIFT	$S \mid x$	B	n
$S \mid (\mathrm{X} \mid \tau_1 \mid \ldots \mid \tau_\ell)$	B	n	REDUCE	$S \mid (\mathrm{X}\, \tau_1\, \ldots\, \tau_\ell)$	B	$n-1$

Figure 1: Parser transitions showing the stack, buffer, and open nonterminal count before and after each action type. S represents the stack, which contains open nonterminals and completed subtrees; B represents the buffer of unprocessed terminal symbols; x is a terminal symbol, X is a nonterminal symbol, and each τ is a completed subtree. The top of the stack is to the right, and the buffer is consumed from left to right. Elements on the stack and buffer are delimited by a vertical bar ($\mid$).

Input: *The hungry cat meows* .

	Stack	Buffer	Action
0		*The* $\mid$ *hungry* $\mid$ *cat* $\mid$ *meows* $\mid$.	NT(S)
1	(S	*The* $\mid$ *hungry* $\mid$ *cat* $\mid$ *meows* $\mid$.	NT(NP)
2	(S $\mid$ (NP	*The* $\mid$ *hungry* $\mid$ *cat* $\mid$ *meows* $\mid$.	SHIFT
3	(S $\mid$ (NP $\mid$ *The*	*hungry* $\mid$ *cat* $\mid$ *meows* $\mid$.	SHIFT
4	(S $\mid$ (NP $\mid$ *The* $\mid$ *hungry*	*cat* $\mid$ *meows* $\mid$.	SHIFT
5	(S $\mid$ (NP $\mid$ *The* $\mid$ *hungry* $\mid$ *cat*	*meows* $\mid$.	REDUCE
6	(S $\mid$ (NP *The hungry cat*)	*meows* $\mid$.	NT(VP)
7	(S $\mid$ (NP *The hungry cat*) $\mid$ (VP	*meows* $\mid$.	SHIFT
8	(S $\mid$ (NP *The hungry cat*) $\mid$ (VP *meows*	.	REDUCE
9	(S $\mid$ (NP *The hungry cat*) $\mid$ (VP *meows*)	.	SHIFT
10	(S $\mid$ (NP *The hungry cat*) $\mid$ (VP *meows*) $\mid$.		REDUCE
11	(S (NP *The hungry cat*) (VP *meows*) .)		

Figure 2: Top-down parsing example.

Stack$_t$	Terms$_t$	Open NTs$_t$	Action	Stack$_{t+1}$	Terms$_{t+1}$	Open NTs$_{t+1}$
S	T	n	NT(X)	$S \mid (\mathrm{X}$	T	$n+1$
S	T	n	GEN(x)	$S \mid x$	$T \mid x$	n
$S \mid (\mathrm{X} \mid \tau_1 \mid \ldots \mid \tau_\ell)$	T	n	REDUCE	$S \mid (\mathrm{X}\, \tau_1\, \ldots\, \tau_\ell)$	T	$n-1$

Figure 3: Generator transitions. Symbols defined as in Fig. 1 with the addition of T representing the history of generated terminals.

	Stack	Terminals	Action
0			NT(S)
1	(S		NT(NP)
2	(S $\mid$ (NP		GEN(*The*)
3	(S $\mid$ (NP $\mid$ *The*	*The*	GEN(*hungry*)
4	(S $\mid$ (NP $\mid$ *The* $\mid$ *hungry*	*The* $\mid$ *hungry*	GEN(*cat*)
5	(S $\mid$ (NP $\mid$ *The* $\mid$ *hungry* $\mid$ *cat*	*The* $\mid$ *hungry* $\mid$ *cat*	REDUCE
6	(S $\mid$ (NP *The hungry cat*)	*The* $\mid$ *hungry* $\mid$ *cat*	NT(VP)
7	(S $\mid$ (NP *The hungry cat*) $\mid$ (VP	*The* $\mid$ *hungry* $\mid$ *cat*	GEN(*meows*)
8	(S $\mid$ (NP *The hungry cat*) $\mid$ (VP *meows*	*The* $\mid$ *hungry* $\mid$ *cat* $\mid$ *meows*	REDUCE
9	(S $\mid$ (NP *The hungry cat*) $\mid$ (VP *meows*)	*The* $\mid$ *hungry* $\mid$ *cat* $\mid$ *meows*	GEN(.)
10	(S $\mid$ (NP *The hungry cat*) $\mid$ (VP *meows*) $\mid$.	*The* $\mid$ *hungry* $\mid$ *cat* $\mid$ *meows* $\mid$.	REDUCE
11	(S (NP *The hungry cat*) (VP *meows*) .)	*The* $\mid$ *hungry* $\mid$ *cat* $\mid$ *meows* $\mid$.	

Figure 4: Joint generation of a parse tree and sentence.

applying a number of pops that is linear in the number of input symbols, the total number of pop operations across an entire parse/generation run will also be linear). Since there is no way to bound the number of output nodes in a parse tree as a function of the number of input words, stating the runtime complexity of the parsing algorithm as a function of the input size requires further assumptions. Assuming our fixed constraint on maximum depth, it is linear.

3.5 Comparison to Other Models

Our generation algorithm algorithm differs from previous stack-based parsing/generation algorithms in two ways. First, it constructs rooted tree structures top down (rather than bottom up), and second, the transition operators are capable of directly generating arbitrary tree structures rather than, e.g., assuming binarized trees, as is the case in much prior work that has used transition-based algorithms to produce phrase-structure trees (Sagae and Lavie, 2005; Zhang and Clark, 2011; Zhu et al., 2013).

4 Generative Model

RNNGs use the generator transition set just presented to define a joint distribution on syntax trees (y) and words (x). This distribution is defined as a sequence model over generator transitions that is parameterized using a continuous space embedding of the algorithm state at each time step ($\mathbf{u}_t$); i.e.,

$$p(x, y) = \prod_{t=1}^{|a(x,y)|} p(a_t \mid a_{<t})$$

$$= \prod_{t=1}^{|a(x,y)|} \frac{\exp \mathbf{r}_{a_t}^{\top} \mathbf{u}_t + b_{a_t}}{\sum_{a' \in \mathcal{A}_G(T_t, S_t, n_t)} \exp \mathbf{r}_{a'}^{\top} \mathbf{u}_t + b_{a'}},$$

and where action-specific embeddings $\mathbf{r}_a$ and bias vector $\mathbf{b}$ are parameters in Θ.

The representation of the algorithm state at time t, $\mathbf{u}_t$, is computed by combining the representation of the generator's three data structures: the output buffer (T_t), represented by an embedding $\mathbf{o}_t$, the stack (S_t), represented by an embedding $\mathbf{s}_t$, and the history of actions ($a_{<t}$) taken by the generator, represented by an embedding $\mathbf{h}_t$,

$$\mathbf{u}_t = \tanh \left(\mathbf{W}[\mathbf{o}_t; \mathbf{s}_t; \mathbf{h}_t] + \mathbf{c} \right),$$

where $\mathbf{W}$ and $\mathbf{c}$ are parameters. Refer to Figure 5 for an illustration of the architecture.

The output buffer, stack, and history are sequences that grow unboundedly, and to obtain representations of them we use recurrent neural networks to "encode" their contents (Cho et al., 2014). Since the output buffer and history of actions are only appended to and only contain symbols from a finite alphabet, it is straightforward to apply a standard RNN encoding architecture. The stack (S) is more complicated for two reasons. First, the elements of the stack are more complicated objects than symbols from a discrete alphabet: open nonterminals, terminals, and full trees, are all present on the stack. Second, it is manipulated using both push and pop operations. To efficiently obtain representations of S under push and pop operations, we use stack LSTMs (Dyer et al., 2015).

4.1 Syntactic Composition Function

When a REDUCE operation is executed, the parser pops a sequence of completed subtrees and/or tokens (together with their vector embeddings) from the stack and makes them children of the most recent open nonterminal on the stack, "completing" the constituent. To compute an embedding of this new subtree, we use a composition function based on bidirectional LSTMs, which is illustrated in Fig. 6.

The first vector read by the LSTM in both the forward and reverse directions is an embedding of the label on the constituent being constructed (in the figure, NP). This is followed by the embeddings of the child subtrees (or tokens) in forward or reverse order. Intuitively, this order serves to "notify" each LSTM what sort of head it should be looking for as it processes the child node embeddings. The final state of the forward and reverse LSTMs are concatenated, passed through an affine transformation and a $\tanh$ nonlinearity to become the subtree embedding.[4] Because each of the child node embeddings ($\mathbf{u}, \mathbf{v}, \mathbf{w}$ in Fig. 6) is computed similarly (if it corresponds to an

---

[4] We found the many previously proposed syntactic composition functions inadequate for our purposes. First, we must contend with an unbounded number of children, and many previously proposed functions are limited to binary branching nodes (Socher et al., 2013b; Dyer et al., 2015). Second, those that could deal with n-ary nodes made poor use of nonterminal information (Tai et al., 2015), which is crucial for our task.

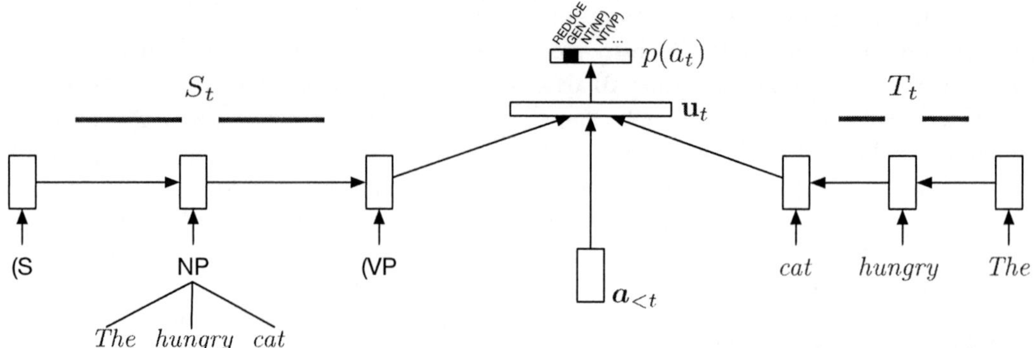

Figure 5: Neural architecture for defining a distribution over a_t given representations of the stack (S_t), output buffer (T_t) and history of actions ($\boldsymbol{a}_{<t}$). Details of the composition architecture of the NP, the action history LSTM, and the other elements of the stack are not shown. This architecture corresponds to the generator state at line 7 of Figure 4.

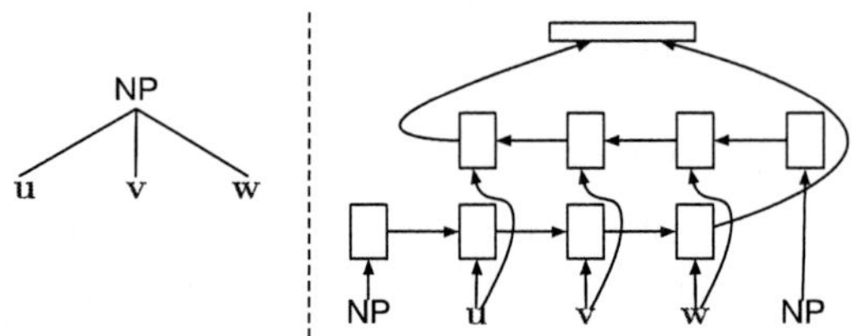

Figure 6: Syntactic composition function based on bidirectional LSTMs that is executed during a REDUCE operation; the network on the right models the structure on the left.

internal node), this composition function is a kind of recursive neural network.

4.2 Word Generation

To reduce the size of $\mathcal{A}_G(S, T, n)$, word generation is broken into two parts. First, the decision to generate is made (by predicting GEN as an action), and then choosing the word, conditional on the current parser state. To further reduce the computational complexity of modeling the generation of a word, we use a class-factored softmax (Baltescu and Blunsom, 2015; Goodman, 2001). By using $\sqrt{|\Sigma|}$ classes for a vocabulary of size $|\Sigma|$, this prediction step runs in time $O(\sqrt{|\Sigma|})$ rather than the $O(|\Sigma|)$ of the full-vocabulary softmax. To obtain clusters, we use the greedy agglomerative clustering algorithm of Brown et al. (1992).

4.3 Training

The parameters in the model are learned to maximize the likelihood of a corpus of trees.

4.4 Discriminative Parsing Model

A discriminative parsing model can be obtained by replacing the embedding of T_t at each time step with an embedding of the input buffer B_t. To train this model, the conditional likelihood of each sequence of actions given the input string is maximized.[5]

5 Inference via Importance Sampling

Our generative model $p(\boldsymbol{x}, \boldsymbol{y})$ defines a joint distribution on trees ($\boldsymbol{y}$) and sequences of words ($\boldsymbol{x}$). To evaluate this as a language model, it is necessary to compute the marginal probability $p(\boldsymbol{x}) = \sum_{\boldsymbol{y}' \in \mathcal{Y}(\boldsymbol{x})} p(\boldsymbol{x}, \boldsymbol{y}')$. And, to evaluate the model as a parser, we need to be able to find the MAP parse tree, i.e., the tree $\boldsymbol{y} \in \mathcal{Y}(\boldsymbol{x})$ that maximizes $p(\boldsymbol{x}, \boldsymbol{y})$. However, because of the unbounded dependencies across the sequence of parsing actions in our model, exactly solving either of these inference problems is intractable. To obtain estimates of these, we use a variant of importance sampling (Doucet and Johansen, 2011).

Our importance sampling algorithm uses a conditional proposal distribution $q(\boldsymbol{y} \mid \boldsymbol{x})$ with the following properties: (i) $p(\boldsymbol{x}, \boldsymbol{y}) > 0 \implies q(\boldsymbol{y} \mid \boldsymbol{x}) > 0$; (ii) samples $\boldsymbol{y} \sim q(\boldsymbol{y} \mid \boldsymbol{x})$ can be obtained efficiently; and (iii) the conditional probabilities $q(\boldsymbol{y} \mid \boldsymbol{x})$ of these samples are known. While many such distributions are available, the discrim-

---

[5]For the discriminative parser, the POS tags are processed similarly as in (Dyer et al., 2015); they are predicted for English with the Stanford Tagger (Toutanova et al., 2003) and Chinese with Marmot (Mueller et al., 2013).

inatively trained variant of our parser (§4.4) fulfills these requirements: sequences of actions can be sampled using a simple ancestral sampling approach, and, since parse trees and action sequences exist in a one-to-one relationship, the product of the action probabilities is the conditional probability of the parse tree under q. We therefore use our discriminative parser as our proposal distribution.

Importance sampling uses **importance weights**, which we define as $w(\boldsymbol{x}, \boldsymbol{y}) = p(\boldsymbol{x}, \boldsymbol{y})/q(\boldsymbol{y} \mid \boldsymbol{x})$, to compute this estimate. Under this definition, we can derive the estimator as follows:

$$p(\boldsymbol{x}) = \sum_{\boldsymbol{y} \in \mathcal{Y}(\boldsymbol{x})} p(\boldsymbol{x}, \boldsymbol{y}) = \sum_{\boldsymbol{y} \in \mathcal{Y}(\boldsymbol{x})} q(\boldsymbol{y} \mid \boldsymbol{x}) w(\boldsymbol{x}, \boldsymbol{y})$$
$$= \mathbb{E}_{q(\boldsymbol{y}|\boldsymbol{x})} w(\boldsymbol{x}, \boldsymbol{y}).$$

We now replace this expectation with its Monte Carlo estimate as follows, using N samples from q:

$$\boldsymbol{y}^{(i)} \sim q(\boldsymbol{y} \mid \boldsymbol{x}) \quad \text{for } i \in \{1, 2, \ldots, N\}$$
$$\mathbb{E}_{q(\boldsymbol{y}|\boldsymbol{x})} w(\boldsymbol{x}, \boldsymbol{y}) \overset{\text{MC}}{\approx} \frac{1}{N} \sum_{i=1}^{N} w(\boldsymbol{x}, \boldsymbol{y}^{(i)})$$

To obtain an estimate of the MAP tree $\hat{\boldsymbol{y}}$, we choose the sampled tree with the highest probability under the joint model $p(\boldsymbol{x}, \boldsymbol{y})$.

6 Experiments

We present results of our two models both on parsing (discriminative and generative) and as a language model (generative only) in English and Chinese.

Data. For English, §2–21 of the Penn Treebank are used as training corpus for both, with §24 held out as validation, and §23 used for evaluation. Singleton words in the training corpus with unknown word classes using the the Berkeley parser's mapping rules.[6] Orthographic case distinctions are preserved, and numbers (beyond singletons) are not normalized. For Chinese, we use the Penn Chinese Treebank Version 5.1 (CTB) (Xue et al., 2005).[7] For

the Chinese experiments, we use a single unknown word class. Corpus statistics are given in Table 1.[8]

Table 1: Corpus statistics.

	PTB-train	PTB-test	CTB-train	CTB-test
Sequences	39,831	2,416	50,734	348
Tokens	950,012	56,684	1,184,532	8,008
Types	23,815	6,823	31,358	1,637
UNK-Types	49	42	1	1

Model and training parameters. For the discriminative model, we used hidden dimensions of 128 and 2-layer LSTMs (larger numbers of dimensions reduced validation set performance). For the generative model, we used 256 dimensions and 2-layer LSTMs. For both models, we tuned the dropout rate to maximize validation set likelihood, obtaining optimal rates of 0.2 (discriminative) and 0.3 (generative). For the sequential LSTM baseline for the language model, we also found an optimal dropout rate of 0.3. For training we used stochastic gradient descent with a learning rate of 0.1. All parameters were initialized according to recommendations given by Glorot and Bengio (2010).

English parsing results. Table 2 (last two rows) gives the performance of our parser on Section 23, as well as the performance of several representative models. For the discriminative model, we used a greedy decoding rule as opposed to beam search in some shift-reduce baselines. For the generative model, we obtained 100 independent samples from a flattened distribution of the discriminative parser (by exponentiating each probability by $\alpha = 0.8$ and renormalizing) and reranked them according to the generative model.[9]

Chinese parsing results. Chinese parsing results were obtained with the same methodology as in English and show the same pattern (Table 6).

Language model results. We report held-out per-word perplexities of three language models, both sequential and syntactic. Log probabilities are normalized by the number of words (excluding the stop

---

[6]http://github.com/slavpetrov/berkeleyparser

[7]§001–270 and 440–1151 for training, §301–325 development data, and §271–300 for evaluation.

[8]This preprocessing scheme is more similar to what is standard in parsing than what is standard in language modeling. However, since our model is both a parser and a language model, we opted for the parser normalization.

[9]The value $\alpha = 0.8$ was chosen based on the diversity of the samples generated on the development set.

Table 2: Parsing results on PTB §23 (D=discriminative, G=generative, S=semisupervised).

Model	type	F_1
Henderson (2004)	D	89.4
Socher et al. (2013a)	D	90.4
Zhu et al. (2013)	D	90.4
Vinyals et al. (2015) – WSJ only	D	90.5
Petrov and Klein (2007)	G	90.1
Bod (2003)	G	90.7
Shindo et al. (2012) – single	G	91.1
Shindo et al. (2012) – ensemble	G	92.4
Zhu et al. (2013)	S	91.3
McClosky et al. (2006)	S	92.1
Vinyals et al. (2015) – single	S	92.5
Vinyals et al. (2015) – ensemble	S	92.8
Discriminative, $q(\boldsymbol{y} \mid \boldsymbol{x})$	D	89.8
Generative, $\hat{p}(\boldsymbol{y} \mid \boldsymbol{x})$	G	92.4

Table 3: Parsing results on CTB 5.1.

Model	type	F_1
Zhu et al. (2013)	D	82.6
Wang et al. (2015)	D	83.2
Huang and Harper (2009)	D	84.2
Charniak (2000)	G	80.8
Bikel (2004)	G	80.6
Petrov and Klein (2007)	G	83.3
Zhu et al. (2013)	S	85.6
Wang and Xue (2014)	S	86.3
Wang et al. (2015)	S	86.6
Discriminative, $q(\boldsymbol{y} \mid \boldsymbol{x})$	D	80.7
Generative, $\hat{p}(\boldsymbol{y} \mid \boldsymbol{x})$	G	82.7

Table 4: Language model perplexity results.

Model	test ppl (PTB)	test ppl (CTB)
IKN 5-gram	169.3	255.2
LSTM LM	113.4	207.3
RNNG	102.4	171.9

symbol), inverted, and exponentiated to yield the perplexity. Results are summarized in Table 4.

7 Discussion

It is clear from our experiments that the proposed generative model is quite effective both as a parser and as a language model. This is the result of (i) relaxing conventional independence assumptions (e.g., context-freeness) and (ii) inferring continuous representations of symbols alongside non-linear models of their syntactic relationships. The most significant question that remains is why the discriminative model—which has more information available to it than the generative model—performs worse than the generative model. This pattern has been observed before in neural parsing by Henderson (2004), who hypothesized that larger, unstructured conditioning contexts are harder to learn from, and provide opportunities to overfit. Our discriminative model conditions on the entire history, stack, and buffer, while our generative model only accesses the history and stack. The fully discriminative model of Vinyals et al. (2015) was able to obtain results similar to those of our generative model (albeit using much larger training sets obtained through semisupervision) but similar results to those of our discriminative parser using the same data. In light of their results, we believe Henderson's hypothesis is correct, and that generative models should be considered as a more statistically efficient method for learning neural networks from small data.

8 Related Work

Our language model combines work from two modeling traditions: (i) recurrent neural network language models and (ii) syntactic language modeling. Recurrent neural network language models use RNNs to compute representations of an unbounded history of words in a left-to-right language model (Zaremba et al., 2015; Mikolov et al., 2010; Elman, 1990). Syntactic language models jointly generate a syntactic structure and a sequence of words (Baker, 1979; Jelinek and Lafferty, 1991). There is an extensive literature here, but one strand of work has emphasized a bottom-up generation of the tree, using variants of shift-reduce parser actions to define the probability space (Chelba and Jelinek, 2000; Emami and Jelinek, 2005). The neural-network–based model of Henderson (2004) is particularly similar to ours in using an unbounded history in a neural network architecture to parameterize generative parsing based on a left-corner model. Dependency-only language models have also been explored (Titov and Henderson, 2007;

Buys and Blunsom, 2015a,b). Modeling generation top-down as a rooted branching process that recursively rewrites nonterminals has been explored by Charniak (2000) and Roark (2001). Of particular note is the work of Charniak (2010), which uses random forests and hand-engineered features over the entire syntactic derivation history to make decisions over the next action to take.

The neural networks we use to model sentences are structured according to the syntax of the sentence being generated. Syntactically structured neural architectures have been explored in a number of applications, including discriminative parsing (Socher et al., 2013a; Kiperwasser and Goldberg, 2016), sentiment analysis (Tai et al., 2015; Socher et al., 2013b), and sentence representation (Socher et al., 2011; Bowman et al., 2006). However, these models have been, without exception, discriminative; this is the first work to use syntactically structured neural models to generate language. Earlier work has demonstrated that sequential RNNs have the capacity to recognize context-free (and beyond) languages (Sun et al., 1998; Siegelmann and Sontag, 1995). In contrast, our work may be understood as a way of incorporating a context-free inductive bias into the model structure.

9 Outlook

RNNGs can be combined with a particle filter inference scheme (rather than the importance sampling method based on a discriminative parser, §5) to produce a left-to-right marginalization algorithm that runs in expected linear time. Thus, they could be used in applications that require language models.

A second possibility is to replace the sequential generation architectures found in many neural network transduction problems that produce sentences conditioned on some input. Previous work in machine translation has showed that conditional syntactic models can function quite well without the computationally expensive marginalization process at decoding time (Galley et al., 2006; Gimpel and Smith, 2014).

A third consideration regarding how RNNGs, human sentence processing takes place in a left-to-right, incremental order. While an RNNG is not a processing model (it is a grammar), the fact that it is

left-to-right opens up several possibilities for developing new sentence processing models based on an explicit grammars, similar to the processing model of Charniak (2010).

Finally, although we considered only the supervised learning scenario, RNNGs are joint models that could be trained without trees, for example, using expectation maximization.

10 Conclusion

We introduced recurrent neural network grammars, a probabilistic model of phrase-structure trees that can be trained generatively and used as a language model or a parser, and a corresponding discriminative model that can be used as a parser. Apart from out-of-vocabulary preprocessing, the approach requires no feature design or transformations to treebank data. The generative model outperforms every previously published parser built on a single supervised generative model in English, and a bit behind the best-reported generative model in Chinese. As language models, RNNGs outperform the best single-sentence language models.

Acknowledgments

We thank Brendan O'Connor, Swabha Swayamdipta, and Brian Roark for feedback on drafts of this paper, and Jan Buys, Phil Blunsom, and Yue Zhang for help with data preparation. This work was sponsored in part by the Defense Advanced Research Projects Agency (DARPA) Information Innovation Office (I2O) under the Low Resource Languages for Emergent Incidents (LORELEI) program issued by DARPA/I2O under Contract No. HR0011-15-C-0114; it was also supported in part by Contract No. W911NF-15-1-0543 with the DARPA and the Army Research Office (ARO). Approved for public release, distribution unlimited. The views expressed are those of the authors and do not reflect the official policy or position of the Department of Defense or the U.S. Government. Miguel Ballesteros was supported by the European Commission under the contract numbers FP7-ICT-610411 (project MULTISENSOR) and H2020-RIA-645012 (project KRISTINA).

References

Steven Abney, David McAllester, and Fernando Pereira. 1999. Relating probabilistic grammars and automata. In *Proc. ACL*.

Dzmitry Bahdanau, Kyunghyun Cho, and Yoshua Bengio. 2015. Neural machine transation by jointly learning to align and translate. In *Proc. ICLR*.

James K. Baker. 1979. Trainable grammars for speech recognition. *The Journal of the Acoustical Society of America*, 65(S1):S132–S132.

Paul Baltescu and Phil Blunsom. 2015. Pragmatic neural modelling in machine translation. In *Proc. NAACL*.

Dan Bikel. 2004. *On the parameter space of generative lexicalized statistical parsing models*. Ph.D. thesis, University of Pennsylvania.

Rens Bod. 2003. An efficient implementation of a new DOP model. In *Proc. EACL*.

Samuel R. Bowman, Jon Gauthier, Abhinav Rastogi, Raghav Gupta, Christopher D. Manning, and Christopher Potts. 2006. A fast unified model for parsing and sentence understanding. *CoRR*, abs/1603.06021.

Peter F. Brown, Peter V. deSouza, Robert L. Mercer, Vincent J. Della Pietra, and Jenifer C. Lai. 1992. Class-based n-gram models of natural language. *Computational Linguistics*, 18(4):467–479.

Jan Buys and Phil Blunsom. 2015a. A Bayesian model for generative transition-based dependency parsing. *CoRR*, abs/1506.04334.

Jan Buys and Phil Blunsom. 2015b. Generative incremental dependency parsing with neural networks. In *Proc. ACL*.

Eugene Charniak. 2000. A maximum-entropy-inspired parser. In *Proc. NAACL*.

Eugene Charniak. 2010. Top-down nearly-context-sensitive parsing. In *Proc. EMNLP*.

Ciprian Chelba and Frederick Jelinek. 2000. Structured language modeling. *Computer Speech and Language*, 14(4).

Kyunghyun Cho, Bart van Merriënboer, Caglar Gulcehre, Dzmitry Bahdanau, Fethi Bougares, Holger Schwenk, and Yoshua Bengio. 2014. Learning phrase representations using rnn encoder–decoder for statistical machine translation. In *Proc. EMNLP*.

Noam Chomsky. 1957. *Syntactic Structures*. Mouton, The Hague/Paris.

Arnaud Doucet and Adam M. Johansen. 2011. A tutorial on particle filtering and smoothing: Fifteen years later. In *Handbook of Nonlinear Filtering*. Oxford.

Chris Dyer, Miguel Ballesteros, Wang Ling, Austin Matthews, and Noah A. Smith. 2015. Transition-based dependency parsing with stack long short-term memory. In *Proc. ACL*.

Jay Earley. 1970. An efficient context-free parsing algorithm. *Communications of the ACM*, 13(2):94–102.

Jeffrey L. Elman. 1990. Finding structure in time. *Cognitive Science*, 14:179–211.

Ahmad Emami and Frederick Jelinek. 2005. A neural syntactic language model. *Machine Learning*, 60:195–227.

Michel Galley, Jonathan Graehl, Kevin Knight, Daniel Marcu, Steve DeNeefe, Wei Wang, and Ignacio Thayer. 2006. Scalable inference and training of context-rich syntactic translation models. In *Proc. ACL*.

Kevin Gimpel and Noah A. Smith. 2014. Phrase dependency machine translation with quasi-synchronous tree-to-tree features. *Computational Linguistics*, 40(2).

Xavier Glorot and Yoshua Bengio. 2010. Understanding the difficulty of training deep feedforward neural networks. In *Proc. ICML*.

Joshua Goodman. 2001. Classes for fast maximum entropy training. *CoRR*, cs.CL/0108006.

James Henderson. 2003. Inducing history representations for broad coverage statistical parsing. In *Proc. NAACL*.

James Henderson. 2004. Discriminative training of a neural network statistical parser. In *Proc. ACL*.

Zhongqiang Huang and Mary Harper. 2009. Self-training PCFG grammars with latent annotations across languages. In *Proc. EMNLP*.

Frederick Jelinek and John D. Lafferty. 1991. Computation of the probability of initial substring generation by stochastic context-free grammars. *Computational Linguistics*, 17(3):315–323.

Mark Johnson. 2001. Joint and conditional estimation of tagging and parsing models. In *Proc. ACL*.

Eliyahu Kiperwasser and Yoav Goldberg. 2016. Easy-first dependency parsing with hierarchical tree LSTMs. ArXiv:1603.00375.

David McClosky, Eugene Charniak, and Mark Johnson. 2006. Effective self-training for parsing. In *Proc. NAACL*.

Tomáš Mikolov, Martin Karafiát, Lukáš Burget, Jan Černocký, and Sanjeev Khudanpur. 2010. Recurrent neural network based language model. In *Proc. Interspeech*.

Thomas Mueller, Helmut Schmid, and Hinrich Schütze. 2013. Efficient higher-order CRFs for morphological tagging. In *Proceedings of the 2013 Conference on Empirical Methods in Natural Language Processing*.

ing, pages 322–332. Association for Computational Linguistics, Seattle, Washington, USA. URL `http://www.aclweb.org/anthology/D13-1032`.

Terence Parr and Kathleen Fisher. 2011. LL(*): The foundation of the ANTLR parser generator. In *Proc. PLDI*.

Slav Petrov and Dan Klein. 2007. Improved inference for unlexicalized parsing. In *Proc. NAACL*.

Brian Roark. 2001. Probabilistic top-down parsing and language modeling. *Computational Linguistics*, 27(2).

Brian Roark. 2004. Robust garden path parsing. *JNLE*, 10(1):1–24.

Kenji Sagae and Alon Lavie. 2005. A classifier-based parser with linear run-time complexity. In *Proc. IWPT*.

Hiroyuki Shindo, Yusuke Miyao, Akinori Fujino, and Masaaki Nagata. 2012. Bayesian symbol-refined tree substitution grammars for syntactic parsing. In *Proc. ACL*.

Hava T. Siegelmann and Eduardo D. Sontag. 1995. On the computational power of neural nets. *Journal of Computer and System Sciences*, 50.

Richard Socher, John Bauer, Christopher D. Manning, and Andrew Y. Ng. 2013a. Parsing with compositional vectors. In *Proc. ACL*.

Richard Socher, Eric H. Huang, Jeffrey Pennington, Andrew Y. Ng, and Christopher D. Manning. 2011. Dynamic pooling and unfolding recursive autoencoders for paraphrase detection. In *Proc. NIPS*.

Richard Socher, Alex Perelygin, Jean Y. Wu, Jason Chuang, Christopher D. Manning, Andrew Y. Ng, and Christopher Potts. 2013b. Recursive deep models for semantic compositionality over a sentiment treebank. In *Proc. EMNLP*.

Guo-Zheng Sun, C. Lee Giles, and Hsing-Hen Chen. 1998. The neural network pushdown automaton: Architecture, dynamics and training. In *Adaptive Processing of Sequences and Data Structures*, volume 1387 of *Lecture Notes in Computer Science*, pages 296–345.

Kai Sheng Tai, Richard Socher, and Christopher D. Manning. 2015. Improved semantic representations from tree-structured long short-term memory networks. In *Proc. ACL*.

Ivan Titov and James Henderson. 2007. A latent variable model for generative dependency parsing. In *Proc. IWPT*.

Kristina Toutanova, Dan Klein, Christopher D. Manning, and Yoram Singer. 2003. Feature-rich part-of-speech tagging with a cyclic dependency network. In *Proc. NAACL*.

Oriol Vinyals, Lukasz Kaiser, Terry Koo, Slav Petrov, Ilya Sutskever, and Geoffrey Hinton. 2015. Grammar as a foreign language. In *Proc. ICLR*.

Zhiguo Wang, Haitao Mi, and Nianwen Xue. 2015. Feature optimization for constituent parsing via neural networks. In *Proc. ACL-IJCNLP*.

Zhiguo Wang and Nianwen Xue. 2014. Joint POS tagging and transition-based constituent parsing in Chinese with non-local features. In *Proc. ACL*.

Tsung-Hsien Wen, Milica Gašić, Nikola Mrkšić, Pei-Hao Su, David Vandyke, and Steve Young. 2015. Semantically conditioned LSTM-based natural language generation for spoken dialogue systems. In *Proc. EMNLP*.

Kelvin Xu, Jimmy Lei Ba, Ryan Kiros, Kyunghyun Cho, Aaron Courville, Ruslan Salakhutdinov, Richard S. Zemel, and Yoshua Bengio. 2015. Show, attend and tell: Neural image caption generation with visual attention. In *Proc. ICML*.

Naiwen Xue, Fei Xia, Fu-dong Chiou, and Marta Palmer. 2005. The Penn Chinese TreeBank: Phrase structure annotation of a large corpus. *Nat. Lang. Eng.*, 11(2).

Wojciech Zaremba, Ilya Sutskever, and Oriol Vinyals. 2015. Recurrent neural network regularization. In *Proc. ICLR*.

Yue Zhang and Stephen Clark. 2011. Syntactic processing using the generalized perceptron and beam search. *Computational Linguistics*, 37(1).

Muhua Zhu, Yue Zhang, Wenliang Chen, Min Zhang, and Jingbo Zhu. 2013. Fast and accurate shift-reduce constituent parsing. In *Proc. ACL*.

Expected F-Measure Training for Shift-Reduce Parsing with Recurrent Neural Networks

Wenduan Xu[†] **Michael Auli**[‡] **Stephen Clark**[†]

[†]Computer Laboratory, Cambridge University

[‡]Facebook AI Research

wx217@cam.ac.uk, michaelauli@fb.com, sc609@cam.ac.uk

Abstract

We present expected F-measure training for shift-reduce parsing with RNNs, which enables the learning of a global parsing model optimized for sentence-level F1. We apply the model to CCG parsing, where it improves over a strong greedy RNN baseline, by 1.47% F1, yielding state-of-the-art results for shift-reduce CCG parsing.

1 Introduction

Shift-reduce parsing is a popular parsing paradigm, one reason being the potential for fast parsers based on the linear number of parsing actions needed to analyze a sentence (Nivre and Scholz, 2004; Sagae and Lavie, 2006; Zhang and Clark, 2011; Goldberg et al., 2013; Zhu et al., 2013; Xu et al., 2014). Recent work has shown that by combining distributed representations and neural network models (Chen and Manning, 2014), accurate and efficient shift-reduce parsing models can be obtained with little feature engineering, largely alleviating the feature sparsity problem of linear models.

In practice, the most common objective for optimizing neural network shift-reduce parsing models is maximum likelihood. In the greedy search setting, the log-likelihood of each target action is maximized during training, and the most likely action is committed to at each step of the parsing process during inference (Chen and Manning, 2014; Dyer et al., 2015). In the beam search setting, Zhou et al. (2015) show that sentence-level likelihood, together with contrastive learning (Hinton, 2002), can be used to derive a global model which incorporates beam search at both training and inference time (Zhang and Clark, 2008), giving significant accuracy gains over a fully greedy model. However, despite the effectiveness of optimizing likelihood, it is often desirable to directly optimize for task-specific metrics, which often leads to higher accuracies for a variety of models and applications (Goodman, 1996; Och, 2003; Smith and Eisner, 2006; Rosti et al., 2010; Auli and Lopez, 2011; He and Deng, 2012; Auli et al., 2014; Auli and Gao, 2014; Gao et al., 2014).

In this paper, we present a global neural network parsing model, optimized for a task-specific loss based on expected F-measure. The model naturally incorporates beam search during training, and is globally optimized, to learn shift-reduce action *sequences* that lead to parses with high expected F-scores. In contrast to Auli and Lopez (2011), who optimize a CCG parser for F-measure via softmax-margin (Gimpel and Smith, 2010), we directly optimize an expected F-measure objective, derivable from only a set of shift-reduce action sequences and sentence-level F-scores. More generally, our method can be seen as an alternative approach for training a neural beam search parsing model (Watanabe and Sumita, 2015; Weiss et al., 2015; Zhou et al., 2015), combining the benefits of global learning and task-specific optimization.

We also introduce a simple recurrent neural network (RNN) model to shift-reduce parsing on which the greedy baseline and the global model is based. Compared with feed-forward networks, RNNs have the potential to capture and use an *unbounded* history, and they have been used to learn explicit representations for parser states as well as actions

Proceedings of NAACL-HLT 2016, pages 210–220,
San Diego, California, June 12-17, 2016. ©2016 Association for Computational Linguistics

performed on the stack and queue in shift-reduce parsers (Dyer et al., 2015; Watanabe and Sumita, 2015), following Miikkulainen (1996) and Mayberry and Miikkulainen (1999). In comparison, our model is a natural extension of the feed-forward architecture in Chen and Manning (2014) using Elman RNNs (Elman, 1990).

We apply our models to CCG, and evaluate the resulting parsers on standard CCGBank data (Hockenmaier and Steedman, 2007). More specifically, by combining the global RNN parsing model with a bidirectional RNN CCG supertagger that we have developed (§4) — building on the supertagger of Xu et al. (2015), we obtain accuracies higher than the shift-reduce CCG parsers of Zhang and Clark (2011) and Xu et al. (2014). Finally, although we choose to focus on shift-reduce parsing for CCG, we expect the methods to generalize to other shift-reduce parsers.

2 RNN Models

In this section, we start by describing the baseline model, which is also taken as the pretrained model to train the global model (§2.4). We abstract away from the details of CCG and present the models in a canonical shift-reduce parsing framework (Aho and Ullman, 1972), which is henceforth assumed: partially constructed derivations are maintained on a *stack*, and a *queue* stores remaining words from the input string; the initial parse item has an empty stack and no input has been consumed on the queue. Parsing proceeds by applying a sequence of shift-reduce actions to transform the input until the queue has been exhausted and no more actions can be applied.

2.1 Model

Our recurrent neural network model is a standard Elman network (Elman, 1990) which is factored into an input layer, a hidden layer with recurrent connections, and an output layer. Similar to Chen and Manning (2014), the input layer x_t encodes stack and queue contexts of a parse item through concatenation of feature embeddings. The output layer y_t represents a probability distribution over possible parser actions for the current item.

The current state of the hidden layer is determined by the current input and the previous hidden layer state. The weights between the layers are repre-

sented by a number of matrices: matrix $\mathbf{U}$ contains weights between the input and hidden layers, $\mathbf{V}$ contains weights between the hidden and output layers, and $\mathbf{W}$ contains weights between the previous hidden layer and the current hidden layer.

The hidden and output layers at time step t are computed via a series of vector-matrix products and non-linearities:

$$h_t = f(x_t \mathbf{U} + h_{t-1}\mathbf{W}),$$
$$y_t = g(h_t \mathbf{V}),$$

where

$$f(z) = \frac{1}{1 + e^{-z}}, \quad g(z_m) = \frac{e^{z_m}}{\sum_k e^{z_k}}$$

are sigmoid[1] and softmax functions, respectively.

2.2 Feature Embeddings

Given a parse item, we first extract features using a set of predefined feature templates; each template belongs to a feature type f (such as word or POS tag), which has an associated look-up table, denoted as L_f, to project a feature to its distributed representation; and $L_f \in \mathbb{R}^{n_f \times d_f}$, where n_f is the vocabulary size of feature type f and d_f is its embedding dimension. The embedding for a concrete feature is obtained by retrieving the corresponding row from L_f. At time step t, the input layer x_t is:

$$x_t = [e_{f_{1,1}}; \ldots; e_{f_{1,|f_1|}}; \ldots; e_{f_{k,1}}; \ldots; e_{f_{k,|f_k|}}],$$

where ";" denotes concatenation, $|f_k|$ is the number of feature templates for the kth feature type and $x_t \in \mathbb{R}^{1 \times (d_{f_1}|f_1| + \ldots + d_{f_k}|f_k|)}$. For each feature type, a special embedding is used for unknown features.

2.3 Greedy Training

To train a greedy model, we extract gold-standard actions from the training data and minimize cross-entropy loss with stochastic gradient descent (SGD) using backpropagation through time (BPTT; Rumelhart et al., 1988). Similar to Chen and Manning (2014), we compute the softmax over only feasible actions at each step.

Unfortunately, although we use an RNN, which keeps a representation of previous parse items in its

---

[1] We also experimented with tanh, and found no difference in resulting performance.

hidden state and has the potential to capture long-term dependencies, the resulting model is still fully greedy: a locally optimal action is taken at each step given the current input x_t and the previous hidden state h_{t-1}. Therefore, once a sub-optimal action has been committed to by the parser at any step, it has no means to recover and has to continue from that mistake. Such mistakes accumulate until the goal is reached, and they are referred to as *search errors*.

In order to enlarge the search space of the greedy model thereby alleviating some search errors, we experiment with applying beam search decoding during inference; and we observe some accuracy improvements by taking the highest scored action sequence as the output (Table 3). However, since the greedy model itself is only optimized locally, as expected, the improvements diminish after a certain beam size. Instead, we show below that by using the greedy model weights as a starting point, we can train a global model optimized for an expected F-measure loss, which gives further significant accuracy improvements (§5).

2.4 Expected F1 Training

The RNN we use to train the global model has the same Elman architecture as the greedy model. Given the greedy model, we summarize its weights as $\theta = \{\mathbf{U}, \mathbf{V}, \mathbf{W}\}$ and initialize the weights of the global model to θ, and training proceeds as follows:

1. We use a beam-search decoder to parse a sentence x_n in the training data and let the decoder generate a k-best list[2] of output parses using the *current* θ, denoted as $\Lambda(x_n)$. Similar to other structured training approaches that use inexact beam search (Zhang and Clark, 2008; Weiss et al., 2015; Watanabe and Sumita, 2015; Zhou et al., 2015), $\Lambda(x_n)$ is as an approximation to the set of all possible parses of an input sentence.

2. Let y_i be the shift-reduce action sequence of a parse in the k-best list $\Lambda(x_n)$, and let $|y_i|$ be its total number of actions and y_{ij} be the jth action in y_i, for $1 \leq j \leq |y_i|$. We compute the log-linear action sequence score of y_i, $\rho(y_i)$, as a sum of individual action scores in that

sequence: $\rho(y_i) = \sum_{j=1}^{|y_i|} \log s_\theta(y_{ij})$, where $s_\theta(y_{ij})$ is the softmax action score of y_{ij} given by the RNN model. For each y_i, we also compute its sentence-level F1 using the set of labeled, directed dependencies, denoted as Δ, associated with its parse item. (We assume F1 over labeled, directed dependencies is also the parser evaluation metric.)

3. We compute the negative expected F1 objective (-xF1, defined below) for x_n using the scores obtained in the above step and minimize this objective using SGD (maximizing the expected F1 for x_n). These three steps repeat for other sentences in the training data, updating θ after processing each sentence, and training iterates in epochs until convergence.

We note that the above process is different from parse reranking (Collins, 2000; Charniak and Johnson, 2005), in which $\Lambda(x_n)$ would stay the same for each x_n in the training data across all epochs, and a reranker is trained on all fixed $\Lambda(x_n)$; whereas the xF1 training procedure is on-line learning with parameters updated after processing each sentence and each $\Lambda(x_n)$ is generated with a new θ.

More formally, we define the loss $J(\theta)$, which incorporates all action scores in each action sequence, and all action sequences in $\Lambda(x_n)$, for each x_n as

$$
\begin{aligned}
J(\theta) &= -\text{xF1}(\theta) \\
&= - \sum_{y_i \in \Lambda(x_n)} p(y_i|\theta)\text{F1}(\Delta_{y_i}, \Delta_{x_n}^G),
\end{aligned} \tag{1}
$$

where $\text{F1}(\Delta_{y_i}, \Delta_{x_n}^G)$ is the sentence level F1 of the parse derived by y_i, with respect to the gold-standard dependency structure $\Delta_{x_n}^G$ of x_n; $p(y_i|\theta)$ is the normalized probability score of the action sequence y_i, computed as

$$
p(y_i|\theta) = \frac{\exp\{\rho(y_i)\}}{\sum_{y \in \Lambda(x_n)} \exp\{\rho(y)\}}. \tag{2}
$$

To apply SGD, we derive the error gradients used for backpropagation. First, by applying the chain

---

[2]We do not put a limit on k, and whenever an item is finished, it is appended to the k-best list. We found the size of the k-best lists were on average twice the size of a given beam size.

rule to $J(\theta)$, we have

$$\frac{\partial J(\theta)}{\partial \theta} = -\sum_{y_i \in \Lambda(x_n)} \sum_{y_{ij} \in y_i} \frac{\partial J(\theta)}{\partial s_\theta(y_{ij})} \frac{\partial s_\theta(y_{ij})}{\partial \theta}$$

$$= -\sum_{y_i \in \Lambda(x_n)} \sum_{y_{ij} \in y_i} \delta_{y_{ij}} \frac{\partial s_\theta(y_{ij})}{\partial \theta},$$

where $\frac{\partial s_\theta(y_{ij})}{\partial \theta}$ is the standard softmax gradients. Next, to compute $\delta_{y_{ij}}$, which are the error gradients propagated from the loss to the softmax layer, we rewrite the loss in (1) as

$$J(\theta) = -\text{xF1} = -\frac{G(\theta)}{Z(\theta)} \tag{3}$$

$$= -\frac{\sum_{y_i \in \Lambda(x_n)} \exp\{\rho(y_i)\}\text{F1}(\Delta_{y_i}, \Delta_{x_n}^G)}{\sum_{y_i \in \Lambda(x_n)} \exp\{\rho(y_i)\}},$$

and by simplifying:

$$\frac{\partial G(\theta)}{\partial s_\theta(y_{ij})} = \frac{1}{s_\theta(y_{ij})}\exp\{\rho(y_i)\}\text{F1}(\Delta_{y_i}, \Delta_{x_n}^G),$$

$$\frac{\partial Z(\theta)}{\partial s_\theta(y_{ij})} = \frac{1}{s_\theta(y_{ij})}\exp\{\rho(y_i)\},$$

since

$$\frac{\partial \rho(y_i)}{\partial s_\theta(y_{ij})} = \frac{1}{s_\theta(y_{ij})}.$$

Finally, using (2) and (3) plus the above simplifications, the error term $\delta_{y_{ij}}$ can be derived using the quotient rule:

$$\begin{aligned}
\delta_{y_{ij}} &= -\frac{\partial \text{xF1}(\theta)}{\partial s_\theta(y_{ij})} \\
&= -\frac{\partial(G(\theta)/Z(\theta))}{\partial s_\theta(y_{ij})} \\
&= \frac{G(\theta)Z'(\theta) - G'(\theta)Z(\theta)}{Z^2(\theta)} \\
&= \frac{\exp\{\rho(y_i)\}}{Z(\theta)}(\text{xF1}(\theta) - \text{F1}(\Delta_{y_i}, \Delta_{x_n}^G))\frac{1}{s_\theta(y_{ij})} \\
&= p(y_i|\theta)(\text{xF1}(\theta) - \text{F1}(\Delta_{y_i}, \Delta_{x_n}^G))\frac{1}{s_\theta(y_{ij})},
\end{aligned} \tag{4}$$

which has a simple closed form.

A naive implementation of the xF1 training procedure would backpropagate the error gradients individually for each y_i in $\Lambda(x_n)$. To make it efficient,

we observe that the unfolded network in the beam containing all y_i becomes a DAG (with one hidden state leading to one or more resulting hidden states) and apply backpropagation through structure (Goller and Kuchler, 1996) to obtain the gradients.

3 Shift-Reduce CCG Parsing

We explain the application of the RNN models to CCG by first describing the CCG mechanisms used in our parser, followed by details of the shift-reduce transition system.

3.1 Combinatory Categorial Grammar

A *lexicon*, together with a set of CCG *rules*, formally constitute a CCG. The former defines a mapping from words to sets of lexical categories representing syntactic types, and the latter gives schemas which dictate whether two categories can be combined. Given the lexicon and the rules, the syntactic types of complete constituents can be obtained by recursive combination of categories using the rules.

More generally, both lexical and non-lexical CCG categories can be either *atomic* or *complex*: atomic categories are categories without any slashes, and complex categories are constructed recursively from atomic ones using forward ($/$) and backward slashes ($\backslash$) as two binary operators. As such, all categories can be represented as follows (Vijay-Shanker and Weir, 1993; Kuhlmann and Satta, 2014):

$$x := \alpha|_1 z_1|_2 z_2 \ldots |_m z_m,$$

where $m \geq 0$, α is an atomic category, $|_1, \ldots, |_m \in \{\backslash, /\}$ and z_i are meta-variables for categories.

CCG *rules* have the following two schematic forms, each a generalized version of *functional composition* (Vijay-Shanker and Weir, 1993):

$$x/y \quad y|_1 z_1 \ldots |_m z_m \to x|_1 z_1 \ldots |_m z_m,$$
$$y|_1 z_1 \ldots |_m z_m \quad x\backslash y \to x|_1 z_1 \ldots |_m z_m.$$

The first schematic form above instantiates into a forward application rule ($>$) for $m = 0$, and forward composition rules ($>_\mathbf{B}$) for $m > 0$. Similarly, the second schematic form, which is symmetric to the first, instantiates into backward application ($<$) and composition ($<_\mathbf{B}$) rules.

Fig.1 shows an example CCG derivation. All the *rule instances* in this derivation are instantiated from

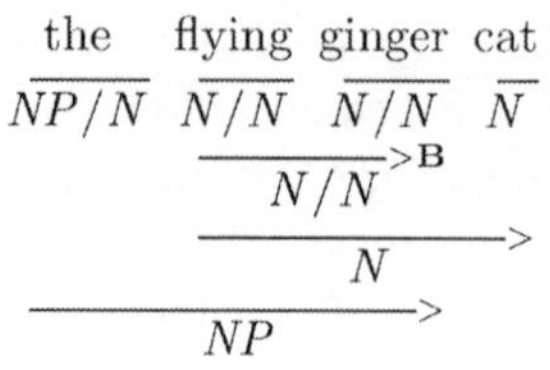

$$\frac{\overline{NP/N} \quad \overline{N/N} \quad \overline{N/N} \quad \overline{N}}{\cfrac{\cfrac{N/N}{}^{>\mathbf{B}}}{\cfrac{N}{NP}^{>}}^{>}}$$

the   flying ginger cat

Figure 1: An example CCG derivation.

forward rules; for example, $N/N\ N/N \to N/N$ is an instance of forward composition and $N/N\ N \to N$ is an instance of forward application.

Given CCGBank (Hockenmaier and Steedman, 2007), there are two approaches to extract a grammar from this data. The first is to treat all CCG derivations as phrase-structure trees, and a binary, context-free "cover" grammar, consisting of all CCG rule instances in the treebank, is extracted from local trees in all the derivations (Fowler and Penn, 2010; Zhang and Clark, 2011). In contrast, one can extract the lexicon from the treebank and define only the rule schemas, without explicitly enumerating any rule instances (Hockenmaier, 2003). This is the approach taken in the C&C parser (Clark and Curran, 2007) and the one we use here. Moreover, following Zhang and Clark (2011), our CCG parsing model is also a normal-form model, which models action sequences of normal-form derivations in CCGBank.

3.2 The Transition System

The transition system we use in this work is based on the CCG transition system of Zhang and Clark (2011). We denote parse items as $(j, \delta, \beta, \Delta)^3$, where δ is the stack (with top element $\delta|s_0$), β is the queue (with top element $x_{w_j}|\beta$), j is the positional index of the word at the front of the queue, and Δ is the set of CCG dependencies realized for the input consumed so far (needed to calculate the expected F-score). We also assume a set of lexical categories has been assigned to each word using a supertagger (Bangalore and Joshi, 1999; Clark and Curran, 2004). The transition system is specified using three action types:

- SHIFT (sh) removes one of the lexical categories x_{w_j} of the front word w_j in the queue, and pushes it onto the stack; and removes w_j from the queue.

---

[3]We partly adopt standard notations from dependency parsing (Nivre, 2008).

input: $w_0 \ldots w_{n-1}$

axiom: $0 : (0, \epsilon, \beta, \phi)$

goal: $2n - 1 + \mu : (n, \delta, \epsilon, \Delta)$

$$\frac{\omega : (j, \delta, x_{w_j}|\beta, \Delta)}{\omega + 1 : (j + 1, \delta|x_{w_j}, \beta, \Delta)} \quad (\mathsf{sh}; 0 \le j < n)$$

$$\frac{\omega : (j, \delta|s_1|s_0, \beta, \Delta)}{\omega + 1 : (j, \delta|x, \beta, \Delta \cup \langle x \rangle))} \quad (\mathsf{re}; s_1 s_0 \to x)$$

$$\frac{\omega : (j, \delta|s_0, \beta, \Delta)}{\omega + 1 : (j, \delta|x, \beta, \Delta)} \quad (\mathsf{un}; s_0 \to x)$$

Figure 2: The shift-reduce deduction system.

- REDUCE (re) combines the top two subtrees s_0 and s_1 on the stack using a CCG rule ($s_1 s_0 \to x$) and replaces them with a subtree rooted in x. It also appends the set of newly created dependencies on x, denoted as $\langle x \rangle$, to Δ.

- UNARY (un) applies either a type-raising or type-changing rule ($s_0 \to x$) to the stack-top element and replaces it with a unary subtree rooted in x.

The deduction system (Fig. 2) of our shift-reduce parser follows from the transition system.[4] Each parse item is associated with a step indicator ω, which denotes the number of actions used to build it. Given a sentence of length n, a full derivation requires $2n - 1 + \mu$ steps to terminate, where μ is the total number of un actions applied. In Zhang and Clark (2011), a *finish* action is used to indicate termination, which we do not use in our parser: an item finishes when no further action can be taken. Another difference between the transition systems is that Zhang and Clark (2011) omit the Δ field in each parse item, due to their use of a context-free, phrase-structure cover, and dependencies are recovered at a post-processing step; in our system, we build dependencies as parsing proceeds.

---

[4]We abuse notation slightly for the sh deduction, using $x_{w_j}|\beta$ to denote that the lexical category x_{w_j} is available for the front word on the queue.

s_0.w	s_1.w	s_2.w	s_3.w
s.w$_0$	s.w$_1$	s.w$_2$	s.w$_3$
s_0.l.w	s_1.l.w	s_o.r.w	s_1.r.w
q_0.w	q_1.w	q_2.w	q_3.w
s_0.c	s_0.l.c	s_0.r.c	
s_1.c	s_1.l.c	s_1.r.c	
s_2.c	s_3.c		

Table 1: Atomic feature templates.

3.3 RNN CCG Parsing

We use the same set of CCG rules as in Clark and Curran (2007) and the total number of output units in our RNN model is equal to the number of lexical categories (i.e., all possible sh actions), plus 10 units for re[5] and 18 units for un actions.

All features in our model fall into three types: word, POS tag and CCG category. Table 1 shows the atomic feature templates and we have $|f_w| = 16$, $|f_p| = 16$ and $|f_c| = 8$ (all word-based features are generalized to POS features). Each template has two parts: the first part denotes parse item context and the second part denotes the feature type. s denotes stack contexts and q denotes queue contexts; e.g., s_0 is the top subtree on the stack, and s_o.l is its left child. w represents head words of constituents and w$_0$ is the right-most word of the input string that has been shifted onto the stack.

4   Bidirectional Supertagging

We extend the RNN supertagging model of Xu et al. (2015) by using a bidirectional RNN (BRNN). The BRNN processes an input in both directions with two separate hidden layers, which are then fed to one output layer to make predictions. At each time step t, we compute the *forward* hidden state h_t for $t = (0, 1, \ldots, n - 1)$; the *backward* hidden state h'_t is computed similarly but from the reverse direction for $t = (n - 1, n - 2, \ldots, 0)$ as

$$h'_t = f(x_t \mathbf{U}' + h_{t+1} \mathbf{W}'), \quad (5)$$

and the output layer, for $t = (0, 1, \ldots, n - 1)$, is computed as

$$y_t = f([h_t; h'_t] \mathbf{V}'). \quad (6)$$

The BRNN introduces two new parameter matrices $\mathbf{U}'$ and $\mathbf{W}'$ and replaces the old hidden-to-output

matrix $\mathbf{V}$ with $\mathbf{V}'$ to take two hidden layers as input. We use the same three feature embedding types as Xu et al. (2015), namely word, suffix and capitalization, and all features are extracted from a context window size of 7 surrounding the current word.

5   Experiments

Setup. All experiments were performed on CCG-Bank (Hockenmaier and Steedman, 2007) with the standard split.[6] We used the C&C supertagger (Clark and Curran, 2007) and the RNN supertagger model of Xu et al. (2015) as two supertagger baselines. For the parsing experiments, the baselines were the shift-reduce CCG parsers of Zhang and Clark (2011) and Xu et al. (2014) and the C&C parser of (Clark and Curran, 2007).

To train the RNN parser, we used 10-fold cross validation for both POS tagging and supertagging. For both development and test parsing experiments, we used the C&C POS tagger and automatically assigned POS tags. The BRNN supertagging model was used as the supertagger by all RNN parsing models for both training and testing. F-score over directed, labeled CCG predicate-argument dependencies was used as the parser evaluation metric, obtained using the script from C&C.

Hyperparameters. For the BRNN supertagging model, we used identical hyperparameter settings as in Xu et al. (2015). For all RNN parsing models, the weights were uniformly initialized using the interval $[-2.0, 2.0]$, and scaled by their fan-in (Bengio, 2012); the hidden layer size was 220, and 50-dimensional embeddings were used for all feature types and scaled Turian embeddings were used (Turian et al., 2010) for word embeddings. We also pretrained CCG lexical category and POS embeddings by using the GENSIM word2vec implementation.[7] The data used for this was obtained by parsing a Wikipedia dump using the C&C parser and concatenating the output with CCGBank Sections 02-21. Embeddings for unknown words and CCG categories outside of the lexical category set were uniformly initialized ($[-2.0, 2.0]$) without scaling.

---

[5]In principle, only 1 re unit is needed, but we use 9 additional units to handle non-standard CCG rules in the treebank.

[6]Training: Sections 02-21; development: Section 00; test Section 23.

[7]https://radimrehurek.com/gensim/

Supertagger	Dev	Test
C&C (gold POS)	92.60	93.32
C&C (auto POS)	91.50	92.02
RNN	93.07	93.00
BRNN	**93.49**	**93.52**

Table 2: 1-best supertagging accuracy comparison.

	Supertagger β			
	0.09	0.08	0.07	0.06
$b = 1$	84.61	84.58	84.55	84.50
$b = 2$	84.94	84.86	84.86	84.81
$b = 4$	85.01	84.95	84.92	84.92
$b = 6$	**85.02**	84.96	84.94	84.93
$b = 8$	**85.02**	84.99	84.96	84.95
$b = 16$	85.01	84.95	84.97	84.98

Table 3: The effect on dev F1 by varying the beam size and supertagger β value for the greedy RNN model.

To train all the models, we used a fixed learning rate of 0.0025 and did not truncate the gradients for BPTT, except for training the greedy RNN parsing model where we used a BPTT step size of 9. We applied dropout at the input layer (Legrand and Collobert, 2015), with a dropout rate of 0.25 for the supertagger and 0.30 for the parser.

5.1 Supertagging Results

Table 2 shows 1-best supertagging results. The MaxEnt C&C supertagger uses POS tag features and a tag dictionary, neither of which are used by the RNN supertaggers. For all supertaggers, the same set of 425 lexical categories is used (Clark and Curran, 2007). On the test set, our BRNN supertagger achieves a 1-best accuracy of 93.52%, an absolute improvement of 0.52% over the RNN model, demonstrating the usefulness of contextual information from both input directions.

Fig. 3a shows multi-tagging accuracy comparison for the three supertaggers by varying the variable-width beam probability cut-off value β for each supertagger. The β value determines the average number of supertags (ambiguity) assigned to each word by pruning supertags whose probabilities are not within β times the probability of the 1-best supertag; for this experiment we used β values ranging from 0.09 to 2×10^{-4} and it can be seen that the BRNN supertagger consistently achieves better accuracies at similar ambiguity levels.

Finally, all shift-reduce CCG parsers mentioned in this paper take multi-tagging output obtained with a *fixed* β for training and testing; and in general, a smaller β value can be used by a shift-reduce CCG parser than by the C&C parser. This is because a β value too small may explode the dynamic program of the C&C parser, and it thus relies on an adaptive supertagging strategy (Clark and Curran, 2007), by starting from a large β value and backing off to smaller values if no spanning analysis can found with the current β.

5.2 Parsing Results

To pretrain the greedy model, we trained 10 cross-validated BRNN supertagging models to supply supertags for the parsing model, and used a supertagger β value of 0.00025 which gave on average 5.02 supertags per word. We ran SGD training for 60 epochs, observing no accuracy gains after that, and the best greedy model was obtained after the 52nd epoch (Fig. 3b).

Furthermore, we found that using a relatively smaller supertagger β value (higher ambiguity) for training, and a larger β value (lower ambiguity) for testing, resulted in more accurate models; and we chose the final β value used for the greedy model to be 0.09 using the dev set (Table 3). This observation was different from Zhang and Clark (2011) and Xu et al. (2014), which are two shift-reduce CCG parsers using the averaged perceptron and beam search (Collins, 2002; Collins and Roark, 2004; Zhang and Clark, 2008): they used the same β values for training and testing, which resulted in lower accuracy for our greedy model.

Table 3 also shows the effect on dev F1 by using different beam sizes at test time for the greedy model: with $b = 6$, we obtained an accuracy of 85.02%, an improvement of 0.41% over $b = 1$ (with a β value of 0.09); we saw accuracy gains up to $b = 8$ (with very minimal gains with $b = 16$ for β values 0.06 and 0.07), after which the accuracy started to drop. F1 on dev with $b = 6$ across all training epochs are shown in Fig. 3b as well, and the best model was obtained after the 43rd epoch.

For the xF1 model, we used $b = 8$ and a supertagger β value of 0.09 for both training and testing. Fig.3c shows dev F1 versus the number of training epochs. The best dev F1 was obtained after the 54th epoch with an accuracy of 85.73%, 1.12%

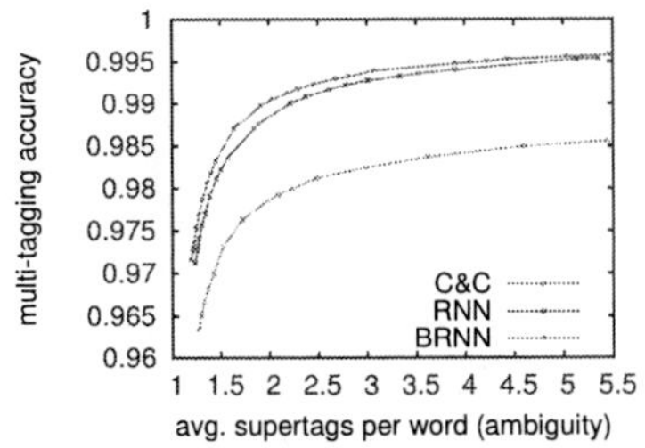

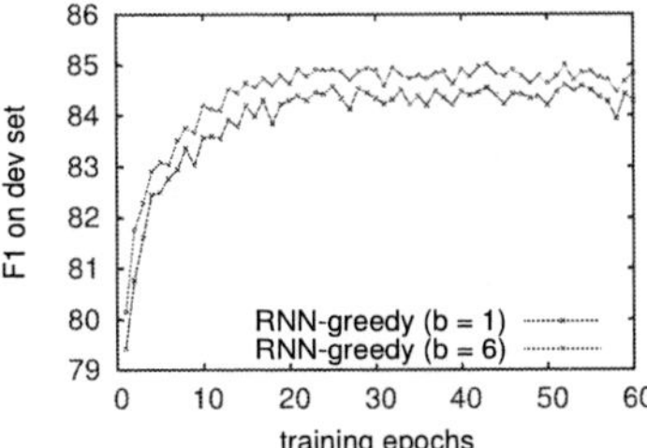

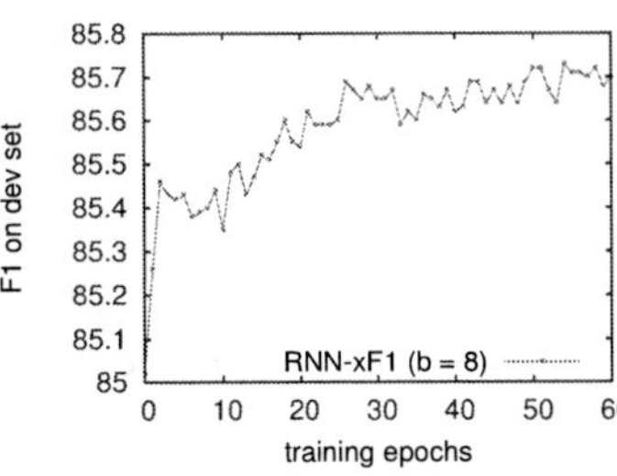

(a) multi-tagging accuracy on dev   (b) F1 on dev with RNN-greedy   (c) F1 on dev with RNN-xF1

Figure 3: Experiment results on the dev set. (a) shows multi-tagging accuracy using the best tagging model. (b) shows F1 scores for the greedy RNN parsing models with beam size $b \in \{1, 6\}$. (c) shows F1 scores for the xF1 models with $b = 8$.

Model	Section 00				Section 23				Speed
	LP	LR	LF	CAT	LP	LR	LF	CAT	
C&C (normal)	85.18	82.53	83.83	92.39	85.45	83.97	84.70	92.83	97.90
C&C (hybrid)	86.07	82.77	84.39	92.57	86.24	84.17	85.19	93.00	95.25
Zhang and Clark (2011) ($b = 16$)	87.15	82.95	85.00	92.77	87.43	83.61	85.48	93.12	-
Zhang and Clark (2011)* ($b = 16$)	86.76	83.15	84.92	92.64	87.04	84.14	85.56	92.95	49.54
Xu et al. (2014) ($b = 128$)	86.29	**84.09**	85.18	92.75	87.03	**85.08**	86.04	93.10	12.85
RNN-greedy ($b = 1$)	88.12	81.38	84.61	93.42	88.53	81.65	84.95	93.57	337.45
RNN-greedy ($b = 6$)	87.96	82.27	85.02	93.47	88.54	82.77	85.56	93.68	96.04
RNN-xF1 ($b = 8$)	**88.20**	83.40	**85.73**	**93.56**	**88.74**	84.22	**86.42**	**93.87**	67.65

Table 4: Final parsing results on Section 00 and Section 23 (100% coverage). Zhang and Clark (2011)* is a reimplementation of the original. All speed results (sents/sec) are obtained using Section 23 and precomputation is used for all RNN parsers. LP (labeled precision); LR (labeled recall); LF (labeled F-score over CCG dependencies); CAT (lexical category assignment accuracy). All experiments using auto POS.

higher than that of the greedy model with $b = 1$ and 0.71% higher than the greedy model with $b \in \{6, 8\}$. This result improves over shift-reduce CCG models of Zhang and Clark (2011) and Xu et al. (2014) by 0.73% and 0.55%, respectively (Table 4).

Table 4 summarizes final results.[8] RNN-xF1, the xF1 trained beam-search model, is currently the most accurate shift-reduce CCG parser, achieving a final F-score of 86.42%, and gives an F-score improvement of 1.47% over the greedy RNN baseline. We show the results for the model of Xu et al. (2014) for reference only, since it uses a more sophisticated dependency, rather than normal-form derivation, model.

At test time, we also used the precomputation trick of Devlin et al. (2014) to speed up the RNN models by caching the top 20K word embeddings and all POS embeddings,[9] and this made the greedy RNN parser more than 3 times faster than the C&C parser (all speed experiments were measured on a workstation with an Intel Core i7 4.0GHz CPU).[10]

6 Related Work

Optimizing for Task-specific Metrics. Our training objective is largely inspired by task-specific optimization for parsing and MT. Goodman (1996) proposed algorithms for optimizing a parser for various constituent matching criteria, and it was one of the earliest work that we are aware of on optimizing a parser for evaluation metrics. Smith and Eisner (2006) proposed a framework for minimizing expected loss for log-linear models and applied it to dependency parsing by optimizing for labeled attachment scores, although they obtained little per-

---

[8]The C&C parser fails to produce spanning analyses for a very small number of sentences (Clark and Curran, 2007) on both dev and test sets, which is not the case for any of the shift-reduce parsers; and for brevity, we omit C&C coverage results.

[9]We used $b = 8$ to do the precomputation.

[10]The speed results for the C&C parser were obtained using the per-compiled C&C binary for Linux available from `http://svn.ask.it.usyd.edu.au/trac/candc/wiki/Download`.

formance improvements. Auli and Lopez (2011) optimized the C&C parser for F-measure. However, they used the softmax-margin (Gimpel and Smith, 2010) objective, which required decomposing precision and recall statistics over parse forests. Instead, we directly optimize for an F-measure loss. In MT, task-specific optimization has also received much attention (e.g., see Och (2003)). Closely related to our work, Gao and He (2013) proposed training a Markov random field translation model as an additional component in a log-linear phrase-based translation system using a k-best list based expected BLEU objective; using the same objective, Auli et al. (2014) and Auli and Gao (2014) trained a large scale phrase-based reordering model and a RNN language model respectively, all as additional components within a log-linear translation model. In contrast, our RNN parsing model is trained in an end-to-end fashion with an expected F-measure loss and all parameters of the model are optimized using backpropagation and SGD.

Parsing with RNNs. A line of work is devoted to parsing with RNN models, including using RNNs (Miikkulainen, 1996; Mayberry and Miikkulainen, 1999; Legrand and Collobert, 2015; Watanabe and Sumita, 2015) and LSTM (Hochreiter and Schmidhuber, 1997) RNNs (Vinyals et al., 2015; Ballesteros et al., 2015; Dyer et al., 2015; Kiperwasser and Goldberg, 2016). Legrand and Collobert (2015) used RNNs to learn conditional distributions over syntactic rules; Vinyals et al. (2015) explored sequence-to-sequence learning (Sutskever et al., 2014) for parsing; Ballesteros et al. (2015) utilized character-level representations and Kiperwasser and Goldberg (2016) built an easy-first dependency parser using tree-structured compositional LSTMs. However, all these parsers use greedy search and are trained using the maximum likelihood criterion (except Kiperwasser and Goldberg (2016), who used a margin-based objective). For learning global models, Watanabe and Sumita (2015) used a margin-based objective, which was not optimized for the evaluation metric; although not using RNNs, Weiss et al. (2015) proposed a method using the averaged perceptron with beam search (Collins, 2002; Collins and Roark, 2004; Zhang and Clark, 2008), which required fixing the neural network representations, and

thus their model parameters were not learned using end-to-end backpropagation.

Finally, a number of recent work (Bengio et al., 2015; Vaswani and Sagae, 2016) explored training neural network models for parsing and other tasks such that the network learns from the oracle as well as its own predictions, and are hence more robust to search errors during inference. In principle, these techniques are largely orthogonal to both global learning and task-based optimization, and we would expect further accuracy gains are possible by combining these techniques in a single model.

7 Conclusion

Neural network shift-reduce parsers are often trained by maximizing likelihood, which does not optimize towards the final evaluation metric. In this paper, we addressed this problem by developing expected F-measure training for an RNN shift-reduce parsing model. We have demonstrated the effectiveness of our method on shift-reduce parsing for CCG, achieving higher accuracies than all shift-reduce CCG parsers to date and the de facto C&C parser.[11] We expect the general framework will be applicable to models using other types of neural networks such as feed-forward or LSTM nets, and to shift-reduce parsers for constituent and dependency parsing.

Acknowledgments

We thank the anonymous reviewers for their detailed comments. Xu acknowledges the Carnegie Trust for the Universities of Scotland and the Cambridge Trusts for funding. Clark is supported by ERC Starting Grant DisCoTex (306920) and EPSRC grant EP/I037512/1.

References

Alfred V Aho and Jeffrey D Ullman. 1972. *The theory of parsing, translation, and compiling*. Prentice-Hall.

Michael Auli and Jianfeng Gao. 2014. Decoder integration and expected BLEU training for recurrent neural network language models. In *Proc. of ACL (Volume 2)*.

---

[11] Auli and Lopez (2011) present higher accuracies but on a different coverage to enable a comparison to Fowler and Penn (2010). Their results are thus not directly comparable to ours.

Michael Auli and Adam Lopez. 2011. Training a log-linear parser with loss functions via softmax-margin. In *Proc. of EMNLP*.

Michael Auli, Michel Galley, and Jianfeng Gao. 2014. Large-scale expected BLEU training of phrase-based reordering models. In *Proc. of EMNLP*.

Miguel Ballesteros, Chris Dyer, and Noah A Smith. 2015. Improved transition-based parsing by modeling characters instead of words with LSTMs. In *Proc. of EMNLP*.

Srinivas Bangalore and Aravind K Joshi. 1999. Supertagging: An approach to almost parsing. In *Computational linguistics*. MIT Press.

Samy Bengio, Oriol Vinyals, Navdeep Jaitly, and Noam M. Shazeer. 2015. Scheduled sampling for sequence prediction with recurrent neural networks. In *Proc. of NIPS*.

Yoshua Bengio. 2012. Practical recommendations for gradient-based training of deep architectures. In *Neural Networks: Tricks of the Trade*. Springer.

Eugene Charniak and Mark Johnson. 2005. Coarse-to-fine n-best parsing and MaxEnt discriminative reranking. In *Proc. of ACL*.

Danqi Chen and Christopher D Manning. 2014. A fast and accurate dependency parser using neural networks. In *Proc. of EMNLP*.

Stephen Clark and James R Curran. 2004. The importance of supertagging for wide-coverage CCG parsing. In *Proc. of COLING*.

Stephen Clark and James R. Curran. 2007. Wide-coverage efficient statistical parsing with CCG and log-linear models. In *Computational Linguistics*. MIT Press.

Michael Collins and Brian Roark. 2004. Incremental parsing with the perceptron algorithm. In *Proc. of ACL*.

Michael Collins. 2000. Discriminative reranking for natural language parsing. In *Proc. of ICML*.

Michael Collins. 2002. Discriminative training methods for hidden Markov models: Theory and experiments with perceptron algorithms. In *Proc. of EMNLP*.

Jacob Devlin, Rabih Zbib, Zhongqiang Huang, Thomas Lamar, Richard Schwartz, and John Makhoul. 2014. Fast and robust neural network joint models for statistical machine translation. In *Proc. of ACL*.

Chris Dyer, Miguel Ballesteros, Wang Ling, Austin Matthews, and Noah A. Smith. 2015. Transition-based dependency parsing with stack long short-term memory. In *Proc. of ACL*.

Jeffrey L Elman. 1990. Finding structure in time. In *Cognitive science*. Elsevier.

Timothy A.D. Fowler and Gerald Penn. 2010. Accurate context-free parsing with Combinatory Categorial Grammar. In *Proc. of ACL*.

Jianfeng Gao and Xiaodong He. 2013. Training MRF-based phrase translation models using gradient ascent. In *Proc. of NAACL*.

Jianfeng Gao, Xiaodong He, Wen-tau Yih, and Li Deng. 2014. Learning continuous phrase representations for translation modeling. In *Proc. of ACL*.

Kevin Gimpel and Noah Smith. 2010. Softmax-margin CRFs: training log-linear models with cost functions. In *Proc. of NAACL*.

Yoav Goldberg, Kai Zhao, and Liang Huang. 2013. Efficient implementation for beam search incremental parsers. In *Proc. of ACL (Volume 2)*.

Christoph Goller and Andreas Kuchler. 1996. Learning task-dependent distributed representations by back-propagation through structure. In *Proc. of IEEE International Conference on Neural Networks*.

Joshua Goodman. 1996. Parsing algorithms and metrics. In *Proc. of ACL*.

Xiaodong He and Li Deng. 2012. Maximum expected BLEU training of phrase and lexicon translation models. In *Proc. of ACL*.

Geoffrey E Hinton. 2002. Training products of experts by minimizing contrastive divergence. In *Neural computation*. MIT Press.

Sepp Hochreiter and Jürgen Schmidhuber. 1997. Long short-term memory. In *Neural computation*. MIT Press.

Julia Hockenmaier and Mark Steedman. 2007. CCG-Bank: A corpus of CCG derivations and dependency structures extracted from the Penn Treebank. In *Computational Linguistics*. MIT Press.

Julia Hockenmaier. 2003. *Data and Models for Statistical Parsing with Combinatory Categorial Grammar*. Ph.D. thesis, University of Edinburgh.

Eliyahu Kiperwasser and Yoav Goldberg. 2016. Easy-first dependency parsing with hierarchical tree LSTMs. *arXiv:1603.00375*.

Marco Kuhlmann and Giorgio Satta. 2014. A new parsing algorithm for combinatory categorial grammar. In *Transactions of the Association for Computational Linguistics*. ACL.

Joël Legrand and Ronan Collobert. 2015. Joint RNN-based greedy parsing and word composition. In *Proc. of ICLR*.

Marshall R. Mayberry and Risto Miikkulainen. 1999. Sardsrn: A neural network shift-reduce parser. In *Proc. of IJCAI*.

Risto Miikkulainen. 1996. Subsymbolic case-role analysis of sentences with embedded clauses. In *Cognitive Science*. Elsevier.

Tomáš Mikolov. 2012. *Statistical Language Models Based on Neural Networks*. Ph.D. thesis, Brno University of Technology.

J. Nivre and M Scholz. 2004. Deterministic dependency parsing of English text. In *Proc. of COLING*.

Joakim Nivre. 2008. Algorithms for deterministic incremental dependency parsing. In *Computational Linguistics*. MIT Press.

Franz Josef Och. 2003. Minimum error rate training in statistical machine translation. In *Proc. of ACL*.

Antti-Veikko I Rosti, Bing Zhang, Spyros Matsoukas, and Richard Schwartz. 2010. BBN system description for WMT10 system combination task. In *Proc. of the Joint Fifth Workshop on Statistical Machine Translation and MetricsMATR*.

David E Rumelhart, Geoffrey E Hinton, and Ronald J Williams. 1988. Learning representations by back-propagating errors. In *Nature*.

Kenji Sagae and Alon Lavie. 2006. A best-first probabilistic shift-reduce parser. In *Proc. of COLING/ACL*.

David A. Smith and Jason Eisner. 2006. Minimum-risk annealing for training log-linear models. In *Proc. of COLING-ACL*.

Ilya Sutskever, Oriol Vinyals, and Quoc Le. 2014. Sequence to sequence learning with neural networks. In *Proc. of NIPS*.

Joseph Turian, Lev Ratinov, and Yoshua Bengio. 2010. Word representations: a simple and general method for semi-supervised learning. In *Proc. of ACL*.

Ashish Vaswani and Kenji Sagae. 2016. Efficient structured inference for transition-based parsing with neural networks and error states. In *Transactions of the Association for Computational Linguistics*. ACL.

Krishnamurti Vijay-Shanker and David J Weir. 1993. Parsing some constrained grammar formalisms. In *Computational Linguistics*. MIT Press.

Oriol Vinyals, Lukasz Kaiser, Terry Koo, Slav Petrov, Ilya Sutskever, and Geoffrey Hinton. 2015. Grammar as a foreign language. In *Proc. of NIPS*.

Taro Watanabe and Eiichiro Sumita. 2015. Transition-based neural constituent parsing. In *Proc. of ACL*.

David Weiss, Chris Alberti, Michael Collins, and Slav Petrov. 2015. Structured training for neural network transition-based parsing. In *Proc. of ACL*.

Wenduan Xu, Stephen Clark, and Yue Zhang. 2014. Shift-Reduce CCG parsing with a dependency model. In *Proc. of ACL*.

Wenduan Xu, Michael Auli, and Stephen Clark. 2015. CCG supertagging with a recurrent neural network. In *Proc. of ACL (Volume 2)*.

Yue Zhang and Stephen Clark. 2008. A tale of two parsers: investigating and combining graph-based and transition-based dependency parsing using beam-search. In *Proc. of EMNLP*.

Yue Zhang and Stephen Clark. 2011. Shift-Reduce CCG parsing. In *Proc. of ACL*.

Hao Zhou, Yue Zhang, Shujian Huang, and Jiajun Chen. 2015. A neural probabilistic structured-prediction model for transition-based dependency parsing. In *Proc. of ACL*.

Muhua Zhu, Yue Zhang, Wenliang Chen, Min Zhang, and Jingbo Zhu. 2013. Fast and accurate shift-reduce constituent parsing. In *Proc. of ACL*.

LSTM CCG Parsing

Mike Lewis   **Kenton Lee**   **Luke Zettlemoyer**
Computer Science & Engineering
University of Washington
Seattle, WA 98195
{mlewis,kentonl,lsz}@cs.washington.edu

Abstract

We demonstrate that a state-of-the-art parser can be built using only a lexical tagging model and a deterministic grammar, with no explicit model of bi-lexical dependencies. Instead, all dependencies are implicitly encoded in an LSTM supertagger that assigns CCG lexical categories. The parser significantly outperforms all previously published CCG results, supports efficient and optimal A* decoding, and benefits substantially from semi-supervised tri-training. We give a detailed analysis, demonstrating that the parser can recover long-range dependencies with high accuracy and that the semi-supervised learning enables significant accuracy gains. By running the LSTM on a GPU, we are able to parse over 2600 sentences per second while improving state-of-the-art accuracy by 1.1 F1 in domain and up to 4.5 F1 out of domain.

1   Introduction

Combinatory Categorial Grammar (CCG) is a strongly lexicalized formalism—the vast majority of attachment decisions during parsing are specified by the selection of lexical entries for words (see Figure 1 for examples). State-of-the-art parsers typically include a supertagging model, to select possible lexical categories, and a bi-lexical dependency model, to resolve the remaining parse attachment ambiguities. In this paper, we introduce a long short-term memory (LSTM) CCG parsing model that has no explicit model of bi-lexical dependencies, but instead relies on a bi-directional recurrent neural network (RNN) supertagger to capture all long distance dependencies. This approach has a number of advantages: it is conceptually simple, allows for the reuse of existing optimal and efficient parsing algorithms, benefits significantly from semi-supervised learning, and is highly accurate both in and out of domain. The parser is publicly released.[1]

Neural networks have shown strong performance in a range of NLP tasks; however they can break the dynamic programs for structured prediction problems, such as parsing, when vector embeddings are recursively computed for subparts of the output. Existing neural net parsers either (1) use greedy inference techniques including shift-reduce parsing (Henderson et al., 2013; Chen and Manning, 2014; Weiss et al., 2015; Dyer et al., 2015), constituency parse re-ranking (Socher et al., 2013), and string-to-string transduction (Vinyals et al., 2015), or (2) avoid recursive computations entirely (Durrett and Klein, 2015). Our approach gives a simple alternative: we only train a model for tagging decisions, where we can easily use recurrent architectures such as LSTMs (Hochreiter and Schmidhuber, 1997), and rely on the highly lexicalized nature of the CCG grammar to allow this tagger to specify nearly every aspect of the complete parse.

Our LSTM supertagger is bi-directional and includes a softmax potential over tags for each word in the sentence. During training, we jointly optimize all LSTM parameters, including the word embeddings, to maximize the conditional likelihood of supertag sequences. For inference, we use a recently introduced A* CCG parsing algorithm (Lewis and Steedman, 2014a), which efficiently searches for the

---

[1] http://github.com/mikelewis0/EasySRL

Proceedings of NAACL-HLT 2016, pages 221–231,
San Diego, California, June 12-17, 2016. ©2016 Association for Computational Linguistics

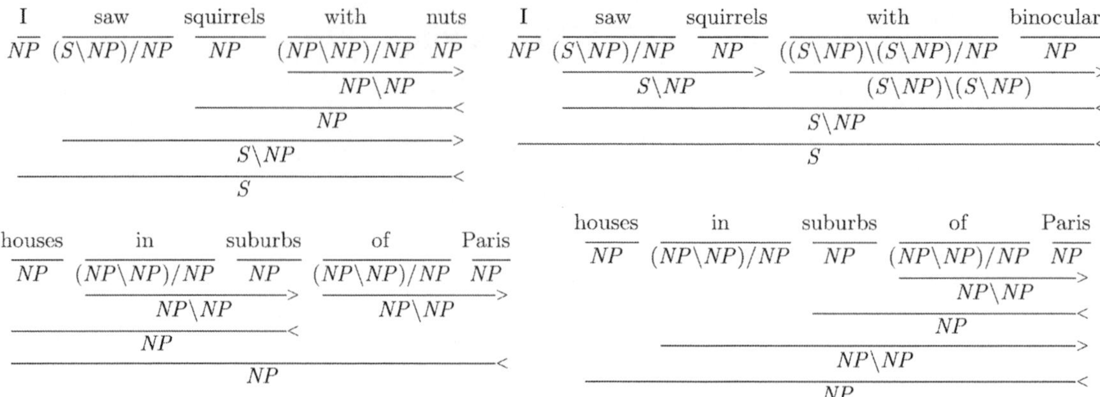

Figure 1: Four examples of prepositional phrase attachment in CCG. In the upper two parses, the attachment decision is determined by the choice of supertags. In the lower parses, the attachment is ambiguous given the supertags. In such cases, our parser deterministically attaches low (i.e. preferring the lower-right parse).

highest probability sequence of tags that combine to produce a complete parse tree. Whenever there is parsing ambiguity not specified by the supertags, the model attaches low (see Figure 1).

This approach is not only conceptually simple but also highly effective, as we demonstrate with extensive experiments. Because the A* algorithm is extremely efficient and the LSTMs can be run in parallel on GPUs, the end-to-end parser can process over 2600 sentences per second. This is more than three times the speed of any publicly available parser for any formalism. Apart from Hall et al. (2014), we are not aware of efficient algorithms for running other state-of-art-parsers on GPUs. The LSTM parameters also benefit from semi-supervised training, which we demonstrate by employing a recently introduced tri-training scheme (Weiss et al., 2015). Finally, the recurrent nature of the LSTM allows for effective modelling of long distance dependencies, as we show empirically. Our approach significantly advances the state-of-the-art on benchmark datasets—improving accuracy by 1.1 F1 in domain and up to 4.5 F1 out of domain.

2 Background

Combinatory Categorial Grammar (CCG)
Compared to a phrase-structure grammar, CCG contains a much smaller set of binary rules (we use 11), but a much larger set of lexical tags (we use 425). The binary rules are conjectured to be language-universal, and most language-specific

information is lexicalized (Steedman, 2000). The large tag set means that most (but not all) attachment decisions are determined by tagging decisions. Figure 1 shows how a prepositional phrase attachment decision can be encoded in the choice of tags.

The process of assigning CCG categories to words is called *supertagging*. All supertaggers used in practice are probabilistic, providing a distribution over possible tags for each word. Parsing models either use these scores directly (Auli and Lopez, 2011b), or as a form of beam search (Clark and Curran, 2007), typically in conjunction with models of the dependencies or derivation.

Supertag-Factored A* CCG Parsing Lewis and Steedman (2014a) introduced supertag-factored CCG parsers, in which the score for a parse is simply the sum of the scores of its supertags. The parser takes in a distribution over supertags for each word, and outputs the highest scoring parse—subject to the hard constraint that the parse only uses standard CCG combinators (resolving any remaining ambiguity by attaching low). One advantage of the supertag-factored model is that it allows a simple A* parsing algorithm, which provably finds the highest scoring supertag sequence that can be combined to construct a complete parse.

In A* parsing, partial parses $y_{i,j}$ of span $i \ldots j$ are maintained in a sorted agenda and added to the chart in order of their cost, which is the sum of their Viterbi inside score $g(y_{i,j})$ and an upper bound on their Viterbi outside score $h(y_{i,j})$. When $y_{i,j}$ is

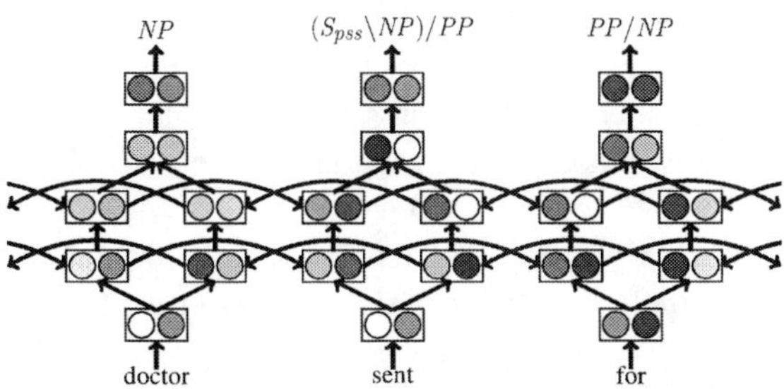

Figure 2: Visualization of our supertagging model, based on stacked bi-directional LSTMs. Each word is fed into stacked LSTMs reading the sentence in each direction, the outputs of the LSTMs are combined, and there is a final softmax over categories.

added to the chart, the agenda is updated with any new partial parses that can be created by combining $y_{i,j}$ with existing chart items (Algorithm 1). If h is a monotonic upper bound on the outside score, the first chart entry for a span with a given category is guaranteed to be optimal—all other possible completions of the competing partial parses provably have lower scores, due to the outside score bounds. There is no guarantee this certificate of optimality is achieved efficiently for parses of the whole sentence, and in the worst case the algorithm could fill the entire parse chart. However, as we will see later, A* parsing is very efficient in practice for the models we present in this paper.

In the supertag-factored model, g and h are computed as follows, where $g(y_k)$ is the score for word k having tag y_k.

$$g(y_{i,j}) = \sum_{k=i}^{j} g(y_k) \qquad (1)$$

$$h(y_{i,j}) = \sum_{k=1}^{i-1} \max_{y_k} g(y_k) + \sum_{k=j+1}^{N} \max_{y_k} g(y_k) \qquad (2)$$

where Eq. 1 follows from the definition of the supertag factored model and Eq. 2 combines this definition with the fact that the max score over all supertags for a word is an upperbound on the score for the actual supertag used in the best parse.

3 LSTM CCG Supertagging Model

Supertagging is *almost parsing* (Bangalore and Joshi, 1999)—consequently the task is very chal-

---

Definitions $x_{1...N}$ is the input words, and y variables denote scored partial parses. TAG($x_{1...N}$) returns a set of scored pre-terminals for every word. ADD(C, y) adds partial parse y to chart C. RULES(C, y) returns the set of scored partial parses that can be created by combining y with existing entries in C. The agenda A is ordered as described in Section 2.

```
1: function PARSE(x_{1...N})
2:     A ← ∅                         ▷ Empty agenda A
3:     for y ∈ TAG(x_{1...N}) do
4:         PUSH(A, y)
5:     C ← ∅                          ▷ Empty chart C
6:     while C_{1,N} = ∅ ∧ A ≠ ∅ do
7:         y ← EXTRACT_MAX(A)
8:         if y ∉ C then
9:             ADD(C, y)
10:            for y' ∈ RULES(C, y) do
11:                INSERT(A, y')
12:    return C_{1,N}
```

lenging, with hundreds of tags, and the correct assignment often depending on long-range dependencies. For example, in *The doctor sent for the patient arrived*, the category for *sent* depends on the final word. Recent work has made dramatic progress, using feed-forward neural networks (Lewis and Steedman, 2014b) and RNNs (Xu et al., 2015).

We make several extensions to previous work on supertagging. Firstly, we use bi-directional models, to capture both previous and subsequent sentence context into supertagging decisions. Secondly, we use LSTMs, rather than RNNs. Many tagging decisions rely on long-range context, and RNNs typically struggle to account for sequences of longer than a few words (Hochreiter and Schmidhuber, 1997). Finally, we use a deep architecture, to allow the modelling of complex interactions in the context.

Our supertagging model is summarized in Figure 2. Each word is mapped to an embedding vector. This vector is a concatenation of an embedding for the word (lower-cased), and embeddings for features of the word (we use 1 to 4 character prefixes and suffixes). The embedding vector is used as input to two stacked LSTMs (with depth 2), one processing the sentence left-to-right, and the other right-to-left.

The outputs from the LSTMs are projected into a further hidden layer, a bias is added, and a RELU non-linearity is applied. This layer gives a context-dependent representation of the word that is fed into a softmax over supertags.

We use a variant on the standard LSTM with coupled 'input' and 'forget' gates, and peephole connections. Each LSTM cell at position t takes three inputs: a cell state vector c_{t-1} and hidden state vector h_{t-1} from the cell at position $t - 1$, and x_t from the layer below. It outputs h_t to the layer above, and c_t and h_t to the cell at $t + 1$. c_t and h_t are computed as follows, where σ is the component-wise logistic sigmoid, and $\circ$ is the component-wise product:

$$i_t = \sigma(W_i[c_{t-1}, h_{t-1}, x_t] + b_i) \tag{3}$$

$$\tilde{c}_t = \tanh(W_c[h_{t-1}, x_t] + b_{\tilde{c}}) \tag{4}$$

$$o_t = \sigma(W_o[\tilde{c}_t, h_{t-1}, x_t] + b_o) \tag{5}$$

$$c_t = i_t \circ \tilde{c}_t + (1 - i_t)c_{t-1} \tag{6}$$

$$h_t = o_t \circ \tanh(c_t) \tag{7}$$

We train the model using stochastic gradient descent, with a minibatch size of 1, a learning rate of 0.01, and using momentum with $\mu = 0.7$. We then fine-tune models using a larger minibatch size of 32. Gradients whose L_2 norm exceeds 5 are clipped. Training was run for 30 epochs, shuffling the order of sentences after each epoch, and we used the model parameters with the highest development supertagging accuracy. The input layer uses dropout with a rate of 0.5. All trainable parameters have L_2 regularization of $\Lambda = 10^{-6}$. Word embedding are initialized using 50-dimensional pre-trained values from Turian et al. (2010). For prefix and suffix embeddings, we use randomly initialized 32-dimensional vectors—features occurring less than 3 times are replaced with an 'unknown' embedding. We add special start and end tokens to each sentence, with trainable parameters. The LSTM state size is 128 and the RELU layer has a size of 64.

4 Parsing Models

Our experiments focus on two parsing models:

Supertag-Factored We use the supertagging model described in Section 3 to build a supertag-factored parser, closely following the approach described in Section 2. We also add a penalty of 0.1 (tuned on development data) for every time a unary rule is applied in a parse. The attach-low heuristic is implemented by adding a small penalty of $-\epsilon d$ at every binary rule instantiation, where d is the absolute distance between the heads of the left and right children, and ϵ is a small constant. We increase the penalty to 10ϵ for clitics, to encourage these to attach locally. Because these penalties are ≤ 0, they do not affect the A* upper bound calculations.

Dependencies We also train a model with dependency features, to investigate how much they improve accuracy beyond the supertag-factored model. We adapt a joint CCG and SRL model (Lewis et al., 2015) to CCGbank parsing, by assigning every CCGbank dependency a role based on its argument number (i.e., the first argument of every category has role *ARG0*). A global log-linear model is trained to maximize the marginal likelihood of the gold dependencies. We use the same features and hyperparameters as Lewis et al. (2015), except that we do not use the supertagger score feature (to separate the effect of the dependencies features from the supertagger). We choose this model because it has an A* parsing algorithm, meaning that we do not need to use aggressive beam search.

5 Semi-supervised Learning

A number of papers have shown that strong parsers can be improved by exploiting text without gold-standard annotations. Recent work suggests *tri-training*, in which the output of two parsers is intersected to create training data for a third parser, is highly effective (Weiss et al., 2015).

We perform the first application of tri-training to a lexicalized formalism. Following Weiss et al., we parse the corpus of Chelba et al. (2013) with a shift-reduce parser and a chart-based model. We use the shift-reduce parser from Ambati et al. (2016) and our dependency model (without using a supertagger feature, to limit the correlation with our tagging model). On development sentences where the parsers produce the same supertags (40%), supertagging accuracy is 98.0%. This subset is considerably easier than general text—our CCGbank-trained supertagger is 97.4% accurate on this data—but tri-training still provides useful additional training data.

In total, we include 43 million words of text that

the parsers annotate with the same supertags and 15 copies of the gold CCGbank training data. Our experiments show that tri-training improves both supertagging and parsing accuracy.

6   GPU Parsing

Our parser makes an unusual trade-off, by combining a complex tagging model with a deterministic parsing model. The A^* parsing algorithm is extremely efficient, and the overall time required to process a sentence is dominated by the supertagger.

GPUs can improve performance over CPUs by computing many vector operations in parallel. There are two major obstacles to using GPUs for parsing. First, most models use sparse rather than dense features, which are difficult to compute efficiently on GPUs. The most successful implementation we are aware of exploits the fact that the Berkeley parser is unlexicalized to run parsing operations in parallel (Hall et al., 2014). Second, most neural models have features that depend on the current parse or stack state (e.g. Chen and Manning (2014)). This makes it difficult to exploit the parallelism of GPUs, because these data structures are typically built incrementally on CPU. It may be possible to write GPU-specific code that maintains the entire parse state on GPU, but we are not aware of any such implementations.

In contrast, our supertagger only uses matrix operations, and does not take any parse state as input—meaning it is straightforward to run on a GPU. To exploit the parallelism of GPUs, we process thousands of sentences simultaneously—improving parsing efficiency by an order-of-magnitude over CPU. A major advantage of our model is that it allows all of the computationally intensive decisions to occur on GPUs. Unlike existing GPU parsers, the LSTM can be run with generic library code.[2]

7   Experiments

7.1   Experimental setup

We trained our parser on Sections 02-21 of CCGbank (Hockenmaier and Steedman, 2007), using Section 00 for development, and Section 23 for test. Our experiments use a supertagger beam of 10^{-4}—which does not affect the final scores, but reduces overheads such as building the initial agenda.

---

[2]We use TensorFlow (Abadi et al., 2015).

Model	Dev	Test
C&C tagger	91.5	92.0
NN	91.3	91.6
RNN	93.1	93.0
LSTM	94.1	94.3
LSTM + Tri-training	**94.9**	**94.7**

Table 1: Supertagging accuracy on CCGbank.

Model	P	R	F1
C&C	86.2	84.2	85.2
C&C + RNN	87.7	86.4	87.0
EASYCCG	83.7	83.0	83.3
Dependencies	86.5	85.8	86.1
LSTM	87.7	86.7	87.2
LSTM + Dependencies	88.2	87.3	87.8
LSTM + Tri-training	**88.6**	**87.5**	**88.1**
LSTM + Tri-training + Dependencies	88.2	87.3	87.8

Table 2: Labelled F1 for CCGbank dependencies on the CCGbank test set (Section 23).

Where results are available, we compare our work with the following models: EASYCCG, which has the same parsing model as our parser, but uses a feed-forward neural-network supertagger (NN); the C&C parser (Clark and Curran, 2007), and C&C+RNN (Xu et al., 2015), which is the C&C parser with an RNN supertagger. All results are for 100% coverage of the test data.

We refer to the models described in Section 4 as LSTM and DEPENDENCIES respectively. We also report the performance of LSTM+DEPENDENCIES, which combines the model scores (weighting the LSTM score by 1.8, tuned on development data).

7.2   Supertagging Results

The most direct measure of the effectiveness of our LSTM and tri-training is on the supertagging task. Results are shown in Table 1. The improvement of our deep LSTM over the RNN model is greater than the improvement of the RNN over C&C model. Further gains follow from tri-training, improving the state-of-the-art by 1.7%.

7.3   English Parsing Results

Parsing results are shown in Figure 2. Surprisingly, our CCGBank-trained LSTM outperforms any previous approach.[3] The ensemble of the LSTM

---

[3]We cannot compare directly with Fowler and Penn (2010)'s adaptation of the Berkeley parser to CCG, or Auli and Lopez

Model	QUESTIONS			BIOINFER		
	P	R	F1	P	R	F1
C&C	-	-	86.6	77.8	71.4	74.5
EASYCCG	78.1	78.2	78.1	76.8	77.6	77.2
C&C + RNN	-	-	-	80.1	75.5	77.7
LSTM	87.6	87.4	87.5	80.1	80.9	80.5
LSTM + Dependencies	**88.2**	**87.9**	**88.0**	77.8	80.1	79.4
LSTM + Tri-training	-	-	-	**81.8**	**82.6**	**82.2**

Table 3: Out-of-domain experiments.

and the Dependency model outperforms the LSTM alone, showing that dependency features are capturing some generalizations that the LSTM does not. However, semi-supervised learning substantially improves the LSTM, matching the accuracy of the ensemble—showing that the LSTM is expressive enough to compensate given sufficient data.

7.4 Out-of-domain Experiments

We also evaluate on two out-of-domain datasets used by Rimell and Clark (2008), but did no development on this data. In both cases, we use Rimell and Clark's scripts for converting CCG parses to the target dependency representations. The datasets are:

QUESTIONS 500 questions from TREC (Rimell and Clark, 2008). Questions frequently contain very long range dependencies, providing an interesting test of the LSTM supertagger's ability to capture unbounded dependencies. We follow Rimell and Clark by re-training the supertagger on the concatenation of the CCGbank training data and 10 copies of the QUESTIONS training data.

BIOINFER 500 sentences from biomedical abstracts. This dataset tests the parser's robustness to a large amount of unseen vocabulary.

Results are shown in Table 3. Our LSTM parser outperforms existing work on question parsing, showing that it can successfully model the long-range dependencies found in questions. Adding dependency features yields only a small improvement.

On the BIOINFER corpus, our tri-trained LSTM parser is 4.5 F1 better than the previous state-of-the-art. Dependency features appear to be much

Parser	Sentences per second
SpaCy*[4]	778
Berkeley GPU* (Hall et al., 2014)	687
Chen and Manning (2014)*	391
C&C	66
EASYCCG	606
LSTM	214
LSTM + Dependencies	58
LSTM GPU	2670

Table 4: Sentences parsed per second on our hardware. Parsers marked * use non-CCG formalisms but are the fastest available CPU and GPU parsers.

less robust to unseen words than the LSTM tagging model, and are unhelpful. Because the parser was not trained or developed on this domain, it is likely to perform similarly well on other domains.

7.5 Efficiency Experiments

In contrast to standard parsing algorithms, the efficiency of our model depends directly on the accuracy of the supertagger in guiding the search. We therefore measure the efficiency empirically.

Results are shown in Table 4.[5] Our parser runs more slowly than EASYCCG on CPU, due to the more complex tagging model (but is 4.8 F1 more accurate). Adding dependencies substantially reduces efficiency, due to calculating sparse features. Without dependencies, the run time is dominated by the LSTM supertagger. Running the supertagger on a GPU reduces parsing times dramatically—outperforming SpaCy, the fastest publicly available parser (Choi et al., 2015). Roughly half the parsing time is spent on GPU supertagging, and half on CPU parsing. To better exploit batching in the GPU, our implementation dynamically buckets sentences by length (bins of width 10), and tags batches when the bucket size reaches 3072 (the number of threads on our GPU). We are not aware of any GPU implementations of shift-reduce parsers or lexicalized chart parsers, so it is unclear if most other state-of-the-art parsers can be adapted to exploit GPUs.

(2011b)'s joint parsing and supertagging model, due to differences in the experimental setup. These models are 0.3 and 1.5 F1 more accurate than the C&C baseline respectively, which is well within the margin of improvement obtained by our model.

[4]`honnibal.github.io/spaCy`
[5]All timing experiments use a single 3.5GHz core and (where applicable) a single NVIDIA TITAN X GPU.

Supertagger	Accuracy
Bidirectional RNNs	93.4
Forward LSTM only	83.5
Backward LSTM only	89.5
Bidirectional LSTMs	**94.1**

Table 5: Development supertagging accuracy.

Word Class	NN	LSTM	LSTM+ Tri-training
All	91.32	94.14	**94.90**
Unseen Words	90.39	94.21	**95.26**
Unseen Usages	45.80	59.37	**62.46**
Prepositions	78.11	84.40	**85.98**
Verbs	82.55	87.85	**89.24**
Wh-words	90.47	92.09	**94.16**
Long range	74.80	83.99	**86.31**

Table 6: Development supertagging accuracy on several classes of words. *Long range* refers to words taking an argument at least 5 words away.

8 Ablations

We also measure performance while removing different aspects of the full parsing model.

8.1 Supertagger Model Architecture

Numerous variations are possible on our supertagging architecture. Apart from tri-training, the major differences from the previous state-of-the-art (Xu et al., 2015) are that we use LSTMs rather than RNNs, and that we use bidirectional networks rather than only a forward-directional RNN. These modifications lead to a 1.3% improvement in accuracy. Table 5 shows performance while ablating these changes; they all contribute substantially to tagging accuracy.

Table 6 shows several classes of words where the LSTM model outperforms the baseline neural network that uses only local context (NN). The performance increase on unseen words is likely due to the fact that the LSTM can model more context to determine the category for a word. Unsurprisingly, this leads to a large improvement in accuracy for words taking non-local arguments. Finally, we see a large improvement in prepositional phrase attachment. This improvement is likely to be due to the deep architecture, which can better take into account the interaction between the preposition, its argument

Relaxation	LSTM+ Tri-train F1	LSTM+ Dependencies F1
-	87.9	87.9
$\{NP, N\}$	87.8	87.7
$\{NP, PP\}$	87.7	87.6
$\{NP, PP, N, N_{num}\}$	87.4	87.2
*	78.3	79.3

Table 7: Effect of simulating weaker grammars, by allowing the specified atomic categories to unify. * allows all atomic categories to unify, except conjunctions and punctuation. Results are on development sentences of length ≤ 40.

noun phrase, and its nominal or verbal attachment.

8.2 Semi-supervised learning

Table 6 also shows cases where the semi-supervised models perform better. Accuracy improves on unseen words—showing that tri-training can be a more effective way of generalizing to unseen words than pre-trained word embeddings alone. We also see improvement in accuracy on wh-words, which we attribute to the training data containing more examples of rare categories used for wh-words in pied-piping and similar constructions. One case where performance remains weak for all models is on unseen usages—where words occur in the CCGbank training data, but not with the category required in the test data. The improvement from tri-training is limited, likely due to the weakness of the baseline parses, and new techniques will be required to correct such errors.

8.3 Effect of Grammar

A subtle but crucial point is that our method depends on the strictness of the CCGbank grammar to exclude ungrammatical derivations. Because there is no dependency model, we rely on the deterministic CCG grammar as a hard constraint. There is a trade-off between restrictive grammars which may be brittle on noisy text, and weaker grammars that may overgenerate ungrammatical sentences.

We measure this trade-off by testing weaker grammars, which merge categories that are normally distinct. For example, if we merge PP and NP, then an $S\backslash NP$ can take either a PP or NP argument.

Table 7 shows that relaxing the grammar significantly hurts performance; the deterministic constraints are crucial to training a high quality LSTM

CCG parser. With a very relaxed grammar in which all atoms can unify, dependencies features help compensate for the weakened grammar. Future work should explore further strengthening the grammar—-e.g. marking plurality on *NPs* to enforce plural agreement, or using slash-modalities to prevent over-generation arising from composition (Baldridge and Kruijff, 2003).

8.4 Effect of Dependency Features

Perhaps our most surprising result is that high accuracy can be achieved with a rule-based grammar and no dependency features. We performed several experiments to verify whether the model can capture long-range dependencies, and the extent to which dependency features are required to further improve parsing performance.

Supertagging accuracy is still the bottleneck A natural question is whether further improvements to our model will require a more powerful parsing model (such as adding dependency or derivation features), or if future work should focus on the supertagger. We found that on sentences where all the supertags are correct in the final parse (51%), the F1 is very high: 97.7. On parses containing supertag errors, the F1 drops to just 80.3. This result suggests that parsing accuracy can be significantly increased by improving the supertagger, and that very high performance could be attained only using a supertagging model.

'Attach low' heuristic is surprisingly effective Given a sequence of supertags, our grammar is still ambiguous. As explained in Section 2, we resolve these ambiguities by attaching low. To investigate the accuracy of this heuristic, we performed oracle decoding given the highest scoring supertags—and found that F1 improved by 1.3, showing that there are limits to what can be achieved with a rule-based grammar. In contrast, an 'attach high' heuristic scores 5.2 F1 less than attaching low, suggesting that these decisions are reasonably frequent, but that attaching low is much more common.

Would adding a dependency model help here? We consider several dependencies whose attachment is often ambiguous given the supertags. Results are shown in Table 8. Any improvements from the dependency model are small—it is difficult to improve

Dependency	Attach Low Heuristic	Dependencies Model
Relative clause	84.66	**85.44**
Adnominal PP	91.67	**93.67**
Adverbial PP	**97.78**	95.86
Adverb	**99.09**	98.09

Table 8: Per-relation accuracy for several dependencies whose attachments are often ambiguous given the supertags. Results are only on sentences where the parsers assign the correct supertags.

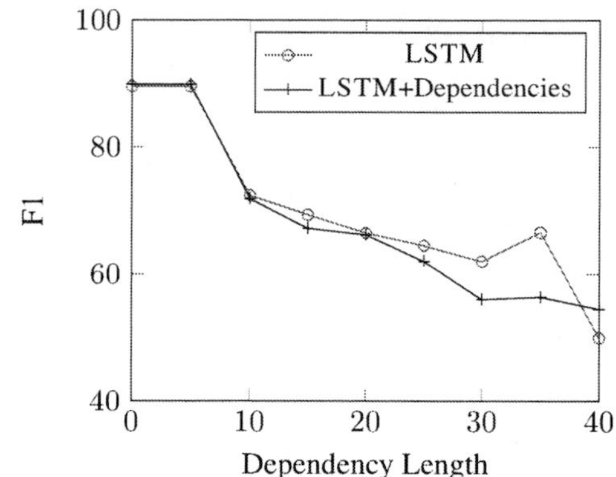

Figure 3: F1 on dependencies of various lengths.

on the 'attach low' heuristic with current models.

Supertag-factored model is accurate on long-range dependencies One motivation for CCG parsing is to recover long-range dependencies. While we do not explicitly model these dependencies, they can still be extracted from the parse. Instead, we rely on the LSTM supertagger to implicitly model the dependencies—a task that becomes more challenging with longer dependencies. We investigate the accuracy of our parser for dependencies of different lengths. Figure 3 shows that adding dependencies features does not improve the recovery of long-range dependencies over the LSTM alone; the LSTM accurately models long-range dependencies.

9 Related Work

Recent work has applied neural networks to parsing, mostly using neural classifiers in shift-reduce parsers (Henderson et al., 2013; Chen and Manning, 2014; Dyer et al., 2015; Weiss et al., 2015). Unlike our approach, none of these report both state-of-the-art speed and accuracy. Vinyals et al. (2015) instead propose embedding entire sentences in a vector space, and then generating parse trees as strings. Our model achieves state-of-the-art accuracy with a non-ensemble model trained on the standard training data, whereas their model requires ensembles or extra supervision to match the state of the art.

Most work on CCG parsing has either used CKY chart parsing (Hockenmaier, 2003; Clark and Curran, 2007; Fowler and Penn, 2010; Auli and Lopez, 2011a) or shift-reduce algorithms (Zhang and Clark, 2011; Xu et al., 2014; Ambati et al., 2015). These methods rely on beam-search to cope with the huge space of possible CCG parses. Instead, we use Lewis and Steedman (2014a)'s A* algorithm. By using a semi-supervised LSTM supertagger, we improved over Lewis and Steedman's parser by 4.8 F1.

CCG supertagging was first attempted with maximum-entropy Markov models (Clark, 2002)—in practice, the combination of sparse features and a large tag set makes such models brittle. Lewis and Steedman (2014b) applied feed-forward neural networks to supertagging, motivated by using pre-trained work embeddings to reduce sparsity. Xu et al. (2015) showed further improvements by using RNNs to condition on non-local context. Concurrently with this work, Xu et al. (2016) explored bidirectional RNN models, and Vaswani et al. (2016) use bidirectional LSTMs with a different training procedure.

Our tagging model is closely related to the bidirectional LSTM POS tagging model of Ling et al. (2015). We see larger gains over the state-of-the-art—likely because supertagging involves more long-range dependencies than POS tagging.

Other work has successfully applied GPUs to parsing, but has required GPU-specific code and algorithms (Yi et al., 2011; Johnson, 2011; Canny et al., 2013; Hall et al., 2014). GPUs have also been used for machine translation (He et al., 2015).

10 Conclusions and Future Work

We have shown that a combination of deep learning, linguistics and classic AI search can be used to build a parser with both state-of-the-art speed and accuracy. Future work will explore using our parser to recover other representations from CCG, such as Universal Dependencies (McDonald et al., 2013) or semantic roles. The major obstacle is the mismatch between these representations and CCGbank—we will therefore investigate new techniques for obtaining other representations from CCG parses. We will also explore new A* parsing algorithms that explicitly model the global parse structure using neural networks, while maintaining optimality guarantees.

Acknowledgements

We thank Bharat Ram Ambati, Greg Coppola, Chloé Kiddon, Luheng He, Yannis Konstas and the anonymous reviewers for comments on an earlier version, and Mark Yatskar for helpful discussions.

This research was supported in part by the NSF (IIS-1252835), DARPA under the DEFT program through the AFRL (FA8750-13-2-0019), an Allen Distinguished Investigator Award, and a gift from Google.

References

Martın Abadi, Ashish Agarwal, Paul Barham, Eugene Brevdo, Zhifeng Chen, Craig Citro, Greg S Corrado, Andy Davis, Jeffrey Dean, Matthieu Devin, et al. 2015. TensorFlow: Large-scale Machine Learning on Heterogeneous Systems. *Software available from tensorflow.org*.

Bharat Ram Ambati, Tejaswini Deoskar, Mark Johnson, and Mark Steedman. 2015. An Incremental Algorithm for Transition-based CCG Parsing. In *Proceedings of the 2015 Conference of the North American Chapter of the Association for Computational Linguistics: Human Language Technologies*. Association for Computational Linguistics.

Bharat Ram Ambati, Tejaswini Deoskar, and Mark Steedman. 2016. Shift-Reduce CCG Parsing using Neural Network Models. In *Proceedings of the Human Language Technology Conference of the NAACL, Companion Volume: Short Papers*.

Michael Auli and Adam Lopez. 2011a. A Comparison of Loopy Belief Propagation and Dual Decomposition for Integrated CCG Supertagging and Parsing. In *Proceedings of the 49th Annual Meeting of the Association for Computational Linguistics: Human Language Technologies-Volume 1*.

Michael Auli and Adam Lopez. 2011b. Training a log-linear parser with loss functions via softmax-margin. In *Proceedings of the Conference on Empirical Methods in Natural Language Processing*.

Jason Baldridge and Geert-Jan M Kruijff. 2003. Multimodal Combinatory Categorial Grammar. In *Proceed-*

ings of the tenth conference on European chapter of the Association for Computational Linguistics-Volume 1.

Srinivas Bangalore and Aravind K. Joshi. 1999. Supertagging: An approach to almost parsing. *Computational Linguistics*, 25(2).

John Canny, David Hall, and Dan Klein. 2013. A multi-teraflop constituency parser using gpus. *Architecture*, 3:3–5.

Ciprian Chelba, Tomas Mikolov, Mike Schuster, Qi Ge, Thorsten Brants, Phillipp Koehn, and Tony Robinson. 2013. One Billion Word Benchmark for Measuring Progress in Statistical Language Modeling. Technical report, Google.

Danqi Chen and Christopher D Manning. 2014. A Fast and Accurate Dependency Parser using Neural Networks. In *Proceedings of the 2014 Conference on Empirical Methods in Natural Language Processing (EMNLP)*, volume 1, pages 740–750.

Jinho D. Choi, Joel Tetreault, and Amanda Stent. 2015. It Depends: Dependency Parser Comparison Using A Web-based Evaluation Tool. In *Proceedings of the 53rd Annual Meeting of the Association for Computational Linguistics and the 7th International Joint Conference on Natural Language Processing (Volume 1: Long Papers)*, pages 387–396, Beijing, China, July. Association for Computational Linguistics.

Stephen Clark and James R Curran. 2007. Wide-coverage Efficient Statistical Parsing with CCG and Log-Linear Models. *Computational Linguistics*, 33(4).

Stephen Clark. 2002. Supertagging for Combinatory Categorial Grammar. In *Proceedings of the 6th International Workshop on Tree Adjoining Grammars and Related Frameworks (TAG+ 6)*, pages 19–24.

Greg Durrett and Dan Klein. 2015. Neural CRF Parsing. In *Proceedings of the Association for Computational Linguistics*.

Chris Dyer, Miguel Ballesteros, Wang Ling, Austin Matthews, and Noah A. Smith. 2015. Transition-based Dependency Parsing with Stack Long Short-Term Memory. In *Proc. ACL*.

Timothy AD Fowler and Gerald Penn. 2010. Accurate Context-free Parsing with Combinatory Categorial Grammar. In *Proceedings of the 48th Annual Meeting of the Association for Computational Linguistics*.

David Hall, Taylor Berg-Kirkpatrick, and Dan Klein. 2014. Sparser, better, faster gpu parsing. In *Proceedings of the 52nd Annual Meeting of the Association for Computational Linguistics (Volume 1: Long Papers)*, pages 208–217, Baltimore, Maryland, June. Association for Computational Linguistics.

Hua He, Jimmy Lin, and Adam Lopez. 2015. Gappy Pattern Matching on GPUs for On-Demand Extraction of Hierarchical Translation Grammars. *TACL*, 3:87–100.

James Henderson, Paola Merlo, Ivan Titov, and Gabriele Musillo. 2013. Multi-lingual Joint Parsing of Syntactic and Semantic Dependencies with a Latent Variable Model. *Computational Linguistics*.

Sepp Hochreiter and Jürgen Schmidhuber. 1997. Long Short-term Memory. *Neural computation*, 9(8):1735–1780.

Julia Hockenmaier and Mark Steedman. 2007. CCG-bank: a Corpus of CCG derivations and Dependency Structures Extracted from the Penn Treebank. *Computational Linguistics*, 33(3).

Julia Hockenmaier. 2003. *Data and models for statistical parsing with Combinatory Categorial Grammar*. Ph.D. thesis, University of Edinburgh. College of Science and Engineering. School of Informatics.

Mark Johnson. 2011. Parsing in Parallel on Multiple Cores and GPUs. In *Proceedings of the Australasian Language Technology Association Workshop 2011*, pages 29–37, Canberra, Australia, December.

Mike Lewis and Mark Steedman. 2014a. A* CCG Parsing with a Supertag-factored Model. In *Proceedings of the 2014 Conference on Empirical Methods in Natural Language Processing*.

Mike Lewis and Mark Steedman. 2014b. Improved CCG parsing with Semi-supervised Supertagging. *Transactions of the Association for Computational Linguistics*.

Mike Lewis, Luheng He, and Luke Zettlemoyer. 2015. Joint A* CCG Parsing and Semantic Role Labelling. In *Empirical Methods in Natural Language Processing*.

Wang Ling, Chris Dyer, Alan W. Black, Isabel Trancoso, Ramon Fermandez, Silvio Amir, Luís Marujo, and Tiago Luís. 2015. Finding function in form: Compositional character models for open vocabulary word representation. In *EMNLP*, pages 1520–1530. The Association for Computational Linguistics.

Ryan T McDonald, Joakim Nivre, Yvonne Quirmbach-Brundage, Yoav Goldberg, Dipanjan Das, Kuzman Ganchev, Keith B Hall, Slav Petrov, Hao Zhang, Oscar Täckström, et al. 2013. Universal Dependency Annotation for Multilingual Parsing. In *ACL (2)*, pages 92–97.

Laura Rimell and Stephen Clark. 2008. Adapting a Lexicalized-grammar Parser to Contrasting Domains. In *Proceedings of the Conference on Empirical Methods in Natural Language Processing*.

Richard Socher, John Bauer, Christopher D Manning, and Andrew Y Ng. 2013. Parsing with Compositional Vector Grammars. In *Proceedings of the ACL conference*.

Mark Steedman. 2000. *The Syntactic Process*. MIT Press.

Joseph Turian, Lev Ratinov, and Yoshua Bengio. 2010. Word representations: A Simple and General Method for Semi-supervised Learning. In *Proceedings of the 48th Annual Meeting of the Association for Computational Linguistics*.

Ashish Vaswani, Yonatan Bisk, Kenji Sagae, and Ryan Musa. 2016. Supertagging With LSTMs . In *Proceedings of the Human Language Technology Conference of the NAACL*.

Oriol Vinyals, Lukasz Kaiser, Terry Koo, Slav Petrov, Ilya Sutskever, and Geoffrey Hinton. 2015. Grammar as a Foreign Language. In *Advances in Neural Information Processing Systems*.

David Weiss, Chris Alberti, Michael Collins, and Slav Petrov. 2015. Structured Training for Neural Network Transition-Based Parsing. In *Proceedings of ACL 2015*, pages 323–333.

Wenduan Xu, Stephen Clark, and Yue Zhang. 2014. Shift-Reduce CCG Parsing with a Dependency Model. In *Proceedings of the 52nd Annual Meeting of the Association for Computational Linguistics (ACL 2014)*.

Wenduan Xu, Michael Auli, and Stephen Clark. 2015. CCG Supertagging with a Recurrent Neural Network. *Volume 2: Short Papers*, page 250.

Wenduan Xu, Michael Auli, and Stephen Clark. 2016. Shift-Reduce CCG Parsing with Recurrent Neural Networks and Expected F-Measure Training. In *Proceedings of the Human Language Technology Conference of the NAACL*.

Youngmin Yi, Chao-Yue Lai, Slav Petrov, and Kurt Keutzer. 2011. Efficient parallel cky parsing on gpus. In *Proceedings of the 12th International Conference on Parsing Technologies*, IWPT '11, pages 175–185, Stroudsburg, PA, USA. Association for Computational Linguistics.

Yue Zhang and Stephen Clark. 2011. Shift-reduce CCG Parsing. In *Proceedings of the 49th Annual Meeting of the Association for Computational Linguistics: Human Language Technologies-Volume 1*.

Supertagging with LSTMs

Ashish Vaswani[1], Yonatan Bisk[1], Kenji Sagae[2], and Ryan Musa[3]
[1]University of Southern California, [2]Kitt.ai
[3]University of Illinois at Urbana-Champaign
vaswani@usc.edu, ybisk@isi.edu
sagae@kitt.ai, ramusa2@illinois.edu

Abstract

In this paper we present new state-of-the-art performance on CCG supertagging and parsing. Our model outperforms existing approaches by an absolute gain of 1.5%. We analyze the performance of several neural models and demonstrate that while feed-forward architectures can compete with bidirectional LSTMs on POS tagging, models that encode the complete sentence are necessary for the long range syntactic information encoded in supertags.

1 Introduction

Morphosyntactic labels for words are commonly used in a variety of NLP applications. For this reason, part-of-speech (POS) tagging and supertagging have drawn significant attention from the community. Combinatory Categorial Grammar is a lexicalized grammar formalism that is widely used for syntactic and semantic parsing. Supertagging (Clark, 2002; Bangalore and Joshi, 2010) assigns complex syntactic labels to words to enable fast and accurate parsing. The disambiguation of correctly labeling a word with one of over 1,200 CCG labels is difficult compared to choosing on of the 45 POS labels in the Penn Treebank (Marcus et al., 1993). In addition to the large label space of CCG supertags, labeling a word correctly depends on knowledge of syntactic phenomena arbitrarily far in the sentence (Hockenmaier and Steedman, 2007). This is because supertags encode highly specific syntactic information (e.g. types and locations of arguments) about a word's usage in a sentence.

In this paper, we show that Bidirectional Long Short-Term Memory recurrent neural networks (bi–LSTMs) (Graves, 2013; Zaremba et al., 2014), which can use information from the entire sentence,

are a natural and powerful architecture for CCG supertagging. In addition to the bi–LSTM, we create a simple yet novel model that outperforms the previous state-of-the-art RNN model that uses hand-crafted features (Xu et al., 2015) by 1.5%. Concurrent to this work (Lewis et al., 2016) introduced a different training methodology for bi-LSTM for supertagging. We provide a detailed analysis of the quality of various LSTM architectures, forward, backward, and bi-directional, shedding light over the ability of the bi–LSTM to exploit rich sentential context necessary for performing supertagging. We also show that a baseline feed-forward neural network (NN) architecture significantly outperforms previous feed-forward NN baselines, with slightly fewer features, achieving better accuracy than the RNN model from (Xu et al., 2015).

Recently, bi–LSTMs have achieved high accuracies in a simpler sequence labeling task: part-of-speech tagging (Wang et al., 2015; Ling et al., 2015) on the Penn treebank, with small improvements over local models. However, we achieve strong accuracies compared to (Wang et al., 2015) using feed-forward neural network model trained on local context, showing that this task does not require bi–LSTMs. Our strong feed-forward NN baselines show the power of feed-forward NNs for some tasks.

Our main contributions are the introduction of a new bi–LSTM model for CCG supertagging that achieves state-of-the-art, on both CCG supertagging and parsing, and a detailed analysis of our results, including a comparison of bi–LSTMs and simpler feed forward NN models for supertagging and POS tagging, which suggests that the added complexity of bi–LSTMs may not be necessary for POS tagging, where local contexts suffice to a much greater extent than in supertagging.

Proceedings of NAACL-HLT 2016, pages 232–237,
San Diego, California, June 12-17, 2016. ©2016 Association for Computational Linguistics

2 Models And Training

We use feed-forward neural network models and bidirectional LSTM (bi–LSTM) based models in this work.

2.1 Feed-Forward

For both POS tagging and our baseline supertagging model, we use feed-forward neural networks with two hidden layers of rectified linear units (Nair and Hinton, 2010). For supertagging, we use a slightly smaller set than Lewis and Steedman (2014a), using a left and right 3-word window with suffix and capitalization features for the center word. However, unlike them, we train on the full set of supertag categories observed during training.

In POS tagging, when tagging word w_i, we consider only features from a window of five words, with w_i at the center. For each w_j with $i - 2 \le j \le i + 2$, we add w_j lowercased and a string that encodes the basic "word shape" of w_j. This is computed by replacing all sequences of uppercase letters with A, all sequences of lowercase letters with a, all sequences of digits with 9, and all sequences of other characters with $*$. Finally, we add two and three letter suffixes and two letter prefix for w_i only.

2.2 LSTM models

We experiment with two kinds of bi–LSTM models. We train a basic bi–LSTM where the forward and backward LSTMs take input words w_i and produce hidden state $\overrightarrow{h}_i$ and $\overleftarrow{h}_i$. For each position, we produce $\tilde{h}_i$, where

$$\tilde{h}_i = \sigma(W_{\overleftarrow{h}} \overleftarrow{h}_i^T + W_{\overrightarrow{h}} \overrightarrow{h}_i^T), \qquad (1)$$

where $\sigma(x) = \max(0, x)$ is a rectifier nonlinearity, and where $W_{\overleftarrow{h}}$ and $W_{\overrightarrow{h}}$ are parameters to be learned. The unnormalized likelihood of an output supertag is computed using supertag embeddings D_{t_i} and biases b_{t_i} as $p(t_i \mid \tilde{h}_i) = D_{t_i} \tilde{h}_i^T + b_{t_i}$. The final softmax layer computes normalized supertag probabilities.

Although bidirectional LSTMs can capture long distance interactions between words, each output label is predicted independently. To explicitly model supertag interactions, our next model combines two models, the bi–LSTM and a LSTM language model (LM) over the supertags (Figure 1). At position

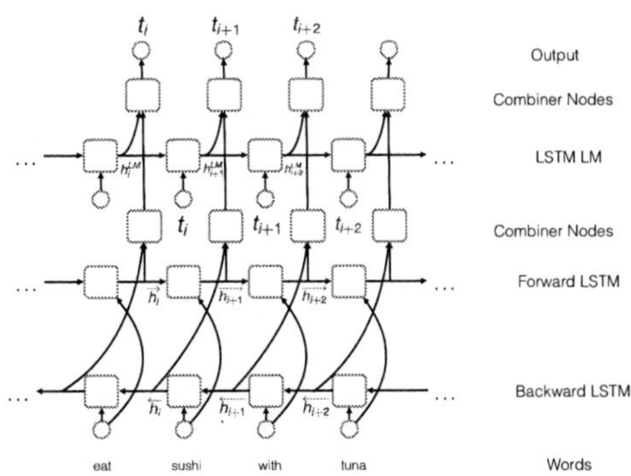

Figure 1: We add a language model between supertags.

i, the LM accepts an input supertag t_{i-1} producing hidden state h_i^{LM}, and a second combiner layer, parametrized by matrices W_{LM} and $W_{\tilde{h}}$ transforms $\tilde{h}_i$ and h_i^{LM} to h_i similar to the combiner for $\tilde{h}_i$ (Equation 1). Output supertag probabilities are computed just as before, replacing replacing $\tilde{h}_i$ with h_i. We refer to this model as bi–LSTM–LM. For all our LSTM models, we only use words as input features.

2.3 Training

We train our models to maximize the log-likelihood of the data with minibatch gradient ascent. Gradients of the models are computed with backpropagation (Chauvin and Rumelhart, 1995). Since gold supertags are available during training time and not while decoding, a bi–LSTM–LM trained on gold supertags might not recover from errors caused by using incorrectly predicted supertags. This results in the bi–LSTM–LM slightly underperforming the bi–LSTM (we refer to training with gold supertags as g–train in Table 1). To bridge this gap between training and testing we also experiment with a sampling training regime in addition to training.

Scheduled sampling: Following (Bengio et al., 2015; Ranzato et al., 2015), for each output token, with some probability p, we use the most likely predicted supertag ($arg\ max_{t_i} P(t_i \mid h_i)$) from the model in position $i-1$ as input to the supertag LSTM LM in position i and use the gold supertag with probability $1 - p$. We denote this training as ss–train–1. We also experiment with using the 5-best previous predicted supertags from the output distribution at position $i - 1$ and feed them to the LM as input in position i as a bit vector. Additionally, we

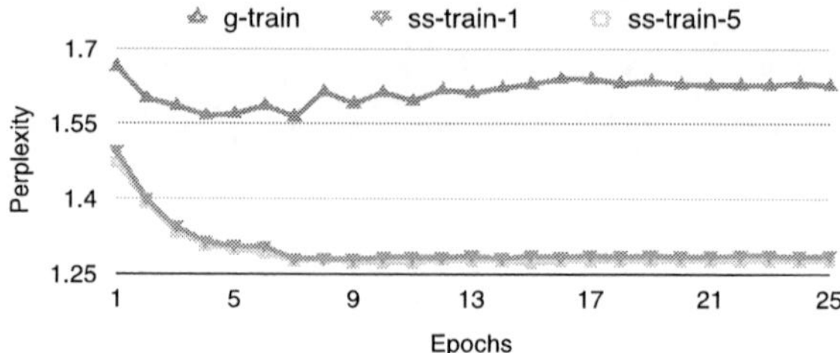

Figure 2: Scheduled sampling improves the perplexity of the gold sequence under predicted tags. We see that the perplexity of the gold supertag sequence when using predicted tags for the LM is lower for ss–train–1 and ss–train–5 than with g–train.

use their probabilities (re-normalized over the 5-best tags) and scale the input supertag embeddings with their re-normalized probability during look-up. We refer to this setting as ss–train–5. In this work, we use an inverse sigmoid schedule to compute p,

$$p = \frac{k}{k + e^{\frac{s}{k}}},$$

where s is the epoch number and k is a hyperparameter that is tuned.[1] In Figure 2, we see that for the development set training with scheduled sampling improves the perplexity of the gold supertag sequence when using predicted supertags, indicating better recovery from conditioning on erroneous supertags. For both ss-train and g-train, we use gold supertags for the output layer and train the model to maximize the log-likelihood of the data.[2]

2.4 Architectures

Our feed-forward models use 2048 rectifier units in the first hidden layer, 50 and 128 rectifier units in the second hidden layer for POS tagging and Supertagging respectively, and 64 dim. input embeddings.

Our LSTM based models use 512 hidden states. We pre-train our word embeddings with a 7-gram feed-forward neural language model using the NPLM toolkit[3] on a concatenation of the BLLIP corpus (Charniak et al., 2000) and WSJ sections 02–21 of the Penn Treebank.

---

[1] The reader should refer to (Bengio et al., 2015) for details.

[2] We use dropout for all our feed-forward (Srivastava, 2013) and bi-LSTM based models (Zaremba et al., 2014). We carry out a grid search over dropout probabilities and sampling schedules. We train the LSTMs for 25 epochs and the feed-forward models for 30 epochs, tuning on the development data.

[3] http://nlg.isi.edu/software/nplm/

Model	Supertag Accuracy			
	All	Seen	Novel	% P
Lewis et al. (2014)	91.30			
Wenduan et al. (2015)	93.07			
Feed Forward + g–train	93.29	93.77	**91.53**	70.3
Forward LSTM + g–train	83.70	85.76	46.22	20.7
Backward LSTM + g–train	88.82	90.06	66.22	40.6
bi–LSTM	94.08	95.03	76.36	81.1
bi–LSTM–LM + g–train	93.89	94.93	76.83	96.5
bi–LSTM–LM + ss–train–1	**94.24**	**95.22**	76.70	87.8
bi–LSTM–LM + ss–train–5	94.23	95.20	76.62	94.5

Table 1: Accuracies on the development section. The language model provides a boost in performance, and large gains on the parseability of the sequence (%P). The numbers for bi–LSTM–LM + ss–train–1 and + g–train are with beam decoding. All others use greedy decoding. Interestingly, greedy decoding with ss–train–5 works as well as beam decoding with ss–train–1.

2.5 Decoding

We perform greedy decoding. For each position i, we select the most probable supertag from the output distribution. For the bi–LSTM–LM models trained with g–train and ss–train–1, we feed the most likely supertag from the output distribution as LM input in the next position. We decode with beam search (size 12) for bi–LSTM–LMs trained with g–train and ss–train–1. For the bi–LSTM–LMs trained with ss–train–5, we perform greedy decoding similar to training, feeding the k-best supertags from the output supertag distribution in position $i - 1$ as input to the LM in position i, along with the renormalized probabilities. We don't perform beam decoding for ss–train–5, as the previous k-best inputs already capture different paths through the network.[4]

3 Data

For supertagging, experiments were run with the standard splits of CCGbank. Unlike previous work no features were extracted for the LSTM models and rare categories were not thresholded. Words were lowercased and digits replaced with @.

CCGbank's training section contains 1,284 lexical categories (394 in Dev). The distribution of categories has a long tail, with only a third of those cate-

---

[4] Code and supertags for our models can be downloaded here: `https://bitbucket.org/ashish_vaswani/lstm_supertagger`

Supertag	F-For	Forward	Backward	bi–LSTM	+LM(g–train)	ss–train–1	ss–train–5
(NP\NP)/NP	90.00	88.89	81.91	92.09	92.18	91.72	**92.31**
((S\NP)\(S\NP))/NP	75.75	69.53	61.60	**80.38**	78.21	79.91	78.77
S[dcl]\NP	77.29	61.14	58.52	**84.28**	83.41	82.97	80.35
(S[dcl]\NP)/NP	91.39	56.58	69.86	92.34	92.46	92.46	**92.82**
((S[dcl]\NP)/PP)/NP	42.30	30.77	42.31	56.41	**64.10**	62.82	60.26
(S[dcl]\NP)/(S[adj]\NP)	86.80	22.84	83.25	87.31	**88.83**	87.82	86.80
((S[dcl]\NP)/(S[to]\NP))/NP	86.49	56.76	75.68	**94.59**	91.89	91.89	91.89

The header spans an "LSTM" label over the bi–LSTM, +LM(g–train), ss–train–1, ss–train–5 columns.

Table 2: Prediction accuracy for our models on several common and difficult supertags.

	Architecture	Test Acc
Ling et al. (2015)	Bi-LSTM	97.36
Wang et al. (2015)	Bi-LSTM	97.78
Søgaard (2011)	SCNN	97.50
This work	Feed-Forward	97.40

Table 3: Our new POS tagging results show a strong Feed-Forward baseline can perform as well as or better than more sophisticated models (e.g. Bi-LSTMs).

	Dev F1	Test F1
Wenduan et al. (2015)	86.25	87.04
+ new POS Tags & C&C	86.99	87.50
bi–LSTM–LM +ss–train–1	**87.75**	**88.32**

Table 4: Parsing at 100% coverage with our new Feed-Forward POS tagger and the Java implementation of C&C. We show both the published and improved results for Wenduan et al.

gories having a frequency count ≥ 10 (the threshold used by existing literature). Following (Lewis and Steedman, 2014b), we allow the model to predict all categories for a word, not just those with which the word was observed to co-occur in the training data. Accuracies on these unseen (word, cat) pairs are presented in the third column of Table 1.

4 Results

Table 3 presents our Feed-Forward POS tagging results. We achieve 97.28% on the development set and 97.4% on test. Although slightly below state-of-the-art, we approach existing work with bi–LSTMs, and our models are much simpler and faster to train.[5]

Table 1 shows a steady increase in performance as the model is provided additional context. The forward and backward models are presented with information that may be arbitrarily far away in the sentence, but only in a specific direction. This yields weaker results than the Feed Forward model which can see in both directions within a small window. The real gains are achieved by the Bidirectional LSTM which incorporates knowledge from the entire sentence. Our addition of a language model and changes to training, further improve the perfor-

mance. Our final model (bi–LSTM–LM+ss–train–1 model with beam decoding) has a test accuracy of 94.5%, 1.5% above state-of-the-art.

4.1 Parsing

Our primary goal in this paper was to demonstrate how a bi–LSTM captures new and different information from uni-directional or feed-forward approaches. This advantage also translates to gains in parsing. Table 4 presents new state-of-the-art parsing results for both (Xu et al., 2015) and our bi–LSTM–LM +ss–train–1. These results were attained using our part-of-speech tags (Table 3) and the Java implementation (Clark et al., 2015) of the C&C parser (Clark and Curran, 2007)[6].

4.2 Error Analysis

Our analysis indicates that the information following a word is more informative than what preceded it. Table 2 compares how well our models recover common and syntactically interesting supertags. In particular, the Forward and Backward models, motivate the need for a Bi-directional approach.

---

[5]We use train, dev, and test splits of WSJ sections 00–18, 19–21, and 22–24, for POS tagging.

[6]Results are presented on the standard development and test splits (Section 00 and 23), and with a beam threshold of 10^{-6}. For a fair comparison to prior work we report results without the skimmer, so no partial credit is given to parse failures. The skimmer boosts performance to 87.91/88.39 for Dev and Test.

	$(S[dcl]\backslash NP)/(S[adj]\backslash NP)$	
Forward	**Backward**	**Bidirectional**
$((S[dcl]\backslash NP)/PP)/(S[adj]\backslash NP)$	$((S[dcl]\backslash NP)/PP)/(S[adj]\backslash NP)$	$(S[dcl]\backslash NP)/(S[pss]\backslash NP)$
$((S[dcl]\backslash NP)/(S[to]\backslash NP))/(S[adj]\backslash NP)$	$((S[b]\backslash NP)\backslash NP)/(S[adj]\backslash NP)$	$(S[dcl]\backslash NP)/PP/(S[adj]\backslash NP)$
$((S[dcl]\backslash NP)/PP)/PP$	$(S[dcl]\backslash S[qem])/(S[adj]\backslash NP)$	$(S[b]\backslash NP)\backslash NP/(S[adj]\backslash NP)$
$(S[dcl]\backslash NP)/S$	$((S[dcl]\backslash NP)/(S[to]\backslash NP))/(S[adj]\backslash NP)$	$(S[dcl]\backslash NP)/(S[to]\backslash NP))/(S[adj]\backslash NP)$
$(S[dcl]\backslash NP)/(S[pss]\backslash NP)$	$((S[dcl]\backslash NP)/(S[adj]\backslash NP))/(S[adj]\backslash NP)$	$(S[dcl]\backslash NP)/(S[adj]\backslash NP))/(S[adj]\backslash NP)$

Table 5: "Neighbor" categories as determined by embedding-based vector similarity for each class of model. As expected for this category, the Backward model captures the argument preference while the Forward model correctly predicts the result.

The first two rows show prepositional phrase attachment decisions (noun and verb attaching categories are in rows one and two, respectively). Here the forward model outperforms the backward model, presumably because knowing the word to be modified and the preposition, is more important than observing the object of the prepositional phrase (the information available to the backward model).

Conversely, the backward model outperforms the forward model in most of the remaining categories. (Di-)transitive verbs (lines 4 & 5) require knowledge of future arguments in the sentence (e.g. separated by a relative clause). Because English has strict SVO word-order, the presence of a subject is more predictable than the presence of an (in-)direct object. It is therefore not surprising that the backward model is often comparable to the Feed Forward model.

If the information missing from either the forward or backward models were local, the bidirectional model should perform the same as the Feed-Forward model, instead it surpasses it, often by a large margin. This implies there is long range information necessary for choosing a supertag.

Embeddings In addition, we can visualize the information captured by our models by investigating a category's nearest neighbors based on the learned embeddings. Table 5 shows nearest neighbor categories for $(S[dcl]\backslash NP)/(S[adj]\backslash NP)$ under the Forward, Backward, and Bidirectional models.

We see see that the forward model learns internal structure with the query category, but the list of arguments is nearly random. In contrast, the backward model clusters categories primarily based on the final argument, perhaps sharing similarities in the subject argument only because of the predictable SVO nature of English text. However, due to its lack of forward context the model incorrectly associates categories with less-common first arguments (e.g. $S[qem]$). Finally, the bidirectional embeddings appear to cleanly capture the strengths of both the forward and backward models.

Consistency and Internal Structure Because supertags are highly structured their co-occurence in a sentence must be permitted by the combinators of CCG. Without encoding this explicitly, the language model dramatically increases the percent of predicted sequences that result in a valid parse by up to 15% (last column of Table 2).

Sparsity One consideration of our approach is that we do not threshold rare categories or use any tag dictionaries; our models are presented with the full space of CCG categories, despite the long tail. This did not did not hurt performance and the models learned to successfully use several categories which were outside the set of traditionally-thresholded frequent categories. Additionally, the total number of categories used correctly at least once by the bidirectional models was substantially higher than the other models ($\sim$270 vs. $\sim$220 of 394), though the large number of unused categories ($\geq$120) indicates that there is still substantial room for improvement.

5 Conclusions and Future Work

Because bi–LSTMs with a language model encode an entire sentence at decision time, we demonstrated large gains in supertagging and parsing. Future work will investigate improving performance on rare categories.

Acknowledgements

This work was supported by the U.S. DARPA LORELEI Program No. HR0011-15-C-0115. We would like to thank Wenduan Xu for his help.

References

Srinivas Bangalore and Aravind K. Joshi. 2010. *Supertagging: Using Complex Lexical Descriptions in Natural Language Processing*. The MIT Press.

Samy Bengio, Oriol Vinyals, Navdeep Jaitly, and Noam Shazeer. 2015. Scheduled sampling for sequence prediction with recurrent neural networks. In *Advances in Neural Information Processing Systems*, pages 1171–1179.

Eugene Charniak, Don Blaheta, Niyu Ge, Keith Hall, John Hale, and Mark Johnson. 2000. Bllip 1987-89 wsj corpus release 1. *Linguistic Data Consortium, Philadelphia*, 36.

Yves Chauvin and David E Rumelhart. 1995. *Backpropagation: theory, architectures, and applications*. Psychology Press.

Stephen Clark and James Curran. 2007. Wide-Coverage Efficient Statistical Parsing with CCG and Log-Linear Models. *Computational Linguistics*, 33(4):493–552.

Stephen Clark, Darren Foong, Luana Bulat, and Wenduan Xu. 2015. The Java Version of the C&C Parser: Version 0.95. Technical report, University of Cambridge Computer Laboratory, August.

Stephen Clark. 2002. Supertagging for combinatory categorial grammar. In *Proceedings of the 6th International Workshop on Tree Adjoining Grammars and Related Formalisms (TAG+6)*, pages 19–24.

A. Graves. 2013. Generating sequences with recurrent neural networks. *arXiv preprint arXiv:1308.0850*.

Julia Hockenmaier and Mark Steedman. 2007. CCGbank: A Corpus of CCG Derivations and Dependency Structures Extracted from the Penn Treebank. *Computational Linguistics*, 33:355–396, September.

Mike Lewis and Mark Steedman. 2014a. A* ccg parsing with a supertag-factored model. In *Proceedings of the Conference on Empirical Methods in Natural Language Processing (EMNLP-2014)*.

Mike Lewis and Mark Steedman. 2014b. Improved ccg parsing with semi-supervised supertagging. *Transactions of the Association for Computational Linguistics*, 2:327–338.

Mike Lewis, Kenton Lee, and Luke Zettlemoyer. 2016. LSTM CCG Parsing. In *Proceedings of the 15th Annual Conference of the North American Chapter of the Association for Computational Linguistics*.

Wang Ling, Tiago Luís, Luís Marujo, Ramón Fernandez Astudillo, Silvio Amir, Chris Dyer, Alan W Black, and Isabel Trancoso. 2015. Finding function in form: Compositional character models for open vocabulary word representation. *arXiv preprint arXiv:1508.02096*.

Mitchell P Marcus, Beatrice Santorini, and Mary Ann Marcinkiewicz. 1993. Building a Large Annotated Corpus of English: The Penn Treebank. *Computational Linguistics*, 19:313–330, June.

Vinod Nair and Geoffrey E. Hinton. 2010. Rectified linear units improve restricted Boltzmann machines. In *Proceedings of ICML*, pages 807–814.

Marc'Aurelio Ranzato, Sumit Chopra, Michael Auli, and Wojciech Zaremba. 2015. Sequence Level Training with Recurrent Neural Networks. *arXiv preprint arXiv:1511.06732*.

Anders Søgaard. 2011. Semisupervised condensed nearest neighbor for part-of-speech tagging. In *Proceedings of the 49th Annual Meeting of the Association for Computational Linguistics: Human Language Technologies: short papers-Volume 2*, pages 48–52. Association for Computational Linguistics.

Nitish Srivastava. 2013. *Improving neural networks with dropout*. Ph.D. thesis, University of Toronto.

Peilu Wang, Yao Qian, Frank K Soong, Lei He, and Hai Zhao. 2015. Part-of-speech tagging with bidirectional long short-term memory recurrent neural network. *arXiv preprint arXiv:1510.06168*.

Wenduan Xu, Michael Auli, and Stephen Clark. 2015. Ccg supertagging with a recurrent neural network. *Volume 2: Short Papers*, page 250.

W. Zaremba, I. Sutskever, and O. Vinyals. 2014. Recurrent neural network regularization. *arXiv preprint arXiv:1409.2329*.

An Empirical Study of Automatic Chinese Word Segmentation for Spoken Language Understanding and Named Entity Recognition

Wencan Luo[*]
University of Pittsburgh
Pittsburgh, PA 15260
wencan@cs.pitt.edu

Fan Yang
Nuance Communications, Inc.
Seattle, WA 98104
fan.yang@nuance.com

Abstract

Word segmentation is usually recognized as the first step for many Chinese natural language processing tasks, yet its impact on these subsequent tasks is relatively under-studied. For example, how to solve the *mismatch* problem when applying an existing word segmenter to new data? Does a better word segmenter yield a better subsequent NLP task performance? In this work, we conduct an initial attempt to answer these questions on two related subsequent tasks: semantic slot filling in spoken language understanding and named entity recognition. We propose three techniques to solve the mismatch problem: using word segmentation outputs as additional features, adaptation with partial-learning and taking advantage of n-best word segmentation list. Experimental results demonstrate the effectiveness of these techniques for both tasks and we achieve an error reduction of about 11% for spoken language understanding and 24% for named entity recognition over the baseline systems.

1 Introduction

Unlike English text in which sentences are sequences of words separated by white spaces, in Chinese text (as are some other languages including Arabic, Japanese, etc.), sentences are represented as strings of characters without similar natural delimiters. Therefore, it is generally claimed that the first step in a Chinese language processing task is to identify the sequence of words in a sentence and mark

boundaries in appropriate places, which is refereed to as the task of Chinese Word Segmentation (CWS).

(1) Input: 能穿多少穿多少
　　CWS 1: 能|穿|多少|穿|多少[1]
　　　　　(Put on as **much** clothes as possible.)
　　CWS 2: 能|穿|多|少|穿|多|少
　　　　　(Put on as **little** clothes as possible.)

Word segmentations in Chinese text do reduce ambiguities. In the example (1), the same span of text (the input) can convey entirely opposite meanings (the English sentences in parentheses) depending on how word boundaries (CWS 1 and CWS 2) are labeled. Therefore, it is generally believed that more accurate word segmentations should benefit more the subsequent Chinese language processing tasks, such as part-of-speech tagging, named entity recognition, etc. There has been quite a number of research in the field of CWS to improve segmentation accuracy, yet its impact on the subsequent processing is relatively under-studied. Chang et al. (2008) explore how word segmentation improves machine translation; and Ni and Leung (2014) explore how word segmentation impacts automatic speech recognition yet do not have conclusive findings. In this research, we aim to better understand how CWS benefits the subsequent NLP tasks, using semantic slot filling in spoken language understanding (SLU) and named entity recognition (NER) as two case studies.

In particular, we investigate the impact of Chinese word segmentation in three different situations.

---

[*]Work done at Nuance during an internship.

[1]We use '|' to indicate a word boundary. Example is borrowed and revised from (Chen et al., 2015).

Proceedings of NAACL-HLT 2016, pages 238–248,
San Diego, California, June 12-17, 2016. ©2016 Association for Computational Linguistics

First, assuming domain data (the data for a particular subsequent task, e.g. SLU or NER) having no word boundary annotation (§4), we can apply word segmenters trained with publicly-available data to the domain data to get the word boundary. However, existing word segmenters may have a domain mismatch problem due to the fact that they may have different genre from the subsequent task and are usually segmented with different standards (Huang and Zhao, 2007). Therefore, we propose three techniques to solve this problem. Note, these techniques can be used together.

1) We use word segmentation outputs as additional features in subsequent tasks (§3.2), which is more robust against error propagation than using segmented word units.

2) We adapt existing word segmenters with partially-labeled data derived from the subsequent task training data (§3.3), further improving the end-to-end performance.

3) We take advantage of the n-best list of word segmentation outputs (§3.4), making the subsequent task less sensitive to word segmentation errors.

Second, assuming domain training data (e.g., NER) is already segmented with word boundary (§5), we are able to train a domain word segmenter with the data itself and apply it to the testing data. This allows us to see the differences between a word segmenter trained with in-domain data and one trained with publicly-available data.

Last, assuming both domain training and testing data have word boundary information (§5), it allows to explore the upper bound performance of the subsequent task with a perfect word segmenter.

Experimental results show that the proposed techniques do improve the end-to-end performance and we achieve an error rate reduction of 11% for SLU and 24% for NER over their corresponding baseline systems. In addition, we found that even a word segmenter that is only moderately reliable is still able to improve the end-to-end performance, and a word segmenter trained with in-domain data is not necessarily better compared to a word segmenter trained with out-domain data in terms of the end-to-end performance.

2 Related Work

Word segmentation has received steady attention over the past two decades. People have shown that models trained with limited text can have a reasonable accuracy (Li and Sun, 2009; Zhang et al., 2013a; Li et al., 2013; Cheng et al., 2015). However, the fact is that none of existing algorithms is robust enough to reliably segment unfamiliar types of texts without fine-tuning (Huang et al., 2007). Several approaches have proposed to eliminate this issue, for example the use of unlabeled data (Sun and Xu, 2011; Wang et al., 2011; Zhang et al., 2013b) and partially-labeled data (Yang and Vozila, 2014; Takahasi and Mori, 2015). In our work, we encounter the same issue when applying word segmentation to the subsequent tasks and thus we propose three approaches to solve this problem.

Word segmentation has been applied in several subsequent tasks, e.g. NER (Zhai et al., 2004), information retrieval (Peng et al., 2002), automatic speech recognition (Ni and Leung, 2014), machine translation (Xu et al., 2008; Chang et al., 2008; Zhang et al., 2008; Zeng et al., 2014), etc. In general, there are two types of approaches to utilize word segmentation in subsequent tasks: *pipeline* and *joint-learning*. The pipeline approach creates word segmentation first and then feeds the segmented words into subsequent task(s). It is straightforward, but suffers from error propagation since an incorrect word segmentation would cause an error in the subsequent task. The joint-learning approach trains a model to learn both word segmentation and the subsequent task(s) at the same time. A number of subsequent tasks have been unified into joint models, including disambiguation (Wang et al., 2012), part-of-speech tagging (Jiang et al., 2008a; Jiang et al., 2008b; Zhang and Clark, 2010; Sun, 2011), NER (Gao et al., 2005; Xu et al., 2014; Peng and Dredze, 2015), and parsing (Hatori et al., 2012; Qian and Liu, 2012). However, the joint-learning process generally assumes the availability of manual word segmentations for the training data, which limits the use of this approach. Thus in this work, we focus on the pipeline approach, but instead of feeding the segmented words, we use word segmentation results as additional features in the subsequent tasks, which is more robust against error propagation.

3 Applying CWS to Subsequent Tasks

In this section, we describe how to integrate word segmentation information when domain data having no word boundary information, using SLU and NER as two case studies.

We first introduce the baseline system, and then describe the techniques that we propose to solve the domain mismatch problem when applying automatic CWS to the subsequent NLP tasks.

3.1 Baseline system

Both of the SLU and NER can be formulated as sequence labeling tasks, and can be solved using machine learning techniques such as Conditional Random Field (CRF), Recurrent Neural Network, or their combinations (Wan et al., 2011; Mesnil et al., 2015; Rondeau and Su, 2015). We adopt the tool wapiti (Lavergne et al., 2010), which is an implementation of CRF. In the baseline system, each Chinese character is treated as a labeling unit. Here is an example of our training sentences for SLU:'三|division 元|division 里|division 莫|street 干|street 山|street 路|street 周|locref 围|locref 的|unk 餐|query 厅|query' (Find the restaurants near Sanyuanli Mogan Mountain road). The input features for training the baseline CRF model are character ngrams in the K-window and label bigrams. For computational efficiency, we use trigram within 5-character window. Given the current character c_0, we extract the following character ngram features: c_{-2}, c_{-1}, c_0, c_1, c_2, $c_{-2}c_{-1}$, $c_{-1}c_0$, c_0c_1, c_1c_2, $c_{-2}c_{-1}c_0$, $c_{-1}c_0c_1$, and $c_0c_1c_2$.

3.2 Using CWS as features

When word segmentation information is not available within the domain data, we can use publicly-available corpora such as the Chinese Tree Bank (Levy and Manning, 2003), to train an automatic word segmenter.

A dominant approach for supervised CWS is to formulate it as a character sequence labeling problem, and label each character with its location in a word (Xue, 2003). A popular labeling scheme is 'BIES': 'B' for the beginning character of a word, 'I' for the internal characters, 'E' for the ending character, and 'S' for single-character word. Following (Yang and Vozila, 2014), we train our au-

tomatic word segmenter with CRF using the input features of character unigrams and bigrams, consecutive character equivalence, separated character equivalence, punctuation, character sequence pattern, anchor of word unigram and bigram. This word segmenter achieves state-of-the-art or comparable performance.

A straightforward way to integrate word segmentation is the traditional pipeline approach. It uses word segmentation first and feeds the segmented words to subsequent task(s), named as **Word Unit**. However, this method suffers from the error propagation problem since an incorrect word segmentation would cause an error in the subsequent task. Therefore, we proposed to use word segmentation outputs as additional features (**As Features**) in the subsequent tasks, as introduced below. We hypothesize the **As Features** is less sensitive to word segmentation errors since the CRF model can still rely on the character features when a word segmentation is not perfect.

Word Unit We can use segmented words instead of characters as labeling units for the CRF learning. During training we can run *forced-decoding* (Lavergne et al., 2010) on word segmentation so that word boundaries are consistent with semantic slot or named entity boundaries. During testing we simply apply the word segmenter to the sentences.

As Features We can still keep using characters as the labeling units, but add the word segmentation information as additional features. Given the current character c_0 and word segmentation output represented as 'BIES' tag t_0, we extract the character ngram features together with the following word segmentation tag ngram features: t_{-2}, t_{-1}, t_0, t_1, t_2, $t_{-2}t_{-1}$, $t_{-1}t_0$, t_0t_1, t_1t_2, $t_{-2}t_{-1}t_0$, $t_{-1}t_0t_1$, and $t_0t_1t_2$. The tag ngram features provide word segmentation information indirectly. For example, t_0t_1='BE' indicates c_0 initiates a two-character word, while $t_0t_1t_2$='BII' means that c_0 is probably a beginning of a long word.

3.3 Adaptation with Partial-learning

The publicly-available corpora for word segmentation, however, may create a domain-mismatch prob-

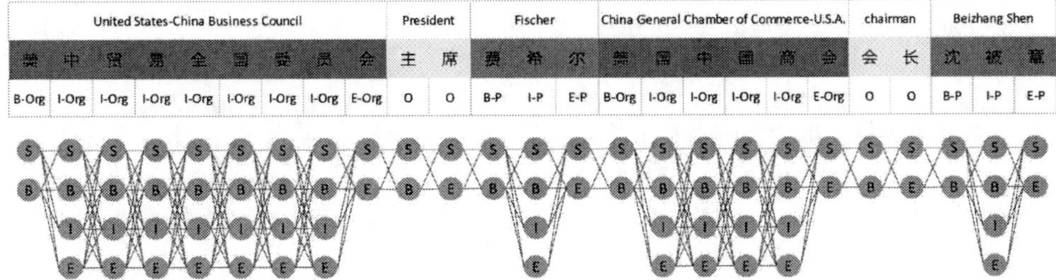

Figure 1: Partially-labeled word segmentations derived from named entity labels. The first character in a name ('美' in the organization name '美中贸易全国委员会') can only be labeled as 'S' or 'B', while the last one ('会') can only be labeled as 'S' or 'E'; similarly, a character after a name ('主') can only be labeled as 'S' or 'B', while a character before a slot ('席') can only be labeled as 'S' or 'E'.

lem (especially for the SLU data). First, these corpora tend to be news articles and thus have different genre in content. Second, these corpora are usually segmented with different standards (Huang and Zhao, 2007) and it is unclear which one would serve the purpose of the subsequent task.

Even if the NER/SLU task training data is not word segmented, the semantic slot and named entity labels actually provide valuable information on word boundaries. As illustrated in Fig. 1, the first character in an organization/person/location name can only be labeled as 'S' or 'B', while the last one can only be labeled as 'S' or 'E'; similarly, a character after a name can only be labeled as 'S' or 'B', while a character before a name can only be labeled as 'S' or 'E'. We can thus create partially-labeled CWS data from SLU and NER labels. These partially-labeled data can then be used to adapt the out-of-domain word segmenter trained from publicly-available corpus.

Täckström et al. (2013) propose the approach *partial-label learning* to learn from partially-labeled data, and Yang and Vozila (2014) apply it to Chinese word segmentation. In partial-label training, each item in the sequence receives multiple labels, and each sequence has a lattice constraint, as shown in Fig. 1. The basic idea is to marginalize the probability mass of the constrained lattice in a cost function. The marginal probability of the lattice is defined as Equation 1, where C denotes the input character sequence, L denotes the label sequence, and $\hat{Y}(C, \tilde{L})$ denotes the constrained lattice (with regard to the input sequence C and the partial-labels $\tilde{L}$).

$$p_\theta(\hat{Y}(C, \tilde{L})|C) = \sum_{L \in \hat{Y}(C,\tilde{L})} p_\theta(L|C) \quad (1)$$

The optimization objective function is to maximize the log-likelihood of the training set, in which likelihood is calculated via the probability mass of the constrained lattice, as shown in Equation 2. Here n denotes the number of sentences in the training set.

$$L(\theta) = \sum_{i=1}^{n} \log p_\theta(\hat{Y}(C_i, \tilde{L}_i)|C_i) \quad (2)$$

With CRF[2], a gradient-based approach such as L-BFGS can be used to optimize Equation 2. We expect that this adaptation process should help to provide better word segmentation information that further improves the subsequent task performance.

3.4 N-best CWS

Only using the best word segmentation output as features for the subsequent tasks might not be sufficient (as we will show in our experiments). Indeed we can make use of the n-best word segmentation outputs. The task of SLU or NER is to find the best label sequence L, given the character sequence C, represented as $\arg\max_L P(L|C)$. By including the word segmentation information, we can rewrite it by marginalizing over all possible word segmentations.

$$\arg\max_L P(L|C) = \arg\max_L \sum_j P(L, W_j|C)$$
$$= \arg\max_L \sum_j P(L|W_j, C) \cdot P(W_j|C) \quad (3)$$

---

[2]We modified wapiti to implement partial learning.

Where, W_j is each possible word segmentation. This formula can be understood as two components: $P(W_j|C)$ is the word segmentation model and $P(L|W_j, C)$ is the SLU/NER model. In practice, we can use the n-best outputs associated posterior probabilities from the wapiti, for both $P(W_j|C)$ and $P(L|W_j, C)$.[3]

4 CWS for SLU

In this section, we investigate the impact of CWS to the task of spoken language understanding (SLU) by making use of existing word segmenters trained with publicly-available data (1st situation in §1). This is motivated by the fact that our SLU training and testing data are not pre-segmented by semantic word units.

We choose semantic slot filling in SLU because it is becoming popular as it is a critical component to support conversational virtual assistants, such as Apple Siri, Samsung S Voice, Microsoft Cortana, Nuance Nina, just to name a few. The task of SLU is to convert a user utterance into a machine-readable semantic representation, which typically includes two sub-tasks: intent recognition and semantic slot filling (Tur et al., 2013). Intent recognition is to determine the intention of the user utterance. For example, for the input utterance 'book a ticket from Boston to Seattle', SLU will determine that its intent is *ticket-booking* as opposed to *music-playing*. Semantic slot filling is to extract the designated slot values for the recognized intent from the input utterance. For example, SLU will extract 'depart:Boston' and 'arrive:Seattle' from the above user utterance. In this paper, we assume the availability and correctness of intent recognition, and focus only on semantic slot filling.

4.1 SLU experiments setting

As described above, intent recognition is the first step in SLU, and the availability of which is assumed in this research work. We organize our training and testing data for semantic slot filling according to their intents. A single model for semantic slot filling is trained for each individual intent because different

	CTB6	PKU
number of sentences	23,458	19,058
number of unique character	4,223	4,685
number of unique word	42,127	55,302
average sentence length	45.0	95.8
average word length	1.7	1.7

Table 1: Statistics of two publicly-available corpus for CWS training.

intents have different designated slots. For example, for the intent *ticket-booking*, the designated slots are the arrival and departure city/airport, airline, date, etc.; While the *local-search* intent is more interested in the city, address, street name, type of point of interest, etc. For evaluation, each model is applied to the corresponding intent's testing data. At the end, we gather the automatic semantic labels of all intents in a pool and calculate F-measure.

Our SLU data consists of about 2 million sentences for training and 260 thousand sentences for testing, distributing into 170 intents.

4.2 Results and discussion

We build two word segmenters from two public corpora, the Chinese Tree Bank 6 (CTB6) and the PKU corpus from the SIGHAN Bakeoff 2005, respectively. The data statistics of the two corpora are shown in Table 1.

The SLU performances are summarized in Table 2. **Baseline** using only character ngram features gives an F-measure of 93.92%. When switching to using automatic segmented words as the labeling units (**Word Unit**), the performance is a lot worse in both cases (87.10% for CTB6 and 88.68% for PKU). This indeed is not too surprising because errors in CWS propagate into SLU semantic slot filling. If an error results in a word crossing the boundary of semantic slots, it will definitely lead to an error in SLU semantic slot filling.

On the other hand, when supplying the automatic 'BIES' ngrams from CWS to SLU semantic slot filling (**As Features**), we observe a nice gain in both cases, 94.41% for CTB6 and 94.13% for PKU. Using the ngram 'BIES' as input features provides useful information of word segmentation to SLU semantic slot filling, while it is less sensitive to word segmentation errors.

---

[3]During training we build the SLU/NER model with 1-best word segmentation; during evaluation, we use n-best word segmentation and n-best SLU/NER.

	CTB6			PKU		
	R (%)	P (%)	F (%)	R (%)	P (%)	F (%)
Baseline	94.10	93.73	93.92	94.10	93.73	93.92
Word Unit	89.42	84.90	87.10	90.29	87.12	88.68
As Features	94.13	94.70	94.41*	94.10	94.16	94.13*
Partial Learning	94.18	94.76	94.47*	94.19	94.77	94.48*
N-best	**94.36**	**94.84**	**94.60***	**94.37**	**94.85**	**94.61***

Table 2: SLU Results in Recall (R), Precision (P), and F-measure (F). * means it is statistically significant better than **Baseline** using a Z-test with a confidence level of 99%.

(2) Input: 查找[湖南财政经济学院][附近]的[餐厅][4]
CWS: 查找|湖南|财政|经济|学院|附近|的|餐厅
(Find the restaurants near Hunan College of Finance and Economics)

Example (2) illustrates that how CWS helps SLU semantic slot filling. For the sentence, the baseline system extracts '湖南财' as a location name. However, the word segmentation separates the words '湖南' (Hunan) and '财政' (Finance), which reduces the probability score of '湖南财' being a slot value because it crosses word boundaries. With CWS information, the system is able to extract '湖南财政经济学院' (Hunan College of Finance and Economics) as a slot value.

(3) Input: 转发[淘宝网的链接]
CWS 1: 转发|淘|宝网|的|链接
(Forward the link of bao.com)
CWS 2: 转发|淘宝网|的|链接
(Forward the link of taobao.com)
(4) Input: 亲[四季酒店]在哪里
CWS 1: 亲四季酒店|在|哪里
(Where is the Kiss Four Seasons Hotel)
CWS 2: 亲|四季酒店|在|哪里
(Dear, where is the Four Seasons Hotel)

Adapting the word segmentation with SLU partially-labeled data gives further gain to semantic slot filling. In the case of CTB6 it reaches an F-measure of 94.47%, and 94.48% in PKU, using the ngram of 'BIES' labels from the adapted segmenters. Here are two examples showing how the adaptation process further improves SLU. In the example (3), we have the incorrect word segmentation (CWS 1) before adaptation. It splits a word '淘宝

网' (taobao.com) and thus labels '宝网的链接' as a semantic slot. From the adaptation the system learns that '淘宝网' is a word, and it generates the correct word segmentation (CWS 2) and thus is able to create the correct semantic slot value '淘宝网的链接' (the link of taobao.com). Similarly, in the example (4), the sentence is initially under-segmented (CWS 1) and it creates the incorrect semantic slot value '亲四季酒店'. From the adaptation the system learns to put a word boundary between '亲' and '四' and then the correct slot value '四季酒店' (Four Seasons Hotel) is extracted.

Finally, we take 10-best outputs from the adapted word segmenter, for each word segmentation generate 10-best SLU outputs, sum up the probabilities, and search for the best semantic label sequence following Equation 3. We further push the performance to an F-measure of 94.60% for CTB6 and 94.61% for PKU. Compared with the baseline system that uses character ngrams as input features, the information of CWS helps us achieve an error reduction of about 11%.

5 CWS for NER

In our experiments on SLU, we showed how CWS helps the subsequent task when no in-domain word segmentation data is available (1st situation in §1). In this section, we investigate the impact of CWS to another important subsequent task: named entity recognition (NER). For the NER data we use, both the domain training and testing data have word boundary information, which allows us to explore the differences between word segmenters trained with in-domain data and publicly-available data (2nd situation). It also allows us to see the performance of the subsequent task using manual word segmen-

---

[4] Semantic slots in the input sentence are marked by '[]'.

tation (3rd situation). Moreover, it allows us to see the relationship between the performance of word segmentation and the end-to-end subsequent task.

5.1 NER experiments setting

For NER experiments, we use the benchmark NER data from the third SIGHAN Chinese language processing Bakeoff (SIGHAN-3) (Levow, 2006). It consists of 46,364 sentences in the training set and 4,365 sentences in the testing set. These data are annotated with both word boundaries and NER information.

5.2 Results and discussion

Baseline system which only uses character ngram features (same configuration as the SLU task) gives the performance of 85.81% in F-measure, as shown in Table 3.[5]

Oracle system uses character ngram features together with manual in-domain word boundary information during both training and testing, showing that *perfect* word segmentation information does help NER a lot. Again this suggests that *good* word segmentation does reduce ambiguities for the subsequent NLP tasks, as we argue in the introduction. Of course, since manual word segmentation is not generally available (esp. on testing), this raises the motivation of our research work: what is the impact of automatic CWS on NER and how to make the best out of it.

To understand the impact of automatic CWS on NER, we discard the manual word segmentations in the NER data, and build two word segmenters from two public corpora, CTB6 and PKU respectively, same as we did for the SLU experiments. We also adapt them to NER with partial-label learning, and finally apply n-best CWS to NER decoding. Here we only report the results for **As Features**, as summarized in Table 3. Similar to SLU, when supplying the automatic 'BIES' ngrams from CWS to NER (**As Features**), we observe a nice gain in both cases

---

[5]We also train a model to learn both word segmentation and NER at the same time (**Joint-learning**) using char ngram features, and then during decoding we marginalize all possible CWS sequences to search for the best NER labels. The performance, however, is only 85.39% in F-measure, suggesting it is non-trivial to leverage the gain from joint-training and the comparison between joint-training and our approaches is out of the scope of this paper.

of **CTB6** and **PKU**. The NER F-measure improves to 86.40% and 87.05% respectively. In addition, adapting the word segmentation with NER partially-labeled data gives a further gain for both CTB6 and PKU, with an F-measure of 86.96% and 87.64% respectively. Note that, the adaptation process does improve the CWS performances for both CTB6 and PKU.

In-domain CWS

NER system uses the NER training data to build a word segmenter and then apply it to the NER training and testing data to extract the word segmentation features. A naive thought is that it will result in a better NER performance than **CTB6** and **PKU** since a word segmenter trained with the in-domain data should be better than one trained with publicly-available data due to the domain mismatch issue. As shown in Table 3, it is true that the word segmentation F-measures of **NER** are much better than **CTB6** and **PKU**. However, to our surprise, the NER F-measure is only 83.45%, which is even worse than **Baseline**.

We hypothesize that this is due to the mismatch of the training CWS and testing CWS (as shown in Table 3, CWS F (train) and F (test)). When CWS accuracy is high on the training data, the NER model trained with such data puts more weight on word segmentation features rather than character features. However, during testing, the performance of CWS drops, resulting in more word segmentation errors, with a high chance to propagate to NER errors; even worse, a lot of these CWS errors are around NERs since a lot of NERs are OOVs and thus are challenging to segment correctly. To test this hypothesis, we use 3-fold cross-validation to get the word boundary information during the CWS training, and thus the model is named as **NER 3-fold**. Note, although the performance of CWS decreases in the training, it has a more balanced CWS performance between training and testing, which gives a better NER performance (improving 83.45% from **NER** to 86.80%).

N-best CWS

The model **N-best** takes N-best outputs from the adapted word segmenter, for each word segmentation generate K-best NER outputs, sums up the probabilities and searches for the best named-entity

	CWS		NER		
	F (Train) (%)	F (Test) (%)	R (%)	P (%)	F (%)
Baseline	-	-	81.63	90.44	85.81
Oracle	100	100	92.01	96.39	94.15*
CTB6 — As Features	84.16	84.71	82.91	90.20	86.40
CTB6 — Partial Learning	85.21	85.21	83.78	90.39	86.96*
CTB6 — N-best	-	-	86.88	90.36	88.59*
PKU — As Features	86.53	87.37	84.04	90.29	87.05*
PKU — Partial Learning	87.56	87.57	84.81	90.66	87.64*
PKU — N-best			87.44	90.59	88.99*
NER — As Features	99.64	95.70	80.88	86.19	83.45
NER — N-best	-	-	84.55	87.47	85.98
NER 3-fold — As Features	94.69	95.70	83.61	90.25	86.80*
NER 3-fold — N-best	-	-	87.22	91.30	89.21*
SIGHAN-3 Best System	-	-	84.20	88.94	86.51

Table 3: CWS and NER Results in F-measure. **CWS F (Train)** and **CWS F (Test)** are the word segmentation F-measure in the training and testing data respectively. **NER F** is the named-entity testing F-measure. '-' means that the metric does not apply. For example, **Baseline** has no word segmentation model and F-measure cannot be calculated for N-best models. For **N-best**, we set N=10 and K=2. '*' means it is statistically significant better than **Baseline** using a Z-test with a confidence level of 99%.

label sequence following Equation 3. We can see a big jump in **N-best** performances for all the models in Table 3. This verifies our hypothesis that 1-best CWS is not sufficient.

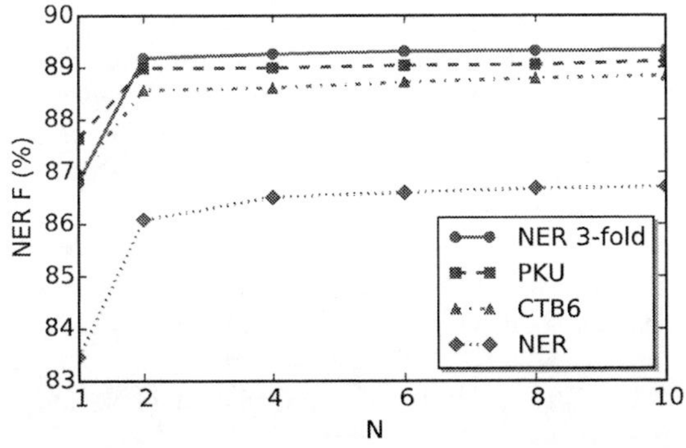

Figure 2: N-best results when varying N ($K = 1$)

To better understand how **N-best** helps NER, we vary the parameter N and the performance of NER (K=1) is shown in Fig. 2. The N-best performance improves dramatically when N jumps from 1 to 2. After that the performance seems to quickly saturate. We also found that the performance does not change much when changing K. These results show that in practice we can set N=2 and K=1, which is cost-efficient.

SIGHAN-3 evaluation

In the closed track evaluation of SIGHAN-3 (Levow, 2006), participants could only use the information found in the provided training data. Our best model (**NER 3-fold**) belongs to this track since it uses only the word segmentation annotation in the training data set. Our model outperforms all the submissions as shown in Table 3. Furthermore, even if manual word segmentation does not exist in the data, the model **CTB6 N-best** and **PKU N-best** which using existing word segmenters trained from publicly-available data can still outperform all the submissions in SIGHAN-3. Note that, these models use only character and word segmentation features without requiring additional name lists, part-of-speech taggers, etc.

6 Conclusion and future work

Chinese word segmentation is an important research topic and usually is the first step in Chinese natural language processing, yet its impact on the subsequent processing is relatively under-studied. To our knowledge, this research work is the first attempt to understand in depth how automatic CWS impacts the two related subsequent tasks: SLU semantic slot filling and named entity recognition.

In this work, we proposed three techniques to

solve the domain mismatch problem when applying CWS to other tasks: using word segmentation outputs as additional features, adaptation with partial-learning and taking advantage of n-best list. All three techniques work for both tasks.

We also examined the impact of CWS in three different situations: First, when domain data has no word boundary information, we showed that a word segmenter built from public out-of-domain data is able to improve the end-to-end performance. In addition, adapting it with the partially-labeled data derived from human annotation can further improve the performance. Moreover, marginalizing n-best word segmentations leads to further improvement. Second, when domain word segmentation is available, the word segmenter trained with the domain data itself has a better CWS performance but it does not necessarily have a better end-to-end task performance. A word segmenter with more balanced performance on the training and testing data may obtain a better end-to-end performance. Third, when testing data is manually segmented, word segmentation does help the task a lot. This is not a typical use case in reality, but it does suggest that word segmentation does reduce ambiguities for the subsequent NLP tasks.

In the future, we can try to sequentially stack two CRFs (one for word segmentation and one of subsequent task). We also would like to explore more subsequent tasks beyond sequence labeling problems.

Acknowledgments

The authors would like to thank Paul Vozila, Xin Lu, Xi Chen, and Xiang Li for helpful discussions, and the anonymous reviewers for insightful comments.

References

Pi-Chuan Chang, Michel Galley, and Christopher D. Manning. 2008. Optimizing Chinese word segmentation for machine translation performance. In *Proceedings of the Third Workshop on Statistical Machine Translation*, StatMT '08, pages 224–232, Stroudsburg, PA, USA. Association for Computational Linguistics.

Xinchi Chen, Xipeng Qiu, and Xuanjing Huang. 2015. Long short-term memory neural networks for chinese word segmentation. In *Proceedings of the 2015 Conference on Empirical Methods in Natural Language Processing (EMNLP)*, pages 1197–1206, Lisbon, Portugal, September. Association for Computational Linguistics.

Fei Cheng, Kevin Duh, and Yuji Matsumoto. 2015. Synthetic word parsing improves chinese word segmentation. In *Proceedings of the 53rd Annual Meeting of the Association for Computational Linguistics and the 7th International Joint Conference on Natural Language Processing (Volume 2: Short Papers)*, pages 262–267, Beijing, China, July. Association for Computational Linguistics.

Jianfeng Gao, Mu Li, Andi Wu, and Chang-Ning Huang. 2005. Chinese word segmentation and named entity recognition: A pragmatic approach. *Computational Linguistics*, 31(4):531–574, December.

Jun Hatori, Takuya Matsuzaki, Yusuke Miyao, and Jun'ichi Tsujii. 2012. Incremental joint approach to word segmentation, pos tagging, and dependency parsing in Chinese. In *Proceedings of the 50th Annual Meeting of the Association for Computational Linguistics: Long Papers - Volume 1*, ACL '12, pages 1045–1053, Stroudsburg, PA, USA. Association for Computational Linguistics.

Changning Huang and Hai Zhao. 2007. Chinese word segmentation: A decade review. *Journal of Chinese Information Processing*, 21(3):8–19, May.

Chu-Ren Huang, Petr Šimon, Shu-Kai Hsieh, and Laurent Prévot. 2007. Rethinking chinese word segmentation: Tokenization, character classification, or wordbreak identification. In *Proceedings of the 45th Annual Meeting of the Association for Computational Linguistics Companion Volume Proceedings of the Demo and Poster Sessions*, pages 69–72, Prague, Czech Republic, June. Association for Computational Linguistics.

Wenbin Jiang, Liang Huang, Qun Liu, and Yajuan Lü. 2008a. A cascaded linear model for joint chinese word segmentation and part-of-speech tagging. In *Proceedings of ACL-08: HLT*, pages 897–904, Columbus, Ohio, June. Association for Computational Linguistics.

Wenbin Jiang, Haitao Mi, and Qun Liu. 2008b. Word lattice reranking for chinese word segmentation and part-of-speech tagging. In *Proceedings of the 22nd International Conference on Computational Linguistics (Coling 2008)*, pages 385–392, Manchester, UK, August. Coling 2008 Organizing Committee.

Thomas Lavergne, Olivier Cappé, and François Yvon. 2010. Practical very large scale CRFs. In *Proceedings the 48th Annual Meeting of the Association for Computational Linguistics (ACL)*, pages 504–513. Association for Computational Linguistics, July.

Gina-Anne Levow. 2006. The third international Chinese language processing bakeoff: Word segmentation and named entity recognition. In *Proceedings of the Fifth SIGHAN Workshop on Chinese Language Processing*, pages 108–117, Sydney, Australia, July. Association for Computational Linguistics.

Roger Levy and Christopher Manning. 2003. Is it harder to parse Chinese, or the Chinese treebank? In *Proceedings of the 41st Annual Meeting on Association for Computational Linguistics - Volume 1*, ACL '03, pages 439–446, Stroudsburg, PA, USA. Association for Computational Linguistics.

Zhongguo Li and Maosong Sun. 2009. Punctuation as implicit annotations for chinese word segmentation. *Computational Linguistics*, 35(4):505–512.

Xiaoqing Li, Chengqing Zong, and Keh-Yih Su. 2013. A study of the effectiveness of suffixes for chinese word segmentation. *Sponsors: National Science Council, Executive Yuan, ROC Institute of Linguistics, Academia Sinica NCCU Office of Research and Development*, page 118.

Grégoire Mesnil, Yann Dauphin, Kaisheng Yao, Yoshua Bengio, Li Deng, Dilek Hakkani-Tur, Xiaodong He, Larry Heck, Gokhan Tur, Dong Yu, and Geoffrey Zweig. 2015. Using recurrent neural networks for slot filling in spoken language understanding. *Trans. Audio, Speech and Lang. Proc.*, 23(3):530–539, March.

Chongjia Ni and Cheung-Chi Leung. 2014. Investigation of using different Chinese word segmentation standards and algorithms for automatic speech recognition. In *International Symposium on Chinese Spoken Language Processing*, pages 44–48.

Nanyun Peng and Mark Dredze. 2015. Named entity recognition for Chinese social media with jointly trained embeddings. In *Proceedings of the 2015 Conference on Empirical Methods in Natural Language Processing (EMNLP)*, pages 548–554, Lisbon, Portugal, September. Association for Computational Linguistics.

Fuchun Peng, Xiangji Huang, Dale Schuurmans, and Nick Cercone. 2002. Investigating the relationship between word segmentation performance and retrieval performance in chinese ir. In *Proceedings of the 19th international conference on Computational linguistics-Volume 1*, pages 1–7. Association for Computational Linguistics.

Xian Qian and Yang Liu. 2012. Joint chinese word segmentation, pos tagging and parsing. In *Proceedings of the 2012 Joint Conference on Empirical Methods in Natural Language Processing and Computational Natural Language Learning*, pages 501–511, Jeju Island, Korea, July. Association for Computational Linguistics.

Marc-Antoine Rondeau and Yi Su. 2015. Full-rank linear-chain neurocrf for sequence labeling. In *IEEE International Conference on Acoustics, Speech and Signal Processing, ICASSP 2015*, pages 5281–5285.

Weiwei Sun and Jia Xu. 2011. Enhancing chinese word segmentation using unlabeled data. In *Proceedings of the 2011 Conference on Empirical Methods in Natural Language Processing*, pages 970–979, Edinburgh, Scotland, UK., July. Association for Computational Linguistics.

Weiwei Sun. 2011. A stacked sub-word model for joint Chinese word segmentation and part-of-speech tagging. In *Proceedings of the 49th Annual Meeting of the Association for Computational Linguistics: Human Language Technologies - Volume 1*, HLT '11, pages 1385–1394, Stroudsburg, PA, USA. Association for Computational Linguistics.

Oscar Täckström, Dipanjan Das, Slav Petrov, Ryan McDonald, and Joakim Nivre. 2013. Token and type constraints for cross-lingual part-of-speech tagging. *Transactions of the Association for Computational Linguistics*, 1:1–12.

Fumihiko Takahasi and Shinsuke Mori. 2015. Keyboard logs as natural annotations for word segmentation. In *Proceedings of the 2015 Conference on Empirical Methods in Natural Language Processing*, pages 1186–1196, Lisbon, Portugal, September. Association for Computational Linguistics.

Gokhan Tur, Anoop Deoras, and Dilek Hakkani-Tur. 2013. Semantic parsing using word confusion networks with conditional random fields. In *Annual Conference of the International Speech Communication Association (Interspeech)*, September.

Xiaojun Wan, Liang Zong, Xiaojiang Huang, Tengfei Ma, Houping Jia, Yuqian Wu, and Jianguo Xiao. 2011. Named entity recognition in Chinese news comments on the web. In *Proceedings of 5th International Joint Conference on Natural Language Processing*, pages 856–864, Chiang Mai, Thailand, November. Asian Federation of Natural Language Processing.

Yiou Wang, Jun'ichi Kazama, Yoshimasa Tsuruoka, Wenliang Chen, Yujie Zhang, and Kentaro Torisawa. 2011. Improving Chinese word segmentation and pos tagging with semi-supervised methods using large auto-analyzed data. In *Proceedings of 5th International Joint Conference on Natural Language Processing*, pages 309–317, Chiang Mai, Thailand, November. Asian Federation of Natural Language Processing.

Longyue Wang, Shuo Li, Derek F. Wong, and Lidia S. Chao. 2012. A joint chinese named entity recognition and disambiguation system. In *Proceedings of the Second CIPS-SIGHAN Joint Conference on Chinese Language Processing*, pages 146–151, Tianjin, China, December. Association for Computational Linguistics.

Jia Xu, Jianfeng Gao, Kristina Toutanova, and Hermann Ney. 2008. Bayesian semi-supervised chinese word segmentation for statistical machine translation. In *Proceedings of the 22nd International Conference on Computational Linguistics (Coling 2008)*, pages 1017–1024, Manchester, UK, August. Coling 2008 Organizing Committee.

Yan Xu, Yining Wang, Tianren Liu, Jiahua Liu, Yubo Fan, Yi Qian, Junichi Tsujii, and Eric I Chang. 2014. Joint segmentation and named entity recognition using dual decomposition in Chinese discharge summaries. *Journal of the American Medical Informatics Association*, 21(e1):84–92, February.

Nianwen Xue. 2003. Chinese word segmentation as character tagging. *Computational Linguistics and Chinese Language Processing*, 8(1):29–48.

Fan Yang and Paul Vozila. 2014. Semi-supervised Chinese word segmentation using partial-label learning with conditional random fields. In *Proceedings of the 2014 Conference on Empirical Methods in Natural Language Processing (EMNLP)*, pages 90–98, Doha, Qatar, October. Association for Computational Linguistics.

Xiaodong Zeng, Lidia S. Chao, Derek F. Wong, Isabel Trancoso, and Liang Tian. 2014. Toward better chinese word segmentation for smt via bilingual constraints. In *Proceedings of the 52nd Annual Meeting of the Association for Computational Linguistics (Volume 1: Long Papers)*, pages 1360–1369, Baltimore, Maryland, June. Association for Computational Linguistics.

Lufeng Zhai, Pascale Fung, Richard Schwartz, Marine Carpuat, and Dekai Wu. 2004. Using n-best lists for named entity recognition from Chinese speech. In Daniel Marcu Susan Dumais and Salim Roukos, editors, *HLT-NAACL 2004: Short Papers*, pages 37–40, Boston, Massachusetts, USA, May 2 - May 7. Association for Computational Linguistics.

Yue Zhang and Stephen Clark. 2010. A fast decoder for joint word segmentation and POS-tagging using a single discriminative model. In *Proceedings of the 2010 Conference on Empirical Methods in Natural Language Processing*, pages 843–852, Cambridge, MA, October. Association for Computational Linguistics.

Ruiqiang Zhang, Keiji Yasuda, and Eiichiro Sumita. 2008. Improved statistical machine translation by multiple Chinese word segmentation. In *Proceedings of the Third Workshop on Statistical Machine Translation*, pages 216–223, Columbus, Ohio, June. Association for Computational Linguistics.

Longkai Zhang, Li Li, Zhengyan He, Houfeng Wang, and Ni Sun. 2013a. Improving chinese word segmentation on micro-blog using rich punctuations. In *Proceedings of the 51st Annual Meeting of the Association for Computational Linguistics (Volume 2: Short Papers)*, pages 177–182, Sofia, Bulgaria, August. Association for Computational Linguistics.

Longkai Zhang, Houfeng Wang, Xu Sun, and Mairgup Mansur. 2013b. Exploring representations from unlabeled data with co-training for Chinese word segmentation. In *Proceedings of the 2013 Conference on Empirical Methods in Natural Language Processing*, pages 311–321, Seattle, Washington, USA, October. Association for Computational Linguistics.

Name Tagging for Low-resource Incident Languages based on Expectation-driven Learning

Boliang Zhang[1], Xiaoman Pan[1], Tianlu Wang[2], Ashish Vaswani[3],
Heng Ji[1], Kevin Knight[3], Daniel Marcu[3]
[1] Computer Science Department, Rensselaer Polytechnic Institute
{zhangb8,panx2,jih}@rpi.edu
[2] Computer Science Department, Zhejiang University
[3] Information Sciences Institute, University of Southern California
{vaswani,knight,marcu}@isi.edu

Abstract

In this paper we tackle a challenging name tagging problem in an emergent setting - the tagger needs to be complete within a few hours for a new incident language (IL) using very few resources. Inspired by observing how human annotators attack this challenge, we propose a new expectation-driven learning framework. In this framework we rapidly acquire, categorize, structure and zoom in on IL-specific expectations (rules, features, patterns, gazetteers, etc.) from various non-traditional sources: consulting and encoding linguistic knowledge from native speakers, mining and projecting patterns from both mono-lingual and cross-lingual corpora, and typing based on cross-lingual entity linking. We also propose a cost-aware combination approach to compose expectations. Experiments on seven low-resource languages demonstrate the effectiveness and generality of this framework: we are able to setup a name tagger for a new IL within two hours, and achieve 33.8%-65.1% F-score [1].

1 Introduction: "Tibetan Room"

In many emergent situations such as disease outbreaks and natural disasters, there is great demand to rapidly develop a Natural Language Processing (NLP) system, such as name tagger, for a "surprise" Incident Language (IL) with very few resources. Traditional supervised learning methods that rely on large-scale manual annotations would be too costly.

Let's start by investigating how a human would discover information in a foreign IL environment. When we are in a foreign country, even if we don't know the language, we would still be able to guess the word *"gate"* from the airport broadcast based on its frequency and position in a sentence; guess the word *"station"* by pattern mining of many subway station labels; and guess the word *"left"* or *"right"* from a taxi driver's GPS speaker by matching movement actions. We designed a *"**Tibetan Room**"* game, similar to *"Chinese Room"* (Searle, 1980), by asking a human user who doesn't know Tibetan to find persons, locations and organizations from some Tibetan documents. We designed an interface where test sentences are presented to the player one by one. When the player clicks token, the interface will display up to 100 manually labeled Tibetan sentences that include this token. The player can also see translations of some common words and a small gazetteer of common names (800 entries) in the interface.

14 players who don't know Tibetan joined the game. Their name tagging F-scores ranged from 0% to 94%. We found that good players usually bring in some kind of *"**expectations**"* derived from their own native languages, or general linguistic knowledge, or background knowledge about the scenario. Then they actively search, confirm, adjust and update these expectations during tagging. For example, they know from English that location names are often ended with suffix words such as *"city"* and *"country"*, so they search for phrases starting or ending with the translations of these suffix words. After they successfully tag some seeds, they will continue to discover more names based on more expectations.

---

[1] The resources developed in this paper, including the survey, patterns and gazetteers, are available at http://nlp.cs.rpi.edu/data/elisaienaacl16.zip

Proceedings of NAACL-HLT 2016, pages 249–259,
San Diego, California, June 12-17, 2016. ©2016 Association for Computational Linguistics

For example, if they already tagged an organization name *A*, and now observe a sequence matching a common English pattern "*[A (Organization)]' s [Title] [B (Person)]*", they will tag *B* as a person name. And if they know the scenario is about Ebola, they will be looking for a phrase with translation similar to "*West Africa*" and tag it as a location. Similarly, based on the knowledge that names appear in a conjunction structure often have the same type, they propagate high-confidence types across multiple names. They also keep gathering and synthesizing common contextual patterns and rules (such as position, frequency and length information) about names and non-names to expand their expectations. For example, after observing a token frequently appearing between a subsidiary and a parent organization, they will predict it as a preposition similar to "*of*" in English, and tag the entire string as a nested organization.

Based on these lessons learned from this game, we propose to automatically acquire and encode expectations about what will appear in IL data (names, patterns, rules), and encode those expectations to drive IL name tagging. We explored various ways of systematically discovering and unifying latent and expressed expectations from nontraditional resources:

- **Language Universals**: Language-independent rules and patterns;
- **Native Speaker**: Interaction with native speakers through a machine-readable survey and supervised active learning;
- **Prior Mining**: IL entity prior knowledge mining from both mono-lingual and cross-lingual corpora and knowledge bases;

Furthermore, in emergent situations these expectations might not be available at once, and they may have different costs, so we need to organize and prioritize them to yield optimal performance within given time bounds. Therefore we also experimented with various **cost-aware** composition methods with the input of acquired expectations, plus a time bound for development (1 hour, 2 hours), and the output as a wall-time schedule that determines the best sequence of applying modules and maximizes the use of all available resources. Experiments on seven low-resource languages demonstrate that our frame-

work can create an effective name tagger for an IL within a couple of hours using very few resources.

2 Starting Time: Language Universals

First we use some language universal rules, gazetteers and patterns to generate a binary feature vector $F = \{f_1, f_2, ...\}$ for each token. Table 1 shows these features along with examples. An identification rule is $r_I = \langle T_I, f = \{f_a, f_b, ...\}\rangle$ where T_I is a "B/I/O" tag to indicate the beginning, inside or outside of a name, and $\{f_a, f_b, ...\}$ is a set of selected features. If the features are all matched, the token will be tagged as T_I. Similarly, a classification rule is $r_C = \langle T_C, f = \{f_a, f_b, ...\}\rangle$, where T_C is "Person/Organization/Location". These rules are triggered in order, and some examples are as follows: $\langle B, \{AllUppercased\}\rangle$, $\langle PER, \{PersonGaz\}\rangle$, $\langle ORG, \{Capitalized, LongLength\}\rangle$, etc.

3 Expectation Learning

3.1 Approach Overview

Figure 1 illustrates our overall approach of acquiring various expectations, by simulating the strategies human players adopted during the Tibetan Room game. Next we will present details about discovering expectations from each source.

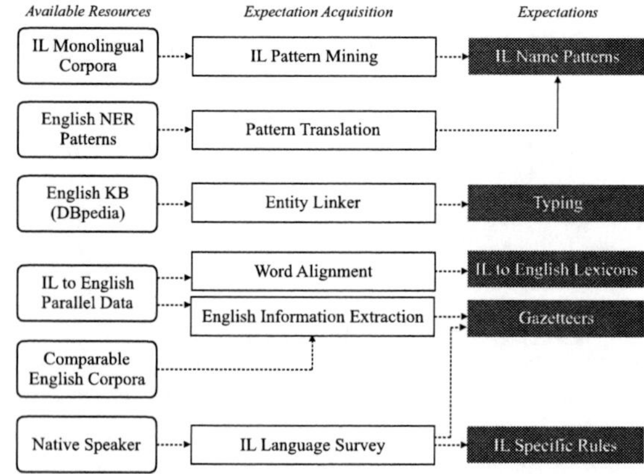

Figure 1: Expectation Driven Name Tagger Overview

3.2 Survey with Native Speaker

The best way to understand a language is to consult people who speak it. We introduce a human-in-

Features	Examples (Feature name is underlined)
in English Gazetteer	- **PerGaz**: person $(472, 765)$; **LocGaz**: location $(211, 872)$; **OrgGaz**: organization $(124, 403)$; **Title** (889); **NoneName** $(2, 380)$.
Case	- **Capitalized**; - **AllUppercased**; - **MixedCase**
Punctuation	- **IternalPeriod**: includes an internal period
Digit	- **Digits**: consisted of digits
Length	- **LongLength**: a name including more than 4 tokens is likely to be an ORG
TF-IDF	- **TF-IDF**: if a capitalized word appears at the beginning of a sentence, and has a low TF-IDF, then it's unlikely to be a name
Patterns	- **Pattern1**: "*Title* $\langle$ PER Name $\rangle$"
	- **Pattern2**: "$\langle PERName \rangle, 00*$," where 00 are two digits
	- **Pattern3**: "$[\langle Name_i \rangle ...], \langle Name_n - 1 \rangle \langle singleterm \rangle \langle Name_n \rangle$" where all names have the same type.
Multi-occurrences	- **MultipleOccurrence**: If a word appears in both uppercased and lowercased forms in a single document, it's unlikely to be a name.

Table 1: Universal Name Tagger Features

the-loop process to acquire knowledge from native speakers. To meet the needs in the emergent setting, we design a comprehensive survey that aims to acquire a wide-range of IL-specific knowledge from native speakers in an efficient way. The survey categorizes questions and organizes them into a tree structure, so that the order of questions is chosen based on the answers of previous questions. The survey answers are then automatically translated into rules, patterns or gazetteers in the tagger. Some example questions are shown in Table 2.

3.3 Mono-lingual Expectation Mining

We use a bootstrapping method to acquire IL patterns from unlabeled mono-lingual IL documents. Following the same idea in (Agichtein and Gravano, 2000; Collins and Singer, 1999), we first use names identified by high-confident rules as seeds, and generalize patterns from the contexts of these seeds. Then we evaluate the patterns and apply high-quality ones to find more names as new seeds. This process is repeated iteratively [2].

We define a pattern as a triple $\langle left, name, right \rangle$, where *name* is a name, left and right[3] are context vectors with weighted terms (the weight is computed based on each token's tf-idf score). For example, from a Hausa sentence "***gwamnatin kasar Sin ta*** *samar wa kasashen yammacin Afirka ... (the Government of China has given ... products to the West African countries)*", we can discover a pattern:

- *left*: $\langle$**gwamnatin** (goevernment), $0.5\rangle$, $\langle$**kasar** (country), $0.6\rangle$
- *name*: $\langle$**Sin** (China), $0.5\rangle$
- *right*: $\langle$**ta** (by), $0.2\rangle$

This pattern matches strings like "*gwamnatin kasar Fiji ta (by the government of Fiji)*".

For any two triples $t_i = \langle l_i, name_i, r_i \rangle$ and $t_j = \langle l_j, name_j, r_j \rangle$, we comput e their similarity by:

$$Sim(t_i, t_j) = l_i \cdot l_j + r_i \cdot r_j$$

We use this similarity measurement to cluster all triples and select the centroid triples in each cluster as candidate patterns.

Similar to (Agichtein and Gravano, 2000), we evaluate the quality of a candidate pattern P by:

$$Conf(P) = \frac{P_{positive}}{(P_{positive} + P_{negative})}$$

,where $P_{positive}$ is the number of positive matches for P and $P_{negative}$ is the number of negative matches. Due to the lack of syntactic and semantic resources to refine these lexical patterns, we set a conservative confidence threshold 0.9.

3.4 Cross-lingual Expectation Projection

Name tagging research has been done for high-resource languages such as English for over twenty years, so we have learned a lot about them. We collected 1,362 patterns from English name tagging literature. Some examples are listed below:

- $\langle \{\}, \{PER\}, \{< say >, < . >\} \rangle$
- $\langle \{< headquarter >, < in >\}, \{LOC\}, \{\} \rangle$
- $\langle \{< secretary >, < of >\}, \{ORG\}, \{\} \rangle$
- $\langle \{< in >, < the >\}, \{LOC\}, \{< area >\} \rangle$

---

[2] We empirically set the number of iterations as 2 in this paper.

[3] *left* and *right* are the context three tokens before and after the name

True/False Questions
1. The letters of this language have upper and lower cases
2. The names of people, organizations and locations start with a capitalized (uppercased) letter
3. The first word of a sentence starts with a capitalized (uppercased) letter
4. Some periods indicate name abbreviations, e.g., St. = Saint, I.B.M. = International Business Machines.
5. Locations usually include designators, e.g., in a format like "country United states", "city Washington"
6. Some prepositions are part of names
Text input
1. Morphology: please enter preposition suffixes as many as you can (e.g. "'da" in "Ankara'da yaşıyorum (I live in Ankara)" is a preposition suffix which means "in").
Translation
1. Please translate the following English words and phrases:
- organization suffix: agency, group, council, party, school, hospital, company, office, ...
- time expression: January, ..., December; Monday, ..., Sunday; ...

Table 2: Survey Question Examples

Besides the static knowledge like patterns, we can also dynamically acquire expected names from topically-related English documents for a given IL document. We apply the Stanford name tagger (Finkel et al., 2005) to the English documents to obtain a list of expected names. Then we translate the English patterns and expected names to IL. When there is no human constructed English-to-IL lexicon available, we derive a word-for-word translation table from a small parallel data set using the GIZA++ word alignment tool (Och and Ney, 2003). We also convert IL text to Latin characters based on Unicode mapping[4], and then apply Soundex code (Mortimer and Salathiel, 1995; Raghavan and Allan, 2004) to find the IL name equivalent that shares the most similar pronunciation as each English name. For example, the Bengali name "টনি ব্লেয়ার" and *"Tony Blair"* have the same Soundex code *"T500 B460"*.

3.5 Mining Expectations from KB

In addition to unstructured documents, we also try to leverage structured English knowledge bases (KBs) such as DBpedia[5]. Each entry is associated with a set of types such as `Company`, `Actor` and `Agent`. We utilize the Abstract Meaning Representation corpus (Banarescu et al., 2013) which contains both entity type and linked KB title annotations, to automatically map $9,514$ entity types in DBPedia to three main entity types of interest: Person (PER), Location (LOC) and Organization (ORG).

Then we adopt a language-independent cross-lingual entity linking system (Wang et al., 2015)

to link each IL name mention to English DBPedia. This linker is based on an unsupervised quantified collective inference approach. It constructs knowledge networks from the IL source documents based on entity mention co-occurrence, and knowledge networks from KB. Each IL name is matched with candidate entities in English KB using name translation pairs derived from inter-lingual KB links in Wikipedia and DBPedia. We also apply the word-for-word translation tables constructed from parallel data as described in Section 3.4 to translate some uncommon names. Then it performs semantic comparison between two knowledge networks based on three criteria: salience, similarity and coherence. Finally we map the DBPedia types associated with the linked entity candidates to obtain the entity type for each IL name.

4 Supervised Active Learning

We anticipated that not all expectations can be encoded as explicit rules and patterns, or covered by projected names, therefore for comparison we introduce a supervised method with pool-based active learning to learn implicit expectations (features, new names, etc.) directly from human data annotation. We exploited basic lexical features including ngrams, adjacent tokens, casing information, punctuations and frequency to train a Conditional Random Fields (CRFs) (Lafferty et al., 2001) based model through active learning (Settles, 2010).

We segment documents into sentences and use each sentence as a training unit. Let $\mathbf{x}_b^*$ be the most informative instance according to a query strategy

---

[4]http://www.ssec.wisc.edu/ tomw/java/unicode.html
[5]http://dbpedia.org

$\phi(\mathbf{x})$, which is a function used to evaluate each instance $\mathbf{x}$ in the unlabeled pool U. Algorithm 1 illustrates the procedure.

Algorithm 1 Pool-based Active Learning

1: $L \leftarrow$ labeled set, $U \leftarrow$ unlabeled pool
2: $\phi(\cdot) \leftarrow$ query strategy, $B \leftarrow$ query batch size
3: $M \leftarrow$ maximum number of tokens
4: **while** Length(L)$< M$ **do**
5:    $\theta = \text{train}(L)$;
6:    **for** $b \in \{1, 2, ..., B\}$ **do**
7:       $\mathbf{x}_b^* = \arg\max_{x \in U} \phi(\mathbf{x})$
8:       $L = L \cup \{\mathbf{x}_b^*, \text{label}(\mathbf{x}_b^*)\}$
9:       $U = U - \mathbf{x}_b^*$
10:    **end for**
11: **end while**

Jing et al. (2004) proposed an entropy measure for active learning for image retrieval task. We compared it with other measures proposed by (Settles and Craven, 2008) and found that **sequence entropy (SE)** is most effective for our name tagging task. We use ϕ^{SE} to represent how informative a sentence is:

$$\phi^{SE}(\mathbf{x}) = -\sum_{t=1}^{T} \sum_{m=1}^{M} P_\theta(y_t = m) log P_\theta(y_t = m)$$

, where T is the length of $\mathbf{x}$, m ranges over all possible token labels and $P_\theta(y_t = m)$ is the probability when y_t is tagged as m.

5 Cost-aware Combination

A new requirement for IL name tagging is a **Linguistic Workflow Generator**, which can generate an activity schedule to organize and maximize the use of acquired expectations to yield optimal F-scores within given time bounds. Therefore, the input to the IL name tagger is not only the test data, but also a time bound for development (1 hour, 2 hours, 24 hours, 1 week, 1 month, etc.).

Figure 2 illustrates our cost-aware expectation composition approach. Given some IL documents as input, as the clock ticks, the system delivers name tagging results at time 0 (immediately), time 1 (e.g., in one hour) and time 2 (e.g., in two hours). At time 0, name tagging results are provided by the universal tagger described in Section 2. During the first hour, we can either ask the native speaker to annotate a small amount of data for supervised active learning of a CRFs model, or fill in the survey to build a rule-based tagger. We estimate the confidence value of

Language	IL Test Docs	Name	Unique Name	IL Dev. Docs	IL-English Docs
Bengali	100	4,713	2,820	12,495	169
Hausa	100	1,619	950	13,652	645
Tagalog	100	6,119	3,375	1,616	145
Tamil	100	4120	2,871	4,597	166
Thai	100	4,954	3,314	10,000	191
Turkish	100	2,694	1,323	10,000	484
Yoruba	100	3,745	2,337	427	252

Table 3: Data Statistics

each expectation-driven rule based on its precision score on a small development set of ten documents. Then we apply these rules in the priority order of their confidence values. When the results of two taggers are conflicting on either mention boundary or type, if the applied rule has high confidence we will trust its output, otherwise adopt the CRFs model's output.

6 Experiments

In this section we will present our experimental details, results and observations.

6.1 Data

We evaluate our framework on seven low-resource incident languages: Bengali, Hausa, Tagalog, Tamil, Thai, Turkish and Yoruba, using the ground-truth name tagging annotations from the DARPA LORELEI program [6]. Table 3 shows data statistics.

6.2 Cost-aware Overall Performance

We test with three checking points: starting time, within one hour, and within two hours. Based on the combination approach described in Section 5, we can have three possible combinations of the expectation-driven learning and supervised active learning methods during two hours: (1) expectation-driven learning + supervised active learning; (2) supervised active learning + expectation-driven learning; and (3) supervised active learning for two hours. Figure 3 compares the overall performance of these combinations for each language.

We can see that our approach is able to rapidly set up a name tagger for an IL and achieves promising performance. During the first hour, there is no clear winner between expectation-driven learning or

---

[6]http://www.darpa.mil/program/low-resource-languages-for-emergent-incidents

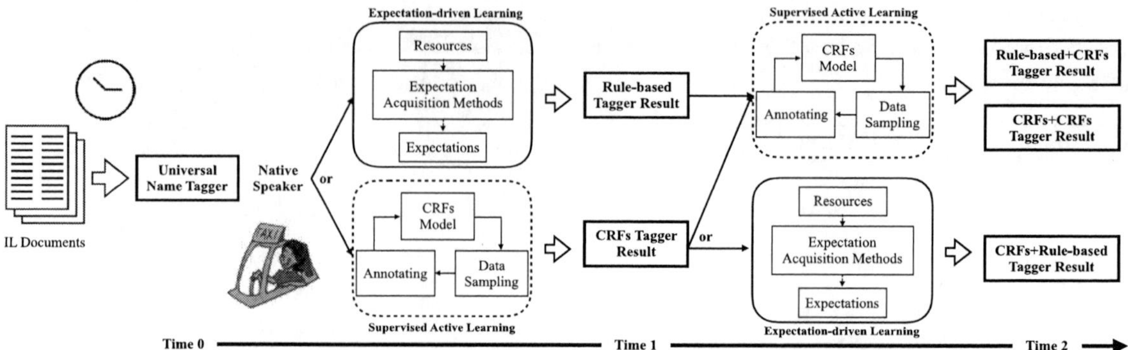

Figure 2: Cost-aware Expectation Composition

supervised active learning. But it's clear that supervised active learning for two hours is generally not the optimal solution. Using Hausa as a case study, we take a closer look at the supervised active learning curve as shown in Figure 4. We can see that supervised active learning based on simple lexical features tends to converge quickly. As time goes by it will reach its own upper-bound of learning and generalizing linguistic features. In these cases our proposed expectation-driven learning method can compensate by providing more explicit and deeper IL-specific linguistic knowledge.

6.3 Comparison of Expectation Discovery Methods

Table 4 shows the performance gain of each type of expectation acquisition method. IL gazetteers covered some common names, especially when the universal case-based rules failed at identifying names from non-Latin languages. IL name patterns were mainly effective for classification. For example, the Tamil name "கத்தோலிக்கன் சிரியன் வங்கியில (Catholic Syrian Bank)" was classified as an organization because it ends with an organization suffix word "வங்கியில(bank)". The patterns projected from English were proven very effective at identifying name boundaries. For example, some non-names such as titles are also capitalized in Turkish, so simple case-based patterns produced many spurious names. But projected patterns can fix many of them. In the following Turkish sentence, "*Ancak Avrupa Birliği Dış İlişkiler Sorumlusu Catherine Ashton,...(But European Union foreign policy chief Catherine Ashton,...)*", among all these capitalized

tokens, after we confirmed "*Avrupa Birliği (European Union)*" as an organization and "*Dış İlişkiler Sorumlusu (foreign policy chief)*" as a title, we applied a pattern projected from English "*[Organization] [Title] [Person]*" and successfully identified "*Catherine Ashton*" as a person. Cross-lingual entity linking based typing successfully enhanced classification accuracy, especially for languages where names often appear the same as their English forms and so entity linking achieved high accuracy. For example, "*George Bush*" keeps the same in Hausa, Tagalog and Yoruba as English.

6.4 Impact of Supervised Active Learning

Figure 5 shows the comparison of supervised active learning and passive learning (random sampling in training data selection). We asked a native speaker to annotate Chinese news documents in one hour, and estimated the human annotation speed approximately as 7,000 tokens per hour. Therefore we set the number of tokens as 7,000 for one hour, and 14,000 for two hours. We can clearly see that supervised active learning significantly outperforms passive learning for all languages, especially for Tamil, Tagalog and Yoruba. Because of the rich morphology in Turkish, the gain of supervised active learning is relatively small because simple lexical features cannot capture name-specific characteristics regardless of the size of labeled data. For example, some prepositions (e.g., "*nin (in)*") can be part of the names, so it's difficult to determine name boundaries, such as "*<ORG Ludian bölgesi **hastanesi**>**nin** (in <ORG Ludian Hospital>)*"

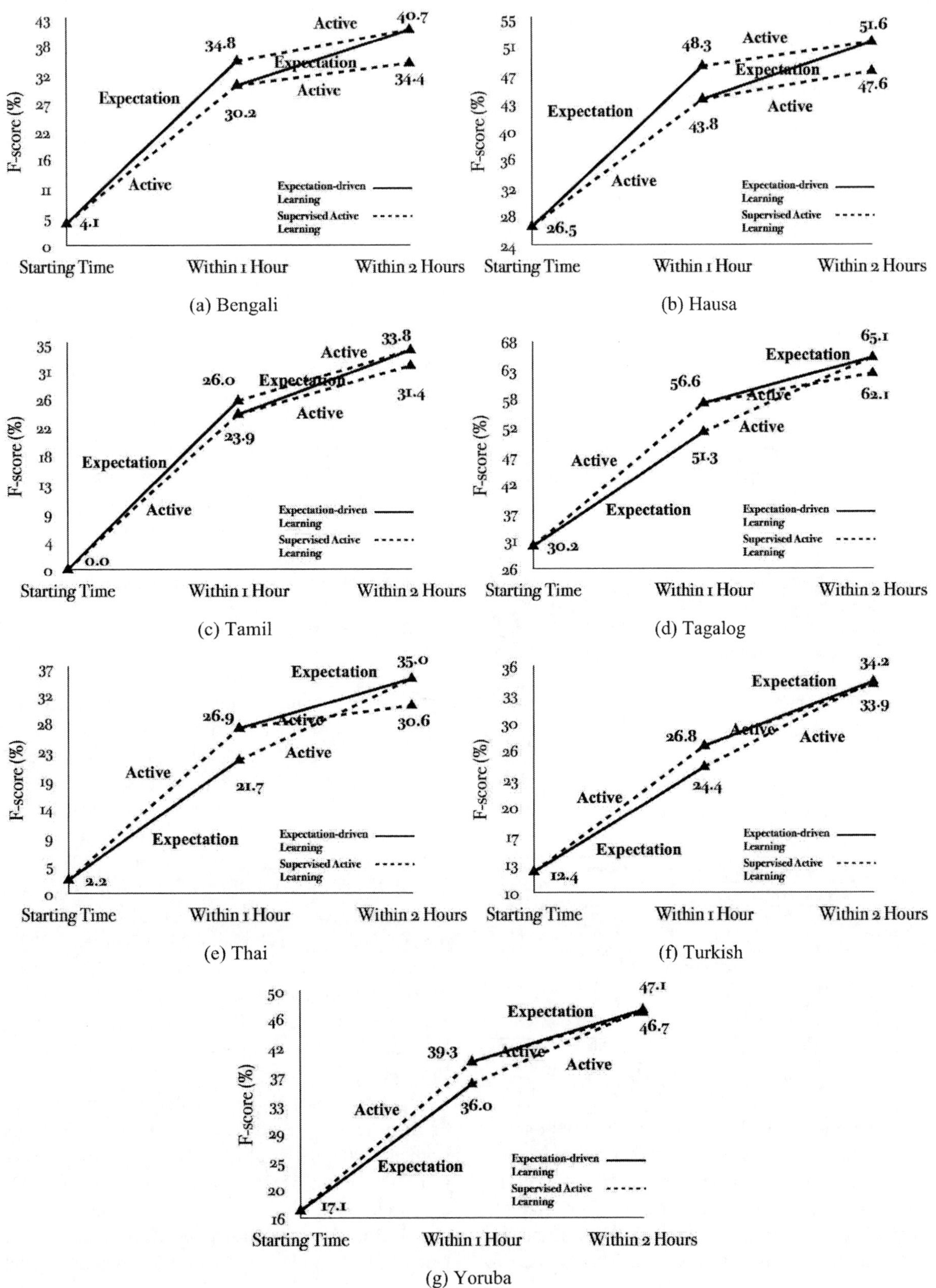

Figure 3: Comparison of methods combining e   tion-driven learning and supervised active learning given various time bounds

Methods	Bengali	Hausa	Tamil	Tagalog	Thai	Turkish	Yoruba
Universal Rules	4.1	26.5	0.0	30.2	2.2	12.4	17.1
+IL Gazetteers	29.7	32.1	21.8	34.3	18.9	17.3	26.9
+IL Name Patterns	31.2	33.8	22.9	35.1	18.9	19.1	28.0
+IL to English Lexicons	31.3	35.2	24.0	38.0	20.5	19.6	29.4
+IL Survey with Native Speaker	34.1	40.6	25.6	45.9	21.6	39.3	30.2
+KB Linking based Typing	34.8	48.3	26.0	51.3	21.7	43.6	36.0

Table 4: Contributions of Various Expectation Discovery Methods (F-score %)

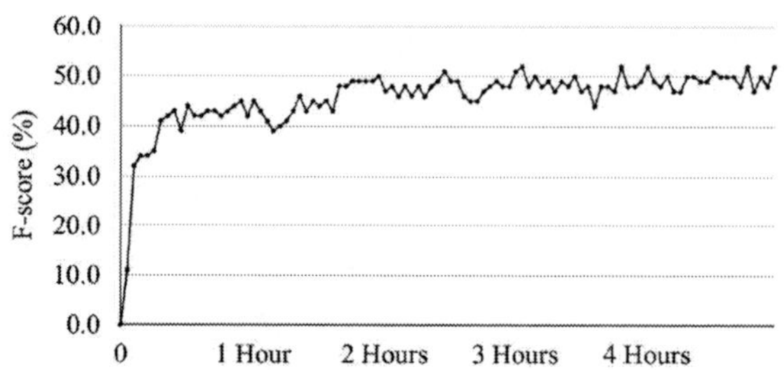

Figure 4: Hausa Supervised Active Learning Curve

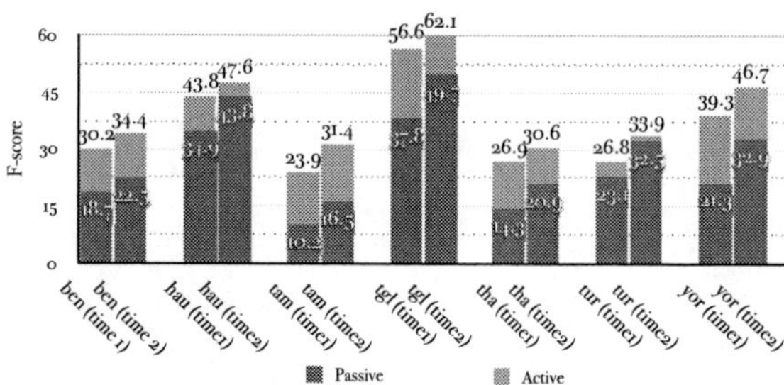

Figure 5: Active Learning vs. Passive Learning (%)

6.5 Remaining Error Analysis

Language	Identification F-score				Typing Accuracy*	Overall F-score
	PER	ORG	LOC	All		
Bengali	51.0	32.7	54.3	48.5	84.1	40.7
Hausa	51.8	36.6	63.3	55.1	93.6	51.6
Tamil	40.4	16.4	46.8	39.2	86.2	33.8
Tagalog	71.6	65.2	73.9	70.1	92.8	65.1
Thai	48.5	21.8	72.8	48.6	72.0	35.0
Turkish	64.3	41.3	73.0	63.1	69.1	43.6
Yoruba	69.3	38.3	60.0	57.2	82.3	47.1

* typing accuracy is computed on correctly identified names

Table 5: Breakdown Scores

Table 5 presents the detailed break-down scores for all languages. We can see that name identification, especially organization identification is the main bottleneck for all languages. For example, many organization names in Hausa are often very long, nested or all low-cased, such as "*makaran-tar horas da Malaman makaranta ta Bawa Jan Gwarzo (Bawa Jan Gwarzo Memorial Teachers College)*" and "*kungiyar masana'antu da tattalin arziki ta kasar Sin (China's Association of Business and Industry)*". Our name tagger will further benefit from more robust universal word segmentation, rich morphology analysis and IL-specific knowledge. For example, in Tamil "ஃ" is a visarga used as a diacritic to write foreign sounds, so we can infer a phrase including it (e.g., "ஹஃபைகபாவின் (Haifa)") is likely to be a foreign name. Therefore our survey should be enriched by exercising with many languages to capture more categories of linguistic phenomena.

7   Related Work

Name Tagging is a well-studied problem. Many types of frameworks have been used, including rules (Farmakiotou et al., 2000; Nadeau and Sekine, 2007), supervised models using monolingual labeled data (Zhou and Su, 2002; Chieu and Ng, 2002; Rizzo and Troncy, 2012; McCallum and Li, 2003; Li and McCallum, 2003), bilingual labeled data (Li et al., 2012; Kim et al., 2012; Che et al., 2013; Wang et al., 2013) or naturally partially annotated data such as Wikipedia (Nothman et al., 2013), bootstrapping (Agichtein and Gravano, 2000; Niu et al., 2003; Becker et al., 2005; Wu et al., 2009; Chiticariu et al., 2010), and unsupervised learning (Mikheev et al., 1999; McCallum and Li, 2003; Etzioni et al., 2005; Nadeau et al., 2006; Nadeau and Sekine, 2007; Ji and Lin, 2009).

Name tagging has been explored for many non-English languages such as in Chinese (Ji and Grishman, 2005; Li et al., 2014), Japanese (Asahara and Matsumoto, 2003; Li et al., 2014), Arabic (Maloney and Niv, 1998), Catalan (Carreras et al., 2003), Bulgarian (Osenova and Kolkovska, 2002), Dutch (De Meulder et al., 2002), French (Béchet et al., 2000), German (Thielen, 1995), Italian (Cucchiarelli et al., 1998), Greek (Karkaletsis et al., 1999), Spanish (Arévalo et al., 2002), Portuguese (Hana et al., 2006), Serbo-croatian (Nenadić and Spasić, 2000), Swedish (Dalianis and Åström, 2001) and Turkish (Tür et al., 2003). However, most of previous work relied on substantial amount of resources such as language-specific rules, basic tools such as part-of-speech taggers, a large amount of labeled data, or a huge amount of Web ngram data, which are usually unavailable for low-resource ILs. In contrast, in this paper we put the name tagging task in a new emergent setting where we need to process a surprise IL within very short time using very few resources.

The TIDES 2003 Surprise Language Hindi Named Entity Recognition task (Li and McCallum, 2003) had a similar setting. A name tagger was required to be finished within a time bound (five days). However, 628 labeled documents were provided in the TIDES task, while in our setting no labeled documents are available at the starting point. Therefore we applied active learning to efficiently annotate about 40 documents for each language and proposed new methods to learn expectations. The results of the tested ILs are still far from perfect, but we hope our detailed comparison and result analysis can introduce new ideas to balance the quality and cost of name tagging.

8   Conclusions and Future Work

Name tagging for a new IL is a very important but also challenging task. We conducted a thorough study on various ways of acquiring, encoding and composing expectations from multiple non-traditional sources. Experiments demonstrate that this framework can be used to build a promising name tagger for a new IL within a few hours. In the future we will exploit broader and deeper entity prior knowledge to improve name identification. We will aim to make the framework more transparent for native speakers so the survey can be done in an automatic interactive question-answering fashion. We will also develop methods to make the tagger capable of active self-assessment to produce the best workflow within time bounds.

Acknowledgments

This work was supported by the U.S. DARPA LORELEI Program No. HR0011-15-C-0115 and ARL/ARO MURI W911NF-10-1-0533. The views and conclusions contained in this document are those of the authors and should not be interpreted as representing the official policies, either expressed or implied, of the U.S. Government. The U.S. Government is authorized to reproduce and distribute reprints for Government purposes notwithstanding any copyright notation here on.

References

Eugene Agichtein and Luis Gravano. 2000. Snowball: Extracting relations from large plain-text collections. In *Proceedings of the fifth ACM conference on Digital libraries*.

Montse Arévalo, Xavier Carreras, Lluís Màrquez, María Antònia Martí, Lluís Padró, and María José Simón. 2002. A proposal for wide-coverage spanish named entity recognition. *Procesamiento del lenguaje natural*.

Masayuki Asahara and Yuji Matsumoto. 2003. Japanese named entity extraction with redundant morphological analysis. In *Proceedings of the 2003 Conference of the North American Chapter of the Association for Computational Linguistics on Human Language Technology*.

Laura Banarescu, Claire Bonial, Shu Cai, Madalina Georgescu, Kira Griffitt, Ulf Hermjakob, Kevin Knight, Philipp Koehn, Martha Palmer, and Nathan Schneider. 2013. Abstract meaning representation for sembanking. In *ACL Workshop on Linguistic Annotation and Interoperability with Discourse*.

Frédéric Béchet, Alexis Nasr, and Franck Genet. 2000. Tagging unknown proper names using decision trees. In *Proceedings of the 38th Annual Meeting on Association for Computational Linguistics*.

Markus Becker, Ben Hachey, Beatrice Alex, and Claire Grover. 2005. Optimising selective sampling for bootstrapping named entity recognition. In *Proceedings of ICML-2005 Workshop on Learning with Multiple Views*.

Xavier Carreras, Lluís Màrquez, and Lluís Padró. 2003. Named entity recognition for catalan using spanish resources. In *Proceedings of the tenth conference on European chapter of the Association for Computational Linguistics*.

Wanxiang Che, Mengqiu Wang, Christopher D Manning, and Ting Liu. 2013. Named entity recognition with bilingual constraints. In *Proceedings of HLT-NAACL*.

Hai Leong Chieu and Hwee Tou Ng. 2002. Named entity recognition: a maximum entropy approach using global information. In *Proceedings of the 19th international conference on Computational linguistics*.

Laura Chiticariu, Rajasekar Krishnamurthy, Yunyao Li, Frederick Reiss, and Shivakumar Vaithyanathan. 2010. Domain adaptation of rule-based annotators for named-entity recognition tasks. In *Proceedings of the 2010 Conference on Empirical Methods in Natural Language Processing*.

Michael Collins and Yoram Singer. 1999. Unsupervised models for named entity classification. In *Proceedings of the joint SIGDAT conference on empirical methods in natural language processing and very large corpora*.

Alessandro Cucchiarelli, Danilo Luzi, and Paola Velardi. 1998. Automatic semantic tagging of unknown proper names. In *Proceedings of the 17th international conference on Computational linguistics*.

Hercules Dalianis and Erik Åström. 2001. Swenam— a swedish named entity recognizer. Technical report, Technical Report. Department of Numerical Analysis and Computing Science.

Fien De Meulder, Walter Daelemans, and Véronique Hoste. 2002. A named entity recognition system for dutch. *Language and Computers*.

Oren Etzioni, Michael Cafarella, Doug Downey, Ana-Maria Popescu, Tal Shaked, Stephen Soderland, Daniel S Weld, and Alexander Yates. 2005. Unsupervised named-entity extraction from the web: An experimental study. *Artificial intelligence*.

Dimitra Farmakiotou, Vangelis Karkaletsis, John Koutsias, George Sigletos, Constantine D Spyropoulos, and Panagiotis Stamatopoulos. 2000. Rule-based named entity recognition for greek financial texts. In *Proceedings of the Workshop on Computational lexicography and Multimedia Dictionaries (COMLEX 2000)*.

Jenny Rose Finkel, Trond Grenager, and Christopher Manning. 2005. Incorporating non-local information into information extraction systems by gibbs sampling. In *Proceedings of the 43rd Annual Meeting on Association for Computational Linguistics*.

Jirka Hana, Anna Feldman, Chris Brew, and Luiz Amaral. 2006. Tagging portuguese with a spanish tagger using cognates. In *Proceedings of the International Workshop on Cross-Language Knowledge Induction*.

Heng Ji and Ralph Grishman. 2005. Improving name tagging by reference resolution and relation detection. In *Proceedings of ACL2005*.

Heng Ji and Dekang Lin. 2009. Gender and animacy knowledge discovery from web-scale n-grams for unsupervised person mention detection. In *Proceedings of PACLIC2009*.

Feng Jing, Mingjing Li, HongJiang Zhang, and Bo Zhang. 2004. Entropy-based active learning with support vector machines for content-based image retrieval. In *Proceedings of ICMCS2004*.

Vangelis Karkaletsis, Georgios Paliouras, Georgios Petasis, Natasa Manousopoulou, and Constantine D Spyropoulos. 1999. Named-entity recognition from greek and english texts. *Journal of Intelligent and Robotic Systems*.

Sungchul Kim, Kristina Toutanova, and Hwanjo Yu. 2012. Multilingual named entity recognition using parallel data and metadata from wikipedia. In *Proceedings of the 50th Annual Meeting of the Association for Computational Linguistics*.

John D. Lafferty, Andrew McCallum, and Fernando C. N. Pereira. 2001. Conditional random fields: Probabilistic models for segmenting and labeling sequence data. In *Proceedings of the Eighteenth International Conference on Machine Learning*.

Wei Li and Andrew McCallum. 2003. Rapid development of hindi named entity recognition using conditional random fields and feature induction. *ACM Transactions on Asian and Low-Resource Language Information Processing*.

Qi Li, Haibo Li, Heng Ji, Wen Wang, Jing Zheng, and Fei Huang. 2012. Joint bilingual name tagging for parallel corpora. In *Proceedings of the 21st ACM international conference on Information and knowledge management*.

Haibo Li, Masato Hagiwara, Qi Li, and Heng Ji. 2014. Comparison of the impact of word segmentation on name tagging for chinese and japanese. In *Proceedings of LREC2014*.

John Maloney and Michael Niv. 1998. Tagarab: a fast, accurate arabic name recognizer using high-precision morphological analysis. In *Proceedings of the Workshop on Computational Approaches to Semitic Languages*.

Andrew McCallum and Wei Li. 2003. Early results for named entity recognition with conditional random fields, feature induction and web-enhanced lexicons. In *Proceedings of the seventh conference on Natural language learning at HLT-NAACL 2003*.

Andrei Mikheev, Marc Moens, and Claire Grover. 1999. Named entity recognition without gazetteers. In *Proceedings of the ninth conference on European chapter of the Association for Computational Linguistics*.

JY Mortimer and JA Salathiel. 1995. 'soundex'codes of surnames provide confidentiality and accuracy in a national hiv database. *Communicable disease report. CDR review*.

David Nadeau and Satoshi Sekine. 2007. A survey of named entity recognition and classification. *Lingvisticae Investigationes*.

David Nadeau, Peter Turney, and Stan Matwin. 2006. Unsupervised named-entity recognition: Generating gazetteers and resolving ambiguity.

Goran Nenadić and Irena Spasić. 2000. Recognition and acquisition of compound names from corpora. In *Natural Language Processing—NLP 2000*.

Cheng Niu, Wei Li, Jihong Ding, and Rohini K Srihari. 2003. Bootstrapping for named entity tagging using concept-based seeds. In *Proceedings of the 2003 Conference of the North American Chapter of the Association for Computational Linguistics on Human Language Technology*.

Joel Nothman, Nicky Ringland, Will Radford, Tara Murphy, and James R Curran. 2013. Learning multilingual named entity recognition from wikipedia. *Artificial Intelligence*.

Franz Josef Och and Hermann Ney. 2003. A systematic comparison of various statistical alignment models. *Computational linguistics*.

Petya Osenova and Sia Kolkovska. 2002. Combining the named-entity recognition task and np chunking strategy for robust pre-processing. In *Proceedings of the Workshop on Treebanks and Linguistic Theories, September*.

Hema Raghavan and James Allan. 2004. Using soundex codes for indexing names in asr documents. In *Proceedings of the Workshop on Interdisciplinary Approaches to Speech Indexing and Retrieval at HLT-NAACL 2004*.

Giuseppe Rizzo and Raphaël Troncy. 2012. Nerd: a framework for unifying named entity recognition and disambiguation extraction tools. In *Proceedings of the Demonstrations at the 13th Conference of the European Chapter of the Association for Computational Linguistics*.

John Searle. 1980. Minds, brains, and programs. *Journal of the Association for Computing Machinery*.

Burr Settles and Mark Craven. 2008. An analysis of active learning strategies for sequence labeling tasks. In *Proceedings of the conference on empirical methods in natural language processing*.

Burr Settles. 2010. Active learning literature survey. *University of Wisconsin, Madison*.

Christine Thielen. 1995. An approach to proper name tagging for german. *arXiv preprint cmp-lg/9506024*.

Gökhan Tür, Dilek Hakkani-Tür, and Kemal Oflazer. 2003. A statistical information extraction system for turkish. *Natural Language Engineering*.

Mengqiu Wang, Wanxiang Che, and Christopher D Manning. 2013. Joint word alignment and bilingual named entity recognition using dual decomposition. In *Proceedings of the Association for Computational Linguistics*.

Han Wang, Jin Guang Zheng, Xiaogang Ma, Peter Fox, and Heng Ji. 2015. Language and domain independent entity linking with quantified collective validation. In *Proceedings of Conference on Empirical Methods in Natural Language Processing (EMNLP2015)*.

Dan Wu, Wee Sun Lee, Nan Ye, and Hai Leong Chieu. 2009. Domain adaptive bootstrapping for named entity recognition. In *Proceedings of the 2009 Conference on Empirical Methods in Natural Language Processing*.

GuoDong Zhou and Jian Su. 2002. Named entity recognition using an hmm-based chunk tagger. In *Proceedings of the 40th Annual Meeting on Association for Computational Linguistics*.

Neural Architectures for Named Entity Recognition

Guillaume Lample♠   Miguel Ballesteros♣♠
Sandeep Subramanian♠   Kazuya Kawakami♠   Chris Dyer♠
♠Carnegie Mellon University   ♣NLP Group, Pompeu Fabra University
`{glample,sandeeps,kkawakam,cdyer}@cs.cmu.edu,`
`miguel.ballesteros@upf.edu`

Abstract

State-of-the-art named entity recognition systems rely heavily on hand-crafted features and domain-specific knowledge in order to learn effectively from the small, supervised training corpora that are available. In this paper, we introduce two new neural architectures—one based on bidirectional LSTMs and conditional random fields, and the other that constructs and labels segments using a transition-based approach inspired by shift-reduce parsers. Our models rely on two sources of information about words: character-based word representations learned from the supervised corpus and unsupervised word representations learned from unannotated corpora. Our models obtain state-of-the-art performance in NER in four languages without resorting to any language-specific knowledge or resources such as gazetteers. [1]

1   Introduction

Named entity recognition (NER) is a challenging learning problem. One the one hand, in most languages and domains, there is only a very small amount of supervised training data available. On the other, there are few constraints on the kinds of words that can be names, so generalizing from this small sample of data is difficult. As a result, carefully constructed orthographic features and language-specific knowledge resources, such as gazetteers, are widely used for solving this task. Unfortunately, language-specific resources and features are costly to develop in new languages and new domains, making NER a challenge to adapt. Unsupervised learning from unannotated corpora offers an alternative strategy for obtaining better generalization from small amounts of supervision. However, even systems that have relied extensively on unsupervised features (Collobert et al., 2011; Turian et al., 2010; Lin and Wu, 2009; Ando and Zhang, 2005b, *inter alia*) have used these to augment, rather than replace, hand-engineered features (e.g., knowledge about capitalization patterns and character classes in a particular language) and specialized knowledge resources (e.g., gazetteers).

In this paper, we present neural architectures for NER that use no language-specific resources or features beyond a small amount of supervised training data and unlabeled corpora. Our models are designed to capture two intuitions. First, since names often consist of multiple tokens, reasoning jointly over tagging decisions for each token is important. We compare two models here, (i) a bidirectional LSTM with a sequential conditional random layer above it (LSTM-CRF; §2), and (ii) a new model that constructs and labels chunks of input sentences using an algorithm inspired by transition-based parsing with states represented by stack LSTMs (S-LSTM; §3). Second, token-level evidence for "being a name" includes both orthographic evidence (what does the word being tagged as a name look like?) and distributional evidence (where does the word being tagged tend to occur in a corpus?). To capture orthographic sensitivity, we use character-based word representation model (Ling et al., 2015b) to capture distributional sensitivity, we combine these representations with distributional representations (Mikolov et al., 2013b). Our word representations combine both of these, and dropout training is used to encourage the model to learn to trust both sources of evidence (§4).

Experiments in English, Dutch, German, and Spanish show that we are able to obtain state-

---

Proceedings of NAACL-HLT 2016, pages 260–270,
San Diego, California, June 12-17, 2016. ©2016 Association for Computational Linguistics

of-the-art NER performance with the LSTM-CRF model in Dutch, German, and Spanish, and very near the state-of-the-art in English without any hand-engineered features or gazetteers (§5). The transition-based algorithm likewise surpasses the best previously published results in several languages, although it performs less well than the LSTM-CRF model.

2 LSTM-CRF Model

We provide a brief description of LSTMs and CRFs, and present a hybrid tagging architecture. This architecture is similar to the ones presented by Collobert et al. (2011) and Huang et al. (2015).

2.1 LSTM

Recurrent neural networks (RNNs) are a family of neural networks that operate on sequential data. They take as input a sequence of vectors $(\mathbf{x}_1, \mathbf{x}_2, \ldots, \mathbf{x}_n)$ and return another sequence $(\mathbf{h}_1, \mathbf{h}_2, \ldots, \mathbf{h}_n)$ that represents some information about the sequence at every step in the input. Although RNNs can, in theory, learn long dependencies, in practice they fail to do so and tend to be biased towards their most recent inputs in the sequence (Bengio et al., 1994). Long Short-term Memory Networks (LSTMs) have been designed to combat this issue by incorporating a memory-cell and have been shown to capture long-range dependencies. They do so using several gates that control the proportion of the input to give to the memory cell, and the proportion from the previous state to forget (Hochreiter and Schmidhuber, 1997). We use the following implementation:

$$\mathbf{i}_t = \sigma(\mathbf{W}_{xi}\mathbf{x}_t + \mathbf{W}_{hi}\mathbf{h}_{t-1} + \mathbf{W}_{ci}\mathbf{c}_{t-1} + \mathbf{b}_i)$$
$$\mathbf{c}_t = (1 - \mathbf{i}_t) \odot \mathbf{c}_{t-1} +$$
$$\mathbf{i}_t \odot \tanh(\mathbf{W}_{xc}\mathbf{x}_t + \mathbf{W}_{hc}\mathbf{h}_{t-1} + \mathbf{b}_c)$$
$$\mathbf{o}_t = \sigma(\mathbf{W}_{xo}\mathbf{x}_t + \mathbf{W}_{ho}\mathbf{h}_{t-1} + \mathbf{W}_{co}\mathbf{c}_t + \mathbf{b}_o)$$
$$\mathbf{h}_t = \mathbf{o}_t \odot \tanh(\mathbf{c}_t),$$

where σ is the element-wise sigmoid function, and $\odot$ is the element-wise product.

For a given sentence $(\mathbf{x}_1, \mathbf{x}_2, \ldots, \mathbf{x}_n)$ containing n words, each represented as a d-dimensional vector, an LSTM computes a representation $\overrightarrow{\mathbf{h}_t}$ of the left context of the sentence at every word t. Naturally, generating a representation of the right context $\overleftarrow{\mathbf{h}_t}$ as well should add useful information. This can be achieved using a second LSTM that reads the same sequence in reverse. We will refer to the former as the forward LSTM and the latter as the backward LSTM. These are two distinct networks with different parameters. This forward and backward LSTM pair is referred to as a bidirectional LSTM (Graves and Schmidhuber, 2005).

The representation of a word using this model is obtained by concatenating its left and right context representations, $\mathbf{h}_t = [\overrightarrow{\mathbf{h}_t}; \overleftarrow{\mathbf{h}_t}]$. These representations effectively include a representation of a word in context, which is useful for numerous tagging applications.

2.2 CRF Tagging Models

A very simple—but surprisingly effective—tagging model is to use the $\mathbf{h}_t$'s as features to make independent tagging decisions for each output y_t (Ling et al., 2015b). Despite this model's success in simple problems like POS tagging, its independent classification decisions are limiting when there are strong dependencies across output labels. NER is one such task, since the "grammar" that characterizes interpretable sequences of tags imposes several hard constraints (e.g., I-PER cannot follow B-LOC; see §2.4 for details) that would be impossible to model with independence assumptions.

Therefore, instead of modeling tagging decisions independently, we model them jointly using a conditional random field (Lafferty et al., 2001). For an input sentence

$$\mathbf{X} = (\mathbf{x}_1, \mathbf{x}_2, \ldots, \mathbf{x}_n),$$

we consider $\mathbf{P}$ to be the matrix of scores output by the bidirectional LSTM network. $\mathbf{P}$ is of size $n \times k$, where k is the number of distinct tags, and $P_{i,j}$ corresponds to the score of the jth tag of the ith word in a sentence. For a sequence of predictions

$$\mathbf{y} = (y_1, y_2, \ldots, y_n),$$

we define its score to be

$$s(\mathbf{X}, \mathbf{y}) = \sum_{i=0}^{n} A_{y_i, y_{i+1}} + \sum_{i=1}^{n} P_{i, y_i}$$

where $\mathbf{A}$ is a matrix of transition scores such that $A_{i,j}$ represents the score of a transition from the tag i to tag j. y_0 and y_n are the *start* and *end* tags of a sentence, that we add to the set of possible tags. $\mathbf{A}$ is therefore a square matrix of size $k+2$.

A softmax over all possible tag sequences yields a probability for the sequence $\mathbf{y}$:

$$p(\mathbf{y}|\mathbf{X}) = \frac{e^{s(\mathbf{X},\mathbf{y})}}{\sum_{\widetilde{\mathbf{y}} \in \mathbf{Y}_{\mathbf{X}}} e^{s(\mathbf{X},\widetilde{\mathbf{y}})}}.$$

During training, we maximize the log-probability of the correct tag sequence:

$$\log(p(\mathbf{y}|\mathbf{X})) = s(\mathbf{X}, \mathbf{y}) - \log \left(\sum_{\widetilde{\mathbf{y}} \in \mathbf{Y}_{\mathbf{X}}} e^{s(\mathbf{X},\widetilde{\mathbf{y}})} \right)$$
$$= s(\mathbf{X}, \mathbf{y}) - \operatorname*{logadd}_{\widetilde{\mathbf{y}} \in \mathbf{Y}_{\mathbf{X}}} s(\mathbf{X}, \widetilde{\mathbf{y}}), \quad (1)$$

where $\mathbf{Y}_{\mathbf{X}}$ represents all possible tag sequences (even those that do not verify the IOB format) for a sentence $\mathbf{X}$. From the formulation above, it is evident that we encourage our network to produce a valid sequence of output labels. While decoding, we predict the output sequence that obtains the maximum score given by:

$$\mathbf{y}^* = \operatorname*{argmax}_{\widetilde{\mathbf{y}} \in \mathbf{Y}_{\mathbf{X}}} s(\mathbf{X}, \widetilde{\mathbf{y}}). \quad (2)$$

Since we are only modeling bigram interactions between outputs, both the summation in Eq. 1 and the maximum a posteriori sequence $\mathbf{y}^*$ in Eq. 2 can be computed using dynamic programming.

2.3 Parameterization and Training

The scores associated with each tagging decision for each token (i.e., the $P_{i,y}$'s) are defined to be the dot product between the embedding of a word-in-context computed with a bidirectional LSTM— exactly the same as the POS tagging model of Ling et al. (2015b) and these are combined with bigram compatibility scores (i.e., the $A_{y,y'}$'s). This architecture is shown in figure 1. Circles represent observed variables, diamonds are deterministic functions of their parents, and double circles are random variables.

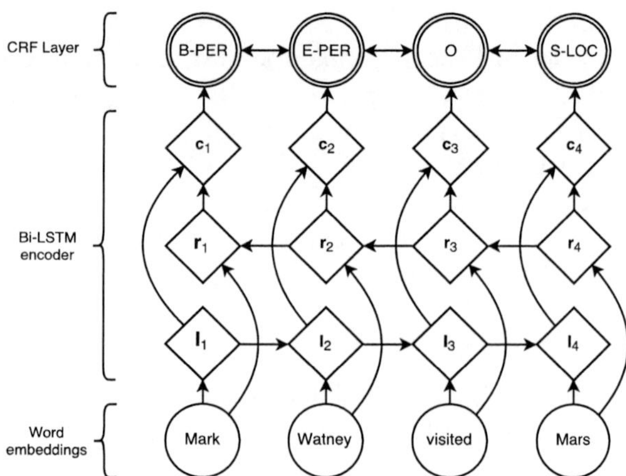

Figure 1: Main architecture of the network. Word embeddings are given to a bidirectional LSTM. l_i represents the word i and its left context, r_i represents the word i and its right context. Concatenating these two vectors yields a representation of the word i in its context, c_i.

The parameters of this model are thus the matrix of bigram compatibility scores $\mathbf{A}$, and the parameters that give rise to the matrix $\mathbf{P}$, namely the parameters of the bidirectional LSTM, the linear feature weights, and the word embeddings. As in part 2.2, let $\mathbf{x}_i$ denote the sequence of word embeddings for every word in a sentence, and y_i be their associated tags. We return to a discussion of how the embeddings $\mathbf{x}_i$ are modeled in Section 4. The sequence of word embeddings is given as input to a bidirectional LSTM, which returns a representation of the left and right context for each word as explained in 2.1.

These representations are concatenated ($\mathbf{c}_i$) and linearly projected onto a layer whose size is equal to the number of distinct tags. Instead of using the softmax output from this layer, we use a CRF as previously described to take into account neighboring tags, yielding the final predictions for every word y_i. Additionally, we observed that adding a hidden layer between $\mathbf{c}_i$ and the CRF layer marginally improved our results. All results reported with this model incorporate this extra-layer. The parameters are trained to maximize Eq. 1 of observed sequences of NER tags in an annotated corpus, given the observed words.

2.4 Tagging Schemes

The task of named entity recognition is to assign a named entity label to every word in a sentence. A single named entity could span several tokens within a sentence. Sentences are usually represented in the IOB format (Inside, Outside, Beginning) where every token is labeled as B-*label* if the token is the beginning of a named entity, I-*label* if it is inside a named entity but not the first token within the named entity, or O otherwise. However, we decided to use the IOBES tagging scheme, a variant of IOB commonly used for named entity recognition, which encodes information about singleton entities (S) and explicitly marks the end of named entities (E). Using this scheme, tagging a word as I-*label* with high-confidence narrows down the choices for the subsequent word to I-*label* or E-*label*, however, the IOB scheme is only capable of determining that the subsequent word cannot be the interior of another label. Ratinov and Roth (2009) and Dai et al. (2015) showed that using a more expressive tagging scheme like IOBES improves model performance marginally. However, we did not observe a significant improvement over the IOB tagging scheme.

3 Transition-Based Chunking Model

As an alternative to the LSTM-CRF discussed in the previous section, we explore a new architecture that chunks and labels a sequence of inputs using an algorithm similar to transition-based dependency parsing. This model directly constructs representations of the multi-token names (e.g., the name *Mark Watney* is composed into a single representation).

This model relies on a stack data structure to incrementally construct chunks of the input. To obtain representations of this stack used for predicting subsequent actions, we use the Stack-LSTM presented by Dyer et al. (2015), in which the LSTM is augmented with a "stack pointer." While sequential LSTMs model sequences from left to right, stack LSTMs permit embedding of a stack of objects that are both added to (using a push operation) and removed from (using a pop operation). This allows the Stack-LSTM to work like a stack that maintains a "summary embedding" of its contents. We refer to this model as Stack-LSTM or S-LSTM model for simplicity.

Finally, we refer interested readers to the original paper (Dyer et al., 2015) for details about the Stack-LSTM model since in this paper we merely use the same architecture through a new transition-based algorithm presented in the following Section.

3.1 Chunking Algorithm

We designed a transition inventory which is given in Figure 2 that is inspired by transition-based parsers, in particular the arc-standard parser of Nivre (2004). In this algorithm, we make use of two stacks (designated *output* and *stack* representing, respectively, completed chunks and scratch space) and a *buffer* that contains the words that have yet to be processed. The transition inventory contains the following transitions: The SHIFT transition moves a word from the buffer to the stack, the OUT transition moves a word from the buffer directly into the output stack while the REDUCE(y) transition pops all items from the top of the stack creating a "chunk," labels this with label y, and pushes a representation of this chunk onto the output stack. The algorithm completes when the stack and buffer are both empty. The algorithm is depicted in Figure 2, which shows the sequence of operations required to process the sentence *Mark Watney visited Mars*.

The model is parameterized by defining a probability distribution over actions at each time step, given the current contents of the stack, buffer, and output, as well as the history of actions taken. Following Dyer et al. (2015), we use stack LSTMs to compute a fixed dimensional embedding of each of these, and take a concatenation of these to obtain the full algorithm state. This representation is used to define a distribution over the possible actions that can be taken at each time step. The model is trained to maximize the conditional probability of sequences of reference actions (extracted from a labeled training corpus) given the input sentences. To label a new input sequence at test time, the maximum probability action is chosen greedily until the algorithm reaches a termination state. Although this is not guaranteed to find a global optimum, it is effective in practice. Since each token is either moved directly to the output (1 action) or first to the stack and then the output (2 actions), the total number of actions for a sequence of length n is maximally $2n$.

It is worth noting that the nature of this algorithm

Out$_t$	Stack$_t$	Buffer$_t$	Action	Out$_{t+1}$	Stack$_{t+1}$	Buffer$_{t+1}$	Segments
O	S	$(\mathbf{u}, u), B$	SHIFT	O	$(\mathbf{u}, u), S$	B	—
O	$(\mathbf{u}, u), \ldots, (\mathbf{v}, v), S$	B	REDUCE(y)	$g(\mathbf{u}, \ldots, \mathbf{v}, \mathbf{r}_y), O$	S	B	$(u \ldots v, y)$
O	S	$(\mathbf{u}, u), B$	OUT	$g(\mathbf{u}, \mathbf{r}_\varnothing), O$	S	B	—

Figure 2: Transitions of the Stack-LSTM model indicating the action applied and the resulting state.   Bold symbols indicate (learned) embeddings of words and relations, script symbols indicate the corresponding words and relations.

Transition	Output	Stack	Buffer	Segment
	[]	[]	[Mark, Watney, visited, Mars]	
SHIFT	[]	[Mark]	[Watney, visited, Mars]	
SHIFT	[]	[Mark, Watney]	[visited, Mars]	
REDUCE(PER)	[(Mark Watney)-PER]	[]	[visited, Mars]	(Mark Watney)-PER
OUT	[(Mark Watney)-PER, visited]	[]	[Mars]	
SHIFT	[(Mark Watney)-PER, visited]	[Mars]	[]	
REDUCE(LOC)	[(Mark Watney)-PER, visited, (Mars)-LOC]	[]	[]	(Mars)-LOC

Figure 3: Transition sequence for *Mark Watney visited Mars* with the Stack-LSTM model.

model makes it agnostic to the tagging scheme used since it directly predicts labeled chunks.

3.2 Representing Labeled Chunks

When the REDUCE(y) operation is executed, the algorithm shifts a sequence of tokens (together with their vector embeddings) from the stack to the output buffer as a single completed chunk. To compute an embedding of this sequence, we run a bidirectional LSTM over the embeddings of its constituent tokens together with a token representing the type of the chunk being identified (i.e., y). This function is given as $g(\mathbf{u}, \ldots, \mathbf{v}, \mathbf{r}_y)$, where $\mathbf{r}_y$ is a learned embedding of a label type. Thus, the output buffer contains a single vector representation for each labeled chunk that is generated, regardless of its length.

4 Input Word Embeddings

The input layers to both of our models are vector representations of individual words. Learning independent representations for word types from the limited NER training data is a difficult problem: there are simply too many parameters to reliably estimate. Since many languages have orthographic or morphological evidence that something is a name (or not a name), we want representations that are sensitive to the spelling of words. We therefore use a model that constructs representations of words from representations of the characters they are composed of (4.1). Our second intuition is that names, which may individually be quite varied, appear in regular contexts in large corpora. Therefore we use embed-

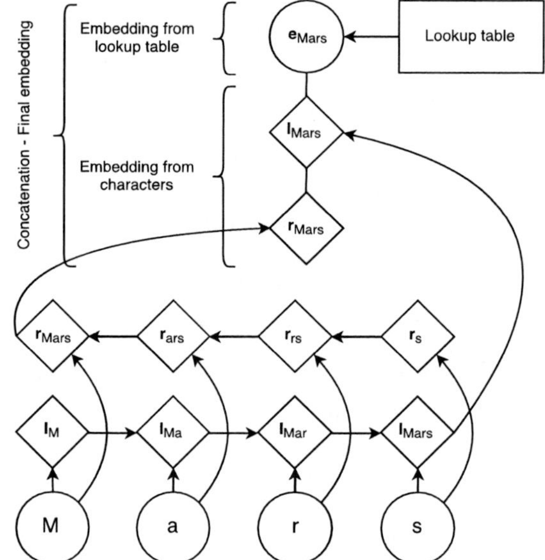

Figure 4: The character embeddings of the word "Mars" are given to a bidirectional LSTMs. We concatenate their last outputs to an embedding from a lookup table to obtain a representation for this word.

dings learned from a large corpus that are sensitive to word order (4.2). Finally, to prevent the models from depending on one representation or the other too strongly, we use dropout training and find this is crucial for good generalization performance (4.3).

4.1 Character-based models of words

An important distinction of our work from most previous approaches is that we learn character-level features while training instead of hand-engineering prefix and suffix information about words. Learning character-level embeddings has the advantage of learning representations specific to the task and domain at hand. They have been found useful for morphologically rich languages and to handle the out-of-vocabulary problem for tasks like part-of-speech tagging and language modeling (Ling et al., 2015b) or dependency parsing (Ballesteros et al., 2015).

Figure 4 describes our architecture to generate a word embedding for a word from its characters. A character lookup table initialized at random contains an embedding for every character. The character embeddings corresponding to every character in a word are given in direct and reverse order to a forward and a backward LSTM. The embedding for a word derived from its characters is the concatenation of its forward and backward representations from the bidirectional LSTM. This character-level representation is then concatenated with a word-level representation from a word lookup-table. During testing, words that do not have an embedding in the lookup table are mapped to a UNK embedding. To train the UNK embedding, we replace singletons with the UNK embedding with a probability 0.5. In all our experiments, the hidden dimension of the forward and backward character LSTMs are 25 each, which results in our character-based representation of words being of dimension 50.

Recurrent models like RNNs and LSTMs are capable of encoding very long sequences, however, they have a representation biased towards their most recent inputs. As a result, we expect the final representation of the forward LSTM to be an accurate representation of the suffix of the word, and the final state of the backward LSTM to be a better representation of its prefix. Alternative approaches—most notably like convolutional networks—have been proposed to learn representations of words from their characters (Zhang et al., 2015; Kim et al., 2015). However, convnets are designed to discover position-invariant features of their inputs. While this is appropriate for many problems, e.g., image recognition (a cat can appear anywhere in a picture), we argue that important information is position dependent (e.g., prefixes and suffixes encode different information than stems), making LSTMs an *a priori* better function class for modeling the relationship between words and their characters.

4.2 Pretrained embeddings

As in Collobert et al. (2011), we use pretrained word embeddings to initialize our lookup table. We observe significant improvements using pretrained word embeddings over randomly initialized ones. Embeddings are pretrained using skip-n-gram (Ling et al., 2015a), a variation of word2vec (Mikolov et al., 2013a) that accounts for word order. These embeddings are fine-tuned during training.

Word embeddings for Spanish, Dutch, German and English are trained using the Spanish Gigaword version 3, the Leipzig corpora collection, the German monolingual training data from the 2010 Machine Translation Workshop and the English Gigaword version 4 (with the LA Times and NY Times portions removed) respectively.[2] We use an embedding dimension of 100 for English, 64 for other languages, a minimum word frequency cutoff of 4, and a window size of 8.

4.3 Dropout training

Initial experiments showed that character-level embeddings did not improve our overall performance when used in conjunction with pretrained word representations. To encourage the model to depend on both representations, we use dropout training (Hinton et al., 2012), applying a dropout mask to the final embedding layer just before the input to the bidirectional LSTM in Figure 1. We observe a significant improvement in our model's performance after using dropout (see table 5).

5 Experiments

This section presents the methods we use to train our models, the results we obtained on various tasks and the impact of our networks' configuration on model performance.

5.1 Training

For both models presented, we train our networks using the back-propagation algorithm updating our parameters on every training example, one at a time, using stochastic gradient descent (SGD) with

---

[2](Graff, 2011; Biemann et al., 2007; Callison-Burch et al., 2010; Parker et al., 2009)

a learning rate of 0.01 and a gradient clipping of 5.0. Several methods have been proposed to enhance the performance of SGD, such as Adadelta (Zeiler, 2012) or Adam (Kingma and Ba, 2014). Although we observe faster convergence using these methods, none of them perform as well as SGD with gradient clipping.

Our LSTM-CRF model uses a single layer for the forward and backward LSTMs whose dimensions are set to 100. Tuning this dimension did not significantly impact model performance. We set the dropout rate to 0.5. Using higher rates negatively impacted our results, while smaller rates led to longer training time.

The stack-LSTM model uses two layers each of dimension 100 for each stack. The embeddings of the actions used in the composition functions have 16 dimensions each, and the output embedding is of dimension 20. We experimented with different dropout rates and reported the scores using the best dropout rate for each language.[3] It is a greedy model that apply locally optimal actions until the entire sentence is processed, further improvements might be obtained with beam search (Zhang and Clark, 2011) or training with exploration (Ballesteros et al., 2016).

5.2 Data Sets

We test our model on different datasets for named entity recognition. To demonstrate our model's ability to generalize to different languages, we present results on the CoNLL-2002 and CoNLL-2003 datasets (Tjong Kim Sang, 2002; Tjong Kim Sang and De Meulder, 2003) that contain independent named entity labels for English, Spanish, German and Dutch. All datasets contain four different types of named entities: locations, persons, organizations, and miscellaneous entities that do not belong in any of the three previous categories. Although POS tags were made available for all datasets, we did not include them in our models. We did not perform any dataset preprocessing, apart from replacing every digit with a zero in the English NER dataset.

---

[3]English (D=0.2), German, Spanish and Dutch (D=0.3)

5.3 Results

Table 1 presents our comparisons with other models for named entity recognition in English. To make the comparison between our model and others fair, we report the scores of other models with and without the use of external labeled data such as gazetteers and knowledge bases. Our models do not use gazetteers or any external labeled resources. The best score reported on this task is by Luo et al. (2015). They obtained a F_1 of 91.2 by jointly modeling the NER and entity linking tasks (Hoffart et al., 2011). Their model uses a lot of hand-engineered features including spelling features, WordNet clusters, Brown clusters, POS tags, chunks tags, as well as stemming and external knowledge bases like Freebase and Wikipedia. Our LSTM-CRF model outperforms all other systems, including the ones using external labeled data like gazetteers. Our Stack-LSTM model also outperforms all previous models that do not incorporate external features, apart from the one presented by Chiu and Nichols (2015).

Tables 2, 3 and 4 present our results on NER for German, Dutch and Spanish respectively in comparison to other models. On these three languages, the LSTM-CRF model significantly outperforms all previous methods, including the ones using external labeled data. The only exception is Dutch, where the model of Gillick et al. (2015) can perform better by leveraging the information from other NER datasets. The Stack-LSTM also consistently presents state-the-art (or close to) results compared to systems that do not use external data.

As we can see in the tables, the Stack-LSTM model is more dependent on character-based representations to achieve competitive performance; we hypothesize that the LSTM-CRF model requires less orthographic information since it gets more contextual information out of the bidirectional LSTMs; however, the Stack-LSTM model consumes the words one by one and it just relies on the word representations when it chunks words.

5.4 Network architectures

Our models had several components that we could tweak to understand their impact on the overall performance. We explored the impact that the CRF, the character-level representations, pretraining of our

Model	F_1
Collobert et al. (2011)*	89.59
Lin and Wu (2009)	83.78
Lin and Wu (2009)*	90.90
Huang et al. (2015)*	90.10
Passos et al. (2014)	90.05
Passos et al. (2014)*	90.90
Luo et al. (2015)* + gaz	89.9
Luo et al. (2015)* + gaz + linking	**91.2**
Chiu and Nichols (2015)	90.69
Chiu and Nichols (2015)*	90.77
LSTM-CRF (no char)	90.20
LSTM-CRF	**90.94**
S-LSTM (no char)	87.96
S-LSTM	90.33

Table 1: English NER results (CoNLL-2003 test set). * indicates models trained with the use of external labeled data

Model	F_1
Florian et al. (2003)*	72.41
Ando and Zhang (2005a)	75.27
Qi et al. (2009)	75.72
Gillick et al. (2015)	72.08
Gillick et al. (2015)*	76.22
LSTM-CRF – no char	75.06
LSTM-CRF	**78.76**
S-LSTM – no char	65.87
S-LSTM	75.66

Table 2: German NER results (CoNLL-2003 test set). * indicates models trained with the use of external labeled data

Model	F_1
Carreras et al. (2002)	77.05
Nothman et al. (2013)	78.6
Gillick et al. (2015)	78.08
Gillick et al. (2015)*	**82.84**
LSTM-CRF – no char	73.14
LSTM-CRF	**81.74**
S-LSTM – no char	69.90
S-LSTM	79.88

Table 3: Dutch NER (CoNLL-2002 test set). * indicates models trained with the use of external labeled data

Model	F_1
Carreras et al. (2002)*	81.39
Santos and Guimarães (2015)	82.21
Gillick et al. (2015)	81.83
Gillick et al. (2015)*	82.95
LSTM-CRF – no char	83.44
LSTM-CRF	**85.75**
S-LSTM – no char	79.46
S-LSTM	83.93

Table 4: Spanish NER (CoNLL-2002 test set). * indicates models trained with the use of external labeled data

word embeddings and dropout had on our LSTM-CRF model. We observed that pretraining our word embeddings gave us the biggest improvement in overall performance of +7.31 in F_1. The CRF layer gave us an increase of +1.79, while using dropout resulted in a difference of +1.17 and finally learn-

ing character-level word embeddings resulted in an increase of about +0.74. For the Stack-LSTM we performed a similar set of experiments. Results with different architectures are given in table 5.

Model	Variant	F_1
LSTM	char + dropout + pretrain	89.15
LSTM-CRF	char + dropout	83.63
LSTM-CRF	pretrain	88.39
LSTM-CRF	pretrain + char	89.77
LSTM-CRF	pretrain + dropout	90.20
LSTM-CRF	pretrain + dropout + char	**90.94**
S-LSTM	char + dropout	80.88
S-LSTM	pretrain	86.67
S-LSTM	pretrain + char	89.32
S-LSTM	pretrain + dropout	87.96
S-LSTM	pretrain + dropout + char	90.33

Table 5: English NER results with our models, using different configurations. "pretrain" refers to models that include pretrained word embeddings, "char" refers to models that include character-based modeling of words, "dropout" refers to models that include dropout rate.

6   Related Work

In the CoNLL-2002 shared task, Carreras et al. (2002) obtained among the best results on both Dutch and Spanish by combining several small fixed-depth decision trees. Next year, in the CoNLL-2003 Shared Task, Florian et al. (2003) obtained the best score on German by combining the output of four diverse classifiers. Qi et al. (2009) later improved on this with a neural network by doing unsupervised learning on a massive unlabeled corpus.

Several other neural architectures have previously been proposed for NER. For instance, Collobert et al. (2011) uses a CNN over a sequence of word embeddings with a CRF layer on top. This can be thought of as our first model without character-level embeddings and with the bidirectional LSTM being replaced by a CNN. More recently, Huang et al. (2015) presented a model similar to our LSTM-CRF, but using hand-crafted spelling features. Zhou and Xu (2015) also used a similar model and adapted it to the semantic role labeling task. Lin and Wu (2009) used a linear chain CRF with L_2 regularization, they added phrase cluster features extracted from the web data and spelling features. Passos et al. (2014) also used a linear chain CRF with spelling features and gazetteers.

Language independent NER models like ours have also been proposed in the past. Cucerzan and Yarowsky (1999; 2002) present semi-supervised bootstrapping algorithms for named entity recognition by co-training character-level (word-internal) and token-level (context) features. Eisenstein et al. (2011) use Bayesian nonparametrics to construct a database of named entities in an almost unsupervised setting. Ratinov and Roth (2009) quantitatively compare several approaches for NER and build their own supervised model using a regularized average perceptron and aggregating context information.

Finally, there is currently a lot of interest in models for NER that use letter-based representations. Gillick et al. (2015) model the task of sequence-labeling as a sequence to sequence learning problem and incorporate character-based representations into their encoder model. Chiu and Nichols (2015) employ an architecture similar to ours, but instead use CNNs to learn character-level features, in a way similar to the work by Santos and Guimarães (2015).

7 Conclusion

This paper presents two neural architectures for sequence labeling that provide the best NER results ever reported in standard evaluation settings, even compared with models that use external resources, such as gazetteers.

A key aspect of our models are that they model output label dependencies, either via a simple CRF architecture, or using a transition-based algorithm to explicitly construct and label chunks of the input. Word representations are also crucially important for success: we use both pre-trained word representations and "character-based" representations that capture morphological and orthographic information. To prevent the learner from depending too heavily on one representation class, dropout is used.

Acknowledgments

This work was sponsored in part by the Defense Advanced Research Projects Agency (DARPA) Information Innovation Office (I2O) under the Low Resource Languages for Emergent Incidents (LORELEI) program issued by DARPA/I2O under Contract No. HR0011-15-C-0114. Miguel Ballesteros is supported by the European Commission under the contract numbers FP7-ICT-610411 (project MULTISENSOR) and H2020-RIA-645012 (project KRISTINA).

References

Rie Kubota Ando and Tong Zhang. 2005a. A framework for learning predictive structures from multiple tasks and unlabeled data. *The Journal of Machine Learning Research*, 6:1817–1853.

Rie Kubota Ando and Tong Zhang. 2005b. Learning predictive structures. *JMLR*, 6:1817–1853.

Miguel Ballesteros, Chris Dyer, and Noah A. Smith. 2015. Improved transition-based dependency parsing by modeling characters instead of words with LSTMs. In *Proceedings of EMNLP*.

Miguel Ballesteros, Yoav Goldberg, Chris Dyer, and Noah A. Smith. 2016. Training with Exploration Improves a Greedy Stack-LSTM Parser. In *arXiv:1603.03793*.

Yoshua Bengio, Patrice Simard, and Paolo Frasconi. 1994. Learning long-term dependencies with gradient descent is difficult. *Neural Networks, IEEE Transactions on*, 5(2):157–166.

Chris Biemann, Gerhard Heyer, Uwe Quasthoff, and Matthias Richter. 2007. The leipzig corpora collection-monolingual corpora of standard size. *Proceedings of Corpus Linguistic*.

Chris Callison-Burch, Philipp Koehn, Christof Monz, Kay Peterson, Mark Przybocki, and Omar F Zaidan. 2010. Findings of the 2010 joint workshop on statistical machine translation and metrics for machine translation. In *Proceedings of the Joint Fifth Workshop on Statistical Machine Translation and MetricsMATR*, pages 17–53. Association for Computational Linguistics.

Xavier Carreras, Lluís Màrquez, and Lluís Padró. 2002. Named entity extraction using adaboost, proceedings of the 6th conference on natural language learning. *August*, 31:1–4.

Jason PC Chiu and Eric Nichols. 2015. Named entity recognition with bidirectional lstm-cnns. *arXiv preprint arXiv:1511.08308*.

Ronan Collobert, Jason Weston, Léon Bottou, Michael Karlen, Koray Kavukcuoglu, and Pavel Kuksa. 2011. Natural language processing (almost) from scratch. *The Journal of Machine Learning Research*, 12:2493–2537.

Silviu Cucerzan and David Yarowsky. 1999. Language independent named entity recognition combining morphological and contextual evidence. In *Proceedings of the 1999 Joint SIGDAT Conference on EMNLP and VLC*, pages 90–99.

Silviu Cucerzan and David Yarowsky. 2002. Language independent ner using a unified model of internal and contextual evidence. In *proceedings of the 6th conference on Natural language learning-Volume 20*, pages 1–4. Association for Computational Linguistics.

Hong-Jie Dai, Po-Ting Lai, Yung-Chun Chang, and Richard Tzong-Han Tsai. 2015. Enhancing of chemical compound and drug name recognition using representative tag scheme and fine-grained tokenization. *Journal of cheminformatics*, 7(Suppl 1):S14.

Chris Dyer, Miguel Ballesteros, Wang Ling, Austin Matthews, and Noah A. Smith. 2015. Transition-based dependency parsing with stack long short-term memory. In *Proc. ACL*.

Jacob Eisenstein, Tae Yano, William W Cohen, Noah A Smith, and Eric P Xing. 2011. Structured databases of named entities from bayesian nonparametrics. In *Proceedings of the First Workshop on Unsupervised Learning in NLP*, pages 2–12. Association for Computational Linguistics.

Radu Florian, Abe Ittycheriah, Hongyan Jing, and Tong Zhang. 2003. Named entity recognition through classifier combination. In *Proceedings of the seventh conference on Natural language learning at HLT-NAACL 2003-Volume 4*, pages 168–171. Association for Computational Linguistics.

Dan Gillick, Cliff Brunk, Oriol Vinyals, and Amarnag Subramanya. 2015. Multilingual language processing from bytes. *arXiv preprint arXiv:1512.00103*.

David Graff. 2011. Spanish gigaword third edition (ldc2011t12). *Linguistic Data Consortium, University of Pennsylvania, Philadelphia, PA*.

Alex Graves and Jürgen Schmidhuber. 2005. Framewise phoneme classification with bidirectional LSTM networks. In *Proc. IJCNN*.

Geoffrey E Hinton, Nitish Srivastava, Alex Krizhevsky, Ilya Sutskever, and Ruslan R Salakhutdinov. 2012. Improving neural networks by preventing co-adaptation of feature detectors. *arXiv preprint arXiv:1207.0580*.

Sepp Hochreiter and Jürgen Schmidhuber. 1997. Long short-term memory. *Neural Computation*, 9(8):1735–1780.

Johannes Hoffart, Mohamed Amir Yosef, Ilaria Bordino, Hagen Fürstenau, Manfred Pinkal, Marc Spaniol, Bilyana Taneva, Stefan Thater, and Gerhard Weikum. 2011. Robust disambiguation of named entities in text. In *Proceedings of the Conference on Empirical Methods in Natural Language Processing*, pages 782–792. Association for Computational Linguistics.

Zhiheng Huang, Wei Xu, and Kai Yu. 2015. Bidirectional LSTM-CRF models for sequence tagging. *CoRR*, abs/1508.01991.

Yoon Kim, Yacine Jernite, David Sontag, and Alexander M. Rush. 2015. Character-aware neural language models. *CoRR*, abs/1508.06615.

Diederik Kingma and Jimmy Ba. 2014. Adam: A method for stochastic optimization. *arXiv preprint arXiv:1412.6980*.

John Lafferty, Andrew McCallum, and Fernando CN Pereira. 2001. Conditional random fields: Probabilistic models for segmenting and labeling sequence data. In *Proc. ICML*.

Dekang Lin and Xiaoyun Wu. 2009. Phrase clustering for discriminative learning. In *Proceedings of the Joint Conference of the 47th Annual Meeting of the ACL and the 4th International Joint Conference on Natural Language Processing of the AFNLP: Volume 2-Volume 2*, pages 1030–1038. Association for Computational Linguistics.

Wang Ling, Lin Chu-Cheng, Yulia Tsvetkov, Silvio Amir, Rámon Fernandez Astudillo, Chris Dyer, Alan W Black, and Isabel Trancoso. 2015a. Not all contexts are created equal: Better word representations with variable attention. In *Proc. EMNLP*.

Wang Ling, Tiago Luís, Luís Marujo, Ramón Fernandez Astudillo, Silvio Amir, Chris Dyer, Alan W Black, and Isabel Trancoso. 2015b. Finding function in form: Compositional character models for open vocabulary word representation. In *Proceedings of the Conference on Empirical Methods in Natural Language Processing (EMNLP)*.

Gang Luo, Xiaojiang Huang, Chin-Yew Lin, and Zaiqing Nie. 2015. Joint named entity recognition and disambiguation. In *Proc. EMNLP*.

Tomas Mikolov, Kai Chen, Greg Corrado, and Jeffrey Dean. 2013a. Efficient estimation of word representations in vector space. *arXiv preprint arXiv:1301.3781*.

Tomas Mikolov, Ilya Sutskever, Kai Chen, Greg S Corrado, and Jeff Dean. 2013b. Distributed representations of words and phrases and their compositionality. In *Proc. NIPS*.

Joakim Nivre. 2004. Incrementality in deterministic dependency parsing. In *Proceedings of the Workshop on Incremental Parsing: Bringing Engineering and Cognition Together*.

Joel Nothman, Nicky Ringland, Will Radford, Tara Murphy, and James R Curran. 2013. Learning multilingual named entity recognition from wikipedia. *Artificial Intelligence*, 194:151–175.

Robert Parker, David Graff, Junbo Kong, Ke Chen, and Kazuaki Maeda. 2009. English gigaword fourth edition (ldc2009t13). *Linguistic Data Consortium, Univer-sity of Pennsylvania, Philadelphia, PA*.

Alexandre Passos, Vineet Kumar, and Andrew McCallum. 2014. Lexicon infused phrase embeddings for named entity resolution. *arXiv preprint arXiv:1404.5367*.

Yanjun Qi, Ronan Collobert, Pavel Kuksa, Koray Kavukcuoglu, and Jason Weston. 2009. Combining labeled and unlabeled data with word-class distribution learning. In *Proceedings of the 18th ACM conference on Information and knowledge management*, pages 1737–1740. ACM.

Lev Ratinov and Dan Roth. 2009. Design challenges and misconceptions in named entity recognition. In *Proceedings of the Thirteenth Conference on Computational Natural Language Learning*, pages 147–155. Association for Computational Linguistics.

Cicero Nogueira dos Santos and Victor Guimarães. 2015. Boosting named entity recognition with neural character embeddings. *arXiv preprint arXiv:1505.05008*.

Erik F. Tjong Kim Sang and Fien De Meulder. 2003. Introduction to the conll-2003 shared task: Language-independent named entity recognition. In *Proc. CoNLL*.

Erik F. Tjong Kim Sang. 2002. Introduction to the conll-2002 shared task: Language-independent named entity recognition. In *Proc. CoNLL*.

Joseph Turian, Lev Ratinov, and Yoshua Bengio. 2010. Word representations: A simple and general method for semi-supervised learning. In *Proc. ACL*.

Matthew D Zeiler. 2012. Adadelta: An adaptive learning rate method. *arXiv preprint arXiv:1212.5701*.

Yue Zhang and Stephen Clark. 2011. Syntactic processing using the generalized perceptron and beam search. *Computational Linguistics*, 37(1).

Xiang Zhang, Junbo Zhao, and Yann LeCun. 2015. Character-level convolutional networks for text classification. In *Advances in Neural Information Processing Systems*, pages 649–657.

Jie Zhou and Wei Xu. 2015. End-to-end learning of semantic role labeling using recurrent neural networks. In *Proceedings of the Annual Meeting of the Association for Computational Linguistics*.

Dynamic Feature Induction:
The Last Gist to the State-of-the-Art

Jinho D. Choi
Department of Mathematics and Computer Science
Emory University
Atlanta, GA 30322, USA
jinho.choi@emory.edu

Abstract

We introduce a novel technique called dynamic feature induction that keeps inducing high dimensional features automatically until the feature space becomes 'more' linearly separable. Dynamic feature induction searches for the feature combinations that give strong clues for distinguishing certain label pairs, and generates joint features from these combinations. These induced features are trained along with the primitive low dimensional features. Our approach was evaluated on two core NLP tasks, part-of-speech tagging and named entity recognition, and showed the state-of-the-art results for both tasks, achieving the accuracy of 97.64 and the F1-score of 91.00 respectively, with about a 25% increase in the feature space.

1 Introduction

Feature engineering typically involves two processes: the process of discovering novel features with domain knowledge, and the process of optimizing combinations between existing features. Discovering novel features may require linguistic background as well as good understanding in machine learning such that it is often difficult to do. Optimizing feature combinations can be also difficult but usually requires less domain knowledge and more importantly, it can be as effective as discovering new features. It has been shown for many tasks that approaches using simple machine learning with extensive feature engineering outperform ones using more advanced machine learning with less intensive feature engineering (Xue and Palmer, 2004; Bengtson and Roth, 2008; Ratinov and Roth, 2009; Zhang and Nivre, 2011).

Recently, people have tried to automate the second part of feature engineering, the optimization of feature combinations, through leading-edge models such as neural networks (Collobert et al., 2011). Coupled with embedding approaches (Mikolov et al., 2013; Le and Mikolov, 2014; Pennington et al., 2014), neural networks can find the optimal feature combinations using techniques such as random weight initialization and back-propagation, and have established the new state-of-the-art for several tasks (Socher et al., 2013; Devlin et al., 2014; Yu et al., 2014). However, neural networks are not as good at optimizing combinations between sparse features, which are still the most dominating factors in natural language processing.

This paper introduces a new technique called dynamic feature induction that automates the optimization of feature combinations (Section 3), and can be easily adapted to any NLP task using sparse features. Dynamic feature induction allows humans to focus on the first part of feature engineering, the discovery of novel features, while machines handle the second part. Our approach was experimented with two core NLP tasks, part-of-speech tagging (Section 4) and named entity recognition (Section 5) and showed the state-of-the-art results for both tasks.

2 Background

2.1 Nonlinearity in NLP

Linear classification algorithms such as Perceptron, Winnow, or Support Vector Machines with a linear kernel have performed exceptionally well for various NLP tasks (Collins, 2002; Zhang and Johnson, 2003; Pradhan et al., 2005). This is not because our feature space is linearly separable by nature, but sparse fea-

Proceedings of NAACL-HLT 2016, pages 271–281,
San Diego, California, June 12-17, 2016. ©2016 Association for Computational Linguistics

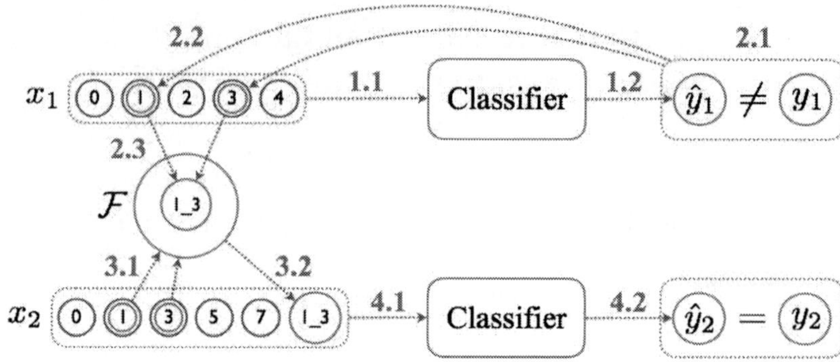

Figure 1: Overview of dynamic feature induction.

tures introduced to NLP yield very high dimensional vector space such that it is rather forced to be linearly separable. For example, NLP features for a word w_i typically involve the word forms of w_{i-1} and w_i (e.g., f_{i-1}, f_i). If the feature space is not linearly separable with these features, a common trick is to introduce 'higher' dimension features by joining 'lower' dimension features together (e.g., f_{i-1}_f_i). The more joint features we introduce, the higher chance we get for the feature space being linearly separable although these joint features can be very overfitted.

Let us define low dimensional features as the primitive features such as f_{i-1} or f_i, and high dimensional features as the joint features such as f_i_f_{i+1}. [1] Low dimensional features are well explored for most NLP tasks; it is the high dimensional features that are quite sensitive to specific tasks. Finding high dimensional features can be a manual intensive work and this is what dynamic feature induction intends to take over.

2.2 Related Work

Kudo and Matsumoto (2003) introduced the polynomial kernel expansion that explicitly enumerated the feature combinations. Our approach is distinguished because they used a frequency-based PrefixSpan algorithm (Pei et al., 2001) whereas we used the online learning weights for finding the feature combinations. Goldberg and Elhadad (2008) suggested an efficient algorithm for computing polynomial kernel SVMs by combining inverted indexing and kernel expansion. Their work is focused more on improving support vector machines whereas our work is generalized to any linear classification algorithm.

Okanohara and Tsujii (2009) introduced an approach for generating feature combinations using ℓ_1 regularization and grafting (Perkins et al., 2003). Although we share similar ideas, their grafting algorithm starts with an empty feature set whereas ours starts with low dimensional features, and their correlation parameters $\alpha_{i,y}$ are pre-computed whereas ours are dynamically determined. Strubell et al. (2015) suggested an algorithm that dynamically selected strong features during decoding. Our work is distinguished because we do not run multiple training phases as they do for figuring our strong features.

3 Dynamic Feature Induction

The intuition behind dynamic feature induction is to keep populating high dimensional features by joining low dimensional features together until the feature space becomes 'more' linearly separable.[2] Figure 1 shows how features are induced during training:

1. Given a training instance (x_1, y_1), where x_1 is a feature set consisting of 5 features and y_1 is the gold label, the classifier predicts the label $\hat{y}_1$.

2. Let us refer "strong features for y against $\hat{y}$" to features that give strong clues for distinguishing y from $\hat{y}$. If $\hat{y}_1$ is not equal to y_1 (2.1), strong features for y_1 against $\hat{y}_1$ in x_1 are selected (2.2), and combinations of these features are added to the induced feature set $\mathcal{F}$ (2.3).

3. Given a new training instance (x_2, y_2), combinations of features in x_2 are checked by $\mathcal{F}$ (3.1), and appended to x_2 if allowed (3.2).

---

[1] The joint features tend to yield a much higher dimensional feature space than the primitive features.

[2] The term 'more' is used because dynamic feature induction does not guarantee for the feature space to be linearly separable.

4. The extended feature set x_2 is fed into the classifier. If $\hat{y}_2$ is equal to y_2, no feature combination is induced from x_2.

Thus, high dimensional features in $\mathcal{F}$ are incrementally induced and learned along with low dimensional features during training. During decoding, each feature set is extended by the induced features in $\mathcal{F}$, and the prediction is made using the extended feature set. The size of $\mathcal{F}$ can grow up to $|\mathcal{X}|^2$, where $|\mathcal{X}|$ is the size of low dimensional features. However, we found that $|\mathcal{F}|$ is more like $1/4 \cdot |\mathcal{X}|$ in practice.

The following sections explain our approach in details. Sections 3.1, 3.2, and 3.3 describe how features are induced and learned during training. Sections 3.4 and 3.5 describe how the induced features are stored and expanded during decoding.

3.1 Feature Induction

Algorithm 1 shows an online learning algorithm that induces and learns high dimensional features during training. It takes the set of training instances D and the learning rate η, and returns the weight vector $\mathbf{w}$ and the set of induced features $\mathcal{F}$.

Algorithm 1 Feature Induction

   Input: D: training set, η: learning rate.
   Output: $\mathbf{w}$: weight vector, $\mathcal{F}$: induced feature set.

1:   $\mathbf{w} \leftarrow \mathbf{g} \leftarrow 0$
2:   $\mathcal{F} \leftarrow \varnothing$
3:   **until** max epoch is reached **do**
4:     **foreach** $(x, y) \in D$ **do**
5:       $\hat{y} \leftarrow \arg\max_{y' \in \mathcal{Y}}(\mathbf{w} \cdot \phi(x, y', \mathcal{F}) - I_y(y'))$
6:       **if** $y \neq \hat{y}$ **then**
7:         $\partial \leftarrow \phi(x, y, \mathcal{F}) - \phi(x, \hat{y}, \mathcal{F})$
8:         $\mathbf{g} \leftarrow \mathbf{g} + \partial \circ \partial$
9:         $\mathbf{w} \leftarrow \mathbf{w} + (\eta/(\rho + \sqrt{\mathbf{g}})) \cdot \partial$
10:      $\mathbf{v} \leftarrow [\mathbf{w} \circ \phi(x, y, \varnothing)]_y - [\mathbf{w} \circ \phi(x, \hat{y}, \varnothing)]_{\hat{y}}$
11:      $\mathcal{L} \leftarrow \arg k \max_{\forall i} \mathbf{v}_i$
12:      **for** $i = 2$ **to** $|\mathcal{L}|$ **do**
13:         $\mathcal{F} \leftarrow \mathcal{F} \cup \{(\mathcal{L}_1, \mathcal{L}_i)\}$
14:   **return** $\mathbf{w}, \mathcal{F}$

The algorithm begins by initializing the weight vector $\mathbf{w}$, the diagonal vector $\mathbf{g}$, and the induced feature set $\mathcal{F}$ (lines 1-2). For each instance $(x, y) \in D$ where y is the gold-label for the feature set x, it predicts $\hat{y}$ maximizing $\mathbf{w} \cdot \phi(x, y', \mathcal{F}) - I_y(y')$, where I is defined as follows (lines 4-5):

$$I_y(y') \leftarrow \begin{cases} 1, & \text{if } y = y'. \\ 0, & \text{otherwise.} \end{cases}$$

The feature map ϕ takes $(x, y, \mathcal{F})$, and returns a $d \times l$-dimensional vector, where d and l are the sizes of features and labels, respectively; each dimension contains the value for a particular feature and a label.[3] If certain combinations between features in x exist in $\mathcal{F}$, they are appended to the feature vector along with the low dimensional features (see Section 3.5 for more details). The indicator function I allows our algorithm to be optimized for the hinge loss for multiclass classification (Crammer and Singer, 2002):

$$\ell_h = \max[0, 1 + \mathbf{w} \cdot (\phi(x, \hat{y}, \mathcal{F}) - \phi(x, y, \mathcal{F}))]$$

If y is not equal to $\hat{y}$ (line 6), the partial vector ∂ is measured (line 7), and $\mathbf{g}$ and $\mathbf{w}$ are updated (lines 8-9) by AdaGrad (Duchi et al., 2011), where the learning rate η is adjusted by $\mathbf{g}$ (in our case, $\rho =$1E-5). Once $\mathbf{w}$ is updated, the d-dimensional vector $\mathbf{v}$ is generated by subtracting $[\mathbf{w} \circ \phi(x, \hat{y}, \varnothing)]_{\hat{y}}$ from $[\mathbf{w} \circ \phi(x, y, \varnothing)]_y$ (line 10), where $[\ldots]_y$ returns only the portion of the values relevant to y (Figure 2).

The i'th element in $\mathbf{v}$ represents the strength of the i'th feature for y against $\hat{y}$; the greater $\mathbf{v}_i$ is, the stronger the i'th feature is. Next, indices of the top-k entries in $\mathbf{v}$ are collected in the ordered list $\mathcal{L}$ (line 11), representing the strongest features for y against $\hat{y}$.[4] Finally, the pairs of the first index in $\mathcal{L}$, representing the strongest feature, and the other indices in $\mathcal{L}$ are added to the induced feature set $\mathcal{F}$ (lines 12-13). For example, if $\mathcal{L} = [i, j, k]$ such that $\mathbf{v}_i \geq \mathbf{v}_j \geq \mathbf{v}_k > 0$, two pairs, (i, j) and (i, k), are added to $\mathcal{F}$.

For all our experiments, $k = 3$ is used; increasing k beyond this cutoff did not show much improvement. Notice that all induced features in $\mathcal{F}$ are derived by joining only low dimensional features together. Our algorithm does not join a high dimensional feature with either a low dimensional feature or another high dimensional feature. This was done intentionally to prevent from the feature space being exploded; such features can be induced by replacing $\varnothing$ with $\mathcal{F}$ in the line 10 as follows:

$$\mathbf{v} \leftarrow [\mathbf{w} \circ \phi(x, y, \mathcal{F})]_y - [\mathbf{w} \circ \phi(x, \hat{y}, \mathcal{F})]_{\hat{y}}$$

---

[3] In most cases, these values are either 0 or 1.

[4] 'arg k max' returns the ordered list of indices whose values in $\mathbf{v}$ are [1] k-largest and [2] greater than 0.

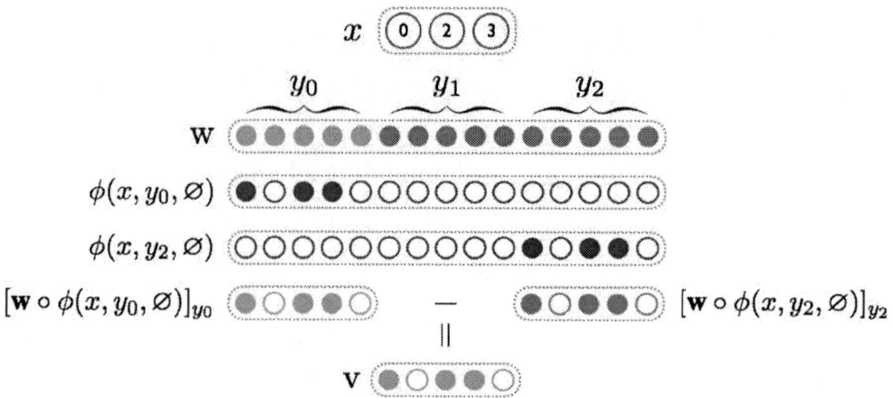

Figure 2: Given the weight vector $\mathbf{w}$ and the feature map ϕ, $[\mathbf{w} \circ \phi(x, y, \varnothing)]_y$ takes the Hadamard product between $\mathbf{w}$ and $\phi(x, y, \varnothing)$, then truncates the resulting vector with respect to the label y.

It is worth mentioning that we did not find it useful for joining intermediate features together (e.g., (j, k) in the above example). It is possible to utilize these combinations by weighting them differently, which we will explore in the future. Additionally, we experimented with the combinations between strong and weak features (joining i'th and j'th features, where $\mathbf{v}_i > 0$ and $\mathbf{v}_j < 0$), which again was not so useful. We are planning to evaluate our approach on more tasks and data, which will give us better understanding of what combinations are the most effective.

3.2 Regularized Dual Averaging

Each high dimensional feature in $\mathcal{F}$ is induced for making classification between two labels, y and $\hat{y}$, but it may or may not be helpful for distinguishing labels other than those two. Our algorithm can be modified to learn the weights of the induced features only for their relevant labels by adding the label information to $\mathcal{F}$, which would change the line 13 in Algorithm 1 as follows:

$$\mathcal{F} \leftarrow \mathcal{F} \cup \{(\mathcal{L}_1, \mathcal{L}_i, y, \hat{y})\}$$

However, introducing features targeting specific label pairs potentially confuses the classifier, especially when they are trained with the low dimensional features targeting all labels. Instead, it is better to apply a feature selection technique such as ℓ_1 regularization so the induced features can be selectively learned for labels that find those features useful. We adapt regularized dual averaging (Xiao, 2010), which efficiently finds the convergence rates for online convex

optimization, and works most effectively with sparse feature vectors. To apply regularized dual averaging, the line 1 in Algorithm 1 is changed to:

$$\mathbf{w} \leftarrow \mathbf{g} \leftarrow \mathbf{c} \leftarrow 0; \ t \leftarrow 1$$

$\mathbf{c}$ is a $d \times l$-dimensional vector consisting of accumulative penalties. t is the number of weight vectors generated during training. Although $\mathbf{w}$ is technically not updated when $y = \hat{y}$, it is still considered a new vector. Thus, t is incremented for every training instance, so $t \leftarrow t + 1$ is inserted after the line 5. $\mathbf{c}$ is updated by adding the partial vector ∂ as follows (to be inserted after the line 7):

$$\mathbf{c} \leftarrow \mathbf{c} + \partial$$

Thus, each dimension in $\mathbf{c}$ represents the accumulative penalty (or reward) for a particular feature and a label. At last, the line 9 is changed to:

$$\mathbf{w} \leftarrow (\eta/(\rho+\sqrt{\mathbf{g}})) \cdot \ell_1(\mathbf{c}, t, \lambda)$$

$$\ell_1(\mathbf{c}, t, \lambda) \leftarrow \begin{cases} \mathbf{c}_i - \mathrm{sgn}(\mathbf{c}_i) \cdot \lambda \cdot t, & |\mathbf{c}_{\vee i}| > \lambda \cdot t. \\ 0, & \text{otherwise.} \end{cases}$$

The function ℓ_1 takes $\mathbf{c}$, t, and the regularizer parameter λ tuned during development. If the absolute value of the accumulative penalty $\mathbf{c}_i$ is greater than $\lambda \cdot t$, the weight $\mathbf{w}_i$ is updated by λ and t; otherwise, it is assigned to 0. For our experiments, RDA was able to throw out irrelevant features successfully, and showed improvement in accuracy; in fact, dynamic feature induction without RDA did not show as much improvement over low dimensional features.

3.3 Locally Optimal Learning to Search

Features in most NLP tasks are extracted from structures (e.g., sequence, tree). For structured learning, we adapt "locally optimal learning to search" (Chang et al., 2015b), that is a member of imitation learning similar to DAGGER (Ross et al., 2011). LOLS not only performs well relative to the reference policy, but also can improve upon the reference policy, showing very good results for tasks such as part-of-speech tagging and dependency parsing. We adapt LOLS by setting the reference policy as follows:

1. The reference policy π determines how often the gold label y is picked over the predicted label $\hat{y}$ to build a structure. For all our experiments, π is initialized to 0.95.

2. For the first epoch, since π is 0.95, y is randomly picked over $\hat{y}$ for 95% of the time.

3. After every epoch, π is multiplied by 0.95. This allows the next epoch to pick y less often than the previous epoch (e.g., π becomes $0.95^2 = 0.9025$ for the 2nd epoch so y is picked about 90% of the time instead of 95%).

For our experiments, LOLS gave only marginal improvement, probably because the tasks we evaluated, part-of-speech tagging and named entity recognition, did not yield complex structures. However, we still included this in our framework because we wanted to evaluate our approach on more tasks such as dependency parsing where learning to search algorithms show a clear advantage (Goldberg and Nivre, 2012; Choi and McCallum, 2013; Chang et al., 2015a).

3.4 Feature Hashing

Feature hashing is a technique of converting string features to vectors (Ganchev and Dredze, 2008; Weinberger et al., 2009). Given a string feature f and a hash function h, the index of f in the vector space is determined by taking the remainder of the hash code:

$$k \leftarrow h_{\text{string}\rightarrow\text{int}}(f) \bmod \delta$$

The divisor δ is tuned during development. Feature hashing allows to convert string features into sparse vectors without reserving an extra space for a map whose keys and values are the string features and their

indices. Given a feature index pair (i, j) representing strong features for y against $\hat{y}$ (Section 3.1), the index of the induced feature can be measured as follows:

$$k \leftarrow h_{\text{int}\rightarrow\text{int}}(i \cdot |\mathcal{X}| + j) \bmod \delta$$

For efficiency, feature hashing is adapted to our system such that the induced feature set $\mathcal{F}$ is actually not a set but a δ-dimensional boolean array, where each dimension represents the validity of the corresponding induced feature. Thus, the line 13 in Algorithm 1 is changed to:

$$k \leftarrow h_{\text{int}\rightarrow\text{int}}(\mathcal{L}_1 \cdot |\mathcal{X}| + \mathcal{L}_i) \bmod \delta$$
$$\mathcal{F}_k \leftarrow \texttt{True}$$

For the choice of h, $\texttt{xxHash}$ is used, that is a fast non-cryptographic hash algorithm showing the perfect score on the Q.Score.[5]

3.5 Feature Expansion

Algorithm 2 describes how high dimensional features are expanded from low dimensional features during training and decoding. It takes the sparse vector $\mathbf{x}^l$ containing only low dimensional features and returns a new sparse vector $\mathbf{x}^{l+h}$ containing both low and high dimensional features.

Algorithm 2 Feature Expansion

Input:	$\mathbf{x}^l$: sparse feature vector containing only low dimensional features.
Output:	$\mathbf{x}^{l+h}$: sparse feature vector containing both low and high dimensional features.

1:    $\mathbf{x}^{l+h} \leftarrow \text{copy}(\mathbf{x}^l)$
2:    **for** $i \leftarrow 1$ **to** $|\mathbf{x}^l|$ **do**
3:       **for** $j \leftarrow i + 1$ **to** $|\mathbf{x}^l|$ **do**
4:          $k \leftarrow h_{\text{int}\rightarrow\text{int}}(i \cdot |\mathcal{X}| + j) \bmod \delta$
5:          **if** $\mathcal{F}_k$ **then** $\mathbf{x}^{l+h}$.append(k)
6:    **return** $\mathbf{x}^{l+h}$

The algorithm begins by copying $\mathbf{x}^l$ to $\mathbf{x}^{l+h}$ (line 1). For every combination $(i, j) \in \mathbf{x}^l \times \mathbf{x}^l$, where i and j represent the corresponding feature indices (lines 2-3), it first measures the index k of the feature combination (line 4), then checks if this combination is valid (Section 3.4). If the combination is valid, meaning that ($\mathcal{F}_k = \texttt{True}$), k is added to $\mathbf{x}^{l+h}$ (line 5). Finally, $\mathbf{x}^{l+h}$ is returned with the expanded high dimensional features.

---

[5] $\texttt{https://github.com/Cyan4973/xxHash}$

4 Part-of-Speech Tagging

4.1 Corpus

The Wall Street Journal corpus from the Penn Treebank III is used (Marcus et al., 1993) with the standard split for part-of-speech tagging experiments.

Set	Sections	Sentences	ALL	OOV
TRN	0-18	38,219	912,344	0
DEV	19-21	5,527	131,768	4,467
TST	22-24	5,462	129,654	3,649

Table 1: Distributions of the Wall Street Journal corpus. TRN: training, DEV: development, TST: evaluation, ALL: all words, OOV: out-of-vocabulary words.

4.2 Tagging and Learning Algorithms

A one-pass, left-to-right tagging algorithm is used for our experiments. Such a simple algorithm is chosen because we want to see the performance gain purely from our approach, not by a more sophisticated tagging algorithm (Toutanova et al., 2003; Shen et al., 2007), which may improve the performance further.

For learning, the final algorithm from Section 3 is used. Additionally, mini-batch is applied, where each batch consists of training instances from k-number of sentences, causing the sizes of these batches different. We found that grouping instances with respect to the sentence boundary was more effective than batching them across arbitrary sentences. For all our experiments, the learning rate $\eta = 0.02$ and the mini-batch boundary $k = 5$ were used without tuning.

4.3 Ambiguity Classes

The ambiguity class of a word is the concatenation of all possible tags for that word. For example, if the word 'study' can be tagged by NN (common noun) or VB (base verb), its ambiguity class becomes NN_VB. Instead of building ambiguity classes only from the training dataset, we automatically tagged a mixture of large datasets, the English Wikipedia articles[6] and the New York Times corpus,[7] and pre-constructed ambiguity classes using the automatic tags before training. This was motivated by Moore (2015), who showed extraordinary results on the out-of-vocabulary words by limiting the classification to the ambiguity classes collected from such large corpora.

---

[6] dumps.wikimedia.org/enwiki
[7] catalog.ldc.upenn.edu/LDC2008T19

We used the ClearNLP POS tagger (Choi and Palmer, 2012) for tagging the data (about 141M words), threw away tags appearing less than a certain threshold, and created the ambiguity classes. For each word, tags appearing less than 20% of the time for that word were discarded. As the result, about 2M ambiguity classes were collected from these datasets.

4.4 Feature Template

Table 2 shows the template for low dimensional features. Digits inside the curly brackets imply the context windows with respect to the word w_i to be tagged. For example, $f_{\{0,\pm1\}}$ represents the word-forms of w_i, w_{i-1}, and w_{i+1}. No joint features (e.g., $f_0\text{-}f_1$) are included in this template; they should be automatically induced by dynamic feature induction.

Orthographic (Giménez and Màrquez, 2004) and word shape (Finkel et al., 2005) features are adapted from the previous work. The positional features indicate whether w_i is the first or the last word in the sentence. Word clusters are trained on the same datasets in Section 4.3 using Brown et al. (1992).

$$f_{:\{0,\pm1,\pm2\}}, f_{u:\{0,\pm1,\pm2\}}, s_{:\{0,\pm1\}}, c_{:\{0,\pm1\}},$$
$$\pi_{2:\{0\}}, \pi_{3:\{0\}}, \sigma_{1:\{0\}}, \sigma_{2:\{0\}}, \sigma_{3:\{0\}}, \sigma_{4:\{0\}},$$
$$p_{:\{0,-1,-2,-3\}}, a_{:\{0,1,2,3\}}, \mathcal{O}_{:\{0\}}, \mathcal{P}_{:\{0\}}$$

Table 2: Feature template for part-of-speech tagging. f: word-form, f_u: uncapitalized word-form, s: word shape, c: word cluster, π_k: k'th prefix, σ_k: k'th suffix, p: part-of-speech tag, a: ambiguity class, $\mathcal{O}$: orthographic feature set, $\mathcal{P}$: positional feature set.

4.5 Development

The regularization parameter λ (Section 3.2) and the modulo divisor δ (Section 3.4) are tuned during development through grid search on $\lambda \in$ [1E-9, 1E-6] and $\delta \in$ [1.5M, 5M]. Table 3 shows the accuracies achieved by our models on the development set.

Model	ALL	OOV	FEAT
M_0: baseline	97.09	86.14	365,400
M_1: M_0 + ext. ambi.	97.37	91.92	365,409
M_2: M_1 + clusters	97.45	91.96	372,181
M_3: M_1 + dynamic	97.42	92.10	468,378
M_4: M_2 + dynamic	97.48	92.21	473,134

Table 3: Part-of-speech tagging accuracies on the development set. FEAT: the number of features generated by each model.

M_0 used the tagging and the learning algorithms in Section 4.2 and the feature template in Section 4.4, where the ambiguity classes were collected only from the training dataset; dynamic feature induction was not used for M_0. By applying the external ambiguity classes in Section 4.3, M_1 achieved about a 5.8% improvement on OOV. M_2 gained small improvements by adding word clusters. Coupled with dynamic feature induction, M_3 and M_4 gained about 0.04% and 0.2% improvements on average for ALL and OOV.

For both M_3 and M_4, about 100K more features were generated from M_1 and M_2, implying that about 25% of the features were automatically induced by dynamic feature induction. It is worth pointing out that improving upon M_1 was a difficult task because it was already reaching near the state-of-the-art. The external ambiguity classes by themselves were strong enough to make accurate predictions such that the induced features did not find a critical role in the classification.

4.6 Evaluation

Table 4 shows the accuracies achieved by the models from Section 4.5 and the previous state-of-the-art approaches on the evaluation set.

Approach	ALL	OOV	EXT
Manning (2011)	97.29	89.70	
Manning (2011)	97.32	90.79	✓
Shen et al. (2007)	97.33	89.61	
Sun (2014)	97.36	-	
Moore (2015)	97.36	91.09	✓
Spoustová et al. (2009)	97.44	-	✓
Søgaard (2011)	97.50	-	✓
Tsuboi (2014)	97.51	91.64	✓
This work: M_0	97.18	86.35	
This work: M_1	97.37	91.34	✓
This work: M_2	97.46	91.23	✓
This work: M_3	97.52	91.53	✓
This work: M_4	**97.64**	**92.03**	✓

Table 4: Part-of-speech tagging accuracies on the evaluation set. EXT: whether or not the approach used external data.

The results on the evaluation set appear much more promising. Still, the biggest gain was made by M_1, but our final model M_4 was able to achieve a 0.8% improvement on OOV over M_2, and showed the state-of-the-art results on both ALL and OOV. Interestingly,

M_2 showed a slightly lower accuracy on OOV than M_1 even with the additional word cluster features. On the other hand, M_2 did show a slightly higher accuracy on ALL, indicating that the model was probably too overfitted to the in-vocabulary words.[8] However, M_4 was still able to achieve improvements over M_2 on both ALL and OOV, implying that dynamic feature induction facilitated the classifier to be trained more robustly.

5 Named Entity Recognition

5.1 Corpus

The English corpus from the CoNLL'03 shared task is used (Tjong Kim Sang and De Meulder, 2003) for named entity recognition experiments.

Set	Articles	Sentences	Words
TRN	946	14,987	203,621
DEV	216	3,466	51,362
TST	231	3,684	46,435

Table 5: Distributions of the English corpus from the CoNLL'03 shared task. TRN: training, DEV: development, TST: evaluation.

5.2 Feature Template

Table 6 shows the feature template for NER, adapting the specifications in Table 2. Following the state-of-the-art approaches (Table 8), word clusters are trained on the Reuters Corpus Volume I (Lewis et al., 2004) using Brown et al. (1992). Named entity gazetteers are collected from DBPedia.[9] Word embeddings are trained on the datasets in Section 4.3 using Mikolov et al. (2013) and appended to the sparse feature vectors as dense vectors. Note that the word embedding features did not participate in dynamic feature induction; it was not intuitive how to combine sparse and dense features together so we left it as a future work.

$$f_{:\{0,\pm1\}},\ f_{u:\{0,\pm1,\pm2\}},\ s_{:\{0,\pm1\}},\ l_{:\{0\}},\ c_{:\{0,1,2\}},$$
$$e_{:\{0,\pm1,\pm2,\pm3,\pm4\}},\ \pi_{1:\{0\}},\ \pi_{3:\{1\}},\ \sigma_{1:\{0\}},\ \sigma_{3:\{-1,0\}},$$
$$p_{:\{0,\pm1,\pm2\}},\ n_{:\{-1,-2,-3\}},\ z_{:\{\pm1,0,2,3\}},\ \mathcal{O}_{:\{0\}},\ \mathcal{O}_{:\{1\}}$$

Table 6: Feature template for named entity recognition. f: word-form, f_u: uncapitalized word-form, s: word shape, l: lemma, c: word cluster, e: word embedding, π_k: k'th prefix, σ_k: k'th suffix, p: part-of-speech tag, n: named entity tag, z: named entity gazetteer, $\mathcal{O}$: orthographic feature set.

---

[8] A similar trend is shown in Table 3 for M_1 and M_2.
[9] `wiki.dbpedia.org/downloads2015-04`

5.3 Development

The regularization parameter and the modulo divisor are tuned during development through the same grid search in Section 4.5. Table 7 shows the precisions and the recalls achieved by our models on the development set (the F1-scores are shown in Table 8).

Model	P	R	FEAT
M_0: baseline	90.87	89.15	164,440
M_1: M_0 + gazetteers	92.30	90.61	164,720
M_2: M_1 + clusters	93.66	91.79	169,232
M_3: M_2 + embeddings	94.14	92.43	169,682
M_4: M_3 + dynamic	94.50	93.10	208,860

Table 7: Precision and recall on the development set for named entity recognition. P: precision, R: recall.

M_0 used the tagging and the learning algorithms in Section 4.2 and the feature template in Section 5.2, excluding the gazetteer, cluster, and embedding features; dynamic feature induction was not applied to M_0. $M_{\{1,2,3\}}$ gained incremental improvements from the gazetteer, cluster, and embedding features, respectively. M_4 showed 0.36% and 0.67% improvements on precision and recall respectively, and generated about 40K more features compared to M_3. This is about 23% increase in features that is similar to the increase shown in Table 3.

5.4 Evaluation

Table 8 shows the F1-scores achieved by our models and the previous state-of-the-art approaches.[10]

Approach	DEV	TST
Turian et al. (2010)	93.25	89.41
Suzuki and Isozaki (2008)	**94.48**	89.92
Ratinov and Roth (2009)	93.50	90.57
Lin and Wu (2009)	-	90.90
Passos et al. (2014)	94.46	90.90
This work: M_0	90.00	84.44
This work: M_1	91.45	86.85
This work: M_2	92.72	89.64
This work: M_3	93.27	90.57
This work: M_4	93.79	**91.00**

Table 8: F1-scores on the development and the evaluation sets for named entity recognition.

---

[10]Ratinov and Roth (2009) reported the F1-score of 90.80 on the evaluation set, but that model was trained on both the training and the development sets so not compared in this table.

All models showed improvements over their predecessors; the improvements made in TST were more dramatic than the ones made in DEV although they followed a very similar trend. Notice that M_3, not using dynamic feature induction, showed very similar scores to Ratinov and Roth (2009). This was not surprising because M_3 adapted many features suggested by them, except for the non-local features.[11]

M_4 achieved about 0.5% improvements over M_3, showing the state-of-the-art result on TST. Considering that M_3 was already near state-of-the-art, this improvement was meaningful. It was interesting that Suzuki and Isozaki (2008) achieved the state-of-the-art result on DEV although their score on TST was much lower than the other approaches. This might be because features extracted from the huge external data they used were overfitted to DEV, but more thorough analysis needs to be done. On the other hand, Passos et al. (2014) achieved the near state-of-the-art result on DEV while it also got a very high score on TST by utilizing phrase embeddings, which we will look into in the future.

6 Conclusion

In this paper, we introduced a novel technique called dynamic feature induction that automatically induces high dimensional features so the feature space can be more linearly separable. Our approach was evaluated on two NLP tasks, part-of-speech tagging and named entity recognition, and showed the state-of-the-art results on both tasks. The improvements achieved by dynamic feature induction might not be statistically significant, but important because they gave the last gist to the state-of-the-art; without this last gist, our system would have not reached the bar.

It is worth mentioning that we also experimented with several feature templates including many joint features without applying dynamic feature induction. The results we got from these manually induced features were not any better (often worse) than the ones achieved by dynamic feature induction, which was very encouraging. In the future, we will experiment our approach on more NLP tasks such as dependency parsing and conference resolution where induced features should play a more critical role.

---

[11]We transformed the original data into the BILOU notation, which was also suggested by Ratinov and Roth (2009).

We concede that our approach is more empirically motivated than theoretically justified. For instance, the choice of k (line 11) or the combination configuration for $\mathcal{L}$ (line 13) in Algorithm 1 are rather empirically derived. All the parameters are automatically tuned by running grid searches on the development sets (Sections 4.5 and 5.3); it would be intellectually intriguing to find a more principled way of adjusting these hyper-parameters than just brute-force search.

The locally optimal learning to search is used to help structured learning although it gives a relatively smaller impact to the tasks involving sequence classification such as part-of-speech tagging and named entity recognition. This framework is used because we plan to apply our approach on more structurally oriented tasks such as dependency parsing and AMR parsing. Our work is also related to feature grouping, which has been shown to be beneficial in learning high-dimensional data (Zhong and Kwok, 2011; Suzuki and Nagata, 2013). It will be interesting to compare our work to the previous work and see the strengths and weaknesses of our approach.

Acknowledgments

We gratefully acknowledge the support of the Yahoo Academic Career Enhancement Award, the IPsoft Development Enhancement Grant, the University Research Committee Award, and the Infosys Research Enhancement Grant. Any contents expressed in this material are those of the authors and do not necessarily reflect the views of these awards and grants.

References

Eric Bengtson and Dan Roth. 2008. Understanding the Value of Features for Coreference Resolution. In *Proceedings of the 2008 Conference on Empirical Methods in Natural Language Processing*, EMNLP'08, pages 294–303.

Peter F. Brown, Peter V. deSouza, Robert L. Mercer, Vincent J. Della Pietra, and Jenifer C. Lai. 1992. Class-based n-gram Models of Natural Language. *Computational Linguistics*, 18(4):467–480.

Kai-Wei Chang, He He, Hal Daumé III, and John Langford. 2015a. Learning to Search for Dependencies. *arXiv:1503.05615*.

Kai-Wei Chang, Akshay Krishnamurthy, Alekh Agarwal, Hal Daume, and John Langford. 2015b. Learning to Search Better than Your Teacher. In *Proceedings of the 32nd International Conference on Machine Learning*, ICML'15, pages 2058–2066.

Jinho D. Choi and Andrew McCallum. 2013. Transition-based Dependency Parsing with Selectional Branching. In *Proceedings of the 51st Annual Meeting of the Association for Computational Linguistics*, ACL'13, pages 1052–1062.

Jinho D. Choi and Martha Palmer. 2012. Fast and Robust Part-of-Speech Tagging Using Dynamic Model Selection. In *Proceedings of the 50th Annual Meeting of the Association for Computational Linguistics*, ACL'12, pages 363–367.

Michael Collins. 2002. Discriminative Training Methods for Hidden Markov Models: Theory and Experiments with Perceptron Algorithms. In *Proceedings of the conference on Empirical methods in natural language processing*, EMNLP'02, pages 1–8.

Ronan Collobert, Jason Weston, Léon Bottou, Michael Karlen, Koray Kavukcuoglu, and Pavel Kuksa. 2011. Natural Language Processing (Almost) from Scratch. *Journal of Machine Learning Research*, 12:2493–2537.

Koby Crammer and Yoram Singer. 2002. On the Algorithmic Implementation of Multiclass Kernel-based Vector Machines. *Journal of Machine Learning Research*, 2:265–292.

Jacob Devlin, Rabih Zbib, Zhongqiang Huang, Thomas Lamar, Richard Schwartz, and John Makhoul. 2014. Fast and Robust Neural Network Joint Models for Statistical Machine Translation. In *Proceedings of the 52nd Annual Meeting of the Association for Computational Linguistics*, ACL'14, pages 1370–1380.

John Duchi, Elad Hazan, and Yoram Singer. 2011. Adaptive Subgradient Methods for Online Learning and Stochastic Optimization. *The Journal of Machine Learning Research*, 12(39):2121–2159.

Jenny Finkel, Shipra Dingare, Christopher Manning, Malvina Nissim, and Beatrice Alex. 2005. Exploring the Boundaries: Gene and Protein Identification in Biomedical Text. *BMC Bioinformatics*, 6:S5.

Kuzman Ganchev and Mark Dredze. 2008. Small Statistical Models by Random Feature Mixing. In *Proceedings of the ACL Workshop on Mobile NLP*, pages 604–613.

Jesús Giménez and Lluís Màrquez. 2004. SVMTool: A general POS tagger generator based on Support Vector Machines. In *Proceedings of the 4th International Conference on Language Resources and Evaluation*, LREC'04.

Yoav Goldberg and Michael Elhadad. 2008. splitSVM: Fast, Space-Efficient, non-Heuristic, Polynomial Kernel Computation for NLP Applications. In *Proceedings of the Annual Conference of the Association for Computational Linguistics*, ACL:HLT'08, pages 237–240.

Yoav Goldberg and Joakim Nivre. 2012. A Dynamic Oracle for Arc-Eager Dependency Parsing. In *Proceedings* of the 24th International Conference on Computational Linguistics, COLING'12.

Taku Kudo and Yuji Matsumoto. 2003. Fast Methods for Kernel-Based Text Analysis. In *Proceedings of the 41st Annual Meeting of the Association for Computational Linguistics*, ACL'04, pages 24–31.

Quoc V. Le and Tomas Mikolov. 2014. Distributed Representations of Sentences and Documents. In *Proceedings of the 31th International Conference on Machine Learning*, ICML'14, pages 1188–1196.

David D. Lewis, Yiming Yang, Tony G. Rose, and Fan Li. 2004. RCV1: A New Benchmark Collection for Text Categorization Research. *Journal of Machine Learning Research*, 5:361–397.

Dekang Lin and Xiaoyun Wu. 2009. Phrase Clustering for Discriminative Learning. In *Proceedings of the 47th Annual Meeting of the Association for Computational Linguistics*, ACL'09, pages 1030–1038.

Christopher D. Manning. 2011. Part-of-Speech Tagging from 97% to 100%: Is It Time for Some Linguistics? In *Proceedings of the 12th international conference on Computational linguistics and intelligent text processing*, CICLing'11, pages 171–189.

Mitchell P. Marcus, Mary Ann Marcinkiewicz, and Beatrice Santorini. 1993. Building a Large Annotated Corpus of English: The Penn Treebank. *Computational Linguistics*, 19(2):313–330.

Tomas Mikolov, Kai Chen, Greg Corrado, and Jeff Dean. 2013. Efficient Estimation of Word Representations in Vector Space. *arXiv:1301.3781*.

Robert Moore. 2015. An Improved Tag Dictionary for Faster Part-of-Speech Tagging. In *Proceedings of the Conference on Empirical Methods in Natural Language Processing*, EMNLP'15, pages 1303–1308.

Daisuke Okanohara and Jun'ichi Tsujii. 2009. Learning Combination Features with L1 Regularization. In *Proceedings of Human Language Technologies: The 2009 Annual Conference of the North American Chapter of the Association for Computational Linguistics, Companion Volume: Short Papers*, NAACL'09, pages 97–100.

Alexandre Passos, Vineet Kumar, and Andrew McCallum. 2014. Lexicon Infused Phrase Embeddings for Named Entity Resolution. In *Proceedings of the 18th Conference on Computational Natural Language Learning*, CoNLL'14, pages 78–86.

Jian Pei, Jiawei Han, Behzad Mortazavi-Asl, Helen Pinto, Qiming Chen, Umeshwar Dayal, and Meichun Hsu. 2001. PrefixSpan: Mining Sequential Patterns by Prefix-Projected Growth. In *Proceedings of the 17th International Conference on Data Engineering*, pages 215–224.

Jeffrey Pennington, Richard Socher, and Christopher D. Manning. 2014. GloVe: Global Vectors for Word Representation. In *Proceedings of the 2014 Conference on Empirical Methods in Natural Language Processing*, EMNLP'14, pages 1532–1543.

Simon Perkins, Kevin Lacker, and James Theiler. 2003. Grafting: Fast, Incremental Feature Selection by Gradient Descent in Function Space. *Journal of Machine Learning Research*, 3:1333–1356.

Sameer Pradhan, Kadri Hacioglu, Valerie Krugler, Wayne Ward, James H. Martin, and Daniel Jurafsky. 2005. Support Vector Learning for Semantic Argument Classification. *Machine Learning*, 60(1):11–39.

Lev Ratinov and Dan Roth. 2009. Design Challenges and Misconceptions in Named Entity Recognition. In *Proceedings of the Thirteenth Conference on Computational Natural Language Learning*, CoNLL'09, pages 147–155.

Stéphane Ross, Geoffrey J. Gordon, and Drew Bagnell. 2011. A Reduction of Imitation Learning and Structured Prediction to No-Regret Online Learning. In *Proceedings of the Workshop on Artificial Intelligence and Statistics*, AI-STATS'11, pages 627–635.

Libin Shen, Giorgio Satta, and Aravind Joshi. 2007. Guided Learning for Bidirectional Sequence Classification. In *Proceedings of the 45th Annual Meeting of the Association of Computational Linguistics*, ACL'07, pages 760–767.

Richard Socher, Alex Perelygin, Jean Wu, Jason Chuang, Christopher D. Manning, Andrew Ng, and Christopher Potts. 2013. Recursive deep models for semantic compositionality over a sentiment treebank. In *Proceedings of the 2013 Conference on Empirical Methods in Natural Language Processing*, EMNLP'13, pages 1631–1642.

Anders Søgaard. 2011. Semi-supervised condensed nearest neighbor for part-of-speech tagging. In *Proceedings of the 49th Annual Meeting of the Association for Computational Linguistics: Human Language Technologies*, ACL:HLT'11, pages 48–52.

Drahomíra "johanka" Spoustová, Jan Hajič, Jan Raab, and Miroslav Spousta. 2009. Semi-supervised Training for the Averaged Perceptron POS Tagger. In *Proceedings of the 12th Conference of the European Chapter of the Association for Computational Linguistics*, EACL'09, pages 763–771.

Emma Strubell, Luke Vilnis, Kate Silverstein, and Andrew McCallum. 2015. Learning Dynamic Feature Selection for Fast Sequential Prediction. In *Proceedings of the 53rd Annual Meeting of the Association for Computational Linguistics*, ACL'16, pages 146–155.

Xu Sun. 2014. Structure Regularization for Structured Prediction. In *Proceedings of Advances in Neural Information Processing Systems.*, NIPS'14, pages 2402—2410.

Jun Suzuki and Hideki Isozaki. 2008. Semi-Supervised Sequential Labeling and Segmentation Using Giga-Word Scale Unlabeled Data. In *Proceedings of the 46th Annual Meeting of the Association for Computational Linguistics: Human Language Technologies*, ACL:HLT'08, pages 665–673.

Jun Suzuki and Masaaki Nagata. 2013. Supervised Model Learning with Feature Grouping based on a Discrete Constraint. In *Proceedings of the 51st Annual Meeting of the Association for Computational Linguistics (Volume 2: Short Papers)*, pages 18–23.

Erik F. Tjong Kim Sang and Fien De Meulder. 2003. Introduction to the CoNLL-2003 Shared Task: Language-independent Named Entity Recognition. In *Proceedings of the Seventh Conference on Natural Language Learning at HLT-NAACL 2003 - Volume 4*, CONLL '03, pages 142–147. Association for Computational Linguistics.

Kristina Toutanova, Dan Klein, Christopher D. Manning, and Yoram Singer. 2003. Feature-Rich Part-of-Speech Tagging with a Cyclic Dependency Network. In *Proceedings of the Annual Conference of the North American Chapter of the Association for Computational Linguistics on Human Language Technology*, NAACL'03, pages 173–180.

Yuta Tsuboi. 2014. Neural Networks Leverage Corpus-wide Information for Part-of-speech Tagging. In *Proceedings of the Conference on Empirical Methods in Natural Language Processing*, EMNLP'14, pages 938–950.

Joseph Turian, Lev-Arie Ratinov, and Yoshua Bengio. 2010. Word Representations: A Simple and General Method for Semi-Supervised Learning. In *Proceedings of the 48th Annual Meeting of the Association for Computational Linguistics*, ACL'10, pages 384–394.

Kilian Weinberger, Anirban Dasgupta, John Langford, Alex Smola, and Josh Attenberg. 2009. Feature Hashing for Large Scale Multitask Learning. In *Proceedings of the 26th Annual International Conference on Machine Learning*, ICML'09, pages 1113–1120.

Lin Xiao. 2010. Dual Averaging Methods for Regularized Stochastic Learning and Online Optimization. *Journal of Machine Learning Research*, 11:2543–2596.

Nianwen Xue and Martha Palmer. 2004. Calibrating Features for Semantic Role Labeling. In *Proceedings of the Conference on Empirical Methods in Natural Language Processing*, EMNLP'04, pages 88–94.

Lei Yu, Karl Moritz Hermann, Phil Blunsom, and Stephen Pulman. 2014. Deep Learning for Answer Sentence Selection. In *Proceedings of the NIPS Deep Learning Workshop*.

Tong Zhang and David Johnson. 2003. A Robust Risk Minimization Based Named Entity Recognition Sys-tem. In *Proceedings of the 7th Conference on Natural Language Learning*, CONLL'03, pages 204–207.

Yue Zhang and Joakim Nivre. 2011. Transition-based Dependency Parsing with Rich Non-local Features. In *Proceedings of the 49th Annual Meeting of the Association for Computational Linguistics: Human Language Technologies*, ACL'11, pages 188–193.

Wenliang Zhong and James Kwok. 2011. Efficient Sparse Modeling with Automatic Feature Grouping. In Lise Getoor and Tobias Scheffer, editors, *Proceedings of the 28th International Conference on Machine Learning (ICML-11)*, ICML '11, pages 9–16, New York, NY, USA, June. ACM.

Drop-out Conditional Random Fields for Twitter with Huge Mined Gazetteer

Eunsuk Yang[‡§]   **Young-Bum Kim**[†§]   **Ruhi Sarikaya**[†]   **Yu-Seop Kim**[‡]

[†]Microsoft Corporation, Redmond, WA
[‡]Hallym University, South Korea
esyang219@gmail.com
{ybkim, ruhi.sarikaya}@microsoft.com
yskim01@hallym.ac.kr

Abstract

In named entity recognition task especially for massive data like Twitter, having a large amount of high quality gazetteers can alleviate the problem of training data scarcity. One could collect large gazetteers from knowledge graph and phrase embeddings to obtain high coverage of gazetteers. However, large gazetteers cause a side-effect called "feature under-training", where the gazetteer features overwhelm the context features. To resolve this problem, we propose the dropout conditional random fields, which decrease the influence of gazetteer features with a high weight. Our experiments on named entity recognition with Twitter data lead to higher F1 score of 69.38%, about 4% better than the strong baseline presented in Smith and Osborne (2006).

1 Introduction

Nowadays, people are generating tremendous amount of information on social websites. For example, more than 200 million tweets are generated everyday on Twitter (Ritter et al., 2011). Twitter has become a key news source, in addition to standard news channels. As such, social scientists are starting to pay attention to it in recent years (Bollen et al., 2011; Chung and Mustafaraj, 2011; Xu et al., 2014; Calvin et al., 2015; Baldwin et al., 2015; Bellmore et al., 2015). The traditional machine learned modeling approaches trained with small and clean general text, such as news articles, perform poorly when applied to tweets, because tweets are structurally very different from general text. Thus, it

is necessary to build new models for Twitter. One could label a reasonable size of tweets to train a model for a natural language processing (NLP) application. The problem is that it is very expensive to refresh the annotated data to keep the model up-to-date, because users generate tweets in a unprecedented rate (Hachman, 2011).

An obvious solution to the problem is to develop methods of utilizing a large amount of unlabeled data. One way is to induce word embeddings in a real-valued vector space from a large number of tweets (Kim et al., 2015a; Mikolov et al., 2013; Pennington et al., 2014). It is shown that the task-specific embeddings induced on tweets provide more powerful than those created from out-of-domain texts (Owoputi et al., 2012; Anastasakos et al., 2014).

Another method is to build the task-specific gazetteers. Task-specific gazetteers make the models more general and increase their coverage for unseen events. They have been proven to be useful on a number of tasks (Smith and Osborne, 2006; Li et al., 2009; Liu and Sarikaya, 2014; Kim et al., 2015b; Kim et al., 2015c). Since gazetteers can improve modeling performance, here we more focus on how to use gazetteer more effectively. To build gazetteers with sufficient coverage for our task, we first expand gazetteers from knowledge graph and phrase embeddings.

However, since the expanded gazetteers cover significant proportions of the entities in the training data, the weight of gazetteers features are easily inflated and thus the model tends to rely too much on lexical features extracted from the gazetteers fea-

---

§ Both authors contributed equally.

tures to assign a tag rather than the contextual features such as n-gram, a phenomenon called "feature under-training". As a result, we often observe noticeable performance degradation at test time when the entity value does not exist in the training set or the entity dictionary.

To solve this problem, we introduce a model called dropout CRFs [1] and compare to the combination model proposed by Smith and Osborne (2006). In our experiments, we show that the proposed method significantly improves the F1 score from 65.54% to 69.38%, compared to the baseline.

2 Model

For the named entity recognition (NER) task, the input is a sentence consisting of a sequence of words, $x = (x_1 \ldots x_n)$ and the output is a sequence of corresponding named entity tags $y = (y_1 \ldots y_n)$. We model the conditional probability $p(y|x; \theta)$ using linear-chain CRFs (Lafferty et al., 2001):

$$p(y|x; \theta) = \frac{\exp(\theta \cdot \Phi(x, y))}{\sum_{y' \in \mathcal{Y}(x)} \exp(\theta \cdot \Phi(x, y'))}$$

where θ is a set of model parameters. $\mathcal{Y}$ contains all possible label sequences of x, and Φ maps (x, y) into a feature vector that is a linear combination of local feature vectors: $\Phi(x, y) = \sum_{j=1}^{n} \phi(x_j, y_{j-1}, y_j)$. Given fully observed training data, $\{(x^{(i)}, y^{(i)})\}_{i=1}^{N}$, the objective of the training is to find θ that maximizes the log likelihood of the training data under the model with l_2-regularization:

$$\theta^* = \operatorname*{argmax}_{\theta} \sum_{i=1}^{N} \log p(y^{(i)}|x^{(i)}; \theta) \\ - \frac{\lambda}{2} ||\theta||^2. \quad (1)$$

CRFs have benefited from having a rich set of gazetteers as features in the model (Smith and Osborne, 2006; Liu and Sarikaya, 2014; Hillard et al., 2011; Kim et al., 2014; Kim et al., 2015c; Kim et al., 2015b; Kim et al., 2015d). Smith and Osborne (2006) point out that common gazetteer features fire

often enough to overwhelm other features during inference. They address this problem by building a combination of two models: one without gazetteers and another with gazetteers. Instead of combining two models, we propose a simple model by having a new penalty term to the equation (1):

$$\theta^* = \operatorname*{argmax}_{\theta} \sum_{i=1}^{N} \log p(y^{(i)}|x^{(i)}; \theta) \\ - \frac{\lambda_1}{2} ||\theta||^2 - \lambda_2 \sum_{g \in G} \theta_g \operatorname{freq}(g), \quad (2)$$

where G is a set of gazetteers and $\operatorname{freq}(g)$ counts how many times words appear in gazetteer g from training data. In our experiments, we tuned both penalty weights for local features and for gazetteer features based on a small held-out validation set. The θ_g is a member of model parameter θ and each gazetteer has its own parameter θ_g. The introduced penalty decreases common gazetteers' influence on model's decisions. By this term, we call our model *dropout CRFs*. The original dropout technique removes features randomly - for each training instance, only a random subset of the features will be activated (Hinton et al., 2012; Xu and Sarikaya, 2014). While it can be perceived as a general treatment to the under-training problem, it is not specifically directed at the problem we are facing in named entity recognition (NER) task. In NER, the under-training problem is more specific - the contextual features may not get large enough weights due to the strong influence of the gazetteer features. The negative impact of such under-training is also more measurable - if a named entity is unseen, the chance of a detection error becomes much higher. Therefore, we focus on decreasing influence of specific features. For specific features, we reduce the coverage of dropout from all features to gazetteer feature through *feature dependent regularization*. Also, the objective function of dropout CRFs, given in equation (2), is still convex because the equation (1) is convex and the new penalty term is linear with respect to θ. Therefore, a standard optimization algorithm finds optimal θ without sacrificing any abilities, which original CRFs have.

---

[1] The original dropout technique is to inactivate features randomly. Here, we consider to decrease the weight of a specific feature.

3 Features

In this section, we detail the feature templates used for our experiments. Besides basic features, we also employ part-of-speech (POS) tags, chunks, word representations and gazetteers. We run task-specific POS-tagger and chunker, which are trained on tweets annotated with Twitter-specific tags (Ritter et al., 2011) as well as standard Penn Treebank tags, of Owoputi et al. (2012) to produce POS tags and chunks. We explain the word representations and gazetteer features in the following subsections.

3.1 Basic Features

The model of Ritter et al. (2011) employs the features described in this subsection. They are composed of the following features: (1) n-grams: unigrams and bigrams, (2) capitalization, (3) three character suffix and prefix presence, (4) binary features that indicate presence of hyphen, punctuation mark, single-digit and double-digit, (5) gazetteers (6) topics inferred by LabeledLDA (Ramage et al., 2009), and (7) brown cluster (Brown et al., 1992) produced by Ritter et al. (2011).

To alleviate the problem of word sparsity, we also use task-specific latent continuous word representations, induced on 65 million unlabeled tweets with 1.3 billion tokens. We create three sets of word representations: CCA (Dhillon et al., 2012; Kim et al., 2015a) based on matrix factorization, word2vec (Mikolov et al., 2013) and glove (Pennington et al., 2014), which are gradient based. All word representation algorithms produce 50-dimensional word vectors for all words occurring at least 40 times in the data. We use left and right word of the target word as context for learning the word representations.

We also use compounding embeddings as an additional feature. Combining multiple sets of features has been proven to be effective (Koo et al., 2008; Kim and Snyder, 2013; Yu et al., 2013). We explore four different ways of combining the word representations: element-wise averaging, element-wise multiplication, concatenation and hierarchical clustering. We empirically determined that the element-wise averaging achieves better performance than single embeddings and other combination methods. We do not describe the results for embedding combinations in detail here.

4 Gazetteers

NER models degrades when they encounter unseen words during training. To make the problem worse, tweets contain many rare words and it is prohibitively expensive to create a training set with sufficient lexical coverage. To alleviate the problem, we extend the original gazetteers with two methods: gathering data from knowledge graph and constructing task-specific gazetteer with phrase embeddings.

4.1 Expansion from Knowledge Graph

To expand gazetteers from knowledge graph, we apply the following processing steps. We first extract the seed words from training data. With seed words, we then collect the relevant lexicons from knowledge graph such as Freebase, Wikipedia and Yelp. For example, "Dior" is related to *company* and *product* from knowledge graph. We collect all lexicons associated with seed words. In addition, we postprocess gazetteers for variance: i) organization: it is composed with full name with abbreviation, such as "Indigenous Land Corporation (ILC)". We also generate variants of full names ("Indigenous Land Corporation") and abbreviation ("ILC"), respectively, ii) facility: because the term *elementary* indicates a school, we add a lexicon removing the word *school* of "tedder elementary school". At the end of the processing, we end up with 2.7 millions lexicon items.

4.2 Constructing Gazetteers with Phrase Embeddings

We now describe how to construct task-specific gazetteer with phrase embeddings. We use canonical correlation analysis (CCA) (Hotelling, 1936) to induce vector representations for phrase embeddings. To extract candidate phrases from unlabeled Twitter data, we first count the frequency of the context words set for each token. The size of context words set ranges from 1 to 3. The context words set occurring more than 100 are used as a rule to extract candidate phrases.

Let n be the number of candidate phrases extracted by rules. Let $x_1 \dots x_n$ be the original representations of the candidate phrases itself and $y_1 \dots y_n$ be the original representations of two words to the left and right of the candidate phrases.

We use the following definition for the original representations. Let d be the number of distinct candidate phrases and d' be the number of distinct context words set.

- $x_l \in \mathbb{R}^d$ is a zero vector, in which the entry corresponding to the candidate phrases of the l-th instance is set to 1.

- $y_l \in \mathbb{R}^{d'}$ is a zero vector, in which the entries corresponding to context words set surrounding candidate phrases are set to 1.

Using CCA, we obtain phrase embeddings U with k-dimensional space. To train a classifier, we manually construct a training data with 5 positive and 5 negative samples, for each gazetteer. With this data, we learn a binary classifier with the phrase embeddings as a feature. Using this classifier, we predict whether the phrases fit to the gazetteers; we refer the readers to Neelakantan and Collins (2014) for details.

5 Experiments

To demonstrate the effectiveness of the dropout CRFs, we run experiments on named entity recognition task on the Twitter dataset of Baldwin et al. (2015). We refer the readers to Baldwin et al. (2015) for the details of the dataset. We split the data into 70% for training, 10% for tuning, and 20% for testing. For all the experiments presented in this section, both CRFs and dropout CRFs are trained using the L-BFGS (Liu and Nocedal, 1989).

5.1 Effectiveness of the Gazetteers

One of our contributions is to augment the size of gazetteers with knowledge graph and phrase embeddings. Table 1 represents the performance of a model with original gazetteers, which are collected by Ritter et al. (2011) from freebase (Base Gazet) and with gazetteers we extended (Our Gazet). The size of *Base Gazet* is 2.9 million and the size of *Our Gazet* is 6.6 million, which has an additional 3.7 million entries compared to the *Base Gazet*. The model trained *Our Gazet* improves the F1 score from 62.76% to 64.67%, compared to the baseline. As shown in Table 1, we believe that larger gazetteers can mitigate the "unseen words" problem by increasing the coverage of the gazetteers.

	F1
Base Gazet	62.76
Our Gazet	64.67

Table 1: Comparison of models with or without new gazetteers. **Base Gazet** is a model with gazetteers collected by Ritter et al. (2011) and **Our gazet** is a model with gazetteers we constructed by augmenting the *Base Gazet* with additional items, using knowledge graph and phrase embeddings.

5.2 Effectiveness of the Dropout CRFs

We conducted additional experiments with the CRF model that uses *Our Gazet*. Table 2 shows the overall results for models with and without dropout. We compare three models: the vanilla CRFs ($\text{CRFs}_{vanilla}$), the combination model as described in Smith and Osborne (2006) (CRFs_{LOP}) and our dropout model ($\text{CRFs}_{dropout}$). To avoid model parameters for gazetteer features getting over-regularized, Smith and Osborne (2006) propose to train separate models with and without gazetteers. They combine predictions from the two models by using logarithmic opinion pool (LOP). We refer the reader to Smith et al. (2005) for further details.

The CRFs_{vanila} yields 64.03% F1 score and the CRFs_{LOP} improves the performance to 65.54%. The $\text{CRFs}_{dropout}$, which reduces the influence of gazetteer features, improves the F1 score to 69.38%, which corresponds to a 13% decrease in error relative to vanilla CRFs.

	F1
CRFs_{vanila}	64.67
CRFs_{LOP}	65.54
$\text{CRFs}_{dropout}$	69.38

Table 2: Comparison of models with or without dropout. $\text{CRFs}_{vanilla}$ is the vanilla CRFs with all features. CRFs_{LOP} is a combination of CRFs with all features except for gazetteers and CRFs with gazetteers only, using logarithmic opinion pool (LOP). $\text{CRFs}_{dropout}$ is the dropout CRFs with all features.

5.3 Analysis

While previous NER tasks mostly focus on reporting numbers on the original data set (Baldwin et al., 2015; Yang and Kim, 2015; Kim et al., 2015c), we further investigate how the tagging performance may change, if entities are unseen at test time. To enable such analysis, we create additional test set based on the original test set by replacing each word in `person` and `company` entities with a special token, *XXXXX*, indicating unseen words. This new test set represents an extreme case, where none of the words contained in the gazetteers are observed in the training data.

Table 3 represents the comparison of vanilla CRF model and dropout model for unseen test. Gazetteer is helpful to resolve "unseen words" problem. Unfortunately, frequent appearance of gazetteer makes a model learn weak context feature and strong gazetteer feature. By forcing a weight of gazetteer feature low, the dropout model allows the weak context features to become strong and the large weight of gazetteer feature to become smaller. Consequently, $CRF_{dropout}$ shows the significant improvement compared to $CRF_{vanilla}$.

Tags	$\mathbf{CRF}_{dropout}$	$\mathbf{CRF}_{vanilla}$
person	74.43	65.81
company	65.74	57.19

Table 3: Comparison of vanilla CRF model and dropout model for unseen test

To see a change of feature weight when we apply dropout technique, we show the feature weights for the word "cahill" of vanilla CRFs and dropout CRFs in Table 4. In vanilla CRFs, gazetteers have a strong weight compared to the context features. However, our dropout CRFs decrease the weight of gazetteer features, while making the context features larger, to steer the models' decision in the right direction.

6 Conclusion

In this paper, we showed how to improve the CRF based NER model for Twitter by exploiting a large number of gazetteers. Using gazetteers in modeling helps the coverage and generalization but simply incorporating gazetteers of all of large sizes into the model may lead to "under-training" of parameters corresponding to the context features. We addressed this problem by adding the dropout penalty term in the CRF training, which improves better parameter. The proposed technique results in significant improvements over the baseline.

cahill (answer: geo-loc prediction: person)

$CRFs_{vanila}$
people.person $\rightarrow$ I-person : 7.46
lastname.5000 $\rightarrow$ I-person: 9.63
lastname.5000 $\rightarrow$ I-geo-loc: 4.01
people.person.lastnames $\rightarrow$ I-person : 6.6
w[-1]|w[0]='s|Cahill $\rightarrow$ I-person : -1.24
w[-1]|w[0]='s|Cahill $\rightarrow$ I-geo-loc : 0.28
w[-1]='s $\rightarrow$ I-person : 0.97
w[-1]='s $\rightarrow$ I-geo-loc : -0.13

$CRFs_{dropout}$
people.person $\rightarrow$ I-person : 5.2
lastname.5000 $\rightarrow$ I-person: 4.67
lastname.5000 $\rightarrow$ I-geo-loc: 4.19
people.person.lastnames $\rightarrow$ I-person : 4.36
w[-1]|w[0]='s|Cahill $\rightarrow$ I-person : 1.98
w[-1]|w[0]='s|Cahill $\rightarrow$ I-geo-loc : 3.02
w[-1]='s $\rightarrow$ I-person : 1.41
w[-1]='s $\rightarrow$ I-geo-loc : 1.82

Table 4: Snapshot of feature weights for the word "cahill", given sentence *tonight 's cahill event*. The vanilla CRFs predict it to `person` and dropout CRFs predict it to `geo-loc` correctly.

One of the future directions of research is to extend the same idea to various sequence learning problems: part-of-speech tagging and slot tagging.

Acknowledgments

We thank Do Kook Choe, Puyang Xu, Alan Ritter and Karl Startos for helpful discussion and feedback.

References

Tasos Anastasakos, Young-Bum Kim, and Anoop Deoras. 2014. Task specific continuous word representations for mono and multi-lingual spoken language understanding. In *Acoustics, Speech and Signal Processing (ICASSP), 2014 IEEE International Conference on*, pages 3246–3250. IEEE.

Timothy Baldwin, Young-Bum Kim, Marie Catherine de Marneffe, Alan Ritter, Bo Han, and Wei Xu. 2015. Shared tasks of the 2015 workshop on noisy user-generated text: Twitter lexical normalization and named entity recognition. *ACL-IJCNLP 2015*, page 126.

Amy Bellmore, Angela J Calvin, Jun-Ming Xu, and Xi-aojin Zhu. 2015. The five ws of bullying on twitter: Who, what, why, where, and when. *Computers in Human Behavior*, 44:305–314.

Johan Bollen, Huina Mao, and Xiaojun Zeng. 2011. Twitter mood predicts the stock market. *Journal of Computational Science*, 2(1):1–8.

Peter F Brown, Peter V Desouza, Robert L Mercer, Vincent J Della Pietra, and Jenifer C Lai. 1992. Class-based n-gram models of natural language. *Computational linguistics*, 18(4):467–479.

Angela J Calvin, Amy Bellmore, Jun-Ming Xu, and Xi-aojin Zhu. 2015. # bully: Uses of hashtags in posts about bullying on twitter. *Journal of School Violence*, 14(1):133–153.

Jessica Elan Chung and Eni Mustafaraj. 2011. Can collective sentiment expressed on twitter predict political elections? In *AAAI*.

Paramveer Dhillon, Jordan Rodu, Dean Foster, and Lyle Ungar. 2012. Two step cca: A new spectral method for estimating vector models of words. *arXiv preprint arXiv:1206.6403*.

Mark Hachman. 2011. Humanitys tweets: Just 20 terabytes. *PCMAG. COM*.

Dustin Hillard, Asli Celikyilmaz, Dilek Z Hakkani-Tür, and Gökhan Tür. 2011. Learning weighted entity lists from web click logs for spoken language understanding. In *INTERSPEECH*, pages 705–708.

Geoffrey E Hinton, Nitish Srivastava, Alex Krizhevsky, Ilya Sutskever, and Ruslan R Salakhutdinov. 2012. Improving neural networks by preventing co-adaptation of feature detectors. *arXiv preprint arXiv:1207.0580*.

Harold Hotelling. 1936. Relations between two sets of variates. *Biometrika*, 28(3/4):321–377.

Young-Bum Kim and Benjamin Snyder. 2013. Unsupervised consonant-vowel prediction over hundreds of languages. In *ACL (1)*, pages 1527–1536.

Young-Bum Kim, Heemoon Chae, Benjamin Snyder, and Yu-Seop Kim. 2014. Training a korean srl system with rich morphological features. In *ACL (2)*, pages 637–642.

Young-Bum Kim, Benjamin Snyder, and Ruhi Sarikaya. 2015a. Part-of-speech taggers for low-resource languages using cca features. In *Proceedings of the 2015 Conference on Empirical Methods in Natural Language Processing*, pages 1292–1302.

Young-Bum Kim, Karl Stratos, Xiaohu Liu, and Ruhi Sarikaya. 2015b. Compact lexicon selection with spectral methods. In *Proceedings of Association for Computational Linguistics (ACL)*, pages 806–811.

Young-Bum Kim, Karl Stratos, and Ruhi Sarikaya. 2015c. Pre-training of hidden-unit crfs. *ACL. Association for Computational Linguistics*.

Young-Bum Kim, Karl Stratos, Ruhi Sarikaya, and Minwoo Jeong. 2015d. New transfer learning techniques for disparate label sets. *ACL. Association for Computational Linguistics*.

Terry Koo, Xavier Carreras, and Michael Collins. 2008. Simple semi-supervised dependency parsing.

John Lafferty, Andrew McCallum, and Fernando CN Pereira. 2001. Conditional random fields: Probabilistic models for segmenting and labeling sequence data.

Xiao Li, Ye-Yi Wang, and Alex Acero. 2009. Extracting structured information from user queries with semi-supervised conditional random fields. In *Proceedings of the 32nd international ACM SIGIR conference on Research and development in information retrieval*.

D.C. Liu and J. Nocedal. 1989. On the limited memory bfgs method for large scale optimization. *Mathematical programming*, 45(1):503–528.

Xiaohu Liu and Ruhi Sarikaya. 2014. A discriminative model based entity dictionary weighting approach for spoken language understanding.

Tomas Mikolov, Ilya Sutskever, Kai Chen, Greg S Corrado, and Jeff Dean. 2013. Distributed representations of words and phrases and their compositionality. In *Advances in Neural Information Processing Systems*, pages 3111–3119.

Arvind Neelakantan and Michael Collins. 2014. Learning dictionaries for named entity recognition using minimal supervision. *EACL 2014*, page 452.

Olutobi Owoputi, Brendan OConnor, Chris Dyer, Kevin Gimpel, and Nathan Schneider. 2012. Part-of-speech tagging for twitter: Word clusters and other advances. *School of Computer Science, Carnegie Mellon University, Tech. Rep.*

Jeffrey Pennington, Richard Socher, and Christopher D Manning. 2014. Glove: Global vectors for word representation. *Proceedings of the Empiricial Methods in Natural Language Processing (EMNLP 2014)*, 12.

Daniel Ramage, David Hall, Ramesh Nallapati, and Christopher D Manning. 2009. Labeled lda: A supervised topic model for credit attribution in multi-labeled corpora. In *Proceedings of the 2009 Conference on Empirical Methods in Natural Language Processing: Volume 1-Volume 1*, pages 248–256. Association for Computational Linguistics.

Alan Ritter, Sam Clark, Oren Etzioni, et al. 2011. Named entity recognition in tweets: an experimental study. In *Proceedings of the Conference on Empirical Methods in Natural Language Processing*, pages 1524–1534. Association for Computational Linguistics.

Andrew Smith and Miles Osborne. 2006. Using gazetteers in discriminative information extraction. In *Proceedings of the Tenth Conference on Computational Natural Language Learning*, pages 133–140. Association for Computational Linguistics.

Andrew Smith, Trevor Cohn, and Miles Osborne. 2005. Logarithmic opinion pools for conditional random fields. In *Proceedings of the 43rd Annual Meeting on Association for Computational Linguistics*, pages 18–25. Association for Computational Linguistics.

Puyang Xu and Ruhi Sarikaya. 2014. Targeted feature dropout for robust slot filling in natural language understanding. In *Fifteenth Annual Conference of the International Speech Communication Association*.

Jun-Ming Xu, Hsun-Chih Huang, Amy Bellmore, and Xiaojin Zhu. 2014. School bullying in twitter and weibo: a comparative study. *Reporter*, 7(16):10–14.

Eun-Suk Yang and Yu-Seop Kim. 2015. Hallym: Named entity recognition on twitter with induced word representation. *ACL-IJCNLP 2015*, page 72.

Mo Yu, Tiejun Zhao, Daxiang Dong, Hao Tian, and Dianhai Yu. 2013. Compound embedding features for semi-supervised learning. In *HLT-NAACL*, pages 563–568.

Joint Extraction of Events and Entities within a Document Context

Bishan Yang
Carnegie Mellon University
5000 Forbes Avenue
Pittsburgh, PA, 15213
bishan@cs.cmu.edu

Tom Mitchell
Carnegie Mellon University
5000 Forbes Avenue
Pittsburgh, PA, 15213
tom.mitchell@cs.cmu.edu

Abstract

Events and entities are closely related; entities are often actors or participants in events and events without entities are uncommon. The interpretation of events and entities is highly contextually dependent. Existing work in information extraction typically models events separately from entities, and performs inference at the sentence level, ignoring the rest of the document. In this paper, we propose a novel approach that models the dependencies among variables of events, entities, and their relations, and performs joint inference of these variables across a document. The goal is to enable access to document-level contextual information and facilitate context-aware predictions. We demonstrate that our approach substantially outperforms the state-of-the-art methods for event extraction as well as a strong baseline for entity extraction.

1 Introduction

Events are things that happen or occur; they involve entities (people, objects, etc.) who perform or are affected by the events and spatio-temporal aspects of the world. Understanding events and their descriptions in text is necessary for any generally-applicable machine reading systems. It is also essential in facilitating practical applications such as news summarization, information retrieval, and knowledge base construction.

The interpretation of event descriptions is highly contextually dependent. To make correct predictions, a model needs to account for mentions of events and entities together with the discourse context. Consider, for example, the following excerpt from a news report:

> "On *Thursday*, there was a massive
> *U.S.* **aerial bombardment** in which more
> than 300 *Tomahawk cruise missiles* rained
> down on *Baghdad*.   *Earlier Saturday*,
> *Baghdad* was again **targeted**. ..."

The excerpt describes two U.S. attacks on Baghdad. The two event anchors (triggers) are boldfaced and the mentions of entities and spatio-temporal information are italicized. The first event anchor "aerial bombardment" along with its surrounding entity mentions — "U.S.", "Tomahawk cruise missiles", and "Baghdad", describe an attack from the U.S. on Baghdad with Tomahawk cruise missiles being the weapon. The second sentence on its own contains little event-related information, but together with the context of the previous sentence, it indicates another U.S. attack on Baghdad.

State-of-the-art event extraction systems have difficulties inferring such information due to two main reasons. First, they extract events and entities in separate stages: entities such as people, organization, and locations are first extracted by a named entity tagger, and then these extracted entities are used as inputs for extracting events and their arguments (Li et al., 2013). This often causes errors to propagate. In the above example, if the entity tagger mistakenly identifies "Baghdad" as a person, then the event extractor will fail to extract "Baghdad" as the place where the attack happened. In fact, previous work (Li et al., 2013) observes that using previously extracted entities in event extraction results in

Proceedings of NAACL-HLT 2016, pages 289–299,
San Diego, California, June 12-17, 2016. ©2016 Association for Computational Linguistics

a substantial decrease in performance compared to using gold-standard entity information.

Second, most existing work extracts events independently from each individual sentence, ignoring the rest of the document (Li et al., 2013; Judea and Strube, 2015; Nguyen and Grishman, 2015). Very few attempts have been made to incorporate document context for event extraction. Ji and Grishman (2008) model the information flow in two stages: the first stage trains classifiers for event triggers and arguments within each sentence; the second stage applies heuristic rules to adjust the classifiers' outputs to satisfy document-wide (or document-cluster-wide) consistency. Liao and Grishman (2010) further improved the rule-based inference by training additional classifiers for event triggers and arguments using document-level information. Both approaches only propagate the highly confident predictions from the first stage to the second stage. To the best of our knowledge, there is no unified model that jointly extracts events from sentences across the whole document.

In this paper, we propose a novel approach that simultaneously extracts events and entities within a document context.[1] We first decompose the learning problem into three tractable subproblems: (1) learning the dependencies between a single event and all of its potential arguments, (2) learning the co-occurrence relations between events across the document, and (3) learning for entity extraction. Then we combine the learned models for these subproblems into a joint optimization framework that simultaneously extracts events, semantic roles, and entities in a document. In summary, our main contributions are:

1. We propose a structured model for learning within-event structures that can effectively capture the dependencies between an event and its arguments, and between the semantic roles and entity types for the arguments.

2. We introduce a joint inference framework that combines probabilistic models of within-event structures, event-event relations, and entity ex-

traction for joint extraction of the set of entities and events over the whole document.

3. We conduct extensive experiments on the Automatic Content Extraction (ACE) corpus, and show that our approach significantly outperforms the state-of-the-art methods for event extraction and a strong baseline for entity extraction.

2 Task Definition

We adopt the ACE definition for entities ((LDC), 2005a) and events ((LDC), 2005b):

- **Entity mention**: An entity is an object or set of objects in the world. An entity mention is a reference to an entity in the form of a noun phrase or a pronoun.

- **Event trigger**: the word or phrase that clearly expresses its occurrence. Event triggers can be verbs, nouns, and occasionally adjectives like "dead" or "bankrupt".

- **Event argument**: event arguments are entities that fill specific roles in the event. They mainly include participants (i.e., the entities that are involved in the event) and general event attributes such as place and time, and some event-type-specific attributes that have certain values (e.g., JOB-TITLE, CRIME).

We are interested in extracting entity mentions, event triggers, and event arguments. We consider ACE entity types PER, ORG, GPE, LOC, FAC, VEH, WEA and ACE VALUE and TIME expressions[2], and focus on 33 ACE event subtypes, each of which has its own set of semantic roles for the potential arguments. There are 35 such roles in total, but we collapse 8 of them that are time-related (e.g., TIME-HOLDS, TIME-AT-END) into one, because most of these roles have very few training examples. Figure 2 shows an example of ACE annotations for events and entities in a sentence. Note that not every entity mention in the sentence is involved in events and a single entity mention can be associated with multiple events.

---

[1]The code for our system is available at https://github.com/bishanyang/EventEntityExtractor.

[2]To simplify notation, we include values and times when referring to entities in the rest of the paper.

Figure 1: An example of ACE annotations of events and entities. The event triggers and the entity mentions are marked in different colors. Each event trigger has an event subtype marked above it and each entity mention has an entity type marked above it. Each event trigger evokes an event with semantic roles that are filled by entity mentions. The roles are marked on the links between event trigger and entity mentions. For example, "conviction" evokes a CONVICT event, and has the CRIME and DEFENDANT roles filled by "blasphemy" and "Christian man" respectively.

3 Approach

In this section, we describe our approach for joint extraction of events and entities within a document context. We first decompose the learning problem into three tractable subproblems: learning within-event structures, learning event-event relations, and learning for entity extraction. We will describe the probabilistic models for learning these subproblems. Then we present a joint inference framework that integrates these learned models into a single model to jointly extract events and entities across a document.

3.1 Learning Within-event Structures

As described in Section 2, a mention of an event consists of an event trigger and a set of event arguments. Each event argument is also an entity mention with an entity type. In the following, we develop a probabilistic model to learn such dependency structure for each individual event mention.

Given a document x, we first generate a set of event trigger candidates $\mathcal{T}$ and a set of entity candidates $\mathcal{N}$.[3] For each trigger candidate $i \in \mathcal{T}$, we associate it with a discrete variable t_i that takes values from the 33 ACE event types and a NONE class indicating other events or no events. Denote the set of entity candidates that are potential arguments for trigger candidate i as $\mathcal{N}_i$.[4] For each $j \in \mathcal{N}_i$, we associate it with a discrete variable r_{ij} which models the event-argument relation between trigger candidate i and entity candidate j. It takes values from 28 semantic roles and a NONE class indicating invalid

---

[3]We describe how to extract these candidates in Section 4.

[4]In this paper we only consider entity mentions that are in the same sentence as the trigger to be potential event arguments due to the ACE annotations. However, our model is general and can handle event-argument relations across sentences with appropriate features.

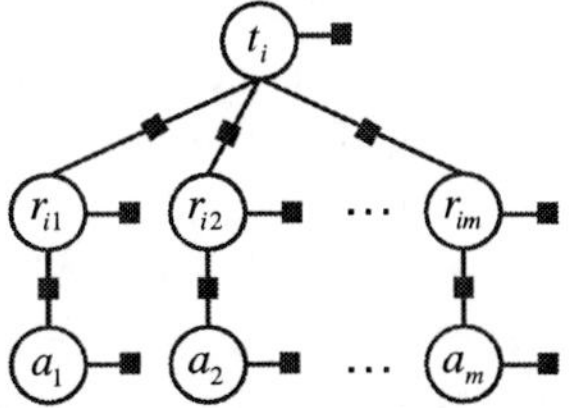

Figure 2: A factor graph representation of the within-event model, relating the event type t_i of trigger candidate i to the role type r_{ij} of each argument candidate j along with its entity type a_j.

roles. Each argument candidate j is also associated with an entity type variable a_j, which takes values from 9 entity types and a NONE class indicating invalid entity types.

We define the joint distribution of variables t_i, $\mathbf{r}_{i\cdot} = \{r_{ij}\}_{j \in \mathcal{N}_i}$, and $\mathbf{a}_\cdot = \{a_j\}_{j \in \mathcal{N}_i}$ conditioned on the observations, which can be factorized according to the factor graph shown in Figure 2:

$$p_{\boldsymbol{\theta}}(t_i, \mathbf{r}_{i\cdot}, \mathbf{a}_\cdot | i, \mathcal{N}_i, x) \propto \exp\left(\boldsymbol{\theta}_1^T f_1(t_i, i, x) + \right.$$
$$\sum_{j \in \mathcal{N}_i} \boldsymbol{\theta}_2^T f_2(r_{ij}, i, j, x) + \sum_{j \in \mathcal{N}_i} \boldsymbol{\theta}_3^T f_3(t_i, r_{ij}, i, j, x) +$$
$$\left. \sum_{j \in \mathcal{N}_i} \boldsymbol{\theta}_4^T f_4(a_j, j, x) + \sum_{j \in \mathcal{N}_i} \boldsymbol{\theta}_5^T f_5(r_{ij}, a_j, j, x) \right)$$

$$(1)$$

where $\boldsymbol{\theta}_1, ..., \boldsymbol{\theta}_5$ are vectors of parameters that need to be estimated, and $f_1, ..., f_5$ are different forms of feature functions which we will describe later.

Note that not all configurations of the variables are valid in our model. Based on the definitions in Section 2, each event type takes arguments with certain semantic roles. For example, the arguments of the event MARRY can only play the roles of

PERSON, TIME, and PLACE. In addition, a NONE event type should not take any arguments. Similarly, each semantic role should be filled with entities with compatible types. For example, the PERSON role type can only be filled with an entity of type PER. However, a NONE role type can be filled with an entity of any type. To account for these compatibility constraints, we enforce the probabilities of all invalid configurations to be zero.

Features. f_1, f_2, and f_4 are unary feature functions that depend on trigger variable t_i, argument variable r_{ij}, and entity variable a_j respectively. We construct a set of features for each feature function (see Table 1). Many of these features overlap with those used in previous work (Li et al., 2013; Li et al., 2014), except for the word embedding features for triggers and the features for entities which are derived from multiple entity resources. f_3 and f_5 are pairwise feature functions that depend on trigger-argument pair (t_i, r_{ij}) and argument-entity pair (r_{ij}, a_j) respectively. We consider simple indicator functions $\mathbb{1}_{t,r}$ and $\mathbb{1}_{r,a}$ as features ($\mathbb{1}_y(x)$ equals 1 when $x = y$ and 0 otherwise).

Training. For model training, we find the optimal parameters θ using the maximum-likelihood estimates with an L2 regularization:

$$\theta^* = \arg\max_{\theta} \mathcal{L}(\theta) - \lambda ||\theta||_2^2$$

$$\mathcal{L}(\theta) = \sum_i \log p(t_i, \mathbf{r}_{i\cdot}, \mathbf{a}_{\cdot} | i, \mathcal{N}_i, x)$$

We use L-BFGS to optimize the training objective. To calculate the gradient, we use the sum-product algorithm to compute the exact marginals for the unary cliques t_i, r_{ij}, a_j and the pairwise cliques (t_i, r_{ij}), (r_{ij}, a_j). Typically the training complexity for graphical models with unary and pairwise cliques is quadratic in the size of the label set. However, the complexity of our model is much lower than that since we only need to compute the joint distributions over valid variable configurations. Denote the number of event subtypes as T, the number of event argument roles as N, the average number of argument roles for each event subtype as k_1, the average number of entity types for each event argument as k_2, and the average number of argument candidates for each trigger candidate as M. The complexity of computing the joint distribution

is $O(M \times (k_1 T + k_2 N))$, and k_1 and k_2 are expected to be small in practice ($k_1 = 6$, $k_2 = 3$ in ACE).

3.2 Learning Event-Event Relations

So far we have described a model for learning structures for a single event. However, the inference of the event types for individual events may depend on other events that are mentioned in the document. For example, an ATTACK event is more likely to occur with INJURE and DIE events than with life events like MARRY and BORN. In order to capture this intuition, we develop a pairwise model of event-event relations in a document.

Our training data consists of all pairs of trigger candidates that co-occur in the same sentence or are connected by a coreferent subject/object if they are in different sentences.[5] We want to propagate information between these trigger pairs since they are more likely to be related.

Formally, given a trigger candidate pair (i, i'), we estimate the probabilities for their event types $(t_i, t_{i'})$ as

$$p_\phi(t_i, t_{i'} | x, i, i') \propto \exp\left(\phi^T g(t_i, t_{i'}, x, i, i')\right) \quad (2)$$

where ϕ is a vector of parameters and g is a feature function that depends on the trigger candidate pair and their context. We consider both trigger-specific features and relational features. For trigger-specific features, we use the same trigger features listed in Table 1. For relational features, we consider for each pair of trigger candidates: (1) whether they are connected by a conjunction dependency relation (based on dependency parsing); (2) whether they share a subject or an object (based on dependency parsing and coreference resolution); (3) whether they have the same head word lemma; (4) whether they share a semantic frame based on FrameNet. During training, we use L-BFGS to compute the maximum-likelihood estimates of ϕ.

3.3 Entity Extraction

For entity extraction, we trained a standard linear-chain Conditional Random Field (CRF) (Lafferty et al., 2001) using the BIO scheme (i.e., identifying the **B**eginning, the **I**nside and the **O**utside of the

---

[5]We use the Stanford coreference system (Lee et al., 2013) for within-document entity coreference.

Category	Type	Features
Trigger	*Lexical resources:* WordNet Nomlex FrameNet Word2Vec	1. lemmas of the words in the trigger mention 2. nominalization of the words based on Nomlex (Macleod et al., 1998) 3. context words within a window of size 2 4. similarity features between the head word and a list of trigger seeds based on WordNet (Bronstein et al., 2015) 5. semantic frames that associate with the head word and its p-o-s tag based on FrameNet (Li et al., 2014) 6. pre-trained vector for the head word (Mikolov et al., 2013)
	Syntactic resources: Stanford parser	7. dependency edges involving the head word, both lexicalized and unlexicalized 8. whether the head word is a pronoun
Argument	*Lexical resources:* WordNet	1. lemmas of the words in the entity mention 2. lemmas of the words in the trigger mention 3. words between the entity mention and the trigger mention
	Syntactic resources: Stanford parser	4. the relative position of the entity mention to the trigger mention (before, after, or contain) 5. whether the entity mention and the trigger mention are in the same clause 6. the shortest dependency paths between the entity mention and the trigger mention
Entity	*Entity resources:* Stanford NER NELL KB	1. Gender and animacy attributes of the entity mention 2. Stanford NER type for the entity mention 3. Semantic type for the entity mention based on the NELL knowledge base (Mitchell et al., 2015) 4. Predicted entity type and confidence score for the entity mention output by the entity extractor described in Section 3.3

Table 1: Features for event triggers, event arguments, and entity mentions.

text segments). We use features that are similar to those from previous work (Ratinov and Roth, 2009): (1) current words and part-of-speech tags; (2) context words in a window of size 2; (3) word type such as all-capitalized, is-capitalized, and all-digits; (4) Gazetteer-based entity type if the current word matches an entry in the gazetteers collected from Wikipedia (Ratinov and Roth, 2009). In addition, we consider pre-trained word embeddings (Mikolov et al., 2013) as dense features for each word in order to improve the generalizability of the model.

3.4 Joint Inference

Our end goal is to extract coherent event mentions and entity mentions across a document. To achieve this, we propose a joint inference approach that allows information flow among the three local models and finds globally-optimal assignments of all variables, including the trigger variables $\mathbf{t}$, the argument role variables $\mathbf{r}$, and the entity variables $\mathbf{a}$. Specifically, we define the following objective:

$$\max_{\mathbf{t},\mathbf{r},\mathbf{a}} \sum_{i \in \mathcal{T}} E(t_i, \mathbf{r}_{i\cdot}, \mathbf{a}.) + \sum_{i,i' \in \mathcal{T}} R(t_i, t_{i'}) + \sum_{j \in \mathcal{N}} D(a_j) \quad (3)$$

The first term is the sum of confidence scores for individual event mentions based on the parameter estimates from the within-event model. $E(t_i, \mathbf{r}_{i\cdot}, \mathbf{a}.)$ can be further decomposed into three parts.

$$E(t_i, \mathbf{r}_{i\cdot}, \mathbf{a}.) =$$
$$\log p_{\boldsymbol{\theta}}(t_i|i, \mathcal{N}_i, x) + \sum_{j \in \mathcal{N}_i} \log p_{\boldsymbol{\theta}}(t_i, r_{ij}|i, \mathcal{N}_i, x)$$
$$+ \sum_{j \in \mathcal{N}_i} \log p_{\boldsymbol{\theta}}(r_{ij}, a_j|i, \mathcal{N}_i, x)$$

The second term is the sum of confidence scores for event relations based on the parameter estimates from the pairwise event model, where $R(t_i, t_{i'}) = \log p_{\boldsymbol{\phi}}(t_i, t_{i'}|i, i', x)$. The third term is the sum of confidence scores for entity mentions, where $D(a_j) = \log p_{\boldsymbol{\psi}}(a_j|j, x)$ and $p_{\boldsymbol{\psi}}(a_j|j, x)$ is the marginal probability derived from the linear-chain CRF described in Section 3.3. The optimization is subjected to agreement constraints that enforce the overlapping variables among the three components to agree on their values.

The joint inference problem can be formulated as an integer linear program (ILP). To solve it efficiently, we find solutions for the relaxation of the problem using a dual decomposition algorithm AD^3 (Martins et al., 2011). AD^3 has been shown to be orders of magnitude faster than a general purpose ILP solver in practice (Das et al., 2012). It is also particularly suitable for our problem since it involves decompositions that have many overlapping simple factors. We observed that AD^3 recovers the exact solutions for all the test documents in our experiments and the runtime for labeling each document is only three seconds in average in a 64-bit machine with two 2GHz CPUs and 8GB of RAM.

4 Experiments

We conduct experiments on the ACE2005 corpus.[6] It contains text documents from a variety of sources such as newswire reports, weblogs, and discussion forums. We use the same data split as in Li et al. (2013). Table 2 shows the data statistics.

We adopt the evaluation metrics for events as defined in Li et al. (2013). An event trigger is correctly identified if its offsets match those of a gold-standard trigger; and it is correctly classified if its event subtype (33 in total) also match the subtype of the gold-standard trigger. An event argument is correctly identified if its offsets and event subtype match those of any of the reference argument mentions in the document; and it is correctly classified if its semantic role (28 in total) is also correct. For entities, a predicted mention is correctly extracted if its head offsets and entity type (9 in total) match those of the reference entity mention.

Note that our approach requires entity mention candidates and event trigger candidates as input. Instead of enumerating all possible text spans, we generate high-quality entity mentions from the k-best predictions of our CRF entity extractor (in Section 3.3).[7] Similarly, we train a CRF for event trigger extraction using the same features except for the gazetteers, and generate trigger candidates based on the k-best predictions. We set $k = 50$ for entities and $k = 10$ for event triggers based on performance on the development set. They cover 92.3% of the gold-standard entity mentions and 96.3% of the gold-standard event triggers in the test set.

	Train	Dev	Test
Documents	529	40	30
Sentences	14,837	863	672
Triggers	4,337	497	438
Arguments	7,768	933	911
Entity Mentions	48,797	3,917	4,184

Table 2: Statistics of the ACE2005 dataset.

4.1 Results

Event Extraction. We compare the proposed models WITHINEVENT (in Section 3.1) and JOINTEVENTENTITY (in Section 3.4) with two strong baselines. One is JOINTBEAM (Li et al., 2013), a state-of-the-art event extractor that uses a structured perceptron with beam search for sentence-level joint extraction of event triggers and arguments. The other is STAGEDMAXENT, a typical two-stage approach that detects event triggers first and then event arguments. We use the same event trigger candidates and entity mention candidates as input to all the comparing models except for JOINTBEAM, because JOINTBEAM only extracts event mentions and assumes entity mentions are given. We consider a realistic experimental setting where no gold-standard annotations are available for entities during testing. To obtain results from JOINTBEAM, we ran the actual system[8] used in Li et al. (2013) using the entity mentions output by our CRF-based entity extractor.

Table 3 shows the average[9] precision, recall, and F1 score for event triggers and event arguments. We can see that our WITHINEVENT model, which explicitly models the trigger-argument dependencies and argument-role-entity-type dependencies, outperforms the MaxEnt pipeline, especially in event argument extraction. This shows that modeling the trigger-argument dependencies is effective in reducing error propagation.

Comparing to the state-of-the-art event extractor JOINTBEAM, the improvements introduced by WITHINEVENT are substantial in both event triggers and event arguments. We believe there are two main reasons: (1) WITHINEVENT considers all possible joint trigger/argument label assignments, whereas

---

[6] http://www.itl.nist.gov/iad/mig/tests/ace/2005/

[7] During training, we randomly split the training data into 10 parts and consider the k-best predictions for each part.

[8] https://github.com/oferbr/BIU-RPI-Event-Extraction-Project

[9] We report the micro-average scores as in previous work (Li et al., 2013).

Model	Event Trigger Identification			Event Trigger Classification			Event Argument Identification			Argument Role Classification		
	P	R	F1	P	R	F1	P	R	F1	P	R	F1
JOINTBEAM (Li et al., 2013)	76.6	58.7	66.5	74.0	56.7	64.2	74.6	25.5	38.0	68.8	23.5	35.0
STAGEDMAXENT	73.9	**66.5**	70.0	70.4	63.3	66.7	**75.7**	20.2	31.9	**71.2**	19.0	30.0
WITHINEVENT	76.9	63.8	69.7	74.7	62.0	67.7	72.4	37.2	49.2	69.9	35.9	47.4
JOINTEVENTENTITY	**77.6**	65.4	**71.0**[*]	**75.1**	63.3	**68.7**	73.7	**38.5**	**50.6**[*]	70.6	**36.9**	**48.4**[*]

Table 3: Event extraction results on the ACE2005 test set. ∗ indicates that the difference in F1 compared to the second best model (WITHINEVENT) is statistically significant ($p < 0.05$).

Model	Trigger	Arg
CROSS-DOC (Ji and Grishman, 2008)	67.3	42.6
CNN (Nguyen and Grishman, 2015)	67.6	-
JOINTEVENTENTITY	**68.7**	**48.4**

Table 4: Comparison of the results (F1 score) of JOINTEVEN-TENTITY and the best known results on ACE event trigger classification and argument role classification.

Model	P	R	F1
CRFENTITY	**85.5**	73.5	79.1
JOINTEVENTENTITY	82.4	**79.2**	**80.7**[*]

Table 5: Entity extraction results on the ACE2005 test set. ∗ indicates statistical significance ($p < 0.05$).

Model	PER	GPE	ORG	TIME
CRFENTITY	85.1	87.0	65.4	78.4
JOINTEVENTENTITY	**87.1**	87.0	**70.2**	**80.2**

Table 6: Entity extraction results (F1 score) per entity type.

JOINTBEAM considers only a subset of the possible assignments based on a heuristic beam search. More specifically, when predicting labels for token i, JointBeam considers only the K-best ($K = 4$ in their paper) partial trigger/argument label configurations for the previous $i - 1$ tokens. As the length of the sentence increases, a large amount of information will be thrown away. (2) WITH-INEVENT models argument-role-entity-type dependencies, whereas JOINTBEAM assumes the entity types are given. This can cause error propagation.

JOINTEVENTENTITY provides the best performance among all the models on all evaluation categories. It boosts both precision and recall compared to WITHINEVENT.[10] This demonstrates the advantages of JOINTEVENTENTITY in allowing information propagation across event mentions and entity mentions and making more context-aware and semantically coherent predictions.

We also compare the results of JOINTEVENTEN-TITY with the best known results on the ACE event

extraction task in Table 4. CROSS-DOC (Ji and Grishman, 2008) performs cross-document inference of events using document clustering information, and CNN (Nguyen and Grishman, 2015) is a convolutional neural network for extracting event triggers at the sentence level. We see that JOINTEVENTEN-TITY outperforms both models and achieves new state-of-the-art results for event trigger and argument extraction in an end-to-end evaluation setting.

Entity Extraction. In addition to extracting event mentions, JOINTEVENTENTITY also extracts entity mentions. We compare its output with the output of a strong entity extraction baseline CRFENTITY (described in Section 3.3). Table 5 shows the (micro-)average precision, recall, and F1 score. We see that JOINTEVENTENTITY introduces a significant improvement in recall and F1. Table 6 further shows the F1 score for four major entity types PER, GPE, ORG, and TIME in ACE. The promising improvements indicate that joint modeling of events and entities allows for more accurate predictions about not only events but also entities.

4.2 Error Analysis

Table 7 divides the errors made by JOINTEVEN-TENTITY based on different subtasks and the classification error types in each task. For event triggers, the majority of the errors relates to missing triggers and only 3.7% involves misclassified event types (e.g., a DEMONSTRATION event is mistaken for a TRANSPORT event). Among the missing triggers, we examine the cases where the event types are correctly identified in a sentence but with in-

---

[10]All significance tests reported in this paper were computed using the paired bootstrap procedure (Berg-Kirkpatrick et al., 2012) with 10,000 samples of the test documents.

Error Type	Missing	Spurious	Misclassified
TRIGGER	62.1%	34.2%	3.7%
ARGUMENT	71.2%	24.7%	4.1%
ENTITY	43.4%	30.5%	26.1%

Table 7: Classification of errors made by JOINTEVENTEN-TITY.

correct triggers and find that there are only 5% of such cases. For event arguments, the majority of the errors relates to missing arguments and only 4.1% is about misclassified argument roles. Among the missing event arguments, 10% of them has correctly identified entity types.

In general, the errors for event extraction are commonly due to three reasons: (1) Lexical sparsity. For example, in the sentence "At least three members of a family ... were **hacked** to death ...", our model fails to detect that "hacked" triggers an AT-TACK event, because it has never seen "hacked" with this sense during training. Using WordNet and pre-trained word vectors may alleviate the sparsity issue. It is also important to disambiguate word senses in context. (2) Shallow understanding of context, especially long-range context. For example, given the sentence "**She** is being held on 50,000 dollars bail on a charge of first-degree reckless **homicide** ...", the model detects that "homicide" triggers an event, but fails to detect that "She" refers to the AGENT who committed the homicide. This is mainly due to the complex long-distance dependency between the trigger and the argument. (3) Use of complex language such as metaphor, idioms, and sarcasm. Addressing these phenomena is in general difficult since it requires richer background knowledge and more sophisticated inference.

For entity extraction, we find that integrating event information into entity extraction successfully improves recall and F1. However, since the ACE dataset is restricted to a limited set of events, a large portion of the sentences does not contain any event triggers and event arguments that are of interest. For these sentences, there is little or no benefit of joint modeling. We also find that some entity misclassification errors can be avoided if entity coreference information is available. We plan to investigate coreference resolution as an additional component to our joint model in future work.

5   Related Work

Event extraction has been mainly studied using the ACE data (Doddington et al., 2004) and biomedical data for the BioNLP shared tasks (Kim et al., 2009). To reduce task complexity, early work employs a pipeline of classifiers that extracts event triggers first, and then determines their arguments (Ahn, 2006; Björne et al., 2009). Recently, Convolutional Neural Networks have been used to improve the pipeline classifiers (Nguyen and Grishman, 2015; Chen et al., 2015). As pipeline approaches suffer from error propagation, researchers have proposed methods for joint extraction of event triggers and arguments, using either structured perceptron (Li et al., 2013), Markov Logic (Poon and Vanderwende, 2010), or dependency parsing algorithms (McClosky et al., 2011). However, existing joint models largely rely on heuristic search to aggressively shrink the search space. One exception is work in Riedel and McCallum (2011), which uses dual decomposition to solve joint inference with runtime guarantees. Our work is similar to Riedel and McCallum (2011). However, there are two main differences: first, our model extracts both event mentions and entity mentions; second, it performs joint inference across sentence boundaries. Although our approach is evaluated on ACE, it can be easily adapted to BioNLP data by using appropriate features for events triggers, argument roles, and entities. We consider this as future work.

There has been work on improving event extraction by exploiting document-level context. Berant et al. (2014) exploits event-event relations, e.g., causality, inhibition, which frequently occur in biological texts. For general texts most work focuses on exploiting temporal event relations (Chambers and Jurafsky, 2008; Do et al., 2012; McClosky and Manning, 2012). For the ACE domain, there is work on utilizing event type co-occurrence patterns to propagation event classification decisions (Ji and Grishman, 2008; Liao and Grishman, 2010). Our model is similar to their work. It models the co-occurrence relations between event types (e.g., a DIE event tends to co-occur with ATTACK events and TRANS-PORT events). It can be extended to handle other types of event relations (e.g., causal and temporal) by designing appropriate features. Chambers and

Jurafsky (2009; 2011) learn narrative schemas by linking event verbs that have coreferring syntactic arguments. Our model also adopts this intuition to relate event triggers across sentences. In addition, each event argument is grounded by its entity type (e.g., an entity mention of type PER can only fill roles that can be played by a person).

6 Conclusion

In this paper, we introduce a new approach for automatic extraction of events and entities across a document. We first decompose the learning problem into three tractable subproblems: learning within-event structures, learning event-event relations, and learning for entity extraction. We then integrate these learned models into a single model that performs joint inference of all event triggers, semantic roles for events, and entities across the whole document. Experimental results demonstrate that our approach outperforms the state-of-the-art event extractors by a large margin and substantially improves a strong entity extraction baseline. For future work, we plan to integrate entity and event coreference as additional components into the joint inference framework. We are also interested in investigating the integration of more sophisticated event-event relation models of causality and temporal ordering.

Acknowledgments

This work was supported in part by NSF grant IIS-1250956, and in part by the DARPA DEFT program under contract FA87501320005. We would like to thank members of the CMU NELL group for helpful comments. We also thank the anonymous reviewers for insightful suggestions.

References

David Ahn. 2006. The stages of event extraction. In *Proceedings of the Workshop on Annotating and Reasoning about Time and Events*, pages 1–8. Association for Computational Linguistics.

Jonathan Berant, Vivek Srikumar, Pei-Chun Chen, Brad Huang, Christopher D Manning, Abby Vander Linden, Brittany Harding, and Peter Clark. 2014. Modeling biological processes for reading comprehension. In *Proceedings of the 2014 Conference on Empirical Methods in Natural Language Processing (EMNLP)*,

pages 1499–1510. Association for Computational Linguistics.

Taylor Berg-Kirkpatrick, David Burkett, and Dan Klein. 2012. An empirical investigation of statistical significance in nlp. In *Proceedings of the 2012 Joint Conference on Empirical Methods in Natural Language Processing and Computational Natural Language Learning (EMNLP-CoNLL)*, pages 995–1005. Association for Computational Linguistics.

Jari Björne, Juho Heimonen, Filip Ginter, Antti Airola, Tapio Pahikkala, and Tapio Salakoski. 2009. Extracting complex biological events with rich graph-based feature sets. In *Proceedings of the Workshop on Current Trends in Biomedical Natural Language Processing: Shared Task*, pages 10–18. Association for Computational Linguistics.

Ofer Bronstein, Ido Dagan, Qi Li, Heng Ji, and Anette Frank. 2015. Seed-based event trigger labeling: How far can event descriptions get us? In *ACL Volume 2: Short Papers*, pages 372–376. Association for Computational Linguistics.

Nathanael Chambers and Dan Jurafsky. 2008. Jointly combining implicit constraints improves temporal ordering. In *Proceedings of the Conference on Empirical Methods in Natural Language Processing (EMNLP)*, pages 698–706. Association for Computational Linguistics.

Nathanael Chambers and Dan Jurafsky. 2009. Unsupervised learning of narrative schemas and their participants. In *Proceedings of the Joint Conference of the 47th Annual Meeting of the ACL and the 4th International Joint Conference on Natural Language Processing of the AFNLP: Volume 2-Volume 2*, pages 602–610. Association for Computational Linguistics.

Nathanael Chambers and Dan Jurafsky. 2011. Template-based information extraction without the templates. In *Proceedings of the 49th Annual Meeting of the Association for Computational Linguistics: Human Language Technologies-Volume 1*, pages 976–986. Association for Computational Linguistics.

Yubo Chen, Liheng Xu, Kang Liu, Daojian Zeng, and Jun Zhao. 2015. Event extraction via dynamic multi-pooling convolutional neural networks. In *Proceedings of the 53rd Annual Meeting of the Association for Computational Linguistics and the 7th International Joint Conference on Natural Language Processing (ACL-IJCNLP)*, volume 1, pages 167–176. Association for Computational Linguistics.

Dipanjan Das, André FT Martins, and Noah A Smith. 2012. An exact dual decomposition algorithm for shallow semantic parsing with constraints. In *Proceedings of the First Joint Conference on Lexical and Computational Semantics-Volume 1: Proceedings of the main conference and the shared task, and Volume*

2: Proceedings of the Sixth International Workshop on Semantic Evaluation, pages 209–217. Association for Computational Linguistics.

Quang Xuan Do, Wei Lu, and Dan Roth. 2012. Joint inference for event timeline construction. In *Proceedings of the 2012 Joint Conference on Empirical Methods in Natural Language Processing and Computational Natural Language Learning (EMNLP-CoNLL)*, pages 677–687. Association for Computational Linguistics.

George R Doddington, Alexis Mitchell, Mark A Przybocki, Lance A Ramshaw, Stephanie Strassel, and Ralph M Weischedel. 2004. The automatic content extraction (ace) program-tasks, data, and evaluation. In *Proceedings of the Fourth International Conference on Language Resources and Evaluation (LREC-2004)*. European Language Resources Association (ELRA).

Heng Ji and Ralph Grishman. 2008. Refining event extraction through cross-document inference. In *Proceedings of ACL-08: HLT*, pages 254–262. Association for Computational Linguistics.

Alex Judea and Michael Strube. 2015. Event extraction as frame-semantic parsing. *Proceedings of the Fourth Joint Conference on Lexical and Computational Semantics (*SEM 2015)*, pages 159–164.

Jin-Dong Kim, Tomoko Ohta, Sampo Pyysalo, Yoshinobu Kano, and Jun'ichi Tsujii. 2009. Overview of bionlp'09 shared task on event extraction. In *Proceedings of the Workshop on Current Trends in Biomedical Natural Language Processing: Shared Task*, pages 1–9. Association for Computational Linguistics.

John Lafferty, Andrew McCallum, and Fernando CN Pereira. 2001. Conditional random fields: Probabilistic models for segmenting and labeling sequence data. In *Proc. 18th International Conf. on Machine Learning (ICML)*, pages 282–289.

Linguistic Data Consortium (LDC). 2005a. English annotation guidelines for entities. `https://www.ldc.upenn.edu/sites/www.ldc.upenn.edu/files/english-entities-guidelines-v5.6.6.pdf`.

Linguistic Data Consortium (LDC). 2005b. English annotation guidelines for events. `https://www.ldc.upenn.edu/sites/www.ldc.upenn.edu/files/english-events-guidelines-v5.4.3.pdf`.

Heeyoung Lee, Angel Chang, Yves Peirsman, Nathanael Chambers, Mihai Surdeanu, and Dan Jurafsky. 2013. Deterministic coreference resolution based on entity-centric, precision-ranked rules. *Computational Linguistics*, 39(4):885–916.

Qi Li, Heng Ji, and Liang Huang. 2013. Joint event extraction via structured prediction with global features. In *Proceedings of the 51st Annual Meeting of the Association for Computational Linguistics (ACL)*, pages 73–82. Association for Computational Linguistics.

Qi Li, Heng Ji, Yu Hong, and Sujian Li. 2014. Constructing information networks using one single model. In *Proceedings of the Conference on Empirical Methods on Natural Language Processing (EMNLP)*, pages 1846–1851. Association for Computational Linguistics.

Shasha Liao and Ralph Grishman. 2010. Using document level cross-event inference to improve event extraction. In *Proceedings of the 48th Annual Meeting of the Association for Computational Linguistics (ACL)*, pages 789–797. Association for Computational Linguistics.

Catherine Macleod, Ralph Grishman, Adam Meyers, Leslie Barrett, and Ruth Reeves. 1998. Nomlex: A lexicon of nominalizations. In *Proceedings of EURALEX*, volume 98, pages 187–193. Citeseer.

André FT Martins, Mario AT Figeuiredo, Pedro MQ Aguiar, Noah A Smith, and Eric P Xing. 2011. An augmented lagrangian approach to constrained map inference. In *Proceedings of the International Conference on Machine Learning (ICML)*.

David McClosky and Christopher D Manning. 2012. Learning constraints for consistent timeline extraction. In *Proceedings of the 2012 Joint Conference on Empirical Methods in Natural Language Processing and Computational Natural Language Learning (EMNLP-CoNLL)*, pages 873–882. Association for Computational Linguistics.

David McClosky, Mihai Surdeanu, and Christopher D Manning. 2011. Event extraction as dependency parsing. In *Proceedings of the 49th Annual Meeting of the Association for Computational Linguistics: Human Language Technologies (ACL)*, pages 1626–1635. Association for Computational Linguistics.

Tomas Mikolov, Ilya Sutskever, Kai Chen, Greg S Corrado, and Jeff Dean. 2013. Distributed representations of words and phrases and their compositionality. In *Advances in neural information processing systems (NIPS)*, pages 3111–3119.

T. Mitchell, W. Cohen, E. Hruschka, P. Talukdar, J. Betteridge, A. Carlson, B. Dalvi, M. Gardner, B. Kisiel, J. Krishnamurthy, N. Lao, K. Mazaitis, T. Mohamed, N. Nakashole, E. Platanios, A. Ritter, M. Samadi, B. Settles, R. Wang, D. Wijaya, A. Gupta, X. Chen, A. Saparov, M. Greaves, and J. Welling. 2015. Never-ending learning. In *Proceedings of the Twenty-Ninth AAAI Conference on Artificial Intelligence (AAAI-15)*.

Thien Huu Nguyen and Ralph Grishman. 2015. Event detection and domain adaptation with convolutional neural networks. In *Proceedings of ACL-IJCNLP 2015 Volume 2: Short Papers*, pages 365–371. Association for Computational Linguistics.

Hoifung Poon and Lucy Vanderwende. 2010. Joint inference for knowledge extraction from biomedical literature. In *Human Language Technologies: The 2010 Annual Conference of the North American Chapter of the Association for Computational Linguistics (NAACL)*, pages 813–821. Association for Computational Linguistics.

Lev Ratinov and Dan Roth. 2009. Design challenges and misconceptions in named entity recognition. In *Proceedings of the Thirteenth Conference on Computational Natural Language Learning*, pages 147–155. Association for Computational Linguistics.

Sebastian Riedel and Andrew McCallum. 2011. Fast and robust joint models for biomedical event extraction. In *Proceedings of the Conference on Empirical Methods in Natural Language Processing (EMNLP)*, pages 1–12. Association for Computational Linguistics.

Joint Event Extraction via Recurrent Neural Networks

Thien Huu Nguyen, Kyunghyun Cho and Ralph Grishman
Computer Science Department, New York University, New York, NY 10003, USA
`thien@cs.nyu.edu,kyunghyun.cho@nyu.edu,grishman@cs.nyu.edu`

Abstract

Event extraction is a particularly challenging problem in information extraction. The state-of-the-art models for this problem have either applied convolutional neural networks in a pipelined framework (Chen et al., 2015) or followed the joint architecture via structured prediction with rich local and global features (Li et al., 2013). The former is able to learn hidden feature representations automatically from data based on the continuous and generalized representations of words. The latter, on the other hand, is capable of mitigating the error propagation problem of the pipelined approach and exploiting the inter-dependencies between event triggers and argument roles via discrete structures. In this work, we propose to do event extraction in a joint framework with bidirectional recurrent neural networks, thereby benefiting from the advantages of the two models as well as addressing issues inherent in the existing approaches. We systematically investigate different memory features for the joint model and demonstrate that the proposed model achieves the state-of-the-art performance on the ACE 2005 dataset.

1 Introduction

We address the problem of event extraction (EE): identifying event triggers of specified types and their arguments in text. Triggers are often single verbs or normalizations that evoke some events of interest while arguments are the entities participating into such events. This is an important and challenging task of information extraction in natural language processing (NLP), as the same event might be present in various expressions, and an expression might expresses different events in different contexts.

There are two main approaches to EE: (i) the joint approach that predicts event triggers and arguments for sentences *simultaneously* as a structured prediction problem, and (ii) the pipelined approach that first performs trigger prediction and then identifies arguments in *separate* stages.

The most successful joint system for EE (Li et al., 2013) is based on the structured perceptron algorithm with a large set of local and global features[1]. These features are designed to capture the *discrete* structures that are intuitively helpful for EE using the NLP toolkits (e.g., part of speech tags, dependency and constituent tags). The advantages of such a joint system are twofold: (i) mitigating the error propagation from the upstream component (trigger identification) to the downstream classifier (argument identification), and (ii) benefiting from the the inter-dependencies among event triggers and argument roles via global features. For example, consider the following sentence (taken from Li et al. (2013)) in the ACE 2005 dataset:

In Baghdad, a <u>cameraman</u> **died** *when an American tank* **fired** *on the Palestine hotel.*

In this sentence, **died** and **fired** are the event triggers for the events of types *Die* and *Attack*, respectively. In the pipelined approach, it is often simple for the argument classifiers to realize that *camera-*

---

[1]Local features encapsulate the characteristics for the individual tasks (i.e, trigger and argument role labeling) while global features target the dependencies between triggers and arguments and are only available in the joint approach.

Proceedings of NAACL-HLT 2016, pages 300–309,
San Diego, California, June 12-17, 2016. ©2016 Association for Computational Linguistics

man is the *Target* argument of the *Die* event due to the proximity between *cameraman* and *died* in the sentence. However, as *cameraman* is far away from *fired*, the argument classifiers in the pipelined approach might fail to recognize *cameraman* as the *Target* argument for the event *Attack* with their local features. The joint approach can overcome this issue by relying on the global features to encode the fact that a *Victim* argument for the *Die* event is often the *Target* argument for the *Attack* event in the same sentence.

Despite the advantages presented above, the joint system by Li et al. (2013) suffers from the lack of generalization over the unseen words/features and the inability to extract the underlying structures for EE (due to its *discrete* representation from the handcrafted feature set) (Nguyen and Grishman, 2015b; Chen et al., 2015).

The most successful pipelined system for EE to date (Chen et al., 2015) addresses these drawbacks of the joint system by Li et al. (2013) via dynamic multi-pooling convolutional neural networks (DMCNN). In this system, words are represented by the *continuous* representations (Bengio et al., 2003; Turian et al., 2010; Mikolov et al., 2013a) and features are automatically learnt from data by the DMCNN, thereby alleviating the unseen word/feature problem and extracting more effective features for the given dataset. However, as the system by Chen et al. (2015) is pipelined, it still suffers from the inherent limitations of error propagation and failure to exploit the inter-dependencies between event triggers and argument roles (Li et al., 2013). Finally, we notice that the discrete features, shown to be helpful in the previous studies for EE (Li et al., 2013), are not considered in Chen et al. (2015).

Guided by these characteristics of the EE systems by Li et al. (2013) and Chen et al. (2015), in this work, we propose to solve the EE problem with the joint approach via recurrent neural networks (RNNs) (Hochreiter and Schmidhuber, 1997; Cho et al., 2014) augmented with the discrete features, thus inheriting all the benefits from both systems as well as overcoming their inherent issues. To the best of our knowledge, this is the first work to employ neural networks to do joint EE.

Our model involves two RNNs that run over the sentences in both forward and reverse directions to learn a richer representation for the sentences. This representation is then utilized to predict event triggers and argument roles jointly. In order to capture the inter-dependencies between triggers and argument roles, we introduce memory vectors/matrices to store the prediction information during the course of labeling the sentences.

We systematically explore various memory vector/matrices as well as different methods to learn word representations for the joint model. The experimental results show that our system achieves the state-of-the-art performance on the widely used ACE 2005 dataset.

2 Event Extraction Task

We focus on the EE task of the Automatic Context Extraction (ACE) evaluation[2]. ACE defines an event as something that happens or leads to some change of state. We employ the following terminology:

- **Event mention**: a phrase or sentence in which an event occurs, including one trigger and an arbitrary number of arguments.
- **Event trigger**: the main word that most clearly expresses an event occurrence.
- **Event argument**: an entity mention, temporal expression or value (e.g. *Job-Title*) that servers as a participant or attribute with a specific role in an event mention.

ACE annotates 8 types and 33 subtypes (e.g., *Attack*, *Die*, *Start-Position*) for event mentions that also correspond to the types and subtypes of the event triggers. Each event subtype has its own set of roles to be filled by the event arguments. For instance, the roles for the *Die* event include *Place*, *Victim* and *Time*. The total number of roles for all the event subtypes is 36.

Given an English text document, an event extraction system needs to recognize event triggers with specific subtypes and their corresponding arguments with the roles for each sentence. Following the previous work (Liao and Grishman, 2011; Li et al., 2013; Chen et al., 2015), we assume that the argument candidates (i.e, the entity mentions, temporal expressions and values) are provided (by the ACE annotation) to the event extraction systems.

---

[2] http://projects.ldc.upenn.edu/ace

3   Model

We formalize the EE task as follow. Let $W = w_1 w_2 \ldots w_n$ be a sentence where n is the sentence length and w_i is the i-th token. Also, let $E = e_1, e_2, \ldots, e_k$ be the entity mentions[3] in this sentence (k is the number of the entity mentions and can be zero). Each entity mention comes with the offsets of the head and the entity type. We further assume that $i_1, i_2, \ldots, i_k$ be the indexes of the last words of the mention heads for $e_1, e_2, \ldots, e_k$, respectively.

In EE, for every token w_i in the sentence, we need to predict the event subtype (if any) for it. If w_i is a trigger word for some event of interest, we then need to predict the roles (if any) that each entity mention e_j plays in such event.

The joint model for event extraction in this work consists of two phases: (i) the *encoding phase* that applies recurrent neural networks to induce a more abstract representation of the sentence, and (ii) the *prediction phase* that uses the new representation to perform event trigger and argument role identification simultaneously for W. Figure 1 shows an overview of the model.

3.1   Encoding

3.1.1   Sentence Encoding

In the encoding phase, we first transform each token w_i into a real-valued vector x_i using the concatenation of the following three vectors:

1. The word embedding vector of w_i: This is obtained by looking up a pre-trained word embedding table D (Collobert and Weston, 2008; Turian et al., 2010; Mikolov et al., 2013a).

2. The real-valued embedding vector for the entity type of w_i: This vector is motivated from the prior work (Nguyen and Grishman, 2015b) and generated by looking up the entity type embedding table (initialized randomly) for the entity type of w_i. Note that we also employ the BIO annotation schema to assign entity type labels to each token in the sentences using the heads of the entity mentions as do Nguyen and Grishman (2015b).

3. The binary vector whose dimensions correspond to the possible relations between words in the dependency trees. The value at each dimension of

---

[3]From now on, when mentioning entity mentions, we always refer to the ACE entity mentions, times and values.

this vector is set to 1 only if there exists one edge of the corresponding relation connected to w_i in the dependency tree of W. This vector represents the dependency features that are shown to be helpful in the previous research (Li et al., 2013).

Note that we do not use the relative position features, unlike the prior work on neural networks for EE (Nguyen and Grishman, 2015b; Chen et al., 2015). The reason is we predict the whole sentences for triggers and argument roles jointly, thus having no fixed positions for anchoring in the sentences.

The transformation from the token w_i to the vector x_i essentially converts the input sentence W into a sequence of real-valued vectors $X = (x_1, x_2, \ldots, x_n)$, to be used by recurrent neural networks to learn a more effective representation.

3.1.2   Recurrent Neural Networks

Consider the input sequence $X = (x_1, x_2, \ldots, x_n)$. At each step i, we compute the hidden vector α_i based on the current input vector x_i and the previous hidden vector α_{i-1}, using the non-linear transformation function Φ: $\alpha_i = \Phi(x_i, \alpha_{i-1})$. This recurrent computation is done over X to generate the hidden vector sequence $(\alpha_1, \alpha_2, \ldots, \alpha_n)$, denoted by $\overrightarrow{\text{RNN}}(x_1, x_2, \ldots, x_n) = (\alpha_1, \alpha_2, \ldots, \alpha_n)$.

An important characteristics of the recurrent mechanism is that it adaptively accumulates the context information from position 1 to i into the hidden vector α_i, making α_i a rich representation. However, α_i is not sufficient for the event trigger and argument predictions at position i as such predictions might need to rely on the context information in the future (i.e, from position i to n). In order to address this issue, we run a second RNN in the reverse direction from X_n to X_1 to generate the second hidden vector sequence: $\overleftarrow{\text{RNN}}(x_n, x_{n-1}, \ldots, x_1) = (\alpha'_n, \alpha'_{n-1}, \ldots, \alpha'_1)$ in which α'_i summarizes the context information from position n to i. Eventually, we obtain the new representation $(h_1, h_2, \ldots, h_n)$ for X by concatenating the hidden vectors in $(\alpha_1, \alpha_2, \ldots, \alpha_n)$ and $(\alpha'_n, \alpha'_{n-1}, \ldots, \alpha'_1)$: $h_i = [\alpha_i, \alpha'_i]$. Note that h_i essentially encapsulates the context information over the whole sentence (from 1 to n) with a greater focus on position i.

Regarding the non-linear function, the simplest

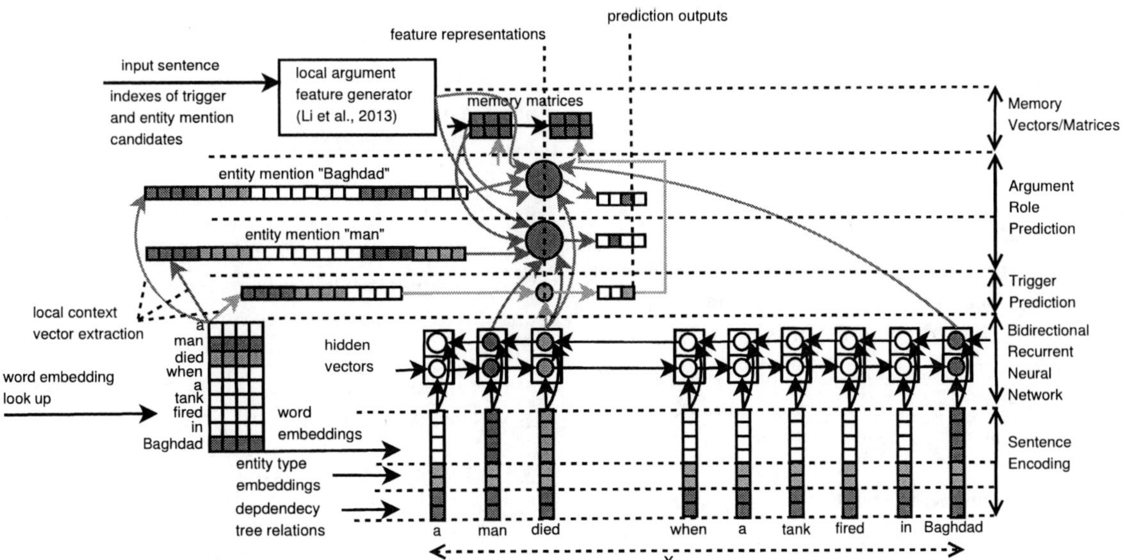

Figure 1: The joint EE model for the input sentence *"a man died when a tank fired in Baghdad"* with local context window $d = 1$. We only demonstrate the memory matrices $G_i^{\text{arg/trg}}$ in this figure. Green corresponds to the trigger candidate *"died"* at the current step while violet and red are for the entity mentions *"man"* and *"Baghdad"* respectively.

form of Φ in the literature considers it as a one-layer feed-forward neural network. Unfortunately, this function is prone to the *"vanishing gradient"* problem (Bengio et al., 1994), making it challenging to train RNNs properly. This problem can be alleviated by long-short term memory units (LSTM) (Hochreiter and Schmidhuber, 1997; Gers, 2001). In this work, we use a variant of LSTM; called the *Gated Recurrent Units* (GRU) from Cho et al. (2014). GRU has been shown to achieve comparable performance (Chung et al., 2014; Józefowicz et al., 2015).

3.2 Prediction

In order to jointly predict triggers and argument roles for W, we maintain a binary memory vector G_i^{trg} for triggers, and binary memory matrices G_i^{arg} and $G_i^{\text{arg/trg}}$ for arguments (at each time i). These vector/matrices are set to zeros initially ($i = 0$) and updated during the prediction process for W.

Given the bidirectional representation $h_1, h_2, \ldots, h_n$ in the encoding phase and the initialized memory vector/matrices, the joint prediction procedure loops over n tokens in the sentence (from 1 to n). At each time step i, we perform the following three stages in order:

(i) *trigger prediction* for w_i.

(ii) *argument role prediction* for all the entity mentions $e_1, e_2, \ldots, e_k$ with respect to the current token w_i.

(iii) *compute* G_i^{trg}, G_i^{arg} and $G_i^{\text{arg/trg}}$ for the current step using the previous memory vector/matrices G_{i-1}^{trg}, G_{i-1}^{arg} and $G_{i-1}^{\text{arg/trg}}$, and the prediction output in the earlier stages.

The output of this process would be the predicted trigger subtype t_i for w_i, the predicted argument roles $a_{i1}, a_{i2}, \ldots, a_{ik}$ and the memory vector/matrices G_i^{trg}, G_i^{arg} and $G_i^{\text{arg/trg}}$ for the current step. Note that t_i should be the event subtype if w_i is a trigger word for some event of interest, or *"Other"* in the other cases. a_{ij}, in constrast, should be the argument role of the entity mention e_j with respect to w_i if w_i is a trigger word and e_j is an argument of the corresponding event, otherwise a_{ij} is set to *"Other"* ($j = 1$ to k).

3.2.1 Trigger Prediction

In the trigger prediction stage for the current token w_i, we first compute the feature representation vector R_i^{trg} for w_i using the concatenation of the following three vectors:

- h_i: the hidden vector to encapsulate the global context of the input sentence.

- L_i^{trg}: the local context vector for w_i. L_i^{trg} is generated by concatenating the vectors of the words in a context window d of w_i:
  $L_i^{\text{trg}} = [D[w_{i-d}], \ldots, D[w_i], \ldots, D[w_{i+d}]]$.
- G_{i-1}^{trg}: the memory vector from the previous step.

The representation vector $R_i^{\text{trg}} = [h_i, L_i^{\text{trg}}, G_{i-1}^{\text{trg}}]$ is then fed into a feed-forward neural network F^{trg} with a softmax layer in the end to compute the probability distribution $P_{i;t}^{\text{trg}}$ over the possible trigger subtypes: $P_{i;t}^{\text{trg}} = P_i^{\text{trg}}(l = t) = F_t^{\text{trg}}(R_i^{\text{trg}})$ where t is a trigger subtype. Finally, we compute the predicted type t_i for w_i by: $t_i = \text{argmax}_t(P_{i;t}^{\text{trg}})$.

3.2.2 Argument Role Prediction

In the argument role prediction stage, we first check if the predicted trigger subtype t_i in the previous stage is "*Other*" or not. If yes, we can simply set a_{ij} to "*Other*" for all $j = 1$ to k and go to the next stage immediately. Otherwise, we loop over the entity mentions $e_1, e_2, \ldots, e_k$. For each entity mention e_j with the head index of i_j, we predict the argument role a_{ij} with respect to the trigger word w_i using the following procedure.

First, we generate the feature representation vector R_{ij}^{arg} for e_j and w_i by concatenating the following vectors:

- h_i and h_{i_j}: the hidden vectors to capture the global context of the input sentence for w_i and e_j, respectively.
- L_{ij}^{arg}: the local context vector for w_i and e_j. L_{ij}^{arg} is the concatenation of the vectors of the words in the context windows of size d for w_i and w_{i_j}:
  $L_{ij}^{\text{arg}} = [D[w_{i-d}], \ldots, D[w_i], \ldots, D[w_{i+d}], D[w_{i_j-d}], \ldots, D[w_{i_j}], \ldots, D[w_{i_j+d}]]$.
- B_{ij}: the hidden vector for the binary feature vector V_{ij}. V_{ij} is based on the local argument features between the tokens i and i_j from (Li et al., 2013). B_{ij} is then computed by feeding V_{ij} into a feed-forward neural network F^{binary} for further abstraction: $B_{ij} = F^{\text{binary}}(V_{ij})$.
- $G_{i-1}^{\text{arg}}[j]$ and $G_{i-1}^{\text{arg/trg}}[j]$: the memory vectors for e_j that are extracted out of the memory matrices G_{i-1}^{arg} and $G_{i-1}^{\text{arg/trg}}$ from the previous step.

In the next step, we again use a feed-forward neural network F^{arg} with a soft-max layer in the end to transform $R_{ij}^{\text{arg}} = [h_i, h_{i_j}, L_{ij}^{\text{arg}}, B_{ij}, G_{i-1}^{\text{arg}}[j], G_{i-1}^{\text{arg/trg}}[j]]$ into the probability distribution $P_{ij;a}^{\text{trg}}$ over the possible argument roles: $P_{ij;a}^{\text{arg}} = P_{ij}^{\text{arg}}(l = a) = F_a^{\text{arg}}(R_{ij}^{\text{arg}})$ where a is an argument role. Eventually, the predicted argument role for w_i and e_j is $a_{ij} = \text{argmax}_a(P_{ij;a}^{\text{arg}})$.

Note that the binary vector V_{ij} enriches the feature representation R_{ij}^{arg} for argument labeling with the discrete structures discovered in the prior work on feature analysis for EE (Li et al., 2013). These features include the shortest dependency paths, the entity types, subtypes, etc.

3.2.3 The Memory Vector/Matrices

An important characteristics of EE is the existence of the dependencies between trigger labels and argument roles within the same sentences (Li et al., 2013). In this work, we encode these dependencies into the memory vectors/matrices G_i^{trg}, G_i^{arg} and $G_i^{\text{arg/trg}}$ ($i = 0$ to n) and use them as features in the trigger and argument prediction explicitly (as shown in the representation vectors R_i^{trg} and R_{ij}^{arg} above). We classify the dependencies into the following three categories:

1. The **dependencies among trigger subtypes**: are captured by the memory vectors G_i^{trg} ($G_i^{\text{trg}} \in \{0,1\}^{n_T}$ for $i = 0, \ldots, n$, and n_T is the number of the possible trigger subtypes). At time i, G_i^{trg} indicates which event subtypes have been recognized before i. We obtain G_i^{trg} from G_{i-1}^{trg} and the trigger prediction output t_i at time i: $G_i^{\text{trg}}[t] = 1$ if $t = t_i$ and $G_{i-1}^{\text{trg}}[t]$ otherwise.

A motivation for such dependencies is that if a *Die* event appears somewhere in the sentences, the possibility for the later occurrence of an *Attack* event would be likely.

2. The **dependencies among argument roles**: are encoded by the memory matrix G_i^{arg} ($G_i^{\text{arg}} \in \{0,1\}^{k \times n_A}$ for $i = 0, \ldots, n$, and n_A is the number of the possible argument roles). At time i, G_i^{arg} summarizes the argument roles that the entity mentions has played with some event in the past. In particular, $G_i^{\text{arg}}[j][a] = 1$ if and only if e_j has the role of a with some event before time i. G_i^{arg} is computed from G_{i-1}^{arg}, and the prediction outputs t_i and $a_{i1}, \ldots, a_{ik}$ at time i: $G_i^{\text{arg}}[j][a] = 1$ if $t_i \neq$ "*Other*" and $a = a_{ij}$, and $G_{i-1}^{\text{arg}}[j][a]$ otherwise (for $j = 1$ to k).

3. The **dependencies between argument roles and trigger subtypes**: are encoded by the memory matrix $G_i^{\text{arg/trg}}$ ($G_i^{\text{arg/trg}} \in \{0,1\}^{k \times n_T}$ for $i = 0$ to n). At time i, $G_i^{\text{arg/trg}}$ specifies which entity mentions have been identified as arguments for which event subtypes before. In particular, $G_i^{\text{arg/trg}}[j][t] = 1$ if and only if e_j has been detected as an argument for some event of subtype t before i. $G_i^{\text{arg/trg}}$ is computed from $G_{i-1}^{\text{arg/trg}}$ and the trigger prediction output t_i at time i: $G_i^{\text{arg/trg}}[j][t] = 1$ if $t_i \neq$ *"Other"* and $t = t_i$, and $G_{i-1}^{\text{arg/trg}}[j][t]$ otherwise (for all $j = 1$ to k).

3.3 Training

Denote the given trigger subtypes and argument roles for W in the training time as $T = t_1^*, t_2^*, \ldots, t_n^*$ and $A = (a_{ij}^*)_{i=1,n}^{j=1,k}$. We train the network by minimizing the joint negative log-likelihood function C for triggers and argument roles:

$$
\begin{aligned}
C(T, A, X, E) &= - \log P(T, A | X, E) \\
&= - \log P(T | X, E) - \log P(A | T, X, E) \\
&= - \sum_{i=1}^{n} \log P_{i;t_i^*}^{\text{trg}} \\
&\quad - \sum_{i=1}^{n} I(t_i \neq \text{"Other"}) \sum_{j=1}^{k} \log P_{ij;a_{ij}^*}^{\text{arg}}
\end{aligned}
$$

where I is the indicator function.

We apply the stochastic gradient descent algorithm with mini-batches and the AdaDelta update rule (Zeiler, 2012). The gradients are computed using back-propagation. During training, besides the weight matrices, we also optimize the word and entity type embedding tables to achieve the optimal states. Finally, we rescale the weights whose Frobenius norms exceed a hyperparameter (Kim, 2014; Nguyen and Grishman, 2015a).

4 Word Representation

Following the prior work (Nguyen and Grishman, 2015b; Chen et al., 2015), we pre-train word embeddings from a large corpus and employ them to initialize the word embedding table. One of the models to train word embeddings have been proposed in Mikolov et al. (2013a; 2013b) that introduce two log-linear models, i.e the continuous bag-of-words model (CBOW) and the continuous skip-gram model (SKIP-GRAM). The CBOW model attempts to predict the current word based on *the average of the context word vectors* while the SKIP-GRAM model aims to predict the surrounding words in a sentence given the current word. In this work, besides the CBOW and SKIP-GRAM models, we examine a concatenation-based variant of CBOW (C-CBOW) to train word embeddings and compare the three models to understand their effectiveness for EE. The objective of C-CBOW is to predict the target word using *the concatenation of the vectors of the words surrounding it*.

5 Experiments

5.1 Resources, Parameters and Dataset

For all the experiments below, in the encoding phase, we use 50 dimensions for the entity type embeddings, 300 dimensions for the word embeddings and 300 units in the hidden layers for the RNNs.

Regarding the prediction phase, we employ the context window of 2 for the local features, and the feed-forward neural networks with one hidden layer for F^{trg}, F^{arg} and F^{binary} (the size of the hidden layers are 600, 600 and 300 respectively).

Finally, for training, we use the mini-batch size = 50 and the parameter for the Frobenius norms = 3.

These parameter values are either inherited from the prior research (Nguyen and Grishman, 2015b; Chen et al., 2015) or selected according to the validation data.

We pre-train the word embeddings from the English Gigaword corpus utilizing the word2vec toolkit[4] (modified to add the C-CBOW model). Following Baroni et al. (2014), we employ the context window of 5, the subsampling of the frequent words set to $1e$-05 and 10 negative samples.

We evaluate the model with the ACE 2005 corpus. For the purpose of comparison, we use the same data split as the previous work (Ji and Grishman, 2008; Liao and Grishman, 2010; Li et al., 2013; Nguyen and Grishman, 2015b; Chen et al., 2015). This data split includes 40 newswire articles (672 sentences) for the test set, 30 other documents (836 sentences) for the development set and 529 remaining documents (14,849 sentences) for the training set. Also,

---

[4] https://code.google.com/p/word2vec/

we follow the criteria of the previous work (Ji and Grishman, 2008; Liao and Grishman, 2010; Li et al., 2013; Chen et al., 2015) to judge the correctness of the predicted event mentions.

5.2 Memory Vector/Matrices

This section evaluates the effectiveness of the memory vector and matrices presented in Section 3.2.3. In particular, we test the joint model on different cases where the memory vector for triggers G^{trg} and the memory matrices for arguments $G^{\text{arg/trg}}$ and G^{arg} are included or excluded from the model. As there are 4 different ways to combine $G^{\text{arg/trg}}$ and G^{arg} for argument labeling and two options to to employ G^{trg} or not for trigger labeling, we have 8 systems for comparison in total. Table 1 reports the identification and classification performance (F1 scores) for triggers and argument roles on the development set. Note that we are using the word embeddings trained with the C-CBOW technique in this section.

System		*No*	$G^{\text{arg/trg}}$	G^{arg}	$G^{\text{arg/trg}}+G^{\text{arg}}$
No	Trigger	67.9	**68.0**	64.6	64.2
	Argument	55.6	**58.1**	55.2	53.1
G^{trg}	Trigger	63.8	61.0	61.3	66.8
	Argument	55.2	56.6	54.7	53.6

Table 1: Performance of the Memory Vector/Matrices on the development set. *No* means not using the memory vector/matrices.

We observe that the memory vector G^{trg} is not helpful for the joint model as it worsens both trigger and argument role performance (considering the same choice of the memory matrices $G^{\text{arg/trg}}$ and G^{arg} (i.e, the same row in the table) and except in the row with $G^{\text{arg/trg}} + G^{\text{arg}}$).

The clearest trend is that $G^{\text{arg/trg}}$ is very effective in improving the performance of argument labeling. This is true in both the inclusion and exclusion of G^{trg}. G^{arg} and its combination with $G^{\text{arg/trg}}$, on the other hand, have negative effect on this task. Finally, $G^{\text{arg/trg}}$ and G^{arg} do not contribute much to the trigger labeling performance in general (except in the case where G^{t}, $G^{\text{arg/trg}}$ and G^{arg} are all applied).

These observations suggest that the dependencies *among trigger subtypes* and *among argument roles* are not strong enough to be helpful for the joint model in this dataset. This is in contrast to the dependencies *between argument roles and trigger subtypes* that improve the joint model significantly.

The best system corresponds to the application of the memory matrix $G^{\text{arg/trg}}$ and will be used in all the experiments below.

5.3 Word Embedding Evaluation

We investigate different techniques to obtain the pre-trained word embeddings for initialization in the joint model of EE. Table 2 presents the performance (for both triggers and argument roles) on the development set when the CBOW, SKIP-GRAM and C-CBOW techniques are utilized to obtain word embeddings from the same corpus. We also report the performance of the joint model when it is initialized with the Word2Vec word embeddings from Mikolov et al. (2013a; 2013b) (trained with the Skip-gram model on Google News) (WORD2VEC). Finally, for comparison, the performance of the random word embeddings (RANDOM) is also included. All of these word embeddings are updated during the training of the model.

Word Embeddings	Trigger	Argument
RANDOM	59.9	50.1
SKIP-GRAM	66.7	57.1
CBOW	66.5	53.8
WORD2VEC	66.9	56.4
C-CBOW	**68.0**	**58.1**

Table 2: Performance of the Word Embedding Techniques.

The first observation from the table is that RANDOM is not good enough to initialize the word embeddings for joint EE and we need to borrow some pre-trained word embeddings for this purpose. Second, SKIP-GRAM, WORD2VEC and CBOW have comparable performance on trigger labeling while the argument labeling performance of SKIP-GRAM and WORD2VEC is much better than that of CBOW for the joint EE model. Third and most importantly, among the compared word embeddings, it is clear that C-CBOW significantly outperforms all the others. We believe that the better performance of C-CBOW stems from its concatenation of the multiple context word vectors, thus providing more information to learn better word embeddings than SKIP-GRAM and WORD2VEC. In addition, the concate-

Model	Trigger Identification (%)			Trigger Identification + Classification (%)			Argument Identification (%)			Argument Role (%)		
	P	R	F	P	R	F	P	R	F	P	R	F
Li's basline	76.2	60.5	67.4	74.5	59.1	65.9	74.1	37.4	49.7	65.4	33.1	43.9
Liao's cross-event†	N/A			68.7	68.9	68.8	50.9	49.7	50.3	45.1	44.1	44.6
Hong's cross-entity†	N/A			72.9	64.3	68.3	53.4	52.9	53.1	51.6	45.5	48.3
Li's structure	76.9	65.0	70.4	73.7	62.3	67.5	69.8	47.9	56.8	64.7	44.4	52.7
DMCNN	80.4	67.7	**73.5**	75.6	63.6	69.1	68.8	51.9	59.1	62.2	46.9	53.5
JRNN	68.5	75.7	71.9	66.0	73.0	**69.3**	61.4	64.2	**62.8**	54.2	56.7	**55.4**

Table 3: Overall Performance on the Blind Test Data. "†" designates the systems that employ the evidences beyond sentence level.

nation mechanism essentially helps to assign different weights to different context words, thereby being more flexible than CBOW that applies a single weight for all the context words.

From now on, for consistency, C-CBOW would be utilized in all the following experiments.

5.4 Comparison to the State of the art

The state-of-the-art systems for EE on the ACE 2005 dataset have been the pipelined system with dynamic multi-pooling convolutional neural networks by Chen et al. (2015) (**DMCNN**) and the joint system with structured prediction and various discrete local and global features by Li et al. (2013) (**Li's structure**).

Note that the pipelined system in Chen et al. (2015) is also the best-reported system based on neural networks for EE. Table 3 compares these state-of-the-art systems with the joint RNN-based model in this work (denoted by **JRNN**). For completeness, we also report the performance of the following representative systems:

1) **Li's baseline**: This is the pipelined system with local features by Li et al. (2013).

2) **Liao's cross event**: is the system by Liao and Grishman (2010) with the document-level information.

3) **Hong's cross-entity** (Hong et al., 2011): This system exploits the cross-entity inference, and is also the best-reported pipelined system with discrete features in the literature.

From the table, we see that JRNN achieves the best F1 scores (for both trigger and argument labeling) among all of the compared models. This is significant with the argument role labeling performance (an improvement of 1.9% over the best-reported model DMCNN in Chen et al. (2015)), and demonstrates the benefit of the joint model with RNNs and memory features in this work. In addition, as JRNN significantly outperforms the joint model with discrete features in Li et al. (2013) (an improvement of 1.8% and 2.7% for trigger and argument role labeling respectively), we can confirm the effectiveness of RNNs to learn effective feature representations for EE.

5.5 Sentences with Multiple Events

In order to further prove the effectiveness of JRNN, especially for those sentences with multiple events, we divide the test data into two parts according to the number of events in the sentences (i.e, single event and multiple events) and evaluate the performance separately, following Chen et al. (2015). Table 4 shows the performance (F1 scores) of JRNN, DMCNN and two other baseline systems, named **Embeddings+T** and **CNN** in Chen et al. (2015). Embeddings+T uses word embeddings and the traditional sentence-level features in (Li et al., 2013) while CNN is similar to DMCNN, except that it applies the standard pooling mechanism instead of the dynamic multi-pooling method (Chen et al., 2015).

The most important observation from the table is that JRNN significantly outperforms all the other methods with large margins when the input sentences contain more than one events (i.e, the row labeled with **1/N** in the table). In particular, JRNN is 13.9% better than DMCNN on trigger labeling while the corresponding improvement for argument role labeling is 6.5%, thereby further suggesting the benefit of JRNN with the memory features. Regard-

Stage	Model	1/1	1/N	all
Trigger	Embedding+T	68.1	25.5	59.8
	CNN	72.5	43.1	66.3
	DMCNN	74.3	50.9	69.1
	JRNN	**75.6**	**64.8**	**69.3**
Argument	Embedding+T	37.4	15.5	32.6
	CNN	51.6	36.6	48.9
	DMCNN	**54.6**	48.7	53.5
	JRNN	50.0	**55.2**	**55.4**

Table 4: System Performance on Single Event Sentences (**1/1**) and Multiple Event Sentences (**1/N**).

ing the performance on the single event sentences, JRNN is still the best system on trigger labeling although it is worse than DMCNN on argument role labeling. This can be partly explained by the fact that DMCNN includes the position embedding features for arguments and the memory matrix $G^{\text{arg/trg}}$ in JRNN is not functioning in this single event case.

6 Related Work

Early research on event extraction has primarily focused on local sentence-level representations in a pipelined architecture (Grishman et al., 2005; Ahn, 2006). After that, higher level features has been investigated to improve the performance (Ji and Grishman, 2008; Gupta and Ji, 2009; Patwardhan and Riloff, 2009; Liao and Grishman, 2010; Liao and Grishman, 2011; Hong et al., 2011; McClosky et al., 2011; Huang and Riloff, 2012; Li et al., 2013). Besides, some recent research has proposed joint models for EE, including the methods based on Markov Logic Networks (Riedel et al., 2009; Poon and Vanderwende, 2010; Venugopal et al., 2014), structured perceptron (Li et al., 2013; Li et al., 2014b), and dual decomposition (Riedel et al. (2009; 2011a; 2011b)).

The application of neural networks to EE is very recent. In particular, Nguyen and Grishman (2015b) study domain adaptation and event detection via CNNs while Chen et al. (2015) apply dynamic multi-pooling CNNs for EE in a pipelined framework. However, none of these work utilizes RNNs to perform joint EE as we do in this work.

7 Conclusion

We present a joint model to do EE based on bidirectional RNN to overcome the limitation of the previous models for this task. We introduce the memory matrix that can effectively capture the dependencies between argument roles and trigger subtypes. We demonstrate that the concatenation-based variant of the CBOW word embeddings is very helpful for the joint model. The proposed joint model is empirically shown to be effective on the sentences with multiple events as well as yields the state-of-the-art performance on the ACE 2005 dataset. In the future, we plan to apply this joint model on the event argument extraction task of the KBP evaluation as well as extend it to other joint tasks such as mention detection together with relation extraction etc.

References

David Ahn. 2006. The stages of event extraction. In *Proceedings of the Workshop on Annotating and Reasoning about Time and Events*.

Marco Baroni, Georgiana Dinu, and Germán Kruszewski. 2014. Don't count, predict! a systematic comparison of context-counting vs. context-predicting semantic vectors. In *ACL*.

Yoshua Bengio, Patrice Simard, and Paolo Frasconi. 1994. Learning long-term dependencies with gradient descent is difficult. In *Journal of Machine Learning Research 3*.

Yoshua Bengio, Réjean Ducharme, Pascal Vincent, and Christian Jauvin. 2003. A neural probabilistic language model. In *Journal of Machine Learning Research 3*.

Yubo Chen, Liheng Xu, Kang Liu, Daojian Zeng, and Jun Zhao. 2015. Event extraction via dynamic multi-pooling convolutional neural networks. In *ACL-IJCNLP*.

Kyunghyun Cho, Bart van Merrienboer, Caglar Gulcehre, Dzmitry Bahdanau, Fethi Bougares, Holger Schwenk, and Yoshua Bengio. 2014. Learning phrase representations using rnn encoder–decoder for statistical machine translation. In *EMNLP*.

Junyoung Chung, Caglar Gulcehre, KyungHyun Cho, and Yoshua Bengio. 2014. Empirical evaluation of gated recurrent neural networks on sequence modeling. In *arXiv preprint arXiv:1412.3555*.

Ronan Collobert and Jason Weston. 2008. A unified architecture for natural language processing: deep neural networks with multitask learning. In *ICML*.

Felix Gers. 2001. Long short-term memory in recurrent neural networks. In *PhD Thesis*.

Ralph Grishman, David Westbrook, and Adam Meyers. 2005. Nyus english ace 2005 system description. In *ACE 2005 Evaluation Workshop*.

Prashant Gupta and Heng Ji. 2009. Predicting unknown time arguments based on cross-event propagation. In *ACL-IJCNLP*.

Sepp Hochreiter and Jurgen Schmidhuber. 1997. Long short-term memory. In *Neural Computation*.

Yu Hong, Jianfeng Zhang, Bin Ma, Jianmin Yao, Guodong Zhou, and Qiaoming Zhu. 2011. Using cross-entity inference to improve event extraction. In *ACL*.

Ruihong Huang and Ellen Riloff. 2012. Modeling textual cohesion for event extraction. In *AAAI*.

Heng Ji and Ralph Grishman. 2008. Refining event extraction through cross-document inference. In *ACL*.

Rafal Józefowicz, Wojciech Zaremba, and Ilya Sutskever. 2015. An empirical exploration of recurrent network architectures. In *ICML*.

Yoon Kim. 2014. Convolutional neural networks for sentence classification. In *EMNLP*.

Qi Li, Heng Ji, and Liang Huang. 2013. Joint event extraction via structured prediction with global features. In *ACL*.

Qi Li, Heng Ji, Yu Hong, and Sujian Li. 2014b. Constructing information networks using one single model. In *EMNLP*.

Shasha Liao and Ralph Grishman. 2010. Using document level cross-event inference to improve event extraction. In *ACL*.

Shasha Liao and Ralph Grishman. 2011. Acquiring topic features to improve event extraction: in pre-selected and balanced collections. In *RANLP*.

David McClosky, Mihai Surdeanu, and Christopher Manning. 2011. Event extraction as dependency parsing. In *BioNLP Shared Task Workshop*.

Tomas Mikolov, Kai Chen, Greg Corrado, and Jeffrey Dean. 2013a. Efficient estimation of word representations in vector space. In *ICLR*.

Tomas Mikolov, Ilya Sutskever, Kai Chen, Greg Corrado, and Jeffrey Dean. 2013b. Distributed representations of words and phrases and their compositionality. In *NIPS*.

Thien Huu Nguyen and Ralph Grishman. 2015a. Relation extraction: Perspective from convolutional neural networks. In *The NAACL Workshop on Vector Space Modeling for NLP (VSM)*.

Thien Huu Nguyen and Ralph Grishman. 2015b. Event detection and domain adaptation with convolutional neural networks. In *ACL-IJCNLP*.

Siddharth Patwardhan and Ellen Riloff. 2009. A unified model of phrasal and sentential evidence for information extraction. In *EMNLP*.

Hoifung Poon and Lucy Vanderwende. 2010. Joint inference for knowledge extraction from biomedical literature. In *NAACL-HLT*.

Sebastian Riedel and Andrew McCallum. 2011a. Fast and robust joint models for biomedical event extraction. In *EMNLP*.

Sebastian Riedel and Andrew McCallum. 2011b. Robust biomedical event extraction with dual decomposition and minimal domain adaptation. In *BioNLP Shared Task 2011 Workshop*.

Sebastian Riedel, Hong-Woo Chun, Toshihisa Takagi, and Jun'ichi Tsujii. 2009. A markov logic approach to bio-molecular event extraction. In *BioNLP 2009 Workshop*.

Joseph Turian, Lev-Arie Ratinov, and Yoshua Bengio. 2010. Word representations: A simple and general method for semi-supervised learning. In *ACL*.

Deepak Venugopal, Chen Chen, Vibhav Gogate, and Vincent Ng. 2014. Relieving the computational bottleneck: Joint inference for event extraction with high-dimensional features. In *EMNLP*.

Matthew D. Zeiler. 2012. Adadelta: An adaptive learning rate method. In *CoRR, abs/1212.5701*.

Top-down Tree Long Short-Term Memory Networks

Xingxing Zhang, Liang Lu and **Mirella Lapata**
School of Informatics, University of Edinburgh
10 Crichton Street, Edinburgh EH8 9AB, UK
{x.zhang,liang.lu}@ed.ac.uk,mlap@inf.ed.ac.uk

Abstract

Long Short-Term Memory (LSTM) networks, a type of recurrent neural network with a more complex computational unit, have been successfully applied to a variety of sequence modeling tasks. In this paper we develop Tree Long Short-Term Memory (TREELSTM), a neural network model based on LSTM, which is designed to predict a tree rather than a linear sequence. TREELSTM defines the probability of a sentence by estimating the generation probability of its dependency tree. At each time step, a node is generated based on the representation of the generated subtree. We further enhance the modeling power of TREELSTM by explicitly representing the correlations between left and right dependents. Application of our model to the MSR sentence completion challenge achieves results beyond the current state of the art. We also report results on dependency parsing reranking achieving competitive performance.

1 Introduction

Neural language models have been gaining increasing attention as a competitive alternative to n-grams. The main idea is to represent each word using a real-valued feature vector capturing the contexts in which it occurs. The conditional probability of the next word is then modeled as a smooth function of the feature vectors of the preceding words and the next word. In essence, similar representations are learned for words found in similar contexts resulting in similar predictions for the next word. Previous approaches have mainly employed feed-forward

(Bengio et al., 2003; Mnih and Hinton, 2007) and recurrent neural networks (Mikolov et al., 2010; Mikolov, 2012) in order to map the feature vectors of the context words to the distribution for the next word. Recently, RNNs with Long Short-Term Memory (LSTM) units (Hochreiter and Schmidhuber, 1997; Hochreiter, 1998) have emerged as a popular architecture due to their strong ability to capture long-term dependencies. LSTMs have been successfully applied to a variety of tasks ranging from machine translation (Sutskever et al., 2014), to speech recognition (Graves et al., 2013), and image description generation (Vinyals et al., 2015).

Despite superior performance in many applications, neural language models essentially predict sequences of words. Many NLP tasks, however, exploit syntactic information operating over tree structures (e.g., dependency or constituent trees). In this paper we develop a novel neural network model which combines the advantages of the LSTM architecture and syntactic structure. Our model estimates the probability of a sentence by estimating the generation probability of its dependency tree. Instead of explicitly encoding tree structure as a set of features, we use four LSTM networks to model four types of dependency edges which altogether specify how the tree is built. At each time step, one LSTM is activated which predicts the next word conditioned on the sub-tree generated so far. To learn the representations of the conditioned sub-tree, we force the four LSTMs to share their hidden layers. Our model is also capable of generating trees just by sampling from a trained model and can be seamlessly integrated with text generation applications.

Proceedings of NAACL-HLT 2016, pages 310–320,
San Diego, California, June 12-17, 2016. ©2016 Association for Computational Linguistics

Our approach is related to but ultimately different from recursive neural networks (Pollack, 1990) a class of models which operate on structured inputs. Given a (binary) parse tree, they recursively generate parent representations in a bottom-up fashion, by combining tokens to produce representations for phrases, and eventually the whole sentence. The learned representations can be then used in classification tasks such as sentiment analysis (Socher et al., 2011b) and paraphrase detection (Socher et al., 2011a). Tai et al. (2015) learn distributed representations over syntactic trees by generalizing the LSTM architecture to tree-structured network topologies. The key feature of our model is not so much that it can learn semantic representations of phrases or sentences, but its ability to predict tree structure and estimate its probability.

Syntactic language models have a long history in NLP dating back to Chelba and Jelinek (2000) (see also Roark (2001) and Charniak (2001)). These models differ in how grammar structures in a parsing tree are used when predicting the next word. Other work develops dependency-based language models for specific applications such as machine translation (Shen et al., 2008; Zhang, 2009; Sennrich, 2015), speech recognition (Chelba et al., 1997) or sentence completion (Gubbins and Vlachos, 2013). All instances of these models apply Markov assumptions on the dependency tree, and adopt standard n-gram smoothing methods for reliable parameter estimation. Emami et al. (2003) and Sennrich (2015) estimate the parameters of a structured language model using feed-forward neural networks (Bengio et al., 2003). Mirowski and Vlachos (2015) re-implement the model of Gubbins and Vlachos (2013) with RNNs. They view sentences as sequences of words over a tree. While they ignore the tree structures themselves, we model them explicitly.

Our model shares with other structured-based language models the ability to take dependency information into account. It differs in the following respects: (a) it does not artificially restrict the depth of the dependencies it considers and can thus be viewed as an infinite order dependency language model; (b) it not only estimates the probability of a string but is also capable of generating dependency trees; (c) finally, contrary to previous dependency-based language models which encode syntactic information as features, our model takes tree structure into account more directly via representing different types of dependency edges explicitly using LSTMs. Therefore, there is no need to manually determine which dependency tree features should be used or how large the feature embeddings should be.

We evaluate our model on the MSR sentence completion challenge, a benchmark language modeling dataset. Our results outperform the best published results on this dataset. Since our model is a general tree estimator, we also use it to rerank the top K dependency trees from the (second order) MSTPasrser and obtain performance on par with recently proposed dependency parsers.

2 Tree Long Short-Term Memory Networks

We seek to estimate the probability of a sentence by estimating the generation probability of its dependency tree. Syntactic information in our model is represented in the form of dependency paths. In the following, we first describe our definition of dependency path and based on it explain how the probability of a sentence is estimated.

2.1 Dependency Path

Generally speaking, a dependency path is the path between ROOT and w consisting of the nodes on the path and the edges connecting them. To represent dependency paths, we introduce four types of edges which essentially define the "shape" of a dependency tree. Let w_0 denote a node in a tree and $w_1, w_2, \ldots, w_n$ its left dependents. As shown in Figure 1, LEFT edge is the edge between w_0 and its first left dependent denoted as (w_0, w_1). Let w_k (with $1 < k \leq n$) denote a non-first left dependent of w_0. The edge from w_{k-1} to w_k is a NX-LEFT edge (NX stands for NEXT), where w_{k-1} is the right adjacent sibling of w_k. Note that the NX-LEFT edge (w_{k-1}, w_k) replaces edge (w_0, w_k) (illustrated with a dashed line in Figure 1) in the original dependency tree. The modification allows information to flow from w_0 to w_k through $w_1, \ldots, w_{k-1}$ rather than directly from w_0 to w_k. RIGHT and NX-RIGHT edges are defined analogously for right dependents.

Given these four types of edges, dependency paths (denoted as $\mathcal{D}(w)$) can be defined as follows

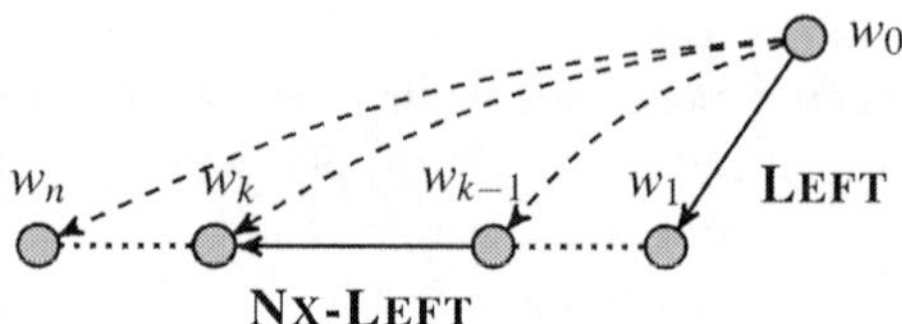

Figure 1: LEFT and NX-LEFT edges. Dotted line between w_1 and w_{k-1} (also between w_k and w_n) indicate that there may be ≥ 0 nodes inbetween.

bearing in mind that the first right dependent of ROOT is its only dependent and that w^p denotes the parent of w. We use $\langle\ldots\rangle$ to denote a sequence, where $()$ is an empty sequence and $\|$ is an operator for concatenating two sequences.

(1) if w is ROOT, then $\mathcal{D}(w) = ()$

(2) if w is a **left dependent** of w^p

    (a) if w is the first left dependent, then
$$\mathcal{D}(w) = \mathcal{D}(w^p)\|(\langle w^p, \text{LEFT}\rangle)$$

    (b) if w is not the first left dependent and w^s is its right adjacent sibling, then
$$\mathcal{D}(w) = \mathcal{D}(w^s)\|(\langle w^s, \text{NX-LEFT}\rangle)$$

(3) if w is a **right dependent** of w^p

    (a) if w is the first right dependent, then
$$\mathcal{D}(w) = \mathcal{D}(w^p)\|(\langle w^p, \text{RIGHT}\rangle)$$

    (b) if w is not the first right dependent and w^s is its left adjacent sibling, then
$$\mathcal{D}(w) = \mathcal{D}(w^s)\|(\langle w^s, \text{NX-RIGHT}\rangle)$$

A dependency tree can be represented by the set of its dependency paths which in turn can be used to reconstruct the original tree.[1]

Dependency paths for the first two levels of the tree in Figure 2 are as follows (ignoring for the moment the subscripts which we explain in the next section). $\mathcal{D}(\text{sold}) = (\langle\text{ROOT},\text{RIGHT}\rangle)$ (see definitions (1) and (3a)), $\mathcal{D}(\text{year}) = \mathcal{D}(\text{sold})\|(\langle\text{sold},\text{LEFT}\rangle)$ (see (2a)), $\mathcal{D}(\text{manufacturer}) = \mathcal{D}(\text{year})\|(\langle\text{year},\text{NX-LEFT}\rangle)$ (see (2b)), $\mathcal{D}(\text{cars}) = \mathcal{D}(\text{sold})\|(\langle\text{sold},\text{RIGHT}\rangle)$ (see (3a)), $\mathcal{D}(\text{in}) = \mathcal{D}(\text{cars})\|(\langle\text{cars},\text{NX-RIGHT}\rangle)$ (according to (3b)).

2.2 Tree Probability

The core problem in syntax-based language modeling is to estimate the probability of sentence S given

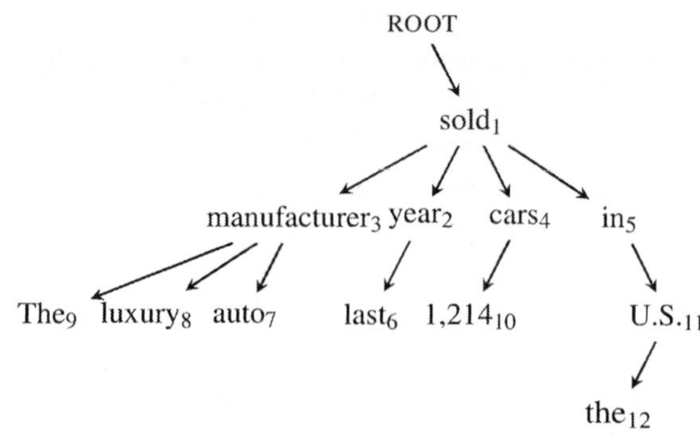

Figure 2: Dependency tree of the sentence *The luxury auto manufacturer last year sold 1,214 cars in the U.S.* Subscripts indicate breadth-first traversal. ROOT has only one dependent (i.e., *sold*) which we view as its first right dependent.

its corresponding tree T, $P(S|T)$. We view the probability computation of a dependency tree as a generation process. Specifically, we assume dependency trees are constructed top-down, in a breadth-first manner. Generation starts at the ROOT node. For each node at each level, first its left dependents are generated from closest to farthest and then the right dependents (again from closest to farthest). The same process is applied to the next node at the same level or a node at the next level. Figure 2 shows the breadth-first traversal of a dependency tree.

Under the assumption that each word w in a dependency tree is *only* conditioned on its *dependency path*, the probability of a sentence S given its dependency tree T is:

$$P(S|T) = \prod_{w \in \text{BFS}(T)\backslash\text{ROOT}} P(w|\mathcal{D}(w)) \qquad (1)$$

where $\mathcal{D}(w)$ is the dependency path of w. Note that each word w is visited according to its breadth-first search order (BFS(T)) and the probability of ROOT is ignored since every tree has one. The role of ROOT in a dependency tree is the same as the begin of sentence token (BOS) in a sentence. When computing $P(S|T)$ (or $P(S)$), the probability of ROOT (or BOS) is ignored (we assume it always exists), but is used to predict other words. We explain in the next section how TREELSTM estimates $P(w|\mathcal{D}(w))$.

2.3 Tree LSTMs

A dependency path $\mathcal{D}(w)$ is subtree which we denote as a sequence of $\langle$*word, edge-type*$\rangle$ tuples. Our

---

[1] Throughout this paper we assume all dependency trees are projective.

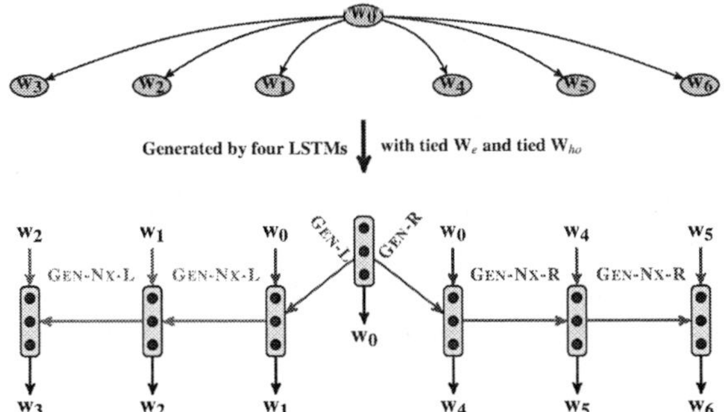

Figure 3: Generation process of left (w_1, w_2, w_3) and right (w_4, w_5, w_6) dependents of tree node w_o (top) using four LSTMs (GEN-L, GEN-R, GEN-NX-L and GEN-NX-R). The model can handle an arbitrary number of dependents due to GEN-NX-L and GEN-NX-R.

innovation is to learn the representation of $\mathcal{D}(w)$ using four LSTMs. The four LSTMs (GEN-L, GEN-R, GEN-NX-L and GEN-NX-R) are used to represent the four types of edges (LEFT, RIGHT, NX-LEFT and NX-RIGHT) introduced earlier. GEN, NX, L and R are shorthands for GENERATE, NEXT, LEFT and RIGHT. At each time step, an LSTM is chosen according to an edge-type; then the LSTM takes a word as input and predicts/generates its dependent or sibling. This process can be also viewed as adding an edge and a node to a tree. Specifically, LSTMs GEN-L and GEN-R are used to generate the first left and right dependent of a node (w_1 and w_4 in Figure 3). So, these two LSTMs are responsible for going deeper in a tree. While GEN-NX-L and GEN-NX-R generate the remaining left/right dependents and therefore go wider in a tree. As shown in Figure 3, w_2 and w_3 are generated by GEN-NX-L, whereas w_5 and w_6 are generated by GEN-NX-R. Note that the model can handle any number of left or right dependents by applying GEN-NX-L or GEN-NX-R multiple times.

We assume time steps correspond to the steps taken by the breadth-first traversal of the dependency tree and the sentence has length n. At time step t ($1 \leq t \leq n$), let $\langle w_{t'}, z_t \rangle$ denote the last tuple in $\mathcal{D}(w_t)$. Subscripts t and t' denote the breadth-first search order of w_t and $w_{t'}$, respectively. $z_t \in \{\text{LEFT}, \text{RIGHT}, \text{NX-LEFT}, \text{NX-RIGHT}\}$ is the edge type (see the definitions in Section 2.1). Let $\mathbf{W}_e \in \mathbb{R}^{s \times |V|}$ denote the word embedding matrix and

$\mathbf{W}_{ho} \in \mathbb{R}^{|V| \times d}$ the output matrix of our model, where $|V|$ is the vocabulary size, s the word embedding size and d the hidden unit size. We use tied $\mathbf{W}_e$ and tied $\mathbf{W}_{ho}$ for the four LSTMs to reduce the number of parameters in our model. The four LSTMs also share their hidden states. Let $\mathbf{H} \in \mathbb{R}^{d \times (n+1)}$ denote the *shared* hidden states of all time steps and $e(w_t)$ the one-hot vector of w_t. Then, $\mathbf{H}[:, t]$ represents $\mathcal{D}(w_t)$ at time step t, and the computation[2] is:

$$\mathbf{x}_t = \mathbf{W}_e \cdot e(w_{t'}) \tag{2a}$$

$$\mathbf{h}_t = \text{LSTM}^{z_t}(\mathbf{x}_t, \mathbf{H}[:, t']) \tag{2b}$$

$$\mathbf{H}[:, t] = \mathbf{h}_t \tag{2c}$$

$$\mathbf{y}_t = \mathbf{W}_{ho} \cdot \mathbf{h}_t \tag{2d}$$

where the initial hidden state $\mathbf{H}[:, 0]$ is initialized to a vector of small values such as 0.01. According to Equation (2b), the model selects an LSTM based on edge type z_t. We describe the details of LSTM^{z_t} in the next paragraph. The probability of w_t given its dependency path $\mathcal{D}(w_t)$ is estimated by a *softmax* function:

$$P(w_t | \mathcal{D}(w_t)) = \frac{\exp(\mathbf{y}_{t, w_t})}{\sum_{k'=1}^{|V|} \exp(\mathbf{y}_{t, k'})} \tag{3}$$

We must point out that although we use four jointly trained LSTMs to encode the hidden states, the training and inference complexity of our model is no different from a regular LSTM, since at each time step only one LSTM is working.

We implement LSTM^z in Equation (2b) using a deep LSTM (to simplify notation, from now on we write z instead of z_t). The inputs at time step t are $\mathbf{x}_t$ and $\mathbf{h}_{t'}$ (the hidden state of an earlier time step t') and the output is $\mathbf{h}_t$ (the hidden state of current time step). Let L denote the layer number of LSTM^z and $\hat{\mathbf{h}}_t^l$ the internal hidden state of the l-th layer of the LSTM^z at time step t, where $\mathbf{x}_t$ is $\hat{\mathbf{h}}_t^0$ and $\mathbf{h}_{t'}$ is $\hat{\mathbf{h}}_{t'}^L$. The LSTM architecture introduces multiplicative gates and memory cells $\hat{\mathbf{c}}_t^l$ (at l-th layer) in order to address the *vanishing gradient* problem which makes it difficult for the standard RNN model to learn long-distance correlations in a sequence. Here, $\hat{\mathbf{c}}_t^l$ is a linear combination of the current input signal $\mathbf{u}_t$ and an earlier memory cell $\hat{\mathbf{c}}_{t'}^l$. How much input information $\mathbf{u}_t$ will flow into $\hat{\mathbf{c}}_t^l$ is controlled

---

[2] We ignore all bias terms for notational simplicity.

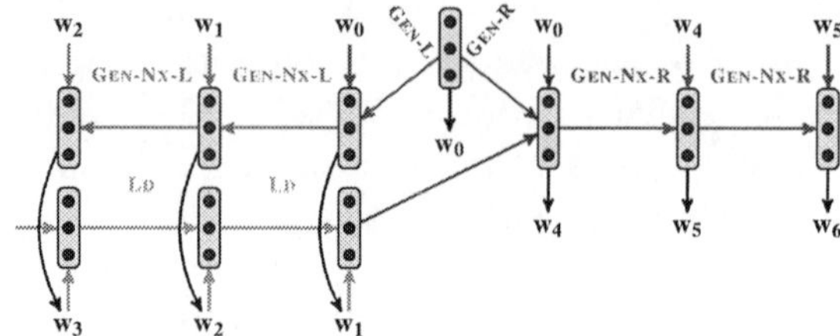

Figure 4: Generation of left and right dependents of node w_0 according to LDTREELSTM.

by input gate $\mathbf{i}_t$ and how much of the earlier memory cell $\hat{\mathbf{c}}_{t'}^l$ will be forgotten is controlled by forget gate $\mathbf{f}_t$. This process is computed as follows:

$$\mathbf{u}_t = \tanh(\mathbf{W}_{ux}^{z,l} \cdot \hat{\mathbf{h}}_t^{l-1} + \mathbf{W}_{uh}^{z,l} \cdot \hat{\mathbf{h}}_{t'}^l) \tag{4a}$$

$$\mathbf{i}_t = \sigma(\mathbf{W}_{ix}^{z,l} \cdot \hat{\mathbf{h}}_t^{l-1} + \mathbf{W}_{ih}^{z,l} \cdot \hat{\mathbf{h}}_{t'}^l) \tag{4b}$$

$$\mathbf{f}_t = \sigma(\mathbf{W}_{fx}^{z,l} \cdot \hat{\mathbf{h}}_t^{l-1} + \mathbf{W}_{fh}^{z,l} \cdot \hat{\mathbf{h}}_{t'}^l) \tag{4c}$$

$$\hat{\mathbf{c}}_t^l = \mathbf{f}_t \odot \hat{\mathbf{c}}_{t'}^l + \mathbf{i}_t \odot \mathbf{u}_t \tag{4d}$$

where $\mathbf{W}_{ux}^{z,l} \in \mathbb{R}^{d \times d}$ ($\mathbf{W}_{ux}^{z,l} \in \mathbb{R}^{d \times s}$ when $l = 1$) and $\mathbf{W}_{uh}^{z,l} \in \mathbb{R}^{d \times d}$ are weight matrices for $\mathbf{u}_t$, $\mathbf{W}_{ix}^{z,l}$ and $\mathbf{W}_{ih}^{z,l}$ are weight matrices for $\mathbf{i}_t$ and $\mathbf{W}_{fx}^{z,l}$, and $\mathbf{W}_{fh}^{z,l}$ are weight matrices for $\mathbf{f}_t$. σ is a sigmoid function and $\odot$ the element-wise product.

Output gate $\mathbf{o}_t$ controls how much information of the cell $\hat{\mathbf{c}}_t^l$ can be seen by other modules:

$$\mathbf{o}_t = \sigma(\mathbf{W}_{ox}^{z,l} \cdot \hat{\mathbf{h}}_t^{l-1} + \mathbf{W}_{oh}^{z,l} \cdot \hat{\mathbf{h}}_{t'}^l) \tag{5a}$$

$$\hat{\mathbf{h}}_t^l = \mathbf{o}_t \odot \tanh(\hat{\mathbf{c}}_t^l) \tag{5b}$$

Application of the above process to all layers L, will yield $\hat{\mathbf{h}}_t^L$, which is $\mathbf{h}_t$. Note that in implementation, all $\hat{\mathbf{c}}_t^l$ and $\hat{\mathbf{h}}_t^l$ ($1 \leq l \leq L$) at time step t are stored, although we only care about $\hat{\mathbf{h}}_t^L$ ($\mathbf{h}_t$).

2.4 Left Dependent Tree LSTMs

TREELSTM computes $P(w|\mathcal{D}(w))$ based on the dependency path $\mathcal{D}(w)$, which ignores the interaction between left and right dependents on the same level. In many cases, TREELSTM will use a verb to predict its object directly without knowing its subject. For example, in Figure 2, TREELSTM uses ⟨ROOT, RIGHT⟩ and ⟨ *sold*, RIGHT ⟩ to predict *cars*. This information is unfortunately not specific to *cars* (many things can be sold, e.g., *chocolates*, *candy*). Considering *manufacturer*, the left dependent of *sold* would help predict *cars* more accurately.

In order to jointly take left and right dependents into account, we employ yet another LSTM, which goes from the furthest left dependent to the closest left dependent (LD is a shorthand for left dependent). As shown in Figure 4, LD LSTM learns the representation of all left dependents of a node w_0; this representation is then used to predict the first right dependent of the same node. Non-first right dependents can also leverage the representation of left dependents, since this information is injected into the hidden state of the first right dependent and can percolate all the way. Note that in order to retain the generation capability of our model (Section 3.4), we only allow right dependents to leverage left dependents (they are generated before right dependents).

The computation of the LDTREELSTM is almost the same as in TREELSTM except when $z_t = $ GEN-R. In this case, let $\mathbf{v}_t$ be the corresponding left dependent sequence with length K ($\mathbf{v}_t = (w_3, w_2, w_1)$ in Figure 4). Then, the hidden state ($\mathbf{q}_k$) of $\mathbf{v}_t$ at each time step k is:

$$\mathbf{m}_k = \mathbf{W}_e \cdot e(\mathbf{v}_{t,k}) \tag{6a}$$

$$\mathbf{q}_k = \mathrm{LSTM}^{\mathrm{LD}}(\mathbf{m}_k, \mathbf{q}_{k-1}) \tag{6b}$$

where $\mathbf{q}_K$ is the representation for all left dependents. Then, the computation of the current hidden state becomes (see Equation (2) for the original computation):

$$\mathbf{r}_t = \begin{bmatrix} \mathbf{W}_e \cdot e(w_{t'}) \\ \mathbf{q}_K \end{bmatrix} \tag{7a}$$

$$\mathbf{h}_t = \mathrm{LSTM}^{\mathrm{GEN\text{-}R}}(\mathbf{r}_t, \mathbf{H}[:, t']) \tag{7b}$$

where $\mathbf{q}_K$ serves as additional input for $\mathrm{LSTM}^{\mathrm{GEN\text{-}R}}$. All other computational details are the same as in TreeLSTM (see Section 2.3).

2.5 Model Training

On small scale datasets we employ Negative Log-likelihood (NLL) as our training objective for both TREELSTM and LDTREELSTM:

$$\mathcal{L}^{\mathrm{NLL}}(\theta) = -\frac{1}{|S|} \sum_{S \in \mathcal{S}} \log P(S|T) \tag{8}$$

where S is a sentence in the training set $\mathcal{S}$, T is the dependency tree of S and $P(S|T)$ is defined as in Equation (1).

On large scale datasets (e.g., with vocabulary size of 65K), computing the output layer activations and the *softmax* function with NLL would become prohibitively expensive. Instead, we employ Noise Contrastive Estimation (NCE; Gutmann and Hyvärinen (2012), Mnih and Teh (2012)) which treats the normalization term $\hat{Z}$ in $\hat{P}(w|\mathcal{D}(w_t)) = \frac{\exp(\mathbf{W}_{ho}[w,:] \cdot \mathbf{h}_t)}{\hat{Z}}$ as constant. The intuition behind NCE is to discriminate between samples from a data distribution $\hat{P}(w|\mathcal{D}(w_t))$ and a known noise distribution $P_n(w)$ via binary logistic regression. Assuming that noise words are k times more frequent than real words in the training set (Mnih and Teh, 2012), then the probability of a word w being from our model $P_d(w, \mathcal{D}(w_t))$ is $\frac{\hat{P}(w|\mathcal{D}(w_t))}{\hat{P}(w|\mathcal{D}(w_t))+kP_n(w)}$. We apply NCE to large vocabulary models with the following training objective:

$$\mathcal{L}^{\mathrm{NCE}}(\theta) = -\frac{1}{|\mathcal{S}|} \sum_{T \in \mathcal{S}} \sum_{t=1}^{|T|} \left(\log P_d(w_t, \mathcal{D}(w_t)) \right.$$
$$\left. + \sum_{j=1}^{k} \log[1 - P_d(\tilde{w}_{t,j}, \mathcal{D}(w_t))] \right)$$

where $\tilde{w}_{t,j}$ is a word sampled from the noise distribution $P_n(w)$. We use smoothed unigram frequencies (exponentiating by 0.75) as the noise distribution $P_n(w)$ (Mikolov et al., 2013b). We initialize $\ln \hat{Z} = 9$ as suggested in Chen et al. (2015), but instead of keeping it fixed we also learn $\hat{Z}$ during training (Vaswani et al., 2013). We set $k = 20$.

3 Experiments

We assess the performance of our model on two tasks: the Microsoft Research (MSR) sentence completion challenge (Zweig and Burges, 2012), and dependency parsing reranking. We also demonstrate the tree generation capability of our models. In the following, we first present details on model training and then present our results. We implemented our models using the Torch library (Collobert et al., 2011) and our code is available at https://github.com/XingxingZhang/td-treelstm.

3.1 Training Details

We trained our model with back propagation through time (Rumelhart et al., 1988) on an Nvidia GPU Card with a mini-batch size of 64. The objective (NLL or NCE) was minimized by stochastic gradient descent. Model parameters were uniformly initialized in $[-0.1, 0.1]$. We used the NCE objective on the MSR sentence completion task (due to the large size of this dataset) and the NLL objective on dependency parsing reranking. We used an initial learning rate of 1.0 for all experiments and when there was no significant improvement in log-likelihood on the validation set, the learning rate was divided by 2 per epoch until convergence (Mikolov et al., 2010). To alleviate the exploding gradients problem, we rescaled the gradient g when the gradient norm $\|g\| > 5$ and set $g = \frac{5g}{\|g\|}$ (Pascanu et al., 2013; Sutskever et al., 2014). Dropout (Srivastava et al., 2014) was applied to the 2-layer TREELSTM and LDTREELSTM models. The word embedding size was set to $s = d/2$ where d is the hidden unit size.

3.2 Microsoft Sentence Completion Challenge

The task in the MSR Sentence Completion Challenge (Zweig and Burges, 2012) is to select the correct missing word for 1,040 SAT-style test sentences when presented with five candidate completions. The training set contains 522 novels from the Project Gutenberg which we preprocessed as follows. After removing headers and footers from the files, we tokenized and parsed the dataset into dependency trees with the Stanford Core NLP toolkit (Manning et al., 2014). The resulting training set contained 49M words. We converted all words to lower case and replaced those occurring five times or less with UNK. The resulting vocabulary size was 65,346 words. We randomly sampled 4,000 sentences from the training set as our validation set.

The literature describes two main approaches to the sentence completion task based on word vectors and language models. In vector-based approaches, all words in the sentence and the five candidate words are represented by a vector; the candidate which has the highest average similarity with the sentence words is selected as the answer. For language model-based methods, the LM computes the probability of a test sentence with each of the five candidate words, and picks the candidate completion which gives the highest probability. Our model belongs to this class of models.

Model	d	$|\theta|$	Accuracy
Word Vector based Models			
LSA	—	—	49.0
Skip-gram	640	102M	48.0
IVLBL	600	96.0M	55.5
Language Models			
KN5	—	—	40.0
UDepNgram	—	—	48.3
LDepNgram	—	—	50.0
RNN	300	48.1M	45.0
RNNME	300	1120M	49.3
depRNN+3gram	100	1014M	53.5
ldepRNN+4gram	200	1029M	50.7
LBL	300	48.0M	54.7
LSTM	300	29.9M	55.00
LSTM	400	40.2M	57.02
LSTM	450	45.3M	55.96
Bidirectional LSTM	200	33.2M	48.46
Bidirectional LSTM	300	50.1M	49.90
Bidirectional LSTM	400	67.3M	48.65
Model Combinations			
RNNMEs	—	—	55.4
Skip-gram + RNNMEs	—	—	58.9
Our Models			
TREELSTM	300	31.6M	55.29
LDTREELSTM	300	32.5M	57.79
TREELSTM	400	43.1M	56.73
LDTREELSTM	400	44.7M	**60.67**

Table 1: Model accuracy on the MSR sentence completion task. The results of KN5, RNNME and RNNMEs are reported in Mikolov (2012), LSA and RNN in Zweig et al. (2012), UDep-Ngram and LDepNgram in Gubbins and Vlachos (2013), de-pRNN+3gram and depRNN+4gram in Mirowski and Vlachos (2015), LBL in Mnih and Teh (2012), Skip-gram and Skip-gram+RNNMEs in Mikolov et al. (2013a), and IVLBL in Mnih and Kavukcuoglu (2013); d is the hidden size and $|\theta|$ the number of parameters in a model.

Table 1 presents a summary of our results together with previoulsy published results. The best performing word vector model is IVLBL (Mnih and Kavukcuoglu, 2013) with an accuracy of 55.5, while the best performing single language model is LBL (Mnih and Teh, 2012) with an accuracy of 54.7. Both approaches are based on the log-bilinear language model (Mnih and Hinton, 2007). A combination of several recurrent neural networks and the skip-gram model holds the state of the art with an accuracy of 58.9 (Mikolov et al., 2013b). To fairly compare with existing models, we restrict the layer

Parser	Development		Test	
	UAS	LAS	UAS	LAS
MSTParser-2nd	92.20	88.78	91.63	88.44
TREELSTM	92.51	89.07	91.79	88.53
TREELSTM*	92.64	89.09	91.97	88.69
LDTREELSTM	**92.66**	**89.14**	**91.99**	**88.69**
NN parser*	92.00	89.70	91.80	89.60
S-LSTM*	**93.20**	**90.90**	**93.10**	**90.90**

Table 2: Performance of TREELSTM and LDTREELSTM on reranking the top dependency trees produced by the 2nd order MSTParser (McDonald and Pereira, 2006). Results for the NN and S-LSTM parsers are reported in Chen and Manning (2014) and Dyer et al. (2015), respectively. * indicates that the model is initialized with pre-trained word vectors.

size of our models to 1. We observe that LDTREEL-STM consistently outperforms TREELSTM, which indicates the importance of modeling the interaction between left and right dependents. In fact, LDTREELSTM ($d = 400$) achieves a new state-of-the-art on this task, despite being a single model. We also implement LSTM and bidirectional LSTM language models.[3] An LSTM with $d = 400$ outperforms its smaller counterpart ($d = 300$), however performance decreases with $d = 450$. The bidirectional LSTM is worse than the LSTM (see Mnih and Teh (2012) for a similar observation). The best performing LSTM is worse than a LDTREEL-STM ($d = 300$). The input and output embeddings ($\mathbf{W}_e$ and $\mathbf{W}_{ho}$) dominate the number of parameters in all neural models except for RNNME, de-pRNN+3gram and ldepRNN+4gram, which include a ME model that contains 1 billion sparse n-gram features (Mikolov, 2012; Mirowski and Vlachos, 2015). The number of parameters in TREELSTM and LDTREELSTM is not much larger compared to LSTM due to the tied $\mathbf{W}_e$ and $\mathbf{W}_{ho}$ matrices.

3.3 Dependency Parsing

In this section we demonstrate that our model can be also used for parse reranking. This is not possible for sequence-based language models since they cannot estimate the probability of a tree. We use our models to rerank the top K dependency trees produced by the second order MSTParser (McDon-

---

[3]LSTMs and BiLSTMs were also trained with NCE ($s = d/2$; hyperparameters were tuned on the development set).

ald and Pereira, 2006).[4] We follow closely the experimental setup of Chen and Manning (2014) and Dyer et al. (2015). Specifically, we trained TREELSTM and LDTREELSTM on Penn Treebank sections 2–21. We used section 22 for development and section 23 for testing. We adopted the Stanford basic dependency representations (De Marneffe et al., 2006); part-of-speech tags were predicted with the Stanford Tagger (Toutanova et al., 2003). We trained TREELSTM and LDTREELSTM as language models (singletons were replaced with UNK) and did not use any POS tags, dependency labels or composition features, whereas these features are used in Chen and Manning (2014) and Dyer et al. (2015). We tuned d, the number of layers, and K on the development set.

Table 2 reports unlabeled attachment scores (UAS) and labeled attachment scores (LAS) for the MSTParser, TREELSTM ($d = 300$, 1 layer, $K = 2$), and LDTREELSTM ($d = 200$, 2 layers, $K = 4$). We also include the performance of two neural network-based dependency parsers; Chen and Manning (2014) use a neural network classifier to predict the correct transition (NN parser); Dyer et al. (2015) also implement a transition-based dependency parser using LSTMs to represent the contents of the stack and buffer in a continuous space. As can be seen, both TREELSTM and LDTREELSTM outperform the baseline MSTParser, with LDTREELSTM performing best. We also initialized the word embedding matrix $\mathbf{W}_e$ with pre-trained GLOVE vectors (Pennington et al., 2014). We obtained a slight improvement over TREELSTM (TREELSTM* in Table 2; $d = 200$, 2 layer, $K = 4$) but no improvement over LDTREELSTM. Finally, notice that LDTREELSTM is slightly better than the NN parser in terms of UAS but worse than the S-LSTM parser. In the future, we would like to extend our model so that it takes labeled dependency information into account.

3.4 Tree Generation

This section demonstrates how to use a trained LDTREELSTM to generate tree samples. The generation starts at the ROOT node. At each time step t, for each node w_t, we add a new edge and node to

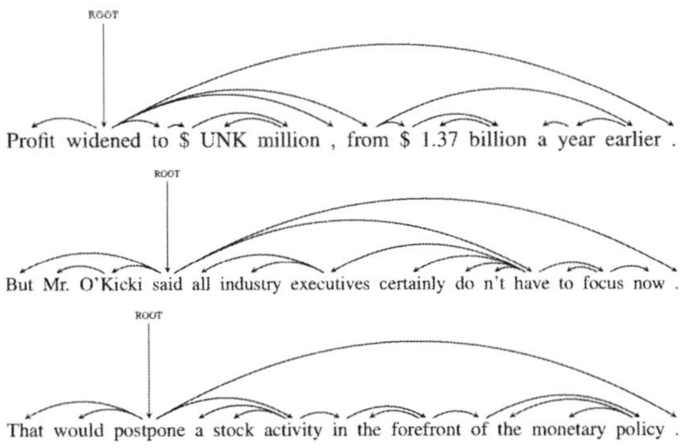

Figure 5: Generated dependency trees with LDTREELSTM trained on the PTB.

the tree. Unfortunately during generation, we do not know which type of edge to add. We therefore use four binary classifiers (ADD-LEFT, ADD-RIGHT, ADD-NX-LEFT and ADD-NX-RIGHT) to predict whether we should add a LEFT, RIGHT, NX-LEFT or NX-RIGHT edge.[5] Then when a classifier predicts true, we use the corresponding LSTM to generate a new node by sampling from the predicted word distribution in Equation (3). The four classifiers take the previous hidden state $\mathbf{H}[:,t']$ and the output embedding of the current node $\mathbf{W}_{ho} \cdot e(w_t)$ as features.[6] Specifically, we use a trained LDTREELSTM to go through the training corpus and generate hidden states and embeddings as input features; the corresponding class labels (true and false) are "read off" the training dependency trees. We use two-layer rectifier networks (Glorot et al., 2011) as the four classifiers with a hidden size of 300. We use the same LDTREELSTM model as in Section 3.3 to generate dependency trees. The classifiers were trained using AdaGrad (Duchi et al., 2011) with a learning rate of 0.01. The accuracies of ADD-LEFT, ADD-RIGHT, ADD-NX-LEFT and ADD-NX-RIGHT are 94.3%, 92.6%, 93.4% and 96.0%, respectively. Fig-

---

[5]It is possible to get rid of the four classifiers by adding START/STOP symbols when generating left and right dependents as in (Eisner, 1996). We refrained from doing this for computational reasons. For a sentence with N words, this approach will lead to $2N$ additional START/STOP symbols (with one START and one STOP symbol for each word). Consequently, the computational cost and memory consumption during training will be three times as much rendering our model less scalable.

[6]The input embeddings have lower dimensions and therefore result in slightly worse classifiers.

---

[4]http://www.seas.upenn.edu/ strctlrn/MSTParser

ure 5 shows examples of generated trees.

4 Conclusions

In this paper we developed TREELSTM (and LDTREELSTM), a neural network model architecture, which is designed to predict tree structures rather than linear sequences. Experimental results on the MSR sentence completion task show that LDTREELSTM is superior to sequential LSTMs. Dependency parsing reranking experiments highlight our model's potential for dependency parsing. Finally, the ability of our model to generate dependency trees holds promise for text generation applications such as sentence compression and simplification (Filippova et al., 2015). Although our experiments have focused exclusively on dependency trees, there is nothing inherent in our formulation that disallows its application to other types of tree structure such as constituent trees or even taxonomies.

Acknowledgments

We would like to thank Adam Lopez, Frank Keller, Iain Murray, Li Dong, Brian Roark, and the NAACL reviewers for their valuable feedback. Xingxing Zhang gratefully acknowledges the financial support of the China Scholarship Council (CSC). Liang Lu is funded by the UK EPSRC Programme Grant EP/I031022/1, Natural Speech Technology (NST).

References

Yoshua Bengio, Réjean Ducharme, Pascal Vincent, and Christian Janvin. 2003. A neural probabilistic language model. *The Journal of Machine Learning Research*, 3:1137–1155.

Eugene Charniak. 2001. Immediate-head parsing for language models. In *Proceedings of the 39th Annual Meeting on Association for Computational Linguistics*, pages 124–131. Association for Computational Linguistics.

Ciprian Chelba and Frederick Jelinek. 2000. Structured language modeling. *Computer Speech and Language*, 14(4):283–332.

Ciprian Chelba, David Engle, Frederick Jelinek, Victor Jimenez, Sanjeev Khudanpur, Lidia Mangu, Harry Printz, Eric Ristad, Ronald Rosenfeld, Andreas Stolcke, et al. 1997. Structure and performance of a dependency language model. In *EUROSPEECH*. Citeseer.

Danqi Chen and Christopher Manning. 2014. A fast and accurate dependency parser using neural networks. In *Proceedings of the 2014 Conference on Empirical Methods in Natural Language Processing (EMNLP)*, pages 740–750, Doha, Qatar, October. Association for Computational Linguistics.

X Chen, X Liu, MJF Gales, and PC Woodland. 2015. Recurrent neural network language model training with noise contrastive estimation for speech recognition. In *In 40th IEEE International Conference on Acoustics, Speech and Signal Processing*, pages 5401–5405, Brisbane, Australia.

Ronan Collobert, Koray Kavukcuoglu, and Clément Farabet. 2011. Torch7: A matlab-like environment for machine learning. In *BigLearn, NIPS Workshop*, number EPFL-CONF-192376.

Marie-Catherine De Marneffe, Bill MacCartney, Christopher D Manning, et al. 2006. Generating typed dependency parses from phrase structure parses. In *Proceedings of LREC*, volume 6, pages 449–454.

John Duchi, Elad Hazan, and Yoram Singer. 2011. Adaptive subgradient methods for online learning and stochastic optimization. *The Journal of Machine Learning Research*, 12:2121–2159.

Chris Dyer, Miguel Ballesteros, Wang Ling, Austin Matthews, and Noah A. Smith. 2015. Transition-based dependency parsing with stack long short-term memory. In *Proceedings of the 53rd Annual Meeting of the Association for Computational Linguistics and the 7th International Joint Conference on Natural Language Processing (Volume 1: Long Papers)*, pages 334–343, Beijing, China, July. Association for Computational Linguistics.

Jason M Eisner. 1996. Three new probabilistic models for dependency parsing: An exploration. In *Proceedings of the 16th conference on Computational linguistics-Volume 1*, pages 340–345. Association for Computational Linguistics.

Ahmad Emami, Peng Xu, and Frederick Jelinek. 2003. Using a connectionist model in a syntactical based language model. In *Proceedings of the IEEE International Conference on Acoustics, Speech, and Signal Processing*, pages 372–375, Hong Kong, China.

Katja Filippova, Enrique Alfonseca, Carlos A Colmenares, Lukasz Kaiser, and Oriol Vinyals. 2015. Sentence compression by deletion with lstms. In *EMNLP*, pages 360–368.

Xavier Glorot, Antoine Bordes, and Yoshua Bengio. 2011. Deep sparse rectifier neural networks. In *International Conference on Artificial Intelligence and Statistics*, pages 315–323.

Alan Graves, Abdel-rahman Mohamed, and Geoffrey Hinton. 2013. Speech recognition with deep recurrent neural networks. In *Acoustics, Speech and Signal Processing (ICASSP), 2013 IEEE International Conference on*, pages 6645–6649. IEEE.

Joseph Gubbins and Andreas Vlachos. 2013. Dependency language models for sentence completion. In *EMNLP*, pages 1405–1410, Seattle, Washington, USA, October. Association for Computational Linguistics.

Michael U Gutmann and Aapo Hyvärinen. 2012. Noise-contrastive estimation of unnormalized statistical models, with applications to natural image statistics. *The Journal of Machine Learning Research*, 13(1):307–361.

Sepp Hochreiter and Jürgen Schmidhuber. 1997. Long short-term memory. *Neural computation*, 9(8):1735–1780.

Sepp Hochreiter. 1998. Vanishing gradient problem during learning recurrent neural nets and problem solutions. *International Journal of Uncertainty, Fuzziness and Knowledge-based Systems*, 6(2):107–116.

Christopher D Manning, Mihai Surdeanu, John Bauer, Jenny Finkel, Steven J Bethard, and David McClosky. 2014. The stanford corenlp natural language processing toolkit. In *Proceedings of 52nd Annual Meeting of the Association for Computational Linguistics: System Demonstrations*, pages 55–60.

Ryan T McDonald and Fernando CN Pereira. 2006. Online learning of approximate dependency parsing algorithms. In *EACL*.

Tomas Mikolov, Martin Karafiát, Lukas Burget, Jan Cernockỳ, and Sanjeev Khudanpur. 2010. Recurrent neural network based language model. In *INTERSPEECH 2010, 11th Annual Conference of the International Speech Communication Association, Makuhari, Chiba, Japan, September 26-30, 2010*, pages 1045–1048.

Tomas Mikolov, Kai Chen, Greg Corrado, and Jeffrey Dean. 2013a. Efficient estimation of word representations in vector space. In *Proceedings of the 2013 International Conference on Learning Representations*, Scottsdale, Arizona, USA.

Tomas Mikolov, Ilya Sutskever, Kai Chen, Greg S Corrado, and Jeff Dean. 2013b. Distributed representations of words and phrases and their compositionality. In *Advances in Neural Information Processing Systems 26*, pages 3111–3119.

Tomas Mikolov. 2012. *Statistical Language Models based on Neural Networks*. Ph.D. thesis, Brno University of Technology.

Piotr Mirowski and Andreas Vlachos. 2015. Dependency recurrent neural language models for sentence completion. In *ACL*, pages 511–517, Beijing, China, July. Association for Computational Linguistics.

Andriy Mnih and Geoffrey Hinton. 2007. Three new graphical models for statistical language modelling. In *Proceedings of the 24th International Conference on Machine Learning*, pages 641–648.

Andriy Mnih and Koray Kavukcuoglu. 2013. Learning word embeddings efficiently with noise-contrastive estimation. In *Advances in Neural Information Processing Systems 26*, pages 2265–2273.

Andriy Mnih and Yee Whye Teh. 2012. A fast and simple algorithm for training neural probabilistic language models. In *Proceedings of the 29th International Conference on Machine Learning*, pages 1751–1758, Edinburgh, Scotland.

Razvan Pascanu, Tomas Mikolov, and Yoshua Bengio. 2013. On the difficulty of training recurrent neural networks. In *Proceedings of the 31st International Conference on Machine Learning*, pages 1310–1318, Atlanta, Georgia, USA.

Jeffrey Pennington, Richard Socher, and Christopher D Manning. 2014. Glove: Global vectors for word representation. *EMNLP*, 12:1532–1543.

Jordan B. Pollack. 1990. Recursive distributed representations. *Artificial Intelligence*, 1–2(46):77–105.

Brian Roark. 2001. Probabilistic top-down parsing and language modeling. *Computational linguistics*, 27(2):249–276.

David E Rumelhart, Geoffrey E Hinton, and Ronald J Williams. 1988. Learning representations by back-propagating errors. *Cognitive modeling*, 5:3.

Rico Sennrich. 2015. Modelling and optimizing on syntactic n-grams for statistical machine translation. *Transactions of the Association for Computational Linguistics*, 3:169–182.

Libin Shen, Jinxi Xu, and Ralph Weischedel. 2008. A new string-to-dependency machine translation algorithm with a target dependency language model. In *Proceedings of ACL-08: HLT*, pages 577–585, Columbus, Ohio, USA.

Richard Socher, Eric H. Huang, Jeffrey Pennington, Christopher D. Manning, and Andrew Ng. 2011a. Dynamic pooling and unfolding recursive autoencoders for paraphrase detection. In *Advances in Neural Information Processing Systems*, pages 801–809.

Richard Socher, Jeffrey Pennington, Eric H. Huang, Andrew Y. Ng, and Christopher D. Manning. 2011b. Semi-supervised recursive autoencoders for predicting sentiment distributions. In *Proceedings of the 2011 Conference on Empirical Methods in Natural Language Processing*, pages 151–161, Edinburgh, Scotland, UK.

Nitish Srivastava, Geoffrey Hinton, Alex Krizhevsky, Ilya Sutskever, and Ruslan Salakhutdinov. 2014. Dropout: A simple way to prevent neural networks from overfitting. *The Journal of Machine Learning Research*, 15(1):1929–1958.

Ilya Sutskever, Oriol Vinyals, and Quoc VV Le. 2014. Sequence to sequence learning with neural networks. In *Advances in Neural Information Processing Systems*, pages 3104–3112.

Kai Sheng Tai, Richard Socher, and Christopher D. Manning. 2015. Improved semantic representations from tree-structured long short-term memory networks. In *Proceedings of the 53rd Annual Meeting of the Association for Computational Linguistics and the 7th International Joint Conference on Natural Language Processing (Volume 1: Long Papers)*, pages 1556–1566, Beijing, China, July. Association for Computational Linguistics.

Kristina Toutanova, Dan Klein, Christopher D Manning, and Yoram Singer. 2003. Feature-rich part-of-speech tagging with a cyclic dependency network. In *Proceedings of the 2003 Conference of the North American Chapter of the Association for Computational Linguistics on Human Language Technology-Volume 1*, pages 173–180. Association for Computational Linguistics.

Ashish Vaswani, Yinggong Zhao, Victoria Fossum, and David Chiang. 2013. Decoding with large-scale neural language models improves translation. In *Proceedings of the 2013 Conference on Empirical Methods in Natural Language Processing*, pages 1387–1392, Seattle, Washington, USA.

Oriol Vinyals, Alexander Toshev, Samy Bengio, and Dumitru Erhan. 2015. Show and tell: A neural image caption generator. In *The IEEE Conference on Computer Vision and Pattern Recognition*, Boston, Massachusetts, USA.

Ying Zhang. 2009. *Structured language models for statistical machine translation*. Ph.D. thesis, Johns Hopkins University.

Geoffrey Zweig and Chris J.C. Burges. 2012. A challenge set for advancing language modeling. In *Proceedings of the NAACL-HLT 2012 Workshop: Will We Ever Really Replace the N-gram Model? On the Future of Language Modeling for HLT*, pages 29–36, Montréal, Canada.

Geoffrey Zweig, John C Platt, Christopher Meek, Christopher JC Burges, Ainur Yessenalina, and Qiang Liu. 2012. Computational approaches to sentence completion. In *Proceedings of the 50th Annual Meeting of the Association for Computational Linguistics: Long Papers-Volume 1*, pages 601–610. Association for Computational Linguistics.

Recurrent Memory Networks for Language Modeling

Ke Tran   Arianna Bisazza   Christof Monz
Informatics Institute, University of Amsterdam
Science Park 904, 1098 XH Amsterdam, The Netherlands
`{m.k.tran,a.bisazza,c.monz}@uva.nl`

Abstract

Recurrent Neural Networks (RNNs) have obtained excellent result in many natural language processing (NLP) tasks. However, understanding and interpreting the source of this success remains a challenge. In this paper, we propose Recurrent Memory Network (RMN), a novel RNN architecture, that not only amplifies the power of RNN but also facilitates our understanding of its internal functioning and allows us to discover underlying patterns in data. We demonstrate the power of RMN on language modeling and sentence completion tasks. On language modeling, RMN outperforms Long Short-Term Memory (LSTM) network on three large German, Italian, and English dataset. Additionally we perform indepth analysis of various linguistic dimensions that RMN captures. On Sentence Completion Challenge, for which it is essential to capture sentence coherence, our RMN obtains 69.2% accuracy, surpassing the previous state of the art by a large margin.[1]

1   Introduction

Recurrent Neural Networks (RNNs) (Elman, 1990; Mikolov et al., 2010) are remarkably powerful models for sequential data. Long Short-Term Memory (LSTM) (Hochreiter and Schmidhuber, 1997), a specific architecture of RNN, has a track record of success in many natural language processing tasks such as language modeling (Józefowicz et al., 2015), dependency parsing (Dyer et al., 2015), sentence compression (Filippova et al., 2015), and machine translation (Sutskever et al., 2014).

Within the context of natural language processing, a common assumption is that LSTMs are able to capture certain linguistic phenomena. Evidence supporting this assumption mainly comes from evaluating LSTMs in downstream applications: Bowman et al. (2015) carefully design two artificial datasets where sentences have explicit recursive structures. They show empirically that while processing the input linearly, LSTMs can implicitly exploit recursive structures of languages. Filippova et al. (2015) find that using explicit syntactic features within LSTMs in their sentence compression model hurts the performance of overall system. They then hypothesize that a basic LSTM is powerful enough to capture syntactic aspects which are useful for compression.

To understand and explain which linguistic dimensions are captured by an LSTM is non-trivial. This is due to the fact that the sequences of input histories are compressed into several dense vectors by the LSTM's components whose purposes with respect to representing linguistic information is not evident. To our knowledge, the only attempt to better understand the reasons of an LSTM's performance and limitations is the work of Karpathy et al. (2015) by means of visualization experiments and cell activation statistics in the context of character-level language modeling.

Our work is motivated by the difficulty in understanding and interpreting existing RNN architectures from a linguistic point of view. We propose Recurrent Memory Network (RMN), a novel RNN architecture that combines the strengths of both LSTM

---

[1]Our code and data are available at `https://github.com/ketranm/RMN`

Proceedings of NAACL-HLT 2016, pages 321–331,
San Diego, California, June 12-17, 2016. ©2016 Association for Computational Linguistics

and Memory Network (Sukhbaatar et al., 2015). In RMN, the Memory Block component—a variant of Memory Network—accesses the most recent input words and selectively attends to words that are relevant for predicting the next word given the current LSTM state. By looking at the attention distribution over history words, our RMN allows us not only to interpret the results but also to discover underlying dependencies present in the data.

In this paper, we make the following contributions:

1. We propose a novel RNN architecture that complements LSTM in language modeling. We demonstrate that our RMN outperforms competitive LSTM baselines in terms of perplexity on three large German, Italian, and English datasets.

2. We perform an analysis along various linguistic dimensions that our model captures. This is possible only because the Memory Block allows us to look into its internal states and its explicit use of additional inputs at each time step.

3. We show that, with a simple modification, our RMN can be successfully applied to NLP tasks other than language modeling. On the Sentence Completion Challenge (Zweig and Burges, 2012), our model achieves an impressive 69.2% accuracy, surpassing the previous state of the art 58.9% by a large margin.

2   Recurrent Neural Networks

Recurrent Neural Networks (RNNs) have shown impressive performances on many sequential modeling tasks due to their ability to encode unbounded input histories. However, training simple RNNs is difficult because of the vanishing and exploding gradient problems (Bengio et al., 1994; Pascanu et al., 2013). A simple and effective solution for exploding gradients is gradient clipping proposed by Pascanu et al. (2013). To address the more challenging problem of vanishing gradients, several variants of RNNs have been proposed. Among them, Long Short-Term Memory (Hochreiter and Schmidhuber, 1997) and Gated Recurrent Unit (Cho et al., 2014) are widely regarded as the most successful variants. In this work, we focus on LSTMs because they have

been shown to outperform GRUs on language modeling tasks (Józefowicz et al., 2015). In the following, we will detail the LSTM architecture used in this work.

Long Short-Term Memory

Notation: Throughout this paper, we denote matrices, vectors, and scalars using bold uppercase (e. g., $\mathbf{W}$), bold lowercase (e. g., $\mathbf{b}$) and lowercase (e. g., α) letters, respectively.

The LSTM used in this work is specified as follows:

$$\mathbf{i}_t = \mathrm{sigm}(\mathbf{W}_{xi}\mathbf{x}_t + \mathbf{W}_{hi}\mathbf{h}_{t-1} + \mathbf{b}_i)$$
$$\mathbf{j}_t = \mathrm{sigm}(\mathbf{W}_{xj}\mathbf{x}_t + \mathbf{W}_{hj}\mathbf{h}_{t-1} + \mathbf{b}_j)$$
$$\mathbf{f}_t = \mathrm{sigm}(\mathbf{W}_{xf}\mathbf{x}_t + \mathbf{W}_{hf}\mathbf{h}_{t-1} + \mathbf{b}_f)$$
$$\mathbf{o}_t = \tanh(\mathbf{W}_{xo}\mathbf{x}_t + \mathbf{W}_{ho}\mathbf{h}_{t-1} + \mathbf{b}_o)$$
$$\mathbf{c}_t = \mathbf{c}_{t-1} \odot \mathbf{f}_t + \mathbf{i}_t \odot \mathbf{j}_t$$
$$\mathbf{h}_t = \tanh(\mathbf{c}_t) \odot \mathbf{o}_t$$

where $\mathbf{x}_t$ is the input vector at time step t, $\mathbf{h}_{t-1}$ is the LSTM hidden state at the previous time step, $\mathbf{W}_*$ and $\mathbf{b}_*$ are weights and biases. The symbol $\odot$ denotes the Hadamard product or element-wise multiplication.

Despite the popularity of LSTM in sequential modeling, its design is not straightforward to justify and understanding why it works remains a challenge (Hermans and Schrauwen, 2013; Chung et al., 2014; Greff et al., 2015; Józefowicz et al., 2015; Karpathy et al., 2015). There have been few recent attempts to understand the components of an LSTM from an empirical point of view: Greff et al. (2015) carry out a large-scale experiment of eight LSTM variants. The results from their 5,400 experimental runs suggest that forget gates and output gates are the most critical components of LSTMs. Józefowicz et al. (2015) conduct and evaluate over ten thousand RNN architectures and find that the initialization of the forget gate bias is crucial to the LSTM's performance. While these findings are important to help choosing appropriate LSTM architectures, they do not shed light on what information is captured by the hidden states of an LSTM.

Bowman et al. (2015) show that a vanilla LSTM, such as described above, performs reasonably well compared to a recursive neural network (Socher et al., 2011) that explicitly exploits tree structures on two artificial datasets. They find that LSTMs can effectively exploit recursive structure in the artificial datasets. In contrast to these simple datasets containing a few logical operations in their experiments, natural languages exhibit highly complex patterns. The extent to which linguistic assumptions about syntactic structures and compositional semantics are reflected in LSTMs is rather poorly understood. Thus it is desirable to have a more principled mechanism allowing us to inspect recurrent architectures from a linguistic perspective. In the following section, we propose such a mechanism.

3 Recurrent Memory Network

It has been demonstrated that RNNs can retain input information over a long period. However, existing RNN architectures make it difficult to analyze what information is exactly retained at their hidden states at each time step, especially when the data has complex underlying structures, which is common in natural language. Motivated by this difficulty, we propose a novel RNN architecture called Recurrent Memory Network (RMN). On linguistic data, the RMN allows us not only to qualify which linguistic information is preserved over time and why this is the case but also to discover dependencies within the data (Section 5). Our RMN consists of two components: an LSTM and a *Memory Block* (MB) (Section 3.1). The MB takes the hidden state of the LSTM and compares it to the most recent inputs using an attention mechanism (Gregor et al., 2015; Bahdanau et al., 2014; Graves et al., 2014). Thus, analyzing the attention weights of a trained model can give us valuable insight into the information that is retained over time in the LSTM.

In the following, we describe in detail the MB architecture and the combination of the MB and the LSTM to form an RMN.

3.1 Memory Block

The Memory Block (Figure 1) is a variant of Memory Network (Sukhbaatar et al., 2015) with one hop (or a single-layer Memory Network). At time step t, the MB receives two inputs: the hidden state $\mathbf{h}_t$ of the LSTM and a set $\{x_i\}$ of n most recent words including the current word x_t. We refer to n as the memory size. Internally, the MB consists of

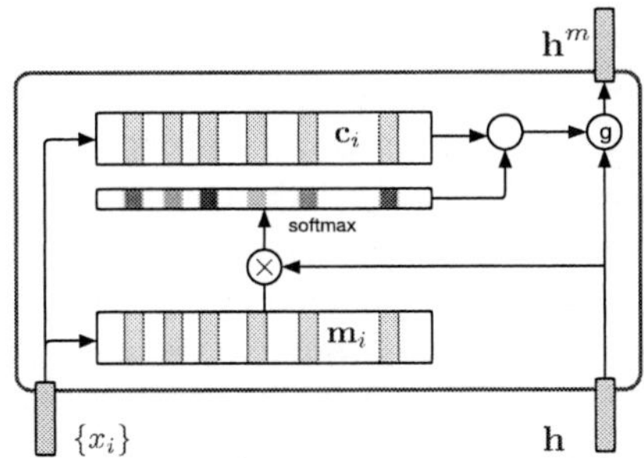

Figure 1: A graphical representation of the MB.

two lookup tables $\mathbf{M}$ and $\mathbf{C}$ of size $|V| \times d$, where $|V|$ is the size of the vocabulary. With a slight abuse of notation we denote $\mathbf{M}_i = \mathbf{M}(\{x_i\})$ and $\mathbf{C}_i = \mathbf{C}(\{x_i\})$ as $n \times d$ matrices where each row corresponds to an input memory embedding $\mathbf{m}_i$ and an output memory embedding $\mathbf{c}_i$ of each element of the set $\{x_i\}$. We use the matrix $\mathbf{M}_i$ to compute an attention distribution over the set $\{x_i\}$:

$$\mathbf{p}_t = \mathrm{softmax}(\mathbf{M}_i\mathbf{h}_t) \tag{1}$$

When dealing with data that exhibits a strong temporal relationship, such as natural language, an additional temporal matrix $\mathbf{T} \in \mathbb{R}^{n \times d}$ can be used to bias attention with respect to the position of the data points. In this case, equation 1 becomes

$$\mathbf{p}_t = \mathrm{softmax}\big((\mathbf{M}_i + \mathbf{T})\mathbf{h}_t\big) \tag{2}$$

We then use the attention distribution $\mathbf{p}_t$ to compute a context vector representation of $\{x_i\}$:

$$\mathbf{s}_t = \mathbf{C}_i^\top \mathbf{p}_t \tag{3}$$

Finally, we combine the context vector $\mathbf{s}_t$ and the hidden state $\mathbf{h}_t$ by a function $g(\cdot)$ to obtain the output $\mathbf{h}_t^m$ of the MB. Instead of using a simple addition function $g(\mathbf{s}_t, \mathbf{h}_t) = \mathbf{s}_t + \mathbf{h}_t$ as in Sukhbaatar et al. (2015), we propose to use a gating unit that decides how much it should trust the hidden state $\mathbf{h}_t$ and context $\mathbf{s}_t$ at time step t. Our gating unit is a form of Gated Recurrent Unit (Cho et al., 2014; Chung et al., 2014):

$$\mathbf{z}_t = \mathrm{sigm}(\mathbf{W}_{sz}\mathbf{s}_t + \mathbf{U}_{hz}\mathbf{h}_t) \tag{4}$$

$$\mathbf{r}_t = \mathrm{sigm}(\mathbf{W}_{sr}\mathbf{s}_t + \mathbf{U}_{hr}\mathbf{h}_t) \tag{5}$$

$$\tilde{\mathbf{h}}_t = \tanh(\mathbf{W}\mathbf{s}_t + \mathbf{U}(\mathbf{r}_t \odot \mathbf{h}_t)) \tag{6}$$

$$\mathbf{h}_t^m = (\mathbf{1} - \mathbf{z}_t) \odot \mathbf{h}_t + \mathbf{z}_t \odot \tilde{\mathbf{h}}_t \tag{7}$$

where $\mathbf{z}_t$ is an update gate, $\mathbf{r}_t$ is a reset gate.

The choice of the composition function $g(\cdot)$ is crucial for the MB especially when one of its input comes from the LSTM. The simple addition function might overwrite the information within the LSTM's hidden state and therefore prevent the MB from keeping track of information in the distant past. The gating function, on the other hand, can control the degree of information that flows from the LSTM to the MB's output.

3.2 RMN Architectures

As explained above, our proposed MB receives the hidden state of the LSTM as one of its input. This leads to an intuitive combination of the two units by stacking the MB on top of the LSTM. We call this architecture Recurrent-Memory (RM). The RM architecture, however, does not allow interaction between Memory Blocks at different time steps. To enable this interaction we can stack one more LSTM layer on top of the RM. We call this architecture Recurrent-Memory-Recurrent (RMR).

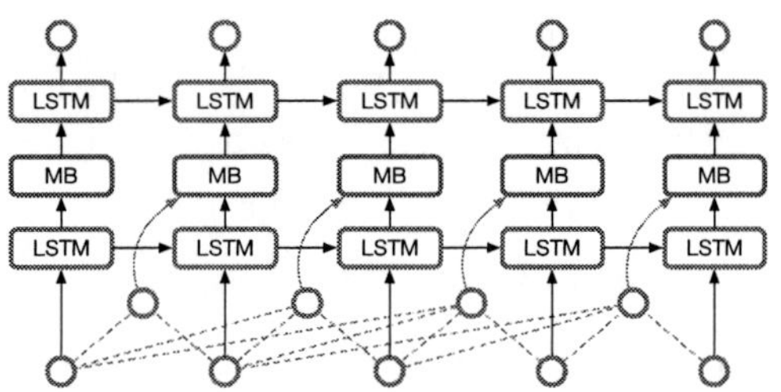

Figure 2: A graphical illustration of an unfolded RMR with memory size 4. Dashed line indicates concatenation. The MB takes the output of the bottom LSTM layer and the 4-word history as its input. The output of the MB is then passed to the second LSTM layer on top. There is no direct connection between MBs of different time steps. The last LSTM layer carries the MB's outputs recurrently.

4 Language Model Experiments

Language models play a crucial role in many NLP applications such as machine translation and speech recognition. Language modeling also serves as a standard test bed for newly proposed models (Sukhbaatar et al., 2015; Kalchbrenner et al., 2015). We conjecture that, by explicitly accessing history words, RMNs will offer better predictive power than

the existing recurrent architectures. We therefore evaluate our RMN architectures against state-of-the-art LSTMs in terms of perplexity.

4.1 Data

We evaluate our models on three languages: English, German, and Italian. We are especially interested in German and Italian because of their larger vocabularies and complex agreement patterns. Table 1 summarizes the data used in our experiments.

Lang	Train	Dev	Test	$|s|$	$|V|$
En	26M	223K	228K	26	77K
De	22M	202K	203K	22	111K
It	29M	207K	214K	29	104K

Table 1: Data statistics. $|s|$ denotes the average sentence length and $|V|$ the vocabulary size.

The training data correspond to approximately 1M sentences in each language. For English, we use all the News Commentary data (8M tokens) and 18M tokens from News Crawl 2014 for training. Development and test data are randomly drawn from the concatenation of the WMT 2009-2014 test sets (Bojar et al., 2015). For German, we use the first 6M tokens from the News Commentary data and 16M tokens from News Crawl 2014 for training. For development and test data we use the remaining part of the News Commentary data concatenated with the WMT 2009-2014 test sets. Finally, for Italian, we use a selection of 29M tokens from the PAISÀ corpus (Lyding et al., 2014), mainly including Wikipedia pages and, to a minor extent, Wikibooks and Wikinews documents. For development and test we randomly draw documents from the same corpus.

4.2 Setup

Our baselines are a 5-gram language model with Kneser-Ney smoothing, a Memory Network (MemN) (Sukhbaatar et al., 2015), a vanilla single-layer LSTM, and two stacked LSTMs with two and three layers respectively. N-gram models have been used intensively in many applications for their excellent performance and fast training. Chen et al. (2015) show that n-gram model outperforms a popular feed-forward language model (Bengio et al.,

2003) on a one billion word benchmark (Chelba et al., 2013). While taking longer time to train, RNNs have been proven superior to n-gram models.

We compare these baselines with our two model architectures: RMR and RM. For each of our models, we consider two settings: with or without temporal matrix (+tM or –tM), and linear vs. gating composition function. In total, we experiment with eight RMN variants.

For all neural network models, we set the dimension of word embeddings, the LSTM hidden states, its gates, the memory input, and output embeddings to 128. The memory size is set to 15. The bias of the LSTM's forget gate is initialized to 1 (Józefowicz et al., 2015) while all other parameters are initialized uniformly in $(-0.05, 0.05)$. The initial learning rate is set to 1 and is halved at each epoch after the forth epoch. All models are trained for 15 epochs with standard stochastic gradient descent (SGD). During training, we rescale the gradients whenever their norm is greater than 5 (Pascanu et al., 2013).

Sentences with the same length are grouped into buckets. Then, mini-batches of 20 sentences are drawn from each bucket. We do not use truncated back-propagation through time, instead gradients are fully back-propagated from the end of each sentence to its beginning. When feeding in a new mini-batch, the hidden states of LSTMs are reset to zeros, which ensures that the data is properly modeled at the sentence level. For our RMN models, instead of using padding, at time step $t < n$, we use a slice $\mathbf{T}[1:t] \in \mathbb{R}^{t \times d}$ of the temporal matrix $\mathbf{T} \in \mathbb{R}^{n \times d}$.

4.3 Results

Perplexities on the test data are given in Table 2. All RMN variants largely outperform n-gram and MemN models, and most RMN variants also outperform the competitive LSTM baselines. The best results overall are obtained by RM with temporal matrix and gating composition (+tM-g).

Our results agree with the hypothesis of mitigating prediction error by explicitly using the last n words in RNNs (Karpathy et al., 2015). We further observe that using a temporal matrix always benefits the RM architectures. This can be explained by seeing the RM as a principled way to combine an LSTM and a neural n-gram model. By contrast, RMR works better without temporal matrix but its

Model		De	It	En
5-gram	–	225.8	167.5	219.0
MemN	1 layer	169.3	127.5	188.2
LSTM	1 layer	135.8	108.0	145.1
	2 layers	128.6	105.9	139.7
	3 layers	125.1	106.5	136.6
RMR	+tM-l	127.5	109.9	133.3
	–tM-l	126.4	106.1	134.5
	+tM-g	126.2	99.5	135.2
	–tM-g	**122.0**	**98.6**	**131.2**
RM	+tM-l	121.5	92.4	**127.2**
	–tM-l	122.9	94.0	130.4
	+tM-g	**118.6**	**88.9**	128.8
	–tM-g	129.7	96.6	135.7

Table 2: Perplexity comparison including RMN variants with and without temporal matrix (tM) and linear (l) versus gating (g) composition function.

overall performance is not as good as RM. This suggests that we need a better mechanism to address the interaction between MBs, which we leave to future work. Finally, the proposed gating composition function outperforms the linear one in most cases.

For historical reasons, we also run a stacked three-layer LSTM and a RM(+tM-g) on the much smaller Penn Treebank dataset (Marcus et al., 1993) with the same setting described above. The respective perplexities are 126.1 and 123.5.

5 Attention Analysis

The goal of our RMN design is twofold: (i) to obtain better predictive power and (ii) to facilitate understanding of the model and discover patterns in data. In Section 4, we have validated the predictive power of the RMN and below we investigate the source of this performance based on linguistic assumptions of word co-occurrences and dependency structures.

5.1 Positional and lexical analysis

As a first step towards understanding RMN, we look at the average attention weights of each history word position in the MB of our two best model variants (Figure 3). One can see that the attention mass tends to concentrate at the rightmost position (the current

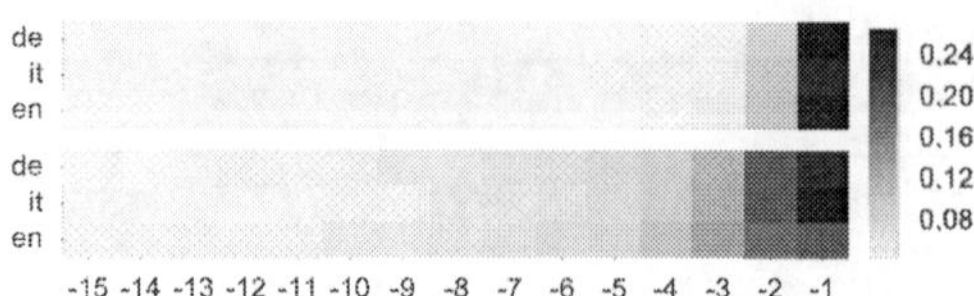

Figure 3: Average attention per position of RMN history. Top: RMR(–tM-g), bottom: RM(+tM-g). Rightmost positions represent most recent history.

word) and decreases when moving further to the left (less recent words). This is not surprising since the success of n-gram language models has demonstrated that the most recent words provide important information for predicting the next word. Between the two variants, the RM average attention mass is less concentrated to the right. This can be explained by the absence of an LSTM layer on top, meaning that the MB in the RM architecture has to pay more attention to the more distant words in the past. The remaining analyses described below are performed on the RM(+tM-g) architecture as this yields the best perplexity results overall.

Beyond average attention weights, we are interested in those cases where attention focuses on distant positions. To this end, we randomly sample 100 words from test data and visualize attention distributions over the last 15 words. Figure 4 shows the attention distributions for random samples of German and Italian. Again, in many cases attention weights concentrate around the last word (bottom row). However, we observe that many long distance words also receive noticeable attention mass. Interestingly, for many predicted words, attention is distributed evenly over memory positions, possibly in-

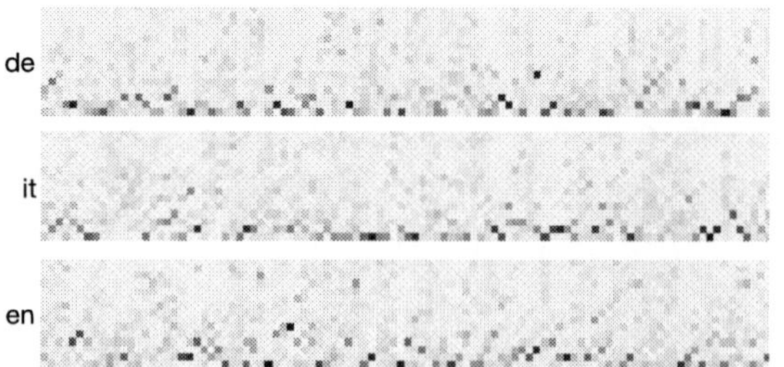

Figure 4: Attention visualization of 100 word samples. Bottom positions in each plot represent most recent history. Darker color means higher weight.

dicating cases where the LSTM state already contains enough information to predict the next word.

To explain the long-distance dependencies, we first hypothesize that our RMN mostly memorizes frequent co-occurrences. We run the RM(+tM-g) model on the German development and test sentences, and select those pairs of (*most-attended-word, word-to-predict*) where the MB's attention concentrates on a word more than six positions to the left. Then, for each set of pairs with equal distance, we compute the mean frequency of corresponding co-occurrences seen in the training data (Table 3). The lack of correlation between frequency and memory location suggests that RMN does more than simply memorizing frequent co-occurrences.

d	7	8	9	10	11	12	13	14	15
μ	54	63	42	67	87	47	67	44	24

Table 3: Mean frequency (μ) of (*most-attended-word, word-to-predict*) pairs grouped by relative distance (d).

Previous work (Hermans and Schrauwen, 2013; Karpathy et al., 2015) studied this property of LSTMs by analyzing simple cases of closing brackets. By contrast RMN allows us to discover more interesting dependencies in the data. We manually inspect those high-frequency pairs to see whether they display certain linguistic phenomena. We observe that RMN captures, for example, *separable verbs* and *fixed expressions* in German. Separable verbs are frequent in German: they typically consist of preposition+verb constructions, such *ab+hängen* ('to depend') or *aus+schließen* ('to exclude'), and can be spelled together (*abhängen*) or apart as in '*hängen von der Situation ab*' ('depend on the situation'), depending on the grammatical construction. Figure 5a shows a long-dependency example for the separable verb *abhängen (to depend)*. When predicting the verb's particle *ab*, the model correctly attends to the verb's core *hängt* occurring seven words to the left. Figure 5b and 5c show fixed expression examples from German and Italian, respectively: *schlüsselrolle ... spielen (play a key role)* and *insignito ... titolo (awarded title)*. Here too, the model correctly attends to the key word despite its long distance from the word to predict.

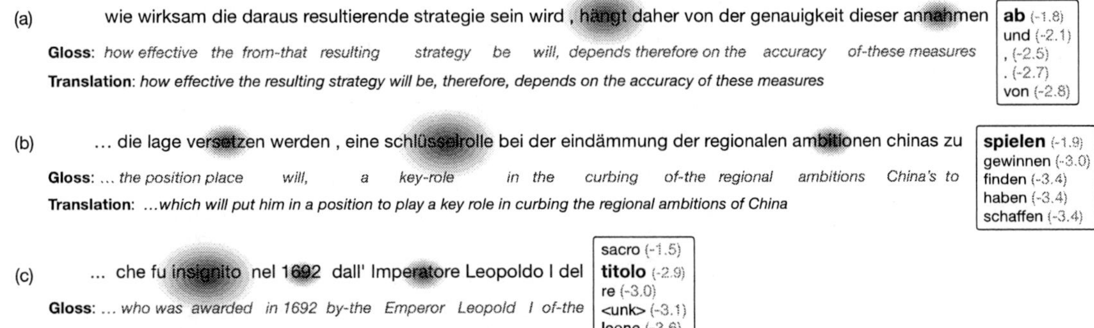

Figure 5: Examples of distant memory positions attended by RMN. The resulting top five word predictions are shown with the respective log-probabilities. The correct choice (in bold) was ranked first in sentences (a,b) and second in (c).

Other interesting examples found by the RMN in the test data include:

German: findet *statt* (takes *place*), kehrte *zurück* (came *back*), fragen *antworten* (questions *answers*), kämpfen *gegen* (fight *against*), bleibt *erhalten* (remains *intact*), verantwortung *übernimmt* (*takes* responsibility);

Italian: sinistra *destra* (left *right*), latitudine *longitudine* (latitude *longitude*), collegata *tramite* (connected *through*), sposò *figli* (got-married *children*), insignito *titolo* (awarded *title*).

5.2 Syntactic analysis

It has been conjectured that RNNs, and LSTMs in particular, model text so well because they capture syntactic structure implicitly. Unfortunately this has been hard to prove, but with our RMN model we can get closer to answering this important question.

We produce dependency parses for our test sets using (Sennrich et al., 2013) for German and (Attardi et al., 2009) for Italian. Next we look at how much attention mass is concentrated by the RM(+tM-g) model on different dependency types. Figure 6 shows, for each language, a selection of ten dependency types that are often long-distance.[2] Dependency direction is marked by an arrow: e.g. →*mod* means that the word to predict is a modifier of the attended word, while *mod*← means that the attended word is a modifier of the word to predict.[3] White cells denote combinations of position and dependency type that were not present in the test data.

While in most of the cases closest positions are attended the most, we can see that some dependency types also receive noticeably more attention than the average (ALL) on the long-distance positions. In German, this is mostly visible for the head of separable verb particles (→*avz*), which nicely supports our observations in the lexical analysis (Section 5.1). Other attended dependencies include: auxiliary verbs (→*aux*) when predicting the second element of a complex tense (*hat ... gesagt / has said*); subordinating conjunctions (*konj*←) when predicting the clause-final inflected verb (*dass sie sagen sollten / that they should say*); control verbs (→*obji*) when predicting the infinitive verb (*versucht ihr zu helfen / tries to help her*). Out of the Italian dependency types selected for their frequent long-distance occurrences (bottom of Figure 6), the most attended are argument heads (→*arg*), complement heads (→*comp*), object heads (→*obj*) and subjects (*subj*←). This suggests that RMN is mainly capturing predicate argument structure in Italian. Notice that syntactic annotation is never used to train the model, but only to analyze its predictions.

We can also use RMN to discover which complex dependency paths are important for word prediction. To mention just a few examples, high attention on

---

[2]The full plots are available at https://github.com/ketranm/RMN. The German and Italian tag sets are explained in (Simi et al., 2014) and (Foth, 2006) respectively.

[3]Some dependency directions, like *obj*← in Italian, are almost never observed due to order constraints of the language.

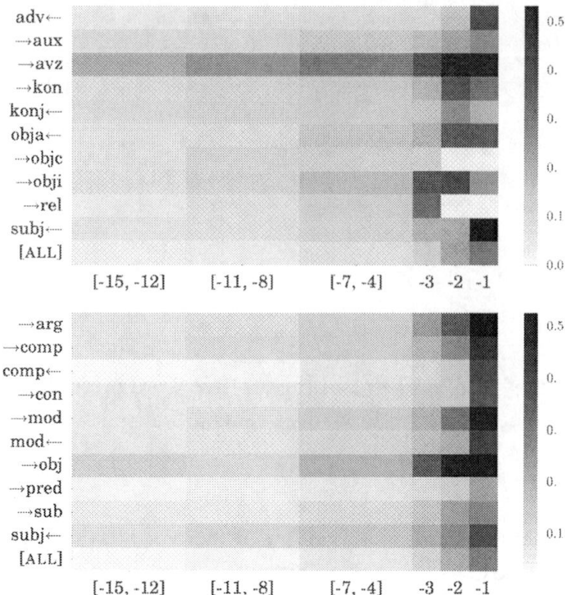

Figure 6: Average attention weights per position, broken down by dependency relation type+direction between the attended word and the word to predict. Top: German. Bottom: Italian. More distant positions are binned.

the German path *[subj←,→kon,→cj]* indicates that the model captures morphological agreement between coordinate clauses in non-trivial constructions of the kind: *spielen die Kinder im Garten und singen / the children play in the garden and sing*. In Italian, high attention on the path *[→obj,→comp,→prep]* denotes cases where the semantic relatedness between a verb and its object does not stop at the object's head, but percolates down to a prepositional phrase attached to it (*passò buona parte della sua vita / spent a large part of his life*). Interestingly, both local n-gram context and immediate dependency context would have missed these relations.

While much remains to be explored, our analysis shows that RMN discovers patterns far more complex than pairs of opening and closing brackets, and suggests that the network's hidden state captures to a large extent the underlying structure of text.

6 Sentence Completion Challenge

The Microsoft Research Sentence Completion Challenge (Zweig and Burges, 2012) has recently be-

come a test bed for advancing statistical language modeling. We choose this task to demonstrate the effectiveness of our RMN in capturing sentence coherence. The test set consists of 1,040 sentences selected from five Sherlock Holmes novels by Conan Doyle. For each sentence, a content word is removed and the task is to identify the correct missing word among five given candidates. The task is carefully designed to be non-solvable for local language models such as n-gram models. The best reported result is 58.9% accuracy (Mikolov et al., 2013)[4] which is far below human accuracy of 91% (Zweig and Burges, 2012).

As baseline we use a stacked three-layer LSTM. Our models are two variants of RM(+tM-g), each consisting of three LSTM layers followed by a MB. The first variant (unidirectional-RM) uses n words preceding the word to predict, the second (bidirectional-RM) uses the n words preceding *and* the n words following the word to predict, as MB input. We include bidirectional-RM in the experiments to show the flexibility of utilizing future context in RMN.

We train all models on the standard training data of the challenge, which consists of 522 novels from Project Gutenberg, preprocessed similarly to (Mnih and Kavukcuoglu, 2013). After sentence splitting, tokenization and lowercasing, we randomly select 19,000 sentences for validation. Training and validation sets include 47M and 190K tokens respectively. The vocabulary size is about 64,000.

We initialize and train all the networks as described in Section 4.2. Moreover, for regularization, we place dropout (Srivastava et al., 2014) after each LSTM layer as suggested in (Pham et al., 2014). The dropout rate is set to 0.3 in all the experiments.

Table 4 summarizes the results. It is worth to mention that our LSTM baseline outperforms a dependency RNN making explicit use of syntactic information (Mirowski and Vlachos, 2015) and performs on par with the best published result (Mikolov et al., 2013). Our unidirectional-RM sets a new state of the art for the Sentence Completion Challenge with 69.2% accuracy. Under the same setting of d we observe that using bidirectional context does not

---

[4]The authors use a weighted combination of skip-ngram and RNN without giving any technical details.

The stage lost a fine ____ , even as science lost an acute reasoner , when he became a specialist in crime
a) linguist   b) hunter   c) **actor**♣   d) estate   e) horseman◇

What passion of hatred can it be which leads a man to ____ in such a place at such a time
a) **lurk**♣   b) dine◇   c) luxuriate   d) grow   e) wiggle

My heart is ____ already since i have confided my trouble to you
a) falling   b) distressed◇   c) soaring   d) **lightened**♣   e) punished

My morning's work has not been ____ , since it has proved that he has the very strongest motives for standing in the way of anything of the sort
a) invisible   b) neglected◇♣   c) overlooked   d) **wasted**   e) deliberate

That is his ____ fault , but on the whole he's a good worker
a) **main**   b) successful   c) mother's♣   d) generous   e) favourite◇

Figure 7: Examples of sentence completion. The correct option is in boldface. Predictions by the LSTM baseline and by our best RMN model are marked by ◇ and ♣ respectively.

Model	n	d	Accuracy
LSTM	–	256	56.0
unidirectional-RM	15	256	64.3
	15	512	**69.2**
bidirectional-RM	7	256	59.6
	10	512	67.0

Table 4: Accuracy on 1,040 test sentences. We use perplexity to choose the best model. Dimension of word embeddings, LSTM hidden states, and gate g parameters are set to d.

bring additional advantage to the model. Mnih and Kavukcuoglu (2013) also report a similar observation. We believe that RMN may achieve further improvements with hyper-parameter optimization.

Figure 7 shows some examples where our best RMN beats the already very competitive LSTM baseline, or where both models fail. We can see that in some sentences the necessary clues to predict the correct word occur only to its *right*. While this seems to conflict with the worse result obtained by the bidirectional-RM, it is important to realize that prediction corresponds to the whole sentence probability. Therefore a badly chosen word can have a negative effect on the score of future words. This appears to be particularly true for the RMN due to its ability to directly access (distant) words in the history. The better performance of unidirectional ver-

sus bidirectional-RM may indicate that the attention in the memory block can be distributed reliably only on words that have been already seen and summarized by the current LSTM state. In future work, we may investigate whether different ways to combine two RMNs running in opposite directions further improve accuracy on this challenging task.

7   Conclusion

We have proposed the Recurrent Memory Network (RMN), a novel recurrent architecture for language modeling. Our RMN outperforms LSTMs in terms of perplexity on three large dataset and allows us to analyze its behavior from a linguistic perspective. We find that RMNs learn important co-occurrences regardless of their distance. Even more interestingly, our RMN implicitly captures certain dependency types that are important for word prediction, despite being trained without any syntactic information. Finally RMNs obtain excellent performance at modeling sentence coherence, setting a new state of the art on the challenging sentence completion task.

Acknowledgments

This research was funded in part by the Netherlands Organization for Scientific Research (NWO) under project numbers 639.022.213 and 612.001.218.

References

Giuseppe Attardi, Felice Dell'Orletta, Maria Simi, and Joseph Turian. 2009. Accurate dependency parsing with a stacked multilayer perceptron. In *Proceedings of Evalita'09, Evaluation of NLP and Speech Tools for Italian*, Reggio Emilia, Italy.

Dzmitry Bahdanau, Kyunghyun Cho, and Yoshua Bengio. 2014. Neural machine translation by jointly learning to align and translate. In *ICLR 2015*, San Diego, CA, USA, May.

Yoshua Bengio, Patrice Simard, and Paolo Frasconi. 1994. Learning long-term dependencies with gradient descent is difficult. *Transaction on Neural Networks*, 5(2):157–166, March.

Yoshua Bengio, Réjean Ducharme, Pascal Vincent, and Christian Janvin. 2003. A neural probabilistic language model. *J. Mach. Learn. Res.*, 3:1137–1155, March.

Ondřej Bojar, Rajen Chatterjee, Christian Federmann, Barry Haddow, Matthias Huck, Chris Hokamp, Philipp Koehn, Varvara Logacheva, Christof Monz, Matteo Negri, Matt Post, Carolina Scarton, Lucia Specia, and Marco Turchi. 2015. Findings of the 2015 workshop on statistical machine translation. In *Proceedings of the Tenth Workshop on Statistical Machine Translation*, pages 1–46, Lisbon, Portugal, September. Association for Computational Linguistics.

Samuel R. Bowman, Christopher D. Manning, and Christopher Potts. 2015. Tree-structured composition in neural networks without tree-structured architectures. In *Proceedings of Proceedings of the NIPS 2015 Workshop on Cognitive Computation: Integrating Neural and Symbolic Approaches*, December.

Ciprian Chelba, Tomas Mikolov, Mike Schuster, Qi Ge, Thorsten Brants, Phillipp Koehn, and Tony Robinson. 2013. One billion word benchmark for measuring progress in statistical language modeling. Technical report, Google.

Welin Chen, David Grangier, and Michael Auli. 2015. Strategies for Training Large Vocabulary Neural Language Models. *ArXiv e-prints*, December.

Kyunghyun Cho, Bart van Merrienboer, Dzmitry Bahdanau, and Yoshua Bengio. 2014. On the properties of neural machine translation: Encoder–decoder approaches. In *Proceedings of SSST-8, Eighth Workshop on Syntax, Semantics and Structure in Statistical Translation*, pages 103–111, Doha, Qatar, October. Association for Computational Linguistics.

Junyoung Chung, Caglar Gulcehre, KyungHyun Cho, and Yoshua Bengio. 2014. Empirical evaluation of gated recurrent neural networks on sequence modeling. In *NIPS Deep Learning and Representation Learning Workshop*.

Chris Dyer, Miguel Ballesteros, Wang Ling, Austin Matthews, and Noah A. Smith. 2015. Transition-based dependency parsing with stack long short-term memory. In *Proceedings of the 53rd Annual Meeting of the Association for Computational Linguistics and the 7th International Joint Conference on Natural Language Processing*, pages 334–343, Beijing, China, July. Association for Computational Linguistics.

Jeffrey L. Elman. 1990. Finding structure in time. *Cognitive Science*, 14(2):179–211.

Katja Filippova, Enrique Alfonseca, Carlos A. Colmenares, Lukasz Kaiser, and Oriol Vinyals. 2015. Sentence compression by deletion with lstms. In *Proceedings of the 2015 Conference on Empirical Methods in Natural Language Processing*, pages 360–368, Lisbon, Portugal, September. Association for Computational Linguistics.

Kilian A. Foth. 2006. *Eine umfassende Constraint-Dependenz-Grammatik des Deutschen*. Fachbereich Informatik.

Alex Graves, Greg Wayne, and Ivo Danihelka. 2014. Neural turing machines. *CoRR*, abs/1410.5401.

Klaus Greff, Rupesh Kumar Srivastava, Jan Koutník, Bas R. Steunebrink, and Jürgen Schmidhuber. 2015. LSTM: A search space odyssey. *CoRR*, abs/1503.04069.

Karol Gregor, Ivo Danihelka, Alex Graves, Danilo Jimenez Rezende, and Daan Wierstra. 2015. DRAW: A recurrent neural network for image generation. In *Proceedings of the 32nd International Conference on Machine Learning, ICML 2015, Lille, France, 6-11 July 2015*, pages 1462–1471.

Michiel Hermans and Benjamin Schrauwen. 2013. Training and analysing deep recurrent neural networks. In C.J.C. Burges, L. Bottou, M. Welling, Z. Ghahramani, and K.Q. Weinberger, editors, *Advances in Neural Information Processing Systems 26*, pages 190–198. Curran Associates, Inc.

Sepp Hochreiter and Jürgen Schmidhuber. 1997. Long short-term memory. *Neural Computation*, 9(8):1735–1780, November.

Rafal Józefowicz, Wojciech Zaremba, and Ilya Sutskever. 2015. An empirical exploration of recurrent network architectures. In *Proceedings of the 32nd International Conference on Machine Learning, ICML 2015, Lille, France, 6-11 July 2015*, pages 2342–2350.

Nal Kalchbrenner, Ivo Danihelka, and Alex Graves. 2015. Grid long short-term memory. *CoRR*, abs/1507.01526.

Andrej Karpathy, Justin Johnson, and Fei-Fei Li. 2015. Visualizing and understanding recurrent networks. *CoRR*, abs/1506.02078.

Verena Lyding, Egon Stemle, Claudia Borghetti, Marco Brunello, Sara Castagnoli, Felice Dell'Orletta, Henrik

Dittmann, Alessandro Lenci, and Vito Pirrelli. 2014. The PAISÀ corpus of italian web texts. In *Proceedings of the 9th Web as Corpus Workshop (WaC-9)*, pages 36–43, Gothenburg, Sweden, April. Association for Computational Linguistics.

Mitchell P. Marcus, Mary Ann Marcinkiewicz, and Beatrice Santorini. 1993. Building a large annotated corpus of english: The penn treebank. *Comput. Linguist.*, 19(2):313–330, June.

Tomas Mikolov, Martin Karafiát, Lukás Burget, Jan Cernocký, and Sanjeev Khudanpur. 2010. Recurrent neural network based language model. In *INTERSPEECH 2010, 11th Annual Conference of the International Speech Communication Association, Makuhari, Chiba, Japan, September 26-30, 2010*, pages 1045–1048.

Tomas Mikolov, Kai Chen, Greg Corrado, and Jeffrey Dean. 2013. Efficient estimation of word representations in vector space. In *ICLR*.

Piotr Mirowski and Andreas Vlachos. 2015. Dependency recurrent neural language models for sentence completion. In *Proceedings of the 53rd Annual Meeting of the Association for Computational Linguistics and the 7th International Joint Conference on Natural Language Processing (Volume 2: Short Papers)*, pages 511–517, Beijing, China, July. Association for Computational Linguistics.

Andriy Mnih and Koray Kavukcuoglu. 2013. Learning word embeddings efficiently with noise-contrastive estimation. In C.J.C. Burges, L. Bottou, M. Welling, Z. Ghahramani, and K.Q. Weinberger, editors, *Advances in Neural Information Processing Systems 26*, pages 2265–2273. Curran Associates, Inc.

Razvan Pascanu, Tomas Mikolov, and Yoshua Bengio. 2013. On the difficulty of training recurrent neural networks. In *ICML (3)*, volume 28 of *JMLR Proceedings*, pages 1310–1318.

Vu Pham, Christopher Bluche, Théodore Kermorvant, and Jérôme Louradour. 2014. Dropout improves recurrent neural networks for handwriting recognition. In *International Conference on Frontiers in Handwriting Recognition (ICFHR)*, pages 285–290, Sept.

Rico Sennrich, Martin Volk, and Gerold Schneider. 2013. Exploiting synergies between open resources for german dependency parsing, pos-tagging, and morphological analysis. In *Recent Advances in Natural Language Processing (RANLP 2013)*, pages 601–609, September.

Maria Simi, Cristina Bosco, and Simonetta Montemagni. 2014. Less is more? towards a reduced inventory of categories for training a parser for the italian stanford dependencies. In *Proceedings of the Ninth International Conference on Language Resources and Evaluation (LREC'14)*, Reykjavik, Iceland, may. European Language Resources Association (ELRA).

Richard Socher, Jeffrey Pennington, Eric H. Huang, Andrew Y. Ng, and Christopher D. Manning. 2011. Semi-supervised recursive autoencoders for predicting sentiment distributions. In *Proceedings of the Conference on Empirical Methods in Natural Language Processing*, EMNLP '11, pages 151–161, Stroudsburg, PA, USA. Association for Computational Linguistics.

Nitish Srivastava, Geoffrey Hinton, Alex Krizhevsky, Ilya Sutskever, and Ruslan Salakhutdinov. 2014. Dropout: A simple way to prevent neural networks from overfitting. *J. Mach. Learn. Res.*, 15(1):1929–1958, January.

Sainbayar Sukhbaatar, Arthur Szlam, Jason Weston, and Rob Fergus. 2015. End-to-end memory networks. In C. Cortes, N.D. Lawrence, D.D. Lee, M. Sugiyama, R. Garnett, and R. Garnett, editors, *Advances in Neural Information Processing Systems 28*, pages 2431–2439. Curran Associates, Inc.

Ilya Sutskever, Oriol Vinyals, and Quoc V Le. 2014. Sequence to sequence learning with neural networks. In Z. Ghahramani, M. Welling, C. Cortes, N.D. Lawrence, and K.Q. Weinberger, editors, *Advances in Neural Information Processing Systems 27*, pages 3104–3112. Curran Associates, Inc.

Geoffrey Zweig and Chris J. C. Burges. 2012. A challenge set for advancing language modeling. In *Proceedings of the NAACL-HLT 2012 Workshop: Will We Ever Really Replace the N-gram Model? On the Future of Language Modeling for HLT*, WLM '12, pages 29–36, Stroudsburg, PA, USA. Association for Computational Linguistics.

A Latent Variable Recurrent Neural Network
for Discourse Relation Language Models

Yangfeng Ji
Georgia Institute of Technology
Atlanta, GA 30308, USA
jiyfeng@gatech.edu

Gholamreza Haffari
Monash University
Clayton, VIC, Australia
gholamreza.haffari
@monash.edu

Jacob Eisenstein
Georgia Institute of Technology
Atlanta, GA 30308, USA
jacobe@gatech.edu

Abstract

This paper presents a novel latent variable recurrent neural network architecture for jointly modeling sequences of words and (possibly latent) discourse relations between adjacent sentences. A recurrent neural network generates individual words, thus reaping the benefits of discriminatively-trained vector representations. The discourse relations are represented with a latent variable, which can be predicted or marginalized, depending on the task. The resulting model can therefore employ a training objective that includes not only discourse relation classification, but also word prediction. As a result, it outperforms state-of-the-art alternatives for two tasks: implicit discourse relation classification in the Penn Discourse Treebank, and dialog act classification in the Switchboard corpus. Furthermore, by marginalizing over latent discourse relations at test time, we obtain a discourse informed language model, which improves over a strong LSTM baseline.

1 Introduction

Natural language processing (NLP) has recently experienced a neural network "tsunami" (Manning, 2016). A key advantage of these neural architectures is that they employ discriminatively-trained distributed representations, which can capture the meaning of linguistic phenomena ranging from individual words (Turian et al., 2010) to longer-range linguistic contexts at the sentence level (Socher et al., 2013) and beyond (Le and Mikolov, 2014). Because they are discriminatively trained, these methods can learn representations that yield very accurate predictive models (e.g., Dyer et al, 2015).

However, in comparison with the probabilistic graphical models that were previously the dominant machine learning approach for NLP, neural architectures lack flexibility. By treating linguistic annotations as random variables, probabilistic graphical models can marginalize over annotations that are unavailable at test or training time, elegantly modeling multiple linguistic phenomena in a joint framework (Finkel et al., 2006). But because these graphical models represent uncertainty for every element in the model, adding too many layers of latent variables makes them difficult to train.

In this paper, we present a hybrid architecture that combines a recurrent neural network language model with a latent variable model over shallow discourse structure. In this way, the model learns a discriminatively-trained distributed representation of the local contextual features that drive word choice at the intra-sentence level, using techniques that are now state-of-the-art in language modeling (Mikolov et al., 2010). However, the model treats shallow discourse structure — specifically, the relationships between pairs of adjacent sentences — as a latent variable. As a result, the model can act as both a discourse relation classifier and a language model. Specifically:

- If trained to maximize the conditional likelihood of the discourse relations, it outperforms state-of-the-art methods for both implicit discourse relation classification in the Penn Discourse Treebank (Rutherford and Xue, 2015) and dialog act classification in Switch-

Proceedings of NAACL-HLT 2016, pages 332–342,
San Diego, California, June 12-17, 2016. ©2016 Association for Computational Linguistics

board (Kalchbrenner and Blunsom, 2013). The model learns from both the discourse annotations as well as the language modeling objective, unlike previous recursive neural architectures that learn only from annotated discourse relations (Ji and Eisenstein, 2015).

- If the model is trained to maximize the joint likelihood of the discourse relations and the text, it is possible to marginalize over discourse relations at test time, outperforming language models that do not account for discourse structure.

In contrast to recent work on continuous latent variables in recurrent neural networks (Chung et al., 2015), which require complex variational autoencoders to represent uncertainty over the latent variables, our model is simple to implement and train, requiring only minimal modifications to existing recurrent neural network architectures that are implemented in commonly-used toolkits such as Theano, Torch, and CNN.

We focus on a class of *shallow discourse relations*, which hold between pairs of adjacent sentences (or utterances). These relations describe how the adjacent sentences are related: for example, they may be in CONTRAST, or the latter sentence may offer an answer to a question posed by the previous sentence. Shallow relations do not capture the full range of discourse phenomena (Webber et al., 2012), but they account for two well-known problems: implicit discourse relation classification in the Penn Discourse Treebank, which was the 2015 CoNLL shared task (Xue et al., 2015); and dialog act classification, which characterizes the structure of interpersonal communication in the Switchboard corpus (Stolcke et al., 2000), and is a key component of contemporary dialog systems (Williams and Young, 2007). Our model outperforms state-of-the-art alternatives for implicit discourse relation classification in the Penn Discourse Treebank, and for dialog act classification in the Switchboard corpus.

2 Background

Our model scaffolds on recurrent neural network (RNN) language models (Mikolov et al., 2010), and recent variants that exploit multiple levels of linguistic detail (Ji et al., 2015; Lin et al., 2015).

RNN Language Models Let us denote token n in a sentence t by $y_{t,n} \in \{1 \ldots V\}$, and write $\boldsymbol{y}_t = \{y_{t,n}\}_{n \in \{1 \ldots N_t\}}$ to indicate the sequence of words in sentence t. In an RNN language model, the probability of the sentence is decomposed as,

$$p(\boldsymbol{y}_t) = \prod_{n}^{N_t} p(y_{t,n} \mid \boldsymbol{y}_{t,<n}), \qquad (1)$$

where the probability of each word $y_{t,n}$ is conditioned on the entire preceding sequence of words $\boldsymbol{y}_{t,<n}$ through the summary vector $\boldsymbol{h}_{t,n-1}$. This vector is computed recurrently from $\boldsymbol{h}_{t,n-2}$ and from the *embedding* of the current word, $\mathbf{X}_{y_{t,n-1}}$, where $\mathbf{X} \in \mathbb{R}^{K \times V}$ and K is the dimensionality of the word embeddings. The language model can then be summarized as,

$$\boldsymbol{h}_{t,n} = \boldsymbol{f}(\mathbf{X}_{y_{t,n}}, \boldsymbol{h}_{t,n-1}) \qquad (2)$$
$$p(y_{t,n} \mid \boldsymbol{y}_{t,<n}) = \text{softmax}\left(\mathbf{W}_o \boldsymbol{h}_{t,n-1} + \boldsymbol{b}_o\right), \qquad (3)$$

where the matrix $\mathbf{W}_o \in \mathbb{R}^{V \times K}$ defines the *output embeddings*, and $\boldsymbol{b}_o \in \mathbb{R}^V$ is an offset. The function $\boldsymbol{f}(\cdot)$ is a deterministic non-linear transition function. It typically takes an element-wise non-linear transformation (e.g., $\tanh$) of a vector resulting from the sum of the word embedding and a linear transformation of the previous hidden state.

The model as described thus far is identical to the recurrent neural network language model (RNNLM) of Mikolov et al. (2010). In this paper, we replace the above simple hidden state units with the more complex Long Short-Term Memory units (Hochreiter and Schmidhuber, 1997), which have consistently been shown to yield much stronger performance in language modeling (Pham et al., 2014). For simplicity, we still use the term RNNLM in referring to this model.

Document Context Language Model One drawback of the RNNLM is that it cannot propagate long-range information between the sentences. Even if we remove sentence boundaries, long-range information will be attenuated by repeated application of the non-linear transition function. Ji et al. (2015) propose the Document Context Language Model (DCLM) to address this issue. The core idea is to represent context with *two* vectors: $\boldsymbol{h}_{t,n}$, representing *intra*-sentence word-level context, and c_t, representing *inter*-sentence context. These two vectors

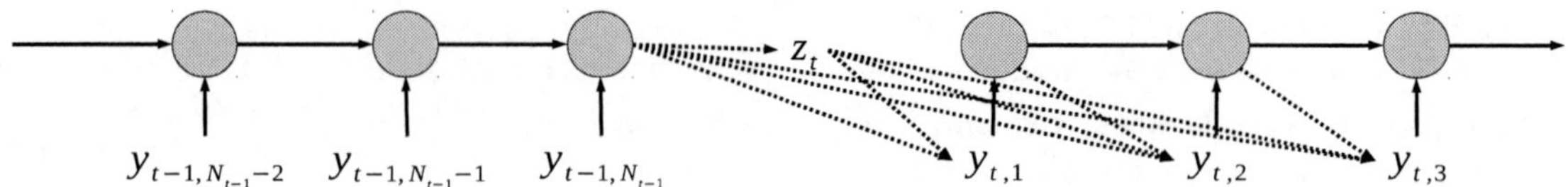

Figure 1: A fragment of our model with latent variable z_t, which only illustrates discourse information flow from sentence $(t-1)$ to t. The information from sentence $(t-1)$ affects the distribution of z_t and then the words prediction within sentence t.

$$p(y_{t,n+1} \mid z_t,\, \boldsymbol{y}_{t,<n},\, \boldsymbol{y}_{t-1}) = g\left(\underbrace{\mathbf{W}_o^{(z_t)} \boldsymbol{h}_{t,n}}_{\substack{\text{relation-specific} \\ \text{intra-sentential context}}} + \underbrace{\mathbf{W}_c^{(z_t)} \boldsymbol{c}_{t-1}}_{\substack{\text{relation-specific} \\ \text{inter-sentential context}}} + \underbrace{\boldsymbol{b}_o^{(z_t)}}_{\substack{\text{relation-specific} \\ \text{bias}}} \right) \quad (4)$$

Figure 2: Per-token generative probabilities in the discourse relation language model

are then linearly combined in the generation function for word $y_{t,n}$,

$$p(y_{t,n} \mid \boldsymbol{y}_{t,<n}, \boldsymbol{y}_{<t})$$
$$= \text{softmax}\left(\mathbf{W}_o \boldsymbol{h}_{t,n-1} + \mathbf{W}_c \boldsymbol{c}_{t-1} + \boldsymbol{b}_o\right), \quad (5)$$

where $\boldsymbol{c}_{t-1}$ is set to the last hidden state of the previous sentence. Ji et al. (2015) show that this model can improve language model perplexity.

3 Discourse Relation Language Models

We now present a probabilistic neural model over sequences of words and shallow discourse relations. Discourse relations z_t are treated as latent variables, which are linked with a recurrent neural network over words in a *latent variable recurrent neural network* (Chung et al., 2015).

3.1 The Model

Our model (see Figure 1) is formulated as a two-step generative story. In the first step, context information from the sentence $(t-1)$ is used to generate the discourse relation between sentences $(t-1)$ and t,

$$p(z_t \mid \boldsymbol{y}_{t-1}) = \text{softmax}\left(\boldsymbol{U}\boldsymbol{c}_{t-1} + \boldsymbol{b}\right), \quad (6)$$

where z_t is a random variable capturing the discourse relation between the two sentences, and $\boldsymbol{c}_{t-1}$ is a vector summary of the contextual information from sentence $(t-1)$, just as in the DCLM (Equation 5). The model maintains a default context vector $\boldsymbol{c}_0$ for the first sentences of documents, and treats it as a parameter learned with other model parameters during training.

In the second step, the sentence $\boldsymbol{y}_t$ is generated, conditioning on the preceding sentence $\boldsymbol{y}_{t-1}$ and the discourse relation z_t:

$$p(\boldsymbol{y}_t \mid z_t, \boldsymbol{y}_{t-1}) = \prod_n^{N_t} p(y_{t,n} \mid \boldsymbol{y}_{t,<n}, \boldsymbol{y}_{t-1}, z_t), \quad (7)$$

The generative probability for the sentence $\boldsymbol{y}_t$ decomposes across tokens as usual (Equation 7). The per-token probabilities are shown in Equation 4, in Figure 2. Discourse relations are incorporated by parameterizing the output matrices $\mathbf{W}_o^{(z_t)}$ and $\mathbf{W}_c^{(z_t)}$; depending on the discourse relation that holds between $(t-1)$ and t, these matrices will favor different parts of the embedding space. The bias term $\boldsymbol{b}_o^{(z_t)}$ is also parametrized by the discourse relation, so that each relation can favor specific words.

Overall, the joint probability of the text and discourse relations is,

$$p(\boldsymbol{y}_{1:T}, \boldsymbol{z}_{1:T}) = \prod_t^T p(z_t \mid \boldsymbol{y}_{t-1}) \times p(\boldsymbol{y}_t \mid z_t, \boldsymbol{y}_{t-1}). \tag{8}$$

If the discourse relations z_t are not observed, then our model is a form of latent variable recurrent neural network (LVRNN). Connections to recent work on LVRNNs are discussed in § 6; the key difference is that the latent variables here correspond to linguistically meaningful elements, which we may wish to predict or marginalize, depending on the situation.

Parameter Tying As proposed, the Discourse Relation Language Model has a large number of parameters. Let K, H and V be the input dimension, hidden dimension and the size of vocabulary in language modeling. The size of each prediction matrix $\mathbf{W}_o^{(z)}$ and $\mathbf{W}_c^{(z)}$ is $V \times H$; there are two such matrices for each possible discourse relation. We reduce the number of parameters by factoring each of these matrices into two components:

$$\mathbf{W}_o^{(z)} = \mathbf{W}_o \cdot \mathbf{V}^{(z)}, \quad \mathbf{W}_c^{(z)} = \mathbf{W}_c \cdot \mathbf{M}^{(z)}, \quad (9)$$

where $\mathbf{V}^{(z)}$ and $\mathbf{M}^{(z)}$ are relation-specific components for intra-sentential and inter-sentential contexts; the size of these matrices is $H \times H$, with $H \ll V$. The larger $V \times H$ matrices $\mathbf{W}_o$ and $\mathbf{W}_c$ are shared across all relations.

3.2 Inference

There are two possible inference scenarios: inference over discourse relations, conditioning on words; and inference over words, marginalizing over discourse relations.

Inference over Discourse Relations The probability of discourse relations given the sentences $p(\boldsymbol{z}_{1:T} \mid \boldsymbol{y}_{1:T})$ is decomposed into the product of probabilities of individual discourse relations conditioned on the adjacent sentences $\prod_t p(z_t \mid \boldsymbol{y}_t, \boldsymbol{y}_{t-1})$. These probabilities are computed by Bayes' rule:

$$p(z_t \mid \boldsymbol{y}_t, \boldsymbol{y}_{t-1}) = \frac{p(\boldsymbol{y}_t \mid z_t, \boldsymbol{y}_{t-1}) \times p(z_t \mid \boldsymbol{y}_{t-1})}{\sum_{z'} p(\boldsymbol{y}_t \mid z', \boldsymbol{y}_{t-1}) \times p(z' \mid \boldsymbol{y}_{t-1})}.$$
$$(10)$$

The terms in each product are given in Equations 6 and 7. Normalizing involves only a sum over a small finite number of discourse relations. Note that inference is easy in our case because all words are observed and there is no probabilistic coupling of the discourse relations.

Inference over Words In discourse-informed language modeling, we marginalize over discourse relations to compute the probability of a sequence of sentence $\boldsymbol{y}_{1:T}$, which can be written as,

$$p(\boldsymbol{y}_{1:T}) = \prod_t^T \sum_{z_t} p(z_t \mid \boldsymbol{y}_{t-1}) \times p(\boldsymbol{y}_t \mid z_t, \boldsymbol{y}_{t-1}),$$
$$(11)$$

because the word sequences are observed, decoupling each z_t from its neighbors z_{t+1} and z_{t-1}. This decoupling ensures that we can compute the overall marginal likelihood as a product over local marginals.

3.3 Learning

The model can be trained in two ways: to maximize the joint probability $p(\boldsymbol{y}_{1:T}, \boldsymbol{z}_{1:T})$, or to maximize the conditional probability $p(\boldsymbol{z}_{1:T} \mid \boldsymbol{y}_{1:T})$. The joint training objective is more suitable for language modeling scenarios, and the conditional objective is better for discourse relation prediction. We now describe each objective in detail.

Joint likelihood objective The joint likelihood objective function is directly adopted from the joint probability defined in Equation 8. The objective function for a single document with T sentences or utterances is,

$$\ell(\boldsymbol{\theta}) = \sum_t^T \log p(z_t \mid \boldsymbol{y}_{t-1})$$
$$+ \sum_n^{N_t} \log p(y_{t,n} \mid \boldsymbol{y}_{t,<n}, \boldsymbol{y}_{t-1}, z_t), \quad (12)$$

where $\boldsymbol{\theta}$ represents the collection of all model parameters, including the parameters in the LSTM units and the word embeddings.

Maximizing the objective function $\ell(\boldsymbol{\theta})$ will jointly optimize the model on both language language and discourse relation prediction. As such, it can be viewed as a form of multi-task learning (Caruana, 1997), where we learn a shared representation that works well for discourse relation prediction and for language modeling. However, in practice, the large vocabulary size and number of tokens means that the language modeling part of the objective function tends to dominate.

Conditional objective This training objective is specific to the discourse relation prediction task, and based on Equation 10 can be written as:

$$\ell_r(\boldsymbol{\theta}) = \sum_t^T \log p(z_t \mid \boldsymbol{y}_{t-1}) + \log p(\boldsymbol{y}_t \mid z_t, \boldsymbol{y}_{t-1})$$
$$- \log \sum_{z'} p(z' \mid \boldsymbol{y}_{t-1}) \times p(\boldsymbol{y}_t \mid z', \boldsymbol{y}_{t-1})$$
$$(13)$$

The first line in Equation 13 is the same as $\ell(\boldsymbol{\theta})$, but the second line reflects the normalization over all possible values of z_t. This forces the objective function to attend specifically to the problem of maximizing the conditional likelihood of the discourse relations and treat language modeling as an auxiliary task (Collobert et al., 2011).

3.4 Modeling limitations

The discourse relation language model is carefully designed to decouple the discourse relations from each other, after conditioning on the words. It is clear that text documents and spoken dialogues have sequential discourse structures, and it seems likely that modeling this structure could improve performance. In a traditional hidden Markov model (HMM) generative approach (Stolcke et al., 2000), modeling sequential dependencies is not difficult, because training reduces to relative frequency estimation. However, in the hybrid probabilistic-neural architecture proposed here, training is already expensive, due to the large number of parameters that must be estimated. Adding probabilistic couplings between adjacent discourse relations $\langle z_{t-1}, z_t \rangle$ would require the use of dynamic programming for both training and inference, increasing time complexity by a factor that is quadratic in the number of discourse relations. We did not attempt this in this paper; we do compare against a conventional HMM on the dialogue act prediction task in § 5.

Ji et al. (2015) propose an alternative form of the document context language model, in which the contextual information c_t impacts the hidden state h_{t+1}, rather than going directly to the outputs y_{t+1}. They obtain slightly better perplexity with this approach, which has fewer trainable parameters. However, this model would couple z_t with *all* subsequent sentences $y_{>t}$, making prediction and marginalization of discourse relations considerably more challenging. Sequential Monte Carlo algorithms offer a possible solution (de Freitas et al., ; Gu et al., 2015), which may be considered in future work.

4 Data and Implementation

We evaluate our model on two benchmark datasets: (1) the Penn Discourse Treebank (Prasad et al., 2008, PDTB), which is annotated on a corpus of Wall Street Journal acticles; (2) the Switchboard dialogue act corpus (Stolcke et al., 2000, SWDA), which is annotated on a collections of phone conversations. Both corpora contain annotations of discourse relations and dialogue relations that hold between adjacent spans of text.

The Penn Discourse Treebank (PDTB) provides a low-level discourse annotation on written texts. In the PDTB, each discourse relation is annotated between two argument spans, `Arg1` and `Arg2`. There are two types of relations: explicit and implicit. Explicit relations are signalled by discourse markers (e.g., *"however"*, *"moreover"*), and the span of `Arg1` is almost totally unconstrained: it can range from a single clause to an entire paragraph, and need not be adjacent to either `Arg2` nor the discourse marker. However, automatically classifying these relations is considered to be relatively easy, due to the constraints from the discourse marker itself (Pitler et al., 2008). In addition, explicit relations are difficult to incorporate into language models which must generate each word exactly once. On the contrary, *implicit* discourse relations are annotated only between adjacent sentences, based on a semantic understanding of the discourse arguments. Automatically classifying these discourse relations is a challenging task (Lin et al., 2009; Pitler et al., 2009; Rutherford and Xue, 2015; Ji and Eisenstein, 2015). We therefore focus on implicit discourse relations, leaving to the future work the question of how to apply our modeling framework to explicit discourse relations. During training, we collapse all relation types other than implicit (explicit, ENTREL, and NOREL) into a single dummy relation type, which holds between all adjacent sentence pairs that do not share an implicit relation.

As in the prior work on first-level discourse relation identification (e.g., Park and Cardie, 2012), we use sections 2-20 of the PDTB as the training set, sections 0-1 as the development set for parameter tuning, and sections 21-22 for testing. For preprocessing, we lower-cased all tokens, and substituted all numbers with a special token *"NUM"*. To build the vocabulary, we kept the 10,000 most frequent words from the training set, and replaced low-frequency words with a special token *"UNK"*. In prior work that focuses on detecting individual relations, balanced training sets are constructed so that there are an equal number of instances with and without each relation type (Park and Cardie, ; Biran and McKeown, 2013; Rutherford and Xue, 2014). In this paper, we target the more challenging multi-way classification problem, so this strategy is not applicable; in any case, since our method deals with entire documents, it is not possible to balance the training set in this way.

The Switchboard Dialog Act Corpus (SWDA) is annotated on the Switchboard Corpus of human-human conversational telephone speech (Godfrey et al., 1992). The annotations label each utterance with one of 42 possible speech acts, such as AGREE, HEDGE, and WH-QUESTION. Because these speech acts form the structure of the dialogue, most of them pertain to both the preceding and succeeding utterances (e.g., AGREE). The SWDA corpus includes 1155 five-minute conversations. We adopted the standard split from Stolcke et al. (2000), using 1,115 conversations for training and nineteen conversations for test. For parameter tuning, we randomly select nineteen conversations from the training set as the development set. After parameter tuning, we train the model on the full training set with the selected configuration. We use the same preprocessing techniques here as in the PDTB.

4.1 Implementation

We use a single-layer LSTM to build the recurrent architecture of our models, which we implement in the CNN package.[1] Our implementation is available on `https://github.com/jiyfeng/drlm`. Some additional details follow.

Initialization Following prior work on RNN initialization (Bengio, 2012), all parameters except the relation prediction parameters $\mathbf{U}$ and b are initialized with random values drawn from the range $[-\sqrt{6/(d_1 + d_2)}, \sqrt{6/(d_1 + d_2)}]$, where d_1 and d_2 are the input and output dimensions of the parameter matrix respectively. The matrix $\mathbf{U}$ is initialized with random numbers from $[-10^{-5}, 10^{-5}]$ and b is initialized to $\mathbf{0}$.

Learning Online learning was performed using AdaGrad (Duchi et al., 2011) with initial learning rate $\lambda = 0.1$. To avoid the exploding gradient problem, we used norm clipping trick with a threshold of $\tau = 5.0$ (Pascanu et al., 2012). In addition, we used value dropout (Srivastava et al., 2014) with rate 0.5, on the input $\mathbf{X}$, context vector c and hidden state h, similar to the architecture proposed by Pham et al. (2014). The training procedure is monitored by the performance on the development set. In our experiments, 4 to 5 epochs were enough.

Hyper-parameters Our model includes two tunable hyper-parameters: the dimension of word representation K, the hidden dimension of LSTM unit H. We consider the values $\{32, 48, 64, 96, 128\}$ for both K and H. For each corpus in experiments, the best combination of K and H is selected via grid search on the development set.

5 Experiments

Our main evaluation is discourse relation prediction, using the PDTB and SWDA corpora. We also evaluate on language modeling, to determine whether incorporating discourse annotations at training time and then marginalizing them at test time can improve performance.

5.1 Implicit discourse relation prediction on the PDTB

We first evaluate our model with implicit discourse relation prediction on the PDTB dataset. Most of the prior work on first-level discourse relation prediction focuses on the "one-versus-all" binary classification setting, but we attack the more general four-way classification problem, as performed by Rutherford and Xue (2015). We compare against the following methods:

Rutherford and Xue (2015) build a set of feature-rich classifiers on the PDTB, and then augment these classifiers with additional automatically-labeled training instances. We compare against their published results, which are state-of-the-art.

Ji and Eisenstein (2015) employ a recursive neural network architecture. Their experimental setting is different, so we re-run their system using the same setting as described in § 4.

---

[1] `https://github.com/clab/cnn`

Model	Accuracy	Macro F_1
Baseline		
1. Most common class	54.7	—
Prior work		
2. (Rutherford and Xue, 2015)	55.0	38.4
3. (Rutherford and Xue, 2015) with extra training data	57.1	40.5
4. (Ji and Eisenstein, 2015)	56.4	40.0
Our work - DRLM		
5. Joint training	57.1	40.5
6. Conditional training	**59.5***	**42.3**

* significantly better than lines 2 and 4 with $p < 0.05$

Table 1: Multiclass relation identification on the first-level PDTB relations.

1. Model	Accuracy
Baseline	
2. Most common class	31.5
Prior work	
3. (Stolcke et al., 2000)	71.0
4. (Kalchbrenner and Blunsom, 2013)	73.9
Our work - DRLM	
5. Joint training	74.0
6. Conditional training	**77.0***

* significantly better than line 4 with $p < 0.01$

Table 2: The results of dialogue act tagging.

Results As shown in Table 1, the conditionally-trained discourse relation language models (DRLM) outperforms all alternatives, on both metrics. While the jointly-trained DRLM is at the same level as the previous state-of-the-art, conditional training on the same model provides a significant additional advantage, indicated by a binomial test.

5.2 Dialogue Act tagging

Dialogue act tagging has been widely studied in both NLP and speech communities. We follow the setup used by Stolcke et al. (2000) to conduct experiments, and adopt the following systems for comparison:

Stolcke et al. (2000) employ a hidden Markov model, with each HMM state corresponding to a dialogue act.

Kalchbrenner and Blunsom (2013) employ a complex neural architecture, with a convolutional network at each utterance and a recurrent network over the length of the dialog. To our knowledge, this model attains state-of-the-art accuracy on this task, outperforming other prior work such as (Webb et al., 2005; Milajevs and Purver, 2014).

Results As shown in Table 2, the conditionally-trained discourse relation language model (DRLM) outperforms all competitive systems on this task. A binomial test shows the result in line 6 is significantly better than the previous state-of-the-art (line 4). All comparisons are against published results, and Macro-F_1 scores are not available. Accuracy is more reliable on this evaluation, since no single class dominates, unlike the PDTB task.

5.3 Discourse-aware language modeling

As a joint model for discourse and language modeling, DRLM can also function as a language model, assigning probabilities to sequences of words while marginalizing over discourse relations. To determine whether discourse-aware language modeling can improve performance, we compare against the following systems:

RNNLM+LSTM This is the same basic architecture as the RNNLM proposed by (Mikolov et al., 2010), which was shown to outperform a Kneser-Ney smoothed 5-gram model on modeling Wall Street Journal text. Following Pham et al. (2014), we replace the Sigmoid nonlinearity with a long short-term memory (LSTM).

DCLM We compare against the Document Context Language Model (DCLM) of Ji et al. (2015). We use the "context-to-output" variant, which is identical to the current modeling approach, except that it is not parametrized by discourse relations. This model achieves strong results on language modeling for small and medium-sized corpora, outperforming RNNLM+LSTM.

Results The perplexities of language modeling on the PDTB and the SWDA are summarized in Table 3. The comparison between line 1 and line 2 shows the benefit of considering multi-sentence context information on language modeling. Line 3 shows that adding discourse relation information

| | PDTB | | | SWDA | | |
Model	K	H	PPLX	K	H	PPLX
Baseline						
1. RNNLM	96	128	117.8	128	96	56.0
2. DCLM	96	96	112.2	96	96	45.3
Our work						
3. DRLM	64	96	108.3	128	64	39.6

Table 3: Language model perplexities (PPLX), lower is better. The model dimensions K and H that gave best performance on the dev set are also shown.

yields further improvements for both datasets. We emphasize that discourse relations in the test documents are marginalized out, so no annotations are required for the test set; the improvements are due to the disambiguating power of discourse relations in the training set.

Because our training procedure requires discourse annotations, this approach does not scale to the large datasets typically used in language modeling. As a consequence, the results obtained here are somewhat academic, from the perspective of practical language modeling. Nonetheless, the positive results here motivate the investigation of training procedures that are also capable of marginalizing over discourse relations at training time.

6 Related Work

This paper draws on previous work in both discourse modeling and language modeling.

Discourse and dialog modeling Early work on discourse relation classification utilizes rich, handcrafted feature sets (Joty et al., 2012; Lin et al., 2009; Sagae, 2009). Recent representation learning approaches attempt to learn good representations jointly with discourse relation classifiers and discourse parsers (Ji and Eisenstein, 2014; Li et al., 2014). Of particular relevance are applications of neural architectures to PDTB implicit discourse relation classification (Ji and Eisenstein, 2015; Zhang et al., 2015; Braud and Denis, 2015). All of these approaches are essentially classifiers, and take supervision only from the 16,000 annotated discourse relations in the PDTB training set. In contrast, our approach is a probabilistic model over the entire text.

Probabilistic models are frequently used in dialog act tagging, where hidden Markov models have been a dominant approach (Stolcke et al., 2000). In this work, the emission distribution is an n-gram language model for each dialogue act; we use a conditionally-trained recurrent neural network language model. An alternative neural approach for dialogue act tagging is the combined convolutional-recurrent architecture of Kalchbrenner and Blunsom (2013). Our modeling framework is simpler, relying on a latent variable parametrization of a purely recurrent architecture.

Language modeling There are an increasing number of attempts to incorporate document-level context information into language modeling. For example, Mikolov and Zweig (2012) introduce LDA-style topics into RNN based language modeling. Sordoni et al. (2015) use a convolutional structure to summarize the context from previous two utterances as context vector for RNN based language modeling. Our models in this paper provide a unified framework to model the context and current sentence. Wang and Cho (2015) and Lin et al. (2015) construct bag-of-words representations of previous sentences, which are then used to inform the RNN language model that generates the current sentence. The most relevant work is the Document Context Language Model (Ji et al., 2015, DCLM); we describe the connection to this model in § 2. By adding discourse information as a latent variable, we attain better perplexity on held-out data.

Latent variable neural networks Introducing latent variables to a neural network model increases its representational capacity, which is the main goal of prior efforts in this space (Kingma and Welling, 2014; Chung et al., 2015). From this perspective, our model with discourse relations as latent variables shares the same merit. Unlike this prior work, in our approach, the latent variables carry a linguistic interpretation, and are at least partially observed. Also, these prior models employ continuous latent variables, requiring complex inference techniques such as variational autoencoders (Kingma and Welling, 2014; Burda et al., 2016; Chung et al., 2015). In contrast, the discrete latent variables in our model are easy to sum and maximize over.

7 Conclusion

We have presented a probabilistic neural model over sequences of words and shallow discourse relations between adjacent sequences. This model combines positive aspects of neural network architectures with probabilistic graphical models: it can learn discriminatively-trained vector representations, while maintaining a probabilistic representation of the targeted linguistic element: in this case, shallow discourse relations. This method outperforms state-of-the-art systems in two discourse relation detection tasks, and can also be applied as a language model, marginalizing over discourse relations on the test data. Future work will investigate the possibility of learning from partially-labeled training data, which would have at least two potential advantages. First, it would enable the model to scale up to the large datasets needed for competitive language modeling. Second, by training on more data, the resulting vector representations might support even more accurate discourse relation prediction.

Acknowledgments

Thanks to Trevor Cohn, Chris Dyer, Lingpeng Kong, and Quoc V. Le for helpful discussions, and to the anonymous reviewers for their feedback. This work was supported by a Google Faculty Research award to the third author. It was partially performed during the 2015 Jelinek Memorial Summer Workshop on Speech and Language Technologies at the University of Washington, Seattle, and was supported by Johns Hopkins University via NSF Grant No IIS 1005411, DARPA LORELEI Contract No HR0011-15-2-0027, and gifts from Google, Microsoft Research, Amazon and Mitsubishi Electric Research Laboratory.

References

Yoshua Bengio. 2012. Practical recommendations for gradient-based training of deep architectures. In *Neural Networks: Tricks of the Trade*, pages 437–478. Springer.

Or Biran and Kathleen McKeown. 2013. In *Proceedings of the Association for Computational Linguistics (ACL)*, pages 69–73, Sophia, Bulgaria.

Chloé Braud and Pascal Denis. 2015. Comparing word representations for implicit discourse relation classification. In *Proceedings of Empirical Methods for Natural Language Processing (EMNLP)*, pages 2201–2211, Lisbon, September.

Yuri Burda, Roger Grosse, and Ruslan Salakhutdinov. 2016. Importance weighted autoencoders. In *Proceedings of the International Conference on Learning Representations (ICLR)*.

Rich Caruana. 1997. Multitask learning. *Machine learning*, 28(1):41–75.

Junyoung Chung, Kyle Kastner, Laurent Dinh, Kratarth Goel, Aaron Courville, and Yoshua Bengio. 2015. A recurrent latent variable model for sequential data. In *Neural Information Processing Systems (NIPS)*, Montréal.

R. Collobert, J. Weston, L. Bottou, M. Karlen, K. Kavukcuoglu, and P. Kuksa. 2011. Natural language processing (almost) from scratch. *Journal of Machine Learning Research*, 12:2493–2537.

João FG de Freitas, Mahesan Niranjan, Andrew H. Gee, and Arnaud Doucet. Sequential monte carlo methods to train neural network models. *Neural computation*, 12(4):955–993.

John Duchi, Elad Hazan, and Yoram Singer. 2011. Adaptive subgradient methods for online learning and stochastic optimization. *The Journal of Machine Learning Research*, 12:2121–2159.

Chris Dyer, Miguel Ballesteros, Wang Ling, Austin Matthews, and Noah A. Smith. 2015. Transition-based dependency parsing with stack long short-term memory. In *Proceedings of the Association for Computational Linguistics (ACL)*, pages 334–343, Beijing, China.

Jenny Rose Finkel, Christopher D Manning, and Andrew Y Ng. 2006. Solving the problem of cascading errors: Approximate bayesian inference for linguistic annotation pipelines. In *Proceedings of Empirical Methods for Natural Language Processing (EMNLP)*, pages 618–626.

John J Godfrey, Edward C Holliman, and Jane McDaniel. 1992. Switchboard: Telephone speech corpus for research and development. In *ICASSP*, volume 1, pages 517–520. IEEE.

Shixiang Gu, Zoubin Ghahramani, and Richard E Turner. 2015. Neural adaptive sequential monte carlo. In *Neural Information Processing Systems (NIPS)*, Montréal.

Sepp Hochreiter and Jürgen Schmidhuber. 1997. Long short-term memory. *Neural computation*, 9(8):1735–1780.

Yangfeng Ji and Jacob Eisenstein. 2014. Representation learning for text-level discourse parsing. In *Proceedings of the Association for Computational Linguistics (ACL)*, Baltimore, MD.

Yangfeng Ji and Jacob Eisenstein. 2015. One vector is not enough: Entity-augmented distributional semantics for discourse relations. *Transactions of the Association for Computational Linguistics (TACL)*, June.

Yangfeng Ji, Trevor Cohn, Lingpeng Kong, Chris Dyer, and Jacob Eisenstein. 2015. Document context language models. In *International Conference on Learning Representations, Poster Paper*, volume abs/1511.03962.

Shafiq Joty, Giuseppe Carenini, and Raymond Ng. 2012. A novel discriminative framework for sentence-level discourse analysis. In *Proceedings of Empirical Methods for Natural Language Processing (EMNLP)*.

Nal Kalchbrenner and Phil Blunsom. 2013. Recurrent convolutional neural networks for discourse compositionality. In *Proceedings of the Workshop on Continuous Vector Space Models and their Compositionality*, pages 119–126, Sofia, Bulgaria, August. Association for Computational Linguistics.

Diederik P Kingma and Max Welling. 2014. Auto-encoding variational bayes. In *Proceedings of the International Conference on Learning Representations (ICLR)*.

Quoc Le and Tomas Mikolov. 2014. Distributed representations of sentences and documents. In *Proceedings of the International Conference on Machine Learning (ICML)*.

Jiwei Li, Rumeng Li, and Eduard Hovy. 2014. Recursive deep models for discourse parsing. In *Proceedings of Empirical Methods for Natural Language Processing (EMNLP)*.

Ziheng Lin, Min-Yen Kan, and Hwee Tou Ng. 2009. Recognizing implicit discourse relations in the penn discourse treebank. In *Proceedings of Empirical Methods for Natural Language Processing (EMNLP)*, pages 343–351, Singapore.

Rui Lin, Shujie Liu, Muyun Yang, Mu Li, Ming Zhou, and Sheng Li. 2015. Hierarchical recurrent neural network for document modeling. In *Proceedings of Empirical Methods for Natural Language Processing (EMNLP)*, pages 899–907, Lisbon, September.

Christopher D. Manning. 2016. Computational linguistics and deep learning. *Computational Linguistics*, 41(4).

Tomas Mikolov and Geoffrey Zweig. 2012. Context dependent recurrent neural network language model. In *Proceedings of Spoken Language Technology (SLT)*, pages 234–239.

Tomas Mikolov, Martin Karafiát, Lukas Burget, Jan Cernockỳ, and Sanjeev Khudanpur. 2010. Recurrent neural network based language model. In *INTERSPEECH*, pages 1045–1048.

Dmitrijs Milajevs and Matthew Purver. 2014. Investigating the contribution of distributional semantic information for dialogue act classification. In *Proceedings of the 2nd Workshop on Continuous Vector Space Models and their Compositionality (CVSC)*, pages 40–47.

Joonsuk Park and Claire Cardie. Improving implicit discourse relation recognition through feature set optimization. In *Proceedings of the 13th Annual Meeting of the Special Interest Group on Discourse and Dialogue*, pages 108–112, Seoul, South Korea, July. Association for Computational Linguistics.

Razvan Pascanu, Tomas Mikolov, and Yoshua Bengio. 2012. On the difficulty of training recurrent neural networks. *arXiv preprint arXiv:1211.5063*.

Vu Pham, Théodore Bluche, Christopher Kermorvant, and Jérôme Louradour. 2014. Dropout improves recurrent neural networks for handwriting recognition. In *Frontiers in Handwriting Recognition (ICFHR), 2014 14th International Conference on*, pages 285–290. IEEE.

Emily Pitler, Mridhula Raghupathy, Hena Mehta, Ani Nenkova, Alan Lee, and Aravind Joshi. 2008. Easily identifiable discourse relations. In *Proceedings of the International Conference on Computational Linguistics (COLING)*, pages 87–90, Manchester, UK.

Emily Pitler, Annie Louis, and Ani Nenkova. 2009. Automatic sense prediction for implicit discourse relations in text. In *Proceedings of the Association for Computational Linguistics (ACL)*, Suntec, Singapore.

Rashmi Prasad, Nikhil Dinesh, Alan Lee, Eleni Miltsakaki, Livio Robaldo, Aravind Joshi, and Bonnie Webber. 2008. The Penn Discourse Treebank 2.0. In *Proceedings of LREC*.

Attapol T Rutherford and Nianwen Xue. 2014. Discovering implicit discourse relations through brown cluster pair representation and coreference patterns. In *Proceedings of the European Chapter of the Association for Computational Linguistics (EACL)*.

Attapol Rutherford and Nianwen Xue. 2015. Improving the inference of implicit discourse relations via classifying explicit discourse connectives. pages 799–808, May–June.

Kenji Sagae. 2009. Analysis of discourse structure with syntactic dependencies and data-driven shift-reduce parsing. In *Proceedings of the 11th International Conference on Parsing Technologies (IWPT'09)*, pages 81–84, Paris, France, October. Association for Computational Linguistics.

Richard Socher, Alex Perelygin, Jean Y Wu, Jason Chuang, Christopher D Manning, Andrew Y Ng, and Christopher Potts. 2013. Recursive deep models for semantic compositionality over a sentiment treebank.

In *Proceedings of Empirical Methods for Natural Language Processing (EMNLP)*, Seattle, WA.

Alessandro Sordoni, Michel Galley, Michael Auli, Chris Brockett, Yangfeng Ji, Meg Mitchell, Jian-Yun Nie, Jianfeng Gao, and Bill Dolan. 2015. A neural network approach to context-sensitive generation of conversational responses. In *Proceedings of the North American Chapter of the Association for Computational Linguistics (NAACL)*, Denver, CO, May.

Nitish Srivastava, Geoffrey Hinton, Alex Krizhevsky, Ilya Sutskever, and Ruslan Salakhutdinov. 2014. Dropout: A simple way to prevent neural networks from overfitting. *The Journal of Machine Learning Research*, 15(1):1929–1958.

Andreas Stolcke, Klaus Ries, Noah Coccaro, Elizabeth Shriberg, Rebecca Bates, Daniel Jurafsky, Paul Taylor, Rachel Martin, Carol Van Ess-Dykema, and Marie Meteer. 2000. Dialogue act modeling for automatic tagging and recognition of conversational speech. *Computational linguistics*, 26(3):339–373.

Joseph Turian, Lev Ratinov, and Yoshua Bengio. 2010. Word representations: A simple and general method for semi-supervised learning. pages 384–394.

Tian Wang and Kyunghyun Cho. 2015. Larger-context language modelling. *arXiv preprint arXiv:1511.03729*.

Nick Webb, Mark Hepple, and Yorick Wilks. 2005. Dialogue act classification based on intra-utterance features. In *Proceedings of the AAAI Workshop on Spoken Language Understanding*.

Bonnie Webber, Markus Egg, and Valia Kordoni. 2012. Discourse structure and language technology. *Journal of Natural Language Engineering*, 1.

Jason D Williams and Steve Young. 2007. Partially observable markov decision processes for spoken dialog systems. *Computer Speech & Language*, 21(2):393–422.

Nianwen Xue, Hwee Tou Ng, Sameer Pradhan, Rashmi Prasad, Christopher Bryant, and Attapol T Rutherford. 2015. The CoNLL-2015 shared task on shallow discourse parsing. In *Proceedings of the Conference on Natural Language Learning (CoNLL)*.

Biao Zhang, Jinsong Su, Deyi Xiong, Yaojie Lu, Hong Duan, and Junfeng Yao. 2015. Shallow convolutional neural network for implicit discourse relation recognition. In *Proceedings of Empirical Methods for Natural Language Processing (EMNLP)*, pages 2230–2235, Lisbon, September.

Questioning Arbitrariness in Language:
a Data-Driven Study of Conventional Iconicity

Ekaterina Abramova
Radboud University Nijmegen
e.abramova@ftr.ru.nl

Raquel Fernández
University of Amsterdam
raquel.fernandez@uva.nl

Abstract

This paper presents a data-driven investigation of *phonesthemes*, phonetic units said to carry meaning associations, thus challenging the traditionally assumed arbitrariness of language. Phonesthemes have received a substantial amount of attention within the cognitive science literature on sound iconicity, but nevertheless remain a controversial and understudied phenomenon. Here we employ NLP techniques to address two main questions: How can the existence of phonesthemes be tested at a large scale with quantitative methods? And how can the meaning arguably carried by a phonestheme be induced automatically from word embeddings? We develop novel methods to make progress on these fronts and compare our results to previous work, obtaining substantial improvements.

1 Introduction

It has long been held in linguistics that since the same concept can be expressed with words whose forms do not resemble each other (e.g., English *dog* vs. Italian *cane* vs. German *Hund*), there is no intrinsic link between how words sound and what they mean. This feature—*arbitrariness*—is often considered a hallmark of human language (Saussure, 1916; Hockett, 1959). At the same time, however, over the last decades, mounting evidence from psycholinguistic studies (Markel and Hamp, 1960; Ohala, 1984; Fordyce, 1989) has shown that speakers do in fact associate words that contain a particular form with certain meaning—that is, there is a degree of *iconicity* in language in addition to arbitrari-

ness, which has been claimed to benefit language learning (Monaghan and Christiansen, 2006; Monaghan et al., 2014).

Non-arbitrary form-meaning associations come in two basic varieties: primary iconicity (also called 'true') and secondary (or 'conventional') iconicity. In the former, the sound is thought to directly resemble the meaning, as in onomatopoeia.[1] In the latter, the relationship is a statistical regularity according to which words that share similar sounds tend to be also similar in meaning, such as a large proportion of English words that end with the sound /-æʃ/ (e.g., *crash, slash, mash, trash, dash*) being related to destructive action or collision (Hutchins, 1998). The phonetic units that exhibit conventional meaning regularities of this latter kind are called *phonesthemes* and are the focus of the present paper. In particular, we investigate two main questions: (1) how can the existence of phonesthemes be tested at a large scale by means of a data-driven method? and (2) how can the meaning arguably conveyed by a phonestheme be derived automatically?

Phonesthemes are traditionally distinguished from morphemes in being non-compositional. That is, *unthinkable* can be thought of as being composed of morphemes *un-* (meaning *not*), *think*, and *-able* (meaning *capable of*), all contributing to the overall meaning of "incapable of being thought" and susceptible of being combined with other units with predictable semantic effects (e.g., *un-drinkable, think-er*). On the other hand, *crash* is not con-

---

[1]Although, the relationship can still be modified by phonetic features of a particular language, e.g., the rooster says *cock-a-doodle-doo* in English but *kikiriki* in German.

Proceedings of NAACL-HLT 2016, pages 343–352,
San Diego, California, June 12-17, 2016. ©2016 Association for Computational Linguistics

sidered to be formed compositionally from *cr-* and *-ash*, since these components do not possesses an easily identifiable independent meaning that can be combined productively with other morphemes.

Because phonesthemes challenge defining features of language such as arbitrariness and compositionality, they remain a rather controversial and poorly understood phenomenon. To a large extent, this is due to methodological issues. Early evidence for the existence of phonesthemes consisted primarily in linguists pointing out instances of intuitive correlations between a phonetic unit and the meaning of words containing that unit (Marchand, 1959; Reid, 1967), while early psycholinguistic experiments attempted to elicit meaning definitions for predefined lists of (real or nonsense) words sharing a phonetic unit traditionally considered to be a phonestheme (Fordyce, 1989; Abelin, 1999; Magnus, 2000). More systematic studies have subsequently been carried out by Hutchins (1998) and Bergen (2004), but overall the phenomenon of conventional linguistic iconicity as reflected in phonesthemes remains largely understudied, certainly within the computational linguistics community.

In this paper, we investigate phonesthemes by analyzing their orthographic correlates in a large corpus of written English, leveraging word embeddings constructed with `word2vec` and made available by Baroni et al. (2014). In particular, we make the following contributions:

- We develop a stricter test than previously done in the literature for deciding whether a unit exhibits conventional iconicity.

- We propose a new unsupervised method to induce the meaning conveyed by a phonesthemic unit.

- We evaluate our meaning induction method with new automatic evaluation techniques and compare its performance to a WordNet-based method proposed by Abramova et al. (2013), obtaining a very substantial improvement.

- We additionally evaluate our automatically derived meanings with human judgments collected via a crowdsourcing experiment.

We believe phonesthemes deserve thorough investigation for both theoretical and practical reasons. Theoretically, adding more data-driven methods can substantially enhance work in linguistics and psycholinguistics. Within computational linguistics itself, cross-fertilization with computational morphology (Wang et al., 2012; Marelli and Baroni, 2015), is an exciting avenue to be pursued. With respect to potential applications of automatic phonestheme meaning induction, creative brand naming (Klink, 2000; Özbal and Strapparava, 2012), sentiment analysis (Sokolova and Bobicev, 2009) and construction of more appropriate language teaching materials (Imai et al., 2008) are viable possibilities.

2   Related Work

Psycholinguistic studies on the nature of phonesthemes have shown that people tend to associate certain sounds with a particular meaning. Such studies were conducted on different languages, employing different methods and exhibiting various degrees of scale and systematicity (Fordyce, 1989; Abelin, 1999; Magnus, 2000; Hutchins, 1998). Recently, it has also been shown that phonesthemes affect online implicit language processing (Bergen, 2004) and language learning (Parault and Schwanenflugel, 2006).

What also emerged from these studies is that phonesthemes are not a homogeneous phenomenon. They can vary in terms of the number of words that contain a given phonestheme, their frequencies, the strength of their association with the core meaning of a phonestheme (for example measured as an average of human ratings for all the words that comprise the given phonesthemic cluster) and the regularity of that association (what proportion of words in the whole cluster are highly related to the predicted meaning). However, psycholinguistic data is to some extent ambiguous on how these features of phonesthemes affect their productivity, learnability and their effect on language processing, which could partly be due the methods being employed. For example, in order to determine the regularity of sound-meaning association, Bergen (2004) consults word definitions in Websters 7th collegiate dictionary and counts how many of those words bear the required meaning for a given phonestheme. The procedure requires an intuitive judgment from the experimenter in determining the meaning of a phonestheme and estimating whether a given word has that meaning, and as a result is prone to experimenter bias and does not allow for large-scale testing. Finding a more automatic method for assessing phonestheme features and determining their meaning could thus alleviate this type of research liabilities.

Otis and Sagi (2008) and Abramova et al. (2013) are two studies that attempted to test for the existence of phonesthemes in a corpus-based automatic manner. For both the guiding question was: are words that contain a given phonetic unit, thought to be a phonestheme, more semantically similar than would be expected by chance? Using distributional models they compared the average cosine similarity of the vectors that correspond to phonestheme-bearing words to similarly sized groups of random words. Both studies found support for a sizable proportion of phonetic units tested. However, it could still be questioned whether the comparison was sufficiently strict, given that sets of random words which do not overlap in form have a priori lower chance of being semantically related than sets of words that share a phonestheme. Therefore, in the first part of our study (Section 4) we present a stricter validation method for candidate phonesthemes that also includes considerations related to morphological diversity, which were ignored in previous work.

Abramova et al. (2013) presented the first attempt to automatically assign meaning to sets of phonestheme-bearing words. The authors viewed the task as an instance of unsupervised ontology acquisition in the style of Widdows (2003) and used WordNet to assign over-arching labels to phonesthemic groups of words. While the approach was moderately successful in inducing WordNet labels that were in the direction predicted by the literature for a few phonesthemes (e.g., *gl*-containing words were assigned light-related labels), most phonesthemes did not receive meaningful labels according to the meanings typically associated with phonesthemes in the sound iconicity literature. The authors surmise that the failure could be due to the nature of WordNet, e.g., that it reflects only one type of semantic relation (hypernymy) which might not exhaust the links between words that share a phonestheme. In Section 5, we present a different approach to phonestheme meaning induction that exploits the properties of word embeddings in a fully unsupervised manner and yields substantially better results.

3 Data

Candidate phonesthemes. Following the studies of Hutchins (1998), we compile a list of possible phonesthemes of interest and their respective semantic glosses (more on the latter in Section 5). We will refer to these units as "candidate phonesthemes" because they all have been considered phonesthemes by previous qualitative studies and our aim is to investigate whether their alleged phenesthemic status is warranted quantitatively. Specifically, we focus on two-consonant units in word-initial position, which we will often call prefixes.[2] We focus on the 16 prefix candidate phonesthemes listed in Table 1. Since we work with orthographic correlates of phonetic units, we restrict ourselves to prefixes that have clear orthographic–phonetic mappings, discarding prefixes that allow for variation, such as *sc-/sk-*.[3]

bl-	*cl-*	*cr-*	*dr-*	*fl-*	*gl -*	*gr-*	*sl-*
sm-	*sn-*	*sp-*	*st-*	*sw-*	*tr-*	*tw-*	*wr-*

Table 1: Candidate phonesthemes considered.

Word embeddings. For our experiments, we use existing, high-quality word embeddings created and made available by Baroni et al. (2014).[4] We use the best performing model amongst those tested by Baroni and colleagues, which has been constructed with word2vec[5] using the CBOW approach proposed by Mikolov et al. (2013). The model contains 400-dimension vectors generated by considering the 300K most frequent word tokens (without lemmatization) in a large corpus comprising the English Wikipedia, the web-based corpus ukWaC (Baroni et al., 2009), and the BNC (Burnard, 2007).

Unfamiliar or very technical words are unlikely to contribute to the formation of sound-meaning associations (Hutchins, 1998). Accordingly, from the 300K target words present in the distributional model, we discard those that are not recognized by a

---

[2]Recall, however, that they do not correspond to morphological prefixes.

[3]Such alternation-susceptible prefixes are excluded from all analyses, including the baseline clusters introduced later on in Section 4.

[4]`http://clic.cimec.unitn.it/composes/semantic-vectors.html`

[5]`https://code.google.com/p/word2vec/`

comprehensive off-the-shelf English spell-checking dictionary. This results in a substantial reduction of the target vocabulary: 61,122 tokens remain after the filtering.[6] We use this restricted set of words and corresponding embeddings in all our experiments.

4 Phonestheme Validation

The aim of the first experiment is to investigate which of the candidate prefixes in Table 1 have phonesthemic character and thus evince conventional iconicity.

4.1 Methods

For a prefix to exhibit conventional iconicity, the words sharing that prefix must be semantically similar, while being morphologically diverse—i.e., their semantic relatedness must stem from their shared sound (as captured by the prefix's orthographic form), and not from their sharing of a common morpheme.

Semantic similarity factors. We start by assessing the degree of semantic similarity exhibited by all the words in the vocabulary that share a candidate phonestheme, which we refer to as candidate *phonesthemic clusters*. Our aim is to conduct a stricter test than previously done in the literature. Therefore, rather than comparing candidate phonesthemic clusters to sets of random words, as done by Otis and Sagi (2008) and Abramova et al. (2013), we compare them to words that share a random two-consonant prefix that is non-phonesthemic, i.e., not present in our list of candidate phonesthemes. Our vocabulary contains a total of 307 non-phonesthemic two-consonant prefixes. We refer to the sets of words sharing these prefixes as *baseline clusters*. For our subsequent analyses we use only 191 baseline clusters which contain between 10 and 2000 words. Naturally, such baseline clusters will contain words that are morphologically and hence semantically related, which offers a more challenging baseline.

____

[6]In particular, we use the spell-checking Python library PyEnchant for English; see https://pythonhosted.org/pyenchant/api/enchant.html. Many of the terms removed with this filtering mechanism correspond to non-words or named entities present in the corpus.

In our first similarity test, we compute cosine similarities for all possible pairs of words within every phonesthemic and baseline cluster. We then run 191 independent-samples one-tailed Welch's t-tests for each candidate phonestheme, comparing its pair-wise similarity to the pair-wise similarity of each of the baseline clusters. For each candidate phonesthemic cluster, we record how many t-tests indicated significantly higher similarity than the baseline (using a Bonferroni-corrected threshold of $\alpha = .05/191$) as well as the effect size (Cohen's d) of the successful t-tests. Based on the binomial distribution (with $\alpha=.05$), we obtain a significance threshold of 108—we hence judge a candidate prefix to exhibit significantly higher similarity than the baseline if more than 108 out of 191 t-tests are successful.

Our second similarity test is a check on the overall semantic cohesiveness of the candidate phonesthemic clusters. We calculate the average of all the pairwise similarities within our 191 baseline clusters. We then compare the average pairwise similarity of each candidate phonesthemic cluster to the distribution of the average similarity of the baseline clusters. We expect a positive correlation between the number of successful t-test per candidate phonestheme and their average similarity.

Morphological diversity factors. Since high semantic similarity could be due to the presence of a large proportion of morphologically related words rather than to a sound-meaning association, we want to balance similarity-based factors with considerations about the morphological diversity of the word clusters we investigate. In general, the larger the size of a cluster, the higher the chance for morphological diversity and the lower the chance for finding high semantic cohesiveness. Hence, we would expect a negative correlation between cluster size and semantic similarity.

In previous studies (Hutchins, 1998; Otis and Sagi, 2008) the impact of morphology is counteracted by manually removing morphologically related words before testing for semantic cohesiveness. Since one of our aims is to minimize manual intervention, we instead take into account morphological relatedness at the validation phase. To that end, we implement a crude lemmatization procedure and use the ratio between the number of words and the number of lemmas in a cluster to estimate morphological diversity.[7]

The higher this ratio, the lower the morphological diversity—with the maximum value being equal to the size of the cluster when all words are reducible to a single lemma. We calculate this proxy of morphological diversity for candidate phonesthemic clusters and baseline clusters.

Validation constraints. Given the factors described above, we judge a candidate prefix to be a phonestheme if all the following conditions hold:

- *pairwise semantic similarity* is significantly higher than the baseline (according to our first semantic similarity analysis test)
- *average effect size* (Cohen's d) of pairwise similarity tests is at least 0.2
- *average semantic similarity* is higher than 2 standard errors above the average baseline similarity ($\mu = 0.1260, SE = 0.0038$)
- *ratio words/lemmas* is lower than 3 standard errors above the average ratio calculated for baseline clusters ($\mu = 2.93, SE = 0.0615$)

We have chosen each of the thresholds to be reasonably strong but not too restrictive since we rely on a combination of constraints. We deemed an average effect size of 0.2 sufficient given the strictness of our comparison method. The average semantic similarity of the phonesthemic cluster was required to be at least 2 standard errors above average similarity of the baseline clusters to approximate the conventional one-tailed alpha level of 0.025. Finally, a stricter threshold of 3 standard errors was chosen for the lemma ratio just to exclude cases of prefixes that have abnormally low morphological diversity. A stricter condition (requiring high diversity) does not seem justified since there is no reason to expect phonestheme-bearing words to be *more* morphologically diverse than average. The candidate phonestheme was judged to be significant when all constraints were simultaneously satisfied.

---

[7]Since our data consists of word embeddings (generalizing over contexts), an off-the-shelf lemmatizer is not effective. Instead we implement a lemmatizer dictionary based on the raw and lemmatized versions of the British National Corpus (Burnard, 2007). The lemma is retrieved if a given word is in the dictionary. Otherwise, we apply two state-of-the-art stemmers, first Lancaser, then Porter (this order was chosen after qualitative examination of a few examples).

4.2 Results

We apply the validation methods to our data. As a sanity check, we test whether the information encoded in the word embeddings is consistent with the data used in previous experiments: Indeed, the average similarity of the 16 candidate prefixes tested is positively correlated with the human ratings for semantic cohesiveness collected by Hutchins (1998) ($r = .46$), and with the similarity values reported by Otis and Sagi (2008) ($r = .68$) and Abramova et al. (2013) ($r = .58$).[8]

As predicted, the correlation between the average number of successful t-tests and average similarity is high ($r = .93$), suggesting that both methods are equally valid for evaluating semantic cohesiveness of phonesthemic clusters. Cluster size (both raw and as the number of lemmas) is negatively correlated with all semantic similarity measures, i.e. average pairwise similarity, average number of successful t-tests, and average effect size ($r \approx -.7$). This is consistent with the experimental finding by Hutchins (1998), who obtained lower human ratings for larger clusters of words.

Regarding evidence for conventional iconicity, the following six prefixes meet all our validation constraints: *bl-*, *gl-*, *sm-*, *sn-*, *sw-*, and *tw-*. Of the remaining 10 prefixes tested, 3 fail all constraints (*cl-*, *cr-*, *tr-*), 3 fail only the morphological diversity constraint (*gr-*, *sp-*, *st-*), and the rest fail some combination of constraints.[9] The 6 validated prefixes are a proper subset of the candidate phonesthemes validated according to the less strict methods used in earlier approaches: Otis and Sagi (2008) found support for *dr-* and *wr-* in addition to our 6 supported phonesthemes and Abramova et al. (2013) discarded only *cr-*, *sp-*, and *tr-* amongst our 16 candidates. This shows that our proposed validation procedure provides a compatible as well as stricter test for evidence of phonesthemic conventional iconicity.

5 Phonestheme Meaning Induction

The quantitative results presented so far show that, according to our validation constraints, some can-

---

[8]Recall that each of these studies uses a different corpus.

[9]Supplementary material including full details of the validation results for all candidate phonesthemes is available at `http://tinyurl.com/phonesthemes-naacl2016`.

bl-	to blow, swell, inflate; or to be round, swollen, or globular in shape	*bloat, blob, blow*
gl-	having to do with light or with vision; or something visually salient	*glow, glitter, glimmer*
sm-	a belittling, insulting, or pejorative term	*smirk, smother, smug*
sn-	related to the nose, or breathing; also snobbishness, inquisitiveness	*snout, sniff, sneeze*
sw-	to oscillate, undulate, or move rhythmically to and fro	*sway, swing, swoosh*
tw-	to turn, distort, entangle, or oscillate; or the result of such an action	*twist, twitch, tweak*

Table 2: Meaning glosses from Hutchins (1998, pp. 66–70) for the six validated phonesthemic prefixes, with example words.

didate phonesthemes do have phonesthemic character: they are present in words that are semantically similar while not being highly morphologically related. But what is the 'meaning' that these phonetic units convey? In this section, we aim at investigating whether the kind of meanings that have been informally proposed for these units in the sound iconicity literature can be derived using fully unsupervised methods.

In addition, we present ways for automatically evaluating the derived meanings, and finally conduct a human evaluation experiment via crowdsourcing.

5.1 Methods

Gold standard. We construct a set of gold standard meaning labels for each validated phonestheme by taking as a starting point the informal glosses provided by Hutchins (1998), who, in turn, compiled them by inspecting previous literature by Firth (1930), Marchand (1959), Wescott (1971) and others. The glosses for our validated phonesthemes are given in Table 2.[10] From each gloss, we extract the content words (ignoring words that bear the given phonestheme to avoid circular results) and manually discard words that play only an instrumental role in the definition. For example, in the following gloss for the phonestheme *sn-*, we keep the words in italics and discard the rest: "related to the *nose*, or *breathing*; or by metaphorical extension to snobbishness, *inquisitiveness*". Since the resulting lists of words are to some extent arbitrary (derived from intuitions of a single scholar), we extend them by manually adding synonyms of each of the initial seed words

until each phonestheme is associated with 25 gold labels.[11]

Meaning induction. We generate an abstract meaning representation for a phonestheme by computing the centroid of the phonestheme-bearing word cluster. Our method for inducing the core meaning conveyed by a phonestheme is then very simple: We extract the nearest neighbors of the phonestheme centroid, with the constraint that these neighboring words cannot be members of the cluster themselves (i.e., must not exhibit the prefix in question). This method outputs an ordered set of words or *meaning labels*, which we can then evaluate against the gold standard labels.

As described in Section 2, the only previous attempt at automatically deriving the meaning of phonesthemes is due to Abramova et al. (2013). Their approach is inspired by the work of Widdows (2003) on ontology acquisition and it consists in assigning to a phonesthemic cluster the WordNet synsets that subsume as many as possible of the cluster words as closely as possible (i.e., within as few as possible intervening levels in the WordNet hierarchy). As discussed in that paper, this method does not only have the disadvantage of relying on a hand-crafted ontology. Other shortcomings include Word-Net's limited coverage in terms of vocabulary and type of semantic relations considered (mostly, hyponymy and synonymy).

For comparison purposes, we apply the Word-Net meaning induction method of Abramova et al. (2013) and compare its performance to the unsupervised centroid method we propose.

---

[10]The semantic glosses for the remaining candidate phonesthemes can be found at `http://tinyurl.com/phonesthemes-naacl2016`.

[11]We consult an online edition of Roget's thesaurus (`thesaurus.com`) and retrieve only the synonyms that correspond to the relevant sense of a seed word, e.g., *light* in the sense of *illuminated*, not in the sense of *blond*.

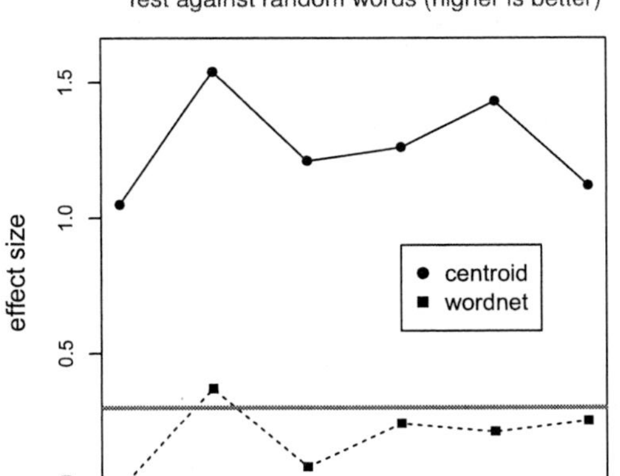
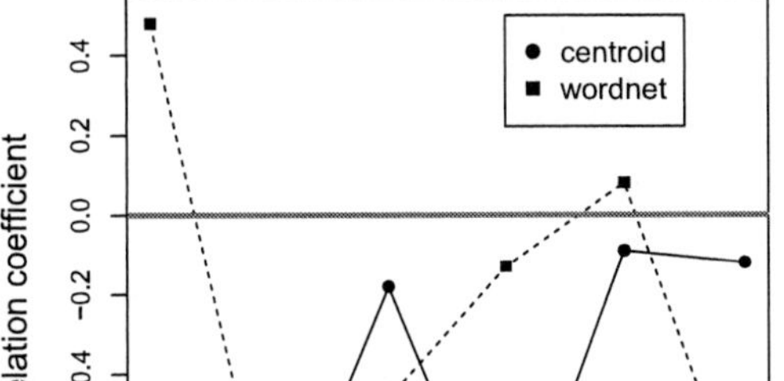

Figure 1: Evaluation of meaning induction methods. Left: only labels induced for prefixes above the horizontal line are significantly better than random labels. Right: negative coefficient scores shown below the line indicate better labels at the top of the list.

Automatic evaluation measures. Abramova et al. (2013) only offer an informal qualitative evaluation of their WordNet-based meaning labels. Here we propose two complementary ways of quantitatively evaluating induced phonesthemic meanings.

For our first meaning label evaluation test, we use a Monte Carlo analysis to determine whether generated labels are closer in vector space to gold labels than random sets of words. More specifically, for each phonesthemic cluster, we compute the *generated–gold similarities*, i.e., pairwise cosine similarities between all the generated labels and the gold set. We then create 100 sets of words, each composed of 25 words randomly drawn from the vocabulary and compute the *random–gold similarities*, i.e., pairwise cosine similarities between these sets of random words and the gold set. Next, we run 100 independent-samples one-tailed Welch's t-tests recording how many t-tests indicated significantly higher generated-gold similarity than random-gold (using a Bonferroni-corrected threshold of $\alpha = .05/100$). We also record the effect sizes (Cohen's d) of the successful t-tests. We repeat the procedure 3 times and take the average of these measures. Based on the binomial distribution (with $\alpha = .05$ and $p = .5$), we judge obtaining at least 59 successful t-tests to indicate that the generated labels are better than random baseline at capturing the phonesthemic meaning.

Our second evaluation test exploits the fact that both our centroid method and the WordNet method output ordered sets of labels (from more to less suitable). We are interested in testing whether the generated meaning labels are more similar to the gold labels the closer they are to the top of the list. To that end, we again compute the pairwise average similarity of each generated label with the gold label set and look at the correlation of that measure with the position k of the generated label. We expect similarity to decrease as k increases: Hence a strongly negative correlation indicates that the method retrieves the best labels first.

5.2 Results

Automatic analysis. We compare the meaning labels induced with our unsupervised centroid method to those generated with the WordNet method. An overview of the results can be seen in Figure 1. Regarding the first label evaluation test (*generated–gold similarities* vs. *random–gold similarities*; left plot in the figure), centroid overwhelmingly outperforms WordNet: Our method obtains significant results with high effect size for all phonestheme prefixes considered, while with the WordNet method only the labels derived for *gl-* are significantly more similar to the gold standard than random words.[12]

Regarding the order-sensitive evaluation measure

---

[12]In line with the informal evaluation by Abramova et al. (2013), who find that their meaning labels only seem to make sense for *gl-*.

(ranking of induced labels, right plot in Figure 1), with the centroid method we obtain negative correlations for all phonesthemes, although rather weak for *sw- tw-*, and *sm-*. This shows that the top induced labels tend to be closer to the gold meaning. Although the WordNet method again obtains results that are poorer overall, there are strong negative correlations for two phonesthemes: *gl-* and *tw-*.

Taken together, the results indicate that the WordNet method might be able to generate a few of good labels at the top of the list, especially when these labels are associated with the phonestheme-bearing words by hypernymy (e.g., the top *gl-* labels are *brightness, flash, radiance, lightness, look*). However, the remaining labels are mostly generic concepts such as *entity* and *object*, which do not produce significant results when compared as a group to the gold labels. The centroid method produces better labels overall as well as better labels at the top of the list. For example, the top *gl-* labels are *shimmered, twinkled, satiny* but it is also able to capture the meaning of other phonesthemes: the pejorative *sm-* receives *stunk* and *leered* as the top two and twisting and oscillating *tw-*'s top label is *waggled*.

Human evaluation. In addition to the automatic label evaluation procedures we have developed, we test our induced meaning labels against human judgments. What we aim at testing here is whether the semantic closeness to the gold standard meaning that we have been able to detect in vector space can actually be perceived by speakers.

We conducted a data collection study using the crowdsourcing platform CrowdFlower.[13] To prepare the stimuli, for each of the six validated phonesthemes we selected the 10 most frequent gold labels,[14] the 10 top labels induced with our centroid method, and 10 words randomly drawn from the vocabulary, with a BNC frequency of at least 100 to try to minimize the presence of words possibly unknown to the participants. The 100 cut-off is justified given that the average frequency of the gold labels is not significantly higher than the average frequency of all words above this threshold ($t = 1.876$, $p < 0.05$).

Prefix	AvgCount	Stats
bl-	5.53	$t(29) = 1.35$
gl-	6.57	$t(29) = 4.37$**
sm-	5.93	$t(29) = 2.04$*
sn-	6.7	$t(29) = 4.12$**
sw-	4.93	$t(29) = -0.18$
tw-	7.8	$t(29) = 5.66$**

Table 3: Results of human evaluation: avg. number of times an induced label was selected (N=30). *=p<0.05, **=p<0.001

An annotation item consisted of the set of gold words and 10 pairs of induced-vs-random labels (randomized in order). The participants were asked to judge which of the words in each pair was more related to the set of gold words.[15] We constructed 10 annotation items per phonestheme (including the same top 10 induced labels but paired with different random words) and for each annotation item we collected judgments from three different subjects (thus $N = 30$ items per phonestheme).

To analyze the results, we counted how many times an automatically induced label was selected as more similar to the gold label set than a random word. We performed a t-test with an alternative hypothesis that the mean number of selected induced labels per item is greater than 5 (i.e., greater than chance since there were 10 pairs to be judged per item). Automatically induced labels for 4 out of 6 phonesthemes (*gl-*, *sm-*, *sn-* and *tw-*) were judged to be related to the gold meaning to a higher degree than random words. Detailed results are in Table 3.

The fact that we obtain significant results indicates that our generated labels are meaningful not only according to automatic evaluation measures but also in terms of what speakers can perceive. However, the pattern of which phonesthemic labels receive better human judgments is somewhat less clear. For example, the appropriateness of the *gl-* labels is highly significant according to human judgment as well as both automatic tests (effect size and average similarity correlation with k). At the same time, while the *sw-* labels achieve a high effect size (see left plot in Figure 1), they are not judged signif-

---

[13]http://www.crowdflower.com/

[14]According to the BNC frequency lists: https://www.kilgarriff.co.uk/bnc-readme.html

[15]A screenshot of the instructions given to the participants can be found at http://tinyurl.com/phonesthemes-naacl2016.

icant in our human study. The pattern is reversed for *tw-*. Whether this exposes a real difference in sensitivity to phonesthemic meanings in human judgments compared to vector-based methods, remains an open question.

6 Conclusions

The analysis we have presented in this paper confirms that the connection between sound and meaning is not always entirely arbitrary and shows that this can be detected using the properties of word embeddings. We find, in line with previous computational and psycholinguistic studies, that words that share certain phonetic prefixes without being morphologically related are more semantically similar that would be expected by chance. In particular, our phonestheme validation procedure is stricter compared to previous work since we use sets of words that share a random two-consonant prefix as baseline and, importantly, take into account morphological relatedness. According to our more principled and stricter constraints, the following six consonant prefixes exhibit symptoms of conventional sound iconicity: *bl-*, *gl-*, *sm-*, *sn-*, *sw-*, and *tw-*. The validation method we employ could serve as a starting point for discovering new phonesthemes. For example, we could inquire whether any of the two-consonant clusters that we consider a baseline is in fact a previously unrecognized phonestheme.

The second aspect we have addressed concerns the automatic induction of the meaning conveyed by a phonestheme. Up to now, the arguable meanings of phonesthemes have been approximated informally by scholars (Hutchins, 1998; Bergen, 2004). To make progress on this front, we have proposed a fully unsupervised meaning induction method that relies on extracting semantic nearest neighbors of a phonesthemic cluster centroid in vector space. We have shown that this method achieves substantially better results than the WordNet-based method of our previous work (Abramova et al., 2013), generating meaning labels that are closer to the meanings proposed in the theoretical literature. For a subset of phonesthemes (4 out of 6: *gl-*, *sm-*, *sn-* and *tw-*), the higher suitability of the centroid-based meaning labels (as compared to random words) was also detected by human evaluators. Although there is ob-

viously room for improvement, we think that these results are very promising given that this is the first data-driven study addressing this problem in an unsupervised manner.

References

Åsa Abelin. 1999. *Studies in sound symbolism*. Ph.D. thesis, Göteborg: Göteborg University.

Ekaterina Abramova, Raquel Fernández, and Federico Sangati. 2013. Automatic labeling of phonesthemic senses. In *Proceedings of the 35th Annual Conference of the Cognitive Science Society*, pages 1696–1701. Cognitive Science Society.

Marco Baroni, Silvia Bernardini, Adriano Ferraresi, and Eros Zanchetta. 2009. The wacky wide web: a collection of very large linguistically processed web-crawled corpora. *Language resources and evaluation*, 43(3):209–226.

Marco Baroni, Georgiana Dinu, and Germán Kruszewski. 2014. Don't count, predict! a systematic comparison of context-counting vs. context-predicting semantic vectors. In *Proceedings of ACL-2014*, volume 1, pages 238–247.

Benjamin K. Bergen. 2004. The psychological reality of phonaesthemes. *Language*, 80(2):290–311.

Lou Burnard, editor. 2007. *Reference Guide for the British National Corpus (XML Edition)*. Oxford Universtity Computing Services.

John R. Firth. 1930. *Speech*. Ernest Benn, London.

James Forrest Fordyce. 1989. *Studies in sound symbolism with special reference to English*. University Microfilm International.

Charles F. Hockett. 1959. Animal "languages" and human language. *Human Biology*, 31(1):32–39.

Sharon S. Hutchins. 1998. *The psychological reality, variability, and compositionality of English phonesthemes*. Ph.D. thesis, Atlanta: Emory University.

Mutsumi Imai, Sotaro Kita, Miho Nagumo, and Hiroyuki Okada. 2008. Sound symbolism facilitates early verb learning. *Cognition*, 109(1):54–65.

Richard R. Klink. 2000. Creating brand names with meaning: The use of sound symbolism. *Marketing Letters*, 11:5–20.

Margaret Magnus. 2000. *What's in a word? Evidence for phonosemantics*. Ph.D. thesis, Trondheim, Norway: University of Trondheim.

Hans Marchand. 1959. Phonetic symbolism in english word formations. *Indogermanische Forschungen*, 64:146–168.

Marco Marelli and Marco Baroni. 2015. Affixation in semantic space: Modeling morpheme meanings with compositional distributional semantics. *Psychological Review*, in press.

Norman N. Markel and Eric P. Hamp. 1960. Connotative meanings of certain phoneme sequences. *Studies in Linguistics*, 15(1):47–61.

Tomas Mikolov, Ilya Sutskever, Kai Chen, Greg S Corrado, and Jeff Dean. 2013. Distributed representations of words and phrases and their compositionality. In *Proceedings of NIPS*, pages 3111–3119.

Padraic Monaghan and Morten H. Christiansen. 2006. Why form-meaning mappings are not entirely arbitrary in language. *Proceedings of the 28th annual conference of the Cognitive Science Society*, pages 1838–1843.

Padraic Monaghan, Richard C. Shillcock, Morten H. Christiansen, and Simon Kirby. 2014. How arbitrary is language? *Philosophical Transactions of the Royal Society of London B: Biological Sciences*, 369(1651).

John J. Ohala. 1984. An ethological perspective on common Cross-Language utilization of fo of voice1. *Phonetica*, 41:1–16.

Katya Otis and Eyal Sagi. 2008. Phonaesthemes: A corpus-based analysis. In *Proceedings of the 30th Annual Meeting of the Cognitive Science Society*, pages 65–70.

Gözde Özbal and Carlo Strapparava. 2012. A computational approach to the automation of creative naming. In *Proceedings of the 50th Annual Meeting of the Association for Computational Linguistics: Long Papers - Volume 1*, ACL '12, pages 703–711, Stroudsburg, PA, USA. Association for Computational Linguistics.

Susan J Parault and Paula J Schwanenflugel. 2006. Sound-symbolism: A piece in the puzzle of word learning. *Journal of Psycholinguistic Research*, 35(4):329–351.

David Reid. 1967. *Sound Symbolism*. T&A Constable.

Ferdinand de Saussure. 1916. Course in general linguistics.

Marina Sokolova and Victoria Bobicev. 2009. Classification of emotion words in russian and romanian languages. In *RANLP*, pages 416–420.

Hsueh-Cheng Wang, Li-Chuan Hsu, Yi-Min Tien, and Marc Pomplun. 2012. Estimating semantic transparency of constituents of english compounds and two-character chinese words using latent semantic analysis. In *Proceedings of CogSci*.

Roger Wescott. 1971. Linguistic iconism. *Language*, 47:416–428.

Dominic Widdows. 2003. Unsupervised methods for developing taxonomies by combining syntactic and statistical information. In *Proc. HLT-NAACL*.

Distinguishing Literal and Non-Literal Usage of German Particle Verbs

Maximilian Köper   **Sabine Schulte im Walde**
Institut für Maschinelle Sprachverarbeitung
Universität Stuttgart, Germany
`{maximilian.koeper,schulte}@ims.uni-stuttgart.de`

Abstract

This paper provides a binary, token-based classification of German particle verbs (PVs) into literal vs. non-literal usage. A random forest improving standard features (e.g., bag-of-words; affective ratings) with PV-specific information and abstraction over common nouns significantly outperforms the majority baseline. In addition, PV-specific classification experiments demonstrate the role of shared particle semantics and semantically related base verbs in PV meaning shifts.

1 Introduction

Automatic detection of non-literal expressions (including metaphors and idioms) is critical for many natural language processing (NLP) tasks such as information extraction, machine translation, and sentiment analysis. For this reason, the last decade has seen an increase in research on identifying literal vs. non-literal meaning (Birke and Sarkar, 2006; Birke and Sarkar, 2007; Li and Sporleder, 2009; Sporleder and Li, 2009; Turney et al., 2011; Shutova et al., 2013; Tsvetkov et al., 2014), as well as the establishment of workshops on metaphorical language in NLP.[1]

In this paper, we explore the prediction of literal vs. non-literal language usage of a computationally challenging class of multiword expressions: German particle verbs (PVs) such as *anlachen* (laugh at) are compositions of a base verb

(BV) such as *lachen* (smile/laugh) and a verb particle such as *an*. German PVs are highly productive (Springorum et al., 2013b; Springorum et al., 2013a), and the particles are notoriously ambiguous (Lechler and Roßdeutscher, 2009; Haselbach, 2011; Springorum, 2011). Furthermore, the particles often trigger (regular) meaning shifts when they combine with base verbs (Springorum et al., 2013b), so the resulting PVs represent frequent cases of non-literal meaning. The contributions of this paper are as follows:

1. We present a random forest classifier that correctly identifies 86.8% of literal vs. non-literal language usage within a novel dataset of 6436 annotated sentences, in comparison to a majority baseline of 64.9%.

2. We successfully incorporate salient PV-specific features and noun clusters in addition to standard bag-of-words features and affective ratings.

3. We demonstrate that PVs with semantically similar particles and semantically similar base verbs can predict each others' literal vs. non-literal language usage.

4. We illustrate the potential and the limits of the most salient classification features in predicting PV non-literal language usage.

In the remainder of this paper we describe previous work on non-literal language identification and computational models of German particle verbs (Section 2), before we introduce our dataset

---

[1] `sites.google.com/site/metaphorinnlp2016/`

Proceedings of NAACL-HLT 2016, pages 353–362,
San Diego, California, June 12-17, 2016. ©2016 Association for Computational Linguistics

on German particle verbs (Section 3), the particle verb features (Section 4), and the experiments, results and analyses (Section 5).

2 Related Work

Previous work relevant to this paper includes research on identifying non-literal language usage, and computational work on (German) particle verb meaning.

Identification of non-literal language usage: Birke and Sarkar (2006), Birke and Sarkar (2007), Li and Sporleder (2009) and Sporleder and Li (2009) performed binary token-based classifications for English datasets, relying on various contextual indicators. Birke & Sarkar exploited seed sets of literal vs. non-literal sentences, and used distributional similarity to classify English verbs. Li & Sporleder defined two models of text cohesion (a cohesion chain and a cohesion graph) to classify V+NP and V+PP combinations. Shutova et al. (2013) performed both metaphor identification and interpretion (by paraphrasing), focusing on English verbs. She relied on a seed set of annotated metaphors and standard verb and noun clustering, to classify literal vs. metaphorical verb senses. Gedigian et al. (2006) also predicted metaphorical meanings of English verb tokens, however heavily relying on manual rather than unsupervised data (i.e. labeled sentences and PropBank annotation) and a maximum entropy classifier. Turney et al. (2011) assumed that metaphorical word usage is correlated with the degree of abstractness of the word's context, and classified word senses in a given context as either literal or metaphorical. Their targets were adjective–noun combinations and verbs. Tsvetkov et al. (2014) presented a language-independent approach to metaphor identification. They used affective ratings, WordNet categories and vector-space word representations to train a metaphor-detecting classifier on English samples, and then applied it to a different target language using bilingual dictionaries.

Computational research on particle verbs was initially concerned with the automatic acquisition of particle verbs from corpora (Baldwin and Villavicencio, 2002; Baldwin, 2005; Villavicencio, 2005).

Afterwards, the main focus has been on modelling the degree of compositionality of particle verbs as based on distributional features (McCarthy et al., 2003; Baldwin et al., 2003; Bannard, 2005). All these approaches were type-based, and predicting the compositionality was mainly concerned with PV–BV similarity, not taking the contribution of the particle into account. In cases where the particle semantics was respected (such as Bannard (2005)), the results were disappointing because modelling particle senses is still an unsolved problem.

Regarding German particle verbs, there has also been a focus on modelling PV compositionality (Kühner and Schulte im Walde, 2010; Bott and Schulte im Walde, 2014; Bott and Schulte im Walde, 2015). As in English, the approaches were all type-based and mainly concerned with PV–BV similarity. Another line of research categorized particle meanings by relating formal semantic definitions to automatic classifications (Rüd, 2012; Springorum et al., 2012). Furthermore, Springorum et al. (2013b) recently provided a corpus-based study on regular meaning shift conditions for German particle verbs.

3 Particle Verb Dataset

We selected 165 particle verbs across 10 particles, based on previous experiments and datasets that incorporated German particle verbs with regular meaning shifts, various degrees of ambiguity, and across frequency ranges (Springorum et al., 2013b; Springorum et al., 2013a; Bott and Schulte im Walde, 2015). For the 165 PVs, we randomly extracted 50 sentences from *DECOW14AX*, a German web corpus containing 12 billion tokens (Schäfer and Bildhauer, 2012; Schäfer, 2015). The sentences were morphologically annotated and parsed using *SMOR* (Faaß et al., 2010), *MarMoT* (Müller et al., 2013) and the MATE dependency parser (Bohnet, 2010). Combining part-of-speech and dependency information, we were able to reliably sample both separated and non-separated PV occurrences ("Der␣Ast␣**bricht␣ab**" vs. "Der␣Ast␣ist␣**abgebrochen**").

Three German native speakers with a linguistic background annotated each of the 8 128 sentences[2] on a 6-point scale [0,5], ranging from clearly literal (0) to clearly non-literal (5) usage. The total agreement of the annotators on all six categories was 43%, Fleiss' κ = 0.35. Dividing the scale into two disjunctive ranges with three categories each ([0,2] and [3,5]), the total agreement of the annotators on the two categories was 79%, Fleiss' κ = 0.70. In the experiments we used the binary-class distinction, and disregarded all cases of disagreement. This final dataset comprises 6436 sentences: 4174 literal and 2262 non-literal uses across 159 particle verbs and 10 particles.[3] Figure 1 shows the distribution of literal and non-literal sentences across the particles.

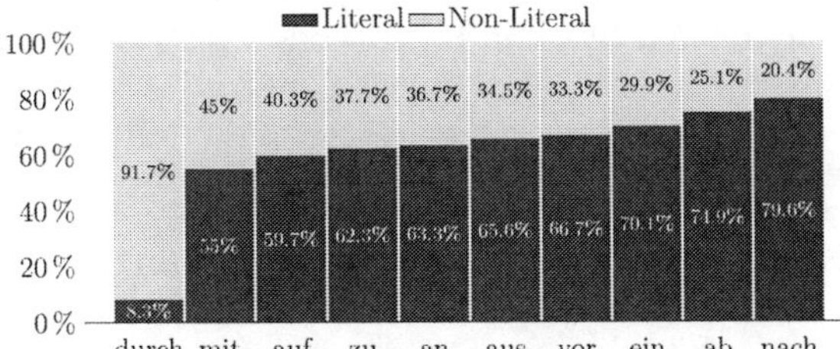

Figure 1: Lit/Non-lit distribution across particles.

4 Particle Verb Features

Our feature space includes standard features to detect non-literal language uses (bags-of-words and affective ratings) as well as PV-specific features and abstraction over common nouns.

4.1 Unigrams

As a standard feature in vector space models, we used all words in the particle verb sentences, i.e., a bag-of-words model relying on unigrams. We expected this standard information to be useful, because some words such as the abstract noun *Hoffnung* (hope) and the concrete noun *Geld* (money) frequently occur with non-literal rather than literal language usage:

1. (non-lit.) "Die Hoffnung **keimte** früh **auf**." *That hope **arose (lit: sprouted)** early.*

2. (non-lit.) "Er versucht das Geld **abzugraben**." *He tries to **demand (lit: dig off)** the money.*

---

[2]Some PVs appeared < 50 times in the corpus.

[3]The dataset is accessible from `http://www.ims.uni-stuttgart.de/data/pv_nonlit`.

To overcome data sparseness, we did not use the unigrams as individual features ($|V|$ = feature space), but implemented this feature as the output of a text-classifier. We relied on the Multinomial Naive Bayes (MNB) classifier by McCallum and Nigam (1998). While the classifier was designed for document classification, we considered a sentence as a document and the possible class outcomes were literal and non-literal.

Noun Clusters Because of the severe data sparseness in our PV feature sets, we performed noun generalization and applied the generalized information to all nouns in our PV contexts. Using all approx. 430000 nouns that appeared >100 times in the *DECOW14AX* corpus, we applied k-Means clustering with $k \in [2, 10000]$. As an alternative to the standard unigrams, we then replaced every noun in the PV sentences with its corresponding cluster tag.

4.2 Affective Ratings

Previous work on detecting non-literal language often makes use of psycholinguistic attributes, namely abstractness and concreteness ratings (Turney et al., 2011), and imageability ratings (Tsvetkov et al., 2014). Words with high abstractness ratings refer to entities that cannot be perceived with our senses; a large subset of which are non-visual (i.e., receive low imageability). It has been shown that non-literal expressions tend to occur with abstract words (*dark humor* versus *dark hair*). We thus expected affective ratings to be useful for particle verbs as well:

1. (lit.) "Den Lippenstift kannst du dir **abschminken**." *You can **remove** the lipstick.*

2. (non-lit.) "Den Job kannst du dir **abschminken**." *You can **forget about** the job.*

We reimplemented the algorithm from (Turney and Littman, 2003) to create large-scale abstractness and imageability ratings for German (Köper and Schulte im Walde, 2016). Based on these ratings, we defined the following (partially redundant) features for the PV sentential contexts:

1. Rating of the PV subject

2. Rating of the PV object

3. Average rating of all nouns (excluding proper names)

4. Average rating of all proper names

5. Average rating of all verbs, excluding the PV

6. Average rating of all adjectives

7. Average rating of all adverbs

While features 3–7 have been adopted from (Turney et al., 2011), features 1–2 represent additional, PV-specific features.

4.3 Distributional Fit of PV, BV and Context

Particle verbs with a meaning shift are non-compositional regarding their base verbs. We thus implemented a PV-specific feature that measures the distributional fit of PVs and their BVs in the PV contexts. For example, looking at the following two PV sentences containing the BV *klingen* (to sound), the context of the first, literal sentence fits well to the BV meaning, but the context of the second, non-literal sentence does not. The distributional fit of the BV in the literal context should therefore be high, but the distributional fit of the BV in the non-literal context should be low.

1. (lit.) "Der Ton der Gitarre **klingt aus.**"
   *The tone of the guitar **fades**.*

2. (non-lit.) "Den Abend lassen wir mit Wein **ausklingen.**" *We **end** the evening with wine.*

To measure the distributional fit of PVs and BVs to PV contexts, we created 400-dimensional word representations using the *hyperwords* toolkit (Levy et al., 2015) and the *DECOW14AX* corpus. We relied on a symmetrical window of size 3 and applied positive pointwise mutual (PPMI) feature weighting together with singular value decomposition (SVD). Based on the word representations, we calculated cosine similarities between the PVs and their contexts, and likewise between the respective BVs and the PV contexts. The contexts we used were the same seven dimensions we used for the affective ratings (cf. Section 4.2). For example, regarding the sentence "Die Katze **springt** auf den Tisch" (*The cat **jumps** on the table*), we calculated the distributional similarity between the PV

"aufspringen" and the subject "Katze", and the distributional similarity between the BV "springen" and the subject "Katze", etc. Each PV–context and each BV–context dimension represents an individual feature.

5 Classification Experiments

In this section, we present a series of binary classification experiments to distinguish literal and non-literal PV usage. Section 5.1 presents the main experiments comparing our features in a global classification setup, and Section 5.2 presents PV-specific additional experiments that zoom into the role of particle types and into the role of semantically related PVs and BVs. Section 5.3 provides a qualitative analysis of the features.

5.1 Main Experiments

We used a random forest with multiple (in our case 100) random decision trees,[4] with each tree voting for an overall classification result. The unigram information was represented by stacking the output of a multinomial naive bayes text classifier as a single feature into the random forest. For all machine learning algorithms we relied on the WEKA toolkit (Witten et al., 2011).

The experiments were performed in two modes, (a) without knowledge of the particle (i.e., the individual particle was not provided as a feature), and (b) with explicit knowledge of the particle. In this way, we could identify the contribution of the particle.

The classification results are shown in Table 1. We report on the feature type, and on the size[5] of the feature set f. We further present literal and non-literal f-scores F_1, and accuracy with and without particle knowledge. We compare against the majority baseline (literal). The right-most columns indicate whether the differences in performance are statistically significant, using the χ^2

---

[4]Experiments with other classification methods showed similar but inferior performance. Simple Logistic Regression performed 2nd best.

[5]Remember from Section 4.1 that the unigram information is based on all tokens (12 427) but we implemented the unigrams as a single feature (using the output of a classifier), thus the combined setting is only based on 22 features.

	Feature Type	$|f|$	Lit. F_1	Non-Lit. F_1	Acc.	Acc.$+P$
1	Majority Baseline	0	78.7	0.0	64.9	-
2	Unigram	12 427	83.2	55.5	75.6	76.5
3	Unigram + NN Clusters	6 305	81.6	66.7	76.3	79.3
4	AC Ratings	7	81.3	60.7	74.7	76.3
5	IMG Ratings	7	77.5	48.1	68.6	71.6
6	Distributional Fit	14	83.0	61.8	76.5	80.2
7	Comb. (2+4+6)	22	88.6	77.1	84.8	86.6
8	Comb. (3+4+6) + NN Clusters	22	88.8	77.3	85.0	86.8

(a) Results across feature types and their combinations.

	1	2	3	4	5	6	7	8
1								
2	*/*							
3	*/*	-/*						
4	*/*	-/-	o/*					
5	*/*	*/*	*/*	*/*				
6	*/*	*/*	-/-	o/*	*/*			
7	*/*	*/*	*/*	*/*	*/*	*/*		
8	*/*	*/*	*/*	*/*	*/*	*/*	-/-	

(b) Statistical significance of differences Acc/Acc+P.

Table 1: Main classification results.

test and $*$ for $p < 0.001$ and o for $p < 0.05$ to mark significance.

The results demonstrate that the classification results across all feature types are significantly better than the majority baseline. The single best performing feature type (cf. lines 1–6) is the unigram information; in combination with the particle information ($+P$), the distributional PV/BV–context fit is best. Combining the best feature types (2+4+6) once more improves the results, and ditto when adding noun cluster information.[6] We can also see that abstractness (AC) ratings outperform imageability (IMG) ratings.

So overall, the best performing feature set successfully combines unigrams that incorporate clusters for noun generalization; abstractness ratings; and PV-specific information regarding the distributional PV/BV–context fit and knowledge about the particle. This setup correctly classifies literal sentences with an f-score of 88.8 and non-literal sentences with an f-score of 77.3; overall accuracy is 86.8 over a baseline of 64.9.

It is difficult to compare our results against previous approaches on different datasets and in different languages. Regarding the closest approaches to our work, Tsvetkov et al. (2014) report an accuracy score of 82.0 using 10-fold cross-validation on a training dataset with a majority baseline of 59.2, combining multiple lexical semantic features on a dataset of 1 609 English subject–verb–object triples. Birke and Sarkar (2007) trained a single classifier for each of twenty-five verbs in the English TROFI verb dataset and reported only an average f-score: 64.9 against a

majority baseline of 62.9. Turney et al. (2011) obtained an average f-score of 63.9 and additionally report an accuracy score of 73.4 on the same dataset, using abstractness ratings.

In contrast to our work, the two approaches by Birke and Sarkar (2007) and Turney et al. (2011) treated each group of sentences for a given target verb as a separate learning problem, while we learn one classifier across different verbs. Our method 4 (AC Ratings) can be considered a German re-implementation of the approach by Turney et al. (2011). In comparison to the results of previous work, our approach can safely be considered state-of-the-art.

5.2 PV-Specific Experiments

5.2.1 Incorporating Standard Measures of Multiword Idiomaticity

One traditional line of research to identify type-based multiword collocations or idiomatic expressions relies on the association strength between the multiword parts (Evert and Krenn, 2001; Krenn and Evert, 2001; Stevenson et al., 2004): The stronger the association between the parts of a multiword expression (as determined by raw frequency, some variant of mutual information, etc.), the stronger the collocation/idiomaticity of the combination of the parts. Based on this assumption, we calculated the association strength between PVs and their contextual subjects/objects, using *local mutual information (LMI)*, cf. Evert (2005). The LMI scores were based on type-based frequency counts in the *DECOW14AX* corpus and added as features to the respective contexts, assuming that large LMI scores indicate non-literal PV usage.

---

[6]The best cluster analysis in our experiments contained 750 noun clusters.

Adding the LMI values to the overall best feature set from the main experiments decreased accuracy from 86.8 → 86.0. Using the LMI association strength values of the PV–subject and PV–object pairs by themselves provided slightly but non-significantly better results in comparison to the majority baseline: 65.9 > 64.9.[7] Manual investigations revealed that verb–noun pairs with high LMI scores represent collocations in many cases, but the collocations are not only used in non-literal language but also in literal language, e.g., "Sendung ausstrahlen" ("broadcast a program").

5.2.2 Non-Literality across Particles

In order to explore the predicability of literal vs. non-literal uses with respect to specific particles, we trained the best classifier from the main experiments on all particle verbs with particle X and applied the classifier to all particle verbs with particle Y. Our hypothesis was that pairs of particles with similar ambiguities might predict each other better than pairs with different particle meanings.

This PV-specific setup could also be applied within a PV group with the same particle: We trained the classifier on all PVs with particle X except for one, and then applied the trained classifier to the missing PV with particle X. The setup was repeated for all PVs with particle X, and the average accuracy was calculated.

Figure 2 provides the results as a heat map, with red indicating high and blue indicating low accuracy scores. The vertical particles on the left correspond to the training particles, and the horizontal particles at the bottom correspond to the test particles. The bottom line shows the majority baseline. For example, training a classifier on "ein" PVs and evaluating it on "aus" PVs results in an accuracy of 76.56, which is significantly better ($* * *$ for $p < 0.001$) than the baseline for "aus" (65.55).

The diagonal in the heat map (showing the within-particle setup) provides particularly high accuracy scores, so the PVs with the same particle predict (non-)literality within the group very well. This demonstrates that the meanings and the meaning shifts across PVs with the same particle (e.g., *aufdecken* and *auftischen*) are quite reg-

ular. A comparably strong prediction is found between "vor" (before/in front of) and "nach" (after/behind), with both particles carrying highly similar temporal and local senses. Other examples of strongly related antonymous particle pairs are "auf"/"zu", "ein"/"aus", and "aus"/"an". Examples of strongly related synonymous particle pairs are "an"/"ein", and "aus"/"zu". "durch" correlates poorly with all other particles, which is probably due to the few sentences we collected from the corpus. "mit" also correlates poorly with all other particles, because it is the only particle with little ambiguity. So overall, the heat map corresponds to intuitions about semantic relatedness across particle pairs.

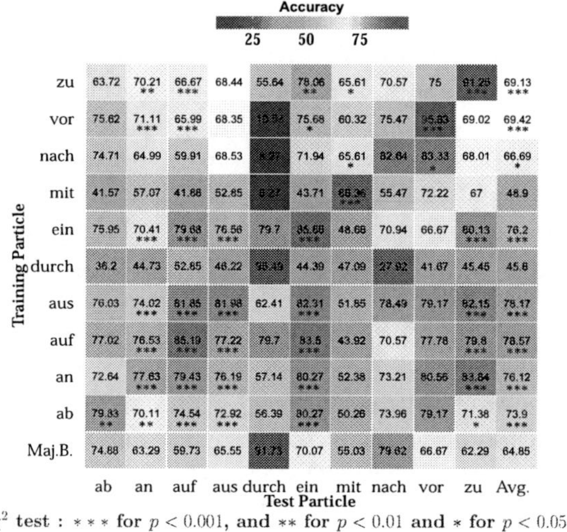

Training Particle	ab	an	auf	aus	durch	ein	mit	nach	vor	zu	Avg.
zu	63.72	70.21 **	66.67 ***	68.44	55.64	78.06 **	65.61 *	70.57	75	91.25 ***	69.13 ***
vor	75.62	71.11 ***	65.99 ***	68.35	19.54	75.68 *	60.32	75.47	95.83 ***	69.02	69.42 ***
nach	74.71	64.99	59.91	68.53	6.27	71.94	65.61 *	82.64	83.33 *	68.01	66.69 *
mit	41.57	57.07	41.88	52.85	6.27	43.71	66.36 ***	55.47	72.22	67	48.9
ein	75.95	70.41 ***	79.68 ***	76.56 ***	79.7	85.68 ***	48.68	70.94	66.67	80.13 ***	76.2 ***
durch	36.2	44.73	52.85	46.22	98.49	44.39	47.09	27.92	41.67	45.45	45.8
aus	76.03	74.02 ***	81.85 ***	81.98 ***	62.41	82.31 ***	51.85	78.49	79.17	82.15 ***	78.17 ***
auf	77.02	76.53 ***	85.19 ***	77.22 ***	79.7	83.5 ***	43.92	70.57	77.78	79.8 ***	78.57 ***
an	72.64	77.63 ***	79.43 ***	76.19 ***	57.14	80.27 ***	52.38	73.21	80.56	93.84 ***	76.12 ***
ab	79.83 **	70.11 **	74.54 ***	72.92 ***	56.39	80.27 ***	50.26	73.96	79.17	71.38 *	73.9 ***
Maj.B.	74.88	63.29	59.73	65.55	91.73	70.07	55.03	79.62	66.67	62.29	64.85

χ^2 test : $* * *$ for $p < 0.001$, and $* *$ for $p < 0.01$ and $*$ for $p < 0.05$.

Figure 2: Train a classifier on PVs with particle X and test it on PVs with particle Y.

5.2.3 Non-Literality across Particle Verbs

An even more fine-grained experiment setting explored the predictability of a specific particle verb based on the classifier trained on a different particle verb. Our hypothesis was that pairs of PVs that predict each other particularly well share some meaning aspects, either (i) because the training and the test verb share the same BV (**SameBV**: ab*graben*:auf*graben*), or (ii) the PVs are synonymous according to the German *Duden*[8]

---

[7] We also experimented with the other five contextual feature dimensions, but the results were even worse.

[8] http://www.duden.de

dictionary (**PVSyn**: *auftragen:auftischen*), or (iii) because the BVs of two PVs with identical particles are synonymous according to the *Duden* (**BVSyn**: auf*reissen*:auf*platzen*).

Figure 3 shows the f-scores for predicting literality and non-literality across the three settings, in comparison to the main experiments ("All"). The number of PV pairs in the settings and the majority accuracy for these PV pairs are also provided, because the experiment sets differ in size. We can see that PVs with the same BV (**SameBV**) predict each other's classifications well regarding literal but not regarding non-literal sentences. This behaviour illustrates the contribution of the particle to the PV meaning: The same BVs with different particles potentially differ strongly, if the particles do not agree on one or more senses. Synonymous PVs (**PVSyn**) predict each other as well in literal as in non-literal cases. Since the PVs in all cases are supposed to have the same meaning, this behaviour is also reasonable. An increase in both literal and non-literal F1 is reached for PV pairs with the same particle and synonymous BVs (**BVSyn**), because the BVs are supposed to carry the same meaning, and the identical particles trigger similar meaning shifts. Overall, the experiment demonstrates that synonymous verbs undergo similar meaning shifts, and that a particle initiates similar meaning shifts when applied to synonymous BVs.

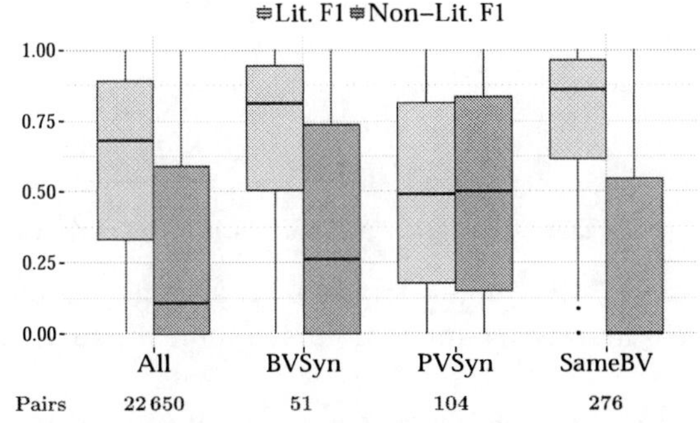

Figure 3: Prediction for semantically related PVs.

5.3 Indicators of Non-Literality

In the final part of the paper, we perform a qualitative analysis of the most salient features.

5.3.1 Information Gain

First of all, we looked into the feature space by computing the information gain within the best random forest classifier. The information gain (*I-Gain*) provides the improvement in information entropy regarding our feature space and the class labels, as defined by equation (1).

$$I\text{-}Gain(Class, Feat) = H(Class) - H(Class|Feat) \quad (1)$$

The information gain does not take feature interaction into account, but determines the importance of the individual features. Applying this method reveals the three most salient features: unigrams (0.31), abstractness ratings of the context nouns (0.17), and distributional fit of the base verbs (0.11). The information gain therefore confirms our results from the main experiments, where these three features worked best.

In addition, we noticed that for all features higher weights were given to dimensions that depend on nouns (such as the common nouns in the PV contexts, and the subject and object nouns), in comparison to proper names, verbs, adjectives and adverbs. For example, the abstractness ratings of the adverbs were ranked second lowest with a score of 0.005, and the distributional fit between BVs and adjectives was ranked last with a zero score, indicating that this feature provides no additional information for our dataset.

5.3.2 Distributional Fit

We now take a look at the distributional fit feature, which was the best performing feature in the main experiments, when combined with particle knowledge. Figure 4 focusing on the distributional fit between BVs and common nouns (as determined third best by the information gain) confirms that the feature is helpful in distinguishing literal vs. non-literal PV sentences across particles: The medians in the boxplots for literal sentences are clearly above those for non-literal sentences. The plots confirm that BVs can be exploited to identify compositional uses of PVs (which in turn refer to literal usage).

Looking into individual PVs confirms that this feature distinguishes well between the literal and non-literal sentences. On the other hand, we also find PVs where this feature is not able to identify non-literal language use. Figure 5 presents the boxplots with cosine values for *aufblühen* (blossom out) and *auflodern* (burn up), where the feature works well, in comparison to *absaufen* (drown), where the feature cannot distinguish (non-)literal language usage.

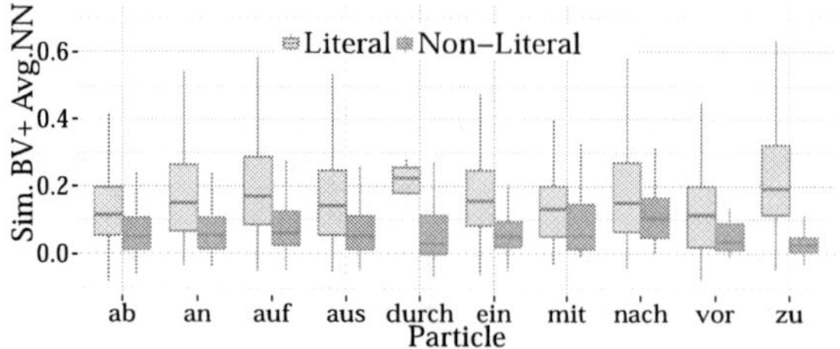

Figure 4: Distributional fit of BVs and context nouns in (non-)literal sentences across particles.

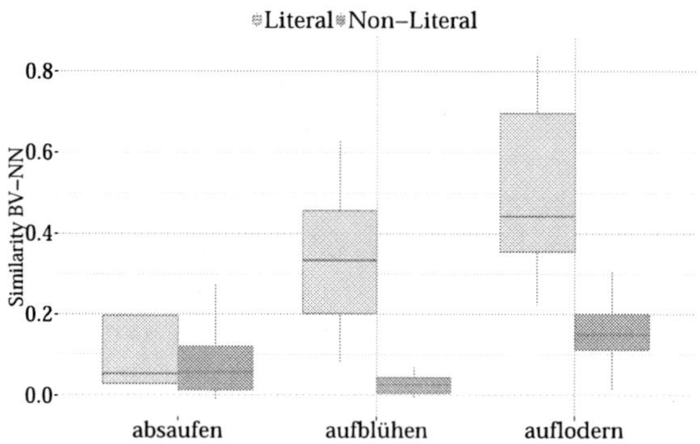

Figure 5: Example PVs and their distributional fit of BVs and context nouns in (non-)literal use.

5.3.3 Abstractness of Contexts

Finally, we take a look at the abstractness feature, which was also among the best performing features in the main experiments, and which is generally assumed to represent a salient indicator of non-literal language usage. Figure 6 focusing on the abstractness of common nouns in the PV sentences[9] (as determined second best by the information gain) confirms that the feature is also helpful in distinguishing literal vs. non-literal PV sentences across particles: Again, the medians in the boxplots for literal sentences are clearly above those for non-literal sentences. The plots confirm

____
[9]High values indicate concreteness.

that contextual abstractness is a salient indicator of non-literal language usage.

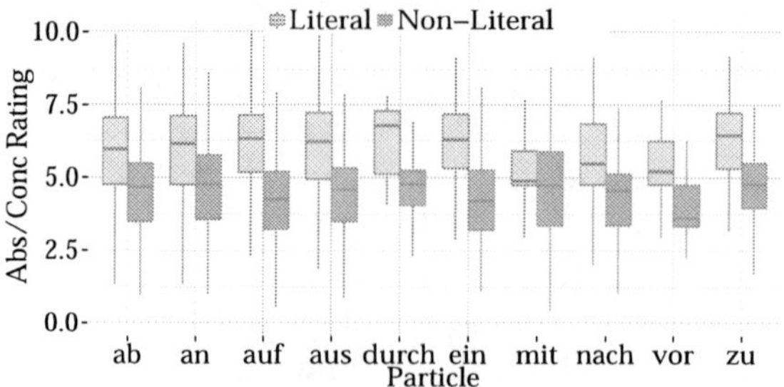

Figure 6: Average abstractness ratings of context nouns in (non-)literal sentences across particles.

Looking into individual PVs again confirms that this feature distinguishes well between the literal and non-literal sentences but also that there are PVs where this feature is not able to identify non-literal language use. Figure 7 presents the boxplots with abstractness ratings for *anstauen* (accumulate) and *durchsickern* (leak through), where the feature works well, in comparison to *antanzen* (waltz in) and especially *ausklingen* (fade/finish), where the feature cannot distinguish (non-)literal language usage.

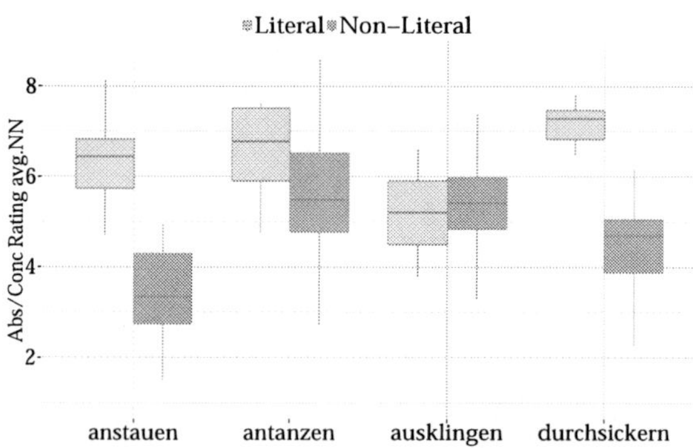

Figure 7: Example PVs and their average abstractness ratings of context nouns in (non-)literal use.

Two example sentences where the abstractness feature goes wrong for a good reason are as follows. In (1) "Aber wir sollten doch um fünf zum Essen **antanzen**." (*But we should **show up (lit: waltz in)** for dinner at five*), the context nouns are concrete (*we; dinner*) but the language usage is non-literal. In contrast, in (2) "Ich liebe Emotionen, deshalb **summen** alle **mit**." (*I love emotions, there-*

*fore everyone **hums along***), the object noun in the sentence is highly abstract (*emotion*), but the language usage is literal. These examples illustrate that contextual abstractness is not a perfect indicator of non-literal language usage.

6 Conclusion

We presented a classifier that predicts literal vs. non-literal language usage for German particle verbs, a semantically challenging type of multiword expressions. The classifier significantly outperformed the baseline by improving standard features with noun clusters and a PV-specific distributional fit feature. PV-specific experiments indicated that PVs whose particles share aspects of ambiguity and which incorporate semantically related BVs seem to undergo similar meaning shifts.

7 Acknowledgements

The research was supported by the DFG Collaborative Research Centre SFB 732 (Maximilian Köper) and the DFG Heisenberg Fellowship SCHU-2580/1 (Sabine Schulte im Walde).

References

Timothy Baldwin and Aline Villavicencio. 2002. Extracting the Unextractable: A Case Study on Verb Particles. In *Proceedings of the 6th Conference on Computational Natural Language Learning*, pages 98–104, Taipei, Taiwan.

Timothy Baldwin, Colin Bannard, Takaaki Tanaka, and Dominic Widdows. 2003. An Empirical Model of Multiword Expression Decomposability. In *Proceedings of the ACL Workshop on Multiword Expressions: Analysis, Acquisition and Treatment*, pages 89–96, Sapporo, Japan.

Timothy Baldwin. 2005. Deep Lexical Acquisition of Verb–Particle Constructions. *Computer Speech and Language*, 19:398–414.

Collin Bannard. 2005. Learning about the Meaning of Verb–Particle Constructions from Corpora. *Computer Speech and Language*, 19:467–478.

Julia Birke and Anoop Sarkar. 2006. A Clustering Approach for the Nearly Unsupervised Recognition of Nonliteral Language. In *Proceedings of the 11th Conference of the European Chapter of the ACL*, pages 329–336, Trento, Italy.

Julia Birke and Anoop Sarkar. 2007. Active Learning for the Identification of Nonliteral Language. In *Proceedings of the Workshop on Computational Approaches to Figurative Language*, pages 21–28, Rochester, NY.

Bernd Bohnet. 2010. Top Accuracy and Fast Dependency Parsing is not a Contradiction. In *Proceedings of the 23rd International Conference on Computational Linguistics*, pages 89–97, Beijing, China.

Stefan Bott and Sabine Schulte im Walde. 2014. Optimizing a Distributional Semantic Model for the Prediction of German Particle Verb Compositionality. In *Proceedings of the 9th International Conference on Language Resources and Evaluation*, pages 509–516, Reykjavik, Iceland.

Stefan Bott and Sabine Schulte im Walde. 2015. Exploiting Fine-grained Syntactic Transfer Features to Predict the Compositionality of German Particle Verbs. In *Proceedings of the 11th Conference on Computational Semantics*, pages 34–39, London, UK.

Stefan Evert and Brigitte Krenn. 2001. Methods for the Qualitative Evaluation of Lexical Association Measures. In *Proceedings of the 39th Annual Meeting of the Association for Computational Linguistics*, pages 188–195, Toulouse, France.

Stefan Evert. 2005. *The Statistics of Word Co-Occurrences: Word Pairs and Collocations*. Ph.D. thesis, Institut für Maschinelle Sprachverarbeitung, Universität Stuttgart.

Gertrud Faaß, Ulrich Heid, and Helmut Schmid. 2010. Design and Application of a Gold Standard for Morphological Analysis: SMOR in Validation. In *Proceedings of the 7th International Conference on Language Resources and Evaluation*, pages 803–810, Valletta, Malta.

Matt Gedigian, John Bryant, Srini Narayanan, and Branimir Ciric. 2006. Catching Metaphors. In *Proceedings of the 3rd Workshop on Scalable Natural Language Understanding*, pages 41–48, New York City, NY.

Boris Haselbach. 2011. Deconstructing the Meaning of the German Temporal Verb Particle 'nach' at the Syntax-Semantics Interface. In *Proceedings of Generative Grammar in Geneva*, pages 71–92, Geneva, Switzerland.

Maximilian Köper and Sabine Schulte im Walde. 2016. Automatically generated affective norms of abstractness, arousal, imageability and valence for 350000 german lemmas. In *Proceedings of the 10th International Conference on Language Resources and Evaluation*, Portorož, Slovenia.

Brigitte Krenn and Stefan Evert. 2001. Can we do better than Frequency? A Case Study on Extracting PP-Verb Collocations. In *Proceedings of the ACL Workshop on Collocations*, pages 39–46, Toulouse, France.

Natalie Kühner and Sabine Schulte im Walde. 2010. Determining the Degree of Compositionality of German Particle Verbs by Clustering Approaches. In *Proceedings of the 10th Conference on Natural Language Processing*, pages 47–56, Saarbrücken, Germany.

Andrea Lechler and Antje Roßdeutscher. 2009. German Particle Verbs with *auf*. Reconstructing their Composition in a DRT-based Framework. *Linguistische Berichte*, 220:439–478.

Omer Levy, Yoav Goldberg, and Ido Dagan. 2015. Improving Distributional Similarity with Lessons learned from Word Embeddings. *Transactions of the Association for Computational Linguistics*, 3:211–225.

Linlin Li and Caroline Sporleder. 2009. Classifier Combination for Contextual Idiom Detection Without Labelled Data. In *Proceedings of the Conference on Empirical Methods in Natural Language Processing*, pages 315–323, Singapore.

Andrew McCallum and Kamal Nigam. 1998. A Comparison of Event Models for Naive Bayes Text Classification. In *Proceedings of the AAAI Workshop on Learning for Text Categorization*.

Diana McCarthy, Bill Keller, and John Carroll. 2003. Detecting a Continuum of Compositionality in Phrasal Verbs. In *Proceedings of the ACL Workshop on Multiword Expressions: Analysis, Acquisition and Treatment*, pages 73–80, Sapporo, Japan.

Thomas Müller, Helmut Schmid, and Hinrich Schütze. 2013. Efficient Higher-Order CRFs for Morphological Tagging. In *Proceedings of the Conference on Empirical Methods in Natural Language Processing*, pages 322–332, Seattle, WA, USA.

Stefan Rüd. 2012. Untersuchung der distributionellen Eigenschaften der Lesarten der Partikel *'auf'* mittels Clustering-Methoden. Master's thesis, Institut für Maschinelle Sprachverarbeitung, Universität Stuttgart.

Roland Schäfer and Felix Bildhauer. 2012. Building Large Corpora from the Web Using a New Efficient Tool Chain. In *Proceedings of the 8th International Conference on Language Resources and Evaluation*, pages 486–493, Istanbul, Turkey.

Roland Schäfer. 2015. Processing and Querying Large Web Corpora with the COW14 Architecture. In Piotr Bański, Hanno Biber, Evelyn Breiteneder, Marc Kupietz, Harald Lüngen, and Andreas Witt, editors, *Proceedings of the 3rd Workshop on Challenges in the Management of Large Corpora*, pages 28 – 34.

Ekaterina Shutova, Simone Teufel, and Anna Korhonen. 2013. Statistical Metaphor Processing. *Computational Linguistics*, 39(2):301–353.

Caroline Sporleder and Linlin Li. 2009. Unsupervised Recognition of Literal and Non-Literal Use of Idiomatic Expressions. In *Proceedings of the 12th Conference of the European Chapter of the ACL*, pages 754–762, Athens, Greece.

Sylvia Springorum, Sabine Schulte im Walde, and Antje Roßdeutscher. 2012. Automatic Classification of German *an* Particle Verbs. In *Proceedings of the 8th International Conference on Language Resources and Evaluation*, pages 73–80, Istanbul, Turkey.

Sylvia Springorum, Sabine Schulte im Walde, and Antje Roßdeutscher. 2013a. Sentence Generation and Compositionality of Systematic Neologisms of German Particle Verbs. Talk at the Conference on Quantitative Investigations in Theoretical Linguistics.

Sylvia Springorum, Jason Utt, and Sabine Schulte im Walde. 2013b. Regular Meaning Shifts in German Particle Verbs: A Case Study. In *Proceedings of the 10th International Conference on Computational Semantics*, pages 228–239, Potsdam, Germany.

Sylvia Springorum. 2011. DRT-based Analysis of the German Verb Particle *"an"*. *Leuvense Bijdragen*, 97:80–105.

Suzanne Stevenson, Afsaneh Fazly, and Ryan North. 2004. Statistical Measures of the Semi-Productivity of Light Verb Constructions. In *Proceedings of the 2nd Workshop on Multiword Expressions: Integrating Processing*, pages 1–8, Barcelona, Spain.

Yulia Tsvetkov, Leonid Boytsov, Anatole Gershman, Eric Nyberg, and Chris Dyer. 2014. Metaphor Detection with Cross-Lingual Model Transfer. In *Proceedings of the 52nd Annual Meeting of the Association for Computational Linguistics*, pages 248–258.

Peter D. Turney and Michael L. Littman. 2003. Measuring Praise and Criticism: Inference of Semantic Orientation from Association. *ACM Transactions on Information Systems*, 21(4):315–346.

Peter Turney, Yair Neuman, Dan Assaf, and Yohai Cohen. 2011. Literal and Metaphorical Sense Identification through Concrete and Abstract Context. In *Proceedings of the Conference on Empirical Methods in Natural Language Processing*, pages 680–690, Edinburgh, UK.

Aline Villavicencio. 2005. The Availability of Verb-Particle Constructions in Lexical Resources: How much is enough? *Computer Speech and Language*, 19:415–432.

Ian H. Witten, Eibe Frank, and Mark A. Hall. 2011. *Data Mining: Practical Machine Learning Tools and Techniques*. Morgan Kaufmann Publishers.

Phrasal Substitution of Idiomatic Expressions

Changsheng Liu and **Rebecca Hwa**
Computer Science Department
University of Pittsburgh
Pittsburgh, PA 15260, USA
{changsheng,hwa}@cs.pitt.edu

Abstract

Idioms pose a great challenge to natural language understanding. A system that can automatically paraphrase idioms in context has applications in many NLP tasks. This paper proposes a phrasal substitution method to replace idioms with their figurative meanings in literal English. Our approach identifies relevant replacement phrases from an idiom's dictionary definition and performs appropriate grammatical and referential transformations to ensure that the idiom substitution fits seamlessly into the original context. The proposed method has been evaluated both by automatic metrics and human judgments. Results suggest that high quality paraphrases of idiomatic expressions can be achieved.

1 Introduction

An idiom is a combination of words that has a figurative meaning which differs from its literal meaning. Idioms pose a great challenge to many NLP tasks, such as machine translation, word sense disambiguation, and sentiment analysis (Volk, 1998; Korkontzelos et al., 2013; Zanzotto et al., 2010; Williams et al., 2015). Previous work (Salton et al., 2014) has shown that a typical statistical machine translation system might achieve only half of the BLEU score (Papineni et al., 2002) on sentences that contain idiomatic expressions than on those that do not. Idioms are also problematic for second language learners. In a pilot study we have surveyed seven non-native speakers on 100 Tweets containing idioms; we have found that, on average, the partici-

pants had trouble understanding 70% of them due to the inclusion of idioms.

This work explores the possibility of automatically replacing idiomatic expressions in sentences. The full pipeline of a successful system has to solve many problems. First, it has to determine that an expression is, in fact, being used as an idiom in a sentence (Fazly et al., 2009; Korkontzelos et al., 2013; Sporleder and Li, 2009). Moreover, the system has to *sense disambiguate* the idiom – it has to pick the correct interpretation when more than one is possible. Second, it has to generate an appropriate phrasal replacement for the idiom using literal English. Third, it has to ensure that the replacement phrase will fit seamlessly back into the original sentence. This paper focuses on the second and third problem, which have not been studied as extensively in previous works.

We propose to extract the phrasal replacement for an idiom from its definition, assuming the existence of an up-to-date dictionary of broad coverage and high quality.[1] Because a typical definition is quite long, it cannot directly serve as a replacement for the idiom. A major challenge of our work is in identifying the right nugget to extract from the definition. Another major challenge is the smooth integration of the substitution phrase into the sentence. We consider both grammatical fluency as well as references resolution in our automatic Post-Editing technique. These phrasal challenges set our goals apart from related work on lexical simplification and substitution (Specia et al., 2012; Jauhar and Specia, 2012; McCarthy, 2002; McCarthy and Navigli, 2007) and

---

[1] This work uses TheFreeDictionary.com.

Proceedings of NAACL-HLT 2016, pages 363–373,
San Diego, California, June 12-17, 2016. ©2016 Association for Computational Linguistics

from general sentence simplification (Wubben et al., 2012; Siddharthan, 2014; Zhu et al., 2010; Coster and Kauchak, 2011) methods.

We validate the plausibility of the proposed methods with empirical experiments on a manually annotated corpus.[2] Results from both automatic evaluations and user studies show that the proposed approach can generate high-quality paraphrases of sentences containing idiomatic expressions. A successful idiom paraphrase generator may not only benefit non-native speakers, but may also facilitate other NLP applications.

2 Background

The main idea of this work is to produce a fluent and meaningful paraphrase of the original sentence similar to how a human non-native reader might approach the problem. Suppose the reader encounters the following sentence:

> **Sentence:** This kind of language really barfs me out and *gets my blood up.*[3]

If they do not understand the expression *gets my blood up*, they may look it up in a dictionary:

> **Definition:** Fig. to get someone or oneself angry. (Fixed order.)[4]

Then they might try to reconcile the definition with the context of the sentence and arrive at:

> **Paraphrased :** This kind of language really barfs me out and *gets me angry.*

In the example above, only a portion of the full definition is needed. One possible way to identify this relevant nugget is to apply sentence compression techniques (McDonald, 2006; Siddharthan, 2011; Štajner et al., 2013; Filippova et al., 2015; Filippova and Strube, 2008; Narayan and Gardent, 2014; Cohn and Lapata, 2009). However, all these methods have been developed for standard texts with complete sentences, and it is not clear whether they are suited to dictionary definitions. Consider Table 1, in which a corpus of 1000 randomly selected

Corpus	Average length	Punctuation density
CLspoken	17	2.16
CLwritten	18	2.07
Definition	12	2.86

Table 1: Some statistics over normal text corpora and an idiom definition corpus.

idiom definitions is compared with samples from two normal text corpora (CLwritten and CLspoken) used by Clarke and Lapata (2008). The CLwritten corpus comes from written sources in the British National Corpus and the American News Text corpus; the CLspoken corpus comes from transcribed broadcast news stories. We see that on average, definitions are shorter than complete sentences; arguably, each word in a definition carries more information. The density of punctuation per sentence shows that definitions are more fragmented. These factors are problematic for sentence compression techniques that rely heavily on the syntactic parse trees of complete, well-formed sentences (Cohn and Lapata, 2009; Narayan and Gardent, 2014). One recent compression method that does not rely as heavily on syntax is the work of Filippova et al. (2015). However, their approach requires a training set of considerable size, which is not practical for the domain of idiom definitions. The most likely to succeed text compression method for our domain is the work of McDonald (2006) as they only use syntactic information as soft evidence to compress target sentences. We choose this method as a comparative baseline in our experimental evaluation.

After obtaining an appropriately shortened definition, *get someone angry*, more operations are needed to properly replace the idiom with it in the original sentence. First, we need to convert *get* to *gets* to make the tense consistent. Second, we need to resolve the reference *someone* to the appropriate person in the context of the original sentence: *me*. These operations are important to fit the shortened definition seamlessly into the original context, which will be covered in the Post Editing section.

3 Our Method

As outlined in the previous section, our proposed method consists of two components: *substitution*

---

generation and *post editing*.

3.1 Substitution Generation

This component aims to extract relevant replacement phrases from an idiom's dictionary definition. Rather than using generic sentence compression techniques, we argue that the taxonomy of a definition follows certain conventions that can be exploited. In most definitions, the *core meaning* is presented first; it is then optionally followed by additional information that supports, explains, and/or exemplifies the main point. The relationship between the core meaning and different types of addition information is akin to relationships between nucleus and surrounding sentences as described by the rhetorical structure theory (Mann and Thompson, 1988). Using a development set of idiom definition, we have identified four types of additional information:

Type	Example
Coordination	to discover **or apprehend** someone with something
Reason	to be feeling happy **because you are satisfied with your life**
Supplement	time is very important.**(Used especially when time is limited)**
Example	to apply thick soapsuds to something, **such as part of the body**

Table 2: Different types of additional information.

Below, we present two methods for extracting the core meaning from a full definition. We first consider a rule-based approach, under the assumption that definitions can be fully described by a small set of regular patterns. We also present a supervised machine-learning approach, showing that these regular patterns do not have to be predefined, thus opening up for possibilities of adapting the method to different dictionaries and languages.

3.1.1 A Rule-based Method

Analyzing the development set, we observe that additional information are often signaled by a small sets of lexical cues[5]; we call them *boundary words*.

Using these boundary words and some shallow syntactic features[6], we have hand-crafted a small set of rules to pare down the definition. Below are five main types of rules:

1. **Delete coordinated phrase after the word "or" or "and"**. We consider that phrase to be an equivalent alternative and discard it.

2. **Delete subordinate clause after "because" or "since"**. The subordinate clause is used to elaborate the reason for a fact or event.

3. **Delete the clause after words such as "so that", "when", "if" and "especially"**. These are often extraneous supplemental information.

4. **Delete sentence after words such as "for instance", "e.g.", etc.**. The clause following these words usually gives further examples.

5. **Delete sentences in bracket**. This is often just supplemental information.

If multiple rules are applicable, we start from the rule that covers the widest range first, then to rules covering smaller ranges. After all these steps, if the output has more than one sentence, we always keep the first sentence for simplicity.

There is also a case of keyword ambiguity with respect to the word "as:" it could signal an explanation (like "because") or an example (like "such as"). Because TheFree Dictionary rarely use "as" by itself to signal an explanation, we have only encoded the "such as" sense in our rule-set to avoid the ambiguity.

3.1.2 A ML-based Method

Not every definition follows the schema expected by the rule-based system. To generalize the patterns, we cast substitution generation as a binary classification problem. The most straightforward way is to decide whether each word in a definition should be deleted or kept, but this will degrade the sequential fluency of the shortened definition.

A better alternative is to segment the definition into syntactic chunks such as non-embedded NP, VP, ADJP, ADVP and PP phrases using off-the-shelf

---

[5]We have identified 23 words and punctuation marks: and, or, because, since, 'cause, especially, if, for example, for instance, such as, e.g., i.e., etc., in particular, like, particularly, namely, viz. , specifically, so that, when, (,).

[6]These are obtained by using the shallow parser in Natural Language Tool Kit (NLTK) (Bird, 2006) and the parts-of-speech tagger in Stanford Parser (De Marneffe et al., 2006).

shallow parsers (e.g., NLTK). Chunks have been shown to minimize the generation of discontinuous sentences in previous works in machine translation (Zhang et al., 2007; Watanabe et al., 2003). We apply a trained binary Support Vector Machine (SVM) classifier to each chunk to predict whether it should be kept or discarded. The shortened definition consists of only chunks that are kept.

Lexical and syntactical features are extracted from definition chunks as well as the sentence containing the original idiom. We have also incorporated features that related previous works have found to be beneficial (Štajner et al., 2013; Narayan and Gardent, 2014). The following is a brief description of our feature set.

Features from the Sentence: These features encode the syntactic context of the idiom. One feature is the constituent label of the entire idiom from the sentence's full parse. It aims to show the big picture of the grammatical function of the idiom in the original sentence. Another feature is the part-of-speech (POS) tag of the word preceding the idiom. These features help to select definition chunks that fit better into the sentence context in which the idiom is used. Due to data sparsity and overfitting concerns, we do not extract lexical features from the sentences.

Features from the Definition: These features encode the syntactic information extracted from all the chunks that made up the definition. In addition to chunking, we also apply a full parser on the definition to obtain its dependency and constituency tree. Although the parse trees may not be reliable enough to serve as hard constraints, they offer useful syntactic information as soft evidences. For example, the dependency tree helps us to identify the head word of every chunk (denoted here as w_h). The constituency tree helps us to determine whether w_h is a node in a subordinate clause (subtree with its root labeled as 'SBAR'). This feature is useful because two adjacent chunks in a relative clause tend to be kept or discarded together. We also include features indicating the relation of the typed dependency of the chunks. Thus, if a verb chunk is kept, its arguments are also likely to be kept. Other features includes whether w_h is the root, whether w_h is the leaf node in the dependency tree. Since certain adjacent words tend to be discarded or kept together, we reinforce this property by adding a bigram POS feature of w_h

to encode its context. Additionally, we extract various surface features from the chunks such as their lengths, their positions in the definition, POS of w_h, etc. Some definitions are very long and have several sub-sentences, while a good shortened definition is usually extracted from one sub-sentence. Thus, we have also included a feature indicating whether the definition has more than one sub-sentence, and if the definition has more than one sub-sentence, whether the chunk is in the first sub-sentence.

Features adapted from the Rule-Based method: These include: whether the chunk contains a boundary word, whether the preceding word of the chunk is a boundary word, whether the following word of the chunk is a boundary word, whether the chunk is in a bracket.

3.2 Post Editing

To ensure that the shortened definition is a fluent replacement for the idiom in the context of the original sentence, we must make grammatical adjustments, resolve references, and smooth over the replacement boundaries.

3.2.1 Grammatical Adjustments

We perform several agreement checks. For example, when replacing a noun phrase idiom, we need to make sure that the grammatical number of the replacement phrase agrees with how it is used in the sentence. Similarly, when replacing a verb phrase idiom, we need to perform verb tense, person and number agreement checks, such as converting *get someone angry* to *gets someone angry* in the example mentioned in Section 2.

3.2.2 Reference Resolution

Reference expression is common in definition of idiom. For example, the idiom *see eye to eye* has a shortened definition of *they agree with each other*. The referent *they* has to be resolved when we substitute the idiom with it. The general reference resolution problem is a long-standing challenge in NLP (Mitkov, 1998; Hobbs, 1978; Hobbs, 1979); even in the limited context of our idiom substitution problem, it is not trivial. While regular expression matching may work for idioms that contain simple slot replacements (e.g., the idiom *lather something up* with the definition *to apply thick soapsuds to something*), further analyses on the idiom's sentential context are necessary for many idioms (e.g., *see eye to eye* has no obvious slot).

Typical reference expressions in a definition include *something, someone, somebody, you, they*, which often refer to noun phrases (NPs) in and around the idiom in the sentence. When the sentence context contains multiple NPs, we need to choose the right one to resolve the reference. To do so, we rely on two commonly used factors: recency and syntactic agreement (Lappin and Leass, 1994). Similar to the work of Siddharthan (2006), we extract all NPs in the original sentence with their agreement types and grammatical functions; for each NP, we assign it a score with equal weights of recency and syntactic factors. We choose the NP that satisfy the agreements and grammatical functions with the highest score, breaking ties by selecting the closest NP. When no contextual NP is suitable, we replace the reference expression with generics such as "it," "people," or "person" instead.

There is one subtle difference between reference resolution in our work and typical cases. In addition to deriving the correct interpretation of a reference expression, our system has to actually insert the referent to the shortened definition and make the paraphrased sentence grammatical. This means that we need to make the appropriate PRP (personal pronoun) and PRP$ (possessive pronouns) conversions. Consider the example from Section 2 again. the *someone* in the shortened definition is initially resolved to *my* in the original sentence, but to make the substitution grammatical, it has to be transformed to *me*. In addition, special processing is also needed when the substitution is in the form of *subordinate clause*. For example:

> **Tweet:** Maybe if the NFL stopped treating him as such, he wouldn't act like *a prima Donna*.[7]
> **Substitution:** *someone* who demands to be treated in a special way[8]

Although *someone* refers to *he* in the original sentence, no pronoun substitution is plausible. Therefore, *someone* is replaced by a generic expression,

<hr>

[7] https://twitter.com/KingKylino/status/678931385608966144

[8] http://idioms.thefreedictionary.com/a+prima+donna

"a person."

3.2.3 Boundary Smoothing

Boundary smoothing is the last step of the Post-Editing process to improve the fluency of the resulting sentence. We rely on a standard n-gram language model to evaluate the "smoothness" of the transitions between the original sentence and the substitution phrase. For the left boundary, we begin by checking the bigram probability of the word immediately before the substitution and the first word of the substitution. If it is 0, we would drop the first word and recheck until we find a bigram with non-zero probability or until we have reached the fourth word, whichever occurs first. If a non-zero bigram cannot be found within the first three words, we substitute the original shortened definition as is, without any word deletion. The range of three word is chosen based on our analysis of the development set. A mirror image process is applied to the right boundary. The language model is trained via NLTK using the Brown corpus[9].

4 Evaluation

To determine the performance of the definition shortening methods and post editing operations, we have carried out two experiments. The first (Section 4.2) evaluates the quality of the substitution generation methods; we also argument the evaluation with statistical analysis of post-editing as a reference for future work. The second (Section 4.3) evaluates whether the resulting paraphrased sentence is grammatical and preserves the original meaning.

4.1 Corpus

To evaluate our method on real data, we chose to select Tweets that contain idioms. The reasons are twofold. First, the inspiration for our problem formulation was to help non-native speakers understand social media contents. The limited context of a Tweet makes it harder for someone who does not know an embedded idiom to induce its meaning from the rest of the text. Second, Tweet are self-contained, making the paraphrase task as well as its evaluation (by human judges) more stand-alone. The short context limits the set of mentioned en-

<hr>

[9] http://www.hit.uib.no/icame/brown/bcm.html

367

Dataset	Agree	MED$_{avg}$	
		Disagree	Total
Training	32.9%	**3.25**	2.18
Testing	36.9%	3.42	**2.15**
All data	34.8%	3.33	2.17

Table 3: Agreement between the two annotators. MED$_{avg}$ represents the average minimum edit distance (by word).

tities, which helps with pronoun resolution; otherwise, we foresee no significant hurdles in applying our system to regular sentences.

To build the dataset, we randomly selected 200 idioms (100 for train and 100 for test) and automatically collected tweets in which they appeared using the query API[10]. There were six idioms for which no exact match was found; so we included the usage examples from TheFreeDictionary.com instead. We presented these sentences along with each idiom's definition and asked a volunteer native speaker (Annotator #1) to manually shorten the definition. After filtering out sentences that do not exemplify the idioms[11], we had a total of 88 instances for training and 84 for testing. Next, a near-native speaker (Annotator #2) also performed the same task so that we may compute the inter-annotator agreement. The shortened definitions from Annotator #1 are used as the gold standard.

Table 3 shows the agreement between two annotators. The overall average edit distance is 2.17 words; since the average length of the definitions is about twelve words long (cf. Table 1), the annotators have significant overlaps with each other (the Cohen's kappa is 0.64, suggesting that the inter-annotator agreement is within an acceptable range (Viera et al., 2005)). However, although the annotators extracted the exact same phrase 34.8% of the times, in general they do not completely agree. Some people may select more words to convey a more precise meaning while others sacrifice some precision in meaning for a greater fluency. Thus, in addition to measuring against the gold standard (Annotator #1) using automatic metrics, we also need to perform a human

evaluation to directly judge the qualities of the paraphrases.

4.2 Automatic evaluation

In this experiment, we compare different approaches for substitution generation using automatic metrics. We wish to determine: 1) How well does each method replicate human annotators' phrasal extractions? 2) Do we need specialized methods for extracting core meanings from idiom definitions? 3) Is the ML-based method more general and flexible?

The training data contains 88 definitions for a total of 645 chunks that have been labeled as "keep" or "discard" according to the gold standards. The test data consists of 84 unique idioms used in tweets. The evaluation metric is the minimum edit distance of each proposed substitution from the gold standard. We also calculate the *compression rate*, the ratio between numbers of tokens kept with total numbers of tokens in original sentence.

We compare our proposed methods with McDonald (2006). Specifically we use an adapted version described in Filippova et al. (2015). We also implemented two simpler baselines:

Equal-POS: Extract those words from the definition that have the same POS tags as the idiom. For example, if the idiom consists of a VB and an NN, then the first two words tagged as VB and NN in the definition are returned as the substitution. When POS matching fails, the whole definition is returned.

First-Six: Always return the first six words. We choose six because the average length of the gold standard extractions from the training set is six words long.

From the results presented in Table 4, we see that the problem of extracting the core explanation from a long definition is not trivial. The average minimum edit distances from the gold standard are high for the two simple baselines (6.29 for First-Six, 4.92 for Equal-POS). The text compression baseline, McDonald, is only a little better, at 4.86. Because the proposed methods are developed especially for idiom definitions, they are closer to the gold standard. Considering the inter-annotator agreement as an upper-bound (with an average minimum edit distance of 2.15 for the test set), the ML-based approach comes the closest to the upper-bound (with an average distance of 2.75).

---

[10]https://dev.twitter.com/rest/public/search

[11]For example, "the bitter end" was used in reference to the name of a club.

Method	Agree	MED_{avg}		Compression Rate
		Disagree	Total	
First-Six	0%	6.29	6.29	37%
Equal-POS	6.0%	5.10	4.92	49%
McDonald	6.0%	5.14	4.86	**22%**
Rule-Based	23.8%	4.04	3.27	59%
ML-based	25.0%	**3.5**	**2.75**	51%

Table 4: A comparison of different substitution generation methods with gold standard. MED_{avg} denotes the average minimum edit distance of the method's extraction from the gold standard.

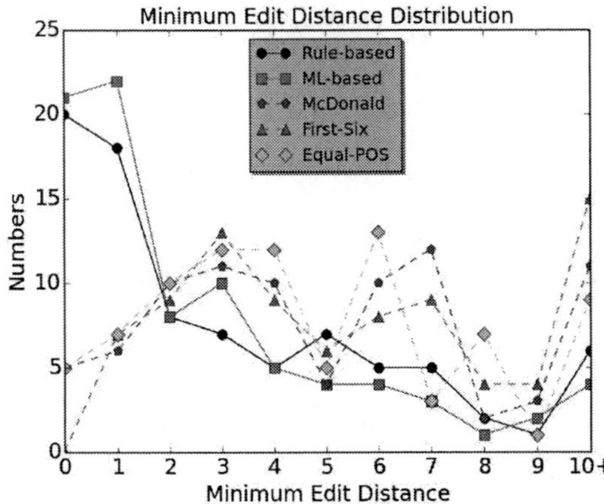

Figure 1: A distribution of edit distances for individual instances.

	Method	Grammaticality	Meaning
	McDonald	3.74	3.32
Def	Rule-Based	**4.92**	**4.71**
	ML-based	4.79	4.68
	McDonald	3.44	3.27
Sen	Rule-Based	4.25	4.31
	ML-based	**4.61**	**4.64**

Table 5: Human evaluation of the different methods in terms of the grammaticality and meaning preservation. In *Def* only the shortened definition are evaluated; in *Sen* the final paraphrased sentences are evaluated.

Figure 1 plots a distribution of each method's minimum edit distances for the instances in the test set. While the rule-based approach has a similar distribution as the trained classifier, it is almost always slightly worse. We see that half of the extractions based on the keep/discard classification are within a one word difference from the gold standard, and there are fewer than five instances for which the edit distance is at least 10; in contrast, the rule-based approach has fewer cases of (nearly) perfect matches and more cases of large mismatches (with the exception of an edit distance of 9). These results suggest that specialized methods are necessary for processing idiom definitions and that an ML-based approach is more general and flexible.

We have also measured the compression rate (CR) of each method; however, this may not be an appropriate metric for our domain in the sense that lower is not necessarily better. The CR of gold standard is 45%, while the ML-based method is 51%. Although the McDonald method has the lowest CR, at 22%, it is lower than that of the gold standard; this suggests that its approach is too aggressive.

To evaluate the contribution of the post-editing component, we have performed data analyses on each step individually: grammatical adjustment, reference resolution and boundary smoothing (using the outputs of the ML-based method). In terms of grammatical adjustments, there are two cases of noun number adjustment and five verb related adjustment.

In terms of reference resolution, we need to address not only the typical reference expressions, but also special cases relating to PRP and PRP$ conversions and subordinate clauses that was discussed in section 3.2.2. We have found fifteen cases of typical reference resolution and nine special cases, out of which, seven were related to subordinate clause (cf. Example 2 in Table 6). Finally, there are three cases for which reference expression cannot be resolved due to the lack of an appropriate noun phrase (cf. Example 5 in Table 6).

Sentence	French and British police are working *in harness* to solve the problem.
Definition	*if two or more people work in harness, they work together to achieve something*
ML-based	French and British police are *working together* to solve the problem.
Rule-Based	French and British police are *working together to achieve it* to solve the problem.
McDonald	French and British police are *working to achieve* to solve the problem.
Sentence	Don't buy *a pig in a poke*.
Definition	*something that you buy without knowing if it is good or not*
ML-based	Don't buy *something without knowing if it is good*.
Rule-Based	Don't buy *something that you buy without knowing if it is good*.
McDonald	Don't buy *without is good*.
Sentence	*Band-Aid solutions* for a homeless Senate worker.
Definition	*a temporary solution to a problem, or something that seems to be a solution but has no real effect*
ML-based	*Temporary solutions* for a homeless Senate worker.
Rule-Based	*Temporary solutions to a problem* for a homeless Senate worker.
McDonald	Or to be a for a homeless Senate worker.
Sentence	I've said all I had to say, *the ball is in your court* .
Definition	*if the ball is in someone's court, they have to do something before any progress can be made in a situation.*
ML-based	I've said all I had to say, *you have to do something*.
Rule-Based	I've said all I had to say, *you have to do something before any progress can be made in a situation.*
McDonald	I've said all I had to say, *do before can made*.
Sentence	I had to *spill my guts* about the broken window.
Definition	*to tell someone all about yourself, especially your problems*
ML-based	I had to *tell me all about myself* about the broken window .
Rule-Based	I had to *tell me all about myself* about the broken window .
McDonald	I had to *tell* about the broken window .

Table 6: Example of paraphrased sentences. The underlined pronouns in Examples 4&5 have to be resolved. Example 5 shows a failure of reference resolution.

With respect to boundary smoothing, there are many more cases of left boundary smoothing than right boundary smoothing (39 vs. 2 cases). Although many of the left boundary cases simply involve deleting the word "to" from the shortened definitions, some boundary smoothing cases do address the more severe redundancy disfluencies (cf. Example 1 in Table 6).

4.3 Human evaluation

Minimum edit distance to the gold standard cannot fully indicate the grammaticality and meaning preservation of the extracted phrase. In this experiment, we follow standard human evaluation procedures (McDonald, 2006) to verify our findings from the first experiment. The results will answer two questions: 1) Are the shortened definitions grammatical and are they representative of the core meanings? 2) Are the final paraphrased sentences grammatical and do they retain their original meanings?

We used the same 84 idioms which were the test set in the automatic evaluation. Four native speakers were recruited to evaluate the grammaticality and meaning of the shortened definitions and paraphrased sentences on a five-point scale. Each person took approximately 90 minutes to finish the study. We did not evaluate the simple baselines (First-Six and Equal-POS) because their qualities were obviously low; including them may bias the human subjects to give inflated scores to the better methods. The results are presented in Table 5.

In terms of shortening the definition, the rule-based method obtains the highest scores in both grammaticality and meaning; this is because it tends to be relatively conservative. The compression rate is 59%, while the ML-based method is 51%. Keeping more words in the definition reduces the chance of introducing grammar error and meaning loss; however, a longer definition makes poorer substitution in the full sentence because it introduces redundancy and thwarts post-editing efforts. This is validated in our experimental results – in terms of the paraphrased sentences, the rule-based method is outperformed by the ML-based method, which achieves the best result, with 4.61 in grammaticality and 4.64 in meaning.

Table 6 shows some typical examples of the paraphrases produced using substitution generation from the ML-based method, the rule-based method, and the McDonald method followed by processing with the proposed post-editing techniques. The first example features the effect of boundary smoothing. The shortened definition from the ML-based method is *work together to*. Direct replacement into the original sentence creates a disfluent bigram "working work", which has a probability of 0; thus the first word in the shortened definition (*work*) is deleted automatically. Similarly, the word *to* is deleted for the right boundary. In the third example, an automatic grammar adjustment is applied during substitution: *a temporary solution* is converted to *Temporary solutions* to keep the number consistent. In the forth example, the reference *they* is successfully resolved to *you* in the definition. The fifth example features a challenging rare case that results in a failed reference resolution.

Shortening the definition is a trade off between length and meaning. In these examples, the rule-based method keeps as many words as possible from the definition and leads to redundancy in the final output. It has a negative impact on the readability of the paraphrase. The McDonald method is too aggressive for short text such as definition, so the outputs are often discontinuous. The ML-based method offers a reasonable balance between length and meaning, and produces paraphrases that people seem to prefer.

5 Conclusion

We have proposed a phrasal substitution method for paraphrasing idiomatic expressions. Our system extracts the core meaning of an idiom from its dictionary definition and replaces the idiom with it. Empirical evaluations shows that the proposed method produces grammatical paraphrases that preserves the idioms' meanings, and it outperforms other methods such as sentence compression. In the future, we will explore the uses of the idiom paraphrases in NLP applications such as machine translation and intelligent tutor for second-language learners.

Acknowledgments

We would like to thank Ric Crabbe, Xiaobing Shi and Huichao Xue for the helpful discussions and suggestions. We also would like to thank the anonymous reviewers for their feedback.

References

Steven Bird. 2006. NLTK: the natural language toolkit. In *Proceedings of the COLING/ACL on Interactive presentation sessions*, pages 69–72. Association for Computational Linguistics.

James Clarke and Mirella Lapata. 2008. Global inference for sentence compression: An integer linear programming approach. *Journal of Artificial Intelligence Research*, pages 399–429.

Trevor Anthony Cohn and Mirella Lapata. 2009. Sentence compression as tree transduction. *Journal of Artificial Intelligence Research*, pages 637–674.

William Coster and David Kauchak. 2011. Learning to simplify sentences using wikipedia. In *Proceedings of the workshop on monolingual text-to-text generation*, pages 1–9. Association for Computational Linguistics.

Marie-Catherine De Marneffe, Bill MacCartney, Christopher D Manning, et al. 2006. Generating typed dependency parses from phrase structure parses. In *Proceedings of LREC*, volume 6, pages 449–454.

Afsaneh Fazly, Paul Cook, and Suzanne Stevenson. 2009. Unsupervised type and token identification of idiomatic expressions. *Computational Linguistics*, 35(1):61–103.

Katja Filippova and Michael Strube. 2008. Dependency tree based sentence compression. *INLG '08: Proceedings of the Fifth International Natural Language Generation Conference*, pages 25–32.

Katja Filippova, Enrique Alfonseca, Carlos A Colmenares, Lukasz Kaiser, and Oriol Vinyals. 2015. Sentence Compression by Deletion with LSTMs. In *Proceedings of the 2015 Conference on Empirical Methods in Natural Language Processing*, pages 360–368.

Jerry R Hobbs. 1978. Resolving pronoun references. *Lingua*, 44(4):311–338.

Jerry R Hobbs. 1979. Coherence and coreference. *Cognitive science*, 3(1):67–90.

Sujay Kumar Jauhar and Lucia Specia. 2012. Uow-shef: Simplex–lexical simplicity ranking based on contextual and psycholinguistic features. In *Proceedings of the First Joint Conference on Lexical and Computational Semantics-Volume 1: Proceedings of the main conference and the shared task, and Volume 2: Proceedings of the Sixth International Workshop on Semantic Evaluation*, pages 477–481. Association for Computational Linguistics.

Ioannis Korkontzelos, Torsten Zesch, Fabio Massimo Zanzotto, and Chris Biemann. 2013. Semeval-2013 task 5: Evaluating phrasal semantics. In *Second Joint Conference on Lexical and Computational Semantics (* SEM)*, volume 2, pages 39–47.

Shalom Lappin and Herbert J Leass. 1994. An algorithm for pronominal anaphora resolution. *Computational linguistics*, 20(4):535–561.

William C Mann and Sandra A Thompson. 1988. Rhetorical structure theory: Toward a functional theory of text organization. *Text-Interdisciplinary Journal for the Study of Discourse*, 8(3):243–281.

Diana McCarthy and Roberto Navigli. 2007. Semeval-2007 task 10: English lexical substitution task. In *Proceedings of the 4th International Workshop on Semantic Evaluations*, pages 48–53. Association for Computational Linguistics.

Diana McCarthy. 2002. Lexical substitution as a task for wsd evaluation. In *Proceedings of the ACL-02 workshop on Word sense disambiguation: recent successes and future directions-Volume 8*, pages 109–115. Association for Computational Linguistics.

Ryan T McDonald. 2006. Discriminative sentence compression with soft syntactic evidence. In *Proc. of EACL-06*, pages 297–304.

Ruslan Mitkov. 1998. Robust pronoun resolution with limited knowledge. In *Proceedings of the 36th Annual Meeting of the Association for Computational Linguistics and 17th International Conference on Computational Linguistics-Volume 2*, pages 869–875. Association for Computational Linguistics.

Shashi Narayan and Claire Gardent. 2014. Hybrid Simplification using Deep Semantics and Machine Translation. *Acl*, pages 435–445.

Kishore Papineni, Salim Roukos, Todd Ward, and Wei-Jing Zhu. 2002. BLEU: a method for automatic evaluation of machine translation. In *Proceedings of the 40th annual meeting on association for computational linguistics*, pages 311–318. Association for Computational Linguistics.

Giancarlo D Salton, Robert J Ross, and John D Kelleher. 2014. An Empirical Study of the Impact of Idioms on Phrase Based Statistical Machine Translation of English to Brazilian-Portuguese. *The Third Workshop on Hybrid Approaches to Translation (HyTra 2014)*.

Advaith Siddharthan. 2006. Syntactic simplification and text cohesion. *Research on Language & Computation*, 4(1):77–109.

Advaith Siddharthan. 2011. Text simplification using typed dependencies: a comparison of the robustness of different generation strategies. *Proceedings of the 13th European Workshop on Natural Language Generation*, (September):2–11.

Advaith Siddharthan. 2014. A survey of research on text simplification. *International Journal of Applied Linguistics*, 165(2):259–298.

Lucia Specia, Sujay Kumar Jauhar, and Rada Mihalcea. 2012. Semeval-2012 task 1: English lexical simplification. In *Proceedings of the First Joint Conference* on *Lexical and Computational Semantics-Volume 1: Proceedings of the main conference and the shared task, and Volume 2: Proceedings of the Sixth International Workshop on Semantic Evaluation*, pages 347–355. Association for Computational Linguistics.

Caroline Sporleder and Linlin Li. 2009. Unsupervised recognition of literal and non-literal use of idiomatic expressions. In *Proceedings of the 12th Conference of the European Chapter of the Association for Computational Linguistics*, pages 754–762. Association for Computational Linguistics.

Anthony J Viera, Joanne M Garrett, et al. 2005. Understanding interobserver agreement: the kappa statistic. *Fam Med*, 37(5):360–363.

Martin Volk. 1998. The automatic translation of idioms. machine translation vs. translation memory systems. *Machine Translation: Theory, Applications, and Evaluation, An Assessment of the State-of-the-art, St. Augustin, Gardez Verlag*.

Sanja Štajner, Biljana Drndarevíc, and Horacio Saggion. 2013. Corpus-based sentence deletion and split decisions for Spanish text simplification. *Computacion y Sistemas*, 17(2):251–262.

Taro Watanabe, Eiichiro Sumita, and Hiroshi G Okuno. 2003. Chunk-based statistical translation. In *Proceedings of the 41st Annual Meeting on Association for Computational Linguistics-Volume 1*, pages 303–310. Association for Computational Linguistics.

Lowri Williams, Christian Bannister, Michael Arribas-Ayllon, Alun Preece, and Irena Spasić. 2015. The role of idioms in sentiment analysis. *Expert Systems with Applications*.

Sander Wubben, Antal Van Den Bosch, and Emiel Krahmer. 2012. Sentence simplification by monolingual machine translation. In *Proceedings of the 50th Annual Meeting of the Association for Computational Linguistics: Long Papers-Volume 1*, pages 1015–1024. Association for Computational Linguistics.

Fabio Massimo Zanzotto, Ioannis Korkontzelos, Francesca Fallucchi, and Suresh Manandhar. 2010. Estimating linear models for compositional distributional semantics. In *Proceedings of the 23rd International Conference on Computational Linguistics*, pages 1263–1271. Association for Computational Linguistics.

Yuqi Zhang, Richard Zens, and Hermann Ney. 2007. Chunk-level reordering of source language sentences with automatically learned rules for statistical machine translation. In *Proceedings of the NAACL-HLT 2007/AMTA Workshop on Syntax and Structure in Statistical Translation*, pages 1–8. Association for Computational Linguistics.

Zhemin Zhu, Delphine Bernhard, and Iryna Gurevych. 2010. A monolingual tree-based translation model for sentence simplification. In *Proceedings of the 23rd international conference on computational linguistics*, pages 1353–1361. Association for Computational Linguistics.

Leverage Financial News to Predict Stock Price Movements Using Word Embeddings and Deep Neural Networks

Yangtuo Peng and **Hui Jiang**

Department of Electrical Engineering and Computer Science,
York University, 4700 Keele Street, Toronto, Ontario, M3J 1P3, Canada
emails: tim@cse.yorku.ca, hj@cse.yorku.ca

Abstract

Financial news contains useful information on public companies and the market. In this paper we apply the popular word embedding methods and deep neural networks to leverage financial news to predict stock price movements in the market. Experimental results have shown that our proposed methods are simple but very effective, which can significantly improve the stock prediction accuracy on a standard financial database over the baseline system using only the historical price information.

1 Introduction

In the past few years, deep neural networks (DNNs) have achieved huge successes in many data modelling and prediction tasks, ranging from speech recognition, computer vision to natural language processing. In this paper, we are interested in applying the powerful deep learning methods to financial data modelling to predict stock price movements.

Traditionally neural networks have been used to model stock prices as time series for the forecasting purpose, such as in (Kaastra and Boyd, 1991; Adya and Collopy, 1991; Chan et al., 2000; Skabar and Cloete, 2002; Zhu et al., 2008). In these earlier work, due to the limited training data and computing power available back then, normally shallow neural networks were used to model various types of features extracted from stock price data sets, such as historical prices, trading volumes, etc, in order to predict future stock yields and market returns.

More recently, in the community of natural language processing, many methods have been proposed to explore additional information (mainly on-line text data) for stock forecasting, such as financial news (Xie et al., 2013; Ding et al., 2014), twitter sentiments (Si et al., 2013; Si et al., 2014), financial reports (Lee et al., 2014). For example, (Xie et al., 2013) has proposed to use semantic frame parsers to generalize from sentences to scenarios to detect the roles of specific companies (positive or negative), where support vector machines with tree kernels are used as predictive models. On the other hand, (Ding et al., 2014) has proposed to use various lexical and syntactic constraints to extract event features for stock forecasting, where they have investigated both linear classifiers and deep neural networks as predictive models.

In this paper, we propose to use the recent word embedding methods (Mikolov et al., 2013b; Liu et al., 2015; Chen et al., 2015) to select features from on-line financial news corpora, and employ deep neural networks (DNNs) to predict the future stock movements based on the extracted features. Experimental results have shown that the features derived from financial news are very useful and they can significantly improve the prediction accuracy over the baseline system that only relies on the historical price information.

2 Our Approach

In this paper, we use deep neural networks (DNNs) as our predictive models, which provide us with the advantage of easily combining various types of features from different domains with the minimum

Proceedings of NAACL-HLT 2016, pages 374–379,
San Diego, California, June 12-17, 2016. ©2016 Association for Computational Linguistics

pre-processing and normalization effort. The DNN model takes as input the features extracted from both historical price information and on-line financial news to predict the stock movements in the future (either up or down) (Peng and Jiang, 2015).

2.1 Deep Neural Networks

The structure of DNNs used in this paper is a conventional multi-layer perceptron with many hidden layers. An L-layer DNN consisting of $L-1$ hidden nonlinear layers and one output layer. The output layer is used to model the posterior probability of each output target. In this paper, we use the rectified linear activation function, i.e., $f(x) = \max(0, x)$, to compute from activations to outputs in each hidden layer, which are in turn fed to the next layer as inputs. For the output layer, we use the *softmax* function to compute posterior probabilities between two nodes, standing for *stock-up* and *stock-down*.

2.2 Features from historical price data

In this paper, for each target stock on a target date, we choose the previous five days' closing prices and concatenate them to form an input feature vector for DNNs: $P = (p_{t-5}, p_{t-4}, p_{t-3}, p_{t-2}, p_{t-1})$, where t denotes the target date, and p_m denotes the closing price on the date m. We then normalize all prices by the mean and variance calculated from all closing prices of this stock in the training set. In addition, we also compute first and second order differences among the five days' closing prices, which are appended as extra feature vectors. For example, we compute the first order difference as follows: $\Delta P = (p_{t-4}, p_{t-3}, p_{t-2}, p_{t-1}) - (p_{t-5}, p_{t-4}, p_{t-3}, p_{n-2})$. In the same way, the second order difference is calculated by taking the difference between two adjacent values in each ΔP: $\Delta\Delta P = (\Delta P_{t-3}, \Delta P_{t-2}, \Delta P_{t-1}) - (\Delta P_{t-4}, \Delta P_{t-3}, \Delta P_{t-2})$. Finally, for each target stock on a particular date, the feature vector representing the historical price information consists of P, ΔP and $\Delta\Delta P$.

2.3 Financial news features

In order to extract fixed-size features suitable to DNNs from financial news corpora, we need to pre-process the text data. For all financial articles, we first split them into sentences. We only keep those sentences that mention at least a stock name or a public company. Each sentence is labelled by the publication date of the original article and the mentioned stock name. It is possible that multiple stocks are mentioned in one sentence. In this case, this sentence is labeled several times for each mentioned stock.

We then group these sentences by the publication dates and the underlying stock names to form the samples. Each sample contains a list of sentences that were published on the same date and mention the same stock or company. Moreover, each sample is labelled as *positive* ("price-up") or *negative* ("price-down") based on its next day's closing price consulted from the CRSP financial database (Booth, 2012). In the following, we introduce our method to extract three types of features from each sample.

(1) Bag of keywords (BoK): We first select the keywords based on the recent word embedding methods in (Mikolov et al., 2013a; Mikolov et al., 2013b). Using the popular word2vec method [1], we first compute the vector representations for all words occurring in the training set. Secondly, we manually select a small set of seed words, namely, nine seed words of {*surge, rise, shrink, jump, drop, fall, plunge, gain, slump*} in this work, which are believed to have a strong indication to the stock price movements. Next, we will repeat an iterative searching process to collect other useful keywords. In each iteration, we compute the cosine distance between other words occurring in the training set and each seed word. The cosine distance represents the similarity between two words in the word vector space. For example, based on the pre-calculated word vectors, we have found other words, such as *rebound, decline, tumble, slowdown, climb*, which are very close to at least one of the above seed words. The top 10 most similar words are chosen and added back into the set of seed words at the end of each iteration. The updated seed words will be used to repeat the searching process again to find another top 10 most similar words, the size of the seed words will increase as we repeat the procedure. In this way, we have searched all words occurring in training set and finally selected 1,000 words (including the nine initial seed words) as the keywords for our prediction

---

[1] https://code.google.com/p/word2vec/

task. In this iterative process to collect keywords, we have found that the final set of the derived keywords is usually very similar as long as we start from a small set of seed words that all strongly indicate the stock price movements.

Finally, a 1000-dimension feature vector, called *bag-of-keywords* or *BoK*, is generated for each sample. Each dimension of the *BoK* vector is the *TFIDF* score computed for each selected keyword from the whole training corpus.

(2) Polarity score (PS): We further compute so-called *polarity* scores (Turney and Littman, 2003; Turney and Pantel, 2010) to measure how each keyword is related to stock movements and how each keyword applies to a target stock in each sentence. To do this, we first compute the point-wise mutual information for each keyword w:

$$\mathrm{PMI}(w, pos) = \log \frac{\mathrm{freq}(w, pos) \times N}{\mathrm{freq}(w) \times \mathrm{freq}(pos)},$$

where $\mathrm{freq}(w, pos)$ denotes the frequency of the keyword w occurring in all positive samples, N denotes the total number of samples in the training set, $\mathrm{freq}(w)$ denotes the total number of keyword w occurring in the whole training set and $\mathrm{freq}(pos)$ denotes the total number of positive samples in the training set. Furthermore, we calculate the polarity score for each keyword w as:

$$\mathrm{PS}(w) = \mathrm{PMI}(w, pos) - \mathrm{PMI}(w, neg).$$

Obviously, the above polarity score $\mathrm{PS}(w)$ measures how each keyword is related to stock movements (either positively or negatively) and by how much.

Next, for each sentence in all samples, we need to detect how each keyword is related to the mentioned stock. To do this, we use the Stanford parser (Marneffe et al., 2006) to detect whether the target stock is a subject of the keyword or not. If the target stock is the direct object of the keyword, we assume the keyword is *oppositely* related to the underlying stock. As a result, we need to flip the sign of the polarity score. Otherwise, if the target stock is the subject of the keyword, we keep the keyword's polarity score as it is. For example, in a sentence like *"Apple slipped behind Samsung and Microsoft in a 2013 customer experience survey from Forrester Research"*, which contains an identified keyword *slip*.

Based on the parsing result, we know *Apple* is the subject of *slip* while *Samsung* and *Microsoft* are the object of *slip*. Therefore, if this sentence is used as a sample for *Apple*, the above polarity score of *slip* is directly used. However, if this sentence is used as a sample for *Samsung* or *Microsoft*, the polarity score of *slipped* is flipped by multiplying -1. Finally, the resultant polarity scores are multiplied to the *TFIDF* scores to generate another 1000-dimension feature vector for each sample.

(3) Category tag (CT): During the preprocessing of the financial news data, we have discovered that certain type of events are frequently described in the financial news, and the stock price will change significantly after the publication of such financial news. In order to discover the impact of these specific events on the stock price, we further define a list of categories that may indicate the specific events or activities of a public company, which we call as category tags. In this paper, the defined category tags include: *new-product, acquisition, price-rise, price-drop, law-suit, fiscal-report, investment, bankrupt, government, analyst-highlights*. Each category is first manually assigned with a few words that are closely related to the category. For example, we have chosen *released, publish, presented, unveil* as a list of seed words for the category *new-product*, which indicates the company's announcement of new products. Similarly, we use the above word embedding model to automatically expand the word list by searching for more words that have closer cosine distances with the selected seed words. At last, we choose the top 100 words to assign to each category tag.

After we have collected all key words for each category, for each sample, we count the total number of occurrences of all words under each category, and then we take the logarithm to obtain a feature vector as $V = (\log N_1, \log N_2, \log N_3, ..., \log N_c)$, where N_c denotes the total number of times the words in category c appear in the sample. In the case where N_c is zero, it is replaced by a large negative number, for example -99.0 in this work.

2.4 Predicting Unseen Stocks via Correlation Graph

There are a large number of stocks trading in the market. However, we normally can only find a

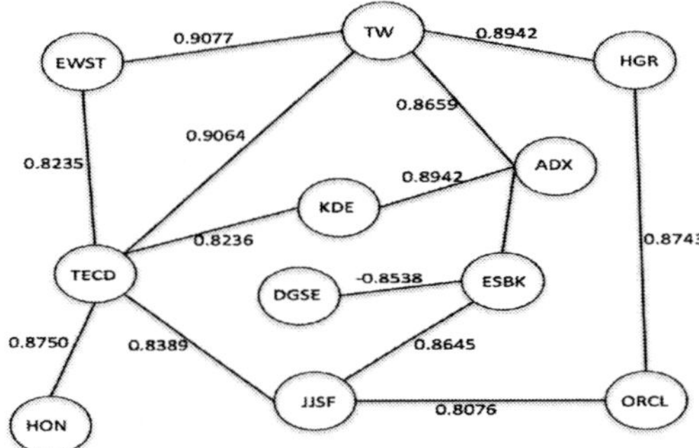

Figure 1: Illustration of a part of correlation graph

fraction of them mentioned in daily financial news. Hence, for each date, the above method can only predict those stocks mentioned in the news. In this section, we propose a new method to extend to predict more stocks that may not be directly mentioned in the financial news. Here we propose to use a stock correlation graph, shown in Figure 1, to predict those unseen stocks. The stock correlation graph is an undirected graph, where each node represents a stock and the arc between two nodes represents the correlation between these two stocks. In this way, if some stocks in the graph are mentioned in the news on a particular day, we first use the above method to predict these mentioned stocks. Afterwards, the predictions are propagated along the arcs in the graph to generate predictions for those unseen stocks.

(1) Build the graph: We choose the top 5,000 stocks from the CRSP database (Booth, 2012) to construct the correlation graph. At each time, any two stocks in the collection are selected to align their closing prices based on the related dates (between 2006/01/01 - 2012/12/31), and we only keep the stock pairs that have an overlapped trading period of at least 252 days (number of trading days in one year). Then we calculate the correlation coefficients between the closing prices of these two stocks. The computed correlation coefficients (between -1 and 1) are attached to the arc connecting these two stocks in the graph, indicating their price correlation. The correlation coefficients are calculated for all stock pairs from the collection of 5,000 stocks. In this paper, we only keep the arcs with an absolute correlation value greater than 0.8, all other edges are considered to be unreliable and pruned from the graph.

(2) Predict unseen stocks: In order to predict

price movements of unseen stocks, we first take the prediction results of those mentioned stocks from the DNN outputs, by which we construct a 5000-dimension vector $\mathbf{x}$. The value of each dimension in this vector is set to indicate the probability of price moving up or down. For the dimensions corresponding to the stocks that are mentioned in the financial news, we set the values using the prediction outputs of the DNN. Since the DNN has two outputs, each of which represents the probabilities of two categories, i.e. stock price moving up or down. If a sample is recognized as price-up, we set this dimension as its probability. Otherwise, if it is recognized as price-down, we set this dimension as its probability multiplied by -1.0. Next, we set zeros for all other dimensions corresponding to unseen stocks. The graph propagation process can be mathematically represented as a matrix multiplication:

$$\mathbf{x}' = \mathbf{A}\mathbf{x}$$

where $\mathbf{A}$ is a symmetric 5000-by-5000 matrix denoting all arc correlation weights in the graph. Of course, this graph propagation may be repeated for several times until the prediction $\mathbf{x}'$ converges.

3 Dataset

The financial news data we used in this paper are provided by (Ding et al., 2014), which contains 106,521 articles from Reuters and 447,145 from Bloomberg. The news articles were published in the time period from October 2006 to December 2013. The historical stock security data are obtained from the Centre for Research in Security Prices (CRSP) database (Booth, 2012), which is published by the Chicago Business School and is widely used in the financial modelling. The CRSP database is properly adjusted for all special price events such as stock splits as well as dividend yields. We only use the security data from 2006 to 2013 to match the time period of the financial news. Base on the samples' publication dates, we split the dataset into three sets: a training set (all samples between 2006-10-01 and 2012-12-31), a validation set (2013-01-01 and 2013-06-15) and a test set (2013-06-16 to 2013-12-31). The training set contains 65,646 samples, the validation set contains 10,941 samples, and the test set contains 9,911 samples.

4 Experiments

4.1 Stock Prediction using DNNs

In the first set of experiments, we use DNNs to predict stock price movements based on a variety of features, namely producing a polar prediction of the price movement on next day (either *price-up* or *price-down*). Here we have trained a set of DNNs using different combinations of feature vectors and found that the DNN structure of 4 hidden layers (with 1024 hidden nodes in each layer) yields the best performance in the validation set. We use the historical price feature alone to create the baseline and various features derived from the financial news are added on top of it. We measure the final performance by calculating the error rate on the test set. As shown in Table 1, the features derived from financial news can significantly improve the prediction accuracy and we have obtained the best performance (an error rate of 43.13%) by using all the features discussed in Sections 2.2 and 2.3. We have also applied the structured event features proposed in (Ding et al., 2014) to our samples and the result is also listed in Table 1, which shows that our proposed features produce better performance in predicting a pool of individual stock prices.

feature combination	error rate
price	48.12%
price + BoK	46.02%
price + BoK + PS	43.96%
price + BoK + CT	45.86%
price + PS	45.00%
price + CT	46.10%
price + PS +CT	46.03%
price + BoK + PS + CT	**43.13%**
structured events (Ding et al., 2014)	44.79%

Table 1: Stock prediction error rates on the test set.

4.2 Predict Unseen Stocks via Correlation

Here we group all outputs from DNNs based on the dates of all samples on the test set. For each date, we create a vector $\mathbf{x}$ based on the DNN prediction results for all observed stocks and zeros for all unseen stocks, as described in section 2.4. Then, the vector is propagated through the correlation graph to generate another set of stock movement prediction. Dur-

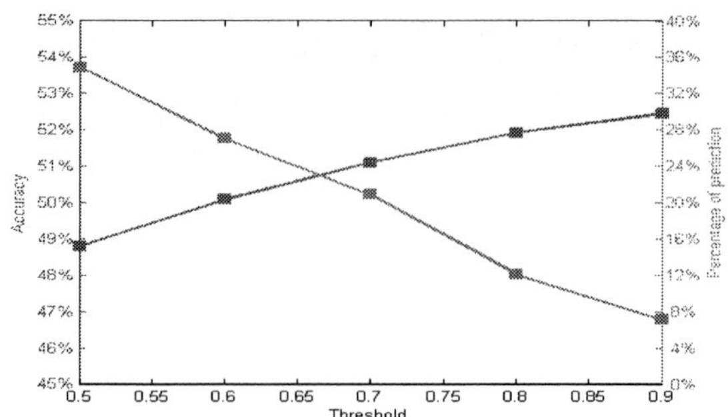

Figure 2: Predict unseen stocks via correlation

ing the propagation, we compute the results from different iterations by multiplying the vector with the correlation matrix ($\mathbf{x}' = \mathbf{A}\mathbf{x}$). Our experimental results show that the prediction accuracy stops to increase after the 4th iteration. After the propagation converges, we may apply a threshold on the propagated vector to prune all low-confidence predictions. The remaining ones may be used to predict some stocks unseen on the test set. The prediction of all unseen stocks is compared with the actual stock movement on next day. Experimental results are shown in Figure 2, where the left y-axis denotes the prediction accuracy and the right y-axis denotes the percentage of stocks predicted out of all 5000 per day under various pruning thresholds. For example, using a large threshold (0.9), we may predict with an accuracy of 52.44% on 354 extra unseen stocks per day, in addition to predicting only 110 stocks per day on the test set.

5 Conclusion

In this paper, we have proposed a simple method to leverage financial news to predict stock movements based on the popular word embedding and deep learning techniques. Our experiments have shown that the financial news is very useful in stock prediction and the proposed methods can improve the prediction accuracy on a standard financial data set.

Acknowledgement

This work is partially supported by a Discovery Grant and an Engage Grant from Natural Sciences and Engineering Research Council (NSERC) of Canada.

References

Monica Adya and Fred Collopy. 1991. How effective are neural networks at forecasting and prediction? a review and evaluation. *Journal of Forecasting*, 17:481–495.

Chicago Booth. 2012. *CRSP Data Description Guide for the CRSP US Stock Database and CRSP US Indices Database*. Center for Research in Security Prices, The University of Chicago Graduate School of Business.

Man-Chung Chan, Chi-Cheong Wong, and Chi-Chung Lam. 2000. Financial time series forecasting by neural network using conjugate gradient learning algorithm and multiple linear regression weight initialization. *Computing in Economics and Finance*, 61.

Zhigang Chen, Wei Lin, Qian Chen, Xiaoping Chen, Si Wei, Xiaodan Zhu, and Hui Jiang. 2015. Revisiting word embedding for contrasting meaning. In *Proceedings of the 53th Annual Meeting of the Association for Computational Linguistics (ACL)*. Association for Computational Linguistics.

Xiao Ding, Yue Zhang, Ting Liu, and Junwen Duan. 2014. Using structured events to predict stock price movement: An empirical investigation. In *Proceedings of the 2014 Conference on Empirical Methods in Natural Language Processing (EMNLP)*, pages 1415–1425. Association for Computational Linguistics.

Iebeling Kaastra and Milton Boyd. 1991. Designing a neural network for forecasting financial and economic time series. *Neurocomputing*, 10:215–236.

Heeyoung Lee, Mihai Surdeanu, Bill Maccartney, and Dan Jurafsky. 2014. On the importance of text analysis for stock price prediction. In *Proceedings of the Ninth International Conference on Language Resources and Evaluation (LREC)*.

Quan Liu, Hui Jiang, Si Wei, Zhenhua Ling, and Yu Hu. 2015. Learning semantic word embeddings based on ordinal knowledge constraints. In *Proceedings of the 53th Annual Meeting of the Association for Computational Linguistics (ACL)*. Association for Computational Linguistics.

Marie-Catherine Marneffe, Bill MacCartney, and Christopher D. Manning. 2006. Generating typed dependency parses from phrase structure parses. In *Proceedings of LREC*.

Tomas Mikolov, Kai Chen, Greg Corrado, and Jeffrey Dean. 2013a. Efficient estimation of word representations in vector space. In *Proceedings of ICLR Workshop*.

Tomas Mikolov, Ilya Sutskever, Kai Chen, Greg S Corrado, and Jeff Dean. 2013b. Distributed representations of words and phrases and their compositionality. In *Proceedings of NIPS*, pages 3111–3119.

Yangtuo Peng and Hui Jiang. 2015. Leverage financial news to predict stock price movements using word embeddings and deep neural networks. In *arXiv:1506.07220*.

Jianfeng Si, Arjun Mukherjee, Bing Liu, Qing Li, Huayi Li, and Xiaotie Deng. 2013. Exploiting topic based twitter sentiment for stock prediction. In *Proceedings of the 51st Annual Meeting of the Association for Computational Linguistics (ACL)*, pages 24–29. Association for Computational Linguistics.

Jianfeng Si, Arjun Mukherjee, Bing Liu, Sinno Jialin Pan, Qing Li, and Huayi Li. 2014. Exploiting social relations and sentiment for stock prediction. In *Proceedings of the 2014 Conference on Empirical Methods in Natural Language Processing (EMNLP)*, pages 1139–1145. Association for Computational Linguistics.

Andrew Skabar and Ian Cloete. 2002. Neural networks, financial trading and the efficient markets hypothesis. In *Proc. of the Twenty-Fifth Australasian Computer Science Conference (ACSC)*.

Peter D. Turney and Michael L. Littman. 2003. Measuring praise and criticism: Inference of semantic orientation from association. *ACM Trans. Inf. Syst.*, 21(4):315–346.

Peter D. Turney and Patrick Pantel. 2010. From frequency to meaning: Vector space models of semantics. *Journal of Artificial Intelligence Research*, 37(1):141–188.

Boyi Xie, Rebecca Passonneau, Leon Wu, and Germán G. Creamer. 2013. Semantic frames to predict stock price movement. In *Proceedings of the 51st Annual Meeting of the Association for Computational Linguistics (ACL)*, pages 873–883. Association for Computational Linguistics.

Xiaotian Zhu, Hong Wang, Li Xu, and Huaizu Li. 2008. Predicting stock index increments by neural networks: The role of trading volume under different horizons. *Expert Systems with Applications*, 34:3043–3054.

Grammatical error correction using neural machine translation

Zheng Yuan and **Ted Briscoe**
The ALTA Institute
Computer Laboratory
University of Cambridge
{zy249,ejb}@cam.ac.uk

Abstract

This paper presents the first study using neural machine translation (NMT) for grammatical error correction (GEC). We propose a two-step approach to handle the rare word problem in NMT, which has been proved to be useful and effective for the GEC task. Our best NMT-based system trained on the CLC outperforms our SMT-based system when testing on the publicly available FCE test set. The same system achieves an $F_{0.5}$ score of 39.90% on the CoNLL-2014 shared task test set, outperforming the state-of-the-art and demonstrating that the NMT-based GEC system generalises effectively.

1 Introduction

Grammatical error correction (GEC) is the task of detecting and correcting grammatical errors in text written by non-native English writers. Unlike building machine learning classifiers for specific error types (e.g. determiner or preposition errors) (Tetreault and Chodorow, 2008; Rozovskaya and Roth, 2011; Dahlmeier and Ng, 2011), the idea of 'translating' a grammatically incorrect sentence into a correct one has been proposed to handle all error types simultaneously (Felice et al., 2014; Junczys-Dowmunt and Grundkiewicz, 2014). Statistical machine translation (SMT) has been successfully used for GEC, as demonstrated by the top-performing systems in the CoNLL-2014 shared task (Ng et al., 2014).

Recently, several neural machine translation (NMT) models have been developed with promising results (Kalchbrenner and Blunsom, 2013; Cho

et al., 2014; Sutskever et al., 2014; Bahdanau et al., 2014). Unlike SMT, which consists of components that are trained separately and combined during decoding (i.e. the translation model and language model) (Koehn, 2010), NMT learns a single large neural network which inputs a sentence and outputs a translation. NMT is appealing for GEC as it may be possible to correct erroneous word phrases and sentences that have not been seen in the training set more effectively (Luong et al., 2015). NMT-based systems thus may help ameliorate the lack of large error-annotated learner corpora for GEC.

However, NMT models typically limit vocabulary size on both source and target sides due to the complexity of training (Sutskever et al., 2014; Bahdanau et al., 2014; Luong et al., 2015; Jean et al., 2015). Therefore, they are unable to translate rare words, and out-of-vocabulary (OOV) words are replaced with *UNK* symbol. This problem is more serious for GEC as non-native text contains not only rare words (e.g. proper nouns), but also misspelled words (i.e. spelling errors). By replacing all the OOV words with the same *UNK* symbol, useful information is discarded, resulting in systems that are not able to correct misspelled words or even keep some of the error-free original words, as in the following examples (OOV words are underlined):

Original sentence

*... I am **goign** to make a plan ...*

System hypothesis

... I am UNK to make a plan ...

Gold standard

Proceedings of NAACL-HLT 2016, pages 380–386,
San Diego, California, June 12-17, 2016. ©2016 Association for Computational Linguistics

*... I am **going** to make a plan ...*

Original sentence

I suggest you visit first the cathedral of " Le <u>Seu</u> d'Mrgell </u> " because it is the most <u>emblematic</u> building in the area .

System hypothesis

I suggest you visit first the cathedral of " Le UNK UNK " because it is the most UNK building in the area .

Gold standard

I suggest you visit first the cathedral of " Le <u>Seu</u> d'Mrgell " because it is the most <u>emblematic</u> building in the area . (unchanged)

Inspired by the work of Luong et al. (2015), we propose a similar but much simpler two-step approach to address the rare word problem: rather than annotating the training data with alignment information, we apply unsupervised alignment models to find the sources of the words in the target sentence. Once we know the source words that are responsible for the unknown target words, a word level translation model learnt from parallel sentences is used to translate these source words.

This paper makes the following contributions. First, we present the first study using NMT for GEC, outperforming the state-of-the-art. Second, we propose a two-step approach to address the rare word problem in NMT for GEC, which we show yields a substantial improvement. Finally, we report results on two well-known publicly available test sets that can be used for cross-system comparisons.

2   Neural machine translation

NMT systems apply the so-called *encoder-decoder* mechanism proposed by Cho et al. (2014) and Sutskever et al. (2014). An encoder reads and encodes an entire source sentence $\mathbf{x} = (x_1, x_2, ..., x_T)$ into a vector c:

$$c = q(h_1, h_2, ..., h_T) \tag{1}$$

where a hidden state h_t at time t is defined as:

$$h_t = f(x_t, h_{t-1}) \tag{2}$$

A decoder then outputs a translation $\mathbf{y} = (y_1, y_2, ..., y_{T'})$ by predicting the next word y_t based on the encoded vector c and all the previously predicted words $\{y_1, y_2, ..., y_{t-1}\}$:

$$p(\mathbf{y}) = \prod_{t=1}^{T'} p(y_t | \{y_1, y_2, ..., y_{t-1}\}, c) = \prod_{t=1}^{T'} g(y_{t-1}, s_t, c) \tag{3}$$

where s_t is the hidden state of the decoder.

Different neural network models have been proposed, for example, Kalchbrenner and Blunsom (2013) proposed a hybrid of a recurrent neural network (RNN) and a convolutional neural network, Sutskever et al. (2014) used a Long Short-Term Memory (LSTM) model, Cho et al. (2014) proposed a similar but simpler gated RNN model, and Bahdanau et al. (2014) introduced an attentional-based architecture.

In this work, we use the *RNNsearch* model of Bahdanau et al. (Bahdanau et al., 2014), which contains a bidirectional RNN as an encoder and an attention-based decoder. The bidirectional RNN encoder has a forward and a backward RNN. The forward RNN reads the source sentence from the first word to the last, and the backward RNN reads the source sentence in reverse order. By doing this, it captures both historical and future information. The attention-based model allows the decoder to focus on the most relevant information in the source sentence, rather than remembering the entire source sentence.

3   Handling rare words

The rare word problem in NMT has been noticed by (Sutskever et al., 2014; Bahdanau et al., 2014; Luong et al., 2015; Jean et al., 2015). Jean et al. (2015) proposed a method based on importance sampling that uses a very large target vocabulary without increasing training complexity. However, no matter how large the target vocabulary size is, there are still OOV words. We also notice that in GEC, the source side vocabulary size is much larger than that of the target side as there are many incorrect words in the source (e.g. spelling mistakes and word form errors) (see Section 4.1). Luong et al. (2015) introduced three new annotation strategies to annotate the training data, so that unknown words in the output can be traced back to their origins. The training data was first re-annotated using the output of a word alignment algorithm. NMT systems were then built using this new data. Finally, information about the OOV words in the target sentence and their corresponding words in the source sentence was extracted from the NMT systems and used in a post-processing step to translate these OOV words using a dictionary.

We propose a similar two-step approach: 1) aligning the unknown words (i.e. *UNK* tokens) in the target sentence to their origins in the source sentence with an unsupervised aligner; 2) building a word level translation model to translate those words in a post-processing step. In order to locate the source words that are responsible for the unknown target words, we apply unsupervised aligners directly and use only the NMT model output instead of first re-annotating training data, and then building new NMT models using this newly annotated data as proposed by Luong et al. (2015). Our approach is much simpler as we avoid re-annotating any data and train only one NMT model. Due to the nature of error correction (i.e. both source and target sentences are in the same language), most words translate as themselves, and errors are often similar to their correct forms. Thus, unsupervised aligners can be successfully used to align the unknown target words. Two automatic alignment tools are used: GIZA++ (Och and Ney, 2003) and METEOR (Banerjee and Lavie, 2005). GIZA++ is an implementation of IBM Models 1-5 (Brown et al., 1993) and a Hidden-Markov alignment model (HMM) (Vogel et al., 1996), which can align two sentences from any languages. Unlike GIZA++, METEOR aligns two sentences from the same language. The latest METEOR 1.5 only supports a few languages, and English is one of them. METEOR identifies not only words with exact matches, but also words with identical stems, synonyms, and unigram paraphrases. This is useful for GEC as it can deal with word form, noun number, and verb form corrections that share identical stems, as well as word choice corrections with synonyms or unigram paraphrases. To build a word level translation model for translating the source words that are responsible for the target unknown words, we need word-aligned data. The IBM Models are used to learn word alignment from parallel sentences.

4 Experiments

4.1 Dataset

We use the publicly available FCE dataset (Yannakoudakis et al., 2011), which is a part of the Cambridge Learner Corpus (CLC) (Nicholls, 2003). The FCE dataset contains 1,244 scripts produced by learners taking the First Certificate in English (FCE) examination between 2000 and 2001. The texts have been manually annotated by linguists using a taxonomy of approximately 80 error types. The publicly available FCE dataset contains about 30,995 pairs of parallel sentences for training (approx. 496,567 tokens on the target side) and about 2,691 pairs of parallel sentences for testing (approx. 41,986 tokens on the target side). Since the FCE training set is too small to build good MT systems, we add training examples extracted from the CLC. Overall, there are 1,965,727 pairs of parallel sentences in our training set. The source side contains 28,823,615 words with 248,028 unique words, and the target side contains 29,219,128 words with 143,852 unique words. As we can see, the source side vocabulary size is much larger than that of the target side. Training and test data is pre-processed using RASP (Briscoe et al., 2006).

4.2 Evaluation

System performance is evaluated using three automatic evaluation metrics: I-measure (Felice and Briscoe, 2015), M^2 Scorer (Dahlmeier and Ng, 2012) and GLEU (Napoles et al., 2015). In the I-measure, an Improvement (I) score is computed by comparing system performance with that of a baseline which leaves the original text uncorrected (i.e. the source). The M^2 Scorer was the official scorer in the CoNLL shared tasks (Ng et al., 2013; Ng et al., 2014), with $F_{0.5}$ being the reported metric in the 2014 edition. GLEU is a simple variant of BLEU (Papineni et al., 2002), which shows better correlation with human judgments on the CoNLL-2014 shared task test set.

4.3 SMT baseline

Following previous work (e.g. Brockett et al. (2006), Yuan and Felice (2013)), we build a phrase-based SMT error correction system as the baseline. Pialign (Neubig et al., 2011) is used to create a phrase translation table. In addition to default features, we add character-level Levenshtein distance to each mapping in the phrase table as proposed by Felice et al. (2014). Decoding is performed using Moses (Koehn et al., 2007). The language model used during decoding is built from the corrected sentences in the learner corpus, to make sure that the final system outputs fluent English sentences. The IRSTLM Toolkit (Federico et al., 2008) is used to buid a 5-gram language model with modified Kneser-Ney smoothing (Kneser and Ney, 1995).

4.4 NMT training details

Our training procedure and hyper-parameters for the NMT system are similar to those used by Bahdanau et al. (2014). We train models with sentences of length up to 100 words, which covers about 99.96% of all the training examples. In terms of vocabulary size, we limit the target vocabulary size to 30K, and experiment with three different source vocabulary sizes: 30K, 50K and 80K.[1] Each model is trained for approximately 5 days using a Tesla K20 GPU.

The output sentences from the NMT systems are aligned with their source sentences using GIZA++. In addition, alignment information learnt by METEOR is used by GIZA++ during aligning. All the *UNK* tokens in the output sentences are replaced with the translation of the source words that are responsible for those *UNK* tokens. The translation is performed using a word level model learnt from IBM Model 4.

4.5 Results

From the results in Table 1, we can see that NMT-based systems alone are not able to achieve comparable results to an SMT-based system. It is probably because of the rare word problem, as increasing the source side vocabulary size helps. The performance of the best NMT system alone (*NMT 80K-30K*), without replacing *UNK* tokens, is still worse than the SMT baseline. When we replace the *UNK* tokens in the NMT output, using GIZA++ for unknown word alignment improves the system performance for all three NMT systems in all three evaluation metrics. We can see that our proposed approach is more useful for NMT systems trained

---

[1]Preliminary experiments show that increasing the source side vocabulary size is more useful than target side.

System	GLEU	$F_{0.5}$ (M^2)	I-measure
Source	60.39	0	0
SMT baseline	70.15	52.90	2.87
NMT-based systems			
NMT 30K-30K	69.04	46.10	-1.30
+ GIZA++	70.89	52.79	3.89
+ METEOR	**71.16**	**53.49**	**3.94**
NMT 50K-30K	68.95	46.78	-1.14
+ GIZA++	70.31	52.02	2.86
+ METEOR	70.40	52.35	2.89
NMT 80K-30K	70.02	49.17	-1.04
+ GIZA++	71.18	53.48	2.40
+ METEOR	71.18	53.49	2.41

Table 1: System performance on the FCE test set (in percentages). The results of our best system are marked in **bold**.

on a small source side vocabulary (e.g. 30K) than a large vocabulary (e.g. 50K, 80K). The larger the vocabulary size, the smaller the gain after replacing *UNK* tokens. The introduction of the METEOR alignment information to GIZA++ yields further improvements. Our best system (*NMT 30K-30K + GIZA++ + METEOR*) achieves an $F_{0.5}$ score of 53.49%, an I score of 3.94%, and a GLEU score of 71.16%, outperforming the SMT baseline in all three evaluation metrics.

Comparing the output of the SMT baseline with that of the NMT system reveals that there are some learner errors which are missed by the SMT system but are captured by the NMT system. One possible reason is that the phrase-based SMT system is trained on surface forms and therefore unaware of syntactic structure. In order to make a correction, it has to have seen the exact correction rule in the training data. Since the NMT system does not rely on any correction rules, in theory, it should be able to make any changes as long as it has seen the words in the training data. For example:

Original sentence

*There are **kidnaps** everywhere and not all of the family can afford the ransom ...*

SMT hypothesis

*There are **kidnaps** everywhere and not all of the families can afford the ransom ...*

NMT hypothesis

*There are **kidnappings** everywhere and not all of the **families** can afford the ransom ...*

Gold standard

*There are **kidnappings** everywhere and not all of the **families** can afford the ransom ...*

The SMT system fails to correct the word form error as the correction rule (*kidnaps $\rightarrow$ kidnappings*) is not in the SMT phrase table learnt from the training data. Since these two words (*kidnaps* and *kidnappings*) have been seen in the training data, the NMT system corrects this error successfully.

5 CoNLL-2014 shared task

The CoNLL-2014 shared task on grammatical error correction required participating systems to correct all errors present in learner English text. The official training and test data comes from the National University of Singapore Corpus of Learner English (NUCLE) (Dahlmeier et al., 2013). $F_{0.5}$ was adopted as the evaluation metric, as reported by the M^2 Scorer. In order to test how well our system generalises, we apply our best system trained on the CLC to the CoNLL-2014 shared task test data directly without adding the NUCLE training data or tuning for the NUCLE. The state-of-the-art $F_{0.5}$ score was reported by Susanto et al. (2014) after the shared task. By combining the outputs from two classification-based systems and two SMT-based systems, they achieved an $F_{0.5}$ score of 39.39%. Results of the uncorrected baseline, our best NMT-based system, Susanto et al. (2014)'s system and the top three systems in the shared task are presented in Table 2. We can see that our NMT-based system outperforms the top three teams, achieving the highest $F_{0.5}$, I and GLEU scores. It also outperforms the state-of-the-art combined system from Susanto et al. (2014). Our system achieves the best $F_{0.5}$ score of 39.90% even though it is not trained on the NUCLE data. This result shows that our system generalises well to other datasets. We expect these results might be further improved by retokenising the test data to be consistent with the tokenisation of the CLC.[2]

---

[2]The NUCLE data was preprocessed using the NLTK toolkit, whereas the CLC was tokenised with RASP.

System	GLEU	$F_{0.5}$ (M^2)	I-measure
Source	64.19	0	0
Our NMT-based system			
30K-30K + GIZA++ + METEOR	65.59	39.90	-3.11
Top 3 systems in CoNLL-2014			
CAMB (Felice et al., 2014)	64.32	37.33	-5.58
CUUI (Rozovskaya et al., 2014)	64.64	36.79	-3.91
AMU (Junczys-Dowmunt and Grundkiewicz, 2014)	64.56	35.01	-3.31
State-of-the-art			
Susanto et al. (2014)	n/a	39.39	n/a

Table 2: System performance on the CoNLL-2014 test set without alternative answers (in percentages).

6 Conclusions

We have shown that NMT can be successfully applied to GEC once we address the rare word problem. Our proposed two-step approach for *UNK* replacement has been proved to be effective, and to provide a substantial improvement. We have developed an NMT-based system that generalises well to another dataset. Our NMT system achieves an $F_{0.5}$ score of 53.49%, an I score of 3.94%, and a GLEU score of 71.16% on the publicly available FCE test set, outperforming an SMT-based system in all three metrics. When testing on the official CoNLL-2014 test set without alternative answers, our system achieves an $F_{0.5}$ score of 39.90%, outperforming the current state-of-the-art. In future work, we would like to explore other ways to address the rare word problem in NMT-based GEC, such as incorporating the soft-alignment information generated by the attention-based decoder, or using character-based models instead of word-based ones.

Acknowledgements

We would like to thank Cambridge English Language Assessment and Cambridge University Press for granting us access to the CLC for research purposes as well as the anonymous reviewers for their comments and suggestions. We acknowledge NVIDIA for an Academic Hardware Grant. This work also used the Wilkes GPU cluster at the University of Cambridge High Performance Computing Service, provided by Dell Inc., NVIDIA and Mellanox, and part funded by STFC with industrial sponsorship from Rolls Royce and Mitsubishi Heavy Industries.

References

Dzmitry Bahdanau, Kyunghyun Cho, and Yoshua Bengio. 2014. Neural Machine Translation by Jointly Learning to Align and Translate. *CoRR*, abs/1409.0473.

Satanjeev Banerjee and Alon Lavie. 2005. METEOR: an automatic metric for MT evaluation with improved correlation with human judgments. In *Proceedings of the ACL Workshop on Intrinsic and Extrinsic Evaluation Measures for Machine Translation and/or Summarization*, pages 65–72.

Ted Briscoe, John Carroll, and Rebecca Watson. 2006. The second release of the RASP system. In *Proceedings of the COLING/ACL 2006 Interactive Presentation Sessions*, pages 77–80.

Chris Brockett, William B. Dolan, and Michael Gamon. 2006. Correcting ESL errors using phrasal SMT techniques. In *Proceedings of the COLING/ACL 2006*, pages 249–256.

Peter F. Brown, Vincent J. Della Pietra, Stephen A. Della Pietra, and Robert L. Mercer. 1993. The mathematics of statistical machine translation: parameter estimation. *Computational Linguistics*, 19(2):263–311.

Kyunghyun Cho, Bart van Merrienboer, Caglar Gulcehre, Dzmitry Bahdanau, Fethi Bougares, Holger Schwenk, and Yoshua Bengio. 2014. Learning Phrase Representations using RNN Encoder-Decoder for Statistical Machine Translation. In *Proceedings of the 2014 Conference on Empirical Methods in Natural Language Processing*, pages 1724–1734.

Daniel Dahlmeier and Hwee Tou Ng. 2011. Grammatical error correction with alternating structure optimization. In *Proceedings of the 49th Annual Meeting of the Association for Computational Linguistics*, pages 915–923.

Daniel Dahlmeier and Hwee Tou Ng. 2012. Better evaluation for grammatical error correction. In *Proceedings of the 2012 Conference of the North American Chapter of the Association for Computational Linguistics: Human Language Technologies*, pages 568–572.

Daniel Dahlmeier, Hwee Tou Ng, and Siew Mei Wu. 2013. Building a large annotated corpus of learner english: the NUS Corpus of Learner English. In *Proceedings of the 8th Workshop on Innovative Use of NLP for Building Educational Applications*, pages 22–31.

Marcello Federico, Nicola Bertoldi, and Mauro Cettolo. 2008. IRSTLM: an open source toolkit for handling large scale language models. In *Proceedings of the 9th Annual Conference of the International Speech Communication Association*, pages 1618–1621.

Mariano Felice and Ted Briscoe. 2015. Towards a standard evaluation method for grammatical error detection and correction. In *Proceedings of the 2015 Conference of the North American Chapter of the Association for Computational Linguistics: Human Language Technologies*, pages 578–587.

Mariano Felice, Zheng Yuan, Øistein E. Andersen, Helen Yannakoudakis, and Ekaterina Kochmar. 2014. Grammatical error correction using hybrid systems and type filtering. In *Proceedings of the 18th Conference on Computational Natural Language Learning: Shared Task*, pages 15–24.

Sébastien Jean, Kyunghyun Cho, Roland Memisevic, and Yoshua Bengio. 2015. On Using Very Large Target Vocabulary for Neural Machine Translation. In *Proceedings of the 53rd Annual Meeting of the Association for Computational Linguistics and the 7th International Joint Conference on Natural Language Processing*, pages 1–10.

Marcin Junczys-Dowmunt and Roman Grundkiewicz. 2014. The AMU system in the CoNLL-2014 shared task: grammatical error correction by data-intensive and feature-rich statistical machine translation. In *Proceedings of the 18th Conference on Computational Natural Language Learning: Shared Task*, pages 25–33.

Nal Kalchbrenner and Phil Blunsom. 2013. Recurrent Continuous Translation Models. In *Proceedings of the 2013 Conference on Empirical Methods in Natural Language Processing*, pages 1700–1709.

Reinhard Kneser and Hermann Ney. 1995. Improved backing-off for M-gram language modeling. In *Proceedings of the IEEE International Conference on Acoustics, Speech, and Signal Processing*, pages 181–184.

Philipp Koehn, Hieu Hoang, Alexandra Birch, Chris Callison-Burch, Marcello Federico, Nicola Bertoldi, Brooke Cowan, Wade Shen, Christine Moran, Richard Zens, Chris Dyer, Ondřej Bojar, Alexandra Constantin, and Evan Herbst. 2007. Moses: open source toolkit for statistical machine translation. In *Proceedings of the 45th Annual Meeting of the ACL on Interactive Poster and Demonstration Sessions*, pages 177–180.

Philipp Koehn. 2010. *Statistical Machine Translation*. Cambridge University Press.

Thang Luong, Ilya Sutskever, Quoc Le, Oriol Vinyals, and Wojciech Zaremba. 2015. Addressing the Rare Word Problem in Neural Machine Translation. In *Proceedings of the ACL-IJCNLP*, pages 11–19.

Courtney Napoles, Keisuke Sakaguchi, Matt Post, and Joel Tetreault. 2015. Ground truth for grammatical error correction metrics. In *Proceedings of the 53rd Annual Meeting of the Association for Computational Linguistics and the 7th International Joint Conference on Natural Language Processing*, pages 588–593.

Graham Neubig, Taro Watanabe, Eiichiro Sumita, Shinsuke Mori, and Tatsuya Kawahara. 2011. An unsupervised model for joint phrase alignment and extraction. In *Proceedings of the 49th Annual Meeting of the Association for Computational Linguistics: Human Language Technologies*, pages 632–641.

Hwee Tou Ng, Siew Mei Wu, Yuanbin Wu, Christian Hadiwinoto, and Joel Tetreault. 2013. The CoNLL-2013 shared task on grammatical error correction. In *Proceedings of the Seventeenth Conference on Computational Natural Language Learning: Shared Task*, pages 1–12.

Hwee Tou Ng, Siew Mei Wu, Ted Briscoe, Christian Hadiwinoto, Raymond Hendy Susanto, and Christopher Bryant. 2014. The CoNLL-2014 shared task on grammatical error correction. In *Proceedings of the 18th Conference on Computational Natural Language Learning: Shared Task*, pages 1–14.

Diane Nicholls. 2003. The Cambridge Learner Corpus - error coding and analysis for lexicography and ELT. In *Proceedings of the Corpus Linguistics 2003 Conference*, pages 572–581.

Franz Josef Och and Hermann Ney. 2003. A systematic comparison of various statistical alignment models. *Computational Linguistics*, 29(1):19–51.

Kishore Papineni, Salim Roukos, Todd Ward, and Wei-Jing Zhu. 2002. BLEU: a method for automatic evaluation of machine translation. In *Proceedings of the 40th Annual Meeting of the Association for Computational Linguistics*, pages 311–318.

Alla Rozovskaya and Dan Roth. 2011. Algorithm selection and model adaptation for ESL correction tasks. In *Proceedings of the 49th Annual Meeting of the Association for Computational Linguistics*, pages 924–933.

Alla Rozovskaya, Kai-Wei Chang, Mark Sammons, Dan Roth, and Nizar Habash. 2014. The Illinois-Columbia System in the CoNLL-2014 Shared Task. In *Proceedings of the 18th Conference on Computational Natural Language Learning: Shared Task*, pages 34–42.

Hendy Raymond Susanto, Peter Phandi, and Tou Hwee Ng. 2014. System combination for grammatical error correction. In *Proceedings of the 2014 Conference on Empirical Methods in Natural Language Processing (EMNLP)*, pages 951–962.

Ilya Sutskever, Oriol Vinyals, and Quoc V. Le. 2014. Sequence to Sequence Learning with Neural Networks. In *Advances in Neural Information Processing Systems*, pages 3104–3112.

Joel R. Tetreault and Martin Chodorow. 2008. The ups and downs of preposition error detection in ESL writing. In *Proceedings of the 22nd International Conference on Computational Linguistics*, volume 1, pages 865–872.

Stephan Vogel, Hermann Ney, and Christoph Tillmann. 1996. HMM-based word alignment in statistical translation. In *Proceedings of the 16th International Conference on Computational linguistics*, volume 2, pages 836–841.

Helen Yannakoudakis, Ted Briscoe, and Ben Medlock. 2011. A new dataset and method for automatically grading ESOL texts. In *Proceedings of the 49th Annual Meeting of the Association for Computational Linguistics: Human Language Technologies*, pages 180–189.

Zheng Yuan and Mariano Felice. 2013. Constrained grammatical error correction using statistical machine translation. In *Proceedings of the 17th Conference on Computational Natural Language Learning: Shared Task*, pages 52–61.

Multimodal Semantic Learning from Child-Directed Input

Angeliki Lazaridou
University of Trento
`angeliki.lazaridou@unitn.it`

Grzegorz Chrupała
Tilburg University
`g.chrupala@uvt.nl`

Raquel Fernández
University of Amsterdam
`raquel.fernandez@uva.nl`

Marco Baroni
University of Trento
`marco.baroni@unitn.it`

Abstract

Children learn the meaning of words by being exposed to perceptually rich situations (linguistic discourse, visual scenes, etc). Current computational learning models typically simulate these rich situations through impoverished symbolic approximations. In this work, we present a *distributed* word learning model that operates on child-directed speech paired with realistic *visual scenes*. The model integrates linguistic and extra-linguistic information (visual and social cues), handles referential uncertainty, and correctly learns to associate words with objects, even in cases of limited linguistic exposure.

1 Introduction

Computational models of word learning typically approximate the perceptual context that learners are exposed to through artificial proxies, e.g., representing a visual scene via a collection of symbols such as `cat` and `dog`, signaling the presence of a cat, a dog, etc. (Yu and Ballard, 2007; Fazly et al., 2010, *inter alia*).[1] While large amounts of data can be generated in this way, they will not display the complexity and richness of the signal found in the natural environment a child is exposed to. We take a step towards a more realistic setup by introducing a model that operates on naturalistic images of the objects present in a communicative episode. Inspired by recent computational models of meaning (Bruni et al., 2014; Kiros et al., 2014; Silberer

and Lapata, 2014), that integrate distributed linguistic and visual information, we build upon the Multimodal Skip-Gram (MSG) model of Lazaridou et al. (2015). and enhance it to handle cross-referential uncertainty. Moreover, we extend the cues commonly used in multimodal learning (e.g., objects in the environment) to include *social cues* (e.g., eyegaze, gestures, body posture, etc.) that reflect speakers' intentions and generally contribute to the unfolding of the communicative situation (Stivers and Sidnell, 2005). As a first step towards developing full-fleged learning systems that leverage all signals available within a communicative setup, in our extended model we incorporate information regarding the objects that caregivers are holding.

2 Attentive Social MSG Model

Like the original MSG, our model learns multimodal word embeddings by reading an utterance sequentially and making, for each word, two sets of predictions: (a) the preceding and following words, and (b) the visual representations of objects co-occurring with the utterance. However, unlike Lazaridou et al. (2015), we do not assume we know the right object to be associated with a word. We consider instead a more realistic scenario where multiple words in an utterance co-occur with multiple objects in the corresponding scene. Under this *referential uncertainty*, the model needs to induce word-object associations as part of learning, relying on current knowledge about word-object affinities as well as on any social clues present in the scene.

Similar to the standard skipgram, the model's parameters are context word embeddings $\mathbf{W}'$ and tar-

---

[1] See Kádár et al. (2015) for a recent review of this line of work, and another learning model using, like ours, real visual input.

Proceedings of NAACL-HLT 2016, pages 387–392,
San Diego, California, June 12-17, 2016. ©2016 Association for Computational Linguistics

get word embeddings $\mathbf{W}$. The model aims at optimizing these parameters with respect to the following multi-task loss function for an utterance w with associated set of objects U:

$$L(w, U) = \sum_{t=1}^{T} (\ell_{ling}(w, t) + \ell_{vis}(w_t, U)) \quad (1)$$

where t ranges over the positions in the utterance w, such that w_t is t^{th} word. The linguistic loss function is the standard skip-gram loss (Mikolov et al., 2013). The visual loss is defined as:

$$\ell_{vis}(w_t, U) = \sum_{s=1}^{S} \lambda\alpha(\mathbf{w}_t, \mathbf{u}_s)g(\mathbf{w}_t, \mathbf{u}_s) \\ +(1 - \lambda)h(\mathbf{u}_s)g(\mathbf{w}_t, \mathbf{u}_s) \quad (2)$$

where $\mathbf{w}_t$ stands for the column of $\mathbf{W}$ corresponding to word w_t, $\mathbf{u}_s$ is the vector associated with object U_s, and g the penalty function

$$g(\mathbf{w}_t, \mathbf{u}_s) = \sum_{\mathbf{u}'} \max(0, \gamma - \cos(\mathbf{w}_t, \mathbf{u}_s) \\ + \cos(\mathbf{w}_t, \mathbf{u}')), \quad (3)$$

which is small when projections to the visual space $\mathbf{w}_t$ of words from the utterance are similar to the vectors representing co-occurring objects, and at the same time they are dissimilar to vectors $\mathbf{u}'$ representing randomly sampled objects. The first term in Eq. 2 is the penalty g weighted by the current word-object affinity α, inspired by the "attention" of Bahdanau et al. (2015). If α is set to a constant 1, the model treats all words in an utterance as equally relevant for each object. Alternatively it can be used to encourage the model to place more weight on words which it already knows are likely to be related to a given object, by defining it as the (exponentiated) cosine similarity between word and object normalized over all words in the utterance:

$$\alpha(\mathbf{w}_t, \mathbf{u}_s) = \frac{\exp(\cos(\mathbf{w}_t, \mathbf{u}_s))}{\sum_r \exp(\cos(\mathbf{w}_r, \mathbf{u}_s))} \quad (4)$$

The second term of Eq. 2 is the penalty weighted by the social salience h of the object, which could be based on various cues in the scene. In our experiments we set it to 1 if the caregiver holds the object, 0 otherwise.

We experiment with three versions of the model. With $\lambda = 1$ and α frozen to 1, the model reduces

Figure 1: Fragment of the IFC corpus where symbolic labels `ring` and `hat` have been replaced by real images. Red frames mark objects being touched by the caregiver.

to the original **MSG**, but now trained with referential uncertainty. The **Attentive MSG** sets $\lambda = 1$ and calculates $\alpha(\mathbf{w}_t, \mathbf{u}_s)$ using Equation 4 (we use the term "attentive" to emphasize the fact that, when processing a word, the model will pay more attention to the more relevant objects). Finally, **Attentive Social MSG** further sets $\lambda = \frac{1}{2}$, boosting the importance of socially salient objects.

All other hyperparameters are set to the values found by Lazaridou et al. (2015) to be optimal after tuning, except hidden layer size that we set to 200 instead of 300 due to the small corpus (see Section 3). We train the MSG models with stochastic gradient descent for one epoch.

3 The Illustrated Frank et al. Corpus

Frank et al. (2007) present a Bayesian cross-situational learning model for simulating early word learning in first language acquisition. The model is tested on a portion of the Rollins section of the CHILDES Database (MacWhinney, 2000) consisting of two transcribed video files (`me03` and `di06`), of approximately 10 minutes each, where a mother and a pre-verbal infant play with a set of toys. By inspecting the video recordings, the authors manually annotated each utterance in the transcripts with a list of object labels (e.g., `ring`, `hat`, `cow`) corresponding to all midsize objects judged to be visible to the infant while the utterance took place, as well as various social cues. The dataset includes a gold-standard lexicon consisting of 36 words paired with 17 object labels (e.g., *hat*=`hat`, *pig*=`pig`, *piggie*=`pig`).[2]

---

[2] `http://langcog.stanford.edu/materials/nipsmaterials.html`

Aiming at creating a more realistic version of the original dataset, akin to simulating a real visual scene, we replaced symbolic object labels with actual visual representations of objects. To construct such visual representations, we sample for each object 100 images from the respective ImageNet (Deng et al., 2009) entry, and from each image we extract a 4096-dimensional visual vector using the Caffe toolkit (Jia et al., 2014), together with the pretrained convolutional neural network of Krizhevsky et al. (2012).[3] These vectors are finally averaged to obtain a single visual representation of each object. Concerning social cues, since infants rarely follow the caregivers' eye gaze but rather attend to objects held by them (Yu and Smith, 2013), we include in our corpus only information on whether the caregiver is holding any of the objects present in the scene. Note however that this signal, while informative, can also be ambiguous or even misleading with respect to the actual referents of a statement. Figure 1 exemplifies our version of the corpus, the Illustrated Frank et al. Corpus (IFC).

Several aspects make IFC a challenging dataset. Firstly, we are dealing with language produced in an interactive setting rather than written discourse. For example, compare the first sentence in the Wikipedia entry for *hat* (*"A hat is a head covering"*) to the third utterance in Figure 1, corresponding to the first occurrence of *hat* in our corpus. Secondly, there is a large amount of referential uncertainty, with up to 7 objects present per utterance (2 on average) and with only 33% of utterances explicitly including a word directly associated with a possible referent (i.e., not taking into account pronouns). For instance, the first, second and last utterances in Figure 1 do not explicitly mention any of the objects present in the scene. This uncertainty also extends to social cues: only in 23% of utterances does the mother explicitly name an object that she is holding in her hands. Finally, models must induce word–object associations from minimal exposure to input rather than from large amounts of training data. Indeed, the IFC is extremely small by any standards: 624 utterances making up 2,533 words in total, with 8/37 test words occurring only once.

---

[3]To match the hidden layer size, we average every k = 4096/200 original non-overlapping visual dimensions into a single dimension.

Model	Best-F
MSG	.64 (.04)
AttentiveMSG	.70 (.04)
AttentiveSocialMSG	.73 (.03)
ASMSG+shuffled visual vectors	.65 (.06)
ASMSG+randomized sentences	.59 (.03)
BEAGLE	.55
PMI	.53
Bayesian CSL	.54
BEAGLE+PMI	.83

Table 1: Best-F results for the MSG variations and alternative models on word-object matching. For all MSG models, we report Best-F mean and standard deviation over 100 iterations.

4 Experiments

We follow the evaluation protocol of Frank et al. (2007) and Kievit-Kylar et al. (2013). Given 37 test words and the corresponding 17 objects (see Table 2), all found in the corpus, we rank the objects with respect to each word. A mean *Best-F* score is then derived by computing, for each word, the top F score across the precision-recall curve, and averaging it across the words. MSG rankings are obtained by directly ordering the visual representations of the objects by cosine similarity to the MSG word vectors.

Table 1 reports our results compared to those in earlier studies, all of which did not use actual visual representations of objects but rather arbitrary symbolic IDs. Bayesian CSL is the original Bayesian cross-situational model of Frank et al. (2007), also including social cues (not limited, like us, to mother's touch). BEAGLE is the best semantic-space result across a range of distributional models and word-object matching methods from Kievit-Kylar et al. (2013). Their distributional models were trained in a *batch mode*, and by treating object IDs as words so that standard word-vector-based similarity methods could be used to rank objects with respect to words. Plain MSG is outperforming nearly all earlier approaches by a large margin. The only method bettering it is the BEAGLE+PMI combination of Kievit-Kylar et al. (PMI measures direct co-occurrence of test words and object IDs). The latter was obtained through a grid search of all possible model combinations performed directly on the test set, and relied on a weight parameter optimized on the corpus by assuming access to gold annotation.

It is thus not comparable to the untuned MSG.

Plain MSG, then, performs remarkably well, even without any mechanism attempting to track word-object matching across scenes. Still, letting the model pay more attention to the objects currently most tightly associated to a word (AttentiveMSG) brings a large improvement over plain MSG, and a further improvement is brought about by giving more weight to objects touched by the mother (AttentiveSocialMSG). As concrete examples, plain MSG associated the word *cow* with a pig, whereas AttentiveMSG correctly shifts attention to the cow. In turn, AttentiveSocialMSG associates to the right object several words that AttentiveMSG wrongly pairs with the hand holding them, instead.

One might fear the better performance of our models might be due to the skip-gram method being superior to the older distributional semantic approaches tested by Kievit-Kylar et al. (2013), independently of the extra visual information we exploit. In other words, it could be that MSG has simply learned to treat, say, the *lamb* visual vector as an arbitrary signature, functioning as a semantically opaque ID for the relevant object, without exploiting the visual resemblance between lamb and sheep. In this case, we should obtain similar performance when arbitrarily shuffling the visual vectors across object types (e.g., consistently replacing each occurrence of the *lamb* visual vector with, say, the *hand* visual vector). The lower results obtained in this control condition (ASMSG+shuffled visual vector) confirm that our performance boost is largely due to exploitation of genuine visual information.

Since our approach is incremental (unlike the vast majority of traditional distributional models that operate on batch mode), it can in principle exploit the fact that the linguistic and visual flows in the corpus are meaningfully ordered (discourse and visual environment will evolve in a coherent manner: a hat appears on the scene, it's there for a while, in the meantime a few statements about hats are uttered, etc.). The dramatic quality drop in the ASMSG+randomized sentences condition, where AttentiveSocialMSG was trained on IFC after randomizing sentence order, confirms the coherent situation flow is crucial to our good performance.

word	*gold object*	*17 objects*		*5.1K objects*	
		nearest	*r*	*nearest*	*r*
bunny	bunny	bunny	**1**	bunny	**1**
cows	cow	cow	**1**	lea	**7**
duck	duck	duck	**1**	mallard	**4**
duckie	duck	duck	**1**	mallard	**3**
kitty	kitty	book	**2**	bookcase	**66**
lambie	lamb	lamb	**1**	lamb	**1**
moocows	cow	cow	**1**	ranch	**4**
rattle	rattle	rattle	**1**	rattle	**1**

Table 2: Test words occurring only once in IFC, together with corresponding gold objects, AttentiveSocialMSG top visual neighbours among the test items and in a larger 5.1K-objects set, and ranks of gold object in the two confusion sets.

Minimal exposure. Given the small size of the input corpus, good performance on the word-object association already counts as indirect evidence that MSG, like children, can learn from small amounts of data. In Table 2 we take a more specific look at this challenge by reporting AttentiveSocialMSG performance on the task of ranking object visual representations for test words that occurred *only once* in IFC, considering both the standard evaluation set and a much larger confusion set including visual vectors for 5.1K distinct objects (those of Lazaridou et al. (2015)). Remarkably, in all but one case, the model associates the test word to the right object from the small set, and to either the right object or another relevant visual concept (e.g., a ranch for *moocows*) when the extended set is considered. The exception is *kitty*, and even for this word the model ranks the correct object as second in the smaller set, and well above chance for the larger one. Our approach, just like humans (Trueswell et al., 2013), can often get a word meaning right based on a single exposure to it.

Generalization. Unlike the earlier models relying on arbitrary IDs, our model is learning to associate words to actual feature-based visual representations. Thus, once the model is trained on IFC, we can test its generalization capabilities to associate known words with new object instances that belong to the right category. We focus on 19 words in our test set corresponding to objects that were normed for visual similarity to other objects by Silberer and Lapata (2014). Each test word was paired with 40 ImageNet pictures evenly divided between images of the gold object (*not* used in IFC), of a highly visually similar object, of a mildly visually similar object and of a dissimilar one (for *duck*: *duck*, *chicken*, *finch* and *garage*, respectively). The pictures were represented by vectors obtained with the same method outlined in Section 3, and were ranked by similarity to a test word AttentiveSocialMSG representation.

Average Precision@10 for retrieving gold object instances is at 62% (chance: 25%). In the majority of cases the top-10 intruders are instances of the most visually related concepts (60% of intruders, vs. 33% expected by chance). For example, the model retrieves pictures of sheep for the word *lamb*, or bulls for *cow*. Intriguingly, this points to classic overextension errors that are commonly reported in child language acquisition (Rescorla, 1980).

5 Related Work

While there is work on learning from multimodal data (Roy, 2000; Yu, 2005, a.o.) as well as work on learning distributed representations from child-directed speech (Baroni et al., 2007; Kievit-Kylar and Jones, 2011, a.o.), to the best of our knowledge ours is the first method which learns distributed representations from multimodal child-directed data. For example, in comparison to Yu (2005)'s model, our approach (1) induces distributed representations for words, based on linguistic and visual context, and (2) operates entirely on distributed representations through similarity measures without positing a categorical level on which to learn word-symbol/category-symbol associations. This leads to rich multimodal conceptual representations of words in terms of distributed multimodal features, while in Yu's approach words are simply distributions over categories. It is therefore not clear how Yu's approach could capture phenomena such as predicting appearance from a verbal description or representing abstract words–all tasks that our model is at least in principle well-suited for. Note also that Frank et al. (2007)'s Bayesian model we compare against could be extended to include realistic visual data in a similar vein to Yu's, but it would then have the same limitations.

Our work is also related to research on reference resolution in dialogue systems, such as Kennington and Schlangen (2015). However, unlike Kennington and Schlangen, who explicitly train an object recognizer associated with each word of interest, with at least 65 labeled positive training examples per word, our model does not have any comparable form of supervision and our data exhibits much lower frequencies of object and word (co-)occurrence. Moreover, reference resolution is only an aspect of what we do: Besides being able to associate a word with a visual extension, our model is simultaneously learning word representations that allow us to deal with a variety of other tasks—for example, as mentioned above, guessing the appearance of the object denoted by a new word from a purely verbal description, grouping concepts into categories by their similarity, or having both abstract and concrete words represented in the same space.

6 Conclusion

Our very encouraging results suggest that multimodal distributed models are well-suited to simulating human word learning. We think the most pressing issue to move ahead in this direction is to construct larger corpora recording the linguistic and visual environment in which children acquire language, in line with the efforts of the Human Speechome Project (Roy, 2009; Roy et al., 2015). Having access to such data will enable us to design agents that acquire semantic knowledge by leveraging all available cues present in multimodal communicative setups, such as learning agents that can automatically predict eye-gaze (Recasens* et al., 2015) and incorporate this knowledge into the semantic learning process.

Acknowledgments

We thank Marco Marelli for useful advice and Brent Kievit-Kylar for help implementing the Best-F measure. We acknowledge the European Network on Integrating Vision and Language for a Short-Term Scientific Mission grant, awarded to Raquel Fernández to visit the University of Trento.

References

Dzmitry Bahdanau, Kyunghyun Cho, and Yoshua Bengio. 2015. Neural machine translation by jointly learning to align and translate. In *Proceedings of ICLR Conference Track*, San Diego, CA. Published online: `http://www.iclr.cc/doku.php?id=iclr2015:main`.

Marco Baroni, Alessandro Lenci, and Luca Onnis. 2007. ISA meets Lara: An incremental word space model for cognitively plausible simulations of semantic learning. In *Proceedings of the ACL Workshop on Cognitive Aspects of Computational Language Acquisition*, pages 49–56.

Elia Bruni, Nam Khanh Tran, and Marco Baroni. 2014. Multimodal distributional semantics. *Journal of Artificial Intelligence Research*, 49:1–47.

Jia Deng, Wei Dong, Richard Socher, Lia-Ji Li, and Li Fei-Fei. 2009. Imagenet: A large-scale hierarchical image database. In *Proceedings of CVPR*, pages 248–255, Miami Beach, FL.

Afsaneh Fazly, Afra Alishahi, and Suzanne Stevenson. 2010. A probabilistic computational model of cross-situational word learning. *Cognitive Science*, 34:1017–1063.

Michael Frank, Noah Goodman, and Joshua Tenenbaum. 2007. A Bayesian framework for cross-situational word-learning. In *Proceedings of NIPS*, pages 457–464, Vancouver, Canada.

Yangqing Jia, Evan Shelhamer, Jeff Donahue, Sergey Karayev, Jonathan Long, Ross Girshick, Sergio Guadarrama, and Trevor Darrell. 2014. Caffe: Convolutional architecture for fast feature embedding. *arXiv preprint arXiv:1408.5093*.

Ákos Kádár, Afra Alishahi, and Grzegorz Chrupała. 2015. Learning word meanings from images of natural scenes. *Traitement Automatique des Langues*. In press, preprint available at `http://grzegorz.chrupala.me/papers/tal-2015.pdf`.

Casey Kennington and David Schlangen. 2015. Simple learning and compositional application of perceptually grounded word meanings for incremental reference resolution. In *Proceedings of the Conference for the Association for Computational Linguistics (ACL)*.

Brent Kievit-Kylar and Michael Jones. 2011. The Semantic Pictionary project. In *Proceedings of CogSci*, pages 2229–2234, Austin, TX.

Brent Kievit-Kylar, George Kachergis, and Michael Jones. 2013. Naturalistic word-concept pair learning with semantic spaces. In *Proceedings of CogSci*, pages 2716–2721, Berlin, Germany.

Ryan Kiros, Ruslan Salakhutdinov, and Richard Zemel. 2014. Unifying visual-semantic embeddings with multimodal neural language models. In *Proceedings of the NIPS Deep Learning and Representation Learning Workshop*, Montreal, Canada. Published online: `http://www.dlworkshop.org/accepted-papers`.

Alex Krizhevsky, Ilya Sutskever, and Geoffrey Hinton. 2012. ImageNet classification with deep convolutional neural networks. In *Proceedings of NIPS*, pages 1097–1105, Lake Tahoe, Nevada.

Angeliki Lazaridou, Nghia The Pham, and Marco Baroni. 2015. Combining language and vision with a multimodal skip-gram model. In *Proceedings of NAACL*, pages 153–163, Denver, CO.

Brian MacWhinney. 2000. *The CHILDES Project: Tools for analyzing talk*. Lawrence Erlbaum Associates, 3rd edition.

Tomas Mikolov, Kai Chen, Greg Corrado, and Jeffrey Dean. 2013. Efficient estimation of word representations in vector space. `http://arxiv.org/abs/1301.3781/`.

Adria Recasens*, Aditya Khosla*, Carl Vondrick, and Antonio Torralba. 2015. Where are they looking? In *Advances in Neural Information Processing Systems (NIPS)*. * indicates equal contribution.

Leslie Rescorla. 1980. Overextension in early language development. *Journal of Child Language*, 7(2):321–335.

Brandon C. Roy, Michael C. Frank, Philip DeCamp, Matthew Miller, and Deb Roy. 2015. Predicting the birth of a spoken word. *Proceedings of the National Academy of Sciences*, 112(41):12663–12668.

Deb Roy. 2000. A computational model of word learning from multimodal sensory input. In *Proceedings of the International Conference of Cognitive Modeling (ICCM2000), Groningen, Netherlands*.

Deb Roy. 2009. New horizons in the study of child language acquisition. In *Proceedings of Interspeech*.

Carina Silberer and Mirella Lapata. 2014. Learning grounded meaning representations with autoencoders. In *Proceedings of ACL*, pages 721–732, Baltimore, Maryland.

Tanya Stivers and Jack Sidnell. 2005. Introduction: Multimodal interaction. *Semiotica*, pages 1–20.

John Trueswell, Tamara Medina, Alon Hafri, and Lila Gleitman. 2013. Propose but verify: Fast mapping meets cross-situational word learning. *Cognitive Psychology*, 66(1):126–156.

Chen Yu and Dana H. Ballard. 2007. A unified model of early word learning: Integrating statistical and social cues. *Neurocomputing*, 70(13-15):2149–2165.

Chen Yu and Linda B. Smith. 2013. Joint attention without gaze following: human infants and their parents coordinate visual attention to objects through eye-hand coordination. *PLoS ONE*, 8(11).

C. Yu. 2005. The emergence of links between lexical acquisition and object categorization: A computational study. *Connection Science*, 17(3):381–397.

Recurrent Support Vector Machines For Slot Tagging In Spoken Language Understanding

Yangyang Shi and **Kaisheng Yao** and **Hu Chen** and **Dong Yu**
Yi-Cheng Pan and **Mei-Yuh Hwang**
Microsoft
{yanshi,kaisheng.yao,huch,dong.yu,ycpan,mehwang}@microsoft.com

Abstract

We propose recurrent support vector machine (RSVM) for slot tagging. This model is a combination of the recurrent neural network (RNN) and the structured support vector machine. RNN extracts features from the input sequence. The structured support vector machine uses a sequence-level discriminative objective function. The proposed model therefore combines the sequence representation capability of an RNN with the sequence-level discriminative objective. We have observed new state-of-the-art results on two benchmark datasets and one private dataset. RSVM obtained statistical significant 4% and 2% relative average F1 score improvement on ATIS dataset and Chunking dataset, respectively. Out of eight domains in Cortana live log dataset, RSVM achieved F1 score improvement on seven domains. Experiments also show that RSVM significantly speeds up the model training by skipping the weight updating for non-support vector training samples, compared against training using RNN with CRF or minimum cross-entropy objectives.

1 Introduction

One of the key tasks in natural language understanding (Hemphill et al., 1990a; He and Young, 2003; De Mori, 2007; Dinarelli et al., 2008; Wang et al., 2005) is slot tagging that labels user queries with semantic tags. It is a sequence labeling problem that transcribes a sequence of observations $X = [x(1), x(2), ..., x(M)]$ to a sequence of discrete labels $Y = [y(1), y(2), ..., y(M)]$. For example, in the query "show me flights from Seattle to Boston", the words "Seattle" and "Boston" should be labeled, respectively, as the *from-city-name* slot and the *to-city-name* slot.

Recently recurrent neural networks (RNNs) and their variants achieved state-of-the-art performances on slot tagging tasks (Yao et al., 2013; Yao et al., 2014b; Yao et al., 2014a; Graves, 2012; Shi et al., 2015; Mesnil et al., 2015; Peng and Yao, 2015). One direction to improve the sequence labeling is to strengthen the model memorization capability by designing dedicated special structures, for example, using long-short-term-memory (LSTM) networks (Hochreiter and Schmidhuber, 1997; Graves et al., 2013; Yao et al., 2014a), gated RNN and RNN with external memory (RNN-em) (Peng and Yao, 2015). The other direction is to optimize the sequence-level discrimination criterion. For example, recurrent conditional random fields (RCRFs) (Yao et al., 2014b) is trained to optimize the sequence conditional likelihood rather than minimizing frame level cross-entropy applied in conventional RNN based sequence labeling (Prez-ortiz et al., 2001; Yao et al., 2013; Mikolov et al., 2010; Shi et al., 2015; Mesnil et al., 2015).

In this paper, we propose recurrent support vector machines (RSVMs) to improve the discrimination ability of RNNs. Different from RCRFs and conventional RNNs that in essence apply the multinomial logistic regression on the output layer, RSVMs optimize the sequence-level max-margin training criterion used by structured support vector machines (Tsochantaridis et al., 2005) on the output layer of RNNs. There are several advantages of using sequence-level max-margin training over maximum likelihood or minimum cross-entropy. Firstly, the sequence-level max-margin criterion is a *global un-normalized* criterion in which there is no computation cost for normalization. Secondly, using max-margin training, only training samples from support vectors generate non zero errors. In other words, model training can be sped up by skipping the weight updating for non-support vector training samples. Finally, as proven in (Vapnik, 1995), margin maximization is equivalent to minimization of an upper bound on the generalization errors. Max-margin training has no assumption about the model distribution. To use maximum likelihood or minimum cross-entropy, it assumes that the model distribution is peaked. However, especially in natural language processing where the ambiguity is ubiquitous, this assumption does not hold.

Proceedings of NAACL-HLT 2016, pages 393–399,
San Diego, California, June 12-17, 2016. ©2016 Association for Computational Linguistics

For example, "seven eleven" can be labeled as time tag or place name (super market name) tag. The conditional probability of tag given "seven eleven" should not be sharp for time or place name.

Recently, SVM is also applied on top of a deep neural network for speech recognition (Zhang et al., 2015). In their work, a cutting-plane algorithm (Joachims et al., 2009) is used, which is computationally expensive for speech recognition tasks. In this paper, we use the stochastic gradient descent algorithm (SGD) (Panagiotakopoulos and Tsampouka, 2013) for model training. The loss function is critical to the sequence level max-margin training criterion, which defines the margin. In this paper, we apply the sequence level hard loss function rather than traditional Hamming loss function (Nguyen and Guo, 2007). In sequence level hard loss function, the wrong sequence is assigned loss one without considering the number of wrong slot labels in the sequence. In the experiments on two bench mark datasets, namely the ATIS (Airline Travel Information Systems) dataset (Hemphill et al., 1990b; Yao et al., 2014b) and the CoNLL 2000 Chunking dataset [1], and private Cortana live log dataset, RSVMs outperformed previous results.

2   Recurrent Support Vector Machines

In this section, we propose RSVM that uses the structured SVM algorithm (Tsochantaridis et al., 2005) to estimate the weights for RNN and label transition probabilities based on the entire training sequence. The training objective in RSVM is the following constrained optimization.

$$\min_{W,A} \frac{1}{2}||W||_2^2 + \frac{1}{2}||A||_2^2 + C\sum_{k=1}^{K} \zeta_k$$

$$s.t.\, f(Y^{(k)^*}) + \zeta_k \geq f(Y^{(k)}) + L(Y^{(k)}) \quad \forall Y^{(k)} \qquad (1)$$

$$L(Y^{(k)}) \geq 0 \quad \forall Y^{(k)} \qquad (2)$$

$$\zeta_k \geq 0 \qquad (3)$$

where

$$f(Y^{(k)}) = \sum_{t=1}^{T} a_{y_k(t-1)y_k(t)} + W_{y_k(t)}^T H(t) \qquad (4)$$

where C is regularization weight for empirical loss. $Y^{(k)}$ represents the slot label sequence $y^{(k)}(1:T)$ for training sample $X^{(k)}$. $Y^{(k)^*}$ is the ground truth slot sequence $y^{(k)^*}(1:T)$ for $X^{(k)}$. $a_{y^{(k)}(t-1)y^{(k)}(t)}$ is one element in matrix A, representing the weight for the slot label transition features from $y^{(k)}(t-1)$ to $y^{(k)}(t)$. $L(Y^{(k)})$ defines the loss function of a possible slot label sequence for a training sample $X^{(k)}$, which is actually used as a margin to

separate the score $f(Y^{(k)^*})$ for ground truth slot label sequence with all other possible slot sequences in Eq. (1). $\zeta^{(k)}$ is the slack variable that penalize the slot label sequence that violates the margin constraint.

The constrained optimization problem can be transformed to an unconstrained optimization problem as

$$\min_{W,A} \quad F(W,A) = \frac{1}{2C}||W||_2^2 + \frac{1}{2C}||A||_2^2$$

$$+ \sum_{k=1}^{K} [\max_{Y^{(k)} \neq Y^{(k)^*}} (f(Y^{(k)}) + L(Y^{(k)})) - f(Y^{(k)^*})]_+. \qquad (5)$$

where $[x]_+$ is the Hinge function that maps x to zero when x is smaller than zero, otherwise $[x]_+ = x$.

The loss function $L(Y^{(k)})$ is critical to the structured SVM training. The following two types of loss functions have been investigated:

$$L(Y^{(k)}) = \sum_{t=1}^{T} 1\left(y^{(k)}(t) \neq y^{(k)^*}(t)\right) \qquad (6)$$

$$L(Y^{(k)}) = 1\left(y^{(k)}(1:T) \neq y^{(k)^*}(1:T)\right) \qquad (7)$$

Eq. (6) is Hamming loss that is applied by (Nguyen and Guo, 2007) for structured SVM sequence labeling. Eq. (7) is sequence level hard loss function that always give loss one to wrong slot label sequences no matter how many words are labeled with wrong slot labels. In our experiment, we find that the margin defined by Eq. (7) gives the best performance.

2.1   Training Procedure For Recurrent Support Vector Machines

Fig. 1 depicts the architecture of RSVM that can be viewed as the conventional RNN unrolled over the sequence $x(1:T)$. For each single training sample $x(1:T)$, a forward inference and a backward learning are carried out to sweep over the network shown in Fig. 1.

In the forward inference, an unnormalized slot score vector $y(t)$ is computed based on each word input $x(t)$ and its corresponding auxiliary feature $Cx(t)$. The word input and auxiliary feature are encoded in one-hot representation. As shown in Fig. 1, a slot label lattice is generated for the training sample $x(1:T)$. Using Viterbi algorithm, two best slot label sequences $Y^{(k)^{top}}$ and $Y^{(k)^{second}}$ are derived from the lattice. In the decoding phase, only the best slot label sequence is computed.

In backward learning, the sub-gradient (Ratliff et al., 2007) are calculated to update the weights for RSVMs. When $Y^{(k)^{top}} \neq Y^{(k)^*}$ the sub-gradient is

$$\frac{\partial \zeta_k}{\partial \theta} = \frac{\partial f(Y^{(k)^{top}})}{\partial \theta} - \frac{\partial f(Y^{(k)^*})}{\partial \theta}. \qquad (8)$$

When $Y^{(k)^{top}} = y^{(k)^*}$ and $y^{(k)^*} - Y^{(k)^{second}} < L(Y^{(k)})$, the

---

[1] See http://www.cnts.ua.ac.be/conll2000/chunking.

sub-gradient is

$$\frac{\partial \zeta_k}{\partial \theta} = \frac{\partial f(Y^{(k)\,\mathrm{second}})}{\partial \theta} - \frac{\partial f(Y^{(k)*})}{\partial \theta}. \quad (9)$$

When $Y^{(k)\,\mathrm{top}} = Y^{(k)*}$ and $y^{(k)*} - Y^{(k)\,\mathrm{second}} \geq L(Y^{(k)})$, the subgradient is zero. Our experiment show that the RSVM training can be substantially sped up by skipping the backward weight updating for non-support vector training samples that obtain zero subgradient.

In Eq. (8) and (9), θ represents the weights in RSVMs. Specifically, the weights W, A, U and V are updated using sequence level mini-batch method. The weights O connecting hidden layers are updated using Backpropagation Through Time (BPTT) (Werbos, 1990).

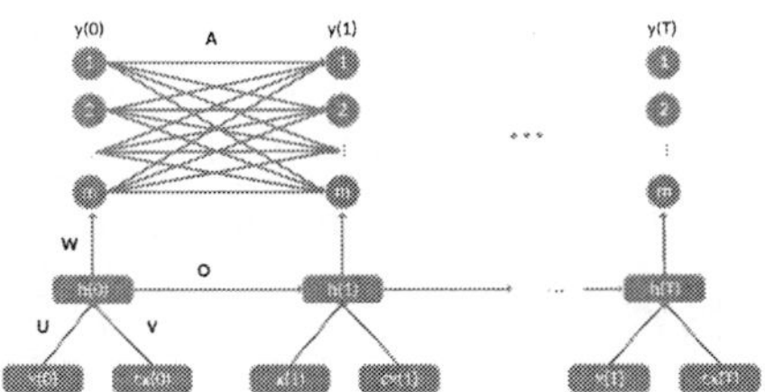

Figure 1: Recurrent support vector machines for slot tagging. U is the weight matrix connecting the word input to the hidden layer, V is the weight matrix connecting auxiliary feature input to the hidden layer, O is the weight matrix connecting previous hidden state to the current hidden state and W is the weight matrix connecting the hidden layer to the output layer. A represents the weight for slot label transition features.

3 Experiments

3.1 Data

To evaluate performances of the proposed model, three sets of experiments were conducted. The first set of experiments are based on ATIS dataset (Hemphill et al., 1990b; Yao et al., 2014b). There are 893 queries from ATIS-III, Nov93 and Dec94 for testing, and 4978 utterances from the rest of ATIS-III and ATIS-II used for training. The training data contains 127 unique slot tags.

The second dataset used in the experiment is CoNLL 2000 Chunking dataset. Chunking is also called shallow parsing that assigns syntactic labels to segments of a sequence of words. Chunking and slot tagging are typical sequence labeling problems. In this paper, we use the chunking task to further verify the performance of the proposed RSVM model. In the CoNLL 2000 Chunking task, the training data are from sections 15-18 of WSJ data and the test data are from section 20. In the training data, there are 220663 tokens with 19123 unique words and additional 45 different types of Part-Of-Speech (POS).

The last dataset is Cortana live log dataset which is constituted by 8 domains, namely alarm, calender, communication, note, ondevice, places, reminder and weather. In total, there are 71 slots. There are 42506 queries used for training and 5290 queries for testing. The data distribution is described in Table. 1. The last column of Table. 1 shows the average query length (the number of words in one query) on different domains.

domain	train	test	length
alarm	3816	452	4.3
calendar	4138	475	4.5
communication	9551	1262	3.8
note	829	139	4.6
ondevice	4384	572	2.4
places	6167	753	4.7
reminder	5359	720	4.1
weather	8270	917	3.4

Table 1: Cortana live log data distribution.

3.2 Settings

In this paper, we use a predefined maximum iteration number to terminate the training. The learning rate is dynamically adjusted using AdaGrad (Duchi et al., 2011).

In all the experiments, we set the hidden layer size to 300 and initial learning rate to 0.1. In RSVMs, the surrounding two words of the current word are used as auxiliary feature which is represented as bag of words. We set the maximum iteration to 20 for ATIS and 30 for Chunking and Cortana live log. For each dataset, we trained 10 models with the same parameter settings except using different random initialization.

3.3 Results on ATIS

ATIS is a well studied benchmark dataset. Table. 2 gives the slot tagging F1 scores achieved by different models in the literature, using the same data settings. There are three blocks in Table. 2. The top block gives the F1 score obtained by CRF and simple RNN. The middle block gives the results obtained by applying advanced RNN architectures such as LSTM, Gated RNN and RNN with external memories (RNN-em) (Peng and Yao, 2015). These advanced RNNs improves RNN by enhancing its memory (sequence representation capability). The bottom block gives results using the proposed RSVMs.

The bottom part gives F1 scores of the proposed RSVM method. We show results generated by 10 models with different random seeds. The average F1 score of RSVM is similar to the best score of RNN-em. F1 score distribution of 10 RSVM models gets significant improvement over the average score of RNN-em (z-test $p - value = 0.0002 \ll 0.05$). Fundamentally, the proposed RSVM

model	F1(%)
CRF (Mesnil et al., 2015)	92.9
DBN (Deoras and Sarikaya, 2013)	93.2
RNN (Yao et al., 2013)	94.1
RNN-Jordan(Mesnil et al., 2015)	94.3
RNN-embed(Xu and Sarikaya, 2013)	94.4
RNN-joint (Shi et al., 2015)	94.6
RNN-hybrid(Mesnil et al., 2015)	95.1
deep-LSTM (Yao et al., 2014a)	95.0
GRNN-max(Peng and Yao, 2015)	94.7
RNN-em-min(Peng and Yao, 2015)	94.7
RNN-em-average(Peng and Yao, 2015)	95.0
RNN-em-max(Peng and Yao, 2015)	95.2
RSVM-min	94.9
RSVM-average	95.2
RSVM-max	95.5

Table 2: F1 score (in %) for slot tagging on ATIS achieved by different models using only lexical feature. "-min", "-max", and "-average" each denotes mininum, maximum and average F1 scores for a corresponding method.

is based on simple RNN. Comparing LSTM and RNN-em, the proposed model has simpler topology. Note that in (Yao et al., 2014a) and (Peng and Yao, 2015), their advanced models are trained using local normalization method without using sequence level optimization. So the superiority of the proposed RSVM may come from the sequence training and the powerful discriminant capability of SVM. Applying the proposed RSVM method to LSTM or other advanced RNN can be a promising direction for future work.

3.4 Results on CoNLL 2000 Chunking

Table. 3 gives the F1 scores of different models on CoNLL 2000 chunking experiment. To our best knowledge, the first neural network (NN) based chunking model is proposed in (Collobert et al., 2011). Using four basic natural language processing tasks, namely POS tagging, chunking, name entity recognition and semantic role labeling, they demonstrate the ability of NN to discover hidden representations. In their work, only simple input feature is used. There is not any task-specific feature engineering work in their proposed system. Their model purely relies on the NN feature representation that are learned from large amount of unlabeled data. As shown in Table. 3, their system performs better than all the previous systems on CoNLL 2000 chunking dataset.

The performance of Bidirectional LSTM (BLSTM), RCRF and the proposed RSVM on chunking task further confirms the conclusion in (Collobert et al., 2011) that NN is able to discover the internal representations that are useful for different natural language processing tasks. Additionally, the results of BLSTM, RCRF and

RSVM, indicate that RNNs have better capabilities to discover the sequence representation than NN. The average F1 score of RCRF and RSVM are 94.9% and 95.0%, respectively. Comparing the F1 score distribution, RSVM achieves the significant improvement over RCRF (paired t-test $p - value = 0.012 < 0.05$). As shown in Table. 3, replacing the CRF objective function with structured SVM max-margin criterion could generate further improvement. The average performance of RSVM is better than the best result of RCRF shown in the table.

model	F1(%)
SVM (Kudo and Matsumoto, 2000)	93.5
gen-Winnow(Zhang et al., 2001)	93.9
SVM (Kudo and Matsumoto, 2001)	93.9
CRF (McDonald et al., 2005)	94.3
CRF (Sun et al., 2008)	94.3
CRF (Sha and Pereira, 2005)	94.4
NN (Collobert et al., 2011)	94.5
BLSTM (Wang et al., 2015)	94.6
RCRF-min	94.7
RCRF-average	94.9
RCRF-max	94.9
RSVM-min	94.7
RSVM-average	95.0
RSVM-max	95.1

Table 3: F1 score (in %) for chunking on CoNLL 2000 shared task using different models. All these models use word features as well as POS features. "-min", "-max", and "-average" each denotes minimum, maximum and average F1 scores for a corresponding method.

3.5 Results on Internal Live dataset

In this section, we compare different slot models on different domains based on Cortana live log data.

Table. 4 compares the F1 score on CRF, RNN, RCRF, joint-RNN and the proposed RSVM on alarm, calendar, communication, and note. Table. 5 presents the F1 score of different models on the rest domains. "RNN" denotes the Elman type of RNN for slot tagging which uses current word information, previous slot output information and context window information (surrounding four words) (Yao et al., 2013). "RCRF" represents the RCRF slot tagging models that use the same feature as "RNN" (Yao et al., 2014b). "joint-RNN" (Shi et al., 2015) also uses the same features as "RNN" and "RCRF". However, "joint-RNN" implicitly makes use of query domain, intent and slot information by training the domain classifier, intent classifier and slot labeling jointly via multi-task learning.

Overall, the proposed RSVM obtains significant improvement over CRF, RNN,RCRF and joint-RNN on alarm, communication, note and reminder (z-test $p - value < 5E - 5$). On the calendar, places and weather, RSVM achieves similar performance as joint-RNN. Even joint-

RNN is built on the basis of conventional RNN using local normalization, it actually takes the sequence representation information implicitly from domain and intent classification. However, in ondevice domain, RCRF performs the best and the proposed RSVM model performs even worse than CRF. We notice that, in ondevice model, user queries tend to be short, with on average 2.4 words in a query, shown in Table. 1. Also the loss function in the proposed model only uses the top and the second most hypothesis, which may be less informative, especially with short sentences, as compared to using all hypothesis in RCRF.

model	alarm	calen	commu	note
CRF	93.2	93.7	91.6	76.5
RNN	93.8	95.2	92.5	77.0
RCRF	93.9	95.9	93.2	76.9
joint-RNN	94.9	96.4	92.9	74.9
RSVM-min	95.8	95.8	93.3	86.9
RSVM-aver	95.9	96.3	93.9	88.3
RSVM-max	96.2	96.6	94.9	89.7

Table 4: F1 score comparison on different slot tagging models on alarm, calendar, communication and note.

model	ondev	place	remin	weath
CRF	98.2	87.5	93.3	95.7
RNN	98.4	88.4	90.5	95.0
RCRF	98.8	88.3	91.9	94.6
joint-RNN	98.6	90.6	92.4	96.7
RSVM-min	97.4	88.2	94.3	96.2
RSVM-aver	97.7	89.7	94.5	96.6
RSVM-max	97.9	90.8	95.1	96.8

Table 5: F1 score comparison on different slot tagging models on on-device, places, reminder and weather.

Table. 6 gives the overall performance comparison of different models in internal live log dataset using the weighted average F1 score over all domains. In this table, we can find that the proposed RSVM on average can achieve 0.6% and 0.7% F1 score improvement over joint-RNN and RCRF, respectively.

3.6 Training Speed Up In RSVM

Using max-margin criteria, backward weight updating only happens to support vector samples. While using cross-entropy or maximum likelihood based training criteria, backward weight updating has to sweep over the whole training data. Fig. 2 shows that RSVM can substantially speed up the model training by skipping the backward weight updating for non-support vector samples. As depicted in Fig. 2, RSVM only executes backward weight updating for 337 training samples (7% of whole training data) at epoch 20.

model	F1(%)
CRF	92.6
RNN	92.8
RCRF	93.9
joint-RNN	94.0
RSVM-min	94.0
RSVM-average	94.6
RSVM-max	95.2

Table 6: The weighted average F1 score of different slot tagging models over all the domains.

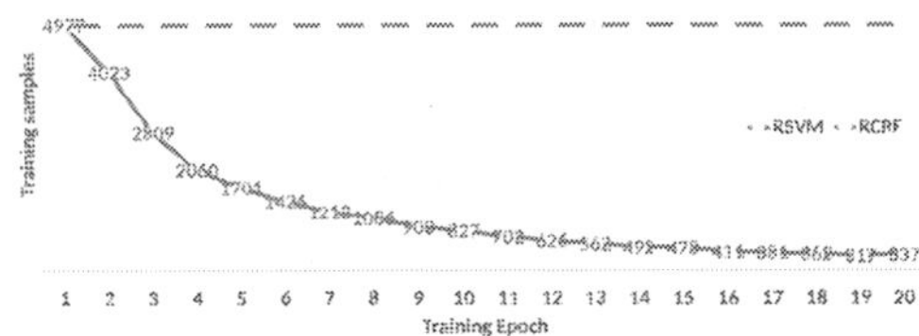

Figure 2: Training sample usage comparison for RSVM and RCRF on ATIS data in backward weight updating in each training epoch.

4   Conclusions

We have proposed a recurrent support vector machine (RSVM) which applies the structured SVM on top of the conventional RNN for slot tagging. Different from previous RNN sequence training approaches that use maximum conditional likelihood as objective function, the proposed method uses sequence level max-margin criterion with hard loss function. The model is trained to discriminate the score of ground-truth slot sequences with respect to other competing slot sequences by a margin. Viterbi algorithm is used in decoding to select a slot sequence that gives the largest score. To verify the performance of the proposed method, three datasets, namely ATIS dataset, CoNLL 2000 Chunking dataset and Cortana live log dataset, were used. The proposed RSVM achieved a new state-of-the-art performances on these datasets. In addition, RSVM showed substantial training speed up by skipping the weight updating for non-support vector training samples. On ATIS data, after 20 epoches, backward weight updating only happened for almost 7% of whole training samples.

The proposed RSVM is built on top of conventional RNN structure. Though RSVM doesn't have advanced topology used in LSTM and RNN-em, it achieves comparable or better performances. Therefore, the improvement comes from its sequence level max-margin criterion. For future works, we plan to apply the structured SVM on top of other advanced models.

References

Ronan Collobert, Jason Weston, Léon Bottou, Michael Karlen, Koray Kavukcuoglu, and Pavel Kuksa. 2011. Natural language processing (almost) from scratch. *Journal of Machine Learning Research*, 12:2493–2537.

Renato De Mori. 2007. Spoken language understanding: a survey. In *The Proceedings of IEEE Workshop on Automatic Speech Recognition Understanding*, pages 365–376.

Anoop Deoras and Ruhi Sarikaya. 2013. Deep belief network based semantic taggers for spoken language understanding. In *ISCA Interspeech*. ISCA, September.

Marco Dinarelli, Alessandro Moschitti, and Giuseppe Riccardi. 2008. Joint generative and discriminative models for spoken language understanding. In *The Proceeding of Spoken Language Technology Workshop*, pages 61–64.

John Duchi, Elad Hazan, and Yoram Singer. 2011. Adaptive subgradient methods for online learning and stochastic optimization. *Journal of Machine Learning Research*, 12:2121–2159.

Alex Graves, Abdel-rahman Mohamed, and Geoffrey E. Hinton. 2013. Speech recognition with deep recurrent neural networks. In *The Proceedings of IEEE International Conference on Acoustics, Speech and Signal Processing*, pages 6645–6649.

Alex Graves. 2012. *Supervised Sequence Labelling with Recurrent Neural Networks*, volume 385. Springer.

Yulan He and S. Young. 2003. A data-driven spoken language understanding system. In *The Proceedings of Automatic Speech Recognition and Understanding*, pages 583–588.

Charles T. Hemphill, John J. Godfrey, and George R. Doddington. 1990a. The atis spoken language systems pilot corpus. In *The Proceedings of the DARPA Speech and Natural Language Workshop*, pages 96–101.

Charles T. Hemphill, John J. Godfrey, and George R. Doddington. 1990b. The atis spoken language systems pilot corpus. In *The Proceedings of the Workshop on Speech and Natural Language*, pages 96–101.

Sepp Hochreiter and Jürgen Schmidhuber. 1997. Long short-term memory. *Neural Comput.*, 9(8):1735–1780.

Thorsten Joachims, Thomas Finley, and Chun-Nam John Yu. 2009. Cutting-plane training of structural svms. *Machine Learning*, 77(1):27–59.

Taku Kudo and Yuji Matsumoto. 2000. Use of support vector learning for chunking identification. In *The proceedings of Conference on Natural Language Learning (CoNLL) and Second Learning Language In Logic WorkShop*.

Taku Kudo and Yuji Matsumoto. 2001. Chunking with support vector machines. In *The Proceedings of the Second Meeting of the North American Chapter of the Association for Computational Linguistics on Language Technologies*, pages 1–8.

Ryan McDonald, Koby Crammer, and Fernando Pereira. 2005. Flexible text segmentation with structured multilabel classification. In *The Proceedings of the Conference on Human Language Technology and Empirical Methods in Natural Language Processing*, pages 987–994.

Grégoire Mesnil, Yann Dauphin, Kaisheng Yao, Yoshua Bengio, Li Deng, Dilek Hakkani-Tur, Xiaodong He, Larry Heck, Gokhan Tur, Dong Yu, and Geoffrey Zweig. 2015. Using recurrent neural networks for slot filling in spoken language understanding. *IEEE/ACM Transactions on Audio, Speech, and Language Processing*, pages 530–539.

Tomas Mikolov, Martin Karafiát, Lukas Burget, Jan Cernocký, and Sanjeev Khudanpur. 2010. Recurrent neural network based language model. In *The Proceedings of Interspeech*, pages 1045–1048.

Nam Nguyen and Yunsong Guo. 2007. Comparisons of sequence labeling algorithms and extensions. *International Conference on Machine Learning*, pages 681–688.

Constantinos Panagiotakopoulos and Petroula Tsampouka. 2013. The stochastic gradient descent for the primal l1-svm optimization revisited. *CoRR*.

Baolin Peng and Kaisheng Yao. 2015. Recurrent neural networks with external memory for language understanding. *CoRR*, abs/1506.00195.

Juan Antonio Prez-ortiz, Mikel L. Forcada, and Departament De Llenguatges I Sistemes. 2001. Part-ofspeech tagging with recurrent neural networks. In *The Proceedings of the International Joint Conference on Neural Networks*.

Nathan Ratliff, J. Andrew (Drew) Bagnell, and Martin Zinkevich. 2007. (online) subgradient methods for structured prediction. In *Eleventh International Conference on Artificial Intelligence and Statistics (AIStats)*.

Fei Sha and Fernando Pereira. 2005. Shallow parsing with conditional random fields. In *The Proceedings of the Conference of the North American Chapter of the Association for Computational Linguistics and Human Language Technologies*.

Yangyang Shi, Kaisheng Yao, Hu Chen, Yi-Cheng Pan, Mei-Yuh Hwang, and Baolin Peng. 2015. Contextual spoken language understanding using recurrent neural networks. In *The Proceedings of International Conference on Acoustics, Speech and Signal Processing*.

Xu Sun, Louis-Philippe Morency, Daisuke Okanohara, and Jun'ichi Tsujii. 2008. Modeling latent-dynamic in shallow parsing: A latent conditional model with improved inference. In *The Proceedings of the 22Nd International Conference on Computational Linguistics - Volume 1*, COLING '08, pages 841–848.

Ioannis Tsochantaridis, Thorsten Joachims, Thomas Hofmann, and Yasemin Altun. 2005. Large margin methods for structured and interdependent output variables. *Journal Of Machine Learning Research*, 6:1453–1484.

Vladimir N. Vapnik. 1995. *The Nature of Statistical Learning Theory*.

Ye-Yi Wang, Li Deng, and Alex Acero. 2005. Spoken language understanding — an introduction to the statistical framework. *IEEE Signal Processing Magazine*, 22(5):16–31.

Peilu Wang, Yao Qian, Frank K. Soong, Lei He, and Hai Zhao. 2015. A unified tagging solution: Bidirectional LSTM recurrent neural network with word embedding. *CoRR*.

P.J. Werbos. 1990. Backpropagation through time: what it does and how to do it. *The Proceedings of the IEEE*, 78(10):1550–1560.

Puyang Xu and Ruhi Sarikaya. 2013. Convolutional neural network based triangular CRF for joint intent detection and slot filling. In *The Proceedings of IEEE Workshop on Automatic Speech Recognition and Understanding*, pages 78–83.

Kaisheng Yao, Geoffrey Zweig, Mei-Yuh Hwang, Yangyang Shi, and Dong Yu. 2013. Recurrent neural networks for language understanding. In *The Proceedings of Interspeech*, pages 2524–2528.

Kaisheng Yao, Baolin Peng, Yu Zhang, Dong Yu, Geoffrey Zweig, and Yangyang Shi. 2014a. Spoken language understanding using long short-term memory neural networks. In *The Proceedings of IEEE workshop on Spoken Language Technology*, pages 189–194.

Kaisheng Yao, Baolin Peng, Geoffrey Zweig, Dong Yu, Xiaolong Li, and Feng Gao. 2014b. Recurrent conditional random field for language understanding. In *The Proceedings of International Conference of Acoustic, Speech and Signal Processing*, pages 4105–4109.

Tong Zhang, Fred Damerau, and David Johnson. 2001. Text chunking based on a generalization of winnow. *Journal of Machine Learning Research*, 2:615–637.

Shi-Xiong Zhang, Chaojun Liu, Kaisheng Yao, and Yifan Gong. 2015. Deep neural support vector machines for speech recognition. In *The Proceedings of IEEE International Conference on Acoustics, Speech and Signal Processing*, pages 4275 – 4279, April.

Expectation-Regulated Neural Model for Event Mention Extraction

Ching-Yun Chang and **Zhiyang Teng** and **Yue Zhang**
Singapore University of Technology and Design
8 Somapah Road, Singapore 487372
{chingyun_chang, yue_zhang}@sutd.edu.sg
zhiyang_teng@mymail.sutd.edu.sg

Abstract

We tackle the task of extracting tweets that mention a specific event from all tweets that contain relevant keywords, for which the main challenges include unbalanced positive and negative cases, and the unavailability of manually labeled training data. Existing methods leverage a few manually given seed events and large unlabeled tweets to train a classifier, by using expectation regularization training with discrete ngram features. We propose a LSTM-based neural model that learns tweet-level features automatically. Compared with discrete ngram features, the neural model can potentially capture non-local dependencies and deep semantic information, which are more effective for disambiguating subtle semantic differences between true event mentions and false cases that use similar wording patterns. Results on both tweets and forum posts show that our neural model is more effective compared with a state-of-the-art discrete baseline.

1 Introduction

A Distributed Denial of Service (DDoS) attack employs multiple compromised systems to interrupt or suspend services of a host connected to the Internet. Victims are often high-profile web servers such as banks or credit card payment gateways, and therefore a single attack may cause considerable loss. The aim of this paper is to build an automatic system which can extract DDoS event mentions from social media, a timely information source for events taking place around the world, so that the mined emerging incidents can serve as early DDoS warnings or signs for Internet service providers.

Ritter et al. (2015) proposed the first work to extract cybersecurity event mentions from raw Twitter stream. They investigated three different event categories, namely *DDoS attacks*, *data breaches* and *account hijacking*, by tracking the keywords *ddos*, *breach* and *hacked*, respectively. Not all tweets containing the keywords describe events. For example, the tweet "give me paypall or i will tell my mum and *ddos* u" shows a metaphor rather than a DDoS event. As a result, the event mention extraction task involves a classification task that filters out true events from all tweets that contain event keywords. Two main challenges exist for this task. First, the numbers of positive and negative examples are typically unbalanced. In our datasets, only about 22% of the tweets that contain the term *ddos* are mentions to DDoS attack events. Second, there is typically little manual annotation available. Ritter et al. (2015) tackled the challenges by weakly supervising a classification model with a small number of human-provided seed events.

In particular, Ritter et al. exploit expectation regularization (ER; Mann and McCallum (2007)) for semi-supervised learning from large amounts of raw tweets that contain the event keyword. They show that the ER approach outperforms semi-supervised expectation-maximization and one-class support vector machine on the task. They build a logistic regression classifier, using few human-labeled seed events and domain knowledge on the ratio between positive and negative examples for ER in training. Results show that the regulariza-

Proceedings of NAACL-HLT 2016, pages 400–410,
San Diego, California, June 12-17, 2016. ©2016 Association for Computational Linguistics

tion method was effective on classifying unbalanced datasets.

Ritter et al. use manually-defined discrete features. However, the event mention extraction task is highly semantic-driven, and simple textual patterns may suffer limitations in representing subtle semantic differences between true event mentions and false cases with similar word patterns. Recently, deep learning received increasing research attention in the NLP community (Bengio, 2009; Mikolov et al., 2013; Pennington et al., 2014; Kalchbrenner et al., 2014; Vo and Zhang, 2015). One important advantage of deep learning is automatic representation learning, which can effectively encodes syntactic and information about words, phrases and sentences in low-dimensional dense vectors.

In this paper we exploit a deep neural model for event mention extraction, using word embeddings and a novel LSTM-based neural network structure to automatically obtain features for a tweet. Results on two human-annotated datasets show that the proposed LSTM-based representation yields significant improvements over Ritter et al. (2015).

2   Related Work

In terms of scope, our work falls into the area of information extraction from social media (Guo et al., 2013; Li et al., 2015). The proposed event mention extraction system is domain-specific, similar to works that aim at detecting categorized events such as disaster outbreak (Sakaki et al., 2010; Neubig et al., 2011; Li and Cardie, 2013) and cybersecurity events (Ritter et al., 2015). Such work typically trains semi-supervised classifiers to determine events of interest due to the limitation of annotated data. On the other hand, a few studies devote to open domain event extraction (Benson et al., 2011; Ritter et al., 2012; Petrović et al., 2010; Diao et al., 2012; Chierichetti et al., 2014; Li et al., 2014; Qiu and Zhang, 2014), in which an event category is not predefined, and clustering models are applied to automatically induce event types.

In terms of method, the proposed model is in line with recent methods on deep learning for neural feature representations, which have seen success in some NLP tasks (Collobert and Weston, 2008; Collobert et al., 2011; Chen and Manning, 2014).

Competitive results have been obtained in sentiment analysis (Kalchbrenner et al., 2014; Kim, 2014; Socher et al., 2013b), semantic relation classification (Hashimoto et al., 2013; Liu et al., 2015), and question answering (Dong et al., 2015; Iyyer et al., 2014). In addition, deep learning models have shown promising results on syntactic parsing (Dyer et al., 2015; Zhou et al., 2015) and machine translation (Cho et al., 2014). Compared to syntactic problems, semantic tasks see relatively larger improvements by using neural architectures, possible because of the capability of neural features in better representing semantic information, which is relatively more difficult to capture by discrete indicator features. We consider event mention extraction as a semantic-heavy task and demonstrate that it can benefit significantly from neural feature representations.

3   Baseline

We take the method of Ritter et al. (2015) as a baseline. Given a tweet containing the keyword *ddos*, the task is to determine whether a DDoS attack event is mentioned in the tweet. A logistic regression classifier is used, which is trained by maximum-likelihood with ER on unlabeled tweets, and automatically generated positive examples from a few seed events.

3.1   Seed Events

Ritter et al. (2015) manually pick seed events, represented as (ENTITY, DATE) tuples, and treated tweets published on DATE referencing ENTITY as positive training instances. For example, (*GitHub*, 2013 July 29)[1] is defined as a seed DDoS event, and the tweet "@amosie *GitHub* is experiencing a large DDos https://t.co/cqEIR6Rz6t" posted on 2013 July 29 is seen as an event mention since it contains the ENTITY *GitHub* as well as matches the DATE 2013 July 29. Those tweets with the word *ddos* but not matching any seed events are grouped as unlabeled data.

3.2   Sparse Feature Representation

Each tweet is represented by a sparse binary vector for feature extraction, where the features consist of bi- to five-grams containing a name entity or the event keyword. For better generalization, all

---

[1] https://status.github.com/messages/2013-07-29

NE: GitHub	keyword: DDoS
USR NE	JJ DDoS
NE is	DDoS URL
USR NE is	DT JJ DDoS
NE is experiencing	JJ DDoS URL
USR NE is experiencing	experiencing DT JJ DDoS
NE is experiencing DT	DT JJ DDoS URL
USR NE is experiencing DT	is experiencing DT JJ DDoS
NE is experiencing DT JJ	experiencing DT JJ DDoS URL

Table 1: Features of a tweet by Ritter et al. (2015).

words other than common nouns and verbs are replaced with their part-of-speech (POS) tags. Table 1 shows an example of contextual features extracted from the tweet "@amosie GitHub is experiencing a large DDos https://t.co/cqEIR6Rz6t". As can be seen from the table, the features contain shallow wording patterns from a tweet, which are local to a 5-word window. In contrast, the observed average tweet length is 16 words, with the longest tweet containing 48 words, which is difficult to fully represent using only a local window. Our neural model addresses the limitations by learning global tweet-level syntactic and semantic features automatically.

3.3 Logistic Regression Classification with Expectation Regularization

With the feature vector $\vec{f}_s \in \mathbb{R}^d$ defined for a given tweet s, the probability of s being an event mention is defined as:

$$p_\theta(y = 1|s) = \frac{1}{1 + e^{-\vec{\theta}\vec{f}_s}} \qquad (1)$$

where $\vec{\theta} \in \mathbb{R}^d$ is a weight vector.

Given a set of event mentions $M = \langle m_1, m_2, ..., m_j \rangle$ and a set of unlabeled instances $U = \langle u_1, u_2, ..., u_k \rangle$, Ritter et al. (2015) train an ER model that maximizes the log-likelihood of positive data while keeping the conditional probabilities on unlabeled data consistent with the human-provided expectations. The objective function is defined as:

$$O(\theta; M, U) = \underbrace{\sum_{m \in M} \log p_\theta(y = 1|m)}_{Log\ Likelihood}$$

$$- \underbrace{\lambda^U \Delta(\tilde{p}, \hat{p}_\theta^U)}_{Expectation\ Regularization} \qquad (2)$$

$$- \underbrace{\lambda^{L^2} \|\theta\|^2}_{L^2\ Regularization}$$

The expectation regularization term $\Delta(\tilde{p}, \hat{p}_\theta^U)$ is defined as the KL divergence between the model's posterior predictions on unlabeled data, $\hat{p}_\theta^U$, and the human-provided label expectation priors, $\tilde{p}$:

$$\Delta(\tilde{p}, \hat{p}_\theta^U) = D(\tilde{p}||\hat{p}_\theta^U)$$

$$= \tilde{p} \log \frac{\tilde{p}}{\hat{p}_\theta^U} + (1 - \tilde{p}) \log \frac{1 - \tilde{p}}{1 - \hat{p}_\theta^U} \qquad (3)$$

4 Distant Seed Event Extraction

We follow Ritter et al. (2015), using a set of seed events and large raw tweets for ER. However, we take a fully-automated approach to find seed events, since manual listing of seed DDoS events can be a costly and time consuming process, and requires a certain level of expert knowledge.

We leverage news articles to collect seed events, representing events as (ENTITY, DATE RANGE) tuples. The ENTITY in our seed events is defined as a name entity that appears in either the *assailant* or *victim* role of an *attack* event labeled by frame-semantic parsing, and the DATE RANGE is a date window around the news publication date. We use a date window rather than a definite news publication date because news articles are not always published on the day a DDoS attack happened. Some examples are given in Figure 1.

We parse DDoS attack news collected from http://www.ddosattacks.net[2] with a state-of-the-art frame-semantic parsing system (SEMAFOR; Das et al. (2010)). Tweets are gathered using the Twitter Streaming API[3] with a case-insensitive track keyword *ddos*. Name entities are extracted from both news articles and tweets using a Twitter-tuned NLP pipeline (Ritter et al., 2011).[4]

Table 2 shows two example DDoS attack news, where the ENTITY values are included in the victim roles, *RBS*, *Ulster Bank*, *GovCERT* and *FBI* in the first news, and *Essex* in the second. It is worth noting that the DDoS attack on RBS, Ulster Bank and Natwest was actually on 2015 July 31. The correlation between tweet mentions and news reports are shown in Figure 1, where each bar indicates the

---

[2]Most of the articles are about DDoS attack events, while a smaller number discusses the nature of DDoS attacks and related issues.

[3]https://dev.twitter.com/streaming/overview

[4]https://github.com/aritter/twitter_nlp

News Title	DDoS Attacks Take Down RBS, Ulster Bank, and Natwest Online Systems
Date	2015 August 02
Sentences	But as can be seen from the attacks *against RBS, NatWest, and Ulster Bank, and the warnings from GovCERT.ch and the FBI*, these attacks are coming back into vogue again.
News Title	Bored Brazilian skiddie claims DDoS against Essex Police
Date	2015 September 04
Sentences	A teenager from Brazil has claimed responsibility for a distributed denial of service (DDoS) attack *on Essex Police's website*, following a similar attack on another force earlier this week.
	They added: "Officers investigating the suspected denial of service attack *on the Essex Police website* ... are liaising with other law enforcement agencies to identify any investigative leads"

Table 2: Example news sentences where victim roles are in italic and ENTITY is in bold.

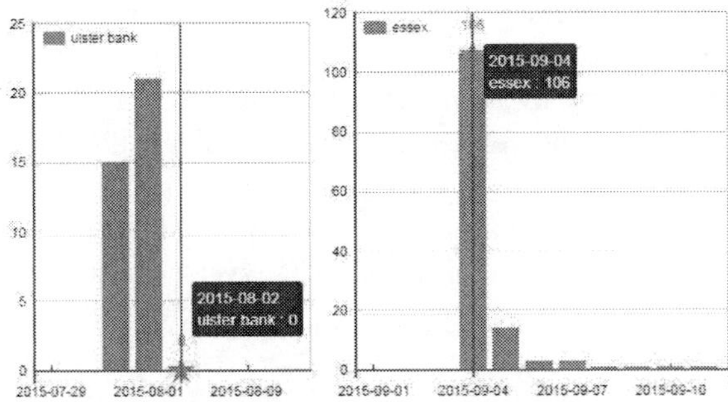

Figure 1: Visualization of the numbers of tweets mentioning Ulster bank (on the left) and Essex (on the right) around the news publication dates.

number of tweets (y-axis) containing a certain ENTITY posted on a certain DATE (x-axis). According to these, we used a 11-day (-3,7) window centered at the news publication date for extracting positive training instances. Experiments show that our method can find seed events with 97% accuracy.

5 Neural Event Mention Extraction

The overall structure of our representation learning model is shown in Figure 2. Given a tweet, two LSTM models (Section 5.1) are used to capture its sequential semantic information in the left-to-right and right-to-left directions, respectively. For deep

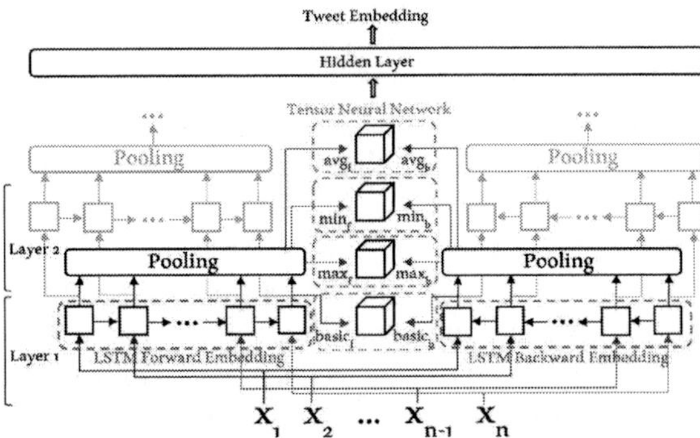

Figure 2: Architecture of the proposed neural tweet representation model.

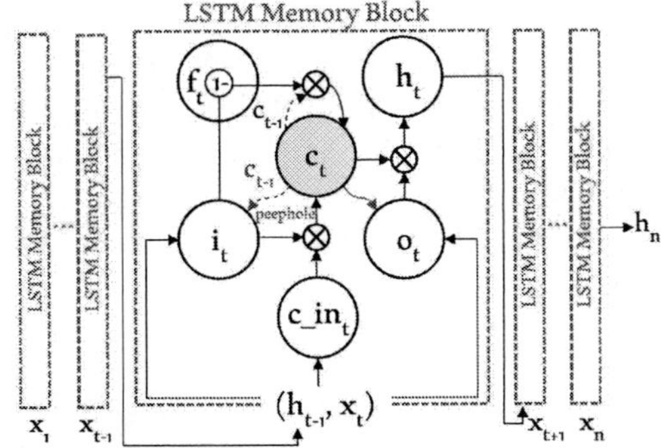

Figure 3: LSTM-based text embedding for word vectors $x_1, x_2, \ldots, x_n$.

semantic representation, each LSTM model can include multiple stacked layers. Neural pooling (Section 5.2) is performed on each LSTM layer to extract rich features. Finally, features from the left-to-right and right-to-left components are combined using neural tensors (Section 5.3), and the resulting features are used as inputs to a feed-forward neural network for classification (Section 5.4).

5.1 LSTM Models

The main goal of our neural model is to find dense vector representations for tweets, which are effective features for event mention extraction. Starting from word embeddings (Mikolov et al., 2013; Pennington et al., 2014), a natural way of modeling a tweet is to treat it as a sequence and use a recurrent neural network (RNN) structure (Pearlmutter, 1989). LSTM (Hochreiter and Schmidhuber, 1997) is a variant of RNNs, which is better at exploiting long range context thanks to purpose-built units called *memory blocks* to store history information.

LSTM has shown improvements over conventional RNN in many NLP tasks (Jozefowicz et al., 2015; Graves et al., 2013b; Cho et al., 2014).

A typical LSTM memory block consists of three gates (i.e. *input*, *forget* and *output*), which control the flow of information, and a *memory cell* to store the temporal state of the network (Gers et al., 2000). While traditionally the values of gates are decided by the input and hidden states in a RNN, we take a variation with *peephole connections* (Gers and Schmidhuber, 2000), which allows gates in the same memory block to learn from the current cell state. In addition, to simplify model complexity, we use coupled *forget* and *input* gates (Cho et al., 2014).

Figure 3 illustrates the memory block used for our tweet representation. The network unit activations for input x_t at time step t are defined by the following set of equations:

Gates at step t:

$$i_t = \sigma(W_{ix}x_t + W_{ih}h_{t-1} + W_{ic}c_{t-1} + b_i) \quad (4)$$

$$f_t = 1 - i_t \quad (5)$$

$$o_t = \sigma(W_{ox}x_t + W_{oh}h_{t-1} + W_{oc}c_t + b_o) \quad (6)$$

Cell:

$$c_t = f_t \otimes c_{t-1}$$
$$+ \; i_t \otimes tanh(W_{cx}x_t + W_{ch}h_{t-1} + b_{c\_in}) \quad (7)$$

Hidden State:

$$h_t = o_t \otimes tanh(c_t) \quad (8)$$

The W terms in Equations 4–7 are the weight matrices (W_{ic} and W_{oc} are diagonal weight matrices for peephole connections); the b terms denote bias vectors; σ is the logistic sigmoid function; and $\otimes$ computes element-wise multiplication of two vectors. i_t, f_t and o_t are *input*, *forget* and *output* gates, respectively; c_t stores the cell state, and h_t is the output of the current memory block.

Inputs For the inputs $x_1, x_2, ..., x_n$, we learn 50-dimension word representations using the skip-gram algorithm (Mikolov et al., 2013). The training corpus was collected from the tweet archive site, and a total of 604,926,764 tweets were used. Each tweet was tokenized using a tweet-adapted tokenizer (Owoputi et al., 2013), and stopwords and punctuations are removed. The trained model contains 5,251,332 words.

Layers Recent research has shown that both RNNs and LSTMs can benefit from depth in space (Graves et al., 2013a; Graves et al., 2013b; Sak et al., 2014; Sak et al., 2015). A deep LSTM is built by stacking multiple LSTM layers, with the output sequence of one layer forming the input sequence for the next, as shown in Figure 2. At each time step the input goes through multiple non-linear layers, which progressively build up higher level representations from the current level. In our tweet representation model, we embody a deep LSTM architecture with up to 3 layers.

5.2 Pooling

Given a LSTM and an input sequence $x_1, x_2, ..., x_n$, using the last state h_n as features is a *basic* representation strategy for the sequence. Apart from this approach, another common feature extraction strategy is to apply pooling (Boureau et al., 2011) over all the states $h_1, h_2, ..., h_n$ to capture the most characteristic information. Pooling extracts fixed dimensional features from $h_1, h_2, ..., h_n$, which has variable length. In our model we consider different pool strategies, including *max*, *average* and *min* poolings. For convenience of writing, we refer to the *basic* feature strategy also as *basic* pooling in later sections. When there are multiple LSTM layers, the features consist of the pooling results from each layer, concatenated to give a single vector.

5.3 Neural Tensor Network for Feature Combination

Given the pooling methods, we extract features r_f and r_b for the forward and backward multi-layer LSTMs, respectively. Inspired by Socher et al. (2013a), we use a neural tensor network (NTN) to combine the bi-directional r_f and $r_b \in \mathbb{R}^d$. The network can be formalized as follows:

$$V = tanh(r_f^T \, T^{[1:q]} \, r_b + W_{ntn} \begin{bmatrix} r_f \\ r_b \end{bmatrix} + b_{ntn}) \quad (9)$$

where $T^{[1:q]} \in \mathbb{R}^{d \times d \times q}$ is a tensor, $W_{ntn} \in \mathbb{R}^{q \times 2d}$ and $b_{ntn} \in \mathbb{R}^q$ are the weight matrix and bias vector, respectively, as that in the standard form of a neural network. The bilinear tensor product $r_f^T \, T^{[1:q]} \, r_b$ is a vector $v \in \mathbb{R}^q$, where each entry is computed by one slice of the tensor:

$$v_i = r_f^T \, T^{[i]} \, r_b \qquad (i = 1, 2, \ldots, q) \quad (10)$$

1. **NSA** site went down due to 'internal error', not DDoS attack, agency claims http://t.co/B7AzoLPsKf $<$ isn't that the same thing
2. **NSA** denies DDOS attack took place on website, claims internal error http://t.co/WW7uFM4Xk5
3. @HostingSocial True Shikha,**Enterprises** are at a greater risk with increased DDoS attacks & #cloud solns need to take measures for prevention

Table 3: The three false positives in the 100 automatically extracted mentions, where EVENT ENTITIES are in bold.

The NTN combined features are concatenated, and fed into a *tanh* hidden layer. The output of the layer, $\vec{f}_s$, becomes the final representation of a tweet, and is used to compute the probability of the tweet being an event mention, as shown in Equation 1.

5.4 Classification

The final classifier of the neural network model is Equation 1, consistent with the baseline model. As a result, ER is applied in the same way as Equation 2. The main difference between our model and the baseline is in the definition of $\vec{f}_s$, the former being a deep neural network and the latter being manual features. Consequently, Equation 1 can be regarded as a softmax layer in our deep neural model, for which all the features and parameters are trained automatically and consistently.

For training, the parameters are initialized uniformly within the interval $[-a,a]$, where

$$a = \sqrt{\frac{6}{H_k + H_{k+1}}} \qquad (11)$$

H_k and H_{k+1} are the numbers of rows and columns of the parameter, respectively (Glorot and Bengio, 2010). The parameters are learned using stochastic gradient descent with momentum (Rumelhart et al., 1988). The model is trained by 500 iterations, in each of which unlabeled instances are randomly sampled so that the same numbers of positives and unlabeled data are used.

6 Experiments and Results

6.1 Data

We streamed tweet with the track kayword *ddos* for five months from April 13 to September 13,

	Training	Dev	Test	Dark Web Test
Positive	930	43	160	82
Negative	–	157	640	318
Unlabeled	127,774	–	–	–

Table 4: Statistics of the datasets.

2015. In addition, we extracted tweets containing the word *ddos* from a tweet archive[5] in the period from September 2011 to September 2014. Using the distant seed event extraction scheme described in Section 4, a total number of 930 mentions covering 45 ENTITY were automatically derived. In order to examine whether the automatically-collected instances are true positives and hence form a useful training set, an author of this paper annotated 100 extracted mentions finding that that 3 are false positives, as listed in Table 3. The result suggests that the automatically extracted mentions are reliable.

The remaining tweets were randomly split into a 200-instance development set, a 800-instance test set, and an unlabeled training set.[6] Both the development and test sets were annotated by a human judge and an author of this paper. The inter-annotator agreement on the binary labeled 1000 instances was measured by using Fleiss' kappa (Fleiss et al., 2013), and the score, which is 0.85 for the data, represents *almost perfect agreement* according to Landis and Koch (1977). There were 47 out of the 1,000 tweets that received different labels, for which another human judge made the final decision.

To test the applicability of the proposed mention extraction system on other domains, we collected 400 sentences containing the keyword *ddos* from dark web. Again each sentence was annotated by two human judges, and the third person made the final decision on conflicting cases. The inter-annotator agreement kappa score on this dataset is 0.85, consistent with the tweet annotation. Table 4 presents the statistics of the datasets.

6.2 Evaluation

We follow Ritter et al. (2015) and evaluate the performance by the area under the precision-recall curve (AUC), where *precision* is the fraction of retrieved instances that are event mentions, and *re-*

---

[5]https://archive.org/details/twitterstream
[6]http://people.sutd.edu.sg/~yue_zhang/pub/naacl16.cyc.zip

	basic	max	avg	min
1-LSTM-layer+concat	0.41	0.39	0.38	0.39
1-LSTM-layer+NTN	0.43	0.43	0.44	0.42
2-LSTM-layer+NTN	0.44	0.42	0.44	0.44
3-LSTM-layer+NTN	0.45	**0.47**	0.46	0.46

Table 5: AUCs of different model architectures.

Pooling	AUC
max+avg	0.48
max+min	0.50
max+basic	**0.51**
max+basic+min	0.50
max+basic+min+avg	0.47

Table 6: AUCs of different pooling methods.

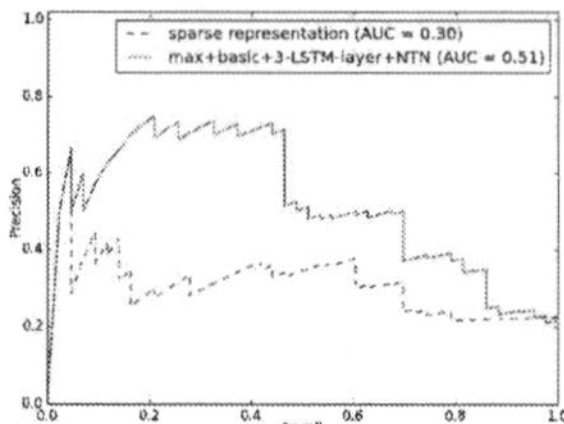

Figure 4: Development PR curves.

call is the fraction of gold event mention instances that are retrieved. Precision-recall (PR) curves offer informative pictures on the classification of unbalanced classes (Davis and Goadrich, 2006).

6.3 Development Experiments

For the proposed model, we empirically set the LSTM output vector h_t, the NTN output V, and the size of the hidden layer to 32.[7] For the ER model, the human-provided label expectation prior $\tilde{p}$ is set to 0.22 since the percentage of positives in the development set is 22%, and the parameter λ^U is set to one-tenth of the positive training data.[8]

6.3.1 Feature Combination

We first test whether using a NTN to combine the bi-directional representations can give a better performance compared to simply concatenating the two representation vectors. Table 5 gives AUCs of one-layer *basic*, *max*, *avg* and *min* pooling strategies tested on the tweet development set. We can see that all the four different pooling strategies perform better when the NTN combination is used. As a result, for the following experiments we only consider using NTNs to combine bi-directional representations.

Next we observe the effect of using different numbers of LSTM layers in our model. AUCs of *basic*, *max*, *avg* and *min* pooling strategies with respect to 1, 2 and 3 LSTM layers are presented in Table 5. In most of the cases, the performance of the model increases when the LSTM architecture goes deeper, and we build our final models using 3 LSTM layers.

6.3.2 Pooling Strategies

In the previous experiments, *max* pooling achieves the highest AUC with the architecture 3-LSTM-layer+NTN, we are interested in whether combining *max* with other pooling strategies would further increase the performance. Table 6 summarizes the AUC of various combinations, according to which we choose *max+basic* for final tests.

Finally, we test the performance of sparse feature representations as used in the model of Ritter et al. (2015). Figure 4 shows the PR curves of the sparse representation and the best setting *max+basic* evaluated on the development set. The AUC of using sparse representation is 0.30 while that of the *max+basic* model is 0.51. The runtime performances of training with sparse feature representations and neural feature representations are 276.17 and 1137.87 seconds, respectively, running on a single thread of an Intel Core i7-4790 3.60GHz CPU.

6.4 Final Test

Figure 5 presents the PR curves of the baseline sparse feature representation and the final neural model evaluated on the datasets, and Table 7 gives the AUC for these test-set evaluations. From the curves we can see that the sparse representation is comparatively less efficient in picking out negative examples, since at a lower recall the model does not gain a higher precision. In contrast, LSTM-based representation demonstrates a better trade-off between recall and precision. We do not have a strong intuition on why the performance on dark web test set is better than that on tweet test set for the proposed model.

---

[7]The hidden layer size is chosen by comparing development test scores using the sizes of 16, 32 and 64.

[8]Mann and McCallum (2007) found that λ^U does not require tuning for different data set.

Discrete Baseline Model (Ritter et al., 2015)	LSTM-based Model
Top 5:	**Top 5:**
N|0.9|0.0 They dealt with the ddos attacks with grace and confidence.	P|0.7|1.0 Until we have proof I don't think we can say who is responsiblemaybe it wasnt tor market who did the ddos, but check this out:http://silkroad5v7dywlc.onion/index.php?topic=8598.0maybe they did initate the ddos in the hopes of proving that their site is superior because they "fended off" a ddos attack faster than SRTM is super sketchy!
P|0.9|1.0 Thank you.And now, this is my hypothesis, only is a personal thinking, my thought of what happening (or something similar, at least): I think that Agora is under DDOS attacks constantly, maybe for another markets (probably Nucleus if I had to bet for one: right now they have the monopoly, practically, it's one of the three and more knowns and used DM's now (Agora, Nucleus, and Middle-Earth, at least this is my thought) all the vendors of Agora are going to Nucleus too and all publishing their listings there.	P|0.7|1.0 what's the status?you find it in the first post i set it to GREEN/ORANGE as the site is still under DDOS attack but temporarily accessable.greets
N|0.9|0.8 But it was basically explaining how the DDOS attacks on SR earlier in the year were the NSA triangulating its position by measuring PING return times and likes.	P|0.7|1.0 It seems their idea of a "hack" is a DDoS attack on the server (which does indeed go on right now, and as all DoS attacks, can result in denial of service) and a brute-force attack on the login system to try to find out users' passwords.
N|0.9|0.1 unforgiven I remember from sr2, many of the sr2 fanboys were all for DDOS attacks on Agora and tormarket if people remember.	P|0.6|1.0 One of the other markets (Nucleus) is paying some blackhat to DDOS most of the other markets, it's all over Reddit.Support here is asleep, I don't know how you can run a market with a daily uptime of 25%.I agree with OP.
N|0.8|0.2 you know things be stressful for admins and dev team right now :/keep your heads up guys, the work you do is the front line of our revolution for personal freedoms being regained.everyone here is a freedom fighter, you guys are our captainsthank you ALL for this wonderful community and sense of freedom you have brought us!so get this DDoS attack under control and keep on truckin!!!	P|0.7|1.0 He also said he was involved in helping DPR hack into Tormarket's database and launch the DDoS against the Russian cyberattackers.
Bottom 5:	**Bottom 5:**
N|0.5|0.0 I only words I could understand were "DDoS" and "Bastard".	N|0.5|0.0 I only words I could understand were "DDoS" and "Bastard".
N|0.5|0.9 In general, it seems like they have set the site up to accommodate all parties: escrow, vendor ratings, buyer ratings, quick wallet transactions, etc.Guess we'll see how they deal with the growing pains, DDOS, & hack attempts that will certainly come their way in the near future.	N|0.9|0.0 They dealt with the ddos attacks with grace and confidence.
N|0.5|0.0 Please ddos him.	N|0.5|0.0 DDOS IS PURE BULLSHIT.
N|0.5|0.0 Next fucking day, ddos dildos and damage....LEGs wares hit my drop while the market was still floundering like guppies on hot concrete, yeah, that's why.	N|0.5|0.0 can you guys ddos this guy?
N|0.5|0.2 child pornography, spamm, DDOS etc.	N|0.5|0.0 The DDoS has nothing to do with this problem.

Table 8: Top 5 and bottom 5 ranked dark web sentences as determined by the baseline and the proposed LSTM-based model. Format: class label\|baseline score\|neural score.

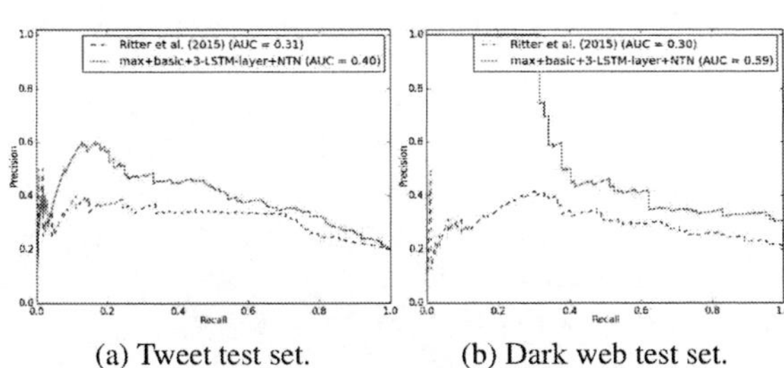

(a) Tweet test set. (b) Dark web test set.

Figure 5: Final PR curves.

	Tweet	Dark Web
Ritter et al. (2015)	0.31	0.30
max+basic+3-LSTM-layer+NTN	0.40	0.59

Table 7: Final AUCs.

6.5 Analysis

Table 8 shows the top 5 and bottom 5 ranked dark web sentences[9] as scored by the baseline and the proposed LSTM-based model, respectively. For each sentence, the human judgment (P for event mentions and N for non-event mentions) is given, followed by the probability values output by the baseline and the proposed system.

Only one of the top five most probable event-mentioning sentences as decided by the baseline is true positive. On the other hand, all of the top five sentences indicated by the proposed model are true positives. We investigate the contextual features that contribute to the false positive case "They dealt with the ddos attacks with grace and confidence." determined by the baseline, and find that the patterns "DT ddos", "ddos attack\|NN", "DT ddos attack\|NN IN" and "IN DT ddos" are ranked 2nd, 18th, 111th, 127th among the 15,355 contextual patterns, respectively, which have relatively high weights but only carry

---

[9]The sentence boundary was detected by NLTK PunktSentenceTokenizer.

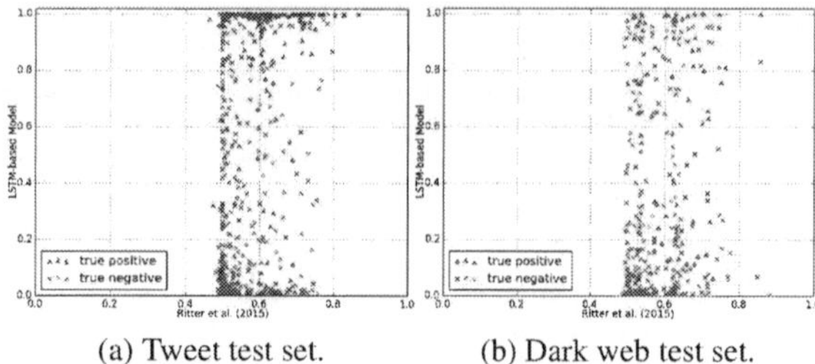

(a) Tweet test set.   (b) Dark web test set.

Figure 6: Probability distributions on the test sets.

limited information. In contrast, the LSTM-based model can capture global syntactic and semantic features other than words surrounding *ddos* to distinguish mentions from non-mentions. From the table we can see that those high-confidence sentences determined by the LSTM-based model are more informative compared with those lower ranked sentences.

Figure 6 presents the probability distributions of positive and negative test cases as obtained by the baseline (x-axis) and the LSTM-based model (y-axis), respectively. It can be seen from the figures that the probabilities determined by the LSTM-based model are scattered between 0.0 and 1.0, while those by the baseline are gathered between 0.5 and 0.9, which shows that the proposed neural model can achieve better confidence on classifying event mentions. This demonstrates its stronger differentiating power as compared with discrete indicator features, as hypothesized in the introduction. In addition, for the proposed model a large portion of true positives (▲) are close to the top in both test sets, while more negatives (×) gather at the bottom of the dark web test set plot, compared to that in the tweet test set. As for the baseline model, many negatives locate around the horizontal centre, with a probability of 0.5, in the tweet test set, which explains why the baseline is relatively less effective on the precision-recall trade-off.

7   Conclusion

We investigated LSTM-based text representation for event mention extraction, finding that automatic features from the deep neural network largely improve the sparse representation method on the task. The model performance can further benefit by exploiting deep LSTM structures and tensor combination of bi-directional features. Results on tweets and dark web forum posts show the effectiveness of the method.

Acknowledgments

We would like to thank Geoffrey Williams for data annotation, Lin Li for data processing, and anonymous reviewers for their informative comments. Yue Zhang is the corresponding author.

References

Yoshua Bengio. 2009. Learning deep architectures for AI. *Foundations and trends® in Machine Learning*, 2(1):1–127.

Edward Benson, Aria Haghighi, and Regina Barzilay. 2011. Event discovery in social media feeds. In *Proceedings of the Annual Meeting of the ACL*, pages 389–398, Portland, Oregon.

Y-Lan Boureau, Nicolas Le Roux, Francis Bach, Jean Ponce, and Yann LeCun. 2011. Ask the locals: multi-way local pooling for image recognition. In *ICCV, IEEE International Conference on*, pages 2651–2658.

Danqi Chen and Christopher D Manning. 2014. A fast and accurate dependency parser using neural networks. In *Proceedings of the Conference on EMNLP*, pages 740–750.

Flavio Chierichetti, Jon Kleinberg, Ravi Kumar, Mohammad Mahdian, and Sandeep Pandey. 2014. Event detection via communication pattern analysis. In *International AAAI Conference on Weblogs and Social Media*.

Kyunghyun Cho, Bart Van Merriënboer, Çalar Gülçehre, Dzmitry Bahdanau, Fethi Bougares, Holger Schwenk, and Yoshua Bengio. 2014. Learning phrase representations using RNN encoder-decoder for statistical machine translation. In *Proceedings of the Conference on EMNLP*, pages 1724–1734, Doha, Qatar.

Ronan Collobert and Jason Weston. 2008. A unified architecture for natural language processing: Deep neural networks with multitask learning. In *Proceedings of the 25th ICML*, pages 160–167.

Ronan Collobert, Jason Weston, Léon Bottou, Michael Karlen, Koray Kavukcuoglu, and Pavel Kuksa. 2011. Natural language processing (almost) from scratch. *The Journal of Machine Learning Research*, 12:2493–2537.

Dipanjan Das, Nathan Schneider, Desai Chen, and Noah A. Smith. 2010. Probabilistic frame-semantic parsing. In *Human Language Technologies: The Annual Conference of NAACL*, pages 948–956, Los Angeles, California.

Jesse Davis and Mark Goadrich. 2006. The relationship between precision-recall and ROC curves. In *Proceedings of the 23rd ICML*, pages 233–240, Pittsburgh, Pennsylvania.

Qiming Diao, Jing Jiang, Feida Zhu, and Ee-Peng Lim. 2012. Finding bursty topics from microblogs. In *Proceedings of the Annual Meeting of the ACL*, pages 536–544, Jeju Island, South Korea.

Li Dong, Furu Wei, Ming Zhou, and Ke Xu. 2015. Question answering over freebase with multi-column convolutional neural networks. In *Proceedings of the Annual Meeting of the ACL and the 7th International Joint Conference on NLP*, pages 260–269.

Chris Dyer, Miguel Ballesteros, Wang Ling, Austin Matthews, and Noah A Smith. 2015. Transition-based dependency parsing with stack long short-term memory. In *Proceedings of the Annual Meeting of the ACL and the 7th International Joint Conference on NLP*, pages 334–343.

Joseph L Fleiss, Bruce Levin, and Myunghee Cho Paik. 2013. *Statistical methods for rates and proportions.* Wiley-Interscience, 3 edition.

Felix Gers and Jürgen Schmidhuber. 2000. Recurrent nets that time and count. In *Neural Networks, 2000. IJCNN 2000, Proceedings of the IEEE-INNS-ENNS International Joint Conference on*, pages 189–194.

Felix A Gers, Jürgen Schmidhuber, and Fred Cummins. 2000. Learning to forget: Continual prediction with LSTM. *Neural computation*, 12(10):2451–2471.

Xavier Glorot and Yoshua Bengio. 2010. Understanding the difficulty of training deep feedforward neural networks. In *International conference on artificial intelligence and statistics*, pages 249–256.

Alan Graves, Navdeep Jaitly, and Abdel-rahman Mohamed. 2013a. Hybrid speech recognition with deep bidirectional LSTM. In *ASRU, 2013 IEEE Workshop on*, pages 273–278.

Alan Graves, Abdel-rahman Mohamed, and Geoffrey Hinton. 2013b. Speech recognition with deep recurrent neural networks. In *ICASSP, 2013 IEEE International Conference on*, pages 6645–6649.

Weiwei Guo, Hao Li, Heng Ji, and Mona T Diab. 2013. Linking tweets to news: A framework to enrich short text data in social media. In *Proceedings of the Annual Meeting of the ACL*, pages 239–249.

Kazuma Hashimoto, Makoto Miwa, Yoshimasa Tsuruoka, and Takashi Chikayama. 2013. Simple customization of recursive neural networks for semantic relation classification. In *EMNLP*, pages 1372–1376.

Sepp Hochreiter and Jürgen Schmidhuber. 1997. Long short-term memory. *Neural computation*, 9(8):1735–1780.

Mohit Iyyer, Jordan Boyd-Graber, Leonardo Claudino, Richard Socher, and Hal Daumé III. 2014. A neural network for factoid question answering over paragraphs. In *Proceedings of the Conference on EMNLP*, pages 633–644.

Rafal Jozefowicz, Wojciech Zaremba, and Ilya Sutskever. 2015. An empirical exploration of recurrent network architectures. In *Proceedings of the 32nd ICML*.

Nal Kalchbrenner, Edward Grefenstette, and Phil Blunsom. 2014. A convolutional neural network for modelling sentences. In *Proceedings of the 52nd Annual Meeting of the ACL*.

Yoon Kim. 2014. Convolutional neural networks for sentence classification. In *Proceedings of the Conference on EMNLP*, pages 1746–1751, Doha, Qatar.

J Richard Landis and Gary G Koch. 1977. The measurement of observer agreement for categorical data. *biometrics*, pages 159–174.

Jiwei Li and Claire Cardie. 2013. Early stage influenza detection from Twitter. *arXiv preprint arXiv:1309.7340.*

Jiwei Li, Alan Ritter, Claire Cardie, and Eduard Hovy. 2014. Major life event extraction from twitter based on congratulations/condolences speech acts. In *Proceedings of the Conference on EMNLP*, pages 1997–2007, Doha, Qatar.

Hao Li, Heng Ji, and Lin Zhao. 2015. Social event extraction: Task, challenges and techniques. In *Proceedings of the IEEE/ACM International Conference on ASONAM*, pages 526–532.

Yang Liu, Furu Wei, Sujian Li, Heng Ji, Ming Zhou, and Houfeng Wang. 2015. A dependency-based neural network for relation classification. In *Proceedings of the Annual Meeting of the ACL and the 7th International Joint Conference on NLP*, pages 285–290, Beijing, China.

Gideon S Mann and Andrew McCallum. 2007. Simple, robust, scalable semi-supervised learning via expectation regularization. In *Proceedings of the 24th ICML*, pages 593–600.

Tomas Mikolov, Kai Chen, Greg Corrado, and Jeffrey Dean. 2013. Efficient estimation of word representations in vector space. In *Proceedings of Workshop at ICLR*.

Graham Neubig, Masato Hagiwara, and Koji Murakami. 2011. Safety information mining — what can NLP do in a disaster —. In *Proceedings of the 5th International Joint Conference on NLP*, pages 965–973.

Olutobi Owoputi, Brendan O'Connor, Chris Dyer, Kevin Gimpel, Nathan Schneider, and Noah A Smith. 2013. Improved part-of-speech tagging for online conversational text with word clusters. In *Proceedings of the Conference of NAACL*.

Barak A Pearlmutter. 1989. Learning state space trajectories in recurrent neural networks. *Neural Computation*, 1(2):263–269.

Jeffrey Pennington, Richard Socher, and Christopher D Manning. 2014. Glove: Global vectors for word representation. In *Proceedings of the Conference on EMNLP*, pages 1532–1543.

Saša Petrović, Miles Osborne, and Victor Lavrenko. 2010. Streaming first story detection with application to twitter. In *Human Language Technologies: The Annual Conference of NAACL*.

Likun Qiu and Yue Zhang. 2014. ZORE: A syntax-based system for Chinese open relation extraction. In *Proceedings of the Conference on EMNLP*, pages 1870–1880, Doha, Qatar.

Alan Ritter, Sam Clark, Mausam, and Oren Etzioni. 2011. Named entity recognition in tweets: An experimental study. In *Proceedings of the Conference on EMNLP*, pages 1524–1534.

Alan Ritter, Mausam, Oren Etzioni, and Sam Clark. 2012. Open domain event extraction from twitter. In *Proceedings of ACM SIGKDD*, pages 1104–1112.

Alan Ritter, Evan Wright, William Casey, and Tom Mitchell. 2015. Weakly supervised extraction of computer security events from twitter. In *Proceedings of the 24th International Conference on World Wide Web*, pages 896–905.

David E Rumelhart, Geoffrey E Hinton, and Ronald J Williams. 1988. Learning representations by back-propagating errors. *Cognitive modeling*, 5:3.

Hasim Sak, Andrew Senior, and Françoise Beaufays. 2014. Long short-term memory recurrent neural network architectures for large scale acoustic modeling. In *Proceedings of the Annual Conference of INTERSPEECH*.

Hasim Sak, Andrew Senior, Kanishka Rao, Ozan Irsoy, Alex Graves, Françoise Beaufays, and Johan Schalkwyk. 2015. Learning acoustic frame labeling for speech recognition with recurrent neural networks. In *ICASSP, 2015 IEEE International Conference on*, pages 4280–4284.

Takeshi Sakaki, Makoto Okazaki, and Yutaka Matsuo. 2010. Earthquake shakes twitter users: real-time event detection by social sensors. In *Proceedings of the international conference on WWW*, pages 851–860. ACM.

Richard Socher, Danqi Chen, Christopher D Manning, and Andrew Ng. 2013a. Reasoning with neural tensor networks for knowledge base completion. In *NIPS*, pages 926–934.

Richard Socher, Alex Perelygin, Jean Y Wu, Jason Chuang, Christopher D Manning, Andrew Y Ng, and Christopher Potts. 2013b. Recursive deep models for semantic compositionality over a sentiment treebank. In *Proceedings of the conference on EMNLP*.

Duy-Tin Vo and Yue Zhang. 2015. Deep learning for event-driven stock prediction. In *Proceedings of IJCAI*, BueNos Aires, Argentina, August.

Hao Zhou, Yue Zhang, and Jiajun Chen. 2015. A neural probabilistic structured-prediction model for transition-based dependency parsing. In *Proceedings of the Annual Meeting of the ACL*, pages 1213–1222.

Agreement on Target-bidirectional Neural Machine Translation

Lemao Liu, Masao Utiyama, Andrew Finch, Eiichiro Sumita
National Institute of Information and Communications Technology (NICT)
3-5 Hikari-dai, Seika-cho, Soraku-gun, Kyoto, Japan
{lmliu, first.last}@nict.go.jp

Abstract

Neural machine translation (NMT) with recurrent neural networks, has proven to be an effective technique for end-to-end machine translation. However, in spite of its promising advances over traditional translation methods, it typically suffers from an issue of unbalanced outputs, that arise from both the nature of recurrent neural networks themselves, and the challenges inherent in machine translation. To overcome this issue, we propose an agreement model for neural machine translation and show its effectiveness on large-scale Japanese-to-English and Chinese-to-English translation tasks. Our results show the model can achieve improvements of up to 1.4 BLEU over the strongest baseline NMT system. With the help of an ensemble technique, this new end-to-end NMT approach finally outperformed phrase-based and hierarchical phrase-based Moses baselines by up to 5.6 BLEU points.

1 Introduction

Recurrent neural network (RNN) has achieved great successes on several structured prediction tasks (Graves, 2013; Watanabe and Sumita, 2015; Dyer et al., 2015), in which RNNs are required to make a sequence of dependent predictions. One of its advantages is that an unbounded *history* is available to enrich the context for the prediction at the current time-step.

Despite its successes, recently, (Liu et al., 2016) pointed out that the RNN suffers from a fundamental issue of generating unbalanced outputs: that is to say the suffixes of its outputs are typically worse than the prefixes. This is due to the fact that later predictions directly depend on the accuracy of previous predictions. They empirically demonstrated this issue on two simple sequence-to-sequence learning tasks: machine transliteration and grapheme-to-phoneme conversion.

On the more general sequence-to-sequence learning task of machine translation (MT), neural machine translation (NMT) based on RNNs has recently become an active research topic (Sutskever et al., 2014; Bahdanau et al., 2014). Compared to those two simple tasks, MT involves in much larger vocabulary and frequent reordering between input and output sequences. This makes the prediction at each time-step far more challenging. In addition, sequences in MT are much longer, with averaged length of 36.7 being about 5 times longer than that in grapheme-to-phoneme conversion. Therefore, we believe that the history is more likely to contain incorrect predictions and the issue of unbalanced outputs may be more serious. This hypothesis is supported later (see Table 1 in §4.1), by an analysis that shows the quality of the prefixes of translation hypotheses is much higher than that of the suffixes.

To address this issue for NMT, in this paper we extend the agreement model proposed in (Liu et al., 2016) to the task of machine translation. Its key idea is to encourage the agreement between a pair of target-directional (left-to-right and right-to-left) NMT models in order to produce more balanced translations and thus improve the overall translation quality. Our contribution is two-fold:

- We introduce a simple and general method to address the issue of unbalanced outputs for

Proceedings of NAACL-HLT 2016, pages 411–416,
San Diego, California, June 12-17, 2016. ©2016 Association for Computational Linguistics

NMT (§3). This method is robust without any extra hyperparameters to tune and is easy to implement. In addition, it is general enough to be applied on top of any of the existing RNN translation models, although it was implemented on top of the model in (Bahdanau et al., 2014) in this paper.

- We provide an empirical evaluation of the technique on large scale Japanese-to-English and Chinese-to-English translation tasks. The results show our model can generate more balanced translation results, and achieves substantial improvements (of up to 1.4 BLEU points) over the strongest NMT baseline (§4). With the help of an ensemble technique, our new end-to-end NMT gains up to 5.6 BLEU points over phrase-based and hierarchical phrase-based Moses (Koehn et al., 2007) systems. [1]

2 Overview of Neural Machine Translation

Suppose $\mathbf{x} = \langle x_1, x_2, \cdots, x_m \rangle$ denotes a source sentence, $\mathbf{y} = \langle y_1, y_2, \cdots, y_n \rangle$ denotes a target sentence. In addition, let $x_{<t} = \langle x_1, x_2, \cdots, x_{t-1} \rangle$ denote a prefix of $\mathbf{x}$. Neural Machine Translation (NMT) directly maps a source sentence into a target within a probabilistic framework. Formally, it defines a conditional probability over a pair of sequences $\mathbf{x}$ and $\mathbf{y}$ via a recurrent neural network as follows:

$$
\begin{aligned}
p(\mathbf{y} \mid \mathbf{x}; \theta) &= \prod_{t=1}^{n} p(y_t \mid y_{<t}, \mathbf{x}; \theta) \\
&= \prod_{t=1}^{n} \mathbf{softmax}\big(g(h_t)\big)[y_t]
\end{aligned}
\tag{1}
$$

where θ is the set of model parameters; h_t denotes a hidden state (i.e. a vector) of $\mathbf{y}$ at timestep t; g is a transformation function from a hidden state to a vector with dimension of the target-side vocabulary size; $\mathbf{softmax}$ is the softmax function, and $[i]$ denotes the i_{th} component in a vector.[2] Furthermore,

$h_t = f(h_{t-1}, c(\mathbf{x}, y_{<t}))$ is defined by a recurrent function over both the previous hidden state h_{t-1} and the context $c(\mathbf{x}, y_{<t})$. [3] Note that both h_t and $c(\mathbf{x}, y_{<t})$ have dimension d for all t.

In this paper, we develop our model on top of the neural machine translation approach of (Bahdanau et al., 2014), and we refer the reader this paper for a complete description of the model, for example, the definitons of f and c. The proposed method could just as easily been implemented on top of any other RNN models such as that in (Sutskever et al., 2014).

3 Agreement on Target-bidirectional NMT

In this section, we extend the method in (Liu et al., 2016) to address this issue of unbalanced outputs for NMT. The key idea is to: 1) train two kinds of NMT, i.e. one generating targets from *left-to-right* while the other from *right-to-left*; 2) encourage the agreement between them by joint search.

3.1 Training

The training objective function for our **agreement** (or **joint**) model is formalized as follows:

$$
\ell = \sum_{\langle \mathbf{x}, \mathbf{y} \rangle} \log p(\mathbf{y} \mid \mathbf{x}; \theta_1) + \log p(\mathbf{y}^r \mid \mathbf{x}; \theta_2)
\tag{2}
$$

where $\mathbf{y}^r = \langle y_n, y_{n-1} \cdots, y_1 \rangle$ is the reverse of sequence $\mathbf{y}$; $p(\mathbf{y} \mid \mathbf{x}; \theta_1)$ denotes the **left-to-right** model with parameters θ_1, while $p(\mathbf{y}^r \mid \mathbf{x}; \theta_2)$ denotes the **right-to-left** model with parameters θ_2, as defined in Eq.(1); and $\langle \mathbf{x}, \mathbf{y} \rangle$ ranges over a given training dataset. Following (Bahdanau et al., 2014), we employ AdaDelta (Zeiler, 2012) to minimize the loss ℓ.

Note that, in parallel to our efforts, Cheng et al. (2016) has explored the agreement idea for NMT close to ours. However, unlike their work on the agreement between source and target sides in the spirit of the general idea in (Liang et al., 2006), we focus on the agreement between left and right directions on the target side oriented to the natural issue of NMT itself. Although our model is orthogonal to theirs, one of our advantage is that our model does not rely on any additional hyperparameters to

---

[1] The absolute gains of our model can be expected to be further increased by applying the well-known techniques in (Jean et al., 2015; Luong et al., 2015) that address the problems presented by unknown words, but these techniques are beyond the scope of this paper.

[2] In that sense, y_t in Eq.(1) also denotes the index of this word in its vocabulary.

[3] Both hidden states and context vectors are dependent on the model parameter θ, but we remove it from the expressions here for simplicity.

encourage agreement, given that tuning such hyper-parameters for NMT is too costly.

3.2 Approximate Joint Search

Given a source sentence $\mathbf{x}$ and model parameters $\langle \theta_1, \theta_2 \rangle$, decoding can be formalized as follows:

$$\hat{\mathbf{y}} = \underset{\mathbf{y}}{\mathbf{argmax}}\, p(\mathbf{y} \mid \mathbf{x}; \theta_1) \times p(\mathbf{y}^r \mid \mathbf{x}; \theta_2)$$

As pointed out by (Liu et al., 2016), it is NP-hard to perform an exact search, and so we adapt one of their approximate search methods for the machine translation scenario. The basic idea consists of two steps: 1) run beam search for forward and reverse models independently to obtain two k-best lists; 2) re-score the union of two k-best lists using the joint model to find the best candidate. We refer to the reader to (Liu et al., 2016) for further details.

4 Experiments

We conducted experiments on two challenging translation tasks: Japanese-to-English (JP-EN) and Chinese-to-English (CH-EN), using case-insensitive BLEU for evaluation.

For the JP-EN task, we use the data from NTCIR-9 (Goto et al., 2011): the training data consisted of 2.0M sentence pairs, The development and test sets contained 2K sentences with a single referece, respectively. For the CH-EN task, we used the data from the NIST2008 Open Machine Translation Campaign: the training data consisted of 1.8M sentence pairs, the development set was nist02 (878 sentences), and the test sets are were nist05 (1082 sentences), nist06 (1664 sentences) and nist08 (1357 sentences).

Four baselines were used. The first two were the conventional state-of-the-art translation systems, phrase-based and hierarchical phrase-based systems, which are from the latest version of well-known Moses (Koehn et al., 2007) and are respectively denoted as Moses and Moses-hier. The other two were neural machine translation systems implemented using the open source NMT toolkit (Bahdanau et al., 2014):[4] left-to-right NMT (**NMT-l2r**) and right-to-left NMT (**NMT-r2l**). The proposed joint model

Systems	Prefix	Suffix
NMT-l2r	29.4	25.4
NMT-r2l	26.2	26.7
NMT-J	29.5	28.6

Table 1: Quality of 5-word prefixes and suffices of translations in the JP-EN test set, evaluated using partial BLEU.

(**NMT-J**) was also implemented using NMT (Bahdanau et al., 2014).

We followed the standard pipeline to train and run Moses. GIZA++ (Och and Ney, 2000) with grow-diag-final-and was used to build the translation model. We trained 5-gram target language models using the training set for JP-EN and the Gigaword corpus for CH-EN, and used a lexicalized distortion model. All experiments were run with the default settings except for a distortion-limit of 12 in the JP-EN experiment, as suggested by (Goto et al., 2013).[5] To alleviate the negative effects of randomness, the final reported results are averaged over five runs of MERT.

To ensure a fair comparison, we employed the same settings for all NMT systems. Specifically, except for the maximum sequence length (seqlen, which was to 80), and the stopping iteration which was selected using development data, we used the default settings set out in (Bahdanau et al., 2014) for all NMT-based systems: the dimension of word embedding was 620, the dimension of hidden units was 1000, the batch size was 80, the source and target side vocabulary sizes were 30000, and the beam size for decoding was 12. Training was conducted on a single Tesla K80 GPU, and it took about 6 days to train a single NMT system on our large-scale data.

4.1 Results and Analysis on the JP-EN Task

In §1, it was claimed that NMT generates unbalanced outputs. To demostrate this, we have to evaluate the partial translations, which is not trivial (Liu and Huang, 2014). Inspired by (Liu and Huang, 2014), we employ the idea of partial BLEU rather than potential BLEU, as there is no future string concept during NMT decoding. In addition, since the lower n-gram (for example, 1-gram) is easier to be aligned to the uncovered words in source side,

---

[4]See https://github.com/lisa-groundhog/GroundHog/tree/master/experiments/nmt.

[5]This configuration achieved the significant improvements over the default setting on JP-EN.

Systems	dev	test
Moses	27.9	29.4
Moses-hier	28.6	30.2
NMT-l2r	31.5	32.4
NMT-r2l	31.5	32.6
NMT-J	33.0	34.1
NMT-l2r-5	32.6	33.7
NMT-r2l-5	33.0	34.3
NMT-J-5	**33.8**	**35.0**
NMT-l2r-10	32.5	33.6
NMT-r2l-10	33.0	34.2

Table 2: BLEU comparison of the proposed model NMT-Joint with three baselines on JP-EN task.

Systems	nist05	nist06	nist08
Moses	35.4	33.7	25.0
Moses-hier	35.6	33.8	25.3
NMT-l2r	34.2	34.9	27.7
NMT-r2l	34.0	34.1	26.9
NMT-J	36.8	36.9	28.5
NMT-l2r-5	37.0	37.5	28.2
NMT-r2l-5	36.9	37.1	27.3
NMT-J-5	**37.5**	**38.9**	**28.8**

Table 3: BLEU comparison of the proposed model NMT-Joint with baselines on CH-EN task.

which might negatively affect the absolute statistics of evaluation,[6] we employ the partial 4-gram as the metric to evaluate the quality of partial translations (both prefixes and suffixes). In Table 1, we can see that the prefixes are of higher quality than the suffixes for a single left-to-right model (NMT-l2r). In contrast to this, it can be seen that our joint model (NMT-J) that includes one left-to-right and one right-to-left model, successfully addresses this issue, producing balanced outputs.

Table 2 shows the main results on the JP-EN task. From this table, we can see that, although a single NMT model (either left-to-right or right-to-left) comfortably outperforms the Moses and Moses-hier baselines, our simple NMT-J (with one l2r and one r2l NMT model) obtain gains of 1.5 BLEU points over a single NMT. In addition, the more powerful joint model NMT-J-5, which is an ensemble of five l2r and five r2l NMT models, gains 0.7 BLEU points over the strongest NMT ensemble NMT-r2l-5, i.e. an ensemble of five r2l NMT models. The ensemble of joint models achieved considerable gains of 5.6 and 4.8 BLEU points over the state-of-the-art Moses and Moses-hier, respectively. To the best of our knowlege, it is the first time that an end-to-end neural machine translation system has achieved such improvements on the very challenging task of JP-EN translation.

One might argue that our NMT-J-5 contained ten NMT models in total, while the NMT-l2r-5 or NMT-r2l-5 only used five models, and thus such a comparison is unfair. Therefore, we integrated ten NMT models into the NMT-r2l-10 ensemble. In Table 2, we can see that NMT-r2l-10 is not necessarily better than NMT-r2l-5, which is consistent with the findings reported in (Zhou et al., 2002).

4.2 Results on the CH-EN Task

Table 3 shows the comparison between our method and the baselines on the CH-EN task.[7] The results were similar in character to the results for JP-EN. The proposed joint model (NMT-J-5) consistently outperformed the strongest neural baseline (NMT-l2r-5), an ensemble of five l2r NMT models, on all the test sets with gains up to 1.4 BLEU points. Furthermore, our model again achieved substantial gains over the Moses and Moses-hier systems, in the range 1.9~5.2 BLEU points, depending on the test set.

5 Related Work

Target-bidirectional transduction techniques were pioneered in the field of machine translation (Watanabe and Sumita, 2002; Finch and Sumita, 2009; Zhang et al., 2013). They used the techniques for traditional SMT models, under the IBM framework (Watanabe and Sumita, 2002) or the feature-driven linear models (Finch and Sumita, 2009; Zhang et al., 2013). However, the target-bidirectional techniques

---

[6]In training SMT (Liu and Huang, 2014), we update weights towards higher BLEU translations and thus we care more about the relative statistics of BLEU; but in this paper, we care more about the absolute statistics, in order to show how severe the problem of unbalanced outputs is.

[7]We did not run NMT-l2r-10 and NMT-r2l-10, because it is too time-consuming to train 10 NMT models on both target directions and especially NMT-r2l-10 is not necessarily better than NMT-r2l-5 as shown in Table 2.

we have developed for the unified neural network framework, target a pressing need directly motivated by a fundamental issue suffered by recurrent neural networks.

Target-directional neural network models have also been successfully employed in (Devlin et al., 2014). However, their approach was concerned with feedforward networks, which can not make full use of rich contextual information. As a result, their models could only be used as features (i.e. submodels) to augment traditional translation techniques in contrast to the end-to-end neural network framework for machine translation in our proposal.

Our approach is related to that in (Bengio et al., 2015) in some sense. Both approaches can alleviate the mismatch between the training and testing stages: the history predictions are always correct in training while may be incorrect in testing. Bengio et al. (2015) introduce noise into history predictions in training to balance the mistmatch, while we try to make the history predictions in testing as accurate as those in training by using of two directional models. Therefore, theirs focuses on this problem from the view of training instead of both modeling and training as ours, but it is possible and promising to apply their approach to optimize our joint model.

6 Conclusion

In this paper, we investigate the issue of unbalanced outputs suffered by recurrent neural networks, and empirically show its existence in the context of machine translation. To address this issue, we propose an easy to implement agreement model that extends the method of (Liu et al., 2016) from simple sequence-to-sequence learning tasks to machine translation.

On two challenging JP-EN and CH-EN translation tasks, our approach was empirically shown to be effective in addressing the issue; by generating balanced outputs, it was able to consistently outperform a respectable NMT baseline on all test sets, delivering gains of up to 1.4 BLEU points. To put these results in the broader context of machine translation research, our approach (even without special handling of unknown words) achieved gains of up to 5.6 BLEU points over strong phrase-based and hierarchical phrase-based Moses baselines, with the help of an ensemble technique.

Acknowledgments

We would like to thank the three anonymous reviewers for helpful comments and suggestions. In addition, we would like to thank Rico Sennrich for fruitful discussions.

References

[Bahdanau et al.2014] Dzmitry Bahdanau, Kyunghyun Cho, and Yoshua Bengio. 2014. Neural machine translation by jointly learning to align and translate. *CoRR*, abs/1409.0473.

[Bengio et al.2015] Samy Bengio, Oriol Vinyals, Navdeep Jaitly, and Noam Shazeer. 2015. Scheduled sampling for sequence prediction with recurrent neural networks. In *Advances in Neural Information Processing Systems*, pages 1171–1179.

[Cheng et al.2016] Yong Cheng, Shiqi Shen, Zhongjun He, Wei He, Hua Wu, Maosong Sun, and Yang Liu. 2016. Agreement-based joint training for bidirectional attention-based neural machine translation. *CoRR*, abs/1512.04650.

[Devlin et al.2014] Jacob Devlin, Rabih Zbib, Zhongqiang Huang, Thomas Lamar, Richard Schwartz, and John Makhoul. 2014. Fast and robust neural network joint models for statistical machine translation. In *Proceedings of ACL*.

[Dyer et al.2015] Chris Dyer, Miguel Ballesteros, Wang Ling, Austin Matthews, and Noah A. Smith. 2015. Transition-based dependency parsing with stack long short-term memory. In *Proceedings of ACL-IJCNLP*.

[Finch and Sumita2009] Andrew Finch and Eiichiro Sumita. 2009. Bidirectional phrase-based statistical machine translation. In *Proceedings of EMNLP*.

[Goto et al.2011] Isao Goto, Bin Lu, Ka-Po Chow, Eiichiro Sumita, and Benjamin K. Tsou. 2011. Overview of the patent machine translation task at the NTCIR-9 workshop. In *Proceedings of NTCIR-9*.

[Goto et al.2013] Isao Goto, Masao Utiyama, Eiichiro Sumita, Akihiro Tamura, and Sadao Kurohashi. 2013. Distortion model considering rich context for statistical machine translation. In *Proceedings of ACL*.

[Graves2013] Alex Graves. 2013. Generating sequences with recurrent neural networks. *CoRR*.

[Jean et al.2015] Sébastien Jean, Kyunghyun Cho, Roland Memisevic, and Yoshua Bengio. 2015. On using very large target vocabulary for neural machine translation. In *Proceedings of ACL-IJCNLP*.

[Koehn et al.2007] P. Koehn, H. Hoang, A. Birch, C. Callison-Burch, M. Federico, N. Bertoldi,

B. Cowan, W. Shen, C. Moran, R. Zens, C. Dyer, O. Bojar, A. Constantin, and E. Herbst. 2007. Moses: open source toolkit for statistical machine translation. In *Proceedings of ACL: Demonstrations*.

[Liang et al.2006] Percy Liang, Ben Taskar, and Dan Klein. 2006. Alignment by agreement. In *Proceedings of HLT-NAACL*.

[Liu and Huang2014] Lemao Liu and Liang Huang. 2014. Search-aware tuning for machine translation. In *Proceedings of EMNLP*.

[Liu et al.2016] Lemao Liu, Andrew Finch, Masao Utiyama, and Eiichiro Sumita. 2016. Agreement on target-bidirectional lstms for sequence-to-sequence learning. In *Proceedings of AAAI*.

[Luong et al.2015] Thang Luong, Ilya Sutskever, Quoc Le, Oriol Vinyals, and Wojciech Zaremba. 2015. Addressing the rare word problem in neural machine translation. In *Proceedings of ACL-IJCNLP*.

[Och and Ney2000] Franz Josef Och and Hermann Ney. 2000. Improved statistical alignment models. In *Proceedings of ACL*, pages 440–447.

[Sutskever et al.2014] Ilya Sutskever, Oriol Vinyals, and Quoc V. V Le. 2014. Sequence to sequence learning with neural networks. In *Proceedings of NIPS*.

[Watanabe and Sumita2002] Taro Watanabe and Eiichiro Sumita. 2002. Bidirectional decoding for statistical machine translation. In *Proceeding of COLING*.

[Watanabe and Sumita2015] Taro Watanabe and Eiichiro Sumita. 2015. Transition-based neural constituent parsing. In *Proceedings of ACL-IJCNLP*.

[Zeiler2012] Matthew D. Zeiler. 2012. ADADELTA: an adaptive learning rate method. *CoRR*.

[Zhang et al.2013] Hui Zhang, Kristina Toutanova, Chris Quirk, and Jianfeng Gao. 2013. Beyond left-to-right: Multiple decomposition structures for smt. In *HLT-NAACL*, pages 12–21.

[Zhou et al.2002] Zhi-Hua Zhou, Jianxin Wu, and Wei Tang. 2002. Ensembling neural networks: Many could be better than all. *Artif. Intell.*

Psycholinguistic Features for Deceptive Role Detection in Werewolf [*]

Codruta Girlea
University of Illinois
Urbana, IL 61801, USA
girlea2@illinois.edu

Roxana Girju
University of Illinois
Urbana, IL 61801, USA
girju@illinois.edu

Eyal Amir
University of Illinois
Urbana, IL 61801, USA
eyal@illinois.edu

Abstract

We tackle the problem of identifying deceptive agents in highly-motivated high-conflict dialogues. We consider the case where we only have textual information. We show the usefulness of psycho-linguistic deception and persuasion features on a small dataset for the game of Werewolf. We analyse the role of syntax and we identify some characteristics of players in deceptive roles.

1 Introduction

Deception detection has gained some attention in the NLP community (Mihalcea and Strapparava, 2009; Ott et al., 2011; Jindal and Liu, 2008). The focus has mostly been on detecting insincere reviews or arguments. However, there has been little work (Hung and Chittaranjan, 2010) in detecting deception and manipulation in dialogues.

When the agents involved in a dialogue have conflicting goals, they are often motivated to use deception and manipulation in order to reach those goals. Examples include trials and negotiations. The high motivation for using deception and the possiblity of tracking the effects on participants throughout the dialogue sets this problem apart from identifying deception in nonce text fragment where motivation is not immediately relevant.

The Werewolf game is an instance of such a dialogue where people are motivated to deceive and manipulate in order to reach their goals. The setting is a village where at least one of the villagers is secretly a werewolf. Each night, a villager falls prey to the werewolves. Each day, the remaining villagers discuss to find the most likely werewolf to execute.

Players are assigned roles that define their goals and available actions. For our purpose, all roles are collapsed together as either werewolf or non-werewolf. There are other important roles in Werewolf, such as seer, vigilante, etc, the goals and available actions of which are not the focus of this paper. (Barnwell, 2012) provides a broader description of the game and roles.

Each player only knows her own role, as assigned by an impartial judge who overlooks the game. The players with a *werewolf* role learn each other's roles in the first round of the game. Every round, they pick another non-werewolf player to be removed from the game. This happens during a *night phase*, and is hidden from the other players. The judge announces the identity and role of the removed player.

All players are then allowed to remove one other player from the game before the next night phase. They discuss and vote during a *day phase*. The *non-werewolves* are motivated to remove the werewolves from the game. The werewolves are motivated to hide their roles, as in every round there is a majority of non-werewolves. Any time werewolves become a majority, they win the game. Any time all werewolves are eliminated, they lose the game.

In this paper we define the task as binary classification of deceptive and non-deceptive roles in Werewolf. Werewolf roles are deceptive, as they rely on deception to win the game, whereas all the

[*]This research was partially funded owing to a collaboration between Adobe Research and the University of Illinois. We thank Julia Hockenmaier, Dan Roth, Dafna Shahaf, Walter Chang, Trung Bui, and our reviewers for their helpful comments and feedback.

Proceedings of NAACL-HLT 2016, pages 417–422,
San Diego, California, June 12-17, 2016. ©2016 Association for Computational Linguistics

other roles are nondeceptive (Hung and Chittaran-jan, 2010). For our purpose, all these roles are col-lapsed together according to whether they help the werewolves or not. We consider all the utterances of each player in each game as one distinct instance.

This is a first step towards building a model of deception in the Werewolf game, and more generally in scenarios where deception can be used to achieve goals. The model can then be used to predict future actions, e.g. the vote outcomes in Werewolf.

We show that by analyzing this dialogue genre we can gain some insights into the dynamics of manip-ulation and deception. These insights would then be useful in detecting hidden intentions and predicting decisions in important, real-life scenarios.

2 Previous Work

There has been little work on deception detection in written language and most of it has focused on either discriminating between sincere and insincere argu-ments (Mihalcea and Strapparava, 2009) or opinion spam (Ott et al., 2011; Jindal and Liu, 2008). One method of data collection has been to ask subjects to argue for both sides of a debate (Mihalcea and Strap-parava, 2009). While lies about one's beliefs are also present, the manipulative behaviour and the motiva-tion are missing. Since none of the previous work focuses on dialogue, the change in participants' be-liefs, intentions, and plans reflected in the interac-tion between players is also absent.

More related is the work of (Hung and Chittaran-jan, 2010), who recorded a total of 81.17 hours of people playing the Werewolf game, and used pho-netic features to detect werewolves. While their re-sults are promising, our focus is on written text only.

We have also been inspired by psycho-linguistic studies of deception detection (Porter and Yuille, 1996) as well as by psycho-linguistic research on persuasive or powerless language (Greenwald et al., 1968; Hosman, 2002; Sparks and Areni, 2008). We build upon findings from both of these lines of re-search, as Werewolf players use both deception, to hide their roles and intentions, and persuasion, to manipulate other players' beliefs and intentions.

3 Experiments

3.1 Data

The raw data consists of 86 game transcripts col-lected by Barnwell (Barnwell, 2012). The tran-scripts have an average length of 205 messages per transcript, including judge comments.

In the transcripts, the judge is a bot, which means there is a small fixed set of phrases it uses to make announcements. As part of the system, the judge knows all the roles as they are assigned. It reveals those roles in an annoucement as follows: every time a player is removed from the game, their role is made known; and the roles of the remaining players are revealed after the game is concluded.

We automatically extracted role assignments by looking for phrases such as *was a, is a, turns out to have been, carried wolfsbane.* We manually checked the assignments and found the werewolf roles were correctly assigned for 72 out of the 86 transcripts. The remaining 14 games end before they should because the judge bot breaks down. How-ever, the players do reveal their own roles after the game ends. By looking at their comments, we man-ually annotated these remaining games.

All the utterances from each player in each tran-script translate to one data instance. The label is 1 or 0, for whether the player is or isn't a werewolf. We do not consider the judge as part of the data. The resulting data set consists of 701 instances, of which 116 are instances of a werewolf role.

Given the small size and the skewed distribution of the dataset, we balanced the data with resampling so that we have enough instances to learn from.

3.2 Features

3.2.1 Psycholinguistic Features

(Tausczik and Pennebaker, 2010) suggest word count and use of negative emotions, motion, and sense words are indicative of deception.

We counted the negative emotion words using the MPQA subjectivity lexicon of (Wilson et al., 2005). We also experimented with the NRC word-emotion association lexicon of (Mohammad and Yang, 2011), but found the MPQA lexicon to per-form better. Since we didn't have access to LIWC (Tausczik and Pennebaker, 2010), we used manually created lists of motion (*arrive, run, walk*) and sense (*see, sense, appearance*) words. The lists are up to 50 words long. We also considered the number of verbs, based on our intuition that heavy use of verbs can be associated to motion. However, we don't expect the number of motion words to be as important in our domain. This is because deception in the Werewolf game does not refer to a fabricated story that other players have to be convinced to believe, but rather to hiding one's identity and intentions.

(Tausczik and Pennebaker, 2010) also talk about honesty features : number of exclusion words (*but, without, exclude, except, only, just, either*) and number of self references (we used a list of first person singular pronoun forms). They claim that cognitive complexity is also correlated with honesty. This is because maintaining the coherence of a fabricated story is cognitively taxing. Cognitive complexity manifests in the use of: long words (longer than 6 letters), exclusion words (differentiating between competing solutions), conjunctions, disjunctions, connectives (integrating different aspects of a task), and cognitive words (*think, plan, reason*).

(Porter and Yuille, 1996) observe that for highly motivated deception, people use longer utterances, more self references, and more negative statements. We used those as features, as the average number of words per utterance and the number of dependencies of type *negation* from the Stanford parser.

Another set of features cited by (Porter and Yuille, 1996) comes for ex-polygrapher Sapir's training program for police investigators. He notes that liars use too many unneeded connectors, and display deviations in pronoun usage – most of the times by avoiding first-person singular. This seems to contradict the discussion on highly motivated deception (Porter and Yuille, 1996), and is aligned with (Tausczik and Pennebaker, 2010)'s findings. It is possible that the natural tendency of a liar is to avoid self references (e.g. due to cognitive dissonance), but that a strong motivation can cause one to purposefully act against this tendency, ignoring any mental discomfort it may cause. In our experiments, we didn't observe any tendency of werewolf to either avoid or increase use of self references.

There are differences in language when used to recount a true memory versus a false one (reality monitoring) (Porter and Yuille, 1996). In this context, a true memory means a memory of reality, i.e. of a story that actually happened, whereas a false memory is a mental representation of a fabricated story. People talking about a true memory tend to focus on the attributes of the stimulus that generated the memory (e.g. shape, location, color), whereas people talking about a false memory tend to use more cognitive words (e.g. *believe, think, recall*) and hedges (e.g. *kind of, maybe, a little*). An explanation is that the process of fabricating a story engages reasoning more than it does memory, and people tend to resist committing to a lie. We used the noun and adjective count as a rough approximation of the number of stimulus attributes, as adjectives and nouns in prepositional phrases can be used to enrich a description, e.g. of a memory. However, it is important to note that Werewolf players do not actively lie, in the sense that the discussion does not involve events not directly accessible to all players. Therefore it's impossible for players to lie about the course of events, so there is no false memory to recount.

Another characteristic of the game is that the werewolves actively try to *persuade* other players that their intentions are not harmful. (Hosman, 2002) notes that language complexity is indicative of persuasive power. A measure of language complexity is the type-token ratio (TTR). On the other hand, hesitations (*um, er, uh*), hedges (*sort of, kind of, almost*), and polite forms are markers of powerless language (Sparks and Areni, 2008). We did not find any polite forms in our data, the context being a game where players adopt a familiar tone.

The complete list of features is as follows (words are stemmed): *TTR* (type-token ratio), *number of hesitations, number of negative emotions, number of words, number of words longer than 6 letters, number of self references, number of negations, number of hedges* (50 hedge words), *number of cognitive words* (50 words), *number of motion words* (20 words), *number of sense words* (17 words), *number of exclusion words, number of connectors* (prepositions and conjunctions), *number of pronouns, number of adjectives, number of nouns, number of verbs, number of conjunctions, number of prepositions*.

3.2.2 POS and Syntactic Features

Following the intuition that cognitive complexity can also be reflected in sentence structure, we decided to look beyond lexical level for markers of deception and persuasion and experimented with POS and syntactic features. We used the Stanford POS parser (Lee et al., 2011) to extract part of speech labels as well as dependencies and production rules.

The syntactic features are based on both constituency and dependency parses, i.e. both production rules and dependency types.

3.3 Results

We used Weka and 10-fold cross-validation. We experimented with: logistic regression (LR, 10^8 ridge), SVM, Naive Bayes, perceptron, decision trees (DT), voted perceptron (VP), and random forest (RF).

The results are summarized in Table 1. DT and LR performed best among basic classifiers. DT outperforms LR, and the ensemble methods (VP and RF) far outperform both. An explanation is that there are deeper nonlinear dependencies between features. We believe such dependencies are worth further investigation beyond the scope of this paper. We plan to address this in future work.

In Table 1, we underlined the results for the two best *basic* classifiers, since we further analyze the features for these. Given space constraints, ensemble methods (VP and RF) are left to future work as analyzing the features and interactions based on their internal structure needs special attention.

Table 2 summarizes the feature selection results. We used Weka's feature selection. The selected features (with a positive/negative association with a deceptive role) were: number of words (negative); number of pronouns, adjectives, nouns (positive).

In order to observe each feature's individual contribution, we also performed manual feature selection, removing one feature at a time. Removing the following features improved or did not affect the performance, increasing the F1 score from 64.9 to 66.1 : number of self references, number of adjectives, number of long words, number of conjunctions or of connectors (but not both), number of cognitive words, number of pronouns.

3.4 POS and Syntactic Features

We repeated the experiments with POS tags as features (POS model), and then with syntactic features, i.e. dependency types and production rules (POS+dep, POS+con, and POS+syn models). For

Model	Acc.	F1	Prec.	Rec.	AUC
SVM	57.2	56.2	58.9	57.2	57.9
Perc	62.77	62.6	63.5	62.8	67
LR	**64.91**	**64.9**	**65.1**	**64.9**	66.8
NB	55.92	53.7	58.9	55.9	68.6
DT	**84.45**	**84.4**	**84.9**	**84.5**	**87.4**
VP	65.34	62.2	70.7	65.3	65.6
RF	90.87	90.8	91.2	90.9	98.1

Table 1: **Werewolf classification:** *Perc* - Perceptron, *LR* - Logistic Regression, *NB* - Naive Bayes, *DT* - Decision Tree, *VP* - Voted Perceptron, *RF* - Random Forest

Model	Acc.	F1	Prec.	Rec.	AUC
bfs	64.91	64.9	65.1	64.9	66.8
afs	62.625	62.4	62.6	63.4	63.4
mfs	**66.76**	**66.8**	**66.9**	**66.8**	**68.9**

Table 2: **Experimental results using logistic regression:** *bfs* - baseline feature set; *afs* - model on a subset of features generated with CFS-BFS feature selection; *mfs* - model on a manually selected subset of features

each model, the *baseline* feature set is the set of psycholinguistic features used in the previous section. The subsequent models use both the baseline features and the syntactic features, e.g. POS+con uses lexical-level psycholinguistic features, POS tags, and production rules. We also used tf-idf weighting.

Table 3 suggests that production rules highly improve performance. An explanation is that complex syntax reflects cognitive complexity. For example, the utterance: *Player A said that I was innocent, which I know to be true* has many subordinates (SBAR nodes , SBAR $\rightarrow$ IN S, SBAR $\rightarrow$ WHNP S), whereas *Anyone feeling particularly lupine?* has elliptical structure (missing S $\rightarrow$ NP VP). There is also overlap with lexical features (IN nodes).

4 Discussion and Conclusions

Inspecting the decision tree, we found that most non-werewolf players used few words, no connectors, and no negations. Most werewolves use more words, adjectives, few negative emotion words, and not many words greater than 6 letters. Some werewolves use sense words and few negative emotion words, whereas others use no sense words and few or no hedges, self references, or cognitive words.

Feature set	Acc.	F1	Prec.	Rec.	AUC
baseline	64.91	64.9	65.1	64.9	66.8
POS	67.33	67.3	67.3	67.3	72.1
POS+dep	76.87	76.8	76.9	76.9	79.9
POS+con	**90.59**	**90.6**	**90.8**	**90.6**	**92.1**
POS+syn	**91.58**	**91.6**	**91.8**	**91.6**	**91.2**
POS+syn (tf-idf)	**92.287**	**92.3**	**92.3**	**92.3**	**91.8**

Table 3: POS and Syntactic Features (Logistic Regression): *baseline* - lexical psycholinguistic features, also used in subsequent models together with new features; *POS* - POS features; *dep* - dependency features; *con* - constituency features (production rules); *syn* - syntactic features; *POS+dep/con/syn* - POS and dependency/constituency/syntactic features

The conclusion is that werewolves are more verbose and moderately emotional, whereas non-werewolves are usually quiet, non-confrontational players. Werewolves also use moderately complex language, which can be explained by the fact that they are both actively trying to persuade other players, and under the cognitive load of constantly adjusting their plans to players' comments, and maintaining a false image of themselves and others.

This aligns with previous findings on low cognitive complexity for maintaining a lie (Tausczik and Pennebaker, 2010) and verbosity for highly motivated deception (Porter and Yuille, 1996).

Inspecting the odds ratios (OR) of the features in the logistic regression classifier, we found the following features to be most relevant: *TTR* (3.49), *number of hesitations* (0.91), *number of negative emotions* (1.16), *number of motion words* (1.25), *number of sense words* (0.76), *number of exclusions* (1.31), *number of connectors* (0.92), *number of conjunctions* (0.92), *number of prepositions* (1.32).

On the connection between werewolf roles and persuasion, TTR is indicative of persuasive power as well as of a werewolf, and the number of hesitations is a marker of powerless language, and is negatively associated with a werewolf role.

The fact that the number of prepositions is indicative of a werewolf role aligns with Sapir's findings, whereas the positive influence of negative emotion and motion words and the negative influence of connectors and conjunctions is as predicted by (Tausczik and Pennebaker, 2010). However, (Tausczik and Pennebaker, 2010) cite the number of sense words as highly associated with deception and the number of exclusions, with honesty. We found that in our case these associations are reversed.

One possible explanation regarding the number of sense words can be the fact that *seeing*, a family of sense words, is overloaded in this data set, since *seer* is a legitimate game role, with actions (*seeing*) that carry a specific meaning. Another explanation is that, since the transcripts are from online game, there is no actual sensing involved.

As for the number of exclusions, (Tausczik and Pennebaker, 2010) list it as a marker of cognitive complexity, which should be affected by any attempt to maintain a false story. But here most players do not actively lie, so there is no false story to maintain, and therefore no toll on cognitive complexity.

Another observation is that features suggested for highly motivated deception (longer utterances, more self references, and more negations) are not important for this data set. It is possible that we do not have highly motivated deception, since any motivation is mitigated by the context, which is a game. This suggests that deception in dialogue contexts as well as game contexts is different than in the storytelling contexts analyzed in previous work in psycholinguistics (Hosman, 2002; Porter and Yuille, 1996). On the other hand, *identity concealment* is different than other kinds of highly motivated deception – in this particular case it might be more helpful to appear logical, rather than emotional.

In this paper we presented a simple model to serve as a baseline for further models of deception detection in dialogues. We did not consider word sequence, player interaction, individual characteristics of players, or non-literal meaning. However, the data set is too small for any more complex models. We believe our results shed light on some mechanisms of deception in the Werewolf game in particular, and of deception and manipulation in dialogues in general. We plan to collect more data on which we can employ richer models that also take into account utterance sequence and dialogue features.

References

Brendan Barnwell. 2012. brenbarn.net. http://www.brenbarn.net/werewolf/. [Online; accessed 1-April-2016].

Anthony G. Greenwald, Rosita Daskal Albert, Dallas Cullen, Robert Love, and Joseph Sakumura Who Have. 1968. Cognitive learning, cognitive response to persuasion, and attitude change. pages 147–170. Academic Press.

M. A. Hall. 1998. *Correlation-based Feature Subset Selection for Machine Learning*. Ph.D. thesis, University of Waikato, Hamilton, New Zealand.

Lawrence A. Hosman. 2002. Language and persuasion. In James Price Dillard and Michael Pfau, editors, *The Persuasion Handbook: Developments in Theory and Practice*. Sage Publications.

Hayley Hung and Gokul Chittaranjan. 2010. The idiap wolf corpus: Exploring group behaviour in a competitive role-playing game. In *Proceedings of the 18th ACM International Conference on Multimedia*, MM '10, pages 879–882, New York, NY, USA. ACM.

Nitin Jindal and Bing Liu. 2008. Opinion spam and analysis. In *Proceedings of the Conference on Web Search and Web Data Mining (WSDM)*, pages 219–230.

Heeyoung Lee, Yves Peirsman, Angel Chang, Nathanael Chambers, Mihai Surdeanu, and Dan Jurafsky. 2011. Stanford's multi-pass sieve coreference resolution system at the conll-2011 shared task. In *Proceedings of the CoNLL-2011 Shared Task*.

Rada Mihalcea and Carlo Strapparava. 2009. The lie detector: Explorations in the automatic recognition of deceptive language. In *Proceedings of the ACL-IJCNLP 2009 Conference Short Papers*, ACLShort '09, pages 309–312, Stroudsburg, PA, USA. Association for Computational Linguistics.

Saif M Mohammad and Tony Wenda Yang. 2011. Tracking sentiment in mail: how genders differ on emotional axes. In *Proceedings of the 2nd Workshop on Computational Approaches to Subjectivity and Sentiment Analysis (ACL-HLT 2011*, pages 70–79.

Myle Ott, Yejin Choi, Claire Cardie, and Jeffrey T. Hancock. 2011. Finding deceptive opinion spam by any stretch of the imagination. In *Proceedings of the 49th Annual Meeting of the Association for Computational Linguistics: Human Language Technologies*, pages 309–319, Portland, Oregon, USA, June. Association for Computational Linguistics.

Stephen Porter and John C. Yuille. 1996. The language of deceit: An investigation of the verbal clues to deception in the interrogation context. *Law and Human Behavior*, 20(4):443–458.

John R. Sparks and Charles S. Areni. 2008. Style versus substance: Multiple roles of language power in persuasion. *Journal of Applied Social Psychology*, 38(1):37–60.

Yla R Tausczik and James W Pennebaker. 2010. The psychological meaning of words: Liwc and computerized text analysis methods. *Journal of language and social psychology*, 29(1):24–54.

Theresa Wilson, Janyce Wiebe, and Paul Hoffmann. 2005. Recognizing contextual polarity in phrase-level sentiment analysis. In *Proceedings of the Conference on Human Language Technology and Empirical Methods in Natural Language Processing*, HLT '05, pages 347–354, Stroudsburg, PA, USA. Association for Computational Linguistics.

Individual Variation in the Choice of Referential Form

Thiago Castro Ferreira and **Emiel Krahmer** and **Sander Wubben**
Tilburg center for Cognition and Communication (TiCC)
Tilburg University
The Netherlands
{tcastrof,e.j.krahmer,s.wubben}@uvt.nl

Abstract

This study aims to measure the variation between writers in their choices of referential form by collecting and analysing a new and publicly available corpus of referring expressions. The corpus is composed of referring expressions produced by different participants in identical situations. Results, measured in terms of normalized entropy, reveal substantial individual variation. We discuss the problems and prospects of this finding for automatic text generation applications.

1 Introduction

Automatic text generation is the process of automatically converting data into coherent text - practical applications range from weather reports (Goldberg et al., 1994) to neonatal intensive care reports (Portet et al., 2009). One important way to achieve coherence in texts is by generating appropriate referring expressions throughout the text (Krahmer and van Deemter, 2012). In this generation process, the choice of referential form is a crucial task (Reiter and Dale, 2000): when referring to a person or object in a text, should the system use a proper name ("Phillip Anschutz"), a definite description ("the American entrepreneur") or a pronoun ("he")?

Despite the large amount of algorithms developed for deciding upon the form of a referring expression (Callaway and Lester, 2002; Greenbacker and McCoy, 2009; Gupta and Bandopadhyay, 2009; Orăsan and Dornescu, 2009; Greenbacker et al., 2010), it is difficult to know how well these algorithms actually perform. Typically, such algorithms are evaluated against a corpus of human written texts, predicting what form each reference should have in a given context. Now consider a situation in which the algorithm predicts that a reference should be a description, while this same reference is a pronoun in the corpus text. Should this count as an error? The answer is: it depends. The use of a pronoun does not necessarily mean that the use of a description is incorrect. In fact, other writers might have used a description as well.

In general, corpora of referring expressions have only *one* gold standard referential form for each situation, while different writers may conceivably vary in the referential form they would use. This complicates the development and evaluation of text generation algorithms, since these will typically attempt to predict the corpus gold standard, which may not always be representative of the choices of different writers. Although recent work in text generation has explored individual variation in the content determination of definite descriptions (Viethen and Dale, 2010; Ferreira and Paraboni, 2014), to the best of our knowledge this has not been systematically explored for choosing referential forms.

In this paper, we collect and analyze a new corpus to address this issue. In the collection, we presented different writers with texts in which all references to the main topic of the text have been replaced with gaps. The task of the participants was to fill each of those gaps with a reference to the topic. In the analysis, we estimated to what extent different writers agree with each other in terms of normalized entropy. In addition, we study whether this variation depends on the text genre, comparing encyclopedic texts with news and product reports. Moreover, we discuss the implications of our findings for automatic text generation, exploring whether factors such as syntactic structure, referential status and recency affect the variation between the writers' choices. The annotated corpus is made publicly available[1].

2 Data Gathering

2.1 Material

For our study, we used 36 English texts, equally distributed over three different genres: news texts, reviews of commercial products and encyclopedic texts. The encyclopedic texts were selected from the GREC corpus (Belz et al., 2010), which is a standard corpus for testing and evaluating models for choice of referential form. The news and review texts were selected from the AQUAINT-2 corpus[2] and the SFU Review corpus (Konstantinova et al., 2012), respectively.

Note that, depending on the genre, texts may address different kinds of topics. For instance, the news texts usually are about a person, a company or a group; the product reviews may be about a book, a movie or a phone; and the encyclopedic texts about a mountain, a river or a country. In all texts, all expressions referring to the topic were replaced with gaps, which the participants should fill in.

2.2 Participants

Participants were recruited through CrowdFlower[3]. 78 participants completed the survey. 53 were female and 25 were male. Their average age was 37 years old. Most were native speakers (73 participants) or fluent in English (5 participants).

2.3 Procedure

The participants were first presented with an introduction to the experiment, explaining the procedure and asking their consent. Next, they were asked for their age, demographic information and English language proficiency. After this, participants were randomly assigned to a list, containing 9 texts (3 per genre).

The task of the participants was to fill in each gap with a reference to the topic of the text. To inform the participants about the entities, a short description - extracted from the Wikipedia page about the topic - was provided before each text.

Participants were encouraged to fill in the gaps according to their preferences, so that they felt the texts would be easy to understand. We made sure that participants did not fill all the gaps in a text with only one referring expression (to avoid copy/paste behaviour). Participants could also not leave any gap empty (they were instructed to use the "-" symbol for empty references).

2.4 Annotation

The first author of this study annotated the referring expressions produced by participants for referential form, syntactic position, referential status, and recency. Coding was straightforward, and the few difficult cases were resolved in discussions between the co-authors.

The referring expressions were assigned to one of five forms: **proper names** ("*Philip Anschutz*, 66, will have no trouble keeping busy."); **pronouns** ("*It* is the highest peak [...]", "Huffman, *who* spoke at the sentencing phase [...]"); **definite descriptions** ("[...] *the Russian President* defended the country's contribution [...]"); **demonstratives** ("You'll probably have screaming kids who want to see *this movie*."); and **empty references** ("He rarely grants on-the-record media interviews and __ seldom allows himself to be photographed.").

Following the GREC Project scheme (Belz et al., 2010), referring expressions were annotated for three syntactic positions: subject noun phrases, object noun phrases, and genitive noun phrases that function as determiners (***Google's** stock*). Referential status refers to whether a referring expression is a first mention to the topic (new) or not (old). We annotated this at the level of the text, paragraph and sentence, so that a reference can be new in paragraph, but old in the text. Recency, finally, is the distance between a given referring expression and the last, previous reference to the same topic, measured in terms of number of words within a paragraph. If the referring expression was the first mention to the topic in the paragraph, its recency is set to 0.

In total, 10,977 referring expressions were col-

---

[1]http://ilk.uvt.nl/~tcastrof/vareg
[2]http://catalog.ldc.upenn.edu/LDC2008T25
[3]http://www.crowdflower.com/

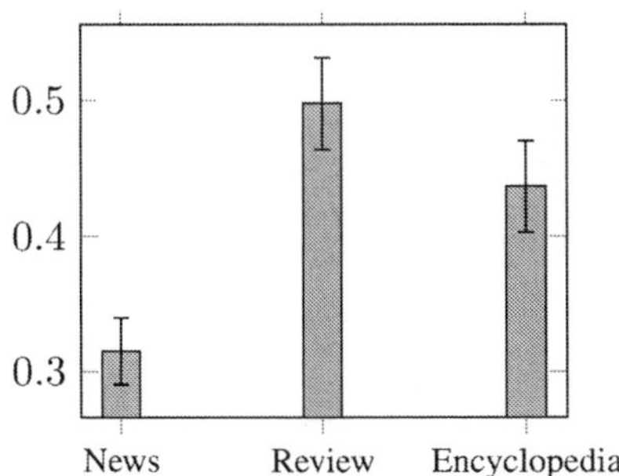

Figure 1: Average entropy per gap as a function of text genre. The error bars represent the 95% confidence intervals.

lected in 563 referential gaps. 3,682 were annotated as proper names, 4,662 as pronouns, 768 as definite descriptions, 318 as demonstratives and 158 as empty references. The remaining 1,389 were ruled out of the corpus, since they did not consist of a reference to the target entity or changed the meaning of the original sentence.

2.5 Analysis

We measured variation between participants' choices for each gap, using the normalized entropy measure, defined in Equation 1, where X corresponds to the references in a given gap, and $n = 5$ the number of referential forms annotated.

$$H(X) = -\sum_{i=1}^{n=5} \frac{p(x_i) \log(p(x_i))}{\log(n)} \tag{1}$$

The measure ranges from 0 to 1, where 0 indicates the complete agreement among the participants for a particular referential form, and 1 indicates the complete variation among their choices.

3 Results

Figure 1 presents the main result, depicting the amount of individual variation in referential forms, measured in terms of entropy, as a function of text genre. The averaged entropies are significantly higher than 0 for all three genres according to a Wilcoxon signed-rank test (News: $V = 20,910.0$, $p < .001$; Reviews: $V = 11,476.0$, $p < .001$; and Encyclopedic texts: $V = 10,153.0$, $p < .001$). This clearly shows that different writers can vary substantially in their choices for a referential form. Com-

paring the three different genres, we find that writers' choices of referential form varied most in review texts and least in news texts, with encyclopedic texts sandwiched in between (Kruskal-Wallis $H = 70.73$, $p < .001$).

In comparison with the original texts, 44% of the referring expressions produced by the writers differ from the original ones in a same referential gap. Furthermore, the form of the original referring expressions differs from the major choice of the writers in 38% of the referential gaps.

To get a better understanding of factors potentially influencing individual variation, we investigate the effects of three linguistic factors: syntactic position, referential status and recency. Figure 2 depicts the average entropies for each of these.

Comparing the three syntactic positions, Figure 2a suggests that the highest variation is found when writers need to choose referential forms in the object position of a sentence, whereas the lowest variation is found for references that function as a genitive noun phrase determiner (Kruskal-Wallis $H = 52.53$, $p < .001$).

Figure 2b depicts individual variation in the choice of referential form for old and new references in the text, paragraph and sentence. The data suggests a higher amount of individual variation when writers need to refer to a topic already mentioned in the text rather than a first mention (Mann-Whitney $U = 3,916.0$, $p < .001$), presumably because for a topic which is new in the text, writers were more likely to agree to use proper names (91% of the choices). Looking at old and new references within paragraphs reveals no significant differences in individual variation (Mann-Whitney $U = 32,669.5$, $p < .094$). At the sentence level, finally, there is more individual variation for references to a new topic than for references to a previously mentioned one (Mann-Whitney $U = 21,873.0$, $p < .001$). When writers referred to a previously mentioned referent in the sentence, they tended to agree on the use of a pronoun (76% of the choices).

Figure 2c shows the individual variation in referential form as a function of recency. Except for the relatively nearby intervals (between 0 and 10 words, and between 11 and 20 words), the data suggests that when the distance between two consecutive references gets larger, the variation among writ-

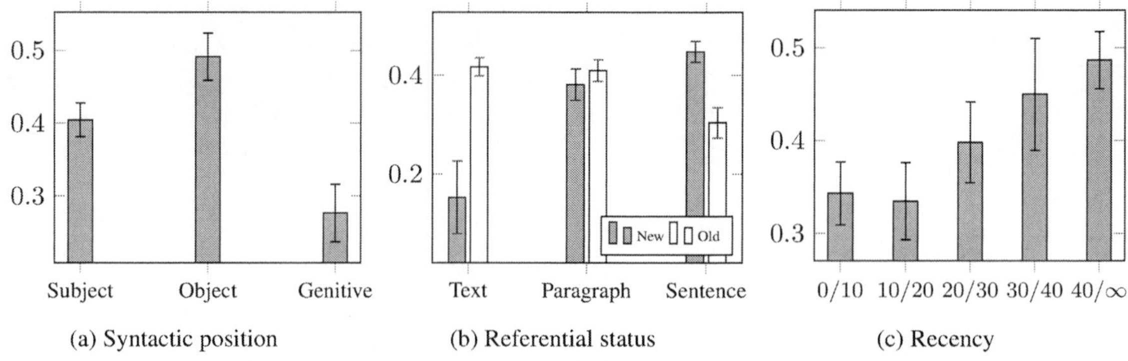

(a) Syntactic position　　　(b) Referential status　　　(c) Recency

Figure 2: Average entropy per gap as a function of: (2a) syntactic position, (2b) referential status, (2c) recency. Error bars represent 95% confidence intervals. In Figure 2c, the bars represent the average entropies for the group of references where the most recent prior reference is 10 or less words away, between 11 and 20 words, between 21 and 30 words, between 31 and 40 words and more than 40 words away.

ers' choices increases (Kruskal-Wallis $H = 35.31$, $p < .001$).

4 Discussion

In this paper, we studied individual variation in the choice of referential form by collecting a new (and publicly available) dataset in which different participants (writers) were asked to refer to the same referent throughout a text. This was done for different genres (news, product review and encyclopedic texts) by measuring the variation between participants in terms of normalized entropy. If participants would all use the same referential form in the same gap, we would expect entropy values of 0 (no individual variation), but instead we found a clearly different pattern in all three text genres. Moreover, we also saw a considerably difference in form among the original referring expressions and the ones generated by the participants. This reveals that substantial individual variation between writers exists in terms of referential form.

To get a better understanding of which factors influence individual variation, we analysed to what extent three linguistic factors had an impact on the entropy scores: syntactic position, referential status and recency. We found a higher amount of individual variation when writers had to choose referential forms in the direct object position, referring to previously mentioned topics in the text and first mentioned ones in the sentence, and references that were relatively distant from the most recent antecedent

reference to the same topic.

These findings can be related to theories of reference involving the salience of a referent (Gundel et al., 1993; Grosz et al., 1995, among others). Brennan (1995), for example, argued that references in the role of the subject of a sentence are more likely to be salient than references in the role of the object. Chafe (1994), to give a second example, pointed out that references to previously mentioned referents in the discourse and ones that are close to their antecedent are more likely to be salient than references to new referents or ones that are distant from their antecedents. Note, incidentally, that none of these earlier studies address the issue of individual variation in referential form.

Arguably, the amount of individual variation is even larger than the data reported here suggest. To illustrate this, consider, for instance, that different participants referred to *Phillip Frederick Anschutz* - the main topic of one of the texts used - as *Phillip Frederick Anschutz, Mr. Phillip Frederick Anschutz, Anschutz, Mr. Anschutz* and *Phillip Anschutz*. Even though these all have the same referential form (proper names), there is also a lot of variation *within* this category. Indeed, it would be interesting in future research to explore which factors account for this within-form variation.

The current findings are important for automatic text generation algorithms in two ways. First, they are beneficial for developers of text generation systems, since they allow for a better understanding of the range of variation that is possible in referring expression generation. Second, they allow for a more principled evaluation of algorithms predicting referential form. In fact, the collected corpus paves the way for developing models which predict frequency distributions over referential forms, rather than merely predicting a single form in particular context (as current models do).

Acknowledgments

This work has been supported by the National Council of Scientific and Technological Development from Brazil (CNPq).

We would also like to thank the members of the JUGO group from TiCC by their insightful comments on the manuscript.

References

Anja Belz, Eric Kow, Jette Viethen, and Albert Gatt. 2010. Empirical methods in natural language generation. chapter Generating Referring Expressions in Context: The GREC Task Evaluation Challenges, pages 294–327. Springer-Verlag, Berlin, Heidelberg.

Susan E. Brennan. 1995. Centering attention in discourse. *Language and Cognitive Processes*, 10(2):137–167.

Charles B. Callaway and James C. Lester. 2002. Pronominalization in generated discourse and dialogue. In *Proceedings of the 40th Annual Meeting on Association for Computational Linguistics*, ACL '02, pages 88–95, Stroudsburg, PA, USA. Association for Computational Linguistics.

Wallace L. Chafe. 1994. *Discourse, Consciousness, and Time: The Flow and Displacement of Conscious Experience in Speaking and Writing*. University of Chicago Press.

Thiago Castro Ferreira and Ivandré Paraboni. 2014. Referring expression generation: Taking speakers preferences into account. In Petr Sojka, Aleš Horák, Ivan KopeČek, and Karel Pala, editors, *Text, Speech and Dialogue*, volume 8655 of *Lecture Notes in Computer Science*, pages 539–546. Springer International Publishing.

Eli Goldberg, Norbert Driedger, and Richard I. Kittredge. 1994. Using natural-language processing to produce weather forecasts. *IEEE Expert: Intelligent Systems and Their Applications*, 9(2):45–53, April.

Charles F Greenbacker and Kathleen F McCoy. 2009. Feature selection for reference generation as informed by psycholinguistic research. In *Proceedings of the CogSci 2009 Workshop on Production of Referring Expressions (PRE-Cogsci 2009)*.

Charles F. Greenbacker, Nicole L. Sparks, Kathleen F. McCoy, and Che-Yu Kuo. 2010. Udel: Refining a method of named entity generation. In *Proceedings of the 6th International Natural Language Generation Conference*, INLG '10, pages 239–240, Stroudsburg, PA, USA. Association for Computational Linguistics.

Barbara J. Grosz, Scott Weinstein, and Aravind K. Joshi. 1995. Centering: A framework for modeling the local coherence of discourse. *Comput. Linguist.*, 21(2):203–225.

Jeanette K Gundel, Nancy Hedberg, and Ron Zacharski. 1993. Cognitive status and the form of referring expressions in discourse. *Language*, pages 274–307.

Samir Gupta and Sivaji Bandopadhyay. 2009. Junlgmsr: A machine learning approach of main subject reference selection with rule based improvement. In *Proceedings of the 2009 Workshop on Language Generation and Summarisation*, UCNLG+Sum '09, pages 103–104, Stroudsburg, PA, USA. Association for Computational Linguistics.

Natalia Konstantinova, Sheila C. M. de Sousa, Noa P. Cruz Díaz, Manuel J. Maña López, Maite Taboada, and Ruslan Mitkov. 2012. A review corpus annotated for negation, speculation and their scope. In *Proceedings of the Eighth International Conference on Language Resources and Evaluation (LREC-2012), Istanbul, Turkey, May 23-25, 2012*, pages 3190–3195.

Emiel Krahmer and Kees van Deemter. 2012. Computational generation of referring expressions: A survey. *Computational Linguistics*, 38(1):173–218.

Constantin Orăsan and Iustin Dornescu. 2009. Wlv: A confidence-based machine learning method for the grec-neg'09 task. In *Proceedings of the 2009 Workshop on Language Generation and Summarisation*, UCNLG+Sum '09, pages 107–108, Stroudsburg, PA, USA. Association for Computational Linguistics.

Franois Portet, Ehud Reiter, Albert Gatt, Jim Hunter, Somayajulu Sripada, Yvonne Freer, and Cindy Sykes. 2009. Automatic generation of textual summaries from neonatal intensive care data. *Artificial Intelligence*, 173(78):789 – 816.

Ehud Reiter and Robert Dale. 2000. *Building natural language generation systems*. Cambridge University Press, New York, NY, USA.

Jette Viethen and Robert Dale. 2010. Speaker-dependent variation in content selection for referring expression generation. In *Proceedings of the Australasian Language Technology Association Workshop 2010*, pages 81–89, Melbourne, Australia, December.

Joint Learning Templates and Slots for Event Schema Induction

Lei Sha, Sujian Li, Baobao Chang, Zhifang Sui
Key Laboratory of Computational Linguistics, Ministry of Education
School of Electronics Engineering and Computer Science, Peking University
Collaborative Innovation Center for Language Ability, Xuzhou 221009 China
`shalei, lisujian, chbb, szf@pku.edu.cn`

Abstract

Automatic event schema induction (*AESI*) means to extract meta-event from raw text, in other words, to find out what types (templates) of event may exist in the raw text and what roles (slots) may exist in each event type. In this paper, we propose a joint entity-driven model to learn templates and slots simultaneously based on the constraints of templates and slots in the same sentence. In addition, the entities' semantic information is also considered for the inner connectivity of the entities. We borrow the *normalized cut* criteria in image segmentation to divide the entities into more accurate template clusters and slot clusters. The experiment shows that our model gains a relatively higher result than previous work.

1 Introduction

Event schema is a high-level representation of a bunch of similar events. It is very useful for the traditional information extraction (*IE*)(Sagayam et al., 2012) task. An example of event schema is shown in Table 1. Given the bombing schema, we only need to find proper words to fill the slots when extracting a bombing event.

There are two main approaches for *AESI* task. Both of them use the idea of clustering the potential event arguments to find the event schema. One of them is probabilistic graphical model (Chambers, 2013; Cheung, 2013). By incorporating templates and slots as latent topics, probabilistic graphical models learns those templates and slots that best explains the text. However, the graphical models

Bombing Template

Perpetrator:	person
Victim:	person
Target:	public
Instrument:	bomb

Table 1: The event schema of bombing event in MUC-4, it has a bombing template and four main slots

considers the entities independently and do not take the interrelationship between entities into account. Another method relies on ad-hoc clustering algorithms (Filatova et al., 2006; Sekine, 2006; Chambers and Jurafsky, 2011). (Chambers and Jurafsky, 2011) is a pipelined approach. In the first step, it uses pointwise mutual information(PMI) between any two clauses in the same document to learn events, and then learns syntactic patterns as fillers. However, the pipelined approach suffers from the error propagation problem, which means the errors in the template clustering can lead to more errors in the slot clustering.

This paper proposes an entity-driven model which jointly learns templates and slots for event schema induction. The main contribution of this paper are as follows:

- To better model the inner connectivity between entities, we borrow the normalized cut in image segmentation as the clustering criteria.

- We use constraints between templates and between slots in one sentence to improve *AESI* result.

Proceedings of NAACL-HLT 2016, pages 428–434,
San Diego, California, June 12-17, 2016. ©2016 Association for Computational Linguistics

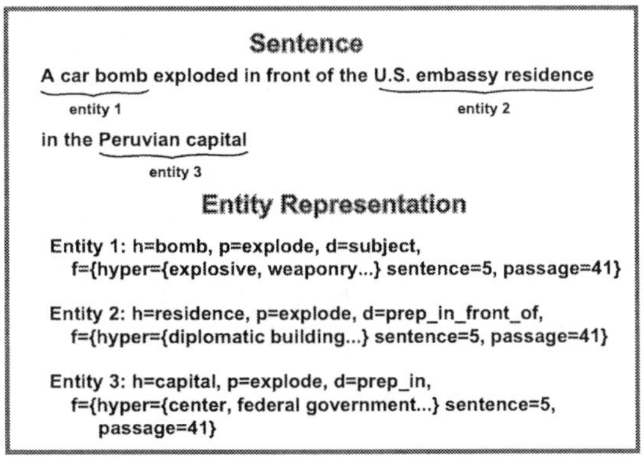

Figure 1 shows the entity representation box:

Sentence

A car bomb exploded in front of the U.S. embassy residence

entity 1   entity 2

in the Peruvian capital

entity 3

Entity Representation

Entity 1: h=bomb, p=explode, d=subject,
f={hyper={explosive, weaponry...} sentence=5, passage=41}

Entity 2: h=residence, p=explode, d=prep_in_front_of,
f={hyper={diplomatic building...} sentence=5, passage=41}

Entity 3: h=capital, p=explode, d=prep_in,
f={hyper={center, federal government...} sentence=5,
passage=41}

Figure 1: An entity example

2 Task Definition

Our model is an entity-driven model. This model represents a document d as a series of entities $E_d = \{e_i | i = 1, 2, \cdots \}$. Each entity is a quadruple $e = (h, p, d, f)$. Here, h represents the head word of an entity, p represents its predicate, and d represents the dependency path between the predicate and the head word, f contains the features of the entity (such as the **direct** hypernyms of the head word), the sentence id where e occurred and the document id where e occurred. A simple example is Fig 1.

Our ultimate goal is to assign two labels, a slot variable s and a template variable t, to each entity. After that, we can summarize all of them to get event schemas.

3 Automatic Event Schema Induction

3.1 Inner Connectivity Between Entities

We focus on two types of inner connectivity: (1) the likelihood of two entities to belong to the same template; (2) the likelihood of two entities to belong to the same slot;

3.1.1 Template Level Connectivity

It is easy to understand that entities occurred near each other are more likely to belong to the same template. Therefore, (Chambers and Jurafsky, 2011) uses PMI to measure the correlation of two words in the same document, but it cannot put two words from different documents together. In the Bayesian model of (Chambers, 2013), p(predicate) is the key factor to decide the template, but it ignores the fact that entities occurring nearby should belong to the same template. In this paper, we try to put two measures together. That is, if two entities occurred nearby, they can belong to the same template; if they have similar meaning, they can also belong to the same template. We use PMI to measure the distance similarity and use word vector (Mikolov et al., 2013) to calculate the semantic similarity.

A word vector can well represent the meaning of a word. So we concatenate the word vector of the j-th entity's head word and its predicate, denoted as $vec_{hp}(i)$. We use the cosine distance $\cos_{hp}(i, j)$ to measure the difference of two vectors.

Then we can get the template level connectivity formula as shown in Eq 1. The $PMI(i, j)$ is calculated by the head words of entity mention i and j.

$$W_T(i, j) = PMI(i, j) + \cos_{hp}(i, j) \qquad (1)$$

3.1.2 Slot Level Connectivity

If two entities can play similar role in an event, they are likely to fill the same slot. We know that if two entities can play similar role, their head words may have the same hypernyms. We only consider the **direct** hypernyms here. Also, their predicates may have similar meaning and the entities may have the same dependency path to their predicate. Therefore, we give the factors equal weights and add them together to get the slot level similarity.

$$W_S(i, j) = \cos_p(i, j) + \delta(depend_i = depend_j)$$
$$+ \delta(hypernym_i \cap hypernym_j \neq \phi)$$
$$\qquad (2)$$

Here, the $\delta(\cdot)$ has value 1 when the inner expression is true and 0 otherwise. The "hypernym" is derived from Wordnet(Miller, 1995), so it is a set of direct hypernyms. If two entities' head words have at least one common direct hypernym, then they may belong to the same slot. And again $\cos_p(i, j)$ represents the cosine distance between the predicates' word vector of entity i and entity j.

3.2 Template and Slot Clustering Using Normalized Cut

Normalized cut intend to maximize the intra-class similarity while minimize the inter class similarity, which deals well with the connectivity between entities.

We represent each entity as a point in a high-dimension space. The edge weight between two points is their template level similarity / slot level similarity. Then the larger the similarity value is, the more likely the two entities (point) belong to the same template / slot, which is also our basis intuition.

For simplicity, denote the entity set as $E = \{e_1, \cdots, e_{|E|}\}$, and the template set as T. We use the $|E| \times |T|$ partition matrix X_T to represent the template clustering result. Let $X_T = [X_{T_1}, \cdots, X_{T_{|T|}}]$, where X_{T_l} is a binary indicator for template $l(T_l)$.

$$X_T(i, l) = \begin{cases} 1 & e_i \in T_l \\ 0 & otherwise \end{cases} \quad (3)$$

Usually, we define the degree matrix D_T as: $D_T(i, i) = \sum_{j \in E} W_T(i, j), i = 1, \cdots, |E|$. Obviously, D_T is a diagonal matrix. It contains information about the weight sum of edges attached to each vertex. Then we have the template clustering optimization as shown in Eq 4 according to (Shi and Malik, 2000).

$$\max \quad \varepsilon_1(X_T) = \frac{1}{|T|} \sum_{l=1}^{|T|} \frac{X_{T_l}^T W_T X_{T_l}}{X_{T_l}^T D_T X_{T_l}} \quad (4)$$

$$s.t. \quad X_T \in \{0, 1\}^{|E| \times |T|} \quad X_T \mathbf{1}_{|T|} = \mathbf{1}_{|E|}$$

where $\mathbf{1}_{|E|}$ represents the $|E| \times 1$ vector of all 1's.

For the slot clustering, we have a similar optimization as shown in Eq 5.

$$\max \quad \varepsilon_2(X_S) = \frac{1}{|S|} \sum_{l=1}^{|S|} \frac{X_{S_l}^T W_S X_{S_l}}{X_{S_l}^T D_S X_{S_l}} \quad (5)$$

$$s.t. \quad X_S \in \{0, 1\}^{|E| \times |S|} \quad X_S \mathbf{1}_{|S|} = \mathbf{1}_{|E|}$$

where S represents the slot set, X_S is the slot clustering result with $X_S = [X_{S_1}, \cdots, X_{S_{|S|}}]$, where X_{S_l} is a binary indicator for slot $l(S_l)$.

$$X_S(i, l) = \begin{cases} 1 & e_i \in S_l \\ 0 & otherwise \end{cases} \quad (6)$$

3.3 Joint Model With Sentence Constraints

For event schema induction, we find an important property and we name it "Sentence constraint". The entities in one sentence often belong to one template but different slots.

The sentence constraint contains two types of constraint, "template constraint" and "slot constraint".

1. **Template constraint**: Entities in the same sentence are usually in the same template. Hence we should make the templates taken by a sentence as few as possible.

2. **Slot constraint**: Entities in the same sentence are usually in different slots. Hence we should make the slots taken by a sentence as many as possible.

Based on these consideration, we can add an extra item to the optimization object. Let $N_{sentence}$ be the number of sentences. Define $N_{sentence} \times |E|$ matrix J as the sentence constraint matrix, the entries of J is as following:

$$J(i, j) = \begin{cases} 1 & e_i \in Sentence_j \\ 0 & otherwise \end{cases} \quad (7)$$

Easy to show, the product $G_T = J^T X_T$ represents the relation between sentences and templates. In matrix G_T, the (i, j)-th entry represents how many entities in sentence i are belong to T_j.

Using G_T, we can construct our objective. To represent the two constraints, the best objective we have found is the trace value: $tr(G_T G_T^T)$. Each entry on the diagonal of matrix $G_T G_T^T$ is the square sum of all the entries in the corresponding line in G_T, and the larger the trace value is, the less templates the sentence would taken. Since $tr(G_T G_T^T)$ is the sum of the diagonal elements, we only need to maximize the value $tr(G_T G_T^T)$ to meet the template constraint. For the same reason, we need to minimize the value $tr(G_S G_S^T)$ to meet the slot constraint.

Generally, we have the following optimization objective:

$$\varepsilon_3(X_T, X_S) = \frac{tr(X_T^T J J^T X_T)}{tr(X_S^T J J^T X_S)} \quad (8)$$

The whole joint model is shown in Eq 9. The detailed derivation[1] is shown in the supplement file.

$$X_T, X_S = \underset{X_T, X_S}{\operatorname{argmax}} \, \varepsilon_1(X_T) + \varepsilon_2(X_S) + \varepsilon_3(X_T, X_S)$$

$$s.t. \; X_T \in \{0,1\}^{|E| \times |T|} \quad X_T \mathbf{1}_{|T|} = \mathbf{1}_{|E|}$$

$$X_S \in \{0,1\}^{|E| \times |S|} \quad X_S \mathbf{1}_{|S|} = \mathbf{1}_{|E|}$$

$$(9)$$

4 Experiment

4.1 Dataset

In this paper, we use MUC-4(Sundheim, 1991) as our dataset, which is the same as previous works (Chambers and Jurafsky, 2011; Chambers, 2013). MUC-4 corpus contains 1300 documents in the training set, 200 in development set (TS1, TS2) and 200 in testing set (TS3, TS4) about Latin American news of terrorism events. We ran several times on the 1500 documents (training/dev set) and choose the best $|T|$ and $|S|$ as $|T| = 6$, $|S| = 4$. Then we report the performance of test set. For each document, it provides a series of hand-constructed event schemas, which are called gold schemas. With these gold schemas we can evaluate our results. The MUC-4 corpus contains six template types: **Attack, Kidnapping, Bombing, Arson, Robbery, and Forced Work Stoppage**, and for each template, there are 25 slots. Since most previous works do not evaluate their performance on all the 25 slots, they instead focus on 4 main slots like Table 1, we will also focus on these four slots. We use the Stanford CoreNLP toolkit to parse the MUC-4 corpus.

4.2 Performance

Fig 2 shows two examples of our learned schemas: Bombing and Attacking. The five words in each slot are the five randomly picked entities from the mapped slots. The templates and slots that were joint learned seem reasonable.

Induced schemas need to map to gold schemas before evaluation. Previous works used two methods of mapping. The first ignores the schema type, and simply finds the best performing slot for each gold template slot. For instance, a perpetrator of a bombing and a perpetrator of an attack are treated

---

[1] At https://github.com/shalei120/ESL_1_2 can the code be found.

Bombing

Perpetrator	Victim	Target	Instrument
El salvador	The police chief	ministry	explosives
The guerrillas	Students	The embassy	car bomb
The drag mafia	The Peruvian embassy	The police station	dynamite
Drug traffickers	The diplomat	organization	incendiary bomb
The Atlacatl battalion	soldiers	bridge	vehicle bomb

Attack

Perpetrator	Victim	Target	Instrument
troops	driver	organization	rifles
criminals	soldiers	helicopter	weapons
combat	children	person	gun
murder	civilians	livestock ministray building	explosives
person	journalists	vehicles	machinegun

Figure 2: Part of the result

	Prec	Recall	F1
C&J (2011)	**0.48**	0.25	0.33
Cheung (2013)	0.32	0.37	0.34
Chambers (2013)	0.41	0.41	0.41
Nguyen et al. (2015)	0.36	0.54	0.43
Our Model-SC	0.38	0.68	0.49
Our Model	0.39	**0.70**	**0.50**

Table 2: Slot-only mapping comparison to state-of-the-art unsupervised systems, "-SC" means without sentence constraint

the same. We call this the **slot-only mapping** evaluation. The second approach is to map each template t to the best gold template g, and limit the slot mapping so that only the slots under t can map to slots under g. We call this the **strict template mapping** evaluation. The slot-only mapping can result in higher scores since it is not constrained to preserve schema structure in the mapping.

We compare our results with four works (Chambers and Jurafsky, 2011; Cheung, 2013; Chambers, 2013; Nguyen et al., 2015) as is shown in Table 2 and Table 3. Our model has outperformed all of the previous methods. The improvement of recall is due to the normalized cut criteria, which can better use the inner connectivity between entities. The sentence constraint improves the result one step further.

Note that after adding the sentence constraint, the slot-only performance has increased a little, but the strict *template mapping* performance has increased a lot as is shown in Table 3. This phenomenon can be explained by the following facts: We count the

	Prec	Recall	F1
Chambers (2013)	**0.42**	0.27	0.33
Our Model-SC	0.26	**0.55**	0.35
Our Model	0.33	0.50	**0.40**

Table 3: strict template mapping comparison to state-of-the-art unsupervised systems, "-SC" means without sentence constraint

amount of entities which has been assigned different templates or different slots in "Our Model-SC" and "Our Model". Of all the 11465 entities, 2305 entities has been assigned different templates in the two methods while only 108 entities has different slots. This fact illustrates that the sentence constraint can affect the assignment of templates much more than the slots. Therefore, the sentence constraint leads largely improvement to the strict mapping performance and very little increase to the slot-only performance.

5 Related Works

The traditional information extraction task is to fill the event schema slots. Many slot filling algorithms requires the full information of the event schemas and the labeled corpus. Among them, there are rule-based method (Rau et al., 1992; Chinchor et al., 1993), supervised learning method (Baker et al., 1998; Chieu et al., 2003; Bunescu and Mooney, 2004; Patwardhan and Riloff, 2009; Maslennikov and Chua, 2007), bootstrapping method (Yangarber et al., 2000) and cross-document inference method (Ji and Grishman, 2008). Also there are many semi-supervised solutions, which begin with unlabeled, but clustered event-specific documents, and extract common word patterns as extractors (Riloff and Schmelzenbach, 1998; Sudo et al., 2003; Riloff et al., 2005; Patwardhan and Riloff, 2007; Filatova et al., 2006; Surdeanu et al., 2006)

Other traditional information extraction task learns binary relations and atomic facts. Models can learn relations like "Jenny is married to Bob" with unlabeled data (Banko et al., 2007; Etzioni et al., 2008; Yates et al., 2007; Fader et al., 2011), or ontology induction (dog is an animal) and attribute extraction (dogs have tails) (Carlson et al., 2010a; Carlson et al., 2010b; Huang and Riloff, 2010; Van Durme and Pasca, 2008), or rely on pre-defined patterns (Hearst, 1992).

Shinyama and Sekine (2006) proposed an approach to learn templates with unlabeled corpus. They use *unrestricted relation discovery* to discover relations in unlabeled corpus as well as extract their fillers. Their constraints are that they need redundant documents and their relations are binary over repeated named entities. (Chen et al., 2011) also extract binary relations using generative model.

Kasch and Oates (2010), Chambers and Jurafsky (2008), Chambers and Jurafsky (2009), Balasubramanian et al. (2013) captures template-like knowledge from unlabeled text by large-scale learning of scripts and narrative schemas. However, their structures are limited to frequent topics in a large corpus. Chambers and Jurafsky (2011) uses their idea, and their goal is to characterize a specific domain with limited data using a three-stage clustering algorithm.

Also, there are some state-of-the-art works using probabilistic graphic model (Chambers, 2013; Cheung, 2013; Nguyen et al., 2015). They use the Gibbs sampling and get good results.

6 Conclusion

This paper presented a joint entity-driven model to induct event schemas automatically.

This model uses word embedding as well as PMI to measure the inner connection of entities and uses normalized cut for more accurate clustering. Finally, our model uses sentence constraint to extract templates and slots simultaneously. The experiment has proved the effectiveness of our model.

Acknowledgments

This research is supported by National Key Basic Research Program of China (No.2014CB340504) and National Natural Science Foundation of China (No.61375074,61273318). The contact authors of this paper are Sujian Li and Baobao Chang.

References

Collin F Baker, Charles J Fillmore, and John B Lowe. 1998. The berkeley framenet project. In *Proceedings of the 36th Annual Meeting of the Association for Computational Linguistics and 17th International Conference on Computational Linguistics-Volume*

1, pages 86–90. Association for Computational Linguistics.

Niranjan Balasubramanian, Stephen Soderland, and Oren Etzioni Mausam. 2013. Generating coherent event schemas at scale. *Proceedings of the Empirical Methods in Natural Language Processing. ACM.*

Michele Banko, Michael J Cafarella, Stephen Soderland, Matt Broadhead, and Oren Etzioni. 2007. Open information extraction from the web. In *Proceedings of the 20th international joint conference on Artifical intelligence*, pages 2670–2676. Morgan Kaufmann Publishers Inc.

Razvan Bunescu and Raymond J Mooney. 2004. Collective information extraction with relational markov networks. In *Proceedings of the 42nd Annual Meeting on Association for Computational Linguistics*, page 438. Association for Computational Linguistics.

Andrew Carlson, Justin Betteridge, Bryan Kisiel, Burr Settles, Estevam R Hruschka Jr, and Tom M Mitchell. 2010a. Toward an architecture for never-ending language learning. In *AAAI*.

Andrew Carlson, Justin Betteridge, Richard C Wang, Estevam R Hruschka Jr, and Tom M Mitchell. 2010b. Coupled semi-supervised learning for information extraction. In *Proceedings of the third ACM international conference on Web search and data mining*, pages 101–110. ACM.

Nathanael Chambers and Daniel Jurafsky. 2008. Unsupervised learning of narrative event chains. In *ACL*, pages 789–797.

Nathanael Chambers and Dan Jurafsky. 2009. Unsupervised learning of narrative schemas and their participants. In *Proceedings of the Joint Conference of the 47th Annual Meeting of the ACL and the 4th International Joint Conference on Natural Language Processing of the AFNLP: Volume 2-Volume 2*, pages 602–610. Association for Computational Linguistics.

Nathanael Chambers and Dan Jurafsky. 2011. Template-based information extraction without the templates. pages 976–986.

Nathanael Chambers. 2013. Event schema induction with a probabilistic entity-driven model. EMNLP.

Harr Chen, Edward Benson, Tahira Naseem, and Regina Barzilay. 2011. In-domain relation discovery with meta-constraints via posterior regularization. In *Proceedings of the 49th Annual Meeting of the Association for Computational Linguistics: Human Language Technologies-Volume 1*, pages 530–540. Association for Computational Linguistics.

Jackie Chi Kit Cheung. 2013. Probabilistic frame induction. *arXiv preprint arXiv:1302.4813.*

Hai Leong Chieu, Hwee Tou Ng, and Yoong Keok Lee. 2003. Closing the gap: Learning-based information extraction rivaling knowledge-engineering methods. In *Proceedings of the 41st Annual Meeting on Association for Computational Linguistics-Volume 1*, pages 216–223. Association for Computational Linguistics.

Nancy Chinchor, David D Lewis, and Lynette Hirschman. 1993. Evaluating message understanding systems: an analysis of the third message understanding conference (muc-3). *Computational linguistics*, 19(3):409–449.

Oren Etzioni, Michele Banko, Stephen Soderland, and Daniel S Weld. 2008. Open information extraction from the web. *Communications of the ACM*, 51(12):68–74.

Anthony Fader, Stephen Soderland, and Oren Etzioni. 2011. Identifying relations for open information extraction. In *Proceedings of the Conference on Empirical Methods in Natural Language Processing*, pages 1535–1545. Association for Computational Linguistics.

Elena Filatova, Vasileios Hatzivassiloglou, and Kathleen McKeown. 2006. Automatic creation of domain templates. In *Proceedings of the COLING/ACL on Main conference poster sessions*, pages 207–214. Association for Computational Linguistics.

Marti A Hearst. 1992. Automatic acquisition of hyponyms from large text corpora. In *Proceedings of the 14th conference on Computational linguistics-Volume 2*, pages 539–545. Association for Computational Linguistics.

Ruihong Huang and Ellen Riloff. 2010. Inducing domain-specific semantic class taggers from (almost) nothing. In *Proceedings of the 48th Annual Meeting of the Association for Computational Linguistics*, pages 275–285. Association for Computational Linguistics.

Heng Ji and Ralph Grishman. 2008. Refining event extraction through cross-document inference. In *ACL*, pages 254–262.

Niels Kasch and Tim Oates. 2010. Mining script-like structures from the web. In *Proceedings of the NAACL HLT 2010 First International Workshop on Formalisms and Methodology for Learning by Reading*, pages 34–42. Association for Computational Linguistics.

Mstislav Maslennikov and Tat-Seng Chua. 2007. Automatic acquisition of domain knowledge for information extraction. In *Proceedings of the Association of Computational Linguistics (ACL)*.

Tomas Mikolov, Kai Chen, Greg Corrado, and Jeffrey Dean. 2013. Efficient estimation of word representations in vector space. *arXiv preprint arXiv:1301.3781.*

George A Miller. 1995. Wordnet: a lexical database for english. *Communications of the ACM*, 38(11):39–41.

Kiem-Hieu Nguyen, Xavier Tannier, Olivier Ferret, and Romaric Besançon. 2015. Generative event schema induction with entity disambiguation. In *Proceedings of the 53rd Annual Meeting of the Association for Computational Linguistics and the 7th International Joint Conference on Natural Language Processing (Volume 1: Long Papers)*, pages 188–197, Beijing, China, July. Association for Computational Linguistics.

Siddharth Patwardhan and Ellen Riloff. 2007. Effective information extraction with semantic affinity patterns and relevant regions. In *EMNLP-CoNLL*, volume 7, pages 717–727.

Siddharth Patwardhan and Ellen Riloff. 2009. A unified model of phrasal and sentential evidence for information extraction. In *Proceedings of the 2009 Conference on Empirical Methods in Natural Language Processing: Volume 1-Volume 1*, pages 151–160. Association for Computational Linguistics.

Lisa Rau, George Krupka, Paul Jacobs, Ira Sider, and Lois Childs. 1992. Ge nltoolset: Muc-4 test results and analysis. In *Proceedings of the 4th conference on Message understanding*, pages 94–99. Association for Computational Linguistics.

Ellen Riloff and Mark Schmelzenbach. 1998. An empirical approach to conceptual case frame acquisition. In *Proceedings of the Sixth Workshop on Very Large Corpora*, pages 49–56.

Ellen Riloff, Janyce Wiebe, and William Phillips. 2005. Exploiting subjectivity classification to improve information extraction. In *Proceedings of the National Conference On Artificial Intelligence*, volume 20, page 1106. Menlo Park, CA; Cambridge, MA; London; AAAI Press; MIT Press; 1999.

R Sagayam, S Srinivasan, and S Roshni. 2012. A survey of text mining: Retrieval, extraction and indexing techniques. *International Journal Of Computational Engineering Research*, 2(5).

Satoshi Sekine. 2006. On-demand information extraction. In *Proceedings of the COLING/ACL on Main conference poster sessions*, pages 731–738. Association for Computational Linguistics.

Jianbo Shi and Jitendra Malik. 2000. Normalized cuts and image segmentation. *Pattern Analysis and Machine Intelligence, IEEE Transactions on*, 22(8):888–905.

Yusuke Shinyama and Satoshi Sekine. 2006. Preemptive information extraction using unrestricted relation discovery. In *Proceedings of the main conference on Human Language Technology Conference of the North American Chapter of the Association of Computational Linguistics*, pages 304–311. Association for Computational Linguistics.

Kiyoshi Sudo, Satoshi Sekine, and Ralph Grishman. 2003. An improved extraction pattern representation model for automatic ie pattern acquisition. In *Proceedings of the 41st Annual Meeting on Association for Computational Linguistics-Volume 1*, pages 224–231. Association for Computational Linguistics.

Beth Sundheim. 1991. Third message understanding evaluation and conference (muc-3): Phase 1 status report. In *HLT*.

Mihai Surdeanu, Jordi Turmo, and Alicia Ageno. 2006. A hybrid approach for the acquisition of information extraction patterns. *Adaptive Text Extraction and Mining (ATEM 2006)*, page 48.

Benjamin Van Durme and Marius Pasca. 2008. Finding cars, goddesses and enzymes: Parametrizable acquisition of labeled instances for open-domain information extraction. In *AAAI*, volume 8, pages 1243–1248.

Roman Yangarber, Ralph Grishman, Pasi Tapanainen, and Silja Huttunen. 2000. Automatic acquisition of domain knowledge for information extraction. In *Proceedings of the 18th conference on Computational linguistics-Volume 2*, pages 940–946. Association for Computational Linguistics.

Alexander Yates, Michael Cafarella, Michele Banko, Oren Etzioni, Matthew Broadhead, and Stephen Soderland. 2007. Textrunner: open information extraction on the web. In *Proceedings of Human Language Technologies: The Annual Conference of the North American Chapter of the Association for Computational Linguistics: Demonstrations*, pages 25–26. Association for Computational Linguistics.

Inferring Psycholinguistic Properties of Words

Gustavo Henrique Paetzold and **Lucia Specia**
Department of Computer Science
University of Sheffield, UK
{ghpaetzold1,l.specia}@sheffield.ac.uk

Abstract

We introduce a bootstrapping algorithm for regression that exploits word embedding models. We use it to infer four psycholinguistic properties of words: Familiarity, Age of Acquisition, Concreteness and Imagery and further populate the MRC Psycholinguistic Database with these properties. The approach achieves 0.88 correlation with human-produced values and the inferred psycholinguistic features lead to state-of-the-art results when used in a Lexical Simplification task.

1 Introduction

Throughout the last three decades, much has been found on how the psycholinguistic properties of words influence cognitive processes in the human brain when a subject is presented with either written or spoken forms. A word's Age of Acquisition is an example. The findings in (Carroll and White, 1973) reveal that objects whose names are learned earlier in life can be named faster in later stages of life. Zevin and Seidenberg (2002) show that words learned in early ages are orthographically or phonologically very distinct from those learned in adult life.

Other examples of psycholinguistic properties, such as Familiarity and Concreteness, influence one's proficiency in word recognition and text comprehension. The experiments in (Connine et al., 1990; Morrel-Samuels and Krauss, 1992) show that words with high Familiarity yield lower reaction times in both visual and auditory lexical decision, and require less hand gesticulation in order to be described. Begg and Paivio (1969) found that humans are less sensitive to changes in wording made to sentences with high Concreteness words.

When quantified, these aspects can be used as features for various Natural Language Processing (NLP) tasks. The Lexical Simplification approach in (Jauhar and Specia, 2012) is an example. By combining various collocational features and psycholinguistic measures extracted from the MRC Psycholinguistic Database (Coltheart, 1981), they trained a ranker (Joachims, 2002) that reached first place in the English Lexical Simplification task at SemEval 2012. Semantic Classification tasks have also benefited from the use of such features: by combining Concreteness with other features, (Hill and Korhonen, 2014) reached the state-of-the-art performance in Semantic Composition (*denotative/connotative*) and Semantic Modification (*intersective/subsective*) prediction.

Despite the evident usefulness of psycholinguistic properties of words, resources describing such properties are rare. The most extensively developed resource for English is the MRC Psycholinguistic Database (Section 2). However, it is far from complete, most likely due to the inherent cost of manually entering such properties. In this paper we propose a method to automatically infer these missing properties. We train regressors by performing bootstrapping (Yarowsky, 1995) over the existing features in the MRC database, exploiting word embedding models and other linguistic resources for that (Section 3). This approach outperform various strong baselines (Section 4) and the resulting properties lead to significant improvements when used in Lexical Simplification models (Section 5).

Proceedings of NAACL-HLT 2016, pages 435–440,
San Diego, California, June 12-17, 2016. ©2016 Association for Computational Linguistics

2 The MRC Psycholinguistic Database

Introduced by Coltheart (1981), the MRC (Machine Readable Dictionary) Psycholinguistic Database is a digital compilation of lexical, morphological and psycholinguistic properties for 150,837 words. The 27 psycholinguistic properties in the resource range from simple frequency measures (Rudell, 1993) to elaborate measures estimated by humans, such as Age of Acquisition and Imagery (Gilhooly and Logie, 1980). However, despite various efforts to populate the MRC Database, these properties are only available for small subsets of the 150,837 words.

We focus on four manually estimated psycholinguistic properties in the MRC Database:

- **Familiarity**: The frequency with which a word is seen, heard or used daily. Available for 9,392 words.

- **Age of Acquisition**: The age at which a word is believed to be learned. Available for 3,503 words.

- **Concreteness**: How "palpable" the object the word refers to is. Available for $8,228$ words.

- **Imagery**: The intensity with which a word arouses images. Available for 9,240 words.

All four properties are real values, determined based on different quantifiable metrics. We focus on these properties since they have been proven useful and are some of the most scarce in the MRC Database. As we discussed in Section 1, these properties have been successfully used in various approaches for Lexical Simplification and Semantic Classification, and yet are available for no more than 6% of the words in the MRC Database.

3 Bootstrapping with Word Embeddings

In order to automatically estimate missing psycholinguistic properties in the MRC Database, we resort to bootstrapping. We base our approach on that by (Yarowsky, 1995), a bootstrapping algorithm which aims to learn a classifier over a reduced set of annotated training instances (or "seeds"). It does so by performing the following five steps:

1. Initialise training set S with the seeds available.

2. Train a classifier over S.

3. Predict values for a set of unlabelled instances U.

4. Add to S all instances from U for which the prediction confidence c is equal or greater than ζ.

5. If at least one instance was added to S, go to step 2, otherwise, return the resulting classifier.

One critical difference between this approach and ours is that our task requires regression algorithms instead of classifiers. In classification, the prediction confidence c is often calculated as the maximum signed distance between an instance and the estimated hyperplanes. There is, however, no analogous confidence estimation technique for regression problems. We address this problem by using word embedding models.

Embedding models have been proved effective in capturing linguistic regularities of words (Mikolov et al., 2013b). In order to exploit these regularities, we assume that the quality of a regressor's prediction on an instance is directly proportional to how similar the instance is to the ones in the labelled set. Since the input for the regressors are words, we compute the similarity between a test word and the words in the labelled dataset as the maximum cosine similarity between the test word's vector and the vectors in the labelled set.

Let M be an embeddings model trained over vocabulary V, S a set of training seeds, ζ a minimum confidence threshold, $sim(w, S, M)$ the maximum cosine similarity between word w and S with respect to model M, R a regression model, and $R(w)$ its prediction for word w. Our bootstrapping algorithm is depicted in Algorithm 1.

Algorithm 1: Regression Bootstrapping

input: M, V, S, ζ;
output: R;

repeat
    Train R over S;
    for $w \in V - S$ **do**
        if $sim(w, S, M) \geq \zeta$ **then**
            Add $\langle w, R(w) \rangle$ to S;
        end
    end
until $\|S\|$ converges ;

We found that 64,895 out of the 150,837 words in the MRC database were not present in either Word-Net or our word embedding models. Since our boot-strappers use features extracted from both these re-sources, we were only able to predict the Familiarity, Age of Acquisition, Concreteness and Imagery values of the remaining 85,942 words in MRC.

4 Evaluation

Since we were not able to find previous work for this task, in these experiments, we compare the performance of our bootstrapping strategy to various baselines. For training, we use the Ridge regression algorithm (Tikhonov, 1963). As features, our regressor uses the word's raw embedding values, along with the following 15 lexical features:

- Word's length and number of syllables, as determined by the Morph Adorner module of LEXenstein (Paetzold and Specia, 2015).

- Word's frequency in the Brown (Francis and Kucera, 1979), SUBTLEX (Brysbaert and New, 2009), SubIMDB (Paetzold and Specia, 2016), Wikipedia and Simple Wikipedia (Kauchak, 2013) corpora.

- Number of senses, synonyms, hypernyms and hyponyms for word in WordNet (Fellbaum, 1998).

- Minimum, maximum and average distance between the word's senses in WordNet and the thesaurus' root sense.

- Number of images found for word in the Getty Images database[1].

We train our embedding models using word2vec (Mikolov et al., 2013a) over a corpus of 7 billion words composed by the SubIMDB corpus, UMBC webbase[2], News Crawl[3], SUBTLEX (Brysbaert and New, 2009), Wikipedia and Simple Wikipedia (Kauchak, 2013). We use 5-fold cross-validation to optimise parameters: ζ, embeddings model architecture (CBOW or Skip-Gram), and word vector size (from 300 to 2,500 in intervals of 200). We include four strong baseline systems in the comparison:

[1] http://developers.gettyimages.com/
[2] http://ebiquity.umbc.edu/resource/html/id/351
[3] http://www.statmt.org/wmt11/translation-task.html

- **Max. Similarity**: Test word is assigned the property value of the closest word in the training set, i.e. the word with the highest cosine similarity according to the word embeddings model.

- **Avg. Similarity**: Test word is assigned the average property value of the n closest words in the training set, i.e. the words with the highest cosine similarity according to the word embeddings model. The value of n is decided through 5-fold cross validation.

- **Simple SVM**: Test word is assigned the property value as predicted by an SVM regressor (Smola and Vapnik, 1997) with a polynomial kernel trained with the 15 aforementioned lexical features.

- **Simple Ridge**: Test word is assigned the property value as predicted by a Ridge regressor trained with the 15 aforementioned lexical features.

- **Super Ridge**: Identical to Simple Ridge, the only difference being that it also includes the words embeddings in the feature set. We note that this baseline uses the exact same features and regression algorithm as our bootstrapped regressors.

The parameters of all baseline systems are optimised following the same method as with our approach. We also measure the correlation between each of the aforementioned lexical features and the psycholinguistic properties. For each psycholinguistic property, we create a training and a test set by splitting the labelled instances available in the MRC Database in two equally sized portions. All training instances are used as seeds in our approach. As evaluation metrics, we use Spearman's (ρ) and Pearson's (r) correlation. Pearson's correlation is the most important indicator of performance: an effective regressor would predict values that change linearly with a given psycholinguistic property.

The results are illustrated in Table 1. While the similarity-based approaches tend to perform well for Concreteness and Imagery, typical regressors capture Familiarity and Age of Acquisition more effectively. Our approach, on the other hand, is consistently superior for all psycholinguistic properties, with both Spearman's and Pearson's correlation

System	Familiarity		Age of Acquisition		Concreteness		Imagery	
	ρ	r	ρ	r	ρ	r	ρ	r
Word Length	-0.238	-0.171	0.501	0.497	-0.170	-0.195	-0.190	-0.193
Syllables	-0.168	-0.114	0.464	0.458	-0.207	-0.238	-0.218	-0.224
Freq: SubIMDB	0.798	**0.725**	**-0.679**	**-0.699**	0.048	0.003	0.208	0.170
Freq: SUBTLEX	**0.827**	0.462	-0.646	-0.251	0.028	0.137	0.187	0.265
Freq: SimpleWiki	0.725	0.488	-0.453	-0.306	0.015	0.145	0.119	0.247
Freq: Wikipedia	0.694	0.283	-0.349	-0.112	-0.076	0.081	0.027	0.134
Freq: Brown	0.706	0.608	-0.380	-0.395	-0.155	-0.214	-0.054	-0.107
Sense Count	0.471	0.363	-0.429	-0.391	0.020	-0.017	0.119	0.059
Synonym Count	0.411	0.336	-0.381	-0.357	-0.036	-0.047	0.070	0.035
Hypernym Count	0.307	0.295	-0.411	-0.387	0.167	0.088	0.268	0.160
Hyponym Count	0.379	0.245	-0.324	-0.196	0.120	0.002	0.196	0.023
Min. Sense Depth	-0.347	-0.072	0.366	0.055	0.151	-0.185	0.127	-0.224
Max. Sense Depth	-0.021	-0.008	-0.197	-0.196	**0.447**	**0.455**	**0.415**	**0.414**
Avg. Sense Depth	-0.295	-0.256	0.215	0.183	0.400	0.428	0.345	0.347
Img. Search Count	0.544	0.145	-0.325	-0.033	-0.037	-0.073	0.117	-0.059
Max. Similarity	0.406	0.402	0.445	0.443	0.742	0.743	0.618	0.605
Avg. Similarity	0.528	0.527	0.536	0.535	0.826	0.819	0.733	0.707
Simple SVM	0.835	0.815	0.778	0.770	0.548	0.477	0.555	0.528
Simple Ridge	0.832	0.815	0.785	0.778	0.603	0.591	0.620	0.613
Super Ridge	**0.847**	**0.833**	**0.827**	**0.820**	**0.859**	**0.852**	**0.813**	**0.800**
Bootstrapping	<u>**0.863**</u>	<u>**0.846**</u>	<u>**0.871**</u>	<u>**0.862**</u>	<u>**0.876**</u>	<u>**0.869**</u>	<u>**0.835**</u>	<u>**0.823**</u>

Table 1: Regression correlation scores. In bold are the highest scores within a group (features, baselines, proposed approach), and underlined the highest scores overall.

scores varying between 0.82 and 0.88. The difference in performance between the Super Ridge baseline and our approach confirm that our bootstrapping algorithm can in fact improve on the performance of a regressor.

The parameters used by our bootstrappers, which are reported below, highlight the importance of parameter optimization in out bootstrapping strategy: its performance peaked with very different configurations for most psycholinguistic properties:

- **Familiarity**: 300 word vector dimensions with a Skip-Gram model, and $\zeta = 0.9$.

- **Age of Acquisition**: 700 word vector dimensions with a CBOW model, and $\zeta = 0.7$.

- **Concreteness**: 1,100 word vector dimensions with a Skip-Gram model, and $\zeta = 0.7$.

- **Imagery**: 1,100 word vector dimensions with a Skip-Gram model, and $\zeta = 0.7$.

Interestingly, frequency in the SubIMDB corpus[4], composed of over 7 million sentences extracted from subtitles of "family" movies and series, has good linear correlation with Familiarity and Age of Acquisition, much higher than any other feature. For Concreteness and Imagery, on the other hand, the results suggest something different: the further a word is from the root of a thesaurus, the most likely it is to refer to a physical object or entity.

5 Psycholinguistic Features for LS

Here we assess the effectiveness of our bootstrappers in the task of Lexical Simplification (LS). As shown in (Jauhar and Specia, 2012), psycholinguistic features can help supervised ranking algorithms capture word simplicity. Using the parameters described in Section 4, we train bootstrappers for these two properties using all instances in the MRC Database as seeds. We then train three rankers with (W) and without (W/O) psycholinguistic features:

---

[4]http://ghpaetzold.github.io/subimdb

- **Horn** (Horn et al., 2014): Uses an SVM ranker trained on various n-gram probability features.

- **Glavas** (Glavaš and Štajner, 2015): Ranks candidates using various collocational and semantic metrics, and then re-ranks them according to their average rankings.

- **Paetzold** (Paetzold and Specia, 2015): Ranks words according to their distance to a decision boundary learned from a classification setup inferred from ranking examples. Uses n-gram frequencies as features.

We use data from the English Lexical Simplification task of SemEval 2012 to assess systems' performance. The goal of the task is to rank words in different contexts according to their simplicity. The training and test sets contain 300 and 1,710 instances, respectively. The official metric from the task – TRank (Specia et al., 2012) – is used to measure systems' performance. As discussed in (Paetzold, 2015), this metric best represents LS performance in practice. The results in Table 2 show that the addition of our features lead to performance increases with all rankers. Performing F-tests over the rankings estimated for the simplest candidate in each instance, we have found these differences to be statistically significant ($p < 0.05$). Using our features, the **Paetzold** ranker reaches the best published results for the dataset, significantly superior to the best system in SemEval (Jauhar and Specia, 2012).

Ranker	TRank	
	W/O	W
Best SemEval	-	0.602
Horn	0.625	**0.635**
Glavas	0.623	**0.636**
Paetzold	0.653	**0.657**

Table 2: Results on SemEval 2012 LS task dataset

6 Conclusions

Overall, the proposed bootstrapping strategy for regression has led to very positive results, despite its simplicity. It is therefore a cheap and reliable alternative to manually producing psycholinguistic properties of words. Word embedding models have proven to be very useful in bootstrapping, both as surrogates for confidence predictors and as regression features. Our findings also indicate the usefulness of individual features and resources: word frequencies in the SubIMDB corpus have a much stronger correlation with Familiarity and Age of Acquisition than previously used corpora, while the depth of a word's in a thesaurus hierarchy correlates well with both its Concreteness and Imagery.

In future work we plan to employ our bootstrapping solution in other regression problems, and to further explore potential uses of automatically learned psycholinguistic features.

The updated version of the MRC resource can be downloaded from http://ghpaetzold.github.io/data/BootstrappedMRC.zip.

References

Ian Begg and Allan Paivio. 1969. Concreteness and imagery in sentence meaning. *Journal of Verbal Learning and Verbal Behavior*, 8(6):821–827.

Marc Brysbaert and Boris New. 2009. Moving beyond kučera and francis: A critical evaluation of current word frequency norms and the introduction of a new and improved word frequency measure for american english. *Behavior research methods*, 41:977–990.

John B Carroll and Margaret N White. 1973. Word frequency and age of acquisition as determiners of picture-naming latency. *The Quarterly Journal of Experimental Psychology*, 25(1):85–95.

Max Coltheart. 1981. The mrc psycholinguistic database. *The Quarterly Journal of Experimental Psychology*, 33(4):497–505.

Cynthia M Connine, John Mullennix, Eve Shernoff, and Jennifer Yelen. 1990. Word familiarity and frequency in visual and auditory word recognition. *Journal of Experimental Psychology: Learning, Memory, and Cognition*, 16(6):1084.

Christiane Fellbaum. 1998. *WordNet: An Electronic Lexical Database*. Bradford Books.

W Nelson Francis and Henry Kucera. 1979. Brown corpus manual. *Brown University*.

Kenneth J Gilhooly and Robert H Logie. 1980. Age-of-acquisition, imagery, concreteness, familiarity, and ambiguity measures for 1,944 words. *Behavior Research Methods & Instrumentation*, 12(4):395–427.

Goran Glavaš and Sanja Štajner. 2015. Simplifying lexical simplification: Do we need simplified corpora? In *Proceedings of the 53rd ACL*.

Felix Hill and Anna Korhonen. 2014. Concreteness and subjectivity as dimensions of lexical meaning. In *Proceedings of ACL*, pages 725–731.

Colby Horn, Cathryn Manduca, and David Kauchak. 2014. Learning a Lexical Simplifier Using Wikipedia. In *Proceedings of the 52nd ACL*, pages 458–463.

S. Jauhar and L. Specia. 2012. Uow-shef: Simplex–lexical simplicity ranking based on contextual and psycholinguistic features. In *Proceedings of the 1st SemEval*, pages 477–481.

Thorsten Joachims. 2002. Optimizing search engines using clickthrough data. In *Proceedings of the 8th ACM*, pages 133–142.

David Kauchak. 2013. Improving text simplification language modeling using unsimplified text data. In *Proceedings of the 51st ACL*, pages 1537–1546.

Tomas Mikolov, Kai Chen, Greg Corrado, and Jeffrey Dean. 2013a. Efficient estimation of word representations in vector space. *arXiv preprint arXiv:1301.3781*.

Tomas Mikolov, Wen-tau Yih, and Geoffrey Zweig. 2013b. Linguistic regularities in continuous space word representations. In *HLT-NAACL*, pages 746–751.

Palmer Morrel-Samuels and Robert M Krauss. 1992. Word familiarity predicts temporal asynchrony of hand gestures and speech. *Journal of Experimental Psychology: Learning, Memory, and Cognition*, 18(3):615.

Gustavo Henrique Paetzold and Lucia Specia. 2015. Lexenstein: A framework for lexical simplification. In *Proceedings of The 53rd ACL*.

Gustavo Henrique Paetzold and Lucia Specia. 2016. Unsupervised lexical simplification for non-native speakers. In *Proceedings of The 30th AAAI*.

Gustavo Henrique Paetzold. 2015. Reliable lexical simplification for non-native speakers. In *Proceedings of the 2015 NAACL Student Research Workshop*.

Allan P. Rudell. 1993. Frequency of word usage and perceived word difficulty: Ratings of Kuera and Francis words. *Behavior Research Methods*.

Alex Smola and Vladimir Vapnik. 1997. Support vector regression machines. *Advances in neural information processing systems*, 9:155–161.

Lucia Specia, Sujay Kumar Jauhar, and Rada Mihalcea. 2012. Semeval-2012 task 1: English lexical simplification. In *Proceedings of the 1st SemEval*, pages 347–355.

Andrey Tikhonov. 1963. Solution of incorrectly formulated problems and the regularization method. In *Soviet Math. Dokl.*, volume 5, pages 1035–1038.

David Yarowsky. 1995. Unsupervised word sense disambiguation rivaling supervised methods. In *Proceedings of the 33rd annual meeting on Association for Computational Linguistics*, pages 189–196. Association for Computational Linguistics.

Jason D Zevin and Mark S Seidenberg. 2002. Age of acquisition effects in word reading and other tasks. *Journal of Memory and language*, 47(1):1–29.

Intra-Topic Variability Normalization based on Linear Projection for Topic Classification

Quan Liu[†], Wu Guo[†], Zhen-Hua Ling[†], Hui Jiang[‡], Yu Hu[†§]
[†] National Engineering Laboratory for Speech and Language Information Processing
University of Science and Technology of China, Hefei, Anhui, China
[‡] Department of Electrical Engineering and Computer Science
York University, 4700 Keele Street, Toronto, Ontario, M3J 1P3, Canada
[§] iFLYTEK Research, Hefei, China
emails: quanliu@mail.ustc.edu.cn, guowu@ustc.edu.cn, zhling@ustc.edu.cn
hj@cse.yorku.ca, yuhu@iflytek.com

Abstract

This paper proposes a variability normalization algorithm to reduce the variability between intra-topic documents for topic classification. Firstly, an optimization problem is constructed based on linear variability removable assumption. Secondly, a new feature space for document representation is found by solving the optimization problem with kernel principle component analysis (KPCA). Finally, effective feature transformation is taken through linear projection. As for experiments, state-of-the-art SVM and KNN algorithm are adopted for topic classification respectively. Experimental results on a free-style conversational corpus show that the proposed variability normalization algorithm for topic classification achieves 3.8% absolute improvement for micro-F_1 measure.

1 Introduction

Topic classification is now faced with the problem of enormous variability between documents due to the exponential growth of free-style unstructured texts in recent years. This paper treats variability as differences between text documents and aims at reducing the intra-topic document variability for better topic classification. There are various factors to cause the intra-topic variability problem, such as the different language usages of different persons (Chambers, 1995; Fillmore et al., 2014). In free-style conversations experimented in this paper, different people would use very different words to express their opinions. Therefore, documents in a same topic could be quite different because of the intra-topic variability problem.

In this work, we are interested in finding a robust document representation strategy to address the intra-topic variability problem. Traditional method represents document by a high-dimensional TF-IDF vector based on the bag-of-word approach (Salton and McGill, 1986; Salton and Buckley, 1988). However, the TF-IDF feature reveals little semantic similarity information between terms, which would increase the differences between intra-topic documents when different words are used. Beyond the TF-IDF strategy, there are two class of techniques, i.e., unsupervised technique and supervised technique for document representations. The unsupervised technique includes some latent semantic analysis methods. The typical method is Latent Semantic Indexing (LSI) while the features estimated by LSI are linear combinations of the original features (Deerwester et al., 1990; Wang et al., 2013). Meanwhile, the popular Latent Dirichlet Allocation (Blei et al., 2003; Morchid et al., 2014) algorithm was proposed to represent document by a generative probabilistic model (Blei et al., 2003). Moreover, in recent years, many neural network based methods have been investigated for document representations (Hinton and Salakhutdinov, 2006; Srivastava et al., 2013; Le and Mikolov, 2014). For example, in (Le and Mikolov, 2014), a model called *paragraph vector* was designed to represent each document by a dense vector while the vector is trained by predicting all words in the corresponding document. On the other hand, supervised technique for document representation includes some discrim-

Proceedings of NAACL-HLT 2016, pages 441–446,
San Diego, California, June 12-17, 2016. ©2016 Association for Computational Linguistics

inative approaches, e.g., Linear Discriminant Analysis (Berry et al., 1995; Chakrabarti et al., 2003; Torkkola, 2004) and supervised latent semantic indexing (Sun et al., 2004; Chakraborti et al., 2007; Bai et al., 2009). Meanwhile, some improved linear analysis methods were proposed for encoding documents with a reliable similarity information (Yih et al., 2011; Chang et al., 2013). However, all those works for document representation paid little attention to the variability of intra-topic documents. Therefore, they could hardly solve the intra-topic variability problem in a direct way.

This paper makes a preliminary investigation to deal with the intra-topic variability problem. The main purpose of this work is to find a new feature space with minimized intra-topic variability. An objective criterion is constructed for optimization. Mathematically, we make use of the topic label information of the training set to create a weighting matrix, and then sum over all the differences of intra-topic documents. Then a robust feature space with minimized intra-topic variability is generated by solving the optimization problem with effective KPCA based algorithm. Finally, we accomplish the variability normalization operations for the baseline features. We also employ the linear discriminant analysis as a supplementary algorithm. As for experiments, state-of-the-art SVM and KNN algorithms are employed for topic classification. System performances are evaluated on a challenging free-style conversational database.

The rest of this paper is organized as follows. In section 2, we introduce the proposed variability normalization algorithm for topic classification in detail. After it, section 3 presents experimental setup and results. Finally, conclusions and future work would be given in section 4.

2 Variability Normalization Algorithm

2.1 Motivation for variability normalization

This work aims to find a robust document representation strategy for topic classification. The proposed algorithm is motivated by the Nuisance Attribute Projection (NAP) algorithm in speaker verification field (Solomonoff et al., 2005; Solomonoff et al., 2007). We firstly make a **linear variability removable assumption** for document representation.

Mathematically, given a document, it could be denoted by a column vector $\mathbf{x}$ with dimensionality of d as follows

$$\mathbf{x} = \mathbf{x}_t + \mathbf{x}_v \tag{1}$$

where $\mathbf{x}_t$ denotes the useful signal information in current document, $\mathbf{x}_v$ stands for the remaining noise. It is very difficult to model the noise signal in a document since it could come from various sources. Therefore, in this paper, we focus on the noise created by the variability among intra-topic documents. Our goal is to find a new document representation through linear projection:

$$\tilde{\mathbf{x}} = \mathbf{P}\mathbf{x} \tag{2}$$

where $\mathbf{P}$ is the projection matrix. Since the goal of this paper is not dimensionality reduction, the dimensionality of the new document representation is the same as the source document representation. Therefore, the size of $\mathbf{P}$ is $d \times d$. This paper proposes to learn $\mathbf{P}$ by minimizing the following intra-topic variability

$$\mathcal{Q} = \sum_{i,j} w_{ij} \|\mathbf{P}(\mathbf{x}_i - \mathbf{x}_j)\|^2 \tag{3}$$

where w_{ij} is the i-th row and j-th column element of a weighting matrix $\mathbf{W}$ created in this work. The matrix is determined by the topic label information of training set as follows

$$w_{ij} = \begin{cases} 1 & \text{if } \mathbf{x}_i \text{ and } \mathbf{x}_j \text{ belong to a same topic} \\ 0 & \text{othervise} \end{cases} \tag{4}$$

2.2 Variability normalization algorithm

For deriving the variability normalization algorithm, we follow the work of (Solomonoff et al., 2007) and re-write the projection matrix $\mathbf{P}$ by the variability space (denoted as a unit vector $\mathbf{v}$ here) as follows

$$\mathbf{P} = \mathbf{I} - \mathbf{v}\mathbf{v}^{\mathrm{T}} \tag{5}$$

where $\mathbf{I}$ is a $(d \times d)$ dimensional identity matrix. Combining (3) and (5), we get

$$\mathcal{Q} = \sum_{i,j} w_{ij} (\|\mathbf{x}_i - \mathbf{x}_j\|^2 - (\mathbf{v}^{\mathrm{T}}(\mathbf{x}_i - \mathbf{x}_j))^2). \tag{6}$$

Since the first part of $\mathcal{Q}$ in (6) is independent on $\mathbf{v}$, we discard it and create the final criterion

$$\mathcal{Q} = -\sum_{i,j} w_{ij}(\mathbf{v}^{\mathrm{T}}(\mathbf{x}_i - \mathbf{x}_j))^2). \qquad (7)$$

Unfolding (7) by linear operation, we get

$$\mathcal{Q} = 2\mathbf{v}^{\mathrm{T}}\mathbf{X} \cdot (\mathbf{W} - \mathrm{diag}(\mathbf{W} \cdot \mathbf{1})) \cdot \mathbf{X}^{\mathrm{T}}\mathbf{v}. \qquad (8)$$

where $\mathbf{X}$ denotes the training set matrix, each row of $\mathbf{X}$ represents one document vector, $\mathbf{1}$ is a vector with all elements equal to 1. Minimizing (8) is equivalent to solving the flowing eigenvalue decomposition problem

$$\mathbf{X} \cdot (\mathrm{diag}(\mathbf{W} \cdot \mathbf{1}) - \mathbf{W})\mathbf{X}^{\mathrm{T}}\mathbf{v} = \lambda \mathbf{v}. \qquad (9)$$

Here we apply the idea of KPCA (Solomonoff et al., 2007; Schölkopf et al., 1997) to solve (9). Denoting $\mathbf{v}$ by a new vector $\mathbf{Xu}$, finding $\mathbf{u}$ turns to solving a generalized eigenvalue problem in kernel space as

$$\begin{cases} \mathbf{KZKu} = \lambda \mathbf{Ku} \\ \mathbf{K} = \mathbf{X}^{\mathrm{T}}\mathbf{X} \\ \mathbf{Z} = \mathrm{diag}(\mathbf{W} \cdot \mathbf{1}) - \mathbf{W}. \end{cases} \qquad (10)$$

The variability space is then constructed by selecting a set of eigenvectors corresponding to the d_1 largest eigenvalues.

$$\mathbf{U} = [\mathbf{u}_1, \mathbf{u}_2, ..., \mathbf{u}_{d_1}] \qquad (11)$$

Finally, a $(d \times d)$ projection matrix is obtained by combining (5), (11) and $\mathbf{v} = \mathbf{Xu}$.

Based on this variability normalization algorithm, the baseline document vectors could be transformed to a new feature space with minimized intra-topic variability. The main procedure to implement intra-topic variation normalization could be divided into the following steps:

- Generate sample matrix $\mathbf{X}$ using the whole n documents of training set.

- Construct weighting matrix $\mathbf{W}$ according to (4) with the use of topic label information.

- Estimate a projection matrix $\mathbf{P}$ by solving the aforementioned eigenvalue problem.

- Transform all documents to new feature space through linear projection according to (2).

It should be noticed that after making feature transformation by the proposed variability normalization algorithm, the dimensionality of document representation has not been changed. This is different with all the existing dimensionality reduction methods since our goal is to re-define the feature representation space for topic document representation. To prove the effectiveness of the proposed algorithm, this paper presents experimental results on a challenging conversational dataset.

3 Experiments

In this section, we evaluate the proposed variability normalization method in a typical topic classification problem. We will firstly introduce the experimental setup, including dataset, evaluation criteria and system description. After it, all the experimental results would be reported in detail.

3.1 Experimental setup

3.1.1 Dataset

The data set used in this paper is the text transcripts of free-style conversational speech database, Fisher English corpus released by LDC, which contains 11699 recorded conversations (Cieri et al., 2004). This corpus is collected from 40 different topics, and each document includes relatively a distinct topic (e.g. "Comedy", "Smoking", "Terrorism", etc.) as well as topics covering similar subject areas (e.g. "Airport Security", "Bioterrorism", "Issues in the Middle East"). This paper randomly chooses 60 documents and 50 documents per topic for the training set and testing set respectively. Another 50 documents for each topic are randomly selected to for the development set.

3.1.2 Evaluation criteria

We use two types of criteria to make a comprehensive evaluations for this work. The first evaluation creterion is F_1 measure corresponding to the recall and precision rates for a typical classification system. In detail, we would report micro-average F_1 and macro-average F_1 results. In consideration of topic classification is similar to topic verification, we choose equal error rate (EER) to be the second criterion, which is the equal value of miss probability and false probability.

3.1.3 System description

Module	Methods
Text processing	stop-word removal, stemming
Representation	TF-IDF feature
Classification	KNN, SVM algorithm

Table 1: Baseline system modules for topic classification.

This paper constructs several systems for comparison. The configurations of our baseline system are shown in Table 1. Porter algorithm (Porter, 1980) is adopted for word stemming after stop-words removal. Then a vocabulary with 19534 unique words is determined according to the occurrence frequency information of training set. Documents in the baseline system are represented by using the popular TF-IDF term weighting strategy (Salton and Buckley, 1988). Two popular algorithms SVM and KNN are used for classification separately. The SVM classification is implemented using the LIBSVM toolkit (Chang and Lin, 2011).

Based on the baseline system, descriptions of other systems are given as below.

(1) *LSI*: documents are represented in latent semantic space estimated by the LSI algorithm (Deerwester et al., 1990) based on the baseline features.

(2) *LDA*: document features are transformed by linear discriminant analysis. We select 50 eigenvectors for the low dimensional feature space.

(3) *VarNorm*: document features are transformed from the baseline TF-IDF vectors by the approach proposed in this paper. We select 60 eigenvectors for generating the project matrix.

(4) *VarNorm-LDA*: system combined *VarNorm* with *LDA*, which employs feature transformation operations twice on the original TF-IDF document features. The number of eigenvectors for *VarNorm* and *LDA* are set to 60 and 50 respectively.

All the parameters suggested in this paper are tuned on the development set. However, the eigenvector number is not restricted to 50 or 60. It is recommended to set the eigenvector num from 45 to 75 since we have 40 topics for experiments.

3.2 Experimental Results

3.2.1 Variability normalization performance

According to (3), we compare the intra-topic variability for the baseline and the *VarNorm* system. The difference for variability calculation is whether to use the projection matrix $\mathbf{P}$ or not. Figure 1 shows the intra-topic variability on 40 topics of the training set. The vertical axis represents the variability for each topic, while the horizontal axis stands for 40 topics in the conversation corpus. As we can see clearly, the variability of baseline system is high. After conducting variability normalization, it could be reduced effectively.

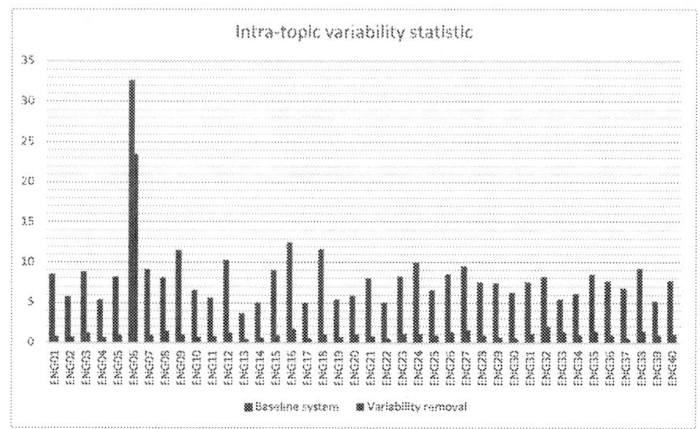

Figure 1: Variability normalization performance.

After making detailed analysis, we find for the topic ENG06, the theme is *"Hypothetical Situations: Perjury – Do either of you think that you would commit perjury for a close friend or family member?"*, the variability among documents from this topic is largest in the whole corpus. However, for the topic ENG13, *"Movies: Do each of you enjoy going to the movies in a theater, or would you rather rent a movie and stay home? What was the last movie that you saw? Was it good or bad and why?"*, the variability is the lowest. This is the difference between common topics and infrequent topics. Since people would use various words to express their ideas, it is reasonable to find the variability problem is more serious for infrequent topics than common topics.

3.2.2 Classification Results using KNN

Experimental results using KNN classification algorithm are given in Table 2. The results show that, compared to the baseline system, the variability normalization system *VarNorm* achieves 2% absolute F_1 improvement, and 29% relative improvement for EER. When taking the variability removing as a preliminary process, and employing LDA as the secondary transformation, the system *VarNorm-LDA* achieves the best performance. The EER is im-

Table 2: Classification results using KNN algorithm

System	EER	macro-F_1	micro-F_1
Baseline	6.10	84.72	83.15
LSI	4.25	86.24	85.45
LDA	4.49	88.94	88.15
VarNorm	4.30	86.46	85.60
VarNorm-LDA	**2.51**	**90.29**	**90.00**

Table 3: Classification results using SVM algorithm

System	EER	macro-F_1	micro-F_1
Baseline	3.40	88.86	88.40
LSI	3.35	89.59	89.25
LDA	3.05	90.81	90.55
VarNorm	**2.90**	**91.04**	**90.80**
VarNorm-LDA	**2.50**	**92.28**	**92.15**

proved by 65% relatively, and the micro-F_1 measure is improved by 6.85% absolutely. The reason for this performance is straightforward. Since the proposed algorithm effectively reduce the differences among intra-topic documents, the LDA algorithm would be more easier and effective to maximize the ratio of between-class-variance to within-class-variance.

3.2.3 Classification Results using SVM

Similarly, the experimental results using SVM classification algorithm are shown in Table 3. The baseline performance is better than system using KNN algorithm. The improvements achieved by *LSI* in KNN sytem almost vanish here, while the *VarNorm* system keeps its improvement. The *VarNorm* system even works better than the *LDA* system, with nearly 15% relative improvement on EER, and 3.4% absolute improvement on micro-F_1 measure. The best results are obtained by the *VarNorm-LDA* system. There are 36% relative improvement for EER, and 3.75% absolute improvement for micro-F_1 measure.

4 Conclusions and Future Work

In this paper, we investigated the intra-topic variability problem for topic classification. The major contribution of this work is that we proposed a effective variability normalization approach for robust document representation. An optimization problem was constructed after making a linear variability removable assumption. In order to take a deep insight into the performance of the proposed variability normalization algorithm, we conducted experiments on a challenge free-style conversation corpus. Experimental results based on the SVM and KNN classification algorithm all confirmed the robustness of the proposed approach. As a conclusion, the variability normalization algorithm could be used as a front-end feature transformation strategy, and we also suggest to combine it with linear discriminant analysis algorithm or some other algorithms to further improve system performances.

Further study will investigate the adaptive methods for constructing robust feature spaces. We would also combine this work with more document representations methods as well. Moreover, it would be very interesting to extend and combine our work to some novel unsupervised machine learning techniques, like the work of (Zhang and Jiang, 2015) while they proposed a model for high-dimensional data by combineing a linear orthogonal projection and a finite mixture model under a unified generative modeling framework.

Acknowledgments

This work was supported in part by the Science and Technology Development of Anhui Province, China (Grants No. 2014z02006) and the Fundamental Research Funds for the Central Universities (Grant No. WK2350000001). At the same time, we want to give special thanks to the anonymous reviewers for their insightful comments as well as suggestions.

References

Bing Bai, Jason Weston, David Grangier, Ronan Collobert, Kunihiko Sadamasa, Yanjun Qi, Olivier Chapelle, and Kilian Weinberger. 2009. Supervised semantic indexing. In *Proceedings of the 18th ACM conference on Information and knowledge management*, pages 187–196. ACM.

Michael W Berry, Susan T Dumais, and Gavin W O'Brien. 1995. Using linear algebra for intelligent information retrieval. *SIAM review*, 37(4):573–595.

D. M. Blei, A. Y. Ng, and M. I. Jordan. 2003. Latent dirichlet allocation. *the Journal of machine Learning research*, 3:993–1022.

Soumen Chakrabarti, Shourya Roy, and Mahesh V Soundalgekar. 2003. Fast and accurate text classification via multiple linear discriminant projections. *The VLDB Journal*, 12(2):170–185.

Sutanu Chakraborti, Rahman Mukras, Robert Lothian, Nirmalie Wiratunga, Stuart NK Watt, and David J Harper. 2007. Supervised latent semantic indexing using adaptive sprinkling. In *IJCAI*, pages 1582–1587.

Jack K Chambers. 1995. *Sociolinguistic theory*. Blackwell.

Chih-Chung Chang and Chih-Jen Lin. 2011. LIBSVM: a library for support vector machines. *ACM Transactions on Intelligent Systems and Technology (TIST)*, 2(3):27.

Kai-Wei Chang, Wen-tau Yih, and Christopher Meek. 2013. Multi-relational latent semantic analysis. In *EMNLP*, pages 1602–1612.

C. Cieri, D. Miller, and K. Walker. 2004. The Fisher corpus: a resource for the next generations of speech-to-text. In *LREC*, pages 69–71.

S. C. Deerwester, S. T. Dumais, T. K. Landauer, G. W. Furnas, and R. A. Harshman. 1990. Indexing by latent semantic analysis. *JASIS*, 41(6):391–407.

Charles J Fillmore, Daniel Kempler, and William SY Wang. 2014. *Individual differences in language ability and language behavior*. Academic Press.

Geoffrey E Hinton and Ruslan R Salakhutdinov. 2006. Reducing the dimensionality of data with neural networks. *Science*, 313(5786):504–507.

Quoc V Le and Tomas Mikolov. 2014. Distributed representations of sentences and documents. *arXiv preprint arXiv:1405.4053*.

Mohamed Morchid, Richard Dufour, and Georges Linares. 2014. A lda-based topic classification approach from highly imperfect automatic transcriptions. *LREC14*.

Martin F Porter. 1980. An algorithm for suffix stripping. *Program*, 14(3):130–137.

Gerard Salton and Christopher Buckley. 1988. Term-weighting approaches in automatic text retrieval. *Information processing & management*, 24(5):513–523.

Gerard Salton and Michael J McGill. 1986. Introduction to modern information retrieval.

B. Schölkopf, A. Smola, and KR. Müller. 1997. Kernel principal component analysis. In *Artificial Neural Networks-ICANN'97*, pages 583–588. Springer.

Alex Solomonoff, William M Campbell, and Ian Boardman. 2005. Advances in channel compensation for svm speaker recognition. In *ICASSP*, pages 629–632.

A. Solomonoff, W. M. Campbell, and C. Quillen. 2007. Nuisance attribute projection. *Speech Communication*.

Nitish Srivastava, Ruslan R Salakhutdinov, and Geoffrey E Hinton. 2013. Modeling documents with deep boltzmann machines. *arXiv preprint arXiv:1309.6865*.

Jian-Tao Sun, Zheng Chen, Hua-Jun Zeng, Yu-Chang Lu, Chun-Yi Shi, and Wei-Ying Ma. 2004. Supervised latent semantic indexing for document categorization. In *Data Mining, 2004. ICDM'04. Fourth IEEE International Conference on*, pages 535–538. IEEE.

K. Torkkola. 2004. Discriminative features for text document classification. *Formal Pattern Analysis & Applications*, 6(4):301–308.

Quan Wang, Jun Xu, Hang Li, and Nick Craswell. 2013. Regularized latent semantic indexing: A new approach to large-scale topic modeling. *ACM Transactions on Information Systems (TOIS)*, 31(1):5.

Wen-tau Yih, Kristina Toutanova, John C Platt, and Christopher Meek. 2011. Learning discriminative projections for text similarity measures. In *CoNLL*, pages 247–256. Association for Computational Linguistics.

Shiliang Zhang and Hui Jiang. 2015. Hybrid orthogonal projection and estimation (hope): A new framework to probe and learn neural networks. *arXiv preprint arXiv:1502.00702*.

Shift-Reduce CCG Parsing using Neural Network Models

Bharat Ram Ambati and **Tejaswini Deoskar** and **Mark Steedman**
Institute for Language, Cognition and Computation
School of Informatics, University of Edinburgh
bharat.ambati@ed.ac.uk, {tdeoskar,steedman}@inf.ed.ac.uk

Abstract

We present a neural network based shift-reduce CCG parser, the first neural-network based parser for CCG. We also study the impact of neural network based tagging models, and greedy versus beam-search parsing, by using a structured neural network model. Our greedy parser obtains a labeled F-score of 83.27%, the best reported result for greedy CCG parsing in the literature (an improvement of 2.5% over a perceptron based greedy parser) and is more than three times faster. With a beam, our structured neural network model gives a labeled F-score of 85.57% which is 0.6% better than the perceptron based counterpart.

1 Introduction

Shift-reduce parsing is interesting for practical real-world applications like parsing the web, since parsing can be achieved in linear time. Although greedy parsers are fast, accuracies of these parsers are typically much lower than graph-based parsers. Conversely, beam-search parsers achieve accuracies comparable to graph-based parsers (Zhang and Nivre, 2011) but are much slower than their greedy counterparts. Recently, Chen and Manning (2014) have showed that fast and accurate parsing can be achieved using neural network based parsers. Improving their work, Weiss et al. (2015) presented a structured neural network model which gave state-of-the-art results for English dependency parsing.

There has been increasing interest in Combinatory Categorial Grammar (CCG) (Steedman, 2000) parsing due to the simplicity of its interface between syntax and semantics. In addition to predicate-argument structure, CCG captures the unbounded dependencies found in grammatical constructions like relativization, coordination, etc. We present a neural network based shift-reduce CCG parser, the first neural network based parser for CCG. We first adapt Chen and Manning (2014)'s shift-reduce dependency parser for CCG parsing. We then develop a structured neural network model based on Weiss et al. (2015), in order to explore the impact of a beam-search on the parser. We also analyze the impact of neural network taggers (for both POS-tagging and CCG supertagging) as compared to maximum entropy taggers. Our greedy neural network parser achieves unlabeled and labeled F-scores of 89.78% and 83.27% respectively, an improvement of around 2.5% over a perceptron based greedy parser, and is more than three times faster. Due to its relevance for large-scale parsing, we make this parser available for public usage. By using a beam search, our structured neural network model gave even better results of 91.95% and 85.57% unlabeled and labeled F-scores respectively. To the best of our knowledge, ours is the first neural network based parser for CCG and also the first work on exploring neural network taggers for shift-reduce CCG parsing.

2 Related Work

2.1 CCG Parsers

Due to the availability of English CCGbank (Hockenmaier and Steedman, 2007), several wide-coverage CCG parsers have been developed (Hockenmaier and Steedman, 2002; Clark and Curran, 2007; Auli and Lopez, 2011; Zhang and Clark,

Proceedings of NAACL-HLT 2016, pages 447–453,
San Diego, California, June 12-17, 2016. ©2016 Association for Computational Linguistics

2011; Lewis and Steedman, 2014a). While the majority of CCG parsers are chart-based (Clark and Curran, 2007; Lewis and Steedman, 2014a), there has been some work on shift-reduce CCG parsing (Zhang and Clark, 2011; Xu et al., 2014; Ambati et al., 2015). Zhang and Clark (2011) used a global linear model trained discriminatively with the averaged perceptron (Collins, 2002) and beam search for their shift-reduce CCG parser. A dependency model for shift-reduce CCG parsing using a dynamic oracle technique (Goldberg and Nivre, 2012) was developed by Xu et al. (2014). Ambati et al. (2015) presented an incremental algorithm for transition based CCG parsing which introduced two novel revealing actions to overcome the consequences of the greedy nature of the previous parsers.

2.2 Neural Network Parsers

Neural Network parsers are attracting interest for both speed and accuracy. There has been some work on neural networks for constituent based parsing (Collobert, 2011; Socher et al., 2013; Watanabe and Sumita, 2015). Chen and Manning (2014) developed a neural network architecture for dependency parsing. This parser was fast and accurate, parsing around 1000 sentences per second and achieving an unlabeled attachment score of 92.0% on the standard Penn Treebank test data for English. Chen and Manning (2014)'s parser used a feed forward neural network. Several improvements were made to this architecture in terms of using Long Short-Term Memory (LSTM) networks (Dyer et al., 2015), deep neural networks (Weiss et al., 2015) and structured neural networks (Weiss et al., 2015; Zhou et al., 2015; Alberti et al., 2015).

3 Our Neural Network Parser (NNPar)

The architecture of our neural network based shift-reduce CCG parser is similar to that of Chen and Manning (2014). We present the details of the network and the model settings in this section. We also discuss our structured neural network model.

3.1 Architecture

Figure 1 shows the architecture of our neural network parser. There are three layers in the parser: input, hidden and output layers. We first extract discrete features like words, POS-tags and CCG su-

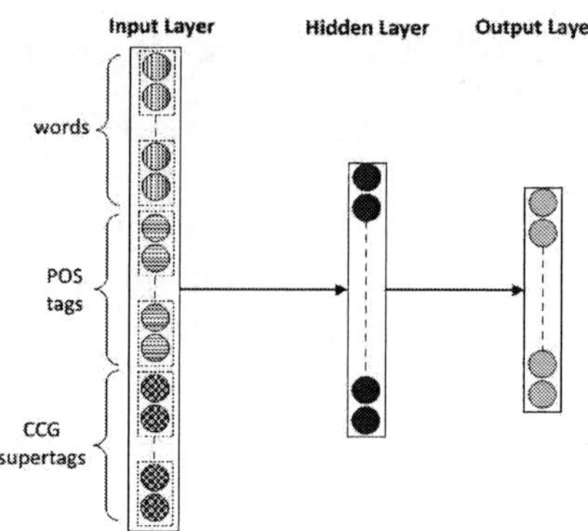

Figure 1: Our Neural Network Architecture (adapted from Chen and Manning (2014)).

pertags from the parser configuration. For each of these discrete features we obtain a continuous vector representation in the form of their corresponding embeddings and use them in the input layer. Following Chen and Manning (2014), we use a cube activation function and softmax for output layer.

3.2 Feature and Model Settings

We extract features from a) top four nodes in the stack, b) next four nodes in the input and c) left and right children of the top two nodes in the stack. We obtain words and POS-tags of all these 12 nodes. In case of CCG supertags, in addition to the CCG categories of the nodes in the stack (top four nodes, left and right children of top two nodes), we also obtain the lexical head categories for the top two nodes. We use a special token 'NULL' if a feature is not present in the parser configuration. So, in total we have 34 features: 12 word, 12 POS-tag and 10 CCG supertag features. For each of these 34 features we obtain their corresponding embeddings. We use Turian embeddings of dimensionality 50 (Turian-50)[1]. For the words which are not in the word embeddings dictionary, embeddings of '-UNKNOWN-' token are used as a backoff. For POS-tags and CCG supertags, the parameters are randomly initialized with values between -0.01 and 0.01.

Our input layer is a 34 (feature templates) X 50 (embedding size) dimensional vector. We use 200

---

[1]Lewis and Steedman (2014b) explored different publicly available word embeddings (Mnih and Hinton, 2009; Turian et al., 2010; Collobert et al., 2011; Mikolov et al., 2013) for CCG supertagging and showed that Turian-50 gave best results.

hidden units in the the hidden layer. For the output layer we compute softmax probabilities only for the actions which are possible in a particular parser configuration instead of all the actions. We use the training settings of Chen and Manning (2014) for our parser. The training objective is to minimize the cross-entropy loss with an l_2-regularization and the training error derivatives are backpropagated during training. For optimization we use AdaGrad (Duchi et al., 2011). 10^{-8} and 0.01 are the values for regularization parameter and Adagrad initial learning rate respectively. Parameters that give the best labeled F-score on the development data are used for testing data.

3.3 Structured Neural Network

Chen and Manning (2014)'s parser is a greedy parser and it is not straight forward to add a beam during training into their parser. As a way of introducing a beam, Weiss et al. (2015) presented a structured perceptron training for the neural network parser. They first pre-trained their neural network model. For the final layer, they trained a structured perceptron using beam search decoding which takes the neural network hidden and output layers as the input. This method, known as a structured neural network, gave the state-of-the-art results for English dependency parsing. In addition to using a softmax for the output layer, we also applied this structured neural network approach for our experiments using a beam. Unlike Weiss et al. (2015)'s neural network architecture, which consists of two hidden layers with 2048 hidden units each, we use the Chen and Manning (2014) style architecture described in the previous sections.

3.4 Comparison to Chen and Manning (2014)

Our neural network parser differs from Chen and Manning (2014) in a number of respects. We use CCG supertags in the input layer rather than dependency labels. For word embeddings, we use Turian embeddings (Turian et al., 2010) whereas they use Collobert et al. (2011). We have a slightly smaller set of 34 feature templates as compared to their 48 templates. Our parser has 2296 actions when instantiated by specific categorial types: 1285 `Shift`, 340 `Reduce-Left`, 593 `Reduce-Right` and 78 `Reduce-Unary` actions. In comparison, Chen and Manning (2014) have a much smaller number of actions (35 for CoNLL and 91 for Stanford dependencies). Because there are many more CCG categories (~ 500) compared to dependency labels, there are relatively more operations in a CCG parser.

4 Experiments and Results

We first compare our neural network parser (NNPar)[2] with a perceptron based parser in the greedy settings. Then we analyze the impact of beam using neural network (NNPar) and structured neural network (Structured NNPar) models.

The perceptron based parser is a re-implementation of Zhang and Clark (2011)'s parser (Z&C*). A global linear model trained with the averaged perceptron (Collins, 2002) is used for this parser and an early-update (Collins and Roark, 2004) strategy is used during training. In the greedy setting (beam=1), when the predicted action differs from the gold action, decoding stops and weights are updated accordingly. When a beam is used (beam=16), weights are updated when the gold parse configuration falls out of the beam. For Z&C*, the feature set of Zhang and Clark (2011), which comprises of 64 feature templates is used. For NNPar, the 34 feature templates described in section 3.2 are used. We employ an arc-standard style shift-reduce algorithm for CCG parsing, similar to Zhang and Clark (2011), for all our experiments.

4.1 Data and Settings

We use the standard CCGbank training (sections 02 − 21), development (section 00) and testing (section 23) splits for our experiments. All the experiments are performed using automatic POS-tags and CCG supertags. We compare performance using two types of taggers: maximum entropy and neural network based taggers (NNT). The C&C taggers [3] (Clark and Curran, 2004) are used for maximum entropy taggers. For neural network taggers, SENNA tagger[4] (version 3.0) (Collobert et al., 2011) is used

---

[2]We used Chen and Manning (2014)'s classifier for implementing our NNPar

[3]`http://svn.ask.it.usyd.edu.au/trac/candc/wiki`

[4]`http://ronan.collobert.com/senna/`

for POS-tagging and EasyCCG tagger[5] (Lewis and Steedman, 2014a) is used for supertagging. Both these taggers use a feed-forward neural network architecture with a single hidden layer similar to our NNPar architecture.

In the case of POS-tags, we consider the first best tag given by the POS tagger. For CCG supertags, we use a multitagger which gives n-best supertags for a word. Following Zhang and Clark (2011) and Xu et al. (2014), only during training, the gold CCG lexical category is added to the list of supertags for a word if it is not present in the list assigned by the multitagger.

4.2 Greedy Setting

In this section, we compare the performance of perceptron (Z&C*) and neural network (NNPar) parsers in the greedy setting. Table 1 presents the unlabeled F-score (UF), labeled F-score (LF) and lexical category accuracy (Cat.) for the Z&C* and NNPar on the CCGbank development data.

NNPar outperformed Z&C* on all the metrices. There is an improvement of 2.14% in UF and 2.4% in LF, when both the parsers used maximum-entropy (C&C) taggers. We also experimented with the revealing based incremental algorithm of Ambati et al. (2015). Neural network parser gave better results than the perceptron parser for the incremental algorithm as well. Using the incremental algorithm, our NNPar obtained UF and LF of 89.08% and 81.07% which is 0.3% and 1.6% respectively lower than the results with the non-incremental algorithm. So, for the rest of the experiments we use non-incremental parsing algorithm of Z&C*.

Using neural network based taggers (NNT) didn't give any improvement for Z&C* in the greedy settings. Performance of NNT is slightly lower than C&C tagger which could be the reason for this (Lewis and Steedman, 2014a). But for NNPar, NNT improved the performance over C&C by 0.7%. Lewis and Steedman (2014a) and Xu et al. (2015) showed improvements in the performance of C&C, a graph based parser, by using neural network taggers. Our result with NNPar is in line with theirs and shows that neural network taggers

[5] http://homepages.inf.ed.ac.uk/s1049478/easyccg.html

can improve the performance of shift-reduce CCG parsers as well. We obtained final unlabeled and labeled F-scores of 90.09% and 83.33% respectively on the development data. To the best of our knowledge these are the best reported results for greedy shift-reduce CCG parsing.

Model	Tagger	UF	LF	Cat.
Z&C*	C&C	87.24	80.25	91.09
Our NNPar	C&C	89.38	82.65	91.72
Z&C*	NNT	87.00	79.78	90.52
Our NNPar	NNT	**90.09**	**83.33**	**92.03**

Table 1: Performance of greedy CCG parsers on CCGbank development data (Sec. 00).

4.3 Beam Search

We next analyze the impact of beam-search on the various parsers. For Z&C* and Structured NNPar, we use a beam of size 16 both during training and testing; for NNPar, a beam (of 16) can be used only during testing. Table 2 presents the results using a beam size of 16. Results are presented with a beam of size 16 to enable direct comparison with Zhang and Clark (2011), since our parsing algorithm is similar to theirs.

The top 3 rows of the table show the results of our experiments and the last 2 rows contain published results of Zhang and Clark (2011) and Xu et al. (2014). Using a beam improved the performance of both the perceptron and neural network parsers. Since NNPar uses a beam only during testing, there is only slight improvement in the f-score. Using a structured neural network gave a significant boost in performance. Structured NNPar is better than NNPar on all the metrices which shows that Structured NNPar is a stronger model than NNPar. We obtained a final LF of 85.69% on the development data which is 1.3% better than the Z&C*, the structured perceptron counter part, and 1.1% better than NNPar. This is the best published result on the development data for shift-reduce CCG parsing.

4.4 Final Test Results

Table 3 presents the results for the final test data. The top 2 rows of the table present the results in the greedy settings. The middle 3 rows of the table show the results with a beam. The last 2 rows give the published results of Zhang and Clark (2011)

Model	Beam	UF	LF	Cat.
Z&C*	1	87.28	80.78	91.44
Our NNPar	1	89.78	83.27	91.89
Z&C*	16	91.28	85.00	92.79
Our NNPar	16	91.14	84.44	92.22
Our Structured NNPar	16	**91.95**	85.57	**92.86**
Zhang and Clark (2011)	16	-	85.48	92.77
Xu et al. (2014)	128	-	**86.00**	92.75

Table 3: Results on CCGbank test data (Sec. 23).

Model	UF	LF	Cat.
Z&C*	91.17	84.34	92.42
Our NNPar	91.46	84.55	92.35
Our Structured NNPar	**92.19**	**85.69**	**93.02**
Zhang and Clark (2011)		85.00	92.77
Xu et al. (2014)		85.18	92.75

Table 2: Impact of the beam on CCGbank development data (Sec. 00).

and Xu et al. (2014). With the greedy setting, our NNPar outperformed Z&C* by around 2.5%, obtaining 89.78% and 83.27% UF and LF respectively. These are the best reported result for greedy shift-reduce CCG parsing.

In the case of the beam search parsers, we achieved final best scores of 91.95% in UF and 85.57% in LF with our Structured NNPar. Structured NNPar gave improvements of 1.1% over the NNPar and 0.6% over the structured perceptron model, Z&C*. Structured NNPar gets better category accuracy, but lower LF than Xu et al.(2014). Note however that we use a much smaller beam size of 16 (similar to Z&C) as compared to theirs (128). Increasing the beam size improved the accuracy but significantly reduced the parsing speed. Testing with a beam of size 128 gave 0.2% improvement in labelled F-score but slowed the parser by ten times.

4.5 Speed

Beam-search parsers are more accurate than greedy parsers but are very slow. With neural network models we can build parsers which give a nice trade-off between speed and accuracy. Table 4 present the speed comparison for both Z&C* and our NNPar in greedy settings. NNPar is much faster, parsing 350 sentences per second compared to Z&C*

which parses 110 sentences per second. Parsers with a beam of size 16 parse around 10 sentences per second and parsers with a beam of size 128 parse around 1 sentence per second. These numbers don't include POS tagging and supertagging time.

Model	Sentences/Second
Z&C*	110
NNPar	350

Table 4: Speed comparison of perceptron and neural network based greedy parsers.

5 Conclusion

We presented the first neural network based shift-reduce parsers for CCG, a greedy and a beam-search parser. On the standard CCGbank test data, we achieved a labeled F-score of 85.57% with our structured neural network parser, an improvement of 0.6% over the structured perceptron parser (Z&C*). Our greedy parser gets UF and LF of 89.78% and 83.27% respectively, the best reported results for a greedy CCG parser, and is more than three times faster. In future we plan to explore more sophisticated tagging and parsing models like deep neural networks (Weiss et al., 2015), recurrent neural networks (Dyer et al., 2015), and bi-directional LSTMs (Lewis et al., 2016) for shift-reduce CCG parsing.

The parser code can be downloaded at `https://github.com/bharatambati/tranccg`.

Acknowledgments

We thank Mike Lewis, Greg Coppola and Siva Reddy for helpful discussions. We also thank the three anonymous reviewers for their useful suggestions. This work was supported by ERC Advanced

Fellowship 249520 GRAMPLUS and EU IST Cognitive Systems IP Xperience.

References

Chris Alberti, David Weiss, Greg Coppola, and Slav Petrov. 2015. Improved Transition-Based Parsing and Tagging with Neural Networks. In *Proceedings of the 2015 Conference on Empirical Methods in Natural Language Processing*, pages 1354–1359, Lisbon, Portugal, September.

Bharat Ram Ambati, Tejaswini Deoskar, Mark Johnson, and Mark Steedman. 2015. An Incremental Algorithm for Transition-based CCG Parsing. In *Proceedings of the 2015 Conference of the North American Chapter of the Association for Computational Linguistics: Human Language Technologies*, pages 53–63, Denver, Colorado, May–June.

Michael Auli and Adam Lopez. 2011. A Comparison of Loopy Belief Propagation and Dual Decomposition for Integrated CCG Supertagging and Parsing. In *Proceedings of the 49th Annual Meeting of the Association for Computational Linguistics: Human Language Technologies*, pages 470–480, Portland, Oregon, USA, June.

Danqi Chen and Christopher Manning. 2014. A Fast and Accurate Dependency Parser using Neural Networks. In *Proceedings of the 2014 Conference on Empirical Methods in Natural Language Processing (EMNLP)*, pages 740–750, Doha, Qatar, October.

Stephen Clark and James R. Curran. 2004. The Importance of Supertagging for Wide-Coverage CCG Parsing. In *Proceedings of Coling 2004*, pages 282–288, Geneva, Switzerland, Aug 23–Aug 27. COLING.

Stephen Clark and James R. Curran. 2007. Wide-Coverage Efficient Statistical Parsing with CCG and Log-Linear Models. *Computational Linguistics*, 33:493–552.

Michael Collins and Brian Roark. 2004. Incremental Parsing with the Perceptron Algorithm. In *Proceedings of the 42nd Meeting of the Association for Computational Linguistics (ACL'04), Main Volume*, pages 111–118, Barcelona, Spain, July.

Michael Collins. 2002. Discriminative Training Methods for Hidden Markov Models: Theory and Experiments with Perceptron Algorithms. In *Proceedings of the 2002 Conference on Empirical Methods in Natural Language Processing*, pages 1–8, July.

R. Collobert, J. Weston, L. Bottou, M. Karlen, K. Kavukcuoglu, and P. Kuksa. 2011. Natural Language Processing (Almost) from Scratch. *Journal of Machine Learning Research*, 12:2493–2537.

Ronan Collobert. 2011. Deep learning for efficient discriminative parsing. In *International Conference on Artificial Intelligence and Statistics*.

John Duchi, Elad Hazan, and Yoram Singer. 2011. Adaptive subgradient methods for online learning and stochastic optimization. *The Journal of Machine Learning Research*, 12:2121–2159.

Chris Dyer, Miguel Ballesteros, Wang Ling, Austin Matthews, and Noah A. Smith. 2015. Transition-Based Dependency Parsing with Stack Long Short-Term Memory. In *Proceedings of the 53rd Annual Meeting of the Association for Computational Linguistics and the 7th International Joint Conference on Natural Language Processing (Volume 1: Long Papers)*, pages 334–343, Beijing, China, July.

Yoav Goldberg and Joakim Nivre. 2012. A Dynamic Oracle for Arc-Eager Dependency Parsing. In *Proceedings of COLING 2012*, pages 959–976, Mumbai, India, December. The COLING 2012 Organizing Committee.

Julia Hockenmaier and Mark Steedman. 2002. Generative Models for Statistical Parsing with Combinatory Categorial Grammar. In *Proceedings of 40th Annual Meeting of the Association for Computational Linguistics*, pages 335–342, Philadelphia, Pennsylvania, USA, July.

Julia Hockenmaier and Mark Steedman. 2007. CCGbank: A Corpus of CCG Derivations and Dependency Structures Extracted from the Penn Treebank. *Computational Linguistics*, 33(3):355–396.

Mike Lewis and Mark Steedman. 2014a. A* CCG Parsing with a Supertag-factored Model. In *Proceedings of the 2014 Conference on Empirical Methods in Natural Language Processing*, Doha, Qatar, October.

Mike Lewis and Mark Steedman. 2014b. Improved CCG parsing with Semi-supervised Supertagging. *Transactions of the Association for Computational Linguistics (TACL)*, 2:327–338.

Mike Lewis, Kenton Lee, and Luke Zettlemoyer. 2016. LSTM CCG Parsing. In *Proceedings of the 2016 Conference of the North American Chapter of the Association for Computational Linguistics: Human Language Technologies*, San Diego, California, June.

Tomas Mikolov, Kai Chen, Greg Corrado, and Jeffrey Dean. 2013. Efficient Estimation of Word Representations in Vector Space. In *Proceedings of Workshop at ICLR*.

Andriy Mnih and Geoffrey Hinton. 2009. A Scalable Hierarchical Distributed Language Model. In *Advances in Neural Information Processing Systems*, volume 21, pages 1081–1088.

Richard Socher, John Bauer, Christopher D. Manning, and Ng Andrew Y. 2013. Parsing with Compositional

Vector Grammars. In *Proceedings of the 51st Annual Meeting of the Association for Computational Linguistics (Volume 1: Long Papers)*, pages 455–465, Sofia, Bulgaria, August.

Mark Steedman. 2000. *The Syntactic Process*. MIT Press, Cambridge, MA, USA.

Joseph Turian, Lev-Arie Ratinov, and Yoshua Bengio. 2010. Word Representations: A Simple and General Method for Semi-Supervised Learning. In *Proceedings of the 48th Annual Meeting of the Association for Computational Linguistics*, pages 384–394, Uppsala, Sweden, July.

Taro Watanabe and Eiichiro Sumita. 2015. Transition-based Neural Constituent Parsing. In *Proceedings of the 53rd Annual Meeting of the Association for Computational Linguistics and the 7th International Joint Conference on Natural Language Processing (Volume 1: Long Papers)*, pages 1169–1179, Beijing, China, July.

David Weiss, Chris Alberti, Michael Collins, and Slav Petrov. 2015. Structured Training for Neural Network Transition-Based Parsing. In *Proceedings of the 53rd Annual Meeting of the Association for Computational Linguistics and the 7th International Joint Conference on Natural Language Processing (Volume 1: Long Papers)*, pages 323–333, Beijing, China, July.

Wenduan Xu, Stephen Clark, and Yue Zhang. 2014. Shift-Reduce CCG Parsing with a Dependency Model. In *Proceedings of the 52nd Annual Meeting of the Association for Computational Linguistics (Volume 1: Long Papers)*, pages 218–227, Baltimore, Maryland, June.

Wenduan Xu, Michael Auli, and Stephen Clark. 2015. CCG Supertagging with a Recurrent Neural Network. In *Proceedings of the 53rd Annual Meeting of the Association for Computational Linguistics and the 7th International Joint Conference on Natural Language Processing (Volume 2: Short Papers)*, pages 250–255, Beijing, China, July.

Yue Zhang and Stephen Clark. 2011. Shift-Reduce CCG Parsing. In *Proceedings of the 49th Annual Meeting of the Association for Computational Linguistics: Human Language Technologies*, pages 683–692, Portland, Oregon, USA, June.

Yue Zhang and Joakim Nivre. 2011. Transition-based Dependency Parsing with Rich Non-local Features. In *Proceedings of the 49th Annual Meeting of the Association for Computational Linguistics: Human Language Technologies*, pages 188–193, Portland, Oregon, USA.

Hao Zhou, Yue Zhang, Shujian Huang, and Jiajun Chen. 2015. A Neural Probabilistic Structured-Prediction Model for Transition-Based Dependency Parsing. In *Proceedings of the 53rd Annual Meeting of the Association for Computational Linguistics and the 7th International Joint Conference on Natural Language Processing (Volume 1: Long Papers)*, pages 1213–1222, Beijing, China, July.

Online Multilingual Topic Models with Multi-Level Hyperpriors

Kriste Krstovski[†,§]**, David A. Smith**[‡] **and Michael J. Kurtz** [†]
[†]Harvard-Smithsonian Center for Astrophysics, Cambridge, MA
[§]College of Information and Computer Sciences, University of Massachusetts Amherst, Amherst, MA
[‡]College of Computer and Information Science, Northeastern University, Boston, MA
kkrstovski@cfa.harvard.edu, dasmith@ccs.neu.edu, kurtz@cfa.harvard.edu

Abstract

For topic models, such as LDA, that use a bag-of-words assumption, it becomes especially important to break the corpus into appropriately-sized "documents". Since the models are estimated solely from the term cooccurrences, extensive documents such as books or long journal articles lead to diffuse statistics, and short documents such as forum posts or product reviews can lead to sparsity. This paper describes practical inference procedures for hierarchical models that smooth topic estimates for smaller sections with hyperpriors over larger documents. Importantly for large collections, these online variational Bayes inference methods perform a single pass over a corpus and achieve better perplexity than "flat" topic models on monolingual and multilingual data. Furthermore, on the task of detecting document translation pairs in large multilingual collections, polylingual topic models (PLTM) with multi-level hyperpriors (mlhPLTM) achieve significantly better performance than existing online PLTM models while retaining computational efficiency.

1 Introduction

Bag of words models simplify the representation of documents by discarding grammatical information and simply relying on document-level word cooccurrence statistics. Topic models, such as latent Dirichlet allocation (LDA) (Blei et al., 2003), use this representation. A major drawback of the bag of words representation, especially in collections of large documents, is that the word co-occurrence statistics are computed on a document level and as such they do not capture the effect of words co-occurring close to each other versus words co-occurring further apart.

One alternative approach to longer documents that has received attention in the past has been to directly model local—i.e., Markov—dependencies among tokens. For example, the topical n-gram model (TNG) introduced by Wang et al. (2007) models unigram and n-gram phrases as mixture of topics based on the nearby word context. More recently, Jameel & Lam (2013) proposed an LDA extension that uses word sequence information to generate topic distribution over n-grams and performs topic segmentation using segment and paragraph information. While these and many other approaches offer a better and more realistic modeling of word sequences, they don't model topical variations across document sections either in mono- or multilingual collections.

In this paper, we focus on hierarchical models for improving topic models of long documents. In the past, document-topic based hierarchical prior structures have been explored for LDA. For example, Wallach et al. (2009) showed that Gibbs sampling implementation of asymmetric Dirichlet priors provide better modeling of documents, across the whole collection, compared to the original LDA approach. More recently, Kim et al. (2013) introduced tiLDA, a topic model of monolingual document collections with nested hierarchies. In order to achieve reasonable performance over large document collections with deep hierarchies, tiLDA utilizes parallel variational Bayes (VB) inference. While VB is known to converge faster than Gibbs sampling, and paral-

Proceedings of NAACL-HLT 2016, pages 454–459,
San Diego, California, June 12-17, 2016. ©2016 Association for Computational Linguistics

lel implementations are even faster, they, as with Gibbs sampling, still require multiple iterations over the whole collection besides the overhead of parallelizing the model parameters. Furthermore these approaches focus on monolingual collections.

We propose an online VB inference approach for topic models that captures the document specific effect of local and long range word co-occurrence by modeling individual document sections using multi-level Dirichlet prior structure. The proposed models assign Dirichlet priors to individual document sections that are coupled by a document level hierarchical Dirichlet prior which facilitates explicit modeling of the variation in topics across documents in mono- and multilingual collections. This in turn streamlines the use of topic models in collections of large documents where there is a predetermined section structure. Our contribution is twofold: (1) we present an online VB inference approach for topic models with multi-level Dirchlet prior structure and more importantly (2) introduce a polylingual topic model (PLTM) with multi-level hyperpriors (mlhPLTM) which is capable of efficiently modeling topical variations across document sections in large multilingual collections.

2 Efficient Multi-level Hyperpriors

The original LDA model and its multilingual variant, PLTM, use symmetric Dirichlet priors over the document-topic distributions θ_d and topic-word distributions φ_k which means that the concentration parameter α of the Dirichlet distribution is fixed and that the base measure u across all topics is uniform. Symmetric Dirichlet priors assume that all documents in the collection are drawn from the same family of distributions. This assumption is not suitable for collections of documents that cover a diverse set of topics. In the past this issue has been addressed with asymmetric priors where the base measures are non-uniform. One way to assign asymmetric priors to individual documents is to treat the base measures vector u as a hidden variable and assign a symmetric Dirichlet prior to it which creates a hierarchical Dirichlet prior structure over all document-topic distributions in the collection. This approach was used by Wallach et al. (2009). Unlike Wallach et al. (2009), who use a single document-

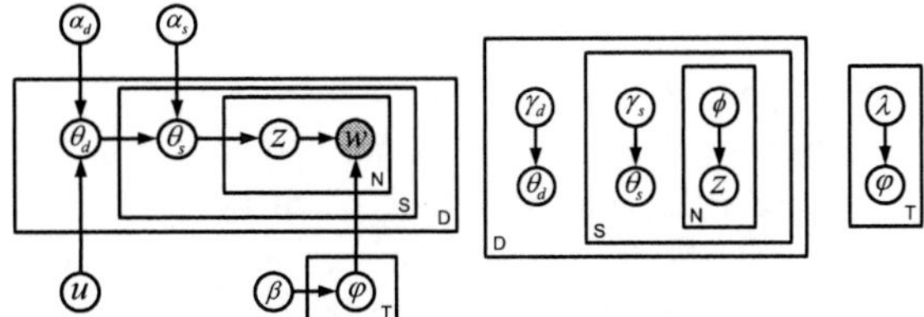

Figure 1: mlhLDA: Graphical representation (left); Free variational parameters for the online VB approximation (right).

topic distribution θ_d, we introduce section-topic distributions θ_s. The existing symmetric Dirichlet prior over θ_d creates a hierarchical Dirichlet prior over θ_s ($\theta = \theta_d, \theta_{s_1}, \theta_{s_2}, ..., \theta_{s_S}$):

$$p(\theta|\alpha_d u, \alpha_s) \propto p(\theta_d|\alpha_d u) \prod_s p(\theta_s|\alpha_s \theta_d) \quad (1)$$

In this setting the most widely used approach for estimating θ_d is Minka's (2000) fixed-point iteration approach which is also used in (Kim et al., 2013). Instead we use a more efficient approach for estimating the Dirichlet-multinomial hyperparameters by approximating the digamma differences in Minka's approach which was showcased in (Wallach, 2008) to be more efficient. Figure 1 shows the graphical model representation (left) of our model, which we refer to as multi-level hyperpriors LDA (mlhLDA), along with the free variational parameters for approximating the posteriors (right).

2.1 Inference using Online VB

Due to its ease of implementation, the most widely used approach for inferring LDA posterior distributions is Gibbs sampling (Griffiths and Steyvers, 2004). For example, this approach was used by Wallach et al. (2009) and was originally used for PLTM. On the other hand the VB approach (Blei et al., 2003) offers more efficient computation but as in the case of Gibbs sampling requires iterating over the whole collection multiple times (e.g. Kim et al. (2013)). More recently Hoffman et al. (2010) introduced online LDA (oLDA) that relies on online stochastic optimization and requires a single pass over the whole collection. The same approach was also extended to PLTM (oPLTM) (Krstovski and Smith, 2013). In our work we also utilize online VB to implement multi-level hyperprior (mlh) structure in LDA and PLTM. Similar to batch VB, in online

VB locally optimal values of the free variational parameters γ and ϕ, which are used to approximate the posterior θ and z, are computed in the E step of the algorithm but on a batch b of documents d_i (rather than the whole collection D as in the case of batch VB) while holding the topic-word variational parameter λ fixed. In the M step, λ is updated using stochastic gradient algorithm by first computing the optimal values of $\tilde{\lambda}$ using the batch optimal values of ϕ^b: $\tilde{\lambda}_{kw} = \eta + \frac{D}{|b|} \sum_{i=1}^{|b|} n_{d_i w} \phi_{wk}^{d_i}$. This value is then combined with value of λ computed on the previous batch through weighted average:

$$\lambda_{kw}^b \leftarrow (1 - \rho_b) \lambda_{kw}^{b-1} + \rho_b \tilde{\lambda}_{kw} \qquad (2)$$

When computing the section-topic variational parameters we follow the proof of the lower bound which was derived by Kim et al. (2013). This lower bound, which is looser than the original VB Evidence Lower Bound (ELBO), allows for the batch VB approach to be used with asymmetric priors. More specifically, given the document-topic variational parameter γ_{dk} in the E step of our online VB approach the update for the section-topic variational parameter γ_{sk} becomes:

$$\gamma_{sk} = \alpha_s \left(\frac{\gamma_{dk}}{\sum_k \gamma_{dk}} \right) + \sum_w n_w^s \, \phi_{wk}^s \qquad (3)$$

3 Online PLTM with multi-level Dirichlet Priors

Given an aligned multilingual document tuple, PLTM assumes that: (1) there exists a single tuple-specific distribution across topics and (2) sets of language specific topic-word distributions. Each word is generated from a language- and topic-specific multinomial distribution φ_k^l as selected by the topic assignment variable z_n^l:

$$w_n^l \sim p \left(w_n^l \mid z_n^l, \varphi_k^l \right) \qquad (4)$$

We extend this model by introducing sections specific topic distributions θ_s across the different languages in the tuple which are coupled by the tuple specific document-topic distribution θ_d.

Given a collection of document tuples d where each tuple contains l documents that are translations of each other in different languages, mlhPLTM assumes the following generative process. For each language l in the collection the model first generates a set of $k \in \{1, 2, ..., K\}$ topic-word distribu-

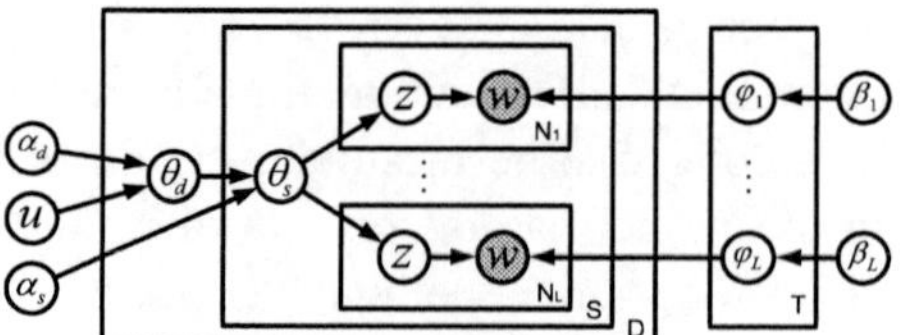

Figure 2: mlhPLTM: Graphical model representation.

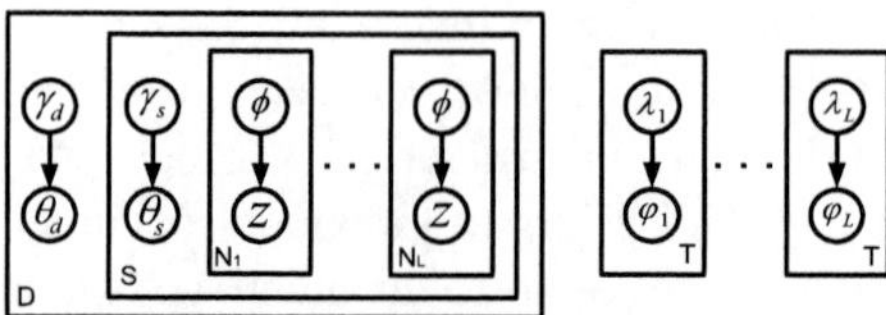

Figure 3: mlhPLTM: Graphical representation of the free variational parameters for the online VB approximation.

tions, φ_k^l which are drawn from a Dirichlet prior with language specific hyperparameter β^l: $\varphi_k^l \sim Dirichlet(\beta^l)$. For each document d^l with s_d sections in tuple d, mlhPLTM then assumes the following generative process:

- Choose $\theta_d \sim Dir.(\alpha_d)$
- For each section s_d in document tuple d:
- Choose $\theta_s \sim Dir.(\alpha_s \theta_d)$
  - For each language l in section s:
    * For each word w in section s_d^l:
      · Choose a topic $z \sim Multi.(\theta_s^l)$
      · Choose a word $w \sim Multi.(\varphi_z^l)$

Figure 2 shows the graphical representation of mlhPLTM. The free variational parameters for the online VB approximation of the posteriors are shown in Figure 3.

4 Modeling Sections in Scientific Articles

We explore the ability of mlhLDA to model variations across document sections found in scientific articles using a collection of journal articles from the Astrophysics Data System (ADS) (Kurtz et al., 2000). Our collection consists of 130k training articles (888,346 sections) and a held-out set of 8,078 articles (54,502 sections). Figure 4 shows an example mlhLDA representation of an ApJ article with 100 topics. Shown on the top is the inferred topic representation of the whole document (θ_d) which, in the mlhLDA model, serves as a prior for the section-topic distributions (θ_s). Shown on the bottom are ex-

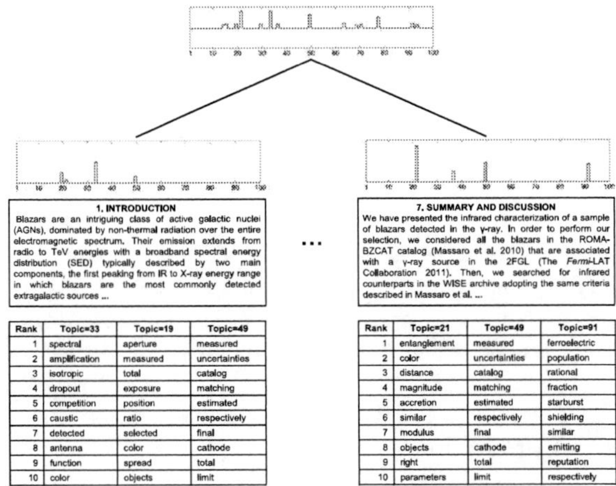

1. INTRODUCTION

Blazars are an intriguing class of active galactic nuclei (AGNs), dominated by non-thermal radiation over the entire electromagnetic spectrum. Their emission extends from radio to TeV energies with a broadband spectral energy distribution (SED) typically described by two main components, the first peaking from IR to X-ray energy range in which blazars are the most commonly detected extragalactic sources ...

Rank	Topic=33	Topic=19	Topic=49
1	spectral	aperture	measured
2	amplification	measured	uncertainties
3	isotropic	total	catalog
4	dropout	exposure	matching
5	competition	position	estimated
6	caustic	ratio	respectively
7	detected	selected	final
8	antenna	color	cathode
9	function	spread	total
10	color	objects	limit

7. SUMMARY AND DISCUSSION

We have presented the infrared characterization of a sample of blazars detected in the γ-ray. In order to perform our selection, we considered all the blazars in the ROMA-BZCAT catalog (Massaro et al. 2010) that are associated with a γ-ray source in the 2FGL (The *Fermi*-LAT Collaboration 2011). Then, we searched for infrared counterparts in the WISE archive adopting the same criteria described in Massaro et al. ...

Rank	Topic=21	Topic=49	Topic=91
1	entanglement	measured	ferroelectric
2	color	uncertainties	population
3	distance	catalog	rational
4	magnitude	matching	fraction
5	accretion	estimated	starburst
6	similar	respectively	shielding
7	modulus	final	similar
8	objects	cathode	emitting
9	right	total	reputation
10	parameters	limit	respectively

Figure 4: mlhLDA representation of the ApJ article "Infrared Colors of the Gamma-Ray Detected Blazers".

amples of 2 article sections (out of 7), their inferred topic distributions along with the top 10 words for each of the top 3 section topics.

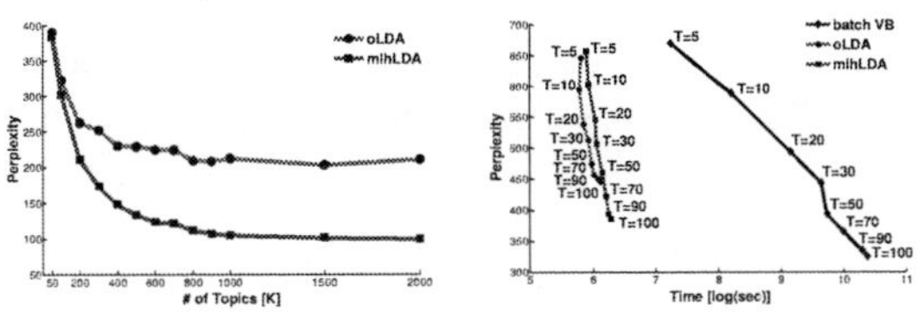

Figure 5: oLDA vs. mlhLDA: perplexity comparison (left); speed vs. perplexity comparisons with batch VB (right).

The left side of Figure 5 shows the held-out perplexity comparison between oLDA and mlhLDA across 13 different topic configurations. For this set of experiments we used the above training set of 130k articles and the set of 8,078 held-out articles. From these comparisons we clearly see the advantage of using the multi-level Dirchlet prior structure. Another way of evaluating topic models is through an extrinsic evaluation task which was not available for this collection. In the case of oLDA, article sections were treated as individual documents. In the original oLDA[1] implementation the per document concentration parameter α_d was set to $\frac{1}{K}$ which we also use in our case for both the symmetric θ_d and asymmetric θ_s (same goes for PLTM

and mlhPLTM). Since in our case we perform relative comparison between oLDA and mlhLDA we weren't concerned with experimenting with different concentration parameters but we rather used the default one implemented in oLDA.

With a random subset of 10k training and 1k held-out articles we compared the performance of oLDA and mlhLDA with the original batch VB[2] implementation of Blei et al. (2003). Unlike the implementations of oLDA and mlhLDA which are written in Python the original VB algorithm is written in C and requires multiple iterations over the whole collection. The right side of Figure 5 shows the speed (in natural log scale) vs. perplexity comparison across the three models.

5 Modeling and Retrieving Speeches in Europarl Sessions

We compared the modeling performance of oPLTM and mlhPLTM on a subset of the English-Spanish Europarl collection (Koehn, 2005). The subset consists of ∼64k training pairs of English-Spanish speeches that are translations of each other which originate from 374 sessions of the European Parliament (Europarl) and a test set of ∼14k speech translation pairs from 112 sessions. With oPLTM we modeled individual speech pairs while with mlh-PLTM we utilized the session hierarchy and modeled pairs of speeches as document sections. Comparisons were performed intrinsically (using perplexity) and extrinsically on a cross-language information retrieval (CLIR) task. This task, along with the Europarl subset, have been previously defined by Mimno et al. (2009) and used across other publications (Platt et al., 2010; Krstovski and Smith, 2013). Given a query English speech, the CLIR task is to retrieve its Spanish translation equivalent. It involves performing comparison across topic representations of all Spanish speeches using Jensen-Shannon divergence and sorting the results. Models are evaluated using precision at rank one (P@1). Figure 6 shows the CLIR task performance comparisons results using 13 different topic configurations. We performed comparisons across three different settings of the concentration parameters α_d and α_s ($\alpha_d=\alpha_s=\frac{1}{K}$, 0.4 and 1.0).

---

[1] http://www.cs.princeton.edu/~mdhoffma

[2] http://www.cs.princeton.edu/~blei/lda-c

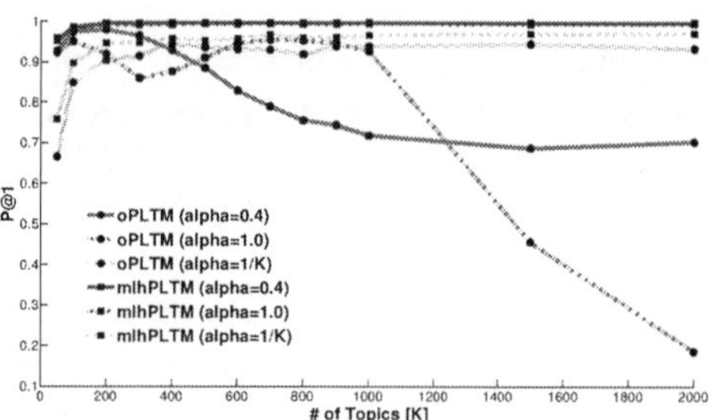

Figure 6: oPLTM vs. mlhPLTM: Performance comparison on the CLIR task using chronological ordering of sessions across different hyperparameter settings, $\alpha_d=\alpha_s=\frac{1}{K}$, 0.4 and 1.0 .

Across the different concentration parameter values and across the 13 different topic configurations we observe that the performance of oPLTM fluctuates as we increase the numbers of topics. On the other hand, across the three different concentration parameter settings, mlhPLTM performance is very steady and tends to increase with the number of topics. Across the different topic configurations both models provide the best performance with $\alpha_d = \alpha_s = 0.4$. Setting the concentration parameters to $\frac{1}{K}$ gives the overall worst performance.

In our initial experiments we unintentionally reordered our set of training Europarl sessions based on two digit years which was different from the experimental setup in (Mimno et al., 2009) and (Krstovski and Smith, 2013) where the order of the presentation data (Europarl speeches) was chronological. This emphasized the fact that in online VB, order of presentation of documents plays an important role especially in the training step where the model learns the per topic-word distributions. Figure 7 shows the performance comparison results between oPLTM and mlhPLTM when documents in the training and test steps are ordered numerically. In our initial experimental setup concentration parameters where set to $\alpha_d = \alpha_s = \frac{1}{K}$. To the left is the perplexity comparison between the two models. The CLIR task performance comparisons results are shown on the right. Unordered mlhPLTM achieves high P@1 after 2,000 topics. While it takes much longer in terms of the number of topics unordered mlhPLTM ultimately achieves similar performance results as ordered mlhPLTM.

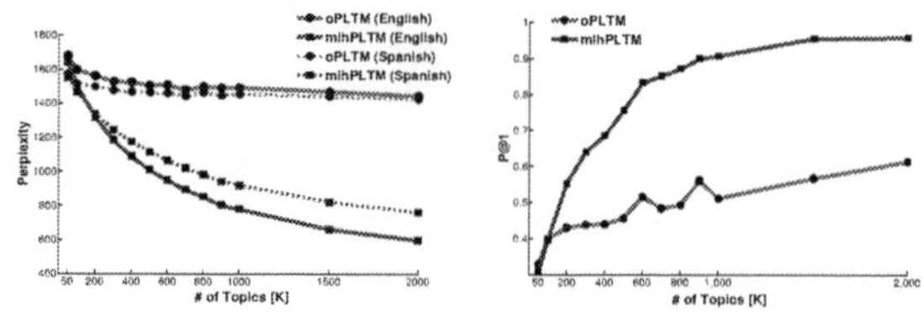

Figure 7: oPLTM vs. mlhPLTM: perplexity comparison (left); performance comparison on the CLIR task (right). Documents were presented out of chronological order and thus performance is lower, especially for oPLTM.

6 Conclusion

We presented online topic models with multi-level Dirichlet prior structure that provide better modeling of topical variations across document sections in mono- and multilingual collections. We showed that documents with rich sub-document level structure could be modeled with higher likelihood compared to regular online LDA and PLTM models while offering the same efficiency. Furthermore on the task of retrieving document translations we showed that mlhPLTM achieves significantly better retrieval results compared to online PLTM.

Acknowledgments

This work was supported in part by the Harvard-Smithsonian CfA predoctoral fellowship, in part by the Center for Intelligent Information Retrieval and in part by NSF grant #IIS-0910884. Any opinions, findings and conclusions or recommendations expressed in this material are those of the authors and do not necessarily reflect those of the sponsor.

References

David M. Blei, Andrew Y. Ng, and Michael I. Jordan. 2003. Latent Dirichlet allocation. *JMLR*, 3:993–1022.

T. L. Griffiths and M. Steyvers. 2004. Finding scientific topics. *Proceedings of the National Academy of Sciences*, 101(Suppl. 1):5228–5235.

Matthew Hoffman, David Blei, and Francis Bach. 2010. Online learning for latent Dirichlet allocation. In *NIPS*, pages 856–864.

Shoaib Jameel and Wai Lam. 2013. An unsupervised topic segmentation model incorporating word order. In *SIGIR*, pages 203–212.

Do-Kyum Kim, Geoffrey Voelker, and Lawrence K. Saul. 2013. A variational approximation for topic modeling of hierarchical corpora. In *ICML*, pages 55–63.

Philipp Koehn. 2005. Europarl: A parallel corpus for statistical machine translation. In *MT Summit*, pages 79–86.

Kriste Krstovski and David A. Smith. 2013. Online polylingual topic models for fast document translation detection. In *WMT*, pages 252–261.

Michael J. Kurtz, Guenther Eichhorn, Alberto Accomazzi, Carolyn S. Grant, Stephen S. Murray, and Joyce M. Watson. 2000. The nasa astrophysics data system: Overview. *Astronomy and Astrophysics Supplement Series*, 143:41–59.

David Mimno, Hanna Wallach, Jason Naradowsky, David A. Smith, and Andrew McCallum. 2009. Polylingual topic models. In *EMNLP*, pages 880–889.

Thomas P. Minka. 2000. Estimating a dirichlet distribution. Technical report, MIT.

John Platt, Kristina Toutanova, and Wen tau Yih. 2010. Translingual document representations from discriminative projections. In *EMNLP*, pages 251–261.

Hanna M. Wallach, David Mimno, and Andrew McCallum. 2009. Rethinking LDA: Why priors matter. In *NIPS*, pages 1973–1981.

Hanna M. Wallach. 2008. *Structured Topic Models for Language*. Ph.D. thesis, University of Cambridge.

Xuerui Wang, Andrew McCallum, and Xing Wei. 2007. Topical n-grams: Phrase and topic discovery, with an application to information retrieval. In *ICDM*, pages 697–702.

STransE: a novel embedding model of entities and relationships in knowledge bases

Dat Quoc Nguyen[1]**, Kairit Sirts**[1]**, Lizhen Qu**[2] **and Mark Johnson**[1]

[1] Department of Computing, Macquarie University, Sydney, Australia
`dat.nguyen@students.mq.edu.au, {kairit.sirts, mark.johnson}@mq.edu.au`
[2] NICTA, ACT 2601, Australia
`lizhen.qu@nicta.com.au`

Abstract

Knowledge bases of real-world facts about entities and their relationships are useful resources for a variety of natural language processing tasks. However, because knowledge bases are typically incomplete, it is useful to be able to perform *link prediction*, i.e., predict whether a relationship not in the knowledge base is likely to be true. This paper combines insights from several previous link prediction models into a new embedding model *STransE* that represents each entity as a low-dimensional vector, and each relation by two matrices and a translation vector. STransE is a simple combination of the SE and TransE models, but it obtains better link prediction performance on two benchmark datasets than previous embedding models. Thus, STransE can serve as a new baseline for the more complex models in the link prediction task.

1 Introduction

Knowledge bases (KBs), such as WordNet (Fellbaum, 1998), YAGO (Suchanek et al., 2007), Freebase (Bollacker et al., 2008) and DBpedia (Lehmann et al., 2015), represent relationships between entities as triples (head entity, relation, tail entity). Even very large knowledge bases are still far from complete (Socher et al., 2013; West et al., 2014). *Link prediction* or *knowledge base completion* systems (Nickel et al., 2015) predict which triples not in a knowledge base are likely to be true (Taskar et al., 2004; Bordes et al., 2011). A variety of different kinds of information is potentially useful here,

including information extracted from external corpora (Riedel et al., 2013; Wang et al., 2014a) and the other relationships that hold between the entities (Angeli and Manning, 2013; Zhao et al., 2015). For example, Toutanova et al. (2015) used information from the external ClueWeb-12 corpus to significantly enhance performance.

While integrating a wide variety of information sources can produce excellent results, there are several reasons for studying simpler models that directly optimize a score function for the triples in a knowledge base, such as the one presented here. First, additional information sources might not be available, e.g., for knowledge bases for specialized domains. Second, models that don't exploit external resources are simpler and thus typically much faster to train than the more complex models using additional information. Third, the more complex models that exploit external information are typically extensions of these simpler models, and are often initialized with parameters estimated by such simpler models, so improvements to the simpler models should yield corresponding improvements to the more complex models as well.

Embedding models for KB completion associate entities and/or relations with dense feature vectors or matrices. Such models obtain state-of-the-art performance (Nickel et al., 2011; Bordes et al., 2011; Bordes et al., 2012; Bordes et al., 2013; Socher et al., 2013; Wang et al., 2014b; Guu et al., 2015) and generalize to large KBs (Krompa et al., 2015). Table 1 summarizes a number of prominent embedding models for KB completion.

Let (h, r, t) represent a triple. In all of the models

Proceedings of NAACL-HLT 2016, pages 460–466,
San Diego, California, June 12-17, 2016. ©2016 Association for Computational Linguistics

Model	Score function $f_r(h, t)$	Opt.
SE	$\|\mathbf{W}_{r,1}\mathbf{h} - \mathbf{W}_{r,2}\mathbf{t}\|_{\ell_{1/2}}$; $\mathbf{W}_{r,1}, \mathbf{W}_{r,2} \in \mathbb{R}^{k \times k}$	SGD
Unstructured	$\|\mathbf{h} - \mathbf{t}\|_{\ell_{1/2}}$	SGD
TransE	$\|\mathbf{h} + \mathbf{r} - \mathbf{t}\|_{\ell_{1/2}}$; $\mathbf{r} \in \mathbb{R}^k$	SGD
DISTMULT	$\mathbf{h}^\top \mathbf{W}_r \mathbf{t}$; $\mathbf{W}_r$ is a diagonal matrix $\in \mathbb{R}^{k \times k}$	AdaGrad
NTN	$\mathbf{u}_r^\top \, tanh(\mathbf{h}^\top \mathbf{M}_r \mathbf{t} + \mathbf{W}_{r,1}\mathbf{h} + \mathbf{W}_{r,2}\mathbf{t} + \mathbf{b}_r)$; $\mathbf{u}_r, \mathbf{b}_r \in \mathbb{R}^d$; $\mathbf{M}_r \in \mathbb{R}^{k \times k \times d}$; $\mathbf{W}_{r,1}, \mathbf{W}_{r,2} \in \mathbb{R}^{d \times k}$	L-BFGS
TransH	$\|(\mathbf{I} - \mathbf{r}_p\mathbf{r}_p^\top)\mathbf{h} + \mathbf{r} - (\mathbf{I} - \mathbf{r}_p\mathbf{r}_p^\top)\mathbf{t}\|_{\ell_{1/2}}$; $\mathbf{r}_p, \mathbf{r} \in \mathbb{R}^k$; $\mathbf{I}$: Identity matrix size $k \times k$	SGD
TransD	$\|(\mathbf{I} + \mathbf{r}_p\mathbf{h}_p^\top)\mathbf{h} + \mathbf{r} - (\mathbf{I} + \mathbf{r}_p\mathbf{t}_p^\top)\mathbf{t}\|_{\ell_{1/2}}$; $\mathbf{r}_p, \mathbf{r} \in \mathbb{R}^d$; $\mathbf{h}_p, \mathbf{t}_p \in \mathbb{R}^k$; $\mathbf{I}$: Identity matrix size $d \times k$	AdaDelta
TransR	$\|\mathbf{W}_r\mathbf{h} + \mathbf{r} - \mathbf{W}_r\mathbf{t}\|_{\ell_{1/2}}$; $\mathbf{W}_r \in \mathbb{R}^{d \times k}$; $\mathbf{r} \in \mathbb{R}^d$	SGD
Our STransE	$\|\mathbf{W}_{r,1}\mathbf{h} + \mathbf{r} - \mathbf{W}_{r,2}\mathbf{t}\|_{\ell_{1/2}}$; $\mathbf{W}_{r,1}, \mathbf{W}_{r,2} \in \mathbb{R}^{k \times k}$; $\mathbf{r} \in \mathbb{R}^k$	SGD

Table 1: The score functions $f_r(h, t)$ and the optimization methods (Opt.) of several prominent embedding models for KB completion. In all of these the entities h and t are represented by vectors $\mathbf{h}$ and $\mathbf{t} \in \mathbb{R}^k$ respectively.

discussed here, the head entity h and the tail entity t are represented by vectors $\mathbf{h}$ and $\mathbf{t} \in \mathbb{R}^k$ respectively. The *Unstructured* model (Bordes et al., 2012) assumes that $\mathbf{h} \approx \mathbf{t}$. As the Unstructured model does not take the relationship r into account, it cannot distinguish different relation types. The *Structured Embedding* (SE) model (Bordes et al., 2011) extends the unstructured model by assuming that h and t are similar only in a relation-dependent subspace. It represents each relation r with two matrices $\mathbf{W}_{r,1}$ and $\mathbf{W}_{r,2} \in \mathbb{R}^{k \times k}$, which are chosen so that $\mathbf{W}_{r,1}\mathbf{h} \approx \mathbf{W}_{r,2}\mathbf{t}$. The *TransE* model (Bordes et al., 2013) is inspired by models such as Word2Vec (Mikolov et al., 2013) where relationships between words often correspond to translations in latent feature space. The TransE model represents each relation r by a translation vector $\mathbf{r} \in \mathbb{R}^k$, which is chosen so that $\mathbf{h} + \mathbf{r} \approx \mathbf{t}$.

The primary contribution of this paper is that two very simple relation-prediction models, SE and TransE, can be combined into a single model, which we call *STransE*. Specifically, we use relation-specific matrices $\mathbf{W}_{r,1}$ and $\mathbf{W}_{r,2}$ as in the SE model to identify the relation-dependent aspects of both h and t, and use a vector $\mathbf{r}$ as in the TransE model to describe the relationship between h and t in this subspace. Specifically, our new KB completion model STransE chooses $\mathbf{W}_{r,1}$, $\mathbf{W}_{r,2}$ and $\mathbf{r}$ so that $\mathbf{W}_{r,1}\mathbf{h} + \mathbf{r} \approx \mathbf{W}_{r,2}\mathbf{t}$. That is, a TransE-style relationship holds in some relation-dependent subspace, and crucially, this subspace may involve very different projections of the head h and tail t. So $\mathbf{W}_{r,1}$ and $\mathbf{W}_{r,2}$ can highlight, suppress, or even change the

sign of, relation-specific attributes of h and t. For example, for the "purchases" relationship, certain attributes of individuals h (e.g., age, gender, marital status) are presumably strongly correlated with very different attributes of objects t (e.g., sports car, washing machine and the like).

As we show below, STransE performs better than the SE and TransE models and other state-of-the-art link prediction models on two standard link prediction datasets WN18 and FB15k, so it can serve as a new baseline for KB completion. We expect that the STransE will also be able to serve as the basis for extended models that exploit a wider variety of information sources, just as TransE does.

2 Our approach

Let $\mathcal{E}$ denote the set of entities and $\mathcal{R}$ the set of relation types. For each triple (h, r, t), where $h, t \in \mathcal{E}$ and $r \in \mathcal{R}$, the STransE model defines a *score function* $f_r(h, t)$ of its implausibility. Our goal is to choose f such that the score $f_r(h, t)$ of a plausible triple (h, r, t) is smaller than the score $f_{r'}(h', t')$ of an implausible triple (h', r', t'). We define the STransE score function f as follows:

$$f_r(h, t) \;=\; \|\mathbf{W}_{r,1}\mathbf{h} + \mathbf{r} - \mathbf{W}_{r,2}\mathbf{t}\|_{\ell_{1/2}}$$

using either the ℓ_1 or the ℓ_2-norm (the choice is made using validation data; in our experiments we found that the ℓ_1 norm gave slightly better results). To learn the vectors and matrices we minimize the following margin-based objective function:

$$\mathcal{L} = \sum_{\substack{(h,r,t)\in\mathcal{G} \\ (h',r,t')\in\mathcal{G}'_{(h,r,t)}}} [\gamma + f_r(h,t) - f_r(h',t')]_+$$

where $[x]_+ = \max(0, x)$, γ is the margin hyper-parameter, $\mathcal{G}$ is the training set consisting of correct triples, and $\mathcal{G}'_{(h,r,t)} = \{(h',r,t) \mid h' \in \mathcal{E}, (h',r,t) \notin \mathcal{G}\} \cup \{(h,r,t') \mid t' \in \mathcal{E}, (h,r,t') \notin \mathcal{G}\}$ is the set of incorrect triples generated by corrupting a correct triple $(h,r,t) \in \mathcal{G}$.

We use Stochastic Gradient Descent (SGD) to minimize $\mathcal{L}$, and impose the following constraints during training: $\|\mathbf{h}\|_2 \leqslant 1$, $\|\mathbf{r}\|_2 \leqslant 1$, $\|\mathbf{t}\|_2 \leqslant 1$, $\|\mathbf{W}_{r,1}\mathbf{h}\|_2 \leqslant 1$ and $\|\mathbf{W}_{r,2}\mathbf{t}\|_2 \leqslant 1$.

3 Related work

Table 1 summarizes related embedding models for link prediction and KB completion. The models differ in the score functions $f_r(h,t)$ and the algorithms used to optimize the margin-based objective function, e.g., SGD, AdaGrad (Duchi et al., 2011), AdaDelta (Zeiler, 2012) and L-BFGS (Liu and Nocedal, 1989).

DISTMULT (Yang et al., 2015) is based on a Bilinear model (Nickel et al., 2011; Bordes et al., 2012; Jenatton et al., 2012) where each relation is represented by a diagonal rather than a full matrix. The neural tensor network (NTN) model (Socher et al., 2013) uses a bilinear tensor operator to represent each relation. Similar quadratic forms are used to model entities and relations in KG2E (He et al., 2015) and TATEC (Garcia-Duran et al., 2015b).

The TransH model (Wang et al., 2014b) associates each relation with a relation-specific hyperplane and uses a projection vector to project entity vectors onto that hyperplane. TransD (Ji et al., 2015) and TransR/CTransR (Lin et al., 2015b) extend the TransH model using two projection vectors and a matrix to project entity vectors into a relation-specific space, respectively. TransD learns a relation-role specific mapping just as STransE, but represents this mapping by projection vectors rather than full matrices, as in STransE. Thus STransE can be viewed as an extension of the TransR model, where head and tail entities are associated with their own project matrices, rather than using the same matrix for both, as in TransR and CTransR.

Dataset	#E	#R	#Train	#Valid	#Test
WN18	40,943	18	141,442	5,000	5,000
FB15k	14,951	1,345	483,142	50,000	59,071

Table 2: Statistics of the experimental datasets used in this study (and previous works). #E is the number of entities, #R is the number of relation types, and #Train, #Valid and #Test are the numbers of triples in the training, validation and test sets, respectively.

Recently, Lao et al. (2011), Neelakantan et al. (2015), Gardner and Mitchell (2015), Luo et al. (2015), Lin et al. (2015a), Garcia-Duran et al. (2015a) and Guu et al. (2015) showed that relation paths between entities in KBs provide richer information and improve the relationship prediction. Nickel et al. (2015) reviews other approaches for learning from KBs and multi-relational data.

4 Experiments

For link prediction evaluation, we conduct experiments and compare the performance of our STransE model with published results on the benchmark WN18 and FB15k datasets (Bordes et al., 2013). Information about these datasets is given in Table 2.

4.1 Task and evaluation protocol

The link prediction task (Bordes et al., 2011; Bordes et al., 2012; Bordes et al., 2013) predicts the head or tail entity given the relation type and the other entity, i.e. predicting h given $(?, r, t)$ or predicting t given $(h, r, ?)$ where ? denotes the missing element. The results are evaluated using the ranking induced by the score function $f_r(h,t)$ on test triples.

For each test triple (h, r, t), we corrupted it by replacing either h or t by each of the possible entities in turn, and then rank these candidates in ascending order of their implausibility value computed by the score function. Following the protocol described in Bordes et al. (2013), we remove any corrupted triples that appear in the knowledge base, to avoid cases where a correct corrupted triple might be ranked higher than the test triple. We report the mean rank and the Hits@10 (i.e., the proportion of test triples in which the target entity was ranked in the top 10 predictions) for each model. Lower mean rank or higher Hits@10 indicates better link prediction performance.

Following TransR/CTransR (Lin et al., 2015b), TransD (Ji et al., 2015), TATEC (Garcia-Duran et al., 2015b), RTransE (Garcia-Duran et al., 2015a) and PTransE (Lin et al., 2015a), we used the entity and relation vectors produced by TransE (Bordes et al., 2013) to initialize the entity and relation vectors in STransE, and we initialized the relation matrices with identity matrices. Following Wang et al. (2014b), Lin et al. (2015b), He et al. (2015), Ji et al. (2015) and Lin et al. (2015a), we applied the "*Bernoulli*" trick for generating head or tail entities when sampling incorrect triples. We ran SGD for 2,000 epochs to estimate the model parameters. Following Bordes et al. (2013) we used a grid search on validation set to choose either the l_1 or l_2 norm in the score function f, as well as to set the SGD learning rate $\lambda \in \{0.0001, 0.0005, 0.001, 0.005, 0.01\}$, the margin hyper-parameter $\gamma \in \{1, 3, 5\}$ and the number of vector dimensions $k \in \{50, 100\}$. The lowest mean rank on the validation set was obtained when using the l_1 norm in f on both WN18 and FB15k, and when $\lambda = 0.0005, \gamma = 5$, and $k = 50$ for WN18, and $\lambda = 0.0001, \gamma = 1$, and $k = 100$ for FB15k.

4.2 Main results

Table 3 compares the link prediction results of our STransE model with results reported in prior work, using the same experimental setup. The first twelve rows report the performance of models that do not exploit information about alternative paths between head and tail entities. The next two rows report results of the RTransE and PTransE models, which are extensions of the TransE model that exploit information about relation paths. The last row presents results for the log-linear model Node+LinkFeat (Toutanova and Chen, 2015) which makes use of textual mentions derived from the large external ClueWeb-12 corpus.

It is clear that Node+LinkFeat with the additional external corpus information obtained best results. In future work we plan to extend the STransE model to incorporate such additional information. Table 3 also shows that models RTransE and PTransE employing path information achieve better results than models that do not use such information. In terms of models not exploiting path information or external information, the STransE model scores better than

Method	WN18		FB15k	
	MR	H10	MR	H10
SE (Bordes et al., 2011)	985	80.5	162	39.8
Unstructured (Bordes et al., 2012)	304	38.2	979	6.3
TransE (Bordes et al., 2013)	251	89.2	125	47.1
TransH (Wang et al., 2014b)	303	86.7	87	64.4
TransR (Lin et al., 2015b)	225	92.0	77	68.7
CTransR (Lin et al., 2015b)	218	92.3	75	70.2
KG2E (He et al., 2015)	348	93.2	59	74.0
TransD (Ji et al., 2015)	212	92.2	91	77.3
TATEC (Garcia-Duran et al., 2015b)	-	-	**58**	76.7
NTN (Socher et al., 2013)	-	66.1^+	-	41.4^+
DISTMULT (Yang et al., 2015)	-	94.2^+	-	57.7^+
Our STransE model	**206**	**93.4**	69	**79.7**
RTransE (Garcia-Duran et al., 2015a)	-	-	**50**	76.2
PTransE (Lin et al., 2015a)	-	-	58	84.6
NLFeat (Toutanova and Chen, 2015)	-	**94.3**	-	**87.0**

Table 3: Link prediction results. MR and H10 denote evaluation metrics of mean rank and Hits@10 (in %), respectively. "NLFeat" abbreviates Node+LinkFeat. The results for NTN (Socher et al., 2013) listed in this table are taken from Yang et al. (2015) since NTN was originally evaluated on different datasets. The results marked with $^+$ are obtained using the optimal hyper-parameters chosen to optimize Hits@10 on the validation set; trained in this manner, STransE obtains a mean rank of 244 and Hits@10 of **94.7**% on WN18, while producing the same results on FB15k.

the other models on WN18 and produces the highest Hits@10 score on FB15k. Compared to the closely related models SE, TransE, TransR, CTransR and TransD, STransE does better than these models on both WN18 and FB15k.

Following Bordes et al. (2013), Table 4 analyzes Hits@10 results on FB15k with respect to the relation categories defined as follows: for each relation type r, we computed the averaged number a_h of heads h for a pair (r, t) and the averaged number a_t of tails t for a pair (h, r). If $a_h < 1.5$ and $a_t < 1.5$, then r is labeled **1-1**. If $a_h \geq 1.5$ and $a_t < 1.5$, then r is labeled **M-1**. If $a_h < 1.5$ and $a_t \geq 1.5$, then r is labeled as **1-M**. If $a_h \geq 1.5$ and $a_t \geq 1.5$, then r is labeled as **M-M**. 1.4%, 8.9%, 14.6% and 75.1% of the test triples belong to a relation type classified as **1-1**, **1-M**, **M-1** and **M-M**, respectively.

Table 4 shows that in comparison to prior models not using path information, STransE obtains highest Hits@10 result for **M-M** relation category at $(80.1\% + 83.1\%)/2 = 81.6\%$. In addition, STransE

Method	Predicting head h				Predicting tail t			
	1-1	1-M	M-1	M-M	1-1	1-M	M-1	M-M
SE	35.6	62.6	17.2	37.5	34.9	14.6	68.3	41.3
Unstr.	34.5	2.5	6.1	6.6	34.3	4.2	1.9	6.6
TransE	43.7	65.7	18.2	47.2	43.7	19.7	66.7	50.0
TransH	66.8	87.6	28.7	64.5	65.5	39.8	83.3	67.2
TransR	78.8	89.2	34.1	69.2	79.2	37.4	90.4	72.1
CTransR	81.5	89.0	34.7	71.2	80.8	38.6	90.1	73.8
KG2E	**92.3**	94.6	**66.0**	69.6	**92.6**	**67.9**	**94.4**	73.4
TransD	86.1	**95.5**	39.8	78.5	85.4	50.6	**94.4**	81.2
TATEC	79.3	93.2	42.3	77.2	78.5	51.5	92.7	80.7
STransE	82.8	94.2	50.4	**80.1**	82.4	56.9	93.4	**83.1**

Table 4: Hits@10 (in %) by the relation category on FB15k. "Unstr." abbreviates Unstructured.

also performs better than TransD for **1-M** and **M-1** relation categories. We believe the improved performance of the STransE model is due to its use of full matrices, rather than just projection vectors as in TransD. This permits STransE to model diverse and complex relation categories (such as **1-M**, **M-1** and especially **M-M**) better than TransD and other similiar models. However, STransE is not as good as TransD for the **1-1** relations. Perhaps the extra parameters in STransE hurt performance in this case (note that 1-1 relations are relatively rare, so STransE does better overall).

5   Conclusion and future work

This paper presented a new embedding model for link prediction and KB completion. Our STransE combines insights from several simpler embedding models, specifically the Structured Embedding model (Bordes et al., 2011) and the TransE model (Bordes et al., 2013), by using a low-dimensional vector and two projection matrices to represent each relation. STransE, while being conceptually simple, produces highly competitive results on standard link prediction evaluations, and scores better than the embedding-based models it builds on. Thus it is a suitable candidate for serving as future baseline for more complex models in the link prediction task.

In future work we plan to extend STransE to exploit relation path information in knowledge bases, in a manner similar to Lin et al. (2015a), Garcia-Duran et al. (2015a) or Guu et al. (2015).

Acknowledgments

This research was supported by a Google award through the Natural Language Understanding Focused Program, and under the Australian Research Council's *Discovery Projects* funding scheme (project number DP160102156).

NICTA is funded by the Australian Government through the Department of Communications and the Australian Research Council through the ICT Centre of Excellence Program. The first author is supported by an International Postgraduate Research Scholarship and a NICTA NRPA Top-Up Scholarship.

References

Gabor Angeli and Christopher Manning. 2013. Philosophers are Mortal: Inferring the Truth of Unseen Facts. In *Proceedings of the Seventeenth Conference on Computational Natural Language Learning*, pages 133–142.

Kurt Bollacker, Colin Evans, Praveen Paritosh, Tim Sturge, and Jamie Taylor. 2008. Freebase: A Collaboratively Created Graph Database for Structuring Human Knowledge. In *Proceedings of the 2008 ACM SIGMOD International Conference on Management of Data*, pages 1247–1250.

Antoine Bordes, Jason Weston, Ronan Collobert, and Yoshua Bengio. 2011. Learning Structured Embeddings of Knowledge Bases. In *Proceedings of the Twenty-Fifth AAAI Conference on Artificial Intelligence*, pages 301–306.

Antoine Bordes, Xavier Glorot, Jason Weston, and Yoshua Bengio. 2012. A Semantic Matching Energy Function for Learning with Multi-relational Data. *Machine Learning*, 94(2):233–259.

Antoine Bordes, Nicolas Usunier, Alberto Garcia-Duran, Jason Weston, and Oksana Yakhnenko. 2013. Translating Embeddings for Modeling Multi-relational Data. In *Advances in Neural Information Processing Systems 26*, pages 2787–2795.

John Duchi, Elad Hazan, and Yoram Singer. 2011. Adaptive Subgradient Methods for Online Learning and Stochastic Optimization. *The Journal of Machine Learning Research*, 12:2121–2159.

Christiane D. Fellbaum. 1998. *WordNet: An Electronic Lexical Database*. MIT Press.

Alberto Garcia-Duran, Antoine Bordes, and Nicolas Usunier. 2015a. Composing Relationships with Translations. In *Proceedings of the 2015 Conference on Empirical Methods in Natural Language Processing*, pages 286–290.

Alberto Garcia-Duran, Antoine Bordes, Nicolas Usunier, and Yves Grandvalet. 2015b. Combining Two And Three-Way Embeddings Models for Link Prediction in Knowledge Bases. *CoRR*, abs/1506.00999.

Matt Gardner and Tom Mitchell. 2015. Efficient and Expressive Knowledge Base Completion Using Subgraph Feature Extraction. In *Proceedings of the 2015 Conference on Empirical Methods in Natural Language Processing*, pages 1488–1498.

Kelvin Guu, John Miller, and Percy Liang. 2015. Traversing Knowledge Graphs in Vector Space. In *Proceedings of the 2015 Conference on Empirical Methods in Natural Language Processing*, pages 318–327.

Shizhu He, Kang Liu, Guoliang Ji, and Jun Zhao. 2015. Learning to Represent Knowledge Graphs with Gaussian Embedding. In *Proceedings of the 24th ACM International on Conference on Information and Knowledge Management*, pages 623–632.

Rodolphe Jenatton, Nicolas L. Roux, Antoine Bordes, and Guillaume R Obozinski. 2012. A latent factor model for highly multi-relational data. In *Advances in Neural Information Processing Systems 25*, pages 3167–3175.

Guoliang Ji, Shizhu He, Liheng Xu, Kang Liu, and Jun Zhao. 2015. Knowledge Graph Embedding via Dynamic Mapping Matrix. In *Proceedings of the 53rd Annual Meeting of the Association for Computational Linguistics and the 7th International Joint Conference on Natural Language Processing (Volume 1: Long Papers)*, pages 687–696.

Denis Krompa, Stephan Baier, and Volker Tresp. 2015. Type-Constrained Representation Learning in Knowledge Graphs. In *Proceedings of the 14th International Semantic Web Conference*, pages 640–655.

Ni Lao, Tom Mitchell, and William W. Cohen. 2011. Random Walk Inference and Learning in a Large Scale Knowledge Base. In *Proceedings of the Conference on Empirical Methods in Natural Language Processing*, pages 529–539.

Jens Lehmann, Robert Isele, Max Jakob, Anja Jentzsch, Dimitris Kontokostas, Pablo N. Mendes, Sebastian Hellmann, Mohamed Morsey, Patrick van Kleef, Sören Auer, and Christian Bizer. 2015. DBpedia - A Large-scale, Multilingual Knowledge Base Extracted from Wikipedia. *Semantic Web*, 6(2):167–195.

Yankai Lin, Zhiyuan Liu, Huanbo Luan, Maosong Sun, Siwei Rao, and Song Liu. 2015a. Modeling Relation Paths for Representation Learning of Knowledge Bases. In *Proceedings of the 2015 Conference on Empirical Methods in Natural Language Processing*, pages 705–714.

Yankai Lin, Zhiyuan Liu, Maosong Sun, Yang Liu, and Xuan Zhu. 2015b. Learning Entity and Relation Embeddings for Knowledge Graph Completion. In *Proceedings of the Twenty-Ninth AAAI Conference on Artificial Intelligence Learning*, pages 2181–2187.

D. C. Liu and J. Nocedal. 1989. On the Limited Memory BFGS Method for Large Scale Optimization. *Mathematical Programming*, 45(3):503–528.

Yuanfei Luo, Quan Wang, Bin Wang, and Li Guo. 2015. Context-Dependent Knowledge Graph Embedding. In *Proceedings of the 2015 Conference on Empirical Methods in Natural Language Processing*, pages 1656–1661.

Tomas Mikolov, Wen-tau Yih, and Geoffrey Zweig. 2013. Linguistic Regularities in Continuous Space Word Representations. In *Proceedings of the 2013 Conference of the North American Chapter of the Association for Computational Linguistics: Human Language Technologies*, pages 746–751.

Arvind Neelakantan, Benjamin Roth, and Andrew McCallum. 2015. Compositional Vector Space Models for Knowledge Base Completion. In *Proceedings of the 53rd Annual Meeting of the Association for Computational Linguistics and the 7th International Joint Conference on Natural Language Processing (Volume 1: Long Papers)*, pages 156–166.

Maximilian Nickel, Volker Tresp, and Hans-Peter Kriegel. 2011. A Three-Way Model for Collective Learning on Multi-Relational Data. In *Proceedings of the 28th International Conference on Machine Learning*, pages 809–816.

Maximilian Nickel, Kevin Murphy, Volker Tresp, and Evgeniy Gabrilovich. 2015. A Review of Relational Machine Learning for Knowledge Graphs. *Proceedings of the IEEE, to appear.*

Sebastian Riedel, Limin Yao, Andrew McCallum, and Benjamin M. Marlin. 2013. Relation Extraction with Matrix Factorization and Universal Schemas. In *Proceedings of the 2013 Conference of the North American Chapter of the Association for Computational Linguistics: Human Language Technologies*, pages 74–84.

Richard Socher, Danqi Chen, Christopher D Manning, and Andrew Ng. 2013. Reasoning With Neural Tensor Networks for Knowledge Base Completion. In *Advances in Neural Information Processing Systems 26*, pages 926–934.

Fabian M. Suchanek, Gjergji Kasneci, and Gerhard Weikum. 2007. YAGO: A Core of Semantic Knowledge. In *Proceedings of the 16th International Conference on World Wide Web*, pages 697–706.

Ben Taskar, Ming fai Wong, Pieter Abbeel, and Daphne Koller. 2004. Link Prediction in Relational Data. In

Advances in Neural Information Processing Systems 16, pages 659–666.

Kristina Toutanova and Danqi Chen. 2015. Observed Versus Latent Features for Knowledge Base and Text Inference. In *Proceedings of the 3rd Workshop on Continuous Vector Space Models and their Compositionality*, pages 57–66.

Kristina Toutanova, Danqi Chen, Patrick Pantel, Hoifung Poon, Pallavi Choudhury, and Michael Gamon. 2015. Representing Text for Joint Embedding of Text and Knowledge Bases. In *Proceedings of the 2015 Conference on Empirical Methods in Natural Language Processing*, pages 1499–1509.

Zhen Wang, Jianwen Zhang, Jianlin Feng, and Zheng Chen. 2014a. Knowledge Graph and Text Jointly Embedding. In *Proceedings of the 2014 Conference on Empirical Methods in Natural Language Processing (EMNLP)*, pages 1591–1601.

Zhen Wang, Jianwen Zhang, Jianlin Feng, and Zheng Chen. 2014b. Knowledge Graph Embedding by Translating on Hyperplanes. In *Proceedings of the Twenty-Eighth AAAI Conference on Artificial Intelligence*, pages 1112–1119.

Robert West, Evgeniy Gabrilovich, Kevin Murphy, Shaohua Sun, Rahul Gupta, and Dekang Lin. 2014. Knowledge Base Completion via Search-based Question Answering. In *Proceedings of the 23rd International Conference on World Wide Web*, pages 515–526.

Bishan Yang, Wen-tau Yih, Xiaodong He, Jianfeng Gao, and Li Deng. 2015. Embedding Entities and Relations for Learning and Inference in Knowledge Bases. In *Proceedings of the International Conference on Learning Representations*.

Matthew D. Zeiler. 2012. ADADELTA: An Adaptive Learning Rate Method. *CoRR*, abs/1212.5701.

Yu Zhao, Sheng Gao, Patrick Gallinari, and Jun Guo. 2015. Knowledge Base Completion by Learning Pairwise-Interaction Differentiated Embeddings. *Data Mining and Knowledge Discovery*, 29(5):1486–1504.

An Unsupervised Model of Orthographic Variation
for Historical Document Transcription

Dan Garrette
Computer Science & Engineering
University of Washington
dhg@cs.washington.edu

Hannah Alpert-Abrams
Comparative Literature Program
University of Texas at Austin
halperta@gmail.com

Abstract

Historical documents frequently exhibit extensive orthographic variation, including archaic spellings and obsolete shorthand. OCR tools typically seek to produce so-called *diplomatic* transcriptions that preserve these variants, but many end tasks require transcriptions with *normalized* orthography. In this paper, we present a novel joint transcription model that learns, unsupervised, a probabilistic mapping between modern orthography and that used in the document. Our system thus produces dual diplomatic and normalized transcriptions simultaneously, and achieves a 35% relative error reduction over a state-of-the-art OCR model on diplomatic transcription, and a 46% reduction on normalized transcription.

1 Introduction

Optical Character Recognition (OCR) for historical texts, a challenging problem due to unknown fonts and deteriorating documents, is made even more difficult by the fact that orthographic conventions including spelling, accent usage, and shorthands have not been consistent across the history of printing. For this reason, modern language models (LMs) yield poor performance when trying to recognize characters on the pages of these documents. Furthermore, transcription of the actual printed characters may not always be the most desirable output.

Greg (1950) describes two types of transcription: one that preserves variants and typographical errors, and another that records the *substantive* content, with this noise removed. Though in 1950 the substantive version was the norm, today these have become two distinct but equally valid tasks. *Diplomatic* transcription, the standard in contemporary OCR, preserves the variants of the document valuable to book historians and linguists. *Normalized* or modernized transcription recovers the substantive content, producing a text that adheres to modern standards. Normalized transcriptions are easier for users to read, and make large collections of historical texts indexable and searchable (Driscoll, 2006).

The current ideal for digital editions of historical texts has been described as a combination of diplomatic and normalized transcription (Pierazzo, 2014). This is generally achieved with a pipeline: first OCR is used to transcribe the document, then an (often manual) post-hoc normalization is performed. However, such a pipeline will result in cascading errors from OCR mistakes, and fails to make use of knowledge about modern language during the initial transcription. Additionally, post-processing tools are typically cumbersome language-specific, hand-built systems (Baron and Rayson, 2008; Burns, 2013; Hendrickx and Marquilhas, 2011).

In this work, we introduce a novel OCR model designed to jointly produce both diplomatic and normalized transcriptions. The model is an extension of Berg-Kirkpatrick et al.'s (2013) *Ocular*, the state of the art in historical OCR. Ocular's innovative ability to handle the material challenges of OCR (unknown fonts, uneven inking, etc.) depends on its use of a character n-gram LM. Our model improves the quality of Ocular's transcriptions by automatically learning a probabilistic mapping between the LM, which is trained on modern text, and the unique orthography of the document. This results in both an

Proceedings of NAACL-HLT 2016, pages 467–472,
San Diego, California, June 12-17, 2016. ©2016 Association for Computational Linguistics

improved orthographically-correct diplomatic transcription and a modern-style normalized transcription. To our knowledge, this represents the first OCR system that jointly produces both diplomatic and normalized transcriptions.

We evaluate our model on a multilingual collection of books exemplifying a high degree of orthographic variation. For diplomatic transcription, our unsupervised joint model achieves an error reduction of 35% over the baseline Ocular system without support for orthographic variation, and nearly matches the error rate of an approach proposed by earlier work that uses a hand-constructed ruleset of orthographic rewrites. However, for the new task of normalized transcription, we achieve a 46% error reduction over the baseline, as well as a 28% reduction over the hand-built ruleset approach.

2 Data

The *Primeros Libros* corpus dataset introduced in our previous work consists of multilingual (Spanish/Latin/Nahuatl) books printed in Mexico in the 1500s (Garrette et al., 2015). The original dataset includes gold diplomatic transcriptions of pages from five books of different time periods, regions, languages, and fonts. We additionally include two new monolingual Spanish *Primeros Libros* books annotated with both diplomatic and normalized transcriptions. Spanish-only texts were needed in order to find language-competent annotators skilled enough to create the more challenging normalized transcriptions. We used each of the seven books in isolation since they each have a different font. For each book, we used 20 pages for training and 10 for testing. For two of the books, an additional 10 pages were held out for tuning hyperparameters with grid search.

To produce the Spanish and Latin LMs, we used texts from Project Gutenberg; these documents were written during the target historical period, but all follow modernization standards including substitution for obsolete characters and expansion of shorthand. These texts were chosen because they are a realistic sample set that is freely and publicly available. In the Nahuatl case, scarce online resources made it necessary to supplement Project Gutenberg text with that from a private collection.

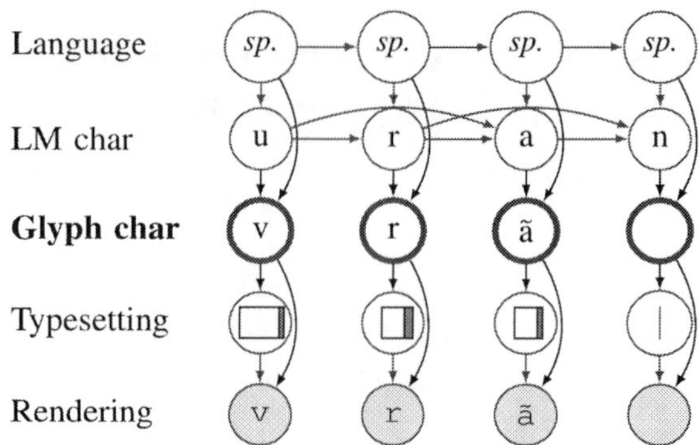

Figure 1: Our generative OCR model with the new *glyph* layer (bolded). The Spanish (*sp.*) n-gram language model (LM) generates a sequence of characters according to standard Spanish spellings, *uran* in this case, from the word *procurando* which may be written *procvrãdo*. Language-specific character-replacement probabilities are used to generate a *glyph char* from each LM char, producing *vrã* and a zero-width (elided) *n*. Finally, the model generates a bounding box and right-side padding (the typesetting) and a pixel-rendering of the glyph character.

3 Model

We extend Ocular, the generative model of Berg-Kirkpatrick et al. (2013), and its EM training procedure, to support our unsupervised approach to jointly modeling both diplomatic and normalized transcription. Ocular works by modeling the operation of a hand press in order to learn unknown fonts in the presence of the visual noise of the printing process: uneven inking and spacing in particular. Briefly, Ocular's generative story is as follows. First, a sequence of language states ℓ_i is generated according to $P^{\text{LANG}}(\ell_i \mid \ell_{i-1})$, where ℓ_{i-1} and ℓ_i may only differ on the start of a word. For each state, a character c_i is generated according to its language-specific n-gram LM: $P^{\text{CHAR}}_{\ell_i}(c_i \mid c_{i-n+1} \ldots c_{i-1})$. Next, a state's *typesetting* t_i, consisting of a character's bounding box, vertical offset, and between-character padding, is generated according to $P^{\text{TYPE}}(t_i \mid c_i)$. Finally, the character image is rendered as a pixel-matrix inside the bounding box: $P^{\text{REND}}(x_i \mid c_i, t_i)$.[1]

A major downside to the Ocular model is that ren-

---

[1] See previous work for fuller detail including how a typesetting is composed of its parts, and how pixels are generated.

| | char sub. | char sub. | elision | accent drop | doubled | typo |
	$(c \rightarrow q)$	$(s \rightarrow \text{long } s)$	$(\text{que} \rightarrow \tilde{q})$	$(\acute{o} \rightarrow o)$	$(c \rightarrow cc)$	$(e \rightarrow r)$
Original image	qual	**efta**	a͂ql	confideracion	peccados	Primeramrnte
Baseline trans.	qual	eña	á ól	confideracion	peccados	Primeraminte
Our diplomatic trans.	qual	efta	a͂ql	confideracion	peccados	Primeramrnte
Our normalized trans.	cual	esta	aquel	consideración	pecados	Primeramente

Table 1: Examples of automatic diplomatic and normalized transcriptions taken from actual system output.

dered image x_i is always generated directly from LM character c_i, resulting in transcription errors when printed characters don't follow the spellings in the LM. Our model (Figure 1) adds an additional layer to the generative model that de-couples the LM from the rendering by allowing the LM-generated character c_i to be replaced by a possibly different *glyph character* g_i which is rendered instead.

For the generative story of our new model, we again begin by generating pairs (ℓ_i, c_i). However, instead of typesetting c_i, we generate a distinct glyph character g_i as its replacement, according to $P^{\text{GLYPH}}_{\ell_i}(g_i \mid c_i)$. Orthographic substitution patterns are language-specific, and thus P^{GLYPH} is as well. Finally, we typeset and render g_i (instead of c_i) using $P^{\text{TYPE}}(t_i \mid g_i)$ and $P^{\text{REND}}(x_i \mid g_i, t_i)$.

We follow the previous Ocular work for the definitions of P^{LANG}, $P^{\text{CHAR}}_{\ell_i}$, P^{TYPE}, and P^{REND}. We define the new conditional distribution $P^{\text{GLYPH}}_{\ell_i}$, specifying the probability of rendering g when the LM generated c, given that the language is ℓ, as follows:

$$P^{\text{GLYPH}}_{\ell}(g \mid c) = \begin{cases} (1-\kappa) + \kappa \cdot p(g \mid c, \ell) & \text{if } g = c \\ \kappa \cdot p(g \mid c, \ell) & \text{else} \end{cases}$$

Constant κ defines a Bernoulli parameter specifying the fixed probability of deterministically choosing to render c_i directly (i.e., $g_i = c_i$). We set $\kappa = 0.9$ to bias the model away from substitutions in general. The remaining $(1 - \kappa)$ probability mass is then divided among all potential output glyph characters.

Table 1 shows some of the common substitution patterns that our model addresses. For a direct rendering of c_i, a letter substitution, or the dropping of an accent, g_i will be a simple character drawn from the language's set of valid characters (each language may have a different set of permitted characters, e.g. accented letters). In order to support the tilde-elision shorthand, we permit g_i to be a tilde-annotated version of c_i, and for doubled letters, we permit g_i to be

$c_i c_i$, for which we typeset and render c_i twice. Finally, to allow for elided letters, including the dropping of a line-break hyphen, we allow g_i to be a special ELISION glyph that renders only as a zero-width space character.

The parameters of the glyph substitution model are learned in an unsupervised fashion as part of Ocular's EM procedure via a hard parameter update:

$$p(g \mid c, \ell) = \frac{\mathit{freq}(\ell, c, g) + 1}{\sum_{g'}(\mathit{freq}(\ell, c, g') + 1)}$$

where $\mathit{freq}(\ell, c, g)$ is the number of times in the training iteration that the model chose to replace c with g in a word (automatically) determined to be of language ℓ. The $+1$ term is Laplace smoothing.

To guide the model and improve efficiency, we employ a number of constraints governing which kinds of substitutions are valid. Among these, we stipulate that substitutions must be letter-to-letter, diacritics may only be added to lowercase letters, only s can replace long-s, and elision-tilde-marked letters must be followed by one or more elisions.

4 Experiments

As a first baseline, we compare against Ocular with no orthographic variation handling, in which characters generated by the LM are rendered directly.

As a second baseline, we compare to our previous work, which improved Ocular's diplomatic transcription accuracy by introducing orthographic variation directly into the LM with hand-constructed language-specific orthographic rules to rewrite the LM training data prior to n-gram estimation (Garrette et al., 2015). However, this rule-based preprocessing approach is inadequate in many ways. First, annotators do not know the full range of orthographic variations, or their frequencies, in each document, and it is impossible to write rules to handle typos. Furthermore, a highly language-proficient

Original image	**dias**	ſuplicar	ſalꝰ	alabã	tí pues	Jeſuxpo
Baseline trans.	dias	fuplicar	faltro	alaba	tí pues	Nefuxpo
Our diplomatic trans.	*días	ſuplicar	*faliio	alabã	ti pues	*Jeſuxpo
Our normalized trans.	días	*súplicar	*salió	*alabar	*te pues	*Jesuxpo
Gold diplomatic trans.	dias	ſuplicar	ſaluo	alabã	ti pues	Jeſu xp̃o
Gold normalized trans.	días	suplicar	salvo	alaban	ti pues	Jesu Cristo

Table 2: Actual system outputs containing transcription errors. Our incorrect outputs are starred (*).

Orthographic variation strategy	Diplomatic		Normalized	
	CER	WER	CER	WER
No handling	13.2	45.7	17.4	47.6
Hand-written rules	**8.5**	**30.8**	13.1	37.9
Unsupv. joint model	8.6	32.7	**9.5**	**27.6**

Table 3: Experimental results for both Diplomatic (preserving variation) and Normalized (modern orthography) transcription tasks. Results given as both character error rate (CER, including punctuation) and word error rate (WER, without punctuation).

c	g	$freq(sp., c, g)$	$P^{\mathrm{GLYPH}}_{spanish}(g \mid c)$
-	ELIDED	52	0.0881
ó	o	31	0.0526
s	ſ (long s)	325	0.0352
q	q̃	9	0.0222
n	ELIDED	57	0.0136
v	u	55	0.0129
o	õ	20	0.0091
c	cc	23	0.0028

Table 4: A sample of high-probability Spanish substitution rules learned by our unsupervised model.

annotator is required, which is not always feasible with, e.g, rare indigenous languages.

Each baseline model has a single output, evaluated against both diplomatic and normalized gold.

Our source code and evaluation data are freely available at *https://github.com/tberg12/ocular* and *https://github.com/dhgarrette/ocr-evaluation-data.*

5 Results and Discussion

Our results are shown in Table 3 and some correct example system outputs can be seen in Table 1.

Our model's accuracy in producing diplomatic transcriptions is substantially better than baseline Ocular performance, yielding a 35% relative character error rate reduction. Further, our model's diplomatic transcription accuracy is comparable to the LM replacement-rule approach of our previous work, but achieves this result with only unsupervised learning, as opposed to expert-produced rules. We can see in Table 4 that our model is able to discover and apply appropriate probabilities to relevant substitution rules. For the new normalized-transcription task, even larger gains were achieved: a 46% relative error reduction over Ocular, and a 28% reduction over the rule-based approach.

5.1 Error Analysis

Table 2 displays a sample of errors in our system output. (1) The word *días* is printed without an accent though it has one in modern Spanish. Our system is unable to distinguish between a dot and an accent above the *i*, and thus it opts to output the accented version since it is preferred by the LM. (2) The word *suplicar* does not have any accents in modern Spanish, but the model is over-eager in this case and attempts to revive an accent where there should not be one. (3) The word *salvo* is printed here as the variant *saluo*, but its under-inking leaves the *u* in disconnected pieces, resembling a pair of *i* characters. The LM model believes this to be the (valid) word *salió* with the accent dropped and the *i* doubled. (4) The model guesses incorrectly that the elision at the end of *alabã* is an *r* since *alabar* is a valid word. (5) The model correctly recognizes that the letters *ti* are printed, but the LM believes the normalized form is *te* even though *te pues* is not valid Spanish, perhaps because *te puedo* is a very common phrase and the six-gram context isn't enough to make that distinction. (6) Finally, there are some special idiomatic shorthands that our model is simply unable to understand because they have no clear

Original Image

de las dos que ſe ſiguen en las quales aprꝰ
uecha mucho acoſtũbrar el anima a ſe le-
uantar hazia arriba poneſe aqui vn modo
el qual pareçe mas cõforme alo ꝗ ſe ſigue

Diplomatic

de las dos que ſe figuen en las quales apro
uecha mucho acoſtũbrar el anima á ſe le-
pantar hazia arriba poneſe aqui vn modo
el qual parece más cõforme á lo ꝗ ſe figue

Normalized

de las dos que se siguen en las quales
aprovecha mucho acostumbrar el ánima á se
levantar hacia arriba pónese aquí un modo
el cual parece más conforme á lo que se sigue

Table 5: A document excerpt along with actual system outputs for both diplomatic and normalized transcriptions. Note that the normalization recovers the first line's missing line-break hyphen, allowing the full word *aprovecha* to be reassembled.

connection to what they are replacing. Here, *xp̃o* (from Greek letters *chi rho*) is shorthand for *Cristo*.

6 Conclusion

In this paper we presented a novel unsupervised OCR model for the joint production of diplomatic (variant-preserving) and normalized transcriptions of historical documents. The model is able to automatically learn a probabilistic mapping from a LM trained on modern text to the orthographic variants present in the document. This has the dual result of both considerably improving diplomatic transcription accuracy, while also enabling the model to simultaneously produce a normalized transcription.

Our model has the potential to significantly impact the work of scholars and librarians who wish to make digital texts easier to read, index, search, and study. Our approach also has the fortunate side-effect of producing metadata about orthographic variation in printed documents that may be valuable to scholars of book history. With our model, we are able to automatically induce sets of variation patterns used by printers, and the locations in the texts where those variants appear, without the need for labor-intensive page-by-page reading. Further, these induced mappings have probabilities attached, and are not simple rulebanks like those used in existing normalization work (Garrette et al., 2015; Baron and Rayson, 2008). Table 4, above, shows a sample of rules and their frequencies that resulted from training our model on Spanish documents.

Finally, our work helps to bridge the gap between historical text and mainline NLP. Orthographic variation lowers the accuracy of NLP tools due to high out-of-vocabulary rates and mismatched morphological features (Piotrowski, 2012). This is especially true when these tools are trained on the modern texts of the standard corpora used in NLP (Yang and Eisenstein, 2016). Normalization of historical texts have been shown to improve the quality of, for example, taggers (Rayson et al., 2007; Yang and Eisenstein, 2016) and parsers (Rayson et al., 2007). These techniques mirror those applied to the processing of text in social media, such as Twitter, where there is a high degree of slang and shorthand (Gimpel et al., 2011; Eisenstein, 2013; Yang and Eisenstein, 2013). Most approaches train off-the-shelf NLP tools on modern text and then apply normalization techniques to historical texts to transform them into something resembling the modern training input (Scheible et al., 2011). A joint model such as ours that automatically learns orthographic variations while training the NLP model might overcome some of the limitations of using such a pipeline approach.

Acknowledgments

We would like to thank Stephanie Wood, Kelly McDonough, Albert Palacios, Adam Coon, Sergio Romero, and Kent Norsworthy for their input, advice, and assistance on this project. We would also like to thank Taylor Berg-Kirkpatrick, Dan Klein, and Luke Zettlemoyer for their valuable feedback on earlier drafts of this paper. This work is supported in part by a Digital Humanities Implementation Grant from the National Endowment for the Humanities for the project Reading the First Books: Multilingual, Early-Modern OCR for Primeros Libros.

References

Alistair Baron and Paul Rayson. 2008. VARD2: A tool for dealing with spelling variation in historical corpora. In *Proceedings of The Postgraduate Conference in Corpus Linguistics*.

Taylor Berg-Kirkpatrick and Dan Klein. 2014. Improved typesetting models for historical OCR. In *ACL*.

Taylor Berg-Kirkpatrick, Greg Durrett, and Dan Klein. 2013. Unsupervised transcription of historical documents. In *Proceedings of ACL*.

Philip R. Burns. 2013. MorphAdorner v2: A Java library for the morphological adornment of English language texts. https://morphadorner. northwestern.edu/morphadorner/ download/morphadorner.pdf.

Arthur P. Dempster, Nan M. Laird, and Donald. B. Rubin. 1977. Maximum likelihood from incomplete data via the EM algorithm. *Journal of the Royal Statistical Society: Series B (Statistical Methodology)*, 39.

Thomas G. Dolan. 2012. The Primeros Libros Project. *The Hispanic Outlook in Higher Education*, 22:20–22, March.

M. J. Driscoll. 2006. Electronic textual editing: Levels of transcription. In Lou Burnard, Katherine O'Brien O'Keeffe, and John Unsworth, editors, *Electronic Textual Editing*. Modern Language Association.

Jacob Eisenstein. 2013. What to do about bad language on the internet. In *Proceedings of NAACL*.

Dan Garrette, Hannah Alpert-Abrams, Taylor Berg-Kirkpatrick, and Dan Klein. 2015. Unsupervised code-switching for multilingual historical document transcription. In *Proceedings of NAACL*.

Kevin Gimpel, Nathan Schneider, Brendan OConnor, Dipanjan Das, Daniel Mills, Jacob Eisenstein, Michael Heilman, Dani Yogatama, Jeffrey Flanigan, , and Noah A. Smith. 2011. Part-of-speech tagging for twitter: annotation, features, and experiments. In *Proceedings of ACL*.

W. W. Greg. 1950. The rationale of copy-text. *Studies in Bibliography*, 3:19–36.

Iris Hendrickx and Rita Marquilhas. 2011. From old texts to modern spellings: An experiment in automatic normalisation. *Journal of Language Technology and Computational Linguistics*, 26(2):65–76.

Reinhard Kneser and Hermann Ney. 1995. Improved backing-off for m-gram language modeling. In *Proceedings of the International Conference on Acoustics, Speech, and Signal Processing*.

Elena Pierazzo. 2014. Digital documentary editions and the Others. *Scholarly Editing*, 35:1–23.

Michael Piotrowski. 2012. Natural language processing for historical texts. *Synthesis Lectures on Human Language Technologies*, 5:1–157.

Primeros Libros. 2010. Los Primeros Libros de las Américas: Impresos Americanos del siglo XVI en las bibliotecas del mundo. *http://primeroslibros.org/*.

Paul Rayson, Dawn Archer, Alistair Baron, Jonathan Culpeper, and Nicholas Smith. 2007. Tagging the bard: Evaluating the accuracy of a modern POS tagger on early modern English corpora. In *Corpus Linguistics Conference*.

Silke Scheible, Richard J Whitt, Martin Durrell, and Paul Bennett. 2011. Evaluating an 'off-the-shelf' POS-tagger on early modern German text. In *Proceedings of the 5th ACL-HLT Workshop on Language Technology for Cultural Heritage, Social Sciences, and Humanities*.

Yi Yang and Jacob Eisenstein. 2013. A log-linear model for unsupervised text normalization. In *Proceedings of EMNLP*.

Yi Yang and Jacob Eisenstein. 2016. Part-of-speech tagging for historical English. In *Proceedings of NAACL*.

Bidirectional RNN for Medical Event Detection in Electronic Health Records

Abhyuday N Jagannatha[1], Hong Yu[1,2]
[1] University of Massachusetts, MA, USA
[2] Bedford VAMC and CHOIR, MA, USA
abhyuday@cs.umass.edu, hong.yu@umassmed.edu

Abstract

Sequence labeling for extraction of medical events and their attributes from unstructured text in Electronic Health Record (EHR) notes is a key step towards semantic understanding of EHRs. It has important applications in health informatics including pharmacovigilance and drug surveillance. The state of the art supervised machine learning models in this domain are based on Conditional Random Fields (CRFs) with features calculated from fixed context windows. In this application, we explored recurrent neural network frameworks and show that they significantly outperformed the CRF models.

1 Introduction

EHRs report patient's health, medical history and treatments compiled by medical staff at hospitals. It is well known that EHR notes contain information about medical events including medication, diagnosis (or Indication), and adverse drug events (ADEs) etc. A medical event in this context can be described as a change in patient's medical status. Identifying these events in a structured manner has many important clinical applications such as discovery of abnormally high rate of adverse reaction events to a particular drug, surveillance of drug efficacy, etc. In this paper we treat EHR clinical event detection as a task of sequence labeling.

Sequence labeling in the context of machine learning refers to the task of learning to predict a label for each data-point in a sequence of data-points. This learning framework has wide applications in many disciplines such as genomics, intrusion detection, natural language processing, speech recognition etc. However, sequence labeling in EHRs is a challenging task. Unlike text in the open domain, EHR notes are frequently noisy, containing incomplete sentences, phrases and irregular use of language. In addition, EHR notes incorporate abundant abbreviations, rich medical jargons, and their variations, which make recognizing semantically similar patterns in EHR notes difficult. Additionally, different events exhibit different patterns and possess different prevalences. For example, while a medication comprises of at most a few words of a noun, an ADE (e.g., "has not felt back to his normal self") may vary to comprise of a significant part of a sentence. While medication information is frequently described in EHRs, ADEs are typically rare events.

Rule-based and learning-based approaches have been developed to identify and extract information from EHR notes (Haerian et al., 2012), (Xu et al., 2010), (Friedman et al., 1994), (Aronson, 2001), (Polepalli Ramesh et al., 2014). Learning-based approaches use sequence labeling algorithms like Conditional Random Fields (Lafferty et al., 2001), Hidden Markov Models (Collier et al., 2000), and Max-entropy Markov Models (McCallum et al., 2000). One major drawback of these graphical models is that the label prediction at any time point only depends on its data instance and the immediate neighboring labels.

While this approach performs well in learning the distribution of the output labels, it has some limitations. One major limitation is that it is not designed to learn from dependencies which lie in the

Proceedings of NAACL-HLT 2016, pages 473–482,
San Diego, California, June 12-17, 2016. ©2016 Association for Computational Linguistics

surrounding but not quite immediate neighborhood. Therefore, the feature vectors have to be explicitly modeled to include the surrounding contextual information. Traditionally, bag of words representation of surrounding context has shown reasonably good performance. However, the information contained in the bag of words vector is very sensitive to context window size. If the context window is too short, it will not include all the information. On the other hand if the context window is too large, it will compress the vital information with other irrelevant words. Usually a way to tackle this problem is to try different context window sizes and use the one that gives the highest validation performance. However, this method cannot be easily applied to our task, because different medical events like medication, diagnosis or adverse drug reaction require different context window sizes. For example, while a medication can be determined by a context of two or three words containing the drug name, an adverse drug reaction would require the context of the entire sentence. As an example, this is a sentence from one of the EHRs, "The follow-up needle biopsy results were consistent with *bronchiolitis obliterans*, which was likely due to the Bleomycin component of his *ABVD chemo*". In this sentence, the true labels are *Adverse Drug Event(ADE)* for "*bronchiolitis obliterans*" and *Drugname* for "*ABVD chemo*". However the ADE , "*bronchiolitis obliterans*" could be mislabeled as just another disease or symptom, if the entire sentence is not taken into context.

Recent advancements in Recurrent Neural Networks (RNNs) have opened up new avenues of research in sequence labeling. Traditionally, recurrent neural networks have been hard to train through Back-Propagation, because learning long term dependencies using simple recurrent neurons lead to problems like exploding or vanishing gradients (Bengio et al., 1994), (Hochreiter et al., 2001). Recent approaches have modified the simple neuron structure in order to learn dependencies over longer intervals more efficiently. In this study, we evaluate the performance of two such neural networks, namely, Long Short Term Memory (LSTM) and Gated Recurrent Units (GRU).

Timely identification of new drug toxicities is an unresolved clinical and public health problem, costing people's lives and billions of US dollars. In this study, we empirically evaluated LSTM and GRU on EHR notes, focusing on the clinically important task of detecting medication, diagnosis, and adverse drug event. To our knowledge, we are the first group reporting the uses of RNN frameworks for information extraction in EHR notes.

2 Related Work

Medication and ADE detection is an important NLP task in biomedicine. Related existing NLP approaches can be grouped into knowledge or rule-based, supervised machine learning, and hybrid approaches. For example, Hazlehurst et al. (2005) developed MediClass, a knowledge-based system that deploys a set of domain-specific logical rules for medical concept extraction. Wang et al. (2015) , Humphreys et.al. (1993) and others map EHR notes to medical concepts to an external knowledge resource using hybrid rule-based and syntactic parsing approaches. Gurulingappa et al. (2010) detect two medical entities (*disease* and *adverse events*) in a corpus of annotated Medline abstracts. In contrast, our work uses a corpus of actual medical notes and detects additional events and attributes.

Rochefort et al. (2015) developed document classifiers to classify whether a clinical note contains deep venous thromboembolisms and pulmonary embolism. Haerian et al. (2012) applied distance supervision to identify terms (e.g., including "suicidal", "self harm", and "diphenhydramine overdose") associated with suicide events. Zuofeng Li et al. (2010) extracted medication information using CRFs.

Many named entity recognition systems in the biomedical domain have been driven by the Shared tasks of BioNLP (Kim et al., 2009), BioCreAtivE (Hirschman et al., 2005) i2b2 shared NLP tasks (Li et al., 2009) and ShARe/CLEF evaluation tasks (Pradhan et al., 2014). The best performing clinical NLP systems for named entity recognition includes Tang et al (2013) which applied CRF and structured SVM.

Neural Network models like Convolutional Neural Networks and Recurrent Neural Networks (LSTM, GRU) have recently been been successfully used to tackle various sequence labeling problems in NLP. Collobert (2011) used Convolutional

Labels	Annotations	Avg. Words / Annotations
ADE	905	1.51
Indication	1988	2.34
Other SSD	26013	2.14
Severity	1928	1.38
Drugname	9917	1.20
Duration	562	2.17
Dosage	3284	2.14
Route	1810	1.14
Frequency	2801	2.35

Table 1: Annotation statistics for the corpus.

Neural Network for sequence labeling problems like POS tagging, NER etc. . Later, Huang et al. (2015) achieved comparable or better scores using bi-directional LSTM based models.

3 Dataset

The annotated corpus contains 780 English EHR notes or 613,593 word tokens (an average of 786 words per note) from cancer patients who have been diagnosed with hematological malignancy. Each note was annotated by at least two annotators with inter-annotator agreement of 0.93 kappa. The annotated events and attributes and their instances in the annotated corpus are shown in Table 1.

The annotated events can be broadly divided into two groups, *Medication*, and *Disease*. The *Medication* group contains *Drugname*, *Dosage*, *Frequency*, *Duration* and *Route*. It corresponds to information about medication events and their attributes. The attributes (Route, Frequency, Dosage, and Duration) of a medication (Drug name) occur less frequently than the Drugname tag itself, because few EHRs report complete attributes of an event.

The *Disease* group contains events related to diseases (*ADE*, *Indication*, *Other SSD*) and their attributes (*Severity*). An injury or disease can be labeled as *ADE*, *Indication*, or *Other SSD* depending on the semantic context. It is marked as *ADE* if it is the side effect of a drug. It is marked as *Indication* if it is being diagnosed currently by the doctor and a medication has been prescribed for it. Any sign, symptom or disease that does not fall into the aforementioned two categories is labeled as *Other SSD*. *Other SSD* is the most common label in our corpus, because it is frequently used to label conditions in

the past history of the patient.

For each note, we removed special characters that do not serve as punctuation and then split the note into sentences using regular expressions.

4 Methods

4.1 Long Short Term Memory

Long Short Term Memory Networks (Hochreiter and Schmidhuber, 1997) are a type of Recurrent Neural Networks (RNNs). RNNs are modifications of feed-forward neural networks with recurrent connections. In a typical NN, the neuron output at time t is given by:

$$y_i^t = \sigma(W_i x_t + b_i) \tag{1}$$

Where W_i is the weight matrix, b_i is the bias term and σ is the sigmoid activation function. In an RNN, the output of the neuron at time $t - 1$ is fed back into the neuron. The new activation function now becomes:

$$y_i^t = \sigma(W_i x_t + U_i y_i^{t-1} + b_i) \tag{2}$$

Since these RNNs use the previous outputs as recurrent connections, their current output depends on the previous states. This property remembers previous information about the sequence, making them useful for sequence labeling tasks. RNNs can be trained through back-propagation through time. Bengio et al. (1994) showed that learning long term dependencies in recurrent neural networks through gradient decent is difficult. This is mainly because the back-propagating error can frequently "blow-up" or explode which makes convergence infeasible, or it can vanish which renders the network incapable of learning long term dependencies (Hochreiter et al., 2001).

In contrast, LSTM networks were proposed as solutions for the vanishing gradient problem and were designed to efficiently learn long term dependencies. LSTMs accomplish this by keeping an internal state that represents the memory cell of the LSTM neuron. This internal state can only be read and written through gates which control the information flowing through the cell state. The updates of various gates can be computed as:

$$i_t = tanh(W_{xi} x_t + W_{hi} h_{t-1}) \tag{3}$$

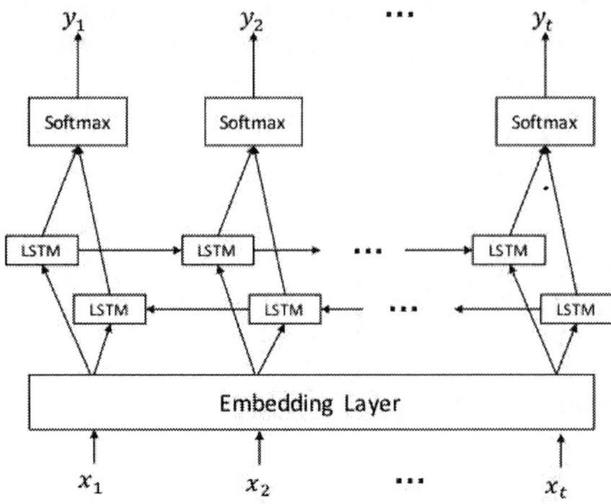

Figure 1: Sequence Labeling model for LSTM network

$$f_t = \sigma(W_{xf}x_t + W_{hf}h_{t-1}) \qquad (4)$$

$$o_t = \sigma(W_{xo}x_t + W_{ho}h_{t-1}) \qquad (5)$$

Here i_t , f_t and o_t denote input, forget and output gate respectively. The forget and input gate determine the contributions of the previous output and the current input, in the new cell state c_t. The output gate controls how much of c_t is exposed as the output. The new cell state c_t and the output h_t can be calculated as follows:

$$c_t = f_t \odot c_{t-1} + i_t \odot tanh(W_{xc}x_t + W_{hc}h_{t-1}) \quad (6)$$

$$h_t = o_t \odot tanh(c_t) \qquad (7)$$

The cell state stores relevant information from the previous time-steps. It can only be modified in an additive fashion via the input and forget gates. Simplistically, this can be viewed as allowing the error to flow back through the cell state unchecked till it back propagates to the time-step that added the relevant information. This nature allows LSTM to learn long term dependencies.

We use LSTM cells in the Neural Network setup shown in figure 1. Here x_k, y_k are the input word, and the predicted label for the kth word in the sentence. The embedding layer contains the word vector mapping from words to dense n-dimensional vector representations. We initialize the embedding layer at the start of the training with word vectors

calculated on the larger data corpus described in section 4.4. This ensures that words which are not seen frequently in the labeled data corpus still have a reasonable vector representation. This step is necessary because our unlabeled corpus is much larger than the labeled one.

The words are mapped into their corresponding vector representations and fed into the LSTM layer. The LSTM layer consists of two LSTM chains, one propagating in the forward direction and other in the backward direction. We concatenate the output from the two chains to form a combined representation of the word and its context. This concatenated vector is then fed into a feed-forward neuron with Softmax activation function. The Softmax activation function normalizes the outputs to produce probability like outputs for each label type j as follows:

$$P(l_t = j | u_t) = \frac{exp(u_t W_j)}{\sum_{k=1}^{K} exp(u_t W_k)} \qquad (8)$$

Here l_t and u_t are the label and the concatenated vector for each time step t. The most likely label at each word position is selected. The entire network is trained through back-propagation. The embedding vectors are also updated based on the back-propagated errors.

4.2 Gated Recurrent Units

Gated Recurrent Unit (GRU) is another type of recurrent neural network which was recently proposed for the purposes of Machine Translation by Cho et. al. (2014). Similar to LSTMs, Gated Recurrent Units also have an additive mechanism to update the cell state, with the current update. However, GRUs have a different mechanism to create the update. The candidate activation $\tilde{h}_t$ is computed based on the previous cell state and the current input .

$$\tilde{h}_t = \sigma(W_{xh}x_t + W_{hh}(r_t \odot h_{t-1})) \qquad (9)$$

Here r_t is the reset gate and it controls the use of previous cell state while calculating the input activation. The reset gate itself is also computed based on the previous cell activation h_{t-1} and the current candidate activation .

$$\tilde{r}_t = \sigma(W_{xr}x_t + W_{hr}h_{t-1}) \qquad (10)$$

Models	Recall	Precision	F-score
CRF-nocontext	0.6562	0.7330	0.6925
CRF-context	0.6806	0.7711	0.7230
LSTM-sentence	0.8024	0.7803	0.7912
GRU-sentence	0.8013	0.7802	0.7906
LSTM-document	0.8050	0.7796	0.7921
GRU-document	**0.8126**	**0.7938**	**0.8031**

Table 2: Cross validated micro-average of Precision, Recall and F-score for all medical tags

The current cell state or activation is a linear combination of previous cell activation and the candidate activation.

$$h_t = (1 - z_t) \odot h_{t-1} + z_t \odot \tilde{h}_t \qquad (11)$$

Here, z_t is the update gate which decides how much contribution the candidate activation and the previous cell state should have in the cell activation. The update gate is computed using the following equation:

$$z_t = (W_{hz} h_{t-1} + W_{xz} x_t) \qquad (12)$$

Gated recurrent units have some fundamental differences with LSTM. For example, there is no mechanism like the output gate which controls the exposure of the cell activation, instead the entire current cell activation is used as output. The mechanisms for using the previous output for the calculation of the current activation are also very different. Recent experiments (Chung et al., 2014), (Jozefowicz et al., 2015) comparing both these architectures have shown GRUs to have comparable or sometimes better performance than LSTM in several tasks with long term dependencies.

We use GRU with the same Neural Network structure as shown in Figure 1 by replacing the LSTM nodes with GRU. The embedding layer used here is also initialized in a similar fashion as the LSTM network.

4.3 The Baseline System

CRFs have been widely used for sequence labeling tasks in NLP. CRFs model the complex dependence of the outputs in a sequence using Probabilistic Graphical Models. Probabilistic Graphical Models represent relationships between variables through a product of factors where each factor is only influenced by a smaller subset of the variables. A particular factorization of the variables provides a specific set of independence relations enforced on the data. Unlike Hidden Markov Models which model the joint $p(x, y)$, CRFs model the posterior probability $p(y|x)$ directly. The conditional can be written as a product of factors as follows:

$$p(y|x) = \frac{1}{Z(x)} \prod_{t=1}^{T} \psi_t(y_t, y_{t-1}, x_t) \qquad (13)$$

Here Z is the partition function used for normalization, ψ_t are the local factor functions.

CRFs are fed the word inputs and their corresponding skip-gram word embedding (section 4.4). To compare CRFs with RNN, we add extra context feature for each word. This is done because our aim is to show that RNNs perform better than CRFs using context windows. This extra feature consists of two vectors that are bag of words representation of the sentence sections before and after the word respectively. We add this feature to explicitly provide a mechanism that is somewhat similar to the surrounding context that is generated in a Bi-directional RNN as shown in Figure 1. This CRF model is referred to as CRF-context in our paper. We also evaluate a CRF-nocontext model, which trains a CRF without the context features.

The tagging scheme used with both CRF models is BIO (Begin, Inside and Outside). We did not use the more detailed BILOU scheme (Begin, Inside, Last, Outside, Unit) due to data sparsity in some of the rarer labels.

4.4 Skip-Gram Word Embeddings

We use skip-gram word embeddings trained through a shallow neural network as shown by Mikolov et al., (2013) to initialize the embedding layer of the RNNs. This embedding is also used in the baseline CRF model as a feature. The embeddings are trained on a large unlabeled biomedical dataset, compiled from three sources, the English Wikipedia, an unlabeled EHR corpus, and PubMed Open Access articles. The English Wikipedia consists of text extracted from all the articles of English Wikipedia 2015. The unlabeled EHR corpus contains 99,700 electronic health record notes. PubMed Open Access articles are obtained by extracting the raw text from all openly available PubMed articles. This

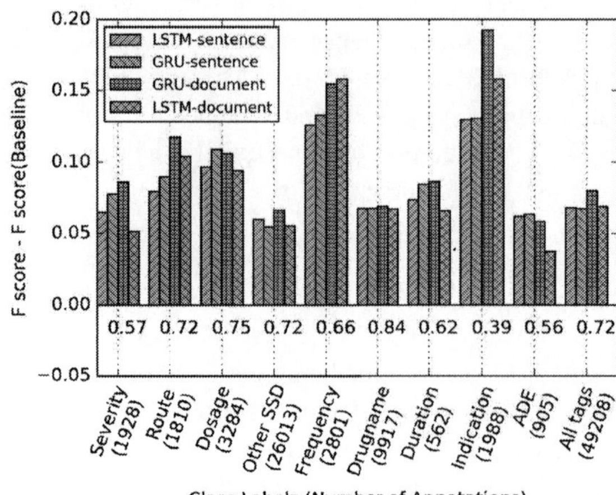

Figure 2: Change in F-score for RNN models with respect to CRF-context (baseline). The values below the plotted bars represent the baseline f-scores for each class label.

combined raw text corpus contains more than 3 billion word tokens. We convert all words to lowercase and use a context window of 10 words to train a 200 dimensional skip gram word embedding.

5 Experiments and Evaluation Metrics

For each word, the models were trained to predict either one of the nine medically relevant tags described in section 3, or the *Outside* label. The CRF tagger was run in two modes. The first mode (CRF–nocontext) used only the current word and its corresponding skip-gram representation. The second mode (CRF– context) used the extra context feature described in section 4.3. The extra features are basically the bag of words representation of the preceding and following sections of the sentence. The first mode was used to compare the performance of CRF and RNN models when using the same input data. It also serves as a method of contrasting with CRF's performance when context features are explicitly added. CRF Tagger uses L-BFGS optimizer with L2- regularization.

The RNN frameworks are trained on sentence level and document level. The sentence level neural networks are fed only one sentence at a time. This means that the LSTM and GRU states are only preserved and propagated within a sentence. The networks cell states are re-initialized before each sen-

tence. The document level neural networks are fed one document at a time, so they can learn context cues that reside outside of the sentence boundary. We use 100 dimensional hidden layer for each directional RNN chain. Since we use bi-directional LSTMs and GRUs, this essentially amounts to a 200 dimensional recurrent hidden layer. The hidden layer activation functions for both RNN models are $tanh$. Output of this hidden layer is fed into a Softmax output layer which emits probabilities for each of the nine medical labels and the *Outside* label. We use categorical cross entropy as the objective function. Similar to the CRF implementation, the Neural Net cost function also contains an L2-regularization component. We also use dropout (Srivastava et al., 2014) as an additional measure to avoid over-fitting. Fifty percent dropout is used to manipulate the inputs to the RNN and the Softmax layer. We use AdaGrad (Duchi et al., 2011) to optimize the network cost.

We use ten-fold cross validation to calculate the performance metric for each model. The dataset is divided at the note level. We separate out 10 % of the training set to form the validation set. This validation set is used to evaluate the different parameter combinations for CRF and RNN models. We employ early stopping to terminate the training run if the validation error increases consistently. We use a maximum of 40 epochs to train each network. The batch sizes used were kept constant at 128 for sentence level RNNs and 16 for document level RNNs.

We report micro-averaged recall, precision and f-score. We use exact phrase matching to calculate the evaluation score for our experiments. Each phrase labeled by the learned models is considered a true positive only if it matches the exact true boundary of the phrase and correctly labels all the words in the phrase.

We use CRFsuite (Okazaki, 2007) for implementing the CRF tagger. We use Lasagne to setup the Neural Net framework. Lasagne[1] is a machine learning library focused towards neural networks that is build on top of Theano (Bergstra et al., 2010).

---

[1] https://github.com/Lasagne/Lasagne

Figure 3 — Heat-maps of Confusion Matrices.

CRF-nocontext

	ADE	Outside	Dosage	Drugname	Duration	Frequency	Indication	Other SSD	Route	Severity
ADE	19	30	0	1.4	0	0.3	0.4	49	0.1	0
Outside	0	98	0.1	0.1	0	0.1	0	1.2	0	0.1
Dosage	0	13	85	0.5	0.1	0.9	0	0.1	0.3	0
Drugname	0.1	11	1.2	86	0.2	0.7	0.1	0.8	0.3	0
Duration	0	50	1	0.1	45	2.7	0	0.3	0.1	0
Frequency	0	31	0.8	0.8	0.3	66	0.1	0	0.3	0
Indication	0.1	17	0	1.3	0	0.3	18	62	0	0.7
Other SSD	0.3	26	0	0.1	0	0	1.3	73	0	0.2
Route	0	17	2.4	2.8	0	0.6	0	0.6	77	0
Severity	0	41	0	0	0	0	0.6	8.1	0	50

CRF-context

	ADE	Outside	Dosage	Drugname	Duration	Frequency	Indication	Other SSD	Route	Severity
ADE	39	29	0	0.7	0	0.1	3.7	28	0	0
Outside	0	98	0.1	0.1	0	0.2	0.2	1.9	0	0.1
Dosage	0	12	80	2.8	0.3	3.5	0.8	0.2	0.6	0
Drugname	0	11	1.6	82	0.2	1.9	1.4	1.5	0.2	0
Duration	0	38	0.9	0.8	56	3.8	0.1	0.8	0	0
Frequency	0	19	1.2	0.9	0.5	77	1.1	0.1	0.3	0
Indication	0.4	18	0.1	1.4	0.1	0.6	44	34	0.1	0.6
Other SSD	0.2	21	0	0.1	0	0	1.5	77	0	0.2
Route	0	14	1.8	3.5	0.1	2.9	1	0.4	76	0
Severity	0.1	35	0	0.2	0	0	1.7	10	0	52

GRU-sentence

	ADE	Outside	Dosage	Drugname	Duration	Frequency	Indication	Other SSD	Route	Severity
ADE	46	21	0	0.3	0	0	5.6	27	0.1	0
Outside	0	99	0	0.1	0	0.1	0	1.1	0	0.1
Dosage	0	5.5	93	0.7	0.2	0.4	0.1	0	0.3	0
Drugname	0	6.7	0.4	92	0	0.1	0.1	0.4	0.1	0
Duration	0	23	0.7	0.1	72	3.8	0.1	0	0	0.2
Frequency	0	8	0.3	0.1	0.4	91	0.1	0	0	0
Indication	0.5	9.6	0	0.5	0	0.1	56	30	0	0.8
Other SSD	0.2	13	0	0	0	0	1.3	85	0	0.2
Route	0	9.4	0.5	0.7	0	0.1	0.1	0.1	89	0
Severity	0	25	0	0	0.1	0	0.6	5.3	0	69

LSTM-sentence

	ADE	Outside	Dosage	Drugname	Duration	Frequency	Indication	Other SSD	Route	Severity
ADE	48	19	0	0.6	0	0	5.1	26	0.1	0.1
Outside	0	99	0	0.1	0	0.1	0	1.1	0	0.1
Dosage	0	4.8	93	0.9	0.1	0.7	0.1	0.1	0.2	0
Drugname	0.1	6.2	0.5	93	0	0.1	0.2	0.4	0.1	0
Duration	0	23	0.8	0.1	72	4.8	0.1	0	0	0
Frequency	0	7.1	0.5	0.1	0.3	92	0.1	0	0	0
Indication	0.6	10	0	0.6	0	0	59	28	0.1	0.7
Other SSD	0.2	14	0	0	0	0	1.6	84	0	0.2
Route	0	8	0.8	0.7	0	0.3	0.1	0.1	90	0
Severity	0	26	0.1	0	0.1	0	0.4	5.1	0	68

LSTM-document

	ADE	Outside	Dosage	Drugname	Duration	Frequency	Indication	Other SSD	Route	Severity
ADE	49	21	0	0.4	0	0	5	24	0.2	0.1
Outside	0	99	0	0.1	0	0.1	0	1	0	0.1
Dosage	0	5.1	93	0.8	0.1	0.5	0	0.1	0.2	0.1
Drugname	0.1	6	0.6	93	0	0.1	0.1	0.5	0.1	0
Duration	0	25	0.5	0.1	68	6.5	0.1	0	0	0.1
Frequency	0	6.1	0.3	0.1	0.3	93	0.1	0	0	0
Indication	0.9	10	0	0.6	0	0	64	24	0.1	0.9
Other SSD	0.3	13	0	0	0	0	1.1	85	0	0.2
Route	0	9.6	0.6	0.8	0	1.2	0	0	88	0
Severity	0	26	0.4	0	0	0	0.4	5.8	0	67

GRU-document

	ADE	Outside	Dosage	Drugname	Duration	Frequency	Indication	Other SSD	Route	Severity
ADE	48	22	0	0.4	0	0	5.1	25	0.1	0.1
Outside	0	99	0	0.1	0	0.1	0	1	0	0.1
Dosage	0	4.9	93	0.8	0.1	0.5	0	0	0.2	0
Drugname	0	5.8	0.7	93	0	0.1	0.1	0.3	0.1	0
Duration	0	23	0.4	0.1	71	6	0.1	0	0	0
Frequency	0	6.1	0.4	0.1	0.1	93	0.1	0	0.1	0
Indication	0.8	9.8	0	0.5	0	0.1	65	23	0	0.8
Other SSD	0.2	13	0	0	0	0	1	85	0	0.2
Route	0	8.8	0.5	0.4	0	0.3	0.2	0.1	90	0
Severity	0	24	0	0.1	0	0	0.5	4.7	0	70

Figure 3: Heat-maps of Confusion Matrices of each method for the different class Labels. Rows are reference and columns are predictions. The value in cell (i, j) denotes the percentage of words in label i that were predicted as label j.

6 Results

Table 2 shows the micro averaged scores for each method. All RNN models significantly outperform the baseline (CRF-context). Compared to the baseline system, our best system (GRU-document) improved the recall (0.8126), precision (0.7938) and F-score (0.8031) by 19% , 2% and 11 % respectively. Clearly the improvement in recall contributes more to the overall increase in system performance. The performance of different RNN models is almost similar, except for the GRU model which exhibits an F-score improvement of at least one percentage point over the rest.

The changes (gain or loss) in label wise F-score for each RNN model relative to the baseline CRF-context method are plotted in Figure 2. GRU-document exhibits the highest gain overall in six of the nine tags: *indication* or diagnosis, *route*, *duration*, *severity*, *drug name*, and *other SSD*. For indication, its gain is about 0.19, a near 50% increase over the baseline. While the overall system performance of GRU-sentence, LSTM-sentence and LSTM-document are very similar, they do exhibit somewhat varied performance for different labels. The sentence level models clearly outperform the document level RNNs (both GRU and LSTM) for *ADE* and *Dosage*. Additionally, GRU sentence model shows the highest gain in *ADE* f-score.

Figure 3 shows the word level confusion matrix of different models for each label. Each cell shows the percentage of word tokens in row label i that were classified as column label j. The consistent increase of diagonal entries of RNN models for all ten labels, indicates an increase in the overall system accuracy when compared to the baseline. The most densely populated column in this figure is the *Outside* column, which denotes percentage of words that were erroneously labeled as *Outside*.

Figure 4 shows the change in average F-scores for each method with changing percentage of training data used. The setup for training, development and test data is kept the same as the ten-fold cross validation setup mentioned in Section 5. Only the training data is randomly down-sampled to achieve the reduced training data size. The figure shows that Recurrent Neural Network models perform better than traditional CRF models even with smaller training data sizes.

7 Discussion

We already discussed in the previous section how improved recall seems to be the major reason behind improvements in the RNN F-score. This trend can be observed in Figure 3 where RNN models lead to significant decreases in confusion values present in *Outside* column.

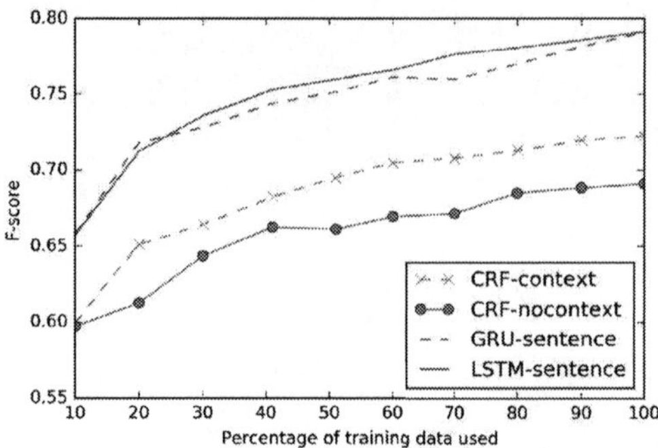

Figure 4: Change in F-score for all sentence models with respect to increasing training data size.

Further examination of Figure 3 shows two major sources of error in the CRF systems. The largest source of error is caused by confusing the relevant medical words as *Outside* (false negatives) and vice versa (false positives). The extent of false positives is not clear from Figure 3, but can be estimated if one takes into account that even a 1 % confusion in the *Outside* row represents about 5000 words. The second largest source of error is the confusion among *ADE*, *Indication* and *Other SSD* labels. As we discuss in the following paragraphs, RNNs manage to significantly reduce both these type of errors.

The large improvement in recall of all labels for RNN models seems to suggest that RNNs are able to recognize a larger set of relevant patterns than CRF baselines. This supports our hypothesis that learning dependencies with variable context ranges is crucial for our task of medical information extraction from EHR notes. This is also evident from the reduced confusion among *ADE*, *Indication* and *Other SSD*. Since these tags share a common vocabulary of Sign, Symptom and Disease Names, identifying the underlying word or phrase is not enough to distinguish between the three. Use of relevant patterns from surrounding context is often needed as a discriminative cue. Consequently, *ADE*, *Indication* confusion values in the *Other SSD* column for RNNs exhibit significant decreases when compared to CRF-nocontext and CRF-context. We also see large improvements in detecting *Duration*, *Frequency* and *Severity*. The vocabulary of these labels often lack specific medical jargon terms. Ex-

amples of these labels include "seven days", "one week" for *duration*, "some", "small", "no significant" for *severity* and "as needed", "twice daily" for *frequency*. Therefore, they are most likely to be confused with *Outside* label. This is indeed the case, as they have the highest confusion values in the *Outside* column of CRF-nocontext. Including context in CRF improves the performance, but not as much as RNN models which decrease the confusion by almost half or more in all cases. For example, GRU-document only confuses Frequency as an unlabeled word about 6.1 % of the time as opposed to 31 % and 19 % for CRF-nocontext and CRF-context respectively.

Document level models benefit by using context from outside the sentence. Since the label *Indication* requires the most use of surrounding context, it is clear that its performance would improve by using information from several sentences. Indications are diseases that are diagnosed by the medical staff, and the entire picture of the diagnosis is usually distributed across multiple sentences. Analysis of ADE is more complicated. Several ADE instances in a sentence also contain explicit cues similar to "secondary to" and "caused by". When coupled with *Drugnames* this is enough to classify the ADE. Sentence level models might depend more on these local cues which leads to improved performance. Document models, on the other hand, have to recognize patterns from a larger context, using a very small dataset (total ADE annotations are just 905) which is quite difficult.

The LSTM-document model does not show the same improvement over the sentence models as GRU-document. One possible reason for this might be the simpler recurrence structure of GRU neuron as compared to LSTM. Since there are only 780 document sequences in the dataset, the GRU model with a smaller number of trainable parameters might learn faster than LSTM. It is possible that with a larger dataset, LSTM might perform comparable to or better than GRU. However, our experiments with reducing the hidden layer size of LSTM-document model to control for the number of trainable parameters did not produce any significant improvements.

Moreover, figure 4 seems to indicate that there is not much difference between the performances of LSTM and GRU with different data sizes. However it is clearly surprising that RNN models with a larger number of parameters can still perform better than CRF models on smaller dataset sizes. This might be because the embedding layer, which contributes to a very large section of the trainable parameters, is initialized with a suitably good estimate using skipgram word embeddings described in section 4.4.

8 Conclusion

We have shown that RNNs models like LSTM and GRU are valuable tools for extracting medical events and attributes from noisy natural language text of EHR notes. We believe that the significant improvement provided by gated RNN models is due to their ability to remember information across different range of dependencies as and when required. As mentioned previously in the introduction, this is very important for our task because different labels have different contextual dependencies. CRF models with hand crafted features like bag of words representation, use fixed context windows and lose a lot of information in the process.

RNNs are excellent in extracting relevant patterns from sequence data. However, they do not explicitly enforce constraints or dependencies over the output labels. We believe that adding a probabilistic graphical model framework for structured output prediction would further improve the performance of our system. This experiment remains as our future work.

Acknowledgments

We thank the UMassMed annotation team, including Elaine Freund, Wiesong Liu and Steve Belknap, for creating the gold standard evaluation set used in this work. We also thank the anonymous reviewers for their comments and suggestions.

This work was supported in part by the grant 5U01CA180975 from the National Institutes of Health (NIH). We also acknowledge the support from the United States Department of Veterans Affairs (VA) through Award 1I01HX001457. The contents of this paper do not represent the views of the NIH, VA or United States Government.

References

Alan R Aronson. 2001. Effective mapping of biomedical text to the UMLS Metathesaurus: the MetaMap program. In *Proceedings of the AMIA Symposium*, page 17.

Y. Bengio, P. Simard, and P. Frasconi. 1994. Learning long-term dependencies with gradient descent is difficult. *IEEE Transactions on Neural Networks*, 5(2):157–166, March.

James Bergstra, Olivier Breuleux, Frdric Bastien, Pascal Lamblin, Razvan Pascanu, Guillaume Desjardins, Joseph Turian, David Warde-Farley, and Yoshua Bengio. 2010. Theano: a CPU and GPU math expression compiler. *Proceedings of the Python for Scientific Computing Conference (SciPy)*.

Kyunghyun Cho, Bart van Merrienboer, Dzmitry Bahdanau, and Yoshua Bengio. 2014. On the Properties of Neural Machine Translation: Encoder-Decoder Approaches. *ArXiv e-prints*, 1409:arXiv:1409.1259, September.

Junyoung Chung, Caglar Gulcehre, KyungHyun Cho, and Yoshua Bengio. 2014. Empirical Evaluation of Gated Recurrent Neural Networks on Sequence Modeling. *arXiv:1412.3555 [cs]*, December. arXiv: 1412.3555.

N. H Collier, C. Nobata, and J. Tshjii. 2000. Extracting the names of genes and gene products with a hidden markov model. *Proceedings of the 18th International Conference on Computational Linguistics (COLING'2000)*, pages 201–7.

Ronan Collobert, Jason Weston, Lon Bottou, Michael Karlen, Koray Kavukcuoglu, and Pavel Kuksa. 2011. Natural language processing (almost) from scratch. *The Journal of Machine Learning Research*, 12:2493–2537.

Lindberg Da, Humphreys Bl, and McCray At. 1993. The Unified Medical Language System. *Methods of information in medicine*, 32(4):281–291, August.

John Duchi, Elad Hazan, and Yoram Singer. 2011. Adaptive subgradient methods for online learning and stochastic optimization. *The Journal of Machine Learning Research*, 12:2121–2159.

C Friedman, P O Alderson, J H Austin, J J Cimino, and S B Johnson. 1994. A general natural-language text processor for clinical radiology. *Journal of the American Medical Informatics Association*, 1(2):161–174.

Harsha Gurulingappa, Roman Klinger, Martin Hofmann-Apitius, and Juliane Fluck. 2010. An Empirical Evaluation of Resources for the Identification of Diseases and Adverse Effects in Biomedical Literature. In *2nd Workshop on Building and evaluating resources for biomedical text mining (7th edition of the Language Resources and Evaluation Conference)*.

K Haerian, H Salmasian, and C Friedman. 2012. Methods for Identifying Suicide or Suicidal Ideation in EHRs. *AMIA Annual Symposium Proceedings*, 2012:1244–1253, November.

Brian Hazlehurst, H. Robert Frost, Dean F. Sittig, and Victor J. Stevens. 2005. MediClass: A System for Detecting and Classifying Encounter-based Clinical Events in Any Electronic Medical Record. *Journal of the American Medical Informatics Association : JAMIA*, 12(5):517–529.

L. Hirschman, A. Yeh, C. Blaschke, and A. Valencia. 2005. Overview of BioCreAtIvE: critical assessment of information extraction for biology. *BMC Bioinformatics*, 6 Suppl 1:S1.

Sepp Hochreiter and Jrgen Schmidhuber. 1997. Long Short-Term Memory. *Neural Computation*, 9(8):1735–1780.

Sepp Hochreiter, Yoshua Bengio, Paolo Frasconi, and Jrgen Schmidhuber. 2001. *Gradient Flow in Recurrent Nets: the Difficulty of Learning Long-Term Dependencies.*

Zhiheng Huang, Wei Xu, and Kai Yu. 2015. Bidirectional LSTM-CRF Models for Sequence Tagging. *arXiv:1508.01991 [cs]*, August. arXiv: 1508.01991.

Rafal Jozefowicz, Wojciech Zaremba, and Ilya Sutskever. 2015. An Empirical Exploration of Recurrent Network Architectures. pages 2342–2350.

J. D Kim, T. Ohta, S. Pyysalo, Y. Kano, and J. Tsujii. 2009. Overview of BioNLP'09 shared task on event extraction. In *Proceedings of the Workshop on BioNLP: Shared Task*, pages 1–9.

John D. Lafferty, Andrew McCallum, and Fernando C. N. Pereira. 2001. Conditional Random Fields: Probabilistic Models for Segmenting and Labeling Sequence Data. In *Proceedings of the Eighteenth International Conference on Machine Learning*, ICML '01, pages 282–289, San Francisco, CA, USA. Morgan Kaufmann Publishers Inc.

Z Li, Y Cao, L Antieau, S Agarwal, Q Zhang, and H Yu. 2009. Extracting Medication Information from Patient Discharge Summaries. In *Third i2b2 Shared-Task Workshop*.

Z. Li, F. Liu, L. Antieau, Y. Cao, and H. Yu. 2010. Lancet: a high precision medication event extraction system for clinical text. *Journal of the American Medical Informatics Association*, 17(5):563–567.

Andrew McCallum, Dayne Freitag, and Fernando C. N. Pereira. 2000. Maximum Entropy Markov Models for Information Extraction and Segmentation. In *Proceedings of the Seventeenth International Conference on Machine Learning*, pages 591–598. Morgan Kaufmann Publishers Inc.

Tomas Mikolov, Ilya Sutskever, Kai Chen, Greg S. Corrado, and Jeff Dean. 2013. Distributed representations of words and phrases and their compositionality. In *Advances in Neural Information Processing Systems*, pages 3111–3119.

Naoaki Okazaki. 2007. CRFsuite: a fast implementation of Conditional Random Fields (CRFs).

Balaji Polepalli Ramesh, Steven M Belknap, Zuofeng Li, Nadya Frid, Dennis P West, and Hong Yu. 2014. Automatically Recognizing Medication and Adverse Event Information From Food and Drug Administrations Adverse Event Reporting System Narratives. *JMIR Medical Informatics*, 2(1):e10, June. 00001.

Sameer Pradhan, Nomie Elhadad, Brett R. South, David Martinez, Lee Christensen, Amy Vogel, Hanna Suominen, Wendy W. Chapman, and Guergana Savova. 2014. Evaluating the state of the art in disorder recognition and normalization of the clinical narrative. *Journal of the American Medical Informatics Association: JAMIA*, August. 00002.

Christian M. Rochefort, Aman D. Verma, Tewodros Eguale, Todd C. Lee, and David L. Buckeridge. 2015. A novel method of adverse event detection can accurately identify venous thromboembolisms (VTEs) from narrative electronic health record data. *Journal of the American Medical Informatics Association: JAMIA*, 22(1):155–165, January.

Nitish Srivastava, Geoffrey Hinton, Alex Krizhevsky, Ilya Sutskever, and Ruslan Salakhutdinov. 2014. Dropout: A Simple Way to Prevent Neural Networks from Overfitting. *J. Mach. Learn. Res.*, 15(1):1929–1958, January.

Buzhou Tang, Yonghui Wu, Min Jiang, Joshua C. Denny, and Hua Xu. 2013. Recognizing and Encoding Disorder Concepts in Clinical Text using Machine Learning and Vector Space Model. 00004.

Chang Wang, Liangliang Cao, and Bowen Zhou. 2015. Medical Synonym Extraction with Concept Space Models. *arXiv:1506.00528 [cs]*, June. arXiv: 1506.00528.

H. Xu, S. P. Stenner, S. Doan, K. B. Johnson, L. R. Waitman, and J. C. Denny. 2010. MedEx: a medication information extraction system for clinical narratives. *J Am Med Inform Assoc*, 17:19–24. 1.

The Sensitivity of Topic Coherence Evaluation
to Topic Cardinality

Jey Han Lau[1,2] and **Timothy Baldwin**[2]
[1] IBM Research
[2] Dept of Computing and Information Systems,
The University of Melbourne
`jeyhan.lau@gmail.com, tb@ldwin.net`

Abstract

When evaluating the quality of topics generated by a topic model, the convention is to score topic coherence — either manually or automatically — using the top-N topic words. This hyper-parameter N, or the *cardinality* of the topic, is often overlooked and selected arbitrarily. In this paper, we investigate the impact of this cardinality hyper-parameter on topic coherence evaluation. For two automatic topic coherence methodologies, we observe that the correlation with human ratings decreases systematically as the cardinality increases. More interestingly, we find that performance can be improved if the system scores and human ratings are aggregated over several topic cardinalities before computing the correlation. In contrast to the standard practice of using a fixed value of N (e.g. $N = 5$ or $N = 10$), our results suggest that calculating topic coherence over several different cardinalities and averaging results in a substantially more stable and robust evaluation. We release the code and the datasets used in this research, for reproducibility.[1]

1 Introduction

Latent Dirichlet Allocation ("LDA": Blei et al. (2003)) is an approach to document clustering, in which "topics" (multinomial distributions over terms) and topic allocations (multinomial distributions over topics per document) are jointly learned. When the topic model output is to be presented

___
[1]`https://github.com/jhlau/`
`topic-coherence-sensitivity`

to humans, optimisation of the number of topics is a non-trivial problem. In the seminal paper of Chang et al. (2009), e.g., the authors showed that — contrary to expectations — extrinsically measured topic coherence correlates negatively with model perplexity. They introduced the word intrusion task, whereby a randomly selected "intruder" word is injected into the top-N words of a given topic and users are asked to identify the intruder word. Low reliability in identifying the intruder word indicates low coherence (and vice versa), based on the intuition that the more coherent the topic, the more clearly the intruder word should be an outlier.

Since then, several methodologies have been introduced to automate the evaluation of topic coherence. Newman et al. (2010) found that aggregate pairwise PMI scores over the top-N topic words correlated well with human ratings. Mimno et al. (2011) proposed replacing PMI with conditional probability based on co-document frequency. Aletras and Stevenson (2013) showed that coherence can be measured by a classical distributional similarity approach. More recently, Lau et al. (2014) proposed a methodology to automate the word intrusion task directly. Their results also reveal the differences between these methodologies in their assessment of topic coherence.

A hyper-parameter in all these methodologies is the number of topic words, or its *cardinality*. These methodologies evaluate coherence over the top-N topic words, where N is selected arbitrarily: for Chang et al. (2009), $N = 5$, whereas for Newman et al. (2010), Aletras and Stevenson (2013) and Lau et al. (2014), $N = 10$.

Proceedings of NAACL-HLT 2016, pages 483–487,
San Diego, California, June 12-17, 2016. ©2016 Association for Computational Linguistics

The germ of this paper came when using the automatic word intrusion methodology (Lau et al., 2014), and noticing that introducing one extra word to a given topic can dramatically change the accuracy of intruder word prediction. This forms the kernel of this paper: to better understand the impact of the topic cardinality hyper-parameter on the evaluation of topic coherence.

To investigate this, we develop a new dataset with human-annotated coherence judgements for a range of cardinality settings ($N = \{5, 10, 15, 20\}$). We experiment with the automatic word intrusion (Lau et al., 2014) and discover that correlation with human ratings decreases systematically as cardinality increases. We also test the PMI methodology (Newman et al., 2010) and make the same observation. To remedy this, we show that performance can be substantially improved if system scores and human ratings are aggregated over different cardinality settings before computing the correlation. This has broad implications for topic model evaluation.

2 Dataset and Gold Standard

To examine the relationship between topic cardinality and topic coherence, we require a dataset that has topics for a range of cardinality settings. Although there are existing datasets with human-annotated coherence scores (Newman et al., 2010; Aletras and Stevenson, 2013; Lau et al., 2014; Chang et al., 2009), these topics were annotated using a fixed cardinality setting (e.g. 5 or 10). We thus develop a new dataset for this experiment.

Following Lau et al. (2014), we use two domains: (1) WIKI, a collection of 3.3 million English Wikipedia articles (retrieved November 28th 2009); and (2) NEWS, a collection of 1.2 million New York Times articles from 1994 to 2004 (English Gigaword). We sub-sample approximately 50M tokens (100K and 50K articles for WIKI and NEWS respectively) from both domains to create two smaller document collections. We then generate 300 LDA topics for each of the sub-sampled collection.[2]

There are two primary approaches to assessing topic coherence: (1) via word intrusion (Chang et

al., 2009); and (2) by directly measuring observed coherence (Newman et al., 2010; Lau et al., 2014). With the first method, Chang et al. (2009) injects an intruder word into the top-5 topic words, shuffles the topic words, and sets the task of selecting the single intruder word out of the 6 words. In preliminary experiments, we found that the word intrusion task becomes unreasonably difficult for human annotators when the topic cardinality is high, e.g. when $N = 20$. As such, we use the second approach as the means for generating our gold standard, asking users to judge topic coherence directly over different topic cardinalities.[3]

To collect the coherence judgements, we used Amazon Mechanical Turk and asked Turkers to rate topics in terms of coherence using a 3-point ordinal scale, where 1 indicates incoherent and 3 very coherent (Newman et al., 2010). For each topic (600 topics in total) we experiment with 4 cardinality settings: $N = \{5, 10, 15, 20\}$. For example, for $N = 5$, we display the top-5 topic words for coherence judgement.

For annotation quality control, we embed a bad topic generated using random words into each HIT. Workers who fail to consistently rate these bad topics low are filtered out.[4] On average, we collected

Domain	N			
	5	10	15	20
WIKI	2.42 (±0.54)	2.37 (±0.53)	2.35 (±0.51)	2.29 (±0.50)
NEWS	2.49 (±0.53)	2.46 (±0.53)	2.42 (±0.51)	2.39 (±0.51)

Table 1: Mean rating across different N (numbers in parentheses denote standard deviations)

Cardinality Pair	WIKI	NEWS
5 vs. 10	0.834	0.849
5 vs. 15	0.777	0.834
5 vs. 20	0.826	0.815
10 vs. 15	0.841	0.876
10 vs. 20	0.853	0.854
15 vs. 20	0.831	0.871
Mean	0.827	0.850

Table 2: Correlation between different pairwise cardinality settings.

---

[2]The sub-sampled document collections are lemmatised using OpenNLP and Morpha (Minnen et al., 2001) before topic modelling.

[3]This is not a major limitation, however, as Lau et al. (2014) found a strong correlation between the judgements generated by the two methodologies.

[4]We filter workers who rate bad topics with a rating > 1 in more than 30% of their HITs.

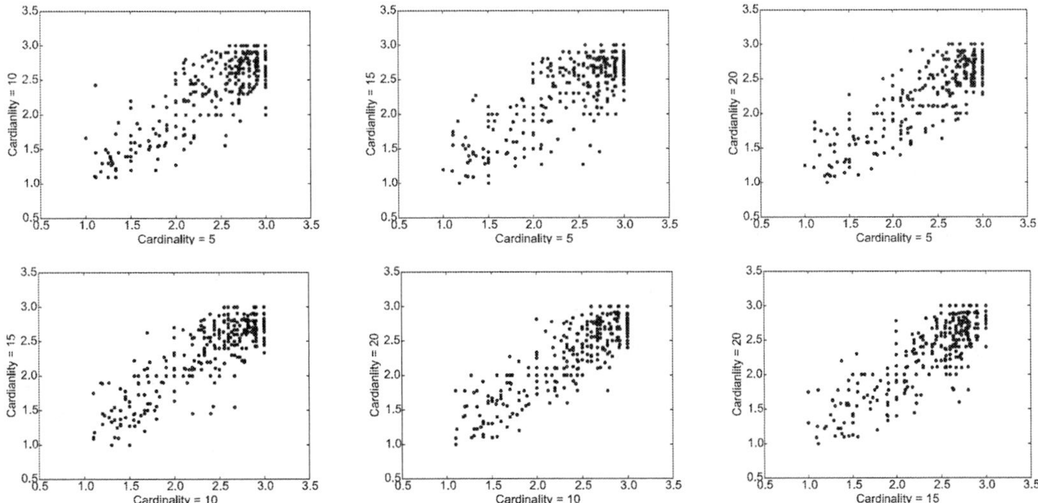

Figure 1: Scatter plots of human ratings for different pairwise cardinality settings for the WIKI topics.

approximately 9 ratings per topic in each cardinality setting (post-filtered), from which we generate the gold standard via the arithmetic mean.

To understand the impact of cardinality (N) on topic coherence, we analyse: (a) the mean topic rating for each N (Table 1), and (b) the pairwise Pearson correlation coefficient between the same topics for different values of N (Table 2).

Coherence decreases slightly but systematically as N increases, suggesting that users find topics less coherent (but marginally more consistently interpretable, as indicated by the slight drop in standard deviation) when more words are presented in a topic. The strong pairwise correlations, however, indicate that the ratings are relatively stable across different cardinality settings.

To better understand the data, in Figure 1 we present scatter plots of the ratings for all pairwise cardinality settings (where a point represents a topic). Note the vertical lines for $x = 3.0$ (cf. the weaker effect of horizontal lines for $y = 3.0$), in particular for the top 3 plots where we are comparing $N = 5$ against higher cardinality settings. This implies that topics that are rated as perfectly coherent (3.0) for $N = 5$ exhibit some variance in coherence ratings when N increases. Intuitively, it means that a number of perfectly coherent 5-word topics become less coherent as more words are presented.

3   Automated Method — Word Intrusion

Lau et al. (2014) proposed an automated approach to the word intrusion task. The methodology computes pairwise word association features for the top-N words, and trains a support vector regression model to rank the words. The top-ranked word is then selected as the predicted intruder word. Note that even though it is supervised, no manual annotation is required as the identity of the true intruder word is known. Following the original paper, we use as features normalised PMI (NPMI) and two conditional probabilities (CP1 and CP2), computed over the full collection of WIKI (3.3 million articles) and NEWS (1.2 million articles), respectively. We use 10-fold cross validation to predict the intruder words for all topics.

To generate an intruder for a topic, we select a random word that has a low probability ($P < 0.0005$) in the topic but high probability ($P > 0.01$) in another topic. We repeat this ten times to generate 10 different intruder words for a topic. The 4 cardinalities of a given topic share the same set of intruder words.

To measure the coherence of a topic, we compute *model precision*, or the accuracy of intruder word prediction. For evaluation we compute the Pearson correlation coefficient r of model precisions and human ratings for each cardinality setting. Results are summarised in Table 3.

Domain	N	In-domain Features	Out-of-Domain Features
	5	0.46	0.66
	10	0.41	0.54*
WIKI	15	0.32*	0.51*
	20	0.33*	0.43*
	Avg	0.46	0.65
	5	0.45*	0.65
	10	0.40*	0.60*
NEWS	15	0.38*	0.54*
	20	0.43*	0.47*
	Avg	0.50	0.65

Table 3: Pearson correlation between system model precision and human ratings across different values of N for word intrusion. '*' denotes statistical significance compared to aggregate correlation.

Domain	N	In-domain Features	Out-of-Domain Features
	5	0.02	0.59*
	10	−0.05*	0.58*
WIKI	15	0.00	0.56*
	20	0.06	0.55*
	Avg	0.00	0.63
	5	0.22*	0.62*
	10	0.27*	0.68*
NEWS	15	0.35	0.68*
	20	0.35	0.65*
	Avg	0.31	0.71

Table 4: Pearson correlation between system topic coherence and human ratings across different values of N for NPMI. "*" denotes statistical significance compared to aggregate correlation.

Each domain has 2 sets of correlation figures, based on in-domain and out-of-domain features. In-domain (out-of-domain) features are word association features computed using the same (different) domain as the topics, e.g. when we compute coherence of WIKI topics using word association features derived from WIKI (NEWS).

The correlations using in-domain features are in general lower than for out-of-domain features. This is due to idiosyncratic words that are closely related in the collection, e.g. remnant Wikipedia markup tags. The topic model discovers them as topics and the word statistics derived from the same collection supports the association, but these topics are generally not coherent, as revealed by out-of-domain statistics. This result is consistent with previous studies (Lau et al., 2014).

We see that correlation decreases systematically as N increases, implying that N has high impact on topic coherence evaluation and that if a single value of N is to be used, a lower value is preferable.

To test whether we can leverage the additional information from the different values of N, we aggregate the model precision values and human ratings per-topic before computing the correlation (Table 3: Cardinality = "Avg"). We also test the significance of difference for each N with the aggregate correlation using the Steiger Test (Steiger, 1980); they are marked with '*' in the table.[5]

---

[5]The test measures if the aggregate correlation is significantly higher ($p < 0.1$) than a non-aggregate correlation using a one-tailed test.

The correlation improves substantially. In fact, for NEWS using in-domain features, the correlation is higher than that of any individual cardinality setting. This observation suggests that a better approach to automatically computing topic coherence is to aggregate coherence scores over different cardinality settings, and that it is sub-optimal to evaluate a topic by only assessing a single setting of N. Instead, we should repeat it several times, varying N.

4 Automated Method — NPMI

The other mainstream approach to evaluating topic coherence is to directly measure the average pairwise association between the top-N words. Newman et al. (2010) found PMI to be the best association measure, and later studies (Aletras and Stevenson, 2013; Lau et al., 2014) found that normalised PMI (NPMI: Bouma (2009)) improves PMI further.

To see if the benefit of aggregating coherence measures over several cardinalities transfers across to other methodologies, we test the NPMI methodology. We compute the topic coherence using the full collection of WIKI and NEWS, respectively, for varying N. Results are presented in Table 4.

The in-domain features perform much worse, especially for the WIKI topics. NPMI assigns very high scores to several incoherent topics, thereby reducing the correlation to almost zero. These topics consist predominantly of Wikipedia markup tags, and the high association is due to word statistics idiosyncratic to the collection.

Once again, aggregating the topic coherence over

multiple N values boosts results further. The correlations using aggregation and out-of-domain features again produce the best results for both WIKI and NEWS.

It is important to note that, while these findings were established based on manual annotation of topic coherence, for practical applications, topic coherence would be calculated in a fully-unsupervised manner (averaged over different topic cardinalities), without the use of manual annotations.

5 Conclusion

We investigate the impact of the cardinality of topic words on topic coherence evaluation. We found that human ratings decrease systematically when cardinality increases, although pairwise correlations are relatively high. We discovered that the performance of two automated methods — word intrusion and pairwise NPMI — can be substantially improved if the system scores and human ratings are aggregated over several cardinality settings before computing the correlation. Contrary to the standard practice of using a fixed cardinality setting, our findings suggest that we should assess topic coherence using several cardinality settings and then aggregate over them. The human-judged coherence ratings, along with code to compute topic coherence, are available online.

6 Acknowledgements

This research was supported in part by funding from the Australian Research Council.

References

Nikos Aletras and Mark Stevenson. 2013. Evaluating topic coherence using distributional semantics. In *Proceedings of the Tenth International Workshop on Computational Semantics (IWCS-10)*, pages 13–22, Potsdam, Germany.

David M. Blei, Andrew Y. Ng, and Michael I. Jordan. 2003. Latent Dirichlet allocation. *Journal of Machine Learning Research*, 3:993–1022.

Gosse Bouma. 2009. Normalized (pointwise) mutual information in collocation extraction. In *Proceedings of the Biennial GSCL Conference*, pages 31–40, Potsdam, Germany.

Jonathan Chang, Sean Gerrish, Chong Wang, Jordan L. Boyd-Graber, and David M. Blei. 2009. Reading tea leaves: How humans interpret topic models. In *Advances in Neural Information Processing Systems 21 (NIPS-09)*, pages 288–296, Vancouver, Canada.

Jey Han Lau, David Newman, and Timothy Baldwin. 2014. Machine reading tea leaves: Automatically evaluating topic coherence and topic model quality. In *Proceedings of the 14th Conference of the EACL (EACL 2014)*, pages 530–539, Gothenburg, Sweden.

David Mimno, Hanna Wallach, Edmund Talley, Miriam Leenders, and Andrew McCallum. 2011. Optimizing semantic coherence in topic models. In *Proceedings of the 2011 Conference on Empirical Methods in Natural Language Processing (EMNLP 2011)*, pages 262–272, Edinburgh, UK.

Guido Minnen, John Carroll, and Darren Pearce. 2001. Applied morphological processing of English. *Natural Language Engineering*, 7(3):207–223.

David Newman, Jey Han Lau, Karl Grieser, and Timothy Baldwin. 2010. Automatic evaluation of topic coherence. In *Proceedings of Human Language Technologies: The 11th Annual Conference of the North American Chapter of the Association for Computational Linguistics (NAACL HLT 2010)*, pages 100–108, Los Angeles, USA.

James H. Steiger. 1980. Tests for comparing elements of a correlation matrix. *Psychological Bulletin*, 87:245–251.

Transition-Based Syntactic Linearization with Lookahead Features

Ratish Puduppully †*, **Yue Zhang ‡**, **Manish Shrivastava †**
†Kohli Center on Intelligent Systems (KCIS),
International Institute of Information Technology, Hyderabad (IIIT Hyderabad)
‡Singapore University of Technology and Design
ratish.surendran@research.iiit.ac.in   yue_zhang@sutd.edu.sg
m.shrivastava@iiit.ac.in

Abstract

It has been shown that transition-based methods can be used for syntactic word ordering and tree linearization, achieving significantly faster speed compared with traditional best-first methods. State-of-the-art transition-based models give competitive results on abstract word ordering and unlabeled tree linearization, but significantly worse results on labeled tree linearization. We demonstrate that the main cause for the performance bottleneck is the sparsity of SHIFT transition actions rather than heavy pruning. To address this issue, we propose a modification to the standard transition-based feature structure, which reduces feature sparsity and allows lookahead features at a small cost to decoding efficiency. Our model gives the best reported accuracies on all benchmarks, yet still being over 30 times faster compared with best-first-search.

1 Introduction

Word ordering is the abstract language modeling task of making a grammatical sentence by ordering a bag of words (White, 2004; Zhang and Clark, 2015; De Gispert et al., 2014; Bohnet et al., 2010; Filippova and Strube, 2007; He et al., 2009), which is practically relevant to text-to-text applications such as summarization (Wann et al., 2009) and machine translation (Blackwood et al., 2010). Zhang (2013) built a discriminative word ordering model, which takes a bag of words, together with optional POS and dependency arcs on a subset of input words, and

yields a sentence together with its dependency parse tree that conforms to input syntactic constraints. The system is flexible with respect to input constraints, performing abstract word ordering when no constraints are given, but gives increasingly confined outputs when more POS and dependency relations are specified. It has been applied to syntactic linearization (Song et al., 2014) and machine translation (Zhang et al., 2014).

One limitation of Zhang (2013) is relatively low time efficiency, due to the use of time-constrained best-first-search (White and Rajkumar, 2009) for decoding. In practice, the system can take seconds to order a bag of words in order to obtain reasonable output quality. Recently, Liu et al. (2015) proposed a transition-based model to address this issue, which uses a sequence of state transitions to build the output. The system of Liu et al. (2015) achieves significant speed improvements without sacrificing accuracies when working with unlabeled dependency trees. With labeled dependency trees as input constraints, however, the system of Liu et al. (2015) gives much lower accuracies compared with Zhang (2013).

While the low accuracy can be attributed to heavy pruning, we show that it can be mitigated by modifying the feature structure of the standard transition-based framework, which scores the output transition sequence by summing the scores of each transition action. Transition actions are treated as an *atomic* output component in each feature instance. This works effectively for most structured prediction tasks, including parsing (Zhang and Clark, 2011a). For word ordering, however, transition actions are significantly more complex and sparse compared

---

*Part of the work was done when the author was a visiting student at Singapore University of Technology and Design.

with parsing, which limits the power of the traditional feature model.

We instead break down complex actions into smaller components, merging some components into configuration features which reduces sparsity in the output action and allows flexible lookahead features to be defined according to the next action to be applied. On the other hand, this change in the feature structure prevents legitimate actions to be scored simultaneously for each configuration state, thereby reducing decoding efficiency. Experiments show that our method is slightly slower compared with Liu et al. (2015), but achieves significantly better accuracies. It gives the best results for all standard benchmarks, being over thirty times faster than Zhang (2013). The new feature structures can be applied to other transition-based systems also.

2 Transition-based linearization

Liu et al. (2015) uses a transition-based model for word ordering, building output sentences using a sequence of state transitions. Instead of scoring output syntax trees directly, it scores the transition action sequence for structural disambiguation. Liu et al.'s transition system extends from transition-based parsers (Nivre and Scholz, 2004; Chen and Manning, 2014), where a *state* consists of a *stack* to hold partially built outputs. Transition-based parsers use a *queue* to maintain input word sequences. However, for word ordering, the input is a set without order. Accordingly, Liu et al. uses a *set* to maintain the input. The transition actions are:

- SHIFT-*Word*-POS, which removes *Word* from the *set*, assigns POS to it and pushes it onto the *stack* as the top word S_0;
- LEFTARC-LABEL, which removes the second top of *stack* S_1 and builds a dependency arc $S_1 \xleftarrow{LABEL} S_0$;
- RIGHTARC-LABEL, which removes the top of *stack* S_0 and builds a dependency arc $S_1 \xrightarrow{LABEL} S_0$.

Using the state transition system, the bag of words {*John, loves, Mary*} can be ordered by (SHIFT-*John*-NNP, SHIFT-*loves*-VBZ, LEFTARC-SBJ, SHIFT-*Mary*-NNP, RIGHTARC-OBJ).

Liu et al. (2015) use a discriminative perceptron model with beam search (Zhang and Clark, 2011a),

Unigrams
S_0w; S_0p; $S_{0,l}w$; $S_{0,l}p$; $S_{0,r}w$; $S_{0,r}p$; $S_{0,l2}w$; $S_{0,l2}p$; $S_{0,r2}w$; $S_{0,r2}p$;
S_1w; S_1p; $S_{1,l}w$; $S_{1,l}p$; $S_{1,r}w$; $S_{1,r}p$; $S_{1,l2}w$; $S_{1,l2}p$; $S_{1,r2}w$; $S_{1,r2}p$;

Bigram
$S_0wS_{0,l}w$; $S_0wS_{0,l}p$; $S_0pS_{0,l}w$; $S_0pS_{0,l}p$; $S_0wS_{0,r}w$; $S_0wS_{0,r}p$; $S_0pS_{0,r}w$; $S_0pS_{0,r}p$;
$S_1wS_{1,l}w$; $S_1wS_{1,l}p$; $S_1pS_{1,l}w$; $S_1pS_{1,l}p$; $S_1wS_{1,r}w$; $S_1wS_{1,r}p$; $S_1pS_{1,r}w$; $S_1pS_{1,r}p$;
S_0wS_1w; S_0wS_1p; S_0pS_1w; S_0pS_1p

Trigram
$S_0wS_0pS_{0,l}w$; $S_0wS_{0,l}wS_{0,l}p$; $S_0wS_0pS_{0,l}p$; $S_0pS_{0,l}wS_{0,l}p$; $S_0wS_0pS_{0,r}w$; $S_0wS_{0,l}wS_{0,r}p$; $S_0wS_0pS_{0,r}p$; $S_0pS_{0,r}wS_{0,r}p$;
$S_1wS_1pS_{1,l}w$; $S_1wS_{1,l}wS_{1,l}p$; $S_1wS_1pS_{1,l}p$; $S_1pS_{1,l}wS_{1,l}p$; $S_1wS_1pS_{1,r}w$; $S_1wS_{1,l}wS_{1,r}p$; $S_1wS_1pS_{1,r}p$; $S_1pS_{1,r}wS_{1,r}p$;

Linearization
w_0; p_0; $w_{-1}w_0$; $p_{-1}p_0$; $w_{-2}w_{-1}w_0$; $p_{-2}p_{-1}p_0$; $S_{0,l}wS_{0,l2}w$; $S_{0,l}pS_{0,l2}p$; $S_{0,r2}wS_{0,r}w$; $S_{0,r2}pS_{0,r}p$; $S_{1,l}wS_{1,l2}w$; $S_{1,l}pS_{1,l2}p$; $S_{1,r2}wS_{1,r}w$; $S_{1,r2}pS_{1,r}p$;

Table 1: Base feature templates.

designing decoding algorithms that accommodate flexible constraints. The features include word(w), pos(p) and dependency label(l) information of words on the stack (S_0, S_1, ... from the top). For example, the word on top of stack is S_0w and the POS of the stack top is S_0p. The full set of feature templates can be found in Table 2 of Liu et al. (2015), reproduced here in Table 1. These templates are called *configuration features*. When instantiated, they are combined with each legal output *action* to score the action. Therefore, actions are atomic in feature instances.

Formally, given a configuration C, the score of a possible action a is calculated as:

$$Score(a) = \vec{\theta} \cdot \Phi(\vec{C}, a),$$

where $\vec{\theta}$ is the model parameter vector of the model and $\Phi(\vec{C}, a)$ denotes a sparse feature vector that consists of features with *configuration* and *action* components i.e $\Phi(\vec{C}, a)$ is sparse. $\vec{\theta}$ has to be loaded for each a.

For efficiency considerations and following transition-based models, Liu et al. (2015) scores all possible actions given a configuration simultaneously. This is effectively the same as formulating the score into

$$Score(a) = \vec{\theta_a} \cdot \Phi(\vec{C}), a \in A.$$

Here A is the full set of actions and $\Phi(\vec{C})$ is fixed, and $\vec{\theta_a}$ for all a can be loaded simultaneously. In a hash-based parameter model, it significantly improves the time efficiency.

3 Feature structure modification

3.1 Two limitations of the baseline model

There are two major limitations in the feature structure of Liu et al. (2015). First, the SHIFT actions, which consist of the word to shift and its POS, are highly sparse. Since the action is combined with all configuration features, there will be no active feature for disambiguating the shift actions for OOV words. This issue does not exist in transition-based parsers because words are not a part of their transition actions. Second, input constraints are not leveraged by the feature model. Although the dependency relations of the word to shift can be given as inputs, they are used only as constraints to the decoder, but not as features to guide the shift action. Such lookahead information on the to-be-shifted word can be highly useful for disambiguation.

For example, consider the bag of words {*John, loves, Mary*}. Without constraints, both '*John loves Mary*' and '*Mary loves John*' are valid word ordering results. However, given the constraint (*John*, SBJ, *loves*), the correct answer is reduced to the former. The first action to build the two examples are (SHIFT-*John*-NNP) and (SHIFT-*Mary*-NNP), respectively. According to Liu et al.'s feature model, there is no feature to disambiguate the first SHIFT action if both '*John*' and '*Mary*' are OOV words. The system has to maintain both hypotheses and rely on the search algorithm to disambiguate them after the dependency arcs (*John*, SBJ, *loves*) and (*Mary*, OBJ, *loves*) are built. However, given the syntactic constraint that '*John*' is the subject, the disambiguation can be done right when performing the first SHIFT action. This requires the dependency arc label to be extracted for the word to shift e.g.(*John, Mary*), which is a lookahead feature. In addition, the OOV word '*John*' must be excluded from the feature instance, which implies that the SHIFT-*John*-NNP action must be simplified.

set of label and POS of child nodes of L
$L_{cls}; L_{clns}; L_{cps}; L_{cpns};$ $S_0 w L_{cls}; S_0 p L_{cls}; S_1 w L_{cls}; S_1 p L_{cls};$ $S_0 w L_{clns}; S_0 p L_{clns}; S_1 w L_{clns}; S_1 p L_{clns};$ $S_0 w L_{cps}; S_0 p L_{cps}; S_1 w L_{cps}; S_1 p L_{cps};$ $S_0 w L_{cpns}; S_0 p L_{cpns}; S_1 w L_{cpns}; S_1 p L_{cpns};$
set of label and POS of siblings of L
$L_{sls}; L_{slns}; L_{sps}; L_{spns};$ $S_0 w L_{sls}; S_0 p L_{sls}; S_1 w L_{sls}; S_1 p L_{sls};$ $S_0 w L_{slns}; S_0 p L_{slns}; S_1 w L_{slns}; S_1 p L_{slns};$ $S_0 w L_{sps}; S_0 p L_{sps}; S_1 w L_{sps}; S_1 p L_{sps};$ $S_0 w L_{spns}; S_0 p L_{spns}; S_1 w L_{spns}; S_1 p L_{spns};$
parent label, POS and word of L
$L_{ps} L_{lp}; L_{ps} L_{pp}; L_{ps} L_{wp};$ $S_0 w L_{ps} L_{lp}; S_0 p L_{ps} L_{lp}; S_1 w L_{ps} L_{lp}; S_1 p L_{ps} L_{lp};$ $S_0 w L_{ps} L_{pp}; S_0 p L_{ps} L_{pp}; S_1 w L_{ps} L_{pp}; S_1 p L_{ps} L_{pp};$ $S_0 w L_{ps} L_{wp}; S_0 p L_{ps} L_{wp}; S_1 w L_{ps} L_{wp}; S_1 p L_{ps} L_{wp};$
set of label and POS of child nodes of S_0
$S_{cls}; S_{clns}; S_{cps}; S_{cpns};$ $S_0 w S_{cls}; S_0 p S_{cls}; S_1 w S_{cls}; S_1 p S_{cls};$ $S_0 w S_{clns}; S_0 p S_{clns}; S_1 w S_{clns}; S_1 p S_{clns};$ $S_0 w S_{cps}; S_0 p S_{cps}; S_1 w S_{cps}; S_1 p S_{cps};$ $S_0 w S_{cpns}; S_0 p S_{cpns}; S_1 w S_{cpns}; S_1 p S_{cpns};$
set of label and POS of siblings of S_0
$S_{sls}; S_{slns}; S_{sps}; S_{spns};$ $S_0 w S_{sls}; S_0 p S_{sls}; S_1 w S_{sls}; S_1 p S_{sls};$ $S_0 w S_{slns}; S_0 p S_{slns}; S_1 w S_{slns}; S_1 p S_{slns};$ $S_0 w S_{sps}; S_0 p S_{sps}; S_1 w S_{sps}; S_1 p S_{sps};$ $S_0 w S_{spns}; S_0 p S_{spns}; S_1 w S_{spns}; S_1 p S_{spns};$
parent label and POS of S_0
$S_{ps} S_{lp}; S_{ps} S_{pp};$ $S_0 w S_{ps} S_{lp}; S_0 p S_{ps} S_{lp}; S_1 w S_{ps} S_{lp}; S_1 p S_{ps} S_{lp};$ $S_0 w S_{ps} S_{pp}; S_0 p S_{ps} S_{pp}; S_1 w S_{ps} S_{pp}; S_1 p S_{ps} S_{pp};$

Table 2: Lookahead feature templates

As a second example, information about dependents can also be useful for disambiguating SHIFT actions. In the above case, the fact that the *subject* has not been shifted onto the stack can be a useful indicator for not shifting the verb '*loves*' onto the stack in the beginning. Inspired by the above, we exploit a range of lookahead features from syntactic constraints.

3.2 New feature structure for SHIFT actions

We modify the feature structure of Liu et al. (2015) by breaking down the SHIFT-*Word-POS* action into three components, namely SHIFT, *Word* and *POS*, using only the action type SHIFT as the output action component in feature instances, while combin-

	no pos no dep		50% pos no dep		all pos no dep		no pos 50% dep		50% pos 50% dep		all pos 50% dep		no pos all dep		50% pos all dep		all pos all dep	
	BL	SP	BL	SP	BL	SP	BL	SP	BL	SP	BL	SP	BL	SP	BL	SP	BL	SP
Z13	42.9	4872	43.4	4856	44.7	4826	50.5	4790	51.4	4737	52.2	4720	73.3	4600	74.7	4431	76.3	4218
L15	47.5	155	47.9	119	48.8	74	54.8	132	55.2	91	56.2	41	77.8	40	79.1	28	81.1	22
Ours	48.0	175	49.0	156	51.5	148	59.0	144	62.0	160	67.1	171	82.8	62	86.2	68	89.9	70

Table 3: Development partial-tree linearization results. *BL* – BLEU score; *SP* – number of milliseconds per sentence. Z13 – best-first system of Zhang (2013) and L15 – transition-based system of Liu et al. (2015).

ing *Word* and *POS* with other configuration features to form a set of lookahead features.

For example, consider the configuration feature S_0w, which captures the word on the top of the stack. Under the feature structure of Liu et al., it is combined with each possible action to form features for scoring the action. As a result, for scoring the action SHIFT-Lw-Lp, S_0w is instantiated into S_0w-SHIFT-Lw-Lp, where Lw is the word to shift and Lp is its POS. Under our new feature structure, the action component is reduced to SHIFT only, while Lw and Lp should be used in lookahead features. Now a effectively equivalent configuration feature to Liu et al.'s S_0w is S_0w-Lw-Lp, with the lookahead Lw and Lp. It gives S_0w-Lw-Lp-SHIFT when combined with the action SHIFT.

This new feature structure reformulates the SHIFT action features only. The LEFTARC/ RIGHTARC actions remain LEFTARC/ RIGHTARC-LABEL since they are not sparse. Note that the change is in the *action features* rather than the *actions* themselves. Given the bag of words {*John, loves, Mary*}, the action SHIFT-*John*-NNP is still different from the action SHIFT-*Mary*-NNP. However, the *action component* of the features becomes SHIFT only, and the words *John/ Mary* must be used as lookahead *configuration features* for their disambiguation.

The new feature structure can reduce feature sparsity by allowing lookahead features without word information. For example, a configuration feature S_0w-Lp, which contains only the stack top word and the POS of the lookahead word, can still fire even if the word to shift is OOV, thereby disambiguating OOV words of different POS. In addition, the lookahead Lw and Lp do not have to be combined with every other configuration feature, as with Liu et al. (2015), thereby allowing more flexible feature combination and a leaner model.

3.3 The new features

The new feature structure includes two types of features. The first is the same feature set as Liu et al. (2015), but with the SHIFT action component not having *Word* and *POS* information. We call this type of features as *base features*. The second is a set of *lookahead features*, which are shown in Table 2. Here L_{cls} represents set of arc labels on child nodes (of the word L to shift) that have been shifted on to the stack, L_{clns} represents set of labels on child nodes that have not been shifted, L_{sls} the label set of shifted sibling nodes, L_{slns} the label set of unshifted sibling nodes, L_{cps} the POS set of shifted child nodes, L_{cpns} the POS set of unshifted child nodes, L_{sps} the POS set of shifted sibling nodes and L_{spns} the POS set of unshifted sibling nodes. L_{ps} is a binary feature indicating if the parent has been shifted. L_{lp} represents label on the parent, L_{pp} POS of parent and L_{wp} the parent word form. We define similar lookahead features for S_0. These features are instantiated only for SHIFT actions.

The new feature structure prevents all possible actions from being scored simultaneously, because the lookahead *Word* and *POS* are now in configuration features, rather than output actions, making it necessary to score the shifting of different words or POS separately. This leads to reduced search speed. Nevertheless, our experiments show that they give a desirable tradeoff between efficiency and accuracy.

Note that the new features are much less than a full Cartesian product of lookahead features and the original features. This is a result of manual feature engineering, which allows similar accuracies to be achieved using a much smaller model, thereby increasing the time efficiency.

	unlabeled		labeled	
	no pos no dep	all pos no dep	all pos all dep	all pos all dep
W09	-	33.7	-	-
Z11	-	40.1	-	-
Z13	44.7	46.8	76.2	89.3
L15	49.4	50.8	82.3	82.9
This paper	**50.5**	**53.0**	**91.0**	**91.8**

Table 4: Final results. W09 – Wann et al. (2009), Z11 – Zhang and Clark (2011b)

4 Experiments

Following previous work we conduct experiments on the Penn TreeBank (PTB), using Wall Street Journal sections 2-21 for training, 22 for development and 23 for testing. Gold-standard dependency trees are derived from bracketed sentences using Penn2Malt, and base noun phrases are treated as a single word. The BLEU score is used to evaluate the performance of linearization.

Table 4 shows a difference in scores between transition-based linearization system of Liu et al. (2015) (L15) and best-first system of Zhang (2013) (Z13). L15 performs better for word ordering with unlabeled dependency arcs, but poorly for the task of labeled syntactic linearization.

Table 3 shows a series of development experiments comparing our system with Z13 and L15. We vary the amount of input syntactic constraints by randomly sampling from POS and dependency labels of the development set. Our system gives consistently higher accuracies when compared with both Z13 and L15. Compared to L15, the increase in scores for unconstrained word ordering is due to the introduction of reduced feature sparsity. The improvements on tree linearization tasks involving partial to full dependency constraints are also due to lookahead features that leverage tree information to reduce ambiguity early. Though slower than L15, our system is over 30 times faster compared to Z13.

We compare final test scores with previous methods in the literature in Table 4. Our system improves upon the previous best scores by 8.7 BLEU points for the task of unlabeled syntactic linearization. For the task of labeled syntactic linearization, we achieve the score of 91.8 BLEU points, the highest results reported so far.

Table 5 contains examples of fully constrained

	Fully constrained output
ref.	The spinoff also will compete with Fujitsu
L15	The spinoff with Fujitsu compete also will
Ours	The spinoff also will compete with Fujitsu
ref.	Dr. Talcott led a team of researchers from the National Cancer Institute .
L15	a team of researchers from the National Cancer Institute led Dr. Talcott .
Ours	Dr. Talcott led a team of researchers from the National Cancer Institute .

Table 5: Example outputs.

output . In the first example '*will*' is the ROOT node with two child nodes '*also*' and '*compete*'. Lookahead feature for child dependency labels L_{cls}, L_{clns} on the node '*will*' can help order the segment '*also will compete*' correctly in our system. Without such features, the system of L15 yields an output that starts with '*The spinoff with Fujitsu*' which is locally fluent, but leaving the words '*also*' and '*will*' difficult to handle. In the second example, '*Dr. Talcott*' is OOV. Hence system of L15 is not able to score it and thus order it correctly. Our system makes use of both POS and dependency label of '*Dr. Talcott*' to order it correctly.

5 Conclusion

We identified a feature sparsity issue in state-of-the-art transition-based word ordering, proposing a solution by redefining the feature structure and introducing lookahead features. The new method gives the best accuracies on a set of benchmarks, which show that transition-based methods are a fast and accurate choice for syntactic linearization. Future work include the testing of this model in a linearization shared task (Belz et al., 2011) and investigating the integration of large scale training data (Zhang et al., 2012; Liu and Zhang, 2015).

We release our source code under GPL at `https://github.com/SUTDNLP/ZGen/releases/tag/v0.2`.

Acknowledgments

We thank Yijia Liu for helpful discussions and for sharing the Latex templates and the anonymous reviewers for their constructive comments. This work was supported by the Singapore Ministry of Education (MOE) AcRF Tier 2 grant T2MOE201301.

References

Anja Belz, Michael White, Dominic Espinosa, Eric Kow, Deirdre Hogan, and Amanda Stent. 2011. The first surface realisation shared task: Overview and evaluation results. In *Proceedings of the 13th European workshop on natural language generation*, pages 217–226. Association for Computational Linguistics.

Graeme Blackwood, Adrià De Gispert, and William Byrne. 2010. Fluency constraints for minimum bayes-risk decoding of statistical machine translation lattices. In *Proceedings of the 23rd International Conference on Computational Linguistics*, pages 71–79. Association for Computational Linguistics.

Bernd Bohnet, Leo Wanner, Simon Mille, and Alicia Burga. 2010. Broad coverage multilingual deep sentence generation with a stochastic multi-level realizer. In *Proceedings of the 23rd International Conference on Computational Linguistics*, pages 98–106. Association for Computational Linguistics.

Danqi Chen and Christopher D Manning. 2014. A fast and accurate dependency parser using neural networks. *Proceedings of the 2014 Conference on Empirical Methods in Natural Language Processing (EMNLP)*, 1:740–750.

A De Gispert, M Tomalin, and W Byrne. 2014. Word ordering with phrase-based grammars. *14th Conference of the European Chapter of the Association for Computational Linguistics 2014, EACL 2014*, pages 259–268.

Katja Filippova and Michael Strube. 2007. Generating constituent order in german clauses. In *Annual Meeting-Association for Computational Linguistics*, volume 45, page 320.

Wei He, Haifeng Wang, Yuqing Guo, and Ting Liu. 2009. Dependency based chinese sentence realization. In *Proceedings of the Joint Conference of the 47th Annual Meeting of the ACL and the 4th International Joint Conference on Natural Language Processing of the AFNLP: Volume 2*, pages 809–816.

Jiangming Liu and Yue Zhang. 2015. An empirical comparison between n-gram and syntactic language models for word ordering. In *Proceedings of the 2015 Conference on Empirical Methods in Natural Language Processing*, pages 369–378, Lisbon, Portugal, September. Association for Computational Linguistics.

Yijia Liu, Yue Zhang, Wanxiang Che, and Bing Qin. 2015. Transition-based syntactic linearization. In *NAACL HLT 2015, The 2015 Conference of the North American Chapter of the Association for Computational Linguistics: Human Language Technologies, Denver, Colorado, USA, May 31 - June 5, 2015*, pages 113–122.

Joakim Nivre and Mario Scholz. 2004. Deterministic dependency parsing of english text. In *Proceedings of the 20th international conference on Computational Linguistics*, page 64. Association for Computational Linguistics.

Linfeng Song, Yue Zhang, Kai Song, and Qun Liu. 2014. Joint morphological generation and syntactic linearization. *Proceedings of the Twenty-Eighth AAAI Conference on Artificial Intelligence*, pages 1522–1528.

Stephen Wann, Mark Dras, Robert Dale, and Cécile Paris. 2009. Improving grammaticality in statistical sentence generation: Introducing a dependency spanning tree algorithm with an argument satisfaction model. In *Proceedings of the 12th Conference of the European Chapter of the Association for Computational Linguistics*, pages 852–860.

Michael White and Rajakrishnan Rajkumar. 2009. Perceptron reranking for ccg realization. In *Proceedings of the 2009 Conference on Empirical Methods in Natural Language Processing: Volume 1-Volume 1*, pages 410–419. Association for Computational Linguistics.

Michael White. 2004. Reining in ccg chart realization. In *Natural Language Generation*, pages 182–191. Springer Berlin Heidelberg.

Yue Zhang and Stephen Clark. 2011a. Syntactic processing using the generalized perceptron and beam search. *Computational linguistics*, 37(1):105–151.

Yue Zhang and Stephen Clark. 2011b. Syntax-based grammaticality improvement using ccg and guided search. In *Proceedings of the Conference on Empirical Methods in Natural Language Processing*, pages 1147–1157. Association for Computational Linguistics.

Yue Zhang and Stephen Clark. 2015. Discriminative syntax-based word ordering for text generation. *Computational Linguistics*, 41(3):503–538.

Yue Zhang, Graeme Blackwood, and Stephen Clark. 2012. Syntax-based word ordering incorporating a large-scale language model. In *Proceedings of the 13th Conference of the European Chapter of the Association for Computational Linguistics*, pages 736–746. Association for Computational Linguistics.

Yue Zhang, Kai Song, Linfeng Song, Jingbo Zhu, and Qun Liu. 2014. Syntactic smt using a discriminative text generation model. In *Proceedings of the 2014 Conference on Empirical Methods in Natural Language Processing (EMNLP)*, pages 177–182, Doha, Qatar, October. Association for Computational Linguistics.

Yue Zhang. 2013. Partial-tree linearization: generalized word ordering for text synthesis. In *Proceedings of the Twenty-Third international joint conference on Artificial Intelligence*, pages 2232–2238. AAAI Press.

A Recurrent Neural Networks Approach
for Estimating the Quality of Machine Translation Output

Hyun Kim
Creative IT Engineering,
Pohang University of Science and
Technology (POSTECH),
Pohang, Republic of Korea
`hkim.postech@gmail.com`

Jong-Hyeok Lee
Computer Science and Engineering,
Pohang University of Science and
Technology (POSTECH),
Pohang, Republic of Korea
`jhlee@postech.ac.kr`

Abstract

This paper presents a novel approach using recurrent neural networks for estimating the quality of machine translation output. A sequence of vectors made by the prediction method is used as the input of the final recurrent neural network. The prediction method uses bi-directional recurrent neural network architecture both on source and target sentence to fully utilize the bi-directional quality information from source and target sentence. Our experiments show that the proposed recurrent neural networks approach achieves a performance comparable to the existing state-of-the-art models for estimating the sentence-level quality of English-to-Spanish translation.

1 Introduction

Estimating the quality of machine translation output, called *quality estimation* (QE) (Specia et al., 2009; Blatz et al., 2004), is to predict quality scores/categories for unseen machine-translated sentences without reference translations at various granularity levels (sentence-level/word-level/document-level). Quality estimation is of growing importance in the field of machine translation (MT) since MT systems are widely used and the quality of each machine-translated sentence is able to vary considerably.

Previous research on QE, addressed as a regression/classification problem to compute quality scores/categories, has mainly focused on feature extraction and feature selection. Feature extraction is

to find the relevant features, such as baseline features (Specia et al., 2013) and latent semantic indexing (LSI) based features (Langlois, 2015), capturing various aspects of quality from source and target sentences[1] and external resources. Feature selection is to select the best features by using selection algorithms, such as Gaussian processes (Shah et al., 2015) and heuristic (González-Rubio et al., 2013), among already extracted features. Finding desirable features has played a key role in the QE research.

In this paper we present a recurrent neural networks approach for estimating the quality of machine translation output at sentence level, which does not require manual effort for finding the best relevant features. The remainder of this paper is organized as follows. In Section 2, we propose a recurrent neural networks approach using a sequence of vectors made by the prediction method as input for quality estimation. And we describe the prediction method using bi-directional recurrent neural networks architecture in Section 3. In Section 4, we report evaluation results, and conclude our paper in Section 5.

2 Recurrent Neural Networks Approach for Estimating Quality Score

Because recurrent neural networks (RNNs) have the strength for handling sequential data (Goodfellow et al., 2015), we apply RNNs to estimate the quality score of translation.

The input of the final RNN is a sequence of vectors that have quality information about whether tar-

---

[1]In this paper, a 'target sentence' means the machine-translated sentence from a source sentence.

Proceedings of NAACL-HLT 2016, pages 494–498,
San Diego, California, June 12-17, 2016. ©2016 Association for Computational Linguistics

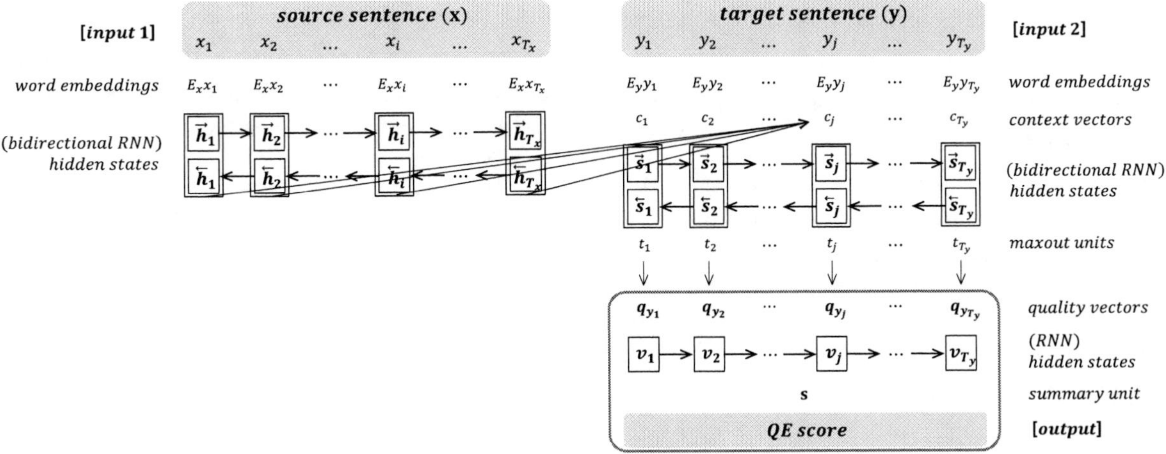

Figure 1: An illustration of the proposed recurrent neural networks model for quality estimation

get words in a target sentence are properly translated from a source sentence. We will refer to this sequence of vectors as *quality vectors* $(q_{y_1}, \dots, q_{y_{T_y}})$. Each quality vector $q_{y_j}{}^2$ has the quality information about how well a target word y_j in a target sentence $\mathbf{y} = (y_1, \dots, y_{T_y})$ is translated from a source sentence[3] $\mathbf{x} = (x_1, \dots, x_{T_x})$. Quality vectors are generated from the prediction method (of Section 3).

To predict a quality estimation score (QE score) as an HTER score (Snover et al., 2006) in [0,1] for each target sentence, a logistic sigmoid function is used such that

$$
\begin{aligned}
\mathrm{QE\,score}(\mathbf{y}, \mathbf{x}) \\
= \mathrm{QE\,score}'(q_{y_1}, \dots, q_{y_{T_y}}) \quad (1) \\
= \sigma(W_{QE}^{\top}\, \mathbf{s})
\end{aligned}
$$

where $\mathbf{s}$ is a summary unit of the whole quality vectors and $W_{QE} \in \mathbb{R}^r$. r is the dimensionality of summary unit.

To get the summary unit $\mathbf{s}$, the hidden state v_j employing p gated hidden units for the target word y_j is computed by

$$
v_j = f(q_{y_j}, v_{j-1}). \quad (2)
$$

The gated hidden unit (Cho et al., 2014) for the activation function f is used to learn long-term dependencies of translation qualities for target words. We consider the QE score as the integrated/condensed value reflecting the sequential quality information of sequential target words. Because the last hidden state v_{T_y} is a summary of the sequential quality vectors, we fix the summary unit $\mathbf{s}$ to the last hidden state v_{T_y}.

3 Prediction method using Bi-directional RNN Architecture to Make Quality Vectors

In this section, we detail the ways to get the quality vectors $(q_{y_1}, \dots, q_{y_{T_y}})$ for computing QE score.

Since the training data for QE[4] are not enough to use a neural networks approach for making quality vectors, we use an alternative based on large-scale parallel corpora such as Europarl. We modify the word prediction method of RNN Encoder-Decoder (Cho et al., 2014) using parallel corpora to make the quality vectors.

In subsection 3.1, we describe the underlying word prediction method of RNN Encoder-Decoder. We i) extend the prediction method to use the additional backward RNN architecture on target sentence in subsection 3.2 and ii) modify to get the quality vectors $(q_{y_1}, \dots, q_{y_{T_y}})$ in subsection 3.3.

---

[2] $1 \leq j \leq T_y$ where T_y is the length of target sentence.

[3] Source(Target) sentence consists of 1-of-$K_x(K_y)$ coded word vectors. $K_x(K_y)$ is the vocabulary sizes of source(target) language.

[4] These data, provided in WMT Quality Estimation Shared Task, consist of source sentences, target sentences, and quality scores.

Figure 1 is the graphical illustration of the proposed RNNs approach.

3.1 Word Prediction Method of RNN Encoder-Decoder

RNN Encoder-Decoder proposed by Cho et al. (2014) is able to predict the target word y_j given a source sentence $\mathbf{x}$ and all preceding target words $\{y_1, ..., y_{j-1}\}$ by using a softmax function. And it is extended by Bahdanau et al. (2015) to use information of relevant source words for predicting the target word y_j such that

$$
\begin{aligned}
p(y_j | \{y_1, ..., y_{j-1}\}, \mathbf{x}) \\
= g(y_{j-1}, \vec{s}_{j-1}, c_j).
\end{aligned}
\tag{3}
$$

g is a nonlinear function predicting the probability of y_j. $\vec{s}_{j-1}$ is the hidden state of the forward RNN on target sentence and contains information of preceding target words $\{y_1, ..., y_{j-1}\}$. c_j is the context vector which means relevant parts of source sentence associated with the target word y_j. $\vec{s}_{j-1}$ and y_{j-1} are related to all preceding target words $\{y_1, ..., y_{j-1}\}$, and c_j is related to $\mathbf{x}$ in the word prediction function of (3).

3.2 Additional Backward RNN Architecture on Target Sentence

Bahdanau et al. (2015) introduce bi-directional RNN architecture only on source sentence to extend RNN Encoder-Decoder. In our proposed QE model, bi-directional RNN architecture is used both on source and target sentence. By applying bi-directional RNN architecture both on source and target sentence, we can fully and bi-directionally utilize source and target sentence for predicting target words, such that

$$
\begin{aligned}
p(y_j | \mathbf{y}_{\not{=} y_j}, \mathbf{x}) \\
= g([y_{j-1}; y_{j+1}], [\vec{s}_{j-1}; \overleftarrow{s}_{j+1}], c_j) \\
= \frac{\exp(y_j^\top W_{o_1} W_{o_2} t_j)}{\sum_{k=1}^{K_y} \exp(y_k^\top W_{o_1} W_{o_2} t_j)},
\end{aligned}
\tag{4}
$$

which is the extended version of (3) using the additional backward RNN architecture.[5]

---

[5]The additional backward RNN on target sentence use the context vectors shared by the forward RNN on target sentence.

To reflect further all following target words $\{y_{j+1}, ..., y_{T_y}\}$ when predicting the target word y_j, the hidden state $\overleftarrow{s}_{j+1}$ of the backward RNN and the next target word y_{j+1} are added. $[\vec{s}_{j-1}; \overleftarrow{s}_{j+1}]$ and $[y_{j-1}; y_{j+1}]$ are related to $\mathbf{y}_{\not{=} y_j}$[6], and c_j is related to $\mathbf{x}$ in the word prediction function of (4).

$W_{o_1} \in \mathbb{R}^{K_y \times q}$ and $W_{o_2} \in \mathbb{R}^{q \times l}$ are weight matrices of softmax function. K_y is the vocabulary sizes of target language and q is the dimensionality of quality vectors. l is the dimensionality of maxout units such that

$$
t_j = [max\{\tilde{t}_{j,2k-1}, \tilde{t}_{j,2k}\}]_{k=1,...,l}^\top,
\tag{5}
$$

where $\tilde{t}_{j,k}$ is the k-th element of a vector $\tilde{t}_j$. And

$$
\tilde{t}_j = S_o'[\vec{s}_{j-1}; \overleftarrow{s}_{j+1}] + V_o'[E_\mathbf{y} y_{j-1}; E_y y_{j+1}] + C_o c_j,
\tag{6}
$$

where $S_o' \in \mathbb{R}^{2l \times 2n}$, $V_o' \in \mathbb{R}^{2l \times 2m}$, and $C_o \in \mathbb{R}^{2l \times 2n}$. $E_\mathbf{y} \in \mathbb{R}^{m \times K_y}$ is the word embedding matrix on target sentence. m and n are the dimensionality of word embedding and hidden states of forward and backward RNNs. The hidden state $\overleftarrow{s}_{j+1}$ of the backward RNN and next target word y_{j+1} are used in (6).[7]

From the extended prediction method of (4), the probability of the target word y_j is computed by using information of relevant source words in source sentence $\mathbf{x}$ and all target words $\mathbf{y}_{\not{=} y_j}$ surrounding the target word y_j in target sentence.

3.3 Quality Vectors on Target Sentence

Word prediction method predicts the probability of target words as a number between 0 and 1. But we want to get quality vectors of q-dimensionality which have the more intrinsic quality information for target words.

To make quality vectors, we regard that the probability of the target word y_j involves the quality information about whether the target word y_j in target sentence is properly translated from source sentence. Thus, by decomposing the softmax function[8] of (4),

---

[6]$\mathbf{y}_{\not{=} y_j} = \{y_1, ..., y_{j-1}, y_{j+1}, ..., y_{T_y}\}$

[7]Original $\tilde{t}_j$ (Bahdanau et al., 2015) is
$$\tilde{t}_j = S_o \vec{s}_{j-1} + V_o E_\mathbf{y} y_{j-1} + C_o c_j.$$

[8]In this softmax function, the bias term is not used for the simplicity of deriving the quality vectors. Generally, bias terms are visually omitted in other equations to make the equations uncluttered.

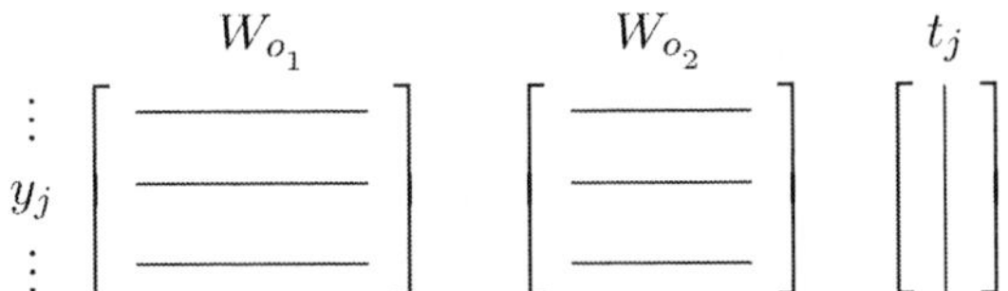

Figure 2: Weight matrices (W_{o_1} and W_{o_2}) of softmax function and maxout unit t_j for the target word y_j

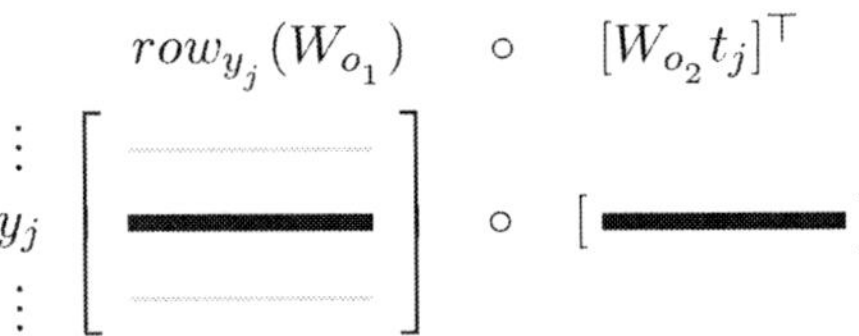

Figure 3: The ways of computing the quality vector q_{y_j} ($\circ$ is an element-wise multiplication)

the quality vector q_{y_j} for the target word y_j is computed by

$$q_{y_j} = \left[\ row_{y_j}(W_{o_1}) \circ [W_{o_2} t_j]^\top\ \right]^\top, \quad (7)$$

where $\circ$ is an element-wise multiplication. All of quality information about possible K_y target words at position j of target sentence is encoded in t_j. Thus, by decoding t_j, we are able to get quality vector q_{y_j} for the target word $y_j \in \mathbb{R}^{K_y}$ at position j of target sentence. Figure 2 and 3 show the ways to compute the quality vector q_{y_j}.

4 Experiments

The proposed RNNs approach was evaluated on the WMT15 Quality Estimation Shared Task[9] at sentence level of English-Spanish.

We trained[10] the proposed model through a two-step process. First, by using English-Spanish parallel corpus of Europarl v7 (Koehn, 2005), we trained bi-directional RNNs having 1000 hidden units on source and target sentence to make quality vectors. Next, by using the training set of WMT15 QE task, to predicte QE scores we trained the final RNN that

---

[9]http://www.statmt.org/wmt15/quality-estimation-task.html

[10]Stochastic gradient descent (SGD) algorithm with adaptive learning rate (Adadelta) (Zeiler, 2012) is used to train the proposed model.

System ID	MAE ↓	RMSE ↓
• RTM-DCU/RTM-FS+PLS-SVR	0.1325	0.1748
• LORIA/17+LSI+MT+FILTRE	0.1334	0.1735
• RTM-DCU/RTM-FS-SVR	0.1335	0.1768
• LORIA/17+LSI+MT	0.1342	0.1745
Bi-RNN	**0.1359**	**0.1765**
• UGENT-LT3/SCATE-SVM	0.1371	0.1745
Baseline SVM	0.1482	0.1913

Table 1: Proposed approach (Bi-RNN) results and official results for the **scoring variant** of WMT15 Quality Estimation Shared Task at sentence level. A total of 5 tied official winning systems are indicated by a •. Two standard metrics is used: Mean Average Error (MAE) as a primary metric, and Root of Mean Squared Error (RMSE) as a secondary metric (Bojar et al., 2015).

System ID	DeltaAvg ↑	Spearman's ρ ↑
• LORIA/17+LSI+MT+FILTRE	6.51	0.36
• LORIA/17+LSI+MT	6.34	0.37
• RTM-DCU/RTM-FS+PLS-SVR	6.34	0.37
• RTM-DCU/RTM-FS-SVR	6.09	0.35
Bi-RNN	**6.08**	**0.33**
Baseline SVM	2.16	0.13

Table 2: Proposed approach (Bi-RNN) results and official results for the **ranking variant** of WMT15 Quality Estimation Shared Task at sentence level. A total of 4 tied official winning systems are indicated by a •. DeltaAvg metric is used as a primary metric (Bojar et al., 2015).

use the quality vectors generated in previous step as the input and have 100 hidden units.

Table 1 and 2 present the results of the proposed approach (Bi-RNN) and the official results for the scoring and ranking[11] variants of the WMT15 Quality Estimation Shared Task at sentence level. At both variants of the task, the proposed RNNs approach achieved the performance over the baseline performance. Also our experiments showed that the performance of the proposed RNNs approach is included to the best performance group (at the scoring variant of Table 1) or is close to the best performance group (at the ranking variant of Table 2).

5 Conclusion

This paper proposed a recurrent neural networks approach using quality vectors for estimating the quality of machine translation output at sentence level.

---

[11]The ranking variant of the QE task measures how close a proposed ranking of target translations from best to worst is to the true ranking.

This approach does not require manual effort for finding the best relevant features which the previous QE research has mainly focused on.

To make quality vectors we used an alternative prediction method based on large-scale parallel corpora, because the QE training data were not enough. By extending the prediction method to use bi-directional RNN architecture both on source and target sentence, we were able to fully utilize the bi-directional quality information from source and target sentence for quality estimation.

The proposed RNNs approach achieved a performance comparable to the existing state-of-the-art models at sentence-level QE. Our experiments have showed that RNNs approach is a meaningful step for QE research. Applying RNNs approach to word-level QE and studying other ways to make quality vectors better are remained for the future study.

Acknowledgments

This research was supported by the MSIP (Ministry of Science, ICT and Future Planning), Korea, under the "ICT Consilience Creative Program" (IITP-2015-R0346-15-1007) supervised by the IITP (Institute for Information & communications Technology Promotion)

References

Dzmitry Bahdanau, Kyunghyun Cho, and Yoshua Bengio. 2015. Neural machine translation by jointly learning to align and translate. In *ICLR 2015*.

John Blatz, Erin Fitzgerald, George Foster, Simona Gandrabur, Cyril Goutte, Alex Kulesza, Alberto Sanchis, and Nicola Ueffing. 2004. Confidence estimation for machine translation. In *Proceedings of the 20th international conference on Computational Linguistics*, page 315. Association for Computational Linguistics.

Ondřej Bojar, Rajen Chatterjee, Christian Federmann, Barry Haddow, Matthias Huck, Chris Hokamp, Philipp Koehn, Varvara Logacheva, Christof Monz, Matteo Negri, Matt Post, Carolina Scarton, Lucia Specia, and Marco Turchi. 2015. Findings of the 2015 workshop on statistical machine translation. In *Proceedings of the Tenth Workshop on Statistical Machine Translation*, pages 1–46, Lisbon, Portugal, September. Association for Computational Linguistics.

Kyunghyun Cho, Bart van Merrienboer, Caglar Gulcehre, Fethi Bougares, Holger Schwenk, and Yoshua Bengio. 2014. Learning phrase representations using rnn encoder-decoder for statistical machine translation. In *Conference on Empirical Methods in Natural Language Processing (EMNLP 2014)*.

Jesús González-Rubio, J Ramón Navarro-Cerdán, and Francisco Casacuberta. 2013. Dimensionality reduction methods for machine translation quality estimation. *Machine translation*, 27(3-4):281–301.

Ian Goodfellow, Aaron Courville, and Yoshua Bengio. 2015. Deep learning. Book in preparation for MIT Press.

Philipp Koehn. 2005. Europarl: A parallel corpus for statistical machine translation. In *MT summit*, volume 5, pages 79–86. Citeseer.

David Langlois. 2015. Loria system for the wmt15 quality estimation shared task. In *Proceedings of the Tenth Workshop on Statistical Machine Translation*, pages 323–329, Lisbon, Portugal, September. Association for Computational Linguistics.

Kashif Shah, Trevor Cohn, and Lucia Specia. 2015. A bayesian non-linear method for feature selection in machine translation quality estimation. *Machine Translation*, pages 1–25.

Matthew Snover, Bonnie Dorr, Richard Schwartz, Linnea Micciulla, and John Makhoul. 2006. A study of translation edit rate with targeted human annotation. In *Proceedings of association for machine translation in the Americas*, pages 223–231.

Lucia Specia, Marco Turchi, Nicola Cancedda, Marc Dymetman, and Nello Cristianini. 2009. Estimating the sentence-level quality of machine translation systems. In *13th Conference of the European Association for Machine Translation*, pages 28–37.

Lucia Specia, Kashif Shah, José GC De Souza, and Trevor Cohn. 2013. Quest-a translation quality estimation framework. In *ACL (Conference System Demonstrations)*, pages 79–84. Citeseer.

Matthew D Zeiler. 2012. Adadelta: An adaptive learning rate method. *arXiv preprint arXiv:1212.5701*.

Symmetric Patterns *and* Coordinations:
Fast *and* Enhanced Representations of Verbs *and* Adjectives

Roy Schwartz,[1]   **Roi Reichart,**[2]   **Ari Rappoport**[1]

[1]Institute of Computer Science, The Hebrew University

[2]Faculty of Industrial Engineering and Management, Technion, IIT

`{roys02|arir}@cs.huji.ac.il   roiri@ie.technion.ac.il`

Abstract

State-of-the-art word embeddings, which are often trained on bag-of-words (*BOW*) contexts, provide a high quality representation of aspects of the semantics of nouns. However, their quality decreases substantially for the task of verb similarity prediction. In this paper we show that using symmetric pattern contexts (*SPs*, e.g., "X and Y") improves word2vec verb similarity performance by up to 15% and is also instrumental in adjective similarity prediction. The unsupervised *SP* contexts are even superior to a variety of dependency contexts extracted using a supervised dependency parser. Moreover, we observe that *SPs* and dependency coordination contexts (*Coor*) capture a similar type of information, and demonstrate that *Coor* contexts are superior to other dependency contexts including the set of all dependency contexts, although they are still inferior to *SPs*. Finally, there are substantially fewer *SP* contexts compared to alternative representations, leading to a massive reduction in training time. On an 8G words corpus and a 32 core machine, the *SP* model trains in 11 minutes, compared to 5 and 11 hours with *BOW* and all dependency contexts, respectively.

1   Introduction

In recent years, vector space models (VSMs) have become prominent in NLP. VSMs are often evaluated by measuring their ability to predict human judgments of lexical semantic relations between pairs of words, mostly association or similarity. While many datasets for these tasks are limited to pairs of nouns, the recent SimLex999 word similarity dataset (Hill et al., 2014) also consists of similarity scores for *verb* and *adjective* pairs. State-of-the-art VSMs such as word2vec skip-gram (*w2v-SG*, (Mikolov et al., 2013a)) and GloVe (Pennington et al., 2014) excel at noun-related tasks. However, their performance substantially decreases on *verb* similarity prediction in SimLex999, and their adjective representations have rarely been evaluated (Section 2).

In this paper we show that a key factor in the reduced performance of the *w2v-SG* model on verb representation is its reliance on bag-of-words (*BOW*) contexts: contexts of the represented words that consist of words in their physical proximity. We investigate a number of alternative contexts for this model, including various dependency contexts, and show that simple, automatically acquired symmetric patterns (*SPs*, e.g., "X or Y", (Hearst, 1992; Davidov and Rappoport, 2006)) are the most useful contexts for the representation of verbs and also adjectives. Moreover, the *SP*-based model is much more compact than the alternatives, making its training an order of magnitude faster.

In particular, we train several versions of the *w2v-SG* model, each with a different context type, and evaluate the resulting word embeddings on the task of predicting the similarity scores of the verb and adjective portions of SimLex999. Our results show that *SP* contexts (SG-*SP*) obtain the best results on both tasks: Spearman's ρ scores of 0.459 on verbs and 0.651 on adjectives. These results are 15.2% and 4.7% better than *BOW* contexts and 7.3% and 6.5% better than all dependency contexts (*DepAll*). Moreover, the number of *SP* contexts is substantially

Proceedings of NAACL-HLT 2016, pages 499–505,

San Diego, California, June 12-17, 2016. ©2016 Association for Computational Linguistics

smaller than the alternatives, making it extremely fast to train: 11 minutes only on an 8G word corpus using a 32 CPU core machine, compared to 5 and 11 hours for *BOW* and *DepAll*, respectively.

Recently, Schwartz et al. (2015) presented a count-based VSM that utilizes *SP* contexts (SRR15). This model excels on verb similarity, outperforming VSMs that use other contexts (e.g., *BOW* and *DepAll*) by more than 20%. In this paper we show that apart from its *SP* contexts, the success of SRR15 is attributed in large to its explicit representation of antonyms (*live/die*); turning this feature off reduces its performance to be on par with SG-*SP*. As opposed to Schwartz et al. (2015), we keep our VSM fixed across experiments (*w2v-SG*), changing only the context type. This allows us to attribute our improved results to one factor: *SP* contexts.

We further observe that *SP* contexts are tightly connected to syntactic *coordination* contexts (*Coor*, Section 3). Following this observation, we compare the *w2v-SG* model with three dependency-based context types: (a) *Coor* contexts; (b) all dependency links (*DepAll*); and (c) all dependency links excluding *Coor* links (*Coor^C*).[1] Our results show that training with *Coor* contexts is superior to training with the other context types, leading to improved similarity prediction of 2.7-4.1% and 4.3-6.9% on verbs and adjectives respectively.

These results demonstrate the prominence of *Coor* contexts in verb and adjective representation: these contexts are even better than their combination with the rest of the dependency-based contexts (the *DepAll* contexts). Nonetheless, although *Coor* contexts are extracted using a supervised dependency parser, they are still inferior to *SP* contexts, extracted automatically from plain text (Section 3), by 4.6% and 2.2% for verb and adjective pairs.

2   Background

Word Embeddings for Verbs and Adjectives. A number of evaluation sets consisting of word pairs scored by humans for semantic relations (mostly association and similarity) are in use for VSM evaluation. These include: RG-65 (Rubenstein and Goodenough, 1965), MC-30 (Miller and Charles, 1991), WordSim353 (Finkelstein et al., 2001), MEN (Bruni

et al., 2014) and SimLex999 (Hill et al., 2014).[2]

Nouns are dominant in almost all of these datasets. For example, RG-65, MC-30 and WordSim353 consist of noun pairs almost exclusively. A few datasets contain pairs of verbs (Yang and Powers, 2006; Baker et al., 2014). The MEN dataset, although dominated by nouns, also contains verbs and adjectives. Nonetheless, the human judgment scores in these datasets reflect *relatedness* between words. In contrast, the recent SimLex999 dataset (Hill et al., 2014) contains word *similarity* scores for nouns (666 pairs), verbs (222 pairs) and adjectives (111 pairs). We use this dataset to study the effect of context type on VSM performance in a verb and adjective similarity prediction task.

Context Type in Word Embeddings. Most VSMs (e.g., (Collobert et al., 2011; Mikolov et al., 2013b; Pennington et al., 2014)) define the context of a target word to be the words in its physical proximity (bag-of-words contexts). Dependency contexts, consisting of the words connected to the target word by dependency links (Grefenstette, 1994; Padó and Lapata, 2007; Levy and Goldberg, 2014), are another well researched alternative. These works did not recognize the importance of syntactic coordination contexts (*Coor*).

Patterns have also been suggested as VSM contexts, but mostly for representing *pairs* of words (Turney, 2006; Turney, 2008). While this approach has been successful for extracting various types of word relations, using patterns to represent *single* words is useful for downstream applications. Recently, Schwartz et al. (2015) explored the value of *symmetric* pattern contexts for word representation, an idea this paper develops further.

A recently published approach (Melamud et al., 2016) also explored the effect of the type of context on the performance of word embedding models. Nonetheless, while they also explored bag-of-words and dependency contexts, they did not experiment with *SPs* or coordination contexts, which we find to be most useful for predicting word similarity.

Limitations of Word Embeddings. Recently, a few papers examined the limitations of word embedding models in representing different types of se-

---

[1] *Coor* $\cup$ *Coor^C* = *DepAll*, *Coor* $\cap$ *Coor^C* = $\emptyset$

[2] For a comprehensive list see: `wordvectors.org/`

mantic information. Levy et al. (2015) showed that word embeddings do not capture semantic relations such as hyponymy and entailment. Rubinstein et al. (2015) showed that while state-of-the-art embeddings are successful at capturing taxonomic information (e.g., *cow* is an animal), they are much less successful in capturing attributive properties (*bananas* are yellow). In (Schwartz et al., 2015), we showed that word embeddings are unable to distinguish between pairs of words with opposite meanings (antonyms, e.g., good/bad). In this paper we study the difficulties of bag-of-words based word embeddings in representing verb similarity.

3 Symmetric Patterns (*SPs*)

Lexico-syntactic patterns are templates of text that contain both words and wildcards (Hearst, 1992), e.g., "X *and* Y" and "X *for a* Y". Pattern *instances* are sequences of words that match a given pattern, such that concrete words replace each of the wildcards. For example, "**John** *and* **Mary**" is an instance of the pattern "X *and* Y". Patterns have been shown useful for a range of tasks, including word relation extraction (Lin et al., 2003; Davidov et al., 2007), knowledge extraction (Etzioni et al., 2005), sentiment analysis (Davidov et al., 2010) and authorship attribution (Schwartz et al., 2013).

Symmetric patterns (*SPs*) are lexico-syntactic patterns that comply to two constraints: (a) Each pattern has exactly two wildcards (e.g., **X** *or* **Y**); and (b) When two words (*X,Y*) co-occur in an *SP*, they are also likely to co-occur in this pattern in opposite positions, given a large enough corpus (e.g., "**X** *or* **Y**" and "**Y** *or* **X**"). For example, the pattern "**X** *and* **Y**" is symmetric as for a large number of word pairs (e.g., (*eat,drink*)) both members are likely to occur in both of its wildcard positions (e.g., "eat *and* drink", "drink *and* eat").

SPs have shown useful for tasks such as word clustering (Widdows and Dorow, 2002; Davidov and Rappoport, 2006), semantic class learning (Kozareva et al., 2008) and word classification (Schwartz et al., 2014). In this paper we demonstrate the value of *SP*-based contexts in vector representations of verbs and adjectives. The rationale behind this context type is that two words that co-occur in an *SP* tend to take the same semantic role in the sentence, and are thus likely to be similar in meaning (e.g., "(John and Mary) sang").

SP **Extraction.** Many works that applied *SPs* in NLP tasks employed a hand-crafted list of patterns (Widdows and Dorow, 2002; Dorow et al., 2005; Feng et al., 2013). Following Schwartz et al. (2015) we employ the DR06 algorithm (Davidov and Rappoport, 2006), an unsupervised algorithm that extracts *SPs* from plain text. We apply this algorithm to our corpus (Section 4) and extract 11 *SPs*: "X *and* Y", "X *or* Y", "X *and the* Y", "X *or the* Y", "X *or a* Y", "X *nor* Y", "X *and one* Y", "*either* X *or* Y", "X *rather than* Y", "X *as well as* Y", "*from* X *to* Y". A description of the DR06 algorithm is beyond the scope of this paper; the interested reader is referred to (Davidov and Rappoport, 2006).

SP **Contexts.** We generate *SP* contexts by taking the co-occurrence counts of pairs of words in *SPs*. For example, in the *SP* token "*boys and girls*", the term *girls* is taken as an *SP* context of the word *boys*, and *boys* is taken as an *SP* context of *girls*.

We do not make a distinction between the different *SPs*. E.g., "*boys* **and** *girls*" and "*boys* **or** *girls*" are treated the same. However, we distinguish between left and right contexts. For example, we generate different contexts for the word *girls*, one for left-hand contexts ("**girls** *and boys*") and another for right-hand contexts ("*boys and* **girls**").

SPs **and Coordinations.** *SPs* and syntactic coordinations (*Coors*) are intimately related. For example, of the 11 *SPs* extracted in this paper by the DR06 algorithm (listed above), the first eight represent coordination structures. Moreover, these *SPs* account for more than 98% of the *SP* instances in our corpus. Indeed, due to the significant overlap between *SPs* and *Coors*, the former have been proposed as a simple model of the latter (Nakov and Hearst, 2005).[3]

Despite their tight connection, *SPs* sometimes fail to properly identify the components of *Coors*. For example, while *SPs* are instrumental in capturing shallow *Coors*, they fail in capturing coordination between phrases. Consider the sentence *John*

---

[3]Note though that the exact syntactic annotation of coordination is debatable both in the linguistic community (Tesnière, 1959; Hudson, 1980; Mel'čuk, 1988) and also in the NLP community (Nilsson et al., 2006; Schwartz et al., 2011; Schwartz et al., 2012).

walked and Mary ran: the *SP* "X *and* Y" captures the phrase *walked and Mary*, while the *Coor* links the heads of the connected phrases ("*walked*" and "*ran*"). *SPs*, on the other hand, can go beyond *Coors* and capture other types of symmetric structures like "*from* X *to* Y" and "X *rather than* Y".

Our experiments reveal that both *SPs* and *Coors* are highly useful contexts for verb and adjective representation, at least with respect to word similarity. Interestingly, *Coor* contexts, extracted using a supervised dependency parser, are less effective than *SP* contexts, which are extracted from plain text.

4 Experiments

Model. We keep the VSM fixed throughout our experiments, changing only the context type. This methodology allows us to evaluate the impact of different contexts on the VSM performance, as context choice is the only modeling decision that changes across experimental conditions.

Our VSM is the word2vec skip-gram model (*w2v-SG*, Mikolov et al. (2013a)), which obtains state-of-the-art results on a variety of NLP tasks (Baroni et al., 2014). We employ the word2vec toolkit.[4] For all context types other than *BOW* we use the word2vec package of (Levy and Goldberg, 2014),[5] which augments the standard word2vec toolkit with code that allows arbitrary context definition.

Experimental Setup. We experiment with the verb pair (222 pairs) and adjective pair (111 pairs) portions of SimLex999 (Hill et al., 2014). We report the Spearman ρ correlation between the ranks derived from the scores of the evaluated models and the human scores provided in SimLex999.[6]

We train the *w2v-SG* model with five different context types: (a) *BOW* contexts (SG-*BOW*); (b) all dependency links (SG-*DepAll*) (c) dependency-based coordination contexts (i.e., those labeled with *conj*, SG-*Coor*); (d) all dependency links except for coordinations (SG-*Coor*[C]); and (e) *SP* contexts. Our training corpus is the 8G words corpus gener-

---

[4]https://code.google.com/p/word2vec/

[5]https://bitbucket.org/yoavgo/word2vecf

[6]Model scores are computed in the standard way: applying the cosine similarity metric to the vectors learned for the words participating in the pair.

Model	Verb	Adj.	Noun	Time	#Cont.
SG-*BOW*	0.307	0.604	**0.501**	320	13G
SG-*DepAll*	0.386	0.586	0.499	551	14.5G
SG-*Coor*	0.413	0.629	0.428	23	550M
SG-*Coor*[C]	0.372	0.56	0.494	677	14G
SG-*SP*	**0.459**	**0.651**	0.415	11	270M
SRR15	0.578	0.663	0.497	—	270M
SRR15[−]	0.441	0.68	0.421	—	270M

Table 1:
Spearman's ρ scores on the different portions of SimLex999. The top part presents results for the word2vec skip-gram model (*w2v-SG*) with various context types (see text). The bottom lines present the results of the count *SP*-based model of Schwartz et al. (2015), with (SRR15) and without (SRR15[−]) its antonym detection method. The two rightmost columns present the run time of the *w2v-SG* models in minutes (Time) and the number of context instances used by the model (#Cont.).[10] For each SimLex999 portion, the score of the best *w2v-SG* model across context types is highlighted in bold font.

ated by the word2vec script.[7]

Models (b)-(d) require the dependency parse trees of the corpus as input. To generate these trees, we employ the Stanford POS Tagger (Toutanova et al., 2003)[8] and the stack version of the MALT parser (Nivre et al., 2009).[9] The *SP* contexts are generated using the *SPs* extracted by the DR06 algorithm from our training corpus (see Section 3).

For *BOW* contexts, we experiment with three window sizes (2, 5 and 10) and report the best results (window size of 2 across conditions). For dependency based contexts we follow the standard convention in the literature: we consider the immediate heads and modifiers of the represented word. All models are trained with 500 dimensions, the default value of the word2vec script. Other hyperparameters were also set to the default values of the code packages.

Results. Table 1 presents our results. The SG-*SP* model provides the most useful verb and adjective representations among the *w2v-SG* models. Compared to *BOW* (SG-*BOW*), the most commonly used

---

[7]code.google.com/p/word2vec/source/
browse/trunk/demo-train-big-model-v1.sh

[8]nlp.stanford.edu/software/tagger.shtml

[9]http://www.maltparser.org/index.html

context type, SG-*SP* results are 15.2% and 4.7% higher on verbs and adjectives respectively. Compared to dependency links (SG-*DepAll*), the improvements are 7.3% and 6.5%. For completeness, we compare the models on the noun pairs portion, observing that SG-*BOW* and SG-*DepAll* are $\sim$8.5% better than SG-*SP*. This indicates that different word classes require different representations.

The results for SG-*Coor*, which is trained with syntactic coordination (*Coor*) contexts, show that these contexts are superior to all the other dependency links (SG-$Coor^C$) by 4.1% and 6.9% on verbs and adjectives. Importantly, comparing the SG-*Coor* model to the SG-*DepAll* model, which augments the *Coor* contexts with the other syntactic dependency contexts, reveals that SG-*DepAll* is actually inferior by 2.7% and 4.3% in Spearman ρ on verbs and adjectives respectively. Interestingly, *Coor* contexts, which are extracted using a supervised parser, are still inferior by 4.6% and 2.2% to *SPs*, which capture similar contexts but are extracted from plain text.

Table 1 also shows the training times of the various *w2v-SG* models on a 32G memory, 32 CPU core machine. SG-*SP* and SG-*Coor*, which take 11 minutes and 23 minutes respectively to train, are substantially faster than the other *w2v-SG* models. For example, they are more than an order of magnitude faster than SG-*BOW* (320 minutes) and SG-$Coor^C$ (677 minutes). This is not surprising, as there are far fewer *SP* contexts (270M) and *Coor* contexts (550M) than *BOW* contexts (13G) and $Coor^C$ contexts (14G) (#Cont. column).

Finally, the performance of the SG-*SP* model is still substantially inferior to the SRR15 *SP*-based model (Schwartz et al., 2015). As both models use the same *SP* contexts, this result indicates that other modeling decisions in SRR15 lead to its superior performance. We show that this difference is mostly attributed to one feature of SRR15: its method for detecting antonym pairs (*good/bad*). Indeed, the SRR15 model without its antonym detection method ($SRR15^-$) obtains a Spearman ρ of 0.441, compared to 0.459 of SG-*SP* on verb pairs. For adjectives, however, $SRR15^-$ is 1.7% better than SRR15, in-

creasing the difference from SG-*SP* to 2.9%.[11]

5 Conclusions

We demonstrated the effectiveness of symmetric pattern contexts in word embedding induction. Experiments with the word2vec model showed that these contexts are superior to various alternatives for verb and adjective representation. We further pointed at the connection between symmetric patterns and syntactic coordinations. We showed that coordinations are superior to other syntactic contexts, but are still inferior to symmetric patterns, although the extraction of symmetric patterns requires less supervision.

Future work includes developing a model that successfully combines the various context types explored in this paper. We are also interested in the representation of other word classes such as adverbs for which no evaluation set currently exists. Finally, the code for generating the SG-*SP* embeddings, as well as the vectors experimented with in this paper, are released and can be downloaded from `http://www.cs.huji.ac.il/~roys02/papers/sp_sg/sp_sg.html`

Acknowledgments

This research was funded (in part) by the Intel Collaborative Research Institute for Computational Intelligence (ICRI-CI), the Israel Ministry of Science and Technology Center of Knowledge in Machine Learning and Artificial Intelligence (Grant number 3-9243). The second author was partially funded by the Microsoft/Technion research center for electronic commerce and the Google faculty research award.

References

Simon Baker, Roi Reichart, and Anna Korhonen. 2014. An unsupervised model for instance level subcategorization acquisition. In *Proc. of EMNLP*.

Marco Baroni, Georgiana Dinu, and Germán Kruszewski. 2014. Don't count, predict! a systematic comparison of context-counting vs. context-predicting semantic vectors. In *Proc. of ACL*.

---

[10]We compare the *w2v-SG* models training time only. SRR15 and $SRR15^-$ are count-based models and have no training step.

[11]We report results for our reimplementation of SRR15 and $SRR15^-$.

Elia Bruni, Nam-Khanh Tran, and Marco Baroni. 2014. Multimodal distributional semantics. *JAIR*.

Ronan Collobert, Jason Weston, Léon Bottou, Michael Karlen, Koray Kavukcuoglu, and Pavel Kuksa. 2011. Natural language processing (almost) from scratch. *JMLR*, 12:2493–2537.

Dmitry Davidov and Ari Rappoport. 2006. Efficient unsupervised discovery of word categories using symmetric patterns and high frequency words. In *Proc. of ACL-COLING*.

Dmitry Davidov, Ari Rappoport, and Moshe Koppel. 2007. Fully unsupervised discovery of concept-specific relationships by web mining. In *Proc. of ACL*.

Dmitry Davidov, Oren Tsur, and Ari Rappoport. 2010. Enhanced sentiment learning using twitter hashtags and smileys. In *Proc. of COLING*.

Beate Dorow, Dominic Widdows, Katarina Ling, Jean-Pierre Eckmann, Danilo Sergi, and Elisha Moses. 2005. Using Curvature and Markov Clustering in Graphs for Lexical Acquisition and Word Sense Discrimination.

Oren Etzioni, Michael Cafarella, Doug Downey, Ana-Maria Popescu, Tal Shaked, Stephen Soderland, Daniel S Weld, and Alexander Yates. 2005. Unsupervised named-entity extraction from the web: An experimental study. *Artificial intelligence*, 165(1):91–134.

Song Feng, Jun Seok Kang, Polina Kuznetsova, and Yejin Choi. 2013. Connotation lexicon: A dash of sentiment beneath the surface meaning. In *Proc. of ACL*.

Lev Finkelstein, Evgeniy Gabrilovich, Yossi Matias, Ehud Rivlin, Zach Solan, Gadi Wolfman, and Eytan Ruppin. 2001. Placing search in context: The concept revisited. In *Proc. of WWW*.

Gregory Grefenstette. 1994. *Explorations in automatic thesaurus discovery*. Boston: Kluwer.

Marti A. Hearst. 1992. Automatic acquisition of hyponyms from large text corpora. In *Proc. of COLING – Volume 2*.

Felix Hill, Roi Reichart, and Anna Korhonen. 2014. Simlex-999: Evaluating semantic models with (genuine) similarity estimation. *arXiv:1408.3456 [cs.CL]*.

Richard A. Hudson. 1980. *Arguments for a Non-transformational Grammar*. Chicago: University of Chicago Press.

Zornitsa Kozareva, Ellen Riloff, and Eduard Hovy. 2008. Semantic class learning from the web with hyponym pattern linkage graphs. In *Proc. of ACL-HLT*.

Omer Levy and Yoav Goldberg. 2014. Dependency-based word embeddings. In *Proc. of ACL*.

Omer Levy, Steffen Remus, Chris Biemann, and Ido Dagan. 2015. Do supervised distributional methods really learn lexical inference relations? In *Proc. of NAACL*.

Dekang Lin, Shaojun Zhao, Lijuan Qin, and Ming Zhou. 2003. Identifying synonyms among distributionally similar words. In *Proc. of IJCAI*.

Oren Melamud, David McClosky, Siddharth Patwardhan, and Mohit Bansal. 2016. The role of context types and dimensionality in learning word embeddings. In *Proc. of NAACL*.

Igor Mel'čuk. 1988. *Dependency Syntax: Theory and Practice*. State University of New York Press.

Tomas Mikolov, Ilya Sutskever, Kai Chen, Greg S Corrado, and Jeff Dean. 2013a. Distributed representations of words and phrases and their compositionality. In *Proc. of NIPS*.

Tomas Mikolov, Wen-tau Yih, and Geoffrey Zweig. 2013b. Linguistic regularities in continuous space word representations. In *Proc. of NAACL-HLT*.

George A Miller and Walter G Charles. 1991. Contextual correlates of semantic similarity. *Language and cognitive processes*.

Preslav Nakov and Marti Hearst. 2005. Using the web as an implicit training set: application to structural ambiguity resolution. In *Proc. of HLT-EMNLP*.

Jens Nilsson, Joakim Nivre, and Johan Hall. 2006. Graph transformations in data-driven dependency parsing. In *Proc. of ACL-COLING*.

Joakim Nivre, Marco Kuhlmann, and Johan Hall. 2009. An improved oracle for dependency parsing with online reordering. In *Proc. of IWPT*.

Sebastian Padó and Mirella Lapata. 2007. Dependency-based construction of semantic space models. *Computational Linguistics*.

Jeffrey Pennington, Richard Socher, and Christopher D. Manning. 2014. Glove: Global vectors for word representation. In *Proc. of EMNLP*.

Herbert Rubenstein and John B. Goodenough. 1965. Contextual correlates of synonymy. *Communications of the ACM*.

Dana Rubinstein, Effi Levi, Roy Schwartz, and Ari Rappoport. 2015. How well do distributional models capture different types of semantic knowledge? In *Proc. of ACL*.

Roy Schwartz, Omri Abend, Roi Reichart, and Ari Rappoport. 2011. Neutralizing linguistically problematic annotations in unsupervised dependency parsing evaluation. In *Proc. of ACL-HLT*.

Roy Schwartz, Omri Abend, and Ari Rappoport. 2012. Learnability-based syntactic annotation design. In *Proc. of COLING*.

Roy Schwartz, Oren Tsur, Ari Rappoport, and Moshe Koppel. 2013. Authorship attribution of micro-messages. In *Proc. of EMNLP*.

Roy Schwartz, Roi Reichart, and Ari Rappoport. 2014. Minimally supervised classification to semantic categories using automatically acquired symmetric patterns. In *Proc. of COLING*.

Roy Schwartz, Roi Reichart, and Ari Rappoport. 2015. Symmetric pattern based word embeddings for improved word similarity prediction. In *Proc. of CoNLL*.

Lucien Tesnière. 1959. *Éléments de syntaxe structurale*. Paris: Klincksieck.

Kristina Toutanova, Dan Klein, Christopher D Manning, and Yoram Singer. 2003. Feature-rich part-of-speech tagging with a cyclic dependency network. In *Proc. of NAACL*.

Peter D. Turney. 2006. Similarity of semantic relations. *Computational Linguistics*.

Peter D. Turney. 2008. A uniform approach to analogies, synonyms, antonyms, and associations. In *Proc. of COLING*.

Dominic Widdows and Beate Dorow. 2002. A graph model for unsupervised lexical acquisition. In *Proc. of COLING*.

Dongqiang Yang and David M. W. Powers. 2006. Verb similarity on the taxonomy of wordnet. In *Proc. of GWC*.

Breaking the Closed World Assumption in Text Classification

Geli Fei and **Bing Liu**
Department of Computer Science
University of Illinois at Chicago
gfei2@uic.edu, liub@cs.uic.edu

Abstract

Existing research on multiclass text classification mostly makes the *closed world* assumption, which focuses on designing accurate classifiers under the assumption that all test classes are known at training time. A more realistic scenario is to expect unseen classes during testing (*open world*). In this case, the goal is to design a learning system that classifies documents of the known classes into their respective classes and also to reject documents from unknown classes. This problem is called *open (world) classification*. This paper approaches the problem by reducing the open space risk while balancing the empirical risk. It proposes to use a new learning strategy, called *center-based similarity* (CBS) *space learning* (or *CBS learning*), to provide a novel solution to the problem. Extensive experiments across two datasets show that CBS learning gives promising results on multiclass open text classification compared to state-of-the-art baselines.

1 Introduction

With the rapid growth of online information, text classifiers have become one of the most important tools for people to track and organize information. And the emergence of social media platforms has brought increasing diversity and dynamics to the Web. Many social science researchers rely on the collected online user generated content to carry out research on different social phenomenon. In this case, multiclass text classifiers are widely used to gather information of several topics of interest. However, most existing research on multiclass text classification makes the *closed world* assumption, meaning that all the test classes have been seen in training. However, in a more realistic scenario

where people use a multiclass classifier to collect information of several topics from a data source that covers a much broader range of topics, it is normal to break the closed world assumption and to see the arrival of documents from unknown classes that have never been seen in training. In this case, a multiclass classifier should not always assign a document to one of the known classes. Instead, it should identify unknown classes of documents and label them as unknown or reject. This is called *open (world)* classification.

More precisely, in the traditional multiclass classification setting, the learner assumes a fixed set of classes $Y = \{C_1, C_2, ..., C_m\}$, and the task is to construct a m-class classifier using the training data. The resulting classifier is tested/applied on the data from only the m classes. While in *open* classification, we allow the classifier to predict labels/classes from the set of $C_1, C_2, ..., C_m, C_{m+1}$ classes, where the $(m+1)^{\text{th}}$ class C_{m+1} represents the unknown which covers documents of all unknown or unseen classes or topics. In other words, every test instance may be predicted to belong to either one of the known classes $y_i \in Y$, or C_{m+1} (unknown).

It is thus not sufficient for a classifier to just return the most likely class label among the m known classes. An option to reject must be provided. An obvious approach to predicting the class label $y \in Y \cup \{C_{m+1}\}$ for an n-dimensional data point $x \in R^n$ is to incorporate a posterior probability estimator $p(y|x)$ and a decision threshold into an existing multiclass learning algorithm (Kwok, 1999; Fumera and Roli, 2002; Huang et al., 2006; Bravo et al., 2008). There are many reasons this technique would not achieve good results in open classification. As we will discuss in the following sections, one of the most important reasons is that the underlying classifier is not robust or is not in-

Proceedings of NAACL-HLT 2016, pages 506–514,
San Diego, California, June 12-17, 2016. ©2016 Association for Computational Linguistics

formed enough to reject unseen classes of documents due to its significant open space risk.

Traditional multiclass learners optimize only on the known classes under the closed world assumption, while a potential learner for open classification has to optimize for both the known classes and for the unknown classes. Some recent research in the field of computer vision studied the problem, which they call *open set recognition* (Scheirer et al., 2013; 2014; Jain et al., 2014) for facial recognition. Classic learners define and optimize over empirical risk, which is measured on the training data. For open classification, it is crucial to consider how to extend the model to capture the risk of the unknown by preventing overgeneralization or overspecialization. In order to tackle this problem, Scheirer et al. (2013) introduced the concept of *open space risk* and formulated an extension of existing one-class and binary SVMs to address the open classification problem. However, as we will see in section 3, their proposed method is weak as the positively labeled open space is still an infinite area.

In this work, we propose a solution to reduce the open space risk while also balancing the empirical risk for open classification. Intuitively, given a positive class of documents, our open space for the positive class is considered as the space that is sufficiently far from the center of the positive documents. In the multiclass classification setting, each of the m target classes is surrounded by a ball covering the positively labeled (the target class) area, while any document falling outside of all the m balls is considered belonging to the unknown class.

Recent work by Fei and Liu (2015) proposed a new learning strategy called *center-based similarity space learning* (*CBS learning*) to deal with the problem of covariate shift in binary classification. We found that it is also suitable for open classification. Instead of conducting learning in the traditional document space (or *D-space*) with n-gram features, CBS learning learns in a similarity space. Unlike SVM learning in D-space that bounds the positive class only by an infinite half-space formed with the decision hyperplane, which has a huge open space risk, CBS learning finds a closed boundary for the positive class covering only a finite area, which is a spherical area in the original D-space and thus reduce the open space risk significantly. While discussing CBS learning, we will also describe the underlying assumptions made by it

which were not stated in our earlier paper (Fei and Liu, 2015). Our final multiclass classifier is called *cbsSVM* (based on SVM).

To the best of our knowledge, this is the first attempt to study multiclass open classification in text from the open space risk management perspective. Our experiments show that *cbsSVM* for multiclass open classification produces superior classifiers to existing state-of-the art methods.

2 Related Work

Compared to research on multiclass classification with the closed world assumption, there is relatively less work on open classification. In this section, we review related work on one-class classification, SVM decision score calibration, and others.

One-class classifiers, which only rely on positive training data, are natural starting solutions to the multiclass open classification task. One-class SVM (Scholkopf et al., 2001) and SVDD (Tax and Duin, 2004) are two representative one-class classifiers. One-class SVM treats the origin in the feature space as the only member of the negative class, and maximizes the margin with respect to it. SVDD tries to place a hypersphere with the minimum radius around almost all the positive training points. It has been shown that the use of Gaussian kernel makes SVDD and One-class SVM equivalent, and the results reported in (Khan and Madden, 2014) demonstrate that SVDD and One-class SVM are comparable when the Gaussian kernel is applied. However, as no negative training data is used, one-class classifiers have trouble producing good separations. We will see in Section 4 that their results are poor.

This work is also related to using thresholded probabilities for rejection. As the decision score produced by SVM is not a probability distribution, several techniques have been proposed to convert a raw decision score to a calibrated probability output (Platt, 2000; Zadrozny and Elkan, 2002; Duan and Keerthi, 2005; Huang et al., 2006; Bravo et al., 2008). Usually a parametric distribution is assumed for the underlying distribution, and raw scores are mapped based on the learned model. A variation of Platt's (2000) approach is the most widely used probability estimator for SVM score calibration. It fits a sigmoid function to the SVM scores during training. Provided with a threshold, a test instance can be rejected if the highest probability of this instance belonging to a class is lower than the threshold in multiclass open classification settings.

Recently, researchers in computer vision (Scheirer et al., 2013; 2014; Jain et al., 2014) made some attempts to solve open classification (which they call *open set recognition*) for visual learning from new angles. Scheirer et al. (2013) introduced the concept of open space risk, and defined it as a relative measure. The proposed model reduces the open space risk by replacing the half-space of a binary linear classifier with a positive region bounded by two parallel hyperplanes. While the positively labeled region for a target class is reduced compared to the half-space in the traditional linear SVM, their open space risk is still infinite. In (Jain et al., 2014), the authors proposed to use Extreme Value Theory (EVT) to estimate the unnormalized posterior probability of inclusion for each class by fitting a Weibull distribution over the positive class scores from a 1-vs-rest multiclass RBF SVM classifier. Scheirer et al. (2014) introduced the Compact Abating Probability (CAP) model, which explains how thresholding the probabilistic output of RBF One-class SVM manages the open space risk. Using the probability output from RBF one-class SVM as a conditioner, the authors combine RBF One-class SVM and a Weibull-calibrated SVM similar to the one in (Jain et al., 2014). For both methods (Jain et al., 2014; Scheirer et al., 2014), decision thresholds need to be chosen based on the prior knowledge of the ratio of unseen classes in testing, which is a weakness of the methods.

Dalvi et al. (2013) proposed Exploratory Learning in the multiclass semi-supervised learning (SSL) setting. In their work, an "exploratory" version of expectation-maximization (EM) is proposed to extend traditional multiclass SSL methods, which deals with the scenario when the algorithm is given seeds from only some of the classes in the data. It automatically explores different numbers of new classes in the EM iterations. The underlying assumption is that a new class should be introduced to hold an instance x when the probability of x belonging to the existing classes is close to uniform. This is quite different from our work. First, it works in the semi-supervised setting and assumes that test data is available during training. Second, it only focuses on improving accuracy on the classes with seed examples.

3 Proposed Method

In this section, we propose our solution for the open classification problem. First we discuss our strategy to reduce the open space risk while balancing the empirical risk of the training data. Then we apply a recently proposed SVM-based learning strategy (Fei and Liu, 2015), which yields the same risk management strategy. We will also discuss its underlying assumptions, which was not addressed in the original paper of Fei and Liu (2015). Lastly, we will show why the proposed solution works for open classification.

3.1 Open Space Risk Formulation

Consider the risk formulation by Scheirer et al. (2013), where apart from the empirical risk, there is risk in labeling the open space (space away from positive training examples) as "positive" for any known class. Due to lack of information on a classification function on the open space, open space risk is approximated by a relative Lebesgue measure (Shackel, 2007). Let S_o be a large ball of radius r_o that contains both the positively labeled open space O and all of the positive training examples; and let f be a measurable classification function where $f_y(x) = 1$ for recognition of class y of interest and $f_y(x) = 0$ otherwise. The probabilistic open space risk $R_o(f)$ of function f for a class y is defined as the fraction (in terms of Lebesgue measure) of positively labeled open space compared to the overall measure of positively labeled space (which includes the space close to the positive examples).

$$R_o(f) = \frac{\int_O f_y(x)\,dx}{\int_{S_o} f_y(x)\,dx}$$

The above definition indicates that the more we label open space as positive, the greater open space risk is. However, it does not suggest how to specify the positively labeled open space O.

In this work, we formulate O as the positively labeled area that is sufficiently far from the center of the positive training examples. Let $B_{r_y}(cen_y)$ be a closed ball of radius r_y centered around the center of positive class y (cen_y), which ideally contains all positive examples of class y; S_o be a larger ball $B_{r_o}(cen_y)$ of radius r_o with the same center cen_y. Let classification function $f_y(x) = 1$ when $x \in B_{r_0}(cen_y)$, and $f_y(x) = 0$ otherwise. Also let h be the positive half space defined by a binary SVM decision hyperplane Ω obtained using positive and negative training examples, and let the size of ball B_{r_0} be bounded by Ω, $B_{r_0} \cap h = B_{r_0}$. We define open space as

$$O = S_o - B_{r_y}(cen_y)$$

where radius r_0 needs to be determined from the training data for each known positive class.

This open space formulation greatly reduces the open space risk compared to traditional SVM and 1-vs-Set Machine in (Scheirer et al., 2013). For traditional SVM, whose classification function $f_y^{SVM}(x) = 1$ when $x \in h$, and positive open space being approximately $h - B_{r_y}(cen_y)$, which is only bounded by the SVM decision hyperplane Ω. For 1-vs-Set Machine in (Scheirer et al., 2013), whose classification function $f_y^{1-vs-set}(x) = 1$ when $x \in g$, where g is a slab area with thickness δ bounded by two parallel hyperplanes Ω and Ψ ($\Psi \parallel \Omega$) in h. And its positive open space is approximately $g - B_{r_y}(cen_y)$. Given open space formulations of traditional SVM and 1-vs-Set Machine, we can see that both methods label an unlimited area as positively labeled space, while our formulation reduces it to a bounded spherical area.

Given the above open space definition, the question is how to estimate radius r_0 for the positive class. We show that the center-based similarity space learning (CBS learning) recently proposed in (Fei and Liu, 2015) is suitable for the purpose. It was original proposed to deal with the negative covariate shift problem in binary text classification.

Below, we first introduce CBS learning and then discuss why it is suitable for our problem, as well as its underlying assumptions.

3.2 Center-Based Similarity Space Learning

We now discuss CBS learning for binary text classification. Let $D = \{(\mathbf{d}_1, y_1), (\mathbf{d}_2, y_2), ..., (\mathbf{d}_n, y_n)\}$ be the set of training examples, where $\mathbf{d}_i$ is the feature vector (e.g., with unigram features) representing a document d_i and $y_i \in \{1, -1\}$ is its class label. This feature vector is called a document space vector (*ds-vector*). Traditional classification directly uses D to build a binary classifier. CBS learning transforms each *ds*-vector $\mathbf{d}_i$ (no change to its class) to a center-based similarity space feature vector (CBS vector) $\mathbf{cbs}\text{-}\mathbf{v}_i$. Each feature in the CBS vector is a similarity between a center c_j of the positive class documents and d_i. CBS learning can use multiple document space representations or feature vectors (e.g., one based on unigrams and one based on bigrams) to represent each document, which results in multiple centers for the positive documents. There can also be multiple document similarity functions used to compute similarity values. The detailed learning technique is as follows.

For a document d_i in D, we have a set R_i of p *ds*-vectors $R_i = \{\mathbf{x}_1^i, \mathbf{x}_2^i, ..., \mathbf{x}_p^i\}$. Each *ds*-vector $\mathbf{x}_j^i$ denotes one document space representation of the document d_i, e.g., unigram representation or bigram representation. Then the center of positive training documents can be computed, which is represented as a set of p centroids $C = \{\mathbf{c}_1, \mathbf{c}_2, ..., \mathbf{c}_p\}$, each of which corresponds to one document space representation in R_i. Rocchio method in information retrieval (Rocchio, 1971; Manning et al. 2008) is used to compute each center $\mathbf{c}_j$ (a vector), which uses the corresponding *ds*-vectors of all training positive and negative documents.

$$\mathbf{c}_j = \frac{\alpha}{|D_+|} \sum_{d_i \in D_+} \frac{\mathbf{x}_j^i}{\|\mathbf{x}_j^i\|} - \frac{\beta}{|D - D_+|} \sum_{d_i \in D-D_+} \frac{\mathbf{x}_j^i}{\|\mathbf{x}_j^i\|}$$

where D_+ is the set of documents in the positive class and $|.|$ is the size function. α and β are parameters, which are usually set empirically. It is reported that using *tf-idf* representation, $\alpha = 16$ and $\beta = 4$ usually work quite well (Buckley et al. 1994). The subtraction is used to reduce the influence of those terms that are not discriminative (i.e., terms appearing in both classes).

Based on R_i for any document d_i in both training and testing and the previously computed set C of centers using the training data, we can transform a document d_i from its document space representations R_i to one center-based similarity vector $\mathbf{cbs}\text{-}\mathbf{v}_i$ by applying a similarity function Sim on each element $\mathbf{x}_j^i$ of R_i and its corresponding center $\mathbf{c}_j$ in C.

$$\mathbf{cbs}\text{-}\mathbf{v}_i = Sim(R_i, C)$$

Sim has a set of similarity measures. Each measure m_j is applied to p document representations $\mathbf{x}_j^i$ in R_i and their corresponding centers $\mathbf{c}_j$ in C to generate p similarity features (*cbs*-features) in $\mathbf{cbs}\text{-}\mathbf{v}_i$.

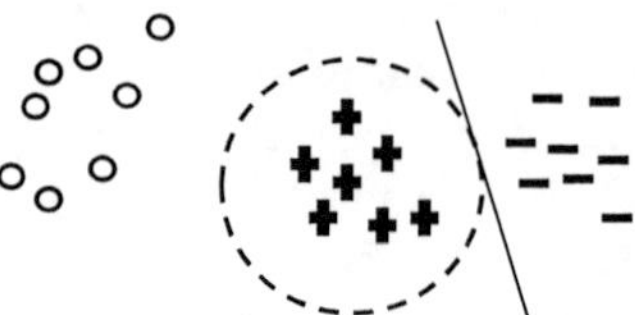

Figure 1: CBS learning reduces open space risk.

For *ds*-features, we use unigrams and bigrams with *tf-idf* weighting as two document representations. We also adopt the five similarity measures in (Fei and Liu, 2015) to gauge the similarity of two vectors. Based on these measures, we produce 10 CBS features to represent a document in the CBS space.

3.3 Why does CBS learning work?

Given the open space definition in Section 3.1, our goal is to estimate the radius r_0 of the positively labeled space for the positive class. Now we explain how CBS learning gives an estimate of r_0.

Due to learning in the similarity space with similarities as features, CBS learning generates a boundary based on similarities to separate the positive and negative training data in the similarity space, which is essentially a ball encompassing the positive training data in the original document space. In other words, instead of explicitly minimizing the positively labeled open space risk, CBS learning approximates the radius r_0 by learning a score based on similarities in the similarity space, which is equivalent to a limited spherical area in the original document space. The generated model thus not only limits the positively labeled open space on the positive side of Ω (SVM decision hyperplane), but also balances the empirical risk from the positive and negative training examples. In fact, r_0 is approximately the distance from the center of positive class to Ω measured in similarities. Figure 1 illustrates the point. The positively labeled/classified region produced by CBS learning is the circle in the original document space, while SVM learning produces a half space bounded by its decision line, which is approximately the tangent line of the circle. Note that as multiple similarity features are used, the spherical area is formed by an integrated similarity produced by SVM, which combines all similarity features.

In order for the method to work well for our multiclass classification, ideally two assumptions should be made about the data. First, the target classes of documents are generated by a mixture model, where each mixture component is responsible for each class of documents. Secondly, after feature normalization each target class of documents is generated by a Gaussian distribution, where the Gaussian mean resides at the center of the class, and its $n \times n$ covariance matrix has equal eigenvalues so that the positive class can have a spherical shape boundary or a ball. Note that we do not make any assumptions about data from non-target classes.

3.4 Multiclass Open Classification

The preceding discussion is based on binary open classification. We follow the standard technique of combining a set of 1-vs-rest binary classifiers to perform multiclass classification with a rejection option for unknown. The SVM scores for each classifier are first converted to probabilities based on a variation of Platt's (2000) algorithm, which is supported in LIBSVM (Chang and Lin, 2011). Let $P(y|\mathbf{x})$ be a probably estimate, where $y \in Y$ is a class label and $\mathbf{x}$ is a feature vector, and let λ be the decision threshold (usually 0.5). Let Y be the set of known classes, C_{m+1} be the unknown class, and y^* is the final predicted class for $\mathbf{x}$. The final classifier (called *cbsSVM*) uses this following for classification.

$$y^* = \begin{cases} argmax_{y \in Y} P(y|\mathbf{x}) & if\ P(y^*|\mathbf{x}) \geq \lambda \\ C_{m+1} & otherwise \end{cases}$$

4 Experiments

In this section, we show the results of the proposed method *cbsSVM* and compare it extensively with state-of-the-art baselines across two datasets.

4.1 Baselines

1-vs-Rest multiclass SVM (*1-vs-rest-SVM*). This is the standard 1-vs-Rest multiclass SVM with Platt Probability Estimation (Platt, 2000), and it is implemented based on LIBSVM[1] (version 3.20) (Chang and Lin, 2011). It works in the same way as the proposed *cbsSVM* (Section 3.4) except that it uses the document space classification. Linear kernel is used as it is shown by many researchers that linear SVM performs the best for text classification

---

[1] http://www.csie.ntu.edu.tw/~cjlin/libsvmtools/

(Joachims, 1998; Colas and Brazdil, 2006).

1-vs-Set Machine (*1-vs-set-linear*). For this baseline (Scheirer et al., 2013), we use all the default parameter settings in the original paper. That is, the near and far plane pressures are set at $p_A = 1.6$ and $p_\Omega = 4$ respectively; regularization constant $\lambda_r = 1$ and no explicit hard constraints are used on the training error ($\alpha = 0, \beta = 1$).

W-SVM (*wsvm-linear* and *wsvm-rbf*). These two baselines combine RBF one-class SVM with binary SVM (Scheirer et al., 2014). Both linear kernel and RBF kernel are tested. For thresholding the output, two parameters δ_τ and δ_R are required. We set $\delta_\tau = 0.001$, which is used to adjust what data the one-class SVM considers to be related. δ_R is a required decision threshold not only for W-SVM, but also for the next two baselines (P$_I$-SVM, P$_I$-OSVM). Two ways of setting δ_R were suggested by the authors. We set it as the prior probability of the number of unseen classes during evaluation (testing). An alternative way is to set it based on an openness score computed using the number of training and testing classes. We tried both methods and found the former gave better results.

P$_I$-SVM (*P$_i$-svm-linear* and *P$_i$-svm-rbf*). This baseline is from (Jain et al., 2014), which estimates the probability of inclusion based on the output of binary SVMs. Two kernels are tested. As stated above, the threshold δ is set as the prior probability of the number of unseen classes in test.

P$_I$-OSVM (*P$_i$-osvm-linear* and *P$_i$-osvm-rbf*). Similar to P$_I$-SVM, P$_I$-OSVM (Jain et al., 2014) uses a multiclass one-class SVM before fitting an Extreme Value Theory distribution to estimate the probability of inclusion. Again, two kernel functions are tested and the prior probability of the number of unseen classes is used to set δ. As P$_I$-OSVM is a variant of the traditional one-class SVM, we do not use one-class SVM as a baseline.

Exploratory Seeded K-Means (Exploratory-EM). In (Dalvi et al., 2013), three well-known multiclass semi-supervised learning methods were extended under the exploratory EM framework. We compare with exploratory version of Seeded K-Means due to its superior performance on 20newsgroup dataset. We also applied the criteria that work the best in the original paper for creating new classes and for model selection, i.e., the MinMax criterion and the AICc criterion. Note that ExploratoryEM works in the semi-supervised setting and uses both the training and test data as labeled and unlabeled data in training. As more than one new class can be introduced during training, for comparison we lump together all instances assigned to new classes as being rejected (unknown). In the experiments, we set the max number of iterations to be 50. Little changes in results are shown after 50 iterations.

All documents use *tf-idf* term weighting scheme with no feature selection. Source code for different baselines (1-vs-Set Machine[2], W-SVM and P$_I$-SVM[3], and Exploratory learning[4]) was provided by the authors of their original papers.

4.2 Datasets

We perform evaluation using two publically available datasets: 20-newsgroup (Rennie, 2008) and Amazon reviews (Jindal and Liu, 2008). The 20-newsgroup data contains 20 non-overlapping classes with a total of 18828 documents. The Amazon reviews dataset has review documents of 50 types of products or domains. Each type of product has 1000 reviews. For each class in both datasets, we randomly sampled 70% of documents for training, and the rest 30% for testing. Although product reviews are used for experiments, we do not perform sentiment classification. Instead, we still perform the traditional topic based classification. That is, given a review, the system decides what type of product the review is about.

4.3 Experiment settings

Following that in (Jain et al., 2013) and (Dalvi et al., 2013), we conduct open world cross-validation style analysis, holding out some classes in training and mixing them back during testing, and varying the number of training and test classes. Since for a given dataset, the number (percentage) of training classes m and the number of test classes n can vary, there are many ways to generate a train-test partition. We report our results using 10 random train-test partitions for each dataset. We vary the number of test classes for Amazon (10, 20, 30, 40, 50), and for 20-newsgroup (10, 20). We use 25%,

---

[2] https://github.com/Vastlab/liblinear.git
[3] https://github.com/ljain2/libsvm-openset
[4] http://www.cs.cmu.edu/~bbd/ExploreEM_package.zip

	25%	50%	75%	100%
cbsSVM	0.450	*0.715*	*0.775*	*0.873*
1-vs-rest-SVM	0.219	0.658	0.715	0.817
ExploratoryEM	0.386	0.647	0.704	0.854
1-vs-set-linear	0.592	0.698	0.700	0.697
wsvm-linear	0.603	0.694	0.698	0.702
wsvm-rbf	0.246	0.587	0.701	0.792
P_i-osvm-linear	0.207	0.590	0.662	0.731
P_i-osvm-rbf	0.061	0.142	0.137	0.148
P_i-svm-linear	*0.600*	0.695	0.701	0.705
P_i-svm-rbf	0.245	0.590	0.718	0.774

Table 1: Amazon 10 Domains.

	25%	50%	75%	100%
cbsSVM	0.566	*0.695*	*0.695*	*0.760*
1-vs-rest-SVM	0.466	0.610	0.616	0.688
ExploratoryEM	*0.571*	0.561	0.573	0.691
1-vs-set-linear	0.506	0.560	0.589	0.620
wsvm-linear	0.553	0.618	0.625	0.641
wsvm-rbf	0.397	0.502	0.574	0.701
P_i-osvm-linear	0.453	0.531	0.589	0.629
P_i-osvm-rbf	0.143	0.079	0.058	0.050
P_i-svm-linear	0.547	0.620	0.628	0.644
P_i-svm-rbf	0.396	0.546	0.675	0.714

Table 2: Amazon 20 Domains.

	25%	50%	75%	100%
cbsSVM	*0.565*	*0.645*	*0.630*	*0.686*
1-vs-rest-SVM	0.463	0.568	0.545	0.627
ExploratoryEM	0.500	0.511	0.569	0.659
1-vs-set-linear	0.462	0.511	0.542	0.585
wsvm-linear	0.521	0.574	0.578	0.598
wsvm-rbf	0.372	0.444	0.502	0.651
P_i-osvm-linear	0.428	0.510	0.553	0.605
P_i-osvm-rbf	0.108	0.047	0.043	0.047
P_i-svm-linear	0.520	0.575	0.581	0.602
P_i-svm-rbf	0.379	0.517	0.629	0.680

Table 3: Amazon 30 Domains.

	25%	50%	75%	100%
cbsSVM	*0.541*	*0.633*	*0.619*	*0.650*
1-vs-rest-SVM	0.463	0.543	0.515	0.584
ExploratoryEM	0.467	0.496	0.562	0.628
1-vs-set-linear	0.429	0.489	0.526	0.558
wsvm-linear	0.499	0.554	0.560	0.565
wsvm-rbf	0.351	0.402	0.464	0.609
P_i-osvm-linear	0.413	0.483	0.533	0.571
P_i-osvm-rbf	0.078	0.043	0.047	0.049
P_i-svm-linear	0.497	0.554	0.563	0.568
P_i-svm-rbf	0.371	0.505	0.602	0.634

Table 4: Amazon 40 Domains.

	25%	50%	75%	100%
cbsSVM	*0.557*	*0.615*	0.586	*0.634*
1-vs-rest-SVM	0.460	0.533	0.502	0.568
ExploratoryEM	0.348	0.467	0.534	0.618
1-vs-set-linear	0.420	0.483	0.514	0.551
wsvm-linear	0.488	0.545	0.549	0.559
wsvm-rbf	0.317	0.367	0.436	0.584
P_i-osvm-linear	0.403	0.489	0.535	0.578
P_i-osvm-rbf	0.066	0.039	0.047	0.050
P_i-svm-linear	0.487	0.546	0.551	0.562
P_i-svm-rbf	0.360	0.509	*0.632*	0.630

Table 5: Amazon 50 Domains.

	25%	50%	75%	100%
cbsSVM	0.417	*0.769*	*0.796*	*0.855*
1-vs-rest-SVM	0.246	0.722	0.784	0.828
ExploratoryEM	0.648	0.706	0.733	0.852
1-vs-set-linear	*0.678*	0.671	0.659	0.567
wsvm-linear	0.666	0.666	0.665	0.679
wsvm-rbf	0.320	0.523	0.675	0.766
P_i-osvm-linear	0.300	0.571	0.668	0.770
P_i-osvm-rbf	0.059	0.074	0.032	0.026
P_i-svm-linear	0.666	0.667	0.667	0.680
P_i-svm-rbf	0.320	0.540	0.705	0.749

Table 6: 20-newsgroup 10 Domains.

	25%	50%	75%	100%
cbsSVM	*0.593*	*0.701*	*0.720*	0.852
1-vs-rest-SVM	0.552	0.683	0.682	0.807
ExploratoryEM	0.555	0.633	0.713	*0.864*
1-vs-set-linear	0.497	0.557	0.550	0.577
wsvm-linear	0.563	0.597	0.602	0.677
wsvm-rbf	0.365	0.469	0.607	0.773
P_i-osvm-linear	0.438	0.534	0.640	0.757
P_i-osvm-rbf	0.143	0.029	0.022	0.009
P_i-svm-linear	0.563	0.599	0.603	0.678
P_i-svm-rbf	0.370	0.494	0.680	0.767

Table 7: 20-newsgroup 20 Domains.

50%, 75% and 100% of the test classes in training.

When 100% of test classes are used in training, the problem reduces to the closed world classification. As most of our baselines such as W-SVM, P_I-OSVM and P_I-SVM all use prior knowledge to set decision threshold to 0 in the closed world setting, for fair comparison, we also set the threshold to 0 for both 1-vs-rest-SVM and our proposed *cbsSVM* for closed world classification. By doing this, we always assign a known class label to a test instance. For Exploratory Seeded K-Means, we use an option supported in the exploratory learning package that does not allow any new classes to be introduced in learning.

For each train-test partition, we first compute precision, recall and F1 score for each class and then macro-average the results across all classes.

Final results are given by averaging the results of 10 random train-test partitions. Due to space limits, we will only show F1 scores in the paper.

For all the methods that use the RBF kernel, the parameters are tuned via cross validation on the training data, yielding $(C = 5, \gamma = 0.2)$ for Amazon and $(C = 10, \gamma = 0.5)$ for 20-newsgroup.

4.4 Results and Discussion

We now show all the results. Results for Amazon is given in Tables 1 to 5, and for 20-newsgroup are given in Tables 6 and 7. As we can see, in most situations (23 of 28 settings) our proposed *cbsSVM* method performs the best. Even when 100% of the test classes are used for training (the traditional closed world classification), *cbsSVM* still performs

rec.motorcycles	comp.graphics	comp.os.ms-windows.misc	alt.atheism	comp.sys.mac.hardware
comp.windows.x	misc.forsale	comp.sys.ibm.pc.hardware	rec.autos	rec.sport.baseball

Table 8: 10 domains for testing.

	comp.windows.x			Unknown (reject)		
	Prec.	Recall	F1	Prec.	Recall	F1
rec.motorcycles	0.260	0.963	0.410	0.972	0.168	0.287
comp.graphics	0.380	0.850	0.525	0.966	0.482	0.643
comp.sys.mac.hardware	0.286	0.972	0.442	0.977	0.356	0.522
comp.os.ms-windows.misc	0.418	0.877	*0.567*	0.976	0.513	*0.672*
misc.forsale	0.244	0.959	0.389	0.966	0.201	0.334
rec.autos	0.226	0.979	0.367	0.976	0.162	0.277

Table 9: Results on comp.windows.x and unknown classes.

	rec.motorcycles			Unknown (reject)		
	Prec.	Recall	F1	Prec.	Recall	F1
comp.sys.mac.hardware	0.284	0.956	0.438	0.962	0.198	0.328
rec.autos	0.459	0.892	*0.606*	0.974	0.470	*0.634*
comp.windows.x	0.260	0.963	0.410	0.972	0.168	0.287
comp.graphics	0.289	0.953	0.444	0.964	0.177	0.299
comp.sys.ibm.pc.hardware	0.284	0.953	0.438	0.958	0.169	0.288
alt.atheism	0.194	0.973	0.324	0.980	0.333	0.498

Table 10: Results on rec.motorcycles and unknown classes.

the best in almost all settings (6 out of 7) except for 20-newsgroup with 20 classes. In this case, it lost to ExploratoryEM by 1.12%. In fact, it is unfair to compare *cbsSVM* with ExploratoryEM because ExploratoryEM uses the test data in training.

We also analyzed the cases where our technique does not perform well. By comparing Table 1 and Table 6, we see that our method loses to 1-vs-set-linear, wsvm-linear and P_i-svm-linear on both datasets when training on 2 classes (25%) and testing on 10 classes, though in other cases training on 25% known classes can still yield good results. By inspecting the results, we found that in both settings our technique achieves very high recall but low precision on the known classes, while achieves high precision but low recall on the unknown classes. After careful investigation, we found this is caused by the relatively poor approximation of radius r_o when positive and negative training examples are far apart.

To verify the cause, we conducted more experiments on the 20-newsgroup data using the same setting (10 classes for test and 2 for training). The 10 classes are listed in Table 8. We show the results for two sets of experiments. In each set of the experiments, we keep one known class unchanged in training and select different classes as the second class. We show how the results change on the unchanged class as well as the unknown (reject) classes. Table 9 gives the precision, recall, and F1 score for *comp.windows.x* and for the unknown classes. Similarly, Table 10 gives the results for *rec.motorcycles* and for the unknown classes. The first column in both tables are the different second classes used in training. We can see that in both sets of experiments, the precision and F1 score on the unchanged known classes (*comp.windows.x* and *rec.motorcycles*) are better when a more similar class (closer in distance) is selected in training. In particular, *comp.windows.x* achieves the best result when *comp.os.ms-windows.misc* is the second known class, and *rec.motorcycles* achieves the best result when *rec.autos* is the second known class. This is because the radius r_o for each positively labeled space is determined based on the distance between the positive and negative training examples. As related classes are closer in distance, a tighter boundary with smaller r_o can be learned. However, our results show in the cases when only 2 known classes are available, a tight boundary is harder to achieve for either class for *cbsSVM*.

5　Conclusion

In this paper, we proposed to study the problem of multiclass open text classification. In particular, we investigated the problem via reducing the open space risk, and proposed a solution based on center-based similarity space learning. The solution reduced the positive labeled area from an infinite space to a finite space compared to previous work. This markedly reduces the open space risk. With extensive experiments across two public multiclass datasets, we demonstrated that the proposed solution is highly promising. Our future work includes designing a more robust solution that still works well when the number of known classes is small.

Acknowledgments

This work was supported in part by a grant from National Science Foundation (NSF) under grant no. IIS-1407927, a NCI grant under grant no. R01CA192240, and a gift from Bosch. The content of the paper is solely the responsibility of the authors and does not necessarily represent the official views of the NSF, NCI, or Bosch.

References

Bravo, C., Lobato, J.L., Weber, R., L'Huillier, G. 2008. A hybrid system for probability estimation in multiclass problems combining svms and neural networks. In: Hybrid Intelligent Systems. pp. 649–654

Chang, C-C. and Lin, C-J. 2011. LIBSVM: a library for support vector machines. ACM Transactions on Intelligent Systems and Technology, 2:27:1--27:27, http://www.csie.ntu.edu. tw/~cjlin/libsvm

Colas, F. and Brazdil. P. 2006. Comparison of SVM and some older classification algorithms in text classification tasks. Artificial Intelligence in Theory and Practice. IFIP International Federation for Information Processing, pp. 169-178.

Dalvi, B., Cohen, W. W. and Callan, J. 2013. Exploratory learning. In ECML.

Duan, K.B. and Keerthi, S.S. 2005. Which is the best multiclass SVM method? An empirical study. In: Proceedings of the 6th International Conference on Multiple Classifier Systems. pp. 278–285

Fei, G. and Liu, B. 2015. Social Media Text Classification under Negative Covariate Shift. Proceedings of the 2015 Conference on Empirical Methods in Natural Language Processing, Lisboa, Portugal, 17-21 September.

Fumera, G., and Roli, F. 2002. Support vector machines with embedded reject option. In: International Workshop on Pattern Recognition with Support Vector Machines (SVM2002). pp. 68–82

Hastie, T. and Tibshirani, R. 1996. Classification by pairwise coupling. In: Annals of Statistics. pp. 507–513. MIT Press

Huang, T.K., Weng, R.C., and Lin, C.J. 2006. Generalized bradley-terry models and multi-class probability estimates. Journal of Machine Learning Research 85–115

Jain, L. P., Scheirer, W. J., and Boult, T. E. 2014. Multiclass open set recognition using probability of inclusion. In Proc. ECCV, pages 393-409. Springer.

Jindal, N. and Liu, B. 2008. Opinion Spam and Analysis. Proceedings of the ACM Conference on Web Search and Data Mining.

Joachims, T. 1998. Text categorization with support vector machines: Learning with many relevant features. ECML.

Khan, S. and Madden, M. 2014. One-Class Classification: Taxonomy of Study and Review of Techniques. The Knowledge Engineering Review, 1-30.

Kwok, J.T.Y. 1999. Moderating the outputs of support vector machine classifiers. IEEE Transactions on Neural Networks 10(5), 1018–1031

Manning, C. D., Prabhakar R., and Hinrich, S. 2008. Introduction to Information Retrieval. Cambridge University Press.

Shackel, N., Bertrand's Paradox and the Principle of Indifference. 2007. Philosophy of Science, vol. 74, no. 2, pp. 150–175.

Platt, J. C. 2000. Probabilistic outputs for support vector machines and comparison to regularized likelihood methods. In Advances in Large Margin Classifiers, A. Smola, P. Bartlett, B. Schölkopf, and D. Schuurmans, Eds. MIT Press, Cambridge, MA.

Rennie, J. 20-newsgroup dataset. 2008

Rocchio, J. 1971. Relevant feedback in information retrieval. In G. Salton (ed.). The smart retrieval system: experiments in automatic document processing.

Scheirer, W., Rocha A., Sapkota A., and Boult T. E. Towards open set recognition. 2013. IEEE Trans. Pattern Analysis and Machine Intelligence, vol. 36, no. 7, pp.1757 -1772

Scheirer, W. J., Jain, L. P., and Boult, T. E. 2014. Probability models for open set recognition, IEEE Trans. Pattern Analysis and Machine Intelligence, vol. 36, no. 11, pp.2317 -2324

Scholkopf, B., Platt, J. C., Shawe-Taylor, J. C., Smola, A. J., Williamson, R. C. 2001. Estimating the support of a high-dimensional distribution. Neural Computation 13, 1443–1471

Tax, D.M.J., Duin, R.P.W. 2004. Support vector data description. Machine Learning 54, 45–66

Vapnik, V.N. 1998. Statistical Learning Theory. Wiley-Interscience

Zadrozny, B. and Elkan, C. 2002. Transforming classifier scores into accurate multiclass probability estimates. In: Proceedings of the Eighth ACM SIGKDD International Conference on Knowledge Discovery and Data Mining. pp. 694–699 (2002)

Sequential Short-Text Classification with Recurrent and Convolutional Neural Networks

Ji Young Lee[*]
MIT
jjylee@mit.edu

Franck Dernoncourt[*]
MIT
francky@mit.edu

Abstract

Recent approaches based on artificial neural networks (ANNs) have shown promising results for short-text classification. However, many short texts occur in sequences (e.g., sentences in a document or utterances in a dialog), and most existing ANN-based systems do not leverage the preceding short texts when classifying a subsequent one. In this work, we present a model based on recurrent neural networks and convolutional neural networks that incorporates the preceding short texts. Our model achieves state-of-the-art results on three different datasets for dialog act prediction.

1 Introduction

Short-text classification is an important task in many areas of natural language processing, including sentiment analysis, question answering, or dialog management. Many different approaches have been developed for short-text classification, such as using Support Vector Machines (SVMs) with rule-based features (Silva et al., 2011), combining SVMs with naive Bayes (Wang and Manning, 2012), and building dependency trees with Conditional Random Fields (Nakagawa et al., 2010). Several recent studies using ANNs have shown promising results, including convolutional neural networks (CNNs) (Kim, 2014; Blunsom et al., 2014; Kalchbrenner et al., 2014) and recursive neural networks (Socher et al., 2012).

Most ANN systems classify short texts in isolation, i.e., without considering preceding short

texts. However, short texts usually appear in sequence (e.g., sentences in a document or utterances in a dialog), and therefore using information from preceding short texts may improve the classification accuracy. Previous works on sequential short-text classification are mostly based on non-ANN approaches, such as Hidden Markov Models (HMMs) (Reithinger and Klesen, 1997; Stolcke et al., 2000; Surendran and Levow, 2006), maximum entropy (Ang et al., 2005), naive Bayes (Lendvai and Geertzen, 2007), and conditional random fields (CRFs) (Kim et al., 2010; Quarteroni et al., 2011).

Inspired by the performance of ANN-based systems for non-sequential short-text classification, we introduce a model based on recurrent neural networks (RNNs) and CNNs for sequential short-text classification, and evaluate it on the dialog act classification task. A dialog act characterizes an utterance in a dialog based on a combination of pragmatic, semantic, and syntactic criteria. Its accurate detection is useful for a range of applications, from speech recognition to automatic summarization (Stolcke et al., 2000). Our model achieves state-of-the-art results on three different datasets.

2 Model

Our model comprises two parts. The first part generates a vector representation for each short text using either the RNN or CNN architecture, as discussed in Section 2.1 and Figure 1. The second part classifies the current short text based on the vector representations of the current as well as a few preceding short texts, as presented in Section 2.2 and Figure 2.

We denote scalars with italic lowercases (e.g.,

---

[*] These authors contributed equally to this work.

Proceedings of NAACL-HLT 2016, pages 515–520,
San Diego, California, June 12-17, 2016. ©2016 Association for Computational Linguistics

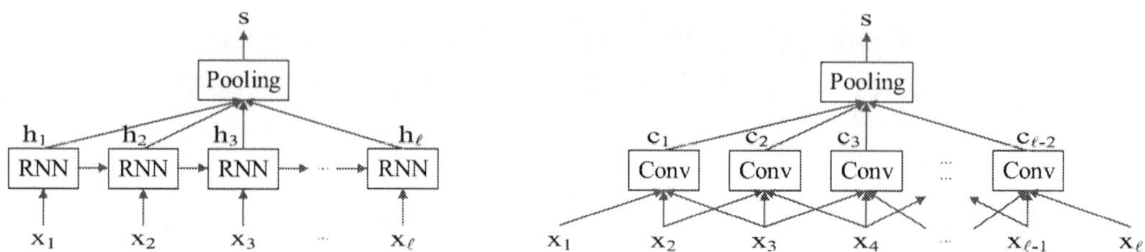

Figure 1: RNN (left) and CNN (right) architectures for generating the vector representation **s** of a short text $\mathbf{x}_{1:\ell}$. For CNN, Conv refers to convolution operations, and the filter height $h = 3$ is used in this figure.

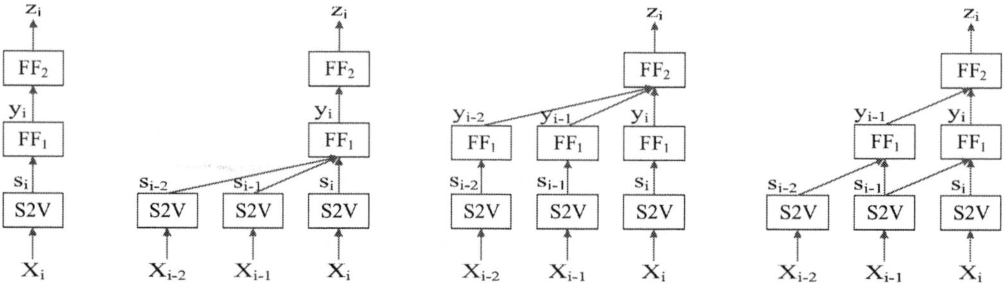

Figure 2: Four instances of the two-layer feedforward ANN used for predicting the probability distribution over the classes $\mathbf{z}_i$ for the ith short-text $\mathbf{X}_i$. S2V stands for short text to vector, which is the RNN/CNN architecture that generates $\mathbf{s}_i$ from $\mathbf{X}_i$. From left to right, the history sizes (d_1, d_2) are $(0, 0)$, $(2, 0)$, $(0, 2)$ and $(1, 1)$. $(0, 0)$ corresponds to the non-sequential classification case.

k, b_f), vectors with bold lowercases (e.g., $\mathbf{s}, \mathbf{x}_i$), and matrices with italic uppercases (e.g., W_f). We use the colon notation $\mathbf{v}_{i:j}$ to denote the sequence of vectors $(\mathbf{v}_i, \mathbf{v}_{i+1}, \ldots, \mathbf{v}_j)$.

2.1 Short-text representation

A given short text of length ℓ is represented as the sequence of m-dimensional word vectors $\mathbf{x}_{1:\ell}$, which is used by the RNN or CNN model to produce the n-dimensional *short-text representation* **s**.

2.1.1 RNN-based short-text representation

We use a variant of RNN called Long Short Term Memory (LSTM) (Hochreiter and Schmidhuber, 1997). For the tth word in the short-text, an LSTM takes as input $\mathbf{x}_t, \mathbf{h}_{t-1}, \mathbf{c}_{t-1}$ and produces $\mathbf{h}_t, \mathbf{c}_t$ based on the following formulas:

$$\mathbf{i}_t = \sigma(W_i \mathbf{x}_t + U_i \mathbf{h}_{t-1} + \mathbf{b}_i)$$
$$\mathbf{f}_t = \sigma(W_f \mathbf{x}_t + U_f \mathbf{h}_{t-1} + \mathbf{b}_f)$$
$$\tilde{\mathbf{c}}_t = \tanh(W_c \mathbf{x}_t + U_c \mathbf{h}_{t-1} + \mathbf{b}_c)$$
$$\mathbf{c}_t = \mathbf{f}_t \odot \mathbf{c}_{t-1} + \mathbf{i}_t \odot \tilde{\mathbf{c}}_t$$
$$\mathbf{o}_t = \sigma(W_o \mathbf{x}_t + U_o \mathbf{h}_{t-1} + \mathbf{b}_o)$$
$$\mathbf{h}_t = \mathbf{o}_t \odot \tanh(\mathbf{c}_t)$$

where $W_j \in \mathbb{R}^{n \times m}$, $U_j \in \mathbb{R}^{n \times n}$ are weight matrices and $\mathbf{b}_j \in \mathbb{R}^n$ are bias vectors, for $j \in \{i, f, c, o\}$. The symbols $\sigma(\cdot)$ and $\tanh(\cdot)$ refer to the element-wise sigmoid and hyperbolic tangent functions, and $\odot$ is the element-wise multiplication. $\mathbf{h}_0 = \mathbf{c}_0 = \mathbf{0}$.

In the pooling layer, the sequence of vectors $\mathbf{h}_{1:\ell}$ output from the RNN layer are combined into a single vector $\mathbf{s} \in \mathbb{R}^n$ that represents the short-text, using one of the following mechanisms: last, mean, and max pooling. Last pooling takes the last vector, i.e., $\mathbf{s} = \mathbf{h}_\ell$, mean pooling averages all vectors, i.e., $\mathbf{s} = \frac{1}{\ell} \sum_{t=1}^{\ell} \mathbf{h}_t$, and max pooling takes the element-wise maximum of $\mathbf{h}_{1:\ell}$.

2.1.2 CNN-based short-text representation

Using a *filter* $W_f \in \mathbb{R}^{h \times m}$ of height h, a convolution operation on h consecutive word vectors starting from t^{th} word outputs the scalar *feature*

$$c_t = \text{ReLU}(W_f \bullet X_{t:t+h-1} + b_f)$$

where $X_{t:t+h-1} \in \mathbb{R}^{h \times m}$ is the matrix whose i^{th} row is $\mathbf{x}_i \in \mathbb{R}^m$, and $b_f \in \mathbb{R}$ is a bias. The symbol $\bullet$ refers to the dot product and $\text{ReLU}(\cdot)$ is the element-wise rectified linear unit function.

We perform convolution operations with n different filters, and denote the resulting features as

$\mathbf{c}_t \in \mathbb{R}^n$, each of whose dimensions comes from a distinct filter. Repeating the convolution operations for each window of h consecutive words in the short-text, we obtain $\mathbf{c}_{1:\ell-h+1}$. The short-text representation $\mathbf{s} \in \mathbb{R}^n$ is computed in the max pooling layer, as the element-wise maximum of $\mathbf{c}_{1:\ell-h+1}$.

2.2 Sequential short-text classification

Let $\mathbf{s}_i$ be the n-dimensional short-text representation given by the RNN or CNN architecture for the ith short text in the sequence. The sequence $\mathbf{s}_{i-d_1-d_2:i}$ is fed into a two-layer feedforward ANN that predicts the class for the ith short text. The hyperparameters d_1, d_2 are the history sizes used in the first and second layers, respectively.

The first layer takes as input $\mathbf{s}_{i-d_1-d_2:i}$ and outputs the sequence $\mathbf{y}_{i-d_2:i}$ defined as

$$\mathbf{y}_j = \tanh\left(\sum_{d=0}^{d_1} W_{-d}\,\mathbf{s}_{j-d} + \mathbf{b}_1\right), \ \forall j \in [i - d_2, i]$$

where $W_0, W_{-1}, W_{-2} \in \mathbb{R}^{k \times n}$ are the weight matrices, $\mathbf{b}_1 \in \mathbb{R}^k$ is the bias vector, $\mathbf{y}_j \in \mathbb{R}^k$ is the *class representation*, and k is the number of classes for the classification task.

Similarly, the second layer takes as input the sequence of class representations $\mathbf{y}_{i-d_2:i}$ and outputs $\mathbf{z}_i \in \mathbb{R}^k$:

$$\mathbf{z}_i = \mathrm{softmax}\left(\sum_{j=0}^{d_2} W_{-j}\,\mathbf{y}_{i-j} + \mathbf{b}_2\right)$$

where $U_0, U_{-1}, U_{-2} \in \mathbb{R}^{k \times k}$ and $\mathbf{b}_2 \in \mathbb{R}^k$ are the weight matrices and bias vector.

The final output $\mathbf{z}_i$ represents the probability distribution over the set of k classes for the ith short-text: the jth element of $\mathbf{z}_i$ corresponds to the probability that the ith short-text belongs to the jth class.

3 Datasets and Experimental Setup

3.1 Datasets

We evaluate our model on the dialog act classification task using the following datasets:

- DSTC 4: Dialog State Tracking Challenge 4 (Kim et al., 2015; Kim et al., 2016).
- MRDA: ICSI Meeting Recorder Dialog Act Corpus (Janin et al., 2003; Shriberg et al., 2004). The 5 classes are introduced in (Ang et al., 2005).

- SwDA: Switchboard Dialog Act Corpus (Jurafsky et al., 1997).

For MRDA, we use the train/validation/test splits provided with the datasets. For DSTC 4 and SwDA, only the train/test splits are provided.[1] Table 1 presents statistics on the datasets.

Dataset	$|C|$	$|V|$	Train	Validation	Test
DSTC 4	89	6k	24 (21k)	5 (5k)	6 (6k)
MRDA	5	12k	51 (78k)	11 (16k)	11 (15k)
SwDA	43	20k	1003 (193k)	112 (23k)	19 (5k)

Table 1: Dataset overview. $|C|$ is the number of classes, $|V|$ the vocabulary size. For the train, validation and test sets, we indicate the number of dialogs (i.e., sequences) followed by the number of utterances (i.e., short texts) in parenthesis.

3.2 Training

The model is trained to minimize the negative log-likelihood of predicting the correct dialog acts of the utterances in the train set, using stochastic gradient descent with the Adadelta update rule (Zeiler, 2012). At each gradient descent step, weight matrices, bias vectors, and word vectors are updated. For regularization, dropout is applied after the pooling layer, and early stopping is used on the validation set with a patience of 10 epochs.

4 Results and Discussion

To find effective hyperparameters, we varied one hyperparameter at a time while keeping the other ones fixed. Table 2 presents our hyperparameter choices.

Hyperparameter	Choice	Experiment Range
LSTM output dim. (n)	100	50 – 1000
LSTM pooling	max	max, mean, last
LSTM direction	unidir.	unidir., bidir.
CNN num. of filters (n)	500	50 – 1000
CNN filter height (h)	3	1 – 10
Dropout rate	0.5	0 – 1
Word vector dim. (m)	200, 300	25 – 300

Table 2: Experiments ranges and choices of hyperparameters. Unidir refers to the regular RNNs presented in Section 2.1.1, and bidir refers to bidirectional RNNs introduced in (Schuster and Paliwal, 1997).

We initialized the word vectors with the 300-dimensional word vectors pretrained with word2vec

---

[1] All train/validation/test splits can be found at `https://github.com/Franck-Dernoncourt/naacl2016`

d_1 \ d_2	LSTM			CNN		
	0	1	2	0	1	2
DSTC4 0	63.1 (62.4, 63.6)	65.7 (65.6, 65.7)	64.7 (63.9, 65.3)	64.1 (63.5, 65.2)	65.4 (64.7, 66.6)	65.1 (63.2, 65.9)
1	**65.8** (65.5, 66.1)	65.7 (65.3, 66.1)	64.8 (64.6, 65.1)	65.3 (64.1, 65.9)	65.1 (62.1, 66.2)	64.9 (64.4, 65.6)
2	65.7 (65.0, 66.2)	65.5 (64.4, 66.1)	64.9 (64.6, 65.2)	65.7 (64.9, 66.3)	**65.8** (65.2, 66.1)	65.4 (64.5, 66.0)
MRDA 0	82.8 (82.4, 83.1)	83.2 (82.9, 83.4)	82.9 (82.4, 83.4)	83.2 (83.0, 83.4)	83.5 (82.9, 84.0)	83.8 (83.4, 84.2)
1	83.2 (82.6, 83.7)	83.8 (83.5, 84.4)	83.6 (83.2, 83.8)	**84.6** (84.5, 84.9)	**84.6** (84.4, 84.8)	84.1 (83.8, 84.4)
2	**84.1** (83.5, 84.4)	83.9 (83.4, 84.7)	83.3 (82.6, 84.2)	84.4 (84.1, 84.8)	**84.6** (84.5, 84.7)	84.4 (84.2, 84.7)
SwDA 0	66.3 (65.1, 68.0)	67.9 (66.3, 68.6)	67.8 (66.7, 69.0)	67.0 (65.3, 68.7)	69.1 (68.5, 70.0)	69.7 (69.2, 70.9)
1	68.4 (67.8, 68.8)	67.8 (65.5, 68.9)	67.3 (65.5, 69.5)	69.9 (69.1, 70.9)	69.8 (69.3, 70.6)	69.9 (68.8, 70.6)
2	**69.5** (68.9, 70.2)	67.9 (66.5, 69.4)	67.7 (66.9, 68.9)	**71.4** (70.4, 73.1)	71.1 (70.2, 72.1)	70.9 (69.7, 71.7)

Table 3: Accuracy (%) on different architectures and history sizes d_1, d_2. For each setting, we report average (minimum, maximum) computed on 5 runs. Sequential classification ($d_1 + d_2 > 0$) outperforms non-sequential classification ($d_1 = d_2 = 0$). Overall, the CNN model outperformed the LSTM model for all datasets, albeit by a small margin except for SwDA. We also tried gated recurrent units (GRUs) (Cho et al., 2014) and the basic RNN, but the results were generally lower than LSTM.

on Google News (Mikolov et al., 2013a; Mikolov et al., 2013b) for DSTC 4, and the 200-dimensional word vectors pretrained with GloVe on Twitter (Pennington et al., 2014) for MRDA and SwDA, as these choices yielded the best results among all publicly available word2vec, GloVe, SENNA (Collobert, 2011; Collobert et al., 2011) and RNNLM (Mikolov et al., 2011) word vectors.

The effects of the history sizes d_1 and d_2 for the short-text and the class representations, respectively, are presented in Table 3 for both the LSTM and CNN models. In both models, increasing d_1 while keeping $d_2 = 0$ improved the performances by 1.3-4.2 percentage points. Conversely, increasing d_2 while keeping $d_1 = 0$ yielded better results, but the performance increase was less pronounced: incorporating sequential information at the short-text representation level was more effective than at the class representation level.

Using sequential information at both the short-text representation level and the class representation level does not help in most cases and may even lower the performances. We hypothesize that short-text representations contain richer and more general information than class representations due to their larger dimension. Class representations may not convey any additional information over short-text representations, and are more likely to propagate errors from previous misclassifications.

Table 4 compares our results with the state-of-the-art. Overall, our model shows competitive results, while requiring no human-engineered features. Rig-orous comparisons are challenging to draw, as many important details such as text preprocessing and train/valid/test split may vary, and many studies fail to perform several runs despite the randomness in some parts of the training process, such as weight initialization.

Model	DSTC 4	MRDA	SwDA
CNN	65.5	**84.6**	**73.1**
LSTM	**66.2**	84.3	69.6
Majority class	25.8	59.1	33.7
SVM	57.0	–	–
Graphical model	–	81.3	–
Naive Bayes	–	82.0	–
HMM	–	–	71.0
Memory-based Learning	–	–	72.3
Interlabeler agreement	–	–	84.0

Table 4: Accuracy (%) of our models and other methods from the literature. The majority class model predicts the most frequent class. SVM: (Dernoncourt et al., 2016). Graphical model: (Ji and Bilmes, 2006). Naive Bayes: (Lendvai and Geertzen, 2007). HMM: (Stolcke et al., 2000). Memory-based Learning: (Rotaru, 2002). All five models use features derived from transcribed words, as well as previous predicted dialog acts except for Naive Bayes. The interlabeler agreement could not be obtained for MRDA, and DSTC 4 was labeled by a single annotator. For the CNN and LSTM models, the presented results are the test set accuracy of the run with the highest accuracy on the validation set.

5 Conclusion

In this article we have presented an ANN-based approach to sequential short-text classification. We demonstrate that adding sequential information improves the quality of the predictions, and the performance depends on what sequential information is used in the model. Our model achieves state-of-the-art results on three different datasets for dialog act prediction.

Acknowledgments

We warmly thank Regina Barzilay, Tommi Jaakkola and the anonymous reviewers for their helpful feedback and suggestions.

References

[Ang et al.2005] Jeremy Ang, Yang Liu, and Elizabeth Shriberg. 2005. Automatic dialog act segmentation and classification in multiparty meetings. In *ICASSP (1)*, pages 1061–1064.

[Blunsom et al.2014] Phil Blunsom, Edward Grefenstette, Nal Kalchbrenner, et al. 2014. A convolutional neural network for modelling sentences. In *Proceedings of the 52nd Annual Meeting of the Association for Computational Linguistics*. Proceedings of the 52nd Annual Meeting of the Association for Computational Linguistics.

[Cho et al.2014] Kyunghyun Cho, Bart van Merriënboer, Dzmitry Bahdanau, and Yoshua Bengio. 2014. On the properties of neural machine translation: Encoder-decoder approaches. *arXiv preprint arXiv:1409.1259*.

[Collobert et al.2011] Ronan Collobert, Jason Weston, Léon Bottou, Michael Karlen, Koray Kavukcuoglu, and Pavel Kuksa. 2011. Natural language processing (almost) from scratch. *The Journal of Machine Learning Research*, 12:2493–2537.

[Collobert2011] Ronan Collobert. 2011. Deep learning for efficient discriminative parsing. In *International Conference on Artificial Intelligence and Statistics*, number EPFL-CONF-192374.

[Dernoncourt et al.2016] Franck Dernoncourt, Ji Young Lee, Trung H. Bui, and Hung H. Bui. 2016. Adobe-MIT submission to the DSTC 4 Spoken Language Understanding pilot task. In *7th International Workshop on Spoken Dialogue Systems (IWSDS)*.

[Hochreiter and Schmidhuber1997] Sepp Hochreiter and Jürgen Schmidhuber. 1997. Long short-term memory. *Neural computation*, 9(8):1735–1780.

[Janin et al.2003] Adam Janin, Don Baron, Jane Edwards, Dan Ellis, David Gelbart, Nelson Morgan, Barbara Peskin, Thilo Pfau, Elizabeth Shriberg, Andreas Stolcke, et al. 2003. The ICSI meeting corpus. In *Acoustics, Speech, and Signal Processing, 2003. Proceedings.(ICASSP'03). 2003 IEEE International Conference on*, volume 1, pages I–364. IEEE.

[Ji and Bilmes2006] Gang Ji and Jeff Bilmes. 2006. Backoff model training using partially observed data: application to dialog act tagging. In *Proceedings of the main conference on Human Language Technology Conference of the North American Chapter of the Association of Computational Linguistics*, pages 280–287. Association for Computational Linguistics.

[Jurafsky et al.1997] Dan Jurafsky, Elizabeth Shriberg, and Debra Biasca. 1997. Switchboard SWBD-DAMSL shallow-discourse-function annotation coders manual. *Institute of Cognitive Science Technical Report*, pages 97–102.

[Kalchbrenner et al.2014] Nal Kalchbrenner, Edward Grefenstette, and Phil Blunsom. 2014. A convolutional neural network for modelling sentences. *arXiv preprint arXiv:1404.2188*.

[Kim et al.2010] Su Nam Kim, Lawrence Cavedon, and Timothy Baldwin. 2010. Classifying dialogue acts in one-on-one live chats. In *Proceedings of the 2010 Conference on Empirical Methods in Natural Language Processing*, pages 862–871. Association for Computational Linguistics.

[Kim et al.2015] Seokhwan Kim, Luis Fernando D'Haro, Rafael E. Banchs, Jason Williams, and Matthew Henderson. 2015. Dialog State Tracking Challenge 4: Handbook.

[Kim et al.2016] Seokhwan Kim, Luis Fernando D'Haro, Rafael E. Banchs, Jason Williams, and Matthew Henderson. 2016. The Fourth Dialog State Tracking Challenge. In *Proceedings of the 7th International Workshop on Spoken Dialogue Systems (IWSDS)*.

[Kim2014] Yoon Kim. 2014. Convolutional neural networks for sentence classification. In *Proceedings of the 2014 Conference on Empirical Methods in Natural Language Processing*, pages 1746–1751. Association for Computational Linguistics.

[Lendvai and Geertzen2007] Piroska Lendvai and Jeroen Geertzen. 2007. Token-based chunking of turn-internal dialogue act sequences. In *Proceedings of the 8th SIGDIAL Workshop on Discourse and Dialogue*, pages 174–181.

[Mikolov et al.2011] Tomas Mikolov, Stefan Kombrink, Anoop Deoras, Lukar Burget, and Jan Cernocky. 2011. Rnnlm-recurrent neural network language modeling toolkit. In *Proc. of the 2011 ASRU Workshop*, pages 196–201.

[Mikolov et al.2013a] Tomas Mikolov, Kai Chen, Greg Corrado, and Jeffrey Dean. 2013a. Efficient estimation of word representations in vector space. *arXiv preprint arXiv:1301.3781*.

[Mikolov et al.2013b] Tomas Mikolov, Ilya Sutskever, Kai Chen, Greg S Corrado, and Jeff Dean. 2013b. Distributed representations of words and phrases and their compositionality. In *Advances in neural information processing systems*, pages 3111–3119.

[Nakagawa et al.2010] Tetsuji Nakagawa, Kentaro Inui, and Sadao Kurohashi. 2010. Dependency tree-based sentiment classification using CRFs with hidden variables. In *Human Language Technologies: The 2010 Annual Conference of the North American Chapter of the Association for Computational Linguistics*, pages 786–794. Association for Computational Linguistics.

[Pennington et al.2014] Jeffrey Pennington, Richard Socher, and Christopher D Manning. 2014. GloVe: global vectors for word representation. *Proceedings of the Empiricial Methods in Natural Language Processing (EMNLP 2014)*, 12:1532–1543.

[Quarteroni et al.2011] Silvia Quarteroni, Alexei V Ivanov, and Giuseppe Riccardi. 2011. Simultaneous dialog act segmentation and classification from human-human spoken conversations. In *Acoustics, Speech and Signal Processing (ICASSP), 2011 IEEE International Conference on*, pages 5596–5599. IEEE.

[Reithinger and Klesen1997] Norbert Reithinger and Martin Klesen. 1997. Dialogue act classification using language models. In *EuroSpeech*. Citeseer.

[Rotaru2002] Mihai Rotaru. 2002. Dialog act tagging using memory-based learning. *Term project, University of Pittsburgh*, pages 255–276.

[Schuster and Paliwal1997] Mike Schuster and Kuldip K Paliwal. 1997. Bidirectional recurrent neural networks. *Signal Processing, IEEE Transactions on*, 45(11):2673–2681.

[Shriberg et al.2004] Elizabeth Shriberg, Raj Dhillon, Sonali Bhagat, Jeremy Ang, and Hannah Carvey. 2004. The ICSI meeting recorder dialog act (MRDA) corpus. Technical report, DTIC Document.

[Silva et al.2011] Joao Silva, Luísa Coheur, Ana Cristina Mendes, and Andreas Wichert. 2011. From symbolic to sub-symbolic information in question classification. *Artificial Intelligence Review*, 35(2):137–154.

[Socher et al.2012] Richard Socher, Brody Huval, Christopher D Manning, and Andrew Y Ng. 2012. Semantic compositionality through recursive matrix-vector spaces. In *Proceedings of the 2012 Joint Conference on Empirical Methods in Natural Language Processing and Computational Natural Language Learning*, pages 1201–1211. Association for Computational Linguistics.

[Stolcke et al.2000] Andreas Stolcke, Klaus Ries, Noah Coccaro, Elizabeth Shriberg, Rebecca Bates, Daniel Jurafsky, Paul Taylor, Rachel Martin, Carol Van Ess-Dykema, and Marie Meteer. 2000. Dialogue act modeling for automatic tagging and recognition of conversational speech. *Computational linguistics*, 26(3):339–373.

[Surendran and Levow2006] Dinoj Surendran and Gina-Anne Levow. 2006. Dialog act tagging with support vector machines and hidden markov models. In *INTERSPEECH*.

[Wang and Manning2012] Sida Wang and Christopher D Manning. 2012. Baselines and bigrams: Simple, good sentiment and topic classification. In *Proceedings of the 50th Annual Meeting of the Association for Computational Linguistics: Short Papers-Volume 2*, pages 90–94. Association for Computational Linguistics.

[Zeiler2012] Matthew D Zeiler. 2012. Adadelta: An adaptive learning rate method. *arXiv preprint arXiv:1212.5701*.

Improved Neural Network-based Multi-label Classification
with Better Initialization Leveraging Label Co-occurrence

Gakuto Kurata
IBM Research
gakuto@jp.ibm.com

Bing Xiang
IBM Watson
bingxia@us.ibm.com

Bowen Zhou
IBM Watson
zhou@us.ibm.com

Abstract

In a multi-label text classification task, in which multiple labels can be assigned to one text, label co-occurrence itself is informative. We propose a novel neural network initialization method to treat some of the neurons in the final hidden layer as dedicated neurons for each pattern of label co-occurrence. These dedicated neurons are initialized to connect to the corresponding co-occurring labels with stronger weights than to others. In experiments with a natural language query classification task, which requires multi-label classification, our initialization method improved classification accuracy without any computational overhead in training and evaluation.

1 Introduction

In multi-label text classification, one text can be associated with multiple labels (*label co-occurrence*) (Zhang and Zhou, 2014). Since label co-occurrence itself contains information, we would like to leverage the label co-occurrence to improve multi-label classification using a neural network (NN). We propose a novel NN initialization method that treats some of the neurons in the final hidden layer as *dedicated neurons* for each pattern of label co-occurrence. These dedicated neurons are initialized to connect to the corresponding co-occurring labels with stronger weights than to others. While initialization of an NN is an important research topic (Glorot and Bengio, 2010; Sutskever et al., 2013; Le et al., 2015), to the best of our knowledge, there has been no attempt to leverage label co-occurrence for NN initialization.

To validate our proposed method, we focus on multi-label Natural Language Query (NLQ) classification in a document retrieval system in which users input queries in natural language and the system returns documents that contain answers to the queries. For NLQ classification, we first train a model from training data that contains pairs of queries and corresponding one or more than one document labels, and then predict the appropriate document labels for new queries with the trained model.

Through experiments with a real-world document retrieval system and publicly available multi-label data set, simply and directly embedding label co-occurrence information into an NN with our proposed method improved accuracy of NLQ classification.

2 Related Work

Along with the recent success in NNs (Collobert et al., 2011; Kim, 2014), NN-based multi-label classification has been proposed. An NN for NLQ classification needs to accept queries with variable length and output their labels. Figure 1 shows a typical NN architecture (Collobert et al., 2011). This NN first transforms words in the input query into word embeddings (Mikolov et al., 2013), then applies Convolutional Neural Network (CNN) and Max-pooling over time to extract fixed-length feature vectors, and feed them into the output layer to predict the label for the query (Collobert and Weston, 2008; Collobert et al., 2011; Yih et al., 2014). To take care of multi-labels, label co-occurrence has been incorporated into loss functions such as *pairwise ranking loss* (Zhang and Zhou, 2006). More recently, Nam et

Proceedings of NAACL-HLT 2016, pages 521–526,
San Diego, California, June 12-17, 2016. ©2016 Association for Computational Linguistics

al. (2014) reported that *binary cross entropy* can outperform the pairwise ranking loss by leveraging rectified linear units (ReLUs) for nonlinearity (Nair and Hinton, 2010), *AdaGrad* for optimization (Duchi et al., 2011), and *dropout* for generalization (Srivastava et al., 2014). Considering the training efficiency and superior performance, we used the binary cross entropy as one of the baselines in our experiments in Section 4 in addition to *negative log-likelihood* and *cross entropy*.

Let x denote the feature vector of a query, y be the vector representation of the label, o be the output value of the NN, and Θ be the parameters of the NN. Note that the representation of y differs depending on the loss function. For simplicity in the following explanation, assume that we have a finite set of labels $\Lambda = \{\lambda_1, \lambda_2, \lambda_3, \lambda_4, \lambda_5\}$ and that a query x has multiple labels $\{\lambda_1, \lambda_4\}$:

Negative Log Probability With minimization of negative log probability, a single label is assumed. To circumvent this limitation, we used *copy transformation* (Tsoumakas et al., 2010) and obtained two training examples $((x, y^{(1)}), (x, y^{(2)}))$, where $y^{(1)} = (1, 0, 0, 0, 0)$ and $y^{(2)} = (0, 0, 0, 1, 0)$. The loss for each example becomes $l(\Theta, (x, y^{(1)})) = -\log(o_1)$ and $l(\Theta, (x, y^{(2)})) = -\log(o_4)$, where softmax activation is used to calculate o in the output layer.

Cross Entropy We assumed multi-labels as probabilistic distribution as $y = (0.5, 0, 0, 0.5, 0)$. The cross entropy loss for the training example (x, y) becomes $l(\Theta, (x, y)) = -y \log(o)$, where softmax activation is used in the output layer.

Binary Cross Entropy As Nam et al. (2014) indicated, minimizing binary cross entropy is superior for handling multi-labels. By representing the target labels as $y = (1, 0, 0, 1, 0)$, the binary cross entropy loss for the training example (x, y) becomes $l(\Theta, (x, y)) = -\sum_{k=1}^{5}(y_k \log(o_k) + (1 - y_k) \log(1 - o_k))$, where sigmoid activation is used in the output layer.

3 Proposed Method

In this section, we explain our proposed method in detail.

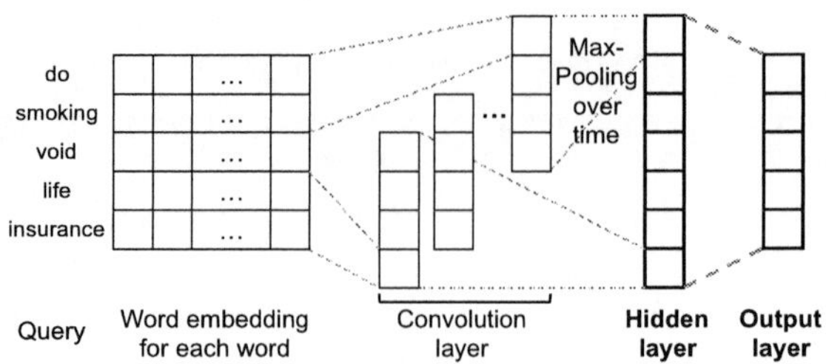

Figure 1: Neural network for NLQ classification. Proposed method is applied to the weight matrix between hidden and output layers as detailed in Figure 2.

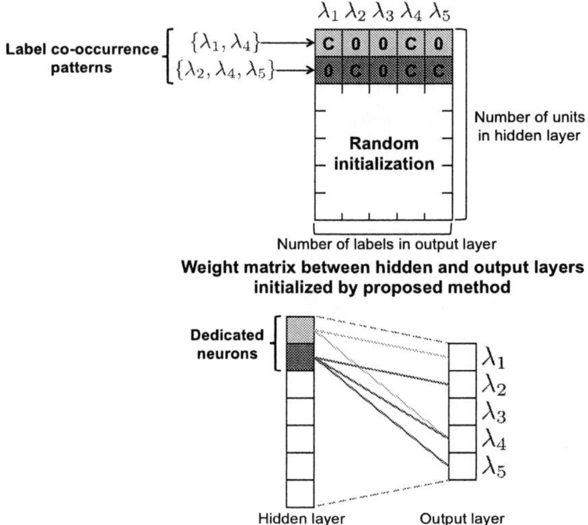

Figure 2: Overview of the proposed method. Label co-occurrence patterns of $\{\lambda_1, \lambda_4\}$ and $\{\lambda_2, \lambda_4, \lambda_5\}$ are used in weight initialization, as shown in the above. This initialization corresponds to preparing dedicated neurons for each label co-occurrence pattern, as shown in the below.

3.1 Weight Initialization Leveraging Label Co-occurrence

We propose an NN initialization method to treat some of the neurons in the final hidden layer as dedicated neurons for each pattern of label co-occurrence. These dedicated neurons simultaneously activate the co-occurring labels. Figure 2 shows the key idea of the proposed method. We first investigate the training data and list up patterns of label co-occurrence. Then, for each pattern of label co-occurrence, we initialize a matrix row so that the columns corresponding to the co-occurring labels have a constant weight C and the other columns

Loss Function	1-best Accuracy			Recall@5			Full Accuracy		
Negative Log Likelihood	49.75	$\rightarrow$	51.27	69.80	$\rightarrow$	71.07	47.03	$\rightarrow$	48.65
Cross Entropy	50.51	$\rightarrow$	**52.54**	71.32	$\rightarrow$	**72.08**	46.96	$\rightarrow$	**48.71**
Binary Cross Entropy	49.75	$\rightarrow$	50.51	70.81	$\rightarrow$	71.32	48.09	$\rightarrow$	48.34

Table 1: 1-best accuracy, recall@5, and full accuracy for evaluation data using different loss functions (Random initialization $\rightarrow$ Proposed initialization). [%]

have a weight of 0, as shown in Figure 2 (above). Note that the remaining rows that are not associated with the pattern of label co-occurrence are randomly initialized. This initialization is equivalent to treating some of the neurons in the final hidden layer as dedicated neurons for each pattern of label co-occurrence, where the dedicated neurons have connections to the corresponding co-occurring labels with an initialized weight C and to others with an initialized weight of 0, as shown in Figure 2 (below). Finally, we conduct normal back-propagation using one of the loss functions, as discussed in the previous section. Note that all the connection weights in the NN including the connection weights between the dedicated neurons and all labels are updated through back-propagation.

Since (1) computation of proposed initialization itself is negligible and (2) computation of back-propagation and the architecture of NN does not change with or without the proposed initialization, our proposed method does not increase computation in training and evaluation.

3.2 Weight Setting for Dedicated Neurons

For the weight value C for initialization, we used the upper bound UB of the normalized initialization (Glorot and Bengio, 2010), which is determined by the number of units in the final hidden layer n_h and output layer n_c as $UB = \frac{\sqrt{6}}{\sqrt{n_h + n_o}}$. Additionally, we changed this value in accordance with the frequency of the label co-occurrence patterns in the training data. The background idea is that the patterns of label co-occurrence that appear frequently (i.e., the number of queries with this pattern of label co-occurrence is large) are more important than less frequent patterns. Assuming that a specific pattern of label co-occurrence appears in the training data f times, we try $f \times UB$ and $\sqrt{f} \times UB$ for initialization to emphasize this pattern.

C	1-best	Recall@5	Full
—	50.51	71.32	46.96
UB	52.54	**72.08**	48.71
$f \times UB$	51.52	70.81	48.39
$\sqrt{f} \times UB$	**53.55**	72.08	**50.04**

Table 2: 1-best accuracy, recall@5, and full accuracy for evaluation data with changing initialization value C. [%]

4 Experiments

We conducted experiments with the real-world NLQ classification data and the publicly available data to confirm the advantage of the proposed method.

4.1 Real-world NLQ classification Data

Experimental Setup We used NLQs for a document retrieval system in the insurance domain for the experiments. Users of the system input queries in natural language, and the system returns the labels of the documents that contain answers. We used $3,133$ queries for training and 394 queries for evaluation, $1,695$ and 158 of which had multiple labels, respectively. The number of unique document labels assigned to the training data was 526.

We used the NN shown in Figure 1. The dimension of word embedding was 100, number of kernels for the CNN was $1,000$, which means $1,000$ units exist in the final hidden layer on top of Max-pooling over time, and number of output units was 526. We used this NN configuration in common for all the experiments. The word embedding was pre-trained with the *skip-gram* model of *word2vec* using the dumped English *Wikipedia* data and the documents of the target insurance domain (Mikolov et al., 2013). The NN except the word embedding layer was randomly initialized in accordance with the normalized initialization (Glorot and Bengio, 2010). We used the ReLU for nonlinearity, AdaGrad for optimization, and dropout for generalization. We fixed

Loss Function	# Survived Neurons (# dedicated neurons:252)	Weights-Dedicated [Mean / Variance]	Weights-All [Mean / Variance]
Negative Log Likelihood	194	0.251 / 0.004	-0.024 / 0.023
Cross Entropy	197	0.267 / 0.005	-0.017 / 0.021
Binary Cross Entropy	168	0.279 / 0.015	-0.007 / 0.011

Table 3: Investigation of neural network after back-propagation training.

the number of training epochs to $1,000$[1].

For the proposed method, we investigated the $1,695$ queries with multiple labels in the training data and found 252 patterns of label co-occurrence. We then embedded this information in a $1,000 \times 526$ weight matrix between the final hidden and output layers. In other words, we treated 252 neurons in the final hidden layer as dedicated neurons in weight initialization.

For the hyper-parameter settings, we first tuned the hyper-parameters including L2-regularization and learning rate so that the accuracy of the baseline system with random initialization was maximized. For the proposed initialization, we used the same hyper-parameters obtained in the former tuning.

We used three evaluation metrics that are closely related to the usability of the document retrieval system: (1) *1-best accuracy* judges if the 1-best result of a system is included in the correct labels[2]. (2) *Recall@5* judges if the 5-best results of a system contain at least one of the correct labels. (3) *Full accuracy* investigates the j-best results of a system and judges if they match the correct labels when j labels are assigned to the query[3].

Different Loss Functions Table 1 shows the experimental results using three different loss functions. Comparing the values to the left of the arrows, which did not use the proposed initialization, superiority of binary cross entropy (Nam et al., 2014) was confirmed in full accuracy, while cross entropy

was the best in 1-best accuracy in this experiment. As shown to the right of the arrows, we obtained improvement for all loss functions with every evaluation metric with the proposed method. Overall, cross entropy training with the proposed initialization achieved the best in all three metrics, where 1-best accuracy improvement from 50.51% to 52.54% was statistically significant ($p < 0.05$).

Different Weight Initialization Table 2 shows the results of emphasizing the frequent patterns of label co-occurrence. We used the cross entropy loss function, which was the best in the previous experiments. Using $\sqrt{f} \times UB$ yielded further improvement in 1-best accuracy and full accuracy, though using $f \times UB$ deteriorated in all metrics compared with UB. This suggests that there is room for improvement if we can appropriately emphasize frequent patterns of label co-occurrence.

Analysis on Trained Neural Network We investigated if the dedicated neurons for patterns of label co-occurrences still simultaneously activate the corresponding labels after back-propagation. Table 3 shows the analysis on the NNs trained in the experiments for Table 1. In the *# Survived Neurons* columns, we investigated if the dedicated neurons initialized for the pattern of k-label co-occurrence still had the k largest weights to the corresponding k labels after back-propagation. Large portions of dedicated neurons "survived" after back-propagation. In the *Weights* columns, we calculated the mean of the connection weights between the dedicated neurons and corresponding co-occurring labels and compared them with the mean of all connections in this weight matrix. The trained weights for the connections between the dedicated neurons and corresponding co-occurring labels (*Weights-Dedicated*) were much stronger than the average weights (*Weights-All*). This analysis suggests that the proposed initialization yields dedicated neurons

---

[1]We confirmed that NN training sufficiently saturated after $1,000$ epochs in preliminary experiments. We also compared the best accuracy achieved in $1,000$ epochs for all experimental conditions and confirmed that the same improvement was achieved with the proposed method.

[2]This metric is comparable with *One-error* (Tsoumakas et al., 2010) by 1-best Accuracy = 100 - One-error.

[3]If a query has three labels, the system needs to return 3-best results that contain the three correct labels of the query to obtain 100% full accuracy.

that simultaneously activate the co-occurring labels even after back-propagation.

There can be an overlap in label co-occurrence patterns. One typical case is "A, B" and "A, B, C", and another case is "D, E", "F, G", and "D, E, F, G". While we prepared the dedicated neurons for each co-occurrence pattern before back-propagation, some overlapped co-occurrences might be explained by the superset or combination of subsets after back-propagation. Table 3 suggests that some of the dedicated neurons did not survive after back-propagation. We confirmed that about half of the label co-occurrence patterns whose dedicated neurons did not survive were covered by the patterns whose neurons survived. "Cover" means that if a neuron for "A, B" did not survive, a neuron for "A, B, C" survived, or if a neuron for "D, E, F, G" did not survive, neurons for "D, E" and "F, G" survived. If we change the network structure by connecting the dedicated neurons only to the corresponding units or preparing the special output units for co-occurring labels (label powerset (Read, 2008)), this flexibility might be lost.

4.2 Publicly Available Data

We used multi-label topic categorization data (*RCV1-v2*) (Lewis et al., 2004) to validate our method. We used the same label assignment and the same training and evaluation data partition with the *LYRL2004* split (Lewis et al., 2004) where $23{,}149$ training texts and $781{,}265$ evaluation texts with 103 topic labels are available. We used the bag-of-word (BoW) feature for each text prepared by Chang and Lin (2011) whose dimension was $47{,}236$ and constructed a feed-forward NN that has an input layer that accepts the BoW feature, hidden layer of $2{,}000$ units, and output layer of 103 output units with the cross entropy loss function. By embedding the label co-occurrence information between the hidden and output layers with the initial weights set to UB, which corresponded to treating 758 neurons out of $2{,}000$ hidden units as the dedicated neurons, we improved 1-best accuracy of topic label classification from 93.95% to 94.60%, which was statistically significant ($p < 0.001$).

To the best of our knowledge, 1-best accuracy

of 94.18% (5.82% one-error)[4] (Rubin et al., 2012) was the best published result with using the standard LYRL2004 split of RCV1-v2. Our proposed method has advantages in a sufficiently competitive setup.

5   Conclusion

We proposed an NN initialization method to leverage label co-occurrence information. Through experiments using the data of a real-world document retrieval system and publicly available data, we confirmed that our proposed method improved NLQ classification accuracy. The advantage of the proposed method also includes no computational overhead during training and evaluation.

When we have large training data, the number of label co-occurrence patterns can be larger than that of hidden units. In such a case, one option is to select an appropriate set of label co-occurrence patterns with certain criteria such as the frequency in the training data. Another option is to make a larger weight matrix using all patterns and then to reduce its dimension with such as Principal Component Analysis (PCA) in advance of NN training. Our future work also includes setting the initialization weight in a more sophisticated way and combining the proposed method with other NN-based methods (Kim, 2014; Johnson and Zhang, 2015).

Acknowledgments

We would like to show our gratitude to Dr. Ramesh M. Nallapati of IBM Watson for supporting the experiments. We are grateful to Dr. Yuta Tsuboi, Dr. Ryuki Tachibana, and Mr. Nobuyasu Itoh of IBM Research - Tokyo for the fruitful discussion and their comments on this and earlier versions of the paper. We thank the anonymous reviewers for their valuable comments.

---

[4]Randomly selected $75{,}000$ texts were used for evaluation, but the results on this subset were confirmed to be almost identical to those on the full evaluation texts (Rubin et al., 2012).

References

Chih-Chung Chang and Chih-Jen Lin. 2011. LIB-SVM: A library for support vector machines. *ACM Transactions on Intelligent Systems and Technology*, 2(3):27:1–27:27.

Ronan Collobert and Jason Weston. 2008. A unified architecture for natural language processing: Deep neural networks with multitask learning. In *Proc. ICML*, pages 160–167. ACM.

Ronan Collobert, Jason Weston, Léon Bottou, Michael Karlen, Koray Kavukcuoglu, and Pavel Kuksa. 2011. Natural language processing (almost) from scratch. *The Journal of Machine Learning Research*, 12:2493–2537.

John Duchi, Elad Hazan, and Yoram Singer. 2011. Adaptive subgradient methods for online learning and stochastic optimization. *The Journal of Machine Learning Research*, 12:2121–2159.

Xavier Glorot and Yoshua Bengio. 2010. Understanding the difficulty of training deep feedforward neural networks. In *Proc. AISTATS*, pages 249–256.

Rie Johnson and Tong Zhang. 2015. Effective use of word order for text categorization with convolutional neural networks. In *Proc. NAACL-HLT*, pages 103–112.

Yoon Kim. 2014. Convolutional neural networks for sentence classification. In *Proc. EMNLP*, pages 1746–1751.

Quoc V Le, Navdeep Jaitly, and Geoffrey E Hinton. 2015. A simple way to initialize recurrent networks of rectified linear units. *arXiv preprint arXiv:1504.00941*.

David D Lewis, Yiming Yang, Tony G Rose, and Fan Li. 2004. RCV1: A new benchmark collection for text categorization research. *The Journal of Machine Learning Research*, 5:361–397.

Tomas Mikolov, Kai Chen, Greg Corrado, and Jeffrey Dean. 2013. Efficient estimation of word representations in vector space. In *Proc. ICLR*.

Vinod Nair and Geoffrey E Hinton. 2010. Rectified linear units improve restricted boltzmann machines. In *Proc. ICML*, pages 807–814.

Jinseok Nam, Jungi Kim, Eneldo Loza Mencía, Iryna Gurevych, and Johannes Fürnkranz. 2014. Large-scale multi-label text classification —– revisiting neural networks. In *Proc. ECML-PKDD*, pages 437–452.

Jesse Read. 2008. A pruned problem transformation method for multi-label classification. In *Proc. NZC-SRS*, pages 143–150.

Timothy N Rubin, America Chambers, Padhraic Smyth, and Mark Steyvers. 2012. Statistical topic models for multi-label document classification. *Machine learning*, 88(1-2):157–208.

Nitish Srivastava, Geoffrey Hinton, Alex Krizhevsky, Ilya Sutskever, and Ruslan Salakhutdinov. 2014. Dropout: A simple way to prevent neural networks from overfitting. *The Journal of Machine Learning Research*, 15(1):1929–1958.

Ilya Sutskever, James Martens, George Dahl, and Geoffrey Hinton. 2013. On the importance of initialization and momentum in deep learning. In *Proc. ICML*, pages 1139–1147.

Grigorios Tsoumakas, Ioannis Katakis, and Ioannis Vlahavas. 2010. Mining multi-label data. In *Data mining and knowledge discovery handbook*, pages 667–685. Springer.

Wen-tau Yih, Xiaodong He, and Christopher Meek. 2014. Semantic parsing for single-relation question answering. In *Proc. ACL*, pages 643–648.

Min-Ling Zhang and Zhi-Hua Zhou. 2006. Multilabel neural networks with applications to functional genomics and text categorization. *IEEE Transactions on Knowledge and Data Engineering*, 18(10):1338–1351.

Min-Ling Zhang and Zhi-Hua Zhou. 2014. A review on multi-label learning algorithms. *IEEE Transactions on Knowledge and Data Engineering*, 26(8):1819–1837.

Learning Distributed Word Representations For
Bidirectional LSTM Recurrent Neural Network[*]

Peilu Wang[1,2][†]**, Yao Qian**[3]**, Hai Zhao**[1][‡]**, Frank K. Soong**[2]**, Lei He**[2]**, Ke Wu**[1]
[1]Shanghai Jiao Tong University, Shanghai, China
[2]Microsoft Research Asia, Beijing, China
[3]Educational Testing Service Research, CA, USA
peiluwang@163.com, yqian@ets.org, zhaohai@cs.sjtu.edu.cn
{frankkps, helei}@microsoft.com,wuke@cs.sjtu.edu.cn

Abstract

Bidirectional long short-term memory (BLSTM) recurrent neural network (RNN) has been successfully applied in many tagging tasks. BLSTM-RNN relies on the distributed representation of words, which implies that the former can be futhermore improved through learning the latter better. In this work, we propose a novel approach to learn distributed word representations by training BLSTM-RNN on a specially designed task which only relies on unlabeled data. Our experimental results show that the proposed approach learns useful distributed word representations, as the trained representations significantly elevate the performance of BLSTM-RNN on three tagging tasks: part-of-speech tagging, chunking and named entity recognition, surpassing word representations trained by other published methods.

1 Introduction

Distributed word representations represent word with a real valued vector, which is also referred to as word embedding. Well learned distributed word representations have been shown capable of capturing semantic and syntactic regularities (Pennington et al., 2014a; Mikolov et al., 2013c) and enhancing neural network model by being used as features (Collobert and Weston, 2008; Bengio and Heigold, 2014; Wang et al., 2015).

Sequence tagging is a basic structure learning task for natural language processing. Many primary processing tasks over sentence such as word segmentation, named entity recognition and part-of-speech tagging can be formalized as a tagging task (Zhao et al., 2006; Huang and Zhao, 2007; Zhao and Kit, 2008b; Zhao and Kit, 2008a; Zhao et al., 2010; Zhao and Kit, 2011). Recently, many state-of-the-art systems of tagging related tasks are implemented with bidirectional long short-term memory (BLSTM) recurrent neural network (RNN), for example, slot filling (Mesnil et al., 2013), part-of-speech tagging (Huang et al., 2015), and dependency parsing (Dyer et al., 2015) etc. All of these systems use distributed representation of words to involve word level information. Better trained word representations would further improve the state-of-the-art performance of these tasks which makes it worthy to research the training methods of word representations.

The existing training methods of word representation can generally be divided into two classes: 1) Matrix factorization methods. These methods utilize low-rank approximation to decompose a large matrix that contains corpus statistics. One typical work is the latent semantic analysis (LSA) (Deerwester et al., 1990) in which the matrix records "term-document" information, i.e., the rows cor-

---

[*]The work was partially supported by the National Natural Science Foundation of China (Grant No. 61170114, and Grant No. 61272248), the National Basic Research Program of China (Grant No. 2013CB329401), the Science and Technology Commission of Shanghai Municipality (Grant No. 13511500200), the European Union Seventh Framework Program (Grant No. 247619), the Cai Yuanpei Program (CSC fund 201304490199, 201304490171), and the art and science interdisciplinary funds of Shanghai Jiao Tong University, No. 14X190040031, and the Key Project of National Society Science Foundation of China, No. 15-ZDA041.

[†]Work performed as an intern in speech group, Microsoft Research Asia

[‡]Corresponding author

respond to words, and the columns correspond to different documents in the corpus. Another work is hyperspace analogue to language (HAL) (Lund and Burgess, 1996) which decomposes the matrix recording "term-term" information, i.e., the rows correspond to words and columns correspond to the number of times that a word occurs in the given context. 2) Window-based methods. This type of methods learn representations by training a neural network model to make prediction within local context windows. For example, (Bengio et al., 2003) learns word representation through a feedforward neural network language model which predicts a word given its previous several words. (Collobert et al., 2011) trains a neural network to judge the validity of a given context. (Mikolov et al., 2013a) proposes skip-gram and continuous bag-of-words (CBOW) models based on a single-layer network architecture. The objective of skip-gram model is to predict the context given the word itself, while the objective of CBOW is to predict a word given its context. Aside from these two sets of methods, distributed representation can also be obtained by training recurrent neural network (RNN) language model proposed by (Mikolov et al., 2010) or GloVe model proposed by (Pennington et al., 2014a) which trains a log-bilinear model on word-word co-occurrence counts.

All of these methods suffer from shortcomings that might limit the quality of trained word distributions. The matrix factorization family only uses the statistics of co-occurrence counts, disregarding of the position of word in sentence and word order. The window-based methods only consider local context, which is incapable of involving information outside the context window. While RNN language model theoretically considers all information of the previous sequence, but fails to involve the information of the posterior sequence. The word-word co-occurence counts that GloVe model relies on also only include information within a limited sized context window.

In this paper, we propose a novel method to obtain word representation by training BLSTM-RNN model on a specifically designed tagging task. Since BLSTM-RNN theoretically involves all information of input sentence, our approach avoids those shortages suffered by most current methods.

We firstly introduce the structure of BLSTM-RNN used to learn word representations in section 2. Then the tagging task for training BLSTM-RNN is described in section 3. Experiments are presented in section 4, followed by conclusion.

2   Model Structure

The structure of BLSTM-RNN to train word representation is illustrated in Figure 1. Each input is composed of a word identity x_i^1 and additional real-valued features x_i^2. x_i^1 is represented with one-hot representation which is a binary vector with dimension $|V|$ where V is the vocabulary. The input vector I_i of the network is computed as:

$$I_i = W_1 x_i^1 + W_2 x_i^2$$

where W_1 and W_2 are weight matrixes connecting two layers and are updated with the neural network during training. $W_1 x_i^1$ is also known as the distributed representation of word or word embedding which is a real-valued vector usually with a much smaller dimension than x_i^1. Distributed representation trained in other tasks can be easily incorporated by initializing W_1 with these external representations.

3   Learning Representation

According to the structure shown in Figure 1, W_1 is a matrix of weights that is updated during training, thus the distributed representations contained in W_1 are learned simultaneously with the training of BLSTM-RNN on any supervised learning tasks. However, all such tasks for BLSTM-RNN, to the best of our knowledge, require labeled data which is usually too small in size and hard to obtain. In this section, we propose a tagging task specially for BLSTM-RNN to train distributed representations with unlabeled data.

In this method, BLSTM-RNN is applied to perform a tagging task with only two types of tags to predict: incorrect/correct. The input is a sequence of words which is a normal sentence with several words replaced by words randomly chosen from vocabulary. The words to be replaced are chosen randomly from the sentence. In practice, we generate a random number for each word, and a word is chosen to be replaced if the number is lower than a given

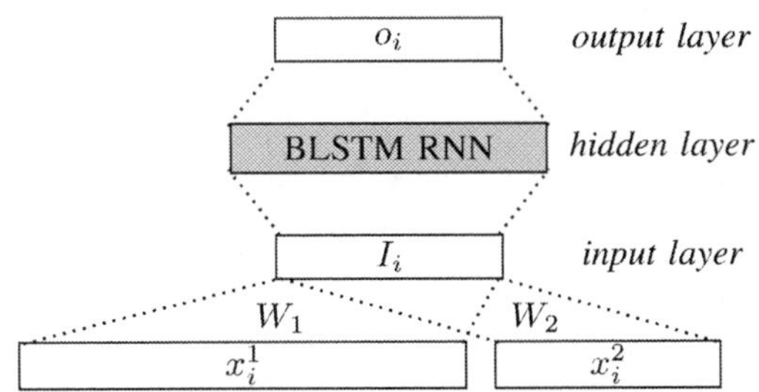

Figure 1: BLSTM-RNN for training word representation.

threshold. For those replaced words, their tags are 0 (incorrect) and for those that are not replaced, their tags are 1 (correct). A simple sample of constructed corpus is shown in Figure 2. Although it is possible that some replaced words are also reasonable in the sentence, they are still considered "incorrect". Then BLSTM-RNN is trained to judge which words have been replaced by minimizing the binary classification error on the training corpus. When the network is trained, W_1 contains all trained word representations. In our experiments, to reduce the vocabulary V, each letter of input word is transferred to its lowercase. The upper case information is kept in an additional features x_i^2 which in practice is a three-dimensional binary vector to indicate if x_i^1 is full lowercase, full uppercase or leading with a capital letter.

Our approach is similar to (Collobert and Weston, 2008) and (Gutmann and Hyvärinen, 2012; Mnih and Teh, 2012; Vaswani et al., 2013). All of these works introduce randomly sampled words and train a neural network on a binary classification task, while (Collobert and Weston, 2008) learns representations for a feedforward network and (Gutmann and Hyvärinen, 2012; Mnih and Teh, 2012; Vaswani et al., 2013) learns normalization parameters instead of representations.

4 Experiments

4.1 Experimental setup

To construct corpus for training word representations, we use North American news (Graff, 2008) which contains about 536 million words as unlabeled data. The North American news data is first tokenized with the Penn Treebank tokenizer script [1]. Consecutive digits occurring within a word are replaced with the symbol "#" . For example, both words "*tel92*" and "*tel6*" are converted into "*tel#*". The vocabulary is limited to the most frequent 100,000 words in North American news corpus (Graff, 2008), plus one single "UNK" symbol for replacing all out of vocabulary words. The threshold to determine whether a word is replaced is 0.2, which means about 20% tokens in corpus are replaced with tokens randomly selected from vocabulary. BLSTM-RNN is implemented based on CURRENNT (Weninger et al., 2014), an open source GPU-based toolkit of BLSTM-RNN. The dimension of word representation as well as input layer size of BLSTM-RNN is 100 and hidden layer size is 128.

Three published methods for training word representations are compared: *Skip-gram* (Mikolov et al., 2013a), *CBOW* (Mikolov et al., 2013a) and *GloVe* (Pennington et al., 2014a). They are reported superior in capturing meaningful latent structures than other previous works in (Mikolov et al., 2013a; Pennington et al., 2014a), thus are regarded as the state-of-the-art approach of training word representations. We train the *Skip-gram* and *CBOW* model using the word2vec tool (Mikolov et al., 2013b) with a context window size of 10 and 10 negative samples. For training *GloVe*, we use the GloVe tool (Pennington et al., 2014b) with a context window size 10. These configurations are set by following (Pennington et al., 2014a). Training corpus, vocabulary and dimension of word representations are set the same as that in experiment for training word representations with BLSTM-RNN[2].

---

[1] https://www.cis.upenn.edu/~treebank/tokenization.html

[2] Our experimental setup are released at: https://github.com/PeiluWang/naacl2016_blstmwe

Original Sentence:
They   seem   to   be   prepared   to   make $\cdots$

Input Sentence:
They   beast   to   be   austere   to   make $\cdots$

Tag Sequence:
1   0   1   1   0   1   1 $\cdots$

Figure 2: Sample of constructed corpus for training word representations. Two words *"seem"* and *"prepared"* are replaced with words randomly chosen from vocabulary.

Sys	POS(Acc.)	CHUNK(F1)	NER(F1)
BLSTM	96.60	91.71	82.52
BLSTM+CBOW	96.73	92.14	84.37
BLSTM+Skip	96.85	92.45	85.80
BLSTM+GloVe	97.02	93.01	87.33
BLSTM+BLSTMWE	**97.26**	**94.44**	**88.38**

Table 1: Performance of BLSTM-RNN with different representations on three tagging tasks

4.2 Evaluation

The quality of trained distributed representation is evaluated by the performance of BLSTM-RNN which uses the trained representations on practical tasks. The representations which lead to better performance are considered containing more useful latent information and are judged better. The structure of BLSTM-RNN to test word representations is the same as that in Figure1. To use trained representation, we initialize the weight matrix W_1 with these external representations. For words without corresponding external representations, their representations are initialized with uniformly distributed random values, ranging from -0.1 to 0.1. Three typical tagging tasks are used for the evaluation: part-of-speech tagging (POS), chunking (CHUNK) and named entity recognition (NER).

- The POS tagging experiment is conducted on the Wall Street Journal data from Penn Treebank III (Marcus et al., 1993). Training, development and test sets are split according to in (Collins, 2002). Performance is evaluated by the accuracy of predicted tags on test set.

- CHUNK experiment is conducted on the data of CoNLL-2000 shared task (Sang and Buchholz, 2000). Performance is assessed by the F1 score computed by the evaluation script re-

leased by the CoNLL-2000 shared task[3].

- NER experiment is conducted on the CoNLL-2003 shared task (Tjong Kim Sang and De Meulder, 2003). Performance is measured by the F1 score calculated by the evaluation script of the CoNLL-2003 shared task [4].

To focus on the effect of word representation, for all tasks, we use the network with the same hidden structure and input features. The size of input layer is 100, size of BLSTM hidden layer is 128 and output layer size is set as the number of tag types according to the specific tagging task. Input features are composed of word identity and three-dimensional binary vector to indicate if the word is full lowercase, full uppercase or leading with a capital letter.

Table 1 presents the performance of BLSTM-RNN with different distributed representations on these three tasks. *BLSTM* is the baseline system that does not involve external word representations. Among all representations, *BLSTMWE* which is trained by our approach gets the best performance on all three tasks. It shows our approach is more helpful for BLSTM-RNN. Besides, all of the three published word representations also significantly en-

---

[3]`http://www.cnts.ua.ac.be/conll2000/chunking`

[4]`http://www.cnts.ua.ac.be/conll2003/ner/`

Sys	POS(Acc.)	CHUNK(F1)	NER(F1)
BLSTMWE (10M)	96.61	91.91	84.66
BLSTMWE (100M)	97.10	93.86	86.47
BLSTMWE (536M)	97.26	94.44	88.38

Table 2: Performance of BLSTMWE trained on corpora with different size

	Skip-gram	*CBOW*	*GloVe*	*BLSTM RNN*
Time (min.)	344	117	127	1393

Table 3: Running time of different training methods

hance BLSTM RNN. It confirms the commonly accepted notion that word representation is a useful feature.

4.3 Analysis

Table 2 shows the performance of word representations trained on corpora with different size. *BLSTMWE* (10M), *BLSTMWE* (100M) and *BLSTMWE* (536M) are word representations respectively trained by BLSTM-RNN on the first 10 million words, first 100 million words and all 536 million words of the North American news corpus. As expected, there is a monotonic increase in performance as the corpus size increases. This observation suggests that the result might be further improved by using even bigger unlabeled data.

Table 3 presents running time with different methods to train word representations on 536 million words corpus. BLSTM-RNN is trained on one NVIDIA Tesla M2090 GPU. The other three methods are trained on a 12 core, 2.53GHz Intel Xeon E5649 machine, using 12 threads. Though with the help of GPU, BLSTM-RNN is still slower than the other methods. However, it should be noted that the speed of our approach is acceptable compared with previous neural network language model based methods, including (Bengio et al., 2003; Mikolov et al., 2010; Mnih and Hinton, 2007), as our model uses a much simpler output layer which only has two nodes, avoiding the time consuming computation of the big softmax output layer in language model.

5   CONCLUSION

In this paper, we propose a novel approach to learn distributed word representations with BLSTM-RNN. Word representations are implemented as the layer weights and are obtained as a byproduct of training BLSTM-RNN on a specially designed task, thus theoretically involve information of the whole sentence. The quality of word representations are evaluated by the performance of BLSTM-RNN which uses these representations on three tagging tasks: part-of-speech tagging, chunking and named entity recognition. In experiments, word representations trained by our approach outperform the word representations trained by other published methods. Our work demonstrates an alternative way to improve BLSTM-RNN's performance by learning useful word representations.

References

Samy Bengio and Georg Heigold. 2014. Word embeddings for speech recognition. In *INTERSPEECH*, pages 1053–1057.

Yoshua Bengio, Rejean Ducharme, Pascal Vincent, and Christian Jauvin. 2003. A neural probabilistic language model. In *Journal of Machine Learning Research (JMLR)*, volume 3, pages 1137–1155.

Michael Collins. 2002. Discriminative training methods for Hidden Markov Models: Theory and experiments with perceptron algorithms. In *Proceedings of Empirical Methods in Natural Language Processing (EMNLP)*, pages 1–8.

Ronan Collobert and Jason Weston. 2008. A unified architecture for natural language processing: Deep neural networks with multitask learning. In *Proceedings of International Conference on Machine Learning (ICML)*, pages 160–167.

Ronan Collobert, Jason Weston, Léon Bottou, Michael Karlen, Koray Kavukcuoglu, and Pavel Kuksa. 2011. Natural language processing (almost) from scratch.

Journal of Machine Learning Research (JMLR), 12:2493–2537.

Scott Deerwester, Susan Dumais, Thomas Landauer, George Furnas, and Richard Harshman. 1990. Indexing by latent semantic analysis. *JASIS*, 41(6):391–407.

Chris Dyer, Miguel Ballesteros, Wang Ling, Austin Matthews, and Noah A. Smith. 2015. Transition-based dependency parsing with stack long short-term memory. In *Proceedings of Association for Computational Linguistics (ACL)*, pages 334–343.

David Graff. 2008. North American News Text, Complete LDC2008T15. `https://catalog.ldc.upenn.edu/LDC2008T15`.

Michael Gutmann and Aapo Hyvärinen. 2012. Noise-contrastive estimation of unnormalized statistical models, with applications to natural image statistics. *Journal of Machine Learning Research (JMLR)*, 13:307–361.

Changning Huang and Hai Zhao. 2007. Chinese word segmentation: A decade review. *Journal of Chinese Information Processing*, 21(3):8–20.

Zhiheng Huang, Wei Xu, and Kai Yu. 2015. Bidirectional LSTM-CRF models for sequence tagging. *arXiv:1508.01991*.

Kevin Lund and Curt Burgess. 1996. Producing high-dimensional semantic spaces from lexical co-occurrence. *Behavior Research Methods, Instruments, & Computers*, 28(2):203–208.

Mitchell Marcus, Mary Ann Marcinkiewicz, and Beatrice Santorini. 1993. Building a large annotated corpus of English: The Penn Treebank. *Computational linguistics (CL)*, 19(2):313–330.

Grégoire Mesnil, Xiaodong He, Li Deng, and Yoshua Bengio. 2013. Investigation of recurrent-neural-network architectures and learning methods for spoken language understanding. In *INTERSPEECH*, pages 3771–3775.

Tomas Mikolov, Martin Karafiát, Lukas Burget, Jan Cernockỳ, and Sanjeev Khudanpur. 2010. Recurrent neural network based language model. In *INTERSPEECH*, pages 1045–1048.

Tomas Mikolov, Kai Chen, Greg Corrado, and Jeffrey Dean. 2013a. Efficient estimation of word representations in vector space. *arXiv preprint arXiv:1301.3781*.

Tomas Mikolov, Kai Chen, Greg Corrado, and Jeffrey Dean. 2013b. word2vec. `https://code.google.com/p/word2vec/`.

Tomas Mikolov, Ilya Sutskever, Kai Chen, Greg Corrado, and Jeff Dean. 2013c. Distributed representations of words and phrases and their compositionality. In *Proceedings of Conference on Neural Information Processing Systems (NIPS)*, pages 3111–3119.

Andriy Mnih and Geoffrey Hinton. 2007. Three new graphical models for statistical language modelling. In *Proceedings of International Conference on Machine Learning (ICML)*, pages 641–648.

Andriy Mnih and Yee Whye Teh. 2012. A fast and simple algorithm for training neural probabilistic language models. In *Proceedings of International Conference on Machine Learning (ICML)*, pages 1751–1758.

Jeffrey Pennington, Richard Socher, and Christopher Manning. 2014a. Glove: Global vectors for word representation. In *Proceedings of Empirical Methods in Natural Language Processing (EMNLP)*, pages 1532–1543.

Jeffrey Pennington, Richard Socher, and Christopher D. Manning. 2014b. GloVe. `http://nlp.stanford.edu/projects/glove/`.

Erik Tjong Kim Sang and Sabine Buchholz. 2000. Introduction to the CoNLL-2000 shared task: Chunking. In *Proceedings of Conference on Natural Language Learning (CoNLL)*, pages 127–132.

Erik Tjong Kim Sang and Fien De Meulder. 2003. Introduction to the CoNLL-2003 shared task: Language-independent named entity recognition. In *Proceedings of Conference on Natural Language Learning (CoNLL)*, pages 142–147.

Ashish Vaswani, Yinggong Zhao, Victoria Fossum, and David Chiang. 2013. Decoding with large-scale neural language models improves translation. In *Proceedings of Empirical Methods in Natural Language Processing (EMNLP)*, pages 1387–1392.

Peilu Wang, Yao Qian, Frank Soong, Lei He, and Hai Zhao. 2015. Word embedding for recurrent neural network based tts synthesis. In *Proceedings of International Conference on Acoustics, Speech, and Signal Processing (ICASSP)*, pages 4879–4883.

Felix Weninger, Johannes Bergmann, and Björn Schuller. 2014. Introducing CURRENNT–the Munich open-source CUDA recurrent Neural Network Toolkit. *Journal of Machine Learning Research (JMLR)*, 16(1):547–551.

Hai Zhao and Chunyu Kit. 2008a. An empirical comparison of goodness measures for unsupervised chinese word segmentation with a unified framework. In *Proceedings of International Joint Conference on Natural Language Processing (IJCNLP)*, volume 1, pages 9–16.

Hai Zhao and Chunyu Kit. 2008b. Unsupervised segmentation helps supervised learning of character tagging for word segmentation and named entity recognition. In *SIGHAN Workshop on Chinese Language Processing*, pages 106–111.

Hai Zhao and Chunyu Kit. 2011. Integrating unsupervised and supervised word segmentation: The role of goodness measures. *Information Sciences*, 181(1):163–183.

Hai Zhao, Chang-Ning Huang, and Mu Li. 2006. An improved chinese word segmentation system with conditional random field. In *SIGHAN Workshop on Chinese Language Processing*, pages 162–165.

Hai Zhao, Chang-Ning Huang, Mu Li, and Bao-Liang Lu. 2010. A unified character-based tagging framework for chinese word segmentation. *ACM Transactions on Asian Language Information Processing (TALIP)*, 9(2):1–32.

Combining Recurrent and Convolutional Neural Networks
for Relation Classification

Ngoc Thang Vu[1,2] and **Heike Adel**[1] and **Pankaj Gupta**[3] and **Hinrich Schütze**[1]

[1]Center for Information and Language Processing, LMU Munich
Oettingenstr. 67, 80538 Munich, Germany
[2]Institute for Natural Language Processing, University of Stuttgart
Pfaffenwaldring 5b, 70569 Stuttgart, Germany
[3]Siemens Corporate Technology - Knowledge Modeling and Retrieval
Otto-Hahn-Ring 6, 81739 Munich, Germany

```
thang.vu@ims.uni-stuttgart.de | heike.adel@cis.lmu.de
gupta.pankaj.ext@siemens.com | inquiries@cislmu.org
```


Abstract

This paper investigates two different neural architectures for the task of relation classification: convolutional neural networks and recurrent neural networks. For both models, we demonstrate the effect of different architectural choices. We present a new context representation for convolutional neural networks for relation classification (extended middle context). Furthermore, we propose connectionist bi-directional recurrent neural networks and introduce ranking loss for their optimization. Finally, we show that combining convolutional and recurrent neural networks using a simple voting scheme is accurate enough to improve results. Our neural models achieve state-of-the-art results on the SemEval 2010 relation classification task.

1 Introduction

Relation classification is the task of assigning sentences with two marked entities to a predefined set of relations. The sentence "We poured the <e1>milk</e1> into the <e2>pumpkin mixture</e2>.", for example, expresses the relation `Entity-Destination(e1,e2)`. While early research mostly focused on support vector machines or maximum entropy classifiers (Rink and Harabagiu, 2010a; Tratz and Hovy, 2010), recent research showed performance improvements by applying neural networks (NNs) (Socher et al., 2012; Zeng et al., 2014; Yu et al., 2014; Nguyen and Grishman, 2015; Dos Santos et al., 2015; Zhang and Wang, 2015) on the benchmark data from SemEval 2010 shared task 8 (Hendrickx et al., 2010) .

This study investigates two different types of NNs: recurrent neural networks (RNNs) and convolutional neural networks (CNNs) as well as their combination. We make the following contributions:

(1) We propose *extended middle context*, a new context representation for CNNs for relation classification. The extended middle context uses all parts of the sentence (the relation arguments, left of the relation arguments, between the arguments, right of the arguments) and pays special attention to the middle part.

(2) We present *connectionist bi-directional RNN models* which are especially suited for sentence classification tasks since they combine all intermediate hidden layers for their final decision. Furthermore, the ranking loss function is introduced for the RNN model optimization which has not been investigated in the literature for relation classification before.

(3) Finally, we combine CNNs and RNNs using a simple voting scheme and achieve new state-of-the-art results on the SemEval 2010 benchmark dataset.

2 Related Work

In 2010, manually annotated data for relation classification was released in the context of a SemEval shared task (Hendrickx et al., 2010). Shared task participants used, i.a., support vector machines or maximum entropy classifiers (Rink and Harabagiu, 2010a; Tratz and Hovy, 2010). Recently, their results on this data set were outperformed by applying NNs (Socher et al., 2012; Zeng et al., 2014; Yu et al., 2014; Nguyen and Grishman, 2015; Dos Santos et al., 2015).

Proceedings of NAACL-HLT 2016, pages 534–539,
San Diego, California, June 12-17, 2016. ©2016 Association for Computational Linguistics

Zeng et al. (2014) built a CNN based only on the context between the relation arguments and extended it with several lexical features. Kim (2014) and others used convolutional filters of different sizes for CNNs. Nguyen and Grishman (2015) applied this to relation classification and obtained improvements over single filter sizes. Dos Santos et al. (2015) replaced the softmax layer of the CNN with a ranking layer. They showed improvements and published the best result so far on the SemEval dataset, to our knowledge.

Socher et al. (2012) used another NN architecture for relation classification: recursive neural networks that built recursive sentence representations based on syntactic parsing. In contrast, Zhang and Wang (2015) investigated a temporal structured RNN with only words as input. They used a bi-directional model with a pooling layer on top.

3   Convolutional Neural Networks (CNN)

CNNs perform a discrete convolution on an input matrix with a set of different filters. For NLP tasks, the input matrix represents a sentence: Each column of the matrix stores the word embedding of the corresponding word. By applying a filter with a width of, e.g., three columns, three neighboring words (trigram) are convolved. Afterwards, the results of the convolution are pooled. Following Collobert et al. (2011), we perform max-pooling which extracts the maximum value for each filter and, thus, the most informative n-gram for the following steps. Finally, the resulting values are concatenated and used for classifying the relation expressed in the sentence.

3.1   Input: Extended Middle Context

One of our contributions is a new input representation especially designed for relation classification. The contexts are split into three disjoint regions based on the two relation arguments: the left context, the middle context and the right context. Since in most cases the middle context contains the most relevant information for the relation, we want to focus on it but not ignore the other regions completely. Hence, we propose to use two contexts: (1) a combination of the left context, the left entity and the middle context; and (2) a combination of the middle context, the right entity and the right context.

Due to the repetition of the middle context, we force the network to pay special attention to it. The two contexts are processed by two independent convolutional and max-pooling layers. After pooling, the results are concatenated to form the sentence representation. Figure 1 depicts this procedure. It shows an examplary sentence: "He had chest pain and `<el>headaches</el>` from `<e2>mold</e2>` in the bedroom." If we only considered the middle context "from", the network might be tempted to predict a relation like `Entity-Origin(e1,e2)`. However, by also taking the left and right context into account, the model can detect the relation `Cause-Effect(e2,e1)`. While this could also be achieved by integrating the whole context into the model, using the whole context can have disadvantages for longer sentences: The max pooling step can easily choose a value from a part of the sentence which is far away from the mention of the relation. With splitting the context into two parts, we reduce this danger. Repeating the middle context increases the chance for the max pooling step to pick a value from the middle context.

3.2   Convolutional Layer

Following previous work (e.g., (Nguyen and Grishman, 2015), (Dos Santos et al., 2015)), we use 2D filters spanning all embedding dimensions. After convolution, a max pooling operation is applied that stores only the highest activation of each filter. We apply filters with different window sizes 2-5 (multiwindows) as in (Nguyen and Grishman, 2015), i.e. spanning a different number of input words.

4   Recurrent Neural Networks (RNN)

Traditional RNNs consist of an input vector, a history vector and an output vector. Based on the representation of the current input word and the previous history vector, a new history is computed. Then, an output is predicted (e.g., using a softmax layer). In contrast to most traditional RNN architectures, we use the RNN for sentence modeling, i.e., we predict an output vector only after processing the whole sentence and not after each word. Training is performed using backpropagation through time (Werbos, 1990) which unfolds the recurrent computations of the history vector for a certain number of time steps. To

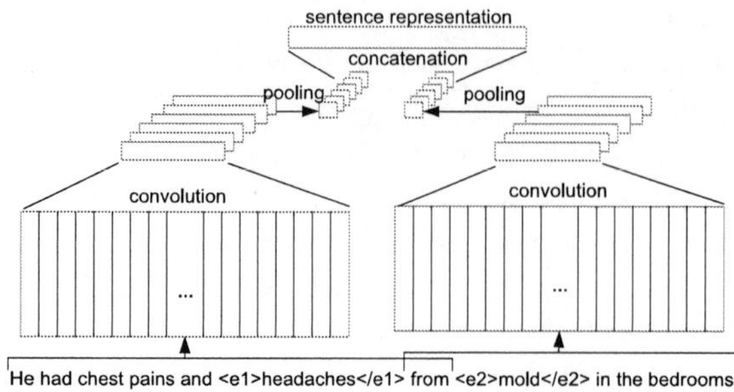

Figure 1: CNN with extended contexts

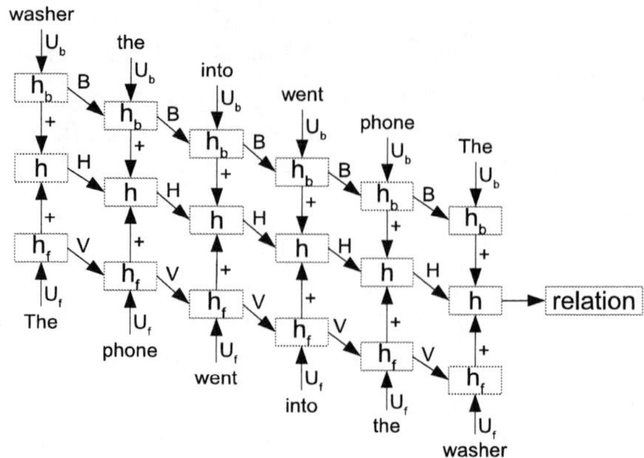

Figure 2: Connectionist bi-directional RNN

avoid exploding gradients, we use gradient clipping with a threshold of 10 (Pascanu et al., 2012).

4.1 Input of the RNNs

Initial experiments showed that using trigrams as input instead of single words led to superior results. Hence, at timestep t we do not only give word w_t to the model but the trigram $w_{t-1}w_tw_{t+1}$ by concatenating the corresponding word embeddings.

4.2 Connectionist Bi-directional RNNs

Especially for relation classification, the processing of the relation arguments might be easier with knowledge of the succeeding words. Therefore in bi-directional RNNs, not only a history vector of word w_t is regarded but also a future vector. This leads to the following conditioned probability for the history h_t at time step $t \in [1, n]$:

$$h_{f_t} = f(U_f \cdot w_t + V \cdot h_{f_{t-1}}) \tag{1}$$
$$h_{b_t} = f(U_b \cdot w_{n-t+1} + B \cdot h_{b_{t+1}}) \tag{2}$$
$$h_t = f(h_{b_t} + h_{f_t} + H \cdot h_{t-1}) \tag{3}$$

Thus, the network can be split into three parts: a forward pass which processes the original sentence word by word (Equation 1); a backward pass which processes the reversed sentence word by word (Equation 2); and a combination of both (Equation 3). All three parts are trained jointly. This is also depicted in Figure 2.

Combining forward and backward pass by adding their hidden layer is similar to (Zhang and Wang, 2015). We, however, also add a connection to the previous combined hidden layer with weight H to be able to include all intermediate hidden layers into the final decision of the network (see Equation 3). We call this "connectionist bi-directional RNN".

In our experiments, we compare this RNN with uni-directional RNNs and bi-directional RNNs without additional hidden layer connections.

5 Model Training

5.1 Word Representations

Words are represented by concatenated vectors: a word embedding and a position feature vector.

Pretrained word embeddings. In this study, we used the word2vec toolkit to train embeddings on an English Wikipedia from May 2014. We only considered words appearing more than 100 times and added a special PADDING token for convolution. This results in an embedding training text of about 485,000 terms and $6.7 \cdot 10^9$ tokens. During model training, the embeddings are updated.

Position features. We incorporate randomly initialized position embeddings similar to Zeng et al. (2014), Nguyen and Grishman (2015) and Dos Santos et al. (2015). In our RNN experiments, we investigate different possibilities of integrating position information: position embeddings, position embeddings with entity presence flags (flags indicating whether the current word is one of the relation arguments), and position indicators (Zhang and Wang, 2015).

5.2 Objective Function: Ranking Loss

Ranking. We applied the ranking loss function proposed in Dos Santos et al. (2015) to train our models. It maximizes the distance between the true label y^+ and the best competitive label c^- given a data point

536

x. The objective function is

$$L = \log(1 + \exp(\gamma(m^+ - s_\theta(x)_{y^+}))) \\ + \log(1 + \exp(\gamma(m^- + s_\theta(x)_{c^-}))) \quad (4)$$

with $s_\theta(x)_{y^+}$ and $s_\theta(x)_{c^-}$ being the scores for the classes y^+ and c^- respectively. The parameter γ controls the penalization of the prediction errors and m^+ and m^- are margins for the correct and incorrect classes. Following Dos Santos et al. (2015), we set $\gamma = 2, m^+ = 2.5, m^- = 0.5$. We do not learn a pattern for the class `Other` but increase its difference to the best competitive label by using only the second summand in Equation 4 during training.

6 Experiments and Results

We used the relation classification dataset of the SemEval 2010 task 8 (Hendrickx et al., 2010). It consists of sentences which have been manually labeled with 19 relations (9 directed relations and one artificial class `Other`). 8,000 sentences have been distributed as training set and 2,717 sentences served as test set. For evaluation, we applied the official scoring script and report the macro F1 score which also served as the official result of the shared task.

RNN and CNN models were implemented with theano (Bergstra et al., 2010; Bastien et al., 2012). For all our models, we use L2 regularization with a weight of 0.0001. For CNN training, we use mini batches of 25 training examples while we perform stochastic gradient descent for the RNN. The initial learning rates are 0.2 for the CNN and 0.01 for the RNN. We train the models for 10 (CNN) and 50 (RNN) epochs without early stopping. As activation function, we apply tanh for the CNN and capped ReLU for the RNN. For tuning the hyperparameters, we split the training data into two parts: 6.5k (training) and 1.5k (development) sentences. We also tuned the learning rate schedule on dev.

Beside of training single models, we also report ensemble results for which we combined the presented single models with a voting process.

6.1 Performance of CNNs

As a baseline system, we implemented a CNN similar to the one described by Zeng et al. (2014). It consists of a standard convolutional layer with filters with only one window size, followed by a softmax

CNN	F1
Baseline (emb dim: 50)	73.0
+ position features	78.6*
+ multi-windows features map	78.7
+ ranking layer	81.9*
+ extended middle context	82.2
+ increase emb dim to 400	83.9*
ensemble	**84.2**

Table 1: F1 score of CNN and its components, * indicates statistical significance compared to the result in the line above (z-test, $p < 0.05$)

layer. As input it uses the middle context. In contrast to Zeng et al. (2014), our CNN does not have an additional fully connected hidden layer. Therefore, we increased the number of convolutional filters to 1200 to keep the number of parameters comparable. With this, we obtain a baseline result of 73.0. After including 5 dimensional position features, the performance was improved to 78.6 (comparable to 78.9 as reported by Zeng et al. (2014) without linguistic features).

In the next step, we investigate how this result changes if we successively add further features to our CNN: multi-windows for convolution (window sizes: 2,3,4,5 and 300 feature maps each), ranking layer instead of softmax and our proposed extended middle context. Table 1 shows the results. Note that all numbers are produced by CNNs with a comparable number of parameters. We also report F1 for increasing the word embedding dimensionality from 50 to 400. The position embedding dimensionality is 5 in combination with 50 dimensional word embeddings and 35 with 400 dimensional word embeddings. Our results show that especially the ranking layer and the embedding size have an important impact on the performance.

6.2 Performance of RNNs

As a baseline for the RNN models, we apply a unidirectional RNN which predicts the relation after processing the whole sentence. With this model, we achieve an F1 score of 61.2 on the SemEval test set.

Afterwards, we investigate the impact of different position features on the performance of unidirectional RNNs (position embeddings, position embeddings concatenated with a flag indicating whether the current word is an entity or not, and

RNN	F1
uni-directional (Baseline, emb dim: 50)	61.2
uni-directional + position embs	68.3*
uni-directional + position embs + entity flag	73.1*
uni-directional + position indicators	73.4
bi-directional + position indicators	74.2*
connectionist-bi-directional+position indicators	78.4*
+ ranking layer	81.4*
+ increase emb dim to 400	82.5*
ensemble	**83.4**

Table 2: F1 score of RNN and its components, * indicates statisticial significance compared to the result in the line above (z-test, $p < 0.05$)

Classifier	F1
SVM (Rink and Harabagiu, 2010b)	82.2
RNN (Socher et al., 2012)	77.6
MVRNN (Socher et al., 2012)	82.4
CNN (Zeng et al., 2014)	82.7
FCM (Yu et al., 2014)	83.0
bi-RNN (Zhang and Wang, 2015)	82.5
CR-CNN (Dos Santos et al., 2015)	84.1
R-RNN	83.4
ER-CNN	84.2
ER-CNN + R-RNN	**84.9**

Table 3: State-of-the-art results for relation classification

position indicators (Zhang and Wang, 2015)). The results indicate that position indicators (i.e. artificial words that indicate the entity presence) perform the best on the SemEval data. We achieve an F1 score of 73.4 with them. However, the difference to using position embeddings with entity flags is not statistically significant.

Similar to our CNN experiments, we successively vary the RNN models by using bi-directionality, by adding connections between the hidden layers ("connectionist"), by applying ranking instead of softmax to predict the relation and by increasing the word embedding dimension to 400.

The results in Table 2 show that all of these variations lead to statistically significant improvements. Especially the additional hidden layer connections and the integration of the ranking layer have a large impact on the performance.

6.3 Combination of CNNs and RNNs

Finally, we combine our CNN and RNN models using a voting process. For each sentence in the test set, we apply several CNN and RNN models presented in Tables 1 and 2 and predict the class with the most votes. In case of a tie, we pick one of the most frequent classes randomly. The combination achieves an F1 score of 84.9 which is better than the performance of the two NN types alone. It, thus, confirms our assumption that the networks provide complementary information: while the RNN computes a weighted combination of all words in the sentence, the CNN extracts the most informative n-grams for the relation and only considers their resulting activations.

6.4 Comparison with State of the Art

Table 3 shows the results of our models ER-CNN (extended ranking CNN) and R-RNN (ranking RNN) in the context of other state-of-the-art models. Our proposed models obtain state-of-the-art results on the SemEval 2010 task 8 data set without making use of any linguistic features.

7 Conclusion

In this paper, we investigated different features and architectural choices for convolutional and recurrent neural networks for relation classification without using any linguistic features. For convolutional neural networks, we presented a new context representation for relation classification. Furthermore, we introduced connectionist recurrent neural networks for sentence classification tasks and performed the first experiments with ranking recurrent neural networks. Finally, we showed that even a simple combination of convolutional and recurrent neural networks improved results. With our neural models, we achieved new state-of-the-art results on the SemEval 2010 task 8 benchmark data.

Acknowledgments

Heike Adel is a recipient of the Google European Doctoral Fellowship in Natural Language Processing and this research is supported by this fellowship.

This research was also supported by Deutsche Forschungsgemeinschaft: grant SCHU 2246/4-2.

References

Frédéric Bastien, Pascal Lamblin, Razvan Pascanu, James Bergstra, Ian J. Goodfellow, Arnaud Bergeron, Nicolas Bouchard, and Yoshua Bengio. 2012. Theano: new features and speed improvements. Deep Learning and Unsupervised Feature Learning NIPS 2012 Workshop.

James Bergstra, Olivier Breuleux, Frédéric Bastien, Pascal Lamblin, Razvan Pascanu, Guillaume Desjardins, Joseph Turian, David Warde-Farley, and Yoshua Bengio. 2010. Theano: a CPU and GPU math expression compiler. In *Proceedings of the Python for Scientific Computing Conference (SciPy)*.

Ronan Collobert, Jason Weston, Léon Bottou, Michael Karlen, Koray Kavukcuoglu, and Pavel Kuksa. 2011. Natural language processing (almost) from scratch. *The Journal of Machine Learning Research*, 12:2493–2537.

Cícero Nogueira Dos Santos, Bing Xiang, and Bowen Zhou. 2015. Classifying relations by ranking with convolutional neural networks. In *Proceedings of ACL*. Association for Computational Linguistics.

Iris Hendrickx, Su Nam Kim, Zornitsa Kozareva, Preslav Nakov, Diarmuid Ó Séaghdha, Sebastian Padó, Marco Pennacchiotti, Lorenza Romano, and Stan Szpakowicz. 2010. Semeval-2010 task 8: Multi-way classification of semantic relations between pairs of nominals. In *Proceedings of the Workshop on SemEval*. Association for Computational Linguistics.

Yoon Kim. 2014. Convolutional neural networks for sentence classification. In *Proceedings of EMNLP*. Association for Computational Linguistics.

Thien Huu Nguyen and Ralph Grishman. 2015. Relation extraction: Perspective from convolutional neural networks. In *Proceedings of the NAACL Workshop on Vector Space Modeling for NLP*. Association for Computational Linguistics.

Razvan Pascanu, Tomas Mikolov, and Yoshua Bengio. 2012. Understanding the exploding gradient problem. *Computing Research Repository*.

Bryan Rink and Sanda Harabagiu. 2010a. Utd: Classifying semantic relations by combining lexical and semantic resources. In *Proceedings of the Workshop on SemEval*. Association for Computational Linguistics.

Bryan Rink and Sanda Harabagiu. 2010b. Utd: Classifying semantic relations by combining lexical and semantic resources. In *Proceedings of the Workshop on SemEval*, pages 256–259. Association for Computational Linguistics.

Richard Socher, Brody Huval, Christopher D Manning, and Andrew Y Ng. 2012. Semantic compositionality through recursive matrix-vector spaces. In *Proceedings of EMNLP / CoNLL*. Association for Computational Linguistics.

Stephen Tratz and Eduard Hovy. 2010. Isi: automatic classification of relations between nominals using a maximum entropy classifier. In *Proceedings of the Workshop on SemEval*. Association for Computational Linguistics.

Paul J Werbos. 1990. Backpropagation through time: what it does and how to do it. *Proceedings of the IEEE*.

Mo Yu, Matthew Gormley, and Mark Dredze. 2014. Factor-based compositional embedding models. In *Proceedings of the NIPS Workshop on Learning Semantics*.

Daojian Zeng, Kang Liu, Siwei Lai, Guangyou Zhou, and Jun Zhao. 2014. Relation classification via convolutional deep neural network. In *Proceedings of COLING*.

Dongxu Zhang and Dong Wang. 2015. Relation classification via recurrent neural network. In *ArXiv*.

Building Chinese Affective Resources in Valence-Arousal Dimensions

Liang-Chih Yu[1,3], Lung-Hao Lee[4], Shuai Hao[5], Jin Wang[2,3,6], Yunchao He[2,3,6],
Jun Hu[5], K. Robert Lai[2,3] and Xuejie Zhang[6]
[1]Department of Information Management, Yuan Ze University, Taiwan
[2]Department of Computer Science & Engineering, Yuan Ze University, Taiwan
[3]Innovation Center for Big Data and Digital Convergence Yuan Ze University, Taiwan
[4]Information Technology Center, National Taiwan Normal University, Taiwan
[5]School of Software, Nanchang University, Jiangxi, P.R. China
[6]School of Information Science and Engineering, Yunnan University, Yunnan, P.R. China
Contact: lcyu@saturn.yzu.edu.tw

Abstract

An increasing amount of research has recently focused on representing affective states as continuous numerical values on multiple dimensions, such as the valence-arousal (VA) space. Compared to the *categorical* approach that represents affective states as several classes (e.g., positive and negative), the *dimensional* approach can provide more fine-grained sentiment analysis. However, affective resources with valence-arousal ratings are still very rare, especially for the Chinese language. Therefore, this study builds 1) an affective lexicon called Chinese valence-arousal words (CVAW) containing 1,653 words, and 2) an affective corpus called Chinese valence-arousal text (CVAT) containing 2,009 sentences extracted from web texts. To improve the annotation quality, a corpus cleanup procedure is used to remove outlier ratings and improper texts. Experiments using CVAW words to predict the VA ratings of the CVAT corpus show results comparable to those obtained using English affective resources.

1 Introduction

Sentiment analysis has emerged as a leading technique to automatically identify affective information from texts (Pang and Lee, 2008; Calvo and D'Mello, 2010; Liu, 2012; Feldman, 2013). In sentiment analysis, affective states are generally represented using either categorical or dimensional approaches.

The categorical approach represents affective states as several discrete classes such as positive, neutral, negative, and Ekman's six basic emotions (e.g., anger, happiness, fear, sadness, disgust and surprise) (Ekman, 1992). Based on this representation, various practical applications have been developed such as aspect-based sentiment analysis (Schouten and Frasincar, 2016; Pontiki et al., 2015), Twitter sentiment analysis (Saif et al., 2013; Rosenthal et al., 2015), deceptive opinion spam detection (Li et al., 2014), and cross-lingual portability (Banea et al., 2013; Xu et al., 2015).

The dimensional approach represents affective states as continuous numerical values in multiple dimensions, such as valence-arousal (VA) space (Russell, 1980), as shown in Fig. 1. The valence represents the degree of pleasant and unpleasant (i.e., positive and negative) feelings, while the arousal represents the degree of excitement and calm. Based on this representation, any affective state can be represented as a point in the VA coordinate plane. For many application domains (e.g., product reviews, political stance detection, etc.), it can be useful to identify highly negative-arousing and highly positive-arousing texts because they are usually of interest to many users and should be given a higher priority. Dimensional sentiment

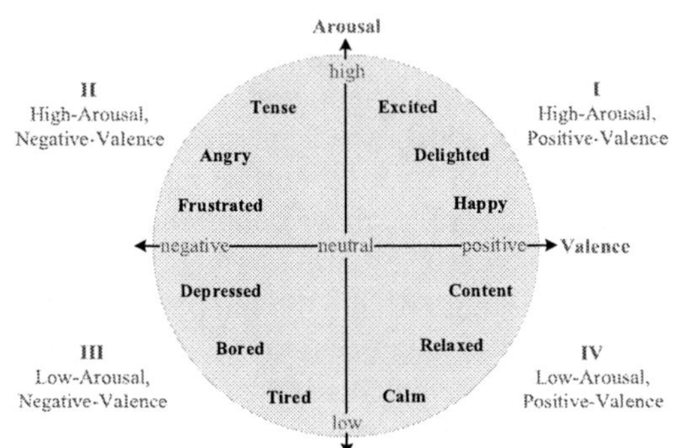

Figure 1: Two-dimensional valence-arousal space.

analysis can accomplish this by recognizing the valence-arousal ratings of texts and ranking them accordingly to provide more intelligent and fine-grained services.

In developing dimensional sentiment applications, affective lexicons and corpora with valence-arousal ratings are useful resources but few exist, especially for the Chinese language. Therefore, this study focuses on building Chinese valence-arousal resources, including an affective lexicon called the Chinese valence-arousal words (CVAW) and an affective corpus called the Chinese valence-arousal text (CVAT). The CVAW contains 1,653 affective words annotated with valence-arousal ratings by five annotators. The CVAT contains 2,009 sentences extracted from web texts annotated with crowd-sourced valence-arousal ratings. To further demonstrate the feasibility of the constructed resources, we conduct an experiment to predict the VA ratings of the CVAT corpus using CVAW words, and compare its performance to a similar evaluation of English affective resources.

To our best knowledge, only one previous study has manually created a small number (162) of Chinese VA words (Wei et al, 2011), and none have focused on creating Chinese VA corpora. This pilot study thus aims to build such resources to enrich the research and development of multi-lingual sentiment analysis in VA dimensions.

The rest of this paper is organized as follows. Section 2 introduces existing affective lexicons and corpora. Section 3 describes the process of building the Chinese affective resource. Section 4 presents the analysis results and feasibility evaluation. Conclusions are finally drawn in Section 5.

2 Related Work

Affective resources are usually obtained by either self-labeling or manual annotation. In the self-labeling approach, users proactively provide their feelings and opinions after browsing the web content. For example, users may read a news article and then offer comments. A user can also review the products available for sale in online stores. In the manual annotation method, trained annotators are asked to create affective annotations for specific language resources for research purposes. Several well-known affective resources are introduced as follows.

SentiWordNet is a lexical resource for opinion mining, which assigns to each synset of WordNet three sentiment ratings: positive, negative, and objective (Esuli and Sebastiani, 2006). Linguistic Inquiry and Word Count (LIWC) calculates the degree to which people use different categories of words across a broad range of texts (Pennebaker et al., 2007). In the LIWC 2007 version, the annotators were asked to note their emotions and thoughts about personally relevant topics. The Affective Norms for English Words (ANEW) provides 1,034 English words with ratings in the dimensions of pleasure, arousal and dominance (Bradley and Lang, 1999). In addition to these English-language sentiment lexicons, a few Chinese lexicons have been constructed. The Chinese LIWC (C-LIWC) dictionary is a Chinese translation of the LIWC with manual revisions to fit the practical characteristics of Chinese usages (Huang et al., 2012). The NTU Sentiment dictionary (NTUSD) has adopted a combination of manual and automatic methods to include positive and negative emotional words (Ku and Chen, 2007). Among the above affective lexicons, only ANEW is dimensional, providing real-valued scores for three dimensions, and the others are categorical, providing information related to sentiment polarity or intensity.

In addition to lexicon resources, several English-language affective corpora have been proposed, such as Movie Review Data (Pang et al. 2002), the MPQA Opinion Corpus (Wiebe et al., 2005), and Affective Norms for English Text (ANET) (Bradley and Lang, 2007). In addition, only ANET provides VA ratings. The above dimensional affective resources ANEW and ANET have been used for both word- and sentence-level VA prediction in previous studies (Wei et al., 2011; Gökçay et al., 2012; Malandrakis et al., 2013; Paltoglou et al., 2013; Yu et al., 2015). In this study, we follow the manual annotation approach to build a Chinese affective lexicon and corpus in the VA dimensions.

3 Affective Resource Construction

This section describes the process of building Chinese affective resources with valence-arousal ratings, including the CVAW and CAVT.

The CVAW is built on the Chinese affective lexicon C-LIWC, and then annotated with VA ratings for each word. Five annotators were trained to rate each word in the valence and arousal dimensions using the Self Assessment Manikin (SAM) model (Lang, 1980). The SAM model provides affective pictures, which can help annotators in determining more precise labels when rating the words. The valence dimension uses a nine degree scale. Values 1 and 9 respectively denote the most negative and positive degrees of affect. Point 5 means a neutral emotion without specific tendency. The arousal dimension uses a similar scale to denote calm and excitement Using this approach, each affective word can be annotated with VA ratings (determined by the average rating values provided by the annotators) to form the CVAW.

To build the CVAT, we first collected 720 web texts from six different categories: news articles, political discussion forums, car discussion forums, hotel reviews, book reviews, and laptop reviews. A total of 2,009 sentences containing the greatest number of affective words found in the C-LIWC lexicon were selected for VA rating. The Google app engine was then used to implement a crowdsourcing annotation platform using the SAM annotation scheme. Volunteer annotators were asked to rate individual sentences from 1 to 9 in terms of valence and arousal. Each sentence was rated by at least 10 annotations. Once the rating process was finished, a corpus cleanup procedure was performed to remove outlier ratings and improper sentences (e.g., those containing abusive or vulgar language). The outlier ratings were identified if they did not fall into the interval of the mean plus/minus 1.5 standard deviations. They were then excluded from the calculation of the average VA ratings for each sentence.

4 Results

4.1 Analysis Results of CVAW

A total of 1,653 words along with the annotated VA ratings were included in the CVAW lexicon, yielding the (mean, standard deviation) = (4.49, 1.81) for valence and (5.48, 1.26) for arousal. To analyze differences between the annotations, we compared the VA values rated by each annotator against their corresponding means across the five annotators to calculate the error rates using the following metrics.

- *Mean Absolute Error* (MAE):

$$MAE = \frac{1}{n}\sum_{i=1}^{n} | A_i - \overline{A_i} |,$$

- *Root Mean Square Error* (RMSE):

$$RMSE = \sqrt{\sum_{i=1}^{n}\left(A_i - \overline{A_i}\right)^2 \Big/ n},$$

where A_i denotes the valence or arousal value of word i rated by an annotator, $\overline{A_i}$ denotes the mean valence or arousal of word i calculated over the five annotators, and n is the total number of words in the CVAW.

	MAE		RMSE	
	Valence	Arousal	Valence	Arousal
Annotator A	0.4934	1.3479	0.6372	1.6411
Annotator B	0.5972	0.7821	0.7488	0.9929
Annotator C	0.5817	1.1393	0.7423	1.4302
Annotator D	0.5188	0.8226	0.6614	1.0374
Annotator E	0.6258	1.0200	0.7970	1.2700
(Mean, SD)	(0.56,0.05)	(1.02, 0.21)	(0.72, 0.06)	(1.27, 0.24)

Table 1: Analysis of error rates of different annotators for building the Chinese VA lexicon.

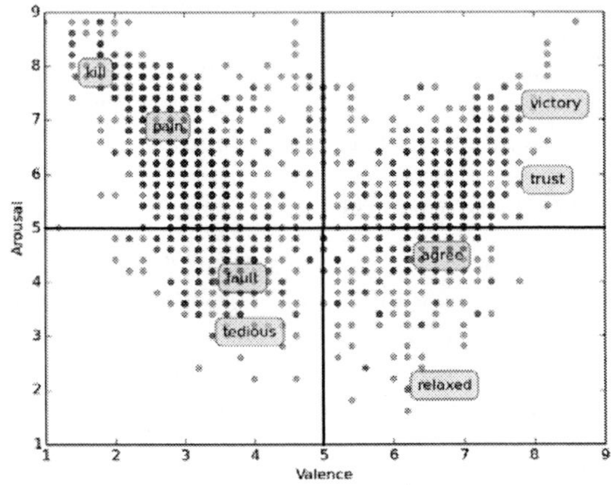

Figure 2: Scatter plot of the CVAW lexicon.

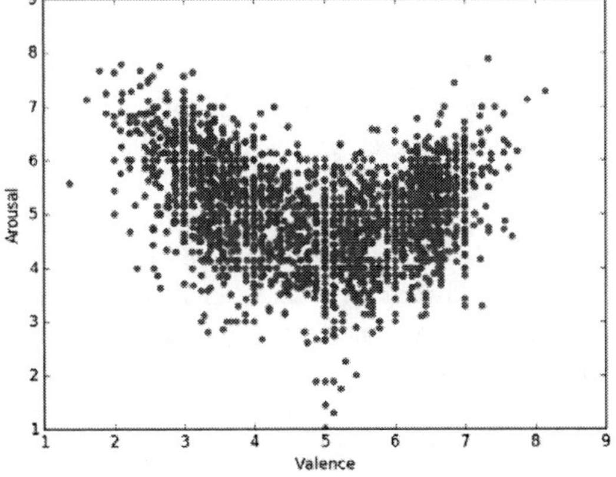

Figure 3: Scatter plot of the CVAT corpus.

	Num. of texts	Num. of tokens	Avg. tokens	Valence			Arousal		
				MAE	RMSE	r	MAE	RMSE	r
ANEW vs Forum	20	15,035	751.75	1.20	1.55	0.77	0.72	0.85	0.27
CVAW vs CVAT	2,009	70,456	35.07	1.20	1.52	0.54	1.01	1.28	0.16
Book Review	287(14%)	8,217	28.63	1.00	1.31	0.41	**0.89**	**1.11**	0.21
Car Forum	257 (13%)	12,261	47.71	1.48	1.77	0.30	0.92	1.15	0.10
Laptop Review	183 (9%)	5,374	29.37	**0.95**	**1.21**	0.55	1.07	1.40	0.04
Hotel Review	301 (15%)	7,268	24.15	1.35	1.73	0.59	0.93	1.17	**0.22**
News Article	542(27%)	21,923	40.45	1.11	1.40	**0.61**	1.11	1.40	0.17
Politics Forum	439 (22%)	15,413	35.11	1.28	1.61	0.51	1.04	1.32	0.19

Table 2: Results of using the CVAW lexicon to predict the VA ratings of the CVAT corpus.

Table 1 shows the error rates of the annotators in rating the VA values of words in the CVAW. Overall, for all metrics the error rates of arousal ratings were greater than those of valence ratings. In addition, the annotators produced more consistent error rates (around 0.49~0.63 for MAE and 0.64~0.80 for RMSE) in the valence dimension than those (around 0.78~1.35 for MAE and 0.99~1.64 for RMSE) in the arousal dimension. These findings indicate that the degree of arousal was more difficult to distinguish than valence.

Figure 2 shows a scatter plot of words in the CVAW, where each point represents the mean of the VA values as rated by the annotators. Several words (translated from Chinese) were marked in the VA space for reference, e.g., *victory* (7.8, 7.2), *trust* (7.8, 5.8), *pain* (2.4, 6.8), *kill* (1.6, 7.8), *tedi-* *ous* (3.4, 3), *fault* (3.6, 4.6), *agree* (6.4, 4.4) and *re-laxed* (6.2, 2.0).

4.2 Analysis Results of CVAT

A total of 2,009 sentences with VA ratings were included in the CVAT corpus, yielding the (mean, standard deviation) = (4.83, 1.37) for valence and (5.05, 0.95) for arousal. The distribution of the six categories and their word counts in CVAT are shown in Table 2. The largest category was News (27%), while the smallest one was Laptop (9%). Figure 3 shows a scatter plot of VA ratings for all sentences in CVAT. It is similar with the plot of the CVAW, indicating that annotators followed similar guidelines for rating affective words and sentences.

4.3 Results of Using CVAW to Predict the VA Ratings of CVAT

To demonstrate the application of the constructed affective resources, this experiment adopted a simple aggregate-and-average method (Taboada et al. 2011) to predict the VA ratings of the CVAT corpus using CVAW words. In this approach, the valence (or arousal) rating of a given sentence was calculated by averaging the valence (or arousal) ratings of the words matched in the CVAW in that sentence. Once the predicted values of the VA ratings for the sentences were obtained, they were compared to the corresponding actual values in the CVAT to calculate MAE, RMSE and Pearson correlation coefficient r, as shown in Table 2. Notice that the sentences which contain no affective words in the CVAW were not included for performance calculation (herein 30 sentences). The results using ANEW to predict the VA rating of 20 English forum discussions were also included for comparison (Paltoglou et al., 2013).

The results show that the average tokens of the CVAT sentences are around 35 which is much smaller than those of the English forum discussions (long texts). Both English and Chinese resources had a similar error rates (MAE and RMSE) for valence, while the English resource outperformed the Chinese resource in terms of arousal rates. In addition, both the English and Chinese resources had a lower correlation for arousal than for valence, indicating again that the arousal dimension is more difficult to predict. Table 2 also shows the performance for each category in CVAT. For valence, Laptop achieved the lowest error rate, while News and Hotel had a higher correlation. The respective ranges of MAE, RMSE and r are 0.95~1.48, 1.21~1.77 and 0.30~0.61. For arousal, Book yielded the lowest error rate, while Hotel and Book yielded a better correlation. The respective ranges of MAE, RMSE and r are 0.89~1.11, 1.11~1.40 and 0.04~0.22.

5 Conclusions and Future Work

This study presents a Chinese affective lexicon with 1,653 words and a corpus of 2,009 sentences with six different categories, both annotated with valence-arousal values. A corpus cleanup procedure was used to remove outlier ratings and improper texts to improve quality. Experimental results provided a feasibility evaluation and baseline performance for VA prediction using the constructed resources. Future work will focus on building useful dimensional sentiment applications based on the constructed resources.

Acknowledgments

This work was supported by the Ministry of Science and Technology, Taiwan, ROC, under Grant No. NSC102-2221-E-155-029-MY3. The authors would like to thank the anonymous reviewers and the area chairs for their constructive comments.

References

Carmen Banea, Rada Mihalcea, and Janyce Wiebe. 2013. Porting multilingual subjectivity resources across languages. *IEEE Trans. Affective Computing*, 4(2):211-225.

Margaret M. Bradley and Peter J. Lang. 1999. Affective norms for English words (ANEW): Instruction manual and affective ratings. Technical Report C-1, University of Florida, Gainesville, FL.

Margaret M. Bradley and Peter J. Lang. 2007. Affective Norms for English Text (ANET): Affective ratings of text and instruction manual. Technical Report D-1, University of Florida, Gainesville, FL.

R. A. Calvo and Sidney. D'Mello. 2010. Affect detection: An interdisciplinary review of models, methods, and their applications. *IEEE Trans. Affective Computing*, 1(1): 18-37.

Paul Ekman. 1992. An argument for basic emotions. *Cognition and Emotion*, 6:169-200.

Andrea Esuli and Fabrizio Sebastiani. 2006. SentiWordNet: a publicly available lexical resource for opinion mining. In *Proc. of LREC-06*, pages 417-422.

Ronen Feldman. 2013. Techniques and applications for sentiment a0nalysis. *Communications of the ACM*, 56(4):82-89.

Didem Gökçay, Erdinç İşbilir and Gülsen Yıldırım. 2012. Predicting the sentiment in sentences based on words: an exploratory study on ANEW and ANET. In *Proc. of CogInfoCom-12*, pages 715-718.

C.-L. Huang, C. K. Chung, N. Hui, Y.-C. Lin, Y.-T. Seih, W.-C. Chen, B. Lam, M. Bond, and James W. Pennebaker. 2012. The development of the Chinese Linguistic Inquiry and Word Count dictionary. *Chinese Journal of Psychology*, 54(2):185-201.

Lun-Wei Ku and Hsin-Hsi Chen. 2007. Mining opinions from the web: beyond relevance retrieval. *Journal of the American Society for Information Science and Technology*, 58(12), 1838-1850.

Peter J. Lang. 1980. Behavioral treatment and biobehavioral assessment: Computer applications. *Tech-*

nology in Mental Health Care Delivery Systems, pp. 119-137, Ablex Publishing, Norwood.

Jiwei Li, Myle Ott, Claire Cardie, and Eduard Hovy. 2014. Towards a general rule for identifying deceptive opinion spam. In *Proc. of ACL-14*, pages 1566-1576.

Bing Liu. 2012. *Sentiment Analysis and Opinion Mining*. Morgan & Claypool, Chicago, IL.

Nikos Malandrakis, Alexandros Potamianos, Elias Iosif, Shrikanth Narayanan. 2013. Distributional semantic models for affective text analysis. *IEEE Trans. Audio, Speech, and Language Processing*, 21(11): 2379-2392.

Georgios Paltoglou, Mathias Theunis, Arvid Kappas, and Mike Thelwall. 2013. Predicting emotional responses to long informal text. *IEEE Trans. Affective Computing*, 4(1):106-115.

Bo Pang and Lillian Lee. 2008. Opinion mining and sentiment analysis. *Foundations and trends in information retrieval*, 2(1-2):1-135.

Bo Pang, Lillian Lee, and Shivakumar Vaithyanathan. 2002. Thumbs up? Sentiment classification using machine learning techniques. In *Proc. of EMNLP-02*, pages 79-86.

James W. Pennebaker, Roger J. Booth, and Martha E. Francis. 2007. Linguistic Inquiry and Word Count: LIWC [Computer software]. Austin, TX: LIWC.net.

Maria Pontiki, Dimitris Galanis, Haris Papageorgiou, Suresh Manandhar and Ion Androutsopoulos. 2015. SemEval-2015 Task 12: Aspect Based Sentiment Analysis. In *Proc. of SemEval-15*, pages 486-495,

Sara Rosenthal, Preslav Nakov, Svetlana Kiritchenko, Saif Mohammad, Alan Ritter and Veselin Stoyanov. 2015. SemEval-2015 Task 10: Sentiment Analysis in Twitter. In *Proc. of SemEval-15*, pages 451-463.

James A. Russell. 1980. A circumplex model of affect. *Journal of Personality and Social Psychology*, 39(6):1161.

Hassan Saif, Miriam Fernandez, Yulan He and Harith Alani. 2013. Evaluation datasets for Twitter sentiment analysis: a survey and a new dataset, the STS-Gold. In *Proc. of ESSEM-13*.

Kim Schouten and Flavius Frasincar. 2016. Survey on Aspect-Level Sentiment Analysis. *IEEE Trans. Knowledge and Data Engineering*, 28(3):813-830.

Maite Taboada, Julian Brooke, Milan Tofiloski, Kimberly Voll, and Manfred Stede. 2011. Lexicon-based methods for sentiment analysis. *Computational Linguistics*, 37(2):267-307.

Wen-Li Wei, Chung-Hsien Wu, and Jen-Chun Lin. 2011. A regression approach to affective rating of Chinese words from ANEW. In *Proc. of ACII-11*, pages 121-131.

Janyce Wiebe, Theresa Wilson, and Claire Cardie. 2005. Annotating expressions of opinions and emotions in language. *Language Resources and Evaluation*, 39(2-3): 165-210.

Ruifeng Xu, Lin Gui, Jun Xu, Qin Lu, and Kam-Fai Wong. 2015. Cross lingual opinion holder extraction based on multi-kernel SVMs and transfer learning. *World Wide Web*, 18:299-316.

Liang-Chih Yu, Jin Wang, K. Robert Lai and Xuejie Zhang. 2015. Predicting valence-arousal ratings of words using a weighted graph method. In *Proc. of ACL/IJCNLP-15*, pages 788-793.

Improving event prediction by representing script participants

Simon Ahrendt and **Vera Demberg**
Saarland University
66123 Saarbrücken
Germany
{simona,vera}@coli.uni-saarland.de

Abstract

Automatically learning script knowledge has proved difficult, with previous work not or just barely beating a most-frequent baseline. Script knowledge is a type of world knowledge which can however be useful for various task in NLP and psycholinguistic modelling. We here propose a model that includes participant information (i.e., knowledge about which participants are relevant for a script) and show, on the Dinners from Hell corpus as well as the InScript corpus, that this knowledge helps us to significantly improve prediction performance on the narrative cloze task.

1   Introduction

Scripts represent knowledge about typical event sequences (Schank and Abelson, 1977), for example the sequence of events happening when eating at a restaurant. Script knowledge thereby includes events like *order*, *bring* and *eat* as well as participants of those events, e.g., *menu*, *waiter*, *food*, *guest*. Script knowledge is a form of structured world knowledge that is useful in NLP applications for natural language understanding tasks (e.g., ambiguity resolution Rahman and Ng, 2012), as well as for psycholinguistic models of human language processing, which need to represent event knowledge to model human expectations (Zwaan et al., 1995; Schütz-Bosbach and Prinz, 2007) of upcoming referents and utterances.

One recent line of research has tried to learn scripts in an unsupervised way from large text collections. The core idea in Chambers and Jurafsky (2008, 2009); Jans et al. (2012) is to use coreference chains to identify events involving the same entity, with the intuition that these events would, if observed in many texts, be likely to represent a prototypical event sequence. Rudinger et al. (2015) show that this method is also applicable for learning specific targeted scripts from a domain-specific corpus, shown at the example of "Dinners From Hell" stories and the restaurant script.

Pichotta and Mooney (2014) (P&M) have demonstrated that using richer event representations containing multiple arguments improves prediciton accuracy on the narrative cloze task over the simpler models by Chambers and Jurafsky (2008). While they represent a script event as a pair of a verb and a dependency (an example of an event chain would be <call,obj>; <bring,subj>; <take,subj>), which is problematic for weak verbs and verb ambiguity, P&M represent events using a multi-argument event representation, e.g., *call(guest,waiter,*)*; *bring(waiter,menu,*)*; *take(waiter,order,*)*.

This richer event representation however still has some shortcomings. As the representation is based on coreference chains, the model runs into difficulties for entities that are in a chain of length one. Entities in a chain are internally mapped onto variables, but all single entities are mapped onto a common category *Other*. This means that all information about such referents is lost, e.g. $enjoy(customer, fish, *)$ can not be distinguished from $enjoy(customer, silence, *)$ when neither fish or silence have appeared before in the text.

The coreference chains provide a good approxi-

Proceedings of NAACL-HLT 2016, pages 546–551,
San Diego, California, June 12-17, 2016. ©2016 Association for Computational Linguistics

mation for identifying events that involve the same participants. But would performance improve substantially if we could represent event participants? This specifically addresses the problem of unlinked coreference chains (e.g., "food", "it", "steak") not appearing in the same coreference chain even though they represent the same role within the script, and the problem of mapping referents which are not part of a chain onto a single "other" representation.

Kampmann et al. (2015) show that referring expressions in a script can be automatically categorized in terms of the role they play within the script by using coreference chains, as well as information from WordNet (telling us e.g., that a *steak* is a kind of *food*).

In this paper, we extend the existing approach by P&M and demonstrate that explicitly labelling participants (instead of using coreference chains) leads to improved event prediction performance. We furthermore provide a systematic evaluation of the effect of automatically-annotated coreference chains vs. gold coreference chains, and automatically-annotated script participants vs. gold participant annotation. We evaluate our approach on the Dinners from Hell corpus (Rudinger et al., 2015), as well as the newly available InScript corpus (Modi et al., 2016).

Following earlier work, we evaluate the quality of script models using the so-called narrative cloze task, where the model has to predict a missing event given surrounding events in the text.

2 Methods

2.1 Participant-labeled Events

In order to capture script-relevant information conveyed by arguments we represent texts as chains of **participant-labeled events (PLEs)**. A PLE is a verb accompanied with the participant labels of its arguments.

The general form of a PLE is $verb(p_{subj}, p_{dobj}, p_{iobj})$, where p_{subj}, p_{dobj} and p_{iobj} are the participant labels of the subject, direct object and indirect object, respectively. For example, in the sentence *The waitress brought us some water*, the corresponding PLE would be $bring(waiter, drink, customer)$.

To automatically create PLEs from our training data, we first extract syntactic relations between verbs and their arguments as well as coreference information using Stanford CoreNLP (Manning et al. (2014)). We then use the max-hypernym heuristic described in Kampmann et al. (2015) to label the arguments with participant roles. This approach assigns to token w the participant label with the highest hyponym-similarity score between the wordnet-synsets associated with the label and one of the synsets of any word present in the coreference chain connected to w.

Where an argument slot of the event is not filled syntactically or the argument is not a participant of the script, a dummy participant O serves as a placeholder to indicate the absence of a labeled argument. Every extracted event that contains at least one participant is included into the chain.

Knowledge about the participants provides a much richer represenation of events. With this representation we are able to generalize from a specific word or entity to its overall role in the script. This way the model can also learn from cases where multiple entities fill one participant role or where a participant occurs in the text only once.

2.2 Predictive Model

Our script model is an adapted version of the bi-gram model in Jans et al. (2012) with an extension of the skip-gram option to skip all possible intervening events. This means we rank an event e to belong to a given ordered event sequence c at insertion point m according to its score as defined by:

$$Score(e) = \sum_{k=0}^{m} logP(e|c_k) + \sum_{k=m+1}^{n} logP(c_k|e), \tag{1}$$

where c_k denotes the kth event in the chain and the conditional probabilties are estimated by skip-all bi-gram counts:

$$P(e_2|e_1) = \frac{freq(e_1, e_2)}{\sum_{e'} freq(e_1, e')} \tag{2}$$

with $freq(e_1, e_2)$ being the the number of times e_1 has been encountered prior to e_2 with an arbitrary number of events between them. This counting method might be noisy in case of long documents or a high number of unrelated events but it significantly reduces data sparsity. In our specialized and rather small data sets of between 87 and 133 stories per scenario, sparsity is more of an issue than unrelatedness, so skip-all performs well, but other counting techniques might prove more suitable for different corpora.

In case our model assigns the same score to several events, we backoff to the simple unigram model described in section 4.2.

3 Data

The Dinners from Hell corpus (Rudinger et al., 2015) contains stories from an internet blog about terrible restaurant experiences. The corpus contains 143 stories (out of which 10 are reserved as a development set), which all have to do with the script of going to a restaurant. All non-copula verbs in this corpus are annotated as to whether they are relevant to the restaurant script.

The InScript corpus is a novel resource (Modi et al., 2016), which contains a total of 910 short stories containing on average 12 sentences each. The stories were collected via Mechanical Turk, instructing workers to describe a specific instance of an activity, as if explaining it to a child. The corpus contains 10 different scenario types, for which there are about 90 stories each. This corpus also contains annotation for whether a verb is script-relevant, coreference annotation and participant type information.

4 Evaluation

4.1 Narrative Cloze Task

The evaluation on the narrative cloze task (originally suggested by Chambers and Jurafsky, 2008) expresses how well a model can predict a missing event in a sequence of events. In order to make the methods comparable, all predictions of our model are mapped onto the encoding used by the simple pair event model, e.g. <order,obj>, as follows:

We map an PLE $v(p_{subj}, p_{dobj}, p_{iobj})$ to a verb-dependency pair $< v, d >$ relating to a participant p if p fills the PLE slot of dependency d. We subsequently define the score of a pair event as the maximum score of all PLEs which are mapped to this pair event. When evaluating on pair events, we rank events according to this redefined score.

4.2 Systems

Unigram Model This baseline is a simple model that ranks any event (whether it is a participant-labeled event or a pair event) by its overall frequency in the training data. It was first used in Pichotta and Mooney (2014) and has proven to be a very competitive baseline on the task.

Verb-dependecy Pair Event Model This is a bigram model over verb-dependency pair events as introduced by Jans et al. (2012) and following the general idea of Chambers and Jurafsky (2008). It has been slightly modified to model not only subjects and objects, but also indirect objects. We use the setting Rudinger et al. (2015) has shown performs best: Skip-all as a counting method, a count threshold of 1, a document threshold of 5 and absolute discounting. Note that their results on the same data set differ from ours as we do not include syntactic relations other than 'subj', 'dobj' and 'iobj' into training and evaluation.

Pichotta and Mooney We re-implemented the approach by Pichotta and Mooney (2014) with the exception that we use $v(e_{subj}, e_{dobj}, e_{iobj})$ instead of $v(e_{subj}, e_{obj}, e_{prep})$ to represent events. That is, we do not model prepositional arguments of an event but discriminate between direct and indirect objects of verbs.

Participant-based model Our model, as described in section 2.2.

4.3 Automatic labels vs. gold standard

Automatic Coreference Chains We evaluate how much the results are effected by the quality of the automatic coreference chains produced by the Stanford Parser vs. annotated gold-chains on our data.

Automatic Participant Labelling We furthermore investigate to what extent our approach suffers from imperfect participant labeling, i.e. how good our model could have been if the labeling process was 100%-accurate. Kampmann et al. (2015) report a 0.59 micro F-score on the DinnersFromHell data, leaving an arguably large room for improvement (although they have a ceiling of 0.84 in terms of micro F-score because of a mismatch between their participant label set and the gold-standard labels they evaluate on). To compare against a perfect participant labeler, we use the participant annotation described in the same paper.

4.4 Testing

Following Rudinger et al. (2015), we perform leave-one-out testing at the document level, i.e., we use 133 folds for Dinners from Hell, and between 87 and 97 for InScript scenarios). We use the annotation provided for the corpora to construct a test set for every document as follows: Every verb that has been annotated as script-relevant is regarded as a test case if it takes an argument in any coreference chain of at least length two, and the dependency between the verb and the argument is either 'subj', 'dobj' or 'iobj'. The test then consists of inferring the verb and dependency, given the model's representation of the remaining events in the document after this held-out event is removed.

5 Results

Methods that encode events in a more complex way have a higher risk of running into sparsity issues, i.e. cases where the model has not encountered any of the events in the current context. Table 1 shows Recall@10 as a measure of prediction precision. We can see that our model beats the baseline models by a large margin on this measure. The core advantage of our model are its participant representations, which allow it to make more correct generalizations, and generate less noisy predictions. This is also reflected in its lower coverage: our model does not predict events when the context (including participant labels) has not been observed, while other models may predict based on non-matching participant types, and hence generalize incorrectly.

We also report the Recall@10 with respect to predicting the entire PLE in Table 1 (shown as

Model	Coverage	R@10	R@10full
this	0.757	0.41	0.18
P&M	0.957	0.26	
Jans	0.809	0.25	
MostFreq	0.936	0.27	0.13

Table 1: Performance for our model is reported with both automatic coreference chains and participant labels; R@10full refers to the evaluation on PLE's instead of pair events.

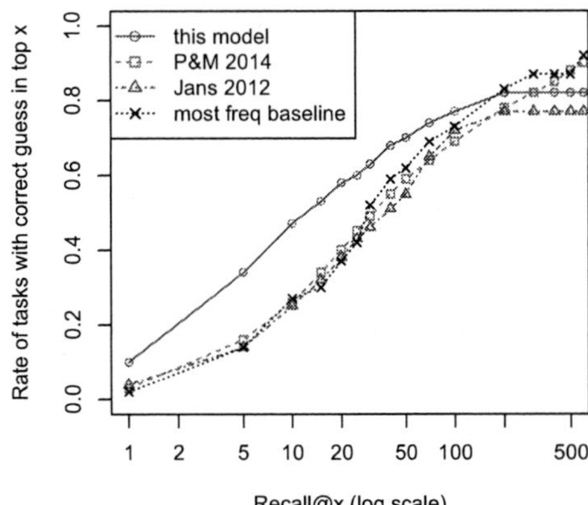

Figure 1: The participant-based method outperforms the other models and most frequent baseline. Performance shown for automatic chains and automatic participants.

R@10full), as we believe that inferring more structured events makes for a qualitative improvement on script modelling, we here provide a baseline for later work.

Figure 1 shows that the participant model succeeds in ranking the correct event high up more frequently than the other models. If the model cannot make any prediction due to coverage problems, it has to guess from unigram frequencies. This is reflected in our model's lower performance for Recall in sets larger than the top 500. We would however argue that performance at small Recall@x values is much more relevant for most applications, as it may matter little for most tasks where exactly in the low ranks 500-1000 a model manages to rank the correct solution. For future work, this lack of coverage could be compensated for by backing off to the P&M model.

Next, we'd like to see how the automatic versions of the models compare to a setting where the models have access to gold coreference chains and participants given by the annotation. Figure 2 shows that using automatic or gold corefernce chains makes no significant difference, but that there is quite a bit of scope for performance improvements if one can improve on the automatic participant labelling task.

Finally, we evaluated all models also on the 10 scenarios of the InScript dataset, to check whether the good performance of our model generalizes also to other datasets. We find that our model consis-

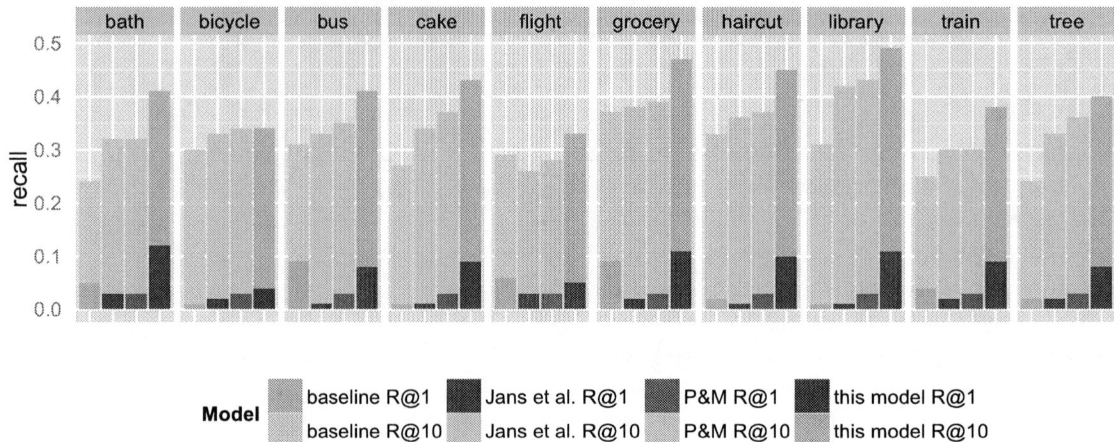

Figure 3: Performance of the different models with automatic participant labelling and automatic coreference chain annotation, on the stories for InScript dataset, showing results by scenario.

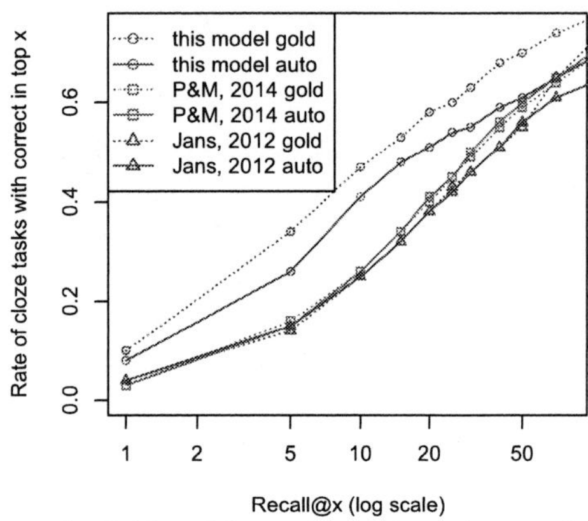

Figure 2: Gold models employ gold coreference chains and participants. There is little to no difference between using gold or automatic corefernce chains, but improving on participant labeling would help to further improve the model.

tently outperforms prior work also on this dataset, in particular with respect to succeeding to rank the correct event very high up on the list in the narrative cloze task. Figure 3 shows the Recall@1 and the Recall@10 measure separately for each of the scenarios from the InScript corpus.

6   Discussion and Conclusions

We have shown that the participant-based model can make much more accurate predictions in the narrative cloze task than previous models which do not have access to participant information; this even holds for automatic participant labelling, where we use a simple WordNet based method suggested in Kampmann et al. (2015). Our evaluation showed that the participant-based model substantially outperforms the state-of-the-art on the narrative cloze task, and that this performance holds for a set of naturalistic texts from blogs as well as for a corpus of narratives collected via crowd-sourcing. The present results hence represent an important step towards automatic inferencing for domains where knowledge of event sequences is relevant.

The automatic participant labeller takes as input a set of script participants, which can for example be acquired using the method of Regneri et al. (2010). The current approach therefore represents a way of combining the existing Mturk-based script acquisition methods by Regneri et al. (2010) with the unsupervised methods suggested in Chambers and Jurafsky (2008); Jans et al. (2012); Pichotta and Mooney (2014). Future work should further develop automated methods for participant labelling.

Acknowledgments

This research was funded by the German Research Foundation (DFG) as part of SFB 1102 'Information Density and Linguistic Encoding' and the Cluster of Excellence 'Multimodal Computing and Interaction' (EXC 284).

References

Chambers, N. and Jurafsky, D. (2008). Unsupervised learning of narrative event chains. In *Proceedings of ACL-08: HLT*, pages 789–797, Columbus, Ohio. Association for Computational Linguistics.

Chambers, N. and Jurafsky, D. (2009). Unsupervised learning of narrative schemas and their participants. In *Proceedings of the Joint Conference of the 47th Annual Meeting of the ACL and the 4th International Joint Conference on Natural Language Processing of the AFNLP*, pages 602–610, Suntec, Singapore. Association for Computational Linguistics.

Jans, B., Bethard, S., Vulić, I., and Moens, M.-F. (2012). Skip n-grams and ranking functions for predicting script events. In *Proceedings of the 13th Conference of the European Chapter of the Association for Computational Linguistics*, pages 336–344, Avignon, France. Association for Computational Linguistics.

Kampmann, A., Thater, S., and Pinkal, M. (2015). A case-study of automatic participant labeling. In *Proceedings of the International Conference of the German Society for Computational Linguistics and Language Technology*, pages 97–105.

Manning, C. D., Surdeanu, M., Bauer, J., Finkel, J., Bethard, S. J., and McClosky, D. (2014). The Stanford CoreNLP natural language processing toolkit. In *Proceedings of 52nd Annual Meeting of the Association for Computational Linguistics: System Demonstrations*, pages 55–60.

Modi, A., Anikina, T., Ostermann, S., and Pinkal, M. (2016). Inscript: Narrative texts annotated with script information. In *Proceedings of the 10th edition of the Language Resources and Evaluation Conference*.

Pichotta, K. and Mooney, R. (2014). Statistical script learning with multi-argument events. In *Proceedings of the 14th Conference of the European Chapter of the Association for Computational Linguistics*, pages 220–229, Gothenburg, Sweden. Association for Computational Linguistics.

Rahman, A. and Ng, V. (2012). Resolving complex cases of definite pronouns: the winograd schema challenge. In *Proceedings of the 2012 Joint Conference on Empirical Methods in Natural Language Processing and Computational Natural Language Learning*, pages 777–789. Association for Computational Linguistics.

Regneri, M., Koller, A., and Pinkal, M. (2010). Learning script knowledge with web experiments. In *Proceedings of the 48th Annual Meeting of the Association for Computational Linguistics*, pages 979–988, Uppsala, Sweden. Association for Computational Linguistics.

Rudinger, R., Demberg, V., Modi, A., Van Durme, B., and Pinkal, M. (2015). Learning to predict script events from domain-specific text. *Lexical and Computational Semantics (* SEM 2015)*, pages 205–210.

Schank, R. and Abelson, R. (1977). *Scripts, plans, goals and understanding: An inquiry into human knowledge structures*. Lawrence Erlbaum Associates, Hillsdale, NJ.

Schütz-Bosbach, S. and Prinz, W. (2007). Prospective coding in event representation. *Cognitive processing*, 8(2):93–102.

Zwaan, R. A., Langston, M. C., and Graesser, A. C. (1995). The construction of situation models in narrative comprehension: An event-indexing model. *Psychological science*, pages 292–297.

Structured Prediction with Output Embeddings
for Semantic Image Annotation

Ariadna Quattoni[1], Arnau Ramisa[2], Pranava Swaroop Madhyastha[3]
Edgar Simo-Serra[4], Francesc Moreno-Noguer[2]
[1]Xerox Research Center Europe, `ariadna.quattoni@xrce.xerox.com`
[2] Institut de Robòtica i Informàtica Industrial (CSIC-UPC), `{aramisa,fmoreno}@iri.upc.edu`
[3]TALP Research Center, Universitat Politècnica de Catalunya, `pranava@cs.upc.edu`
[4]Waseda University, `esimo@aoni.waseda.jp`

Abstract

We address the task of annotating images with semantic tuples. Solving this problem requires an algorithm able to deal with hundreds of classes for each argument of the tuple. In such contexts, data sparsity becomes a key challenge. We propose handling this sparsity by incorporating feature representations of both the inputs (images) and outputs (argument classes) into a factorized log-linear model.

1 Introduction

Many important problems in machine learning can be framed as structured prediction tasks where the goal is to learn functions that map inputs to structured outputs such as sequences, trees or general graphs. A wide range of applications involve learning over large state spaces, e.g., if the output is a labeled graph, each node of the graph may take values over a potentially large set of labels. Data sparsity then becomes a challenge, as there will be many classes with very few training examples.

Within this context, we are interested in the task of predicting semantic tuples for images. That is, given an input image we seek to predict what are the events or actions (referred here as *predicates*), who and what are the participants (referred here as *actors*) of the actions and where is the action taking place (referred here as *locatives*). For example, an image might be annotated with the semantic tuples: $\langle run, dog, park \rangle$ and $\langle play, dog, grass \rangle$. We call each field of a tuple an *argument*.

To handle the data sparsity challenge imposed by the large state space, we will leverage an approach that has proven to be useful in multiclass and multilabel prediction tasks (Weston et al., 2010; Akata et al., 2013). The idea is to represent a value for an argument a using a feature vector representation $\phi \in I\!R^n$. We will integrate this argument representation into the structured prediction model.

In summary, our main contribution is to propose an approach that incorporates feature representations of the outputs into a structured prediction model, and apply it to the problem of annotating images with semantic tuples. We present an experimental study using different output feature representations and analyze how they affect performance for different argument types.

2 Semantic Tuple Image Annotation

Task: We will address the task of predicting semantic tuples for images. Following Farhadi et al. (2010), we will focus on a simple semantic representation that considers three basic arguments: predicate, actors and locatives. For example, in the tuple $\langle play, dog, grass \rangle$, "*play*" is the predicate, "*dog*" is the actor and "*grass*" is the locative.

Given this representation, we can formally define our problem as that of learning a function $\theta : X \times P \times A \times L \rightarrow I\!R$ that scores the compatibility between images and semantic tuples. Here X is the space of images; P, A and L are discrete sets of predicate, actor and locative arguments respectively, and $\langle p\ a\ l \rangle$ is a specific tuple instance. The overall learning process is illustrated in Fig. 1.

Dataset: For our experiments we used a subset of the Flickr8k dataset, proposed in Hodosh et al. (2013). This dataset (subset $\mathcal{B}$ in Fig. 1) consists of 8,000 images from Flickr of people and animals

Proceedings of NAACL-HLT 2016, pages 552–557,
San Diego, California, June 12-17, 2016. ©2016 Association for Computational Linguistics

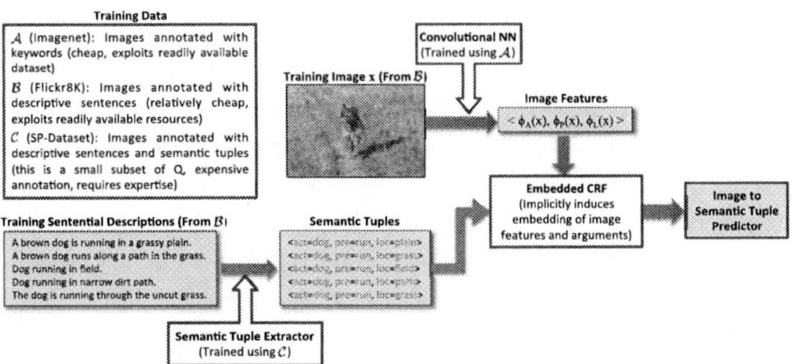

Figure 1: Overview of our approach. First, images $x \in \mathcal{A}$ are represented using image features $\phi_s(x)$, and semantic tuples are obtained applying our semantic tuple extractor (learned from the subset $\mathcal{C}$) to their corresponding captions. The resulting enlarged training set, is used to train our embedded CRF model that maps images to semantic tuples.

(mostly dogs) performing some action, with five crowd-sourced descriptive captions for each one.

We first manually annotated 1,544 captions, corresponding to 311 images (approximately one third of the development set (subset $\mathcal{C}$ in Fig. 1), producing more than 2,000 semantic tuples of predicate, actor and locative. For the experiments we partitioned the images and annotations into training, validation and test sets of 150, 50 and 100 images respectively.

Data augmentation: To enlarge the manually annotated dataset we trained a model able to predict semantic tuples from captions using standard shallow and deep linguistic features (e.g., POS tags, dependency parsing, semantic role labeling). We extract the predicates by looking at the words tagged as verbs by the POS tagger. Then, the extraction of arguments for each predicate is resolved as a classification problem.

More specifically, for each detected predicate in a sentence we regard each noun as a positive or negative training example of a given relation depending on whether the candidate noun is or is not an argument of the predicate. We use these examples to train a SVM classifier that predicts if a candidate noun is an argument of a given predicate based on several linguistic features computed over the syntactic path of the dependency tree that connects them. We run the learned tuple predictor model on all the captions of the Fickr8k dataset to obtain a larger dataset of 8,000 images paired with semantic tuples.

3 Bilinear Models with Output Features

In this section we explain how we incorporate output feature representations into a factorized linear model. For simplicity, we will consider factorized

sequence models over sequences of fixed length. However, it should not be hard to see that all the ideas presented here can be easily generalized to other structured prediction settings.

Let $y = [y_1 \ldots y_T]$ be a set of labels and $S = [S_1, \ldots, S_T]$ be the set of possible label values, where $y_i \in S_i$. We are interested in learning a model that computes $P(y|x)$, i.e., the conditional probability of a sequence y given some input x. We will consider factorized log-linear models that take the form:

$$P(y|x) = \frac{exp^{\theta(x,y)}}{\sum_y exp^{\theta(x,y)}} \quad (1)$$

The scoring function $\theta(x,y)$ is modeled as a sum of unary and binary bilinear potentials and is defined as:

$$\theta(x,y) = \sum_{t=1}^{T} v_{y_t}^{\top} W_t \phi(x,t) + \sum_{t=1}^{T} v_{y_t}^{\top} Z_t v_{y_{t+1}} \quad (2)$$

where $v_{y_t} \in I\!\!R^{n_t}$ is a n_t-dimensional feature representation of label arguments $y_t \in S_t$ and $\phi(x,t) \in I\!\!R^{d_t}$ is a d_t-dimensional feature representation of the tth input factor of x.

The first set of terms in the above equation are usually referred as unary potentials and measure the compatibility between a single state at t and the feature representation of input factor t. The second set of terms are the binary potentials and measure the compatibility between pairs of states at adjacent factors. The scoring $\theta(x,y)$ function is fully parameterized by the unary parameter matrices $W_t \in I\!\!R^{n_t \times d_t}$ and the binary parameter matrices $Z_t \in I\!\!R^{n_t \times n_t}$.

The main idea is to define a feature space where semantically similar labels will be close. Like in the multilabel scenario (Weston et al., 2010; Akata et al., 2013), having full feature representations for arguments will allow us to share information across different classes and generalize better. With a good output feature representation, our model should be able to make sensible predictions about pairs of arguments that it has not observed at training. This is easy to see: consider a case were we have a pair of arguments represented with feature vectors a_1 and a_2 and suppose that we have not observed the factor a_1, a_2 in our training data but we have observed the factor b_1, b_2. Then if a_1 is close in the feature space to argument b_1 and a_2 is close to b_2 our model will predict that a_1 and a_2 are compatible. That is it will assign probability to the factor a_1, a_2 which seems a natural generalization from the observed training data.

Now we show that the rank of W and Z have useful interpretations. Let $W = U\Sigma V$ be the singular value decomposition of W. We can then write unary potentials: $v_y^\top W \phi(x,t)$ as: $v_y^\top U \Sigma [V\phi(x,t)]$ Thus we can regard the bilinear form as a function computing a weighted inner product over some real embedding $v_y^\top U$ representing state y and some real embedding $[V\phi(x,t)]$ representing input factor t. The rank of W gives us the intrinsic dimensionality of the embedding. Thus if we want to induce shared low-dimensional embeddings across different states it seems reasonable to impose a low rank penalty on W. Similarly, let $Z = U\Sigma V$ be now the singular value decomposition of Z. We can write the binary potentials $v_y^\top Z v_{y'}$ as: $v_y^\top U \Sigma V v_{y'}$ and thus the binary potentials compute a weighted inner product between a real embedding of state y and a real embedding of state y'. As before, the rank of Z gives us the intrinsic dimensionality of the embedding and, to induce a low dimensional embedding for binary potentials, we will impose a low rank penalty on Z.

After having described the type of scoring functions we are interested in, we now turn our attention to the learning problem. That is, given a training set $D = \{\langle x \cdot y \rangle\}$ of pairs of inputs x and output sequences y we need to learn the parameters $\{W\}$ and $\{Z\}$. For this purpose we will do standard max-likelihood estimation and find the parameters that minimize the conditional negative log-likelihood of the data in D. That is, we will find the $\{W\}$ and $\{Z\}$ that mini-

mize the following loss function $\mathcal{L}(D, \{W\}, \{Z\})$:
$-\sum_{\langle x \ y \rangle \in D} log P(y|x; \{W\}, \{Z\})$ Recall that we are interested in learning low-rank unary and binary potentials. To achieve this we take a common approach which is to use as the nuclear norm $|W|_*$ and $|Z|_*$ as a convex approximation of the rank function, the final optimization problem becomes:

$$min_{\{W\}}\mathcal{L}(D, \{W\}) + \sum_t \alpha |W_t|_* + \beta |Z_t|_* \quad (3)$$

where $\mathcal{L}(D, \{W\}) = \sum_{d \in D} loss(d, \{W\})$ is the negative log likelihood function and α and β are two constants that control the trade off between minimizing the loss and the implicit dimensionality of the embeddings. We use a simple optimization scheme known as Forward Backward Splitting, or FOBOS (Duchi and Singer, 2009).

For our task we will consider a simple factorized scoring function: $\theta(x, \langle p \ a \ l \rangle)$ that has one factor associated with the *locative-predicate* pair and one factor associated with the *predicate-actor* pair. Since this corresponds to a chain structure, $argmax_{t \in T} \theta(x; \langle p \ a \ l \rangle)$ can be efficiently computed using Viterbi decoding in time $\mathcal{O}(N^2)$, where $N = max(|P|, |A|, |L|)$. Similarly, we can also find the top k predictions in $\mathcal{O}(kN^2)$. Thus for this application the scoring function of the bilinear CRF will take the form of:

$$
\begin{aligned}
\theta(x, \langle p\ a\ l \rangle) = \ & \lambda_{loc}(l)^\top W_{loc}\phi_{loc}(l) \\
& +\lambda_{pre}(p)^\top W_{pre}\phi_{pre}(p) \\
& +\lambda_{act}(a)^\top W_{act}\phi_{act}(a) \\
& +\phi_{loc}(l)^\top W_{pre}^{loc}\phi_{pre}(p) \\
& +\phi_{pre}(p)^\top W_{act}^{pre}\phi_{act}(a) \quad (4)
\end{aligned}
$$

The unary potentials measure the compatibility between an image and a semantic argument, the first binary potential measures the compatibility between a locative and a predicate, and the second binary potential measures the compatibility between a predicate and an actor. The scoring function is fully parameterized by the unary parameter matrices $W_{loc} \in I\!R^{d_l \times n_l}$, $W_{pre} \in I\!R^{d_p \times n_p}$ and $W_a \in I\!R^{d_a \times n_a}$ and the binary parameter matrices $W_{pre}^{loc} \in I\!R^{n_l \times n_p}$ and $W_{act}^{pre} \in I\!R^{n_p \times n_a}$. Where, n_l, n_p and n_a are the dimensionality of the locatives, predicates and actors feature representations, respectively and d_l, d_p and

d_a are the dimensionality of the image representations. Notice that if we let the argument representation $\phi_t(r) \in \mathbb{R}^{|S_t|}$ be an indicator vector for label argument t, we obtain the usual parametrization of a standard factorized linear model, while having a dense feature representations for arguments instead of indicator vectors will allow us to share information across different classes.

4 Representing Semantic Arguments

We will conduct experiments with two different feature representations: 1) Fully unsupervised *Skip-Gram based Continuous Word Representations* (SCWR) representation (Mikolov et al., 2013) and 2) A feature representation computed using the $\langle caption, semantic\text{-}tuples \rangle$ pairs, that we call *Semantic Equivalence Representation* (SER).

We decided to exploit the dataset of captions paired with semantic tuples to induce a useful feature representation for arguments. The idea is quite simple: we wish to leverage the fact that any pair of semantic tuples associated with the same image will be likely describing the same event. Thus, they are in essence different ways of lexicalizing the same underlying concept. Let's look at a concrete example. Imagine that we have an image annotated with the tuples: $\langle play, \ dog, \ water \rangle$ and $\langle play, \ dog, \ river \rangle$. Since both tuples describe the same image, it is quite likely that both "*river*" and "*water*" refer to the same real world entity, i.e, "*river*" and "*water*" are 'semantically equivalent' for this image. Using this idea we can build a representation $\phi_{loc}(i) \in \mathbb{R}^{|L|}$ where the j-th dimension corresponds to the number of times the argument j has been semantically equivalent to argument i. More precisely, we compute the probability that argument j can be exchanged with argument i as: $\frac{[i,j]_{sr}}{\sum_j [i,j]_{sr}}$ Where $[i,j]_{sr}$ is the number of times that i and j have appeared as annotations of the same image and with the same other arguments. For example, for the actor arguments $[i,j]_{sr}$ represents the number of time that actor i and actor j have appeared with the same locative and predicate as descriptions of the same image.

5 Related Work

In recent years, some works have tackled the problem of generating rich textual descriptions of images. One of the pioneers is (Kulkarni et al., 2011), where a CRF model combines the output of several vision systems to produce input for a language generation method. In Farhadi et al. (2010), the authors find the similarity between sentences and images in a "meaning" space, represented by semantic tuples which are very similar to our triplets. Other works focus on a simplified problem: ranking of human-generated captions for images. Hodosh et al. (2013) propose to use Kernel Canonical Correlation Analysis to project images and their captions into a joint representation space, in which images and captions can be related and ranked to perform illustration and annotation tasks. Socher et al. (2014) also address the ranking of images given a sentence and vice-versa using a common subspace learned via Recursive Neural Networks. Other recent works also exploit deep networks to address the problem (Vinyals et al., 2015; Karpathy and Fei-Fei, 2015). Using label embeddings combined with bilinear forms has been previously proposed in the context of multi-class and multilabel image classification (Weston et al., 2010; Akata et al., 2013).

6 Experiments

For image features we use the 4,096-dimensional second to last layer of BVLC implementation of 'AlexNet' ImageNet model, a Convolutional Neural Network (CNN) as described in Jia et al. (2014). To test our method we used the 100 test images that were annotated with ground-truth semantic tuples. To measure performance we first predict the top tuple for each image and then measure accuracy for each argument type (i.e. the number of correct predictions among the top 1 triplets). The regularization parameters of each model were set using the validation set. We compare the performance of the following models: 1) Baseline Separate Predictors (S-Pred): We consider a baseline made of independent predictors for each argument type.

More specifically we train one-vs-all SVMs (we also tried multi-class SVMs but they did not improve performance) to independently predict locatives, predicates and actors. For each argument type and candidate label we have a score computed by the corresponding SVM. Given an image we generate the top tuples that maximize the sum of scores for each argument type; 2) Baseline KCCA: This model implements the Kernel Canonical Correlation Anal-

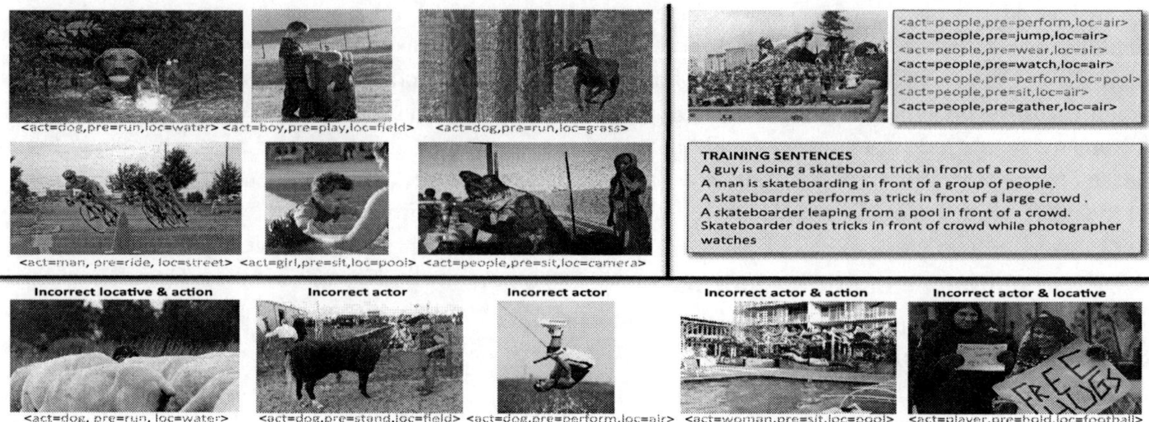

Figure 2: Samples of predicted tuples. **Top-left:** Examples of visually correct predictions. **Bottom:** Typical errors on one or several arguments. **Top-right:** Sample image and its top predicted tuples. The tuples in blue were not observed neither in the SP-Dataset nor in the automatically enlarged dataset. Note that all of them are descriptive of what is occurring in the scene.

ysis approach of Hodosh et al. (2013). We first note that this approach is able to rank a list of candidate captions but cannot directly generate tuples. To generate tuples for test images, we first find the caption in the training set that has the highest ranking score for that image and then extract the corresponding semantic tuples from that caption; 3) Indicator Features (IND), this is a standard factorized log-linear model that does not use any feature representation for the outputs; 4) A model that uses the skip-gram continuous word representation of outputs (SCWR); 5) A model that uses that semantic equivalence representation of outputs (SER); 6) A combined model that makes predictions using the best feature representation for each argument type (COMBO).

	S-Pred	KCCA	IND	SCWR	SER	COMBO
LOC	15	23	32	28	**33**	
PRED	11	20	24	**33**	25	
ACT	30	25	**52**	51	50	
MEAN	18.6	22.6	36	37.3	36	**39.3**

Table 1: Comparison of Output Feature Representation.

Table 1 shows the results. We observe that our proposed method performs significantly better than the baselines. The second observation is that the best performing output feature representation is different for different argument types, for the locatives the best representation is SER, for the predicates is the SCWR and for the actors using an output feature representation actually hurts performance. The biggest improvement we get is on the predicate arguments, where we improve almost by 10% in average precision over the baseline using the skip-gram word representation. Overall, the model that uses the best representation performs better than the indicator baseline.

Regarding the rank of the parameter matrices, we observed that the learned models can work well even if we drop the rank to 10% of its maximum rank. This shows that the learned models are efficient in the sense that they can work well with low-dimensional projections of the features.

7   Conclusion

In this paper we have presented a framework for exploiting input and output embeddings in the context of structured prediction. We have applied this framework to the problem of predicting compositional semantic descriptions of images. Our results show the advantages of using output embeddings and inducing low-dimensional embeddings for handling large state spaces in structured prediction problems. The framework we propose is general enough to consider additional sources of information.

8   Acknowledgments

This work was partly funded by the Spanish MINECO project RobInstruct TIN2014-58178-R and by the ERA-net CHISTERA projects VISEN PCIN- 2013-047 and I-DRESS PCIN-2015-147. The authors are grateful to the Nvidia donation program for its support with GPU cards.

References

[Akata et al.2013] Zeynep Akata, Florent Perronnin, Zaid Harchaoui, and Cordelia Schmid. 2013. Label-embedding for attribute-based classification. In *Proc. IEEE Conference on Computer Vision and Pattern Recognition (CVPR)*.

[Duchi and Singer2009] John Duchi and Yoram Singer. 2009. Efficient online and batch learning using forward backward splitting. *Journal of Machine Learning Research (JMLR)*, 10:2899–2934.

[Farhadi et al.2010] Ali Farhadi, Mohsen Hejrati, MohammadAmin Sadeghi, Peter Young, Cyrus Rashtchian, Julia Hockenmaier, and David Forsyth. 2010. Every picture tells a story: Generating sentences from images. In *Proc. European Conference on Computer Vision (ECCV)*.

[Hodosh et al.2013] Micah Hodosh, Peter Young, and Julia Hockenmaier. 2013. Framing image description as a ranking task: Data, models and evaluation metrics. *Journal of Artificial Intelligence Research (JAIR)*, 47:853–899.

[Jia et al.2014] Yangqing Jia, Evan Shelhamer, Jeff Donahue, Sergey Karayev, Jonathan Long, Ross Girshick, Sergio Guadarrama, and Trevor Darrell. 2014. Caffe: Convolutional architecture for fast feature embedding. *arXiv preprint arXiv:1408.5093*.

[Karpathy and Fei-Fei2015] Andrej Karpathy and Li Fei-Fei. 2015. Deep visual-semantic alignments for generating image descriptions. In *Proc. IEEE Conference on Computer Vision and Pattern Recognition (CVPR)*.

[Kulkarni et al.2011] Girish Kulkarni, Visruth Premraj, Sagnik Dhar, Siming Li, Yejin Choi, Alexander C Berg, and Tamara L Berg. 2011. Baby talk: Understanding and generating image descriptions. In *Proc. IEEE Conference on Computer Vision and Pattern Recognition (CVPR)*.

[Mikolov et al.2013] Tomas Mikolov, Kai Chen, Greg Corrado, and Jeffrey Dean. 2013. Efficient estimation of word representations in vector space. In *Proc. International Conference on Learning Representations (ICLR)*.

[Socher et al.2014] Richard Socher, Andrej Karpathy, Quoc V. Le, Christopher D. Manning, and Andrew Y. Ng. 2014. Grounded compositional semantics for finding and describing images with sentences. *Transactions of the Association of Computational Linguistics (TACL)*, 2:207–218.

[Vinyals et al.2015] Oriol Vinyals, Alexander Toshev, Samy Bengio, and Dumitru Erhan. 2015. Show and tell: A neural image caption generator. In *Proc. IEEE Conference on Computer Vision and Pattern Recognition (CVPR)*.

[Weston et al.2010] Jason Weston, Samy Bengio, and Nicolas Usunier. 2010. Large scale image annotation: Learning to rank with joint word-image embeddings. In *Proc. European Conference on Computer Vision (ECCV)*.

Large-scale Multitask Learning for Machine Translation Quality Estimation

Kashif Shah and **Lucia Specia**
Department of Computer Science
University of Sheffield, UK
`{kashif.shah,l.specia}@sheffield.ac.uk`

Abstract

Multitask learning has been proven a useful technique in a number of Natural Language Processing applications where data is scarce and naturally diverse. Examples include learning from data of different domains and learning from labels provided by multiple annotators. *Tasks* in these scenarios would be the domains or the annotators. When faced with limited data for each task, a framework for the learning of tasks in parallel while using a shared representation is clearly helpful: what is learned for a given task can be transferred to other tasks while the peculiarities of each task are still modelled. Focusing on machine translation quality estimation as application, in this paper we show that multitask learning is also useful in cases where data is abundant. Based on two large-scale datasets, we explore models with multiple annotators and multiple languages and show that state-of-the-art multitask learning algorithms lead to improved results in all settings.

1 Introduction

Quality Estimation (QE) models predict the quality of Machine Translation (MT) output based on the source and target texts only, without reference translations. This task is often framed as a supervised machine learning problem using various features indicating fluency, adequacy and complexity of the source-target text pair, and annotations on translation quality given by human translators. Various kernel-based regression and classification algorithms have been explored to learn prediction models.

The application of QE we focus on here is that of guiding professional translators during the post-editing of MT output. QE models can provide translators with information on how much editing/time will be necessary to fix a given segment, or on whether it is worth editing it at all, as opposed to translating it from scratch. For this application, models are learnt from quality annotations that reflect post-editing effort, for instance, 1-5 judgements on estimated post-editing effort (Callison-Burch et al., 2012) or actual post-editing effort measured as post-editing time (Bojar et al., 2013) or edit distance between the MT output and its post-edited version (Bojar et al., 2014; Bojar et al., 2015).

One of the biggest challenges in this field is to deal with the inherent subjectivity of quality labels given by humans. Explicit judgements (e.g. the 1-5 point scale) are affected the most, with previous work showing that translators' perception of post-editing effort differs from actual effort (Koponen, 2012). However, even objective annotations of actual post-editing effort are subject to natural variance. Take, for example, post-editing time as a label: Different annotators have different typing speeds and may require more or less time to deal with the same edits depending on their level of experience, familiarity with the domain, etc. Post-editing distance also varies across translators as there are often multiple ways of producing a good quality translation from an MT output, even when strict guidelines are given.

In order to address variance among multiple translators, three strategies have been applied: (i) models are built by averaging annotations from multiple

Proceedings of NAACL-HLT 2016, pages 558–567,
San Diego, California, June 12-17, 2016. ©2016 Association for Computational Linguistics

translators on the same data points, as was done in the first shared task on the topic (Callison-Burch et al., 2012); (ii) models are built for individual translators by collecting labelled data for each translator (Shah and Specia, 2014); and (iii) models are built using multitask learning techniques (Caruana, 1997) to put together annotations from multiple translators while keeping track of the translators' identification to account for their individual biases (Cohn and Specia, 2013; de Souza et al., 2015).

The first approach is sensible because, in the limit, the models built should reflect the "average" strategies/preferences of translators. However, its cost makes it prohibitive. The second approach can lead to very accurate models but it requires sufficient training data for each translator, and that all translators are known at model building time. The last approach is very attractive. It is a *transfer learning* (a.k.a. *domain-adaptation*) approach that allows the modelling of data from each individual translator while also modelling correlations between translators such that "similar" translators can mutually inform one another. As such, it does not require multiple annotations of the same data points and can be effective even if only a few data points are available for each translator. In fact, previous work on multitask learning for quality estimation has concentrated on the problem of learning prediction models from little data provided by different annotators.

In this paper we take a step further to investigate multitask learning for quality estimation in settings where data may be abundant for some or most annotators. We explore a multitask learning approach that provides a general, scalable and robust solution regardless of the amount of data available. By testing models on single translator data, we show that while building models for individual translators is a sensible decision when large amounts of data are available, the multitask learning approach can outperform these models by learning from data by multiple annotators. Additionally, besides having translators as "tasks", we address the problem of learning from data for multiple language pairs.

We devise our multitaslk approach within the Bayesian non-parametric machine learning framework of Gaussian Processes (Rasmussen and Williams, 2006). Gaussian Processes have shown very good results for quality estimation in previous

work (Cohn and Specia, 2013; Beck et al., 2013; Shah et al., 2013). Our datasets – annotated for post-editing distance – contain nearly 100K data points, two orders of magnitude larger than those used in previous work. To cope with scalability issues resulting from the size of these datasets, we apply a sparse version of Gaussian Processes. We perform extensive experiments on this large-scale data aiming to answer the following research questions:

- What is the best approach to build models to be used by **individual translators**? How much data is necessary to build independent models (one per translator) that can be as accurate as (or better than) models using data from multiple translators?

- When large amounts of data are available, can we still improve over independent and pooled models by learning from metadata to exploit **transfer across translators**?

- Can crosslingual data help improve model performance by exploiting **transfer across language pairs**?

In the remainder of the paper we start with an overview on related work in the area of multitask learning for quality estimation (Section 2), to then describe our approach to multitask learning in the context of Gaussian Processes (Section 3). In Section 4 we introduce our data and experimental settings. Finally in Sections 5 and 6 we present the results of our experiments to answer the above mentioned questions for cross-annotator and crosslingual transfer, respectively.

2 Related Work

As was discussed in Section 1, the problem of variance among multiple translators in QE has recently been approached in three ways. The first two approaches essentially refer to preparation of the data. At WMT12, the first shared task on QE (Callison-Burch et al., 2012), the official dataset was created by collecting three 1-5 (worst-best) discrete judgements on "perceived" post-editing effort for each translated segment. The final score was a scaled average of the three scores, and about 15% of the labelled data was discarded as annotators diverged in their judgemetns by more than one point. While this type of data proved useful and certainly reliable in the limit of the number of annotators, it is too expensive to collect.

Shah and Specia (2014) built QE models using data from n annotators by either pooling all the data together or splitting it into n datasets for n individual annotator models. These models were tested in blind versus non-blind settings, where the former refers to test sets whose annotator identifiers were unknown. They observed a substantial difference in the error scores for each of the individual models. They showed that the task is much more challenging for QE models trained independently when training data for each annotator is scarce. In other words, sufficient data needs to be available to build individual models for all possible translators.

The approach of using multitask learning to build models addresses the data scarcity issue and has been shown effective in previous work. Cohn and Specia (2013) first introduced multitask learning for QE. Their goal was to allow the modelling of various perspectives on the data, as given by multiple annotators, while also recognising that they are rarely independent of one another (annotators often agree) by explicitly accounting for inter-annotator correlations. A set of task-specific regression models were built from data labelled with post-editing time and perceived post-editing effort (1-5). "Tasks" included annotators, the MT system and the actual source sentence, as their data included same source segments translated/edited by multiple systems/editors.

Similarly, de Souza et al. studied multitask learning to deal with data coming from different training/test set distributions or domains, and generally scenarios in which training data is scarce. Offline multitask (de Souza et al., 2014a) and online multitask (de Souza et al., 2015; de Souza et al., 2014b) learning methods for QE were proposed. The later focused on continuous model learning and adaptation from new post-edits in a computer-aided translation environment. For that, they adapted an online passive-aggressive algorithm (Cavallanti et al., 2010) to the multitask scenario. While their setting is interesting and could be considered more challenging because of the online adaptation requirements, ours is different as we can take advantage of already having collected large volumes of data.

Multitask learning has also been used for other classification and regression tasks in language processing, mostly for domain adaptation (Daume III, 2007; Finkel and Manning, 2009), but also more recently for tasks such as multi-emotion analysis (Beck et al., 2014), where the each emotion explaining a text is defined as a task. However, in all previous work the focus has been on addressing task variance coupled with data scarcity, which makes them different from the work we describe in this paper.

3 Gaussian Processes

Gaussian Processes (GPs) (Rasmussen and Williams, 2006) are a Bayesian non-parametric machine learning framework considered the state-of-the-art for regression. GPs have been used successfully for MT quality prediction (Cohn and Specia, 2013; Beck et al., 2013; Shah et al., 2013), among other tasks.

GPs assume the presence of a latent function $f : \mathbb{R}^F \to \mathbb{R}$, which maps a vector $\mathbf{x}$ from feature space F to a scalar value. Formally, this function is drawn from a GP prior:

$$f(\mathbf{x}) \sim \mathcal{GP}(\mathbf{0}, k(\mathbf{x}, \mathbf{x}')),$$

which is parameterised by a mean function (here, $\mathbf{0}$) and a covariance kernel function $k(\mathbf{x}, \mathbf{x}')$. Each response value is then generated from the function evaluated at the corresponding input, $y_i = f(\mathbf{x}_i) + \eta$, where $\eta \sim \mathcal{N}(0, \sigma_n^2)$ is added white-noise.

Prediction is formulated as a Bayesian inference under the posterior:

$$p(y_*|\mathbf{x}_*, \mathcal{D}) = \int_f p(y_*|\mathbf{x}_*, f) p(f|\mathcal{D}),$$

where $\mathbf{x}_*$ is a test input, y_* is the test response value and $\mathcal{D}$ is the training set. The predictive posterior can be solved analitically, resulting in:

$$y_* \sim \mathcal{N}(\mathbf{k}_*^T (\mathbf{K} + \sigma_n^2 I)^{-1} \mathbf{y},$$
$$k(x_*, x_*) - \mathbf{k}_*^T (\mathbf{K} + \sigma_n^2 I)^{-1} \mathbf{k}_*),$$

where $\mathbf{k}_* = [k(\mathbf{x}_*, \mathbf{x}_1) k(\mathbf{x}_*, \mathbf{x}_2) \dots k(\mathbf{x}_*, \mathbf{x}_n)]^T$ is the vector of kernel evaluations between the training set and the test input and $\mathbf{K}$ is the kernel matrix over the training inputs (the Gram matrix).

3.1 Multitask Learning

The GP regression framework can be extended to multiple outputs by assuming $f(\mathbf{x})$ to be a vector valued function. These models are commonly referred as *Intrinsic Coregionalization Models (ICM)* in the GP literature (Álvarez et al., 2012).

In this work, we employ a separable multitask kernel, similar to the one used by Bonilla et al. (2008) and Cohn and Specia (2013). Considering a set of D tasks, we define the corresponding multitask kernel as:

$$k((\mathbf{x}, d), (\mathbf{x}', d')) = k_{\text{data}}(\mathbf{x}, \mathbf{x}') \times \mathbf{M}_{d,d'},$$

where k_{data} is a kernel (Radial Basis Function, in our experiments) on the input points, d and d' are task or metadata information for each input and $\mathbf{M} \in \mathbb{R}^{D \times D}$ is the multitask matrix, which encodes task covariances. In our experiments, we first consider each post-editor as a different task, and then use crosslingual data to treat each combination of language and post-editor as a task.

An adequate parametrisation of the multitask matrix is required to perform learning process. We follow the parameterisations proposed by Cohn and Specia (2013) and Beck et al. (2014):

Individual: $\mathbf{M} = \mathbf{I}$. In this setting each task is modelled independently by keeping corresponding task identity.

Pooled: $\mathbf{M} = \mathbf{1}$. Here the task identity is ignored. This is equivalent to pooling all datasets in a single task model.

Multitask: $\mathbf{M} = \tilde{\mathbf{H}}\tilde{\mathbf{H}}^T + \text{diag}(\boldsymbol{\alpha})$, where $\tilde{\mathbf{H}}$ is a $D \times R$ matrix. The vector $\boldsymbol{\alpha}$ enables the degree of independence for each task with respect to the global task. The choice of R defines the *rank* ($= 1$ in our case) which can be understood as the capacity of the manifold with which we model the D tasks. We refer readers to see Beck et al. (2014) for a more detailed explanation of this setting.

3.2 Sparse Gaussian Processes

The performance bottleneck for GP models is the Gram matrix inversion, which is $O(n^3)$ for standard GPs, with n being the number of training instances. For multitask settings this becomes an issue for large datasets as the models replicate the instances for each task and the resulting Gram matrix has dimensionality $nd \times nd$, where d is the number of tasks.

Sparse GPs (Snelson and Ghahramani, 2006) tackle this problem by approximating the Gram matrix using only a subset of m inducing inputs. Without loss of generalisation, consider these m points as the first instances in the training data. We can then expand the Gram matrix in the following way:

$$\mathbf{K} = \begin{bmatrix} \mathbf{K}_{mm} & \mathbf{K}_{m(n-m)} \\ \mathbf{K}_{(n-m)m} & \mathbf{K}_{(n-m)(n-m)} \end{bmatrix}.$$

Following the notation in (Rasmussen and Williams, 2006), we refer $\mathbf{K}_{m(n-m)}$ as $\mathbf{K}_{mn}$ and its transpose as $\mathbf{K}_{nm}$. The block structure of $\mathbf{K}$ forms the basis of the so-called Nyström approximation:

$$\tilde{\mathbf{K}} = \mathbf{K}_{nm}\mathbf{K}_{mm}^{-1}\mathbf{K}_{mn},$$

which results in the following predictive posterior:

$$y_* \sim \mathcal{N}(\mathbf{k}_{m*}^T \tilde{\mathbf{G}}^{-1}\mathbf{K}_{mn}\mathbf{y},$$
$$k(\mathbf{x}_*, \mathbf{x}_*) - \mathbf{k}_{m*}^T \mathbf{K}_{mm}^{-1}\mathbf{k}_{m*} +$$
$$\sigma_n^2 \mathbf{k}_{m*}^T \tilde{\mathbf{G}}^{-1}\mathbf{k}_{m*}),$$

where $\tilde{\mathbf{G}} = \sigma_n^2 \mathbf{K}_{mm} + \mathbf{K}_{mn}\mathbf{K}_{nm}$ and $\mathbf{k}_{m*}$ is the vector of kernel evaluations between test input $\mathbf{x}_*$ and the m inducing inputs. The resulting training complexity is $O(m^2 n)$.

In our experiments, the number of inducing points was set empirically by inspecting where the learning curves (in terms of Pearson's correlation gains) flatten, as shown in Figure 1. We used 300 inducing points in experiments with all the settings (see Section 4.3).

4 Experimental Settings

4.1 Data

Our experiments are based on data from two language pairs: English-Spanish (en-es) and English-French (en-fr). The data was collected and made available by WIPO's (World Intellectual Property Organization) Brands and Design Sector. The domain of the data is trademark applications in English, using one or more of the 45 categories of the

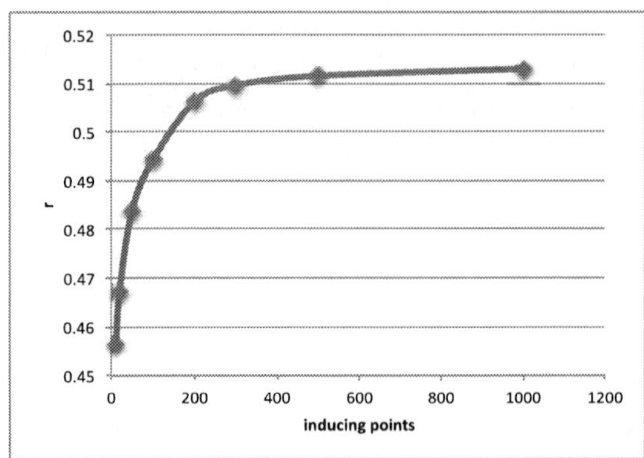

Figure 1: Number of inducing points versus Pearson's correlation

Lang. Pair	ID	Total	Train	Test
en-es	1	28,423	21,317	7,105
	2	12,904	9,678	3,226
	3	3,939	2,954	984
	4	16,518	12,388	4,129
	5	14,187	10,640	3,546
	6	9,395	7,046	2,348
	7	402	301	100
	8	9,294	6,970	2,323
	9	845	633	211
	10	2,756	2,067	689
	All	98,663	73,997	24,665
en-fr	1	65,280	48,960	16,320
	2	6,336	4,752	1,584
	3	769	576	192
	4	5,271	3,953	1,317
	All	77,656	58,241	19,413

Table 1: Number of en-es and en-fr segments

NICE[1] goods and services (e.g. furniture, clothing), and their translations into one of the two languages.

An in-house phrase-based statistical MT system was built by WIPO (Pouliquen et al., 2011), trained on domain-specific data, to translate the English segments. The quality of the translations produced is considered high, with BLEU scores on a 1K-single reference test set reaching 0.71. This is partly attributed to the short length and relative simplicity of the segments in the sub-domains of goods and services. The post-editing was done mostly internally and systematically collected between November 2014 and August 2015. The quality label for each segment is post-editing distance, calculated as the HTER (Snover et al., 2006) between the target segment and its post-edition using the TERCOM tool.[2]

The data was split into 75% for training and 25% for test, with each split maintaining the original data distribution by post-editor. The number of training and test <source, MT output, post-edited MT, HTER score> tuples for each of the post-editors (ID) and language pair is given in Table 1. There are 63,763 overlapping English source segments out of 77,656 entries for en-fr and 98,663 entries for en-es. This information is relevant for the crosslingual data experiments, as we discuss in Section 6.

It should be noted that the total number of segments as well as the number of segments per post-editor is significantly higher than those used in previous work. For example, (Cohn and Specia, 2013) used datasets of 6,762 instances (2,254 for each of three translator) and 1,624 instances (299 for each of eight translators), while (Beck et al., 2014) had access to 1000 instances annotated with six emotions.

4.2 Algorithms

For all tasks we used the QuEst framework (Specia et al., 2013) to extract a set of 17 baseline black-box features[3] (Shah et al., 2013) for which we had all the necessary resources for the WIPO domain. These baseline features have shown to perform well in the WMT shared tasks on QE. They include simple counts, e.g. number of tokens in source and target segments, source and target language model probabilities and perplexities, average number of possible translations for source words, number of punctuation marks in source and target segments, among other features reflecting the complexity of the source segment and the fluency of the target segment.

All our models were trained using the GPy[4] toolkit, an open source implementation of GPs written in Python.

4.3 Settings

We built and tested models in the following conditions:

[1] http://www.wipo.int/classifications/nice/en/

[2] http://www.cs.umd.edu/~snover/tercom/

[3] http://www.quest.dcs.shef.ac.uk/quest_files/features_blackbox_baseline_17

[4] http://sheffieldml.github.io/GPy/

One language	Setting-1 ind_trn-ind_tst	Setting-2 pol_trn-ind_tst	Setting-3 mtl_trn-ind_tst	Setting-4 ind_trn-pol_tst	Setting-5 pol_trn-pol_tst	Setting-6 mtl_trn-pol_tst
Model	Individual	Pooled	Multitask	Individual	Pooled	Multitask
Test	Individual	Individual	Individual	Pooled	Pooled	Pooled
Crosslingual (cl)	Setting-7 cl_pol_trn-ind_tst	Setting-8 cl_mtl_trn-ind_tst	Setting-9 cl_pol_trn-pol_tst	Setting-10 cl_mtl_trn-pol_tst		
Model	Pooled	Multitask	Pooled	Multitask		
Test	Individual	Individual	Pooled	Pooled		
Non-overlapping (no)	Setting-11 no_cl_pol_trn-pol_tst	Setting-12 no_mtl_trn-pol_tst	Setting-13 no_cl_mtl_trn-pol_tst			
Model	Pooled	Multitask	Multitask			
Test	Pooled	Pooled	Pooled			

Table 2: Various models and test settings in our experiments

- **Setting-1:** Individual models on individual test sets: each model is trained with data from an individual post-editor and tested on the test set for the same individual post-editor.

- **Setting-2:** Pooled model on individual test sets: model trained with data concatenated from all post-editors and tested on test sets of individual post-editors.

- **Setting-3:** Multitask model on individual test sets: multitask models trained with data from all post-editors and tested on test sets of individual post-editors.

- **Setting-4:** Individual models tested on pooled test set: each model is trained with data from an individual post-editor and tested on a test set with data from all post-editors. This setup aims to find out the performance of individual models when the identifier of the post-editor is not known (e.g. in crowdsourcing settings).

- **Setting-5:** Pooled model on pooled test set: model trained with data concatenated from all post-editors and tested on test set of all post-editors.

- **Setting-6:** Multitask model on pooled test set: Multitask model trained with data from all post-editors and tested on test set from all post-editors together.

- **Setting-7 to 10:** Similar to setting-2, 3, 5, 6 but with additional crosslingual data where pooled and multitask models are trained with both en-es and en-fr datasets together.

- **Setting-11-13:** Similar to setting-9, 6, 10 respectively, but with non-overlapping crosslingual data only.

5 Results with Multiple Annotators

We report results in terms of Pearson's correlation between predicted and true quality labels, as was done in the WMT QE shared tasks (Bojar et al., 2015). The multitask learning models consistently led to improvement over pooled models, and over individual models in most cases. We present the comparisons of the models for various settings in the following. The bars marked with * in each comparison are significantly better than all others with $p < 0.01$ according to the Williams significance test (Williams, 1959).

Individual, pooled and multitask models on individual test sets Results for both language pairs are shown in Figure 2. As expected, in cases where a large number of instances is available from an individual post-editor, individual models tested on individual test sets perform better than pooled models. Overall, multitask learning models show improvement over both individual and pooled models, or the same performance in cases where large amounts of data are available for an individual post-editor. For example, in en-es, for post-editors 9 and 3, which have 845 and 3,939 instances in total, respectively, multitask learning models are considerably better. The same goes for post-editor 3 in en-fr, which has only 769 instances. For very few post-editors with a large number of instances (1,2 and 4 in en-es) multitask learning models perform the same as individual or even pooled models. For all other post-editors, multitask models further improve correlation with humans. These results emphasize

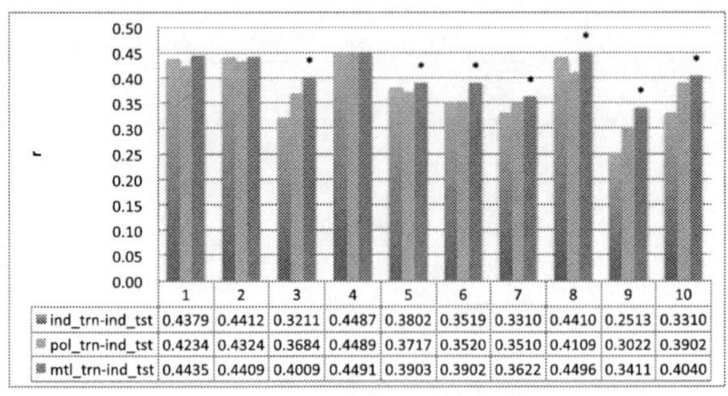

	1	2	3	4	5	6	7	8	9	10
ind_trn-ind_tst	0.4379	0.4412	0.3211	0.4487	0.3802	0.3519	0.3310	0.4410	0.2513	0.3310
pol_trn-ind_tst	0.4234	0.4324	0.3684	0.4489	0.3717	0.3520	0.3510	0.4109	0.3022	0.3902
mtl_trn-ind_tst	0.4435	0.4409	0.4009	0.4491	0.3903	0.3902	0.3622	0.4496	0.3411	0.4040

(a) en-es

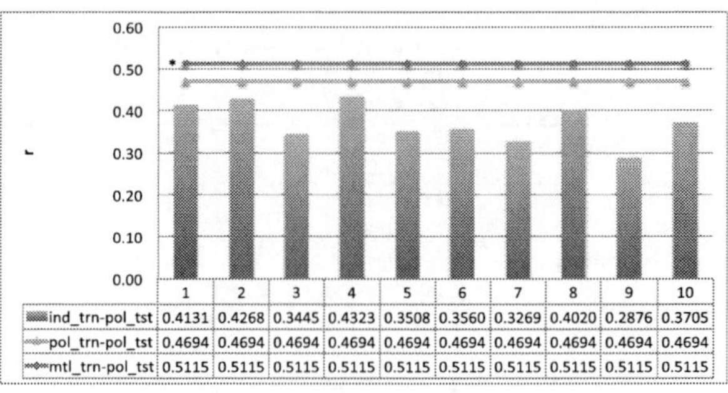

	1	2	3	4	5	6	7	8	9	10
ind_trn-pol_tst	0.4131	0.4268	0.3445	0.4323	0.3508	0.3560	0.3269	0.4020	0.2876	0.3705
pol_trn-pol_tst	0.4694	0.4694	0.4694	0.4694	0.4694	0.4694	0.4694	0.4694	0.4694	0.4694
mtl_trn-pol_tst	0.5115	0.5115	0.5115	0.5115	0.5115	0.5115	0.5115	0.5115	0.5115	0.5115

(a) en-es

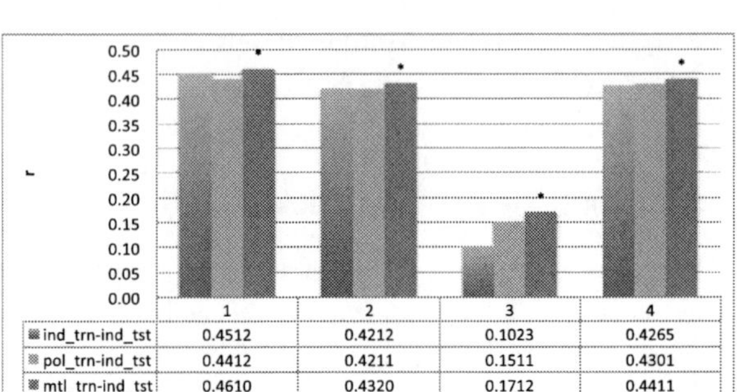

	1	2	3	4
ind_trn-ind_tst	0.4512	0.4212	0.1023	0.4265
pol_trn-ind_tst	0.4412	0.4211	0.1511	0.4301
mtl_trn-ind_tst	0.4610	0.4320	0.1712	0.4411

(b) en-fr

Figure 2: Pearson's correlation with various models on individual test sets

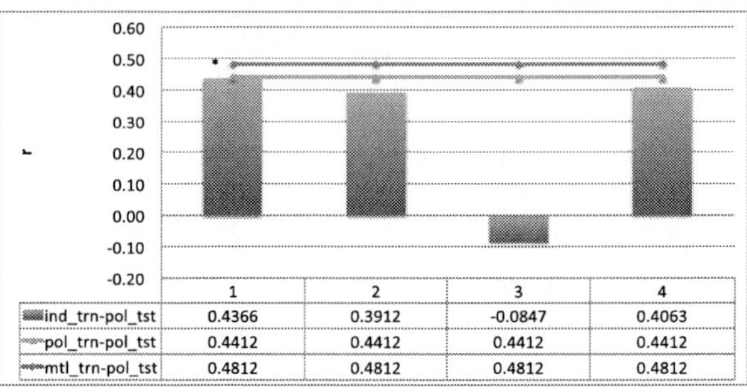

	1	2	3	4
ind_trn-pol_tst	0.4366	0.3912	-0.0847	0.4063
pol_trn-pol_tst	0.4412	0.4412	0.4412	0.4412
mtl_trn-pol_tst	0.4812	0.4812	0.4812	0.4812

(b) en-fr

Figure 3: Pearson's correlation with various models on pooled test set

the advantages of multitask learning models, even in cases where the post-editors that will use the models are known in advance (first research question): Clearly, the models for post-editors with fewer instances benefit from the sharing of information from the larger post-editor data sets. As for post-editors with large numbers of instances, in the worst case the performance remains the same.

Individual, pooled and multitask models on pooled test set Here we focus on cases where models are built to be used by any post-editor (second research question). Results in Figure 3 show that when test sets for all post-editors are put together, individual models perform distinctively worse than pooled and multitask learning models. Multitask learning models are significantly better than pooled models for both languages (0.511 vs 0.469 for en-es, and 0.481 vs 0.441 for en-fr). In the case of post-editor 3 for en-fr, the correlation is negative for individual models given the very low number of instances for this post-editor, which is not sufficient to build a general enough model that also

works for other post-editors.

Relationship among post-editors In order to gain a better insight into the strength of the relationships among various post-editors and thus into the expected benefits from joint modelling, we plot the learned Corregionalisation matrix for all against all post-editors in Figure 4.[5] It can be observed that there exist various degrees of mutual interdependences among post-editors. For instance, in the case of en-es, post-editor 4 shows a strong relationship with post-editors 6 and 7, a relatively weaker relationship with post-editors 1 and 9, and close to nonexisting with post-editors 3, 8 and 10. In the case of en-fr, post-editor 3 shows very weak relationship with all other post-editors, especially 4. This might explain the low Pearson's correlation with individual models for post-editor 3 on pooled test sets.

---

[5]We note that the Corregionalisation matrix cannot be interpreted as a correlation matrix. Rather, it shows the covariance between tasks.

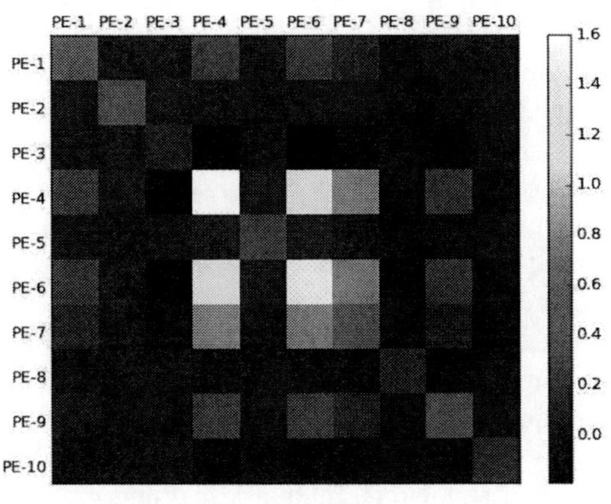

(a) en-es

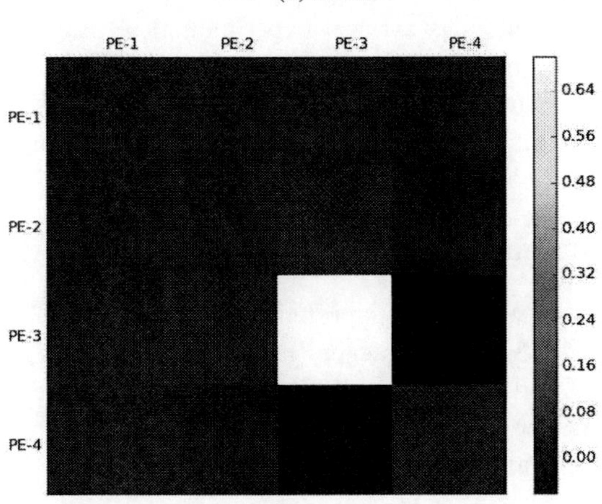

(b) en-fr

Figure 4: Heatmap showing a learned Coregionalisation matrix over all post-editors

6 Results with Multiple Languages

To address the last research question, here we present the results on crosslingual models in comparison to single language pair models. The training models contain data from both en-es and en-fr language pairs in the various settings previously described, where for the multitask settings, tasks can be annotators, languages, or both.

Single versus crosslingual pooled and multitask models on individual test sets Figure 5 shows a performance comparison between single language versus crosslingual models on individual test sets.

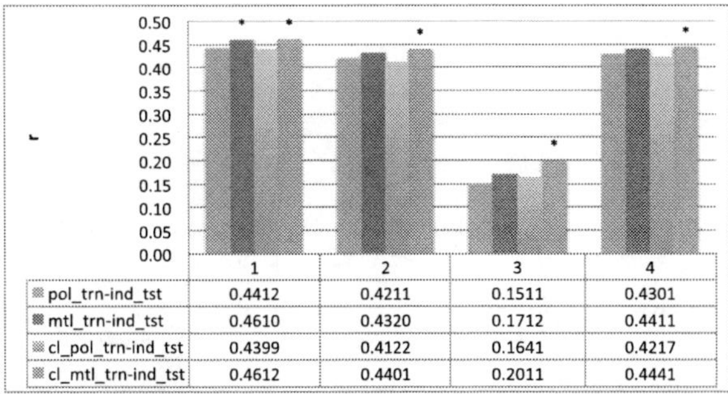

	1	2	3	4
pol_trn-ind_tst	0.4412	0.4211	0.1511	0.4301
mtl_trn-ind_tst	0.4610	0.4320	0.1712	0.4411
cl_pol_trn-ind_tst	0.4399	0.4122	0.1641	0.4217
cl_mtl_trn-ind_tst	0.4612	0.4401	0.2011	0.4441

Figure 5: Pearson's correlation with single versus crosslingual models on individual en-fr test sets

Due to space constraints, we only present results for the en-fr test sets, but those for the en-es test sets follow the same trend. Multitask models lead to further improvements, particularly visible for post-editor 3 (the one with less training data), where the crosslingual multitask learning model reaches 0.201 Pearson's correlation, while the monolingual multitask learning model performs at 0.171. The performance of the pooled models with crosslingual data also improves on this test set over monolingual pooled models, but the overall figures are lower than with multitask learning, showing that the benefit does not only come from adding more data, but from adequate modelling of the additional data. This shows the potential to learn robust prediction models from datasets with multiple languages.

Single versus crosslingual pooled and multitask models on pooled test set Figure 6 compares single language and crosslingual models on the pooled test sets for both languages. A pooled test set with data from different languages presents a more challenging case. Simply building crosslingual pooled models deteriorates the performance over single pooled models, whereas multitask models marginally improve the performance for en-es and keep the performance of the single language models for en-fr. This again shows that multitask learning is an effective technique for robust prediction models over several training and test conditions.

Single versus crosslingual pooled and multitask models on non-overlapping data on pooled test set We posited that the main reason behind the marginal or non-existing improvement of the crosslingual transfer learning shown in Figure 6 is

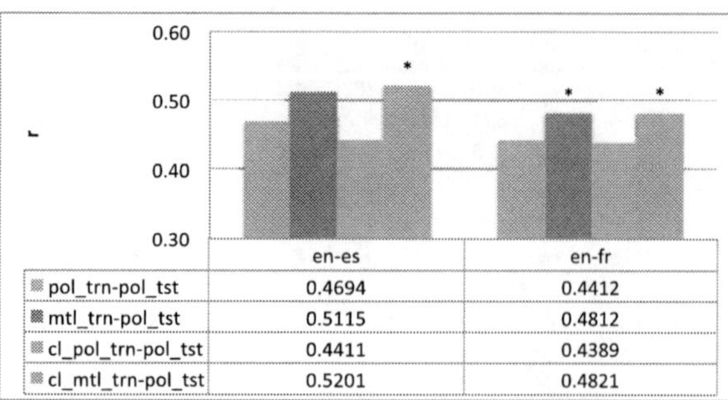

	en-es	en-fr
pol_trn-pol_tst	0.4694	0.4412
mtl_trn-pol_tst	0.5115	0.4812
cl_pol_trn-pol_tst	0.4411	0.4389
cl_mtl_trn-pol_tst	0.5201	0.4821

Figure 6: Pearson's correlation with single vs crosslingual models: en-es and en-fr pooled test sets

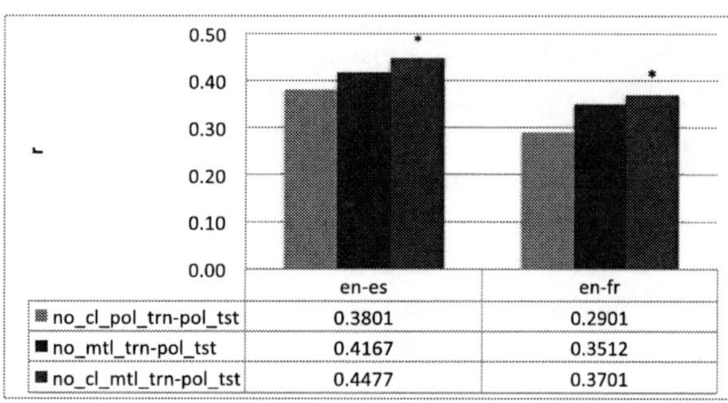

	en-es	en-fr
no_cl_pol_trn-pol_tst	0.3801	0.2901
no_mtl_trn-pol_tst	0.4167	0.3512
no_cl_mtl_trn-pol_tst	0.4477	0.3701

Figure 7: Pearson's correlation with non-overlapping language data: single vs crosslingual models on en-es and en-fr on pooled test sets

the large overlap between the source segments in the datasets for the two language pairs, as mentioned in Section 4: 63,763 instances, which comprise 82% of the en-fr instances, and 65% of the en-es instances. This becomes an issue because nearly half of the quality estimation features are based on the source segments. Therefore, we conducted an experiment with only 41,930 non-overlapping segments in the two languages. This experiment is only possible with pooled test sets, as otherwise too few (if any) instances are left for some post-editors. The results, shown in Figure 7, are much more promising. The Figure compares single language and crosslingual multitask and pooled models on the polled test sets for both languages. It is interesting to note that, while the absolute figures are lower when compared to models trained on all data (Figures 5 and 6), the relative improvements of multitask crosslingual models over multitask single language models are much larger.

7 Conclusions

We investigated multitask learning with GP for QE based on large datasets with multiple annotators and language pairs. The experiments were performed with various settings for training QE models to study the cases where data is available in abundance, versus cases with less data. Our results show that multitask learning leads to improved results in all settings against individual and pooled models. Individual models perform reasonably well in cases where a large amount of training data for individual annotators is available. Yet, by learning from data by multiple annotators, multitask learning models still perform better (in most cases) or at least the same as these models. Testing models on data for individual annotators is a novel experimental setting that we explored in this paper. Another novel finding was the advantage of multitask models in crosslingual settings, where individual models performed poorly and pooled models brought little gain.

Acknowledgments

This work was supported by the QT21 (H2020 No. 645452) and Cracker (H2020 No. 645357). We would like to thank Bruno Pouliquen and Peter Baker for providing the WIPO data, resources and revising the details in Section 4.1.

References

Mauricio A. Álvarez, Lorenzo Rosasco, and Neil D. Lawrence. 2012. Kernels for Vector-Valued Functions: a Review. *Foundations and Trends in Machine Learning*, pages 1–37.

Daniel Beck, Kashif Shah, Trevor Cohn, and Lucia Specia. 2013. SHEF-Lite: When less is more for translation quality estimation. In *Eighth Workshop on Statistical Machine Translation*, WMT, pages 337–342, Sofia, Bulgaria.

Daniel Beck, Trevor Cohn, and Lucia Specia. 2014. Joint emotion analysis via multi-task gaussian processes. In *Conference on Empirical Methods in Natural Language Processing*, EMNLP, pages 1798–1803, Doha, Qatar.

Ondej Bojar, Christian Buck, Chris Callison-Burch, Christian Federmann, Barry Haddow, Philipp Koehn, Christof Monz, Matt Post, Radu Soricut, and Lucia Specia. 2013. Findings of the 2013 Workshop on Statistical Machine Translation. In *Eigth Workshop on Statistical Machine Translation*, pages 1–44.

Ondrej Bojar, Christian Buck, Christian Federmann, Barry Haddow, Philipp Koehn, Johannes Leveling, Christof Monz, Pavel Pecina, Matt Post, Herve Saint-Amand, Radu Soricut, Lucia Specia, and Aleš Tamchyna. 2014. Findings of the 2014 Workshop on Statistical Machine Translation. In *Ninth Workshop on Statistical Machine Translation*, pages 12–58, Baltimore, Maryland.

Ondrej Bojar, Barry Haddow, Matthias Huck, and Philipp Koehn. 2015. Findings of the 2015 workshop on statistical machine translation. In *Tenth Workshop on Statistical Machine Translation*, pages 1–42, Lisboa, Portugal.

Edwin V. Bonilla, Kian Ming A. Chai, and Christopher K. I. Williams. 2008. Multi-task Gaussian Process Prediction. *Advances in Neural Information Processing Systems*.

Chris Callison-Burch, Philipp Koehn, Christof Monz, Matt Post, Radu Soricut, and Lucia Specia. 2012. Findings of the 2012 Workshop on Statistical Machine Translation. In *Seventh Workshop on Statistical Machine Translation*.

Rich Caruana. 1997. Multitask Learning. *Machine Learning*, 28:41–75.

Giovanni Cavallanti, Nicolo Cesa-Bianchi, and Claudio Gentile. 2010. Linear algorithms for online multitask classification. *The Journal of Machine Learning Research*, 11:2901–2934.

Trevor Cohn and Lucia Specia. 2013. Modelling annotator bias with multi-task gaussian processes: An application to machine translation quality estimation. In *51st Annual Meeting of the Association for Computational Linguistics*, ACL, pages 32–42, Sofia, Bulgaria.

Hal Daume III. 2007. Frustratingly easy domain adaptation. In *Proceedings of the 45th Annual Meeting of the Association of Computational Linguistics*, pages 256–263, Prague, Czech Republic, June. Association for Computational Linguistics.

José G.C. de Souza, Marco Turchi, and Matteo Negri. 2014a. Machine translation quality estimation across domains. In *Proceedings of COLING 2014, the 25th International Conference on Computational Linguistics: Technical Papers*, pages 409–420, Dublin, Ireland, August. Dublin City University and Association for Computational Linguistics.

José G.C. de Souza, Marco Turchi, and Matteo Negri. 2014b. Towards a combination of online and multitask learning for mt quality estimation: a preliminary study. In *Workshop on Interactive and Adaptive Machine Translation*.

José G.C. de Souza, Matteo Negri, Elisa Ricci, and Marco Turchi. 2015. Online multitask learning for machine translation quality estimation. In *Proceedings of the 53rd Annual Meeting of the Association for Computational Linguistics and the 7th International Joint Conference on Natural Language Processing (Volume 1: Long Papers)*, pages 219–228, Beijing, China.

Jenny Rose Finkel and Christopher D Manning. 2009. Hierarchical bayesian domain adaptation. In *Proceedings of Human Language Technologies: The 2009 Annual Conference of the North American Chapter of the Association for Computational Linguistics*, pages 602–610. Association for Computational Linguistics.

Maarit Koponen. 2012. Comparing human perceptions of post-editing effort with post-editing operations. In *Proceedings of the Seventh Workshop on Statistical Machine Translation*, pages 181–190, Montréal, Canada.

Bruno Pouliquen, Christophe Mazenc, and Aldo Iorio. 2011. Tapta: a user-driven translation system for patent documents based on domain-aware statistical machine translation. In *Proceedings of the 15th conference of the European Association for Machine Translation*, pages 5–12, Leuven, Belgium.

Carl Edward Rasmussen and Christopher K. I. Williams. 2006. *Gaussian processes for machine learning*, volume 1. MIT Press Cambridge.

Kashif Shah and Lucia Specia. 2014. Quality estimation for translation selection. In *17th Annual Conference of the European Association for Machine Translation*, EAMT, pages 109–116, Dubrovnik, Croatia.

Kashif Shah, Trevor Cohn, and Lucia Specia. 2013. An Investigation on the Effectiveness of Features for Translation Quality Estimation. In *Proceedings of MT Summit XIV*.

Edward Snelson and Zoubin Ghahramani. 2006. Sparse gaussian processes using pseudo-inputs. In *Advances in neural information processing systems*, pages 1257–1264.

Matthew Snover, Bonnie Dorr, Richard Schwartz, Linnea Micciulla, and John Makhoul. 2006. A study of translation edit rate with targeted human annotation. In *Proceedings of the 7th Conference of the Association for Machine Translation in the Americas (AMTA)*, pages 223–231.

Lucia Specia, Kashif Shah, Jose G.C. de Souza, and Trevor Cohn. 2013. Quest - a translation quality estimation framework. In *51st Annual Meeting of the Association for Computational Linguistics: System Demonstrations*, ACL, pages 79–84, Sofia, Bulgaria.

E. J. Williams. 1959. *Regression analysis*. Wiley New York.

Conversational Markers of Constructive Discussions

Vlad Niculae and **Cristian Danescu-Niculescu-Mizil**

{vlad|cristian}@cs.cornell.edu

Cornell University

Abstract

Group discussions are essential for organizing every aspect of modern life, from faculty meetings to senate debates, from grant review panels to papal conclaves. While costly in terms of time and organization effort, group discussions are commonly seen as a way of reaching better decisions compared to solutions that do not require coordination between the individuals (e.g. voting)—through discussion, the sum becomes greater than the parts. However, this assumption is not irrefutable: anecdotal evidence of wasteful discussions abounds, and in our own experiments we find that over 30% of discussions are unproductive.

We propose a framework for analyzing conversational dynamics in order to determine whether a given task-oriented discussion is worth having or not. We exploit conversational patterns reflecting the *flow of ideas* and the *balance* between the participants, as well as their linguistic choices. We apply this framework to conversations naturally occurring in an online collaborative world exploration game developed and deployed to support this research. Using this setting, we show that linguistic cues and conversational patterns extracted from the first 20 seconds of a team discussion are predictive of whether it will be a wasteful or a productive one.

1 Introduction

Working in teams is a common strategy for decision making and problem solving, as building on effective social interaction and on the abilities of each member can enable a team to outperform lone individuals. Evidence shows that teams often perform better than individuals (Williams and Sternberg, 1988) and even have high chances of reaching

correct answers when all team members were previously wrong (Laughlin and Adamopoulos, 1980). Furthermore, team performance is not a factor of individual intelligence, but of *collective intelligence* (Woolley et al., 2010), with interpersonal interactions and emotional intelligence playing an important role (Jordan et al., 2002).

Yet, as most people can attest from experience, team interaction is not always smooth, and poor coordination can lead to unproductive meetings and wasted time. In fact, Romano Jr and Nunamaker Jr (2001) report that one third of work-related meetings in the U. S. are considered unproductive, while a 2005 Microsoft employee survey reports that 69% of meetings are ineffective.[1] As such, many grow cynical of meetings.

Computational methods with the ability to reliably recognize unproductive discussions could have an important impact on our society. Ideally, such a system could provide actionable information as a discussion progresses, indicating whether it is likely to turn out to be productive, rather than a waste of time. In this paper we focus on the conversational aspects of productive interactions and take the following steps:

- introduce a *constructiveness* framework that allows us to characterize teams where discussion enables better performance than the individuals could reach, and, conversely, teams better off not having discussed at all (Section 3);

- create a setting that is conducive to decision-making discussions, where all steps of the process (e.g., individual answers, intermediate guesses) are observable to researchers: the *StreetCrowd* game (Sections 4–5);

---

[1] money.cnn.com/2005/03/16/technology/survey/

Proceedings of NAACL-HLT 2016, pages 568–578,
San Diego, California, June 12-17, 2016. ©2016 Association for Computational Linguistics

- develop a novel framework for conversational analysis in small group discussions, studying aspects such as the flow of ideas, conversational dynamics, and group balance (Sections 6–7).

We reveal differences in the collective decision process characteristic of productive and unproductive teams, and show that these differences are reflected in their conversational patterns. For example, the language used when new ideas are introduced and adopted encodes important discriminative cues. Measures of interactional balance and language matching (Niederhoffer and Pennebaker, 2002; Danescu-Niculescu-Mizil et al., 2011) also prove to be informative, suggesting that more balanced discussions are most productive. Our results underline the potential held by computational approaches to conversational dynamics. To encourage further work in this direction, we render our dataset of task-oriented discussions and our feature-extraction code publicly available.[2]

2 Related Work

Existing computational work on task-oriented group interaction is largely focused on how well the team performs. Coetzee et al. (2015) deployed and studied the impact of a chat-based team interaction platform in massive open online courses, finding that teams reach more correct answers than individuals, and that the experience is more enjoyable. One often studied experimental setting is the HCRC Map Task Corpus (Anderson et al., 1991), consisting of 128 conversations between pairs of people, where a designated one gives directions to the other. This simplified setting avoids issues like role establishment and leadership. Reitter and Moore (2007) find that successful dialogs are characterized by long-term adaptation and alignment of linguistic structures at syntactic, lexical and character level. A notable feature of this work is the *success prediction* task attempted using only the first 5 minutes of conversation. Other attempts use authority level features inspired from negotiation theory, experimental meta-features, task-specific features (Mayfield et al., 2011), and sociolinguistic spelling differences (Mayfield et al., 2012). Another research path

uses negotiation tasks from the Inspire dataset (Kersten and Zhang, 2003), a collection of 1525 online bilateral negotiations where roles are fixed (buyer and seller) and success is defined by the sale going through. Sokolova et al. (2008) use a bag-of-words model and investigate the importance of temporal aspects. Sokolova and Lapalme (2012) measure informativeness, quantified by lexical sets of degrees, scalars and comparatives.

Research on success in groups with more than two members is less common. Friedberg et al. (2012) model the grades of 27 group assignments from a class using measures of average entrainment, finding task-specific words to be a strong cue. Jung (2011) shows how the affective balance expressed in teams correlates with performance on engineering tasks, in 30 teams of up to 4 students. In a related study the balance in the first 5 minutes of an interaction is found predictive of performance (Jung et al., 2012). None of the research we are aware of controls for initial skill or potential of the team members.

In management science, network analysis reveals that certain subgraphs found in long-term, structured teams indicate better performance, as rated by senior managers (Cummings and Cross, 2003); controlled experiments show that optimal structures depend on the complexity of the task (Guetzkow and Simon, 1955; Bavelas, 1950). These studies, as well as much of the research on effective team crowdsourcing (Lasecki et al., 2012; Wang et al., 2011, *inter alia*), do not focus on linguistic and conversational factors.

3 Constructive Discussions

The first hurdle is to reliably quantify how productive group conversations are. In problem-solving, the ultimate goal is to find the correct answer, or, failing that, to come as close to it as possible. To quantify closeness to the correct answer, a *score* is often used, such that better guesses get higher scores; for example, school grades.

In contrast, our goal is to measure how productive a team's interaction is. Scores are measures of correctness, so using them as a proxy for interaction quality is not ideal: a team of straight A students can manage to get an A on a project without exchanging ideas, while a group of D students getting a B is

---

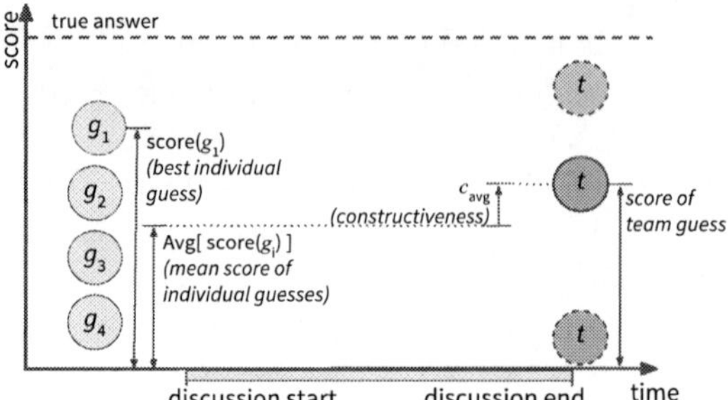

Figure 1: Intuitive sketch for constructiveness. The solid green circle corresponds a team guess following a constructive discussion ($c_{avg} > 0$), the dashed green circle corresponds to the scenario of a team that outperforms its best member ($c_{best} > 0$), while the dashed red circle corresponds to a team that underperforms its worst member ($c_{worst} < 0$).

more interesting. In the latter case, the team's improved performance is likely to come from a good discussion and an efficient exchange of complementary ideas—making the sum greater than the parts.

To capture this intuition we say a team discussion is *constructive* if it results in an improvement over the potential of the individuals. We can then quantify the degree of constructiveness c_{avg} as the improvement of the team score t over the mean of the initial scores g_i of the N individuals in the team:

$$c_{avg} = \text{score}(t) - \frac{\sum_{i=1}^{N} \text{score}(g_i)}{N}.$$

The higher c_{avg} is, the more the team's answer, *after discussion*, improves upon the individuals' average performance *before discussion*; zero constructiveness ($c_{avg} = 0$) means the team performed no better than its members did before discussing, while negative constructiveness ($c_{avg} < 0$) corresponds to non-constructive discussions.[3] Figure 1 sketches the idea visually: the dark green circle corresponds to the team's score after a constructive discussion ($c_{avg} > 0$), being above the average individual score.

Since individuals answers can sometimes vary widely, we also consider the extreme cases of teams

that perform better than the best team member ($c_{best} > 0$) and worse than the worst member ($c_{worst} < 0$), where:

$$c_{best} = \text{score}(t) - \max_i \text{score}(g_i)$$

$$c_{worst} = \text{score}(t) - \min_i \text{score}(g_i).$$

One way to think of the extreme cases is to imagine a team supervisor that collects the individual answers and aggregates them, without any external information. An oracle supervisor can do no better than choosing the best answer. The discussion and interaction of teams where $c_{best} > 0$ leads to a better answer than such an oracle could achieve. (One such scenario is illustrated by the dashed light green circle in Figure 1.) Similarly, teams where $c_{worst} < 0$ waste their time completely, as simply picking one of their members' answers at random is guaranteed to do better. (The dashed red circle in Figure 1 illustrates this scenario.)

The most important aspect of the constructiveness framework, in contrast to traditional measures of correctness or success, is that all constructiveness measures are designed to control for initial performance or potential of the team members, in order to focus on the effect of the discussion.[4]

In settings of importance, the true answer is not known a priori, and this constructiveness cannot be calculated directly. We therefore seek out to model constructiveness using observable conversational and linguistic correlates (Sections 6–7). To develop such a model, we design a large-scale experimental setting where the true answer is available to researchers, but unknown by the players (Section 4).

4 Experimental setting

4.1 StreetCrowd

In order to study the constructiveness of task-oriented group discussion, we need a setting that is conducive to decision-making discussions, where all steps of the process (individual answers, intermediate guesses, group discussions and decisions) are observable. Furthermore, to study at scale, we need to

---

[3] From an operational perspective, a team can choose, instead of having a discussion, to aggregate individual guesses, e.g., by majority voting or averaging. Non-constructive discussions roughly correspond to cases where such an aggregate guess would actually be better than what the team discussion would accomplish.

[4] Due to its relative nature, constructiveness also accounts for variation in task difficulty in most scenarios. For example, in terms of c_{worst}, when a team cannot even match its worst performing member, this is a sign of poor team interaction even if the task is particularly challenging.

find a class of complex tasks with known solutions that can be automatically generated, but that cannot be easily solved by simply querying search engines.

With these constraints in mind, we built *StreetCrowd*, an online multi-player world exploration game.[5] *StreetCrowd* is played in teams of at least two players and is built around a geographic puzzle: determining your location based on first-person images from the ground level.[6] Each location generates a new puzzle.

Solo phase. Each player has 3 minutes to navigate the surroundings, explore, and try to find clues. This happens independently and without communicating. At the end, the player is asked to make a guess by placing a marker on the world's map, and is prompted for an explanation and for a confidence level. The answer is not yet revealed.

Team phase. The team must then decide on a single, common guess. To accomplish this, all teammates are placed in a chatroom and are provided with a map and a shared marker. Any player can move the marker at any point during the discussion. The game ends when all players agree on the answer, or when the time limit is reached. An example discussion is given in Figure 4.

Guesses are scored according to their distance to the true location using the spherical law of cosines:

$$\text{score}(\text{guess}, \text{true}) = -Rd(\text{guess}, \text{true})$$

where d is the arc distance on a sphere, and R denotes the radius of the earth, assumed spherical. The score is given by the negative distance in kilometers, such that higher means better. To motivate players and emphasize collaboration, the main *StreetCrowd* page displays a leaderboard consisting of the best team players.

The key aspects of the *StreetCrowd* design are:

- The puzzles are complex and can be generated automatically in large numbers;

- The true answers are known to researchers, but hard to obtain without solving the puzzle, allowing for objective evaluation of both individual and group performance;

- Scoring is continuous rather than discrete, allowing us to quantify degrees of improvement and capture incremental effects;

- Each teammate has a different *solo phase* experience and background knowledge, making it possible for the group discussion to shed light on new ideas;

- The puzzles are engaging and naturally conducive to collaboration, avoiding the use of monetary incentives that can bias behavior.

4.2 Preprocessing

In the first 8 months, over 1400 distinct players participated in over 2800 *StreetCrowd* games. We tokenize and part-of-speech tag the conversations.[7] Before analysis, due to the public nature of the game, we perform several filtering and quality check steps. **Discarding trivial games.** We remove all games that the developers took part in. We filter games where the team fails to provide a guess, where fewer than two team members engage in the team chat, and puzzles with insufficient samples. **Preventing and detecting cheating.** The *StreetCrowd* tutorial asks players to avoid using external resources to look up clues and get an unfair advantage. To prevent cheating, we detect and block chat messages that link to websites, and we employ cookies and user accounts to prevent people from playing the same puzzle multiple times. To identify games that slip through this net, we flag cases where the team, or any individual player, guesses within 10 km of the correct answer, and leaves the window while playing. We further remove a small set of games where the players confess to cheating in the chat.

After filtering, our dataset consists of 1450 games on 70 different puzzles, with an average of 3.9 games per unique player, and 12.1 messages and 64.5 words in an average conversation.

5 Constructiveness in StreetCrowd

We find that, indeed, most of the games are constructive. There are, however, 32% non-constructive

---

[5] http://streetcrowd.us/log_in
(the experiment was approved by the IRB).
[6] We embed Google Street View data.

[7] We use the *TweetNLP* toolkit (Owoputi et al., 2013) with a tag set developed for Twitter data. Manual examination reveals this approach to be well suited for online chat data.

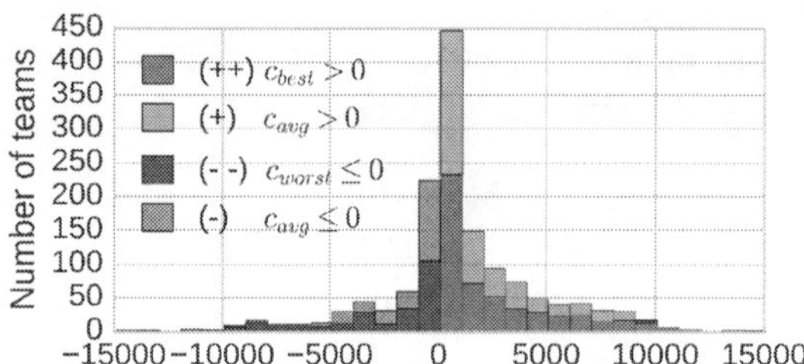

Figure 2: Distribution of team constructiveness.

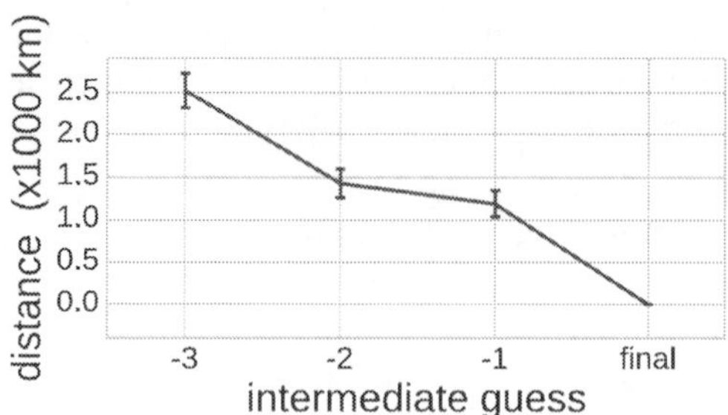

(a) Distance between the last three intermediate guesses and the final guess.

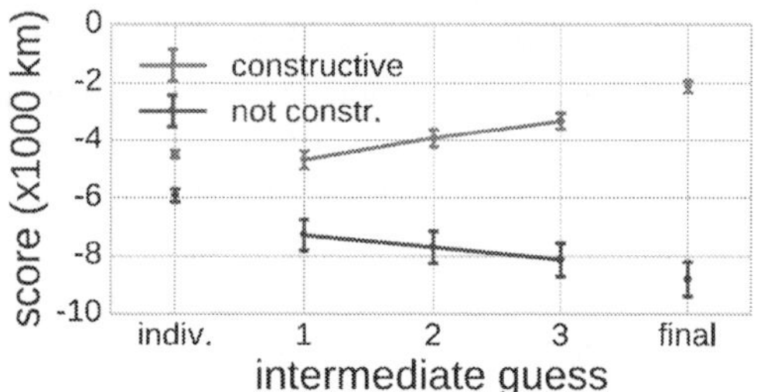

(b) Score of the first three intermediate guesses; the mean score of the initial individual guesses and the score of the final team guess are shown for reference.

Figure 3: Intermediate guesses offer a glimpse at the decision process: (a) guesses converge rather than zig-zag (b) in constructive games, guesses get incrementally better than the mean individual score, while in non-constructive games, they get worse. (Games with ≥ 3 intermediate guesses.)

games ($c_{\text{avg}} < 0$); this reflects very closely the survey by Romano Jr and Nunamaker Jr (2001). Interestingly, in 36% of games, the team arrives at a better answer than any of the individual guesses ($c_{\text{best}} > 0$). The flip side is also remarkably common, with 17% of teams performing even worse than the worst individual ($c_{\text{worst}} < 0$). The distribution of constructiveness is shown in Figure 2: the fat tails indicate that cases of large improvements and large deterioration are not uncommon.

Collective decision process. Due to the full instrumentation of the game interface, we can investigate how constructiveness emerges out of the team's interaction. The team's intermediate guesses during discussion confirm that a meaningful process leads to the final team decision: guesses get closer and closer to the final submitted guess (Figure 3a); in other words, the team *converges* to their final guess.

Notably, when considering how *correct* the intermediate guesses are, we notice an important difference between the way constructive and non-constructive teams converge to their final guess (Figure 3b). During their collaborative decision process, constructive teams make guesses that get closer and closer to the correct answer; in contrast, non-constructive teams make guesses that take them farther from the correct answer. This observation has two important consequences. First, it shows that the two types of teams behave differently throughout, suggesting we could potentially detect non-constructive discussions early on, using interaction patterns. Second, it emphasizes the potential practical value of such a task: stopping a non-constructive team early could lead to a better answer than if they would carry on.

6 Conversation analysis

The process of team convergence revealed in the previous section suggests a relation between the interaction leading to the final group decision and the relative quality of the outcome. In this section, we develop a conversation analysis framework aimed at characterizing this relation. This framework relies on conversational patterns and linguistic features, while steering away from lexicalized cues that might not generalize well beyond our experimental setting. To enable reproducibility, we make available the feature extraction code and the hand-crafted resources on which it relies.[8]

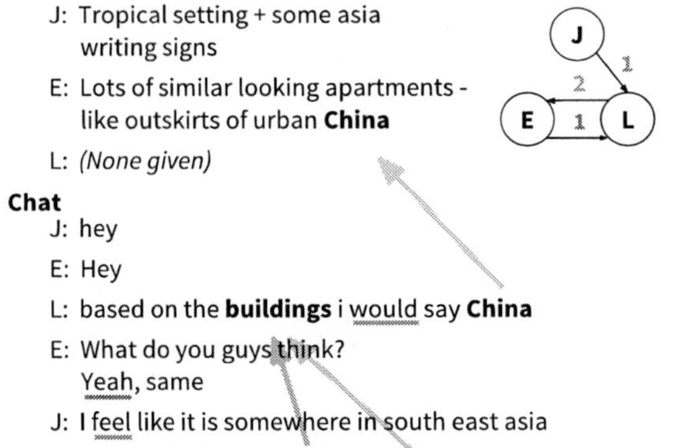

Figure 4: Example (constructive) conversation and the corresponding flow of ideas. Idea mentions are in bold, and relevant word classess are underlined. Arrow colors map to introducer–adopter pairs, matching the edges in the top-right graph.

6.1 Idea flow

Task-oriented discussions are the the primary way of exchanging ideas and opinions between the group members; some are quickly discarded while others prove useful to the final guess. The arrows in Figure 4 show how ideas are introduced and discussed in that example conversation. We attempt to capture the shape in which the ideas flow in the discussion. In particular, we are interested in how many ideas are discussed, how widely they are adopted, who tends to introduce them, and how.

We consider as candidate ideas all nouns, proper nouns, adjectives and verbs that are not stopwords. As soon as a candidate idea introduced by a player is *adopted* by another, we count it. Henceforth, we'll refer to such adopted ideas simply as *ideas*. In general chat domains, state-of-the-art models of conver-

sation structure use unsupervised probabilistic models (Ritter et al., 2010; Elsner and Charniak, 2010). Since *StreetCrowd* conversations are short and focused, the *adoption* filter is sufficient to accurately capture what ideas are being discussed; a manual examination of the ideas reveals almost exclusively place names and words such as *flag*, *sign*, *road*—highly relevant clues in the context of *StreetCrowd*. In Figure 4, three ideas are adopted: *China*, *buildings* and *Shanghai*. The only idea adopted by all players is *buildings*, a good signal that this was the most important clue. A notable limitation is that this approach cannot capture the connections between *Shanghai* and *China*, or *buildings* and *apartments*. Further work is needed to robustly capture such variations in idea flow, as they could reveal trajectories (discussion getting more specific or more vague) or lexical choice disagreement.

Balance in idea contributions between the team members is a good indicator of productive discussions. In particular, in the best teams (the ones that outperform the best player, i.e., $c_{best} > 0$) the most idea-prolific player introduces fewer ideas, on average, than in the rest of the games (Figure 5a, $p = 0.01$).[9] In Figure 4, E is the most prolific player and only introduces two ideas. To further capture the balance in contribution between the team members, we use the entropy of the number ideas introduced by each player. We also count the number of ideas adopted unanimously as an indicator of convergence in the conversation.

In terms of the overall number of ideas discussed, both the best teams (the ones that outperform the best player) and the worst teams (the ones that perform worse than the worst player) discuss fewer ideas than the rest (Figure 5b, $p = 0.006$). Indeed, an ideal interaction would avoid distracting ideas, but in teams with communication breakdowns, members might fail to adequately discuss the ideas that led them to their individual guesses.

The language used to introduce new ideas can indicate confidence or hesitation; in Figure 4, a hedge (*would*) is used when introducing the *buildings* cue. We find that, in teams that outperform the best player, ideas are less likely to be accom-

---

[9] All p-values reported reported in this section are based on one-sided Mann-Whitney rank statistical significance tests.

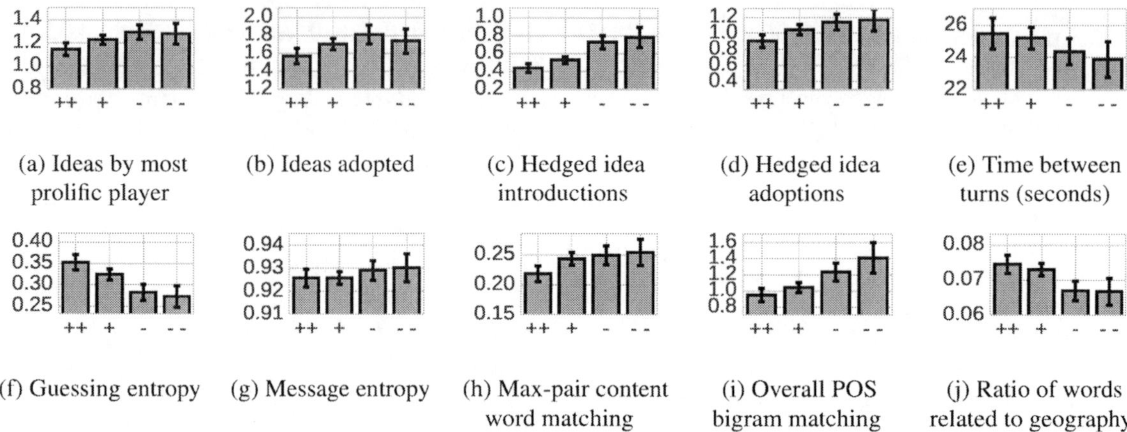

<table>
<tr><td>(a) Ideas by most prolific player</td><td>(b) Ideas adopted</td><td>(c) Hedged idea introductions</td><td>(d) Hedged idea adoptions</td><td>(e) Time between turns (seconds)</td></tr>
<tr><td>(f) Guessing entropy</td><td>(g) Message entropy</td><td>(h) Max-pair content word matching</td><td>(i) Overall POS bigram matching</td><td>(j) Ratio of words related to geography</td></tr>
</table>

Figure 5: Averages for some of the predictive features, based on idea flow (a-d), balance (e-i), and lexicons (j). Error bars denote standard errors. Legend: (++): teams that do better than their best member ($N = 525$), (+): constructive ($N = 986$), (-): non-constructive ($N = 464$), (- -): worse than worst member ($N = 248$).

panied by hedge words when introduced (Figure 5c, $p < 10^{-4}$), showing less hesitation. Furthermore, the level of confidence used when players adopt others' ideas is also informative (Figure 5d). Interestingly, overall occurrences of certainty and hedge words (detailed in Section 6.3) are not predictive, suggesting that ideas are good selectors for important discussion segments.

6.2 Interaction dynamics

Balance. Interpersonal balance has been shown to be predictive of team performance (Jung, 2011; Jung et al., 2012) and, similarly, forms of linguistic balance have been shown to characterize stable relationships (Niculae et al., 2015). Here we focus on balance in contributions to the discussion and the decision process. In search of measures applicable to teams of arbitrary sizes, we use binary indicators of whether all players participate in the discussion and in moving the marker, as well as whether at least two players move the marker. To measure team balance with respect to continuous user-level features, we use the entropy of these features:

$$\text{balance}(S) = -\sum_{\bar{s} \in S} \bar{s} \log_{|S|} \bar{s},$$

where, for a given feature, S is the set of its values for each user, normalized to sum to 1. For instance, the chat message entropy is 1 if everybody chats equally, and decreases toward 0 as one or more

players dominate. We use the entropy of the number of messages, words per message, and number of intermediate guesses. In teams that outperform the best player, users take turns controlling the marker more uniformly (Figure 5f, $p = 0.006$), adding further evidence that well-balanced teams perform best.

Language matching. We investigate matching at stopword, content word, and POS tag bigram level: the stopword matching at a turn is given by the number of stopwords from the earlier message repeated in the reply, divided by the total number of distinct stopwords to choose from; similarly for the rest. We micro-average over the conversation:

$$\text{match} = \frac{\sum_{(\text{msg},\text{reply}) \in \text{Turns}} |\text{msg} \cap \text{reply}|}{\sum_{(\text{msg},\text{reply}) \in \text{Turns}} |\text{msg}|}.$$

We also micro-average at the player-pair level, and use the maximum pair value as a feature. This gives an indication of how cohesive the closest pair is, which can be a sign of the level of power imbalance between the two (Danescu-Niculescu-Mizil et al., 2012). Figure 5h shows that in teams that outperform the best individual the most cohesive pair matches fewer content words ($p = 0.023$). Overall matching is also significant, notably in terms of part-of-speech bigrams; in teams that outperform the best individual there is less overall matching (Figure 5i, $p = 0.007$). These results suggest that in constructive teams the relationships between the members are less subordinate.

Agreement and confidence. We capture the amount of agreement and disagreement using high-precision keywords and filters validated on a subset of the data. (For instance, the word *sure* marks agreement if found at the beginning of a message, but not otherwise.) In Figure 4, agreement signals are underlined with purple; the team exhibits no disagreement.

The relative position of successive guesses made can also indicate whether the team is refining a guess or contradicting each other. We measure the median distance between intermediate guesses, as well as between guesses made by different players; in constructive teams, the jumps between different player guesses are smaller ($p < 10^{-16}$).

Before the discussion starts, players are asked to self-evaluate their confidence in their individual guesses. Constructive teams have more confident members on average ($p < 10^{-5}$).

6.3 Other linguistic features

Length and variation. We measure the average number of words per message, the total number of words used to express the *solo phase* reasons, and the overall type/token ratio of the conversation. We also measure responsiveness in terms of the mean time between turns and the total number of turns.

Psycholinguistic lexicons. We use hand-crafted lexicons inspired from LIWC (Tausczik and Pennebaker, 2010) to capture certainty and pronoun use. For example, the conversation in Figure 4 has two confident phrases, underlined in red. We also use a custom hedging lexicon adapted from Hyland (2005) for conversational data; hedging words are underlined in blue in Figure 4. To estimate how grounded the conversation is, we measure the average *concreteness* of all content nouns, adjectives, adverbs and verbs, using scalar word and bigram ratings from Brysbaert et al. (2014).[10] Concreteness reflects the degree to which a word denotes something perceptible, as opposed to ideas and concepts. Words like *soil* and *coconut* are highly concrete, while words like *trust* have low concreteness.

Game-specific words. We put together a lexicon of geography terms and place names, to capture task-

Features	Full conversation			First 20s		
	(++)	(+)	(- -)	(++)	(+)	(- -)
Baseline	.51	.52	.55	.52	.50	.54
Linguistic	.54	.52	.50	.50	.51	.50
Interaction	.55†	.56†	.53	.55†	.57*	.56
POS	.55†	.59*	.55	.54	.54	.53
All	.56*	.60*	.56	.56*	.57*	.57†

Table 1: Cross-validation AUC scores. Significantly better than chance scores after 5000 permutations denoted with $\star$ ($p < 0.05$) and $\dagger$ ($p < 0.1$).

specific discussion. We use a small set of words specific to the *StreetCrowd* interface, such as *map, marker,* and *game*, to capture phatic communication. Figure 5j shows that constructive teams tend to use more geography terms ($p = 0.008$), possibly because of more on-topic discussion and a more focused vocabulary.

Part-of-speech patterns. We use n-grams of coarse part-of-speech tags as a general way of capturing common syntactic patterns.

7 Predicting constructiveness

7.1 Experimental setup

So far we have characterized the relation between a team's interaction patterns and its level of productivity. This opens the door towards recognizing constructive and non-constructive interactions in realistic settings where the true answer is not known. Ideally, such an automatic system could prompt unproductive teams to reconsider their approach, or to aggregate their individual answers instead. With *early detection*, non-constructive discussions could be stopped or steered on the right track. In order to assess the feasibility of such a challenging task and to compare the predictive power of our features, we consider three classification objectives:

(++): Team outperforms its best member ($c_{\text{best}} > 0$)?

(+): Team is constructive ($c_{\text{avg}} > 0$)?

(- -): Team underperforms its worst member ($c_{\text{worst}} < 0$)?

To investigate *early detection*, we evaluate the classification performance when using data from only the first 20 seconds of the team's interaction.[11]

---

[10]We scale the ratings to lie in $[0, 1]$. We extrapolate to out-of-vocabulary words by regressing on dependency-based word embeddings (Levy and Goldberg, 2014); this approach is highly accurate (median absolute error of about 0.1).

[11]Measured from the first chat message or guess. For this evaluation, we remove teams where the first 20 seconds contain over 75% of the interaction, to avoid distorting the results with

Since all three objectives are imbalanced (Figure 2), we use the area under the ROC curve (AUC) as the performance metric, and we use logistic regression models. We perform 20 iterations of puzzle-aware shuffled train-validation splitting, followed by 5000 iterations on the best models, to estimate variance. This ensures that the models don't learn to overfit puzzle-specific signals. The combined model uses weighted model averaging. We use grid search for regularization parameters, feature extraction parameters, and combination weights.

7.2   Discussion of the results (Table 1)

We compare to a baseline consisting of the team size, average number of messages per player, and conversation duration. For comparison, a bag-of-words classifier does no better than chance and is on par with the baseline. We refer to idea flow and interaction dynamics features (Section 6.2) as *Interaction*, and to linguistic and lexical features (Section 6.3) as *Linguistic*. The combination model including baseline, interaction, linguistic and part-of-speech n-gram features, is consistently the best and significantly outperforms random guessing (AUC .50) in nearly all settings. While overall scores are modest, the results confirm that our conversational analysis framework has predictive power, and that the high-stakes task of *early prediction* is feasible. The language used when introducing and adopting ideas, together with balance and language matching features, are selected in nearly all settings. The least represented class (- -) has the highest variance in prediction, suggesting that more data collection is needed to successfully capture extreme cases. Useful POS patterns capture the amount of proper nouns and their contexts: proper nouns at the end of messages are indicative of constructiveness, while proper nouns followed by verbs are a negative feature. (The constructive discussion shown in Figure 4 has most proper nouns at the end of messages.)

A manual error analysis of the false positives and false negatives where our best model is most confident points to games with very short conversations and spelling mistakes, confirming that the noisy data problem causes learning and modeling difficulties.

teams who make their decision early, but take longer to submit. The 20 second threshold was chosen as a trade-off in terms of how much interaction it covers in the games.

8   Conclusions and Future Work

We developed a framework based on conversational dynamics in order to distinguish between productive and unproductive task-oriented discussions. By applying it to an online collaborative game we designed for this study, we reveal new interactions with conversational patterns. Constructive teams are generally well-balanced on multiple aspects, with team-members participating equally in proposing ideas and making guesses and showing little asymmetry in language matching. Also, the flow of ideas between teammates marks predictive linguistic cues, with the most constructive teams using fewer hedges when introducing and adopting ideas.

We show that such cues have predictive power even when extracted from the first 20 seconds of the conversations. In future work, improved classifiers could lead to a system that can intervene in non-constructive discussions early on, steering them on track and preventing wasted time.

Further improving classification performance on such a difficult task will hinge on better conversation processing tools, adequate for the domain and robust to the informal language style. In particular, we plan to develop and evaluate models for idea flow and (dis)agreement, using more advanced features (e.g., from dependency relations and knowledge graphs).

The *StreetCrowd* game is continuously accumulating more data, enabling further development on conversation analysis. Our full control over the game permits manipulation and intervention experiments that can further advance research on teamwork. In future work, we envision applying our framework to settings where teamwork takes place online, such as open-source software development, Wikipedia editing, or massive open online courses.

Acknowledgements We are particularly grateful to Bob West for the poolside chat that inspired the design of the game, to Daniel Garay, Jinjing Liang and Neil Parker for participating in its development, and to the numerous passionate players. We are also grateful to Natalya Bazarova, David Byrne, Mala Gaonkar, Lillian Lee, Sendhil Mullainathan, Andreas Veit, Connie Yuan, Justine Zhang and the anonymous reviewers for their insightful suggestions. This work was supported in part by a Google Faculty Research Award.

References

Anne H Anderson, Miles Bader, Ellen Gurman Bard, Elizabeth Boyle, Gwyneth Doherty, Simon Garrod, Stephen Isard, Jacqueline Kowtko, Jan McAllister, and Jim Miller. 1991. The HCRC map task corpus. *Language and speech*, 34(4):351–366.

Alex Bavelas. 1950. Communication patterns in task-oriented groups. *Journal of the Acoustical Society of America*.

Marc Brysbaert, Amy Beth Warriner, and Victor Kuperman. 2014. Concreteness ratings for 40 thousand generally known English word lemmas. *Behavior Research Methods*, 46(3):904–911.

Derrick Coetzee, Seongtaek Lim, Armando Fox, Bjorn Hartmann, and Marti A Hearst. 2015. Structuring interactions for large-scale synchronous peer learning. In *Proceedings of CSCW*.

Jonathon N Cummings and Rob Cross. 2003. Structural properties of work groups and their consequences for performance. *Social Networks*, 25(3):197–210.

Cristian Danescu-Niculescu-Mizil, Michael Gamon, and Susan Dumais. 2011. Mark my words! Linguistic style accommodation in social media. In *Proceedings of WWW*.

Cristian Danescu-Niculescu-Mizil, Lillian Lee, Bo Pang, and Jon Kleinberg. 2012. Echoes of power: Language effects and power differences in social interaction. In *Proceedings of WWW*.

Micha Elsner and Eugene Charniak. 2010. Disentangling chat. *Computational Linguistics*, 36(3):389–409.

Heather Friedberg, Diane Litman, and Susannah BF Paletz. 2012. Lexical entrainment and success in student engineering groups. In *Proceedings of the Spoken Language Technology Workshop*.

Harold Guetzkow and Herbert A Simon. 1955. The impact of certain communication nets upon organization and performance in task-oriented groups. *Management Science*, 1(3-4):233–250.

Ken Hyland. 2005. *Metadiscourse: Exploring interaction in writing*. Continuum.

Peter J Jordan, Neal M Ashkanasy, Charmine EJ Härtel, and Gregory S Hooper. 2002. Workgroup emotional intelligence: Scale development and relationship to team process effectiveness and goal focus. *Human Resource Management Review*, 12(2):195–214.

Malte F Jung, Jan Chong, and Larry Leifer. 2012. Group hedonic balance and pair programming performance: affective interaction dynamics as indicators of performance. In *Proceedings of SIGCHI*.

Malte F Jung. 2011. *Engineering team performance and emotion: Affective interaction dynamics as indicators of design team performance*. Ph.D. thesis, Stanford University.

Gregory E Kersten and Grant Zhang. 2003. Mining inspire data for the determinants of successful internet negotiations. *Central European Journal of Operations Research*, 11(3).

Walter S Lasecki, Christopher D Miller, Adam Sadilek, Andrew Abumoussa, Donato Borrello, Raja Kushalnagar, and Jeffrey P Bigham. 2012. Real-time captioning by groups of non-experts. In *Proceedings of UIST*.

Patrick R Laughlin and John Adamopoulos. 1980. Social combination processes and individual learning for six-person cooperative groups on an intellective task. *Journal of Personality and Social Psychology*, 38(6):941.

Omer Levy and Yoav Goldberg. 2014. Dependency-based word embeddings. In *Proceedings of ACL*.

Elijah Mayfield, Michael Garbus, David Adamson, and Carolyn Penstein Rosé. 2011. Data-driven interaction patterns: Authority and information sharing in dialogue. In *Proceedings of AAAI Fall Symposium on Building Common Ground with Intelligent Agents*.

Elijah Mayfield, David Adamson, Alexander Rudnicky, and Carolyn Penstein Rosé. 2012. Computational representation of discourse practices across populations in task-based dialogue. In *Proceedings of ICIC*.

Vlad Niculae, Srijan Kumar, Jordan Boyd-Graber, and Cristian Danescu-Niculescu-Mizil. 2015. Linguistic harbingers of betrayal: A case study on an online strategy game. In *Proceedings of ACL*.

Kate G Niederhoffer and James W Pennebaker. 2002. Linguistic style matching in social interaction. *Journal of Language and Social Psychology*, 21(4):337–360.

Olutobi Owoputi, Brendan O'Connor, Chris Dyer, Kevin Gimpel, Nathan Schneider, and Noah A Smith. 2013. Improved part-of-speech tagging for online conversational text with word clusters. In *Proceedings of NAACL*.

David Reitter and Johanna D Moore. 2007. Predicting success in dialogue. In *ACL*, volume 45, page 808.

Alan Ritter, Colin Cherry, Bill Dolan, et al. 2010. Unsupervised modeling of Twitter conversations. In *Proceedings of NAACL*.

Nicholas C Romano Jr and Jay F Nunamaker Jr. 2001. Meeting analysis: Findings from research and practice. In *Proceedings of HICSS*.

Marina Sokolova and Guy Lapalme. 2012. How much do we say? Using informativeness of negotiation text records for early prediction of negotiation outcomes. *Group Decision and Negotiation*, 21(3):363–379.

Marina Sokolova, Vivi Nastase, and Stan Szpakowicz. 2008. The telling tail: Signals of success in electronic negotiation texts.

Yla R Tausczik and James W Pennebaker. 2010. The psychological meaning of words: LIWC and computerized text analysis methods. *Journal of Language and Social Psychology*, 29(1):24.

Hao-Chuan Wang, Susan R Fussell, and Dan Cosley. 2011. From diversity to creativity: Stimulating group brainstorming with cultural differences and conversationally-retrieved pictures. In *Proceedings of CSCW*.

Wendy M Williams and Robert J Sternberg. 1988. Group intelligence: Why some groups are better than others. *Intelligence*, 12(4):351–377.

Anita Williams Woolley, Christopher F Chabris, Alex Pentland, Nada Hashmi, and Thomas W Malone. 2010. Evidence for a collective intelligence factor in the performance of human groups. *Science*, 330(6004):686–688.

Vision and Feature Norms: Improving automatic feature norm learning through cross-modal maps

Luana Bulat, Douwe Kiela and Stephen Clark
Computer Laboratory
University of Cambridge
`ltf24,douwe.kiela,stephen.clark@cl.cam.ac.uk`

Abstract

Property norms have the potential to aid a wide range of semantic tasks, provided that they can be obtained for large numbers of concepts. Recent work has focused on text as the main source of information for automatic property extraction. In this paper we examine property norm prediction from visual, rather than textual, data, using cross-modal maps learnt between property norm and visual spaces. We also investigate the importance of having a complete feature norm dataset, for both training and testing. Finally, we evaluate how these datasets and cross-modal maps can be used in an image retrieval task.

1 Introduction

Many cognitive theories of conceptual organisation assume that concepts are distributed representations over semantic primitives, often referred to as features or properties[1] (Tyler et al., 2000; Randall et al., 2004). That is, we can understand the meaning of a concept through its properties. For example, understanding the meaning of BANANA is closely related to understanding that it has properties such as *is a fruit*, *is yellow*, *is long*, *is sweet*, and knowing how these properties overlap with or differ from the properties of other concepts.

A number of property norm datasets, where humans were asked to list attributes of given concepts, have been collected to test this hypothesis (McRae et al., 2005; Vinson and Vigliocco, 2008; Devereux

et al., 2013). After having been used to test models of conceptual representation in cognitive science for decades (Randall et al., 2004; Cree et al., 2006), these datasets have proved to be useful in a wide range of semantic NLP tasks as well, including text simplification for limited vocabulary groups. More recently, property norms have been used as a proxy for perceptual information in a number of studies on multi-modal semantics (Andrews et al., 2009; Riordan and Jones, 2011; Silberer and Lapata, 2012; Roller and Im Walde, 2013; Hill and Korhonen, 2014). Such models aim to addres the grounding problem (Harnad, 1990) that distributional semantic models of language (Turney and Pantel, 2010; Clark, 2015) suffer from.

Property norms are a valuable source of semantic information, and can potentially be applied to a variety of NLP tasks, but are expensive to obtain because they involve intensive human annotation. The largest property norm dataset to date consists of just 638 concepts (Devereux et al., 2013), and the most widely cited one presents properties for only 541 concepts (McRae et al., 2005). If we are to use these datasets in large-scale semantic tasks, we would need to extend the currently available property norms by obtaining annotations for more than just a few hundred words.

The alternative to collecting more data through human annotation is to increase the coverage of property norms datasets by automatically inferring properties of concepts from easily accessible resources, such as textual data. Considering the fact that concepts, as well as their properties, are in linguistic form, the task then becomes a bootstrapping

---

[1]Throughout the paper we will be using the terms *properties*, *features norms* and *attributes* interchangeably.

Proceedings of NAACL-HLT 2016, pages 579–588,
San Diego, California, June 12-17, 2016. ©2016 Association for Computational Linguistics

one where we take advantage of the abundance of freely available textual corpora.

There are two strands of research that attempt to automatically obtain property norm data for new concepts. One approach is to automatically generate feature norms from text corpora by mining text data for a set of generalised property patterns (Kelly et al., 2014; Baroni et al., 2010; Barbu, 2008). Another avenue of research is inspired by Lazaridou et al. (2014) and Mikolov et al. (2013b) and tries to increase the coverage of feature norms through cross-modal mapping from linguistic information (Fagarasan et al., 2015).

Here, we follow recent trends in multi-modal semantics and explore automatic property norm extraction from visual, rather than textual, data. Obtaining property norms from visual information makes intuitive sense: information contained in the property norm datasets can often be attributed to extra-linguistic modalities—a large proportion of relevant properties are visual, auditory or tactile, rather than linguistic (e.g. *is_round, makes_noise, is_yellow*).

We show that such conceptual properties can be more accurately predicted through cross-modal mappings from raw perceptual information (i.e. image data) or multi-modal models (i.e. text and image data combined) rather than from purely textual information (Section 3). Furthermore, we analyse the quality of human collected property norm datasets and conclude that these are sparse and incomplete, meaning that there will be a lot of property annotations missing for a given concept (e.g. *has_legs* is not listed as a property of TORTOISE). We show that having a complete dataset can drastically increase the performance of automatic feature prediction, resulting in a truer evaluation (Section 3.5). Lastly, we demonstrate how property norm datasets could be used in an image retrieval task (Section 4), which opens up intriguing possibilities for retrieving concepts based on their visual properties.

2   Property norms

Property norming studies are set up in the following way: participants are asked to freely write down a list of properties for a given concept, whilst being encouraged to consider different kinds of properties

BANANA	CELLO
is_yellow, 29	a_musical_instrument, 26
a_fruit, 25	has_strings, 16
is_edible, 13	made_of_wood, 16
is_soft, 12	found_in_orchestras, 13
grows_on_trees, 11	is_large, 13
eaten_by_peeling, 10	requires_a_bow, 9

Table 1: Examples of features together with their production frequencies from MCRAE

(how the concept feels, smells, what it is used for *etc*).

Besides collecting lists of properties for the concepts of interest, a number of useful property statistics are also collected during these studies. For example, the number of participants that have produced the same property for a given concept (also called *production frequency*) and the number of concepts for which a particular property is listed in the dataset (number of *concepts per feature*) have been proposed as fundamental organising principles of cognitive models (Cree et al., 2006).

One of the most widely used property norm datasets is the one collected by McRae et al. (2005), henceforth MCRAE. It contains feature norms for a set of 541 concrete nouns. Each concept was seen by 30 participants and only features that were listed by at least 5 participants were recorded. The published dataset contains a total of 2526 features, with a mean of 13.7 features per concept. The numbers of features registered for a given concept range between 6 (for concepts like COLANDER or HARMONICA) and 26 (for FAWN). Table 1 lists some examples of properties that have been produced for BANANA and CELLO, taken from the MCRAE dataset.

The largest feature norm dataset published to date was developed by the Cambridge Centre for Speech, Language and Brain (Devereux et al., 2013). It contains semantic properties for 638 concrete concepts, with 415 of these also appearing in MCRAE. The data collection experiment was done similarly to McRae et al. (2005), using a production frequency cutoff of 5. The final dataset lists a total of 4359 features for the 638 concepts, with an average of 2.15 features per concept more than MCRAE. Although most property norm datasets have only collected property norms for nouns, Vinson and Vigliocco

Property type	Count	Examples
ENCYCLOPAEDIC	739	associated_with_vampires
FUNCTION	794	used_for_cutting
SMELL	7	is_musty, smells_bad
SOUND	55	barks, produces_music
TACTILE	39	is_scaly, is_hot, is_soft
TASTE	12	is_delicious, tastes_sour
TAXONOMIC	207	an_insect, a_vegetable
VISUAL(COLOUR)	34	is_black, is_white
VISUAL(FORM)	544	has_a_motor, made_of_lace
VISUAL(MOTION)	95	flies, jumps, runs_fast
TOTAL	2526	-

Table 2: Property types and associated examples from MCRAE

	is_yellow	a_fruit	is_edible	is_soft
BANANA	29	25	13	12
APPLE	7	24	0	0
BED	0	0	0	13

Table 3: Subspace of PROPNORM. Important to note that MCRAE is not complete, meaning that even though some properties are true of a given concept, they have not been produced by the human participants (e.g. the *is_edible* property for APPLE holds the value 0).

(2008) also include verbs in their study.

All the experiments presented in this paper were conducted on MCRAE. Our choice is motivated by the fact that this dataset has also been used in previous work on automated property norm prediction (Kelly et al., 2014; Fagarasan et al., 2015), besides being one of the largest publicly-available property norm datasets.

One aspect of feature norms that previous work (Kelly et al., 2014; Baroni et al., 2010; Barbu, 2008; Fagarasan et al., 2015) fails to capture is their multimodal nature. Even though the attributes are elicited in a linguistic form, and some properties (e.g. what things look like) are easier to verbalise than others (e.g. what things smell like), these datasets contain a variety of property types, ranging from visual and auditory to encyclopaedic and behavioural. Table 2 shows some examples for each of the 10 property types as defined and annotated in MCRAE. More than 25% of all features are visual (e.g. *is_yellow, is_round, made_of_metal*); hence a natural question that follows is whether images can be used in the property norm prediction task and how their performance compares to that of predicting properties from text.

3 Predicting feature norms from images through cross-modal mapping

Cross-modal maps represent a formalisation of the reference problem. For example, by inducing cross-modal maps between visual vectors and linguistic ones we can learn which images (represented as visual vectors) refer to which concepts (represented as text-based distributional vectors) (Lazaridou et al., 2014). This represents an extension of the object recognition problem, since we want to associate images with semantic representations of their depicted objects, rather than just with their label (Frome et al., 2013; Socher et al., 2014).

The benefit of this approach lies in its generalisation power: once a function between the two semantic spaces is learnt, it can be used to see how an unseen concept relates to other concepts, just by looking at an image of that concept. This is referred to as the zero-shot learning task (Palatucci et al., 2009; Lazaridou et al., 2014). Our task is to increase the coverage of the property norm datasets, meaning that we want to predict properties for new (unseen) concepts. For example, the concept WOLF is not included in MCRAE, but it would be desirable to know which of the properties in the dataset apply to it (e.g. *is_animal, has_4_legs*) and which don't (e.g. *a_bird, made_of_metal*).

3.1 Building modality-specific representations

We obtain distributed representations of concepts in the property-norm semantic space (henceforth PROPNORM) by simply treating MCRAE as a bag of 2526 properties, with the production frequencies representing the "co-occurrence counts" (Table 3).

Our visual space (henceforth VISUAL) consists of visual representations for all the 541 concepts in MCRAE, built as follows. First, we retrieve 10 images per concept from Google Images,[2] following previous work (Bergsma and Goebel, 2011; Kiela and Bottou, 2014). The image representations are then obtained by extracting the pre-softmax layer

---

[2] www.google.com/imghp (images were retrieved on 10 April 2015)

from a forward pass in a convolutional neural network that has been trained on the ImageNet classification task using Caffe (Jia et al., 2014). We aggregate images associated with a concept into an overall visually grounded representation by taking the mean of the individual image representations. The dimensionality of the visual vectors is 4096.

We also build three linguistic spaces (DISTRIB, SVD and EMBED), along the lines of Fagarasan et al. (2015). DISTRIB is a 10K-dimensional "vanilla" distributional semantic space, where the contexts are the top 10K most frequent lemmatised words (excluding stopwords) from the October 2013 Wikipedia dump. We use raw frequency counts with context windows being defined as sentence boundaries. SVD is a 300-dimensional SVD-reduced version of DISTRIB where PPMI has been applied to the raw counts. EMBED stands for the continuous vector representations from the log-linear skipgram model of Mikolov et al. (2013a). We used the publicly-available[3] representations that were trained on part of the Google News dataset (about 100 billion words).

We will also employ three multi-modal semantic spaces (VISUAL+DISTRIB, VISUAL+SVD, VISUAL+EMBED), in which the visual (VISUAL) and respective linguistic representations (DISTRIB, SVD, EMBED) are combined into a multi-modal representation by concatenating their respective L2-normalized representations.

3.2 Method and evaluation

Following previous work (Fagarasan et al., 2015; Kiela et al., 2015) we use partial least squares regression (PLSR)[4] to learn cross-modal maps to the property-norm space (PROPNORM) from the visual (VISUAL), linguistic (DISTRIB, SVD, EMBED) and multi-modal semantic spaces (VISUAL+DISTRIB, VISUAL+SVD, VISUAL+EMBED). At training time, we take advantage of the fact that we possess both visual/linguistic/multi-modal and property norm information for the concepts in MCRAE. Let's consider the VISUAL→PROPNORM setting as an example. We use this cross-modal vocabulary to learn a mapping function between VISUAL and PROP-

NORM: this function will learn to map visual dimensions to property dimensions. During testing, we use the learnt function to map the visual information of a previously unseen concept (e.g. CAT) to the property norm space and obtain a *predicted property vector* for that concept. Ideally, we want this predicted property vector to be closer to the gold-standard property vector for CAT than to any other property vector (i.e. the label of its nearest neighbour in PROPNORM to be CAT).

We use the standard evaluation metric for this task: average percentage correct at N (P@N) (Fagarasan et al., 2015; Lazaridou et al., 2014; Kiela et al., 2015). This measures how many of the test instances were ranked within the top N highest ranked nearest neighbors (using the cosine measure). All the results reported in Table 4 use the zero-shot learning procedure—for each of the 541 concepts in MCRAE, we train a mapping on the remaining 540 concepts and record whether the correct label is retrieved among the top N neighbours—and are averaged over the entire dataset. We also compare to a random baseline, for which a concept's nearest neighbours list is obtained by randomly ranking the list of target words.

Since the cross-modal map allows us to obtain property vectors for any concept, we were also able to evaluate these semantic representations on a standard NLP task, such as the well known conceptual similarity and relatedness task. The MEN test collection (Bruni et al., 2014) contains human similarity ratings for 3000 concept pairs. Performance on this dataset is usually measured by computing the Spearman ρ_s correlation between the ranking produced by the similarity scores of the learnt property vectors and that produced by the human-annotated concept similarity scores. Similarity between concept pairs is calculated using cosine similarity.

For each of the semantic spaces presented in Table 5 we learn a cross-modal map to PROPNORM using all the concepts in MCRAE at training time. During testing, we predict property vectors for all concepts in MEN-NOUNS, a subset of the MEN dataset consisting of 1285 noun pairs that don't occur in MCRAE. Table 5 reports the Spearman ρ_s correlation of the predicted property vectors and the gold-standard relatedness scores on MEN-NOUNS (column →PROPNORM), as well as the correlation of the

---

[3] https://code.google.com/p/word2vec/

[4] The number of components in the linear regression was set to 100 for all experiments.

From	P@1	P@5	P@10	P@20
DISTRIB	1.30	6.88	16.54	26.58
SVD	2.79	22.12	38.10	57.99
EMBED	3.90	23.42	36.80	55.02
VISUAL	3.35	28.44	47.96	64.50
VISUAL+DISTRIB	2.60	23.23	39.41	56.13
VISUAL+SVD	2.97	28.44	50.74	65.43
VISUAL+EMBED	3.16	28.44	51.12	65.06
RANDOM	0.0	0.74	2.42	3.90

Table 4: Zero-shot learning performance when mapping to the property-norm space (PROPNORM)

Semantic space (SS)		SS	→PROPNORM
Linguistic	DISTRIB	**0.68**	0.42
	SVD	**0.68**	0.58
	EMBED	**0.75**	0.69
Visual	VISUAL	0.56	**0.60**
Multi-modal	DISTRIB+VISUAL	**0.56**	0.45
	SVD+VISAL	0.57	**0.60**
	EMBED+VISUAL	0.56	**0.60**

Table 5: Performance (Spearman ρ_s correlation) of various uni-modal and multi-modal semantic spaces (column SS), together with that of the property vectors they predict (column →PROPNORM) on a semantic relatedness task (MEN-NOUNS)

original semantic spaces (e.g. DISTRIB or SVD) and the gold standard scores (column SS).

3.3 Quantitative results

The results presented in Table 4 show that visual information is a overall better predictor of a concept's properties than linguistic information. The cross-modal maps from the visual space VISUAL outperform all those from linguistic spaces DISTRIB, SVD, EMBED, and the addition of linguistic information to the visual one (maps from VISUAL+DISTRIB, VISUAL+SVD, VISUAL+EMBED) seem to only slightly improve the performance.

It is also important to point out that, even though the P@1 numbers may appear small, similar results have been reported for other zero-shot cross-modal maps (Lazaridou et al., 2014; Kiela et al., 2015). Overall results are good for higher values of N and

the qualitative results (Table 6) demonstrate how well the mapping is performing.

A model will achieve a perfect score on this task if it is able to predict, for a given concept, exactly those features (and associated production frequencies) listed in MCRAE. However, close-to-perfect performance in this task is impossible, since almost 30% of the features only occur with one concept, and hence can't be reconstructed for that particular concept. Consider the case of the *a_baby_deer* property: this only occurs in the MCRAE dataset as an attribute of FAWN. When predicting properties of FAWN as part of the zero-shot learning procedure, the *a_baby_deer* property can't be learned, since it doesn't occur with any other concept.

Columns SS and →PROPNORM in Table 5 report correlations with the MEN-NOUNS ratings. The predicted property vectors obtain a high correlation with the MEN scores, showing that the property vectors do capture lexical similarity well, although not as well as the linguistic vectors, which was expected (Bruni et al., 2012). An useful finding is that in some cases, the predicted property vectors obtain a better correlation with the MEN scores than their predictors (i.e. the VISUAL and multi-modal vectors). This shows a potential strength of the attribute-centric semantic representations: their capability to perform better on some lexical similarity/relatedness tasks than representations that contain raw perceptual information.

3.4 Qualitative results

In order to gain more insight into the differences between the *from vision* and *from language* mappings, we performed two types of qualitative analysis: we looked at the differences in nearest neighbours of the predicted property-norm representations (Table 6), as well as the top predicted properties of a concept (Table 6). In the *from language* setting we learned the mapping using the EMBED space, as it was the best performing linguistic space at P@1 and P@5 as shown in Table 4. We obtained the list of nearest neighbours as follows: at test time, we use the learnt cross-modal map to project the visual or linguistic representation of the unseen concept onto a property-norm representation. Using cosine similarity, we then obtain a ranked list of neighbours from all the 541 gold-standard property vectors. By in-

Concept	Nearest neighbours (from VISION)	Nearest neighbours (from LANGUAGE)
banana	**banana**, lemon, corn, pear, grapefruit, pineapple	pear, apple, avocado, plum, peach, lime, pineapple
cabbage	lettuce, asparagus, spinach, celery, broccoli, cucumber	asparagus, turnip, cauliflower, **cabbage**, celery, spinach
crocodile	alligator, **crocodile**, frog, turtle, iguana, toad	alligator, walrus, otter, platypus, **crocodile**, gorilla, buffalo
cello	violin, guitar, banjo, harp, harpsichord, **cello**, flute	harpsichord, harp, clarinet, flute, banjo, guitar, piano
drum	pot, pan, coin, skillet, bucket, peg, cap_(bottle)	tuba, clarinet, trombone, flute, harpsichord, trumpet, harp
fox	**fox**, cougar, coyote, deer, mink, elk, chipmunk	blackbird, raven, sparrow, pigeon, starling, chickadee
harpoon	sword, machete, **harpoon**, dagger, rifle, knife, gun	spear, dagger, harpoon, rifle, bazooka, crossbow, sword
muzzle	donkey, horse, ox, dog, cat, goat, cow	peg, fox, pin, crowbar, gun, dog, harpoon
pants	jeans, trousers, **pants**, shirt, blouse, jacket, coat	shirt, blouse, shawl, coat, sweater, dress, **pants**
prune	plum, blueberry, nectarine, peach, tangerine, raisin	pear, apple, avocado, lime, peach, pineapple, plum
rice	cauliflower, turnip, pie, **rice**, cabbage, biscuit, plate	turnip, lettuce, eggplant, peas, potato, corn, asparagus
stool	**stool_(furniture)**, table, peg, chair, gate, desk, door	chair, couch, **stool_(furniture)**, sofa, bench, desk, peg
swan	pelican, goose, dove, seagull, partridge, raven, falcon	raven, blackbird, goose, sparrow, pelican, partridge
tortoise	turtle, **tortoise**, crocodile, alligator, otter, frog, walrus	cat, fox, cougar, squirrel, hamster, donkey, turtle
worm	eel, rattlesnake, **worm**, shrimp, bat_(baseball), python	plum, tangerine, mandarin, nectarine, minnow, peach

Concept	Top predicted features (from VISION)	Top predicted features (from LANGUAGE)
banana	is_yellow, is_black*, is_round, is_long, a_fruit	a_fruit, is_green*, tastes_sweet*, grows_on_trees, is_edible
cabbage	is_green, a_vegetable, is_edible, eaten_in_salads	a_vegetable, is_green, is_white, is_edible, eaten_in_salads
crocodile	is_green, an_animal, lives_in_water, beh_-_swims	an_animal, is_long, beh_-_swims, lives_in_water, is_large
cello	has_strings, a_musical_instrument, made_of_wood	a_musical_instrument, inbeh_-_produces_music,
drum	made_of_metal, is_round, used_for_cooking*,	a_musical_instrument, is_large*, made_of_metal, is_loud
fox	an_animal, is_fast, is_small, has_fur, has_a_tail	an_animal, a_bird*, beh_-_flies*, has_a_tail, is_green*
harpoon	made_of_metal, a_weapon, is_sharp, is_dangerous*	a_weapon, is_large*, used_for_killing, is_dangerous*
muzzle	an_animal*, has_legs*, has_4_legs*, is_large*	made_of_metal*, an_animal*, is_small*, has_4_legs*
pants	clothing, has_buttons, is_blue*, different_colours	clothing, worn_by_women, worn_for_warmth, has_buttons
prune	a_fruit, is_small, tastes_sweet, is_round*, is_edible*	a_fruit, is_green*, grows_on_trees, tastes_sweet, is_juicy
rice	is_edible, is_white, is_round, a_vegetable*, is_yellow*	is_edible, a_vegetable*, is_yellow*, is_brown, has_wheels*
stool	made_of_wood, made_of_metal, has_4_legs, has_legs,	made_of_metal, used_by_sitting_on, has_legs, has_4_legs
swan	a_bird, is_white, beh_-_flies, has_a_beak, has_feathers	a_bird, an_animal*, has_feathers, beh_-_flies, is_white
tortoise	an_animal, has_a_shell, is_green, lives_in_water	an_animal, has_legs*, is_green, is_large, is_small*
worm	is_long, is_edible*, made_of_wood*, has_strings*	a_fruit*, is_small, an_insect*, is_black*, a_fish*

Table 6: Comparison of the top predicted features and nearest neighbours when mapping from VISION or from LANGUAGE. Properties marked with * don't appear as attributes of the associated concept in MCRAE.

specting the nearest neighbour predictions, we can check where the unseen concept is mapped to (e.g. BANANA is mapped close to yellow fruits). In order to retrieve the top predicted properties of a concept, we rank the dimensions of PROPNORM according to the weights in the predicted property vector (e.g. the predicted property vector for BANANA has high weights for a_fruit and is_green when mapped from language).

By looking at the nearest neighbour predictions, we observe that, when mapping from visual input, the predicted vector will be mapped into a subspace containing visually-similar things. When mapping from linguistic input, the neighbours tend to be concepts that are semantically related or denoted by words that occur in the same context as the target concept (e.g. worms are found in plums and nectarines).

A notable result is that when mapping from vision, the top neighbours tend to share the same colour (top neighbours for BANANA are yellow fruits, for SWAN are white birds) or shape as the target concept (top neighbours for WORM are long things with no legs). One possible clue as to why vision is better at predicting a concept's properties is given by the fact that it obtains better results on concepts such as PANTS or STOOL, where the only difference to very similar concepts like TROUSERS or CHAIR are visual (a STOOL has no backrest as opposed to a CHAIR).

However, there are cases in which the visual attributes of an object are not very useful in predicting its most important features: e.g. DRUM is mapped into a subspace of round objects (from vision), and not instruments (from language).

Besides the difference in top predicted features, Table 6 also indicates a shortcoming of MCRAE, specifically that this is not complete, meaning that not all properties that apply to a given concept were produced by the human annotators. Most of the top predicted attributes that don't occur in the dataset (those marked with * in Table 6) are highly plausible properties for the given concepts: *tastes_sweet* for BANANA or *has_legs* for TORTOISE. This also means that the model is being unfairly penalised.

In order to obtain a *complete* version of MCRAE, every possible (CONCEPT, *property*) pair would have to be checked for validity and annotated accordingly depending on whether *property* is a valid attribute of CONCEPT.

3.5 Importance of complete data

We were interested in measuring the impact that a *complete* dataset of features would have on the performance of the cross-modal zero-shot learning task. Silberer et al. (2013) conducted a study using a subset of the concepts and properties in MCRAE, whereby every property was annotated if it was a plausible attribute of the concept.

The published dataset (SILBERER) consists of visual attribute annotations for 512 concepts (that also occur in MCRAE) and 693 visual properties. The an-

Dataset	#concs	#props	#(conc,prop) pairs
SILBERER	512	693	7743
SILB-VIS	512	283	5335
M-VIS	512	283	2140
MCRAE	541	2526	7259

Table 7: Comparison of various datasets, according to the number of concepts and properties covered, as well as the pairs of (CONCEPT, *property*) contained

Train	Test	P@1	P@5	P@10	P@20
M-VIS	M-VIS	0.59	7.91	15.02	19.97
M-VIS	SILB-VIS	7.11	27.67	43.68	56.92
SILB-VIS	SILB-VIS	5.93	35.77	54.74	71.54

Table 8: Zeroshot learning performance for the vision to norms cross-modal map on different training and test sets

notation was done on a per-concept basis by looking at 10 images retrieved from ImageNet (Deng et al., 2009) and selecting all the attributes that were considered to be generally true for the given concept, even if not depicted in the images. For example, *has_a_pit* is a valid visual attribute for PLUM, even though not all retrieved images of plums show the pit.

Since not all of the 693 visual properties covered in SILBERER can be found in MCRAE, we will only be concerned with the subset of SILBERER which contains only those visual properties that also occur in MCRAE, henceforth SILB-VIS. These datasets are *complete*, since they were exhaustively annotated as explained above.

Let us also define M-VIS as the subset of MCRAE that contains the 512 concepts listed in SILBERER and the 283 properties that are common to SILBERER and MCRAE, together with their production frequencies as in MCRAE. This will act as our *incomplete* dataset. Table 7 lists all the aforementioned datasets, together with statistics related to their number of concepts, features and concept-feature pairs. It also demonstrates the sparsity of MCRAE: it contains fewer (CONCEPT, *property*) pairs than SILBERER, even though it contains 4 times more properties.

All the experiments performed using these

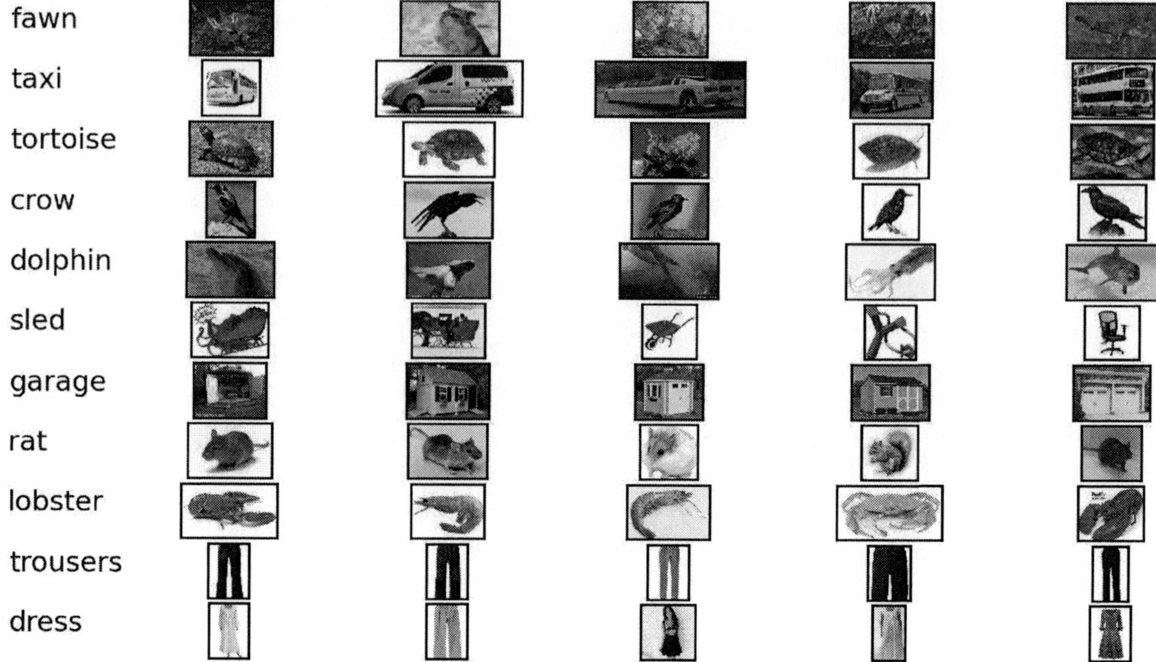

Figure 1: Nearest neighbours of the predicted visual vectors

datasets are listed in Table 8. These are identical in methodology to the zero-shot cross-modal maps from VISUAL to PROPNORM; the only difference being the datasets that these are run on.

The row (train:M-VIS, test:M-VIS) represents the setting where the cross-modal map learning and testing are both done on the incomplete set of data, just like we would do using MCRAE. We notice a huge improvement in performance by using the complete data only at test-time (row (train:M-VIS, test:SILB-VIS)). Note that, in this scenario, the learning is carried out in the same way, but the model can't be penalised for ranking plausible features near the top during test time, since we are testing against a complete dataset. This new setting provides a truer evaluation scenario and demonstrates the weakness in using MCRAE as a test set.

Performance improves even more if the complete dataset is used at training time as well (the row (train:SILB-VIS, test:SILB-VIS)), showing the benefit of also learning the mapping from complete data, as well as evaluating on it.

From	P@1	P@5	P@10	P@20	P@50
PROPNORM	6.13	36.43	54.46	68.40	81.97
DISTRIB	4.08	10.78	17.29	26.21	40.89
SVD	7.81	34.57	47.77	60.60	79.00
EMBED	9.48	31.60	47.21	62.08	78.81

Table 9: Zero-shot learning performance when mapping to the visual space (VISUAL)

4 Property based query engine

An interesting question follows from the good performance of the cross-modal mapping in Section 3, and that is whether we can reliably predict what concepts look like based on their semantic properties. For example, does something that flies, has wings and a beak look like a bird?

This task could be formalised as a property-based query engine, where we can train the cross-modal mapping to learn which concepts refer to which images. We follow the same experimental setup as detailed in Section 3.2 in order to learn a cross-modal map from PROPNORM to VISUAL. We also learn cross-modal maps from the linguistic spaces

(DISTRIB, SVD, EMBED) to VISUAL in order to see whether conceptual properties or linguistic input are better at predicting visual information.

Table 9 shows the results of our quantitative evaluation: the average precentage of correctly retrieved mean visual representations at N.

A qualitative analysis of the PROPNORM to VISUAL cross-modal map is shown in Figure 1. Because there are no images associated with the predicted mean visual representation, we retrieve and display the top neighbouring images. These images look surprisingly good, considering that the representation for TAXI in PROPNORM is a sparse vector where only the features *is_yellow, requires_drivers, used_for_transportation, a_car, requires_money, found_in_New_York, is_expensive, used_for_passengers, a_cab, is_fast* are activated.

5 Conclusions

We have studied the automatic prediction of property norms for unseen concepts, through learning the cross-modal mapping from image data. Following previous work, we evaluated on a zero-shot learning task and show that raw visual information (images) is a better predictor for conceptual properties than linguistic input (text). We also presented a short case study demonstrating the importance of having complete annotations in the property norm datasets, for both testing and training. Lastly, we demonstrated a possible use case for property norm datasets in an image retrieval task.

Our contributions are two-fold: first, we show that property norms can be successfully predicted from non-linguistic modalities and secondly, we quantify the need to have *complete* property norm datasets, where a production frequency of 0 for a (CONCEPT, *property*) pair can always be interpreted as "*property* is not true of CONCEPT".

Acknowledgments

LB is supported by an EPSRC Doctoral Training Grant. DK is supported by EPSRC grant EP/I037512/1. SC is supported by ERC Starting Grant DisCoTex (306920) and EPSRC grant EP/I037512/1. We thank the anonymous reviewers for their helpful comments. A link to the data used for the experiments in this paper is available at http://www.cl.cam.ac.uk/~ltf24/.

References

Mark Andrews, Gabriella Vigliocco, and David Vinson. 2009. Integrating experiential and distributional data to learn semantic representations. *Psychological review*, 116(3):463.

Eduard Barbu. 2008. Combining methods to learn feature-norm-like concept descriptions. In *Proceedings of the ESSLLI Workshop on Distributional Lexical Semantics*, pages 9–16.

Marco Baroni, Brian Murphy, Eduard Barbu, and Massimo Poesio. 2010. Strudel: A corpus-based semantic model based on properties and types. *Cognitive Science*, 34(2):222–254.

Shane Bergsma and Randy Goebel. 2011. Using visual information to predict lexical preference. In *RANLP*, pages 399–405.

Elia Bruni, Gemma Boleda, Marco Baroni, and Nam-Khanh Tran. 2012. Distributional semantics in technicolor. In *Proceedings of the 50th Annual Meeting of the Association for Computational Linguistics: Long Papers-Volume 1*, pages 136–145. Association for Computational Linguistics.

Elia Bruni, Nam-Khanh Tran, and Marco Baroni. 2014. Multimodal distributional semantics. *J. Artif. Intell. Res.(JAIR)*, 49(1-47).

Stephen Clark. 2015. Vector space models of lexical meaning. *Handbook of Contemporary Semantics– second edition. Wiley-Blackwell*.

George S Cree, Chris McNorgan, and Ken McRae. 2006. Distinctive features hold a privileged status in the computation of word meaning: Implications for theories of semantic memory. *Journal of Experimental Psychology: Learning, Memory, and Cognition*, 32(4):643.

Jia Deng, Wei Dong, Richard Socher, Li-Jia Li, Kai Li, and Li Fei-Fei. 2009. Imagenet: A large-scale hierarchical image database. In *Computer Vision and Pattern Recognition, 2009. CVPR 2009. IEEE Conference on*, pages 248–255. IEEE.

Barry J Devereux, Lorraine K Tyler, Jeroen Geertzen, and Billi Randall. 2013. The centre for speech, language and the brain (cslb) concept property norms. *Behavior research methods*, pages 1–9.

Luana Fagarasan, Eva Maria Vecchi, and Stephen Clark. 2015. From distributional semantics to feature norms: grounding semantic models in human perceptual data. In *Proceedings of the 11th International Conference on Computational Semantics*, pages 52–57, London, UK, April. Association for Computational Linguistics.

Andrea Frome, Greg S Corrado, Jon Shlens, Samy Bengio, Jeff Dean, Tomas Mikolov, et al. 2013. Devise: A deep visual-semantic embedding model. In *Advances in Neural Information Processing Systems*, pages 2121–2129.

Stevan Harnad. 1990. The symbol grounding problem. *Physica D: Nonlinear Phenomena*, 42(1):335–346.

Felix Hill and Anna Korhonen. 2014. Learning abstract concept embeddings from multi-modal data: Since you probably cant see what i mean. *Proceedings of EMNLP. ACL*.

Yangqing Jia, Evan Shelhamer, Jeff Donahue, Sergey Karayev, Jonathan Long, Ross Girshick, Sergio Guadarrama, and Trevor Darrell. 2014. Caffe: Convolutional architecture for fast feature embedding. In *Proceedings of the ACM International Conference on Multimedia*, pages 675–678. ACM.

Colin Kelly, Barry Devereux, and Anna Korhonen. 2014. Automatic extraction of property norm-like data from large text corpora. *Cognitive Science*, 38(4):638–682.

Douwe Kiela and Léon Bottou. 2014. Learning image embeddings using convolutional neural networks for improved multi-modal semantics. In *Proceedings of EMNLP*, volume 2014.

Douwe Kiela, Luana Bulat, and Stephen Clark. 2015. Grounding semantics in olfactory perception. In *Proceedings of ACL*, volume 2, pages 231–6.

Angeliki Lazaridou, Elia Bruni, and Marco Baroni. 2014. Is this a wampimuk? Cross-modal mapping between distributional semantics and the visual world. In *Proceedings of the 52nd Annual Meeting of the Association for Computational Linguistics (Volume 1: Long Papers)*, pages 1403–1414, Baltimore, Maryland, June. Association for Computational Linguistics.

Ken McRae, George S Cree, Mark S Seidenberg, and Chris McNorgan. 2005. Semantic feature production norms for a large set of living and nonliving things. *Behavior research methods*, 37(4):547–559.

Tomas Mikolov, Kai Chen, Greg Corrado, and Jeffrey Dean. 2013a. Efficient estimation of word representations in vector space. *arXiv preprint arXiv:1301.3781*.

Tomas Mikolov, Quoc V Le, and Ilya Sutskever. 2013b. Exploiting similarities among languages for machine translation. *arXiv preprint arXiv:1309.4168*.

Mark Palatucci, Dean Pomerleau, Geoffrey E Hinton, and Tom M Mitchell. 2009. Zero-shot learning with semantic output codes. In *Advances in neural information processing systems*, pages 1410–1418.

Billi Randall, Helen E Moss, Jennifer M Rodd, Mike Greer, and Lorraine K Tyler. 2004. Distinctiveness and correlation in conceptual structure: behavioral and computational studies. *Journal of Experimental Psychology: Learning, Memory, and Cognition*, 30(2):393.

Brian Riordan and Michael N Jones. 2011. Redundancy in perceptual and linguistic experience: Comparing feature-based and distributional models of semantic representation. *Topics in Cognitive Science*, 3(2):303–345.

Stephen Roller and Sabine Schulte Im Walde. 2013. A multimodal lda model integrating textual, cognitive and visual modalities. *Seattle, Washington, USA*, pages 1146–1157.

Carina Silberer and Mirella Lapata. 2012. Grounded models of semantic representation. In *Proceedings of the 2012 Joint Conference on Empirical Methods in Natural Language Processing and Computational Natural Language Learning*, pages 1423–1433. Association for Computational Linguistics.

Carina Silberer, Vittorio Ferrari, and Mirella Lapata. 2013. Models of semantic representation with visual attributes. In *ACL (1)*, pages 572–582.

Richard Socher, Andrej Karpathy, Quoc V Le, Christopher D Manning, and Andrew Y Ng. 2014. Grounded compositional semantics for finding and describing images with sentences. *Transactions of the Association for Computational Linguistics*, 2:207–218.

Peter D Turney and Patrick Pantel. 2010. From frequency to meaning: Vector space models of semantics. *Journal of artificial intelligence research*, 37(1):141–188.

Lorraine K Tyler, HE Moss, MR Durrant-Peatfield, and JP Levy. 2000. Conceptual structure and the structure of concepts: A distributed account of category-specific deficits. *Brain and language*, 75(2):195–231.

David P Vinson and Gabriella Vigliocco. 2008. Semantic feature production norms for a large set of objects and events. *Behavior Research Methods*, 40(1):183–190.

Cross-lingual Wikification Using Multilingual Embeddings

Chen-Tse Tsai and **Dan Roth**
University of Illinois at Urbana-Champaign
201 N. Goodwin, Urbana, Illinois, 61801
{ctsai12, danr}@illinois.edu

Abstract

Cross-lingual Wikification is the task of grounding mentions written in non-English documents to entries in the English Wikipedia. This task involves the problem of comparing textual clues across languages, which requires developing a notion of similarity between text snippets across languages. In this paper, we address this problem by jointly training multilingual embeddings for words and Wikipedia titles. The proposed method can be applied to all languages represented in Wikipedia, including those for which no machine translation technology is available. We create a challenging dataset in 12 languages and show that our proposed approach outperforms various baselines. Moreover, our model compares favorably with the best systems on the TAC KBP2015 Entity Linking task including those that relied on the availability of translation from the target language to English.

1 Introduction

Wikipedia has become an indispensable resource in knowledge acquisition and text understanding for both human beings and computers. The task of Wikification or Entity Linking aims at disambiguating mentions (sub-strings) in text to the corresponding titles (entries) in Wikipedia or other Knowledge Bases, such as FreeBase. For English text, this problem has been studied extensively (Bunescu and Pasca, 2006; Cucerzan, 2007; Mihalcea and Csomai, 2007; Ratinov et al., 2011; Cheng and Roth, 2013). It also has been shown to be a valuable component of several natural language processing and information extraction tasks across different domains.

Recently, there has also been interest in the cross-lingual setting of Wikification: given a mention from a document written in a foreign language, the goal is to find the corresponding title in the English Wikipedia. This task is driven partly by the fact that a lot of information around the world may be written in a foreign language for which there are limited linguistic resources and, specifically, no English translation technology. Instead of translating the whole document to English, *grounding* the important entity mentions in the English Wikipedia may be a good solution that could better capture the key message of the text, especially if it can be reliably achieved with fewer resources than those needed to develop a translation system. This task is mainly driven by the Text Analysis Conference (TAC) Knowledge Base Population (KBP) Entity Linking Tracks (Ji et al., 2012; Ji et al., 2015; Ji et al., 2016), where the target languages are Spanish and Chinese.

In this paper, we develop a general technique which can be applied to all languages in Wikipedia even when no machine translation technology is available for them.

The challenges in Wikification are due both to ambiguity and variability in expressing entities and concepts: a given mention in text, e.g., Chicago, may refer to different titles in Wikipedia (Chicago Bulls, the City, Chicago Bears, the band, etc.), and a title can be expressed in the text in multiple ways, such as synonyms and nicknames. These challenges are usually resolved by calculating some similarity between the representation of the mention and candidate titles. For instance, the mention could be represented using its neighboring words, whereas a title is usually represented by the words and entities in the document which introduces the title. In the cross-lingual setting, an additional challenge arises from the need to match words in a foreign language to an English title.

In this paper, we address this problem by using multilingual title and word embeddings. We represent words and Wikipedia titles in both the foreign language and in English in the same continuous vector space, which allows us to compute meaningful similarity between mentions in the foreign language and titles in English. We show that learning these embeddings only requires Wikipedia documents and language links between the titles across different languages, which are quite common in Wikipedia. Therefore, we can learn embeddings for all languages in Wikipedia without any additional annotation or supervision.

Another notable challenge for the cross-lingual setting that we do not address in this paper is that of *generating* English candidate titles given a foreign mention when there is no corresponding title in the foreign language Wikipedia. If a title exists in both the English and the foreign language Wikipedia, there could be examples of using this title in the foreign language Wikipedia text, and this information could help us determine the possible English titles. For example, Vladimir N. Vapnik exists in both the English Wikipedia (en/Vladimir_Vapnik)[1] and the Chinese Wikipedia (zh/弗拉基米·万普尼克). In the Chinese Wikipedia, we may see the use of the mention 萬普尼克 as a reference, that is, 萬普尼克 is linked to the title zh/弗拉基米·万普尼克. Following the inter-language links in Wikipedia, we can reach the English title en/Vladimir_Vapnik. On the other hand, Dan Roth does not have a page in the Chinese Wikipedia, it would have been harder to get to en/Dan_Roth from the Chinese mention. In this case, a transliteration model may be needed. Note that the difference between these two cases is only in generating English title candidates from the given foreign mention. The disambiguation method which identifies the most probable title is conceptually the same, so our method could generalize as is to this case.

---

[1] We use en/Vladimir_Vapnik to refer to the title of en.wikipedia.org/wiki/Vladimir_Vapnik

For evaluation purposes, we focus in this paper on mentions that have corresponding titles in both the English and the foreign language Wikipedia, and concentrate on disambiguating titles across languages. This allows us to evaluate on a large number of Wikipedia documents. Note that under this setting, a natural approach is to do wikification on the foreign language and then follow the language links to obtain the corresponding English titles. However, this approach requires developing a separate wikifier for each foreign language if it uses language-specific features, while our approach is generic and only requires using the appropriate embeddings. Importantly, the aforementioned approach will also not generalize to the cases where the target titles only exist in the English Wikipedia while ours does.

We create a challenging Wikipedia dataset for 12 foreign languages and show that the proposed approach, WikiME (**Wiki**fication using **M**ultilingual **E**mbeddings), consistently outperforms various baselines. Moreover, the results on the TAC KBP2015 Entity Linking dataset show that our approach compares favorably with the best Spanish system and the best Chinese system despite using significantly weaker resources (no need for translation). We note that the need for translation would have prevented the wikification of 12 languages used in this paper.

2   Task Definition and Model Overview

We formalize the problem as follows. We are given a document d in a foreign language, a set of mentions $M_d = \{m_1, \cdots, m_n\}$ in d, and the English Wikipedia. For each mention in the document, the goal is to retrieve the English Wikipedia title that the mention refers to. If the corresponding entity or concept does not exist in the English Wikipedia, "NIL" should be the answer.

Given a mention $m \in M_d$, the first step is to generate a set of title candidates C_m. The goal of this step is to quickly produce a short list of titles which includes the correct answer. We only look at the surface form of the mention in this step, that is, no contextual information is used.

The second and the key is the ranking step where we calculate a score for each title candidate $c \in C_m$, which indicates how relevant it is to the given mention. We represent the mention using various contextual clues and compute several similarity scores between the mention and the English title candidates based on multilingual word and title embeddings. A ranking model learnt from Wikipedia documents is used to combine these similarity scores and output the final score for each title candidate. We then select the candidate with the highest score as the answer, or output NIL if there is no appropriate candidate.

The rest of paper is structured as follows. Section 3 introduces our approach of generating multilingual word and title embeddings for all languages in Wikipedia. Section 4 presents the proposed cross-lingual wikification model which is based on multilingual embeddings. Evaluations and analyses are presented in Section 5. Section 6 discusses related work. Finally, Section 7 concludes the paper.

3   Multilingual Entity and Word Embeddings

In this section, we describe how we generate a vector representation for each word and Wikipedia title in any language.

3.1   Monolingual Embeddings

The first step is to train monolingual embeddings for each language separately. We adopt the "Alignment by Wikipedia Anchors" model proposed in Wang et al. (2014). For each language, we take all documents in Wikipedia and replace the hyperlinked text with the corresponding Wikipedia title. For example, consider the following Wikipedia sentence: "It is led by and mainly composed of **Sunni** Arabs from **Iraq** and **Syria**.", where the three bold faced mentions are linked to some Wikipedia titles. We replace those mentions and the sentence becomes "It is led by and mainly composed of en/Sunni_Islam Arabs from en/Iraq and en/Syria." We then learn the skip-gram model (Mikolov et al., 2013a; Mikolov et al., 2013b) on this newly generated text. Since a title appears as a token in the transformed text, we will obtain an embedding for each word and title from the model.

The skip-gram model maximizes the following objective:

$$\sum_{(w,c)\in D} \log \frac{1}{1 + e^{-v_c' \cdot v_w}} + \sum_{(w,c)\in D'} \log \frac{1}{1 - e^{-v_c' \cdot v_w}},$$

where w is the target token (word or title), c is a context token within a window of w , v_w is the target embedding represents w, v_c' is the embedding of c in context, D is the set of training documents, and D' contains the sampled token pairs which serve as negative examples. This objective is maximized with respect to variables v_w's and v_w''s. In this model, tokens in the context are used to predict the target token. The token pairs in the training documents are positive examples, and the randomly sampled pairs are negative examples.

3.2   Multilingual Embeddings

After getting monolingual embeddings, we adopt the model proposed in Faruqui and Dyer (2014) to project the embeddings of a foreign language and English to the same space. The requirement of this model is a dictionary which maps the words in English to the words in the foreign language. Note that there is no need to have this mapping for every word. The aligned words are used to learn the projection matrices, and the matrices can later be applied to the embeddings of each word to obtain the enhanced new embeddings. Faruqui and Dyer (2014) obtain this dictionary by picking the most frequent translated word from a parallel corpus. However, there is a limited or no parallel corpus for many languages. Since our monolingual embedding model consists also of title embeddings, we can use the Wikipedia title alignments between two languages as the dictionary.

Let $A_{en} \in R^{a \times k_1}$ and $A_{fo} \in R^{a \times k_2}$ be the matrices containing the embeddings of the aligned English and foreign language titles, where a is the number of aligned titles and k_1 and k_2 are the dimensionality of English embeddings and foreign language embeddings respectively (i.e., each row is a title embedding). Canonical correlation analysis (CCA) (Hotelling, 1936) is applied to these two matrices:

$$P_{en}, P_{fo} = CCA(A_{en}, A_{fo}),$$

where $P_{en} \in R^{k_1 \times d}$ and $P_{fo} \in R^{k_2 \times d}$ are the projection matrices for English and foreign language

FEATURE TYPE	DESCRIPTIONS
Basic	$Pr(c|m)$ and $Pr(m|c)$, the fraction of times the title candidate c is the target page given the mention m, and the fraction of times c is referred by m
Other Mentions	Cosine similarity of $e(c)$ and the average of vectors in $other\text{-}mentions(m)$ The maximum and minimum cosine similarity of the vectors in $other\text{-}mentions(m)$ and $e(c)$
Local Context	Cosine similarity of $e(c)$ and $context_j(m)$, for $j = 30, 100,$ and 200
Previous Titles	Cosine similarity of $e(c)$ and the average of vectors in $previous\text{-}titles(m)$ The maximum and minimum cosine similarity of the vectors in $previous\text{-}titles(m)$ and $e(c)$

Table 1: Features for measuring similarity of an English title candidate c and a mention m in the foreign language, where $e(c)$ is the English title embedding of c. $other\text{-}mentions(m)$, $previous\text{-}titles(m)$, and $context_j(m)$ are defined in Section 4.2.

embeddings, and d is the dimensionality of the projected vectors, which is a parameter in CCA.

Let $E_{en} \in R^{n_1 \times k_1}$ be the matrix containing the monolingual embeddings for all words and titles in English, where the number of words and titles is n_1, We obtain the multilingual embeddings of English words and titles by

$$E'_{en} = E_{en}P_{en} \in R^{n_1 \times d}.$$

Similarly, the multilingual embeddings of the foreign words and titles are stored in the rows of

$$E'_{fo} = E_{fo}P_{fo} \in R^{n_2 \times d},$$

where there are n_2 words and titles in the foreign language. The rows of E'_{en} and E'_{fo} are the representations of words and titles that we use to create the similarity features in the ranker.

Faruqui and Dyer (2014) show that the multilingual embeddings perform better than monolingual embeddings on various English word similarity datasets. Since synonyms in English may be translated into the same word in a foreign language, the CCA model could bring the synonyms in English closer in the embedding space. In this paper, we further show that projecting the embeddings of the two languages into the same space helps us computing better similarity between the words and titles across languages and that a bilingual dictionary consisting of pairs of Wikipedia titles is sufficient to induce these embeddings.

4   Cross-lingual Wikification

We now describe the algorithm for finding the English title given a foreign mention.

4.1   Candidate Generation

Given a mention m, the first step is to select a set of English title candidates C_m, a subset of all titles in the English Wikipedia. Ideally the correct title is included in this set. The goal is to produce a manageable number of candidates so that a more sophisticated algorithm can be applied to disambiguate them.

Since we focus on the titles in the intersection of English and the foreign language Wikipedia, we can build indices from the anchor texts in the foreign language Wikipedia. More specifically, we create two dictionaries and apply a two-step approach. The first dictionary maps each hyperlinked mention string in the text to the corresponding English titles. We simply lookup this dictionary by using the query mention m to retrieve all possible titles. The title candidates are initially sorted by $Pr(title|mention)$, the fraction of times the title is the target page of the given mention. This probability is estimated from all Wikipedia documents. The top k title candidates are then returned.

If the first high-precision dictionary fails to generate any candidate, we then lookup the second dictionary. We break each hyperlinked mention string into tokens, and create a dictionary which maps tokens to English titles. The tokens of m are used to query this dictionary. Similarly, the candidates are sorted by $Pr(title|token)$ and the top k candidates are returned.

4.2   Candidate Ranking

Given a mention m and a set of title candidates C_m, we compute a score for each title in C_m which indicates how relevant the title is to m. For a candidate $c \in C_m$, we define the relevance as:

$$s(m, c) = \sum_i w_i \phi_i(m, c), \qquad (1)$$

a weighted sum of the features, ϕ_i, which are based on multilingual title and word embeddings. We represent the mention m by the following contextual clues and use these representation to compute feature values:

- $context_j(m)$: use the tokens within j characters of m to compute the TF-IDF weighted average of their embeddings in the foreign language.
- $other\text{-}mentions(m)$: a set of vectors that represent other mentions. For each mention in the document other than m, we represent it by averaging the embeddings of the tokens in the mention surface string.
- $previous\text{-}titles(m)$: a set of vectors that represent previous entities. For each mention before m, we represent it by the English embedding of the disambiguated title.

Let $e(c)$ be the English embedding of the title candidate c. The features used in Eq. (1) are shown in Table 1. We train a linear ranking SVM model with the proposed features to obtain the weights, w_i, in Eq. (1). Finally, the title which has the highest relevant score is chosen as the answer to m.

5 Experiments

We evaluate the proposed method on the Wikipedia dataset of 12 langugaes and the TAC'15 Entity Linking dataset.

For all experiments, we use the Word2Vec implementation in Gensim[2] to learn the skip-gram model with dimensionality 500 for each language. The CCA code for projecting mono-lingual embeddings is from Faruqui and Dyer (2014)[3] in which the ratio parameter is set to 0.5 (i.e., the resulting multilingual embeddings have dimensionality 250).

We use Stanford Word Segmenter (Chang et al., 2008) for tokenizing Chinese, and use the Java built-in BreakIterator for Thai. For all other languages,

---

[2]https://radimrehurek.com/gensim/
[3]https://github.com/mfaruqui/
crosslingual-cca

LANGUAGE	#TOKENS	#ALIGN. TITLES
German	616,347,668	960,624
Spanish	460,984,251	754,740
French	357,553,957	1,088,660
Italian	342,038,537	836,154
Chinese	179,637,674	469,982
Hebrew	75,076,391	137,821
Thai	68,991,911	72,072
Arabic	67,954,771	255,935
Turkish	47,712,534	162,677
Tamil	12,665,312	50,570
Tagalog	4,925,785	48,725
Urdu	3,802,679	83,665

Table 2: The number of tokens used in training the skip-gram model and the number of titles which can be aligned to the corresponding English titles via the language links in Wikipedia.

tokenization is based on whitespaces. The number of tokens we use to learn the skip-gram model and the number of title alignments used by the CCA are given in Table 2. For learning the weights in Eq. (1), we use the implementation of linear ranking SVM in Lee and Lin (2014). Parameter selection and feature engineering are done by conducting cross-validation on the training data of Spanish Wikipedia dataset.

5.1 Wikipedia Dataset

We create this dataset from the documents in Wikipedia by taking the anchors (hyperlinked texts) as the query mentions and the corresponding English Wikipedia titles as the answers. Note that we only keep the mentions for which we can get the corresponding English Wikipedia titles by the language links. As observed in previous work (Ratinov et al., 2011), most of the mentions in Wikipedia documents are easy, that is, the baseline of simply choosing the title that maximizes $Pr(title|mention)$, the most frequent title given the mention surface string, performs quite well. In order to create a more challenging dataset, we randomly select mentions such that the number of easy mentions is about twice the number of hard mentions (those mentions for which the most common title is not the correct title). This generation process is inspired by (and close to) the distribution generated in the TAC KBP2015 Entity Linking Track. Another problem that occurs when creating a dataset from Wikipedia documents is that even though training documents are different from

LANGUAGE	#TRAINING	#TEST (#HARD)
German	23,124	9,798 (3,266)
Spanish	30,471	12,153 (4,051)
French	37,860	14,358 (4,786)
Italian	34,185	12,775 (4,254)
Chinese	44,246	11,394 (3,798)
Hebrew	20,223	16,146 (5,382)
Thai	16,819	11,381 (3,792)
Arabic	22,711	10,646 (3,549)
Turkish	12,942	13,798 (4,598)
Tamil	21,373	11,346 (3,776)
Tagalog	4,835	1,074 (358)
Urdu	1,413	1,389 (463)

Table 3: The number of training and test mentions of the Wikipedia dataset. The mentions are from the hyperlinked text in randomly selected Wikipedia documents. We ensure that there are at least one-third of test mentions are hard (cannot be solved by the most common title given the mention).

test documents, many mentions and titles actually overlap. To test that the algorithms really generalize from training examples, we ensure that no (mention, title) pair in the test set appear in the training set. Table 3 shows the number of training mentions, test mentions, and hard mentions in the test set of each language. This dataset is publicly available at `http://bilbo.cs.illinois.edu/~ctsai12/xlwikifier-wikidata.zip`.

The performance of the proposed method (WikiME) is shown in Table 4 along with the following approaches:

MonoEmb: In this method, we use the monolingual embeddings before applying CCA while all the other settings are the same as in WikiME. Since the monolingual embeddings are learnt separately for each language, calculating the cosine similarity of the word embedding in the foreign language and an English title embedding does not produce a good similarity function. The ranker, though, learns that the most important feature is $Pr(title|mention)$, and, consequently, performs well on easy mentions but has poor performance on hard mentions.

WordAlign: Instead of using the aligned Wikipedia titles in generating multilingual embeddings, the CCA model operates on the word alignments as originally proposed in Faruqui and Dyer (2014). We use the word alignments provided by Faruqui and Dyer (2014), which are obtained

LANGUAGE	METHOD	HARD	EASY	TOTAL
German	MonoEmb	35.18	**96.92**	76.34
	WordAlign	52.39	95.32	81.01
	WikiME	**53.28**	95.53	**81.45**
	Ceiling	90.20	100	96.73
Spanish	EsWikifier	40.11	**99.28**	79.56
	MonoEmb	38.46	96.12	76.90
	WordAlign	48.75	95.78	80.10
	WikiME	**54.46**	94.83	**81.37**
	Ceiling	93.46	100	97.69
French	MonoEmb	23.17	**97.16**	72.50
	WordAlign	41.70	96.08	77.96
	WikiME	**47.51**	95.72	**79.65**
	Ceiling	89.41	100	96.47
Italian	MonoEmb	32.68	**97.48**	75.90
	WikiME	**48.28**	95.52	**79.79**
	Ceiling	87.99	100	96.00
Chinese	MonoEmb	43.73	97.85	79.81
	WikiME	**57.61**	**98.03**	**84.55**
	Ceiling	94.29	100	98.10
Hebrew	MonoEmb	42.59	**98.16**	79.64
	WikiME	**56.67**	97.71	**84.03**
	Ceiling	96.84	100	98.95
Thai	MonoEmb	53.43	99.08	83.87
	WikiME	**70.02**	**99.17**	**89.46**
	Ceiling	94.49	100	98.16
Arabic	MonoEmb	39.81	**98.99**	79.26
	WikiME	**62.05**	98.17	**86.13**
	Ceiling	93.27	100	97.76
Turkish	MonoEmb	40.47	**98.15**	78.93
	WikiME	**60.18**	97.55	**85.10**
	Ceiling	94.08	100	98.03
Tamil	MonoEmb	34.51	98.65	77.30
	WikiME	**54.13**	**99.13**	**84.15**
	Ceiling	95.60	100	98.54
Tagalog	MonoEmb	35.47	**99.44**	78.12
	WikiME	**56.70**	98.46	**84.54**
	Ceiling	90.78	100	96.93
Urdu	MonoEmb	63.71	98.81	87.11
	WikiME	**74.51**	**99.35**	**91.07**
	Ceiling	90.06	100	96.69

Table 4: Ranking performance (Precision@1) of different approaches on various languages. Since about one-third of the test mentions are non-trivial, a baseline is 66.67 for all languages, if we pick the most common title given the mention. **Bold** signifies highest score for each column.

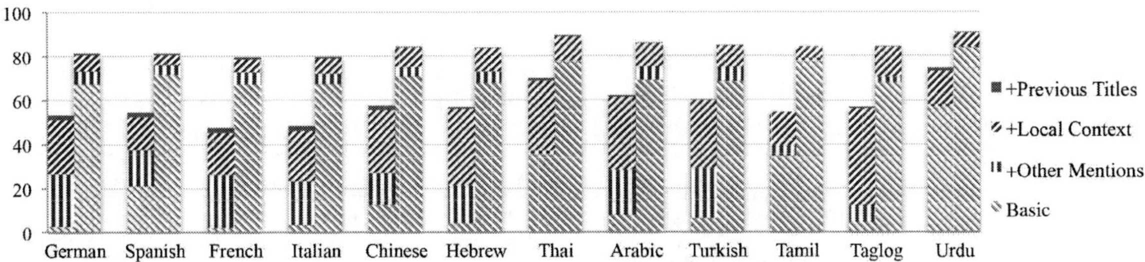

Figure 1: Feature ablation study of WikiME. The left bar of each language shows the performance on hard mentions, whereas the right bar corresponds to the performance of all mentions. The descriptions of feature types are listed in Table 1.

from the parallel news commentary corpora combined with the Europarl corpus for English to German, France, and Spanish. The number of aligned words for German, France, and Spanish are 37,484, 37,582, and 37,554 respectively. WikiME performs statistically significantly better than WordAlign on all three languages.

EsWikifier: We use Illinois Wikifier (Ratinov et al., 2011; Cheng and Roth, 2013) on a Spanish Wikipedia dump and train its ranker on the same set of documents that are used in WikiME.

Ceiling: These rows show the performance of title candidate generation. That is, the numbers indicate the percentage of mentions that have the gold title in its candidate set, therefore upper-bounds the ranking performance.

In sum, WikiME can disambiguate the hard mentions much better than other methods without sacrificing the performance on the easy mentions much. Comparing across different languages, it is important to note that languages which have a smaller size Wikipedia tend to have better performance, despite the degradation in the quality of the embeddings (see below). This is due to the difficulty of the datasets. That is, there is less ambiguity because the number of articles in the corresponding Wikipedia is small.

Figure 1 shows the feature ablation study of WikiME. For each language, we show results on hard mentions (the left bar) and all mentions (the right bar). We do not show the performance on easy mentions since it always stays high and does not change much. We can see that *Local Context* and *Other Mentions* are very effective for most of the languages. In particular, on hard mentions, the performance gain of the three feature groups is from almost 0 to around 50. For the easier dataset such as

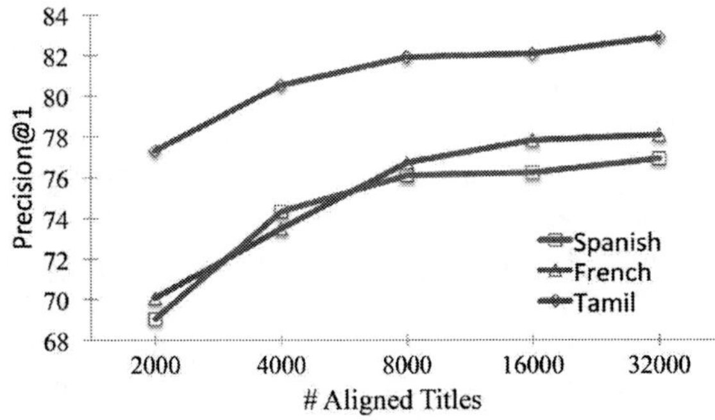

Figure 2: The number of aligned titles used in generating multilingual embeddings versus the performance of WikiME.

Urdu, *Basic features* alone work quite well.

Figure 2 shows the performance of WikiME when we vary the number of aligned titles in generating multilingual embeddings. The performance drops a lot when there are only few aligned titles, especially for Spanish and French, where the results are even worse than MonoEmb when only 2000 titles are aligned. This indicates that the CCA method needs enough aligned pairs in order to produce good embeddings. The performance does not change much when there are more than 16,000 aligned titles.

5.2 TAC KBP2015 Entity Linking

To evaluate our system on documents outside Wikipedia, we conduct an experiment on the evaluation documents in TAC KBP2015 Tri-Lingual Entity Linking Track. In this dataset, there are 166 Chinese documents (84 news and 82 discussion forum articles) and 167 Spanish documents (84 news and 83 discussion forum articles). The mentions in this dataset are all named entities of five types: Person, Geo-political Entity, Organization, Location, and Facility.

Table 5 shows the results. Besides the Spanish Wikifier (EsWikifier) that we used in the previous experiment, we implemented another baseline for Spanish Wikification. In this method, we use Google Translate to translate the whole documents from Spanish to English, and then the English Illinois Wikifier is applied to disambiguate the English gold mentions. Note that the target Knowledge Base of this dataset is FreeBase, therefore we use the FreeBase API to map the resulting English or Spanish Wikipedia titles to the corresponding FreeBase ID. If this conversion fails to find the corresponding FreeBase ID, "NIL" is returned instead.

The ranker models used in all three systems are trained on Wikipedia documents. We can see that WikiME outperforms both baselines significantly on Spanish. It is interesting to see that the translation-based baseline performs slightly better than the Spanish Wikifier, which indicates that the machine translation between Spanish and English is quite reliable. Note that this translation-based baseline got the highest score in this shared task when the mention boundaries were not given.

The row "Top TAC'15 System" lists the best scores of the diagnostic setting in which mention boundaries are given (Ji et al., 2016). Since the official evaluation metric considers not only the linked FreeBase IDs but also the entity types, namely, an answer is counted as correct only if the FreeBase ID and the entity type are both correct, we built two simple 5-class classifiers to classify each mention into the five entity types so that we can compare with the state of the art. One classifier uses FreeBase types of the linked FreeBase ID as features, and this classifier is only applied to mentions that are linked to some entry in FreeBase. For NIL mentions, another classifier which uses word form features (words in the mention, previous word, and next word) is applied. Both classifiers are trained on the training data of this task. From the last two rows of Table 5, we can see that WikiME achieves better results than the best TAC participants.

6   Related Work

Wikification on English documents has been studied extensively. Earlier works (Bunescu and Pasca,

APPROACH	SPANISH	CHINESE
Translation + EnWikifier	79.35	N/A
EsWikifier	79.04	N/A
WikiME	**82.43**	**85.07**
+Typing		
Top TAC'15 System	80.4	83.1
WikiME	**80.93**	**83.63**

Table 5: TAC KBP2015 Entity Linking dataset. All results use gold mentions and the metric is precision@1. The top section only evaluates the linked FreeBase ID. To compare with the best systems in TAC, we also classify each mention into the five entity types. The results which evaluate both FreeBase IDs and entity types are shown in the bottom section.

2006; Mihalcea and Csomai, 2007) focus on local features which compare context words with the content of candidate Wikipedia pages. Later, several works (Cucerzan, 2007; Milne and Witten, 2008; Han and Zhao, 2009; Ferragina and Scaiella, 2010; Ratinov et al., 2011) proposed to explore global features, trying to capture coherence among titles that appear in the text. In our method, we compute local and global features based on multilingual embeddings, which allow us to capture better similarity between words and Wikipedia titles across languages.

The annual TAC KBP Entity Linking Track has used the cross-lingual setting since 2011 (Ji et al., 2012; Ji et al., 2015; Ji et al., 2016), where the target foreign languages are Spanish and Chinese. To our best knowledge, most of the participants use one of the following two approaches: (1) Do entity linking in the foreign language, and then find the corresponding English titles from the resulting foreign language titles; and (2) Translate the query documents to English and do English entity linking. The first approach relies on a large enough Knowledge Base in the foreign language, whereas the second depends on a good machine translation system. The approach developed in this paper makes significantly simpler assumptions on the availability of such resources, and therefore can scale also to lower-resource languages, while doing very well also on high-resource languages.

Wang et al. (2015) proposed an unsupervised method which matches a knowledge graph with a graph constructed from mentions and the corresponding candidates of the query document. This approach performs well on the Chinese dataset of TAC'13, but falls into the category (1). Moro et al. (2014) proposed another graph-based approach which uses Wikipedia and WordNet in multiple languages as lexical resources. However, they only focus on English Wikification.

McNamee et al. (2011) aims at the same cross-lingual Wikification setting as we do, where the challenge is in comparing foreign language words with English titles. They treat this problem as a cross-lingual information retrieval problem. That is, given the context words of the target mention in the foreign language, retrieve the most relevant English Wikipedia page. However, their approach requires parallel text to estimate word translation probabilities. In contrast, our method only needs Wikipedia documents and the inter-language links.

Besides the CCA-based multilingual word embeddings (Faruqui and Dyer, 2014) that we extend in Section 3, several other methods also try to embed words in different languages into the same space. Hermann and Blunsom (2014) use a sentence aligned corpus to learn bilingual word vectors. The intuition behind the model is that representations of aligned sentences should be similar. Unlike the CCA-based method which learns monolingual word embeddings first, this model directly learns the cross-lingual embeddings. Luong et al. (2015) propose Bilingual Skip-Gram which extends the monolingual skip-gram model and learns bilingual embeddings using a parallel copora and word alignments. The model jointly considers within language co-occurrence and meaning equivalence across languages. That is, the monolingual objective for each language is also included in their learning objective. Several recent approaches (Gouws et al., 2014; Coulmance et al., 2015; Shi et al., 2015; Soyer et al., 2015) also require a sentence aligned parallel corpus to learn multilingual embeddings. Unlike other approaches, Vulić and Moens (2015) propose a model that only requires comparable corpora in two languages to induce cross-lingual vectors. Similar to our proposed approach, this model can also be applied to all languages in Wikipedia if we treat documents across two Wikipedia languages as a comparable corpus. However, the quality and quantity of this comparable corpus for low-resource languages will be low, we believe.

We choose the CCA-based model because we can obtain multilingual word and title embeddings for all languages in Wikipedia without any additional data beyond Wikipedia. In addition, by decoupling the training of the monolingual embeddings from the cross-lingual alignment we make it easier to improve the quality of the embeddings by getting more text in the target language or a better dictionary between English and the target language. Nevertheless, as cross-lingul wikification provides another testbed for multilingual embeddings, it would be very interesting to compare these recent models on Wikipedia languages.

7 Conclusion

We propose a new, low-resource, approach to Wikification across multiple languages. Our first step is to train multilingual word and title embeddings jointly using title alignments across Wikipedia collections in different languages. We then show that using features based on these multilingual embeddings, our wikification ranking model performs very well on a newly constructed dataset in 12 languages, and achieves state of the art also on the TAC'15 Entity Linking dataset.

An immediate future direction following our work is to improve the title candidate generation process so that it can handle the case where the corresponding titles only exist in the English Wikipedia. This only requires augmenting our method with a transliteration tool and, together with the proposed disambiguation approach across languages, this will be a very useful tool for low-resource languages which have a small number of articles in Wikipedia.

Acknowledgments

This research is supported by NIH grant U54-GM114838, a grant from the Allen Institute for Artificial Intelligence (allenai.org), and Contract HR0011-15-2-0025 with the US Defense Advanced Research Projects Agency (DARPA). Approved for Public Release, Distribution Unlimited. The views expressed are those of the authors and do not reflect the official policy or position of the Department of Defense or the U.S. Government.)

References

R. Bunescu and M. Pasca. 2006. Using encyclopedic knowledge for named entity disambiguation. In *Proceedings of the European Chapter of the ACL (EACL)*.

P.-C. Chang, M. Galley, and C. D. Manning. 2008. Optimizing chinese word segmentation for machine translation performance. In *Proceedings of the third workshop on statistical machine translation, Association for Computational Linguistics*.

X. Cheng and D. Roth. 2013. Relational inference for wikification. In *Proceedings of the Conference on Empirical Methods for Natural Language Processing (EMNLP)*.

J. Coulmance, J.-M. Marty, G. Wenzek, and A. Benhalloum. 2015. Trans-gram, fast cross-lingual word-embeddings. In *Proceedings of EMNLP*.

S. Cucerzan. 2007. Large-scale named entity disambiguation based on Wikipedia data. In *Proceedings of the 2007 Joint Conference of EMNLP-CoNLL*, pages 708–716.

M. Faruqui and C. Dyer. 2014. Improving vector space word representations using multilingual correlation. Association for Computational Linguistics.

P. Ferragina and U. Scaiella. 2010. Tagme: on-the-fly annotation of short text fragments (by wikipedia entities). In *Proceedings of the 19th ACM international conference on Information and knowledge management*, pages 1625–1628. ACM.

S. Gouws, Y. Bengio, and G. Corrado. 2014. Bilbowa: Fast bilingual distributed representations without word alignments. In *Deep Learning Workshop, NIPS*.

X. Han and J. Zhao. 2009. Named entity disambiguation by leveraging wikipedia semantic knowledge. In *Proceedings of the 18th ACM conference on Information and knowledge management*, pages 215–224. ACM.

K. M. Hermann and P. Blunsom. 2014. Multilingual distributed representations without word alignment. In *Proceedings of ICLR*.

H. Hotelling. 1936. Relations between two sets of variates. *Biometrika*, pages 321–377.

H. Ji, R. Grishman, and H. T. Dang. 2012. Overview of the tac2011 knowledge base population track. In *Text Analysis Conference (TAC2011)*.

H. Ji, J. Nothman, and B. Hachey. 2015. Overview of tac-kbp2014 entity discovery and linking tasks. In *Text Analysis Conference (TAC2014)*.

H. Ji, J. Nothman, B. Hachey, and R. Florian. 2016. Overview of tac-kbp2015 tri-lingual entity discovery and linking. In *Text Analysis Conference (TAC2015)*.

C.-P. Lee and C.-J. Lin. 2014. Large-scale linear RankSVM. *Neural computation*, 26(4):781–817.

T. Luong, H. Pham, and C. D. Manning. 2015. Bilingual word representations with monolingual quality in mind. In *Proceedings of the 1st Workshop on Vector Space Modeling for Natural Language Processing*.

P. McNamee, J. Mayfield, D. Lawrie, D. W. Oard, and D. S. Doermann. 2011. Cross-language entity linking. In *Proceedings of IJCNLP*, pages 255–263.

R. Mihalcea and A. Csomai. 2007. Wikify!: linking documents to encyclopedic knowledge. In *Proceedings of ACM Conference on Information and Knowledge Management (CIKM)*, pages 233–242.

T. Mikolov, K. Chen, G. Corrado, and J. Dean. 2013a. Efficient estimation of word representations in vector space. In *Proceedings of Workshop at ICLR*.

T. Mikolov, I. Sutskever, K. Chen, G. S. Corrado, and J. Dean. 2013b. Distributed representations of words and phrases and their compositionality. In *Advances in neural information processing systems*, pages 3111–3119.

D. Milne and I. H. Witten. 2008. Learning to link with wikipedia. In *Proceedings of ACM Conference on Information and Knowledge Management (CIKM)*, pages 509–518.

A. Moro, A. Raganato, and R. Navigli. 2014. Entity linking meets word sense disambiguation: a unified approach. In *Transactions of the Association for Computational Linguistics*, volume 2, pages 231–244.

L. Ratinov, D. Downey, M. Anderson, and D. Roth. 2011. Local and global algorithms for disambiguation to wikipedia. In *Proceedings of the Annual Meeting of the Association for Computational Linguistics (ACL)*.

T. Shi, Z. Liu, Y. Liu, and M. Sun. 2015. Learning crosslingual word embeddings via matrix cofactorization. In *Proceedings of ACL*.

H. Soyer, P. Stenetorp, and A. Aizawa. 2015. Leveraging monolingual data for crosslingual compositional word representations. In *Proceedings of ICLR*.

I. Vulić and M.-F. Moens. 2015. Bilingual word embeddings from non-parallel document-aligned data applied to bilingual lexicon induction. In *Proceedings of ACL*.

Z. Wang, J. Zhang, J. Feng, and Z. Chen. 2014. Knowledge graph and text jointly embedding. In *Proceedings of EMNLP*.

H. Wang, J. G. Zheng, X. Ma, P. Fox, and H. Ji. 2015. Language and domain independent entity linking with quantified collective validation. In *Proceedings of EMNLP*.

Deconstructing Complex Search Tasks: A Bayesian Nonparametric Approach for Extracting Sub-tasks

Rishabh Mehrotra
Dept. of Computer Science
University College London
London, UK
R.Mehrotra@cs.ucl.ac.uk

Prasanta Bhattacharya
Dept. of Information Systems
National University of Singapore
Singapore
prasanta@comp.nus.edu.sg

Emine Yilmaz
Dept. of Computer Science
University College London
London, UK
emine.yilmaz@ucl.ac.uk

Abstract

Search tasks, comprising a series of search queries serving a common informational need, have steadily emerged as accurate units for developing the next generation of task-aware web search systems. Most prior research in this area has focused on segmenting chronologically ordered search queries into higher level tasks. A more naturalistic viewpoint would involve treating query logs as convoluted structures of tasks-subtasks, with complex search tasks being decomposed into more focused sub-tasks. In this work, we focus on extracting sub-tasks from a given collection of on-task search queries. We jointly leverage insights from Bayesian nonparametrics and word embeddings to identify and extract sub-tasks from a given collection of *on-task* queries. Our proposed model can inform the design of the next generation of task-based search systems that leverage user's task behavior for better support and personalization.

1 Introduction

Search behavior, and information behavior more generally, is often motivated by tasks that prompt search processes that are often lengthy, iterative, and intermittent, and are characterized by distinct stages, shifting goals and multitasking (Kelly et al., 2013; Mehrotra et al., 2016). Current search systems do not provide adequate support for users tackling complex tasks, due to which the cognitive burden of keeping track of such tasks is placed on the searcher. Ideally, a search engine should be able to understand the reason that caused the user to submit a query (i.e., the actual task that caused the query to be issued) and be able to guide users to achieve their tasks by incorporating this information about the actual informational need. Clearly, identifying and analyzing search tasks is an extremely important activity not only for search engine providers but also other web based frameworks like spoken dialogue (Sun et al., 2015) and general recommendation systems (Mehrotra et al., 2014) in their effort to improve user experience on their platforms.

Previous work in the area have proposed a number of methods for identifying and extracting task knowledge from search query sessions (Mehrotra and Yilmaz, 2015b; Wang et al., 2013; Lucchese et al., 2011; Verma and Yilmaz, 2014; Mehrotra and Yilmaz, 2015a). However, while some tasks are fairly trivial and single-shot (e.g. "latest Taylor Swift album"), others are more complex and often involve multiple steps or sub-tasks (e.g. "planning a wedding").

Deciphering sub-tasks from search query logs becomes an important problem since users might exhibit different search preferences as well as expend different amounts of search effort while executing the sub-tasks. For example, while planning a wedding, users might choose to spend more time and effort on searching for a suitable venue, while spending considerably less on the choice of a wedding cake. However, even before we can analyze the variance in search effort across sub-tasks, it becomes imperative to successfully identify and extract sub-tasks for a specific task from search query logs. This turns out to be a complex problem for two reasons. First, the number of sub-tasks in a given task is not a

Proceedings of NAACL-HLT 2016, pages 599–605,
San Diego, California, June 12-17, 2016. ©2016 Association for Computational Linguistics

parameter than can be explicitly defined, and is generally task dependent. Second, while similar sounding queries like "wedding planning checklist" and "wedding dress" belong to the same task, they inherently represent different sub-tasks. This necessitates the use of advanced distancing techniques, beyond the usual bag-of-words or TF-IDF approaches.

In our current study, we propose a method for extracting search sub-tasks from a given collection of queries constituting a complex search task, using a non-parametric Bayes approach. Our generative model is not restricted by a fixed number of sub-task clusters, and assumes an infinite number of latent groups, with each group described by a certain set of parameters. We specify our non-parametric model by defining a Distance-dependent Chinese Restaurant Process (dd-CRP) prior and a Dirichlet multinomial likelihood (Blei and Frazier, 2011). Further, we draw on recent advancements that emphasize the superiority of embedding based distancing approaches over others, especially when comparing documents with less or no common words (Mikolov et al., 2013). We enrich our non-parametric model by working in the vector embedding space and propose a word-embedding based distance measure (Kusner et al., 2015) to encode query distances for efficient sub-task extraction.

2   Related Work

Web search logs have been extensively studied to generate insights and provide explicit cues about the information seeking behavior of users, that would improve their search experiences. There have been attempts to extract in-session tasks (Jones and Klinkner, 2008; Lucchese et al., 2011; Spink et al., 2005), and cross-session tasks (Wang et al., 2013; Kotov et al., 2011; Li et al., 2014) from query sequences based on classification and clustering methods. Hagen *et al.* (Hagen et al., 2013) have recently presented a cascading method for logical session detection that can also be applied to search mission detection. Kotov et al (Kotov et al., 2011) and Agichtein et al (Agichtein et al., 2012) have studied the problem of cross-session task extraction via binary same-task classification. Unfortunately, pairwise predictions alone cannot generate the partition of tasks, and post-processing is needed to obtain the final task partitions (Liao et al., 2012).

Some previous attempts have been made to support people engaged in complex tasks by allowing them to take notes and record results that they already examined (Donato et al., 2010), or to provide task continuation assistance (Morris et al., 2008). Jones et al. (Jones and Klinkner, 2008) was the first work to consider the notion that there may be multiple sub-tasks associated with a user's informational needs. However, they fall short of proposing a method to identify a task from queries. Since most of these task extraction methods are based on relating a user's current query to one of her previous tasks, these methods cannot be directly used in finding and extracting sub-tasks. As a result, while task extraction methods abound, very little has been done to explicitly identify the sub-tasks from within complex search tasks.

3   Extracting Sub-tasks

Consider a collection of queries (Q) issued by search engine users, trying to accomplish certain search tasks. Quite often, these search tasks (e.g. planing a trip) are complex and conceptually decompose into a set of sub-tasks (e.g. booking flights, finding places of interest etc), each of which warrants the user to further issue multiple queries to solve. It is important to note that while the queries are observed, the inherent sub-tasks and their numbers are latent. Given a collection of *on-task* queries, extracted using a standard task extraction algorithm, our goal is to extract these sub-tasks from the *on-task* query collection.

The distance dependent Chinese restaurant process (dd-CRP) (Blei and Frazier, 2011) was recently introduced to model random partitions of non-exchangeable data. To extract sub-tasks, we consider the dd-CRP model in an embedding-space setting and place a dd-CRP prior over the search tasks.

3.1   Nonparametric Priors for Sub-tasks

The Chinese restaurant process (CRP) is a distribution on all possible partitions of a set of objects (in our case, queries). The generative process can be described via a restaurant with an infinite number of tables (in our case, sub-tasks). Customers (queries) i

enter the restaurant in sequence and select a table z_i to join. They pick an occupied table with a probability proportional to the number of customers already sitting there, or a new table with probability proportional to a scaling parameter α. The dd-CRP alters the CRP by modeling customer links not to tables, but to other customers.

In our sub-task extraction problem, each task is associated with a dd-CRP and its tables are embellished with IID draws from a base distribution over mixture component parameters. Let z_i denote the ith query assignment, the index of the query with whom the ith query is linked. Let d_{ij} denote the distance measurement between queries i and j, let D denote the set of all distance measurements between queries, and let f be a decay function. The distance dependent CRP independently draws the query assignments to sub-tasks conditioned on the distance measurements,

$$p(z_i = j|D, \alpha) \propto \begin{cases} f(d_{ij}) & \text{if } j \neq i \\ \alpha & \text{if } j = i \end{cases}$$

Here, d_{ij} is an externally specified distance between queries i and j, and α determines the probability that a customer links to themselves rather than another customer. The monotonically decreasing decay function $f(d)$ mediates how the distance between two queries affects their probability of connecting to each other. The overall link structure specifies a partition: two queries are clustered together in the same sub-task if and only if one can reach the other by traversing the link edges. $R(q_{1:N})$ maps query assignments to sub-task assignments.

Given a decay function f, distances between queries D, scaling parameter α, and an exchangeable Dirichlet distribution with parameter λ, N M-word queries are drawn as follows,

1. For $i \in [1, N]$, draw $z_i \sim dist - CRP(\alpha, f, D)$.

2. For $i \in [1, N]$,

    (a) If $z_i \notin R^*_{q_{1:N}}$, set the parameter for the ith query to $\theta_i = \theta_{q_i}$. Otherwise draw the parameter from the base distribution, $\theta_i \sim Dirichlet(\lambda)$.

    (b) Draw the ith query terms, $w_i \sim Mult(M, \theta_i)$.

We experimented with 3 different values of alpha and reported the best performing results. We next define the distance and decay functions which help us find task-specific query distances.

3.2 Quantifying Task Based Query Distances

Word embeddings capture lexico-semantic regularities in language, such that words with similar syntactic and semantic properties are found to be close to each other in the embedding space. We leverage this insight and propose a novel query-query distance metric based on such embeddings. We train a skip-gram word embeddings model where a query term is used as an input to a log-linear classifier with continuous projection layer and words within a certain window before and after the words are predicted. We next describe how we use these query term embedding vectors to define query distances.

For a search task like "planning a wedding", frequent queries include *wedding checklist, wedding planning* and *bridal dresses*. Ideally, checklist and planning related queries constitute a different sub-task than bridal dresses. Given the overall context of weddings, words like *checklist* and *dresses* are more informative than generic words like *weddings*. To this end, we classify each word as **background word** or **subtask-specific word** using a simple frequency based approach on the given collection of *on-task* query terms and use a weighted combination of their embedding vectors to encode a query's vector:

$$V_q = \frac{1}{n_{terms}} \sum_i \frac{n_{qt_i}}{\Sigma_q n_q} V_{t_i} \tag{1}$$

where t_i is the i-th term in the query q, n_{qt_i} is the number of queries in the current task which contain the term t_i. We encode each query by its corresponding embedding vector representation V_q and take the cosine distance of these vectors while defining d_{ij}. We consider a simple window decay $f(d) = 1[d < a]$ to only considers queries that are separated from the current query for a given sub-task, by a distance of, at most, a .

3.3 Posterior Inference

The posterior of the proposed dd-CRP model is intractable to compute because the dd-CRP places a prior over a combinatorial number of possible customer configurations. We employ a Gibbs sampler,

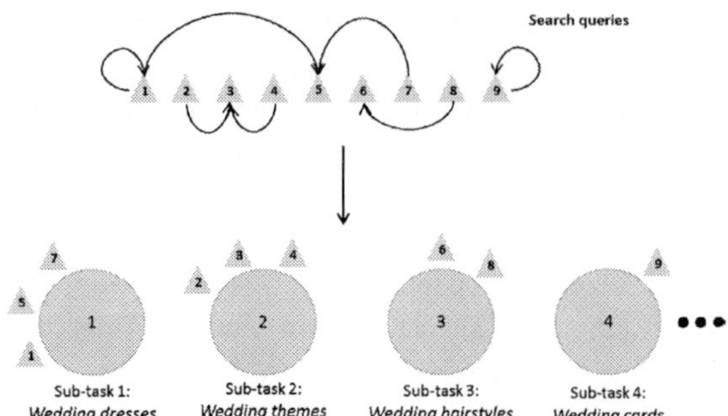

Figure 1: Visual formulation of the proposed approach. The tables represent the different sub-tasks while each triangle represents the search queries. Query assignment leads to sub-task assignments.

wherein we iteratively draw from the conditional distribution of each latent variable, given the other latent variables and observations.

The Gibbs sampler iteratively draws from

$$p(z_i^{new}|z_{-i}, x) \propto p(z_i^{new}|D, \alpha)$$
$$p(x|t(z_{-i} \cup z_i^{new}), G_0) \tag{2}$$

The first term is the dd-CRP prior and the second is the likelihood of observations (x) under the partition, and $t(z)$ is the sub-task formed from the assignments z. We employ a Dirichlet-Multinomial conjugate distribution to model the likelihood of query terms.

Queries are assigned to sub-tasks by considering sets of queries that are reachable from each other through the query assignments. Notice that many configurations of query assignments might lead to the same sub-task assignment. Finally, query assignments can produce a cycle, e.g., query 1 linking with 2 and query 2 linking with 1. This still determines a valid sub-task assignment: all queries linked in a cycle are assigned to the same sub-task. Figure 1 provides a pictorial representation of the sub-task assignment process.

4 Experimental Evaluation

In this section, we evaluate the robustness of the proposed sub-task extraction framework. In addition to qualitative analysis of the extracted sub-tasks, we perform a user judgment study to evaluate the quality of the extracted sub-tasks.

4.1 Dataset & Baselines

We make use of the AOL log dataset which consists of 20M web queries collected over three months (Pass et al., 2006). The dataset comprises of five fields viz. the search query string, the query time stamp, the rank of the selected item (if any), the domain of the selected items URL (if any), and a unique user identifier. We augment on-task queries extracted from the AOL logs with the related searches output from different search engines by making use of their APIs.

To compare the performance of the proposed sub-task extraction algorithm, we baseline against a number of methods including state-of-the-art task extraction systems, in addition to parametric and non-parametric clustering approaches:

1 **QC-HTC** (Lucchese et al., 2011): a frequently used search task identification method.

2 **LDA** (Blei et al., 2003): a topic model based baseline which aggregates queries (similar to tweet aggregation as proposed in (Mehrotra et al., 2013)) in a session to form a document and learns an LDA model on top of it.

3 **vanilla-CRP**: a vanilla non-parametric CRP model (Wang and Blei, 2009).

4 **Proposed Approach**: the proposed embedding based dd-CRP model.

4.2 Qualitative Evaluation

Table 1 shows some exemplar sub-tasks identified by the proposed model and the baseline methods using a CRP, QC-HTC and a LDA process. Each task is visualized using four search queries that were most frequently executed in relation to that sub-task, but not in any specific order among themselves. The task selected for this illustration was that of planning a wedding, and the three sub-tasks identified using our proposed method, for this particular task were wedding hairstyles, wedding dresses, and wedding cards. In comparison, however, the baseline methods failed to identify diagnostic clusters. For instance, LDA grouped wedding insurance, wedding planning books and wedding cards as a single sub-task, while CRP grouped wedding planning kits, wedding dresses and wedding decorations into

Proposed Approach			LDA		
sub-task 1	sub-task 2	sub-task 3	sub-task 1	sub-task 2	sub-task 3
wedding hairstyles	used wedding dresses	wedding card holders	wedding insurance	christian wedding vows	make wedding invitations
wedding hair dos	colorful bridal gowns	indian wedding program	destination wedding	brides	wedding cakes pictures
curly wedding hairstyles	preowned wedding dresses	wedding program	wedding planning book	cheap wedding dresses	planners
pictures of wedding hair	wedding attire	regency wedding cards	party supply stores	tea length wedding dresses	wedding colors
CRP			QC-HTC		
sub-task 1	sub-task 2	sub-task 3	sub-task 1	sub-task 2	sub-task 3
wedding planning kit	wedding theme	wedding insurance	wedding insurance	christian wedding vows	cheap dresses
destination wedding	wedding guide	weddings in vegas	destination wedding	plus size bridesmaid	wedding cakes pictures
wedding table decorations	save the date ideas	wedding cakes pictures	financing wedding rings	wedding colors	pricing weddings
1930s wedding pictures	wedding vacation	planning a wedding	party supply stores	tea length wedding dresses	wedding dresses discounts

Table 1: Qualitative Analysis of Sub-Tasks extracted by different approaches.

a single sub-task. Our proposed method, however, demonstrated remarkably good discriminant validity, as is clear from Table 1.

4.3 User Study

Evaluation of tasks and sub-tasks is an open research question. Owing to the absence of ground truth data on sub-task classification, we resort to user judgments in order to validate the quality of sub-tasks extracted. We select a sub-task at random and then choose a randomly selected pair of queries from that sub-task. Next, we ask the judges, recruited via AMT[1], to affirm or deny if the two queries should be assigned to the same sub-task category. We repeat this process for a total of 100 iterations and compare the results with the ones predicted by our proposed approach, as well as with the ones predicted by the baselines.

We report the proportion of correct matches (i.e. proportion of times our predicted sub-task classifications matched the expert judgments) in Fig. 2. The label agreement among the judges was 85.4% and the performance differences were statistically significant. It is clear that our proposed method outperforms both, task extraction & topic model based baselines in making correct sub-task classifications.

5   Results & Discussion

Web search tasks are often complex and comprise several constituent sub-tasks. In this paper we offer a non-parametric Bayesian approach to identifying sub-tasks by grouping search queries using an embedding based dd-CRP approach. The proposed model combines insights from Bayesian nonparametrics and distributional semantics to extract

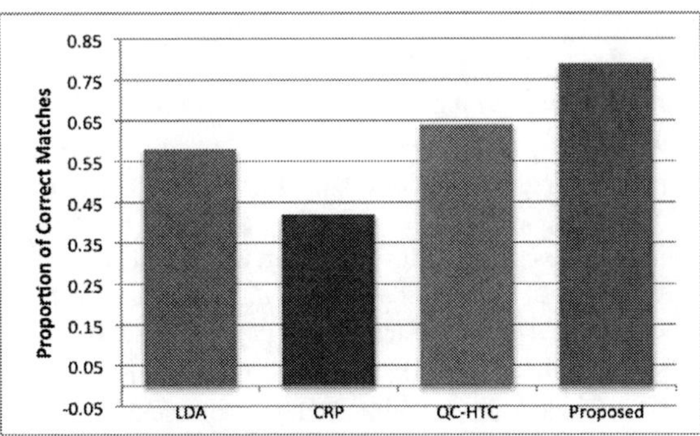

Figure 2: Judgments results for sub-task validity across compared approaches.

sub-tasks which are not only meaningful but are also coherent. We evaluate our proposed method on the popular AOL search log dataset augmented with related search queries and demonstrate superiority over comparable approaches such as LDA and CRP. Further, we contend that our proposed approach is significantly more useful in online environments where the number of sub-tasks is never known apriori and impossible to ascertain or approximate.

In future work, we intend to consider hierarchical extensions for extracting hierarchies of tasks-subtasks. Further, using an embedding based distancing scheme, we offer an improvement in empirical performance over prior clustering approaches that have used either a bag-of-words or TF-IDF based solution. Our method offers search engine providers with a novel method to identify and analyze user task-behavior, and better support task decisions on their platforms.

Acknowledgments

This work was supported in part by a Google Faculty Research Award.

---

[1] https://www.mturk.com/mturk/welcome

References

[Agichtein et al.2012] Eugene Agichtein, Ryen W White, Susan T Dumais, and Paul N Bennet. 2012. Search, interrupted: understanding and predicting search task continuation. In *Proceedings of the 35th international ACM SIGIR conference on Research and development in information retrieval*, pages 315–324. ACM.

[Blei and Frazier2011] David M Blei and Peter I Frazier. 2011. Distance dependent chinese restaurant processes. *The Journal of Machine Learning Research*, 12:2461–2488.

[Blei et al.2003] David M Blei, Andrew Y Ng, and Michael I Jordan. 2003. Latent dirichlet allocation. *the Journal of machine Learning research*, 3:993–1022.

[Donato et al.2010] Debora Donato, Francesco Bonchi, Tom Chi, and Yoelle Maarek. 2010. Do you want to take notes?: identifying research missions in yahoo! search pad. In *Proceedings of the 19th international conference on World wide web*, pages 321–330. ACM.

[Hagen et al.2013] Matthias Hagen, Jakob Gomoll, Anna Beyer, and Benno Stein. 2013. From search session detection to search mission detection. In *Proceedings of the 10th Conference on Open Research Areas in Information Retrieval*, pages 85–92.

[Jones and Klinkner2008] Rosie Jones and Kristina Lisa Klinkner. 2008. Beyond the session timeout: automatic hierarchical segmentation of search topics in query logs. In *Proceedings of the 17th ACM conference on Information and knowledge management*, pages 699–708. ACM.

[Kelly et al.2013] Diane Kelly, Jaime Arguello, and Robert Capra. 2013. Nsf workshop on task-based information search systems. In *ACM SIGIR Forum*, volume 47, pages 116–127. ACM.

[Kotov et al.2011] Alexander Kotov, Paul N Bennett, Ryen W White, Susan T Dumais, and Jaime Teevan. 2011. Modeling and analysis of cross-session search tasks. In *Proceedings of the 34th international ACM SIGIR conference on Research and development in Information Retrieval*, pages 5–14. ACM.

[Kusner et al.2015] M. J. Kusner, Y. Sun, N. I. Kolkin, and K. Q. Weinberger. 2015. From word embeddings to document distances. In *ICML*.

[Li et al.2014] Liangda Li, Hongbo Deng, Anlei Dong, Yi Chang, and Hongyuan Zha. 2014. Identifying and labeling search tasks via query-based hawkes processes. In *Proceedings of the 20th ACM SIGKDD international conference on Knowledge discovery and data mining*, pages 731–740. ACM.

[Liao et al.2012] Zhen Liao, Yang Song, Li-wei He, and Yalou Huang. 2012. Evaluating the effectiveness of search task trails. In *Proceedings of the 21st international conference on World Wide Web*, pages 489–498. ACM.

[Lucchese et al.2011] Claudio Lucchese, Salvatore Orlando, Raffaele Perego, Fabrizio Silvestri, and Gabriele Tolomei. 2011. Identifying task-based sessions in search engine query logs. In *Proceedings of the fourth ACM international conference on Web search and data mining*, pages 277–286. ACM.

[Mehrotra and Yilmaz2015a] Rishabh Mehrotra and Emine Yilmaz. 2015a. Terms, topics & tasks: Enhanced user modelling for better personalization. In *Proceedings of the 2015 International Conference on The Theory of Information Retrieval*, pages 131–140. ACM.

[Mehrotra and Yilmaz2015b] Rishabh Mehrotra and Emine Yilmaz. 2015b. Towards hierarchies of search tasks & subtasks. In *Proceedings of the 24th International Conference on World Wide Web Companion*, pages 73–74. International World Wide Web Conferences Steering Committee.

[Mehrotra et al.2013] Rishabh Mehrotra, Scott Sanner, Wray Buntine, and Lexing Xie. 2013. Improving lda topic models for microblogs via tweet pooling and automatic labeling. In *Proceedings of the 36th international ACM SIGIR conference on Research and development in information retrieval*, pages 889–892. ACM.

[Mehrotra et al.2014] Rishabh Mehrotra, Emine Yilmaz, and Manisha Verma. 2014. Task-based user modelling for personalization via probabilistic matrix factorization. In *RecSys Posters*.

[Mehrotra et al.2016] Rishabh Mehrotra, Prasanta Bhattacharya, and Emine Yilmaz. 2016. Characterizing users' multi-tasking behavior in web search. In *Proceedings of the 2016 ACM on Conference on Human Information Interaction and Retrieval*, CHIIR '16, pages 297–300, New York, NY, USA. ACM.

[Mikolov et al.2013] Tomas Mikolov, Ilya Sutskever, Kai Chen, Greg S Corrado, and Jeff Dean. 2013. Distributed representations of words and phrases and their compositionality. In *Advances in neural information processing systems*, pages 3111–3119.

[Morris et al.2008] Dan Morris, Meredith Ringel Morris, and Gina Venolia. 2008. Searchbar: a search-centric web history for task resumption and information refinding. In *Proceedings of the SIGCHI Conference on Human Factors in Computing Systems*, pages 1207–1216. ACM.

[Pass et al.2006] Greg Pass, Abdur Chowdhury, and Cayley Torgeson. 2006. A picture of search. In *InfoScale*, volume 152, page 1.

[Spink et al.2005] Amanda Spink, Sherry Koshman, Minsoo Park, Chris Field, and Bernard J Jansen. 2005.

Multitasking web search on vivisimo. com. In *Information Technology: Coding and Computing, 2005. ITCC 2005. International Conference on*, volume 2, pages 486–490. IEEE.

[Sun et al.2015] Ming Sun, Yun-Nung Chen, and Alexander I Rudnicky. 2015. Understanding users cross-domain intentions in spoken dialog systems. In *NIPS Workshop on Machine Learning for SLU and Interaction*.

[Verma and Yilmaz2014] Manisha Verma and Emine Yilmaz. 2014. Entity oriented task extraction from query logs. In *Proceedings of the 23rd ACM International Conference on Conference on Information and Knowledge Management*, pages 1975–1978. ACM.

[Wang and Blei2009] Chong Wang and David M Blei. 2009. Variational inference for the nested chinese restaurant process. In *Advances in Neural Information Processing Systems*, pages 1990–1998.

[Wang et al.2013] Hongning Wang, Yang Song, Ming-Wei Chang, Xiaodong He, Ryen W White, and Wei Chu. 2013. Learning to extract cross-session search tasks. In *Proceedings of the 22nd international conference on World Wide Web*, pages 1353–1364. International World Wide Web Conferences Steering Committee.

Probabilistic Models for Learning a Semantic Parser Lexicon

Jayant Krishnamurthy
Allen Institute for Artificial Intelligence
2157 N. Northlake Way, Suite 110
Seattle, WA 98103
jayantk@allenai.org

Abstract

We introduce several probabilistic models for learning the lexicon of a semantic parser. Lexicon learning is the first step of training a semantic parser for a new application domain and the quality of the learned lexicon significantly affects both the accuracy and efficiency of the final semantic parser. Existing work on lexicon learning has focused on heuristic methods that lack convergence guarantees and require significant human input in the form of lexicon templates or annotated logical forms. In contrast, our probabilistic models are trained directly from question/answer pairs using EM and our simplest model has a concave objective that guarantees convergence to a global optimum. An experimental evaluation on a set of 4th grade science questions demonstrates that our models improve semantic parser accuracy (35-70% error reduction) and efficiency (4-25x more sentences per second) relative to prior work despite using less human input. Our models also obtain competitive results on GEO880 without any dataset-specific engineering.

1 Introduction

Semantic parsing has recently gained popularity as a technique for mapping from natural language to a formal meaning representation language, e.g., in order to answer questions against a database (Zelle and Mooney, 1993; Zettlemoyer and Collins, 2005). In order to train a semantic parser, one must first provide a *lexicon*, which is a mapping from words in the language to statements in the meaning representation language. This mapping defines the grammar of

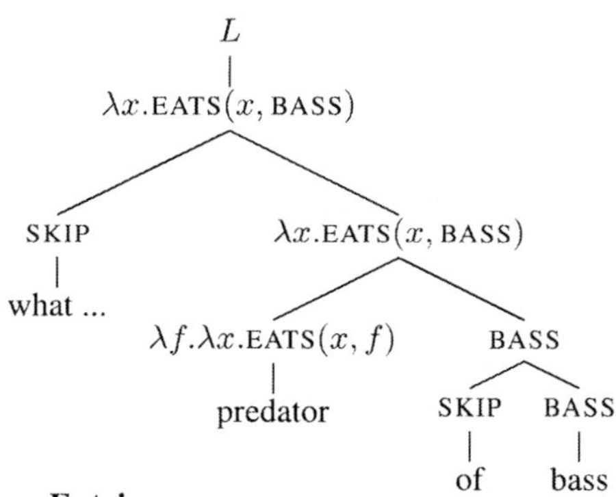

Lexicon Entries:
predator := N/NP : $\lambda f.\lambda x.\text{EATS}(x, f)$
bass := NP : BASS

Figure 1: Parse tree of a training example and the lexicon entries derived from it.

the parser and thereby determines the set of meaning representations that can be produced for any given sentence. Therefore, a good lexicon is necessary to achieve both high accuracy and parsing speed. However, the lexicon is unobserved in real semantic parsing applications, leading us to ask: *how do we learn a lexicon for a semantic parser?*

This paper presents several novel probabilistic models for learning a semantic parser lexicon. Existing lexicon learning algorithms are heuristic in nature and require either annotated logical forms or manually-specified lexicon entry templates during training. In contrast, our models do not require such templates and can be trained from question/answer pairs and other forms of weak supervision. Training consists of optimizing an objective function with Expectation Maximization (EM), thereby guaran-

Proceedings of NAACL-HLT 2016, pages 606–616,
San Diego, California, June 12-17, 2016. ©2016 Association for Computational Linguistics

teeing convergence to a local optimum. Furthermore, the objective function for our simplest model is *concave*, guaranteeing convergence to a global optimum. Our approach generates a probabilistic context-free grammar that represents the space of correct semantic parses for each question; once trained, our approach derives lexicon entries from the most likely parse of each question (Figure 1).

We present an experimental evaluation of our lexicon learning models on a data set of food chain questions from a 4th grade science domain. These questions concern relations between organisms in an ecosystem and have challenging lexical diversity and question length. Our models improve semantic parser accuracy (35-70% error reduction) over prior work despite using less human input. Furthermore, our best model produces a lexicon that contains 40x fewer entries than the most accurate baseline, resulting in a semantic parser that is 4x faster. Our models also obtain competitive results on GEO880 without any dataset-specific engineering.

2 Prior Work

Work on lexicon learning falls into two categories:

Pipelined approaches build a lexicon before training the parser, either by manually defining it (Lee et al., 2014; Angeli et al., 2012) or by using a collection of heuristics. The heuristics often take the form of *lexicon templates*, which are rules that create lexicon entries by pattern-matching training examples (Liang et al., 2011; Krishnamurthy and Mitchell, 2012; Krishnamurthy and Kollar, 2013). These approaches require new lexicon templates for each application. More complex heuristic algorithms have been proposed based on word alignments (Wong and Mooney, 2006; Wong and Mooney, 2007) or common substructures in the meaning representation (Chen and Mooney, 2011); these algorithms all require annotated logical forms.

Joint approaches simultaneously learn a lexicon and the parameters of a semantic parser. Typically, these algorithms use lexicon templates to generate a set of lexicon entries for each example, then heuristically select a subset of these entries to include in the global lexicon while training the parser (Zettlemoyer and Collins, 2005; Zettlemoyer and Collins, 2007; Artzi and Zettlemoyer, 2013b; Artzi et al., 2014).

UBL takes a different approach that performs top-down, iterative splits of an annotated logical form for each training example (Kwiatkowski et al., 2010; Kwiatkowski et al., 2011). Artzi et al. (2015) combine templates with top-down splitting. The heuristic search performed by these algorithms can be difficult to control and we empirically found that these algorithms often selected overly-specific lexicon entries (see Section 4.4).

Other work has avoided the lexicon learning problem altogether by searching over all possible meaning representations (Kate and Mooney, 2006; Clarke et al., 2010; Goldwasser et al., 2011; Berant and Liang, 2014; Pasupat and Liang, 2015; Reddy et al., 2014). The challenge of this approach is that the space of meaning representations for a sentence can be very large, making parsing less efficient and learning more difficult. A practical compromise is to combine a (possibly minimal) lexicon with flexible parsing operations (Liang et al., 2011; Zettlemoyer and Collins, 2007; Poon, 2013; Parikh et al., 2015).

Our lexicon learning models are closely related to machine translation word alignment models (Brown et al., 1993) – our key insight is that *lexicon learning is equivalent to word alignment where the tokenization of one of the sentences is unobserved*. Thus, our models simultaneously "tokenize" the logical form – using a splitting process similar to UBL – and align the resulting logical form "tokens" to words.

3 Probabilistic Models for Lexicon Learning

This section describes our lexicon learning models. For concreteness, we focus on learning a lexicon for a Combinatory Categorial Grammar (CCG) semantic parser with lambda calculus logical forms as the meaning representation; however, our models are applicable to other semantic parsing formalisms and meaning representation languages.

Our models learn a CCG lexicon from a data set of question/label pairs $\{(\mathbf{w}^i, L^i)\}_{i=1}^n$. Each question is a sequence of words, $\mathbf{w}^i = [w_1^i, w_2^i, ...]$, and each label is a *set* of logical forms, $L^i = \{\ell_1^i, ...\}$. Labeling each question with a set of logical forms generalizes many weak supervision settings, including ambiguous supervision (Kate and Mooney, 2007) and ques-

Training Example:

$\mathbf{w}$ = What is the predator of bass ?

L = $\{\lambda x.\text{EATS}(x, \text{BASS}),$

$\quad\quad \lambda x.\text{CAUSE}(\text{INCREASE}(\text{BASS}), \text{INCREASE}(x)),$

$\quad\quad ...\}$

Generated Grammar:

Unary rules:

$L \to \lambda x.\text{EATS}(x, \text{BASS})$

$L \to \lambda x.\text{CAUSE}(\text{INCREASE}(\text{BASS}), \text{INCREASE}(x))$

Nonterminal rules:

$\lambda x.\text{EATS}(x, \text{BASS}) \to \text{BASS} \;\; \lambda f.\lambda x.\text{EATS}(x, f)$

$\lambda x.\text{EATS}(x, \text{BASS}) \to \lambda f.\lambda x.\text{EATS}(x, f) \;\; \text{BASS}$

$\text{BASS} \to \text{SKIP} \;\; \text{BASS}$

...

Terminal rules:

$\lambda x.\text{EATS}(x, \text{BASS}) \to$ what

$\lambda x.\text{EATS}(x, \text{BASS}) \to$ is

$\text{SKIP} \to$ what

...

Figure 2: Training example (top) and several of the rules in its logical form derivation grammar (bottom).

tion/answer pairs (Liang et al., 2011).[1] The output of learning is a collection of lexicon entries $w := C : \ell$ mapping word w to syntactic category C and logical form ℓ.

Our models are generative models of questions given a label, $P(\mathbf{w}|L)$. The key component of each model is a probabilistic context-free grammar (PCFG) over *correct* logical form derivations. A parse tree in this grammar simultaneously represents (1) the choice of a logical form $\ell \in L$, (2) the way ℓ is constructed from smaller parts, and (3) the alignment between these parts and words in the question. Training each model amounts to learning the rule probabilities of this grammar, including which logical forms are likely to generate which words. Parsing an example with the trained grammar produces an alignment between words and logical forms that is used to construct a lexicon.

3.1 Logical Form Derivation Grammar

The logical form derivation grammar is a PCFG constructed to represent the set of correct logical form derivations – i.e., correct semantic parses – of each

---

[1] In the second case, the set L can be generated by enumerating logical forms and evaluating each one to determine if it produces the correct answer. See Section 5 for a discussion of the benefits and limitations of this process.

training example. The grammar's nonterminals are logical forms and its binary production rules represent ways that pairs of logical forms can combine in the semantic parser. The grammar's terminals are words and its terminal production rules represent lexicon entries. The complete grammar is a union of many smaller grammars, each of which is constructed to represent the logical form derivations of a single example. Figure 2 shows a training example and a portion of the grammar generated for it, and Figure 1 shows a parse tree in the grammar.

Our algorithm for constructing the PCFG for a training example $(\mathbf{w}, L)$ uses a top-down approach that iteratively splits logical forms in L. Assume we are given a procedure $\text{SPLIT}(f)$ that outputs a list of ways to split f into a pair of logical forms (g, h). Grammar generation performs the following steps:

1. **Model weak supervision.** Add L to the grammar as a nonterminal and add a unary rule $L \to \ell$ for all $\ell \in L$.

2. **Enumerate logical form splits.** For all $\ell \in L$, perform a depth-first search over logical forms starting at ℓ. To explore a logical form f during the search, use $\text{SPLIT}(f)$ to produce a collection of g, h pairs. For each g, h pair, add the binary rules $f \to g\ h$ and $f \to h\ g$ to the grammar, then add g and h to the search queue for later exploration.

3. **Create lexicon entries.** Add a terminal rule $f \to w$ to G for every word in the question, $w \in \mathbf{w}$, and logical form f encountered during the search above.

4. **Allow word skipping.** Add a special SKIP nonterminal, along with the rules $f \to f\ \text{SKIP}$, $f \to \text{SKIP}\ f$ and $\text{SKIP} \to w$ for all logical forms f and words $w \in \mathbf{w}$.

The SPLIT procedure required above depends on the meaning representation language, but is application-independent. For our lambda calculus representation, $\text{SPLIT}(f)$ returns a list of logical forms g, h such that $f = g(h)$. We use similar constraints as Kwiatkowski et al. (2011) to keep the number of splits manageable. Note that SPLIT could also include composition by returning g, h

pairs such that $f = \lambda x.g(h(x))$; however, we did not explore this possibility in this paper.

An important property of this grammar is that it *excludes many logical form derivations that cannot lead to the label*. For example, the grammar in Figure 2 does not let us apply $\lambda x.\text{EATS}(x, \text{BASS})$ to BASS – even though this operation would be permitted by CCG – because there is no way to reach the label L from the result $\text{EATS}(\text{BASS}, \text{BASS})$. This property reduces the number of possible parses of a question relative to a CCG parser with the same lexicon entries, making parsing more efficient.

The logical form derivation grammar G is constructed by applying the above process to every example in the data set. Let $P(t|L;\theta)$ denote the probability of generating tree t from G given $\text{ROOT}(t) = L$ and parameters θ. This probability factors into a product of production rule probabilities:

$$P(t|L;\theta) = \prod_{(f \to g\ h) \in t} P(f \to g\ h;\theta) \times$$
$$\prod_{(f \to w) \in t} P(f \to w;\theta)$$

In the above equation, $P(f \to g\ h;\theta)$ and $P(f \to w;\theta)$ represent the conditional probability of selecting a production rule given the nonterminal f. We use $P(\mathbf{w}, t|L;\theta)$ to denote $P(t|L;\theta)$ where the terminals of t are equal to the question $\mathbf{w}$. In the following, sums over trees t are implicitly over all trees permitted by G.

3.2 Independent Model

The independent model assumes that each word w_j of a question $\mathbf{w}$ is generated independently from a parse tree t chosen uniformly at random given the label L. This simple model allows two words in the same question to be generated by different trees. The probability of a question given a label is:

$$P(\mathbf{w}|L;\theta) = \prod_{j=1}^{|\mathbf{w}|} \sum_f P(f \to w_j;\theta) \#(f, j, L, |\mathbf{w}|)$$

The final term $\#(f, j, L, |\mathbf{w}|)$ is the fraction of trees with root L and $|\mathbf{w}|$ terminals where the jth terminal symbol is generated by nonterminal f. This

term appears due to the assumption that trees are drawn uniformly at random. The parameters θ of this model are the terminal production rule probabilities, which are modeled as a conditional probability table: $P(f \to w;\theta) = \theta_{f,w}$ where $\sum_w \theta_{f,w} = 1$.

The independent model is a generalization of IBM Model 1 (Brown et al., 1993) to the lexicon learning problem, and – like IBM Model 1 – its loglikelihood function is *concave* (see Appendix A). Therefore, the EM algorithm will converge to a global optimum of the data loglikelihood under this model.

3.3 Coupled Model

The coupled model generates the entire question $\mathbf{w}$ from a single parse tree t that is generated given L. This model removes the previous model's naïve assumption that each word is generated independently. The probability of a question given a label under this model is:

$$P(\mathbf{w}|L;\theta) = \sum_t P(\mathbf{w}, t|L;\theta)$$

Theoretically, we could learn both of the production rule distributions that compose $P(\mathbf{w}, t|L;\theta)$ in this formulation. However, in practice, the large number of nonterminals makes it challenging to learn a conditional probability table for the binary production rules. Therefore, we again assume the trees are drawn uniformly at random and only learn a conditional probability table for the terminal production rules.

3.4 Coupled Loglinear Model

The coupled loglinear model replaces the conditional probability tables of the coupled model with loglinear models. Loglinear models can share parameters across different – but intuitively similar – production rules. For example, both $\lambda x.\text{EATS}(x, \text{BASS})$ and $\lambda x.\text{EATS}(x, \text{FROG})$ should have similar distributions over production rules when BASS is appropriately replaced by FROG. We can produce this effect with loglinear models by assigning similar feature vectors to these rules.

This model uses *three* locally-normalized loglinear models to parameterize the distribution over production rules. First, a rule model decides whether or not to apply a terminal production rule. Next, given this model's response, a second loglinear model decides which of the chosen kind of rules to apply. This approach ensures that each nonterminal symbol has a proper conditional probability distribution over rules. The production rule distributions are parameterized as:

$$P(f \to w; \theta) = \frac{\exp(\theta_r^T \phi_r(f) + \theta_t^T \phi_t(f, w))}{Z_r Z_t(f)}$$

$$P(f \to g \, h; \theta) = \frac{\exp(\theta_n^T \phi_n(f, g, h))}{Z_r Z_n(f)}$$

In the above equation, the r, t and n subscripts indicate terms of the rule, terminal and nonterminal models, respectively. The Z_r, $Z_t(f)$ and $Z_n(f)$ terms denote the partition functions of each model, and ϕ_r, ϕ_n and ϕ_t are functions mapping nonterminals and production rules to feature vectors. We use indicator features for logical form patterns, where each pattern is produced by replacing all of a logical form's subexpressions below a certain depth with their types.

3.5 Training with Expectation Maximization

We train all three models by maximizing data loglikelihood with EM (Dempster et al., 1977). Training the independent model is equivalent to training a mixture of multinomials where each word of each question has its own prior over cluster assignments. Let θ^m represent the model parameters on the mth training iteration. The E-step calculates expected count of each terminal production rule:

$$E_{f,w} \leftarrow \sum_{i,j:w_j^i=w} P(f \to w_j^i; \theta^m) \#(f, j, L^i, |\mathbf{w}^i|)$$

The term $\#(f, j, L^i, |\mathbf{w}^i|)$ – representing the fraction of trees where nonterminal f generates the jth word of question i – can be calculated by parsing each example once using the inside/outside algorithm. The M-step re-estimates the terminal production rule probabilities using these expected counts:

$$\theta_{f,w}^{m+1} \leftarrow \frac{E_{f,w}}{\sum_{w'} E_{f,w'}}$$

Training the coupled models is a standard application of EM to learning the parameters of a latent probabilistic CFG. The E-step calculates the expected number of occurrences of each production rule in each example:

$$E_{f,g,h} \leftarrow \sum_{i,t} \#(f \to g \, h, t) P(t|\mathbf{w}^i, L^i; \theta^m)$$

$$E_{f,w} \leftarrow \sum_{i,t} \#(f \to w, t) P(t|\mathbf{w}^i, L^i; \theta^m)$$

In the above equation, the function $\#(f \to w; t)$ returns the number of occurrences of $f \to w$ in t. These expected counts can be computed efficiently using the inside/outside algorithm.[2] The M-step of the coupled model is the same as that of the independent model above. The M-step of the coupled loglinear model solves an optimization problem to fit the loglinear models to the computed expectations (Berg-Kirkpatrick et al., 2010):

$$\theta^{m+1} \leftarrow \arg\max_{\theta} \sum_{f,w} E_{f,w} \log P(f \to w; \theta) + \\ \sum_{f,g,h} E_{f,g,h} \log P(f \to g \, h; \theta)$$

This problem factors into three separate optimization problems: a binary logistic regression for the rule model, and estimating two conditional distributions over nonterminal and terminal production rules. We use L-BFGS to solve these problems.

3.6 Producing a Lexicon

Given parameters θ and a data set $\{(\mathbf{w}^i, L^i)\}_{i=1}^n$, we produce a CCG lexicon from the terminal production rules of the most probable parse of each example. First, we parse each question $\mathbf{w}^i$ conditioning on the parse tree root being L^i. Second, we generate lexicon entries from the highest scoring parse tree for each example. We identify the nonterminal f that generates each word $w \in \mathbf{w}$ and, if $f \neq$ SKIP, create a lexicon entry $w := C : f$. As in previous work, we derive the syntactic category C from the semantic type of the logical form (Kwiatkowski et

---

[2]A further efficiency improvement is to note that, when parsing an example, it is sufficient to use the subset of G that was generated for it.

w: Which organism in the diagram is eaten by the blackbird?

ℓ: $\lambda x.\text{EATS}(\text{BLACKBIRD}, x)$

c: sun → grains → blackbird → hawk → falcon

a: grains

---

w: The __ is neither a producer or a consumer.

ℓ: $\lambda x.\text{NOT}(\text{ANIMAL}(x) \lor \text{PLANT}(x))$,

c: sun → grasses → hartebeest → lion

a: sun

---

w: If the sun is blocked by clouds for a long period of time, which animal will be most quickly threatened by starvation?

ℓ: $\lambda x.\text{CAUSE}(\text{DECREASE}(\text{SUN}), \text{DECREASE}(x))$

c: sun → algae → shrimp → smelt → salmon

a: algae

---

w: If the seals were killed off, the population of penguin would most likely

ℓ: $\lambda f.\text{CAUSE}(\text{DECREASE}(\text{SEAL}), f(\text{PENGUIN}))$

c: sun → algae → squid → penguin → seal

a: increase

Figure 3: Examples from FOODCHAINS. Each example consists of a question w, logical form ℓ, food chain c and answer a.

al., 2011). The argument directions of C are determined by walking up the tree and noting the relative position of each of its arguments. Figure 1 shows an example of a predicted parse tree and the lexicon entries generated from it.

4 Evaluation

We compare our lexicon learning models against several baselines on two data sets: FOODCHAINS, containing 4th grade science food chain questions, and GEO880, containing geography questions. These data sets each present different challenges for lexicon learning: FOODCHAINS has more difficult language – long questions and more lexical variation – while GEO880 has more complex logical forms. Our results demonstrate that our models perform better than several baselines with difficult language while simultaneously performing reasonably well with complex logical forms.

Code, data and other supplementary material for this paper is available at http://www.allenai.org/paper-appendix/ naacl2016-lexicon.

	FOODCHAINS	GEO880
Examples	774	880
Word types	446	279
Word types w/o entity names	357	157
Tokens per question	11.6	7.56
Predicates in ontology	15	38
Constants per logical form	4.0	7.7

Table 1: Data statistics for FOODCHAINS and GEO880.

4.1 Data

We collected a new data set, FOODCHAINS, that contains 774 food chain questions designed to imitate actual questions from the New York State Grade 4 Regents Exam. Each example in the data set consists of a natural language question and a food chain, which is a list of organisms that eat each other. The questions are multiple choice and the answer options are either animals from the food chain or a direction of change, e.g., "increase." Each question also has a logical form annotated by the first author, which is necessary to train some of the baseline systems. The denotation of each predicate – and therefore logical form – is a deterministic function of the food chain. Figure 3 shows some examples from this data set.

FOODCHAINS was created using Mechanical Turk. We first manually created 25 distinct food chains of various lengths containing different organisms and a set of question templates – questions with a blank – based on real Regents questions. In the first task, Turk workers were shown a randomly-selected food chain, question template, and answer, and were asked to complete the question by filling in the blank. In the second task, workers paraphrased questions from the first task, thereby eliminating the templated structure and increasing lexical variation (similar to Wang et al., (2015)). In the third task, a worker validated each question by answering it.

Statistics of FOODCHAINS are presented in Table 1 alongside corresponding statistics of GEO880 (Zelle and Mooney, 1996; Tang and Mooney, 2001; Zettlemoyer and Collins, 2005). FOODCHAINS differs from GEO880 in two significant and interesting ways. First, although the data set contains relatively few predicates, there are many ways to reference each predicate – for example, consider the diversity in references to DECREASE in Figure 3. Second, the questions are long but contain many uninformative

Model	Accuracy
Independent Model (§3.2)	78.7%
Coupled Model (§3.3)	79.0%
Coupled Loglinear Model (§3.4)	**81.7%**

Table 2: Comparison of semantic parser accuracy on FOOD-CHAINS when trained using our three proposed probabilistic models for lexicon learning.

Model	Logical forms?	Lexicon Templates?	PAL Accuracy	% Err. Red.
PAL	**No**	**No**	**81.7%**	–
POS	**No**	Yes	70.5%	38.0%
UBL	Yes	**No**	40.6%	69.1%
ZC2007	Yes	Yes	49.4%	63.8%
ADP2014	**No**	Yes	32.4%	72.9%

Table 3: Semantic parser accuracy comparison for several lexicon learning algorithms on FOODCHAINS. The middle two columns note the human input required by each algorithm and the final column notes the relative error reduction of PAL over each baseline.

words that can safely be ignored by the parser.

4.2 Methodology

We compare lexicon learning algorithms by performing an end-to-end evaluation, measuring the question answering accuracy of a CCG semantic parser trained with the learned lexicon. The parser has a rich set of features, including lexicon entry features, dependency features, and dependency distance features. The parser is also permitted to skip words in the question for a learned per-word cost. We train the parser by optimizing data loglikelihood with 100 epochs of stochastic gradient descent.

All experiments on FOODCHAINS are performed using 5-fold cross validation. All questions about a single food chain appear in the same fold, ensuring that the questions in the held-out fold reference unseen food chains.

4.3 Comparing Probabilistic Models

Our initial experiment compares the three probabilistic models proposed in Section 3 on FOOD-CHAINS. We generated three lexicons by training each model using 10 iterations of EM. We used a smoothing parameter of 0.1 when estimating conditional probability tables, and an L2 regularization parameter of 10^{-6} when estimating loglinear models. We also initialized the coupled model with the optimum of the independent model. All of these models are trained without labeled logical forms, instead using an automatically enumerated set of logical forms that evaluate to the correct answer.

Table 2 presents the result of this evaluation. All three models perform roughly similarly, with the coupled loglinear model slightly outperforming the others. The competitive performance of the independent model is interesting because its concave objective function is easy to optimize. The remaining experiments compare against the coupled loglinear

model, which we dub PAL, short for "Probabilistic Alignments for Lexicon learning."

4.4 Lexicon Learning Baselines

Our second experiment compares PAL with four baseline lexicon learning algorithms. The first baseline, POS, defines a set of lexicon entries for each word in the training set based on its part-of-speech tag (Liang et al., 2011). We iteratively developed these templates to cover the data set, and the lexicon generated by these templates can correctly parse 96% of the examples in FOODCHAINS. The remaining three baselines, ZC2007 (Zettlemoyer and Collins, 2007), UBL (Kwiatkowski et al., 2011), and ADP2014 (Artzi et al., 2014), are joint lexicon and parameter learning algorithms. We used the UW SPF (Artzi and Zettlemoyer, 2013a) implementations of UBL and ZC2007. For these two models, we trained our parser using the learned lexicon to ensure consistency of implementation details.[3] We initialized UBL's parameters using GIZA++ (Och and Ney, 2003) as in the original paper. The lexicon entry templates for ZC2007 and ADP2014 are derived from the POS templates to ensure coverage of the questions; these algorithms allow each template to apply to 1-4 word phrases.

Table 3 compares the accuracy of semantic parsers trained with these baseline approaches to PAL. Our model outperforms all of the baselines, beating the most accurate baseline, POS, by more

---

[3]We also postprocessed the lexicon entries to improve performance, for example, by removing lexicon entries that skip words. In both cases, our parser was more accurate than the UW SPF parser.

Model	Lexicon Size	Parse Time (ms)
POS	4,282	7.8
UBL	3,356	14.9
ZC2007	2,949	43.4
ADP2014	401	1.1
Independent Model	410	6.7
Coupled Model	318	3.1
PAL	184	1.8

Table 4: Lexicon size excluding entity names and parse time per question on FOODCHAINS averaged across folds per model. Our models produce smaller lexicons that lead to faster semantic parsers.

Model	Accuracy
UBL (Kwiatkowski et al., 2011)	88.6%
ZC2007 (Zettlemoyer and Collins, 2007)	86.1%
PAL	81.8%
w/ factored lexicon	85.4%

Table 5: Logical form accuracy on GEO880 compared to previously reported CCG parsing results. Both UBL and ZC2007 use special CCG extensions to improve performance; adding one of these to PAL brings its accuracy near that of these systems.

than 10 points. Note that all of these baselines also use more human input than our model, either in the form of lexicon templates or logical forms. Table 4 compares the average number of lexicon entries and semantic parser speed of the baselines with our models. PAL produces the most compact lexicon and second fastest parser, which is 4x faster than POS, the baseline with the highest accuracy. The correlation between lexicon size and parse time is imperfect due to word frequency and co-occurrence effects.

The three joint lexicon and parameter learning algorithms perform poorly on our data set for two reasons. First, the long question length increases the difficulty of finding good lexicon entries. The algorithms with lexicon templates were frequently unable to find a correct parse for long questions, even with a large beam size – we ran ADP2014 with a beam size of 10000. (Note that POS does not suffer from this problem because it only generates lexicon entries for a few parts of speech, so most of the words in a question are ignored by default.) Second, these algorithms' discriminative objectives inherently prefer lexicon entries with highly specific word sequences. This preference interacts poorly with the uninformative words in the data set, leading these algorithms to produce many lexicon entries for long phrases that do not generalize well. The lexicon sizes in Table 4 are suggestive of this problem for ZC2007 and UBL; ADP2014 also has this problem, but its voting mechanism prunes lexicon entries much more aggressively. We tried to solve this problem for ZC2007 and ADP2014 by restricting lexicon templates to apply to at most 1 word, but this change actually reduced accuracy. An investigation of this

phenomenon found that reducing the length of the templates made it even more difficult for these models to find correct parses for long questions.

In contrast to these baselines, our models do not suffer from either of these problems because the logical form derivation grammar restricts the search to *correct* derivations and our generative objective prefers frequently-occurring lexicon entries. Our models actually consider a *larger* space of possible lexicon entries than ZC2007 and ADP2014 with 1 word templates, yet find better lexicon entries.

4.5 Geo880 Evaluation

We performed an additional evaluation on GEO880 to demonstrate that our models can work with more complex logical forms. GEO880 is a good data set for this evaluation because its logical forms contain, on average, about twice as many constants as FOODCHAINS. We applied PAL to generate a lexicon for this data set using its included logical form labels, then trained a CCG semantic parser with this lexicon. Table 5 compares the accuracy of this parser with previous CCG lexicon learning results on this data set using the standard 600/280 train/test split. The comparison to PAL is inexact because both prior systems use CCG parsers with special extensions that improve performance on this data set. UBL uses factored lexicon entries that generalize better to certain infrequent entries, and ZC2007 includes relaxed parsing operators that fix common parsing errors. Examining the errors made by our parser, we found many cases where these extensions would help. We therefore trained another CCG parser using a lexicon generated by postprocessing PAL's lexicon to include factored lexicon entries. This parser achieves an accuracy close to previous work.

5 Discussion

We introduce several probabilistic models for learning a semantic parser lexicon that can be trained from question/answer pairs and other forms of weak supervision. Our experimental results demonstrate that our models improve semantic parser accuracy and efficiency relative to prior work on data sets with more challenging language, despite using less human input. Furthermore, we find that our independent model is nearly as effective as more complex models, but has a concave objective function that guarantees training converges to a global optimum.

A possible complaint about our approach is that, when training from question/answer pairs, it is not practical to enumerate all logical forms that produce the correct answer. We believe this complaint is misguided because enumerating logical forms is unavoidable in the question/answer setting. *Every* algorithm uses an enumerate-and-test approach to identify correct logical forms; this process occurs in the gradient computation of semantic parser training and in template-based lexicon learning algorithms such as ADP2014. The critical question is not *whether* enumeration is used, but rather *how* logical forms are enumerated. Many strategies are possible and different strategies are likely to be effective on different data sets. In fact, the failure of template-based algorithms on FOODCHAINS is largely a failure of their template-guided enumeration strategy to find correct logical forms. Choosing an enumeration strategy and related questions – e.g., does semantic parser parameter learning affect the enumeration? – are empirical questions that must be decided on a task-specific basis.

A recent trend in semantic parsing has been to avoid lexicon learning, instead directly searching the space of all possible logical forms. However, we think that lexicon learning still serves a valuable purpose. Fundamentally, a lexicon constrains the space of logical forms searched by a semantic parser; these constraints improve efficiency and can improve accuracy as long as they do not exclude correct logical forms. Thus, a promising approach to building a semantic parser is to automatically learn a lexicon using one of our models, then (perhaps) manually specify new parsing operations to correct any problems with the learned lexicon. We plan to apply this approach in the future to construct semantic parsers for more challenging tasks.

Acknowledgments

We gratefully acknowledge Oyvind Tafjord, Matt Gardner, Peter Turney, Oren Etzioni and the anonymous reviewers for their helpful comments.

References

Gabor Angeli, Christopher D. Manning, and Daniel Jurafsky. 2012. Parsing time: Learning to interpret time expressions. In *Proceedings of the 2012 Conference of the North American Chapter of the Association for Computational Linguistics: Human Language Technologies*.

Yoav Artzi and Luke Zettlemoyer. 2013a. UW SPF: The University of Washington Semantic Parsing Framework.

Yoav Artzi and Luke Zettlemoyer. 2013b. Weakly supervised learning of semantic parsers for mapping instructions to actions. *Transactions of the Association for Computational Linguistics*.

Yoav Artzi, Dipanjan Das, and Slav Petrov. 2014. Learning compact lexicons for CCG semantic parsing. In *Proceedings of the 2014 Conference on Empirical Methods in Natural Language Processing*.

Yoav Artzi, Kenton Lee, and Luke Zettlemoyer. 2015. Broad-coverage CCG semantic parsing with AMR. In *Proceedings of the 2015 Conference on Empirical Methods in Natural Language Processing*.

Jonathan Berant and Percy Liang. 2014. Semantic parsing via paraphrasing. In *Proceedings of the 52nd Annual Meeting of the Association for Computational Linguistics*.

Taylor Berg-Kirkpatrick, Alexandre Bouchard-Côté, John DeNero, and Dan Klein. 2010. Painless unsupervised learning with features. In *Human Language Technologies: The 2010 Annual Conference of the North American Chapter of the Association for Computational Linguistics*.

Peter F. Brown, Vincent J. Della Pietra, Stephen A. Della Pietra, and Robert L. Mercer. 1993. The mathematics of statistical machine translation: Parameter estimation. *Computational Linguistics*.

David L. Chen and Raymond J. Mooney. 2011. Learning to interpret natural language navigation instructions from observations. In *Proceedings of the 25th AAAI Conference on Artificial Intelligence*.

James Clarke, Dan Goldwasser, Ming-Wei Chang, and Dan Roth. 2010. Driving semantic parsing from the world's response. In *Proceedings of the Fourteenth Conference on Computational Natural Language Learning*.

Arthur P. Dempster, Nan M. Laird, and Donald B. Rubin. 1977. Maximum likelihood from incomplete data via the EM algorithm. *Journal of the royal statistical society. Series B (methodological)*, pages 1–38.

Dan Goldwasser, Roi Reichart, James Clarke, and Dan Roth. 2011. Confidence driven unsupervised semantic parsing. In *Proceedings of the 49th Annual Meeting of the Association for Computational Linguistics*.

Rohit J. Kate and Raymond J. Mooney. 2006. Using string-kernels for learning semantic parsers. In *21st International Conference on Computational Linguistics and 44th Annual Meeting of the Association for Computational Linguistics, Proceedings of the Conference*.

Rohit J. Kate and Raymond J. Mooney. 2007. Learning language semantics from ambiguous supervision. In *Proceedings of the 22nd Conference on Artificial Intelligence*.

Jayant Krishnamurthy and Thomas Kollar. 2013. Jointly learning to parse and perceive: Connecting natural language to the physical world. *Transactions of the Association of Computational Linguistics – Volume 1*.

Jayant Krishnamurthy and Tom M. Mitchell. 2012. Weakly supervised training of semantic parsers. In *Proceedings of the 2012 Joint Conference on Empirical Methods in Natural Language Processing and Computational Natural Language Learning*.

Tom Kwiatkowski, Luke Zettlemoyer, Sharon Goldwater, and Mark Steedman. 2010. Inducing probabilistic CCG grammars from logical form with higher-order unification. In *Proceedings of the 2010 Conference on Empirical Methods in Natural Language Processing*.

Tom Kwiatkowski, Luke Zettlemoyer, Sharon Goldwater, and Mark Steedman. 2011. Lexical generalization in CCG grammar induction for semantic parsing. In *Proceedings of the Conference on Empirical Methods in Natural Language Processing*.

Kenton Lee, Yoav Artzi, Jesse Dodge, and Luke Zettlemoyer. 2014. Context-dependent semantic parsing for time expressions. In *Proceedings of the 52nd Annual Meeting of the Association for Computational Linguistics (Volume 1: Long Papers)*.

Percy Liang, Michael I. Jordan, and Dan Klein. 2011. Learning dependency-based compositional semantics. In *Proceedings of the Association for Computational Linguistics*.

Franz Josef Och and Hermann Ney. 2003. A systematic comparison of various statistical alignment models. *Computational Linguistics*.

Ankur P. Parikh, Hoifung Poon, and Kristina Toutanova. 2015. Grounded semantic parsing for complex knowledge extraction. In *Proceedings of the 2015 Conference of the North American Chapter of the Association for Computational Linguistics: Human Language Technologies*.

Panupong Pasupat and Percy Liang. 2015. Compositional semantic parsing on semi-structured tables. In *Proceedings of the 53rd Annual Meeting of the Association for Computational Linguistics and the 7th International Joint Conference on Natural Language Processing (Volume 1: Long Papers)*.

Hoifung Poon. 2013. Grounded unsupervised semantic parsing. In *Proceedings of the 51st Annual Meeting of the Association for Computational Linguistics (Volume 1: Long Papers)*.

Siva Reddy, Mirella Lapata, and Mark Steedman. 2014. Large-scale semantic parsing without question-answer pairs. *Transactions of the Association for Computational Linguistics*.

Lappoon R. Tang and Raymond J. Mooney. 2001. Using multiple clause constructors in inductive logic programming for semantic parsing. In *Proceedings of the 12th European Conference on Machine Learning*.

Yushi Wang, Jonathan Berant, and Percy Liang. 2015. Building a semantic parser overnight. In *Proceedings of the 53rd Annual Meeting of the Association for Computational Linguistics and the 7th International Joint Conference on Natural Language Processing*.

Yuk Wah Wong and Raymond J. Mooney. 2006. Learning for semantic parsing with statistical machine translation. In *Proceedings of the Human Language Technology Conference of the NAACL*.

Yuk Wah Wong and Raymond J. Mooney. 2007. Learning synchronous grammars for semantic parsing with lambda calculus. In *Proceedings of the 45th Annual Meeting of the Association for Computational Linguistics*.

John M. Zelle and Raymond J. Mooney. 1993. Learning semantic grammars with constructive inductive logic programming. In *Proceedings of the 11th National Conference on Artificial Intelligence*.

John M. Zelle and Raymond J. Mooney. 1996. Learning to parse database queries using inductive logic programming. In *Proceedings of the Thirteenth National Conference on Artificial Intelligence*.

Luke S. Zettlemoyer and Michael Collins. 2005. Learning to map sentences to logical form: structured classification with probabilistic categorial grammars. In *UAI '05, Proceedings of the 21st Conference in Uncertainty in Artificial Intelligence*.

Luke S. Zettlemoyer and Michael Collins. 2007. Online learning of relaxed CCG grammars for parsing to logical form. In *Proceedings of the 2007 Joint Conference*

*on Empirical Methods in Natural Language Process-
ing and Computational Natural Language Learning.*

Appendix A: Proof of Concavity

The loglikelihood $O(\theta)$ of the independent model is:

$$O(\theta) = \sum_{i=1}^{n} \log P(\mathbf{w}^i | L^i; \theta)$$

$$= \sum_{i=1}^{n} \sum_{j=1}^{|\mathbf{w}^i|} \log \sum_{f} \theta_{f,w_j^i} \#(f, j, L^i, |\mathbf{w}^i|)$$

Each log term above is concave in θ because log is a
concave function applied to an affine function of θ.
(Note that the $\#(f, j, L^i, |\mathbf{w}^i|)$ terms do not depend
on θ.) Finally, $O(\theta)$ is concave because it is a sum
of concave functions.

Unsupervised Compound Splitting With Distributional Semantics Rivals Supervised Methods

Martin Riedl and **Chris Biemann**
Language Technology
Computer Science Department, Technische Universität Darmstadt
Hochschulstrasse 10, D-64289 Darmstadt, Germany
{riedl,biem}@cs.tu-darmstadt.de

Abstract

In this paper we present a word decompounding method that is based on distributional semantics. Our method does not require any linguistic knowledge and is initialized using a large monolingual corpus. The core idea of our approach is that parts of compounds (like "candle" and "stick") are semantically similar to the entire compound, which helps to exclude spurious splits (like "candles" and "tick"). We report results for German and Dutch: For German, our unsupervised method comes on par with the performance of a rule-based and a supervised method and significantly outperforms two unsupervised baselines. For Dutch, our method performs only slightly below a rule-based optimized compound splitter.

1 Introduction

Germanic and agglutinative languages (e.g. German, Swedish, Finnish, Korean) have a productive morphology that allows the formation of not space-separated compounds in a much larger extent than e.g. in English. The task of separating such compounds into their corresponding single word (sub-) units is called compound splitting or decompounding.

Decompounding showed impact in several NLP applications, e.g. ASR (Adda-Decker and Adda, 2000), MT (Koehn and Knight, 2003) or IR (Monz and de Rijke, 2001), and is generally perceived as a crucial component for the processing of respective languages. However, most existing systems rely on dictionaries or are trained in a supervised fashion. Both approaches require substantial manual work and do not adapt to vocabulary change. In this paper we introduce an unsupervised method for decompounding that relies on distributional semantics. For the computation of the semantic model we solely rely on a tokenized monolingual corpus and do not require any further linguistic processing. Most previous research on compound splitting concentrates on the detection of lemmas that form the compound. Whereas this is important for several tasks, in this work we focus on the splitting of a compound into its word units without any base form reduction, arguing that lemmatization is either part of the task pipeline anyways (e.g. IR) or not required (e.g. for ASR).

2 Related Work

Approaches to automatic decompounding can be classified into corpus-driven approaches and supervised approaches. Corpus-driven approaches are usually informed by a frequency list (Koehn and Knight, 2003), by a probabilistic model (Schiller, 2005), by parallel corpora (Koehn and Knight, 2003; Macherey et al., 2011) or by the existence of periphrases (i.e. reformulations) in large monolingual corpora (Holz and Biemann, 2008). As with other tasks, supervised approaches are usually superior to unsupervised approaches if sufficient training material is provided. A straightforward yet effective supervised decompounding system is contained in the ASV Toolbox (Biemann et al., 2008), which uses trie-based datastructures for recursively splitting compounds based on learned splits. Alfonseca

Proceedings of NAACL-HLT 2016, pages 617–622,
San Diego, California, June 12-17, 2016. ©2016 Association for Computational Linguistics

et al. (2008) combine several signals, including web anchor text, in an SVM-based supervised splitter. A widely used German decompounder is JWordSplitter[1], which is based on word lists of compound parts as well as manually crafted blacklists and whitelists. The NL Splitter[2] uses similar technology for Dutch compound decomposition. An unsupervised approach is presented in (Koehn and Knight, 2003): out of several splits as given by matching parts of the compound to a vocabulary list, they pick the split with the highest geometric mean of word frequencies, which is entirely corpus-driven but ignores semantic relations between the compound and its parts. Another unsupervised system is proposed by Daiber et al. (2015). They propose an analogy-based approach, which relies on word embeddings.

Decompounding is evaluated either intrinsically or in a task that benefits from it, e.g. IR (Monz and de Rijke, 2001), MT (Koehn and Knight, 2003; Macherey et al., 2011) or ASR (Adda-Decker and Adda, 2000; Ordelman et al., 2003).

3 Method

The introduced method, called SECOS (SEmantic COmpound Splitter)[3], is based on the hypothesis that compounds are similar to their constituting word units. Our method is based on a distributional thesaurus (DT) that is computed, based on the distributional hypothesis (Harris, 1951), using a monolingual background corpus and does not require any language-specific rules or preprocessing. We exemplify the method based on the compound noun *Bundesfinanzministerium* (*federal finance ministry*), which is assembled of the words *Bundes* (*federal*), *Finanz* (*finance*) and *Ministerium* (*ministry*).

Our method consists of three stages: First we extract a candidate word set that defines the possible word units of compounds. We present several approaches to generate such candidates. Second, we use a general method that splits the compound based on a candidate word set. Using the different candidate sets, we obtain different compound splits. Fi-

nally, we define a mechanism that ranks these splits and returns the top-ranked one.

3.1 Candidate Extraction

For the extraction of all candidates in C, we use a distributional thesaurus (DT) that is computed on a background corpus. We present three approaches for the generation of candidate sets.

When we retrieve the l most similar terms for a word w from a DT, we observe well-suited candidates that are nested in w. For example *Bundesfinanzministerium* is similar to *Bund*, *Bundes* and *Finanzministerium*. Extracting the most similar terms that are nested in w results in the first split candidate set, called *similar candidate units*.

However, only for few terms we observe nested candidates in the most similar words. Thus, we require methods to generate "back-off" candidates.

First, we introduce the *extended similar candidate units*. Here, we extract the l most similar terms for w and then grow this set by again adding their respective l most similar words. Based on these terms, we extract all words that are nested in w. This results into more but less precise decompounding candidates.

As the coverage might still be insufficient to decompound all words (e.g. entirely unseen compounds), we propose a method to generate a global dictionary of single atomic word units. For this, we iterate over the entire vocabulary of the background corpus, apply the compound splitter (see Section 3.2) to all words where we find *similar candidate units*. Then, we add these detected units to the dictionary. Finally, for word w subject to decompounding, we first extract all nested words NW from this dictionary. Then, we remove all words in NW that are nested itself in NW, resulting in the candidate set we call *generated dictionary*.

3.2 Compound Splitting

Here, we introduce the decompounding algorithm for a given candidate set. For decompounding the word w, we require a set of candidate words C. Each word in the candidate set needs to be a substring of w. We do not include candidates in C that have less than ml characters. Additionally, we apply a frequency threshold of wc. These mechanisms are intended to rule out spurious parts and 'words'

---

[1] https://github.com/danielnaber/jwordsplitter

[2] http://ilps.science.uva.nl/resources/compound-splitter-nl/

[3] An implementation and models for German and Dutch are available at: https://github.com/riedlma/SECOS

word w	Bundesfinanzministerium
candidates C	Finanzministerium, Ministerium,
w. ml=3	Bunde, Bund, Bundes, Minister
split possibilities	Bund-e-s-finanz-minister-ium
Merging character n-grams	
suffix-prefix	Bundes-finanz-ministerium
prefix-suffix	Bund-esfinanz-ministerium

Table 1: Examples of the output of our algorithms for the example term *Bundesfinanzministerium*.

that are in fact short abbreviations. We show candidates, extracted from the *similar candidate unit*, with $ml = 3$ for the example term in Table 1. Then, we iterate over each candidate $c_i \in C$ and add its beginning and ending position within w to the set S. This set is then used to identify possible split positions of w. For this, we iterate from left to right and add all split possibilities to the word w. This approach over-generates split points, as can be observed for the example word, which is split into 6 units: *Bund-e-s-finanz-minister-ium*.

To merge character n-grams, we use a suffix- and prefix-based method. The suffix merging method appends all character n-grams with n below ms to the left word. The prefix method merges all character n-grams with n below mp to the word on the right side. To avoid remaining prefixes/suffixes, we apply the opposite method afterwards. For the German language, the suffix-prefix ordering mostly yields the best output. The suffix-prefix-based approach results to *Bundes-finanz-ministerium* and the prefix-suffix method to *Bund-esfinanz-ministerium*. However for some words, the prefix-suffix generates the correct compound split, e.g. for the word *Zuschauer-er-wartung* (*audience + he + service*), which is correctly decompounded as *Zuschauer-erwartung* (*audience+expectation*).

In order to select the correct split, we compute the geometric mean of the joint probability for each split variation. For this we use word counts from a background corpus. In addition to the geometric mean formula introduced in (Koehn and Knight, 2003), we apply a smoothing factor[4] ϵ to each frequency in order to assign non-zero values to unknown units. This yields the following formula for a compound

w, which is decomposed into the units $w_i, \ldots, w_N$:

$$p(w) = \left(\prod_i^N \frac{wordcount(w_i) + \epsilon}{total\_wordcount + \epsilon * \#words} \right)^{\frac{1}{N}} \quad (1)$$

Here, $\#word$ denotes the total number of words in the background corpus and $total\_wordcount$ is the sum of all word counts. Then, we select the split variation with the highest geometric mean.[5] In our example, this is the prefix-suffix-merged candidate *Bundes-finanz-ministerium*.

3.3 Split Ranking

We have examined schemes of priority ordering for integrating information from different candidate sets, e.g. using the *similar candidate units* first and only apply the other candidate sets if no split was found. However, preliminary experiments revealed that it was always beneficial to generate splits based on all three candidate sets and use the geometric mean scoring as outlined above to select the best split as decomposition of a word.

4 Datasets

For testing the performance of our method, we chose four datasets. The first dataset was manually labeled by Holz and Biemann (2008) and consists of 700 German nouns from different frequency bands. The second dataset consists of 158,653 nouns from the German newspaper magazine c't[6] and was created by Marek (2006). As third dataset we use a noun compound dataset of 54,571 nouns from GermaNet[7], which has been constructed by Henrich and Hinrichs (2011).[8] While converting these datasets for the task of compound splitting, we do not separate words in the gold standard, which comprise of prepositions, e.g. the word *Abgang (outflow)* is not split into *Ab-gang (off walk)*. To show the language independency of our method, we apply it to a

---

[4]We set $\epsilon = 0.01$. Using values in the range of $\epsilon = [0.0001, 1]$ we observe marginally higher scores using smaller values.

[5]Whereas our method mostly does not assume language knowledge, we uppercase the first letter of each w_i, when we apply our method on German texts.

[6]http://heise.de/ct

[7]available at: http://www.sfs.uni-tuebingen.de/lsd/documents/compounds/split_compounds_from_GermaNet10.0.txt

[8]We follow Schiller (2005) and remove all words including dashs. This only affects the GermaNet dataset and reduces the effective test set to 53,118 nouns.

Dutch compound dataset proposed by van Zaanen et al. (2014). This dataset comprises of 21,997 nouns.

5 Experimental Setting

The corpus-based DT is computed following the approach by Biemann and Riedl (2013). For each word, we use the left and the right neighboring word as context representation to compute the DT. For the generation of the split candidates we rely on the $l = 200$ most similar entries for each word.

The German DT is computed based on 70 million newspaper sentences, which are extracted from the Leipzig Corpora Collection (LCC) (Richter et al., 2006). For the generation of the Dutch DT, we use the Dutch web corpus (Schäfer and Bildhauer, 2013), which is composed from 259 million sentences.[9]

We evaluate the performance of the algorithms using precision and recall as defined by Koehn and Knight (2003). As unsupervised baselines we use the split ranking by (Koehn and Knight, 2003), called KK, and the semantic analogy-based splitter (SAS) from Daiber et al. (2015).[10] As advanced systems we apply the lexicon- and rule-based JWord-Splitter (JWS) and the supervised decompounding algorithm (ASV), introduced by Holz and Biemann (2008).[11] For all algorithms, we converted the splits to capture all characters in the words, reverting base forms to full forms. For Dutch, we apply the KK baseline and the NL Splitter.

6 Method Tuning

We use the small dataset with the 700 German nouns to find the best parameter settings of our method. The highest F1-scores are obtained using candidates with a frequency above 50 (wc=50) and that have more than 4 characters (ml=5). Further we append only prefixes and suffixes equal or shorter than 3 characters (ms=3 and mp=3).

The highest precision is achieved with the similar candidate units (see Table 2). However, the recall is lowest as for many words no information is available. Using the extended similarities, the precision

---

[9]available at: http://webcorpora.org/.

[10]https://github.com/jodaiber/semantic_compound_splitting

[11]http://wortschatz.uni-leipzig.de/~cbiemann/software/toolbox/.

	P	R	F1
similar cand.	**0.9880**	0.6798	0.8054
ext. sim. cand.	0.9617	0.7304	0.8303
gen. dictionary	0.9576	**0.9199**	**0.9384**
geom. mean scoring	0.9698	0.9338	0.9515

Table 2: Precision (P), Recall (R) and F1-Measure (F1) for the 700 compound nouns using different split candidates.

decreases and the recall increases. The best overall performance is achieved with the generated dictionary, which yields an F1-measure of 0.9384. The selection mechanism using the geometric mean scoring brings F1-measure up to 0.9515 on this dataset.

7 Results

In this section we compare the performance of our method against the unsupervised baselines and the knowledge-based systems (see Table 3).

		P	R	F1
700	JWS	0.9328	0.9037	0.9180
	ASV	0.9584	0.9238	0.9408
	SAS	0.8723	0.6224	0.7265
	KK	0.9532	0.7513	0.8403
	SECOS	**0.9698**	**0.9338**	**0.9515**
c't	JWS	0.9557	**0.9045**	**0.9294***
	ASV	0.9571	0.8980	0.9266
	SAS	0.9303	0.5428	0.6856
	KK	0.9432	0.8114	0.8723
	SECOS	**0.9606**	0.8809	0.9190
Germa-Net	JWS	0.9248	0.8734	0.8983
	ASV	0.9346	**0.8866**	0.9100
	SAS	0.8861	0.6188	0.7287
	KK	0.9486	0.7361	0.8289
	SECOS	**0.9543**	0.8773	**0.9142***
Dutch	NL Splitter	**0.9706**	**0.8694**	**0.9172***
	KK	0.9579	0.7735	0.8559
	SECOS	0.9624	0.8272	0.8897

Table 3: Results for three German datasets and for one Dutch dataset. The significantly best results are marked with an asterisk (*).

For the 700 nouns we achieve the highest precision, recall and F1-measure using our method. However, we have tuned our parameters on this dataset. Our improvement in terms of F-score is not significant[12] with respect to the ASV system, but with re-

---

[12]We perform a Wilcoxon signed-rank test between the F1-

spect to all other systems on this dataset. Nevertheless, JWS is based on a manually created dictionary and ASV uses a supervised algorithm. On this dataset, ASV outperforms JWS. Due to their low recall, both unsupervised baselines (SAS and KK) achieve significantly lower F1-scores than SECOS.

Using the c't dataset we observe a different trend. Here, the best results are observed by using JWS followed by ASV and our method. Nevertheless, our method yields the highest precision value. Again, SAS and KK score lowest.

For the GermaNet dataset, our method significantly outperforms all others. Similar to the evaluation with the 700 nouns, JWS performs lower than the decompounding method from the ASV toolbox. Whereas our method obtains lower recall than ASV and JWS, it still significantly outperforms the unsupervised baselines and yields the overall highest precision.

In a last experiment, we show the performance on the Dutch dataset. As no trained models for JWS and ASV are available, we did not use these tools but compare to NL splitter, achieving a competitive precision but lower recall. This is caused by many short split candidates that are not detected due to the ml parameter. However, our method still beats the KK baseline significantly.

8   Error Analysis

In order to understand the errors of our method, we analyzed the compounds that have been split incorrectly. Considering the 700 German compounds our method splits 12.17% incorrectly, for the Dutch dataset, we observe the highest percentage of 32.60% incorrectly split compounds (see Table 4).

In addition, we analyzed how many compounds have been split in fewer parts (*under-split*), more parts (*over-split*) than the gold data or have the same number of splits, which, however, are incorrect (*wrongly-split*). For all datasets we observe a general trend: our method tends to suppress splitting compounds, due to the parameters *ms* and *mp* that suppress very short parts. Compounds that are split at entirely incorrect positions constitute the lowest error class. We also analyzed for incorrectly split compounds how often our method missed a split,

---

scores of each candidate assuming $p < 0.01$.

dataset	700	c't	GermaNet	Dutch
number of compounds				
# incorrect	85	35177	12532	7258
% incorrect	12.17	22.17	23.26	32.60
under-split	47	23773	7972	5849
over-split	33	7843	3578	806
wrongly-split	5	3561	982	603
number of splits				
missed	55	29213	8968	6612
wrong	43	12703	4669	1520
correct	43	20381	3777	1743

Table 4: Number of compounds that have been split incorrectly with respect to the gold data. We report numbers of how many of these compounds are split fewer (*under-split*), more often (*over-split*) or equally (*wrongly-split*) in comparison to the gold standard. In addition, we show the total number of missed, wrong and correct splits for these compounds.

performed a wrong split and split correctly (see bottom three lines in Table 4). This analysis supports the previous finding: most errors of our SECOS method consist of missed splits.

9   Conclusion

In this paper we have introduced an unsupervised method for decompounding words that is based on distributional semantics. We show the impact of its components and tune its parameters on a small German dataset. On two large German datasets, we demonstrate a performance of our method that is competitive to supervised and rule-based tools and outperforms two unsupervised baselines by a large margin. Further, we demonstrated its language-independence by achieving a good performance on a Dutch dataset. In the future, we would like to assess the impact of SECOS in task-based settings as well as apply it to other compounding languages.

Acknowledgments

This work has been supported by the Deutsche Forschungsgemeinschaft (DFG) within the SeMSch project. Additionally, we want to thank the anonymous reviewers for their helpful comments.

References

Martine Adda-Decker and Gilles Adda. 2000. Morphological Decomposition for ASR in German. In *In Pro-

ceedings of the Workshop on Phonetics and Phonology in ASR, PHONUS 5, pages 129–143, Saarbrücken, Germany.

Enrique Alfonseca, Slaven Bilac, and Stefan Pharies. 2008. Decompounding Query Keywords from Compounding Languages. In *Proceedings of the 46th Annual Meeting of the Association for Computational Linguistics on Human Language Technologies*, ACL-HLT '08, pages 253–256, Columbus, OH, USA.

Chris Biemann and Martin Riedl. 2013. Text: Now in 2D! A Framework for Lexical Expansion with Contextual Similarity. *Journal of Language Modelling*, 1(1):55–95.

Chris Biemann, Uwe Quasthoff, Gerhard Heyer, and Florian Holz. 2008. ASV Toolbox: a Modular Collection of Language Exploration Tools. In *Proceedings of the International Conference on Language Resources and Evaluation*, LREC '08, pages 1760–1767, Marrakech, Morocco.

Joachim Daiber, Lautaro Quiroz, Roger Wechsler, and Stella Frank. 2015. Splitting Compounds by Semantic Analogy. In *Proceedings of the 1st Deep Machine Translation Workshop*, pages 20–28, Prague, Czech Republic.

Zellig S. Harris. 1951. *Methods in Structural Linguistics*. University of Chicago Press, Chicago.

Verena Henrich and Erhard Hinrichs. 2011. Determining Immediate Constituents of Compounds in GermaNet. In *Proceedings of the International Conference Recent Advances in Natural Language Processing 2011*, pages 420–426, Hissar, Bulgaria.

Florian Holz and Chris Biemann. 2008. Unsupervised and Knowledge-Free Learning of Compound Splits and Periphrases. In *Proceedings of the 9th International Conference on Computational Linguistics and Intelligent Text Processing (CICLING)*, pages 117–127, Haifa, Israel.

Philipp Koehn and Kevin Knight. 2003. Empirical Methods for Compound Splitting. In *In Proceedings of the 10th Conference of the European Chapter of the Association for Computational Linguistics*, EACL '03, pages 187–193, Budapest, Hungary.

Klaus Macherey, Andrew M. Dai, David Talbot, Ashok C. Popat, and Franz Och. 2011. Language-independent Compound Splitting with Morphological Operations. In *Proceedings of the 49th Annual Meeting of the Association for Computational Linguistics: Human Language Technologies*, HLT '11, pages 1395–1404, Portland, OR, USA.

Torsten Marek. 2006. Analysis of German Compounds Using Weighted Finite State Transducers. Bachelor thesis, Universität Tübingen.

Christof Monz and Maarten de Rijke. 2001. Shallow Morphological Analysis in Monolingual Information Retrieval for Dutch, German, and Italian. In *Evaluation of Cross-Language Information Retrieval Systems, Second Workshop of the Cross-Language Evaluation Forum*, CLEF 2001, pages 262–277, Darmstadt, Germany.

Roeland Ordelman, Arjan van Hessen, and Franciska de Jong. 2003. Compound decomposition in Dutch large vocabulary speech recognition. In *Proceedings of the European Conference on Speech Communication and Technology*, EUROSPEECH '03, pages 225–228, Geneva, Switzerland.

Matthias Richter, Uwe Quasthoff, Erla Hallsteinsdóttir, and Chris Biemann. 2006. Exploiting the Leipzig Corpora Collection. In *Proceedings of the Fifth Slovenian and First International Language Technologies Conference*, IS-LTC '06, pages 68–73, Ljubljana, Slovenia.

Roland Schäfer and Felix Bildhauer. 2013. *Web Corpus Construction*. Synthesis Lectures on Human Language Technologies. Morgan and Claypool.

Anne Schiller. 2005. German Compound Analysis with wfsc. In *Proceedings of the 5th International Workshop on Finite-State Methods and Natural Language Processing*, FSMNLP 2005, pages 239–246, Helsinki, Finnland.

Menno van Zaanen, Gerhard van Huyssteen, Suzanne Aussems, Chris Emmery, and Roald Eiselen. 2014. The Development of Dutch and Afrikaans Language Resources for Compound Boundary Analysis. In *Proceedings of the 9th International Conference on Language Resources and Evaluation*, LREC '14, pages 1056–1062, Reykjavík, Iceland.

Weighting Finite-State Transductions With Neural Context

Pushpendre Rastogi and **Ryan Cotterell** and **Jason Eisner**
Department of Computer Science, Johns Hopkins University
{pushpendre,ryan.cotterell,eisner}@jhu.edu

Abstract

How should one apply deep learning to tasks such as morphological reinflection, which stochastically edit one string to get another? A recent approach to such sequence-to-sequence tasks is to compress the input string into a vector that is then used to generate the output string, using recurrent neural networks. In contrast, we propose to keep the traditional architecture, which uses a finite-state transducer to score *all possible output strings*, but to augment the scoring function with the help of recurrent networks. A stack of bidirectional LSTMs reads the input string from left-to-right and right-to-left, in order to summarize the *input context* in which a transducer arc is applied. We combine these learned features with the transducer to define a probability distribution over *aligned* output strings, in the form of a weighted finite-state automaton. This reduces hand-engineering of features, allows learned features to examine unbounded context in the input string, and still permits exact inference through dynamic programming. We illustrate our method on the tasks of morphological reinflection and lemmatization.

1 Introduction

Mapping one character sequence to another is a structured prediction problem that arises frequently in NLP and computational linguistics. Common applications include grapheme-to-phoneme (G2P), transliteration, vowelization, normalization, morphology, and phonology. The two sequences may have different lengths.

Traditionally, such settings have been modeled with weighted finite-state transducers (WFSTs) with parametric edge weights (Mohri, 1997; Eisner, 2002). This requires manual design of the transducer states and the features extracted from those states. Alternatively, deep learning has recently been tried

for sequence-to-sequence transduction (Sutskever et al., 2014). While training these systems could discover contextual features that a hand-crafted parametric WFST might miss, they dispense with important structure in the problem, namely the *monotonic input-output alignment*. This paper describes a natural hybrid approach that marries simple FSTs with features extracted by recurrent neural networks.

Our novel architecture allows efficient modeling of globally normalized probability distributions over string-valued output spaces, simultaneously with automatic feature extraction. We evaluate on morphological reinflection and lemmatization tasks, showing that our approach strongly outperforms a standard WFST baseline as well as neural sequence-to-sequence models with attention. Our approach also compares reasonably with a state-of-the-art WFST approach that uses task-specific latent variables.

2 Notation and Background

Let Σ_x be a discrete input alphabet and Σ_y be a discrete output alphabet. Our goal is to define a conditional distribution $p(\mathbf{y} \mid \mathbf{x})$ where $\mathbf{x} \in \Sigma_x^*$ and $\mathbf{y} \in \Sigma_y^*$ and x and y may be of different lengths.

We use italics for characters and boldface for strings. x_i denotes the ith character of $\mathbf{x}$, and $\mathbf{x}_{i:j}$ denotes the substring $x_{i+1}x_{i+2}\cdots x_j$ of length $j - i \geq 0$. Note that $\mathbf{x}_{i:i} = \varepsilon$, the empty string. Let $n = |\mathbf{x}|$.

Our approach begins by hand-specifying an *unweighted* finite-state transducer (FST), F, that non-deterministically maps any well-formed input $\mathbf{x}$ to all appropriate outputs $\mathbf{y}$. An FST is a directed graph whose vertices are called states, and whose arcs are each labeled with some pair $\mathbf{s}:\mathbf{t}$, representing a possible edit of a source substring $\mathbf{s} \in \Sigma_x^*$ into a target substring $\mathbf{t} \in \Sigma_y^*$. A path π from the FST's initial state to its final state represents an alignment of $\mathbf{x}$ to $\mathbf{y}$, where $\mathbf{x}$ and $\mathbf{y}$ (respectively) are the concatenations of the $\mathbf{s}$ and $\mathbf{t}$ labels of the arcs along π. In

Proceedings of NAACL-HLT 2016, pages 623–633,
San Diego, California, June 12-17, 2016. ©2016 Association for Computational Linguistics

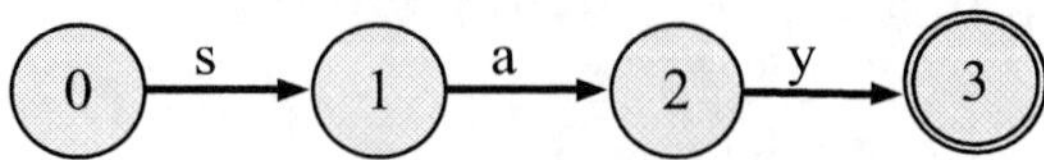

Figure 1: An automaton encoding the English word say.

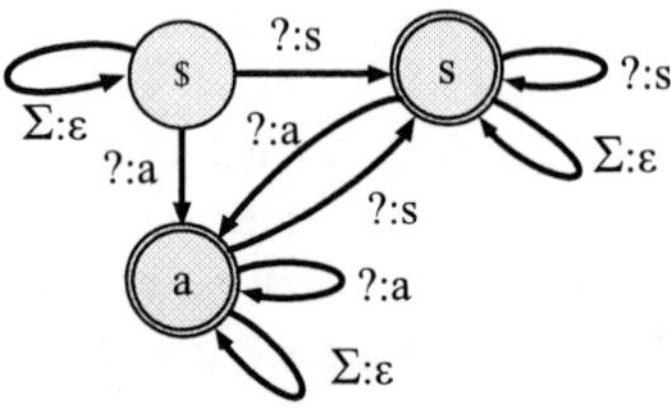

Figure 2: An example transducer F, whose state remembers the most recent *output* character (or $ if none). Only a few of the states are shown, with all arcs among them. The Σ wildcard matches any symbol in Σ_x; the "?" wildcard matches the empty string ε *or any symbol in* Σ_x.

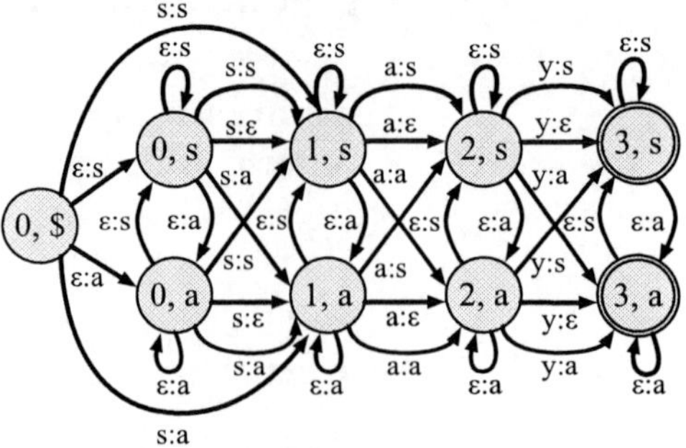

Figure 3: An example of the transducer G, which pairs the string x=say with infinitely many possible strings **y**. This G was created as the composition of the straight-line input automaton (Figure 1) and the transducer F (Figure 2). Thus, the state of G tracks the states of those two machines: the position in **x** and the most recent output character. To avoid a tangled diagram, this figure shows only a few of the states (the start state plus all states of the form (i,s) or (i,a)), with all arcs among them.

general, two strings **x**, **y** can be aligned through exponentially many paths, via different edit sequences.

If we represent **x** as a straight-line finite-state automaton (Figure 1), then composing **x** with F (Figure 2) yields a new FST, G (Figure 3). The paths in G are in 1-1 correspondence with exactly the paths in F that have input **x**. G can have cycles, allowing outputs of unbounded length.

Each path in G represents an alignment of **x** to some string in Σ_y^*. We say $p(\mathbf{y} \mid \mathbf{x})$ is the *total* probability of all paths in G that align **x** to **y** (Figure 4).

But how to define the probability of a path? Traditionally (Eisner, 2002), each arc in F would also be equipped with a weight. The weight of a path in F, or the corresponding path in G, is the sum of its arcs' weights. We would then define the probability $p(\pi)$ of a path π in G as proportional to $\exp w(\pi)$, where $w(\cdot) \in \mathbb{R}$ denotes the weight of an object.

The weight of an arc $(h) \xrightarrow{\mathbf{s:t}} (h')$ in F is traditionally defined as a function of features of the edit $\mathbf{s:t}$ and the names (h, h') of the source and target states. In effect, h summarizes the alignment between the prefixes of **x** and **y** that precede this edit, and h' summarizes the alignment of the suffixes that follow it.

Thus, while the weight of an edit $\mathbf{s:t}$ may depend on context, it traditionally does so only through h and h'. So if F has k states, then the edit weight can only distinguish among k different types of preceding or following context.

3 Incorporating More Context

That limitation is what we aim to correct in this paper, by augmenting our representation of context. Our *contextual weighting* approach will assign weights directly to G's arcs, instead of to F's arcs.

Each arc of G can be regarded as a "token" of an edit arc in F: it "applies" that edit to *a particular substring of* **x**. It has the form $(i,h) \xrightarrow{\mathbf{s:t}} (j,h')$, and represents the replacement of $\mathbf{x}_{i:j} = \mathbf{s}$ by **t**. The finite-state composition construction produced this arc of G by combining the arc $(h) \xrightarrow{\mathbf{s:t}} (h')$ in F with the path $(i) \overset{\mathbf{s}}{\rightsquigarrow} (j)$ in the straight-line automaton representing **x**. The latter automaton uses integers as state names: it is $(0) \xrightarrow{x_1} (1) \xrightarrow{x_2} \ldots \xrightarrow{x_n} (n)$.

Our top-level idea is to make the weight of this arc in G depend also on $(\mathbf{x}, i, j)$, so that it can consider unbounded input context around the edit's location. Arc weights can now consider arbitrary features of the input **x** and the position i, j—exactly like the potential functions of a linear-chain conditional random field (CRF), which also defines $p(\mathbf{y} \mid \mathbf{x})$.

Why not just use a CRF? That would only model a situation that enforced $|\mathbf{y}| = |\mathbf{x}|$ with each character y_i aligned to x_i, since the emissions of a CRF correspond to edits $\mathbf{s : t}$ with $|\mathbf{s}| = |\mathbf{t}| = 1$. An FST can also allow edits with $|\mathbf{s}| \neq |\mathbf{t}|$, if desired, so it can be fit to $(\mathbf{x}, \mathbf{y})$ pairs of different lengths with unknown

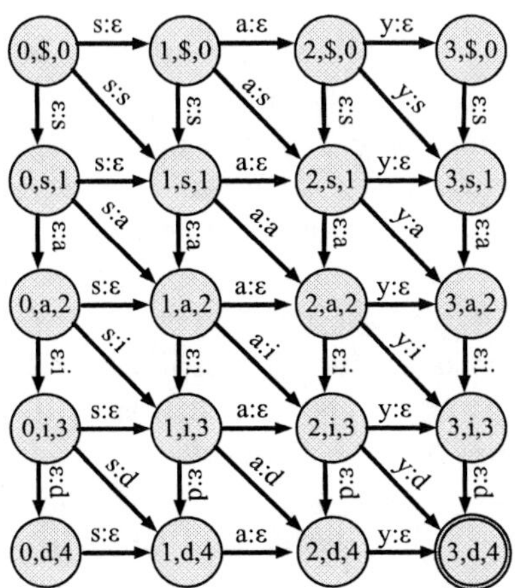

Figure 4: A compact lattice of the exponentially many paths in the transducer G of Figure 3 that align input string x=say with output string y=said. To find $p(\mathbf{y} \mid \mathbf{x})$, we must sum over these paths (i.e., alignments). The lattice is created by composing G with $\mathbf{y}$, which selects all paths in G that output $\mathbf{y}$. Note that horizontal movement makes progress through $\mathbf{x}$; vertical movement makes progress through $\mathbf{y}$. The lattice's states specialize states in G so that they also record a position in $\mathbf{y}$.

alignment, summing over their possible alignments.

A standard weighted FST F is similar to a dynamic linear-chain CRF. Both are unrolled against the input $\mathbf{x}$ to get a dynamic programming lattice G. But they are not equivalent. By weighting G instead of F, we combine the FST's advantage (aligning unequal-length strings $\mathbf{x}, \mathbf{y}$ via a latent path) with the CRF's advantage (arbitrary dependence on $\mathbf{x}$).

To accomplish this weighting in practice, sections 4–5 present a trainable neural architecture for an arc weight function $w = f(\mathbf{s}, \mathbf{t}, h, h', \mathbf{x}, i, j)$. The goal is to extract continuous features from *all* of $\mathbf{x}$. While our specific architecture is new, we are not the first to replace hand-crafted log-linear models with trainable neural networks (see section 9).[1]

Note that as in a CRF, our arc weights cannot consider arbitrary features of $\mathbf{y}$, only of $\mathbf{x}$. Still, a weight's dependence on states h, h' does let it depend on a *finite* amount of information about $\mathbf{y}$ (also possible in CRFs/HCRFs) and its alignment to $\mathbf{x}$.

In short, our model $p(\mathbf{y} \mid \mathbf{x})$ makes the weight of

an s:t edit, applied to substring $\mathbf{x}_{i:j}$, depend *jointly* on s:t and *two* summaries of the edit's context:

- a finite-state summary (h, h') of its context in the aligned $(\mathbf{x}, \mathbf{y})$ pair, as found by the FST F
- a vector-valued summary of the context in $\mathbf{x}$ only, as found by a recurrent neural network

The neural vector is generally a richer summary of the context, but it considers only the *input*-side context. We are able to efficiently extract these rich features from the *single* input $\mathbf{x}$, but not from each of the *very many* possible outputs $\mathbf{y}$. The job of the FST F is to compute additional features that also depend on the output.[2] Thus our model of $p(\mathbf{y} \mid \mathbf{x})$ is defined by an FST together with a neural network.

4   Neural Context Features

Our arc weight function f will make use of a vector $\boldsymbol{\gamma}_{i:j}$ (computed from $\mathbf{x}, i, j$) to characterize the substring $\mathbf{x}_{i:j}$ that is being replaced, in context. We define $\boldsymbol{\gamma}_{i:j}$ as the concatenation of a left vector $\boldsymbol{\alpha}_j$ (describing the prefix $\mathbf{x}_{0:j}$) and a right vector $\boldsymbol{\beta}_i$ (describing the suffix $\mathbf{x}_{i:n}$), which characterize $\mathbf{x}_{i:j}$ jointly with its left or right context. We use $\boldsymbol{\gamma}_i$ to abbreviate $\boldsymbol{\gamma}_{i-1:i}$, just as x_i abbreviates $\mathbf{x}_{i-1:i}$.

To extract $\boldsymbol{\alpha}_j$, we read the string $\mathbf{x}$ one character at a time with an LSTM (Hochreiter and Schmidhuber, 1997), a type of trainable recurrent neural network that is good at extracting relevant features from strings. $\boldsymbol{\alpha}_j$ is the LSTM's output after j steps (which read $\mathbf{x}_{0:j}$). Appendix A reviews how $\boldsymbol{\alpha}_j \in \mathbb{R}^q$ is computed for $j = 1, \ldots, n$ using the recursive, differentiable update rules of the LSTM architecture.

We also read the string $\mathbf{x}$ *in reverse* with a second LSTM. $\boldsymbol{\beta}_i \in \mathbb{R}^q$ is the second LSTM's output after $n - i$ steps (which read reverse($\mathbf{x}_{i:n}$)).

We regard the two LSTMs together as a BiLSTM function (Graves and Schmidhuber, 2005) that reads $\mathbf{x}$ (Figure 5). For each bounded-length substring $\mathbf{x}_{i:j}$, the BiLSTM produces a characterization $\boldsymbol{\gamma}_{i:j}$ of that substring in context, in $O(n)$ *total* time.

We now define a "deep BiLSTM," which stacks up K BiLSTMs. This deepening is aimed at extracting the kind of rich features that Sutskever et al.

---

[1] For CRFs, this sacrifices the convexity of the log-likelihood training objective. But for FSTs, that objective was usually non-convex to begin with, because the alignment path is latent.

[2] Each arc of G is used in a known input context, but could be reused in many output contexts—different *paths* in G. Those contexts are only guaranteed to share h, h'. So the arc weight cannot depend on any *other* features of the output context.

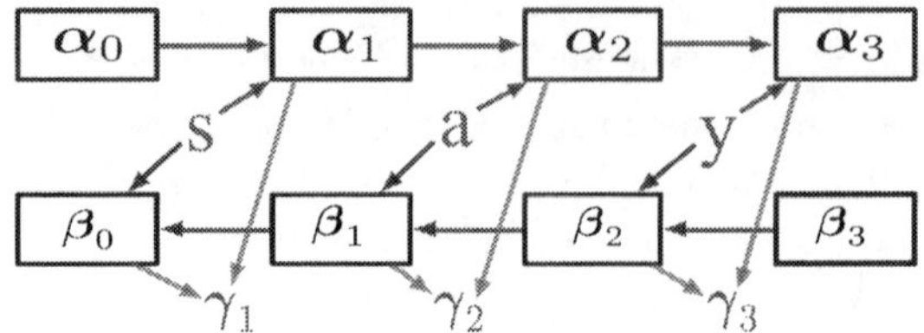

Figure 5: A level-1 BiLSTM reading the word $\mathbf{x}$=say.

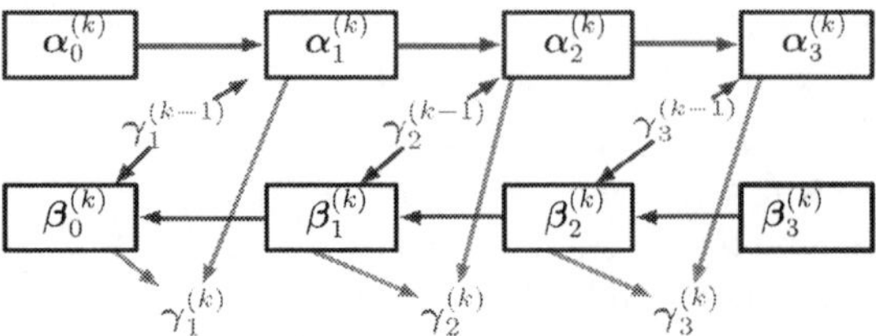

Figure 6: Level $k > 1$ of a deep BiLSTM. (We augment the shown input vectors with level $k - 1$'s input vectors.)

(2014) and Vinyals et al. (2015) found so effective in a different structured prediction architecture.

The kth-level BiLSTM (Figure 6) reads a sequence of input vectors $\mathbf{x}_1^{(k)}, \mathbf{x}_2^{(k)}, \ldots, \mathbf{x}_n^{(k)} \in \mathbb{R}^{d^{(k)}}$, and produces a sequence of vectors $\gamma_1^{(k)}, \gamma_2^{(k)}, \ldots, \gamma_n^{(k)} \in \mathbb{R}^{2q}$. At the initial level $k = 1$, we define $\mathbf{x}_i^{(1)} = \mathbf{e}_{x_i} \in \mathbb{R}^{d^{(1)}}$, a vector embedding of the character $x_i \in \Sigma_{\mathbf{x}}$. For $k > 1$, we take $\mathbf{x}_i^{(k)}$ to be $\gamma_i^{(k-1)}$, concatenated with $\mathbf{x}_i^{(k-1)}$ for good measure. Thus, $d^{(k)} = 2q + d^{(k-1)}$.

After this deep generalization, we define $\gamma_{i:j}$ to be the concatenation of all $\gamma_{i:j}^{(k)}$ (rather than just $\gamma_{i:j}^{(K)}$).

This novel deep BiLSTM architecture has more connections than a pair of deep LSTMs, since $\alpha_i^{(k)}$ depends not only on $\alpha_i^{(k-1)}$ but also on $\beta_i^{(k-1)}$. Thus, while we may informally regard $\alpha_i^{(k)}$ as being a deep summary of the prefix $\mathbf{x}_{0:i}$, it actually depends indirectly on all of $\mathbf{x}$ (except when $k = 1$).

5 The Arc Weight Function

Given the vector $\gamma_{i:j}$, we can now compute the weight of the edit arc $(i,h) \overset{\mathbf{s:t}}{\longrightarrow} (j,h)$ in G, namely $w = f(\mathbf{s}, \mathbf{t}, h, h', \mathbf{x}, i, j)$. Many reasonable functions are possible. Here we use one that is inspired by the log-bilinear language model (Mnih and Hinton, 2007):

$$w = (\mathbf{e_s}, \gamma_{i,j}, \mathbf{e}_{x_i}, \mathbf{e}_{x_{j+1}}) \cdot \mathbf{r}_{\mathbf{t},h,h',\text{type}(\mathbf{s:t})} \qquad (1)$$

The first argument to the inner product is an embedding $\mathbf{e_s} \in R^{d^{(1)}}$ of the source substring $\mathbf{s}$, con-

catenated to the edit's neural context and also (for good measure) its local context.[3] For example, if $|\mathbf{s}| = 1$, i.e. $\mathbf{s}$ is a single character, then we would use the embedding of that character as $\mathbf{e_s}$. Note that the embeddings $\mathbf{e_s}$ for $|\mathbf{s}| = 1$ are also used to encode the local context characters and the level-1 BiLSTM input. We learn these embeddings, and they form part of our model's parameter vector $\boldsymbol{\theta}$.

The second argument is a *joint* embedding of the other properties of the edit: the target substring $\mathbf{t}$, the edit arc's state labels from F, and the type of the edit (INS, DEL, or SUB: see section 8). When replacing $\mathbf{s}$ in a particular context, which fixes the first argument, we will prefer those replacements whose $\mathbf{r}$ embeddings yield a high inner product w. We will learn the $\mathbf{r}$ embeddings as well; note that their dimensionality must match that of the first argument.

The model's parameter vector $\boldsymbol{\theta}$ includes the $O((d^{(K)})^2)$ parameters from the $2K$ LSTMs, where $d^{(K)} = O(d^{(1)} + Kq)$. It also $O(d^{(1)}S)$ parameters for the embeddings $\mathbf{e_s}$ of the S different input substrings mentioned by F, and $O(d^{(K)}T)$ for the embeddings $\mathbf{r}_{\mathbf{t},h,h',\text{type}(\mathbf{s:t})}$ of the T "actions" in F.

6 Training

We train our model by maximizing the conditional log-likelihood objective,

$$\sum_{(\mathbf{x},\mathbf{y}^*) \in \text{dataset}} \log p(\mathbf{y}^* \mid \mathbf{x}) \qquad (2)$$

Recall that $p(\mathbf{y}^* \mid \mathbf{x})$ sums over all alignments. As explained by Eisner (2002), it can be computed as the pathsum of the composition $G \circ \mathbf{y}^*$ (Figure 4), divided by the pathsum of G (which gives the normalizing constant for the distribution $p(\mathbf{y} \mid \mathbf{x})$). The pathsum of a weighted FST is the total weight of all paths from the initial state to a final state, and can be computed by the forward algorithm.[4]

---

[3] Our present implementation handles INS edits (for which $j = i$) a bit differently, using $(\mathbf{e}_{x_{i+1}}, \gamma_{i:i+1}, \mathbf{e}_{x_i}, \mathbf{e}_{x_{i+2}})$ rather than $(\mathbf{e}_\varepsilon, \gamma_{i:i}, \mathbf{e}_{x_i}, \mathbf{e}_{x_{i+1}})$. This is conveniently the same vector that is used for all other competing edits at this i position (as they all have $|\mathbf{s}| = 1$ in our present implementation); it provides an extra character of lookahead.

[4] If an FST has cycles, such as the self-loops in the example of Figure 3, then the forward algorithm's recurrence equations become cyclic, and must be solved as a linear system rather than sequentially. This is true regardless of how the FST's weights

Eisner (2002) and Li and Eisner (2009) also explain how to compute the partial derivatives of $p(\mathbf{y}^* \mid \mathbf{x})$ with respect to the arc weights, essentially by using the forward-backward algorithm. We backpropagate further from these partials to find the gradient of (2) with respect to all our model parameters. We describe our gradient-based maximization procedure in section 10.3, along with regularization.

Our model does not have to be trained with the conditional log likelihood objective. It could be trained with other objectives such as empirical risk or softmax-margin (Li and Eisner, 2009; Gimpel and Smith, 2010), or with error-driven updates such as in the structured perceptron (Collins, 2002).

7 Inference and Decoding

For a new input $\mathbf{x}$ at test time, we can now construct a weighted FST, G, that defines a probability distribution over all *aligned* output strings. This can be manipulated to make various predictions about $\mathbf{y}^*$ and its alignment.

In our present experiments, we find the most probable (highest-weighted) path in G (Dijkstra, 1959), and use its output string $\hat{\mathbf{y}}$ as our prediction. Note that Dijkstra's algorithm is exact; no beam search is required as in some neural sequence models.

On the other hand, $\hat{\mathbf{y}}$ may not be the most probable string—extracting that from a weighted FST is NP-hard (Casacuberta and de la Higuera, 1999). The issue is that the total probability of each $\mathbf{y}$ is split over many paths. Still, this is a well-studied problem in NLP. Instead of the Viterbi approximation, we could have used a better approximation, such as crunching (May and Knight, 2006) or variational decoding (Li et al., 2009). We actually did try crunching the 10000-best outputs but got no significant improvement, so we do not report those results.

8 Transducer Topology

In our experiments, we choose F to be a simple contextual edit FST as illustrated in Figure 2. Just as in Levenshtein distance (Levenshtein, 1966), it allows all edits $\mathbf{s} : \mathbf{t}$ where $|\mathbf{s}| \leq 1, |\mathbf{t}| \leq 1, |\mathbf{s}| + |\mathbf{t}| \neq 0$. We consider the edit type to be INS if $\mathbf{s} = \varepsilon$, DEL if $\mathbf{t} = \varepsilon$, and SUB otherwise. Note that copy is a SUB edit with $\mathbf{s} = \mathbf{t}$.

For a "memoryless" edit process (Ristad and Yianilos, 1996), the FST would require only a single state. By contrast, we use $|\Sigma_{\mathbf{x}}| + 1$ states, where each state records the most recent output character (initially, a special "beginning-of-string" symbol $\$$). That is, the state label h is the "history" output character immediately before the edit $\mathbf{s} : \mathbf{t}$, so the state label h' is the history before the *next* edit, namely the final character of $h\mathbf{t}$. For edits other than DEL, $h\mathbf{t}$ is a bigram of $\mathbf{y}$, which can be evaluated (in context) by the arc weight function $w = f(\mathbf{s}, \mathbf{t}, h, h', \mathbf{x}, i, j)$.

Naturally, a weighted version of this FST F is far too simple to do well on real NLP tasks (as we show in our experiments). The magic comes from instead weighting G so that we can pay attention to the input context $\gamma_{i:j}$.

The above choice of F corresponds to the "$(0, 1, 1)$ topology" in the more general scheme of Cotterell et al. (2014). For practical reasons, we actually modify it to limit the number of consecutive INS edits to 3.[5] This trick bounds $|\mathbf{y}|$ to be $< 4 \cdot (|\mathbf{x}| + 1)$, ensuring that the pathsums in section 6 are finite regardless of the model parameters. This simplifies both the pathsum algorithm and the gradient-based training (Dreyer, 2011). Less importantly, since G becomes acyclic, Dijkstra's algorithm in section 7 simplifies to the Viterbi algorithm.

9 Related Work

Our model adds to recent work on linguistic sequence transduction using deep learning.

Graves and Schmidhuber (2005) combined BiLSTMs with HMMs. Later, "sequence-to-sequence" models were applied to machine translation by Sutskever et al. (2014) and to parsing by Vinyals et al. (2015). That framework did not model any alignment between $\mathbf{x}$ and $\mathbf{y}$, but adding an "attention" mechanism provides a kind of soft alignment that has improved performance on MT (Bahdanau et al., 2015). Faruqui et al. (2016) apply these methods to morphological reinflection (the only other application to morphology we know of). Grefenstette

---

are defined. (For convenience, our experiments in this paper avoid cycles by limiting consecutive insertions: see section 8.)

[5]This multiplies the number of states 4-fold, since each state must also record a count in $[0, 3]$ of immediately preceding INS edits. No INS edit arc is allowed from a state with counter 3. The counter is not considered by the arc weight function.

et al. (2015) recently augmented the sequence-to-sequence framework with a continuous analog of stack and queue data structures, to better handle long-range dependencies often found in linguistic data.

Some recent papers have used LSTMs or BiLSTMs, as we do, to define probability distributions over action sequences that operate directly on an input sequence. Such actions are aligned to the input. For example, Andor et al. (2016) score edit sequences using a globally normalized model, and Dyer et al. (2015) evaluate the local probability of a parsing action given past actions (and their result) and future words. These architectures are powerful because their LSTMs can examine the *output* structure; but as a result they do not permit dynamic programming and must fall back on beam search.

Our use of dynamic programming for efficient exact inference has long been common in non-neural architectures for sequence transduction, including FST systems that allow "phrasal" replacements $s : t$ where $|s|, |t| > 1$ (Chen, 2003; Jiampojamarn et al., 2007; Bisani and Ney, 2008). Our work augments these FSTs with neural networks, much as others have augmented CRFs. In this vein, Durrett and Klein (2015) augment a CRF parser (Finkel et al., 2008) to score constituents with a feedforward neural network. Likewise, FitzGerald et al. (2015) employ feedforward nets as a factor in a graphical model for semantic role labeling. Many CRFs have incorporated feedforward neural networks (Bridle, 1990; Peng et al., 2009; Do and Artieres, 2010; Vinel et al., 2011; Fujii et al., 2012; Chen et al., 2015, and others). Some work augments CRFs with BiLSTMs: Huang et al. (2015) report results on part-of-speech tagging and named entity recognition with a linear-chain CRF-BiLSTM, and Kong et al. (2015) on Chinese word segmentation and handwriting recognition with a semi-CRF-BiLSTM.

10   Experiments

We evaluated our approach on two morphological generation tasks of reinflection (section 10.1) and lemmatization (section 10.2). In the reinflection task, the goal is to transduce verbs from one inflected form into another, whereas the lemmatization task requires the model to reduce an inflected verb to its root form.

We compare our WFST-LSTM against two standard baselines, a WFST with hand-engineered features and the Moses phrase-based MT system (Koehn et al., 2007), as well as the more complex latent-variable model of Dreyer et al. (2008). The comparison with Dreyer et al. (2008) is of noted interest since their latent variables are structured particularly for morphological transduction tasks—we are directly testing the ability of the LSTM to structure its hidden layer as effectively as linguistically motivated latent-variables. Additionally, we provide detailed ablation studies and learning curves which show that our neural-WFSA hybrid model can generalize even with very low amounts of training data.

10.1   Morphological Reinflection

Following Dreyer (2011), we conducted our experiments on the following transduction tasks from the CELEX (Baayen et al., 1993) morphological database: 13SIA $\mapsto$ 13SKE, 2PIE $\mapsto$ 13PKE, 2PKE $\mapsto$ z and rP $\mapsto$ pA.[6] We refer to these tasks as 13SIA, 2PIE, 2PKE and rP, respectively.

Concretely, each task requires us to map a German inflection into another inflection. Consider the 13SIA task and the German verb `abreiben` ("to rub off"). We require the model to learn to map a past tense form `abrieb` to a present tense form `abreibe`—this involves a combination of stem change and affix generation. Sticking with the same verb `abreiben`, task 2PIE requires the model to transduce `abreibt` to `abreiben`— this requires an insertion and a substitution at the end. The tasks 2PKE and rP are somewhat more challenging since performing well on these tasks requires the model to learn complex transduction: `abreiben` to `abzureiben` and `abreibt` to `abgerieben`, respectively. These are complex transductions with phenomenon like infixation in specific contexts (`abzureiben`) and circumfixation (`abgerieben`) along with additional stem and affix changes. See Dreyer (2011) for more details and examples of these tasks.

We use the datasets of Dreyer (2011). Each exper-

---

[6] Glossary: 13SIA=*1st/3rd sg. ind. past*; 13SKE=*1st/3rd sg. subjunct. pres.*; 2PIE=*2nd pl. ind. pres.*; 13PKE=*1st/3rd pl. subjunct. pres.*; 2PKE=*2nd pl. subjunct. pres.*; z=*infinitive*; rP=*imperative pl.*; pA=*past part.*

iment sampled a different dataset of 2500 examples from CELEX, dividing this into 500 training + 1000 validation + 1000 test examples. Like them, we report exact-match accuracy on the test examples, averaged over 5 distinct experiments of this form. We also report results when the training and validation data are swapped in each experiment, which doubles the training size.

10.2 Lemmatization

Lemmatization is a special case of morphological re-inflection where we map an inflected form of a word to its lemma (canonical form), i.e., the target inflection is fixed. This task is quite useful for NLP, as dictionaries typically list only the lemma for a given lexical entry, rather than all possible inflected forms. In the case of German verbs, the lemma is taken to be the infinitive form, e.g., we map the past participle `abgerieben` to the infinitive `abreiben`.

Following Dreyer (2011), we use a subset of the lemmatization dataset created by Wicentowski (2002) and perform 10-fold experiments on four languages: Basque (5843), English (4915), Irish (1376) and Tagalog (9545), where the numbers in parenthesis indicate the total number of data pairs available. For each experimental fold the total data was divided into train, development and test sets in the proportion of 80:10:10 and we report test accuracy averaged across folds.

10.3 Settings and Training Procedure

We set the hyperparameters of our model to $K = 4$ (stacking depth), $d^{(1)} = 10$ (character embedding dimension), and $q = 15$ (LSTM state dimension). The alphabets Σ_x and Σ_y are always equal; their size is language-dependent, typically ≈ 26 but larger in languages like Basque and Irish where our datasets include properly accented characters. With $|\Sigma| = 26$ and the above settings for the hyperparameters, the number of parameters in our models is $352,801$.

We optimize these parameters through stochastic gradient descent of the negative log-likelihood objective, and regularize the training procedure through dropout accompanied with gradient clipping and projection of parameters onto L2-balls with small radii, which is equivalent to adding a group-ridge regularization term to the training objective. The learning rate decay schedule, gradient clipping

Model	13SIA	2PIE	2PKE	rP
Moses15	85.3	94.0	82.8	70.8
Dreyer (Backoff)	82.8	88.7	74.7	69.9
Dreyer (Lat-Class)	84.8	93.6	75.7	81.8
Dreyer (Lat-Region)	**87.5**	93.4	**87.4**	**84.9**
BiLSTM-WFST	85.1	**94.4**	85.5	83.0
Model Ensemble	85.8	**94.6**	86.0	83.8
BiLSTM-WFST (2 × Data)	*87.6*	*94.8*	*88.1*	*85.7*

Table 1: Exact match accuracy on the morphological re-inflection task. All the results in the first half of the table are taken from Dreyer (2011), whose experimental setup we copied exactly. The Moses15 result is obtained by applying the SMT toolkit Moses (Koehn et al., 2007) over letter strings with 15-character context windows. Dreyer (Backoff) refers to the *ngrams+x* model which has access to all the "backoff features." Dreyer (Lat-Class) is the *ngrams+x+latent class* model, and Dreyer (Lat Region) refers to the *ngrams+x+latent class + latent change region* model. The "Model Ensemble" row displays the performance of an ensemble including our full model and the 7 models that we performed ablation on. In each column, we boldfaced the highest result and those that were not significantly worse (sign test, $p < 0.05$). Finally, the last row reports the performance of our BiLSTM-WFST when trained on twice the training data.

threshold, radii of L2-balls, and dropout frequency were tuned by hand on development data.

In our present experiments, we made one change to the architecture. Treating copy edits like other SUB edits led to poor performance: the system was unable to learn that all SUB edits with $s = t$ were extremely likely. In the experiments reported here, we addressed the problem by simply tying the weights of all copy edits regardless of context, bypassing (1) and instead setting $w = c$ where c is a learned parameter of the model. See section 11 for discussion.

10.4 Results

Table 1 and 2 show our results. We can see that our proposed BiLSTM-WFST model always outperforms all but the most complex latent-variable model of Dreyer (2011); it is competitive with that model, but only beats it once individually. All of Dreyer's models include output trigram features, while we only use bigrams.

Figure 7 shows learning curves for the 13SIA and 2PKE tasks: test accuracy when we train on less data. Curiously, at 300 data points the performance of our model is tied to Dreyer (2011). We also note

Model	Basque	English	Irish	Tagalog
Base (W)	85.3	91.0	43.3	0.3
WFAffix (W)	80.1	93.1	70.8	81.7
ngrams (D)	91.0	92.4	96.8	80.5
ngrams + x (D)	91.1	93.4	97.0	83.0
ngrams + x + l (D)	**93.6**	**96.9**	**97.9**	88.6
BiLSTM-WFST	91.5	94.5	**97.9**	**97.4**

Table 2: Lemmatization results on Basque, English, Irish and Tagalog. Comparison systems marked with (W) are taken from Wicentowski (2002) and systems marked with a (D) are taken from Dreyer (2011). We outperform baselines on all languages and are competitive with the latent-variable approach (ngrams + x + l), beating it in two cases: Irish and Tagalog.

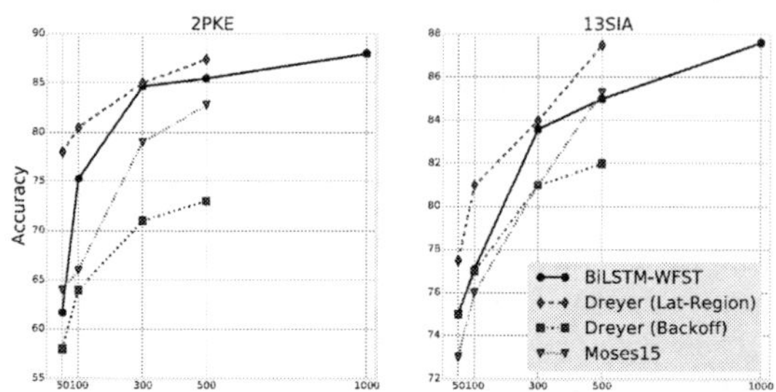

Figure 7: Learning Curves

Systems	13SIA	2PIE	2PKE	rP
Deep BiLSTM w/ Tying	**86.8**	**94.8**	**87.9**	**81.1**
Deep BiLSTM (No Context)	**86.5**	**94.3**	**87.8**	78.8
Deep BiLSTMs w/o Copying	**86.5**	**94.6**	86.5	**80.7**
Shallow BiLSTM	**86.4**	**94.7**	86.1	**80.6**
Bi-Deep LSTM	86.1	94.2	86.5	78.6
Deep MonoLSTM	84.0	93.8	85.6	67.3
Shallow MonoLSTM	84.2	**94.5**	84.9	68.2
No LSTM (Local Context)	83.6	88.5	83.2	68.0
Deep BiLSTM w/o Tying	69.7	78.5	77.9	66.7
No LSTM (No Context)	70.7	84.9	72.4	64.1
Seq2Seq-Att-4Layer	76.0	91.4	81.2	79.3
Seq2Seq-Att-1Layer	77.2	89.6	82.1	79.1
Seq2Seq-4Layer	2.5	5.2	11.5	6.4
Seq2Seq-1Layer	9.1	11.1	14.1	11.9

Table 3: Ablation experiments: Exact-match accuracy of the different systems averaged on 5 folds of validation portions of the morphological induction dataset.

that our model always outperforms the Moses15 baseline on all training set sizes except on the 2PKE task with 50 training samples.

In general, the results from our experiments are a promising indicator that LSTMs are capable of extracting linguistically relevant features for morphology. Our model outperforms all baselines, and is competitive with and sometimes surpasses the latent-variable model of Dreyer et al. (2008) *without* any of the hand-engineered features or linguistically inspired latent variables.

On morphological reinflection, we outperform all of Dreyer et al's models on 2PIE, but fall short of his latent-change region model on the other tasks (outperforming the other models). On lemmatization, we outperform all of Wicentowski's models on all the languages and all of Dreyer et al.'s models on Irish and Tagalog, but, but not on English and Irish. This suggests that perhaps further gains are possible through using something like Dreyer's FST as our F. Indeed, this would be compatible with much recent work that gets best results from a *combination* of automatically learned neural features and hand-

engineered features.

10.5 Analysis of Results

We analyzed our lemmatization errors for all the languages on one fold of the datasets. On the English lemmatization task, 7 of our 27 errors simply copied the input word to the output: `ate`, `kept`, `went`, `taught`, `torn`, `paid`, `strung`. This suggests that our current aggressive parameter tying for copy edits may predict a high probability for a copy edit even in contexts that should not favor it.

Also we found that the FST sometimes produced non-words while lemmatizing the input verbs. For example it mapped `picnicked` $\mapsto$ `picnick`, `happen` $\mapsto$ `hapen`, `exceed` $\mapsto$ `excy` and `lining` $\mapsto$ `lin`. Since these strings would be rare in a corpus, many such errors could be avoided by a reranking approach that combined the FST's path score with a string frequency feature.

In order to better understand our architecture and the importance of its various components, we performed an ablation study on the validation portions of the morphological induction datasets, shown in Table 3. We can see in particular that using a BiLSTM instead of an LSTM, increasing the depth of the network, and including local context all helped to improve the final accuracy.

"Deep BiLSTM w/ Tying" refers to our complete model. The other rows are ablation experiments—architectures that are the same as the first row except in the specified way. "Deep BiLSTM (No Context)" omits local context $\mathbf{e}_{x_i}, \mathbf{e}_{x_{j+1}}$ from (1). "Deep BiL-STMs w/o Copying" does not concatenate a copy of $\mathbf{x}_i^{(k-1)}$ into $\mathbf{x}_i^{(k)}$ and simplifies $\gamma_{i:j}$ to be $\gamma_{i:j}^{(K)}$ only. "Shallow BiLSTM" reduces K from 4 to 1. "Bi-Deep LSTM" replaces our deep BiLSTM with two deep LSTMs that run in opposite directions but do not interact with each other. "Deep MonoLSTM" redefines β_i to be the empty vector,g i.e. it replaces the deep BiLSTM with a deep left-to-right LSTM. "Shallow MonoLSTM" replaces the deep BiLSTM with a shallow left-to-right LSTM. "No LSTM (Local Context)" omits $\gamma_{i:j}$ from the weight function altogether. "Deep BiLSTM w/o Tying" does not use the parameter tying heuristic for copy edits. "No LSTM (No Context)" is the simplest model that we consider. It removes $\gamma_{i:j}, \mathbf{e}_{x_i}$ and $\mathbf{e}_{x_{j+1}}$ and in fact, it is precisely a weighting of the edits in our original FST F, without further considering the context in which an edit is applied.

Finally, to compare the performance of our method to baseline neural encoder-decoder models, we trained 1-layer and 4-layer neural sequence-to-sequence models with and without attention, using the publicly available `morph-trans` toolkit (Faruqui et al., 2016). We show the performance of these models in the lower half of the table. The results consistently show that sequence-to-sequence transduction models that lack the constraints of monotonic alignment perform worse than our proposed models on morphological transduction tasks.

11   Future Work

As neither our FST-LSTM model or the latent-variable WFST model of Dreyer et al. (2008) uniformly outperforms the other, a future direction is to improve the FST we use in our model—e.g., by augmenting its states with explicit latent variables. Other improvements to the WFST would be to increase the amount of history h stored in the states, and to allow $\mathbf{s}, \mathbf{t}$ to be longer than a single character, which would allow the model to segment $\mathbf{x}$.

We are not committed to the arc weight function in (1), and we believe that further investigation here could improve performance. The goal is to define the weight of $\textcircled{h} \xrightarrow{\mathbf{s}:\mathbf{t}} \textcircled{h'}$ in the context summarized by α_i, β_j (the context around $\mathbf{x}_{i:j} = \mathbf{s}$) and/or α_j, β_i (which incorporate $\mathbf{s}$ as well).

Any parametric function of the variables $(\mathbf{s}, \mathbf{t}, h, h', \alpha_i, \alpha_j, \beta_i, \beta_j)$ could be used—for example, a neural network or a multilinear function. This function might depend on learned embeddings of the separate objects $\mathbf{s}, \mathbf{t}, h, h'$, but also on learned joint embeddings of pairs of these objects (which adds finer-grained parameters), or hand-specified properties of the objects such as their phonological features (which adds backoff parameters).

A basic approach along the lines of (1) would use an inner product of some encoding of the arc $(\mathbf{s}, \mathbf{t}, h, h')$ with some encoding of the context $(\mathbf{s}, h, h', \alpha_i, \alpha_j, \beta_i, \beta_j)$. Note that this formulation lets the objects $\mathbf{s}, h, h'$ play a dual role—they may appear as part of the arc and/or as part of the context. This is because we must judge whether $\mathbf{s} = \mathbf{x}_{i:j}$ (with "label" $\textcircled{h} \longrightarrow \textcircled{h'}$) is an appropriate input segment given the string context around $\mathbf{x}_{i:j}$, but if this segment is chosen, in turn it provides additional context to judge whether $\mathbf{t}$ is an appropriate output.

High-probability edits $\mathbf{s} : \mathbf{t}$ typically have $\mathbf{t} \approx \mathbf{s}$: a perfect copy, or a modified copy that changes just one or two features such as phonological voicing or orthographic capitalization. Thus, we are interested in learning a shared set of embeddings for $\Sigma_x \cup \Sigma_y$, and making the arc weight depend on features of the "discrepancy vector" $\mathbf{e}_t - \mathbf{e}_s$, such as this vector's components[7] and their absolute magnitudes, which would signal discrepancies of various sorts.

12   Conclusions

We have presented a hybrid FST-LSTM architecture for string-to-string transduction tasks. This approach combines classical finite-state approaches to transduction and newer neural approaches. We weight the same FST arc *differently* in different contexts, and use LSTMs to *automatically* extract features that determine these weights. This reduces the need to engineer a complex topology for the FST or to hand-engineer its weight features. We evaluated one such model on the tasks of morphological reinflection and lemmatization. Our approach outperforms several baselines and is competitive with (and sometimes surpasses) a latent-variable model hand-crafted for morphological transduction tasks.

---

[7]In various directions—perhaps just the basis directions, which might come to encode distinctive features, via training.

Acknowledgements

This research was supported by the Defense Advanced Research Projects Agency under the Deep Exploration and Filtering of Text (DEFT) Program, agreement number FA8750-13-2-001; by the National Science Foundation under Grant No. 1423276; and by a DAAD fellowship to the second author. We would like to thank Markus Dreyer for providing the datasets and Manaal Faruqui for providing implementations of the baseline sequence-to-sequence models. Finally we would like to thank Mo Yu, Nanyun Peng, Dingquan Wang and Elan Hourticolon-Retzler for helpful discussions and early prototypes for some of the neural network architectures.

References

Daniel Andor, Chris Alberti, David Weiss, Aliaksei Severyn, Alessandro Presta, Kuzman Ganchev, Slav Petrov, and Michael Collins. 2016. Globally normalized transition-based neural networks. Available at arXiv.org as arXiv:1603.06042, March.

R. Harald Baayen, Richard Piepenbrock, and Rijn van H. 1993. The CELEX lexical data base on CD-ROM.

Dzmitry Bahdanau, Kyunghyun Cho, and Yoshua Bengio. 2015. Neural machine translation by jointly learning to align and translate. In *Proceedings of ICLR*.

Maximilian Bisani and Hermann Ney. 2008. Joint-sequence models for grapheme-to-phoneme conversion. *Speech Communication*, 50(5):434–451.

John S. Bridle. 1990. Training stochastic model recognition algorithms as networks can lead to maximum mutual information estimation of parameters. In *Proceedings of NIPS*, pages 211–217.

Francisco Casacuberta and Colin de la Higuera. 1999. Optimal linguistic decoding is a difficult computational problem. *Pattern Recognition Letters*, 20(8):813–821.

Liang-chieh Chen, Alexander Schwing, Alan Yuille, and Raquel Urtasun. 2015. Learning deep structured models. In *Proceedings of ICML*, pages 1785–1794.

Stanley F. Chen. 2003. Conditional and joint models for grapheme-to-phoneme conversion. In *Proceedings of EUROSPEECH*.

Michael Collins. 2002. Discriminative training methods for hidden Markov models: Theory and experiments with perceptron algorithms. In *Proceedings of the Conference on Empirical Methods in Natural Language Processing*, Philadelphia, July.

Ryan Cotterell, Nanyun Peng, and Jason Eisner. 2014. Stochastic contextual edit distance and probabilistic FSTs. In *Proceedings of ACL*, pages 625–630, June.

E. W. Dijkstra. 1959. A note on two problems in connexion with graphs. *Numerische Mathematik*, 1(1).

Trinh-Minh-Tri Do and Thierry Artieres. 2010. Neural conditional random fields. In *Proceedings of AISTATS*. JMLR.

Markus Dreyer, Jason R. Smith, and Jason Eisner. 2008. Latent-variable modeling of string transductions with finite-state methods. In *Proceedings of EMNLP*, pages 1080–1089, October.

Markus Dreyer. 2011. *A Non-Parametric Model for the Discovery of Inflectional Paradigms from Plain Text Using Graphical Models over Strings*. Ph.D. thesis, Johns Hopkins University, Baltimore, MD, April.

Greg Durrett and Dan Klein. 2015. Neural CRF parsing. In *Proceedings of ACL*.

Chris Dyer, Miguel Ballesteros, Wang Ling, Austin Matthews, and Noah A. Smith. 2015. Transition-based dependency parsing with stack long short-term memory. In *Proceedings of ACL-IJCNLP*, pages 334–343, July.

Jason Eisner. 2002. Parameter estimation for probabilistic finite-state transducers. In *Proceedings of ACL*, pages 1–8, July.

Manaal Faruqui, Yulia Tsvetkov, Graham Neubig, and Chris Dyer. 2016. Morphological inflection generation using character sequence to sequence learning. In *Proceedings of NAACL*. Code available at https://github.com/mfaruqui/morph-trans.

Jenny Rose Finkel, Alex Kleeman, and Christopher D. Manning. 2008. Efficient, feature-based, conditional random field parsing. In *Proceedings of ACL*, pages 959–967.

Nicholas FitzGerald, Oscar Täckström, Kuzman Ganchev, and Dipanjan Das. 2015. Semantic role labeling with neural network factors. In *Proceedings of EMNLP*, pages 960–970.

Yasuhisa Fujii, Kazumasa Yamamoto, and Seiichi Nakagawa. 2012. Deep-hidden conditional neural fields for continuous phoneme speech recognition. In *Proceedings of IWSML*.

Kevin Gimpel and Noah A. Smith. 2010. Softmax-margin CRFs: Training log-linear models with cost functions. In *Proceedings of NAACL-HLT*, pages 733–736, June.

Alex Graves and Jürgen Schmidhuber. 2005. Framewise phoneme classification with bidirectional lstm and other neural network architectures. *Neural Networks*, 18(5):602–610.

Alex Graves. 2012. *Supervised Sequence Labelling with Recurrent Neural Networks*. Springer.

Edward Grefenstette, Karl Moritz Hermann, Mustafa Suleyman, and Phil Blunsom. 2015. Learning to transduce with unbounded memory. In *Proceedings of NIPS*, pages 1819–1827.

Sepp Hochreiter and Jürgen Schmidhuber. 1997. Long short-term memory. *Neural Computation*.

Zhiheng Huang, Wei Xu, and Kai Yu. 2015. Bidirectional LSTM-CRF models for sequence tagging. *arXiv preprint arXiv:1508.01991*.

Sittichai Jiampojamarn, Grzegorz Kondrak, and Tarek Sherif. 2007. Applying many-to-many alignments and hidden Markov models to letter-to-phoneme conversion. In *Proceedings of NAACL-HLT*, pages 372–379.

Philipp Koehn, Hieu Hoang, Alexandra Birch, Chris Callison-Burch, Marcello Federico, Nicola Bertoldi, Brooke Cowan, Wade Shen, Christine Moran, Richard Zens, et al. 2007. Moses: Open source toolkit for statistical machine translation. In *Proceedings of ACL (Interactive Poster and Demonstration Sessions)*, pages 177–180.

Lingpeng Kong, Chris Dyer, and Noah A. Smith. 2015. Segmental recurrent neural networks. *arXiv preprint arXiv:1511.06018*.

Vladimir I. Levenshtein. 1966. Binary codes capable of correcting deletions, insertions, and reversals. *Soviet Physics Doklady*, 10(8):707–710.

Zhifei Li and Jason Eisner. 2009. First- and second-order expectation semirings with applications to minimum-risk training on translation forests. In *Proceedings of EMNLP*, pages 40–51, August.

Zhifei Li, Jason Eisner, and Sanjeev Khudanpur. 2009. Variational decoding for statistical machine translation. In *Proceedings of ACL*, pages 593–601.

Jonathan May and Kevin Knight. 2006. A better n-best list: Practical determinization of weighted finite tree automata. In *Proceedings of NAACL*, pages 351–358.

Andriy Mnih and Geoffrey Hinton. 2007. Three new graphical models for statistical language modelling. In *Proceedings of ICML*, pages 641–648. ACM.

Mehryar Mohri. 1997. Finite-state transducers in language and speech processing. *Computational Linguistics*, 23(2):269–311.

Jian Peng, Liefeng Bo, and Jinbo Xu. 2009. Conditional neural fields. In *Proceedings of NIPS*, pages 1419–1427.

Eric Sven Ristad and Peter N. Yianilos. 1996. Learning string edit distance. Technical Report CS-TR-532-96, Princeton University, Department of Computer Science, October. Revised October 1997.

Ilya Sutskever, Oriol Vinyals, and Quoc Le. 2014. Sequence to sequence learning with neural networks. In *Proceedings of NIPS*.

Antoine Vinel, Trinh Minh Tri Do, and Thierry Artieres. 2011. Joint optimization of hidden conditional random fields and non-linear feature extraction. In *Proceedings of ICDAR*, pages 513–517. IEEE.

Oriol Vinyals, Łukasz Kaiser, Terry Koo, Slav Petrov, Ilya Sutskever, and Geoffrey Hinton. 2015. Grammar as a foreign language. In *Proceedings of NIPS*, pages 2755–2763.

Richard Wicentowski. 2002. *Modeling and Learning Multilingual Inflectional Morphology in a Minimally Supervised Framework*. Ph.D. thesis, Johns Hopkins University.

Morphological Inflection Generation Using Character Sequence to Sequence Learning

Manaal Faruqui[1]   **Yulia Tsvetkov**[1]   **Graham Neubig**[2]   **Chris Dyer**[1]

[1]Language Technologies Institute, Carnegie Mellon University, USA

[2]Graduate School of Information Science, Nara Institute of Science and Technology, Japan

{mfaruqui,ytsvetko,cdyer}@cs.cmu.edu neubig@is.naist.jp

Abstract

Morphological inflection generation is the task of generating the inflected form of a given lemma corresponding to a particular linguistic transformation. We model the problem of inflection generation as a character sequence to sequence learning problem and present a variant of the neural encoder-decoder model for solving it. Our model is language independent and can be trained in both supervised and semi-supervised settings. We evaluate our system on seven datasets of morphologically rich languages and achieve either better or comparable results to existing state-of-the-art models of inflection generation.

1 Introduction

Inflection is the word-formation mechanism to express different grammatical categories such as tense, mood, voice, aspect, person, gender, number and case. Inflectional morphology is often realized by the concatenation of bound morphemes (prefixes and suffixes) to a root form or stem, but nonconcatenative processes such as ablaut and infixation are found in many languages as well. Table 1 shows the possible inflected forms of the German stem *Kalb* (calf) when it is used in different cases and numbers. The inflected forms are the result of both ablaut (e.g., $a{\rightarrow}\ddot{a}$) and suffixation (e.g., *+ern*).

Inflection generation is useful for reducing data sparsity in morphologically complex languages. For example, statistical machine translation suffers from data sparsity when translating morphologically-rich languages, since every surface form is considered an

	singular	plural
nominative	Kalb	Kälber
accusative	Kalb	Kälber
dative	Kalb	Kälbern
genitive	Kalbes	Kälber

Table 1: An example of an inflection table from the German noun dataset for the word *Kalb* (calf).

independent entity. Translating into lemmas in the target language, and then applying inflection generation as a post-processing step, has been shown to alleviate the sparsity problem (Minkov et al., 2007; Toutanova et al., 2008; Clifton and Sarkar, 2011; Fraser et al., 2012; Chahuneau et al., 2013a). Modeling inflection generation has also been used to improve language modeling (Chahuneau et al., 2013b), identification of multi-word expressions (Oflazer et al., 2004), among other applications.

The traditional approach to modeling inflection relies on hand-crafted finite state transducers and lexicography, e.g., using *two-level morphology* (Koskenniemi, 1983; Kaplan and Kay, 1994). Such systems are appealing since they correspond to linguistic theories, but they are expensive to create, they can be fragile (Oflazer, 1996), and the composed transducers can be impractically large. As an alternative, machine learning models have been proposed to generate inflections from root forms as string transduction (Yarowsky and Wicentowski, 2000; Wicentowski, 2004; Dreyer and Eisner, 2011; Durrett and DeNero, 2013; Ahlberg et al., 2014; Hulden, 2014; Ahlberg et al., 2015; Nicolai et al., 2015). However, these impose either assumptions about the set of possible morphological processes

Proceedings of NAACL-HLT 2016, pages 634–643,

San Diego, California, June 12-17, 2016. ©2016 Association for Computational Linguistics

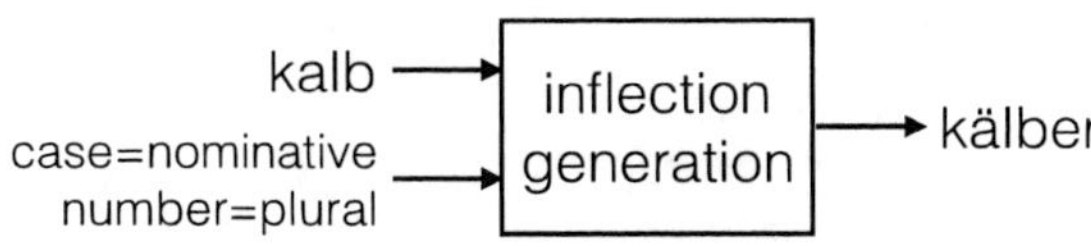

Figure 1: A general inflection generation model.

(e.g. affixation) or require careful feature engineering.

In this paper, we present a model of inflection generation based on a neural network sequence to sequence transducer. The root form is represented as sequence of characters, and this is the input to an encoder-decoder architecture (Cho et al., 2014; Sutskever et al., 2014). The model transforms its input to a sequence of output characters representing the inflected form (§4). Our model makes no assumptions about morphological processes, and our features are simply the individual characters. The model is trained on pairs of root form and inflected forms obtained from inflection tables extracted from Wiktionary.[1] We improve the supervised model with unlabeled data, by integrating a character language model trained on the vocabulary of the language.

Our experiments show that the model achieves better or comparable results to state-of-the-art methods on the benchmark inflection generation tasks (§5). For example, our model is able to learn long-range relations between character sequences in the string aiding the inflection generation process required by Finnish vowel harmony (§6), which helps it obtain the current best results in that language.

2 Inflection Generation: Background

Durrett and DeNero (2013) formulate the task of supervised inflection generation for a given root form, based on a large number of training inflection tables extracted from Wiktionary. Every inflection table contains the inflected form of a given root word corresponding to different linguistic transformations (cf. Table 1). Figure 1 shows the inflection generation framework. Since the release of the Wiktionary dataset, several different models have reported performance on this dataset. As we are also using this dataset, we will now review these models.

We denote the models of Durrett and DeNero

[1]www.wiktionary.org

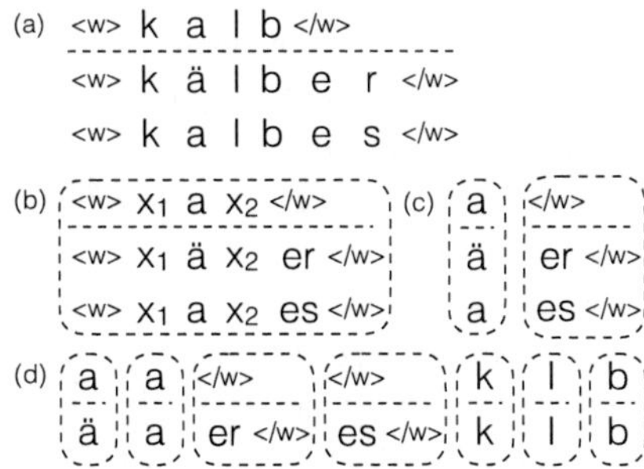

Figure 2: Rule extraction: (a) Character aligned-table; (b) Table-level rule of AFH14, AFH15 (c) Vertical rules of DDN13 and (d) Atomic rules of NCK15.

(2013), Ahlberg et al. (2014), Ahlberg et al. (2015), and Nicolai et al. (2015), by DDN13, AFH14, AFH15, and NCK15 respectively. These models perform inflection generation as string transduction and largely consist of three major components: (1) Character alignment of word forms in a table; (2) Extraction of string transformation rules; (3) Application of rules to new root forms.

The first step is learning character alignments across inflected forms in a table. Figure 2 (a) shows alignment between three word forms of *Kalb*. Different models use different heuristic algorithms for alignments such as edit distance, dynamic edit distance (Eisner, 2002; Oncina and Sebban, 2006), and longest subsequence alignment (Bergroth et al., 2000). Aligning characters across word forms provide spans of characters that have changed and spans that remain unchanged. These spans are used to extract rules for inflection generation for different inflection types as shown in Figure 2 (b)–(d).

By applying the extracted rules to new root forms, inflected words can be generated. DDN13 use a semi-Markov model (Sarawagi and Cohen, 2004) to predict what rules should be applied, using character n-grams ($n = 1$ to 4) as features. AFH14 and AFH15 use substring features extracted from words to match an input word to a rule table. NCK15 use a semi-Markov model inspired by DDN13, but additionally use target n-grams and joint n-grams as features sequences while selecting the rules.

Motivation for our model. Morphology often makes references to segmental features, like place or manner of articulation, or voicing status (Chomsky and Halle, 1968). While these can be encoded as features in existing work, our approach treats segments as vectors of features "natively". Our approach represents every character as a bundle of continuous features, instead of using discrete surface character sequence features. Also, our model uses features as part of the transduction rules themselves, whereas in existing work features are only used to rescore rule applications.

In existing work, the learner implicitly specifies the class of rules that can be learned, such as "delete" or "concatenate". To deal with phenomenona like segment lengthening in English: *run* → *running*; or reduplication in Hebrew: *Kelev* → *Klavlav*, *Chatul* → *Chataltul*; (or consonant gradation in Finnish), where the affixes are induced from characters of the root form, one must engineer a new rule class, which leads to poorer estimates due to data sparsity. By modeling inflection generation as a task of generating a character sequence, one character at a time, we do away with such problems.

3   Neural Encoder-Decoder Models

Here, we describe briefly the underlying framework of our inflection generation model, called the recurrent neural network (RNN) encoder-decoder (Cho et al., 2014; Sutskever et al., 2014) which is used to transform an input sequence $\vec{x}$ to output sequence $\vec{y}$. We represent an item by x, a sequence of items by $\vec{x}$, vectors by $\mathbf{x}$, matrices by $\mathbf{X}$, and sequences of vectors by $\vec{\mathbf{x}}$.

3.1   Formulation

In the encoder-decoder framework, an encoder reads a variable length input sequence, a sequence of vectors $\vec{\mathbf{x}} = \langle \mathbf{x}_1, \cdots, \mathbf{x}_T \rangle$ (corresponding to a sequence of input symbols $\vec{x} = \langle x_1, \cdots, x_T \rangle$) and generates a fixed-dimensional vector representation of the sequence. $\mathbf{x}_t \in \mathbb{R}^l$ is an input vector of length l. The most common approach is to use an RNN such that:

$$\mathbf{h}_t = f(\mathbf{h}_{t-1}, \mathbf{x}_t) \qquad (1)$$

where $\mathbf{h}_t \in \mathbb{R}^n$ is a hidden state at time t, and f is generally a non-linear transformation, producing $\mathbf{e} := \mathbf{h}_{T+1}$ as the input representation. The decoder is trained to predict the next output y_t given the

encoded input vector $\mathbf{e}$ and all the previously predicted outputs $\langle y_1, \cdots y_{t-1} \rangle$. In other words, the decoder defines a probability over the output sequence $\vec{y} = \langle y_1, \cdots, y_{T'} \rangle$ by decomposing the joint probability into ordered conditionals:

$$p(\vec{y}|\vec{x}) = \prod_{t=1}^{T'} p(y_t | \mathbf{e}, \langle y_1, \cdots, y_{t-1} \rangle) \qquad (2)$$

With a decoder RNN, we can first obtain the hidden layer at time t as: $\mathbf{s}_t = g(\mathbf{s}_{t-1}, \{\mathbf{e}, \mathbf{y}_{t-1}\})$ and feed this into a softmax layer to obtain the conditional probability as:

$$p(y_t = i | \mathbf{e}, \vec{y}_{<t}) = \mathrm{softmax}(\mathbf{W}_s \mathbf{s}_t + \mathbf{b}_s)_i \qquad (3)$$

where, $\vec{y}_{<t} = \langle y_1, \cdots, y_{t-1} \rangle$. In recent work, both f and g are generally LSTMs, a kind of RNN which we describe next.

3.2   Long Short-Term Memory (LSTM)

In principle, RNNs allow retaining information from time steps in the distant past, but the nonlinear "squashing" functions applied in the calculation of each $\mathbf{h}_t$ result in a decay of the error signal used in training with backpropagation. LSTMs are a variant of RNNs designed to cope with this "vanishing gradient" problem using an extra memory "cell" (Hochreiter and Schmidhuber, 1997; Graves, 2013). Past work explains the computation within an LSTM through the metaphors of deciding how much of the current input to pass into memory or forget. We refer interested readers to the original papers for details.

4   Inflection Generation Model

We frame the problem of inflection generation as a sequence to sequence learning problem of character sequences. The standard encoder-decoder models were designed for machine translation where the objective is to translate a sentence (sequence of words) from one language to a semantically equivalent sentence (sequence of words) in another language. We can easily port the encoder-decoder translation model for inflection generation. Our model predicts the sequence of characters in the inflected string given the characters in the root word (input).

However, our problem differs from the above setting in two ways: (1) the input and output character

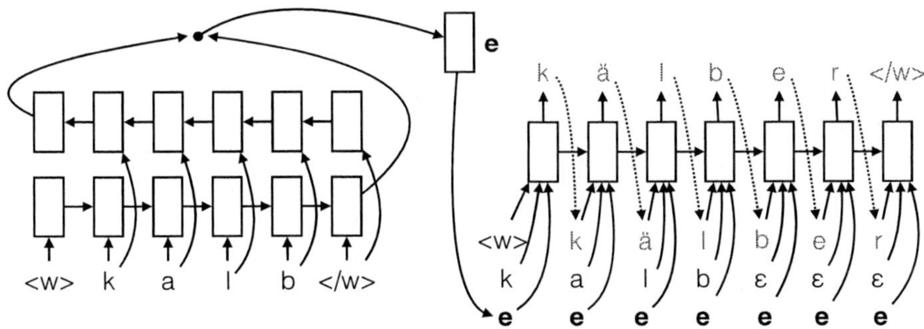

Figure 3: The modified encoder-decoder architecture for inflection generation. Input characters are shown in black and predicted characters are shown in red. • indicates the append operation.

sequences are mostly similar except for the inflections; (2) the input and output character sequences have different semantics. Regarding the first difference, taking the word *play* as an example, the inflected forms corresponding to past tense and continuous forms are *played* and *playing*. To better use this correspondence between the input and output sequence, we also feed the input sequence directly into the decoder:

$$\mathbf{s}_t = g(\mathbf{s}_{t-1}, \{\mathbf{e}, \mathbf{y}_{t-1}, \mathbf{x}_t\}) \qquad (4)$$

where, g is the decoder LSTM, and $\mathbf{x}_t$ and $\mathbf{y}_t$ are the input and output character vectors respectively. Because the lengths of the input and output sequences are not equal, we feed an ϵ character in the decoder, indicating null input, once the input sequence runs out of characters. These ϵ character vectors are parameters that are learned by our model, exactly as other character vectors.

Regarding the second difference, to provide the model the ability to learn the transformation of semantics from input to output, we apply an affine transformation on the encoded vector $\mathbf{e}$:

$$\mathbf{e} \leftarrow \mathbf{W}_{trans}\mathbf{e} + \mathbf{b}_{trans} \qquad (5)$$

where, $\mathbf{W}_{trans}, \mathbf{b}_{trans}$ are the transformation parameters. Also, in the encoder we use a bi-directional LSTM (Graves et al., 2005) instead of a uni-directional LSTM, as it has been shown to capture the sequence information more effectively (Ling et al., 2015; Ballesteros et al., 2015; Bahdanau et al., 2015). Our resultant inflection generation model is shown in Figure 3.

4.1 Supervised Learning

The parameters of our model are the set of character vectors, the transformation parameters ($\mathbf{W}_{trans}, \mathbf{b}_{trans}$), and the parameters of the encoder and decoder LSTMs (§3.2). We use negative log-likelihood of the output character sequence as the loss function:

$$-\log p(\vec{y}|\vec{x}) = -\sum_{t=1}^{T'} \log p(y_t|\mathbf{e}, \vec{y}_{<t}) \qquad (6)$$

We minimize the loss using stochastic updates with AdaDelta (Zeiler, 2012). This is our purely supervised model for inflection generation and we evaluate it in two different settings as established by previous work:

Factored Model. In the first setting, we learn a separate model for each type of inflection independent of the other possible inflections. For example, in case of German nouns, we learn 8, and for German verbs, we learn 27 individual encoder-decoder inflection models (cf. Table 3). There is no parameter sharing across these models. We call these factored models of inflection generation.

Joint Model. In the second setting, while learning a model for an inflection type, we also use the information of how the lemma inflects across all other inflection types i.e., the inflection table of a root form is used to learn different inflection models. We model this, by having the same encoder in the encoder-decoder model across all inflection models.[2] The encoder in our model is learning a

---

[2] We also tried having the same encoder and decoder across inflection types, with just the transformation matrix being dif-

$p_{\text{LM}}(\vec{y})$	$p(\vec{y}|\vec{x})$
len($\vec{y}$) - len($\vec{x}$)	levenshtein($\vec{y}, \vec{x}$)
same-suffix($\vec{y}, \vec{x}$)?	subsequence($\vec{y}, \vec{x}$)?
same-prefix($\vec{y}, \vec{x}$)?	subsequence($\vec{x}, \vec{y}$)?

Table 2: Features used to rerank the inflected outputs. $\vec{x}$, $\vec{y}$ denote the root and inflected character sequences resp.

Dataset	root forms	Infl.
German Nouns (DE-N)	2764	8
German Verbs (DE-V)	2027	27
Spanish Verbs (ES-V)	4055	57
Finnish NN & Adj. (FI-NA)	6400	28
Finnish Verbs (FI-V)	7249	53
Dutch Verbs (NL-V)	11200	9
French Verbs (FR-V)	6957	48

Table 3: The number of root forms and types of inflections across datasets.

representation of the input character sequence. Because all inflection models take the same input but produce different outputs, we hypothesize that having the same encoder can lead to better estimates.

4.2 Semi-supervised Learning

The model we described so far relies entirely on the availability of pairs of root form and inflected word form for learning to generate inflections. Although such supervised models can be used to obtain inflection generation models (Durrett and DeNero, 2013; Ahlberg et al., 2015), it has been shown that unlabeled data can generally improve the performance of such systems (Ahlberg et al., 2014; Nicolai et al., 2015). The vocabulary of the words of a language encode information about what correct sequences of characters in a language look like. Thus, we learn a language model over the character sequences in a vocabulary extracted from a large unlabeled corpus. We use this language model to make predictions about the next character in the sequence given the previous characters, in following two settings.

Output Reranking. In the first setting, we first train the inflection generation model using the supervised setting as described in §4.1. While making predictions for inflections, we use beam search to generate possible output character sequences and rerank them using the language model probability along with other easily extractable features as described in Table 2. We use pairwise ranking optimization (PRO) to learn the reranking model (Hopkins and May, 2011). The reranker is trained on the beam output of dev set and evaluated on test set.

Language Model Interpolation. In the second setting, we interpolate the probability of observing the next character according to the language model with the probability according to our inflection gen-

eration model. Thus, the loss function becomes:

$$-\log p(\vec{y}|\vec{x}) = \frac{1}{Z} \sum_{t=1}^{T'} - \log p(y_t|\mathbf{e}, \vec{y}_{<t}) \\ - \lambda \log p_{\text{LM}}(y_t|\vec{y}_{<t}) \quad (7)$$

where $p_{LM}(y_t|\vec{y}_{<t})$ is the probability of observing the word y_t given the history estimated according to a language model, $\lambda \geq 0$ is the interpolation parameter which is learned during training and Z is the normalization factor. This formulation lets us use any off-the-shelf pre-trained character language model easily (details in §5).

4.3 Ensembling

Our loss functions (equ. 6 & 7) formulated using a neural network architecture are non-convex in nature and are thus difficult to optimize. It has been shown that taking an ensemble of models which were initialized differently and trained independently leads to improved performance (Hansen and Salamon, 1990; Collobert et al., 2011). Thus, for each model type used in this work, we report results obtained using an ensemble of models. So, while decoding we compute the probability of emitting a character as the product-of-experts of the individual models in the ensemble: $p_{ens}(y_t|\cdot) = \frac{1}{Z} \prod_{i=1}^{k} p_i(y_t|\cdot)^{\frac{1}{k}}$ where, $p_i(y_t|\cdot)$ is the probability according to i-th model and Z is the normalization factor.

5 Experiments

We now conduct experiments using the described models. Note that not all previously published models present results on all settings, and thus we compare our results to them wherever appropriate.

Hyperparameters. Across all models described in this paper, we use the following hyperparameters.

---

ferent (equ. 5), and observed consistently worse results.

In both the encoder and decoder models we use single layer LSTMs with the hidden vector of length 100. The length of character vectors is the size of character vocabulary according to each dataset. The parameters are regularized with ℓ_2, with the regularization constant 10^{-5}.[3] The number of models for ensembling are $k = 5$. Models are trained for at most 30 epochs and the model with best result on development set is selected.

5.1 Data

Durrett and DeNero (2013) published the Wiktionary inflection dataset with training, development and test splits. The development and test sets contain 200 inflection tables each and the training sets consist of the remaining data. This dataset contains inflections for German, Finnish and Spanish. This dataset was further augmented by (Nicolai et al., 2015), by adding Dutch verbs extracted from CELEX lexical database (Baayen et al., 1995), French verbs from Verbsite, an online French conjugation dictionary and Czech nouns and verbs from the Prague Dependnecy Treebank (Hajič et al., 2001). As the dataset for Czech contains many incomplete tables, we do not use it for our experiments. These datasets come with pre-specified training/dev/test splits, which we use. For each of these sets, the training data is restricted to 80% of the total inflection tables, with 10% for development and 10% for testing. We list the size of these datasets in Table 3.

For semi-supervised experiments, we train a 5-gram character language model with Witten-Bell smoothing (Bell et al., 1990) using the SRILM toolkit (Stolcke, 2002). We train the character language models on the list of unique word types extracted from the Wikipedia dump for each language after filtering out words with characters unseen in the inflection generation training dataset. We obtained around 2 million unique words for each language.

5.2 Results

Supervised Models. The individual inflected form accuracy for the factored model (§4.1) is shown in Table 4. Across datasets, we obtain either com-

---

[3]Using dropout did not improve our results.

	DDN13	NCK15	Ours
DE-V	94.76	**97.50**	96.72
DE-N	88.31	**88.60**	88.12
ES-V	99.61	99.80	**99.81**
FI-V	97.23	**98.10**	97.81
FI-NA	92.14	93.00	**95.44**
NL-V	90.50	96.10	**96.71**
FR-V	98.80	**99.20**	98.82
Avg.	94.47	96.04	**96.20**

Table 4: Individual form prediction accuracy for **factored supervised** models.

	DDN13	AFH14	AFH15	Ours
DE-V	96.19	97.01	**98.11**	97.25
DE-N	88.94	87.81	**89.88**	88.37
ES-V	99.67	99.52	**99.92**	99.86
FI-V	96.43	96.36	97.14	**97.97**
FI-NA	93.41	91.91	93.68	**94.71**
Avg.	94.93	94.53	**95.74**	95.63
NL-V	93.88	–	–	96.16
FR-V	98.60	–	–	98.74
Avg.	95.30	–	–	**96.15**

Table 5: Individual form prediction accuracy for **joint supervised** models.

parable or better results than NCK15 while obtaining on average an accuracy of 96.20% which is higher than both DDN13 and NCK15. Our factored model performs better than DDN13 and NCK15 on datasets with large training set (ES-V, FI-V, FI-NA, NL-V, FR-V) as opposed to datasets with small training set (DE-N, DE-V). In the joint model setting (cf. Table 5), on average, we perform better than DDN13 and AFH14 but are behind AFH15 by 0.11%. Our model improves in performance over our factored model for DE-N, DE-V, and ES-V, which are the three smallest training datasets. Thus, parameter sharing across different inflection types helps the low-resourced scenarios.[4]

Semi-supervised Models. We now evaluate the utility of character language models in inflection generation, in two different settings as described earlier (§4.2). We use the factored model as our base model in the following experiments as it performed

---

[4]Although NCK15 provide results in the joint model setting, they also use raw data in the joint model which makes it incomparable to our model and other previous models.

	AFH14	NCK15	Interpol	Rerank
DE-V	97.87	**97.90**	96.79	97.11
DE-N	91.81	**89.90**	88.31	89.31
ES-V	99.58	99.90	99.78	**99.94**
FI-V	96.63	**98.10**	96.66	97.62
FI-NA	93.82	93.60	94.60	**95.66**
Avg.	**95.93**	95.88	95.42	**95.93**
NL-V	–	96.60	**96.66**	96.64
FR-V	–	**99.20**	98.81	98.94
Avg.	–	**96.45**	96.08	**96.45**

Table 6: Individual form prediction accuracy for **factored semi-supervised** models.

Model	Accuracy
Encoder-Decoder	79.08
Encoder-Decoder Attention	95.64
Ours W/O Encoder	84.04
Ours	**96.20**

Table 7: Avg. accuracy across datasets of the encoder-decoder, attentional encoder-decoder & our model without encoder.

better than the joint model (cf. Table 4 & 5). Our reranking model which uses the character language model along with other features (cf. Table 2) to select the best answer from a beam of predictions, improves over almost all the datasets with respect to the supervised model and is equal on average to AFH14 and NCK15 semi-supervised models with 96.45% accuracy. We obtain the best reported results on ES-V and FI-NA datasets (99.94% and 95.66% respectively). However, our second semi-supervised model, the interpolation model, on average obtains 96.08% and is surprisingly worse than our supervised model (96.20%).

Comparison to Other Architectures. Finally it is of interest how our proposed model compares to more traditional neural models. We compare our model against a standard encoder-decoder model, and an encoder-decoder model with attention, both trained on root form to inflected form character sequences. In a standard encoder-decoder model (Sutskever et al., 2014), the encoded input sequence vector is fed into the hidden layer of the decoder as input, and is not available at every time step in contrast to our model, where we additionally feed in x_t at every time step as in equ. 4. An attentional model computes a weighted average of the hidden layer of

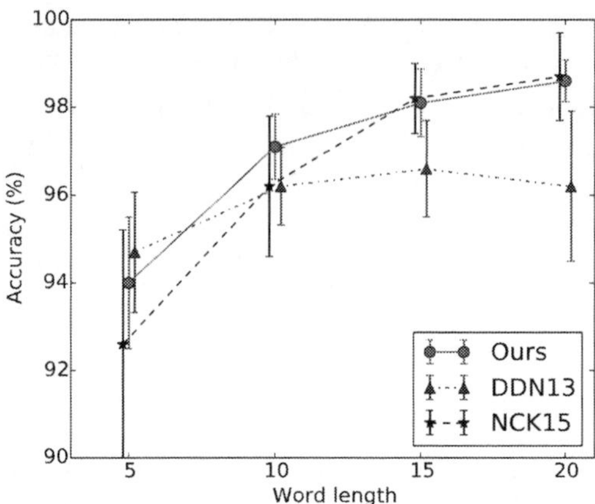

Figure 4: Plot of inflection prediction accuracy against the length of gold inflected forms. The points are shown with minor offset along the x-axis to enhance clarity.

the input sequence, which is then used along with the decoder hidden layer to make a prediction (Bahdanau et al., 2015). These models also do not take the root form character sequence as inputs to the decoder. We also evaluate the utility of having an encoder which computes a representation of the input character sequence in a vector **e** by removing the encoder from our model in Figure 3. The results in Table 7 show that we outperform the encoder-decoder model, and the model without an encoder substantially. Our model is slightly better than the attentional encoder-decoder model, and is simpler as it does not have the additional attention layer.

6   Analysis

Length of Inflected Forms. In Figure 4 we show how the prediction accuracy of an inflected form varies with respect to the length of the correct inflected form.To get stable estimates, we bin the inflected forms according to their length: < 5, $[5, 10)$, $[10, 15)$, and ≥ 15. The accuracy for each bin is macro-averaged across 6 datasets[5] for our factored model and the best models of DDN13 and NCK15. Our model consistently shows improvement in performance as word length increases and is significantly better than DDN13 on words of length more than 20 and is approximately equal to NCK15. On words of length < 5, we perform worse than DDN13

---

[5]We remove DE-N as its the smallest and shows high variance in results.

but better than NCK15. On average, our model has
the least error margin across bins of different word
length as compared to both DDN13 and NCK15.
Using LSTMs in our model helps us make better
predictions for long sequences, since they have the
ability to capture long-range dependencies.

Finnish Vowel Harmony. Our model obtains the
current best result on the Finnish noun and adjective
dataset, this dataset has the longest inflected words,
some of which are > 30 characters long. Finnish exhibits *vowel harmony*, i.e, the occurrence of a vowel
is controlled by other vowels in the word. Finnish
vowels are divided into three groups: front (ä, ö,
y), back (a, o, u), and neutral (e, i). If back vowels are present in a stem, then the harmony is back
(i.e, front vowels will be absent), else the harmony is
front (i.e, back vowels will be absent). In compound
words the suffix harmony is determined by the final
stem in the compound. For example, our model correctly inflects the word *fasisti* (fascist) to obtain *fa-
sisteissa* and the compound *tärkkelyspitoinen* (starch
containing) to *tärkkelyspitoisissa*. The ability of our
model to learn such relations between these vowels
helps capture vowel harmony. For FI-NA, our model
obtains 99.87% for correctly predicting vowel harmony, and NCK15 obtains 98.50%.We plot the character vectors of these Finnish vowels (cf. Figure 5)
using t-SNE projection (van der Maaten and Hinton, 2008) and observe that the vowels are correctly
grouped with visible transition from the back to the
front vowels.

7 Related Work

Similar to the encoder in our framework, Rastogi et
al. (2016) extract sub-word features using a forward-
backward LSTM from a word, and use them in a traditional weighted FST to generate inflected forms.
Neural encoder-decoder models of string transduction have also been used for sub-word level transformations like grapheme-to-phoneme conversion (Yao
and Zweig, 2015; Rao et al., 2015).

Generation of inflectional morphology has been
particularly useful in statistical machine translation, both in translation from morphologically rich
languages (Goldwater and McClosky, 2005), and
into morphologically rich languages (Minkov et al.,
2007; Toutanova et al., 2008; Clifton and Sarkar,

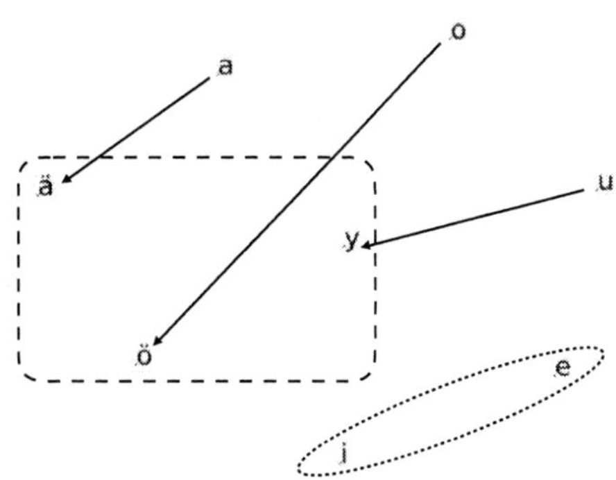

Figure 5: Plot of character vectors of Finnish vowels. Their
organization shows that front, back and neutral vowel groups
have been discovered. The arrows show back and front vowel
correspondences.

2011; Fraser et al., 2012). Modeling the morphological structure of a word has also shown to improve
the quality of word clusters (Clark, 2003) and word
vector representations (Cotterell and Schütze, 2015).

Inflection generation is complementary to the task
of morphological and phonological segmentation,
where the existing word form needs to be segmented
to obtained meaningful sub-word units (Creutz and
Lagus, 2005; Snyder and Barzilay, 2008; Poon et
al., 2009; Narasimhan et al., 2015; Cotterell et al.,
2015; Cotterell et al., 2016). An additional line of
work that benefits from implicit modeling of morphology is neural character-based natural language
processing, e.g., part-of-speech tagging (Santos and
Zadrozny, 2014; Ling et al., 2015) and dependency
parsing (Ballesteros et al., 2015). These models
have been successful when applied to morphologically rich languages, as they are able to capture word
formation patterns.

8 Conclusion

We have presented a model that generates inflected
forms of a given root form using a neural network
sequence to sequence string transducer. Our model
obtains state-of-the-art results and performs at par or
better than existing inflection generation models on
seven different datasets. Our model is able to learn
long-range dependencies within character sequences
for inflection generation which makes it specially
suitable for morphologically rich languages.

Acknowledgements

We thank Mans Hulden for help in explaining Finnish vowel harmony, and Garrett Nicolai for making the output of his system available for comparison. This work was sponsored in part by the National Science Foundation through award IIS-1526745.

References

Malin Ahlberg, Markus Forsberg, and Mans Hulden. 2014. Semi-supervised learning of morphological paradigms and lexicons. In *Proc. of EACL*.

Malin Ahlberg, Markus Forsberg, and Mans Hulden. 2015. Paradigm classification in supervised learning of morphology. *Proc. of NAACL*.

Harald R. Baayen, Richard Piepenbrock, and Leon Gulikers. 1995. *The CELEX Lexical Database. Release 2 (CD-ROM)*. LDC, University of Pennsylvania.

Dzmitry Bahdanau, Kyunghyun Cho, and Yoshua Bengio. 2015. Neural machine translation by jointly learning to align and translate. In *Proc. of ICLR*.

Miguel Ballesteros, Chris Dyer, and Noah A. Smith. 2015. Improved transition-based parsing by modeling characters instead of words with lstms. In *Proc. of EMNLP*.

Timothy C Bell, John G Cleary, and Ian H Witten. 1990. *Text compression*. Prentice-Hall, Inc.

Lasse Bergroth, Harri Hakonen, and Timo Raita. 2000. A survey of longest common subsequence algorithms. In *Proc. of SPIRE*.

Victor Chahuneau, Eva Schlinger, Noah A. Smith, and Chris Dyer. 2013a. Translating into morphologically rich languages with synthetic phrases. In *Proc. of EMNLP*.

Victor Chahuneau, Noah A Smith, and Chris Dyer. 2013b. Knowledge-rich morphological priors for bayesian language models. In *Proc. of NAACL*.

Kyunghyun Cho, Bart van Merrienboer, Caglar Gulcehre, Dzmitry Bahdanau, Fethi Bougares, Holger Schwenk, and Yoshua Bengio. 2014. Learning phrase representations using rnn encoder–decoder for statistical machine translation. In *Proc. of EMNLP*.

N. Chomsky and M. Halle. 1968. *The Sound Pattern of English*. Harper & Row, New York, NY.

Alexander Clark. 2003. Combining distributional and morphological information for part of speech induction. In *Proc. of EACL*.

Ann Clifton and Anoop Sarkar. 2011. Combining morpheme-based machine translation with postprocessing morpheme prediction. In *Proc. of ACL*.

Ronan Collobert, Jason Weston, Léon Bottou, Michael Karlen, Koray Kavukcuoglu, and Pavel Kuksa. 2011. Natural language processing (almost) from scratch. *The Journal of Machine Learning Research*, 12:2493–2537.

Ryan Cotterell and Hinrich Schütze. 2015. Morphological word-embeddings. In *Proc. of NAACL*.

Ryan Cotterell, Nanyun Peng, and Jason Eisner. 2015. Modeling word forms using latent underlying morphs and phonology. *Transactions of the Association for Computational Linguistics*, 3:433–447.

Ryan Cotterell, Tim Vieria, and Hinrich Schütze. 2016. A joint model of orthography and morphological segmentation. In *Proc. of NAACL*.

Mathias Creutz and Krista Lagus. 2005. *Unsupervised morpheme segmentation and morphology induction from text corpora using Morfessor 1.0*. Helsinki University of Technology.

Markus Dreyer and Jason Eisner. 2011. Discovering morphological paradigms from plain text using a dirichlet process mixture model. In *Proc. of EMNLP*.

Greg Durrett and John DeNero. 2013. Supervised learning of complete morphological paradigms. In *Proc. of NAACL*.

Jason Eisner. 2002. Parameter estimation for probabilistic finite-state transducers. In *Proc. of ACL*.

Alexander Fraser, Marion Weller, Aoife Cahill, and Fabienne Cap. 2012. Modeling inflection and word-formation in SMT. In *Proc. of EACL*.

Sharon Goldwater and David McClosky. 2005. Improving statistical MT through morphological analysis. In *Proc. of EMNLP*, pages 676–683.

Alex Graves, Santiago Fernández, and Jürgen Schmidhuber. 2005. Bidirectional lstm networks for improved phoneme classification and recognition. In *Proc. of ICANN*.

Alex Graves. 2013. Generating sequences with recurrent neural networks. *CoRR*, abs/1308.0850.

Jan Hajič, Barbora Vidová-Hladká, and Petr Pajas. 2001. The Prague Dependency Treebank: Annotation structure and support. In *Proc. of the IRCS Workshop on Linguistic Databases*.

Lars Kai Hansen and Peter Salamon. 1990. Neural network ensembles. In *Proc. of PAMI*.

Sepp Hochreiter and Jürgen Schmidhuber. 1997. Long short-term memory. *Neural Computation*, 9(8):1735–1780.

Mark Hopkins and Jonathan May. 2011. Tuning as ranking. In *Proc. of EMNLP*.

Mans Hulden. 2014. Generalizing inflection tables into paradigms with finite state operations. In *Proc. of the Joint Meeting of SIGMORPHON and SIGFSM*.

Ronald M Kaplan and Martin Kay. 1994. Regular models of phonological rule systems. *Computational linguistics*, 20(3):331–378.

Kimmo Koskenniemi. 1983. Two-level morphology: A general computational model for word-form recognition and production. *University of Helsinki*.

Wang Ling, Tiago Luís, Luís Marujo, Rámon Fernandez Astudillo, Silvio Amir, Chris Dyer, Alan W Black, and Isabel Trancoso. 2015. Finding function in form: Compositional character models for open vocabulary word representation. In *Proc. of EMNLP*.

Einat Minkov, Kristina Toutanova, and Hisami Suzuki. 2007. Generating complex morphology for machine translation. In *Proc. of ACL*.

Karthik Narasimhan, Regina Barzilay, and Tommi Jaakkola. 2015. An unsupervised method for uncovering morphological chains. *TACL*.

Garrett Nicolai, Colin Cherry, and Grzegorz Kondrak. 2015. Inflection generation as discriminative string transduction. In *Proc. of NAACL*.

Kemal Oflazer, Özlem çetinoğlu, and Bilge Say. 2004. Integrating morphology with multi-word expression processing in turkish. In *Proc. of the Workshop on Multiword Expressions*.

Kemal Oflazer. 1996. Error-tolerant finite-state recognition with applications to morphological analysis and spelling correction. *Computational Linguistics*, 22(1):73–89.

Jose Oncina and Marc Sebban. 2006. Learning stochastic edit distance: Application in handwritten character recognition. *Pattern recognition*, 39(9):1575–1587.

Hoifung Poon, Colin Cherry, and Kristina Toutanova. 2009. Unsupervised morphological segmentation with log-linear models. In *Proc. of NAACL*.

Kanishka Rao, Fuchun Peng, Hasim Sak, and Françoise Beaufays. 2015. Grapheme-to-phoneme conversion using long short-term memory recurrent neural networks. In *Proc. of ICASSP*.

Pushpendre Rastogi, Ryan Cotterell, and Jason Eisner. 2016. Weighting finite-state transductions with neural context. In *Proc. of NAACL*.

Cicero D. Santos and Bianca Zadrozny. 2014. Learning character-level representations for part-of-speech tagging. In *Proc. of ICML*.

Sunita Sarawagi and William W Cohen. 2004. Semi-markov conditional random fields for information extraction. In *Proc. of NIPS*.

Benjamin Snyder and Regina Barzilay. 2008. Unsupervised multilingual learning for morphological segmentation. In *In The Annual Conference of the*.

Andreas Stolcke. 2002. Srilm-an extensible language modeling toolkit. In *Proc. of Interspeech*.

Ilya Sutskever, Oriol Vinyals, and Quoc VV Le. 2014. Sequence to sequence learning with neural networks. In *Proc. of NIPS*.

Kristina Toutanova, Hisami Suzuki, and Achim Ruopp. 2008. Applying morphology generation models to machine translation. In *Proc. of ACL*, pages 514–522.

Laurens van der Maaten and Geoffrey Hinton. 2008. Visualizing Data using t-SNE. *Journal of Machine Learning Research*, 9:2579–2605.

Richard Wicentowski. 2004. Multilingual noise-robust supervised morphological analysis using the word-frame model. In *Proc. of SIGPHON*.

Kaisheng Yao and Geoffrey Zweig. 2015. Sequence-to-sequence neural net models for grapheme-to-phoneme conversion. In *Proc. of ICASSP*.

David Yarowsky and Richard Wicentowski. 2000. Minimally supervised morphological analysis by multi-modal alignment. In *Proc. of ACL*.

Matthew D Zeiler. 2012. Adadelta: An adaptive learning rate method. *arXiv preprint arXiv:1212.5701*.

Towards Unsupervised and Language-independent Compound Splitting using Inflectional Morphological Transformations

Patrick Ziering
Institute for Natural Language Processing
University of Stuttgart, Germany
`Patrick.Ziering@`
`ims.uni-stuttgart.de`

Lonneke van der Plas
Institute of Linguistics
University of Malta, Malta
`Lonneke.vanderPlas@um.edu.mt`

Abstract

In this paper, we address the task of language-independent, knowledge-lean and unsupervised compound splitting, which is an essential component for many natural language processing tasks such as machine translation. Previous methods on statistical compound splitting either include language-specific knowledge (e.g., linking elements) or rely on parallel data, which results in limited applicability. We aim to overcome these limitations by learning compounding morphology from inflectional information derived from lemmatized monolingual corpora. In experiments for Germanic languages, we show that our approach significantly outperforms language-dependent state-of-the-art methods in finding the correct split point and that word inflection is a good approximation for compounding morphology.

1 Introduction

Compounding represents one of the most productive word formation types in many languages. In particular, Germanic languages (e.g., German or Dutch) show high productivity in closed compounding, i.e., in creating one-word compounds such as the German *Armutsbekämpfungsprogramm* 'poverty elimination program'. Previous studies on German corpora reveal that almost half of the corpus types are compounds, whereas individual compounds are very infrequent (Baroni et al., 2002). Therefore, an automatic compound analysis is indispensable and represents an essential component in many natural language processing (NLP) tasks such as machine translation (MT) or information retrieval (IR).

Besides determining the concatenated constituent forms, i.e., the correct split points (e.g., *Armuts | bekämpfungs | programm*), a compound splitter needs to normalize each part (e.g., *Armut + Bekämpfung + Programm*), because down-stream applications such as MT systems expect lemmatized words as input. However, normalization of constituent forms is non-trivial and usually requires language-specific knowledge (e.g., linking elements). State-of-the-art lemmatizers, designed for regular word inflection, would fail, because constituent forms often contain linking elements leading to a non-paradigmatic word form of the corresponding lexeme (e.g., *Armuts* 'poverty + s' never occurs as an isolated token in German corpora, since the *s*-suffix, often used for genitive or pluralization, is not used with *Armut*). Moreover, morphological operations during compounding vary a lot across languages and lexemes: we find cases that start from the lemma and have additions (e.g., linking elements), truncations (e.g., reductions to a verbal stem), word-internal operations (e.g., Umlautung) and combinations thereof (e.g., the first constituent of the German *Weihnachts|baum* 'Christmas tree', *Weihnachten*, undergoes both the *en*-truncation and the *s*-suffixation).

In this paper, we present a language-independent, unsupervised compound splitter that normalizes constituent forms by tolerantly retrieving candidate lemmas using an Ngram index and weighting string differences with inflectional information derived from lemmatized corpora.

Most previous work on compound splitting includes language-specific knowledge such as large

Proceedings of NAACL-HLT 2016, pages 644–653,
San Diego, California, June 12-17, 2016. ©2016 Association for Computational Linguistics

lexicons and morphological analyzers (Fritzinger and Fraser, 2010) or hand-crafted lists of linking elements and rules for modeling morphological transitions (Koehn and Knight, 2003; Stymne, 2008; Weller and Heid, 2012), which makes the approaches language-dependent. Macherey et al., (2011) were the first to overcome this limitation by learning morphological compounding operations automatically by retrieving compounds and their constituents from parallel corpora including English as support language.

We would like to take this one step further by avoiding the usage of parallel data, which are known to be sparse and frequently domain-specific, while Bretschneider and Zillner (2015) showed that compounding morphology varies between different domains. Instead, we exploit lemmatized corpora and use word inflection as an approximation to compounding morphology. This way, we are able to process compounds of any type of domain.

Our contributions are as follows. Firstly, we develop a language-independent and unsupervised compound splitter that does not rely on parallel data. As we will show, our system significantly outperforms language-dependent, knowledge-rich state-of-the-art methods in predicting the best split point. Secondly, in a controlled experiment, we show that compound splitting based on inflectional morphology performs similarly to splitting based on an extensive hand-crafted set of rules for compounding morphology. Thirdly, we perform a comprehensive, intrinsic evaluation of compound splitting, which is often missing in previous work that focuses on task-based evaluation (e.g., MT), and thus evaluates performance only indirectly. We compare splitting performance for several languages for two disciplines: (1) prediction of the correct split points and (2) normalization of the constituent forms. To the best of our knowledge, we are the first to evaluate these disciplines separately.

The paper is structured as follows. Section 2 outlines previous work on compound splitting. Section 3 discusses some theoretical assumptions on which we base our splitting method. Section 4 shows two efficient and flexible data structures used for our statistical compound splitter, which is described in Section 5. Section 6 presents some splitting experiments performed on German, Dutch and Afrikaans. Finally, Section 7 concludes and points to future work.

2   Related work

In the following discussion, we focus on splitting approaches that address morphological transformations, as these are most relevant for our work. Previous work on compound splitting can be roughly divided into two groups: (1) *statistical* approaches that are mainly based on large corpora and (2) *linguistically based* splitters, usually relying on knowledge-rich morphological analyzers or rules.

Statistical approaches generate all possible splits and rank them according to corpus statistics. Although independent of lexical resources, most methods contain morphological knowledge in terms of linking elements. The most influential statistical splitter is developed by Koehn and Knight (2003) who addressed German compound splitting by scoring splits according to the geometric mean of the potential constituents' frequencies. For normalization, they selected the two fillers $\oplus$s and $\oplus$es. Stymne (2008) performed several experiments to measure the impact of varying parameters of Koehn and Knight's (2003) algorithm for factored statistical MT. Instead of using two single fillers, she implemented the collection of the 20 most frequent morphological transformations for German compounding as presented by Langer (1998). She observed that splitting parameters should not necessarily be the same for translating in different directions. Bretschneider and Zillner (2015) compared the splitting performance between Koehn and Knight's (2003) two fillers and Langer's (1998) collection, illustrating the necessity of an exhaustive set of linking elements. Moreover, they showed that Langer's (1998) data is still not sufficient for domain-specific targets. Macherey et al., (2011) were the first to overcome the need for manual morphological input and the limitation to a fixed set of linking elements by learning morphological operations automatically from parallel corpora including a support language which creates open compounds and has only little inflection, such as English. We take this one step further by avoiding the dependence on such parallel corpora, known to be sparse, and by approximating compounding morphology with word inflection learned from monolingual preprocessed data.

Linguistically based splitters are usually relying on a lexical database or a set of linguistic rules. While these splitters outperform statistical approaches (Escartín, 2014), they are designed for a specific language and thus less applicable to other languages. Nießen and Ney (2000) used the morpho-syntactic analyzer GERTWOL (Mariikka Haapalainen and Ari Majorin, 1995) for splitting compounds. Schmid (2004) developed the morphological analyzer SMOR, that enumerates linguistically motivated compound splits. Fritzinger and Fraser (2010) combined SMOR with Koehn and Knight's (2003) statistical approach and outperformed both individual methods. Weller and Heid (2012) extended the splitter of Koehn and Knight (2003) with a list of PoS-tagged lemmas and a handcrafted set of morphological transition rules. While our approach similarly exploits lemma and PoS information, we avoid the manual input of transition rules.

3 Theoretical preliminaries

The splitting architecture, data structure, features and evaluation we propose in this paper are based on a number of assumptions and considerations that we would like to discuss first.

3.1 Morphological transformation

Closed (or concatenative) compounding is the main spelling form in many languages around the world, e.g., Germanic languages such as *German*, *Dutch*, *Swedish*, *Afrikaans* or *Danish*, Uralic languages such as *Estonian* or *Finnish*, Hellenic languages such as *Modern Greek*, Slavic languages such as *Russian* and many more. Most closed-compounding languages use morphological transformations. German or Dutch often insert a linking element between the constituents while Greek reduces the first constituent to its morphological stem and adds a compound marker. In contrast to conjugations of irregular verbs (such as *to be*), there is only a minor string difference (e.g., in terms of edit distance (ED)) between constituent form and corresponding lemma (usually they differ in at most two characters). This minimal difference makes it possible to interpret constituent normalization as a kind of tolerant string retrieval (which is presented for the case of spelling correction within IR by Manning et al., (2008)). This is why we are using an N gram index for retrieving the candidate lemmas with the highest string similarity to the constituent form.

3.2 Inflectional morphology

Relying exclusively on the highest string similarity for the normalization, would lead to candidate lemmas that result from linguistically unmotivated operations, e.g., the German *Hühner* 'chickens' would be normalized to the most string-similar lemma *Hüne* 'giant' (ED=2) and not to the correct but less string-similar lemma *Huhn* 'chicken' (ED=3). Thus, a linguistic restrictor is indispensable for finding the underlying lemma for a given constituent.

In many languages, inflectional morphology shares operations with compounding morphology, e.g., the German *Hühner* in *Hühner|suppe* 'chicken soup' is equivalent to the plural form of *Huhn*. But even for non-paradigmatic constituent forms (e.g., *Armuts* 'poverty'), we can find cases of inflection that use the transformation at hand (e.g., the genitive form of window: *Fensters*).

We thus decided to approximate compounding morphology by using inflectional morphology as derived from lemmatized corpus tokens. We realize that the inflectional approximation does not work for all closed-compounding languages but it does for a large subset that is known to have a large variety of linking elements and is therefore most in need of unsupervised morphology induction, the Germanic languages. Moreover, our flexible system can be easily supported with morphological information, which is suitable for languages like Greek, that use a special compound marker.

3.3 Compound headedness

Most closed-compounding languages usually follow the **right**hand **head** **r**ule (RHHR), i.e., the head of a compound is the right-most constituent and encodes the principal semantics and the PoS of the compound. As done by previous splitting approaches (Stymne, 2008; Weller and Heid, 2012), we assume the RHHR and allow only splits for which the right-hand side constituents has the same PoS as the compound.

3.4 Splitting depth

The granularity of the morphological analysis needed differs with the type of application. For MT, a compound should not be split deeper than into parts for which a translation is known, whereas for linguistic research, a deeper morphological analysis is desirable.

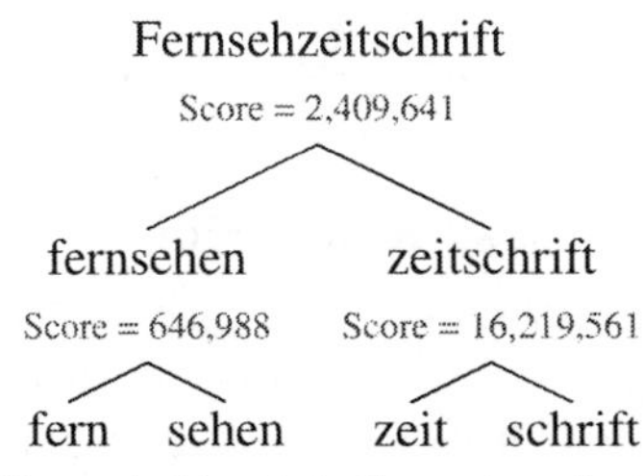

Figure 1: Linguistically motivated split

For example, while an MT system needs a binary split for the German *Fernsehzeitschrift* 'television journal', for a linguistic analysis, a split into four parts as given in Figure 1 is also valid and introduces etymological clues (e.g., how far is *Zeit* 'time' related to *Zeitschrift* 'journal'). Our flexible approach caters for all tasks[1].

3.5 Constituent length balance

While compounds can be build up from almost any semantic concept pair, we observed a bias towards constituent pairs having a similar word length.

For the German, Dutch and Afrikaans compound splitting gold standards (described in Section 6.2) comprising m split compounds, we randomly recombine all modifiers with all heads to a set of m recombinations. For both original compounds and recombined compounds, we measure the character difference in length between modifier and head form.

Compound set	German	Dutch	Afrikaans
Original	2.62	2.26	2.87
Recombination	3.43	2.74	2.92

Table 1: Average constituent length difference in characters

As shown in Table 1, all original compounds have a smaller difference than the recombinations. There-

fore, we decided to promote compound splits with more balanced constituent lengths.

4 Data preparation

4.1 Ngram index

As described in Section 3.1, we tolerantly retrieve candidate lemmas using an N gram index, in order to limit the search space and allow for a quick candidate lookup during splitting.

N gram	Lemma length (LL)	Lemmas
`^hund`	4	hund#13162
`^hund`	11	hundeführer#251, hundehalter#81, hundesteuer#64
`^h*hn`	4	hahn#2078, huhn#1839, hohn#506

Table 2: Examples from the German N gram index

As search key, we use N grams of variable length ($N \leq 15$). Word-initial N grams are indicated by ^ and word-final N grams end on \$. By using N grams, we are able to capture any kind of transformation a lemma can undergo when involved in compounding.

Sometimes, a transformation includes a character replacement within the word (e.g., Umlautung). This leads to a very small set of N grams a constituent has in common with its underlying lemma. For example *Hühner* and *Huhn* only have the bigrams ^h and hn in common, which is also true for many irrelevant words such as *Haarschnitt* 'haircut'. In order to reduce noise and increase efficiency, we include the wildcard * for a single character in N grams[2]. This way, *Hühner* and *Huhn* have the common 5gram `^H*hn`. As a further cue, we consider the lemma length (assuming that there is only a minor difference to the constituent's length).

For a given lemmatized and PoS-tagged corpus, we index all content words (i.e., nouns, adjectives and verbs) by generating all N grams and mapping them to a list of frequency-ranked lemma-freq pairs. Table 2 shows some examples for German[3].

---

[1]As the splitting depth is very dependent on the task at hand and the gold standard we used is not created with a specific task in mind, we do not evaluate our system with respect to splitting depth but treat it as given. Our system cuts off subtrees with the lowest splitting score until the desired splitting depth is achieved.

[2]For efficiency reasons, we add wildcard N grams only for $3 \leq N \leq 7$.

[3]Note that the lemmas include compounds, because these are necessary for our binary recursive splitter, described in Section 5.

Language	MOP	Corpus frequency	Examples
German	u/ü:$/er$	117K	<Huhn, Hühner> 'chicken', <Buch, Bücher> 'book'
German	um$/en$	264K	<Studium, Studien> 'study', <Medium, Medien> 'medium'
Dutch	$/en$	1.6M	<arts, artsen> 'doctor', <band, banden> 'tyre'
Afrikaans	$/se$	34K	<proses, prosesse> 'process'

Table 3: Examples of MOPs for German, Dutch and Afrikaans

4.2 Morphological operation patterns

Macherey et al., (2011) describe a representation of compounding morphology using a single character replacement at either the beginning, the middle or the end of a word. For our experiments, we adopt this format. Since it is possible that a morphological operation takes place at several positions of a word, we combine all atomic replacements into a pattern describing a series of operations. This transformation from a word Σ to a word Ω is referred to as **morphological operation pattern** (MOP). For compiling an MOP, we use the Levenshtein edit distance algorithm including the four operations IN-SERT (adding a character), DELETE (removing a character), REPLACE (exchanging a character σ_i by ω_i) and COPY (retaining a character). In a backtrace step, we determine the first set of operations that lead to a minimum edit distance. Except for COPY, we interpret all operations as replacements (insertion and deletion are replacements of or by an empty element ϵ respectively). We merge all adjacent replacements by concatenating the source and target characters. Word-initial source and target sequences start with ^ and word-final sequences end on $. Sequences of adjacent COPY operations are represented by ':' and separate the merged replacements. For example, in *Hühner|suppe*, the modifier lemma *Huhn* is transformed to *Hühner* by replacing u by ü (i.e., Umlautung) and adding the suffix er. The corresponding MOP is 'u/ü:$/er$'. The second column in Table 3 shows some additional German, Dutch and Afrikaans examples of MOPs.

As discussed in Section 3.2, we try to approximate compounding MOPs using inflectional MOPs. In a lemmatized corpus, for each lemmatized word token, we determine the MOP that represents the transformation from lemma to word form. We collect all inflectional MOPs with their token-based corpus frequency. The third column in Table 3 shows the corpus frequencies for the corresponding MOPs.

5 Compound splitting method

Our compound splitter can process compounds composed of any content word type (i.e., nouns, verbs and adjectives) and of any number of constituents, and provides both the split points (e.g., *Hühner|suppe*) and the normalized constituents (e.g., *Huhn + Suppe*). The splitter is designed recursively, which allows us to represent the compound split both hierarchical (i.e., as a tree structure) and as a linear sequence. Figure 2 shows the architecture of our splitting algorithm. The recursive main method starts with the target word as a single constituent and recursively splits the constituents produced by the binary splitter (Section 5.1) until an atomic result is returned. The binary splitter has two subtasks: (1) for each potential constituent form, a set of candidate lemmas is retrieved (Section 5.2) and (2) all candidate lemma combinations are ranked and the best split is returned (Section 5.3).

5.1 Binary splitter

We first generate all possible binary splits with a minimum constituent length of 2 (e.g., for *Ölpreis* 'oil price', we generate *Öl|preis*, …, *Ölpre|is*) and add a non-split option. For each potential constituent among the generated splits, we retrieve the M most probable lemmas as described in Section 5.2. We consider all M^2 lemma combinations of all possible splits and rank them as described in Section 5.3. The highest-ranked split is returned.

5.2 Candidate lemma retrieval

In this step, we retrieve the M most probable candidate lemmas for a given constituent. For this task, we make use of the Ngram index, described in Section 4.1. Instead of applying MOPs directly which would be the classical and more efficient way, we decided to look up candidates using the Ngram in-

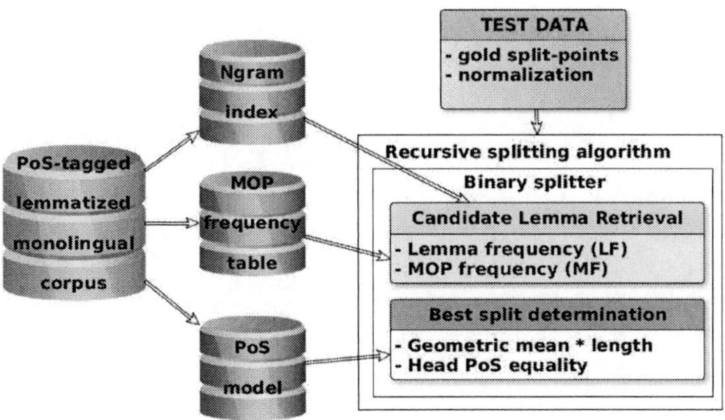

Figure 2: Architecture of our splitting algorithm

dex first, thereby following the assumption that there is only a minor string difference between lemma and constituent form (cf. Section 3.1). In a second step, the inflectional MOPs are used to rank the candidate lemmas. While following this order, we put less weight on our approximation and thereby avoid false lemmas due to irrelevant inflectional MOPs. The pseudocode for the candidate lemma retrieval is given in Algorithm 1.

Algorithm 1 Candidate lemma retrieval

1: Constituent c
2: LLs $\leftarrow$ lemma lengths, $\pm\Delta$ around $len(c)$
3: CLs $\leftarrow$ [ ]   ▷ the candidate lemmas
4: **for** $L \leftarrow len(c)$ to 1 **do**
5:     LGs $\leftarrow$ generate all Lgrams of c
6:     **for** Lg in LGs **do**
7:         CLs $\leftarrow$ CLs + topλ(IDX[Lg][LLs])
8:     **if** len(CLs) > 1 **then**
9:         break   ▷ otherwise, L is decremented
10: **score**(CLs)   ▷ according to a lemma model
11: **rank**(CLs)   ▷ according to the scores
12: **return** top$M$(CLs)

For a given constituent c, we search for lemmas with a minimum lemma length (LL) of 2 which ranges between $\pm\Delta$ around the length of c (lines 1-2). All retrieved candidate lemmas are stored in the list CLs (line 3). Starting with the L = $len(c)$, we inspect all Lgrams of c (lines 4-5). For a given Lgram, we retrieve the top λ most frequent lemmas that have a length $\pm\Delta$ around the length of c (lines

6-7). If there are no lemmas retrieved, we decrement L (lines 8-9)[4]. All retrieved candidate lemmas are scored (line 10) according to our lemma model, for which we present two lemma features.

$$LP(l_i) = cf(l_i) \cdot count(l_i, \text{CLs}) \quad (1)$$

The first feature is based on the lemma prominence (LP) as given in (1), i.e., we multiply the corpus frequency (cf) of a lemma l_i (as given in the Ngram index) with the token number of l_i in CLs (i.e., with the prominence of l_i among all inspected Lgrams).

The second feature estimates the suitability of the MOP (MS) transforming the candidate lemma l_i to the constituent form at hand, c, (represented as '$MOP[l_i, c]$'), as given in (2). As the first component, we use the corpus frequency extracted with the inflectional MOPs as described in Section 4.2. We rescale the MOP frequency with the resulting edit distance between the candidate lemma l_i and the constituent form at hand, c, (represented as $ED(l_i, c)$)[5]. As motivated in Section 3.1, we expect MOPs having a small edit distance to be more prominent in compounding. Such MOPs are not necessarily most frequent in inflection, e.g., the frequent irregular Afrikaans verb *wees* (*to be*) leads to MOPs like MOP[*wees,is*] = ^wee/^i, which has an ED of 3.

$$MS(l_i) = \frac{cf(MOP[l_i, c])}{ED(l_i, c) + 1} \quad (2)$$

---

[4]For noise reduction due to lemmatizer errors, we can predefine a minimum number of L decrements.

[5]For avoiding a division by zero, we add 1.

All candidate lemmas are finally scored as product of lemma prominence and MOP suitability, as given in (3).

$$score(l_i) = LP(l_i) \cdot MS(l_i) \qquad (3)$$

We rank all candidate lemmas and return the top M candidates (lines 11-12).

5.3 Best split determination

In the final step, we determine the best split among all split combinations (i.e., pairs of retrieved candidate lemmas for modifier (l_m) and head (l_h), and corresponding split point) and the non-split option. For this task, we use a combination model, which considers the interaction between l_m and l_h. Inspired by Koehn and Knight (2003), as a first feature, we take the geometric mean of the products of lemma score multiplied by the length of the corresponding constituent form, as given in (4). The length factor promotes splits with more balanced lengths (as motivated in Section 3.5), which mitigates the impact of short and high-frequent words on the overall score. For binary splits, we use the constituent set $con = \{l_m, l_h\}$ and for the non-split option, we use $con = \{l_h\}$.

$$geoLen(con) = \sqrt[|con|]{\prod_{l_i \in con} score(l_i) \cdot len(c_{l_i})} \qquad (4)$$

The second feature is based on the assumption that the PoS of a compound word Ψ usually equals the PoS of its head l_h, as discussed in Section 3.3. Since our splitter works out of context, we try to subsume all possible PoS tags by representing them as a distribution over the PoS probabilities $p(\text{PoS}|word) = \frac{freq(PoS \cap word)}{freq(word)}$ acquired from the monolingual PoS-tagged corpus. The value of the head-PoS-equality (hEQ) feature is defined as the the cosine similarity between the PoS probability distributions of compound word Ψ and head l_h, $hEQ(\Psi, l_h)$. If the PoS tag of the compound is unknown, we take 1.0 as default value.

$$split(con) = geoLen(con) \cdot hEQ(\Psi, l_h) \qquad (5)$$

Finally, all candidate lemma combinations (including the non-split option) are ranked according to the splitting score given in (5). The highest-scored split is returned as output of the binary splitter, being

subject to the recursive process. Figure 3 shows an example of the recursive splitter output for the German compound *Studienbescheinigungsablaufdatum* 'enrollment certification expiration date' with the related MOPs.

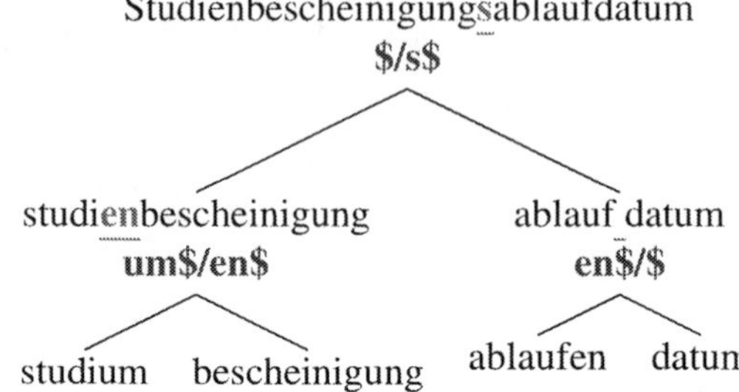

Figure 3: Example of a split tree structure with related MOPs

6 Experiments

In our experiments, we focus on German, Dutch and Afrikaans, but expect to see similar performance for other Germanic languages.

6.1 Data

We use the German and Dutch version of Wikipedia[6] and the Afrikaans Taalkommissie corpus[7]. For tokenizing, PoS-tagging and lemmatizing Wikipedia, we use Treetagger (Schmid, 1995).

Corpus	# tokens	# types		
language	words	words	lemmas	MOPs
German	665M	9.0M	8.8M	1201
Dutch	114M	2.0M	1.9M	920
Afrikaans	57M	748K	696K	459

Table 4: Corpus statistics

We tokenize the Taalkommissie corpus using the approach of Augustinus and Dirix (2013). We PoS-tag the corpus using the tool described in Eiselen and Puttkammer (2014) and use the lemmatizer of Peter Dirix, the second author of the previous paper.

Table 4 shows some statistics of the three preprocessed corpora. Since the Afrikaans corpus is one order of magnitude smaller than the German corpus, we expect a lower performance for the Afrikaans splitter.

---

[6] {de,nl}.wikipedia.org
[7] Taalkommissie van die Suid-Afrikaanse Akademie vir Wetenskap en Kuns (2011)

System	SPAcc			NormAcc		
	@1	@2	@3	@1	@2	@3
(A) LP.MS$_{\text{infl}}$	**95.2%**^{B,C}	**98.9%**^{B,C}	**99.4%**^{B,C}	86.6%	**94.6%**^{B,C}	**96.5%**^{B,C}
(B) WH2012	93.3%	95.6%	95.7%	81.0%	85.9%	86.4%
(C) FF2010	91.4%	92.3%	93.0%	**88.4%**^{A,B}	89.7%	90.2%
(D) LP.$\varnothing$	54.1%	70.5%	78.4%	28.4%	42.6%	50.8%
(E) LP.MS$_{\text{Langer}}$	94.5%	98.7%	99.1%	87.1%	94.2%	95.4%
(F) LP.MS$_{\text{GS}}$	95.4%	99.0%	99.4%	87.8%	95.6%	97.2%

Table 5: German results for binary compound splitting, scores δ^{Φ} outperform the system Φ significantly

6.2 Gold standard

For evaluating our splitting method on **German**, we use the binary split compound set developed for GermaNet[8] by Henrich and Hinrichs (2011). After removing hyphenated compounds[9], it comprises **51,230** binary split samples. For **Dutch** and **Afrikaans**, we use the split point gold standards developed by Verhoeven et al., (2014), which comprise **21,941** samples for Dutch and **17,369** for Afrikaans.

6.3 Evaluation measures

We evaluate the splitting quality with respect to two disciplines: (1) determination of the correct split points and (2) normalization of the resulting modifier constituents[10]. For both disciplines, we use the accuracy measure as described in Koehn and Knight (2003). The split point accuracy (**SPAcc**) refers to the correctness of the split points (on word level) and the normalization accuracy (**NormAcc**) measures the amount of both correct split points and modifier lemmas. All systems presented in this paper provide a ranked list of splits. This allows for a more fine-grained ranking evaluation of the binary splitting decisions with respect to the first n positions. Accuracy@n refers to the amount of correct splits among the top n splits. We stop at $n = 3$, because we do not expect to see a crucial difference in the performance gap for higher values of n.

6.4 Parameter setting and models in comparison

There are three parameters presented in the candidate lemma retrieval. For efficiency reasons, we set the number of lemmas retrieved per Lgram and lemma length (λ) to 20 and the final number of retrieved candidate lemmas (M) to 3. For the maximum difference in length between lemma and constituent form, we observed that $\Delta = 2$ covers all compounding operations for Germanic languages.

For German, we compare our system based on inflectional MOPs (LP.MS$_{\text{infl}}$) against the LP baseline (LP.$\varnothing$), which lacks a linguistic restrictor after candidate lemma lookup from the Ngram index, against an upper bound (LP.MS$_{\text{GS}}$), which uses the MOPs and frequencies derived from the normalizations in the gold standard and against a version that uses a hand-crafted set of MOPs and frequencies derived from Langer's (1998) set of fillers (LP.MS$_{\text{Langer}}$). In addition, we compare our system against previous work: the splitting methods of Fritzinger and Fraser (2010) and of Weller and Heid (2012)[11]. For Dutch and Afrikaans, we compare with the SPAcc numbers of Verhoeven et al., (2014).

6.5 Results and discussion

Table 5 shows the **German** results for the binary compound splitting. We present the split point accuracy (SPAcc) and the normalization accuracy (NormAcc) for the splits ranked @1-3. We first compare LP.MS$_{\text{infl}}$ against the previous work of FF2010 and WH2012. Our system significantly[12] outperforms both systems with respect to SPAcc and reaches

---

[8]sfs.uni-tuebingen.de/GermaNet

[9]We consider hyphenated compounds as trivial cases of splitting that can be disregarded for our purpose.

[10]Since for Germanic languages compounding morphology is exclusively found on the modifier, we disregard the head.

[11]We use an updated version of Weller and Heid (2012) developed and provided to us by Marion Di Marco.

[12]Approximate randomization test (Yeh, 2000), $p < 0.05$

99.4% for SPAcc@3. While for NormAcc@1 our splitter's performance is less than 2 percentage point lower than the system of FF2010, which heavily relies on language-dependent and knowledge-rich resources, we significantly outperform both systems in comparison for NormAcc@2 and NormAcc@3. This proves that one can attain state-of-the-art performance on compound splitting by using language-independent and unsupervised methods, and in particular by means of inflectional information.

In an error analysis, it turned out that FF2010 (i.e., SMOR) cannot process 2% of the gold samples. However on a common processable test set, we still find our system to outperform FF2010 significantly, which indicates that the difference in performance is not just a matter of coverage. WH2012 leaves several compounds unsplit, for which our splitter provides the correct analysis. This is partly due to the hand-crafted transition rules of WH2012, which cannot capture all morphological operations, such as in *Hilfs|bereitschaft* 'cooperativeness', for which the MOP e\$/s\$ (i.e., the combination of *e*-truncation and *s*-suffixation) is not even covered by Langer's (1998) published collection.

To evaluate whether our assumption about the usability of inflectional MOPs holds, we run some controlled experiments with two variants of our system, shown in the last two lines of Table 5. The exhaustive set of inflectional MOPs (LP.MS$_{\text{infl}}$) shows competitive performance in SPAcc with the hand-crafted set of Langer (1998) (LP.MS$_{\text{Langer}}$) and with the upper bound (LP.MS$_{\text{GS}}$). The latter outperforms LP.MS$_{\text{infl}}$ by only 1 percentage point in NormAcc.

Our separate evaluation of SPAcc and NormAcc reveals a lower performance for the normalization across all systems, as this is a much harder discipline. In addition, we can conclude that normalization requires more linguistic knowledge: while the LP-baseline (LP.$\varnothing$) underperforms heavily, both FF2010 and LP.MS$_{Langer}$, systems with a lot of lexical and morphological information, outperform all systems in comparison at NormAcc@1.

For illustrating the multilingual applicability of our splitter, we perform an experiment on Dutch and Afrikaans. Table 6 shows the SPAcc[13] results for

N-ary splits. While Verhoeven et al., (2014) use a supervised approach for predicting the correct split points, our unsupervised splitter outperforms their **Dutch** results significantly[14]. Although Dutch and Afrikaans are similar languages, the SPAcc achieved by our system for **Afrikaans** is 3.6% worse than the method presented by Verhoeven et al., (2014). This result is partly due to the crucial corpus size differences presented in Table 4.

System	Dutch	Afrikaans
LP.MS$_{\text{infl}}$	**93.4%**	84.7%
Verh.et.al.2014	91.5%	**88.3%**

Table 6: SPAcc results for N-ary splits in Dutch and Afrikaans

7 Conclusion

We presented a language-independent, unsupervised compound splitter based on inflectional morphology that significantly outperforms state-of-the-art methods in finding the correct split points, relying only on monolingual PoS-tagged and lemmatized corpora. We provided a comprehensive, intrinsic evaluation of several systems in comparison for several languages on two separate disciplines: split point determination and constituent normalization. As a result, we draw the conclusions that inflectional morphology is a practical approximation for compounding in Germanic languages and overcomes the necessity of manual input, because both hand-crafted sets of compounding operations and operations derived from the gold standard lead to small differences in performance only. In future work, we plan to adapt our methods for learning compounding morphology for languages such as Greek, that have a special compound marker.

Acknowledgments

We thank the anonymous reviewers for their helpful feedback. We also thank our colleague Stefan Müller for the discussions and feedback, and Marion Di Marco and Fabienne Cap for providing their splitting methods. This research was funded by the German Research Foundation (Collaborative Research Centre 732, Project D11).

---

[13]The Dutch and Afrikaans gold standard only provides split points and no reliable normalized constituents.

[14]z-test for proportions; $p < 0.05$

References

Liesbeth Augustinus and Peter Dirix. 2013. The IPP effect in Afrikaans: A Corpus Analysis. In *Proceedings of the 19th Nordic Conference of Computational Linguistics (NODALIDA 2013)*, pages 213–225.

Marco Baroni, Johannes Matiasek, and Harald Trost. 2002. Predicting the Components of German Nominal Compounds. In *ECAI*, pages 470–474. IOS Press.

Claudia Bretschneider and Sonja Zillner. 2015. Semantic Splitting of German Medical Compounds. In *Text, Speech, and Dialogue*. Springer International Publishing.

Roald Eiselen and Martin J. Puttkammer. 2014. Developing Text Resources for Ten South African Languages. In *Proceedings of the 9th International Conference on Language Resources and Evaluation (LREC 2014)*, pages 3698–3703.

Carla Parra Escartín. 2014. Chasing the Perfect Splitter: A Comparison of Different Compound Splitting Tools. In *LREC 2014*.

Fabienne Fritzinger and Alexander Fraser. 2010. How to Avoid Burning Ducks: Combining Linguistic Analysis and Corpus Statistics for German Compound Processing. In *Proceedings of the ACL 2010 Joint 5th Workshop on Statistical Machine Translation and Metrics MATR*, pages 224–234.

Verena Henrich and Erhard W. Hinrichs. 2011. Determining Immediate Constituents of Compounds in GermaNet. In *RANLP 2011*, pages 420–426.

Philipp Koehn and Kevin Knight. 2003. Empirical methods for compound splitting. In *EACL*.

Stefan Langer. 1998. Zur Morphologie und Semantik von Nominalkomposita. In *KONVENS*.

Klaus Macherey, Andrew M. Dai, David Talbot, Ashok C. Popat, and Franz Och. 2011. Language-independent Compound Splitting with Morphological Operations. In *ACL HLT 2011*.

Christopher D. Manning, Prabhakar Raghavan, and Hinrich Schütze. 2008. *Introduction to Information Retrieval*. Cambridge University Press, New York, NY, USA.

Mariikka Haapalainen and Ari Majorin. 1995. GERTWOL und Morphologische Disambiguierung für das Deutsche. Technical report.

Sonja Nießen and Hermann Ney. 2000. Improving SMT quality with morpho-syntactic analysis. In *COLING 2000*, pages 1081–1085.

Helmut Schmid, Arne Fitschen, and Ulrich Heid. 2004. SMOR: A German Computational Morphology Covering Derivation, Composition, and Inflection. In *LREC 2004*, pages 1263–1266.

Helmut Schmid. 1995. Improvements in Part-of-Speech Tagging with an Application to German. In *ACL SIGDAT-Workshop*.

Sara Stymne. 2008. German Compounds in Factored Statistical Machine Translation. In *GoTAL*.

Taalkommissie van die Suid-Afrikaanse Akademie vir Wetenskap en Kuns. 2011. Taalkommissiekorpus 1.1. Technical report, CTexT, North West University, Potchefstroom.

Ben Verhoeven, Menno van Zaanen, Walter Daelemans, and Gerhard B van Huyssteen. 2014. Automatic Compound Processing: Compound Splitting and Semantic Analysis for Afrikaans and Dutch. In *ComAComA 2014*, pages 20–30.

Marion Weller and Ulrich Heid. 2012. Analyzing and Aligning German compound nouns. In *LREC 2012*.

Alexander Yeh. 2000. More Accurate Tests for the Statistical Significance of Result Differences. In *COLING 2000*.

Phonological Pun-derstanding

Aaron Jaech and **Rik Koncel-Kedziorski** and **Mari Ostendorf**
University of Washington
Seattle, WA
{ajaech,kedzior,ostendor}@uw.edu

Abstract

Many puns create humor through the relationship between a pun and its phonologically similar target. For example, in "Don't take geologists for granite" the word "granite" is a pun with the target "granted". The recovery of the target in the mind of the listener is essential to the success of the pun. This work introduces a new model for automatic target recovery and provides the first empirical test for this task. The model draws upon techniques for automatic speech recognition using weighted finite-state transducers, and leverages automatically learned phone edit probabilities that give insight into how people perceive sounds and into what makes a good pun. The model is evaluated on a small corpus where it is able to automatically recover a large fraction of the pun targets.

1 Introduction

From the high culture of Shakespeare's plays (Tanaka, 1992), to the depths of the YouTube comments section, from advertising slogans (Keller, 2009) to conversations with nerdy parents, puns are a versatile rhetorical device and their understanding is essential to any comprehensive approach to computational humor. Humor has been described as "one of the most interesting and puzzling research areas in the field of natural language understanding" (Yang et al., 2015). Puns, in particular, offer an interesting subject for study since their humor derives from wordplay and double-meaning.

An important class of puns, known as paronomasic puns, are those where one entity, the pun, is phonologically similar to another, the target (Joseph, 2008). Consider an example from Crosbie (1977):

> "Sign by gate to nudist colony: Come in. We are Never Clothed."

Here, "clothed" is the pun and "closed" is the target. Paronomasic puns are distinguished from homographic puns such as

> "Two silkworms had a race. They ended up in a tie."

which puns on the two definitions of the word "tie". When the pun and target are homophonic this is called a *perfect* pun, and when nearly homophonic an *imperfect* pun (Zwicky and Zwicky, 1986) (or a *heterophonic* pun (Hempelmann, 2003)). The focus of this work is to propose and evaluate a model for target recovery of both perfect and imperfect paronomasic puns, assuming that the location of the pun word or word sequence.

Ritchie (2005) classifies puns in terms of whether they are *self-contained*, i.e., based on general knowledge and humorous in a variety of circumstances, or *contextually integrated*, i.e. relying on a specific context such as a visual context, knowledge of a recent event or discussion. Many puns of this type are associated with cartoons or images, e.g. a cartoon with pies and cakes in the street having the caption

> "The streets were oddly desserted"

(desserted/deserted). Contextually integrated puns lose their humor out of context because the pun is difficult to detect. However, target recovery is often still possible, and thus this distinction does not play a major role in the current study.

If a listener fails to recover the target of the pun then the statement fails in its humor. The two chief

Proceedings of NAACL-HLT 2016, pages 654–663,
San Diego, California, June 12-17, 2016. ©2016 Association for Computational Linguistics

clues that the listener must rely on to perform target recovery are the phonetic information and language context. This is analogous to the way in which someone listening to speech uses the acoustic information and language context to recover a sequence of words from an audio source. In the words of Hempelmann (2003), "the recovery of the target in heterophonic puns is just a specific case of the complex task of hearing." The similarity between hearing and target recovery suggests the use of methods from automatic speech recognition in building a model for automatic target recovery.

The goal of this paper is to develop and test a computational model for target recovery in puns. Sentences with the position of the pun marked are given as input and the model must output the target word sequence. As the focus is on paronomasic puns, the relationship between the pun and the target is primarily phonological, but surrounding language context is also important for recovering the target. This work has applications in natural language understanding of texts that contain humor. Furthermore, the insights gained from our model are useful for improving pun generation in computational humor systems.

2 Prior Work

Zwicky and Zwicky (1986) provided an analysis of the properties of paronomasic puns, especially with regard to the markedness of phonological segments. They assembled a corpus of 2140 instances of segmental relationships from imperfect pun/target pairs for their analysis. By counting how many times each phoneme was used in a pun or target, the authors observe a behavior they refer to as ousting, a strong asymmetry in phoneme substitution likelihood. For instance, punners will rarely replace a 'T' phoneme (IPA t) in the target word with 'TH' (θ) in the pun, but regularly replace 'TH' with 'T.' An example of such a pun is

"I lost my temper in a fit of whiskey"
(fit/fifth)). Because of this asymmetry, we say that 'T' ousts 'TH.' Zwicky and Zwicky correlate the ousting behavior evident in their pun data with the phonological notion of *markedness*. Markedness can be defined (if oversimplified) as "the tendency for phonetic terms to be pronounced in a simple,

natural way" with regard to physiological, acoustic, and perceptual factors (*marked* segments are more complex) (Anderson and Lightfoot, 2002). They conclude that marked segments tend to oust unmarked segments (e.g. voiced stops oust their voiceless counterparts).

This is followed-up by Sobkowiak (1991), whose manual alignment of the phoneme sequences of 3,850 pun/target pairs allows for a more careful study of the ousting behavior. This corpus, where whole sequences of phonemes are aligned between puns and targets, is a much richer resource for analyzing ousting than the segment-only data used in (Zwicky and Zwicky, 1986). Sobkowiak's improved data provides evidence against the conclusions of Zwicky and Zwicky (1986). Rather, "it seems that it is not the case that 'marked ousts unmarked' in paronomasic puns." Sobkowiak goes on to show that puns more frequently involve changes to vowels than consonants, noting that their information load (i.e. contribution to target recoverability) is lighter. Our data corroborates Sobkowiak's claims regarding the role of markedness in punning as well as the mutability of vowels, and provides more details about the specific nature of substitutions in a large corpus of puns.

Building off of Sobkowiak's work, Hempelmann (2003) studies target recoverability, arguing that a good model for target recovery provides necessary groundwork for effective automatic pun generation. He proposes a preliminary phonetic edit cost table to be one part of a scoring system. The model is based on the phoneme edit counts from Sobkowiak (1991) with an ad-hoc formula for transforming the counts into substitution costs. However, Hempelmann makes no effort to empirically test his model at the recovery task. The model uses a subset of 1,182 puns from the 3,850 identified by Sobkowiak. This subset is the data used for training our phonetic edit models and we use Hempelmann's cost function as a baseline.

The task of automatic target recovery of paronomasic puns has not been previously attempted. Recently, Miller and Gurevych (2015) studied methods for automatic understanding of homographic puns using methods from word-sense disambiguation. Paronomasia is intentionally excluded from their data.

3 Target Recovery

Following the convention of Miller and Gurevych (2015), we assume that the position of the pun in the input sentence is known. The target recovery task is to identify the pun target given the pun and its left and right word contexts.

3.1 Model

The model has three parts: a phonetic edit model, a phonetic lexicon and a language model. The recovered target T^* is the word (or words) with the maximum probability given the pun P according to

$$T^* = \underset{T}{\operatorname{argmax}}\, p(T|P) = \underset{T}{\operatorname{argmax}}\, p(P|T)p(T),$$

where $p(P|T)$ is the phonetic edit model and $p(T)$ is the language model. The factorization into a language model and a phonetic edit model is similar to the classic approach to automatic speech recognition.

The implementation of the model uses weighted finite-state transducers (WFSTs) which have been adopted as a useful structure for speech decoding due to their ability to efficiently represent each of the relevant knowledge sources, i.e. phonetic information, phonetic lexicon and language model, in a single framework (Mohri et al., 2002; Hori et al., 2007). Finite-state transducers are finite-state machines with an input and an output tape. We will use WFSTs for our pun target recovery model. Each of the phonetic edit model (PEM), phonetic lexicon (L) and language model (LM) can be represented as WFSTs, which are joined together by applying the composition operation. The weights on the PEM and LM are negative log-likelihoods, and the lexicon has no weighting. Each of these models will be explained in further detail below. The target is given by the shortest path in the WFST:

$$(\text{LC} \oplus \text{P} \circ \text{L}^{-1} \circ \text{PEM} \circ \text{L} \oplus \text{RC}) \circ \text{LM},$$

where P is the pun and LC and RC are the left and right word contexts. The symbols $^{-1}$, $\circ$ and $\oplus$ denote the inverse, composition, and concatenation operations respectively.

The sequence of operations $\text{P} \circ \text{L}^{-1} \circ \text{PEM} \circ \text{L}$ converts a pun to its phonetic form, expands it to a lattice based on phonetic confusions, and then converts the phone lattice to a lattice of possible target words. By concatenating the left and right word contexts and composing with the language model, each path through the WFST is a target word sequence with a weight equal to the combined phonetic edit and language model scores. The ability to handle multi-word puns and/or targets (e.g., the word sequence "no bell" can be matched to "Nobel", using an example from (Yang et al., 2015)) is made possible because the lexicon WFST L allows multiword sequences.

Since the scores are negative log likelihoods, the target hypothesis is just the shortest path in the WFST. We score the model based on its accuracy at identifying the target which must be an exact match, ignoring punctuation. We disallow the possibility that the pun is hypothesized as a target, i.e. homographic puns, in order to focus on the class of puns whose relationship with their targets is primarily phonological. The OpenFst library is used to perform all of the WFST operations (Allauzen et al., 2007).

3.2 Phonetic Edit Model

The purpose of the phonetic edit model is to estimate the probability of the pun phoneme sequence given a candidate target phoneme sequence. We prefer to learn a model from the data rather than adopt an existing model that relies on phonetic features and edit costs that were derived by hand (Kondrak, 2000). As shown by Ristad and Yianilos (1998), a memoryless WFST model can learn a probability distribution over edit operations with a principled objective, namely, to maximize the likelihood of the source/target sequences in the training data. In our case, the training data is pun/target phoneme sequences. Memoryless, in this context, refers to the fact that the model is not conditioning on previous symbols, i.e. there is only a single state in the WFST. The model assumes that the phoneme sequence of the pun is generated through the stochastic application of insertions, deletions, and substitutions to the target phoneme sequence. During learning, the model estimates the function $p(y|x)$ where y is a phoneme from the pun and x is a phoneme from the target. When $x = \epsilon$ this is an insertion of y and when $y = \epsilon$ it is a deletion of x.

Training uses the expectation-maximization algorithm following the equations given by Oncina and Sebban (2005) to estimate the conditional probability distribution instead of the joint one as originally derived by Ristad and Yianilos. The model is trained to maximize the probability of the pun targets given their sources subject to the constraint that the model encode a probability distribution over all possible string pairs. In the expectation step, puns are aligned with their targets given the current model. Then, the maximization step re-estimates the edit probabilities given the current alignment. Edit probabilities are initialized by giving a high probability to keeping the same phoneme and uniform small probabilities to all possible edits. (We initialized by giving ten times the probability to preserving the same phoneme as to any possible edit operation.) Following the convention of Sobkowiak (1991), vowels can not align with consonants and vice-versa.

The training data consists of the 1,182 target pun pairs taken from Appendix E of Hempelmann (Hempelmann, 2003). These are a subset of the puns that Sobkowiak took mostly from Crosbie's "Dictionary of Puns" and analyzed in his work.

3.3 Phonetic Lexicon

The lexicon models the pronunciation of each word in the vocabulary. Pronunciations come from the CMU pronunciation dictionary (Weide, 1998). This dictionary has an inventory of 39 phonemes. If a pun is not in the vocabulary of the dictionary, for example if it is not a word, then its pronunciation is generated automatically using the LOGIOS lexicon tool.[1] The same is not true for the targets, since they are unknown beforehand. Thus, when the lexicon is used to map puns to phonemes the vocabulary size is essentially unlimited. But, when it is used to map the phoneme lattice into a word lattice of potential targets then the fixed vocabulary from the language model is used.

The CMU dictionary includes multiple pronunciations for some words. All pronunciations are used with unweighted parallel paths. The version of the dictionary used here includes stress markers and syllable boundaries (Bartlett et al., 2009). In the simplest version of our model, this information is ig-

nored in order to reduce the number of learned parameters in the PEM.

After composing with the phonetic edit model and the lexicon, we do a conservative pruning of the WFST to remove highly improbable word sequences based on the phonetic score and run epsilon removal on the resulting lattice. This reduces the memory footprint and allows use of a larger language model.

3.4 Language Model

A 230 million word corpus was formed from comments obtained from Reddit, an online discussion forum. These comments were collected from a wide variety of forums, known as subreddits. Reddit contributors tend to use a casual conversational style that is a good match for the language used in common puns. All of the text data from Reddit was tokenized using the NLTK tokenizer (Bird et al., 2009). The tokenizer splits contractions into two tokens but we kept these as a single token to match the pronunciation dictionary. We remove case information. Punctuation is removed when evaluating the correctness of the hypothesized targets, but punctuation symbols are included in the language model. It provides a useful context break in punning riddles where the pun/target typically follows a question mark or other punctuation.

The vocabulary is set by intersecting the vocabulary from the CMU pronunciation dictionary with the set of tokens that occur at least 30 times in the language model training data. This gives us a 36,175 word vocabulary. As Sobkowiak (1991) observed, the target tends to have a much higher unigram probability than the pun. This means that the vocabulary size need not be too large to cover most of the targets.

The language model is a trigram model with modified Kneser-Ney smoothing (Chen and Goodman, 1999). Entropy pruning is used to reduce the size of the language model (Stolcke, 2000). It is important to perform the determinization and minimization operations on the LM after converting it into the FST representation, in order to reduce the size of the model (Mohri et al., 2008). Because we are using a trigram model, only two words of context are needed on each side of the pun.

---

[1] http://www.speech.cs.cmu.edu/tools/lextool.html

3.5 Extending the Phoneme Edit Model with Syllable Structure and Stress

For a listener to recognize the phonological distinctness of the pun and the target, they should preferably differ in a perceptually salient position such as a stressed syllable. In particular, we expect that puns would take advantage of the increased acoustic energy in the onset and nucleus of a stressed syllable and utilize these positions for phoneme changes.

To analyze this effect we used a syllabified version of the CMU pronunciation dictionary (Bartlett et al., 2009). We took the 1-best phonetic alignment of the training data and split it according to the syllable boundaries of the pun. Then we computed the probability of a phoneme change according to the position in the syllable and the stress. Consonants in the onset of a stressed syllable have a 40.3% probability of changing between the target and pun. The nucleus of a stressed syllable of has a 36.8% probability of substitution. This is compared to a 31.8% probability of substitution for phonemes in unstressed syllables and coda positions.

To incorporate this into an extension of the phonetic edit model, we created a three state model. There is one default state and two special states for the stressed syllable onset and nucleus respectively. The phoneme edit probabilities $p(y|x)$ were scaled according to the state s and renormalized so that $p(y|x, s)$ is a valid probability distribution. When a substitution does occur, we assume that the choice of target phoneme is independent of the syllable position and stress. The net effect of the syllable extension to the PEM is to encourage substitution of onsets and nuclei of stressed syllables and discourage it otherwise.

4 Experiments

4.1 Data

We collected 75 puns from various joke websites such as Tumblr, Reddit, and Twitter and soliciting examples from friends and colleagues.[2] These were collected without reference to the sources used by Sobkowiak to assemble the puns used in building the phonetic edit model. This data was used for test data only and is completely separate from the training

---

[2]Data available at http://ssli.ee.washington.edu/data/puns.

data used by the language model and the phonetic edit model. (It would be nice to have used some of the 1,182 puns from Sobkowiak for test data but only the isolated pun/target pairs were provided without the necessary word contexts.) Pun locations were marked in each sentence as the minimal set of words that change between the pun and the target.

Note that the phonetic edit model is trained on exclusively imperfect puns but it is tested on both perfect and imperfect puns (24 perfect and 51 imperfect). This creates a mismatch between the training data and the test data. Target recovery is harder on imperfect puns but having a mix of both types better reflects what is commonly found in the wild.

4.2 Baseline Model

As a baseline model we replace our phonetic edit model with the cost function proposed by Hempelmann, which we replicated based on details given in Appendix G of his thesis (Hempelmann, 2003). This cost function, which Hempelmann refers to as "preliminary," is the only published phonetic edit model for paronomasic puns. The cost table is based on the phoneme pair alignment counts from the 1,182 training pairs that were aligned by hand. The phoneme alignment counts are converted to costs by using simple ad-hoc equations. Vowel pair counts are transformed to costs using $cost = 0.3 - 0.3 * count/161$ and other pairs use $cost = count^{-0.6}$. Our model improves upon the baseline by avoiding heuristic transformations. Since the phoneme symbol set used by Hempelmann (based on (Sobkowiak, 1991)) differs from that used in the CMU dictionary, the Hempelmann costs are mapped to match the CMU inventory.

4.3 Results

We report the performance of our model in Table 1 using accuracy and mean reciprocal rank as metrics. If the correct target did not appear in our n-best list then we use a value of zero for its reciprocal rank. Ties are broken randomly. The baseline uses Hempelmann's phonetic cost model plus the LM, and we include two ablation models that use just the LM or just the PEM. The other two models use the LM with either the memoryless PEM or the PEM with the syllable extension.

	Accuracy			
Model	**Perfect**	**Imperfect**	**Overall**	**MRR**
LM Only	13.0%	7.7%	9.3%	0.127
PEM Only	43.5%	9.6%	20.0%	0.282
LM + Hempelmann	47.8%	7.7%	29.3%	0.389
LM + PEM	73.9%	65.4%	68.0%	0.729
LM + Syll. PEM	73.9%	65.4%	68.0%	0.733

Table 1: Accuracy and mean reciprocal rank (MRR) for target recovery

Using the language model only gives poor performance. It is only able to recover the target when the target happens to be an idiomatic expression. The PEM-only model does significantly better than using the LM only, highlighting the importance of phonetics in paronomasic puns. In the full system, Hempelmann's cost matrix does not fare well compared to the PEM model. The Hempelmann cost matrix does a poor job of separating likely targets from the rest of the vocabulary. Thus, many times the true target is pruned before the application of the language model.

The LM + PEM model recovers the target more than two-thirds of the time and has a mean reciprocal rank of 0.729. When using the syllable extension to the PEM, the results agree on the rank of the target for all but five puns. For those five, the model with the syllable extension improves the rank compared to the basic PEM. Two puns from that set of five are

"If you've seen one shopping center you've seen a mall"

"How does Moses make his tea? Hebrews it."

(a mall/'em all and Hebrews/he brews, respectively). The hypothesized targets "immoral" and "he abuse" outrank the true target for these puns in the basic PEM model but not in the syllable one because they change more phonemes in unstressed syllables.

Perfect puns are easier to recover than imperfect ones. The LM + PEM model does well on both perfect and imperfect puns. As to be expected, the PEM only model does very poorly on imperfect puns and the LM only model does equally poorly on both perfect and imperfect.

Table 2 shows the top ranked hypothesis for a sample pun using the LM + PEM model, where the cost in this table is the negative log-likelihood. In this case, the top ranked hypothesis was correct. The second highest ranked hypothesis is a misspelling of

the target that is common enough for the language model to also give it a high score.

An example where the model makes a mistake is:

"A Freudian slip is where you say one thing but mean your mother"

The pattern of "one thing . . . another" is common in English but, in this case, the target "another" is too far away from "one thing" for the relationship to be captured by the tri-gram language model.

5   Analysis

A consequence of using a stochastic model for phonetic edit costs is that there is a non-zero edit cost between a phoneme and itself and that cost is different depending on the phoneme. This highlights the fact that we model the edit (or transformation) probabilities of the pun/target corpus rather than phonological similarity (which would be a symmetric cost function). The analysis below shows that the edit model is in fact capturing more than simple phonological similarity.

5.1   Phoneme Edit Probabilities

Figures 1 and 2 show the probability of observing a source phoneme (i.e. a phoneme appearing in the pun) given each target phoneme for the vowel and consonant pairs respectively. The numbers are to be interpreted as percentages and values less than 1 are not shown. The '.' symbol is used for epsilon transitions and indicates segment insertions and deletions.

Vowels.   Regarding vowels, our data corroborates some of the findings of Sobkowiak (1991). The lower numbers along the diagonal in Figure 1 relative to Figure 2 indicates the violability of vowels (39%) relative to consonants (34%) in paronomasic puns. Our data also confirms that, where puns are concerned, marked segments do not necessarily

Rank	Cost	Hypothesis
1	21.0	... ONLY GOT **MYSELF** TO BLAME
2	23.2	... ONLY GOT **MY SELF** TO BLAME
3	24.2	... ONLY GOT **A MYSELF** TO BLAME
4	24.2	... ONLY GOT **MY YOURSELF** TO BLAME
Source		... ONLY GOT **MY SHELF** TO BLAME

Table 2: Top ranked target LM + PEM hypotheses for the pun "A book fell on my head. I've only got my shelf to blame."

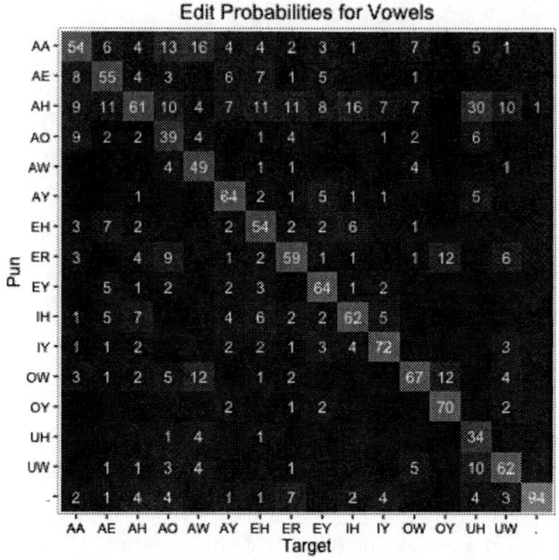

Figure 1: Edit probabilities for vowels based on the LM + PEM model.

oust unmarked. According to Zwicky and Zwicky (1986), if "marked ousts unmarked" we would expect to see that tense vowels oust lax vowels. Rather, what we find in this data is that the majority of vowels and diphthongs are ousted by AH (ə), widely considered an unmarked vowel. Puns demonstrating this phenomenon include

"The pun is mightier than the sword"

"He's an honest geologist, you can trust what he sediment"

(pun/pen and sediment/said he meant, respectively). We hypothesize that the low cost for substituting AH for other vowels is due in part to the fact paronomasic puns originally were a spoken phenomenon, and so the substitution possibilities for a given target vowel depend significantly on the variety of realizations of that vowel in speech. It is well attested cross-linguistically that vowels undergo reduction in unstressed positions (Crosswhite, 2004). In English running speech, this reduced form most

closely resembles AH (Burzio, 2007). The data presented here suggests that punners take advantage of the commonality of running speech vowel reduction when considering target recoverability, resulting in the availability of AH as a replacement for most target vowels. Our model captures this fact by assigning low cost to such a substitution.

Our data provides other insights into the nature of vowel substitutions in puns. For instance, we see that IY (i) is less likely to change in a pun than other monophthongs, indicating a significant perceptual distance between IY and its neighbors. Most likely to change are the vowels AO (ɔ) and UH (ʊ). The violability of AO is likely due to the AO/AA merger present in many American English Dialects (Labov et al., 2006), and in fact we see targets with AO frequently mapping to puns with AA. The mutability of UH is also interesting: while it, like other monophthongs, is ousted by AH, it is also ousted by a closely articulated marked counterpart, UW (u). This seems to be the sole example in our data of marked vowels ousting an unmarked vowel to a significant degree.

Another interesting feature of this data is the substitutability of ER (ɝ) and OY (ɔɪ), as in puns like

"The British used to dress their sandwiches with earl and vinegar"

"In cooking class this week we're loining how to prepare tuna"

(earl/oil and loining/learning, respectively). These edits seem to indicate punners' awareness of rhoticity variation among English dialects (Labov, 1972).

Consonants. In Figure 2, we see several expected trends. D (d) ousting DH (ð), T (t) ousting TH (θ), and V (v) ousting W (w) are all as expected according to the "marked ousting unmarked" hypothesis of Zwicky and Zwicky (1986). Yet we also see S (s) ousting Z (z), which is an instance of the unmarked voiceless alveolar fricative ousting the voiced, as well as N (n) ousting NG (ŋ), an instance of the unmarked coronal ousting the marked velar. These oustings, like the case of AH ousting other vowels, are likely conditioned by segment frequency. For N ousting NG, syllable structure may play a role as well, as NG is restricted to codas whereas N is not.

An interesting feature of our consonant data is the extreme violability of interdentals TH and DH, which are more likely to map to T and D respectively than to retain their identity in a paronomasic pun. In addition to the "fit of whiskey" example mentioned earlier, we have

"Disgusting wind knocked over my trash cans" (disgusting/this gusting). This phenomenon is known as "th-stopping" and is a common dialectal feature of many variants of English, from those of Philadelphia and New York to the Caribbean (Wells, 1982). This substitution supports the hypothesis that the substitution possibilities for a segment depend on the realizations of that segment which are commonly encountered in speech. Notably, T is significantly more likely to replace TH than is F (f), despite that the articulatory and acoustic similarity between TH and F is greater.

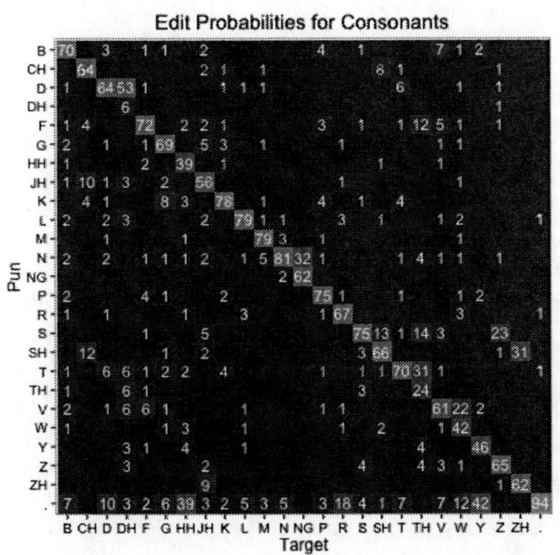

Figure 2: Edit probabilities for consonants based on the LM + PEM model.

5.2 Correlation with Human Ratings

Our phonetic edit model allows us to empirically verify an untested assumption with respect to phonological similarity from Fleischhacker (2002) "that degree of representation in the pun corpus correlates with pun goodness." In another paper, she repeats this assumption and adds the explanation "Truly funny puns are generally those in which the phonological relationship between pun and target is ... subtle but quickly recognizable" (Fleischhacker, 2005). Hempelmann writes that this assumption is "unlikely" to be true.

We conducted a survey of native English speakers where respondents were asked to rate 17 puns on a five point scale: hilarious, funny, okay, bad, terrible. The puns were selected from the test set to have a variety of phonemic edit distances. Respondents also had the option to indicate that they did not understand the pun, in which case their answer was ignored. A phonetic edit score was calculated for each pun-target pair by averaging the log-likelihood value from our model over the phonemes in the pun. The order of the questions was randomized for each respondent. Advertising for the survey was done using /r/SampleSize, a Reddit forum for recruiting survey participants. The 435 respondents gave us 7,135 ratings in total.

The relationship between phonetic edit cost and goodness was measured using ordinal regression, with clustered standard errors to account for the fact that responses from the same person are not independent. We use the RMS package in R (Harrell Jr., 2015). The regression coefficient indicates that decreased phonetic edit cost is indeed associated with higher perceived goodness of the pun with $p < 0.0001$. For visualization purposes we mapped the categorical goodness ratings onto a numeric scale from 1-5 to create an average goodness rating for each pun. In Figure 3, we depict the phonetic edit cost vs. the average goodness rating for each of the 17 puns. The line shown in that figure is an outlier resistant linear regression.

The biggest outlier is

"They say a Freudian slip is when you say one thing but really mean your mother."

The pun is on "your mother" with "another" as the target. This pun has the highest phonetic edit cost in our sample but it makes up for it with more interesting semantics than average.

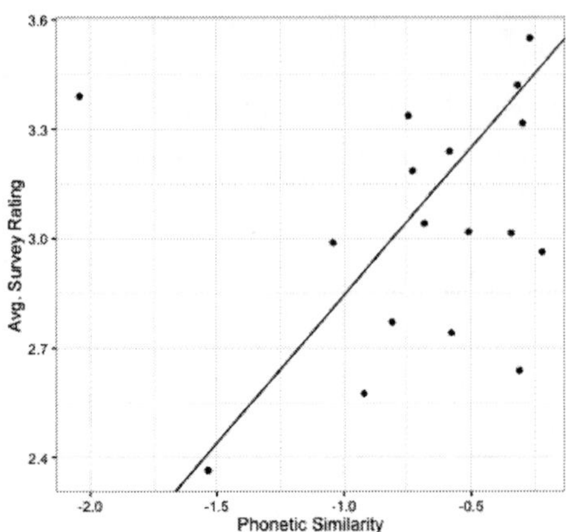

Figure 3: Relationship between the LM + PEM phonetic edit cost and goodness of the pun.

6 Conclusions and Future Work

The quality of our phonetic edit model is evident from its performance at the target recovery task, as well as the fact that it captures known linguistic phenomena such as vowel reduction and dialectal features. Furthermore, by collecting human ratings we are able to empirically verify the previously untested assumption that lower phonetic edit costs in puns correlate with pun goodness.

The strength of the model can be leveraged to improve the quality of pun generation and humor classification systems that have used weaker phonetic edit models (Binsted, 1996; Valitutti, 2011; Raz, 2012). Some pun generation systems are limited to exact homophones. In this work, we did not consider homographic puns. In principle, our algorithm can handle these by introducing an LM weight to control the balance of PEM/LM scores. Pun generation is much more complicated than target recovery as reflected in the complexity of proposed systems for humor generation. However, improved understanding of puns by way of progress in the target recovery task should also lead to corresponding improvements in the task of pun generation.

Our syllable extension to the PEM gave the best performance, but only by a small margin. Extending the edit model further is a fruitful area for future work but will likely require additional data.

In this work, we assume that the pun is given. Of interest for future work is joint recognition of the pun and its target. Preliminary experiments indicate that the unigram word probabilities are a somewhat strong feature for pun recognition but further work is needed. For contextually-integrated puns, identifying the pun is likely to be more difficult, and for some cases it would be useful to integrate image cues.

Acknowledgments

We thank Arjun Sondhi for his assistance in designing and analyzing the survey and Hope Boyarsky for her help assembling our pun corpus. We also would like to thank Nathan Loggins and the anonymous reviewers for their feedback on this work.

References

Cyril Allauzen, Michael Riley, Johan Schalkwyk, Wojciech Skut, and Mehryar Mohri. 2007. OpenFst: A general and efficient weighted finite-state transducer library. In *Implementation and Application of Automata*, pages 11–23. Springer.

Stephen R Anderson and David W Lightfoot. 2002. *The language organ: Linguistics as cognitive physiology*. Cambridge University Press.

Susan Bartlett, Grzegorz Kondrak, and Colin Cherry. 2009. On the syllabification of phonemes. In *Proceedings of Human Language Technologies: The 2009 Annual Conference of the North American Chapter of the Association for Computational Linguistics*, pages 308–316. Association for Computational Linguistics.

Kim Binsted. 1996. Machine humour: An implemented model of puns.

Steven Bird, Ewan Klein, and Edward Loper. 2009. *Natural language processing with Python*. " O'Reilly Media, Inc.".

Luigi Burzio. 2007. Phonology and phonetics of english stress and vowel reduction. *Language Sciences*, 29(2):154–176.

Stanley F Chen and Joshua Goodman. 1999. An empirical study of smoothing techniques for language modeling. *Computer Speech & Language*, 13(4):359–393.

John S Crosbie. 1977. *Crosbie's dictionary of puns*. New York: Harmony Books.

Katherine M. Crosswhite. 2004. Vowel reduction. In Bruce Hayes, Robert Kirchner, and Donca Steriade, editors, *Phonetically based phonology*, pages 191–231. Pearson Education.

Heidi Fleischhacker. 2002. Onset transfer in reduplication. In *LSA annual meeting. San Francisco: January*, pages 3–6.

Heidi Anne Fleischhacker. 2005. *Similarity in phonology: Evidence from reduplication and loan adaptation*. Ph.D. thesis.

Frank E Harrell Jr., 2015. *rms: Regression Modeling Strategies*. R package version 4.3-0.

Christian F Hempelmann. 2003. Paronomasic puns: Target recoverability towards automatic generation.

Takaaki Hori, Chiori Hori, Yasuhiro Minami, and Atsushi Nakamura. 2007. Efficient WFST-based one-pass decoding with on-the-fly hypothesis rescoring in extremely large vocabulary continuous speech recognition. *Audio, Speech, and Language Processing, IEEE Transactions on*, 15(4):1352–1365.

Sister Miriam Joseph. 2008. *Shakespeare's Use of the Arts of Language*. Paul Dry Books.

Stefan Daniel Keller. 2009. *The development of Shakespeare's rhetoric: a study of nine plays*, volume 136.

Grzegorz Kondrak. 2000. A new algorithm for the alignment of phonetic sequences. In *Proceedings of the 1st North American chapter of the Association for Computational Linguistics conference*, pages 288–295. Association for Computational Linguistics.

William Labov, Sharon Ash, and Charles Boberg. 2006. Atlas of north american english: Phonology and phonetics. *Berlin: Mouton de Gruyter*.

William Labov. 1972. *Sociolinguistic patterns*. Number 4. University of Pennsylvania Press.

Tristan Miller and Iryna Gurevych. 2015. Automatic disambiguation of English puns.

M. Mohri, F. Pereira, and M. Riley. 2002. Weighted finite-state transducers in speech recognition. *Computer Speech & Language*, 16(1):69–88.

Mehryar Mohri, Fernando Pereira, and Michael Riley. 2008. Speech recognition with weighted finite-state transducers. In *Springer Handbook of Speech Processing*, pages 559–584. Springer.

Jose Oncina and Marc Sebban. 2005. Learning unbiased stochastic edit distance in the form of a memoryless finite-state transducer. In *International Joint Conference on Machine Learning (2005). Workshop: Grammatical Inference Applications: Successes and Future Challenges*.

Yishay Raz. 2012. Automatic humor classification on Twitter. In *Proceedings of the NAACL Human Language Technologies: Student Research Workshop*, pages 66–70. Association for Computational Linguistics.

Eric Sven Ristad and Peter N Yianilos. 1998. Learning string-edit distance. *Pattern Analysis and Machine Intelligence, IEEE Transactions on*, 20(5):522–532.

Graeme Ritchie. 2005. Computational mechanisms for pun generation. In *Proc. European Natural Language Generation Workshop*.

Włodzimierz Sobkowiak. 1991. *Metaphonology of English paronomasic puns*, volume 26. P. Lang.

Andreas Stolcke. 2000. Entropy-based pruning of backoff language models. *arXiv preprint cs/0006025*.

Keiko Tanaka. 1992. The pun in advertising: A pragmatic approach. *Lingua*, 87(1):91–102.

Alessandro Valitutti. 2011. How many jokes are really funny? towards a new approach to the evaluation. In *Human-Machine Interaction in Translation: Proceedings of the 8th International NLPCS Workshop*, volume 41, page 189.

Robert L Weide. 1998. The cmu pronouncing dictionary. *URL: http://www.speech.cs.cmu.edu/cgibin/cmudict*.

John C Wells. 1982. *Accents of English*, volume 1. Cambridge University Press.

Diyi Yang, Alon Lavie, Chris Dyer, and Eduard Hovy. 2015. Humor recognition and humor anchor extraction. *EMNLP*.

Arnold Zwicky and Elizabeth Zwicky. 1986. Imperfect puns, markedness, and phonological similarity: With fronds like these, who needs anemones. *Folia Linguistica*, 20(3/4):493–503.

A Joint Model of Orthography and Morphological Segmentation

Ryan Cotterell   **Tim Vieira**
Department of Computer Science
Johns Hopkins University, USA
{ryan.cotterell,tim.f.vieira}@gmail.com

Hinrich Schütze
Center for Information and Language Processing
LMU Munich, Germany
inquiries@cis.lmu.org

Abstract

We present a model of morphological segmentation that jointly learns to segment and restore orthographic changes, e.g., *funniest* ↦ *fun-y-est*. We term this form of analysis *canonical segmentation* and contrast it with the traditional *surface segmentation*, which segments a surface form into a sequence of substrings, e.g., *funniest* ↦ *funn-i-est*. We derive an importance sampling algorithm for approximate inference in the model and report experimental results on English, German and Indonesian.

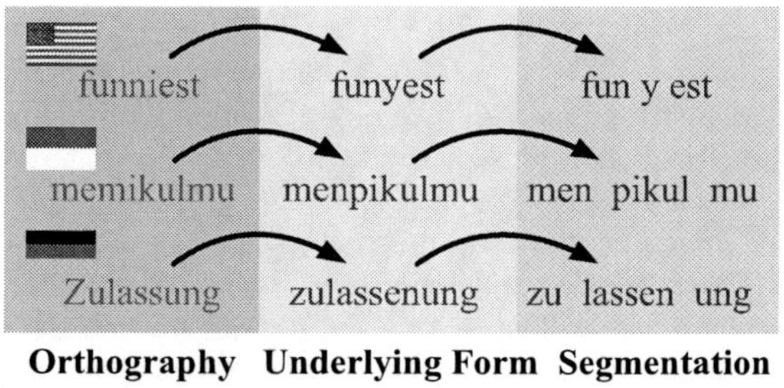

1 Introduction

Morphological segmentation is useful for NLP applications, such as, automatic speech recognition (Afify et al., 2006), keyword spotting (Narasimhan et al., 2014), machine translation (Clifton and Sarkar, 2011) and parsing (Seeker and Çetinoğlu, 2015). Prior work cast the problem as *surface segmentation:* a word form w is segmented into a sequence of substrings whose concatenation is w. In this paper, we introduce the problem of *canonical segmentation:* w is analyzed as a sequence of *canonical morphemes*, based on a set of word forms that have been "canonically" annotated for supervised learning. Each canonical morpheme c corresponds to a *surface morph s*, defined as its orthographic manifestation, i.e., as the substring of w that is generated by applying editing operations like insertion and deletion. Consider the following example: *funniest* has a canonical segmentation *fun-y-est* with three morphs *funn-i-est*. Arriving at the canonical analysis requires two edit operations: delete n in *funn* and replace i with y in

funniest   funyest   fun y est
memikulmu   menpikulmu   men pikul mu
Zulassung   zulassenung   zu lassen ung

Orthography   Underlying Form   Segmentation

Figure 1: Examples of canonical segmentation for English (top), Indonesian (middle) and German (bottom).

i. Figure 1 gives examples of orthography (i.e., the concatenation of surface morphs), underlying form (i.e., the concatenation of canonical morphemes) and canonical segmentation in three languages.

Canonical segmentation is motivated in the following three ways: (i) Computational morphology is the study of how words and their meanings are composed from smaller units. This goal is better supported by canonical morphemes than by surface morphemes because the smaller units are more accurately modeled. For *funniest*, composition can reason with canonical morphemes *fun* and *y*, whereas surface segmentation must work with *funn* and *i*. (ii) Morphological analysis is typically done with attribute-value pairs (AVP), e.g., [lemma=FUNNY, degree=SUPER]. While AVP is a good representation for *inflectional* morphology, it is not powerful enough for *derivational* morphology. If we represent the derivation of *funnier* as [lemma=FUN, deriv-suffix=-Y, degree=SUPER], then it is no longer clear in this fixed representation whether

Proceedings of NAACL-HLT 2016, pages 664–669,
San Diego, California, June 12-17, 2016. ©2016 Association for Computational Linguistics

$\texttt{degree} = \textsc{super}$ applies to *fun* or *fun+y*.[1] Canonical segmentation is more flexible—allowing us to express derivational relations without committing to a fixed attribute-value structure, which are used to study inflection. This point is important due to the fundamental distinction between the creation of words through inflection vs. through derivation. Inflection alters words to express syntactic relations (e.g., tense) with no major change in meaning nor POS. For example, *perturbed* and *perturbs* are inflections of the verb *perturb*. On the other hand, derivation modifies words more drastically—often changing the meaning or POS. For example, the noun *perturbation* derives from the verb stem *perturb* and the suffix *ation* (Haspelmath and Sims, 2013). (iii) Most NLP systems take *word forms* as atomic building blocks. We propose *canonical morphemes*, an alternative representation that models the structure of a language's lexicon and supports applications that benefit from access to the internal structure of words. This includes access to internal *morphological* structure, e.g., canonical morphemes like -*y* and -*ly* are recognized (independent of their orthographic manifestation) as derivational suffixes that cause predictable modifications; as well as access to internal *semantic* structure, e.g., the canonical segmentations of *fun* and *funny* share the canonical morpheme *fun*).

The contributions of this paper are as follows. We present the challenging new task of canonical segmentation. We develop a feature-rich structured joint model for canonical segmentation, which accounts for orthographic variation and segment-level structure. We derive an efficient importance sampling algorithm for approximate inference. We present experiments on three languages: English, German and Indonesian.

2 Model, Inference and Training

Our goal is canonical segmentation: identifying both the canonical morphemes and the morphs (their orthographic manifestations) of a word. This task involves *segmenting* the input as well as accounting for *orthographic* changes occurring in the word formation processes. Let w be the surface form, u the orthographic underlying representation (UR) of w, and s a labeled segmentation of u. Note: all random

---

[1] Note that *funnest* is a word of (colloquial) English.

variables are string-valued (Dreyer and Eisner, 2009). For example, consider the word *unhappiness*:

$$\underbrace{\textit{unhappiness}}_{w} \overset{\text{transduction}}{\mapsto} \underbrace{\textit{unhappyness}}_{u}$$

$$\overset{\text{segmentation}}{\mapsto} \underbrace{[\,\text{prefix } \textit{un}\,][\text{stem } \textit{happy}\,][\text{suffix } \textit{ness}\,]}_{s}.$$

Note that our notion of an orthographic UR closely resembles the phonological concept of a UR (Kenstowicz, 1994) and, indeed, many orthographic variations are manifestations of phonology.

We model this process as a globally normalized log-linear model of the conditional distribution,

$$p(s, u \mid w) = \frac{1}{Z(w)} \exp\left(\boldsymbol{\eta}^{\top} \boldsymbol{f}(s, u) + \boldsymbol{\omega}^{\top} \boldsymbol{g}(u, w)\right),$$

where $\boldsymbol{\theta} = \{\boldsymbol{\eta}, \boldsymbol{\omega}\}$ are the model parameters, $\boldsymbol{f}$ and $\boldsymbol{g}$ are, respectively, feature functions of the segmentation-UR and UR-surface-form pairs and $Z(w) = \sum_{s', u'} \exp\left(\boldsymbol{\eta}^{\top} \boldsymbol{f}(s', u') + \boldsymbol{\omega}^{\top} \boldsymbol{g}(u', w)\right)$ is the partition function. We can view this model as a conjunction of a finite-state transduction factor g (Dreyer et al., 2008) and a semi-Markov segmentation factor f (Sarawagi and Cohen, 2004), relating it to previous semi-CRF models of segmentation.[2] To fit the model, we maximize the log-likelihood of the training data $\{(s_i, u_i, w_i)\}_{i=1}^{N}$, $\mathcal{L}(\boldsymbol{\theta}) = \sum_{i=1}^{N} \log p(s_i, u_i \mid w_i)$, with respect to the model parameters $\boldsymbol{\theta}$. Optimization is done with gradient-based methods—requiring the computation of $\log Z(w)$ and $\nabla \log Z(w)$, which is intractable.[3] Thus, we turn to sampling (Rubinstein and Kroese, 2011) and stochastic gradient methods.

Features Our model includes several simple feature templates. The transduction factor of the model is based on (Cotterell et al., 2014): we include features that fire on individual edit actions as well as conjunctions of edit actions and characters on the surrounding context. For the semi-Markov factor, we use the feature set of Cotterell et al. (2015a), which

---

[2] Our transduction factor maps surface forms w to UR strings u of bounded length by imposing an insertion limit k. Thus, $|u| \leq |w| + k$. Our experiments use $k = 5$.

[3] Since the semi-CRF features fire on substrings, we would need a dynamic programming state for each substring of each of the exponentially many settings of u.

includes indicator features on individual segments, conjunctions of segments and segment labels and conjunctions of segments and left and right context on the input string. We also include a feature that checks whether the segment is a word in ASPELL (or a monolingual corpus).

Importance Sampling To approximately compute the gradient for learning, we employ importance sampling (MacKay, 2003, pp. 361–364). Rather than considering all underlying orthographic forms u, we use samples taken from proposal distribution q—a distribution over Σ^*. In the following equations, we omit the dependence on w for notational brevity. Also, let $h(s, u) = f(s, u) + g(u, w)$. We now provide the derivation of our importance sampling estimate for the gradient of log-partition function, including Rao-Blackwellization (Robert and Casella, 2013).

$$\nabla \log Z = \mathop{\mathbb{E}}_{(s,u)\sim p} [h(s, u)] \tag{1}$$

$$= \sum_{s,u} p(s, u) h(s, u) \tag{2}$$

$$= \sum_{s,u} p(s|u) p(u) h(s, u) \tag{3}$$

$$= \sum_{u} p(u) \sum_{s} p(s|u) h(s, u) \tag{4}$$

$$= \sum_{u} p(u) \mathop{\mathbb{E}}_{s\sim p(\cdot|u)} [h(s, u)] \tag{5}$$

$$= \mathop{\mathbb{E}}_{u\sim q} \left[\frac{p(u)}{q(u)} \mathop{\mathbb{E}}_{s\sim p(\cdot|u)} [h(s, u)] \right]. \tag{6}$$

The expectation $\mathbb{E}_{s\sim p(\cdot|u)} [h(s, u)]$ is efficiently computed with the semi-Markov generalization of the forward-backward algorithm (Sarawagi and Cohen, 2004). The algorithm runs in $\mathcal{O}(n^2 \cdot t^2)$ per sample where n is the length of the string to be segmented and t is the size of the label space. In our case, we have three labels: prefix, stem and suffix so $t = 3$.

So long as q has support everywhere p does (i.e., $p(u) > 0 \Rightarrow q(u) > 0$), the estimate is unbiased. Unfortunately, we can only efficiently compute $p(u) \propto \sum_{s} \exp(\theta^\top h(s, u))$ up to constant factor, $p(u) = \bar{p}(u)/Z_u$. Thus, we use the *indirect importance sampling estimator*,

$$\frac{1}{\sum_{i=1}^{m} \frac{\bar{p}(u^{(i)})}{q(u^{(i)})}} \sum_{i=1}^{m} \frac{\bar{p}(u^{(i)})}{q(u^{(i)})} \mathop{\mathbb{E}}_{s\sim p(\cdot|u^{(i)})} \left[h(s, u^{(i)}) \right], \tag{7}$$

where $u^{(1)} \ldots u^{(m)} \stackrel{\text{i.i.d.}}{\sim} q$. The indirect estimator is biased, but statistically consistent.[4] We also note that the particular instantiation of the indirect estimator leverages an efficient dynamic program to compute the expected features under $p(\cdot|u^{(i)})$. This has the effect of decreasing the number of samples required to get a useful estimate of the gradient. Computing $\bar{p}(u^{(i)})$ is a side effect of the dynamic program, namely the normalization constant. As a proposal distribution q, we use the following locally normalized distribution,

$$q(u) = \frac{\exp(\omega^\top g(u, w))}{\sum_{u'} \exp(\omega^\top g(u', w))}. \tag{8}$$

3 Related Work

Most work on morphological segmentation has been unsupervised. The LINGUISTICA (Goldsmith, 2001) and MORFESSOR (Creutz and Lagus, 2002) models rely on the minimum description length principle (Cover and Thomas, 2012). In short, these methods seek to segment words while at the same time minimizing the number of unique morphs discovered, i.e., the complexity of the model. The MORFESSOR model has additionally been augmented to handle the semi-supervised scenario (Kohonen et al., 2010). Goldwater et al. (2009) proposed a Bayesian non-parametric approach to word and morphological segmentation. Poon et al. (2009) used contrastive estimation (Smith and Eisner, 2005) to learn a log-linear model for segmentation fully unsupervised.

Few supervised techniques have been applied to morphological segmentation. Ruokolainen et al. (2013) applied a linear-chain CRF, showing that with a minimal amount of labeled data the performance of standard unsupervised and semi-supervised baselines are surpassed. In follow-up work (Ruokolainen et al., 2014), they found that incorporating distributional character-level features acquired from large unlabeled corpora improved the earlier model. Cotterell et al. (2015a) showed that modeling morphotactics with a semi-CRF improves results further.

The previously described approaches only attempt to split words into a sequence of stem and affixes— making it difficult to restore the underlying structure

---

[4]Informally, the indirect importance sampling estimate converges to the *true* expectation as $m \to \infty$.

which has been "corrupted" by the orthographic process. Our approach, however, is capable of restoring the underlying morphemes, e.g., *stopping* $\mapsto$ *stop-ing*. We note two exceptions to the above statement. Both Dasgupta and Ng (2007) and Naradowsky and Goldwater (2009) incorporate basic, heuristic spelling rules into *unsupervised* induction algorithms. Relatedly, Cotterell et al. (2015b) induced a phonology in an unsupervised manner. In contrast, our model is fully supervised and supports rich features, which enable accurate prediction on new words.

4 Experiments

We provide canonical segmentation experiments in three languages: English, German and Indonesian.

4.1 Corpora

The English data was extracted from segmentations derived from CELEX (Baayen et al., 1993). The German data was extracted from DerivBase (Zeller et al., 2013), which provides a collection of derived forms and the transformation rules. We manipulated these rules to create canonical segmentations. Lastly, the Indonesian data was created from the output of the MORPHIND analyzer (Larasati et al., 2011), which we ran on an open-source corpus of Indonesian.[5] For each language we selected 10,000 forms at random from a uniform distribution over types to form our corpus. We sampled 5 splits of the data into 8000 training forms, 1000 development forms and 1000 test forms. We have released all train, development and test splits online with additional documentation about their construction.[6]

4.2 Models

We train two versions of our proposed model. First, we train a *pipeline model*, i.e., we train the transduction component and segmentation component independently and decode sequentially. This approach is faster both at train and at test but suffers from cascading errors. Second, we train a *joint model*, the transduction and the segmentation components are trained to work well together.

[5]https://github.com/desmond86/
  Indonesian-English-Bilingual-Corpus
[6]http://ryancotterell.github.io/
  canonical-segmentation/

		Joint	Pipeline	SemiCRF	WFST
error	en	**0.27** (.02)	0.33 (.01)	0.33 (.01)	0.63 (.00)
	de	**0.41** (.03)	0.53 (.02)	0.65 (.01)	0.74 (.01)
	id	**0.10** (.01)	0.22 (.01)	0.27 (.01)	0.71 (.00)
distance	en	0.98 (.34)	**0.63** (.04)	0.68 (.01)	1.35 (.01)
	de	**1.01** (.07)	1.10 (.04)	1.32 (.04)	4.24 (.20)
	id	**0.15** (.02)	0.36 (.03)	0.49 (.02)	2.13 (.00)
F_1	en	**0.76** (.02)	0.70 (.02)	0.68 (.01)	0.53 (.02)
	de	**0.76** (.02)	0.71 (.01)	0.65 (.01)	0.59 (.02)
	id	**0.80** (.01)	0.75 (.01)	0.71 (.01)	0.62 (.02)

Table 1: Top: Error rate. Middle: Average edit distance. Bottom: Mean morpheme F_1 (higher better). Standard deviation in parentheses. Best result on each line in bold.

Baseline: Semi-CRF Segmenter The first baseline is a semi-CRF (Sarawagi and Cohen, 2004) that segments the orthographic form into morphs *without* canonicalization. Earlier work by Cotterell et al. (2015a) applied this model to *supervised* morphological segmentation. We use the feature set as Cotterell et al. (2015a), but we do not incorporate their augmented morphotactic state space.

Baseline: WFST Segmenter Our second baseline is a weighted finite-state transducer (Mohri, 1997) with a log-linear parameterization (Dreyer et al., 2008). We use the stochastic contextual edit model of Cotterell et al. (2014). We employ context n-gram features (up to 6-grams) on the input string to the left and right of the edit location in addition to 2-gram features on the lower string. The context features are then conjoined with the exact edit action. We refer the reader to Cotterell et al. (2014) for more details. The segmentation boundaries are marked as a distinguished symbol in the target string. This model is not entirely suited for the task as it makes it difficult to include the rich features we get through ASPELL.

Training and Decoding Details We train all models with AdaGrad (Duchi et al., 2011; Bottou, 2010). For the joint model, we take 10 samples ($m = 10$) for each gradient estimate. See Algorithm 3 of Bengio et al. (2003) for pseudocode for SGD with importance sampling. The pipeline and segmentation models use ordinary SGD. We use L_2 regularization with the regularization coefficient chosen by based on development set performance.

Exact decoding, $\mathrm{argmax}_{s,u}\, p(s, u \mid w)$, is intractable. Thus, we use a sampling approximation:

$\text{argmax}_{s,u^{(i)}}\, p(s, u^{(i)} \mid w)$ where $u^{(1)} \ldots u^{(m)} \overset{\text{i.i.d.}}{\sim} q$. We use $m = 1000$ in our experiments. Conditioned on each sample value for u, we use exact semi-CRF Viterbi decoding to select s.

4.3 Evaluation Measures

Evaluating morphological segmentation is tricky. The standard measure for the supervised task is border F_1, which measures how often the segmentation boundaries posited by the model are correct. However, this measure assumes that the concatenation of the segments is identical to the input string (i.e., surface segmentation) and is thus not applicable to canonical segmentation. On the other hand, the Morpho Challenge competition (Kurimo et al., 2010) uses a measure that samples a large number of word pairs from a linguistic gold standard. A form is considered correct if the gold standard contains at least one overlapping morph *and* the model posits at least one overlapping morph—this is problematic because for languages with multi-morphemic words (e.g., German), one should consider all morphs. Moreover, we can actually recover the linguistically annotated gold standard in contrast to unsupervised methods.

Instead, we report results under three measures: error rate, edit distance and morpheme F_1. Error rate is the proportion of analyses that are completely correct. Since error rate gives no partial credit, we also report edit distance between the predicted analysis and the gold standard, where both are encoded as strings using a distinguished boundary character at segment boundaries. Finally, morpheme F_1 (van den Bosch and Daelemans, 1999) considers overlap between the *set* of morphemes in the model's analysis and the set of morphemes in the gold standard. In this case, precision asks how often did the predicted segmentation contain morphemes in the gold standard and recall asks how often were the gold standard morphemes in the predicted segmentation.

4.4 Results and Error Analysis

Table 1 gives results for the three measures. Under error rate and morpheme F_1 our joint model performs the best on all three languages, followed by our pipeline model and then the two baselines. In fact, we observe that error rate and F_1 are quite correlated in general. Under edit distance, the joint model is the best model on German and Indonesian, but the

pipeline model is superior on English. Error analysis indicates that the lower performance is due to spurious insertions. For example, our model incorrectly analyzes *ruby* (stone) as *ruble-y*, mistaking the *ruby* as an adjectival form of *ruble* (the Russian currency); the correct analysis is *ruby* $\mapsto$ *ruby*. We believe that a richer transduction component may fix some of these problems. Overall, our joint model performs well; it is on average within one edit operation of the gold segmentation on three languages.

Unsurprisingly, the WFST performs poorly because it cannot leverage segment-level features (e.g., ASPELL features), which are available to the other models. The performance of the semi-CRF is limited by the orthographic changes in the language, which it cannot model. German is rich in such changes, hence the semi-CRF performs poorly and gets more than half the test cases wrong.

5 Conclusion

We presented a joint model for the task of canonical morphological segmentation, which extends existing approaches with the ability to learn orthographic changes. We argue that canonical morphological segmentation provides a useful analysis of linguistic phenomena (e.g., derivational morphology) because the sequence of morphemes is canonical—making it evident, which words share morphemes. Our model outperforms two baselines on three languages.

Acknowledgments

This material is based in part on research sponsored by DARPA under agreement number FA8750-13-2-0017 (the DEFT program) and the National Science Foundation under Grant No. 1423276. RC was funded by a DAAD Long-Term Research Grant. HS was supported by DFG (SCHU 2246/4-2).

References

Mohamed Afify, Ruhi Sarikaya, Hong-Kwang Jeff Kuo, Laurent Besacier, and Yuqing Gao. 2006. On the use of morphological analysis for dialectal Arabic speech recognition. In *INTERSPEECH*.

R Harald Baayen, Richard Piepenbrock, and Rijn van H. 1993. The CELEX lexical data base on CD-ROM.

Yoshua Bengio, Jean-Sébastien Senécal, et al. 2003.

Quick training of probabilistic neural nets by importance sampling. In *AISTATS*.

Léon Bottou. 2010. Large-scale machine learning with stochastic gradient descent. In *Proceedings of COMPSTAT'2010*, pages 177–186. Springer.

Ann Clifton and Anoop Sarkar. 2011. Combining morpheme-based machine translation with post-processing morpheme prediction. In *ACL*.

Ryan Cotterell, Nanyun Peng, and Jason Eisner. 2014. Stochastic contextual edit distance and probabilistic FSTs. In *ACL*.

Ryan Cotterell, Thomas Müller, Alexander Fraser, and Hinrich Schütze. 2015a. Labeled morphological segmentation with semi-Markov models. In *CoNLL*.

Ryan Cotterell, Nanyun Peng, and Jason Eisner. 2015b. Modeling word forms using latent underlying morphs and phonology. *TACL*, 3:433–447.

Thomas M Cover and Joy A Thomas. 2012. *Elements of information theory*. John Wiley & Sons.

Mathias Creutz and Krista Lagus. 2002. Unsupervised discovery of morphemes. In *Proceedings of the ACL-02 workshop on Morphological and phonological learning-Volume 6*, pages 21–30. Association for Computational Linguistics.

Sajib Dasgupta and Vincent Ng. 2007. High-performance, language-independent morphological segmentation. In *NAACL*.

Markus Dreyer and Jason Eisner. 2009. Graphical models over multiple strings. In *EMNLP*.

Markus Dreyer, Jason R Smith, and Jason Eisner. 2008. Latent-variable modeling of string transductions with finite-state methods. In *EMNLP*.

John Duchi, Elad Hazan, and Yoram Singer. 2011. Adaptive subgradient methods for online learning and stochastic optimization. *The Journal of Machine Learning Research*, 12:2121–2159.

John Goldsmith. 2001. Unsupervised learning of the morphology of a natural language. *Computational linguistics*, 27(2):153–198.

Sharon Goldwater, Thomas L Griffiths, and Mark Johnson. 2009. A Bayesian framework for word segmentation: Exploring the effects of context. *Cognition*, 112(1):21–54.

Martin Haspelmath and Andrea Sims. 2013. *Understanding morphology*. Routledge.

Michael Kenstowicz. 1994. *Phonology in Generative Grammar*. Blackwell.

Oskar Kohonen, Sami Virpioja, and Krista Lagus. 2010. Semi-supervised learning of concatenative morphology. In *Proceedings of the 11th Meeting of the ACL Special Interest Group on Computational Morphology and Phonology*.

Mikko Kurimo, Sami Virpioja, Ville Turunen, and Krista Lagus. 2010. Morpho Challenge competition 2005–2010: evaluations and results. In *SIGMORPHON*.

Septina Dian Larasati, Vladislav Kuboň, and Daniel Zeman. 2011. Indonesian morphology tool (morphind): Towards an Indonesian corpus. In *Systems and Frameworks for Computational Morphology*, pages 119–129. Springer.

David JC MacKay. 2003. *Information Theory, Inference and Learning Algorithms*. Cambridge University Press.

Mehryar Mohri. 1997. Finite-state transducers in language and speech processing. *Computational linguistics*, 23(2):269–311.

Jason Naradowsky and Sharon Goldwater. 2009. Improving morphology induction by learning spelling rules. In *IJCAI*.

Karthik Narasimhan, Damianos Karakos, Richard Schwartz, Stavros Tsakalidis, and Regina Barzilay. 2014. Morphological segmentation for keyword spotting. In *EMNLP*.

Hoifung Poon, Colin Cherry, and Kristina Toutanova. 2009. Unsupervised morphological segmentation with log-linear models. In *NAACL*. Association for Computational Linguistics.

Christian Robert and George Casella. 2013. *Monte Carlo statistical methods*. Springer Science & Business Media.

Reuven Y Rubinstein and Dirk P Kroese. 2011. *Simulation and the Monte Carlo method*. John Wiley & Sons.

Teemu Ruokolainen, Oskar Kohonen, Sami Virpioja, and Mikko Kurimo. 2013. Supervised morphological segmentation in a low-resource learning setting using conditional random fields. In *CoNLL*.

Teemu Ruokolainen, Oskar Kohonen, Sami Virpioja, and Mikko Kurimo. 2014. Painless semi-supervised morphological segmentation using conditional random fields. In *EACL*.

Sunita Sarawagi and William W Cohen. 2004. Semi-Markov conditional random fields for information extraction. In *NIPS*.

Wolfgang Seeker and Özlem Çetinoğlu. 2015. A graph-based lattice dependency parser for joint morphological segmentation and syntactic analysis. *TACL*.

Noah A. Smith and Jason Eisner. 2005. Contrastive estimation: Training log-linear models on unlabeled data. In *ACL*.

Antal van den Bosch and Walter Daelemans. 1999. Memory-based morphological analysis. In *ACL*.

Britta D Zeller, Jan Snajder, and Sebastian Padó. 2013. DErivBase: Inducing and evaluating a derivational morphology resource for german. In *ACL*.

Syntactic Parsing of Web Queries with Question Intent

Yuval Pinter[1], Roi Reichart[1,2], and Idan Szpektor[1]

[1]Yahoo Research, Haifa 31905, Israel, {yuvalp, roiri, idan}@yahoo-inc.com
[2]Faculty of Industrial Engineering and Management, Technion, IIT

Abstract

Accurate automatic processing of Web queries is important for high-quality information retrieval from the Web. While the syntactic structure of a large portion of these queries is trivial, the structure of queries with question intent is much richer. In this paper we therefore address the task of statistical syntactic parsing of such queries. We first show that the standard dependency grammar does not account for the full range of syntactic structures manifested by queries with question intent. To alleviate this issue we extend the dependency grammar to account for segments – independent syntactic units within a potentially larger syntactic structure. We then propose two distant supervision approaches for the task. Both algorithms do not require manually parsed queries for training. Instead, they are trained on millions of *(query, page title)* pairs from the *Community Question Answering (CQA)* domain, where the CQA page was clicked by the user who initiated the query in a search engine. Experiments on a new treebank[1] consisting of 5,000 Web queries from the CQA domain, manually parsed using the proposed grammar, show that our algorithms outperform alternative approaches trained on various sources: tens of thousands of manually parsed OntoNotes sentences, millions of unlabeled CQA queries and thousands of manually segmented CQA queries.

1 Introduction

As the World Wide Web grows in volume, it encompasses ever-increasing amounts of text. A major gateway to this invaluable resource is *Web queries* which users compose to guide a search engine in retrieving the information they desire to inspect. Automatic processing of Web queries is therefore of utmost importance.

Previous research (Bergsma and Wang, 2007; Barr et al., 2008) suggested that many Web queries are trivial in structure, usually embodying entity lookup, e.g. *"frozen"* or *"condos in NY"*. However, with the increasing popularity of Community Question Answering (CQA) sites, such as Yahoo Answers, StackOverflow and social QA forums, more Web queries encompass information needs related to questions that these sites can answer. We found that this subcategory of queries, which we call *CQA queries* (following Liu et al. (2011; Carmel et al. (2014)), exhibits a wide range of structures. This suggests that the processing of such queries, which constitute $\sim$10% of all queries issued to search engines (White et al., 2015), may benefit from syntactic analysis (Tsur et al., 2016).

Recent progress in statistical parsing (Choi et al., 2015) has resulted in models that are both fast, parsing several hundred sentences per second, and accurate. These parsers, however, still suffer from the problem of domain adaptation (McClosky et al., 2010), excelling mostly when their training and test domains are similar. This problem is of particular importance in the heterogeneous Web (Petrov and McDonald, 2012) and is expected to worsen when addressing queries, due to their non-standard grammatical conventions.

Some recent work addresses the syntactic analysis of User Generated Content (UGC) (Petrov and McDonald, 2012; Eisenstein, 2013; Kong et al., 2014). Yet, these efforts generally focus on UGC aspects related to grammatical mistakes made by users (Foster et al., 2008) and to the unique writing conventions of specific Web platforms, such as Twitter (Foster et al., 2011; Kong et al., 2014). Our analysis of thousands of CQA queries, however, reveals that regardless of such issues, CQA queries are generated by a well-defined grammar that sometimes deviates from the one used to generate the standard written language of edited resources such as newspapers.

Consequently, this work has two main contributions. First, we extend the standard dependency grammar to de-

---

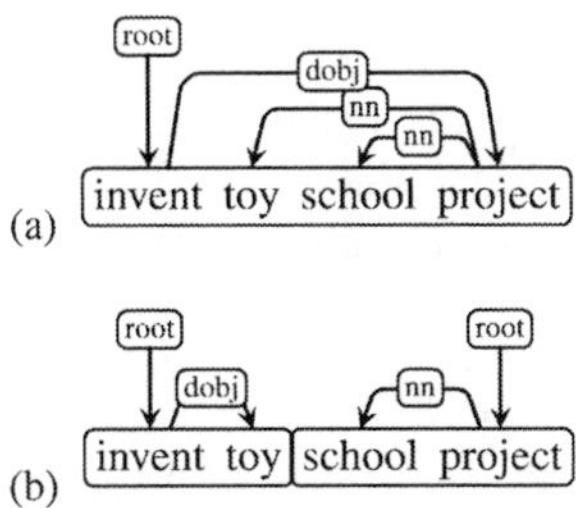

Figure 1: A two-segment query, parsed by an off-the shelf parser: (a) as is, producing an incorrect noun phrase ("toy school project"); (b) after correct segmentation.

scribe the syntax of queries with question intent. The extended grammar is driven by the concept of a *syntactic segment*: an independent syntactic unit within a potentially larger syntactic structure. A query may include several segments, potentially related to each other semantically but lacking an explicit syntactic connection. Hence, query analysis consists of the query's segments and their internal dependency structure, and may be complemented by the inter-segment semantic relationships. Therefore, we constructed a new query treebank consisting of 5,000 CQA queries, manually annotated according to our extended grammar. A comparison of direct application of an off-the-shelf parser (Clear (Choi and McCallum, 2013)) trained on edited text (OntoNotes 5 (Weischedel et al., 2013)) to a raw query with the application of the same parser to the gold-standard segments of that query is given in Fig. 1.

Second, we develop two CQA query parsing algorithms that can adapt any given off-the-shelf dependency parser trained on standard edited text to produce syntactic structures that conform to the extended grammar. Both our algorithms employ *distant supervision* in the form of a training set consisting of millions of *(query, title)* pairs. The *title* is the title of the Yahoo Answers question page that was clicked by the user who initiated the *query*. The alignment between the query and the title provides a valuable training signal for query segmentation and parsing, since the title is usually a grammatical question. Both algorithms employ an off-the-shelf parser, but differ on whether segmentation and parsing are performed in a pipeline or jointly.

We compared our algorithms to several alternatives: (a) Direct application of an off-the-shelf parser to queries; (b) A supervised variant of our pipeline algorithm where thousands of manually segmented queries replace the distant supervision source; and (c) A pipeline algorithm similar to ours where segmentation is based on the predictions of a query language model. We report results on two query treebank tasks: (a) Dependency parsing, reporting Unlabeled Attachment Score (UAS); and (b) Query segmentation, which reflects the core aspect of the extended

grammar compared to the standard one.

In experiments on our new treebank, our joint model outperformed the alternatives on UAS for the full test set and for the subset of single-segment queries. Our pipeline model excelled both on UAS and on segmentation F1 for two large subsets that are automatically identifiable at test time: (a) Queries that consist mostly of content words (42.4% of the test set); and (b) Queries for which the confidence score of the off-the-shelf parser is at most 0.8 (30% of the test set). It also beat all other models on the subset of multi-segment queries.

2 Previous Work

The Web attracts considerable NLP research attention (e.g. Eisenstein (2013)). Here we focus on grammar and parsing of Web data in general and queries in particular.

Syntactic Query Analysis Web queries differ from standard sentences in a number of aspects: they tend to be shorter, not to follow standard grammatical conventions, and to convey more information than can be directly inferred from their words. Consequently, a number of works addressed their syntactic analysis. Allan and Raghavan (2002) use part-of-speech (POS) tag patterns in order to manually map very short queries into clarification questions, which are then presented to the user to help them clarify their intent. Barr et al. (2008) trained POS taggers for Web queries and used a set of rules to map the resulting tagged queries into one of seven syntactic categories, whose merit is tested in the context of information retrieval tasks. Manshadi and Li (2009) and Li (2010) addressed the task of semantic tagging and structural analysis of Web queries, focusing on noun phrase queries. Bendersky et al. (2010) used the POS tags of the top-retrieved documents to enhance the initial POS tagging of query terms. Bendersky et al. (2011) proposed a joint framework for annotating queries with POS tags and phrase chunks. Ganchev et al. (2012) trained a POS tagger on automatically tagged queries. The POS tags of the training queries are projected from sentences containing the query terms within Web pages retrieved for them. The retrieved sentences were POS tagged using an off-the-shelf tagger. These works, as opposed to ours, do not aim to produce a complete syntactic analysis of queries.

Syntactic Parsing of Web Data To the best of our knowledge, only a handful of works have aimed at building syntactic parsers for Web data. Petrov and McDonald (2012) conducted a shared task on parsing Web data from the Google Web Treebank, consisting of texts from the email, weblog, CQA, newsgroup, and review domains. The participating systems relied mostly on existing domain adaptation techniques to adapt parsers trained on existing treebanks of edited text to the Web. Foster et al.

(2011) took a similar approach for tweet parsing. Contrary to our approach, these works rely on existing grammatical frameworks, particularly phrase-structure and dependency grammars, and do not aim at adapting them to domains such as Web queries, where standard grammar does not properly describe the language. This may be the reason Web queries were not included in the shared task.

A work that is more related to ours is Kong et al. (2014), who addressed the task of tweet parsing. Like us, they adapt the grammatical annotation scheme to the target linguistic domain and produce a multi-rooted syntactic structure. However, CQA queries and tweets exhibit different syntactic properties: (1) tweets often consist of multiple sentences, while CQA queries are concise in nature and usually correspond to a phrase, a fragment of a sentence, or several of these concatenated; and (2) queries are generated in order to retrieve information from the Web. Tweets, on the other hand, usually aim to convey a short message. These differences lead us to take approaches substantially different from theirs.

3 CQA Query Grammar

3.1 Motivating Analysis

In this section we define the class of *CQA queries* and analyze their properties in comparison with other writing genres. This analysis will establish the motivation for the extension of standard dependency grammar so that it accounts for CQA queries (§3.2).

The data we analyzed consists of queries randomly sampled from the Yahoo Answers log. In cases where a searcher, after issuing a Web query on a search engine, viewed a question page on Yahoo Answers, a popular CQA site, this query is logged. From this log we sampled 100K queries for our analysis, as well as 5,000 additional queries for constructing a query treebank (see §3.3).

According to Barr et al. (2008), who analyzed queries from Yahoo's search engine, 69.8% of general Web queries are composed of a single noun phrase, leaving little room for a meaningful taxonomy. Focusing on CQA queries removes this bias and allows exploration of additional syntactic categories of queries. Especially, we would like to delve into the categories Barr et al. label as *word salad* (e.g. *"mp3s free"*) and *other-query* (e.g. *"florida reading conference 2006"*), cited as composing 8.1% and 6.8% of all queries respectively and for which no analysis is offered.

To characterize the domain of CQA queries, we compare its properties to those of other Web domain samples: (a) 100K general Web queries; (b) 120K titles of questions posted on Yahoo Answers; and (c) 100K story bodies from Yahoo News. In our analysis, individual sentences were identified using the OpenNLP sentence splitting tool[2], POS-tagged by the Stanford parser (Klein and Manning, 2003)[3] and syntactically parsed using the Clear parser (Choi and McCallum, 2013)[4].

Table 1 presents four measures of syntactic complexity (four leftmost measure columns). The first column reports the average number of word tokens per parsed item. The second column contains the median and mean dependency tree depths, defined as the number of edges in the longest path from the root node to a leaf in the tree. The third and fourth columns present the fraction of dependency tree root edges that go to words POS-tagged as nouns or as verbs, respectively. We use these last two measures as proxies of the syntactic category of the input text, with noun roots often indicating simple noun phrases and verb roots often indicating more complex syntactic forms that include a verb argument structure[5]. Finally, the rightmost column of the table presents the average parser confidence per item provided by Clear, which we use as a proxy for parsing difficulty.

As the table shows, both CQA and general Web queries are harder to parse (according to parser confidence) compared to news article sentences and CQA question titles. Yet, CQA and general Web queries strongly differ with respect to their syntactic complexity. Indeed, CQA queries have substantially more tokens and deeper trees. Moreover, while 62.9% of the root nodes in general query parse trees govern a noun and 30.3% govern a verb, in CQA queries the respective figures are flipped: 32.2% and 62.7%, respectively.

3.2 Dependency Grammar Extension for Queries

Our analysis above reveals the special status of CQA queries. Like general Web queries, CQA queries are hard to parse. However, while the difficulty of parsing general Web queries may result from their short length and shallow syntactic structure, CQA queries are longer and seem to have a deeper syntactic structure.

Based on our manual inspection of thousands of the queries used in the above analysis, we propose an extension of the standard dependency grammar so that it accounts for CQA queries. Our reasoning is that the grammatical structure of CQA queries is a syntactic forest. The query's tokens are partitioned into one or more contiguous *syntactic segments*, each representing a maximal constituent unit syntactically independent of the other units. The final syntactic representation of the query consists of a set of trees produced according to the Stanford Dependency schema (De Marneffe and Manning, 2008),

---

[2]opennlp.apache.org

[3]Manual inspection revealed that this parser outperforms the Stanford tagger (Toutanova et al., 2003) on these sets.

[4]Version 2.0.1, parsing model 1.2. www.clearnlp.com

[5]We verified this hypothesis by manual inspection of the 1,000 development set queries (see §3.3).

Corpus	Average token count	Median (mean) tree depth	$root \rightarrow NN*$ edges (%)	$root \rightarrow VB*$ edges (%)	Average parser confidence
News article sentences	18.4	6 (6.5)	12.0	84.8	0.898
CQA question titles	10.5	4 (4.5)	10.0	86.9	0.991
CQA queries	6.4	4 (3.7)	32.2	62.7	0.809
General queries	4.5	3 (3.0)	62.9	30.3	0.752

Table 1: Syntactic properties of four types of Web domains. The four leftmost properties are proxies of syntactic complexity. The fifth property (parser confidence) is a proxy of parsing difficulty. The "$root \rightarrow NN* \ edges$" and "$root \rightarrow VB* \ edges$" columns present the fraction of edges from the root of the parse tree that go to words POS-tagged as nouns and verbs respectively.

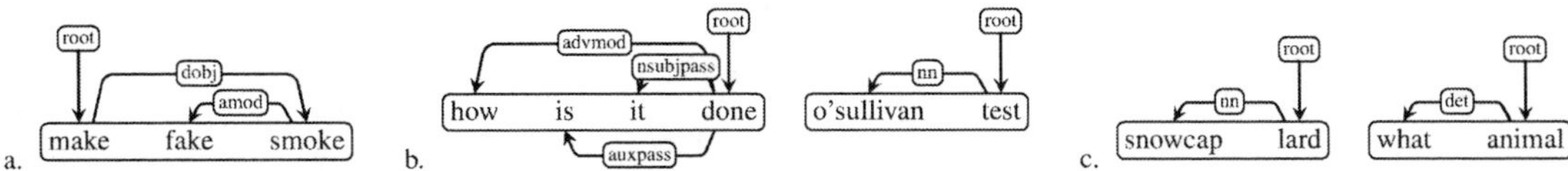

Figure 2: Queries segmented and parsed according to our extended dependency grammar.

one tree per segment. Based on this observation, CQA queries may consist of several syntactically independent segments, as opposed to grammatical sentences which consist of exactly one segment. Importantly, query segments are syntactically independent, although they tend to be semantically related.

Figure 2 provides examples of parsed queries. Query (a) consists of a single segment, a verb phrase rooted by the word *make*. Query (b) is composed of two segments that are syntactically independent, but semantically connected. Particularly, the first segment is an interrogative sentence rooted in the word *done* and the second is a noun phrase which specifies the pronoun *it* from the first segment. Finally, query (c) consists of two segments, each a noun phrase, presumably connected by an *is-made-of* semantic relation. As in query (b), the segments of this query are syntactically independent, but unlike query (b), their semantic connection is more loose. The existence of such loose connections motivates us to exclude semantic subcategorization from the syntactic layer.

We note that the notion of *segment* has another meaning, within the task of *query segmentation* (Bergsma and Wang, 2007; Guo et al., 2008; Tan and Peng, 2008; Mishra et al., 2011; Hagen et al., 2012). This task's goal is to identify words in the query that together form compound concepts or phrases, like *"Chicago Bulls"*. As such, this task differs from ours as it defines segmentation in semantic rather than syntactic terms.

We also note that query segments are distinct from the concept of *fragments* in constituency parsing. Marcus et al. (1993) introduce fragments in order to overcome problems involving the attachment point of various modifying phrases, *e.g.* in the sentence '*In Asia, as [FRAG in Europe], a new order is taking shape*'. While proper treatment of such phrases often requires extra syntactic information, their syntactic connection to other parts of the sentence is present, unlike between query segments.

3.3 Query Treebank

Following our proposed grammar, we constructed a treebank by manually annotating 5,000 queries that landed on Yahoo Answers (see §3.1). These queries were randomly split into a 4,000-query test set and a 1,000-query development set. Four human annotators segmented both sets, and parsed the test set with unlabeled dependency trees (including POS tags). The annotators' sets did not overlap, yet cross-reviews were made in cases deemed difficult by them. On a validation set of 100 queries tagged by all annotators, the agreement scores measured were 0.97 for segmentation and 0.96 for dependency edges.

To evaluate how well out-of-the-box parsers conform with our grammar, we applied seven dependency parsers to the 4,000-query test set. We trained all parsers on the OntoNotes 5 training set [6] and applied them: (a) to each gold-standard segment of each query; and (b) to full, unsegmented, queries. For comparison we also recap the performance of the parsers on the OntoNotes 5 test set as reported in Choi et al. (2015). The same non-gold POS tags were provided to all parsers (see §6.2).

The results, presented in Table 2, establish the difficulty of our task: UAS differences between OntoNotes and full queries range from 13.4% to 18.6%. Moreover, injecting gold segmentation knowledge increases the performance of the parsers by 5.3-5.9%, highlighting the value of accurate segmentation in syntactic query analysis. Finally, the ranking of the parsers with respect to their accuracy on queries differs from their ranking with respect to accuracy on OntoNotes, raising Redshift to first place and dropping RBG to last place.

Since knowledge of segment boundaries consistently improves parsing quality in our analysis, we next present two distant supervision approaches that attempt to discover the segments of an input query and return a parse forest that adheres to the segment boundaries.

---

[6]This parser training convention was kept throughout the paper.

Parser	ON5	Segmented Queries	Full Queries
Redshift (Honnibal et al., 2013)	91.0	**82.5**	**76.6**
Mate (Bohnet and Nivre, 2012)	**91.6**	81.4	75.5
Clear (Choi and McCallum, 2013)	91.3	80.7	75.4
SNN (Chen and Manning, 2014)	88.2	80.7	74.8
GN13 (Goldberg and Nivre, 2013)	89.2	80.5	74.8
Turbo (Martins et al., 2013)	89.6	79.4	73.9
RBG (Lei et al., 2014)	91.4	78.5	72.8

Table 2: UAS of out-of-the-box parsers trained on OntoNotes 5. RBG is reported on its best-performing setting, *basic*.

	Question Title	Associated Query (After segmentation)	Segmentation Cue
1	How many crickets to feed 7 month old leopard gecko?	[leopard gecko] [7 month old] [how many to feed]	Reordering (x2)
2	Does any1 think that Heath Ledger is Cute?	[heath ledger] [cute]	Intruding BE
3	Does Beijing still have license plate restrictions?	[beijing] [license plate restrictions]	Intruding HAVE
4	Do you know the song "Little Sister" by Queens of the Stone Age?	[little sister] [queens]	Intruding IN
5	What came first the jedi or the sith?	[what came first jedi] [sith]	Intruding CC
6	What do you think of a double major in Finance and Marketing?	[double major] [finance] [marketing]	Intruding IN, CC

Table 3: Examples for title-query pairs with the resulting segmentation and the corresponding segmentation cues. Note that they do not necessarily produce correct data.

4 A Pipeline Segmentation-Parsing Model

As our first approach, we present a query segmentation algorithm which can be combined with an off-the-shelf parser in two ways in order to form a pipeline query parsing system: (a) first segmenting the query and then applying the parser to each of the segments; or (b) first parsing the query and then fixing the resulting dependency tree so that it conforms with the segmentation. In the second setup the parser's output is aligned against the segmentation such that dependency edges which cross segment boundaries are re-assigned to become *root* edges. In our experiments we found that, for all our tested pipeline models, the first setup performed slightly better. We therefore report results only for this setup.

Our segmentation algorithm is based on the observation that CQA queries are generated in order to express a searcher's need which is likely to be formulated as a question on the web page that they then visit, and that this paraphrasing can serve as a source for query segmentation cues. The algorithm therefore inspects at training time *(query,title)* pairs where *title* is the title of a Yahoo Answers question page that was clicked by the user who initiated *query*. A query for which a full word-wise alignment to the clicked question can be found is annotated with segmentation markers according to several cues, then added to the training set.

Segmentation Cues The following cues are used for detection of query segment boundaries:

- **Reordering**: a part of the query which appears in the title out of order relative to another part of the query is marked as a segmentation location on both ends (ex. #1 in Table 3). This rule accounted for about 32% of the segmentation cues.

- **Intruding word classes**: if between two words which appear adjacent in the query there are words of certain classes in the question title, the position between them is marked for segmentation. These classes include the verb BE and its conjugations (ex. #2), HAVE and its conjugations (ex. #3), prepositions (ex. #4, #6), and conjunctions (ex. #5, #6). In addition, any multi-word intruding sequence that contains a word of these classes in one of the last three positions is construed as a cue.

Training Set Generation We started with a query log for 60 million Yahoo Answers pages. We filtered out titles of more than 20 words, titles that do not start with a question word, and titles that do not have an associated query which after lowercasing and punctuation removal contains only words from the title (as well as possibly '*site:*' terms or the word '*to*'). The remaining 7.5 million queries were automatically segmented according to the above cues. A sample of 100 queries was found to have a segmentation F1 score (defined in §6.2) of 64.5.

Model and Training We trained a linear chain CRF with pairwise potentials (Lafferty et al., 2001)[7] on the set of 7.5M automatically segmented queries. The model employs the following standard features: (a) unigram and bigram word features (± 2 and ± 1 windows around the represented word respectively); (b) unigram and bigram POS features (in a ± 2 window); (c) unigram word+POS features (± 1 window); and (d) distance of word from start and end of query, as well as each distance combined with word and/or POS.

---

[7]We used CRF++ (crfpp.googlecode.com)

Algorithm 1 Projection-based query parsing

1: **function** FINDPROJECTIONBASEDSEGMENTPARSE-
   TREES(QUERY)
2:     $question \leftarrow$ Q2Q(*query*)
3:     $parse \leftarrow$ OffTheShelfParse(*question*)
4:     **for** Node n in parse **do**
5:         **if** n.text does not match token in *query* **then**
6:             CollapseAllEdges(n, *parse*)
7:             parse.remove(n)
8:     segment-trees $\leftarrow \emptyset$
9:     **for** Node r in *parse*.root.children **do**
10:         segment-trees.add(Tree(r))
        return segment-trees

1: **function** COLLAPSEALLEDGES(N, PARSE)
2:     $in \leftarrow n$.incomingEdge
3:     **for** Edge out in n.outgoingEdges **do**
4:         $label \leftarrow$ GenerateLabel(in.type, out.type)
5:         **if** n.POS is preposition or conjunction **then**
6:             *parse*.addEdge(*parse*.root, out.target, 'root')
7:         **else**
8:             *parse*.addEdge(in.source, out.target, *label*)

---

5   A Joint Projection-based Model

An alternative distant supervision approach is to employ the *(query,title)* pair set in the training of a model that maps queries to natural language questions. These inferred questions are supposedly easier to parse as they follow standard grammatical conventions. A query parsing algorithm that employs such a mapping component has three steps: first, a grammatical question with a similar information need to that of the query is automatically inferred. Then, the inferred question is parsed by an off-the-shelf dependency parser, trained on a grammatical corpus. Finally, the question parse is projected onto the query, inducing the query's multi-rooted syntactic forest. Algorithm 1 presents pseudo-code for the projection-based query parsing algorithm.

The first step maps a given user query to a synthetic natural-language question. For this step we implemented the Query-to-Question (Q2Q) algorithm of Dror et al. (2013). Q2Q maps queries into valid CQA questions by instantiating templates that were extracted out of *(query,title)* pairs taken from the page view log of a CQA site. We trained the Q2Q algorithm on millions of *(query,title)* pairs taken from the Yahoo Answers log, where each *title* starts with a question word and query length ≥ 3.

Our algorithm obtains the top inferred Q2Q question and parses it using an off-the-shelf parser, trained on grammatical English sentences (lines 2-3 in Algorithm 1). It then projects the question parse tree onto the original query to generate its syntactic structure, in accordance with the extended dependency grammar (§3.2), as follows. First (lines 4-7), the algorithm traverses the question parse, removing all question tokens that do not appear in the query and reassigning the dependents of each removed token to be headed by its parent. In addition, as prepositions and conjunctions inserted by the Q2Q templates are strong signals of segmentation, parse subtrees governed by such nodes are also treated as separate segments. Following this phase, all remaining question tokens appear in the query. The algorithm is then left with a syntactic forest, since the root node may have multiple children, each one defining a query segment. Lines 8-10 extract these segments and their parse trees.

Figure 3 shows the projection process for two queries, the second of which demonstrates how an added preposition (*'on'*) invokes segmentation. We emphasize that the only manually annotated data required for the training of our joint model is a treebank of standard edited text (OntoNotes 5), used for training the off-the-shelf parser.

Since we expect the projected query parse to produce trees for contiguous segments, we only accept the top Q2Q result where the query word order is maintained in the question, and use an off-the-shelf parser which produces projective trees. In addition, the projection algorithm may collapse several edges from the question tree into a single edge within a query segment tree, leaving the resulting label unspecified. In this work we evaluate unlabeled parse trees and therefore defer the treatment of this issue to future work (leaving $GenerateLabel()$ in line 4 of Algorithm 1 unspecified).

6   Experiments

6.1   Models

We evaluated the following models (summarized in Table 4) on our new query treebank (§3.3):

Distant Supervision Models   Our proposed pipeline (§4) and joint (§5) models. Our pipeline model, denoted by *DistPipe*, performs query segmentation and then parses each segment. Our projection-based joint model, denoted by *Q2QProj*, parses an inferred question for the query and projects the parse tree on the query. Both models use the Clear parser for parsing. Importantly, both our models do not require any type of manually annotated queries (parsed or segmented) for training.

The Q2Q algorithm employed by our joint model returns a question for only 2954 of the 4000 test set queries. We thus reverted to the full-query parsing baseline when it returned no result.

Baselines   The first natural baseline is the Clear parser, which is employed by our models. We note that while Clear is not constrained to output a single segment tree[8], in practice it generated a multi-segment structure for $\sim$2% of the development queries, compared to $\sim$25% of

---

[8]Personal communication with the authors.

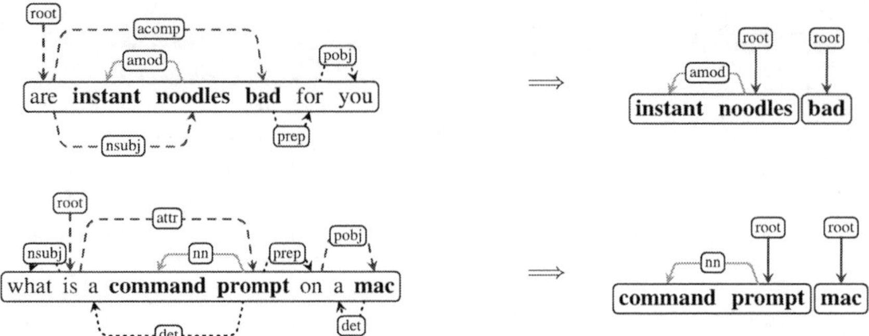

Figure 3: Question parse trees and their projections onto the queries they were generated for. Solid edges are preserved in the projection, dotted edges are removed, and dashed edges are collapsed (in both cases demonstrated, into root edges).

Group	Setup name	Segmentation	Process
Benchmark	*Gold*	gold	pipeline
Ensemble	*Ens*	CRF ensemble	pipeline
Supervised	*Sup*	supervised CRF	pipeline
Distant	*DistPipe*	distant CRF	pipeline
Supervision	*Q2QProj*	from question parse	projection
Baselines	*Lm*	NNLM	pipeline
	Clear	from parse	parser only

Table 4: The algorithms evaluated in this work.

the queries in the gold standard annotation, making it ill-qualified for multi-segment queries.

As a second baseline, denoted by *Lm*, we constructed a pipeline model identical to ours expect that segmentation is performed with a *Language model (LM)* based approach. For this aim we applied a Neural-Network language model (NNLM) (Mikolov, 2012) to each input query. For each word the language model computes its likelihood given the current model state, which is based on previous words. We then used the 1,000-query development set to find the optimal probability threshold for which words with estimated probability under the threshold are considered "surprising" and therefore mark the beginning of a new segment. We learned a language model[9] with 200 dimensions over 20M randomly sampled queries of length ≥ 3.

Supervised Models We further compare our distant supervision approach to an algorithm that does use manually annotated queries for training, denoted by *Sup*. For this aim we implemented a pipeline model identical to ours, except that the pairwise linear-chain CRF is trained on manually-annotated queries. The algorithm is trained and tested following a 5-fold cross-validation protocol over the 4,000-query test set.

Ensemble Model We also tested the complementary aspects of distant and manual supervision by constructing the same pipeline model, except that segmentation is based on both types of supervision sources. We experimented with various ensemble generation techniques, and the one that has shown to work best was a method that unifies the segmentation decisions of the distant-supervised and supervised CRFs: the model, denoted by *Ens*, considers a token to be a segment boundary if it is considered to be so by at least one of the CRFs.

Gold Segmentation An upper-bound benchmark to our pipeline approach. This is a pipeline model, denoted by *Gold*, that is identical to ours, except that the segmentation is taken from the gold standard.

6.2 Evaluation Tasks and Data Pre-Processing

We consider two evaluation tasks: (a) Dependency parsing, reporting Unlabeled Attachment Score (UAS); and (b) Query Segmentation, reporting the F1 score, where each segment is represented by its boundaries: in order for an observed segment to be considered correct, both of its ends must match those of a gold segment.

All tested algorithms, except for our joint model, directly segment and parse queries and hence require these queries to be POS-tagged. Thus, we POS-tagged the test-set queries with the OpenNLP[10] POS tagger which was adapted to queries using the self-training algorithm of Ganchev et al. (2012). Our self-training set consisted of 14M *(query,title)* pairs from the Yahoo Answers log. This

---

[9]NNLM implementation in `rnnlm.org` with default parameters.

[10]`opennlp.apache.org`

tagger reached 88.2% accuracy on our query treebank, compared to 81.3% of the off-the-shelf tagger[11].

Analyzing our development set we noticed that a very strong indicator that a query is a grammatical, and thus consists of a single segment, is when it starts with a WH-word or an auxiliary verb. Hence, in all pipeline models, except *Gold*, we do not segment such queries but rather directly apply the Clear parser to them. In postmortem analysis of the test set we found that this indicator was correct for 93.2% of the 1600 detected queries with 40% recall with respect to the single-segment queries subset.

6.3 Results

Tables 5 and 6 present the results of our experiments. The *All Queries* column in Table 5 reports the performance of the tested models on the full test set. Overall, methods based on distant and manual supervision are superior to the baseline methods in both measures. Interestingly, our *Q2QProj* model performs best in terms of UAS (77.1%) although its segmentation F1 is mediocre (63.5). In terms of UAS, the distant-supervised and supervised models approach the performance of the upper bound gold standard segmentation. For example, *Q2QProj* is outperformed by *Gold* by only 3.6%. The *Clear* parser baseline, which is not trained to identify multiple segments, lags 5.7-5.8 F1 points behind the models that employ CRF segmentation. This is translated to a difference in UAS of up to 1.7%. The *Lm* baseline, on the other hand, scores substantially lower than the other models in both measures. This may be an indication of the syntactic, rather than lexical, nature of our task.

In development set experiments we were able to characterize two subsets of queries on which our distant supervised pipeline model performs particularly well, outperforming even the supervised pipeline algorithm which requires thousands of manually annotated queries for training. One such set is the subset of queries that contain at most one word not tagged with what we define to be a *content word POS*, namely: noun, verb, adjective or adverb ('≤ 1 ncw' column in Table 5). Intuitively, this subset, which accounts for 42.4% of the test set, consists of queries that convey larger amounts of semantic content and are structured less coherently. On this subset, our *DistPipe* model outperforms the supervised *Sup* model by 4.1 segmentation F1 points, and by 1.7% in UAS.

The other subset, which accounts for 30% of the test set, includes those queries for which the confidence score of the Clear parser, when applied to the whole query, is at most 0.8 (*LowConf* column in Table 5). This subset singles out cases deemed difficult by the parser, indicating queries with non-standard syntax. Indeed, the performance of all models substantially drops compared to the

full set or the '≤ 1 ncw' set. Here again, *DistPipe* improves over *Sup* by 5.8 segmentation F1 points and 1.9% in UAS, with additional gain by the ensemble model *Ens*.

Q2QProj performs lower than the pipeline models on both subsets, suggesting that this approach does not work for difficult queries as well as it does for more simple queries. The decreased performance of the *Clear* baseline on both these subsets compared to the entire test set is not surprising, given their challenging syntactic properties.

Altogether, queries belonging to either of the two subsets (or both) account for 50.2% of the full set, emphasizing the benefit of developing more sophisticated ensemble approaches, based on the above characteristics of queries and the individual tested models.

Next, we turn to Table 6, which compares the performance of the various models on the test subsets that consist of single-segment or multi-segment queries only[12]. Our pipeline model, *DistPipe*, excels on the multi-segment subset, achieving a segmentation F1 of 42.2 and UAS of 67.5% compared to only 23.5 and 64.3% respectively of the fully supervised *Sup* model. Our joint model *Q2QProj* achieves a UAS score similar to the supervised model, though its segmentation performance is lower. The ensemble model *Ens* provides additional improvement, hinting that the *Sup* and *DistPipe* models may have learned somewhat different segmentation cues. The segmentation F1 of Clear is as low as 2.2, as its training set contains only single-segment sentences.

We note that the intersection between the multi-segment subset and the '≤ 1 ncw' subset is only 622 queries (63.4% of the multi-seg set, 36.7% of '≤ 1 ncw'), and with *LowConf* it is only 524 queries (53.3% of the multi-seg set, 43.7% of *LowConf*). This demonstrates that our *Dist* model is of merit for a variety of query types.

On Single-segment queries, our joint model, *Q2QProj*, achieves the best UAS. This may be because it provides the parser with more context for telegraphic single-segment queries, so much so, that it even outperforms the *Gold* benchmark. Both the *Q2QProj* and *DistPipe* models over-segment (86.5 and 86.8 F1), compared to the near perfect single-segment detection of the supervised *Sup* model (96.2). Still, these differences are only mildly reflected in the UAS scores for single-segment queries.

6.4 Error Analysis

To better understand our distant-supervised signal, we applied the CRF tagger introduced in §4 (without additional filtering) to the test set and analyzed two cases: 100 *false positives* – single-segment queries which were incorrectly tagged with multiple segments, and 100 *false negatives* – multi-segment queries the tagger was wrong to tag as having a single segment.

---

[11]Several other taggers we experimented with gave similar accuracy figures: ClearNLP, the Stanford tagger and the Stanford parser.

[12]These subsets are extracted using the gold standard and are therefore not available to the models at inference time.

Test Set / Setup	All Queries (N=4000)		$\leq 1\ ncw$ (N=1694)		*LowConf* (N=1199)	
	F1	UAS	F1	UAS	F1	UAS
Gold	100	80.7	100	81.9	100	73.5
Ens	**70.4**	76.4	**63.5**	**73.0**	**59.2**	**64.6**
Sup	70.3	76	59.1	71.1	52.8	62.4
DistPipe	70.3	76.3	63.2	72.8	58.6	64.3
Q2QProj	63.5	**77.1**	53.1	70.5	47.2	61.1
Lm	37.2	66.6	31.6	59.9	30.8	54.4
Clear	64.6	75.4	51.3	69.5	42.9	60.7

Table 5: Performance of the various models on various automatically-extractable subsets of the data. *All Queries* is our test set, the others are its subsets with: $\leq 1\ ncw$ – at most one non-content word according to POS tags; *LowConf* – a Clear parser confidence score of at most 0.8. 'F1' denotes segmentation F1.

Test Set / Setup	Multi-segment (N=984)		Single-segment (N=3016)	
	S. F1	UAS	S. F1	UAS
Gold	100	83.9	100	79.8
Ens	**46.6**	**68.7**	84.8	78.7
Sup	23.5	64.3	96.2	79.4
DistPipe	42.2	67.5	86.8	78.9
Q2QProj	21.2	64.3	86.5	**80.9**
Lm	29.6	60.4	41.6	68.4
Clear	2.2	60.5	**96.9**	79.8

Table 6: Performance on queries which have a single segment or multiple segments according to the gold standard.

Two types of queries cause most false positives cases. The first type, making up 65% of the errors, is a full (or nearly-full) question or sentence. In half of these cases, a word in the middle of the query, which often marks the beginning of a grammatical question, is incorrectly marked as a segment start. Such an example is "*[sherlock is the best show ever]*", where the underlined word *is* is the incorrectly tagged segment start. The other main error is the segmentation of a query consisting of a single noun phrase (19% of the cases), for example "*[clothing product testing]*".

Our false negative analysis discovered four main types of errors, where a multi-segment query is not segmented. The most frequent one (35%) is cases where the tagger did not detect a syntactic cue for a segment start, *e.g.* in "*[grilling pork chops] [seasoning]*", where '*and*' is potentially missing. Another common mistake (24%) is a named entity which is added as its own segment for context (usually in the beginning or the end of the query). Such a query is "*[biotin] [mcg vs mg]*". The third type of errors (17%) is queries for which segmentation detection requires the understanding of the semantics behind the query. One example is "*[movies on youtube] [list]*", where '*youtube list*' was construed as a single noun phrase. The forth type (11%) contains a reference for a preferred content provider by the searcher on its own segment, such as "*[is illuminati good] [yahoo]*".

This analysis shows that the more frequent errors involve semantics and require either a different segmentation approach, or more semantic-oriented features.

7 Conclusions

We studied the syntactic properties of Web queries with question intent. We motivated the need to extend the dependency grammar framework so that it accounts for such queries, and constructed a new Query Treebank, annotated according to the extended grammar. We then developed distant-supervised algorithms that can parse queries according to our grammar. Our algorithms outperform strong baselines, including a supervised model trained on thousands of manually segmented queries.

In future work we would like to improve the query analysis performance of our algorithms. In addition, we plan to assess the contribution of query parsing to IR tasks such as document retrieval and query reformulation.

Acknowledgments

We thank: Bettina Bolla and Shir Givoni, for their annotation work on Query Treebank; Avihai Mejer, for implementing the Q2Q element of the projection algorithm; and Joel Tetreault, for providing the infrastructure for the experiments in Section 3.3.

References

James Allan and Hema Raghavan. 2002. Using part-of-speech patterns to reduce query ambiguity. In *Proceedings of SIGIR*.

Cory Barr, Rosie Jones, and Moira Regelson. 2008. The linguistic structure of english web-search queries. In *Proceedings of the Conference on Empirical Methods in Natural Language Processing*. Association for Computational Linguistics.

Michael Bendersky, W Bruce Croft, and David A Smith. 2010. Structural annotation of search queries using pseudo-relevance feedback. In *Proceedings of the 19th ACM international conference on Information and knowledge management*, pages 1537–1540. ACM.

Michael Bendersky, W Bruce Croft, and David A Smith. 2011. Joint annotation of search queries. In *Proceedings of the 49th Annual Meeting of the Association for Computational Linguistics: Human Language Technologies-Volume 1*. Association for Computational Linguistics.

Shane Bergsma and Qin Iris Wang. 2007. Learning noun phrase query segmentation. In *EMNLP-CoNLL*. Citeseer.

Bernd Bohnet and Joakim Nivre. 2012. A transition-based system for joint part-of-speech tagging and labeled non-projective dependency parsing. In *Proceedings of EMNLP-CoNLL*, pages 1455–1465. Association for Computational Linguistics.

David Carmel, Avihai Mejer, Yuval Pinter, and Idan Szpektor. 2014. Improving term weighting for community question answering search using syntactic analysis. In *Proceedings of the 23rd ACM International Conference on Conference on Information and Knowledge Management, CIKM 2014, Shanghai, China, November 3-7, 2014*, pages 351–360.

Danqi Chen and Christopher D Manning. 2014. A fast and accurate dependency parser using neural networks. In *Proceedings of the 2014 Conference on Empirical Methods in Natural Language Processing (EMNLP)*, volume 1, pages 740–750.

Jinho D Choi and Andrew McCallum. 2013. Transition-based dependency parsing with selectional branching. In *ACL (1)*, pages 1052–1062.

Jino Choi, Joel Tetreault, and Amanda Stent. 2015. It depends: Dependency parser comparison using a web-based evaluation tool. In *Proceedings of ACL-IJCNLP*.

Marie-Catherine De Marneffe and Christopher D Manning. 2008. The stanford typed dependencies representation. In *Coling 2008: Proceedings of the workshop on Cross-Framework and Cross-Domain Parser Evaluation*, pages 1–8. Association for Computational Linguistics.

Gideon Dror, Yoelle Maarek, Avihai Mejer, and Idan Szpektor. 2013. From Query to Question in One Click: Suggesting Synthetic Questions to Searchers. In *Proceedings of WWW 2013*.

Jacob Eisenstein. 2013. What to do about bad language on the internet. In *Proceedings of NAACL-HLT*.

Jennifer Foster, Joachim Wagner, and Josef van Genabith. 2008. Adapting a wsj-trained parser to grammatically noisy text. In *Proceedings of ACL-HLT: Short Papers*.

Jennifer Foster, Özlem Çetinoglu, Joachim Wagner, Joseph Le Roux, Stephen Hogan, Joakim Nivre, Deirdre Hogan, Josef Van Genabith, et al. 2011. # hardtoparse: Pos tagging and parsing the twitterverse. In *proceedings of the Workshop On Analyzing Microtext (AAAI 2011)*, pages 20–25.

Kuzman Ganchev, Keith Hall, Ryan McDonald, and Slav Petrov. 2012. Using search-logs to improve query tagging. In *Proceedings of the 50th Annual Meeting of the Association for Computational Linguistics (Volume 2: Short Papers)*.

Yoav Goldberg and Joakim Nivre. 2013. Training deterministic parsers with non-deterministic oracles. *Transactions of the association for Computational Linguistics*, 1:403–414.

Jiafeng Guo, Gu Xu, Hang Li, and Xueqi Cheng. 2008. A unified and discriminative model for query refinement. In *Proceedings of the 31st annual international ACM SIGIR conference on Research and development in information retrieval*, pages 379–386. ACM.

Matthias Hagen, Martin Potthast, Anna Beyer, and Benno Stein. 2012. Towards optimum query segmentation: in doubt without. In *Proceedings of CIKM*.

Matthew Honnibal, Yoav Goldberg, and Mark Johnson. 2013. A non-monotonic arc-eager transition system for dependency parsing. In *Proceedings of the Seventeenth Conference on Computational Natural Language Learning*, pages 163–172. Citeseer.

Dan Klein and Christopher D. Manning. 2003. Accurate unlexicalized parsing. In *Proceedings of the 41st Annual Meeting on Association for Computational Linguistics - Volume 1*.

Lingpeng Kong, Nathan Schneider, Swabha Swayamdipta, Archna Bhatia, Chris Dyer, and Noah A. Smith. 2014. A dependency parser for tweets. In *Proceedings of the 2014 Conference on Empirical Methods in Natural Language Processing (EMNLP)*.

John Lafferty, Andrew McCallum, and Fernando CN Pereira. 2001. Conditional random fields: Probabilistic models for segmenting and labeling sequence data. In *ICML*.

Tao Lei, Yu Xin, Yuan Zhang, Regina Barzilay, and Tommi Jaakkola. 2014. Low-rank tensors for scoring dependency structures. In *Proceedings of the 52nd Annual Meeting of the Association for Computational Linguistics*, volume 1, pages 1381–1391.

Xiao Li. 2010. Understanding the semantic structure of noun phrase queries. In *Proceedings of the 48th Annual Meeting of the Association for Computational Linguistics*.

Qiaoling Liu, Eugene Agichtein, Gideon Dror, Evgeniy Gabrilovich, Yoelle Maarek, Dan Pelleg, and Idan Szpektor. 2011. Predicting web searcher satisfaction with existing community-based answers. In *Proceeding of the 34th International ACM SIGIR Conference on Research and Development in Information Retrieval, SIGIR 2011, Beijing, China, July 25-29, 2011*, pages 415–424.

Mehdi Manshadi and Xiao Li. 2009. Semantic tagging of web search queries. In *Proceedings of the ACL-IJCNLP*.

Mitchell P Marcus, Mary Ann Marcinkiewicz, and Beatrice Santorini. 1993. Building a large annotated corpus of english: The penn treebank. *Computational linguistics*.

André FT Martins, Miguel Almeida, and Noah A Smith. 2013. Turning on the turbo: Fast third-order non-projective turbo parsers. In *ACL (2)*, pages 617–622. Citeseer.

David McClosky, Eugene Charniak, and Mark Johnson. 2010. Automatic domain adaptation for parsing. In *Human Language Technologies: The 2010 Annual Conference of the North American Chapter of the Association for Computational Linguistics*.

Tomáš Mikolov. 2012. *Statistical Language Models Based on Neural Networks*. Ph.D. thesis, Ph. D. thesis, Brno University of Technology.

Nikita Mishra, Rishiraj Saha Roy, Niloy Ganguly, Srivatsan Laxman, and Monojit Choudhury. 2011. Unsupervised query segmentation using only query logs. In *Proceedings of WWW*, pages 91–92.

Slav Petrov and Ryan McDonald. 2012. Overview of the 2012 shared task on parsing the web. In *Notes of the First Workshop on Syntactic Analysis of Non-Canonical Language (SANCL)*, volume 59. Citeseer.

Bin Tan and Fuchun Peng. 2008. Unsupervised query segmentation using generative language models and wikipedia. In *Proceedings of WWW*.

Kristina Toutanova, Dan Klein, Christopher D. Manning, and Yoram Singer. 2003. Feature-rich part-of-speech tagging with a cyclic dependency network. In *Proceedings of HLT-NAACL*.

Gilad Tsur, Yuval Pinter, Idan Szpektor, and David Carmel. 2016. Identifying web queries with question intent. In *Proceedings of WWW*.

Ralph Weischedel, Martha Palmer, Mitchell Marcus, Eduard Hovy, Sameer Pradhan, Lance Ramshaw, Nianwen Xue, Ann Taylor, Jeff Kaufman, Michelle Franchini, Mohammed El-Bachouti, Robert Belvin, and Ann Houston, 2013. *OntoNotes Release 5.0*.

Ryen W. White, Matthew Richardson, and Wen-tau Yih. 2015. Questions vs. queries in informational search tasks. In *Proceedings of WWW'15 Companion*, pages 135–136. WWW.

Visualizing and Understanding Neural Models in NLP

Jiwei Li[1], Xinlei Chen[2], Eduard Hovy[2] and Dan Jurafsky[1]
[1]Computer Science Department, Stanford University, Stanford, CA 94305, USA
[2]Language Technology Institute, Carnegie Mellon University, Pittsburgh, PA 15213, USA
{jiweil,jurafsky}@stanford.edu   {xinleic,ehovy}@andrew.cmu.edu

Abstract

While neural networks have been successfully applied to many NLP tasks the resulting vector-based models are very difficult to interpret. For example it's not clear how they achieve *compositionality*, building sentence meaning from the meanings of words and phrases. In this paper we describe strategies for visualizing compositionality in neural models for NLP, inspired by similar work in computer vision. We first plot unit values to visualize compositionality of negation, intensification, and concessive clauses, allowing us to see well-known markedness asymmetries in negation. We then introduce methods for visualizing a unit's *salience*, the amount that it contributes to the final composed meaning from first-order derivatives. Our general-purpose methods may have wide applications for understanding compositionality and other semantic properties of deep networks.

1   Introduction

Neural models match or outperform the performance of other state-of-the-art systems on a variety of NLP tasks. Yet unlike traditional feature-based classifiers that assign and optimize weights to varieties of human interpretable features (parts-of-speech, named entities, word shapes, syntactic parse features etc) the behavior of deep learning models is much less easily interpreted. Deep learning models mainly operate on word embeddings (low-dimensional, continuous, real-valued vectors) through multi-layer neural architectures, each layer of which is characterized as an array of hidden neuron units. It is unclear how deep learning models deal with *composition*, implementing functions like negation or intensification, or combining meaning from different parts of the sentence, filtering away the informational chaff from the wheat, to build sentence meaning.

In this paper, we explore multiple strategies to interpret meaning composition in neural models. We employ traditional methods like representation plotting, and introduce simple strategies for measuring how much a neural unit contributes to meaning composition, its 'salience' or importance using first derivatives.

Visualization techniques/models represented in this work shed important light on how neural models work: For example, we illustrate that LSTM's success is due to its ability in maintaining a much sharper focus on the important key words than other models; Composition in multiple clauses works competitively, and that the models are able to capture negative asymmetry, an important property of semantic compositionally in natural language understanding; there is sharp dimensional locality, with certain dimensions marking negation and quantification in a manner that was surprisingly localist. Though our attempts only touch superficial points in neural models, and each method has its pros and cons, together they may offer some insights into the behaviors of neural models in language based tasks, marking one initial step toward understanding how they achieve meaning composition in natural language processing.

The next section describes some visualization models in vision and NLP that have inspired this work. We describe datasets and the adopted neural models in Section 3. Different visualization strategies and correspondent analytical results are presented

Proceedings of NAACL-HLT 2016, pages 681–691,
San Diego, California, June 12-17, 2016. ©2016 Association for Computational Linguistics

separately in Section 4,5,6, followed by a brief conclusion.

2 A Brief Review of Neural Visualization

Similarity is commonly visualized graphically, generally by projecting the embedding space into two dimensions and observing that similar words tend to be clustered together (e.g., Elman (1989), Ji and Eisenstein (2014), Faruqui and Dyer (2014)). (Karpathy et al., 2015) attempts to interpret recurrent neural models from a statical point of view and does deeply touch compositionally of meanings. Other relevant attempts include (Fyshe et al., 2015; Faruqui et al., 2015).

Methods for interpreting and visualizing neural models have been much more significantly explored in vision, especially for Convolutional Neural Networks (CNNs or ConvNets) (Krizhevsky et al., 2012), multi-layer neural networks in which the original matrix of image pixels is convolved and pooled as it is passed on to hidden layers. ConvNet visualizing techniques consist mainly in mapping the different layers of the network (or other features like SIFT (Lowe, 2004) and HOG (Dalal and Triggs, 2005)) back to the initial image input, thus capturing the human-interpretable information they represent in the input, and how units in these layers contribute to any final decisions (Simonyan et al., 2013; Mahendran and Vedaldi, 2014; Nguyen et al., 2014; Szegedy et al., 2013; Girshick et al., 2014; Zeiler and Fergus, 2014). Such methods include:

(1) Inversion: Inverting the representations by training an additional model to project outputs from different neural levels back to the initial input images (Mahendran and Vedaldi, 2014; Vondrick et al., 2013; Weinzaepfel et al., 2011). The intuition behind reconstruction is that the pixels that are reconstructable from the current representations are the content of the representation. The inverting algorithms allow the current representation to align with corresponding parts of the original images.

(2) Back-propagation (Erhan et al., 2009; Simonyan et al., 2013) and Deconvolutional Networks (Zeiler and Fergus, 2014): Errors are back propagated from output layers to each intermediate layer and finally to the original image inputs. Deconvolutional Networks work in a similar way by projecting outputs back to initial inputs layer by layer, each layer associated with one supervised model for projecting upper ones to lower ones These strategies make it possible to spot active regions or ones that contribute the most to the final classification decision.

(3) Generation: This group of work generates images in a specific class from a sketch guided by already trained neural models (Szegedy et al., 2013; Nguyen et al., 2014). Models begin with an image whose pixels are randomly initialized and mutated at each step. The specific layers that are activated at different stages of image construction can help in interpretation.

While the above strategies inspire the work we present in this paper, there are fundamental differences between vision and NLP. In NLP words function as basic units, and hence (word) vectors rather than single pixels are the basic units. Sequences of words (e.g., phrases and sentences) are also presented in a more structured way than arrangements of pixels. In parallel to our research, independent researches (Karpathy et al., 2015) have been conducted to explore similar direction from an error-analysis point of view, by analyzing predictions and errors from a recurrent neural models. Other distantly relevant works include: Murphy et al. (2012; Fyshe et al. (2015) used an manual task to quantify the interpretability of semantic dimensions by presetting human users with a list of words and ask them to choose the one that does not belong to the list. Faruqui et al. (2015). Similar strategy is adopted in (Faruqui et al., 2015) by extracting top-ranked words in each vector dimension.

3 Datasets and Neural Models

We explored two datasets on which neural models are trained, one of which is of relatively small scale and the other of large scale.

3.1 Stanford Sentiment Treebank

Stanford Sentiment Treebank is a benchmark dataset widely used for neural model evaluations. The dataset contains gold-standard sentiment labels for every parse tree constituent, from sentences to phrases to individual words, for 215,154 phrases in 11,855 sentences. The task is to perform both fine-grained (very positive, positive, neutral, negative and very negative) and coarse-grained (positive vs negative) classification at both the phrase and sentence level. For more details about the dataset, please refer to Socher et al. (2013).

While many studies on this dataset use recursive parse-tree models, in this work we employ only standard sequence models (RNNs and LSTMs) since these are the most widely used current neural models, and sequential visualization is more straightforward. We therefore first transform each parse tree node to a sequence of tokens. The sequence is first mapped to a phrase/sentence representation and fed into a softmax classifier. Phrase/sentence representations are built with the following three models: *Standard Recurrent Sequence* with TANH activation functions, *LSTMs* and *Bidirectional LSTMs*. For details about the three models, please refer to Appendix.

Training AdaGrad with mini-batch was used for training, with parameters ($L2$ penalty, learning rate, mini batch size) tuned on the development set. The number of iterations is treated as a variable to tune and parameters are harvested based on the best performance on the dev set. The number of dimensions for the word and hidden layer are set to 60 with 0.1 dropout rate. Parameters are tuned on the dev set. The standard recurrent model achieves 0.429 (fine grained) and 0.850 (coarse grained) accuracy at the sentence level; LSTM achieves 0.469 and 0.870, and Bidirectional LSTM 0.488 and 0.878, respectively.

3.2 Sequence-to-Sequence Models

SEQ2SEQ are neural models aiming at generating a sequence of output texts given inputs. Theoretically, SEQ2SEQ models can be adapted to NLP tasks that can be formalized as predicting outputs given inputs and serve for different purposes due to different inputs and outputs, e.g., machine translation where inputs correspond to source sentences and outputs to target sentences (Sutskever et al., 2014; Luong et al., 2014); conversational response generation if inputs correspond to messages and outputs correspond to responses (Vinyals and Le, 2015; Li et al., 2015). SEQ2SEQ need to be trained on massive amount of data for implicitly semantic and syntactic relations between pairs to be learned.

SEQ2SEQ models map an input sequence to a vector representation using LSTM models and then sequentially predicts tokens based on the pre-obtained representation. The model defines a distribution over outputs (Y) and sequentially predicts tokens given

inputs (X) using a softmax function.

$$P(Y|X) = \prod_{t=1}^{n_y} p(y_t|x_1, x_2, ..., x_t, y_1, y_2, ..., y_{t-1})$$

$$= \prod_{t=1}^{n_y} \frac{\exp(f(h_{t-1}, e_{y_t}))}{\sum_{y'} \exp(f(h_{t-1}, e_{y'}))}$$

where $f(h_{t-1}, e_{y_t})$ denotes the activation function between h_{t-1} and e_{y_t}, where h_{t-1} is the representation output from the LSTM at time $t - 1$. For each time step in word prediction, SEQ2SEQ models combine the current token with previously built embeddings for next-step word prediction.

For easy visualization purposes, we turn to the most straightforward task—autoencoder— where inputs and outputs are identical. The goal of an autoencoder is to reconstruct inputs from the pre-obtained representation. We would like to see how individual input tokens affect the overall sentence representation and each of the tokens to predict in outputs. We trained the auto-encoder on a subset of WMT'14 corpus containing 4 million english sentences with an average length of 22.5 words. We followed training protocols described in (Sutskever et al., 2014).

4 Representation Plotting

We begin with simple plots of representations to shed light on local compositions using Stanford Sentiment Treebank.

Local Composition Figure 1 shows a 60d heatmap vector for the representation of selected words/phrases/sentences, with an emphasis on extent modifications (adverbial and adjectival) and negation. Embeddings for phrases or sentences are attained by composing word representations from the pretrained model.

The intensification part of Figure 1 shows suggestive patterns where values for a few dimensions are strengthened by modifiers like "a lot" (the red bar in the first example) "so much" (the red bar in the second example), and "incredibly". Though the patterns for negations are not as clear, there is still a consistent reversal for some dimensions, visible as a shift between blue and red for dimensions boxed on the left.

We then visualize words and phrases using t-sne (Van der Maaten and Hinton, 2008) in Figure 2, de-

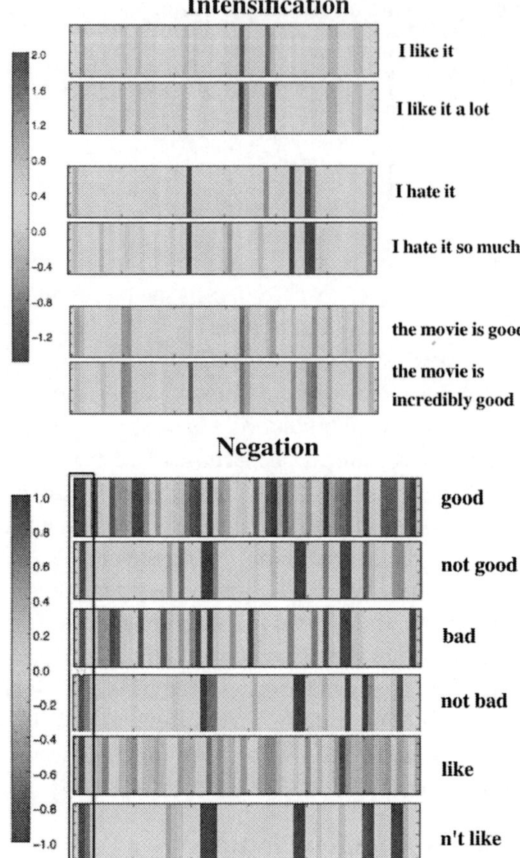

Figure 1: Visualizing intensification and negation. Each vertical bar shows the value of one dimension in the final sentence/phrase representation after compositions. Embeddings for phrases or sentences are attained by composing word representations from the pretrained model.

liberately adding in some random words for comparative purposes. As can be seen, neural models nicely learn the properties of local compositionally, clustering negation+positive words ('not nice', 'not good') together with negative words. Note also the asymmetry of negation: "not bad" is clustered more with the negative than the positive words (as shown both in Figure 1 and 2). This asymmetry has been widely discussed in linguistics, for example as arising from markedness, since 'good' is the unmarked direction of the scale (0; Horn, 1989; Fraenkel and Schul, 2008). This suggests that although the model does seem to focus on certain units for negation in Figure 1, the neural model is not just learning to apply a fixed transform for 'not' but is able to capture the subtle differences in the composition of different words.

Concessive Sentences In concessive sentences, two clauses have opposite polarities, usually related by a contrary-to-expectation implicature. We plot evolving representations over time for two concessives in Figure 3. The plots suggest:

1. For tasks like sentiment analysis whose goal is to predict a specific semantic dimension (as opposed to general tasks like language model word prediction), too large a dimensionality leads to many dimensions non-functional (with values close to 0), causing two sentences of opposite sentiment to differ only in a few dimensions. This may explain why more dimensions don't necessarily lead to better performance on such tasks (For example, as reported in (Socher et al., 2013), optimal performance is achieved when word dimensionality is set to between 25 and 35).

2. Both sentences contain two clauses connected by the conjunction "though". Such two-clause sentences might either work *collaboratively*— models would remember the word "though" and make the second clause share the same sentiment orientation as first—or *competitively*, with the stronger one dominating. The region within dotted line in Figure 3(a) favors the second assumption: the difference between the two sentences is diluted when the final words ("interesting" and "boring") appear.

Clause Composition In Figure 4 we explore this clause composition in more detail. Representations move closer to the negative sentiment region by adding negative clauses like "although it had bad acting" or "but it is too long" to the end of a simply positive "I like the movie". By contrast, adding a concessive clause to a negative clause does not move toward the positive; "I hate X but ..." is still very negative, not that different than "I hate X". This difference again suggests the model is able to capture negative asymmetry (0; Horn, 1989; Fraenkel and Schul, 2008).

5   First-Derivative Saliency

In this section, we describe another strategy which is is inspired by the back-propagation strategy in vision (Erhan et al., 2009; Simonyan et al., 2013). It measures how much each input unit contributes to

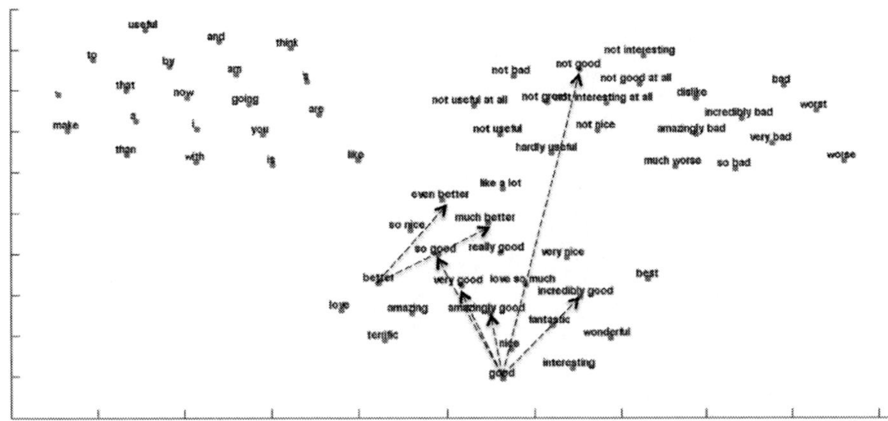

Figure 2: t-SNE Visualization on latent representations for modifications and negations.

the final decision, which can be approximated by first derivatives.

More formally, for a classification model, an input E is associated with a gold-standard class label c. (Depending on the NLP task, an input could be the embedding for a word or a sequence of words, while labels could be POS tags, sentiment labels, the next word index to predict etc.) Given embeddings E for input words with the associated gold class label c, the trained model associates the pair (E, c) with a score $S_c(E)$. The goal is to decide which units of E make the most significant contribution to $S_c(e)$, and thus the decision, the choice of class label c.

In the case of deep neural models, the class score $S_c(e)$ is a highly non-linear function. We approximate $S_c(e)$ with a linear function of e by computing the first-order Taylor expansion

$$S_c(e) \approx w(e)^T e + b \qquad (1)$$

where $w(e)$ is the derivative of S_c with respect to the embedding e.

$$w(e) = \frac{\partial(S_c)}{\partial e}\Big|_e \qquad (2)$$

The magnitude (absolute value) of the derivative indicates the sensitiveness of the final decision to the change in one particular dimension, telling us how much one specific dimension of the word embedding contributes to the final decision. The saliency score is given by

$$S(e) = |w(e)| \qquad (3)$$

5.1 Results on Stanford Sentiment Treebank

We first illustrate results on Stanford Treebank. We plot in Figures 5, 6 and 7 the saliency scores (the absolute value of the derivative of the loss function with respect to each dimension of all word inputs) for three sentences, applying the trained model to each sentence. Each row corresponds to saliency score for the correspondent word representation with each grid representing each dimension. The examples are based on the clear sentiment indicator "hate" that lends them all negative sentiment.

"I hate the movie" All three models assign high saliency to "hate" and dampen the influence of other tokens. LSTM offers a clearer focus on "hate" than the standard recurrent model, but the bi-directional LSTM shows the clearest focus, attaching almost zero emphasis on words other than "hate". This is presumably due to the gates structures in LSTMs and Bi-LSTMs that controls information flow, making these architectures better at filtering out less relevant information.

"I hate the movie that I saw last night" All three models assign the correct sentiment. The simple recurrent models again do poorly at filtering out irrelevant information, assigning too much salience to words unrelated to sentiment. However none of the models suffer from the gradient vanishing problems despite this sentence being longer; the salience of "hate" still stands out after 7-8 following convolutional operations.

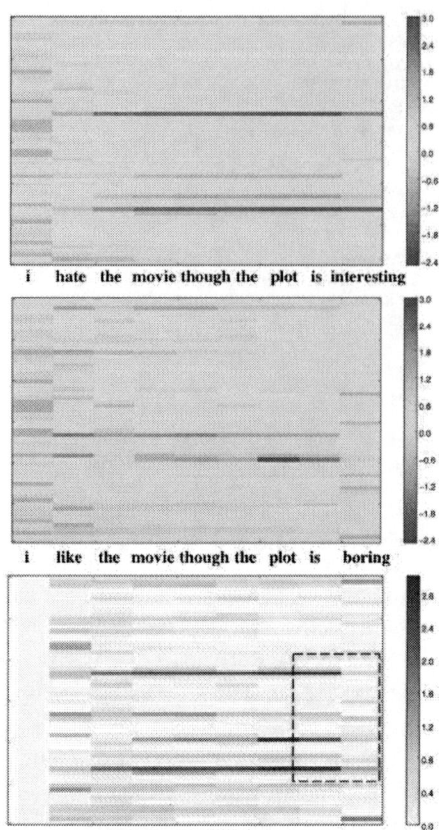

Figure 3: Representations over time from LSTMs. Each column corresponds to outputs from LSTM at each time-step (representations obtained after combining current word embedding with previous build embeddings). Each grid from the column corresponds to each dimension of current time-step representation. The last rows correspond to absolute differences for each time step between two sequences.

"I hate the movie though the plot is interesting"
The simple recurrent model emphasizes only the second clause "the plot is interesting", assigning no credit to the first clause "I hate the movie". This might seem to be caused by a vanishing gradient, yet the model correctly classifies the sentence as very negative, suggesting that it is successfully incorporating information from the first negative clause. We separately tested the individual clause "though the plot is interesting". The standard recurrent model confidently labels it as positive. Thus despite the lower saliency scores for words in the first clause, the simple recurrent system manages to rely on that

clause and downplay the information from the latter positive clause—despite the higher saliency scores of the later words. This illustrates a limitation of saliency visualization. first-order derivatives don't capture all the information we would like to visualize, perhaps because they are only a rough approximate to individual contributions and might not suffice to deal with highly non-linear cases. By contrast, the LSTM emphasizes the first clause, sharply dampening the influence from the second clause, while the Bi-LSTM focuses on both "hate the movie" and "plot is interesting".

5.2 Results on Sequence-to-Sequence Autoencoder

Figure 9 represents saliency heatmap for autoencoder in terms of predicting correspondent token at each time step. We compute first-derivatives for each preceding word through back-propagation as decoding goes on. Each grid corresponds to magnitude of average saliency value for each 1000-dimensional word vector. The heatmaps give clear overview about the behavior of neural models during decoding. Observations can be summarized as follows:

1. For each time step of word prediction, SEQ2SEQ models manage to link word to predict back to correspondent region at the inputs (automatically learn alignments), e.g., input region centering around token "hate" exerts more impact when token "hate" is to be predicted, similar cases with tokens "movie", "plot" and "boring".

2. Neural decoding combines the previously built representation with the word predicted at the current step. As decoding proceeds, the influence of the initial input on decoding (i.e., tokens in source sentences) gradually diminishes as more previously-predicted words are encoded in the vector representations. Meanwhile, the influence of language model gradually dominates: when word "boring" is to be predicted, models attach more weight to earlier predicted tokens "plot" and "is" but less to correspondent regions in the inputs, i.e., the word "boring" in inputs.

6   Average and Variance

For settings where word embeddings are treated as parameters to optimize from scratch (as opposed to using pre-trained embeddings), we propose a second,

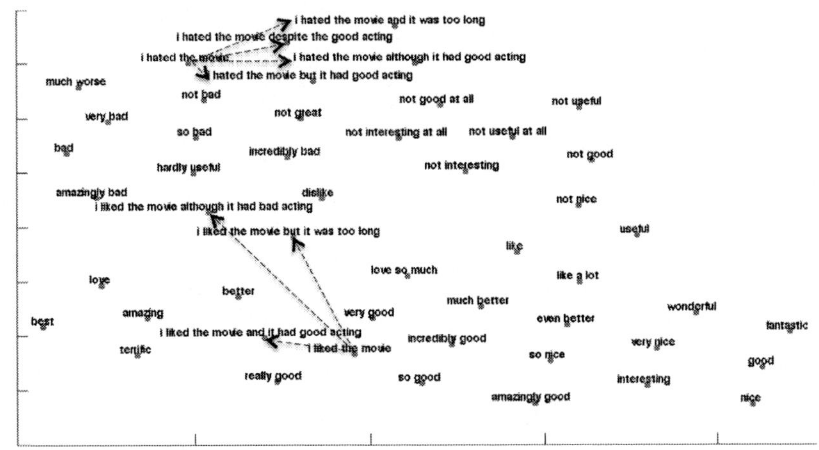

Figure 4: t-SNE Visualization for clause composition.

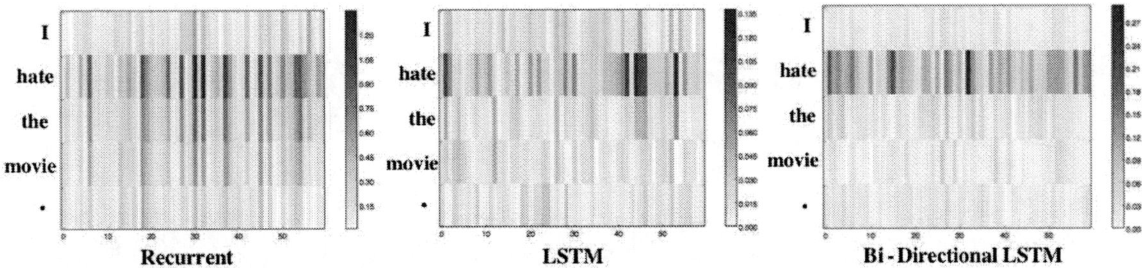

Figure 5: Saliency heatmap for for "I hate the movie ." Each row corresponds to saliency scores for the correspondent word representation with each grid representing each dimension.

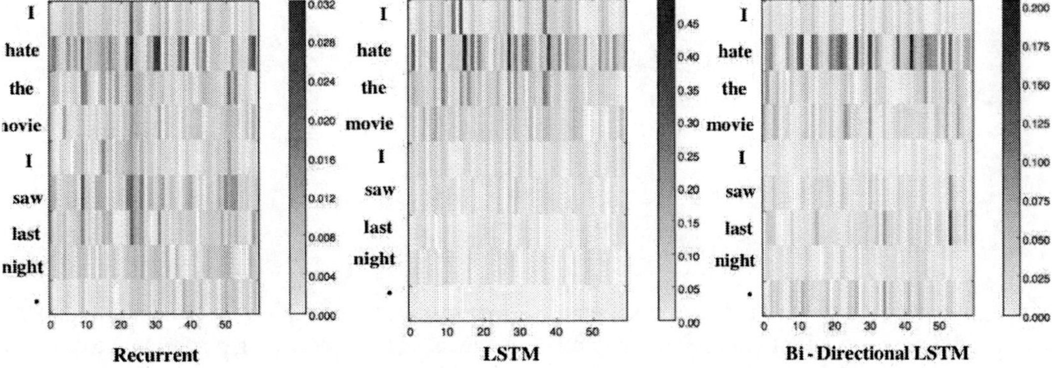

Figure 6: Saliency heatmap for "I hate the movie I saw last night ." .

surprisingly easy and direct way to visualize important indicators. We first compute the average of the word embeddings for all the words within the sentences. The measure of salience or influence for a word is its deviation from this average. The idea is that during training, models would learn to render indicators different from non-indicator words, enabling them to stand out even after many layers of computation.

Figure 8 shows a map of variance; each grid corresponds to the value of $||e_{i,j} - \frac{1}{N_S}\sum_{i' \in N_S} e_{i'j}||^2$ where $e_{i,j}$ denotes the value for j th dimension of word i and N denotes the number of token within the sentences.

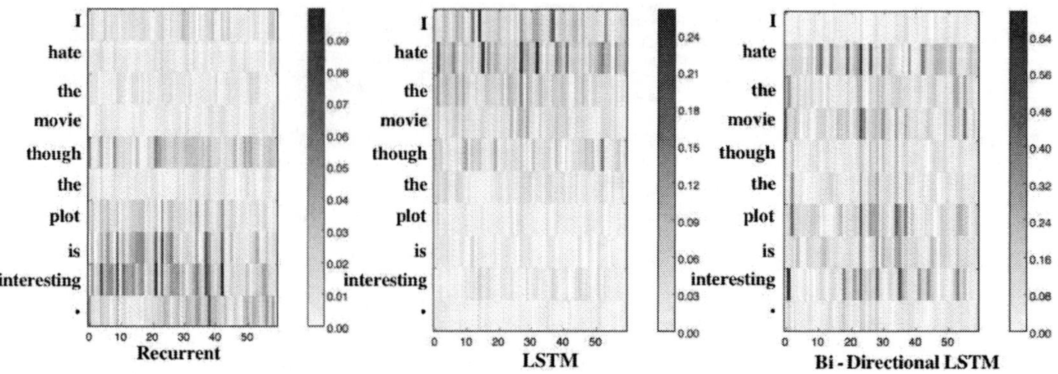

Figure 7: Saliency heatmap for "I hate the movie though the plot is interesting ." .

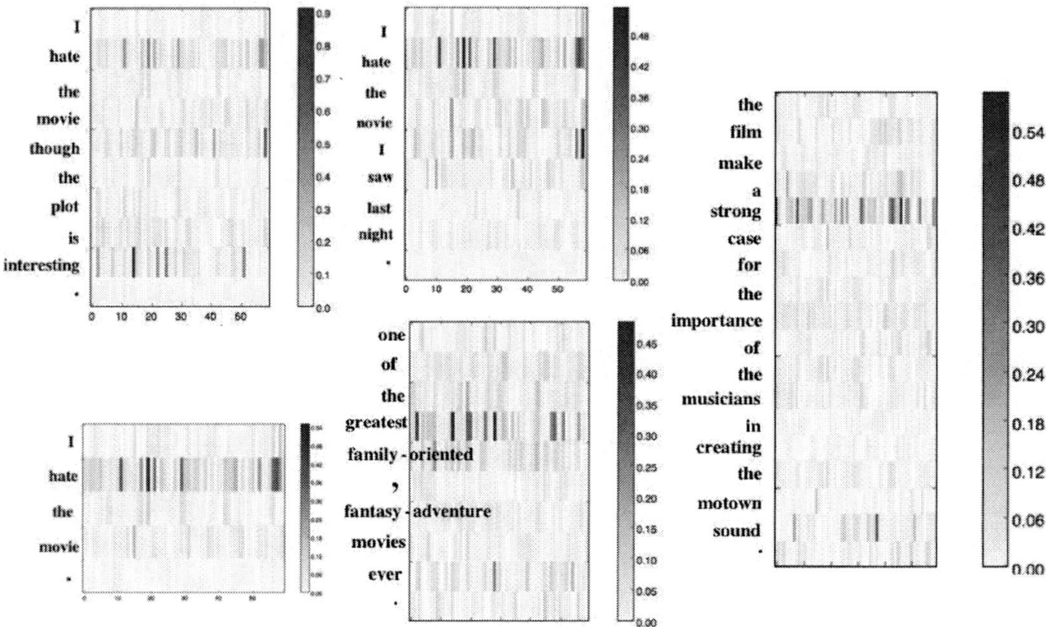

Figure 8: Variance visualization.

As the figure shows, the variance-based salience measure also does a good job of emphasizing the relevant sentiment words. The model does have shortcomings: (1) it can only be used in to scenarios where word embeddings are parameters to learn (2) it's clear how well the model is able to visualize local compositionality.

7 Conclusion

In this paper, we offer several methods to help visualize and interpret neural models, to understand how neural models are able to compose meanings, demonstrating asymmetries of negation and explain some aspects of the strong performance of LSTMs at these tasks.

Though our attempts only touch superficial points in neural models, and each method has its pros and cons, together they may offer some insights into the behaviors of neural models in language based tasks, marking one initial step toward understanding how they achieve meaning composition in natural language processing. Our future work includes using results of the visualization be used to perform error analysis, and understanding strengths limitations of

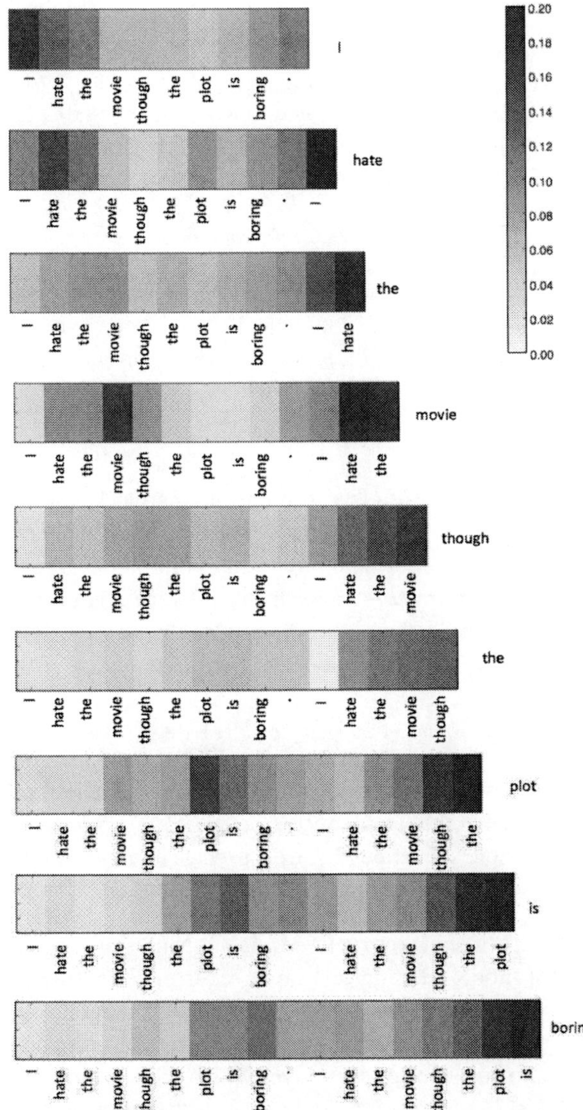

Figure 9: Saliency heatmap for SEQ2SEQ auto-encoder in terms of predicting correspondent token at each time step.

different neural models.

8 Acknowledgement

The authors want to thank Sam Bowman, Percy Liang, Will Monroe, Sida Wang, Chris Manning and other members of the Stanford NLP group, as well as anonymous reviewers for their helpful advice on various aspects of this work. This work partially supported by NSF Award IIS-1514268. Jiwei Li is supported by Facebook fellowship, which we gratefully acknowledge. Any opinions, findings, and conclusions or recommendations expressed in this material are those of the authors and do not necessarily reflect the views of NSF or Facebook.

References

Herbert H. Clark and Eve V. Clark. 1977. *Psychology and language: An introduction to psycholinguistics.* Harcourt Brace Jovanovich.

Navneet Dalal and Bill Triggs. 2005. Histograms of oriented gradients for human detection. In *Computer Vision and Pattern Recognition, 2005. CVPR 2005. IEEE Computer Society Conference on*, volume 1, pages 886–893. IEEE.

Jeffrey L. Elman. 1989. Representation and structure in connectionist models. Technical Report 8903, Center for Research in Language, University of California, San Diego.

Dumitru Erhan, Yoshua Bengio, Aaron Courville, and Pascal Vincent. 2009. Visualizing higher-layer features of a deep network. *Dept. IRO, Université de Montréal, Tech. Rep.*

Manaal Faruqui and Chris Dyer. 2014. Improving vector space word representations using multilingual correlation. In *Proceedings of EACL*, volume 2014.

Manaal Faruqui, Yulia Tsvetkov, Dani Yogatama, Chris Dyer, and Noah Smith. 2015. Sparse overcomplete word vector representations. *arXiv preprint arXiv:1506.02004.*

Tamar Fraenkel and Yaacov Schul. 2008. The meaning of negated adjectives. *Intercultural Pragmatics*, 5(4):517–540.

Alona Fyshe, Leila Wehbe, Partha P Talukdar, Brian Murphy, and Tom M Mitchell. 2015. A compositional and interpretable semantic space. *Proceedings of the NAACL-HLT, Denver, USA.*

Ross Girshick, Jeff Donahue, Trevor Darrell, and Jitendra Malik. 2014. Rich feature hierarchies for accurate object detection and semantic segmentation. In *Computer Vision and Pattern Recognition (CVPR), 2014 IEEE Conference on*, pages 580–587. IEEE.

Sepp Hochreiter and Jürgen Schmidhuber. 1997. Long short-term memory. *Neural computation*, 9(8):1735–1780.

Laurence R. Horn. 1989. *A natural history of negation*, volume 960. University of Chicago Press Chicago.

Yangfeng Ji and Jacob Eisenstein. 2014. Representation learning for text-level discourse parsing. In *Proceedings of the 52nd Annual Meeting of the Association for Computational Linguistics*, volume 1, pages 13–24.

Andrej Karpathy, Justin Johnson, and Fei-Fei Li. 2015. Visualizing and understanding recurrent networks. *arXiv preprint arXiv:1506.02078.*

Alex Krizhevsky, Ilya Sutskever, and Geoffrey E Hinton. 2012. Imagenet classification with deep convolutional neural networks. In *Advances in neural information processing systems*, pages 1097–1105.

Jiwei Li, Michel Galley, Chris Brockett, Jianfeng Gao, and Bill Dolan. 2015. A diversity-promoting objective function for neural conversation models. *arXiv preprint arXiv:1510.03055*.

David G Lowe. 2004. Distinctive image features from scale-invariant keypoints. *International journal of computer vision*, 60(2):91–110.

Thang Luong, Ilya Sutskever, Quoc V Le, Oriol Vinyals, and Wojciech Zaremba. 2014. Addressing the rare word problem in neural machine translation. *arXiv preprint arXiv:1410.8206*.

Aravindh Mahendran and Andrea Vedaldi. 2014. Understanding deep image representations by inverting them. *arXiv preprint arXiv:1412.0035*.

Brian Murphy, Partha Pratim Talukdar, and Tom M Mitchell. 2012. Learning effective and interpretable semantic models using non-negative sparse embedding. In *COLING*, pages 1933–1950.

Anh Nguyen, Jason Yosinski, and Jeff Clune. 2014. Deep neural networks are easily fooled: High confidence predictions for unrecognizable images. *arXiv preprint arXiv:1412.1897*.

Mike Schuster and Kuldip K Paliwal. 1997. Bidirectional recurrent neural networks. *Signal Processing, IEEE Transactions on*, 45(11):2673–2681.

Karen Simonyan, Andrea Vedaldi, and Andrew Zisserman. 2013. Deep inside convolutional networks: Visualising image classification models and saliency maps. *arXiv preprint arXiv:1312.6034*.

Richard Socher, Alex Perelygin, Jean Y Wu, Jason Chuang, Christopher D Manning, Andrew Y Ng, and Christopher Potts. 2013. Recursive deep models for semantic compositionality over a sentiment treebank. In *Proceedings of the conference on empirical methods in natural language processing (EMNLP)*, volume 1631, page 1642. Citeseer.

Ilya Sutskever, Oriol Vinyals, and Quoc VV Le. 2014. Sequence to sequence learning with neural networks. In *Advances in Neural Information Processing Systems*, pages 3104–3112.

Christian Szegedy, Wojciech Zaremba, Ilya Sutskever, Joan Bruna, Dumitru Erhan, Ian Goodfellow, and Rob Fergus. 2013. Intriguing properties of neural networks. *arXiv preprint arXiv:1312.6199*.

Laurens Van der Maaten and Geoffrey Hinton. 2008. Visualizing data using t-sne. *Journal of Machine Learning Research*, 9(2579-2605):85.

Oriol Vinyals and Quoc Le. 2015. A neural conversational model. *arXiv preprint arXiv:1506.05869*.

Carl Vondrick, Aditya Khosla, Tomasz Malisiewicz, and Antonio Torralba. 2013. Hoggles: Visualizing object detection features. In *Computer Vision (ICCV), 2013 IEEE International Conference on*, pages 1–8. IEEE.

Philippe Weinzaepfel, Hervé Jégou, and Patrick Pérez. 2011. Reconstructing an image from its local descriptors. In *Computer Vision and Pattern Recognition (CVPR), 2011 IEEE Conference on*, pages 337–344. IEEE.

Matthew D Zeiler and Rob Fergus. 2014. Visualizing and understanding convolutional networks. In *Computer Vision–ECCV 2014*, pages 818–833. Springer.

Appendix

Recurrent Models A recurrent network successively takes word w_t at step t, combines its vector representation e_t with previously built hidden vector h_{t-1} from time $t-1$, calculates the resulting current embedding h_t, and passes it to the next step. The embedding h_t for the current time t is thus:

$$h_t = f(W \cdot h_{t-1} + V \cdot e_t) \qquad (4)$$

where W and V denote compositional matrices. If N_s denote the length of the sequence, h_{N_s} represents the whole sequence S. h_{N_s} is used as input a softmax function for classification tasks.

Multi-layer Recurrent Models Multi-layer recurrent models extend one-layer recurrent structure by operation on a deep neural architecture that enables more expressivity and flexibly. The model associates each time step for each layer with a hidden representation $h_{l,t}$, where $l \in [1, L]$ denotes the index of layer and t denote the index of time step. $h_{l,t}$ is given by:

$$h_{t,l} = f(W \cdot h_{t-1,l} + V \cdot h_{t,l-1}) \qquad (5)$$

where $h_{t,0} = e_t$, which is the original word embedding input at current time step.

Long-short Term Memory LSTM model, first proposed in (Hochreiter and Schmidhuber, 1997), maps an input sequence to a fixed-sized vector by sequentially convoluting the current representation with the output representation of the previous step. LSTM associates each time epoch with an input, control and memory gate, and tries to minimize the impact of unrelated information. i_t, f_t and o_t denote to gate states at time t. h_t denotes the hidden vector outputted from LSTM model at time t and e_t denotes the word embedding input at time t. We have

$$
\begin{aligned}
i_t &= \sigma(W_i \cdot e_t + V_i \cdot h_{t-1}) \\
f_t &= \sigma(W_f \cdot e_t + V_f \cdot h_{t-1}) \\
o_t &= \sigma(W_o \cdot e_t + V_o \cdot h_{t-1}) \\
l_t &= \tanh(W_l \cdot e_t + V_l \cdot h_{t-1}) \\
c_t &= f_t \cdot c_{t-1} + i_t \times l_t \\
h_t &= o_t \cdot m_t
\end{aligned}
\tag{6}
$$

where σ denotes the sigmoid function. i_t, f_t and o_t are scalars within the range of [0,1]. $\times$ denotes pairwise dot.

A multi-layer LSTM models works in the same way as multi-layer recurrent models by enable multi-layer's compositions.

Bidirectional Models (Schuster and Paliwal, 1997) add bidirectionality to the recurrent framework where embeddings for each time are calculated both forwardly and backwardly:

$$
\begin{aligned}
\overrightarrow{h_t} &= f(W^{\rightarrow} \cdot \overrightarrow{h_{t-1}} + V^{\rightarrow} \cdot e_t) \\
\overleftarrow{h_t} &= f(W^{\leftarrow} \cdot \overleftarrow{h_{t+1}} + V^{\leftarrow} \cdot e_t)
\end{aligned}
\tag{7}
$$

Normally, bidirectional models feed the concatenation vector calculated from both directions $[\overleftarrow{e_1}, \overrightarrow{e_{N_s}}]$ to the classifier. Bidirectional models can be similarly extended to both multi-layer neural model and LSTM version.

Bilingual Word Embeddings from Parallel and Non-parallel Corpora for Cross-Language Text Classification

Aditya Mogadala
Institute AIFB
Karlsruhe Institute of Technology
Karlsruhe, Germany
aditya.mogadala@kit.edu

Achim Rettinger
Institute AIFB
Karlsruhe Institute of Technology
Karlsruhe, Germany
rettinger@kit.edu

Abstract

In many languages, sparse availability of resources causes numerous challenges for textual analysis tasks. Text classification is one of such standard tasks that is hindered due to limited availability of label information in low-resource languages. Transferring knowledge (i.e. label information) from high-resource to low-resource languages might improve text classification as compared to the other approaches like machine translation. We introduce BRAVE (*Bilingual paRAgraph VEctors*), a model to learn bilingual distributed representations (i.e. embeddings) of words without word alignments either from sentence-aligned parallel or label-aligned non-parallel document corpora to support cross-language text classification. Empirical analysis shows that classification models trained with our bilingual embeddings outperforms other state-of-the-art systems on three different cross-language text classification tasks.

1   Introduction

The availability of language-specific annotated resources is crucial for the efficiency of natural language processing tasks. Still, many languages lack rich annotated resources that support various tasks such as part-of-speech tagging, dependency parsing and text classification. While the growth of multilingual information on the web has provided an opportunity to build these missing annotated resources, but still lots of manual effort is required to achieve high quality resources for every language separately.

Another possibility is to utilize the unlabeled data present in those languages or transfer knowl-

edge from annotation-rich languages. For the first alternative, recent advancements made in learning monolingual distributed representations of words (Mikolov et al., 2013a; Pennington et al., 2014; Levy and Goldberg, 2014) (i.e. monolingual word embeddings) capturing syntactic and semantic information in an unsupervised manner was useful in numerous NLP tasks (Collobert et al., 2011). However, this may not be sufficient for several other tasks such as cross-language information retrieval (Grefenstette, 2012), cross-language word semantic similarity (Vulić and Moens, 2014), cross-language text classification (CLTC, henceforth) (Klementiev et al., 2012; Xiao and Guo, 2013; Prettenhofer and Stein, 2010; Tang and Wan, 2014) and machine translation (Zhao et al., 2015) due to irregularities across languages. In these kind of scenarios, transfer of knowledge can be useful.

Several approaches (Hermann and Blunsom, 2014; Sarath Chandar et al., 2014; Gouws et al., 2015; Coulmance et al., 2015) tried to induce monolingual distributed representations into a language independent space (i.e. bilingual or multilingual word embeddings) by jointly training on pair of languages. Although the overall goal of these approaches is to capture linguistic regularities in words that share same semantic and syntactic space across languages, they differ in their implementation. One set of methods either perform offline alignment of trained monolingual embeddings or jointly-train both monolingual and cross-lingual objectives, while the other set uses only cross-lingual objective. Jointly-trained or offline alignment methods can be further divided based on the type of par-

Proceedings of NAACL-HLT 2016, pages 692–702,
San Diego, California, June 12-17, 2016. ©2016 Association for Computational Linguistics

Cross-Language Setups			
Objective	Method	Tasks	Parallel Corpus
Monolingual+ Cross-lingual	(Klementiev et al., 2012)	CLDC	Word-Aligned
	(Zou et al., 2013)	MT,NER	Word-Aligned
	(Mikolov et al., 2013b)	MT	Word-Aligned
	(Faruqui and Dyer, 2014)	Word Similarity	Word-Aligned
	(Lu et al., 2015)	Word Similarity	Word-Aligned
	(Gouws and Søgaard, 2015)	POS,SuS	Word-Aligned
	(Gouws et al., 2015)	CLDC,MT	Sentence-Aligned
	(Coulmance et al., 2015)	CLDC,MT	Sentence-Aligned
Cross-lingual	(Hermann and Blunsom, 2014)	CLDC	Sentence-Aligned
	(Sarath Chandar et al., 2014)	CLDC	Sentence-Aligned
	(Luong et al., 2015)	Word Similarity, CLDC	Sentence-Aligned
	(Pham et al., 2015)	CLDC	Sentence-Aligned

Table 1: Summary of bilingual or multilingual embedding methods that support Cross-language Document Classification (CLDC), Machine Translation (MT), Named Entity Recognition (NER), Part-of-Speech Tagging (POS), Super Sense Tagging (SuS).

allel corpus (e.g. word-aligned, sentence-aligned) they use for learning the cross-lingual objective. Table 1 summarizes different setups to learn bilingual or multilingual embeddings for the various tasks.

Methods in the Table 1 that use word-aligned parallel corpus as offline alignment (Mikolov et al., 2013b; Faruqui and Dyer, 2014) assume single correspondence between the words across languages and ignore polysemy. While, the jointly-train methods (Klementiev et al., 2012) that use word-alignment parallel corpus and consider polysemy perform computationally expensive operation of considering all possible interactions between the pairs of words in vocabulary of two different languages. Methods (Hermann and Blunsom, 2014; Sarath Chandar et al., 2014) that overcame the complexity issues of word-aligned models by using sentence-aligned parallel corpora limits themselves to only cross-lingual objective, thus making these approaches unable to explore monolingual corpora. Jointly-trained models (Gouws et al., 2015; Coulmance et al., 2015) overcame the issues of both word-aligned and purely cross-lingual objective models by using monolingual and sentence-aligned parallel corpora. Nonetheless, these approaches still have certain drawbacks such as usage of only bag-of-words from the parallel sentences ignoring order of words. Thus, they are missing to capture the non-compositional meaning of entire sentence. Also, learned bilingual embeddings were heavily biased towards the sampled sentence-aligned parallel corpora. It is also some-

times hard to acquire sentence-level parallel corpora for every language pair. To subdue this concern, few approaches (Rajendran et al., 2015) used pivot languages like English or comparable document-aligned corpora (Vulić and Moens, 2015) to learn bilingual embeddings specific to only one task.

This major downside can be observed in other aforementioned methods also, which are inflexible to handle different types of parallel corpora and have a tight-binding between cross-lingual objectives and the parallel corpora. For example, a method using sentence-level parallel corpora cannot be altered to leverage document-level parallel corpora (if available) that might have better performance for some tasks. Also, none of the approaches do leverage widely available label/class-aligned non-parallel documents (e.g. sentiment labels, multi-class datasets) across languages which share special semantics such as sentiment or correlation between concepts as opposed to parallel texts.

In this paper, we introduce BRAVE a jointly-trained flexible model that learns bilingual embeddings based on the availability of the type of corpora (e.g. sentence-aligned parallel or label/class-aligned non-parallel document) by just altering the cross-lingual objective. BRAVE leverages paragraph vector embeddings (Le and Mikolov, 2014) of the monolingual corpora to effectively conceal semantics of the text sequences across languages and build a cross-lingual objective. Method closely related to our approach is by Pham et al. (2015) who uses shared context sentence vector across languages to learn multilingual text sequences.

The main contributions of this paper are:

- We jointly train monolingual part of parallel corpora with the improved cross-lingual alignment function that extends beyond bag-of-word models.

- Introduced a novel approach to leverage non-parallel data sets such as label or class aligned documents in different languages for learning bilingual cues.

- Experimental evaluation on three different CLTC tasks, namely cross-language document classification, multi-label classification and cross-language sentiment classification using learned bilingual word embeddings.

2   Related Work

Most of the related work can be associated to the approaches that aim to learn latent topics across languages or distributed representations of the words and larger pieces of text for supporting various cross-lingual tasks.

2.1   Cross-Language Latent Topics

Various approaches have been proposed to identify latent topics in monolingual (Blei, 2012; Rus et al., 2013) and multilingual (Mimno et al., 2009; Fukumasu et al., 2012) scenarios for cross-language semantic word similarity and document comparison. Extraction of cross-language latent topics or concepts use context-insensitive (Zhang et al., 2010) and context-sensitive methods (Vulić and Moens, 2014) to build word co-occurrence statistics for document representations.

2.2   Distributed Representations

Continuous word representations (Bengio et al., 2003; Mikolov et al., 2013a; Pennington et al., 2014) was further extended to multilingual (Hermann and Blunsom, 2014; Kočiský et al., 2014; Coulmance et al., 2015), bilingual (Gouws et al., 2015; Vulić and Moens, 2015; Luong et al., 2015) and polylingual (Al-Rfou et al., 2013) settings by projecting multiple or pair of languages into the shared semantic space. Also, word representations were extended to meet larger textual units like phrases, sentences

and documents either monolingual (Socher et al., 2012; Le and Mikolov, 2014) or bilingual (Pham et al., 2015). Some approaches fine tuned the embeddings for specific tasks such as cross-lingual sentiment analysis (Zhou et al., 2015b), cross-language POS tagging (Gouws and Søgaard, 2015), machine translation (Cho et al., 2014) etc.

3   BRAVE Model

In this section, we present the BRAVE model along with its variations whose aim is to learn bilingual embeddings that can generalize across different languages.

3.1   Bilingual Paragraph Vectors (BRAVE)

Most of the NLP tasks require fixed-length vectors. Tasks like CLTC also require fixed-length vectors to incorporate inherent semantics of sentences or documents. Distributed representation of sentences and documents i.e. paragraph vectors (Le and Mikolov, 2014) are designed to out-perform certain text classification tasks by overcoming constraints posed by the bag-of-words models.

Here, we leverage paragraph vectors distributed memory model (PV-DM) as the monolingual objective $\mathcal{M}(\cdot)$ and jointly optimize with bilingual regularization function $\varphi(\cdot)$ for learning bilingual embeddings similar to the earlier approaches (Gouws et al., 2015; Coulmance et al., 2015). Equation 1 shows the formulation of the overall objective function that is minimized.

$$\mathcal{L} = \min_{\theta^{l_1}, \theta^{l_2}} \sum_{l \in \{l_1, l_2\}} \sum_{C^l} \mathcal{M}^l(w_t, h; \theta^l) + \frac{\lambda \varphi(\theta^{l_1}, \theta^{l_2})}{2}$$

(1)

Here, C^l represent the corpus of individual languages (i.e. l_1 or l_2). Given any sequence of words $(w_1^l, w_2^l ... w_T^l)$ in C^l, w_t is the predicted word in a context h constrained on paragraph p (i.e. sentence or document) and sequence of words.

Formally, the first term (i.e. $\mathcal{M}(\cdot)$) in the Equation 1 maximizes the average log probability based on word vector matrix W^l and a unique paragraph vector matrix P^l. Equation 2 represents the average log probability.

$$\mathcal{M}^l(w_t, h; \theta^l) = \frac{\Sigma_{t=k}^{T-k} y_{w_t}^l - log(\sum_i e^{y_i^l})}{T}$$

(2)

where each y_i^l is log-probability of predicted word i and is given by Equation 3.

$$y^l = b + Uh(w_{t-k}^l....w_{t+k}^l; W^l, P^l) \qquad (3)$$

To optimize for efficiency, hierarchical softmax (Mnih and Hinton, 2009) is used in training with U and b as parameters. Binary Huffmann tree is utilized to represent hierarchial softmax (Mikolov et al., 2013a). Analogous to Pham et al., (2015), we also derive h by concatenating paragraph vector from P^l with the average of word vectors in W^l. This helps to fine tune both word and paragraph vectors independently.

Now, to capture the bilingual cues, the regularization function ($\varphi(\cdot)$) is learned in two different ways. In the first approach a sentence-aligned parallel corpora is used, while in the second approach a label-aligned document corpora.

3.2 BRAVE with Sentence-Aligned Parallel corpora (BRAVE-S)

To compute the bilingual regularization function $\varphi(\cdot)$, we slightly deviate from earlier approaches (Gouws et al., 2015). Instead of simply performing L_2-loss between the mean of word vectors in each sentence pair $(s_j^{l_1}, s_j^{l_2})$ of the sentence-aligned parallel corpus (PC) at each training step. We use the concept of elastic net regularization (Zou and Hastie, 2005) and employ linear combination of L_2-loss between *sentence paragraph vectors* $SP_j^{l_1}$ and $SP_j^{l_2} \in R^d$ precomputed from the monolingual term $\mathcal{M}(\cdot)$ with L_2-loss between the mean of word vectors observed in sentences. This induces a constraint on the usage of monolingual part of parallel training data to learn $\mathcal{M}(\cdot)$. At the same time, it has an advantage of using combination of paragraph and word vectors which combines compositional and non-compositional meanings of sentences.

Also, it eliminates the need for word-alignment and makes an assumption that each word observed in the sentence of language l_1 can potentially find its alignment in the sentence of language l_2. Theoretically, low value of $\varphi(\cdot)$ ensures that words across languages which are similar are embedded closer to each other. Equation 4 shows the regularization term.

$$\alpha||SP_j^{l_1} - SP_j^{l_2}||^2 + (1-\alpha)||\frac{1}{m}\sum_{w_i \epsilon s_j^{l_1}}^{m} W_i^{l_1} - \frac{1}{n}\sum_{w_k \epsilon s_j^{l_2}}^{n} W_k^{l_2}||^2$$

$$(4)$$

Where $W_i^{l_1}$ and $W_k^{l_2}$ represent word embeddings obtained for the words w_i and w_k in each sentence (s_j) of length m and n in languages l_1 and l_2 respectively.

3.3 BRAVE with Non-Parallel Document Corpora (BRAVE-D)

Sometimes it is hard to acquire sentence-aligned parallel corpora for many languages. Availability of non-parallel corpora such as topic-aligned (e.g. Wikipedia) or label/class-aligned document corpora (e.g. sentiment analysis and multi-class classification data sets) in different languages can be leveraged to learn bilingual embeddings for performing CLTC. Earlier approaches like CL-LSI (Dumais et al., 1997) and CL-KCCA (Vinokourov et al., 2003) were used to learn bilingual document spaces for the tasks comparable to CLTC. Although these approaches provide decent results, they face serious scalability issues and are mostly limited to Wikipedia. Cross-lingual latent topic extraction models (Vulić and Moens, 2014) showed promising results for the tasks like word-level or phrase-level translations, but have certain drawbacks for CLTC tasks.

Here, we propose a two step approach to build bilingual embeddings with label/class-aligned document corpora.

- In the first step, we perform manifold alignment using Procrustes analysis (Wang and Mahadevan, 2008) between sets of documents belonging to same class/label in different languages. This will help to identify the closest alignment of a document in language l_1 with a document in another language l_2.

- In the second step, we use the pair of partially aligned documents belonging to same class or label in different languages to extract bilingual cues similar to the approach mentioned in § 3.2. Only difference being paragraph vector is learned for the entire document.

Step-1:

Let S^{l_1} and S^{l_2} be the sets containing languages l_1 and l_2 training documents associated to label or a class. Below, we provide the three step procedure to attain partial alignment between the documents present in these sets.

- Learning low-dimensional embeddings of the sets (S^{l_1}, S^{l_2}) is key for alignment. We use **document paragraph vectors** (Le and Mikolov, 2014) to learn low-dimensional embeddings of the documents in each language. Let X^{l_1} and X^{l_2} be the low-dimensional embeddings of S^{l_1} and S^{l_2} respectively.

- To find the optimal values of transformation, Procrustes superimposition is done by translating, rotating and scaling the objects (i.e. rows of X^{l_2} is transformed to make it similar to the rows of X^{l_1}). Transformation is achieved by

  - **Translation:** Taking mean of all the members of set to make centroids ($\sum_{i=1}^{|S^{l_1}|} \frac{X^{l_1}}{|S^{l_1}|}, \sum_{i=1}^{|S^{l_2}|} \frac{X^{l_2}}{|S^{l_2}|}$) lie at origin.
  - **Scaling and Rotation:** The rotation and scaling that maximizes the alignment is given by orthogonal matrix (Q) and scaling factor (k). They are obtained by minimizing orthogonal Procrustes problem (Schönemann, 1966) and is provided by Equation 5.

$$\arg\min_{k,Q} ||X^{l_1} - X^{l_2}_*||_F \qquad (5)$$

  where $X^{l_2}_*$ a matrix of transformed X^{l_2} values given by $kX^{l_2}Q$ and $||.||_F$ is the Frobenius norm constrained over $Q^T Q = I$.

- If $S^{l_2}_*$ represents the new document set obtained after identifying the close alignment among documents in S^{l_1} and S^{l_2} with cosine similarity between X^{l_1} and $X^{l_2}_*$, then the partially aligned corpora $\{S^{l_1}, S^{l_2}_*\}$ contains one-to-one correspondence between the two languages documents that are used to learn bilingual cues in the second step.

From perturbation theory of spectral spaces (Kostrykin et al., 2003) it can be understood that the difference between low-dimensional

embedding subspaces (i.e. X^{l_1} and $X^{l_2}_*$) is always bounded, thus the new alignment obtained between document sets $\{S^{l_1}, S^{l_2}_*\}$ is insensitive to perturbations. Which also means that Procrustes analysis has provided best possible document alignments.

Step-2:

Now, document pairs $(d_j^{l_1}, d_j^{l_2})$ of the partially-aligned corpus (PAC) is used to compute bilingual regularization function $\varphi(\cdot)$. At each training step, L_2-loss of precomputed *document paragraph vectors* $DP_j^{l_1}$ and $DP_j^{l_2} \in R^d$ obtained from the monolingual term $\mathcal{M}(\cdot)$ is combined with the L_2-loss between vector of words weighted by the probability of their occurrence in a particular label/class of entire **PAC**. Consideration of word probabilities will help to induce label/class specific information. Equation 6 provides the regularization term.

$$\alpha ||DP_j^{l_1} - DP_j^{l_2}||^2$$
$$+ (1-\alpha)|| \sum_{w_i \in d_j^{l_1}} \frac{p_{w_i} W_i^{l_1}}{\sum_m p_{w_i}} - \sum_{w_k \in d_j^{l_2}} \frac{q_{w_k} W_k^{l_2}}{\sum_n q_{w_k}} ||^2 \qquad (6)$$

Where w_i, w_k are words and their embeddings $W_i^{l_1}, W_k^{l_2}$ observed in each document (d_j) of length m and n in languages l_1 and l_2 respectively. While, p_{w_i} and q_{w_k} represents probability of occurrence of words w_i and w_k in a specific label/class of entire **PAC**. Figure- 1 shows overall goal of both the approaches.

4 Experiments

In this section, we report results on three different CLTC tasks to comprehend whether our learned bilingual embeddings are semantically useful across languages. First, cross-language document classification (CLDC) task proposed by Klementiev et al. (2012) using the subset of Reuters RCV1/RCV2 corpora (Lewis et al., 2004). Second, a multi-label CLDC task with more languages using TED corpus[1] of Hermann et al. (2014) . Subsequently, a cross-language sentiment classification (CLSC) proposed by Prettenhofer et al., (2010) on a multi-domain sentiment dataset.

---

[1] http://www.clg.ox.ac.uk/tedcorpus

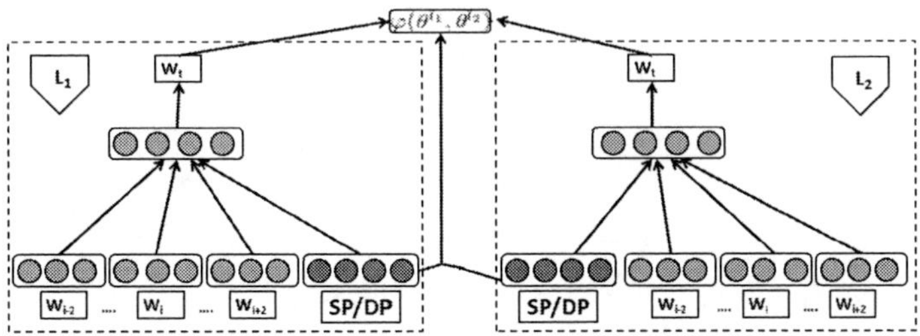

Figure 1: Bilingual word embeddings learned using sentence or document paragraph vectors (SP/DP) along with word vectors.

4.1 Parallel and Non-Parallel Corpora

For sentence-aligned parallel corpora, Europarl-v7 [2](EP) is used as both monolingual and parallel training data. While for label-aligned non-parallel document corpora, only training and testing collections of the cross-language multi-domain Amazon product reviews(CL-APR) (Prettenhofer and Stein, 2010) corpus with sentiment labels is used.

4.2 Implementation

Our implementation launches monolingual paragraph vector (Le and Mikolov, 2014) threads for each language along with bilingual regularization thread. Word and paragraph embeddings matrices are initialized with normal distribution ($\mu = 0$ and $\sigma^2 = 0.1$) for each language and all threads access them asynchronously. Following Pham et al. (2015) suggested combination (P=5*W) of paragraph and word embeddings, we chose paragraph embeddings with dimensionality of 200 and 640 when word embeddings are of 40 and 128 dimensions respectively. Asynchronous stochastic gradient descent (ASGD) is used to update parameters (i.e. P^l, W^l, U and b) and train the model.

For each training pair in parallel or non-parallel corpora, initially monolingual threads sample context h with window size of 8 from a random paragraph (i.e. sentence or document) in each language. Then the bilingual regularization thread along with monolingual threads make update to parameters asynchronously. Learning rate is set to 0.001 which decrease with the increase of epochs, while α is chosen to be 0.6 (can be fine tuned based on empirical analysis) to give more weight to paragraph vectors. All models are trained for 50 epochs.

[2]http://www.statmt.org/europarl/

4.3 Document Representation

Documents are represented with tf-idf weighted sum of embedding vectors of the words that are present in them.

4.4 Results

The experimental results for each of the CLTC tasks are presented separately.

4.4.1 Cross-language Document Classification (CLDC) - RCV1/RCV2

Goal of this task is to classify target language documents with the labeled examples from the source language. To achieve it, we used the subset of Reuters RCV1/RCV2 corpora as the training and evaluation sets and replicated the experimental setting of Klementiev et al. (2012). From the English, German, French and Spanish collection of the dataset, only those documents are selected which was labeled with a single topic (i.e. CCAT, ECAT, GCAT and MCAT). For the classification experiments, 1000 labeled documents from source language are selected to train a multi-class classifier using averaged perceptron (Freund and Schapire, 1999; Collins, 2002) and 5000 documents were used as the testing data.

English-German, English-French and English-Spanish portion of **EP** corpora (i.e. each with around 1.9M sentence-pairs) is used both as monolingual and parallel training data with **BRAVE-S** approach to build vocabulary of around 85k English, 144k German, 119k French and 118k Spanish. While training and testing collections belonging to all domains in English-German, English-French languages of **CL-APR** ((i.e. around 12,000 document-pairs)) was used both as monolingual and partially aligned data with **BRAVE-D** approach to build vocabulary of around 21k English, 22k German and

Model	Dim	en → de	de → en	en → fr	fr → en	en → es	es → en
Majority class	40	46.8	46.8	22.5	25.0	15.3	22.2
MT	40	68.1	67.4	76.3	71.1	52.0	58.4
I-Matrix (Klementiev et al., 2012)	40	77.6	71.1	74.5	61.9	31.3	63.0
BAE-cr (Sarath Chandar et al., 2014)	40	**91.8**	74.2	**84.6**	74.2	49.0	64.4
CVM-Add (Hermann and Blunsom, 2014)	40	86.4	74.7	-	-	-	-
DWA (Kočiský et al., 2014)	40	83.1	75.4	-	-	-	-
BilBOWA (Gouws et al., 2015)	40	86.5	75	-	-	-	-
UnsupAlign (Luong et al., 2015)	40	87.6	77.8	-	-	-	-
Trans-gram (Coulmance et al., 2015)	40	87.8	78.7	-	-	-	-
BRAVE-S(EP)	40	88.1	**78.9**	79.2	**77.8**	**56.9**	**67.6**
BRAVE-D(CL-APR)	40	69.4	67.9	64.1	56.5	-	-
CVM-BI (Hermann and Blunsom, 2014)	128	86.1	79.0	-	-	-	-
UnsupAlign (Luong et al., 2015)	128	88.9	77.4	-	-	-	-
BRAVE-S(EP)	128	89.7	**80.1**	82.5	**79.5**	**60.2**	**70.4**
BRAVE-D(CL-APR)	128	70.4	70.6	66.2	57.6	-	-

Table 2: CLDC Accuracy with 1000 labeled examples on RCV1/RCV2 Corpus. en/de, en/fr and en/es results of Majority class, MT, I-Matrix and BAE-cr are adopted from Sarath Chandar et al., (2014)

18k French. Further, documents in the training and testing data of RCV1/RCV2 corpora are represented as described in § 4.3 with the vocabulary built. Table 2 shows the comparison of our approaches with the existing systems.

4.4.2 Multi-label CLDC - TED Corpus

To understand the applicability of our approaches to wider range of languages[3] and class labels, we perform experiments with the subset of TED corpus (Hermann and Blunsom, 2014). Aim of this task is same as § 4.4.1, but experiments were conducted with larger variety of languages and class labels. TED Corpus contains English transcriptions and their sentence-aligned translations for 12 languages from the TED conference. Entire corpus is further classified into 15 topics (i.e. class labels) based on the most frequent keywords appearing in them.

To conduct our experiments, we follow the *single* mode setting of Hermann et al. (2014) (i.e. embeddings are learned only from a single language pair). Entire language pair (i.e. en→L2) training data of the TED corpus is used both as monolingual and parallel training data to learn bilingual word embeddings with dimensionality of 128 using **BRAVE-S** approach. Bilingual word embeddings of 128 dimensions learned with **EP** and **CL-APR** are also

used for comparison. Documents in the training and testing data of TED corpus are represented as described in § 4.3 using each of these embeddings. A multi-class classifier using averaged perceptron is built using training documents in source language to be applied on target language testing data for predicting the class labels. Table 3 shows the cumulative F1-scores.

4.4.3 Cross-language Sentiment Classification (CLSC)

The objective of the third CLTC task is to identify sentiment polarity (e.g. positive or negative) of the data in target language by exploiting the labeled data in source language. We chose subset of publicly available Amazon product reviews (CL-APR) (Prettenhofer and Stein, 2010) dataset mainly English(E), German(G) and French(F) languages belonging to three different product categories (books(B), dvds(D) and music(M)) to conduct our experiments. For each language-category pair, corpus consists of training, testing sets comprising 1000 positive and 1000 negative reviews each with an additional unlabeled reviews varying from 9,000 to 170,000.

We constructed 12 different CLSC tasks using different languages (i.e. E,G and F) for three categories (i.e. B,D and M). For example, EFM refers English music reviews as source language and French music reviews as target language. Bilingual word embeddings with dimensionality of 128 learned with

---

[3]Our goal is not to evaluate shared multilingual semantic representation.

Method	de	es	fr	it	nl	pt	po	ro	ru	tr
en $\rightarrow$ L2										
MT-*Baseline*	0.465	**0.518**	**0.526**	**0.514**	**0.505**	0.470	0.445	**0.493**	0.432	0.409
DOC/ADD	0.424	0.383	<u>0.476</u>	0.485	0.264	0.354	0.402	0.418	0.448	0.452
DOC/BI	0.428	0.416	0.445	0.473	0.219	0.400	0.403	0.467	0.421	0.457
BRAVE-S(TED)	**0.484**	<u>0.436</u>	0.456	<u>0.507</u>	<u>0.328</u>	**0.506**	**0.453**	<u>0.488</u>	**0.456**	**0.491**
BRAVE-S(EP)	0.418	0.365	0.387	0.418	0.284	0.454	0.412	0.424	-	-
BRAVE-D(CL-APR)	0.385	-	0.212	-	-	-	-	-	-	-
L2 $\rightarrow$ en										
MT-*Baseline*	0.469	0.486	0.358	**0.481**	**0.463**	0.374	**0.460**	**0.486**	0.404	0.441
DOC/ADD	0.476	0.422	0.464	0.461	0.251	0.338	0.400	0.407	0.471	0.435
DOC/BI	0.442	0.365	**0.479**	0.460	0.235	0.380	0.393	0.426	**0.467**	0.477
BRAVE-S(TED)	**0.492**	**0.495**	0.465	<u>0.475</u>	<u>0.384</u>	**0.388**	<u>0.442</u>	<u>0.464</u>	0.457	**0.484**
BRAVE-S(EP)	0.458	0.404	0.437	0.443	0.338	0.312	0.374	0.418	-	-
BRAVE-D(CL-APR)	0.366	-	0.278	-	-	-	-	-	-	-

Table 3: Cumulative F1-scores on TED Corpus using training data in English language and evaluation on other languages (i.e. German (de), Spanish (es), French (fr), Italian (it), Dutch (nl), Portugese (pt), Polish (po), Romanian (ro), Russian (ru) and Turkish (tr)) and vice versa. MT-*Baseline*, DOC/ADD, DOC/BI represents single language pair of Hermann et al., (2014) as document features. Underline shows the best results amongst embedding models.

	Cross-Language Sentiment Classification (en→L2 and Vice versa)						
Task	CL-SCL	CL-SSMC	CL-SLF	CL-DCI$_{100}$	BSE	BRAVE-S (EP)	BRAVE-D (CL-APR)
EFB	79.86±0.22	83.05±0.26	82.61±0.25	82.30	-	72.24±0.31	82.57±0.33
EFD	78.80±0.25	82.70±0.20	82.70±0.45	82.40	-	74.95±0.25	**82.90±0.35**
EFM	75.95±0.31	80.46±0.20	80.19±0.40	81.05	-	72.80±0.20	**80.70±0.45**
FEB	77.26±0.22	80.05±0.26	80.48±0.33	-	-	75.45±0.38	80.28±0.21
FED	76.57±0.20	79.40±0.28	78.76±0.38	-	-	73.75±0.26	**79.80±0.15**
FEM	76.76±0.25	78.82±0.17	79.18±0.33	-	-	73.66±0.17	78.56±0.33
EGB	77.77±0.28	81.88±0.42	79.91±0.47	81.40	80.27±0.50	75.95±0.16	**81.75±0.45**
EGD	79.93±0.23	82.25±0.20	81.86±0.31	79.95	77.16±0.30	78.30±0.42	81.56±0.26
EGM	73.95±0.30	81.30±0.20	79.59±0.42	83.30	77.98±0.51	75.95±0.33	81.20±0.17
GEB	77.85±0.27	79.06±0.23	78.61±0.34	-	-	72.25±0.20	**80.23±0.17**
GED	77.83±0.33	80.89±0.16	80.27±0.35	-	-	73.28±0.23	**80.78±0.20**
GEM	77.37±0.34	79.85±0.17	79.80±0.26	-	-	74.41±0.22	**79.77±0.36**

Table 4: Average classification accuracies and standard deviations for 12 CLSC tasks. Results of other baselines are adopted from CL-SCL (Prettenhofer and Stein, 2010), CL-SSMC (Xiao and Guo, 2002), CL-SLF (Zhou et al., 2015a), CL-DCI$_{100}$ (Esuli and Fernandez, 2015) and BSE (Tang and Wan, 2014)

BRAVE-S and **BRAVE-D** are used to represent each review as described in § 4.3. To have fair comparison with earlier approaches, sentiment classification model is then trained with libsvm[4] default parameter settings using source language training reviews[5] to classify target language test reviews. Table 4 shows the accuracy and standard deviation results after we randomly chose subset of target language testing documents and repeated the experiment for 10 times for all CLSC tasks.

5 Discussion

First CLTC task (i.e. CLDC) results presented in Table 2 shows that BRAVE-S was able to outperform most of the existing systems. Success of BRAVE-S can be attributed to its ability to incorporate both non-compositional and compositional meaning observed in entire sentence and the individual words respectively. Thus making it different from other models which use only bag-of-words (Gouws et al., 2015) or bi-grams (Hermann and Blunsom, 2014).

Similarly, second CLTC task (i.e. multi-label

---

[4]https://www.csie.ntu.edu.tw/ cjlin/libsvm/

[5]We do not use 100 labeled target language reviews in model training, as it was shown by earlier approaches that 100 labeled target language reviews does not have much impact.

Top-3 Nearest Neighbors (Euclidean Distance)			
English Words	Models	German	French
great		wachstum	éminent
	BRAVE-S	super	maintenus
		spielen	m'efforcerai
		schärfe	festival
	BRAVE-D	mögen	interressante
		kraftvolle	attachant
bored		boykottiert	ennuyé
	BRAVE-S	leere	précédera
		ausgehen	compromettent
		ableben	réserve
	BRAVE-D	lichtblick	intensité
		traurigen	consterné

Table 5: Nearest Neighbors for English Words in German and French.

CLDC) results presented in Table 3 shows that BRAVE-S learned with the training data of TED corpus outperformed *single mode* DOC/* embedding models (Hermann and Blunsom, 2014), BRAVE-S learned with **EP** and BRAVE-D. The BRAVE-S(TED) was able to capture better linguistic regularities across languages that is more specific to the corpus, than the general purpose bilingual embeddings learned with **EP**. Though in some cases, all our embedding models could not outperform machine translation baseline. This can be due to the asymmetry between languages induced by the language specific words which could not find its equivalents in English.

Also, it can be apprehended from the Table 2 and Table 3 that BRAVE-D results are not as expected. Though being a general approach like BRAVE-S which can capture both non-compositional and compositional meaning from larger pieces of texts, minimal overlap of vocabulary learned with BRAVE-D using cross-language sentiment label-aligned corpora with other domains (i.e. Reuters and TED) produce unfavorable results. Thus, we understand that the choice of label/class-aligned corpora is crucial.

Final CLTC task (i.e. CLSC) results presented in Table 4 shows that BRAVE-D outperforms other baseline approaches in most of the cases. As BRAVE-D learns bilingual word embeddings using **CL-APR**, it was able to inherently encompass sentiment label information effectively like earlier approaches (Tang and Wan, 2014; Zhou et al., 2015b) than the general purpose embeddings learned using BRAVE-S with **EP** and similar approaches (Meng et al., 2012). Thus making it more suitable for sentiment classification task. Also unlike CL-SSMC (Xiao and Guo, 2002) and CL-SLF (Zhou et al., 2015a), BRAVE-D is not highly parameter dependent where the results of the former approaches show big variance based on the parameter settings. To visualize the difference in embeddings learned with BRAVE-S and BRAVE-D, we selected sentiment words and identified cross-language nearest neighbors in Table 5. It can be observed that BRAVE-D was able to identify better sentiment (either positive or negative) word neighbors than BRAVE-S.

6 Conclusion and Future Work

In this paper, we presented an approach that leverages paragraph vectors to learn bilingual word embeddings with sentence-aligned parallel and label-aligned non-parallel corpora. Empirical analysis exhibited that embeddings learned from both of these types of corpora have shown good impact on CLTC tasks. In future, we aim to extend the approach to learn multilingual semantic spaces with more labels/classes.

Acknowledgments

The research leading to these results has received funding from the European Union Seventh Framework Programme (FP7/2007-2013) under grant agreement no. 611346.

References

R. Al-Rfou, B. Perozzi, and S. Skiena. 2013. Polyglot: Distributed word representations for multilingual nlp. In *CoNLL*.

Y. Bengio, R. Ducharme, P. Vincent, and C. Janvin. 2003. A neural probabilistic language model. *The Journal of Machine Learning Research.*, 3:1137–1155.

D. M. Blei. 2012. Probabilistic topic models. *Communications of the ACM.*, 55(4):77–84.

K. Cho, B. van Merrienboer, C. Gulcehre, F. Bougares, H. Schwenk, and Y. Bengio. 2014. Learning phrase representations using rnn encoder-decoder for statistical machine translation. In *EMNLP*.

M. Collins. 2002. Discriminative training methods for hidden markov models: Theory and experiments with perceptron algorithms. In *ACL-EMNLP.*, pages 1–8.

R. Collobert, J. Weston, L. Bottou, M. Karlen, K. Kavukcuoglu, and P. Kuksa. 2011. Natural language processing (almost) from scratch. *The Journal of Machine Learning Research.*, 12:2493–2537.

J. Coulmance, J. M. Marty, G. Wenzek, and A. Benhalloum. 2015. Trans-gram, fast cross-lingual word-embeddings reyes- mannde= reginait- femmefr. In *EMNLP*.

S. T. Dumais, Todd A. Letsche, Michael L. Littman, and Thomas K. Landauer. 1997. Automatic cross-language retrieval using latent semantic indexing. In *AAAI spring symposium on cross-language text and speech retrieval*.

A. Esuli and A. M. Fernandez. 2015. Distributional correspondence indexing for cross-language text categorization. In *Advances in Information Retrieval.*, pages 104–109.

M. Faruqui and C. Dyer. 2014. Improving vector space word representations using multilingual correlation. In *ACL*.

Y. Freund and R. E. Schapire. 1999. Large margin classification using the perceptron algorithm. *The Journal of Machine Learning Research.*, 37(3):277–296.

K. Fukumasu, Koji Eguchi, and Eric P. Xing. 2012. Symmetric correspondence topic models for multilingual text analysis. In *NIPS*, pages 1295–1303.

S. Gouws and A. Søgaard. 2015. Simple task-specific bilingual word embeddings. In *NAACL-HLT.*, pages 1386–1390.

S. Gouws, Y. Bengio, and G. Corrado. 2015. Bilbowa: Fast bilingual distributed representations without word alignments. In *ICML*.

G. Grefenstette. 2012. Cross-language information retrieval. *Springer Science and Business Media*, 2.

K. M. Hermann and P. Blunsom. 2014. Multilingual models for compositional distributed semantics. In *ACL*.

A. Klementiev, I. Titov, and B. Bhattarai. 2012. Inducing crosslingual distributed representations of words. In *COLING*.

T. Kočiský, K. M. Hermann, and P. Blunsom. 2014. Learning bilingual word representations by marginalizing alignments. In *ACL*, pages 224–229.

V. Kostrykin, K. Makarov, and A. Motovilov. 2003. On a subspace perturbation problem. *American Mathematical Society.*, pages 3469–3476.

Q. Le and T. Mikolov. 2014. Distributed representations of sentences and documents. In *ICML*, pages 1188–1196.

O. Levy and Y. Goldberg. 2014. Dependency based word embeddings. In *ACL.*, pages 302–308.

D. D. Lewis, Y. Yang, T. G. Rose, and F. Li. 2004. Rcv1: A new benchmark collection for text categorization research. *The Journal of Machine Learning Research.*, 5:361–397.

A. Lu, W. Wang, M. Bansal, K. Gimpel, and K. Livescu. 2015. Deep multilingual correlation for improved word embeddings. In *NAACL-HLT*.

T. Luong, H. Pham, and C. D. Manning. 2015. Bilingual word representations with monolingual quality in mind. In *First Workshop on Vector Space Modeling for Natural Language Processing.*, pages 151–159.

X. Meng, F. Wei, X. Liu, M. Zhou, G. Xu, and H. Wang. 2012. Cross-lingual mixture model for sentiment classification. In *ACL.*, pages 572–581.

T. Mikolov, K. Chen, G. Corrado, and J. Dean. 2013a. Efficient estimation of word representations in vector space. In *arXiv preprint arXiv:1301.3781*.

T. Mikolov, Q. V. Le, and I. Sutskever. 2013b. Exploiting similarities among languages for machine translation. In *arXiv preprint arXiv:1309.4168*.

D. Mimno, Hanna M. Wallach, Jason Naradowsky, David A. Smith, and Andrew McCallum. 2009. Polylingual topic models. In *EMNLP*, pages 880–889.

A. Mnih and G. E. Hinton. 2009. A scalable hierarchical distributed language model. In *NIPS.*, pages 1081–1088.

J. Pennington, R. Socher, and C. D. Manning. 2014. Glove: Global vectors for word representation. In *EMNLP*.

H. Pham, M. T. Luong, and C. D. Manning. 2015. Learning distributed representations for multilingual text sequences. In *NAACL-HLT*, pages 88–94.

P. Prettenhofer and B. Stein. 2010. Cross-language text classification using structural correspondence learning. In *ACL.*, pages 1118–1127.

J. Rajendran, M. M. Khapra, S. Chandar, and B. Ravindran. 2015. Bridge correlational neural networks for multilingual multimodal representation learning. In *arXiv preprint arXiv:1510.03519*.

V. Rus, M. C. Lintean, R. Banjade, N. B. Niraula, and D. Stefanescu. 2013. Semilar: The semantic similarity toolkit. In *ACL(Conference System Demonstrations)*, pages 163–168.

A. P. Sarath Chandar, S. Lauly, H. Larochelle, M. Khapra, B. Ravindran, V. C. Raykar, and A. Saha. 2014. An autoencoder approach to learning bilingual word representations. In *NIPS.*, pages 1853–1861.

P. H. Schönemann. 1966. A generalized solution of the orthogonal procrustes problem. *The Journal of Psychometrika.*, 31(1):1–10.

R. Socher, B. Huval, C. D. Manning, and A. Y. Ng. 2012. Semantic compositionality through recursive matrix-vector spaces. In *EMNLP*, pages 1201–1211.

X. Tang and X. Wan. 2014. Learning bilingual embedding model for cross-language sentiment classification. In *Web Intelligence (WI) and Intelligent Agent Technologies (IAT), 2014 IEEE/WIC/ACM International Joint Conferences.*, volume 2, pages 134–141.

A. Vinokourov, J. Shawe-Taylor, and N. Cristianini. 2003. Inferring a semantic representation of text via cross-language correlation analysis. In *NIPS.*, pages 1497–1504.

I. Vulić and M. F. Moens. 2014. Probabilistic models of cross-lingual semantic similarity in context based on latent cross-lingual concepts induced from comparable data. In *EMNLP.*

I. Vulić and M. F. Moens. 2015. Bilingual word embeddings from non-parallel document-aligned data applied to bilingual lexicon induction. In *ACL.*

C. Wang and S. Mahadevan. 2008. Manifold alignment using procrustes analysis. In *ICML.*, pages 1120–1127.

M. Xiao and Y. Guo. 2002. Semi-supervised matrix completion for cross-lingual text classification. In *AAAI.*

M. Xiao and Y. Guo. 2013. Semi-supervised representation learning for cross-lingual text classification. In *EMNLP.*, pages 1465–1475.

D. Zhang, Qiaozhu Mei, and ChengXiang Zhai. 2010. Cross-lingual latent topic extraction. In *ACL*, pages 1128–1137.

K. Zhao, H. Hassan, and M. Auli. 2015. Learning translation models from monolingual continuous representations. In *NAACL-HLT.*

G. Zhou, T. He, J. Zhao, and W. Wu. 2015a. A subspace learning framework for cross-lingual sentiment classification with partial parallel data. In *IJCAI.*

H. Zhou, L. Chen, F. Shi, and D. Huang. 2015b. Learning bilingual sentiment word embeddings for cross-language sentiment classification. In *ACL*, pages 430–440.

H. Zou and T. Hastie. 2005. Regularization and variable selection via the elastic net. *The Journal of the Royal Statistical Society: Series B (Statistical Methodology).*, 67(2):301–320.

W. Y. Zou, R. Socher, D. M. Cer, and C. D. Manning. 2013. Bilingual word embeddings for phrase-based machine translation. In *EMNLP.*, pages 1393–1398.

Joint Learning with Global Inference
for Comment Classification in Community Question Answering

Shafiq Joty, **Lluís Màrquez** and **Preslav Nakov**
ALT Research Group
Qatar Computing Research Institute — HBKU, Qatar Foundation
{sjoty, lmarquez, pnakov}@qf.org.qa

Abstract

This paper addresses the problem of comment classification in community Question Answering. Following the state of the art, we approach the task with a global inference process to exploit the information of all comments in the answer-thread in the form of a fully connected graph. Our contribution comprises two novel joint learning models that are on-line and integrate inference within learning. The first one jointly learns two *node-* and *edge*-level MaxEnt classifiers with stochastic gradient descent and integrates the inference step with loopy belief propagation. The second model is an instance of fully connected pairwise CRFs (FCCRF). The FCCRF model significantly outperforms all other approaches and yields the best results on the task to date. Crucial elements for its success are the global normalization and an Ising-like edge potential.

1 Introduction

Online community fora have been gaining a lot of popularity in recent years. Many of them, such as Stack Exchange[1], are quite open, allowing anybody to ask and anybody to answer a question, which makes them very valuable sources of information. Yet, this same democratic nature resulted in some questions accumulating a large number of answers, many of which are of low quality. While nowadays online fora are typically searched using standard search engines that index entire threads, this is not optimal, as it can be very time-consuming for a user to go through and make sense of a long thread.

Q: *hello guys and gals..could anyone of u knows where to buy a good and originals RC helicopters and toy guns here in qatar..im longin for this toys but its nowhere to find.. thanks*

A$_1$ Go to Doha city center you may get it at 4 floor.
Local: Good, Human: Good

A$_2$ "Hobby Shop" in City center has these toys with original motors. They are super cool.. U will love that shop..and will definetly buy one :) Have fun :)
Local: Good, Human: Good

A$_3$ IM selling all my rc nitro helicopters. call me at 5285113.. (1)TREX 600 new/ (1) TREX500 (1) SHUTTLERG (1) FUTABA ... [truncated]
Local: Good, Human: Bad

A$_4$ Hobby Shop- City Centre
Local: Bad, Human: Good

A$_5$ OMG!! :— Guns and helicopters??!!
Local: Good, Human: Bad

A$_6$ Speed Marine- Salwa Road I think these guys r the best in town...
Local: Good, Human: Good

A$_7$ City center, i've seen wonderful collection.. Its some wer besides the kids fun place..
Local: Bad, Human: Good

A$_8$ try the shop in city center. they have many RC toys for sale there. and for the toy guns, in your talking baout airsoft i think its prohibited here. good luck
Local: Good, Human: Good

Figure 1: Example answer-thread with human annotations and automatic predictions by a local classifier at the comment level.

[1]http://stackexchange.com/

Proceedings of NAACL-HLT 2016, pages 703–713,
San Diego, California, June 12-17, 2016. ©2016 Association for Computational Linguistics

Thus, the creation of automatic systems for Community Question Answering (cQA), which could provide efficient and effective ways to find good answers in a forum, has received a lot of research attention recently (Duan et al., 2008; Li and Manandhar, 2011; dos Santos et al., 2015; Zhou et al., 2015a; Wang and Ittycheriah, 2015; Tan et al., 2015; Feng et al., 2015; Nicosia et al., 2015; Barrón-Cedeño et al., 2015; Joty et al., 2015). There have been also related shared tasks at SemEval-2015[2] and SemEval-2016[3] (Nakov et al., 2015; Nakov et al., 2016).

In this paper, we focus on the particular problem of classifying comments in the answer-thread of a given question as *good* or *bad* answers. Figure 1 presents an excerpt of a real example from the Qatar-Living dataset from SemEval-2015 Task 3. There is a question on top (Q) followed by eight comments $(A_1, A_2, \cdots, A_8)$. According to the human annotations ('Human'), all comments but 3 and 5 are good answers to Q. The comments also contain the predictions of a *good-vs-bad* binary classifier trained with state-of-the-art features on this dataset (Nicosia et al., 2015); its errors are highlighted in red. Many comments are short, making it difficult for the classifier to make the right decisions, but some errors could be corrected using information in the other comments. For instance, comments 4 and 7 are similar to each other, but also to comments 2 and 8 ('Hobby shop', 'City Center', etc.). It seems reasonable to think that similar comments should have the same labels, so comments 2, 4, 7 and 8 should all be labeled consistently as *good* comments.

Indeed, recent work has shown the benefit of using varied thread-level information for answer classification, either by developing features modeling the thread structure and dialogue (Barrón-Cedeño et al., 2015), or by applying global inference mechanisms at the thread level using the predictions of local classifiers (Joty et al., 2015). We follow the second approach, assuming a graph representation of the answer-thread, where nodes are comments and edges represent pairwise (similarity) relations between them. Classification decisions are at the level of nodes and edges, and global inference is used to get the best label assignment to all comments.

Our main contribution is to propose online models for learning the decisions jointly, incorporating the inference inside the joint learning algorithm. Building on the ideas from papers coupling learning and inference for NLP structure prediction problems (Punyakanok et al., 2005; Carreras et al., 2005), we propose joint learning of two MaxEnt classifiers with stochastic gradient descent, integrating global inference based on loopy belief propagation. We also propose a joint model with global normalization, that is an instance of Fully Connected Conditional Random Fields (Murphy, 2012). We compare our joint models with the previous state of the art for the comment classification problem. We find that the coupled learning-and-inference model is not competitive, probably due to the label bias problem. On the contrary, the fully connected CRF model improves results significantly over all rivaling models, yielding the best results on the task to date.

In the remainder of this paper, after discussing related work in Section 2, we introduce our joint models in Section 3. We then describe our experimental settings in Section 4. The experiments and analysis of results are presented in Section 5. Finally, we summarize our contributions with future directions in Section 6.

2 Related Work

The idea of using global inference based on locally learned classifiers has been tried in various settings. In the family of graph-based inference, Pang and Lee (2004) used local classification scores with proximity information as edge weights in a graph-cut inference to collectively identify subjective sentences in a review. Thomas et al. (2006) used the same framework to classify congressional transcribed speeches. They applied a classifier to provide edge weights that reflect the degree of agreement between speakers. Burfoot et al. (2011) extended the framework by including other inference algorithms such as loopy belief propagation and mean-field.

"Learning and inference under structural and linguistic constraints" (Roth and Yih, 2004) is a framework to combine the predictions of local classifiers in a global decision process solved by Integer Linear Programming.

---

[2]http://alt.qcri.org/semeval2015/task3/
[3]http://alt.qcri.org/semeval2016/task3/

The framework has been applied to many NLP structure prediction problems, including shallow parsing (Punyakanok and Roth, 2000), semantic role labeling (Punyakanok et al., 2004), and joint learning of entities and relations (Roth and Yih, 2004). Further work explored the possibility of coupling learning and inference in the previous setting. For instance, Carreras et al. (2005) presented a model for parsing that jointly trains several local decisions with a perceptron-like algorithm that gets feedback after inference. Punyakanok et al. (2005) studied empirically and theoretically the cases in which this *inference-based learning* strategy is superior to the decoupled approach.

On the particular problem of comment classification in cQA, we find some work exploiting thread-level information. Hou et al. (2015) used features about the position of the comment in the thread. Barrón-Cedeño et al. (2015) developed more elaborated global features to model thread structure and the interaction among users. Other work exploited global inference algorithms at the thread-level. For instance, (Zhou et al., 2015c; Zhou et al., 2015b; Barrón-Cedeño et al., 2015) treated the task as sequential classification, using a variety of machine learning algorithms to label the sequence of time-sorted comments: LSTMs, CRFs, SVM^{hmm}, etc. Finally, Joty et al. (2015) showed that exploiting the pairwise relations between comments (at any distance) is more effective than the sequential information. Their results are the best on this task to date. In this paper, we assume the same setting (cf. Section 3) and we experiment with new models to do learning jointly with inference in the same manner as in (Punyakanok et al., 2005), and also using fully connected pairwise CRFs.

3 Our Model

Given a forum question Q and a thread of answers $T = \{A_1, A_2, \cdots, A_n\}$, the task is to classify each answer A_i in the thread into one of K possible classes based on its relevance to the question. We represent each thread as a fully-connected graph, where each node represents an answer in the thread.

Given this setting, there exist at least three fundamentally different approaches to learn classification functions.

First, the traditional approach of learning a local classifier ignoring the structure in the output and using it to predict the label of each node A_i separately. This approach only considers correlations between the label of A_i and features extracted from A_i.

The second approach, adopted by Joty et al. (2015), is to first learn two local classifiers separately: (*i*) a node-level classifier to predict the label for each individual node, and (*ii*) an edge-level classifier to predict whether the two nodes connected by an edge should have the same label or not (assuming a fully connected graph). The predictions of the local classifiers are then used in a global inference algorithm (e.g., graph-cut) to perform collective classification by maintaining structural constraints in the output. There are two issues with this model: (*i*) the local classifiers are trained separately; (*ii*) by decoupling learning from inference, this approach can lead to suboptimal solutions, as Punyakanok et al. (2005) pointed out.

The third approach, which we adopt in this paper, is to model the dependencies between the output variables while learning the classification functions jointly by optimizing a global performance criterion. The dependencies are captured using node-level and edge-level factors defined over a fully connected graph. The idea is that incorporating structural constraints in the form of all-pair relations during training can yield a better solution that directly optimizes an objective function for the target task.

Before we present our models in subsections 3.1 and 3.2, let us first introduce the notation that we will use. Each thread $T = \{A_1, A_2, \cdots, A_n\}$ is represented by a complete graph $G = (V, E)$. Each node $i \in V$ in the graph is associated with an input vector $\mathbf{x}_i$, which represents the features of an answer A_i, and an output variable $y_i \in \{1, 2, \cdots, K\}$, representing the class label. Similarly, each edge $(i, j) \in E$ is associated with an input feature vector $\phi(\mathbf{x}_i, \mathbf{x}_j)$, derived from the node-level features, and an output variable $y_{i,j} \in \{1, 2, \cdots, L\}$, representing the labels for the pair of nodes. We use $\psi_n(y_i | \mathbf{x}_i, \mathbf{v})$ and $\psi_e(y_{i,j} | \phi(\mathbf{x}_i, \mathbf{x}_j), \mathbf{w})$ to denote the node-level and the edge-level classification functions, respectively. We call ψ_n and ψ_e factors, which can be either normalized (e.g., probabilities) or unnormalized quantities. The model parameters $\theta = [\mathbf{v}, \mathbf{w}]$ are to be learned during training.

3.1 Joint Learning of Two Classifiers with Global Thread-Level Inference

Our aim is to train the local classifiers so that they produce correct global classification. To this end, in our first model we train the node- and the edge-level classifiers jointly based on global feedback provided by a global inference algorithm. The global feedback determines how much to adjust the local classifiers so that the classifiers and the inference together produce the desired result. We use log-linear models (aka maximum entropy) for both classifiers:

$$\psi_n(y_i = k|\mathbf{x_i}, \mathbf{v}) \;=\; \frac{\exp(\mathbf{v}_k^T\mathbf{x_i})}{\sum_{k'=1}^{K}\exp(\mathbf{v}_k^T\mathbf{x_i})} \quad (1)$$

$$\psi_e(y_{i,j} = l|\phi(\mathbf{x_i}, \mathbf{x_j}), \mathbf{w}) = \frac{\exp(\mathbf{w}_l^T\phi(\mathbf{x_i}, \mathbf{x_j}))}{\sum_{l'=1}^{L}\exp(\mathbf{w}_{l'}^T\phi(\mathbf{x_i}, \mathbf{x_j}))} \quad (2)$$

The log likelihood (LL) for one data point $(\mathbf{x}, \mathbf{y})$ (i.e., a thread) can be written as follows:

$$f(\theta) = \sum_{i\in V}\sum_{k=1}^{K} y_i^k \left[\mathbf{v}_k^T\mathbf{x_i} - \log Z(\mathbf{v}, \mathbf{x_i})\right] +$$

$$\sum_{(i,j)\in E}\sum_{l=1}^{L} y_{i,j}^l \left[\mathbf{w}_l^T\phi(\mathbf{x_i}, \mathbf{x_j}) - \log Z(\mathbf{w}, \mathbf{x_i}, \mathbf{x_j})\right] \quad (3)$$

where y_i^k and $y_{i,j}^l$ are the gold labels for i-th node and (i, j)-th edge expressed in 1-of-K (or 1-of-L) encoding, respectively, and $Z(\cdot)$ terms are the local normalization constants.

We give a pseudocode in Algorithm 1 that trains this model in an online fashion using feedback from the loopy belief propagation (LBP) inference algorithm (to be described later in Section 3.1.1). Specifically, the marginals from the LBP are used in a stochastic gradient descent (SGD) algorithm, which has the following (minibatch) update rule:

$$\theta_{t+1} = \theta_t - \eta_t \frac{1}{N} f'(\theta_t) \quad (4)$$

where θ_t and η_t are the model parameters and the learning rate at step t, respectively, and $\frac{1}{N}f'(\theta_t)$ is the mean gradient for the minibatch (a thread). For our maximum entropy models, the gradients become

$$f'(\mathbf{v}) \;=\; \sum_{i\in V}\left[\beta_n(y_i) - y_i\right].\mathbf{x}_i \quad (5)$$

$$f'(\mathbf{w}) \;=\; \sum_{(i,j)\in E}\left[\beta_e(y_{i,j}) - y_{i,j}\right].\phi(\mathbf{x_i}, \mathbf{x_j}) \quad (6)$$

Algorithm 1: Joint learning of local classifiers with global thread-level inference

1. Initialize the model parameters $\mathbf{v}$ and $\mathbf{w}$;
2. **repeat**
    for *each thread* $G = (V, E)$ **do**
        a. Compute node and edge probabilities $\psi_n(y_i|\mathbf{x}_i, \mathbf{v})$ and $\psi_e(y_{i,j}|\phi(\mathbf{x}_i, \mathbf{x}_j), \mathbf{w})$;
        b. Infer node and edge marginals $\beta_n(y_i)$ and $\beta_e(y_{i,j})$ using sum-product LBP;
        c. Update: $\mathbf{v} = \mathbf{v} - \frac{\eta}{|V|}f'(\mathbf{v})$;
        d. Update: $\mathbf{w} = \mathbf{w} - \frac{\eta}{|E|}f'(\mathbf{w})$;
    end
until *convergence*;

In the above equations, β and y are the marginals and the gold labels, respectively.

Note that when applying the model to the test threads, we need to perform the same global inference to get the best label assignments.

3.1.1 Inference Using Belief Propagation

Belief Propagation or BP (Pearl, 1988) is a message passing algorithm for inference in probabilistic graphical models. It supports (i) *sum-product,* to compute the marginal distribution for each unobserved variable, i.e., $p(y_i|\mathbf{x}, \theta)$; and (ii) *max-product,* to compute the most likely label configuration, i.e., $\operatorname{argmax}_{\mathbf{y}} p(\mathbf{y}|\mathbf{x}, \theta)$. We describe here the variant that operates on undirected graphs (aka Markov random fields) with pairwise factors, which uses the following equations:

$$\mu_{i\rightarrow j}(y_j) = \sum_{y_i} \psi_n(y_i)\psi_e(y_{i,j})\prod_{k\in N(i)\backslash j}\mu_{k\rightarrow i}(y_i) \quad (7)$$

$$\beta_n(y_i) \;\approx\; \psi_n(y_i)\prod_{j\in N(i)}\mu_{j\rightarrow i}(y_i) \quad (8)$$

where $\mu_{i\rightarrow j}$ is a message from node i to node j, $N(i)$ are the nodes neighbouring i, and $\psi_n(y_i)$ and $\psi_e(y_{i,j})$ are the node and the edge factors.

The algorithm proceeds by sending messages on each edge until the node beliefs $\beta_n(y_i)$ stabilize. The edge beliefs can be written as follows:

$$\beta_e(y_{i,j}) \approx \psi_e(y_{i,j}) \times \mu_{i\rightarrow j}(y_i) \times \mu_{j\rightarrow i}(y_j) \quad (9)$$

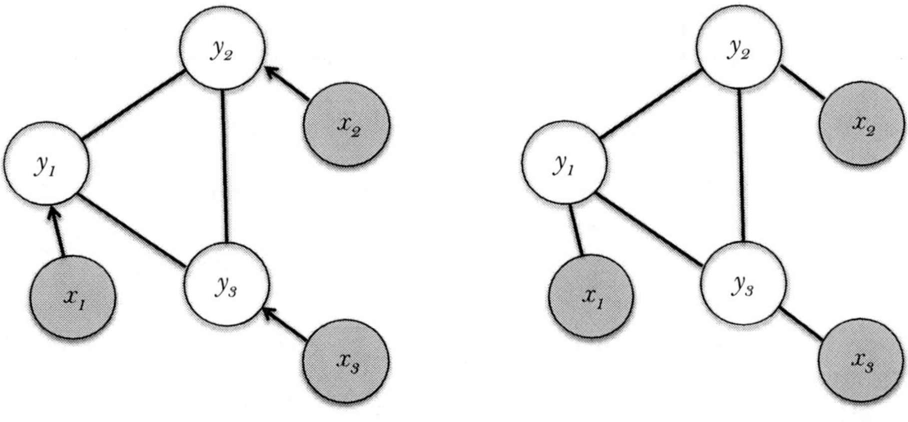

(a) Locally normalized joint model   (b) Globally normalized joint model

Figure 2: Graphical representation of our two joint models: (a) a joint model with locally normalized factors; (b) a joint model with global normalization, i.e., a fully connected conditional random field.

The node and the edge marginals are then computed by normalizing the node and the edge beliefs, respectively. By replacing the summation with a max operation in Equation 7, we can get the most likely label configuration (i.e., argmax over labels).

BP is guaranteed to converge to an exact solution if the graph is a tree. However, exact inference is intractable for general graphs, i.e., graphs with loops. Despite this, it has been advocated by Pearl (1988) to use BP in loopy graphs as an approximation scheme; see also (Murphy, 2012), page 768. The algorithm is then called "loopy" BP, or LBP. Although LBP gives approximate solutions for general graphs, it often works well in practice (Murphy et al., 1999), outperforming other methods such as mean field (Weiss, 2001) and graph-cut (Burfoot et al., 2011).

It is important to mention that the approach presented above (i.e., subsection 3.1) is similar in spirit to the approach of Collins (2002), Carreras and Màrquez (2003) and Punyakanok et al. (2005). The main difference is that they use a Perceptron-like online algorithm, where the updates are done based on the best label configuration (i.e., $\mathrm{argmax}_{\mathbf{y}}\, p(\mathbf{y}|\mathbf{x}, \theta)$) rather than the marginals.

One can use graph-cut (applicable only for binary output variables) or max-product LBP for the decoding task. However, this yields a discontinuous estimate (even with averaged perceptron) for the gradient (see Section 5). For the same reason, we use sum-product LBP rather than max-product LBP.

3.2 A Joint Model with Global Normalization

Although the approach of updating the parameters of the local classifiers based on the global inference might seem like a natural extension to train the classifiers jointly, it suffers from at least two problems. First, since the node and the edge scores are normalized locally (see Equations 1 and 2), this approach leads to the so-called *label bias* problem, previously discussed by Lafferty et al. (2001). Namely, due to the local normalization, local features at any node do not influence states of other nodes in the graph. Second, the two classifiers use their own feature sets. However, the same feature sets that give optimal results locally (i.e., when trained on local objectives), may not work well when the models are trained jointly based on the global feedback. In order to address these issues, below we propose a different model.

In our second approach, we seek to build a joint model with global normalization. We define the following conditional joint distribution:

$$p(\mathbf{y}|\mathbf{v}, \mathbf{w}, \mathbf{x}) = \frac{1}{Z(\mathbf{v}, \mathbf{w}, \mathbf{x})} \prod_{i \in V} \psi_n(y_i|\mathbf{x}, \mathbf{v}) \cdot$$
$$\prod_{(i,j) \in E} \psi_e(y_{i,j}|\mathbf{x}, \mathbf{w}) \quad (10)$$

where ψ_n and ψ_e are the node and edge *factors*, and $Z(\cdot)$ is the global normalization constant that ensures a valid probability distribution.

This model is essentially a fully connected conditional random field or FCCRF (Murphy, 2012). Figure 2 shows the differences between the two models with the standard graphical model representation.[4] The global normalization allows CRFs to take long-range interactions into account. Similar to our previous model, we use a log-linear representation for the factors:

$$\psi_n(y_i|\mathbf{x}, \mathbf{v}) = \exp(\mathbf{v}^T \phi(y_i, \mathbf{x})) \quad (11)$$
$$\psi_e(y_{i,j}|\mathbf{x}, \mathbf{w}) = \exp(\mathbf{w}^T \phi(y_{i,j}, \mathbf{x})) \quad (12)$$

where $\phi(\cdot)$ is a feature vector derived from the inputs and the labels. The LL for one data point becomes

$$f(\theta) = \sum_{i \in V} \mathbf{v}^T \phi(y_i, \mathbf{x}) + \sum_{(i,j) \in E} \mathbf{w}^T \phi(y_{i,j}, \mathbf{x})$$
$$- \log Z(\mathbf{v}, \mathbf{w}, \mathbf{x}) \quad (13)$$

This objective is convex, so we can use gradient-based methods to find the global optimum. The gradients have the following form:

$$f'(\mathbf{v}) = \sum_{i \in V} \phi(y_i, \mathbf{x}) - \mathbb{E}[\phi(y_i, \mathbf{x})] \quad (14)$$
$$f'(\mathbf{w}) = \sum_{(i,j) \in E} \phi(y_{i,j}, \mathbf{x}) - \mathbb{E}[\phi(y_{i,j}, \mathbf{x})] \quad (15)$$

where $\mathbb{E}[\phi(.)]$ terms denote the expected feature vector. Traditionally, CRFs have been trained using offline methods like limited-memory BFGS. Online training of CRFs using SGD was proposed by Vishwanathan et al. (2006). To compare our two methods, we use SGD to train our CRF models. The pseudocode is very similar to Algorithm 1.

3.2.1 Modeling Edge Factors

One crucial aspect in the joint models described above is the modeling of edge factors. The traditional way is to define edge factors, where $y_{i,j}$ spans over all possible state transitions, that is K^2 different transitions, each of which is associated with a weight vector. This method has the advantage that it models transitions in a fine-grained way, but, in doing so, it also increases the number of model parameters, which may result in overfitting.

Alternatively, one can define *Ising-like* edge factors, where we only distinguish between two transitions: (*i*) *same*, when $y_i = y_j$ and (*ii*) *different*, when $y_i \neq y_j$. This modeling involves tying one set of parameters for all *same* transitions, and another set for all *different* transitions.

4   Experimental Setting

In this section, we describe our experimental setting. We first introduce the dataset we use, then we present the features and the models that we compare.

4.1   Datasets and Evaluation

We experimented with the dataset from SemEval-2015 Task 3 on Answer Selection for Community Question Answering (Nakov et al., 2015). The dataset contains question-answer threads from the Qatar Living forum.[5] Each thread consists of a question followed by one or more (up to 143) comments. The dataset is split into training, development and test sets, with 2,600, 300, and 329 questions, and 16,541, 1,645, and 1,976 answers, respectively.

Each comment in the dataset is annotated with one of the following labels, reflecting how well it answers the question: *Good*, *Potential*, *Bad*, *Dialogue*, *Not English*, and *Other*. At SemEval-2015 Task 3, the latter four classes were merged into *BAD* at testing time, and the evaluation measure uses a macro-averaged F_1 over the three classes: *Good*, *Potential*, and *BAD*. Unfortunately, the *Potential* class was both the smallest (covering about 10% of the data), and also the noisiest and the hardest to predict; yet, its impact was magnified by the macro-averaged F_1. Thus, subsequent work has further merged *Potential* under *BAD* (Barrón-Cedeño et al., 2015; Joty et al., 2015), and has used for evaluation F_1 with respect to the *Good* category (or just accuracy). For our experiments below, we also report F_1 for the *Good* class and the overall accuracy. We further perform statistical significance tests using an approximate randomization test based on accuracy.[6] We used SIGF V.2 (Padó, 2006) with 10,000 iterations.

---

[4]Edge level features and output variables are not shown in Figure 2 to avoid visual clutter.

[5]http://www.qatarliving.com/forum

[6]Significance tests operate on individual instances rather than individual classes; thus, they are not applicable for F_1.

4.2 Features

For comparison, we use the features from our previous work (Joty et al., 2015) to implement all classifiers in our models and baselines. There are two sets of features, corresponding to the two main classification problems in the models: node-level (i.e., classifying a comment as *good* or *bad*) and edge-level (i.e., classifying a pair of comments as having the *same* or *different* labels).

The features for node-level classification include three types of information: (*i*) a variety of textual similarity measures computed between the question and the comment, (*ii*) several boolean features capturing the presence of certain relevant words or patterns, e.g., URLs, emails, positive/negative words, acknowledgements, forum categories, presence of long words, etc., and (*iii*) a set of global features modeling dialogue and user interactions in the answer-thread. The features in the last two categories are manually engineered (Nicosia et al., 2015; Barrón-Cedeño et al., 2015).

The features we use for edge-level classification include (*i*) all features from the node classification problem coded as the absolute value of the difference between the two comments, (*ii*) a variety of text similarity features between the two comments, (*iii*) the *good/bad* predictions of the node-level classifier on the two comments involved in the edge decision. See (Joty et al., 2015) and (Barrón-Cedeño et al., 2015) for a detailed description of the features.

4.3 Methods Compared

We experimentally compare our above-described joint models to some baselines and to the state of the art for this problem. We briefly describe all models below, together with the names used in the tables of results.

Independent Comment Classification (ICC) These are binary classifiers to label thread comments independently into *good* and *bad* categories. The simplest baseline (Majority) classifies all examples with the most frequent category. We also train a MaxEnt classifier with stochastic gradient descent (SGD) and a voted perceptron (ICC_{ME} and ICC_{Perc}, respectively).

Learning-and-Inference Models (LI) This is the approach presented by Joty et al. (2015), who report the best results on the task. The model is explained in Section 3. We experiment with MaxEnt classifiers trained on-line with SGD and two different inference strategies, graph-cut and loopy BP (LI_{ME-GC} and LI_{ME-LBP}, in our notation).

Joint Learning and Inference Models These are our new models. First, we experiment with the model for joint learning of two classifiers coupled with thread-level inference (Section 3.1). We have two versions, one using MaxEnt classifiers and the other using averaged Perceptron. The inference algorithm is loopy BP in both cases. We call these methods $Joint_{ME-LBP}$ and $Joint_{Perc-LBP}$, respectively. Second, we experiment with the joint model with global normalization (cf. Section 3.2). We call it FCCRF, for fully connected CRF. We use the *Ising-like* edge factors defined in Section 3.2.1.

5 Evaluation

All results we report below are calculated in the test set, using parameters tuned on the development set.

Our main results are shown in Table 1, where we report accuracy (Acc) as well as precision (P), recall (R) and F_1-score (F_1) for the *good* class.

The models are organized in four blocks. On top, we see that the majority class baseline achieves accuracy of 50.5%, as the dataset is very well balanced between the classes.

In block II, we find the results for the local classifiers, ICC_{ME} and ICC_{Perc}, which achieve very similar results. They are comparable to MaxEnt in Table 2, where we report the best published results on this dataset; yet, our classifiers are trained on-line.

Block III in the table reports results for models that train two local MaxEnt classifiers and then perform thread-level inference using either graph-cut (LI_{ME-GC}) or loopy BP (LI_{ME-LBP}).[7] This yields improvements over the ICC models with the thread-level inference in block II, which is consistent with the findings of (Joty et al., 2015); however, the difference in terms of accuracy is not statistically significant (p-value = 0.09).

---

[7]Given that MaxEnt and Perceptron perform comparably in this setting, we have just used MaxEnt as it provides directly the class probabilities needed for the thread-level inference.

	Model	Learning	Inference	P	R	F_1	Acc
I.	Majority	–	–	50.5	100.0	67.1	50.5
II.	ICC_{ME}	Local, SGD	–	75.1	85.8	80.1	78.5
	ICC_{Perc}	Local, Voted	–	76.6	82.4	79.4	78.4
III.	LI_{ME-GC}	Local, SGD	Graph-cut	**77.4**	83.6	80.4	79.4
	LI_{ME-LBP}	Local, SGD	LBP	76.4	84.6	80.3	79.1
IV.	$Joint_{ME-LBP}$	2 classifiers, Joint, SGD	LBP	76.1	84.4	80.0	78.7
	$Joint_{Perc-LBP}$	2 classifiers, Joint, AVG	LBP	77.1	74.5	75.8	76.0
	FCCRF	Joint, SGD	LBP	77.3	**86.2**	**81.5**	**80.5**

Table 1: Results of all compared models on the test set. The best results are boldfaced.

Model	P	R	F_1	Acc
MaxEnt classifier	75.7	84.3	79.8	78.4
Linear CRF	74.9	83.5	78.9	77.5
MaxEnt+ILP	77.0	83.5	80.2	79.1
MaxEnt+GraphCut	**78.3**	82.9	80.6	79.8
Our method (FCCRF)	77.3	**86.2**	**81.5**	**80.5**

Table 2: Comparison to the best published results on the same datasets, as reported in (Joty et al., 2015).

Comparing our LI_{ME-GC} to MaxEnt+GraphCut in Table 2, we see that we are slightly worse: -0.2 in F_1-score, and -0.4 in accuracy. It turns out that this is due to our on-line MaxEnt classifier for the pairwise classification being slightly worse (-0.4 accuracy points absolute), which could explain the lower performance after the graph-cut inference.

Next, block IV shows that the fully connected CRF model (FCCRF) improves over the models in block III by more than one point absolute in both F_1 and accuracy. The improvement is statistically significant (p-value = 0.04); especially noticeable is the increase in recall (+2.6 points). This result is also an improvement over the state of the art, as Table 2 shows.

Again in block IV, we can see that the two models that perform joint training of two classifiers and then integrate inference in the training loop, $Joint_{ME-LBP}$ and $Joint_{Perc-LBP}$, do not work well and fall below the learning and inference models from block III. As we explained above, these models have two major disadvantages compared to FCCRF: (*i*) the local normalization of node and edge scores is prone to label bias issues; (*ii*) each of the two classifiers uses its own feature set, which might not be optimal when they are trained jointly based on the global feedback.

Notice that the version using Perceptron, $Joint_{Perc-LBP}$, works bad in this setting. Since updates are done after each thread-level inference, we could not use a voted perceptron, but an averaged one (Collins, 2002). Moreover, it did not yield probabilities but real-valued scores, which we had to remap to the [0;1] interval using a sigmoid.

5.1 CRF Variants Analysis

Table 3 compares different variants of CRF. The first two rows show the results for the commonly used linear-chain CRF (LCCRF) of order 1 and 2. We can see that these models fall two accuracy (and F_1) points below FCCRF, which indicates that the pairwise relations between non-consecutive comments provide additional relevant information for the task. The fourth row shows the results when we eliminate the edge-level features and we consider state transitions using the bias features only: the decrease in performance is tiny, which means that what matters is to model the interaction in the first place; the particular features used are less important. More noticeable is the effect of using Ising-like modeling of the edge factors in our FCCRF model. If we use finer-grained edge factors for each of the four combinations (Good-Good, Good-Bad, Bad-Good, and Bad-Bad), the performance decreases significantly, mostly due to a drop in recall (see 'FCCRF (4C)').

5.2 Error Analysis

Next, we get a closer look at the predictions made by our best Local (ICC_{ME}), Inference (LI_{ME-GC}), and Global (FCCRF) models. We focus on questions for which there are at least two comments. There were 280 such test questions (out of 329), with a total of 1,927 comments.

Model	P	R	F_1	Acc
LCCRF (ord=1)	76.1	83.2	79.4	78.3
LCCRF (ord=2)	76.8	82.1	79.3	78.4
FCCRF	77.3	**86.2**	**81.5**	**80.5**
FCCRF-noFeatures	77.2	86.0	81.4	80.1
FCCRF (4C)	**78.8**	79.7	79.3	79.0

Table 3: Results for different variants of the joint CRF model on the test set.

The Local, the Inference, and the Joint models made correct predictions for 78.7%, 79.1% and 80.4% of the comments, respectively. We can see that the Inference model behaves more like Local, and not so much like Joint. This is indeed further confirmed when we look at the agreement between each pair of models: Local vs. Inference has 6.0% disagreement, for Local vs. Joint it is 9.9%, and for Inference vs. Joint it is 8.8%.

Figure 3 compares the three models vs. the gold human labels on a particular test question (ID=Q2908; some long comments are truncated and the four omitted answers were classified correctly by all three classifiers). We can see that the Joint model is more robust than the Local one: while Joint corrects two of the three wrong classifications of Local, Inference makes two further errors instead.

6 Conclusion

We have proposed two learning methods for comment classification in community Question Answering. We depart from the state-of-the-art knowledge that exploiting the interrelations between all the comments in the answer-thread is beneficial for the task. Thus, we take as our baseline the learning and inference model from Joty et al. (2015), in which the answer-thread is modeled as a fully connected graph. Our contribution consists of moving the framework to on-line learning and proposing two models for coupling learning with inference.

Our first model learns jointly the two MaxEnt classifiers with SGD and incorporates the graph inference at every step with loopy belief propagation. This model, due to its local normalization, suffers from the label bias problem. The alternative we proposed is to use an instance of a Fully Connected CRF that operates on the same graph and considers the node and edge factors with a shared set of features.

Q: *I have a female friend who is leaving for a teaching job in Qatar in January. What would be a useful portable gift to give her to take with her?*

$\mathbf{A}_1$ A couple of good best-selling novels. [...]
Loc: Good, Inf: Good, Jnt: Good, Hum: Good

$\mathbf{A}_5$ A big box of decent tea.... like "Scottish blend" or "Tetleys".. [...]
Loc: Good, Inf: Good, Jnt: Good, Hum: Good

$\mathbf{A}_6$ Bacon. Nice bread, bacon, bacon, errmmm bacon and a pork joint..
Loc: Good, Inf: Bad, Jnt: Good, Hum: Good

$\mathbf{A}_8$ Go to Tesco buy some good latest DVD.. [...]
Loc: Good, Inf: Good, Jnt: Good, Hum: Good

$\mathbf{A}_9$ Couple of good novels, All time favorite movies, ..
Loc: Good, Inf: Bad, Jnt: Good, Hum: Good

$\mathbf{A}_{10}$ Agree I do the same Indorachel..But some time you get a good copy some time a bad one.. [...]
Loc: Good, Inf: Good, Jnt: Good, Hum: Bad

$\mathbf{A}_{11}$ Ditto on the books and dvd's. Excedrin.
Loc: Bad, Inf: Bad, Jnt: Good, Hum: Good

$\mathbf{A}_{12}$ Ditto on the bacon, pork sausage, pork chops, ham,..can you tell we miss pork! [...]
Loc: Bad, Inf: Bad, Jnt: Good, Hum: Good

Figure 3: Sample test question with a thread of comments and, for each comment, decisions by the local (Loc), the global inference (Inf), and the global joint (Jnt) classifiers, as well as by the human annotators.

One of the main advantages is that the normalization is global. We experimented with the SemEval-2015 Task 3 dataset and we confirmed the advantage of the FCCRF model, which outperforms all baselines and achieves better results than the state of the art.

In the near future, we plan to apply the FCCRF model to the full cQA task, i.e., finding good answers to newly-asked questions using previously-asked questions and their answer threads. In this setting, we want to experiment with (*i*) ranking comments (instead of classifying them), (*ii*) exploiting the similarities between the new question and the questions in the database and also the relations between comments across different answer-threads.

Acknowledgments

This research was performed by the Arabic Language Technologies (ALT) group at the Qatar Computing Research Institute (QCRI), HBKU, part of Qatar Foundation. It is part of the Interactive sYstems for Answer Search (IYAS) project, which is developed in collaboration with MIT-CSAIL.

References

Alberto Barrón-Cedeño, Simone Filice, Giovanni Da San Martino, Shafiq Joty, Lluís Màrquez, Preslav Nakov, and Alessandro Moschitti. 2015. Thread-level information for comment classification in community question answering. In *Proceedings of the 53rd Annual Meeting of the Association for Computational Linguistics and the 7th International Joint Conference on Natural Language Processing*, ACL-IJCNLP '15, pages 687–693, Beijing, China.

Clinton Burfoot, Steven Bird, and Timothy Baldwin. 2011. Collective classification of congressional floor-debate transcripts. In *Proceedings of the 49th Annual Meeting of the Association for Computational Linguistics: Human Language Technologies - Volume 1*, HLT '11, pages 1506–1515, Portland, Oregon.

Xavier Carreras and Lluís Màrquez. 2003. Online learning via global feedback for phrase recognition. In *Proceedings of the 17th Annual Conference on Neural Information Processing Systems*, NIPS '03, Whistler, Canada. MIT Press.

Xavier Carreras, Lluís Màrquez, and Jorge Castro. 2005. Filtering–ranking perceptron learning for partial parsing. *Machine Learning*, 60:41–71.

Michael Collins. 2002. Discriminative training methods for hidden Markov models: Theory and experiments with perceptron algorithms. In *Proceedings of the 2002 Conference on Empirical Methods in Natural Language Processing*, EMNLP '02, pages 1–8, Philadelphia, Pennsylvania, USA.

Cicero dos Santos, Luciano Barbosa, Dasha Bogdanova, and Bianca Zadrozny. 2015. Learning hybrid representations to retrieve semantically equivalent questions. In *Proceedings of the 53rd Annual Meeting of the Association for Computational Linguistics and the 7th International Joint Conference on Natural Language Processing (Volume 2: Short Papers)*, ACL-IJCNLP '15, pages 694–699, Beijing, China.

Huizhong Duan, Yunbo Cao, Chin-Yew Lin, and Yong Yu. 2008. Searching questions by identifying question topic and question focus. In *Proceedings of the 46th Annual Meeting of the Association for Computational Linguistics and the Human Language Technology Conference*, ACL-HLT '08, pages 156–164, Columbus, Ohio, USA.

Minwei Feng, Bing Xiang, Michael R Glass, Lidan Wang, and Bowen Zhou. 2015. Applying deep learning to answer selection: A study and an open task. In *Proceedings of the 2015 IEEE Workshop on Automatic Speech Recognition and Understanding*, ASRU '15, pages 813–820, Scottsdale, Arizona, USA.

Yongshuai Hou, Cong Tan, Xiaolong Wang, Yaoyun Zhang, Jun Xu, and Qingcai Chen. 2015. HITSZ-ICRC: Exploiting classification approach for answer selection in community question answering. In *Proceedings of the 9th International Workshop on Semantic Evaluation*, SemEval '15, pages 196–202, Denver, Colorado, USA.

Shafiq Joty, Alberto Barrón-Cedeño, Giovanni Da San Martino, Simone Filice, Lluís Màrquez, Alessandro Moschitti, and Preslav Nakov. 2015. Global thread-level inference for comment classification in community question answering. In *Proceedings of the 2015 Conference on Empirical Methods in Natural Language Processing*, EMNLP '15, pages 573–578, Lisbon, Portugal.

John Lafferty, Andrew McCallum, and Fernando Pereira. 2001. Conditional random fields: Probabilistic models for segmenting and labeling sequence data. In *Proceedings of the Eighteenth International Conference on Machine Learning*, ICML '01, pages 282–289, San Francisco, California, USA.

Shuguang Li and Suresh Manandhar. 2011. Improving question recommendation by exploiting information need. In *Proceedings of the 49th Annual Meeting of the Association for Computational Linguistics: Human Language Technologies - Volume 1*, ACL '11, pages 1425–1434, Portland, Oregon, USA.

Kevin P. Murphy, Yair Weiss, and Michael I. Jordan. 1999. Loopy belief propagation for approximate inference: An empirical study. In *Proceedings of the Fifteenth Conference on Uncertainty in Artificial Intelligence*, UAI'99, pages 467–475, Stockholm, Sweden.

Kevin Murphy. 2012. *Machine Learning A Probabilistic Perspective*. The MIT Press.

Preslav Nakov, Lluís Màrquez, Walid Magdy, Alessandro Moschitti, Jim Glass, and Bilal Randeree. 2015. SemEval-2015 task 3: Answer selection in community question answering. In *Proceedings of the 9th International Workshop on Semantic Evaluation*, SemEval '15, pages 269–281, Denver, Colorado, USA.

Preslav Nakov, Lluís Màrquez, Alessandro Moschitti, Walid Magdy, Hamdy Mubarak, Abed Alhakim Freihat, Jim Glass, and Bilal Randeree. 2016. SemEval-2016 task 3: Community question answering. In *Proceedings of the 10th International Workshop on Semantic Evaluation*, SemEval '16, San Diego, California, USA.

Massimo Nicosia, Simone Filice, Alberto Barrón-Cedeño, Iman Saleh, Hamdy Mubarak, Wei Gao, Preslav Nakov, Giovanni Da San Martino, Alessandro Moschitti, Kareem Darwish, Lluís Màrquez, Shafiq Joty, and Walid Magdy. 2015. QCRI: Answer selection for community question answering - experiments for Arabic and English. In *Proceedings of the 9th International Workshop on Semantic Evaluation*, SemEval '15, pages 203–209, Denver, Colorado, USA.

Sebastian Padó, 2006. *User's guide to `sigf`: Significance testing by approximate randomisation.*

Bo Pang and Lillian Lee. 2004. A sentimental education: Sentiment analysis using subjectivity summarization based on minimum cuts. In *Proceedings of the 42nd Annual Meeting on Association for Computational Linguistics*, ACL '04, pages 271–278, Barcelona, Spain.

Judea Pearl. 1988. *Probabilistic Reasoning in Intelligent Systems: Networks of Plausible Inference.* Morgan Kaufmann Publishers Inc., San Francisco, California, USA.

Vasin Punyakanok and Dan Roth. 2000. Shallow parsing by inferencing with classifiers. In *Proceedings of the 2nd Workshop on Learning Language in Logic and the 4th Conference on Computational Natural Language Learning - Volume 7*, ConLL '00, pages 107–110, Lisbon, Portugal.

Vasin Punyakanok, Dan Roth, Wen-tau Yih, and Dav Zimak. 2004. Semantic role labeling via integer linear programming inference. In *Proceedings of the 20th International Conference on Computational Linguistics*, COLING '04, Geneva, Switzerland.

Vasin Punyakanok, Dan Roth, Wen-tau Yih, and Dav Zimak. 2005. Learning and inference over constrained output. In *Proceedings of the 19th International Joint Conference on Artificial Intelligence*, IJCAI' 05, pages 1124–1129, Edinburgh, Scotland.

Dan Roth and Wen-tau Yih. 2004. A linear programming formulation for global inference in natural language tasks. In *Proceedings of the HLT-NAACL 2004 Workshop: Eighth Conference on Computational Natural Language Learning*, CoNLL '04, pages 1–8, Boston, Massachusetts, USA.

Ming Tan, Bing Xiang, and Bowen Zhou. 2015. LSTM-based deep learning models for non-factoid answer selection. *arXiv preprint arXiv:1511.04108.*

Matt Thomas, Bo Pang, and Lillian Lee. 2006. Get out the vote: Determining support or opposition from congressional floor-debate transcripts. In *Proceedings of the 2006 Conference on Empirical Methods in Natural Language Processing*, EMNLP '06, pages 327–335, Sydney, Australia.

S. V. N. Vishwanathan, Nicol N. Schraudolph, Mark W. Schmidt, and Kevin P. Murphy. 2006. Accelerated training of conditional random fields with stochastic gradient methods. In *Proceedings of the 23rd International Conference on Machine Learning*, ICML '06, pages 969–976, Pittsburgh, Pennsylvania, USA.

Zhiguo Wang and Abraham Ittycheriah. 2015. Faq-based question answering via word alignment. *arXiv preprint arXiv:1507.02628.*

Yair Weiss. 2001. Comparing the mean field method and belief propagation for approximate inference in MRFs. *Advanced Mean Field Methods.*

Guangyou Zhou, Tingting He, Jun Zhao, and Po Hu. 2015a. Learning continuous word embedding with metadata for question retrieval in community question answering. In *Proceedings of the 53rd Annual Meeting of the Association for Computational Linguistics and the 7th International Joint Conference on Natural Language Processing (Volume 1: Long Papers)*, ACL-IJCNLP '15, pages 250–259, Beijing, China.

Xiaoqiang Zhou, Baotian Hu, Qingcai Chen, Buzhou Tang, and Xiaolong Wang. 2015b. Answer sequence learning with neural networks for answer selection in community question answering. In *Proceedings of the 53rd Annual Meeting of the Association for Computational Linguistics*, pages 713–718, Beijing, China.

Xiaoqiang Zhou, Baotian Hu, Jiaxin Lin, Yang Xiang, and Xiaolong Wang. 2015c. ICRC-HIT: A deep learning based comment sequence labeling system for answer selection challenge. In *Proceedings of the 9th International Workshop on Semantic Evaluation*, SemEval '15, pages 210–214, Denver, Colorado, USA.

Weak Semi-Markov CRFs for NP Chunking in Informal Text

Aldrian Obaja Muis and **Wei Lu**
Singapore University of Technology and Design
{aldrian_muis, luwei}@sutd.edu.sg

Abstract

This paper introduces a new annotated corpus based on an existing informal text corpus: the NUS SMS Corpus (Chen and Kan, 2013). The new corpus includes 76,490 noun phrases from 26,500 SMS messages, annotated by university students. We then explored several graphical models, including a novel variant of the semi-Markov conditional random fields (semi-CRF) for the task of noun phrase chunking. We demonstrated through empirical evaluations on the new dataset that the new variant yielded similar accuracy but ran in significantly lower running time compared to the conventional semi-CRF.

1 Introduction

Processing user-generated text data is getting more popular recently as a way to gather information, such as collecting facts about certain events (Ritter et al., 2015), gathering and identifying user profiles (Layton et al., 2010; Li et al., 2014; Spitters et al., 2015), or extracting information in open domain (Ritter et al., 2012; Mitchell et al., 2015).

Most recent work focus on the texts generated through Twitter, which, due to the design of Twitter, contain a lot of announcement-like messages mostly intended for general public. In contrast, SMS was designed as a way to communicate short personal messages to a known person, and hence SMS messages tend to be more conversational and more informal compared to tweets.

As conversational texts, SMS data often contains references to named entities such as people and locations relevant to certain events. Recognizing those

Hmm Dr teh says the research presentation should still prepare, butshe's not to sure whether they'd time to present

Figure 1: Sample SMS, with NPs underlined

references will be useful for further NLP tasks. One way to recognize those named entities is to first create a list of candidates, which can be further filtered to get the desired named entities. Nadeau (Nadeau and Sekine, 2007) lists several methods that work upon candidates for NER. As all named entities are nouns, recognizing noun phrases (NP) is therefore a task that can be potentially useful for further steps in the NLP pipeline to build upon. Figure 1 shows an example SMS message within which noun phrases are highlighted. As can be seen from this example, recognizing the NP information on such a dataset presents some additional challenges over conventional NP recognition tasks. Specifically, the texts are highly informal and noisy, with misspelling errors and without grammatical structures. The correct casing and punctuation information is often missing. The lack of spaces between adjacent words makes the detection of NP boundaries more challenging.

Furthermore, the lack of available annotated data for such informal datasets prevents researchers from understanding what effective models can be used to resolve the above issues. In this work, we focus on tackling these issues while making the following two main contributions:

- We build a new corpus of SMS data that is fully annotated with noun phrase information.

- We propose and build a new variant of semi-

Markov CRF (Sarawagi and Cohen, 2004) for the task of NP chunking on our corpus, which is faster and yields a performance similar to the conventional semi-Markov CRF models.

2 NP-annotated SMS Corpus

Our text corpus comes from the NUS SMS Corpus (Chen and Kan, 2013), containing 55,835 SMS messages from university students, mostly in English. We used the 2011 version of the corpus, containing 45,718 messages, as it is more relevant to modern phone models using full keyboard layout.

We note that there are a small portion of the messages written in non-English language, such as Tamil and Chinese. As we are focusing on English, we excluded messages written by non-native English speakers based on the metadata (21.3% of all messages). We also excluded messages which contain only one word (6.1%) and we remove duplicate messages (8.1%). [1]

We assigned the remaining 27,700 messages to 64 university students who conduct annotations, each annotating 500 with 100 messages co-annotated by two other annotators. After manual verification we excluded annotations with low quality from 3 students. We used the resulting 26,500 messages as our dataset. The students were asked to annotate the top-level noun phrases found in each message using the BRAT rapid annotation tool[2], where they were instructed to highlight character spans to be marked as noun phrases. The number of noun phrases per message can be found in Table 1.

Due to the noisy nature of SMS messages, there may not be proper capitalization or punctuation, and in some cases there might be missing spaces between words. Figure 1 shows a sample SMS message taken from the corpus. We can see that "Dr teh" is not properly capitalized and "she" in "butshe's" is missing spaces around it. NPs which do not have clear boundaries (*improper* NPs) constitutes 4.0% of all NPs.

We then use this dataset to evaluate some models on base NP chunking task, where, given a text, the

	#SMS	#NPs	*improper*	#tokens
total	26,500	76,490	3,066 (4.0)	359,009
train	21,200	61,212	2,406 (3.9)	287,590
dev	2,650	7,617	338 (4.4)	35,470
test	2,650	7,661	322 (4.2)	35,949

Table 1: Number of messages, NPs, number of *improper* NPs (as percentage in brackets), which are NPs that end in a middle of a word, and number of tokens.

system should return a list of character spans denoting the noun phrases found in the text.

3 Models

In this paper, we will build our models based on a class of discriminative graphical models, namely conditional random fields (CRFs) (Lafferty et al., 2001), for extracting NPs. The edges in the graph represents the dependencies between states and the features are defined over each edge in the graph. Though CRFs are undirected graphical models, we can use directed acyclic graphs with a root, a leaf, and some inner nodes to represent label sequences[3]. A path in the graph from the root to the leaf represents one possible label assignment to the input. In the labeled instance, there will be only one single path from the root to the leaf, while for the unlabeled instance, the graph will compactly encode all possible label assignments. The learning procedure is essentially the process that tries to tune the feature weights such that the true structures get assigned higher weights as compared to all other alternative structures in the graph.

In general, a CRF tries to maximize the following objective function:

$$\mathcal{L}(\mathcal{T}) = \sum_{(\mathbf{x},\mathbf{y}) \in \mathcal{T}} \left[\sum_{e \in \mathcal{E}(\mathbf{x},\mathbf{y})} \mathbf{w}^T \mathbf{f}(e) - \log Z_{\mathbf{w}}(\mathbf{x}) \right] - \lambda ||\mathbf{w}||^2 \quad (1)$$

where $\mathcal{T}$ is the training set, $(\mathbf{x}, \mathbf{y})$ is a training instance consisting of the sentence $\mathbf{x}$ and the label sequence $\mathbf{y} \in \mathcal{Y}^n$ for a label set $\mathcal{Y}$, $\mathbf{w}$ is the feature weight vector, $\mathcal{E}(\mathbf{x}, \mathbf{y})$ is the set of edges which form the path in the labeled instance, $\mathbf{f}(e)$ is the feature vector of the edge e, $Z_{\mathbf{w}}(\mathbf{x})$ is the normaliza-

---

[1]We also manually excluded some messages (ID 1017-4016) which are mostly not written in English (4.0% of all messages).

[2]http://brat.nlplab.org

---

[3]Extension to directed hypergraphs is possible. See (Lu and Roth, 2015).

tion term which sums over all possible paths from the root to the leaf node, and λ is the regularization parameter.

The set of edges and features defined in each model affects the feature expectation and the normalization term. Computation of the normalization term, being the highest in time complexity, will determine the overall complexity of training the model. The set of edges and the normalization term in each model will be described in the following sections.

3.1 Linear CRF

A linear-chain CRF, or linear CRF is a standard version of CRF which was introduced in (Lafferty et al., 2001), where each word in the sentence is given a set of nodes representing the possible labels, and edges are present between any two nodes from adjacent words, forming a trellis graph. Here we consider only the first-order linear CRF.

The normalization term $Z_{\mathbf{w}}(\mathbf{x})$ is calculated as:

$$\sum_{i=1}^{n}\sum_{y\in\mathcal{Y}}\sum_{y'\in\mathcal{Y}} \mathbf{w}^{T}\mathbf{f}_{\mathbf{x}}(y',y,i) \qquad (2)$$

where $\mathbf{f}_{\mathbf{x}}(y',y,i)$ represents the feature vector on the edge connecting state y' at position $i-1$ to state y at position i. The time complexity of the inference procedure for this model is $O(n\,|\mathcal{Y}|^2)$.

3.2 Semi-CRF

In semi-CRF (Sarawagi and Cohen, 2004), in addition to the edges defined in linear CRF, there are additional edges from a node to all nodes up to L next words away, representing a segment within which the words will be labeled with a single label.

The normalization term $Z_{\mathbf{w}}(\mathbf{x})$ is calculated as:

$$\sum_{i=1}^{n}\sum_{y\in\mathcal{Y}}\sum_{k=1}^{L}\sum_{y'\in\mathcal{Y}} \mathbf{w}^{T}\mathbf{g}_{\mathbf{x}}(y',y,i-k,i) \qquad (3)$$

where $\mathbf{g}_{\mathbf{x}}(y',y,i-k,i)$ represents the feature vector on the edge connecting state y' at position $i-k$ to state y at position i. The time complexity for this model is $O(nL\,|\mathcal{Y}|^2)$.

3.3 Weak Semi-CRF

Note that in semi-CRF, each node is connected to $L \times |\mathcal{Y}|$ next nodes. Intuitively, the model tries to

decide the next segment length and type at the same time. We propose a weaker variant that makes the two decisions separately by restricting each node to connect to either only the nodes of the same label up to L next words away, or to all the nodes only in the next word. We call this *Weak Semi-CRF*.

To implement this, we need to split the original nodes into Begin and End nodes, representing the start and end of a segment. The End nodes connect only to the very next Begin nodes of any label, while the Begin nodes connect only to the End nodes of same label up to next L words. The term $Z_{\mathbf{w}}(\mathbf{x})$ is:

$$\sum_{i=1}^{n}\sum_{y\in\mathcal{Y}}\left[\sum_{y'\in\mathcal{Y}}\mathbf{w}^{T}\mathbf{f}_{\mathbf{x}}(y',y,i)+\sum_{k=1}^{L}\mathbf{w}^{T}\mathbf{g}_{\mathbf{x}}(y,i-k,i)\right]$$
$$(4)$$

where $\mathbf{g}_{\mathbf{x}}(y,i-k,i)$ represents the feature vector on the edge connecting the Begin node with state y at position $i-k$ to the End node with the same state y at position i. Note that, different from the $\mathbf{g}_{\mathbf{x}}$ function defined in Equation (3), this new $\mathbf{g}_{\mathbf{x}}$ function is defined over a single (current) y label only, making the time complexity $O(n\,|\mathcal{Y}|^2 + nL\,|\mathcal{Y}|)$. Theoretically this model is slightly more efficient than the conventional semi-CRF model.

Unlike conventional (first-order) semi-Markov CRF, this new model does not allow us to capture the dependencies between one segment and its adjacent segment's label information. We argue that, however, such dependencies can be less crucial for our task. We will empirically assess this aspect through experiments. Figure 2 illustrates the differences among the three models.

4 Features

In linear CRF, the baseline feature set considers the previous word, current word, and the tag transition.

In semi-CRF, following (Sarawagi and Cohen, 2004) we put all words not part of a noun phrase in its own segment, and put each noun phrase in one segment, possibly spanning over multiple words. Here we set $L = 6$ and ignored NPs with more than six words during training, which is less than 0.5% of all NPs. For each segment, we defined the following features as the baseline: (1) indexed words inside current segment, running from the start and from the end of the segment, (2) the word before and after

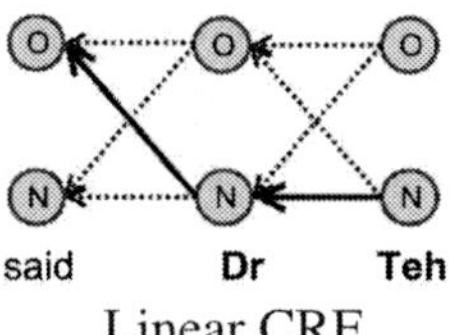

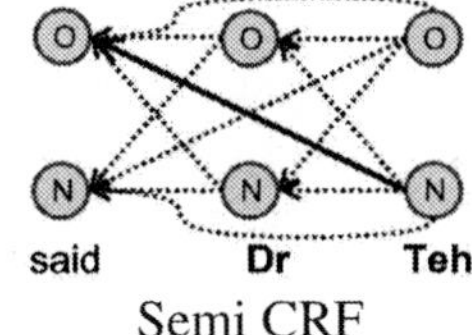

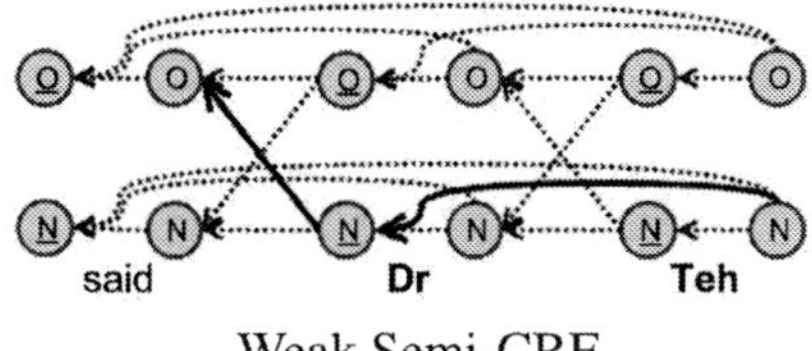

Figure 2: Graphical illustrations of the differences between three models. The bold arrows represent the path in each model to label "Dr Teh" as a noun phrase. For Linear CRF, this is a simplified diagram; in the implementation we used the "BIO" approach to represent text chunks. The underlined nodes in Weak Semi-CRF are the Begin nodes.

current segment, and (3) the labels of last segment and current segment.

In weak semi-CRF we use the same feature set as semi-CRF, adjusting the features accordingly where segment-specific features (1) are defined only in the Begin-End edges, and transition features (3) are defined only in the End-Begin edges.

For each model we then add the character prefixes and suffixes up to length 3 for each word (+a), Brown cluster (Brown et al., 1992) for current word (+b), and word shapes (+s). For Brown cluster features we used 100 clusters trained on the whole NUS SMS Corpus. The cluster information is then used directly as a feature.

Word shapes can be considered a generic representation of words that retains only the "shape" information, such as whether it starts with capital letter or whether it contains digits. The Brown clusters and word shapes features are applied to each of the word features described in each model.

5 Experiments

All models were built by us using Java, and were optimized with L-BFGS. Models are all tuned in the development set for optimal λ. The optimal λ values are noted in Table 2.

Since the models that we consider are all word-based [4], we tokenize the corpus using a regex-based tokenizer similar to the `wordpunct_tokenize` function in Python NLTK package. We also included some rules to consider special anonymization tokens in the SMS dataset (Chen and Kan, 2013).

The gold character spans are converted into word

---

[4]We experimented with character-based models, but they do not perform well. We leave them for future investigations.

	Linear CRF	Semi-CRF	Weak Semi-CRF
base	0.125	2.0	2.0
+s	0.25	1.0	2.0
+b	0.5	1.0	2.0
+b+s	0.5	2.0	2.0
+a	1.0	2.0	2.0
+a +s	2.0	1.0	2.0
+a+b	1.0	2.0	2.0
+a+b+s	2.0	2.0	2.0

Table 2: Tuned regularization parameter λ from the set $\{0.125, 0.25, 0.5, 1.0, 2.0\}$ for various feature sets. +a, +b, and +s refer to the affix, Brown cluster, and word shape features respectively.

labels in BIO format, reducing or extending the character spans as necessary to the closest word boundaries. The converted annotations are regarded as gold word spans. Note that this conversion is lossy due to the presence of *improper* NPs, which makes it impossible for the converted format to represent the original gold standard.

We evaluated the models in the original character-level spans and also in the converted word-level spans, to see the impact of the lossy conversion on the scores. In character-level evaluation, the system output is converted back into character boundaries and compared with the original gold standard, while in the word-level evaluation, the system output is compared directly with the gold word spans. For this reason, we anticipate that the scores in word-level evaluation will be higher than in the character-level evaluation. The results are shown in Table 3. The scores for "Gold" in the character-level evaluation mark the upperbound of word-based models due to the presence of *improper* NPs.

The average time per training iteration on the base models is 1.311s, 2.072s, and 1.811s respectively for Linear CRF, Semi-CRF, and Weak Semi-CRF.

	Character-level Eval.			Word-level Eval.		
	Prec	*Rec*	*F*	*Prec*	*Rec*	*F*
Linear CRF						
base	72.29	70.13	71.19	74.04	71.93	72.97
+s	72.56	70.50	71.52	74.38	72.38	73.36
+b	72.48	71.82	72.15	74.32	73.77	74.04
+b+s	72.90	72.10	72.50	74.70	73.99	74.34
+a	72.56	72.41	72.49	74.66	74.62	74.64
+a +s	72.65	71.93	72.29	74.69	74.07	74.38
+a+b	72.63	72.80	72.71	74.70	75.00	74.85
+a+b+s	72.63	72.74	72.68	74.77	74.99	74.88
Semi-CRF						
base	74.94	73.80	**74.37**	76.50	75.45	75.97
+s	75.14	73.48	74.30	76.81	75.23	76.01
+b	73.95	74.50	74.22	75.82	76.50	76.15
+b+s	73.79	74.08	73.93	75.67	76.09	75.88
+a	74.31	75.08	<u>**74.69**</u>	76.20	77.11	<u>**76.65**</u>
+a +s	74.36	74.49	**74.42**	76.32	76.57	**76.44**
+a+b	74.30	74.88	**74.58**	76.20	76.92	**76.55**
+a+b+s	74.24	74.93	**74.58**	76.23	77.06	**76.64**
Weak Semi-CRF						
base	74.84	73.94	**74.39**	76.47	75.67	76.07
+s	74.84	72.67	73.74	76.50	74.40	75.43
+b	74.13	74.12	74.12	75.97	76.08	76.02
+b+s	74.19	74.21	74.20	76.06	76.19	76.13
+a	74.07	75.13	**74.60**	76.02	77.23	**76.62**
+a +s	74.47	74.49	**74.48**	76.44	76.58	**76.51**
+a+b	74.08	74.57	**74.32**	76.01	76.64	**76.32**
+a+b+s	74.19	74.43	**74.31**	76.15	76.52	**76.33**
Gold	95.96	95.81	95.88	100.0	100.0	100.0

Table 3: Scores on test set (both character-level and word-level evaluation) using optimal λ. +a, +b, and +s refer to the affix, Brown cluster, and word shape features respectively. Best F1 scores are underlined, and values which are not significantly different in 95% confidence interval are in bold

5.1 Discussion

First, we see that the two semi-CRF models perform better compared to the baseline linear CRF model, showing the benefit of using segment features over only single word features.

It is also interesting that, while being a weaker version of the semi-CRF, the weak semi-CRF can actually perform in the same level within 95% confidence interval as the conventional semi-CRF. This shows that some of the dependencies in the conventional semi-CRF do not really contribute to the strength of semi-CRF over standard linear CRF. As noted in Section 3.3, weak semi-CRF makes the decision on the segment type and length separately. This means there is enough information in the local features to decide the segment type and length separately, and so we can remove some combined features while retaining the same performance.

This result, coupled with the fact that the weak semi-CRF requires 12.5% less time than the conven-tional semi-CRF (1.811s vs 2.072s), shows the potentials of using this weak semi-CRF as an alternative of the conventional semi-CRF. With more label types (here only two), the difference will be larger, since the weak semi-CRF is linear in number of label types, while conventional semi-CRF is quadratic.

6 Related Work

Ritter et al. (2011) previously showed that off-the-shelf NP-chunker performs worse on informal text. Then they trained a linear-CRF model on additional in-domain data, reducing the error up to 22%. However no results on semi-CRF was given.

Semi-CRF has proven effective in chunking tasks. Other variants of semi-CRF models also exist. Nguyen et al. (2014) explored the use of higher-order dependencies to improve the performance of semi-CRF models on synthetic data and on hand-writing recognition. They exploited the sparsity of label sequence in order to make the training efficient.

It is also known that feature selection is an important aspect when trying to use semi-CRF models to improve on the linear CRF. Andrew (2006) reported an error reduction of up to 25% when using features that are best exploited by semi-CRF.

7 Conclusion and Future Work

In this paper we present a new NP-annotated SMS corpus, together with a novel variant of the semi-CRF model, which runs in significantly lower time while maintaining similar accuracy on the NP chunking task on the new dataset. Future work includes the application of the weak semi-CRF model to other structured prediction problems, as well as performing investigations on handling other types of informal or noisy texts such as speech transcripts. We make the code and data available for download at `http://statnlp.org/research/ie/`.

Acknowledgements

We would like to thank Alexander Binder, Jie Yang, Dinh Quang Thinh as well as the 64 undergraduate students who helped us with annotations. We would also like to thank the three anonymous reviewers for their helpful comments. This work is supported by SUTD grant SRG ISTD 2013 064 and MOE Tier 1 grant SUTDT12015008.

References

Galen Andrew. 2006. A hybrid Markov/semi-Markov conditional random field for sequence segmentation. In *Proc. EMNLP'06*.

Peter F. Brown, Peter V. DeSouza, Robert L. Mercer, Vincent J. Della Pietra, and Jenifer C. Lai. 1992. Class-Based n-gram Models of Natural Language. *Computational Linguistics*, 18(4):467–479.

Tao Chen and Min-Yen Kan. 2013. Creating a live, public short message service corpus: the NUS SMS corpus. In *Language Resources and Evaluation*, volume 47, pages 299–335. Springer Netherlands.

John Lafferty, Andrew McCallum, and Fernando Pereira. 2001. Conditional Random Fields: Probabilistic Models for Segmenting and Labeling Sequence Data. In *International Conference on Machine Learning (ICML)*, pages 282–289.

Robert Layton, Paul Watters, and Richard Dazeley. 2010. Authorship Attribution for Twitter in 140 Characters or Less. In *2010 Second Cybercrime and Trustworthy Computing Workshop*, pages 1–8.

Jiwei Li, Alan Ritter, and Eduard Hovy. 2014. Weakly Supervised User Profile Extraction from Twitter. In *Association for Computational Linguistics*, pages 165–174.

Wei Lu and Dan Roth. 2015. Joint mention extraction and classification with mention hypergraphs. In *Proceedings of the 2015 Conference on Empirical Methods in Natural Language Processing*, pages 857–867, Lisbon, Portugal, September. Association for Computational Linguistics.

Tom M. Mitchell, William Cohen, Estevam Hruschka, Partha Talukdar, Justin Betteridge, Andrew Carlson, Bhavana Dalvi Mishra, Matthew Gardner, Bryan Kisiel, Jayant Krishnamurthy, Ni Lao, Kathryn Mazaitis, Thahir Mohamed, Ndapa Nakashole, Emmanouil Antonios Platanios, Alan Ritter, Mehdi Samadi, Burr Settles, Richard Wang, Derry Wijaya, Abhinav Gupta, Xinlei Chen, Abulhair Saparov, Malcolm Greaves, and Joel Welling. 2015. Never-Ending Learning. In *AAAI Conference on Artificial Intelligence*, pages 2302–2310.

David Nadeau and Satoshi Sekine. 2007. A survey of named entity recognition and classification. *Lingvisticae Investigationes*, 30(1):3–26.

Viet Cuong Nguyen, Nan Ye, Wee Sun Lee, and Hai Leong Chieu. 2014. Conditional Random Field with High-order Dependencies for Sequence Labeling and Segmentation. *Journal of Machine Learning Research 2014*, 15:981–1009.

Alan Ritter, Sam Clark, and Oren Etzioni. 2011. Named entity recognition in tweets: an experimental study. In *Proceedings of the 2011 Conference on Empirical Methods in Natural Language Processing*, pages 1524–1534, Edinburgh.

Alan Ritter, Oren Etzioni, and Sam Clark. 2012. Open Domain Event Extraction from Twitter. In *Proceedings Workshop on Text Mining, ACM International Conference on Knowledge Discovery and Data Mining 2012 (KDD'12)*.

Alan Ritter, Evan Wright, William Casey, and Tom M. Mitchell. 2015. Weakly Supervised Extraction of Computer Security Events from Twitter. In *Proceedings of the 24th International Conference on World Wide Web*, volume i, pages 896–905.

Sunita Sarawagi and William W. Cohen. 2004. Semi-markov conditional random fields for information extraction. In *Advances in Neural Information Processing Systems 17*, pages 1185–1192.

Martijn Spitters, Femke Klaver, Gijs Koot, and Mark van Staalduinen. 2015. Authorship Analysis on Dark Marketplace Forums. In *Proceedings of the IEEE European Intelligence & Security Informatics Conference 2015 (EISIC 2015)*.

What to talk about and how? Selective Generation using LSTMs with Coarse-to-Fine Alignment

Hongyuan Mei
UChicago, TTI-Chicago
hongyuan@uchicago.edu

Mohit Bansal
TTI-Chicago
mbansal@ttic.edu

Matthew R. Walter
TTI-Chicago
mwalter@ttic.edu

Abstract

We propose an end-to-end, domain-independent neural encoder-aligner-decoder model for selective generation, i.e., the joint task of content selection and surface realization. Our model first encodes a full set of over-determined database event records via an LSTM-based recurrent neural network, then utilizes a novel coarse-to-fine aligner to identify the small subset of salient records to talk about, and finally employs a decoder to generate free-form descriptions of the aligned, selected records. Our model achieves the best selection and generation results reported to-date (with 59% relative improvement in generation) on the benchmark WEATHER-GOV dataset, despite using no specialized features or linguistic resources. Using an improved k-nearest neighbor beam filter helps further. We also perform a series of ablations and visualizations to elucidate the contributions of our key model components. Lastly, we evaluate the generalizability of our model on the ROBOCUP dataset, and get results that are competitive with or better than the state-of-the-art, despite being severely data-starved.

1 Introduction

We consider the important task of producing a natural language description of a rich world state represented as an over-determined database of event records. This task, which we refer to as selective generation, is often formulated as two subproblems: *content selection*, which involves choosing a subset of relevant records to talk about from the exhaustive database, and *surface realization*, which is concerned with generating natural language descriptions for this subset. Learning to perform these tasks

jointly is challenging due to the uncertainty in deciding which records are relevant, the complex dependencies between selected records, and the multiple ways in which these records can be described.

Previous work has made significant progress on this task (Chen and Mooney, 2008; Angeli et al., 2010; Kim and Mooney, 2010; Konstas and Lapata, 2012). However, most approaches solve the two content selection and surface realization subtasks separately, use manual domain-dependent resources (e.g., semantic parsers) and features, or employ template-based generation. This limits domain adaptability and reduces coherence. We take an alternative, neural encoder-aligner-decoder approach to free-form selective generation that jointly performs content selection and surface realization, without using any specialized features, resources, or generation templates. This enables our approach to generalize to new domains. Further, our memory-based model captures the long-range contextual dependencies among records and descriptions, which are integral to this task (Angeli et al., 2010).

We formulate our model as an encoder-aligner-decoder framework that uses recurrent neural networks with long short-term memory units (LSTM-RNNs) (Hochreiter and Schmidhuber, 1997) together with a coarse-to-fine aligner to select and "translate" the rich world state into a natural language description. Our model first encodes the full set of over-determined[1] event records using a bidirectional LSTM-RNN. A novel coarse-to-fine aligner then reasons over multiple abstractions of the input to decide which of the records to discuss. The model next employs an LSTM decoder to gen-

---

[1] By "over-determined", we mean that there are extraneous and redundant records present in the database.

Proceedings of NAACL-HLT 2016, pages 720–730,
San Diego, California, June 12-17, 2016. ©2016 Association for Computational Linguistics

erate natural language descriptions of the selected records.

The use of LSTMs, which have proven effective for similar long-range generation tasks (Sutskever et al., 2014; Vinyals et al., 2015b; Karpathy and Fei-Fei, 2015), allows our model to capture the long-range contextual dependencies that exist in selective generation. Further, the introduction of our proposed variation on alignment-based LSTMs (Bahdanau et al., 2014; Xu et al., 2015) enables our model to learn to perform content selection and surface realization jointly, by aligning each generated word to an event record during decoding. Our novel coarse-to-fine aligner avoids searching over the full set of over-determined records by employing two stages of increasing complexity: a pre-selector and a refiner acting on multiple abstractions (low- and high-level) of the record input. The end-to-end nature of our framework has the advantage that it can be trained directly on corpora of record sets paired with natural language descriptions, without the need for ground-truth content selection.

We evaluate our model on a benchmark weather forecasting dataset (WEATHERGOV) and achieve the best results reported to-date on content selection (12% relative improvement in F-1) and language generation (59% relative improvement in BLEU), despite using no domain-specific resources. We also perform a series of ablations and visualizations to elucidate the contributions of the primary model components, and also show improvements with a simple, k-nearest neighbor beam filter approach. Finally, we demonstrate the generalizability of our model by directly applying it to a benchmark sportscasting dataset (ROBOCUP), where we get results competitive with or better than state-of-the-art, despite being extremely data-starved.

2   Related Work

Selective generation is a task where a natural language description is produced for a salient subset of a rich world state represented as an over-determined database of event records. A good deal of attention in this area has been paid to the individual content selection and selective realization subproblems. With regards to the former, Barzilay and Lee (2004) model the content structure from unanno-

tated documents and apply it to the application of text summarization. Barzilay and Lapata (2005) treat content selection as a collective classification problem and simultaneously optimize the local label assignment and their pairwise relations. Liang et al. (2009) address the related task of aligning a set of records to given textual description clauses. They propose a generative semi-Markov alignment model that jointly segments text sequences into utterances and associates each to the corresponding record.

Surface realization is often treated as a problem of producing text according to a given representation (Reiter et al., 2000). Walker et al. (2001) and Stent et al. (2004) design trainable sentence planners to generate sentences (and their combinations) for context planning and dialog, relying upon various linguistics features. Soricut and Marcu (2006) propose a language generation system that uses the WIDL-representation, a formalism used to compactly represent probability distributions over finite sets of strings. Wong and Mooney (2007) and Lu and Ng (2011) use synchronous context-free grammars to generate natural language sentences from formal meaning representations. Similarly, Belz (2008) employs probabilistic context-free grammars to perform surface realization. Other effective approaches include the use of tree conditional random fields (Lu et al., 2009) and template extraction within a log-linear framework (Angeli et al., 2010).

Recent work seeks to solve the full selective generation problem through a single framework. Chen and Mooney (2008) and Chen et al. (2010) learn alignments between comments and their corresponding event records using a translation model for parsing and generation. Kim and Mooney (2010) implement a two-stage framework that decides what to discuss using a combination of the methods of Lu et al. (2008) and Liang et al. (2009), and then produces the text based on the generation system of Wong and Mooney (2007).

Angeli et al. (2010) propose a unified concept-to-text model that treats joint content selection and surface realization as a sequence of local decisions represented by a log-linear model. Similar to other work, they train their model using external alignments from Liang et al. (2009). Generation then follows as inference over this model, where they first choose an event record, then the record's fields (i.e., attributes), and finally a set of templates that they then fill in with words for the selected fields. Their ability to model long-range dependencies relies on their choice of features for the log-linear model, while the template-based generation further employs some domain-specific features for fluent output.

Konstas and Lapata (2012) propose an alternative method that simultaneously optimizes the content selection and surface realization problems. They employ a probabilistic context-free grammar that specifies the structure of the event records, and then treat generation as finding the best derivation tree according to this grammar. However, their method still selects and orders records in a local fashion via a Markovized chaining of records. Konstas and Lapata (2013) improve upon this approach with global document representations. However, this approach also requires alignment during training, which they estimate using the method of Liang et al. (2009).

We treat the problem of selective generation as end-to-end learning via a recurrent neural network encoder-aligner-decoder model, which enables us to jointly learn content selection and surface realization directly from database-text pairs, without the need for an external aligner or ground-truth selection labels. The use of LSTM-RNNs enables our model to capture the long-range dependencies that exist among the records and natural language output. Additionally, the model does not rely on any manually-selected or domain-dependent features, templates, or parsers, and is thereby generalizable. The alignment-RNN approach has recently proven successful for generation-style tasks, e.g., machine translation (Bahdanau et al., 2014) and image captioning (Xu et al., 2015). Since selective generation requires identifying the small number of salient records among an over-determined database, we avoid performing exhaustive search over the full record set, and instead propose a novel coarse-to-fine aligner that divides the search complexity into pre-selection and refinement stages.

3 Task Definition

We consider the problem of generating a natural language description for a rich world state specified in terms of an over-determined set of records (database). This problem requires deciding which of the records to discuss (content selection) and

$r_{1:N}$:

temperature(time=17-06, min=48, mean=53, max=61)
windSpeed(time=17-06, min=3, mean=6, max=11)
windDir(time=17-06, mode=SSW)
gust(time=17-06, min=0, mean=0, max=0)
skyCover(time=17-21, mode=0-25)
skyCover(time=02-06, mode=75-100)
precipChance(time=17-06, min=2, mean=14, max=20)
rainChance(time=17-06, mode=someChance)

$x_{1:N}$: "a 20 percent chance of showers after midnight. increasing clouds, with a low around 48 southwest wind between 5 and 10 mph"

(a) WEATHERGOV

$r_{1:N}$:

pass(arg1=purple6, arg2=purple3)
kick(arg1=purple3)
badPass(arg1=purple3, arg2=pink9)
turnover(arg1=purple3, arg2=pink9)

$x_{1:N}$: "purple3 made a bad pass that was picked off by pink9"

(b) ROBOCUP

Figure 1: Sample database-text pairs chosen from the (a) WEATHERGOV and (b) ROBOCUP datasets.

how to discuss them (surface realization). Training data consists of *scenario* pairs $(r^{(i)}, x^{(i)})$ for $i = 1, 2, \ldots, n$, where $r^{(i)}$ is the complete set of records and $x^{(i)}$ is the natural language description (Fig. 1). At test time, only the records are given. We evaluate our model in the context of two publicly-available benchmark selective generation datasets.

WEATHERGOV The weather forecasting dataset (see Fig. 1(a)) of Liang et al. (2009) consists of 29528 scenarios, each with 36 weather records (e.g., temperature, sky cover, etc.) paired with a natural language forecast (28.7 avg. word length).

ROBOCUP We evaluate our model's generalizability on the sportscasting dataset of Chen and Mooney (2008), which consists of only 1539 pairs of temporally ordered robot soccer events (e.g., pass, score) and commentary drawn from the four-game 2001–2004 RoboCup finals (see Fig. 1(b)). Each scenario contains an average of 2.4 event records and a 5.7 word natural language commentary.

4 The Model

We formulate selective generation as inference over a probabilistic model $P(x_{1:T}|r_{1:N})$, where

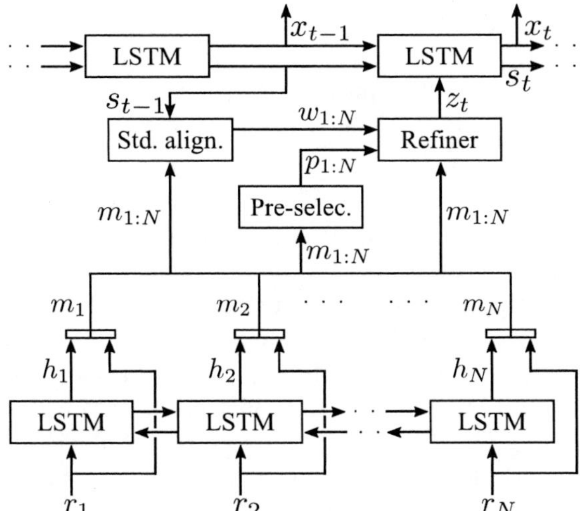

Figure 2: Our model architecture with a bidirectional LSTM encoder, coarse-to-fine aligner, and decoder.

$r_{1:N} = (r_1, r_2, \ldots, r_N)$ is the input set of over-determined event records,[2] $x_{1:T} = (x_1, x_2, \ldots, x_T)$ is the generated description with x_t being the word at time t and x_0 being a special start token:

$$x_{1:T}^* = \arg\max_{x_{1:T}} P(x_{1:T}|r_{1:N}) \tag{1a}$$

$$= \arg\max_{x_{1:T}} \prod_{t=1}^{T} P(x_t|x_{0:t-1}, r_{1:N}) \tag{1b}$$

The goal of inference is to generate a natural language description for a given set of records. An effective means of learning to perform this generation is to use an encoder-aligner-decoder architecture with a recurrent neural network, which has proven effective for related problems in machine translation (Bahdanau et al., 2014) and image captioning (Xu et al., 2015). We propose a variation on this general model with novel components that are well-suited to the selective generation problem.

Our model (Fig. 2) first encodes each input record r_j into a hidden state h_j with $j \in \{1, \ldots, N\}$ using a bidirectional recurrent neural network (RNN). Our novel coarse-to-fine aligner then acts on a concatenation m_j of each record and its hidden state

---

[2]These records may take the form of an unordered set or have a natural ordering (e.g., temporal in the case of ROBOCUP). In order to make our model generalizable, we treat the set as a sequence and use the order specified by the dataset. We note that it is possible that a different ordering will yield improved performance, since ordering has been shown to be important when operating on sets (Vinyals et al., 2015a).

as multi-level representation of the input to compute the selection decision z_t at each decoding step t. The model then employs an RNN decoder to arrive at the word likelihood $P(x_t|x_{0:t-1}, r_{1:N})$ as a function of the multi-level input and the hidden state of the decoder s_{t-1} at time step $t - 1$. In order to model the long-range dependencies among the records and descriptions (which is integral to effectively performing selective generation (Angeli et al., 2010; Konstas and Lapata, 2012; Konstas and Lapata, 2013)), our model employs LSTM units as the nonlinear encoder and decoder functions.

Encoder Our LSTM-RNN encoder (Fig. 2) takes as input the set of event records represented as a sequence $r_{1:N} = (r_1, r_2, \ldots, r_N)$ and returns a sequence of hidden annotations $h_{1:N} = (h_1, h_2, \ldots, h_N)$, where the annotation h_j summarizes the record r_j. This results in a representation that models the dependencies that exist among the records in the database. We adopt an encoder architecture similar to that of Graves et al. (2013)

$$\begin{pmatrix} i_j^e \\ f_j^e \\ o_j^e \\ g_j^e \end{pmatrix} = \begin{pmatrix} \sigma \\ \sigma \\ \sigma \\ \tanh \end{pmatrix} T^e \begin{pmatrix} r_j \\ h_{j-1} \end{pmatrix} \tag{2a}$$

$$c_j^e = f_j^e \odot c_{j-1}^e + i_j^e \odot g_j^e \tag{2b}$$

$$h_j = o_j^e \odot \tanh(c_j^e) \tag{2c}$$

where T^e is an affine transformation, σ is the logistic sigmoid that restricts its input to $[0, 1]$, i_j^e, f_j^e, and o_j^e are the input, forget, and output gates of the LSTM, respectively, and c_j^e is the memory cell activation vector. The memory cell c_j^e summarizes the LSTM's previous memory c_{j-1}^e and the current input, which are modulated by the forget and input gates, respectively. Our encoder operates bidirectionally, encoding the records in both the forward and backward directions, which provides a better summary of the input records. In this way, the hidden annotations $h_j = (\overrightarrow{h}_j^\top; \overleftarrow{h}_j^\top)^\top$ concatenate forward $\overrightarrow{h}_j$ and backward $\overleftarrow{h}_j$ annotations, each determined using Equation (2c).

Coarse-to-Fine Aligner Having encoded the input records $r_{1:N}$ to arrive at the hidden annotations $h_{1:N}$, the model then seeks to select the content at each time step t that will be used for generation. Our model performs content selection using an extension of the alignment mechanism proposed by Bahdanau et al. (2014), which allows for selection and generation that is independent of the ordering of the input.

In selective generation, the given set of event records is over-determined with only a small subset of salient records being relevant to the output natural language description. Standard alignment mechanisms limit the accuracy of selection and generation by scanning the entire range of over-determined records. In order to better address the selective generation task, we propose a coarse-to-fine aligner that prevents the model from being distracted by non-salient records. [3] Our model aligns based on multiple abstractions of the input: both the original input record as well as the hidden annotations $m_j = (r_j^\top; h_j^\top)^\top$, an approach that has previously been shown to yield better results than aligning based only on the hidden state (Mei et al., 2015).

Our coarse-to-fine aligner avoids searching over the full set of over-determined records by using two stages of increasing complexity: a pre-selector and refiner (Fig. 2). The pre-selector first assigns to each record a probability p_j of being selected, while the standard aligner computes the alignment likelihood w_{tj} over all the records at each time step t during decoding. Next, the refiner produces the final selection decision by re-weighting the aligner weights w_{tj} with the pre-selector probabilities p_j:

$$p_j = \text{sigmoid}\left(q^\top \tanh(Pm_j)\right) \tag{3a}$$

$$\beta_{tj} = v^\top \tanh(W s_{t-1} + U m_j) \tag{3b}$$

$$w_{tj} = \exp(\beta_{tj}) / \sum_j \exp(\beta_{tj}) \tag{3c}$$

$$\alpha_{tj} = p_j w_{tj} / \sum_j p_j w_{tj} \tag{3d}$$

$$z_t = \sum_j \alpha_{tj} m_j \tag{3e}$$

where P, q, U, W, v are learned parameters. Ideally, the selection decision would be based on the highest-value alignment $z_t = m_k$ where $k = \arg\max_j \alpha_{tj}$. However, we use the weighted average (Eqn. 3e) as its soft approximation to maintain differentiability of the entire architecture.

---

[3] Our coarse-to-fine nomenclature is based on the alignment inference at successively finer granularities.

The pre-selector assigns large values ($p_j > 0.5$) to a small subset of salient records and small values ($p_j < 0.5$) to the rest. This modulates the standard aligner, which then has to assign a large weight w_{tj} in order to select the j-th record at time t. In this way, the learned prior p_j makes it difficult for the alignment (attention) to be distracted by non-salient records. Further, we can relate the output of the pre-selector to the number of records that are selected. Specifically, the output p_j expresses the extent to which the j-th record should be selected. The summation $\sum_{j=1}^{N} p_j$ can then be regarded as a real-valued approximation to the total number of pre-selected records (denoted as γ), which we regularize towards, based on validation (see Eqn. 5).

Decoder Our architecture uses an LSTM decoder that takes as input the current context vector z_t, the last word x_{t-1}, and the LSTM's previous hidden state s_{t-1}. The decoder outputs the conditional probability distribution $P_{x,t} = P(x_t | x_{0:t-1}, r_{1:N})$ over the next word, represented as a deep output layer (Pascanu et al., 2014),

$$\begin{pmatrix} i_t^d \\ f_t^d \\ o_t^d \\ g_t^d \end{pmatrix} = \begin{pmatrix} \sigma \\ \sigma \\ \sigma \\ \tanh \end{pmatrix} T^d \begin{pmatrix} E x_{t-1} \\ s_{t-1} \\ z_t \end{pmatrix} \tag{4a}$$

$$c_t^d = f_t^d \odot c_{t-1}^d + i_t^d \odot g_t^d \tag{4b}$$

$$s_t = o_t^d \odot \tanh(c_t^d) \tag{4c}$$

$$l_t = L_0(E x_{t-1} + L_s s_t + L_z z_t) \tag{4d}$$

$$P_{x,t} = \text{softmax}\,(l_t) \tag{4e}$$

where E (an embedding matrix), L_0, L_s, and L_z are parameters to be learned.

Training and Inference We train the model using the database-record pairs $(r_{1:N}, x_{1:T})$ from the training corpora so as to maximize the likelihood of the ground-truth language description $x_{1:T}^*$ (Eqn. 1). Additionally, we introduce a regularization term $(\sum_{j=1}^{N} p_j - \gamma)^2$ that enables the model to influence the pre-selector weights based on the aforementioned relationship between the output of the pre-selector and the number of selected records. Moreover, we also introduce the term $(1.0 - \max(p_j))$, which accounts for the fact that at least one record should be pre-selected. Note that when γ is equal to N, the pre-selector is forced to select all the records

$(p_j = 1.0$ for all $j)$, and the coarse-to-fine alignment reverts to the standard alignment introduced by Bahdanau et al. (2014). Together with the negative log-likelihood of the ground-truth description $x_{1:T}^*$, our loss function becomes

$$L = -\log P(x_{1:T}^* | r_{1:N}) + G \tag{5a}$$

$$= -\sum_{t=1}^{T} \log P(x_t^* | x_{0:t-1}, r_{1:N}) + G \tag{5b}$$

$$G = \left(\sum_{j=1}^{N} p_j - \gamma \right)^2 + \left(1 - \max(p_j) \right) \tag{5c}$$

Having trained the model, we generate the natural language description by finding the maximum a posteriori words under the learned model (Eqn. 1).[4] For inference, we perform greedy search starting with the first word x_1. Beam search offers a way to perform approximate joint inference — however, we empirically found that beam search does not perform any better than greedy search on the datasets that we consider, an observation that is shared with previous work (Angeli et al., 2010). We later discuss an alternative k-nearest neighbor-based beam filter (see Sec 6.2).

5 Experimental Setup

Datasets We analyze our model on the benchmark WEATHERGOV dataset, and use the data-starved ROBOCUP dataset to demonstrate the model's generalizability. Following Angeli et al. (2010), we use WEATHERGOV training, development, and test splits of size 25000, 1000, and 3528, respectively. For ROBOCUP, we follow the evaluation methodology of previous work (Chen and Mooney, 2008), performing three-fold cross-validation whereby we train on three games (approximately 1000 scenarios) and test on the fourth. Within each split, we hold out 10% of the training data as the development set to tune the early-stopping criterion and γ. We then report the standard average performance (weighted by the number of scenarios) over these four splits.

Dataset Processing In this section, we present the implementation details regarding our data preprocessing. We use WEATHERGOV as an example here,

since it is our primary dataset, and the same recipe is followed for ROBOCUP.

For tokenization of the textual descriptions, we simply treat as token each string unit delimited by a space, which includes regular words ("sunny"), punctuation (","), and numerical values ("20"). A special token is added to represent the beginning and end of the entire textual description. This operation results in a vocabulary of size 338, and we did not filter out any rare tokens. Moreover, in this setup, numerical values are also generated as any other token during decoding period.

For event record representation, we represent each event as a fixed-length vector, concatenated by multiple "attribute (field) vectors". Each attribute vector represents either a 1) record type (e.g., "rainChance") with a one-hot vector, 2) record time slot (e.g., "06:00–21:00") with a one-hot vector, 3) record mode (e.g., "SSE") with a one-hot vector, or, 4) record value (e.g., "20") with a 0-1 vector. The 0-1 vector for record value is simply the signed binary representation of this number. We choose the usage of 0-1 binary representation vectors for numbers because it allows us to share binning-style information between nearby numbers (whereas a one-hot vector is sparse).

Training Details On WEATHERGOV, we lightly tune the number of hidden units and γ on the development set according to the generation metric (BLEU), and choose 500 units from $\{250, 500, 750\}$ and $\gamma = 8.5$ from $\{6.5, 7.5, 8.5, 10.5, 12.5\}$. For ROBOCUP, we only tune γ on the development set and choose $\gamma = 5.0$ from the set $\{1.0, 2.0, \ldots, 6.0\}$. However, we do not retune the number of hidden units on ROBOCUP. For each iteration, we randomly sample a mini-batch of 100 scenarios during back-propagation and use Adam (Kingma and Ba, 2015) for optimization. Training typically converges within 30 epochs. We select the model according to the BLEU score on the development set.[5]

Evaluation Metrics We consider two metrics as a means of evaluating the effectiveness of our model on the two selective generation subproblems. For content selection, we use the F-1 score of the set of

---

[4]Numerical values are also generated exactly as any other token in the vocabulary.

[5]We implement our model in Theano (Bergstra et al., 2010; Bastien et al., 2012) and will make the code publicly available.

Table 1: Primary WEATHERGOV results

Method	F-1	sBLEU	cBLEU
KL12	–	33.70	–
KL13	–	36.54	–
ALK10	65.40	38.40	51.50
Our model	**73.21**	**61.01**	**70.39**

selected records as defined by the harmonic mean of precision and recall with respect to the ground-truth selection record set. We define the set of selected records as consisting of the record with the largest selection weight α_{ti} computed by our aligner at each decoding step t.

We evaluate the quality of surface realization using the BLEU score[6] (a 4-gram matching-based precision) (Papineni et al., 2001) of the generated description with respect to the human-created reference. To be comparable to previous results on WEATHERGOV, we also consider a modified BLEU score (cBLEU) that does not penalize numerical deviations of at most five (Angeli et al., 2010) (i.e., to not penalize "low around 58" compared to a reference "low around 60"). On ROBOCUP, we also evaluate the BLEU score in the case that ground-truth content selection is known (sBLEU$_G$), to be comparable to previous work.

6   Results and Analysis

We analyze the effectiveness of our model on the benchmark WEATHERGOV (as primary) and ROBOCUP (as generalization) datasets. We also present several ablations to illustrate the contributions of the primary model components.

6.1   Primary Results (WEATHERGOV)

We report the performance of content selection and surface realization using F-1 and two BLEU scores (standard sBLEU and the customized cBLEU of Angeli et al. (2010)), respectively (Sec. 5). Table 1 compares our test results against previous methods that include KL12 (Konstas and Lapata, 2012), KL13 (Konstas and Lapata, 2013), and ALK10 (Angeli et al., 2010). Our method achieves the best results reported to-date on all three metrics, with relative improvements of 11.94% (F-1), 58.88%

---

[6]We compute BLEU using the publicly available evaluation provided by Angeli et al. (2010).

(sBLEU), and 36.68% (cBLEU) over the previous state-of-the-art.

6.2   Beam Filter with k-Nearest Neighbors

We perform greedy search as an approximation to full inference over the set of decision variables (Eqn. 1). We considered beam search as an alternative, but as with previous work on this dataset (Angeli et al., 2010), we found that greedy search still yields better BLEU performance (Table 2).

Table 2: Effect of beam width

Beam width M	1	2	5	10
dev sBLEU	65.58	64.70	57.02	47.07
dev cBLEU	75.78	74.91	65.83	54.19

As an alternative, we consider a beam filter based on a k-nearest neighborhood. First, we generate the M-best description candidates (i.e., a beam width of M) for a given input record set (database) using standard beam search. Next, we find the K nearest neighbor database-description pairs from the training data, based on the cosine similarity of each neighbor database with the given input record. We then compute the BLEU score for each of the M description candidates relative to the K nearest neighbor descriptions (as references) and select the candidate with the highest BLEU score. We tune K and M on the development set and report the results in Table 3. Table 4 presents the test results with this tuned setting ($M = 2$, $K = 1$), where we achieve BLEU scores better than our primary greedy results.

Table 3: k-NN beam filter (dev set)

sBLEU	$M = 2$	$M = 5$	$M = 10$
$K = 1$	**65.99**	65.88	65.65
$K = 2$	65.89	65.98	65.83
$K = 5$	65.64	65.45	65.41
$K = 10$	65.91	65.89	65.12

cBLEU	$M = 2$	$M = 5$	$M = 10$
$K = 1$	**76.21**	76.13	75.98
$K = 2$	75.99	76.03	75.82
$K = 5$	75.90	75.63	75.41
$K = 10$	75.95	75.87	75.23

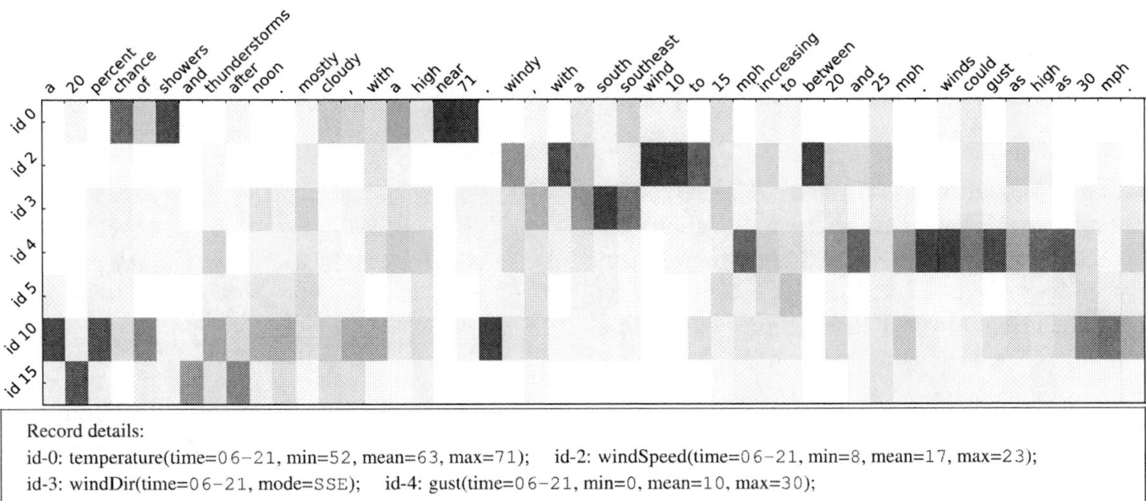

Figure 3: An example generation for a set of records from WEATHERGOV.

Table 4: k-NN beam filter (test set)

	Primary	k-NN ($M = 2, K = 1$)
sBLEU	61.01	**61.76**
cBLEU	70.39	**71.23**

6.3 Ablation Analysis (WEATHERGOV)

Next, we present several ablations to analyze the contribution of our model components.[7]

Aligner Ablation First, we evaluate the contribution of our proposed coarse-to-fine aligner by comparing our model with the basic encoder-aligner-decoder model introduced by Bahdanau et al. (2014) (which we originally started with). Table 5 reports the results demonstrating that our two-level aligner yields superior F-1 and BLEU scores relative to a standard aligner.[8]

Table 5: Coarse-to-fine aligner ablation (dev set)

Aligner	F-1	sBLEU	cBLEU
Basic	60.35	63.54	74.90
Coarse-to-fine	76.28	65.58	75.78

---

[7]These results are based on our primary model of Sec. 6.1 and on the development set.

[8]The same improvement trends hold on the test set. Moreover, our two-level aligner (and the basic aligner) model is substantially better than having no aligner at all, i.e., a simple encoder-decoder model of Sutskever et al. (2014).

Encoder Ablation Next, we consider the effectiveness of the encoder. Table 6 compares the results with and without the encoder on the development set, and demonstrates that there is a significant gain from encoding the event records using the LSTM-RNN. We attribute this improvement to the LSTM-RNN's ability to capture the relationships that exist among the records, which is known to be essential to selective generation (Barzilay and Lapata, 2005; Angeli et al., 2010).

Table 6: Encoder ablation (dev set)

Encoder	F-1	sBLEU	cBLEU
With	76.28	65.58	75.78
Without	57.45	56.47	68.63

6.4 Qualitative Analysis (WEATHERGOV)

Output Examples Fig. 3 shows an example record set with its output description and record-word alignment heat map. As shown, our model learns to align records with their corresponding words (e.g., windDir and "southeast," temperature and "71," windSpeed and "wind 10," and gust and "winds could gust as high as 30 mph"). It also learns the subset of salient records to talk about (matching the ground-truth description perfectly for this example, i.e., a standard BLEU of 100.00). We also see some word-level mismatch, e.g., "cloudy" misaligns to id-0 temp and id-10 precipChance, which we attribute to the high correlation between these types of records ("garbage collection" in Liang et al. (2009)).

Word Embeddings (Trained & Pretrained)
Training our decoder has the effect of learning embeddings for the words in the training set (via the embedding matrix E in Eqn. 4). Here, we explore the extent to which these learned embeddings capture semantic relationships among the training words. Table 7 presents nearest neighbor words for some of the common words from the WEATHER-GOV dataset (according to cosine similarity in the embedding space).

Table 7: Nearest neighbor word for example words

Word	Nearest neighbor
gusts	gust
clear	sunny
isolated	scattered
southeast	northeast
storms	winds
decreasing	falling

We also consider different ways of using pre-trained word embeddings (Mikolov et al., 2013) to bootstrap the quality of our learned embeddings. One approach initializes our embedding matrix with the pre-trained vectors and then refines the embedding based on our training corpus. The second concatenates our learned embedding matrix with the pre-trained vectors in an effort to simultaneously exploit general similarities as well as those learned for the domain. As shown previously for other tasks (Vinyals et al., 2014; Vinyals et al., 2015b), we find that the use of pre-trained embeddings results in negligible improvements (on the development set).

6.5 Out-of-Domain Results (ROBOCUP)

We use the ROBOCUP dataset to evaluate the domain-independence of our model. The dataset is severely data-starved with only 1000 (approx.) training pairs, which is much smaller than is typically necessary to train RNNs. This results in higher variance in the trained model distributions, and we thus adopt the standard denoising method of ensembles (Sutskever et al., 2014; Vinyals et al., 2015b;

Zaremba et al., 2014).[9]

Table 8: ROBOCUP results

Method	F-1	sBLEU	sBLEU$_G$
CM08	72.00	–	28.70
LJK09	75.70	–	–
CKM10	79.30	–	–
ALK10	79.90	–	28.80
KL12	–	24.88	**30.90**
Our model	**81.58**	**25.28**	29.40

Following previous work, we perform two experiments on the ROBOCUP dataset (Table 8), the first considering full selective generation and the second assuming ground-truth content selection at test time. On the former, we obtain a standard BLEU score (sBLEU) of 25.28, which exceeds the best score of 24.88 (Konstas and Lapata, 2012). Additionally, we achieve an selection F-1 score of 81.58, which is also the best result reported to-date. In the case of assumed (known) ground-truth content selection, our model attains an sBLEU$_G$ score of 29.40, which is competitive with the state-of-the-art.[10]

7 Conclusion

We presented an encoder-aligner-decoder model for selective generation that does not use any specialized features, linguistic resources, or generation templates. Our model employs a bidirectional LSTM-RNN model with a novel coarse-to-fine aligner that jointly learns content selection and surface realization. We evaluate our model on the benchmark WEATHERGOV dataset and achieve state-of-the-art selection and generation results. We achieve further improvements via a k-nearest neighbor beam filter. We also present several model ablations and visualizations to elucidate the effects of the primary components of our model. Moreover, our model generalizes to a different, data-starved domain (ROBOCUP), where it achieves results competitive with or better than the state-of-the-art.

Acknowledgments

We thank Gabor Angeli, David Chen, Ioannis Konstas, and the reviewers for their helpful comments.

---

[9]We use an ensemble of five randomly initialized models.

[10]The Chen and Mooney (2008) sBLEU$_G$ result is from Angeli et al. (2010).

References

Gabor Angeli, Percy Liang, and Dan Klein. 2010. A simple domain-independent probabilistic approach to generation. In *Proceedings of the Conference on Empirical Methods in Natural Language Processing (EMNLP)*, pages 502–512.

Dzmitry Bahdanau, Kyunghyun Cho, and Yoshua Bengio. 2014. Neural machine translation by jointly learning to align and translate. *arXiv preprint arXiv:1409.0473*.

Regina Barzilay and Mirella Lapata. 2005. Collective content selection for concept-to-text generation. In *Proceedings of the Human Language Technology Conference and the Conference on Empirical Methods in Natural Language Processing (HLT/EMNLP)*, pages 331–338.

Regina Barzilay and Lillian Lee. 2004. Catching the drift: Probabilistic content models, with applications to generation and summarization. In *Proceedings of the Conference of the North American Chapter of the Association for Computational Linguistics Human Language Technologies (NAACL HLT)*, pages 113–120.

Frédéric Bastien, Pascal Lamblin, Razvan Pascanu, James Bergstra, Ian J. Goodfellow, Arnaud Bergeron, Nicolas Bouchard, and Yoshua Bengio. 2012. Theano: new features and speed improvements. NIPS Workshop on Deep Learning and Unsupervised Feature Learning.

Anja Belz. 2008. Automatic generation of weather forecast texts using comprehensive probabilistic generation-space models. *Natural Language Engineering*, 14(04):431–455.

James Bergstra, Olivier Breuleux, Frédéric Bastien, Pascal Lamblin, Razvan Pascanu, Guillaume Desjardins, Joseph Turian, David Warde-Farley, and Yoshua Bengio. 2010. Theano: a CPU and GPU math expression compiler. In *Proceedings of the Scientific Computing with Python Conference (SciPy)*.

David L. Chen and Raymond J. Mooney. 2008. Learning to sportscast: a test of grounded language acquisition. In *Proceedings of the International Conference on Machine Learning (ICML)*, pages 128–135.

David L. Chen, Joohyun Kim, and Raymond J. Mooney. 2010. Training a multilingual sportscaster: Using perceptual context to learn language. *Journal of Artificial Intelligence Research*, 37:397–435.

Alex Graves, Mohamed Abdel-rahman, and Geoffrey Hinton. 2013. Speech recognition with deep recurrent neural networks. In *Proceedings of the IEEE International Conference on Acoustics, Speech and Signal Processing (ICASSP)*, pages 6645–6649.

Sepp Hochreiter and Jürgen Schmidhuber. 1997. Long short-term memory. *Neural Computation*, 9(8):1735–1780.

Andrej Karpathy and Li Fei-Fei. 2015. Deep visual-semantic alignments for generating image descriptions. In *Proceedings of the IEEE Conference on Computer Vision and Pattern Recognition (CVPR)*, pages 3128–3137.

Joohyun Kim and Raymond J Mooney. 2010. Generative alignment and semantic parsing for learning from ambiguous supervision. In *Proceedings of the International Conference on Computational Linguistics (COLING)*, pages 543–551.

Diederik Kingma and Jimmy Ba. 2015. Adam: A method for stochastic optimization. In *Proceedings of the International Conference on Learning Representations (ICLR)*.

Ioannis Konstas and Mirella Lapata. 2012. Unsupervised concept-to-text generation with hypergraphs. In *Proceedings of the Conference of the North American Chapter of the Association for Computational Linguistics Human Language Technologies (NAACL HLT)*, pages 752–761.

Ioannis Konstas and Mirella Lapata. 2013. Inducing document plans for concept-to-text generation. In *Proceedings of the Conference on Empirical Methods in Natural Language Processing (EMNLP)*, pages 1503–1514.

Percy Liang, Michael I. Jordan, and Dan Klein. 2009. Learning semantic correspondences with less supervision. In *Proceedings of the Joint Conference of the Annual Meeting of the Association for Computational Linguistics and the International Joint Conference on Natural Language Processing (ACL/IJCNLP)*, pages 91–99.

Wei Lu and Hwee Tou Ng. 2011. A probabilistic forest-to-string model for language generation from typed lambda calculus expressions. In *Proceedings of the Conference on Empirical Methods in Natural Language Processing (EMNLP)*, pages 1611–1622.

Wei Lu, Hwee Tou Ng, Wee Sun Lee, and Luke S Zettlemoyer. 2008. A generative model for parsing natural language to meaning representations. In *Proceedings of the Conference on Empirical Methods in Natural Language Processing (EMNLP)*, pages 783–792.

Wei Lu, Hwee Tou Ng, and Wee Sun Lee. 2009. Natural language generation with tree conditional random fields. In *Proceedings of the Conference on Empirical Methods in Natural Language Processing (EMNLP)*, pages 400–409.

Hongyuan Mei, Mohit Bansal, and Matthew R. Walter. 2015. Listen, attend, and walk: Neural mapping of navigational instructions to action sequences. *arXiv preprint arXiv:1506.04089*.

Tomas Mikolov, Kai Chen, Greg Corrado, and Jeffrey Dean. 2013. Efficient estimation of word representations in vector space. In *Proceedings of the International Conference on Learning Representations (ICLR)*.

Kishore Papineni, Salim Roukos, Todd Ward, and Wei-Jing Zhu. 2001. BLEU: a method for automatic evaluation of machine translation. In *Proceedings of the Annual Meeting of the Association for Computational Linguistics (ACL)*, pages 311–318.

Razvan Pascanu, Caglar Gulcehre, Kyunghyun Cho, and Yoshua Bengio. 2014. How to construct deep recurrent neural networks. In *Proceedings of the International Conference on Learning Representations (ICLR)*.

Ehud Reiter, Robert Dale, and Zhiwei Feng. 2000. *Building natural language generation systems*, volume 33. MIT Press.

Radu Soricut and Daniel Marcu. 2006. Stochastic language generation using WIDL-expressions and its application in machine translation and summarization. In *Proceedings of the International Conference on Computational Linguistics and the Annual Meeting of the Association for Computational Linguistics (COLING/ACL)*, pages 1105–1112.

Amanda Stent, Rashmi Prasad, and Marilyn Walker. 2004. Trainable sentence planning for complex information presentation in spoken dialog systems. In *Proceedings of the 42nd annual meeting on association for computational linguistics*, page 79. Association for Computational Linguistics.

Ilya Sutskever, Oriol Vinyals, and Quoc V. Lee. 2014. Sequence to sequence learning with neural networks. In *Advances in Neural Information Processing Systems (NIPS)*.

Oriol Vinyals, Lukasz Kaiser, Terry Koo, Slav Petrov, Ilya Sutskever, and Geoffrey Hinton. 2014. Grammar as a foreign language. *arXiv preprint arXiv:1412.7449*.

Oriol Vinyals, Samy Bengio, and Manjunath Kudlur. 2015a. Order matters: Sequence to sequence for sets. *arXiv preprint arXiv:1511.06391*.

Oriol Vinyals, Alexander Toshev, Samy Bengio, and Dumitru Erhan. 2015b. Show and tell: A neural image caption generator. In *Proceedings of the IEEE Conference on Computer Vision and Pattern Recognition (CVPR)*, pages 3156–3164.

Marilyn A Walker, Owen Rambow, and Monica Rogati. 2001. Spot: A trainable sentence planner. In *Proceedings of the second meeting of the North American Chapter of the Association for Computational Linguistics on Language technologies*, pages 1–8. Association for Computational Linguistics.

Yuk Wah Wong and Raymond J Mooney. 2007. Generation by inverting a semantic parser that uses statistical machine translation. In *Proceedings of the Conference of the North American Chapter of the Association for Computational Linguistics Human Language Technologies (NAACL HLT)*, pages 172–179.

Kelvin Xu, Jimmy Ba, Ryan Kiros, Kyunghyun Cho, Aaron Courville, Ruslan Salakhutdinov, Richard Zemel, and Yoshua Bengio. 2015. Show, attend and tell: Neural image caption generation with visual attention. In *Proceedings of the International Conference on Machine Learning (ICML)*.

Wojciech Zaremba, Ilya Sutskever, and Oriol Vinyals. 2014. Recurrent neural network regularization. *arXiv preprint arXiv:1409.2329*.

Generation from Abstract Meaning Representation using Tree Transducers

Jeffrey Flanigan♠ **Chris Dyer**♠ **Noah A. Smith**♡ **Jaime Carbonell**♠
♠School of Computer Science, Carnegie Mellon University, Pittsburgh, PA, USA
♡Computer Science & Engineering, University of Washington, Seattle, WA, USA
`{jflanigan,cdyer,jgc}@cs.cmu.edu, nasmith@cs.washington.edu`

Abstract

Language generation from purely semantic representations is a challenging task. This paper addresses generating English from the Abstract Meaning Representation (AMR), consisting of re-entrant graphs whose nodes are concepts and edges are relations. The new method is trained statistically from AMR-annotated English and consists of two major steps: (i) generating an appropriate spanning tree for the AMR, and (ii) applying tree-to-string transducers to generate English. The method relies on discriminative learning and an argument realization model to overcome data sparsity. Initial tests on held-out data show good promise despite the complexity of the task. The system is available open-source as part of JAMR at:
`http://github.com/jflanigan/jamr`

1 Introduction

We consider natural language generation from the Abstract Meaning Representation (AMR; Banarescu et al., 2013). AMR encodes the meaning of a sentence as a rooted, directed, acyclic graph, where concepts are nodes, and edges are relationships among the concepts.

Because AMR models propositional meaning[1] while abstracting away from surface syntactic realizations, and is designed with human annotation in mind, it suggests a separation of (i) engineering the application-specific propositions that need to be

communicated about from (ii) general-purpose realization details, modeled by a generator shareable across many applications. The latter is our focus here.

Because any AMR graph has numerous valid realizations, and leaves underspecified many important details—including tense, number, definiteness, whether a concept should be referred to nominally or verbally, and more—transforming an AMR graph into an English sentence is a nontrivial problem.

To our knowledge, our system is the first for generating English from AMR. The approach is a statistical natural language generation (NLG) system, trained discriminatively using sentences in the AMR bank (Banarescu et al., 2013). It first transforms the graph into a tree, then decodes into a string using a weighted tree-to-string transducer and a language model (Graehl and Knight, 2004). The decoder bears a strong similarity to state-of-the-art machine translation systems (Koehn et al., 2007; Dyer et al., 2010), but with a rule extraction approach tailored to the NLG problem.

2 Overview

Generation of English from AMR graphs is accomplished as follows: the input graph is converted to a tree, which is input into the weighted intersection of a tree-to-string transducer (§4) with a language model. The output English sentence is the (approximately) highest-scoring sentence according to a feature-rich discriminatively trained linear model. After discussing notation (§3), we describe our approach in §4. The transducer's rules are extracted from the limited AMR corpus and learned general-

---

[1]In essence, AMR handles semantic roles, entity types, within-sentence coreference, discourse connectives, modality, negation, and some other phenomena.

Proceedings of NAACL-HLT 2016, pages 731–739,
San Diego, California, June 12-17, 2016. ©2016 Association for Computational Linguistics

izations; they are of four types: **basic rules** (§5), **synthetic rules** created using a specialized model (§6), **abstract rules** (§7), and a small number of **handwritten rules** (§8).

3   Notation and Definitions

AMR graphs are directed, weakly connected graphs with node labels from the set of **concepts** L_N and edge labels from the set of **relations** L_E.

AMR graphs are transformed to eliminate cycles (details in §4); we refer to the resulting tree as a **transducer input representation (TI representation)**. For a node n with label C and outgoing edges $n \xrightarrow{L_1} n_1, \ldots, n \xrightarrow{L_m} n_m$ sorted lexicographically by L_i (each an element of L_E), the TI representation of the tree rooted at n is denoted:[2]

$$(X\ C\ (L_1\ T_1) \ldots (L_m\ T_m)) \tag{1}$$

where each T_i is the TI representation of the tree rooted at n_i. See Fig. 1 for an example. A LISP-like textual formatting of the TI representation in Fig. 1 is:

$$(X\ \textit{want-01}\ (\textit{ARG0}\ (X\ \textit{boy}))\ (\textit{ARG1}\ (X\ \textit{ride-01}$$
$$(\textit{ARG0}\ (X\ \textit{bicycle}\ (\textit{mod}\ (X\ \textit{red}))))))))$$

To ease notation, we use the function $sort[\,]$ to lexicographically sort edge labels in a TI representation. Using this function, an equivalent way of representing the TI representation in Eq. 1, if the L_i are unsorted, is:

$$(X\ C\ sort[(L_1\ T_1) \ldots (L_m\ T_m)])$$

The TI representation is converted into a word sequence using a tree-to-string transducer. The tree transducer formalism we use is one-state extended linear, non-deleting tree-to-string (**1-xRLNs**) transducers (Huang et al., 2006; Graehl and Knight, 2004).[3]

Definition 1. *(From Huang et al., 2006.) A **1-xRLNs transducer** is a tuple* $(N, \Sigma, W, \mathcal{R})$ *where* N

---

[2]If there are duplicate child edge labels, then the conversion process is ambiguous and any of the conversions can be used. The ordering ambiguity will be handled later in the tree-transducer rules.

[3]Multiple states would be useful for modeling dependencies in the output, but we do not use them here.

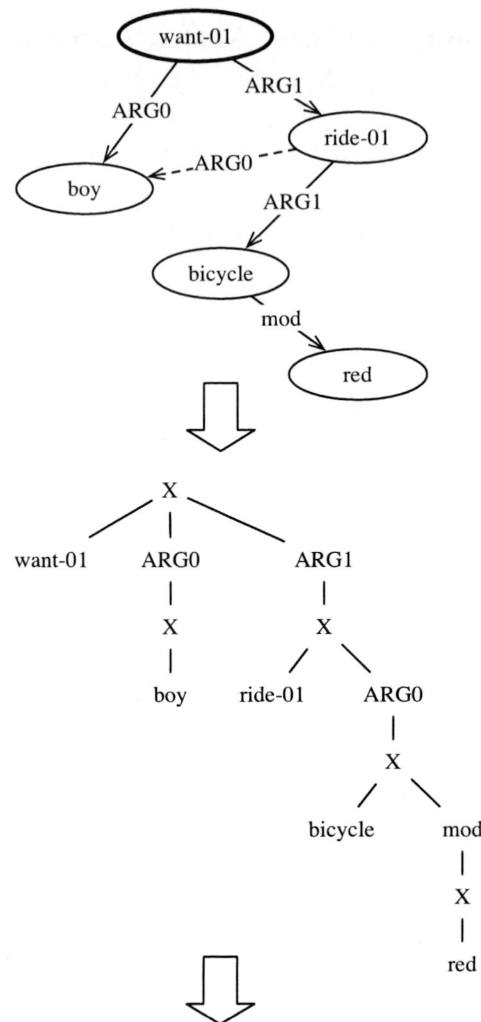

Figure 1: The generation pipeline. An AMR graph (top), with a deleted re-entrancy (dashed), is converted into a transducer input representation (TI representation, middle), which is transduced to a string using a tree-to-string transducer (bottom).

is the set of nonterminals (relation labels and X), Σ *is the input alphabet (concept labels),* W *is the output alphabet (words), and* $\mathcal{R}$ *is the set of rules. A rule in* $\mathcal{R}$ *is a tuple* (t, s, ϕ) *where:*

1. t is the LHS tree, whose internal nodes are labeled by nonterminal symbols, and whose frontier nodes are labeled terminals from Σ or variables from a set $\mathcal{X} = \{X_1, X_2, \ldots\}$;

2. $s \in (\mathcal{X} \cup W)^*$ *is the RHS string;*

3. ϕ *is a mapping from $\mathcal{X}$ to nonterminals N.*

A rule is a **purely lexical rule** if it has no variables.

As an example, the tree-to-string transducer rules which produce the output sentence from the TI representation in Fig. 1 are:

$$(X \text{ } want\text{-}01 \text{ } (ARG0 \text{ } X_1) \text{ } (ARG1 \text{ } X_2)) \rightarrow$$
$$\text{The } X_1 \text{ wants to } X_2 \text{ .}$$
$$(X \text{ } ride\text{-}01 \text{ } (ARG1 \text{ } X_1)) \rightarrow \text{ride the } X_1$$
$$(X \text{ } bicycle \text{ } (mod \text{ } X_1)) \rightarrow X_1 \text{ bicycle}$$
$$(X \text{ } red) \rightarrow \text{red}$$
$$(X \text{ } boy) \rightarrow \text{boy} \qquad (2)$$

Here, all X_i are mapped by a trivial ϕ to the nonterminal X.

The output string of the transducer is the target projection of the derivation, defined as follows:

Definition 2. *(From Huang et al., 2006.) A **derivation** d, its **source and target projections**, denoted $\mathcal{S}(d)$ and $\mathcal{E}(d)$ respectively, are recursively defined as follows:*

1. *If $r = (t, s, \phi)$ is a purely lexical rule, then $d = r$ is a derivation, where $\mathcal{S}(d) = t$ and $\mathcal{E}(d) = s$;*

2. *If $r = (t, s, \phi)$ is a rule, and d_i is a (sub)-derivation with the root symbol of its source projection maching the corresponding substition node in r, i.e., $root(\mathcal{S}(d_i)) = \phi(x_i)$, then $d = r(d_1, \ldots, d_m)$ is also a derivation, where $\mathcal{S}(d) = [x_i \mapsto \mathcal{S}(d_i)]t$ and $\mathcal{E}(d) = [x_i \mapsto \mathcal{E}(d_i)]s$.*

The notation $[x_i \mapsto y_i]t$ is shorthand for the result of substituting y_i for each x_i in t, where x_i ranges over all variables in t.

The set of all derivations of a target string e with a transducer T is denoted

$$\mathcal{D}(e, T) = \{d \mid \mathcal{E}(d) = e\}$$

where d is a derivation in T.

We use a shorthand notation for the transducer rules that will be useful when discussing rule extraction and synthetic rules. Let f_i be a TI representation. The TI representation has the form

$$f_i = (X \text{ } C \text{ } (L_1 \text{ } T_1) \ldots (L_m \text{ } T_m))$$

where $L_i \in L_E$ and $T_1, \ldots, T_m$ are TI representations.[4] Let $A_1, \ldots A_n \in L_E$. We use

$$(f_i, A_1, \ldots, A_n) \rightarrow r \qquad (3)$$

as shorthand for the rule:

$$(X \text{ } C \text{ } sort[(L_1 \text{ } T_1) \text{ } \ldots \text{ } (L_m \text{ } T_m)$$
$$(A_1 \text{ } X_1) \text{ } \ldots \text{ } (A_n \text{ } X_n)]]) \rightarrow r \qquad (4)$$

Note r must contain the variables $X_1 \ldots X_n$. In (3) and (4), argument slots with relation labels A_i have been added as children to the root node of the TI representation f_i.

For example, the shorthand for the transducer rules in (2) is:

$$((X \text{ } want\text{-}01), ARG0, ARG1) \rightarrow$$
$$\text{The } X_1 \text{ wants to } X_2 \text{ .}$$
$$((X \text{ } ride\text{-}01), ARG1) \rightarrow \text{ride the } X_1$$
$$((X \text{ } bicycle), mod) \rightarrow X_1 \text{ bicycle}$$
$$((X \text{ } red)) \rightarrow \text{red} \qquad (5)$$

4 Generation

To generate a sentence e from an input AMR graph G, a spanning tree G' of G is computed, then transformed into a string using a tree-to-string transducer.

Spanning tree. The choice of the graph G's spanning tree G' could have a big effect on the output, since the transducer's output will always be a projective reordering of the tree's leaves. Our spanning tree results from a breadth-first-search traversal, visiting child nodes in lexicographic order of the relation label (inverse relations are visited last). The edges traversed are included in the tree. This simple heuristic is a baseline which can potentially be improved in future work.

Decoding. Let $T = (N, \Sigma, W, \mathcal{R})$ be a tree-to-string transducer. The output sentence is the highest scoring transduction of G':

$$e = \mathcal{E}\left(\underset{d \in \mathcal{D}(G', T)}{\arg\max} \text{ } score(d; \boldsymbol{\theta})\right) \qquad (6)$$

---

[4]If f_i is just a single concept with no children, then $m = 0$ and $f_i = (X \text{ } C)$.

Eq. 6 is solved approximately using the cdec decoder for machine translation (Dyer et al., 2010). The score of the transduction is a linear function (with coefficients $\boldsymbol{\theta}$) of a vector of features including the output sequence's language model log-probability and features associated with the rules in the derivation (denoted $\mathbf{f}$; Table 1):

$$score(d; \boldsymbol{\theta}) = \theta_{LM} \log(p_{LM}(\mathcal{E}(d))) + \sum_{r \in d} \boldsymbol{\theta}^\top \mathbf{f}(r)$$

The feature weights are trained on a development dataset using MERT (Och, 2003).

In the next four sections, we describe the rules extracted and generalized from the training corpus.

5 Inducing Basic Rules

The basic rules, denoted $\mathcal{R}_B$, are extracted from the training AMR data using an algorithm similar to extracting tree transucers from tree-string aligned parallel corpora (Galley et al., 2004). Informally, the rules are extracted from a sentence $\boldsymbol{w} = \langle w_1, \ldots, w_n \rangle$ with AMR graph G as follows:

1. The AMR graph and the sentence are aligned; we use the JAMR aligner from Flanigan et al. (2014), which aligns non-overlapping subgraphs of the graph to spans of words. The subgraphs that JAMR aligns are called **fragments**. In JAMR's aligner, all fragments are trees.

2. G is replaced by its spanning tree by deleting relations that use a variable in the AMR annotation.

3. In the spanning tree, for each node i, we keep track of the word indices $b(i)$ and $e(i)$ in the original sentence that trap all of i's descendents. (This is calculated using a simple bottom-up propagation from the leaves to the root.)

4. For each aligned fragment i, a rule is extracted by taking the subsequence $\langle w_{b(i)} \ldots w_{e(i)} \rangle$ and "punching out" the spans of the child nodes (and their descendants) and replacing them with argument slots.

See Fig. 2 for examples.

More formally, assume the nodes in G are numbered $1, \ldots, N$ and the fragments are numbered

$1, \ldots, F$. Let nodes $: \{1, \ldots, F\} \to 2^{\{1, \ldots, N\}}$ and root $: \{1, \ldots, F\} \to \{1, \ldots, N\}$ be functions that return the nodes in a fragment and the root of a fragment, respectively, and let children $: \{1, \ldots, N\} \to 2^{\{1, \ldots, N\}}$ return the child nodes of a node. We consider a node aligned if it belongs to an aligned fragment. Let the span of an aligned node i be denoted by endpoints a_i and a_i'; for unaligned nodes, $a_i = \infty$ and $a_i' = -\infty$ (depicted with superscripts in Fig. 2). The node alignments are propagated by defining $b(\cdot)$ and $e(\cdot)$ recursively, bottom up:

$$b(i) = \min(a_j, \min_{j \in \text{children}(i)} b(j))$$

$$e(i) = \max(a_j', \max_{j \in \text{children}(i)} e(j))$$

Also define functions $\tilde{b}$ and $\tilde{e}$, from fragment indices to integers, as:

$$\tilde{b}(i) = b(\text{root}(i))$$

$$\tilde{e}(i) = e(\text{root}(i))$$

For fragment i, let $C_i = \text{children}(\text{root}(i)) - \text{nodes}(i)$, which is the children of the fragment's root concept that are not included in the fragment. Let f_i be the TI representation for fragment i.[5] If C_i is empty, then the rule extracted for fragment i is:

$$r_i : (f_i) \to w_{\tilde{b}(i):\tilde{e}(i)} \tag{7}$$

Otherwise, let $m = |C_i|$, and denote the edge labels from $\text{root}(i)$ to elements of C_i as $A_1(i) \ldots A_m(i)$. For $j \in \{1, \ldots, m\}$, let k_j select the elements c_{k_j} of C_i in ascending order of $b(k_j)$. Then the rule extracted for fragment i is:

$$r_i : (f_i, A_{k_1}(i), \ldots A_{k_m}(i)) \to$$
$$w_{\tilde{b}(i):\tilde{b}(k_1)} \ X_1 \ w_{\tilde{e}(k_1):\tilde{b}(k_2)} \ X_2 \ldots$$
$$\ldots w_{\tilde{e}(k_{m-1}):\tilde{b}(k_m)} X_m \ w_{\tilde{e}(k_m):\tilde{e}(i)} \tag{8}$$

A rule is only extracted if the fragment i is aligned and the child spans do not overlap. Fig. 2 gives an example of a tree annotated with alignments, b and e, and the extracted rules.

---

[5]I.e., the nodes in fragment i, with the edges between them, represented as a TI representation.

Name	Description
Rule	1 for every rule
Basic	1 for basic rules, else 0
Synthetic	1 for synthetic rules, else 0
Abstract	1 for abstract rules, else 0
Handwritten	1 for handwritten rules, else 0
Rule given concept	log(number of times rule extracted / number of times concept observed in training data) (only for basic rules, 0 otherwise)
… without sense	same as above, but with sense tags for concepts removed
Synthetic score	model score for the synthetic rule (only for synthetic rules, 0 otherwise)
Word count	number of words in the rule
Stop word count	number of words not in a stop word list
Bad stop word	number of words in a list of meaning-changing stop words, such as "all, can, could, only, so, too, until, very"
Negation word	number of words in "no, not, n't"

Table 1: Rule features in the transducer. There is also an indicator feature for every handwritten rule.

6 Modeling Synthetic Rules

The synthetic rules, denoted $\mathcal{R}_S(G)$, are created to generalize the basic rules and overcome data sparseness resulting from our relatively small training dataset. Our synthetic rule model considers an AMR graph G and generates a set of rules for each node in G. S synthetic rule's LHS is a TI representation f with argument slots $A_1 \ldots A_m$ (this is the same form as the LHS for basic rules). For each node in G, one or more LHS are created (we will discuss this further below), and for each LHS, a set of k-best synthetic rules are produced. The simplest case of a LHS is just a concept and argument slots corresponding to each of its children.

For a given LHS, the synthetic rule model creates a RHS by concatenating together a string in W^* (called a **concept realization** and corresponding to the concept fragment) with strings in $W^* \mathcal{X} W^*$ (called an **argument realization** and corresponding to the argument slots). See the top of Fig. 3 for a synthetic rule with concept and argument realizations highlighted.

Synthetic rules have the form:

$$r : (f, A_1, \ldots A_m) \to \qquad (9)$$
$$\mathbf{l}_{k_1} X_{k_1} \mathbf{r}_{k_1} \ldots \mathbf{l}_{k_c} X_{k_c} \mathbf{r}_{k_c} \; \mathbf{c}$$
$$\mathbf{l}_{k_{c+1}} X_{k_{c+1}} \mathbf{r}_{k_{c+1}} \ldots \mathbf{l}_{k_m} X_{k_m} \mathbf{r}_{k_m}$$

where:

- f is a TI representation.

- Each $A_i \in L_E$.

- $\langle k_1, \ldots, k_m \rangle$ is a permutation of $\langle 1, \ldots, m \rangle$

- $\mathbf{c} \in W^*$ is the **realization** of TI representation f.

- Each $\mathbf{l}_i, \mathbf{r}_i \in W^*$ and $X_i \in \mathcal{X}$. Let $R_i = \langle \mathbf{l}_i, \mathbf{r}_i \rangle$ denote the **realization of argument** i.

- $c \in [0, m]$ is the position of $\mathbf{c}$ among the realizations of the arguments.

Let $\mathcal{F}$ be the space of all possible TI representations. Synthetic rules make use of three lookup tables (which are partial functions) to provide candidate realizations for concepts and arguments: a table for concept realizations $lex : \mathcal{F} \to 2^{W^*}$, a table for argument realizations when the argument is on the left $left_{lex} : \mathcal{F} \times L_E \to 2^{W^*}$, and a table for argument realizations when the argument is on the right $right_{lex} : \mathcal{F} \times L_E \to 2^{W^*}$. These tables are constructed during basic rule extraction, the details of which are discussed below .

Synthetic rules are selected using a linear model with features $\mathbf{g}$ and coefficients ϕ, which scores each RHS for a given LHS. For LHS = $(f, A_1, \ldots A_m)$, the RHS is specified completely by $\mathbf{c}, c, R_1, \ldots, R_m$ and a permutation $k_1, \ldots, k_m$. For each node in G, and for each TI representation f in the domain of lex that matches the node, a LHS is created, and a set of K synthetic rules is produced for each $\mathbf{c} \in lex(f)$. The rules produced are the

$_0$ The $_1$ ((boy) $_2$ wants $_3$ to $_4$ (ride $_5$ the $_6$ ((red) $_7$ bicycle))) $_8$

(a) Sentence annotated with indexes, and bracketed according to $b(i)$ and $e(i)$ from the graph in (b).

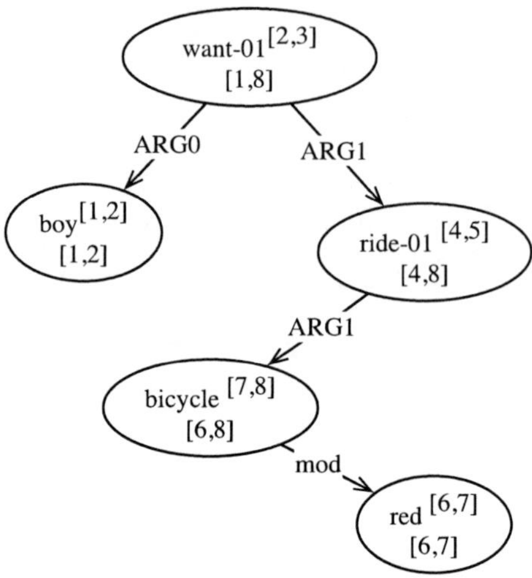

(b) Tree annotated with a_i, a'_i (superscripts) and $b(i)$, $e(i)$ (subscripts).

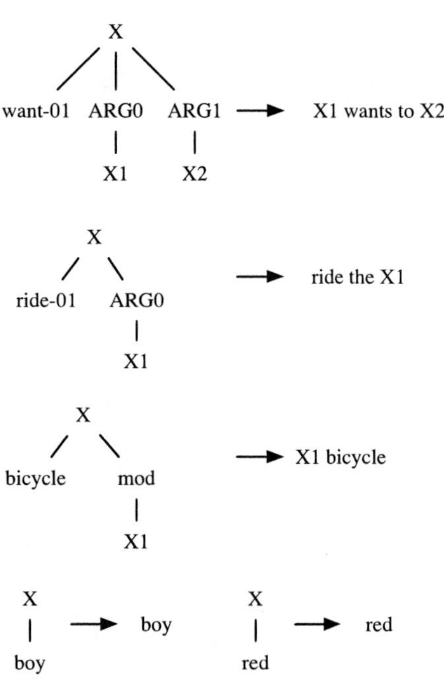

(c) Extracted rules.

Figure 2: Example rule extraction from an AMR-annotated sentence.

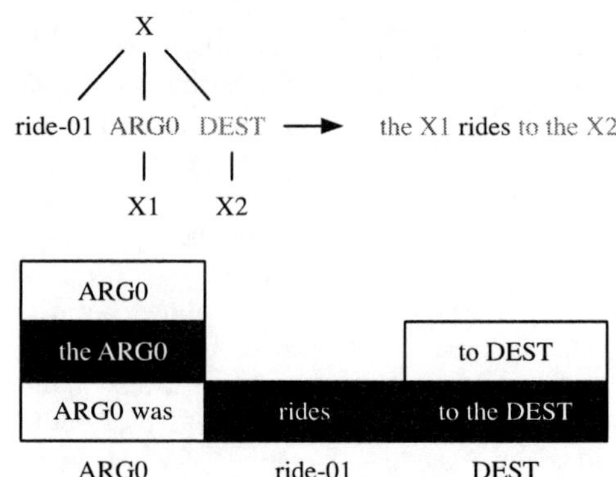

Figure 3: Synthetic rule generation for the rule shown at top. In the rule RHS, the realization for ARG0 is blue, the realization for DEST is red, and the realization for ride-01 is black. For a fixed permutation of the concept and arguments, choosing the argument realizations can be seen as a sequence labeling problem (bottom). The highlighted sequence corresponds to the rule at top.

K-best solutions to:

$$\underset{c, k_1 \ldots k_m, R_1, \ldots, R_m}{\arg\max} \Big(\sum_{i=1}^{c} \boldsymbol{\psi}^\top \mathbf{g}(R_{k_i}, A_{k_i}, \mathbf{c}, i, c)$$
$$+ \boldsymbol{\psi}^\top \mathbf{g}(\langle \epsilon, \epsilon \rangle, *, \mathbf{c}, c+1, c)$$
$$+ \sum_{i=c+1}^{m} \boldsymbol{\psi}^\top \mathbf{g}(R_{k_i}, A_{k_i}, \mathbf{c}, i+1, c) \Big) \quad (10)$$

where the max is over $c \in 0 \ldots m$, $k_1, \ldots, k_m$ is any permutation of $1, \ldots, m$, and $R_i \in \mathit{left}_{lex}(A_i)$ for $i < c$ and $R_i \in \mathit{right}_{lex}(A_i)$ for $i > c$. $*$ is used to denote the concept position. ϵ is the empty string.

The best solution to Eq. 10 is found exactly by brute force search over concept position $c \in [0, m+1]$ and the permutation $k_1, \ldots, k_m$. With fixed concept position and permutation, each R_i for the $\arg\max$ is found independently. To obtain the exact K-best solutions, we use dynamic programming with a K-best semiring (Goodman, 1999) to keep track of the K best sequences for each concept position and permutation, and take the best K sequences over all values of c and k..

The synthetic rule model's parameters are estimated using basic rules extracted from the training data. Basic rules are put into the form of Eq. 9 by

Feature name	Value
POS + A_i + "dist"	$\lvert c-i \rvert$
POS + A_i + side	1.0
POS + A_i + side + "dist"	$\lvert c-i \rvert$
POS + A_i + R_i + side	1.0
$\mathbf{c}$ + A_i + "dist"	$\lvert c-i \rvert$
$\mathbf{c}$ + A_i + side	1.0
$\mathbf{c}$ + A_i + side + "dist"	$\lvert c-i \rvert$
$\mathbf{c}$ + POS + A_i + side + "dist"	$\lvert c-i \rvert$

Table 2: Synthetic rule model features. POS is the most common part-of-speech tag sequence for $\mathbf{c}$, "dist" is the string "dist", and side is "L" if $i < c$, "R" otherwise. + denotes string concatenation.

segmenting the RHS into the form

$$\mathbf{l}_1 X_1 \mathbf{r}_1 \ \ldots \ \mathbf{c} \ \ldots \ \mathbf{l}_m X_m \mathbf{r}_m \tag{11}$$

by choosing $\mathbf{c}, \mathbf{l}_i, \mathbf{r}_i \in W^*$ for $i \in \{1, \ldots, m\}$. An example segmentation is the rule RHS in Fig. 3.

Segmenting the RHS of the basic rules into the form of Eq. 11 is done as follows: $\mathbf{c}$ is the aligned span for f. For the argument realizations, arguments to the left of $\mathbf{c}$ pick up words to their right, and arguments to the right pick up words to their left. Specifically, for $i < c$ (R_i to the left of $\mathbf{c}$ but not next to $\mathbf{c}$), $\mathbf{l}_i$ is empty and $\mathbf{r}_i$ contains all words between a_i and a_{i+1}. For $i = c$ (R_i directly to the left of $\mathbf{c}$), $\mathbf{l}_i$ is empty and $\mathbf{r}_i$ contains all words between a_c and $\mathbf{c}$. For $i > c+1$, $\mathbf{l}_i$ contains all words between a_{i-1} and a_i, and for $i = c + 1$, $\mathbf{l}_i$ contains all words between $\mathbf{c}$ and a_i.

The tables for lex, $left_{lex}$, and $right_{lex}$ are populated using the segmented basic rules. For each basic rule extracted from the training corpus and segmented according to the previous paragraph, $f \to \mathbf{c}$ is added to lex, and $A_{k_i} \to \langle \mathbf{l}_i, \mathbf{r}_i \rangle$ is added to $left_{lex}$ for $i \le c$ and $right_{lex}$ for $i > c$. The permutation k_i is known during extraction in Eq. 8.

The parameters ψ are trained using Ada-Grad (Duchi et al., 2011) with the perceptron loss function (Rosenblatt, 1957; Collins, 2002) for 10 iterations over the basic rules. The features $\mathbf{g}$ are listed in Table 2.

7 Abstract Rules

Like the synthetic rules, the abstract rules $\mathcal{R}_A(G)$ generalize the basic rules. However, abstract rules

Split	Sentences	Tokens
Train	10,000	210,000
Dev.	1,400	29,000
Test	1,400	30,000
MT09	204	5,000

Table 3: Train/dev./test/MT09 split.

are much simpler generalizations which use part-of-speech (POS) tags to generalize. Abstract rules make use of a **POS abstract rule table**, which is a table listing every combination of the POS of the concept realization, the child arguments' labels, and rule RHS with the concept realization removed and replaced with $*$. This table is populated from the basic rules extracted from the training corpus. An example entry in the table is:

$$(\text{VBD}, \text{ARG0}, \text{DEST}) \to$$
$$X_1 \langle * \rangle \text{ to the } X_2$$

For the LHS $(f, A_1, \ldots A_m)$, an abstract rule is created for each member of $\mathbf{c} \in lex(f)$ and the most common POS tag p for $\mathbf{c}$ by looking up p, $A_1, \ldots A_m$ in the POS abstract rule table, finding the common RHS, and filling in the concept position with $\mathbf{c}$. The set of all such rules is returned.

8 Handwritten Rules

We have handwritten rules for dates, conjunctions, multiple sentences, and the concept have-org-role-91. We also create pass-through rules for concepts by removing sense tags and quotes (for string literals).

9 Experiments

We evaluate on the AMR Annotation Release version 1.0 (LDC2014T12) dataset. We follow the recommended train/dev./test splits, except that we remove MT09 data (204 sentences) from the training data and use it as another test set. Statistics for this dataset and splits are given in Table 3. We use a 5-gram language model trained with KenLM (Heafield et al., 2013) on Gigaword (LDC2011T07), and use 100-best synthetic rules.

We evaluate with the Bleu scoring metric (Papineni et al., 2002) (Table 4). We report single ref-

Rules	Test	MT09
Full	22.1	21.2
Full − basic	22.1	20.9
Full − synthetic	9.1	7.8
Full − abstract	22.0	21.2
Full − handwritten	21.9	20.5

Table 4: Uncased Bleu scores with various types of rules removed from the full system.

erence Bleu for the LCD2014T12 test set, and four-reference Bleu for the MT09 set. We report ablation experiments for different sources of rules. When ablating handwritten rules, we do not ablate pass-through rules.

The full system achieves 22.1 Bleu on the test set, and 21.2 on MT09. Removing the synthetic rules drops the results to 9.1 Bleu on test and 7.8 on MT09. Removing the basic and abstract rules has little impact on the results. This may be because the synthetic rule model already contains much of the information in the basic and abstract rules. Removing the handwritten rules has a slightly larger effect, demonstrating the value of handwritten rules in this statistical system.

10   Related Work

There is a large body of work for statistical and non-statistical NLG from a variety of input representations. Statistical NLG systems have been built for input representations such as HPSG (Nakanishi et al., 2005), LFG (Cahill and Van Genabith, 2006; Hogan et al., 2007), and CCG (White et al., 2007), as well as surface and deep syntax (Belz et al., 2011). The deep syntax representations in Bohnet et al. (2010) and Belz et al. (2011) share similarities with AMR: the representations are graphs with re-entrancies, and have an concept inventory from PropBank (Palmer et al., 2005).

The Nitrogen and Halogen systems (Langkilde and Knight, 1998; Langkilde, 2000) used an input representation that was a precursor to the modern version of AMR, which was also called AMR, although it was not the same representation as Banarescu et al. (2013).

Techniques from statistical machine translation have been applied to the problem of NLG (Wong

and Mooney, 2006), and many grammar-based approaches can be formulated as weighted tree-to-string transducers. Jones et al. (2012) developed technology for generation and translation with synchronous hyperedge replacement (SHRG) grammars applied to the GeoQuery corpus (Wong and Mooney, 2006), which in principle could be applied to AMR generation.

11   Conclusion

We have presented a two-stage method for natural language generation from AMR, setting a baseline for future work. We have also demonstrated the importance of modeling argument realization for good performance. Our feature-based, tree-transducer approach can be easily extended with rules and features from other sources, allowing future improvements.

Acknowledgments

The authors would like to thank Adam Lopez and Nathan Schneider for valuable feedback, and Sam Thomson and the attendees of the Fred Jelinek Memorial Workshop in 2014 in Prague for helpful discussions. This work is supported by the U.S. Army Research Office under grant number W911NF-10-1-0533. Any opinion, findings, and conclusions or recommendations expressed in this material are those of the author(s) and do not necessarily reflect the view of the U.S. Army Research Office or the United States Government.

References

Laura Banarescu, Claire Bonial, Shu Cai, Madalina Georgescu, Kira Griffitt, Ulf Hermjakob, Kevin Knight, Philipp Koehn, Martha Palmer, and Nathan Schneider. 2013. Abstract meaning representation for sembanking. In *Proc. of the 7th Linguistic Annotation Workshop and Interoperability with Discourse*.

Anja Belz, Michael White, Dominic Espinosa, Eric Kow, Deirdre Hogan, and Amanda Stent. 2011. The first surface realisation shared task: Overview and evaluation results. In *Proc. of the 13th European Workshop on Natural Language Generation*.

Bernd Bohnet, Leo Wanner, Simon Mille, and Alicia Burga. 2010. Broad coverage multilingual deep sentence generation with a stochastic multi-level realizer. In *Proc. of COLING*.

Aoife Cahill and Josef Van Genabith. 2006. Robust pcfg-based generation using automatically acquired LFG approximations. In *Proc. of COLING-ACL*.

Michael Collins. 2002. Discriminative training methods for hidden Markov models: Theory and experiments with perceptron algorithms. In *Proc. of EMNLP*.

John Duchi, Elad Hazan, and Yoram Singer. 2011. Adaptive subgradient methods for online learning and stochastic optimization. *JMLR*, 12.

Chris Dyer, Adam Lopez, Juri Ganitkevitch, Johnathan Weese, Ferhan Ture, Phil Blunsom, Hendra Setiawan, Vladimir Eidelman, and Philip Resnik. 2010. cdec: A decoder, alignment, and learning framework for finite-state and context-free translation models. In *Proc. of ACL*.

Jeffrey Flanigan, Sam Thomson, Jaime Carbonell, Chris Dyer, and Noah A. Smith. 2014. A discriminative graph-based parser for the abstract meaning representation. In *Proc. of ACL*.

Michel Galley, Mark Hopkins, Kevin Knight, and Daniel Marcu. 2004. What's in a translation rule? In *Proc. of HLT-NAACL*.

Joshua Goodman. 1999. Semiring parsing. *CL*, 25(4).

Jonathan Graehl and Kevin Knight. 2004. Training tree transducers. In *Proc. of HLT-NAACL*.

Kenneth Heafield, Ivan Pouzyrevsky, Jonathan H. Clark, and Philipp Koehn. 2013. Scalable modified Kneser-Ney language model estimation. In *Proc. of ACL*.

Deirdre Hogan, Conor Cafferkey, Aoife Cahill, and Josef Van Genabith. 2007. Exploiting multi-word units in history-based probabilistic generation. In *Proc. of ACL*.

Liang Huang, Kevin Knight, and Aravind Joshi. 2006. Statistical syntax-directed translation with extended domain of locality. In *Proc. of AMTA*.

Bevan Jones, Jacob Andreas, Daniel Bauer, Karl Moritz Hermann, and Kevin Knight. 2012. Semantics-based machine translation with hyperedge replacement grammars. In *Proc. of COLING*.

Philipp Koehn, Hieu Hoang, Alexandra Birch, Chris Callison-Burch, Marcello Federico, Nicola Bertoldi, Brooke Cowan, Wade Shen, Christine Moran, Richard Zens, et al. 2007. Moses: Open source toolkit for statistical machine translation. In *Proc. of ACL*.

Irene Langkilde and Kevin Knight. 1998. Generation that exploits corpus-based statistical knowledge. In *Proc. of COLING-ACL*.

Irene Langkilde. 2000. Forest-based statistical sentence generation. In *Proc. of NAACL 2000*.

Hiroko Nakanishi, Yusuke Miyao, and Jun'ichi Tsujii. 2005. Probabilistic models for disambiguation of an HPSG-based chart generator. In *Proc. of IWPT*.

Franz Josef Och. 2003. Minimum error rate training in statistical machine translation. In *Proc. of ACL*.

Martha Palmer, Daniel Gildea, and Paul Kingsbury. 2005. The proposition bank: An annotated corpus of semantic roles. *CL*, 31(1).

Kishore Papineni, Salim Roukos, Todd Ward, and Wei-Jing Zhu. 2002. Bleu: a method for automatic evaluation of machine translation. In *Proc. of ACL*.

Frank Rosenblatt. 1957. The perceptron—a perceiving and recognizing automaton. Technical Report 85-460-1, Cornell Aeronautical Laboratory.

Michael White, Rajakrishnan Rajkumar, and Scott Martin. 2007. Towards broad coverage surface realization with CCG. In *Proc. of the Workshop on Using Corpora for NLG: Language Generation and Machine Translation*.

Yuk Wah Wong and Raymond J Mooney. 2006. Learning for semantic parsing with statistical machine translation. In *Proc. of HLT-NAACL*.

A Corpus and Semantic Parser for
Multilingual Natural Language Querying of OpenStreetMap

Carolin Haas
Computational Linguistics
Heidelberg University
69120 Heidelberg, Germany
haas1@cl.uni-heidelberg.de

Stefan Riezler
Computational Linguistics & IWR
Heidelberg University
69120 Heidelberg, Germany
riezler@cl.uni-heidelberg.de

Abstract

We present a corpus of 2,380 natural language queries paired with machine readable formulae that can be executed against world wide geographic data of the OpenStreetMap (OSM) database. We use the corpus to learn an accurate semantic parser that builds the basis of a natural language interface to OSM. Furthermore, we use response-based learning on parser feedback to adapt a statistical machine translation system for multilingual database access to OSM. Our framework allows to map fuzzy natural language expressions such as "nearby", "north of", or "in walking distance" to spatial polygons on an interactive map. Furthermore, it combines syntactic complexity and compositionality with a reasonable lexical variability of queries, making it an interesting new publicly available dataset for research on semantic parsing.

1 Introduction

OpenStreetMap[1] (OSM) is a community-built database of geographic data, containing user-contributed local and up-to-date information about landmarks all over the world. Currently, the database contains over 3 billion data objects and is continuously growing with contributions from over 2 million registered users. While the main API is optimized for editing map data, there exists an API that allow to filter map data based on search criteria such as location, type of objects, or features with which objects are tagged. However, issuing a query that is

executable against the OSM database still requires detailed knowledge of database internals, something that cannot be expected from a layman user.

The goal of our work is the development of an interface to OSM that lets a user ask a question in natural language, which is then parsed into a database query that is executable against a web-based filtering tool and returns OSM data on an interactive map. For example, we want a user without detailed knowledge of OSM to be able to ask questions that embrace the "fuzziness" of natural language, for example, *"What are the locations, names and telephone numbers of hotels in Paris with wheelchair access that are close to the station Gare du Nord?"*. To find such information one would have to issue a query that requires detailed knowledge of the database and the query language: *"area[name='Paris']→.a;node(area.a) [name='Gare du Nord']→.b;node(around.b:1000) [tourism='hotel'][wheelchair='yes'];out;"*. Additionally, we present an adaptation of a statistical machine translation (SMT) system for multilingual access to OSM by response-based learning from parser executability of translated queries.

As a starting point for our natural language interface we built a corpus of 2,380 natural language queries paired with machine readable language (MRL) formulae that we used to extract a semantic parser. We chose to manually creating a corpus of MRLs from which structure and weights of a semantic parser can be learned for three reasons:

Online availability: We want to be able to present the OSM community with a set of sample questions that can be executed and whose database

---

[1] http://www.openstreetmap.org

Proceedings of NAACL-HLT 2016, pages 740–750,
San Diego, California, June 12-17, 2016. ©2016 Association for Computational Linguistics

query representation can be inspected. We hope it will be inspiring and helpful for OSM users and developers to see how complex geographical facts can be issued as simple natural language queries that are parsed into executable filters on OSM objects.

Accuracy: For an online natural language interface, high accuracy of semantic parsing is crucial. So far, semi-automatic methods of constructing semantic parsers without bootstrapping from MRLs could not reach the accuracy of semantic parsers extracted from manually created MRLs (Wang et al., 2015). The semantic parser we extracted by simple monolingual machine translation (Andreas et al., 2013) achieves a F1 score of 77.3% for answer retrieval on our data.

Complexity: Our corpus adds a new and complex domain for research on semantic parsing: Compared to existing corpora such as GEOQUERY (Wong and Mooney, 2006) or FREE917 (Cai and Yates, 2013), our corpus combines the compositionality and syntactic complexity of the former corpus with a lexical variation that constitutes a healthy middle ground between closed and open domains.

Our contributions in this paper are threefold: First, we introduce OSM as a new knowledge base that has not, to the best of our knowledge, been used for question answering, and offer a new corpus to the research community. Second, we show that a parser read off the corpus achieves promising parsing accuracy and can be used to adapt SMT to multilingual database access. Third, our work builds the basis of a natural language interface to OSM that will be enabling for interesting directions of future research, e.g., response-based learning to improve semantic parsing and multilingual database access.

2   Related Work

The common approach to semantic parsing is a manual annotation of a corpus with natural language utterances and machine readable formulae which are then used to learn the structure and weights of a semantic parser. Corpora that have been used for training and testing a number of semantic parsers are GEOQUERY (Zelle and Mooney, 1996; Kate et al.,

# users	2,389,374
# objects	3,464,399,738
# nodes	3,139,787,926
# ways	320,775,580
# relations	3,836,232
# tags	1,259,132,137
# distinct tags	76,204,309
# distinct keys	57,159

Table 1: Statistics of OSM as of December 14th, 2015

2005) and FREE917 (Cai and Yates, 2013). While GEOQUERY queries are restricted to the closed domain of US geography, the structural complexity of the questions is higher than for FREE917, which focuses on open domain queries. Seminal work on building semantic parsers from the GEOQUERY meaning representations are Zettlemoyer and Collins (2005) or Wong and Mooney (2006). Later approaches try to learn semantic parsers from question-answer pairs only, for example, Liang et al. (2009) for GEOQUERY, or Kwiatkowski et al. (2013) or Berant et al. (2013) for FREE917. Newer research attempts to close the gap between lexical variability and structural complexity (Vlachos and Clark, 2014; Artzi et al., 2015; Pasupat and Liang, 2015), however, answer retrieval accuracy is low if semantic parsers cannot be bootstrapped from a corpus of queries and MRLs (Wang et al., 2015; Pasupat and Liang, 2015).

Our approach treats semantic parsing as a monolingual machine translation problem in which natural language is translated into the machine readable language. This approach is convenient because one can make use of the efficient and robust decoders that are freely available for SMT. Despite the simplicity of the approach, Andreas et al. (2013) have shown that highly accurate semantic parsers can be trained from annotated data.

OSM has previously been used by Boye et al. (2014) for pedestrian routing using a dialogue system, however, no details on semantic parsing and no resource are provided.

Our SMT tuning experiment builds on the work of Riezler et al. (2014) and Haas and Riezler (2015) who applied response-based learning for SMT to the GEOQUERY and FREE917 domains, respectively.

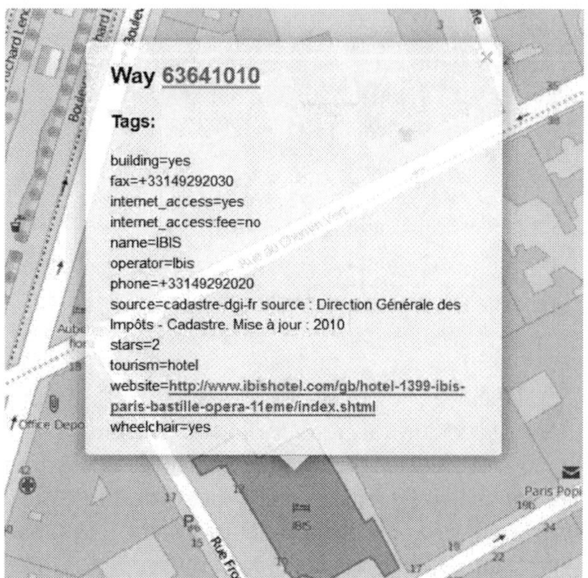

Figure 1: Illustration of a possible entity (here: way) on the Overpass turbo website for the query *"area[name='Paris']→.a;node(area.a)[name='Gare du Nord']→.b;node(around.b:1000[tourism='hotel'][wheelchair='yes'] ;out;"*. The way consists of several nodes that together span the outline of the relevant building. Clicking on the way gives all the key-value pairs registered for this way in the database.

3 OpenStreetMap

OpenStreetMap is a freely available map of the world, annotated by volunteers and editable by anyone. Entered GPS points, referred to as *nodes*, constitute the basis of the database and currently amount to over 3 billion examples (see Figure 1 for more statistics on the OSM database). Nodes can be given tags which are key-value pairs, such as *"amenity=restaurant"*, *"highway=living_street"* or *"abandoned:tourism=theme_park"*. In total there are over 76 million distinct tags which are based on 57,159 unique keys. Nodes may be grouped together to form *ways*. Ways can be given their own set of tags and are for example used to display roads or building outlines. Both nodes and ways may be joined to be part of a *relation* which is used to model the interdependence of several objects. A relation can for example be employed to delineate bus lines or to define administrative boundaries. As relations can also be part of other relations, one can even ex-press hierarchical structures.

The Overpass API[2] can be used to query the database made up of the aforementioned nodes, ways and relations. It can efficiently extract the correct subset of database objects that satisfy the entered constraints. The following constraints are most relevant for our corpus creation later on:

- The simplest constraints require the database objects to have certain keys or key-value pairs. For example to search for hotels, one would use *"node[tourism='hotel'];out;"*.

- Overpass can find ways and relations that form a filled polygon. Based on this, Overpass is able to search for database objects in only the specified *area*, such as a town or country. To search for hotels in Paris, the corresponding Overpass would be: *"area[name='Paris']→.a; node(area.a)[tourism='hotel'];out;"*.

- The operator called *around* allows the user to search for a database object in a certain radius around another object. For hotels in a radius of 1,000 metres around Gare du Nord in Paris, the Overpass query would be: *"area[name='Paris']→.a; node(area.a)[name='Gare du Nord']→.b; node(around.b:1000)[tourism='hotel'];out;"*.

Further tools related to OSM are Overpass turbo[3], a web interface that allows users to run Overpass queries, and the Overpass turbo Query Wizard, which supports querying by predefined human readable shorthands to executable Overpass queries. A screenshot of the map and an example database entry for an Overpass query is shown in Figure 1.

4 Query Creation

Since even the Overpass Query Wizard requires users to be familiar with the tag set of OSM key-value pairs, it unusable for users with only casual or no knowledge of OSM's internal structure. Nonetheless, we could use parts of the user query log to formulate natural language questions. For example users would enter the query *"(node["abandoned:tourism"="theme_park"]; way["abandoned:tourism"="theme_park"]; rela-*

---

[2] http://wiki.openstreetmap.org/wiki/
Overpass_API
[3] http://overpass-turbo.eu/

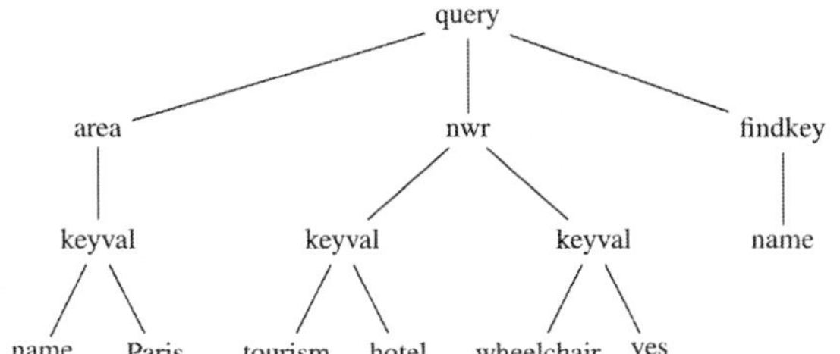

Figure 2: The question *"Which hotels in Paris have wheelchair access?"* with MRL *"query(area(keyval(name,'Paris')), nwr(keyval(tourism,'hotel'),keyval(wheelchair,'yes')), findkey(name))"* can be presented as a tree. A preorder traversal gives: *"query@3 area@1 keyval@2 name@0 Paris@s nwr@2 keyval@2 tourism@0 hotel@s keyval@2 wheelchair@0 yes@s findkey@1 name@0"*

tion["abandoned:tourism"="theme_park"];);out;" which we then extended to *"When did the abandoned theme parks close?"* and added the corresponding MRL *"query(nwr(keyval('abandoned:tourism','theme_park')),qtype(findkey('end_date')))"*. Additionally we often had to provide a reference point for the queries, as users usually searched their current map cut-out and while all abandoned theme parks in the world is a short list, all restaurants for example would be too many to realistically handle. Thus we fell back to 3 chosen cities in those cases, Heidelberg, Paris and Edinburgh. In sum, most of the queries are based on OSM user queries that were issued to the Overpass turbo Query Wizard and shared among users; others were written by the first author with an utilization of the underlying Overpass API in mind.

5   Machine Readable Language (MRL)

Our corpus creation process was guided by the goal to pair a diverse range of questions with machine readable language (MRL) formulae. These should include the most important OSM tags so that the parser is able to learn a mapping between these tags and the different corresponding natural language expressions.

To answer concise questions without including superfluous details, the MRL needs to be able to extract more specific information instead of a list of all database objects as in the underlying Overpass

result. The MRL thus wraps around Overpass and contains additional indicators about what information should be returned from a database object, for example just its GPS coordinates, or a website address, or the number of returned objects.

Given the above consideration, we define our MRL as a variable free language that focuses on practicality and speed, akin in style to the GEO-QUERY MRL language. It is unambiguously defined via a context-free grammar (CFG) so that one can always ascertain whether or not a formula is valid. While the written form of the MRL is a bracket structure, this structure can easily be encoded as a tree by taking a pre-order traversal which makes it easy and efficient to work with. An example CFG tree for a MRL is given in Figure 2. In the following, we list the operators of our MRL.

Query Operator. A single database query is encoded in the operator **query()** which will hold the Overpass query as well as further specifications about what kind of answer should be retrieved. A few operators are directly derived from Overpass, merely re-written as a tree structure. As such OSM key-value pairs are encoded using the operator **keyval()** which takes 2 arguments, the first being the *key* and the second the *value*. The area operator from Overpass directly translates to the operator **area()**. Nodes, ways and relations are grouped together under the **nwr()** operator which will supply the union of the query run with the 3 types in turn. This is necessary because often buildings, e.g. schools, may be represented as any of the 3 types depending on how specific the annotator wanted to be. Both *area()* and *nwr()* then take one ore more **keyval()** arguments. If *area()* and *nwr()* appear as siblings in the tree (for an example see Figure 2), then only the objects that lie within *area()* will be searched to determine if they fulfil the *nwr()* constraints.

Meta Operators. In order to add specificity beyond the lists returned by Overpass, each MRL formula needs one or more of the following meta parameters to be valid; the meta parameters in turn are held by the operator **qtype()**. The operator **latlong()** retrieves the geographical coordinates of the database objects. For a node this is simply its recorded GPS point. In the case of ways and relations the centre of the associated nodes is calcu-

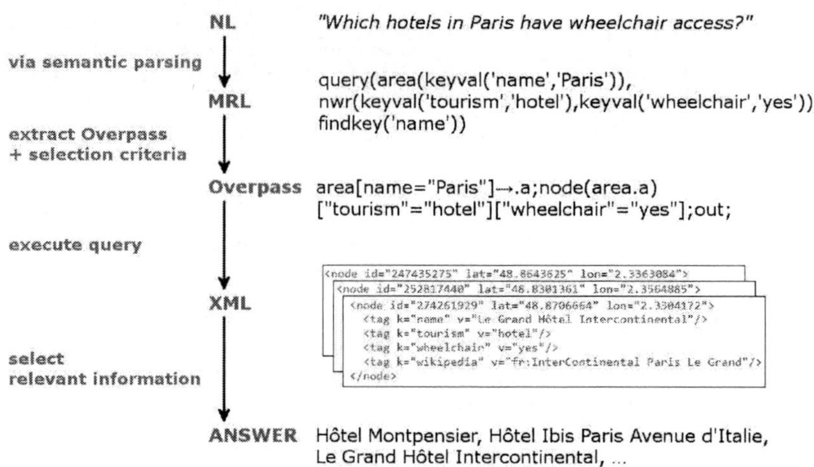

Figure 3: Mapping of natural language question to MRL (via semantic parsing) and to structured database query, returning a set of database objects (via Overpass API) which may be represented as XML documents, from which the correct answer is retrieved.

lated. **findkey()** searches for a specific key (such as *name* or *website*) in the database objects of the retrieved set and returns its value. **count()** simply counts the number of elements in the retrieved set. **least()** checks for the existence of at least x elements in the returned set, whereas x is defined in a second meta function **topx()** which returns the top x elements of a set. *topx()* may also be used in conjunction with *latlong()* and *findkey()*.

Additionally the user can ask for the distance between two points of interests. This operator, **dist()** needs to be supplied with two separate *query()* operators using the *latlong()* meta operator, and can return the value in either kilometres or miles (*unit(mi/km)*). In conjunction with that the user can inquire if the point of interest is still within walking distance (*for("walk")*), or if a car is recommended (*for("car")*).

Fuzzy Language Operators. Fuzzy terms such as "nearby", "within walking distance" and "closest" can be modelled by making use of the *around* operator from Overpass. **around()** searches for points of interest (supplied via **search()**) in the vicinity of another (supplied using **center()**). If only the x closest points are to be returned, *topx()* can be added. The radius is defined via *dist()*. This information can occur either explicitly (*"No further than 200m away"*), or implicitly (*"Give me a cinema with a car park close by"* implies that the car park should be in

walking distance). For the implicit case 4 options are available: walking distance, within town distance, out of town distance, and day trip distance. Choosing the appropriate distance in the implicit case is of particular difficulty because often a term such as *"close by"* implies a different distance depending on the surrounding context. For example, *"a close by airport"* may imply day trip distance, while *"a close by restaurant"* at most implies a just out of town distance (see also Minock and Mollevik (2013)).

Another set of fuzzy terms are the cardinal directions, either within an *area()* operator (*"Where are hotels in the north of Paris?"*), or beyond an *nwr()* operator (*"Where are hotels north of Gare du Nord in Paris?"*). The correct operator, **north()**, **east()**, **south()** or **west()**, follows after *query()*, if present.

Further Operators. Some further operators were needed to model the MRL formula for complex questions. **and()** is used when the user asks for two different nuggets of information (*"Where is the closest bakery and the closest butcher?"* or *"Give me the website and name of ..."*). **or()** is used to create unions, as for example, needed in a sentence such as *"Give me the closest bar or restaurant."* "*"** can be used as a wild card in a value position, e.g. *['historic'=*]* will returned any historic objects, be it a castle, a monument or something else. **nodup()** returns a set with no duplicates. This is, for example, needed in *"Which cuisines are there?"*.

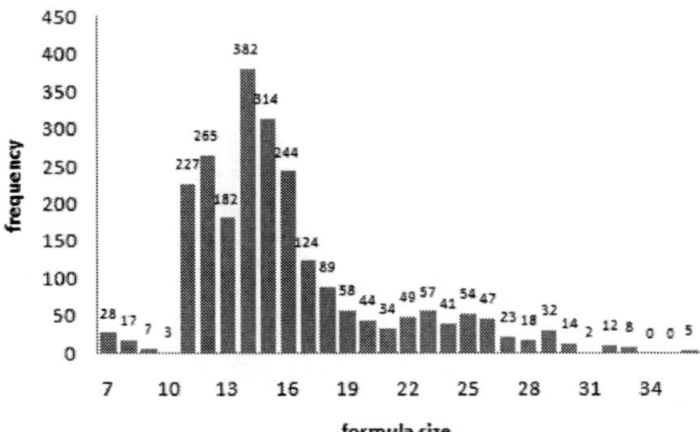

Figure 4: Histogram of the gold formulae sizes

	NLMAPS	GEOQUERY	FREE917
# sent.	2,380	880	917
tokens	25,906	6,660	6,785
types	1002	296	2,038
avg. sent. length.	10.88	7.57	7.4
avg. types per sent.	0.42	0.34	2.22
avg. singleton per sent.	0.1	0.1	1.52
avg. NT per sent.	21	16	16
FRES	82.18	86.61	83.77

Figure 5: Corpus statistics of the corpora NLMAPS, GEOQUERY, FREE917. NT stands for non-terminal and FRES is the Flesch Reading Ease Score (Flesch, 1974).

The complete pipeline process leading from natural language question to an appropriate answer can be seen in Figure 3. The natural language question is first translated by the semantic parser into a MRL, from which the Overpass query is deterministically extracted, while keeping a list of the relevant further indicators. These indicators then operate on the database objects returned by the Overpass query to form the answer.

6   Corpus Statistics

Our corpus, called NLMAPS, is more than twice as large as GEOQUERY or FREE917. In the following, we present a comparison of the lexical and syntactic complexity of the three corpora. All statistics reported in Figure 5 are normalized by the number of sentences.

Lexically, NLMAPS is more diverse than GEOQUERY, as can be seen by the average number of types, but less so compared to FREE917 due to the fact that the OSM database is still a somewhat more closed domain compared to Freebase. Syntactically however, NLMAPS is with 3 more words on average per sentence more complex than GEOQUERY and FREE917, which have nearly identical sentence length. As a further test, we ran the Stanford Parser (Klein and Manning, 2003) on the queries to generate syntactic parse trees. We then counted the number of non-terminals required to produce the parse tree. This result reaffirms what the simpler sentence length already reported: the language in NLMAPS is more complex than in the other two corpora, which have identical complexity.

In Figure 4 we report the number of operators and values needed to construct the different gold formulae. While there are a few questions that need a formula shorter than 10, the vast majority needs a length of around 15, followed by a long tail of sizes with decreasing frequency of up to 36. The fact that many of the gold formulae are in fact longer than the average sentence length shows that the questions are far from trivial and require elaborate database queries to be answered. The last measure we report is the Flesch Reading Ease Score (Flesch, 1974) which is usually used to asses the text difficulty for readers. In this score, a lower number indicates a harder text. NLMAPS receives the lowest number, indicating it as the most complex corpus.

Overall we can infer that NLMAPS provides a good balance between lexical diversity as well as stability for a machine learning algorithm to learn. With regards to syntactic complexity, NLMAPS easily supersedes the other two corpora. We conclude this section with a few example sentences:

```
What are the websites and
names of the museums or art
centers in walking distance of
the Eiffel Tower?

What are the opening times of
the Sainsbury's Local closest
to the Edinburgh Waverley in
Edinburgh?

What are the peaks in the
north of Languedoc-Roussillon
called and how high are they?
```

7   Semantic Parsing

We treat semantic parsing as an SMT problem, using our own implementation of the framework in-

		Precision	Recall	F1
1	+intersect +stem +cdec	84.69	62.42	71.87
2	+intersect +stem +cdec +sparse	84.40	65.8	73.95[1]
3	+intersect +stem +cdec +pass +cfg	**89.45**	65.19	75.41[1]
4	+intersect +stem +cdec +sparse +pass +cfg	89.04	**68.3**	**77.3**[1,2,3]

Table 2: Semantic Parsing results on NLMAPS (split 1500/880 for train/test set) using different settings. Tuning was carried out on the training set. In the case of MERT tuning, the results are averaged over 3 runs due to the randomness MERT introduces. Best results are indicated in **bold face**. Statistical significance in terms of F1 of system differences at $p < 0.05$ are indicated by experiment number in superscript.

troduced by Andreas et al. (2013) who have shown that this approach achieves state-of-the-art performance on GEOQUERY. In this framework it is crucial that the MRL can be represented as a tree. A pre-order tree traversal can give a unique string in which each node is a word (i.e. surrounded by white space). Once the MRL has been converted into such a structure (for an example see Figure 2), a word aligner, here GIZA++ (Och and Ney, 2003), can be used to generate word-to-word alignments in both translation directions which can then be combined with various heuristics (Koehn, 2010, Chapter 4.5.3). From the next step onwards we use the freely available SMT framework CDEC (Dyer et al., 2010). After building a language model for the target (MRL) side, SCFG grammars for hierarchical phrases for tuning and testing were extracted. Experiments in n-gram order showed that 5-gram models are sufficient for language modelling.

At test time, a critical issue is the fact that monolingual SMT does not ensure that the translations are valid MRL formulae. Thus a k-best list (sorted from most probable to least) is generated which needs to be traversed until a valid formula is found. Experimentation with the k-best list size showed that 100 is a good trade-off between speed and performance. A bigger size of k might enable us to find a valid (and correct) formula further down the k-best, however, we verified experimentally that in most cases no option in the extended k-best list contained a valid formula either.

Once a valid formula is found, it is executed against a database and the resulting answer is compared to the answer the gold formula provides. Only exact matches are considered correct. We report *Precision*, *Recall* and *F1-score* to evaluate the se-

mantic parser.[4]

Table 2 shows experimental results for different settings of semantic parsing on NLMAPS. Statistical significance of system differences in terms of F1 was assessed by an Approximate Randomization test (Noreen, 1989). For the word-alignment step, we found that the choice of the strategy for combining word alignments from both translation directions is crucial to the semantic parser's performance. The *intersect* strategy performs significantly better than any other, suggesting that high precision alignments are very important when using a monolingual SMT approach for semantic parsing. Further, stemming the words on the NL side is also always significantly better than not doing so. In a next step we compare the use of dense features (Dyer et al., 2010) in conjunction with the tuning algorithm MERT (Och, 2003) and additional sparse features (Simianer et al., 2012). As MERT cannot handle such a large amount of features, we paired the sparse features with the tuning algorithm MIRA (Crammer and Singer, 2003). Because MERT suffers from optimizer instability (Clark et al., 2011) due to random initialization, the experiments 1 & 3 in Table 2 report the average result based on 3 different MERT runs. Another variation we tested is the use of the NLMAPS CFG to check whether or not a translation is a valid MRL, instead of a quicker check that only ensures that a translation can be parsed as a tree. This variation is indicated with "+*cfg*". Lastly, while the system was able to directly learn the mapping of named entities previously seen dur-

---

[4]*Recall* is defined as the percentage of correct answers out of all examples, *Precision* the percentage of correct answers out of all examples with an answer, and *F1-score* the harmonic mean between the two aforementioned.

ing training, this is not possible for new named entities. These unknown named entities will automatically be passed through by the SMT system but they will be missing the marker of where in the tree they belong. As named entities always have to be in a value position in the corresponding MRL and values are always leave nodes, this can easily be rectified by appending the marker for a leave node to passed through words ("+*pass*"). Of course, when stemming is used, one has to also keep track of the unstemmed form. The decision of which route to go with named entities is left up to the SMT system.

Overall, the modules tested in Table 2 add up to a total F1 score of 77.3%. Given the complexity of our corpus and the simplicity of the semantic parser, this is a promising result.

8 Multilingual Parsing

Riezler et al. (2014) and Haas and Riezler (2015) have shown how to use semantic parsers for GEO-QUERY and FREE917, respectively, to adapt an SMT system for multilingual database access. In this section we show that our semantic parser can be used for response-based learning of an SMT system to allow multilingual natural language queries to OSM, here German. To this end, a SMT system first translates the question from German to English and then the translation is passed to the semantic parser to answer the question. The SMT system uses the feedback from the parser, i.e. the knowledge whether or not the question could be parsed to the correct answer, to improve translations.

More formally, assume an SMT system with a joint feature representation $\phi(x, y)$ for input sentences x and output translations $y \in Y(x)$, that uses a linear scoring function to predict the most likely translation $\hat{y} = \arg\max_{y \in Y(x)} w^\top \phi(x, y)$. We define a cost function $c(y^{(i)}, y) = (1 - \mathrm{BLEU}(y^{(i)}, y))$ based on sentence-wise BLEU (Nakov et al., 2012) and a binary feedback function $e(y) \in \{1, 0\}$. The binary function evaluates to 1 if and only if a natural language's semantic parse receives the same answer as the corresponding gold parse. Training is performed by moving w closer to a *hope* translation y^+ while pushing it away from a *fear* translation y^-. Both y^+ and y^- have a high model score. y^+ incorporates the *hope* for a best translation to have a low

cost and positive feedback. y^- is *feared* due to a high cost and negative feedback, thus we define:

$$y^+ = \underset{y \in Y(x^{(i)}):e(y)=1}{\arg\max} \left(s(x^{(i)}, y; w) - c(y^{(i)}, y) \right),$$

$$y^- = \underset{y \in Y(x^{(i)}):e(y)=0}{\arg\max} \left(s(x^{(i)}, y; w) + c(y^{(i)}, y) \right).$$

The algorithm, called REBOL (Riezler et al., 2014), proceeds by iterating over the training data, predicting the top translation $\hat{y}$, and receiving feedback for this translation from a semantic parser. If the feedback is positive, $\hat{y}$ is set equal to y^+, otherwise to y^-. The algorithm then searches the k-best list for the missing y^- or y^+, respectively, and performs an update that adds the feature vector of y^+ onto w, and subtracts the feature vector of y^-.

For our experiment, the NLMAPS questions were translated by the first author into German. As parser we chose to use number 3 (+intersect +stem +cdec +pass +cfg) from Table 2, deciding against the use of sparse features due speed reasons. The CDEC (Dyer et al., 2010) decoder was used for machine translation from German to English. Here we employ its standard features plus additional sparse features[5] and the COMMON CRAWL[6] (Smith et al., 2013) corpus to built the baseline SMT system.

REBOL is compared to a baseline system without discriminative training (CDEC) and to a stochastic (sub)gradient descent variant of RAMPION (Gimpel and Smith, 2012). Both baseline systems do not make use of the feedback from the semantic parser. While both REBOL and RAMPION assume the availability of both a reference translation and a gold parse, response-based learning can also succeed without any access to reference translations or even to gold standard parses. Riezler et al. (2014) introduced an algorithm, called EXEC, that only relies on task-based feedback and omits the cost function based on sentence-wise BLEU. Collecting real world data for this algorithm is realistic for an online interface to OSM since it only requires a user to pose a question and then indicate if it was answered to their satisfaction.

---

[5] https://github.com/pks/cdec-dtrain
[6] http://www.statmt.org/wmt13/
training-parallel-commoncrawl.tgz

method	P	R	F1	BLEU
[1]CDEC	67.8	24.89	36.41	38.3
[2]EXEC	75.2	31.36	44.27[1]	40.85[1]
[3]RAMPION	78.21	38.75	51.82[1,2]	51.82[1,2]
[4]REBOL	80.76	41.02	**54.41**[1,2,3]	**51.88**[1,2]

Table 3: SMT results on NLMAPS, reporting Precision (P), Recall (R) and their harmonic mean (F1). Best results are indicated in **bold face**. Statistical significance of result differences at $p < 0.05$ are indicated by algorithm number in superscript.

While we do report BLEU (Papineni et al., 2002), the primary goal in our work is to achieve highest possible F1 score. This is vital because our ultimate aim is to give users asking German questions the correct answer, whereas the English translation from which BLEU is be calculated is only an intermediate result that is irrelevant for the task goal.

To test significance of F1 and BLEU, we again use Approximate Randomization. Before training, we split of 200 sentences from the training set to use as held out data (dev set). RAMPION, REBOL and EXEC ran for 50 epochs and then the dev set was used to pinpoint the best epoch for each algorithm. In the case of RAMPION, the best epoch equalled the epoch in which the dev set achieved the highest BLEU score (epoch 20). For REBOL and EXEC, on the other hand, this decision was made by the highest F1 score on the dev set (epoch 40 and 6 respectively). The learning rate for both algorithms was set on a per feature basis using Adadelta (Zeiler, 2012).

As shown in Table 3, REBOL can significantly improve in terms of F1 and BLEU over the CDEC baseline. It is also significantly better than RAMPION in terms of F1 while being able to keep up in BLEU. Should reference translations not be available, EXEC shows that it can still significantly outperform the CDEC baseline, it however cannot keep up with REBOL or RAMPION which have a more detailed supervision signal available to them.

9 Conclusion

We presented an approach to query the OSM database for complex geographical facts via natural language questions. The key technology is a semantic parser that is trained in supervised fashion from a large set of questions annotated with executable MRLs. Our corpus is larger than previous annotated question-answer corpora, while including a wide variety of challenging questions.

Terms such as *"nearby"*, *"in the south of"*, *"within x miles"* are particularly well-suited for a natural language query interface that allows to map the fuzziness of natural language to flexible spatial polygons. Our corpus is publicly available[7] and a website where users can query OSM using natural language is under development[8]. This in turn will give us new and more realistic data which we can use to extend the corpus and to improve the semantic parser.

An online version of our natural language interface to OSM will be enabling for various interesting directions of future research: Besides the possibility to gain new and more realistic data which we can use to extend the corpus, the semantic parser can be improved itself by response-based learning, where supervision signals can be extracted from the executed parses of new user queries against the database (Kwiatowski et al. (2013), Berant et al. (2013), Goldwasser and Roth (2013), *inter alia*). In a similar way, multilingual database access can be enhanced by adapting an SMT system by response-based learning, using executability of a parse of a translated query as supervision signal (Riezler et al., 2014). Both cases of response-based learning only require a user who issues a query and gives feedback on whether the proposed OSM object was the intended answer. Such an interactive scenario enables further research on alternative algorithms for learning from partial feedback (Szepesvári, 2009; Bubeck and Cesa-Bianchi, 2012).

Acknowledgments

We would like to thank the OSM developers Roland Olbricht and Martin Raifer for their support and for contributing a dataset of shared user queries. The research reported in this paper was supported in part by DFG grant RI-2221/2-1 "Grounding Statistical Machine Translation in Perception and Action".

---

[7]`www.cl.uni-heidelberg.de/nlmaps`
[8]`nlmaps.cl.uni-heidelberg.de`

References

Jacob Andreas, Andreas Vlachos, and Stephen Clark. 2013. Semantic parsing as machine translation. In *Proceedings of the 51st Annual Meeting of the Association for Computational Linguistics (ACL)*, Sofia, Bulgaria.

Yoav Artzi, Kenton Lee, and Luke Zettlemoyer. 2015. Broad-coverage CCG semantic parsing with AMR. In *Proceedings of the Conference on Empirical Methods on Natural Language Processing (EMNLP)*, Lisbon, Portugal.

Jonathan Berant, Andrew Chou, Roy Frostig, and Percy Liang. 2013. Semantic parsing on Freebase from question-answer pairs. In *Proceedings of the 2013 Conference on Empirical Methods in Natural Language Processing (EMNLP)*, Seattle, WA.

Johan Boye, Morgan Fredriksson, Jana Gtze, and Jrgen Knigsmann. 2014. A demonstration of a natural-language pedestrian routing system. In *Proceedings of the 5th international workshop on spoken dialogue systems (IWSDS)*, Napa, USA.

Sébastian Bubeck and Nicolò Cesa-Bianchi. 2012. Regret analysis of stochastic and nonstochastic multi-armed bandit problems. *Foundations and Trends in Machine Learning*, 5(1):1–122.

Qingqing Cai and Alexander Yates. 2013. Large-scale semantic parsing via schema matching and lexicon extenstion. In *Proceedings of the 51st Annual Meeting of the Association for Computational Linguistics (ACL)*, Sofia, Bulgaria.

Jonathan Clark, Chris Dyer, Alon Lavie, and Noah Smith. 2011. Better hypothesis testing for statistical machine translation: Controlling for optimizer instability. In *Proceedings of the 49th Annual Meeting of the Association for Computational Linguistics (ACL)*, Portland, OR.

Koby Crammer and Yoram Singer. 2003. Ultraconservative online algorithms for multiclass problems. *Journal of Machine Learning Research*, 3:951–991.

Chris Dyer, Adam Lopez, Juri Ganitkevitch, Johnathan Weese, Ferhan Ture, Phil Blunsom, Hendra Setiawan, Vladimir Eidelman, and Philip Resnik. 2010. cdec: A decoder, alignment, and learning framework for finite-state and context-free translation models. In *Proceedings of the 48th Annual Meeting of the Association for Computational Linguistics (ACL)*, Uppsala, Sweden.

Rudolf Flesch. 1974. *The Art of Readable Writing: With the Flesch Readability Formula*. Harper & Row.

Kevin Gimpel and Noah A. Smith. 2012. Structured ramp loss minimization for machine translation. In *Proceedings of the 2012 Conference of the North American Chapter of the Association for Computational Linguistics: Human Language Technologies (HLT-NAACL)*, Stroudsburg, PA.

Dan Goldwasser and Dan Roth. 2013. Learning from natural instructions. *Machine Learning*, 94(2):205–232.

Carolin Haas and Stefan Riezler. 2015. Response-based learning for machine translation of open-domain database queries. In *Proceedings of the North American Chapter of the Association for Computational Linguistics (NAACL)*, Denver, CO.

Rohit J. Kate, Yuk Wah Wong, and Raymond J. Mooney. 2005. Learning to transform natural to formal languages. In *Proceedings of AAAI*, Pittsburgh, PA.

Dan Klein and Christopher D. Manning. 2003. Accurate unlexicalized parsing. In *Proceedings of the 41st Annual Meeting of the Association for Computational Linguistics (ACL)*, pages 423–430.

Philipp Koehn. 2010. *Statistical Machine Translation*. Cambridge University Press.

Tom Kwiatkowski, Eunsol Choi, Yoav Artzi, and Luke Zettlemoyer. 2013. Scaling semantic parsers with on-the-fly ontology matching. In *Proceedings of the 2013 Conference on Empirical Methods in Natural Language Processing (EMNLP)*, Seattle, WA.

Tom Kwiatowski, Eunsol Choi, Yoav Artzi, and Luke Zettlemoyer. 2013. Scaling semantic parsers with on-the-fly ontology matching. In *Proceedings of the Conference on Empirical Methods in Natural Language Processing (EMNLP)*, Seattle, WA.

Percy Liang, Michael I. Jordan, and Dan Klein. 2009. Learning dependency-based compositional semantics. In *Proceedings of the 59th Annual Meeting of the Association for Computational Linguistics: Human Language Technologies (ACL-HLT)*, Portland, OR.

Michael Minock and Johan Mollevik. 2013. Context-dependent 'near' and 'far' in spatial databases via supervaluation. *Data Knowl. Eng.*, 86:295–305.

Preslav Nakov, Francisco Guzmán, and Stephan Vogel. 2012. Optimizing for sentence-level bleu+1 yields short translations. In *Proceedings of the 24th International Conference on Computational Linguistics (COLING)*, Bombay, India.

Eric W. Noreen. 1989. *Computer Intensive Methods for Testing Hypotheses: An Introduction*. Wiley, New York.

Franz Josef Och and Hermann Ney. 2003. A systematic comparison of various statistical alignment models. *Computational Linguistics*, 29(1):19–51.

Franz Josef Och. 2003. Minimum error rate training in statistical machine translation. In *Proceedings of the Human Language Technology Conference and the 3rd Meeting of the North American Chapter of the Association for Computational Linguistics (HLT-NAACL)*, Edmonton, Cananda.

Kishore Papineni, Salim Roukos, Todd Ward, and Wei-Jing Zhu. 2002. Bleu: A method for automatic evaluation of machine translation. In *Proceedings of the 40th Annual Meeting on Association for Computational Linguistics (ACL)*, Stroudsburg, PA.

Panupong Pasupat and Percy Liang. 2015. Compositional semantic parsing on semi-structured tables. In *Proceedings of the 53rd Annual Meeting of the Association for Computational Linguistics and the 7th International Joint Conference on Natural Language Processing (ACL-IJCNLP)*, Beijing, China.

Stefan Riezler, Patrick Simianer, and Carolin Haas. 2014. Response-based learning for grounded machine translation. In *Proceedings of the 52nd Annual Meeting of the Association for Computational Linguistics (ACL)*, Baltimore, MD.

Patrick Simianer, Stefan Riezler, and Chris Dyer. 2012. Joint feature selection in distributed stochastic learning for large-scale discriminative training in SMT. In *Proceedings of the 50th Annual Meeting of the Association for Computational Linguistics (ACL)*, Jeju Island, South Korea.

Jason Smith, Herve Saint-Amand, Magdalena Plamada, Philipp Koehn, Chris Callison-Burch, and Adam Lopez. 2013. Dirt cheap web-scale parallel text from the Common Crawl. In *Proceedings of the 51st Annual Meeting of the Association for Computational Linguistics (ACL)*, Sofia, Bulgaria.

Csaba Szepesvári. 2009. *Algorithms for Reinforcement Learning*. Synthesis Lectures on Artificial Intelligence and Machine Learning. Morgan & Claypool.

Andreas Vlachos and Stephen Clark. 2014. A new corpus and imitation learning framework for context-dependent semantic parsing. *Transactions of the Association for Computational Linguistics (TACL)*, 2:547–559.

Yushi Wang, Jonathan Berant, and Percy Liang. 2015. Building a semantic parser overnight. In *Proceedings of the 53rd Annual Meeting of the Association for Computational Linguistics and the 7th International Joint Conference on Natural Language Processing (ACL-IJCNLP)*, Beijing, China.

Yuk Wah Wong and Raymond J. Mooney. 2006. Learning for semantic parsing with statistical machine translation. In *Proceedings of the Human Language Technology Conference of the North American Chapter of the Association for Computational Linguistics (HLT/NAACL)*.

Matthew D. Zeiler. 2012. ADADELTA: An adaptive learning rate method. arXiv:1212.5701 [cs.LG].

John M. Zelle and Raymond J. Mooney. 1996. Learning to parse database queries using inductive logic programming. In *Proceedings of AAAI*, Portland, OR.

Luke S. Zettlemoyer and Michael Collins. 2005. Learning to map sentences to logical form: Structured classification with probabilistic categorial grammars. In *Proceedings of the Conference on Uncertainty in Artificial Intelligence (UAI)*, Edinburgh, Scotland, UK.

Natural Language Communication with Robots

Yonatan Bisk
Information Sciences Institute
Univ. of Southern California
`ybisk@isi.edu`

Deniz Yuret
Koç University
Computer Engineering
`dyuret@ku.edu.tr`

Daniel Marcu
Information Sciences Institute &
Department of Computer Science
Univ. of Southern California
`marcu@isi.edu`

Abstract

We propose a framework for devising empirically testable algorithms for bridging the communication gap between humans and robots. We instantiate our framework in the context of a problem setting in which humans give instructions to robots using unrestricted natural language commands, with instruction sequences being subservient to building complex goal configurations in a blocks world. We show how one can collect meaningful training data and we propose three neural architectures for interpreting contextually grounded natural language commands. The proposed architectures allow us to correctly understand/ground the blocks that the robot should move when instructed by a human who uses unrestricted language. The architectures have more difficulty in correctly understanding/grounding the spatial relations required to place blocks correctly, especially when the blocks are not easily identifiable.

1 Motivation

Much of the progress in Natural Language Processing can be attributed to defining problems of broad interest (e.g. parsing and machine translation); collecting or creating publicly available corpora that encode meaningful ⟨input, output⟩ samples (e.g. Penn TreeBank and LDC Parallel Corpora); and devising simple, objective and computable evaluation metrics to automatically assess the performance of algorithms designed to solve the problems of interest, independent of the approach or technology used (e.g. ParseEval and Bleu).

As robots become increasingly ubiquituous, we need to learn to interact with them intelligently, in the same manner we interact with members of our own species. To make rapid progress in this area, we propose to use an intellectual framework that has the same ingredients that have transformed our field: appealing science problem definitions; publicly available datasets; and easily computable, objective evaluation metrics.

In this paper, we study the problem of Human-Robot Natural Language Communication in a setting inspired by a traditional AI problem – blocks world (Winograd, 1972). After reviewing previous work (Section 2), we propose a novel Human-Robot Communication Problem that is testable empirically (Section 3.1) and we describe the publicly available datasets (Section 3.2) and evaluation metric that we devised to support our research (Section 6). We then introduce a set of algorithms for solving our problem and we evaluate their performance both objectively and subjectively (Sections 4–8).

2 Previous work

Most research on Human-Robot Interaction (Klingspor et al., 1997; Thompson et al., 1993; Mavridis, 2015) bridges the gap between natural language commands and the physical world via a set of pre-defined templates characterized by a small vocabulary and grammar. Progress on language in this area has largely focused on grounding visual attributes (Kollar et al., 2013; Matuszek et al., 2014) and on learning spatial relations and actions for small vocabularies with hard-coded abstract concepts (Steels and Vogt, 1997; Roy, 2002;

Proceedings of NAACL-HLT 2016, pages 751–761,
San Diego, California, June 12-17, 2016. ©2016 Association for Computational Linguistics

Guadarrama et al., 2013). Language is sometimes grounded into simple actions (MacMahon et al., 2006; Yu and Siskind, 2013) but the data, while multimodal, is relatively formulaic, the vocabularies are small, and the grammar is constrained. Although robots have significantly increased their autonomy and ability to plan, that has not resulted, to date, in more flexible human-robot communication protocols that would enable robots to understand free-er form language and/or acquire simple and complex concepts via human-robot interactions.

Recently the connection between less formulaic language and simple actions has been explored successfully in the context of simulated worlds (Branavan et al., 2009; Goldwasser and Roth, 2011; Branavan et al., 2011; Artzi and Zettlemoyer, 2013; Andreas and Klein, 2015) and videos (Malmaud et al., 2015; Venugopalan et al., 2015). However, to our knowledge, there is no body of work that focuses on understanding the relation between natural language and complex actions and goals or on explaining flexibly the actions taken by a robot in natural language utterances. As observed by Klingspor (1997), there is a big gap between the formulaic interactions that are typical of state-of-the-art human-robot communications and human-human interactions, which are more abstract.

3 A Framework for Human-Robot Natural Language Communication Research

3.1 Problem Definition

Problem-Solution Sequences. In order to build models that understand the ambiguous and complex language used by people when communicating to solve a task, we adopt the Problem-Solution Sequence (PSS) framework proposed by Bisk et al. (2016). Problem-Solution Sequences provide high and low level descriptions of actions in service of a goal; more specifically, they are sequences of images that encode what a robot might see as it goes about accomplishing a goal. In this paper, we work with PSSs specific to a simple world that has blocks placed on a table and a robot that can visually inspect the table and manipulate the blocks on it.

Figure 1 shows four intermediate block configurations of a PSS the robot observes as it transforms the initial state block configuration (random) into the fi-

1	coca cola , hp , nvidia .
2	nvidia , to the right of hp
3	place the nvidia block east of the hp block .
4	move the nvidia block to the right of the hp block
5	place the nvidia block to the east of the hp block .
6	move the nvidia block directly to the right of the hp block .
7	move the nvidia block just to the right of the hp block in line with the mercedes block .
8	put the nvidia block on the right end of the row of blocks that includes the coca cola and hp blocks .
9	put the nvidia block on the same row as the coca cola block , in the first open space to the right of the coca cola block .

Table 1: Examples of the type of natural language instructions seen in our corpus that verbalize the action needed to transition from t_8 to t_9 in Figure 1.

nal one (the number five). The PSS makes explicit the natural language instructions that a human may give to a robot in order to transform the configuration in an Image$_i$ into the configuration in an Image$_j$ - the two configurations may correspond to one robot action (for adjacent states in the sequence) or to a sequence of robot actions (for non-adjacent states). To account for language variance, each simple action or sequence of actions is associated with a set of alternative natural language instructions. For example, nine descriptions of the same action ($t_8 \rightarrow t_9$) from Figure 1 are shown in Table 1.

We see some structural similarity between the utterances, but they require different amounts of inference to understand, use different (potentially synonymous) language, and choose different blocks as contextual anchors for proper interpretation. Despite this, they each describe the action with equal precision. The natural language instructions encode implicitly partial or full descriptions of the world ("in line with" or "first open space").

Simple Instruction/Command Understanding. The problem definition we focus on in this paper is that of simple instruction/command understanding: given a state of the world, Image$_i$, and a human-like natural language command, C, we would like to infer the target world, Image$_{i+1}$, that a robot should construct if it understood C. If we assume, for simplicity, that only one block can be moved at a time, command understanding has a straightforward se-

t_0: Initial state t_8 t_9 t_{20}: Final drawing

Figure 1: Above are four states in a 20-action sequence for drawing the digit 5. The world state can be encoded for the learner as IDs and locations or raw images. Annotations are provided between every adjacent state (See Table 1) or between sequences (e.g. $t_8 \rightarrow t_{20}$: *Create a four-line diagonal which moves to the southeast. Starting with Heineken ...*) to describe multi-action plans.

mantics: understanding a command amounts to inferring that the block at location $(x, y, z)_S$ needs to be moved and the location $(x, y, z)_T$ where the block needs to be moved. The rest of the blocks are not affected by the move.

3.2 Data

We follow Bisk et al. (2016)'s methodology and collect PSSs specific to both goal oriented and random actions.[1] Our discussion focuses primarily on the goal oriented data, wherein blocks are used to draw configurations/scenes that look like the digits zero through nine. To create these abstract drawings in a diverse and natural manner, configurations are derived from actual hand-written digits in the MNIST corpus (LeCun et al., 1998). These digits provide an easily recognizable target goal when arranging blocks. To create a sequence of actions that draws out these digits, the MNIST images were sharpened and down-sampled until each had at most 20 active pixels which could be replaced with blocks. The blocks were either decorated with brands (as shown above) or with the numbers one through twenty.

These block configurations were placed into a virtual world and scrambled until the board's initial state was unrecognizable. This was achieved by randomly relocating adjacent blocks to new locations in the world. Once every block had been placed at a new location, the world appears random (for example, Image$_0$ in Figure 1), but when these random actions are played in reverse, the sequence of moves recreates the digit in a deliberate and ordered manner. Each of these actions are then shown to Amazon Mechanical Turkers. To ensure that our robot

learns to understand human-like commands, turkers were asked to provide instructions they would give to another person in order to transform a block configuration corresponding to a first image (t_i) into a second block configuration corresponding to an image (t_{i+1}). Each image pair was presented to three turkers, each of whom had to provide three different instructions for achieving the same goal.

A total of 100 digits sequences were annotated (10 drawings for every digits). The sequences were split so that half were decorated with numbers and half with logos. The sides of every block have a different color and a logo or number is overlayed on every side. Eight sequences for every digit are included in Training, one for development and two for testing. Overall, the training data has 11,871 commands, while the development and test corpora each have 1,719 and 3,177 commands, respectively.

For each learning example, we thus have access to an input that consists of an Image$_i$ (what the robot sees), the (x, y, z) coordinates of each block in Image$_i$ (a discrete representation of the world corresponding to the image), and a natural language command that a robot needs to understand in order to operate on the world in Image$_i$. The output consists of an Image$_{i+1}$ (what the robot should build) and the (x, y, z) coordinates of each block in Image$_{i+1}$.

The training/development/test sections of the data contain ∼177K/31K/48K tokens for the decorated blocks. The overall lexical type and token counts for our data are presented in Table 2. To compute statistics all text was lower-cased and tokenized using Stanford's CoreNLP (Manning et al., 2014). For the MNIST configurations, digits 0-9 are present in the test data as drawn with both logos and numbered blocks. In contrast, only half the digits appear with

---

[1] All data (both single actions and sequences) and links to code are available at `http://nlg.isi.edu/language-grounding/`

	MNIST		Blank	
	Types	Tokens	Types	Tokens
Train	1,506	177K	961	58K
Dev	583	31K	444	8K
Test	645	48K	575	17K
Total	1,359 / 257K		1,172 / 84K	

Table 2: Type and token counts for the Logo and Number decorated block data sets (left) and the Blank blocks (right).

	# of Commands	
Command Length (l)	MNIST	Random
$1 \leq l \leq 5$	81	0
$5 < l \leq 10$	3,817	61
$10 < l \leq 20$	5,752	995
$20 < l \leq 40$	2,028	1,329
$40 < l \leq 80$	192	107

Table 3: A breakdown of the number of commands in the training data by the number of tokens per sentence.

a given decoration in the development data.

Perhaps because annotators were not constrained or told they were giving instructions to a robot, the breadth of constructions and variance in command length is substantial. For example, the length of the commands varies wildly. Table 3 shows the number of training commands in a given length range. Some commands span multiple sentences. The average command length is 15 tokens with a standard deviation of 8.

The free form nature of the language and task allows for both utilitarian descriptions as well as more flowery instructions which utilize the full three-dimensional world:

> *take a plunger . plunge the top of the adidas block . lift it into the air , and place it directly to the left of the burgerking block , making sure the right edge of the adidas block and the left edge of the burgerking block are touching . remove the plunger .*

Random Blank Blocks. In both Table 2 and 3 we also present statistics on a second much more challenging dataset of blank blocks used to build random configurations. For this data, blocks were randomly placed alongside each other, on top of one another, or randomly scattered in the space. Additionally, these blocks have no identifying labels so they are more difficult to describe, making the grounding problem difficult. This leads to more interesting language with more spatial cues and counting (e.g. *third block from the top...*). This manifests as much longer descriptions averaging 23.5 words with a standard deviation of 9 words. We see this length bias in Table 3. Finally, this data also presents the challenge of stack creation in the third-dimension. As capturing the language and phenomena of this data is largely out of the scope of our current work, we present baseline results to demonstrate its dif-

ficulty in the hope of motivating future research. The complete blank blocks corpus consists of 2,493 training commands, 360 for development and 720 for testing or a total of ~58K/8K/17K tokens.

4 Learning Problems of Interest

Implicitly encoded in our data are three tasks with varying amounts of abstraction and context-specific language: Entity grounding, Spatial Relation grounding, and Planning.

Entity Grounding. As one would expect based on Gricean maxims, there are many ways an object might be referred to in everyday speech. These are context specific and depend on the perceived ambiguity of a scene. For example, the decoration of blocks with logos allows for easy indexing ("nvidia block") which uniquely identifies the referent. If a human feels the brand is not sufficiently recognizable they may choose to describe *Texaco* as "the star block", or *Mercedes* as "three lines in a circle". In these cases, the speaker is appealing to more basic geometric knowledge in lieu of brand recognition.

The introduction of numbered blocks complicates the grounding as many actions also contain measures of how far to move a block:

> *put block 10 four spaces below block 9 .*

In this case, the user has decided to denote the block IDs with the numerals 0-9, but distances by spelling out the number. As is to be expected, most strategies do not hold across users, and an individual user may be very inconsistent:

> *move block seven two spaces to the right of block 6*

This inconsistency, while difficult for a learner, introduces no actual ambiguity for a fluent speaker.

Finally, blank block descriptions use lots of spacial references the involve often complicated recursive structure:

Move the block that is to the [left of [the block closest to [the right side of the table]]] so that it is on top of the block that is at the [top of the [group of blocks [closest to the [left side of the table]]]].

It follows that an important subtask for our models/algorithms is to correctly ground the entities referenced in naturally occurring commands. In general this may require a thorough understanding of syntax and scoping.

Spatial Relation Grounding. Another subtask is that of understanding spacial relations. Again, we are presented with lots of linguistic ambiguity which can be resolved by the shared context and references of the speaker and listener. For example, the first command in Table 1 is simply a list of three brands:

coca cola, hp, nvidia.

This statement on its own is meaningless, but in the context of an image that contains the first two brands in sequence from left to right, the list implies that the final logo should be appended to the existing line.

Naturally occurring commands also assume basic knowledge of physics. The final description in Table 1, asks that we place a block in the "first open space to the right ...". Implicit in this statement is a shared understanding that two blocks cannot occupy the same space. This implies that a human or robot knows to search for the open space, which may be arbitrarily far away. Knowledge of physics or basic geometric shapes appears to be common in the instructions and injecting this knowledge into our models may be helpful.

use block 2 as a bridge to complete the diagonal line formed by blocks 17 , 8 , 6 , 4 and 1 .

Finally, when analyzing the data, we found that command givers would often create an ad hoc grid to assist in specifying where a block should be placed. This was particularly common when placing the first block ($t_0 \rightarrow t_1$) to start the drawing. This initial block may need to be placed in a position that is not near any existing blocks. Common solutions include specifying midpoints between blocks to center a conversation:

place the adidas block in the column between the columns that contain the mercedes and esso blocks , but two block spaces below either .

Often the referenced blocks may be very far apart but appear opposite one another and equidistant from a useful reference point in space.

Plan Recognition. The third problem of interest is plan recognition. The annotation of sequences of actions shows that natural commands are also used in a manner that assumes the ability to plan and execute individual and complex actions:

slide the adidas block 2 blocks straight up . then slide it 6 block spaces to the left .

The models we introduce in this paper have difficulty dealing with these kind of commands.

5 Models

In order to correctly interpret commands in context, we need models that ground entities and understand spatial relations, shapes, and the compositionality of language. This is a large and fertile space for exploration. In contrast with previous work which attempts to produce deep semantic interpretations of commands (Kim and Mooney, 2012; Dukes, 2014), in this paper we explore the degree to which we can solve our communication problem using semantic free models. We are quick to note though that our framework can also assess the performance of semantic-heavy approaches.

We outline here three basic neural models that provide a set of reasonable baselines for other researchers interested in solving this problem. Each approach assumes less knowledge injection than the previous. As discussed in Section 3.1, in all three models, the eventual output is a tuple specifying where to find the block to move and where to move it: $(x, y, z)_S$ and $(x, y, z)_T$. For each model presented below we will try both simple feed-forward and recurrent neural network architectures for encoding the input utterance.

5.1 Model Architecture

The goal of our models is to convert an utterance and world state into a location prediction in the world. We tackle this problem by breaking the problem into four steps: Encoding, Representation, Grounding, Prediction. Components of this pipeline

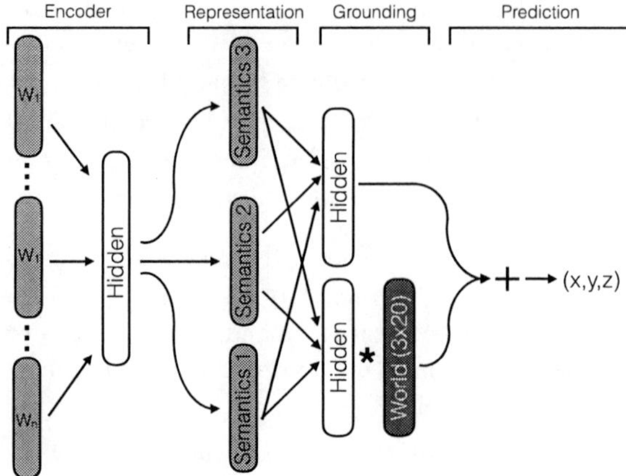

Figure 2: Our models all follow the above architecture. 1-Hot word vectors (orange) are fed as input to a Feed-Forward or Recurrent Neural Network for encoding. A semantic representation is extracted (green), which in conjunction with knowledge of the world (blue) is grounded to predict an action.

can be trained independently (Sections 5.2 and 5.3) or jointly as a single End-to-End model (Section 5.4). This division of labor also allows for differing amounts of human intervention both during training and in the interpretation of actions and bears some resemblance to (Andreas et al., 2016). Specifically, we will first present results where the model predicts a fixed semantic interpretation of actions which are easily human interpretable (Encoder + Representation). In this setting, the experimenter/human then must convert the semantics to actions in the world. Second, we remove the human interpreter and train a model for Grounding and Predicting from our semantic representation. Finally, we maintain our architecture but remove the human entirely, forcing the model to both converge to and interpret its own internal semantic representation.

The model architecture, regardless of how it is trained, at least implicitly, encodes our beliefs about the best way to solve the learning problem: performing single actions requires identifying anchors in the world that can be used as spacial referents from which a target location can be offset.

5.2 Discrete Predictions of a Fixed Semantics

Our first model assumes a setup with very simple semantics. Despite all blocks existing in a real-valued world, we will assume that a final location is parameterized by knowledge of a reference block and the

direction from the reference to the target position.

Move the Adidas block to the right of the BMW.

For example, in the simple command above, we can distill three pieces of relevant information:

```
Source:       Adidas
Reference:    BMW
Direction:    right (east)
```

By assuming a grid world, BMW can be converted to its location in the world $(x, y, z)_{\text{BMW}}$, which we shift *east* by changing the y component to yield: $(x, y + \delta, z)$. In practice we define a set of nine relative positions:

NW $(x\text{-}\delta, y\text{+}\delta, z)$	N $(x, y\text{+}\delta, z)$	NE $(x\text{+}\delta, y\text{+}\delta, z)$
NW $(x\text{-}\delta, y, z)$	TOP $(x, y, z\text{+}\delta)$	E $(x\text{+}\delta, y, z)$
SW $(x\text{-}\delta, y\text{-}\delta, z)$	S $(x, y\text{-}\delta, z)$	SE $(x\text{+}\delta, y\text{-}\delta, z)$

First our model produces an encoding of the sentence. We present two approaches:

Feed-Forward Neural Network (FFN): This model produces a sentence encoding by concatenating one-hot word vectors as input to a hidden layer. We pad sentences so all inputs are the same length.

Recurrent Neural Network (RNN): In contrast, the RNN encoder consumes the full sentence, each word passing through a hidden layer one at a time, before returning a final representation.

Additionally, in both encoding approaches, words which only occur a single time during training are replaced with an UNK token.

We use a single hidden layer architecture with a softmax for prediction and and train with cross entropy loss. We train a separate model for each prediction (The Encoder and Representation stages of Figure 2). Once three versions of the model have been used to predict the Source, Reference and Direction, this triple is used to compute both the source $(x, y, z)_S$ and target $(x, y, z)_T$ locations. The former is computed via a simple look-up table, while the latter amends the reference look-up with the appropriate offset from the aforementioned grid.

When the model predicts a reference block which is not on the board (not all configurations use all 20 blocks) we set the reference location to the center of the board and then apply the relative position transformation to this hallucinated block location.

5.3 Continuous Valued Predictions From a Semantic Triple

At this point, we have constructed a model for predicting a specific semantic triple, but rely on the human to convert its output to physical locations given the current state of the world. To address this, we train a simple architecture which is shown the world and automatically learn direction offsets (the Grounding and Prediction stages of Figure 2).

The model takes knowledge of the Source, Reference and Direction and passes them to two hidden layers. One is multiplied by the world (a 3×20 matrix of coordinates) and then both are summed to produce a final (x, y, z) prediction. The world matrix columns are the locations of each block, with a fixed ordering. If any block is missing from the configuration the matrix is padded with [-1,-1,-1]. This component of the network is then trained with a mean-square error regression loss.

Running this model on the predicted representation of Section 5.2 creates a simple pipeline from Sentence and World representations to location predictions, with no human intervention. We are particularly interested in this model's performance because its intermediary representation is forced to conform to the simple, interpretable semantics we chose for this domain and task.

5.4 End-to-End Model

Finally, we present a single model which takes as input the sentence and world as before and predicts either the location of the block to move or its final location. This corresponds to training the neural architecture (Figure 2). We train the model twice, once to predict the source location $(x, y, z)_S$ and a second time to predict the target location $(x, y, z)_T$. While the model architecture implicitly assumes the presence of an internal semantics we do not train it directly, but rather rely on the model to discover one based solely on its prediction error in the world. This approach is likely to allow for easier future extensions that encode finer-grained direction information and scaling (see analysis in Section 8).

6 Evaluation Metric

In our formulation, understanding a command C in the context of a world configuration Image$_i$ amounts to inferring the block $(x, y, z)_S$ that needs to be moved and the target location $(x, y, z)_T$ where the block needs to be moved to. Given that we control the manner in which the data is generated, we always have access to the gold interpretation of command C. Therefore, it is trivial to measure the performance of various command understanding algorithms by tracking two metrics: (i) we measure our ability to identify the block to be moved (and reference/direction information when available) using standard accuracy figures; (ii) and we measure our ability to select and place the block to be moved by measuring the distance between our predicted locations and the gold locations.

The first evaluation is presented in Table 4 under the S, R, and D columns. The distance errors are computed in terms of block lengths and we present the mean and median errors both for the source block's initial and final location.

7 Baselines and Human Performance

Since the gold annotations make explicit only the block to move and its target location, the Fixed Semantics models do not have gold training data for predicting the reference block used for anchoring or the direction to offset. To remedy this, we use a simple string matching heuristic that chooses a reference block during training and that computes a "gold" direction from its location. The reference is chosen as the closest block mentioned in the sentence, other than the source.

Oracle. To evaluate the strength of this heuristic, we perform an oracle evaluation (Table 4): we assume perfect knowledge of the source block that is moved; we apply our string matching heuristic to choose a reference block; and then assume perfect knowledge of the quadrant in which we place the block that is moved. For the blank blocks, our string matching heuristic fails, so we simply use the closest block to the target location to the reference location. This, unsurprisingly, leads to higher error.

Human Performance. We randomly sampled 50 utterances from each dataset to evaluate human performance. The participants in our experiment were not affiliated with the project and were not provided any guidance about the task; for example, they were

| | MNIST Patterns with labeled blocks | | | | | | | Random Patterns with blank blocks | | | | | | |
| | Source | | Target | | | | | Source | | Target | | | | |
	Med	Mean	Med	Mean	S	R	D	Med	Mean	Med	Mean	S	R	D
Human Performance	0.00	0.00	0.21	0.53	100			0.00	0.30	0.37	1.39	93		
Oracle	–	–	0.00	0.45	100	100	100	–	–	1.00	1.09	100	100	100
FFN Discrete Predictions	**0.00**	0.49	**1.09**	2.17	93	69	63	5.28	5.09	5.51	5.46	9	15	32
Continuous Predictions	0.49	1.00	1.59	2.42				4.25	4.04	3.86	**3.93**			
End-to-End	0.02	**0.38**	1.14	**1.81**				**3.45**	**3.52**	**3.60**	3.94			
RNN Discrete Predictions	**0.00**	**0.14**	**0.00**	**0.98**	98	92	78	5.29	5.00	5.51	5.57	10	7	46
Continuous Predictions	0.47	0.64	1.23	1.60				4.16	4.05	3.71	3.87			
End-to-End	0.03	0.19	0.53	1.05				**3.29**	**3.47**	**3.60**	**3.70**			
Center Baseline	–	–	3.46	3.43	100			–	–	4.09	4.06	100		
Random Baseline	6.37	6.49	6.12	6.21	5	5	11	4.90	4.97	5.51	5.44	10	11	12

Table 4: Model error when trained on only the subset of the data with decorated blocks or blank blocks. Where appropriate S, R, and D are the model's predictive accuracy at identifying the Source, Reference and Direction. All models are evaluated on the Median and Mean prediction error the source block and its final target location. Distances are presented in block-lengths.

not told about the high-level goal of drawing a number. Despite this, Table 4 shows human performance is very similar to Oracle performance. Although humans did not place blocks in line "perfectly", they were comparable to or outperformed the oracle.

Baselines. Finally, Table 4 also shows the results obtained by two baseline models. One (Center) has perfect knowledge of the source block to move, but always places it in the center of the table. The second baseline (Random), chooses random values for the source, reference, and direction. As expected, the performance of these baselines is abysmal.

8 Results

The results in Table 4 show that there is a massive difference in performance between block configurations that use blocks marked with identifiers (logos and digits) and those without. When the blocks are marked with clearly identifiable logos, all models outperform our baselines by a wide margin. However, when blocks are blank the situation is flipped.

The results in Table 4 also highlight a noticeable gap in performance between the simplest Discrete model and the two location predicting models. The comparable performance of the Continuous and End-to-End models on labeled blocks seems to imply that the End-to-End model is capturing/discovering similar anchoring information without being explicitly told to do so. On the blank block

data, the End-to-End model performs best by learning its own more appropriate representation.

Parameters. Where appropriate, we used 256 unit hidden-layers, 0.5 dropout, and the Adam optimizer with a learning rate of 0.001. With the exception of the FFN Discrete Predictions model, SGD parameter grid-search did not yield an improvement.

8.1 Subjective Error Analysis

In Table 5, we collected 50 of our models worst errors on the decorated blocks data and categorized them into five classes of error. Eliminating most of these errors require more knowledge or a richer representation than currently afforded by our simple semantic triples. This is often due to the use of multiple reference blocks, but grammatical ambiguity and a knowledge of some basic geometric primitives also account for many of the mistakes.

8.2 Future Work on Blank Blocks

One of the most jarring results we present is the the clear performance gap between easily grounded blocks (MNIST data) and the Blank blocks (Random) which require a much richer understanding of the world. We do not believe this is due to additional complexity in the types of relations present in the data, but rather the difficulty in grounding the references. When analyzing the data we see that much of the data still follow a very simple (Source, Ref-

Error Type	Count	Example
Multi-Relation Actions	20	Place block 20 parallel with the 8 block and slightly to the right of the 6 block. Place block 15 on the same vertical column as blocks 16 and 17, and two rows above blocks 11 and 3.
Geometric Understanding	10	Continue the diagonal row of 20, 19 and 15 downward with 13. Put block 12 in the column between the columns with blocks 4 and 13, and on the same row as the lowest block on the board.
Grammatical Ambiguity	10	19 moved from behind the 8 to under the 18th block. Burger King tile should be directly above the Coca Cola tile. Move Coca Cola.
Grounding Names	5	Put the block that looks like a taurus symbol just above the bird.
Understanding Distance	5	move the texaco block 5 block lengths above the BMW block

Table 5: We performed a subjective error analysis of the results of our Fixed Semantics model using the RNN encoder. Example sentences and the frequency of each type of error are reported above from the worst 50 errors on the development data.

Scene	Utterance
	Move the block that is currently located closest to the top left corner to the bottom left of the table, slightly higher than the block in the bottom right corner.
Error:	`7.29 Block lengths`
	Move the block closest to the top left corner so it is above half a block length to the right of the blocks near the lower left corner of the table.
Error:	`0.94 Block lengths`

Table 6: Above are two commands and the worlds they apply to. Below we see the prediction error of our best model.

erence, Direction) paradigm, but automatically extracting that semantics is now more difficult and the purview for future work with scene understanding.

To remove the possibility that this performance difference is due to sparsity, we down-sampled the training data from the decorated blocks to match that of the blank ones. We found the development errors grew (Average 0.27 and 1.35 on source and target, respectively) but were still substantially lower than those observed with blank block data.

Because extracting the semantics for training is so difficult, a particularly nice result is that while the End-to-End model was slightly weaker than the others on the MNIST based data, it actually performs best in this domain, where we cannot provide an ex-plicit training signal for the representation.

The nature of the language in the blank blocks differs quite dramatically due to this grounding difficulty. Table 6 shows the two sentences we perform best (and worst) on in the development data and that make use of a reference and direction.

9 Conclusion

We showed how human-robot communication can be attacked within an empirical framework that supports alternative models to be evaluated and compared using objective metrics. We introduced a set of simple algorithms for human-robot, in-context command/instruction understanding that should serve as strong baselines for future research in this field. The datasets present unique and important challenges for NLU, in which the interpretation of the language has varying amounts of dependence on the world in which it is uttered. The datasets we created in support of this work are made publicly available and should support the development of increasingly sophisticated models and algorithms for solving the problem defined in this paper, as well as additional problems that concern human-robot communication.

Acknowledgments

This work was supported by Contract W911NF-15-1-0543 with the US Defense Advanced Research Projects Agency (DARPA) and the Army Research Office (ARO).

References

Jacob Andreas and Dan Klein. 2015. Alignment-based compositional semantics for instruction following. In *Proceedings of the 2015 Conference on Empirical Methods in Natural Language Processing*, pages 1165–1174, Lisbon, Portugal, September. Association for Computational Linguistics.

Jacob Andreas, Marcus Rohrbach, Trevor Darrell, and Dan Klein. 2016. Learning to compose neural networks for question answering. *arXiv preprint arXiv:1601.01705*.

Yoav Artzi and Luke S Zettlemoyer. 2013. Weakly Supervised Learning of Semantic Parsers for Mapping Instructions to Actions. *Transactions of the Association for Computational Linguistics*, pages 49–62.

Yonatan Bisk, Daniel Marcu, and William Wong. 2016. Towards a dataset for human computer communication via grounded language acquisition. In *Proceedings of the AAAI'16 Workshop on Symbiotic Cognitive Systems*.

SRK Branavan, Harr Chen, Luke S Zettlemoyer, and Regina Barzilay. 2009. Reinforcement Learning for Mapping Instructions to Actions. In *Proceedings of the Joint Conference of the 47th Annual Meeting of the ACL and the 4th International Joint Conference on Natural Language Processing of the AFNLP*, Suntec, Singapore, August.

S R K Branavan, David Silver, and Regina Barzilay. 2011. Learning to Win by Reading Manuals in a Monte-Carlo Framework. In *Proceedings of the 49th Annual Meeting of the Association for Computational Linguistics: Human Language Technologies*, pages 268–277, Portland, Oregon, USA, June.

Kais Dukes. 2014. Semeval-2014 task 6: Supervised semantic parsing of robotic spatial commands. In *Proceedings of the 8th International Workshop on Semantic Evaluation (SemEval 2014)*, pages 45–53, Dublin, Ireland, August.

Dan Goldwasser and Dan Roth. 2011. Learning From Natural Instructions. In *Twenty-Second International Joint Conferences on Artificial Intelligence*.

Sergio Guadarrama, Lorenzo Riano, Dave Golland, Daniel Göhring, Jia Yangqing, Dan Klein, Pieter Abbeel, and Trevor Darrell. 2013. Grounding Spatial Relations for Human-Robot Interaction . In *IEEE/RSJ International Conference on Intelligent Robots and Systems (IROS)*, pages 1640–1647.

Joohyun Kim and Raymond Mooney. 2012. Unsupervised pcfg induction for grounded language learning with highly ambiguous supervision. In *Proceedings of the 2012 Joint Conference on Empirical Methods in Natural Language Processing and Computational Natural Language Learning*, pages 433–444, Jeju Island, Korea, July.

Volker Klingspor, John Demiris, and Michael Kaiser. 1997. Human-Robot-Communication and Machine Learning. *Applied Artificial Intelligence Journal*, 11:719–746.

Thomas Kollar, Jayant Krishnamurthy, and Grant Strimel. 2013. Toward Interactive Grounded Language Acquisition. In *Robotics: Science and Systems*.

Y. LeCun, L. Bottou, Y. Bengio, and P. Haffner. 1998. Gradient-based learning applied to document recognition. *Proceedings of the IEEE*, 86(11):2278–2324, November.

Matt MacMahon, Brian Stankiewicz, and Benjamin Kuipers. 2006. Walk the talk: Connecting language, knowledge, and action in route instructions. In *Proceedings of the 21st National Conference on Artificial Intelligence - Volume 2*, AAAI'06, pages 1475–1482. AAAI Press.

Jonathan Malmaud, Jonathan Huang, Vivek Rathod, Nicholas Johnston, Andrew Rabinovich, and Kevin Murphy. 2015. Whats cookin? interpreting cooking videos using text, speech and vision. In *Proceedings of the 2015 Conference of the North American Chapter of the Association for Computational Linguistics: Human Language Technologies*, pages 143–152, Denver, Colorado, May–June.

Christopher D. Manning, Mihai Surdeanu, John Bauer, Jenny Finkel, Steven J. Bethard, and David McClosky. 2014. The Stanford CoreNLP natural language processing toolkit. In *Association for Computational Linguistics (ACL) System Demonstrations*, pages 55–60.

Cynthia Matuszek, Liefeng Bo, Luke S Zettlemoyer, and Dieter Fox. 2014. Learning from Unscripted Deictic Gesture and Language for Human-Robot Interactions. In *Proceedings of the Twenty-Eighth AAAI Conference on Artificial Intelligence*.

Nikolaos Mavridis. 2015. A review of verbal and non-verbal human–robot interactive communication. *Robotics and Autonomous Systems*, 63:22–35, January.

Deb K Roy. 2002. Learning visually grounded words and syntax for a scene description task. *Computer speech & language*, 16(3-4):353–385, July.

Luc Steels and Paul Vogt. 1997. Grounding Adaptive Language Games in Robotic Agents. *Proceedings of the Fourth European Conference on Artificial Life*.

H. Thompson, A. Anderson, E. Bard, G. Doherty-Sneddon, A. Newlands, and C. Sotillo. 1993. The HCRC map task corpus: natural dialogue for speech recognition. In *HLT '93: Proc. of the workshop on Human Language Technology*, pages 25–30. ACL.

Subhashini Venugopalan, Huijuan Xu, Jeff Donahue, Marcus Rohrbach, Raymond Mooney, and Kate

Saenko. 2015. Translating videos to natural language using deep recurrent neural networks. In *Proceedings of the 2015 Conference of the North American Chapter of the Association for Computational Linguistics: Human Language Technologies*, pages 1494–1504, Denver, Colorado, May–June.

Terry Winograd. 1972. *Understanding Natural Language*. Academic Press.

Haonan Yu and Jeffrey Mark Siskind. 2013. Grounded language learning from video described with sentences. In *Proceedings of the 51st Annual Meeting of the Association for Computational Linguistics (Volume 1: Long Papers)*, pages 53–63, Sofia, Bulgaria, August.

Inter-document Contextual Language Model

Quan Hung Tran and **Ingrid Zukerman** and **Gholamreza Haffari**
Faculty of Information Technology
Monash University, Australia
`hung.tran,ingrid.zukerman,gholamreza.haffari@monash.edu`

Abstract

In this paper, we examine the impact of employing contextual, structural information from a tree-structured document set to derive a language model. Our results show that this information significantly improves the accuracy of the resultant model.

1   Introduction

Conventional Language Models (LMs) are based on n-grams, and thus rely upon a limited number of preceding words to assign a probability to the next word in a document. Recently, Mikolov *et al.* (2010) proposed a Recurrent Neural Network (RNN) LM which uses a vector representation of all the preceding words in a sentence as the context for language modeling. This model, which theoretically can utilize an infinite context window within a sentence, yields an LM with lower perplexity than that of n-gram-based LMs. However, the model does not leverage the wider contextual information provided by words in other sentences in a document or in related documents.

Several researchers have explored extending the contextual information of an RNN-based LM. Mikolov and Zweig (2012) proposed a context-dependent RNN LM that employs Latent Dirichlet Allocation for modeling a long span of context. Wang and Cho (2015) offered a bag-of-words representation of preceding sentences as the context for the RNN LM. Ji *et al.* (2015) used a Document-Context LM (DCLM) to leverage both intra- and inter-sentence context.

These works focused on contextual information at the document level for LM, but did not consider information at the inter-document level. Many document sets on the Internet are structured, which means there are connections between different documents. This phenomenon is prominent in social media, where all the posts are directly linked to several other posts. We posit that these related documents could hold important information about a particular post, including the topic and language use, and propose an RNN-based LM architecture that utilizes both intra- and inter-document contextual information. Our approach, which was tested on the social media dataset `reddit`, yielded promising results, which significantly improve on the state of the art.

2   Dataset

We used pre-collected `reddit` data,[1] which as of December, 2015, consists of approximately 1.7 billion comments in JSON format. A comment thread starts with a "topic", which might be a link or an image. The users then begin to comment on the topic, or reply to previous comments. Over time, this process creates a tree-structured document repository (Figure 1), where a level indicator is assigned to each comment, e.g., a response to the root topic is assigned level 1, and the reply to a level n comment is assigned level $n + 1$. We parsed the raw data in JSON format into a tree structure, removing threads that have less than three comments, contain deleted comments, or do not have comments above

---

[1] `https://www.reddit.com/r/datasets/` `comments/3bxlg7/i_have_every_publicly_` `available_reddit_comment`

Proceedings of NAACL-HLT 2016, pages 762–766,
San Diego, California, June 12-17, 2016. ©2016 Association for Computational Linguistics

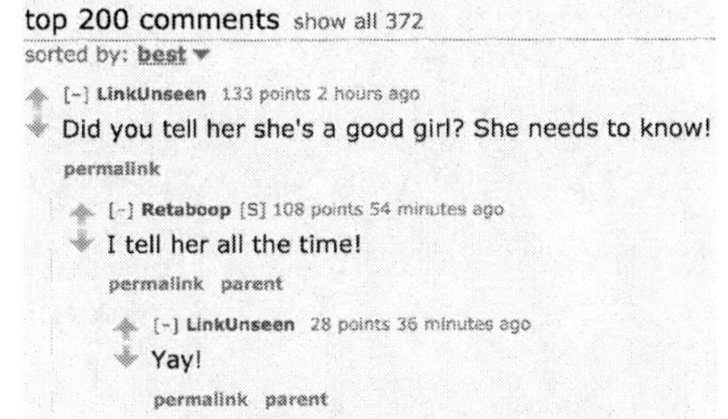

Figure 1: `reddit` example

Table 1: Dataset statistics

	# of threads	# of posts	# of sentences	# of tokens
training	1500	14592	40709	648624
testing	500	5007	13612	217164
validation	100	968	2762	44575

level 2. We randomly selected 2100 threads that fit these criteria. The data were then split into training/testing/validation sets. Table 1 displays some statistics of our dataset.

3 Baseline Neural Language Models

Our inter-document contextual language model scaffolds on the RNN LM (Mikolov et al., 2010) and DCLMs (Ji et al., 2015), as described below.

RNN-LSTM. Given a sentence $\{x_t\}_{t\in[1,\dots,N]}$, where x_t is the vector representation of the t-th word in the sentence, and N is the length of the sentence, Mikolov *et al.*'s (2010) RNN LM can be defined as:

$$h_t = f(h_{t-1}, x_t) \tag{1}$$
$$y_t \sim \text{softmax}(W_o h_{t-1} + b_o) \tag{2}$$

where h_t is the hidden unit at word t, and y_t is the prediction of the t-th word given the previous hidden unit h_{t-1}. The function f in Equation 1 can be any non-linear function. Following the approach in (Sundermeyer et al., 2012) and (Ji et al., 2015), we make use of Long Short-Term Memory (LSTM) units (Hochreiter and Schmidhuber, 1997) rather than the simple hidden units used in the original RNN LM. In our work, the word representation

x_t is obtained from the one-hot representation using an affine transformation, as follows:

$$x_t = W_p o_t + b_p \tag{3}$$

where o_t is the one-hot representation, W_p is the projection matrix, and b_p is a bias term.

Document Context LMs (DCLMs). We re-implemented two of Ji *et al.*'s (2015) DCLMs as our baselines,[2] viz Context-to-context (Figure 2a) and Context-to-output (Figure 2b). These models extend the RNN-LSTM model by leveraging information from preceding sentences.

The context-to-context model (ccDCLM) concatenates the final hidden unit of the previous sentence with the word vectors of the current sentence. Thus, Equation 1 becomes:

$$h_t^i = f(h_{t-1}^i, x_{i,t}') \tag{4}$$
$$x_{i,t}' = \text{concat}\left(x_{i,t}, h_{N_{i-1}}^{i-1}\right) \tag{5}$$

where N_{i-1} is the length of the previous sentence in the document, $x_{i,t}$ is the vector representation of the t-th word in the i-th sentence, $x_{i,t}'$ is the concatenation of the vector representation $x_{i,t}$ and the previous sentence's final hidden unit $h_{N_{i-1}}^{i-1}$.

The context-to-output model (coDCLM) applies the additional information directly to the word-decoding phase. Thus, Equation 2 becomes:

$$y_{i,t} \sim \text{softmax}\left(W_o h_{t-1}^i + W_o' h_{N_{i-1}}^{i-1} + b_o\right) \tag{6}$$

4 Inter-document Context Language Model

We now extend the DCLM by leveraging the information at the inter-document level, taking advantage of the structure of the repository — a tree in `reddit`. Specifically, by harnessing the information in documents related to a target document, i.e., its siblings and parent, the LM is expected to contain additional relevant information, and hence lower perplexity. Formally, let's call the sentence-level context vector h_s, the parent document context

---

[2] Ji *et al.*'s three options performed similarly.

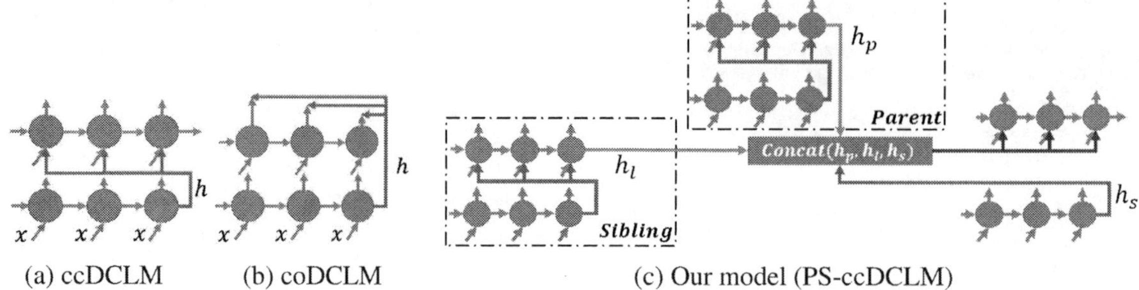

(a) ccDCLM   (b) coDCLM   (c) Our model (PS-ccDCLM)

Figure 2: Contextual language models; see Sections 3 and 4 for detailed descriptions.

vector h_p, the sibling context vector h_l, and the overall context vector h_c. Our framework is defined as:

$$h_c = g_h(h_s, h_l, h_p) \quad (7)$$
$$x'_{i,t} = g_i(x_{i,t}, h_c) \quad (8)$$
$$h_t = f(h_{t-1}, x'_t) \quad (9)$$
$$y_t \sim \text{softmax}\left(g_o(h_{t-1}, x'_t, h_c)\right) \quad (10)$$

We use the last hidden vector of the RNNs as the representation of the parent post, the older-sibling, and the previous sentence. The definition of the context function (g_h), the input function (g_i), and the word-decoding function (g_o) yields different configurations.

We also explored two strategies of training the models: *Disconnected (disC)* and *Fully Connected (fulC)*. In the disC-trained models, the error signal within a time step (i.e. a post or sentence) only affects the parameters in that time step. This is in contrast to the fulC-trained models, where the error signal is propagated to the previous time steps, hence influencing parameters in those time steps too.

4.1 Analysis of our modelling approach

In this section, we empirically analyze different training and modelling decisions within our framework, namely DC vs FC training, as well as contextual information from parent vs sibling.

The Setup. For our analysis, we employed a subset of the data described in Table 1 which contains 450 threads split into training/testing/validation sets with 300/100/50 threads respectively. The hidden-vector and word-vector dimensions were set to 50 and 70, respectively. The models were implemented in Theano (Bastien et al., 2012; Bergstra et al., 2010), and trained with RMSProp (Tieleman and Hinton, 2012).

Table 2: disC/fulC-trained models vs the baselines.

Model	Training	Perplexity
6-gram	na	205
RNN-LSTM	na	182
ccDCLM	disC	185
coDCLM	disC	181
ccDCLM	fulC	176
coDCLM	fulC	172

disC vs fulC. We first compared the disC and fulC strategies, at the sentence level only, in order to select the best strategy in a known setting. To this effect, we re-implemented Ji *et al.*'s (2015) DCLMs with the disC strategy, noting that Ji *et al.*'s original sentence-based models are fulC-trained. The results of this experiment appear in Table 2 which further compares these models with the following baselines: (1) vanila RNN-LSTM, and (2) a 6-gram LM with Kneser-Ney smoothing[3] (Kneser and Ney, 1995). The disC-trained models showed no improvement over the RNN-LSTM, and lagged behind their fulC-trained counterparts. The lower performance of the disC-trained models may be due to not fully leveraging the contextual information; disC-training lose information, as the error signal from the current time step is not used to calibrate the parameters of previous time steps. Therefore, we make use of fulC strategy to train our models in the rest of this paper.

Parent vs Sibling Context. The inter-document information in `reddit`'s case may come from a parent post, sibling posts or both. We tested our models with different combinations of inter-document con-

---

[3]Tested with the SRILM toolkit (Stolcke et al., 2011).

text information to reflect these options. At present, we consider only the closest older-sibling of a post, as it is deemed the most related; different combinations of sibling posts are left for future work. We tested the following three context-to-context configurations: parent only (P-ccDCLM), sibling only (S-ccDCLM), and parent and sibling (PS-ccDCLM), which define the context function as Equation 11, 12 and 13 respectively. The three configurations use the same word-decoding function (Equation 15) and the same input function (Equation 14).

$$\begin{aligned} h_c &= \text{concat}\,(h_s, h_p) & (11) \\ h_c &= \text{concat}\,(h_s, h_l) & (12) \\ h_c &= \text{concat}\,(h_s, h_l, h_p) & (13) \\ x'_{i,t} &= \text{concat}\,(x_{i,t}, h_c) & (14) \\ y_{i,t} &\sim \text{softmax}\,(W_o h_{t-1} + b_o) & (15) \end{aligned}$$

The results of this experiment appear in the first three rows of Table 3, which shows that the best-performing model is PS-ccDCLM.

As discussed by Ji *et al.* (2015), the coDCLM makes the hidden units of the previous sentence have no effect on the hidden units of the current sentence. While this configuration might have some advantages (Ji et al., 2015), applying it directly to a larger context may lead to complications. Suppose we use the last hidden unit of the previous document as the context for the next document. With the context-to-output approach, the last hidden unit summarizes only the information in the last sentence of the previous document, and doesn't reflect the entire document. We address this problem by not using the context-to-output approach in isolation. Instead, we use the context-to-output approach in tandem with the context-to-context approach of ccDCLM. This approach was tested in an additional parent-sibling configuration (PS-ccoDCLM), as an alternative to the best performing context-to-context configuration. The PS-ccoDCLM is similar to the PS-ccDCLM except for the decoding equation, which is changed into Equation 16.

$$y_{i,t} \sim \text{softmax}\left(W_o h^i_{t-1} + W'_o h_c + b_o\right) \quad (16)$$

Based on the results of these trials, we chose the best-performing PS-ccDCLM (Figure 2c) as our final system.

Table 3: Comparing models incorporating parent (P) and/or sibling (S) contextual information.

Systems	Perplexity
P-ccDCLM	172
S-ccDCLM	174
PS-ccDCLM	**168**
PS-ccoDCLM	175

Table 4: Results on the entire dataset.

Systems	Perplexity
6-gram	209
RNN-LSTM	184
ccDCLM	168
coDCLM	176
PS-ccDCLM	**159**

4.2 Results

The model perplexity obtained by the baselines and our best-performing model for the test set (Table 1) is shown in Table 4 — our system (PS-ccDCLM) statistically significantly outperforms the best baseline (ccDCLM), with $\alpha = 0.01$, using the Friedman test. The inter-sentence contextual information under the context-to-context regime (ccDCLM) decreases model perplexity by 9% compared to the original RNN-LSTM, while the inter-document contextual information (PS-ccDCLM) reduces perplexity by a further 5% compared to ccDCLM.

5 Discussion and Future Work

Our results show that including inter-document contextual information yields additional improvements to those obtained from inter-sentence information. However, as expected, the former are smaller than the latter, as sentences in the same post are more related than sentences in different posts. At present, we rely on the final hidden-vector of the sentences and the posts for contextual information. In the future, we propose to explore other options, such as additional models to combine the contextual information from all siblings in the tree structure, and extending our model to structures beyond trees.

References

Frédéric Bastien, Pascal Lamblin, Razvan Pascanu, James Bergstra, Ian J. Goodfellow, Arnaud Bergeron, Nicolas Bouchard, and Yoshua Bengio. 2012. Theano: new features and speed improvements. Deep Learning and Unsupervised Feature Learning NIPS 2012 Workshop.

James Bergstra, Olivier Breuleux, Frédéric Bastien, Pascal Lamblin, Razvan Pascanu, Guillaume Desjardins, Joseph Turian, David Warde-Farley, and Yoshua Bengio. 2010. Theano: a CPU and GPU math expression compiler. In *Proceedings of the Python for Scientific Computing Conference (SciPy)*, June. Oral Presentation.

Sepp Hochreiter and Jürgen Schmidhuber. 1997. Long short-term memory. *Neural computation*, 9(8):1735–1780.

Yangfeng Ji, Trevor Cohn, Lingpeng Kong, Chris Dyer, and Jacob Eisenstein. 2015. Document context language models. *arXiv preprint arXiv:1511.03962*.

Reinhard Kneser and Hermann Ney. 1995. Improved backing-off for M-gram language modeling. In *ICASSP-95*, volume 1, pages 181–184. IEEE.

Tomas Mikolov and Geoffrey Zweig. 2012. Context dependent recurrent neural network language model. In *SLT*, pages 234–239.

Tomas Mikolov, Martin Karafiát, Lukas Burget, Jan Cernockỳ, and Sanjeev Khudanpur. 2010. Recurrent neural network based language model. In *INTERSPEECH 2010*, pages 1045–1048.

Andreas Stolcke, Jing Zheng, Wen Wang, and Victor Abrash. 2011. SRILM at sixteen: Update and outlook. In *Proceedings of IEEE Automatic Speech Recognition and Understanding Workshop*, page 5.

Martin Sundermeyer, Ralf Schlüter, and Hermann Ney. 2012. LSTM neural networks for language modeling. In *INTERSPEECH*, pages 194–197.

Tijmen. Tieleman and Geoffrey Hinton. 2012. Neural Networks for Machine Learning. `http://www.youtube.com/watch?v=O3sxAc4hxZU`. [Online].

Tian Wang and Kyunghyun Cho. 2015. Larger-context language modelling. *arXiv preprint arXiv:1511.03729*.

Ultradense Word Embeddings by Orthogonal Transformation

Sascha Rothe and **Sebastian Ebert** and **Hinrich Schütze**
Center for Information and Language Processing
LMU Munich, Germany
`{sascha|ebert}@cis.lmu.de`

Abstract

Embeddings are *generic* representations that
are useful for many NLP tasks. In this paper,
we introduce DENSIFIER, a method that learns
an *orthogonal transformation* of the embedding space that focuses the information relevant for a task in an *ultradense subspace* of a
dimensionality that is smaller by a factor of
100 than the original space. We show that
ultradense embeddings generated by DENSIFIER reach state of the art on a lexicon creation
task in which words are annotated with three
types of lexical information – sentiment, concreteness and frequency. On the SemEval2015
10B sentiment analysis task we show that no
information is lost when the ultradense subspace is used, but training is an order of magnitude *more efficient* due to the compactness
of the ultradense space.

1 Introduction

Embeddings are useful for many tasks, including
word similarity (e.g., Pennington et al. (2014)),
named entity recognition (NER) (e.g., Collobert et
al. (2011)) and sentiment analysis (e.g., Kim (2014),
Kalchbrenner et al. (2014), Severyn and Moschitti
(2015)). Embeddings are generic representations,
containing different types of information about a
word. Statistical models can be trained to make best
use of these generic representations for a specific application like NER or sentiment analysis (Ebert et
al., 2015).

Our hypothesis in this paper is that the information useful for any given task is contained in an *ultradense subspace* E_u. We propose the new method
DENSIFIER to identify E_u. Given a set of word embeddings, DENSIFIER learns an *orthogonal transformation* of the original space E_o on a task-specific
training set. The orthogonality of the transformation
can be considered a hard regularizer.

The benefit of the proposed method is that embeddings are most useful if learned on unlabeled corpora and performance-enhanced on a broad array of
tasks. This means we should try to keep all information offered by them. Orthogonal transformations
"reorder" the space without adding or removing information and preserve the bilinear form, i.e., Euclidean distance and cosine. The transformed embeddings concentrate all information relevant for the
task in E_u.

The benefits of E_u compared to E_o are (i) *high-quality* and (ii) *efficient* representations. (i) DENSIFIER moves non-task-related information outside of
E_u, i.e., into the orthogonal complement of E_u. As
a result, E_u provides *higher-quality representations*
for the task than E_o; e.g., noise that could result in
overfitting is reduced in E_u compared to E_o. (ii) E_u
has a *dimensionality smaller by a factor of 100* in our
experiments. As a result, training statistical models
on these embeddings is much faster. These models
also have many fewer parameters, thus again helping
to prevent overfitting, especially for complex, deep
neural networks.

We show the benefits of ultradense representations in two text polarity classification tasks (SemEval2015 Task 10B, Czech movie reviews).

In the most extreme form, ultradense representations – i.e., E_u – have a single dimension. We exploit this for creating lexicons in which words are

Proceedings of NAACL-HLT 2016, pages 767–777,
San Diego, California, June 12-17, 2016. ©2016 Association for Computational Linguistics

annotated with lexical information, e.g., with sentiment. Specifically, we create high-coverage lexicons with up to 3 million words (i) for three lexical properties: for *sentiment*, *concreteness* and *frequency*; (ii) for five languages: *Czech*, *English*, *French*, *German* and *Spanish*; (iii) for two domains, *Twitter* and *News*, in a domain adaptation setup.

The main advantages of this method of lexicon creation are: (i) We need a training lexicon of only a few hundred words, thus making our method effective for new domains and languages and requiring only a minimal manual annotation effort. (ii) The method is applicable to any set of embeddings, including phrase and sentence embeddings. Assuming the availability of a small hand-labeled lexicon, DENSIFIER automatically creates a domain dependent lexicon based on a set of embeddings learned on a large corpus of the domain. (iii) While the input lexicon is *discrete* – e.g., positive (+1) and negative (-1) sentiment – the output lexicon is *continuous* and this more fine-grained assessment is potentially more informative than a simple binary distinction.

We show that lexicons created by DENSIFIER beat the state of the art on SemEval2015 Task 10E (determining association strength).

One of our goals is to make embeddings more interpretable. The work on sentiment, concreteness and frequency we present in this paper is a first step towards a *general decomposition of embedding spaces into meaningful, dense subspaces*. This would lead to cleaner and more easily interpretable representations – as well as representations that are more effective and efficient.

2 Model

Let $Q \in \mathbb{R}^{d \times d}$ be an orthogonal matrix that transforms the original word embedding space into a space in which certain types of information are represented by a small number of dimensions. Concretely, we learn Q such that the dimensions $D^s \subset \{1, \ldots, d\}$ of the resulting space correspond to a word's sentiment information and the $\{1, \ldots, d\} \setminus D^s$ remaining dimensions correspond to non-sentiment information. Analogously, the sets of dimensions D^c and D^f correspond to a word's concreteness information and frequency information, respectively. In this paper, we assume that these

properties do not correlate and therefore the ultradense subspaces do not overlap, e.g., $D^s \cap D^c = \emptyset$. However, this might not be true for other settings, e.g., sentiment and semantic information.

If $e_w \in E_o \subset \mathbb{R}^d$ is the original embedding of word w, the transformed representation is Qe_w. We use $*$ as a placeholder for s, c and f and call $d^* = |D^*|$ the dimensionality of the ultradense subspace of $*$. For each ultradense subspace, we create $P^* \in \mathbb{R}^{d^* \times d}$, an identity matrix for the dimensions in $D^* \subset \{1, \ldots, d\}$. Thus, the ultradense representation $u_w^* \in E_u \subset \mathbb{R}^{d^*}$ of e_w is defined as:

$$u_w^* := P^* Q e_w \tag{1}$$

2.1 Separating Words of Different Groups

We assume to have a lexicon resource l in which each word w is annotated for a certain information as either $l^*(w) = +1$ (positive, concrete, frequent) or $l^*(w) = -1$ (negative, abstract, infrequent). Let $L_{\not\sim}^*$ be a set of word index pairs (v, w) for which $l^*(v) \neq l^*(w)$ holds. We want to maximize:

$$\sum_{(v,w) \in L_{\not\sim}^*} \|u_v^* - u_w^*\| \tag{2}$$

Thus, our objective is given by:

$$\underset{Q}{\operatorname{argmax}} \sum_{(v,w) \in L_{\not\sim}^*} \|P^* Q(e_w - e_v)\| \tag{3}$$

or, equivalently, by:

$$\underset{Q}{\operatorname{argmin}} \sum_{(v,w) \in L_{\not\sim}^*} -\|P^* Q(e_w - e_v)\| \tag{4}$$

subject to Q being an orthogonal matrix.

2.2 Aligning Words of the Same Group

Another goal is to minimize the distance of two words of the same group. Let $L_{\sim}^*$ be a set of word index pairs (v, w) for which $l^*(v) = l^*(w)$ holds. In contrast to Eq. 3, we now want to minimize each distance. Thus, the objective is given by:

$$\underset{Q}{\operatorname{argmin}} \sum_{(v,w) \in L_{\sim}^*} \|P^* Q(e_w - e_v)\| \tag{5}$$

subject to Q being an orthogonal matrix.

The intuition behind the two objectives is graphically depicted in Figure 1.

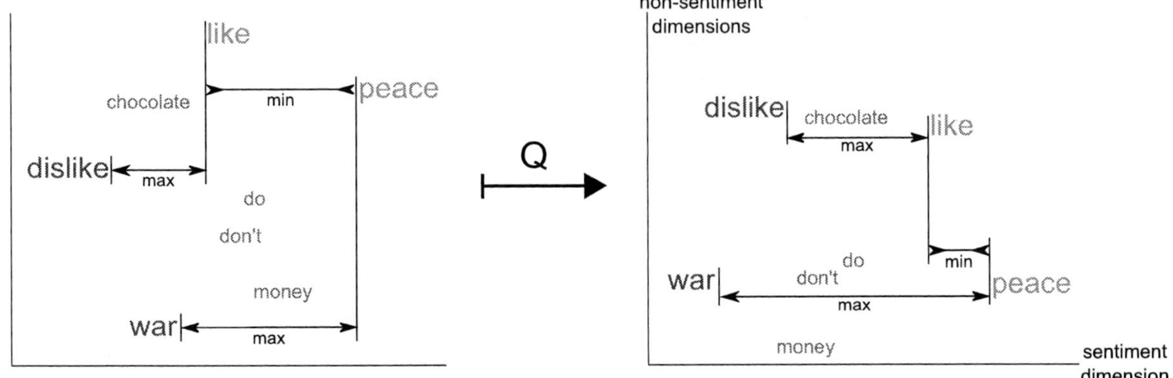

Figure 1: The original word embedding space (left) and the transformed embedding space (right). The training objective for Q is to *minimize* the distances in the sentiment dimension between words of the same group (e.g., positive/green: "like" & "peace") and to *maximize* the distances between words of different groups (e.g., negative/red & positive/green: "war" & "peace"; not necessarily antonyms).

2.3 Training

We combine the two objectives in Eqs. 3/5 for each subspace, i.e., for sentiment, concreteness and frequency, and weight them with α^* and $1-\alpha^*$. Hence, there is one hyperparameter α^* for each subspace. We then perform stochastic gradient descent (SGD). Batch size is 100 and starting learning rate is 5, multiplied by .99 in each iteration.

2.4 Orthogonalization

Each step of SGD updates Q. The updated matrix Q' is in general no longer orthogonal. We therefore reorthogonalize Q' in each step based on singular value decomposition:

$$Q' = USV^T$$

where S is a diagonal matrix, and U and V are orthogonal matrices. The matrix

$$Q := UV^T$$

is the nearest orthogonal matrix to Q' in both the 2-norm and the Frobenius norm (Fan and Hoffman, 1955). (Formalizing our regularization directly as projected gradient descent would be desirable. However, gradient descent includes an additive operation and orthogonal matrices are not closed under summation.)

SGD for this problem is sensitive to the learning rate. If the learning rate is too large, a large jump results and the reorthogonalized matrix Q basically is a random new point in the parameter space. If the learning rate is too small, then learning can take long. We found that our training regime of starting at a high learning rate (5) and multiplying by .99 in each iteration is effective. Typically, the cost initially stays about constant (random jumps in parameter space), then cost steeply declines in a small number of about 50 iterations (sweet spot); the curve flattens after that. Training Q took less than 5 minutes per experiment for all experiments in this paper.

3 Lexicon Creation

For lexicon creation, the input is a set of *embeddings* and a lexicon *resource* l, in which words are annotated for a lexical information such as sentiment, concreteness or frequency. DENSIFIER is then trained to produce a *one-dimensional ultra-dense subspace*. The output is an *output lexicon*. It consists of all words covered by the embedding set, each associated with its one-dimensional ultra-dense subspace representation (which is simply a real number), an indicator of the word's strength for that information.

The embeddings and lexicon resources used in this paper cover five languages and three domains (Table 1). The Google News embeddings for English[1] and the FrWac embeddings for French[2] are

---

[1] https://code.google.com/p/word2vec/
[2] http://fauconnier.github.io/

		#tokens	#types	train			test			τ
				resource	$\cap$	#words	resource	$\cap$	#words	
1	sent CZ web	2.44	3.3	SubLex 1.0	2,492	4,125	SubLex 1.0	319	500	.580
2	sent DE web	1.34	8.0	German PC	10,718	37,901	German PC	573	1,000	.654
3	sent ES web	0.37	3.7	full-strength	824	1,147	full-strength	185	200	.563
4	sent FR web	0.12	1.6	FEEL	7,496	10,979	FEEL	715	1,000	.544
5	sent EN twitter	3.34	5.4	WHM all	12,601	19,329	Trial 10E	198	200	.661
6	sent EN news	3.00	100.0	WHM train	7,633	10,270	WHM val	952	1,000	.622
7	conc EN news	3.00	100.0	BWK	14,361	29,954	BWK	8,694	10,000	.623
8	freq EN news	3.00	100.0	word2vec order	4,000	4,000	word2vec order	1,000	1,000	.361
9	freq FR web	0.12	1.6	word2vec order	4,000	4,000	word2vec order	1,000	1,000	.460

Table 1: Results for lexicon creation. #tokens: size of embedding training corpus (in billion). #types: size of output lexicon (in million). For each resource, we give its size ("#words") and the size of the intersection of resource and embedding set ("$\cap$"). Kendall's τ is computed on "$\cap$".

publicly available. We use word2vec to train 400-dimensional embeddings for English on a 2013 Twitter corpus of size 5.4×10^9. For Czech, German and Spanish, we train embeddings on web data of sizes 3.3, 8.0 and 3.8×10^9, respectively. We use the following lexicon resources for sentiment: SubLex 1.0 (Veselovská and Bojar, 2013) for Czech; WHM for English [the combination of MPQA (Wilson et al., 2005), Opinion Lexicon (Hu and Liu, 2004) and NRC Emotion lexicons (Mohammad and Turney, 2013)]; FEEL (Abdaoui et al., 2014) for French; German Polarity Clues (Waltinger, 2010) for German; and the sentiment lexicon of Pérez-Rosas et al. (2012) for Spanish. For concreteness, we use BWK, a lexicon of 40,000 English words (Brysbaert et al., 2014). For frequency, we exploit the fact that word2vec stores words in frequency order; thus, the ranking provided by word2vec is our lexicon resource for frequency.

For a resource/embedding-set pair (l, E), we intersect the vocabulary of l with the top 80,000 words of E to filter out noisy, infrequent words that tend to have low quality embeddings and we do not want them to introduce noise when training the transformation matrix.

For the sentiment and concreteness resources, $l^*(w) \in \{-1, 1\}$ for all words w covered. We create a resource l^f for frequency by setting $l^f(w) = 1$ for the 2000 most frequent words and $l^f(w) = -1$ for words at ranks 20000-22000. 1000 words randomly selected from the 5000 most frequent are the test set.[3] We designate three sets of dimen-

sions D^s, D^c and D^f to represent sentiment, concreteness and frequency, respectively, and arbitrarily set (i) $D^c = \{11\}$ for English and $D^c = \emptyset$ for the other languages since we do not have concreteness resources for them, (ii) $D^s = \{1\}$ and (iii) $D^f = \{21\}$. Referring to the lines in Table 1, we then learn six orthogonal transformation matrices Q: for CZ-web (1), DE-web (2), ES-web (3), FR-web (4, 9), EN-twitter (5) and EN-news (6, 7, 8).

4 Evaluation

4.1 Top-Ranked Words

Table 2 shows the top 10 positive/negative words (i.e., most extreme values on dimension D^s) when we apply the transformation to the corpora EN-twitter, EN-news and DE-web and the top 10 concrete/abstract words (i.e., most extreme values on dimension D^c) for EN-news. For EN-twitter (leftmost double column), the selected words look promising: they contain highly domain-specific words such as hashtags (e.g., #happy). This is surprising because there is not a single hashtag in the lexicon resource WHM that DENSIFIER was trained on. Results for the other three double columns show likewise extreme examples for the corresponding information and language. This initial evaluation indicates that our method effectively learns high quality lexicons for new domains. Figure 3 depicts values for selected words for the three properties. Illustrative examples are "brother" / "brotherhood" for concreteness and "hate" / "love" for sentiment.

---

[3]The main result of the frequency experiment below is that

τ is low even in a setup that is optimistic due to train/test overlap; presumably it would be even lower without overlap.

EN-twitter		EN-news		EN-news		DE-web	
positive	negative	positive	negative	concrete	abstract	positive	negative
#blessed	rape	expertise	angry	tree	fundamental	herzlichen	gesperrt
inspiration	racist	delighted	delays	truck	obvious	kenntnisse	droht
blessed	horrible	honored	worse	kitchen	legitimate	hervorragende	verurteilt
inspiring	nasty	thank	anger	dog	reasonable	ideale	gefahr
foundation	jealousy	wonderful	foul	bike	optimistic	bestens	falsche
provide	murder	commitment	blamed	bat	satisfied	glückwunsch	streit
wishes	waste	affordable	blame	garden	surprising	optimale	angst
dedicated	mess	passion	complained	homer	honest	anregungen	krankheit
offers	disgusting	exciting	bad	bed	regard	freuen	falschen
#happy	spam	flexibility	deaths	gallon	extraordinary	kompetenzen	verdacht

Table 2: Top 10 words in the output lexicons for the domains Twitter and News (English) and Web (German).

4.2 Quality of Predictions

Table 1 presents experimental results. In each case, we split the resource into train/test, except for Twitter where we used the trial data of SemEval2015 Task 10E for test. We train DENSIFIER on train and compute Kendall's τ on test. The size of the lexicon resource has no big effect; e.g., results for Spanish (small resource; line 3) and French (large resource; line 4) are about the same. See Section 5.2 for a more detailed analysis of the effect of resource size.

The quality of the output lexicon depends strongly on the quality of the underlying word embeddings; e.g., results for French (small embedding training corpus; line 4) are worse than results for English (large embedding training corpus; line 6) even though the lexicon resources have comparable size.

In contrast to sentiment/concreteness, τ values for frequency are low (lines 8-9). For the other three languages we obtain $\tau \in [.34, .46]$ for frequency (not shown). This suggests that word embeddings represent sentiment and concreteness much better than frequency. The reason for this likely is the learning objective of word embeddings: modeling the context. Infrequent words can occur in frequent contexts. Thus, the frequency information in a single word embedding is limited. In contrast negative words are likely to occur in negative contexts.

The nine output lexicons in Table 1 – each a list of words annotated with predicted strength on one of three properties – are available at `www.cis.lmu.de/~sascha/Ultradense/`.

	system	all	τ $\cap$
1	Amir et al. (2015)	.626[†]	
2	Hamdan et al. (2015)	.621[†]	
3	Zhang et al. (2015)	.591[†]	
4	Özdemir and Bergler (2015)	.584[†]	
5	Plotnikova et al. (2015)	.577[†]	
6	DENSIFIER	**.654**	**.650**
7	Sentiment140	.508[†]	.538[†]
8	DENSIFIER, trial only	.627[†]	

Table 3: Results for Lexicon Creation. The first column gives the correlation with the entire test lexicon of SemEval2015 10E, the last column only on the intersection of our output lexicon and Sentiment140. Of the 1315 words of task 10E, 985 and 1308 are covered by DENSIFIER and Sentiment140, respectively. †: significantly worse than the best (bold) result in the same column ($\alpha = .05$, Fisher z-transformation).

4.3 Determining Association Strength

We also evaluate lexicon creation on SemEval2015 Task 10E. As before, the task is to predict the sentiment score of words/phrases. We use the trial data of the task to tune the hyperparameter, $\alpha^s = .4$. Out-of-vocabulary words were predicted as neutral (7/1315). Table 3 shows that the lexicon computed by DENSIFIER (line 5, Table 1) has a τ of .654 (line 6, column *all*), significantly better than all other systems, including the winner of SemEval 2015 ($\tau = .626$, line 1). DENSIFIER also beats Sentiment140 (Mohammad et al., 2013), a widely used semi-automatic sentiment lexicon. The last column is τ on the intersection of DENSIFIER and Sentiment140. It shows that DENSIFIER again performs significantly better than Sentiment140.

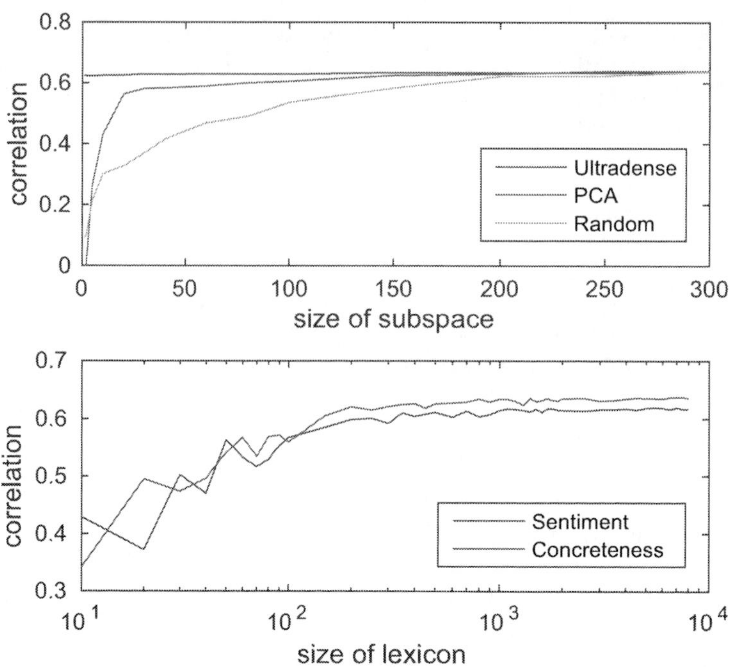

Figure 2: Kendall's τ versus subspace size (top) and training resource size (bottom). See lines 6 & 8, Table 1, for train/test split.

4.4 Text Polarity Classification

We now show that ultradense embeddings decrease model training times without any noticeable decrease in performance compared to the original embeddings. We evaluate on SemEval2015 Task 10B, classification of Twitter tweets as positive, negative or neutral. We reimplement the linguistically-informed convolutional neural network (lingCNN) of Ebert et al. (2015) that has close to state-of-the-art performance on the task. We do not use sentence-based features to focus on the evaluation of the embeddings. We initialize the first layer of lingCNN, the embedding layer, in three different ways: (i) 400-dimensional Twitter embeddings (Section 3); (ii) 40-dimensional ultradense embeddings derived from (i); (iii) 4-dimensional ultradense embeddings derived from (i). The objective weighting is $\alpha^s = .4$, optimized on the development set.

The embedding layer converts a sentence into a matrix of word embeddings. We also add linguistic features for words, such as sentiment lexicon scores. The combination of embeddings and linguistic features is the input for a convolution layer with filters spanning 2-5 words (100 filters each). This is fol-lowed by a max pooling layer, a rectifier nonlinearity (Nair and Hinton, 2010) and a fully connected softmax layer predicting the final label. The model is trained with SGD using AdaGrad (Duchi et al., 2011) and ℓ_2 regularization ($\lambda = 5 \times 10^{-5}$). Learning rate is 0.01. Mini-batch size is 100.

We follow the official guidelines and use the SemEval2013 training and development sets as training set, the SemEval2013 test set as development set and the SemEval2015 test set to report final scores (Nakov et al., 2013; Rosenthal et al., 2015). We report macro F_1 of positive and negative classes (the official SemEval evaluation metric) and accuracy over the three classes. Table 4 shows that 40-dimensional ultradense embeddings perform almost as well as the full 400-dimensional embeddings (no significant difference according to sign test). Training time is shorter by a factor of 21 (85/4 examples/second). The 4-dimensional ultradense embeddings lead to only a small loss of 1.5% even though the size of the embeddings is smaller by a factor of 100 (again not a significant drop). Training time is shorter by a factor of 44 (178/4).

We perform the same experiment on CSFD, a

lang.	embeddings	#dim	acc	F_1	ex./sec
en	original	400	.666	.623	4
en	DENSIFIER	40	.662	.620	85
en	DENSIFIER	4	.646	.608	178
cz	original	400	.803	.802	1
cz	DENSIFIER	40	.803	.801	24
cz	DENSIFIER	4	.771	.769	83

Table 4: Performance on Text Polarity Classification

Czech movie review dataset (Habernal et al., 2013), to show the benefits of ultradense embeddings for a low-resource language where only one rather small lexicon is available. As original word embeddings we train new 400 dimensional embeddings on a large Twitter corpus (3.3×10^9 tokens). We use DENSIFIER to create 40 and 4 dimensional embeddings out of these embeddings and SubLex 1.0 (Veselovská and Bojar, 2013). Word polarity features are also taken from SubLex. A simple binary negation indicator is implemented by searching for all tokens beginning with "ne". Since that includes superlative forms having the prefix "nej", we remove them with the exception of common negated words, such as "nejsi" – "you are not". We randomly split the 91,000 dataset instances into 90% train and 10% test and report accuracy and macro F_1 score over all three classes.

Table 4 shows that what we found for English is also true for Czech. There is only a small performance drop when using ultradense embeddings (not significant for 40 dimensional embeddings) while the speed improvement is substantial.

5 Parameter Analysis

In this section, we analyze two parameters: size of ultradense subspace and size of lexicon resource. We leave an evaluation of another parameter, the size of the embedding training corpus, for future work, but empirical results suggest that this corpus should ideally have a size of several billion tokens.

5.1 Size of Subspace

With the exception of the two text polarity classification experiments, all our subspaces have dimensionality $d^* = 1$. The question arises: does a one-dimensional space perhaps have too low a capacity to encode all relevant information and could we further improve our results by increasing the dimen-

sionality of the subspace to values $d^* > 1$? The lexicon resources that we train and test on are all binary; thus, if we use values $d^* > 1$, then we need to map the subspace embeddings to a one-dimensional scale for evaluation. We do this by training, on the train part of the resource, a linear transformation from the ultradense subspace to the one-dimensional scale (e.g., to the sentiment scale).

Figure 2 compares different values of d^s for three different types of subspaces in this setup, i.e., the setup in which the subspace representations are mapped via linear transformation to a one-dimensional sentiment value: (i) *Random*: we take the first d^s dimensions of the original embeddings; (ii) *PCA*: we compute a PCA and take the first d^s principal components; (iii) *Ultradense* subspace of dimensionality d^s. We use the word embeddings and lexicon resources of line 6 in Table 1. For random, the performance starts dropping when the subspace is smaller than 200 dimensions. For PCA, the performance is relatively stable until the subspace becomes smaller than 100. In contrast, ultradense subspaces have almost identical performance for all values of d^s, even for $d^s = 1$. This suggests that a single dimension is sufficient to encode all sentiment information needed for sentiment lexicon creation. However, for other sentiment tasks more dimensions may be needed, e.g., for modeling different emotional dimensions of polarity: fear, sadness, anger etc.

An alternative approach to create a low-dimensional space is to simply train low-dimensional word2vec embeddings. The following experiment suggests that this does not work very well. We used word2vec to train 60-dimensional twitter embeddings with the same settings as on line 5 in Table 1. While the correlation for 400-dimensional embeddings shown in Table 1 is .661, the correlation of 60-dimensional embeddings is only .568. Thus, even though we show that the information in 400-dimensional embeddings that is relevant for sentiment can be condensed into a single dimension, hundreds of dimensions seem to be needed if we use word2vec to collect sentiment information. If we run word2vec with a small dimensionality, only a subset of available sentiment information is "harvested" from the corpus.

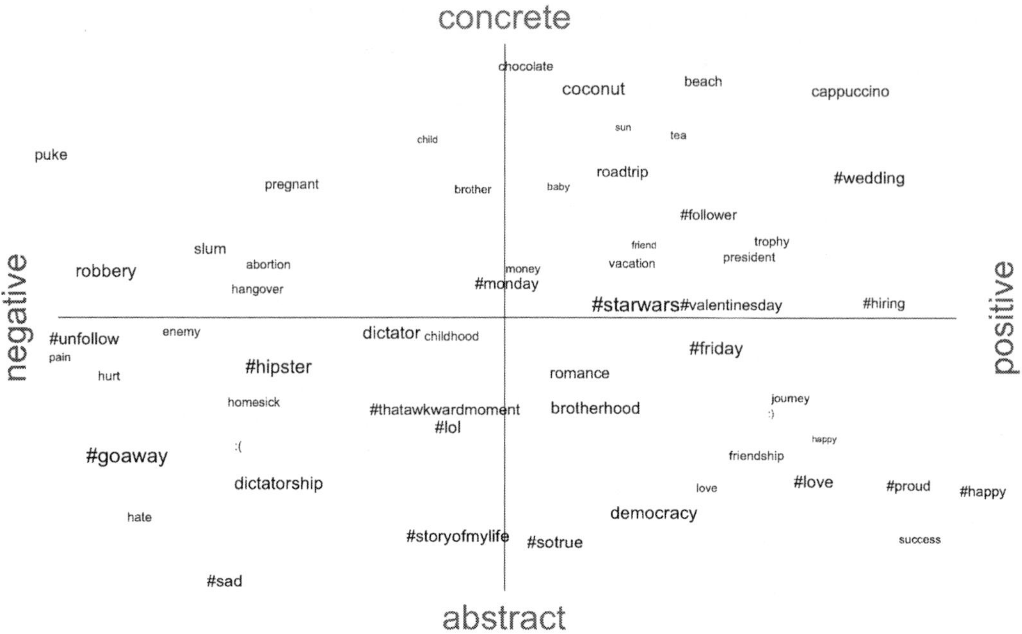

Figure 3: Illustration of EN-twitter output lexicon: DENSIFIER values are x coordinate (sentiment), y coordinate (concreteness) and font size (frequency)

5.2 Size of Training Resource

Next, we analyze what size of training resource is required to learn a good transformation Q. Labeled resources covering many words may not be available or suffer from lack of quality. We use the settings of lines 6 (sentiment) and 7 (concreteness) in Table 1. Figure 2 shows that a small training resource of 300 entries is sufficient for high performance. This suggests that DENSIFIER can create a high quality output lexicon for a new language by hand-labeling only 300 words; and that a small, high-quality resource may be preferable to a large lower-quality resource (semi-automatic or out of domain).

To provide further evidence for this, we train DENSIFIER on only the trial data of SemEval2015 task 10E. To convert the continuous trial data to binary -1 / 1 labels, we discard all words with sentiment values between -0.5 and 0.5 and round the remaining values, giving us 39 positive and 38 negative training words. The resulting lexicon has $\tau = .627$ (Table 3, line 8).[4] This is worse than $\tau = $ .654 (line 6) for the setup in which we used several large resources, but still better than all previous work. This indicates that DENSIFIER is especially suited for languages or domains for which little training data is available.

6 Related Work

To the best of our knowledge, this paper is the first to train an orthogonal transformation to reorder word embedding dimensions into ultradense subspaces. However, there is much prior work on postprocessing word embeddings.

Faruqui et al. (2015) perform postprocessing based on a semantic lexicon with the goal of fine-tuning word embeddings. Their transformation is not orthogonal and therefore does not preserve distances. They show that their approach optimizes word embeddings for a given application, i.e., word similarity, but also that it worsens them for other applications like detecting syntactic relations. Faruqui et al. (2015)'s approach also does not have the bene-

---

[4]Here, we tune α^s on train (equals trial data of SemEval2015 task 10E). This seems to work due to the different objectives for training (maximize/minimize difference) and development (correlation).

fit of ultradense embeddings, in particular the benefit of increased efficiency.

In a tensor framework, Rothe and Schütze (2015) transform the word embeddings to sense (synset) embeddings. In their work, all embeddings live in the same space whereas we explicitly want to change the embedding space to create ultradense embeddings with several desirable properties.

Xing et al. (2015) restricted the work of Mikolov et al. (2013) to an orthogonal transformation to ensure that normalized embeddings stay normalized. This transformation is learned between two embedding spaces of different languages to exploit similarities. They normalized word embeddings in a first step, something that did not improve our results.

As a reviewer pointed out, our method is also related to Oriented PCA (Diamantaras and Kung, 1996). However in contrast to PCA a solution for Oriented PCA is not orthogonal.

Sentiment lexicons are often created semi-automatically, e.g., by extending manually labeled seed sets of sentiment words or adding for each word its syno-/antonyms. Alternatively, words frequently cooccurring with a seed set of manually labeled sentiment words are added (Turney, 2002; Kiritchenko et al., 2014). Heerschop et al. (2011) used Word-Net together with a PageRank-based algorithm to propagate the sentiment of the seed set to unknown words. Scheible (2010) presented a semi-automatic approach based on machine translation of sentiment lexicons. The winning system of SemEval2015 10E (Amir et al., 2015) was based on structured skip-gram embeddings with 600 dimensions and support vector regression with RBF kernels. Hamdan et al. (2015), the second ranked team, used the average of six sentiment lexicons as a final sentiment score, a method that cannot be applied to low resource languages. We showed that the lexicons created by DENSIFIER achieve better performance than other semi-automatically created lexicons.

Tang et al. (2014b) train sentiment specific embeddings by extending Collobert & Weston's model and Tang et al. (2014a)'s skip-gram model. The first model automatically labels tweets as positive/negative based on emoticons, a process that cannot be easily transferred to other domains like news. The second uses the Urban Dictionary to expand a small list of 350 sentiment seeds. In our work, we

showed that a training resource of about the same size is sufficient without an additional dictionary. DENSIFIER differs from this work in that it does not need a text corpus, but can transform existing, publicly available word embeddings. DENSIFIER is independent of the embedding learning algorithm and therefore extensible to other word embedding models like GloVe (Pennington et al., 2014), to phrase embeddings (Yu and Dredze, 2015) and even to sentence embeddings (Kiros et al., 2015).

7 Conclusion

We have introduced DENSIFIER, a method that is trained to focus embeddings used for an application to an ultradense subspace that contains the information relevant for the application. In experiments on SemEval, we demonstrate two benefits of the ultradense subspace. (i) Information is preserved even if we focus on a subspace that is smaller by a factor of 100 than the original space. This means that unnecessary noisy information is removed from the embeddings and robust learning without overfitting is better supported. (ii) Since the subspace is 100 times smaller, models that use the embeddings as their input representation can be trained more efficiently and have a much smaller number of parameters. The subspace can be learned with just $80 - 300$ training examples, achieving state-of-the-art results on lexicon creation.

We have shown in this paper that up to three orthogonal ultradense subspaces can be created. Many training datasets can be restructured as sets of similar/dissimilar pairs. For instance, in part-of-speech tasks verb/verb pairs would be similar, verb/noun pairs dissimilar. Hence, our objective is widely applicable. In future work, we will explore the possibility of factoring all information present in an embedding into a dozen or so orthogonal subspaces. This factorization would not change the information embeddings contain, but it would make them more compact for any given application, more meaningful and more interpretable.

The nine large DENSIFIER lexicons shown in Table 1 are publicly available.[5]

Acknowledgments. We gratefully acknowledge the support of DFG: grant SCHU 2246/10-1.

---

[5] `www.cis.lmu.de/~sascha/Ultradense/`

References

Amine Abdaoui, Jérôme Azé, Sandra Bringay, and Pascal Poncelet. 2014. FEEL: French Extended Emotional Lexicon: ISLRN: 041-639-484-224-2.

Silvio Amir, Ramón Astudillo, Wang Ling, Bruno Martins, Mario J. Silva, and Isabel Trancoso. 2015. Inescid: A regression model for large scale twitter sentiment lexicon induction. In *Proceedings of SemEval*.

Marc Brysbaert, Amy Beth Warriner, and Victor Kuperman. 2014. Concreteness ratings for 40 thousand generally known english word lemmas. *Behavior research methods*, 46(3):904–911.

Ronan Collobert, Jason Weston, Léon Bottou, Michael Karlen, Koray Kavukcuoglu, and Pavel Kuksa. 2011. Natural language processing (almost) from scratch. *JMLR*, 12:2493–2537.

K. I. Diamantaras and S. Y. Kung. 1996. *Principal Component Neural Networks: Theory and Applications*. John Wiley & Sons, Inc.

John C. Duchi, Elad Hazan, and Yoram Singer. 2011. Adaptive subgradient methods for online learning and stochastic optimization. *JMLR*, 12:2121–2159.

Sebastian Ebert, Ngoc Thang Vu, and Hinrich Schütze. 2015. A Linguistically Informed Convolutional Neural Network. In *Proceedings of WASSA*.

Ky Fan and Alan J Hoffman. 1955. Some metric inequalities in the space of matrices. volume 6, pages 111–116.

Manaal Faruqui, Jesse Dodge, Sujay Kumar Jauhar, Chris Dyer, Eduard Hovy, and Noah A. Smith. 2015. Retrofitting word vectors to semantic lexicons. In *Proceedings of NAACL*.

Ivan Habernal, Tomáš Ptáček, and Josef Steinberger. 2013. Sentiment Analysis in Czech Social Media Using Supervised Machine Learning. In *Proceedings of WASSA*.

Hussam Hamdan, Patrice Bellot, and Frederic Bechet. 2015. Lsislif: Feature extraction and label weighting for sentiment analysis in twitter. In *Proceedings of SemEval*.

Bas Heerschop, Alexander Hogenboom, and Flavius Frasincar. 2011. Sentiment lexicon creation from lexical resources. In *Business Information Systems*.

Minqing Hu and Bing Liu. 2004. Mining and Summarizing Customer Reviews. In *Proceedings of KDD*.

Nal Kalchbrenner, Edward Grefenstette, and Phil Blunsom. 2014. A Convolutional Neural Network for Modelling Sentences. In *Proceedings of ACL*.

Yoon Kim. 2014. Convolutional Neural Networks for Sentence Classification. In *Proceedings of EMNLP*.

Svetlana Kiritchenko, Xiaodan Zhu, and Saif M Mohammad. 2014. Sentiment analysis of short informal texts. *JAIR*, pages 723–762.

Ryan Kiros, Yukun Zhu, Ruslan R Salakhutdinov, Richard Zemel, Raquel Urtasun, Antonio Torralba, and Sanja Fidler. 2015. Skip-thought vectors. In *Proceedings of NIPS*.

Tomas Mikolov, Quoc V Le, and Ilya Sutskever. 2013. Exploiting similarities among languages for machine translation. *arXiv preprint arXiv:1309.4168*.

Saif M. Mohammad and Peter D. Turney. 2013. Crowdsourcing a Word-Emotion Association Lexicon. *Computational Intelligence*, 29(3).

Saif M. Mohammad, Svetlana Kiritchenko, and Xiaodan Zhu. 2013. NRC-Canada: Building the State-of-the-Art in Sentiment Analysis of Tweets. In *Proceedings of SemEval*.

Vinod Nair and Geoffrey E. Hinton. 2010. Rectified Linear Units Improve Restricted Boltzmann Machines. In *Proceedings of ICML*.

Preslav Nakov, Sara Rosenthal, Zornitsa Kozareva, Veselin Stoyanov, Alan Ritter, and Theresa Wilson. 2013. SemEval-2013 Task 2: Sentiment Analysis in Twitter. In *Proceedings of SemEval*.

Canberk Özdemir and Sabine Bergler. 2015. Clacsentipipe: Semeval2015 subtasks 10 b,e, and task 11. In *Proceedings of SemEval*.

Jeffrey Pennington, Richard Socher, and Christopher D. Manning. 2014. GloVe: Global Vectors for Word Representation. In *Proceedings of EMNLP*.

Verónica Pérez-Rosas, Carmen Banea, and Rada Mihalcea. 2012. Learning Sentiment Lexicons in Spanish. In *Proceedings of LREC*.

Nataliia Plotnikova, Micha Kohl, Kevin Volkert, Stefan Evert, Andreas Lerner, Natalie Dykes, and Heiko Ermer. 2015. Klueless: Polarity classification and association. In *Proceedings of SemEval*.

Sara Rosenthal, Preslav Nakov, Svetlana Kiritchenko, Saif M. Mohammad, Alan Ritter, and Veselin Stoyanov. 2015. SemEval-2015 Task 10: Sentiment Analysis in Twitter. In *Proceedings of SemEval*.

Sascha Rothe and Hinrich Schütze. 2015. Autoextend: Extending word embeddings to embeddings for synsets and lexemes. In *Proceedings of ACL*.

Christian Scheible. 2010. Sentiment translation through lexicon induction. In *Proceedings of ACL, Student Research Workshop*.

Aliaksei Severyn and Alessandro Moschitti. 2015. UNITN: Training Deep Convolutional Neural Network for Twitter Sentiment Classification. In *Proceedings of SemEval*.

Duyu Tang, Furu Wei, Bing Qin, Ming Zhou, and Ting Liu. 2014a. Building large-scale twitter-specific sentiment lexicon : A representation learning approach. In *Proceedings of COLING*.

Duyu Tang, Furu Wei, Nan Yang, Ming Zhou, Ting Liu, and Bing Qin. 2014b. Learning Sentiment-Specific Word Embedding for Twitter Sentiment Classification. In *Proceedings of ACL*.

Peter D. Turney. 2002. Thumbs Up or Thumbs Down? Semantic Orientation Applied to Unsupervised Classification of Reviews. In *Proceedings of ACL*.

Kateřina Veselovská and Ondřej Bojar. 2013. Czech SubLex 1.0.

Ulli Waltinger. 2010. GermanPolarityClues: A Lexical Resource for German Sentiment Analysis. In *Proceedings of LREC*.

Theresa Wilson, Janyce Wiebe, and Paul Hoffmann. 2005. Recognizing contextual polarity in phrase-level sentiment analysis. In *Proceedings of HLT/EMNLP*.

Chao Xing, Dong Wang, Chao Liu, and Yiye Lin. 2015. Normalized word embedding and orthogonal transform for bilingual word translation. In *Proceedings of NAACL*.

Mo Yu and Mark Dredze. 2015. Learning composition models for phrase embeddings. *TACL*, 3:227–242.

Zhihua Zhang, Guoshun Wu, and Man Lan. 2015. Ecnu: Multi-level sentiment analysis on twitter using traditional linguistic features and word embedding features. In *Proceedings of SemEval*.

AUTHOR INDEX

AUTHOR INDEX

AUTHOR INDEX

Association for Computational Linguistics
209 N. Eighth Street
Stroudsburg, Pennsylvania 18360

ISBN 978-1-5108-2512-3

Conference of the North American Chapter of the Association for Computational Linguistics: Human Language Technologies 2016 (NAACL HLT 2016)

San Diego, California, USA
12 - 17 June 2016

Volume 2 of 2

Conference of the North American Chapter of the Association for Computational Linguistics: Human Language Technologies 2016 (NAACL HLT 2016)

San Diego, California, USA
12 - 17 June 2016

Volume 2 of 2

ISBN: 978-1-5108-2512-3

NAACL HLT 2016

**The 2016 Conference of the
North American Chapter of the
Association for Computational Linguistics:
Human Language Technologies**

Proceedings of the Conference

June 12-17, 2016
San Diego, California, USA

This page intentionally left blank.

Message from the General Chair

Greetings,

Welcome to NAACL HLT 2016! This year's conference is held in San Diego, California, where we have assembled an exciting program of computational linguistics research.

The main program features a wide array of topics, and it includes excellent invited talks by Prof. Regina Barzilay and Prof. Ehud Reiter. In addition, we have six tutorials on the day before the main program, plus fifteen workshops on the following two days. Some of these workshops are back for their 10th or 11th incarnation, while others are brand-new. In parallel, we have a live demonstration track, and a Student Research Workshop that showcases work by the junior members of our research community.

This NAACL HLT meeting takes place only through the hard work of many people who deserve our gratitude.

Thanks to Priscilla Rasmussen for making local arrangements, handling registration, setting up social events, writing visa invitation letters, and solving a myriad of issues. Priscilla, your experience is a great asset to any conference!

The NAACL HLT organizing committee took all the steps to bring you a great conference. Many thanks to Ani Nenkova and Owen Rambow (Program Co-chairs), Mohit Bansal and Alexander M. Rush (Tutorial Co-chairs), Radu Soricut and Adrià de Gispert (Workshop Co-chairs), Jacob Andreas, Eunsol Choi, and Angeliki Lazaridou (Student Research Workshop Co-Chairs) and their faculty advisors Jacob Eisenstein and Nianwen Xue, Aliya Deri (Student Volunteer Coordinator), Julie Medero (Local Sponsorship Chair), Mark Finlayson, Sravana Reddy, and John DeNero (Demonstration Co-chairs), Adam Lopez and Margaret Mitchell (Publications Co-chairs), Jason Riesa (Website Chair), Wei Xu (Publicity Chair), and Jonathan May (Social Media Chair).

Thanks also to the NAACL Board for providing excellent advice, and thanks to previous chairs for their suggestions and timelines.

Sponsors of NAACL HLT 2016 include Baidu and Google (Platinum Sponsors), Amazon, Bloomberg, eBay, Microsoft Research, and UnitedHealth Group (Gold Sponsors), Huawei (Silver Sponsors), Civis Analytics, Facebook, @newsela, and Nuance (Bronze Sponsors), and the University of Washington (Supporter). Thanks for your extremely valuable contributions!

Finally, thanks to the scientists, engineers, authors, and attendees who come to share and learn at this leading venue for computational linguistics research!

Kevin Knight
Information Sciences Institute, University of Southern California
NAACL HLT 2016 General Chair

Message from the Program Co-Chairs

Welcome to San Diego for the 15th Annual Conference of the North American Chapter of the Association for Computational Linguistics: Human Language Technologies!

The conference has grown remarkably in the past five years: we had 698 submissions this year, despite our deadline right after the end-of-the-year holidays. As we worked on organizing the conference program, we made many changes to reflect the growth of the NAACL community, the increasing diversity of topics covered by the field, and the acceleration of the pace of the publication cycle.

We had a record short time between paper submission and author notification—less than two months. We settled on such compressed timeline in order to avoid spreading the reviewing period over the winter holidays, to ensure that papers spend only a short time under submission, and to coordinate submission deadlines with ACL. Our incredible team of area chairs and reviewers ensured that the planned schedule went smoothly.

As the computational linguistics field has expanded, it has become increasingly difficult to recruit a sufficient number of knowledgeable reviewers. We decided to reach out to the largest possible pool of computational linguists and provide convenient ways for the area chairs to control which reviewers they end up working with: we invited all researchers actively working in the area of computational linguistics/language processing to review for the conference. We defined "active researchers" to be those who have published at least five papers in the last ten years in the ACL, NAACL, EMNLP, EACL or COLING conferences. In order to be inclusive of the amazing young researchers who became active in the field only more recently, we also included everyone who had published at least three papers in the same venues for the last five years. This yielded a list of over 1,400 researchers that we invited to serve as reviewers for the conference. Of these, 685 agreed and participated in the review process. This is another record for NAACL HLT 2016, no previous NAACL has had such a large program committee. Among these, the area chairs recognized 120 as best reviewers.

Working with the reviewers were the 42 area chairs. We asked the area chairs to work in pairs, so they can have a back-up in case other obligations need their attention during the review period and to ensure that all decisions about reviewer assignment and paper recommendation are discussed in detail. All area chairs and reviewers submitted a list of keywords that describe their area of expertise (the full list appears in the conference call for papers). The area chairs were paired based on the keyword overlap.

To match reviewers to area chairs, we used a bidding system. For bidding, each area received a list of the 140 reviewers with best matching keyword profiles. If the area chairs did not know the work of a potential reviewer on their bidding list, they looked him or her up on DBLP or Google Scholar before making their final bid. Areas were assigned only reviewers for which the area chairs bid positively. Area chairs were free as usual to recruit additional reviewers they wished to work with.

Submissions were assigned to areas by taking into account the match between the paper keywords and the area chair keywords. Areas were capped at 40 submissions maximum (long and short combined). As in the past, reviewers bid on papers they wanted to review. 69% of the reviews were written by reviewers who had bid indicating that they want to review the paper; 29% of the reviews were written by reviewers who had bid indicating they are ok with reviewing the paper. The remaining 2% of reviews were written by reviewers who did not bid on the paper but were asked by an area chair to review it. Three reviewers were assigned a paper that they did not want to review according to their bid. The average reviewer load was 3 papers, which included a mix of long and short submissions. Only 43 reviewers had more than four papers to review.

Area chairs wrote meta-reviews, for use only by us, justifying their accept/reject recommendation. In making difficult decisions, we drew on these meta-reviews, the reviews themselves, the discussion among the reviewers, and the author response to the initial reviews.

We are happy with our changes to the review process: area chairs had control over the reviewers they worked with, reviewers were assigned papers they wanted to review and the overall reviewing load was low. Needless to say, there is room for further improvements. The reviewing process is crucial to the quality of this conference; only if the community has confidence in the quality of the reviewing process will this conference continue to be a leading conference in our field. Our goal has been to make sure that every single submission receives a complete and fair review and decision, and to make sure that the authors of every single submission understand why their paper was accepted or declined for the conference. We would like to thank our 685 reviewers, and we would especially like to thank our 42 area chairs, who were patient in allowing us to pursue some of the innovative aspects of this year's reviewing cycle.

Eighteen of the 698 initial submissions were withdrawn by the authors or rejected without review because of formatting violations. A total of 396 long and 284 short papers underwent review; 100 long and 82 short papers were accepted, for an acceptance rate of 25% and 29% respectively. In addition, ten TACL papers will be presented at the conference.

This year we decided to have shorter slots for oral presentations, in order to have more of the accepted papers presented as talks. In the program, long papers are allotted 20-minute slots (15 min presentation + 5 min questions). Short papers are allotted 10-minute slots (6 min presentation + 4 min questions).

The best paper award committee consisted of NAACL general and program chairs from the last three years. Not all past chairs could participate in the selection. The final best paper committee included Joyce Chai, Katrin Kirchhoff, Rada Mihalcea, Kristina Toutanova, Lucy Vanderwende and Hua Wu. They selected two best long papers and one best short paper, along with two runner-ups in each category.

Best Short Paper
Improving sentence compression by learning to predict gaze
Sigrid Klerke, Yoav Goldberg and Anders Søgaard

Short Paper, Runners Up
Patterns of Wisdom: Discourse-Level Style in Multi-Sentence Quotations
Kyle Booten and Marti A. Hearst

A Joint Model of Orthography and Morphological Segmentation
Ryan Cotterell, Tim Vieira and Hinrich Schütze

Best Long Papers
Feuding Families and Former Friends: Unsupervised Learning for Dynamic Fictional Relationships
Mohit Iyyer, Anupam Guha, Snigdha Chaturvedi, Jordan Boyd-Graber and Hal Daumé III

Learning to Compose Neural Networks for Question Answering
Jacob Andreas, Marcus Rohrbach, Trevor Darrell and Dan Klein

Long Paper, Runners Up
Multi-way, Multilingual Neural Machine Translation with a Shared Attention Mechanism
Orhan Firat, Kyunghyun Cho and Yoshua Bengio

Black Holes and White Rabbits: Metaphor Identification with Visual Features
Ekaterina Shutova, Douwe Kiela and Jean Maillard

The conference program includes two inspiring invited talks by Regina Barzilay and Ehud Reiter. Both push the boundaries of the field, discussing the potential for real-world impact of language technologies.

Finally we would like to thank all other people who supported us in the past year in our work for NAACL HLT 2016. Last year's program chairs, Anoop Sarkar and Joyce Chai shared their valuable advice and promptly answered the many questions we had throughout the process. The NAACL board chair for 2015 (Hal Daumé III) and 2016 (Emily Bender) were our effective link with the NAACL board. The conference general chair, Kevin Knight, was always available to us when we needed to consult about decisions we were making. The conference business manager, Priscilla Rasmussen, gave us details about the venue and coordinated with us at the final stages of making the conference schedule. The ACL treasurer, Greame Hirst, answered questions about the venue. The conference webmaster, Jason Riesa, put content on the conference webpage as soon as we made it available to him. The publication chairs, Meg Mitchell and Adam Lopez, answered all lingering author questions about formatting for submission and final versions. Many talks to all of them!

We look forward to an exciting conference!

NAACL HLT 2016 Program Co-Chairs
Ani Nenkova, University of Pennsylvania
Owen Rambow, Columbia University

Organizing Committee

General Chair
Kevin Knight, USC Information Sciences Institute

Program Co-chairs
Ani Nenkova, University of Pennsylvania
Owen Rambow, Columbia University

Workshop Co-chairs
Radu Soricut, Google
Adrià de Gispert, SDL

Local Sponsorship Chair
Julie Medero, Harvey Mudd College

Tutorial Co-chairs
Mohit Bansal, TTI Chicago
Alexander M. Rush, Harvard University

Demonstration Co-chairs
Mark Finlayson, Florida International University
Sravana Reddy, Wellesley College
John DeNero, University of California, Berkeley

Publication Co-chairs
Adam Lopez, University of Edinburgh
Margaret Mitchell, Microsoft Research

Local Arrangements Chair
Priscilla Rasmussen, ACL Business Manager

Student Research Workshop Co-chairs
Student Co-chairs
    Jacob Andreas, University of California, Berkeley
    Eunsol Choi, University of Washington
    Angeliki Lazaridou, University of Trento
Faculty Advisors
    Jacob Eisenstein, Georgia Tech
    Nianwen Xue, Brandeis University

Publicity Chair
Wei Xu, University of Pennsylvania

Social Media Chair
Jonathan May, USC Information Sciences Institute

Website Chair
Jason Riesa, Google

Student Volunteer Coordinator
Aliya Deri, USC Information Sciences Institute

Program Committee

Program Co-chairs
Ani Nenkova, University of Pennsylvania
Owen Rambow, Columbia University

Area Chairs
Mohit Bansal, TTI-Chicago
Regina Barzilay, MIT
Eduardo Blanco, University of North Texas
Asli Celikyilmaz, Microsoft
Cristian Danescu-Niculescu-Mizil, Cornell University
Markus Dreyer, Amazon
Chris Dyer, Carnegie Mellon University
Jacob Eisenstein, Georgia Institute of Technology
Micha Elsner, The Ohio State University
Eric Fosler-Lussier, The Ohio State University
Alexander Fraser, University of Munich
Michel Galley, Microsoft Research
Kevin Gimpel, Toyota Technological Institute at Chicago
Dilek Hakkani-Tür, Microsoft Research
Helen Hastie, Heriot-Watt University
Yulan He, Aston University
Dirk Hovy, University of Copenhagen
Heng Ji, Rensselaer Polytechnic Institute
Jing Jiang, Singapore Management University
Annie Louis, University of Essex
Chin-Yew Lin, Microsoft Research
Daniel Marcu, Information Sciences Institute, University of Southern California
Margaret Mitchell, Microsoft Research
Alessandro Moschitti, Qatar Computing Research Institute, HBKU
Hwee Tou Ng, National University of Singapore
Viet-An Nguyen, Facebook
Mari Ostendorf, University of Washington
Marius Pasca, Google
Slav Petrov, Google
Dan Roth, University of Illinois
Alexander Rush, Harvard University
Kenji Sagae, KITT.AI
Giorgio Satta, University of Padua
Hinrich Schuetze, LMU Munich
William Schuler, the Ohio State University
Mihai Surdeanu, University of Arizona
Kristina Toutanova, Microsoft Research
Byron Wallace, University of Texas at Austin

Xiaojun Wan, Peking University
Furu Wei, Microsoft Research
Dekai Wu, Hong Kong University of Science and Technology
Fei Xia, University of Washington

Guzmàn, Carlos Gómez-Rodríguez.

Barry Haddow, Matthias Hagen, Udo Hahn, John Hale, David Hall, Keith Hall, Xianpei Han, Sanda Harabagiu, Christian Hardmeier, Kazi Saidul Hasan, Sadid A. Hasan, Mohammed Hasanuzzaman, Hany Hassan, Hua He, He He, Yifan He, Zhongjun He, Kenneth Heafield, Michael Heilman, Karl Moritz Hermann, Ulf Hermjakob, Felix Hieber, Ryuichiro Higashinaka, Erhard Hinrichs, Tsutomu Hirao, Kai Hong, Yu Hong, Mark Hopkins, Yufang Hou, Yuening Hu, Ruihong Huang, Hen-Hsen Huang, Songfang Huang, Minlie Huang, Xuanjing Huang, Shujian Huang, Fei Huang, Hongzhao Huang, Mans Hulden, Rebecca Hwa, Seung-won Hwang.

Ryu Iida, Kenji Imamura, Abe Ittycheriah, Mohit Iyyer.

Minwoo Jeong, Rahul Jha, Yangfeng Ji, Donghong Ji, Wenbin Jiang, Hui Jiang, Anders Johannsen, Richard Johansson, Gareth Jones, Mahesh Joshi, Shafiq Joty, Dan Jurafsky, David Jurgens.

Nobuhiro Kaji, Min-Yen Kan, Dimitri Kartsaklis, David Kauchak, Daisuke Kawahara, Anna Kazantseva, Simon Keizer, Frank Keller, Casey Kennington, Mitesh M. Khapra, Douwe Kiela, Seokhwan Kim, Young-Bum Kim, Katrin Kirchhoff, Svetlana Kiritchenko, Dietrich Klakow, Alexandre Klementiev, Julien Kloetzer, Kevin Knight, Hayato Kobayashi, Philipp Koehn, Varada Kolhatkar, Mamoru Komachi, Grzegorz Kondrak, Lingpeng Kong, Fang Kong, Ioannis Konstas, Valia Kordoni, Anna Korhonen, Yannis Korkontzelos, Zornitsa Kozareva, Mikhail Kozhevnikov, Emiel Krahmer, Jayant Krishnamurthy, Marco Kuhlmann, Roland Kuhn, Shankar Kumar, Jonathan K. Kummerfeld, Sadao Kurohashi.

Siwei Lai, Wai Lam, Vasileios Lampos, Phillippe Langlais, Ni Lao, Mirella Lapata, Jey Han Lau, Angeliki Lazaridou, Joseph Le Roux, Kenton Lee, John Lee, Young-Suk Lee, Tao Lei, Johannes Leveling, Tomer Levinboim, Rivka Levitan, Omer Levy, Mike Lewis, Peifeng Li, Xiaoli Li, Junhui Li, Hang Li, Sheng Li, Yanran Li, Binyang Li, Chen Li, Fangtao Li, Junyi Jessy Li, Jiwei Li, Peng Li, Chin-Yew Lin, Chu-Cheng Lin, Wang Ling, Diane Litman, Marina Litvak, Bing Liu, Yang Liu, Shujie Liu, Kang Liu, Ting Liu, Qun Liu, Chi-kiu Lo, Adam Lopez, Wei Lu, Michal Lukasik, Xiaoqiang Luo, Minh-Thang Luong.

Yanjun Ma, Xuezhe Ma, Ji Ma, Wolfgang Macherey, Klaus Macherey, Nitin Madnani, Wolfgang Maier, Andreas Maletti, Suresh Manandhar, Christopher D. Manning, David Mareček, Benjamin Marie, Katja Markert, André F. T. Martins, Yuval Marton, Shigeki Matsubara, Mausam, Jonathan May, Diana McCarthy, David McClosky, Ryan McDonald, Kathy McKeown, Yashar Mehdad, Oren Melamud, Arul Menezes, Fandong Meng, Haitao Mi, Rada Mihalcea, Timothy Miller, Bonan Min, Einat Minkov, Margaret Mitchell, Prasenjit Mitra, Makoto Miwa, Daichi Mochihashi, Behrang Mohit, Christof Monz, Raymond Mooney, Shinsuke Mori, Véronique Moriceau, Emmanuel Morin, Hajime Morita, Lili Mou, Arjun Mukherjee, Philippe Muller, Dragos Munteanu, Yugo Murawaki, Brian Murphy.

Masaaki Nagata, Ajay Nagesh, Iftekhar Naim, Ndapandula Nakashole, Preslav Nakov, Karthik Narasimhan, Shashi Narayan, Alexis Nasr, Roberto Navigli, Mark-Jan Nederhof, Arvind Neelakantan, Matteo Negri, Graham Neubig, Vincent Ng, Raymond W. M. Ng, Jun-Ping Ng, Dominick Ng, Dong Nguyen, Thien Huu Nguyen, Garrett Nicolai, Massimo Nicosia, Vlad Niculae, Jian-Yun Nie, Hitoshi Nishikawa, Joakim Nivre, Hiroshi Noji, Joel Nothman.

Timothy O'Donnell, Stephan Oepen, Kemal Oflazer, Jong-Hoon Oh, Kiyonori Ohtake, Naoaki Okazaki, Manabu Okumura, Noam Ordan, Vicente Ordonez, Miles Osborne, Myle Ott, Cecilia Ovesdotter Alm.

Martha Palmer, Siddharth Patwardhan, Michael J. Paul, Adam Pauls, Ellie Pavlick, Gerald Penn, Marco Pennacchiotti, Nghia The Pham, Daniele Pighin, Mohammad Taher Pilehvar, Barbara Plank, Tamara Polajnar, Simone Paolo Ponzetto, Andrei Popescu-Belis, Matt Post, Christopher Potts, Vinodkumar Prabhakaran, Daniel Preoţiuc-Pietro, Emily Prud'hommeaux, Matthew Purver.

Ashequl Qadir, Behrang QasemiZadeh, Longhua Qian, Xian Qian, Lu Qin, Chris Quirk.

Will Radford, Preethi Raghavan, Altaf Rahman, Rohan Ramanath, Vivek Kumar Rangarajan Sridhar, Ari Rappoport, Mohammad Sadegh Rasooli, Marta Recasens, Sravana Reddy, Roi Reichart, Sebastian Riedel, Martin Riedl, Jason Riesa, Verena Rieser, Stefan Riezler, German Rigau, Michael Riley, Ellen Riloff, Eric Ringger, Alan Ritter, Brian Roark, Stephen Roller, Sophie Rosset, Paolo Rosso, Michael Roth, Benjamin Roth, Johann Roturier, Alla Rozovskaya, Josef Ruppenhofer.

Kugatsu Sadamitsu, Markus Saers, Kenji Sagae, Horacio Saggion, Benoît Sagot, Hassan Sajjad, Bahar Salehi, Avneesh Saluja, Ruhi Sarikaya, Anoop Sarkar, Ryohei Sasano, Asad Sayeed, Christian Scheible, Helmut Schmid, Sabine Schulte im Walde, Roy Schwartz, Wolfgang Seeker, Nina Seemann, Satoshi Sekine, Rico Sennrich, Hendra Setiawan, Izhak Shafran, Shuming Shi, Hiroyuki Shindo, Eyal Shnarch, Ekaterina Shutova, Maryam Siahbani, Carina Silberer, Khe Chai Sim, Yanchuan Sim, Khalil Sima'an, Sameer Singh, Noam Slonim, Jan Šnajder Thamar Solorio, Hyun-Je Song, Xuan Song, Radu Soricut, Aitor Soroa, Lucia Specia, Caroline Sporleder, Richard Sproat, Vivek Srikumar, Asher Stern, Mark Stevenson, Veselin Stoyanov, Carlo Strapparava, Karl Stratos, Tomek Strzalkowski, Jinsong Su, Keh-Yih Su, Amarnag Subramanya, Xu Sun, Yoshimi Suzuki, Jun Suzuki, Hisami Suzuki, Stan Szpakowicz, Anders Søgaard.

Hiroya Takamura, David Talbot, Partha Talukdar, Akihiro Tamura, Chenhao Tan, Xavier Tannier, Joel Tetreault, Kapil Thadani, Stefan Thater, Sam Thomson, Jörg Tiedemann, Ivan Titov, Tomoki Toda, Marc Tomlinson, Sara Tonelli, Kentaro Torisawa, Isabel Trancoso, Reut Tsarfaty, Yoshimasa Tsuruoka, Yulia Tsvetkov, Zhaopeng Tu, Marco Turchi, Ferhan Ture, Oscar Täckström.

Kiyotaka Uchimoto, Raghavendra Udupa, Lyle Ungar, Masao Utiyama.

Tim Van de Cruys, Lonneke van der Plas, Benjamin Van Durme, Marten van Schijndel, Lucy Vanderwende, Ashish Vaswani, Sriram Venkatapathy, David Vilar, Martin Villalba, Veronika Vincze, Andreas Vlachos, Svitlana Volkova, Clare Voss, Ivan Vulić.

Henning Wachsmuth, Marilyn Walker, Tong Wang, Xiaolin Wang, Baoxun Wang, Yiou Wang, Zhiguo Wang, Zhongqing Wang, William Yang Wang, Chang Wang, Hongning Wang, Leo Wanner, Taro Watanabe, Andy Way, Wouter Weerkamp, Zhongyu Wei, Gerhard Weikum, David Weir, Michael White, Michael Wiegand, Theresa Wilson, Shuly Wintner, Guillaume Wisniewski, Travis Wolfe, Kam-Fai Wong, Jian Wu, Hua Wu, Joern Wuebker.

Rui Xia, Bing Xiang, Min Xiao, Xinyan Xiao, Tong Xiao, Shasha Xie, Deyi Xiong, Ruifeng Xu, Wenduan Xu.

Ichiro Yamada, Elif Yamangil, Bishan Yang, Diyi Yang, Yaqin Yang, Min Yang, Wen-tau Yih, Wenpeng Yin, Dani Yogatama, Naoki Yoshinaga, Dianhai Yu, Liang-Chih Yu, Dian Yu, Mo Yu, François Yvon.

Roberto Zamparelli, Fabio Massimo Zanzotto, Klaus Zechner, Daojian Zeng, Xiaodong Zeng, Richard Zens, Torsten Zesch, Luke Zettlemoyer, Feifei Zhai, Jiajun Zhang, Wei Zhang, Min Zhang, Dongdong

Zhang, Jianwen Zhang, Congle Zhang, Yongfeng Zhang, Dongyan Zhao, Bing Zhao, Yaqian Zhou, Muhua Zhu, Imed Zitouni, Chengqing Zong, Bowei Zou, Diarmuid Ó Séaghdha, Gözde Özbal.

Best Reviewers

Yaser Al-Onaizan, Enrique Alfonseca, Daniel Andrade, Jacob Andreas, Ion Androutsopoulos, Gabor Angeli.

David Bamman, Ritmiek Banerjee, Emily Bender, Taylor Berg-Kirkpatrick, Chris Biemann, Arianna Bisazza, Graeme Blackwood, Gemma Boleda, Florian Boudin.

Jose Camacho-Collados, Marie Candito, Taylor Cassidy, Colin Cherry, Christos Christodopoulos, Alina Maria Ciobanu, Jon Clark, Trevor Cohn, Danilo Croce.

Hal Daumé III, Marie-Catherine de Marneffe, Jose G. C. de Souza, John DeNero, Jacob Devlin, Doug Downey, Gabe Doyle, Mark Dras, Greg Durrett.

Steffen Eger, Jason Eisner, Michael Elhadad.

Francis Ferraro, Mikel Forcada, James Foulds.

Matt Gardner, Dan Garrette, Yvette Graham, Dmitriy Genzel.

Barry Haddow, Matthias Hagen, David Hall, Mohammed Hasanuzzaman, Kai Hong.

Mohit Iyyer.

Yangfeng Ji, Anders Johannsen, Mahesh Joshi, Dan Jurafsky.

Dimitri Karsaklis, Daisuke Kawahara, Alexandre Klementiev, Grzegorz Kondrak, Ioannis Konstas, Yannis Korkontzelos, Roland Kuhn, Shankar Kumar, Jonathan K. Kummerfeld.

Tomer Levinboim, Rivka Levitan, Omer Levy, Junyi Jessy Li.

Klaus Macherey, Wolfgang Macherey, Wolfgang Maier, Andreas Maletti, Christopher D. Manning, Diana McCarthy, David McClosky, Lili Mou, Philippe Muller, Dragos Munteanu, Yugo Murawaki.

Masaki Nagaata, Ajay Nagesh, Mark-Jan Nederhof, Dominick Ng, Vincent Ng, Vlad Niculae, Jian-Yin Nie, Joel Nothman.

Stephan Oepen, Myle Ott.

Adam Pauls, Daniele Pighin, Andrei Popescu Belis, Matt Post, Vinod Prabhakaran, Matt Purver.

Ashequl Qadir.

Rohan Ramanath, Jason Riesa, Verena Rieser, Eric Ringger, Brian Roark, Stephen Roller, Sophie Rosset.

Wolfgang Seeker, Thamar Solorio, Vivek Kumar Rangarajan Sridhar, Vivek Srikumar, Jun Suzuki.

Akihiro Tamura, Joel Tetreault, Kapil Thadani, Ivan Titov, Marco Turchi.

Raghavendra Udupa.

Clare Voss, Ivan Vulic.

Henning Wachsmuth, Marilyn Walker, Taro Watanabe, Wouter Weerkamp, Michael Wiegand.

Min Yang.

Invited Talk: How can NLP help cure cancer?

Regina Barzilay

Massachusetts Institute of Technology

Abstract

Cancer inflicts a heavy toll on our society. One out of seven women will be diagnosed with breast cancer during their lifetime, a fraction of them contributing to about 450,000 deaths annually worldwide. Despite billions of dollars invested in cancer research, our understanding of the disease, treatment, and prevention is still limited.

Majority of cancer research today takes place in biology and medicine. Computer science plays a minor supporting role in this process if at all. In this talk, I hope to convince you that NLP as a field has a chance to play a significant role in this battle. Indeed, free-form text remains the primary means by which physicians record their observations and clinical findings. Unfortunately, this rich source of textual information is severely underutilized by predictive models in oncology. Current models rely primarily only on structured data.

In the first part of my talk, I will describe a number of tasks where NLP-based models can make a difference in clinical practice. For example, these include improving models of disease progression, preventing over-treatment, and narrowing down to the cure. This part of the talk draws on active collaborations with oncologists from Massachusetts General Hospital (MGH).

In the second part of the talk, I will push beyond standard tools, introducing new functionalities and avoiding annotation-hungry training paradigms ill-suited for clinical practice. In particular, I will focus on interpretable neural models that provide rationales underlying their predictions, and semi-supervised methods for information extraction.

Biography

Regina Barzilay is a professor in the Department of Electrical Engineering and Computer Science and a member of the Computer Science and Artificial Intelligence Laboratory at the Massachusetts Institute of Technology. Her research interests are in natural language processing. She is a recipient of various awards including of the NSF Career Award, the MIT Technology Review TR-35 Award, Microsoft Faculty Fellowship and several Best Paper Awards at NAACL and ACL. She received her Ph.D. in Computer Science from Columbia University, and spent a year as a postdoc at Cornell University.

Invited Talk: Evaluating Natural Language Generation Systems

Ehud Reitter

University of Aberdeen and Arria NLG

Abstract

Natural Language Generation (NLG) systems have different characteristics than other NLP systems, which effects how they are evaluated. In particular, it can be difficult to meaningfully evaluate NLG texts by comparing them against gold- standard reference texts, because (A) there are usually many possible texts which are acceptable to users and (B) some NLG systems produce texts which are better (as judged by human users) than human-written corpus texts. Partially because of these reasons, the NLG community places much more emphasis on human-based evaluations than most areas of NLP.

I will discuss the various ways in which NLG systems are evaluated, focusing on human-based evaluations. These typically either measure the success of generated texts at achieving a goal (eg, measuring how many people change their behaviour after reading behaviour-change texts produced by an NLG system); or ask human subjects to rate various aspects of generated texts (such as readability, accuracy, and appropriateness), often on Likert scales. I will use examples from evaluations I have carried out, and highlight some of the lessons I have learnt, including the importance of reporting negative results, the difference between laboratory and real-world evaluations, and the need to look at worse-case as well as average-case performance. I hope my talk will be interesting and relevant to anyone who is interested in the evaluation of NLP systems.

Biography

Ehud Reiter is a Professor of Computing Science at the University of Aberdeen and also Chief Scientist of Arria NLG. He has worked on natural language generation for the past 30 years, on methodology (including evaluation) and resources as well as algorithms, and is one of the most cited authors in NLG. His 2000 book Building Natural Language Generation Systems is widely used as an NLG textbook. Dr Reiter currently spends most of his time trying to commercialise NLG at Arria (one of the largest specialist NLG companies), which grew out of a startup he cofounded in 2009.

Table of Contents

"

xxix

Conference Program

Sunday, June 12, 2016

18:00–21:00 *Welcome reception, Pavilion*

Monday, June 13, 2016

7:30–8:45 *Breakfast, Pavilion*

9:00–9:15 *Welcome, Grande Ballroom*
Kevin Knight, Ani Nenkova, Owen Rambow

9:15–10:30 *Invited talk: "How can NLP help cure cancer?"*
Regina Barzilay

10:30–11:00 *Coffee break, Pavilion*

11:00–12:30 *Session 1*

1A. Machine translation

11:00–11:20 *Achieving Accurate Conclusions in Evaluation of Automatic Machine Translation Metrics*
Yvette Graham and Qun Liu

11:20–11:40 *Flexible Non-Terminals for Dependency Tree-to-Tree Reordering*
John Richardson, Fabien Cromierès, Toshiaki Nakazawa and Sadao Kurohashi

11:40–12:00 *Selecting Syntactic, Non-redundant Segments in Active Learning for Machine Translation*
Akiva Miura, Graham Neubig, Michael Paul and Satoshi Nakamura

12:00–12:10 *Multi-Source Neural Translation*
Barret Zoph and Kevin Knight

12:10–12:20 *Controlling Politeness in Neural Machine Translation via Side Constraints*
Rico Sennrich, Barry Haddow and Alexandra Birch

12:20–12:30 *An Empirical Evaluation of Noise Contrastive Estimation for the Neural Network Joint Model of Translation*
Colin Cherry

1B. Summarization

11:00–11:20 *Neural Network-Based Abstract Generation for Opinions and Arguments*
Lu Wang and Wang Ling

11:20–11:40 *A Low-Rank Approximation Approach to Learning Joint Embeddings of News Stories and Images for Timeline Summarization*
William Yang Wang, Yashar Mehdad, Dragomir R. Radev and Amanda Stent

11:40–12:00 *Entity-balanced Gaussian pLSA for Automated Comparison*
Danish Contractor, Parag Singla and Mausam

12:00–12:10 *Automatic Summarization of Student Course Feedback*
Wencan Luo, Fei Liu, Zitao Liu and Diane Litman

12:10–12:20 *Knowledge-Guided Linguistic Rewrites for Inference Rule Verification*
Prachi Jain and Mausam

12:20–12:30 *Abstractive Sentence Summarization with Attentive Recurrent Neural Networks*
Sumit Chopra, Michael Auli and Alexander M. Rush

1C. Dialog

11:00–11:20 *Integer Linear Programming for Discourse Parsing*
Jérémy Perret, Stergos Afantenos, Nicholas Asher and Mathieu Morey

11:20–11:40 *A Diversity-Promoting Objective Function for Neural Conversation Models*
Jiwei Li, Michel Galley, Chris Brockett, Jianfeng Gao and Bill Dolan

11:40–12:00 *Multi-domain Neural Network Language Generation for Spoken Dialogue Systems*
Tsung-Hsien Wen, Milica Gašić, Nikola Mrkšić, Lina M. Rojas-Barahona, Pei-Hao Su, David Vandyke and Steve Young

12:00–12:10 *A Long Short-Term Memory Framework for Predicting Humor in Dialogues*
Dario Bertero and Pascale Fung

12:10–12:20   *Conversational Flow in Oxford-style Debates*
Justine Zhang, Ravi Kumar, Sujith Ravi and Cristian Danescu-Niculescu-Mizil

12:20–12:30   *Counter-fitting Word Vectors to Linguistic Constraints*
Nikola Mrkšić, Diarmuid Ó Séaghdha, Blaise Thomson, Milica Gašić, Lina M.
Rojas-Barahona, Pei-Hao Su, David Vandyke, Tsung-Hsien Wen and Steve Young

12:30–2:00   Lunch break

2:00–3:30   Session 2

2A. Language and Vision

2:00–2:20   *Grounded Semantic Role Labeling*
Shaohua Yang, Qiaozi Gao, Changsong Liu, Caiming Xiong, Song-Chun Zhu and
Joyce Y. Chai

2:20–2:40   *Black Holes and White Rabbits: Metaphor Identification with Visual Features*
Ekaterina Shutova, Douwe Kiela and Jean Maillard

2:40–3:00   *Bridge Correlational Neural Networks for Multilingual Multimodal Representation
Learning*
Janarthanan Rajendran, Mitesh M. Khapra, Sarath Chandar and Balaraman Ravin-
dran

3:00–3:20   *Unsupervised Visual Sense Disambiguation for Verbs using Multimodal Embeddings*
Spandana Gella, Mirella Lapata and Frank Keller

3:20–3:30   *Stating the Obvious: Extracting Visual Common Sense Knowledge*
Mark Yatskar, Vicente Ordonez and Ali Farhadi

2B. Parsing

2:00–2:20   *Efficient Structured Inference for Transition-Based Parsing with Neural Networks and Error States [TACL]*
Ashish Vaswani and Kenji Sagae

2:20–2:40   *Recurrent Neural Network Grammars*
Chris Dyer, Adhiguna Kuncoro, Miguel Ballesteros and Noah A. Smith

2:40–3:00   *Expected F-Measure Training for Shift-Reduce Parsing with Recurrent Neural Networks*
Wenduan Xu, Michael Auli and Stephen Clark

3:00–3:20   *LSTM CCG Parsing*
Mike Lewis, Kenton Lee and Luke Zettlemoyer

3:20–3:30   *Supertagging With LSTMs*
Ashish Vaswani, Yonatan Bisk, Kenji Sagae and Ryan Musa

2C. Named Entity Recognition

2:00–2:20   *An Empirical Study of Automatic Chinese Word Segmentation for Spoken Language Understanding and Named Entity Recognition*
Wencan Luo and Fan Yang

2:20–2:40   *Name Tagging for Low-resource Incident Languages based on Expectation-driven Learning*
Boliang Zhang, Xiaoman Pan, Tianlu Wang, Ashish Vaswani, Heng Ji, Kevin Knight and Daniel Marcu

2:40–3:00   *Neural Architectures for Named Entity Recognition*
Guillaume Lample, Miguel Ballesteros, Sandeep Subramanian, Kazuya Kawakami and Chris Dyer

3:00–3:20   *Dynamic Feature Induction: The Last Gist to the State-of-the-Art*
Jinho D. Choi

3:20–3:30   *Drop-out Conditional Random Fields for Twitter with Huge Mined Gazetteer*
Eunsuk Yang, Young-Bum Kim, Ruhi Sarikaya and Yu-Seop Kim

3:30–4:00   ***Coffee break, Pavilion***

4:00–5:00   *Session 3*

3A. Event detection

4:00–4:20   *Joint Extraction of Events and Entities within a Document Context*
Bishan Yang and Tom M. Mitchell

4:20–4:40   *A Hierarchical Distance-dependent Bayesian Model for Event Coreference Resolution [TACL]*
Bishan Yang, Claire Cardie, and Peter Frazier

4:40–5:00   *Joint Event Extraction via Recurrent Neural Networks*
Thien Huu Nguyen, Kyunghyun Cho and Ralph Grishman

3B. Language Models

4:00–4:20   *Top-down Tree Long Short-Term Memory Networks*
Xingxing Zhang, Liang Lu and Mirella Lapata

4:20–4:40   *Recurrent Memory Networks for Language Modeling*
Ke Tran, Arianna Bisazza and Christof Monz

4:40–5:00   *A Latent Variable Recurrent Neural Network for Discourse-Driven Language Models*
Yangfeng Ji, Gholamreza Haffari and Jacob Eisenstein

3C. Non Literal Language

4:00–4:20   *Questioning Arbitrariness in Language: a Data-Driven Study of Conventional Iconicity*
Ekaterina Abramova and Raquel Fernández

4:20–4:40   *Distinguishing Literal and Non-Literal Usage of German Particle Verbs*
Maximilian Köper and Sabine Schulte im Walde

4:40–5:00   *Phrasal Substitution of Idiomatic Expressions*
Changsheng Liu and Rebecca Hwa

5:00–5:15   ***Break***

5:15–6:00   ***One Minute Madness***

6:00–8:00   ***Posters and Dinner***

Posters

Leverage Financial News to Predict Stock Price Movements Using Word Embeddings and Deep Neural Networks
Yangtuo Peng and Hui Jiang

Grammatical error correction using neural machine translation
Zheng Yuan and Ted Briscoe

Multimodal Semantic Learning from Child-Directed Input
Angeliki Lazaridou, Grzegorz Chrupała, Raquel Fernández and Marco Baroni

Recurrent Support Vector Machines For Slot Tagging In Spoken Language Understanding
Yangyang Shi, Kaisheng Yao, Hu Chen, Dong Yu, Yi-Cheng Pan and Mei-Yuh Hwang

Expectation-Regulated Neural Model for Event Mention Extraction
Ching-Yun Chang, Zhiyang Teng and Yue Zhang

Cross-lingual Wikification Using Multilingual Embeddings
Chen-Tse Tsai and Dan Roth

Deconstructing Complex Search Tasks: a Bayesian Nonparametric Approach for Extracting Sub-tasks
Rishabh Mehrotra, Prasanta Bhattacharya and Emine Yilmaz

6:00–8:00   ***System Demonstrations***

rstWeb - A Browser-based Annotation Interface for Rhetorical Structure Theory and Discourse Relations
Amir Zeldes

Instant Feedback for Increasing the Presence of Solutions in Peer Reviews
Huy Nguyen, Wenting Xiong and Diane Litman

Farasa: A Fast and Furious Segmenter for Arabic
Ahmed Abdelali, Kareem Darwish, Nadir Durrani and Hamdy Mubarak

iAppraise: A Manual Machine Translation Evaluation Environment Supporting Eye-tracking
Ahmed Abdelali, Nadir Durrani and Francisco Guzmán

Linguistica 5: Unsupervised Learning of Linguistic Structure
Jackson Lee and John Goldsmith

TransRead: Designing a Bilingual Reading Experience with Machine Translation Technologies
François Yvon, Yong Xu, Marianna Apidianaki, Clément Pillias and Pierre Cubaud

New Dimensions in Testimony Demonstration
Ron Artstein, Alesia Gainer, Kallirroi Georgila, Anton Leuski, Ari Shapiro and David Traum

ArgRewrite: A Web-based Revision Assistant for Argumentative Writings
Fan Zhang, Rebecca Hwa, Diane Litman and Homa B. Hashemi

Scaling Up Word Clustering
Jon Dehdari, Liling Tan and Josef van Genabith

Task Completion Platform
A self-serve multi-domain goal oriented dialogue platform: Paul Crook, Alex Marin, Vipul Agarwal, Khushboo Aggarwal, Tasos Anastasakos, Ravi Bikkula, Daniel Boies, Asli Celikyilmaz, Senthilkumar Chandramohan, Zhaleh Feizollahi, Roman Holenstein, Minwoo Jeong, Omar Khan, Young-Bum Kim, Elizabeth Krawczyk, Xiaohu Liu, Danko Panic, Vasiliy Radostev, Nikhil Ramesh, Jean-Phillipe Robichaud, Alexandre Rochette, Logan Stromberg and Ruhi Sarikaya

Student Workshop Posters

An End-to-end Approach to Learning Semantic Frames with Feedforward Neural Network
Yukun Feng, Yipei Xu and Dong Yu

Analogy-based detection of morphological and semantic relations with word embeddings
what works and what doesn't: Anna Gladkova, Aleksandr Drozd and Satoshi Matsuoka

Argument Identification in Chinese Editorials
Marisa Chow

Automatic tagging and retrieval of E-Commerce products based on visual features
Vasu Sharma and Harish Karnick

Combining syntactic patterns and Wikipedia's hierarchy of hyperlinks to extract relations: The case of meronymy extraction
Debela Tesfaye Gemechu, Michael Zock and Solomon Teferra

Cross-Lingual Question Answering Using Profile HMM & Unified Semantic Space
Amir Pouran Ben Veyseh

Data-driven Paraphrasing and Stylistic Harmonization
Gerold Hintz

Detecting "Smart" Spammers on Social Network
A Topic Model Approach: Linqing Liu, Yao Lu, Ye Luo, Renxian Zhang, Laurent Itti and Jianwei Lu

Developing language technology tools and resources for a resource-poor language: Sindhi
Raveesh Motlani

Tuesday, June 14, 2016

7:30–8:45   *Breakfast, Pavilion*

9:00–10:30   *Session 4*

4A. Semantic Parsing

9:00–9:20   *Transforming Dependency Structures to Logical Forms for Semantic Parsing [TACL]*
Siva Reddy, Oscar Täckström, Michael Collins, Tom Kwiatkowski, Dipanjan Das, Mark Steedman, and Mirella Lapata

9:20–9:40   *Imitation Learning of Agenda-based Semantic Parsers [TACL]*
Jonathan Berant and Percy Liang

9:40–10:00   *Probabilistic Models for Learning a Semantic Parser Lexicon*
Jayant Krishnamurthy

10:00–10:20   *Semantic Parsing of Ambiguous Input through Paraphrasing and Verification [TACL]*
Philip Arthur, Graham Neubig, Sakriani Sakti, Tomoki Toda, and Satoshi Nakamura

10:20–10:30   *Unsupervised Compound Splitting With Distributional Semantics Rivals Supervised Methods*
Martin Riedl and Chris Biemann

4B. Morphology and Phonology

9:00–9:20   *Weighting Finite-State Transductions With Neural Context*
Pushpendre Rastogi, Ryan Cotterell and Jason Eisner

9:20–9:40   *Morphological Inflection Generation Using Character Sequence to Sequence Learning*
Manaal Faruqui, Yulia Tsvetkov, Graham Neubig and Chris Dyer

9:40–10:00   *Towards Unsupervised and Language-independent Compound Splitting using Inflectional Morphological Transformations*
Patrick Ziering and Lonneke van der Plas

10:00–10:20   *Phonological Pun-derstanding*
Aaron Jaech, Rik Koncel-Kedziorski and Mari Ostendorf

10:20–10:30   *A Joint Model of Orthography and Morphological Segmentation*
Ryan Cotterell, Tim Vieira and Hinrich Schütze

4C. Various

9:00–9:20   *Syntactic Parsing of Web Queries with Question Intent*
Yuval Pinter, Roi Reichart and Idan Szpektor

9:20–9:40   *Visualizing and Understanding Neural Models in NLP*
Jiwei Li, Xinlei Chen, Eduard Hovy and Dan Jurafsky

9:40–10:00   *Bilingual Word Embeddings from Parallel and Non-parallel Corpora for Cross-Language Text Classification*
Aditya Mogadala and Achim Rettinger

10:00–10:20   *Joint Learning with Global Inference for Comment Classification in Community Question Answering*
Shafiq Joty, Lluís Màrquez and Preslav Nakov

10:20–10:30   *Weak Semi-Markov CRFs for Noun Phrase Chunking in Informal Text*
Aldrian Obaja Muis and Wei Lu

10:30–11:00   *Coffee break, Pavilion*

11:00–12:30   *Session 5*

5A. Generation

11:00–11:20   *What to talk about and how? Selective Generation using LSTMs with Coarse-to-Fine Alignment*
Hongyuan Mei, Mohit Bansal and Matthew R. Walter

11:20–11:40   *Generation from Abstract Meaning Representation using Tree Transducers*
Jeffrey Flanigan, Chris Dyer, Noah A. Smith and Jaime Carbonell

11:40–12:00   *A Corpus and Semantic Parser for Multilingual Natural Language Querying of OpenStreetMap*
Carolin Haas and Stefan Riezler

12:00–12:20   *Natural Language Communication with Robots*
Yonatan Bisk, Deniz Yuret and Daniel Marcu

12:20–12:30   *Inter-document Contextual Language model*
Quan Hung Tran, Ingrid Zukerman and Gholamreza Haffari

5B. Sentiment

11:00–11:20   *Ultradense Word Embeddings by Orthogonal Transformation*
Sascha Rothe, Sebastian Ebert and Hinrich Schütze

11:20–11:40   *Separating Actor-View from Speaker-View Opinion Expressions using Linguistic Features*
Michael Wiegand, Marc Schulder and Josef Ruppenhofer

11:40–12:00   *Clustering for Simultaneous Extraction of Aspects and Features from Reviews*
Lu Chen, Justin Martineau, Doreen Cheng and Amit Sheth

12:00–12:20   *Opinion Holder and Target Extraction on Opinion Compounds – A Linguistic Approach*
Michael Wiegand, Christine Bocionek and Josef Ruppenhofer

12:20–12:30   *Capturing Reliable Fine-Grained Sentiment Associations by Crowdsourcing and Best–Worst Scaling*
Svetlana Kiritchenko and Saif M. Mohammad

5C. Knowledge Acquisition

11:00–11:20   *Concept Grounding to Multiple Knowledge Bases via Indirect Supervision [TACL]*
Chen-Tse Tsai and Dan Roth

11:20–11:40   *Mapping Verbs in Different Languages to Knowledge Base Relations using Web Text as Interlingua*
Derry Tanti Wijaya and Tom M. Mitchell

11:40–12:00   *Comparing Convolutional Neural Networks to Traditional Models for Slot Filling*
Heike Adel, Benjamin Roth and Hinrich Schütze

12:00–12:20   *A Corpus and Cloze Evaluation for Deeper Understanding of Commonsense Stories*
Nasrin Mostafazadeh, Nathanael Chambers, Xiaodong He, Devi Parikh, Dhruv Batra, Lucy Vanderwende, Pushmeet Kohli and James Allen

12:20–12:30   *Dynamic Entity Representation with Max-pooling Improves Machine Reading*
Sosuke Kobayashi, Ran Tian, Naoaki Okazaki and Kentaro Inui

12:30–1:15   *Lunch*

1:15–2:15   *Panel Discussion: How Will Deep Learning Change Computational Linguistics?*

2:30–3:30   *Session 6*

6A. Machine Translation II

2:30–2:50   *Speed-Constrained Tuning for Statistical Machine Translation Using Bayesian Optimization*
Daniel Beck, Adrià de Gispert, Gonzalo Iglesias, Aurelien Waite and Bill Byrne

2:50–3:10   *Multi-Way, Multilingual Neural Machine Translation with a Shared Attention Mechanism*
Orhan Firat, Kyunghyun Cho and Yoshua Bengio

3:10–3:30   *Incorporating Structural Alignment Biases into an Attentional Neural Translation Model*
Trevor Cohn, Cong Duy Vu Hoang, Ekaterina Vymolova, Kaisheng Yao, Chris Dyer and Gholamreza Haffari

6B. Relation Extraction

2:30–2:50   *Multilingual Relation Extraction using Compositional Universal Schema*
Patrick Verga, David Belanger, Emma Strubell, Benjamin Roth and Andrew McCallum

2:50–3:10   *Effective Crowd Annotation for Relation Extraction*
Angli Liu, Stephen Soderland, Jonathan Bragg, Christopher H. Lin, Xiao Ling and Daniel S. Weld

3:10–3:30   *A Translation-Based Knowledge Graph Embedding Preserving Logical Property of Relations*
Hee-Geun Yoon, Hyun-Je Song, Seong-Bae Park and Se-Young Park

6C. Semantic Similarity

2:30–2:50   *DAG-Structured Long Short-Term Memory for Semantic Compositionality*
Xiaodan Zhu, Parinaz Sobhani and Hongyu Guo

2:50–3:10   *Bayesian Supervised Domain Adaptation for Short Text Similarity*
Md Arafat Sultan, Jordan Boyd-Graber and Tamara Sumner

3:10–3:30   *Pairwise Word Interaction Modeling with Deep Neural Networks for Semantic Similarity Measurement*
Hua He and Jimmy Lin

3:30–4:00   ***Break***

4:00–5:00 *Session 7*

7A. Machine Translation III

4:00–4:20 *An Attentional Model for Speech Translation Without Transcription*
Long Duong, Antonios Anastasopoulos, David Chiang, Steven Bird and Trevor
Cohn

4:20–4:40 *Information Density and Quality Estimation Features as Translationese Indicators*
for Human Translation Classification
Raphael Rubino, Ekaterina Lapshinova-Koltunski and Josef van Genabith

4:40–4:50 *Interpretese vs. Translationese: The Uniqueness of Human Strategies in Simultane-*
ous Interpretation
He He, Jordan Boyd-Graber and Hal Daumé III

4:50–5:00 *LSTM Neural Reordering Feature for Statistical Machine Translation*
Yiming Cui, Shijin Wang and Jianfeng Li

7B. Anaphora Resolution

4:00–4:20 *A Novel Approach to Dropped Pronoun Translation*
Longyue Wang, Zhaopeng Tu, Xiaojun Zhang, Hang Li, Andy Way and Qun Liu

4:20–4:40 *Learning Global Features for Coreference Resolution*
Sam Wiseman, Alexander M. Rush and Stuart M. Shieber

4:40–4:50 *Search Space Pruning: A Simple Solution for Better Coreference Resolvers*
Nafise Sadat Moosavi and Michael Strube

4:50–5:00 *Unsupervised Ranking Model for Entity Coreference Resolution*
Xuezhe Ma, Zhengzhong Liu and Eduard Hovy

7C. Word Embeddings I

4:00–4:20   *Embedding Lexical Features via Low-Rank Tensors*
Mo Yu, Mark Dredze, Raman Arora and Matthew R. Gormley

4:20–4:40   *The Role of Context Types and Dimensionality in Learning Word Embeddings*
Oren Melamud, David McClosky, Siddharth Patwardhan and Mohit Bansal

4:40–5:00   *Improve Chinese Word Embeddings by Exploiting Internal Structure*
Jian Xu, Jiawei Liu, Liangang Zhang, Zhengyu Li and Huanhuan Chen

5:00–5:15   ***Break***

5:15–6:00   ***One-Minute Madness***

6:00–8:00   ***Posters, Demos, and Snacks***

Posters

Assessing Relative Sentence Complexity using an Incremental CCG Parser
Bharat Ram Ambati, Siva Reddy and Mark Steedman

Frustratingly Easy Cross-Lingual Transfer for Transition-Based Dependency Parsing
Ophélie Lacroix, Lauriane Aufrant, Guillaume Wisniewski and François Yvon

Geolocation for Twitter: Timing Matters
Mark Dredze, Miles Osborne and Prabhanjan Kambadur

Fast and Easy Short Answer Grading with High Accuracy
Md Arafat Sultan, Cristobal Salazar and Tamara Sumner

Interlocking Phrases in Phrase-based Statistical Machine Translation
Ye Kyaw Thu, Andrew Finch and Eiichiro Sumita

Eyes Don't Lie: Predicting Machine Translation Quality Using Eye Movement
Hassan Sajjad, Francisco Guzmán, Nadir Durrani, Ahmed Abdelali, Houda Bouamor, Irina Temnikova and Stephan Vogel

Making Dependency Labeling Simple, Fast and Accurate
Tianxiao Shen, Tao Lei and Regina Barzilay

Deep Lexical Segmentation and Syntactic Parsing in the Easy-First Dependency Framework
Matthieu Constant, Joseph Le Roux and Nadi Tomeh

Sentiment Composition of Words with Opposing Polarities
Svetlana Kiritchenko and Saif M. Mohammad

Learning to Recognize Ancillary Information for Automatic Paraphrase Identification
Simone Filice and Alessandro Moschitti

Learning a POS tagger for AAVE-like language
Anna Jørgensen, Dirk Hovy and Anders Søgaard

PIC a Different Word: A Simple Model for Lexical Substitution in Context
Stephen Roller and Katrin Erk

Bootstrapping Translation Detection and Sentence Extraction from Comparable Corpora
Kriste Krstovski and David Smith

Discriminative Reranking for Grammatical Error Correction with Statistical Machine Translation
Tomoya Mizumoto and Yuji Matsumoto

Patterns of Wisdom: Discourse-Level Style in Multi-Sentence Quotations
Kyle Booten and Marti A. Hearst

Right-truncatable Neural Word Embeddings
Jun Suzuki and Masaaki Nagata

MAWPS: A Math Word Problem Repository
Rik Koncel-Kedziorski, Subhro Roy, Aida Amini, Nate Kushman and Hannaneh Hajishirzi

Cross-genre Event Extraction with Knowledge Enrichment
Hao Li and Heng Ji

Student Workshop Posters

Effects of Communicative Pressures on Novice L2 Learners' Use of Optional Formal Devices
Yoav Binoun

Explicit Argument Identification for Discourse Parsing In Hindi: A Hybrid Pipeline
Rohit Jain and Dipti Sharma

Exploring Fine-Grained Emotion Detection in Tweets
Jasy Suet Yan Liew and Howard Turtle

Extraction of Bilingual Technical Terms for Chinese-Japanese Patent Translation
Wei Yang, Jinghui Yan and Yves Lepage

Hateful Symbols or Hateful People? Predictive Features for Hate Speech Detection on Twitter
Zeerak Waseem and Dirk Hovy

Non-decreasing Sub-modular Function for Comprehensible Summarization
Litton JKurisinkel, Pruthwik Mishra, Vigneshwaran Muralidaran, Vasudeva Varma and Dipti Misra Sharma

Phylogenetic simulations over constraint-based grammar formalisms
Andrew Lamont and Jonathan Washington

Question Answering over Knowledge Base using Weakly Supervised Memory Networks
Sarthak Jain

Using Related Languages to Enhance Statistical Language Models
Anna Currey, Alina Karakanta and Jon Dehdari

8:00–10:00   *Bayview Lawn Beach Social*

Wednesday, June 15, 2016

7:30–8:45   *Breakfast, Pavilion*

9:00–10:15   *Invited talk: "Human-based evaluations of language generation systems"*
Ehud Reiter

10:15–10:45   *Coffee break, Pavilion*

10:45–12:15   *Session 8*

8A. Question Answering

10:45–11:05   *A Joint Model for Answer Sentence Ranking and Answer Extraction [TACL]*
Md Arafat Sultan, Vittorio Castelli, and Radu Florian

11:05–11:25   *Convolutional Neural Networks vs. Convolution Kernels: Feature Engineering for Answer Sentence Reranking*
Kateryna Tymoshenko, Daniele Bonadiman and Alessandro Moschitti

11:25–11:45   *Semi-supervised Question Retrieval with Gated Convolutions*
Tao Lei, Hrishikesh Joshi, Regina Barzilay, Tommi Jaakkola, Kateryna Tymoshenko, Alessandro Moschitti and Lluís Màrquez

11:45–12:05   *Parsing Algebraic Word Problems into Equations [TACL]*
Rik Koncel-Kedziorski, Hannaneh Hajishirzi, Ashish Sabharwal, Oren Etzioni, and Siena Dumas Ang

12:05–12:15   *This is how we do it: Answer Reranking for Open-domain How Questions with Paragraph Vectors and Minimal Feature Engineering*
Dasha Bogdanova and Jennifer Foster

8B. Multilingual Processing

10:45–11:05   *Multilingual Language Processing From Bytes*
Dan Gillick, Cliff Brunk, Oriol Vinyals and Amarnag Subramanya

11:05–11:25   *Ten Pairs to Tag – Multilingual POS Tagging via Coarse Mapping between Embeddings*
Yuan Zhang, David Gaddy, Regina Barzilay and Tommi Jaakkola

11:25–11:45   *Part-of-Speech Tagging for Historical English*
Yi Yang and Jacob Eisenstein

11:45–12:05   *Statistical Modeling of Creole Genesis*
Yugo Murawaki

12:05–12:15   *Shallow Parsing Pipeline - Hindi-English Code-Mixed Social Media Text*
Arnav Sharma, Sakshi Gupta, Raveesh Motlani, Piyush Bansal, Manish Shrivastava, Radhika Mamidi and Dipti M. Sharma

8C. Word Embeddings II

10:45–11:05   *Bilingual Learning of Multi-sense Embeddings with Discrete Autoencoders*
Simon Šuster, Ivan Titov and Gertjan van Noord

11:05–11:25   *Polyglot Neural Language Models: A Case Study in Cross-Lingual Phonetic Representation Learning*
Yulia Tsvetkov, Sunayana Sitaram, Manaal Faruqui, Guillaume Lample, Patrick Littell, David Mortensen, Alan W Black, Lori Levin and Chris Dyer

11:25–11:45   *Learning Distributed Representations of Sentences from Unlabelled Data*
Felix Hill, Kyunghyun Cho and Anna Korhonen

11:45–12:05   *Learning to Understand Phrases by Embedding the Dictionary [TACL]*
Felix Hill, KyungHyun Cho, Anna Korhonen, and Yoshua Bengio

12:05–12:15   *Retrofitting Sense-Specific Word Vectors Using Parallel Text*
Allyson Ettinger, Philip Resnik and Marine Carpuat

12:15–1:00   ***Lunch***

1:00–2:00   *NAACL business meeting, Grande Ballroom A*

2:15–3:45   *Session 9*

9A. Argumentation and Discourse

2:15–2:35   *End-to-End Argumentation Mining in Student Essays*
Isaac Persing and Vincent Ng

2:35–2:55   *Cross-Domain Mining of Argumentative Text through Distant Supervision*
Khalid Al-Khatib, Henning Wachsmuth, Matthias Hagen, Jonas Köhler and Benno Stein

2:55–3:15   *A Study of the Impact of Persuasive Argumentation in Political Debates*
Amparo Elizabeth Cano-Basave and Yulan He

3:15–3:35   *Lexical Coherence Graph Modeling Using Word Embeddings*
Mohsen Mesgar and Michael Strube

3:35–3:45   *Using Context to Predict the Purpose of Argumentative Writing Revisions*
Fan Zhang and Diane Litman

9B. Misc Semantics

2:15–2:35   *Automatic Generation and Scoring of Positive Interpretations from Negated Statements*
Eduardo Blanco and Zahra Sarabi

2:35–2:55   *Learning Natural Language Inference with LSTM*
Shuohang Wang and Jing Jiang

2:55–3:15   *Activity Modeling in Email*
Ashequl Qadir, Michael Gamon, Patrick Pantel and Ahmed Hassan Awadallah

3:15–3:35   *Clustering Paraphrases by Word Sense*
Anne Cocos and Chris Callison-Burch

3:35–3:45   *Unsupervised Learning of Prototypical Fillers for Implicit Semantic Role Labeling*
Niko Schenk and Christian Chiarcos

9C. Text Categorization

2:15–2:35   *Hierarchical Attention Networks for Document Classification*
Zichao Yang, Diyi Yang, Chris Dyer, Xiaodong He, Alex Smola and Eduard Hovy

2:35–2:55   *Dependency Based Embeddings for Sentence Classification Tasks*
Alexandros Komninos and Suresh Manandhar

2:55–3:15   *Deep LSTM based Feature Mapping for Query Classification*
Yangyang Shi, Kaisheng Yao, Le Tian and Daxin Jiang

3:15–3:35   *Dependency Sensitive Convolutional Neural Networks for Modeling Sentences and Documents*
Rui Zhang, Honglak Lee and Dragomir R. Radev

3:35–3:45   *MGNC-CNN: A Simple Approach to Exploiting Multiple Word Embeddings for Sentence Classification*
Ye Zhang, Stephen Roller and Byron C. Wallace

3:45–4:15   ***Coffee break, Pavilion***

4:15–5:45   ***Best paper awards***

4:15–4:35   *Improving sentence compression by learning to predict gaze*
Sigrid Klerke, Yoav Goldberg and Anders Søgaard

4:35–5:05   *Feuding Families and Former Friends: Unsupervised Learning for Dynamic Fictional Relationships*
Mohit Iyyer, Anupam Guha, Snigdha Chaturvedi, Jordan Boyd-Graber and Hal Daumé III

5:05–5:35   *Learning to Compose Neural Networks for Question Answering*
Jacob Andreas, Marcus Rohrbach, Trevor Darrell and Dan Klein

5:35–5:45   ***Closing remarks***

Separating Actor-View from Speaker-View Opinion Expressions using Linguistic Features

Michael Wiegand and **Marc Schulder**
Spoken Language Systems
Saarland University
D-66123 Saarbrücken, Germany
michael.wiegand@lsv.uni-saarland.de
marc.schulder@lsv.uni-saarland.de

Josef Ruppenhofer
Dept. of Information Science
and Language Technology
Hildesheim University
D-31141 Hildesheim, Germany
ruppenho@uni-hildesheim.de

Abstract

We examine different features and classifiers for the categorization of opinion words into actor and speaker view. To our knowledge, this is the first comprehensive work to address sentiment views on the word level taking into consideration opinion verbs, nouns and adjectives. We consider many high-level features requiring only few labeled training data. A detailed feature analysis produces linguistic insights into the nature of sentiment views. We also examine how far global constraints between different opinion words help to increase classification performance. Finally, we show that our (prior) word-level annotation correlates with contextual sentiment views.

1 Introduction

While there has been much research in sentiment analysis on the tasks of subjectivity detection and polarity classification, there has been less work on other types of categorizations that can be imposed upon subjective expressions.

In this paper, we focus on the *views* that an opinion expression evokes. By views, we understand the perspective of the holder of some opinion. We distinguish between the two most common types: expressions conveying sentiment of the entities participating in the event denoted by the opinion word, referred to as **actor views** (e.g. *disappointed* in (1) or *praised* in (2)), and expressions conveying sentiment of the speaker of the utterance, referred to as **speaker views** (e.g. *excelled* in (3) or *wasted* in (4)).

(1) Party members were **disappointed**$_{actor}$ at the election outcome.

(2) All representatives **praised**$_{actor}$ the final agreement.

(3) Sarah **excelled**$_{speaker}$ in virtually every subject.

(4) The government **wasted**$_{speaker}$ a lot of money.

The distinction between those categories is relevant for related tasks in sentiment analysis, most importantly, opinion holder and target extraction. This has already been demonstrated for verbs (Wiegand and Ruppenhofer, 2015). For example, even though the noun *Peter* has the same grammatical relation to the opinion verb in (5) & (6), in the former sentence it is a holder but in the latter it is a target. Similar cases can be observed for opinion nouns (7) & (8) and opinion adjectives (9) & (10). Only the knowledge of sentiment views helps us to assign opinion roles correctly.

(5) [Peter]$_{Holder}$ **criticizes**$_{actor}^{verb}$ Mary.

(6) [Peter]$_{Target}$ **cheated**$_{speaker}^{verb}$ in the exam.

(7) [Peter's]$_{Holder}$ **belief**$_{actor}^{noun}$ is that all people should be treated equally.

(8) [Peter's]$_{Target}$ **misbehaviour**$_{speaker}^{noun}$ is unbearable.

(9) [Peter]$_{Holder}$ is **disappointed**$_{actor}^{adj}$.

(10) [Peter]$_{Target}$ is **intelligent**$_{speaker}^{adj}$.

While the distinction of sentiment views is not new, we put a different emphasis on this task. Our focus is on the prior meaning that opinion words evoke. Hence we consider this as a **word-level** task. Every opinion word from a sentiment lexicon is to be categorized as conveying either an actor or a speaker view. Our aim is to find comprehensive methods to automatically categorize opinion words of various parts of speech (verbs, nouns, adjectives). The resulting lexical resources are indispensable for open-domain categorization. Previous work focused on contextual classification of sentiment views (Johans-

Proceedings of NAACL-HLT 2016, pages 778–788,
San Diego, California, June 12-17, 2016. ©2016 Association for Computational Linguistics

son and Moschitti, 2013). Wiegand and Ruppenhofer (2015) showed that while prior lexical knowledge of sentiment views is effective in transferring opinion role extractors to other domains, this does not apply to contextual classifiers.

In this work, we focus on linguistic properties for predicting sentiment views. We examine in how far morphological information can be used. Distributional and syntactic information is also considered. In terms of lexical resources, we examine WordNet and FrameNet. We show that information from a sentiment lexicon can give some additional clues.

In order to combine the different features to predict the sentiment views evoked by opinion words we employ supervised classification. As a classifier, we use Markov Logic Networks (Richardson and Matthew, 2006) since they do not only allow us to define features for instances (i.e. opinion words) but also to formulate global constraints between different instances. The latter cannot be expressed by traditional classifiers (e.g. SVM). We examine two types of constraints: consistency between instances that are distributionally similar and consistency between morphologically related instances.

Finally, we also examine the relationship between prior lexical information (i.e. our approach) and contextual annotation in the MPQA corpus.

2 Related Work

The annotation scheme of the MPQA corpus (Wiebe et al., 2005) was the first work to address the distinction between different sentiment views. The two sentiment views are referred to as *direct subjectivity* (=actor view) and *expressive subjectivity* (=speaker view). In subsequent research, some approaches have been proposed to distinguish these two categories in the MPQA corpus. The most extensive work is Johansson and Moschitti (2013). Since MPQA provides annotation regarding sentiment in context, sentiment views are exclusively considered in *contextual* classification. The fact that it is the opinion words that convey those views, as we do in this paper, is not addressed. Unlike in this paper, the focus of Johansson and Moschitti (2013) is also on optimizing a machine-learning classifier, in particular to model the interaction between different subjective phrases within the same sentence.

Part of Speech	Actor View		Speaker View	
	Freq	Perc	Freq	Perc
adjective	223	8.9	2279	91.1
noun	487	29.1	1189	70.9
verb	618	52.6	557	47.4

Table 1: Distribution of the different sentiment views.

Some of the lexical resources we examine, i.e. WordNet (§4.1) and FrameNet (§4.2), have also been employed in Breck et al. (2007) who, like Johansson and Moschitti (2013), also deal with contextual (sentiment) classification. However, the authors do not examine in how far these individual resources separate speaker and actor views.

Maks and Vossen (2012b) link sentiment views to opinion words as part of a lexicon model for sentiment analysis. Maks and Vossen (2012a) also examine a corpus-driven method to induce opinion words for the different sentiment views. The authors, however, conclude that their approach, which sees news articles as a source for actor views and news comments as a source for speaker views, is not sufficiently effective.

The work most closely related to our research is Wiegand and Ruppenhofer (2015). Opinion words are categorized according to their sentiment view. Our work substantially goes beyond that previous research: Firstly, Wiegand and Ruppenhofer (2015) only consider distributional similarity for inducing opinion views. In this work, we consider various linguistic features and also compare this with distributional information. Secondly, Wiegand and Ruppenhofer (2015) only consider opinion verbs, while we also consider opinion nouns and opinion adjectives.

Wiegand and Ruppenhofer (2015) distinguish between two types of actor views, *agent views* and *patient views*. The former take their opinion holder as an agent and their target as a patient (typical verbs are *criticize*, *love*, *believe*), while the latter align their roles inversely (typical verbs are *disappoint*, *please*, *interest*). Since this distinction between actor views does not exist among nouns or adjectives, we consider one merged (actor-view) category for all three parts of speech in this paper.

3 Data

We manually annotated all verbs, nouns and adjectives contained in the Subjectivity Lexicon (Wilson et al., 2005) for view type. The dataset comprises 2502 adjectives, 1676 nouns and 1175 verbs. Since our new dataset[1] is an extension of the dataset from Wiegand and Ruppenhofer (2015), we adhere to the annotation process proposed in that paper. That is, the basis of the annotation were online dictionaries (e.g. *Macmillan Dictionary*) which provide both a word definition and example sentences. Each word is either labeled as primarily conveying an actor or a speaker view. (Our categorization is binary.) On a subset of 250 words for each part of speech, we computed an interannotation agreement (Cohen's κ) of 61.9, 71.9 and 60.1 for verbs, nouns and adjectives, respectively. This agreement can be considered substantial (Landis and Koch, 1977). Table 1 shows the distribution of the different sentiment views among the different parts of speech.

The expressions comprising our gold standard do not represent anywhere near the full set of English subjective words with these parts of speech. Otherwise, an automatic categorization would not be necessary in the presence of our gold standard. The classification approach that we propose in this paper, which works well with few labeled training data, would also be helpful for categorizing sentiment views on much larger sets of subjective expressions.

4 Feature Design

4.1 WordNet

WordNet (Miller et al., 1990) is the largest lexical ontology for the English language. It is organized in synsets. However, we want to assign categories to words. Due to the lack of robust word sense disambiguation, in order to use this resource, we consider the union of synsets in which a word with the same part of speech to be categorized is contained.

4.1.1 Gloss Information (GLOSS)

One common way to harness WordNet is by taking into account its glosses. A gloss represents some explanatory text for each synset, usually some definition of the concept. We use the words from those glosses as features in a supervised classifier. We assume that opinion words conveying the same sentiment view also contain similar glosses.

Glosses are a special type of feature. It is basically a bag-of-words feature set, i.e. a *low-level* feature set, which is known to be sparse yet effective when sufficient training data are used. All the other features presented in this paper are *high-level* features, i.e. more frequently occurring features already being effective if only few labeled data are used. Glosses are one of the most frequently used features for lexicon induction tasks in sentiment analysis (Esuli and Sebastiani, 2005; Andreevskaia and Bergler, 2006; Gyamfi et al., 2009; Choi and Wiebe, 2014; Kang et al., 2014). We will consider them as a baseline, showing that our proposed high-level features are more suitable for our task.

4.1.2 Lexicographer Files (LEX)

Lexicographer files organize the synset inventory of WordNet into a coarse-grained set of semantic categories. In total, there are 45 categories for the three parts of speech we consider.[2] The advantage of such a coarse-grained inventory is that it should require only few labeled training data in supervised classification.

4.2 FrameNet (FN)

FrameNet (Baker et al., 1998) is a semantic resource that has been found useful for subtasks of sentiment analysis related to ours, i.e. opinion holder/target extraction (Bethard et al., 2004; Kim and Hovy, 2006). It includes a large set of more than $1,200$ semantic frames that comprise words with similar semantic behaviour. As a feature we use the frame-membership of the opinion words, assuming that different frames are associated with different sentiment views. We use FrameNet version 1.5.

4.3 Subcategorization Frames (SUB)

Subcategorization frames could also be predictive. For example, actor views demand the presence of an

---

[1]available at: www.coli.uni-saarland.de/~miwieg/naacl_2016_views_data.tgz

[2]For adjectives there exist only two categories. These are too general for our task. Instead we use the lexicographer files of all nouns and verbs occurring in the glosses of those adjectives.

Type	Affixes Used
Sentiment	*-able, dis-, mis-, over-, under-, -(i)sm*
Neutral	adj → noun: *-cy, -ity, -ness*; adj/noun → verb: *-ize*; verb → adj: *-ed, -ing*; verb → noun: *-ion, -ing*

Table 2: Affixes used as features.

explicit entity that utters some opinion, i.e. the opinion holder. For a speaker view, this entity remains implicit. This should be reflected in the argument valence of the respective opinion words. We employ the subcategorization frames encoded in *COMLEX* (Grishman et al., 1994) for verbs and adjectives, and *NOMLEX* (Macleod et al., 1998) for nouns.

4.4 Morphological Information (MORPH)

As morphological information, we consider derivational affixes. Table 2 lists our choice of prefixes and suffixes. We only included affixes that occurred at least 10 times in our dataset.

We distinguish between sentiment and neutral affixes. The *sentiment affixes* are affixes which, due to their meaning, suggest a sentiment view. For example, *mis-* as in *misinterpret* indicates that the speaker believes that a given interpretation is incorrect. *-able* as in *admirable* has the meaning of *capable of* which corresponds to an evaluation of the speaker. We could only find sentiment affixes for speaker views.

The *neutral affixes* that we use specify which kinds of bases they can combine with. For example, the noun suffix *-ness* as in *foolishness* indicates that the word originates from an adjective (i.e. *foolish*). Even though this knowledge is syntactic, it may give us some clue as to what sentiment view an opinion word conveys. Table 1 shows that adjectives predominantly carry speaker views. Therefore, a noun ending in *-ness* (thus originating from an adjective) may be similarly likely to convey a speaker view.

4.5 Context Patterns (PATT)

Wiegand and Ruppenhofer (2015) proposed patterns for actor-view and speaker-view <u>verbs</u>. For actor views (PATT_actor), they rely on *prototypical opinion holders (protoOHs)*, i.e. common nouns, such as *opponents* or *critics*, that act like opinion holders (Wiegand and Klakow, 2011). If a verb often co-occurs with an opinion holder – Wiegand and Ruppenhofer (2015) take protoOHs as a proxy – then this is a good indicator of being an actor view

(speaker views, per definition, do not have any opinion holder as their dependent). ProtoOHs can similarly be used to extract actor-view nouns and adjectives. For speaker views (PATT_speaker), Wiegand and Ruppenhofer introduced *reproach patterns*, e.g. *blamed for X* as in (11). These patterns can also be applied to nouns (12) but not to adjectives. For the latter, we did not find any pattern. The patterns were applied to the North American News Text Corpus (LDC95T21).

(11) The UN was **blamed for** $misinterpreting_{verb}$ climate data.

(12) The UN was **blamed for** the $misinterpretation_{noun}$ of climate data.

4.6 Polarity Information (POLAR)

We also investigate in how far polarity information correlates with sentiment views. This information is obtained from the Subjectivity Lexicon (Wilson et al., 2005). Each opinion word is assigned a polarity type, i.e. *positive*, *negative* or *neutral*.

5 Markov Logic Networks and Global Constraints

Markov Logic Networks (MLNs) are a supervised classifier combining first-order logic with probabilities. MLNs are a set of pairs (F_i, w_i) where F_i is a first-order logic formula and w_i a real valued weight associated with F_i. They build a template for constructing a Markov network given a set of constants C. The probability distribution that is estimated is a log-linear model

$$P(X = x) = \frac{1}{Z} exp \left(\sum_{i=1}^{k} w_i n_i(x) \right) \qquad (1)$$

where $n_i(x)$ is the number of groundings in F_i in x and Z is a normalization constant. As an implementation, we use *thebeast* (Riedel, 2008).

We employ MLNs since they allow us (in addition to including ordinary features, i.e. §4.1-§4.6) to formulate constraints holding between individual instances. Such *global constraints* have been effectively exploited with MLNs in related tasks, such as semantic-role labeling (Meza-Ruiz and Riedel, 2009), anaphora resolution (Hou et al., 2013), question answering (Khot et al., 2015) and discourse-based sentiment analysis (Zirn et al., 2011). We formulate three such constraints. Two of them are

Abbrev.	Constraint as Logic Formula
w2v	$\forall x[\forall y[\forall z[\forall u[[Opin.Word(x) \wedge Opin.Word(y) \wedge Word2Vec\text{-}Similar(x,y) \wedge ViewOf(z,x) \wedge ViewOf(u,y)] \rightarrow (z{==}u)]]]]$
lin	$\forall x[\forall y[\forall z[\forall u[[Opin.Word(x) \wedge Opin.Word(y) \wedge DekangLin\text{-}Similar(x,y) \wedge ViewOf(z,x) \wedge ViewOf(u,y)] \rightarrow (z{==}u)]]]]$
morph	$\forall x[\forall y[\forall z[\forall u[[Opin.Word(x) \wedge Opin.Word(y) \wedge MorphRelated(x,y) \wedge ViewOf(z,x) \wedge ViewOf(u,y)] \rightarrow (z{==}u)]]]]$

Table 3: Global constraints enforcing sentiment view consistency as incorporated in MLNs.

based on the two most effective types of word similarities from Wiegand and Ruppenhofer (2015). The first word similarity measures the cosine of word vectors representing opinion words produced by *Word2Vec*-embeddings (Mikolov et al., 2013). The second word similarity is represented by the metric of Lin (1998), which exploits the rich set of dependency-relation labels in the context of distributional similarity.[3] The third type of consistency considers morphological relatedness by which we understand two words deriving from two different parts of speech but belonging to the same lexical root and therefore carrying similar meaning (e.g. *happiness.noun* and *happy.adj*). We obtain that type of relatedness from WordNet (Miller et al., 1990).

Table 3 lists our constraints. They state that if for two opinion words some similarity or morphological relatedness holds, then these words should convey the same sentiment view. For the two types of word-similarity consistencies we considered the top 3 most similar words for each noun, and the top 5 most similar words for each verb and adjective. These values were determined empirically. For the generation of word vectors, we used 200 dimensions along the default configuration of *Word2Vec*. Word similarity and word vectors were generated from the North American News Text Corpus.

6 Experiments

For our evaluation of supervised classification, we focus on a setting in which only few labeled training data are available. We sampled from our gold standard 20% of the labeled training data. The remaining 80% are used as test data. This process was repeated five times. We report performance averaged over these five (test) samples. We focus on small training sizes since we think that for the given lexicon induction task, we should pursue an approach that requires little human annotation. Moreover, we

---

[3]WordNet is not a good option for measuring similarity, as many synonyms of the same synset have different sentiment views, e.g. *comment.noun* (actor) vs. *gossip.noun* (speaker).

show that our approach yields good results despite the absence of large amounts of training data.

6.1 High-Precision Features

Before we evaluate supervised classification, we look for each part of speech at the 10 features with the highest precision (for each of the two views) as displayed in Table 4. This provides a good overview of the quality of different features. Since we do not have an equal class distribution, we also list a baseline-precision that always predicts the sentiment view under consideration. Since this is just an exploratory experiment, we measure precision on the entire dataset. We exclude the WordNet glosses (§4.1.1) from our analysis as we found individual words from glosses too difficult to interpret.

Table 4 shows that features from all feature groups (§4.1-§4.6) achieve a high precision. Subcategorization features (§4.3) are very predictive for verbs conveying actor views. The frame types that are predictive mostly have in common that one of their arguments is some proposition (13)-(17). This is also true for adjectives (18).

(13) PP-HOW-TO-INF: They $\underline{agree}_{actor}$ [with him]$_{PP}$ [how to solve the problem]$_{HOW\text{-}TO\text{-}INF}$.

(14) NP-TOBE: They $\underline{believe}_{actor}$ [him]$_{NP}$ [to be honest]$_{TOBE}$.

(15) NP-ADJP-PRED: They $\underline{consider}_{actor}$ [him]$_{NP}$ [foolish]$_{ADJP\text{-}PRED}$.

(16) NP-TO-INF: He $\underline{allowed}_{actor}$ [her]$_{NP}$ [to go]$_{TO\text{-}INF}$.

(17) S: They $\underline{thought}_{actor}$ [he was always late]$_{S}$.

(18) THAT-S-ADJ: They were $\underline{aware}_{actor}$ [that he was sick]$_{THAT\text{-}S\text{-}ADJ}$.

FrameNet-frames (§4.2) achieve high precision; but the only frame with good coverage is *Stimulus-focus* for adjectives conveying a speaker view.

There are fewer lexicographer files (§4.1.2) than FrameNet-frames in Table 4, but some of them have high coverage, most notably *LEX_person* for speaker-view nouns and *LEX_feeling* for actor-view nouns. Given the strength of *LEX_person*, we conclude that most opinion nouns denoting persons tend to be speaker views (e.g. *idiot* or *loser*). There are also several predictive lexicographer files whose label seems fairly unintuitive, e.g. *LEX_weather* for

<table>
<tr><td colspan="9" align="center">Speaker View</td></tr>
<tr><td colspan="3">adj (always-predict-this-view prec: 91.1)</td><td colspan="3">noun (always-predict-this-view prec: 70.9)</td><td colspan="3">verb (always-predict-this-view prec: 47.4)</td></tr>
<tr><td>Feature</td><td>Prec</td><td>Freq</td><td>Feature</td><td>Prec</td><td>Freq</td><td>Feature</td><td>Prec</td><td>Freq</td></tr>
<tr><td>SUB_EXTRAP-FOR-TO-INF</td><td>100.0</td><td>104</td><td>FN_Killing</td><td>100.0</td><td>11</td><td>MORPH_mis-</td><td>92.3</td><td>13</td></tr>
<tr><td>FN_Desirability</td><td>100.0</td><td>48</td><td>LEX_animal</td><td>91.7</td><td>24</td><td>LEX_weather</td><td>84.2</td><td>19</td></tr>
<tr><td>FN_Expertise</td><td>100.0</td><td>31</td><td>FN_Catastrophe</td><td>90.9</td><td>11</td><td>FN_Prevarication</td><td>81.8</td><td>11</td></tr>
<tr><td>FN_Morality-evaluation</td><td>100.0</td><td>30</td><td>LEX_body</td><td>90.9</td><td>11</td><td>MORPH_over-</td><td>78.6</td><td>14</td></tr>
<tr><td>FN_Candidness</td><td>100.0</td><td>20</td><td>MORPH_-cy</td><td>90.6</td><td>32</td><td>FN_Killing</td><td>76.9</td><td>13</td></tr>
<tr><td>FN_Usefulness</td><td>100.0</td><td>19</td><td>MORPH_-ity</td><td>90.2</td><td>132</td><td>FN_Self-motion</td><td>75.0</td><td>16</td></tr>
<tr><td>FN_Praiseworthiness</td><td>100.0</td><td>15</td><td>MORPH_mis-</td><td>90.0</td><td>20</td><td>MORPH_-ize</td><td>73.5</td><td>200</td></tr>
<tr><td>FN_Stimulus-focus</td><td>99.1</td><td>113</td><td>LEX_substance</td><td>87.0</td><td>23</td><td>LEX_change</td><td>64.8</td><td>270</td></tr>
<tr><td>LEX_plant</td><td>98.7</td><td>79</td><td>LEX_food</td><td>84.2</td><td>19</td><td>PATT_speaker</td><td>62.7</td><td>252</td></tr>
<tr><td>MORPH_-able</td><td>98.3</td><td>172</td><td>LEX_person</td><td>83.5</td><td>267</td><td>FN_Communication-noise</td><td>62.5</td><td>16</td></tr>
<tr><td colspan="9" align="center">Actor View</td></tr>
<tr><td colspan="3">adj (always-predict-this-view prec: 8.9)</td><td colspan="3">noun (always-predict-this-view prec: 29.1)</td><td colspan="3">verb (always-predict-this-view prec: 52.6)</td></tr>
<tr><td>Feature</td><td>Prec</td><td>Freq</td><td>Feature</td><td>Prec</td><td>Freq</td><td>Feature</td><td>Prec</td><td>Freq</td></tr>
<tr><td>FN_Experiencer-focus</td><td>81.8</td><td>11</td><td>FN_Emotion-directed</td><td>95.1</td><td>41</td><td>FN_Experiencer-focus</td><td>100.0</td><td>21</td></tr>
<tr><td>SUB_THAT-S-ADJ</td><td>75.9</td><td>54</td><td>FN_Experiencer-focus</td><td>92.9</td><td>14</td><td>SUB_PP-HOW-TO-INF</td><td>100.0</td><td>13</td></tr>
<tr><td>FN_Emotion-directed</td><td>74.6</td><td>67</td><td>PATT_actor</td><td>83.0</td><td>53</td><td>SUB_NP-TOBE</td><td>100.0</td><td>12</td></tr>
<tr><td>SUB_ADJ-TO-INF</td><td>38.7</td><td>31</td><td>FN_Judgment</td><td>73.3</td><td>15</td><td>SUB_NP-ADVP-PRED</td><td>100.0</td><td>11</td></tr>
<tr><td>MORPH_-ed</td><td>29.2</td><td>288</td><td>LEX_feeling</td><td>65.7</td><td>268</td><td>SUB_NP-ADJP-PRED</td><td>94.4</td><td>18</td></tr>
<tr><td>PATT_actor</td><td>26.3</td><td>335</td><td>FN_Medical-conditions</td><td>61.5</td><td>13</td><td>FN_Judgment-direct-address</td><td>92.8</td><td>14</td></tr>
<tr><td>MORPH_dis-</td><td>25.4</td><td>71</td><td>FN_Hostile-encounter</td><td>58.3</td><td>12</td><td>SUB_NP-TO-NP</td><td>92.3</td><td>13</td></tr>
<tr><td>LEX_weather</td><td>22.2</td><td>18</td><td>SUB_NOM-INTRANS-RECIP</td><td>57.1</td><td>14</td><td>SUB_NP-TO-INF</td><td>91.7</td><td>12</td></tr>
<tr><td>LEX_feeling</td><td>18.1</td><td>695</td><td>POLAR_neutral</td><td>54.8</td><td>93</td><td>SUB_NP-ING-OC</td><td>90.9</td><td>11</td></tr>
<tr><td>SUB_ADJ-PP</td><td>17.2</td><td>548</td><td>LEX_relation</td><td>53.8</td><td>26</td><td>SUB_S</td><td>90.4</td><td>52</td></tr>
</table>

Table 4: High-precision features (*minimal frequency* > 10).

speaker-view verbs or *LEX_animal* for speaker-view nouns. These are not errors, however. They actually concern words that convey opinions in metaphorical usage. For instance, *cloud* (a typical weather verb) conveys a speaker view if it is used metaphorically as in *The stroke clouded memories of her youth.* Nouns denoting animals, such as *bull* and *dragon*, convey a speaker view if they are meant to describe a human being (*She is a real dragon!*). Other noun classes follow this pattern, e.g. *body (parts)* with terms such as *backbone* or *bum*.

Simple morphological features (§4.4) also seem to be meaningful. In particular, the noun suffix *-ity* (occurring 132 times in our set of opinion nouns) is indicative of speaker views. The relevant nouns are derived from adjectives (Table 2) and the set of adjectives predominantly conveys speaker views (Table 1).

Even plain polarity information (§4.6) has some significance. *Neutral* sentiment verbs often convey an actor view, such as *opinion*, *utterance* or *view*.

The fact that the pattern-feature (§4.5) also appears on the list of actor-view nouns and adjectives suggests that it is not only effective for verbs as shown in Wiegand and Ruppenhofer (2015) but also for nouns and adjectives.

Classifier(s)	Description
graph	graph-based induction approach as proposed in Wiegand and Ruppenhofer (2015)
mln$_{local}$	Markov Logic Networks with only local features, i.e. features from §4
svm	Support Vector Machines using exactly the same features as *mln$_{local}$*
mln$_{w2v}$, mln$_{lin}$, mln$_{morph}$	Markov Logic Networks with global constraints from Table 3
mln+graph	Markov Logic Networks that uses the output of *graph* as a further feature

Table 5: Description of the different classifiers.

Finally, we performed an ablation experiment in which we trained a classifier with all of these features in MLNs and compared it to another classifier in which each of the feature groups (*POLAR*, *LEX*, *MORPH* etc.) was removed, one by one. We computed statistical significance (t-test), testing whether the classifier trained on a feature set in which one feature group was removed performs significantly worse than a classifier with all features. We found that, at a significance level $p < 0.05$, this is always the case, with the exception of *LEX* (here, the significance level is $p = 0.0552$). This is proof that features from most feature groups contain information that is to some extent complementary.

6.2 Classification

Table 5 lists the different types of classifiers we consider. As one baseline, we consider the graph-based approach *graph* from Wiegand and Ruppenhofer (2015) which starts with the seeds gained by the surface patterns (§4.5)[4] and then runs label propagation (Talukdar et al., 2008) based on a distributional similarity graph (using the metric by Lin (1998)). *graph* is the only classifier not depending on manually labeled training data. So far, it has only been examined on verbs. As a further baseline, we consider our features from §4 on an SVM. (We use SVM^{light} (Joachims, 1999).) It should be considered as a state-of-the-art classifier that, unlike *mln*, cannot incorporate global constraints (Table 3).

Table 6 shows the results. Both *graph* and *svm* are significantly outperformed. *graph* performs better on verbs (in terms of F-score) than on nouns and adjectives. It is also for these parts of speech that the global constraints *w2v* and *lin* notably improve the performance of *mln*. Global constraints have a lesser impact on verbs. However, a combination of global constraints is effective, as well as a combination of *graph* and *mln*. The best overall results are obtained by the combination of *mln* with global constraints and *graph*. These results suggest that our new features (including global constraints) are useful and complementary to previous work, i.e. *graph*.

Figure 1 compares the feature derived from WordNet glosses (§4.1.1), a standard feature for lexicon induction, with the remaining features we use on a learning curve. This feature performs poorly if only few labeled training data are used. Our proposed feature set is consistently better. The combination of glosses and our proposed features is only helpful if many labeled training instances are used ($> 60\%$).

6.3 Prior Labels and Context Labels

So far, we have considered sentiment views as prior information of words. Now we relate those labels to sentiment views annotated in context. For that, we consider the view annotation in the MPQA corpus.

Table 7 shows that prior labels of opinion words largely coincide with the respective context labels.

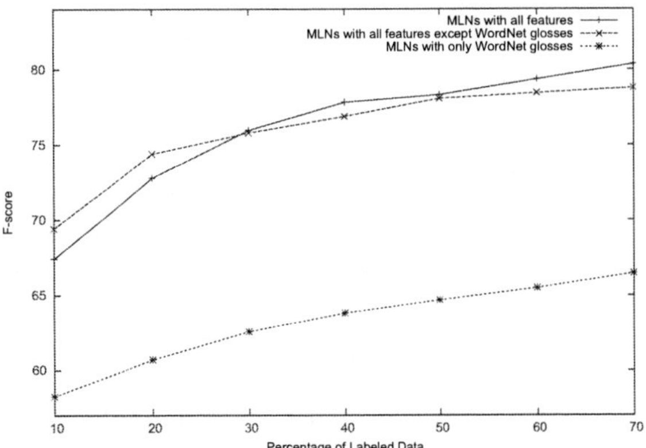

Figure 1: WordNet gloss feature vs. the remaining features *(results averaged over all three parts of speech).*

	context					
	verbs		nouns		adjectives	
prior	actor	speaker	actor	speaker	actor	speaker
actor	**2926**	834	**1671**	802	**269**	81
speaker	119	**810**	151	**2150**	354	**3489**

Table 7: Comparison of prior labels and context labels.

This proves that it is a valid approach to compile lexicons with sentiment views, which can subsequently be used in contextual sentiment-view classification.

However, in Table 7, we still observe mismatches between prior and contextual labels. This mostly concerns actor-view words in speaker-view contexts. We examine this mismatch more closely on nouns *(highlighted in gray)* where this confusion is greatest. In MPQA, most subjective expressions that are annotated are sequences of tokens rather than individual words. We found that the largest set of disagreements derives from the nature of MPQA's contextual annotation. The annotators were asked to label spans that expressed opinions that are salient in the document context. Often these are larger spans composed of multiple smaller subjective expressions. The component expressions were not kept track of because the opinion expressed by the larger span was more salient on the document level.

For example, the annotation of the subjective phrase *this must be a **warning*** as a speaker view (containing the actor noun *warning*), in our opinion is primarily triggered by the epistemic modal verb *must*, which signals that the speaker feels compelled to come to the conclusion that *this is a warn-*

---

[4]Since the surface patterns for speaker views from Wiegand and Ruppenhofer (2015) cannot be applied to adjectives (§4.5), we instead used the effective suffix feature MORPH_-*able* (Table 4) for generating speaker-view seeds of opinion adjectives.

| | | graph | svm | $\mathbf{mln}_{local}$ | $\mathbf{mln}_{morph}$ | $\mathbf{mln}_{w2v}$ | $\mathbf{mln}_{lin}$ | $\mathbf{mln}_{morph+lin}$ | $\mathbf{mln}_{morph+w2v+lin}$ | graph | |
										$\mathbf{+mln}_{local}$	$\mathbf{+mln}_{morph+w2v+lin}$
adj	**F1**	53.1	54.2	69.0°	69.0°	71.1°	72.3$^{\circ\bullet\diamond}$	73.0$^{\circ\bullet\diamond\dagger}$	70.8°	70.4$^{\circ\bullet\diamond}$	**73.6**$^{\circ\bullet\diamond}$
	Acc	91.4$^{\bullet\diamond}$	91.6$^{\bullet}$	89.8	89.7	92.8$^{\circ\bullet\diamond}$	93.3$^{\circ\bullet\diamond\dagger}$	93.3$^{\circ\bullet\diamond\dagger}$	93.3$^{\circ\bullet\diamond\dagger}$	90.6	**93.6**$^{\circ\bullet\diamond\dagger}$
noun	**F1**	66.1	69.6	72.4°	73.3$^{\circ\bullet}$	74.7$^{\circ\bullet\diamond\ddagger}$	73.9$^{\circ\bullet}$	75.3$^{\circ\bullet\diamond\ddagger}$	75.4$^{\circ\bullet\diamond\ddagger}$	73.9$^{\circ\bullet}$	**76.9**$^{\circ\bullet\diamond\dagger\ddagger}$
	Acc	70.7	78.2	77.7	79.0$^{\bullet}$	80.2$^{\circ\bullet\diamond}$	79.9$^{\circ\bullet\diamond}$	81.1$^{\circ\bullet\diamond\dagger\ddagger}$	81.6$^{\circ\bullet\diamond\dagger\ddagger}$	78.7°	**82.2**$^{\circ\bullet\diamond\dagger\ddagger}$
verb	**F1**	71.0$^{\circ\bullet\diamond\dagger\ddagger}$	69.6	69.1	69.6	69.6	69.8	70.2$^{\bullet}$	70.4$^{\bullet}$	71.8$^{\circ\bullet\diamond\dagger\ddagger}$	**72.7**$^{\circ\bullet\diamond\dagger\ddagger*}$
	Acc	71.1$^{\circ\bullet\diamond\dagger\ddagger}$	69.7	69.2	69.6	69.7	69.9	70.3$^{\bullet}$	70.5$^{\bullet}$	71.9$^{\circ\bullet\diamond\dagger\ddagger}$	**72.8**$^{\circ\bullet\diamond\dagger\ddagger*}$

statistical significance testing (paired t-test, significance level $p < 0.05$) $^{\circ}$: better than *svm*; $^{\bullet}$: better than *mln*$_{local}$; $^{\diamond}$: better than *mln*$_{morph}$; †: better than *mln*$_{w2v}$; ‡: better than *mln*$_{lin}$; *: better than *graph* (measured for verbs only)

Table 6: Comparison of different classifiers *(for training, 20% of the labeled data were sampled; the test data are the remaining 80%; this procedure is repeated 5 times; results represent averages over the 5 test samples).*

ing. The actor view of *warning* is not invalidated by this: it is just backgrounded relative to the speaker view introduced by the modal verb, which, going in parallel with its greater prominence, is also the syntactic governor of the verb phrase *be a warning*, of which the actor view *warning* is part. Our evaluation scheme might thus detect a match between our prior annotation for the modal *must* and the MPQA's larger phrase. But since the less prominent actor view was not picked up by the MPQA annotators, our prior annotation has no counterpart. Copula constructions similarly represent instances, where the speaker performs a speech act (e.g. a warning) by using the copular construction (e.g. *This is a warning*). Here, the speaker is identical to the actor of the warning. Practically, it makes no difference whether we call such a case speaker or actor view, as long as we can recognize that the actor is the speaker.

In order to show that the annotation of MPQA focuses on the more salient opinions and thus sentiment views as conveyed by less prominent expressions are not considered (and largely account for the mismatches in Table 7), we designed a supervised classifier whose features indicate whether a mention of an actor-view expression in a subjective phrase is salient. The features are displayed in Table 8.

The key salience features regarding speaker views, i.e. *modal* and *copular*, were already discussed above. Features indicating the salience of the actor-view word address the subcategorization frame of the word. Cases in which there is a person as some subcategorized argument (*personArg*) often imply an opinion holder. The presence of an (explicit) opinion holder indicates an actor view. A proposition as argument of an opinion word is typically the proposition of some opinion holder

(*propArg*) and not of the speaker of the utterance.

For this experiment we take the detection of subjective phrases as given. (Only the information regarding contextual sentiment views is withheld.) This allows us to define features that explicitly look into the entire text span constituting the subjective phrase in which each opinion word is contained. The two length features (*shortPhrase* and *longPhrase*) make use of this information. If a phrase is long, chances are high that there are other more salient opinion words contained than the one under consideration. In short subjective phrases, the presence of other salient words in it is unlikely. This is supported by the fact that the average length of subjective phrases with a speaker view (in which an actor-view opinion noun occurs) are 5.4 tokens while actor-view phrases (that include an actor-view noun) only have an average length of 2.3 tokens.

The majority features (*majActor* and *majSpeaker*) also exploit the information of the entire subjective phrase. We argue that the sentiment view of the phrase is likely to coincide with the view of the majority of the opinion words contained in that phrase.

Table 9 shows how these features separate the mentions of an actor-view opinion noun into contextual actor views and speaker views. We report classification using an SVM (10-fold cross-validation). With only those few features, we largely outperform the baseline always classifying an instance as an actor view (i.e. the majority class). Table 10 displays the precision of each individual feature, supporting that these features are effective. These experiments show that there is indeed a systematic relationship between salience and contextual sentiment views.

Abbreviation	Features Indicating Contextual ACTOR View
personArg	a person is argument of opinion word; persons may indicate opinion holders; (explicit) opinion holders indicate absence of speaker view (*his warning of a catastrophe*)
propArg	a proposition is argument of the opinion word (*warning that this fish is not fit to eat*); propositions are typically arguments of actor-views words
lightVerb	opinion word is governed by light verb (*they issued/gave a warning*), light verbs indicate the presence of an actor outside of the maximal phrase of a subjective noun
shortPhrase	opinion word is part of short subjective phrase ($<$ 3 tokens); short phrases make embedding of another more salient (speaker-view) word unlikely
majActor	majority of other opinion words in subjective phrase are actor-view words
Abbreviation	**Features Indicating Contextual SPEAKER View**
copula	opinion word is part of copula construction (*this is a warning*) – see discussion in §6.3
modal	opinion word is in modal scope (*this must be a warning*) – see discussion in §6.3
emphasis	opinion word is accompanied by emphatic cue, e.g. *!*, quotation (*they gave him a "warning"*), (rhetoric) question; emphases typically originate from speaker
precededByAs	preceded by *as* (*this was regarded [as an urgent warning]$_{as\text{-}phrase}$*), *as*-phrase typically occurs as an argument of categorization predicates *regard, view, see, consider* etc. – with these predicates an *as*-phrase often conveys a speaker view, especially since the predicates often have no explicit holder
longPhrase	opinion word is part of long subjective phrase ($>$ 4 tokens); long phrases make embedding of another more salient (speaker-view) word likely
majSpeaker	majority of other opinion words in subjective phrase are speaker-view words

Table 8: Salience features for detecting contextual views (given a mention of a prior actor-view opinion noun).

Majority Class.		Proposed Features	
Acc 65.9	F1 39.7	Acc 78.7	F1 73.5

Table 9: Contextual classification of opinion nouns with a prior actor view (using feature set from Table 8).

Actor View	shortPhrase: 88.5; lightVerb: 85.8; personArg: 81.0; propArg: 74.6; majActor: 72.9
Speaker View	precededByAs: 90.9; majSpeaker: 90.0; modal: 79.6; longPhrase: 73.3; copula: 61.9; emphasis: 57.5

Table 10: Precision of features from Table 8.

7 Conclusion

We examined different types of features and classifiers for the categorization of sentiment views that opinion words convey. We found that many features are effective for this task. A detailed feature analysis provided linguistic insights into the nature of sentiment views. As a classifier, MLNs performed best. This classifier has the advantage that global constraints can be incorporated, which raises classification performance on nouns and adjectives. Our approach outperforms a previously proposed graph-based approach evaluated on opinion verbs. We also demonstrated that prior sentiment views correlate with contextual sentiment views on MPQA.

Acknowledgements

The authors would like to thank Stephanie Köser for annotating the dataset presented in this paper. We are also grateful to Sebastian Riedel, Manfred Klenner, Don Tuggener and Cäcilia Zirn for advising us on Markov Logic Networks. The authors were partially supported by the German Research Foundation (DFG) under grants RU 1873/2-1 and WI 4204/2-1.

References

Alina Andreevskaia and Sabine Bergler. 2006. Mining WordNet for a Fuzzy Sentiment: Sentiment Tag Extraction from WordNet Glosses. In *Proceedings of the Conference on European Chapter of the Association for Computational Linguistics (EACL)*, pages 209–216, Trento, Italy.

Collin F. Baker, Charles J. Fillmore, and John B. Lowe. 1998. The Berkeley FrameNet Project. In *Proceedings of the International Conference on Computational Linguistics and Annual Meeting of the Association for Computational Linguistics (COLING/ACL)*, pages 86–90, Montréal, Quebec, Canada.

Steven Bethard, Hong Yu, Ashley Thornton, Vasileios Hatzivassiloglou, and Dan Jurafsky. 2004. Extracting Opinion Propositions and Opinion Holders using Syntactic and Lexical Cues. In *Computing Attitude and Affect in Text: Theory and Applications*. Springer-Verlag.

Eric Breck, Yejin Choi, and Claire Cardie. 2007. Identifying Expressions of Opinion in Context. In *Proceedings of the International Joint Conference on Artificial Intelligence (IJCAI)*, pages 2683–2688, Hyderabad, India.

Yoonjung Choi and Janyce Wiebe. 2014. +/-EffectWordNet: Sense-level Lexicon Acquisition for Opinion Inference. In *Proceedings of the Conference on Empirical Methods in Natural Language Processing (EMNLP)*, pages 1181–1191, Doha, Qatar.

Andrea Esuli and Fabrizio Sebastiani. 2005. Determining the semantic orientation of terms through gloss classification. In *Proceedings of the ACM International Conference on Information and Knowledge Management (CIKM)*, pages 617–624, Bremen, Germany.

Ralph Grishman, Catherine McKeown, and Adam Meyers. 1994. COMLEX Syntax: Building a Computational Lexicon. In *Proceedings of the International Conference on Computational Linguistics (COLING)*, pages 268–272, Kyoto, Japan.

Yaw Gyamfi, Janyce Wiebe, Rada Mihalcea, and Cem Akkaya. 2009. Integrating Knowledge for Subjectivity Sense Labeling. In *Proceedings of the Human Language Technology Conference of the North American Chapter of the ACL (HLT/NAACL)*, pages 10–18, Boulder, CO, USA.

Yufang Hou, Katja Markert, and Michael Strube. 2013. Global Inference for Bridging Anaphora Resolution. In *Proceedings of the Human Language Technology Conference of the North American Chapter of the ACL (HLT/NAACL)*, pages 907–917, Atlanta, GA, USA.

Thorsten Joachims. 1999. Making Large-Scale SVM Learning Practical. In B. Schölkopf, C. Burges, and A. Smola, editors, *Advances in Kernel Methods - Support Vector Learning*, pages 169–184. MIT Press.

Richard Johansson and Alessandro Moschitti. 2013. Relational Features in Fine-Grained Opinion Analysis. *Computational Linguistics*, 39(3):473–509.

Jun Seok Kang, Song Feng, Leman Akoglu, and Yejin Choi. 2014. ConnotationWordNet: Learning Connotation over the Word+Sense Network. In *Proceedings of the Annual Meeting of the Association for Computational Linguistics (ACL)*, pages 1544–1554, Baltimore, MD, USA.

Tushar Khot, Niranjan Balasubramanian, Eric Gribkoff, Ashish Sabharwal, Peter Clark, and Oren Etzioni. 2015. Exploring Markov Logic Networks for Question Answering. In *Proceedings of the Conference on Empirical Methods in Natural Language Processing (EMNLP)*, pages 685–694, Lisbon, Portugal.

Soo-Min Kim and Eduard Hovy. 2006. Extracting Opinions, Opinion Holders, and Topics Expressed in Online News Media Text. In *Proceedings of the ACL Workshop on Sentiment and Subjectivity in Text*, pages 1–8, Sydney, Australia.

J. Richard Landis and Gary G. Koch. 1977. The Measurement of Observer Agreement for Categorical Data. *Biometrics*, 33(1):159–174.

Dekang Lin. 1998. Automatic Retrieval and Clustering of Similar Words. In *Proceedings of the Annual Meeting of the Association for Computational Linguistics and International Conference on Computational Linguistics (ACL/COLING)*, pages 768–774, Montreal, Quebec, Canada.

Catherine Macleod, Ralph Grishman, Adam Meyers, Leslie Barrett, and Ruth Reeves. 1998. NOMLEX: A Lexicon of Nominalizations. In *Proceedings of EURALEX*, pages 187–193, Liège, Belgium.

Isa Maks and Piek Vossen. 2012a. Building a fine-grained subjectivity lexicon from a web corpus. In *Proceedings of the Conference on Language Resources and Evaluation (LREC)*, pages 3070–3076, Istanbul, Turkey.

Isa Maks and Piek Vossen. 2012b. A lexicon model for deep sentiment analysis and opinion mining applications. *Decision Support Systems*, 53:680–688.

Ivan Meza-Ruiz and Sebastian Riedel. 2009. Jointly Identifying Predicates, Arguments and Senses using Markov Logic. In *Proceedings of the Human Language Technology Conference of the North American Chapter of the ACL (HLT/NAACL)*, pages 155–163, Boulder, CO, USA.

Tomas Mikolov, Kai Chen, Greg Corrado, and Jeffrey Dean. 2013. Efficient Estimation of Word Representations in Vector Space. In *Proceedings of Workshop at the International Conference on Learning Representations (ICLR)*, Scottsdale, AZ, USA.

George Miller, Richard Beckwith, Christiane Fellbaum, Derek Gross, and Katherine Miller. 1990. Introduction to WordNet: An On-line Lexical Database. *International Journal of Lexicography*, 3:235–244.

Matthew Richardson and Pedro Matthew. 2006. Markov Logic Networks. *Machine Learning*, 62(1–2):107–136.

Sebastian Riedel. 2008. Improving the Accuracy and Efficiency of MAP Inference for Markov Logic. In *Proceedings of the Annual Conference on Uncertainty in AI (UAI)*, pages 468–475, Helsinki, Finland.

Partha Pratim Talukdar, Joseph Reisinger, Marius Pasca, Deepak Ravichandran, Rahul Bhagat, and Fernando Pereira. 2008. Weakly-Supervised Acquisition of Labeled Class Instances using Graph Random Walks. In *Proceedings of the Conference on Empirical Methods in Natural Language Processing (EMNLP)*, pages 582–590, Honolulu, HI, USA.

Janyce Wiebe, Theresa Wilson, and Claire Cardie. 2005. Annotating Expressions of Opinions and Emotions in Language. *Language Resources and Evaluation*, 39(2/3):164–210.

Michael Wiegand and Dietrich Klakow. 2011. Prototypical Opinion Holders: What We can Learn from

Experts and Analysts. In *Proceedings of Recent Advances in Natural Language Processing (RANLP)*, pages 282–288, Hissar, Bulgaria.

Michael Wiegand and Josef Ruppenhofer. 2015. Opinion Holder and Target Extraction based on the Induction of Verbal Categories. In *Proceedings of the Conference on Computational Natural Language Learning (CoNLL)*, pages 215–225, Beijing, China.

Theresa Wilson, Janyce Wiebe, and Paul Hoffmann. 2005. Recognizing Contextual Polarity in Phrase-level Sentiment Analysis. In *Proceedings of the Conference on Human Language Technology and Empirical Methods in Natural Language Processing (HLT/EMNLP)*, pages 347–354, Vancouver, BC, Canada.

Cäcilia Zirn, Mathias Niepert, Heiner Stuckenschmidt, and Michael Strube. 2011. Fine-Grained Sentiment Analysis with Structural Features. In *Proceedings of the International Joint Conference on Natural Language Processing (IJCNLP)*, pages 336–344, Chiang Mai, Thailand.

Clustering for Simultaneous Extraction of Aspects and Features from Reviews

Lu Chen[1], **Justin Martineau[2]**, **Doreen Cheng[2]**, **Amit Sheth[1]**

[1] Kno.e.sis Center, Wright State University
Fairborn, OH 45435 USA
[2] Samsung Research America, Silicon Valley
San Jose, CA 95134 USA
{chen, amit}@knoesis.org
justin.m@samsung.com
doreenycheng@yahoo.com

Abstract

This paper presents a clustering approach that simultaneously identifies product features and groups them into aspect categories from online reviews. Unlike prior approaches that first extract features and then group them into categories, the proposed approach combines feature and aspect discovery instead of chaining them. In addition, prior work on feature extraction tends to require seed terms and focus on identifying explicit features, while the proposed approach extracts both *explicit* and *implicit* features, and does not require seed terms. We evaluate this approach on reviews from three domains. The results show that it outperforms several state-of-the-art methods on both tasks across all three domains.

1 Introduction

If you are thinking of buying a TV for watching football, you might go to websites such as Amazon to read customer reviews on TV products. However, there are many products and each of them may have hundreds of reviews. It would be helpful to have an aspect-based sentiment summarization for each product. Based on other customers' opinions on multiple aspects such as size, picture quality, motion-smoothing, and sound quality, you might be able to make the decision without going through all the reviews. To support such summarization, it is essential to have an algorithm that extracts product features and aspects from reviews.

Features are components and attributes of a product. A feature can be directly mentioned as an opinion target (i.e., explicit feature) or implied by opinion words (i.e., implicit feature). Different feature expressions may be used to describe the same *aspect* of a product. Aspect can be represented as a group of features. Consider the following review sentences, in which we denote **explicit** and *implicit* features in boldface and italics, respectively.

1. This phone has great **display** and perfect **size**. It's very *fast* with all great **features**.
2. Good **features** for an *inexpensive* android. The **screen** is *big* and *vibrant*. Great **speed** makes *smooth* viewing of tv programs or sports.
3. The phone runs *fast* and *smooth*, and has great **price**.

In review 1, *display* is an explicit feature, and opinion word "fast" implies implicit feature *speed*. The task is to identify both explicit and implicit features, and group them into aspects, e.g., {speed, fast, smooth}, {size, big}, {price, inexpensive}.

Many existing studies (Hu and Liu, 2004; Su et al., 2006; Qiu et al., 2009; Hai et al., 2012; Xu et al., 2013) have focused on extracting features without grouping them into aspects. Some methods have been proposed to group features given that feature expressions have been identified beforehand (Zhai et al., 2010; Moghaddam and Ester, 2011; Zhao et al., 2014), or can be learned from semi-structured Pros and Cons reviews (Guo et al., 2009; Yu et al., 2011). In recent years, topic models have been widely studied for their use in aspect discovery with the advantage that they extract features and group them simultaneously. However, researchers have found some

---

This author's research was done during an internship with Samsung Research America.

limitations of such methods, e.g., the produced topics may not be coherent or directly interpretable as aspects (Chen et al., 2013; Bancken et al., 2014), the extracted aspects are not fine-grained (Zhang and Liu, 2014), and it is ineffective when dealing with aspect sparsity (Xu et al., 2014).

In this paper, we present a clustering algorithm that extracts features and groups them into aspects from product reviews. Our work differs from prior studies in three ways. First, it identifies both features and aspects simultaneously. Existing clustering-based solutions (Su et al., 2008; Lu et al., 2009; Bancken et al., 2014) take a two-step approach that first identifies features and then employs standard clustering algorithms (e.g., k-means) to group features into aspects. We propose that these two steps can be combined into a single clustering process, in which different words describing the same aspect can be automatically grouped into one cluster, and features and aspects can be identified at the same time. Second, both explicit and implicit features are extracted and grouped into aspects. While most existing methods deal with explicit features (e.g., "speed", "size"), much less effort has been made to identify implicit features implied by opinion words (e.g., "fast", "big"), which is challenging because many general opinion words such as "good" or "great" do not indicate product features, therefore they should not be identified as features or grouped into aspects. Third, it is unsupervised and does not require seed terms, hand-crafted patterns, or any other labeling efforts.

Specifically, the algorithm takes a set of reviews on a product (e.g., TV, cell phone) as input and produces aspect clusters as output. It first uses a part-of-speech tagger to identify nouns/noun phrases, verbs and adjectives as candidates. Instead of applying the clustering algorithm to all the candidates, only the frequent ones are clustered to generate *seed clusters*, and then the remaining candidates are placed into the closest seed clusters. This does not only speed up the algorithm, but it also reduces the noise that might be introduced by infrequent terms in the clustering process. We propose a novel *domain-specific similarity measure* incorporating both statistical association and semantic similarity between a pair of candidates, which recognizes features referring to the same aspects in a particular domain. To further

improve the quality of clusters, several problem-specific *merging constraints* are used to prevent the clusters referring to different aspects from being merged during the clustering process. The algorithm stops when it cannot find another pair of clusters satisfying these constraints.

This algorithm is evaluated on reviews from three domains: cell phone, TV and GPS. Its effectiveness is demonstrated through comparison with several state-of-the-art methods on both tasks of feature extraction and aspect discovery. Experimental results show that our method consistently yields better results than these existing methods on both tasks across all the domains.

2 Related Work

Feature and aspect extraction is a core component of aspect-based opinion mining systems. Zhang and Liu (2014) provide a broad overview of the tasks and the current state-of-the-art techniques.

Feature identification has been explored in many studies. Most methods focus on explicit features, including unsupervised methods that utilize association rules (Hu and Liu, 2004; Liu et al., 2005), dependency relations (Qiu et al., 2009; Xu et al., 2013), or statistical associations (Hai et al., 2012) between features and opinion words, and supervised ones that treat it as a sequence labeling problem and apply Hidden Markov Model (HMM) or Conditional Random Fields (CRF) (Jin et al., 2009; Yang and Cardie, 2013) to it. A few methods have been proposed to identify implicit features, e.g., using co-occurrence associations between implicit and explicit features (Su et al., 2006; Hai et al., 2011; Zhang and Zhu, 2013), or leveraging lexical relations of words in dictionaries (Fei et al., 2012). Many of these techniques require seed terms, hand-crafted rules/patterns, or other annotation efforts.

Some studies have focused on grouping features and assumed that features have been extracted beforehand or can be extracted from semi-structured Pros and Cons reviews. Methods including similarity matching (Carenini et al., 2005), topic modeling (Guo et al., 2009; Moghaddam and Ester, 2011), Expectation-Maximization (EM) based semi-supervised learning (Zhai et al., 2010; Zhai et al., 2011), and synonym clustering (Yu et al., 2011) have been explored in this context.

To extract features and aspects at the same time, topic model-based approaches have been explored by a large number of studies in recent years. Standard topic modeling methods such as pLSA (Hofmann, 2001) and LDA (Blei et al., 2003) are extended to suit the peculiarities of the problem, e.g., capturing local topics corresponding to ratable aspects (Titov and McDonald, 2008a; Titov and McDonald, 2008b; Brody and Elhadad, 2010), jointly extracting both topic/aspect and sentiment (Lin and He, 2009; Jo and Oh, 2011; Kim et al., 2013; Wang and Ester, 2014), incorporating prior knowledge to generate coherent aspects (Mukherjee and Liu, 2012; Chen et al., 2013; Chen et al., 2014), etc.

Very limited research has focused on exploring clustering-based solutions. Su et al. (2008) presented a clustering method that utilizes the mutual reinforcement associations between features and opinion words. It employs standard clustering algorithms such as k-means to iteratively group feature words and opinion words separately. The similarity between two feature words (or two opinion words) is determined by a linear combination of their intra-similarity and inter-similarity. Intra-similarity is the traditional similarity, and inter-similarity is calculated based on the degree of association between feature words and opinion words. To calculate the inter-similarity, a feature word (or an opinion word) is represented as a vector where each element is the co-occurrence frequency between that word and opinion words (or feature words) in sentences. Then the similarity between two items is calculated by cosine similarity of two vectors. In each iteration, the clustering results of one type of data items (feature words or opinion words) are used to update the pairwise similarity of the other type of items. After clustering, the strongest links between features and opinion words form the aspect groups. Mauge et al. (2012) first trained a maximum-entropy classifier to predict the probability that two feature expressions are synonyms, then construct a graph based on the prediction results and employ greedy agglomerative clustering to partition the graph to clusters. Bancken et al. (2014) used k-medoids clustering algorithm with a WordNet-based similarity metric to cluster semantically similar aspect mentions.

These existing clustering methods take two steps.

In the first step, features are extracted based on association rules or dependency patterns, and in the second step features are grouped into aspects using clustering algorithms. In contrast, our method extracts features and groups them at the same time. Moreover, most of these methods extract and group only explicit features, while our method deals with both explicit and implicit features. The method proposed in (Su et al., 2008) also handles implicit features (opinion words), but their similarity measure largely depends on co-occurrence between features and opinion words, which may not be efficient in identifying features that are semantically similar but rarely co-occur in reviews.

3   The Proposed Approach

Let $X = \{x_1, x_2, ..., x_n\}$ be a set of candidate features extracted from reviews of a given product (e.g., TV, cell phone). Specifically, by using a part-of-speech tagger[1], nouns (e.g., "battery") and two consecutive nouns (e.g., "battery life") are identified as candidates of *explicit* features, and adjectives and verbs are identified as candidates of *implicit* features. Stop words are removed from X. The algorithm aims to group similar candidate terms so that the terms referring to the same aspect are put into one cluster. At last, the important aspects are selected from the resulting clusters, and the candidates contained in these aspects are identified as features.

3.1   A Clustering Framework

Algorithm 1 illustrates the clustering process. The algorithm takes as input a set X that contains n candidate terms, a natural number k indicating the number of aspects, a natural number s ($0 < s \leq n$) indicating the number of candidates that will be grouped first to generate the *seed clusters*, and a real number δ indicating the upper bound of the distance between two mergeable clusters. Instead of applying the *agglomerative clustering* to all the candidates, it first selects a set $X' \subseteq X$ of s candidates that appear most frequently in the corpus for clustering. The reasons for this are two-fold. First, the frequently mentioned terms are more likely the actual features of customers' interests. By clustering these terms first, we can generate high quality seed clusters.

---

[1] http://nlp.stanford.edu/software/tagger.shtml

Second, as the clustering algorithm requires pairwise distances between candidates/clusters, it could be very time-consuming if there are a large number of candidates. We can speed up the process by clustering only the most frequent ones.

Algorithm 1: Clustering for Aspect Discovery

Input: $X = \{x_1, ..., x_n\}$, k, s, δ
Output: $\{A_j\}_{j=1}^k$

1 Select the top s most frequent candidates from X: $X' = \{x'_1, ..., x'_s\}$;
2 Set $C_1 \leftarrow \{x'_1\}, ..., C_s \leftarrow \{x'_s\}$;
3 Set $\Theta \leftarrow \{C_1, ..., C_s\}$;
4 **while** *there exist a pair of mergeable clusters from Θ* **do**
5   Select a pair of closest clusters C_l and C_m such that VIOLATE-CONSTRAINTS(C_l, C_m, δ) is false;
6     $C_m \leftarrow C_l \cup C_m$;
7     $\Theta \leftarrow \Theta - \{C_l\}$;
8 **for** $x_i \in X - X'$ **do**
9   Select the closest clusters C_d from Θ such that VIOLATE-CONSTRAINTS($\{x_i\}$, C_d, δ) is false;
10   **if** *there exist such cluster C_d* **then**
11         $C_d \leftarrow C_d \cup \{x_i\}$;
12 $\{A_j\}_{j=1}^k \leftarrow$ SELECT(Θ, k);

The clustering starts with every frequent term x'_i in its own cluster C_i, and Θ is the set of all clusters. In each iteration, a pair of clusters C_l and C_m that are most likely composed of features referring to the same aspect are merged into one. Both a similarity measure and a set of constraints are used to select such pair of clusters. We propose a *domain-specific similarity measure* that determines how similar the members in two clusters are regarding the particular domain/product. Moreover, we add a set of *merging constraints* to further ensure that the terms from different aspects would not be merged. The clustering process stops when it cannot find another pair of clusters that satisfy the constraints. We call the obtained clusters in Θ the *seed clusters*. Next, the algorithm assigns each of the remaining candidate $x_i \in X - X'$ to its closest seed cluster that satisfies the merging constraints. At last, k clusters are se-

lected from Θ as aspects[2]. Based on the idea that the frequent clusters are usually the important aspects of customers' interests, we select the top k clusters having the highest sum of members' frequencies of occurrence. From the k aspects, the nouns and noun phrases (e.g., "speed", "size") are recognized as explicit features, and the adjectives and verbs (e.g., "fast", "big"), are recognized as implicit features.

3.2 Domain-specific Similarity

The similarity measure aims to identify terms referring to the same aspect of a product. Prior studies (Zhai et al., 2010; Zhai et al., 2011) have shown that general semantic similarities learned from thesaurus dictionaries (e.g., WordNet) do not perform well in grouping features, mainly because the similarities between words/phrases are domain dependent. For example, "ice cream sandwich" and "operating system" are not relevant in general, but they refer to the same aspect in *cell phone* reviews[3]; "smooth" and "speed" are more similar in *cell phone* domain than they are in *hair dryer* domain. Methods based on distributional information in a domain-specific corpus are usually used to determine the domain-dependent similarities between words/phrases. However, relying completely on the corpus may not be sufficient either. For example, people usually use "inexpensive" or "great price" instead of "inexpensive price"; similarly, they use "running fast" or "great speed" instead of "fast speed". Though "inexpensive" and "price" or "fast" and "speed" refer to the same aspect, we may not find they are similar based on their context or co-occurrences in the corpus.

We propose to estimate the domain-specific similarities between candidates by incorporating both general semantic similarity and corpus-based statistical association. Formally, let G be a $n \times n$ similarity matrix, where G_{ij} is the *general semantic similarity* between candidates x_i and x_j, $G_{ij} \in [0, 1]$, $G_{ij} = 1$ when $i = j$, and $G_{ij} = G_{ji}$. We use UMBC Semantic Similarity Service[4] to get G. It combines both WordNet knowledge and statistics

---

[2]If k is larger than the number of clusters obtained, all the clusters are selected as aspects.

[3]*Ice Cream Sandwich* is a version of the Android mobile operating system.

[4]http://swoogle.umbc.edu/SimService/index.html

from a large web corpus to compute the semantic similarity between words/phrases (Han et al., 2013).

Let T be a $n \times n$ association matrix, where T_{ij} is the pairwise *statistical association* between x_i and x_j in the domain-specific corpus, $T_{ij} \in [0,1]$, $T_{ij} = 1$ when $i = j$, and $T_{ij} = T_{ji}$. We use normalized pointwise mutual information (NPMI) (Bouma, 2009) as the measure of association to get T, that is,

$$NPMI(x_i, x_j) = \frac{\log \frac{Nf(x_i, x_j)}{f(x_i)f(x_j)}}{-\log \frac{f(x_i, x_j)}{N}},$$

where $f(x_i)$ (or $f(x_j)$) is the number of documents where x_i (or x_j) appears, $f(x_i, x_j)$ is the number of documents where x_i and x_j co-occur in a sentence, and N is the total number of documents in the domain-specific corpus. NPMI is the normalization of pointwise mutual information (PMI), which has the pleasant property $NPMI(x_i, x_j) \in [-1, 1]$ (Bouma, 2009). The values of NPMI are rescaled to the range of $[0, 1]$, because we want $T_{ij} \in [0, 1]$.

A candidate x_i can be represented by the i-th row in G or T, i.e., the row vector $g_{i:}$ or $t_{i:}$, which tells us what x_i is about in terms of its general semantic similarities or statistical associations to other terms. The cosine similarity between two vectors $\vec{u}$ and $\vec{v}$ can be calculated as:

$$cosine(\vec{u}, \vec{v}) = \frac{\vec{u} \cdot \vec{v}}{\| \vec{u} \| \| \vec{v} \|} = \frac{\sum_{i=1}^n u_i v_i}{\sqrt{\sum_{i=1}^n u_i^2} \sqrt{\sum_{i=1}^n v_i^2}}.$$

By calculating the cosine similarity between two vectors of x_i and x_j ($i \neq j$), we get the following similarity metrics:

$$sim_g(x_i, x_j) = cosine(g_{i:}, g_{j:}),$$
$$sim_t(x_i, x_j) = cosine(t_{i:}, t_{j:}),$$
$$sim_{gt}(x_i, x_j) = max(cosine(g_{i:}, t_{j:}), cosine(t_{i:}, g_{j:})).$$

$sim_g(x_i, x_j)$ provides the comparison between $g_{i:}$ and $g_{j:}$. Similar row vectors in G indicate similar semantic meanings of two terms (e.g., "price" and "inexpensive"). $sim_t(x_i, x_j)$ provides the comparison between $t_{i:}$ and $t_{j:}$. Similar row vectors in T indicate similar context of two terms in the domain, and terms that occur in the same contexts tend to have similar meanings (Harris, 1954) (e.g., "ice cream sandwich" and "operating system"). $sim_{gt}(x_i, x_j)$ provides the comparison between the row vector in G and the row vector in T

of two terms. $sim_{gt}(x_i, x_j)$ is designed to get high value when the terms strongly associated with x_i (or x_j) are semantically similar to x_j (or x_i). By this measure, the domain-dependent synonyms such as "smooth" and "speed" (in *cell phone* domain) can be identified because the word "smooth" frequently co-occurs with some other words (e.g., "fast", "run") that are synonymous with the word "speed".

Because $G_{ij} \in [0, 1]$ and $T_{ij} \in [0, 1]$, the values of $sim_g(x_i, x_j)$, $sim_t(x_i, x_j)$, and $sim_{gt}(x_i, x_j)$ range from 0 to 1. In addition, $sim_g(x_i, x_j) = sim_g(x_j, x_i)$, $sim_t(x_i, x_j) = sim_t(x_j, x_i)$ and $sim_{gt}(x_i, x_j) = sim_{gt}(x_j, x_i)$. When $i = j$, we set all the similarity metrics between x_i and x_j to 1. Finally, the domain-specific similarity between x_i and x_j ($i \neq j$) is defined as the weighted sum of the above three similarity metrics: $sim(x_i, x_j) = w_g sim_g(x_i, x_j) + w_t sim_t(x_i, x_j) + w_{gt} sim_{gt}(x_i, x_j)$, where w_g, w_t and w_{gt} denote the relative weight of importance of the three similarity metrics, respectively. The values of the weight ranges from 0 to 1, and $w_g + w_t + w_{gt} = 1$.

Based on the domain-specific similarities between candidates, we now define the distance measures of clustering as:

$$dist_{avg}(C_l, C_m) = \frac{\sum_{x_{i'} \in C_l} \sum_{x_{j'} \in C_m} (1 - sim(x_{i'}, x_{j'}))}{|C_l| \times |C_m|},$$
$$r(C_l) = argmax_{x_{i'} \in C_l} f(x_{i'}),$$
$$dist_{rep}(C_l, C_m) = 1 - sim(r(C_l), r(C_m)),$$

where $dist_{avg}(C_l, C_m)$ is the average of candidate distances between clusters C_l and C_m, $r(C_l)$ is the most frequent member (i.e., *representative term*) in cluster C_l, and $dist_{rep}(C_l, C_m)$ is the distance between the representative terms of two clusters. The two clusters describing the same aspect should be close to each other in terms of both average distance and representative distance, thus the final distance is defined as the maximum of these two:

$$dist(C_l, C_m) = max(dist_{avg}(C_l, C_m), dist_{rep}(C_l, C_m)).$$

3.3 Merging Constraints

Prior studies (Wagstaff et al., 2001) have explored the idea of incorporating background knowledge as constraints on the clustering process to further improve the performance. Two types of constraints are usually considered: must-link constraints specifying that two objects (e.g., words) must be placed in the same cluster, and cannot-link constraints specifying that two objects cannot be placed in the same cluster. We also add problem-specific constraints that specify which clusters cannot be merged together, but instead of manually creating the cannot-links between specific words, our cannot-link constraints are automatically calculated during the clustering process.

Specifically, two clusters cannot be merged if they violate any of the three merging constraints: (1) The distance between two clusters must be less than a given value δ (see Algorithm 1). (2) There must be at least one noun or noun phrase (candidate of explicit feature) existing in one of the two clusters. Because we assume an aspect should contain at least one explicit feature, and we would not get an aspect by merging two non-aspect clusters. (3) The sum of frequencies of the candidates from two clusters co-occurring in the same sentences must be higher than the sum of frequencies of them co-occurring in the same documents but different sentences. The idea is that people tend to talk about different aspects of a product in different sentences in a review, and talk about the same aspect in a small window (e.g., the same sentence).

4 Experiments

In this section, we evaluate the effectiveness of the proposed approach on feature extraction and aspect discovery. Table 1 describes the datasets from three different domains that were used in the experiments. The cell phone reviews were collected from the on-line shop of a cell phone company, and the GPS and TV reviews were collected from Amazon.

Three human annotators manually annotate the datasets to create gold standards of features and aspects. These annotators first identify feature expressions from reviews independently. The expressions that were agreed by at least two annotators were selected as features. Then the authors manually specified a set of aspects based on these features, and asked three annotators to label each feature with an aspect category. The average inter-annotator agreement on aspect annotation was $\kappa = 0.687$ ($stddev = 0.154$) according to Cohen's Kappa statistic. To obtain the gold standard annotation of aspects, the annotators discussed to reach an agreement when there was a disagreement on the aspect category of a feature. *We are making the datasets and annotations publicly available[5].*

Table 1 shows the number of reviews, aspects, unique explicit/implicit features manually identified by annotators, and candidates of explicit (i.e., noun and noun phrase) and implicit (i.e., adjective and verb) features extracted from the datasets in three domains.

	Cell phone	GPS	TV
# Reviews	500	500	500
# Aspects	46	37	34
# Features (expl.)	419	637	485
# Features (impl.)	339	492	277
# Candidates (expl.)	1,248	2,078	2,333
# Candidates (impl.)	1,115	1,779	1,690

Table 1: Data sets and gold standards.

We use "CAFE" (**C**lustering for **A**spect and **F**eature **E**xtraction) to denote the proposed method. We assume the number of aspects k is specified by the users, and set $k = 50$ throughout all the experiments. We use $s = 500$, $\delta = 0.8$, $w_g = w_t = 0.2$, $w_{gt} = 0.6$ as the default setting of CAFE, and study the effect of parameters in Section "Influence of Parameters". In addition, we evaluate each individual similarity metric – "CAFE-g", "CAFE-t" and "CAFE-gt" denote the variations of "CAFE" that use $sim_g(x_i, x_j)$, $sim_t(x_i, x_j)$, and $sim_{gt}(x_i, x_j)$ as the similarity measure, respectively. We empirically set $\delta = 0.4$ for "CAFE-g", $\delta = 0.84$ for "CAFE-t" and $\delta = 0.88$ for "CAFE-gt".

4.1 Evaluations on Feature Extraction

We compared CAFE against the following two state-of-the-art methods on feature extraction:

- **PROP**: A double propagation approach (Qiu et al., 2009) that extracts features using hand-crafted rules based on dependency relations between features and opinion words.
- **LRTBOOT**: A bootstrapping approach (Hai et al., 2012) that extracts features by mining pairwise feature-feature, feature-opinion, opinion-opinion associations between terms in the corpus, where the association is measured by the likelihood ratio tests (LRT).

Both methods require seeds terms. We ranked the feature candidates by descending document fre-

---

[5]http://knoesis.wright.edu/researchers/luchen/download/naacl16_aspects.zip

	Cell-phone			GPS			TV			macro-averaged F-score
Method	Precision	Recall	F-score	Precision	Recall	F-score	Precision	Recall	F-score	
PROP	0.3489	0.6503	0.4541	0.3157	**0.8222**	0.4562	0.2851	**0.8454**	0.4264	0.4456
LRTBOOT	0.3819	**0.8112**	0.5193	0.5342	0.7488	0.6235	0.4572	0.7340	0.5635	0.5688
CAFE	0.6421	0.5929	0.6165	**0.7197**	0.7064	**0.7130**	**0.6086**	0.7155	**0.6577**	**0.6624**
CAFE-g	**0.6822**	0.5667	**0.6191**	0.6831	0.6154	0.6475	0.5959	0.6330	0.6139	0.6268
CAFE-t	0.4761	0.5833	0.5243	0.5765	0.6845	0.6259	0.4892	0.7175	0.5817	0.5773
CAFE-gt	0.5519	0.6000	0.5749	0.6512	0.6028	0.6261	0.5445	0.7320	0.6245	0.6085

Table 2: Experimental results of feature extraction.

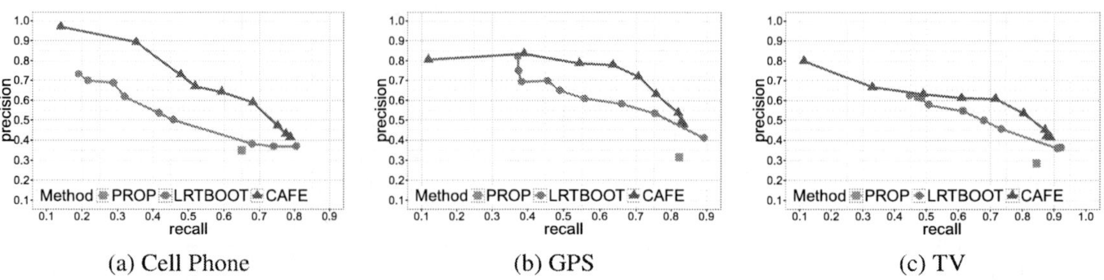

(a) Cell Phone   (b) GPS   (c) TV

Figure 1: Precision-recall curves at various parameter settings for three feature extraction methods.

quency and manually selected the top 10 genuine features as seeds for them. According to the study (Hai et al., 2012), the performance for LRTBOOT remained almost constant when increasing the seeds from 1 to 50. Three association thresholds need to be specified for LRTBOOT. Following the original study in which the experiments were conducted on cell-phone reviews, we set $ffth = 21.0$, $ooth = 12.0$, and performed grid search for the value of $foth$. The best results were achieved at $foth = 9.0$ for cell-phone reviews, and at $foth = 12.0$ for GPS and TV reviews.

The results were evaluated by precision $= \frac{N_{agree}}{N_{result}}$, recall $= \frac{N_{agree}}{N_{gold}}$, and F-score $= \frac{2 \times precision \times recall}{precision + recall}$, where N_{result} and N_{gold} are the number of features in the result and the gold standard, respectively, and N_{agree} is the number of features that are agreed by both sides. Because PROP and LRTBOOT extract only explicit features, the evaluation was conducted on the quality of explicit features. The performance of identifying implicit features will be examined by evaluation on aspect discovery, because implicit features have to be merged into aspects to be detected.

Table 2 shows the best results (in terms of F-score) of feature extraction by different methods. Both PROP and LRTBOOT obtain high recall and relatively low precision. CAFE greatly improves precision, with a relatively small loss of recall, resulting in 21.68% and 9.36% improvement in macro-averaged F-score over PROP and LRTBOOT,

respectively. We also plot precision-recall curves at various parameter settings for CAFE and LRT-BOOT in Figure 1. For CAFE, we kept $s = 500$, $w_g = w_t = 0.2, w_{gt} = 0.6$, and increased δ from 0.64 to 0.96. For LRTBOOT, we kept $ffth = 21.0$, $ooth = 12.0$, and increased $foth$ from 6.0 to 30.0. For PROP, only one precision-recall point was obtained. From Figure 1, we see that the curve of CAFE lies well above those of LRTBOOT and PROP across three datasets. Though LRTBOOT achieved similar precision as CAFE did at the recall rate of approximately 0.37 for GPS reviews and at the recall rate of approximately 0.49 for TV reviews, it performed worse than CAFE at increasing recall levels for both datasets.

The key difference between CAFE and the baselines is that CAFE groups terms into clusters and identifies the terms in the selected aspect clusters as features, while both baselines enlarge a feature seed set by mining syntactical or statistical associations between features and opinion words. The results suggest that features can be more precisely identified via aspect clustering. Generally, CAFE is superior to its variations, and CAFE-g outperforms CAFE-gt and CAFE-t.

4.2 Evaluations on Aspect Discovery

For comparison with CAFE on aspect discovery, we implemented the following three methods:

- **MuReinf**: A clustering method (Su et al., 2008) that utilizes the mutual reinforcement association between features and opinion words to iteratively group them into clusters. Similar to the proposed method, it is unsupervised, clustering-based, and handling implicit features.

- **L-EM**: A semi-supervised learning method (Zhai et al., 2011) that adapts the Naive Bayesian-based EM algorithm to group synonym features into categories. Because semi-supervised learning needs some labeled examples, the proposed method first automatically generates some labeled examples (i.e., the groups of synonym feature expressions) based on features sharing common words and lexical similarity.
- **L-LDA**: A baseline method (Zhai et al., 2011) that is based on LDA. The same labeled examples generated by L-EM are used as seeds for each topic in topic modeling.

These three methods require features to be extracted beforehand, and focus on grouping features into aspects. Both LRTBOOT and CAFE are used to provide the input features to them. We set $\alpha = 0.6$ for MuReinf, because their study (Su et al., 2008) showed that the method achieved best results at $\alpha > 0.5$. All three methods utilize dictionary-based semantic similarity to some extent. Since CAFE uses the UMBC Semantic Similarity Service, we use the same service to provide the semantic similarity for all the methods.

	Cell-phone	GPS	TV	macro-average
LRTBOOT + MuReinf	0.7182	0.8031	0.7747	0.7653
LRTBOOT + L-EM	0.6633	0.6893	0.7138	0.6888
LRTBOOT + L-LDA	0.7653	0.7198	0.7664	0.7505
CAFE + MuReinf	0.7973	0.8212	**0.8334**	0.8173
CAFE + L-EM	0.7581	0.7772	0.7879	0.7744
CAFE + L-LDA	0.7904	0.8144	0.8247	0.8098
CAFE	0.8041	**0.8238**	0.8326	**0.8202**
CAFE-g	0.7382	0.7534	0.8205	0.7707
CAFE-t	0.7868	0.8050	0.7965	0.7961
CAFE-gt	**0.8073**	0.7716	0.7906	0.7898

Table 3: Rand Index of aspect identification.

The results were evaluated using Rand Index (Rand, 1971), a standard measure of the similarity between the clustering results and a gold standard. Given a set of n objects and two partitions of them, the Rand Index is defined as $\frac{2(a+b)}{n \times (n-1)}$. The idea is that the agreements/disagreements between two partitions are checked on $n \times (n-1)$ pairs of objects.

Among all the pairs, there are a pairs belonging to the same cluster in both partitions, and b pairs belonging to different clusters in both partitions. In this study, the gold standard and the aspect clusters may not share the exact same set of features due to the noise in feature extraction, therefore we consider n the number of expressions in the union of two sets.

Table 3 shows the Rand Index achieved by different methods. Among the methods that generate partitions of the same features provided by CAFE, CAFE achieves the best macro-averaged Rand Index, followed by CAFE + MuReinf, CAFE + L-LDA, and CAFE + L-EM. CAFE outperforms the variations using the single similarity metric, i.e., CAFE-g, CAFE-t and CAFE-gt. The results imply the effectiveness of our domain-specific similarity measure in identifying synonym features in a particular domain. Using the input features from LRT-BOOT, the performance of MuReinf, L-EM and L-LDA decrease on all three domains, compared with using the input features from CAFE. The decrease is more significant for L-EM and L-LDA than for MuReinf, which suggest that the semi-supervised methods L-EM and L-LDA are more dependent on the quality of input features.

Table 4 illustrates a sample of the discovered aspects and features by CAFE. The algorithm identifies the important *aspects* in general sense as well as the important aspects that are not so obvious thus could be easily missed by human judges, e.g., *suction cup* for GPS and *glare* for TV. In addition, both explicit and implicit features are identified and grouped into the aspects, e.g., *expensive* and *price*, *big* and *size*, *sensitive* and *signal*, etc.

4.3 Influence of Parameters

We varied the value of δ (distance *upper bound*), s (the number of frequent candidates selected to generate seed clusters) and w_{gt} (the weight of sim_{gt}) to see how they impact the results of CAFE, for both feature extraction (in terms of F-Score) and aspect discovery (in terms of Rand Index). Both F-score and Rand Index increases rapidly at first and then slowly decreases as we increase δ from 0.64 to 0.96 (see the left subplot in Figure 2). Because more clusters are allowed to be merged as we increase δ, which is good at first but then it introduces more noise than benefit. Based on the experiments on

Cell-phone	GPS	TV
screen, display, touch, button, pixel screen, icon, amold display, *pressed, click, navigate*	**direction, route, road, instructions, streets, highway, side, lane, exit, intersection, track**	**picture, hd picture, image, scene, photo, action scenes, view**, *visual, show, present*
battery, life, battery life, power, backup battery, *spare, recharge, powered, plug, lasted*	**map, point, information, interest, info, data, map loading**, *accurate, search, locate, listed*	**cable, channel, cable box, station, wire, antenna tuner, format, transmission**
camera, picture, video, photo, zoom, motion videos, gallery, *fuzzy, grainy, shooting, recorded*	**signal, satellite, antenna, receiver, radio, fm transmitter, traffic receiver, sensor**, *sensitive*	**sound, speaker, volume, noise, hum, echo**, *audible, tinny, muffled, hissing, loud, pitched*
call, car, speaker, call quality, call reminder, *drop, connect, answered, clear, hear, speak*	**voice, voice recognition, microphone, speaker, volume, guy voice, robot voice**, *repeat, loud*	**price, market, cost, tax, credit, sale, discount**, *purchase, expensive, worth, saved, cheap*
size, hand, screen size, finger, font size, width, *tiny, huge, bigger, larger, big, carry, small, large*	**suction cup, windshield, bean bag, mount, attachment**, *unit fall, attaching, pulling, break*	**glare, reflection, sunlight, lamp, daylight**, *blind, flickering, dim, fluorescent, dark, reflective*

Table 4: Examples of discovered aspects and features by the proposed approach CAFE. Explicit and implicit features are denoted in boldface and italics, respectively. The first term in each cluster is the representative term of that aspect.

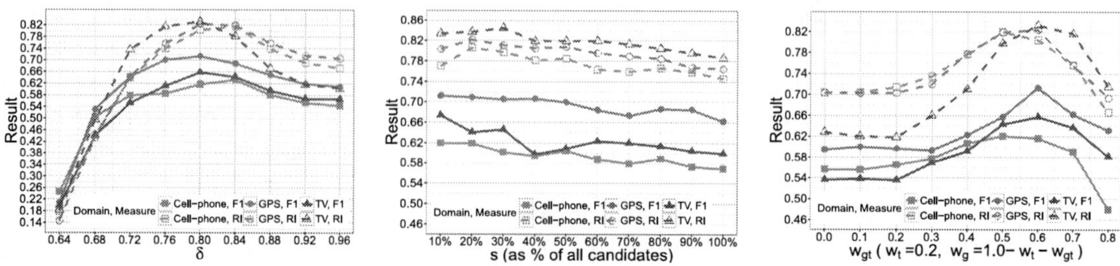

Figure 2: CAFE parameter tuning: feature quality in terms of F-score (F1) and aspect quality in terms of Rand Index (RI). The default setting is $s = 500$, $\delta = 0.8$, $w_g = w_t = 0.2$, $w_{gt} = 0.6$. We keep other parameters as the default setting when we tune an individual parameter.

three domains, the best results can be achieved when δ is set to a value between 0.76 and 0.84. The middle subplot illustrates the impact of s, which shows that CAFE generates better results by first clustering the top 10%-30% most frequent candidates. Infrequent words/phrases are usually more noisy, and the results could be affected more seriously if the noises are included in the clusters in the early stage of clustering. Experiments were also conducted to study the impact of the three similarity metrics. Due to the space limit, we only display the impact of w_{gt} and w_g given $w_t = 0.2$. As we can see from the right subplot in Figure 2, setting w_{gt} or w_g to zero evidently decreases the performance, indicating both similarity metrics are useful. The best F-score and Rand Index can be achieved when we set w_{gt} to 0.5 or 0.6 across all three domains.

5 Conclusion

In this paper, we proposed a clustering approach that simultaneously extracts features and aspects of a given product from reviews. Our approach groups the feature candidates into clusters based on their domain-specific similarities and merging constraints, then selects the important aspects and identifies features from these aspects. This approach has the following advantages: (1) It identifies both aspects and features simultaneously. The evaluation shows its accuracy on both tasks outperforms the competitors. (2) Both explicit and implicit features can be identified and grouped into aspects. The mappings of implicit features into explicit features are accomplished naturally during the clustering process. (3) It does not require labeled data or seed words, which makes it easier to apply and broader in application. In our future work, instead of selecting aspects based on frequency, we will leverage domain knowledge to improve the selection.

Acknowledgments

We would like to thank Lushan Han and UMBC Ebiquity Lab for kindly allowing us to access their Semantic Similarity Service. This research was partially supported by NSF awards CNS-1513721 "Context-Aware Harassment Detection on Social Media" and EAR-1520870 "Hazards SEES: Social and Physical Sensing Enabled Decision Support for Disaster Management and Response".

References

Wouter Bancken, Daniele Alfarone, and Jesse Davis. 2014. Automatically detecting and rating product aspects from textual customer reviews. In *DMNLP Workshop at ECML/PKDD*.

David M Blei, Andrew Y Ng, and Michael I Jordan. 2003. Latent dirichlet allocation. *the Journal of machine Learning research*, 3:993–1022.

Gerlof Bouma. 2009. Normalized (pointwise) mutual information in collocation extraction. *GSCL*, pages 31–40.

Samuel Brody and Noemie Elhadad. 2010. An unsupervised aspect-sentiment model for online reviews. In *NAACL*, pages 804–812.

Giuseppe Carenini, Raymond T Ng, and Ed Zwart. 2005. Extracting knowledge from evaluative text. In *K-CAP*, pages 11–18.

Zhiyuan Chen, Arjun Mukherjee, Bing Liu, Meichun Hsu, Malu Castellanos, and Riddhiman Ghosh. 2013. Exploiting domain knowledge in aspect extraction. In *EMNLP*, pages 1655–1667.

Zhiyuan Chen, Arjun Mukherjee, and Bing Liu. 2014. Aspect extraction with automated prior knowledge learning. In *ACL*, pages 347–358.

Geli Fei, Bing Liu, Meichun Hsu, Malu Castellanos, and Riddhiman Ghosh. 2012. A dictionary-based approach to identifying aspects im-plied by adjectives for opinion mining. In *COLING*, page 309.

Honglei Guo, Huijia Zhu, Zhili Guo, XiaoXun Zhang, and Zhong Su. 2009. Product feature categorization with multilevel latent semantic association. In *CIKM*, pages 1087–1096.

Zhen Hai, Kuiyu Chang, and Jung-jae Kim. 2011. Implicit feature identification via co-occurrence association rule mining. In *Computational Linguistics and Intelligent Text Processing*, pages 393–404.

Zhen Hai, Kuiyu Chang, and Gao Cong. 2012. One seed to find them all: mining opinion features via association. In *CIKM*, pages 255–264.

Lushan Han, Abhay Kashyap, Tim Finin, James Mayfield, and Jonathan Weese. 2013. Umbc ebiquity-core: Semantic textual similarity systems. In *the Second Joint Conference on Lexical and Computational Semantics*, pages 44–52.

Zellig S Harris. 1954. Distributional structure. *Word*.

Thomas Hofmann. 2001. Unsupervised learning by probabilistic latent semantic analysis. *Machine learning*, 42(1-2):177–196.

Minqing Hu and Bing Liu. 2004. Mining opinion features in customer reviews. In *AAAI*, pages 755–760.

Wei Jin, Hung Hay Ho, and Rohini K Srihari. 2009. Opinionminer: a novel machine learning system for web opinion mining and extraction. In *SIGKDD*, pages 1195–1204.

Yohan Jo and Alice H Oh. 2011. Aspect and sentiment unification model for online review analysis. In *WSDM*, pages 815–824.

Suin Kim, Jianwen Zhang, Zheng Chen, Alice H Oh, and Shixia Liu. 2013. A hierarchical aspect-sentiment model for online reviews. In *AAAI*.

Chenghua Lin and Yulan He. 2009. Joint sentiment/topic model for sentiment analysis. In *CIKM*, pages 375–384.

Bing Liu, Minqing Hu, and Junsheng Cheng. 2005. Opinion observer: analyzing and comparing opinions on the web. In *WWW*, pages 342–351.

Yue Lu, ChengXiang Zhai, and Neel Sundaresan. 2009. Rated aspect summarization of short comments. In *WWW*, pages 131–140.

Samaneh Moghaddam and Martin Ester. 2011. Ilda: interdependent lda model for learning latent aspects and their ratings from online product reviews. In *SIGIR*, pages 665–674.

Arjun Mukherjee and Bing Liu. 2012. Aspect extraction through semi-supervised modeling. In *ACL*, pages 339–348.

Guang Qiu, Bing Liu, Jiajun Bu, and Chun Chen. 2009. Expanding domain sentiment lexicon through double propagation. In *IJCAI*, pages 1199–1204.

William M Rand. 1971. Objective criteria for the evaluation of clustering methods. *Journal of the American Statistical association*, 66(336):846–850.

Qi Su, Kun Xiang, Houfeng Wang, Bin Sun, and Shiwen Yu. 2006. Using pointwise mutual information to identify implicit features in customer reviews. In *ICCPOL*, pages 22–30.

Qi Su, Xinying Xu, Honglei Guo, Zhili Guo, Xian Wu, Xiaoxun Zhang, Bin Swen, and Zhong Su. 2008. Hidden sentiment association in chinese web opinion mining. In *WWW*, pages 959–968.

Ivan Titov and Ryan McDonald. 2008a. Modeling online reviews with multi-grain topic models. In *WWW*, pages 111–120.

Ivan Titov and Ryan T McDonald. 2008b. A joint model of text and aspect ratings for sentiment summarization. In *ACL*, pages 308–316.

Kiri Wagstaff, Claire Cardie, Seth Rogers, Stefan Schrödl, et al. 2001. Constrained k-means clustering with background knowledge. In *ICML*, volume 1, pages 577–584.

Hao Wang and Martin Ester. 2014. A sentiment-aligned topic model for product aspect rating prediction. In *EMNLP*, pages 1192–1202.

Liheng Xu, Kang Liu, Siwei Lai, Yubo Chen, and Jun Zhao. 2013. Mining opinion words and opinion targets in a two-stage framework. In *ACL*, pages 1764–1773.

Yinqing Xu, Tianyi Lin, Wai Lam, Zirui Zhou, Hong Cheng, and Anthony Man-Cho So. 2014. Latent aspect mining via exploring sparsity and intrinsic information. In *CIKM*, pages 879–888.

Bishan Yang and Claire Cardie. 2013. Joint inference for fine-grained opinion extraction. In *ACL*, pages 1640–1649.

Jianxing Yu, Zheng-Jun Zha, Meng Wang, and Tat-Seng Chua. 2011. Aspect ranking: identifying important product aspects from online consumer reviews. In *ACL*, pages 1496–1505.

Zhongwu Zhai, Bing Liu, Hua Xu, and Peifa Jia. 2010. Grouping product features using semi-supervised learning with soft-constraints. In *COLING*, pages 1272–1280.

Zhongwu Zhai, Bing Liu, Hua Xu, and Peifa Jia. 2011. Clustering product features for opinion mining. In *WSDM*, pages 347–354.

Lei Zhang and Bing Liu. 2014. Aspect and entity extraction for opinion mining. In *Data Mining and Knowledge Discovery for Big Data*, pages 1–40.

Yu Zhang and Weixiang Zhu. 2013. Extracting implicit features in online customer reviews for opinion mining. In *WWW companion*, pages 103–104.

Li Zhao, Minlie Huang, Haiqiang Chen, Junjun Cheng, and Xiaoyan Zhu. 2014. Clustering aspect-related phrases by leveraging sentiment distribution consistency. In *EMNLP*, pages 1614–1623.

Opinion Holder and Target Extraction on Opinion Compounds – A Linguistic Approach

Michael Wiegand and **Christine Bocionek**
Spoken Language Systems
Saarland University
D-66123 Saarbrücken, Germany
michael.wiegand@lsv.uni-saarland.de
cbocionek@lsv.uni-saarland.de

Josef Ruppenhofer
Dept. of Information Science
and Language Technology
Hildesheim University
D-31141 Hildesheim, Germany
ruppenho@uni-hildesheim.de

Abstract

We present an approach to the new task of opinion holder and target extraction on opinion compounds. Opinion compounds (e.g. *user rating* or *victim support*) are noun compounds whose head is an opinion noun. We do not only examine features known to be effective for noun compound analysis, such as paraphrases and semantic classes of heads and modifiers, but also propose novel features tailored to this new task. Among them, we examine paraphrases that jointly consider holders and targets, a verb detour in which noun heads are replaced by related verbs, a global head constraint allowing inferencing between different compounds, and the categorization of the sentiment view that the head conveys.

1 Introduction

One of the key subtasks in sentiment analysis is opinion role extraction. It can be divided into the extraction of *opinion holders (OH)*, i.e. entities expressing an opinion, and the extraction of *opinion targets (OT)*, i.e. entities or propositions at which sentiment is directed. This task is vital for various applications involving sentiment analysis, e.g. opinion summarization or opinion question answering.

Opinion role extraction is commonly regarded as a task in lexical semantics. An opinion is evoked by some opinion word, e.g. *criticized* in (1), *skeptical* in (2) or *intentions* in (3), and its opinion roles are usually realized as syntactic dependents. Opinion words come in many shapes, the most frequent types being opinion verbs (1), opinion adjectives (2) and opinion nouns (3). These types of opinion words

have extensively been studied in various sentiment-related corpora, such as MPQA (Wiebe et al., 2005).

(1) [Peter $_{OH}$] **criticized**$_{verb}$ [Mary $_{OT}$].
(2) [Mary $_{OH}$] was **skeptical**$_{adj}$ [about the plan $_{OT}$].
(3) [Peter $_{OH}$] had firm **intentions**$_{noun}$ [to quit his job $_{OT}$].

In this work, we examine opinion roles that are realized in opinion compounds. We define an opinion compound (Table 1) as a noun compound, i.e. a sequence of two nouns, where the second noun, i.e. the *head*, is an opinion expression. The first noun, i.e. the *modifier*, can represent an opinion holder (4)-(5), an opinion target (6)-(7) or neither (8)-(9). Our aim is to automatically classify the modifier into these categories. This task is challenging as, unlike with opinion roles expressed in the syntax (1)-(3), the immediate context of compounds does not contain explicit cues as to the relation between head and modifier. Moreover, due to the high productivity of compounding, this task cannot be solved by compiling a (finite) compound lexicon that encodes for each compound the category of its modifier.

(4) [user $_{OH}$] **rating** *(i.e. user rates something)*
(5) [consumer $_{OH}$] **uncertainty** *(i.e. consumers are uncertain)*
(6) [victim $_{OT}$] **support** *(i.e. support for victims)*
(7) [test $_{OT}$] **anxiety** *(i.e. having anxiety towards test taking)*
(8) spring **upswing** *(i.e. economic upswing in spring)*
(9) phone **harassment** *(i.e. harassment inflicted via phone)*

Notice that we focus exclusively on opinion role extraction. We do not try to detect the polarity associated with the compound. Neither do we consider implicature-related information about effects (Deng and Wiebe, 2014), but only inherent sentiment.

We study opinion role extraction on opinion compounds in German. German is known for its frequent

Proceedings of NAACL-HLT 2016, pages 800–810,
San Diego, California, June 12-17, 2016. ©2016 Association for Computational Linguistics

compounds	*user rating*; *victim support*; *spring upswing*	
immediate constituents	*user*; *victim*; *spring*	*rating*; *support*; *upswing*
grammatical function	modifier	head

Table 1: Internal structure of opinion compounds.

	Dataset I		Dataset II	
	2000 compounds 389 (unique) heads		1000 compounds 247 (unique) heads	
category of modifier	role	no role	holder	target
frequency	937	1063	450	580
proportion (in %)	46.85	53.15	45.00	58.00

Table 2: The two different datasets.

use of noun compounds. In the STEPS-corpus, the benchmark dataset for German opinion role extraction (Ruppenhofer et al., 2014), almost every other sentence contains an opinion compound.

Compounds can also be commonly found in other key languages, such as English. Since the methods we apply to this task and the issues that they address are not language specific, our approach can be replicated on other languages.

Apart from examining traditional features from noun compound analysis, in this paper, we also introduce novel features specially designed for the analysis of opinion compounds.

We also created a new gold standard for this task (see also §3). The STEPS-corpus, as such, is fairly small and only contains about 200 unique compounds. We considered this amount insufficient for producing a gold standard. Also, none of the existing datasets on noun compounds (Lauer, 1995; Barker and Szpakowicz, 1998; Nastase and Szpakowicz, 2003; Girju et al., 2009; Kim and Baldwin, 2005; Tratz and Hovy, 2010; Dima et al., 2014) contain any information regarding opinion roles.

2 Related Work

With regard to opinion role extraction, many features for supervised learning have been explored. They typically address the relationship between opinion word and opinion role on the basis of surface patterns (Choi et al., 2005), part-of-speech information (Wiegand and Klakow, 2010), syntactic information (Kessler and Nicolov, 2009; Jakob and Gurevych, 2010) or semantic role labeling (Johansson and Moschitti, 2013; Deng and Wiebe, 2015). The majority of those features cannot be applied to our task since for opinion compounds, there is no context between opinion role and opinion word.

In the area of noun compound analysis, there are two predominant approaches. On the one hand, lexical resources, such as WordNet (Miller et al., 1990), are employed in order to assign semantic categories to head and modifier and infer from those labels the

underlying relation (Rosario and Hearst, 2001; Kim and Baldwin, 2005; Girju et al., 2005; Girju et al., 2009). On the other hand, paraphrases that contain co-occurrences of head and modifier are exploited (Girju et al., 2009; Nakov and Hearst, 2013). In order to increase coverage, paraphrases can be automatically acquired (Butnariu and Veale, 2008; Kim and Nakov, 2011). Cross-lingual information has also been harnessed for this task (Girju, 2007).

3 Data & Annotation

We created a new dataset[1] by retrieving opinion compounds from the *deWaC*-corpus (Baroni et al., 2009) comprising 1.7 billion words. (Word embeddings (§5.2 & §5.6) and word similarity graphs (§5.7 & §6.4) were also created from this corpus.)

In German, noun compounds are typically realized as single tokens. In order to obtain a set of opinion compounds, we extracted all noun compounds from *deWaC* whose second morpheme is an opinion noun. Morphological analysis was carried out using *morphisto* (Zielinski and Simon, 2009).[2] As opinion nouns, we used the nouns from the **PolArt sentiment lexicon** (Klenner et al., 2009). Unfortunately, this lexicon is lacking in *neutral* opinion nouns, such as *Meinung (opinion)* or *Erwartung (expectation)* which frequently occur in compounds, e.g. *Expertenmeinung (expert opinion)* or *Kundenerwartungen (customer expectations)*. Therefore, we translated the 235 neutral opinion nouns from the (English) Subjectivity Lexicon (Wilson et al., 2005) into German.

From the opinion compounds extracted from *deWaC*, we created two manually annotated datasets (Table 2). We use more than one dataset as we consider our task as a multi-stage task as shown in Figure 1. We believe that this is necessary as differ-

---

[1]available at: www.coli.uni-saarland.de/~miwieg/naacl_2016_op_compounds_data.tgz

[2]*The data release provides more details regarding the gold standard, e.g. how compound instances were sampled.*

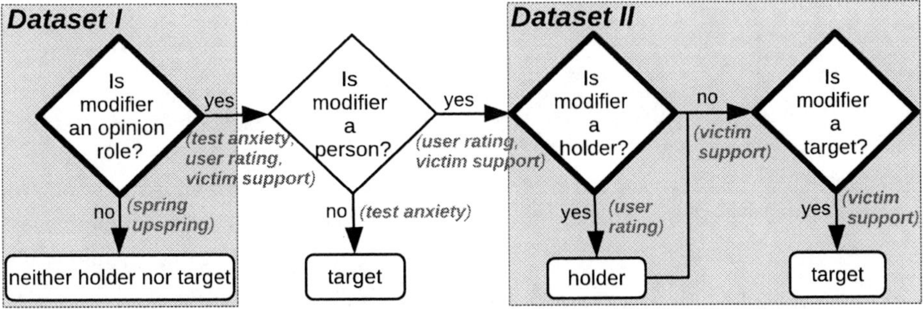

Example opinion compounds are listed in brackets.

Each question (indicated by a rhombus) can be modeled with one binary supervised classifier. We build 3 classifiers, thus excluding the second question because of its simplicity.

Figure 1: Generic pipeline for processing opinion compounds.

ent types of knowledge are required for the different steps. In the first step (**Dataset I**), the compounds containing some opinion role (4)-(7) are separated from those not containing any role at all (8)-(9). At this stage, holders are <u>not</u> distinguished from targets. This is done in the second step which exclusively focuses on opinion roles. This step is further divided into two substeps. First, one checks whether the modifier denotes a person. A modifier representing an opinion role but not denoting a person (e.g. *test anxiety*) can only be a target. Since this is a simple classification step (provided a lexical resource is available which tells persons apart from non-persons, e.g. WordNet), we have no dataset for it. The greater challenge lies in all those compounds whose modifier is a person and for which we already know that it is either holder or target (e.g. *user rating* or *victim support*). Only for those cases do we produce another dataset (**Dataset II**). Note that in this dataset the two roles are not completely disjoint. In 3% of the compounds, the modifier represents both holder and target. Prominent examples are reciprocal relationships, e.g. *Geschwisterneid (sibling jealousy)*.

On a sample of 200 compounds extracted from each of the two datasets we measured inter-annotation agreement. On the first dataset, we obtained Cohen's $\kappa = 0.60$, while on the second, we obtained $\kappa = 0.60$ for holders and $\kappa = 0.62$ for targets, respectively. These scores can be interpreted as substantial agreement (Landis and Koch, 1977).

4 Classifiers and the Three Different Tasks

We solve the given task as a supervised classification problem. As a classifier, we employ Markov Logic Networks (MLNs). We use this classifier because it allows us to integrate all of our features, including global constraints (see discussion in §5.5).

We consider **3 different tasks** (bold rhombuses in Figure 1): the detection of opinion **roles** (Dataset I), the detection of opinion **holders** (Dataset II) and the detection of opinion **targets** (Dataset II). Each task is modeled as a binary classifier. Even though the latter two tasks use the same dataset, we cannot train just one single binary classifier as there are compounds whose modifiers represent both holder and target, e.g. *Geschwisterneid (sibling jealousy)*.[3]

5 Feature Design

Our core **global features**, which are used for all three tasks (§4), include the two predominant approaches for compound analysis, i.e. (plain) paraphrases (§5.1) and semantic knowledge (§5.4). We extend the paraphrase approach with two major innovations. First, we examine a verb detour (§5.2) by which we gain important information regarding the syntactic relationship between the modifier and the head of the compound. Secondly, we show that joint paraphrases (§5.3) considering both holder and

---

[3]For the holder-detection task, the modifier of such compounds are considered a holder, while for the target-detection task, they are considered a target. For the holder-detection task, we have the two classes *holder* and *no holder*, while for the target-detection task, the classes are *target* and *no target*.

Global Features	
features used on all three tasks (i.e. Datasets I and II)	PARA (§5.1-5.3), SEM (§5.4), HEAD (§5.5)
Local Features	
feature used only on task *Role* (i.e. Dataset I)	SUBJ (§5.6)
feature used only on task *Holder* and task *Target* (i.e. Dataset II)	VIEW (§5.7)

Table 3: Division of global and local features.

target are better than paraphrases focusing on only one role. We argue that for our task, (syntactic) ambiguity rather than lack of coverage is the pressing problem. Therefore, we do not focus on paraphrase acquisition but introduce new disambiguation features. Beside the extensions to paraphrases mentioned above, we introduce a global head constraint (§5.5) as an additional global feature. As a **local feature** for the initial role classification, we perform subjectivity detection on the compound (§5.6). And finally, we use the sentiment view that the head of the compound evokes (§5.7) as a local feature in the holder and target classification tasks.

Table 3 lists which feature is used in which task. If a feature is restricted to a specific task (i.e. it is a local feature), then this is motivated below in the relevant subsection introducing the respective feature.

5.1 Plain Paraphrases ($PARA_{plain}$)

An established method for computing the relation expressed by a compound is to consider paraphrases, that is, co-occurrences of the head and modifier as individual constituents accompanied by some predictive context. For example, the compound *Expertenauffassung (expert view)* can be paraphrased by *Auffassung unter Experten (view among experts)*. The preposition *unter (among)* is an explicit lexical clue for the (implicit) relation holding between head and modifier in the compound. As paraphrases we manually collected 18 frequent dependency relations that typically hold between an opinion noun and its opinion holder (10) or its opinion target (11).[4] *(The data release provides more information including a full list of all paraphrases.)* For each compound, we check in *deWaC* whether head and modifier can be observed in any of those relations.

(10) $objp_{unter(among)}$(<opinion noun>, <holder>): Auffassung

---

[4] We obtain dependency parses by *ParZu* (Sennrich et al., 2009).

unter Experten (view among experts)

(11) $objp_{auf(towards)}$(<opinion noun>, <target>): Hass auf Christen (hatred towards Christians)

We consider each of those selected dependency relations as an individual feature, i.e. we do not explicitly group the chosen relations to *holder* and *target*. Assuming that the predictiveness of the different relations varies, this encoding allows a supervised classifier to appropriately weight each relation.

5.2 Verb Detour Paraphrases ($PARA_{verb}$)

Some of the paraphrases from §5.1 are ambiguous. This particularly concerns $objp_{von(of)}$ which occurs with approx. 40% of the compounds of our dataset. On the first reading illustrated by (12)a), we observe a modifier being a holder, while, on the second reading shown by (13)a), the modifier is a target.

For heads being deverbal nouns (e.g. *comment* or *assessment*), this ambiguity can often be resolved by considering morphologically related verbs. In (12)b) and (13)b), the two modifiers no longer share the same dependency relation to the opinion word. Opinion holders tend to occur in subject position (12)b) while targets occur in object position (13)b). Wiegand and Klakow (2012) identify these dependency relations for the two different opinion roles as the most frequent ones. So for deverbal nouns, which make up 57% of the heads of our compounds, we add a feature that checks in *deWaC* whether the modifier is more often observed as a subject or an object of a verb related to the head. (Wiegand and Klakow (2012) actually consider semantic roles, i.e. *agent* and *patient*, instead of dependency relations. Due to the lack of robust semantic role-labeling for German, we use dependency relations as a proxy. That is, we identify agents with the dependency relation *subj* and patients with the relation *obj*.)

(12) *paraphrases for* <u>Leser</u>kommentar (reader comments):
- a) Kommentar$_{noun}$ [von Lesern $_{objp_{von}}$] (comment$_{noun}$ [of readers $_{objp_{of}}$]).
- b) Leser$_{subj}$ kommentieren$_{verb}$ ein Ereignis. (Readers$_{subj}$ comment$_{verb}$ on an event.)

(13) *paraphrases for* <u>Schüler</u>beurteilung (student assessment):
- a) Beurteilung$_{noun}$ [von Schülern $_{objp_{von}}$] (assessment$_{noun}$ [of students $_{objp_{of}}$])
- b) Lehrer beurteilen$_{verb}$ Schüler$_{obj}$. (Teachers assess$_{verb}$ students$_{obj}$.)

Even though the disambiguation of deverbal noun compounds with the help of verb relations has been examined before (Lapata, 2002), it has not been exploited for an actual application, such as opinion role extraction. Neither has it been compared against plain paraphrases, which use the head noun of the compound directly (§5.1).

Our use of verb semantics for compound analysis is also different from its predominant use in previous work (Kim and Baldwin, 2006; Nakov and Hearst, 2013) where noun compounds are considered whose parts represent arguments of an abstract verbal relation (e.g. *malaria mosquito* are arguments of relation '*mosquito causes malaria*'). Thus, the aim has been to predict verbs for those compounds that match those abstract relations (e.g. *to cause*). We are looking for different verbs, namely those that are the morphological basis for the head noun.

For this verb detour, we produce a mapping from nouns (i.e. the heads of our opinion compounds) to verbs by combining distributional and string similarity. We extracted the verbs most similar to each of these nouns (we use top 100). For that we induce vector representations of all head nouns of our gold standard and all existing German verbs using the embedding toolkit *Word2Vec* (Mikolov et al., 2013).[5] For each noun, we select the verb with the highest cosine-similarity that has at least a *Levenshtein (string) similarity* (Levenshtein, 1966) of 3. This high threshold ensures that nouns which are not deverbal nouns are not mapped to any verb. Against a manual mapping, our automatic method produced an F-score of 76.1 (at a precision of 77.1).

5.3 Joint Paraphrases (PARA$_{joint}$)

Another way of reducing the ambiguity of paraphrases is to employ paraphrases that jointly consider opinion holder and target (Table 4). We assume that the presence of one ambiguous dependency relation is less problematic in the presence of another less ambiguous relation. The ambiguity can be resolved by method of elimination. For instance, even though $objp_{von/of}$ (*Widerstand/resistance, Bauern/farmers*) is ambiguous, in the first example of Table 4, it can only represent a holder, since the second relation $objp_{gegen/against}$ (*Widerstand/resistance, Gesetz/regulation*) implies a target.

---

[5]We used the `cbow`-model with 200 dimensions. All remaining parameters are set to their respective default values.

We also use paraphrases in which the compound itself occurs (second and third pattern type of Table 4). Since, in the first example of the second pattern type, only the relation $objp_{mit/with}$ (*Zufriedenheit/satisfaction, Unternehmen/company*) is indicative of a target, the modifier is likely to be a holder. (The example of the third pattern type follows an analogous pattern to extract a target.) The second example (of the second pattern type) *Sprengstoffanschlag (bomb attack)* illustrates that paraphrases can also be used to infer the absence of opinion roles. *Sprengstoff (explosive)* cannot be a target because of the other target relation that is present. It cannot be a holder either as it is not a person.

The fourth pattern type in Table 4 considers patterns involving possessive pronouns. They typically represent holders, so the remaining dependency relation can only represent a target.

Similar to §5.1, we encode the joint-paraphrase patterns by their individual dependency relations. That is, the first example in Table 4 would be represented as the feature $objp_{von}^{\textbf{modifier}}\_objp_{gegen}$.

5.4 Semantic Knowledge (SEM)

We use GermaNet (Hamp and Feldweg, 1997), the German version of WordNet, to look up the hypernyms of each modifier and each head. The hypernymy relation is the most frequently used semantic relation employed for noun compound analysis (Girju et al., 2005; Nastase et al., 2006; Girju et al., 2009; Tratz and Hovy, 2010). Hypernyms allow some generalization over the lexical units representing the heads and modifiers of our compounds. By manual inspection, we found that there are several hypernyms that correlate with a category we want to predict. For example, heads having the hypernym *politische Handlung (political act)* typically indicate holders as in *Arbeiterunruhe (worker unrest)* or *Studentenrebellion (student rebellion)*. Hypernyms may also serve as negative cues. For example, heads having the hypernym *Verbrechen (crime)* are typically contained in compounds whose modifiers represent neither a holder nor a target, such as *Steuervergehen (tax offense)* or *Autodiebstahl (car theft)*.

Pattern Type	Example Compound	Label	Example Sentence
<head> <holder> <target>	Bauern**widerstand** (farmer **resistance**)	holder	**Widerstand** [von Bauern $_{objp_{von}}$] [gegen das Gesetz $_{objp_{gegen}}$] (**resistance** [of farmers $_{objp_{of}}$] [against the regulation $_{objp_{against}}$])
	Schüler**beurteilung** (student **assessment**)	target	**Beurteilung** [der Lehrer $_{gmod}$] [von Schülern $_{objp_{von}}$] ([teachers' $_{possessive}$] **assessment** [of students $_{objp_{of}}$])
<compound> <target>	Mitarbeiter**zufriedenheit** (staff **satisfaction**)	holder	Mitarbeiter**zufriedenheit** [mit dem Unternehmen $_{objp_{mit}}$] (staff **satisfaction** [with their company $_{objp_{with}}$])
	Sprengstoff**anschlag** (bomb **attack**)	no role	Sprengstoff**anschlag** [auf Touristen $_{objp_{auf}}$] (bomb **attack** [on tourists $_{objp_{on}}$])
<compound> <holder>	Prüfungs**angst** (test **anxiety**)	target	Prüfungs**angst** [unter Schülern $_{objp_{unter}}$] (test **anxiety** [among students $_{objp_{among}}$])
<possessive> <head> <target>	Kinder**freundlichkeit** (child **friendliness**)	target	[seine $_{possessive}$] **Freundlichkeit** [gegenüber Kindern $_{objp_{gegenueber}}$] ([his $_{possessive}$] **friendliness** [towards children $_{objp_{towards}}$])

Table 4: Illustration of patterns for joint paraphrases.

Head	Preference	Examples
Haltung (attitude)	holder	Arbeitgeberhaltung (employer attitude), Autorenhaltung (author attitude), Konsumentenhaltung (consumer attitude), Verbraucherhaltung (customer attitude), Zuschauerhaltung (viewer attitude)
Verehrung (worship)	target	Ahnenverehrung (ancestor worship), Heldenverehrung (hero worship), Ikonenverehrung (icon worship), Kaiserverehrung (emperor worship), Märtyrerverehrung (martyr worship)
Attentat (attack)	no role	Bombenattentat (bombing attack), Flugzeugattentat (aircraft attack), Selbstmordattentat (suicide attack), Sprengstoffattentat (explosive attack), Säureattentat (acid attack)

Table 5: Illustration of selectional preferences of heads of opinion compounds.

5.5 Head Constraint (HEAD)

We observed that many heads have a strong selectional preference as to what type they select as a modifier. This is illustrated in Table 5. There are heads that prefer opinion holders as modifiers (e.g. *Haltung (attitude)*), heads that prefer targets (e.g. *Verehrung (worship)*) or heads that prefer no role (e.g. *Attentat (attack)*). This is further substantiated by Table 6 showing the high average role-purity of compound groups sharing the same head. Purity is measured by the proportion of the most frequent role occurring within each group of compounds sharing the same head.[6] Given this selectional preference, we formulate a *global head constraint* (Table 7) that if two compounds have the same head, their modifiers should convey the same opinion role.

In order to implement this constraint in a supervised classifier we employ Markov Logic Networks (MLNs), which combine first-order logic with probabilities. As a tool, we use *thebeast* (Riedel, 2008). MLNs have been effectively used in various related NLP tasks, such as discourse-based sentiment analysis (Zirn et al., 2011), semantic-role labeling (Meza-Ruiz and Riedel, 2009), anaphora resolution (Hou et al., 2013) or question answering (Khot et al., 2015).

---

[6]On average, a head occurs in 5 different compounds on Dataset I, and in 4 different compounds on Dataset II.

Dataset I	88.86	Dataset II	91.36

Table 6: Role-purity of compounds with the same head.

MLNs are a set of pairs (F_i, w_i) where F_i is a first-order logic formula and w_i an associated real-valued weight. They build a template for constructing a Markov network given a set of constants C. The probability distribution that is estimated is a log-linear model

$$P(X = x) = \frac{1}{Z} exp \left(\sum_{i=1}^{k} w_i n_i(x) \right) \qquad (1)$$

where $n_i(x)$ is the number of groundings in F_i in x and Z is some normalization constant.

5.6 Subjectivity Disambiguation (SUBJ)

Many opinion words are known to be ambiguous. Some of their senses convey subjectivity while others do not (Akkaya et al., 2009). 13% of the compounds in Dataset I (Figure 1) are not subjective due to an ambiguous head. The modifier of such compounds neither represents a holder or a target. Examples are *Luftdruck (air pressure)* or *Strömungswiderstand (flow resistance)*. Dataset II exclusively contains compounds whose modifiers are holders or targets. By definition, all those compounds are subjective. So a subjectivity feature may only be useful for the *role*-detection task, which uses Dataset I.

$$\forall c_1 [\forall c_2 [\forall h [\forall r_1 [\forall r_2 [[isCompound(c_1) \land isCompound(c_2) \land isHeadOf(h, c_1) \land isHeadOf(h, c_2) \land isRoleOfModifierOf(r_1, c_1) \land isRoleOfModifierOf(r_2, c_2)] \rightarrow (r_1 == r_2)]]]]]$$

Table 7: Head constraint as logic formula.

For a feature indicating the subjectivity of a compound, we cannot look up the compounds in a sentiment lexicon since they are rarely included. Instead, we compute the 100 most similar German nouns for every compound and use as a feature the proportion of opinion nouns (according to the PolArt sentiment lexicon) on that list. Opinion nouns on that similarity list are less likely to be compounds and therefore more likely to be found in a sentiment lexicon. As in §5.2, similarity is measured by the cosine between two *Word2Vec*-vector embeddings. As a result, we find, for example, for *Luftdruck (air pressure)*, other non-subjective terms, such as *Temperatur (temperature)* or *Luftfeuchtigkeit (humidity)*, while for the subjective compound *Hexenglaube (witch belief)*, we find the subjective expressions *Aberglaube (superstition)* or *Häresie (heresy)*.

5.7 Sentiment Views (VIEW)

Our final feature considers the sentiment view (Wiegand and Ruppenhofer, 2015) that an opinion noun, in our case the head of the compound, conveys. We distinguish between *speaker views*, expressions conveying sentiment of the speaker of the utterance (e.g. *mistake, finesse, noise*), and *actor views*, expressions conveying sentiment of the entities participating in the event denoted by the opinion noun (e.g. *support, criticism, rating*). Nouns conveying speaker views have an implicit opinion holder (i.e. the speaker). Therefore, if such a noun is the head of an opinion compound, the modifier cannot be a holder but only a target, e.g. *Arztfehler (doctor's mistake), Kinderlärm (children's noise)* or *Neonazipropaganda (neonazi propaganda)*. Only heads conveying an actor view can take modifiers to represent a holder *(Nutzerwertung/user rating)* or a target *(Opferunterstützung/victim support)*. Sentiment views may be helpful on Dataset II (Figure 1), where we have to decide between holders and targets. 40.3% of those heads convey a speaker view.

So far, the detection of sentiment views on a *lexical* level has only been examined for opinion verbs. Wiegand and Ruppenhofer (2015) propose a boot-strapping approach in which seed verbs for the different sentiment views are automatically extracted.[7] Then, a label propagation algorithm (Talukdar et al., 2008) is run on a word-similarity graph generated from the opinion verbs. Thus labels from the seeds can be expanded to the remaining opinion verbs. The nodes in the graph correspond to the opinion verbs. The best performing graph is based on the similarity metric introduced in Lin (1998).

A critical step is the seed generation. Wiegand and Ruppenhofer (2015) extract seeds representing actor views by looking for opinion words frequently co-occurring with *prototypical opinion holders (protoOHs)*. These are common nouns, such as *opponents* or *critics*, that typically act as opinion holders (Wiegand and Klakow, 2011). By definition, such explicit opinion holders indicate an actor view. Seeds for speaker-view verbs are obtained by extracting verbs co-occurring with *reproach-patterns*, such as *obji(beschuldigt/blamed for, <verb>)* (14) that matches in (15).

(14) *Pattern*: obji(*beschuldigt/blamed for,* <**speaker-view verb**>)
(15) Die UNO wurde *beschuldigt,* [die Klimadaten **fehlgedeutet**$_{verb}$ zu haben $_{obji}$]. (The UN was *blamed for* **misinterpreting**$_{verb}$ climate data.)
(16) *Pattern*: objg(*beschuldigt/blamed for,* <**speaker-view noun**>)
(17) Die UNO wurde [der **Fehldeutung**$_{noun\ objg}$] von Klimadaten *beschuldigt*. (The UN was *blamed for* the **misinterpretation**$_{noun}$ of climate data.)

This bootstrapping approach can be immediately applied to our setting. In the word-similarity graph, the opinion verbs are replaced by opinion nouns. With protoOHs, not only actor-view verbs but also actor-view nouns can be extracted. Similarly, the reproach-patterns work for both verbs (15) and nouns (17). (Only the dependency relation changes from *obji* (14) to *objg* (16).) ProtoOHs and reproach patterns are simply translated from English to German.

---

[7]Wiegand and Ruppenhofer (2015) consider two types of actor views, *agent view* and *patient view*. The former take their opinion holder as an agent (typical verbs are *criticize* or *support*), while the latter align holders to patients (typical verbs are *disappoint* or *please*). Since this distinction of actor views does not exist among nouns, we combine them into a single category in this paper.

6 Experiments

We consider one binary MLN classifier for each of our three tasks (§4). Most of our features are frequently occurring features (e.g. paraphrases (§5.1), subjectivity feature (§5.6), sentiment views (§5.7)). Supervised classifiers only require few training data in order to assign appropriate weights to such features. Therefore, we sample 20% of the instances for each task of the respective dataset as training data. We test on the remaining 80% of the dataset. This procedure is repeated 5 times. The 5 training samples within each task are disjoint. We report macro-average F-score averaged over the 5 test samples.

We will first evaluate global features and then proceed to the local features. A division of our feature set into these groups was presented in Table 3.

6.1 Evaluation of Global Features

Table 8 compares the features that can be applied on all three tasks. On average, PARA (§5.1-§5.3) is slightly better than SEM (§5.4). Since their combination always results in a significant improvement, we conclude that these features contain complementary information. In the majority of cases, HEAD (§5.5) also yields significant improvement.

Table 9 compares the different subtypes of paraphrases (§5.1-§5.3). For all tasks, notable improvements are obtained by adding the other types of paraphrases to the plain paraphrases. While the joint paraphrases improve the plain paraphrases on all tasks, for the verb detour, improvements can be observed only for the extraction of holders and targets. However, this improvement is significantly better than that of the joint paraphrases. In summary, in order to obtain best possible results on all three types of classifications, we need all types of paraphrases.

6.2 Evaluation of the Local Feature for Role Detection

Table 10 examines the impact of the subjectivity feature (§5.6). We closely compare this feature with the head constraint since we found both features only working in combination with other features. In terms of statistical significance, the head constraint is more effective than the subjectivity feature.

| | Tasks | | |
Features	Role	Holder	Target
SEM	54.75	58.82	58.10
SEM+HEAD	56.33°	60.88°	60.33°
PARA	62.62	57.01	57.46
PARA+HEAD	63.82*†	59.07*	60.64*
PARA+SEM	63.92†	60.28	62.20‡
PARA+SEM+HEAD	**65.26***†‡	**61.58***†	**63.27**°‡

statistical significance testing (paired t-test): °: better than w/o **+HEAD** ($p < 0.1$); *: better than w/o **+HEAD** ($p < 0.05$); †: better than **SEM+HEAD** ($p < 0.05$); ‡: better than **PARA+HEAD** ($p < 0.05$)

Table 8: F-scores of features applicable to all tasks.

| | Tasks | | |
Features	Role	Holder	Target
PARA$_{plain}$	58.34	52.55	51.64
PARA$_{plain+joint}$	62.34*	54.87*	54.96*
PARA$_{plain+verb}$	58.85	**57.51***†	**58.43***†
PARA$_{plain+joint+verb}$	**62.62***	57.01*†	57.46*†

statistical significance testing (paired t-test, significance level $p < 0.05$) *: better than **PARA**$_{plain}$; †: better than **PARA**$_{plain+joint}$

Table 9: F-scores of paraphrase features.

6.3 Evaluation of the Local Feature for the Detection of Holders and Targets

Table 11 examines the impact of the sentiment-view feature (§5.7). We evaluate two variants of this feature. **VIEW**$_{gold}$ is a manual view annotation of all opinion head nouns. It should be considered an upper bound. The second variant, **VIEW**$_{boot}$, employs the views as produced automatically by the bootstrapping approach outlined in §5.7.[8]

Table 11 shows that this feature has a notable impact on both PARA$_{plain}$ (i.e. the simplest feature set) and SEM+PARA+HEAD (i.e. the most complex feature set). This underlines that sentiment views are an important aspect for opinion role extraction.

---

[8]Note that unlike Wiegand and Ruppenhofer (2015) we manually removed incorrect seeds from the set of automatically generated seeds (this affects less than 9% of the seeds).

| Features | SEM | | PARA | | PARA+SEM | |
		+HEAD		+HEAD		+HEAD
	54.75	56.33†	62.62	63.82‡	63.92	65.26‡
+SUBJ	56.37°	58.57°†	63.07	64.76*‡	64.57	66.42°‡

statistical significance testing (paired t-test) °: better than w/o **+SUBJ** ($p < 0.1$); *: better than w/o **+SUBJ** ($p < 0.05$); †: better than w/o **+HEAD** ($p < 0.1$); ‡: better than w/o **+HEAD** ($p < 0.05$)

Table 10: Comparison of SUBJ and HEAD evaluated on task *Role* (Dataset I); *evaluation measure: F-score.*

Task	$VIEW_{gold}$	$PARA_{plain}$			PARA+SEM+HEAD		
			+VIEW			+VIEW	
			boot	gold		boot	gold
Holder	42.4	52.6	59.5*	64.8*	61.6	64.7*	**71.2***†
Target	43.6	51.6	61.7*	65.1*	63.3	66.5*	**73.4***†

statistical significance testing (paired t-test, significance level $p < 0.05$) *: better than w/o **+VIEW**; †: better than **+VIEW**$_{boot}$

Table 11: F-scores of sentiment view features.

all words in the sentences (bag of words)
brown clusters of all words in the sentences (bag of clusters)
part-of-speech sequences between head and modifier mentions
part-of-speech tags before/after modifier mentions
part-of-speech tags before/after head mentions
dependency paths between head and modifier mentions
proportion of opinion words in the sentences

each training/test instance represents the set of all sentences in which head and modifier of a specific compound co-occur

Table 12: Features for distant supervision (baseline) classifier.

6.4 Comparison against Baselines

Table 13 compares the best result from our previous experiments against **3 baselines**. The first is a **majority classifier** predicting the majority class.

The second baseline is a classifier inspired by **distant supervision** (Mintz et al., 2009). As in our paraphrase features, this classifier considers the context in which modifier and head of a compound occur as separate constituents. The difference is, however, that we consider <u>every</u> such co-occurrence (within the same sentence) as a context that conveys the same relation as the one that is (implicitly) conveyed by the compound. Even though such an assumption is naive, it has been shown to produce quite reasonable performance in relation extraction (Mintz et al., 2009). The advantage of such an approach is that a *generic* relation extraction/opinion role extraction classifier can be trained on the resulting data. Unlike our proposed method, it does not require features tailored to the specific task (e.g. *manually* written paraphrases). Since the result-

Features		Tasks		
		Role	Holder	Target
BASELINES	Majority	34.70	35.49	36.71
	Distant Superv.	54.85	47.71	45.72
	Distributional	58.15	52.91	52.72
our approach *(best feature sets)*		**66.42***	**64.71***	**66.50***

*: better than all baselines according to statistical significance testing (paired t-test, significance level at $p < 0.05$)

Table 13: Comparison of our approach against baselines; *evaluation measure: F-score.*

ing feature set (see also Table 12) is fairly high-dimensional, we employ a support vector machine. As an implementation, we use SVM^{light} (Joachims, 1999).

The third baseline is a **distributional approach** in which label propagation is performed on a word-similarity graph for compounds. The fundamental difference between that baseline and our proposed approach is that no relationship between head and modifier is modeled but just the contexts of the compounds themselves. We use the same (distributional) similarity metric to form the word-similarity graph and the same label propagation algorithm for this task as we did for bootstrapping sentiment views in §5.7. The only difference is that the nodes in the graph are opinion compounds instead of opinion nouns. The training data for the second and third baseline are the same compounds as in our previous experiments.

Table 13 shows that our proposed method substantially outperforms the baselines.

7 Conclusion

We presented an approach to the new task of opinion role extraction on opinion compounds. We produced a gold standard and proposed a method for classification. We did not only consider established features for noun compound analysis, i.e. paraphrases and semantic classes of heads and modifiers, but also proposed useful new features tailored to our task. We examined paraphrases that jointly consider holders and targets, a verb detour in which noun heads are replaced by related verbs, a global head constraint, and an auxiliary classification categorizing the sentiment view of the head of the compound. None of these features is language-specific.

Acknowledgements

We would like to thank Ines Rehbein for interesting discussions and helpful feedback on earlier drafts of the paper. The authors were partially supported by the German Research Foundation (DFG) under grants RU 1873/2-1 and WI 4204/2-1.

References

Cem Akkaya, Janyce Wiebe, and Rada Mihalcea. 2009. Subjectivity Word Sense Disambiguation. In *Proceedings of EMNLP*, pages 190–199.

Ken Barker and Stan Szpakowicz. 1998. Semi-Automatic Recognition of Noun ModifierRelationships. In *Proceedings of COLING/ACL*, pages 96–102.

Marco Baroni, Silvia Bernardini, Adriano Ferraresi, and Eros Zanchetti. 2009. The WaCky Wide Web: A Collection of Very Large Linguistically Processed Web-Crawled Corpora. *Language Resources and Evaluation*, 43(3):209–226.

Cristina Butnariu and Tony Veale. 2008. A Concept-Centered Approach to Noun-Compound Interpretation. In *Proceedings of COLING*, pages 81–88.

Yejin Choi, Claire Cardie, Ellen Riloff, and Siddharth Patwardhan. 2005. Identifying Sources of Opinions with Conditional Random Fields and Extraction Patterns. In *Proceedings of HLT/EMNLP*, pages 355–362.

Lingjia Deng and Janyce Wiebe. 2014. Sentiment Propagation via Implicature Constraints. In *Proceedings of EACL*, pages 377–385.

Lingjia Deng and Janyce Wiebe. 2015. Joint Prediction for Entity/Event-Level Sentiment Analysis using Probabilistic Soft Logic Models. In *Proceedings of EMNLP*, pages 179–189.

Corina Dima, Verena Henrich, Erhard Hinrichs, and Christina Hoppermann. 2014. How to Tell a Schneemann from a Milchmann: An Annotation Scheme for Compound-Internal Relations. In *Proceedings of LREC*, pages 1194–1201.

Roxana Girju, Dan Moldovan, Marta Tatu, and Daniel Antohe. 2005. On the semantics of noun compounds. *Computer Speech and Language*, 19:479–496.

Roxana Girju, Preslav Nakov, Vivi Nastase, Stan Szpakowicz, Peter Turney, and Deniz Yuret. 2009. Classification of semantic relations between nominals. *Language Resources and Evaluation*, 43(2):105–121.

Roxana Girju. 2007. Improving the Interpretation of Noun Phrases with Cross-linguistic Information. In *Proceedings of ACL*, pages 568–575.

Birgit Hamp and Helmut Feldweg. 1997. GermaNet - a Lexical-Semantic Net for German. In *Proceedings of ACL workshop Automatic Information Extraction and Building of Lexical Semantic Resources for NLP Applications*, pages 9–15.

Yufang Hou, Katja Markert, and Michael Strube. 2013. Global Inference for Bridging Anaphora Resolution. In *Proceedings of HLT/NAACL*, pages 907–917.

Niklas Jakob and Iryna Gurevych. 2010. Extracting Opinion Targets in a Single- and Cross-Domain Setting with Conditional Random Fields. In *Proceedings of EMNLP*, pages 1035–1045.

Thorsten Joachims. 1999. Making Large-Scale SVM Learning Practical. In B. Schölkopf, C. Burges, and A. Smola, editors, *Advances in Kernel Methods - Support Vector Learning*, pages 169–184. MIT Press.

Richard Johansson and Alessandro Moschitti. 2013. Relational Features in Fine-Grained Opinion Analysis. *Computational Linguistics*, 39(3):473–509.

Jason S. Kessler and Nicolas Nicolov. 2009. Targeting Sentiment Expressions through Supervised Ranking of Linguistic Configurations. In *Proceedings of ICWSM*.

Tushar Khot, Niranjan Balasubramanian, Eric Gribkoff, Ashish Sabharwal, Peter Clark, and Oren Etzioni. 2015. Exploring Markov Logic Networks for Question Answering. In *Proceedings of EMNLP*, pages 685–694.

Su Nam Kim and Timothy Baldwin. 2005. Automatic Interpretation of Noun Compounds Using Wordnet Similarity. In *Proceedings of IJCNLP*, pages 945–956. Springer.

Su Nam Kim and Timothy Baldwin. 2006. Interpreting Semantic Relations in Noun Compounds via Verb. In *Proceedings of COLING/ACL*, pages 491–498.

Su Nam Kim and Preslav Nakov. 2011. Large-Scale Noun Compound Interpretation Using Bootstrapping and the Web as a Corpus. In *Proceedings of EMNLP*, pages 648–658.

Manfred Klenner, Angela Fahrni, and Stefanos Petrakis. 2009. PolArt: A Robust Tool for Sentiment Analysis. In *Proceedings of NoDaLiDa*, pages 235–238.

J. Richard Landis and Gary G. Koch. 1977. The Measurement of Observer Agreement for Categorical Data. *Biometrics*, 33(1):159–174.

Maria Lapata. 2002. The Disambiguation of Nominalizations. *Computational Linguistics*, 28(3):357–388.

Mark Lauer. 1995. *Designing Statistical Language Learners: Experiments on Noun Compounds*. Ph.D. thesis, Department of Computing, Macquarie University, Australia.

Vladimir I. Levenshtein. 1966. Binary codes capable of correcting deletions, insertions, and reversals. *Soviet Physics Doklady*, 10(8):707–710.

Dekang Lin. 1998. Automatic Retrieval and Clustering of Similar Words. In *Proceedings of ACL/COLING*, pages 768–774.

Ivan Meza-Ruiz and Sebastian Riedel. 2009. Jointly Identifying Predicates, Arguments and Senses using Markov Logic. In *Proceedings of HLT/NAACL*, pages 155–163.

Tomas Mikolov, Kai Chen, Greg Corrado, and Jeffrey Dean. 2013. Efficient Estimation of Word Representations in Vector Space. In *Proceedings of Workshop at the International Conference on Learning Representations (ICLR)*.

George Miller, Richard Beckwith, Christiane Fellbaum, Derek Gross, and Katherine Miller. 1990. Introduction to WordNet: An On-line Lexical Database. *International Journal of Lexicography*, 3:235–244.

Mike Mintz, Steven Bills, Rion Snow, and Dan Jurafsky. 2009. Distant Supervision for Relation Extraction without Labeled Data. In *Proceedings of ACL/IJCNLP*, pages 1003–1011.

Preslav I. Nakov and Marti A. Hearst. 2013. Semantic Interpretation of Nouns Compounds Using Verbal and Other Paraphrases. *ACM Transactions on Speech and Language Processing*, 10(3).

Vivi Nastase and Stan Szpakowicz. 2003. Exploring Noun-Modifier Semantic Relations. In *Proceedings of IWCS*, pages 285–301.

Vivi Nastase, Jelber Sayyad-Shirabad, Marina Sokolova, and Stan Szpakowicz. 2006. Learning Noun-Modifier Semantic Relations with Corpus-based and WordNet-based Features. In *Proceedings of AAAI*, pages 781–786.

Sebastian Riedel. 2008. Improving the Accuracy and Efficiency of MAP Inference for Markov Logic. In *Proceedings of UAI*, pages 468–475.

Barbara Rosario and Marti Hearst. 2001. Classifying the Semantic Relations in Noun Compounds via a Domain-Specific Lexical Hierarchy. In *Proceedings of EMNLP*.

Josef Ruppenhofer, Julia Maria Struß, Jonathan Sonntag, and Stefan Gindl. 2014. IGGSA-STEPS: Shared Task on Source and Target Extraction from Political Speeches. *Journal for Language Technology and Computational Linguistics*, 29(1):33–46.

Rico Sennrich, Gerold Schneider, Martin Volk, and Martin Warin. 2009. A New Hybrid Dependency Parser for German. In *Proceedings of GSCL*, pages 115–124.

Partha Pratim Talukdar, Joseph Reisinger, Marius Pasca, Deepak Ravichandran, Rahul Bhagat, and Fernando Pereira. 2008. Weakly-Supervised Acquisition of Labeled Class Instances using Graph Random Walks. In *Proceedings of EMNLP*, pages 582–590.

Stephen Tratz and Eduard Hovy. 2010. A Taxonomy, Dataset, and Classifier for Automatic Noun Compound Interpretation. In *Proceedings of ACL*, pages 678–687.

Janyce Wiebe, Theresa Wilson, and Claire Cardie. 2005. Annotating Expressions of Opinions and Emotions in Language. *Language Resources and Evaluation*, 39(2/3):164–210.

Michael Wiegand and Dietrich Klakow. 2010. Convolution Kernels for Opinion Holder Extraction. In *Proceedings of HLT/NAACL*, pages 795–803.

Michael Wiegand and Dietrich Klakow. 2011. Prototypical Opinion Holders: What We can Learn from Experts and Analysts. In *Proceedings of RANLP*, pages 282–288.

Michael Wiegand and Dietrich Klakow. 2012. Generalization Methods for In-Domain and Cross-Domain Opinion Holder Extraction. In *Proceedings of EACL*, pages 325–335.

Michael Wiegand and Josef Ruppenhofer. 2015. Opinion Holder and Target Extraction based on the Induction of Verbal Categories. In *Proceedings of CoNLL*, pages 215–225.

Theresa Wilson, Janyce Wiebe, and Paul Hoffmann. 2005. Recognizing Contextual Polarity in Phrase-level Sentiment Analysis. In *Proceedings of HLT/EMNLP*, pages 347–354.

Andrea Zielinski and Christian Simon. 2009. Morphisto – An Open Source Morphological Analyzer for German. In *Proceedings of the 2009 Conference on Finite-State Methods and Natural Language Processing: Post-proceedings of the 7th International Workshop FSMNLP 2008*, pages 224–231. IOS Press Amsterdam, The Netherlands.

Cäcilia Zirn, Mathias Niepert, Heiner Stuckenschmidt, and Michael Strube. 2011. Fine-Grained Sentiment Analysis with Structural Features. In *Proceedings of IJCNLP*, pages 336–344.

Capturing Reliable Fine-Grained Sentiment Associations
by Crowdsourcing and Best–Worst Scaling

Svetlana Kiritchenko and **Saif M. Mohammad**
National Research Council Canada
{svetlana.kiritchenko,saif.mohammad}@nrc-cnrc.gc.ca

Abstract

Access to word–sentiment associations is useful for many applications, including sentiment analysis, stance detection, and linguistic
analysis. However, manually assigning fine-
grained sentiment association scores to words
has many challenges with respect to keeping
annotations consistent. We apply the annotation technique of Best–Worst Scaling to obtain real-valued sentiment association scores
for words and phrases in three different domains: general English, English Twitter, and
Arabic Twitter. We show that on all three domains the ranking of words by sentiment remains remarkably consistent even when the
annotation process is repeated with a different
set of annotators. We also, for the first time,
determine the minimum difference in sentiment association that is perceptible to native
speakers of a language.

1 Introduction

Word–sentiment associations, commonly captured
in sentiment lexicons, are useful in automatic sentiment prediction (Pontiki et al., 2014; Rosenthal
et al., 2014), stance detection (Mohammad et al.,
2016a; Mohammad et al., 2016b), literary analysis
(Hartner, 2013; Kleres, 2011; Mohammad, 2012),
detecting personality traits (Grijalva et al., 2015;
Mohammad and Kiritchenko, 2015), and other applications. Manually created sentiment lexicons are
especially useful because they tend to be more accurate than automatically generated lexicons; they can
be used to automatically generate large-scale lexicons (Tang et al., 2014; Esuli and Sebastiani, 2006);

they can be used to evaluate different methods of
automatically creating sentiment lexicons; and they
can be used for linguistic analyses such as examining how sentiment is composed in phrases and sentences.

The sentiment of a phrase can differ significantly
from the sentiment of its constituent words. Sentiment composition is the determining of sentiment
of a multi-word linguistic unit, such as a phrase or
a sentence, from its constituents. Lexicons that include sentiment associations for phrases as well as
for their constituent words are useful in studying
sentiment composition. We refer to them as *sentiment composition lexicons (SCLs)*. We created SCLs
for three domains, and all three were used in recent
SemEval shared tasks. We refer to the lexicon created for the English Twitter domain as the *SemEval-
2015 English Twitter Sentiment Lexicon*; for the general English domain as the *SemEval-2016 General
English Sentiment Modifiers Lexicon*; and for the
Arabic Twitter domain as the *SemEval-2016 Arabic Twitter Sentiment Lexicon*. Note that the English
Twitter lexicon was first described in (Kiritchenko et
al., 2014), whereas the other two are novel contributions presented in this paper.

Most existing manually created sentiment lexicons tend to provide only lists of positive and
negative words with very coarse levels of sentiment (Stone et al., 1966; Hu and Liu, 2004; Wilson et al., 2005; Mohammad and Turney, 2013).
The coarse-grained distinctions may be less useful in downstream applications than having access
to fine-grained (real-valued) sentiment association
scores. Only a small number of manual lexicons

Proceedings of NAACL-HLT 2016, pages 811–817,
San Diego, California, June 12-17, 2016. ©2016 Association for Computational Linguistics

capture sentiment associations at a fine-grained level (Bradley and Lang, 1999; Warriner et al., 2013). This is not surprising because obtaining real-valued sentiment annotations has several challenges. Respondents are faced with a higher cognitive load when asked for real-valued sentiment scores for terms as opposed to simply classifying terms as either positive or negative. Besides, it is difficult for an annotator to remain consistent with his/her annotations. Further, the same sentiment association may map to different sentiment scores in the minds of different annotators; for example, one annotator may assign a score of 0.6 and another 0.8 for the same degree of positive association. One could overcome these problems by providing annotators with pairs of terms and asking which is more positive (a comparative approach), however that requires a much larger set of annotations (order N^2, where N is the number of terms to be annotated). Best–Worst Scaling (BWS) is an annotation technique, commonly used in marketing research (Louviere and Woodworth, 1990), that exploits the comparative approach to annotation while keeping the number of required annotations small.

In this work, we investigate the applicability and reliability of the Best–Worst Scaling annotation technique in capturing word–sentiment associations via crowdsourcing. Our main contributions are as follows:

1. We create fine-grained sentiment composition lexicons for Arabic Twitter and general English (in addition to our earlier work on English Twitter) using Best–Worst Scaling. The lexicons include entries for single words as well as multi-word phrases. The sentiment scores are real values between -1 (most negative) and +1 (most positive).

2. We show that the annotations on all three domains are reliable; re-doing the annotation with different sets of annotators produces a very similar order of terms—an average Spearman rank correlation of 0.98. Furthermore, we show that reliable rankings can be obtained with just two or three annotations per BWS question. (Warriner et al. (2013) and Graham et al. (2015) have shown that conventional rating-scale methods require a much higher number of responses (15 to 20)).

3. We examine the relationship between 'difference in the sentiment scores between two terms' and 'agreement amongst annotators' when asked which term is more positive. We show that agreement grows rapidly and reaches 90% when the difference in sentiment scores is about 0.4 (20% of interval between -1 and 1).

4. We calculate the minimum difference in sentiment scores of two terms that is perceptible to native speakers of a language. For sentiment scores between -1 (most negative) and 1 (most positive), we show that the perceptible difference is about 0.08 for English and Arabic speakers. Knowing the least perceptible difference helps researchers better understand sentiment composition. For example, consider the task of determining whether an adjective significantly impacts the sentiment of the noun it qualifies. This can be accomplished by determining whether the difference in sentiment scores between the combined phrase and the constituent noun alone is greater than the least perceptible difference.

The data and code created as part of this project (the lexicons, the annotation questionnaire, and the code to generate BWS questions) are made available.[1]

2 Capturing Fine-Grained Sentiment Associations By Manual Annotation

We now describe how we created three lexicons, through manual annotation, that each provide real-valued sentiment association scores.

2.1 Best–Worst Scaling Method of Annotation

Best–Worst Scaling (BWS), also sometimes referred to as Maximum Difference Scaling (MaxDiff), is an annotation scheme that exploits the comparative approach to annotation (Louviere and Woodworth, 1990; Cohen, 2003; Louviere et al., 2015). Annotators are given four items (4-tuple) and asked which item is the Best (highest in terms of the property of interest) and which is the Worst (least in terms of the property of interest). These annotations can then be easily converted into real-valued scores of association between the items and the property, which eventually allows for creating a ranked list of items as per their association with the property of interest.

---

[1] www.saifmohammad.com/WebPages/BestWorst.html

Given n terms to be annotated, the first step is to randomly sample this set (with replacement) to obtain sets of four terms each, *4-tuples*, that satisfy the following criteria:

1. no two 4-tuples have the same four terms;

2. no two terms within a 4-tuple are identical;

3. each term in the term list appears approximately in the same number of 4-tuples;

4. each pair of terms appears approximately in the same number of 4-tuples.

In practice, around $1.5 \times n$ to $2 \times n$ BWS questions, where n is the number of items, are sufficient to obtain reliable scores. We annotated terms for the three lexicons separately, and generated $2 \times n$ 4-tuples for each set.

Next, the sets of 4-tuples were annotated through a crowdsourcing platform, CrowdFlower. The annotators were presented with four terms at a time, and asked which term is the most positive (or least negative) and which is the most negative (or least positive). Below is an example annotation question.[2] (The Arabic data was annotated through a similar questionnaire in Arabic.)

Focus terms:
1. th*nks 2. doesn't work 3. w00t 4. #theworst

Q1: Identify the term that is associated with the most amount of positive sentiment (or least amount of negative sentiment) – **the most positive term**:
1. th*nks 2. doesn't work 3. w00t 4. #theworst

Q2: Identify the term that is associated with the most amount of negative sentiment (or least amount of positive sentiment) – **the most negative term**:
1. th*nks 2. doesn't work 3. w00t 4. #theworst

Each 4-tuple was annotated by ten respondents.

The responses were then translated into real-valued scores and also a ranking of terms by sentiment for all the terms through a simple counting procedure: For each term, its score is calculated as the percentage of times the term was chosen as the most positive minus the percentage of times the term was chosen as the most negative (Orme, 2009; Flynn and Marley, 2014). The scores range from -1 (the most negative) to 1 (the most positive).

2.2 Lexicons Created With Best–Worst Scaling

SEMEVAL-2015 ENGLISH TWITTER LEXICON: This lexicon is comprised of 1,515 high-frequency English single words and simple negated expressions commonly found in tweets. The set includes regular English words as well as some misspelled words (e.g., *parlament*), creatively-spelled words (e.g., *happeee*), hashtagged words (e.g., *#loveumom*), and emoticons.

SEMEVAL-2016 ARABIC TWITTER LEXICON: This lexicon was created in a similar manner as the English Twitter Lexicon but using Arabic words and negated expressions commonly found in Arabic tweets. It has 1,367 terms.

SEMEVAL-2016 GENERAL ENGLISH SENTIMENT MODIFIERS LEXICON aka SENTIMENT COMPOSITION LEXICON FOR NEGATORS, MODALS, AND DEGREE ADVERBS (SCL-NMA): This lexicon consists of all 1,621 positive and negative single words from Osgood's seminal study on word meaning (Osgood et al., 1957) available in General Inquirer (Stone et al., 1966). In addition, it includes 1,586 high-frequency phrases formed by the Osgood words in combination with simple negators such as *no*, *don't*, and *never*, modals such as *can*, *might*, and *should*, or degree adverbs such as *very* and *fairly*. More details on the lexicon creation and an analysis of the effect of different modifiers on sentiment can be found in (Kiritchenko and Mohammad, 2016).

Table 1 shows example entries from each lexicon. The complete lists of modifiers used in the three lexicons are available online.[3] Details on the use of these lexicons in SemEval shared tasks can be found in (Rosenthal et al., 2015; Kiritchenko et al., 2016).

3 Quality of Annotations

3.1 Agreement and Reproducibility

Let *majority answer* refer to the option chosen most often for a BWS question. The percentage of responses that matched the majority answer were as follows: 82% for the English Twitter Lexicon, 80% for the Arabic Twitter Lexicon, and 80% for the General English Lexicon.

---

[2]The full sets of instructions for both English and Arabic datasets are available at:
http://www.saifmohammad.com/WebPages/BestWorst.html

[3]www.saifmohammad.com/WebPages/SCL.html#ETSL
www.saifmohammad.com/WebPages/SCL.html#ATSL
www.saifmohammad.com/WebPages/SCL.html#NMA

Table 1: Example entries from the three lexicons.

Lexicon, Term	Sentiment
SemEval-2015 English Twitter Lexicon	
yummm	0.813
cant waitttt	0.656
#feelingsorryformyself	-0.547
:'(	-0.563
SemEval-2016 Arabic Twitter Lexicon	
‏#السعادة_الزوجية‎ (marital happiness)	0.800
‏#يقين‎ (certainty)	0.675
‏لا امكن‎ (not possible)	-0.400
‏ارهاب‎ (terrorism)	-0.925
SemEval-2016 General English Lexicon	
would be very easy	0.431
did not harm	0.194
increasingly difficult	-0.583
severe	-0.833

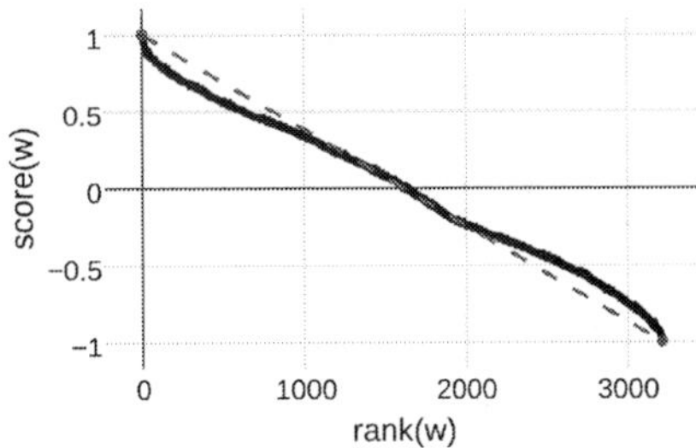

Figure 1: Rank vs. sentiment scores in SCL-NMA.

with $2 \times n$ BWS questions (for n terms), each term occurs in eight 4-tuples on average, and so even just one annotation per BWS question means that each term is assessed eight times.

3.2 Distribution of Sentiment Scores

Figure 1 gives an overview of the sentiment scores in SCL-NMA. Each term in the lexicon is shown as a dot in the corresponding plot. The x-axis is the rank of each term in the lexicon when the terms are ordered from most positive to least positive. The y-axis is the real-valued sentiment score obtained from the BWS annotations. Observe that the lexicon has entries for the full range of sentiment scores (-1 to 1); that is, there are no significant gaps—ranges of sentiment scores for which the lexicon does not include any terms. The dashed red line indicates a uniform spread of scores, i.e., the same number of terms are expected to fall into each same-size interval of scores. Observe that the lexicon has slightly fewer terms in the intervals with very high and very low sentiment scores. Similar figures (not shown here) were obtained for the other two lexicons.

3.3 Perception of Sentiment Difference

The created lexicons capture sentiment associations at a fine level of granularity. Thus, these annotations can help answer key questions such as: (1) If native speakers of a language are given two terms and asked which is more positive, how does human agreement vary with respect to the amount of difference in sentiment between the two focus terms? It is expected that the greater the difference in sentiment, the higher the agreement, but the exact shape of this increase in agreement has not been shown till now. (2) What least amount of difference in sentiment is perceptible to native speakers of a language?

Annotations are reliable if similar results are obtained from repeated trials. To test the reliability of our annotations, we randomly divided the sets of ten responses to each question into two halves and compared the rankings obtained from these two groups of responses. The Spearman rank correlation coefficient between the two sets of rankings produced for each of the three lexicons was found to be at least 0.98. (The Pearson correlation coefficient between the two sets of sentiment scores for each lexicon was also at least 0.98.) Thus, even though annotators might disagree about answers to individual questions, the aggregated scores produced by applying the counting procedure on the BWS annotations are remarkably reliable at ranking terms.

Number of annotations needed: Even though we obtained ten annotations per BWS question, we wanted to determine the least number of annotations needed to obtain reliable sentiment scores. For every k (where k ranges from 1 to 10), we made the following calculations: for each BWS question, we randomly selected k annotations and calculated sentiment scores based on the selected subset of annotations. We will refer to these sets of scores for the different values of k as S_1, S_2, and so on until S_{10}. This process was repeated ten times for each k. The average Spearman rank correlation coefficient between S_1 and S_{10} was 0.96, between S_2 and S_{10} was 0.98, and S_3 and S_{10} was 0.99. This shows that as few as two or three annotations per BWS question are sufficient to obtain reliable sentiment scores. Note that

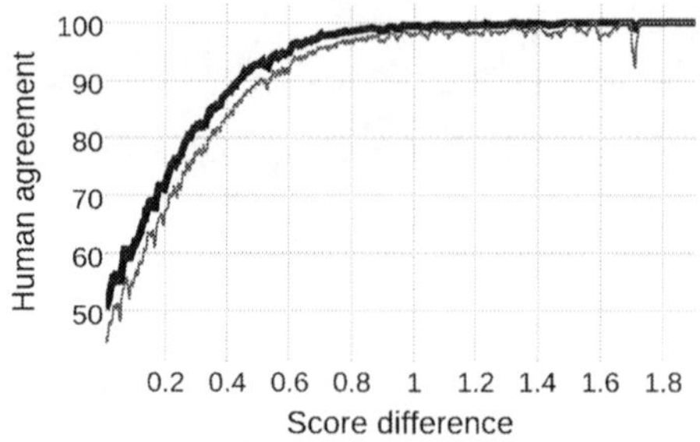

Figure 2: SCL-NMA: Human agreement on annotating term w_1 as more positive than term w_2 for pairs with difference in scores $d = score(w_1) - score(w_2)$. The x-axis represents d. The y-axis plots the avg. percentage of human annotations that judge term w_1 as more positive than term w_2 (thick line) and the corresponding 99.9%-confidence lower bound (thin blue line).

Agreement vs. Sentiment Difference: For each word pair w_1 and w_2 such that $score(w_1) - score(w_2) \geq 0$, we count the number of BWS annotations from which we can infer that w_1 is more positive than w_2 and divide this number by the total number of BWS annotations from which we can infer either that w_1 is more positive than w_2 or that w_2 is more positive than w_1. (We can infer that w_1 is more positive than w_2 if in a 4-tuple that has both w_1 and w_2 the annotator selected w_1 as the most positive or w_2 as the least positive. The case for w_2 being more positive than w_1 is similar.) This ratio is the human agreement for w_1 being more positive than w_2, and we expect that it is correlated with the sentiment difference $d = score(w_1) - score(w_2)$. To get more reliable estimates, we average the human agreement for all pairs of terms whose sentiment differs by $d \pm 0.01$. Figure 2 shows the resulting average human agreement on SCL-NMA. Similar figures (not shown here) were obtained for the English and Arabic Twitter data. Observe that the agreement grows rapidly with the increase in score differences. Given two terms with sentiment differences of 0.4 or higher, more than 90% of the annotators correctly identify the more positive term.

Least Difference in Sentiment that is Perceptible to Native Speakers: In psychophysics, there is a notion of *least perceptible difference* (aka *just-noticeable difference*)—the amount by which something that can be measured (e.g., weight or sound intensity) needs to be changed in order for the differ-

ence to be noticeable by a human (Fechner, 1966). Analogously, we can measure the least perceptible difference in sentiment. If two words have close to identical sentiment associations, then it is expected that native speakers will choose each of the words about the same number of times when forced to pick a word that is more positive. However, as the difference in sentiment starts getting larger, the frequency with which the two terms are chosen as most positive begins to diverge. At one point, the frequencies diverge so much that we can say with high confidence that the two terms do not have the same sentiment associations. The average of this minimum difference in sentiment score is the least perceptible difference for sentiment. To determine the least perceptible difference, we first obtain the 99.9%-confidence lower bounds on the human agreement (see the thin blue line in Figure 2). The least perceptible difference is the point starting at which the lower bound consistently exceeds 50% threshold (i.e., the point starting at which we observe with 99.9% confidence that the human agreement is higher than chance). The least perceptible difference when calculated from SCL-NMA is 0.069, from the English Twitter Lexicon is 0.080, and from the Arabic Twitter Lexicon is 0.087. Observe, that the estimates are very close to each other despite being calculated from three completely independent datasets. Kiritchenko and Mohammad (2016) use the least perceptible difference to determine whether a modifier significantly impacts the sentiment of the word it composes with.

4   Conclusions

We obtained real-valued sentiment association scores for single words and multi-word phrases in three domains (general English, English Twitter, and Arabic Twitter) by manual annotation and Best–Worst Scaling. Best–Worst Scaling exploits the comparative approach to annotation while keeping the number of annotations small. Notably, we showed that the procedure when repeated produces remarkably consistent rankings of terms by sentiment. This reliability allowed us to determine the value of the psycho-linguistic concept—least perceptible difference in sentiment. We hope these findings will encourage further use of Best–Worst Scaling in linguistic annotation.

References

Margaret M Bradley and Peter J Lang. 1999. Affective norms for English words (ANEW): Instruction manual and affective ratings. Technical report, The Center for Research in Psychophysiology, University of Florida.

Steven H. Cohen. 2003. Maximum difference scaling: Improved measures of importance and preference for segmentation. Sawtooth Software, Inc.

Andrea Esuli and Fabrizio Sebastiani. 2006. SENTI-WORDNET: A publicly available lexical resource for opinion mining. In *Proceedings of the 5th Conference on Language Resources and Evaluation (LREC)*, pages 417–422.

Gustav Fechner. 1966. *Elements of psychophysics. Vol. I.* New York: Holt, Rinehart and Winston.

T. N. Flynn and A. A. J. Marley. 2014. Best-worst scaling: theory and methods. In Stephane Hess and Andrew Daly, editors, *Handbook of Choice Modelling*, pages 178–201. Edward Elgar Publishing.

Yvette Graham, Nitika Mathur, and Timothy Baldwin. 2015. Accurate evaluation of segment-level machine translation metrics. In *Proceedings of the Annual Conference of the North American Chapter of the ACL (NAACL)*, pages 1183–1191.

Emily Grijalva, Daniel A. Newman, Louis Tay, M. Brent Donnellan, P.D. Harms, Richard W. Robins, and Taiyi Yan. 2015. Gender differences in narcissism: A meta-analytic review. *Psychological bulletin*, 141(2):261–310.

Marcus Hartner. 2013. The lingering after-effects in the reader's mind – an investigation into the affective dimension of literary reading. *Journal of Literary Theory Online*.

Minqing Hu and Bing Liu. 2004. Mining and summarizing customer reviews. In *Proceedings of the 10th ACM SIGKDD International Conference on Knowledge Discovery and Data Mining (KDD)*, pages 168–177, New York, NY, USA.

Svetlana Kiritchenko and Saif M. Mohammad. 2016. The effect of negators, modals, and degree adverbs on sentiment composition. In *Proceedings of the Workshop on Computational Approaches to Subjectivity, Sentiment and Social Media Analysis (WASSA)*.

Svetlana Kiritchenko, Xiaodan Zhu, and Saif M. Mohammad. 2014. Sentiment analysis of short informal texts. *Journal of Artificial Intelligence Research*, 50:723–762.

Svetlana Kiritchenko, Saif M. Mohammad, and Mohammad Salameh. 2016. SemEval-2016 Task 7: Determining sentiment intensity of English and Arabic phrases. In *Proceedings of the International Workshop on Semantic Evaluation (SemEval)*, San Diego, California, June.

Jochen Kleres. 2011. Emotions and narrative analysis: A methodological approach. *Journal for the Theory of Social Behaviour*, 41(2):182–202.

Jordan J. Louviere and George G. Woodworth. 1990. Best-worst analysis. Working Paper. Department of Marketing and Economic Analysis, University of Alberta.

Jordan J. Louviere, Terry N. Flynn, and A. A. J. Marley. 2015. *Best-Worst Scaling: Theory, Methods and Applications*. Cambridge University Press.

Saif M. Mohammad and Svetlana Kiritchenko. 2015. Using hashtags to capture fine emotion categories from tweets. *Computational Intelligence*, 31(2):301–326.

Saif M. Mohammad and Peter D. Turney. 2013. Crowdsourcing a word–emotion association lexicon. *Computational Intelligence*, 29(3):436–465.

Saif M. Mohammad, Svetlana Kiritchenko, Parinaz Sobhani, Xiaodan Zhu, and Colin Cherry. 2016a. A dataset for detecting stance in tweets. In *Proceedings of 10th edition of the the Language Resources and Evaluation Conference (LREC)*, Portorož, Slovenia.

Saif M. Mohammad, Parinaz Sobhani, and Svetlana Kiritchenko. 2016b. Stance and sentiment in tweets. *Special Section of the ACM Transactions on Internet Technology on Argumentation in Social Media*, Submitted.

Saif M Mohammad. 2012. From once upon a time to happily ever after: Tracking emotions in mail and books. *Decision Support Systems*, 53(4):730–741.

Bryan Orme. 2009. Maxdiff analysis: Simple counting, individual-level logit, and HB. Sawtooth Software, Inc.

Charles E Osgood, George J Suci, and Percy Tannenbaum. 1957. *The measurement of meaning*. University of Illinois Press.

Maria Pontiki, Harris Papageorgiou, Dimitrios Galanis, Ion Androutsopoulos, John Pavlopoulos, and Suresh Manandhar. 2014. SemEval-2014 Task 4: Aspect based sentiment analysis. In *Proceedings of the 8th International Workshop on Semantic Evaluation (SemEval)*, Dublin, Ireland.

Sara Rosenthal, Alan Ritter, Preslav Nakov, and Veselin Stoyanov. 2014. SemEval-2014 Task 9: Sentiment analysis in Twitter. In *Proceedings of the 8th International Workshop on Semantic Evaluation (SemEval)*, pages 73–80, Dublin, Ireland, August.

Sara Rosenthal, Preslav Nakov, Svetlana Kiritchenko, Saif Mohammad, Alan Ritter, and Veselin Stoyanov. 2015. SemEval-2015 Task 10: Sentiment analysis in Twitter. In *Proceedings of the 9th International Workshop on Semantic Evaluation (SemEval)*, pages 450–462, Denver, Colorado.

Philip Stone, Dexter C. Dunphy, Marshall S. Smith, Daniel M. Ogilvie, and associates. 1966. *The General*

Inquirer: A Computer Approach to Content Analysis. The MIT Press.

Duyu Tang, Furu Wei, Bing Qin, Ming Zhou, and Ting Liu. 2014. Building large-scale Twitter-specific sentiment lexicon: A representation learning approach. In *Proceedings of the International Conference on Computational Linguistics (COLING)*, pages 172–182.

Amy Beth Warriner, Victor Kuperman, and Marc Brysbaert. 2013. Norms of valence, arousal, and dominance for 13,915 English lemmas. *Behavior Research Methods*, 45(4):1191–1207.

Theresa Wilson, Janyce Wiebe, and Paul Hoffmann. 2005. Recognizing contextual polarity in phrase-level sentiment analysis. In *Proceedings of the Joint Conference on HLT and EMNLP*, pages 347–354, Stroudsburg, PA, USA.

Mapping Verbs In Different Languages to Knowledge Base Relations using Web Text as Interlingua

Derry Tanti Wijaya
Carnegie Mellon University
5000 Forbes Avenue
Pittsburgh, PA, 15213
dwijaya@cs.cmu.edu

Tom M. Mitchell
Carnegie Mellon University
5000 Forbes Avenue
Pittsburgh, PA, 15213
tom.mitchell@cs.cmu.edu

Abstract

In recent years many knowledge bases (KBs) have been constructed, yet there is not yet a verb resource that maps to these growing KB resources. A resource that maps verbs in different languages to KB relations would be useful for extracting facts from text into the KBs, and to aid alignment and integration of knowledge across different KBs and languages. Such a multi-lingual verb resource would also be useful for tasks such as machine translation and machine reading. In this paper, we present a scalable approach to automatically construct such a verb resource using a very large web text corpus as a kind of interlingua to relate verb phrases to KB relations. Given a text corpus in any language and any KB, it can produce a mapping of that language's verb phrases to the KB relations. Experiments with the English NELL KB and ClueWeb corpus show that the learned English verb-to-relation mapping is effective for extracting relation instances from English text. When applied to a Portuguese NELL KB and a Portuguese text corpus, the same method automatically constructs a verb resource in Portuguese that is effective for extracting relation instances from Portuguese text.

1   Introduction

In recent years a variety of large knowledge bases (KBs) have been constructed e.g., Freebase (Bollacker et al., 2008), DBpedia (Auer et al., 2007), NELL (Carlson et al., 2010), and Yago (Suchanek et al., 2007). These KBs consist of (1) an ontology that defines a set of categories (e.g., *Sport-sTeam, City*), (2) another part of the ontology that defines relations with these categories as argument types (e.g., *teamPlaysInCity(SportsTeam, City)*), (3) KB entities which instantiate these categories (e.g., *Steelers* ∈ *SportsTeam*), and (4) KB entity pairs which instantiate these relations (e.g., (*Steelers, Pittsburgh*) ∈ *teamPlaysInCity*). The KB ontology also specifies constraints (e.g., mutual exclusion, subset) among KB categories and relations.

Despite recent progress in KB construction, there is not yet a verb resource that maps to these KBs: one that contains verb phrases[1] that identify KB relations. Such a verb resource can be useful to aid KB relation extraction. A distribution of verb phrases associated with any given KB relation is also a KB-independent representation of that relation's semantics which can form the basis of aligning ontologies across arbitrary KBs (Wijaya et al., 2013). Given a KB and verb resources in different languages that map to the KB, we can also begin to align knowledge expressed in different languages.

We introduce here an approach to mapping verb phrases to KB relations using a very large ClueWeb corpus (Callan et al., 2009) as a kind of interlingua. Our approach grounds each KB relation instance (e.g., *teamPlaysInCity(Steelers, Pittsburgh)*) in mentions of its argument pair in this text, then represents the relation in terms of the verb phrases that connect these paired mentions (see Fig. 1). For a high coverage mapping, we train on both labelled and unlabelled data using expectation maximization (EM). We introduce argument type checking during

---

[1]In this paper we use the term "verb phrase" and "verb" interchangeably; both referring to either verb or verb+preposition

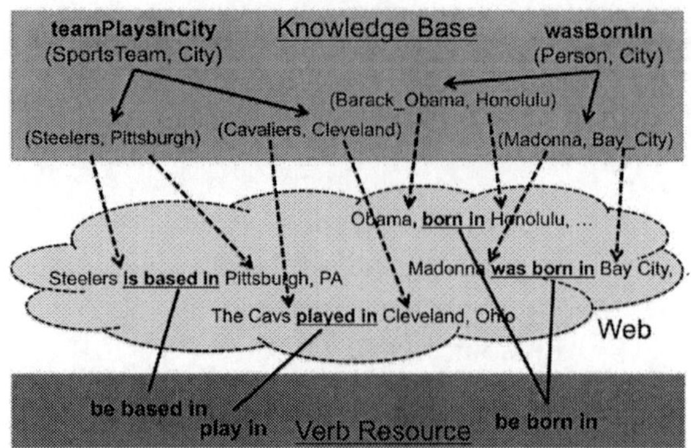

Figure 1: Mapping verb phrases to relations in KB through Web-text as interlingua. Each relation instance is grounded by its mentions in the Web-text. The verbs that co-occur with mentions of the relation's instances are mapped to that relation.

the EM process to ensure only verbs whose argument types match the relation's argument types are mapped to the relation. We also incorporate constraints defined in the KB ontology to find a verb to relation mapping consistent with these constraints.

Our contributions are: (1) We propose a scalable EM-based method that automatically maps verb phrases to KB relations by using the mentions of the verb phrases with the relation instances in a very large unlabeled text corpus. (2) We demonstrate the effectiveness of the resource for extracting relation instances in NELL KB. Specifically, it improves the recall of both the supervised- and the unsupervised- verb-to-relation mapping; demonstrating the benefit of semi-supervised learning on unlabeled Web-scale text. (3) We demonstrate the flexibility of the method, which is both KB- and language-independent, by using the same method for constructing English verb resource to automatically construct a Portuguese verb resource. (4) We make our verb resources publicly available [2].

2 Method

2.1 Terminology

We define a NELL KB to be a 6-tuple $(C, I_C, R, I_R, Subset, Mutex)$. C is the set of categories e.g., *SportsTeam* i.e., $c_j \in C = \{c_1, ..., c_{|C|}\}$. I_C is the set of category instances which are

entity-category pairs e.g., (*Cleveland*, *City*) i.e., $I_C = \{(e_m, c_j) \mid e_m \in c_j, \; c_j \in C\}$.

R is the set of relations e.g., *teamPlaysInCity* i.e., $r_i \in R = \{r_1, ..., r_{|R|}\}$. We also define f_{type} to be a function that when applied to a relation r_i returns the argument type signature of the relation $f_{type}(r_i) = (c_j, c_k)$ for some $c_j, c_k \in C$ e.g., $f_{type}(\textbf{\textit{teamPlaysInCity}}) = (\textit{SportsTeam}, \textit{City})$.

I_R is the set of relation instances which are entity-relation-entity triples e.g., (*Cavaliers*, *teamPlaysInCity*, *Cleveland*) i.e., $I_R = \{(e_m, r_i, e_n) \mid (e_m, e_n) \in r_i, \; r_i \in R, \; e_m \in c_j, \; e_n \in c_k, \; f_{type}(r_i) = (c_j, c_k)\}; I_R = I_{r_1} \cup I_{r_2} \cup ... I_{r_{|R|}}$.

Subset is the set of all subset constraints among relations in R i.e., $Subset = \{(i, k) : I_{r_i} \subseteq I_{r_k}\}$. For example $\{(person, \textbf{\textit{ceoOf}}, company)\} \subseteq \{(person, \textbf{\textit{worksFor}}, company)\}$.

Mutex is the set of all mutual exclusion constraints among relations in R i.e., $Mutex = \{(i, k) : I_{r_i} \cap I_{r_k} = \phi\}$. For example $\{(drug, \textbf{\textit{hasSideEffect}}, physiologicalCondition)\} \cap \{(drug, \textbf{\textit{possiblyTreats}}, physiologicalCondition)\} = \phi$.

Each KB entity e_m can be referred to by one or more noun phrases (NPs). For example, the entity *Cavaliers*, can be referred to in text using either the NP *"Cleveland Cavaliers"* or the NP *"The Cavs"*[3]. We define $N_{en}(e_m)$ to be the set of English NPs corresponding to entity e_m.

We define SVO to be the English Subject-Verb-Object (SVO) interlingua[4] consisting of tuples of the form (np_s, v_p, np_o, w), where np_s and np_o are noun phrases (NP) corresponding to subject and object, respectively, v_p is a verb phrase that connects them, and w is the count of the tuple.

2.2 Data Construction

We construct a dataset D for mapping English verbs to NELL KB relations. First, we convert each tuple in SVO to its equivalent entity pair tuple(s) in $SVO' = \{(e_m, v_p, e_n, w) \mid np_s \in N_{en}(e_m), \; np_o \in N_{en}(e_n), \; (np_s, v_p, np_o, w) \in SVO\}$. Then, we construct D from SVO' as a collection of labeled and unlabeled instances.

---

[2] http://www.cs.cmu.edu/%7Edwijaya/mapping.html

[3] defined by the *canReferTo* relation in NELL KB

[4] We use 600 million SVO triples collected from the entire ClueWeb (Callan et al., 2009) of about 230 billion tokens with some filtering described in Section 3.1.

The set of labeled instances is $D^\ell = \{(\mathbf{y}_{(e_m,e_n)}, \mathbf{v}_{(e_m,e_n)})\}$ where $\mathbf{y}_{(e_m,e_n)} \in \{0,1\}^{|R|}$ is a bit vector of label assignment, each bit representing whether the instance belongs to a particular relation i.e., $y^i_{(e_m,e_n)} = 1 \iff (e_m, e_n) \in r_i$ and 0 otherwise. $\mathbf{v}_{(e_m,e_n)} \in \mathbb{R}^{|V|}$ is a $|V|$-dimensional vector of verb phrase counts that connect e_m and e_n in SVO' (V is the set of all verb phrases) i.e., $v^p_{(e_m,e_n)}$ is the number of times the verb phrase v_p connects e_m and e_n in SVO'.

The collection of unlabeled instances is constructed from entity pairs in SVO' whose label assignment $\mathbf{y}$ are unknown (its bits are all zero) i.e., $D^u = \{(\mathbf{y}_{(e_m,e_n)}, \mathbf{v}_{(e_m,e_n)}) \mid (e_m, *, e_n, *) \in SVO', (e_m, *, e_n) \notin I_R\}$.

An instance in our dataset $d_{(e_m,e_n)} \in D$ is therefore either a labeled or unlabeled tuple i.e., $d_{(e_m,e_n)} = (\mathbf{y}_{(e_m,e_n)}, \mathbf{v}_{(e_m,e_n)})$.

We let $f_{type}(d_{(e_m,e_n)})$ return the argument type of the instance i.e., $f_{type}(d_{(e_m,e_n)}) = (c_j, c_k)$ where (e_m, c_j) and $(e_n, c_k) \in I_C$.

We let $f_{verb}(d_{(e_m,e_n)})$ return the set of all verb phrases that co-occur with the instance in SVO' i.e., $f_{verb}(d_{(e_m,e_n)}) = \{v_p \mid (e_m, v_p, e_n, *) \in SVO'\}$.

When applied to a relation r_i, we let $f_{verb}(r_i)$ return the set of all verb phrases that co-occur with instances in D whose types match that of the relation i.e., $f_{verb}(r_i) = \{v_p \mid \exists\, d_{(e_m,e_n)} \in D, v_p \in f_{verb}(d_{(e_m,e_n)}), f_{type}(d_{(e_m,e_n)}) = f_{type}(r_i)\}$.

2.3 Model

We train a Naive Bayes classifier on our dataset. Given as input a collection D^ℓ of labeled instances and D^u of unlabeled instances, it outputs a classifier, $\hat{\theta}$, that takes an unlabeled instance and predicts its label assignment i.e., for each unlabeled instance $d_{(e_m,e_n)} \in D^u$ the classifier predicts the label assignment $\mathbf{y}_{(e_m,e_n)}$ using $\mathbf{v}_{(e_m,e_n)}$ as features:

$$P(y^i_{(e_m,e_n)} = 1 \mid d_{(e_m,e_n)}; \hat{\theta})$$
$$= \frac{P(r_i|\hat{\theta})P(d_{(e_m,e_n)} \mid r_i; \hat{\theta})}{P(d_{(e_m,e_n)}|\hat{\theta})}$$
$$= \frac{P(r_i|\hat{\theta}) \prod_{p=1}^{|V|} P(v_p|r_i; \hat{\theta})^{v^p_{(e_m,e_n)}}}{\sum_{k=1}^{|R|} P(r_k|\hat{\theta}) \prod_{p=1}^{|V|} P(v_p|r_k; \hat{\theta})^{v^p_{(e_m,e_n)}}} \quad (1)$$

If the task is to classify the unlabeled instance into a single relation, only the bit of the relation with the highest posterior probability is set i.e, $y^k_{(e_m,e_n)} = 1$ where $k = \arg\max_i P(y^i_{(e_m,e_n)} = 1 \mid d_{(e_m,e_n)}; \hat{\theta})$.

2.3.1 Parameter Estimation

To estimate model parameters (the relation prior probabilities $\hat{\theta}_{r_i} \equiv P(r_i|\hat{\theta})$ and probabilities of a verb given a relation $\hat{\theta}_{v_p|r_i} \equiv P(v_p|r_i; \hat{\theta})$) from both labeled and unlabeled data, we use an Expectation Maximization (EM) algorithm (Nigam et al., 2006). The estimates are computed by calculating a maximum a posteriori estimate of θ, i.e. $\hat{\theta} = \arg\max_\theta \mathcal{L}(\theta|D) = \arg\max_\theta log(P(D \mid \theta)P(\theta))$.

The first term, $P(D \mid \theta)$ is calculated by the product of all the instance likelihoods:

$$P(D|\theta)$$
$$= \prod_{d_{(e_m,e_n)} \in D^u} \sum_{i=1}^{|R|} P(r_i|\theta)P(d_{(e_m,e_n)}|r_i; \theta)$$
$$\times \prod_{d_{(e_m,e_n)} \in D^\ell} \sum_{\{i | y^i_{(e_m,e_n)} = 1\}} P(r_i|\theta)P(d_{(e_m,e_n)}|r_i; \theta)$$
$$(2)$$

The second term, $P(\theta)$, the prior distribution over parameters is represented by Dirichlet priors:

$$P(\theta) \propto \prod_{i=1}^{|R|}((\theta_{r_i})^{\alpha_1 - 1} \prod_{p=1}^{|V|} (\theta_{v_p|r_i})^{\alpha_2 - 1}) \text{ where } \alpha_1$$

and α_2 are parameters that effect the strength of the priors. In this paper we set $\alpha_1 = 2$ and $\alpha_2 = 1 + \sigma(P^e(v_p|r_i))$, where $P^e(v_p|r_i)$ is the initial bias of the verb-to-relation mapping. Thus, in this paper we define $P(\theta)$ as:

$$P(\theta) = \prod_{i=1}^{|R|}(P(r_i|\theta) \prod_{p=1}^{|V|} (P(v_p|r_i; \theta)^{\sigma(P^e(v_p|r_i))}) \quad (3)$$

We can see from this that $\sigma(P^e(v_p|r_i))$ is a conjugate prior on $P(v_p|r_i; \theta)$ with σ as the confidence parameter. This conjugate prior allows incorporation of any existing knowledge (Section 2.3.2) we may have about the verb-to-relation mapping.

From Equation 2, we see that $log\ P(D|\theta)$ contains a log of sums, which makes a maximization by partial derivatives computationally intractable. Using EM, we instead maximize the *expected* log likelihood of the data with respect to the posterior distribution of the y labels given by: $\arg\max_\theta E_{(\mathbf{y}|D;\theta)}[log\ P(D|\theta)]$.

In the E-step, we use the current estimates of the parameters $\hat{\theta}^t$ to compute $\hat{\mathbf{y}}^t = E[\mathbf{y}|D;\hat{\theta}^t]$ the expected label assignments according to the current model. In practice it corresponds to calculating the posterior distribution over the y labels for unlabeled instances $P(y^i_{(e_m,e_n)} = 1 \mid d_{(e_m,e_n)}; \hat{\theta}^t)$ (Equation 1) and using the estimates to compute its expected label assignment $\hat{\mathbf{y}}^t_{(e_m,e_n)}$.

In the M-step, we calculate a new maximum a posteriori estimate for $\hat{\theta}^{(t+1)}$ which maximizes the expected log likelihood of the complete data, $\mathcal{L}_c(\theta|D;\hat{\mathbf{y}}^t) = log(P(\theta^t)) + \hat{\mathbf{y}}^t [log\ P(D|\theta^t)]$:

$$\mathcal{L}_c(\theta|D;\hat{\mathbf{y}}^t) = log(P(\theta^t))$$
$$+ \sum_{d_{(e_m,e_n)} \in D} \sum_{i=1}^{|R|} y^{ti}_{(e_m,e_n)}\ log\ P(r_i|\theta)P(d_{(e_m,e_n)}|r_i;\theta)$$
$$(4)$$

$\mathcal{L}_c(\theta|D;\mathbf{y})$ bounds $\mathcal{L}(\theta|D)$ from below (by application of Jensen's inequality $E[log(X)] \leq log(EX)$). The EM algorithm produces parameter estimates $\hat{\theta}$ that correspond to a local maximum of $\mathcal{L}_c(\theta|D;\mathbf{y})$. The relation prior probabilities are thus estimated using current label assignments as:

$$P(r_i|\hat{\theta}^{(t+1)}) = \frac{1 + \sum_{d_{(e_m,e_n)} \in D} y^{ti}_{(e_m,e_n)}}{|R| + |D|} \quad (5)$$

The verb-to-relation mapping probabilities are estimated in the same manner:

$$P(v_p \mid r_i; \hat{\theta}^{(t+1)}) =$$
$$\frac{\sigma_i^{(t+1)}\left(P^e(v_p \mid r_i)\right) + \sum_{d_{(e_m,e_n)} \in D} v^p_{(e_m,e_n)}\ y^{ti}_{(e_m,e_n)}}{\sigma_i^{(t+1)} + \sum_{s=1}^{|V|} \sum_{d_{(e_m,e_n)} \in D} v^s_{(e_m,e_n)}\ y^{ti}_{(e_m,e_n)}} \quad (6)$$

We start with $\sigma = |V|$ and gradually reduce the impact of prior by decaying σ with a decay parameter of 0.8 at each iteration in the manner of (Lu and Zhai, 2008)). This will allow the EM to gradually pick up more verbs from the data to map to relations.

EM iteratively computes parameters θ^1, ..., θ^t using the above E-step and M-step update rule at each iteration t, halting when there is no further improvement in the value of $\mathcal{L}_c(\theta|D;\mathbf{y})$.

2.3.2 Prior Knowledge

In our prior $P(\theta)$, we incorporate knowledge about verb-to-relation mappings from the text patterns learned by NELL to extract relations. This is our way of *aligning* our verb-to-relation mappings with NELL's current extractions. Coupled Pattern Learner (CPL) (Carlson et al., 2010) is a component in NELL that learns these contextual patterns for extracting instances of relations and categories.

We consider only CPL's extraction patterns that contain verb phrases. Given a set E_{r_i} of CPL's extraction patterns for a relation r_i, and E_{r_i,v_p} as the set of extraction patterns in E_{r_i} that contains the verb phrase v_p, we compute $P^e(v_p \mid r_i) = \frac{|E_{r_i,v_p}|}{|E_{r_i}|}$ and use them as priors in our classifier (Equation 3).[5]

2.3.3 Argument Type Checking

Although some verbs are ambiguous (e.g., the verb "play" may express several relations: *musicianPlaysMusicalInstrument*, *athletePlaysSport*, *actorPlaysMovie*, etc), knowing the types of the verbs' arguments can help disambiguate the verbs (e.g., the verb "play" that takes a *musicalInstrument* type as object is more likely to express the *musicianPlaysMusicalInstrument* relation). Therefore, we incorporate argument type checking in our EM process to ensure that it maps verbs to relations whose argument types match:

- In the E-Step, we make sure that unlabeled instances are only labeled with relations that have the same argument types as the instance *and* that share some verbs with the instance. In other words, in the E-step we compute $P(y^i_{(e_m,e_n)} = 1 \mid d_{(e_m,e_n)})$ if $f_{type}(r_i) = f_{type}(d_{(e_m,e_n)})$ *and* $\left(f_{(verb)}(r_i) \cup \{v_p|E_{r_i,v_p} \neq \emptyset\}\right) \cap f_{(verb)}(d_{(e_m,e_n)}) \neq \emptyset$.

- In the M-step, we make sure that verbs are only mapped to relations whose argument types match at least one of the instances that co-occur with the verbs in SVO'. In other words, in the M-step we compute $P(v_p \mid r_i)$ if $v_p \in f_{verb}(r_i)$ or $E_{r_i,v_p} \neq \emptyset$.

---

[5] We manually add a few verb phrases for relations whose E_r is an empty set when possible, to set the EM process on these relations with good initial guesses of the parameters. In average, each relation has about 6 verb patterns in total as priors.

2.3.4 Incorporating Constraints

In the E-step, for each unlabeled instance, given the probabilities over relation labels $P(y^i_{(e_m,e_n)} = 1 \mid d_{(e_m,e_n)}; \hat{\theta}^t)$, and $Subset$ and $Mutex$ constraints[6], similar to (Dalvi et al., 2015), we use a Mixed-Integer Program (MIP) to produce its bit vector of label assignment as output: $\hat{\mathbf{y}}^t_{(e_m,e_n)}$.

The constraints among relations are incorporated as constraints on bits in this bit vector. For example, if for an unlabeled instance (*Jeff Bezos, Amazon*), a bit corresponding to the relation **ceoOf** is set then the bit corresponding to the relation **worksFor** should also be set due to the subset constraint: **ceoOf** $\subseteq$ **worksFor**. For the same instance, the bit corresponding to **competesWith** should not be set due to the mutual exclusion constraint **ceoOf** $\cap$ **competesWith** $= \phi$. The MIP formulation for each unlabeled instance thus tries to maximize the sum of probabilities of selected relation labels after penalizing for violation of constraints (Equation 7), where ζ_{ik} are slack variables for $Subset$ constraints and δ_{ik} are slack variables for $Mutex$ constraints:

$$\underset{\mathbf{y}_{(e_m,e_n)},\zeta_{ik},\delta_{ik}}{\text{maximize}} \left(\sum_{i=1}^{|R|} y^i_{(e_m,e_n)} \times P(y^i_{(e_m,e_n)} = 1|d_{(e_m,e_n)};\hat{\theta}^t) \right.$$
$$\left. - \sum_{(i,k)\in Subset} \zeta_{ik} - \sum_{(i,k)\in Mutex} \delta_{ik} \right)$$

subject to,

$$y^i_{(e_m,e_n)} \leq y^k_{(e_m,e_n)} + \zeta_{ik}, \forall(i,k) \in Subset$$
$$y^i_{(e_m,e_n)} + y^k_{(e_m,e_n)} \leq 1 + \delta_{ik}, \forall(i,k) \in Mutex$$
$$\zeta_{ik}, \delta_{ik} \geq 0, y^i_{(e_m,e_n)} \in \{0,1\}, \forall i,k \quad (7)$$

Our algorithm that includes argument type checking and constraints is summarized in Algorithm 1.

2.4 Portuguese Verb Mapping

To map Portuguese verbs to relations in Portuguese NELL, which is an automatically and independently constructed KB separate from English NELL, we use the Portuguese NELL and Portuguese text corpus SVO_{pt}[7] and construct a dataset D_{pt}. Given

---

[6]The *Subset* and *Mutex* constraints are obtained as part of the NELL KB ontology, which is publicly available at the NELL Read The Web project website: http://rtw.ml.cmu.edu/resources/.

[7]We obtain the Portuguese SVO from the NELL-Portuguese team at Federal University of Sao Carlos.

Algorithm 1 The EM Algorithm for Verb-to-Relation Mapping

Input: $D = D^\ell \cup D^u$ and an initial naive Bayes classifier θ^1 from labeled documents D^ℓ only (using Equations 5 and 6)

Output: θ^T that include verbs to relations mappings given by $P(v_p|r_i;\theta^T)$

1: **for** $t = 1 \ldots T$ **do**
2:   **E-Step:**
3:   **for** $d_{(e_m,e_n)} \in D^u$ **do**
4:     Compute $P(y^i_{(e_m,e_n)} = 1|d_{(e_m,e_n)};\theta^t)$ $\forall r_i \in R$ that satisfy argument types checking (Equation 1)
5:     Find a consistent label assignment $\mathbf{y}^t_{(e_m,e_n)}$ by solving MIP (Equation 7)
6:   **end for**
7:   **M-step:** Recompute model parameters θ^{t+1} based on current label assignments (Equation 5 and 6) respecting argument type checking
8:   **if** convergence $(\mathcal{L}_c(\theta^{t+1}), \mathcal{L}_c(\theta^t))$ **then**
9:     **break**
10:   **end if**
11: **end for**
12: **return** θ^T

	English NELL	Portuguese NELL	Portuguese NELL^{+en}
$|R|$	317	302	302
$|I_R|$	135,267	5,675	12,444
$|D^\ell|$	85,192	2,595	5,412
$|D^u|$	240,490	595,274	1,186,329

Table 1: Statistics of KB facts and dataset constructed

D_{pt}, we follow the same approach as before to find a mapping of Portuguese verbs to relations. Since Portuguese NELL is newly constructed, it contains fewer facts (category and relation instances) than English NELL, and hence its dataset D^ℓ_{pt} has fewer labeled instances (see Table 1).

Adding more relation instances to Portuguese NELL can result in more labeled instances in the dataset D_{pt}, a more productive EM, and a better verb-to-relation mapping. Since each category and each relation in Portuguese NELL ontology has a one-to-one mapping in English NELL ontology, we can add relation instances to Portuguese NELL from the corresponding English NELL relations.

English NELL however, has only English noun phrases (NPs) to refer to entities in its relation instances. To add more labeled instances in D_{pt} using English relation instances, we need to find instantiations of these English relation instances in Portuguese SVO_{pt}, which translates to finding Portuguese NPs that refer to English NELL entities. For example, Portuguese NP: "Artria torcica interna" for English NELL entity: *internal mammary artery*.

To automatically translate English NELL enti-

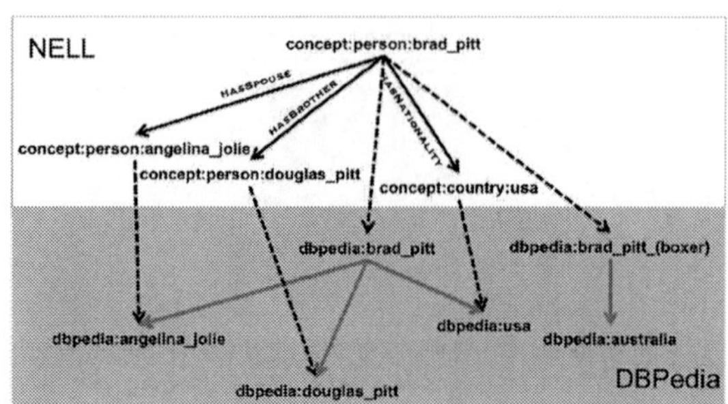

Figure 2: Mapping NELL entity *Brad Pitt* to DBPedia.

ties to Portuguese NPs, we use DBPedia (Auer et al., 2007) which has structured information about Wikipedia pages in many languages. The idea is to map each English NELL entity e_m to its corresponding English DBPedia page and therefore its Portuguese DBPedia page[8]. We use the structured information of the Portuguese page in DBPedia: its title and label as the set of Portuguese NPs corresponding to the English entity, $N_{pt}(e_m)$.

More specifically, for each English NELL entity e_m with English NPs that can refer to it, $N_{en}(e_m)$, we find *candidate* English DBPedia pages that can refer to the entity. We do this by computing Jaccard similarities (Jaccard, 1912; Chapman, 2009) of the entity's NPs with titles and labels of English DBPedia pages. We select pages with Jaccard similarities of more than 0.6 as candidates e.g., for English NELL entity *Brad Pitt* we find candidate English pages: `http://dbpedia.org/page/Brad_Pitt` (*Brad Pitt,* the US actor) and `http://dbpedia.org/page/Brad_Pitt_(boxer)` (*Brad Pit,* the Australian boxer).

Then, we construct a graph containing nodes that are: (1) the NELL entity that we want to map to DBPedia, (2) its candidate DBPedia pages, (3) other entities that have relations to the entity in NELL KB, and (4) the candidate DBPedia pages of these other entities (see Fig. 2 for the NELL entity *Brad Pitt*).

We add as edges to this graph: (1) the can-refer-to edges between entities in NELL and their candidate pages in DBPedia (dashed edges in Fig. 2), (2) the relation edges between the entities in NELL KB (black edges), and (3) the hyperlink edges be-

tween the pages in DBPedia (gray edges). In this graph we want to use the knowledge that NELL has already learned about the entity to narrow its candidates down to the page that the entity refers to. The idea is that relatedness among the entities in NELL implies relatedness among the DBPedia pages that refer to the entities. We use Personalized Page Rank (Page et al., 1999) to rank candidate DBPedia pages in this graph and pick the top ranked page as the page that can refer to the NELL entity.

For example, to find the DBPedia page that can refer to our NELL entity *Brad Pitt*, we use NELL's knowledge about this entity to rank its candidate pages. As seen in Fig. 2, DBPedia page of *Brad Pitt*, the US actor (*dbpedia:brad_pitt*) is highly connected to other pages (*dbpedia:angelina_jolie, dbpedia:douglas_pitt, dbpedia:usa*) that are in turn connected to the NELL entity *Brad Pitt*. *dbpedia:brad_pitt* is thus ranked highest and picked as the page that can refer to the NELL entity *Brad Pitt*.

Once we have an English DBPedia page that can refer to the NELL entity e_m, we can obtain the corresponding Portuguese page from DBPedia. The title and label of the Portuguese page becomes the set of Portuguese NPs that can refer to the NELL entity i.e., $N_{pt}(e_m)$ (see Table 2 for examples). Using $N_{pt}(e_m)$ we find instantiations of English relation instances in SVO_{pt} to add as labeled instances in D_{pt}. Portuguese NELL enriched with English NELL (i.e., Portuguese NELL^{+en}) has more than double the amount of relation instances, labeled and unlabeled instances (Table 1) than Portuguese NELL. In the experiments, we observe that this translates to a better verb-to-relation mapping.

Mapping NELL to DBPedia is also useful because it can align existing knowledge and add new knowledge to NELL. For example, by mapping to DBPedia, we can resolve abbreviations (e.g., the NELL entity: *COO* as "Chief Operations Officer" in English or "Diretor de Operações" in Portuguese), or resolve a person entity (e.g., the NELL entity: *Utamaro* as "Kitagawa Utamaro", the virtual artist).

3 Experiments

3.1 Pre-processing

For better coverage of verbs, we lemmatize verbs in the English SVO (using Stanford CoreNLP (Man-

---

[8]Almost every DBPedia English page has a corresponding Portuguese page

English NELL entity	Portuguese NPs
Amazonian Brown Brocket	"Veado-Roxo", "Fuboca"
COO	"Diretor de Operações"
Utamaro	"Kitagawa Utamaro"
Notopteridae	"Peixe-faca"
1967 Arab Israeli War	"Guerra dos Seis Dias", "Guerra de 1967"
Food Products	"Produtos Alimenticios", "Alimento", "Comida", ...

Table 2: Example Portuguese NPs learned for NELL entities

ning et al., 2014)). We lemmatize verbs in Portuguese SVO_{pt} (using LemPORT (Rodrigues et al., 2014)) and expand contracted prepositions.

For better precision and to make our method scale to a large text corpus, we focus on mapping verbs that are important for a relation based on how often the verbs co-occur with entity pairs that match the relation's argument type. For each argument type in the English SVO we consider only the top 50 verbs (in terms of *tf-idf* scores) for mapping. We use *tf-idf* scores to adjust for the fact that some verbs appear more frequently in general. For each of these verbs, we also use only the top 50 entity pairs that co-occur with the verb in the SVO (in terms of co-occurrence counts) to construct our dataset D.

For Portuguese verb-to-relation mapping, since SVO_{pt} is much smaller than the English SVO (i.e., it contains only about 22 million entity pair-verb triples compared to the 600 million triples in the English SVO), we use all the Portuguese entity pairs and verbs for mapping. To adjust for the fact that some verbs appear more frequently in general, we use *tf-idf* scores instead of co-occurrence counts for the values of $\mathbf{v}_{(e_m,e_n)}$ in the M-step (Equation 6).

3.2 Evaluation

We set aside 10% of D^ℓ for testing. Given a test instance $t_{(e_m,e_n)}$ and the trained model, we can predict the label assignment $\mathbf{y}_{(e_m,e_n)}$ using Eq. 1. This simulates the task of relation extraction where we predict relation(s) that exist between the entity pair in $t_{(e_m,e_n)}$.

We compare predicted labels of these test instances to the actual labels and measure precision, recall and F1 values of the prediction. We evaluate NELL relations that have more than one labeled instances in D^ℓ (constructed using the method described in section 2.2). For experiments on the English NELL, we evaluate 77 relations, with an aver-

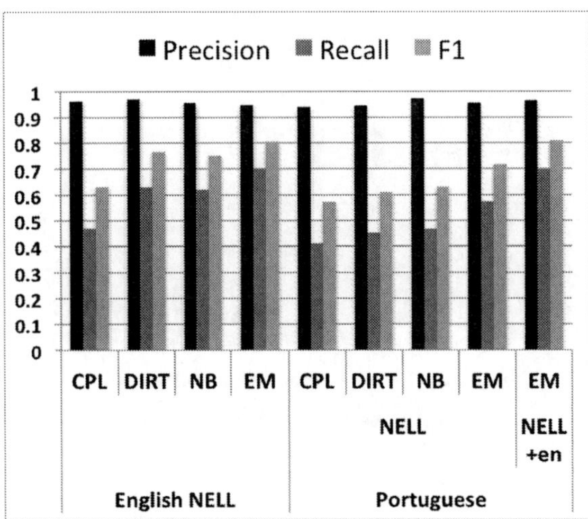

Figure 3: Performance on leaf relations.

age of 23 (and a median of 11) *training* instances per relations. For experiments on the Portuguese $NELL^{+en}$, which is Portuguese NELL enriched with relation instances from English NELL, we evaluate 85 relations, with an average of 31 (and a median of 10) *training* instances per relations. We compare the prediction produced by our approach: **EM** with that of other systems: **CPL**, **DIRT**, and **NB**.

In **CPL**, we obtain verb-to-relation mapping weights from NELL's CPL patterns and hand-labeled verb phrases (see Section 2.3.2). In **DIRT**, we obtain verb-to-relation mapping weights in an unsupervised manner (Lin and Pantel, 2001) based on their mutual information over labeled training instances. In Naive Bayes (**NB**) we learn the verb-to-relation mapping weights from labeled training instances. In contrast to the other systems, **EM** allows learning from both labeled and unlabeled instances.

To make other systems comparable to our proposed method, For **NB** and **DIRT** we add **CPL** weights as priors to their verb-to-relation mapping weights. For all these other systems, we also incorporate type-checking during prediction in that unlabeled instances are only labeled with relations that have the same argument types as the instance.

We show the micro-averaged performance of the systems on *leaf* relations of English NELL and Portuguese NELL (Fig. 3), where we do not incorporate constraints and classify each test instance into a single relation. We observe in both English and

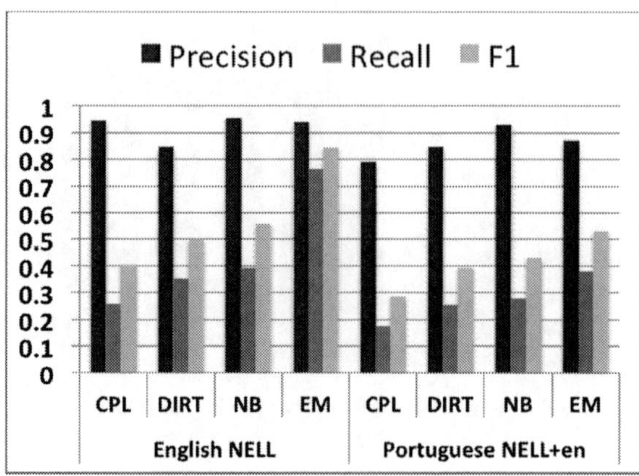

Figure 4: Performance on all relations.

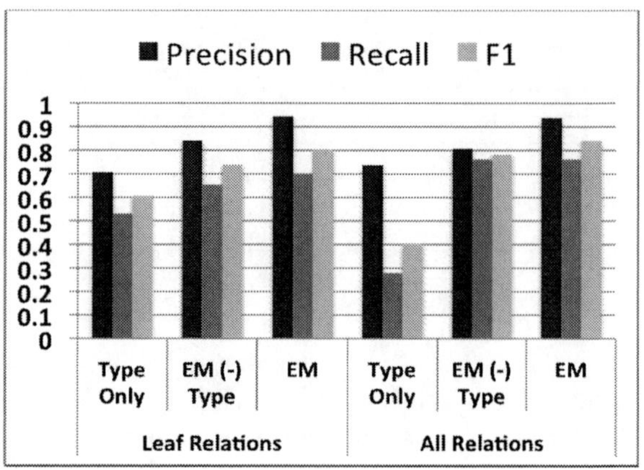

Figure 5: Performance on English NELL relations with and without type-checking.

Portuguese NELL that the verb-to-relation mapping obtained by **EM** results in predictions that have a much higher recall and comparable precision.

In Figure 3, we also observe a gain in performance when we run **EM** on Portuguese NELL^{+en} which is Portuguese NELL enriched with relation instances from English NELL obtained using our DBPedia linking in section 2.4. More labeled instances results in higher recall and precision. This shows the usefulness of aligning and merging knowledge from many different KBs to improve verb-to-relation mapping and relation extraction in general.

We show the micro-averaged performance of the systems on *all* relations of English NELL and Portuguese NELL (Fig. 4). Here, we incorporate hierarchical and mutual exclusive constraints between relations in our **EM**, allowing a test instance to be classified into more than one relation while respecting these constraints. Like before, we observe that the verb-to-relation mapping obtained by **EM** results in predictions with a much higher recall and comparable precision to other systems which do not incorporate constraints between relations.

In the experiments we also observe that **NB** performs comparably or better than **DIRT**. We hypothesize that it is because **NB** obtains its verb-to-relation mapping in a supervised manner while **DIRT** obtains its mapping in an unsupervised manner.

We also conduct experiments to investigate how much influence type-checking has on prediction. We show performance over instances whose types alone are not enough to disambiguate their assignments

Relation	Verbs	Proposed New Instances
bookWriter	a_1 be written by a_2, a_2 write a_1	*(Dracula, Bram Stoker),* *(Divine Comedy, Dante)*
city-Also-KnownAs	a_1 be known as a_2, a_2 be known as a_1, a_2 be renamed a_1,	*(Amman, Philadelphia),* *(Chennai, Madras),* *(Southport, Smithville)*
liderDe-Organizacao	a_1 fundador a_2, a_1 ceo de/em a_2	*(Jimmy Wales, Wikipedia),* *(Chad Hurley, Youtube)*
pessoa-Acusada-DoCrime	a_1 ser condenar aa_2, a_1 ser acusar de a_2, a_1 ser prender por a_2	*(Pedrinho Matador,* *Homicidios),* *(Omid Tahvili,* *Trafico de Drogaso)*

Table 3: Some relations' verbs and proposed new instances

(i.e., when more than one relation shares their argument type signatures) to see the merits of verb-to-relation mapping on prediction (Fig. 5). We observe that verbs learned by **EM** results in a better prediction even when used without type-checking (**EM (-) Type**) than using type-checking alone (by picking majority class among relations that have the correct type) (**Type Only**). Adding type checking improves performance even further (**EM**). This shows how verbs learning is complementary to type-checking.

The results of our experiments also highlight the merit of learning from a large, though unlabeled corpus to improve the coverage of verb-to-relation mapping and hence the recall of predictions. We also observe the usefulness of incorporating constraints and for merging knowledge from multiple KBs to improve performance. Another advantage of **EM** is that it produces relation labels for unlabeled data not yet in NELL KB. We show some of these new proposed relation instances as well as some of the verb-to-relation mapping obtained by **EM** (Table 3).

EM learns in average 177 English verbs and 3310 Portuguese verbs per relation; and propose in average 1695 new instances per relation for English NELL, and 6426 new instances per relation for Portuguese NELL. It learns less English verbs than Portuguese due to the filtering of English data (Section 3.1) and a high degree of inflection in Portuguese verbs. The smaller size of Portuguese KB also means more of its proposed instances are new.

4 Related Work

Existing verb resources are limited in their ability to map to KBs. Some existing resources classify verbs into semantic classes either manually (e.g. WordNet (Miller et al., 1990)) or automatically (e.g. DIRT (Lin and Pantel, 2001)). However, these classes are not directly mapped to KB relations. Other resources provide relations between verbs and their arguments in terms of semantic roles (e.g. PropBank (Kingsbury and Palmer, 2002), VerbNet (Kipper et al., 2000), FrameNet (Ruppenhofer et al., 2006)). However, it is not directly clear how the verbs map to relations in specific KBs.

Most existing verb resources are also manually constructed and not scalable. A verb resource that maps to KBs should grow in coverage with the KBs, possibly by leveraging large corpora such as the Web for high coverage mapping. One system that leverages Web-text as an interlingua is (Wijaya et al., 2013). However, they use it to map KBs to KBs, and obtain a verb-to-relation mapping only indirectly. They also compute heuristic confidences in verb-to-relation mappings from label propagation scores, which are not probabilities. In contrast, we map verbs directly to relations, and obtain $P(v_p|r_i)$ as an integral part of our EM process.

In terms of systems that learn mappings of textual patterns to KB relations, CPL (Carlson et al., 2010) is one system that is most similar to our proposed approach in that it also learns text patterns for KB relations in a semi-supervised manner and uses constraints in KB ontology to couple the learning to produce extractors consistent with these constraints. However, CPL uses a combination of heuristics in its learning, while we use EM. In our experiments, we use CPL patterns that contain verbs as priors and

show that our approach outperforms CPL in terms of effectiveness for extracting relation instances.

In terms of the relation extraction, there are distantly-supervised methods that can produce verb groupings as a by product of relation extraction. One state-of-the-art uses matrix factorization and universal schemas to extract relations (Riedel et al., 2013). In this work, they populate a database of a universal schema (which involves surface form predicates and relations from pre-existing KBs such as Freebase) by using matrix factorization models that learn latent feature vectors for relations and entity tuples. One can envision obtaining a verb grouping for a particular relation by predicting verb surface forms that occur between entity tuples that are instances of the relation. However, unlike our proposed method that learns mapping between typed-verbs to relations, they do not incorporate argument types in their learning, preferring to learn latent entity representation from data. Although this improves relation extraction, they observe that it hurts performance of surface form prediction because a single surface pattern (like "visit") can have multiple argument types (person-visit-location, person-visit-person, etc). Unlike our method, it is not clear in their method how argument types of surface patterns can be dealt with. Furthermore, it is not clear how useful prior constraints between relations (subset, mutex, etc.) can be incorporated in their method.

5 Conclusion

In this paper, we introduce an EM-based approach with argument type checking and ontological constraints to automatically map verb phrases to KB relations. We demonstrate that our verb resource is effective for extracting KB relation instances while improving recall; highlighting the value of learning from large scale unlabeled Web text. We also show the flexibility of our method. Being KB-, and language-independent, our method is able to construct a verb resource for any language, given a KB and a text corpus in that language. We illustrate this by building a verb resource in Portuguese and in English which are both effective for extracting KB relations. Future work will explore the use of our multilingual verb resource for relation extraction by reading natural language text in multiple languages.

Acknowledgments

We thank members of the NELL team at CMU and Federal University of Sao Carlos for their helpful datasets, comments, and suggestions. This research was supported by DARPA under contract number FA8750-13-2-0005.

References

Sören Auer, Christian Bizer, Georgi Kobilarov, Jens Lehmann, Richard Cyganiak, and Zachary Ives. 2007. Dbpedia: A nucleus for a web of open data. In *The semantic web*.

Kurt Bollacker, Colin Evans, Praveen Paritosh, Tim Sturge, and Jamie Taylor. 2008. Freebase: a collaboratively created graph database for structuring human knowledge. In *SIGMOD*.

J. Callan, M. Hoy, C. Yoo, and L. Zhao. 2009. Clueweb09 data set. *boston.lti.cs.cmu.edu*.

Andrew Carlson, Justin Betteridge, Bryan Kisiel, Burr Settles, Estevam R Hruschka Jr, and Tom M Mitchell. 2010. Toward an architecture for never-ending language learning. In *AAAI*, volume 5, page 3.

Sam Chapman. 2009. Simmetrics. *URL http://sourceforge. net/projects/simmetrics/. SimMetrics is a Similarity Metric Library, eg from edit distance's (Levenshtein, Gotoh, Jaro etc) to other metrics,(eg Soundex, Chapman). Work provided by UK Sheffield University funded by (AKT) an IRC sponsored by EPSRC, grant number GR N*, 15764.

Bhavana Dalvi, Einat Minkov, Partha P Talukdar, and William W Cohen. 2015. Automatic gloss finding for a knowledge base using ontological constraints. In *Proceedings of the Eighth ACM International Conference on Web Search and Data Mining*, pages 369–378. ACM.

Paul Jaccard. 1912. The distribution of the flora in the alpine zone. *New phytologist*, 11(2):37–50.

Paul Kingsbury and Martha Palmer. 2002. From treebank to propbank. In *LREC*. Citeseer.

Karin Kipper, Hoa Trang Dang, and Martha Palmer. 2000. Class-based construction of a verb lexicon. In *AAAI/IAAI*, pages 691–696.

Dekang Lin and Patrick Pantel. 2001. Discovery of inference rules for question-answering. *Natural Language Engineering*, 7(04):343–360.

Yue Lu and Chengxiang Zhai. 2008. Opinion integration through semi-supervised topic modeling. In *Proceedings of the 17th international conference on World Wide Web*, pages 121–130. ACM.

Christopher D. Manning, Mihai Surdeanu, John Bauer, Jenny Finkel, Steven J. Bethard, and David McClosky. 2014. The Stanford CoreNLP natural language processing toolkit. In *Proceedings of 52nd Annual Meeting of the Association for Computational Linguistics: System Demonstrations*, pages 55–60.

George A Miller, Richard Beckwith, Christiane Fellbaum, Derek Gross, and Katherine J Miller. 1990. Introduction to wordnet: An on-line lexical database*. *International journal of lexicography*, 3(4):235–244.

Kamal Nigam, Andrew McCallum, and Tom Mitchell. 2006. Semi-supervised text classification using em. *Semi-Supervised Learning*, pages 33–56.

Lawrence Page, Sergey Brin, Rajeev Motwani, and Terry Winograd. 1999. The pagerank citation ranking: bringing order to the web.

Sebastian Riedel, Limin Yao, Andrew McCallum, and Benjamin M Marlin. 2013. Relation extraction with matrix factorization and universal schemas.

Ricardo Rodrigues, Hugo Gonçalo Oliveira, and Paulo Gomes. 2014. Lemport: a high-accuracy crossplatform lemmatizer for portuguese. *Maria João Varanda Pereira José Paulo Leal*, page 267.

Josef Ruppenhofer, Michael Ellsworth, Miriam RL Petruck, Christopher R Johnson, and Jan Scheffczyk. 2006. Framenet ii: Extended theory and practice.

Fabian M Suchanek, Gjergji Kasneci, and Gerhard Weikum. 2007. Yago: a core of semantic knowledge. In *Proceedings of the 16th international conference on World Wide Web*, pages 697–706. ACM.

Derry Wijaya, Partha Pratim Talukdar, and Tom Mitchell. 2013. Pidgin: ontology alignment using web text as interlingua. In *Proceedings of the 22nd ACM international conference on Conference on information & knowledge management*, pages 589–598. ACM.

Comparing Convolutional Neural Networks
to Traditional Models for Slot Filling

Heike Adel and **Benjamin Roth** and **Hinrich Schütze**
Center for Information and Language Processing (CIS)
LMU Munich
Oettingenstr. 67, 80538 Munich, Germany
heike@cis.lmu.de

Abstract

We address relation classification in the context of slot filling, the task of finding and evaluating fillers like "Steve Jobs" for the slot X in "X founded Apple". We propose a convolutional neural network which splits the input sentence into three parts according to the relation arguments and compare it to state-of-the-art and traditional approaches of relation classification. Finally, we combine different methods and show that the combination is better than individual approaches. We also analyze the effect of genre differences on performance.

1 Introduction

Structured knowledge about the world is useful for many natural language processing (NLP) tasks, such as disambiguation, question answering or semantic search. However, the extraction of structured information from natural language text is challenging because one relation can be expressed in many different ways. The TAC Slot Filling (SF) Shared Task defines slot filling as extracting fillers for a set of predefined relations ("slots") from a large corpus of text data. Exemplary relations are the city of birth of a person or the employees or founders of a company. Participants are provided with an evaluation corpus and a query file consisting of pairs of entities and slots. For each entity slot pair (e.g. "Apple" and "founded_by"), the systems have to return the second argument ("filler") of the relation (e.g. "Steve Jobs") as well as a supporting sentence from the evaluation corpus. The key challenge in slot

filling is relation classification: given a sentence s of the evaluation corpus containing the name of a queried entity (e.g., "Apple") and a filler candidate (e.g., "Steve Jobs"), we need to decide whether s expresses the relation ("founded_by", in this case). We will refer to the mentions of the two arguments of the relation as *name* and *filler*. Performance on relation classification is crucial for slot filling since its effectiveness directly depends on it.

In this paper, we investigate three complementary approaches to relation classification.

The first approach is pattern matching, a leading approach in the TAC evaluations. Fillers are validated based on patterns. In this work, we consider patterns learned with distant supervision and patterns extracted from Universal Schema relations.

The second approach is support vector machines. We evaluate two different feature sets: a bag-of-word feature set (BOW) and more sophisticated skip n-gram features.

Our third approach is a convolutional neural network (CNN). CNNs have been applied to NLP tasks like sentiment analysis, part-of-speech tagging and semantic role labeling. They can recognize phrase patterns independent of their position in the sentence. Furthermore, they make use of word embeddings that directly reflect word similarity (Mikolov et al., 2013). Hence, we expect them to be robust models for the task of classifying filler candidates and to generalize well to unseen test data. In this work, we train different variants of CNNs: As a baseline, we reimplement the recently developed piecewise CNN (Zeng et al., 2015). Then, we extend this model by splitting the contexts not only for

Proceedings of NAACL-HLT 2016, pages 828–838,
San Diego, California, June 12-17, 2016. ©2016 Association for Computational Linguistics

pooling but also for convolution (contextwise CNN).

Currently, there is no benchmark for slot filling. Therefore, it is not possible to directly compare results that were submitted to the Shared Task to new results. Comparable manual annotations for new results, for instance, cannot be easily obtained. There are also many different system components, such as document retrieval from the evaluation corpus and coreference resolution, that affect Shared Task performance and that are quite different in nature from relation classification. Even in the subtask of relation classification, it is not possible to directly use existing relation classification benchmarks (e.g. Riedel et al. (2013), Hendrickx et al. (2010)) since data and relations can be quite different. Many benchmark relations, for instance, correspond to Freebase relations but not all slots are modeled in Freebase and some slots even comprise more than one Freebase relation. While most relation classification benchmarks either use newswire or web data, the SF task includes documents from both domains (and discussion fora). Another difference to traditional relation classification benchmarks arises from the pipeline aspect of slot filling. Depending on the previous steps, the input for the relation classification models can be incomplete, noisy, include coreferent mentions, etc.

The official SF Shared Task evaluations only assess whole systems (with potential subsequent faults in their pipelines (Pink et al., 2014)). Thus, we expect component wise comparisons to be a valuable addition to the Shared Task: With comparisons of single components, teams would be able to improve their modules more specifically. To start with one of the most important components, we have created a benchmark for slot filling relation classification, based on 2012 – 2014 TAC Shared Task data. It will be described below and published along with this paper.[1] In addition to presenting model results on this benchmark dataset, we also show that these results correlate with end-to-end SF results. Hence, optimizing a model on this dataset will also help improving results in the end-to-end setting.

In our experiments, we found that our models suffer from large genre differences in the TAC data. Hence, the SF Shared Task is a task that conflates an

investigation of domain (or genre) adaptation with the one of slot filling. We argue that both problems are important NLP problems and provide datasets and results for both within and across genres. We hope that this new resource will encourage others to test their models on our dataset and that this will help promote research on slot filling.

In summary, our contributions are as follows. (i) We investigate the complementary strengths and weaknesses of different approaches to relation classification and show that their combination can better deal with a diverse set of problems that slot filling poses than each of the approaches individually. (ii) We propose to split the context at the relation arguments before passing it to the CNN in order to better deal with the special characteristics of a sentence in relation classification. This outperforms the state-of-the-art piecewise CNN. (iii) We analyze the effect of genre on slot filling and show that it is an important conflating variable that needs to be carefully examined in research on slot filling. (iv) We provide a benchmark for slot filling relation classification that will facilitate direct comparisons of models in the future and show that results on this dataset are correlated with end-to-end system results.

Section 2 gives an overview of related work. Section 3 discusses the challenges that slot filling systems face. In Section 4, we describe our slot filling models. Section 5 presents experimental setup and results. Section 6 analyzes the results. We present our conclusions in Section 7 and describe the resources we publish in Section 8.

2   Related Work

Slot filling. The participants of the SF Shared Task (Surdeanu, 2013) are provided with a large text corpus. For evaluation, they get a collection of queries and need to provide fillers for predefined relations and an offset of a context which can serve as a justification. Most participants apply pipeline based systems. Pink et al. (2014) analyzed sources of recall losses in these pipelines. The results of the systems show the difficulty of the task: In the 2014 evaluation, the top-ranked system had an F_1 of .37 (Angeli et al., 2014a). To train their models, most groups use distant supervision (Mintz et al., 2009). The top-ranked systems apply machine learning based ap-

---

[1] http://cistern.cis.lmu.de

proaches rather than manually developed patterns or models (Surdeanu and Ji, 2014). The methods for extracting and scoring candidates range from pattern based approaches (Gonzàlez et al., 2012; Liu and Zhao, 2012; Li et al., 2012; Qiu et al., 2012; Roth et al., 2014) over rule based systems (Varma et al., 2012) to classifiers (Malon et al., 2012; Roth et al., 2013). The top ranked system from 2013 used SVMs and patterns for evaluating filler candidates (Roth et al., 2013); their results suggest that n-gram based features are sufficient to build reliable classifiers for the relation classification module. They also show that SVMs outperform patterns.

CNNs for relation classification. Zeng et al. (2014) and Dos Santos et al. (2015) apply CNNs to the relation classification SemEval Shared Task data from 2010 and show that CNNs outperform other models. We train CNNs on noisy distant supervised data since (in contrast to the SemEval Shared Task) clean training sets are not available. Malon et al. (2012) describe a CNN for slot filling that is based on the output of a parser. We plan to explore parsing for creating a more linguistically motivated input representation in the future.

Baseline models. In this paper, we will compare our methods against traditional relation classification models: Mintz++ (Mintz et al., 2009; Surdeanu et al., 2012) and MIMLRE (Surdeanu et al., 2012). Mintz++ is a model based on the Mintz features (lexical and syntactic features for relation extraction). It was developed by Surdeanu et al. (2012) and used as a baseline model by them. MIMLRE is a graphical model designed to cope with multiple instances and multiple labels in distant supervised data. It is trained with Expectation Maximization.

Another baseline model which we use in this work is a piecewise convolutional neural network (Zeng et al., 2015). This recently published network is designed especially for the relation classification task which allows to split the context into three parts around the two relation arguments. While it uses the whole context for convolution, it performs max pooling over the three parts individually. In contrast, we propose to split the context even earlier and apply the convolutional filters to each part separately.

Genre dependency. There are many studies showing the genre dependency of machine learning models. In 2012, the SANCL Shared Task fo-

cused on evaluating models on web data that have been trained on news data (Petrov and McDonald, 2012). The results show that POS tagging performance can decline a lot when the genre is changed. For other NLP tasks like machine translation or sentiment analysis, this is also a well-known challenge and domain adaptation has been extensively studied (Glorot et al., 2011; Foster and Kuhn, 2007). We do not investigate domain adaptation per se, but show that the genre composition of the slot filling source corpus poses challenges to genre independent models.

3 Challenges of Slot Filling

Slot filling includes NLP challenges of various natures. Given a large evaluation corpus, systems first need to find documents relevant to the entity of the query. This involves challenges like alternate names for the same entity, misspellings of names and ambiguous names (different entities with the same name). Then for each relevant document, sentences with mentions of the entity need to be extracted, as well as possible fillers for the given slot. In most cases, coreference resolution and named entity recognition tools are used for these tasks. Finally, the systems need to decide which filler candidate to output as the solution for the given slot. This step can be reduced to relation classification. It is one of the most crucial parts of the whole pipeline since it directly influences the quality of the final output. The most important challenges for relation classification for slot filling are little or noisy (distant supervised) training data, data from different domains and test sentences which have been extracted with a pipeline of different NLP components. Thus, their quality directly depends on the performance of the whole pipeline. If, for example, sentence splitting fails, the input can be incomplete or too long. If coreference resolution or named entity recognition fails, the relation arguments can be wrong or incomplete.

4 Models for Relation Classification

Patterns. The first approach we evaluate for relation classification is pattern matching. For a given sentence, the pattern matcher classifies the relation as correct if one of the patterns matches; otherwise the candidate is rejected. In particular, we apply two different pattern sets: The first set consists of patterns learned using distant supervision (*PATdist*). They have been used in the SF challenge by the top-ranked system in the 2013 Shared Task (Roth et al., 2013). The second set contains patterns from universal schema relations for the SF task (*PATuschema*). Universal schema relations are extracted based on matrix factorization (Riedel et al., 2013). In this work, we apply the universal schema patterns extracted for slot filling by Roth et al. (2014).

Support vector machines (SVMs). Our second approach is support vector machines. We evaluate two different feature sets: bag-of-word features (*SVMbow*) and skip n-gram features (*SVMskip*). Based on the results of Roth et al. (2013), we will not use additional syntactic or semantic features for our classifiers. For SVMbow, the representation of a sentence consists of a flag and four bag-of-word vectors. Let m_1 and m_2 be the mentions of name and filler (or filler and name) in the sentence, with m_1 occurring before m_2. The binary flag indicates in which order name and filler occur. The four BOW vectors contain the words in the sentence to the left of m_1, between m_1 and m_2, to the right of m_2 and all words of the sentence. For SVMskip, we use the previously described BOW features and additionally a feature vector which contains skip n-gram features. They wildcard tokens in the middle of the n-gram (cf. Roth et al. (2013)). In particular, we use skip 3-grams, skip 4-grams and skip 5-grams. A possible skip 4-gram of the context ", founder and director of", for example, would be the string "founder of", a pattern that could not have been directly extracted from this context otherwise. We train one linear SVM (Fan et al., 2008) for each relation and feature set and tune parameter C on dev.

Convolutional neural networks (CNNs). CNNs are increasingly applied in NLP (Collobert et al., 2011; Kalchbrenner et al., 2014). They extract n-gram based features independent of the position in the sentence and create (sub-)sentence representations. The two most important aspects that make this possible are convolution and pooling. Max pooling (Collobert et al., 2011) detects the globally most relevant features obtained by local convolution.

Another promising aspect of CNNs for relation classification is that they use an embedding based in-put representation. With word embeddings, similar words are represented by similar vectors and, thus, we can recognize (near-)synonyms – synonyms of relation triggers as well as of other important context words. If the CNN has learned, for example, that the context "is based in" triggers the relation location_of_headquarters and that "based" has a similar vector representation as "located", it may recognize the context "is located in" correctly as another trigger for the same relation even if it has never seen it during training. In the following paragraphs, we describe the different variants of CNNs which we evaluate in this paper. For each variant, we train one binary CNN per slot and optimize the number of filters ($\in \{300, 1000, 3000\}$), the size of the hidden layer ($\in \{100, 300, 1000\}$) and the filter width ($\in \{3, 5\}$) on dev. We use word2vec (Mikolov et al., 2013) to pre-train word embeddings (dimensionality $d = 50$) on a May-2014 English Wikipedia corpus.

Piecewise CNN. Our baseline CNN is the model developed by Zeng et al. (2015). It represents the input sentence by a matrix of word vectors, applies several filters for convolution and then divides the resulting n-gram representation into left, middle and right context based on the positions m_1 and m_2 of name and filler (see SVM description). For each of the three parts, one max value is extracted by pooling. The results are passed to a softmax classifier.

Contextwise CNN. In contrast to the piecewise CNN, we propose to split the context before convolution as shown in Figure 1. Hence, similar to our BOW vectors for the SVM, we split the original context words into left, middle and right context. Then, we apply convolution and pooling to each of the contexts separately. In contrast to the piecewise CNN, there is no convolution across relation arguments. Thus, the network learns to focus on the context words and cannot be distracted by the presence of (always present) relation arguments. The filter weights W are shared for the three contexts. Our intuition is that the most important sequence features we want to extract by convolution can appear in two or three of the regions. Weight sharing also reduces the number of parameters and increases robustness. We also found in initial experiments that sharing filter weights across left, middle, right outperformed not sharing weights. The results of convolution are pooled using k-max pooling (Kalchbrenner et al.,

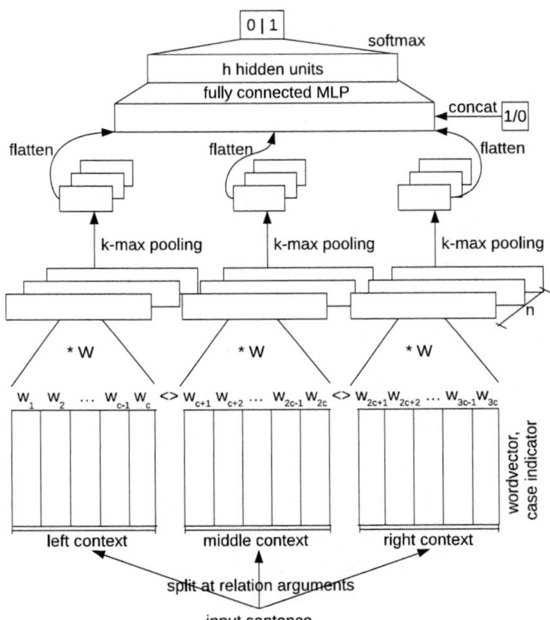

Figure 1: Contextwise CNN for relation classification

2014): only the $k = 3$ maximum values of each filter application are kept. The pooling results are then concatenated to a single vector and extended by a flag indicating whether the name or the filler appeared first in the sentence.

In initial experiments, we found that a fully connected hidden layer after convolution and pooling leads to a more powerful model. It connects the representations of the three contexts and, thus, can draw conclusions based on cooccurring patterns across contexts. Therefore, the result vector after convolution and pooling is fed into a fully connected hidden layer. A softmax layer makes the final decision.

For a fair comparison of models, we also add a hidden layer to the piecewise CNN and apply k-max pooling there as well. Thus, the number of parameters to learn is the same for both models. We call this model *CNNpieceExt*. The key difference between CNNpieceExt and CNNcontext is the time when the context is split into three parts: before or after convolution. This affects the windows of words to which the convolutional filters are applied.

Model combination (CMB). To combine a set M of models for classification, we perform a simple linear combination of the scores of the models:

$$q_{\text{CMB}} = \sum_{m=1\ldots M} \alpha_m q_m$$

where q_m is the score of model m and α_m is its weight (optimized on dev using grid search). All weights sum to 1.

For a comparison of different combination possibilities, see, for example, (Viswanathan et al., 2015).

5 Experiments and Results

5.1 Training Data

We used distant supervision for generating training data. We created a set of (subject, relation, object) tuples by querying Freebase (Bollacker et al., 2008) for relations that correspond to the slot relations. Then we scanned the following corpora for sentences containing both arguments of a relation in the tuple set: (i) the TAC source corpus (TAC, 2014), (ii) a snapshot of Wikipedia (May 2014), (iii) the Freebase description fields, (iv) a subset of Clueweb[2], (v) a New York Times corpus (LDC2008T19). The resulting sentences are positive training examples. Based on the tuple set, we selected negative examples by scanning the corpora for sentences that (i) contain a mention of a name occurring in a tuple, (ii) do not contain the correct filler, (iii) contain a mention different from the correct filler, but with the same named entity type (based on CoreNLP NER (Manning et al., 2014)). All negative examples for date slots, for instance, are sentences containing an incorrect date.

This procedure gave us a large but noisy training set for most slots. In order to reduce incorrect labels, we applied a self-training procedure: We trained SVMs on the SF dataset created by Angeli et al. (2014b). With the resulting SVMs, we predicted labels for our training set. If the predicted label did not match the distant supervised label, we deleted the corresponding training example (Min et al., 2012). This procedure was conducted in several iterations on different chunks of the training set. Finally, the SF dataset and the filtered training examples were merged. (We do not use the SF dataset directly because (i) it provides few examples per slot

---

[2]`http://lemurproject.org/clueweb12`

(min: 1, max: 4960) and (ii) it consists of examples for which the classifiers of Angeli et al. (2014b) were indecisive, i.e., presumably contexts that are hard to classify.) Since their contexts are similar, we also merged city, state-or-province and country slots to one location slot.

5.2 Evaluation Data

One of the main challenges in building and evaluating relation classification models for SF is the shortage of training and evaluation data. Each group has their own datasets and comparisons across groups are difficult. Therefore, we have developed a script that creates a clean dataset based on manually annotated system outputs from previous Shared Task evaluations. In the future, it can be used by all participants to evaluate components of their slot filling systems.[3] The script only extracts sentences that contain mentions of both name and filler. It conducts a heuristic check based on NER tags to determine whether the name in the sentence is a valid mention of the query name or is referring to another entity. In the latter case, the example is filtered out. One difficulty is that many published offsets are incorrect. We tried to match these using heuristics. In general, we apply filters that ensure high quality of the resulting evaluation data even if that means that a considerable part of the TAC system output is discarded. In total, we extracted 39,386 high-quality evaluation instances out of the 59,755 system output instances published by TAC and annotated as either completely correct or completely incorrect.

A table in the supplementary material[4] gives statistics: the number of positive and negative examples per slot and year (without duplicates). For 2013, the most examples were extracted. The lower number for 2014 is probably due to the newly introduced inference across documents. This limits the number of sentences with mentions of both name and filler. The average ratio of positive to negative examples is 1:4. The number of positive examples per slot and year ranges from 0 (org:member_of, 2014) to 581 (per:title, 2013), the number of negative examples from 5 (org:website, 2014) to 1886 (per:title, 2013).

---

[3]http://cistern.cis.lmu.de. We publish scripts since we cannot distribute data.

[4]also available at http://cistern.cis.lmu.de

In contrast to other relation classification benchmarks, this dataset is not based on a knowledge base (such as Freebase) and unrelated text (such as web documents) but directly on the SF assessments. Thus, it includes exactly the SF relations and addresses the challenges of the end-to-end task: noisy data, possibly incomplete extractions of sentences and data from different domains.

We use the data from 2012/2013 as development and the data from 2014 as evaluation set.

5.3 Experiments

We evaluate the models described in Section 4, select the best models and combine them.

Experiments with patterns. First, we compare the performance of PATdist and PATuschema on our dataset. We evaluate the pattern matchers on all slots presented in Table 1 and calculate their average F_1 scores on dev. PATdist achieves a score of .35, PATuschema of .33. Since it performs better, we use PATdist in the following experiments.

Experiments with SVMs. Second, we train and evaluate SVMbow and SVMskip. Average F_1 of SVMskip and SVMbow are .62 and .59, respectively. Thus, we use SVMskip. We expected that SVMskip beats SVMbow due to its richer feature set, but SVMbow performs surprisingly well.

Experiments with CNNs. Finally, we compare the performance of CNNpiece, CNNpieceExt and CNNcontext. While the baseline network CNNpiece (Zeng et al., 2015) achieves F_1 of .52 on dev, CNNpieceExt has an F_1 score of .55 and CNNcontext an F_1 of .60. The difference of CNNpiece and CNNpieceExt is due to the additional hidden layer and k-max pooling. The considerable difference in performance of CNNpieceExt and CNNcontext shows that splitting the context for convolution has a positive effect on the performance of the network.

Overall results. Table 1 shows the slot wise results of the best patterns (PATdist), SVMs (SVMskip) and CNNs (CNNcontext). Furthermore, it provides a comparison with two baseline models: Mintz++ and MIMLRE. SVM and CNN clearly outperform these baselines. They also outperform PAT for almost all slots. The difference between dev and eval results varies a lot among the slots. We suspect that this is a result of genre differences in the data and analyze this in Section 6.4.

	Mintz++		MIMLRE		PATdist		SVMskip		CNNcontext		CMB	
	dev	eval	dev	eval	dev	eval	dev	eval	dev	eval	dev	eval
per:age	.84	.71	.83	.73	.69	**.80**	**.86**	.74	.83	.76	**.86**	.77
per:alternate_names	.29	.03	.29	.03	**.50**	**.50**	.35	.02	.32	.04	**.50**	**.50**
per:children	.76	.43	.77	.48	.10	.07	.81	.68	.82	.61	**.87**	**.76**
per:cause_of_death	.76	.42	.75	.36	.44	.11	**.82**	.32	.77	**.52**	**.82**	.31
per:date_of_birth	**1.0**	.60	.99	.60	.67	.57	**1.0**	.67	**1.0**	**.77**	**1.0**	.67
per:date_of_death	.67	.45	.67	.45	.30	.32	**.79**	**.54**	.72	.48	**.79**	**.54**
per:empl_memb_of	.38	.36	.41	.37	.24	.22	.42	.36	.41	.37	**.47**	**.39**
per:location_of_birth	.56	.22	.56	.22	.30	.30	.59	.27	.59	.23	**.74**	**.36**
per:loc_of_death	.65	.41	.66	**.43**	.13	.00	.64	.34	.63	.28	**.70**	.35
per:loc_of_residence	.14	.11	.15	.18	.10	.03	**.31**	**.33**	.20	.23	**.31**	.31
per:origin	.40	.48	.42	.46	.13	.11	**.65**	**.64**	.43	.39	**.65**	.59
per:parents	.64	.59	.68	.65	.27	.38	.65	**.79**	.65	.78	**.72**	.71
per:schools_att	.75	**.78**	.76	.75	.27	.26	.78	.71	.72	.55	**.79**	.71
per:siblings	**.66**	.59	.64	.59	.14	.50	.60	.68	.63	**.70**	.65	**.70**
per:spouse	.58	.23	.59	.27	.40	.53	.67	.32	.67	.30	**.78**	**.57**
per:title	.49	.39	.49	.40	.48	.42	.54	**.48**	.57	.46	**.59**	.46
org:alternate_names	.49	.46	.50	.48	.70	**.71**	.62	.62	.65	.66	**.72**	.67
org:date_founded	.41	.71	.42	**.73**	.47	.40	.57	.70	.64	.71	**.68**	.68
org:founded_by	.60	.62	.70	.65	.39	.62	.77	.74	.80	.68	**.85**	**.77**
org:loc_of_headqu	.13	.19	.14	.20	.39	.30	.43	.42	.43	.45	**.50**	**.46**
org:members	.58	.06	.55	.16	.03	**.29**	.70	.13	.65	.04	**.76**	.13
org:parents	.32	.14	.36	.17	.31	.18	.37	.20	.41	.16	**.52**	**.21**
org:subsidiaries	.32	.43	.35	.35	.32	**.56**	.38	.37	.36	.44	**.42**	.49
org:top_memb_empl	.35	.44	.37	.46	.53	.46	.43	**.55**	.43	.53	**.58**	.51
average	.53	.41	.54	.42	.35	.36	.62	.48	.60	.46	**.68**	**.53**

Table 1: Performance on Slot Filling benchmark dataset (dev: data from 2012/2013, eval: from 2014). CMB denotes the combination of PATdist, SVMskip and CNNcontext.

Slot wise results of the other models (PATuschema, SVMbow, CNNpiece, CNNpieceExt) can be found in the supplementary material.

Comparing PAT, SVM and CNN,[5] different patterns emerge for different slots. Each is best on a subset of the slots (see bold numbers). This indicates that relation classification for slot filling is not a uniform problem: each slot has special properties and the three approaches are good at modeling a different subset of these properties. Given the big differences, we expect to gain performance by combining the three approaches. Indeed, CMB (PATdist + SVMskip + CNNcontext), the combination of the three best performing models, obtains the best results in average (in bold).

Section 6.3 shows that the performance on our dataset is highly correlated with SF end-to-end per-

formance. Thus, our results indicate that a combination of different models ist the most promising approach to getting good performance on slot filling.

6 Analysis

6.1 Contribution of Each Model

To see how much each model contributes to CMB, we count how often each weight between 0.0 and 1.0 is selected for the linear interpolation. The results are plotted as a histogram (Figure 2). A weight of 0.0 means that the corresponding model does not contribute to CMB. We see that all three models contribute to CMB for most of the slots. The CNN, for instance, is included in the combination for 14 of 24 slots.

6.2 Comparison of CNN to Traditional Models

Our motivation for using a CNN is that convolution and max pooling can recognize important n-grams independent of their position in the sentence. To in-

---

[5]In prior experiments, we also compared with recurrent neural networks. RNN performance was comparable to CNNs, but required much more training time and parameter tuning. Therefore, we focus on CNNs in this paper. See also Vu et al. (2016).

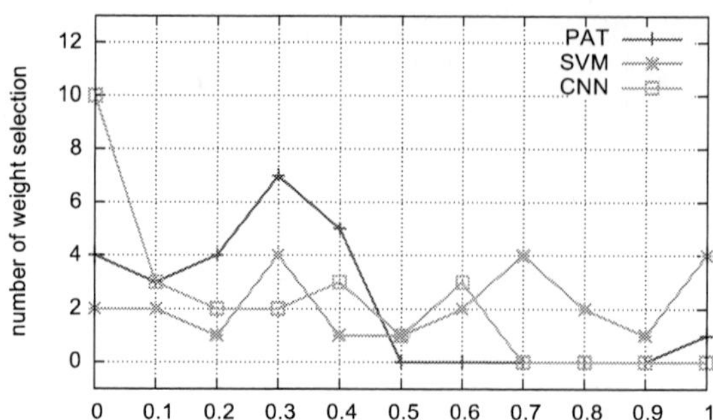

Figure 2: # times each weight is selected in CMB

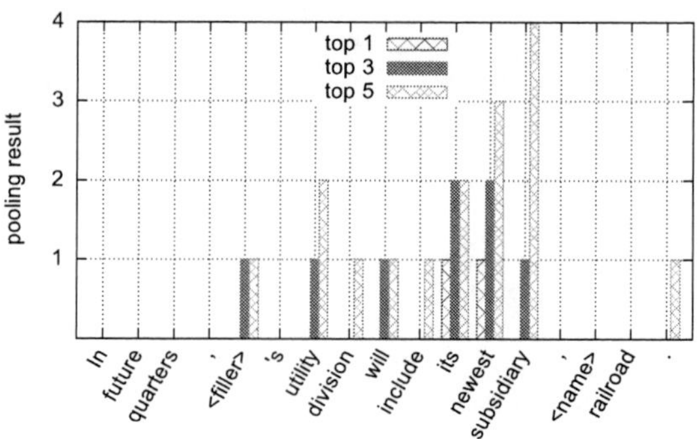

Figure 3: Analysis of convolution and pooling

vestigate this effect, we select for each CNN the top five kernels whose activations are the most correlated with the final score of the positive class. Then we calculate which n-grams are selected by these kernels in the max pooling step. This corresponds to those n-grams which are recognized by the kernel to be the most informative for the given slot. Figure 3 shows the result for an example sentence expressing the slot relation org:parents. The height of a bar is the number of times that the 3-gram around the corresponding word was selected by k-max pooling; e.g., the bar above "newest" corresponds to the trigram "its newest subsidiary". The figure shows that the convolutional filters are able to learn phrases that trigger a relation, e.g., "its subsidiary". In contrast to patterns, they do not rely on exact matches. The first reason is embeddings. They generalize similar words and phrases by assigning similar word vectors to them. For PAT and SVM, this type of generalization is more difficult. The second type of generalization that the CNN learns concerns insertions, similar to skip n-gram features. The recognition of important phrases in convolution is robust against insertions. An example is "newest" in Figure 3, a word that is not important for the slot.

A direct comparison of results with PAT shows that the CNN has better eval scores for about 67% of the slots (see Table 1). Our reasoning above can explain this. Compared to the SVM, the CNN generalizes better to unseen data in only 42% of all cases. The fact that this does not happen in more cases shows the power of the skip n-gram features of the SVM: they also provide a kind of generalization against insertions. The SVM might also need less data to train than the CNN. Nevertheless, the

final scores show that the CNN performs almost as well as the SVM in average (.60 vs .62 on dev, .46 vs .48 on eval) and contributes to a better combination score.

6.3 Correlation with End-to-end Results

In this section, we show that using the dataset we provide with this paper allows tuning classification models for the end-to-end SF task. For each model and each possible combination of models, we calculate average results on our evaluation set as well as final F_1 scores when running the whole slot filling pipeline with our in-house system. The best results of our slot filling system are an F_1 of .29 on the 2013 queries and of .25 on the 2014 queries. We calculate Pearson's correlation coefficient to assess correlation of relation classification and end-to-end performances for the n different system configurations (i.e., model combinations). The correlation of the results on our eval dataset with the SF results on 2013 queries is .89, the correlation with the SF results on 2014 queries is .82. This confirms that good results on the dataset we propose lead to good results on the slot filling end-to-end task.

6.4 Effect of Genre and Time

The TAC source corpus consists of about 1M news documents, 1M web documents and 100K documents from discussion forums (TAC, 2014). The distribution of these different genres in the extracted assessment data is as shown in Table 2.

The proportion of non-news more than doubled from 12.5% to 26.6%. Thus, when using 2012/2013 as the development and 2014 as the test set, we are faced with a domain adaptation problem.

	2012/3	2014
news	87.5%	73.4%
web + forums	12.5%	26.6%

Table 2: Distribution of genres

In this section, we show the effect of domain differences on our models in more detail. For our genre analysis, we retrain our models on genre specific training sets WEB and $\text{NEWS}_\subset$ and show within-genre as well as cross-genre evaluations. To avoid performance differences due to different training set sizes, we reduced the news training set to the same size as the web training set. We refer to this subset as $\text{NEWS}_\subset$.

Cross-genre evaluation. Table 3 shows results of testing models trained on genre-specific data: on data of the same genre and on data of the other genre. We present results only for a subset of relations in this paper, however, the numbers for the other slots follow the same trends.

Models trained on news (left part) show clearly higher performance in the within-genre evaluation than cross-genre. For models trained on web (right part), this is different. We suspect that the reason is that web data is much noiser and thus less predictable, even for models trained on web. For all evaluations, the differences among dev and eval are quite large. Especially for slot filling on web (bottom part of Table 3), the results on dev do not seem much related to the results on eval. This domain effect increases the difficulties of training robust relation classification models for slot filling. It can also explain why optimizing models for unseen data (with unknown genre distributions) as in Table 1 is challenging. Since slot filling by itself is a challenging task, even in the absence of domain differences, we will distribute two splits: a split by year and a split by genre. For training and tuning models for the slot filling research challenge, the year split can be used to cover the challenge of mixing different genres. For experiments on domain adaptation or genre-specific effects, our genre split can be used.

7 Conclusion

In this paper, we presented different approaches to slot filling relation classification: patterns, support vector machines and convolutional neural networks.

		Train on $\text{NEWS}_\subset$				Train on WEB			
		SVM		CNN		SVM		CNN	
		dev	ev	dev	ev	dev	ev	dev	ev
Test on news	per:age	.79	.80	**.88**	**.87**	.78	.76	**.85**	**.83**
	per:children	**.85**	**.86**	.78	.78	**.75**	**.80**	.00	.07
	per:spouse	.74	.64	**.76**	**.71**	.77	.65	.73	**.67**
	org:alt_names	.22	.32	**.69**	**.67**	.65	**.70**	**.66**	.66
	org:loc_headqu	.51	.50	**.53**	**.51**	.51	**.53**	**.53**	.50
	org:parents	**.30**	.32	.29	**.34**	.26	.33	**.30**	**.34**
Test on web	per:age	.33	.73	**.57**	**.83**	.00	.67	**.57**	**.83**
	per:children	.59	**.33**	**.70**	**.33**	**.63**	**.57**	.00	.00
	per:spouse	.52	.50	**.60**	**.57**	.56	.57	**.67**	**.62**
	org:alt_names	.27	.19	**.51**	**.37**	**.60**	**.49**	.56	.38
	org:loc_headqu	.39	**.46**	**.43**	.44	**.44**	**.48**	.36	.47
	org:parents	.09	**.08**	**.11**	.07	.10	**.08**	**.15**	**.08**

Table 3: Genre specific F_1 scores. Genre specific training data (of the same sizes). Top: news results. Bottom: web results.

We investigated their complementary strengths and weaknesses and showed that their combination can better deal with a diverse set of problems that slot filling poses than each of the approaches individually. We proposed a contextwise CNN which outperforms the recent state-of-the-art piecewise CNN. Furthermore, we analyzed the effect of genre on slot filling and showed that it needs to be carefully examined in research on slot filling. Finally, we provided a benchmark for slot filling relation classification that will facilitate direct comparisons of approaches in the future.

8 Additional Resources

We publish the scripts that we developed to extract the annotated evaluation data and our splits by genre and by year as well as the dev/eval splits.

Acknowledgments

Heike Adel is a recipient of the Google European Doctoral Fellowship in Natural Language Processing and this research is supported by this fellowship.

This research was also supported by Deutsche Forschungsgemeinschaft: grant SCHU 2246/4-2.

We would like to thank Gabor Angeli for his help with the Mintz++ and MIMLRE models.

References

Gabor Angeli, Sonal Gupta, Melvin Jose, Christopher D. Manning, Christopher Re, Julie Tibshirani, Jean Y. Wu, Sen Wu, and Ce Zhang. 2014a. Stanfords 2014 slot filling systems. In *TAC*.

Gabor Angeli, Julie Tibshirani, Jean Y. Wu, and Christopher D. Manning. 2014b. Combining distant and partial supervision for relation extraction. In *EMNLP*.

Kurt Bollacker, Colin Evans, Praveen Paritosh, Tim Sturge, and Jamie Taylor. 2008. Freebase: a collaboratively created graph database for structuring human knowledge. In *ACM SIGMOD*.

Ronan Collobert, Jason Weston, Léon Bottou, Michael Karlen, Koray Kavukcuoglu, and Pavel Kuksa. 2011. Natural language processing (almost) from scratch. *JMLR*.

Cícero Nogueira Dos Santos, Bing Xiang, and Bowen Zhou. 2015. Classifying relations by ranking with convolutional neural networks. In *ACL*.

Rong-En Fan, Kai-Wei Chang, Cho-Jui Hsieh, Xiang-Rui Wang, and Chih-Jen Lin. 2008. LIBLINEAR: A library for large linear classification. *JMLR*.

George Foster and Roland Kuhn. 2007. Mixture-model adaptation for SMT. In *Workshop on SMT*.

Xavier Glorot, Antoine Bordes, and Yoshua Bengio. 2011. Domain adaptation for large-scale sentiment classification: A deep learning approach. In *ICML*.

E. Gonzàlez, H. Rodríguez, J. Turmo, P. R. Comas, A. Naderi, A. Ageno, E. Sapena, M. Vila, and M. A. Martí. 2012. The TALP participation at TAC-KBP 2012. In *TAC*.

Iris Hendrickx, Su Nam Kim, Zornitsa Kozareva, Preslav Nakov, Diarmuid Ó Séaghdha, Sebastian Padó, Marco Pennacchiotti, Lorenza Romano, and Stan Szpakowicz. 2010. Semeval-2010 task 8: Multi-way classification of semantic relations between pairs of nominals. In *SemEval*. ACL.

Nal Kalchbrenner, Edward Grefenstette, and Phil Blunsom. 2014. A convolutional neural network for modelling sentences. In *ACL*.

Yan Li, Sijia Chen, Zhihua Zhou, Jie Yin, Hao Luo, Liyin Hong, Weiran Xu, Guang Chen, and Guo Jun. 2012. PRIS at TAC 2012 KBP track. In *TAC*.

Fang Liu and Jun Zhao. 2012. Sweat2012: Pattern based English slot filling system for knowledge base population at TAC 2012. In *TAC*.

Christopher Malon, Bing Bai, and Kazi Saidul Hasan. 2012. Slot-filling by substring extraction at TAC KBP 2012 (team papelo). In *TAC*.

Christopher D. Manning, Mihai Surdeanu, John Bauer, Jenny Finkel, Steven J. Bethard, and David McClosky. 2014. The Stanford CoreNLP natural language processing toolkit. In *ACL: System Demonstrations*.

Tomas Mikolov, Kai Chen, Greg Corrado, and Jeffrey Dean. 2013. Efficient estimation of word representations in vector space. In *Workshop at ICLR*.

Bonan Min, Xiang Li, Ralph Grishman, and Ang Sun. 2012. New york university 2012 system for KBP slot filling. In *TAC*.

Mike Mintz, Steven Bills, Rion Snow, and Dan Jurafsky. 2009. Distant supervision for relation extraction without labeled data. In *ACL-IJCNLP*.

Slav Petrov and Ryan McDonald. 2012. Overview of the 2012 shared task on parsing the web. In *SANCL*.

Glen Pink, Joel Nothman, and James R Curran. 2014. Analysing recall loss in named entity slot filling. In *EMNLP*.

Xin Ying Qiu, Xiaoting Li, Weijian Mo, Manli Zheng, and Zhuhe Zheng. 2012. GDUFS at slot filling TAC-KBP 2012. In *TAC*.

Sebastian Riedel, Limin Yao, Andrew McCallum, and Benjamin M Marlin. 2013. Relation extraction with matrix factorization and universal schemas. In *HLT-NAACL*.

Benjamin Roth, Tassilo Barth, Michael Wiegand, Mittul Singh, and Dietrich Klakow. 2013. Effective slot filling based on shallow distant supervision methods. In *TAC*.

Benjamin Roth, Emma Strubell, John Sullivan, Lakshmi Vikraman, Kate Silverstein, and Andrew McCallum. 2014. Universal schema for slot-filling, cold-start KBP and event argument extraction: UMAss IESL at TAC KBP 2014. In *TAC*.

Mihai Surdeanu and Heng Ji. 2014. Overview of the English slot filling track at the TAC 2014 knowledge base population evaluation. In *TAC*.

Mihai Surdeanu, Julie Tibshirani, Ramesh Nallapati, and Christopher D Manning. 2012. Multi-instance multi-label learning for relation extraction. In *EMNLP-CoNLL*.

Mihai Surdeanu. 2013. Overview of the TAC 2013 knowledge base population evaluation: English slot filling and temporal slot filling. In *TAC*.

TAC. 2014. Task description for English slot filling at TAC KBP 2014. `http://surdeanu. info/kbp2014/KBP2014_TaskDefinition_ EnglishSlotFilling_1.1.pdf`.

Vasudeva Varma, Bhaskar Ghosh, Mohan Soundararajan, Deepti Aggarwal, and Priya Radhakrishnan. 2012. IIIT Hyderabad at TAC 2012. In *TAC*.

Vidhoon Viswanathan, Nazneen Fatema Rajani, Yinon Bentor, and Raymond Mooney. 2015. Stacked ensembles of information extractors for knowledge-base population. In *ACL*.

Ngoc Thang Vu, Heike Adel, Pankaj Gupta, and Hinrich Schütze. 2016. Combining recurrent and convolutional neural networks for relation classification. In *HLT-NAACL*.

Daojian Zeng, Kang Liu, Siwei Lai, Guangyou Zhou, and Jun Zhao. 2014. Relation classification via convolutional deep neural network. In *COLING*.

Daojian Zeng, Kang Liu, Yubo Chen, and Jun Zhao. 2015. Distant supervision for relation extraction via piecewise convolutional neural networks. In *EMNLP*.

A Corpus and Cloze Evaluation for Deeper Understanding of Commonsense Stories

Nasrin Mostafazadeh[1], Nathanael Chambers[2], Xiaodong He[3], Devi Parikh[4],
Dhruv Batra[4], Lucy Vanderwende[3], Pushmeet Kohli[3], James Allen[1,5]

1 University of Rochester, 2 United States Naval Academy, 3 Microsoft Research, 4 Virginia Tech,

5 The Institute for Human & Machine Cognition

`{nasrinm,james}@cs.rochester.edu, nchamber@usna.edu,`

`{parikh,dbatra}@vt.edu, {xiaohe,lucyv,pkohli}@microsoft.com`

Abstract

Representation and learning of commonsense knowledge is one of the foundational problems in the quest to enable deep language understanding. This issue is particularly challenging for understanding casual and correlational relationships between events. While this topic has received a lot of interest in the NLP community, research has been hindered by the lack of a proper evaluation framework. This paper attempts to address this problem with a new framework for evaluating story understanding and script learning: the 'Story Cloze Test'. This test requires a system to choose the correct ending to a four-sentence story. We created a new corpus of 50k five-sentence commonsense stories, ROCStories, to enable this evaluation. This corpus is unique in two ways: (1) it captures a rich set of causal and temporal commonsense relations between daily events, and (2) it is a high quality collection of everyday life stories that can also be used for story generation. Experimental evaluation shows that a host of baselines and state-of-the-art models based on shallow language understanding struggle to achieve a high score on the Story Cloze Test. We discuss these implications for script and story learning, and offer suggestions for deeper language understanding.

1 Introduction

Story understanding is an extremely challenging task in natural language understanding with a long-running history in AI (Charniak, 1972; Winograd, 1972; Turner, 1994; Schubert and Hwang, 2000).

Recently, there has been a renewed interest in story and narrative understanding based on progress made in core NLP tasks. This ranges from generic story telling models to building systems which can compose meaningful stories in collaboration with humans (Swanson and Gordon, 2008). Perhaps the biggest challenge of story understanding (and story generation) is having commonsense knowledge for the interpretation of narrative events. The question is how to provide commonsense knowledge regarding daily events to machines.

A large body of work in story understanding has focused on learning scripts (Schank and Abelson, 1977). Scripts represent structured knowledge about stereotypical event sequences together with their participants. It is evident that various NLP applications (text summarization, co-reference resolution, question answering, etc.) can hugely benefit from the rich inferential capabilities that structured knowledge about events can provide. Given that developing hand-built scripts is extremely time-consuming, there is a serious need for automatically induced scripts. Most relevant to this issue is work on unsupervised learning of 'narrative chains' (Chambers and Jurafsky, 2008) and event schemas (Chambers and Jurafsky, 2009; Balasubramanian et al., 2013; Cheung et al., 2013; Nguyen et al., 2015). The first requirement of any learner is to decide on a corpus to drive the learning process. We are foremost interested in a resource that is full of temporal and causal relations between events because causality is a central component of coherency. Personal stories from daily weblogs are good sources of commonsense causal information (Gordon and Swanson, 2009; Manshadi et al., 2008), but teasing out useful information from noisy blog entries is a problem of its own. Consider the following snippet from ICWSM 2011 Spinn3r Dataset of Weblog entries (Burton et al., 2009):

> "I had an interesting day in the studio today. It was so interesting that I took pictures along the way to describe it to you. Sometimes I like to read an autobiography/biography to discover how someone got from there to here.....how they started, how they traveled in mind and spirit, what made them who they are now. Well, today, my work was a little like that."

This text is full of discourse complexities. A host of challenging language understanding tasks are required to get at the commonsense knowledge embedded within such text snippets. What is needed is a simplified version of these narratives. This paper introduces a new corpus of such short commonsense stories. With careful prompt design and multiple phases of quality control, we collected 50k high quality five-sentence stories that are full of stereotypical causal and temporal relations between events. The corpus not only serves as a resource for learning commonsense narrative schemas, but is also suitable for training story generation models. We describe this corpus in detail in Section 3.

This new corpus also addresses a problem facing script learning over the past few years. Despite the attention scripts have received, progress has been inhibited by the lack of a systematic evaluation framework. A commonly used evaluation is the 'Narrative Cloze Test' (Chambers and Jurafsky, 2008) in which a system predicts a held-out event (a verb and its arguments) given a set of observed events. For example, the following is one such test with a missing event: {X threw, pulled X, told X, ???, X completed}[1]. As is often the case, several works now optimize to this specific test, achieving higher scores with shallow techniques. This is problematic because the models often are not learning commonsense knowledge, but rather how to beat the shallow test.

This paper thus introduces a new evaluation framework called the Story Cloze Test. Instead of predicting an event, the system is tasked with choosing an entire sentence to complete the given story.

---

[1]Narrative cloze tests were not meant to be human solvable.

We collected 3,742 doubly verified Story Cloze Test cases. The test is described in detail in Section 4.

Finally, this paper proposes several models, including the most recent state-of-the-art approaches for the narrative cloze test, for tackling the Story Cloze Test. The results strongly suggest that achieving better than random or constant-choose performance requires richer semantic representation of events together with deeper levels of modeling the semantic space of stories. We believe that switching to the Story Cloze Test as the empirical evaluation framework for story understanding and script learning can help direct the field to a new direction of deeper language understanding.

2 Related Work

Several lines of research have recently focused on learning narrative/event representations. Chambers and Jurafsky first proposed narrative chains (Chambers and Jurafsky, 2008) as a partially ordered set of narrative events that share a common actor called the 'protagonist'. A narrative event is a tuple of an event (a verb) and its participants represented as typed dependencies. Several expansions have since been proposed, including narrative schemas (Chambers and Jurafsky, 2009), script sequences (Regneri et al., 2010), and relgrams (Balasubramanian et al., 2013). Formal probabilistic models have also been proposed to learn event schemas and frames (Cheung et al., 2013; Bamman et al., 2013; Chambers, 2013; Nguyen et al., 2015). These are trained on smaller corpora and focus less on large-scale learning. A major shortcoming so far is that these models are mainly trained on news articles. Little knowledge about everyday life events are learned.

Several groups have directly addressed script learning by focusing exclusively on the narrative cloze test. Jans et al. (Jans et al., 2012) redefined the test to be a text ordered sequence of events, whereas the original did not rely on text order (Chambers and Jurafsky, 2008). Since then, others have shown language-modeling techniques perform well (Pichotta and Mooney, 2014a; Rudinger et al., 2015). This paper shows that these approaches struggle on the richer Story Cloze evaluation.

There has also been renewed attention toward natural language comprehension and commonsense reasoning (Levesque, 2011; Roemmele et al., 2011; Bowman et al., 2015). There are a few recent frameworks for evaluating language comprehension (Hermann et al., 2015; Weston et al., 2015), including the MCTest (Richardson et al., 2013) as a notable one. Their framework also involves story comprehension, however, their stories are mostly fictional, on average 212 words, and geared toward children in grades 1-4. Some progress has been made in story understanding by limiting the task to the specific domains and question types. This includes research on understanding newswire involving terrorism scripts (Mueller, 2002), stories about people in a restaurant where a reasonable number of questions about time and space can be answered (Mueller, 2007), and generating stories from fairy tales (McIntyre and Lapata, 2009). Finally, there is a rich body of work on story plot generation and creative or artistic story telling (Méndez et al., 2014; Riedl and León, 2008). This paper is unique to these in its corpus of short, simple stories with a wide variety of commonsense events. We show these to be useful for learning, but also for enabling a rich evaluation framework for narrative understanding.

3   A Corpus of Short Commonsense Stories

We aimed to build a corpus with two goals in mind:

1. The corpus contains a *variety* of commonsense causal and temporal relations between everyday events. This enables learning narrative structure across a range of events, as opposed to a single domain or genre.

2. The corpus is a high quality collection of non-fictional daily short life stories, which can be used for training rich coherent story-telling models.

In order to narrow down our focus, we carefully define a narrative or story as follows: 'A narrative or story is anything which is told in the form of a causally (logically) linked set of events involving some shared characters'. The classic definition of a story requires having a plot, (e.g., a character following a goal and facing obstacles), however, here we are not concerned with how entertaining or dramatic the stories are. Instead, we are concerned with the essence of actually being a logi-

cally meaningful story. We follow the notion of 'storiness' (Forster, 1927; Bailey, 1999), which is described as "the expectations and questions that a reader may have as the story develops", where expectations are 'common-sense logical inferences' made by the imagined reader of the story.

We propose to satisfy our two goals by asking hundreds of workers on Amazon Mechanical Turk (AMT) to write novel five-sentence stories. The five-sentence length gives enough context to the story without allowing room for sidetracks about less important or irrelevant information in the story. In this Section we describe the details about how we collected this corpus, and provide statistical analysis.

3.1   Data Collection Methodology

Crowdsourcing this corpus makes the data collection scalable and adds to the diversity of stories. We tested numerous pilots with varying prompts and instructions. We manually checked the submitted stories in each pilot and counted the number of submissions which did not have our desired level of coherency or were specifically fictional or offensive. Three people participated in this task and they iterated over the ratings until everyone agreed with the next pilot's prompt design. We achieved the best results when we let the workers write about anything they have in mind, as opposed to mandating a pre-specified topic. The final crowdsourcing prompt can be found in supplementary material.

The key property that we had enforced in our final prompt was the following: the story should read like a coherent story, with a specific *beginning* and *ending*, where *something happens* in between. This constraint resulted in many causal and temporal links between events. Table 1 shows the examples we provided to the workers for instructing them about the constraints. We set a limit of 70 characters to the length of each sentence. This prevented multi-part sentences that include unnecessary details. The workers were also asked to provide a title that best describes their story. Last but not least, we instructed the workers not to use quotations in their sentences and avoid using slang or informal language.

Collecting high quality stories with these constraints gives us a rich collection of commonsense stories which are full of stereotypical inter-event re-

✗	The little puppy thought he was a great basketball player. He challenged the kitten to a friendly game. The kitten agreed. Kitten started to practice really hard. Eventually the kitten beat the puppy by 40 points.
✓	Bill thought he was a great basketball player. He challenged Sam to a friendly game. Sam agreed. Sam started to practice really hard. Eventually Sam beat Bill by 40 points.
✗	I am happy with my life. I have been kind. I have been successful. I work out. Why not be happy when you can?
✗	The city is full of people and offers a lot of things to do. One of my favorite things is going to the outdoor concerts. I also like visiting the different restaurants and museums. There is always something exciting to do in the city.
✓	The Smith family went to the family beach house every summer. They loved the beach house a lot. Unfortunately there was a bad hurricane once. Their beach house was washed away. Now they lament the loss of their beach house every summer.
✗	Miley was in middle school. ~~She lived in an apartment.~~ Once Miley made a mistake and cheated in one of her exams. She tried to hide the truth from her parents. After her parents found out, they grounded her for a month.
✓	Miley was in middle school. She usually got good grades in school . Once Miley made a mistake and cheated in one of her exams. She tried to hide the truth from her parents. After her parents found out, they grounded her for a month.

Table 1: Examples of good and bad stories provided to the crowd-sourced workers. Each row emphasizes one of the three properties that each story should satisfy: (1) being realistic, (2) having clear beginning and ending, and (3) not stating anything irrelevant to the story.

X *challenge* Y – Y *agree* play —— Y *practice* —— Y *beat* X

Figure 1: An example narrative chain with characters X and Y.

lations. For example, from the good story in first row of Table 1, one can extract the narrative chain represented in Figure 1. Developing a better semantic representation for narrative chains which can capture rich inter-event relations in these stories is a topic of future work.

Quality Control: One issue with crowdsourcing is how to instruct non-expert workers. This task is a type of creative writing, and is trickier than classification and tagging tasks. In order to ensure we get qualified workers, we designed a qualification test on AMT in which the workers had to judge whether or not a given story (total five stories) is an acceptable one. We used five carefully selected stories to be a part of the qualification test. This not only eliminates any potential spammers on AMT, but also provides us with a pool of creative story writers. Furthermore, we qualitatively browsed through the submissions and gave the workers detailed feedback before approving their submissions. We often bonused our top workers, encouraging them to write new stories on a daily basis.

Statistics: Figure 2 shows the distribution of number of tokens of different sentence positions. The first sentence tends to be shorter, as it usually introduces characters or sets the scene, and the fifth

sentence is longer, providing more detailed conclusions to the story. Table 2 summarizes the statistics of our crowdsourcing effort. Figure 3 shows the distribution of the most frequent 50 events in the corpus. Here we count event as any hyponym of 'event' or 'process' in WordNet (Miller., 1995). The top two events, 'go' and 'get', each comprise less than 2% of all the events, which illustrates the rich diversity of the corpus.

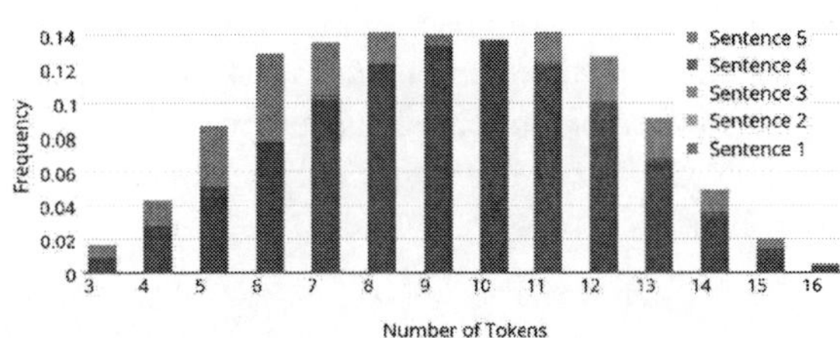

Figure 2: Number of tokens in each sentence position.

# submitted stories	49,895
# approved stories	**49,255**
# workers participated	932
Average # stories by one worker	52.84
Max # stories written by one worker	3,057
Average work time among workers (minute)	4.80
Median work time among workers (minute)	2.16
Average payment per story (cents)	26

Table 2: Crowdsourcing worker statistics.

Figure 4 visualizes the n-gram distribution of our story titles, where each radial path indicates an n-

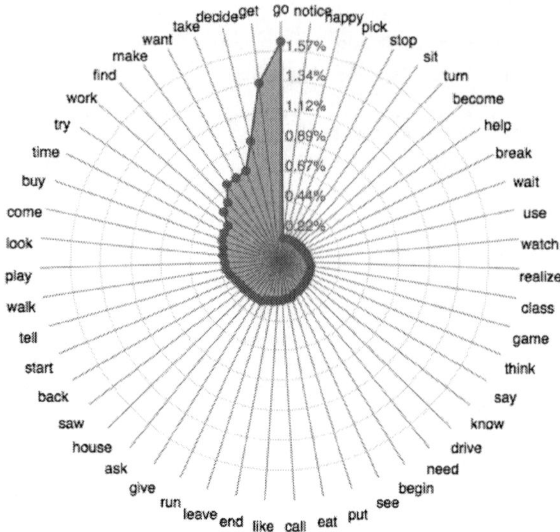

Figure 3: Distribution of top 50 events in our corpus.

gram sequence. For this analysis we set n=5, where the mean number of tokens in titles is 9.8 and median is 10. The 'end' token distinguishes the actual ending of a title from five-gram cut-off. This figure demonstrates the range of topics that our workers have written about. The full circle reflects on 100% of the title n-grams and the n-gram paths in the faded 3/4 of the circle comprise less than 0.1% of the n-grams. This further demonstrates that the range of topics covered by our corpus is quite diverse. A full dynamic visualization of these n-grams can be found here: http://goo.gl/Qhg60B.

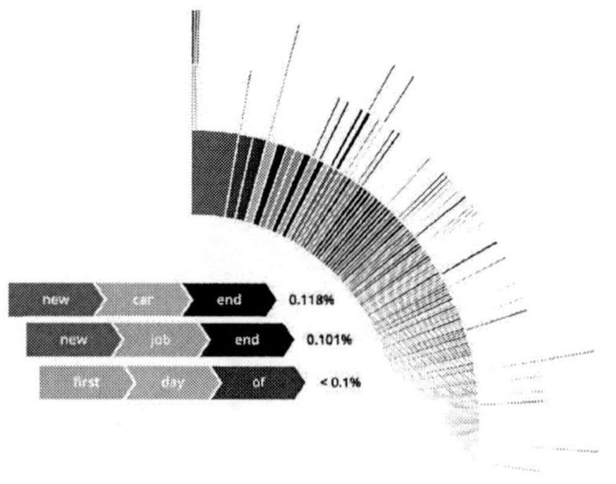

Figure 4: N-gram distribution of story titles.

3.2 Corpus Release

The corpus is publicly available to the community and can be accessed through http://cs.rochester.edu/nlp/rocstories, which will be grown even further over the coming years. Given the quality control pipeline and the creativity required from workers, data collection goes slowly.

We are also making available semantic parses of these stories. Since these stories are not newswire, off-the-shelf syntactic and shallow semantic parsers for event extraction often fail on the language. To address this issue, we customized search parameters and added a few lexical entries[2] to TRIPS broad-coverage semantic parser[3], optimizing its performance on our corpus. TRIPS parser (Allen et al., 2008) produces state-of-the-art logical forms for input stories, providing sense disambiguated and ontology-typed rich deep structures which enables event extraction together with semantic roles and coreference chains throughout the five sentences.

3.3 Temporal Analysis

Being able to temporally order events in the stories is a pre-requisite for complete narrative understanding. Temporal analysis of the events in our short commonsensical stories is an important topic of further research on its own. In this Section, we summarize two of our analyses regarding the nature of temporal ordering of events in our corpus.

Shuffling Experiment: An open question in any text genre is how text order is related to temporal order. Do the sentences follow the real-world temporal order of events? This experiment shuffles the stories and asks AMT workers to arrange them back to a coherent story. This can shed light on the correlation between the original position of the sentences and the position when another human rearranges them in a commonsensically meaningful way. We set up this experiment as follows: we sampled two sets of 50 stories from our corpus: *Good-Stories*$_{50}$ and *Random-Stories*$_{50}$. *Good-Stories*$_{50}$[4] is sampled from a set of stories written by top workers

---

[2]For example, new informal verbs such as 'vape' or 'vlog' have been added to the lexicon of this semantic parser.

[3]http://trips.ihmc.us/parser/cgi/step

[4]This set can be found here: https://goo.gl/VTnJ9s

	Good-Stories$_{50}$	Random-Stories$_{50}$
% perfectly ordered, taking majority ordering for each of the 50 stories	100	86
% all sentences perfectly ordered, out of 250 orderings	95.2	82.4
% ≤ 1 sentences misplaced, rest flow correctly, out of 250 orderings	98.0	96.0
% correct placements of each position, 1 to 5	**98.8**, 97.6, 96, 96, **98.8**	**95.6**, 86, 86.8, 91.2, **96.8**

Table 3: Results from the human temporal shuffling experiment.

who have shown shown consistent quality throughout their submissions. *Random-Stories*$_{50}$[5] is a random sampling from all the stories in the corpus. Then we randomly shuffled the sentences in each story and asked five crowd workers on AMT to rearrange the sentences.

Table 3 summarizes the results of this experiment. The first row shows the result of ordering if we take the absolute majority ordering of the five crowd workers as the final ordering. The second row shows the result of ordering if we consider each of the 250 (50 stories x 5 workers ordering each one) ordering cases independently. As shown, the good stories are perfectly ordered with very high accuracy. It is important to note that this specific set rarely had any linguistic adverbials such as 'first', 'then', etc. to help human infer the ordering, so the main factors at play are the following: (1) the commonsensical temporal and causal relation between events (narrative schemas), e.g., human knows that first someone loses a phone then starts searching; (2) the natural way of narrating a story which starts with introducing the characters and concludes the story at the end. The role of the latter factor is quantified in the misplacement rate of each position reported in Table 3, where the first and last sentences are more often correctly placed than others. The high precision of ordering in sentences 2 up to 4 further verifies the richness of our corpus in terms of logical relation between events.

TimeML Annotation: TimeML-driven analysis of these stories can give us finer-grained insight about temporal aspect of the events in this corpus. We performed a simplified TimeML-driven (Pustejovsky et al., 2003) expert annotation of a sample of 20 stories[6]. Among all the temporal links (TLINK) annotated, 62% were 'before' and 10% were 'simultaneous'. We were interested to know if the actual text order mirrors real-world order of events. We found that sentence order matches TimeML order 55% of the time. A more comprehensive study of temporal and causal aspects of these stories requires defining a specific semantic annotation framework which covers not only temporal but also causal relations between commonsense events. This is captured in a recent work which introduces a Causal and Temporal Relation Scheme (CaTeRS) for semantic annotation of event structures (Mostafazadeh et al., 2016).

4 A New Evaluation Framework

As described earlier in the introduction, the common evaluation framework for script learning is the 'Narrative Cloze Test' (Chambers and Jurafsky, 2008), where a system generates a ranked list of guesses for a missing event, given some observed events. The original goal of this test was to provide a comparative measure to evaluate narrative knowledge. However, gradually, the community started optimizing towards the performance on the test itself, achieving higher scores without demonstrating narrative knowledge learning. For instance, generating the ranked list according to the event's corpus frequency (e.g., always predicting 'X said') was shown to be an extremely strong baseline (Pichotta and Mooney, 2014b). Originally, narrative cloze test chains were extracted by hand and verified as gold chains. However, the cloze test chains used in all of the most recent works are not human verified as gold.

It is evident that there is a need for a more systematic automatic evaluation framework which is more in line with the original deeper script/story understanding goals. It is important to note that reordering of temporally shuffled stories (Section 3.3) can serve as a framework to evaluate a system's story understanding. However, reordering can be achieved to a degree by using various surface features such as adverbials, so this cannot be a foolproof story understanding evaluation framework. Our ROCStories corpus enables a brand new framework for evaluating story understanding, called the '*Story Cloze*

---

[5]This set can be found here: `https://goo.gl/pgm2KR`
[6]The annotation is available: `http://goo.gl/7qdNsb`

Test'.

4.1 Story Cloze Test

The cloze task (Taylor, 1953) is used to evaluate a human (or a system) for language understanding by deleting a random word from a sentence and having a human fill in the blank. We introduce 'Story Cloze Test', in which a system is given a four-sentence 'context' and two alternative endings to the story, called 'right ending' and 'wrong ending'. Hence, in this test the fifth sentence is blank. Then the system's task is to choose the right ending. The 'right ending' can be viewed as 'entailing' hypothesis in a classic Recognizing Textual Entailment (RTE) framework (Giampiccolo et al., 2007), and 'wrong' ending can be seen as the 'contradicting' hypothesis. Table 4 shows three example Story Cloze Test cases.

Story Cloze Test will serve as a generic story understanding evaluation framework, also applicable to evaluation of story generation models (for instance by computing the log-likelihoods assigned to the two ending alternatives by the story generation model), which does not necessarily imply requirement for explicit narrative knowledge learning. However, it is safe to say that any model that performs well on Story Cloze Test is demonstrating some level of deeper story understanding.

4.2 Data Collection Methodology

We randomly sampled 13,500 stories from ROCStories Corpus and presented only the first four sentences of each to AMT workers. For each story, a worker was asked to write a 'right ending' and a 'wrong ending'. The workers were prompted to satisfy two conditions: (1) the sentence should follow up the story by sharing at least one of the characters of the story, and (2) the sentence should be entirely realistic and sensible when read in isolation. These conditions make sure that the Story Cloze Test cases are not trivial. More details on this setup is described in the supplementary material.

Quality Control: The accuracy of the Story Cloze Test can play a crucial role in directing the research community in the right trajectory. We implemented the following two-step quality control:

1. Qualification Test: We designed a qualification

test for this task, where the workers had to choose whether or not a given 'right ending' and 'wrong ending' satisfy our constraints. At this stage we collected 13,500 cloze test cases.

2. Human Verification: In order to further validate the cloze test cases, we compiled the 13,500 Story Cloze Test cases into $2 \times 13,500 = 27,000$ full five-sentence stories. Then for each story we asked three crowd workers to verify whether or not the given sequence of five sentences makes sense as a meaningful and coherent story, rating within $\{-1, 0, 1\}$. Then we filtered cloze test cases which had 'right ending' with all ratings 1 and 'wrong ending' with all ratings 0. This process ensures that there are no boundary cases of 'right ending' and 'wrong ending'. This resulted in final 3,742 test cases, which was randomly divided into validation and test Story Cloze Test sets. We also made sure to remove the original stories used in the validation and test set from our ROCStories Corpus.

Statistics: Table 5 summarizes the statistics of our crowdsourcing effort. The Story Cloze Test sets can also be accessed through our website.

5 Story Cloze Test Models

In this Section we demonstrate that Story Cloze Test cannot be easily tackled by using shallow techniques, without actually understanding the underlying narrative. Following other natural language inference frameworks such as RTE, we evaluate system performance according to basic accuracy measure, which is defined as $\frac{\#correct}{\#test\ cases}$. We present the following baselines and models for tackling Story Cloze Test. All of the models are tested on the validation and test Story Cloze sets, where only the validation set could be used for any tuning purposes.

1. Frequency: Ideally, the Story Cloze Test cases should not be answerable without the context. For example, if for some context the two alternatives are 'He was mad after he won'[7] and 'He was cheerful after he won', the first alternative is simply less probable in real world than the other one. This baseline chooses the alternative with higher

---

[7] Given our prompt that the 'wrong ending' sentences should make sense in isolation, such cases should be rare in our dataset.

Context	Right Ending	Wrong Ending
Tom and Sheryl have been together for two years. One day, they went to a carnival together. He won her several stuffed bears, and bought her funnel cakes. When they reached the Ferris wheel, he got down on one knee.	Tom asked Sheryl to marry him.	He wiped mud off of his boot.
Karen was assigned a roommate her first year of college. Her roommate asked her to go to a nearby city for a concert. Karen agreed happily. The show was absolutely exhilarating.	Karen became good friends with her roommate.	Karen hated her roommate.
Jim got his first credit card in college. He didn't have a job so he bought everything on his card. After he graduated he amounted a $10,000 debt. Jim realized that he was foolish to spend so much money.	Jim decided to devise a plan for repayment.	Jim decided to open another credit card.

Table 4: Three example Story Cloze Test cases, completed by our crowd workers.

# cases collected	13,500
# workers participated	282
Average # cases written by one worker	47.8
Max # cases written by one worker	1461
Average payment per test case (cents)	10
Size of the final set (verified by human)	**3,744**

Table 5: Statistics for crowd-sourcing Story Cloze Test instances.

search engine[8] hits of the main event (verb) together with its semantic roles (e.g., 'I*poison*flowers' vs 'I*nourish*flowers'). We extract the main verb and its corresponding roles using TRIPS semantic parser.

2. N-gram Overlap: Simply chooses the alternative which shares more n-grams with the context. We compute Smoothed-BLEU (Lin and Och, 2004) score for measuring up to four-gram overlap of an alternative and the context.

3. GenSim: Average Word2Vec: Choose the hypothesis with closer average word2vec (Mikolov et al., 2013) embedding to the average word2vec embedding of the context. This is basically an enhanced word overlap baseline, which accounts for semantic similarity.

4. Sentiment-Full: Choose the hypothesis that matches the average sentiment of the context. We use the state-of-the-art sentiment analysis model (Manning et al., 2014) which assigns a numerical value from 1 to 5 to a sentence.

5. Sentiment-Last: Choose the hypothesis that matches the sentiment of the last context sentence.

[8] https://developers.google.com/custom-search/

6. Skip-thoughts Model: This model uses Skip-thoughts' Sentence2Vec embedding (Kiros et al., 2015) which models the semantic space of novels. This model is trained on the 'BookCorpus' (Zhu et al., 2015) (containing 16 different genres) of over 11,000 books. We use the skip-thoughts embedding of the alternatives and contexts for making decision the same way as with GenSim model.

7. Narrative Chains-AP: Implements the standard approach to learning chains of narrative events based on Chambers and Jurafsky (2008). An event is represented as a verb and a typed dependency (e.g., the *subject* of *runs*). We computed the PMI between all event pairs in the Associate Press (AP) portion of the English Gigaword Corpus that occur at least 2 times. We run coreference over the given story, and choose the hypothesis whose coreferring entity has the highest average PMI score with the entity's chain in the story. If no entity corefers in both hypotheses, it randomly chooses one of the hypotheses.

8. Narrative Chains-Stories: The same model as above, but trained on ROCStories.

9. Deep Structured Semantic Model (DSSM): This model (Huang et al., 2013) is trained to project the four-sentences context and the fifth sentence into the same vector space. It consists of two separate deep neural networks for learning jointly the embedding of the four-sentences context and the fifth sentence, respectively. As suggested in Huang et al. (2013), the input of the DSSM is based on context-dependent characters, e.g., the distribution count of letter-trigrams in the context and in the fifth sentence, respectively. The hyper parameters of the DSSM is determined on the validation set, while the

	Constant-choose-first	Frequency	N-gram-overlap	GenSim	Sentiment-Full	Sentiment-Last	Skip-thoughts	Narrative-Chains-AP	Narrative-Chains-Stories	DSSM	Human
Validation Set	0.514	0.506	0.477	0.545	0.489	0.514	0.536	0.472	0.510	0.604	1.0
Test Set	0.513	0.520	0.494	0.539	0.492	0.522	0.552	0.478	0.494	**0.585**	1.0

Table 6: The accuracy of various models on The Story Cloze validation and test sets.

model's parameters are trained on the ROCStories corpus. In our experiment, each of the two neural networks in the DSSM has two layers: the dimension of the hidden layer is 1000, and the dimension of the embedding vector is 300. At runtime, this model picks the candidate with the largest cosine similarity between its vector representation and the context's vector representation.

The results of evaluating these models on the Story Cloze validation and test sets are shown in Table 6. The constant-choose-first (51%) and human performance (100%) is also provided for comparison. Note that these sets were doubly verified by human, hence it does not have any boundary cases, resulting in 100% human performance. The DSSM model achieves the highest accuracy, but only 7.2 points higher than constant-choose-first. Error analysis on the narrative chains model shows why this and other event-based language models are not sufficient for the task: often, the final sentences of our stories contain complex events beyond the main verb, such as 'Bill was highly unprepared' or 'He had to go to a homeless shelter'. Event language models only look at the verb and syntactic relation like 'was-object' and 'go-to'. In that sense, going to a homeless shelter is the same as going to the beach. This suggests the requirement of having richer semantic representation for events in narratives. Our proposed Story Cloze Test offers a new challenge to the community.

6 Discussion

There are three core contributions in this paper: (1) a new corpus of commonsense stories, called ROC-Stories, (2) a new evaluation framework to evaluate script/story learners, called Story Cloze Test, and (3) a host of first approaches to tackle this new test framework. ROCStories Corpus is the first crowd-sourced corpus of its kind for the community. We have released about 50k stories, as well as validation and test sets for Story Cloze Test. This dataset will eventually grow to 100k stories, which will be released through our website. In order to continue making meaningful progress on this task, although it is possible to keep increasing the size of the training data, we expect the community to develop models that will learn to generalize to unseen commonsense concepts and situations.

The Story Cloze Test proved to be a challenge to all of the models we tested. We believe it will serve as an effective evaluation for both story understanding and script knowledge learners. We encourage the community to benchmark their progress by reporting their results on Story Cloze test set. Compared to the previous Narrative Cloze Test, we found that one of the early models for that task actually performs worse than random guessing. We can conclude that Narrative Cloze test spurred interest in script learning, however, it ultimately does not evaluate deeper knowledge and language understanding.

Acknowledgments

We would like to thank the amazing crowd workers whose endless hours of daily story writing made this research possible. We thank William de Beaumont and Choh Man Teng for their work on TRIPS parser. We thank Alyson Grealish for her great help in the quality control of our corpus. This work was supported in part by Grant W911NF-15-1-0542 with the US Defense Advanced Research Projects Agency (DARPA), the Army Research Office (ARO) and the Office of Naval Research (ONR). Our data collection effort was sponsored by Nuance Foundation.

References

James F. Allen, Mary Swift, and Will de Beaumont. 2008. Deep semantic analysis of text. In *Proceedings of the 2008 Conference on Semantics in Text Processing*, STEP '08, pages 343–354, Stroudsburg, PA, USA. Association for Computational Linguistics.

Paul Bailey. 1999. Searching for storiness: Story-generation from a reader's perspective. In *AAAI Fall Symposium on Narrative Intelligence*.

Niranjan Balasubramanian, Stephen Soderland, Oren Etzioni Mausam, and Oren Etzioni. 2013. Generating coherent event schemas at scale. In *EMNLP*, pages 1721–1731.

David Bamman, Brendan OConnor, and Noah Smith. 2013. Learning latent personas of film characters. ACL.

Samuel R Bowman, Gabor Angeli, Christopher Potts, and Christopher D Manning. 2015. Learning natural language inference from a large annotated corpus. In *Proceedings of the 2015 Conference on Empirical Methods in Natural Language Processing*, pages 632–642, Stroudsburg, PA. Association for Computational Linguistics.

K. Burton, A. Java, , and I. Soboroff. 2009. The icwsm 2009 spinn3r dataset. In *In Proceedings of the Third Annual Conference on Weblogs and Social Media (ICWSM 2009)*, San Jose, CA.

Nathanael Chambers and Daniel Jurafsky. 2008. Unsupervised learning of narrative event chains. In Kathleen McKeown, Johanna D. Moore, Simone Teufel, James Allan, and Sadaoki Furui, editors, *ACL*, pages 789–797. The Association for Computer Linguistics.

Nathanael Chambers and Dan Jurafsky. 2009. Unsupervised learning of narrative schemas and their participants. In *Proceedings of the Joint Conference of the 47th Annual Meeting of the ACL and the 4th International Joint Conference on Natural Language Processing of the AFNLP: Volume 2 - Volume 2*, ACL '09, pages 602–610, Stroudsburg, PA, USA. Association for Computational Linguistics.

Nathanael Chambers. 2013. Event schema induction with a probabilistic entity-driven model. In *EMNLP*, volume 13, pages 1797–1807.

Eugene Charniak. 1972. Toward a model of children's story comprehension. December.

Jackie Cheung, Hoifung Poon, and Lucy Vanderwende. 2013. Probabilistic frame induction. In *ACL*.

E.M. Forster. 1927. *Aspects of the Novel*. Edward Arnold, London.

Danilo Giampiccolo, Bernardo Magnini, Ido Dagan, and Bill Dolan. 2007. The third pascal recognizing textual entailment challenge. In *Proceedings of the ACL-PASCAL Workshop on Textual Entailment and Paraphrasing*, RTE '07, pages 1–9, Stroudsburg, PA, USA. ACL.

Andrew S. Gordon and Reid Swanson. 2009. Identifying Personal Stories in Millions of Weblog Entries. In *Third International Conference on Weblogs and Social Media, Data Challenge Workshop*, San Jose, CA, May.

Karl Moritz Hermann, Tomas Kocisky, Edward Grefenstette, Lasse Espeholt, Will Kay, Mustafa Suleyman, and Phil Blunsom. 2015. Teaching machines to read and comprehend. In C. Cortes, N. D. Lawrence, D. D. Lee, M. Sugiyama, and R. Garnett, editors, *Advances in Neural Information Processing Systems 28*, pages 1693–1701. Curran Associates, Inc.

Po-Sen Huang, Xiaodong He, Jianfeng Gao, Li Deng, Alex Acero, and Larry Heck. 2013. Learning deep structured semantic models for web search using click-through data. In *Proceedings of the 22Nd ACM International Conference on Information & Knowledge Management*, CIKM '13, pages 2333–2338, New York, NY, USA. ACM.

Bram Jans, Steven Bethard, Ivan Vulić, and Marie Francine Moens. 2012. Skip n-grams and ranking functions for predicting script events. In *Proceedings of the 13th Conference of the European Chapter of the Association for Computational Linguistics*, pages 336–344. Association for Computational Linguistics.

Ryan Kiros, Yukun Zhu, Ruslan Salakhutdinov, Richard S Zemel, Antonio Torralba, Raquel Urtasun, and Sanja Fidler. 2015. Skip-thought vectors. *NIPS*.

Hector J. Levesque. 2011. The winograd schema challenge. In *AAAI Spring Symposium: Logical Formalizations of Commonsense Reasoning*. AAAI.

Chin-Yew Lin and Franz Josef Och. 2004. Automatic evaluation of machine translation quality using longest common subsequence and skip-bigram statistics. In *Proceedings of the 42Nd Annual Meeting on Association for Computational Linguistics*, ACL '04, Stroudsburg, PA, USA. Association for Computational Linguistics.

Christopher D. Manning, Mihai Surdeanu, John Bauer, Jenny Finkel, Steven J. Bethard, and David McClosky. 2014. The Stanford CoreNLP natural language processing toolkit. In *Proceedings of 52nd Annual Meeting of the Association for Computational Linguistics: System Demonstrations*, pages 55–60.

Mehdi Manshadi, Reid Swanson, and Andrew S. Gordon. 2008. Learning a Probabilistic Model of Event Sequences From Internet Weblog Stories. In *21st Conference of the Florida AI Society, Applied Natural Language Processing Track*, Coconut Grove, FL, May.

Neil McIntyre and Mirella Lapata. 2009. Learning to tell tales: A data-driven approach to story generation. In

Proceedings of the Joint Conference of the 47th Annual Meeting of the ACL and the 4th International Joint Conference on Natural Language Processing of the AFNLP, pages 217–225, Singapore.

Gonzalo Méndez, Pablo Gervás, and Carlos León. 2014. A model of character affinity for agent-based story generation. In *9th International Conference on Knowledge, Information and Creativity Support Systems*, Limassol, Cyprus, 11/2014. Springer-Verlag, Springer-Verlag.

Tomas Mikolov, Ilya Sutskever, Kai Chen, Gregory S. Corrado, and Jeffrey Dean. 2013. Distributed representations of words and phrases and their compositionality. In *Advances in Neural Information Processing Systems 26: 27th Annual Conference on Neural Information Processing Systems 2013. Proceedings of a meeting held December 5-8, 2013, Lake Tahoe, Nevada, United States.*, pages 3111–3119.

G. Miller. 1995. Wordnet: A lexical database for english. In *In Communications of the ACM*.

Nasrin Mostafazadeh, Alyson Grealish, Nathanael Chambers, James F. Allen, and Lucy Vanderwende. 2016. Caters: Causal and temporal relation scheme for semantic annotation of event structures. In *Proceedings of the The 4th Workshop on EVENTS: Definition, Detection, Coreference, and Representation*, San Diego, California, June. Association for Computational Linguistics.

Erik T. Mueller. 2002. Understanding script-based stories using commonsense reasoning. *Cognitive Systems Research*, 5:2004.

Erik T. Mueller. 2007. Modeling space and time in narratives about restaurants. *LLC*, 22(1):67–84.

Kiem-Hieu Nguyen, Xavier Tannier, Olivier Ferret, and Romaric Besançon. 2015. Generative event schema induction with entity disambiguation. In *Proceedings of the 53rd annual meeting of the Association for Computational Linguistics (ACL-15)*.

Karl Pichotta and Raymond J Mooney. 2014a. Statistical script learning with multi-argument events. *EACL 2014*, page 220.

Karl Pichotta and Raymond J. Mooney. 2014b. Statistical script learning with multi-argument events. In *Proceedings of the 14th Conference of the European Chapter of the Association for Computational Linguistics (EACL 2014)*, Gothenburg, Sweden, April.

James Pustejovsky, Jos Castao, Robert Ingria, Roser Saur, Robert Gaizauskas, Andrea Setzer, and Graham Katz. 2003. Timeml: Robust specification of event and temporal expressions in text. In *in Fifth International Workshop on Computational Semantics (IWCS-5*.

Michaela Regneri, Alexander Koller, and Manfred Pinkal. 2010. Learning script knowledge with web experiments. In *Proceedings of the 48th Annual Meeting of the Association for Computational Linguistics*, pages 979–988. Association for Computational Linguistics.

Matthew Richardson, Christopher J. C. Burges, and Erin Renshaw. 2013. Mctest: A challenge dataset for the open-domain machine comprehension of text. In *EMNLP*, pages 193–203. ACL.

M. Riedl and Carlos León. 2008. Toward vignette-based story generation for drama management systems. In *Workshop on Integrating Technologies for Interactive Stories - 2nd International Conference on INtelligent TEchnologies for interactive enterTAINment*, 8-10/1.

Melissa Roemmele, Cosmin Adrian Bejan, and Andrew S. Gordon. 2011. Choice of Plausible Alternatives: An Evaluation of Commonsense Causal Reasoning. In *AAAI Spring Symposium on Logical Formalizations of Commonsense Reasoning*, Stanford University, March.

Rachel Rudinger, Pushpendre Rastogi, Francis Ferraro, and Benjamin Van Durme. 2015. Script induction as language modeling. In *Proceedings of the 2015 Conference on Empirical Methods in Natural Language Processing (EMNLP-15)*.

Roger C. Schank and Robert P. Abelson. 1977. *Scripts, Plans, Goals and Understanding: an Inquiry into Human Knowledge Structures*. L. Erlbaum, Hillsdale, NJ.

Lenhart K. Schubert and Chung Hee Hwang. 2000. Episodic logic meets little red riding hood: A comprehensive, natural representation for language understanding. In *Natural Language Processing and Knowledge Representation: Language for Knowledge and Knowledge for Language*. MIT/AAAI Press.

Reid Swanson and Andrew S. Gordon. 2008. Say Anything: A Massively collaborative Open Domain Story Writing Companion. In *First International Conference on Interactive Digital Storytelling*, Erfurt, Germany, November.

Wilson L Taylor. 1953. Cloze procedure: a new tool for measuring readability. *Journalism quarterly*.

Scott R. Turner. 1994. The creative process: A computer model of storytelling. *Hillsdale: Lawrence Erlbaum*.

Jason Weston, Antoine Bordes, Sumit Chopra, and Tomas Mikolov. 2015. Towards ai-complete question answering: A set of prerequisite toy tasks. *CoRR*, abs/1502.05698.

Terry Winograd. 1972. *Understanding Natural Language*. Academic Press, Inc., Orlando, FL, USA.

Yukun Zhu, Ryan Kiros, Richard Zemel, Ruslan Salakhutdinov, Raquel Urtasun, Antonio Torralba, and Sanja Fidler. 2015. Aligning books and movies: Towards story-like visual explanations by watching movies and reading books. In *arXiv preprint arXiv:1506.06724*.

Dynamic Entity Representation with Max-pooling Improves Machine Reading

Sosuke Kobayashi and **Ran Tian** and **Naoaki Okazaki** and **Kentaro Inui**
Tohoku University, Japan
{sosuke.k, tianran, okazaki, inui}@ecei.tohoku.ac.jp

Abstract

We propose a novel neural network model for machine reading, *DER Network*, which explicitly implements a reader building dynamic meaning representations for entities by gathering and accumulating information around the entities as it reads a document. Evaluated on a recent large scale dataset (Hermann et al., 2015), our model exhibits better results than previous research, and we find that max-pooling is suited for modeling the accumulation of information on entities. Further analysis suggests that our model can put together multiple pieces of information encoded in different sentences to answer complicated questions. Our code for the model is available at https://github.com/soskek/der-network

1 Introduction

Machine reading systems (Poon et al., 2010; Richardson et al., 2013) can be tested on their ability to answer queries about contents of documents that they read, thus a central problem is how the information of documents should be organized in the system and retrieved by the queries. Recently, large scale datasets of document-query-answer triples have been constructed from online newspaper articles and their summaries (Hermann et al., 2015), by replacing named entities in the summaries with placeholders to form Cloze (Taylor, 1953) style questions (Figure 1). These datasets have enabled training and testing of complicated neural network models of hypothesized machine readers (Hermann et al., 2015; Hill et al., 2015).

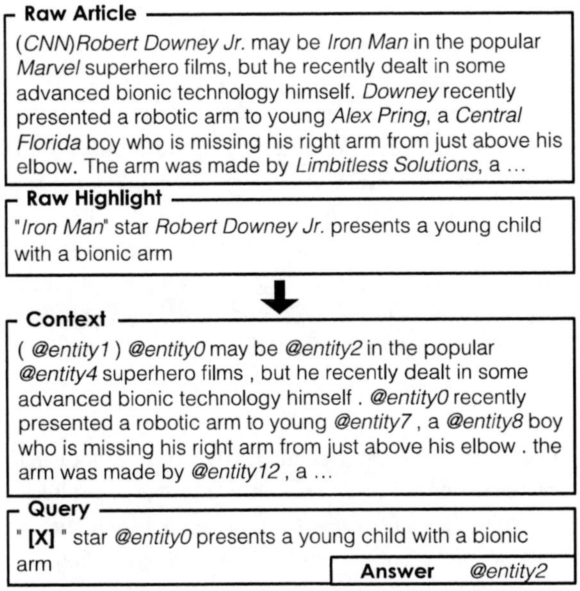

Figure 1: A document-query-answer triple constructed from a news article and its bullet point summary. An entity in the summary (*Robert Downey Jr.*) is replaced by the placeholder [**X**] to form a query. All entities are anonymized to exclude world knowledge and focus on reading comprehension.

In this paper, we hypothesize that a reader without world knowledge can only understand a named entity by dynamically constructing its meaning from the contexts. For example, in Figure 1, a reader reading the sentence *"Robert Downey Jr. may be Iron Man ..."* can only understand *"Robert Downey Jr."* as something that *"may be Iron Man"* at this stage, given that it does not know Robert Downey Jr. *a priori*. Information about this entity can only

Proceedings of NAACL-HLT 2016, pages 850–855,
San Diego, California, June 12-17, 2016. ©2016 Association for Computational Linguistics

be accumulated by its subsequent occurrence, such as *"Downey recently presented a robotic arm ..."*. Thus, named entities basically serve as anchors to link multiple pieces of information encoded in different sentences. This insight has been reflected by the anonymization process in construction of the dataset, in which coreferent entities (e.g. *"Robert Downey Jr."* and *"Downey"*) are replaced by randomly permuted abstract entity markers (e.g. *"@entity0"*), in order to prevent additional world knowledge from being attached to the surface form of the entities (Hermann et al., 2015). We, however, take it as a strong motivation to implement a reader that dynamically builds meaning representations for each entity, by gathering and accumulating information on that entity as it reads a document (Section 2).

Evaluation of our model, *DER Network*, exhibits better results than previous research (Section 3). In particular, we find that max-pooling of entity representations, which is intended to model the accumulation of information on entities, can drastically improve performance. Further analysis suggests that max-pooling can help our model draw multiple pieces of information from different sentences.

2 Model

Following Hermann et al. (2015), our model estimates the conditional probability $p(e|D, q)$, where q is a query and D is a document. A candidate answer for the query is denoted by e, which in this paper is any named entity. Our model can be factorized as:

$$p(e|D, q) \propto \exp(v(e; D, q)^{\mathrm{T}} u(q)) \quad (1)$$

in which $u(q)$ is the learned meaning for the query and $v(e; D, q)$ the dynamically constructed meaning for an entity, depending on the document D and the query q. We note that (1) is in contrast to the factorization used by Hermann et al. (2015):

$$p(a|D, q) \propto \exp(v(a)^{\mathrm{T}} u(D, q)) \quad (2)$$

in which a vector $u(D, q)$ is learned to represent the status of a reader after reading a document and a query, and this vector is used to retrieve an answer by coupling with the answer vector $v(a)$.[1]

Factorization (2) relies on the hypothesis that there exists a fixed vector for each candidate answer representing its meaning. However, as we argued in Section 1, an entity surface does not possess meaning; rather, it serves as an anchor to link pieces of information about it. Therefore, we hypothesize that the meaning representation $v(e; D, q)$ of an entity e should be dynamically constructed from its surrounding contexts, and the meanings are "accumulated" through the reader reading the document D. We explain the construction of $v(e; D, q)$ in Section 2.1, and propose a max-pooling process for modeling information accumulation in Section 2.2.

2.1 Dynamic Entity Representation

For any entity e, we take its context c as any sentence that includes a token of e. Then, we use bidirectional single-layer LSTMs (Hochreiter and Schmidhuber, 1997; Graves et al., 2005) to encode c into vectors. LSTM is a neural cell that outputs a vector $h_{c,t}$ for each token t in the sentence c; taking the word vector $x_{c,t}$ of the token as input, each $h_{c,t}$ is calculated recurrently from its precedent vector $h_{c,t-1}$ or $h_{c,t+1}$, depending on the direction of the encoding. Formally, we write forward and backward LSTMs as:

$$\vec{h}_{c,t} = \overrightarrow{LSTM}(x_{c,t}, \vec{h}_{c,t-1}) \quad \text{(forward)} \quad (3)$$
$$\overleftarrow{h}_{c,t} = \overleftarrow{LSTM}(x_{c,t}, \overleftarrow{h}_{c,t+1}) \quad \text{(backward)} \quad (4)$$

Then, denoting the length of the sentence c as T and the index of the entity e token as τ, we define the dynamic entity representation $d_{e,c}$ as the concatenation of the vectors $[\vec{h}_{c,T}, \overleftarrow{h}_{c,1}, \vec{h}_{c,\tau}, \overleftarrow{h}_{c,\tau}]$ encoded by a feed-forward layer (Figure 2):

$$d_{e,c} = \tanh(W_{hd}[\vec{h}_{c,T}, \overleftarrow{h}_{c,1}, \vec{h}_{c,\tau}, \overleftarrow{h}_{c,\tau}] + b_d)$$

in which W_{hd} and b_d respectively stand for the learned weight matrix and bias vector of that feed-forward layer. Index hd denotes that W_{hd} is a matrix mapping h-vectors to d-vectors. Index d shows that b_d has the same dimension as d-vectors. We use this convention throughout this paper.

Having $d_{e,c}$ as the dynamic representation of an entity e occurring in context c, we define vector

---

[1] Hermann et al. (2015) models $p(a|D, q)$ for every word token a in a document. While the approach could be more general because it has the potential to answer other types of questions given appropriate training data, our approach is arguably suitable for the specific task and natural for testing our hypothesis.

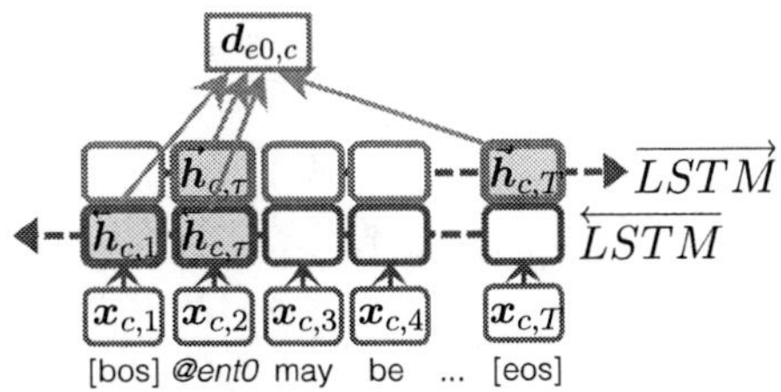

Figure 2: Dynamic entity representation $d_{e,c}$ encodes LSTM outputs, modeling surrounding context.

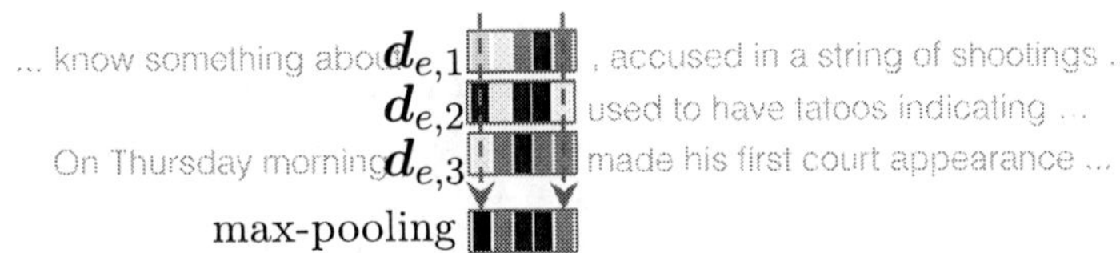

Figure 3: Max-pooling takes the max value of each dimension of dynamic entity representations, modeling accumulation of context information. It is then fed to $x_{c,\tau}$ as input to LSTMs.

$v(e; D, q)$ for each entity as a weighted sum [2]:

$$v(e; D, q) = W_{dv}\Big[\sum_{c \in D} s_{e,c}(q) d_{e,c}\Big] + b_v \qquad (5)$$

in which $s_{e,c}(q)$ is calculated by the attention mechanism (Bahdanau et al., 2015), modeling the degree to which our reader should attend to a particular occurrence of an entity, given the query q. More precisely, $s_{e,c}(q)$ is defined as the following:

$$s_{e,c}(q) = \frac{\exp(s'_{e,c}(q))}{\sum_{c'} \exp(s'_{e,c'}(q))} \qquad (6)$$

$$s'_{e,c'}(q) = m^{\mathrm{T}} \tanh(W_{dm} d_{e,c'} + q) + b_s \qquad (7)$$

where $s_{e,c}(q)$ is calculated by taking the softmax of $s'_{e,c'}(q)$, which is calculated from the dynamic entity representation $d_{e,c'}$ and the query vector q. The vector m, matrix W_{dm}, and the bias b_s in (7) are learned parameters in the attention mechanism. Vector m is used here to map a vector value to a scalar.

The query vector[3] $u(q)$ is constructed similarly as dynamic entity representations, using bidirectional LSTMs[4] to encode the query and then encoding the output vectors. More precisely, if we denote the length of the query as T and the index of the placeholder as τ, the query vector is calculated as:

$$u(q) = W_{hq}[\vec{h}_{q,T}, \overleftarrow{h}_{q,1}, \vec{h}_{q,\tau}, \overleftarrow{h}_{q,\tau}] + b_q \qquad (8)$$

Then, $v(e; D, q)$ and $u(q)$ are used in (1) to calculate probability $p(e|D, q)$.

---

[2] Following a heuristic used in Hill et al. (2015), we add a secondary bias b'_v to $v(e; D, q)$ if the entity e already appears in the query q.

[3] $u(q)$ and another query vector q, are calculated respectively, in the same way (8) with unshared model parameters, while sharing the parameters is also promising.

[4] The parameters of the bi-LSTM for queries are not shared with the ones for entity contexts.

2.2 Max-pooling

We expect the dynamic entity representation to capture information about an entity mentioned in a sentence. However, as an entity occurs multiple times in a document, information is accumulated as subsequent occurrences of the entity draw information from previous mentions. For example, in Figure 1, the first sentence mentioning "*Robert Downey Jr.*" relates *Downey* to *Iron Man*, whereas a subsequent mention of "*Downey*" also relates him to a robotic arm. Both of the two pieces of information are necessary to answer the query "*Iron Man star [X] presents ... with a bionic arm*". Therefore, the dynamic entity representations as constructed individually from single sentences may not provide enough information for our reader model. We thus propose the use of max-pooling to model information accumulation of dynamic entity representations.

More precisely, for each entity e, max-pooling takes the max value of each dimension of the vectors $d_{e,c'}$ from all preceding contexts c' (Figure 3). Then, in a subsequent sentence c where the entity occurs again at index τ, we use the vector

$$x_{c,\tau} = W_{dx} \max_{c' \prec c}\text{-pooling}(d_{e,c'}) + b_x$$

as input for the LSTMs in (3) and (4) for encoding the context. This vector $x_{c,\tau}$ draws information from preceding contexts, and is regarded as the meaning of the entity e that the reader understands so far, before reading the sentence c. It is used in place of a vector previously randomly initialized as a notion of e, in the construction of the new dynamic entity representation $d_{e,c}$.

3 Evaluation

We use the CNN-QA dataset (Hermann et al., 2015) for evaluating our model's ability to answer questions about named entities. The dataset consists of (D, q, e)-triples, where the document D is taken from online news articles, and the query q is formed by hiding a named entity e in a summarizing bullet point of the document (Figure 1). The training set has 90k articles and 380k queries, and both validation and test sets have 1k articles and 3k queries. An average article has about 25 entities and 700 word tokens. One trains a machine reading system on the data by maximizing likelihood of correct answers. We use `Chainer`[5] (Tokui et al., 2015) to implement our model[6].

Experimental Settings Named entities in CNN-QA are already recognized. For preprocessing, we segment sentences at punctuation marks ".", "!", and "?".[7] We train our model[8] with hyper-parameters lightly tuned on the validation set[9], and we conduct ablation test on several techniques that improve our basic model.

Results As shown in Table 1, Max-pooling described in Section 2.2 drastically improves performance, showing the effect of accumulating information on entities. Another technique, called "Byway", is based on the observation that the attention mechanism (5) must always promote some entity occurrences (since all weights sum to 1), which could be difficult if the entity does not answer the query. To counter this, we make an artificial occurrence for each entity with no contexts, which serves as a byway to attend when no other occurrences can be reasonably related to the query. This simple trick shows

---

[5]`http://chainer.org/`

[6]The implementation is available at `https://github.com/soskek/der-network`.

[7]Text in CNN-QA are tokenized without any sentence segmentations.

[8]Training process takes roughly a week (3-5 passes of the training data) on a 6-core 2.4GHz Xeon CPU.

[9]Vector dimension: 300, Dropout: 0.3, Batch: 50, Optimization: RMSProp with momentum (Tieleman and Hinton, 2012; Graves, 2013) (momentum: 0.9, decay: 0.95), Learning rate: 1e-4 divided by 2.0 per epoch, Gradient clipping factor: 10. We initialize word vectors by uniform distribution [-0.05, 0.05], and other matrix parameters by Gaussians of mean 0 and variance $2/(\#\text{ rows} + \#\text{ columns})$.

Models	Valid	Test
Basic Proposed Model (Basic)	0.614	0.623
Basic + Max-pooling	**0.712**	0.707
Basic + Byway	0.691	0.706
Basic + Byway, Max-pooling (Full)	0.708	**0.720**
Full + w2v-initialization	**0.713**	**0.729**
Deep LSTMs*	0.550	0.570
Attentive Reader*	0.616	0.630
Impatient Reader*	0.618	0.638
Memory Networks**	0.635	0.684
+ Ensemble (11 models)**	0.662	0.694

Table 1: Accuracy on CNN-QA dataset. Results marked by $*$ are cited from Hermann et al. (2015) and $**$ from Hill et al. (2015).

Max / Basic
e2 / e2 / e7

" [X] " star @entity0 presents a young child with a bionic arm

.58 .75 — (@entity1) @entity0 may be @entity2 in the popular @entity4 superhero films , but he recently dealt in some advanced bionic technology himself .

...

1.00 — @entity7 received his robotic arm in the summer , then later had it upgraded to resemble a " @entity26 " arm .

.31 .25 — this past saturday , @entity7 received an even more impressive gift , from " @entity2 " himself .

...

.11 .00 — the actor showed the child two arms , one from @entity0 's movies and one for @entity7 : a real , working robotic @entity2 arm .

...

Figure 4: A correct answer found by max-pooling. Attention to each entity occurrence shown on left.

clear effects, suggesting that the attention mechanism plays a key role in our model. Combining these two techniques helps more. Further, we note that initializing our model with pre-trained word vectors[10] is helpful, though world knowledge of entities has been prevented by the anonymization process. This suggests that pre-trained word vectors may still bring extra linguistic knowledge encoded in ordinary words. Finally, we note that our model, full *DER Network*, shows the best results compared to several previous reader models (Hermann et al., 2015; Hill et al., 2015), endorsing our approach as promising. The 99% confidence intervals of the results of full DER Network and the one initialized by word2vec on the test set were $[0.700, 0.740]$ and $[0.708, 0.749]$, respectively (measured by bootstrap tests).

---

[10]We use GoogleNews vectors from `http://code.google.com/p/word2vec/` (Mikolov et al., 2013).

Analysis In the example shown in Figure 4, our basic model missed by paying little attention to the second and third sentences, probably because it does not mention *@entity0* (*Downey*). In contrast, max-pooling of *@entity2* (*Iron Man*) draws attention to the second and third sentences because *Iron Man* is said related to *Downey* in the first sentence. This helps *Iron Man* surpass *@entity26* (*Transformers*), which is the name of a different movie series in which robots appear but *Downey* doesn't. Quantitatively, in the 479 samples in test set correctly answered by max-pooling but missed by basic model, the average occurrences of answer entities (8.0) is higher than the one (7.2) in the 1782 samples correctly answered by both models. This suggests that max-pooling especially helps samples with more entity mentions.

4 Discussion

It is actually a surprise for us that deep learning models, despite their vast amount of parameters, seem able to learn as intended by the designers. This also indicates a potential that additional linguistic intuitions modeled by deep learning methods can improve performances, as in the other work using max-pooling (LeCun et al., 1998; Socher et al., 2011; Le et al., 2012; Collobert et al., 2011; Kalchbrenner et al., 2014), attention (Bahdanau et al., 2015; Luong et al., 2015; Xu et al., 2015; Rush et al., 2015), etc. In this work, we have focused on modeling a reader that dynamically builds meanings for entities. We believe the methodology can be inspiring to other problems as well.

Acknowledgments

This work was supported by CREST, JST and JSPS KAKENHI Grant Number 15H01702 and 15H05318. We would like to thank members of Preferred Infrastructure, Inc. and Preferred Networks, Inc. for useful discussions. We also thank the anonymous reviewers for comments on earlier version of this paper.

References

Dzmitry Bahdanau, Kyunghyun Cho, and Yoshua Bengio. 2015. Neural machine translation by jointly learning to align and translate. In *Proceedings of the 3rd International Conference on Learning Representations*.

Ronan Collobert, Jason Weston, Léon Bottou, Michael Karlen, Koray Kavukcuoglu, and Pavel Kuksa. 2011. Natural language processing (almost) from scratch. *Journal of Machine Learning Research*, 12:2493–2537.

Alex Graves, Santiago Fernández, and Jürgen Schmidhuber. 2005. Bidirectional lstm networks for improved phoneme classification and recognition. In *Proceedings of the 15th International Conference on Artificial Neural Networks: Formal Models and Their Applications - Volume Part II*, pages 799–804.

Alex Graves. 2013. Generating sequences with recurrent neural networks. *CoRR*, abs/1308.0850.

Karl Moritz Hermann, Tomas Kocisky, Edward Grefenstette, Lasse Espeholt, Will Kay, Mustafa Suleyman, and Phil Blunsom. 2015. Teaching machines to read and comprehend. In *Advances in Neural Information Processing Systems 28*, pages 1684–1692.

Felix Hill, Antoine Bordes, Sumit Chopra, and Jason Weston. 2015. The goldilocks principle: Reading children's books with explicit memory representations. *CoRR*, abs/1511.02301.

Sepp Hochreiter and Jürgen Schmidhuber. 1997. Long short-term memory. *Neural computation*, 9(8):1735–1780.

Nal Kalchbrenner, Edward Grefenstette, and Phil Blunsom. 2014. A convolutional neural network for modelling sentences. In *Proceedings of the 52nd Annual Meeting of the Association for Computational Linguistics (Volume 1: Long Papers)*, pages 655–665.

Quoc Le, Marc'Aurelio Ranzato, Rajat Monga, Matthieu Devin, Kai Chen, Greg Corrado, Jeff Dean, and Andrew Ng. 2012. Building high-level features using large scale unsupervised learning. In *Proceedings of the 29th International Conference on Machine Learning*, pages 81–88.

Yann LeCun, Léon Bottou, Yoshua Bengio, and Patrick Haffner. 1998. Gradient-based learning applied to document recognition. *Proceedings of the IEEE*, 86(11):2278–2324.

Thang Luong, Hieu Pham, and Christopher D. Manning. 2015. Effective approaches to attention-based neural machine translation. In *Proceedings of the 2015 Conference on Empirical Methods in Natural Language Processing*, pages 1412–1421.

Tomas Mikolov, Ilya Sutskever, Kai Chen, Gregory S. Corrado, and Jeffrey Dean. 2013. Distributed representations of words and phrases and their compositionality. In *Advances in Neural Information Processing Systems 26*, pages 3111–3119.

Hoifung Poon, Janara Christensen, Pedro Domingos, Oren Etzioni, Raphael Hoffmann, Chloe Kiddon, Thomas Lin, Xiao Ling, Mausam, Alan Ritter, Stefan Schoenmackers, Stephen Soderland, Dan Weld, Fei Wu, and Congle Zhang. 2010. Machine reading at the university of washington. In *Proceedings of the NAACL HLT 2010 First International Workshop on Formalisms and Methodology for Learning by Reading*, pages 87–95.

Matthew Richardson, Christopher J.C. Burges, and Erin Renshaw. 2013. MCTest: A challenge dataset for the open-domain machine comprehension of text. In *Proceedings of the 2013 Conference on Empirical Methods in Natural Language Processing*, pages 193–203.

Alexander M. Rush, Sumit Chopra, and Jason Weston. 2015. A neural attention model for abstractive sentence summarization. In *Proceedings of the 2015 Conference on Empirical Methods in Natural Language Processing*, pages 379–389.

Richard Socher, Eric H. Huang, Jeffrey Pennington, Andrew Y. Ng, and Christopher D. Manning. 2011. Dynamic pooling and unfolding recursive autoencoders for paraphrase detection. In *Advances in Neural Information Processing Systems 24*, pages 801–809.

Wilson L. Taylor. 1953. "cloze procedure": a new tool for measuring readability. *Journalism Quarterly*, 30:415–433.

Tijmen Tieleman and Geoffrey Hinton. 2012. Lecture 6.5 - msprop: Divide the gradient by a running average of its recent magnitude. *COURSERA: Neural Networks for Machine Learning.*

Seiya Tokui, Kenta Oono, Shohei Hido, and Justin Clayton. 2015. Chainer: a next-generation open source framework for deep learning. In *Proceedings of Workshop on Machine Learning Systems (LearningSys) in The 29th Annual Conference on Neural Information Processing Systems.*

Kelvin Xu, Jimmy Ba, Ryan Kiros, Kyunghyun Cho, Aaron Courville, Ruslan Salakhudinov, Rich Zemel, and Yoshua Bengio. 2015. Show, attend and tell: Neural image caption generation with visual attention. In *Proceedings of the 32nd International Conference on Machine Learning*, pages 2048–2057.

Speed-Constrained Tuning for Statistical Machine Translation Using Bayesian Optimization

Daniel Beck[†*]   **Adrià de Gispert**[‡]   **Gonzalo Iglesias**[‡]   **Aurelien Waite**[‡]   **Bill Byrne**[‡]

[†]Department of Computer Science, University of Sheffield, United Kingdom
`debeckl@sheffield.ac.uk`
[‡]SDL Research, Cambridge, United Kingdom
`{agispert,giglesias,rwaite,bbyrne}@sdl.com`

Abstract

We address the problem of automatically finding the parameters of a statistical machine translation system that maximize BLEU scores while ensuring that decoding speed exceeds a minimum value. We propose the use of Bayesian Optimization to efficiently tune the speed-related decoding parameters by easily incorporating speed as a noisy constraint function. The obtained parameter values are guaranteed to satisfy the speed constraint with an associated confidence margin. Across three language pairs and two speed constraint values, we report overall optimization time reduction compared to grid and random search. We also show that Bayesian Optimization can decouple speed and BLEU measurements, resulting in a further reduction of overall optimization time as speed is measured over a small subset of sentences.

1 Introduction

Research in Statistical Machine Translation (SMT) aims to improve translation quality, typically measured by BLEU scores (Papineni et al., 2001), over a baseline system. Given a task defined by a language pair and its corpora, the quality of a system is assessed by contrasting choices made in rule/phrase extraction criteria, feature functions, decoding algorithms and parameter optimization techniques.

Some of these choices result in systems with significant differences in performance. For example, in phrase-based translation (PBMT) (Koehn et al.,

2003), decoder parameters such as pruning thresholds and reordering constraints can have a dramatic impact on both BLEU and decoding speed. However, unlike feature weights, which can be optimized by MERT (Och and Ney, 2004), it is difficult to optimize decoder parameters either for speed or for BLEU.

We are interested in the problem of automatically finding the decoder parameters and feature weights that yield the best BLEU at a specified minimum decoding speed. This is potentially very expensive because each change in a decoder parameter requires re-decoding to assess both BLEU and translation speed. This is under-studied in the literature, despite its importance for real-life commercial SMT engines whose speed and latency can be as significant for user satisfaction as overall translation quality.

We propose to use Bayesian Optimization (Brochu et al., 2010b; Shahriari et al., 2015) for this constrained optimization task. By using prior knowledge of the function to be optimized and by exploring the most uncertain and the most promising regions of the parameter space, Bayesian Optimization (BO) is able to quickly find optimal parameter values. It is particularly well-suited to optimize expensive and non-differentiable functions such as the BLEU score of a decoder on a tuning set. The BO framework can also incorporate noisy constraints, such as decoder speed measurements, yielding parameters that satisfy these constraints with quantifiable confidence values.

For a set of fixed feature weights, we use BO to optimize phrase-based decoder parameters for speed and BLEU. We show across 3 different language

---

* This work was done during an internship of the first author at SDL Research, Cambridge.

Proceedings of NAACL-HLT 2016, pages 856–865,
San Diego, California, June 12-17, 2016. ©2016 Association for Computational Linguistics

pairs that BO can find fast configurations with high BLEU scores much more efficiently than other tuning techniques such as grid or random search. We also show that BLEU and decoding speed can be treated as decoupled measurements by BO. This results in a further reduction of overall optimization time, since speed can be measured over a smaller set of sentences than is needed for BLEU.

Finally, we discuss the effects of feature weights reoptimization after speed tuning, where we show that further improvements in BLEU can be obtained. Although our analysis is done on a phrase-based system with standard decoder parameters (decoding stack size, distortion limit, and maximum number of translations per source phrase), BO could be applied to other decoding paradigms and parameters.

The paper is organized as follows. Section 2 gives a brief overview of Bayesian Optimization and describes how it can be applied to our problem, Section 3 reports our speed-constrained tuning experiments, Section 4 reviews related work, and Section 5 concludes.

2 Bayesian Optimization

We are interested in finding a global maximizer of an objective function f:

$$\theta_\star = \arg\max_{\theta \in \Theta} f(\theta) \tag{1}$$

where θ is a parameter vector from a search space Θ. It is assumed that f has no simple closed form but can be evaluated at an arbitrary θ point. In this paper, we take f as the BLEU score produced by an SMT system on a tuning set, and θ will be the PBMT decoder parameters.

Bayesian Optimization is a powerful framework to efficiently address this problem. It works by defining a prior model over f and evaluating it sequentially. Evaluation points are chosen to maximize the utility of the measurement, as estimated by an acquisition function that trades off exploration of uncertain regions in Θ versus exploitation of regions that are promising, based on function evaluations over all x points gathered so far. BO is particularly well-suited when f is non-convex, non-differentiable and costly to evaluate (Shahriari et al., 2015).

2.1 Prior Model

The first step in performing BO is to define the prior model over the function of interest. While a number of different approaches exist in the literature, in this work we follow the concepts presented in Snoek et al. (2012) and implemented in the Spearmint[1] toolkit, which we detail in this Section.

The prior over f is defined as a Gaussian Process (GP) (Rasmussen and Williams, 2006):

$$f \sim \mathcal{GP}(m(\theta), k(\theta, \theta')) \tag{2}$$

where m and k are the mean and kernel (or covariance) functions. The mean function is fixed to the zero constant function, as usual in GP models. This is not a large restriction because the *posterior* over f will have non-zero mean in general. We use the Matèrn52 kernel, which makes little assumptions about the function smoothness.

The observations, BLEU scores in our work, are assumed to have additive Gaussian noise over f evaluations. In theory we do not expect variations in BLEU for a fixed set of decoding parameters but in practice assuming some degree of noise helps to make the posterior calculation more stable.

2.2 Adding Constraints

The optimization problem of Equation 1 can be extended to incorporate an added constraint on some measurement $c(\theta)$:

$$\theta_\star = \arg\max_{\theta \in \Theta} f(\theta) \quad \text{s.t. } c(\theta) > t \tag{3}$$

In our setup, $c(\theta)$ is the decoding speed of a configuration θ, and t is the minimum speed we wish the decoder to run at. This formulation assumes c is deterministic given a set of parameters θ. However, as we show in Section 3.2, speed measurements are inherently noisy, returning different values when using the same decoder parameters.

So, we follow Gelbart et al. (2014) and redefine Equation 3 by assuming a probabilistic model p over $c(\theta)$:

$$\theta_\star = \arg\max_{\theta \in \Theta} f(\theta) \quad \text{s.t. } p(c(\theta) > t) \geq 1 - \delta \tag{4}$$

where δ is a user-defined tolerance value. For our problem, the formulation above states that we wish

---

[1] https://github.com/HIPS/Spearmint

to optimize the BLEU score for decoders that run at speeds faster than t with probability $1 - \delta$. Like f, c is also assumed to have a GP prior with zero mean, Matèrn52 kernel and additive Gaussian noise.

2.3 Acquisition Function

The prior model combined with observations gives rise to a posterior distribution over f. The posterior mean gives information about potential optima in Θ, in other words, regions we would like to *exploit*. The posterior variance encodes the uncertainty in unknown regions of Θ, i.e., regions we would like to *explore*. This exploration/exploitation trade-off is a fundamental aspect not only in BO but many other global optimization methods.

Acquisition functions are heuristics that use information from the posterior to suggest new evaluation points. They naturally encode the exploration/exploitation trade-off by taking into account the full posterior information. A suggestion is obtained by maximizing this function, which can be done using standard optimization techniques since they are much cheaper to evaluate compared to the original objective function.

Most acquisition functions used in the literature are based on improving the best evaluation obtained so far. However, it has been shown that this approach has some pathologies in the presence of constrained functions (Gelbart et al., 2014). Here we employ Predictive Entropy Search with Constraints (PESC) (Hernández-Lobato et al., 2015), which aims to maximize the information about the global optimum $\theta_\star$. This acquisition function has been empirically shown to obtain better results when dealing with constraints and it can easily take advantage of a scenario known as *decoupled constraints* (Gelbart et al., 2014), where the objective (BLEU) and the constraint (speed) values can come from different sets of measurements. This is explained in the next Section.

Algorithm 1 summarizes the BO procedure under constraints. It starts with a set $\mathcal{D}_0$ of data points (selected at random, for instance), where each data point is a (θ, f, c) triple made of parameter values, one function evaluation (BLEU) and one constraint evaluation (decoding speed). Initial posteriors over the objective and the constraint are calculated[2]. At

every iteration, the algorithm selects a new evaluation point by maximizing the acquisition function α, measures the objective and constraint values on this point and updates the respective posterior distributions. It repeats this process until it reaches a maximum number of iterations N, and returns the best set of parameters obtained so far that is valid according to the constraint.

Algorithm 1 Constrained Bayesian Optimization

Input max. number of iterations N, acquisition function α, initial evaluations $\mathcal{D}_0$, min. constraint value t, tolerance δ

1: $\Theta = \emptyset$
2: **for** $i = 1, \ldots, N$ **do**
3:    select new θ_i by maximizing α:
$$\theta_i = \arg\max_{\theta} \alpha(\theta, p(f|\mathcal{D}_{i-1}), p(c|\mathcal{D}_{i-1}))$$
4:    $\Theta = \Theta \cup \theta_i$
5:    query objective $f(\theta_i)$
6:    query constraint $c(\theta_i)$
7:    augment data $\mathcal{D}_i = \mathcal{D}_i \cup (\theta, f, c)_i$
8:    update objective posterior $p(f|\mathcal{D}_i)$
9:    update constraint posterior $p(c|\mathcal{D}_i)$
10: **end for**
11: return $\theta_\star$ as per Equation 4

2.4 Decoupling Constraints

Translation speed can be measured on a much smaller tuning set than is required for reliable BLEU scores. In speed-constrained BLEU tuning, we can decouple the constraint by measuring speed on a small set of sentences, while still measuring BLEU on the full tuning set. In this scenario, BO could spend more time querying values for the speed constraint (as they are cheaper to obtain) and less time querying the BLEU objective.

We use PESC as the acquisition function because it can easily handle decoupled constraints (Gelbart, 2015, Sec. 4.3). Effectively, we modify Algorithm 1 to update *either* the objective *or* the constraint posterior at each iteration, according to what is obtained by maximizing PESC at line 3. This kind of decoupling is not allowed by standard acquisition functions used in BO.

---

[2]Note that the objective posterior $p(f|\mathcal{D})$ does not depend on the constraint measurements, and the constraint posterior $p(c|\mathcal{D})$ does not depend on the objective measurements.

The decoupled scenario makes good use of heterogeneous computing resources. For example, we are interested in measuring decoding speed on a specific machine that will be deployed. But translating the tuning set to measure BLEU can be parallelized over whatever computing is available.

3   Speed Tuning Experiments

We report translation results in three language pairs, chosen for the different challenges they pose for SMT systems: Spanish-to-English, English-to-German and Chinese-to-English. For each language pair, we use generic parallel data extracted from the web. The data sizes are 1.7, 1.1 and 0.3 billion words, respectively.

For Spanish-to-English and English-to-German we use mixed-domain tuning/test sets, which have about 1K sentences each and were created to evenly represent different domains, including world news, health, sport, science and others. For Chinese-to-English we use in-domain sets (2K sentences) created by randomly extracting unique parallel sentences from in-house parallel text collections; this in-domain data leads to higher BLEU scores than in the other tasks, as will be reported later. In all cases we have one reference translation.

We use an in-house implementation of a phrase-based decoder with lexicalized reordering model (Galley and Manning, 2008). The system uses 21 features, whose weights are optimized for BLEU via MERT (Och and Ney, 2004) at very slow decoder parameter settings in order to minimize search errors in tuning. The feature weights remain fixed during the speed tuning process.

3.1   Decoder Parameters

We tune three standard decoder parameters $\theta = (d, s, n)$ that directly affect the translation speed. We describe them next.

d: distortion limit. The maximum number of source words that may be skipped by the decoder as it generates phrases left-to-right on the target side.

s: stack size. The maximum number of hypotheses allowed to survive histogram pruning in each decoding stack.

n: number of translations. The maximum number of alternative translations per source phrase considered in decoding.

3.2   Measuring Decoding Speed

To get a better understanding of the speed measurements we decode the English-German tuning set 100 times with a slow decoder parameter setting, *i.e.* $\theta = (5, 100, 100)$, and repeat for a fast setting with $\theta = (0, 1, 1)$. We collect speed measurements in number of translated words per minute (wpm)[3].

The plots in Figure 1 show histograms containing the measurements obtained for both slow and fast settings. While both fit in a Gaussian distribution, the speed ranges approximately from 750 to 950 wpm in the slow setting and from 90K to 120K wpm in the fast setting. This means that speed measurements exhibit heteroscedasticity: they follow Gaussian distributions with different variances that *depend on* the decoder parameter values. This is a problem for our BO setting because the GP we use to model the constraint assumes homoscedasticity, or constant noise over the support set Θ.

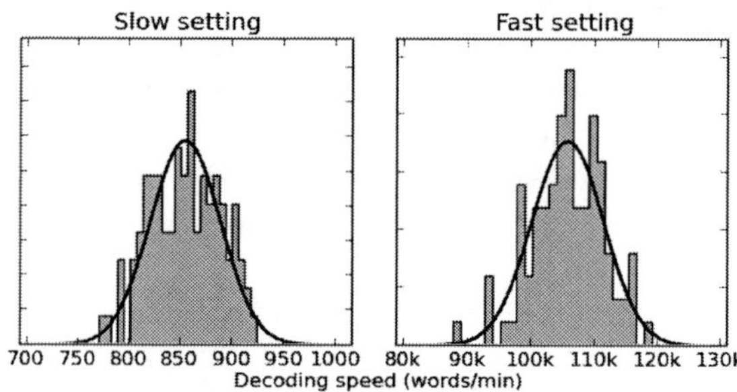

Figure 1: Histograms of speed measurements. The solid line shows a Gaussian fit with the empirical mean and variance. Note the difference in scale between the two settings, showing the heteroscedasticity.

A simple way to reduce the effect of heteroscedasticity is to take the logarithm of the speed measurements, which is also a standard practice when modeling non-negative measures in a GP (Gelbart et al., 2014). Table 1 shows the values for mean and standard deviation before and after the log transformation. Using the logarithm keeps the GP inference

---

[3]Measured on an Intel Xeon E5-2450 at 2.10GHz.

	Slow setting		Fast setting	
	Mean	Std	Mean	Std
speed	854.23	33.88	105.7k	5.6k
log speed	6.75	0.0398	11.57	0.0541

Table 1: Speed means and standard deviations in words per minute before and after the logarithmic transformation.

formulas tractable so we use this solution in our experiments.

3.3 BO Details and Baselines

All BO experiments use Spearmint (Snoek et al., 2012) with default values unless explicitly stated otherwise. We set the minimum and maximum values for d, s and n as $[0, 10]$, $[1, 500]$ and $[1, 100]$, respectively. We model d in linear scale but s and n in logarithmic scale for both BO and the baselines. This scaling is based on the intuition that optimal values for s and n will be in the lower interval values, which was confirmed in preliminary experiments on all three datasets.

We run two sets of experiments, using 2000wpm and 5000wpm as minimum speed constraints. In addition, we use the following BO settings:

Standard (BO-S): in this setting each BO iteration performs a full decoding of the tuning set in order to obtain both the BLEU score and the decoding speed jointly. We use $\delta = 0.01$ as the constraint tolerance described in Section 2.2.

Decoupled (BO-D): here we decouple the objective and the constraint as explained in Section 2.4. We still decode the full tuning set to get BLEU scores, but speed measurements are taken from a smaller subset of 50 sentences. Since speed measurements are faster in this case, we enforce BO to query for speed more often by modeling the task duration as described by Snoek et al. (2012). We use a higher constraint tolerance ($\delta = 0.05$), as we found that BO otherwise focused on the speed constraints at the expense of optimizing BLEU.

We compare these settings against two baselines: grid search and random search (Bergstra and Bengio, 2012). Grid search and random search seek parameter values in a similar way: a set of parameter values is provided; the decoder runs over the tuning set for all these values; the parameter value that

yields the highest BLEU at a speed above the constraint is returned. For grid search, parameter values are chosen to cover the allowed value range in even splits given a budget of a permitted maximum number of decodings. For random search, parameters are chosen from a uniform distribution over the ranges specified above. BO-S, grid search and random search use a maximum budget of 125 decodings. BO-D is allowed a larger budget of 250 iterations, as the speed measurements can be done quickly. This is not a bias in favour of BO-D, as the overall objective is to find the best, fast decoder in as little CPU time as possible.

3.4 Results

Our results using the 2000wpm speed constraint are shown in Figure 2. The solid lines in the figure show the tuning set BLEU score obtained from the current best parameters θ, as suggested by BO-S, as a function of CPU time (in logarithmic scale). Given that $\delta = 0.01$, we have a 99% confidence under the GP model that the speed constraint is met.

Figure 2 also shows the best BLEU scores of fast systems found by grid and random search at increasing budgets of 8, 27, and 125 decodings of the tuning set[4]. These results are represented by squares/circles of different sizes in the plot: the larger the square/circle, the larger the budget. For grid and random search we report only the single highest BLEU score found amongst the sufficiently fast systems; the CPU times reported are the total time spent decoding the batch. For BO, the CPU times include both decoding time and the time spent evaluating the acquisition function for the next decoder parameters to evaluate (see Section 3.5).

In terms of CPU time, BO-S finds optimal parameters in less time than either grid search or random search. For example, in Spanish-to-English, BO-S takes $\sim$70 min (9 iterations) to achieve 36.6 BLEU score. Comparing to the baselines using a budget of 27 decodings, random search and grid search need $\sim$160 min and $\sim$6 hours, respectively, to achieve 36.5 BLEU. Note that, for a given budget, grid search proves always slower than random search because it always considers parameters val-

---

[4]For grid search, these correspond to 2, 3 and 5 possible values per parameter.

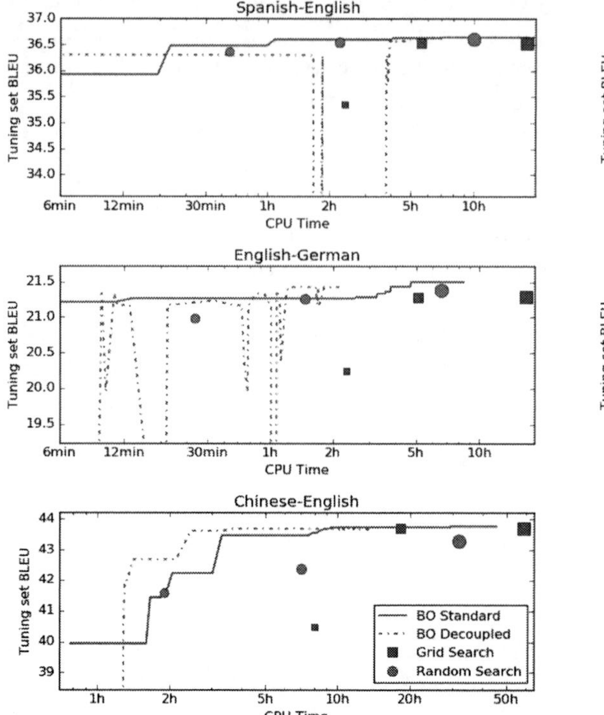 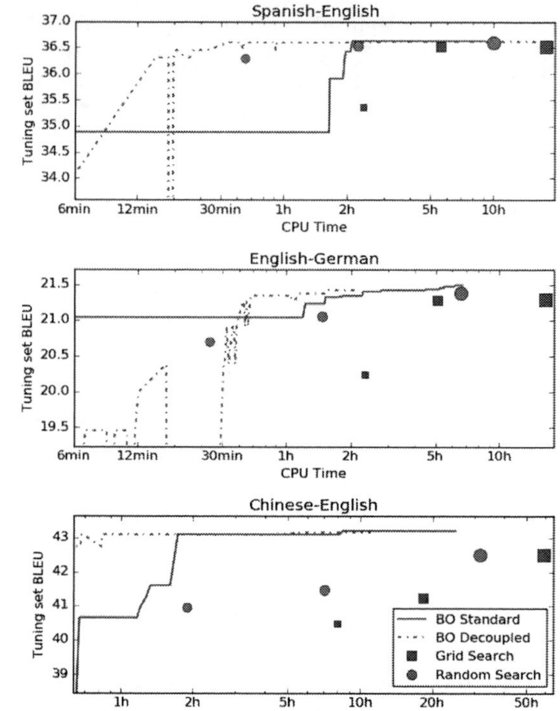

Figure 2: BLEU scores at 2000wpm. Squares and circles with increasing sizes correspond to searches with increasing evaluation budgets (8, 27, 125). For example: in Spanish-English, a random search with a budget of 125 evaluations required 10 CPU hours to run, and the highest BLEU score found among the sufficiently fast ($>=$2000wpm) systems was 36.2. For BO-D and BO-S, BLEU scores are plotted only if the speed is above 2000wpm and for BO-S only if the full dev set is decoded.

ues at the high end of the ranges (which are the slowest decoding settings).

In terms of translation quality, we find that BO-S reaches the best BLEU scores across all language pairs, although all approaches eventually achieve similar scores, except in Chinese-to-English where random search is unable to match the BO-S BLEU score even after 125 decodings.

The dotted lines show the results obtained by the decoupled BO-D approach. BO-D does manage to find good BLEU scores, but it proceeds somewhat erratically. As the figure shows, BO-D spends a good deal of time testing systems at parameter values that are too slow. There are also negative excursions in the BLEU score, which we observed were due to updates of the posterior constraint model. For

Figure 3: BLEU scores at 5000wpm. Squares and circles with increasing sizes correspond to baselines with increasing evaluation budgets (8, 27, 125).

each new iteration, the confidence on the best parameter values may decrease, and if the confidence drops below $1 - \delta$, then BO suggests parameter values which are more likely to satisfy the speed constraint; this potentially hurts BLEU by decoding too fast. Interestingly, this instability is not seen on the Chinese-to-English pair. We speculate this is due to the larger tuning set for this language pair. Because the task time difference between BLEU and speed measurements is higher compared to the other language pairs, BO-D tends to query speed more in this case, resulting in a better posterior for the constraint.

Our results using the stricter 5000 wpm speed constraint are shown in Figure 3. As in the 2000wpm case, BO-S tends to find better parameter values faster than any of the baselines. One exception is found in Spanish-to-English after ∼40 min, when random search finds a better BLEU after 8 iterations when compared to BO-S. However, later BO-S catches up and finds parameters that yield the same score. In Chinese-to-English BO is able to find parameters that yield significantly better BLEU scores than any of the baselines. It appears that the harsher the speed constraint, the more difficult the optimization task, and the more chances BO will beat the baselines.

Interestingly, the decoupled BO-D approach is more stable than in the less strict 2000wpm case. After some initial oscillations in BLEU for English-to-German, BO-D curves climb to optimal parameters in much less CPU time than BO-S. This is clearly seen in Spanish-to-English and Chinese-to-English. We conclude that the harsher the speed constraint, the more benefit in allowing BO to query for speed separately from BLEU.

Tables 2 and 3 report the final parameters θ found by each method after spending the maximum allowed budget, and the BLEU and speed measured (average of 3 runs) when translating the tuning and test using θ. These show how different each language pair behaves when optimizing for speed and BLEU. For Spanish-to-English and English-to-German it is possible to find fast decoding configurations (well above 5K wpm) that nearly match the BLEU score of the slow system used for MERT tuning, *i.e.* $\theta_{MERT} = (10, 1000, 500)$. In contrast, significant degradation in BLEU is observed at 5000wpm for Chinese-to-English, a language pair with complicated reordering requirements – notice that all methods consistently keep a very high distortion limit for this language pair. However, both BO-S and BO-D strategies yield better performance on test (at least +0.5BLEU improvement) than the grid and random search baselines.

Only BO is able to find optimal parameters across all tasks faster. The optimum parameters yield similar performance on the tuning and test sets, allowing for the speed variations discussed in Section 3.2. All the optimization procedures guarantee that the constraint is always satisfied over the tuning set. However, this strict guarantee does not necessarily extend to other data in the same way that there might be variations in BLEU score. This can be seen in the Chinese-English experiments. Future work could focus on improving the generalization of the confidence over constraints.

	Tuning		Test		θ		
	BLEU	speed	BLEU	speed	d	s	n
Spanish-English							
MERT	36.9	93	37.9	95	10	1K	500
Grid	36.5	8.1K	37.9	8.1K	5	22	31
Random	36.6	4.1K	37.8	4.1K	4	64	27
BO-S	36.6	2.7K	37.8	2.7K	4	95	68
BO-D	36.6	2.6K	37.8	2.6K	4	110	24
English-German							
MERT	21.1	72	18.0	70	10	1K	500
Grid	21.3	12.4K	18.2	12.4K	2	22	31
Random	21.4	18.4K	18.1	18.4K	2	13	43
BO-S	21.5	14.7K	18.1	14.3K	3	13	34
BO-D	21.5	14.4K	18.1	14.7K	3	13	35
Chinese-English							
MERT	44.3	50	42.5	51	10	1K	500
Grid	43.7	2.3K	41.8	2.1K	10	22	100
Random	43.3	3.0K	41.4	2.9K	9	19	46
BO-S	43.8	2.0K	41.9	1.9K	10	25	100
BO-D	43.7	2.2K	41.8	2.1K	10	24	44

Table 2: Results obtained after reaching the full evaluation budget (2000 words/min constraint). Speed is reported in translated words per minute.

	Tuning		Test		θ		
	BLEU	speed	BLEU	speed	d	s	n
Spanish-English							
MERT	36.9	93	37.9	95	10	1K	500
Grid	36.5	8.1K	37.9	8.1K	5	22	31
Random	36.6	8.0K	37.8	7.9K	4	28	43
BO-S	36.6	11.9K	37.8	12.0K	4	19	24
BO-D	36.6	11.0K	37.8	10.9K	4	19	73
English-German							
MERT	21.1	72	18.0	70	10	1K	500
Grid	21.3	12.4K	18.2	12.4K	2	22	31
Random	21.4	18.4K	18.1	18.4K	2	13	43
BO-S	21.5	14.7K	18.1	14.3K	3	13	34
BO-D	21.5	14.6K	18.1	14.4K	3	13	33
Chinese-English							
MERT	44.3	50	42.5	51	10	1K	500
Grid	42.5	10.7K	40.9	10.1K	10	4	100
Random	42.5	10.6K	40.5	10.4K	9	7	14
BO-S	43.2	5.4K	41.4	5.3K	10	13	15
BO-D	43.2	5.8K	41.4	5.7K	10	12	15

Table 3: Results obtained after reaching the full evaluation budget (5000 words/min constraint).

3.5 BO Time Analysis

The complexity of GP-based BO is $O(n^3)$, n being the number of GP observations, or function evaluations (Rasmussen and Williams, 2006). As the objective function f is expected to be expensive, this

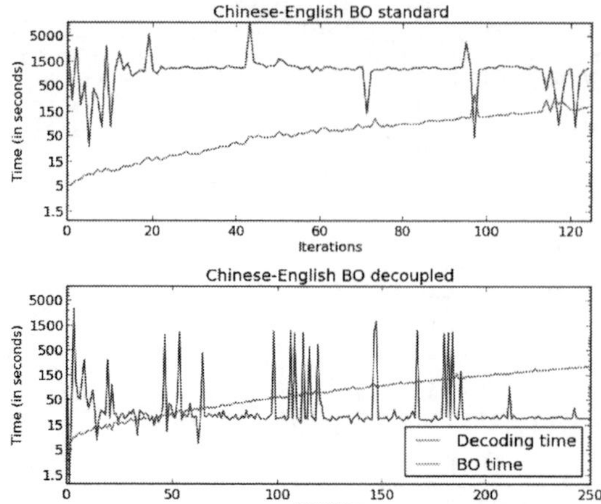

Figure 4: Time spent at each iteration in decoding and in BO (Chinese-to-English, 2000 wpm). BO-S (top), BO-D (bottom)

	Tuning		Test		θ		
	BLEU	speed	BLEU	speed	d	s	n
MERT	44.3	–	42.5	51	10	1K	500
BO-S	43.8	2.0K	41.9	1.9K	10	25	100
MERT-flat	43.8	2.0K	41.4	1.9K	10	25	100
MERT-opt	**44.3**	**2.0K**	**42.4**	**1.9K**	10	25	100

Table 4: Chinese-to-English results of re-running MERT using parameters that satisfy the 2K wpm speed constraint.

should not be an issue for low budgets. However, as the number of iterations grows there might reach a point at the time spent on the GP calculations surpasses the time spent evaluating the function.

This is investigated in Figure 4, where the time spent in decoding versus BO (in logarithmic scale) for Chinese-to-English using the 2K wpm constraint is reported, as a function of the optimization iteration. For BO-S (top), decoding time is generally constant but can peak upwards or downwards depending on the chosen parameters. For BO-D (bottom), most of the decoding runs are faster (when BO is querying for speed), and shoot up significantly only when the full tuning set is decoded (when BO is querying for BLEU). For both cases, BO time increases with the number of iterations, becoming nearly as expensive as decoding when a high maximum budget is considered. As shown in the previous section, this was no problem for our speed-tuning experiments because optimal parameters could be found with few iterations, but more complex settings (for example, with more decoder parameters) might require more iterations to find good solutions. For these cases the time spent in BO could be significant.

3.6 Reoptimizing Feature Weights

We have used BO to optimize decoder parameters for feature weights that had been tuned for BLEU using MERT. However, there is no reason to believe

that the best feature weights for a slow setting are also the best weights at the fast settings we desire.

To assess this we now fix the decoder parameters θ and re-run MERT on Chinese-to-English with 2000 wpm using the fast settings found by BO-S: $\theta_{BO} = (10, 25, 100)$ in Table 2. We run MERT starting from flat weights (MERT-flat) and from the optimal weights (MERT-opt), previously tuned for the MERT baseline with θ_{MERT}. Table 4 reports the results.

We find that MERT-opt is able to recover from the BLEU drops observed during speed-constrained tuning and close the gap with the slow baseline (from 41.9 to 42.4 BLEU at 1.8 Kwpm, versus 42.5 for MERT at only 51 wpm). Note that this performance is not achieved using MERT-flat, so rather than tune from flat parameters in a fixed fast setting, we conclude that it is better to: (1) use MERT to find feature weights in slow settings; (2) optimize decoder parameters for speed; (3) run MERT again with the fast decoder parameters from the feature weights found at the slow settings. As noted earlier, this may reduce the impact of search errors encountered in MERT when decoding at fast settings. However, this final application MERT is unconstrained and there is no guarantee that it will yield a decoder configuration that satisfies the constraints. This must be verified through subsequent testing.

Ideally, one should *jointly* optimize decoder parameters, feature weights and all decisions involved in building an SMT system, but this can be very challenging to do using only BO. We note anecdotally that we have attempted to replicate the feature weight tuning procedure of Miao et al. (2014) but obtained mixed results on our test sets. Effective ways to combine BO with well-established feature tuning algorithms such as MERT could be a promising research direction.

4 Related Work

Bayesian Optimization has been previously used for hyperparameter optimization in machine learning systems (Snoek et al., 2012; Bergstra et al., 2011), automatic algorithm configuration (Hutter et al., 2011) and for applications in which system tuning involves human feedback (Brochu et al., 2010a). Recently, it has also been used successfully in several NLP applications. Wang et al. (2015) use BO to tune sentiment analysis and question answering systems. They introduce a multi-stage approach where hyperparameters are optimized using small datasets and then used as starting points for subsequent BO stages using increasing amounts of data. Yogatama et al. (2015) employ BO to optimize text representations in a set of classification tasks. They find that there is no representation that is optimal for all tasks, which further justifies an automatic tuning approach. Wang et al. (2014) use a model based on optimistic optimization to tune parameters of a term extraction system. In SMT, Miao et al. (2014) use BO for feature weight tuning and report better results in some language pairs when compared to traditional tuning algorithms.

Our approach is heavily based on the work of Gelbart et al. (2014) and Hernández-Lobato et al. (2015) which uses BO in the presence of unknown constraints. They set speed and memory constraints on neural network trainings and report better results compared to those of naive models which explicitly put high costs on regions that violate constraints. A different approach based on augmented Lagrangians is proposed by Gramacy et al. (2014). The authors apply BO in a water decontamination setting where the goal is to find the optimal pump positioning subject to restrictions on water and contaminant flows. All these previous work in constrained BO use GPs as the prior model.

Optimizing decoding parameters for speed is an understudied problem in the MT literature. Chung and Galley (2012) propose direct search methods to optimize feature weights and decoder parameters jointly but aiming at the traditional goal of maximizing translation quality. To enable search parameter optimization they enforce a deterministic time penalty on BLEU scores, which is not ideal due to the stochastic nature of time measurements shown on Section 3.2 (this issue is also cited by the authors in their manuscript). It would be interesting to incorporate their approach into BO for optimizing translation quality under speed constraints.

5 Conclusion

We have shown that Bayesian Optimisation performs well for translation speed tuning experiments and is particularly suited for low budgets and for tight constraints. There is much room for improvement. For better modeling of the speed constraint and possibly better generalization in speed measurements across tuning and test sets, one possibility would be to use randomized sets of sentences. Warped GPs (Snelson et al., 2003) could be a more accurate model as they can learn transformations for heteroscedastic data without relying on a fixed transformation, as we do with log speed measurements.

Modelling of the objective function could also be improved. In our experiments we used a GP with a Matèrn52 kernel, but this assumes f is doubly-differentiable and exhibits Lipschitz-continuity (Brochu et al., 2010b). Since that does not hold for the BLEU score, using alternative smoother metrics such as linear corpus BLEU (Tromble et al., 2008) or expected BLEU (Rosti et al., 2010) could yield better results. Other recent developments in Bayesian Optimisation could be applied to our settings, like multi-task optimization (Swersky et al., 2013) or freeze-thaw optimization (Swersky et al., 2014).

In our application we treat Bayesian Optimisation as a sequential model. Parallel approaches do exist (Snoek et al., 2012; González et al., 2015), but we find it easy enough to harness parallel computation in decoding tuning sets and by decoupling BLEU measurements from speed measurements. However for more complex optimisation scenarios or for problems that require lengthy searches, parallelization might be needed to keep the computations required for optimisation in line with what is needed to measure translation speed and quality.

References

James Bergstra and Yoshua Bengio. 2012. Random Search for Hyper-Parameter Optimization. *Journal of Machine Learning Research*, 13:281–305.

James Bergstra, Rémi Bardenet, Yoshua Bengio, and Balázs Kégl. 2011. Algorithms for Hyper-Parameter Optimization. In *Proceedings of NIPS*.

Eric Brochu, Tyson Brochu, and Nando de Freitas. 2010a. A Bayesian Interactive Optimization Approach to Procedural Animation Design. In *Proceedings of ACM SIGGRAPH/Eurographics Symposium on Computer Animation*.

Eric Brochu, Vlad M. Cora, and Nando de Freitas. 2010b. A Tutorial on Bayesian Optimization of Expensive Cost Functions, with Application to Active User Modeling and Hierarchical Reinforcement Learning. *arXiv:1012.2599v1 [cs.LG]*.

Tagyoung Chung and Michel Galley. 2012. Direct Error Rate Minimization for Statistical Machine Translation. In *Proceedings of WMT*, pages 468–479.

Michel Galley and Christopher D. Manning. 2008. A Simple and Effective Hierarchical Phrase Reordering Model. In *Proceedings of EMNLP*, pages 847–855.

Michael A. Gelbart, Jasper Snoek, and Ryan P. Adams. 2014. Bayesian Optimization with Unknown Constraints. In *Proceedings of UAI*.

Michael A. Gelbart. 2015. *Constrained Bayesian Optimization and Applications*. Ph.D. thesis, Harvard University.

Javier González, Zhenwen Dai, Philipp Hennig, and Neil D. Lawrence. 2015. Batch Bayesian Optimization via Local Penalization.

Robert B. Gramacy, Genetha A. Gray, Sebastien Le Digabel, Herbert K. H. Lee, Pritam Ranjan, Garth Wells, and Stefan M. Wild. 2014. Modeling an Augmented Lagrangian for Blackbox Constrained Optimization. *arXiv preprint arXiv:1403.4890*.

José Miguel Hernández-Lobato, Michael A. Gelbart, Matthew W. Hoffman, Ryan P. Adams, and Zoubin Ghahramani. 2015. Predictive Entropy Search for Bayesian Optimization with Unknown Constraints. In *Proceedings of ICML*.

Frank Hutter, Holger H. Hoos, and Kevin Leyton-Brown. 2011. Sequential Model-based Optimization for General Algorithm Configuration. In *Proceedings of LION 5*.

Philipp Koehn, Franz Josef Och, and Daniel Marcu. 2003. Statistical phrase-based translation. In *Proceedings of NAACL*, pages 48–54.

Yishu Miao, Ziyu Wang, and Phil Blunsom. 2014. Bayesian Optimisation for Machine Translation. In *NIPS Workshop on Bayesian Optimization*, pages 1–5.

Franz Josef Och and Hermann Ney. 2004. The Alignment Template Approach to Statistical Machine Translation. *Computational Linguistics*, 30(4):417–449.

Kishore Papineni, Salim Roukos, Todd Ward, and Wei-Jing Zhu. 2001. Bleu: a method for automatic evaluation of machine translation. In *Proceedings of ACL*, pages 311–318.

Carl Edward Rasmussen and Christopher K. I. Williams. 2006. *Gaussian processes for machine learning*, volume 1. MIT Press Cambridge.

Antti-Veikko Rosti, Bing Zhang, Spyros Matsoukas, and Richard Schwartz. 2010. Bbn system description for wmt10 system combination task. In *Proceedings of WMT and MetricsMATR*, pages 321–326.

Bobak Shahriari, Kevin Swersky, Ziyu Wang, Ryan P. Adams, and Nando de Freitas. 2015. Taking the Human Out of the Loop : A Review of Bayesian Optimization. Technical Report 1, Universities of Harvard, Oxford, Toronto, and Google DeepMind.

Edward Snelson, Carl Edward Rasmussen, and Zoubin Ghahramani. 2003. Warped Gaussian Processes. In *Proceedings of NIPS*, pages 337–344.

Jasper Snoek, Hugo Larochelle, and Ryan P. Adams. 2012. Practical Bayesian optimization of Machine Learning Algorithms. In *Proceedings of NIPS*.

Kevin Swersky, Jasper Snoek, and Ryan P. Adams. 2013. Multi-task Bayesian Optimization. In *Proceedings of NIPS*.

Kevin Swersky, Jasper Snoek, and Ryan P. Adams. 2014. Freeze-Thaw Bayesian Optimization. *arXiv:1406.3896v1 [stat.ML]*.

Roy Tromble, Shankar Kumar, Franz Och, and Wolfgang Macherey. 2008. Lattice Minimum Bayes-Risk decoding for statistical machine translation. In *Proceedings of EMNLP*, pages 620–629.

Ziyu Wang, Babak Shakibi, Lin Jin, and Nando de Freitas. 2014. Bayesian Multi-Scale Optimistic Optimization. In *Proceedings of AISTATS*.

Lidan Wang, Minwei Feng, Bowen Zhou, Bing Xiang, and Sridhar Mahadevan. 2015. Efficient Hyperparameter Optimization for NLP Applications. In *Proceedings of EMNLP*, pages 2112–2117.

Dani Yogatama, Lingpeng Kong, and Noah A. Smith. 2015. Bayesian Optimization of Text Representations. In *Proceedings of EMNLP*, pages 2100–2105.

Multi-Way, Multilingual Neural Machine Translation
with a Shared Attention Mechanism

Orhan Firat
Middle East Technical University
`orhan.firat@ceng.metu.edu.tr`

Kyunghyun Cho
New York University

Yoshua Bengio
University of Montreal
CIFAR Senior Fellow

Abstract

We propose multi-way, multilingual neural machine translation. The proposed approach enables a single neural translation model to translate between multiple languages, with a number of parameters that grows only linearly with the number of languages. This is made possible by having a single attention mechanism that is shared across all language pairs. We train the proposed multi-way, multilingual model on ten language pairs from WMT'15 simultaneously and observe clear performance improvements over models trained on only one language pair. In particular, we observe that the proposed model significantly improves the translation quality of low-resource language pairs.

1 Introduction

Neural Machine Translation It has been shown that a deep (recurrent) neural network can successfully learn a complex mapping between variable-length input and output sequences on its own. Some of the earlier successes in this task have, for instance, been handwriting recognition (Bottou et al., 1997; Graves et al., 2009) and speech recognition (Graves et al., 2006; Chorowski et al., 2015). More recently, a general framework of encoder-decoder networks has been found to be effective at learning this kind of sequence-to-sequence mapping by using two recurrent neural networks (Cho et al., 2014b; Sutskever et al., 2014).

A basic encoder-decoder network consists of two recurrent networks. The first network, called an encoder, maps an input sequence of variable length into a point in a continuous vector space, resulting in a fixed-dimensional context vector. The other recurrent neural network, called a decoder, then generates a target sequence again of variable length starting from the context vector. This approach however has been found to be inefficient in (Cho et al., 2014a) when handling long sentences, due to the difficulty in learning a complex mapping between an arbitrary long sentence and a single fixed-dimensional vector.

In (Bahdanau et al., 2014), a remedy to this issue was proposed by incorporating an *attention mechanism* to the basic encoder-decoder network. The attention mechanism in the encoder-decoder network frees the network from having to map a sequence of arbitrary length to a single, fixed-dimensional vector. Since this attention mechanism was introduced to the encoder-decoder network for machine translation, neural machine translation, which is purely based on neural networks to perform full end-to-end translation, has become competitive with the existing phrase-based statistical machine translation in many language pairs (Jean et al., 2015; Gulcehre et al., 2015; Luong et al., 2015b).

Multilingual Neural Machine Translation Existing machine translation systems, mostly based on a phrase-based system or its variants, work by directly mapping a symbol or a subsequence of symbols in a source language to its corresponding symbol or subsequence in a target language. This kind of mapping is strictly specific to a given language *pair*, and it is not trivial to extend this mapping to work on multiple pairs of languages.

A system based on neural machine translation, on the other hand, can be decomposed into two mod-

Proceedings of NAACL-HLT 2016, pages 866–875,
San Diego, California, June 12-17, 2016. ©2016 Association for Computational Linguistics

ules. The encoder maps a source sentence into a continuous representation, either a fixed-dimensional vector in the case of the basic encoder-decoder network or a set of vectors in the case of attention-based encoder-decoder network. The decoder then generates a target translation based on this source representation. This makes it possible conceptually to build a system that maps a source sentence in any language to a common continuous representation space and decodes the representation into any of the target languages, allowing us to make a *multilingual machine translation* system.

This possibility is straightforward to implement and has been validated in the case of basic encoder-decoder networks (Luong et al., 2015a). It is however not so, in the case of the attention-based encoder-decoder network, as the attention mechanism, or originally called the alignment function in (Bahdanau et al., 2014), is conceptually language pair-specific. In (Dong et al., 2015), the authors cleverly avoided this issue of language pair-specific attention mechanism by considering only a one-to-many translation, where each target language decoder embedded its own attention mechanism. Also, we notice that both of these works have only evaluated their models on relatively small-scale tasks, making it difficult to assess whether multilingual neural machine translation can scale beyond low-resource language translation.

Multi-Way, Multilingual Neural Machine Translation   In this paper, we first step back from the currently available multilingual neural translation systems proposed in (Luong et al., 2015a; Dong et al., 2015) and ask the question of whether the attention mechanism can be shared across multiple language pairs. As an answer to this question, we propose an attention-based encoder-decoder network that admits a shared attention mechanism with multiple encoders and decoders. We use this model for all the experiments, which suggests that it is indeed possible to share an attention mechanism across multiple language pairs.

The next question we ask is the following: in which scenario would the proposed multi-way, multilingual neural translation have an advantage over the existing, single-pair model? Specifically, we consider a case of the translation between a low-resource language pair. The experiments show that the proposed multi-way, multilingual model generalizes better than the single-pair translation model, when the amount of available parallel corpus is small. Furthermore, we validate that this is not only due to the increased amount of target-side, monolingual corpus.

Finally, we train a single model with the proposed architecture on all the language pairs from the WMT'15; English, French, Czech, German, Russian and Finnish. The experiments show that it is indeed possible to train a single attention-based network to perform multi-way translation.

2   Background: Attention-based Neural Machine Translation

The attention-based neural machine translation was proposed in (Bahdanau et al., 2014). It was motivated from the observation in (Cho et al., 2014a) that a basic encoder-decoder translation model from (Cho et al., 2014b; Sutskever et al., 2014) suffers from translating a long source sentence efficiently. This is largely due to the fact that the encoder of this basic approach needs to compress a whole source sentence into a single vector. Here we describe the attention-based neural machine translation.

Neural machine translation aims at building a single neural network that takes as input a source sequence $X = (x_1, \ldots, x_{T_x})$ and generates a corresponding translation $Y = (y_1, \ldots, y_{T_y})$. Each symbol in both source and target sentences, x_t or y_t, is an integer index of the symbol in a vocabulary.

The encoder of the attention-based model encodes a source sentence into a set of context vectors $C = \{\mathbf{h}_1, \mathbf{h}_2, \ldots, \mathbf{h}_{T_x}\}$, whose size varies w.r.t. the length of the source sentence. This context set is constructed by a bidirectional recurrent neural network (RNN) which consists of a forward RNN and reverse RNN. The forward RNN reads the source sentence from the first token until the last one, resulting in the forward context vectors $\left\{\overrightarrow{\mathbf{h}}_1, \ldots, \overrightarrow{\mathbf{h}}_{T_x}\right\}$, where

$$\overrightarrow{\mathbf{h}}_t = \overrightarrow{\Psi}_{\text{enc}}\left(\overrightarrow{\mathbf{h}}_{t-1}, \mathbf{E}_x\left[x_t\right]\right),$$

and $\mathbf{E}_x \in \mathbb{R}^{|V_x| \times d}$ is an embedding matrix containing row vectors of the source symbols. The reverse RNN in an opposite direction, resulting in $\left\{ \overleftarrow{\mathbf{h}}_1, \ldots, \overleftarrow{\mathbf{h}}_{T_x} \right\}$, where

$$\overleftarrow{\mathbf{h}}_t = \overleftarrow{\Psi}_{\text{enc}} \left(\overleftarrow{\mathbf{h}}_{t+1}, \mathbf{E}_x \left[x_t \right] \right).$$

$\overrightarrow{\Psi}_{\text{enc}}$ and $\overleftarrow{\Psi}_{\text{enc}}$ are recurrent activation functions such as long short-term memory units (LSTM, (Hochreiter and Schmidhuber, 1997)) or gated recurrent units (GRU, (Cho et al., 2014b)). At each position in the source sentence, the forward and reverse context vectors are concatenated to form a full context vector, i.e.,

$$\mathbf{h}_t = \left[\overrightarrow{\mathbf{h}}_t; \overleftarrow{\mathbf{h}}_t \right]. \tag{1}$$

The decoder, which is implemented as an RNN as well, generates one symbol at a time, the translation of the source sentence, based on the context set returned by the encoder. At each time step t in the decoder, a time-dependent context vector $\mathbf{c}_t$ is computed based on the previous hidden state of the decoder $\mathbf{z}_{t-1}$, the previously decoded symbol $\tilde{y}_{t-1}$ and the whole context set C.

This starts by computing the relevance score of each context vector as

$$e_{t,i} = f_{\text{score}}(\mathbf{h}_i, \mathbf{z}_{t-1}, \mathbf{E}_y \left[\tilde{y}_{t-1} \right]), \tag{2}$$

for all $i = 1, \ldots, T_x$. f_{score} can be implemented in various ways (Luong et al., 2015b), but in this work, we use a simple single-layer feedforward network. This relevance score measures how relevant the i-th context vector of the source sentence is in deciding the next symbol in the translation. These relevance scores are further normalized:

$$\alpha_{t,i} = \frac{\exp(e_{t,i})}{\sum_{j=1}^{T_x} \exp(e_{t,j})}, \tag{3}$$

and we call $\alpha_{t,i}$ the attention weight.

The time-dependent context vector $\mathbf{c}_t$ is then the weighted sum of the context vectors with their weights being the attention weights from above:

$$\mathbf{c}_t = \sum_{i=1}^{T_x} \alpha_{t,i} \mathbf{h}_i. \tag{4}$$

With this time-dependent context vector $\mathbf{c}_t$, the previous hidden state $\mathbf{z}_{t-1}$ and the previously decoded symbol $\tilde{y}_{t-1}$, the decoder's hidden state is updated by

$$\mathbf{z}_t = \Psi_{\text{dec}} \left(\mathbf{z}_{t-1}, \mathbf{E}_y \left[\tilde{y}_{t-1} \right], \mathbf{c}_t \right), \tag{5}$$

where Ψ_{dec} is a recurrent activation function.

The initial hidden state $\mathbf{z}_0$ of the decoder is initialized based on the last hidden state of the reverse RNN:

$$\mathbf{z}_0 = f_{\text{init}} \left(\overleftarrow{\mathbf{h}}_{T_x} \right), \tag{6}$$

where f_{init} is a feedforward network with one or two hidden layers.

The probability distribution for the next target symbol is computed by

$$p(y_t = k | \tilde{y}_{<t}, X) \propto e^{g_k(\mathbf{z}_t, \mathbf{c}_t, \mathbf{E}[\tilde{y}_{t-1}])}, \tag{7}$$

where g_k is a parametric function that returns the unnormalized probability for the next target symbol being k.

Training this attention-based model is done by maximizing the conditional log-likelihood

$$\mathcal{L}(\boldsymbol{\theta}) = \frac{1}{N} \sum_{n=1}^{N} \sum_{t=1}^{T_y} \log p(y_t = y_t^{(n)} | y_{<t}^{(n)}, X^{(n)}), \tag{8}$$

where the log probability inside the inner summation is from Eq. (7). It is important to note that the ground-truth target symbols $y_t^{(n)}$ are used during training. The entire model is differentiable, and the gradient of the log-likelihood function with respect to all the parameters $\boldsymbol{\theta}$ can be computed efficiently by backpropagation. This makes it straightforward to use stochastic gradient descent or its variants to train the whole model jointly to maximize the translation performance.

3 Multi-Way, Multilingual Translation

In this section, we discuss issues and our solutions in extending the conventional *single-pair* attention-based neural machine translation into *multi-way, multilingual* model.

Problem Definition We assume $N > 1$ source languages $\{X^1, X^2, \ldots, X^N\}$ and $M > 1$ target languages $\{Y^1, Y^2, \ldots, Y^M\}$, and the availability of $L \leq M \times N$ *bilingual* parallel corpora $\{D_1, \ldots, D_L\}$, each of which is a set of sentence pairs of one source and one target language. We use $s(D_l)$ and $t(D_l)$ to indicate the source and target languages of the l-th parallel corpus.

For each parallel corpus l, we can directly use the log-likelihood function from Eq. (8) to define a pair-specific log-likelihood $\mathcal{L}^{s(D_l),t(D_l)}$. Then, the goal of multi-way, multilingual neural machine translation is to build a model that maximizes the joint log-likelihood function $\mathcal{L}(\boldsymbol{\theta}) = \frac{1}{L}\sum_{l=1}^{L}\mathcal{L}^{s(D_l),t(D_l)}(\boldsymbol{\theta})$. Once the training is over, the model can do translation from any of the source languages to any of the target languages included in the parallel training corpora.

3.1 Existing Approaches

Neural Machine Translation without Attention In (Luong et al., 2015a), the authors extended the basic encoder-decoder network for multitask neural machine translation. As they extended the basic encoder-decoder network, their model effectively becomes a set of encoders and decoders, where each of the encoder projects a source sentence into a common vector space. The point in the common space is then decoded into different languages.

The major difference between (Luong et al., 2015a) and our work is that we extend the attention-based encoder-decoder instead of the basic model. This is an important contribution, as the attention-based neural machine translation has become *de facto* standard in neural translation literatures recently (Jean et al., 2014; Jean et al., 2015; Luong et al., 2015b; Sennrich et al., 2015b; Sennrich et al., 2015a), by opposition to the basic encoder-decoder.

There are two minor differences as well. First, they do not consider multilinguality in depth. The authors of (Luong et al., 2015a) tried only a single language pair, English and German, in their model. Second, they only report translation perplexity, which is not a widely used metric for measuring translation quality. To more easily compare with other machine translation approaches it would be important to evaluate metrics such as BLEU, which counts the number of matched n-grams between the generated and reference translations.

One-to-Many Neural Machine Translation The authors of (Dong et al., 2015) earlier proposed a multilingual translation model based on the *attention-based neural machine translation*. Unlike this paper, they only tried it on one-to-many translation, similarly to earlier work by (Collobert et al., 2011) where one-to-many natural language processing was done. In this setting, it is trivial to extend the single-pair attention-based model into multilingual translation by simply having a single encoder for a source language and pairs of a decoder and attention mechanism (Eq. (2)) for each target language. We will shortly discuss more on why, with the attention mechanism, one-to-many translation is trivial, while multi-way translation is not.

3.2 Challenges

A quick look at neural machine translation seems to suggest a straightforward path toward incorporating multiple languages in both source and target sides. As described earlier already in the introduction, the basic idea is simple. We assign a separate encoder to each source language and a separate decoder to each target language. The encoder will project a source sentence in its own language into a common, language-agnostic space, from which the decoder will generate a translation in its own language.

Unlike training multiple single-pair neural translation models, in this case, the encoders and decoders are shared across multiple pairs. This is computationally beneficial, as the number of parameters grows only linearly with respect to the number of languages ($O(L)$), in contrary to training separate single-pair models, in which case the number of parameters grows quadratically ($O(L^2)$.)

The attention mechanism, which was initially called a soft-alignment model in (Bahdanau et al., 2014), aligns a (potentially non-contiguous) source phrase to a target word. This alignment process is largely specific to a language pair, and it is not clear whether an alignment mechanism for one language pair can also work for another pair.

The most naive solution to this issue is to have $O(L^2)$ attention mechanisms that are *not* shared across multiple language pairs. Each attention mechanism takes care of a single pair of source and

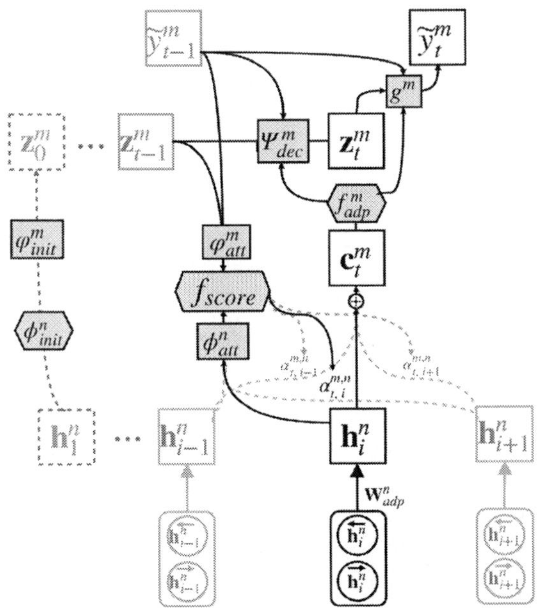

Figure 1: One step of the proposed multi-way. multilingual Neural Machine Translation model, for the n-th encoder and the m-th decoder at time step t. Shaded boxes are parametric functions and square boxes represent intermediate variables of the model. Initializer network is also illustrated as the left-most network with dashed boxes. Notice, all the shared components are drawn with diamond boxes. See Sec. 4 for details.

target languages. This is the approach employed in (Dong et al., 2015), where each decoder had its own attention mechanism.

There are two issues with this naive approach. First, unlike what has been hoped initially with multilingual neural machine translation, the number of parameters again grows quadratically w.r.t. the number of languages. Second and more importantly, having separate attention mechanisms makes it less likely for the model to fully benefit from having multiple tasks (Caruana, 1997), especially for transfer learning towards resource-poor languages.

In short, the major challenge in building a multi-way, multilingual neural machine translation is in avoiding independent (i.e., quadratically many) attention mechanisms. There are two questions behind this challenge. The first one is whether it is even possible to share a single attention mechanism across multiple language pairs. The second question immediately follows: how can we build a neural translation model to share a single attention mecha-

nism for all the language pairs in consideration?

4 Multi-Way, Multilingual Model

We describe in this section, the proposed *multi-way, multilingual attention-based neural machine translation*. The proposed model consists of N encoders $\{\Psi^n_{\mathrm{enc}}\}_{n=1}^N$ (see Eq. (1)), M decoders $\{(\Psi^m_{\mathrm{dec}}, g^m, f^m_{\mathrm{init}})\}_{m=1}^M$ (see Eqs. (5)–(7)) and a shared attention mechanism f_{score} (see Eq. (2) in the single language pair case).

Encoders Similarly to (Luong et al., 2015b), we have one encoder per source language, meaning that a single encoder is shared for translating the language to multiple target languages. In order to handle different source languages better, we may use for each source language a different type of encoder, for instance, of different size (in terms of the number of recurrent units) or of different architecture (convolutional instead of recurrent.)[1] This allows us to efficiently incorporate varying types of languages in the proposed multilingual translation model.

This however implies that the dimensionality of the context vectors in Eq. (1) may differ across source languages. Therefore, we add to the original bidirectional encoder from Sec. 2, a linear transformation layer consisting of a weight matrix $\mathbf{W}^n_{\mathrm{adp}}$ and a bias vector $\mathbf{b}^n_{\mathrm{adp}}$, which is used to project each context vector into a common dimensional space:

$$\mathbf{h}^n_t = \mathbf{W}^n_{\mathrm{adp}}\left[\overrightarrow{\mathbf{h}}_t; \overleftarrow{\mathbf{h}}_t\right] + \mathbf{b}^n_{\mathrm{adp}}, \qquad (9)$$

where $\mathbf{W}^n_{\mathrm{adp}} \in \mathbb{R}^{d \times (\dim \overrightarrow{\mathbf{h}}_t + \dim \overleftarrow{\mathbf{h}}_t)}$ and $\mathbf{b}^n_{\mathrm{adp}} \in \mathbb{R}^d$.

In addition, each encoder exposes two transformation functions ϕ^n_{att} and ϕ^n_{init}. The first transformer ϕ^n_{att} transforms a context vector to be compatible with a shared attention mechanism:

$$\tilde{\mathbf{h}}^n_t = \phi^n_{\mathrm{att}}(\mathbf{h}^n_t). \qquad (10)$$

This transformer can be implemented as any type of parametric function, and in this paper, we simply apply an element-wise tanh to $\mathbf{h}^n_t$.

---

[1] For the pairs without enough parallel data, one may also consider using smaller encoders to prevent over-fitting.

The second transformer ϕ_{init}^n transforms the first context vector $\mathbf{h}_1^n$ to be compatible with the initializer of the decoder's hidden state (see Eq. (6)):

$$\hat{\mathbf{h}}_1^n = \phi_{\text{init}}^n(\mathbf{h}_1^n). \tag{11}$$

Similarly to ϕ_{att}^n, it can be implemented as any type of parametric function. In this paper, we use a feedforward network with a single hidden layer and share one network ϕ_{init} for all encoder-decoder pairs.

Decoders We first start with an initialization of the decoder's hidden state. Each decoder has its own parametric function φ_{init}^m that maps the last context vector $\hat{\mathbf{h}}_{T_x}^n$ of the source encoder from Eq. (11) into the initial hidden state:

$$\mathbf{z}_0^m = \varphi_{\text{init}}^m(\hat{\mathbf{h}}_{T_x}^n) = \varphi_{\text{init}}^m(\phi_{\text{init}}^n(\mathbf{h}_1^n))$$

φ_{init}^m can be any parametric function, and in this paper, we used a feedforward network with a single tanh hidden layer.

Each decoder exposes a parametric function φ_{att}^m that transforms its hidden state and the previously decoded symbol to be compatible with a shared attention mechanism. This transformer is a parametric function that takes as input the previous hidden state $\mathbf{z}_{t-1}^m$ and the previous symbol $\tilde{y}_{t-1}^m$ and returns a vector for the attention mechanism:

$$\tilde{\mathbf{z}}_{t-1}^m = \varphi_{\text{att}}^m\left(\mathbf{z}_{t-1}^m, \mathbf{E}_y^m\left[\tilde{y}_{t-1}^m\right]\right) \tag{12}$$

which replaces $\mathbf{z}_{t-1}$ in Eq. 2. In this paper, we use a feedforward network with a single tanh hidden layer for each φ_{att}^m.

Given the previous hidden state $\mathbf{z}_{t-1}^m$, previously decoded symbol $\tilde{y}_{t-1}^m$ and the time-dependent context vector $\mathbf{c}_t^m$, which we will discuss shortly, the decoder updates its hidden state:

$$\mathbf{z}_t = \Psi_{\text{dec}}\left(\mathbf{z}_{t-1}^m, \mathbf{E}_y^m\left[\tilde{y}_{t-1}^m\right], f_{\text{adp}}^m(\mathbf{c}_t^m)\right),$$

where f_{adp}^m affine-transforms the time-dependent context vector to be of the same dimensionality as the decoder. We share a single affine-transformation layer f_{adp}^m, for all the decoders in this paper.

Once the hidden state is updated, the probability distribution over the next symbol is computed exactly as for the pair-specific model (see Eq. (7).)

| | # Symbols | | # Sentence |
	# En	Other	Pairs
En-Fr	1.022b	2.213b	38.85m
En-Cs	186.57m	185.58m	12.12m
En-Ru	50.62m	55.76m	2.32m
En-De	111.77m	117.41m	4.15m
En-Fi	52.76m	43.67m	2.03m

Table 1: Statistics of the parallel corpora from WMT'15. Symbols are BPE-based sub-words.

Attention Mechanism Unlike the encoders and decoders of which there is an instance for each language, there is only a single attention mechanism, shared across all the language pairs. This shared mechanism uses the *attention-specific* vectors $\tilde{\mathbf{h}}_t^n$ and $\tilde{\mathbf{z}}_{t-1}^m$ from the encoder and decoder, respectively.

The relevance score of each context vector $\mathbf{h}_t^n$ is computed based on the decoder's previous hidden state $\mathbf{z}_{t-1}^m$ and previous symbol $\tilde{y}_{t-1}^m$:

$$e_{t,i}^{m,n} = f_{\text{score}}\left(\tilde{\mathbf{h}}_t^n, \tilde{\mathbf{z}}_{t-1}^m, \tilde{y}_{t-1}^m\right)$$

These scores are normalized according to Eq. (3) to become the attention weights $\alpha_{t,i}^{m,n}$.

With these attention weights, the time-dependent context vector is computed as the weighted sum of the *original* context vectors: $\mathbf{c}_t^{m,n} = \sum_{i=1}^{T_x} \alpha_{t,i}^{m,n} \mathbf{h}_i^n$.

See Fig. 1 for the illustration.

5 Experiment Settings

5.1 Datasets

We evaluate the proposed multi-way, multilingual translation model on all the pairs available from WMT'15–English (En) $\leftrightarrow$ French (Fr), Czech (Cs), German (De), Russian (Ru) and Finnish (Fi)–, totalling ten directed pairs. For each pair, we concatenate all the available parallel corpora from WMT'15 and use it as a training set. We use newstest-2013 as a development set and newstest-2015 as a test set, in all the pairs other than Fi-En. In the case of Fi-En, we use newsdev-2015 and newstest-2015 as a development set and test set, respectively.

Data Preprocessing Each training corpus is tokenized using the tokenizer script from the Moses decoder.[2] The tokenized training corpus is cleaned fol-

[2]`https://github.com/moses-smt/mosesdecoder/blob/master/scripts/tokenizer/tokenizer.perl`

lowing the procedure in (Jean et al., 2015). Instead of using space-separated tokens, or words, we use sub-word units extracted by byte pair encoding, as recently proposed in (Sennrich et al., 2015b). For each and every language, we include 30k sub-word symbols in a vocabulary. See Table 1 for the statistics of the final, preprocessed training corpora.

Evaluation Metric   We mainly use BLEU as an evaluation metric using the multi-bleu script from Moses.[3] BLEU is computed on the tokenized text after merging the BPE-based sub-word symbols. We further look at the average log-probability assigned to reference translations by the trained model as an additional evaluation metric, as a way to measure the model's density estimation performance free from any error caused by approximate decoding.

5.2   Two Scenarios

Low-Resource Translation   First, we investigate the effect of the proposed multi-way, multilingual model on low-resource language-pair translation. Among the six languages from WMT'15, we choose En, De and Fi as source languages, and En and De as target languages. We control the amount of the parallel corpus of each pair out of three to be 5%, 10%, 20% and 40% of the original corpus. In other words, we train four models with different sizes of parallel corpus for each language pair (En-De, De-En, Fi-En.)

As a baseline, we train a single-pair model for each multi-way, multilingual model. We further finetune the single-pair model to incorporate the target-side monolingual corpus consisting of all the target side text from the other language pairs (e.g., when a single-pair model was trained on Fi-En, the target-side monolingual corpus consists of the target sides from De-En.) This is done by the recently proposed deep fusion (Gulcehre et al., 2015). The latter is included to tell whether any improvement from the multilingual model is simply due to the increased amount of target-side monolingual corpus.

Large-scale Translation   We train one multi-way, multilingual model that has six encoders and six decoders, corresponding to the six languages from

<hr>

[3]`https://github.com/moses-smt/`
`mosesdecoder/blob/master/scripts/generic/`
`multi-bleu.perl`

	Size	Single	Single+DF	Multi
Fi→En	100k	5.06/3.96	4.98/3.99	6.2/**5.17**
	200k	7.1/6.16	7.21/6.17	8.84/**7.53**
	400k	9.11/7.85	9.31/8.18	11.09/**9.98**
	800k	11.08/9.96	11.59/10.15	12.73/**11.28**
De→En	210k	14.27/13.2	14.65/13.88	16.96/**16.26**
	420k	18.32/17.32	18.51/17.62	19.81/**19.63**
	840k	21/19.93	21.69/20.75	22.17/**21.93**
	1.68m	23.38/23.01	23.33/22.86	23.86/**23.52**
En→De	210k	11.44/11.57	11.71/11.16	12.63/**12.68**
	420k	14.28/14.25	14.88/15.05	15.01/**15.67**
	840k	17.09/17.44	17.21/17.88	17.33/**18.14**
	1.68m	19.09/19.6	19.36/20.13	19.23/**20.59**

Table 2: BLEU scores where the target pair's parallel corpus is constrained to be 5%, 10%, 20% and 40% of the original size. We report the BLEU scores on the development and test sets (separated by /) by the single-pair model (Single), the single-pair model with monolingual corpus (Single+DF) and the proposed multi-way, multilingual model (Multi).

WMT'15; En, Fr, De, Cs, Ru, Fi → En, Fr, De, Cs, Ru, Fi. We use the full corpora for all of them.

5.3   Model Architecture

Each symbol, either source or target, is projected on a 620-dimensional space. The encoder is a bidirectional recurrent neural network with 1,000 gated recurrent units (GRU) in each direction, and the decoder is a recurrent neural network with also 1,000 GRU's.   The decoder's output function g_k from Eq. (7) is a feedforward network with 1,000 $\tanh$ hidden units.   The dimensionalities of the context vector $\mathbf{h}_t^n$ in Eq. (9), the attention-specific context vector $\tilde{\mathbf{h}}_t^n$ in Eq. (10) and the attention-specific decoder hidden state $\tilde{\mathbf{h}}_{t-1}^m$ in Eq. (12) are all set to 1,200.

We use the same type of encoder for every source language, and the same type of decoder for every target language.   The only difference between the single-pair models and the proposed multilingual ones is the numbers of encoders N and decoders M. We leave those multilingual translation specific components, such as the ones in Eqs. (9)–(12), in the single-pair models in order to keep the number of shared parameters constant.

5.4   Training

Basic Settings   We train each model using stochastic gradient descent (SGD) with Adam (Kingma and

		Dir	Fr (39m)		Cs (12m)		De (4.2m)		Ru (2.3m)		Fi (2m)	
			$\to$ En	En $\to$	$\to$ En	En $\to$	$\to$ En	En $\to$	$\to$ En	En $\to$	$\to$ En	En $\to$
(a) BLEU	Dev	Single	27.22	26.91	21.24	15.9	24.13	20.49	21.04	18.06	13.15	9.59
		Multi	26.09	25.04	21.23	14.42	23.66	19.17	21.48	17.89	12.97	8.92
	Test	Single	27.94	**29.7**	20.32	**13.84**	24	**21.75**	22.44	**19.54**	12.24	**9.23**
		Multi	**28.06**	27.88	**20.57**	13.29	**24.20**	20.59	**23.44**	19.39	**12.61**	8.98
(b) LL	Dev	Single	-50.53	-53.38	-60.69	-69.56	-54.76	-61.21	-60.19	-65.81	-88.44	-91.75
		Multi	-50.6	-56.55	-54.46	-70.76	-54.14	-62.34	-54.09	-63.75	-74.84	-88.02
	Test	Single	-43.34	**-45.07**	-60.03	**-64.34**	-57.81	**-59.55**	-60.65	-60.29	-88.66	-94.23
		Multi	**-42.22**	-46.29	**-54.66**	-64.80	**-53.85**	-60.23	**-54.49**	**-58.63**	**-71.26**	**-88.09**

Table 3: (a) BLEU scores and (b) average log-probabilities for all the five languages from WMT'15.

Ba, 2015) as an adaptive learning rate algorithm. We use the initial learning rate of $2 \cdot 10^{-4}$ and leave all the other hyperparameters as suggested in (Kingma and Ba, 2015). Each SGD update is computed using a minibatch of 80 examples, unless the model is parallelized over two GPUs, in which case we use a minibatch of 60 examples. We only use sentences of length up to 50 symbols during training. We clip the norm of the gradient to be no more than 1 (Pascanu et al., 2012). All training runs are early-stopped based on BLEU on the development set. As we observed in preliminary experiments better scores on the development set when finetuning the shared parameters and output layers of the decoders in the case of multilingual models, we do this for all the multilingual models. During finetuning, we clip the norm of the gradient to be no more than 5. [4]

Schedule As we have access only to bilingual corpora, each sentence pair updates only a subset of the parameters. Excessive updates based on a single language pair may bias the model away from the other pairs. To avoid it, we cycle through all the language pairs, one pair at a time, in Fi⇆En, De⇆En, Fr⇆En, Cs⇆En, Ru⇆En order. [5] Initial experiments on random scheduling across pairs and increasing the number of consecutive updates for a pair did not give better results and left as a future work.

Model Parallelism The size of the multilingual model grows linearly w.r.t. the number of languages. We observed that a single model that handles six source and six target languages does not fit in a single GPU[6] during training. We address this by distributing computational paths according to different translation pairs over multiple GPUs, following (Ding et al., 2014). The shared parameters, mainly related to the attention mechanism, is duplicated on both GPUs.

In more detail, we distribute language pairs across multiple GPUs such that those pairs in each GPU shares either an encoder or decoder. This allows us to avoid synchronizing a large subset of the parameters across multiple GPUs. Only the shared attention mechanism, which has substantially less parameters, is duplicated on all the GPUs. Before each update, we build a minibatch to contain an approximately equal number of examples per GPU in order to minimize any discrepancy in computation among multiple GPUs. Each GPU then computes the gradient w.r.t. the parameters on its own board and updates the local parameters. The gradients w.r.t. the attention mechanism are synchronized using direct memory access (DMA). In this way, we achieve near-linear speed-up.

6 Results and Analysis

Low-Resource Translation It is clear from Table 2 that the proposed model (Multi) outperforms the single-pair one (Single) in all the cases. This is true even when the single-pair model is strengthened with a target-side monolingual corpus (Single+DF). This suggests that the benefit of generalization from having multiple languages goes beyond that of simply having more target-side monolingual corpus. The performance gap grows as the size of target parallel corpus decreases.

---

[4] All the training details as well as the code is available at `http://github.com/nyu-dl/dl4mt-multi`.

[5] ⇆ indicates simultaneous updates on two GPUs.

[6] NVidia Titan X with 12GB on-board memory

Further, directly adding monolingual data from all languages during training, e.g. like an auto-encoder, En→ En, De→ De etc. is straightforward. In fact, experiments based on the autoencoder reconstruction criterion resulted in rapid memorization, copying source tokens without capturing semantics, resulting in worse performance. Exploring ways to leverage unlabeled data and regularizing the monolingual paths in the multi-way, multilingual architecture, is therefore left as a future work.

Large-Scale Translation In Table 3, we observe that the proposed multilingual model outperforms or is comparable to the single-pair models for the majority of the all ten pairs/directions considered. This happens in terms of both BLEU and average log-probability. This is encouraging, considering that there are twice more parameters in the whole set of single-pair models than in the multilingual model.

Note that, the numbers are below state-of-the-art neural MT systems, which use large vocabularies, unknown replacements techniques and ensembling. We mainly focused on comparing the proposed model against single-pair models without these techniques in order to carefully control and analyze the effect of having multiple languages. It is indeed required in the future to analyze the consequence of having both multiple languages and other such techniques in a single model.

It is worthwhile to notice that the benefit is more apparent when the model translates from a foreign language to English. This may be due to the fact that all of the parallel corpora include English as either a source or target language, leading to a better parameter estimation of the English decoder. In the future, a strategy of using a pseudo-parallel corpus to increase the amount of training examples for the decoders of other languages (Sennrich et al., 2015a) should be investigated to confirm this conjecture.

7   Conclusion

In this paper, we proposed multi-way, multilingual attention-based neural machine translation. The proposed approach allows us to build a single neural network that can handle multiple source and target languages simultaneously. The proposed model is a step forward from the recent works on multilingual neural translation, in the sense that we support attention mechanism, compared to (Luong et al., 2015a) and multi-way translation, compared to (Dong et al., 2015). Furthermore, we evaluate the proposed model on large-scale experiments, using the full set of parallel corpora from WMT'15.

We empirically evaluate the proposed model in large-scale experiments using all five languages from WMT'15 with the full set of parallel corpora and also in the settings with artificially controlled amount of the target parallel corpus. In both of the settings, we observed the benefits of the proposed multilingual neural translation model over having a set of single-pair models. The improvement was especially clear in the cases of translating low-resource language pairs.

We observed the larger improvements when translating to English. We conjecture that this is due to a higher availability of English in most parallel corpora, leading to a better parameter estimation of the English decoder. More research on this phenomenon in the future will result in further improvements from using the proposed model. Also, all the other techniques proposed recently, such as ensembling and large vocabulary tricks, need to be tried together with the proposed multilingual model to improve the translation quality even further. Finally, an interesting future work is to use the proposed model to translate between a language pair not included in a set of training corpus.

Acknowledgments

We acknowledge the support of the following agencies for research funding and computing support: NSERC, Calcul Québec, Compute Canada, the Canada Research Chairs, CIFAR and Samsung. OF thanks the support by TUBITAK (2214/A). KC thanks the support by Facebook and Google (Google Faculty Award 2016).

References

Dzmitry Bahdanau, Kyunghyun Cho, and Yoshua Bengio. 2014. Neural machine translation by jointly learning to align and translate. In *ICLR 2015*.

Léon Bottou, Yoshua Bengio, and Yann Le Cun. 1997. Global training of document processing systems using graph transformer networks. In *Computer Vision and Pattern Recognition, 1997. Proceedings., 1997*

IEEE Computer Society Conference on, pages 489–494. IEEE.

Rich Caruana. 1997. Multitask learning. *Machine learning*, 28(1):41–75.

Kyunghyun Cho, Bart van Merriënboer, Dzmitry Bahdanau, and Yoshua Bengio. 2014a. On the properties of neural machine translation: Encoder–Decoder approaches. In *Eighth Workshop on Syntax, Semantics and Structure in Statistical Translation*, October.

Kyunghyun Cho, Bart Van Merriënboer, Caglar Gulcehre, Dzmitry Bahdanau, Fethi Bougares, Holger Schwenk, and Yoshua Bengio. 2014b. Learning phrase representations using rnn encoder-decoder for statistical machine translation. *arXiv preprint arXiv:1406.1078*.

Jan K Chorowski, Dzmitry Bahdanau, Dmitriy Serdyuk, Kyunghyun Cho, and Yoshua Bengio. 2015. Attention-based models for speech recognition. In *Advances in Neural Information Processing Systems*, pages 577–585.

Ronan Collobert, Jason Weston, Léon Bottou, Michael Karlen, Koray Kavukcuoglu, and Pavel Kuksa. 2011. Natural language processing (almost) from scratch. *The Journal of Machine Learning Research*, 12:2493–2537.

Weiguang Ding, Ruoyan Wang, Fei Mao, and Graham W. Taylor. 2014. Theano-based large-scale visual recognition with multiple gpus. *arXiv:1412.2302*.

Daxiang Dong, Hua Wu, Wei He, Dianhai Yu, and Haifeng Wang. 2015. Multi-task learning for multiple language translation. ACL.

Alex Graves, Santiago Fernández, Faustino Gomez, and Jürgen Schmidhuber. 2006. Connectionist temporal classification: labelling unsegmented sequence data with recurrent neural networks. In *Proceedings of the 23rd international conference on Machine learning*, pages 369–376. ACM.

Alex Graves, Marcus Liwicki, Santiago Fernández, Roman Bertolami, Horst Bunke, and Jürgen Schmidhuber. 2009. A novel connectionist system for unconstrained handwriting recognition. *Pattern Analysis and Machine Intelligence, IEEE Transactions on*, 31(5):855–868.

Caglar Gulcehre, Orhan Firat, Kelvin Xu, Kyunghyun Cho, Loic Barrault, Huei-Chi Lin, Fethi Bougares, Holger Schwenk, and Yoshua Bengio. 2015. On using monolingual corpora in neural machine translation. *arXiv preprint arXiv:1503.03535*.

Sepp Hochreiter and Jürgen Schmidhuber. 1997. Long short-term memory. *Neural computation*, 9(8):1735–1780.

Sébastien Jean, Kyunghyun Cho, Roland Memisevic, and Yoshua Bengio. 2014. On using very large target vocabulary for neural machine translation. In *ACL 2015*.

Sébastien Jean, Orhan Firat, Kyunghyun Cho, Roland Memisevic, and Yoshua Bengio. 2015. Montreal neural machine translation systems for wmt'15. In *Proceedings of the Tenth Workshop on Statistical Machine Translation*, pages 134–140, Lisbon, Portugal, September. Association for Computational Linguistics.

Diederik Kingma and Jimmy Ba. 2015. Adam: A method for stochastic optimization. *The International Conference on Learning Representations (ICLR)*.

Minh-Thang Luong, Quoc V Le, Ilya Sutskever, Oriol Vinyals, and Lukasz Kaiser. 2015a. Multi-task sequence to sequence learning. *arXiv preprint arXiv:1511.06114*.

Minh-Thang Luong, Hieu Pham, and Christopher D Manning. 2015b. Effective approaches to attention-based neural machine translation. *arXiv preprint arXiv:1508.04025*.

Razvan Pascanu, Tomas Mikolov, and Yoshua Bengio. 2012. On the difficulty of training recurrent neural networks. *arXiv preprint arXiv:1211.5063*.

Rico Sennrich, Barry Haddow, and Alexandra Birch. 2015a. Improving neural machine translation models with monolingual data. *arXiv preprint arXiv:1511.06709*.

Rico Sennrich, Barry Haddow, and Alexandra Birch. 2015b. Neural machine translation of rare words with subword units. *arXiv preprint arXiv:1508.07909*.

Ilya Sutskever, Oriol Vinyals, and Quoc VV Le. 2014. Sequence to sequence learning with neural networks. In *Advances in neural information processing systems*, pages 3104–3112.

Incorporating Structural Alignment Biases into an Attentional Neural Translation Model

Trevor Cohn and **Cong Duy Vu Hoang** and **Ekaterina Vymolova**
University of Melbourne
Melbourne, VIC, Australia
`tcohn@unimelb.edu.au` and `{vhoang2,evylomova}@student.unimelb.edu.au`

Kaisheng Yao
Microsoft Research
Redmond, WA, USA
`kaisheng.YAO@microsoft.com`

Chris Dyer
Carnegie Mellon University
Pittsburgh, PA, USA
`cdyer@cmu.edu`

Gholamreza Haffari
Monash University
Clayton, VIC, Australia
`gholamreza.haffari@monash.edu`

Abstract

Neural encoder-decoder models of machine translation have achieved impressive results, rivalling traditional translation models. However their modelling formulation is overly simplistic, and omits several key inductive biases built into traditional models. In this paper we extend the attentional neural translation model to include structural biases from word based alignment models, including positional bias, Markov conditioning, fertility and agreement over translation directions. We show improvements over a baseline attentional model and standard phrase-based model over several language pairs, evaluating on difficult languages in a low resource setting.

1 Introduction

Recently, models of end-to-end machine translation based on neural network classification have been shown to produce excellent translations, rivalling or in some cases surpassing traditional statistical machine translation systems (Kalchbrenner and Blunsom, 2013; Sutskever et al., 2014; Bahdanau et al., 2015). This is despite the neural approaches using an overall simpler model, with fewer assumptions about the learning and prediction problem.

Broadly, neural approaches are based around the notion of an *encoder-decoder* (Sutskever et al., 2014), in which the source language is *encoded* into a distributed representation, followed by a *decoding* step which generates the target translation. We focus on the *attentional model* of translation (Bahdanau et al., 2015) which uses a dynamic representation of the source sentence while allowing the decoder to *attend* to different parts of the source as it generates the target sentence. The attentional model raises intriguing opportunities, given the correspondence between the notions of attention and alignment in traditional word-based machine translation models (Brown et al., 1993).

In this paper we map modelling biases from word based translation models into the attentional model, such that known linguistic elements of translation can be better captured. We incorporate *absolute positional bias* whereby word order tends to be similar between the source sentence and its translation (e.g., IBM Model 2 and (Dyer et al., 2013)), *fertility* whereby each instance of a source word type tends to be translated into a consistent number of target tokens (e.g., IBM Models 3, 4, 5), *relative position bias* whereby prior preferences for monotonic alignments/attention can be encouraged (e.g., IBM Model 4, 5 and HMM-based Alignment (Vogel et al., 1996)), and *alignment consistency* whereby the attention in *both* translation directions are encouraged to agree (e.g. symmetrisation heuristics (Och and Ney, 2003) or joint modelling (Liang et al., 2006; Ganchev et al., 2008)).

We provide an empirical analysis of incorporating the above structural biases into the attentional model, considering low resource translation scenario over four language-pairs. Our results demonstrate consistent improvements over vanilla encoder-

Proceedings of NAACL-HLT 2016, pages 876–885,
San Diego, California, June 12-17, 2016. ©2016 Association for Computational Linguistics

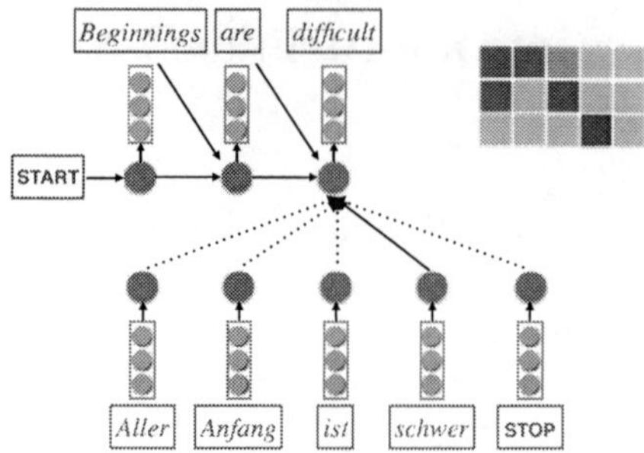

Figure 1: Attentional model of translation (Bahdanau et al., 2015). The encoder is shown below the decoder, and the edges connecting the two corresponding to the attention mechanism. Heavy edges denote a higher attention weight, and these values are also displayed in matrix form, with one row for each target word.

decoder and attentional model in terms of the perplexity and BLEU score, e.g. up to 3.5 BLEU points when re-ranking the candidate translations generated by a state-of-the-art phrase based model.

2 The attentional model of translation

We start by reviewing the attentional model of translation (Bahdanau et al., 2015), as illustrated in Fig. 1, before presenting our extensions in §3.

Encoder The encoding of the source sentence is formulated using a pair of RNNs (denoted *bi-RNN*) one operating left-to-right over the input sequence and another operating right-to-left,

$$\boldsymbol{h}_i^{\rightarrow} = \mathrm{RNN}(\boldsymbol{h}_{i-1}^{\rightarrow}, \boldsymbol{r}_{s_i}^{(\mathrm{s})})$$

$$\boldsymbol{h}_i^{\leftarrow} = \mathrm{RNN}(\boldsymbol{h}_{i+1}^{\leftarrow}, \boldsymbol{r}_{s_i}^{(\mathrm{s})})$$

where $\boldsymbol{h}_i^{\rightarrow}$ and $\boldsymbol{h}_i^{\leftarrow}$ are the RNN hidden states. The left-to-right RNN function is defined as

$$\boldsymbol{h}_i^{\rightarrow} = \tanh\left(\boldsymbol{W}_{si}^{\rightarrow}\boldsymbol{r}_{s_i}^{(\mathrm{s})} + \boldsymbol{W}_{sh}^{\rightarrow}\boldsymbol{h}_{i-1}^{\rightarrow} + \boldsymbol{b}_s^{\rightarrow}\right) \quad (1)$$

where $\boldsymbol{h}_0^{\rightarrow} \in \mathbb{R}^H$ is a learned parameter vector, as are $\mathbf{R}^{(\mathrm{s})} \in \mathbb{R}^{V_S \times E}$, $\boldsymbol{W}_{si}^{\rightarrow} \in \mathbb{R}^{H \times E}$, $\boldsymbol{W}_{sh}^{\rightarrow} \in \mathbb{R}^{H \times H}$ and $\boldsymbol{b}_s^{\rightarrow} \in \mathbb{R}^H$, with H the number of hidden units, V_S the size of the source vocabulary and E the word embedding dimensionality.[1] Each source word is

---

[1]Similarly, $\boldsymbol{h}_0^{\leftarrow} \in \mathbb{R}^H, \boldsymbol{W}_{si}^{\leftarrow} \in \mathbb{R}^{H \times E}, \boldsymbol{W}_{sh}^{\leftarrow} \in \mathbb{R}^{H \times H}, \boldsymbol{b}_s^{\leftarrow} \in \mathbb{R}^H$ are the parameters of the right-to-left RNN. Note that we use a long short term memory unit (Hochreiter and Schmidhuber, 1997) in place of the RNN, shown here for simplicity of exposition.

then represented as a pair of hidden states, one from each RNN, $\boldsymbol{e}_i = \begin{bmatrix} \boldsymbol{h}_i^{\rightarrow} \\ \boldsymbol{h}_i^{\leftarrow} \end{bmatrix}$. This encodes not only the word but also its left and right context, which can provide important evidence for its translation.

A crucial question is how this dynamic sized matrix $\mathbf{E} = [\boldsymbol{e}_1, \boldsymbol{e}_2, \ldots, \boldsymbol{e}_I] \in \mathbb{R}^{I \times H}$ can be used in the decoder to generate the target sentence. As with Sutskever's encoder-decoder, the target sentence is created left-to-right using an RNN, while the encoded source is used to bias the process as an auxiliary input. The mechanism for this bias is by attentional vectors, i.e. vectors of scores over each source sentence location, which are used to aggregate the dynamic source encoding into a fixed length vector.

Decoder The decoder operates as a standard RNN over the translation $\boldsymbol{t}$, formulated as follows

$$\boldsymbol{g}_j = \tanh\left(\mathbf{W}^{(\mathrm{th})}\boldsymbol{g}_{j-1} + \mathbf{W}^{(\mathrm{ti})}\boldsymbol{r}_{t_{j-1}}^{(\mathrm{t})} + \mathbf{W}^{(\mathrm{ta})}\boldsymbol{c}_j\right) \quad (2)$$

$$\boldsymbol{u}_j = \tanh\left(\boldsymbol{g}_j + \mathbf{W}^{(\mathrm{uc})}\boldsymbol{c}_j + \mathbf{W}^{(\mathrm{ui})}\boldsymbol{r}_{t_{j-1}}^{(\mathrm{t})}\right) \quad (3)$$

$$\boldsymbol{t}_j \sim \mathrm{softmax}\left(\mathbf{W}^{(\mathrm{ou})}\boldsymbol{u}_j + \boldsymbol{b}^{(\mathrm{to})}\right) \quad (4)$$

where the decoder RNN is defined analogously to Eq 1 but with an additional input, the source attention component $\boldsymbol{c}_j \in \mathbb{R}^{2H}$ and weighting matrix $\mathbf{W}^{(\mathrm{ta})} \in \mathbb{R}^{H \times 2H}$. The hidden state of the recurrence is then passed through a single hidden layer[2] (Eq 3) in combination with the source attention and target word using weighting matrices $\mathbf{W}^{(\mathrm{uc})} \in \mathbb{R}^{H \times 2H}$ and $\mathbf{W}^{(\mathrm{ui})} \in \mathbb{R}^{H \times E}$. In Eq 4 this vector is transformed to be target vocabulary sized, using weight matrix $\mathbf{W}^{(\mathrm{ou})} \in \mathbb{R}^{V_T \times H}$ and bias $\boldsymbol{b}^{(\mathrm{to})} \in \mathbb{R}^{V_T}$, after which a softmax is taken, and the resulting normalised vector used as the parameters of a Categorical distribution in generating the next target word.

The presentation above assumes a simple RNN is used to define the recurrence over hidden states, however we can easily use alternative formulations of recurrent networks including multiple-layer RNNs, gated recurrent units (GRU; Cho et al. (2014)), or long short-term memory (LSTM; Hochreiter and Schmidhuber (1997)) units. These more advanced methods allow for more efficient learning of more complex concepts, particularly

---

[2]In Bahdanau et al. (2015) they use a max-out layer for this final step, however we found this to be a needless complication, and instead use a standard hidden layer with tanh activation.

long distance effects. Empirically we found LSTMs to be the best performing, and therefore use these units herein.

The last key detail is the attentional component c_j in Eqs 2 and 3, which is defined as follows

$$f_{ji} = \boldsymbol{v}^\top \tanh\left(\mathbf{W}^{(\mathrm{ae})}\boldsymbol{e}_i + \mathbf{W}^{(\mathrm{ah})}\boldsymbol{g}_{j-1}\right) \quad (5)$$

$$\boldsymbol{\alpha}_j = \mathrm{softmax}\left(\boldsymbol{f}_j\right)$$

$$\boldsymbol{c}_j = \sum_i \alpha_{ji}\boldsymbol{e}_i$$

with the scalars f_{ji} denoting the compatibility between the target hidden state $\boldsymbol{g}_{j-1}$ and the source encoding $\boldsymbol{e}_i$. This is defined as a neural network with one hidden layer of size A and a single output, parameterised by $\mathbf{W}^{(\mathrm{ae})} \in \mathbb{R}^{A\times 2H}$, $\mathbf{W}^{(\mathrm{ah})} \in \mathbb{R}^{A\times H}$ and $\boldsymbol{v} \in \mathbb{R}^A$. The softmax then normalises the scalar compatibility values such that for a given target word j, the values of α_j can be interpreted as alignment probabilities to each source location. Finally, these alignments are used to to reweight the source components E to produce a fixed length context representation.

Training of this model is done by minimising the cross-entropy of the target sentence, measured word-by-word as for a language model. We use standard stochastic gradient optimisation using the back-propagation technique for computation of partial derivatives according to the chain rule.

3 Incorporating Structural Biases

The attentional model, as described above, provides a powerful and elegant model of translation in which alignments between source and target words are learned through the implicit conditioning context afforded by the attention mechanism. Despite its elegance, the attentional model omits several key components of a traditional alignment models such as the IBM models (Brown et al., 1993) and Vogel's hidden Markov Model (Vogel et al., 1996) as implemented in the GIZA++ toolkit (Och and Ney, 2003). Combining the strengths of this highly successful body of research into a neural model of machine translation holds potential to further improve modelling accuracy of neural techniques. Below we outline methods for incorporating these factors as structural biases into the attentional model.

3.1 Position bias

First we consider position bias, based on the observation that a word at a given relative position in the source tends to align to a word at a similar relative position in the target, $\frac{i}{I} \approx \frac{j}{J}$ (Dyer et al., 2013). Related, the IBM model 2 learns discrete mappings between positions i and j conditioned on sentence lengths I and J.

We include a position bias through redefining the pre-normalised attention scalars f_{ji} in Eq 5 as:

$$f_{ji} = \boldsymbol{v}^\top \tanh\left(\mathbf{W}^{(\mathrm{ae})}\boldsymbol{e}_i + \mathbf{W}^{(\mathrm{ah})}\boldsymbol{g}_{j-1} + \right.$$
$$\left. \mathbf{W}^{(\mathrm{ap})}\psi(j,i,I)\right) \quad (6)$$

where the new component in the input is a simple feature function of the positions in the source and target sentences and the source length,

$$\psi(j,i,I) = \left[\log(1+j), \log(1+i), \log(1+I)\right]^\top$$

and $\mathbf{W}^{(\mathrm{ap})} \in \mathbb{R}^{A\times 3}$. We exclude the target length J as this is unknown during decoding, as a partial translation can have several (infinite) different lengths. The use of the $\log(1+\cdot)$ function is to avoid numerical instabilities from widely varying sentence lengths. The non-linearity in Eq 6 allows for complex functions of these inputs to be learned, such as relative positions and approximate distance from the diagonal, as well as their interactions with the other inputs (e.g., to learn that some words are exceptional cases where a diagonal bias should not apply).

3.2 Markov condition

The HMM model of translation (Vogel et al., 1996) is based on a Markov condition over alignment random variables, to allow the model to learn local effects such as when $i \leftarrow j$ is aligned then it is likely that $i + 1 \leftarrow j + 1$ or $i \leftarrow j + 1$. These correspond to local diagonal alignments or one-to-many alignments, respectively. In general, there are many correlations between the alignments of a word and the alignments of the preceding word.

Markov conditioning can also be incorporated in a similar manner to positional bias, by augmenting the attentional input from Eqs 5 and 6 to include:

$$f_{ji} = \boldsymbol{v}^\top \tanh\left(\ldots + \mathbf{W}^{(\mathrm{am})}\xi_1(\boldsymbol{\alpha}_{j-1}; i)\right) \quad (7)$$

where ... abbreviates the e_i, g_{j-1} and ψ components from Eq 6, and $\xi_1(\alpha_{j-1})$ provides a fixed dimensional representation of the attention state for the preceding word. It is not immediately obvious how to incorporate the previous attention vector as α is dynamically sized to match the source sentence length, thus using it directly would not generalise over sentences of different lengths. For this reason, we make a simplification by just considering local moves offset by $\pm k$ positions, that is,

$$\xi_1(\alpha_{j-1}; i) = \left[\alpha_{j-1,i-k}, .., \alpha_{j-1,i}, .., \alpha_{j-1,i+k} \right]^\top$$

with $\mathbf{W}^{(\mathrm{am})} \in \mathbb{R}^{A \times (2k+1)}$. Our approach is likely to capture the most important alignments patterns forming the backbone of the alignment HMM, namely monotone, 1-to-many, and local inversions.

3.3 Fertility

Fertility is the propensity for a word to be translated as a consistent number of words in the other language, e.g., *Iseseisvusdeklaratsioon* (Et) translates as 3-4 words in English, namely *(the) Declaration of Independence*. Fertility is a central component in the IBM models 3–5 (Brown et al., 1993). Incorporating fertility into the attentional model is a little more involved, and we present two techniques for doing so.

Local fertility First we consider a feature-based technique, which includes the following features

$$\xi_2(\alpha_{<j}; i) = \left[\sum_{j'<j} \alpha_{j',i-k}, .., \sum_{j'<j} \alpha_{j',i}, .., \sum_{j'<j} \alpha_{j',i+1} \right]^\top$$

and the corresponding feature weights, i.e., $\mathbf{W}^{(\mathrm{af})} \in \mathbb{R}^{A \times (2k+1)}$. These sums represent the total alignment score for the surrounding source words, similar to fertility in a traditional latent variable model, which is the sum over binary alignment random variables. A word which already has several alignments can be excluded from participating in more alignments, thus combating the garbage collection problem. Conversely words that tend to need high fertility can be learned through the interactions between these features and the word and context embeddings in Eq 7.

Global fertility A second, more explicit, technique for incorporating fertility is to include this as a modelling constraint. Initially we considered a soft constraint based on the approach in (Xu et al., 2015), where an image captioning model was biased to attend to every pixel in the image exactly once. In our setting, the same idea can be applied through adding a regularisation term to the training objective of the form $\sum_i \left(1 - \sum_j \alpha_{j,i} \right)^2$. However this method is overly restrictive: enforcing that every word is used exactly once is not appropriate in translation where some words are likely to be dropped (e.g., determiners and other function words), while others might need to be translated several times to produce a phrase in the target language.[3] For this reason we develop an alternative method, based around a contextual fertility model, $p(f_i|\boldsymbol{s}, i) = \mathcal{N}\left(\mu(e_i), \sigma^2(e_i) \right)$ which scores the fertility of source word i, defined as $f_i = \sum_j \alpha_{j,i}$, using a normal distribution[4] parameterised by μ and σ^2, both positive scalar valued non-linear functions of the source word encoding e_i. This is incorporated into the training objective as an additional additive term, $\sum_i \log p(f_i|\boldsymbol{s}, i)$, for each training sentence.

This formulation allows for greater consistency in translation, through e.g., learning which words tend to be omitted from translation, or translate as several words. Compared to the fertility model in IBM 3–5 (Brown et al., 1993), ours uses many fewer parameters through working over vector embeddings, and moreover, the BiRNN encoding of the source means that we learn context-dependent fertilities, which can be useful for dealing with fixed syntactic patterns or multi-word expressions.

3.4 Bilingual Symmetry

So far we have considered a conditional model of the target given the source, modelling $p(\boldsymbol{t}|\boldsymbol{s})$. However it is well established for latent variable translation models that the alignments improve if $p(\boldsymbol{s}|\boldsymbol{t})$ is

---

[3] Modern decoders (Koehn et al., 2003) often impose the restriction of each word being translated exactly once, however this is tempered by their use of phrases as translation units rather than words, which allow for higher fertility within phrases.

[4] The normal distribution is deficient, as it has support for all scalar values, despite f_i being bounded above and below ($0 \leq f_i \leq J$). This could be corrected by using a truncated normal, or various other choices of distribution.

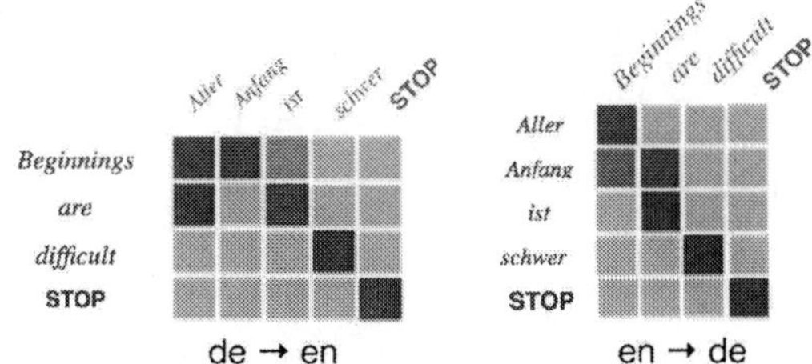

Figure 2: Symmetric training with trace bonus, computed as matrix multiplication, $-\operatorname{tr}(\boldsymbol{\alpha}^{s \leftarrow t} \boldsymbol{\alpha}^{s \rightarrow t \top})$. Dark shading indicates higher values.

lang-pair	# tokens (K)		# types (K)	
Zh-En	422	454	3.44	3.12
Ru-En	1639	1809	145	65
Et-En	1411	1857	90	25
Ro-En	1782	1806	39	24

Table 1: Statistics of the training sets, showing in each cell the count for the source language (left) and target language (right).

also modelled and the inferences of both directional models are combined – evidenced by the symmetrisation heuristics used in most decoders (Koehn et al., 2005), and also by explicit joint agreement training objectives (Liang et al., 2006; Ganchev et al., 2008). The rationale is that both models make somewhat independent errors, so an ensemble stands to gain from variance reduction.

We propose a method for joint training of two directional models as pictured in Figure 2. Training twinned models involves optimising $\mathcal{L} = -\log p(\boldsymbol{t}|\boldsymbol{s}) - \log p(\boldsymbol{s}|\boldsymbol{t}) + \gamma B$ where, as before, we consider only a single sentence pair, for simplicity of notation. This corresponds to a pseudo-likelihood objective, with the B linking the two models.[5] The B component considers the alignment (attention) matrices, $\boldsymbol{\alpha}^{s \rightarrow t} \in \mathbb{R}^{J \times I}$ and $\boldsymbol{\alpha}^{t \leftarrow s} \in \mathbb{R}^{I \times J}$, and attempts to make these close to one another for both translation directions (see Fig. 2). To achieve this, we use a 'trace bonus', inspired by (Levinboim et al., 2015), formulated as

$$B = -\operatorname{tr}(\boldsymbol{\alpha}^{s \leftarrow t \top} \boldsymbol{\alpha}^{s \rightarrow t}) = \sum_j \sum_i \alpha_{i,j}^{s \leftarrow t} \alpha_{j,i}^{s \rightarrow t} .$$

As the alignment cells are normalised using the softmax and thus take values in [0,1], the trace term is bounded above by $\min(I, J)$ which occurs when the two alignment matrices are transposes of each other, representing perfect one-to-one alignments in both directions

4 Experiments

Datasets. We conducted our experiments with four language pairs, translating between English $\leftrightarrow$ Romanian, Estonian, Russian and Chinese. These languages were chosen to represent a range of translation difficulties, including languages with significant morphological complexity (Estonian, Russian). We focus on a (simulated) low resource setting, where only a limited amount of training data is available. This serves to demonstrate the robustness and generalisation of our model on sparse data – something that has not yet been established for neural models with millions of parameters with vast potential for over-fitting.

Table 1 shows the statistics of the training sets.[6] For Chinese-English, the data comes from the BTEC corpus, where the number of training sentence pairs is 44,016. We used 'devset1_2' and 'devset_3' as the development and test sets, respectively, and in both cases used only the first reference for evaluation. For Romanian and Estonian, the data come from the Europarl corpus (Koehn, 2005), where we used 100K sentence pairs for training, and 3K for development and 2K for testing.[7] The Russian-English data was taken from a web derived corpus (Antonova and Misyurev, 2011). The dataset is split into three parts using the same technique as for the Europarl sets. During the preprocessing stage we lower-cased and tokenized the data, and excluded sentences longer than 30 words. For the Europarl

---

[5]We could share some parameters, e.g., the word embedding matrices, however we found this didn't make much difference versus using disjoint parameter sets. We set $\gamma = 1$ herein.

[6]For all datasets words were thresholded for training frequency ≥ 5, with uncommon training and unseen testing words replaced by an $\langle$unk$\rangle$ symbol.

[7]The first 100K sentence pairs were used for training, while the development and test were drawn from the last 100K sentence pairs, taking the first 2K for testing and the last 3K for development.

data, we also removed sentences containing headings and other meeting formalities.[8]

Models and Baselines. We have implemented our neural translation model with linguistic features in C++ using the CNN library.[9] We compared our proposed model against our implementations of the attentional model (Bahdanau et al., 2015) and encoder-decoder architecture (Sutskever et al., 2014). As the baseline, we used a state-of-the-art phrase-based statistical machine translation model built using Moses (Koehn et al., 2007) with the standard features: relative-frequency and lexical translation model probabilities in both directions; distortion model; language model and word count. We used KenLM (Heafield, 2011) to create 3-gram language models with Kneser-Ney smoothing on the target side of the bilingual training corpora.

Evaluation Measures. Following previous work (Kalchbrenner and Blunsom, 2013; Sutskever et al., 2014; Bahdanau et al., 2015; Neubig et al., 2015), we evaluated all neural models using test set perplexities and translation results, as well as in an additional re-ranking setting, using BLEU (Papineni et al., 2002) measure. We applied bootstrap resampling (Koehn, 2004) to measure statistical significance, $p < 0.05$, of our models compared to a baseline. For re-ranking, we generated 100-best translations using the baseline phrase-based model, to which we added log probability features from our neural models alongside all the features of the underlying phrase-based model. We trained the re-ranking models using MERT (Och, 2003) on development sets with 100-best translations.

4.1 Analysis of Alignment Biases

We start by investigating the effect of various linguistic constraints, described in Section 3, on the attentional model. Table 2 presents the perplexity of trained models for Chinese→English translation. For comparison, we report the results of an encoder-decoder-based neural translation model (Sutskever et al., 2014) as the baseline. All other results are for the attentional model with a single-layer LSTM as encoder and two-layer LSTM as decoder, using 512

---

configuration	test	#param (M)
Sutskever encdec	5.35	8.7
Attentional	4.77	15.0
+align	4.56	15.0
+align+glofer	5.20	15.5
+align+glofer-pre	4.31	15.5
+align+sym	4.44	30.1
+align+sym+glofer-pre	4.43	31.2

Table 2: Perplexity results for attentional model variants evaluated on BTEC zh→en, and number of model parameters (in millions).

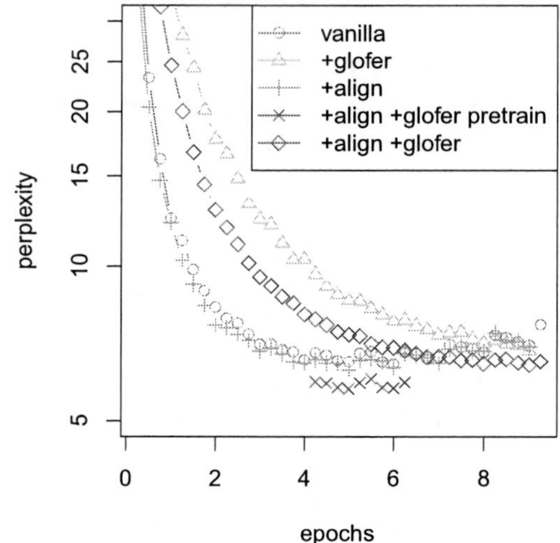

Figure 3: Perplexity with training epochs on ro-en translation, comparing several model variants.

embedding, 512 hidden, and 256 alignment dimensions. For each model, we also report the number of its parameters. Models are trained end-to-end using stochastic gradient descent (SGD), allowing up to 20 epochs. We use a held-out development set for regularisation by early stopping, which terminated the training after 5-10 epochs for most cases.

As expected, the vanilla attentional model greatly improves over encoder-decoder (perplexity of 4.77 vs. 5.35), clearly making good use of the additional context. Adding the combined positional bias, local fertility, and Markov structure (denoted by +align) further decreases the perplexity to 4.56. Adding the global fertility (+glofer) is detrimental, however, increases perplexity to 5.20. Interestingly, global fertility helps to reduce the perplexity (to 4.31) when used with the pre-training setting (+align+glofer-

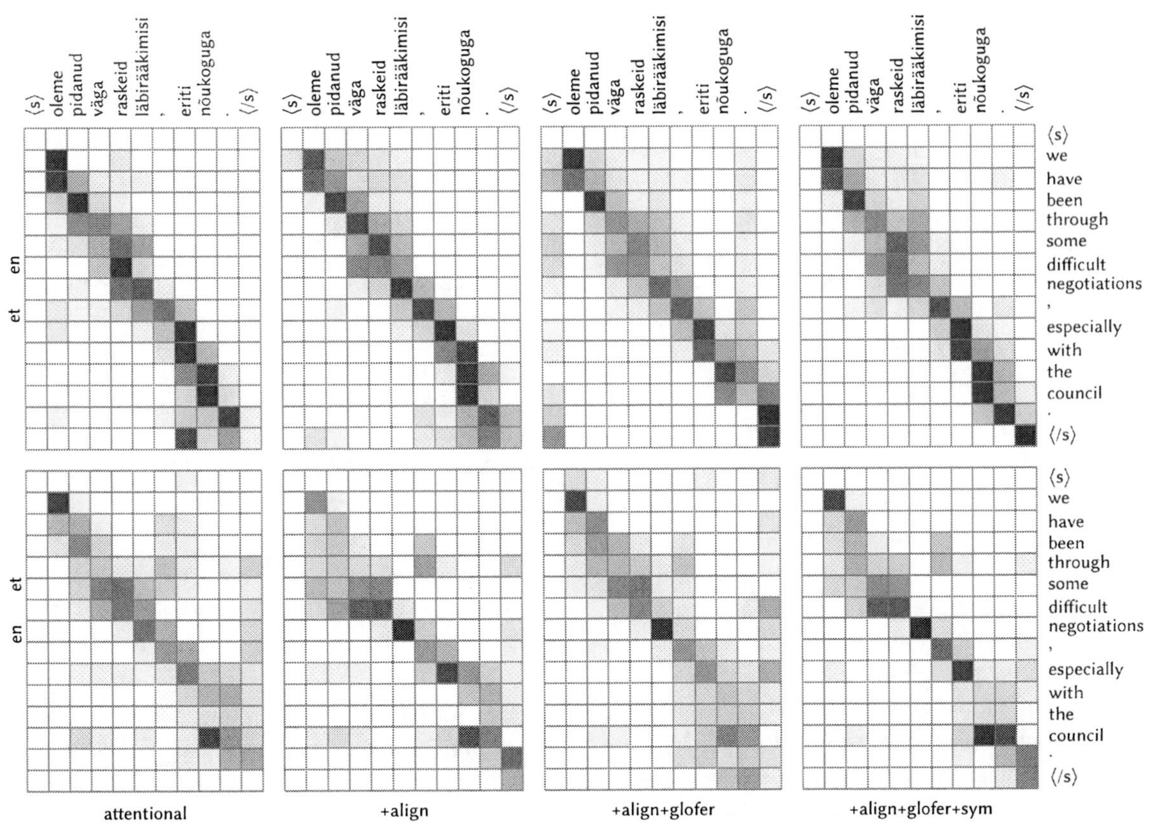

Figure 4: Example development sentence, showing the inferred attention matrix for various models for Et ↔ En. Rows correspond to the translation direction and columns correspond to different models: attentional, with alignment features (+align), global fertility (+glofer), and symmetric joint training (+sym). Darker shades denote higher values and white denotes zero.

pre). In this case, it is refining an already excellent model from which reliable global fertility estimates can be obtained. This finding is consistent with the other languages, see Figure 3 which shows typical learning curves of different variants of the attentional model. Note that when global fertility is added to the vanilla attentional model with alignment features, it significantly slows down training as it limits exploration in early training iterations, however it does bring a sizeable win when used to fine-tune a pre-trained model. Finally, the bilingual symmetry also helps to reduce the perplexity scores when used with the alignment features, however, does not combine well with global fertility (+align+sym+glofer-pre). This is perhaps an unsurprising result as both methods impose a often-times similar regularising effect over the attention matrix.

Figure 4 illustrates the different attention matri-

ces inferred by the various model variants. Note the difference between the base attentional model and its variant with alignment features ('+align'), where more weight is assigned to diagonal and 1-to-many alignments. Global fertility pushes more attention to the sentinel symbols ⟨s⟩ and ⟨/s⟩. Determiners and prepositions in English show much lower fertility than nouns, while Estonian nouns have even higher fertility. This accords with Estonian morphology, wherein nouns are inflected with rich case marking, e.g., *nõukoguga* has the cogitative *-ga* suffix, meaning 'with', and thus translates as several English words (*with the council*). The right-most column corresponds to joint symmetric training, with many more confident attention values especially for consistent 1-to-many alignments (*difficult* in English and *raskeid* in Estonian, an adjective in partitive case meaning *some difficult*).

Lang. Pair	Zh-En	Ru-En	Et-En	Ro-En
Enc-Dec	5.35	61.9	18.2	10.3
Attentional	4.77	41.7	12.8	6.62
Our Work	**4.31**	**39.9**	**11.8**	**5.89**

Lang. Pair	En-Zh	En-Ru	En-Et	En-Ro
Enc-Dec	8.60	67.3	31.4	11.5
Attentional	7.49	43.0	19.4	7.30
Our Work	**6.24**	**40.6**	**17.0**	**6.35**

Table 3: Perplexity on the test sets for the two translation directions. Our work includes: bidirectional LSTM attentional model combined with positional bias, Markov, local fertility, and global fertility (pre-trained setting).

4.2 Experimental Results

The perplexity results of the neural models for the two translation directions across the four language pairs are presented in Table 3. In all cases, our work achieves lower perplexities compared to the vanilla attentional model and the encoder-decoder architecture, owing to the linguistic constraints. We also obtained similar patterns of improvements when decoding, using a greedy decoding strategy, as shown in Table 4. The exception was for en→ru, where the addition of the global fertility (in addition to the other aligment features) was detrimental, resulting in a decrease in BLEU score (5.94→5.26). This may be due to highly noisy nature of the web text corpus of Russian-English language pair, compared to the much cleaner sources for the other language pairs.

Greedy decoding does not appear to be competitive for neural models trained on small parallel corpora, not reaching the level of a phrase-based baseline (see Table 5). Despite this, however, these models still provide substantial gains when used for re-ranking (as shown in Table 5) for translating into English from the other four languages. We compare re-ranking settings using the log probabilities produced by our model as additional features[10] vs. using log probabilities from the vanilla attentional model and the encoder-decoder. The re-rankers based on our model are significantly better than the rest for Chinese and Estonian, and on par with the other for Russian and Romanian→English. In all cases our model has performance at least 1 BLEU point better than the baseline phrase-based system. It is worth not-

---

[10]We include two features: the normalised log-probability of the translation, evaluated in both translation directions.

Lang. Pair	Zh-En	Ru-En	Et-En	Ro-En
Enc-Dec	17.4	3.63	12.5	21.2
Attentional	29.9	8.11	19.7	33.0
Our Work	**31.56♠**	**9.14♠**	**20.44♠**	**34.16♠**

Lang. Pair	En-Zh	En-Ru	En-Et	En-Ro
Enc-Dec	14.6	2.08	7.97	16.6
Attentional	20.9	5.26	12.5	28.1
Our Work	**23.45♠**	5.26	**13.40♠**	**30.07♠**

Table 4: BLEU scores on the test sets for the two translation directions, using greedy decoding. **bold:** Best performance, ♠: Statistically significantly better than Attentional.

Lang. Pair	Zh-En	Ru-En	Et-En	Ro-En
Phrase-based	40.63	18.70	31.99	45.21
Enc-Dec	40.41	18.83	32.20	45.36
Attentional	41.16	**19.79**	32.78	46.83
Our Work	**43.50♠**	19.73	**33.26♠**	**46.88**

Table 5: BLEU scores on the test sets for re-ranking. **bold:** Best performance, ♠: Statistically significantly better than Attentional.

ing that for Chinese-English, our re-ranker leads to a substantial increase of almost 3 BLEU points.

5 Related Work

Kalchbrenner and Blunsom (2013) were the first to propose a full neural model of translation, using a convolutional network as the source encoder, followed by an RNN decoder to generate the target translation. This was extended in Sutskever et al. (2014), who replaced the source encoder with an RNN using a Long Short-Term Memory (LSTM) and leveraged the last hidden RNN states as source context for generating the output. Inspired by this, Bahdanau et al. (2015) introduced the notion of "attention" to the model, whereby the source context can dynamically change during the decoding process to attend to the most relevant parts of the source sentence. Further, Luong et al. (2015) refined the attention mechanism to be more local, by constraining attention to a text span, whose words' representations are averaged.

Similar in spirit to our work, recent research has proposed different ways of leveraging the attention history to incorporate alignment structural biases. (Luong et al., 2015) made use of the attention vector of the previous position when generating the attention vector for the next position. Feng et al. (2016)

added another recurrent structure for the attention mechanism to enhance its memorization capabilities and capture long-range dependencies between the attention vectors. Tu et al. (2016) proposed a coverage vector to keep track of the attention history, hence refining future attentions. Finally, Cheng et al. (2015) proposed a similar agreement-based joint training for bidirectional attention-based neural machine translation, and showed significant improvements in BLEU for the large data French↔English translation.

6 Conclusion

We have shown that the attentional model of translation does not capture many well known properties of traditional word-based translation models, and proposed several ways of imposing these as structural biases on the model. We show improvements across several challenging language pairs in a low-resource setting, as well as in perplexity, translation and re-ranking evaluations. In future work we intend to investigate the model performance on larger-scale datasets, and incorporate further linguistic information, such as morphological representations.

Acknowledgements

The work reported here was started at JSALT 2015 in UW, Seattle, and was supported by JHU via grants from NSF (IIS), DARPA (LORELEI), Google, Microsoft, Amazon, Mitsubishi Electric, and MERL. Dr Cohn was supported by the ARC (Future Fellowship).

References

Alexandra Antonova and Alexey Misyurev. 2011. Building a web-based parallel corpus and filtering out machine-translated text. In *Proceedings of the 4th Workshop on Building and Using Comparable Corpora: Comparable Corpora and the Web*, pages 136–144.

Dzmitry Bahdanau, Kyunghyun Cho, and Yoshua Bengio. 2015. Neural machine translation by jointly learning to align and translate. In *Proceedings of the International Conference on Learning Representations (ICLR)*, San Diego, CA.

Peter E. Brown, Stephen A. Della Pietra, Vincent J. Della Pietra, and Robert L. Mercer. 1993. The mathematics of statistical machine translation: Parameter estimation. *Computational Linguistics*, 19(2).

Yong Cheng, Shiqi Shen, Zhongjun Zhongjun He, Wei He, Hua Wu, Maosong Sun, and Yang Liu. 2015. Agreement-based joint training for bidirectional attention-based neural machine translation. In *arXiv: 1512.04650 [cs.CL]*.

K. Cho, B. van Merrienboer, D. Bahdanau, and Y. Bengio. 2014. On the properties of neural machine translation. In *arXiv:1409.1259 [cs.CL]*.

Chris Dyer, Victor Chahuneau, and Noah A. Smith. 2013. A simple, fast, and effective reparameterization of ibm model 2. In *Proceedings of the 2013 Conference of the North American Chapter of the Association for Computational Linguistics: Human Language Technologies*, pages 644–648, Atlanta, Georgia, June. Association for Computational Linguistics.

S. Feng, S. Liu, M. Li, and M. Zhou. 2016. Implicit Distortion and Fertility Models for Attention-based Encoder-Decoder NMT Model. *ArXiv e-prints*, January.

Kuzman Ganchev, João V. Graça, and Ben Taskar. 2008. Better alignments = better translations? In *Proceedings of ACL-08: HLT*, pages 986–993, Columbus, Ohio, June. Association for Computational Linguistics.

Kenneth Heafield. 2011. KenLM: faster and smaller language model queries. In *Proceedings of the EMNLP 2011 Sixth Workshop on Statistical Machine Translation*, pages 187–197, Edinburgh, Scotland, United Kingdom, July.

S. Hochreiter and J. Schmidhuber. 1997. Long short-term memory. *Neural Computation*, 9:1735–1780.

Nal Kalchbrenner and Phil Blunsom. 2013. Recurrent continuous translation models. In *Proceedings of the 2013 Conference on Empirical Methods in Natural Language Processing*, Seattle, October.

Philipp Koehn, Franz Josef Och, and Daniel Marcu. 2003. Statistical phrase-based translation. In *Proceedings of North American Chapter of the Association for Computational Linguistics on Human Language Technology*, pages 48–54.

Philipp Koehn, Amittai Axelrod, Alexandra Birch, Chris Callison-Burch, Miles Osborne, David Talbot, and Michael White. 2005. Edinburgh system description for the 2005 IWSLT speech translation evaluation. In *IWSLT*, pages 68–75.

Philipp Koehn, Hieu Hoang, Alexandra Birch, Chris Callison-Burch, Marcello Federico, Nicola Bertoldi, Brooke Cowan, Wade Shen, Christine Moran, Richard Zens, et al. 2007. Moses: Open source toolkit for statistical machine translation. In *Proc. ACL Interactive Poster and Demonstration Sessions*, pages 177–180.

Philipp Koehn. 2004. Statistical significance tests for machine translation evaluation. In Dekang Lin and Dekai Wu, editors, *Proceedings of EMNLP 2004*, pages 388–395, Barcelona, Spain, July. Association for Computational Linguistics.

Philipp Koehn. 2005. Europarl: A Parallel Corpus for Statistical Machine Translation. In *Conference Proceedings: the tenth Machine Translation Summit*, pages 79–86. AAMT.

Tomer Levinboim, Ashish Vaswani, and David Chiang. 2015. Model invertibility regularization: Sequence alignment with or without parallel data. In *Proceedings of the North American Chapter of the Association for Computational Linguistics (NAACL)*, pages 609–618, Denver, CO.

Percy Liang, Ben Taskar, and Dan Klein. 2006. Alignment by agreement. In *Proceedings of the North American Chapter of the Association for Computational Linguistics (NAACL)*, pages 104–111, New York, NY.

Minh-Thang Luong, Hieu Pham, and Christopher D. Manning. 2015. Effective approaches to attention-based neural machine translation. In *Proceedings of the 2015 Conference on Empirical Methods in Natural Language Processing*, pages 1412–1421, Lisbon, Portugal, September. Association for Computational Linguistics.

Graham Neubig, Makoto Morishita, and Satoshi Nakamura. 2015. Neural reranking improves subjective quality of machine translation: NAIST at WAT2015. In *Proceedings of the 2nd Workshop on Asian Translation (WAT2015)*, Kyoto, Japan, October.

Franz Josef Och and Hermann Ney. 2003. A systematic comparison of various statistical alignment models. *Computational Linguistics*, 29(1):19–51.

Franz Josef Och. 2003. Minimum error rate training in statistical machine translation. In *Proceedings of the 41st Annual Meeting on Association for Computational Linguistics - Volume 1*, ACL.

Kishore Papineni, Salim Roukos, Todd Ward, and Wei-Jing Zhu. 2002. Bleu: A method for automatic evaluation of machine translation. In *Proceedings of the 40th Annual Meeting on Association for Computational Linguistics*, ACL.

Ilya Sutskever, Oriol Vinyals, and Quoc VV Le. 2014. Sequence to sequence learning with neural networks. In *Neural Information Processing Systems (NIPS)*, pages 3104–3112, Montréal.

Z. Tu, Z. Lu, Y. Liu, X. Liu, and H. Li. 2016. Modeling Coverage for Neural Machine Translation. *ArXiv e-prints*, January.

Stephan Vogel, Hermann Ney, and Christoph Tillmann. 1996. HMM-based word alignment in statistical translation. In *Proceedings of the International Conference on Computational Linguistics (COLING)*, pages 836–841.

Kelvin Xu, Jimmy Ba, Ryan Kiros, Kyunghyun Cho, Aaron Courville, Ruslan Salakhudinov, Rich Zemel, and Yoshua Bengio. 2015. Show, attend and tell: Neural image caption generation with visual attention. In *Proceedings of the 32nd International Conference on Machine Learning (ICML-15)*, pages 2048–2057.

Multilingual Relation Extraction using Compositional Universal Schema

Patrick Verga, David Belanger, Emma Strubell, Benjamin Roth & Andrew McCallum
College of Information and Computer Sciences
University of Massachusetts Amherst
{pat, belanger, strubell, beroth, mccallum}@cs.umass.edu

Abstract

Universal schema builds a knowledge base (KB) of
entities and relations by jointly embedding all relation types from input KBs as well as textual patterns observed in raw text. In most previous applications of universal schema, each textual pattern is
represented as a single embedding, preventing generalization to unseen patterns. Recent work employs
a neural network to capture patterns' compositional
semantics, providing generalization to all possible
input text. In response, this paper introduces significant further improvements to the coverage and
flexibility of universal schema relation extraction:
predictions for entities unseen in training and multilingual transfer learning to domains with no annotation. We evaluate our model through extensive
experiments on the English and Spanish TAC KBP
benchmark, outperforming the top system from TAC
2013 slot-filling using no handwritten patterns or additional annotation. We also consider a multilingual
setting in which English training data entities overlap with the seed KB, but Spanish text does not.
Despite having no annotation for Spanish data, we
train an accurate predictor, with additional improvements obtained by tying word embeddings across
languages. Furthermore, we find that multilingual
training improves English relation extraction accuracy. Our approach is thus suited to broad-coverage
automated knowledge base construction in a variety
of languages and domains.

1   Introduction

The goal of automatic knowledge base construction
(AKBC) is to build a structured knowledge base (KB)
of facts using a noisy corpus of raw text evidence, and
perhaps an initial seed KB to be augmented (Carlson et
al., 2010; Suchanek et al., 2007; Bollacker et al., 2008).
AKBC supports downstream reasoning at a high level
about extracted entities and their relations, and thus has
broad-reaching applications to a variety of domains.

One challenge in AKBC is aligning knowledge from
a structured KB with a text corpus in order to perform
supervised learning through *distant supervision*. *Universal schema* (Riedel et al., 2013) along with its extensions (Yao et al., 2013; Gardner et al., 2014; Neelakantan
et al., 2015; Rocktaschel et al., 2015), avoids alignment
by jointly embedding KB relations, entities, and surface
text patterns. This propagates information between KB
annotation and corresponding textual evidence.

The above applications of universal schema express
each text relation as a distinct item to be embedded. This
harms its ability to generalize to inputs not precisely seen
at training time. Recently, Toutanova et al. (2015) addressed this issue by embedding text patterns using a deep
sentence encoder, which captures the compositional semantics of textual relations and allows for prediction on
inputs never seen before.

This paper further expands the coverage abilities of
universal schema relation extraction by introducing techniques for forming predictions for new entities unseen in
training and even for new domains with no associated annotation. In the extreme example of domain adaptation
to a completely new language, we may have limited linguistic resources or labeled data such as treebanks, and
only rarely a KB with adequate coverage. Our method
performs multilingual transfer learning, providing a predictive model for a language with no coverage in an existing KB, by leveraging common representations for shared
entities across text corpora. As depicted in Figure 1, we
simply require that one language have an available KB
of seed facts. We can further improve our models by tying a small set of word embeddings across languages using only simple knowledge about word-level translations,
learning to embed semantically similar textual patterns
from different languages into the same latent space.

In extensive experiments on the TAC Knowledge Base
Population (KBP) slot-filling benchmark we outperform
the top 2013 system with an F1 score of 40.7 and perform relation extraction in Spanish with no labeled data
or direct overlap between the Spanish training corpus and

Proceedings of NAACL-HLT 2016, pages 886–896,
San Diego, California, June 12-17, 2016. ©2016 Association for Computational Linguistics

the training KB, demonstrating that our approach is well-suited for broad-coverage AKBC in low-resource languages and domains. Interestingly, joint training with Spanish improves English accuracy.

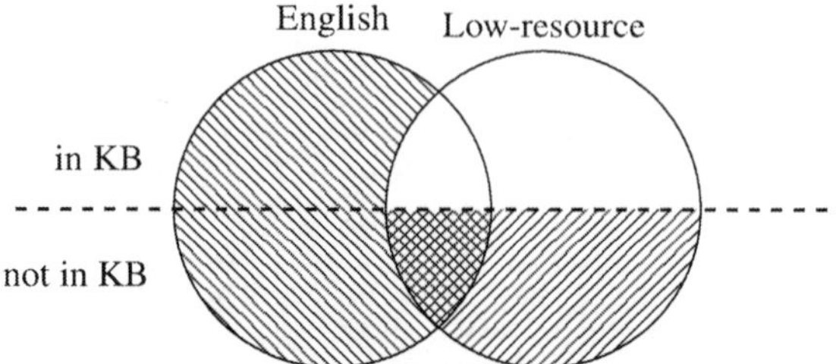

Figure 1: Splitting the entities in a multilingual AKBC training set into parts. We only require that entities in the two corpora overlap. Remarkably, we can train a model for the low-resource language even if entities in the low-resource language do not occur in the KB.

2 Background

AKBC extracts unary attributes of the form (*subject, attribute*), typed binary relations of the form (*subject, relation, object*), or higher-order relations. We refer to subjects and objects as *entities*. This work focuses solely on extracting binary relations, though many of our techniques generalize naturally to unary prediction. Generally, for example in Freebase (Bollacker et al., 2008), higher-order relations are expressed in terms of collections of binary relations.

We now describe prior work on approaches to AKBC. They all aim to predict (*s, r, o*) triples, but differ in terms of: (1) input data leveraged, (2) types of annotation required, (3) definition of relation label schema, and (4) whether they are capable of predicting relations for entities unseen in the training data. Note that all of these methods require pre-processing to detect entities, which may result in additional KB construction errors.

2.1 Relation Extraction as Link Prediction

A knowledge base is naturally described as a graph, in which entities are nodes and relations are labeled edges (Suchanek et al., 2007; Bollacker et al., 2008). In the case of *knowledge graph completion*, the task is akin to link prediction, assuming an initial set of (*s, r, o*) triples. See Nickel et al. (2015) for a review. No accompanying text data is necessary, since links can be predicted using properties of the graph, such as transitivity. In order to generalize well, prediction is often posed as low-rank matrix or tensor factorization. A variety of model variants have been suggested, where the probability of a given edge existing depends on a multi-linear form (Nickel et al., 2011; García-Durán et al., 2015; Yang

et al., 2015; Bordes et al., 2013; Wang et al., 2014; Lin et al., 2015), or non-linear interactions between s, r, and o (Socher et al., 2013). Other approaches model the compositionality of multi-hop paths, typically for question answering (Bordes et al., 2014; Gu et al., 2015; Neelakantan et al., 2015).

2.2 Relation Extraction as Sentence Classification

Here, the training data consist of (1) a text corpus, and (2) a KB of seed facts with provenance, i.e. supporting evidence, in the corpus. Given individual an individual sentence, and pre-specified entities, a classifier predicts whether the sentence expresses a relation from a target schema. To train such a classifier, KB facts need to be aligned with supporting evidence in the text, but this is often challenging. For example, not all sentences containing Barack and Michelle Obama state that they are married. A variety of one-shot and iterative methods have addressed the alignment problem (Bunescu and Mooney, 2007; Mintz et al., 2009; Riedel et al., 2010; Yao et al., 2010; Hoffmann et al., 2011; Surdeanu et al., 2012; Min et al., 2013; Zeng et al., 2015). An additional degree of freedom in these approaches is whether they classify individual sentences or predicting at the corpus level by aggregating information from all sentences containing a given pair of entities before prediction. The former approach is often preferable in practice, due to the simplicity of independently classifying individual sentences and the ease of associating each prediction with a provenance. Prior work has applied deep learning to small-scale relation extraction problems, where functional relationships are detected between common nouns (Li et al., 2015; dos Santos et al., 2015). Xu et al. (2015) apply an LSTM to a parse path, while Zeng et al. (2015) use a CNN on the raw text, with a special temporal pooling operation to separately embed the text around each entity.

2.3 Open-Domain Relation Extraction

In the previous two approaches, prediction is carried out with respect to a fixed schema R of possible relations r. This may overlook salient relations that are expressed in the text but do not occur in the schema. In response, *open-domain* information extraction (OpenIE) lets the text speak for itself: R contains all possible patterns of text occurring between entities s and o (Banko et al., 2007; Etzioni et al., 2008; Yates and Etzioni, 2007). These are obtained by filtering and normalizing the raw text. The approach offers impressive coverage, avoids issues of distant supervision, and provides a useful exploratory tool. On the other hand, OpenIE predictions are difficult to use in downstream tasks that expect information from a fixed schema.

Table 1 provides examples of OpenIE patterns. The examples in row two and three illustrate relational contexts for which similarity is difficult to be captured by an OpenIE approach because of their syntactically complex constructions. This motivates the technique in Section 3.2, which uses a deep architecture applied to raw tokens, instead of rigid rules for normalizing text to obtain patterns.

Sentence (context tokens italicized)	OpenIE pattern
Khan *'s younger sister,* **Annapurna Devi,** who later married Shankar, developed into an equally accomplished master of the surbahar, but custom prevented her from performing in public.	*arg1*'s * sister *arg2*
A professor emeritus at Yale, **Mandelbrot** *was born in Poland but as a child moved with his family to* **Paris** where he was educated.	*arg1* * moved with * family to *arg2*
Kissel *was born in Provo, Utah, but her family also lived in* **Reno**.	*arg1* * lived in *arg2*

Table 1: Examples of sentences expressing relations. Context tokens (italicized) consist of the text occurring between entities (bold) in a sentence. OpenIE patterns are obtained by normalizing the context tokens using handcoded rules. The top example expresses the per:siblings relation and the bottom two examples both express the per:cities_of_residence relation.

2.4 Universal Schema

When applying Universal Schema (Riedel et al., 2013) (USchema) to relation extraction, we combine the OpenIE and link-prediction perspectives. By jointly modeling both OpenIE patterns and the elements of a target schema, the method captures broader relational structure than multi-class classification approaches that just model the target schema. Furthermore, the method avoids the distant supervision alignment difficulties of Section 2.2.

Riedel et al. (2013) augment a knowledge graph from a seed KB with additional edges corresponding to OpenIE patterns observed in the corpus. Even if the user does not seek to predict these new edges, a joint model over all edges can exploit regularities of the OpenIE edges to improve modeling of the labels from the target schema.

The data still consist of (s, r, o) triples, which can be predicted using link-prediction techniques such as low-rank factorization. Riedel et al. (2013) explore a variety of approximations to the 3-mode (s, r, o) tensor. One such probabilistic model is:

$$\mathbb{P}\left((s, r, o)\right) = \sigma\left(u_{s,o}^{\top} v_r\right), \tag{1}$$

where $\sigma()$ is a sigmoid function, $u_{s,o}$ is an embedding of the entity pair (s, o), and v_r is an embedding of the relation r, which may be an OpenIE pattern or a relation from the target schema. All of the exposition and results in this paper use this factorization, though many of the techniques we present later could be applied easily to

the other factorizations described in Riedel et al. (2013). Note that learning unique embeddings for OpenIE relations does not guarantee that similar patterns, such as the final two in Table 1, will be embedded similarly.

As with most of the techniques in Section 2.1, the data only consist of positive examples of edges. The absence of an annotated edge does not imply that the edge is false. In fact, we seek to predict some of these missing edges as true. Riedel et al. (2013) employ the Bayesian Personalized Ranking (BPR) approach of Rendle et al. (2009), which does not explicitly model unobserved edges as negative, but instead seeks to rank the probability of observed triples above unobserved triples.

Recently, Toutanova et al. (2015) extended USchema to not learn individual pattern embeddings v_r, but instead to embed text patterns using a deep architecture applied to word tokens. This shares statistical strength between OpenIE patterns with similar words. We leverage this approach in Section 3.2. Additional work has modeled the regularities of multi-hop paths through knowledge graph augmented with text patterns (Lao et al., 2011; Lao et al., 2012; Gardner et al., 2014; Neelakantan et al., 2015).

2.5 Multilingual Embeddings

Much work has been done on multilingual word embeddings. Most of this work uses aligned sentences from the Europarl dataset (Koehn, 2005) to align word embeddings across languages (Gouws et al., 2015; Luong et al., 2015; Hermann and Blunsom, 2014). Others (Mikolov et al., 2013; Faruqui et al., 2014) align separate single-language embedding models using a word-level dictionary. Mikolov et al. (2013) use translation pairs to learn a linear transform from one embedding space to another.

However, very little work exists on multilingual relation extraction. Faruqui and Kumar (2015) perform multilingual OpenIE relation extraction by projecting all languages to English using Google translate. However, as explained in Section 2.3 the OpenIE paradigm is not amenable to prediction within a fixed schema. Further, their approach does not generalize to low-resource languages where translation is unavailable – while we use translation dictionaries to improve our results, our experiments demonstrate that our method is effective even without this resource.

3 Methods

3.1 Universal Schema as Sentence Classifier

Similar to many link prediction approaches, (Riedel et al., 2013) perform transductive learning, where a model is learned jointly over train and test data. Predictions are made by using the model to identify edges that were unobserved in the test data but likely to be true. The approach is vulnerable to the *cold start* problem in collab-

Figure 2: Universal Schema jointly embeds KB and textual relations from Spanish and English, learning dense representations for entity pairs and relations using matrix factorization. Cells with a 1 indicate triples observed during training (left). The bold score represents a test-time prediction by the model (right). Using transitivity through KB/English overlap and English/Spanish overlap, our model can predict that a text pattern in Spanish evidences a KB relation despite no overlap between Spanish/KB entity pairs. At train time we use BPR loss to maximize the inner product of entity pairs with KB relations and text patterns encoded using a bidirectional LSTM. At test time we score compatibility between embedded KB relations and encoded textual patterns using cosine similarity. In our Spanish model we treat embeddings for a small set of English/Spanish translation pairs as a single word, e.g. casado and married.

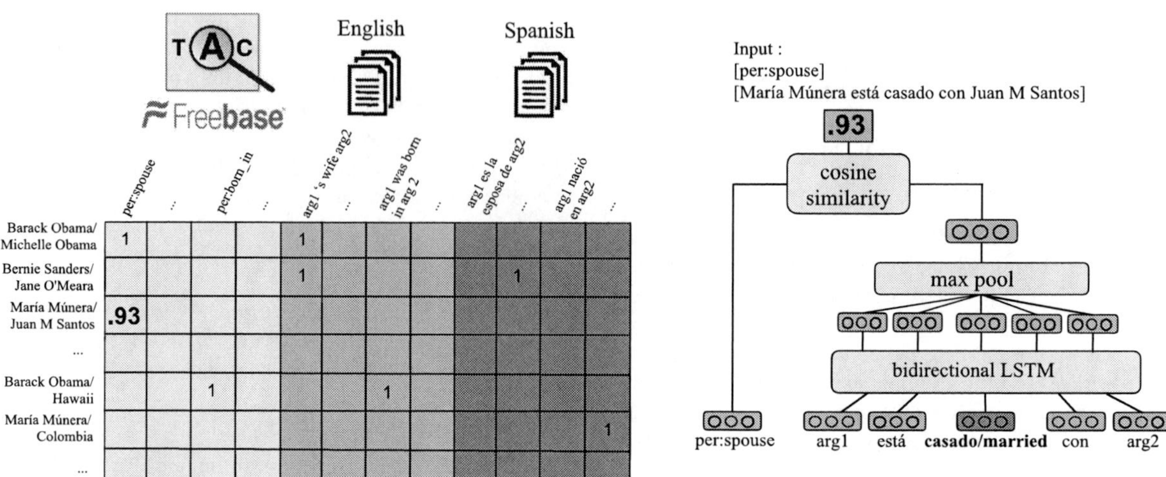

orative filtering (Schein et al., 2002): it is unclear how to form predictions for unseen entity pairs, without refactorizing the entire matrix or applying heuristics.

In response, this paper re-purposes USchema as a means to train a sentence-level relation classifier, like those in Section 2.2. This allows us to avoid errors from aligning distant supervision to the corpus, but is more deployable for real world applications. It also provides opportunities in Section 3.4 to improve multilingual AKBC.

We produce predictions using a very simple approach: (1) scan the corpus and extract a large quantity of triplets (s, r_{text}, o), where r_{text} is an OpenIE pattern. For each triplet, if the similarity between the embedding of r_{text} and the embedding of a target relation r_{schema} is above some threshold, we predict the triplet $(s, r_{\text{schema}}, o)$, and its provenance is the input sentence containing (s, r_{text}, o). We refer to this technique as *pattern scoring*. In our experiments, we use the cosine distance between the vectors (Figure 2). In Section 7.3, we discuss details for how to make this distance well-defined.

3.2 Using a Compositional Sentence Encoder to Predict Unseen Text Patterns

The pattern scoring approach is subject to an additional cold start problem: input data may contain patterns unseen in training. This section describes a method for us-

ing USchema to train a relation classifier that can take arbitrary context tokens (Section 2.3) as input.

Fortunately, the cold start problem for context tokens is more benign than that of entities since we can exploit statistical regularities of text: similar sequences of context tokens should be embedded similarly. Therefore, following Toutanova et al. (2015), we embed raw context tokens compositionally using a deep architecture. Unlike Riedel et al. (2013), this requires no manual rules to map text to OpenIE patterns and can embed any possible input string. The modified USchema likelihood is:

$$\mathbb{P}\left((s,r,o)\right) = \sigma\left(u_{s,o}^{\top}\text{Encoder}(r)\right). \qquad (2)$$

Here, if r is raw text, then $\text{Encoder}(r)$ is parameterized by a deep architecture. If r is from the target schema, $\text{Encoder}(r)$ is a produced by a lookup table (as in traditional USchema). Though such an encoder increases the computational cost of test-time prediction over straightforward pattern matching, evaluating a deep architecture can be done in large batches in parallel on a GPU.

Both convolutional networks (CNNs) and recurrent networks (RNNs) are reasonable encoder architectures, and we consider both in our experiments. CNNs have been useful in a variety of NLP applications (Collobert et al., 2011; Kalchbrenner et al., 2014; Kim, 2014). Unlike Toutanova et al. (2015), we also consider RNNs, specifically Long-Short Term Memory Networks

(LSTMs) (Hochreiter and Schmidhuber, 1997). LSTMs have proven successful in a variety of tasks requiring encoding sentences as vectors (Sutskever et al., 2014; Vinyals et al., 2014). In our experiments, LSTMs outperform CNNs.

There are two key differences between our sentence encoder and that of Toutanova et al. (2015). First, we use the encoder at test time, since we process the context tokens for held-out data. On the other hand, Toutanova et al. (2015) adopt the transductive approach where the encoder is only used to help train better representations for the relations in the target schema; it is ignored when forming predictions. Second, we apply the encoder to the raw text between entities, while Toutanova et al. (2015) first perform syntactic dependency parsing on the data and then apply an encoder to the path between the two entities in the parse tree. We avoid parsing, since we seek to perform multilingual AKBC, and many languages lack linguistic resources such as treebanks. Even parsing non-newswire English text, such as tweets, is extremely challenging.

3.3 Modeling Frequent Text Patterns

Despite the coverage advantages of using a deep sentence encoder, separately embedding each OpenIE pattern, as in Riedel et al. (2013), has key advantages. In practice, we have found that many high-precision patterns occur quite frequently. For these, there is sufficient data to model them with independent embeddings per pattern, which imposes minimal inductive bias on the relationship between patterns. Furthermore, some discriminative phrases are idiomatic, i.e.. their meaning is not constructed compositionally from their constituents. For these, a sentence encoder may be inappropriate.

Therefore, pattern embeddings and deep token-based encoders have very different strengths and weaknesses. One values specificity, and models the head of the text distribution well, while the other has high coverage and captures the tail. In experimental results, we demonstrate that an ensemble of both models performs substantially better than either in isolation.

3.4 Multilingual Relation Extraction with Zero Annotation

The models described in previous two sections provide broad-coverage relation extraction that can generalize to all possible input entities and text patterns, while avoiding error-prone alignment of distant supervision to a corpus. Next, we describe techniques for an even more challenging generalization task: relation classification for input sentences in completely different languages.

Training a sentence-level relation classifier, either using the alignment-based techniques of Section 2.2, or the alignment-free method of Section 3.1, requires an available KB of seed facts that have supporting evidence in the corpus. Unfortunately, available KBs have low overlap with corpora in many languages, since KBs have cultural and geographical biases. In response, we perform multilingual relation extraction by jointly modeling a high-resource language, such as English, and an alternative language with no KB annotation. This approach provides transfer learning of a predictive model to the alternative language, and generalizes naturally to modeling more languages.

Extending the training technique of Section 3.1 to corpora in multiple languages can be achieved by factorizing a matrix that mixes data from a KB and from the two corpora. In Figure 1 we split the entities of a multilingual training corpus into sets depending on whether they have annotation in a KB and what corpora they appear in. We can perform transfer learning of a relation extractor to the low-resource language if there are entity pairs occurring in the two corpora, even if there is no KB annotation for these pairs. Note that we do not use the entity pair embeddings at test time: They are used only to bridge the languages during training. To form predictions in the low-resource language, we can simply apply the pattern scoring approach of Section 3.1.

In Section 5, we demonstrate that jointly learning models for English and Spanish, with no annotation for the Spanish data, provides fairly accurate Spanish AKBC, and even improves the performance of the English model. Note that we are not performing *zero-shot* learning of a Spanish model (Larochelle et al., 2008). The relations in the target schema are language-independent concepts, and we have supervision for these in English.

3.5 Tied Sentence Encoders

The sentence encoder approach of Section 3.2 is complementary to our multilingual modeling technique: we simply use a separate encoder for each language. This approach is sub-optimal, however, because each sentence encoder will have a separate matrix of word embeddings for its vocabulary, despite the fact that there may be considerable shared structure between the languages. In response, we propose a straightforward method for tying the parameters of the sentence encoders across languages.

Drawing on the dictionary-based techniques described in Section 2.5, we first obtain a list of word-word translation pairs between the languages using a translation dictionary. The first layer of our deep text encoder consists of a word embedding lookup table. For the aligned word types, we use a single cross-lingual embedding. Details of our approach are described in Appendix 7.5.

4 Task and System Description

We focus on the TAC KBP slot-filling task. Much related work on embedding knowledge bases evaluates on the FB15k dataset (Bordes et al., 2013; Wang et al., 2014; Lin et al., 2015; Yang et al., 2015; Toutanova et al., 2015). Here, relation extraction is posed as link prediction on a subset of Freebase. This task does not capture the particular difficulties we address: (1) evaluation on entities and text unseen during training, and (2) zero-annotation learning of a predictor for a low-resource language.

Also, note both Toutanova et al. (2015) and Riedel et al. (2013) explore the pros and cons of learning embeddings for entity pairs vs. separate embeddings for each entity. As this is orthogonal to our contributions, we only consider entity pair embeddings, which performed best in both works when given sufficient data.

4.1 TAC Slot-Filling Benchmark

The aim of the TAC benchmark is to improve both coverage and quality of relation extraction evaluation compared to just checking the extracted facts against a knowledge base, which can be incomplete and where the provenances are not verified. In the slot-filling task, each system is given a set of paired query entities and relations or 'slots' to fill, and the goal is to correctly fill as many slots as possible along with provenance from the corpus. For example, given the query entity/relation pair (*Barack Obama, per:spouse*), the system should return the entity *Michelle Obama* along with sentence(s) whose text expresses that relation. The answers returned by all participating teams, along with a human search (with time-out), are judged manually for correctness, i.e. whether the provenance specified by the system indeed expresses the relation in question.

In addition to verifying our models on the 2013 and 2014 English slot-filling task, we evaluate our Spanish models on the 2012 TAC Spanish slot-filling evaluation. Because this TAC track was never officially run, the coverage of facts in the available annotation is very small, resulting in many correct predictions being marked incorrectly as precision errors. In response, we manually annotated all results returned by the models considered in Table 4. Precision and recall are calculated with respect to the union of the TAC annotation and our new labeling[1].

4.2 Retrieval Pipeline

Our retrieval pipeline first generates all valid slot filler candidates for each query entity and slot, based on entities extracted from the corpus using FACTORIE (Mc-Callum et al., 2009) to perform tokenization, segmentation, and entity extraction. We perform entity linking by heuristically linking all entity mentions from our text corpora to a Freebase entity using anchor text in Wikipedia. Making use of the fact that most Freebase entries contain a link to the corresponding Wikipedia page, we link all

entity mentions from our text corpora to a Freebase entity by the following process: First, a set of candidate entities is obtained by following frequent link anchor text statistics. We then select that candidate entity for which the cosine similarity between the respective Wikipedia and the sentence context of the mention is highest, and link to that entity if a threshold is exceeded.

An entity pair qualifies as a candidate prediction if it meets the type criteria for the slot.[2] The TAC 2013 English and Spanish newswire corpora each contain about 1 million newswire documents from 2009–2012. The document retrieval and entity matching components of our relation extraction pipeline are based on RelationFactory (Roth et al., 2014), the top-ranked system of the 2013 English slot-filling task. We also use the English distantly supervised training data from this system, which aligns the TAC 2012 corpus to Freebase. More details on alignment are described in Appendix 7.4.

As discussed in Section 3.3, models using a deep sentence encoder and using a pattern lookup table have complementary strengths and weaknesses. In response, we present results where we ensemble the outputs of the two models by simply taking the union of their individual outputs. Slightly higher results might be obtained through more sophisticated ensembling schemes.

4.3 Model Details

All models are implemented in Torch (code publicly available[3]). Models are tuned to maximize F1 on the 2012 TAC KBP slot-filling evaluation. We additionally tune the thresholds of our pattern scorer on a per-relation basis to maximize F1 using 2012 TAC slot-filling for English and the 2012 Spanish slot-filling development set for Spanish. As in Riedel et al. (2013), we train using the BPR loss of Rendle et al. (2009). Our CNN is implemented as described in Toutanova et al. (2015), using width-3 convolutions, followed by tanh and max pool layers. The LSTM uses a bi-directional architecture where the forward and backward representations of each hidden state are averaged, followed by max pooling over time. See Section 7.2

We also report results including an alternate names (AN) heuristic, which uses automatically-extracted rules to detect the TAC 'alternate name' relation. To achieve this, we collect frequent Wikipedia link anchor texts for

---

[1] Following Surdeanu et al. (2012) we remove facts about undiscovered entities to correct for recall.

[2] Due to the difficulty of retrieval and entity detection, the maximum recall for predictions is limited. For this reason, Surdeanu et al. (2012) restrict the evaluation to answer candidates returned by their system and effectively rescaling recall. We do not perform such a re-scaling in our English results in order to compare to other reported results. Our Spanish numbers are rescaled. All scores reflect the 'anydoc' (relaxed) scoring to mitigate penalizing effects for systems not included in the evaluation pool.

[3] https://github.com/patverga/
torch-relation-extraction

Model	Recall	Precision	F1
CNN	31.6	36.8	34.1
LSTM	32.2	39.6	**35.5**
USchema	29.4	42.6	34.8
USchema+LSTM	34.4	41.9	37.7
USchema+LSTM+Es	38.1	40.2	**39.2**
USchema+LSTM+AN	36.7	43.1	39.7
USchema+LSTM+Es+AN	40.2	41.2	**40.7**
Roth et al. (2014)	35.8	45.7	40.2

Table 2: Precision, recall and F1 on the English TAC 2013 slot-filling task. AN refers to alternative names heuristic and Es refers to the addition of Spanish text at train time. LSTM+USchema ensemble outperforms any single model, including the highly-tuned top 2013 system of Roth et al. (2014), despite using no handwritten patterns.

Model	Recall	Precision	F1
CNN	28.1	29.0	28.5
LSTM	27.3	32.9	**29.8**
USchema	24.3	35.5	28.8
USchema+LSTM	34.1	29.3	31.5
USchema+LSTM+Es	34.4	31.0	**32.6**

Table 3: Precision, recall and F1 on the English TAC 2014 slot-filling task. Es refers to the addition of Spanish text at train time. The AN heuristic is ineffective on 2014 adding only 0.2 to F1. Our system would rank 4/18 in the official TAC 2014 competition behind systems that use hand-written patterns and active learning despite our system using neither of these additional annotations (Surdeanu and Ji., 2014).

each query entity. If a high probability anchor text co-occurs with the canonical name of the query in the same document, we return the anchor text as a slot filler.

5 Experimental Results

In experiments on the English and Spanish TAC KBC slot-filling tasks, we find that both USchema and LSTM models outperform the CNN across languages, and that the LSTM tends to perform slightly better than USchema as the only model. Ensembling the LSTM and USchema models further increases final F1 scores in all experiments, suggesting that the two different types of model compliment each other well. Indeed, in Section 5.3 we present quantitative and qualitative analysis of our results which further confirms this hypothesis: the LSTM and USchema models each perform better on different pattern lengths and are characterized by different precision-recall tradeoffs.

Model	Recall	Precision	F1
LSTM	9.3	12.5	10.7
LSTM+Dict	14.7	15.7	15.2
USchema	15.2	17.5	16.3
USchema+LSTM	21.7	14.5	17.3
USchema+LSTM+Dict	26.9	15.9	**20.0**

Table 4: Zero-annotation transfer learning F1 scores on 2012 Spanish TAC KBP slot-filling task. Adding a translation dictionary improves all encoder-based models. Ensembling LSTM and USchema models performs the best.

5.1 English TAC Slot-filling Results

Tables 2 and 3 present the performance of our models on the 2013 and 2014 English TAC slot-filling tasks. Ensembling the LSTM and USchema models improves F1 by 2.2 points for 2013 and 1.7 points for 2014 over the strongest single model on both evaluations, LSTM. Adding the alternative names (AN) heuristic described in Section 4.3 increases F1 by an additional 2 points on 2013, resulting in an F1 score that is competitive with the state-of-the-art. We also demonstrate the effect of jointly learning English and Spanish models on English slot-filling performance. Adding Spanish data improves our F1 scores by 1.5 points on 2013 and 1.1 on 2014 over using English alone. This places are system higher than the top performer at the 2013 TAC slot-filling task even though our system uses no hand-written rules.

The state of the art systems on this task all rely on matching handwritten patterns to find additional answers while our models use only automatically generated, indirect supervision; even our AN heuristics (Section 4.2) are automatically generated. The top two 2014 systems were Angeli et al. (2014) and RPI Blender (Surdeanu and Ji., 2014) who achieved F1 scores of 39.5 and 36.4 respectively. Both of these systems used additional active learning annotation. The third place team (Lin et al., 2014) relied on highly tuned patterns and rules and achieved an F1 score of 34.4.

Our model performs substantially better on 2013 than 2014 for two reasons. First, our RelationFactory (Roth et al., 2014) retrieval pipeline was a top retrieval pipeline on the 2013 task, but was outperformed on the 2014 task which introduced new challenges such as confusable entities. Second, improved training using active learning gave the top 2014 systems a boost in performance. No 2013 systems, including ours, use active learning. Bentor et al. (2014), the 4th place team in the 2014 evaluation, used the same retrieval pipeline (Roth et al., 2014) as our model and achieved an F1 score of 32.1.

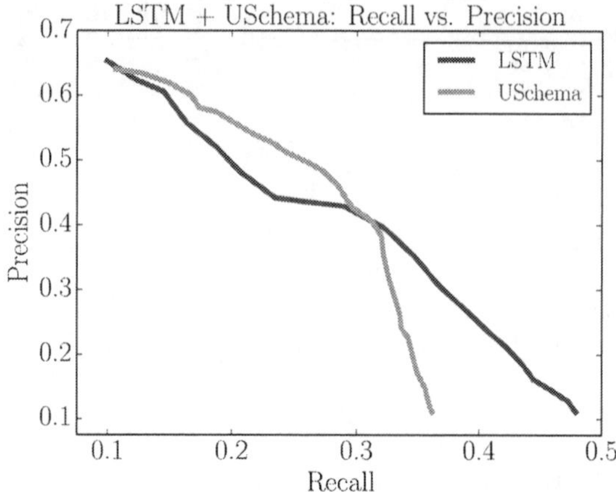

Figure 3: Precision-Recall curves for USchema and LSTM on 2013 TAC slot-filling. USchema achieves higher precision values whereas LSTM has higher recall.

5.2 Spanish TAC Slot-filling Results

Table 4 presents 2012 Spanish TAC slot-filling results for our multilingual relation extractors trained using zero-annotation transfer learning. Tying word embeddings between the two languages results in substantial improvements for the LSTM. We see that ensembling the non-dictionary LSTM with USchema gives a slight boost over USchema alone, but ensembling the dictionary-tied LSTM with USchema provides a significant increase of nearly 4 F1 points over the highest-scoring single model, USchema. Clearly, grounding the Spanish data using a translation dictionary provides much better Spanish word representations. These improvements are complementary to the baseline USchema model, and yield impressive results when ensembled.

In addition to embedding semantically similar phrases from English and Spanish to have high similarity, our models also learn high-quality multilingual word embeddings. In Table 5 we compare Spanish nearest neighbors of English query words learned by the LSTM with dictionary ties versus the LSTM with no ties, using no unsupervised pre-training for the embeddings. Both approaches jointly embed Spanish and English word types, using shared entity embeddings, but the dictionary-tied model learns qualitatively better multilingual embeddings.

5.3 USchema vs LSTM

We further analyze differences between USchema and LSTM in order to better understand why ensembling the models results in the best performing system. Figure 3 depicts precision-recall curves for the two models on the 2013 slot-filling task. As observed in earlier results, the LSTM achieves higher recall at the loss of

CEO	
Dictionary	No Ties
jefe (chief)	CEO
CEO	director (principle)
ejecutivo (executive)	directora (director)
cofundador (co-founder)	firma (firm)
president (chairman)	magnate (tycoon)
headquartered	
Dictionary	No Ties
sede (headquarters)	Geológico (Geological)
situado (located)	Treki (Treki)
selectivo (selective)	Geofísico(geophysical)
profesional (vocational)	Normandía (Normandy)
basándose (based)	emplea (uses)
hubby	
Dictionary	No Ties
matrimonio (marriage)	esposa (wife)
casada (married)	esposo (husband)
esposa (wife)	casada(married)
casó (married)	embarazada (pregnant)
embarazada (pregnant)	embarazo (pregnancy)
alias	
Dictionary	No Ties
simplificado (simplified)	Weaver (Weaver)
sabido (known)	interrogación (question)
seudónimo (pseudonym)	alias
privatización (privatization)	reelecto (reelected)
nombre (name)	conocido (known)

Table 5: Example English query words (not in translation dictionary) in bold with their top nearest neighbors by cosine similarity listed for the dictionary and no ties LSTM variants. Dictionary-tied nearest neighbors are consistently more relevant to the query word than untied.

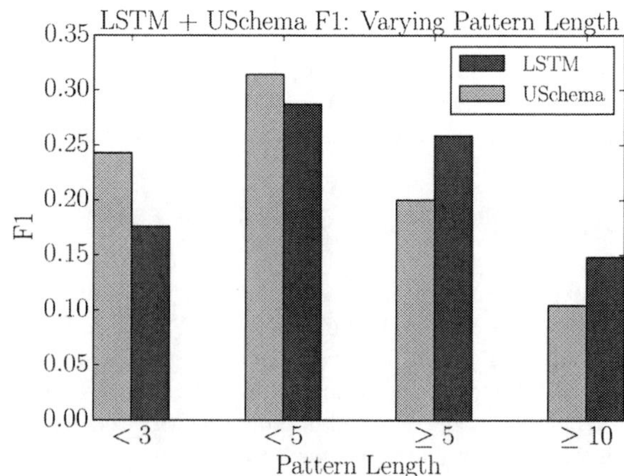

Figure 4: F1 achieved by USchema vs. LSTM models for varying pattern token lengths on 2013 TAC slot-filling. LSTM performs better on longer patterns whereas USchema performs better on shorter patterns.

some precision, whereas USchema can make more precise predictions at a lower threshold for recall. In Figure 4 we observe evidence for these different precision-recall trade-offs: USchema scores higher in terms of F1 on shorter patterns whereas the LSTM scores higher on longer patterns. As one would expect, USchema successfully matches more short patterns than the LSTM, making more precise predictions at the cost of being unable to predict on patterns unseen during training. The LSTM can predict using any text between entities observed at test time, gaining recall at the loss of precision. Combining the two models makes the most of their strengths and weaknesses, leading to the highest overall F1.

Qualitative analysis of our English models also suggests that our encoder-based models (LSTM) extract relations based on a wide range of semantically similar patterns that the pattern-matching model (USchema) is unable to score due to a lack of exact string match in the test data. For example, Table 6 lists three examples of the *per:children* relation that the LSTM finds which USchema does not, as well as three patterns that USchema does find. Though the LSTM patterns are all semantically and syntactically similar, they each contain different specific noun phrases, e.g. *Lori, four children, toddler daughter, Lee and Albert*, etc. Because these specific nouns weren't seen during training, USchema fails to find these patterns whereas the LSTM learns to ignore the specific nouns in favor of the overall pattern, that of a parent-child relationship in an obituary. USchema is limited to finding the relations represented by patterns observed during training, which limits the patterns matched at test-time to short and common patterns; all the USchema patterns matched at test time were similar to those listed in Table 6: variants of *'s son, '*.

LSTM
McGregor *is survived by his wife, Lori, and four children, daughters Jordan,* **Taylor** *and Landri, and a son, Logan.*
In addition to his wife, **Mays** *is survived by a toddler daughter and a son,* **Billy Mays Jr.,** *who is in his 20s.*
Anderson *is survived by his wife Carol, sons Lee and Albert, daughter* **Shirley Englebrecht** *and nine grandchildren.*

USchema
Dio *'s son,* **Dan Padavona,** cautioned the memorial crowd to be screened regularly by a doctor and take care of themselves, something he said his father did not do.
But **Marshall** *'s son,* **Philip,** told a different story.
"I'd rather have Sully doing this than some stranger, or some hotshot trying to be the next Billy Mays," said the guy who actually is the next **Billy Mays,** *his son* **Billy Mays III.**

Table 6: Examples of the *per:children* relation discovered by the LSTM and Universal Schema. Entities are bold and patterns italicized. The LSTM models a richer set of patterns

6 Conclusion

By jointly embedding English and Spanish corpora along with a KB, we can train an accurate Spanish relation extraction model using no direct annotation for relations in the Spanish data. This approach has the added benefit of providing significant accuracy improvements for the English model, outperforming the top system on the 2013 TAC KBC slot filling task, without using the hand-coded rules or additional annotations of alternative systems. By using deep sentence encoders, we can perform prediction for arbitrary input text and for entities unseen in training. Sentence encoders also provides opportunities to improve cross-lingual transfer learning by sharing word embeddings across languages. In future work we will apply this model to many more languages and domains besides newswire text. We would also like to avoid the entity detection problem by using a deep architecture to both identify entity mentions and identify relations between them.

Acknowledgments

Many thanks to Arvind Neelakantan for good ideas and discussions. We also appreciate a generous hardware grant from nVidia. This work was supported in part by the Center for Intelligent Information Retrieval, in part by Defense Advanced Research Projects Agency (DARPA) under agreement #FA8750-13-2-0020 and contract #HR0011-15-2-0036, and in part by the National Science Foundation (NSF) grant numbers DMR-1534431, IIS-1514053 and CNS-0958392. The U.S. Government is authorized to reproduce and distribute reprints for Governmental purposes notwithstanding any copyright notation thereon, in part by DARPA via agreement #DFA8750-13-2-0020 and NSF grant #CNS-0958392. Any opinions, findings and conclusions or recommendations expressed in this material are those of the authors and do not necessarily reflect those of the sponsor.

References

[Angeli et al.2014] Gabor Angeli, Sonal Gupta, Melvin Jose, Christopher D Manning, Christopher Ré, Julie Tibshirani, Jean Y Wu, Sen Wu, and Ce Zhang. 2014. Stanfords 2014 slot filling systems. *TAC KBP*.

[Banko et al.2007] Michele Banko, Michael J Cafarella, Stephen Soderland, Matt Broadhead, and Oren Etzioni. 2007. Open information extraction from the web. In *International Joint Conference on Artificial Intelligence*.

[Bentor et al.2014] Yinon Bentor, Vidhoon Viswanathan, and Raymond Mooney. 2014. University of texas at austin kbp 2014 slot filling system: Bayesian logic programs for textual inference. In *Proceedings of the Seventh Text Analysis Conference: Knowledge Base Population (TAC 2014)*.

[Bollacker et al.2008] Kurt Bollacker, Colin Evans, Praveen Paritosh, Tim Sturge, and Jamie Taylor. 2008. Freebase: a collaboratively created graph database for structuring human knowledge. In *Proceedings of the ACM SIGMOD International Conference on Management of Data*.

[Bordes et al.2013] Antoine Bordes, Nicolas Usunier, Alberto García-Durán, Jason Weston, and Oksana Yakhnenko. 2013. Translating embeddings for modeling multi-relational data. In *Advances in Neural Information Processing Systems*.

[Bordes et al.2014] Antoine Bordes, Sumit Chopra, and Jason Weston. 2014. Question answering with subgraph embeddings. *arXiv preprint arXiv:1406.3676*.

[Bunescu and Mooney2007] Razvan Bunescu and Raymond Mooney. 2007. Learning to extract relations from the web using minimal supervision. In *Annual meeting-association for Computational Linguistics*, volume 45, page 576.

[Carlson et al.2010] Andrew Carlson, Justin Betteridge, Bryan Kisiel, Burr Settles, Estevam R. Hruschka, and A. 2010. Toward an architecture for never-ending language learning. In *In AAAI*.

[Collobert et al.2011] Ronan Collobert, Jason Weston, Léon Bottou, Michael Karlen, Koray Kavukcuoglu, and Pavel Kuksa. 2011. Natural language processing (almost) from scratch. *The Journal of Machine Learning Research*, 12:2493–2537.

[dos Santos et al.2015] Cıcero Nogueira dos Santos, Bing Xiang, and Bowen Zhou. 2015. Classifying relations by ranking with convolutional neural networks. In *Proceedings of the 53rd Annual Meeting of the Association for Computational Linguistics and the 7th International Joint Conference on Natural Language Processing*, volume 1, pages 626–634.

[Etzioni et al.2008] Oren Etzioni, Michele Banko, Stephen Soderland, and Daniel S Weld. 2008. Open information extraction from the web. *Communications of the ACM*, 51(12):68–74.

[Faruqui and Kumar2015] Manaal Faruqui and Shankar Kumar. 2015. Multilingual open relation extraction using cross-lingual projection. *arXiv preprint arXiv:1503.06450*.

[Faruqui et al.2014] Manaal Faruqui, Jesse Dodge, Sujay K Jauhar, Chris Dyer, Eduard Hovy, and Noah A Smith. 2014. Retrofitting word vectors to semantic lexicons. *arXiv preprint arXiv:1411.4166*.

[García-Durán et al.2015] Alberto García-Durán, Antoine Bordes, Nicolas Usunier, and Yves Grandvalet. 2015. Combining two and three-way embeddings models for link prediction in knowledge bases. *CoRR*, abs/1506.00999.

[Gardner et al.2014] Matt Gardner, Partha Talukdar, Jayant Krishnamurthy, and Tom Mitchell. 2014. Incorporating vector space similarity in random walk inference over knowledge bases. In *Empirical Methods in Natural Language Processing*.

[Gouws et al.2015] Stephan Gouws, Yoshua Bengio, and Greg Corrado. 2015. B IL BOWA : Fast Bilingual Distributed Representations without Word Alignments. *Icml*, pages 1–10.

[Gu et al.2015] Kelvin Gu, John Miller, and Percy Liang. 2015. Traversing knowledge graphs in vector space. *arXiv preprint arXiv:1506.01094*.

[Hermann and Blunsom2014] Karl Moritz Hermann and Phil Blunsom. 2014. Multilingual models for compositional distributed semantics. *arXiv preprint arXiv:1404.4641*.

[Hochreiter and Schmidhuber1997] Sepp Hochreiter and Jürgen Schmidhuber. 1997. Long short-term memory. In *Neural Computation*.

[Hoffmann et al.2011] Raphael Hoffmann, Congle Zhang, Xiao Ling, Luke Zettlemoyer, and Daniel S Weld. 2011. Knowledge-based weak supervision for information extraction of overlapping relations. In *Proceedings of the 49th Annual Meeting of the Association for Computational Linguistics: Human Language Technologies-Volume 1*, pages 541–550. Association for Computational Linguistics.

[Kalchbrenner et al.2014] Nal Kalchbrenner, Edward Grefenstette, and Phil Blunsom. 2014. A convolutional neural network for modelling sentences. *Proceedings of the 52nd Annual Meeting of the Association for Computational Linguistics*, June.

[Kim2014] Yoon Kim. 2014. Convolutional neural networks for sentence classification. *EMNLP*.

[Kingma and Ba2015] Diederik Kingma and Jimmy Ba. 2015. Adam: A method for stochastic optimization. In *3rd International Conference for Learning Representations (ICLR)*.

[Koehn2005] Philipp Koehn. 2005. Europarl: A parallel corpus for statistical machine translation. In *MT summit*, volume 5, pages 79–86. Citeseer.

[Lao et al.2011] Ni Lao, Tom Mitchell, and William W. Cohen. 2011. Random walk inference and learning in a large scale knowledge base. In *Conference on Empirical Methods in Natural Language Processing*.

[Lao et al.2012] Ni Lao, Amarnag Subramanya, Fernando Pereira, and William W. Cohen. 2012. Reading the web with learned syntactic-semantic inference rules. In *Joint Conference on Empirical Methods in Natural Language Processing and Computational Natural Language Learning*.

[Larochelle et al.2008] Hugo Larochelle, Dumitru Erhan, and Yoshua Bengio. 2008. Zero-data learning of new tasks. In *National Conference on Artificial Intelligence*.

[Li et al.2015] Jiwei Li, Dan Jurafsky, and Eudard Hovy. 2015. When are tree structures necessary for deep learning of representations? *arXiv preprint arXiv:1503.00185*.

[Lin et al.2014] Hailun Lin, Zeya Zhao, Yantao Jia, Yuanzhuo Wang, Jinhua Xiong, and Xiaojing Li. 2014. OpenKN at TAC KBP 2014.

[Lin et al.2015] Yankai Lin, Zhiyuan Liu, Maosong Sun, Yang Liu, and Xuan Zhu. 2015. Learning entity and relation embeddings for knowledge graph completion. In *Proceedings of AAAI*.

[Luong et al.2015] Thang Luong, Hieu Pham, and Christopher D Manning. 2015. Bilingual word representations with monolingual quality in mind. In *Proceedings of the 1st Workshop on Vector Space Modeling for Natural Language Processing*, pages 151–159.

[McCallum et al.2009] Andrew McCallum, Karl Schultz, and Sameer Singh. 2009. FACTORIE: Probabilistic programming via imperatively defined factor graphs. In *Neural Information Processing Systems (NIPS)*.

[Mikolov et al.2013] Tomas Mikolov, Quoc V Le, and Ilya Sutskever. 2013. Exploiting Similarities among Languages for Machine Translation. In *arXiv preprint arXiv:1309.4168v1*, pages 1–10.

[Min et al.2013] Bonan Min, Ralph Grishman, Li Wan, Chang Wang, and David Gondek. 2013. Distant supervision for relation extraction with an incomplete knowledge base. In *HLT-NAACL*, pages 777–782.

[Mintz et al.2009] Mike Mintz, Steven Bills, Rion Snow, and Dan Jurafsky. 2009. Distant supervision for relation extraction without labeled data. In *Association for Computational Linguistics and International Joint Conference on Natural Language Processing*.

[Neelakantan et al.2015] Arvind Neelakantan, Benjamin Roth, and Andrew McCallum. 2015. Compositional vector space models for knowledge base completion. *Proceedings of the 53rd Annual Meeting of the Association for Computational Linguistics*.

[Nickel et al.2011] Maximilian Nickel, Volker Tresp, and Hans-Peter Kriegel. 2011. A three-way model for collective learning on multi-relational data. In *International Conference on Machine Learning*.

[Nickel et al.2015] Maximilian Nickel, Kevin Murphy, Volker Tresp, and Evgeniy Gabrilovich. 2015. A review of relational machine learning for knowledge graphs: From multi-relational link prediction to automated knowledge graph construction. *arXiv preprint arXiv:1503.00759*.

[Rendle et al.2009] Steffen Rendle, Christoph Freudenthaler, Zeno Gantner, and Lars Schmidt-Thieme. 2009. Bpr: Bayesian personalized ranking from implicit feedback. In *Proceedings of the Twenty-Fifth Conference on Uncertainty in Artificial Intelligence*, pages 452–461. AUAI Press.

[Riedel et al.2010] Sebastian Riedel, Limin Yao, and Andrew McCallum. 2010. Modeling relations and their mentions without labeled text. In *Machine Learning and Knowledge Discovery in Databases*, pages 148–163. Springer.

[Riedel et al.2013] Sebastian Riedel, Limin Yao, Andrew McCallum, and Benjamin M. Marlin. 2013. Relation extraction with matrix factorization and universal schemas. In *HLT-NAACL*.

[Rocktaschel et al.2015] Tim Rocktaschel, Sameer Singh, and Sebastian Riedel. 2015. Injecting logical background knowledge into embeddings for relation extraction. In *Annual Conference of the North American Chapter of the Association for Computational Linguistics (NAACL)*.

[Roth et al.2014] Benjamin Roth, Tassilo Barth, Grzegorz Chrupała, Martin Gropp, and Dietrich Klakow. 2014. Relationfactory: A fast, modular and effective system for knowledge base population. *EACL 2014*, page 89.

[Schein et al.2002] Andrew I Schein, Alexandrin Popescul, Lyle H Ungar, and David M Pennock. 2002. Methods and metrics for cold-start recommendations. In *Proceedings of the 25th annual international ACM SIGIR conference on Research and development in information retrieval*, pages 253–260. ACM.

[Socher et al.2013] Richard Socher, Danqi Chen, Christopher D Manning, and Andrew Ng. 2013. Reasoning with neural tensor networks for knowledge base completion. In *Advances in Neural Information Processing Systems*.

[Suchanek et al.2007] Fabian M. Suchanek, Gjergji Kasneci, and Gerhard Weikum. 2007. Yago: A core of semantic knowledge. In *Proceedings of the 16th International Conference on World Wide Web*.

[Surdeanu and Ji.2014] Mihai Surdeanu and Heng Ji. 2014. Overview of the english slot filling track at the tac2014 knowledge base population evaluation. *Proc. Text Analysis Conference (TAC2014)*.

[Surdeanu et al.2012] Mihai Surdeanu, Julie Tibshirani, Ramesh Nallapati, and Christopher D Manning. 2012. Multi-instance multi-label learning for relation extraction. In *Proceedings of the 2012 Joint Conference on Empirical Methods in Natural Language Processing and Computational Natural Language Learning*, pages 455–465. Association for Computational Linguistics.

[Sutskever et al.2014] Ilya Sutskever, Oriol Vinyals, and Quoc V. V Le. 2014. Sequence to sequence learning with neural networks. In *Advances in Neural Information Processing Systems*.

[Toutanova et al.2015] Kristina Toutanova, Danqi Chen, Patrick Pantel, Hoifung Poon, Pallavi Choudhury, and Michael Gamon. 2015. Representing text for joint embedding of text and knowledge bases. In *Empirical Methods in Natural Language Processing (EMNLP)*.

[Vinyals et al.2014] Oriol Vinyals, Lukasz Kaiser, Terry Koo, Slav Petrov, Ilya Sutskever, and Geoffrey Hinton. 2014. Grammar as a foreign language. In *CoRR*.

[Wang et al.2014] Zhen Wang, Jianwen Zhang, Jianlin Feng, and Zheng Chen. 2014. Knowledge graph embedding by translating on hyperplanes. In *Proceedings of the Twenty-Eighth AAAI Conference on Artificial Intelligence*, pages 1112–1119. Citeseer.

[Xu et al.2015] Yan Xu, Lili Mou, Ge Li, Yunchuan Chen, Hao Peng, and Zhi Jin. 2015. Classifying relations via long short term memory networks along shortest dependency paths. In *Proceedings of Conference on Empirical Methods in Natural Language Processing (to appear)*.

[Yang et al.2015] Bishan Yang, Wen-tau Yih, Xiaodong He, Jianfeng Gao, and Li Deng. 2015. Embedding entities and relations for learning and inference in knowledge bases. *International Conference on Learning Representations 2014*.

[Yao et al.2010] Limin Yao, Sebastian Riedel, and Andrew McCallum. 2010. Collective cross-document relation extraction without labelled data. In *Proceedings of the 2010 Conference on Empirical Methods in Natural Language Processing*, pages 1013–1023. Association for Computational Linguistics.

[Yao et al.2013] Limin Yao, Sebastian Riedel, and Andrew McCallum. 2013. Universal schema for entity type prediction. In *Proceedings of the 2013 workshop on Automated knowledge base construction*, pages 79–84. ACM.

[Yates and Etzioni2007] Alexander Yates and Oren Etzioni. 2007. Unsupervised resolution of objects and relations on the web. In *North American Chapter of the Association for Computational Linguistics*.

[Zeng et al.2015] Daojian Zeng, Kang Liu, Yubo Chen, and Jun Zhao. 2015. Distant supervision for relation extraction via piecewise convolutional neural networks. *EMNLP*.

Effective Crowd Annotation for Relation Extraction

Angli Liu, Stephen Soderland, Jonathan Bragg,
Christopher H. Lin, Xiao Ling, and Daniel S. Weld
Turing Center, Department of Computer Science and Engineering
Box 352350
University of Washington
Seattle, WA 98195, USA
{anglil, soderlan, jbragg, chrislin, xiaoling, weld} at cs.washington.edu

Abstract

Can crowdsourced annotation of training data
boost performance for relation extraction over
methods based solely on distant supervision?
While crowdsourcing has been shown effective for many NLP tasks, previous researchers
found only minimal improvement when applying the method to relation extraction. This
paper demonstrates that a much larger boost
is possible, e.g., raising F1 from 0.40 to 0.60.
Furthermore, the gains are due to a simple, generalizable technique, *Gated Instruction*, which combines an interactive tutorial,
feedback to correct errors during training, and
improved screening.

1 Introduction

Relation extraction (RE) is the task of identifying
instances of relations, such as *nationality (person,
country)* or *place_of_birth (person, location)*, in passages of natural text. Since RE enables a broad range
of applications — including question answering and
knowledge base population — it has attracted attention from many researchers. Many approaches to RE
use supervised machine learning, e.g., (Soderland et
al., 1995; Califf and Mooney, 1997; Lafferty et al.,
2001), but these methods require a large, human-
annotated training corpus that may be unavailable.

In response, researchers developed methods for
distant supervision (DS) in which a knowledge base
such as Wikipedia or Freebase is used to automatically tag training examples from a text corpus (Wu
and Weld, 2007; Mintz et al., 2009). Indeed, virtually all entries to recent TAC KBP relation extraction

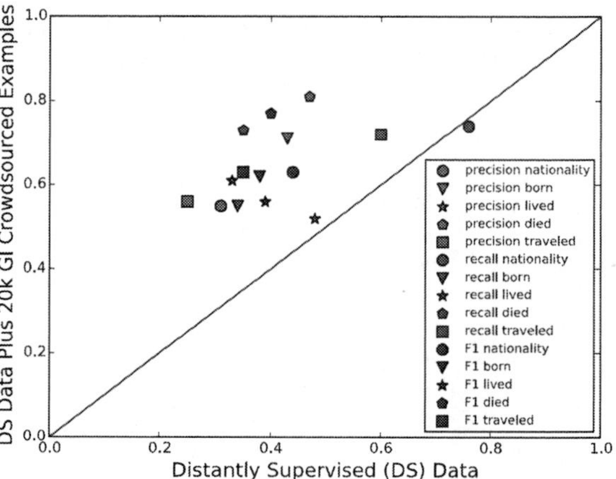

Figure 1: Adding 20K crowdsourced instances, acquired using
Gated Instruction, to 700K examples from distant supervision
raises precision, recall, and F1 for nearly all relations and raises
overall F1 from 0.40 to 0.60 with MIML-RE learning.

competitions use distant supervision (Ji and Grishman, 2011). However, distant supervision provides
noisy training data with many false positives, and
this limits the precision of the resulting extractors
(see Section 2). A natural assumption is that human-
annotated training data, either alone or in conjunction with distant supervision, would give better precision. In particular, Snow et al. (2008) showed that,
for many NLP tasks, crowdsourced data is as good
as or better than that annotated by experts.

It is quite surprising, therefore, that researchers
who have applied crowdsourced annotation to relation extraction argue the *opposite*, that crowdsourcing provides only minor improvement:

Proceedings of NAACL-HLT 2016, pages 897–906,
San Diego, California, June 12-17, 2016. ©2016 Association for Computational Linguistics

- Zhang et al. (2012) conclude that "Human feedback has relatively small impact on precision and recall." Instead, they advise applying distant supervision to vastly more data.

- Pershina et al. (2014) assert "Simply taking the union of the hand-labeled data and the corpus labeled by distant supervision is not effective since hand-labeled data will be swamped by a larger amount of distantly labeled data." Instead, they introduce a complex feature-creation approach which improves the F1-score of MIML-RE, a state-of-the-art extractor (Surdeanu et al., 2012), just 4%, from 0.28 to 0.32 on a set of 41 TAC KBP relations.

- Angeli et al. (2014) explored a novel active learning method to control crowdsourcing, but found no improvement from adding the crowdsourced training to distant supervision using the default settings of MIML-RE, and only a 0.04 improvement in F1 when they initialized MIML-RE using the crowdsourced training.

This paper reports quite a different result, showing up to a 0.20 boost to F1. By carefully designing a quality-controlled crowdsourcing workflow that uses *Gated Instruction* (GI), we are able to create much more accurate annotations than those produced by previous crowdsourcing methods. GI (summarized in Figure 2) includes an interactive tutorial to train workers, providing immediate feedback to correct mistakes during training. Workers are then screened by their accuracy on gold-standard questions while doing the annotation. We show that GI generates much better training data than crowdsourcing used by other researchers, and that this leads to dramatically improved extractors.

Adding GI-crowdsourced annotations of the example sentences selected by Angeli et al.'s active learning method provides a much larger boost to the performance of the learned extractors than when their traditional crowdsourcing methods are used. In fact, the improvement due to our crowdsourcing method substantially outweighs the benefits of Angeli et al.'s active learning strategy as well. In total, this paper makes the following contributions:

- We present the design of the Gated Instruction crowdsourcing workflow with worker training and screening that ensures high-precision annotations for relation extraction training data in the presence of unreliable workers.

- We demonstrate that Gated Instruction increases the annotation quality of crowdsourced training data, raising precision from 0.50 to 0.77 and recall from 0.70 to 0.78, compared to Angeli et al.'s crowdsourced tagging of the same sentences. We make the data available for future research (Section 4.1).

- Augmenting distant supervision with 10K of Angeli et al.'s training examples annotated using Gated Instruction boosts F1 from 0.40 to 0.47, compared to 0.43, the result from using Angeli et al.'s crowdsourced annotations.

- We demonstrate that improved crowdsourcing has a greater effect than Angeli et al.'s active learning approach. Adding 10K *randomly selected* sentences, labeled using Gated Instruction, to distantly supervised data raises F1 by 6 points, compared to the 3 point gain from adding Angeli et al.'s crowdsourced labels on their active-learning sample.

- In contradiction to Zhang et al.'s prior claims, we show that increasing amounts of crowdsourced data can dramatically improve extractor performance. When we augmented distant supervision with 20K instances using Gated Instruction, we show that F1 is raised from 0.40 to 0.60.

- Gated Instruction may also reduce the cost of crowdsourcing. We show that with the high quality Gated Instruction annotations, a single annotation is more effective than majority vote over multiple annotators.

Our results provide a clear lesson for future researchers hoping to use crowdsourced data for NLP tasks. Extreme care must be exercised in the details of the workflow design to ensure quality data and useful results.

2 Background and Related Work

Distant supervision (DS) is a method for training extractors that obviates the need for human-labeled training data by heuristically matching facts from a background knowledge base (KB) to a large textual corpus. Originally developed to extract biological relations (Craven and Kumlien, 1999), DS was later extended to extract relations from Wikipedia infoboxes (Wu and Weld, 2007) and Freebase (Mintz et al., 2009). Specifically, distant supervision uses the KB to find pairs of entities E_1 and E_2 for which a relation R holds. Distant supervision then makes that assumption that any sentence that contains a mention of both E_1 and E_2 is a positive training instance for $R(E_1, E_2)$.

Unfortunately, this assumption leads to a large proportion of false positive training instances. For example, Freebase asserts that Nicolas Sarkozy was born in Paris, but nearly all sentences in a news corpus that mention Sarkozy and Paris do not give evidence for a *place_of_birth* relation. To address this shortcoming, there have been attempts to model the relation dependencies as multi-instance multi-class (Bunescu and Mooney, 2007; Riedel et al., 2010) leading to state-of-the art extraction learners MultiR (Hoffmann et al., 2011) and MIML-RE (Surdeanu et al., 2012).

Additionally, other techniques developed to study the relation extraction problem have achieved certain success, including universal schemas (Riedel et al., 2013), and deep learning (Nguyen and Grishman, 2014). Despite these technical innovations, the best systems at the TAC-KBP evaluation[1] still require substantial human effort, typically handwritten extraction rules (Surdeanu and Ji, 2014).

Recently researchers have explored the idea of augmenting distant supervision with a small amount of crowdsourced annotated data in an effort to improve relation extraction performance (Angeli et al., 2014; Zhang et al., 2012; Pershina et al., 2014).

Zhang et al. (2012) studied how the size of the crowdsourcing training corpus and distant supervision corpus affect the performance of the relation extractor. They considered the 20 TAC KBP relations that had a corresponding Freebase relation. They added up to 20K instances of crowd data to 1.8M DS instances using sparse logistic regression, tuning the relative weight of crowdsourced and DS training. However, they saw only a marginal improvement from F1 0.20 to 0.22 when adding crowdsourced training to DS training, and conclude that human feedback has little impact.

Angeli et al. (2014) also investigated methods for infusing distant supervision with crowdsourced annotations in the Stanford TAC-KBP sys-

tem. They experimented with several methods, including adding a random sample of annotated sentences to the training mix, and using active learning to select which sentences should be annotated by humans. Their best results were what they termed "Sample JS," training a committee of MIML-RE classifiers and then sampling the sentences to be crowdsourced weighted by the divergence of classifications.

Surprisingly, they found that the simple approach of just adding crowdsourced data to the training mix *hurt* extractor performance slightly. They conclude that the most important use for crowdsourced annotations is as a way to *initialize* MIML-RE, mitigating the problem of local minima during learning. When they initialized MIML-RE with 10K Sample JS crowdsourced instances and then trained on a combination of Sample JS crowdsourced and DS instances, this raised F1 from 0.34 to 0.38.

Pershina et al. (2014) also exploited a small set of highly informative hand-labeled training data to improve distant supervision. Rather than crowdsourcing, they used the set of 2,500 labeled instances from the KBP 2012 assessment data. They state that "Simply taking the union of the hand-labeled data and the corpus labeled by distant supervision is not effective since hand-labeled data will be swamped by a larger amount of distantly labeled data." Instead they use the hand-annotated data to learn *guidelines* that are included in a graphical prediction model that extends MIML-RE, trained using distant supervision. This raised F1 from 0.28 to 0.32 over a comparison system without the learned guidelines.

Gormley et al. (2010) filtered crowdsourced workers by agreement with gold questions and by noting which workers took fewer than three seconds per question. They reported good inter-annotator agreement, but did not build a relation extractor from their data.

Both Zhang et al. and Angeli et al. used trad{}tional methods to ensure the quality of their crowdsourced data. Zhang et al. replicated each question three times and included a gold question (i.e., one with a known answer) in each set of five questions. They only used answers from workers who answered at least 80% of the gold-standard questions correctly.

---

[1]http://www.nist.gov/tac/

Angeli et al. included two gold-standard questions in every set of 15. They discarded sets in which both controls were answered incorrectly, and additionally discarded all submissions from workers who failed the controls on more than one third of their submissions. They collected five annotations for each example, and used the majority vote as the ground truth in their training. They did not report the resulting quality of their crowdsourced annotations, but did release their data, allowing us to measure its precision and recall (see Section 4.1).

We argue that all these systems would have gotten better performance by focusing attention on the quality of their crowdsourced annotation. We demonstrate that by improving the crowdsourcing workflow, we achieve a higher F1 score, both with the crowdsourced training alone and in combination with distant supervision.

Our work adds to the existing large body of work that shows that crowdsourcing can be and is an effective and efficient method for training machine learning algorithms. Snow et al. (2008) showed that multiple workers can simulate an expert worker in a variety of natural language tasks. Many researchers (e.g., (Dawid and Skene, 1979; Whitehill et al., 2009)) have designed methods to aggregate crowd labels in order to reduce noise, and Sheng et al. (2008) showed that paying multiple crowd workers to relabel examples, as opposed to labeling new ones, can increase the accuracy of a classifier.

The effectiveness of crowdsourcing is dependent on a number of human factors. Several researchers have studied how worker retention is affected by payment schemes (Mao et al., 2013), recruitment techniques (Ipeirotis and Gabrilovich, 2014), or attention diversions (Dai et al., 2015). Ipeirotis and Gabrilovich show that volunteer workers may provide higher quality work. By contrast, we show that paid workers, too, can produce high quality work through careful attention to worker training and testing.

3 Gated Instruction Crowdsourcing

We used Amazon Mechanical Turk for our crowdsourcing, but designed our own website to implement the Gated Instruction (GI) protocol, rather than use the platform Amazon provides directly. This allowed us greater control over the UI and the worker

Gated Instruction Crowdsourcing Protocol

Phase I: Interactive tutorial
1. Give a clear definition of each relation and tagging criteria.
2. Worker annotates practice sentences that illustrate each relation.
3. Give immediate feedback after each practice sentence.

Phase II: Screening questions
1. Worker annotates representative set of 5 gold questions.
2. Give feedback to worker on each question.
3. Eliminate workers who fail a majority of these questions.

Phase III: Batches of questions (with continued screening)
1. Include gold questions without feedback.
2. Sets of 5 gold questions in batches (20 questions) with exponentially decreasing frequency.
3. Eliminate workers with accuracy lower than 80% on last 10 gold questions.

General Principles
1. Accept only workers with AMT reputation above threshold.
2. Provide a link to definitions of relations during the task.
3. Worker may not proceed before correcting mistakes shown in feedback.
4. Give feedback on how much earned so far and performance on gold questions after each batch.
5. Remind of a bonus from completing all 10 batches.

Figure 2: Architecture of the Gated Instruction protocol.

experience. The primary benefit of GI is worker training, which is necessary across platforms, so we expect to see comparable results on other platforms, such as CrowdFlower.

The ideas behind Gated Instruction are summarized in Figure 2. The workflow proceeds in three phases: tutorial, weed-out, and work (described below) with a focus on well-known user interface principles (rapid feedback and availability of extra help). While conceptually simple, we show this approach has a much bigger effect on the resulting learned NLP system than a more complex graphical model.

3.1 Interactive Tutorial Design

The most important step in crowdsourcing is ensuring that workers understand the task. To this end we required workers to complete an interactive tutorial to learn the criteria for the relations to be annotated.

Since we wanted to test our extractor against official answers for the TAC-KBP Slot Filling evaluation, our tutorial taught workers to follow the official KBP guidelines. These guidelines require tagging only relations directly stated in the sentence, and discourage plausible inferences. For example, if a sentence states only that a person works in a city, then annotating a *place_of_residence* relation with

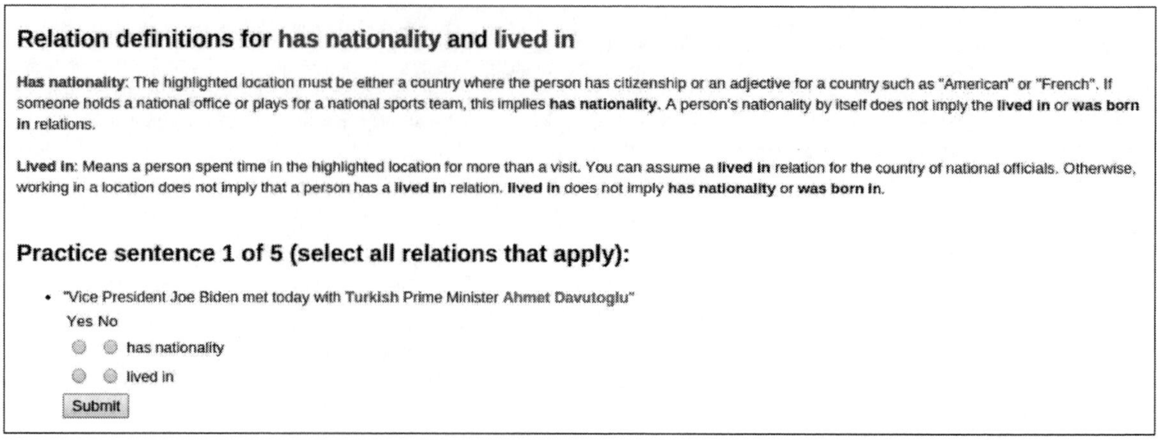

Relation definitions for has nationality and lived in

Has nationality: The highlighted location must be either a country where the person has citizenship or an adjective for a country such as "American" or "French". If someone holds a national office or plays for a national sports team, this implies **has nationality**. A person's nationality by itself does not imply the **lived in** or **was born in** relations.

Lived in: Means a person spent time in the highlighted location for more than a visit. You can assume a **lived in** relation for the country of national officials. Otherwise, working in a location does not imply that a person has a **lived in** relation. **lived in** does not imply **has nationality** or **was born in**.

Practice sentence 1 of 5 (select all relations that apply):

- "Vice President Joe Biden met today with Turkish Prime Minister Ahmet Davutoglu"

Yes No

  ◉ ◉ has nationality

  ◉ ◉ lived in

[Submit]

Figure 3: Tutorial page that teaches guidelines for *nationality* and *lived_in*. The worker answers practice sentences with immediate feedback that teach each relation.

that city is counted as an error, even if it is probable that the person lives there.

Figure 3 shows a page from the tutorial that explains annotation guidelines for *nationality* and *lived_in* (i.e., *place_of_residence*). This figure shows the first page of the tutorial — as more relations are taught, those relations are added to the question. The real questions are asked in the same format later on for consistency. The worker can click on a link to see the relation definitions at any time during the tutorial or while doing the actual task. If workers make a mistake during the tutorial, they are given immediate feedback along with an explanation for the correct answer. The workers cannot proceed without correcting all errors on all problems in the tutorial.

3.2 Adaptive Worker Screening

After examining worker mistakes in a preliminary experiment, we manually selected a set of gold questions (i.e., questions with unambiguous, known answers) that workers are likely to get wrong if they don't clearly understand the annotation criteria. The gold questions are grouped into sets of 5 questions that represent all relations being annotated. The first 5 questions (the screening phase) are used to eliminate spammers and careless workers early on. These questions look no different from normal questions, but we give feedback to workers with the right answers if workers give wrong answers to any of these questions. If a worker fails a majority of such questions, the worker is disqualified from the task.

We then place additional sets of gold questions among real test questions without feedback in order to spot-check workers' responses. In our experience, workers who start out with high accuracy maintain that accuracy throughout the entire session. Therefore, we place the gold questions in exponentially decreasing frequency among the batches of 20 questions (5 gold questions in batches 2, 4, 8, etc.), and allow only workers who maintain at least 80% accuracy on the most recent 10 gold questions to continue with the task. Our task was not large enough to attract problems of collusion, but more lucrative or long-running tasks may require continual generation of new gold questions in order to combat sharing of answers among workers (Oleson et al., 2011). Techniques such as expectation maximization (Dawid and Skene, 1979) can be used to produce new gold questions based on worker answers.

3.3 Motivational Feedback

We want workers to stay motivated, so our crowdsourcing system also provides feedback to workers. In particular, workers receive adaptive per-batch message feedback at the end of each batch of questions (every 20 questions) about how well they did on the gold questions in the past batches, how much they have earned so far, and a reminder of the bonus for finishing all 10 batches. We paid workers $0.50 for each batch of 20 questions with a bonus of $1.00 for finishing 10 batches.

4   Experimental Results

In this section, we address the following questions:

- Does Gated Instruction produce training data with higher precision and recall than other research in crowdsourcing for relation extraction?

- Does higher quality crowdsourced training data result in higher extractor performance when adding crowdsourcing to distant supervision?

- How does the boost in extractor performance on random training instances labeled with Gated Instruction compare to that with instances labeled using traditional crowdsourcing techniques selected with active learning?

- How does extractor performance increase with larger amounts of Gated Instruction training data?

- What's the most cost-effective way to aggregate worker votes? Are multiple annotations needed, given high quality crowdsourcing?

4.1   Quality of Gated Instruction Training

We took the best training set of 10,000 instances from Angeli et al.'s 2014 system that selected training instances using active learning (their Sample JS data). In order to focus on the effect of crowdsourcing, we restricted our attention to four distinct relations between *person* and *location* that were used by previous researchers: *nationality*, *place_of_birth*, *place_of_residence*, and *place_of_death*[2]. We then sent these sentences to crowdsourced workers using the Gated Instruction protocol.

To evaluate the crowdsourced training data quality, we hand-tagged the crowdsourced annotations from both our Gated Instruction system and Angeli et al.'s work on 200 random instances. Annotations were considered correct if they followed the TAC-KBP annotation guidelines. Two authors tagged the sample with 87% agreement and then reconciled opinions to agree on consensus labels.

The training precision, recall, and F1 are shown in Figure 4. In this and all other experiments, aggregate statistics are macro-averaged across relations. We also include the training quality from Zhang et

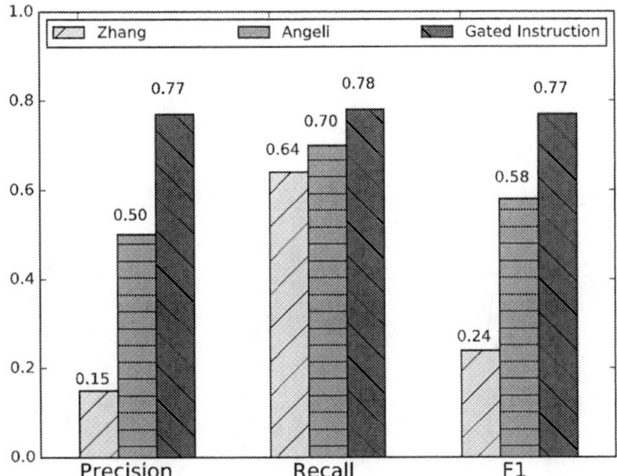

Figure 4: The training data produced by Gated Instruction has much higher precision and somewhat higher recall than that of Angeli et al. or Zhang et al.

al., although this is on a different set of sentences and only for *place_of_birth*, *place_of_residence*, and *place_of_death*.

Our Gated Instruction protocol gives higher F1 for the training set of each of the four relations we compared with Angeli's crowdsourcing on the same sentences. Our overall F1 was 0.77, compared to 0.58 for Angeli et al. and 0.24 for Zhang et al. The difference in precision is most dramatic, with our system achieving 0.77 compared to 0.50 and 0.15.

Worker agreement with GI was surprisingly high. Two workers agreed on between 78% to 97% of the instances, depending on the relation. The average agreement was 88%. The data is available for research purposes.[3]

4.2   Integrating Crowdsourced Data with the Relation Extraction Pipeline

The pipeline of our relation extraction system is as follows. First we collected sentences of training data from the TAC-KBP newswire corpus that contain a person and a location according to the Stanford NER tagger (Finkel et al., 2005). We represent them using the features described by Mintz et al. (2009). These features include NER tags of the two arguments, the dependency path between two designated arguments, the sequence of tokens between the ar-

---

[2]We collapsed the KBP relations *per:city_of_*, *per:stateorprovince_of_*, and *per:country_of_* into a single relation *place_of_*.

[3]https://www.cs.washington.edu/ai/gated_instructions/naacl_data.zip

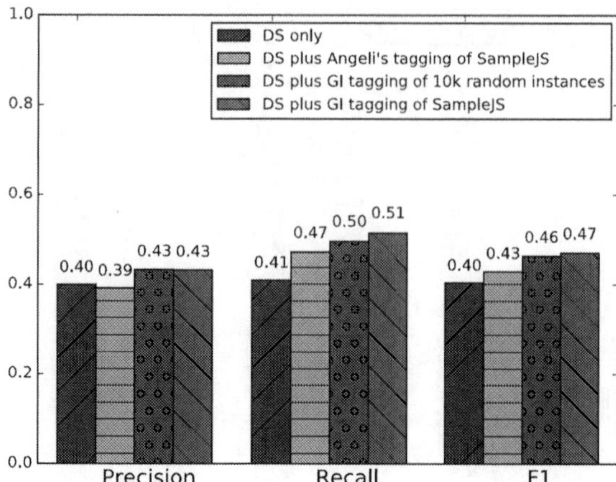

Figure 5: Adding 10K instances with Gated Instruction to 700K DS instances boosts F1 more than that of the original Sample JS annotations. Furthermore, GI applied to 10K randomly-selected instances outperforms active learning with traditional annotation.

guments, and the order of the arguments in the sentence.

We then split the data into 700K used for distant supervision and much smaller sets for crowdsourcing and for a held-out test set. For the experiments presented, unless otherwise noted, we used a variant of majority vote to create a training set. We obtained annotations from two workers for each example sentence and kept the instances where both agreed as our training data.

Finally, we ran a learning algorithm on the distant supervision training data, the crowdsourced training data, and a combination of the two. The results were evaluated on the hand-labeled test set.

4.3 Effect of Data Quality on Extractor Performance

We now study how the higher quality training data from our crowdsourcing protocol affects extractor performance, when it is added to a large amount of distantly-supervised data.

We compared adding the 10K crowdsourced instances from the previous experiment to 700K instances from distant supervision, where the crowdsourced data had tags from either Gated Instruction or the original crowdsourcing from Angeli et al. We compare only with Angeli et al. as we did not have

annotations from Zhang et al. for the same training sentences.

We experimented using three learning algorithms: logistic regression, MultiR, and MIML-RE. We found that logistic regression gives the best results when applied to the crowdsourced training alone. With logistic regression, training on the 10K Sample JS instances gave F1 of 0.31 with Angeli et al.'s crowdsourced labels and 0.40 with Gated Instruction. Logistic regression is not a good fit for distant supervision — we had F1 of 0.34 from logistic regression trained on DS only.

MultiR and MIML-RE gave the best results for *combining* crowdsourcing with distant supervision. Each of these multi-instance multi-class learners had similar results, so we present results only for MIML-RE in the remainder of our experiments, as it is the learning algorithm used by other researchers.

We included no special mechanisms to prevent distant supervision data from swamping the smaller amount of crowdsourced data. MIML-RE has a built-in mechanism to combine supervised and distant supervision. It automatically builds a classifier from the supervised instances, uses this to initialize the distant supervision instance labels, and locks the supervised labels. With MultiR, we put the crowdsourced instances in separate singleton "bags" of training instances, since MultiR always takes at least one instance in each bag as truth.

As Angeli et al. found, it is important to use the crowdsourced training to initialize MIML-RE. With the default initialization, Angeli et al. report no gain in F1. We found a small gain in F1 even with the default initialization, but larger gains with crowdsourced initialization, which we use for the following experiments.

To see how much of the boost over distant supervision comes from the active learning that went into Angeli et al.'s sample JS training, we also used Gated Instruction on a *randomly selected* set of 10K newswire instances from the TAC KBP 2010 corpus (LDC2010E12) that contained at least one NER tag for *person* and one for *location*.

As Figure 5 shows, adding the Sample JS training with Gated Instruction crowdsourcing had a positive impact on performance, increasing precision from 0.40 to 0.43, recall from 0.41 to 0.51, and F1 from 0.40 to 0.47. With the original crowdsourced tag-

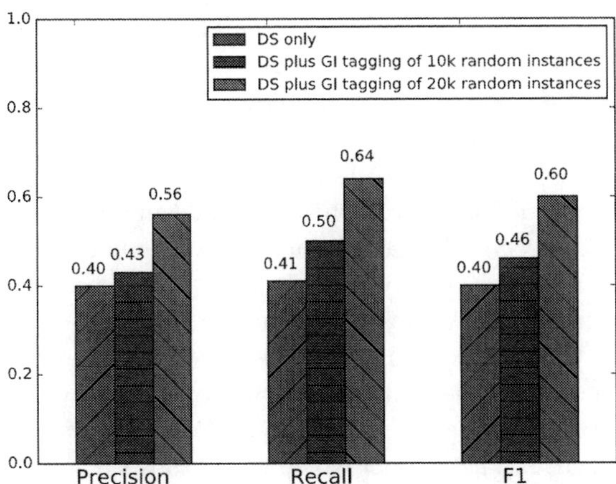

Figure 6: Adding 20K instances with Gated Instruction to DS gives a large boost to both precision and recall, raising F1 from 0.40 to 0.60.

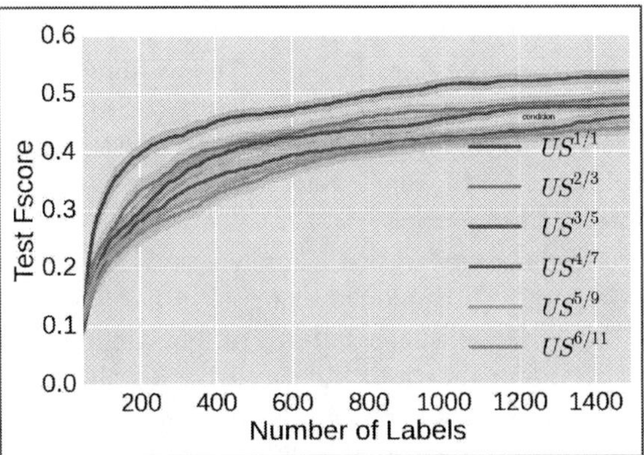

Figure 7: With high quality crowdsourcing, the simple policy of requesting a single annotation performs better than majority-vote of 3, 5, 7, 9, or 11 annotations (holding the annotation budget constant), since the increase in the *number* of data points outweighs the reduction in noise.

ging from Angeli et al., adding the crowdsourced instances actually caused a small *drop* in precision, a smaller gain in recall than Gated Instruction, and F1 of 0.43 — substantially less than achieved with labels from Gated Instruction.

Furthermore, in an apples-to-oranges comparison, we found that our improved crowdsourcing protocol had a much bigger impact than Angeli et al.'s active learning mechanism. Adding 10K *randomly* selected newswire instances tagged with Gated Instruction gave higher precision (0.43), recall (0.51), and F1 (0.46) than adding instances selected by active learning (Sample JS) when labeled using Angeli et al.'s protocol. In fact Gated Instruction gave double the improvement (6 points gain in F1 vs. 3). Of course, both of these numbers are small — bigger gains come from using the techniques together, and especially from using more crowdsourced data.

4.4 Effect of Data Quantity on Extractor Performance

Zhang et al. reported negligible improvement in F1 from adding 20K instances with their crowdsourcing to distant supervision, and Angeli et al. reported a gain of 0.04 F1 from adding 10K instances with active learning and their crowdsourcing.

As Figure 6 shows, Gated Instruction can raise F1 from 0.40 to 0.60 over distant supervision alone from adding 20K random newswire instances. This experiment uses all five relations that we crowd-

sourced, adding *travel_to* to the relations from Figure 5 that we had in common with Angeli et al. The results for DS only and 10K random instances are not significantly different from those in Figure 5 in which *travel_to* was omitted.

4.5 Comparison between Ways to Aggregate Annotations

In this section we explore the cost-effectiveness of alternate methods of creating training from Gated Instruction annotations. We compare a policy of using the majority vote of two out of three, or three out of five workers, and so forth, as opposed to soliciting a single annotation for each training sentence (unilabeling). Lin et al. (2014) show that in many settings, unilabeling is better because some classifiers are able to learn more accurately with a larger, noisier training set than a smaller, cleaner one.

With a given budget, single annotation gives three times as many training instances as the policy that uses three votes and five times as many as the policy that requires five votes, and so forth. Is the quality of data produced by Gated Instruction high enough to rely on just one annotation per instance?

We randomly select 2K examples from the 20K newswire instances and use Gated Instruction to acquire labels from 10 workers for each sentence. Figure 7 shows that when training a logistic regression classifier with high quality crowdsourcing data, a single annotation is, indeed, more cost effective than using a simple majority of three, five, or more annotations (given a fixed budget). The learning curves in Figure 7 use uncertainty sampling (US) to select examples from the 2000 available with the curves labeled US 1/1 for single votes, US 2/3 for two out of three, and so forth.

This is not to say that a single vote is always the best policy. It is another example of the impact of GI's high quality annotation. In the same domain of relation extraction, Lin et al. (2016) also show that with a more intelligent and dynamic relabeling policy, relabeling certain examples can still help.

5   Conclusion

This paper describes the design of Gated Instruction, a crowdsourcing protocol that produces high quality training data. GI uses an interactive tutorial to teach the annotation task, provides feedback during training so workers understand their errors, refuses to let workers annotate new sentences until they have demonstrated competence, and adaptively screens low-accuracy workers with a schedule of test questions. While we demonstrate GI for the task of relation extraction, the method is general and may improve annotation for many other NLP tasks.

Higher quality training data produces higher extractor performance for a variety of learning algorithms: logistic regression, MultiR, and MIML-RE. Contrary to past claims, augmenting distant supervision with a relatively small amount of high-quality crowdsourced training data gives a sizeable boost in performance. Adding 10K instances that Angeli et al. selected by active learning, annotated with Gated Instruction, raised F1 from 0.40 to 0.47 — substantially higher than the 0.43 F1 provided by Angeli et al.'s annotations. We also find that Gated Instruction is more effective than a complicated active learning strategy. Adding 10K randomly selected instances raises F1 to 0.46, and adding 20K random instances gave F1 of 0.60.

Our experimental results yield two main takeaway messages. First, we show that in contrast to prior work, adding crowdsourced training data substantially improves the performance of the resulting extractor as long as care is taken to ensure high quality crowdsourced annotations. We haven't yet experimented beyond person-location relations, but we believe that Gated Instruction is generalizable, particularly where there are clear criteria to be taught. We believe that Gated Instruction can greatly improve training data for other NLP tasks beside relation extraction as well.

Second, we provide practical and easily instituted guidelines for a novel crowdsourcing protocol, Gated Instruction, as an effective method for acquiring high-quality training data. It's important to break complex annotation guidelines into small, digestible chunks and to use tests (gates) to ensure that the worker reads and understands each chunk of the instructions before work begins. Without these extra checks, many poor workers pass subsequent gold tests by accident, polluting results.

Acknowledgment

This work was supported by NSF grant IIS-1420667, ONR grant N00014-15-1-2774, DARPA contract FA8750-13-2-0019, the WRF/Cable Professorship, and a gift from Google. We are very grateful to Chris Re and Ce Zhang who generously supplied their annotated data. Likewise, Masha Pershina and Ralph Grishman allowed us an early look at their paper and gave us their data. Similarly, Gabor Angeli and Chris Manning not only provided their data, but provided many insights about the best ways to combine crowd and distantly supervised annotations. Without this cooperation it would have been impossible to have done our work. We appreciate Natalie Hawkins, who helped prepare the data used in our study. We further thank Shih-Wen Huang and Congle Zhang for their suggestions on the design of the crowdsourcing system and the experiments.

References

Gabor Angeli, Julie Tibshirani, Jean Y. Wu, and Christopher D. Manning. 2014. Combining distant and partial supervision for relation extraction. In *EMNLP*.

Razvan Bunescu and Raymond Mooney. 2007. Learning to extract relations from the web using minimal supervision. In *Proceedings of the 45th Annual Meeting of the Association for Computational Linguistics*.

M. Califf and R. Mooney. 1997. Relational learning of pattern-match rules for information extraction. In *Workshop in Natural Language Learning, Conf. Assoc. Computational Linguistics*.

Mark Craven and Johan Kumlien. 1999. Constructing biological knowledge bases by extracting information from text sources. In *ISMB*.

Peng Dai, Jeffrey M Rzeszotarski, Praveen Paritosh, and Ed H Chi. 2015. And Now for Something Completely Different : Improving Crowdsourcing Workflows with Micro-Diversions. In *CSCW*.

A.P. Dawid and A. M. Skene. 1979. Maximum likelihood estimation of observer error-rates using the EM algorithm. *Applied Statistics*, 28(1):20–28.

Jenny Rose Finkel, Trond Grenager, and Christopher Manning. 2005. Incorporating non-local information into information extraction systems by Gibbs sampling. In *Proceedings of the 43rd Annual Meeting on Association for Computational Linguistics*, pages 363–370. Association for Computational Linguistics.

Matthew R. Gormley, Adam Gerber, Mary Harper, and Mark Dredze. 2010. Non-expert correction of automatically generated relation annotations. In *Proceedings of NAACL and HLT 2010*.

Raphael Hoffmann, Congle Zhang, Xiao Ling, Luke Zettlemoyer, and Daniel S Weld. 2011. Knowledge-based weak supervision for information extraction of overlapping relations. In *Proceedings of ACL*. Association for Computational Linguistics.

Panagiotis G. Ipeirotis and Evgeniy Gabrilovich. 2014. Quizz: targeted crowdsourcing with a billion (potential) users. In *WWW '14: Proceedings of the 23rd International Conference on the World Wide Web*.

Heng Ji and Ralph Grishman. 2011. Knowledge base population: Successful approaches and challenges. In *Proceedings of the 49th Annual Meeting of the Association for Computational Linguistics: Human Language Technologies - Volume 1*, HLT '11, pages 1148–1158, Stroudsburg, PA, USA. Association for Computational Linguistics.

John D. Lafferty, Andrew McCallum, and Fernando C. N. Pereira. 2001. Conditional random fields: Probabilistic models for segmenting and labeling sequence data. In *Proceedings of the Eighteenth International Conference on Machine Learning*, ICML '01.

Christopher H. Lin, Mausam, and Daniel S. Weld. 2014. To re(label), or not to re(label). In *HCOMP*.

Christopher H. Lin, Mausam, and Daniel S. Weld. 2016. Reactive learning: Active learning with relabeling. In *AAAI*.

Andrew Mao, Yiling Chen, Eric Horvitz, Megan E Schwamb, Chris J Lintott, and Arfon M Smith. 2013. Volunteering Versus Work for Pay: Incentives and Tradeoffs in Crowdsourcing. In *HCOMP*.

Mike Mintz, Steven Bills, Rion Snow, and Dan Jurafsky. 2009. Distant supervision for relation extraction without labeled data. In *Proceedings of ACL*. Association for Computational Linguistics.

Thien Huu Nguyen and Ralph Grishman. 2014. Employing word representations and regularization for domain adaptation of relation extraction. In *Proceedings of the 52nd Annual Meeting of the Association for Computational Linguistics*, volume 2, pages 68–74.

David Oleson, Alexander Sorokin, Greg P Laughlin, Vaughn Hester, John Le, and Lukas Biewald. 2011.

Programmatic gold: Targeted and scalable quality assurance in crowdsourcing. In *Human Computation Workshop*, page 11.

Maria Pershina, Bonan Min, Wei Xu, and Ralph Grishman. 2014. Infusion of labeled data into distant supervision for relation extraction. In *Proceedings of ACL*.

Sebastian Riedel, Limin Yao, and Andrew McCallum. 2010. Modeling relations and their mentions without labeled text. In *Proceedings of the Sixteenth European Conference on Machine Learning (ECML-2010)*, pages 148–163.

Sebastian Riedel, Limin Yao, Andrew McCallum, and Benjamin M Marlin. 2013. Relation extraction with matrix factorization and universal schemas. *NAACL HLT 2013*, pages 74–84.

Victor S. Sheng, Foster Provost, and Panagiotis G. Ipeirotis. 2008. Get another label? improving data quality and data mining using multiple, noisy labelers. In *Proceedings of the Fourteenth ACM SIGKDD International Conference on Knowledge Discovery and Data Mining*.

Rion Snow, Brendan O'Connor, Daniel Jurafsky, and Andrew Y Ng. 2008. Cheap and fast—but is it good?: evaluating non-expert annotations for natural language tasks. In *Proceedings of the conference on empirical methods in natural language processing*, pages 254–263. Association for Computational Linguistics.

S. Soderland, D. Fisher, J. Aseltine, and W. Lehnert. 1995. CRYSTAL: Inducing a conceptual dictionary. In *Proceedings of the Fourteenth International Joint Conference on Artificial Intelligence*, pages 1314–21.

Mihai Surdeanu and Heng Ji. 2014. Overview of the English slot filling track at the TAC2014 knowledge base population evaluation.

Mihai Surdeanu, Julie Tibshirani, Ramesh Nallapati, and Christopher D Manning. 2012. Multi-instance multi-label learning for relation extraction. In *Proceedings of EMNLP*, pages 455–465. Association for Computational Linguistics.

Jacob Whitehill, Ting-fan Wu, Jacob Bergsma, Javier R Movellan, and Paul L Ruvolo. 2009. Whose vote should count more: Optimal integration of labels from labelers of unknown expertise. In *NIPS'09*.

F. Wu and D. Weld. 2007. Autonomously semantifying Wikipedia. In *Proceedings of the ACM Sixteenth Conference on Information and Knowledge Management (CIKM-07)*, Lisbon, Portugal.

Ce Zhang, Feng Niu, Christopher Ré, and Jude Shavlik. 2012. Big data versus the crowd: Looking for relationships in all the right places. In *Proceedings of the 50th Annual Meeting of the Association for Computational Linguistics: Long Papers-Volume 1*, pages 825–834. Association for Computational Linguistics.

A Translation-Based Knowledge Graph Embedding
Preserving Logical Property of Relations

Hee-Geun Yoon, Hyun-Je Song, Seong-Bae Park, Se-Young Park

School of Computer Science and Engineering

Kyungpook National University

Daegu, 41566, Korea

`{hkyoon, hjsong, sbpark, sypark}@sejong.knu.ac.kr`

Abstract

This paper proposes a novel translation-based knowledge graph embedding that preserves the logical properties of relations such as transitivity and symmetricity. The embedding space generated by existing translation-based embeddings do not represent transitive and symmetric relations precisely, because they ignore the role of entities in triples. Thus, we introduce a role-specific projection which maps an entity to distinct vectors according to its role in a triple. That is, a head entity is projected onto an embedding space by a head projection operator, and a tail entity is projected by a tail projection operator. This idea is applied to TransE, TransR, and TransD to produce lppTransE, lppTransR, and lppTransD, respectively. According to the experimental results on link prediction and triple classification, the proposed logical property preserving embeddings show the state-of-the-art performance at both tasks. These results prove that it is critical to preserve logical properties of relations while embedding knowledge graphs, and the proposed method does it effectively.

1 Introduction

Representing knowledge as a graph is one of the most effective ways to utilize human knowledge with a machine, and various large-scale knowledge graphs such as Freebase (Bollacker et al., 2008) and Yago (Suchanek et al., 2007) are available these days. However, the sparsity of the graphs makes it difficult to utilize them in real world applications. In spite of their huge volume, the relations among entities in the graphs are insufficient, which results in very limited inference of the knowledge of the graphs. Therefore, it is of importance to resolve such sparsity of knowledge graphs.

One of the most promising methods to complete knowledge graphs is to embed the graphs in a low-dimensional continuous vector space. This method learns a vector representation of a knowledge graph, and the plausibility of a certain knowledge within the graph is measured with algebraic operations in the vector space. Thus, new knowledge can be harvested from the space by finding knowledge instances with high plausibility.

The translation-based model among various knowledge-embedding models shows the state-of-the-art performance of knowledge graph completion (Bordes et al., 2013; Wang et al., 2014; Lin et al., 2015; Ji et al., 2015). TransE (Bordes et al., 2013) is one of the well-known translation-based approaches to this problem. When a set of knowledge triples (h, r, t) composed of a relation (r) and two entities (h and t) is given, it finds vector representations of h, t, and r by compelling the vector of t to be same with the sum of the vectors of h and r. While TransE embeds all relations in a single vector space, TransH (Wang et al., 2014) and TransR (Lin et al., 2015) assume that each relation has its own embedding space. On the other hand, Ji et al. (2015) found out that even a single relation or a single entity usually has multiple types. Thus, they have proposed TransD which allows multiple mapping matrices of entities and relations.

Even though these translation-based models achieve high performance in knowledge graph completion, they all ignore logical properties of rela-

Proceedings of NAACL-HLT 2016, pages 907–916,

San Diego, California, June 12-17, 2016. ©2016 Association for Computational Linguistics

tions. That is, transitive relations and symmetric relations lose their transitivity or symmetricity in the vector space generated by the translation-based models. As a result, the models can not complete only new knowledge with such relations, but also new knowledge with a relation affected by the relations. In most knowledge graphs, transitive or symmetric relations are common. For instance, FB15K, one of the benchmark datasets for knowledge graph completion, has a number of transitive and symmetric relations. About 20% of triples in FB15K have a transitive or a symmetric relation. Therefore, the ignorance of logical properties of relations becomes a serious problem in knowledge graph completion.

The main reason why existing translation-based embeddings can not reflect logical properties of relations is that they do not consider the role of entities. An entity should be a different vector in the embedding space according to its role. Therefore, the solution to preserve the logical properties of relations in the embedding space is to distinguish the role of entities while embedding entities and relations.

In this paper, we propose a role-specific projection to preserve logical properties of relations in an embedding space. This can be implemented by projecting a head entity onto an embedding space by a head projection operator and a tail entity by a tail projection operator. As a result, an identical entity is represented as two distinct vectors. This idea can be applied to various translation-based models including TransE, TransR, and TransD. Therefore, we also propose how to modify existing translation-based models to preserve logical properties. The effectiveness of the proposed idea is verified with two tasks of link prediction and triple classification using standard benchmark datasets of WordNet and Freebase. According to the experimental results, the logical property preserving embeddings achieve the state-of-the-art performance in both tasks.

2 Related Work

The sparsity of knowledge graphs is one of the most critical issues in utilizing them in real-world applications. Thus, there have been a number of studies on completing knowledge graphs as a solution to overcome the sparsity. Link prediction is one of the promising ways for knowledge graph comple-

tion. This task predicts new relations between entities on a knowledge graph by investigating existing relations of the graph (Nickel et al., 2015; Neelakantan and Chang, 2015). The methods used for link prediction can be categorized into three groups. One group consists of the methods based on graph features. The observable features used in these methods are the paths between entity pairs (Lao and Cohen, 2010; Lao et al., 2011) and subgraphs (Gardner and Mitchell, 2015). The other group is composed of the methods based on Markov random fields. The studies belonging to this group inference new relations by probabilistic soft logic (Pujara et al., 2013) and first-order logic (Jiang et al., 2012).

Knowledge graph embedding is another prominent method for link prediction (Bordes et al., 2011; Nickel et al., 2011; Guo et al., 2015; Neelakantan et al., 2015). It embeds entities of a knowledge graph into a continuous low dimensional space as vectors, and embeds relations as vectors or matrices. These vectors are optimized by a score function of each knowledge graph embedding model. The Semantic Matching Energy (SME) model proposed by Bordes et al. (2014) finds vector representations of entities and relations using a neural network. When a triple (h, r, t) is given, SME makes two relation-dependent embeddings of (h, r) and (r, t). Its score function for a triple is the similarity between the embeddings. Since relations are expressed as vectors instead of matrices, the complexity of SME is relatively low compared to other embedding methods. Jenatton et al. (2012) suggested Latent Factor Model (LFM). In order to capture both the first-order and the second-order interactions between two entities, LFM adopts a bilinear function as its score function. In addition, it represents a relation as a weighted sum of sparse latent factors to work with a large number of relations. Socher et al. (2013) proposed the Neural Tensor Network (NTN) model. NTN is a highly expressive embedding model which has a bilinear tensor layer instead of a standard linear neural network layer. As a result, it can process various interactions between entity vectors. However, it is difficult to process large-scale knowledge graphs with NTN due to its high complexity.

The current main stream of knowledge graph embedding is a translation-based embedding approach. The basic idea of this embedding is that entities and

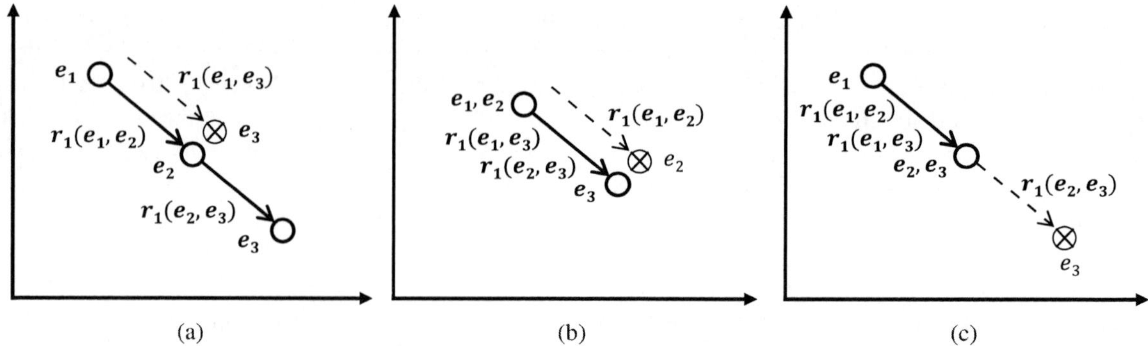

Figure 1: An example of entity vectors trained wrong by a transitive relation.

relations are represented as vectors, and relations are treated as operators to translate entities into other positions on an embedding space. Thus, they try to find vector representations of h, t, and r so that the vector of t becomes the sum of the vectors of h and r. TransE (Bordes et al., 2013) is the simplest translation-based graph embedding. It assumes that all vectors of entities and relations lie on a single vector space. As a result, it fails in dealing with the reflexivity and the multiplicities of relations except 1-to-1. The solution to this problem is to allow the entities to play different roles according to relations, but TransE is unable to do it.

An entity plays multiple roles in TransH (Wang et al., 2014), since TransH allows entities to have multiple vector representations. In order to obtain multiple representations of an entity, TransH projects an entity vector into relation-specific hyperplanes. TransR (Lin et al., 2015) also solves the problems of TransE by introducing relation spaces. It allows an entity to have various vector representations by mapping an entity vector into relation-specific spaces rather than relation-specific hyperplanes. Although both TransH and TransR overcome the limitations of TransE, they are still not able to handle multiple types of relations which is determined by head and tail entities of each relation. For example, let us consider two triples of (*California, part_of, USA*) and (*arm, part_of, body*). Both triples have a relation *part_of* in common, but the relation should be interpreted differently in each triple. Ji et al. (2015) have proposed TransD in which a relation can have multiple relation spaces according to its entities. TransD constructs relation mapping matrices

dynamically by considering entities and a relation simultaneously. For this, it introduces projection vectors for entities and relations, and then constructs the mapping matrices by multiplying these entity and relation projection vectors. As a result, every relation in TransD has multiple entity-specific spaces.

3   Loss of Logical Properties in Translation-Based Embeddings

Translation-based embeddings aim to find vector representations of knowledge graph entities in an embedding space by regarding relations as translation of entities in the space. Since they map the entities onto a vector space regardless of the role of the entities, they do not express logical properties of relations such as transitivity and symmetricity. That is, the vectors of transitive or symmetric relations do not deliver transitivity or symmetricity in the embedding spaces from translation-based embeddings.

For instance, let us consider a transitive relation. Assume that we have three triples (e_1, r_1, e_2), (e_2, r_1, e_3), and (e_1, r_1, e_3) and r_1 is a transitive relation. When the vector of r_1 is not a zero vector, there could be three types of entity vectors as shown in Figure 1. In Figure 1-(a), e_1, e_2, and e_3 are placed linearly. In this case, (e_1, r_1, e_3) can not be expressed in this figure. When e_1 and e_2 are placed at the same point like Figure 1-(b), (e_1, r_1, e_2) can not be expressed. In Figure 1-(c), (e_2, r_1, e_3) can not be expressed when e_2 and e_3 are same. In a similar way, translation-based embeddings can not express symmetric relations perfectly.

The problems caused by wrong expression of transitive and symmetric relations are two-folds.

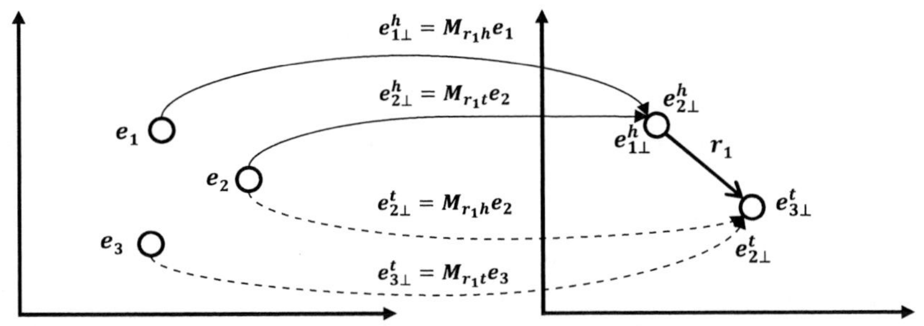

Figure 2: Simple illustration on a transitive relation with role-specific projections.

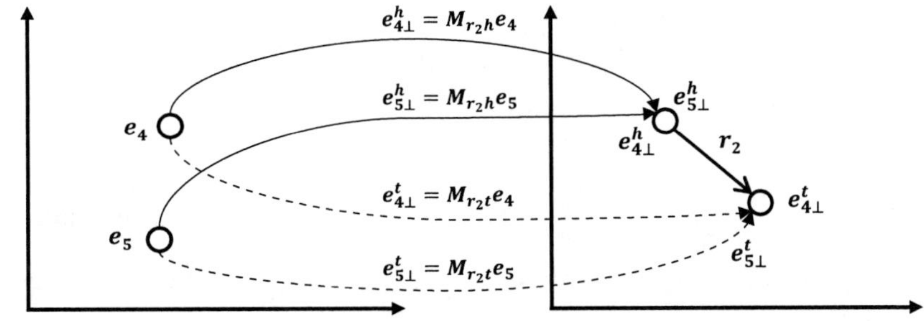

Figure 3: Simple illustration on a symmetric relation with role-specific projections.

One fold is that the relations with logical properties are common in knowledge bases. Two benchmark datasets of FB15K and WN18 in Table 2 prove it. There are 483,142 triples in FB15K, and 84,172 (= 47,841 + 36,331) triples among them have a transitive or symmetric relation. That is, the translation-based embeddings do not express triples precisely for about 17% of triples in FB15K. 22.4% of triples in another dataset WN18 also have a transitive or symmetric relation. The other is that transitive or symmetric relations do not affect the entities that are directly connected by the relations, but affect also other entities shared by non-transitive and non-symmetric relations through the entities. Therefore, it is of importance in translation-based embeddings to represent transitive and symmetric relations precisely.

4 Logical Property Preserving Embedding

4.1 Role-Specific Projection of Entity Vectors

The main reason why transitive or symmetric relations are not represented precisely by existing translation-based embeddings is that they ignore the role of entities in embedding them onto a vector space. That is, when a triple (h, r, t) is given, h and t plays different roles. However, the existing embeddings treat them equally and embed them into a space in the same way. Therefore, in order to express entities and relations more precisely, entities should be represented differently according to their role in a triple.

Figure 2 shows how entities can be represented according to their role. In this figure, solid lines represent entity mappings as head roles and dotted lines mean that entities are mapped as tails. Assume that three triples of (e_1, r_1, e_2), (e_2, r_1, e_3), and (e_1, r_1, e_3) are given with a transitive relation r_1. e_1 plays only a head role and e_3 plays only a tail role, while e_2 plays both roles. Then, the entity vectors in the entity space are mapped into the space of r_1 using two mapping matrices $\mathbf{M}_{r_1h}$ and $\mathbf{M}_{r_1t}$. That is, head entities are mapped by $\mathbf{M}_{r_1h}$, while tail entities are projected by $\mathbf{M}_{r_1t}$. Let $e_{1\perp}^h$ and $e_{2\perp}^h$ be the projected vectors of e_1 and e_2 respectively by $\mathbf{M}_{r_1h}$, and let $e_{2\perp}^t$ and $e_{3\perp}^t$ be the projected vectors of e_2 and e_3 respectively by $\mathbf{M}_{r_1t}$. $e_{1\perp}^h$ and $e_{2\perp}^h$ are placed at the same point in the space of r_1 from (e_2, r_1, e_3) and (e_1, r_1, e_3). Similarly, $e_{2\perp}^t$ and $e_{3\perp}^t$ are same from (e_1, r_1, e_2) and (e_1, r_1, e_3). Since e_2 is used as both a head and a tail, it is mapped differently as $e_{2\perp}^h$ and $e_{2\perp}^t$, respectively. Note that all three triples are well expressed in this space.

Symmetric relations also can be expressed precisely by logical property preserving knowledge graph embedding. Assume that two triples of (e_4, r_2, e_5) and (e_5, r_2, e_4) are given with a symmetric relation r_2. Figure 3 shows how the triples are well represented. The solid lines imply that entities are mapped by $\mathbf{M}_{r_2 h}$ while the dotted lines mean that entities are mapped by $\mathbf{M}_{r_2 t}$. By placing $e_{4\perp}^h$ and $e_{5\perp}^h$ at the same point and imposing $e_{4\perp}^t$ and $e_{5\perp}^t$ at the same point, r_2 is precisely expressed as a symmetric relation in the embedding space.

4.2 Realization of Logical Property Preserving Embedding

Due to the simplicity of role-specific projection of entity vectors, it can be applied to various translation-based embeddings. In this paper, we apply it to TransE, TransR, and TransD.

4.2.1 TransE

The score function of TransE is

$$f_r^E(h, t) = \|\mathbf{h} + \mathbf{r} - \mathbf{t}\|_{l_{1/2}},$$

where $\mathbf{h}, \mathbf{t} \in \mathbb{R}^n$, and $\mathbf{r} \in \mathbb{R}^n$ are the vectors of a head entity, a tail entity, and a relation on a single embedding space. In the logical property preserving TransE (lppTransE), $\mathbf{h}$ and $\mathbf{t}$ should be mapped differently. For this purpose, we adopt a head and a tail space mapping matrices of $\mathbf{M}_h \in \mathbb{R}^{n \times n}$ and $\mathbf{M}_t \in \mathbb{R}^{n \times n}$. As a result, the score function of lppTransE becomes

$$f_r^{lppE}(h, t) = \|\mathbf{M}_h \mathbf{h} + \mathbf{r} - \mathbf{M}_t \mathbf{t}\|_{l_{1/2}}.$$

This is similar to the score function of TransR. The difference between lppTransE and TransR is that both h and t are mapped by a single mapping matrix for r in TransR, while h is mapped by $\mathbf{M}_h$ and t is by $\mathbf{M}_t$ in lppTransE.

4.2.2 TransR

The entities in TransR are mapped into vectors in different relation space according to a relation. Thus, its score function is defined as

$$f_r^R(h, t) = \|\mathbf{M}_r \mathbf{h} + \mathbf{r} - \mathbf{M}_r \mathbf{t}\|_{l_{1/2}},$$

where $\mathbf{M}_r \in \mathbb{R}^{m \times n}$ is a mapping matrix for a relation r which is represented as $\mathbf{r} \in \mathbb{R}^m$. Thus, in the logical property preserving TransR (lppTransR), the mapping matrix of each relation is split into a head mapping matrix $\mathbf{M}_{r_h} \in \mathbb{R}^{m \times n}$ and a tail mapping matrix $\mathbf{M}_{r_t} \in \mathbb{R}^{m \times n}$. Then, the score function of lppTransR is

$$f_r^{lppR}(h, t) = \|\mathbf{M}_{r_h} \mathbf{h} + \mathbf{r} - \mathbf{M}_{r_t} \mathbf{t}\|_{l_{1/2}}.$$

With these two distinct mapping matrices, entities can have two different vector representations in the same relation space.

4.2.3 TransD

TransD maps entity vectors into different vectors in relation spaces according to entity and relation types. That is, the entity vectors are mapped by entity-relation specific mapping matrices. Thus, its score function is defined as

$$f_r^D(h, t) = \|\mathbf{M}_{rh} \mathbf{h} + \mathbf{r} - \mathbf{M}_{rt} \mathbf{t}\|_{l_{1/2}},$$

where $\mathbf{M}_{rh} \in \mathbb{R}^{m \times n}$ and $\mathbf{M}_{rt} \in \mathbb{R}^{m \times n}$ are entity-relation specific mapping matrices. These mapping matrices are computed by multiplying projection vectors of an entity and a relation as follows.

$$\mathbf{M}_{rh} = \mathbf{r}_p \mathbf{h}_p^\top + \mathbf{I}^{m \times n},$$
$$\mathbf{M}_{rt} = \mathbf{r}_p \mathbf{t}_p^\top + \mathbf{I}^{m \times n},$$

where $\mathbf{h}_p, \mathbf{t}_p$ and $\mathbf{r}_p$, are the projection vectors for a head, a tail and a relation.

The logical property preserving TransD (lppTransD) divides $\mathbf{r}_p$ into two projection vectors $\mathbf{r}_{p_h}$ and $\mathbf{r}_{p_t}$ to reflect the role of entities. The mapping matrices then becomes

$$\mathbf{M}'_{rh} = \mathbf{r}_{p_h} \mathbf{h}_p^\top + \mathbf{I}^{m \times n},$$
$$\mathbf{M}'_{rt} = \mathbf{r}_{p_t} \mathbf{t}_p^\top + \mathbf{I}^{m \times n}.$$

Then, its score function is

$$f_r^{lppD}(h, t) = \|\mathbf{M}'_{rh} \mathbf{h} + \mathbf{r} - \mathbf{M}'_{rt} \mathbf{t}\|_{l_{1/2}}.$$

Table 2: A simple statistics on datasets.

Dataset	#Rel	#Ent	#Train	#Valid	#Test	#Transitive	#Symmetric	Ratio
WN11	11	38,696	112,581	2,609	10,544	822	1,597	2.2%
FB13	13	75,043	316,232	5,908	23,733	262	4,152	1.4%
WN18	18	40,943	141,442	5,000	5,000	2,001	29,667	22.4%
FB15K	1,345	14,951	483,142	50,000	59,071	47,841	36,331	17.4%

Table 1: Complexity of knowledge graph embedding models.

Model	No. of parameters
TransE	$\mathcal{O}\left(N_e n + N_r n\right)$
TransR	$\mathcal{O}\left(N_e n + N_r\left(m+1\right)n\right)$
TransD	$\mathcal{O}\left(2N_e n + 2N_r m\right)$
lppTransE	$\mathcal{O}\left(N_e n + N_r n + n^2\right)$
lppTransR	$\mathcal{O}\left(N_e n + N_r\left(2m+1\right)n\right)$
lppTransD	$\mathcal{O}\left(2N_e n + 3N_r m\right)$

4.3 Training Logical Property Preserving Embeddings

Since all logical property preserving embeddings are based on the score function used by previous translation-based knowledge graph embeddings, they can be trained using a margin-based ranking loss defined as

$$L = \sum_{(h,r,t)\in P} \sum_{(h',r,t')\in N} \max(0, f_r^*(h,t)+\gamma-f_r^*(h',t')),$$

where f_r^* is the score function of a corresponding logical property preserving embedding. Here, P and N are sets of correct and incorrect triples, and γ is a margin. N is constructed by replacing a head or a tail entity in an existing triple because a knowledge graph has only correct triples. All logical property preserving embeddings are optimized by stochastic gradient descent.

The complexities of the logical property preserving embeddings are shown in Table 1. N_e and N_r in this table are the number of entities and relations, and n and m are the dimensions of entity and relation embedding spaces. Their complexity mainly depends on the number of relations. Thus, the increased complexities of the logical property preserving embeddings is not significant, when compared with TransE, TransR, and TransD.

5 Experiments

The superiority of the proposed logical property preserving embeddings is shown through two kinds of tasks. The first task is *link prediction* (Bordes et al., 2013). This task predicts the missing entity when there is a missing entity in a given triple. The other is *triple classification* (Socher et al., 2013). This task aims to decide whether a given triple is correct or not.

5.1 Data Sets

Two popular knowledge graphs of WordNet (Miller, 1995) and Freebase (Bollacker et al., 2008) are used for evaluating embeddings. WordNet provides the semantic relations among words, and there exist its two widely-used subsets which are WN11 (Socher et al., 2013) and WN18 (Bordes et al., 2014). WN18 is used for link prediction, and WN11 is adopted for triple classification. Freebase represents general facts about the world. It has two subsets of FB13 (Socher et al., 2013) and FB15K (Bordes et al., 2014). FB15K is used for both triple classification and link prediction, while FB13 is employed only for triple classification.

Table 2 summarizes a simple statistics of each dataset. #Triples is the number of training triples in each benchmark dataset. #Transitive and #Symmetric are the number of triples which have transitive and symmetric relations, respectively. Ratio denotes the proportion of triples of which relation is transitive or symmetric. As shown in this table, the triples with a transitive or symmetric relation take a large proportion in WN18 and FB15K.

5.2 Link Prediction

For the evaluation of link prediction, we followed the evaluation protocols and metrics used in previous studies (Socher et al., 2013; Bordes et al., 2013; Lin et al., 2015; Ji et al., 2015). To compare the

Table 4: Experimental results on link prediction.

Dataset	WN18				FB15K			
Metric	Mean Rank		Hits@10 (%)		Mean Rank		Hits@10 (%)	
	Raw	Filter	Raw	Filter	Raw	Filter	Raw	Filter
TransE	263	251	75.4	89.2	243	125	34.9	47.1
TransH (unif)	318	301	75.4	86.7	211	84	42.5	58.5
TransH (bern)	401	388	73.0	82.3	212	87	45.7	64.4
TransR (unif)	232	219	78.3	91.7	226	78	43.8	65.5
TransR (bern)	238	225	79.8	92.0	198	77	48.2	68.7
TransD (unif)	242	229	79.2	92.5	211	**67**	49.4	74.2
TransD (bern)	224	212	79.6	92.2	194	91	**53.4**	77.3
lppTransE (unif)	336	323	**77.7** (+2.3)	**89.5** (+0.3)	228	78	**47.4** (+12.5)	**72.9** (+25.8)
lppTransE (bern)	342	329	**79.5** (+4.1)	**92.7** (+3.5)	215	95	**48.9** (+14.0)	**73.1** (+26.0)
lppTransR (unif)	331	317	**79.2** (+0.9)	**92.7** (+1.0)	238	79	**47.2** (+3.4)	**74.4** (+8.9)
lppTransR (bern)	334	321	79.6 (-0.2)	**92.8** (+0.8)	219	92	**50.4** (+2.2)	**77.2** (+8.5)
lppTransD (unif)	342	328	**79.3** (+0.1)	**93.6** (+1.1)	218	69	**49.6** (+0.2)	**77.4** (+3.2)
lppTransD (bern)	283	270	**80.5** (+0.9)	**94.3** (+2.1)	195	78	53.0 (-0.4)	**78.7** (+1.4)

Table 3: Parameter values in link prediction.

Dataset	Model	α	B	γ	n, m	D.S
	lppTransE	0.001	1,440	1	50	L_1
WN18	lppTransR	0.001	1,440	1	50	L_1
	lppTransD	0.001	1,440	2	50	L_1
	lppTransE	0.001	480	1	100	L_1
FB15K	lppTransR	0.001	4,800	1	100	L_1
	lppTransD	0.0001	4,800	2	100	L_1

methods for this task, two metrics of mean rank and Hits@10 are used. The mean rank measures the average rank of all correct entities, and Hits@10 is the proportion of correct triples ranked in top 10. Since there are two evaluation settings of "raw" and "filter" in this task (Bordes et al., 2013), we report both results. In addition, we report the results for two sampling methods of "bern" and "unif" (Wang et al., 2014) as the previous studies did.

There are five parameters in the proposed property preserving embeddings. They are a learning rate α, the number of training triples in each mini-batch B[1], a margin γ, the embedding dimension for entities and relations (n and m), and a dissimilarity measure in embedding score functions (D.S). The parameter values used in our experiments are given at Table 3. The iteration number of stochastic gradient descent is 1,000.

Table 4 shows the results on link prediction. The results of previous studies are referred from their report, since the same datasets are used. The val-

ues between parentheses are the improvement over their base models. The logical property preserving embeddings outperform all other methods for both "bern" and "unif" on WN18 except lppTransR with "bern" in the raw setting. In the raw setting, lppTransE, lppTransR, and lppTransD achieve 79.5%, 79.6%, and 80.5% of Hits@10 respectively in "bern", which are 4.1%, -0.2%, and 0.9% higher than those of TransE, TransR, and TransD. The logical property preserving embeddings show even higher performance in the filter setting. Hits@10 of lppTransD in "bern" is 94.3%, while that of TransD in "unif" is 92.5% and that in "bern" is 92.2%. Thus, lppTransD improves 2.1% over TransD in "bern". Especially, this performance of lppTransD is 1.8% higher than that of TransD in "unif", the previous state-of-the-art performance.

The logical property preserving embeddings outperform their base models also on FB15K. TransE is improved most significantly with this dataset. The improvements by lppTransE in the raw setting are 12.5% in "unif" and 14.0% in "bern", while those in the filter setting are 25.8% in "unif" and 26.0% in "bern". In addition, its Hits@10 exceeds those of TransH and TransR. That is, even if TransH and TransR were proposed to tackle the problem of TransE, the proposed lppTransE solves the problem better than TransH and TransR. lppTransD achieves just a little bit lower Hits@10 than TransD in "bern", but the improvements in the filter setting are notice-

---

[1]α and B are related with stochastic gradient descent.

Table 6: Parameter values in triple classification.

Dataset	Model	α	B	γ	n, m	D.S
WN11	lppTransE	0.01	120	2	20	L_1
	lppTransR	0.001	120	4	20	L_1
	lppTransD	0.0001	1,000	1	100	L_2
FB13	lppTransE	0.001	30	1	100	L_1
	lppTransR	0.0001	300	1	100	L_1
	lppTransD	0.0001	300	1	100	L_2
FB15K	lppTransE	0.001	480	1	100	L_1
	lppTransR	0.001	4,800	1	100	L_1
	lppTransD	0.0001	4,800	2	100	L_1

Table 7: Accuracies on triple classification. (%)

Dataset	WN11	FB13	FB15K
TransE (unif)	75.9	70.9	80.3
TransE (bern)	75.9	81.5	80.8
TransH (unif)	77.7	76.5	81.9
TransH (bern)	78.8	83.3	82
TransR (unif)	85.5	74.7	82.6
TransR (bern)	85.9	82.5	82.7
TransD (unif)	85.6	85.9	84.2
TransD (bern)	86.4	**89.1**	84.8
lppTransE (unif)	81.3 (+5.4)	72.3 (+1.4)	83.2 (+2.9)
lppTransE (bern)	81.3 (+5.4)	83.4 (+1.9)	83.6 (+2.8)
lppTransR (unif)	85.5 (+0.0)	79.5 (+4.8)	83.4 (+0.8)
lppTransR (bern)	85.5 (-0.4)	83.1 (+0.6)	84.6 (+1.9)
lppTransD (unif)	86.1 (+0.5)	86.6 (+0.7)	84.7 (+0.5)
lppTransD (bern)	86.2 (-0.2)	88.6 (-0.5)	**85.3** (+0.5)

able. Since Hits@10 of TransD in "bern" is the best performance ever reported, that of lppTransD in "bern" becomes a new state-of-the-art performance.

Table 5 exhibits Hits@10s according to mapping property of the relations of FB15K. The notable trend of this table is that the logical property preserving embeddings show much higher Hits@10 than their base models in N-to-1 and N-to-N, while their Hits@10s are similar to those of their base models in 1-to-1 and 1-to-N. This is notable with TransD and lppTransD. lppTransD improves TransD, the previous state-of-the-art method by 7.3% (N-to-1) and 3.7% (N-to-N) in predicting head, and by 0.9% (N-to-1) and 0.3% (N-to-N). Note that it is important to verify if logical property preserving embeddings achieve good performances in N-to-N, since all transitive relations and some symmetric relations are, in general, N-to-N. According to this table, Hits@10s of most logical property preserving embeddings are improved significantly in N-to-N, which proves that the proposed method solves transitivity and symmetricity problem of previous embeddings.

5.3 Triple Classification

Three datasets of WN11, FB13, and FB15K are used in this task. WN11 and FB13 have negative triples, but FB15K has only positives. Thus, we generated negative triples for FB15K by following the strategy of (Socher et al., 2013). As a result, the classification accuracies on FB15K can not be compared directly with previous studies, and the accuracies on FB15K in this table are those obtained with our dataset. The parameter values for training TransE, TransH, TransR, and TransD are borrowed from their reports, and those for logical property preserving embeddings are shown in Table 6.

Table 7 shows the accuracies of triple classifi-

cation on the three datasets. The logical property preserving embeddings in general outperform their base models. lppTransE always shows higher accuracy than TransE, lppTransR than TransR except for WN11, and lppTransD than TransD in FB15K. One thing to note is that the improvements by the logical property preserving embeddings are always observed in FB15K, while those in WN11 and FB13 are small or slightly negative. This can be explained with the number of triples with a transitive or symmetric relation in the datasets. As shown in Table 2, the triples with such a relation take just a small portion of WN11 and FB13. The ratio of those triples is less than 2.3% in these datasets. However, as noted before, more than 17% triples are such ones in FB15K. Thus, the improvement in FB15K is remarkable. The other thing to note is that lppTransD shows the best accuracy in FB15K. These results imply that the proposed logical property preserving embeddings solve the problems of existing translation-based embeddings effectively.

6 Conclusion

This paper has proposed a new translation-based knowledge graph embedding that preserves logical properties of relations. Transitivity and symmetricity are very important characteristics of relations for representing and inferring knowledge, and the triples with such a relation take a large proportion of real-world knowledge graphs. In order to preserve the logical properties in an embedding space, an entity is forced to have multiple vector represen-

Table 5: Experimental results on FB15K according to mapping properties of relations. (%)

Tasks	Predicting Head (Hits@10)				Predicting Tail (Hits@10)			
Relation Category	1-to-1	1-to-N	N-to-1	N-to-N	1-to-1	1-to-N	N-to-1	N-to-N
TransE	43.7	65.7	18.2	47.2	43.7	19.7	66.7	50.0
TransH (unif)	66.7	81.7	30.2	57.4	63.7	30.1	83.2	60.8
TransH (bern)	66.8	87.6	28.7	64.5	65.5	39.8	83.3	67.2
TransR (unif)	76.9	77.9	38.1	66.9	76.2	38.4	76.2	69.1
TransR (bern)	78.8	89.2	34.1	69.2	79.2	37.4	90.4	72.1
TransD (unif)	80.7	85.8	47.1	75.6	80.0	**54.5**	80.7	77.9
TransD (bern)	**86.1**	**95.5**	39.8	78.5	**85.4**	50.6	94.4	81.2
lppTransE (unif)	77.5	86.5	43.1	75.9	76.7	46.4	79.4	75.5
lppTransE (bern)	78.3	93.5	35.4	74.7	78.1	45.9	80.3	76.6
lppTransR (unif)	75.2	88.1	41.5	75.2	76.6	44.9	82.7	72.6
lppTransR (bern)	84.3	94.2	49.7	79.2	84.3	46.9	91.9	79.6
lppTransD (unif)	82.7	89.5	53.2	81.6	82.3	52.6	84.8	**81.5**
lppTransD (bern)	86.0	94.2	**54.4**	**82.2**	79.7	43.2	**95.3**	79.7

tations according to its role in a triple. This idea has been applied to TransE, TransR, and TransD, and they are called as lppTransE, lppTransR, and lpp-TransD. Their superiority was shown through two tasks of link prediction and triple classification. The logical property preserving embeddings showed the improved performance over their base models[2]. Especially, lppTransD showed the state-of-the-art performance in both tasks. These results imply that the proposed role-specific projection is plausible to preserve logical properties of relations.

Acknowledgments

This work was supported by Institute for Information & communications Technology Promotion (IITP) grant funded by the Korea government (MSIP) (No. R0101-15-0054, WiseKB: Big data based self-evolving knowledge base and reasoning platform).

References

[Bollacker et al.2008] Kurt Bollacker, Colin Evans, Praveen Paritosh, Tim Sturge, and Jamie Taylor. 2008. Freebase: a collaboratively created graph database for structuring human knowledge. In *Proceedings of the 2008 ACM SIGMOD International Conference on Management of Data*, pages 1247–1250.

[Bordes et al.2011] Antoine Bordes, Jason Weston, Ronan Collobert, and Yoshua Bengio. 2011. Learning structured embeddings of knowledge bases. In *Proceedings of the 28th AAAI Conference on Artificial Intelligence*, pages 301–306.

[Bordes et al.2013] Antoine Bordes, Nicolas Usunier, Alberto Garcia-Duran, Jason Weston, and Oksana Yakhnenko. 2013. Translating embeddings for modeling multi-relational data. In *Advances in Neural Information Processing Systems*, pages 2787–2795.

[Bordes et al.2014] Antoine Bordes, Xavier Glorot, Jason Weston, and Yoshua Bengio. 2014. A semantic matching energy function for learning with multi-relational data. *Machine Learning*, 94(2):233–259.

[Gardner and Mitchell2015] Matt Gardner and Tom Mitchell. 2015. Efficient and expressive knowledge base completion using subgraph feature extraction. In *Proceedings of the 2015 Conference on Empirical Methods in Natural Language Processing*, pages 1488–1498.

[Guo et al.2015] Shu Guo, Quan Wang, Bin Wang, Lihong Wang, and Li Guo. 2015. Semantically smooth knowledge graph embedding. In *Proceedings of the 53rd Annual Meeting of the Association for Computational Linguistics and the 7th International Joint Conference on Natural Language Processing*, pages 84–94.

[Jenatton et al.2012] Rodolphe Jenatton, Nicolas L. Roux, Antoine Bordes, and Guillaume R. Obozinski. 2012. A latent factor model for highly multi-relational data. In *Advances in Neural Information Processing Systems*, pages 3167–3175.

---

[2] The source codes and resources can be downloaded from `http://ml.knu.ac.kr/lppKE`.

[Ji et al.2015] Guoliang Ji, Shizhu He, Liheng Xu, Kang Liu, and Jun Zhao. 2015. Knowledge graph embedding via dynamic mapping matrix. In *Proceedings of the 53rd Annual Meeting of the Association for Computational Linguistics and the 7th International Joint Conference on Natural Language Processing*, pages 687–696.

[Jiang et al.2012] Shangpu Jiang, Daniel Lowd, and Dejing Dou. 2012. Learning to refine an automatically extracted knowledge base using markov logic. In *Proceedings of the IEEE International Conference on Data Mining*, pages 912–917.

[Lao and Cohen2010] Ni Lao and William W. Cohen. 2010. Relational retrieval using a combination of path-constrained random walks. *Machine Learning*, 81(1):53–67.

[Lao et al.2011] Ni Lao, Tom Mitchell, and William W. Cohen. 2011. Random walk inference and learning in a large scale knowledge base. In *Proceedings of the 2011 Conference on Empirical Methods in Natural Language Processing*, pages 529–539.

[Lin et al.2015] Yankai Lin, Zhiyuan Liu, Maosong Sun, Yang Liu, and Xuan Zhu. 2015. Learning entity and relation embeddings for knowledge graph completion. In *Proceedings of the 29th AAAI Conference on Artificial Intelligence*, pages 2181–2187.

[Miller1995] George A. Miller. 1995. WordNet: A lexical database for english. *Communications of the ACM*, 38(11):39–41.

[Neelakantan and Chang2015] Arvind Neelakantan and Ming-Wei Chang. 2015. Inferring missing entity type instances for knowledge base completion: New dataset and methods. In *Proceedings of the 2015 Conference of the North American Chapter of the Association for Computational Linguistics: Human Language Technologies*, pages 515–525.

[Neelakantan et al.2015] Arvind Neelakantan, Benjamin Roth, and Andrew McCallum. 2015. Compositional vector space models for knowledge base completion. In *Proceedings of the 53rd Annual Meeting of the Association for Computational Linguistics and the 7th International Joint Conference on Natural Language Processing*, pages 156–166.

[Nickel et al.2011] Maximilian Nickel, Volker Tresp, and Hans peter Kriegel. 2011. A three-way model for collective learning on multi-relational data. In *Proceedings of the 28st International Conference on Machine Learning*, pages 809–816.

[Nickel et al.2015] Maximilian Nickel, Kevin Murphy, Volker Tresp, and Evgeniy Gabrilovich. 2015. A review of relational machine learning for knowledge graphs: From multi-relational link prediction to automated knowledge graph construction. *CoRR*, abs/1503.00759.

[Pujara et al.2013] Jay Pujara, Hui Miao, Lise Getoor, and William Cohen. 2013. Knowledge graph identification. In *Proceedings of the 12th International Semantic Web Conference*, pages 542–557.

[Socher et al.2013] Richard Socher, Danqi Chen, Christopher D. Manning, and Andrew Ng. 2013. Reasoning with neural tensor networks for knowledge base completion. In *Advances in Neural Information Processing Systems*, pages 926–934.

[Suchanek et al.2007] Fabian M. Suchanek, Gjergji Kasneci, and Gerhard Weikum. 2007. YAGO: A core of semantic knowledge unifying wordnet and wikipedia. In *Proceedings of the 16th International Conference on World Wide Web*, pages 697–706.

[Wang et al.2014] Zhen Wang, Jianwen Zhang, Jianlin Feng, and Zheng Chen. 2014. Knowledge graph embedding by translating on hyperplanes. In *Proceedings of the 28th AAAI Conference on Artificial Intelligence*, pages 1112–1119.

DAG-Structured Long Short-Term Memory for Semantic Compositionality

Xiaodan Zhu
National Research Council Canada
1200 Montreal Road, M50
Ottawa, ON K1A 0R6, Canada
zhu2048@gmail.com

Parinaz Sobhani
EECS, University of Ottawa
800 King Edward Avenue
Ottawa, ON K1N 6N5, Canada
psobh090@uottawa.ca

Hongyu Guo
National Research Council Canada
1200 Montreal Road, M50
Ottawa, ON K1A 0R6, Canada
hongyu.guo@nrc-cnrc.gc.ca

Abstract

Recurrent neural networks, particularly long short-term memory (LSTM), have recently shown to be very effective in a wide range of sequence modeling problems, core to which is effective learning of distributed representation for subsequences as well as the sequences they form. An assumption in almost all the previous models, however, posits that the learned representation (e.g., a distributed representation for a sentence), is fully compositional from the atomic components (e.g., representations for words), while non-compositionality is a basic phenomenon in human languages. In this paper, we relieve the assumption by extending the chain-structured LSTM to directed acyclic graphs (DAGs), with the aim to endow linear-chain LSTMs with the capability of considering compositionality together with non-compositionality in the same semantic composition framework. From a more general viewpoint, the proposed models incorporate additional prior knowledge into recurrent neural networks, which is interesting to us, considering most NLP tasks have relatively small training data and appropriate prior knowledge could be beneficial to help cover missing semantics. Our experiments on sentiment composition demonstrate that the proposed models achieve the state-of-the-art performance, outperforming models that lack this ability.

1 Introduction

Recurrent neural networks, particularly long short-term memory (LSTM), have recently shown to be very effective in a wide range of sequence modeling problems, including speech recognition (Graves et al., 2013), automatic machine translation (Sutskever et al., 2014; Cho et al., 2014), and image-to-text conversion (Vinyals et al., 2014), among many others. The specific memory copying and gating configurations in LSTM's memory blocks render an effective mechanism in capturing both short and distant interplays in an input sequence.

In modeling sequences, core to many problems is to learn effective distributed representations for subsequences and the sequences they form. A strong assumption in most previous models, however, posits that the learned representation (e.g., a distributed representation for a sentence) is fully compositional from the atomic components (e.g., representations for words), while non-compositionality is a basic phenomenon in human languages and other modalities, which does not only include rather rigid cases such as idiomatic expressions (e.g., *kick the bucket*) but also *soft* cases that are harder to make a binary judgment.

A framework with the capability to consider both compositionality and non-compositionality in semantic composition are of theoretic interest. From a more pragmatical viewpoint, if one is able to holistically obtain the representations for a sequence (e.g., for the bigram *must try* in a customer-review corpus for sentiment analysis), it would be desirable that a composition model has the ability to choose the sources of knowledge it can trust more: the composition of subsequences of this sequence, the holistic representation, or a soft combination of them, in the process of semantic composition. In such situations,

Proceedings of NAACL-HLT 2016, pages 917–926,
San Diego, California, June 12-17, 2016. ©2016 Association for Computational Linguistics

whether this sequence (*must try*) is indeed compositional or non-compositional may often be blurry or may not be an explicit concern of applications.

In this paper, we extend the popular chain-structured LSTM to directed acyclic graph (DAG) structures, with the aim to endow conventional LSTM with the capability of considering compositionality and non-compositionality together. From a more general viewpoint, the proposed models are along the line of incorporating external knowledge into recurrent neural models, which is interesting to us, considering that most NLP tasks have relatively limited amount of training data, and external prior knowledge could be beneficial to help cover missing semantics. The proposed models unify the compositional power of recurrent neural networks (RNN) and additional prior knowledge. In general, neural nets are powerful approaches for composition, which can fit very complicated compositional functions underlying the annotated data (Cybenko, 1989; Hornik, 1991). Over that, externally obtained semantics could help cope with missing information in limited training data.

We demonstrated the models' effectiveness in sentiment composition, a popular semantic composition problem that optimizes a sentiment objective. We show that the proposed models achieve the state-of-the-art performance on two benchmark datasets, without any feature engineering, by unifying the compositional strength of LSTM with external semantic knowledge.

2 Related Work

Linear and Structured RNN Linear-chain RNN, particularly LSTM, has been applied to a wide range of problems as in (Graves et al., 2013; Sutskever et al., 2014; Cho et al., 2014; Vinyals et al., 2014), among many others. While the models take a linear encoding process to absorb input symbols, they are capable of implicitly capturing rather complicated structures embedded in the input sequences.

Recent research has also moved beyond linear-chain LSTM. For example, in (Tai et al., 2015; Zhu et al., 2015b; Le and Zuidema, 2015), LSTM was extended to tree structures. The results show that tree-structured LSTM achieves the-state-of-the-art performance on semantic tasks such as paraphrasing detection and sentiment analysis, due to its abilities in capturing both local and long-distance interplay over the structures.

In this work, we proposed DAG-structured LSTM for modeling sequences of text. Unlike the tree-structured LSTM, where the structures are used for considering syntax, the proposed models leverage DAG structures to incorporate external semantics including non-compositional or holistically learned semantics.

Compositionality Semantic composition exists in multiple modalities, including images and vision (Lake, 2014; Hummel, 2001; Socher et al., 2011; van der Velde and de Kamps, 2006). In human languages, the recent years have seen extensive interests on distributional approaches. The research includes the influential pioneering work that examined a number of explicit forms of compositional functions (Mitchell and Lapata, 2008).

More recent works explored neural networks, e.g., (Socher et al., 2013; Irsoy and Cardie, 2014; Kalchbrenner et al., 2014; Tai et al., 2015; Le and Zuidema, 2015; Zhu et al., 2015c) among many others, which extended the success of word-level embeddings (Collobert et al., 2011; Mikolov et al., 2013; Chen et al., 2015) and modeled sentences through semantic composition. In general, neural models can fit very complicated functions and can be a universal approximator (Cybenko, 1989; Hornik, 1991).

In obtaining the distributed representation for longer spans of text from its subsequences, previous neural models assume full compositionality from the atomic components and disregard non-compositionality and in general prior semantics. Some very recent work (Zhu et al., 2015a) has started to address this problem in recursive neural networks with the assumption of the availability of parse information. In this work, we extend the general sequence models, chain-structured LSTM, to directed acyclic graphs (DAGs) in order to consider prior semantics, including non-compositional or holistically learned semantics. We utilize DAG structures to unify different sources of semantics.

From the decomposition direction, modeling non-constitutionality could potentially help learn the representations for the atomic components (e.g., words) as well, by avoiding backpropagating unnecessary errors to the atom level. For example, the errors received by the block *kick the bucket*, may not need to be passed down to the word level and potentially confuse the embedding of the component words *kick* or *bucket*.

3 DAG-Structured LSTM

The DAG-structured LSTM aims to integrate compositional, non-compositional, and in general external semantics in semantic composition. Figure 1 depicts an example of DAG-structured LSTM (referred to as DAG-LSTM in the remainder of the paper) in modeling a sentence.

The proposed DAG-LSTM networks consist of four types of nodes, denoted in Figure 1 with different colors. The blue nodes (0, 1, 2, 6, and 7) correspond to normal chain-structured LSTM memory blocks. The yellow nodes (5 and 8) model non-compositional knowledge. The purple nodes (3 and 4), which we call *fork blocks* or *fork nodes* in this paper, are the modified versions of regular LSTM nodes, summarizing history for different types of outgoing blocks. The merging memory block is depicted in red (node 9), aiming at infusing information from multiple histories and deciding which sources will be considered more. Each category of these four types of memory blocks share its own parameters or weight matrices; e.g., the two yellow blocks share the same parameters.

3.1 Compositional and Non-compositional Memory Blocks

The conventional components of DAG-LSTM in Figure 1 are nodes 0, 1, 2, 6, and 7, which implement linear-chain LSTM memory blocks that we will not discuss in detail here (refer to (Graves, 2012) for a good introduction and discussion.)

The yellow nodes (blocks 5 and 8) model non-compositional knowledge. In general, the goal is incorporating external, holistic knowledge. Specifically for the sentiment composition task that we experiment with in this paper, we leverage two different types of such external knowledge: (1) sentiment of words and ngrams holistically learned from external, larger corpora, and (2) sentiment of words and phrases from human prior, i.e., annotation assigned

by human subjects. We concatenate these two resources (in form of vectors) to be a longer vector for nodes 5 and 8. Note that the models allow both the number of hidden units and the embedding spaces of a non-compositional node to be different from those of a compositional node.

Accordingly, the DAG-LSTM employs two types of paths, compositional path (shortened as c-path) and non-compositional path (nc-path), to incorporate different knowledge sources. For example, the c-path in the figure connects nodes 3, 4, 6, 7, and 9, which model the regular sequential compositional procedure. The two nc-paths explore non-compositional knowledge. The path 4-5-9 considers the composition vector accumulated at node 4 so far with the non-compositional knowledge of the phrase *must try*. Similarly, the path 3-8-9 considers holistic representation for the negated phrase *not must try*. Note that negation by itself has shown to be a rather complicated non-linear function (Zhu et al., 2014a), if being modeled only compositionally. The model here provides the flexibility to consider both compositional and non-compositional representations. All knowledge from these three paths are then merged, to obtain the comprehensive representation so far, at node 9. Later in the experiment section, we will discuss how to obtain prior non-compositional knowledge, from both human heuristics/annotation and from automatically learned resources.

3.2 Fork Memory Blocks

The fork blocks (node 3 and 4) summarize history obtained so far for different types of outgoing blocks (node 5 and 6 from node 4) that are either compositional or non-compositional. More specifically, the cell and output vectors of a fork node will be passed to multiple paths as intuitively shown in Figure 2. While the forward propagation of a fork block is the same as that of a regular LSTM block, during backpropagation, the errors are summed over multiple outgoing blocks and passed back to the memory cell and output layer of the current node.

More specifically, for each memory block, assume that the error passed to the hidden vector is ϵ_t^h. The derivatives of the output gate δ_t^o, forget gate δ_t^f and input gate δ_t^i are computed as follows:

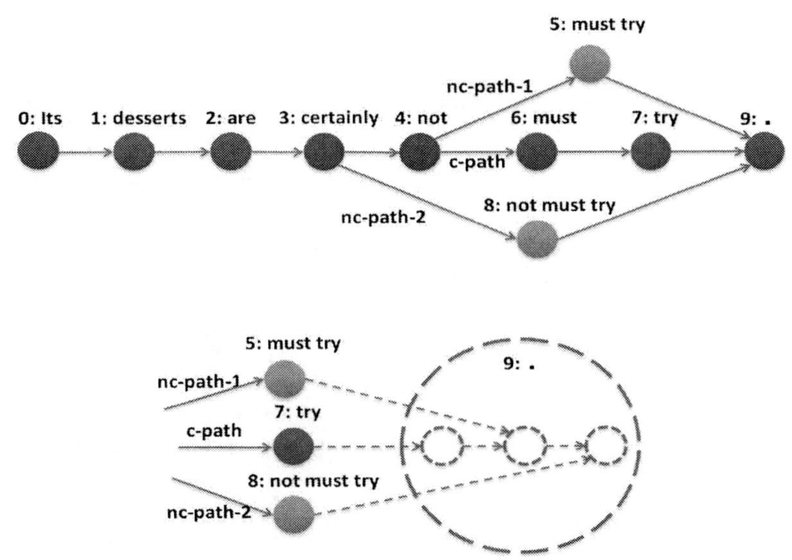

Figure 1: An example of DAG-LSTM in modeling a sentence. Nodes with different colors contain different types of LSTM memory blocks.

$$\epsilon_t^h = \frac{\partial \sum_p O_p}{\partial h_t} \tag{1}$$

$$\delta_t^o = \epsilon_t^h \otimes \tanh(c_t) \otimes \sigma'(o_t) \tag{2}$$

$$\delta_t^f = \epsilon_t^c \otimes c_{t-1} \otimes \sigma'(f_t) \tag{3}$$

$$\delta_t^i = \epsilon_t^c \otimes \tanh(x_t) \otimes \sigma'(i_t) \tag{4}$$

where $\sigma'(x)$ is the element-wise derivative of the logistic function over vector x. Since it can be computed with the activation of x, we relax the notation a bit to write it over the activated vectors in these equations. The underscript p is representative of parent over different paths (both non-compositional paths and compositional path). ϵ_t^c is the derivative over the cell vector and it is calculated as follows:

$$\epsilon_t^c = \epsilon_t^h \otimes o_t \otimes g'(c_t) + (W_{co})^T \delta_t^o$$
$$+ \sum_p [(W_{ci}^L)^T \delta_p^i + \epsilon_p^c \otimes f_p^L + (W_{cf}^L)^T \delta_p^f] \tag{5}$$

where $g'(x)$ is the element-wise derivative of the *tanh* function. It can also be directly calculated from

the *tanh* activation of x. The superscript T over the weight matrices means matrix transpose.

3.3 Merging Blocks

Merging blocks (node 9 in Figure 1) accumulate and summarize multiple histories. For the specific example in Figure 1, the merging block combines information from two non-compositional paths and one compositional path.

Binarization In this paper, we propose to *binarize* the nodes in the merging process. Taking Figure 1 as an example, binarization is performed as depicted in the bottom subfigure. We merge the compositional path (c-path) with one of the non-compositional path (nc-path) and then another. With this binarization trick, we can handle nodes with any number of incoming edges (degrees) with the same architecture of memory block. We made all the binarized merging nodes (the three dotted-lined nodes in the lower subfigure of Figure 1) to share the same parameters (weight matrices), as during merging we should treat compositional and non-compositional history (5, 7, 8) in the same way, by their content but not by how many words they contain. Note that since the dimension of the output vectors and memory cell vectors of different paths are the same, one has the choice of using other variants of memory blocks such as those described in (Tai et al., 2015; Le and Zuidema, 2015; Zhu et al., 2015c).

Again, note that we use merging node to consider noncompositional and prior knowledge in DAG, but the above tree-LSTM was proposed to wire with syntactic structures to consider syntactic information. In addition, in DAG, the merging nodes work together with fork nodes to correctly forward-propagate and back-propagate compositional and non-compositional knowledge jointly.

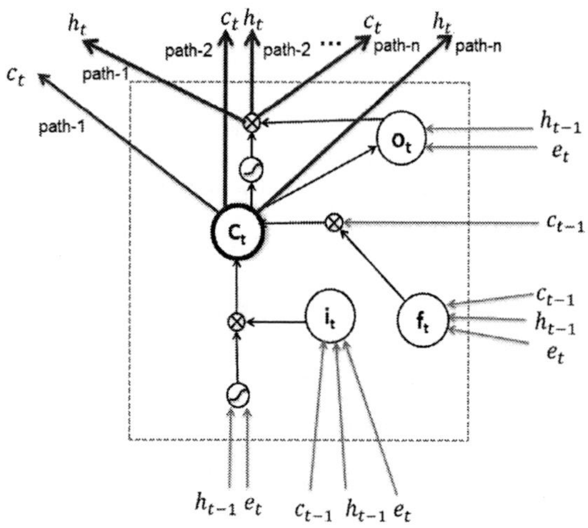

Figure 2: An example of a fork memory block. Both the hidden vectors h_t and cell vectors c_t are passed along multiple outgoing paths to the future blocks. $\otimes$ denotes a Hadamard product, and the "s" shape sign is a squashing function (in this paper the *tanh* function).

4 Experiment Set-Up

In this paper, we study the proposed models on a semantic composition task that determine the sentiment of a piece of text. We use social-media messages from the official SemEval Sentiment Analysis in Twitter competition. Analyzing social-media text has attracted extensive attention (Nakov et al., 2016; Kiritchenko et al., 2014; Mohammad et al., 2014; Mohammad et al., 2015; Zhu et al., 2014b; Mohammad et al., 2013a) and have many applications. Sen-

timental analysis of such data presents a unique set of challenges as well; for example, the tweet posts are often short, use informal languages, and are often not linguistically well-formed. Syntactic analysis such as parsing is much less reliable in such data than in news articles, and sequential models without depending on deep linguistic analysis (e.g., parsing) are adopted by most previous work.

In obtaining the sentiment of a text span, e.g., a sentence, early work often factorized the problem to consider smaller pieces of component words or phrases with bag-of-words or bag-of-phrases models (Liu and Zhang, 2012; Pang and Lee, 2008). More recent work has started to model composition process (Choi and Cardie, 2008; Moilanen and Pulman, 2007; Socher et al., 2012; Socher et al., 2013; Irsoy and Cardie, 2014; Kalchbrenner et al., 2014; Tai et al., 2015; Zhu et al., 2015b; Le and Zuidema, 2015), more closely. In general, the composition process is critical in the formation of the sentiment of a text span, which has not been well modeled yet and more work would be desirable.

4.1 Data and Evaluation Metric

In our experiments, we use the official data from the SemEval-2013 (Wilson et al., 2013) and SemEval-2014 (Rosenthal et al., 2014) Sentiment Analysis in Twitter challenges. The task attempts to determine the sentiment category of a tweet; that is, detecting whether an entire tweet message conveys a positive, negative, or neutral sentiment.

To give a rough idea about the data, the SemEval-2013 tweets were collected through the public streaming Twitter API during a period of one year: between January 2012 and January 2013. The dataset is comprised of 5,192 positive and 2,150 negative and 6,383 neutral tweets split into the training (8,258 tweets), development (1,654 tweets), and test (3,813 tweets) sets. For more details, please refer to (Wilson et al., 2013; Rosenthal et al., 2014). In our experiments, we report our results on the official in-domain (tweets) test data but not out-of-domain (e.g., SMS) test data to better observe the supervised performances of our models but not the domain adaptation performance.

Following the official specification, we use macro-averaged F-score to evaluate the performances.

4.2 Prior Knowledge

As briefly discussed in Section 3, we use two different sources of prior, non-compositional knowledge. These two types of resources encode: (1) sentiment of ngrams automatically learned from an external, much larger corpus, and (2) sentiment of ngrams assigned by human annotators. Below, we introduce them in further details.

Automatically Learned Knowledge Following the method proposed in (Mohammad et al., 2013b), we learn sentimental ngrams from Tweets, e.g., the sentiment knowledge for the bigram *must try*. The unsupervised approach utilizes *hashtags*, which can be regarded as conveying freely available (but noisy) human annotation of sentiment. More specifically, certain words in tweets are specially marked with the hash character (#) to indicate the topic, sentiment polarity, or emotions such as joy, sadness, angry, and surprised. With enough data, such artificial annotation can be used to learn the sentiment of ngrams by their likelihood of co-occurring with such hashtagged words.

More specifically, a collection of 78 seed hashtags closely related to *positive* and *negative* such as *#good*, *#excellent*, *#bad*, and *#terrible* were used (32 positive and 36 negative). These terms were chosen from entries for *positive* and *negative* in the Roget's Thesaurus. A set of 775,000 tweets that contain at least a positive hashtag or a negative hashtag were used as the learning corpus. A tweet was considered positive if it had one of the 32 positive seed hashtags, and negative if it had one of the 36 negative seed hashtags. The association score for an ngram w was calculated from these pseudo-labeled tweets as follows:

$$score(w) = PMI(w, positive) - PMI(w, negative) \tag{6}$$

where PMI stands for pointwise mutual information, and the two terms in the formula calculate the PMI between the target ngram and the pseudo-labeled positive tweets as well as that between the ngram and the negative tweets, respectively. Accordingly, a positive *score(.)* indicates association with positive sentiment, whereas a negative score indicates association with negative sentiment.

We use in our experiments the unigrams, bigrams and trigrams learned from the dataset with the occurrences higher than 5. We assign these ngrams into one of the 5 bins according to their sentiment scores obtained with Formula 6: $(-\infty, -2]$, $(-2, -1]$, $(-1, 1)$, $[1, 2)$, and $[2, +\infty)$. Each ngram is now given a one-hot vector, indicating the polarity and strength of its sentiment. For example, a bigram with a score of -1.5 will be assigned a 5-dimensional vector $[0, 1, 0, 0, 0]$, indicating a weak negative. Note that we can also take into other forms of sentiment embeddings, such as those learned in (Tang et al., 2014).

Manually Encoded Semantics In addition, we also leveraged prior knowledge from human, i.e., manually encoded semantics, for the task here. This includes a widely used sentiment lexicon, the MPQA Subjectivity Lexicon (Wilson et al., 2005), which encodes the prior knowledge that the human annotators have about the sentiment of words. The MPQA, which draws from the General Inquirer and other sources, has sentiment labels for about 8,000 words. The contained words marked with their prior polarity (positive or negative) and a discrete strength of evaluative intensity (strong or weak). We convert them to value -1.0, -0.5, 0, 0.5, 1, corresponding to *strong negative*, *weak negative*, *neutral*, *weak positive*, *strong positive*, respectively.

4.3 Training Details

Our networks aim to minimize the cross-entropy error (Socher et al., 2013). The models learn the weight matrices used in those different memory blocks described above in addition to learning word embedding. For all Twitter messages, the error is calculated as a regularized sum:

$$E(\theta) = \sum_i \sum_j t_j^i \log y^{sen_i}{}_j + \lambda \|\theta\|_2^2 \tag{7}$$

where $y^{sen_i} \in \mathbb{R}^{c \times 1}$ is predicted distribution and $t^i \in \mathbb{R}^{c \times 1}$ the target distribution. c is the number of classes or categories, and $j \in c$ denotes the j-th element of the multinomial target distribution; i iterates over root nodes, θ are model parameters, and λ is a regularization parameter. We tuned our model against the development data set.

The DAG-LSTM and LSTM results reported here are all obtained by setting the size of the hidden units to 10, batch size to 10 and learning rate to 0.1, which achieved the best performance during development.

5   Results

5.1   Overall Performance

Table 1 presents the macro-averaged F-scores of different models on the official test sets of the SemEval-2013 and SemEval-2014 Sentiment Analysis in Twitter. The first row of results show the majority baseline where a majority classifier simply predicts all test cases into the most frequent class observed in training data. SVM is a support vector machine classifier applied to unigram features, as reported in (Nakov et al., 2016). In addition, we list the results of top three models described in the official reports of SemEval-2013 (Wilson et al., 2013) and SemEval-2014 (Rosenthal et al., 2014), respectively.

Method	SemEval-13	SemEval-14
Majority baseline	29.19	34.46
Unigram (SVM)	56.95	58.58
3rd best model	64.86	69.95
2nd best model	65.27	70.14
The best model	69.02	70.96
LSTM-DAG	70.88	71.97

Table 1: Performances of different models in official evaluation metric (macro F-scores) on the test sets of SemEval-2013 and SemEval-2014 Sentiment Analysis in Twitter in predicting the sentiment of the tweet messages.

The results show DAG-LSTM achieves a macro-averaged F-score of 70.88% on the SemEval-2013 test set and 71.97% on the SemEval-2014 test set, which outperform the models officially reported in the competition. Note that DAG-LSTM performs no feature engineering, but unifies LSTM with the external semantic knowledge to perform semantic composition within the DAG structures, where LSTM, as discussed earlier in the paper, possesses strong modeling and composition power through capturing distant interplay and complicated structures embedded in sequences, while prior knowledge used covers missing semantics in the limited training data.

Note that further improvement, including that reported in (Zhu et al., 2014b), is additionally possible, which was achieved by building better resources through discriminating affirmative and negative context. Such improvement could be orthogonally combined with our model, while in this paper, we are interested in the basic modeling problems and leave such engineering as future work. Note also that the external resources we use in this paper is the same or less than the top official system we compare to in Table 1.

5.2   Effect of DAG Paths

To provide a more detailed analysis on the effect of different paths in DAG-LSTM, Table 2 include the ablation results obtained by removing different types of paths gradually. The table show that by removing all the paths that incorporate the prior semantics, a regular LSTM (last row of the table) achieves the f-scores of a 64.0% and 66.4% on the two test sets, which is far less than the best result we have achieved; But the performance of the regular LSTM is still much better than that of unigram-based SVM reported in Table 1, suggesting the usefulness of the LSTM composition compared to bag-of-word models.

Method	SemEval-13	SemEval-14
DAG-LSTM		
Full paths	70.88	71.97
Full − {autoPaths}	69.36	69.27
Full − {triPaths}	70.16	70.77
Full − {triPaths, biPaths}	69.55	69.93
Full − {manuPaths}	69.88	70.58
LSTM without DAG		
Full − {autoPaths, manuPaths}	64.00	66.40

Table 2: Ablation performances (macro-averaged F-scores) of DAG-LSTM with different types of paths being removed.

When removing the paths corresponding to automatic lexicons, the performance dropped to 69.36% and 69.27% on the SemEval-2013 and SemEval-2014 dataset, respectively. If removing all paths corresponding to manual lexicons, the performance dropped to 69.88% and 70.58%. In both test sets, the paths corresponds to automatic lexicon have more impact on the ablation performance than manual-lexicon paths, which agree with the observation reported in previous top systems that use conventional feature-based classifiers (Mohammad et al., 2013a), suggesting the usefulness of the automatically acquired semantics. The table also lists more details of removing trigram and bigram paths.

In addition to the ablation models reported in Table 2, we also created an additional model that incorporated into the basic chain LSTM the external knowledge only for longest n-grams but not for their substrings. This experiment is supposed to investigate the effect of DAG structures that integrate knowledge for different granularities of ngrams in comparison to the LSTM that incorporates the external knowledge only for the longest n-grams. On SemEval-2014 official set, the performance (Macro-F) of this model is 69.37, compared with DAG-LSTM (71.97) and chain LSTM (66.40). On Semeval-2013, Macro-F is 68.81, compared with DAG-LSTM (70.88) and chain LSTM (64.00). After some manual analysis, we observe that in tweets where DAG-LSTM works better than this baseline model, the prior sentiment of the longest n-grams is often noisy and not very reliable; in this case, the weight matrix of DAG-LSTM helps choose more reliable resources, e.g., composition from lower-order ngrams.

6 Conclusions and Discussions

In obtaining the distributed representation for longer text spans from its subsequences, previous neural models assume fully compositionality from the atomic components and often disregard the non-compositionality and in general prior semantics. In this paper, we extend chain-structured LSTM to a directed acyclic graph (DAG) structure, with the aim to provide the popular chain LSTM with the capability of considering both compositionality and non-compositionality in a single semantic composition framework. We demonstrated the models' effectiveness in a sentiment composition task, a popular semantic composition problem that optimizes a sentiment objective. We use two official SemEval datasets to detect the sentiment expressed by social-media messages. The proposed models achieve the state-of-the-art performance without any feature engineering, through unifying the composition strength of LSTM with external holistic semantics.

We consider our work as an attempt towards unifying the strong modeling power of neural models with proper prior or external knowledge. This is an intriguing direction for us, as most NLP tasks lack training data, compared with speech recognition or image classification where neural models have achieved more significant successes.

While we specifically treat LSTM in this paper, it should be rather straightforward to adapt the proposed idea to other architectures of recurrent neural networks.

Acknowledgments

The second author of this paper was supported by the Natural Sciences and Engineering Research Council of Canada under the CREATE program.

References

Zhigang Chen, Wei Lin, Qian Chen, Si Wei, Hui Jiang, and Xiaodan Zhu. 2015. Revisiting word embedding for contrasting meaning. In *Proceedings of ACL*.

Kyunghyun Cho, Bart van Merrienboer, Çaglar Gülçehre, Fethi Bougares, Holger Schwenk, and Yoshua Bengio. 2014. Learning phrase representations using RNN encoder-decoder for statistical machine translation. *CoRR*, abs/1406.1078.

Yejin Choi and Claire Cardie. 2008. Learning with compositional semantics as structural inference for subsentential sentiment analysis. In *Proceedings of the Conference on Empirical Methods in Natural Language Processing*, EMNLP '08, pages 793–801, Honolulu, Hawaii.

R. Collobert, J. Weston, L. Bottou, M. Karlen, K. Kavukcuoglu, and P. Kuksa. 2011. Natural language processing (almost) from scratch. *JMLR*, 12:2493–2537.

George Cybenko. 1989. Approximations by superpositions of sigmoidal functions. *Mathematics of Control, Signals, and Systems*, 2(4):303–314.

Alex Graves, Abdel-rahman Mohamed, and Geoffrey E. Hinton. 2013. Speech recognition with deep recurrent neural networks. *CoRR*, abs/1303.5778.

Alex Graves. 2012. *Supervised sequence labelling with recurrent neural networks*, volume 385. Springer.

Kurt Hornik. 1991. Approximation capabilities of multilayer feedforward networks. *Neural Networks*, 4(2):251–257.

John E Hummel. 2001. Complementary solutions to the binding problem in vision: Implications for shape perception and object recognition. *Visual cognition*, 8(3-5):489–517.

Ozan Irsoy and Claire Cardie. 2014. Deep recursive neural networks for compositionality in language. In Z. Ghahramani, M. Welling, C. Cortes, N.D. Lawrence, and K.Q. Weinberger, editors, *Advances in Neural Information Processing Systems 27*, pages 2096–2104. Curran Associates, Inc.

Nal Kalchbrenner, Edward Grefenstette, and Phil Blunsom. 2014. A convolutional neural network for modelling sentences. *Proceedings of the 52nd Annual Meeting of the Association for Computational Linguistics*, June.

Svetlana Kiritchenko, Xiaodan Zhu, and Saif Mohammad. 2014. Sentiment analysis of short informal texts. *Journal of Artificial Intelligence Research*, 50:724–762, August.

Brenden M Lake. 2014. *Towards more human-like concept learning in machines : compositionality, causality, and learning-to-learn*. Ph.D. thesis, Massachusetts Institute of Technology. Department of Brain and Cognitive Sciences.

Phong Le and Willem Zuidema. 2015. Compositional distributional semantics with long short term memory. *CoRR*, abs/1503.02510.

Bing Liu and Lei Zhang. 2012. A survey of opinion mining and sentiment analysis. In Charu C. Aggarwal and ChengXiang Zhai, editors, *Mining Text Data*, pages 415–463. Springer US.

Tomas Mikolov, Ilya Sutskever, Kai Chen, Greg S Corrado, and Jeff Dean. 2013. Distributed representations of words and phrases and their compositionality. In *Advances in neural information processing systems*, pages 3111–3119.

Jeff Mitchell and Mirella Lapata. 2008. Vector-based models of semantic composition. In *Proceedings of the 46th Annual Meeting of the Association for Computational Linguistics*, June.

S. Mohammad, S. Kiritchenko, and X. Zhu. 2013a. NRC-Canada: Building the state-of-the-art in sentiment analysis of tweets. In *Proceedings of the International Workshop on Semantic Evaluation*, SemEval '13, Atlanta, Georgia, USA, June.

Saif M. Mohammad, Bonnie J. Dorr, Graeme Hirst, and Peter D. Turney. 2013b. Computing lexical contrast. *Computational Linguistics*, 39(3):555–590.

Saif Mohammad, Xiaodan Zhu, and Joel Martin. 2014. Semantic role labeling of emotions in tweets. In *Proceedings of ACL Workshop on Computational Approaches to Subjectivity*, June.

Saif Mohammad, Xiaodan Zhu, Svetlana Kiritchenko, and Joel Martin. 2015. Sentiment, emotion, purpose, and style in electoral tweets. *Information Processing and Management*, 51:480–499.

Karo Moilanen and Stephen Pulman. 2007. Sentiment composition. In *Proceedings of RANLP 2007*, Borovets, Bulgaria.

Preslav Nakov, Sara Rosenthal, Svetlana Kiritchenko, Saif M. Mohammad, Zornitsa Kozareva, Alan Ritter, Veselin Stoyanov, and Xiaodan Zhu. 2016. Developing a successful semeval task in sentiment analysis of twitter and other social media texts. *Language Resources and Evaluation*, 50(1):35–65.

Bo Pang and Lillian Lee. 2008. Opinion mining and sentiment analysis. *Foundations and Trends in Information Retrieval*, 2(1–2):1–135.

Sara Rosenthal, Preslav Nakov, Alan Ritter, and Veselin Stoyanov. 2014. Semeval-2014 task 9: Sentiment analysis in twitter. *Proc. SemEval*, pages 73–80.

Richard Socher, Cliff Chiung-Yu Lin, Andrew Y. Ng, and Christopher D. Manning. 2011. Parsing natural scenes and natural language with recursive neural networks. In *Proceedings of the 28th International Conference on Machine Learning, ICML*, pages 129–136, Washington, USA.

Richard Socher, Brody Huval, Christopher D. Manning, and Andrew Y. Ng. 2012. Semantic compositionality through recursive matrix-vector spaces. In *Proceedings of the Conference on Empirical Methods in Natural Language Processing*, EMNLP '12, Jeju, Korea. Association for Computational Linguistics.

Richard Socher, Alex Perelygin, Jean Y. Wu, Jason Chuang, Christopher D. Manning, Andrew Y. Ng, and Christopher Potts. 2013. Recursive deep models for semantic compositionality over a sentiment treebank. In *Proceedings of the Conference on Empirical Methods in Natural Language Processing*, EMNLP '13, Seattle, USA. Association for Computational Linguistics.

Ilya Sutskever, Oriol Vinyals, and Quoc V. Le. 2014. Sequence to sequence learning with neural networks. *CoRR*, abs/1409.3215.

Kai Sheng Tai, Richard Socher, and C hristopher D. Manning. 2015. Improved semantic representations from tree-structured long short-term memory networks. *CoRR*, abs/1503.00075.

Duyu Tang, Furu Wei, Nan Yang, Ming Zhou, Ting Liu, and Bing Qin. 2014. Learning sentiment-specific word embedding for twitter sentiment classification. In *Proceedings of ACL*, Baltimore, Maryland, USA, June.

F. van der Velde and M. de Kamps. 2006. Neural blackboard architectures of combinatorial structures in cognition. *Behavioral and Brain Sciences*, 29:37–70.

Oriol Vinyals, Alexander Toshev, Samy Bengio, and Dumitru Erhan. 2014. Show and tell: A neural image caption generator. *CoRR*, abs/1411.4555.

Theresa Wilson, Janyce Wiebe, and Paul Hoffmann. 2005. Recognizing contextual polarity in phrase-level sentiment analysis. In *Proceedings of the Conference on Human Language Technology and Empirical Methods in Natural Language Processing*, HLT '05, pages 347–354, Stroudsburg, PA, USA. Association for Computational Linguistics.

Theresa Wilson, Zornitsa Kozareva, Preslav Nakov, Sara Rosenthal, Veselin Stoyanov, and Alan Ritter. 2013. SemEval-2013 Task 2: Sentiment analysis in Twitter. In *Proceedings of the International Workshop on Semantic Evaluation*, SemEval '13, Atlanta, Georgia, USA, June.

Xiaodan Zhu, Hongyu Guo, Saif Mohammad, and Svetlana Kiritchenko. 2014a. An empirical study on the effect of negation words on sentiment. In *Proceedings of ACL*, Baltimore, Maryland, USA, June.

Xiaodan Zhu, Svetlana Kiritchenko, and Saif Mohammad. 2014b. Nrc-canada-2014: Recent improvements in the sentiment analysis of tweets. In *Proceedings of the International Workshop on Semantic Evaluation*, August.

Xiaodan Zhu, Hongyu Guo, and Parinaz Sobhani. 2015a. Neural networks for integrating compositional and non-compositional sentiment in sentiment composition. In *Proceedings of Joint Conference on Lexical and Computational Semantics*, June.

Xiaodan Zhu, Parinaz Sobhani, and Hongyu Guo. 2015b. Long short-term memory over recursive structures. In *Proceedings of International Conference on Machine Learning*, July.

Xiaodan Zhu, Parinaz Sobhani, and Hongyu Guo. 2015c. Long short-term memory over tree structures. *CoRR*, abs/1503.04881.

Bayesian Supervised Domain Adaptation for Short Text Similarity

Md Arafat Sultan[1,2]   **Jordan Boyd-Graber**[2]   **Tamara Sumner**[1,2]
[1]Institute of Cognitive Science
[2]Department of Computer Science
University of Colorado, Boulder, CO
{arafat.sultan,Jordan.Boyd.Graber,sumner}@colorado.edu

Abstract

Identification of short text similarity (STS) is a high-utility NLP task with applications in a variety of domains. We explore adaptation of STS algorithms to different target domains and applications. A two-level hierarchical Bayesian model is employed for domain adaptation (DA) of a linear STS model to text from different sources (e.g., news, tweets). This model is then further extended for multitask learning (MTL) of three related tasks: STS, short answer scoring (SAS) and answer sentence ranking (ASR). In our experiments, the adaptive model demonstrates better overall cross-domain and cross-task performance over two non-adaptive baselines.

1 Short Text Similarity: The Need for Domain Adaptation

Given two snippets of text—neither longer than a few sentences—short text similarity (**STS**) determines how semantically close they are. STS has a broad range of applications: question answering (Yao et al., 2013; Severyn and Moschitti, 2015), text summarization (Dasgupta et al., 2013; Wang et al., 2013), machine translation evaluation (Chan and Ng, 2008; Liu et al., 2011), and grading of student answers in academic tests (Mohler et al., 2011; Ramachandran et al., 2015).

STS is typically viewed as a *supervised* machine learning problem (Bär et al., 2012; Lynum et al., 2014; Hänig et al., 2015). SemEval contests (Agirre et al., 2012; Agirre et al., 2015) have spurred recent progress in STS and have provided valuable training data for these supervised approaches. However, similarity varies across domains, as does the underlying text; e.g., syntactically well-formed academic text versus informal English in forum QA.

Our goal is to effectively use domain adaptation (DA) to transfer information from these disparate STS domains. While "domain" can take a range of meanings, we consider adaptation to different (1) sources of text (e.g., news headlines, tweets), and (2) applications of STS (e.g., QA vs. answer grading). Our goal is to improve performance in a new domain with few in-domain annotations by using many out-of-domain ones (Section 2).

In Section 3, we describe our Bayesian approach that posits that per-domain parameter vectors share a common Gaussian prior that represents the global parameter vector. Importantly, this idea can be extended with little effort to a nested domain hierarchy (domains within domains), which allows us to create a single, unified STS model that *generalizes across domains as well as tasks*, capturing the nuances that an STS system must have for tasks such as short answer scoring or question answering.

We compare our DA methods against two baselines: (1) a domain-agnostic model that uses all training data and does not distinguish between in-domain and out-of-domain examples, and (2) a model that learns only from in-domain examples. Section 5 shows that across ten different STS domains, the adaptive model consistently outperforms the first baseline while performing at least as well as the second across training datasets of different sizes. Our multitask model also yields better overall results over the same baselines across three related tasks: (1) STS, (2) short answer scoring (SAS), and (3) answer sentence ranking (ASR) for question answering.

2 Tasks and Datasets

Short Text Similarity (STS)   Given two short texts, STS provides a real-valued score that represents their degree of semantic similarity. Our STS datasets come from the SemEval 2012–2015 corpora, containing over 14,000 human-annotated sentence pairs (via Amazon Mechanical Turk) from domains like news, tweets, forum posts, and image descriptions.

For our experiments, we select ten datasets from ten different domains, containing 6,450 sentence pairs.[1] This selection is intended to maximize (a) the number of domains, (b) domain uniqueness: of three different news headlines datasets, for example, we select the most recent (2015), discarding older ones (2013, 2014), and (c) amount of per-domain data available: we exclude the FNWN (2013) dataset with 189 annotations, for example, because it limits per-domain training data in our experiments. Sizes of the selected datasets range from 375 to 750 pairs. Average correlation (Pearson's r) among annotators ranges from 58.6% to 88.8% on individual datasets (above 70% for most) (Agirre et al., 2012; Agirre et al., 2013; Agirre et al., 2014; Agirre et al., 2015).

Short Answer Scoring (SAS)   SAS comes in different forms; we explore a form where for a short-answer question, a gold answer is provided, and the goal is to grade student answers based on how similar they are to the gold answer (Ramachandran et al., 2015). We use a dataset of undergraduate data structures questions and student responses graded by two judges (Mohler et al., 2011). These questions are spread across ten different assignments and two examinations, each on a related set of topics (e.g., programming basics, sorting algorithms). Inter-annotator agreement is 58.6% (Pearson's ρ) and 0.659 (RMSE on a 5-point scale). We discard assignments with fewer than 200 pairs, retaining 1,182 student responses to forty questions spread across five assignments and tests.[2]

Answer Sentence Ranking (ASR)   Given a factoid question and a set of candidate answer sentences, ASR orders candidates so that sentences containing the answer are ranked higher. Text similarity is the foundation of most prior work: a candidate sentence's relevance is based on its similarity with the question (Wang et al., 2007; Yao et al., 2013; Severyn and Moschitti, 2015).

For our ASR experiments, we use factoid questions developed by Wang et al. (2007) from Text REtrieval Conferences (TREC) 8–13. Candidate QA pairs of a question and a candidate were labeled with whether the candidate answers the question. The questions are of different types (e.g., *what, where*); we retain 2,247 QA pairs under four question types, each with at least 200 answer candidates in the combined development and test sets.[3] Each question type represents a unique topical domain—*who* questions are about persons and *how many* questions are about quantities.

3 Bayesian Domain Adaptation for STS

We first discuss our base linear models for the three tasks: Bayesian L_2-regularized linear (for STS and SAS) and logistic (for ASR) regression. We extend these models for (1) adaptation across different short text similarity domains, and (2) multitask learning of short text similarity (STS), short answer scoring (SAS), and answer sentence ranking (ASR).

3.1 Base Models

In our base models (Figure 1), the feature vector f combines with the feature weight vector w (including a bias term w_0) to form predictions. Each parameter $w_i \in w$ has its own zero-mean Gaussian prior with its standard deviation σ_{w_i} distributed uniformly in $[0, m_{\sigma_w}]$, the covariance matrix Σ_w is diagonal, and the zero-mean prior L_2 regularizes the model.

In the linear model (Figure 1a), S is the output (similarity score for STS; answer score for SAS) and is normally distributed around the dot product $w^T f$. The model error σ_S has a uniform prior over a pre-specified range $[0, m_{\sigma_S}]$. In the logistic model (Figure 1b) for ASR, the probability p that the candidate sentence answers the question, is (1) the sigmoid of $w^T f$, and (2) the Bernoulli prior of A, whether or not the candidate answers the question.

The common vectors w and f in these models enable joint parameter learning and consequently multitask learning (Section 3.3).

---

[1]2012: MSRpar-test; 2013: SMT; 2014: Deft-forum, OnWN, Tweet-news; 2015: Answers-forums, Answers-students, Belief, Headlines and Images.

[2]Assignments: #1, #2, and #3; Exams: #11 and #12.

[3]*what, when, who* and *how many*.

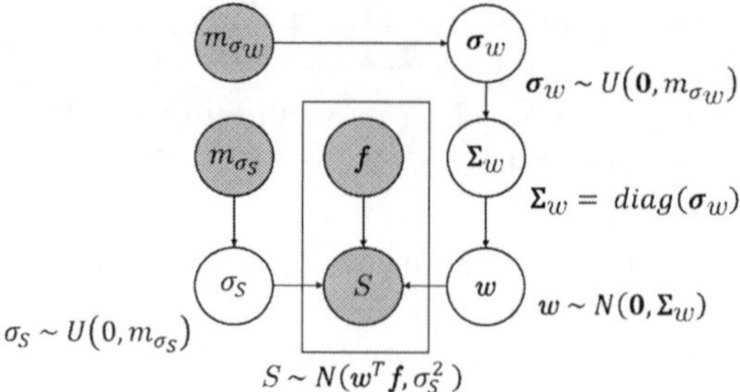

(a) Bayesian ridge regression for STS and SAS.

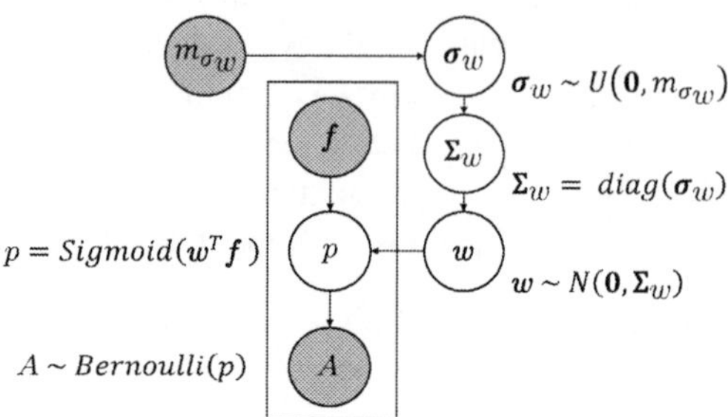

(b) Bayesian logistic regression for ASR.

Figure 1: Base models for STS, SAS and ASR. Plates represent replication across sentence pairs. Each model learns weight vector w. For STS and SAS, the real-valued output S (similarity or student score) is normally distributed around the weight-feature dot product $w^T f$. For ASR, the sigmoid of this dot product is the Bernoulli prior for the binary output A, relevance of the question's answer candidate.

3.2 Adaptation to STS Domains

Domain adaptation for the linear model (Figure 1a) learns a separate weight vector w_d for each domain d (i.e., applied to similarity computations for test pairs in domain d) alongside a common, global domain-agnostic weight vector w_*, which has a zero-mean Gaussian prior and serves as the Gaussian prior mean for each w_d. Figure 2 shows the model. Both w_* and w_d have hyperpriors identical to w in Figure 1a.[4]

Each w_d depends not just on its domain-specific observations but also on information derived from the global, shared parameter w_*. The balance between capturing in-domain information and inductive trans-

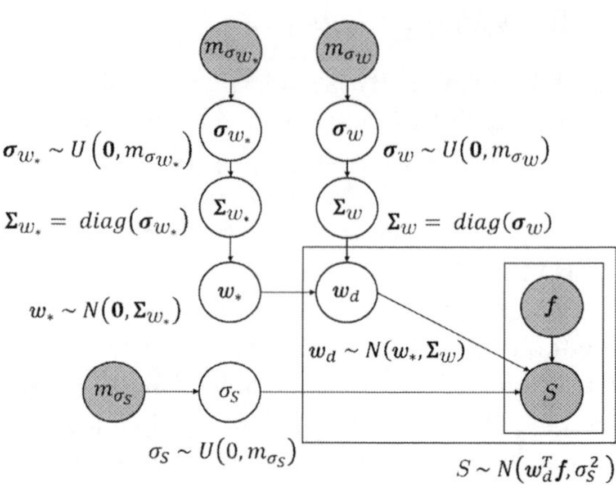

Figure 2: Adaptation to different STS domains. The outer plate represents replication across domains. Joint learning of a global weight vector w_* along with individual domain-specific vectors w_d enables inductive transfer among domains.

fer is regulated by Σ_w; larger variance allows w_d more freedom to reflect the domain.

3.3 Multitask Learning

An advantage of hierarchical DA is that it extends easily to arbitrarily nested domains. Our multitask learning model (Figure 3) models topical domains nested within one of three related tasks: STS, SAS, and ASR (Section 2). This model adds a level to the hierarchy of weight vectors: each domain-level w_d is now normally distributed around a task-level weight vector (e.g., w_{STS}), which in turn has global Gaussian mean w_*.[5] Like the DA model, all weights in the same level share common variance hyperparameters while those across different levels are separate.

Again, this hierarchical structure (1) jointly learns global, task-level and domain-level feature weights enabling inductive transfer among tasks and domains while (2) retaining the distinction between in-domain and out-of-domain annotations. A task-specific model (Figure 1) that only learns from in-domain annotations supports only (2). On the other hand, a non-hierarchical joint model (Figure 4) supports only (1): it learns a single shared w applied to any test pair regardless of task or domain. We compare these models in Section 5.

---

[4]Results do not improve with individual domain-specific instances of σ_S and σ_w, consistent with Finkel and Manning (2009) for dependency parsing and named entity recognition.

[5]We use the same variable for the domain-specific parameter w_d across tasks to simplify notation.

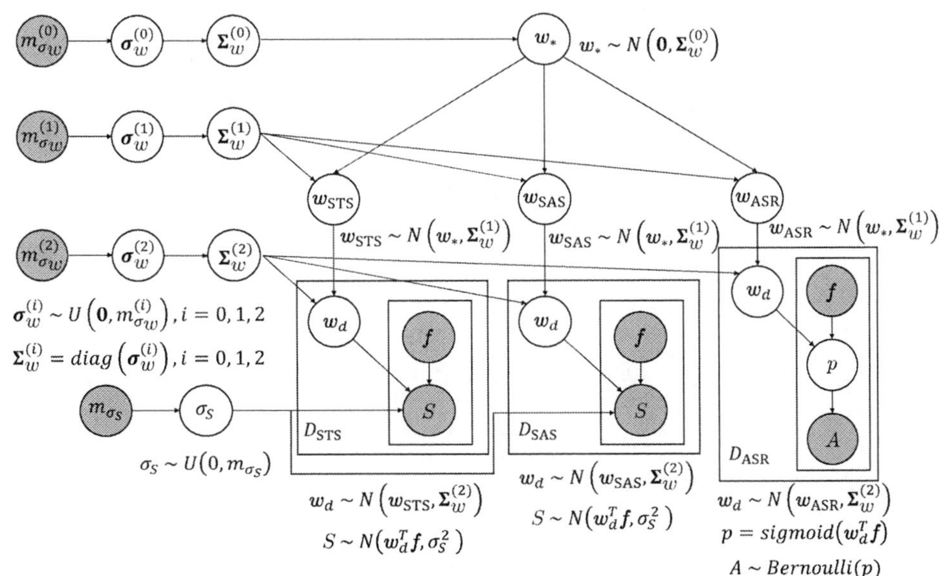

Figure 3: Multitask learning: STS, SAS and ASR. Global (w_*), task-specific (w_{STS}, w_{SAS}, w_{ASR}) and domain-specific (w_d) weight vectors are jointly learned, enabling transfer across domains and tasks.

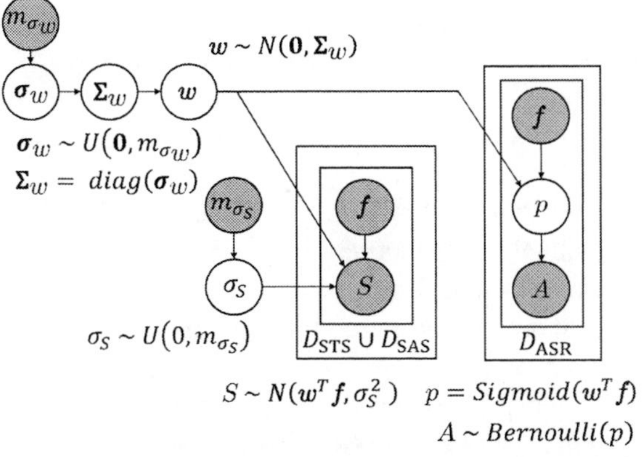

Figure 4: A non-hierarchical joint model for STS, SAS and ASR. A common weight vector w is learned for all tasks and domains.

4 Features

Any feature-based STS model can serve as the base model for a hierarchical Bayesian adaptation framework. For our experiments, we adopt the feature set of the ridge regression model in Sultan et al. (2015), the best-performing system at SemEval-2015 (Agirre et al., 2015).

Input sentences $S^{(1)} = (w_1^{(1)}, ..., w_n^{(1)})$ and $S^{(2)} = (w_1^{(2)}, ..., w_m^{(2)})$ (where each w is a token)

produce two similarity features. The first is the proportion of content words in $S^{(1)}$ and $S^{(2)}$ (combined) that have a semantically similar word—identified using a monolingual word aligner (Sultan et al., 2014)—in the other sentence. The overall semantic similarity of a word pair $(w_i^{(1)}, w_j^{(2)}) \in S^{(1)} \times S^{(2)}$ is a weighted sum of lexical and contextual similarities: a paraphrase database (Ganitkevitch et al., 2013, PPDB) identifies lexically similar words; contextual similarity is the average lexical similarity in (1) dependencies of $w_i^{(1)}$ in $S^{(1)}$ and $w_j^{(2)}$ in $S^{(2)}$, and (2) content words in [-3, 3] windows around $w_i^{(1)}$ in $S^{(1)}$ and $w_j^{(2)}$ in $S^{(2)}$. Lexical similarity scores of pairs in PPDB as well as weights of word and contextual similarities are optimized on an alignment dataset (Brockett, 2007). To avoid penalizing long answer snippets (that still have the desired semantic content) in SAS and ASR, word alignment proportions outside the reference (gold) answer (SAS) and the question (ASR) are ignored.

The second feature captures finer-grained similarities between related words (e.g., cell and organism). Given the 400-dimensional embedding (Baroni et al., 2014) of each content word (lemmatized) in an input sentence, we compute a sentence vector by adding its content lemma vectors. The co-

Task	Current SOA	Our Model
STS	Pearson's $r = 73.6\%$	Pearson's $r = 73.7\%$
SAS	Pearson's $r = 51.8\%$ RMSE $= 19.6\%$	Pearson's $r = 56.4\%$ RMSE $= 18.1\%$
ASR	MAP $= 74.6\%$ MRR $= 80.8\%$	MAP $= 76.0\%$ MRR $= 82.8\%$

Table 1: Our base linear models beat the state of the art in STS, SAS and ASR.

sine similarity between the $S^{(1)}$ and $S^{(2)}$ vectors is then used as an STS feature. Baroni et al. develop the word embeddings using `word2vec`[6] from a corpus of about 2.8 billion tokens, using the Continuous Bag-of-Words (CBOW) model proposed by Mikolov et al. (2013).

5 Experiments

For each of the three tasks, we first assess the performance of our base model to (1) verify our sampling-based Bayesian implementations, and (2) compare to the state of the art. We train each model with a Metropolis-within-Gibbs sampler with 50,000 samples using PyMC (Patil et al., 2010; Salvatier et al., 2015), discarding the first half of the samples as burn-in. The variances m_{σ_w} and m_{σ_S} are both set to 100. Base models are evaluated on the entire test set for each task, and the same training examples as in the state-of-the-art systems are used. Table 1 shows the results.

Following SemEval, we report a weighted sum of correlations (Pearson's r) across all test sets for STS, where the weight of a test set is proportional to its number of pairs. Our model and Sultan et al. (2015) are almost identical on all twenty test sets from SemEval 2012–2015, supporting the correctness of our Bayesian implementation.

Following Mohler et al. (2011), for SAS we use RMSE and Pearson's r with gold scores over all answers. These metrics are complementary: correlation is a measure of consistency across students while error measures deviation from individual scores. Our model beats the state-of-the-art text matching model of Mohler et al. (2011) on both metrics.[7]

---

[6]https://code.google.com/p/word2vec/

[7]Ramachandran et al. (2015) report better results; however, they evaluate on a much smaller random subset of the test data and use in-domain annotations for model training.

Finally, for ASR, we adopt two metrics widely used in information retrieval: mean average precision (MAP) and mean reciprocal rank (MRR). MAP assesses the quality of the ranking as a whole whereas MRR evaluates only the top-ranked answer sentence. Severyn and Moschitti (2015) report a convolutional neural network model of text similarity which shows top ASR results on the Wang et al. (2007) dataset. Our model outperforms this model on both metrics.

5.1 Adaptation to STS Domains

Ideally, our domain adaptation (DA) should allow the application of large amounts of out-of-domain training data along with few in-domain examples to improve in-domain performance. Given data from n domains, two other alternatives in such scenarios are: (1) to train a single *global* model using all available training examples, and (2) to train n *individual* models, one for each domain, using only in-domain examples. We present results from our DA model and these two baselines on the ten STS datasets discussed in Section 2. We fix the training set size per domain and split each domain into train and test folds randomly.

Models have access to training data from all ten domains (thus nine times more out-of-domain examples than in-domain ones). Each model (global, individual, and adaptive) is trained on relevant annotations and applied to test pairs, and Pearson's r with gold scores is computed for each model on each individual test set. Since performance can vary across different splits, we average over 20 splits of the same train/test ratio per dataset. Finally, we evaluate each model with a weighted sum of average correlations across all test sets, where the weight of a test set is proportional to its number of pairs.

Figure 5 shows how models adapt as the training set grows. The global model clearly falters with larger training sets in comparison to the other two models. On the other hand, the domain-specific model (i.e., the ten individual models) performs poorly when in-domain annotations are scarce. Importantly, the adaptive model performs well across different amounts of available training data.

To gain a deeper understanding of model performance, we examine results in individual domains. A single performance score is computed for every model-domain pair by taking the model's average

global	72.08 ±0.14	72.21 ±0.21	72.21 ±0.28	72.27 ±0.31	72.32 ±0.35	72.39 ±0.53	72.39 ±0.63
individual	71.18 ±0.89	72.16 ±0.62	72.21 ±0.54	72.63 ±0.4	72.8 ±0.41	72.98 ±0.53	73.01 ±0.6
adaptive	72.14 ±0.18	72.5 ±0.25	72.43 ±0.34	72.69 ±0.35	72.86 ±0.37	72.98 ±0.55	73.03 ±0.6

Figure 5: Results of adaptation to STS domains across different amounts of training data. Table shows mean±SD from 20 random train/test splits. While the baselines falter at extremes, the adaptive model shows consistent performance.

correlation in that domain over all seven training set sizes of Figure 5. We then normalize each score by dividing by the best score in that domain. Each cell in Table 2 shows this score for a model-domain pair. For example, Row 1 shows that—on average—the individual model performs the best (hence a correlation ratio of 1.0) on QA forum answer pairs while the global model performs the worst.

While the adaptive model is not the best in every domain, it has the best worst-case performance across domains. The global model suffers in domains that have unique parameter distributions (e.g., MSRpar-test: a paraphrase dataset). The individual model performs poorly with few training examples and in domains with noisy annotations (e.g., SMT: a machine translation evaluation dataset). The adaptive model is much less affected in such extreme cases. The summary statistics (weighted by dataset size) confirm that it not only stays the closest to the best model on average, but also deviates the least from its mean performance level.

5.1.1 Qualitative Analysis

We further examine the models to understand *why* the adaptive model performs well in different extreme scenarios, i.e., when one of the two baseline models performs worse than the other. Table 3 shows feature weights learned by each model from a split with

Dataset	Glob.	Indiv.	Adapt.
Answers-forums (2015)	.9847	1	.9999
Answers-students (2015)	.9850	1	.9983
Belief (2015)	1	.9915	.9970
Headlines (2015)	.9971	.9998	1
Images (2015)	.9992	.9986	1
Deft-forum (2014)	1	.9775	.9943
OnWN (2014)	.9946	.9990	1
Tweet-news (2014)	.9998	.9950	1
SMT (2013)	1	.9483	.9816
MSRpar-test (2012)	.9615	1	.9923
Mean	.9918	.9911	**.9962**
SD	.0122	.0165	.0059

Table 2: Correlation ratios of the three models vs. the best model across STS domains. Best scores are **boldfaced**, worst scores are underlined. The adaptive model has the best (1) overall score, and (2) consistency across domains.

Dataset	Var.	Glob.	Indiv.	Adapt.
SMT	w_1	.577	.214	.195
	w_2	.406	-.034	.134
	r	**.4071**	.3866	**.4071**
MSRpar-test	w_1	.577	1.0	.797
	w_2	.406	-.378	.050
	r	.6178	**.6542**	.6469
Answers-students	w_1	.577	.947	.865
	w_2	.406	.073	.047
	r	.7677	**.7865**	.7844

Table 3: Feature weights and correlations of different models in three extreme scenarios. In each case, the adaptive model learns relative weights that are more similar to those in the best baseline model.

seventy-five training pairs per domain and how well each model does.

All three domains have very different outcomes for the baseline models. We show weights for the alignment (w_1) and embedding features (w_2). In each domain, (1) the relative weights learned by the two baseline models are very different, and (2) the adaptive model learns relative weights that are closer to those of the best model. In SMT, for example, the predictor weights learned by the adaptive model have a ratio very similar to the global model's and does just as well. On Answers-students, however, it learns weights similar to those of the in-domain model, again approaching best results for the domain.

Now, the labor of cleaning up at the karaoke parlor is realized.	Gold=.52 ΔG=**.1943**
Up till now on the location the cleaning work is already completed.	ΔI=.2738 ΔA=.2024
The Chelsea defender Marcel Desailly has been the latest to speak out.	Gold=.45 ΔG=.2513
Marcel Desailly, the France captain and Chelsea defender, believes the latter is true.	ΔI=**.2222** ΔA=.2245

Table 4: Sentence pairs from SMT and MSRpar-test with gold similarity scores and model errors (Global, Individual and Adaptive). The adaptive model error is very close to the best model error in each case.

Table 4 shows the effect of this on two specific sentence pairs as examples. The first pair is from SMT; the adaptive model has a much lower error than the individual model on this pair, as it learns a higher relative weight for the embedding feature in this domain (Table 3) via inductive transfer from out-of-domain annotations. The second pair, from MSRpar-test, shows the opposite: in-domain annotations help the adaptive model fix the faulty output of the global model by upweighting the alignment feature and downweighting the embedding feature.

The adaptive model gains from the strengths of both in-domain (higher relevance) and out-of-domain (more training data) annotations, leading to good results even in extreme scenarios (e.g., in domains with unique parameter distributions or noisy annotations).

5.2 Multitask Learning

We now analyze performance of our multitask learning (MTL) model in each of the three tasks: STS, SAS and ASR. Multitask baselines resemble DA's: (1) a global model trained on all available training data (Figure 4), and (2) nineteen task-specific models, each trained on an individual dataset from one of the three tasks (Figure 1). The smallest of these datasets has only 204 pairs (SAS assignment #1); therefore, we use training sets with up to 175 pairs per dataset. Because the MTL model is more complex, we use a stronger regularization for this model (m_{σ_w}=10) while keeping the number of MCMC samples unchanged. As in the DA experiments, we compute average performance over twenty random train/test splits for each training set size.

Figure 6 shows STS results for all models across

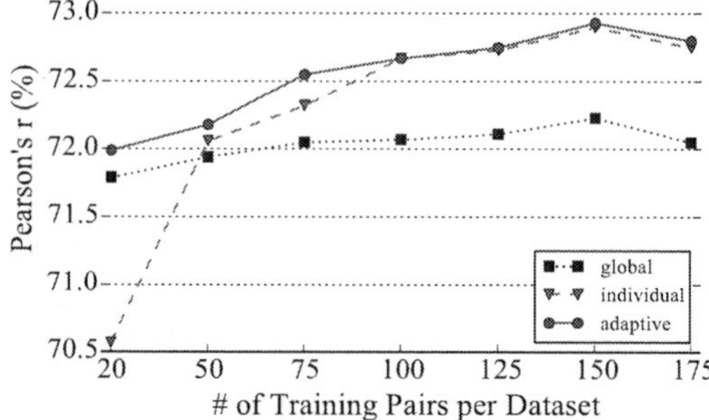

global	71.79 ±0.39	71.94 ±0.34	72.05 ±0.39	72.07 ±0.29	72.11 ±0.38	72.23 ±0.31	72.05 ±0.41
individual	70.57 ±1.45	72.06 ±0.56	72.32 ±0.55	72.67 ±0.44	72.73 ±0.51	72.9 ±0.33	72.75 ±0.41
adaptive	71.99 ±0.43	72.18 ±0.27	72.55 ±0.33	72.67 ±0.35	72.75 ±0.43	72.93 ±0.34	72.8 ±0.37

Figure 6: Multitask learning for STS: mean±SD from twenty random train/test splits. The adaptive model consistently performs well while the baselines have different failure modes.

different training set sizes. Like DA, the adaptive model consistently performs well while the global and individual models have different failure modes. However, the individual model does better than in DA: it overtakes the global model with fewer training examples and the differences with the adaptive model are smaller. This suggests that inductive transfer and therefore adaptation is less effective for STS in the MTL setup than in DA. Later in this section, coarse-grained ASR annotations (binary as opposed to real-valued) in MTL may provide an explanation for this.

The performance drop after 150 training pairs is a likely consequence of the random train/test selection process.

For SAS, the adaptive model again has the best overall performance for both correlation and error (Figure 7). The correlation plot is qualitatively similar to the STS plot, but the global model has a much higher RMSE across all training set sizes, indicating a parameter shift across tasks. Importantly, the adaptive model remains unaffected by this shift.

The ASR results in Figure 8 show a different pattern. Contrary to all results thus far, the global model performs the best in this task. The individual model consistently has lower scores, regardless of the amount of training data. Importantly, the adaptive model stays close to the global model even with very few training examples. The ASR datasets are heavily biased towards negative examples; thus, we

global	58.49 ±1.12	58.84 ±0.88	58.81 ±1.18	58.94 ±1.58	58.59 ±2.39	59.25 ±2.79	60.14 ±2.77
individual	55.8 ±4.65	60.15 ±1.86	60.98 ±1.15	61.38 ±2.0	61.45 ±2.21	61.79 ±2.52	63.02 ±2.51
adaptive	59.64 ±1.74	60.97 ±1.51	61.4 ±1.07	61.59 ±1.89	61.67 ±2.3	61.85 ±2.52	63.16 ±2.49

global	29.01 ±0.92	28.95 ±0.66	29.01 ±0.78	28.9 ±0.52	28.9 ±0.68	28.59 ±0.72	28.06 ±0.8
individual	19.94 ±0.88	19.03 ±0.41	18.76 ±0.33	18.81 ±0.45	18.57 ±0.52	18.65 ±0.58	18.37 ±0.84
adaptive	19.22 ±0.32	18.9 ±0.36	18.68 ±0.3	18.77 ±0.44	18.53 ±0.53	18.64 ±0.59	18.35 ±0.83

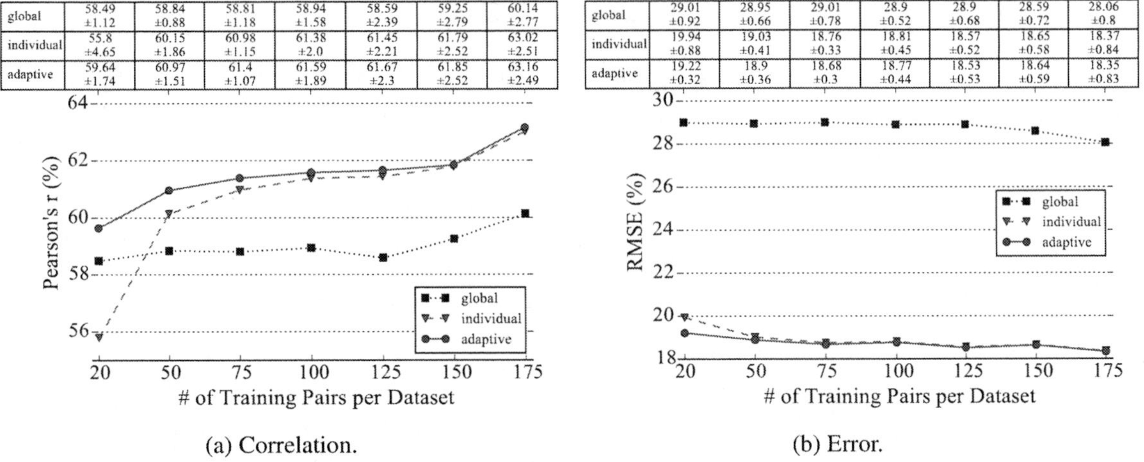

(a) Correlation.   (b) Error.

Figure 7: Multitask learning for SAS: mean±SD from 20 random train/test splits. The adaptive model performs the best, and successfully handles domain shift evident from the global model error.

global	75.86 ±0.39	76.16 ±0.8	76.32 ±0.96	76.3 ±1.31	75.95 ±1.22	76.78 ±1.24	76.41 ±1.31
individual	70.0 ±1.45	74.53 ±1.3	75.15 ±1.25	75.66 ±1.27	75.13 ±1.11	76.21 ±1.2	75.76 ±1.17
adaptive	75.39 ±1.14	75.95 ±0.8	76.0 ±1.07	76.04 ±1.21	75.47 ±1.0	76.35 ±1.26	76.21 ±1.23

global	82.82 ±0.63	82.95 ±0.91	83.23 ±1.15	82.78 ±1.59	82.18 ±1.43	83.1 ±1.3	82.27 ±1.48
individual	76.61 ±4.56	81.23 ±1.64	81.91 ±1.57	82.03 ±1.44	81.36 ±1.37	82.34 ±1.24	81.66 ±1.72
adaptive	82.31 ±1.36	82.71 ±0.86	82.72 ±1.23	82.44 ±1.39	81.66 ±1.26	82.56 ±1.42	82.07 ±1.67

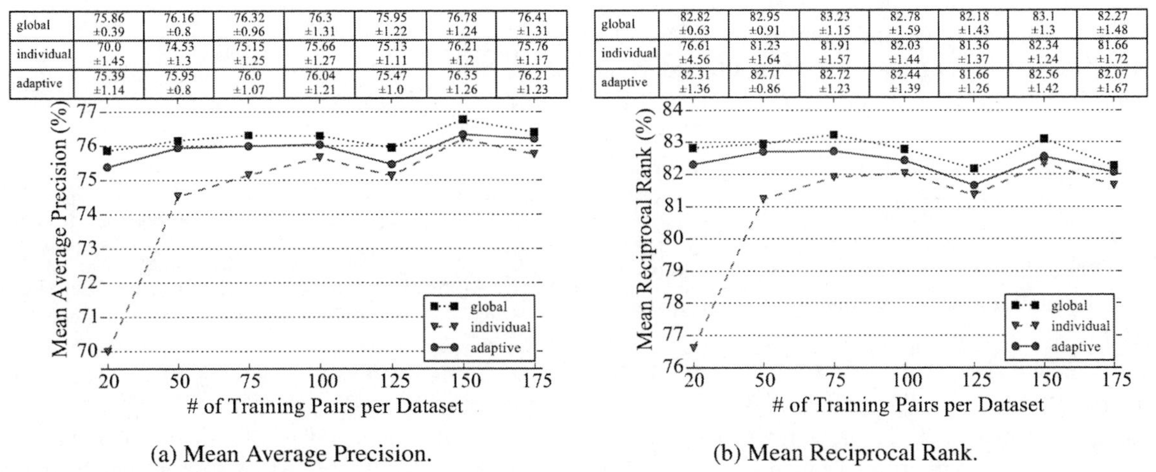

(a) Mean Average Precision.   (b) Mean Reciprocal Rank.

Figure 8: Multitask learning for ASR: mean±SD from 20 random train/test splits. Least affected by coarse-grained in-domain annotations, the global model performs the best; the adaptive model stays close across all training set sizes.

use stratified sampling to ensure each ASR training set has balanced examples.

A reason for the global model's strength at ASR may lie in the finer granularity of the real-valued STS and SAS scores compared to binary ASR annotations. If a fine granularity is indeed desirable in training data, as a model that ignores in-domain and out-of-domain distinction, the global model would be affected the least by coarse-grained ASR annotations. To test this hypothesis, we train a linear model on all STS examples from SemEval 2012–2015 and apply it to the ASR test set via a logistic transformation. This model indeed demonstrates better results (MAP=.766, MRR=.839) than our base model trained on ASR annotations (Table 1). This is an unusual scenario where in-domain training examples matter less than out-of-domain ones, hurting domain-specific and adaptive models.

Going back to STS, this finding also offers an explanation of why adaptation might have been less useful in multitask learning than in domain adaptation, as only the former has ASR annotations.

6 Discussion and Related Work

For a variety of short text similarity tasks, domain adaptation improves average performance across different domains, tasks, and training set sizes. Our adaptive model is also by far the least affected by adverse factors such as noisy training data and scarcity or coarse granularity of in-domain examples. This combination of excellent average-case and very reliable worst-case performance makes it the model of choice for new STS domains and applications.

Although STS is a useful task with sparse data, few domain adaptation studies have been reported. Among those is the supervised model of Heilman and Madnani (2013a; 2013b) based on the multilevel model of Daumé III (2007). Gella et al. (2013) report using a two-level stacked regressor, where the second level combines predictions from n level 1 models, each trained on data from a separate domain. Unsupervised models use techniques such as tagging examples with their source datasets (Gella et al., 2013; Severyn et al., 2013) and computing vocabulary similarity between source and target domains (Arora et al., 2015). To the best of our knowledge, ours is the first systematic study of supervised DA and MTL

techniques for STS with detailed comparisons with comparable non-adaptive baselines.

7 Conclusions and Future Work

We present hierarchical Bayesian models for supervised domain adaptation and multitask learning of short text similarity models. In our experiments, these models show improved overall performance across different domains and tasks. We intend to explore adaptation to other STS applications and with additional STS features (e.g., word and character n-gram overlap) in future. Unsupervised and semi-supervised domain adaptation techniques that do not assume the availability of in-domain annotations or that learn effective domains splits (Hu et al., 2014) provide another avenue for future research.

Acknowledgments

This material is based in part upon work supported by the NSF under grants EHR/0835393 and EHR/0835381. Boyd-Graber is supported by NSF grants IIS/1320538, IIS/1409287, and NCSE/1422492. Any opinions, findings, conclusions, or recommendations expressed here are those of the authors and do not necessarily reflect the view of the sponsor.

References

Eneko Agirre, Daniel Cer, Mona Diab, and Aitor Gonzalez-Agirre. 2012. SemEval-2012 task 6: A pilot on semantic textual similarity. In *SemEval*.

Eneko Agirre, Daniel Cer, Mona Diab, Aitor Gonzalez-Agirre, and Weiwei Guo. 2013. *SEM 2013 shared task: Semantic textual similarity. In *SEM*.

Eneko Agirre, Carmen Banea, Claire Cardie, Daniel Cer, Mona Diab, Aitor Gonzalez-Agirre, Weiwei Guo, Rada Mihalcea, German Rigau, and Janyce Wiebe. 2014. SemEval-2014 Task 10: Multilingual semantic textual similarity. In *SemEval*.

Eneko Agirre, Carmen Banea, Claire Cardie, Daniel Cer, Mona Diab, Aitor Gonzalez-Agirre, Weiwei Guo, Iñigo Lopez-Gazpio, Montse Maritxalar, Rada Mihalcea, German Rigau, Larraitz Uria, and Janyce Wiebe. 2015. SemEval-2015 Task 2: Semantic textual similarity, english, spanish and pilot on interpretability. In *SemEval*.

Piyush Arora, Chris Hokamp, Jennifer Foster, and Gareth J.F.Jones. 2015. DCU: Using distributional semantics and domain adaptation for the semantic textual similarity SemEval-2015 Task 2. In *SemEval*.

Daniel Bär, Chris Biemann, Iryna Gurevych, and Torsten Zesch. 2012. UKP: Computing semantic textual similarity by combining multiple content similarity measures. In *SemEval*.

Marco Baroni, Georgiana Dinu, and Germán Kruszewski. 2014. Don't count and predict! A systematic comparison of context-counting vs. context-predicting semantic vectors. In *Proceedings of the Association for Computational Linguistics*.

Chris Brockett. 2007. Aligning the RTE 2006 corpus. Technical Report MSR-TR-2007-77, Microsoft Research.

Yee Seng Chan and Hwee Tou Ng. 2008. MAXSIM: A maximum similarity metric for machine translation evaluation. In *Proceedings of the Association for Computational Linguistics*.

Anirban Dasgupta, Ravi Kumar, and Sujith Ravi. 2013. Summarization through submodularity and dispersion. In *Proceedings of the Association for Computational Linguistics*.

Hal Daumé III. 2007. Frustratingly easy domain adaptation. In *Proceedings of the Association for Computational Linguistics*.

Jenny Rose Finkel and Christopher D. Manning. 2009. Hierarchical bayesian domain adaptation. In *Conference of the North American Chapter of the Association for Computational Linguistics*, Morristown, NJ, USA.

Juri Ganitkevitch, Benjamin Van Durme, and Chris Callison-Burch. 2013. PPDB: The paraphrase database. In *Conference of the North American Chapter of the Association for Computational Linguistics*.

Spandana Gella, Bahar Salehi, Marco Lui, Karl Grieser, Paul Cook, and Timothy Baldwin. 2013. UniMelb_NLP-CORE: Integrating predictions from multiple domains and feature sets for estimating semantic textual similarity. In **SEM*.

Christian Hänig, Robert Remus, and Xose de la Puente. 2015. ExB Themis: Extensive feature extraction from word alignments for semantic textual similarity. In *SemEval*.

Michael Heilman and Nitin Madnani. 2013a. ETS: Domain adaptation and stacking for short answer scoring. In *SemEval*.

Michael Heilman and Nitin Madnani. 2013b. HENRY-CORE: Domain adaptation and stacking for text similarity. In *SemEval*.

Yuening Hu, Ke Zhai, Vlad Eidelman, and Jordan Boyd-Graber. 2014. Polylingual tree-based topic models for translation domain adaptation. In *Association for Computational Linguistics*.

Chang Liu, Daniel Dahlmeier, and Hwee Tou Ng. 2011. Better evaluation metrics lead to better machine translation. In *Proceedings of Empirical Methods in Natural Language Processing*.

André Lynum, Partha Pakray, Björn Gambäck, and Sergio Jimenez. 2014. NTNU: Measuring semantic similarity with sublexical feature representations and soft cardinality. In *SemEval*.

Tomas Mikolov, Kai Chen, Greg Corrado, and Jeffrey Dean. 2013. Efficient estimation of word representations in vector space. In *Proceedings of the International Conference on Learning Representations Workshop*.

Michael Mohler, Razvan Bunescu, and Rada Mihalcea. 2011. Learning to grade short answer questions using semantic similarity measures and dependency graph alignments. In *Proceedings of the Association for Computational Linguistics*.

Anand Patil, David Huard, and Christopher J. Fonnesbeck. 2010. PyMC: Bayesian stochastic modelling in python. *Journal of Statistical Software*, 35(4).

Lakshmi Ramachandran, Jian Cheng, and Peter Foltz. 2015. Identifying patterns for short answer scoring using graph-based lexico-semantic text matching. In *NAACL-BEA*.

John Salvatier, Thomas V. Wiecki, and Christopher Fonnesbeck. 2015. Probabilistic programming in python using PyMC. *arXiv:1507.08050v1*.

Aliaksei Severyn and Alessandro Moschitti. 2015. Learning to rank short text pairs with convolutional deep neural networks. In *Proceedings of the ACM SIGIR Conference on Research and Development in Information Retrieval*.

Aliaksei Severyn, Massimo Nicosia, and Alessandro Moschitti. 2013. Learning semantic textual similarity with structural representations. In *Proceedings of the Association for Computational Linguistics*.

Md Arafat Sultan, Steven Bethard, and Tamara Sumner. 2014. Back to basics for monolingual alignment: Exploiting word similarity and contextual evidence. *TACL*, 2.

Md Arafat Sultan, Steven Bethard, and Tamara Sumner. 2015. DLS@CU: Sentence similarity from word alignment and semantic vector composition. In *SemEval*.

Mengqiu Wang, Noah A. Smith, and Teruko Mitamura. 2007. What is the Jeopardy model? a quasi-synchronous grammar for QA. In *Proceedings of Empirical Methods in Natural Language Processing*.

Lu Wang, Hema Raghavan, Vittorio Castelli, Radu Florian, and Claire Cardie. 2013. A sentence compression based framework to query-focused multi-document summarization. In *Proceedings of the Association for Computational Linguistics*.

Xuchen Yao, Benjamin Van Durme, Chris Callison-Burch, and Peter Clark. 2013. Answer extraction as sequence tagging with tree edit distance. In *Conference of the North American Chapter of the Association for Computational Linguistics*.

Pairwise Word Interaction Modeling with Deep Neural Networks for Semantic Similarity Measurement

Hua He[1] and **Jimmy Lin**[2]

[1] Department of Computer Science, University of Maryland, College Park
[2] David R. Cheriton School of Computer Science, University of Waterloo

huah@umd.edu, jimmylin@uwaterloo.ca

Abstract

Textual similarity measurement is a challenging problem, as it requires understanding the semantics of input sentences. Most previous neural network models use coarse-grained sentence modeling, which has difficulty capturing fine-grained word-level information for semantic comparisons. As an alternative, we propose to explicitly model pairwise word interactions and present a novel similarity focus mechanism to identify important correspondences for better similarity measurement. Our ideas are implemented in a novel neural network architecture that demonstrates state-of-the-art accuracy on three SemEval tasks and two answer selection tasks.

1 Introduction

Given two pieces of text, measuring their semantic textual similarity (STS) remains a fundamental problem in language research and lies at the core of many language processing tasks, including question answering (Lin, 2007), query ranking (Burges et al., 2005), and paraphrase generation (Xu, 2014).

Traditional NLP approaches, e.g., developing hand-crafted features, suffer from sparsity because of language ambiguity and the limited amount of annotated data available. Neural networks and distributed representations can alleviate such sparsity, thus neural network-based models are widely used by recent systems for the STS problem (He et al., 2015; Tai et al., 2015; Yin and Schütze, 2015).

However, most previous neural network approaches are based on *sentence modeling*, which first maps each input sentence into a fixed-length vector and then performs comparisons on these representations. Despite its conceptual simplicity, researchers have raised concerns about this approach (Mooney, 2014): Will fine-grained word-level information, which is crucial for similarity measurement, get lost in the coarse-grained sentence representations? Is it really effective to "cram" whole sentence meanings into fixed-length vectors?

In contrast, we focus on capturing fine-grained word-level information directly. Our contribution is twofold: First, instead of using sentence modeling, we propose *pairwise word interaction modeling* that encourages explicit word context interactions across sentences. This is inspired by our own intuitions of how people recognize textual similarity: given two sentences $sent_1$ and $sent_2$, a careful reader might look for corresponding semantic units, which we operationalize in our pairwise word interaction modeling technique (Sec. 5). Second, based on the pairwise word interactions, we describe a novel *similarity focus layer* which helps the model selectively identify important word interactions depending on their importance for similarity measurement. Since not all words are created equal, important words that can make more contributions deserve extra "focus" from the model (Sec. 6).

We conducted thorough evaluations on ten test sets from three SemEval STS competitions (Agirre et al., 2012; Marelli et al., 2014; Agirre et al., 2014) and two answer selection tasks (Yang et al., 2015; Wang et al., 2007). We outperform the recent multi-perspective convolutional neural networks of He et al. (2015) and demonstrate state-of-the-art accuracy on all five tasks. In addition, we conducted ablation

Proceedings of NAACL-HLT 2016, pages 937–948,
San Diego, California, June 12-17, 2016. ©2016 Association for Computational Linguistics

studies and visualized our models to show the clear benefits of modeling pairwise word interactions for similarity measurement.

2 Related Work

Feature engineering was the dominant approach in most previous work; different types of sparse features were explored and found useful. For example, n-gram overlap features at the word and character levels (Madnani et al., 2012; Wan et al., 2006), syntax features (Das and Smith, 2009; Xu et al., 2014), knowledge-based features using Word-Net (Fellbaum, 1998; Fern and Stevenson, 2008) and word-alignment features (Sultan et al., 2014).

The recent shift from sparse feature engineering to neural network model engineering has significantly improved accuracy on STS datasets. Most previous work use sentence modeling with a "Siamese" structure (Bromley et al., 1993). For example, Hu et al. (2014) used convolutional neural networks that combine hierarchical structures with layer-by-layer composition and pooling. Tai et al. (2015) and Zhu et al. (2015) concurrently proposed tree-structured long short-term memory networks, which recursively construct sentence representations following their syntactic trees. There are many other examples of neural network-based sentence modeling approaches for the STS problem (Yin and Schütze, 2015; Huang et al., 2013; Andrew et al., 2013; Weston et al., 2011; Socher et al., 2011; Zarrella et al., 2015).

Sentence modeling is coarse-grained by nature. Most recently, despite still using a sentence modeling approach, He et al. (2015) moved toward fine-grained representations by exploiting multiple perspectives of input sentences with different types of convolution filters and pooling, generating a "matrix" representation where rows and columns capture different aspects of the sentence; comparisons over local regions of the representation are then performed. He et al. (2015) achieves highly competitive accuracy, suggesting the usefulness of fine-grained information. However, these multiple perspectives are obtained at the cost of increased model complexity, resulting in slow model training. In this work, we take a different approach by focusing directly on pairwise word interaction modeling.

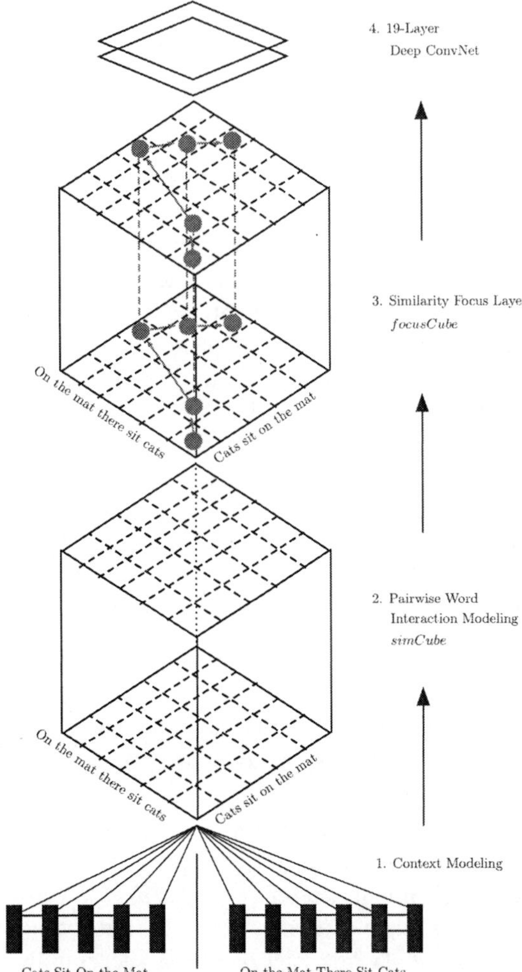

Figure 1: Our end-to-end neural network model, consisting of four major components.

3 Model Overview

Figure 1 shows our end-to-end model with four major components:

1. Bidirectional Long Short-Term Memory Networks (Bi-LSTMs) (Graves et al., 2005; Graves et al., 2006) are used for context modeling of input sentences, which serves as the basis for all following components (Sec. 4).

2. A novel pairwise word interaction modeling technique encourages direct comparisons between word contexts across sentences (Sec. 5).

3. A novel similarity focus layer helps the model identify important pairwise word interactions across sentences (Sec. 6).

4. A 19-layer deep convolutional neural network (ConvNet) converts the similarity measurement problem into a pattern recognition problem for final classification (Sec. 7).

To our best knowledge this is the first neural network model, a novel hybrid architecture combining Bi-LSTMs and a deep ConvNet, that uses a similarity focus mechanism with selective attention to important pairwise word interactions for the STS problem. Our approach only uses pretrained word embeddings, and unlike several previous neural network models (Yin and Schütze, 2015; Tai et al., 2015), we do not use sparse features, unsupervised model pretraining, syntactic parsers, or external resources like WordNet. We describe details of each component in the following sections.

4 Context Modeling

Different words occurring in similar semantic contexts of respective sentences have a higher chance to contribute to the similarity measurement. We therefore need word context modeling, which serves as a basis for all following components of this work.

LSTM (Hochreiter and Schmidhuber, 1997) is a special variant of Recurrent Neural Networks (Williams and Zipser, 1989). It can capture long-range dependencies and nonlinear dynamics between words, and has been successfully applied to many NLP tasks (Sutskever et al., 2014; Filippova et al., 2015). LSTM has a memory cell that can store information over a long history, as well as three gates that control the flow of information into and out of the memory cell. At time step t, given an input x_t, previous output h_{t-1}, input gate i_t, output gate o_t and forget gate f_t, $LSTM(x_t, h_{t-1})$ outputs the hidden state h_t based on the equations below:

$$i_t = \sigma(W^i x_t + U^i h_{t-1} + b^i) \tag{1}$$

$$f_t = \sigma(W^f x_t + U^f h_{t-1} + b^f) \tag{2}$$

$$o_t = \sigma(W^o x_t + U^o h_{t-1} + b^o) \tag{3}$$

$$u_t = tanh(W^u x_t + U^u h_{t-1} + b^u) \tag{4}$$

$$c_t = i_t \cdot u_t + f_t \cdot c_{t-1} \tag{5}$$

$$h_t = o_t \cdot tanh(c_t) \tag{6}$$

$$LSTM(x_t, h_{t-1}) = h_t \tag{7}$$

$$BiLSTMs(x_t, h_{t-1}) = \{LSTM^f, LSTM^b\} \tag{8}$$

where σ is the logistic sigmoid activation, W^*, U^* and b^* are learned weight matrices and biases. LSTMs are better than RNNs for context modeling, in that their memory cells and gating mechanisms handle the vanishing gradients problem in training.

We use bidirectional LSTMs (Bi-LSTMs) for context modeling in this work. Bi-LSTMs consist of two LSTMs that run in parallel in opposite directions: one (forward $LSTM^f$) on the input sequence and the other (backward $LSTM^b$) on the reverse of the sequence. At time step t, the Bi-LSTMs hidden state h_t^{bi} is a concatenation of the hidden state h_t^{for} of $LSTM^f$ and the hidden state h_t^{back} of $LSTM^b$, representing the neighbor contexts of input x_t in the sequence. We define the $unpack$ operation below:

$$h_t^{for}, h_t^{back} = unpack(h_t^{bi}) \tag{9}$$

Context modeling with Bi-LSTMs allows all the following components to be built over word contexts, rather than over individual words.

5 Pairwise Word Interaction Modeling

From our own intuitions, given two sentences in a STS task, a careful human reader might compare words and phrases across the sentences to establish semantic correspondences and from these infer similarity. Our pairwise word interaction model is inspired by such behavior: whenever the next word of a sentence is read, the model would compare it and its context against all words and their contexts in the other sentence. Figure 2 illustrates this model.

We first define a comparison unit for comparing two hidden states $\overrightarrow{h_1}, \overrightarrow{h_2}$ of Bi-LSTMs.

$$coU(\overrightarrow{h_1}, \overrightarrow{h_2}) = \{\cos(\overrightarrow{h_1}, \overrightarrow{h_2}), L_2Euclid(\overrightarrow{h_1}, \overrightarrow{h_2}),$$
$$DotProduct(\overrightarrow{h_1}, \overrightarrow{h_2})\} \tag{10}$$

Cosine distance (cos) measures the distance of two vectors by the angle between them, while L_2 Euclidean distance ($L_2Euclid$) and dot-product distance ($DotProduct$) measure magnitude differences. We use three similarity functions for richer measurement.

Algorithm 1 provides details of the modeling process. Given the input $x_t^a \in sent_a$ at time step t where $a \in \{1, 2\}$, its Bi-LSTMs hidden state h_{at}^{bi} is the concatenation of the forward state h_{at}^{for} and the

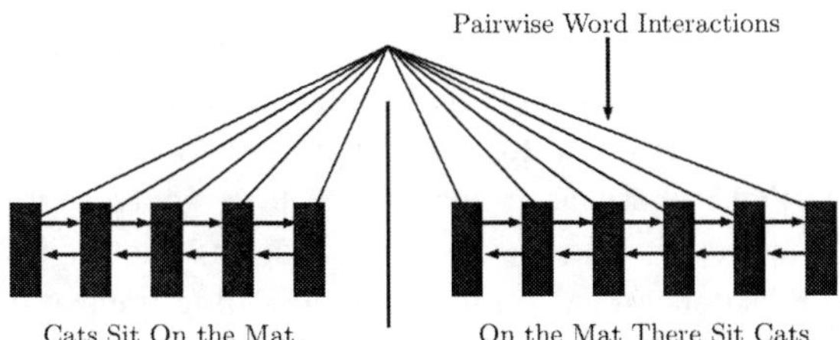

Figure 2: Pairwise word interaction modeling. Sentences are encoded by weight-shared Bi-LSTMs. We construct pairwise word interactions for context comparisons across sentences.

Algorithm 1 Pairwise Word Interaction Modeling

1: Initialize: $simCube \in R^{13 \cdot |sent_1| \cdot |sent_2|}$ to all 1
2: **for** each time step $t = 1...|sent_1|$ **do**
3:     **for** each time step $s = 1...|sent_2|$ **do**
4:        $h_{1t}^{for}, h_{1t}^{back} = unpack(h_{1t}^{bi})$
5:        $h_{2s}^{for}, h_{2s}^{back} = unpack(h_{2s}^{bi})$
6:        $h_{1t}^{add} = h_{1t}^{for} + h_{1t}^{back}$
7:        $h_{2s}^{add} = h_{2s}^{for} + h_{2s}^{back}$
8:        $simCube[1:3][t][s] = coU(h_{1t}^{bi}, h_{2s}^{bi})$
9:        $simCube[4:6][t][s] = coU(h_{1t}^{for}, h_{2s}^{for})$
10:       $simCube[7:9][t][s] = coU(h_{1t}^{back}, h_{2s}^{back})$
11:       $simCube[10:12][t][s] = coU(h_{1t}^{add}, h_{2s}^{add})$
12:     **end for**
13: **end for**
14: **return** $simCube$

---

backward state h_{at}^{back}. Algorithm 1 proceeds as follows: it enumerates all word pairs (s, t) across both sentences, then perform comparisons using the coU unit four times over: 1) Bi-LSTMs hidden states h_{1t}^{bi} and h_{2s}^{bi}; 2) forward hidden states h_{1t}^{for} and h_{2s}^{for}; 3) backward hidden states h_{1t}^{back} and h_{2s}^{back}; and 4) the addition of forward and backward hidden states h_{1t}^{add} and h_{2s}^{add}. The output of Algorithm 1 is a similarity cube $simCube$ with size $R^{13 \cdot |sent_1| \cdot |sent_2|}$, where $|sent_*|$ is the number of words in the sentence $sent_*$. The 13 values collected from each word pair (s, t) are: the 12 similarity distances, plus one extra dimension for the padding indicator. Note that all word interactions are modeled over word contexts in Algorithm 1, rather than individual words.

Our pairwise word interaction model shares similarities with recent popular neural attention models (Bahdanau et al., 2014; Rush et al., 2015). However, there are important differences: For example, we do not use attention weight vectors or weighted

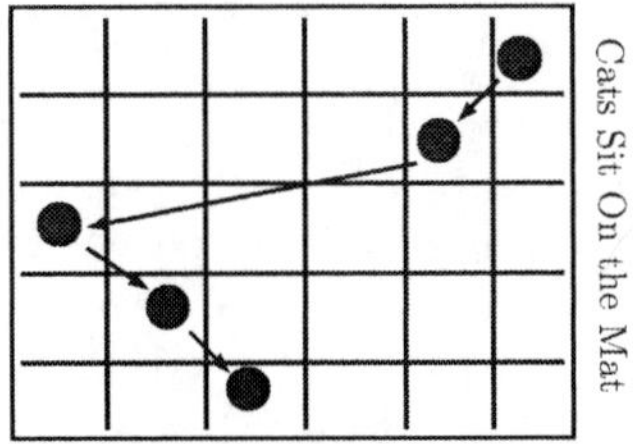

Figure 3: The similarity focus layer helps identify important pairwise word interactions (in black dots) depending on their importance for similarity measurement.

representations, which are the core of attention models. The other difference is that attention weights are typically interpreted as soft degrees with which the model attends to particular words; in contrast, our word interaction model directly utilizes multiple similarity metrics, and thus is more explicit.

6 Similarity Focus Layer

Since not all words are created equal, important pairwise word interactions between the sentences (Sec. 5) that can better contribute to the similarity measurement deserve more model focus. We therefore develop a similarity focus layer which can identify important word interactions and increase their model weights correspondingly. This similarity focus layer is directly incorporated into our end-to-end model and is placed on top of the pairwise word interaction model, as in Figure 1.

Figure 3 shows one example where each cell of the matrix represents a pairwise word interaction. The similarity focus layer introduces re-weightings to word interactions depending on their importance for similarity measurement. The ones tagged with black dots are considered important, and are given higher weights than those without.

Algorithm 2 shows the forward pass of the similarity focus layer. Its input is the similarity cube $simCube$ (Section 5). Algorithm 2 is designed to incorporate two different aspects of similarity based on $cosine$ (angular) and $L2$ (magnitude) similarity, thus it has two symmetric components: the first one is based on $cosine$ similarity (Line 5 to Line 13); and the second one is based on $L2$ similarity (Line 15 to Line 23). We also aim for the goal that similarity values of all found important word in-

Algorithm 2 Forward Pass: Similarity Focus Layer

1: Input: $simCube \in R^{13 \cdot |sent_1| \cdot |sent_2|}$
2: Initialize: $mask \in R^{13 \cdot |sent_1| \cdot |sent_2|}$ to all 0.1
3: Initialize: $s1tag \in R^{|sent_1|}$ to all zeros
4: Initialize: $s2tag \in R^{|sent_2|}$ to all zeros
5: $sortIndex_1 = sort(simCube[10])$
6: **for** each $id = 1...|sent_1| + |sent_2|$ **do**
7:     $pos_{s1}, pos_{s2} = calcPos(id, sortIndex_1)$
8:     **if** $s1tag[pos_{s1}] + s2tag[pos_{s2}] == 0$ **then**
9:         $s1tag[pos_{s1}] = 1$
10:         $s2tag[pos_{s2}] = 1$
11:         $mask[:][pos_{s1}][pos_{s2}] = 1$
12:     **end if**
13: **end for**
14: Re-Initialize: $s1tag, s2tag$ to all zeros
15: $sortIndex_2 = sort(simCube[11])$
16: **for** each $id = 1...|sent_1| + |sent_2|$ **do**
17:     $pos_{s1}, pos_{s2} = calcPos(id, sortIndex_2)$
18:     **if** $s1tag[pos_{s1}] + s2tag[pos_{s2}] == 0$ **then**
19:         $s1tag[pos_{s1}] = 1$
20:         $s2tag[pos_{s2}] = 1$
21:         $mask[:][pos_{s1}][pos_{s2}] = 1$
22:     **end if**
23: **end for**
24: $mask[13][:][:] = 1$
25: $focusCube = mask \cdot simCube$
26: **return** $focusCube \in R^{13 \cdot |sent_1| \cdot |sent_2|}$

---

teractions should be maximized. To achieve this, we sort the similarity values in descending order (Line 5 for $cosine$, Line 15 for $L2$). Note channels 10 and 11 of the $simCube$ contain $cosine$ and $L2$ values, respectively; the padding indicator is in Line 24.

We start with the $cosine$ part first, then $L2$. For each, we check word interaction candidates moving down the sorted list. Function $calcPos$ is used to calculate relative sentence positions pos_{s*} in the $simCube$ given one interaction pair. We follow the constraint that no word in both sentences should be tagged to be important more than once. We increase weights of important word interactions to 1 (in Line 11 based on $cosine$ and Line 21 based on $L2$), while unimportant word interactions receive weights of 0.1 (in Line 2).

We use a mask matrix, $mask$, to hold the weights of each. The final output of the similarity focus layer is a focus-weighted similarity cube $focusCube$, which is the element-wise multiplication (Line 25) of the matrix $mask$ and the input $simCube$.

The similarity focus layer is based on the follow-ing intuition: given each word in one sentence, we look for its semantically similar twin in the other sentence; if found then this word is considered important, otherwise it contributes to a semantic difference. Though technically different, this process shares conceptual similarity with finding translation equivalences in statistical machine translation (Al-onaizan et al., 1999).

The backward pass of the similarity focus layer is straightforward: we reuse the $mask$ matrix as generated in the forward pass and apply the element-wise multiplication of $mask$ and inflow gradients, then propagate the resulting gradients backward.

7 Similarity Classification with Deep Convolutional Neural Networks

The $focusCube$ contains focus-weighted fine-grained similarity information. In the final model component we use the $focusCube$ to compute the final similarity score. If we treat the $focusCube$ as an "image" with 13 channels, then semantic similarity measurement can be converted into a pattern recognition (image processing) problem, where we are looking for patterns of strong pairwise word interactions in the "image". The stronger the overall pairwise word interactions are, the higher similarity the sentence pair will have.

Recent advances from successful systems at ImageNet competitions (Simonyan and Zisserman, 2014; Szegedy et al., 2015) show that the depth of a neural network is a critical component for achieving competitive performance. We therefore use a deep homogeneous architecture which has repetitive convolution and pooling layers.

Our network architecture (Table 1) is composed of spatial max pooling layers, spatial convolutional layers (Conv) with a small filter size of 3×3 plus stride 1 and padding 1. We adopt this filter size because it is the smallest one to capture the space of left/right, up/down, and center; the padding and stride is used to preserve the spatial input resolution. We then use fully-connected layers followed by the final softmax layer for the output. After each spatial convolutional layer, a rectified linear units (ReLU) non-linearity layer (Krizhevsky et al., 2012) is used.

The input to this deep ConvNet is the $focusCube$, which does not always have the same size because

Deep ConvNet Configurations	
Input Size: 32 **by** 32	**Input Size:** 48 **by** 48
Spatial Conv 128: size 3×3, stride 1, pad 1	
ReLU	
Max Pooling: size 2×2, stride 2	
Spatial Conv 164: size 3×3, stride 1, pad 1	
ReLU	
Max Pooling: size 2×2, stride 2	
Spatial Conv 192: size 3×3, stride 1, pad 1	
ReLU	
Max Pooling: size 2×2, stride 2	
Spatial Conv 192: size 3×3, stride 1, pad 1	
ReLU	
Max Pooling: size 2×2, stride 2	
Spatial Conv 128: size 3×3, stride 1, pad 1	
ReLU	
Max Pooling: 2×2, s2	Max Pooling: 3×3, s1
Fully-Connected Layer	
ReLU	
Fully-Connected Layer	
LogSoftMax	

Table 1: Deep ConvNet architecture given two padding size configurations for final classification.

the lengths of input sentences vary. To address this, we use zero padding. For computational reasons we provide two configurations in Table 1, for length padding up to either 32×32 or 48×48. The only difference between the two configurations is the last pooling layer. If sentences are longer than the padding length limit we only use the number of words up to the limit. In our experiments we found the 48×48 padding limit to be acceptable since most sentences in our datasets are only $1 - 30$ words long.

8 Experimental Setup

Datasets. We conducted five separate experiments on ten different datasets: three recent SemEval competitions and two answer selection tasks. Note that the answer selection task, which is to rank candidate answer sentences based on their similarity to the questions, is essentially the similarity measurement problem. The five experiments are as follows:

1. Sentences Involving Compositional Knowledge (SICK) is from Task 1 of the 2014 SemEval competition (Marelli et al., 2014) and consists of 9,927 annotated sentence pairs, with 4,500 for training, 500 as a development set, and 4,927 for

STS2014	Domain	Pairs
deft-forum	discussion forums	450
deft-news	news articles	300
headlines	news headlines	750
images	image descriptions	750
OnWN	word sense definitions	750
tweet-news	social media	750
Total		**3,750**

Table 2: Description of STS2014 test sets.

testing. Each pair has a relatedness score $\in [1, 5]$ which increases with similarity.

2. Microsoft Video Paraphrase Corpus (MSRVID) is from Task 6 of the 2012 SemEval competition (Agirre et al., 2012) and consists of 1,500 annotated pairs of video descriptions, with half for training and the other half for testing. Each sentence pair has a relatedness score $\in [0, 5]$ which increases with similarity.

3. Task 10 of the 2014 SemEval competition on Semantic Textual Similarity (STS2014) (Agirre et al., 2014) provided six different test sets from different domains. Each pair has a similarity score $\in [0, 5]$ which increases with similarity. Following the competition rules, our training data is only drawn from previous STS competitions in 2012 and 2013. We excluded training sentences with lengths longer than the 48 word padding limit, resulting in 7,382 training pairs out of a total of 7,592. Table 2 provides a brief description of the test sets.

4. The open domain question-answering WikiQA data is from Bing query logs by Yang et al. (2015). We followed the same pre-processing steps as Yang et al. (2015), where questions with no correct candidate answer sentences are excluded and answer sentences are truncated to 40 tokens. The resulting dataset consists of 873 questions with 8,672 question-answer pairs in the training set, 126 questions with 1,130 pairs in the development set, and 243 questions with 2,351 pairs in the test set.

5. The TrecQA dataset (Wang et al., 2007) from the Text Retrieval Conferences has been widely used for the answer selection task during the past decade. To enable direct comparison with previous work, we used the same training, development, and test sets as released by Yao et al. (2013).

The TrecQA data consists of 1,229 questions with 53,417 question-answer pairs in the *TRAIN-ALL* training set, 82 questions with 1,148 pairs in the development set, and 100 questions with 1,517 pairs in the test set.

Training. For experiments on SICK, MSRVID, and STS2014, the training objective is to minimize the KL-divergence loss:

$$loss(\theta) = \frac{1}{n} \sum_{k=1}^{n} KL\left(f^k \parallel \widehat{f_\theta^k}\right) \qquad (11)$$

where f is the ground truth, $\widehat{f_\theta}$ is the predicted distribution with model weights θ, and n is the number of training examples.

We used a hinge loss for the answer selection task on WikiQA and TrecQA data. The training objective is to minimize the following loss, summed over examples $\langle x, y_{gold} \rangle$:

$$loss(\theta, x, y_{gold}) =$$
$$\sum_{y' \neq y_{gold}} \max(0, 1 + f_\theta(x, y') - f_\theta(x, y_{gold})) \qquad (12)$$

where y_{gold} is the ground truth label, input x is the pair of sentences $x = \{S_1, S_2\}$, θ is the model weight vector, and the function $f_\theta(x, y')$ is the output of our model.

In all cases, we performed optimization using RMSProp (Tieleman and Hinton, 2012) with back-propagation (Bottou, 1998), with a learning rate fixed to 10^{-4}.

Settings. For the SICK and MSRVID experiments, we used 300-dimension GloVe word embeddings (Pennington et al., 2014). For the STS2014, WikiQA, and TrecQA experiments, we used 300-dimension PARAGRAM-SL999 embeddings from Wieting et al. (2015) and the PARAGRAM-PHRASE embeddings from Wieting et al. (2016), trained on word pairs from the Paraphrase Database (PPDB) (Ganitkevitch et al., 2013). We did not update word embeddings in all experiments.

We used the SICK development set for tuning and then applied exactly the *same* hyperparameters to *all* ten test sets. For the answer selection task (Wiki-QA and TrecQA), we used the official trec_eval scorer to compute the metrics Mean Average Precision (MAP) and Mean Reciprocal Rank (MRR) and

Model	r	ρ	MSE
Socher et al. (2014) DTRNN	0.7863	0.7305	0.3983
Socher et al. (2014) SDTRNN	0.7886	0.7280	0.3859
Lai and Hockenmaier (2014)	0.7993	0.7538	0.3692
Jimenez et al. (2014)	0.8070	0.7489	0.3550
Bjerva et al. (2014)	0.8268	0.7721	0.3224
Zhao et al. (2014)	0.8414	-	-
LSTM	0.8477	0.7921	0.2949
Bi-LSTM	0.8522	0.7952	0.2850
2-layer LSTM	0.8411	0.7849	0.2980
2-layer Bi-LSTM	0.8488	0.7926	0.2893
Tai et al. (2015) Const. LSTM	0.8491	0.7873	0.2852
Tai et al. (2015) Dep. LSTM	0.8676	0.8083	0.2532
He et al. (2015)	0.8686	0.8047	0.2606
This work	**0.8784**	**0.8199**	**0.2329**

Table 3: Test results on SICK grouped as: (1) RNN variants; (2) SemEval 2014 systems; (3) Sequential LSTM variants; (4) Dependency and constituency tree LSTMs. Evaluation metrics are Pearson's r, Spearman's ρ, and mean squared error (MSE). Rows in grey are neural network models.

selected the best development model based on MRR for final testing. Our timing experiments were conducted on an Intel Xeon E5-2680 CPU.

Due to sentence length variations, for the SICK and MSRVID data we padded the sentences to 32 words; for the STS2014, WikiQA, and TrecQA data, we padded the sentences to 48 words.

9 Results

SICK Results (Table 3). Our model outperforms previous neural network models, most of which are based on sentence modeling. The ConvNet work (He et al., 2015) and TreeLSTM work (Tai et al., 2015) achieve comparable accuracy; for example, their difference in Pearson's r is only 0.1%. In comparison, our model outperforms both by 1% in Pearson's r, over 1.1% in Spearman's ρ, and 2-3% in MSE. Note that we used the same word embeddings, sparse distribution targets, and loss function as in He et al. (2015) and Tai et al. (2015), thereby representing comparable experimental conditions.

MSRVID Results (Table 4). Our model outperforms the work of He et al. (2015), which already reports a Pearson's r score of over 0.9,

STS2014 Results (Table 5). Systems in the competition are ranked by the weighted mean (the of-

Model	Pearson's r
Beltagy et al. (2014)	0.8300
Bär et al. (2012)	0.8730
Šarić et al. (2012)	0.8803
He et al. (2015)	0.9090
This work	**0.9112**

Table 4: Test results on MSRVID data.

STS2014	3rd	2nd	1st	This work
deft-forum	0.5305	0.4711	0.4828	**0.5684**
deft-news	**0.7813**	0.7628	0.7657	0.7079
headlines	**0.7837**	0.7597	0.7646	0.7551
image	**0.8343**	0.8013	0.8214	0.8221
OnWN	0.8502	0.8745	0.8589	**0.8847**
tweetnews	0.6755	**0.7793**	0.7639	0.7469
Wt. Mean	0.7549	0.7605	0.7610	**0.7666**

Table 5: Test results on all six test sets in STS2014. We show results of the top three participating systems at the competition in Pearson's r scores.

ficial measure) of Pearson's r scores calculated based on the number of sentence pairs in each test set. We show the 1st ranked (Sultan et al., 2014), 2nd (Kashyap et al., 2014), 3rd (Lynum et al., 2014) systems in the STS2014 competition, all of which are based on heavy feature engineering. Our model does not use any sparse features, WordNet, or parse trees, but still performs favorably compared to the STS2014 winning system (Sultan et al., 2014).

WikiQA Results (Table 6). We compared our model to competitive baselines prepared by Yang et al. (2015) and also evaluated He et al. (2015)'s multi-perspective ConvNet on the same data. The neural network models in the table, paragraph vector (PV) (Le and Mikolov, 2014), CNN (Yu et al., 2014), and PV-Cnt/CNN-Cnt with word matching features (Yang et al., 2015), are mostly based on sentence modeling. Our model outperforms them all.

TrecQA Results (Table 7). This is the largest dataset in our experiments, with over 55,000 question-answer pairs. Only recently have neural network approaches (Yu et al., 2014) started to show promising results on this decade-old dataset. Previous approaches with probabilistic tree-edit techniques or tree kernels (Wang and Manning, 2010; Heilman and Smith, 2010; Yao et al., 2013) have been successful since tree structure information per-

Model	MAP	MRR
Word Cnt (Yang et al., 2015)	0.4891	0.4924
Wgt Word Cnt (Yang et al., 2015)	0.5099	0.5132
PV (Le and Mikolov, 2014)	0.5110	0.5160
PV-Cnt (Yang et al., 2015)	0.5976	0.6058
LCLR (Yih et al., 2013)	0.5993	0.6086
CNN (Yu et al., 2014)	0.6190	0.6281
CNN-Cnt (Yang et al., 2015)	0.6520	0.6652
He et al. (2015)	0.6930	0.7090
This work	**0.7090**	**0.7234**

Table 6: Test results on WikiQA data.

Model	MAP	MRR
Cui et al. (2005)	0.4271	0.5259
Wang et al. (2007)	0.6029	0.6852
Heilman and Smith (2010)	0.6091	0.6917
Wang and Manning (2010)	0.5951	0.6951
Yao et al. (2013)	0.6307	0.7477
Severyn and Moschitti (2013)	0.6781	0.7358
Yih et al. (2013)	0.7092	0.7700
Wang and Nyberg (2015)	0.7134	0.7913
Severyn and Moschitti (2015)	0.7459	0.8078
This work	**0.7588**	**0.8219**

Table 7: Test results on TrecQA data.

mits a fine-grained focus on important words for similarity comparison purposes. Our approach essentially follows this intuition, but in a neural network setting with the use of our similarity focus layer. Our model outperforms previous work.

10 Analysis

Ablation Studies. Table 8 shows the results of ablation studies on SICK and WikiQA data. We removed or replaced one component at a time from the full system and performed re-training and re-testing. We found large drops when removing the context modeling component, indicating that the context information provided by the Bi-LSTMs is crucial for the following components (e.g., interaction modeling). The use of our similarity focus layer is also beneficial, especially on the WikiQA data. When we replaced the entire similarity focus layer with a random dropout layer ($p = 0.3$), the dropout layer hurts accuracy; this shows the importance of directing the model to focus on important pairwise word interactions, to better capture similarity.

Model Efficiency and Storage. He et al. (2015)'s

Ablation on SICK Data	Pearson
Full Model	0.8784
- Remove context modeling (Sec. 4)	-0.1225
- Remove entire focus layer (Sec. 6)	-0.0083
- Replace entire focus layer with dropout	-0.0314
Ablation on WikiQA Data	**MRR**
Full Model	0.7234
- Remove context modeling (Sec. 4)	-0.0990
- Remove entire focus layer (Sec. 6)	-0.0327
- Replace entire focus layer with dropout	-0.0403

Table 8: Ablation studies on SICK and WikiQA data, removing each component separately.

Model	# of Parameters	Timing (s)
He et al. (2015)	10.0 million	2265
This work	**1.7 million**	**664**

Table 9: Comparison of training efficiency and number of tunable model parameters on SICK data. Timing is the average epoch time in seconds for training on a single CPU thread.

ConvNet model uses multiple types of convolution and pooling for sentence modeling. This results in a wide architecture with around 10 million tunable parameters. Our approach only models pairwise word interactions and does not require such a complicated architecture. Compared to that previous work, Table 9 shows that our model is $3.4\times$ faster in training and has 83% fewer tunable parameters.

Visualization. Table 10 visualizes the cosine value channel of the $focusCube$ for pairwise word interactions given two sentence pairs in the SICK test set. Note for easier visualization, the values are multiplied by 10. Darker red areas indicate stronger pairwise word interactions. From these visualizations, we see that our model is able to identify important word pairs (in dark red) and tag them with proper similarity values, which are significantly higher than the ones of their neighboring unimportant pairs. This shows that our model is able to recognize important fine-grained word-level information for better similarity measurement, suggesting the reason why our model performs well.

11 Conclusion

In summary, we developed a novel neural network model based on a hybrid of ConvNet and Bi-LSTMs for the semantic textual similarity measurement problem. Our pairwise word interaction model and the similarity focus layer can better capture fine-grained semantic information, compared to previous sentence modeling approaches that attempt to "cram" all sentence information into a fixed-length vector. We demonstrated the state-of-the-art accuracy of our approach on data from three SemEval competitions and two answer selection tasks.

	A	man	is	playing	the	drum
A	8.99	0.69	0.43	0.32	0.38	0.22
man	0.70	9.93	0.62	0.45	0.46	0.38
is	0.64	0.80	8.50	0.62	0.58	0.36
practicing	0.46	0.67	0.66	6.51	0.62	0.48
the	0.35	0.56	0.66	0.64	7.85	0.52
drum	0.27	0.47	0.46	0.55	0.64	8.82

	A	man	is	carrying	a	tree
A	0.53	0.33	0.32	0.33	5.53	0.49
tree	0.32	0.30	0.19	0.20	0.38	8.73
is	0.35	0.31	0.21	0.06	0.03	0.40
being	0.28	0.37	2.60	0.18	0.13	0.38
picked	0.15	0.18	0.10	1.60	0.07	0.27
up	0.26	0.27	0.06	0.13	0.05	0.21
by	0.43	0.36	0.08	1.33	0.15	0.29
a	6.50	0.45	0.03	0.08	0.16	0.23
man	0.50	8.60	0.45	0.34	0.34	0.34

Table 10: Visualization of cosine values (multiplied by 10) in the $focusCube$ given two sentence pairs in the SICK test set.

Acknowledgments

This work was supported by the U.S. National Science Foundation under awards IIS-1218043 and CNS-1405688. Any opinions, findings, conclusions, or recommendations expressed are those of the authors and do not necessarily reflect the views of the sponsor. We would like to thank Kevin Gimpel, John Wieting and TS for all the support.

References

Eneko Agirre, Mona Diab, Daniel Cer, and Aitor Gonzalez-Agirre. 2012. SemEval-2012 task 6: A pilot on semantic textual similarity. In *Proceedings of the First Joint Conference on Lexical and Computational Semantics*, pages 385–393.

Eneko Agirre, Carmen Banea, Claire Cardie, Daniel Cer, Mona Diab, Aitor Gonzalez-Agirre, Weiwei Guo, Rada Mihalcea, German Rigau, and Janyce Wiebe.

2014. SemEval-2014 task 10: Multilingual semantic textual similarity. In *Proceedings of the 8th International Workshop on Semantic Evaluation*, pages 81–91.

Yaser Al-onaizan, Jan Curin, Michael Jahr, Kevin Knight, John Lafferty, Dan Melamed, Franz-Josef Och, David Purdy, Noah A. Smith, and David Yarowsky. 1999. Statistical machine translation. Final report, JHU Summer Workshop on Language Engineering.

Galen Andrew, Raman Arora, Jeff Bilmes, and Karen Livescu. 2013. Deep canonical correlation analysis. In *Proceedings of the 30th International Conference on Machine Learning*, pages 1247–1255.

Dzmitry Bahdanau, Kyunghyun Cho, and Yoshua Bengio. 2014. Neural machine translation by jointly learning to align and translate. *CoRR*, abs/1409.0473.

Daniel Bär, Chris Biemann, Iryna Gurevych, and Torsten Zesch. 2012. UKP: Computing semantic textual similarity by combining multiple content similarity measures. In *Proceedings of the First Joint Conference on Lexical and Computational Semantics*, pages 435–440.

Islam Beltagy, Katrin Erk, and Raymond Mooney. 2014. Probabilistic soft logic for semantic textual similarity. In *Proceedings of 52nd Annual Meeting of the Association for Computational Linguistics*, pages 1210–1219.

Johannes Bjerva, Johan Bos, Rob van der Goot, and Malvina Nissim. 2014. The meaning factory: Formal semantics for recognizing textual entailment and determining semantic similarity. In *Proceedings of the 8th International Workshop on Semantic Evaluation*, pages 642–646.

Léon Bottou. 1998. Online learning and stochastic approximations. In David Saad, editor, *Online Learning and Neural Networks*. Cambridge University Press.

Jane Bromley, James W Bentz, Léon Bottou, Isabelle Guyon, Yann LeCun, Cliff Moore, Eduard Säckinger, and Roopak Shah. 1993. Signature verification using a "Siamese" time delay neural network. *International Journal of Pattern Recognition and Artificial Intelligence*, 7(4):669–688.

Chris Burges, Tal Shaked, Erin Renshaw, Ari Lazier, Matt Deeds, Nicole Hamilton, and Greg Hullender. 2005. Learning to rank using gradient descent. In *Proceedings of the 22nd International Conference on Machine Learning*, pages 89–96.

Hang Cui, Renxu Sun, Keya Li, Min-Yen Kan, and Tat-Seng Chua. 2005. Question answering passage retrieval using dependency relations. In *Proceedings of the 28th Annual International ACM SIGIR Conference on Research and Development in Information Retrieval*, pages 400–407.

Dipanjan Das and Noah A. Smith. 2009. Paraphrase identification as probabilistic quasi-synchronous recognition. In *Proceedings of the 47th Annual Meeting of the Association for Computational Linguistics*, pages 468–476.

Christiane Fellbaum. 1998. *WordNet: An Electronic Lexical Database*. MIT Press.

Samuel Fern and Mark Stevenson. 2008. A semantic similarity approach to paraphrase detection. In *Proceedings of the 11th Annual Research Colloquium of the UK Special-Interest Group for Computational Lingusitics*, pages 45–52.

Katja Filippova, Enrique Alfonseca, Carlos A. Colmenares, Lukasz Kaiser, and Oriol Vinyals. 2015. Sentence compression by deletion with LSTMs. In *Proceedings of the 2015 Conference on Empirical Methods in Natural Language Processing*, pages 360–368.

Juri Ganitkevitch, Benjamin Van Durme, and Chris Callison-Burch. 2013. PPDB: The Paraphrase Database. In *Proceedings of the 2013 Conference of the North American Chapter of the Association for Computational Linguistics: Human Language Technologies*, pages 758–764.

Alex Graves, Santiago Fernández, and Jürgen Schmidhuber. 2005. Bidirectional LSTM networks for improved phoneme classification and recognition. In *Proceedings of the 15th International Conference on Artificial Neural Networks: Formal Models and Their Applications - Part II*, pages 799–804.

Alex Graves, Santiago Fernández, Faustino Gomez, and Jürgen Schmidhuber. 2006. Connectionist temporal classification: Labelling unsegmented sequence data with recurrent neural networks. In *Proceedings of the 23rd International Conference on Machine Learning*, pages 369–376.

Hua He, Kevin Gimpel, and Jimmy Lin. 2015. Multi-perspective sentence similarity modeling with convolutional neural networks. In *Proceedings of the 2015 Conference on Empirical Methods in Natural Language Processing*, pages 1576–1586.

Michael Heilman and Noah A. Smith. 2010. Tree edit models for recognizing textual entailments, paraphrases, and answers to questions. In *Human Language Technologies: The 2010 Annual Conference of the North American Chapter of the Association for Computational Linguistics*, pages 1011–1019.

Sepp Hochreiter and Jürgen Schmidhuber. 1997. Long short-term memory. *Neural Computation*, 9(8):1735–1780.

Baotian Hu, Zhengdong Lu, Hang Li, and Qingcai Chen. 2014. Convolutional neural network architectures for matching natural language sentences. In *Advances* in *Neural Information Processing Systems 27*, pages 2042–2050.

Po-Sen Huang, Xiaodong He, Jianfeng Gao, Li Deng, Alex Acero, and Larry Heck. 2013. Learning deep structured semantic models for web search using click-through data. In *Proceedings of the 22nd ACM International Conference on Information & Knowledge Management*, pages 2333–2338.

Sergio Jimenez, George Duenas, Julia Baquero, Alexander Gelbukh, Av Juan Dios Bátiz, and Av Mendizábal. 2014. UNAL-NLP: Combining soft cardinality features for semantic textual similarity, relatedness and entailment. In *Proceedings of the 8th International Workshop on Semantic Evaluation*, pages 732–742.

Abhay Kashyap, Lushan Han, Roberto Yus, Jennifer Sleeman, Taneeya Satyapanich, Sunil Gandhi, and Tim Finin. 2014. Meerkat mafia: Multilingual and cross-level semantic textual similarity systems. In *Proceedings of the 8th International Workshop on Semantic Evaluation*, pages 416–423.

Alex Krizhevsky, Ilya Sutskever, and Geoffrey E. Hinton. 2012. ImageNet classification with deep convolutional neural networks. In *Advances in Neural Information Processing Systems 25*, pages 1097–1105.

Alice Lai and Julia Hockenmaier. 2014. Illinois-LH: A denotational and distributional approach to semantics. In *Proceedings of the 8th International Workshop on Semantic Evaluation*, pages 329–334.

Quoc V. Le and Tomas Mikolov. 2014. Distributed representations of sentences and documents. In *Proceedings of the 31th International Conference on Machine Learning*, pages 1188–1196.

Jimmy Lin. 2007. An exploration of the principles underlying redundancy-based factoid question answering. *ACM Transactions on Information Systems*, 25(2):1–55.

André Lynum, Partha Pakray, Björn Gambäck, and Sergio Jimenez. 2014. NTNU: Measuring semantic similarity with sublexical feature representations and soft cardinality. In *Proceedings of the 8th International Workshop on Semantic Evaluation*, pages 448–453.

Nitin Madnani, Joel Tetreault, and Martin Chodorow. 2012. Re-examining machine translation metrics for paraphrase identification. In *Proceedings of the 2012 Conference of the North American Chapter of the Association for Computational Linguistics: Human Language Technologies*, pages 182–190.

Marco Marelli, Luisa Bentivogli, Marco Baroni, Raffaella Bernardi, Stefano Menini, and Roberto Zamparelli. 2014. SemEval-2014 task 1: Evaluation of compositional distributional semantic models on full sentences through semantic relatedness and textual entailment. In *Proceedings of the 8th International Workshop on Semantic Evaluation*, pages 1–8.

Raymond J. Mooney. 2014. Semantic parsing: Past, present, and future. In *ACL Workshop on Semantic Parsing. Presentation slides.*

Jeffrey Pennington, Richard Socher, and Christopher D. Manning. 2014. GloVe: Global vectors for word representation. In *Proceedings of the 2014 Conference on Empirical Methods in Natural Language Processing*, pages 1532–1543.

Alexander M. Rush, Sumit Chopra, and Jason Weston. 2015. A neural attention model for abstractive sentence summarization. *CoRR*, abs/1509.00685.

Frane Šarić, Goran Glavaš, Mladen Karan, Jan Šnajder, and Bojana Dalbelo Bašić. 2012. TakeLab: systems for measuring semantic text similarity. In *Proceedings of the First Joint Conference on Lexical and Computational Semantics*, pages 441–448.

Aliaksei Severyn and Alessandro Moschitti. 2013. Automatic feature engineering for answer selection and extraction. In *Proceedings of the 2013 Conference on Empirical Methods in Natural Language Processing*, pages 458–467.

Aliaksei Severyn and Alessandro Moschitti. 2015. Learning to rank short text pairs with convolutional deep neural networks. In *Proceedings of the 38th International ACM SIGIR Conference on Research and Development in Information Retrieval*, pages 373–382.

Karen Simonyan and Andrew Zisserman. 2014. Very deep convolutional networks for large-scale image recognition. *CoRR*, abs/1409.1556.

Richard Socher, Eric H. Huang, Jeffrey Pennington, Andrew Y. Ng, and Christopher D. Manning. 2011. Dynamic pooling and unfolding recursive autoencoders for paraphrase detection. In *Advances in Neural Information Processing Systems 24*, pages 801–809.

Richard Socher, Andrej Karpathy, Quoc V. Le, Christopher D. Manning, and Andrew Y. Ng. 2014. Grounded compositional semantics for finding and describing images with sentences. *Transactions of the Association for Computational Linguistics*, 2:207–218.

Md Arafat Sultan, Steven Bethard, and Tamara Sumner. 2014. Dls@cu: Sentence similarity from word alignment. In *Proceedings of the 8th International Workshop on Semantic Evaluation*, pages 241–246.

Ilya Sutskever, Oriol Vinyals, and Quoc V Le. 2014. Sequence to sequence learning with neural networks. In *Advances in Neural Information Processing Systems 27*, pages 3104–3112.

Christian Szegedy, Wei Liu, Yangqing Jia, Pierre Sermanet, Scott Reed, Dragomir Anguelov, Dumitru Erhan, Vincent Vanhoucke, and Andrew Rabinovich.

2015. Going deeper with convolutions. In *Proceedings of the IEEE Conference on Computer Vision and Pattern Recognition*, pages 1–9.

Kai Sheng Tai, Richard Socher, and Christopher D. Manning. 2015. Improved semantic representations from tree-structured long short-term memory networks. In *Proceedings of the 53rd Annual Meeting of the Association for Computational Linguistics*, pages 1556–1566.

Tijmen Tieleman and Geoffrey E. Hinton. 2012. Lecture 6.5—RMSProp: Divide the gradient by a running average of its recent magnitude. Coursera: Neural Networks for Machine Learning.

Stephen Wan, Mark Dras, Robert Dale, and Cecile Paris. 2006. Using Dependency-based Features to Take the "Para-farce" out of Paraphrase. In *Australasian Language Technology Workshop*, pages 131–138.

Mengqiu Wang and Christopher D. Manning. 2010. Probabilistic tree-edit models with structured latent variables for textual entailment and question answering. In *Proceedings of the 23rd International Conference on Computational Linguistics*, pages 1164–1172.

Di Wang and Eric Nyberg. 2015. A long short-term memory model for answer sentence selection in question answering. In *Proceedings of the 53rd Annual Meeting of the Association for Computational Linguistics*, pages 707–712.

Mengqiu Wang, Noah A. Smith, and Teruko Mitamura. 2007. What is the Jeopardy model? A quasi-synchronous grammar for QA. In *Proceedings of the 2007 Joint Conference on Empirical Methods in Natural Language Processing and Computational Natural Language Learning*, pages 22–32.

Jason Weston, Samy Bengio, and Nicolas Usunier. 2011. Wsabie: Scaling up to large vocabulary image annotation. In *Proceedings of the 22nd International Joint Conference on Artificial Intelligence*, pages 2764–2770.

John Wieting, Mohit Bansal, Kevin Gimpel, Karen Livescu, and Dan Roth. 2015. From paraphrase database to compositional paraphrase model and back. *Transactions of the Association for Computational Linguistics*, 3:345–358.

John Wieting, Mohit Bansal, Kevin Gimpel, and Karen Livescu. 2016. Towards universal paraphrastic sentence embeddings. In *Proceedings of the 4th International Conference on Learning Representations*.

Ronald J. Williams and David Zipser. 1989. A learning algorithm for continually running fully recurrent neural networks. *Neural Computation*, 1(2):270–280.

Wei Xu, Alan Ritter, Chris Callison-Burch, William B. Dolan, and Yangfeng Ji. 2014. Extracting lexically divergent paraphrases from Twitter. *Transactions of the Association for Computational Linguistics*, 2:435–448.

Wei Xu. 2014. *Data-Drive Approaches for Paraphrasing Across Language Variations*. Ph.D. thesis, Department of Computer Science, New York University.

Yi Yang, Wen-tau Yih, and Christopher Meek. 2015. WikiQA: A challenge dataset for open-domain question answering. In *Proceedings of the 2015 Conference on Empirical Methods in Natural Language Processing*, pages 2013–2018.

Xuchen Yao, Benjamin Van Durme, Chris Callison-burch, and Peter Clark. 2013. Answer extraction as sequence tagging with tree edit distance. In *Proceedings of the 2013 Conference of the North American Chapter of the Association for Computational Linguistics: Human Language Technologies*, pages 858–867.

Wentau Yih, Ming-Wei Chang, Christopher Meek, and Andrzej Pastusiak. 2013. Question answering using enhanced lexical semantic models. In *Proceedings of the 51st Annual Meeting of the Association for Computational Linguistics*, pages 1744–1753.

Wenpeng Yin and Hinrich Schütze. 2015. Convolutional neural network for paraphrase identification. In *Proceedings of the 2015 Conference of the North American Chapter of the Association for Computational Linguistics: Human Language Technologies*, pages 901–911.

Lei Yu, Karl Moritz Hermann, Phil Blunsom, and Stephen Pulman. 2014. Deep Learning for Answer Sentence Selection. In *NIPS Deep Learning Workshop*.

Guido Zarrella, John Henderson, Elizabeth M. Merkhofer, and Laura Strickhart. 2015. MITRE: Seven systems for semantic similarity in tweets. In *Proceedings of the 9th International Workshop on Semantic Evaluation*, pages 12–17.

Jiang Zhao, Tian Tian Zhu, and Man Lan. 2014. ECNU: One stone two birds: Ensemble of heterogenous measures for semantic relatedness and textual entailment. In *Proceedings of the 8th International Workshop on Semantic Evaluation*, pages 271–277.

Xiaodan Zhu, Parinaz Sobhani, and Hongyu Guo. 2015. Long short-term memory over recursive structures. In *Proceedings of the 32nd International Conference on Machine Learning*, pages 1604–1612.

An Attentional Model for Speech Translation Without Transcription

Long Duong,[12] **Antonios Anastasopoulos,**[3] **David Chiang,**[3] **Steven Bird**[14] and **Trevor Cohn**[1]

[1]Department of Computing and Information Systems, University of Melbourne
[2]National ICT Australia, Victoria Research Laboratory
[3]Department of Computer Science and Engineering, University of Notre Dame
[4]International Computer Science Institute, University of California Berkeley

Abstract

For many low-resource languages, spoken language resources are more likely to be annotated with translations than transcriptions. This bilingual speech data can be used for word-spotting, spoken document retrieval, and even for documentation of endangered languages. We experiment with the neural, attentional model applied to this data. On phone-to-word alignment and translation reranking tasks, we achieve large improvements relative to several baselines. On the more challenging speech-to-word alignment task, our model nearly matches GIZA++'s performance on gold transcriptions, but without recourse to transcriptions or to a lexicon.

1 Introduction

For many low-resource languages, spoken language resources are more likely to come with translations than with transcriptions. Most of the world's languages are not written, so there is no orthography for transcription. Phonetic transcription is possible but too costly to produce at scale. Even when a minority language has an official orthography, people are often only literate in the language of formal education, such as the national language. Nevertheless, it is relatively easy to provide written or spoken *translations* for audio sources. Subtitled or dubbed movies are a widespread example.

One application of models of bilingual speech data is documentation of endangered languages. Since most speakers are bilingual in a higher-resource language, they can listen to a source language recording sentence by sentence and provide a spoken translation (Bird, 2010; Bird et al., 2014). By aligning this data at the word level, we hope to automatically identify regions of data where further evidence is needed, leading to a substantial, interpretable record of the language that can be studied even if the language falls out of use (Abney and Bird, 2010; Bird and Chiang, 2012).

We experiment with extensions of the neural, attentional model of Bahdanau et al. (2015), working at the phone level or directly on the speech signal. We assume that the target language is a high-resource language such as English that can be automatically transcribed; therefore, in our experiments, the target side is text rather than the output of an automatic speech recognition (ASR) system.

In the first set of experiments, as a stepping stone to direct modeling of speech, we represent the source as a sequence of phones. For phone-to-word alignment, we obtain improvements of 9–24% absolute F1 over several baselines (Och and Ney, 2000; Neubig et al., 2011; Stahlberg et al., 2012). For phone-to-word translation, we use our model to rerank n-best lists from Moses (Koehn et al., 2007) and observe improvements in BLEU of 0.9–1.7.

In the second set of experiments, we operate directly on the speech signal, represented as a sequence of Perceptual Linear Prediction (PLP) vectors (Hermansky, 1990). Without using transcriptions or a lexicon, the model is able to align the source-language speech to its English translations nearly as well as GIZA++ using gold transcriptions.

Our main contributions are: (i) proposing a new task, alignment of speech with text translations, including a dataset extending the Spanish

Proceedings of NAACL-HLT 2016, pages 949–959,
San Diego, California, June 12-17, 2016. ©2016 Association for Computational Linguistics

Fisher and CALLHOME datasets; (ii) extending the neural, attentional model to outperform existing models at both alignment and translation reranking when working on source-language phones; and (iii) demonstrating the feasibility of alignment directly on source-language speech.

2   Background

To our knowledge, there has been relatively little research on models that operate directly on parallel speech. Typically, speech is transcribed into a word sequence or lattice using ASR, or at least a phone sequence or lattice using a phone recognizer. This normally requires manually transcribed data and a pronunciation lexicon, which can be costly to create. Recent work has introduced models that do not require pronunciation lexicons, but train only on speech with text transcriptions (Lee et al., 2013; Maas et al., 2015; Graves et al., 2006). Here, we bypass phonetic transcriptions completely, and rely only on translations.

Such data can be found, for example, in subtitled or dubbed movies. Some specific examples of corpora of parallel speech are the European Parliament Plenary Sessions Corpus (Van den Heuvel et al., 2006), which includes parliamentary speeches in the 21 official EU languages, as well as their interpretation into all the other languages; and the TED Talks Corpus (Cettolo et al., 2012), which provides speech in one language (usually English) together with translations into other languages.

As mentioned in the introduction, a stepping-stone to model parallel speech is to assume a recognizer that can produce a phonetic transcription of the source language, then to model the transformation from transcription to translation. We compare against three previous models that can operate on sequences of phones. The first is simply to run GIZA++ (IBM Model 4) on a phonetic transcription (without word boundaries) of the source side. Stahlberg et al. (2012) present a modification of IBM Model 3, named Model 3P, designed specifically for phone-to-word alignment. Finally, pialign (Neubig et al., 2011), an unsupervised model for joint phrase alignment and extraction, has been shown to work well at the character level (Neubig et al., 2012) and extends naturally to work on phones.

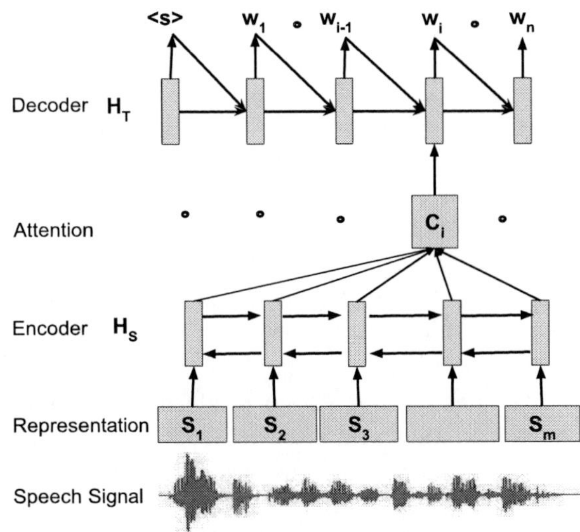

Figure 1: The attentional model as applied to our tasks. We consider two types of input: discrete phone input, or continuous audio, represented as PLP vectors at 10ms intervals

3   Model

We base our approach on the attentional translation model of Cohn et al. (2016), an extension of Bahdanau et al. (2015) which incorporates more fine grained components of the attention mechanism to mimic the structural biases in standard word based translation models. The attentional model encodes a source as a sequence of vectors, then decodes it to generate the output. At each step, it "attends" to different parts of the encoded sequence. This model has been used for translation, image caption generation, and speech recognition (Luong et al., 2015; Xu et al., 2015; Chorowski et al., 2014; Chorowski et al., 2015). Here, we briefly describe the basic attentional model, following Bahdanau et al. (2015), review the extensions for encoding structural biases (Cohn et al., 2016), and then present our novel means for adapting the approach handle parallel speech.

3.1   Base attentional model

The model is shown in Figure 1. The speech signal is represented as a sequence of vectors $S_1, S_2, \ldots, S_m$. For the first set of experiments, each S_i is a 128-dimensional vector-space embedding of a phone. For the second set of experiments, each S_i is the

39-dimensional PLP vector of a single frame of the speech signal. Our model has two main parts: an encoder and a decoder. For the encoder, we used a bidirectional recurrent neural network (RNN) with Long Short-Term Memory (LSTM) units (Hochreiter and Schmidhuber, 1997); we also tried Gated Recurrent Units (Pezeshki, 2015), with similar results. The source speech signal is encoded as sequence of vectors $H_S = (H_S^1, H_S^2, \ldots, H_S^m)$ where each vector H_S^j ($1 \leq j \leq m$) is the concatenation of the hidden states of the forward and backward LSTMs at time j.

The attention mechanism is added to the model through an alignment matrix $\alpha \in \mathbb{R}^{n \times m}$, where n is the number of target words. We add <s> and </s> to mark the start and end of the target sentence. The row $\alpha_i \in \mathbb{R}^m$ shows where the model should attend to when generating target word w_i. Note that $\sum_{j=1}^m \alpha_{ij} = 1$. The "glimpse" vector c_i of the source when generating w_i is $c_i = \sum_j \alpha_{ij} H_S^j$.

The decoder is another RNN with LSTM units. At each time step, the decoder LSTM receives c_i in addition to the previously-output word. Thus, the hidden state[1] at time i of the decoder is defined as $H_T^i = \text{LSTM}(H_T^{i-1}, c_i, w_{i-1})$, which is used to predict word w_i:

$$p(w_i \mid w_1 \cdots w_{i-1}, H_S) = \text{softmax}(g(H_T^i)), \quad (1)$$

where g is an affine transformation. We use 128 dimensions for the hidden states and memory cells in both the source and target LSTMs.

We train this model using stochastic gradient descent (SGD) on the negative log-likelihood for 100 epochs. The gradients are rescaled if their L2 norm is greater than 5. We tried Adagrad (Duchi et al., 2011), AdaDelta (Zeiler, 2012), and SGD with momentum (Attoh-Okine, 1999), but found that simple SGD performs best. We implemented dropout (Srivastava et al., 2014) and the local attentional model (Luong et al., 2015), but did not observe any significant improvements.

3.2 Structural bias components

As we are primarily interested in learning accurate alignments (roughly, attention), we include the mod-

---

[1]The LSTM also carries a memory cell, along with the hidden state; we exclude this from the presentation for clarity of notation.

elling extensions of Cohn et al. (2016) for incorporating structural biases from word-based translation models into the neural attentional model. As shown later, we observe that including these components result in a substantial improvement in measured alignment quality. We now give a brief overview of these components.

Previous attention. In the basic attentional model, the alignment is calculated based on the source encoding H_S and the previous hidden state H_T^{i-1} of the target, $\alpha_i = \text{Attend}(H_T^{i-1}, H_S)$, where Attend is a function that outputs m attention coefficients. This attention mechanism is overly simplistic, in that it is incapable of capturing patterns in the attention over different positions i. Recognising and exploiting these kinds of patterns has proven critical in traditional word based models of translation (Brown et al., 1993; Vogel et al., 1996; Dyer et al., 2013). For this reason Cohn et al. (2016) include explicit features encoding structural biases from word based models, namely absolute and relative position, Markov conditioning and fertility:

1. previous alignment, α_{i-1}
2. sum of previous alignments, $\sum_{j=1}^{i-1} \alpha_j$
3. source index vector, $(1, 2, 3, \ldots, m)$; and
4. target index vector $(i, i, i, \ldots, i)$.

These features are concatenated to form a feature matrix $\beta \in \mathbb{R}^{4 \times m}$, which are added to the alignment calculation, i.e., $\alpha_i = \text{Attend}(H_T^{i-1}, H_S, \beta)$.

Coverage penalty. The sum over previous alignments feature, described above provides a basic fertility mechanism, however as it operates locally it is only partially effective. To address this, Cohn et al. (2016) propose a global regularisation method for implementing fertility.

Recall that the alignment matrix $\alpha \in \mathbb{R}^{n \times m}$, each α_i is normalized, such that $\sum_j \alpha_{ij} = 1$. However, nothing in the model requires that every source element gets used. This is remedied by encouraging the columns of the alignment matrix to also sum to one, that is, $\sum_i \alpha_{ij} = 1$. To do so, we add a regularization penalty, $\lambda \sum_{j=1}^m \left\| \sum_{i=1}^n \alpha_{ij} - 1 \right\|_2^2$ to the objective function where λ controls the regularization strength. We tune λ on the development set and found that $\lambda = 0.05$ gives the best performance.

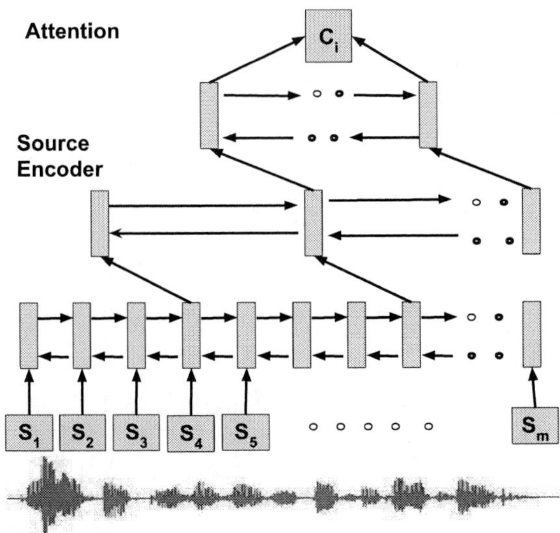

Figure 2: Stacking three layers of LSTM to the source side as in the second set of experiments

4 Extensions for Speech

We can easily apply the attentional model to parallel data, where the source side is represented as a sequence of phones. In cases where no annotated data or lexicon are available, we expect it is difficult to obtain phonetic transcriptions. Instead, we would like to work directly with the speech signal. However, dealing with the speech signal is significantly different than the phone representation, and so we need to modify the base attentional model.

4.1 Stacked and pyramidal RNNs

Both the encoder and decoder can be made more powerful by stacking several layers of LSTMs (Sutskever et al., 2014). For the first set of experiments below, we stack 4 layers of LSTMs on the target side; further layers did not improve performance on the development set.

For the second set of experiments, we work directly with the speech signal as a sequence of PLP vectors, one per frame. Since the frames begin at 10 millisecond intervals, the sequence can be very long. This makes the model slow to train; in our experiments, it seems not to converge at all. Following Chan et al. (2016), we use RNNs stacked into a pyramidal structure to reduce the size of the source speech representation. As illustrated in Fig-

ure 2, we stack 3 layers of bidirectional LSTMs. The first layer is the same as the encoder H_S described in Figure 1. The second layer uses every fourth output of the first layer as its input. The third layer selects every other output of the second layer as its input. The attention mechanism is applied only to the top layer. This reduces the size of the alignment matrix by a factor of eight, giving rise to vectors at the top layer representing 80ms intervals, which roughly correspond in duration to input phones.

4.2 Alignment smoothing

In most bitexts, source and target sentences have roughly the same length. However, for our task of aligning text and speech where the speech is represented as a sequence of phones or PLP vectors, the source can easily be several times larger than the target. Therefore we expect that a target word will commonly align to a run of several source elements. We want to encourage this behavior by smoothing the alignment matrix.

The easiest way to do this is by post-processing the alignment matrix. We train the model as usual, and then modify the learned alignment matrix α by averaging each cell over a window, $\alpha'_{ij} := \frac{1}{3}(\alpha_{i,j-1} + \alpha_{ij} + \alpha_{i,j+1})$. The modified alignment matrix, α', is only used for generating hard alignments in our alignment evaluation experiments. We can smooth further by changing the computation of α_{ij} during training. We flatten the softmax by adding a temperature factor, $T \geq 1$:

$$\alpha_{ij} = \frac{\exp(e_{ij}/T)}{\sum_k \exp(e_{ik}/T)}$$

Note that when $T = 1$ we recover the standard softmax function; we set $T = 10$ in both experiments.

5 Experimental Setup

We work on the Spanish CALLHOME Corpus (LDC96S35), which consists of telephone conversations between Spanish native speakers based in the US and their relatives abroad. While Spanish is not a low-resource language, we pretend that it is by not using any Spanish ASR or resources like transcribed speech or pronunciation lexicons (except in the construction of the "silver" standard for evaluation, described below). We also use the English translations produced by Post et al. (2013).

We treat the Spanish speech as a sequence of 39-dimensional PLP vectors (order 12 with energy and first and second order delta) encoding the power spectrum of the speech signal. We do not have gold standard alignments between the Spanish speech and English words for evaluation, so we produced "silver" standard alignments. We used a forced aligner (Gorman et al., 2011) to align the speech to its transcription, and GIZA++ with the gdfa symmetrization heuristic (Och and Ney, 2000) to align the Spanish transcription to the English translation. We then combined the two alignments to produce "silver" standard alignments between the Spanish speech and the English words.

Cleaning and splitting the data based on dialogue turns, resulted in a set of 17,532 Spanish utterances from which we selected 250 for development and 500 testing. For each utterance we have the corresponding English translation, and for each word in the translation we have the corresponding span of Spanish speech.

The forced aligner produces the phonetic sequences that correspond to each utterance, which we use later in our first set of experiments as an intermediate representation for the Spanish speech.

In order to evaluate an automatic alignment between the Spanish speech and English translation against the "silver" standard alignment, we compute alignment precision, recall, and F1-score as usual, but on links between Spanish PLP vectors and English words.

6 Phone-to-Word Experiments

In our first set of experiments, we represent the source Spanish speech as a sequence of phones. This sets an upper bound for our later experiments working directly on speech.

6.1 Alignment

We compare our model against three baselines: GIZA++, Model 3P, and pialign. For pialign, in order to better accommodate the different phrase lengths of the two alignment sides, we modified the model to allow different parameters for the Poisson distributions for the average phrase length, as well as different null align-

Model	F-score	Δ
GIZA++	29.7	−13.0
Model 3P	31.2	−11.5
Pialign (default)	42.4	−0.3
Pialign (modified)	44.0	+1.3
Base model	42.7	+0
+ alignment features	46.2	+3.5
+ coverage penalty	48.6	+5.9
+ stacking	46.3	+3.6
+ alignment smoothing	47.3	+4.6
+ alignment/softmax smoothing	48.2	+5.5
All modifications	53.6	+10.9

Table 1: On the alignment task, the base model performs much better than GIZA++ and Model 3P, and at roughly the same level as pialign; modifications to the model produce further large improvements. The Δ column shows the score difference compared with the base model.

ment probabilities for each side.[2] We used the settings `-maxsentlen 200 -maxphraselen 20 -avgphraselenF 10 -nullprobF 0.001`, improving performance by 1.6% compared with the default setting. For Model 3P, we used the settings `-maxFertility 15 -maxWordLength 20`, unrestricted `max[Src/Trg]SenLen` and 10 `Model3Iterations`. We chose the iteration with the highest score to report as the baseline.

The attentional model produces a soft alignment matrix, whose entries α_{ij} indicate $p(s_j \mid w_i)$ of aligning source phone s_j to target word w_i. For evaluation, we need to convert this to a hard alignment that we can compare against the "silver" standard. Since each word is likely to align with several phones, we choose a simple decoding algorithm: for each phone s_j, pick the word w_i that maximizes $p(w_i \mid s_j)$, where this probability is calculated from alignment matrix α using Bayes' Rule.

Table 1 shows the results of the alignment experiment. The base attentional model achieved an F-score of 42.7%, which is much better than GIZA++ and Model 3P (by 13% and 11.5% absolute, respectively) and at roughly the same level as pialign. Adding our various modifications one at a time

---

[2]Our modifications have been submitted to the pialign project.

aligner	decoder	reranker none	AM
AM (all mods)		14.6	
GIZA++	Moses	18.2	19.9
pialign	Moses	18.9	19.8
pialign (mod)	Moses	20.2	21.1
Word-based Reference		34.1	

Table 2: BLEU score on the translation task. Using the attentional model (AM) alone (first row) significantly underperformed Moses. However, using the AM as a reranker yielded improvements across several settings. The word-based reference translation provides the upper bound for our phoneme-based systems.

yields improvements ranging from 3.5% to 5.9%. Combining all of them yields a net improvement of 10.9% over the base model, which is 9.4% better than the modified pialign, 22.4% better than Model 3P, and 23.9% better than GIZA++.

6.2 Translation

In this section, we evaluate our model on the translation task. We compare the model against the Moses phrase-based translation system (Koehn et al., 2007), applied to phoneme sequences. We also provide baseline results for Moses applied to word sequences, to serve as an upper bound. Since Moses requires word alignments as input, we used various alignment models: GIZA++, pialign, and pialign with our modifications. Table 2 shows that translation performance roughly correlates with alignment quality.

For the attentional model, we used all of the modifications described above except alignment smoothing. We also used more dimensions (256) for hidden states and memory cells in both encoder and decoder. The decoding algorithm starts with the symbol <s> and uses beam search to generate the next word. The generation process stops when we reach the symbol </s>. We use a beam size of 5, as larger beam sizes make the decoder slower without substantial performance benefits.

As shown in Table 2, the attentional model achieved a BLEU score of 14.6 on the test data, whereas the Moses baselines achieve much better

BLEU scores, from 18.2 to 20.2. We think this is because the attentional model is powerful, but we don't have enough data to train it fully given that the output space is the size of the vocabulary. Moreover, this attentional model has been configured to optimize the alignment quality rather than translation quality.

We then tried using the attentional model to rerank 100-best lists output by Moses. The model gives a score for generating the next word $p(w_i|w_1 \cdots w_{i-1}, H_S)$ as in equation (1). We simply compute the score of a hypothesis by averaging the negative log probabilities of the output words,

$$\text{score}(w_1 \cdots w_n) = -\frac{1}{n} \sum_{i=1}^{n} \log(p(w_i|w_1 \cdots w_{i-1}, H_S)),$$

and then choosing the best scoring hypothesis. Table 2 shows the result using the attentional model as the reranker on top of Moses, giving improvements of 0.9 to 1.7 BLEU over their corresponding baselines. These consistent improvements suggest that the probability estimation part of the attentional model is good, but perhaps the search is not adequate. Further research is needed to improve the attentional model's translation quality. Another possibility, which we leave for future work, is to include the attentional model score as a feature in Moses.

Table 3 shows some example translations comparing different models. In all examples, it appears that using pialign produced better translations than GIZA++. Using the attentional model as a reranker for pialign further corrects some errors. Using the attentional model alone seems to perform the worst, which is evident in the third example where the attentional model simply repeats a text fragment (although all models do poorly here). Despite the often incoherent output, the attentional model still captures the main keywords used in the translation.

We test this hypothesis by applying the attentional model for a cross-lingual keyword spotting task where the input is the English keyword and the outputs are all Spanish sentences (represented as phones) containing a likely translation of the keyword. From the training data we select the top 200 terms as the keyword based on tf.idf. The relevance judgment is based on exact word matching. The attentional model achieved 35.8% precision, 43.3%

recall and 36.0% F-score on average on 200 queries. Table 4 shows the English translations of retrieved Spanish sentences. In the first example, the attentional model identifies *mañana* as the translation of *tomorrow*. In the second example, it does reasonably well by retrieving 2 correct sentences out of 3, correctly identifying *dejamos* and *salgo* as the translation of *leave*.

7 Speech-to-Word Experiments

In this section, we represent the source Spanish speech as a sequence of 39 dimensional PLP vectors. The frame length is 25ms, and overlapping frames are computed every 10ms. As mentioned in Section 4.1, we used a pyramidal RNN to reduce the speech representation size. Other than that, the model used here is identical to the first set of experiments.

Using this model directly for translation from speech does not yield useful output, as is to be expected from the small training data, noisy speech data, and an out-of-domain language model. However, we are able to produce useful results for the ASR and alignment tasks, as presented below.

	PER (%)
Our model	24.3
Our model + monotonic	22.3
Chorowski et al. (2014)	18.6
Graves et al. (2013)	17.7

Table 5: Phone-error-rate (PER) for various models evaluated on TIMIT

7.1 ASR Evaluation

To illustrate the utility of our approach to modelling speech input, first, we evaluate on the more common ASR task of phone recognition. This can be considered as a sub-problem of translation, and moreover, this allows us to benchmark our approach against the state-of-the-art in phone recognition. We experimented on the TIMIT dataset. Following convention, we removed all the SA sentences, evaluated on the 24 speaker core test set and used the 50 auxiliary speaker development set for early stopping. The model was trained to recognize 48 phonemes

and was mapped to 39 phonemes for testing. We extracted 39 dimensional PLP features from the TIMIT dataset and trained the same model without any modification. Table 5 shows the performance of our model. It performs reasonably well compared with the state-of-the-art (Graves et al., 2013), considering that we didn't tune any hyper-parameters or feature representations for the task. Moreover, our model is not designed for the monotonic constraints inherent to the ASR problem, which process the input without reordering. By simply adding a masking function (equation 2 from Chorowski et al. (2014)) to encourage the monotonic constraint in the alignment function, we observe a 2% PER improvement. This is close to the performance reported by Chorowski et al. (2014) (Table 5), despite the fact that they employed user-adapted speech features.

7.2 Alignment Evaluation

We use alignment as a second evaluation, training and testing on parallel data comprising paired Spanish speech input with its English translations (as described in §5), and using the speech-based modelling techniques (see §4.) We compare to a naive baseline where we assume that each English letter (not including spaces) corresponds to an equal number of Spanish frames. The results of our attentional model and the baseline are summarized in Table 6. The attentional model is substantially lower than the scores in Table 1, because the PLP vector representation is much less informative than the gold phonetic transcription. Here, we have to identify phones and their boundaries in addition to phoneword alignment. However, the naive baseline does surprisingly well, presumably because our (unrealistic) choice of Spanish-English does not have very much reordering.

Figure 3 presents some examples of Spanish speech and English text, showing a heat map of the alignment matrix α (before smoothing). Due to the pyramidal structure of the encoder, each column roughly corresponds to 80ms. In the example on the left, the model is confident at aligning *a little* with columns 1–5, which corresponds roughly to their correct Spanish translation *algo*. We misalign the word *of* with columns 8–10, when the correct alignment should be columns 5–6, corresponding

Phones	sil e m e d i h o k e t e i B a a y a m a r sp a y e r o a n t e a y e r sp sil
Transcription	eh , me dijo que te iba a llamar , ayer , o anteayer
AM	eh , he told me that she was going to call , yesterday before yesterday
Giza	oh , he told me that you called yesterday or before yesterday .
Mod. Pialign	eh , she told me that I was going to call yesterday or before yesterday .
Mod. Pialign + AM	eh , he told me that I was going to call , yesterday or before yesterday .
Reference	eh , he told me that he was going to call you , yesterday , or the day before yesterday .
Phones	sil i t u k o m o a s e s t a D o h w a n i t o e s t a s t r a B a h a n d o k e sp e s t a s a s y e n d o sil
Transcription	y tú , cómo has estado , juanito , estás trabajando , qué estás haciendo.
AM	and how have you been working , are working ?
GIZA	and how are you Juanito , are you job , what are you doing ?
Mod. pialign	and how have you been Juanito are you working , what are you doing ?
Mod. pialign + AM	and how have you been Juan , are you working , what are you doing ?
Reference	and how have you been , Juanita , are you working , what are you doing .
Phones	sil t e n g o k e a s e r l e e l a s e o a s i k o m o a u n h a r D i n i n f a n t i l sp sil
Transcription	tengo que hacerle el aseo así como a un jardín infantil –
AM	I have to have to him like to like that to ⟨unkA⟩
GIZA	I have to do the , the how a vegetable information in the .
Mod. pialign	I have to do the that like to a and it was , didn't you don't have the .
Mod. pialign + AM	I have to make the or like to a and it was , didn't you don't have the –
Reference	I have to clean it like a kindergarten

Table 3: Translation examples for various models: the attentional model (AM), the standard Moses with GIZA++ aligner (giza), with modified Pialign aligner (Mod. pialign) and using the attentional model as reranker on top of pialign.

Keyword : **tomorrow**
El va **mañana** para Caracas. A qué va a Caracas él.
Y **mañana** , y **mañana** o pasado te voy a poner un paquete.
Oh , no , Julio no sé a dónde está y va **mañana** a Caracas , está con Richard.
Oye , qué bueno , entonces nos vamos tempranito en la **mañana**
No , aquí la gente se acuesta a las dos de la **mañana**.

Keyword : **leave**
Todo , organizar completo todo , desde los alquileres , la comida , mozo , cantina , todo lo pongo yo aquí
Y entonces dónde lo **dejamos** pagando estacionamiento y pagando seguro
Sí , el veintiuno. yo **salgo** de para aquí el dieciséis para florida , y el veintiuno llego a Caracas.

Table 4: Examples of cross-lingual keyword spotting using the attentional model. The bolded terms in the retrieved text are based on manual inspection.

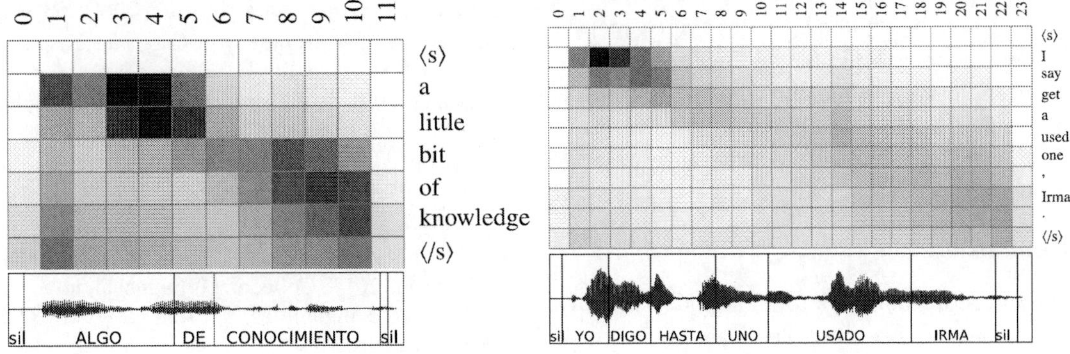

Figure 3: PLP-word alignment examples. The heat maps shows the alignment matrix which is time-aligned with the speech signals and their transcriptions.

ASR	aligner	F1
none	Naive baseline	31.7
none	AM (all mods)	26.4
cz	AM (all mods)	28.0
hu	AM (all mods)	27.9
ru	AM (all mods)	27.4
es	GIZA++	29.7

Table 6: Alignment of Spanish speech to English translations. In the first two rows, no gold or automatic transcriptions of any sort are used. In the next three rows, non-Spanish phone recognizers (cz, hu, ru) are used on the Spanish speech and the attentional model is run on the noisy transcription; this does better than no transcriptions. The last row is an unfair comparison because it uses gold Spanish (es) phonetic transcriptions; nevertheless, our model performs nearly as well.

to Spanish translation *de*. The word *knowledge* is aligned quite well with columns 7–10, corresponding to Spanish *conocimiento*. The example on the right is for a longer sentence. The model is less confident about this example, mostly because there are words that appear infrequently, such as the personal name *Irma*. However, we are still observing diagonal-like alignments that are roughly correct. In both examples, the model correctly leaves silence (`sil`) unaligned.

As a middle ground between assuming gold phonetic transcriptions (cf. Section 6) and no transcriptions at all, we use noisy transcriptions by running speech recognizers for other languages on the Spanish speech: Russian (ru), Hungarian (hu) and Czech (cz) (Vasquez et al., 2012). These distantly related languages were chosen to be a better approximation to the low-resource scenario. All three models perform better than operating directly on the speech signal (Table 6), and notably, the Russian result is nearly as good as GIZA++'s performance on gold phonetic transcriptions.

8 Conclusion

This paper reports our work to train models directly on parallel speech, i.e. source-language speech with English text translations that, in the low-resource setting, would have originated from spoken translations. To our knowledge, it is the first exploration of this type. We augmented the Spanish Fisher and CALLHOME datasets and extended the alignment F1 evaluation metric for this setting. We extended the attentional model of Bahdanau et al. to work on parallel speech and observed improvements relative to all baselines on phone-to-word alignment. On speech-to-word alignment, our model, without using any knowledge of Spanish, performs almost as well as GIZA++ using gold Spanish transcriptions.

Language pairs with word-order divergences and other divergences will of course be more challenging than Spanish-English. This work provides a proof-of-concept that we hope will spur future work towards solving this important problem in a true low-resource language.

Acknowledgments

This work was partly conducted during Duong's internship at ICSI, UC Berkeley and partially supported by the University of Melbourne and National ICT Australia (NICTA). We are grateful for support from NSF Award 1464553 and the DARPA LORELEI Program. Cohn is the recipient of an Australian Research Council Future Fellowship FT130101105.

References

Steven Abney and Steven Bird. 2010. The Human Language Project: Building a universal corpus of the world's languages. In *Proceedings of ACL*, pages 88–97.

Nii O. Attoh-Okine. 1999. Analysis of learning rate and momentum term in backpropagation neural network algorithm trained to predict pavement performance. *Advances in Engineering Software*, 30(4):291–302.

Dzmitry Bahdanau, Kyunghyun Cho, and Yoshua Bengio. 2015. Neural machine translation by jointly learning to align and translate. In *Proceedings of ICLR*.

Steven Bird and David Chiang. 2012. Machine translation for language preservation. In *Proceedings of COLING*, pages 125–134, Mumbai, India.

Steven Bird, Lauren Gawne, Katie Gelbart, and Isaac McAlister. 2014. Collecting bilingual audio in remote indigenous communities. In *Proceedings of COLING*, pages 1015–1024.

Steven Bird. 2010. A scalable method for preserving oral literature from small languages. In *The Role of Digital Libraries in a Time of Global Change: 12th Inter-*

national Conference on Asia-Pacific Digital Libraries*, pages 5–14, Berlin, Heidelberg. Springer-Verlag.

Peter E. Brown, Stephen A. Della Pietra, Vincent J. Della Pietra, and Robert L. Mercer. 1993. The mathematics of statistical machine translation: Parameter estimation. *Computational Linguistics*, 19(2).

Mauro Cettolo, Christian Girardi, and Marcello Federico. 2012. WIT^3: Web inventory of transcribed and translated talks. In *Proceedings of EAMT*, pages 261–268.

William Chan, Navdeep Jaitly, Quoc V. Le, and Oriol Vinyals. 2016. Listen, attend and spell: A neural network for large vocabulary conversational speech recognition. In *Proceedings of ICASSP*.

Jan Chorowski, Dzmitry Bahdanau, Kyunghyun Cho, and Yoshua Bengio. 2014. End-to-end continuous speech recognition using attention-based recurrent NN: first results. In *Proceedings of NIPS Workshop on Deep Learning and Representation Learning*.

Jan K. Chorowski, Dzmitry Bahdanau, Dmitriy Serdyuk, Kyunghyun Cho, and Yoshua Bengio. 2015. Attention-based models for speech recognition. In *Proceedings of NIPS*, pages 577–585.

Trevor Cohn, Cong Duy Vu Hoang, Ekaterina Vymolova, Kaisheng Yao, Chris Dyer, and Gholamreza Haffari. 2016. Incorporating structural alignment biases into an attentional neural translation model. In *Proceedings of NAACL HLT*.

John Duchi, Elad Hazan, and Yoram Singer. 2011. Adaptive subgradient methods for online learning and stochastic optimization. *Journal of Machine Learning Research*, 12:2121–2159.

Chris Dyer, Victor Chahuneau, and Noah A. Smith. 2013. A simple, fast, and effective reparameterization of IBM Model 2. In *Proceedings of NAACL HLT*, pages 644–648.

Kyle Gorman, Jonathan Howell, and Michael Wagner. 2011. Prosodylab-Aligner: A tool for forced alignment of laboratory speech. *Canadian Acoustics*, 39(3):192–193.

Alex Graves, Santiago Fernández, Faustino Gomez, and Jürgen Schmidhuber. 2006. Connectionist temporal classification: labelling unsegmented sequence data with recurrent neural networks. In *Proceedings of ICML*, pages 369–376. ACM.

Alex Graves, Abdel-rahman Mohamed, and Geoffrey E. Hinton. 2013. Speech recognition with deep recurrent neural networks. In *Proceedings of ICASSP*, pages 6645–6649.

Hynek Hermansky. 1990. Perceptual linear predictive (PLP) analysis for speech. *Acoustical Society of America*, pages 1738–1752.

Sepp Hochreiter and Jürgen Schmidhuber. 1997. Long short-term memory. *Neural Computation*, 9(8):1735–1780.

Philipp Koehn, Hieu Hoang, Alexandra Birch, Chris Callison-Burch, Marcello Federico, Nicola Bertoldi, Brooke Cowan, Wade Shen, Christine Moran, Richard Zens, Christ Dyer, Ondřej Bojar, Alexandra Constantin, and Evan Herbst. 2007. Moses: Open source toolkit for statistical machine translation. In *Proceedings of ACL (Interactive Poster and Demonstration Sessions)*, pages 177–180.

Chia-ying Lee, Yu Zhang, and James Glass. 2013. Joint learning of phonetic units and word pronunciations for ASR. In *Proceedings of EMNLP*, pages 182–192.

Thang Luong, Hieu Pham, and Christopher D. Manning. 2015. Effective approaches to attention-based neural machine translation. In *Proceedings of EMNLP*, pages 1412–1421.

Andrew L. Maas, Ziang Xie, Dan Jurafsky, and Andrew Y. Ng. 2015. Lexicon-free conversational speech recognition with neural networks. In *Proceedings of NAACL HLT*, pages 345–354.

Graham Neubig, Taro Watanabe, Eiichiro Sumita, Shinsuke Mori, and Tatsuya Kawahara. 2011. An unsupervised model for joint phrase alignment and extraction. In *Proceedings of NAACL HLT*, pages 632–641.

Graham Neubig, Taro Watanabe, Shinsuke Mori, and Tatsuya Kawahara. 2012. Machine translation without words through substring alignment. In *Proceedings of ACL*, pages 165–174.

Franz Josef Och and Hermann Ney. 2000. Improved statistical alignment models. In *Proceedings of ACL*, pages 440–447.

Mohammad Pezeshki. 2015. Sequence modeling using gated recurrent neural networks. *arXiv preprint arXiv:1501.00299*.

Matt Post, Gaurav Kumar, Adam Lopez, Damianos Karakos, Chris Callison-Burch, and Sanjeev Khudanpur. 2013. Improved speech-to-text translation with the Fisher and Callhome Spanish–English speech translation corpus. In *Proceedings of IWSLT*.

Nitish Srivastava, Geoffrey Hinton, Alex Krizhevsky, Ilya Sutskever, and Ruslan Salakhutdinov. 2014. Dropout: A simple way to prevent neural networks from overfitting. *Journal of Machine Learning Research*, 15:1929–1958.

Felix Stahlberg, Tim Schlippe, Sue Vogel, and Tanja Schultz. 2012. Word segmentation through cross-lingual word-to-phoneme alignment. In *Proceedings of the IEEE Spoken Language Technology Workshop (SLT)*, pages 85–90.

Ilya Sutskever, Oriol Vinyals, and Quoc V. Le. 2014. Sequence to sequence learning with neural networks. In *Proceedings of NIPS*, pages 3104–3112.

Henk Van den Heuvel, Khalid Choukri, Chr Gollan, Asuncion Moreno, and Djamel Mostefa. 2006. Tc-star: New language resources for ASR and SLT purposes. In *Proceedings of LREC*, pages 2570–2573.

Daniel Vasquez, Rainer Gruhn, and Wolfgang Minker. 2012. *Hierarchical Neural Network Structures for Phoneme Recognition*. Springer.

Stephan Vogel, Hermann Ney, and Christoph Tillmann. 1996. HMM-based word alignment in statistical translation. In *Proceedings of COLING*, pages 836–841.

Kelvin Xu, Jimmy Ba, Ryan Kiros, Kyunghyun Cho, Aaron C. Courville, Ruslan Salakhutdinov, Richard S. Zemel, and Yoshua Bengio. 2015. Show, attend and tell: Neural image caption generation with visual attention. In *Proceedings of ICML*, pages 2048–2057.

Matthew D. Zeiler. 2012. ADADELTA: an adaptive learning rate method. *arXiv preprint arXiv:1212.5701*.

Information Density and Quality Estimation Features as Translationese Indicators for Human Translation Classification

Raphael Rubino
Universität des Saarlandes
Saarbrücken, Germany

Ekaterina Lapshinova-Koltunski
Universität des Saarlandes
Saarbrücken, Germany

Josef van Genabith
Universität des Saarlandes
DFKI
Saarbrücken, Germany

`e.lapshinova@mx.uni-saarland.de`
`{raphael.rubino,josef.vangenabith}@uni-saarland.de`

Abstract

This paper introduces information density and machine translation quality estimation inspired features to automatically detect and classify human translated texts. We investigate two settings: discriminating between translations and comparable originally authored texts, and distinguishing two levels of translation professionalism. Our framework is based on delexicalised sentence-level dense feature vector representations combined with a supervised machine learning approach. The results show state-of-the-art performance for mixed-domain translationese detection with information density and quality estimation based features, while results on translation expertise classification are mixed.

1 Introduction

Translations, regardless of the method they were produced with, are different from their source texts and from originally authored comparable texts in the target language. This has been confirmed by many linguistic studies on translation properties commonly called *translationese* (Gellerstam, 1986). These studies show that translations tend to share a set of lexical, syntactic and/or textual features distinguishing them from non-translated texts. As most of these features can be measured quantitatively, we are able to automatically distinguish translations from originals (Baroni and Bernardini, 2006; Ozdowska and Way, 2009; Kurokawa et al., 2009). This is useful for Statistical Machine Translation (SMT), as language and translation models can be improved if

the translation direction and status of the data (translation or original) is known (Lembersky, 2013).

Research on translationese has recently focused on exploring features capturing aspects of translationese such as simplification, explicitation, convergence, normalisation and shining-through (Volansky, 2012; Ilisei, 2012). Here we extend this work as follows: (i) we investigate the impact of information density and surprisal features, (ii) we explore the use of features used in machine translation quality estimation (Blatz et al., 2003; Specia et al., 2010), (iii) we explore classification between originally authored text and trainee and professional translation, as well as between professional and trainee translation. In order to avoid biasing classification by topic content, throughout our experiments we use fully delexicalised features, resulting in dense vector representations (rather than sparse vectors, where the size of the vectors can be up to and in fact exceed the size of the vocabulary). We show that information theory as well as translation quality estimation inspired features achieve state-of-the-art results in mixed-domain original vs. human translation classification.

Languages provide speakers with a large number of possibilities of how they may encode messages. These include the choice of phonemes, words, syntactic structures, as well as arranging sentences in discourse. Speakers' decisions regarding these choices are influenced by diverse factors: cognitive processing limitations can impact variation in linguistic encoding across all linguistic levels. Text production conditions, including monolingual vs. multilingual settings, can influence this variation: in

Proceedings of NAACL-HLT 2016, pages 960–970,
San Diego, California, June 12-17, 2016. ©2016 Association for Computational Linguistics

translation, choices can be shaped by aspects of both the source and the target language.

Contrastive studies have shown that information density is distributed differently in English and German (Doherty, 2006; Fabricius-Hansen, 1996). These contrasts may impact translation, and in case of source language shining through[1], we would expect to observe differences between translations and comparable originals in terms of information density. Additionally, translations are often more specialised and more conventionalised than originals (excluding translation of fictional texts). In this paper we investigate whether and to what extent information density based features are useful in human translation classification.

Quality estimation (QE) (Blatz et al., 2004; Ueffing and Ney, 2005) is the attempt to learn models that predict machine translation quality without access to a reference translation at prediction time. Translation, manual or automatic, is always a process of transforming a source into a target text. This process is prone to error. In this paper we explore whether and to what extent the extensive research on QE can be brought to bear on the problem of human translation vs. originals classification, and in particular the discrimination between novice and professional translation output.

Below we explore the ability of our features to distinguish between 1) non-translated texts and translations by professionals, 2) non-translated texts and translations by translator trainees, and 3) the two translation varieties that diverge in the degree of translation experience. We report results in terms of accuracy and f-score, and provide a feature analysis in order to understand the role of the information density and QE inspired features in the task.

The paper is organised as follows: related work is presented in Section 2. The experimental setup is detailed in Section 3, followed by the results and analysis in Section 4. A discussion about our results compared to previous work is given in Section 5. Finally, conclusion and future work are provided in Section 6.

---

[1]If translations demonstrate features more typical for the source language, see e.g. Teich (2003).

2 Related Work

We briefly review previous work on translationese, information density, machine translation quality estimation and studies on human translation expertise.

2.1 Translationese

A number of corpus-based studies on translation have shown that it is possible to automatically predict whether a text is an original or a translation (Baroni and Bernardini, 2006; Koppel and Ordan, 2011). These approaches are based on the concept of translationese – a term coined to capture the specific language of translations by Gellerstam (1986). The idea is that translations exhibit properties which distinguish them from original texts, both the source texts of the translation and comparable texts originally authored in the target language. Baker (1993; 1995) claimed these properties to be universal, i.e. (source) language-independent, emphasising general effects of the process of translation.

However, translationese includes features involving both source and target language. Most linguistic studies distinguish *explicitation* – a tendency to spell things out rather than leave them implicit and *implicitation* (the opposite effect), *simplification* – a tendency to simplify the language used in translation, *normalisation* – a tendency to exaggerate features of the target language and to conform to its typical patterns, *levelling out* or *convergence* – a relatively higher level of homogeneity of translated texts compared to non-translated ones, and *interference* or *shining through* (e.g. Teich (2003)). While simple lexicalised features including word tokens and character n-grams can produce near perfect classification results for in-domain data (Avner et al., 2014), a significant amount of work has gone into devising features that can capture presumed linguistic aspects of translationese (Volansky, 2012). Rabinovich et al. (2015) explore unsupervised discrimination of translations based on principal components analysis for dimensionality reduction followed by a clustering step. The method is robust to unbalanced and heterogeneous datasets, which may be useful to handle mixed domain, genre and source of data, a common situation when training language and translation models.

Automatic classification of original vs. translated

texts has applications in machine translation, especially in studies showing the impact of the nature (original vs. translation) of the text in translation and language models used in SMT. Kurokawa et al. (2009) show that taking directionality into account when training an English-to-French phrase-based SMT system leads to improved translation performance. Ozdowska & Way (2009) analyse the same language pair and demonstrate that the nature of the original source language has an impact on the quality of SMT output. Lembersky et al. (2012) show that BLEU scores can be improved by language models compiled from translated texts and not from comparable originally authored ones.

2.2 Information Density

In a natural communication situation, speakers tend to exploit variations in their linguistic encoding – modulating the order, density and specificity of their expressions to avoid informational peaks and troughs that may result in inefficient communication. This is often referred to as the *uniform information density* hypothesis (Frank and Jaeger, 2008). The information conveyed by an expression can be quantified by its *surprisal*, a measure of how predictable an expression is given its context. Simplification and explicitation may impact the average information density measured on translated texts compared to comparable originally authored ones in the same language. Source language interference should result in peaks of measured surprisal values in translated texts, while the information density may remain uniform in originals.

According to Hale (2001), a surprisal model allows the estimation of the probability of a parse tree given a sentence prefix. Levy (2008) showed that a lexical-based surprisal measure can be obtained by computing the negative log probability of a word given its preceding context: $S = -\log P(w_{k+1}|w_1 \ldots w_k)$. Following Demberg et al. (2013), we estimate surprisal in three ways, at the word, part-of-speech and syntax levels, based on n-gram language models and language models trained on unlexicalised part-of-speech sequences and flattened syntactic trees. Note that all resulting feature vectors do not represent lexical information but information theoretic surprisal measures.

2.3 Quality Estimation

Machine translation QE is the process of estimating how accurate an automatic translation is through characteristic features of the source and target texts, and (possibly) also the translation engine, with a supervised machine learning setting to estimate quality scores. QE can be applied at the word, sentence and document level (Gandrabur and Foster, 2003; Ueffing et al., 2003; Blatz et al., 2003; Scarton and Specia, 2014).

Many different delexicalised dense features have been explored in previous work on QE, including language and topic models, n-best lists, etc. (Quirk, 2004; Ueffing and Ney, 2004; Specia and Gimenez, 2010; Rubino et al., 2013a). It has been shown that the performance of a supervised classifier to distinguish between originals and automatic translations is correlated with the quality of the machine translated texts (Aharoni et al., 2014): low quality translation, containing grammatical and syntactic errors, as well as incorrect lexical choices, are robust indicators of automatic translations. In the case of human translation, to the best of our knowledge, there are no empirical studies on the level of professional expertise in the translation process and its correlation with the performance of a translationese classifier.

2.4 Translator Experience

Jääskeläinen (1997) describes translational behaviour of professionals and non-professionals who perform translation from English into Finnish. Carl and Buch-Kromann (2010) apply psycholinguistic methods in their analysis. They present a study of translation phases and processes for student and professional translators, relating translators' eye movements and keystrokes to the quality of the translations produced. They show that the translation behaviour of novice and professional translators differs with respect to how they use the translation phases. Englund Dimitrova (2005) develops a combined process and product analysis and compares translators with different levels of translation experience, but concentrates only on cohesive explicitness.

Most of these works are rather process-oriented than product-oriented, which means that features of translated texts are rarely taken into account. However, some of the findings are valuable for the analysis of translated texts. For instance, Göpferich & Jääskeläinen (2009) find that with increasing translation competence, translators focus on larger translation units, which can impact the choice of linguistic encoding translators use.

3 Experimental Setup

Our experiments are designed to investigate underexplored topics focusing on (i) information theoretic and (ii) machine translation QE features in translation classification. We use dense vector representations with fully delexicalised features and investigate three hypotheses:

1. originals & professional translations should be close in terms of quality and thus more difficult to separate automatically,

2. originals & student translations should be distant in terms of quality and thus easier to classify,

3. professional & student translations should both contain translationese features and thus may be very difficult to differentiate.

3.1 Supervised Classification

In order to train a classifier and predict binary labels on unseen data, we use a dense vector sentence-level representation associated with a class $(\mathbf{x}_i, y_i)$, $i = 1, \ldots, l$ (l is the number of training instances) with $\mathbf{x}_i \in R^n$ (n is the size of a dense vector) and $y \in \{-1, 1\}^l$. We train classification models with a support vector machine SVM (the C-SVC implementation in LIBSVM (Chang and Lin, 2011)) as a quadratic optimization problem:

$$\min_{\omega, b, \xi} \quad \frac{1}{2}\omega^T\omega + C\sum_{i=1}^{l} \xi_i \,,$$

$$\text{subject to} \quad y_i(\omega^T\phi(x_i) + b) \geq 1 - \xi_i \,, \quad \xi_i \geq 0 \,.$$

ϕ is a kernel function and allows the projection of training data to a higher dimensional space. We use the radial basis function (RBF) kernel, as it produced the best empirical results compared to linear and polynomial kernels. We predict the class for unseen instances x as follows:

$$f(x) = \text{sgn}(\omega^T\phi(x) + b).$$

Corpus	Token (M)	Sentence (k)
Europarl Originals	4.1	155.5
Literature Originals	1.3	48.1
Literature Translations	1.4	45.8
Politics Originals	0.2	9.7
Politics Translations	0.2	8.7

Table 1: Details of the corpora used to train language and n-gram frequency models for originally authored texts and translations.

Two hyper-parameters have to be set for C-SVC with the RBF kernel: the regularisation parameter (or penalty) C and the kernel parameter γ. We use grid-search to find optimal values, performing a 5-fold cross-validation on the training data. To avoid over-fitting, we use a held-out development set to evaluate the models obtained.

3.2 Datasets

The datasets used in our experiments are separated into two subsets: corpora used to extract features and corpora used to train, tune and test our classifiers. The former are taken from the publicly available bilingual English-German parallel corpora consisting of parliamentary proceedings, literary works and political commentary, compiled by (Rabinovich et al., 2015). These corpora are used individually to train language models and compute n-gram frequency distributions. Basic corpus statistics are presented in Table 1. The latter ones are composed of German texts, taken from the VARTRA corpora (Lapshinova-Koltunski, 2013), which were either originally written in German (originals) or translated from English (translations).

Originals and translations belong to the same genres and registers and can be considered comparable. They include a mixture of literary, tourism and popular-scientific texts, instruction manuals, commercial letters and political essays and speeches. The VARTRA translations are split in two sets: one produced by professional translators, and one produced by translator trainees. Details are presented in Table 2. We extract balanced subsets of training, tuning and testing data containing three, one and two thousands sentences, respectively, of each type.

Corpus	Token (k)	Sentence (k)
Originals	121.7	6.0
Professional Translations	125.2	6.0
Student Translations	126.2	6.0

Table 2: Details of the comparable corpora used as training, development and test sets for the originals versus translation classification experiments.

3.3 Feature Sets

For classification, input text is represented as a set of feature vectors. The features capture aspects of information density and translation QE. Throughout we use unlexicalised lower-dimensional dense vectors rather than high-dimensional lexicalised sparse vectors to minimize the input of specific content on classification results. We extract a total of 778 features[2] and separate them into four subsets corresponding to broad but distinct characteristics of original and translated sentences: surface and distortion features are related to QE, surprisal and complexity features are inspired by information theory.

Surface Features - 13 surface features based on meta representations of sentences' lexical form. Features include sentence and average word length, the number of word tokens and number of punctuation marks. Three case-based features capture the number of upper-cased letters and words, and a binary feature indicates whether a sentence starts with an upper-case character. Another binary value encodes whether the sentence ends with a period. Two features are obtained from the ratio between the number of upper-cased and lower-cased letters, the number of punctuation marks and the length of the sentence. Finally two features capture the number of periods merged with words and words with mixed-case characters.

Surprisal Features - 225 features based on the surprisal measure presented in Section 2.2 are extracted using language models trained on words, delexicalised part-of-speech and flattened syntactic trees. The language models are trained

on individual[3] corpora presented in Table 1. We extract n-gram ($n \in [1; 5]$) log-probabilities and perplexities, with and without the tags indicating the beginning and ending of sentences, using the SRILM toolkit (Stolcke et al., 2011).

Complexity Features - 315 features based on n-gram frequencies, indicating how frequent the lexical choices, part-of-speech and flattened syntactic sequences present in the text to be classified are. As for the surprisal features, we use the same originally authored and translated texts individually to extract n-grams frequency quartiles. We extract the percentage of n-grams ($n \in [1; 5]$) occurring in each quartile. Frequency percentages are averaged at the sentence level, leading to 4 features per sentence (one per quartile) given a value of n, for each corpus used to define the frequency quartiles. This approach allows us to avoid encoding raw n-gram features and keep a dense vector representation (Blatz et al., 2003).

Distortion Features - 225 features based on the possible distortion in lexical, part-of-speech and syntactic structures observed between originals and translations, as well as between different levels of translation experience. These features are extracted the same way as the suprisal features, but based on language models trained on sentence-level reversed text. The backward language model features are popular in translation quality estimation studies and show interesting results (Duchateau et al., 2002; Rubino et al., 2013b).

3.4 Preprocessing and Tools

All data used in our experiments are sentence-split, lower-cased and tokenised using the CORENLP toolkit (Manning et al., 2014). The part-of-speech tags and syntactic trees required to extract some features are obtained with the same set of tools. For parsing, we use the probabilistic context-free grammar model trained on the Negra corpus (Brants et al., 2003) and described in (Rafferty and Manning, 2008), before flattening the trees as illustrated in Figure 1. Both part-of-speech and flattened syntac-

---

[2]Too many to list in the paper, a complete list is provided with the additional material submitted.

[3]Originally authored texts and translations are used separately in order to model their characteristics.

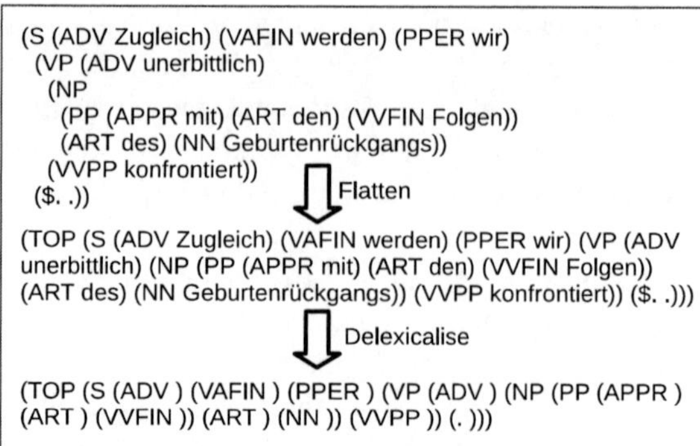

Figure 1: Flattening and delexicalising a syntactic tree.

tic trees are then delexicalised in order to remove all surface forms from the representations.

4 Results and Analysis

Below we provide details on discriminating between originally authored texts and translations, followed by the prediction of translation experience comparing professional translators and students. Finally, we evaluate feature importance with individual and ensemble feature selection techniques.

4.1 Original vs Translated Texts

Two sets of experiments are conducted to discriminate between originals and professional translations (Table 3) and originals and student translations (Table 4). For each classification task, we evaluate feature groups on the test set containing $4,000$ unseen sentences balanced over two classes, reporting overall accuracy, and also precision, recall and f-score. Finally, a classification model is trained and evaluated combining all features.

Originals vs. professional translations reaches a maximum accuracy of 70.0% using the distortion feature set with surprisal a close second at 69.2%. The difference is not statistically significant (bootstrap resampling at $p < 0.05$). They outperform the other types of features, as well as the combination of all feature types. Per class evaluation shows a similar trend with the best performing feature sets. The results show that originals and professional translations exhibit differences in terms of sequences of words, part-of-speech and syntactic tags which are captured by language model based features.

Feature set	Acc (%)	Originals			Professional		
		P	R	F	P	R	F
Surface	54.7	0.54	0.64	0.58	0.56	0.46	0.50
Surprisal	69.2*	0.66	0.77	0.71	0.73	0.61	**0.66**
Complexity	65.3	0.63	0.73	0.68	0.68	0.57	0.62
Distortion	**70.0***	0.66	0.81	**0.73**	0.75	0.59	**0.66**
All	66.5	0.64	0.74	0.69	0.70	0.59	0.64

Table 3: Accuracy, precision, recall and F-measure obtained on the originals versus professional translations classification task. Best results in bold and statistically significant winner marked with $\star$ ($p < 0.05$).

Feature set	Acc (%)	Originals			Student		
		P	R	F	P	R	F
Surface	57.8	0.58	0.58	0.58	0.58	0.58	0.58
Surprisal	69.7*	0.69	0.72	0.70	0.71	0.67	**0.69**
Complexity	65.4	0.62	0.81	0.70	0.73	0.49	0.59
Distortion	70.8*	0.69	0.75	**0.72**	0.73	0.66	**0.69**
All	**71.1***	0.69	0.76	**0.72**	0.73	0.66	**0.69**

Table 4: Accuracy, precision, recall and F-measure obtained on the originals versus student translations classification task. Best results in bold and statistically significant winner marked with $\star$ ($p < 0.05$).

The classification of originals and student translations shows that the combination of the four feature types leads to the most accurate classifier, followed by the distortion and the surprisal sets (with equivalent accuracy results at $p < 0.05$). The two latter feature sets are the best performing ones overall based on the two classification tasks. Comparing the two tasks, originally authored texts are closer to professional translations and more distant to student translations, which validates two of our hypotheses listed in Section 3.

4.2 Translation Expertise

In order to investigate whether our third assumption is correct, we perform binary classification between professional and student translations (Table 5). The results, barely above the 50% baseline, show the proximity of the two types of translations according to our feature sets, which supports our third assumption. The combination of four feature types reaches the highest accuracy, followed by the distortion and complexity sets. However, the surprisal features do not seem to be helpful in differentiating between the professional and the student translations, compared to the two previous binary classification tasks.

This result indicates that the surprisal measure is a reliable source of information to determine whether a sentence is originally authored or a translation, but it is not reliable to separate two translations produced by translators with different levels of expertise. The features inspired by translation quality estimation do not reach high accuracy results: it seems that the difference between professional and student translations cannot be tied to properties of the surface level or lexical choices of the human translators as indirectly captured by our features.

Feature set	Acc (%)	Professional			Students		
		P	R	F	P	R	F
Surface	54.5	0.56	0.43	0.48	0.54	0.66	0.59
Surprisal	55.7	0.57	0.48	0.52	0.55	0.64	0.59
Complexity	56.0	0.56	0.55	0.56	0.56	0.57	0.56
Distortion	57.7	0.58	0.55	0.56	0.57	0.60	0.59
All	**58.7***	0.59	0.57	**0.58**	0.58	0.61	0.59

Table 5: Accuracy, precision, recall and F-measure obtained on the professional versus student translations classification task. Best results in bold and statistically significant winner marked with * ($p < 0.05$).

4.3 3-way Classification

Table 6 shows the confusion matrix obtained with the classifier trained on the combination of the four feature sets. This classifier reaches third position overall in terms of accuracy, behind the distortion and surprisal sets with first and second positions, respectively. This ranking of classifiers trained on different feature sets follows the trend observed in the originals versus professional translation binary classification task.

		Reference		
		Originals	Professional	Student
	Originals	1318	656	544
Prediction	Professional	276	699	491
	Student	406	645	965

Table 6: Confusion matrix obtained using a classifier trained on the four feature sets for the multi-class task, separating originals, professional and student translations.

The training method chosen for the multi-class problem is the *one against one*, where individual classifiers are first trained on each binary classification task before being combined to form the final multi-class classifier (Hsu and Lin, 2002). The results indicate that our feature sets distinguish originally authored texts from professional and student translations (first line of the matrix), while the professional translations are more difficult to separate from the two other types of text. Also, student translations have characteristics differing from originals and professional translations, which can be captured with our feature sets (last line of the matrix). However, the columns of the confusion matrix show that originals are not necessarily closer to professional translations, as indicated by the first column where a larger amount of gold originals are incorrectly classified as student translations. The same trend is observable in the last column. These results go against the hypothesis that originals and student translations are easier to separate, a phenomenon which does not appear for the binary classification task (originals vs. student translations).

4.4 Feature Performance

Evaluating the performance of our feature sets is done by calculating the discriminative power of each feature individually which allows us to rank features according to their correlation with a class given a classification task. We follow the "f-score" measure (1) as proposed by Chen (2006):

$$F(i) \equiv \frac{\left(\bar{x}_i^{(+)} - \bar{x}_i\right)^2 + \left(\bar{x}_i^{(-)} - \bar{x}_i\right)^2}{\frac{1}{n_+ - 1} \sum_{k=1}^{n_+} \left(\bar{x}_{k,i}^{(+)} - \bar{x}_i^{(+)}\right)^2 + \frac{1}{n_- - 1} \sum_{k=1}^{n_-} \left(\bar{x}_{k,i}^{(-)} - \bar{x}_i^{(-)}\right)^2} \tag{1}$$

with training vectors x_k and $k = 1, \ldots, m$, binary classes n_+ and n_- for positive and negative instances, $\bar{x}_i$, $\bar{x}_i^{(+)}$, $\bar{x}_i^{(-)}$ the average of the ith feature of the whole, positive and negative instances, and $\bar{x}_{k,i}^{(+)}$ and $\bar{x}_{k,i}^{(-)}$ the ith feature of the kth positive or negative instance. The measure indicates how discriminative a feature is given a binary classification task. A drawback of the *f-score* is that it does not take into account possible feature complementarity.

We report the distribution of the top 25 features amongst the three levels of analysis: lexical, POS and syntax (Figure 2a), as well as amongst the four

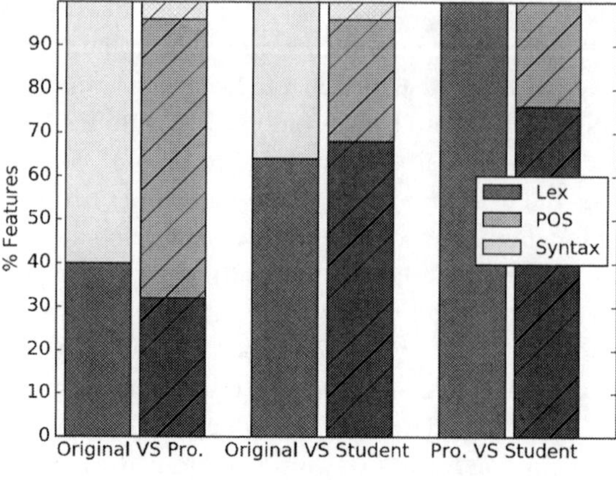

(a) Lexical, POS and syntax.

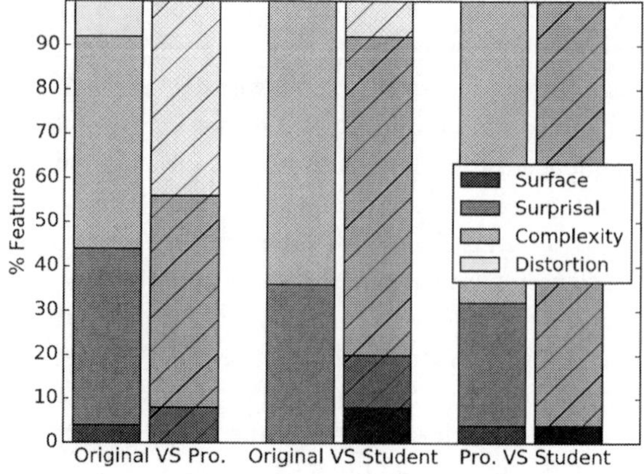

(b) Surface, surprisal, complexity and distortion.

Figure 2: Distributions of the top 25 most important features according to individual discriminative power (left bars) and ensemble of randomised trees (right hatched bars).

feature types: surface, surprisal, complexity and distortion (Figure 2b). The results show that POS features are not ranked as the most discriminant ones when evaluated individually, while syntactic features are the most important ones for the originals vs. professional translation task and lexical features have the highest discriminative power for the two other tasks. When looking at the feature types, we see that complexity features, based on n-gram frequencies, are the most discriminant for the three tasks, followed by the surprisal features, while the distortion and surface features do not have a strong discriminative power. Most of the top n-gram based features rely on sequences between 1 and 3 words, indicating that higher order n-grams are not important features when considered individually. Surprisal, distortion and complexity features are based on external resources (detailed in Table 1) and the corpus of political texts translated into German is the most useful one when used to extract the complexity and surprisal features, which can be explained by the presence of political speeches and essays in the VARTRA corpus.

The results obtained on individual feature discriminative power do not reflect the ones obtained using features grouped by types. Individually, features indicating complexity based on n-gram frequencies are ranked highest. However, only a few of the distortion features appear in the discriminative ranking while this feature type reaches the high-

est accuracy scores on the three binary classification tasks. These results indicate that features are highly complementary within a group of a particular type, but also between different types. To capture possible relationships between features, we conduct a non-linear feature selection using the forest of randomised trees approach (Geurts et al., 2006) and present the results for the top 25 features in Figure 2 (right hatched bars).

The tree-based feature ranking method shows the complementarity of words and POS features, while the syntactic ones appear in the top 25 for the original vs. translation tasks for both levels of expertise. When looking at the feature types, the originals vs. professional task relies mainly on a mixture of distortion and complexity features, and surprisal indicators are totally absent from the top 25 for the professional vs. student task. For both tasks involving student translation, the complexity features are the most important ones, and simple surface features are useful, such as the average words occurrence per sentence or the ratio between the number of punctuation marks and the sentence length. The most useful external resource used to extract n-gram based features is again the political corpus, indicating once more the domain proximity of our datasets.

Individually, syntactic features appear to be highly discriminant when classifying between originals and translations (regardless expertise), which may indicate two translationese phenomena: simplification, translators use less complex constructions, and interference (shining through), source syntax shines through in translated texts. The ensemble ranking shows that surprisal and distortion, although not as important as complexity and distortion, are important indicators of translationese as they appear in both tasks where originals are classified against translations. These feature types are not present in the top 25 if only translated texts are classified.

5   Discussion

Previous research (Baroni and Bernardini, 2006; Volansky, 2012) has shown that high classification accuracy ($>$ 80%) can be achieved using lexicalised token n-gram sparse feature vectors. As a sanity check, we conduct a set of experiments for each of our classification tasks using token unigram frequency as features, normalised by the segment length. The vocabulary defining the feature vector dimensionality is taken from the training sets, using the data presented in Table 2 only, leading to $25,561$ features. The same classification setup as presented in Section 3 is used and we observe accuracy results reaching 78.0%, 83.3% and 65.2% for original vs. professional, originals vs. student and professional vs. student classifications respectively. For the three-way task, an accuracy score of 62.7% is reached. These results are substantially lower than the ones reported by Volansky (2012), mostly because of the text chunks size, which has a strong impact on performance as shown by Rabinovich and Wintner (2015). In our work, we classify each sentence individually as they appear naturally in the corpus, while most previous studies are based on artificial chunks of approximately $2,000$ tokens. An other explanation of the low performing unigram-based features is related to our mixed-domain setting, as it was shown that classifiers' performance drop drastically when trained on this type of features and tested on out-of-domain data (Rabinovich and Wintner, 2015).

6   Conclusion

This paper presented a first step in using information density, and especially surprisal and complexity inspired features, as well as features used in translation quality estimation, as indicators of transla-

tionese for originally authored and manually translated text classification. We focused on separating originals and translations produced by humans with different levels of expertise and showed that translationese features based on information density and quality estimation are useful indicators of whether a text was manually translated or originally produced. We conducted experiments in a mixed-domain setting, including literary, tourism and scientific texts, as well as instruction manuals, commercial letters and political essays and speeches.

Our experiments on feature type evaluation show that the best performing one is a set of quality estimation inspired distortion indicators, extracted from backward language models trained on originally authored and translated texts. When features are evaluated individually according to the "f-score" measure (Chen and Lin, 2006), the most discriminative ones are from the complexity subset, extracted from n-gram frequency quartiles, followed by surprisal features, both extracted at the lexical and syntactic levels. The features ensemble evaluation based on randomised trees reveals feature complementarity and shows that extracting complexity and distortion indicators at the lexical and POS levels leads to the highest performing sets.

The features used in our experiments are extracted at the word-level. As future work, we plan to extend our feature sets to information theoretic aspects of character-level indicators, such as character n-grams frequencies and language models, encoding complexity and surprisal respectively. This approach would allow to capture sub-word information density indicators, such as morphological information (Avner et al., 2014).

Acknowledgments

This research is funded by the German Research Foundation (Deutsche Forschungsgemeinschaft) under grant SFB 1102: Information Density and Linguistic Encoding[4].

We would like to thank the anonymous reviewers for their insightful comments.

---

[4]IDEAL – `http://www.sfb1102.uni-saarland.de/`

References

Roee Aharoni, Moshe Koppel, and Yoav Goldberg. 2014. Automatic detection of machine translated text and translation quality estimation. In *Proceedings of ACL*, pages 289–295.

Ehud Alexander Avner, Noam Ordan, and Shuly Wintner. 2014. Identifying translationese at the word and sub-word level. *Digital Scholarship in the Humanities*.

Mona Baker. 1993. Corpus linguistics and translation studies: Implications and applications. In G. Francis Baker M. and E. Tognini-Bonelli, editors, *Text and Technology: in Honour of John Sinclair*, pages 233–250. Benjamins, Amsterdam.

Mona Baker. 1995. Corpora in translation studies: An overview and some suggestions for future research. *Target*, 7(2):223–243.

Marco Baroni and Silvia Bernardini. 2006. A new approach to the study of translationese: Machine-learning the difference between original and translated text. *Literary and Linguistic Computing*, 21(3):259–274.

John Blatz, Erin Fitzgerald, George Foster, Simona Gandrabur, Cyril Goutte, Alex Kulesza, Alberto Sanchis, and Nicola Ueffing. 2003. Confidence estimation for machine translation. In *JHU/CLSP Summer Workshop Final Report*.

John Blatz, Erin Fitzgerald, George Foster, Simona Gandrabur, Cyril Goutte, Alex Kulesza, Alberto Sanchis, and Nicola Ueffing. 2004. Confidence estimation for machine translation. In *Proceedings of COLING*, pages 315–321.

Thorsten Brants, Wojciech Skut, and Hans Uszkoreit. 2003. Syntactic annotation of a German newspaper corpus. In *Treebanks*, volume 20 of *Text, Speech and Language Technology*, pages 73–87. Springer.

Michael Carl and Matthias Buch-Kromann. 2010. Correlating translation product and translation process data of professional and student translators. In *Proceedings of EAMT*.

Chih-Chung Chang and Chih-Jen Lin. 2011. LIBSVM: A library for support vector machines. *ACM Transactions on Intelligent Systems and Technology (TIST)*, 2(3):27.

Yi-Wei Chen and Chih-Jen Lin. 2006. Combining SVMs with various feature selection strategies. In *Feature extraction*, pages 315–324. Springer.

Vera Demberg, Frank Keller, and Alexander Koller. 2013. Incremental, predictive parsing with psycholinguistically motivated tree-adjoining grammar. *Computational Linguistics*, 39(4):1025–1066.

Monika Doherty. 2006. *Structural propensities: translating nominal word groups from English into German*, volume 65. John Benjamins Publishing.

Jacques Duchateau, Kris Demuynck, and Patrick Wambacq. 2002. Confidence scoring based on backward language models. In *Proceedings of ICASSP*, volume 1.

Birgitta Englund Dimitrova. 2005. *Expertise and explicitation in the translation process*, volume 64. John Benjamins Publishing.

Cathrine Fabricius-Hansen. 1996. Informational density: a problem for translation and translation theory. *Linguistics*, 34(3):521–566.

Austin Frank and T Florian Jaeger. 2008. Speaking rationally: Uniform information density as an optimal strategy for language production. In *Proceedings of the cognitive science society*, pages 933–938.

Simona Gandrabur and George Foster. 2003. Confidence estimation for translation prediction. In *Proceedings of CoNLL*, pages 95–102.

Martin Gellerstam. 1986. Translationese in Swedish novels translated from English. In L. Wollin and H. Lindquist, editors, *Translation Studies in Scandinavia*, pages 88–95. CWK Gleerup, Lund.

Pierre Geurts, Damien Ernst, and Louis Wehenkel. 2006. Extremely randomized trees. *Machine learning*, 63(1):3–42.

Susanne Göpferich and Riitta Jääskeläinen. 2009. Process research into the development of translation competence: Where are we, and where do we need to go? *Across Languages and Cultures*, 10(2):169–191.

John Hale. 2001. A probabilistic Earley parser as a psycholinguistic model. In *Proceedings of NAACL*, pages 1–8.

Chih-Wei Hsu and Chih-Jen Lin. 2002. A comparison of methods for multiclass support vector machines. *Neural Networks, IEEE Transactions on*, 13(2):415–425.

Iustina-Narcisa Ilisei. 2012. *A Machine Learning Approach to the Identification of Translational Language: An Inquiry into Translationese Learning Models*. Ph.D. thesis, University of Wolverhampton.

Riitta Jääskeläinen. 1997. *Tapping the Process: An Explorative Study of the Cognitive and Affective Factors Involved in Translating*. Doctoral dissertation. Ph.D. thesis, University of Joensuu, Joensuu.

Moshe Koppel and Noam Ordan. 2011. Translationese and its dialects. In *Proceedings of ACL*, pages 1318–1326.

David Kurokawa, Cyril Goutte, and Pierre Isabelle. 2009. Automatic detection of translated text and its impact on machine translation. In *Proceedings of MT Summit*.

Ekaterina Lapshinova-Koltunski. 2013. VARTRA: A comparable corpus for analysis of translation variation. In *Proceedings of the Workshop on Building and Using Comparable Corpora*, pages 77–86.

Gennadi Lembersky, Noam Ordan, and Shuly Wintner. 2012. Language models for machine translation: Original vs. translated texts. *Computational Linguistics*, 38(4):799–825.

Gennadi Lembersky. 2013. *The Effect of Translationese on Statistical Machine Translation*. Ph.D. thesis, University of Haifa, Israel.

Roger Levy. 2008. Expectation-based syntactic comprehension. *Cognition*, 106(3):1126–1177.

Christopher D. Manning, Mihai Surdeanu, John Bauer, Jenny Finkel, Steven J. Bethard, and David McClosky. 2014. The stanford CoreNLP natural language processing toolkit. In *Proceedings of ACL: System Demonstrations*, pages 55–60.

Sylwia Ozdowska and Andy Way. 2009. Optimal bilingual data for french-english PB-SMT. In *Proceedings of EAMT*, page 96–103.

Christopher Quirk. 2004. Training a sentence-level machine translation confidence measure. In *Proceedings of LREC*, pages 825–828.

Ella Rabinovich and Shuly Wintner. 2015. Unsupervised identification of translationese. *Transactions of the Association for Computational Linguistics*, 3:419–432.

Ella Rabinovich, Shuly Wintner, and Ofek Luis Lewinsohn. 2015. The Haifa corpus of translationese. *arXiv:1509.03611*.

Anna N Rafferty and Christopher D Manning. 2008. Parsing three German treebanks: Lexicalized and unlexicalized baselines. In *Proceedings of the Workshop on Parsing German*, pages 40–46.

Raphael Rubino, Jose G. C. de Souza, Jennifer Foster, and Lucia Specia. 2013a. Topic models for translation quality estimation for gisting purposes. In *Proceedings of MT Summit*, pages 295–302.

Raphael Rubino, Jennifer Foster, Rasoul Samed Zadeh Kaljahi, Johann Roturier, and Fred Hollowood. 2013b. Estimating the quality of translated user-generated content. In *Proceedings of IJCNLP*, pages 14–18.

Carolina Scarton and Lucia Specia. 2014. Document-level translation quality estimation: exploring discourse and pseudo-references. In *Proceedings of EAMT*.

Lucia Specia and Jesús Gimenez. 2010. Combining confidence estimation and reference-based metrics for segment level MT evaluation. In *Proceedings of AMTA*.

Lucia Specia, Dhwaj Raj, and Marco Turchi. 2010. Machine translation evaluation versus quality estimation. *Machine translation*, 24(1):39–50.

Andreas Stolcke, Jing Zheng, Wen Wang, and Victor Abrash. 2011. SRILM at sixteen: Update and outlook. In *Proceedings of ASRU*.

Elke Teich. 2003. *Cross-linguistic variation in system and text: A methodology for the investigation of translations and comparable texts*, volume 5. Walter de Gruyter.

Nicola Ueffing and Hermann Ney. 2004. Bayes decision rules and confidence measures for statistical machine translation. *Proceedings of Advances in Natural Language Processing*, pages 70–81.

Nicola Ueffing and Hermann Ney. 2005. Word-level confidence estimation for machine translation using phrase-based translation models. In *Proceedings of EMNLP*, pages 763–770.

Nicola Ueffing, Klaus Macherey, and Hermann Ney. 2003. Confidence measures for statistical machine translation. In *Proceedings of MT Summit*.

Vered Volansky. 2012. The features of translationese. Master's thesis, University of Haifa.

Interpretese vs. Translationese:
The Uniqueness of Human Strategies in Simultaneous Interpretation

He He
Computer Science
University of Maryland
hhe@cs.umd.edu

Jordan Boyd-Graber
Computer Science
University of Colorado
Jordan.Boyd.Graber
@colorado.edu

Hal Daumé III
Computer Science and UMIACS
University of Maryland
hal@cs.umd.edu

Abstract

Computational approaches to simultaneous interpretation are stymied by how little we know about the tactics human interpreters use. We produce a parallel corpus of translated and simultaneously interpreted text and study differences between them through a computational approach. Our analysis reveals that human interpreters regularly apply several effective tactics to reduce translation latency, including sentence segmentation and passivization. In addition to these unique, clever strategies, we show that limited human memory also causes other idiosyncratic properties of human interpretation such as generalization and omission of source content.

1 Human Simultaneous Interpretation

Although simultaneous interpretation has a key role in today's international community,[1] it remains underexplored within machine translation (MT). One key challenge is to achieve a good quality/speed trade-off: deciding when, what, and how to translate. In this study, **we take a data-driven, comparative approach and examine:** (i) What distinguishes simultaneously interpreted text (Interpretese[2]) from batch-translated text (Translationese)? (ii) What strategies do human interpreters use?

Most previous work focuses on qualitative analysis (Bendazzoli and Sandrelli, 2005; Camayd-Freixas, 2011; Shimizu et al., 2014) or pattern counting (Tohyama and Matsubara, 2006; Sridhar et al., 2013). In contrast, we use a more systematic approach based on feature selection and statistical tests. In addition, most work ignores *translated* text, making it hard to isolate strategies applied by interpreters as opposed to general strategies needed for any translation. Shimizu et al. (2014) are the first to take a comparative approach; however, they directly train MT systems on the interpretation corpus without explicitly examining interpretation tactics. While some techniques can be learned implicitly, the model may also learn undesirable behavior such as omission and simplification: byproducts of limited human working memory (Section 4).

Prior work studies simultaneous interpretation of Japanese↔English (Tohyama and Matsubara, 2006; Shimizu et al., 2014) and Spanish↔English (Sridhar et al., 2013). We focus on Japanese↔English interpretation. Since information required by the target English sentence often comes late in the source Japanese sentence (e.g., the verb, the noun being modified), we expect it to reveal a richer set of tactics.[3] Our contributions are three-fold. First, we collect new human translations for an existing simultaneous interpretation corpus, which can benefit future comparative research.[4] Second, we use classification and feature selection methods to examine linguistic characteris-

---

[1]Unlike consecutive interpretation (speakers stop after a complete thought and wait for the interpreter), simultaneous interpretation has the interpreter to translate *while* listening to speakers.

[2]Language produced in the process of translation is often considered a dialect of the target language: "Translationese" (Baker, 1993). Thus, "Interpretese" refers to interpreted language.

[3]The tactics are consistent with those discovered on other language pairs in prior work, with additional ones specific to head-final to head-initial languages.

[4]https://github.com/hhexiy/interpretese

Proceedings of NAACL-HLT 2016, pages 971–976,
San Diego, California, June 12-17, 2016. ©2016 Association for Computational Linguistics

tics comparatively. Third, we categorize human interpretation strategies, including word reordering tactics and summarization tactics. Our results help linguists understand simultaneous interpretation and help computer scientists build better automatic interpretation systems.

2 Distinguishing Translationese and Interpretese

In this section, we discuss strategies used in Interpretese, which we detect automatically in the next section. Our hypothesis is that tactics used by interpreters roughly fall in two non-exclusive categories: (i) *delay minimization*, to enable prompt translation by arranging target words in an order similar to the source; (ii) *memory footprint minimization*, to avoid overloading working memory by reducing communicated information.

Segmentation Interpreters often break source sentences into multiple smaller sentences (Camayd-Freixas, 2011; Shimizu et al., 2013), a process we call segmentation. This is different from what is commonly used in speech translation systems (Fujita et al., 2013; Oda et al., 2014), where translations of segments are directly concatenated. Instead, humans try to incorporate new information into the precedent partial translation, e.g., using "which is" to put it in a clause (Table 1, Example 3), or creating a new sentence joined by conjunctions (Table 1, Example 5).

Passivization Passivization is useful for interpreting from head-final languages (e.g., Japanese, German) to head-initial languages (e.g., English, French) (He et al., 2015). Because the verb is needed early in the target sentence but only appears at the end of the source sentence, an obvious strategy is to wait for the final verb. However, if the interpreter uses passive voice, they can start translating immediately and append the verb at the end (Table 1, Examples 4–5). During passivization, the subject is often omitted when obvious from context.

Generalization Camayd-Freixas (2011) and Al-Khanji et al. (2000) observe that interpreters focus on delivering the gist of a sentence rather than duplicating the nuanced meaning of each word. More frequent words are chosen as their retrieval time is faster (Dell and O'Seaghdha, 1992; Cuetos et al.,

Figure 1: A word cloud visualization of Interpretese (black) and Translationese (gold).

2006) (e.g., "honorific" versus "polite" in Table 1, Example 1). Although Volansky et al. (2013) show that generalization happens in translation too, it is likely more frequent in Interpretese given the severe time constraints.

Summarization Faced with overwhelming information, interpreters need efficient ways to encode meaning. Less important words, or even a whole sentence can drop, especially when the interpreter falls behind the speaker. In Table 1, Example 2, the literal translation "as much as possible" is reduced to "very", and the adjective "Japanese" is omitted.

Before we study these characteristics quantitatively in the next section, we visualize Interpretese and Translationese by a word cloud in Figure 1. The size of each word is proportional to the difference between its frequencies in Interpretese and Translationese (Section 3). The word color indicates whether it is more frequent in Interpretese (black) or Translationese (gold). "the" is over-represented in Interpretese, a phenomenon also occurs in Translationese vs. the original text (Eetemadi and Toutanova, 2014). More conjunction words (e.g., "and", "so", "or", "then") are used in Interpretese, likely for segmentation, whereas "that" is more frequent in Translationese—a sign of clauses. In addition, the pronoun "I" occurs more often in Translationese while "be" and "is" occur more often in Interpretese, which is consistent with our passivization hypothesis.

	Source (S), translation (T) and interpretation (I) text	Tactic
1	(S) この日本語の待遇表現の特徴ですが英語から日本語へ直訳しただけでは表現できないといった特徴があります. (T) (One of) the characteristics of *honorific* Japanese is that it can not be *adequately* expressed when using a direct translation (from English to Japanese). (I) Now let me talk about the characteristic of the Japanese *polite* expressions. ⟨‖⟩ And such such expressions can not be expressed *enough* just by translating directly.	*generalize* <u>segment</u> ⟨‖⟩ (omit)
2	(S) で三番目の特徴としてはですねえ出来る限り自然な日本語の話言葉とてその出力をするといったような特徴があります. (T) Its third *characteristic* is that its output is, as much as possible, in the natural language of spoken (Japanese). (I) And the third *feature* is that the translation could be produced in a very natural spoken language.	*generalize* summarize (omit)
3	(S) まとめますと我々は派生文法という従来の学校文法とは違う文法を使った日本語解析を行っています.その結果従来よりも単純な解析が可能となっております. (T) In sum , we've conducted an analysis on the Japanese language , using a grammar different from school grammar, called derivational grammar. (As a result,) we were able to produce a simpler analysis (than the conventional method). (I) So, we are doing Japanese analysis based on derivational grammar, ⟨‖⟩ which is different from school grammar, ⟨‖⟩ which enables us to analyze in simple way.	segment ⟨‖⟩ (omit)
4	(S) つまり例えばこの表現一は認識できますが二から四は認識できない. (T) They might *recognize* expression one but not *expressions* two to four. (I) The phrase number one only is *accepted* ⟨‖⟩ and *phrases* two, three, four were not *accepted*.	*generalize* passivize segment ⟨‖⟩
5	(S) 以上のお話をまとめますと自然な発話というものを扱うことができる音声対話の方法といういうことを考案しました. (T) In summary , we have *devised* a way for voice interaction systems to handle natural speech. (I) And this is the summary of what I have so far stated. The spontaneous speech can be dealt with by the speech dialog method ⟨‖⟩ and that method was *proposed*.	*generalize* passivize segment ⟨‖⟩

Table 1: Examples of tactics used by interpreters to cope with divergent word orders, limited working memory, and the pressure to produce low-latency translations. We show the source input (S), translated sentences (T), and interpreted sentences (I). The tactics are listed in the rightmost column and marked in the text: more general translations are highlighted in *italics*; ⟨‖⟩ marks where new clauses or sentences are created; and passivized verbs in translation are underlined. Information appearing in translation but omitted in interpretation are in (parentheses). Summarized expressions and their corresponding expression in translation are underlined by wavy lines.

3 Classification of Translationese and Interpretese

We investigate the difference between Translationese and Interpretese by creating a text classifier to distinguish between them and then examining the most useful features. We train our classifier on a bilingual Japanese-English corpus of spoken monologues and their simultaneous interpretations (Matsubara et al., 2002). To obtain a three-way parallel corpus of aligned translation, interpretation, and their shared source text, we first align the interpreted sentences to source sentences by dynamic programming following Ma (2006).[5] This step results in 1684 pairs of text chunks, with 33 tokens per chunk on average. We then collect human translations from Gengo[6] for each source text chunk (one translator per monologue). The original corpus has four interpretors per monologue. We use all available interpretation by copying the translation of a text chunk for its additional interpretation.

3.1 Discriminative Features

We use logistic regression as our classifier. Its job is to tell, given a chunk of English text, which translation produced it. We add ℓ_1 regularization to select the non-zero features that best distinguish Interpretese from Translationese. We experiment with three dif-

---

[5] Sentences are defined by sentence boundaries marked in the corpus, thus coherence is preserved during alignment.

[6] http://gengo.com ("standard" quality).

ferent sets of features: (1) **POS:** n-gram features of POS tags (up to trigram);[7] (2) **LEX:** word unigrams; (3) **LING:** features reflecting linguistic hypothese (Section 2), most of which are counts of indicator functions normalized by length of the chunk (Appendix A).

The top linguistic features listed in Table 3 are consistent with our hypotheses. The most prominent ones—also revealed by POS and LEX—are the segmentation features, including counts of conjunction words (CC), content words (nouns, verbs, adjectives, and adverbs) that appear more than once (repeated), demonstratives (demo) such as *this, that, these, those*, segmented sentences (sent), and proper nouns (NNP). More conjunction words and more sentences in a text chunk are signs of segmentation. Repeated words and the frequent use of demonstratives come from transforming clauses to independent sentences. Next are the passivization features, indicating more passivized verbs (passive) and fewer pronouns (pronoun) in Interpretese. The lack of pronouns may be results of either subject omission during passivization or general omission. The last group are the vocabulary features, showing fewer numbers of stem types, token types, and content words in Interpretese, evidence of word generalization. In addition, a smaller number of content words suggests that interpreters may use more function words to manipulate the sentence structure.

3.2 Classification Results

Recall that our goal is to understand Interpretese, not to classify Interpretese and Translationese; however, the ten-fold cross validation accuracy of LING, POS, LEX are 0.66, 0.85, and 0.94. LEX and POS yield high accuracy as some features are overfitting, e.g., in this dataset, most interpreters used "parsing" for "構文解析" while the translator used "syntactic analysis". Therefore, they do not reveal much about the characteristics of Interpretese except for frequent use of "and" and CC, which indicates segmentation. Similarly, Volansky et al. (2013) and Eetemadi and Toutanova (2014) also find lexical features very effective but not generalizable for detecting Translationese and exclude them from analysis. One reason for the relatively low accuracy of LING may be inconsistent

---

[7]We prepend $\langle$S$\rangle$ and append $\langle$E$\rangle$ to all sentences.

LING		POS		LEX	
CC	+	$\langle$S$\rangle$ CC	+	And	+
repeated	+	. CC	+	parsing	+
demo	+	$\langle$S$\rangle$ CC IN	+	gradual	–
sent	+	NN CC PR	+	syntax	–
passive	+	$\langle$S$\rangle$ CC DT	+	keyboard	+
pronoun	–	CC RB DT	+	attitudinal	–
NNP	+	, RB DT	+	text	–
stem type	–	. CC DT	+	adhoc	+
tok type	–	NN FW NN	+	construction	–
content	–	NN CC RB	–	Furthermore	–

Table 3: Top 10 highest-weighted features in each model. The sign shows whether it is indicative of Interpretese (+) or Translationese (–).

use of strategies among humans (Section 4).

4 Strategy Analysis

To better understand under what situations these tactics are used, we apply two-sample t-tests to compare the following quantities between Interpretese and Translationese: (1) number of inversions (non-monotonic translations) on all source tokens (inv-all), verbs (inv-verb) and nouns (inv-noun); (2) number of segmented sentences; (3) number of natural passivization (pass-st), meaning copying a passive construction in the source sentence into the target sentence, and intentional passivization (pass-t), meaning introducing passivization into the target sentence when the source sentence is in active voice; (4) number of omitted words on the source side and inserted words on the target side;[8] (5) average word frequency given by Microsoft Web n-gram—higher means more common.[9] For all pairs of samples, the null hypothesis H_0 is that the means on Interpretese and Translationese are equal; the alternative hypotheses and results are in Table 2.

As expected, segmentation and intentional passivization happen more often during interpretation. Interpretese has fewer inversions, especially for verbs; reducing word order difference is important for delay minimization. Since there are two to four different interpretations for each lecture, we further analyze how consistent humans are on these decisions. All interpreters agree on segmentation 73.7% of the time, while the agreement on passivization is

---

[8]The number of unaligned words in the source or target.
[9]`http://weblm.research.microsoft.com/`

Sample	inv-all	inv-verb	inv-noun	segment	pass-t	pass-st	omit	insert	word freq
H_a		$\mu_I < \mu_T$		$\mu_I > \mu_T$	$\mu_I > \mu_T$		$\mu_I > \mu_T$		$\mu_I > \mu_T$
t-stat	-1.55	**-3.81**	-2.13	**4.21**	**5.67**	1.41	**16.16**	**10.66**	**7.88**
p-value	.12	<.001	.03	<.001	<.001	.16	<.001	<.001	<.001

Table 2: Two-sample t-tests for Interpretese and Translationese. The test statistics are bolded when we reject H_0 at the 0.05 significance level (two-tailed).

only 57.1%—passivization is an acquired skill; not all interpreters use it when it can speed interpretation.

The tests also confirm our hypotheses on generalization and omission. However, these tactics are not inherent to the task of simultaneous interpretation. Instead, they are a byproduct of humans' limited working memory. Computers can load much larger resources into memory and weigh quality of different translations in an instant, thus potentially rendering the speaker's message more accurately. Therefore, directly learning from corpus of human interpretation may lead to suboptimal results (Shimizu et al., 2014).

5 Conclusion

While we describe how Translationese and Interpretese are different and characterize *how* they differ, the contribution of our work is not just examining an interesting, important dialect. Our work provides opportunities to improve conventional simultaneous MT systems by exploiting and modeling human tactics. He et al. (2015) use hand-crafted rules to decrease latency; our data-driven approach could yield additional strategies for improving MT systems. Another strategy—given the scarcity and artifacts of interpretation corpus—is to select references that present delay-minimizing features of Interpretese from translation corpus (Axelrod et al., 2011). Another future direction is to investigate cognitive inference (Chernov, 2004), which is useful for semantic/syntactic prediction during interpretation (Grissom II et al., 2014; Oda et al., 2015).

A Feature Extraction

We use the Berkeley aligner (Liang et al., 2006) for word alignment, the Stanford POS tagger (Toutanova et al., 2003) to tag English sentences, and Kuromoji [10] to tokenize, lemmatize and tag Japanese sen-

tences. Below we describe the features in detail.

Inversion: Let $\{A_i\}$ be the set of indexes of target words to which each source word w_i is aligned. We count A_i and A_j ($i < j$) as an inverted pair if $\max(A_i) > \min(A_j)$. This means that we have to wait until the jth word to translate the ith word.

Segmentation: We use the `punkt` sentence segmenter (Kiss and Strunk, 2006) from NLTK to detect sentences in a text chunk.

Passivization: We compute the number of passive verbs normalized by the total number of verbs. We detect passive voice in English by matching the following regular expression: a *be* verb (be, are, is, was, were etc.) followed by zero to four non-verb words and one verb in its past participle form. We detect passive voice in Japanese by checking that the dictionary form of a verb has the suffix "れる".

Vocabulary To measure variety, we use V_t/N and V_s/N, where V_t and V_s are counts of distinct tokens and stems, and N is the total number of tokens. To measure complexity, we use word length, number of syllables per word, approximated by vowel sequences; and unigram and bigram frequency from Microsoft Web N-gram.

Summarization We use the sentence compression ratio, sentence length, number of omitted source words, approximated by counts of unaligned words, and number of content words.

Acknowledgments

We thank CIAIR (Nagoya University, Japan) for providing the interpretation data which formed the foundation of this research. We also thank Alvin Grissom II, Naho Orita and the reviewers for their insightful comments. This work was supported by NSF grant IIS-1320538. Boyd-Graber is also partially supported by NSF grants CCF-1409287 and NCSE-1422492. Any opinions, findings, conclusions, or recommendations expressed here are those of the authors and do not necessarily reflect the view of the sponsor.

---

[10] `http://www.atilika.org/`

References

Raja Al-Khanji, Said El-Shiyab, and Riyadh Hussein. 2000. On the use of compensatory strategies in simultaneous interpretation. *Journal des Traducteurs*, 45(3):548–577.

Amittai Axelrod, Xiaodong He, and Jianfeng Gao. 2011. Domain adaptation via pseudo in-domain data selection. In *Proceedings of Empirical Methods in Natural Language Processing (EMNLP)*.

Mona Baker. 1993. Corpus linguistics and translation studies: Implications and applications. In Mona Baker, Gill Francis, and Elena Tognini-Bonelli, editors, *Text and Technology: In Honour of John Sinclair*, pages 233–250.

Claudio Bendazzoli and Annalisa Sandrelli. 2005. An approach to corpus-based interpreting studies: Developing EPIC (european parliament interpreting corpus). In *Proceedings of Challenges of Multidimensional Translation*.

Erik Camayd-Freixas. 2011. Cognitive theory of simultaneous interpreting and training. In *Proceedings of the 52nd Conference of the American Translators Association*.

Ghelly V. Chernov. 2004. *Inference and Anticipation in Simultaneous Interpreting. A Probability-prediction Model*. Amsterdam: John Benjamins Publishing Company.

F. Cuetos, B. Alvarez B, M. González-Nosti, A. Méot, and P. Bonin. 2006. Determinants of lexical access in speech production: role of word frequency and age of acquisition. *Mem Cognit*, 34.

G.S. Dell and P.G. O'Seaghdha. 1992. Stages of lexical access in language production. *Cognition*.

Sauleh Eetemadi and Kristina Toutanova. 2014. Asymmetric features of human generated translation. In *Proceedings of Empirical Methods in Natural Language Processing (EMNLP)*.

Tomoki Fujita, Graham Neubig, Sakriani Sakti, Tomoki Toda, and Satoshi Nakamura. 2013. Simple, lexicalized choice of translation timing for simultaneous speech translation. In *Proceedings of Interspeech*.

Alvin C. Grissom II, He He, Jordan Boyd-Graber, John Morgan, and Hal Daumé III. 2014. Don't until the final verb wait: Reinforcement learning for simultaneous machine translation. In *Proceedings of Empirical Methods in Natural Language Processing (EMNLP)*.

He He, Alvin Grissom II, Jordan Boyd-Graber, John Morgan, and Hal Daumé III. 2015. Syntax-based rewriting for simultaneous machine translation. In *Proceedings of Empirical Methods in Natural Language Processing (EMNLP)*.

Tibor Kiss and Jan Strunk. 2006. Unsupervised multilingual sentence boundary detection. *Computational Linguistics*, 32:485–525.

Percy Liang, Ben Taskar, and Dan Klein. 2006. Alignment by agreement. In *Proceedings of the Conference of the North American Chapter of the Association for Computational Linguistics (NAACL)*.

Xiaoyi Ma. 2006. Champollion: A robust parallel text sentence aligner. In *Proceedings of the Language Resources and Evaluation Conference (LREC)*.

Shigeki Matsubara, Akira Takagi, Nobuo Kawaguchi, and Yasuyoshi Inagaki. 2002. Bilingual spoken monologue corpus for simultaneous machine interpretation research. In *Proceedings of the Language Resources and Evaluation Conference (LREC)*.

Yusuke Oda, Graham Neubig, Sakriani Sakti, Tomoki Toda, and Satoshi Nakamura. 2014. Optimizing segmentation strategies for simultaneous speech translation. In *Proceedings of the annual meeting of the Association for Computational Linguistics (ACL)*.

Yusuke Oda, Graham Neubig, Sakriani Sakti, Tomoki Toda, and Satoshi Nakamura. 2015. Syntax-based simultaneous translation through prediction of unseen syntactic constituents. In *The 53rd Annual Meeting of the Association for Computational Linguistics (ACL)*, Beijing, China, July.

Hiroaki Shimizu, Graham Neubig, Sakriani Sakti, Tomoki Toda, and Satoshi Nakamura. 2013. Constructing a speech translation system using simultaneous interpretation data. In *Proceedings of International Workshop on Spoken Language Translation (IWSLT)*.

Hiroaki Shimizu, Graham Neubig, Sakriani Sakti, Tomoki Toda, and Satoshi Nakamura. 2014. Collection of a simultaneous translation corpus for comparative analysis. In *Proceedings of the Language Resources and Evaluation Conference (LREC)*.

Vivek Kumar Rangarajan Sridhar, John Chen, and Srinivas Bangalore. 2013. Corpus analysis of simultaneous interpretation data for improving real time speech translation. In *Proceedings of Interspeech*.

Hitomi Tohyama and Shigeki Matsubara. 2006. Collection of simultaneous interpreting patterns by using bilingual spoken monologue corpus. In *Proceedings of the Language Resources and Evaluation Conference (LREC)*.

Kristina Toutanova, Dan Klein, Christopher Manning, and Yoram Singer. 2003. Feature-rich part-of-speech tagging with a cyclic dependency network. In *Proceedings of the Conference of the North American Chapter of the Association for Computational Linguistics (NAACL)*.

Vered Volansky, Noam Ordan, and Shuly Wintner. 2013. On the features of translationese. *Literary and Linguistic Computing*, pages 98–118.

LSTM Neural Reordering Feature for Statistical Machine Translation

Yiming Cui, Shijin Wang and **Jianfeng Li**
iFLYTEK Research, Beijing, China
{ymcui,sjwang3,jfli3}@iflytek.com

Abstract

Artificial neural networks are powerful models, which have been widely applied into many aspects of machine translation, such as language modeling and translation modeling. Though notable improvements have been made in these areas, the reordering problem still remains a challenge in statistical machine translations. In this paper, we present a novel neural reordering model that directly models word pairs and their alignment. Further by utilizing LSTM recurrent neural networks, much longer context could be learned for reordering prediction. Experimental results on NIST OpenMT12 Arabic-English and Chinese-English 1000-best rescoring task show that our LSTM neural reordering feature is robust, and achieves significant improvements over various baseline systems.

1 Introduction

In statistical machine translation, the language model, translation model, and reordering model are the three most important components. Among these models, the reordering model plays an important role in phrase-based machine translation (Koehn et al., 2004), and it still remains a major challenge in current study.

In recent years, various phrase reordering methods have been proposed for phrase-based SMT systems, which can be classified into two broad categories:

(1) *Distance-based RM*: Penalize phrase displacements with respect to the degree of non-monotonicity (Koehn et al., 2004).

(2) *Lexicalized RM*: Conditions reordering probabilities on current phrase pairs. According to the orientation determinants, lexicalized reordering model can further be classified into word-based RM (Tillman, 2004), phrase-based RM (Koehn et al., 2007), and hierarchical phrase-based RM (Galley and Manning, 2008).

Furthermore, some researchers proposed a reordering model that conditions both current and previous phrase pairs by utilizing recursive auto-encoders (Li et al., 2014).

In this paper, we propose a novel neural reordering feature by including longer context for predicting orientations. We utilize a long short-term memory recurrent neural network (LSTM-RNN) (Graves, 1997), and directly models word pairs to predict its most probable orientation. Experimental results on NIST OpenMT12 Arabic-English and Chinese-English translation show that our neural reordering model achieves significant improvements over various baselines in 1000-best rescoring task.

2 Related Work

Recently, various neural network models have been applied into machine translation.

Feed-forward neural language model was first proposed by Bengio et al. (2003), which was a breakthrough in language modeling. Mikolov et al. (2011) proposed to use recurrent neural network in language modeling, which can include much longer context history for predicting next word. Experimental results show that RNN-based language model significantly outperform standard feed-forward language model.

Proceedings of NAACL-HLT 2016, pages 977–982,
San Diego, California, June 12-17, 2016. ©2016 Association for Computational Linguistics

Devlin et al. (2014) proposed a neural network joint model (NNJM) by conditioning both source and target language context for target word predicting. Though the network architecture is a simple feed-forward neural network, the results have shown significant improvements over state-of-the-art baselines.

Sundermeyer et al. (2014) also put forward a neural translation model, by utilizing LSTM-based RNN and Bidirectional RNN. In bidirectional RNNs, the target word is conditioned on not only the history but also future source context, which forms a full source sentence for predicting target words.

Li et al. (2013) proposed to use a recursive auto-encoder (RAE) to map each phrase pairs into continuous vectors, and handle reordering problems with a classifier. Also, they suggested that by both including current and previous phrase pairs to determine the phrase orientations could achieve further improvements in accuracy (Li et al., 2014).

By far, we have noticed that this is the first time to use LSTM-RNN in reordering model. We could include much longer context information to determine phrase orientations using RNN architecture. Furthermore, by utilizing the LSTM layer, the network is able to capture much longer range dependencies than standard RNNs.

Because we need to record fixed length of history information in SMT decoding step, we only utilize our LSTM-RNN reordering model as a feature in 1000-best rescoring step. As word alignments are known after generating n-best list, it is possible to use LSTM-RNN reordering model to score each hypothesis.

3 Lexicalized Reordering Model

In traditional statistical machine translation, lexicalized reordering models (Koehn et al., 2007) have been widely used. It considers alignments of current and previous phrase pairs to determine the orientation.

Formally, when given source language sentence $f = \{f_1, ..., f_n\}$, target language sentence $e = \{e_1, ..., e_n\}$, and phrase alignment $a = \{a_1, ..., a_n\}$, the lexicalized reordering model can be illustrated in Equation 1, which only conditions on a_{i-1} and a_i, i.e. previous and current alignment.

$$p(\mathbf{o}|\mathbf{e}, \mathbf{f}) = \prod_{i=1}^{n} p(o_i|e_i, f_{a_i}, a_{i-1}, a_i) \quad (1)$$

In Equation 1, the o_i represents the set of phrase orientations. For example, in the most commonly used MSD-based orientation type, o_i takes three values: M stands for *monotone*, S for *swap*, and D for *discontinuous*. The definition of MSD-based orientation is shown in Equation 2.

$$o_i = \begin{cases} M, & a_i - a_{i-1} = 1 \\ S, & a_i - a_{i-1} = -1 \\ D, & |a_i - a_{i-1}| \neq 1 \end{cases} \quad (2)$$

For other orientation types, such as LR and MSLR are also widely used, whose definition can be found on Moses official website [1].

Recent studies on reordering model suggest that by also conditioning previous phrase pairs can improve context sensitivity and reduce reordering ambiguity.

4 LSTM Neural Reordering Model

In order to include more context information for determining reordering, we propose to use a recurrent neural network, which has been shown to perform considerably better than standard feed-forward architectures in sequence prediction (Mikolov et al., 2011). However, RNN with conventional back-propagation training suffers from gradient vanishing issues (Bengio et al., 1994) .

Later, the long short-term memory was proposed for solving gradient vanishing problem, and it could catch longer context than standard RNNs with sigmoid activation functions. In this paper, we adopt LSTM architecture for training neural reordering model.

4.1 Training Data Processing

For reducing model complexity and easy implementation, our neural reordering model is purely lexicalized and trained on word-level.

We will take LR orientation for explanations, while other orientation types (MSD, MSLR) can be induced similarly. Given a sentence pair and

---

its alignment information, we can induce the word-based reordering information by following steps. Note that, we always evaluate the model in the order of target sentence.

(1) If current target word is one-to-one alignment, then we can directly induce its orientations, i.e. $\langle left \rangle$ or $\langle right \rangle$.

(2) If current source/target word is one-to-many alignment, then we judge its orientation by considering its first aligned target/source word, and the other aligned target/source words are annotated as $\langle follow \rangle$ reordering type, which means these word pairs inherent the orientation of previous word pair.

(3) If current source/target word is not aligned to any target/source words, we introduce a $\langle null \rangle$ token in its opposite side, and annotate this word pair as $\langle follow \rangle$ reordering type.

Figure 1 shows an example of data processing.

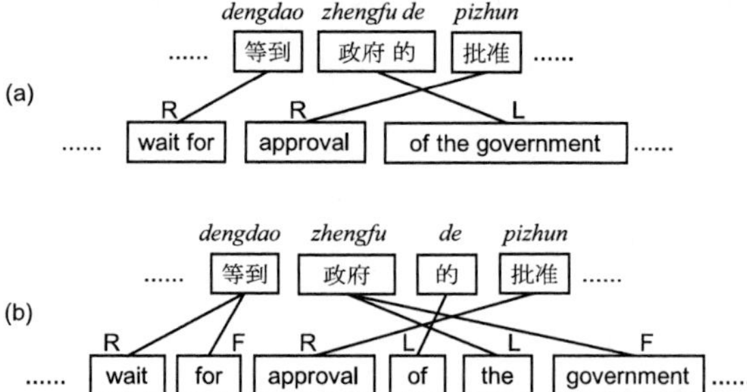

Figure 1: Illustration of data processing. (a) Original reordering (omit alignment inside each phrase); (b) processed reordering, all alignments are regularized to word level, R-right, L-left, F-follow.

4.2 LSTM Network Architecture

After processing the training data, we can directly utilize the word pairs and its orientation to train a neural reordering model.

Given a word pair and its orientation, a neural reordering model can be illustrated by Equation 3.

$$p(\mathbf{o}|\mathbf{e}, \mathbf{f}) = \prod_{i=1}^{n} p(o_i|e_1^i, f_1^{a_i}, a_{i-1}, a_i) \quad (3)$$

Where $e_1^i = \{e_1, ..., e_i\}$, $f_1^{a_i} = \{f_1, ..., f_{a_i}\}$. Inclusion of history word pairs is done with recurrent neural network, which is known for its capability of learning history information.

The architecture of LSTM-RNN reordering model is depicted in Figure 2, and corresponding equations are shown in Equation 4 to 6.

$$y_i = W_1 * f_{a_i} + W_2 * e_i \quad (4)$$

$$z_i = LSTM(y_i, W_3, y_1^{i-1}) \quad (5)$$

$$p(o_i|e_1^i, f_1^{a_i}, a_{i-1}, a_i) = softmax(W_4 * z_i) \quad (6)$$

The input layer consists both source and target language word, which is in one-hot representation. Then we perform a linear transformation of input layer to a projection layer, which is also called embedding layer. We adopt extended-LSTM as our hidden layer implementation, which consists of three gating units, i.e. input, forget and output gates. We omit rather extensive LSTM equations here, which can be found in (Graves and Schmidhuber, 2005). The output layer is composed by orientation types. For example, in LR condition, the output layer contains two units: $\langle left \rangle$ and $\langle right \rangle$ orientation. Finally, we apply softmax function to obtain normalized probabilities of each orientation.

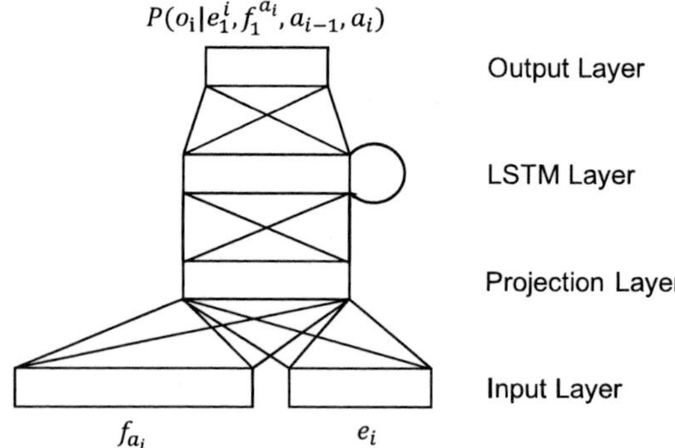

Figure 2: Architecture of LSTM neural reordering model.

5 Experiments

5.1 Setups

We mainly tested our approach on Arabic-English and Chinese-English translation. The training corpus contains 7M words for Arabic, and 4M words for Chinese, which is selected from NIST

System	Dev	Test1	Test2
Ar-En	MT04-05-06 (3795)	MT08 (1360)	MT09 (1313)
Zh-En	MT05-08 (2439)	MT08.prog (1370)	MT12.rd (820)

Table 1: Statistics of development and test set. The number of segments are indicated in brackets.

OpenMT12 parallel dataset. We use the SAMA tokenizer[2] for Arabic word tokenization, and in-house segmenter for Chinese words. The English part of parallel data is tokenized and lowercased. All development and test sets have 4 references for each segment. The statistics of development and test sets are shown in Table 1.

The baseline systems are built with the open-source phrase-based SMT toolkit Moses (Koehn et al., 2007). Word alignment and phrase extraction are done by GIZA++ (Och and Ney, 2000) with L0-normalization (Vaswani et al., 2012), and grow-diag-final refinement rule (Koehn et al., 2004). Monolingual part of training data is used to train a 5-gram language model using SRILM (Stolcke, 2002). Parameter tuning is done by K-best MIRA (Cherry and Foster, 2012). For guarantee of result stability, we tune every system 5 times independently, and take the average BLEU score (Clark et al., 2011). The translation quality is evaluated by case-insensitive BLEU-4 metric (Papineni et al., 2002). The statistical significance test is also carried out with paired bootstrap resampling method with $p < 0.001$ intervals (Koehn, 2004). Our models are evaluated in a 1000-best rescoring step, and all features in 1000-best list as well as LSTM-RNN reordering feature are retuned via K-best MIRA algorithm.

For neural network training, we use all parallel text in the baseline training. As a trade-off between computational cost and performance, the projection layer and hidden layer are set to 100, which is enough for our task (We have not seen significant gains when increasing dimensions greater than 100). We use an initial learning rate of 0.01 with standard SGD optimization without momentum. We trained model for a total of 10 epochs with cross-entropy criterion. Input and output vocabulary are

set to 100K and 50K respectively, and all out-of-vocabulary words are mapped to a $\langle unk \rangle$ token.

5.2 Results on Different Orientation Types

At first, we test our neural reordering model (NRM) on the baseline that contains word-based reordering model with LR orientation. The results are shown in Table 2 and 3.

As we can see that, among various orientation types (LR, MSD, MSLR), our model could give consistent improvements over baseline system. The overall BLEU improvements range from 0.42 to 0.79 for Arabic-English, and 0.31 to 0.72 for Chinese-English systems. All neural results are significantly better than baselines ($p < 0.001$ level).

In the meantime, we also find that "Left-Right" based orientation methods, such as LR and MSLR, consistently outperform MSD-based orientations. The may caused by non-separability problem, which means that MSD-based methods are vulnerable to the change of context, and weak in resolving reordering ambiguities. Similar conclusion can be found in Li et al. (2014) .

Ar-En System	Dev	Test1	Test2
Baseline	43.87	39.84	42.05
+NRM_LR	44.43	40.53	**42.84**
+NRM_MSD	44.29	40.41	42.62
+NRM_MSLR	**44.52**	**40.59**	42.78

Table 2: LSTM reordering model with different orientation types for Arabic-English system.

Zh-En System	Dev	Test1	Test2
Baseline	27.18	26.17	24.04
+NRM_LR	**27.90**	26.58	**24.70**
+NRM_MSD	27.49	26.51	24.39
+NRM_MSLR	27.82	**26.78**	24.53

Table 3: LSTM reordering model with different orientation types for Chinese-English system.

5.3 Results on Different Reordering Baselines

We also test our approach on various baselines, which either contains word-based, phrase-based, or hierarchical phrase-based reordering model. We only show the results of MSLR orientation, which is relatively superior than others according to the results in Section 5.2.

---

[2]https://catalog.ldc.upenn.edu/LDC2010L01

Ar-En System	Dev	Test1	Test2
Baseline_wbe	43.87	39.84	42.05
+NRM_MSLR	44.52	40.59	42.78
Baseline_phr	44.11	40.09	42.21
+NRM_MSLR	44.52	40.73	42.89
Baseline_hier	44.30	40.23	42.38
+NRM_MSLR	44.61	40.82	42.86
Zh-En System	**Dev**	**Test1**	**Test2**
Baseline_wbe	27.18	26.17	24.04
+NRM_MSLR	27.90	26.58	24.70
Baseline_phr	27.33	26.05	24.13
+NRM_MSLR	27.86	26.46	24.73
Baseline_hier	27.56	26.29	24.38
+NRM_MSLR	28.02	26.49	24.67

Table 4: Results on various baselines for Arabic-English and Chinese-English system. "wbe": word-based; "phr": phrase-based; "hier": hierarchical phrase-based reordering model. All NRM results are significantly better than baselines ($p < 0.001$ level).

In Table 4 and 5, we can see that though we add a strong hierarchical phrase-based reordering model in the baseline, our model can still bring a maximum gain of 0.59 BLEU score, which suggest that our model is applicable and robust in various circumstances. However, we have noticed that the gains in Arabic-English system is relatively greater than that in Chinese-English system. This is probably because hierarchical reordering features tend to work better for Chinese words, and thus our model will bring little remedy to its baseline.

6 Conclusions

We present a novel work that build a reordering model using LSTM-RNN, which is much sensitive to the change of context and introduce rich context information for reordering prediction. Furthermore, the proposed model is purely lexicalized and straightforward, which is easy to realize. Experimental results on 1000-best rescoring show that our neural reordering feature is robust, and could give consistent improvements over various baseline systems.

In future, we are planning to extend our word-based LSTM reordering model to phrase-based reordering model, in order to dissolve much more ambiguities and improve reordering accuracy. Further-more, we are also going to integrate our neural reordering model into neural machine translation systems.

Acknowledgments

We sincerely thank the anonymous reviewers for their thoughtful comments on our work.

References

Y. Bengio, P. Simard, and P. Frasconi. 1994. Learning long-term dependencies with gradient descent is difficult. *IEEE Transactions on Neural Networks*, 5(2):157–166.

Yoshua Bengio, Holger Schwenk, Jean Sbastien Sencal, Frderic Morin, and Jean Luc Gauvain. 2003. A neural probabilistic language model. *Journal of Machine Learning Research*, 3(6):1137–1155.

Colin Cherry and George Foster. 2012. Batch tuning strategies for statistical machine translation. In *Proceedings of the 2012 Conference of the North American Chapter of the Association for Computational Linguistics: Human Language Technologies*, pages 427–436, Montréal, Canada, June. Association for Computational Linguistics.

Jonathan H. Clark, Chris Dyer, Alon Lavie, and Noah A. Smith. 2011. Better hypothesis testing for statistical machine translation: Controlling for optimizer instability. In *Proceedings of the 49th Annual Meeting of the Association for Computational Linguistics: Human Language Technologies*, pages 176–181, Portland, Oregon, USA, June. Association for Computational Linguistics.

Jacob Devlin, Rabih Zbib, Zhongqiang Huang, Thomas Lamar, Richard Schwartz, and John Makhoul. 2014. Fast and robust neural network joint models for statistical machine translation. In *Proceedings of the 52nd Annual Meeting of the Association for Computational Linguistics (Volume 1: Long Papers)*, pages 1370–1380, Baltimore, Maryland, June. Association for Computational Linguistics.

Michel Galley and Christopher D. Manning. 2008. A simple and effective hierarchical phrase reordering model. In *Proceedings of the 2008 Conference on Empirical Methods in Natural Language Processing*, pages 848–856, Honolulu, Hawaii, October. Association for Computational Linguistics.

A. Graves and J. Schmidhuber. 2005. Framewise phoneme classification with bidirectional lstm networks. In *Proceedings in 2005 IEEE International Joint Conference on Neural Networks*, pages 2047–2052 vol. 4.

Alex Graves. 1997. Long short-term memory. *Neural Computation*, 9(8):1735–1780.

Philipp Koehn, Franz Josef Och, and Daniel Marcu. 2004. Statistical phrase-based translation. In *Conference of the North American Chapter of the Association for Computational Linguistics on Human Language Technology-volume*, pages 127–133.

Philipp Koehn, Hieu Hoang, Alexandra Birch, Chris Callison-Burch, Marcello Federico, Nicola Bertoldi, Brooke Cowan, Wade Shen, Christine Moran, Richard Zens, Chris Dyer, Ondrej Bojar, Alexandra Constantin, and Evan Herbst. 2007. Moses: Open source toolkit for statistical machine translation. In *Proceedings of the 45th Annual Meeting of the Association for Computational Linguistics Companion Volume Proceedings of the Demo and Poster Sessions*, pages 177–180, Prague, Czech Republic, June. Association for Computational Linguistics.

Philipp Koehn. 2004. Statistical significance tests for machine translation evaluation. In Dekang Lin and Dekai Wu, editors, *Proceedings of EMNLP 2004*, pages 388–395, Barcelona, Spain, July. Association for Computational Linguistics.

Peng Li, Yang Liu, and Maosong Sun. 2013. Recursive autoencoders for ITG-based translation. In *Proceedings of the 2013 Conference on Empirical Methods in Natural Language Processing*, pages 567–577, Seattle, Washington, USA, October. Association for Computational Linguistics.

Peng Li, Yang Liu, Maosong Sun, Tatsuya Izuha, and Dakun Zhang. 2014. A neural reordering model for phrase-based translation. In *Proceedings of COLING 2014, the 25th International Conference on Computational Linguistics: Technical Papers*, pages 1897–1907, Dublin, Ireland, August. Dublin City University and Association for Computational Linguistics.

T. Mikolov, S. Kombrink, L. Burget, and J. H. Cernocky. 2011. Extensions of recurrent neural network language model. In *IEEE International Conference on Acoustics, Speech Signal Processing*, pages 5528–5531.

Franz Josef Och and Hermann Ney. 2000. A comparison of alignment models for statistical machine translation. In *Proceedings of the 18th conference on Computational linguistics - Volume 2*, pages 1086–1090.

Kishore Papineni, Salim Roukos, Todd Ward, and Wei-Jing Zhu. 2002. Bleu: a method for automatic evaluation of machine translation. In *Proceedings of 40th Annual Meeting of the Association for Computational Linguistics*, pages 311–318, Philadelphia, Pennsylvania, USA, July. Association for Computational Linguistics.

Andreas Stolcke. 2002. Srilm — an extensible language modeling toolkit. In *Proceedings of the 7th International Conference on Spoken Language Processing (ICSLP 2002)*, pages 901–904.

Martin Sundermeyer, Tamer Alkhouli, Joern Wuebker, and Hermann Ney. 2014. Translation modeling with bidirectional recurrent neural networks. In *Proceedings of the 2014 Conference on Empirical Methods in Natural Language Processing (EMNLP)*, pages 14–25, Doha, Qatar, October. Association for Computational Linguistics.

Christoph Tillman. 2004. A unigram orientation model for statistical machine translation. In Daniel Marcu Susan Dumais and Salim Roukos, editors, *HLT-NAACL 2004: Short Papers*, pages 101–104, Boston, Massachusetts, USA, May 2 - May 7. Association for Computational Linguistics.

Ashish Vaswani, Liang Huang, and David Chiang. 2012. Smaller alignment models for better translations: Unsupervised word alignment with the l0-norm. In *Proceedings of the 50th Annual Meeting of the Association for Computational Linguistics (Volume 1: Long Papers)*, pages 311–319, Jeju Island, Korea, July. Association for Computational Linguistics.

A Novel Approach to Dropped Pronoun Translation

Longyue Wang[†] **Zhaopeng Tu**[‡] **Xiaojun Zhang**[†] **Hang Li**[‡] **Andy Way**[†] **Qun Liu**[†]

[†]ADAPT Centre, School of Computing, Dublin City University, Ireland

{lwang, xzhang, away, qliu}@computing.dcu.ie

[‡]Noah's Ark Lab, Huawei Technologies, China

{tu.zhaopeng, hangli.hl}@huawei.com

Abstract

Dropped Pronouns (DP) in which pronouns are frequently dropped in the source language but should be retained in the target language are challenge in machine translation. In response to this problem, we propose a semi-supervised approach to recall possibly missing pronouns in the translation. Firstly, we build training data for DP generation in which the DPs are automatically labelled according to the alignment information from a parallel corpus. Secondly, we build a deep learning-based DP generator for input sentences in decoding when no corresponding references exist. More specifically, the generation is two-phase: (1) DP position detection, which is modeled as a sequential labelling task with recurrent neural networks; and (2) DP prediction, which employs a multilayer perceptron with rich features. Finally, we integrate the above outputs into our translation system to recall missing pronouns by both extracting rules from the DP-labelled training data and translating the DP-generated input sentences. Experimental results show that our approach achieves a significant improvement of 1.58 BLEU points in translation performance with 66% F-score for DP generation accuracy.

1 Introduction

In pro-drop languages, certain classes of pronouns can be omitted to make the sentence compact yet comprehensible when the identity of the pronouns can be inferred from the context (Yang et al., 2015). Figure 1 shows an example, in which Chinese is a pro-drop language (Huang, 1984), while English is

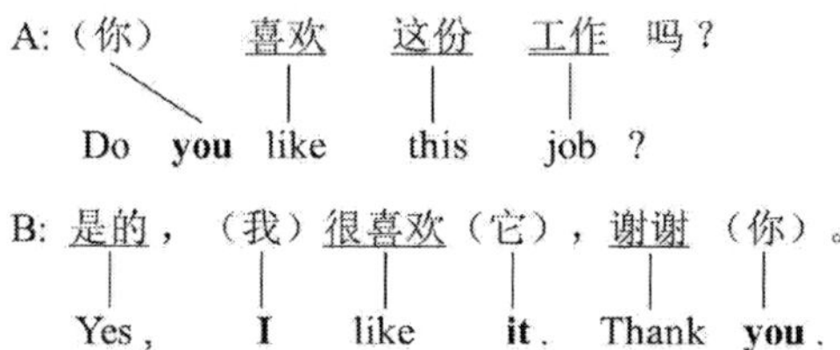

Figure 1: Examples of dropped pronouns in a parallel dialogue corpus. The Chinese pronouns in brackets are dropped.

not (Haspelmath, 2001). On the Chinese side, the subject pronouns {你 (*you*), 我 (*I*)} and the object pronouns {它 (*it*), 你 (*you*)} are omitted in the dialogue between Speakers A and B. These omissions may not be problems for humans since people can easily recall the missing pronouns from the context. However, this poses difficulties for Statistical Machine Translation (SMT) from pro-drop languages (e.g. Chinese) to non-pro-drop languages (e.g. English), since translation of such missing pronouns cannot be normally reproduced. Generally, this phenomenon is more common in informal genres such as dialogues and conversations than others (Yang et al., 2015). We also validated this finding by analysing a large Chinese–English dialogue corpus which consists of 1M sentence pairs extracted from movie and TV episode subtitles. We found that there are 6.5M Chinese pronouns and 9.4M English pronouns, which shows that more than 2.9 million Chinese pronouns are missing.

In response to this problem, we propose to find a general and replicable way to improve translation quality. The main challenge of this research is that training data for DP generation are scarce. Most works either apply manual annotation (Yang et al., 2015) or use existing but small-scale resources such as the Penn Treebank (Chung and Gildea, 2010; Xiang et al., 2013). In contrast, we employ an unsupervised approach to automatically build a large-scale training corpus for DP generation using alignment information from parallel corpora. The idea is that parallel corpora available in SMT can be used to project the missing pronouns from the target side (i.e. non-pro-drop language) to the source side (i.e. pro-drop language). To this end, we propose a simple but effective method: a bi-directional search algorithm with Language Model (LM) scoring.

After building the training data for DP generation, we apply a supervised approach to build our DP generator. We divide the DP generation task into two phases: *DP detection* (from which position a pronoun is dropped), and *DP prediction* (which pronoun is dropped). Due to the powerful capacity of feature learning and representation learning, we model the DP detection problem as sequential labelling with Recurrent Neural Networks (RNNs) and model the prediction problem as classification with Multi-Layer Perceptron (MLP) using features at various levels: from lexical, through contextual, to syntax.

Finally, we try to improve the translation of missing pronouns by explicitly recalling DPs for both parallel data and monolingual input sentences. More specifically, we extract an additional rule table from the DP-inserted parallel corpus to produce a "pronoun-complete" translation model. In addition, we pre-process the input sentences by inserting possible DPs via the DP generation model. This makes the input sentences more consistent with the additional pronoun-complete rule table. To alleviate the propagation of DP prediction errors, we feed the translation system N-best prediction results via confusion network decoding (Rosti et al., 2007).

To validate the effect of the proposed approach, we carried out experiments on a Chinese–English translation task. Experimental results on a large-scale subtitle corpus show that our approach improves translation performance by 0.61 BLEU points (Papineni et al., 2002) using the additional translation model trained on the DP-inserted corpus. Working together with DP-generated input sentences achieves a further improvement of nearly 1.0 BLEU point. Furthermore, translation performance with N-best integration is much better than its 1-best counterpart (i.e. +0.84 BLEU points).

Generally, the contributions of this paper include the following:

- We propose an automatic method to build a large-scale DP training corpus. Given that the DPs are annotated in the parallel corpus, models trained on this data are more appropriate to the translation task;

- Benefiting from representation learning, our deep learning-based generation models are able to avoid ignore the complex feature-engineering work while still yielding encouraging results;

- To decrease the negative effects on translation caused by inserting incorrect DPs, we force the SMT system to arbitrate between multiple ambiguous hypotheses from the DP predictions.

The rest of the paper is organized as follows. In Section 2, we describe our approaches to building the DP corpus, DP generator and SMT integration. Related work is described in Section 3. The experimental results for both the DP generator and translation are reported in Section 4. Section 5 analyses some real examples which is followed by our conclusion in Section 6.

2 Methodology

The architecture of our proposed method is shown in Figure 2, which can be divided into three phases: DP corpus annotation, DP generation, and SMT integration.

2.1 DP Training Corpus Annotation

We propose an approach to automatically annotate DPs by utilizing alignment information. Given a parallel corpus, we first use an unsupervised word alignment method (Och and Ney, 2003; Tu et al., 2012) to produce a word alignment. From observing of the alignment matrix, we found it is possible to detect DPs by projecting misaligned pronouns from the non-pro-drop target side (English) to the pro-drop source side (Chinese). In this work, we focus on nominative and accusative pronouns including personal, possessive and reflexive instances, as listed in Table 1.

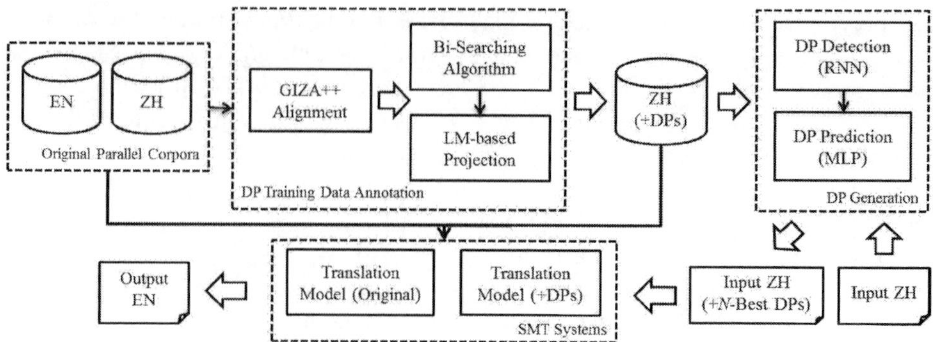

Figure 2: Architecture of proposed method.

Category	Pronouns
Subjective Personal	我 (*I*), 我们 (*we*), 你/你们 (*you*), 他 (*he*), 她 (*she*), 它 (*it*), 他们/她们/它们 (*they*).
Objective Personal	我 (*me*), 我们 (*us*), 你/你们 (*you*), 他 (*him*), 她 (*her*), 它 (*it*), 她们/他们/它们 (*them*).
Possessive	我的 (*my*), 我们的 (*our*), 你的/你们的 (*your*), 他的 (*his*), 她的 (*her*), 它的 (*its*), 他们的/她们的/它们的 (*their*).
Objective Possessive	我的 (*mine*), 我们的 (*ours*), 你的/你们的 (*yours*), 他的 (*his*), 她的 (*hers*), 它的 (*its*), 她们的/他们的/它们的 (*theirs*).
Reflexive	我自己 (*myself*), 我们自己 (*ourselves*), 你自己 (*yourself*), 你们自己 (*yourselves*), 他自己 (*himself*), 她自己 (*herself*), 它自己 (*itself*), 他们自己/她们自己/它们自己 (*themselves*).

Table 1: Pronouns and their categories.

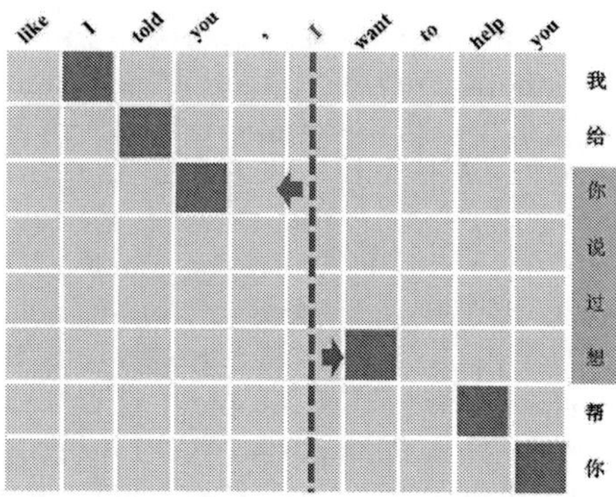

Figure 3: Example of DP projection using alignment results (i.e. blue blocks).

We use an example to illustrate our idea. Figure 3 features a dropped pronoun "我" (not shown) on the source side, which is aligned to the second "*I*" (in red) on the target side. For each pronoun on the target side (e.g. "*I*", "*you*"), we first check whether it has an aligned pronoun on the source side. We find that the second "*I*" is not aligned to any source word and possibly corresponds to a DP_I (e.g. "我"). To determine the possible positions of DP_I on the source side, we employ a *diagonal* heuristic based on the observation that there exists a diagonal rule in the local area of the alignment matrix. For example, the alignment blocks in Figure 3 generally follow a diagonal line. Therefore, the pronoun "*I*" on the target side can be projected to the purple area (i.e. "你 说 过 想") on the source side, according to the preceding and following alignment blocks (i.e. "*you*-你" and "*want*-想").

However, there are still three possible positions to insert DP_I (i.e. the three gaps in the purple area). To further determine the exact position of DP_I, we generate possible sentences by inserting the corresponding Chinese DPs[1] into every possible position. Then we employ an n-gram language model (LM) to score these candidates and select the one with the lowest perplexity as final result. This LM-based projection is based on the observation that the amount and type of DPs are very different in different gen-

---

[1] The Chinese DP can be determined by using its English pronouns according to Table 1. Note that some English pronouns may correspond to different Chinese pronouns, such as "*they* - 他们 / 她们 / 它们". In such cases, we use all the corresponding Chinese pronouns as the candidates.

res. We hypothesize that the DP position can be determined by utilizing the inconsistency of DPs in different domains. Therefore, the LM is trained on a large amount of webpage data (detailed in Section 3.1). Considering the problem of incorrect DP insertion caused by incorrect alignment, we add the original sentence into the LM scoring to reduce impossible insertions (noise).

2.2 DP Generation

In light of the recent success of applying deep neural network technologies in natural language processing (Raymond and Riccardi, 2007; Mesnil et al., 2013), we propose a neural network-based DP generator via the DP-inserted corpus (Section 2.1). We first employ an RNN to predict the DP position, and then train a classifier using multilayer perceptrons to generate our N-best DP results.

2.2.1 DP detection

The task of DP position detection is to label words if there are pronouns missing before the words, which can intuitively be regarded as a sequence labelling problem. We expect the output to be a sequence of labels $y^{(1:n)} = (y^{(1)}, y^{(2)}, \cdots, y^{(t)}, \cdots, y^{(n)})$ given a sentence consisting of words $w^{(1:n)} = (w^{(1)}, w^{(2)}, \cdots, w^{(t)}, \cdots, w^{(n)})$, where $y^{(t)}$ is the label of word $w^{(t)}$. In our task, there are two labels $L = \{NA, DP\}$ (corresponding to non-pro-drop or pro-drop pronouns), thus $y^{(t)} \in L$.

Word embeddings (Mikolov et al., 2013) are used for our generation models: given a word $w^{(t)}$, we try to produce an embedding representation $\mathbf{v}^{(t)} \in \mathbb{R}^d$ where d is the dimension of the representation vectors. In order to capture short-term temporal dependencies, we feed the RNN unit a window of context, as in Equation (1):

$$\mathbf{x_d}^{(t)} = \mathbf{v}^{(t-k)} \oplus \cdots \oplus \mathbf{v}^{(t)} \oplus \cdots \oplus \mathbf{v}^{(t+k)} \quad (1)$$

where k is the window size.

We employ an RNN (Mesnil et al., 2013) to learn the dependency of sentences, which can be formulated as Equation (2):

$$\mathbf{h}^{(t)} = f(\mathbf{U}\mathbf{x_d}^{(t)} + \mathbf{V}\mathbf{h}^{(t-1)}) \quad (2)$$

where $f(x)$ is a sigmoid function at the hidden layer. $\mathbf{U}$ is the weight matrix between the raw input and

ID.	Description
	Lexical Feature Set
1	S surrounding words around p
2	S surrounding POS tags around p
3	preceding pronoun in the same sentence
4	following pronoun in the same sentence
	Context Feature Set
5	pronouns in preceding X sentences
6	pronouns in following X sentences
7	nouns in preceding Y sentences
8	nouns in following Y sentences
	Syntax Feature Set
9	path from current word (p) to the root
10	path from preceding word ($p-1$) to the root

Table 2: List of features.

the hidden nodes, and $\mathbf{V}$ is the weight matrix between the context nodes and the hidden nodes. At the output layer, a softmax function is adopted for labelling, as in Equation (3):

$$y^{(t)} = g(\mathbf{W_d}\mathbf{h}^{(t)}) \quad (3)$$

where $g(z_m) = \frac{e^{z_m}}{\sum_k e^{z_k}}$, and $\mathbf{W_d}$ is the output weight matrix.

2.2.2 DP prediction

Once the DP position is detected, the next step is to determine which pronoun should be inserted based on this result. Accordingly, we train a 22-class classifier, where each class refers to a distinct Chinese pronoun in Table 1. We select a number of features based on previous work (Xiang et al., 2013; Yang et al., 2015), including lexical, contextual, and syntax features (as shown in Table 2). We set p as the DP position, S as the window size surrounding p, and X, Y as the window size surrounding current sentence (the one contains p). For Features 1–4, we extract words, POS tags and pronouns around p. For Features 5–8, we also consider the pronouns and nouns between X/Y surrounding sentences. For Features 9 and 10, in order to model the syntactic relation, we use a path feature, which is the combined tags of the sub-tree nodes from $p/(p-1)$ to the root. Note that Features 3–6 consider all pronouns that were not dropped. Each unique feature is treated as a word, and assigned a "word embedding". The embeddings of the features are then fed to the neural network. We fix the number of features for the variable-length features, where missing ones are tagged as None. Accordingly, all training instances share the same feature length. For the training data, we sample all DP instances from the corpus (annotated by the method in Section 2.1). During decoding, p can be given by our DP detection model.

We employ a feed-forward neural network with four layers. The input $\mathbf{x_p}$ comprises the embeddings of the set of all possible feature indicator names. The middle two layers $\mathbf{a}^{(1)}$, $\mathbf{a}^{(2)}$ use Rectified Linear function R as the activation function, as in Equation (4)–(5):

$$\mathbf{a}^{(1)} = R(\mathbf{b}^{(1)} + \mathbf{W_p}^{(1)}\mathbf{x_p}) \quad (4)$$
$$\mathbf{a}^{(2)} = R(\mathbf{b}^{(2)} + \mathbf{W_p}^{(2)}\mathbf{a}^{(1)}) \quad (5)$$

where $\mathbf{W_p}^{(1)}$ and $\mathbf{b}^{(1)}$ are the weights and bias connecting the first hidden layer to second hidden layer; and so on. The last layer $\mathbf{y_p}$ adopts the softmax function g, as in Equation (6):

$$\mathbf{y_P} = g(\mathbf{W_p}^{(3)}\mathbf{a}^{(2)}) \quad (6)$$

2.3 Integration into Translation

The baseline SMT system uses the parallel corpus and input sentences without inserting/generating DPs. As shown in Figure 2, the integration into SMT system is two fold: DP-inserted translation model (*DP-ins. TM*) and DP-generated input (*DP-gen. Input*).

2.3.1 DP-inserted TM

We train an additional translation model on the new parallel corpus, whose source side is inserted with DPs derived from the target side via the alignment matrix (Section 2.1). We hypothesize that DP insertion can help to obtain a better alignment, which can benefit translation. Then the whole translation process is based on the boosted translation model, i.e. with DPs inserted. As far as TM combination is concerned, we directly feed Moses the multiple phrase tables. The gain from the additional TM is mainly from complementary information about the recalled DPs from the annotated data.

2.3.2 DP-generated input

Another option is to pre-process the input sentence by inserting possible DPs with the DP generation model (Section 2.2) so that the DP-inserted

input (Input ZH+DPs) is translated. The predicted DPs would be explicitly translated into the target language, so that the possibly missing pronouns in the translation might be recalled. This makes the input sentences and DP-inserted TM more consistent in terms of recalling DPs.

2.3.3 N-best inputs

However, the above method suffers from a major drawback: it only uses the 1-best prediction result for decoding, which potentially introduces translation mistakes due to the propagation of prediction errors. To alleviate this problem, an obvious solution is to offer more alternatives. Recent studies have shown that SMT systems can benefit from widening the annotation pipeline (Liu et al., 2009; Tu et al., 2010; Tu et al., 2011; Liu et al., 2013). In the same direction, we propose to feed the decoder N-best prediction results, which allows the system to arbitrate between multiple ambiguous hypotheses from upstream processing so that the best translation can be produced. The general method is to make the input with N-best DPs into a confusion network. In our experiment, each prediction result in the N-best list is assigned a weight of $1/N$.

3 Related Work

There is some work related to DP generation. One is zero pronoun resolution (ZP), which is a subdirection of co-reference resolution (CR). The difference to our task is that ZP contains three steps (namely ZP detection, anaphoricity determination and co-reference link) whereas DP generation only contains the first two steps. Some researchers (Zhao and Ng, 2007; Kong and Zhou, 2010; Chen and Ng, 2013) propose rich features based on different machine-learning methods. For example, Chen and Ng (2013) propose an SVM classifier using 32 features including lexical, syntax and grammatical roles etc., which are very useful in the ZP task. However, most of their experiments are conducted on a small-scale corpus (i.e. OntoNotes)[2] and performance drops correspondingly when using a system-parse tree compared to the gold standard one. Novak and Zabokrtsky (2014) explore cross-language

---

[2]It contains 144K coreference instances, but only 15% of them are dropped subjects.

differences in pronoun behavior to affect the CR results. The experiment shows that bilingual feature sets are helpful to CR. Another line related to DP generation is using a wider range of empty categories (EC) (Yang and Xue, 2010; Cai et al., 2011; Xue and Yang, 2013), which aims to recover long-distance dependencies, discontinuous constituents and certain dropped elements[3] in phrase structure treebanks (Xue et al., 2005). This work mainly focus on sentence-internal characteristics as opposed to contextual information at the discourse level. More recently, Yang et al. (2015) explore DP recovery for Chinese text messages based on both lines of work.

These methods can also be used for DP translation using SMT (Chung and Gildea, 2010; Le Nagard and Koehn, 2010; Taira et al., 2012; Xiang et al., 2013). Taira et al. (2012) propose both simple rule-based and manual methods to add zero pronouns in the source side for Japanese–English translation. However, the BLEU scores of both systems are nearly identical, which indicates that only considering the source side and forcing the insertion of pronouns may be less principled than tackling the problem head on by integrating them into the SMT system itself. Le Nagard and Koehn (2010) present a method to aid English pronoun translation into French for SMT by integrating CR. Unfortunately, their results are not convincing due to the poor performance of the CR method (Pradhan et al., 2012). Chung and Gildea (2010) systematically examine the effects of EC on MT with three methods: pattern, CRF (which achieves best results) and parsing. The results show that this work can really improve the end translation even though the automatic prediction of EC is not highly accurate.

4 Experiments

4.1 Setup

For dialogue domain training data, we extract around 1M sentence pairs (movie or TV episode subtitles) from two subtitle websites.[4] We manually create both development and test data with DP annotation. Note that all sentences maintain their contextual information at the discourse level, which can be used for feature extraction in Section 2.1. The detailed statistics are listed in Table 3. As far as the DP training corpus is concerned, we annotate the Chinese side of the parallel data using the approach described in Section 2.1. There are two different language models for the DP annotation (Section 2.1) and translation tasks, respectively: one is trained on the 2.13TB Chinese Web Page Collection Corpus[5] while the other one is trained on all extracted 7M English subtitle data (Wang et al., 2016).

Corpus	Lang.	Sentents	Pronouns	Ave. Len.
Train	ZH	1,037,292	604,896	5.91
	EN	1,037,292	816,610	7.87
Dev	ZH	1,086	756	6.13
	EN	1,086	1,025	8.46
Test	ZH	1,154	762	5.81
	EN	1,154	958	8.17

Table 3: Statistics of corpora.

We carry out our experiments using the phrase-based SMT model in Moses (Koehn et al., 2007) on a Chinese–English dialogue translation task. Furthermore, we train 5-gram language models using the SRI Language Toolkit (Stolcke, 2002). To obtain a good word alignment, we run GIZA++ (Och and Ney, 2003) on the training data together with another larger parallel subtitle corpus that contains 6M sentence pairs.[6] We use minimum error rate training (Och, 2003) to optimize the feature weights.

The RNN models are implemented using the common Theano neural network toolkit (Bergstra et al., 2010). We use a pre-trained word embedding via a lookup table. We use the following settings: windows = 5, the size of the single hidden layer = 200, iterations = 10, embeddings = 200. The MLP classifier use random initialized embeddings, with the following settings: the size of the single hidden layer = 200, embeddings = 100, iterations = 200.

For end-to-end evaluation, case-insensitive BLEU (Papineni et al., 2002) is used to measure

---

[3]EC includes trace markers, dropped pronoun, big PRO etc, while we focus only on dropped pronoun.

[4]Avaliable at http://www.opensubtitles.org and http://weisheshou.com.

[5]Available at http://www.sogou.com/labs/dl/t-e.html.

[6]Dual Subtitles – Mandarin-English Subtitles Parallel Corpus, extracted by Zhang et al. (2014) without contextual information at the discourse level.

DP	Set	P	R	F1
DP Detection	Dev	0.88	0.84	0.86
	Test	0.88	0.87	0.88
DP Prediction	Dev	0.67	0.63	0.65
	Test	0.67	0.65	0.66

Table 4: Evaluation of DP generation quality.

Systems	Dev Set	Test set
Baseline	20.06	18.76
+DP-ins. TM	20.32 (+0.26)	19.37 (+0.61)
+DP-gen. Input		
1-best	20.49 (+0.43)	19.50 (+0.74)
2-best	20.15 (+0.09)	18.89 (+0.13)
4-best	20.64 (+0.58)	19.68 (+0.92)
6-best	21.61 (+1.55)	20.34 (+1.58)
8-best	20.94 (+0.88)	19.83 (+1.07)
Manual Oracle	24.27 (+4.21)	22.98 (+4.22)
Auto Oracle	23.10 (+3.04)	21.93 (+3.17)

Table 5: Evaluation of DP translation quality.

translation performance and micro-averaged F-score is used to measure DP generation quality.

4.2 Evaluation of DP Generation

We first check whether our DP annotation strategy is reasonable. To this end, we follow the strategy to automatically and manually label the source sides of the development and test data with their target sides. The agreement between automatic labels and manual labels on DP prediction are 94% and 95% on development and test data and on DP generation are 92% and 92%, respectively. This indicates that the automatic annotation strategy is relatively trustworthy.

We then measure the accuracy (in terms of words) of our generation models in two phases. "DP Detection" shows the performance of our sequence-labelling model based on RNN. We only consider the tag for each word (pro-drop or not pro-drop before the current word), without considering the exact pronoun for DPs. "DP Prediction" shows the performance of the MLP classifier in determining the exact DP based on detection. Thus we consider both the detected and predicted pronouns. Table 4 lists the results of the above DP generation approaches. The F1 score of "DP Detection" achieves 88% and 86% on the Dev and Test set, respectively. However, it has lower F1 scores of 66% and 65% for the final pronoun generation ("DP Prediction") on the development and test data, respectively. This indicates that predicting the exact DP in Chinese is a really difficult task. Even though the DP prediction is not highly accurate, we still hypothesize that the DP generation models are reliable enough to be used for end-to-end machine translation. Note that we only show the results of 1-best DP generation here, but in the translation task, we use N-best generation candidates to recall more DPs.

4.3 Evaluation of DP Translation

In this section, we evaluate the end-to-end translation quality by integrating the DP generation results (Section 3.3). Table 5 summaries the results of translation performance with different sources of DP information. "Baseline" uses the original input to feed the SMT system. "+DP-ins. TM" denotes using an additional translation model trained on the DP-inserted training corpus, while "+DP-gen. Input N" denotes further completing the input sentences with the N-best pronouns generated from the DP generation model. "Oracle" uses the input with manual ("Manual") or automatic ("Auto") insertion of DPs by considering the target set. Taking "Auto Oracle" for example, we annotate the DPs via alignment information (supposing the reference is available) using the technique described in Section 2.1.

The baseline system uses the parallel corpus and input sentences without inserting/generating DPs. It achieves 20.06 and 18.76 in BLEU score on the development and test data, respectively. The BLEU scores are relatively low because 1) we have only one reference, and 2) dialogue machine translation is still a challenge for the current SMT approaches.

By using an additional translation model trained on the DP-inserted parallel corpus as described in Section 2.1, we improve the performance consistently on both development (+0.26) and test data (+0.61). This indicates that the inserted DPs are helpful for SMT. Thus, the gain in the "+DP-ins TM" is mainly from the improved alignment quality.

We can further improve translation performance by completing the input sentences with our DP generation model as described in Section 2.2. We test N-best DP insertion to examine the performance, where $N = \{1, 2, 4, 6, 8\}$. Working together with "DP-ins. TM", 1-best generated input already achieves +0.43 and + 0.74 BLEU score improvements on development and test set, respectively. The consistency between the input sentences and the DP-inserted parallel corpus contributes most to these further improvements. As N increases, the BLEU score grows, peaking at 21.61 and 20.34 BLEU points when N=6. Thus we achieve a final improvement of 1.55 and 1.58 BLEU points on the development and test data, respectively. However, when adding more DP candidates, the BLEU score decreases by 0.97 and 0.51. The reason for this may be that more DP candidates add more noise, which harms the translation quality.

The oracle system uses the input sentences with manually annotated DPs rather than "DP-gen. Input". The performance gap between "Oracle" and "+DP-gen. Input" shows that there is still a large space (+4.22 or +3.17) for further improvement for the DP generation model.

5 Case Study

We select sample sentences from the test set to further analyse the effects of DP generation on translation.

In Figure 4, we show an improved case (Case A), an unchanged case (Case B), and a worse case (Case C) of translation no-/using DP insertion (i.e. "+DP-gen. Input 1-best"). In each case, we give (a) the original Chinese sentence and its translation, (b) the DP-inserted Chinese sentence and its translation, and (c) the reference English sentence. In Case A, "*Do you*" in the translation output is compensated by adding DP ⟨你⟩ (you) in (b), which gives a better translation than in (a). In contrast, in case C, our DP generator regards the simple sentence as a compound sentence and insert a wrong pronoun ⟨我⟩ (I) in (b), which causes an incorrect translation output (worse than (a)). This indicates that we need a highly accurate parse tree of the source sentences for more correct completion of the antecedent of the DPs. In Case B, the translation results are the same in (a) and (b). This kind of unchanged case always occurs in "fixed" linguistic chunks such as prepo-

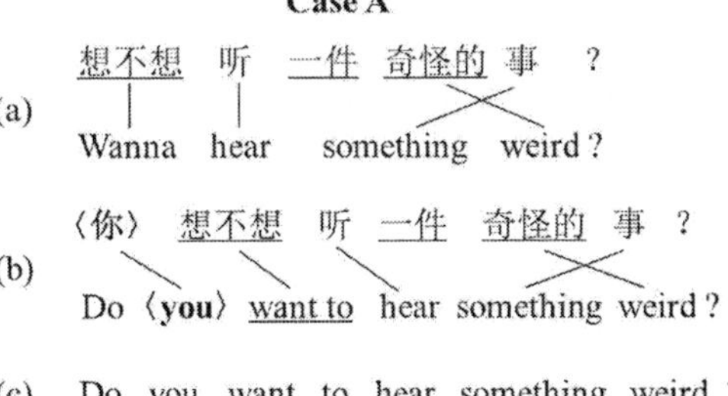

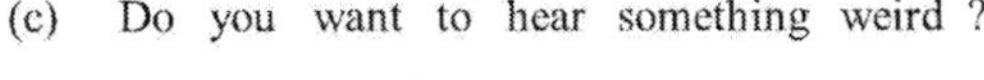

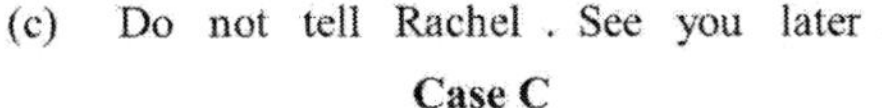

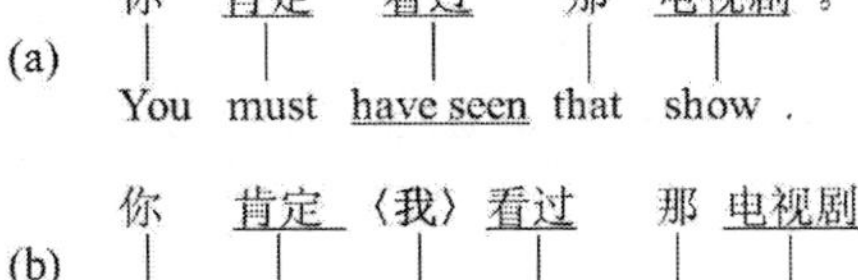

Figure 4: Effects of DP generation for translation.

sition phrases ("on *my* way"), greetings ("see *you* later" , "thank *you*") and interjections ("*My* God"). However, the alignment of (b) is better than that of (a) in this case.

Figure 5 shows an example of "+DP-gen. Input N-best" translation. Here, (a) is the original Chinese sentence and its translation; (b) is the 1-best DP-generated Chinese sentence and its MT output; (c) stands for 2-best, 4-best and 6-best DP-generated Chinese sentences and their MT outputs (which are all the same); (d) is the 8-best DP-generated Chinese sentence and its MT output; (e) is the reference. The N-best DP candidate list is ⟨我⟩ (I), ⟨你⟩ (You), ⟨他⟩ (He), ⟨我们⟩ (We), ⟨他们⟩ (They), ⟨你们⟩ (You), ⟨它⟩ (It) and ⟨她⟩ (She). In (b), when integrating an incorrect 1-best DP into MT, we obtain the wrong translation. However, in (c), when considering more DPs (2-/4-/6-best), the SMT system generates a perfect translation by weighting the DP candidates during decoding. When further increasing N (8-best), (d) shows a wrong translation again due to increased noise.

Case D

(a)
都　不会　想　我　吗　？
Won 't　even　miss　me　?

(b)
〈我〉都　不会　想　我　吗　？
〈I〉 won 't　even　miss　me　?

(c)
〈我|你|...〉都　不会　想　我　吗?
You won 't　even　miss　me　?

(d)
〈我|你|他|...〉都　不会　想　我　吗?
He won 't　even　miss me　?

(e)　You　won 't　even　miss　me　?

Figure 5: Effects of N-best DP generation for translation.

6　Conclusion and Future Work

We have presented a novel approach to recall missing pronouns for machine translation from a pro-drop language to a non-pro-drop language. Experiments show that it is crucial to identify the DP to improve the overall translation performance. Our analysis shows that insertion of DPs affects the translation in a large extent.

Our main findings in this paper are threefold:

- Bilingual information can help to build monolingual models without any manually annotated training data;

- Benefiting from representation learning, neural network-based models work well without complex feature engineering work;

- N-best DP integration works better than 1-best insertion.

In future work, we plan to extend our work to different genres, languages and other kinds of dropped words to validate the robustness of our approach.

Acknowledgments

This work is supported by the Science Foundation of Ireland (SFI) ADAPT project (Grant No.:13/RC/2106), and partly supported by the DCU-Huawei Joint Project (Grant No.:201504032-A (DCU), YB2015090061 (Huawei)). It is partly supported by the Open Projects Program of National Laboratory of Pattern Recognition (Grant 201407353) and the Open Projects Program of Centre of Translation of GDUFS (Grant CTS201501).

References

James Bergstra, Olivier Breuleux, Frederic Bastien, Pascal Lamblin, Razvan Pascanu, Guillaume Desjardins, Joseph Turian, David Warde-Farley, and Yoshua Bengio. 2010. Theano: A cpu and gpu math expression compiler in python. In *Proceedings of Python for Scientific Computing Conference (SciPy)*, pages 3–10, Austin,Texas, USA.

Shu Cai, David Chiang, and Yoav Goldberg. 2011. Language-independent parsing with empty elements. In *Proceedings of the 49th Annual Meeting of the Association for Computational Linguistics: Human Language Technologies: Short Papers - Volume 2*, pages 212–216, Portland, Oregon.

Chen Chen and Vincent Ng. 2013. Chinese zero pronoun resolution: Some recent advances. In *Proceedings of the 2013 Conference on Empirical Methods in Natural Language Processing*, pages 1360–1365, Seattle, Washington, USA.

Tagyoung Chung and Daniel Gildea. 2010. Effects of empty categories on machine translation. In *Proceedings of the 2010 Conference on Empirical Methods in Natural Language Processing*, pages 636–645, Cambridge, Massachusetts, USA.

Martin Haspelmath. 2001. The European linguistic area: standard average European. In *Language typology and language universals. (Handbücher zur Sprach- und Kommunikationswissenschaft)*, volume 2, pages 1492–1510. Berlin: de Gruyter.

C.-T. James Huang. 1984. On the distribution and reference of empty pronouns. *Linguistic Inquiry*, 15(4):531–574.

Philipp Koehn, Hieu Hoang, Alexandra Birch, Chris Callison-Burch, Marcello Federico, Nicola Bertoldi, Brooke Cowan, Wade Shen, Christine Moran, Richard Zens, Chris Dyer, Ondřej Bojar, Alexandra Constantin, and Evan Herbst. 2007. Moses: Open source toolkit for statistical machine translation. In *Proceedings of the 45th Annual Meeting of the Association for*

Computational Linguistics Companion Volume Proceedings of the Demo and Poster Sessions, pages 177–180, Prague, Czech Republic.

Fang Kong and Guodong Zhou. 2010. A tree kernel-based unified framework for chinese zero anaphora resolution. In *Proceedings of the 2010 Conference on Empirical Methods in Natural Language Processing*, pages 882–891, Cambridge, Massachusetts, USA.

Ronan Le Nagard and Philipp Koehn. 2010. Aiding pronoun translation with co-reference resolution. In *Proceedings of the Joint 5th Workshop on Statistical Machine Translation and MetricsMATR*, pages 252–261, Uppsala, Sweden.

Yang Liu, Tian Xia, Xinyan Xiao, and Qun Liu. 2009. Weighted alignment matrices for statistical machine translation. In *Proceedings of the 2009 Conference on Empirical Methods in Natural Language Processing: Volume 2 - Volume 2*, pages 1017–1026, Singapore.

Qun Liu, Zhaopeng Tu, and Shouxun Lin. 2013. A novel graph-based compact representation of word alignment. In *Proceedings of the 51st Annual Meeting of the Association for Computational Linguistics (Volume 2: Short Papers)*, pages 358–363, Sofia, Bulgaria, August. Association for Computational Linguistics.

Grégoire Mesnil, Xiaodong He, Li Deng, and Yoshua Bengio. 2013. Investigation of recurrent-neural-network architectures and learning methods for spoken language understanding. In *Proceedings of the 14th Annual Conference of the International Speech Communication Association*, pages 3771–3775, Lyon, France.

Tomas Mikolov, Ilya Sutskever, Kai Chen, Greg S Corrado, and Jeff Dean. 2013. Distributed representations of words and phrases and their compositionality. In *Proceedings of the 27th Annual Conference on Neural Information Processing Systems*, pages 3111–3119, Lake Tahoe, Nevada, USA.

Michal Novak and Zdenek Zabokrtsky. 2014. Cross-lingual coreference resolution of pronouns. In *Proceedings of the 25th International Conference on Computational Linguistics*, pages 14–24, Dublin, Ireland.

Franz Josef Och and Hermann Ney. 2003. A systematic comparison of various statistical alignment models. *Computational Linguistics*, 29(1):19–51.

Franz Josef Och. 2003. Minimum error rate training in statistical machine translation. In *Proceedings of the 41st Annual Meeting on Association for Computational Linguistics - Volume 1*, pages 160–167, Sapporo, Japan.

Kishore Papineni, Salim Roukos, Todd Ward, and Wei-Jing Zhu. 2002. Bleu: A method for automatic evaluation of machine translation. In *Proceedings of the 40th Annual Meeting on Association for Computational Linguistics*, pages 311–318, Philadelphia, Pennsylvania, USA.

Sameer Pradhan, Alessandro Moschitti, Nianwen Xue, Olga Uryupina, and Yuchen Zhang. 2012. CoNLL-2012 shared task: Modeling multilingual unrestricted coreference in ontonotes. In *Proceedings of the 15th Conference on Computational Natural Language Learning: Shared Task*, pages 1–27, Jeju Island, Korea.

Christian Raymond and Giuseppe Riccardi. 2007. Generative and discriminative algorithms for spoken language understanding. In *Proceedings of 8th Annual Conference of the International Speech Communication Association*, pages 1605–1608, Antwerp, Belgium.

Antti-Veikko I Rosti, Necip Fazil Ayan, Bing Xiang, Spyridon Matsoukas, Richard M Schwartz, and Bonnie J Dorr. 2007. Combining outputs from multiple machine translation systems. In *Proceedings of the Human Language Technology and the 6th Meeting of the North American Chapter of the Association for Computational Linguistics*, pages 228–235, Rochester, NY, USA.

Andreas Stolcke. 2002. Srilm - an extensible language modeling toolkit. In *Proceedings of the 7th International Conference on Spoken Language Processing*, pages 901–904, Colorado, USA.

Hirotoshi Taira, Katsuhito Sudoh, and Masaaki Nagata. 2012. Zero pronoun resolution can improve the quality of j-e translation. In *Proceedings of the 6th Workshop on Syntax, Semantics and Structure in Statistical Translation*, pages 111–118, Jeju, Republic of Korea.

Zhaopeng Tu, Yang Liu, Young-Sook Hwang, Qun Liu, and Shouxun Lin. 2010. Dependency forest for statistical machine translation. In *Proceedings of the 23rd International Conference on Computational Linguistics*, pages 1092–1100, Beijing, China.

Zhaopeng Tu, Yang Liu, Qun Liu, and Shouxun Lin. 2011. Extracting Hierarchical Rules from a Weighted Alignment Matrix. In *Proceedings of the 5th International Joint Conference on Natural Language Processing*, pages 1294–1303, Chiang Mai, Thailand.

Zhaopeng Tu, Yang Liu, Yifan He, Josef van Genabith, Qun Liu, and Shouxun Lin. 2012. Combining multiple alignments to improve machine translation. In *Proceedings of the 24rd International Conference on Computational Linguistics*, pages 1249–1260, Mumbai, India.

Longyue Wang, Xiaojun Zhang, Zhaopeng Tu, Andy Way, and Qun Liu. 2016. The automatic construction of discourse corpus for dialogue translation. In *Proceedings of the 10th Language Resources and Evaluation Conference*, Portorož, Slovenia. (To appear).

Bing Xiang, Xiaoqiang Luo, and Bowen Zhou. 2013. Enlisting the ghost: Modeling empty categories for machine translation. In *Proceedings of the 51st Annual Meeting of the Association for Computational Linguistics (Volume 1: Long Papers)*, pages 822–831, Sofia, Bulgaria.

Nianwen Xue and Yaqin Yang. 2013. Dependency-based empty category detection via phrase structure trees. In *Proceedings of the 2013 Conference of the North American Chapter of the Association for Computational Linguistics: Human Language Technologies*, pages 1051–1060, Atlanta, Georgia, USA.

Naiwen Xue, Fei Xia, Fu-Dong Chiou, and Marta Palmer. 2005. The Penn Chinese Treebank: Phrase structure annotation of a large corpus. *Natural language engineering*, 11(02):207–238.

Yaqin Yang and Nianwen Xue. 2010. Chasing the ghost: recovering empty categories in the Chinese treebank. In *Proceedings of the 23rd International Conference on Computational Linguistics: Posters*, pages 1382–1390, Beijing, China.

Yaqin Yang, Yalin Liu, and Nianwen Xu. 2015. Recovering dropped pronouns from Chinese text messages. In *Proceedings of the 53rd Annual Meeting of the Association for Computational Linguistics and the 7th International Joint Conference on Natural Language Processing (Volume 2: Short Papers)*, pages 309–313, Beijing, China.

Shikun Zhang, Wang Ling, and Chris Dyer. 2014. Dual subtitles as parallel corpora. In *Proceedings of the 10th International Conference on Language Resources and Evaluation*, pages 1869–1874, Reykjavik, Iceland.

Shanheng Zhao and Hwee Tou Ng. 2007. Identification and resolution of Chinese zero pronouns: A machine learning approach. In *Proceedings of the 2007 Joint Conference on Empirical Methods in Natural Language Processing and Computational Natural Language Learning*, pages 541–550, Prague, Czech Republic.

Learning Global Features for Coreference Resolution

Sam Wiseman and **Alexander M. Rush** and **Stuart M. Shieber**
School of Engineering and Applied Sciences
Harvard University
Cambridge, MA, USA
`{swiseman,srush,shieber}@seas.harvard.edu`

Abstract

There is compelling evidence that coreference prediction would benefit from modeling global information about entity-clusters. Yet, state-of-the-art performance can be achieved with systems treating each mention prediction independently, which we attribute to the inherent difficulty of crafting informative cluster-level features. We instead propose to use recurrent neural networks (RNNs) to learn latent, global representations of entity clusters directly from their mentions. We show that such representations are especially useful for the prediction of pronominal mentions, and can be incorporated into an end-to-end coreference system that outperforms the state of the art without requiring any additional search.

1 Introduction

While structured, non-local coreference models would seem to hold promise for avoiding many common coreference errors (as discussed further in Section 3), the results of employing such models in practice are decidedly mixed, and state-of-the-art results can be obtained using a completely local, mention-ranking system.

In this work, we posit that global context is indeed necessary for further improvements in coreference resolution, but argue that informative *cluster*, rather than mention, level features are very difficult to devise, limiting their effectiveness. Accordingly, we instead propose to learn representations of mention clusters by embedding them sequentially using a recurrent neural network (shown in Section 4). Our model has no manually defined cluster features, but

instead learns a global representation from the individual mentions present in each cluster. We incorporate these representations into a mention-ranking style coreference system.

The entire model, including the recurrent neural network and the mention-ranking sub-system, is trained end-to-end on the coreference task. We train the model as a local classifier with fixed context (that is, as a history-based model). As such, unlike several recent approaches, which may require complicated inference during training, we are able to train our model in much the same way as a vanilla mention-ranking model.

Experiments compare the use of learned global features to several strong baseline systems for coreference resolution. We demonstrate that the learned global representations capture important underlying information that can help resolve difficult pronominal mentions, which remain a persistent source of errors for modern coreference systems (Durrett and Klein, 2013; Kummerfeld and Klein, 2013; Wiseman et al., 2015; Martschat and Strube, 2015). Our final system improves over 0.8 points in CoNLL score over the current state of the art, and the improvement is statistically significant on all three CoNLL metrics.

2 Background and Notation

Coreference resolution is fundamentally a clustering task. Given a sequence $(x_n)_{n=1}^{N}$ of (intra-document) mentions – that is, syntactic units that can refer or be referred to – coreference resolution involves partitioning (x_n) into a sequence of clusters $(X^{(m)})_{m=1}^{M}$ such that all the mentions in any particular cluster

Proceedings of NAACL-HLT 2016, pages 994–1004,
San Diego, California, June 12-17, 2016. ©2016 Association for Computational Linguistics

$X^{(m)}$ refer to the same underlying entity. Since the mentions within a particular cluster may be ordered linearly by their appearance in the document,[1] we will use the notation $X_j^{(m)}$ to refer to the j'th mention in the m'th cluster.

A valid clustering places each mention in exactly one cluster, and so we may represent a clustering with a vector $z \in \{1, \dots, M\}^N$, where $z_n = m$ iff x_n is a member of $X^{(m)}$. Coreference systems attempt to find the best clustering $z^* \in \mathcal{Z}$ under some scoring function, with $\mathcal{Z}$ the set of valid clusterings.

One strategy to avoid the computational intractability associated with predicting an entire clustering z is to instead predict a single *antecedent* for each mention x_n; because x_n may not be anaphoric (and therefore have no antecedents), a "dummy" antecedent ϵ may also be predicted. The aforementioned strategy is adopted by "mention-ranking" systems (Denis and Baldridge, 2008; Rahman and Ng, 2009; Durrett and Klein, 2013), which, formally, predict an antecedent $\hat{y} \in \mathcal{Y}(x_n)$ for each mention x_n, where $\mathcal{Y}(x_n) = \{1, \dots, n-1, \epsilon\}$. Through transitivity, these decisions induce a clustering over the document.

Mention-ranking systems make their antecedent predictions with a *local* scoring function $f(x_n, y)$ defined for any mention x_n and any antecedent $y \in \mathcal{Y}(x_n)$. While such a scoring function clearly ignores much structural information, the mention-ranking approach has been attractive for at least two reasons. First, inference is relatively simple and efficient, requiring only a left-to-right pass through a document's mentions during which a mention's antecedents (as well as ϵ) are scored and the highest scoring antecedent is predicted. Second, from a linguistic modeling perspective, mention-ranking models learn a scoring function that requires a mention x_n to be compatible with only *one* of its coreferent antecedents. This contrasts with mention-pair models (e.g., Bengtson and Roth (2008)), which score all pairs of mentions in a cluster, as well as with certain cluster-based models (see discussion in Culotta et al. (2007)). Modeling each mention as having a single antecedent is particularly advantageous for pronominal mentions, which we might like to model

as linking to a single nominal or proper antecedent, for example, but not necessarily to all other coreferent mentions.

Accordingly, in this paper we attempt to maintain the inferential simplicity and modeling benefits of mention ranking, while allowing the model to utilize global, structural information relating to z in making its predictions. We therefore investigate objective functions of the form

$$\arg\max_{y_1, \dots, y_N} \sum_{n=1}^{N} f(x_n, y_n) + g(x_n, y_n, z_{1:n-1}) \quad ,$$

where g is a global function that, in making predictions for x_n, may examine (features of) the clustering $z_{1:n-1}$ induced by the antecedent predictions made through y_{n-1}.

3   The Role of Global Features

Here we motivate the use of global features for coreference resolution by focusing on the issues that may arise when resolving pronominal mentions in a purely local way. See Clark and Manning (2015) and Stoyanov and Eisner (2012) for more general motivation for using global models.

3.1   Pronoun Problems

Recent empirical work has shown that the resolution of pronominal mentions accounts for a substantial percentage of the total errors made by modern mention-ranking systems. Wiseman et al. (2015) show that on the CoNLL 2012 English development set, almost 59% of mention-ranking precision errors and almost 24% of recall errors involve pronominal mentions. Martschat and Strube (2015) found a similar pattern in their comparison of mention-ranking, mention-pair, and latent-tree models.

To see why pronouns can be so problematic, consider the following passage from the "Broadcast Conversation" portion of the CoNLL development set (bc/msnbc/0000/018); below, we enclose mentions in brackets and give the same subscript to co-clustered mentions. (This example is also shown in Figure 2.)

> **DA:** um and [I]$_1$ think that is what's - Go ahead [Linda]$_2$.
>
> **LW:** Well and uh thanks goes to [you]$_1$ and to [the media]$_3$ to help [us]$_4$...So [our]$_4$ hat is off to all of [you]$_5$ as well.

---

[1] We assume nested mentions are ordered by their syntactic heads.

This example is typical of Broadcast Conversation, and it is difficult because local systems learn to myopically link pronouns such as [you]₅ to other instances of the same pronoun that are close by, such as [you]₁. While this is often a reasonable strategy, in this case predicting [you]₁ to be an antecedent of [you]₅ would result in the prediction of an incoherent cluster, since [you]₁ is coreferent with the singular [I]₁, and [you]₅, as part of the phrase "all of you," is evidently plural. Thus, while there is enough information in the text to correctly predict [you]₅, doing so crucially depends on having access to the *history* of predictions made so far, and it is precisely this access to history that local models lack.

More empirically, there are non-local statistical regularities involving pronouns we might hope models could exploit. For instance, in the CoNLL training data over 70% of pleonastic "it" instances and over 74% of pleonastic "you" instances follow (respectively) previous pleonastic "it" and "you" instances. Similarly, over 78% of referential "I" instances and over 68% of referential "he" instances corefer with previous "I" and "he" instances, respectively.

Accordingly, we might expect non-local models with access to global features to perform significantly better. However, models incorporating non-local features have a rather mixed track record. For instance, Björkelund and Kuhn (2014) found that cluster-level features improved their results, whereas Martschat and Strube (2015) found that they did not. Clark and Manning (2015) found that incorporating cluster-level features *beyond* those involving the pre-computed mention-pair and mention-ranking probabilities that form the basis of their agglomerative clustering coreference system did not improve performance. Furthermore, among recent, state-of-the-art systems, mention-ranking systems (which are completely local) perform at least as well as their more structured counterparts (Durrett and Klein, 2014; Clark and Manning, 2015; Wiseman et al., 2015; Peng et al., 2015).

3.2 Issues with Global Features

We believe a major reason for the relative ineffectiveness of global features in coreference problems is that, as noted by Clark and Manning (2015), cluster-level features can be hard to define. Specif-

ically, it is difficult to define discrete, fixed-length features on clusters, which can be of variable size (or shape). As a result, global coreference features tend to be either too coarse or too sparse. Thus, early attempts at defining cluster-level features simply applied the coarse quantifier predicates *all*, *none*, *most* to the mention-level features defined on the mentions (or pairs of mentions) in a cluster (Culotta et al., 2007; Rahman and Ng, 2011). For example, a cluster would have the feature 'most-female=true' if more than half the mentions (or pairs of mentions) in the cluster have a 'female=true' feature.

On the other extreme, Björkelund and Kuhn (2014) define certain cluster-level features by concatenating the mention-level features of a cluster's constituent mentions in order of the mentions' appearance in the document. For example, if a cluster consists, in order, of the mentions (*the president, he, he*), they would define a cluster-level "type" feature 'C-P-P=true', which indicates that the cluster is composed, in order, of a common noun, a pronoun, and a pronoun. While very expressive, these concatenated features are often quite sparse, since clusters encountered during training can be of any size.

4   Learning Global Features

To circumvent the aforementioned issues with defining global features, we propose to learn cluster-level feature representations implicitly, by identifying the state of a (partial) cluster with the hidden state of an RNN that has consumed the sequence of mentions composing the (partial) cluster. Before providing technical details, we provide some preliminary evidence that such learned representations capture important contextual information by displaying in Figure 1 the learned final states of all clusters in the CoNLL development set, projected using T-SNE (van der Maaten and Hinton, 2012). Each point in the visualization represents the learned features for an entity cluster and the head words of mentions are shown for representative points. Note that the model learns to roughly separate clusters by simple distinctions such as predominant type (nominal, proper, pronominal) and number (it, they, etc), but also captures more subtle relationships such as grouping geographic terms and long strings of pronouns.

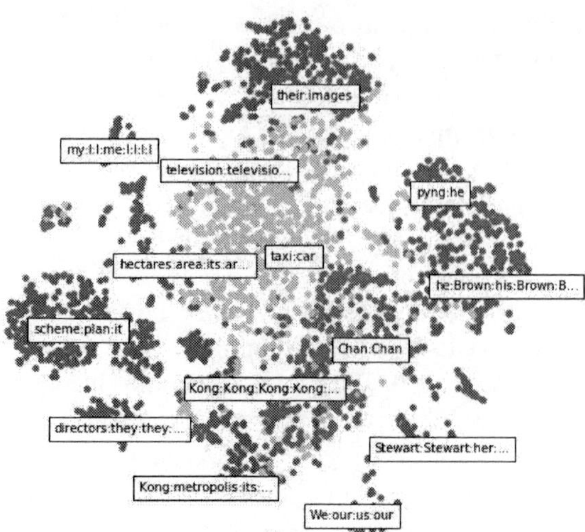

Figure 1: T-SNE visualization of learned entity representations on the CoNLL development set. Each point shows a gold cluster of size > 1. Yellow, red, and purple points represent predominantly common noun, proper noun, and pronoun clusters, respectively. Captions show head words of representative clusters' mentions.

4.1 Recurrent Neural Networks

A recurrent neural network is a parameterized non-linear function $\mathbf{RNN}$ that recursively maps an input sequence of vectors to a sequence of hidden states. Let $(\boldsymbol{m}_j)_{j=1}^{J}$ be a sequence of J input vectors $\boldsymbol{m}_j \in \mathbb{R}^D$, and let $\boldsymbol{h}_0 = \boldsymbol{0}$. Applying an RNN to any such sequence yields

$$\boldsymbol{h}_j \leftarrow \mathbf{RNN}(\boldsymbol{m}_j, \boldsymbol{h}_{j-1}; \boldsymbol{\theta}) \quad ,$$

where $\boldsymbol{\theta}$ is the set of parameters for the model, which are shared over time.

There are several varieties of RNN, but by far the most commonly used in natural-language processing is the Long Short-Term Memory network (LSTM) (Hochreiter and Schmidhuber, 1997), particularly for language modeling (e.g., Zaremba et al. (2014)) and machine translation (e.g., Sutskever et al. (2014)), and we use LSTMs in all experiments.

4.2 RNNs for Cluster Features

Our main contribution will be to utilize RNNs to produce feature representations of entity clusters which will provide the basis of the global term g. Recall that we view a cluster $X^{(m)}$ as a sequence of mentions $(X_j^{(m)})_{j=1}^{J}$ (ordered in linear document or-

der). We therefore propose to embed the state(s) of $X^{(m)}$ by running an RNN over the cluster in order.

In order to run an RNN over the mentions we need an embedding function $\boldsymbol{h}_{\mathrm{c}}$ to map a mention to a real vector. First, following Wiseman et al. (2015) define $\phi_{\mathrm{a}}(x_n) : \mathcal{X} \rightarrow \{0, 1\}^F$ as a standard set of local indicator features on a mention, such as its head word, its gender, and so on. (We elaborate on features below.) We then use a non-linear feature embedding $\boldsymbol{h}_{\mathrm{c}}$ to map a mention x_n to a vector-space representation. In particular, we define

$$\boldsymbol{h}_{\mathrm{c}}(x_n) \triangleq \tanh(\boldsymbol{W}_{\mathrm{c}}\,\phi_{\mathrm{a}}(x_n) + \boldsymbol{b}_{\mathrm{c}}) \quad ,$$

where $\boldsymbol{W}_{\mathrm{c}}$ and $\boldsymbol{b}_{\mathrm{c}}$ are parameters of the embedding.

We will refer to the j'th hidden state of the RNN corresponding to $X^{(m)}$ as $\boldsymbol{h}_j^{(m)}$, and we obtain it according to the following formula

$$\boldsymbol{h}_j^{(m)} \leftarrow \mathbf{RNN}(\boldsymbol{h}_{\mathrm{c}}(X_j^{(m)}), \boldsymbol{h}_{j-1}^{(m)}; \boldsymbol{\theta}) \quad ,$$

again assuming that $\boldsymbol{h}_0^{(m)} = \boldsymbol{0}$. Thus, we will effectively run an RNN over each (sequence of mentions corresponding to a) cluster $X^{(m)}$ in the document, and thereby generate a hidden state $\boldsymbol{h}_j^{(m)}$ corresponding to each step of each cluster in the document. Concretely, this can be implemented by maintaining M RNNs – one for each cluster – that all share the parameters $\boldsymbol{\theta}$. The process is illustrated in the top portion of Figure 2.

5 Coreference with Global Features

We now describe how the RNN defined above is used within an end-to-end coreference system.

5.1 Full Model and Training

Recall that our inference objective is to maximize the score of both a local mention ranking term as well as a global term based on the current clusters:

$$\arg\max_{y_1,\dots,y_N} \sum_{n=1}^{N} f(x_n, y_n) + g(x_n, y_n, \boldsymbol{z}_{1:n-1})$$

We begin by defining the local model $f(x_n, y)$ with the two layer neural network of Wiseman et al. (2015), which has a specialization for the non-anaphoric case, as follows:

$$f(x_n, y) \triangleq \begin{cases} \boldsymbol{u}^{\mathsf{T}} \begin{bmatrix} \boldsymbol{h}_{\mathrm{a}}(x_n) \\ \boldsymbol{h}_{\mathrm{p}}(x_n, y) \end{bmatrix} + u_0 & \text{if } y \neq \epsilon \\ \boldsymbol{v}^{\mathsf{T}} \boldsymbol{h}_{\mathrm{a}}(x_n) + v_0 & \text{if } y = \epsilon \end{cases} \quad .$$

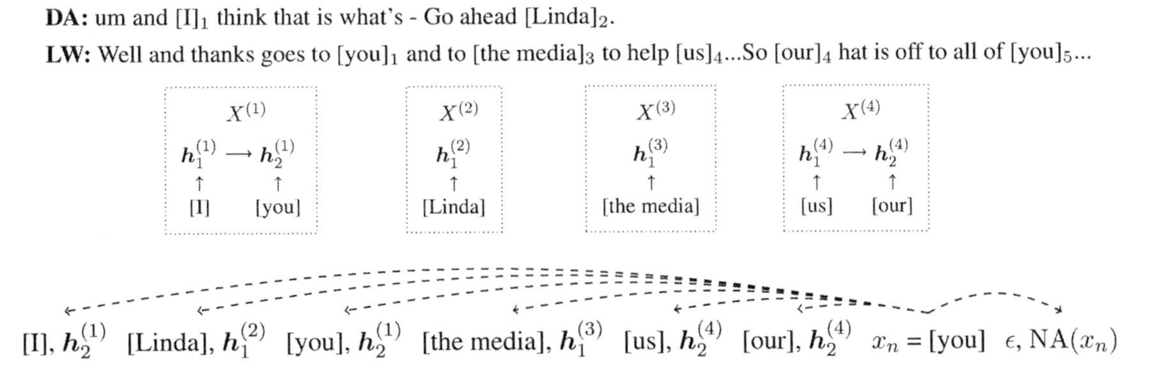

DA: um and [I]$_1$ think that is what's - Go ahead [Linda]$_2$.

LW: Well and thanks goes to [you]$_1$ and to [the media]$_3$ to help [us]$_4$...So [our]$_4$ hat is off to all of [you]$_5$...

Figure 2: Full RNN example for handling the mention $x_n = $ [you]. There are currently four entity clusters in scope $X^{(1)}, X^{(2)}, X^{(3)}, X^{(4)}$ based on unseen previous decisions (y). Each cluster has a corresponding RNN state, two of which ($h^{(1)}$ and $h^{(4)}$) have processed multiple mentions (with $X^{(1)}$ notably including a singular mention [I]). At the bottom, we show the complete mention-ranking process. Each previous mention is considered as an antecedent, and the global term considers the antecedent clusters' current hidden state. Selecting ϵ is treated with a special case $\text{NA}(x_n)$.

Above, u and v are the parameters of the model, and h_a and h_p are learned feature embeddings of the local mention context and the pairwise affinity between a mention and an antecedent, respectively. These feature embeddings are defined similarly to h_c, as

$$h_a(x_n) \triangleq \tanh(W_a \, \phi_a(x_n) + b_a)$$
$$h_p(x_n, y) \triangleq \tanh(W_p \, \phi_p(x_n, y) + b_p) \quad ,$$

where ϕ_a (mentioned above) and ϕ_p are "raw" (that is, unconjoined) features on the context of x_n and on the pairwise affinity between mentions x_n and antecedent y, respectively (Wiseman et al., 2015). Note that h_a and h_c use the same raw features; only their weights differ.

We now specify our global scoring function g based on the history of previous decisions. Define $h_{<n}^{(m)}$ as the hidden state of cluster m before a decision is made for x_n – that is, $h_{<n}^{(m)}$ is the state of cluster m's RNN after it has consumed all mentions in the cluster *preceding* x_n. We define g as

$$g(x_n, y, z_{1:n-1}) \triangleq \begin{cases} h_c(x_n)^\top h_{<n}^{(z_y)} & \text{if } y \neq \epsilon \\ \text{NA}(x_n) & \text{if } y = \epsilon \end{cases} ,$$

where NA gives a score for assigning ϵ based on a non-linear function of all of the current hidden states:

$$\text{NA}(x_n) = q^\top \tanh \left(W_s \left[\begin{smallmatrix} \phi_a(x_n) \\ \sum_{m=1}^{M} h_{<n}^{(m)} \end{smallmatrix} \right] + b_s \right) .$$

See Figure 2 for a diagram. The intuition behind the first case in g is that in considering whether y is a good antecedent for x_n, we add a term to the score that examines how well x_n matches with the mentions already in $X^{(z_y)}$; this matching score is expressed via a dot-product.[2] In the second case, when predicting that x_n is non-anaphoric, we add the NA term to the score, which examines the (sum of) the current states $h_{<n}^{(m)}$ of all clusters. This information is useful both because it allows the non-anaphoric score to incorporate information about potential antecedents, and because the occurrence of certain singleton-clusters often predicts the occurrence of future singleton-clusters, as noted in Section 3.

The whole system is trained end-to-end on coreference using backpropagation. For a given training document, let $z^{(o)}$ be the oracle mapping from mention to cluster, which induces an oracle clustering. While at training time we do have oracle clusters, we do not have oracle antecedents $(y)_{n=1}^N$, so following past work we treat the oracle antecedent as latent (Yu and Joachims, 2009; Fernandes et al., 2012; Chang et al., 2013; Durrett and Klein, 2013). We train with the following slack-rescaled, margin objective:

---

[2] We also experimented with other non-linear functions, but dot-products performed best.

$$\sum_{n=1}^{N} \max_{\hat{y}\in\mathcal{Y}(x_n)} \Delta(x_n,\hat{y})(1 + f(x_n,\hat{y}) + g(x_n,\hat{y},\boldsymbol{z}^{(o)})$$

$$- f(x_n,y_n^{\ell}) - g(x_n,y_n^{\ell},\boldsymbol{z}^{(o)})),$$

where the latent antecedent y_n^{ℓ} is defined as

$$y_n^{\ell} \triangleq \arg\max_{y\in\mathcal{Y}(x_n):z_y^{(o)}=z_n^{(o)}} f(x_n,y) + g(x_n,y,\boldsymbol{z}^{(o)})$$

if x_n is anaphoric, and is ϵ otherwise. The term $\Delta(x_n,\hat{y})$ gives different weight to different error types. We use a Δ with 3 different weights $(\alpha_1,\alpha_2,\alpha_3)$ for "false link" (FL), "false new" (FN), and "wrong link" (WL) mistakes (Durrett and Klein, 2013), which correspond to predicting an antecedent when non-anaphoric, ϵ when anaphoric, and the wrong antecedent, respectively.

Note that in training we use the oracle clusters $\boldsymbol{z}^{(o)}$. Since these are known a priori, we can precompute all the hidden states $\boldsymbol{h}_j^{(m)}$ in a document, which makes training quite simple and efficient. This approach contrasts in particular with the work of Björkelund and Kuhn (2014) — who also incorporate global information in mention-ranking — in that they train against latent *trees*, which are not annotated and must be searched for during training. On the other hand, training on oracle clusters leads to a mismatch between training and test, which can hurt performance.

5.2 Search

When moving from a strictly local objective to one with global features, the test-time search problem becomes intractable. The local objective requires $O(n^2)$ time, whereas the full clustering problem is NP-Hard. Past work with global features has used integer linear programming solvers for exact search (Chang et al., 2013; Peng et al., 2015), or beam search with (delayed) early update training for an approximate solution (Björkelund and Kuhn, 2014). In contrast, we simply use greedy search at test time, which also requires $O(n^2)$ time.[3] The full algorithm

---

is shown in Algorithm 1. The greedy search algorithm is identical to a simple mention-ranking system, with the exception of line 11, which updates the current RNN representation based on the previous decision that was made, and line 4, which then uses this cluster representation as part of scoring.

6 Experiments

6.1 Methods

We run experiments on the CoNLL 2012 English shared task (Pradhan et al., 2012). The task uses the OntoNotes corpus (Hovy et al., 2006), consisting of 3,493 documents in various domains and formats. We use the experimental split provided in the shared task. For all experiments, we use the Berkeley Coreference System (Durrett and Klein, 2013) for mention extraction and to compute features ϕ_a and ϕ_p.

Features We use the raw BASIC+ feature sets described by Wiseman et al. (2015), with the following modifications:

- We remove all features from ϕ_p that concatenate a feature of the antecedent with a feature of the current mention, such as bi-head features.

- We add true-cased head features, a current speaker indicator feature, and a 2-character

---

Algorithm 1 Greedy search with global RNNs

1: **procedure** GREEDYCLUSTER$(x_1,\ldots,x_N)$
2:     Initialize clusters $X^{(1)}\ldots$ as empty lists, hidden states $\boldsymbol{h}^{(0)},\ldots$ as $\boldsymbol{0}$ vectors in $\mathbb{R}^D$, $\boldsymbol{z}$ as map from mention to cluster, and cluster counter $M \leftarrow 0$
3:     **for** $n = 2\ldots N$ **do**
4:         $y^* \leftarrow \arg\max_{y\in\mathcal{Y}(x_n)} f(x_n,y) + g(x_n,y,\boldsymbol{z}_{1:n-1})$
5:         $m \leftarrow z_{y^*}$
6:         **if** $y^* = \epsilon$ **then**
7:             $M \leftarrow M + 1$
8:             $m \leftarrow M$
9:         append x_n to $X^{(m)}$
10:        $z_n \leftarrow m$
11:        $\boldsymbol{h}^{(m)} \leftarrow \text{RNN}(\boldsymbol{h}_c(x_n),\boldsymbol{h}^{(m)})$
12:    **return** $X^{(1)},\ldots,X^{(M)}$

---

[3]While beam search is a natural way to decrease search error at test time, it may fail to help if training involves a *local* margin objective (as in our case), since scores need not be calibrated across local decisions. We accordingly attempted to train various locally normalized versions of our model, but found that they underperformed. We also experimented with training approaches and model variants that expose the model to its own predictions (Daumé III et al., 2009; Ross et al., 2011; Bengio et al., 2015), but found that these yielded a negligible performance improvement.

System	MUC			B^3			CEAF$_e$			CoNLL
	P	R	F$_1$	P	R	F$_1$	P	R	F$_1$	
B&K (2014)	74.3	67.46	70.72	62.71	54.96	58.58	59.4	52.27	55.61	61.63
M&S (2015)	76.72	68.13	72.17	66.12	54.22	59.58	59.47	52.33	55.67	62.47
C&M (2015)	76.12	69.38	72.59	65.64	56.01	60.44	59.44	52.98	56.02	63.02
Peng et al. (2015)	-	-	72.22	-	-	60.50	-	-	56.37	63.03
Wiseman et al. (2015)	76.23	69.31	72.60	66.07	55.83	60.52	59.41	54.88	57.05	63.39
This work	77.49	69.75	**73.42**	66.83	56.95	**61.50**	62.14	53.85	**57.70**	**64.21**

Table 1: Results on CoNLL 2012 English test set. We compare against recent state of the art systems, including (in order) Bjorkelund and Kuhn (2014), Martschat and Strube (2015), Clark and Manning (2015), Peng et al. (2015), and Wiseman et al. (2015). F$_1$ gains are significant ($p < 0.05$ under the bootstrap resample test (Koehn, 2004)) compared with Wiseman et al. (2015) for all metrics.

genre (out of {bc,bn,mz,nw,pt,tc,wb}) indicator to ϕ_p and ϕ_a.

- We add features indicating if a mention has a substring overlap with the current speaker (ϕ_p and ϕ_a), and if an antecedent has a substring overlap with a speaker distinct from the current mention's speaker (ϕ_p).

- We add a single centered, rescaled document position feature to each mention when learning h_c. We calculate a mention x_n's rescaled document position as $\frac{2n-N-1}{N-1}$.

These modifications result in there being approximately 14K distinct features in ϕ_a and approximately 28K distinct features in ϕ_p, which is far fewer features than has been typical in past work.

For training, we use document-size minibatches, which allows for efficient pre-computation of RNN states, and we minimize the loss described in Section 5 with AdaGrad (Duchi et al., 2011) (after clipping LSTM gradients to lie (elementwise) in $(-10, 10)$). We find that the initial learning rate chosen for AdaGrad has a significant impact on results, and we choose learning rates for each layer out of $\{0.1, 0.02, 0.01, 0.002, 0.001\}$.

In experiments, we set $h_a(x_n)$, $h_c(x_n)$, and $h^{(m)}$ to be $\in \mathbb{R}^{200}$, and $h_p(x_n, y) \in \mathbb{R}^{700}$. We use a single-layer LSTM (without "peep-hole" connections), as implemented in the `element-rnn` library (Léonard et al., 2015). For regularization, we apply Dropout (Srivastava et al., 2014) with a rate of 0.4 before applying the linear weights u, and we also apply Dropout with a rate of 0.3 to the LSTM states before forming the dot-product scores.

	MUC	B^3	CEAF$_e$	CoNLL
MR	73.06	62.66	58.98	64.90
Avg, OH	73.30	63.06	58.85	65.07
RNN, GH	73.63	63.23	59.56	65.47
RNN, OH	74.26	63.89	59.54	65.90

Table 2: F$_1$ scores of models described in text on CoNLL 2012 development set. Rows in grey highlight models using oracle history.

Following Wiseman et al. (2015) we use the cost-weights $\alpha = \langle 0.5, 1.2, 1 \rangle$ in defining Δ, and we use their pre-training scheme as well. For final results, we train on both training and development portions of the CoNLL data. Scoring uses the official CoNLL 2012 script (Pradhan et al., 2014; Luo et al., 2014). Code for our system is available at `https://github.com/swiseman/nn_coref`. The system makes use of a GPU for training, and trains in about two hours.

6.2 Results

In Table 1 we present our main results on the CoNLL English test set, and compare with other recent state-of-the-art systems. We see a statistically significant improvement of over 0.8 CoNLL points over the previous state of the art, and the highest F$_1$ scores to date on all three CoNLL metrics.

We now consider in more detail the impact of global features and RNNs on performance. For these experiments, we report MUC, B^3, and CEAF$_e$ F$_1$-scores in Table 2 as well as errors broken down by mention type and by whether the mention is anaphoric or not in Table 3. Table 3 further partitions errors into FL, FN, and WL categories, which

Non-Anaphoric (FL)		
	Nom. HM	Nom. No HM	Pron.
MR	1061	130	1075
Avg, OH	983	140	1011
RNN, GH	914	125	893
RNN, OH	913	130	842
# Mentions	9.0K	22.2K	3.1K

Anaphoric (FN + WL)		
Model	Nom. HM	Nom. No HM	Pron.
MR	665+326	666+56	533+796
Avg, OH	781+300	641+60	578+744
RNN, GH	767+303	648+57	664+727
RNN, OH	750+289	648+52	611+686
# Mentions	4.7K	1.0K	7.3K

Table 3: Number of "false link" (FL) errors on non-anaphoric mentions (top) and number of "false new" (FN) and "wrong link" (WL) errors on anaphoric mentions (bottom) on CoNLL 2012 development set. Mentions are categorized as nominal or proper with (previous) head match (Nom. HM), nominal or proper with no head match (Nom. No HM), and pronominal. Models are described in the text, and rows in grey highlight models using oracle history.

are defined in Section 5.1. We typically think of FL and WL as representing precision errors, and FN as representing recall errors.

Our experiments consider several different settings. First, we consider an oracle setting ("RNN, OH" in tables), in which the model receives $z_{1:n-1}^{(o)}$, the oracle partial clustering of all mentions preceding x_n in the document, and is therefore not forced to rely on its own past predictions when predicting x_n. This provides us with an upper bound on the performance achievable with our model. Next, we consider the performance of the model under a greedy inference strategy (RNN, GH), as in Algorithm 1. Finally, for baselines we consider the mention-ranking system (MR) of Wiseman et al. (2015) using our updated feature-set, as well as a non-local baseline with oracle history (Avg, OH), which averages the representations $h_c(x_j)$ for all $x_j \in X^{(m)}$, rather than feed them through an RNN; errors are still backpropagated through the h_c representations during learning.

In Table 3 we see that the RNN improves performance overall, with the most dramatic improve-

"I had no idea I was getting in so deep," says Mr. Kaye, who founded Justin in 1982. Mr. Kaye had sold Capetronic Inc., a Taiwan electronics Maker, and retired, only to find he was bored. With Justin, he began selling toys and electronics made mostly in Hong Kong, beginning with Mickey Mouse radios. The company has grown -- to about 40 employees, from four initially, Mr. Kaye says. Justin has been profitable since 1986, adds the official, who shares [his] office... (nw/wsj/2418)

Figure 3: Cluster predictions of greedy RNN model; co-clustered mentions are of the same color, and intensity of mention x_j corresponds to $h_c(x_n)^\top h_{<k}^{(i)}$, where $k = j+1$, $i \in \{1, 2\}$, and $x_n =$ "his." See text for full description.

ments on non-anaphoric pronouns, though errors are also decreased significantly for non-anaphoric nominal and proper mentions that follow at least one mention with the same head. While WL errors also decrease for both these mention-categories under the RNN model, FN errors increase. Importantly, the RNN performance is significantly better than that of the Avg baseline, which barely improves over mention-ranking, even with oracle history. This suggests that modeling the sequence of mentions in a cluster is advantageous. We also note that while RNN performance degrades in both precision and recall when moving from the oracle history upper-bound to a greedy setting, we are still able to recover a significant portion of the possible performance improvement.

6.3 Qualitative Analysis

In this section we consider in detail the impact of the g term in the RNN scoring function on the two error categories that improve most under the RNN model (as shown in Table 3), namely, pronominal WL errors and pronominal FL errors. We consider an example from the CoNLL development set in each category on which the baseline MR model makes an error but the greedy RNN model does not.

The example in Figure 3 involves the resolution of the ambiguous pronoun "his," which is bracketed and in bold in the figure. Whereas the baseline MR model *incorrectly* predicts "his" to corefer with the closest gender-consistent antecedent "Justin" — thus making a WL error — the greedy RNN model

> **B:** Yeah, it's not far. Through the S-bahn
> here. I mean it's like twenty minutes.
> **A:** Or something. And so, if I do it, I'd love to
> have you join me . **[It's]** a fancy wedding too.
> (tc/ch/0010)

Figure 4: Magnitudes of gradients of NA score applied to bold "It's" with respect to final mention in three preceding clusters. See text for full description.

correctly predicts "his" to corefer with "Mr. Kaye" in the previous sentence. (Note that "the official" also refers to Mr. Kaye). To get a sense of the greedy RNN model's decision-making on this example, we color the mentions the greedy RNN model has predicted to corefer with "Mr. Kaye" in green, and the mentions it has predicted to corefer with "Justin" in blue. (Note that the model incorrectly predicts the initial "I" mentions to corefer with "Justin.") Letting $X^{(1)}$ refer to the blue cluster, $X^{(2)}$ refer to the green cluster, and x_n refer to the ambiguous mention "his," we further shade each mention x_j in $X^{(1)}$ so that its intensity corresponds to $\boldsymbol{h}_c(x_n)^\top \boldsymbol{h}_{<k}^{(1)}$, where $k = j + 1$; mentions in $X^{(2)}$ are shaded analogously. Thus, the shading shows how highly g scores the compatibility between "his" and a cluster $X^{(i)}$ as each of $X^{(i)}$'s mentions is added. We see that when the initial "Justin" mentions are added to $X^{(1)}$ the g-score is relatively high. However, after "The company" is correctly predicted to corefer with "Justin," the score of $X^{(1)}$ drops, since companies are generally not coreferent with pronouns like "his."

Figure 4 shows an example (consisting of a telephone conversation between "A" and "B") in which the bracketed pronoun "It's" is being used pleonastically. Whereas the baseline MR model predicts "It's" to corefer with a previous "it" — thus making a FL error — the greedy RNN model does not. In Figure 4 the final mention in three preceding clusters is shaded so its intensity corresponds to the magnitude of the gradient of the NA term in g with respect to that mention. This visualization resembles the "saliency" technique of Li et al. (2016), and it attempts to gives a sense of the contribution of a (preceding) cluster in the calculation of the NA score. We see that the potential antecedent "S-Bahn" has a large gradient, but also that the initial, obviously pleonastic use of "it's" has a large gradient, which may suggest that earlier, easier predictions of pleonasm can inform subsequent predictions.

7 Related Work

In addition to the related work noted throughout, we add supplementary references here. Unstructured approaches to coreference typically divide into mention-pair models, which classify (nearly) every pair of mentions in a document as coreferent or not (Soon et al., 2001; Ng and Cardie, 2002; Bengtson and Roth, 2008), and mention-ranking models, which select a single antecedent for each anaphoric mention (Denis and Baldridge, 2008; Rahman and Ng, 2009; Durrett and Klein, 2013; Chang et al., 2013; Wiseman et al., 2015). Structured approaches typically divide between those that induce a clustering of mentions (McCallum and Wellner, 2003; Culotta et al., 2007; Poon and Domingos, 2008; Haghighi and Klein, 2010; Stoyanov and Eisner, 2012; Cai and Strube, 2010), and, more recently, those that learn a latent tree of mentions (Fernandes et al., 2012; Björkelund and Kuhn, 2014; Martschat and Strube, 2015).

There have also been structured approaches that merge the mention-ranking and mention-pair ideas in some way. For instance, Rahman and Ng (2011) rank clusters rather than mentions; Clark and Manning (2015) use the output of both mention-ranking and mention pair systems to learn a clustering.

The application of RNNs to modeling (the trajectory of) the state of a cluster is apparently novel, though it bears some similarity to the recent work of Dyer et al. (2015), who use LSTMs to embed the state of a transition based parser's stack.

8 Conclusion

We have presented a simple, state of the art approach to incorporating global information in an end-to-end coreference system, which obviates the need to define global features, and moreover allows for simple (greedy) inference. Future work will examine improving recall, and more sophisticated approaches to global training.

Acknowledgments

We gratefully acknowledge the support of a Google Research Award.

References

Samy Bengio, Oriol Vinyals, Navdeep Jaitly, and Noam Shazeer. 2015. Scheduled sampling for sequence prediction with recurrent neural networks. In *Advances in Neural Information Processing Systems*, pages 1171–1179.

Eric Bengtson and Dan Roth. 2008. Understanding the Value of Features for Coreference Resolution. In *Proceedings of the 2008 Conference on Empirical Methods in Natural Language Processing*, pages 294–303. Association for Computational Linguistics.

Anders Björkelund and Jonas Kuhn. 2014. Learning structured perceptrons for coreference Resolution with Latent Antecedents and Non-local Features. *ACL, Baltimore, MD, USA, June*.

Jie Cai and Michael Strube. 2010. End-to-end coreference resolution via hypergraph partitioning. In *23rd International Conference on Computational Linguistics (COLING)*, pages 143–151.

Kai-Wei Chang, Rajhans Samdani, and Dan Roth. 2013. A Constrained Latent Variable Model for Coreference Resolution. In *Proceedings of the 2013 Conference on Empirical Methods in Natural Language Processing*, pages 601–612.

Kevin Clark and Christopher D. Manning. 2015. Entity-centric coreference resolution with model stacking. In *Proceedings of the 53rd Annual Meeting of the Association for Computational Linguistics (ACL)*, pages 1405–1415.

Aron Culotta, Michael Wick, Robert Hall, and Andrew McCallum. 2007. First-order Probabilistic Models for Coreference Resolution. In *Human Language Technology Conference of the North American Chapter of the Association of Computational Linguistics (NAACL HLT)*.

Hal Daumé III, John Langford, and Daniel Marcu. 2009. Search-based structured prediction. *Machine Learning*, 75(3):297–325.

Pascal Denis and Jason Baldridge. 2008. Specialized Models and Ranking for Coreference Resolution. In *Proceedings of the 2008 Conference on Empirical Methods in Natural Language Processing*, pages 660–669. Association for Computational Linguistics.

John Duchi, Elad Hazan, and Yoram Singer. 2011. Adaptive Subgradient Methods for Online Learning and Stochastic Optimization. *The Journal of Machine Learning Research*, 12:2121–2159.

Greg Durrett and Dan Klein. 2013. Easy Victories and Uphill Battles in Coreference Resolution. In *Proceedings of the 2013 Conference on Empirical Methods in Natural Language Processing*, pages 1971–1982.

Greg Durrett and Dan Klein. 2014. A Joint Model for Entity Analysis: Coreference, Typing, and Linking. *Transactions of the Association for Computational Linguistics*, 2:477–490.

Chris Dyer, Miguel Ballesteros, Wang Ling, Austin Matthews, and Noah A. Smith. 2015. Transition-based dependency parsing with stack long short-term memory. In *Proceedings of the 53rd Annual Meeting of the Association for Computational Linguistics (ACL)*, pages 334–343.

Eraldo Rezende Fernandes, Cícero Nogueira Dos Santos, and Ruy Luiz Milidiú. 2012. Latent Structure Perceptron with Feature Induction for Unrestricted Coreference Resolution. In *Joint Conference on EMNLP and CoNLL-Shared Task*, pages 41–48. Association for Computational Linguistics.

Aria Haghighi and Dan Klein. 2010. Coreference Resolution in a Modular, Entity-centered Model. In *The 2010 Annual Conference of the North American Chapter of the Association for Computational Linguistics*, pages 385–393. Association for Computational Linguistics.

Sepp Hochreiter and Jürgen Schmidhuber. 1997. Long short-term memory. *Neural Comput.*, 9:1735–1780.

Eduard Hovy, Mitchell Marcus, Martha Palmer, Lance Ramshaw, and Ralph Weischedel. 2006. Ontonotes: the 90% Solution. In *Proceedings of the human language technology conference of the NAACL, Companion Volume: Short Papers*, pages 57–60. Association for Computational Linguistics.

Philipp Koehn. 2004. Statistical Significance Tests for Machine Translation Evaluation. In *Proceedings of the 2004 Conference on Empirical Methods in Natural Language Processing*, pages 388–395. Citeseer.

Jonathan K. Kummerfeld and Dan Klein. 2013. Error-driven Analysis of Challenges in Coreference Resolution. In *Proceedings of the 2013 Conference on Empirical Methods in Natural Language Processing*, Seattle, WA, USA, October.

Nicholas Léonard, Yand Waghmare, Sagar ad Wang, and Jin-Hwa Kim. 2015. rnn: Recurrent Library for Torch. *arXiv preprint arXiv:1511.07889*.

Jiwei Li, Xinlei Chen, Eduard Hovy, and Dan Jurafsky. 2016. Visualizing and understanding neural models in nlp. In *NAACL HLT*.

Xiaoqiang Luo, Sameer Pradhan, Marta Recasens, and Eduard Hovy. 2014. An Extension of BLANC to System Mentions. *Proceedings of ACL, Baltimore, Maryland, June*.

Sebastian Martschat and Michael Strube. 2015. Latent structures for coreference resolution. *TACL*, 3:405–418.

Sebastian Martschat, Thierry Göckel, and Michael Strube. 2015. Analyzing and visualizing coreference resolution errors. In *NAACL HLT*, pages 6–10.

Andrew McCallum and Ben Wellner. 2003. Toward Conditional Models of Identity Uncertainty with Application to Proper Noun Coreference. *Advances in Neural Information Processing Systems 17*.

Vincent Ng and Claire Cardie. 2002. Identifying Anaphoric and Non-anaphoric Noun Phrases to Improve Coreference Resolution. In *Proceedings of the 19th international conference on Computational linguistics-Volume 1*, pages 1–7. Association for Computational Linguistics.

Haoruo Peng, Kai-Wei Chang, and Dan Roth. 2015. A joint framework for coreference resolution and mention head detection. In *Proceedings of the 19th Conference on Computational Natural Language Learning (CoNLL)*, pages 12–21.

Hoifung Poon and Pedro M. Domingos. 2008. Joint unsupervised coreference resolution with markov logic. In *2008 Conference on Empirical Methods in Natural Language Processing (EMNLP)*, pages 650–659.

Sameer Pradhan, Alessandro Moschitti, Nianwen Xue, Olga Uryupina, and Yuchen Zhang. 2012. Conll-2012 Shared Task: Modeling Multilingual Unrestricted Coreference in OntoNotes. In *Joint Conference on EMNLP and CoNLL-Shared Task*, pages 1–40. Association for Computational Linguistics.

Sameer Pradhan, Xiaoqiang Luo, Marta Recasens, Eduard Hovy, Vincent Ng, and Michael Strube. 2014. Scoring Coreference Partitions of Predicted Mentions: A Reference Implementation. In *Proceedings of the Association for Computational Linguistics*.

Altaf Rahman and Vincent Ng. 2009. Supervised Models for Coreference Resolution. In *Proceedings of the 2009 Conference on Empirical Methods in Natural Language Processing: Volume 2-Volume 2*, pages 968–977. Association for Computational Linguistics.

Altaf Rahman and Vincent Ng. 2011. Narrowing the modeling gap: A cluster-ranking approach to coreference resolution. *J. Artif. Intell. Res. (JAIR)*, 40:469–521.

Stéphane Ross, Geoffrey J. Gordon, and Drew Bagnell. 2011. A reduction of imitation learning and structured prediction to no-regret online learning. In *Proceedings of the Fourteenth International Conference on Artificial Intelligence and Statistics*, pages 627–635.

Wee Meng Soon, Hwee Tou Ng, and Daniel Chung Yong Lim. 2001. A Machine Learning Approach to Coreference Resolution of Noun Phrases. *Computational Linguistics*, 27(4):521–544.

Nitish Srivastava, Geoffrey Hinton, Alex Krizhevsky, Ilya Sutskever, and Ruslan Salakhutdinov. 2014. Dropout: A simple way to prevent neural networks from overfitting. *The Journal of Machine Learning Research*, 15(1):1929–1958.

Veselin Stoyanov and Jason Eisner. 2012. Easy-first Coreference Resolution. In *COLING*, pages 2519–2534. Citeseer.

Ilya Sutskever, Oriol Vinyals, and Quoc VV Le. 2014. Sequence to sequence learning with neural networks. In *Advances in Neural Information Processing Systems (NIPS)*, pages 3104–3112.

Laurens van der Maaten and Geoffrey E. Hinton. 2012. Visualizing non-metric similarities in multiple maps. *Machine Learning*, 87(1):33–55.

Sam Wiseman, Alexander M. Rush, Stuart M. Shieber, and Jason Weston. 2015. Learning anaphoricity and antecedent ranking features for coreference resolution. In *Proceedings of the 53rd Annual Meeting of the Association for Computational Linguistics (ACL)*, pages 1416–1426.

Chun-Nam John Yu and Thorsten Joachims. 2009. Learning Structural SVMs with Latent Variables. In *Proceedings of the 26th Annual International Conference on Machine Learning*, pages 1169–1176. ACM.

Wojciech Zaremba, Ilya Sutskever, and Oriol Vinyals. 2014. Recurrent neural network regularization. *CoRR*, abs/1409.2329.

Search Space Pruning: A Simple Solution for Better Coreference Resolvers

Nafise Sadat Moosavi and **Michael Strube**
Heidelberg Institute for Theoretical Studies gGmbH
Schloss-Wolfsbrunnenweg 35
69118 Heidelberg, Germany
`{nafise.moosavi|michael.strube}@h-its.org`

Abstract

There is a significant gap between the performance of a coreference resolution system on gold mentions and on system mentions. This gap is due to the large and unbalanced search space in coreference resolution when using system mentions. In this paper we show that search space pruning is a simple but efficient way of improving coreference resolvers. By incorporating our pruning method in one of the state-of-the-art coreference resolution systems, we achieve the best reported overall score on the CoNLL 2012 English test set. A version of our pruning method is available with the Cort coreference resolution source code.

1 Introduction

Coreference resolution is the task of clustering referring expressions in a text so that each resulting cluster represents an entity. It is a very challenging task in natural language processing and it is still far from being solved, i.e. the best reported overall CoNLL score on the CoNLL 2012 English test set is 63.39 (Wiseman et al., 2015).

Text spans referring to an entity are called mentions. Mentions are the primary objects in a coreference resolution system. As with most previous work on coreference resolution, we only consider mentions that are noun phrases. However, not all of the noun phrases are mentions. A noun phrase may not refer to any entity at all. The pronoun *it* in the sentence *it is raining* is an example of a non-referential noun phrase. Noun phrases which do refer to an entity (mentions) can be further divided into two cat-

egories: mentions referring to entities which only appear once in the discourse (i.e. singletons), and mentions realizing entities that have been referred to more than once in the text (i.e. coreferent mentions). Henceforth, we refer to both singletons and non-referential phrases as non-coreferent mentions. A large number of mentions that appear in a text are non-coreferent. For instance, more than 80% of mentions are singletons in the OntoNotes English development set (Marneffe et al., 2015).

The latent ranking model is the best performing model for coreference resolution to date (Wiseman et al., 2015; Martschat and Strube, 2015). If we use gold mentions, the latent ranking model of Martschat and Strube (2015) achieves an overall score of 80% on the CoNLL 2012 English test set. This result shows that once we have the ideal pruned search space, the ranking model with the current set of features is reasonably capable of finding corresponding entities of mentions. The substantial gap (17%) between the results of the gold mentions and system mentions implies that search space pruning is a promising direction for further improvements in coreference resolution.

Marneffe et al. (2015) examine different search space pruning methods that exist for coreference resolution. Among those, anaphoricity detection is the most popular method (e.g. Ng and Cardie (2002), Denis and Baldridge (2007), Ng (2009), Zhou and Kong (2009), Durrett and Klein (2013), Martschat and Strube (2015), Wiseman et al. (2015), Peng et al. (2015), and Lassalle and Denis (2015)), while singleton detection is a more recent method (Recasens et al., 2013; Ma et al., 2014; Marneffe et al., 2015).

Proceedings of NAACL-HLT 2016, pages 1005–1011,
San Diego, California, June 12-17, 2016. ©2016 Association for Computational Linguistics

Anaphoricity detection examines whether a phrase is anaphoric. Singleton detection examines whether a phrase belongs to a coreference chain regardless of being anaphor or antecedent. Therefore, anaphoricity detection only prunes the search space of anaphors while singleton detection prunes the search space of both anaphors and antecedents.

Except for Clark and Manning (2015), all of the state-of-the-art coreference resolvers explicitly model anaphoricity detection (Martschat and Strube, 2015; Wiseman et al., 2015; Peng et al., 2015). Therefore, modeling search space pruning as singleton detection can provide additional information for the state-of-the-art coreference resolution systems.

In this paper we propose a simple but efficient singleton detection model. We first perform intrinsic evaluations and show that our simple model significantly improves the state-of-the-art results in singleton detection by a large margin. We then evaluate our singleton model extrinsically on coreference resolution showing that search space pruning improves different coreference resolution models.

2 Simple but Efficient Singleton Detection

In this section we show that pruning the coreference resolution search space is not a very difficult task. By using a simple set of features and a standard classifier, we achieve new state-of-the-art results for classifying coreferent and non-coreferent mentions.

Unlike Marneffe et al. (2015) who use both surface (i.e. part-of-speech and n-gram based) features and a large number (123) of carefully designed linguistic features, we select a simple and small set of shallow features:

1. lemmas of all words included in the mention;

2. lemmas of the two previous/next words before/after the mention;

3. part-of-speech tags of all words of the mention;

4. part-of-speech tags of the two previous/next words before/after the mention;

5. complete mention string;

6. length of the mention in words;

7. mention type (proper, nominal, pronominal);

8. whether the whole string of the mention appears again in the document;

9. whether the head of the mention appears again in the document.

We use an anchored SVM (Goldberg and Elhadad, 2007) with a polynomial kernel of degree two for classification. When only few features are available, anchored SVMs generalize much better than soft-margin-SVMs (Goldberg and Elhadad, 2009). In our experiments, we use a count threshold for discarding vary rare lexical features that occur fewer than 10 times.

Similar to Marneffe et al. (2015), we use three different configurations for evaluation. The *Surface* configuration only uses the shallow features. The *Combined* configuration uses the surface features plus the linguistic features introduced by Marneffe et al. (2015). The linguistic features of Marneffe et al. (2015) also include some pairwise combinations of the single features. Since our SVM with a polynomial kernel of degree two implicitly models feature pairs, we only include the single features in our *Combined* configuration. When removing mentions that are classified as non-coreferent during preprocessing, precision matters more than recall in order not to over prune coreferent mentions. To achieve higher precision, the *Confident* configuration uses high confidence predictions of SVM (i.e. classifying a mention as non-coreferent if the SVM output is less or equal to -1, and as coreferent if the output is greater or equal to +1). We use the same set of shallow features as *Surface* for *Confident*. However, Marneffe et al. (2015) use their combined feature set for *Confident*.

2.1 Results

Table 2 shows the results of our singleton detection model in comparison to that of Marneffe et al. (2015). We train our model on the CoNLL 2012 English training set and evaluate it on the development set using recall, precision, F1 measure and accuracy for both coreferent and non-coreferent mentions. Unlike Marneffe et al. (2015) that also use some gold annotations for their features, we extract all of our surface features from `'auto_conll'` files. Therefore, only predicted annotations are used.

The incorporation of linguistic features in Marneffe et al. (2015) improves the classification of both coreferent and non-coreferent mentions by about 1

		#Features	\multicolumn{3}{c}{Non-Coreferent}			\multicolumn{3}{c}{Coreferent}			Accuracy
		#Features	R	P	F1	R	P	F1	Accuracy
Marneffe et al.	Surface	73,393	80.2	79.9	80.0	75.3	75.6	75.4	78.0
	Confident	73,516	56.0	89.8	69.0	48.2	90.7	62.9	52.2
	Combined	73,516	81.1	80.8	80.9	76.4	76.6	76.5	79.0
This work	Surface	8,331	89.37	87.08	88.21	80.32	83.59	81.92	85.73
	Confident	8,331	65.08	94.44	77.06	55.14	93.55	69.38	61.08
	Combined	8,446	89.48	87.16	88.30	80.45	83.76	82.07	85.85

Table 1: Results on the the CoNLL 2012 English development set.

percent in comparison to the *Surface* results. However, in our case, the linguistic features only improve the results by about 0.1 percent.

As the results show, by only using shallow features, we achieve a new state-of-the-art performance for singleton detection that improves the results of Marneffe et al. (2015) by a large margin for classifying both coreferent and non-coreferent mentions.

2.2 Error Analysis

For a singleton detector, precision errors (classifying a coreferent mention as non-coreferent) are more harmful than recall errors. If a coreferent mention is classified as non-coreferent, the recall of the coreference resolver that uses the singleton detector will decrease. On the other hand, recall errors only affect the singleton detector itself and not coreference resolvers.

The precision error ratios of our *Surface* and *Confident* systems for proper name (NAM), nominal (NOM) and pronominal (PRO) mentions are listed in Table 2. For each mention type, Table 2 also shows the precision error ratio by mention type related to the mentions that are first mentions of their corresponding entities. For example, in the *Confident* system 73.45% of the nominal mentions that are incorrectly classified as non-coreferent are first mentions of their corresponding entities. As can be seen, many of the precision errors in both *Surface* and *Confident* systems are errors in which the first mention of an entity is detected as non-coreferent. Detecting whether a mention will be referred to later, is indeed very hard and requires more context information. Features (8) and (9) from our feature set are designed to address the correct detection of the first mentions of entities to a limited degree. These features only address first mentions of entities that are

		NAM	NOM	PRO
Surface	Error rate	23.17	70.61	6.22
	First mentions	57.68	65.54	20.19
Confident	Error rate	23.52	74.70	1.78
	First mentions	62.63	73.45	33.33

Table 2: Precision error ratio.

	NAM	NOM	PRO
Surface	30.48	34.07	35.45
Confident	23.65	58.25	13.50

Table 3: Recall error ratio.

referred to by later mentions with head or complete string match. More features considering properties of other mentions, rather than the examined mention itself, are required in order to improve the correct detection of the first mentions of entities.

Table 3 shows the ratio of recall errors for each mention type. For our *Surface* system, this ratio is more or less the same for different mention types. However, *Confident*'s main source of recall errors is the detection of non-coreferent nominal mentions.

2.3 Discussion

Our results significantly outperform the results of Marneffe et al. (2015) who use both surface features and a set of hand-engineered features targeting different linguistic phenomena related to the task. Our findings are mirrored by Durrett and Klein (2013)'s work on the coreference resolution task. Durrett and Klein (2013) show that a coreference resolution system that uses surface features can outperform those using hand-engineered linguistic features.

Linguistic features like syntactic nearness (on which Hobbs' algorithm (Hobbs, 1978) is based), morpho-syntactic and semantic agreement (e.g. number, gender and semantic class agreements), re-

		MUC			B^3			$CEAF_e$			Avg.
		R	P	F1	R	P	F1	R	P	F1	F1
Stanford	Baseline	64.58	63.65	64.11	49.53	55.21	52.22	53.06	44.82	48.59	54.97
	+Stanford Singleton	64.26	65.19	64.72	49.09	56.84	52.68	52.54	46.55	49.37	55.59
	+Preprocess Pruning	64.27	69.01	66.56	48.65	60.32	53.86	48.71	51.48	50.06	56.83
Cort	Pairwise	68.46	71.01	69.71	54.02	59.47	56.61	51.88	52.17	52.02	59.45
	+Preprocess Pruning	68.19	73.38	70.69	53.62	62.02	57.52	51.42	55.07	53.18	60.46
	Latent Ranking	68.55	77.22	72.63	54.64	66.78	60.11	52.85	60.3	56.33	63.02
	+Pruning Feature	68.81	78.37	73.28	55.46	66.9	60.65	52.07	62.23	56.7	63.54
Wiseman et al. (2015)		69.31	76.23	72.60	55.83	66.07	60.52	54.88	59.41	57.05	63.39

Table 4: Results on the English test set. All the improvements made by our singleton detection models are statistically significant.

cency, focus (Grosz and Sidner, 1986), and centering (Brennan et al., 1987) are examples of useful linguistic features for coreference resolution which have the additional benefit of being applicable to different languages. For example, Hobbs' algorithm and agreement features are being used successfully in the Stanford system (Lee et al., 2013). However, apart from features like these, a large number of linguistically motivated features have been proposed which either do not have a significant impact or are only applicable to a specific language or domain. Therefore, designing general linguistic features which provide information that is not captured by surface features deserve more attention in order to gain higher recall and better generalization.

We combine a simple set of surface features with a standard machine learning model that can handle a large number of surface features. This leads to a new state-of-the-art singleton detection with high precision that can easily be incorporated in a coreference resolution system for pruning non-coreferent mentions.

3   Pruning = Better Coreference Resolvers

In this section, we investigate the effect of search space pruning on coreference resolution. We choose the Stanford rule-based system (Lee et al., 2013) and the Cort[1] system (Martschat and Strube, 2015) as our baselines for coreference resolution. Wiseman et al. (2015) is the best performing coreference resolution system to date. However, we choose Cort as our learning-based baseline because Cort is a framework that allows evaluations on various coreference

---

[1]http://github.com/smartschat/cort

resolution models, i.e. ranking, antecedent trees, and pairwise. The pairwise model is the most commonly used model in coreference resolution, and latent ranking is the best performing model for coreference resolution to date (Wiseman et al., 2015; Martschat and Strube, 2015).

3.1   Results

Table 4 shows the results of integrating singleton detection into different coreference resolution approaches. We evaluate the systems on the CoNLL 2012 English test set using the MUC (Vilain et al., 1995), B^3 (Bagga and Baldwin, 1998), and $CEAF_e$ (Luo, 2005) measures as provided by the CoNLL coreference scorer version 8.01 (Pradhan et al., 2014). According to the approximate randomization test (Noreen, 1989), all of the improvements made by our singleton detection module are statistically significant ($p < 0.05$).

Baseline shows the result of the Stanford system without using singleton detection. *+Stanford Singleton* is the result of the Stanford system including its singleton detection module (Recasens et al., 2013). *+Preprocess Pruning* is the result when our *Confident* model from Section 2 is used.

The singleton detection modules of Recasens et al. (2013) and Marneffe et al. (2015) are incorporated in the Stanford system in a heuristic way: if both anaphor and antecedent are classified as singleton, and none of them is a named entity, then those mentions will be disregarded. However, since our *Confident* model does have a high precision, we use it for removing all non-coreferent mentions in a preprocessing step. As shown in Table 4, our singleton detection improves the overall score of the *Baseline* system by about 2 percent on the test set.

Cort uses a perceptron for learning. Therefore, we use a perceptron in Cort while an anchored SVM would have performed slightly better. We also include all the additional features that are used in Cort for our Cort singleton detection model. SVM accuracy with surface features on the development set is about 0.1 percent better than that of the perceptron with Cort's additional features.

For the pairwise model, singleton detection is performed in a preprocessing step. The singleton detection module improves the overall performance of the pairwise model by about 1 percent on the test set.

The Cort latent model already performs search space pruning in the form of anaphoricity detection. Additional pruning of potential anaphors in the pre-processing step by the singleton model hurts the recall of the latent model. Therefore, we add the output of the singleton model as a new feature for both anaphor and antecedent. For obtaining these features for training, we split the training data into two halves and train a singleton perceptron separately on each half. The values of the singleton feature for the first half are computed based on the model that is trained on the second half, and vice versa. This way, the accuracy of singleton features on both training and testing is similar. If we would train the singleton model on the whole training data, we would overfit the model seriously. The values of the singleton feature would be very accurate on the training data, and the learner would overestimate the importance of this feature.

The new feature improves the overall performance of the latent ranking model by about 0.5 percent on the test set. This result is the best reported overall score for coreference resolution on the CoNLL 2012 English test set to date.

The singleton feature support is added to the Cort source code. It is available at http://github.com/smartschat/cort.

3.2 Discussion

Recent improvements in coreference resolution have been made by exploring more complex learning and inference strategies, a larger number of features, and joint processing. There are also technically viable solutions for improving the performance of a coreference resolver which do not work in practice. For instance, since coreference resolution is a set partitioning problem, entity-based models seem to be more suitable for coreference resolution than mention-pair models. However, entity-based models do not necessarily perform better than mention-pair models (e.g. Ng (2010) and Moosavi and Strube (2014)). The same is true for incorporating more semantic-level information in a coreference resolution system (e.g. Durrett and Klein (2013)).

In this paper, we show that coreference resolution can also simply be improved by performing search space pruning. The significant gap between the performance of the latent ranking model on gold mentions and on system mentions indicates that there is still room for further improvements in search space pruning.

4   Conclusions

We achieve new state-of-the-art results for singleton detection by only using shallow features and simple classifiers. We also show that search space pruning significantly improves different coreference resolution models. The substantial gap between the performance on gold mentions and on system mentions indicates that there is still plenty of room for further improvements in singleton detection. Therefore, search space pruning is a promising direction for further improvements in coreference resolution. The proposed singleton detector as a feature for coreference resolvers is implemented for the Cort coreference resolver. It is available with the Cort source code.

Acknowledgments

The authors would like to thank Sebastian Martschat for his help to use the proposed singleton detector in the Cort coreference resolver. We would also like to thank Mark-Christoph Müller, Benjamin Heinzerling, Mohsen Mesgar, Daraksha Parveen and Alex Judea for their helpful comments. This work has been funded by the Klaus Tschira Foundation, Heidelberg, Germany. The first author has been supported by a Heidelberg Institute for Theoretical Studies PhD. scholarship.

References

Amit Bagga and Breck Baldwin. 1998. Algorithms for scoring coreference chains. In *Proceedings of the 1st International Conference on Language Resources and Evaluation,* Granada, Spain, 28–30 May 1998, pages 563–566.

Susan E. Brennan, Marilyn W. Friedman, and Carl J. Pollard. 1987. A centering approach to pronouns. In *Proceedings of the 25th Annual Meeting of the Association for Computational Linguistics,* Stanford, Cal., 6–9 July 1987, pages 155–162.

Kevin Clark and Christopher D. Manning. 2015. Entity-centric coreference resolution with model stacking. In *Proceedings of the 53rd Annual Meeting of the Association for Computational Linguistics (Volume 1: Long Papers),* Beijing, China, 26–31 July 2015, pages 1405–1415.

Pascal Denis and Jason Baldridge. 2007. Joint determination of anaphoricity and coreference resolution using integer programming. In *Proceedings of Human Language Technologies 2007: The Conference of the North American Chapter of the Association for Computational Linguistics,* Rochester, N.Y., 22–27 April 2007, pages 236–243.

Greg Durrett and Dan Klein. 2013. Easy victories and uphill battles in coreference resolution. In *Proceedings of the 2013 Conference on Empirical Methods in Natural Language Processing,* Seattle, Wash., 18–21 October 2013, pages 1971–1982.

Yoav Goldberg and Michael Elhadad. 2007. SVM model tampering and anchored learning: A case study in Hebrew NP chunking. In *Proceedings of the 45th Annual Meeting of the Association for Computational Linguistics,* Prague, Czech Republic, 23–30 June 2007, pages 224–231.

Yoav Goldberg and Michael Elhadad. 2009. On the role of lexical features in sequence labeling. In *Proceedings of the 2009 Conference on Empirical Methods in Natural Language Processing,* Singapore, 6–7 August 2009, pages 1142–1151.

Barbara J. Grosz and Candace L. Sidner. 1986. Attention, intentions, and the structure of discourse. *Computational Linguistics,* 12(3):175–204.

Jerry R. Hobbs. 1978. Resolving pronominal references. *Lingua,* 44:311–338.

Emmanuel Lassalle and Pascal Denis. 2015. Joint anaphoricity detection and coreference resolution with constrained latent structures. In *Proceedings of the 29th Conference on the Advancement of Artificial Intelligence,* Austin, Texas, 25–30 January 2015, pages 2274–2280.

Heeyoung Lee, Angel Chang, Yves Peirsman, Nathanael Chambers, Mihai Surdeanu, and Dan Jurafsky. 2013. Deterministic coreference resolution based on entity-centric, precision-ranked rules. *Computational Linguistics,* 39(4):885–916.

Xiaoqiang Luo. 2005. On coreference resolution performance metrics. In *Proceedings of the Human Language Technology Conference and the 2005 Conference on Empirical Methods in Natural Language Processing,* Vancouver, B.C., Canada, 6–8 October 2005, pages 25–32.

Chao Ma, Janardhan Rao Doppa, J. Walker Orr, Prashanth Mannem, Xiaoli Fern, Tom Dietterich, and Prasad Tadepalli. 2014. Prune-and-score: Learning for greedy coreference resolution. In *Proceedings of the 2014 Conference on Empirical Methods in Natural Language Processing,* Doha, Qatar, 25–29 October 2014, pages 2115–2126.

Marie-Catherine de Marneffe, Marta Recasens, and Christopher Potts. 2015. Modeling the lifespan of discourse entities with application to coreference resolution. *Journal of Artificial Intelligent Research,* 52:445–475.

Sebastian Martschat and Michael Strube. 2015. Latent structures for coreference resolution. *Transactions of the Association for Computational Linguistics,* 3:405–418.

Nafise Sadat Moosavi and Michael Strube. 2014. Unsupervised coreference resolution by utilizing the most informative relations. In *Proceedings of the 25th International Conference on Computational Linguistics,* Dublin, Ireland, 23–29 August 2014, pages 644–655.

Vincent Ng and Claire Cardie. 2002. Identifying anaphoric and non-anaphoric noun phrases to improve coreference resolution. In *Proceedings of the 19th International Conference on Computational Linguistics,* Taipei, Taiwan, 24 August – 1 September 2002.

Vincent Ng. 2009. Graph-cut-based anaphoricity determination for coreference resolution. In *Proceedings of Human Language Technologies 2009: The Conference of the North American Chapter of the Association for Computational Linguistics,* Boulder, Col., 31 May – 5 June 2009, pages 575–583.

Vincent Ng. 2010. Supervised noun phrase coreference research: The first fifteen years. In *Proceedings of the 48th Annual Meeting of the Association for Computational Linguistics,* Uppsala, Sweden, 11–16 July 2010, pages 1396–1411.

Eric W. Noreen. 1989. *Computer Intensive Methods for Hypothesis Testing: An Introduction.* Wiley, New York, N.Y.

Haoruo Peng, Kai-Wei Chang, and Dan Roth. 2015. A joint framework for coreference resolution and mention head detection. In *Proceedings of the 19th Conference on Computational Natural Language Learning,* Beijing, China, 30–31 July 2015, pages 12–21.

Sameer Pradhan, Xiaoqiang Luo, Marta Recasens, Eduard Hovy, Vincent Ng, and Michael Strube. 2014. Scoring coreference partitions of predicted mentions: A reference implementation. In *Proceedings of the 52nd Annual Meeting of the Association for Computational Linguistics (Volume 2: Short Papers)*, Baltimore, Md., 22–27 June 2014, pages 30–35.

Marta Recasens, Marie-Catherine de Marneffe, and Christopher Potts. 2013. The life and death of discourse entities: Identifying singleton mentions. In *Proceedings of the 2013 Conference of the North American Chapter of the Association for Computational Linguistics: Human Language Technologies*, Atlanta, Georgia, 9–14 June 2013, pages 627–633.

Marc Vilain, John Burger, John Aberdeen, Dennis Connolly, and Lynette Hirschman. 1995. A model-theoretic coreference scoring scheme. In *Proceedings of the 6th Message Understanding Conference (MUC-6)*, pages 45–52, San Mateo, Cal. Morgan Kaufmann.

Sam Wiseman, Alexander M. Rush, Stuart Shieber, and Jason Weston. 2015. Learning anaphoricity and antecedent ranking features for coreference resolution. In *Proceedings of the 53rd Annual Meeting of the Association for Computational Linguistics (Volume 1: Long Papers)*, Beijing, China, 26–31 July 2015, pages 1416–1426.

Guodong Zhou and Fang Kong. 2009. Global learning of noun phrase anaphoricity in coreference resolution via label propagation. In *Proceedings of the 2009 Conference on Empirical Methods in Natural Language Processing*, Singapore, 6–7 August 2009, pages 978–986.

Unsupervised Ranking Model for Entity Coreference Resolution

Xuezhe Ma and **Zhengzhong Liu** and **Eduard Hovy**
Language Technologies Institute
Carnegie Mellon University
Pittsburgh, PA 15213, USA
`{xuezhem, liu}@cs.cmu.edu, ehovy@cmu.edu`

Abstract

Coreference resolution is one of the first stages in deep language understanding and its importance has been well recognized in the natural language processing community. In this paper, we propose a generative, unsupervised ranking model for entity coreference resolution by introducing resolution mode variables. Our unsupervised system achieves 58.44% F1 score of the CoNLL metric on the English data from the CoNLL-2012 shared task (Pradhan et al., 2012), outperforming the Stanford deterministic system (Lee et al., 2013) by 3.01%.

1 Introduction

Entity coreference resolution has become a critical component for many Natural Language Processing (NLP) tasks. Systems requiring deep language understanding, such as information extraction (Wellner et al., 2004), semantic event learning (Chambers and Jurafsky, 2008; Chambers and Jurafsky, 2009), and named entity linking (Durrett and Klein, 2014; Ji et al., 2014) all benefit from entity coreference information.

Entity coreference resolution is the task of identifying mentions (i.e., noun phrases) in a text or dialogue that refer to the same real-world entities. In recent years, several supervised entity coreference resolution systems have been proposed, which, according to Ng (2010), can be categorized into three classes — mention-pair models (McCarthy and Lehnert, 1995), entity-mention models (Yang et al., 2008a; Haghighi and Klein, 2010; Lee et al., 2011) and ranking models (Yang et al., 2008b;

Durrett and Klein, 2013; Fernandes et al., 2014) — among which ranking models recently obtained state-of-the-art performance. However, the manually annotated corpora that these systems rely on are highly expensive to create, in particular when we want to build data for resource-poor languages (Ma and Xia, 2014). That makes unsupervised approaches, which only require unannotated text for training, a desirable solution to this problem.

Several unsupervised learning algorithms have been applied to coreference resolution. Haghighi and Klein (2007) presented a mention-pair nonparametric fully-generative Bayesian model for unsupervised coreference resolution. Based on this model, Ng (2008) probabilistically induced coreference partitions via EM clustering. Poon and Domingos (2008) proposed an entity-mention model that is able to perform joint inference across mentions by using Markov Logic. Unfortunately, these unsupervised systems' performance on accuracy significantly falls behind those of supervised systems, and are even worse than the deterministic rule-based systems. Furthermore, there is no previous work exploring the possibility of developing an unsupervised ranking model which achieved state-of-the-art performance under supervised settings for entity coreference resolution.

In this paper, we propose an unsupervised generative ranking model for entity coreference resolution. Our experimental results on the English data from the CoNLL-2012 shared task (Pradhan et al., 2012) show that our unsupervised system outperforms the Stanford deterministic system (Lee et al., 2013) by 3.01% absolute on the CoNLL official metric. The

Proceedings of NAACL-HLT 2016, pages 1012–1018,

contributions of this work are (i) proposing the first unsupervised ranking model for entity coreference resolution. (ii) giving empirical evaluations of this model on benchmark data sets. (iii) considerably narrowing the gap to supervised coreference resolution accuracy.

2 Unsupervised Ranking Model

2.1 Notations and Definitions

In the following, $D = \{m_0, m_1, \ldots, m_n\}$ represents a generic input document which is a sequence of coreference mentions, including the artificial root mention (denoted by m_0). The method to detect and extract these mentions is discussed later in Section 2.6. Let $C = \{c_1, c_2, \ldots, c_n\}$ denote the coreference assignment of a given document, where each mention m_i has an associated random variable c_i taking values in the set $\{0, i, \ldots, i - 1\}$; this variable specifies m_i's selected antecedent ($c_i \in \{1, 2, \ldots, i - 1\}$), or indicates that it begins a new coreference chain ($c_i = 0$).

2.2 Generative Ranking Model

The following is a straightforward way to build a generative model for coreference:

$$
\begin{aligned}
P(D, C) &= P(D|C)P(C) \\
&= \prod_{j=1}^{n} P(m_j|m_{c_j}) \prod_{j=1}^{n} P(c_j|j)
\end{aligned} \quad (1)
$$

where we factorize the probabilities $P(D|C)$ and $P(C)$ into each position j by adopting appropriate independence assumptions that given the coreference assignment c_j and corresponding coreferent mention m_{c_j}, the mention m_j is independent with other mentions in front of it. This independent assumption is similar to that in the IBM 1 model on machine translation (Brown et al., 1993), where it assumes that given the corresponding English word, the aligned foreign word is independent with other English and foreign words. We do not make any independent assumptions among different features (see Section 2.4 for details).

Inference in this model is efficient, because we can compute c_j separately for each mention:

$$
c_j^* = \underset{c_j}{\operatorname{argmax}} \, P(m_j|m_{c_j})P(c_j|j)
$$

The model is a so-called ranking model because it is able to identify the most probable candidate antecedent given a mention to be resolved.

2.3 Resolution Mode Variables

According to previous work (Haghighi and Klein, 2009; Ratinov and Roth, 2012; Lee et al., 2013), antecedents are resolved by different categories of information for different mentions. For example, the Stanford system (Lee et al., 2013) uses string-matching sieves to link two mentions with similar text and precise-construct sieve to link two mentions which satisfy special syntactic or semantic relations such as apposition or acronym. Motivated by this, we introduce resolution mode variables $\Pi = \{\pi_1, \ldots, \pi_n\}$, where for each mention j the variable $\pi_j \in \{str, prec, attr\}$ indicates in which mode the mention should be resolved. In our model, we define three resolution modes — string-matching (*str*), precise-construct (*prec*), and attribute-matching (*attr*) — and Π is deterministic when D is given (i.e. $P(\Pi|D)$ is a point distribution). We determine π_j for each mention m_j in the following way:

- $\pi_j = str$, if there exists a mention $m_i, i < j$ such that the two mentions satisfy the *String Match* sieve, the *Relaxed String Match* sieve, or the *Strict Head Match A* sieve in the Stanford multi-sieve system (Lee et al., 2013).

- $\pi_j = prec$, if there exists a mention $m_i, i < j$ such that the two mentions satisfy the *Speaker Identification* sieve, or the *Precise Constructs* sieve.

- $\pi_j = attr$, if there is no mention $m_i, i < j$ satisfies the above two conditions.

Now, we can extend the generative model in Eq. 1 to:

$$
\begin{aligned}
P(D, C) &= P(D, C, \Pi) \\
&= \prod_{j=1}^{n} P(m_j|m_{c_j}, \pi_j)P(c_j|\pi_j, j)P(\pi_j|j)
\end{aligned}
$$

where we define $P(\pi_j|j)$ to be uniform distribution. We model $P(m_j|m_{c_j}, \pi_j)$ and $P(c_j|\pi_j, j)$ in the fol-

Mode π	Feature	Description
prec	Mention Type	the type of a mention. We use three mention types: *Proper, Nominal, Pronoun*
str	Mention Type	the same as the mention type feature under *prec* mode.
	Exact Match	boolean feature corresponding to String Match sieve in Stanford system.
	Relaxed Match	boolean feature corresponding to Relaxed String Match sieve in Stanford system.
	Head Match	boolean feature corresponding to Strict Head Match A sieve in Stanford system.
attr	Mention Type	the same as the mention type feature under *prec* mode.
	Number	the number of a mention similarly derived from Lee et al. (2013).
	Gender	the gender of a mention from Bergsma and Lin (2006) and Ji and Lin (2009).
	Person	the person attribute from Lee et al. (2013). We assign person attributes to all mentions, not only pronouns.
	Animacy	the animacy attribute same as Lee et al. (2013).
	Semantic Class	semantic classes derived from WordNet (Soon et al., 2001).
	Distance	sentence distance between the two mentions. This feature is for parameter $q(k|j,\pi)$

Table 1: Feature set for representing a mention under different resolution modes. The *Distance* feature is for parameter q, while all other features are for parameter t.

Algorithm 1: Learning Model with EM

1 **Initialization:** Initialize $\theta_0 = \{t_0, q_0\}$
2 **for** $t = 0$ *to* T **do**
3   set all counts $c(\ldots) = 0$
4   **for** *each document* D **do**
5   **for** $j = 1$ *to* n **do**
6   **for** $k = 0$ *to* $j - 1$ **do**
7 $L_{jk} = \dfrac{t(m_j|m_k,\pi_j)q(k|\pi_j,j)}{\sum_{i=0}^{j-1} t(m_j|m_i,\pi_j)q(i|\pi_j,j)}$
8 $c(m_j, m_k, \pi_j) \mathrel{+}= L_{jk}$
9 $c(m_k, \pi_j) \mathrel{+}= L_{jk}$
10 $c(k, j, \pi_j) \mathrel{+}= L_{jk}$
11 $c(j, \pi_j) \mathrel{+}= L_{jk}$
     // Recalculate the parameters
12 $t(m|m',\pi) = \frac{c(m,m',\pi)}{c(m',\pi)}$
13 $q(k,j,\pi) = \frac{c(k,j,\pi)}{c(j,\pi)}$

Corpora	# Doc	# Sent	# Word	# Entity	# Mention
Gigaword	3.6M	75.4M	1.6B	-	-
ON-Dev	343	9,142	160K	4,546	19,156
ON-Test	348	9,615	170K	4,532	19,764

Table 2: Corpora statistics. "ON-Dev" and "ON-Test" are the development and testing sets of the OntoNotes corpus.

2.4 Features

In this section, we describe the features we use to represent mentions. Specifically, as shown in Table 1, we use different features under different resolution modes. It should be noted that only the *Distance* feature is designed for parameter q, all other features are designed for parameter t.

2.5 Model Learning

For model learning, we run EM algorithm (Dempster et al., 1977) on our Model, treating D as observed data and C as latent variables. We run EM with 10 iterations and select the parameters achieving the best performance on the development data. Each iteration takes around 12 hours with 10 CPUs parallelly. The best parameters appear at around the 5th iteration, according to our experiments. The detailed derivation of the learning algorithm is shown in Appendix A. The pseudo-code is shown is Algorithm 1. We use uniform initialization for all the parameters in our model.

Several previous work has attempted to use EM for entity coreference resolution. Cherry and Bergsma (2005) and Charniak and Elsner (2009) applied EM for pronoun anaphora resolution. Ng (2008) probabilistically induced coreference partitions via EM clustering. Recently, Moosavi and Strube (2014) proposed an unsupervised model uti-

lowing way:

$$P(m_j|m_{c_j}, \pi_j) = t(m_j|m_{c_j}, \pi_j)$$
$$P(c_j|\pi_j, j) = \begin{cases} q(c_j|\pi_j, j) & \pi_j = attr \\ \frac{1}{j} & \text{otherwise} \end{cases}$$

where $\theta = \{t, q\}$ are parameters of our model. Note that in the attribute-matching mode ($\pi_j = attr$) we model $P(c_j|\pi_j, j)$ with parameter q, while in the other two modes, we use the uniform distribution. It makes sense because the position information is important for coreference resolved by matching attributes of two mentions such as resolving pronoun coreference, but not that important for those resolved by matching text or special relations like two mentions referring the same person and matching by the name.

	CoNLL'12 English development data						CoNLL'12 English test data					
	MUC	B^3	$CEAF_m$	$CEAF_e$	Blanc	CoNLL	MUC	B^3	$CEAF_m$	$CEAF_e$	Blanc	CoNLL
MIR	65.39	54.89	–	51.36	–	57.21	64.64	52.52	–	49.11	–	55.42
Stanford	64.96	54.49	59.39	51.24	56.03	56.90	64.71	52.26	56.01	49.32	53.92	55.43
Multigraph	66.22	56.41	60.87	52.61	58.15	58.41	65.41	54.38	58.60	50.21	56.03	56.67
Our Model	**67.89**	**57.83**	**62.11**	**53.76**	**60.58**	**59.83**	**67.69**	**55.86**	**59.66**	**51.75**	**57.78**	**58.44**
IMS	67.15	55.19	58.86	50.94	56.22	57.76	67.58	54.47	58.17	50.21	55.41	57.42
Latent-Tree	69.46	57.83	–	54.43	–	60.57	70.51	57.58	–	53.86	–	60.65
Berkeley	70.44	59.10	–	55.57	–	61.71	70.62	58.20	–	54.80	–	61.21
LaSO	70.74	60.03	65.01	56.80	–	62.52	70.72	58.58	63.45	59.40	–	61.63
Latent-Strc	72.11	60.74	–	57.72	–	63.52	72.17	59.58	–	55.67	–	62.47
Model-Stack	72.59	61.98	–	57.58	–	64.05	72.59	60.44	–	56.02	–	63.02
Non-Linear	72.74	61.77	–	58.63	–	64.38	72.60	60.52	–	57.05	–	63.39

Table 3: F1 scores of different evaluation metrics for our model, together with two deterministic systems and one unsupervised system as baseline (above the dashed line) and seven supervised systems (below the dashed line) for comparison on CoNLL 2012 development and test datasets.

lizing the most informative relations and achieved competitive performance with the Stanford system.

2.6 Mention Detection

The basic rules we used to detect mentions are similar to those of Lee et al. (2013), except that their system uses a set of filtering rules designed to discard instances of pleonastic *it*, partitives, certain quantified noun phrases and other spurious mentions. Our system keeps partitives, quantified noun phrases and *bare NP* mentions, but discards pleonastic *it* and other spurious mentions.

3 Experiments

3.1 Experimental Setup

Datasets. Due to the availability of readily parsed data, we select the APW and NYT sections of Gigaword Corpus (years 1994-2010) (Parker et al., 2011) to train the model. Following previous work (Chambers and Jurafsky, 2008), we remove duplicated documents and the documents which include fewer than 3 sentences. The development and test data are the English data from the CoNLL-2012 shared task (Pradhan et al., 2012), which is derived from the OntoNotes corpus (Hovy et al., 2006). The corpora statistics are shown in Table 2. Our system is evaluated with automatically extracted mentions on the version of the data with automatic preprocessing information (e.g., predicted parse trees).

Evaluation Metrics. We evaluate our model on three measures widely used in the literature: MUC (Vilain et al., 1995), B^3 (Bagga and Baldwin, 1998), and Entity-based CEAF ($CEAF_e$) (Luo, 2005). In addition, we also report results on another two popular metrics: Mention-based CEAF ($CEAF_m$) and BLANC (Recasens and Hovy, 2011). All the results are given by the latest version of CoNLL-2012 scorer [1]

3.2 Results and Comparison

Table 3 illustrates the results of our model together as baseline with two deterministic systems, namely **Stanford**: the Stanford system (Lee et al., 2011) and **Multigraph**: the unsupervised multigraph system (Martschat, 2013), and one unsupervised system, namely **MIR**: the unsupervised system using most informative relations (Moosavi and Strube, 2014). Our model outperforms the three baseline systems on all the evaluation metrics. Specifically, our model achieves improvements of 2.93% and 3.01% on CoNLL F1 score over the Stanford system, the winner of the CoNLL 2011 shared task, on the CoNLL 2012 development and test sets, respectively. The improvements on CoNLL F1 score over the Multigraph model are 1.41% and 1.77% on the development and test sets, respectively. Comparing

---

[1] http://conll.cemantix.org/2012/ software.html

with the MIR model, we obtain significant improvements of 2.62% and 3.02% on CoNLL F1 score.

To make a thorough empirical comparison with previous studies, Table 3 (below the dashed line) also shows the results of some state-of-the-art supervised coreference resolution systems — **IMS**: the second best system in the CoNLL 2012 shared task (Björkelund and Farkas, 2012); **Latent-Tree**: the latent tree model (Fernandes et al., 2012) obtaining the best results in the shared task; **Berkeley**: the Berkeley system with the final feature set (Durrett and Klein, 2013); **LaSO**: the structured perceptron system with non-local features (Björkelund and Kuhn, 2014); **Latent-Strc**: the latent structure system (Martschat and Strube, 2015); **Model-Stack**: the entity-centric system with model stacking (Clark and Manning, 2015); and **Non-Linear**: the non-linear mention-ranking model with feature representations (Wiseman et al., 2015). Our unsupervised ranking model outperforms the supervised IMS system by 1.02% on the CoNLL F1 score, and achieves competitive performance with the latent tree model. Moreover, our approach considerably narrows the gap to other supervised systems listed in Table 3.

4 Conclusion

We proposed a new generative, unsupervised ranking model for entity coreference resolution into which we introduced resolution mode variables to distinguish mentions resolved by different categories of information. Experimental results on the data from CoNLL-2012 shared task show that our system significantly improves the accuracy on different evaluation metrics over the baseline systems.

One possible direction for future work is to differentiate more resolution modes. Another one is to add more precise or even event-based features to improve the model's performance.

Acknowledgements

This research was supported in part by DARPA grant FA8750-12-2-0342 funded under the DEFT program. Any opinions, findings, and conclusions or recommendations expressed in this material are those of the authors and do not necessarily reflect the views of DARPA.

References

Amit Bagga and Breck Baldwin. 1998. Algorithms for scoring coreference chains. In *The first international conference on language resources and evaluation workshop on linguistics coreference*, volume 1, pages 563–566. Citeseer.

Shane Bergsma and Dekang Lin. 2006. Bootstrapping path-based pronoun resolution. In *Proceedings of ACL-2006*, pages 33–40, Sydney, Australia, July. Association for Computational Linguistics.

Anders Björkelund and Richárd Farkas. 2012. Data-driven multilingual coreference resolution using resolver stacking. In *Proceedings of EMNLP-CoNLL-2012 - Shared Task*, pages 49–55, Jeju Island, Korea, July. Association for Computational Linguistics.

Anders Björkelund and Jonas Kuhn. 2014. Learning structured perceptrons for coreference resolution with latent antecedents and non-local features. In *Proceedings of ACL-2014*, pages 47–57, Baltimore, Maryland, June. Association for Computational Linguistics.

Peter F Brown, Vincent J Della Pietra, Stephen A Della Pietra, and Robert L Mercer. 1993. The mathematics of statistical machine translation: Parameter estimation. *Computational linguistics*, 19(2):263–311.

Nathanael Chambers and Dan Jurafsky. 2008. Unsupervised learning of narrative event chains. In *Proceedings of ACL-2008: HLT*, pages 789–797, Columbus, Ohio, June. Association for Computational Linguistics.

Nathanael Chambers and Dan Jurafsky. 2009. Unsupervised learning of narrative schemas and their participants. In *Proceedings of ACL-2009*, pages 602–610, Suntec, Singapore, August. Association for Computational Linguistics.

Eugene Charniak and Micha Elsner. 2009. EM works for pronoun anaphora resolution. In *Proceedings of EACL 2009*, pages 148–156, Athens, Greece, March.

Colin Cherry and Shane Bergsma. 2005. An Expectation Maximization approach to pronoun resolution. In *Proceedings of CoNLL-2005*, pages 88–95, Ann Arbor, Michigan, June.

Kevin Clark and Christopher D. Manning. 2015. Entity-centric coreference resolution with model stacking. In *Proceedings of ACL-IJCNLP-2015*, pages 1405–1415, Beijing, China, July. Association for Computational Linguistics.

Arthur P Dempster, Nan M Laird, and Donald B Rubin. 1977. Maximum likelihood from incomplete data via the em algorithm. *Journal of the royal statistical society. Series B (methodological)*, pages 1–38.

Greg Durrett and Dan Klein. 2013. Easy victories and uphill battles in coreference resolution. In *Proceedings of EMNLP-2013*, pages 1971–1982, Seattle,

Washington, USA, October. Association for Computational Linguistics.

Greg Durrett and Dan Klein. 2014. A joint model for entity analysis: Coreference, typing, and linking. In *Proceedings of the Transactions of the Association for Computational Linguistics*.

Eraldo Fernandes, Cícero dos Santos, and Ruy Milidiú. 2012. Latent structure perceptron with feature induction for unrestricted coreference resolution. In *Proceedings of EMNLP-CoNLL-2012 - Shared Task*, pages 41–48, Jeju Island, Korea, July. Association for Computational Linguistics.

Eraldo Rezende Fernandes, Cícero Nogueira dos Santos, and Ruy Luiz Milidiú. 2014. Latent trees for coreference resolution. *Computational Linguistics*.

Aria Haghighi and Dan Klein. 2007. Unsupervised coreference resolution in a nonparametric bayesian model. In *Proceedings of ACL-2007*, pages 848–855, Prague, Czech Republic, June. Association for Computational Linguistics.

Aria Haghighi and Dan Klein. 2009. Simple coreference resolution with rich syntactic and semantic features. In *Proceedings of EMNLP-2009*, pages 1152–1161, Singapore, August. Association for Computational Linguistics.

Aria Haghighi and Dan Klein. 2010. Coreference resolution in a modular, entity-centered model. In *Proceedings of NAACL-2010*, pages 385–393, Los Angeles, California, June. Association for Computational Linguistics.

Eduard Hovy, Mitchell Marcus, Martha Palmer, Lance Ramshaw, and Ralph Weischedel. 2006. Ontonotes: The 90% solution. In *Proceedings of NAACL-2006*, pages 57–60, New York City, USA, June. Association for Computational Linguistics.

Heng Ji and Dekang Lin. 2009. Gender and animacy knowledge discovery from web-scale n-grams for unsupervised person mention detection. In *Proceedings of PACLIC-2009*, pages 220–229.

Heng Ji, HT Dang, J Nothman, and B Hachey. 2014. Overview of tac-kbp2014 entity discovery and linking tasks. In *Proc. Text Analysis Conference (TAC2014)*.

Heeyoung Lee, Yves Peirsman, Angel Chang, Nathanael Chambers, Mihai Surdeanu, and Dan Jurafsky. 2011. Stanford's multi-pass sieve coreference resolution system at the conll-2011 shared task. In *Proceedings of CoNLL-2011: Shared Task*, pages 28–34, Portland, Oregon, USA, June. Association for Computational Linguistics.

Heeyoung Lee, Angel Chang, Yves Peirsman, Nathanael Chambers, Mihai Surdeanu, and Dan Jurafsky. 2013. Deterministic coreference resolution based on entity-centric, precision-ranked rules. *Comput. Linguist.*, 39(4):885–916, December.

Xiaoqiang Luo. 2005. On coreference resolution performance metrics. In *Proceedings of EMNLP-2005*, pages 25–32, Vancouver, British Columbia, Canada, October. Association for Computational Linguistics.

Xuezhe Ma and Fei Xia. 2014. Unsupervised dependency parsing with transferring distribution via parallel guidance and entropy regularization. In *Proceedings of ACL-2014*, pages 1337–1348, Baltimore, Maryland, June.

Sebastian Martschat and Michael Strube. 2015. Latent structures for coreference resolution. *Transactions of the Association for Computational Linguistics*, 3:405–418.

Sebastian Martschat. 2013. Multigraph clustering for unsupervised coreference resolution. In *ACL-2013: Student Research Workshop*, pages 81–88, Sofia, Bulgaria, August. Association for Computational Linguistics.

Joseph F McCarthy and Wendy G Lehnert. 1995. Using decision trees for conference resolution. In *Proceedings of IJCAI-1995*, pages 1050–1055. Morgan Kaufmann Publishers Inc.

Nafise Sadat Moosavi and Michael Strube. 2014. Unsupervised coreference resolution by utilizing the most informative relations. In *Proceedings of COLING-2014*, pages 644–655.

Vincent Ng. 2008. Unsupervised models for coreference resolution. In *Proceedings of EMNLP-2008*, pages 640–649, Honolulu, Hawaii, October. Association for Computational Linguistics.

Vincent Ng. 2010. Supervised noun phrase coreference research: The first fifteen years. In *Proceedings of ACL-2010*, pages 1396–1411, Uppsala, Sweden, July. Association for Computational Linguistics.

Robert Parker, David Graff, Junbo Kong, Ke Chen, and Kazuaki Maeda. 2011. English gigaword fifth edition. *Linguistic Data Consortium, LDC2011T07*.

Hoifung Poon and Pedro Domingos. 2008. Joint unsupervised coreference resolution with Markov Logic. In *Proceedings of EMNLP-2008*, pages 650–659, Honolulu, Hawaii, October. Association for Computational Linguistics.

Sameer Pradhan, Alessandro Moschitti, Nianwen Xue, Olga Uryupina, and Yuchen Zhang. 2012. Conll-2012 shared task: Modeling multilingual unrestricted coreference in ontonotes. In *Proceedings of EMNLP-CoNLL-2012 - Shared Task*, pages 1–40, Jeju Island, Korea, July. Association for Computational Linguistics.

Lev Ratinov and Dan Roth. 2012. Learning-based multi-sieve co-reference resolution with knowledge. In *Proceedings of EMNLP-CoNLL-2012*, pages 1234–1244, Jeju Island, Korea, July. Association for Computational Linguistics.

Marta Recasens and Eduard Hovy. 2011. Blanc: Implementing the rand index for coreference evaluation. *Natural Language Engineering*, 17(04):485–510.

Wee Meng Soon, Hwee Tou Ng, and Daniel Chung Yong Lim. 2001. A machine learning approach to coreference resolution of noun phrases. *Computational linguistics*, 27(4):521–544.

Marc Vilain, John Burger, John Aberdeen, Dennis Connolly, and Lynette Hirschman. 1995. A model-theoretic coreference scoring scheme. In *Proceedings of the 6th conference on Message understanding*, pages 45–52. Association for Computational Linguistics.

Ben Wellner, Andrew McCallum, Fuchun Peng, and Michael Hay. 2004. An integrated, conditional model of information extraction and coreference with application to citation matching. In *Proceedings of the 20th conference on Uncertainty in artificial intelligence*, pages 593–601. AUAI Press.

Sam Wiseman, Alexander M. Rush, Stuart Shieber, and Jason Weston. 2015. Learning anaphoricity and antecedent ranking features for coreference resolution. In *Proceedings of ACL-IJCNLP-2015*, pages 1416–1426, Beijing, China, July. Association for Computational Linguistics.

Xiaofeng Yang, Jian Su, Jun Lang, Chew Lim Tan, Ting Liu, and Sheng Li. 2008a. An entity-mention model for coreference resolution with inductive logic programming. In *Proceedings of ACL-2008*, pages 843–851.

Xiaofeng Yang, Jian Su, and Chew Lim Tan. 2008b. A twin-candidate model for learning-based anaphora resolution. *Computational Linguistics*, 34(3):327–356.

Appendix A. Derivation of Model Learning

Formally, we iteratively estimate the model parameters θ, employing the following EM algorithm:

E-step: Compute the posterior probabilities of C, $P(C|D; \theta)$, based on the current θ.

M-step: Calculate the new θ' that maximizes the expected complete log likelihood, $E_{P(C|D;\theta)}[\log P(D, C; \theta')]$

For simplicity, we denote:

$$\begin{aligned} P(C|D; \theta) &= \tilde{P}(C|D) \\ P(C|D; \theta') &= P(C|D) \end{aligned}$$

In addition, we use $\tau(\pi_j|j)$ to denote the probability $P(\pi_j|j)$ which is uniform distribution in our model.

Moreover, we use the following notation for convenience:

$$\theta(m_j, m_k, j, k, \pi_j) = t(m_j|m_k, \pi_j)q(k|\pi_j, j)\tau(\pi_j|j)$$

Then, we have

$$\begin{aligned} &E_{\tilde{P}(c|D)}[\log P(D, C)] \\ &= \sum_C \tilde{P}(C|D)\log P(D, C) \\ &= \sum_C \tilde{P}(C|D)\big(\sum_{j=1}^{n} \log t(m_j|m_{c_j}, \pi_j) + \log q(c_j|\pi_j, j) + \log \tau(\pi_j|j)\big) \\ &= \sum_{j=1}^{n} \sum_{k=0}^{j-1} L_{jk}\big(\log t(m_j|m_k, \pi_j) + \log q(k|\pi_j, j) + \log \tau(\pi_j|j)\big) \end{aligned}$$

Then the parameters t and q that maximize $E_{\tilde{P}(c|D)}[\log P(D, C)]$ satisfy that

$$\begin{aligned} t(m_j|m_k, \pi_j) &= \frac{L_{jk}}{\sum_{i=1}^{n} L_{ik}} \\ q(k|\pi_j, j) &= \frac{L_{jk}}{\sum_{i=0}^{j-1} L_{ji}} \end{aligned}$$

where L_{jk} can be calculated by

$$\begin{aligned} L_{jk} &= \sum_{C, c_j=k} \tilde{P}(C|D) = \frac{\sum_{C, c_j=k} \tilde{P}(C,D)}{\sum_C \tilde{P}(C,D)} \\ &= \frac{\sum_{C, c_j=k} \prod_{i=1}^{n} \tilde{\theta}(m_i, m_{c_i}, c_i, i, \pi_i)}{\sum_C \prod_{i=1}^{n} \tilde{\theta}(m_i, m_{c_i}, c_i, i, \pi_i)} \\ &= \frac{\tilde{\theta}(m_j, m_k, k, j, \pi_j) \sum_{C(-j)} \tilde{P}(C(-j)|D)}{\sum_{i=0}^{j-1} \tilde{\theta}(m_j, m_i, i, j, \pi_j) \sum_{C(-j)} \tilde{P}(C(-j)|D)} \\ &= \frac{\tilde{\theta}(m_j, m_k, k, j, \pi_j)}{\sum_{i=0}^{j-1} \tilde{\theta}(m_j, m_i, i, j, \pi_j)} \\ &= \frac{\tilde{t}(m_j|m_k, \pi_j)\tilde{q}(k|\pi_j, j)\tilde{\tau}(\pi_j|j)}{\sum_{i=0}^{j-1} \tilde{t}(m_j|m_i, \pi_j)\tilde{q}(i|\pi_j, j)\tilde{\tau}(\pi_j|j)} \\ &= \frac{\tilde{t}(m_j|m_k, \pi_j)\tilde{q}(k|\pi_j, j)}{\sum_{i=0}^{j-1} \tilde{t}(m_j|m_i, \pi_j)\tilde{q}(i|\pi_j, j)} \end{aligned}$$

where $C(-j) = \{c_1, \ldots, c_{j-1}, c_{j+1}, \ldots, c_n\}$. The above derivations correspond to the learning algorithm in Algorithm 1.

Embedding Lexical Features via Low-Rank Tensors

Mo Yu[*]
Harbin Institute of Technology
IBM Watson
`yum@us.ibm.com`

Mark Dredze
HLTCOE
Johns Hopkins University
`mdredze@cs.jhu.edu`

Raman Arora
Johns Hopkins University
`arora@cs.jhu.edu`

Matthew R. Gormley
Carnegie Mellon University
`mgormley@cs.cmu.edu`

Abstract

Modern NLP models rely heavily on engineered features, which often combine word and contextual information into complex lexical features. Such combination results in large numbers of features, which can lead to overfitting. We present a new model that represents complex lexical features—comprised of parts for words, contextual information and labels—in a tensor that captures conjunction information among these parts. We apply low-rank tensor approximations to the corresponding parameter tensors to reduce the parameter space and improve prediction speed. Furthermore, we investigate two methods for handling features that include n-grams of mixed lengths. Our model achieves state-of-the-art results on tasks in relation extraction, PP-attachment, and preposition disambiguation.

1 Introduction

Statistical NLP models usually rely on hand-designed features, customized for each task. These features typically combine lexical and contextual information with the label to be scored. In relation extraction, for example, there is a parameter for the presence of a specific relation occurring with a feature conjoining a word type (lexical) with dependency path information (contextual). In measuring phrase semantic similarity, a word type is conjoined with its position in the phrase to signal its role. Figure 1b shows an example in dependency parsing, where multiple types (words) are conjoined with POS tags or distance information.

To avoid model over-fitting that often results from features with lexical components, several smoothed lexical representations have been proposed and shown to improve performance on various NLP tasks; for instance, word embeddings (Bengio et al., 2006) help improve NER, dependency parsing and semantic role labeling (Miller et al., 2004; Koo et al., 2008; Turian et al., 2010; Sun et al., 2011; Roth and Woodsend, 2014; Hermann et al., 2014).

However, using only word embeddings is not sufficient to represent complex lexical features (e.g. ϕ in Figure 1c). In these features, the same word embedding conjoined with different non-lexical properties may result in features indicating different labels; the corresponding lexical feature representations should take the above interactions into consideration. Such important interactions also increase the risk of over-fitting as feature space grows exponentially, yet how to capture these interactions in representation learning remains an open question.

To address the above problems,[1] we propose a general and unified approach to reduce the feature space by constructing low-dimensional feature representations, which provides a new way of combining word embeddings, traditional non-lexical properties, and label information. Our model exploits the inner structure of features by breaking the feature into multiple parts: lexical, non-lexical and (optional) label. We demonstrate that the full feature is an outer product among these parts. Thus, a parameter tensor scores each feature to produce a prediction. Our model then reduces the number of param-

---

Paper submitted during Mo Yu's PhD study at HIT.

[1]Our paper only focuses on lexical features, as non-lexical features usually suffer less from over-fitting.

Proceedings of NAACL-HLT 2016, pages 1019–1029,
San Diego, California, June 12-17, 2016. ©2016 Association for Computational Linguistics

"

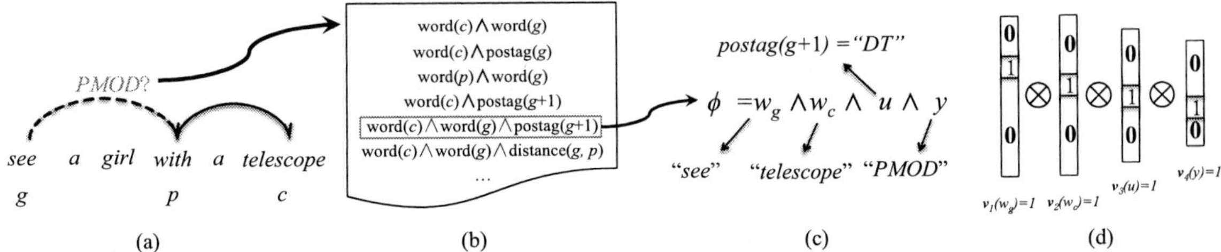

Figure 1: An example of lexical features used in dependency parsing. To predict the "PMOD" arc (the dashed one) between "see" and "with" in (a), we may rely on lexical features in (b). Here p, c, g are indices of the word "with", its child ("telescope") and a candidate head. Figure (c) shows what the fifth feature (ϕ) is like, when the candidate is "see". As is common in multi-class classification tasks, each template generates a different feature for each label y. Thus a feature $\phi = w_g \wedge w_c \wedge u \wedge y$ is the conjunction of the four parts. Figure (d) is the one-hot representation of ϕ, which is equivalent to the outer product (i.e. a 4-way tensor) among the four one-hot vectors. $\mathbf{v}(x) = 1$ means the vector $\mathbf{v}$ has a single non-zero element in the x position.

eters by approximating the parameter tensor with a low-rank tensor: the Tucker approximation of Yu et al. (2015) but applied to each embedding type (view), or the **C**anonical/**P**arallel-Factors Decomposition (CP). Our models use fewer parameters than previous work that learns a separate representation for each feature (Ando and Zhang, 2005; Yang and Eisenstein, 2015). CP approximation also allows for much faster prediction, going from a method that is cubic in rank and exponential in the number of lexical parts, to a method linear in both. Furthermore, we consider two methods for handling features that rely on n-grams of mixed lengths.

Our model makes the following contributions when contrasted with prior work:

Lei et al. (2014) applied CP to combine different views of features. Compared to their work, our usage of CP-decomposition is different in the application to feature learning: (1) We focus on dimensionality reduction of existing, well-verified features, while Lei et al. (2014) generates new features (usually different from ours) by combining some "atom" features. Thus their work may ignore some useful features; it relies on binary features as supplementary but our model needs not. (2) Lei et al. (2014)'s factorization relies on views with explicit meanings, e.g. head/modifier/arc in dependency parsing, making it less general. Therefore its applications to tasks like relation extraction are less obvious.

Compared to our previous work (Gormley et al., 2015; Yu et al., 2015), this work allows for higher-order interactions, mixed-length n-gram features,

lower-rank representations. We also demonstrate the strength of our new model via applications to new tasks.

The resulting method learns smoothed feature representations combining lexical, non-lexical and label information, achieving state-of-the-art performance on several tasks: relation extraction, preposition semantics and PP-attachment.

2 Notation and Definitions

We begin with some background on notation and definitions. Let $\mathcal{T} \in \mathbb{R}^{d_1 \times \cdots \times d_K}$ be a K-way tensor (i.e., a tensor with K views). In this paper, we consider the tensor k-mode product, i.e. multiplying a tensor $\mathcal{T} \in \mathbb{R}^{d_1 \times \cdots \times d_K}$ by a matrix $\mathbf{x} \in \mathbb{R}^{d_k \times J}$ (or a vector if $J = 1$) in mode (view) k. The product is denoted by $\mathcal{T} \times_k \mathbf{x}$ and is of size $d_1 \times \cdots \times d_{k-1} \times J \times d_{k+1} \times \cdots \times d_K$. Element-wise, we have

$$(\mathcal{T} \times_k \mathbf{x})_{i_1 \ldots i_{k-1} j \, i_{k+1} \ldots i_K} = \sum_{i_k=1}^{d_k} \mathcal{T}_{i_1 \ldots i_k \ldots i_K} \mathbf{x}_{i_k j},$$

for $j = 1, \ldots, J$. A mode-k fiber $\mathcal{T}_{i_1 \ldots i_{k-1} \bullet i_{k+1} \ldots i_K}$ of $\mathcal{T}$ is the d_k dimensional vector obtained by fixing all but the kth index. The mode-k unfolding $\mathcal{T}_{(k)}$ of $\mathcal{T}$ is the $d_k \times \prod_{i \neq k} d_i$ matrix obtained by concatenating all the $\prod_{i \neq k} d_i$ mode-k fibers along columns.

Given two matrices $\mathbf{W}_1 \in \mathbb{R}^{d_1 \times r_1}, \mathbf{W}_2 \in \mathbb{R}^{d_2 \times r_2}$, we write $\mathbf{W}_1 \otimes \mathbf{W}_2$ to denote the Kronecker product between $\mathbf{W}_1$ and $\mathbf{W}_2$ (outer product for vectors). We define the Frobenius product (matrix dot product) $\mathbf{A} \odot \mathbf{B} = \sum_{i,j} A_{ij} B_{ij}$ between two matrices with the same sizes; and define element-wise (Hadamard) multiplication $\mathbf{a} \circ \mathbf{b}$ between vectors with the same sizes.

Tucker Decomposition: Tucker Decomposition represents a $d_1 \times d_2 \times \ldots \times d_K$ tensor $\mathcal{T}$ as:

$$\mathcal{T} = g \times_1 \mathbf{W}_1 \times_2 \mathbf{W}_2 \ldots \times_K \mathbf{W}_K \qquad (1)$$

where each $\times_i$ is the tensor i-mode product and each $\mathbf{W}_i$ is a $r_i \times d_i$ matrix. Tensor g with size $r_1 \times r_2 \times \ldots \times r_K$ is called the *core tensor*. We say that $\mathcal{T}$ has a Tucker rank $(r_{(1)}, r_{(2)}, \ldots, r_{(K)})$, where $r_{(i)} = \text{rank}(\mathcal{T}_{(i)})$ is the rank of mode-i unfolding. To simplify learning, we define the Tucker rank as $r_{(i)} = \text{rank}(\mathbf{g}_{(i)})$, which can be bounded simply by the dimensions of g, i.e. $r_{(i)} \leq r_i$; this allows us to enforce a rank constraint on $\mathcal{T}$ simply by restricting the dimensions r_i of g, as described in §6.

CP Decomposition: CP decomposition represents a $d_1 \times d_2 \times \ldots \times d_K$ tensor $\mathcal{T}$ as a sum of rank-one tensors (i.e. a sum of outer products of K vectors):

$$\mathcal{T} = \sum_{j=1}^{r} \mathbf{W}_1[j,:] \otimes \mathbf{W}_2[j,:] \otimes \ldots \otimes \mathbf{W}_K[j,:] \qquad (2)$$

where each $\mathbf{W}_i$ is an $r \times d_i$ matrix and $\mathbf{W}_i[j,:]$ is the vector of its j-th row. For CP decomposition, the rank r of a tensor $\mathcal{T}$ is defined to be the number of rank-one tensors in the decomposition. CP decomposition can be viewed as a special case of Tucker decomposition in which $r_1 = r_2 = \ldots = r_K = r$ and g is a superdiagonal tensor.

3 Factorization of Lexical Features

Suppose we have feature ϕ that includes information from a label y, multiple lexical items $\mathbf{w}_1, \ldots, \mathbf{w}_n$ and non-lexical property u. This feature can be factorized as a conjunction of each part: $\phi = \mathbf{y} \wedge \mathbf{u} \wedge \mathbf{w}_1 \wedge \ldots \wedge \mathbf{w}_n$. The feature fires when all $(n+2)$ parts fire in the instance (reflected by the $\wedge$ symbol in ϕ). The one-hot representation of ϕ can then be viewed as a tensor $e_\phi = \mathbf{y} \otimes \mathbf{u} \otimes \mathbf{w}_1 \otimes \cdots \otimes \mathbf{w}_n$, where each feature part is also represented as a one-hot vector.[2] Figure 1d illustrates this case with two lexical parts.

Given an input instance $\mathbf{x}$ and its associated label y, we can extract a set of features $S(\mathbf{x}, \mathbf{y})$. In

---

[2] $\mathbf{u}, \mathbf{y}, \mathbf{w}_i$ denote one-hot vectors instead of symbols.

a traditional log-linear model, we view the instance $\mathbf{x}$ as a bag-of-features, i.e. a feature vector $F(\mathbf{x}, \mathbf{y})$. Each dimension corresponds to a feature ϕ, and has value 1 if $\phi \in S(\mathbf{x}, \mathbf{y})$. Then the log-linear model scores the instance as $s(\mathbf{x}, \mathbf{y}; \mathbf{w}) = \mathbf{w}^T F(\mathbf{x}, \mathbf{y}) = \sum_{\phi \in S(\mathbf{x}, \mathbf{y})} s(\phi; \mathbf{w})$, where $\mathbf{w}$ is the parameter vector. We can re-write $s(\mathbf{x}, \mathbf{y}; \mathbf{w})$ based on the factorization of the features using tensor multiplication; in which $\mathbf{w}$ becomes a parameter tensor $\mathcal{T}$:

$$s(\mathbf{x}, \mathbf{y}; \mathbf{w}) = s(\mathbf{x}, \mathbf{y}; \mathcal{T}) = \sum_{\phi \in S(\mathbf{x}, \mathbf{y})} s(\phi; \mathcal{T}) \qquad (3)$$

Here each ϕ has the form $(\mathbf{y}, \mathbf{u}, \mathbf{w}_1, \ldots, \mathbf{w}_n)$, and

$$s(\phi; \mathcal{T}) = \mathcal{T} \times_l \mathbf{y} \times_f \mathbf{u} \times_{\mathbf{w}_1} \mathbf{w}_1 \ldots \times_{\mathbf{w}_n} \mathbf{w}_n. \qquad (4)$$

Note that one-hot vectors $\mathbf{w}_i$ of words themselves are large ($|\mathbf{w}_i| > 500\text{k}$), thus the above formulation with parameter tensor $\mathcal{T}$ can be very large, making parameter estimation difficult. Instead of estimating only the values of the dimensions which appear in training data as in traditional methods, we will reduce the size of tensor $\mathcal{T}$ via a low-rank approximation. With different approximation methods, (4) will have different equivalent forms, e.g. (6), (7) in §4.1.

Optimization objective: The loss function ℓ for training the log-linear model uses (3) for scores, e.g., the log-loss $\ell(\mathbf{x}, \mathbf{y}; \mathcal{T}) = -\log \frac{\exp\{s(\mathbf{x}, \mathbf{y}; \mathcal{T})\}}{\sum_{\mathbf{y}' \in L} \exp\{s(\mathbf{x}, \mathbf{y}'; \mathcal{T})\}}$. Learning can be formulated as the following optimization problem:

$$\underset{\mathcal{T}}{\text{minimize:}} \quad \sum_{(\mathbf{x}, y) \in \mathcal{D}} \ell(\mathbf{x}, y; \mathcal{T})$$

$$\text{subject to:} \quad \begin{cases} \text{rank}(\mathcal{T}) \leq (r_1, r_2, \ldots, r_{n+2}) & (5) \\ \qquad\qquad \text{(Tucker-form)} \\ \text{rank}(\mathcal{T}) \leq r \quad \text{(CP-form)} \end{cases}$$

where the constraints on $\text{rank}(\mathcal{T})$ depend on the chosen tensor approximation method (§2).

The above framework has some advantages: First, as discussed in §1 and here, we hope the representations capture rich interactions between different parts of the lexical features; the low-rank tensor approximation methods keep the most important interaction information of the original tensor, while significantly reducing its size. Second, the low-rank structure will encourage weight-sharing among lexical features with similar decomposed parts, leading to better model generalization. Note that there are examples where features have different numbers of multiple lexical parts, such as both unigram and bigram features in PP-attachment. We will use two different methods to handle these features (§5).

Remarks (advantages of our factorization) Compared to prior work, e.g. (Lei et al., 2014; Lei et al., 2015), the proposed factorization has the following advantages:

1. **Parameter explosion** when mapping a view with lexical properties to its representation vector (as will be discussed in 4.3): Our factorization allows the model to treat word embeddings as inputs to the views of lexical parts, dramatically reducing the parameters. Prior work cannot do this since its views are mixtures of lexical and non-lexical properties. Note that Lei et al. (2014) uses embeddings by *concatenating* them to specific views, which increases dimensionality, but the improvement is limited.

2. **No weight-sharing** among conjunctions with same lexical property, like the child-word "word(c)" and its conjunction with head-postag "word(c) $\wedge$ word(g)" in Figure 1(b). The factorization in prior work treats them as *independent* features, greatly increasing the dimensionality. Our factorization builds representations of both features based on the embedding of "word(c)", thus utilizing their connections and reducing the dimensionality.

The above advantages are also key to overcome the problems of prior work mentioned at the end of §1.

4 Feature Representations via Low-rank Tensor Approximations

Using one-hot encodings for each of the parts of feature ϕ results in a very large tensor. This section shows how to compute the score in (4) without constructing the full feature tensor using two tensor approximation methods (§4.1 and §4.2).

We begin with some intuition. To score the original (full rank) tensor representation of ϕ, we need a parameter tensor $\mathcal{T}$ of size $d_1 \times d_2 \times \ldots \times d_{n+2}$, where $d_3 = \cdots = d_{n+2} = |V|$ is the vocabulary size, n is the number of lexical parts in the feature

and $d_1 = |L|$ and $d_2 = |F|$ are the number of different labels and non-lexical properties, respectively. (§5 will handle n varying across features.) Our methods reduce the tensor size by embedding each part of ϕ into a lower dimensional space, where we represent each label, non-lexical property and words with an $r_1, r_2, r_3, \ldots, r_{n+2}$ dimensional vector respectively ($r_i \ll d_i, \forall i$). These embedded features can then be scored by much smaller tensors. We denote the above transformations as matrices $\mathbf{W}_l \in \mathbb{R}^{r_1 \times d_1}$, $\mathbf{W}_f \in \mathbb{R}^{r_2 \times d_2}$, $\mathbf{W}_i \in \mathbb{R}^{r_{i+2} \times d_{i+2}}$ for $i = 1, \ldots, n$, and write corresponding low-dimensional hidden representations as $\mathbf{h}_{\mathbf{y}}^{(l)} = \mathbf{W}_l \mathbf{y}$, $\mathbf{h}_{\mathbf{u}}^{(f)} = \mathbf{W}_f \mathbf{u}$ and $\mathbf{h}_{\mathbf{w}}^{(i)} = \mathbf{W}_i \mathbf{w}$.

In our methods, the above transformations of embeddings are *parts of low-rank tensors* as in (5), so the embeddings of non-lexical properties and labels can be trained simultaneously with the low-rank tensors. Note that for one-hot input encodings the transformation matrices are essentially lookup tables, making the computation of these transformations sufficiently fast.

4.1 Tucker Form

For our first approximation, we assume that tensor $\mathcal{T}$ has a low-rank Tucker decomposition: $\mathcal{T} = g \times_l \mathbf{W}_l \times_f \mathbf{W}_f \times_{\mathbf{w}_1} \mathbf{W}_1 \times_{\mathbf{w}_2} \cdots \times_{\mathbf{w}_n} \mathbf{W}_n$. We can then express the scoring function (4) for a feature $\phi = (\mathbf{y}, \mathbf{u}, \mathbf{w}_1, \ldots \mathbf{w}_n)$ with n-lexical parts, as:

$$s(\mathbf{y}, \mathbf{u}, \mathbf{w}_1, \cdots, \mathbf{w}_n; g, \mathbf{W}_l, \mathbf{W}_f, \{\mathbf{W}_i\}_{i=1}^n)$$
$$= g \times_l \mathbf{h}_{\mathbf{y}}^{(l)} \times_f \mathbf{h}_{\mathbf{u}}^{(f)} \times_{\mathbf{w}_1} \mathbf{h}_{\mathbf{w}_1}^{(1)} \cdots \times_{\mathbf{w}_n} \mathbf{h}_{\mathbf{w}_n}^{(n)}, \quad (6)$$

which amounts to first projecting $\mathbf{u}, \mathbf{y}$, and $\mathbf{w}_i$ (for all i) to lower dimensional vectors $\mathbf{h}_{\mathbf{u}}^{(f)}, \mathbf{h}_{\mathbf{y}}^{(l)}, \mathbf{h}_{\mathbf{w}_i}^{(i)}$, and then weighting these hidden representations using the flattened core tensor g. The low-dimensional representations and the corresponding weights are learned jointly using a discriminative (supervised) criterion. We call the model based on this representation the *Low-Rank Feature Representation with Tucker form*, or LRFR$_n$-TUCKER.

4.2 CP Form

For the Tucker approximation the number of parameters in (6) scale exponentially with the number of lexical parts. For instance, suppose each $\mathbf{h}_{\mathbf{w}_i}^{(i)}$ has dimensionality r, then $|g| \propto r^n$. To address scalability and further control the complexity of our tensor based model, we approximate the parameter tensor using CP decomposition as in (2), resulting in the following scoring function:

$$s(\mathbf{y}, \mathbf{u}, \mathbf{w}_1, \cdots, \mathbf{w}_n; \mathbf{W}_l, \mathbf{W}_f, \{\mathbf{W}_i\}_{i=1}^n) =$$

$$\sum_{j=1}^{r} \left(\mathbf{h}_\mathbf{y}^{(l)} \circ \mathbf{h}_\mathbf{u}^{(f)} \circ \mathbf{h}_{\mathbf{w}_1}^{(1)} \circ \cdots \circ \mathbf{h}_{\mathbf{w}_n}^{(n)} \right)_j . \quad (7)$$

We call this model *Low-Rank Feature Representation with CP form* (LRFR$_n$-CP).

4.3 Pre-trained Word Embeddings

One of the computational and statistical bottlenecks in learning these LRFR$_n$ models is the vocabulary size; the number of parameters to learn in each matrix $\mathbf{W}_i$ scales linearly with $|V|$ and would require very large sets of labeled training data. To alleviate this problem, we use pre-trained continuous word embeddings (Mikolov et al., 2013) as input embeddings rather than the one-hot word encodings. We denote the m-dimensional word embeddings by $e_\mathbf{w}$; so the transformation matrices $\mathbf{W}_i$ for the lexical parts are of size $r_i \times m$ where $m \ll |V|$.

We note that when sufficiently large labeled data is available, our model allows for fine-tuning the pre-trained word embeddings to improve the expressive strength of the model, as is common with deep network models.

Remarks Our LRFRs introduce embeddings for non-lexical properties and labels, making them better suit the common setting in NLP: rich linguistic properties; and large label sets such as open-domain tasks (Hoffmann et al., 2010). The LRFR-CP better suits n-gram features, since when n increases 1, the only new parameters are the corresponding $\mathbf{W}_i$. It is also very efficient during prediction ($O(nr)$), since the cost of transformations can be ignored with the help of look-up tables and pre-computing.

5 Learning Representations for n-gram Lexical Features of Mixed Lengths

For features with n lexical parts, we can train an LRFR$_n$ model to obtain their representations. However, we often have features of varying n (e.g. both unigrams (n=1) and bigrams (n=2) as in Figure 1).

We require representations for features with arbitrary different n simultaneously.

We propose two solutions. The first is a straightforward solution based on our framework, which handles each n with a $(n+2)$-way tensor. This strategy is commonly used in NLP, e.g. Taub-Tabib et al. (2015) have different kernel functions for different order of dependency features. The second is an approximation method which aims to use a single tensor to handle all ns.

Multiple Low-Rank Tensors Suppose that we can divide the feature set $S(\mathbf{x}, \mathbf{y})$ into subsets $S_1(\mathbf{x}, \mathbf{y}), S_2(\mathbf{x}, \mathbf{y}), \ldots, S_n(\mathbf{x}, \mathbf{y})$ which correspond to features with one lexical part (unigram features), two lexical parts (bigram features), $\ldots$ and n lexical parts (n-gram features), respectively. To handle these types of features, we modify the training objective as follows:

$$\underset{\mathcal{T}_1, \mathcal{T}_2, \cdots, \mathcal{T}_n}{\text{minimize}} \sum_{(\mathbf{x}, \mathbf{y}) \in D} \ell(\mathbf{x}, \mathbf{y}; \mathcal{T}_1, \mathcal{T}_2, \ldots, \ldots \mathcal{T}_n), \quad (8)$$

where the score of a training instance $(\mathbf{x}, \mathbf{y})$ is defined as $s(\mathbf{x}, \mathbf{y}; \mathcal{T}) = \sum_{i=1}^{n} \sum_{\phi \in S_i(\mathbf{x}, \mathbf{y})} s(\phi; \mathcal{T}_i)$. We use the Tucker form low-rank tensor for $\mathcal{T}_1$, and the CP form for $\mathcal{T}_i$ ($\forall i > 1$). We refer to this method as LRFR$_1$-TUCKER & LRFR$_2$-CP.

Word Clusters Alternatively, to handle different numbers of lexical parts, we replace some lexical parts with discrete word clusters. Let $c(\mathbf{w})$ denote the word cluster (e.g. from Brown clustering) for word w. For bigram features we have:

$$s(\mathbf{y}, \mathbf{u}, \mathbf{w}_1, \mathbf{w}_2; \mathcal{T})$$
$$= s(\mathbf{y}, \mathbf{u} \wedge c(\mathbf{w}_1), \mathbf{w}_2; \mathcal{T}) + s(\mathbf{y}, \mathbf{u} \wedge c(\mathbf{w}_2), \mathbf{w}_1; \mathcal{T})$$
$$= \mathcal{T} \times_l \mathbf{y} \times_f (\mathbf{u} \wedge c(\mathbf{w}_1)) \times_\mathbf{w} e_{\mathbf{w}_2}$$
$$+ \mathcal{T} \times_l \mathbf{y} \times_f (\mathbf{u} \wedge c(\mathbf{w}_2)) \times_\mathbf{w} e_{\mathbf{w}_1} \quad (9)$$

where for each word we have introduced an additional set of non-lexical properties that are conjunctions of word clusters and the original non-lexical properties. This allows us to reduce an n-gram feature representation to a unigram representation. The advantage of this method is that it uses a single low-rank tensor to score features with different numbers of lexical parts. This is particularly helpful when we have very limited labeled data. We denote this method as LRFR$_1$-BROWN, since we use Brown clusters in practice. In the experiments we use the

Tucker form for LRFR$_1$-BROWN.

6 Parameter Estimation

The goal of learning is to find a tensor $\mathcal{T}$ that solves problem (5). Note that this is a non-convex objective, so compared to the convex objective in a traditional log-linear model, we are trading better feature representations with the cost of a harder optimization problem. While stochastic gradient descent (SGD) is a natural choice for learning representations in large data settings, problem (5) involves rank constraints, which require an expensive proximal operation to enforce the constraints at each iteration of SGD. We seek a more efficient learning algorithm. Note that we fixed the size of each transformation matrix $W_i \in \mathbb{R}^{r_i \times d_i}$ so that the smaller dimension ($r_i < d_i$) matches the upper bound on the rank. Therefore, the rank constants are always satisfied through a run of SGD and we in essence have an unconstrained optimization problem. Note that in this way we do not guarantee orthogonality and full-rank of the learned transformation matrices. These properties are assumed in general, but are not necessary according to (Kolda and Bader, 2009).

The gradients are computed via the chain-rule. We use AdaGrad (Duchi et al., 2011) and apply L2 regularization on all W_is and g, except for the case of $r_i{=}d_i$, where we will start with $W_i = I$ and regularize with $\|W_i - I\|_2$. We use early-stopping on a development set.

7 Experimental Settings

We evaluate LRFR on three tasks: relation extraction, PP attachment and preposition disambiguation (see Table 1 for a task summary). We include detailed feature templates in Table 2.

PP-attachment and relation extraction are two fundamental NLP tasks, and we test our models on the largest English data sets. The preposition disambiguation task was designed for compositional semantics, which is an important application of deep learning and distributed representations. On all these tasks, we compare to the state-of-the-art.

We use the same word embeddings in Belinkov et al. (2014) on PP-attachment for a fair comparison. For the other experiments, we use the same 200-d word embeddings in Yu et al. (2015).

Relation Extraction We use the English portion of the ACE 2005 relation extraction dataset (Walker et al., 2006). Following Yu et al. (2015), we use both gold entity spans and types, train the model on the news domain and test on the broadcast conversation domain. To highlight the impact of training data size we evaluate with all 43,518 relations (entity mention pairs) and a reduced training set of the first 10,000 relations. We report precision, recall, and F1.

We compare to two baseline methods: 1) a log-linear model with a rich binary feature set from Sun et al. (2011) and Zhou et al. (2005) as described in Yu et al. (2015) (BASELINE); 2) the embedding model (FCM) of Gormley et al. (2015), which uses rich linguistic features for relation extraction. We use the same feature templates and evaluate on fine-grained relations (sub-types, 32 labels) (Yu et al., 2015). This will evaluate how LRFR can utilize non-lexical linguistic features.

PP-attachment We consider the prepositional phrase (PP) attachment task of Belinkov et al. (2014),[3] where for each PP the correct head (verbs or nouns) must be selected from content words before the PP (within a 10-word window). We formulate the task as a ranking problem, where we optimize the score of the correct head from a list of candidates with varying sizes.

PP-attachment suffers from data sparsity because of bi-lexical features, which we will model with methods in §5. Belikov et al. show that rich features – POS, WordNet and VerbNet – help this task. The combination of these features give a large number of non-lexical properties, for which embeddings of non-lexical properties in LRFR should be useful.

We extract a dev set from section 22 of the PTB following the description in Belinkov et al. (2014).

Preposition Disambiguation We consider the preposition disambiguation task proposed by Ritter et al. (2014). The task is to determine the spatial relationship a preposition indicates based on the two objects connected by the preposition. For example, "the apple on the refrigerator" indicates the "support by Horizontal Surface" relation, while "the apple on the branch" indicates the "Support from Above" relation. Since the meaning of a preposition depends

---

[3] http://groups.csail.mit.edu/rbg/code/pp

Task	Benchmark	Dataset	Numbers on Each View	
			#Labels (d_1)	#Non-lexical Features (d_2)
Relation Extraction	Yu et al. (2015)	ACE 2005	32	264
PP-attachment	Belinkov et al. (2014)	WSJ	-	1,213 / 607
Preposition Disambiguation	Ritter et al. (2014)	Ritter et al. (2014)	6	9/3

Table 1: Statistics of each task. PP-attachment and preposition disambiguation have both unigram and bigram features. Therefore we list the numbers of non-lexical properties for both types.

Set	Template
HeadEmb	$\{I[i = h_1], I[i = h_2]\}$ (head of M_1/M_2) $\&\{\phi, t_{h_1}, t_{h_2}, t_{h_1}\&t_{h_2}\}$
Context	$I[i = h_1/h_2 \pm 1]$ (left/right token of w_{h_1/h_2})
In-between	$I[i > h_1]\&I[i < h_2]\&\{\phi, t_{h_1}, t_{h_2}, t_{h_1}\&t_{h_2}\}$
On-path	$I[w_i \in P]\&\{\phi, t_{h_1}, t_{h_2}, t_{h_1}\&t_{h_2}\}$

Set	Template
Bag of Words	$w, p \& w$ (w is w_m or w_h)
Word-Position	$w_m, w_h, w_m \& w_h$
Preposition	$p, p \& w_m, p \& w_h, p \& w_m \& w_h$

Set	Template
Bag of Words	w (w is w_m or w_h), $w_m\&w_h$
Distance	$\mathrm{Dis}(w_h, w_m) \& \{w_m, w_h, w_m\&w_h\}$
Prep	$w_p \& \{w_m, w_h, w_m\&w_h\}$
POS	$t(w_h) \& \{w_m, w_h, w_m\&w_h\}$
NextPOS	$t(w_{h+1}) \& \{w_m, w_h, w_m\&w_h\}$
VerbNet	$P = \{p(w_h)\} \& \{w_m, w_h, w_m\&w_h\}$
	$I[w_p \in P] \& \{w_m, w_h, w_m\&w_h\}$
WordNet	$R_h = \{r(w_h)\} \& \{w_m, w_h, w_m\&w_h\}$
	$R_m = \{r(w_m)\} \& \{w_m, w_h, w_m\&w_h\}$

Table 2: **Up-left**: Unigram lexical features (only showing non-lexical parts) for **relation extraction** (from Yu et al. (2014)). We denote the two target entities as M_1, M_2 (with head indices h_1, h_2, NE types t_{h_1}, t_{h_2}), and their dependency path as P. **Right**: Uni/bi-gram feature for **PP-attachment**: Each feature is defined on tuple (w_m, w_p, w_h), where w_p is the preposition word, w_m is the child of the preposition, and w_h is a candidate head of w_p. $t(w)$: POS tag of word w; $p(w)$: a preposition collocation of verb w from VerbNet; $r(w)$: the root hypernym of word w in WordNet. Dis($\cdot, \cdot$): the number of candidate heads between two words. **Down-left**: Uni/bi-gram feature for **preposition disambiguation** (for each preposition word p, its modifier noun w_m and head noun w_h). Since the sentences are different from each other on only p, w_m and w_h, we ignore the words on the other positions.

on the combination of both its head and child word, we expect conjunctions between these word embeddings to help, i.e. features with two lexical parts.

We include three baselines: point-wise addition (SUM) (Mitchell and Lapata, 2010), concatenation (Ritter et al., 2014), and an SVM based on hand-crafted features in Table 2. Ritter et al. show that the first two methods beat other compositional models.

Hyperparameters are all tuned on the dev set. The chosen values are learning rate $\eta = 0.05$ and the weight of L2 regularizer $\lambda = 0.005$ for LRFR, except for the third LRFR in Table 3 which has $\lambda = 0.05$. We select the rank of LRFR-TUCKER with a grid search from the following values: $r_1 = \{10, 20, d_1\}$, $r_2 = \{20, 50, d_2\}$ and $r_3 = \{50, 100, 200\}$. For LRFR-CP, we select $r = \{50, 100, 200\}$. For the *PP-attachement* task there is no r_1 since it uses a ranking model. For the *Preposition Disambiguation* we do not choose r_1 since the number of labels is small.

8 Results

Relation Extraction All LRFR-TUCKER models improve over BASELINE and FCM (Table 3), making

these the best reported numbers for this task. However, LRFR-CP does not work as well on the features with only one lexical part. The Tucker-form does a better job of capturing interactions between different views. In the limited training setting, we find that LRFR-CP does best.

Additionally, the primary advantage of the CP approximation is its reduction in the number of model parameters and running time. We report each model's running time for a single pass on the development set. The LRFR-CP is by far the fastest. The first three LRFR-TUCKER models are slightly slower than FCM, because they work on dense non-lexical property embeddings while FCM benefits from sparse vectors.

PP-attachment Table 4 shows that LRFR (89.6 and 90.3) improves over the previous best standalone system HPCD (88.7) by a large margin, with exactly the same resources. Belinkov et al. (2014) also reported results of parsers and parser re-rankers, which can access to additional resources (complete parses for training and complete sentences as inputs) so it is unfair to compare them with the standalone systems like HPCD and our LRFR. Nonethe-

Method	Parameters			Full Set ($|D|$=43,518)			Reduced Set ($|D|$=10,000)			Prediction Time (ms)
	r_1	r_2	r_3	P	R	F1	P	R	F1	
BASELINE	-	-	-	60.2	**51.2**	55.3	-	-	-	-
FCM	32/N	264/N	200/N	62.9	49.6	55.4	**61.6**	37.1	46.3	2,242
LRFR$_1$-TUCKER	32/N	20/Y	200/Y	62.1	**52.7**	**57.0**	51.5	40.8	45.5	3,076
LRFR$_1$-TUCKER	32/N	20/Y	200/N	**63.5**	51.1	56.6	52.8	40.1	45.6	2,972
LRFR$_1$-TUCKER	20/Y	20/Y	200/Y	62.4	51.0	56.1	52.1	41.2	46.0	2,538
LRFR$_1$-TUCKER	32/Y	20/Y	50/Y	57.4	52.4	54.8	49.7	**46.1**	47.8	1,198
LRFR$_1$-CP		200/Y		61.3	50.7	55.5	58.3	41.6	**48.6**	**502**

Table 3: Results on test for relation extraction. Y(es)/N(o) indicates whether embeddings are updated during training.

System	Resources Used	Acc
SVM (Belinkov et al., 2014)	distance, word, embedding, clusters, POS, WordNet, VerbNet	86.0
HPCD (Belinkov et al., 2014)	distance, embedding, POS, WordNet, VerbNet	88.7
LRFR$_1$-TUCKER & LRFR$_2$-CP	distance, embedding, POS, WordNet, VerbNet	**90.3**
LRFR$_1$-BROWN	distance, embedding, clusters, POS, WordNet, VerbNet	89.6
RBG (Lei et al., 2014)	dependency parser	88.4
Charniak-RS (McClosky et al., 2006)	dependency parser + re-ranker	88.6
RBG + HPCD (combined model)	dependency parser + distance, embedding, POS, WordNet, VerbNet	90.1

Table 4: PP-attachment test accuracy. The baseline results are from Belinkov et al. (2014).

less LRFR$_1$-TUCKER & LRFR$_2$-CP (90.3) still outperforms the state-of-the-art parser RBG (88.4), re-ranker Charniak-RS (88.6), and the combination of the state-of-the-art parser and compositional model RBG + HPCD (90.1). Thus, even with fewer resources, LRFR becomes the new best system.

Not shown in the table: we also tried LRFR$_1$-TUCKER & LRFR$_2$-CP with *postag features only* (89.7), and with grand-head-modifier conjunctions removed (89.3) . Note that compared to LRFR, RBG benefits from binary features, which also exploit grand-head-modifier structures. Yet the above reduced models still work better than RBG (88.4) without using additional resources.[4] Moreover, the results of LRFR can still be potentially improved by combining with binary features. The above results show the advantage of our factorization method, which allows for utilizing pre-trained word embeddings, and thus can benefit from semi-supervised learning.

Preposition Disambiguation LRFR improves (Table 5) over the best methods (SUM and Concatenation) in Ritter et al. (2014) as well as the SVM

Method	Accuracy
SVM - Lexical Features	85.09
SUM	80.55
Concatenation	86.73
LRFR$_1$-TUCKER & LRFR$_2$-CP	87.82
LRFR$_1$-BROWN	**88.18**
LRFR$_1$-BROWN - Control	84.18

Table 5: Accuracy for spatial classification of PPs.

based on the original lexical features (85.1). In this task LRFR$_1$-BROWN better represents the unigram and bigram lexical features, compared to the usage of two low-rank tensors (LRFR$_1$-TUCKER & LRFR$_2$-CP). This may be because LRFR$_1$-BROWN has fewer parameters, which is better for smaller training sets.

We also include a control setting (LRFR$_1$-BROWN - Control), which has a full rank parameter tensor with the same inputs on each view as LRFR$_1$-BROWN, but represented as one hot vectors without transforming to the hidden representations hs. This is equivalent to an SVM with the compound cluster features as in Koo et al. (2008). It performs much worse than LRFR$_1$-BROWN, showing the advantage of using word embeddings and low-rank tensors.

Summary For unigram lexical features, LRFR$_n$-TUCKER achieves better results than LRFR$_n$-CP. However, in settings with fewer training examples,

---

[4]Still this is not a fair comparison since we have different training objectives. Using RBG's factorization and training with our objective will give a fair comparison and we leave it to future work.

features with more lexical parts (n-grams), or when faster predictions are advantageous, LRFR$_n$-CP does best as it has fewer parameters to estimate. For n-grams of variable length, LRFR$_1$-TUCKER & LRFR$_2$-CP does best. In settings with fewer training examples, LRFR$_1$-BROWN does best as it has only one parameter tensor to estimate.

9 Related Work

Dimensionality Reduction for Complex Features is a standard technique to address high-dimensional features, including PCA, alternating structural optimization (Ando and Zhang, 2005), denoising autoencoders (Vincent et al., 2008), and feature embeddings (Yang and Eisenstein, 2015). These methods treat features as atomic elements and ignore the inner structure of features, so they learn separate embedding for each feature without shared parameters. As a result, they still suffer from large parameter spaces when the feature space is very huge.[5]

Another line of research studies the inner structures of lexical features: e.g. Koo et al. (2008), Turian et al. (2010), Sun et al. (2011), Nguyen and Grishman (2014), Roth and Woodsend (2014), and Hermann et al. (2014) used pre-trained word embeddings to replace the lexical parts of features ; Srikumar and Manning (2014), Gormley et al. (2015) and Yu et al. (2015) propose splitting lexical features into different parts and employing tensors to perform classification. The above can therefore be seen as special cases of our model that only embed a certain part (view) of the complex features. This restriction also makes their model parameters form a full rank tensor, resulting in data sparsity and high computational costs when the tensors are large.

Composition Models (Deep Learning) build representations for structures based on their component word embeddings (Collobert et al., 2011; Bordes et al., 2012; Socher et al., 2012; Socher et al., 2013b). When using only word embeddings, these models achieved successes on several NLP tasks, but sometimes fail to learn useful syntactic or semantic patterns beyond the strength of combinations of word embeddings, such as the dependency relation in Figure 1(a). To tackle this problem, some work designed their model structures according to a specific kind of linguistic patterns, e.g. dependency paths (Ma et al., 2015; Liu et al., 2015), while a recent trend enhances compositional models with linguistic features. For example, Belinkov et al. (2014) concatenate embeddings with linguistic features before feeding them to a neural network; Socher et al. (2013a) and Hermann and Blunsom (2013) enhanced Recursive Neural Networks by refining the transformation matrices with linguistic features (e.g. phrase types). These models are similar to ours in the sense of learning representations based on linguistic features and embeddings.

Low-rank Tensor Models for NLP aim to handle the conjunction among different views of features (Cao and Khudanpur, 2014; Lei et al., 2014; Chen and Manning, 2014). Yu and Dredze (2015) proposed a model to compose phrase embeddings from words, which has an equivalent form of our CP-based method under certain restrictions. Our work applies a similar idea to exploiting the inner structure of complex features, and can handle n-gram features with different ns. Our factorization (§3) is general and easy to adapt to new tasks. More importantly, it makes the model benefit from pre-trained word embeddings as shown by the PP-attachment results.

10 Conclusion

We have presented LRFR, a feature representation model that exploits the inner structure of complex lexical features and applies a low-rank tensor to efficiently score features with this representation. LRFR attains the state-of-the-art on several tasks, including relation extraction, PP-attachment, and preposition disambiguation. We make our implementation available for general use.[6]

Acknowledgements

A major portion of this work was done when MY was visiting MD and RA at JHU. This research was supported in part by NSF grant IIS-1546482.

---

[5]For example, a state-of-the-art dependency parser (Zhang and McDonald, 2014) extracts about 10 million features; in this case, learning 100-dimensional feature embeddings involves estimating approximately a billion parameters.

[6]https://github.com/Gorov/LowRankFCM

References

Rie Kubota Ando and Tong Zhang. 2005. A framework for learning predictive structures from multiple tasks and unlabeled data. *The Journal of Machine Learning Research*, 6.

Yonatan Belinkov, Tao Lei, Regina Barzilay, and Amir Globerson. 2014. Exploring compositional architectures and word vector representations for prepositional phrase attachment. *Transactions of the Association for Computational Linguistics*, 2.

Yoshua Bengio, Holger Schwenk, Jean-Sébastien Senécal, Fréderic Morin, and Jean-Luc Gauvain. 2006. Neural probabilistic language models. In *Innovations in Machine Learning*. Springer.

Antoine Bordes, Xavier Glorot, Jason Weston, and Yoshua Bengio. 2012. A semantic matching energy function for learning with multi-relational data. *Machine Learning*.

Yuan Cao and Sanjeev Khudanpur. 2014. Online learning in tensor space. In *Proceedings of the 52nd Annual Meeting of the Association for Computational Linguistics (Volume 1: Long Papers)*.

Danqi Chen and Christopher Manning. 2014. A fast and accurate dependency parser using neural networks. In *Proceedings of EMNLP*.

Ronan Collobert, Jason Weston, Léon Bottou, Michael Karlen, Koray Kavukcuoglu, and Pavel Kuksa. 2011. Natural language processing (almost) from scratch. *JMLR*, 12.

John Duchi, Elad Hazan, and Yoram Singer. 2011. Adaptive subgradient methods for online learning and stochastic optimization. *The Journal of Machine Learning Research*, 12.

Matthew R. Gormley, Mo Yu, and Mark Dredze. 2015. Improved relation extraction with feature-rich compositional embedding models. In *Proceedings of the 2015 Conference on Empirical Methods in Natural Language Processing*.

Karl Moritz Hermann and Phil Blunsom. 2013. The role of syntax in vector space models of compositional semantics. In *Association for Computational Linguistics*.

Karl Moritz Hermann, Dipanjan Das, Jason Weston, and Kuzman Ganchev. 2014. Semantic frame identification with distributed word representations. In *Proceedings of the 52nd Annual Meeting of the Association for Computational Linguistics (Volume 1: Long Papers)*.

Raphael Hoffmann, Congle Zhang, and Daniel S. Weld. 2010. Learning 5000 relational extractors. In *Proceedings of the 48th Annual Meeting of the Association for Computational Linguistics*.

Tamara G Kolda and Brett W Bader. 2009. Tensor decompositions and applications. *SIAM review*, 51(3).

Terry Koo, Xavier Carreras, and Michael Collins. 2008. Simple semi-supervised dependency parsing. In *Proceedings of ACL*.

Tao Lei, Yu Xin, Yuan Zhang, Regina Barzilay, and Tommi Jaakkola. 2014. Low-rank tensors for scoring dependency structures. In *Proceedings of the 52nd Annual Meeting of the Association for Computational Linguistics (Volume 1: Long Papers)*.

Tao Lei, Yuan Zhang, Lluís Màrquez, Alessandro Moschitti, and Regina Barzilay. 2015. High-order low-rank tensors for semantic role labeling. In *Proceedings of the 2015 Conference of the North American Chapter of the Association for Computational Linguistics: Human Language Technologies*.

Yang Liu, Furu Wei, Sujian Li, Heng Ji, Ming Zhou, and Houfeng WANG. 2015. A dependency-based neural network for relation classification. In *Proceedings of the 53rd Annual Meeting of the Association for Computational Linguistics and the 7th International Joint Conference on Natural Language Processing (Volume 2: Short Papers)*.

Mingbo Ma, Liang Huang, Bowen Zhou, and Bing Xiang. 2015. Dependency-based convolutional neural networks for sentence embedding. In *Proceedings of the 53rd Annual Meeting of the Association for Computational Linguistics and the 7th International Joint Conference on Natural Language Processing (Volume 2: Short Papers)*.

David McClosky, Eugene Charniak, and Mark Johnson. 2006. Effective self-training for parsing. In *Proceedings of the main conference on human language technology conference of the North American Chapter of the Association of Computational Linguistics*.

Tomas Mikolov, Ilya Sutskever, Kai Chen, Greg S Corrado, and Jeff Dean. 2013. Distributed representations of words and phrases and their compositionality. In *Advances in neural information processing systems*, pages 3111–3119.

Scott Miller, Jethran Guinness, and Alex Zamanian. 2004. Name tagging with word clusters and discriminative training. In *Proceedings of HLT-NAACL*.

Jeff Mitchell and Mirella Lapata. 2010. Composition in distributional models of semantics. *Cognitive science*, 34(8).

Thien Huu Nguyen and Ralph Grishman. 2014. Employing word representations and regularization for domain adaptation of relation extraction. In *Association for Computational Linguistics (ACL)*.

Samuel Ritter, Cotie Long, Denis Paperno, Marco Baroni, Matthew Botvinick, and Adele Goldberg. 2014.

Leveraging preposition ambiguity to assess representation of semantic interaction in cdsm. In *NIPS Workshop on Learning Semantics*.

Michael Roth and Kristian Woodsend. 2014. Composition of word representations improves semantic role labelling. In *Proceedings of EMNLP*.

Richard Socher, Brody Huval, Christopher D. Manning, and Andrew Y. Ng. 2012. Semantic compositionality through recursive matrix-vector spaces. In *Proceedings of EMNLP-CoNLL 2012*.

Richard Socher, John Bauer, Christopher D Manning, and Andrew Y Ng. 2013a. Parsing with compositional vector grammars. In *Proceedings of ACL*.

Richard Socher, Alex Perelygin, Jean Wu, Jason Chuang, Christopher D. Manning, Andrew Ng, and Christopher Potts. 2013b. Recursive deep models for semantic compositionality over a sentiment treebank. In *Proceedings of EMNLP*.

Vivek Srikumar and Christopher D Manning. 2014. Learning distributed representations for structured output prediction. In *Advances in Neural Information Processing Systems*.

Ang Sun, Ralph Grishman, and Satoshi Sekine. 2011. Semi-supervised relation extraction with large-scale word clustering. In *Proceedings of the 49th Annual Meeting of the Association for Computational Linguistics: Human Language Technologies*.

Hillel Taub-Tabib, Yoav Goldberg, and Amir Globerson. 2015. Template kernels for dependency parsing. In *Proceedings of the 2015 Conference of the North American Chapter of the Association for Computational Linguistics: Human Language Technologies*.

Joseph Turian, Lev Ratinov, and Yoshua Bengio. 2010. Word representations: a simple and general method for semi-supervised learning. In *Association for Computational Linguistics*.

Pascal Vincent, Hugo Larochelle, Yoshua Bengio, and Pierre-Antoine Manzagol. 2008. Extracting and composing robust features with denoising autoencoders. In *Proceedings of the 25th international conference on Machine learning*.

Christopher Walker, Stephanie Strassel, Julie Medero, and Kazuaki Maeda. 2006. ACE 2005 multilingual training corpus. *Linguistic Data Consortium, Philadelphia*.

Yi Yang and Jacob Eisenstein. 2015. Unsupervised multi-domain adaptation with feature embeddings. In *Proceedings of the 2015 Conference of the North American Chapter of the Association for Computational Linguistics: Human Language Technologies*, pages 672–682, Denver, Colorado, May–June. Association for Computational Linguistics.

Mo Yu and Mark Dredze. 2015. Learning composition models for phrase embeddings. *Transactions of the Association for Computational Linguistics*, 3.

Mo Yu, Matthew R. Gormley, and Mark Dredze. 2015. Combining word embeddings and feature embeddings for fine-grained relation extraction. In *North American Chapter of the Association for Computational Linguistics (NAACL)*.

Hao Zhang and Ryan McDonald. 2014. Enforcing structural diversity in cube-pruned dependency parsing. In *Proceedings of ACL*.

GuoDong Zhou, Jian Su, Jie Zhang, and Min Zhang. 2005. Exploring various knowledge in relation extraction. In *Proceedings of ACL*.

The Role of Context Types and Dimensionality in Learning Word Embeddings

Oren Melamud[†*]   **David McClosky**[‡*]   **Siddharth Patwardhan**[◇]   **Mohit Bansal**[§]

[†]Computer Science Department, Bar-Ilan University, Ramat-Gan, Israel
`melamuo@cs.biu.ac.il`

[‡]Google, New York, NY, USA
`dmcc@google.com`

[◇]IBM Watson, Yorktown Heights, NY, USA
`siddharth@us.ibm.com`

[§]Toyota Technological Institute at Chicago, Chicago, IL, 60637, USA
`mbansal@ttic.edu`

Abstract

We provide the first extensive evaluation of how using different types of context to learn skip-gram word embeddings affects performance on a wide range of intrinsic and extrinsic NLP tasks. Our results suggest that while intrinsic tasks tend to exhibit a clear preference to particular types of contexts and higher dimensionality, more careful tuning is required for finding the optimal settings for most of the extrinsic tasks that we considered. Furthermore, for these extrinsic tasks, we find that once the benefit from increasing the embedding dimensionality is mostly exhausted, simple concatenation of word embeddings, learned with different context types, can yield further performance gains. As an additional contribution, we propose a new variant of the skip-gram model that learns word embeddings from weighted contexts of substitute words.

1 Introduction

Word embeddings have become increasingly popular lately, proving to be valuable as a source of features in a broad range of NLP tasks with limited supervision (Turian et al., 2010; Collobert et al., 2011; Socher et al., 2013; Bansal et al., 2014). word2vec[1] skip-gram (Mikolov et al., 2013a)

and `GloVe`[2] (Pennington et al., 2014) are among the most widely used word embedding models today. Their success is largely due to an efficient and user-friendly implementation that learns high-quality word embeddings from very large corpora.

Both `word2vec` and `GloVe` learn low-dimensional continuous vector representations for words by considering window-based contexts, i.e., context words within some fixed distance of each side of the target word. However, the underlying models are equally applicable to different choices of context types. For example, Bansal et al. (2014) and Levy and Goldberg (2014) showed that using syntactic contexts rather than window contexts in `word2vec` captures *functional* similarity (as in *lion:cat*) rather than *topical* similarity or *relatedness* (as in *lion:zoo*). Further, Bansal et al. (2014) and Melamud et al. (2015b) showed the benefits of such modified-context embeddings in dependency parsing and lexical substitution tasks. However, to the best of our knowledge, there has not been an extensive evaluation of the effect of multiple, diverse context types on a wide range of NLP tasks.

Word embeddings are typically evaluated on *intrinsic* and *extrinsic* tasks. Intrinsic tasks mostly include predicting human judgments of semantic relations between words, e.g., as in WordSim-353 (Finkelstein et al., 2001), while extrinsic tasks include various 'real' downstream NLP tasks, such as coreference resolution and sentiment analysis. Re-

---

[1]`http://code.google.com/p/word2vec/`

[2]`http://nlp.stanford.edu/projects/glove/`

Proceedings of NAACL-HLT 2016, pages 1030–1040,
San Diego, California, June 12-17, 2016. ©2016 Association for Computational Linguistics

cent works have shown that while intrinsic evaluations are easier to perform, their correlation with results on extrinsic evaluations is not very reliable (Schnabel et al., 2015; Tsvetkov et al., 2015), stressing the importance of the latter.

In this work, we provide the first extensive evaluation of word embeddings learned with different types of context, on a wide range of intrinsic similarity and relatedness tasks, and extrinsic NLP tasks, namely dependency parsing, named entity recognition, coreference resolution, and sentiment analysis. We employ contexts based of different word window sizes, syntactic dependencies, and a lesser-known substitute words approach (Yatbaz et al., 2012). Finally, we experiment with combinations of the above word embeddings, comparing two approaches: (1) simple vector concatenation that offers a wider variety of features for a classifier to choose and learn weighted combinations from, and (2) dimensionality reduction via either Singular Value Decomposition or Canonical Correlation Analysis, which tries to find a smaller subset of features.

Our results suggest that it is worthwhile to carefully choose the right type of word embeddings for an extrinsic NLP task, rather than rely on intrinsic benchmark results. Specifically, picking the optimal context type and dimensionality is critical. Furthermore, once the benefit from increasing the embedding dimensionality is mostly exhausted, concatenation of word embeddings learned with different context types can yield further performance gains.

2 Word Embedding Context Types

2.1 Learning Corpus

We use a fixed learning corpus for a fair comparison of all embedding types: a concatenation of three large English corpora: (1) English Wikipedia 2015, (2) UMBC web corpus (Han et al., 2013), and (3) English Gigaword (LDC2011T07) newswire corpus (Parker et al., 2011). Our concatenated corpus is diverse and substantial in size with approximately 10B words. This allows us to learn high quality embeddings that cover a large vocabulary. After extracting clean text from these corpora, we used Stanford CoreNLP (Manning et al., 2014) for sentence splitting, tokenization, part-of-speech tagging and

dependency parsing.[3] Then, all tokens were lowercased, and sentences were shuffled to prevent structured bias. When learning word embeddings, we ignored words with corpus frequency lower than 100, yielding a vocabulary of about 500K words.[4]

2.2 Window-based Word Embeddings

We used `word2vec`'s skip-gram model with negative sampling (Mikolov et al., 2013b) to learn window-based word embeddings.[5] This popular method embeds both target words and contexts in the same low-dimensional space, where the embeddings of a target and context are pushed closer together the more frequently they co-occur in a learning corpus. Indirectly, this also results in similar embeddings for target words that co-occur with similar contexts. More formally, this method optimizes the following objective function:

$$L = \sum_{(t,c) \in PAIRS} L_{t,c} \qquad (1)$$

$$L_{t,c} = \log \sigma(v'_c \cdot v_t) + \sum_{neg \in NEGS_{(t,c)}} \log \sigma(-v'_{neg} \cdot v_t) \qquad (2)$$

where v_t and v'_c are the vector representations of target word t and context word c. $PAIRS$ is the set of window-based co-occurring target-context pairs considered by the model that depends on the window size, and $NEGS_{(t,c)}$ is a set of randomly sampled context words used with the pair (t, c).[6]

We experimented with window sizes of 1, 5, and 10, and various dimensionalities. We denote a window-based word embedding with window size of n and dimensionality of m with Wn^m. For example, $W5^{300}$ is a word embedding learned using a window size of 5 and dimensionality of 300.

2.3 Dependency-based Word Embeddings

We used `word2vecf`[7] (Levy and Goldberg, 2014), to learn dependency-based word embeddings from

---

[3]Parses follow the Universal Dependencies formalism and were produced by Stanford CoreNLP, version 3.5.2

[4]Our word embeddings are available at: `www.cs.biu.ac.il/nlp/resources/downloads/embeddings-contexts/`

[5]We used negative sampling = 5 and iterations = 3 in all of the experiments described in this paper.

[6]For more details refer to Mikolov et al. (2013b).

[7]`http://bitbucket.org/yoavgo/word2vecf`

the parsed version of our corpus, similar to the approach of Bansal et al. (2014). `word2vecf` accepts as its input arbitrary target-context pairs. In the case of dependency-based word embeddings, the context elements are the syntactic contexts of the target word, rather than the words in a window around it. Specifically, following Levy and Goldberg (2014), we first 'collapsed' prepositions (as implemented in `word2vecf`). Then, for a target word t with modifiers $m_1,...,m_k$ and head h, we paired the target word with the context elements $(m_1, r_1),...,(m_k, r_k),(h, r_h^{-1})$, where r is the type of the dependency relation between the head and the modifier (e.g., *dobj*, *prep_of*) and r^{-1} denotes an inverse relation. We denote a dependency-based word embedding with dimensionality of m by DEP^m. We note that under this setting `word2vecf` optimizes the same objective function described in Equation (1), with *PAIRS* now comprising dependency-based pairs instead of window-based ones.

2.4 Substitute-based Word Embeddings

Substitute vectors are a recent approach to representing contexts of target words, proposed in Yatbaz et al. (2012). Instead of the neighboring words themselves, a substitute vector includes the potential filler words for the target word slot, weighted according to how 'fit' they are to fill the target slot *given* the neighboring words. For example, the substitute vector representing the context of the word *love* in "I love my job", could look like: [*quit* 0.5, *love* 0.3, *hate* 0.1, *lost* 0.1]. Substitute-based contexts are generated using a language model and were successfully used in distributional semantics models for part-of-speech induction (Yatbaz et al., 2012), word sense induction (Baskaya et al., 2013), functional semantic similarity (Melamud et al., 2014) and lexical substitution tasks (Melamud et al., 2015a).

Similar to Yatbaz et al. (2012), we consider the words in a substitute vector, as a weighted set of contexts 'co-occurring' with the observed target word. For example, the above substitute vector is considered as the following set of weighted target-context pairs: {(*love*, *quit*, 0.5), (*love*, *love*, 0.3), (*love*, *hate*, 0.1), (*love*, *lost*, 0.1)}. To learn word embeddings from such weighted target-context pairs, we extended `word2vecf` by modifying the objective

W10^{300}	DEP^{300}	SUB^{300}
played	play	singing
play	played	rehearsing
plays	understudying	performing
professionally	caddying	composing
player	plays	running

Table 1: The top five words closest to target word *playing* in different embedding spaces.

function in Equation (1) as follows:

$$L = \sum_{(t,c)\in PAIRS} \alpha_{t,c} \cdot L_{t,c} \qquad (3)$$

where $\alpha_{t,c}$ is the weight of the target-context pair (t, c). With this simple modification, the effect of target-context pairs on the learned word representations becomes proportional to their weights.

To generate the substitute vectors we followed the methodology in (Yatbaz et al., 2012; Melamud et al., 2015a). We learned a 4-gram Kneser-Ney language model from our learning corpus using KenLM (Heafield et al., 2013). Then, we used FASTSUBS (Yuret, 2012) with this language model to efficiently generate substitute vectors, where the weight of each substitute s is the conditional probability $p(s|C)$ for this substitute to fill the target slot given the sentential context C. For efficiency, we pruned the substitute vectors to their top-10 substitutes, $s_1..s_{10}$, and normalized their probabilities such that $\sum_{i=1..10} p(s_i|C) = 1$. We also generated only up to 20,000 substitute vectors for each target word type. Finally, we converted each substitute vector into weighted target-substitute pairs and used our extended version of `word2vecf` to learn the substitute-based word embeddings, denoted SUB^m.

2.5 Qualitative Effect of Context Type

To motivate the rest of our work, we first qualitatively inspect the top most-similar words to some target words, using cosine similarity of their respective embeddings. As illustrated in Table 1, in embeddings learned with large window contexts, we see both functionally similar words and topically similar words, sometimes with a different part-of-speech. With small windows and dependency contexts, we generally see much fewer topically similar words, which is consistent with previous findings (Bansal et al., 2014; Levy and Goldberg, 2014). Finally, with substitute-based contexts, there appears to be even a stronger preference for functional similarity, with a tendency to also strictly preserve verb tense.

3 Word Embedding Combinations

As different choices of context type yield word embeddings with different properties, we hypothesize that combinations of such embeddings could be more informative for some extrinsic tasks. We experimented with two alternative approaches to combine different sets of word embeddings: (1) Simple vector concatenation, which is a lossless combination that comes at the cost of increased dimensionality, and (2) SVD and CCA, which are lossy combinations that attempt to capture the most useful information from the different embeddings sets with lower dimensionality. The methods used are described in more detail next.

3.1 Concatenation

Perhaps the simplest way to combine two different sets of word embeddings (sharing the same vocabulary) is to concatenate their word vectors for every word type. We denote such a combination of word embedding set A with word embedding set B using the symbol (+). For example W10+DEP^{600} is the concatenation of W10^{300} with DEP^{300}. Naturally, the dimensionality of the concatenated embeddings is the sum of the dimensionalities of the component embeddings. In our experiments, we only ever combine word embeddings of equal dimensionality.

The motivation behind concatenation relates primarily to supervised models in extrinsic tasks. In such settings, we hypothesize that using concatenated word embeddings as input features to a classifier could let it choose and combine (i.e., via learned weights) the most suitable features for the task. Consider a situation where the concatenated embedding W10+DEP^{600} is used to represent the word inputs to a named entity recognition classifier. In this case, the classifier could choose, for instance, to represent entity words mostly with dependency-based embedding features (reflecting functional semantics), and surrounding words with large window-based embedding features (reflecting topical semantics).

3.2 Singular Value Decomposition

Singular Value Decomposition (SVD) has been shown to be effective in compressing sparse word representations (Levy et al., 2015). In this work, we use this technique in the same way to reduce the dimensionality of concatenated word embeddings.

3.3 Canonical Correlation Analysis

Recent work used Canonical Correlation Analysis (CCA) to derive an improved set of word embeddings. The main idea is that two distinct sets of word embeddings, learned with different types of input data, are considered as multi-views of the same vocabulary. Then, CCA is used to project each onto a lower dimensional space, where correlation between the two is maximized. The correlated information is presumably more reliable. Dhillon et al. (2011) considered their two CCA views as embeddings learned from the left and from the right context of the target words, showing improvements on chunking and named entity recognition. Faruqui and Dyer (2014) and Lu et al. (2015) considered multilingual views, showing improvements in several intrinsic tasks, such as word and phrase similarity.

Inspired by this prior work, we consider pairs of word embedding sets, learned with different types of context, as different views and correlate them using linear CCA.[8] We use either the SimLex-999 or WordSim-353-R intrinsic benchmark (section 4.1) to tune the CCA hyperparameters[9] with the Spearmint Bayesian optimization tool[10] (Snoek et al., 2012). This results in different projections for each of these tuning objectives, where SimLex-999/WordSim-353-R is expected to give some bias towards functional/topical similarity, respectively.

4 Evaluation

4.1 Intrinsic Benchmarks

We employ several commonly used intrinsic benchmarks for assessing how well word embeddings mimic human judgements of semantic similarity of words. The popular **WordSim-353** dataset (Finkelstein et al., 2001) includes 353 word pairs manually

---

[8]See Faruqui and Dyer (2014), Lu et al. (2015) for details.
[9]These are projection dimensionality and regularization.
[10]`github.com/JasperSnoek/spearmint`

annotated with a degree of similarity. For example, *computer:keyboard* is annotated with 7.62, indicating a relatively high degree of similarity. While WordSim-353 does not make a distinction between different 'flavors' of similarity, Agirre et al. (2009) proposed two subsets of this dataset, **WordSim-353-S** and **WordSim-353-R**, which focus on functional and topical similarities, respectively. **SimLex-999** (Hill et al., 2014) is a larger word pair similarity dataset with 999 annotated pairs, purposely built to focus on functional similarity. We evaluate our embeddings on these datasets by computing a score for each pair as the cosine similarity of two word vectors. The Spearman's correlation[11] between the ranking of word pairs induced from the human annotations and that from the embeddings is reported.

The **TOEFL** task contains 80 synonym selection items, where a synonym of a target word is to be selected out of four possible choices. We report the overall accuracy of a system that uses cosine distance between the embeddings of the target word and each of the choices to select the one most similar to the target word as the answer.

4.2 Extrinsic Benchmarks

The following four diverse downstream NLP tasks serve as our extrinsic benchmarks.[12]

1) Dependency Parsing (PARSE) The Stanford Neural Network Dependency (NNDEP) parser (Chen and Manning, 2014) uses dense continuous representations of words, parts-of-speech and dependency labels. While it can learn these representations entirely during the training on labeled data, Chen and Manning (2014) show that initialization with word embeddings, which were pre-trained on unlabeled data, yields improved performance. Hence, we used our different types of embeddings to initialize the NNDEP parser and compared their performance on a standard Penn Treebank benchmark. We used WSJ sections 2–21 for training and 22 for development. We used predicted tags produced via 20-fold jackknifing on sections 2–21 with the Stanford CoreNLP tagger.

2) Named Entity Recognition (NER) We used the NER system of Turian et al. (2010), which allows adding word embedding features (on top of various other features) to a regularized averaged perceptron classifier, and achieves near state-of-the-art results using several off-the-shelf word representations. We varied the type of word embeddings used as features when training the NER model, to evaluate their effect on NER benchmarks results. Following Turian et al. (2010), we used the CoNLL-2003 shared task dataset (Tjong Kim Sang and De Meulder, 2003) with 204K/51K train/dev words, as our main benchmark. We also performed an out-of-domain evaluation, using CoNLL-2003 as the train set and the MUC7 formal run (59K words) as the test set.[13]

3) Coreference Resolution (COREF) We used the Berkeley Coreference System (Durrett and Klein, 2013), which achieves near state-of-the-art results with a log-linear supervised model. Most of the features in this model are associated with pairs of *current* and *antecedent* reference mentions, for which a coreference decision needs to be made. To evaluate the contribution of different word embedding types to this model, we extended it to support the following additional features: $\{a_i\}_{i=1..m}$, $\{c_i\}_{i=1..m}$ and $\{a_i \cdot c_i\}_{i=1..m}$, where a_i or c_i is the value of the ith dimension in a word embedding vector representing the antecedent or current mention, respectively. We considered two different word embedding representations for a mention: (1) the embedding of the head word of the mention and (2) the average embedding of all words in the mention. The features of both types of representations were presented to the learning model as inputs at the same time. They were added on top of Berkeley's full feature list ('FINAL') as described in Durrett and Klein (2013). We evaluated our features on the CoNLL-2012 coreference shared task (Pradhan et al., 2012).

4) Sentiment Analysis (SENTI) Following Faruqui et al. (2014), we used a sentence-level binary decision version of the sentiment analysis task from Socher et al. (2013). In this setting, neutral sentences were discarded and all remaining sentences were labeled coarsely as positive or negative. Maintaining the original split into train/dev

---

[11]We used `spearmanr`, SciPy version 0.15.1.

[12]Since our goal is to explore performance trends, we mostly experimented with the tasks' development sets.

[13]See Turian et al. (2010) for more details on this setting.

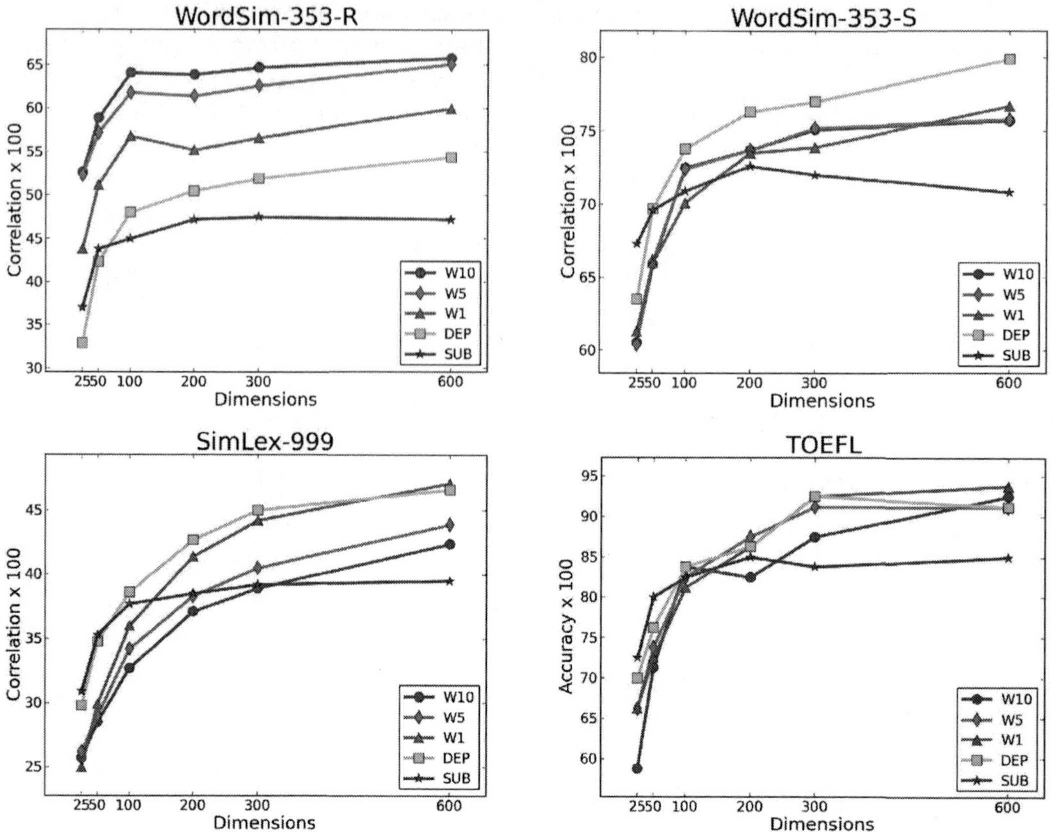

Figure 1: Intrinsic tasks' results for embeddings learned with different types of contexts.

results, we get a dataset containing 6920/872 sentences. To evaluate different types of word embeddings, we represented each sentence as an average of its word embeddings and then used an L2-regularized logistic regression classifier trained on these features to predict the sentiment labels.

5 Results

5.1 Intrinsic Results for Context Types

The results on the intrinsic tasks are illustrated in Figure 1. First, we see that the performance on all tasks generally increases with the number of dimensions, reaching near-optimal performance at around 300 dimensions, for all types of contexts. This is in line with similar observations on skip-gram word embeddings (Mikolov et al., 2013a).

Looking further, we observe that there are significant differences in the results when using different types of contexts. The effect of context choice is perhaps most evident in the WordSim-353-R task, which captures topical similarity. As might be expected, in this benchmark, the largest-window word embeddings perform best. The performance decreases with the decrease in window size and then reaches significantly lower levels for dependency (DEP) and substitute-based (SUB) embeddings. Conversely, in WordSim-353-S and SimLex-999, both of which capture a more functional similarity, the DEP embeddings are the ones that perform best, strengthening similar observations in Levy and Goldberg (2014). Finally, in the TOEFL benchmark, all contexts except for SUB, perform comparably.

5.2 Extrinsic Results for Context Types

The extrinsic tasks results are illustrated in Figure 2. A first observation is that optimal extrinsic results may be reached with as few as 50 dimensions. Furthermore, performance may even degrade when us-

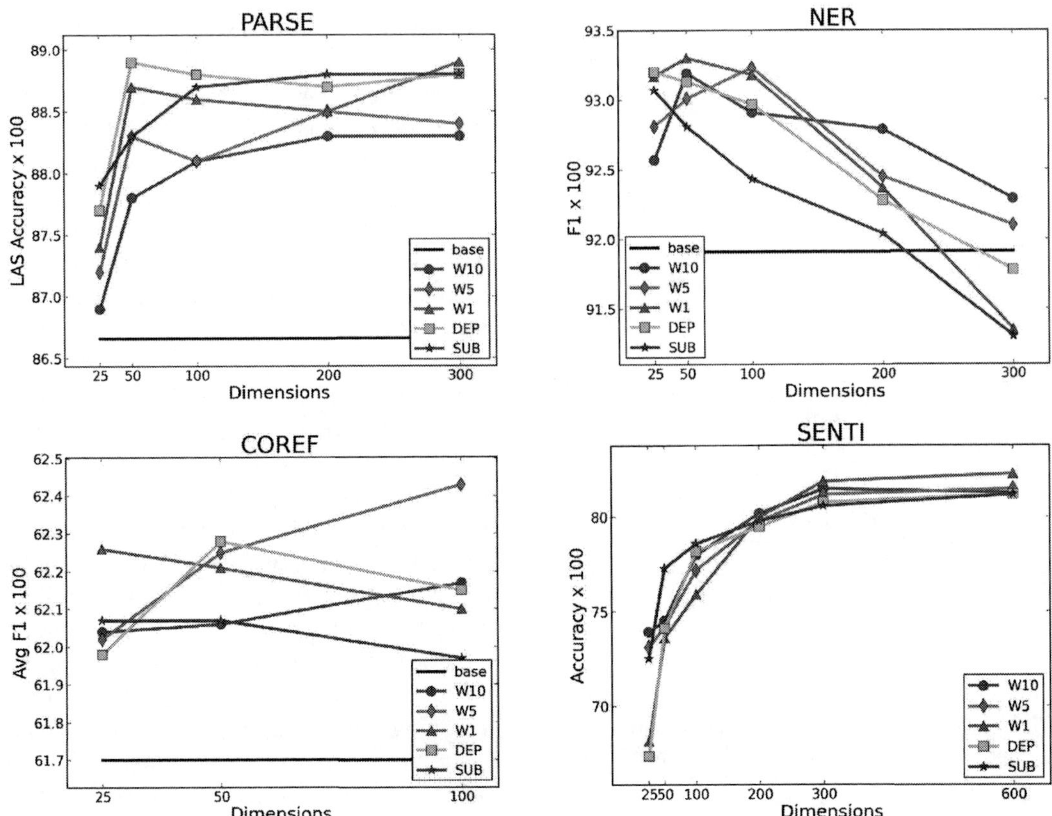

Figure 2: Extrinsic tasks' development set results for embeddings learned with different types of contexts. 'base' denotes the results with no word embedding features. Due to computational limitations we tested NER and PARSE with only up to 300 dimensions embeddings, and COREF with up to 100.

ing too many dimensions, as is most evident in the NER task. This behavior presumably depends on various factors, such as the size of the labeled training data or the type of classifier used, and highlights the importance of tuning the dimensionality of word embeddings in extrinsic tasks. This is in contrast to intrinsic tasks, where higher dimensionality typically yields better results.

Next, comparing the results of different types of contexts, we see, as might be expected, that dependency embeddings work best in the PARSE task. More generally, embeddings that do well in functional similarity intrinsic benchmarks and badly in topical ones (DEP, SUB and W1) work best for PARSE, while large window contexts perform worst, similar to observations in Bansal et al. (2014).

In the rest of the tasks it's difficult to say which context works best for what. One possible expla-

Context type	F1 x 100
DEP	79.8
W1	79.3
SUB	79.0
W10	78.1
W5	77.4
None	71.8

Table 2: NER MUC out-of-domain results for different embeddings with dimensionality = 25.

nation to this in the case of NER and COREF is that the embedding features are used as add-ons to an already competitive learning system. Therefore, the total improvement on top of a 'no embedding' baseline is relatively small, leaving little room for significant differences between different contexts.

We did find a more notable contribution of word

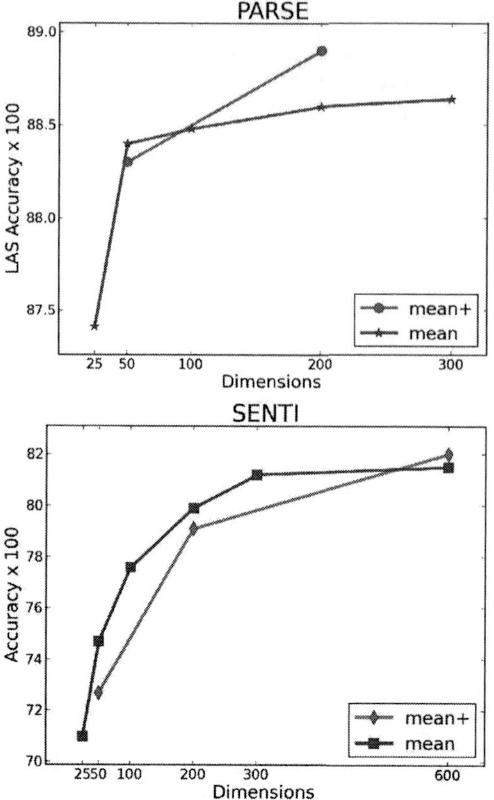

Figure 3: Mean development set results for the tasks PARSE and SENTI. 'mean' and 'mean+' stand for mean results across all single context types and context concatenations, respectively.

embedding features to the overall system performance in the out-of-domain NER MUC evaluation, described in Table 2. In this out-of-domain setting, all types of contexts achieve at least five points improvement over the baseline. Presumably, this is because continuous word embedding features are more robust to differences between train and test data, such as the typical vocabulary used. However, a detailed investigation of out-of-domain settings is out of scope for this paper and left for future work.

5.3 Extrinsic Results for Combinations

A comparison of the results obtained on the extrinsic tasks using the word embedding concatenations (*concats*), described in section 3.1, versus the original single context word embeddings (*singles*), appears in Table 3. To control for dimensionality, concats are always compared against sin-

gles with identical dimensionality. For example, the 200-dimensional concat $W10+DEP^{200}$, which is a concatenation of $W10^{100}$ and DEP^{100}, is compared against 200-dimensional singles, such as $W10^{200}$.

Looking at the results, it seems like the benefit from concatenation depends on the dimensionality and task at hand, as also illustrated in Figure 3. Given task X and dimensionality d, if $\frac{d}{2}$ is in the range where increasing the dimensionality yields significant improvement on task X, then it's better to simply increase dimensionality of singles from $\frac{d}{2}$ to d rather than concatenate. The most evident example for this are the results on the SENTI task with $d = 50$. In this case, the benefit from concatenating two 25-dimensional singles is notably lower than that of using a single 50-dimensional word embedding. On the other hand, if $\frac{d}{2}$ is in the range where near-optimal performance is reached on task X, then concatenation seems to pay off. This can be seen in SENTI with $d = 600$, PARSE with $d = 200$, and NER with $d = 50$. More concretely, looking at the best performing concatenations, it seems like combinations of the topical W10 embedding with one of the more functional ones, SUB, DEP or W1, typically perform best, suggesting that there is added value in combining embeddings of different nature.

Finally, our experiments with the methods using SVD (section 3.2) and CCA (section 3.3) yielded degraded performance compared to single word embeddings for all extrinsic tasks and therefore are not reported for brevity. These results seem to further strengthen the hypothesis that the information captured with varied types of context is different and complementary, and therefore it is beneficial to preserve these differences as in our concatenation approach.

6   Related Work

There are a number of recent works whose goal is a broad evaluation of the performance of different word embeddings on a range of tasks. However, to the best of our knowledge, none of them focus on embeddings learned with diverse context types as we do. Levy et al. (2015), Lapesa and Evert (2014), and Lai et al. (2015) evaluate several design choices when learning word representations. However, Levy et al. (2015) and Lapesa and Evert (2014)

Dimensions	Result	SENTI	PARSE	NER	COREF
50	best+	74.3 (W10+W1)	88.7 (W10+SUB)	**93.6** (W1+DEP)	**62.4** (W10+W1)
	best	**77.3** (SUB)	**88.9** (W1)	93.3 (W1)	62.3 (DEP)
	mean+	72.7	88.3	**93.3**	62.1
	mean	**74.7**	**88.4**	93.1	**62.2**
200	best+	**81.0** (W10+SUB)	**89.1** (W1+DEP)	**93.1** (W10+DEP)	
	best	80.2 (W10)	88.8 (SUB)	92.8 (W10)	
	mean+	79.1	**88.9**	**92.8**	
	mean	**79.9**	88.6	92.4	
600	best+	**82.6** (W10+SUB)			
	best	82.3 (W1)			
	mean+	**82.0**			
	mean	81.5			

Table 3: Extrinsic tasks development set results obtained with word embeddings concatenations. 'best' and 'best+' are the best results achieved across all single context types and context concatenations, respectively (best performing embedding indicated in parenthesis). 'mean' and 'mean+' are the mean results for the same. Due to computational limitations of the employed systems, some of the evaluations were not performed.

perform only intrinsic evaluations and restrict context representation to word windows, while Lai et al. (2015) do perform extrinsic evaluations, but restrict their context representation to a word window with the default size of 5. Schnabel et al. (2015) and Tsvetkov et al. (2015) report low correlation between intrinsic and extrinsic results with different word embeddings (they did not evaluate different context types), which is consistent with differences we found between intrinsic and extrinsic performance patterns in all tasks, except parsing. Bansal et al. (2014) show that functional (dependency-based and small-window) embeddings yield higher parsing improvements than topical (large-window) embeddings, which is consistent with our findings.

Several works focus on particular types of contexts for learning word embeddings. Cirik and Yuret (2014) investigates S-CODE word embeddings based on substitute word contexts. Ling et al. (2015b) and Ling et al. (2015a) propose extensions to the standard window-based context modeling. Alternatively, another recent popular line of work (Faruqui et al., 2014; Kiela et al., 2015) attempts to improve word embeddings by using manually-constructed resources, such as WordNet. These techniques could be complementary to our work. Finally, Yin and Schütze (2015) and Goikoetxea et al. (2016) propose word embeddings combinations, using methods such as concatenation and CCA, but evaluate mostly on intrinsic tasks and do not consider different types of contexts.

7   Conclusions

In this paper we evaluated skip-gram word embeddings on multiple intrinsic and extrinsic NLP tasks, varying dimensionality and type of context. We show that while the best practices for setting skip-gram hyperparameters typically yield good results on intrinsic tasks, success on extrinsic tasks requires more careful thought. Specifically, we suggest that picking the optimal dimensionality and context type are critical for obtaining the best accuracy on extrinsic tasks and are typically task-specific. Further improvements can often be achieved by combining complementary word embeddings of different context types with the right dimensionality.

Acknowledgments

We thank Do Kook Choe for providing us the jack-knifed version of WSJ. We also wish to thank the IBM Watson team for helpful discussions and our anonymous reviewers for their comments. This work was partially supported by the Israel Science Foundation grant 880/12 and the German Research Foundation through the German-Israeli Project Cooperation (DIP, grant DA 1600/1-1).

References

[Agirre et al.2009] Eneko Agirre, Enrique Alfonseca, Keith Hall, Jana Kravalova, Marius Paşca, and Aitor Soroa. 2009. A study on similarity and relatedness using distributional and WordNet-based approaches. In *Proceedings of NAACL*. Association for Computational Linguistics.

[Bansal et al.2014] Mohit Bansal, Kevin Gimpel, and Karen Livescu. 2014. Tailoring continuous word representations for dependency parsing. In *Proceedings of the Annual Meeting of the Association for Computational Linguistics*.

[Baskaya et al.2013] Osman Baskaya, Enis Sert, Volkan Cirik, and Deniz Yuret. 2013. Ai-ku: Using substitute vectors and co-occurrence modeling for word sense induction and disambiguation. In *Proceedings of the SemEval*.

[Chen and Manning2014] Danqi Chen and Christopher D Manning. 2014. A fast and accurate dependency parser using neural networks. In *Proceedings of the 2014 Conference on Empirical Methods in Natural Language Processing (EMNLP)*, volume 1, pages 740–750.

[Cirik and Yuret2014] Volkan Cirik and Deniz Yuret. 2014. Substitute based scode word embeddings in supervised nlp tasks. *arXiv preprint arXiv:1407.6853*.

[Collobert et al.2011] Ronan Collobert, Jason Weston, Léon Bottou, Michael Karlen, Koray Kavukcuoglu, and Pavel Kuksa. 2011. Natural language processing (almost) from scratch. *The Journal of Machine Learning Research*, 12:2493–2537.

[Dhillon et al.2011] Paramveer Dhillon, Dean P Foster, and Lyle H Ungar. 2011. Multi-view learning of word embeddings via cca. In *Advances in Neural Information Processing Systems*, pages 199–207.

[Durrett and Klein2013] Greg Durrett and Dan Klein. 2013. Easy victories and uphill battles in coreference resolution. In *Proc. of EMNLP*.

[Faruqui and Dyer2014] Manaal Faruqui and Chris Dyer. 2014. Improving vector space word representations using multilingual correlation. In *Proceedings of EACL*.

[Faruqui et al.2014] Manaal Faruqui, Jesse Dodge, Sujay K Jauhar, Chris Dyer, Eduard Hovy, and Noah A Smith. 2014. Retrofitting word vectors to semantic lexicons. In *Proceedings of Deep Learning and Representation Learning Workshop, NIPS*.

[Finkelstein et al.2001] Lev Finkelstein, Evgeniy Gabrilovich, Yossi Matias, Ehud Rivlin, Zach Solan, Gadi Wolfman, and Eytan Ruppin. 2001. Placing search in context: The concept revisited. In *Proceedings of the 10th international conference on World Wide Web*, pages 406–414. ACM.

[Goikoetxea et al.2016] Josu Goikoetxea, Eneko Agirre, and Aitor Soroa. 2016. Single or multiple? combining word representations independently learned from text and wordnet. In *Proceedings of AAAI*.

[Han et al.2013] Lushan Han, Abhay L. Kashyap, Tim Finin, James Mayfield, and Johnathan Weese. 2013. UMBC_EBIQUITY-CORE: Semantic Textual Similarity Systems. In *Proceedings of the Second Joint Conference on Lexical and Computational Semantics*. Association for Computational Linguistics, June.

[Heafield et al.2013] Kenneth Heafield, Ivan Pouzyrevsky, Jonathan H. Clark, and Philipp Koehn. 2013. Scalable modified Kneser-Ney language model estimation. In *Proceedings of ACL*.

[Hill et al.2014] Felix Hill, Roi Reichart, and Anna Korhonen. 2014. Simlex-999: Evaluating semantic models with (genuine) similarity estimation. *arXiv preprint arXiv:1408.3456*.

[Kiela et al.2015] Douwe Kiela, Felix Hill, and Stephen Clark. 2015. Specializing word embeddings for similarity or relatedness.

[Lai et al.2015] Siwei Lai, Kang Liu, Liheng Xu, and Jun Zhao. 2015. How to generate a good word embedding? *arXiv preprint arXiv:1507.05523*.

[Lapesa and Evert2014] Gabriella Lapesa and Stefan Evert. 2014. A large scale evaluation of distributional semantic models: Parameters, interactions and model selection. *Transactions of the Association for Computational Linguistics*, 2:531–545.

[Levy and Goldberg2014] Omer Levy and Yoav Goldberg. 2014. Dependencybased word embeddings. In *Proceedings of ACL*.

[Levy et al.2015] Omer Levy, Yoav Goldberg, and Ido Dagan. 2015. Improving distributional similarity with lessons learned from word embeddings. *Transactions of the Association for Computational Linguistics*, 3:211–225.

[Ling et al.2015a] Wang Ling, Lin Chu-Cheng, Yulia Tsvetkov, Silvio Amir, Ramón Fernandez Astudillo, Chris Dyer, Alan W Black, and Isabel Trancoso. 2015a. Not all contexts are created equal: Better word representations with variable attention. In *Proceedings of EMNLP*.

[Ling et al.2015b] Wang Ling, Chris Dyer, Alan Black, and Isabel Trancoso. 2015b. Two/too simple adaptations of word2vec for syntax problems. In *Proceedings of NAACL-HLT*.

[Lu et al.2015] Ang Lu, Weiran Wang, Mohit Bansal, Kevin Gimpel, , and Karen Livescu. 2015. Deep multilingual correlation for improved word embeddings. In *Proceedings of NAACL*.

[Manning et al.2014] Christopher D. Manning, Mihai Surdeanu, John Bauer, Jenny Finkel, Steven J.

Bethard, and David McClosky. 2014. The Stanford CoreNLP natural language processing toolkit. In *Proceedings of 52nd Annual Meeting of the Association for Computational Linguistics: System Demonstrations*, pages 55–60.

[Melamud et al.2014] Oren Melamud, Ido Dagan, Jacob Goldberger, Idan Szpektor, and Deniz Yuret. 2014. Probabilistic modeling of joint-context in distributional similarity. In *Proceedings of CoNLL*.

[Melamud et al.2015a] Oren Melamud, Ido Dagan, and Jacob Goldberger. 2015a. Modeling word meaning in context with substitute vectors. In *Proceedings of NAACL*.

[Melamud et al.2015b] Oren Melamud, Omer Levy, and Ido Dagan. 2015b. A simple word embedding model for lexical substitution. In *Proceedings of the Vector Space Modeling for NLP Workshop, NAACL*.

[Mikolov et al.2013a] Tomas Mikolov, Kai Chen, Greg Corrado, and Jeffrey Dean. 2013a. Efficient estimation of word representations in vector space. In *Proceedings of ICLR*.

[Mikolov et al.2013b] Tomas Mikolov, Ilya Sutskever, Kai Chen, Greg Corrado, and Jeffrey Dean. 2013b. Distributed representations of words and phrases and their compositionality. In *Proceedings of NIPS*.

[Parker et al.2011] Robert Parker, David Graff, Junbo Kong, Ke Chen, and Kazuaki Maeda. 2011. English Gigaword Fifth edition. *Linguistic Data Consortium, LDC2011T07*, June.

[Pennington et al.2014] Jeffrey Pennington, Richard Socher, and Christopher D Manning. 2014. Glove: Global vectors for word representation. In *Proceedings of the Empiricial Methods in Natural Language Processing (EMNLP 2014)*, volume 12.

[Pradhan et al.2012] Sameer Pradhan, Alessandro Moschitti, Nianwen Xue, Olga Uryupina, and Yuchen Zhang. 2012. Conll-2012 shared task: Modeling multilingual unrestricted coreference in ontonotes. In *Joint Conference on EMNLP and CoNLL-Shared Task*, pages 1–40. Association for Computational Linguistics.

[Schnabel et al.2015] Tobias Schnabel, Igor Labutov, David Mimno, and Thorsten Joachims. 2015. Evaluation methods for unsupervised word embeddings. In *Proc. of EMNLP*.

[Snoek et al.2012] Jasper Snoek, Hugo Larochelle, and Ryan P Adams. 2012. Practical bayesian optimization of machine learning algorithms. In *Advances in neural information processing systems*, pages 2951–2959.

[Socher et al.2013] Richard Socher, Alex Perelygin, Jean Y Wu, Jason Chuang, Christopher D Manning, Andrew Y Ng, and Christopher Potts. 2013. Recursive deep models for semantic compositionality over a sentiment treebank. In *Proceedings of the conference on empirical methods in natural language processing (EMNLP)*, volume 1631, page 1642. Citeseer.

[Tjong Kim Sang and De Meulder2003] Erik F Tjong Kim Sang and Fien De Meulder. 2003. Introduction to the conll-2003 shared task: Language-independent named entity recognition. In *Proceedings of the seventh conference on Natural language learning at HLT-NAACL 2003-Volume 4*, pages 142–147. Association for Computational Linguistics.

[Tsvetkov et al.2015] Yulia Tsvetkov, Manaal Faruqui, Wang Ling, Guillaume Lample, and Chris Dyer. 2015. Evaluation of word vector representations by subspace alignment. In *Proc. of EMNLP*.

[Turian et al.2010] J. Turian, L. Ratinov, and Y. Bengio. 2010. Word representations: A simple and general method for semisupervised learning. In *Proc. of ACL*, pages 384–394.

[Yatbaz et al.2012] Mehmet Ali Yatbaz, Enis Sert, and Deniz Yuret. 2012. Learning syntactic categories using paradigmatic representations of word context. In *Proceedings of EMNLP*.

[Yin and Schütze2015] Wenpeng Yin and Hinrich Schütze. 2015. Learning word meta-embeddings by using ensembles of embedding sets. *arXiv preprint arXiv:1508.04257*.

[Yuret2012] Deniz Yuret. 2012. FASTSUBS: An efficient and exact procedure for finding the most likely lexical substitutes based on an n-gram language model. *Signal Processing Letters, IEEE*, 19(11):725–728.

Improve Chinese Word Embeddings by Exploiting Internal Structure

Jian Xu, Jiawei Liu, Liangang Zhang, Zhengyu Li, Huanhuan Chen[*]
Department of Computer Science, University of Science and Technology of China, China
{jianxu1, ustcljw, liangang, lzy0503}@mail.ustc.edu.cn
hchen@ustc.edu.cn

Abstract

Recently, researchers have demonstrated that both Chinese word and its component characters provide rich semantic information when learning Chinese word embeddings. However, they ignored the semantic similarity across component characters in a word. In this paper, we learn the semantic contribution of characters to a word by exploiting the similarity between a word and its component characters with the semantic knowledge obtained from other languages. We propose a similarity-based method to learn Chinese word and character embeddings jointly. This method is also capable of disambiguating Chinese characters and distinguishing non-compositional Chinese words. Experiments on word similarity and text classification demonstrate the effectiveness of our method.

1 Introduction

Distributed representations of knowledge has received wide attention in recent years. Researchers have proposed various models to learn it at different granularity levels. Distributed word representations, also known as word embeddings, were learned in (Rumelhart et al., 1988; Bengio et al., 2006; Mnih and Hinton, 2009; Mikolov et al., 2013a). Larger granularity levels than words have also been investigated, including phrase level (Socher et al., 2010; Zhang et al., 2014; Yu and Dredze, 2015), sentence level (Le and Mikolov, 2014; Socher et al., 2013; Kalchbrenner et al., 2014; Kiros et al., 2015), and

document level (Le and Mikolov, 2014; Hermann and Blunsom, 2014; Srivastava et al., 2013).

For language like Chinese, some smaller units than word also provide rich semantic information. For example, Chinese characters in word, Chinese radicals in character. These internal structures have been proved to be useful for Chinese word and character embeddings (Chen et al., 2015; Li et al., 2015). Chen et al. (2015) took Chinese characters in a word into account when modeling the semantic meaning of the word. They proposed a character-enhanced word embeddings model (CWE) by adding the embedding of component characters in a word with the same weight to the word embedding. However, the internal characters in a Chinese word have different semantic contributions to its meaning. Take Chinese word "青蛙" (frog) as an example. The character "青" (blue or green) is to decorate character "蛙" (frog). It is obvious that the latter character contributes more than the former one to the word meaning. In Li et al. (2015), they proposed a component-enhanced Chinese character embeddings model based on the feature that most Chinese characters are phono-semantic compounds. They considered characters and bi-characters as the basic embedding units. However, some bi-characters are meaningless, and may not form a Chinese word. These bi-characters may undermine embeddings of others.

This paper, motivated by Chen et al. (2015), exploits the internal structures of Chinese word, namely the Chinese characters. We propose a method to calculate the semantic contribution of characters to a word in a cross-lingual manner. The basic

---

[*]Corresponding author

Proceedings of NAACL-HLT 2016, pages 1041–1050,
San Diego, California, June 12-17, 2016. ©2016 Association for Computational Linguistics

idea is that the semantic contribution of Chinese characters in most Chinese words can be learned from their translations in other languages. Such as the word "青蛙" we mentioned above. The word embeddings of other languages are used to calculate semantic contribution of characters to the word they compose. Moreover, Chinese characters are more ambiguous than words. To tackle this problem, multiple-prototype character embeddings is proposed. Different meanings of characters will be represented by different embeddings. Our contributions can be summarized as follows:

1. We provide a method to calculate the semantic contribution of Chinese characters to the word they compose with English translation. Compared with English, there are fewer human-made resources to supervise the learning process of Chinese word and character embeddings. While translation resources are always easy to be accessed on the Internet.

2. We propose a novel way to disambiguate Chinese characters with translating resources. There are some limitations in existing cluster-based algorithms (Huang et al., 2012; Neelakantan et al., 2015; Chen et al., 2015). They either fixed the number of clusters or proposed a nonparametric way to learn it for each word. However, the number of clusters for words varies a lot. For nonparametric method, different hyperparameters have to be tune to control the number of clusters for different datasets.

3. We provide a method to distinguish whether a Chinese word is semantically compositional automatically. Not all Chinese words exhibit semantic compositions from their component characters. For example, entity names, transliterated words like "沙发" (sofa), single-morpheme multi-character words like "徘徊" (wander). In Chen et al. (2015), they performed part-of-speech tagging to identify entity names. The transliterated words are tagged manually, which requires human work and need to be updated when new words are created.

The evaluations on word similarity, text classification, Chinese characters disambiguation, and qualitative analysis of word embeddings demonstrate the effectiveness of our method.

2 Related Work

2.1 Word2vec

Word2vec (Mikolov et al., 2013a) is an algorithm to learn distributed word representations using a neural language model. Word2vec has two models, the continuous bag-of-words model (CBOW) and the skip-gram model. In this paper, we propose a new model based on the CBOW, hence we focus attention on it. CBOW aims at predicting the target word given context words in a slide window. Given a word sequence $D = \{x_1, x_2, \ldots, x_T\}$, the objective of CBOW is to maximize the average log probability

$$L = \frac{1}{T} \sum_{i=1}^{T} \log p(x_i | x_{i-j}^{i+j}), \qquad (1)$$

where x_{i-j}^{i+j} is the context words centered at x_i, $p(x_i | x_{i-j}^{i+j})$ is defined as:

$$\frac{\exp(v_{x_i}^{'T} \sum_{-j \leq k \leq j, k \neq 0} v_{x_{i+k}})}{\sum_{x=1}^{W} \exp(v_x^{'T} \sum_{-j \leq k \leq j, k \neq 0} v_{x_{i+k}})}, \qquad (2)$$

where v_{x_i} and $v_{x_i}^{'}$ are the input and output vector representations of word x_i. Since the size of English vocabulary W may be up to 10^6 scale, hierarchical softmax and negative sampling (Mikolov et al., 2013b) are applied during training to learn the model efficiently. However, using CBOW to learn Chinese word embeddings directly may have some limitations. It fails to capture the internal structure of words. In (Botha and Blunsom, 2014; Luong et al., 2013; Trask et al., 2015; Chen et al., 2015), they demonstrated the usefulness to exploit the internal structure of words, and proposed some morphological-based methods. For example, Chen et al. (2015) exploit the internal structure in Chinese words.

2.2 The CWE model

The basic idea of CWE is that both external context words and internal component characters in words provide rich information in modeling the semantic meaning of the target word. In CWE, they learned word embeddings with its component characters embeddings. Let C denotes the Chinese characters set, and the word x_t in context x_{i-j}^{i+j} is composed by several characters in C, let $x_t = \{c_1, c_2, \ldots, c_{N_t}\}$, c_k denotes the k-th character in x_t,

$$\widehat{v}_{x_t} = v_{x_t} + \frac{1}{N_t} \sum_{k=1}^{N_t} v_{c_k}, \tag{3}$$

where $\widehat{v}_{x_t}$ is the modified word embedding, N_t denotes the number of Chinese characters in x_t. To address the issue of ambiguity in Chinese characters, they proposed several approaches for multiple-prototype character embeddings: position-based, cluster-based, nonparametric methods, and position-cluster-based character embeddings. These methods are denoted as CWE+P, CWE+L, CWE+N, CWE+LP respectively. However, this model has some limitations. The internal characters are of the same contribution to the semantic meaning of the word in CWE, which is not the case for most Chinese words.

3 Methodology

Our method can be described as three stages:

- **Obtain translations of Chinese words and characters**
  Chinese words segmentation tool is used to segment words in Chinese corpus. Then we use an online English-Chinese translation tool to translate all the Chinese characters and segmented words.

- **Perform Chinese character sense disambiguation**
  We train an English corpus with CBOW to get English word embeddings. Then, we merge some meanings of Chinese characters with small difference, and disambiguate the meanings of characters in words by computing the similarity between their English translation words.

- **Learn word and character embeddings with our model**
  Based on the character sense disambiguation process, we modify the objective of CWE to learn Chinese word and character embeddings. Then we analyse the complexity of our model briefly.

3.1 Obtain translations of Chinese words and characters

We use segmentation tools to segment words in Chinese training corpus, and perform part-of-speech tagging to recognize all the entity names. Since entity name words do not exhibit semantic compositions, they are identified as non-compositional words. We count the times of characters appearing in different words. Words with Chinese characters rarely combined with other characters are classified as single-morpheme multi-character words and identified as non-compositional.

Then programming interface of online translation tool is used to translate Chinese words and characters into English. For non-compositional Chinese words, they are not included in the translation list. Table 1 shows the English meanings of Chinese word "音乐", "沙发" and their component characters "音" and " 乐", "沙" and "发".

3.2 Perform Chinese character sense disambiguation

We train an English corpus with CBOW to get English word embeddings. Then, the meanings of characters with small difference are merged.

In Table 1, we observe that the difference between some meanings of character "乐" is very small, some of them differ only in their part-of-speech. In Chinese, the same characters and words are used in different part-of-speech but express the same semantic meaning. Hence these meanings are merged as one semantic meaning. Let $\mathrm{Sim}(\cdot)$ denotes the function to calculate the similarity between meanings of Chinese words and characters, we use cosine distance as the distance metric. The i-th and j-th meanings of Chinese character c are c^i and c^j. Their similarity is defined as:

$$\mathrm{Sim}(c^i, c^j) = \max(cos(v_{x_m}, v_{x_n})),$$
$$s.t. \quad x_m \in \mathrm{Trans}(c^i), x_n \in \mathrm{Trans}(c^j), \tag{4}$$
$$x_m, x_n \notin \mathrm{stop\_words(en)},$$

where $\mathrm{Trans}(c^i)$ denotes the English translation words set of c^i, $\mathrm{stop\_words(en)}$ denotes the stop words in English, x_m and x_n are not in these stop words. For example, the Chinese word "音乐" in Table 1, c_2 denotes the second character

Word	English Explanation
音乐	music;
音	(声音) sound; (消息) news, tidings; (音质) tone; (姓氏) a surname;
乐	N. (音乐) music; (姓氏) a surname; (愉快; 满足) pleasure, enjoyment; JJ. (快乐) happy,glad,joyful,cheerful; V. (喜欢) enjoy, be glad to, love, find pleasure in; (笑) laugh, be amused; RB. (乐意) gladly, happily, willingly;
沙发	sofa, settee;
沙	N. (沙子) sand; (某些呈沙状的食物) granulated, powdered; (姓氏) a surname; JJ. (嗓音不清脆) (of voice) hoarse, husky;
发	N. (头发) hair; V. (送出;交付) send out, distribute, deliver; (发射) launch, discharge, shoot, emit; (产生, 发生) produce, generate, come into existence; (表达) express, utter; (扩大, 开展) expand, develop; (因得财物而兴旺) flourish; (放散, 散开) spread out, disperse, diffuse; etc.;

Table 1: English Translation of Chinese words and characters in ICIBA. V., N., JJ., RB. denote their verb, noun, adjective and adverb meaning respectively. Different meanings of word and character are separated by semicolon.

"乐" in the word. $\text{Trans}(c_2^3)$ is the third translation English words set of character "乐", which is $\{pleasure, enjoyment\}$. Therefore x_m can be pleasure or enjoyment here.

If the $\text{Sim}(c^i, c^j)$ is above a threshold δ, then they are merged as one semantic meaning. For simplicity, we use the union of English translation words set. One character may be translated into several English words. We may average all the translation word embeddings and then compute the similarity, or select the maximum value of the similarity between all English word pairs. In our experiments, maximum method works better.

Finally, we perform Chinese character sense disambiguation. In Chinese, characters may have multiple meanings, but for a certain word, their meanings are determined. For exmaple, the word "音乐", the English translation is music. For character "乐", the first translation "music" matches the meaning of the word. For character "音", the best match is the first translation "sound". For transliterated word like "沙发", the English translations are sofa and settee, neither sofa nor settee have high similarity with English translation words of character "沙" and character "发". Formally, if $\max(\text{Sim}(x_t, c_k)) > \lambda, c_k \in x_t$, then x_t is identified as compositional word, and belongs to the compositional set COMP. For compositional words, we build a set

$$F = \{(x_t, s_t, n_t) \mid x_t \in \text{COMP}\}, \quad (5)$$

where

$$s_t = \{\text{Sim}(x_t, c_k) \mid c_k \in x_t\},$$
$$n_t = \{\max_i \text{Sim}(x_t, c_k^i) \mid c_k \in x_t\} \quad (6)$$

For example, the word "音乐" is defined as ("音乐", {Sim("音乐", "音"), Sim("音乐", "乐")},{1,1}) in F.

3.3 Learn word and character vectors with SCWE

The internal characters in a word make different contributions to its semantic meaning. However, in Chen et al. (2015), the contribution of component characters to the semantic meaning of word are treated equally. They add character embeddings to the word embeddings with the same weight, which may undermine the quality of word embeddings. Based on this point, we propose a similarity-based character-enhanced word embedding model, which takes the contribution of characters into account. We name it SCWE for ease of reference in the later part. The architecture of CWE and SCWE are shown in Fig. 1.

Similarity-Based Character-Enhanced word Embedding In the character sense disambiguation stage, we build a set F, which contains compositional words, the similarity between words and its component characters, and the meaning order number of characters in the word. Suppose x_t in W is a

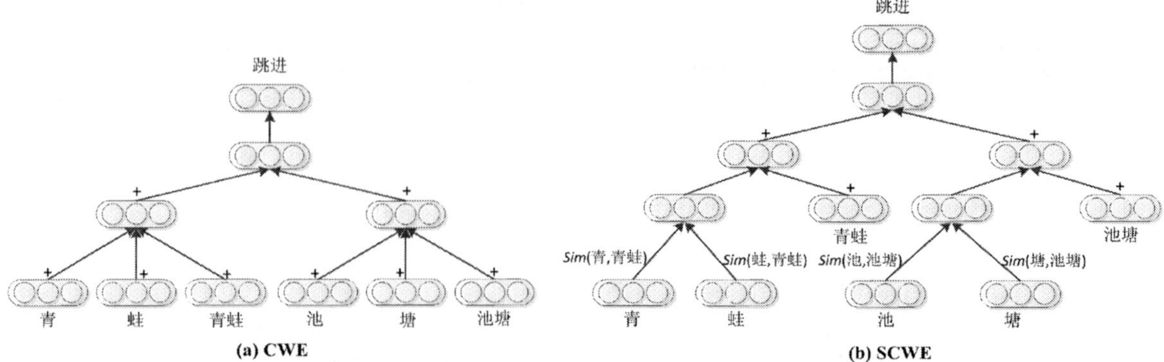

Figure 1: Architecture of models. The left is CWE and right is SCWE. "青蛙 (frog) 跳进 (jump into) 池塘 (pond)" is the word sequence. The word "青蛙" is composed of characters "青 (blue or green)" and "蛙 (frog)", and the word "池塘 (pond) is composed of characters "池 (pond, pool)" and "塘 (pond)".

compositional word, in SCWE,

$$\widehat{v}_{x_t} = \frac{1}{2}\Big\{v_{x_t} + \frac{1}{N_t}\sum_{k=1}^{N_t}\mathrm{Sim}(x_t, c_k)v_{c_k}\Big\} \quad (7)$$

To deal with ambiguity problem of Chinese characters, we propose multiple-prototype character embeddings and denote it as SCWE+M model. Since the meaning of a character is determined in a given word, we utilize the information provided by the last element in set F, and use different character embeddings for different meanings of characters. Then, in SCWE+M,

$$\widehat{v}_{x_t} = \frac{1}{2}\Big\{v_{x_t} + \frac{1}{N_t}\sum_{k=1}^{N_t}\mathrm{Sim}(x_t, c_k)v_{c_k^i}\Big\} \quad (8)$$

Complexity analysis We analyze the complexities of CBOW, CWE, SCWE and SCWE+M. Let S denotes the size of corpus, $|W|$ denotes the size of vocabulary, $|C|$ denotes the number of Chinese characters in corpus. And d is the dimensions of Chinese word and character embeddings, k is the context window size, f is the time spend in computing hierarchical softmax or negative sampling, n is the average number of characters in a Chinese word, m is the average meaning number of Chinese characters. The results are shown in Table 2.

In Chinese, most of words are composed by two Chinese characters, and the meaning number of commonly used characters are usually less than five.

Moreover, according to *CJK Unified Ideographs*[1], the total number of Chinese characters is 20913, the commonly used characters are less than 10000. Therefore, our model is competitive to other methods in model parameters and computational complexity.

Method	Model parameters	Computational complexity
CBOW	$|W|d$	$2kSf$
CWE	$(|W| + |C|)d$	$2kS(f + n)$
SCWE	$(|W| + |C|)d$	$2kS(f + n)$
SCWE + M	$(|W| + m|C|)d$	$2kS(f+n+mn)$

Table 2: Complexity analysis

4 Experiments and Analysis

4.1 Experiments Settings

We select *English Wikipedia Dump*[2] to train English word embeddings with CBOW, and set dimensions to 200. For Chinese word embeddings, we select *Chinese Wikipedia Dump*[3] to train character and word embeddings. Before training, pure digits and non-Chinese characters are removed. We use an open-source Chinese segment tool called *ANSJ*[4] to

[1] https://en.wikipedia.org/wiki/CJK_Unified_Ideographs
[2] http://download.wikipedia.com/enwiki/
[3] http://download.wikipedia.com/zhwiki/
[4] https://github.com/NLPchina/ansj_seg

segment words in corpus. ANSJ is a java implementation of ICTCLAS (Institute of Computing Technology, Chinese Lexical Analysis System). It can process about one million words in a second, and get up to 96 percent accuracy in segmentation task. The part-of-speech tagging and name entity recognition tasks are also done in this process. We select *ICIBA*[5] as English-Chinese translation tool, which provides us with an application programming interface. CBOW and CWE are used as baseline methods. Context window size is set as 5 and both Chinese word and character embeddings are set as 100 dimension. After some cross validation steps, our threshold δ and λ are set as 0.5 and 0.4 in character disambiguation process. The influence of λ and δ is report in the later part.

Model	wordsim-240	wordsim-296
CBOW	51.78	60.82
CWE	52.57	60.36
SCWE	54.92	60.85
SCWE + M	**55.10**	**62.86**

Table 3: Evaluation on wordsim-240 and wordsim-296

4.2 Word Similarity

Word similarity is a task to compute semantic relatedness between given word pairs. The relatedness between word pairs have been scored by human in advance. The correlation between model results and human judgement can be used to evaluate the performance of models. In this paper, wordsim-240 and wordsim-296 (Jin and Wu, 2012) are used as e-valuation datasets. The Spearman's rank correlation (Myers et al., 2010) is applied to compute the correlation. The experimental results are summarized in Table 3.

We observe that on wordsim-240, SCWE and SCWE+M outperform the baseline methods, which indicates the effectiveness of exploiting the internal structure. On dataset wordsim-296, we can see that CBOW, CWE, SCWE perform similarly. This may be explained by some highly ambiguous Chinese characters in this dataset. In SCWE and CWE, representing these ambiguous characters with the same embeddings may undermine word embed-

Fudan-large	Size	Fudan-small	Size
Environment	1218	Education	59
Agriculture	1022	Philosophy	44
Economy	1601	Transport	58
Politics	1025	Medical	52
Sports	1254	Military	75

Table 4: 2 groups datasets of text classification, the first column denotes the category of documents and the second denotes number of documents in each category.

dings. Therefore, SCWE+M achieves a better performance by applying multiple-prototype character embeddings.

4.3 Text Classification

In this experiment, we use *Fudan Corpus*[6] as datasets, which contains 20 categories of documents, including economy, politics, sports and etc.. The number of documents in each category ranges from 27 to 1061. To avoid imbalance, we select 10 categories and organize them into 2 groups. One group is named *Fudan-large* and each category in this group contains more than 1000 documents. The other is named *Fudan-small* and each category contains less than 100 documents. In each category, 80 percent of documents are used as training set, the rest are used as testing set to evaluate the performance. The detailed information for two datasets are reported in Table 4.

Similar to the way we deal with Chinese training corpus, pure digits and non-Chinese characters are removed and ANSJ is used to do word segmentation on these datasets. The publish information of each document is removed. We represent each document by averaging word embeddings in the document. The classifiers are trained using LIBLINEAR package(Fan et al., 2008) with the embeddings obtained from different methods. The performance of each method is evaluated by predicting accuracy on testing set. Experiment results are given in Table 5.

It is observed that our methods outperform the baseline methods on both datasets. This can be explained that the semantic relatedness of a word with the component characters which have more contribution to its semantic meaning is strengthen in our methods. Such as, in sports documents, the word

---

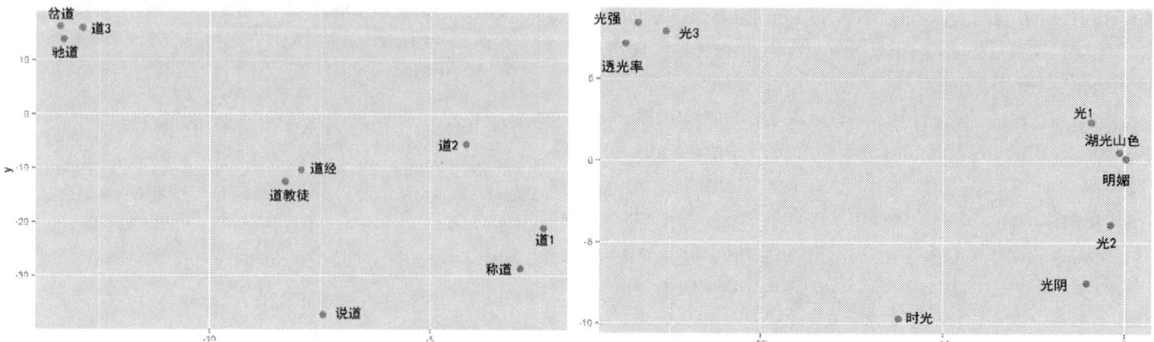

Figure 2: Illustration of words and characters in two dimension plane.

Method	Fudan-small	Fudan-large
CBOW	84.75	91.42
CWE	88.14	91.84
SCWE	91.53	92.68
SCWE + M	**93.22**	**92.89**

Table 5: Evaluation accuracies (%) on text classification.

Characters	Words
道1 (say, speak)	说道 (say) 称道 (speak)
道2 (Taoism, Taoist)	道经 (Taoist scriptures) 道教徒 (Taoist)
道3 (road, path)	岔道 (branch road) 驰道 (royal road)
光1 (scenery)	湖光山色 (a landscape of lakes and mountains) 明媚 (bright and beautiful)
光2 (time)	时光 (time, year) 光阴 (time)
光3 (light, ray)	光强 (light intensity) 透光率 (light transmittance)

Table 6: English explanatory of characters and their nearest words in vector space.

"球" (ball) is used frequently. For Chinese words like "篮球" (basketball) and "网球" (tennis), the character "球" contributes more to their semantic meaning than other characters. Therefore, they lie closer to character "球" in embedding space obtained by our model than CBOW and CWE, and tend to form a cluster in embedding space.

4.4 Multiple Prototype of Chinese Charaters

To tackle the ambiguity of Chinese characters, we propose multiple-prototype character embeddings. To evaluate the effectiveness of our method, we use PCA to conduct dimensionality reduction on word and character embeddings. The results are illustrated in Fig 2. We take 3 different meanings of Chinese characters "道" and "光", and 2 of their top-related words as examples. The character followed by a digit i denotes the i-th meanings of it.

We can observe that characters and words, which have similar meanings are gathered together. For example, "光3", "光强" and "透光率" are all related to the light. Thus, they get closer in the embedding space.

We also develop a dataset to compare our method with the disambiguation methods in Chen et al. (2015). We select some ambiguous Chinese char-

acters, and then use *online Xinhua Dictionary*[7] as our standard to disambiguate the words that contain these ambiguous characters. Each word is assigned a number according to their explanation in the dictionary. We use KNN as classifier to evaluate all the methods. The results are shown in Table 7. It is observed that our method outperforms the methods proposed in Chen et al. (2015).

Model	Accuracy
CWE + P	84.9
CWE + L	81.0
CWE + LP	85.4
CWE + N	73.5
SCWE + M	**91.1**

Table 7: Evaluation accuracies (%) on ambiguous characters.

---

[7] http://xh.5156edu.com/

Words	CWE	SCWE
青蛙 (frog)	青蛇 (green snake) 青蟹 (blue crab) 青椒 (green pepper) 牛蛙 (Rana catesbeiana)	牛蛙 (Rana catesbeiana) 狐狸 (fox) 螃蟹 (crab) 蛙 (frog)
电话 (telephone)	电话网 (telephone network) 电邮 (Email) 电话卡 (phonecard) 长途电话 (toll call)	电讯 (dispatch) 手机 (cellphone) 通讯 (communication) 短信 (message)

Table 8: Nearest words example of Chinese words.

4.5 Qualitative analysis of word embeddings

In this part, we take two Chinese words as examples, and list their nearest words to examine the quality of word embeddings obtained by CWE and SCWE. The results are shown in Table 8. We can observe the most similar words return by CWE and SCWE both tend to share common characters with the given word. In CWE, characters with little semantic contribution to the word may undermine the quality of word embeddings. For example, the character "青" in word "青蛙". The semantic relatedness of words with character "青" to the given word are overestimated in CWE. In our model, by calculating the semantic contribution of internal characters to the word, we alleviate this misjudgement greatly, which demonstrates the effectiveness of our model.

4.6 Parameter Analysis

In this part, the influence of parameters on our model is investigated. The parameters include the compositional word similarity threshold λ, character disambiguation threshold δ.

Compositional word similarity To investigate how λ influence the process of non-compositional word detection, we build a word list of transliterated words manually, which consists of 161 words. Then 161 of most frequent semantic compositional words with more than one Chinese characters are added to the list in the corpus. In Table 9, the performance of our method in classifying transliterated words when λ ranges from 0.25 to 0.55 are reported. From Table 9, we can observe as λ increases, more compositional words will be classified as non-compositional words, while transliterated words are more likely to

be classified correctly. Our method achieves best F-Score when $\lambda = 0.4$.

Character disambiguation threshold In Table 10, we show the performance of our model in disambiguating Chinese characters. We adopted the same datasets in Section 4.4 with different δ. From Table 1, we can observe some meanings of a character are very close, therefore, a high δ are adopted in our model. When $\delta = 0.5$, our model gets the best result in our dataset.

Parameter λ	Precision	Recall	F-Score
0.25	97.0	60.9	74.8
0.30	96.5	68.9	80.4
0.35	94.6	75.8	84.2
0.40	92.0	78.9	**85.0**
0.45	88.9	80.1	84.3
0.50	84.0	84.5	84.2
0.55	82.5	85.1	83.8

Table 9: Precision, recall, F-score of transliterated words when λ ranges from 0.25 to 0.55

Parameter δ	Precision
0.35	87.5
0.40	89.0
0.45	89.5
0.50	**91.1**
0.55	89.9
0.60	89.5
0.65	88.5

Table 10: Evaluation accuracies (%) on ambiguous characters when λ ranges from 0.35 to 0.65.

5 Conclusion

In this paper, we exploit the internal structure in Chinese words by learning the semantic contribution of internal characters to the word. We propose a method to improve Chinese word and character embeddings with a similarity-based character-enhanced word embeddings model. Ambiguity problem of Chinese characters can also be tackled in our method. Moreover, we build a way to classify whether a Chinese word is compositional automatically, which requires to be labelled manually in CWE. We argue that our method may be used to improve word embeddings of other language whose internal structure is similar to Chinese. The code and datasets we use is available at: `https://github.com/JianXu123/SCWE`.

Acknowledgement

This work is supported by NSFC grants 91546116 and 61511130083.

References

[Bengio et al.2006] Yoshua Bengio, Holger Schwenk, Jean-Sébastien Senécal, Fréderic Morin, and Jean-Luc Gauvain. 2006. Neural probabilistic language models. In *Innovations in Machine Learning*, pages 137–186. Springer.

[Botha and Blunsom2014] Jan A Botha and Phil Blunsom. 2014. Compositional morphology for word representations and language modelling. *arXiv preprint arXiv:1405.4273*.

[Chen et al.2015] Xinxiong Chen, Lei Xu, Zhiyuan Liu, Maosong Sun, and Huanbo Luan. 2015. Joint learning of character and word embeddings. *In Proceedings of the 25th International Joint Conference on Artificial Intelligence (IJCAI)*.

[Fan et al.2008] Rong-En Fan, Kai-Wei Chang, Cho-Jui Hsieh, Xiang-Rui Wang, and Chih-Jen Lin. 2008. Liblinear: A library for large linear classification. *The Journal of Machine Learning Research*, 9:1871–1874.

[Hermann and Blunsom2014] Karl Moritz Hermann and Phil Blunsom. 2014. Multilingual models for compositional distributed semantics. *arXiv preprint arXiv:1404.4641*.

[Huang et al.2012] Eric H Huang, Richard Socher, Christopher D Manning, and Andrew Y Ng. 2012. Improving word representations via global context and multiple word prototypes. In *In Proceedings of the 50th Annual Meeting of the Association for Computational Linguistics: Long Papers-Volume 1*, pages 873–882. Association for Computational Linguistics.

[Jin and Wu2012] Peng Jin and Yunfang Wu. 2012. Semeval-2012 task 4: evaluating chinese word similarity. In *In Proceedings of the Sixth International Workshop on Semantic Evaluation*, pages 374–377. Association for Computational Linguistics.

[Kalchbrenner et al.2014] Nal Kalchbrenner, Edward Grefenstette, and Phil Blunsom. 2014. A convolutional neural network for modelling sentences. *arXiv preprint arXiv:1404.2188*.

[Kiros et al.2015] Ryan Kiros, Yukun Zhu, Ruslan R Salakhutdinov, Richard Zemel, Raquel Urtasun, Antonio Torralba, and Sanja Fidler. 2015. Skip-thought vectors. In *Advances in Neural Information Processing Systems*, pages 3276–3284.

[Le and Mikolov2014] Quoc V Le and Tomas Mikolov. 2014. Distributed representations of sentences and documents. *arXiv preprint arXiv:1405.4053*.

[Li et al.2015] Yanran Li, Wenjie Li, Fei Sun, and Sujian Li. 2015. Component-enhanced chinese character embeddings. *arXiv preprint arXiv:1508.06669*.

[Luong et al.2013] Minh-Thang Luong, Richard Socher, and Christopher D Manning. 2013. Better word representations with recursive neural networks for morphology. *CoNLL-2013*, 104.

[Mikolov et al.2013a] Tomas Mikolov, Kai Chen, Greg Corrado, and Jeffrey Dean. 2013a. Efficient estimation of word representations in vector space. *arXiv preprint arXiv:1301.3781*.

[Mikolov et al.2013b] Tomas Mikolov, Ilya Sutskever, Kai Chen, Greg S Corrado, and Jeff Dean. 2013b. Distributed representations of words and phrases and their compositionality. In *Advances in neural information processing systems*, pages 3111–3119.

[Mnih and Hinton2009] Andriy Mnih and Geoffrey E Hinton. 2009. A scalable hierarchical distributed language model. In *Advances in neural information processing systems*, pages 1081–1088.

[Myers et al.2010] Jerome L Myers, Arnold Well, and Robert Frederick Lorch. 2010. *Research design and statistical analysis*. Routledge.

[Neelakantan et al.2015] Arvind Neelakantan, Jeevan Shankar, Alexandre Passos, and Andrew McCallum. 2015. Efficient non-parametric estimation of multiple embeddings per word in vector space. *arXiv preprint arXiv:1504.06654*.

[Rumelhart et al.1988] David E Rumelhart, Geoffrey E Hinton, and Ronald J Williams. 1988. Learning representations by back-propagating errors. *Cognitive modeling*, 5:3.

[Socher et al.2010] Richard Socher, Christopher D Manning, and Andrew Y Ng. 2010. Learning continuous phrase representations and syntactic parsing with recursive neural networks. In *In Proceedings of the NIPS-2010 Deep Learning and Unsupervised Feature Learning Workshop*, pages 1–9.

[Socher et al.2013] Richard Socher, Alex Perelygin, Jean Y Wu, Jason Chuang, Christopher D Manning, Andrew Y Ng, and Christopher Potts. 2013. Recursive deep models for semantic compositionality over a sentiment treebank. In *In Proceedings of the conference on empirical methods in natural language processing (EMNLP)*, volume 1631, page 1642. Citeseer.

[Srivastava et al.2013] Nitish Srivastava, Ruslan R Salakhutdinov, and Geoffrey E Hinton. 2013. Modeling documents with deep boltzmann machines. *arXiv preprint arXiv:1309.6865*.

[Trask et al.2015] Andrew Trask, David Gilmore, and Matthew Russell. 2015. Modeling order in neural word embeddings at scale. *arXiv preprint arXiv:1506.02338*.

[Yu and Dredze2015] Mo Yu and Mark Dredze. 2015. Learning composition models for phrase embeddings. *Transactions of the Association for Computational Linguistics*, 3:227–242.

[Zhang et al.2014] Jiajun Zhang, Shujie Liu, Mu Li, Ming Zhou, and Chengqing Zong. 2014. Bilingually-constrained phrase embeddings for machine translation. In *In Proceedings of the 52th Annual Meeting on Association for Computational Linguistics. Association for Computational Linguistics*.

Assessing Relative Sentence Complexity using an Incremental CCG Parser

Bharat Ram Ambati and **Siva Reddy** and **Mark Steedman**
School of Informatics, University of Edinburgh
10 Crichton Street, Edinburgh EH8 9AB
bharat.ambati@ed.ac.uk, siva.reddy@ed.ac.uk, steedman@inf.ed.ac.uk

Abstract

Given a pair of sentences, we present computational models to assess if one sentence is simpler to read than the other. While existing models explored the usage of phrase structure features using a non-incremental parser, experimental evidence suggests that the human language processor works incrementally. We empirically evaluate if syntactic features from an incremental CCG parser are more useful than features from a non-incremental phrase structure parser. Our evaluation on Simple and Standard Wikipedia sentence pairs suggests that incremental CCG features are indeed more useful than phrase structure features achieving 0.44 points gain in performance. Incremental CCG parser also gives significant improvements in speed (12 times faster) in comparison to the phrase structure parser. Furthermore, with the addition of psycholinguistic features, we achieve the strongest result to date reported on this task. Our code and data can be downloaded from https://github.com/bharatambati/sent-compl.

1 Introduction

The task of assessing text readability aims to classify text into different levels of difficulty, e.g., text comprehensible by a particular age group or second language learners (Petersen and Ostendorf, 2009; Feng, 2010; Vajjala and Meurers, 2014). There have been efforts to automatically simplify Wikipedia to cater its content for children and English language learners (Zhu et al., 2010; Woodsend and Lapata, 2011; Coster and Kauchak, 2011; Wubben et al.,

2012; Siddharthan and Mandya, 2014). A related attempt of Vajjala and Meurers (2016) studied the usage of linguistic features for automatic classification of a pair of sentences – one from Standard Wikipedia and the other its corresponding simplification from Simple Wikipedia – into COMPLEX and SIMPLE. As syntactic features, they use information from phrase structure trees produced by a non-incremental parser, and found them useful.

However, psycholinguistic theories suggest that humans process text incrementally, i.e., humans build syntactic analysis interactively by enhancing current analysis or choosing an alternative analysis on the basis of the plausibility with respect to context (Marslen-Wilson, 1973; Altmann and Steedman, 1988; Tanenhaus et al., 1995). Besides being cognitively possible, incremental parsing has shown to be useful for many real-time applications such as language modeling for speech recognition (Chelba and Jelinek, 2000; Roark, 2001), modeling text reading time (Demberg and Keller, 2008), dialogue systems (Stoness et al., 2004) and machine translation (Schwartz et al., 2011). Furthermore, incremental parsers offer linear time speed. Here we explore the usefulness of incremental parsing for predicting relative sentence readability.

Given a pair of sentences – one sentence a simplified version of the other – we aim to classify the sentences into SIMPLE or COMPLEX. We use the sentences from Standard Wikipedia (WIKI) paired with their corresponding simplifications in Simple Wikipedia (SIMPLEWIKI) as training and evaluation data. We pose this problem as a pairwise classification problem (Section 2). For feature extraction,

Proceedings of NAACL-HLT 2016, pages 1051–1057,
San Diego, California, June 12-17, 2016. ©2016 Association for Computational Linguistics

we use an incremental CCG parser which provides a trace of each step of the parse derivation (Section 3). Our evaluation results show that incremental parse features are more useful than non-incremental parse features (Section 5). With the addition of psycholinguistic features, we attain the best reported results on this task. We make our system available for public usage.

2 Problem Formulation

Initially Vajjala and Meurers (2014) trained a binary classifier to classify sentences in SIMPLEWIKI to the class SIMPLE, and sentences in WIKI to the class COMPLEX. This model performed poorly on relative readability assessment. Noting that not all SIMPLEWIKI sentences are simpler than every other sentence in WIKI, Vajjala and Meurers (2016) reframed the problem as a ranking problem according to which given a pair of parallel SIMPLEWIKI and WIKI sentences, the former must be ranked better than the latter in terms of readability. Inspired by Vajjala and Meurers (2016), we also treat each pair together, and model relative readability assessment as a pairwise classification problem. Let a, b be a pair of parallel sentences. Let $\mathbf{a}$, $\mathbf{b}$ represent their corresponding feature vectors. We define our classifier Φ as

$$\Phi(\mathbf{a} - \mathbf{b}) = \ \ 1 \ \ \text{if } a \in \text{SIMPLE} \ \& \ b \in \text{COMPLEX}$$
$$= -1 \ \ \text{if } b \in \text{SIMPLE} \ \& \ a \in \text{COMPLEX}$$

The motivation for our modelling is that relative features (difference) are more useful than absolute features, e.g., intuitively shorter sentences are simple to read, but length can only be defined in comparison with another sentence.

3 Incremental CCG Parse Features

Below we provide necessary background, and then present the features.

3.1 Combinatory Categorial Grammar (CCG)

CCG (Steedman, 2000) is a lexicalized formalism in which words are assigned syntactic types encoding subcategorization information. Figure 1 displays an incremental CCG derivation. Here, the syntactic type (category) (S\NP)/NP on *ate* indicates that it is a transitive verb looking for a NP

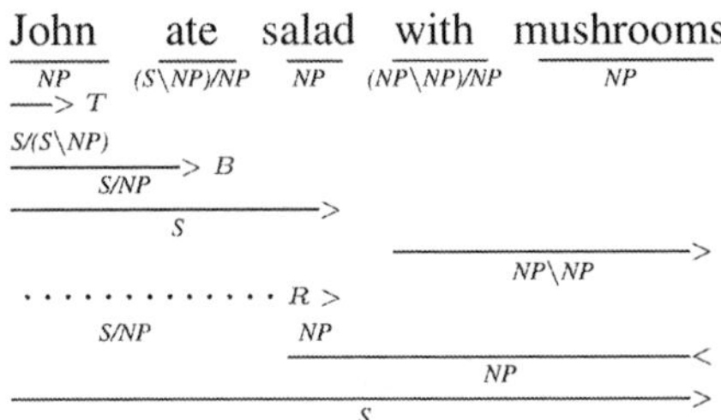

Figure 1: Incremental CCG derivation tree.

(object) on the righthand side and a NP (subject) on the lefthand side. Due to its lexicalized and strongly typed nature, the formalism offers attractive properties like elegant composition mechanisms which impose context-sensitive constraints, efficient parsing algorithms, and a synchronous syntax-semantics interface. In Figure 1, the category of *with* (NP\NP)/NP combines with the category of *mushrooms* NP on its righthand side using the combinatory rule of *forward application* (indicated by >), to form the category NP\NP representing the phrase *with mushrooms*. This phrase in turn combines with other contextual categories using CCG combinators to form new categories representing larger phrases.

In contrast to phrase structure trees, CCG derivation trees encode a richer notion of syntactic type and constituency. For example, in a phrase structure tree, the category (constituency tag) of *ate* would be *VBD* irrespective of whether it is transitive or intransitive, whereas the CCG category distinguishes these types. As the linguistic complexity increases, the complexity of the CCG category may increase, e.g., the relative pronoun has the category (NP\NP)/(S\NP) in relative clause constructions. In addition, CCG derivation trees have combinators annotated at each level which indicate the way in which the category is derived, e.g., in Figure 1 the category S/NP of *John ate* is formed by first *type-raising* (indicated by >T) *John* and then applying *forward composition* (indicated by >B) with *ate*. CCG combinators can throw light into the linguistic complexity of the construction, e.g., *crossed composition* is an indicator of long-range dependency. Phrase structure trees do not have this additional information encoded on their nodes.

3.2 Incremental CCG

Ambati et al. (2015) introduced a shift-reduce in-

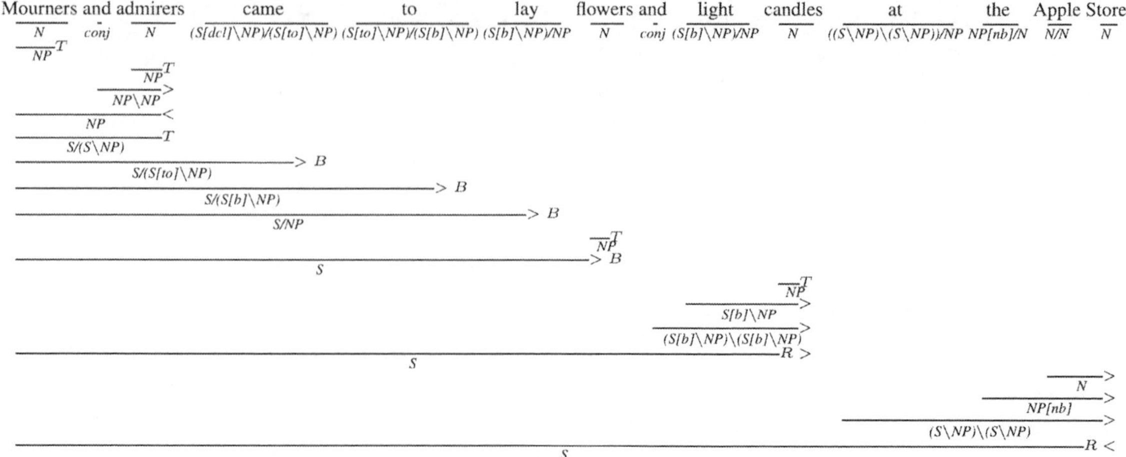

Figure 2: Incremental Derivation for a relatively complex sentence.

cremental CCG parser for English.[1] The main difference between this incremental version and standard non-incremental CCG parsers such as Zhang and Clark (2011) is that as soon as the grammar allows two types to combine, they are greedily combined. For example, in Figure 1, first *John* is pushed on the stack but is immediately reduced when its head *ate* appears on the stack (i.e., *John*'s category combines with *ate*'s category to form a new category), and similarly when *salad* is seen, it is reduced with *ate*. When *with* appears it waits to be reduced until its head *mushrooms* appears on the stack, and later *mushrooms* is reduced with *salad* via *ate* using a special *revealing* operation (indicated by R>) followed by a sequence of operations. The *revealing* operation is performed when a category has greedily consumed a head in advance of a subsequently encountered post-modifier to regenerate the head. In the non-incremental version, *salad* is not reduced with *ate* until *with mushrooms* is reduced with it.

Consider the following sentences (A) and (B) where (B) is a simpler version of (A).

(A)	Mourners and admirers came to lay flowers and light candles at the Apple Store.
(B)	People went to the Apple Store with flowers and candles.

Figures 2 and 3 present the incremental deriva-

tions for both these sentences. Consider the CCG category for *to* in both the sentences. In (A), the category of *to* is (S[dcl]\NP)/(S[to]\NP) which is more complex compared to the category of *to* in (B) which is PP/NP. Both the derivations have one right reveal action (indicated by $R >$). In (A), the depth of this action is two since it is a VP coordination.[2] Whereas in (B) the depth is only one. Such information can be useful in predicting the complexity of a sentence.

3.3 Features

As discussed above, as the complexity of a sentence increases, the complexity of CCG categories, combinators and the number of revealing operations increase in the incremental analysis. We exploit this information to assess the readability of a sentence. For each sentence, we build a feature vector using the features defined below extracted from its incremental CCG derivation.

Sentence Level Features. These features include sentence length, height of the CCG derivation, and the final number of constituents. A CCG derivation may have multiple constituents if none of the combinators allow the constituents to combine. This happens mainly in ungrammatical sentences.

CCG Rule Counts. These features include the number of applications, forward applications, back-

---

[1]This parser is not word by word (strictly) incremental but is incremental with respect to CCG derivational constituents following Strict Competence Hypothesis (Steedman, 2000).

[2]Please see Ambati et al. (2015) for additional information on the *depth* of revealing operations.

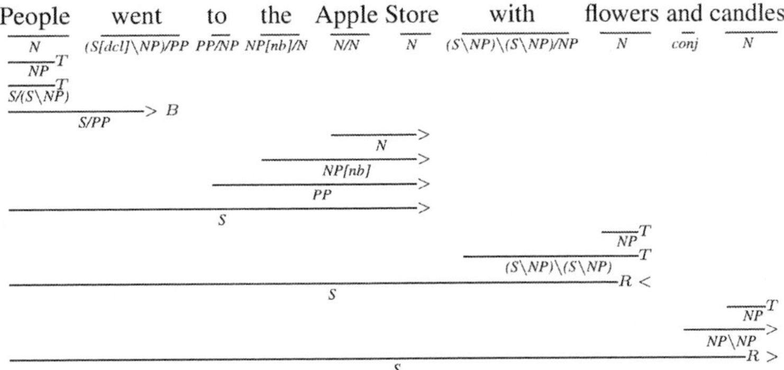

Figure 3: Incremental Derivation for a relatively simple sentence.

ward applications, compositions, forward compositions, backward compositions, left punctuations, right punctuations, coordinations, type-raisings, type-changing, left revealing, right revealing operations used in the CCG derivation. Each combinator is treated as a different feature dimension with its count as the feature value. For the revealing operations, we also add additional features which indicate the depth of the revealing which is analogous to surprisal (Hale, 2001).

CCG Categories. We define the complexity of a CCG category as the number of basic syntactic types used in the category, e.g., the complexity of $(S[pss]\backslash NP)/(S[to]\backslash NP)$ is 4 since it has one $S[pss]$, one $S[to]$, and two NPs. Note that CCG type $S[pss]$ indicates a *sentence* but of the subtype *passive*. We use average complexity of all the CCG categories used in the derivation as a real valued feature. In addition, we define integer-valued features representing the frequency of specific subtypes (we have 21 subtypes each defined as a different dimension) and the frequency of the top 8 syntactic types (each as a different dimension).

4 Experimental Setup

4.1 Evaluation Data

As evaluation data, we use WIKI and SIMPLEWIKI parallel sentence pairs collected by Hwang et al. (2015), a newer and larger version compared to Zhu et al. (2010)'s collection. We only use the pairs from the section GOOD consisting of 150K pairs. We further removed pairs containing identical sentences which resulted in 117K clean pairs. We randomly divided the data into training (60%), development (20%) and test (20%) splits.

4.2 Implementation details

As our classifier (see Section 2) we use SVM with Sequential Minimal Optimization in Weka toolkit (Hall et al., 2009) following its popularity in readability literature (Feng, 2010; Hancke et al., 2012; Vajjala and Meurers, 2014).[3] We use Ambati et al. (2015)'s CCG parser for extracting CCG derivations. This parser requires a CCG supertagger to limit its search space for which we use EasyCCG tagger (Lewis and Steedman, 2014).

4.3 Baseline

NON-INCREMENTAL PST. Following Vajjala and Meurers (2016), we use features extracted from Phrase Structure Trees (PST) produced by the Stanford parser (Klein and Manning, 2003), a nonincremental parser. We use the exact code used by Vajjala and Meurers (2016) to extract these features which include part-of-speech tags, constituency features like the number of noun phrases, verb phrases and preposition phrases, and the average size of the constituent trees. Vajjala and Meurers (2016) used a total of 57 features.[4]

5 Results

First we analyze the impact of incremental CCG features (and so the name INCREMENTAL CCG).

---

[3] We also experimented with Naive Bayes and Logistic Regression and observed similar pattern in the results. But, SVM gave the best results among the classifiers we explored.

[4] Details of the features can be found in Vajjala and Meurers (2016).

Model	Accuracy
NON-INCREMENTAL PST	71.68
INCREMENTAL CCG	**72.12**

Table 1: Impact of different syntactic features.

Table 1 presents the results of predicting relative readability on the test data.[5] INCREMENTAL CCG achieves 72.12% accuracy, a significant[6] improvement of 0.44 points over NON-INCREMENTAL PST (71.68%) indicating that incremental CCG features are empirically more useful than non-incremental phrase structure features. We also evaluate if this result holds for incremental vs. non-incremental CCG parse features. Ambati et al. (2015) can also produce non-incremental CCG parses by turning off a flag. Note that in the non-incremental version, revealing features are absent. This version achieves an accuracy of 72.02%, around 0.1% lower than the winner INCREMENTAL CCG, yet higher than NON-INCREMENTAL PST showing that CCG derivation trees offer richer syntactic information than phrase structure trees. POS taggers used for Stanford and CCG parsers gave similar accuracy. This shows that the improvements are indeed due to the incremental CCG parse features rather than the POS features.

Apart from the syntactic features, Vajjala and Meurers (2016) have also used psycholinguistic features such as age of acquisition of words, word imagery ratings, word familiarity ratings, and ambiguity of a word, collected from the psycholinguistic repositories Celex (Baayen et al., 1995), MRC (Wilson, 1988), AoA (Kuperman et al., 2012) and WordNet (Fellbaum, 1998). These features are found to be highly predictive for assessing readability. We enhance our syntactic models NON-INCREMENTAL PST and INCREMENTAL CCG by adding these psycholinguistic features to build NON-INCREMENTAL PST++ and INCREMENTAL CCG++ respectively. Table 2 presents the final results along with the previous state-of-the-art results of Vajjala and Meurers (2016).[7] Psycholinguistic features gave a boost of

Model	Accuracy
Vajjala and Meurers (2016)	74.58
NON-INCREMENTAL PST++	78.68
INCREMENTAL CCG++	**78.87**

Table 2: Performance of models with both syntactic and psycholinguistic features.

around 6.75 points on the syntactic models.[8] Additionally the performance gap between our models decrease (from 0.44 to 0.19) showing some of the psycholinguistic features also model a subset of the syntactic features. INCREMENTAL CCG++ achieves an accuracy of 78.77% outperforming the previous best system of Vajjala and Meurers (2016) by a wide margin.

Speed. In addition to accuracy, parsing speed is important in real-time applications. The Stanford parser took 204 minutes to parse the test data with a speed of 3.8 sentences per second. The incremental CCG parser took 16 minutes with an average speed of 47.5 sentences per second, a 12X improvement over the Stanford parser. These numbers include POS tagging time for the Stanford parser, and POS tagging and supertagging time for the incremental CCG parser. All the systems are run on the same hardware (Intel i5-2400 CPU @ 3.10GHz).

6 Conclusion

Our empirical evaluation on assessing relative sentence complexity suggests that syntactic features extracted from an incremental CCG parser are more useful than from a non-incremental phrase structure parser. This result aligns with psycholinguistic findings that human sentence processor is incremental. Our incremental model enhanced with psycholinguistic features achieves the best reported results on predicting relative sentence readability. We experimented with Simple Wikipedia and Wikipedia data from Hwang et al. (2015). We can explore the usefulness of our system on other datasets like OneStopEnglish (OSE) corpus (Vajjala and Meurers, 2016) or the dataset from Xu et al. (2015). We are also currently exploring the usefulness of incremental analysis for psycholinguistic data by switching off the lookahead feature.

---

[5]All feature engineering is done on the development data.

[6]Numbers in bold indicate significant results, significance measured using McNemar's test.

[7]We ran Vajjala and Meurers (2016)'s code on our dataset and get similar results reported on Zhu et al. (2010)'s dataset.

[8]Non-incremental CCG achieves an accuracy of 78.77%.

Acknowledgments

We thank Sowmya Vajjala and Dave Howcroft for providing data and settings for the baseline. We also thank the three anonymous reviewers for their useful suggestions. This work was supported by ERC Advanced Fellowship 249520 GRAMPLUS, EU IST Cognitive Systems IP Xperience and a Google PhD Fellowship for the second author.

References

[Altmann and Steedman1988] Gerry Altmann and Mark Steedman. 1988. Interaction with context during human sentence processing. *Cognition*, 30(3):191–238.

[Ambati et al.2015] Bharat Ram Ambati, Tejaswini Deoskar, Mark Johnson, and Mark Steedman. 2015. An Incremental Algorithm for Transition-based CCG Parsing. In *Proceedings of the 2015 Conference of the North American Chapter of the Association for Computational Linguistics: Human Language Technologies*, pages 53–63, Denver, Colorado, May–June. Association for Computational Linguistics.

[Baayen et al.1995] R. H. Baayen, R. Piepenbrock, and L. Gulikers. 1995. *The CELEX Lexical Database (CD-ROM)*. Linguistic Data Consortium, University of Pennsylvania, Philadelphia, PA.

[Chelba and Jelinek2000] Ciprian Chelba and Frederick Jelinek. 2000. Structured language modeling. *Computer Speech & Language*, 14(4):283–332.

[Coster and Kauchak2011] William Coster and David Kauchak. 2011. Simple English Wikipedia: A New Text Simplification Task. In *Proceedings of the 49th Annual Meeting of the Association for Computational Linguistics: Human Language Technologies*, pages 665–669, Portland, Oregon, USA, June. Association for Computational Linguistics.

[Demberg and Keller2008] Vera Demberg and Frank Keller. 2008. Data from eye-tracking corpora as evidence for theories of syntactic processing complexity. *Cognition*, 109(2):193–210.

[Fellbaum1998] Christiane Fellbaum. 1998. *WordNet*. Wiley Online Library.

[Feng2010] Lijun Feng. 2010. *Automatic readability assessment*. Ph.D. thesis, City University of New York.

[Hale2001] John Hale. 2001. A probabilistic Earley parser as a psycholinguistic model. In *Proceedings of the second meeting of the North American Chapter of the Association for Computational Linguistics on Language technologies*, pages 159–166. Association for Computational Linguistics.

[Hall et al.2009] Mark Hall, Eibe Frank, Geoffrey Holmes, Bernhard Pfahringer, Peter Reutemann, and Ian H Witten. 2009. The WEKA Data Mining Software: An Update. *ACM SIGKDD explorations newsletter*, 11(1):10–18.

[Hancke et al.2012] Julia Hancke, Sowmya Vajjala, and Detmar Meurers. 2012. Readability Classification for German using Lexical, Syntactic, and Morphological Features. In *Proceedings of COLING 2012*, pages 1063–1080, Mumbai, India, December. The COLING 2012 Organizing Committee.

[Hwang et al.2015] William Hwang, Hannaneh Hajishirzi, Mari Ostendorf, and Wei Wu. 2015. Aligning Sentences from Standard Wikipedia to Simple Wikipedia. In *Proceedings of the 2015 Conference of the North American Chapter of the Association for Computational Linguistics: Human Language Technologies*, pages 211–217, Denver, Colorado, May–June. Association for Computational Linguistics.

[Klein and Manning2003] Dan Klein and Christopher D. Manning. 2003. Accurate Unlexicalized Parsing. In *Proceedings of the 41st Annual Meeting of the Association for Computational Linguistics*, pages 423–430, Sapporo, Japan, July. Association for Computational Linguistics.

[Kuperman et al.2012] Victor Kuperman, Hans Stadthagen-Gonzalez, and Marc Brysbaert. 2012. Age-of-acquisition ratings for 30,000 English words. *Behavior Research Methods*, 44(4):978–990.

[Lewis and Steedman2014] Mike Lewis and Mark Steedman. 2014. Improved CCG parsing with Semi-supervised Supertagging. *Transactions of the Association for Computational Linguistics (TACL)*, 2:327–338.

[Marslen-Wilson1973] W. Marslen-Wilson. 1973. Linguistic structure and speech shadowing at very short latencies. *Nature*, 244:522–533.

[Petersen and Ostendorf2009] Sarah E Petersen and Mari Ostendorf. 2009. A machine learning approach to reading level assessment. *Computer speech & language*, 23(1):89–106.

[Roark2001] Brian Roark. 2001. Probabilistic Top-Down Parsing and Language Modeling. *Computational Linguistics*, 27:249–276.

[Schwartz et al.2011] Lane Schwartz, Chris Callison-Burch, William Schuler, and Stephen Wu. 2011. Incremental Syntactic Language Models for Phrase-based Translation. In *Proceedings of the 49th Annual Meeting of the Association for Computational Linguistics: Human Language Technologies*, pages 620–631, Portland, Oregon, USA, June. Association for Computational Linguistics.

[Siddharthan and Mandya2014] Advaith Siddharthan and Angrosh Mandya. 2014. Hybrid text simplification using synchronous dependency grammars with handwritten and automatically harvested rules. In *Proceedings of the 14th Conference of the European Chapter of the Association for Computational Linguistics*, pages 722–731, Gothenburg, Sweden, April. Association for Computational Linguistics.

[Steedman2000] Mark Steedman. 2000. *The Syntactic Process*. MIT Press, Cambridge, MA, USA.

[Stoness et al.2004] Scott C Stoness, Joel Tetreault, and James Allen. 2004. Incremental Parsing with Reference Interaction. In *Proceedings of the Workshop on Incremental Parsing: Bringing Engineering and Cognition Together*, pages 18–25.

[Tanenhaus et al.1995] MK Tanenhaus, MJ Spivey-Knowlton, KM Eberhard, and JC Sedivy. 1995. Integration of visual and linguistic information in spoken language comprehension. *Science*, 268(5217):1632–1634.

[Vajjala and Meurers2014] Sowmya Vajjala and Detmar Meurers. 2014. Assessing the relative reading level of sentence pairs for text simplification. In *Proceedings of the 14th Conference of the European Chapter of the Association for Computational Linguistics*, pages 288–297, Gothenburg, Sweden, April. Association for Computational Linguistics.

[Vajjala and Meurers2016] Sowmya Vajjala and Detmar Meurers. 2016. Readability-based Sentence Ranking for Evaluating Text Simplification. In *arXiv preprint*.

[Wilson1988] Michael Wilson. 1988. MRC Psycholinguistic Database: Machine-usable dictionary, version 2.00. *Behavior Research Methods, Instruments, & Computers*, 20(1):6–10.

[Woodsend and Lapata2011] Kristian Woodsend and Mirella Lapata. 2011. WikiSimple: Automatic Simplification of Wikipedia Articles. In *Proceedings of the Twenty-Fifth AAAI Conference on Artificial Intelligence (AAAI)*, pages 927–932, San Francisco, California, USA.

[Wubben et al.2012] Sander Wubben, Antal van den Bosch, and Emiel Krahmer. 2012. Sentence Simplification by Monolingual Machine Translation. In *Proceedings of the 50th Annual Meeting of the Association for Computational Linguistics (Volume 1: Long Papers)*, pages 1015–1024, Jeju Island, Korea, July. Association for Computational Linguistics.

[Xu et al.2015] Wei Xu, Chris Callison-Burch, and Courtney Napoles. 2015. Problems in Current Text Simplification Research: New Data Can Help. *Transactions of the Association for Computational Linguistics*, 3:283–297.

[Zhang and Clark2011] Yue Zhang and Stephen Clark. 2011. Shift-Reduce CCG Parsing. In *Proceedings of*

the 49th Annual Meeting of the Association for Computational Linguistics: Human Language Technologies*, pages 683–692, Portland, Oregon, USA, June. Association for Computational Linguistics.

[Zhu et al.2010] Zhemin Zhu, Delphine Bernhard, and Iryna Gurevych. 2010. A Monolingual Tree-based Translation Model for Sentence Simplification. In *Proceedings of the 23rd International Conference on Computational Linguistics (Coling 2010)*, pages 1353–1361, Beijing, China, August. Coling 2010 Organizing Committee.

Frustratingly Easy Cross-Lingual Transfer for Transition-Based Dependency Parsing

Ophélie Lacroix[1], Lauriane Aufrant[1,2], Guillaume Wisniewski[1] and François Yvon[1]

[1]LIMSI, CNRS, Univ. Paris-Sud, Université Paris-Saclay, F-91405 Orsay

[2]DGA, 60 boulevard du Général Martial Valin, F-75509 Paris

{ophelie.lacroix, lauriane.aufrant, guillaume.wisniewski, francois.yvon}@limsi.fr

Abstract

In this paper, we present a straightforward strategy for transferring dependency parsers across languages. The proposed method learns a parser from partially annotated data obtained through the projection of annotations across unambiguous word alignments. It does not rely on any modeling of the reliability of dependency and/or alignment links and is therefore easy to implement and parameter free. Experiments on six languages show that our method is at par with recent algorithmically demanding methods, at a much cheaper computational cost. It can thus serve as a fair baseline for transferring dependencies across languages with the use of parallel corpora.

1 Introduction

Cross-lingual learning techniques enable to transfer useful supervision information from well-resourced to under-resourced languages, helping the development of NLP tools for a large number of languages. In this work, we present a simple method for transferring dependency parsers between languages.

Two main strategies have been considered to transfer syntactic annotations: (a) direct model transfer and (b) annotation transfer. The first approach assumes a common representation between the source and target languages (e.g. at the level of PoS tags), which enables to train a model on source data and to use it to parse target sentences. The performance of 'pure' delexicalized dependency transfer can be significantly improved using additional techniques such as self-training (Zeman and Resnik, 2008), smart data selection (Søgaard, 2011), relexicalization and/or multi-source model transfer (Cohen et al., 2011; Naseem et al., 2012; Täckström et al., 2013). The second approach (transfer of annotations) requires parallel sentences, in which word alignments are used to infer target syntactic structures from source dependencies. The main difficulty here is to cope with cases of non-isomorphism between the source and target structures as well as with the noise in source annotations and in alignments. Turning source trees into target trees indeed may require to filter poor alignments and to apply various heuristic transformation rules, such as the ones introduced in Hwa et al. (2005), later improved in Tiedemann (2014).

In this study, we consider a simple, yet effective approach to transfer annotations, which entirely dispenses from the transfer rules of Hwa et al. (2005), the sharp filtering of partially annotated trees (Tiedemann, 2014), the inclusion of fake root dependencies for unattached words (Spreyer and Kuhn, 2009), or the multi-step process of Rasooli and Collins (2015). Our proposal is, in fact, quite as straightforward (apart from the use of parallel texts) as the delexicalized transfer method of McDonald et al. (2013) while achieving performances that surpass this state-of-the-art method by a wide margin, and competing with recent algorithmically costly methods: it globally outperforms the scores of (Ma and Xia, 2014) and even achieves the same performance as (2015) for 1 language out of 5. It can thus be used as a fair and simple baseline when evaluating new transfer methodologies.

Proceedings of NAACL-HLT 2016, pages 1058–1063,

San Diego, California, June 12-17, 2016. ©2016 Association for Computational Linguistics

Our method relies on the observation (Section 2) that transition-based dependency parsers using the dynamic oracle strategy can be trained from partially annotated trees (in which some words may not have a governor) *using exactly the same algorithm that is used to train from fully annotated tree*. As explained in Section 3, this observation allows us to design a simple transfer strategy that, first, (partially) projects syntactic annotations from a source language onto a target language via unambiguous word alignments and, second, learns a dependency parser from these partially annotated target data. We then apply this strategy for six language pairs.

2 Training Dependency Parsers on Partially Annotated Data

2.1 Training with a Dynamic Oracle

We consider a transition-based dependency parser based on the arc-eager algorithm (Nivre, 2003): this parser builds a dependency tree incrementally by performing a sequence of *actions*. At each step of the parsing process, a classifier scores each possible action and the highest scoring one is applied.

Training relies on the dynamic oracle of Goldberg and Nivre (2012): for each sentence, a parse tree is built incrementally; at each step, if the predicted action creates an erroneous dependency (or, equivalently, prevents the creation of a gold dependency), a weight vector is updated, according to the perceptron rule. The set of all 'correct' actions is built considering the (potentially wrong) predicted tree and the gold action is defined as the correct action with the highest model score.

It is crucial to notice that the training algorithm is an error-correction learning procedure that solely depends on its ability to detect when an action choice will result in an error: when no error is detected, the construction of the parse tree continues according to the model prediction. Consequently, this training procedure can also be used, unchanged, to train a dependency parser from partially annotated data: when no supervision information is available (no reference dependency is known), all actions are considered as correct; in this case, the predicted action is one of the correct actions, the weight vector is not updated, and the training process goes on.

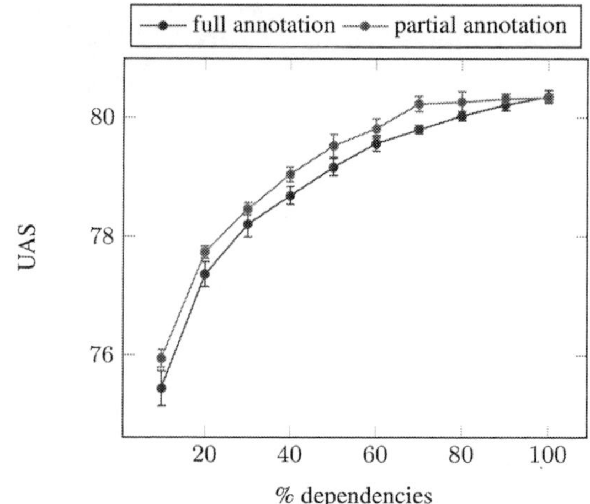

Figure 1: UAS achieved by a parser trained on $n\%$ of the dependencies on German.

This observation can be readily generalized to dependency parsers using a beam search procedure.[1] For the experiments in Section 3, we use a beam-search version of the parser trained with an early-update strategy (Collins and Roark, 2004).

2.2 Experiments on Artificial Datasets

We first carry out a control experiment on datasets in which dependencies have been artificially removed to show that learning from partially annotated data is possible. We compare the performance achieved by a parser trained on $n\%$ of the sentences of the train set with the performance of a parser trained on the whole train set, but in which only $n\%$ of the dependencies of each sentence are known. In both conditions, the total number of dependencies considered during training is roughly the same. Figure 1 plots the parsing performance for German, evaluated by the UAS, with respect to the percentage of dependencies that were kept. To avoid any bias, the reported scores have been averaged over 10 runs. Similar results are observed for 5 other languages of the Universal Dependency Treebank[2] (UDT) (McDonald et al., 2013).

Overall, these results show that learning a parser from partially annotated data is possible. Two other

---

[1] See (Aufrant and Wisniewski, 2016) for a detailed explanation.

[2] See Section 3.2 for more details on datasets.

conclusions can also be drawn. First, it appears that the number of training examples can be reduced without significantly hurting the performance: removing half the training sentences only reduces the UAS by 1.2 absolute. Second, for a similar number of annotations (i.e. number of dependencies known), better results are achieved when more sentences are annotated, even if this annotation is only partial: in Figure 1, the UAS of a parser trained on partially annotated sentences is higher than the UAS of a parser trained from a subset of the training set.

Indeed, in a partial structure, information on unknown dependencies can be inferred from neighbouring dependencies because of the projectivity constraints. Therefore, the set of gold actions is sometimes smaller than the set of possible actions and an update can happen even if the dependency is unknown. For instance, when training a German dependency parser, 35,382 updates are performed when only 60% of the dependencies are known, to be compared with the 31,339 updates that take place when training on 60% of the fully annotated sentences.

3   Application to Dependency Transfer

In this section, we show how learning from partially annotated data can be used for cross-lingual dependency transfer. A partial projection strategy is first applied to infer partially annotated data for a target language from a full-parsed source data. The target annotations are then used to learn an effective parsing model for the target language.

3.1   Partial Projection of Dependencies

Using sentence-aligned bitexts associating an automatically parsed text in a resource-rich language with its translation in target language, dependencies can readily be projected via alignment links, yielding 'cheap', albeit noisy, supervision data. The main difficulties with the projection arise with many-to-many links and un-aligned tokens. Hwa et al. (2005) have proposed several specific heuristics to deal with the different kinds of alignments and project a full dependency tree. However, this solution comes at the expense of deleting words or creating fake dependencies in the target sentence, which may introduce unreliable annotations in the target data.

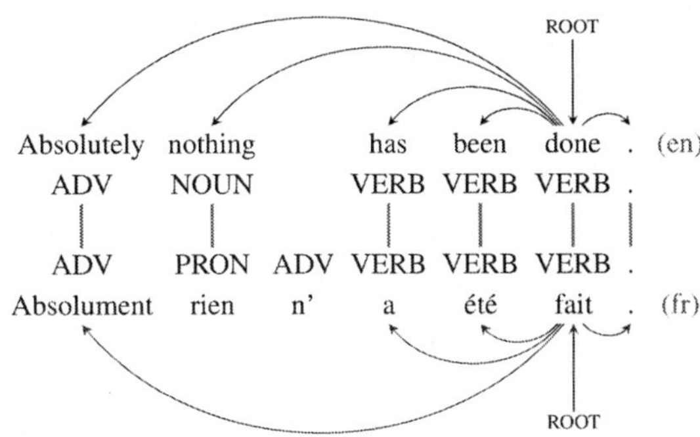

Figure 2: Partial dependency projection from English to French. Only English dependencies compatible with 1 : 1 alignments, and for which the POS of the aligned words are consistent, are transferred to French.

In this work, we advocate another approach and show that it is simpler and more effective to ignore unattached words and many-to-many alignments: we claim that training a parser from a corpus of high-quality annotated (albeit partially) data will result in better parsing performances than a parser trained from fully-annotated but noisy data.

In practice, parallel sentences are aligned in both directions with Giza++ (Och and Ney, 2003) and these alignments are merged with the intersection heuristic. This heuristic only selects 1 : 1 alignment links that occur in the two directional alignments and, intuitively, contains only reliable alignment points, as they have been predicted by two independent models. Note that we do not try to model the reliability of dependency and/or alignment links, making our approach easy to implement and parameter free.

We additionally consider three simple heuristics to filter the transferred annotations and improve their precision: we first remove from the training set target sentences containing non-projective dependencies,[3] as well as sentences for which less than 80% of the words are attached. The latter case indeed corresponds to parallel sentences with few alignment links that are often not perfect translation of each other. Finally, following Rasooli and Collins (2015), we ignore all alignment links that associate words

---

[3] As shown in the work of (Mareček, 2011), sentences containing non-projective dependencies often results in low-quality projected dependency structures.

with different PoS tags. As shown in Figure 2, for each pair of aligned sentences, only the dependencies for which both the head and the dependent are each aligned to exactly one word (PoS-consistent) are projected.[4]

This approach finally produces an automatically annotated corpus for the target language that contains mostly accurate annotations, even if the dependency structure is incomplete.

3.2 Datasets and Experimental Setup

All our experiments are carried out on six languages[5] of the Universal Dependency Treebank Project: German, English, Spanish, French, Italian and Swedish. We considered as parallel corpora a subset of the Europarl corpus (Koehn, 2005) that have exactly the same English sentences, collecting $1,231,216$ parallel sentences for the 6 language pairs.

For training the target partial data, we used our own implementation of the arc-eager dependency parser with a dynamic oracle, using the features described in (Zhang and Nivre, 2011), with a beam size of 8. The beam-search strategy is used for training (20 iterations) and decoding.

3.3 Dependency Transfer Experiments

For each language pair, the source dataset (Europarl) is PoS-tagged and parsed using the transition-based version of the MateParser (Bohnet and Nivre, 2012), trained on the UDT corpus with a beam size of 40.[6] Dependencies are then (partially) projected onto the target side of the corpus and filtered using the method described above. As reported in Table 2, after filtering, the number of sentences in the train set varies between $15,191$ for German and $52,554$ for Swedish and the percentage of tokens receiving a dependency varies from 88.15% for French to 90.84% for German.

Our parser is then trained on the resulting partially annotated dataset and its performance evaluated on

	# sentences		
source	en		multi
filter	100%	80%	80%
de	7,346	15,191	70,905
es	9,293	27,700	178,147
fr	6,626	21,381	144,755
it	7,353	21,204	160,864
sv	20,550	52,554	175,201

Table 2: Number of sentences in projected and filtered target data.

the target UDT test set by the Unlabeled Attachment Score, UAS (excluding punctuation). Gold PoS were used for evaluating in order to make results of our method comparable with state-of-art methods.

The proposed method is compared to three transfer method baselines: the relexicalisation procedure of McDonald et al. (2011), the method of Ma and Xia (2014) for transferring cross-lingual knowledge using entropy regularization, and the recent density-driven approach of Rasooli and Collins (2015) exploiting partially annotated data. The results are first compared for cross-lingual transfer from English and second, applying a voting method[7] for transferring from multiple sources. Note, however, that a direct comparison with these results is not completely fair as systems were not trained with the same exact conditions (less features, lower beam size, etc). As a baseline for comparing parsers, we also report the scores achieved by Rasooli and Collins (2015) and by our method on fully projected sentences ('en-100%').

3.4 Results

Table 1 reports the results of the various transfer methods. Our method achieves significantly better results than the relexicalisation procedure of McDonald et al. (2011) (up to +8.33 in Spanish) and outperforms the method of Ma and Xia (2014) for 3 languages (from +0.91 (fr) to +2.86 (sv)) and equalizes it for one (it). Finally, for Swedish, it achieves performance that are on a par with that of Rasooli

---

[4]To account for the root dependency, we consider that both the source and target sentences contain an additional ROOT token that is always aligned.

[5]These are the languages that are both in Europarl and UDT.

[6]Here are the supervised scores obtained with the MateParser (predicted PoS-tags) on the source languages: 92.4 (en), 80.4 (de), 83.1 (es), 83.8 (fr), 84.2 (it) and 85.7 (sv).

[7]The voting method chooses, for each token of a sentence, the most frequent head among the projected heads from the various source languages if it does not impede the projectivity of the resulted tree (otherwise the next most frequent head is chosen). The most frequent "head" may be null. Finally, the sentence may be partially annotated.

| | M11 | MX14 | RC15 | | | this work | | | sup. |
source	(en)	(en)	(en)	(en-100%)	(multi)	(en)	(en-100%)	(multi)	
de	69.77	74.30	74.32	70.56	79.68	73.40	69.36	75.99	84.43
es	68.72	75.53	78.17	75.69	80.86	77.05	73.98	78.94	85.51
fr	73.13	76.53	79.91	77.03	82.72	77.44	75.89	80.80	85.81
it	70.74	77.74	79.46	77.35	83.67	77.74	75.50	79.39	86.97
sv	75.87	79.27	82.11	78.68	84.06	82.13	77.26	82.97	87.89

(The left margin of the data rows is labeled **target**.)

Table 1: Parsing quality (evaluated in UAS) of our method and previous works: M11 stands for McDonald et al. (2011), MX14 for Ma and Xia (2014), RC15 for Rasooli and Collins (2015) and 'sup' corresponds to the supervised scores. State-of-the-art scores are from (Rasooli and Collins, 2015).

and Collins (2015).

It therefore appears that, while being much simpler, the proposed approach achieves results very competitive with state-of-the-art methods at a much cheaper computational cost: our results have been obtained by training a single parser with a beam size of 8, while Ma and Xia (2014) use a parser with exact inference, the training and inference complexity of which is $\mathcal{O}(n^4)$ and the method of Rasooli and Collins (2015) requires the costly training of 4 different parsers each using a beam size of 64.

Results of Table 1 also show that Rasooli and Collins (2015) achieves better scores than our method when training on fully projected trees. This can be explained by the differing training conditions (as previously mentioned).[8] Finally, these results show the benefits of considering partial dependency trees and not only sentences for which a complete parse tree is transferred: a parser trained with partial dependencies improves the UAS up to 4.8 points.

4 Conclusion

In this paper, we have proposed and evaluated a very simple procedure to train a dependency parser with projected partial annotations. In fact, our training algorithm is virtually unchanged with respect to the fully supervised case. Yet, it has proved extremely effective when combined with an appropriate selection of the transferred annotations.[9]

Further improvements could be obtained using additional tricks, such as better data selection strategies or constrained parsing. Besides that, it is worth noting that our method is not only on a par with the method of Rasooli and Collins (2015) but could also be combined with it. Indeed, their first step can be substituted by our method. Since the latter outperforms the former, the combination of the two should improve their best final scores.

In our future work, we intend to study how this training strategy behaves for other transition-based systems or, more generally, for other NLP scenarios using partially annotated data.

Acknowledgments

This work has been partly funded by a DGA-RAPID project under grant agreement N.°1429060465 (Papyrus) and the French *Direction générale de l'armement*. We thank the reviewers for their accurate comments and suggestions.

References

Lauriane Aufrant and Guillaume Wisniewski. 2016. PanParser: a Modular Implementation for Efficient Transition-Based Dependency Parsing. Technical report, LIMSI, March.

Bernd Bohnet and Joakim Nivre. 2012. A transition-based system for joint part-of-speech tagging and labeled non-projective dependency parsing. In *Proceedings of the 2012 Joint Conference on Empirical Methods in Natural Language Processing and Computational Natural Language Learning*, pages 1455–1465, Jeju Island, Korea, July.

Shay B. Cohen, Dipanjan Das, and Noah A. Smith. 2011. Unsupervised Structure Prediction with Non-Parallel Multilingual Guidance. In *Proceedings of EMNLP 2011, the Conference on Empirical Methods in Natural Language Processing*, pages 50–61, Edinburgh, Scotland, UK., July.

---

[8] Indeed, the supervised scores achieved by Rasooli and Collins (2015) are 1.03 higher than ours.

[9] The external parameters used for filtering and training were selected according to the results of several experiments. The impact of these parameters are examined in Lacroix et al. (2016).

Michael Collins and Brian Roark. 2004. Incremental Parsing with the Perceptron Algorithm. In *Proceedings of ACL 2004, the 42nd Annual Meeting on Association for Computational Linguistics*, page 111. Association for Computational Linguistics.

Yoav Goldberg and Joakim Nivre. 2012. A Dynamic Oracle for Arc-Eager Dependency Parsing. In *Proceedings of COLING 2012, the International Conference on Computational Linguistics*, pages 959–976, Bombay, India.

Rebecca Hwa, Philip Resnik, Amy Weinberg, Clara Cabezas, and Okan Kolak. 2005. Bootstrapping Parsers via Syntactic Projection accross Parallel Texts. *Natural language engineering*, 11:311–325.

Philipp Koehn. 2005. Europarl: A parallel corpus for Statistical Machine Translation. In *2nd Workshop on EBMT of MT-Summit X*, pages 79–86, Phuket, Thailand.

Ophélie Lacroix, Guillaume Wisnewski, and François Yvon. 2016. Cross-lingual Dependency Transfer: What Matters? Assessing the Impact of Pre- and Postprocessing. In *Proceedings of the NAACL-16 Workshop on Multilingual and Crosslingual Methods in NLP*, MLCL 2016, San Diego, CA, USA. Association for Computational Linguistics.

Xuezhe Ma and Fei Xia. 2014. Unsupervised dependency parsing with transferring distribution via parallel guidance and entropy regularization. In *Proceedings of the 52nd Annual Meeting of the Association for Computational Linguistics (Volume 1: Long Papers)*, pages 1337–1348, Baltimore, Maryland, June.

David Mareček. 2011. Combining Diverse Word-Alignment Symmetrizations Improves Dependency Tree Projection. In *Computational Linguistics and Intelligent Text Processing*, pages 144–154. Springer.

Ryan McDonald, Slav Petrov, and Keith Hall. 2011. Multi-source Transfer of Delexicalized Dependency Parsers. In *Proceedings of EMNLP 2011, the Conference on Empirical Methods in Natural Language Processing*, pages 62–72.

Ryan McDonald, Joakim Nivre, Yvonne Quirmbach-Brundage, Yoav Goldberg, Dipanjan Das, Kuzman Ganchev, Keith Hall, Slav Petrov, Hao Zhang, Oscar Täckström, Claudia Bedini, Núria Bertomeu Castelló, and Jungmee Lee. 2013. Universal Dependency Annotation for Multilingual Parsing. In *Proceedings of ACL 2013, the 51st Annual Meeting of the Association for Computational Linguistics (Volume 2: Short Papers)*, pages 92–97, Sofia, Bulgaria, August.

Tahira Naseem, Regina Barzilay, and Amir Globerson. 2012. Selective sharing for multilingual dependency parsing. In *Proceedings of the 50th Annual Meeting of the Association for Computational Linguistics: Long Papers - Volume 1*, ACL '12, pages 629–637.

Joakim Nivre. 2003. An Efficient Algorithm for Projective Dependency Parsing. In *Proceedings of IWPT 2003, the 8th International Workshop on Parsing Technologies*, Nancy, France.

Franz Joseph Och and Hermann Ney. 2003. A systematic comparison of various statistical alignment models. *Computational Linguistics*, 29:19–51.

Mohammad Sadegh Rasooli and Michael Collins. 2015. Density-driven cross-lingual transfer of dependency parsers. In *Proceedings of the 2015 Conference on Empirical Methods in Natural Language Processing*, pages 328–338, Lisbon, Portugal, September. Association for Computational Linguistics.

Anders Søgaard. 2011. Data point selection for cross-language adaptation of dependency parsers. In *Proceedings of ACL 2011, the 49th Annual Meeting of the Association for Computational Linguistics: Human Language Technologies*, pages 682–686, Portland, Oregon, USA, June.

Kathrin Spreyer and Jonas Kuhn. 2009. Data-Driven Dependency Parsing of New Languages Using Incomplete and Noisy Training Data. In *Proceedings of CoNLL 2009, the Thirteenth Conference on Computational Natural Language Learning*, pages 12–20, Boulder, Colorado, June.

Oscar Täckström, Ryan McDonald, and Joakim Nivre. 2013. Target Language Adaptation of Discriminative Transfer Parsers. In *Proceedings of ACL 2013, the Conference of the North American Chapter of the Association for Computational Linguistics: Human Language Technologies*, pages 1061–1071, Atlanta, Georgia.

Jörg Tiedemann. 2014. Rediscovering Annotation Projection for Cross-Lingual Parser Induction. In *Proceedings of COLING 2014, the 25th International Conference on Computational Linguistics: Technical Papers*, pages 1854–1864, Dublin, Ireland, August. Dublin City University and Association for Computational Linguistics.

Daniel Zeman and Philip Resnik. 2008. Cross-Language Parser Adaptation between Related Languages. In *Proceedings of the IJCNLP-08 Workshop on NLP for Less Privileged Languages*, pages 35–42, Hyderabad, India, January. Asian Federation of Natural Language Processing.

Yue Zhang and Joakim Nivre. 2011. Transition-based Dependency Parsing with Rich Non-local Features. In *Proceedings of ACL 2011, the 49th Annual Meeting of the Association for Computational Linguistics: Human Language Technologies*, pages 188–193, Portland, Oregon, USA, June. Association for Computational Linguistics.

Geolocation for Twitter: Timing Matters

Mark Dredze[1,2]**, Miles Osborne**[1]**, Prabhanjan Kambadur**[1]

[1] Bloomberg L.P.
731 Lexington Ave, New York, NY 10022

[2] Human Language Technology Center of Excellence
Johns Hopkins University, Baltimore, MD 21211
`mdredze@cs.jhu.edu   mosborne29,pkambadur@bloomberg.net`

Abstract

Automated geolocation of social media messages can benefit a variety of downstream applications. However, these geolocation systems are typically evaluated without attention to how changes in time impact geolocation. Since different people, in different locations write messages at different times, these factors can significantly vary the performance of a geolocation system over time. We demonstrate cyclical temporal effects on geolocation accuracy in Twitter, as well as rapid drops as test data moves beyond the time period of training data. We show that temporal drift can effectively be countered with even modest online model updates.

1   Introduction

Geolocation – the task of identifying a social media message's location – can support a variety of downstream applications, such as advertising, personalization, event discovery, trend analysis and disease tracking (Watanabe et al., 2011; Hong et al., 2012; Kulshrestha et al., 2012; Broniatowski et al., 2013). Geolocation work has mostly focused on Twitter, since tweets are readily accessible and true location available from user geocoded tweets (*inter alia* (Eisenstein et al., 2010; Han et al., 2014; Rout et al., 2013; Compton et al., 2014; Cha et al., 2015; Jurgens et al., 2015; Osborne et al., 2014; Dredze et al., 2013)).

Most previous work consider the task of author geolocation, the identification of a author's primary (home) location (Eisenstein et al., 2010; Han et al., 2014). Author geolocation systems rely on multiple tweets from each author to identify the location. In this work, we consider the task of tweet geolocation, where a system identifies the location where a single tweet was written (Osborne et al., 2014; Dredze et al., 2013). This approach is necessary when geolocation decisions must be made quickly, with limited resources, or when the location of a specific tweet is required.

When focusing on a single tweet, time becomes relevant. Intuitively, tweets written in the morning might be in different locations (at home) than say tweets written during the day (at work). This information is often ignored but can provide important clues as to a tweet's location. Likewise, models built using historical data never adapt as time evolves. These factors may have a significant impact on geolocation accuracy, and downstream system's should be sensitive to these variations.

For the first time, we consider the impact of time on Twitter geolocation and predict where a post was made (rather than the more usual, and easier task of author location). We take a supervised learning approach, training a multi-class classifier to identify the city of a tweet. We train a system on 250 million tweets sampled from a 45 month period, perhaps the largest evaluation to date. We find that:

- Geolocation accuracy is cyclical, varying significantly with time.

- While access to massive training data improves accuracy, these effects are largely lost when models are deployed on new tweets, in large part due to new users and duplicate tweets.

- Periodically updating geolocation models, even with data available from the free Twitter API, can largely supplant massive training datasets.

Our study is similar to that of Pavalanathan and Eisenstein (2015), who called into question the accuracy of geolocation models due to mismatches between the behavior of users in available training data as compared to users encountered in live data. While our work provides a cautionary tale, it provides a guide for how these models can be used in practice.

2 Dataset

We start with *every geocoded tweet* (based on the "location" field) from January 1, 2012 to September 30, 2015: 8,530,693,792 tweets.[1] These tweets are associated with a specific location by Twitter (the "location" field is populated.)

We took several steps to remove tweets that were not relevant to the task. We removed tweets posted by location sharing services (FourSquare and jSwarm) since these are not written by users. We removed retweets for the same reason. We also remove tweets that do not have a specific latitude/longitude (geo) while nevertheless containing a location. Twitter allows user's to tag a tweet with a location (populating the location field) even when the user's device does not provide a latitude and longitude (geo field). To ensure we know the precise location of the user we only consider tweets with the geo field.

We matched each tweet to a city using the procedure of Han et al. (2014), with 3,709 cities derived from the geonames database[2]. Only 2983 locations contained a tweet; locations without tweets were mostly in Africa and China, which has low Twitter usage. Following Han et al. (2014) we focus on English tweets only, removing non-English tweets based on the metadata language code. We also identified the tweet's country for a country prediction task (161 labels). We divided this dataset into two time periods. We use tweets from January 1, 2012 to March 30, 2015 for a standard train/dev/test evaluation, selecting $\frac{2}{10,000}$ of the data for development and test sets. Data from March 31, 2015 to September 30, 2015 forms an "out of time" sample.

The most common cities were Los Angeles, London, Jakarta, Chicago, Kuala Lumpur and Dallas.

The city clustering procedure of Han et al. (2014) greatly influences this list. For example, Los Angeles ends up as one large city, whereas the New York City area is divided into several smaller cities.

3 Geolocation Model

We treat geolocation as a multi-class task, with each city (or country) a label (Jurgens et al., 2015).

Features All of our features are extracted from a single tweet (text or metadata) without requiring additional queries to the Twitter API.[3] These include: **Text**: We extracted unigrams and bigrams from the text of each tweet after tokenizing with Twokenizer (O'Connor et al., 2010). We removed all punctuation, and replaced unique usernames and urls with placeholder tokens. Numbers were replaced with a NUM token. **Profile location**: Unigrams and bigrams extracted from the user supplied profile location field, as well as a feature for the entire location string. These fields often provide clues as to the user's location, e.g. "New York Living". **Timezone**: Each tweet has a timezone that reflects a specific location, e.g. "Pacific Time (US & Canada)", "Atlantic Time (Canada)", "Casablanca". We also include the UTC offset of the timezone. **Time**: We use a feature indicating the hour of the day (in UTC time) at which the tweet was posted.

Learning We used vowpal wabbit (version 8.1.1) (Agarwal et al., 2011), a linear classifier trained using stochastic gradient descent with adaptive, individual learning rates (Duchi et al., 2011) that minimizes the hinge loss. We used feature hashing with a 31-bit feature space. We selected the best model and parameters based on initial tests using *development data*. All other parameters used default settings.

---

[1] Data is available from third party resellers, such as *Gnip*.

[2] http://www.geonames.org/

[3] Our reliance on text features created a very large feature space, but only a small fraction of these occur with any regularity. Previous work has shown feature selection helpful for geolocation (Han et al., 2014). We tried L1 regularization for feature selection without a significant change to our results. It may be that our larger volume of training data removes the need for feature selection. Alternatively, we use feature hashing (to a 31-bit feature space) which can be a form of regularization as feature collisions mitigate overfitting (Ganchev and Dredze, 2008; Weinberger et al., 2009).

4 Evaluation

We report the four evaluation metrics of Han et al. (2014): city accuracy (AccCi), country accuracy (AccCo), accuracy within 161 km (100 miles) (Acc@161), and the median error in km (Median).

Baselines We include two baselines: (1) the majority predictor: always predicts the most popular label. (2) alias matching: we create a list of aliases for each of the 2983 cities from the genomes dataset, which includes the smaller cities clustered together by Han et al. (2014). We search each tweet and the user's profile location for these aliases, assigning a tweet with a matched alias to the corresponding city; unmatched tweets are assigned the majority label. When multiple cities match a tweet, we selected the correct one (if present) using oracle knowledge. About 90% of matches were in the profile. This strategy is similar to that of Dredze et al. (2013).

Duplicates A tweet may be duplicated in our dataset, appearing in both training and held out data, or appearing multiple times in held out data. We define duplicates as tweets with identical feature representations. We removed duplicates from dev and test splits, to ensure evaluation examples are unseen in training, yielding 22,966 dev and 23,240 test tweets.

5 Baseline Results

We begin by establishing the models' performance with a large training set, as measured on held out evaluation data drawn from the same time period. Here we use a standard setting, where there is no online adaptation. We include results for city and country models trained with the tweet text features alone (content). These evaluations train with a sample of 25,822,353 tweets, similar to previous large scale training for geolocation (Han et al., 2014).

Table 2 shows our model beating both baselines, with the additional features generally improving over content features alone. Interestingly, improvements from adding features appears to be additive: the final model's accuracy is nearly the sum of the individual improvements from each feature set. On the non-deduped test dataset (25,941 tweets), the accuracy was higher (city: 0.2920, country: 0.8777) but the trends of adding features remain unchanged. Our time feature, which captures a temporal prior

over locations, does not seem to help, providing only a small boost.

We consider the impact of training data size in Figure 1, including a model trained on 258,222,490 tweets, an order of magnitude larger than Han et al. (2014), which improves accuracy by roughly 3%. This figure provides guidance on how much data is necessary to do well on this task.

To summarize: our approach yields tweet level geolocation accuracy similar to, or better than, state of the art user level geolocation.[4] We note that for small datasets (tens of millions of training examples, which can be obtained from the Twitter streaming API), one can obtain a reasonable model.

6 Temporal Factors in Geolocation

We now consider factors that influence geolocation temporal accuracy using our largest city model (258M training tweets), which has an accuracy of 0.3302 on test data (0.3062 excluding duplicates).

6.1 Question 1: How do daily and weekly patterns impact geolocation accuracy?

Twitter traffic varies over the course of a day and a week. User behavior may change at different times, and different locations are active at different times.

Figure 3 shows the number of tweets and test geolocation accuracy by the hour of the day (b) and day of the week (c). The day of the week has a minor impact on geolocation accuracy; the standard deviation of the 7 days is 2.7% of the total mean. Tweet volume has a negative correlation with accuracy (-0.435), i.e. more tweets may be indicative of more people from different locations tweeting, which makes the task harder. Notably, Monday is significantly harder, with an accuracy of 1.5 standard deviations below the mean. However, the hour of the day has much more significant impact on accuracy; some times of the day are significantly easier and harder than the average. The standard deviation is 6.8% of the mean, and tweet volume is strongly negatively correlated with accuracy (-0.647). Geolocation is easier during times when there are fewer locations actively tweeting. This is most apparent during

---

[4]Direct comparisons are not possible because of different datasets and tasks. However, our results are on par with the user-level geolocation system of Han et al. (2014).

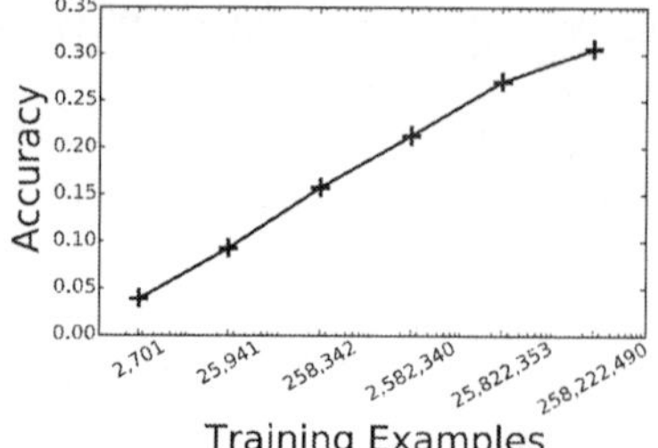

Training Examples

Figure 1: Varying training data size.

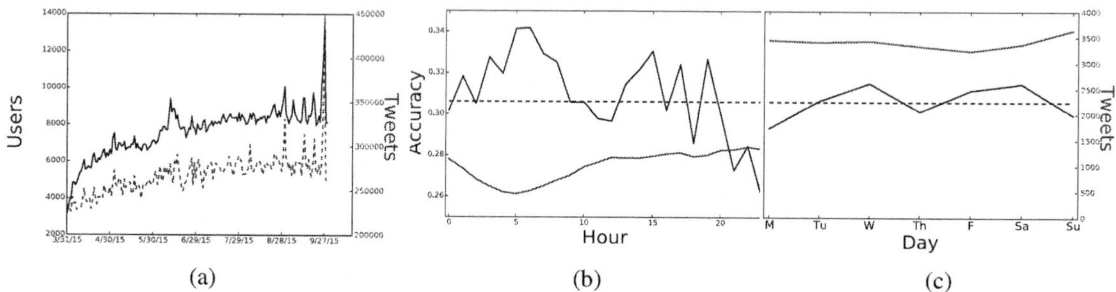

Model		AccCi	AccCo	Acc@161	Median	AccCo
				City		Country
Baselines:	Majority	0.0209	0.6410	0.0402	3582	0.6363
	Alias Match	0.1923	0.7317	0.2096	3169	0.7253
Features:	Content	0.0259	0.4093	0.0602	3216	0.4285
	+ Profile	0.2120	0.5609	0.2917	1659	0.7537
	+ Timezone	0.0415	0.5682	0.0974	1690	0.5273
	+ Time	0.0279	0.4282	0.0598	3074	0.4142
	All features	0.2708	0.5861	0.3612	1008	0.8734

Figure 2: Results for different features sets on test data from the same time period as training data for both city and country prediction tasks.

(a)   (b)   (c)

Figure 3: (a) New users and tweets each day. Accuracy and number of tweets by hour (US eastern) (b) and day (c).

the nighttime in the US, where there are much fewer tweets overall and many fewer active locations. In short, the accuracy of a geolocation system depends on when it is running.

6.2 Question 2: How do changes over time impact a fixed geolocation model?

We now turn to our data sample taken after the training data: a 10% sample of 49,307,720 tweets from 2015/3/31 - 2015/9/30.[5] These tweets will demonstrate the accuracy of a trained model deployed on new data over time.

Evaluating on these tweets (duplicates included), our model yields an accuracy of 0.2661, down from 0.3302, a 19% relative drop. Surprisingly, this isn't a gradual change over time; the drop is quite rapid. The week immediately following the training period has an accuracy of 0.2884. Figure 4 shows the decline in accuracy over time.[6]

---

[5]While training data is taken from the first 39 months, it is biased towards more recent months due to Twitter growth: the last 12 months (30% of the time) account for 37% of tweets. We evaluated with a 10% sample for efficiency.

[6]While accuracy continues to degrade over time, it begins to rise in August 2015. It may be that there are seasonal effects in geolocation accuracy, or recent changes by Twitter are making

What factors contribute to this rapid drop? We consider two: new users and reposted tweets.

New Users One factor affecting geolocation performance might be new users joining, posting a few tweets and then no longer posting. In a sense, users have a temporal lifespan, after which information originating from them is of less predictive value. One measure of this is the number of users encountered in the evaluation data, which have never been previously encountered, either in training or earlier in the evaluation data. Over the six month evaluation period, the number of new tweets from geocoded users per day *increases*, even as a percentage of all tweets (Figure 3(a)).

We remove all tweets in the evaluation period from users that we have previously encountered, either in training or earlier in evaluation data. Accuracy drops to 0.1859, a 30% relative decrease from 0.2661, suggesting that the training data learns features specific to the users it observes. By comparison, the alias match baseline has an accuracy of 0.2113 on this data.

While trained models remain effective on users

---

geolocation easier. However, we were unable to determine the source of this change.

present in training, it has difficulty generalizing to new users. Far from a small percentage of the total, new users make up a significant number of tweets, at a rate that does not appear to be slowing.

Reposted Tweets Users often repost content, which can include repeating simple message (e.g. "feeling good!") or tweeting the same content to multiple users. Users are more likely to repost content shortly after it was first created, making the number of reposts go down over time. For example, while 8% of test tweets from the same time period as training data are duplicates (they appear in the training data), only 3.8% of tweets in the six month evaluation period are duplicates.

How much of an impact do these reposts have on accuracy? For the test data from the same time period, we saw model performance drop from 0.3302 to 0.3062, a fairly large difference. By comparison, removing reposts in the the six month evaluation period drops accuracy from 0.2661 to 0.2541, a more modest change. Reposts help to inflate geolocation accuracy, and their decrease as time progresses from training removes this accuracy inflation.

7   Question 3: Can periodic model updates maintain a trained geolocation system?

Our results so far are sobering: shortly after a static model is deployed performance degrades to a model using *two orders of magnitude less training data* (compare the drop in §6.2 with Figure 1). Increasing the amount of training data might be an option, but given our previous results on new users, etc., this is unlikely to be sufficient.

A simple method for addressing model degradation over time is to continuously update the model over time using online learning on new data as it becomes available. For example, we can continuously download a stream of (at least) 1% of geocoded tweets from the Twitter API to use as training for updating a deployed system. What is the impact on a system's accuracy when it is updated on these geocoded tweets with SGD updates (§3)?

Figure 4 shows the performance of our system in an online setting (dashed black line). This model updates on every 100th example (1% of all geocoded tweets) encountered in the six-month evaluation period. When we update this previously trained static

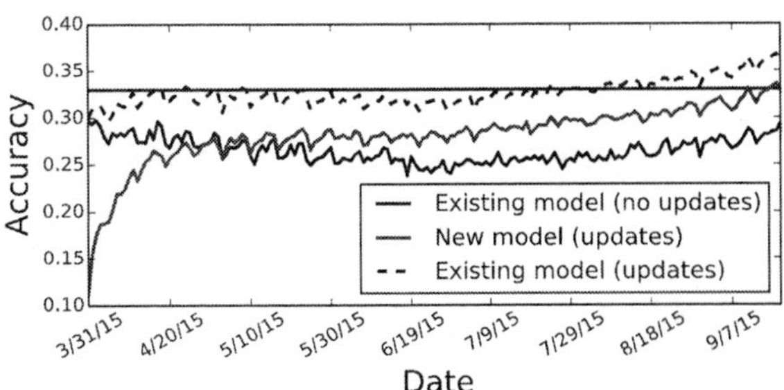

Figure 4: Accuracy over the six months following training. The horizontal line reflects the existing model's performance on test from the same time period as training.

model, we see a quick recovery to accuracy levels that meet or exceed those on the test set from the same time period as training (horizontal line.)

Finally, we consider the case where a practitioner starts from scratch with no training data, but updates using just 1% of geocoded tweets. Can someone with access to no prior training data build an effective model? Encouragingly, within 20 days the new model (solid blue line) catches the previously trained static model (solid black line, "Existing model: no updates"). This is an extremely promising result as it suggests that most practitioners **who do not have access to all geolocated data** can produce geolocation prediction models that approximate models trained using hundred of millions of examples.

8   Conclusion

We have presented a tweet geolocation system that considers an order of magnitude more data than any prior work. Despite hundreds of millions of training examples, the resulting system is sensitive to the time the tweet was authored. Additionally, accuracy suffers when deployed on data beyond the training period. We show that online updates can mitigate problems caused by concept drift. In short, sheer volume of data is not enough: geolocation models should adapt to new data. Encouragingly, starting from no training data and updating on just 1% of geocoded tweets, within 20 days we can recover a model that catches a static model previously trained on hundreds of millions of tweets.

Acknowledgments   We thank Bo Han and Tim Baldwin for their help in reproducing their city labels.

References

Alekh Agarwal, Olivier Chapelle, Miroslav Dudík, and John Langford. 2011. A reliable effective terascale linear learning system. *CoRR*, abs/1110.4198.

David Broniatowski, Michael J. Paul, and Mark Dredze. 2013. National and local influenza surveillance through twitter: An analysis of the 2012-2013 influenza epidemic. *PLOS ONE*, December 9.

Miriam Cha, Youngjune Gwon, and HT Kung. 2015. Twitter geolocation and regional classification via sparse coding. In *Ninth International AAAI Conference on Web and Social Media*.

Ryan Compton, David Jurgens, and David Allen. 2014. Geotagging one hundred million twitter accounts with total variation minimization. In *Big Data (Big Data), 2014 IEEE International Conference on*, pages 393–401. IEEE.

Mark Dredze, Michael J Paul, Shane Bergsma, and Hieu Tran. 2013. Carmen: A twitter geolocation system with applications to public health. In *AAAI Workshop on Expanding the Boundaries of Health Informatics Using AI (HIAI)*.

John Duchi, Elad Hazan, and Yoram Singer. 2011. Adaptive subgradient methods for online learning and stochastic optimization. *Journal of Machine Learning Research*.

Jacob Eisenstein, Brendan O'Connor, Noah A Smith, and Eric P Xing. 2010. A latent variable model for geographic lexical variation. In *Empirical Methods in Natural Language Processing (EMNLP)*.

Kuzman Ganchev and Mark Dredze. 2008. Small statistical models by random feature mixing. In *Proceedings of the ACL08 HLT Workshop on Mobile Language Processing*, pages 19–20.

Bo Han, Paul Cook, and Timothy Baldwin. 2014. Text-based twitter user geolocation prediction. *Journal of Artificial Intelligence Research*, pages 451–500.

Liangjie Hong, Amr Ahmed, Siva Gurumurthy, Alexander J Smola, and Kostas Tsioutsiouliklis. 2012. Discovering geographical topics in the twitter stream. In *Proceedings of the 21st international conference on World Wide Web*, pages 769–778. ACM.

David Jurgens, Tyler Finethy, James McCorriston, Yi Tian Xu, and Derek Ruths. 2015. Geolocation prediction in twitter using social networks: A critical analysis and review of current practice. In *Proceedings of the 9th International AAAI Conference on Weblogs and Social Media (ICWSM)*.

Juhi Kulshrestha, Farshad Kooti, Ashkan Nikravesh, and P Krishna Gummadi. 2012. Geographic dissection of the twitter network. In *ICWSM*.

Brendan O'Connor, Michel Krieger, and David Ahn. 2010. Tweetmotif: Exploratory search and topic summarization for twitter. In *International Conference on Weblogs and Social Media (ICWSM)*.

Miles Osborne, Sean Moran, Richard McCreadie, Alexander Von Lunen, Martin D Sykora, Elizabeth Cano, Neil Ireson, Craig Macdonald, Iadh Ounis, Yulan He, et al. 2014. Real-time detection, tracking, and monitoring of automatically discovered events in social media. In *Association for Computational Linguistics (ACL)*.

Umashanthi Pavalanathan and Jacob Eisenstein. 2015. Confounds and consequences in geotagged twitter data. In *Proceedings of the 2015 Conference on Empirical Methods in Natural Language Processing*, pages 2138–2148, Lisbon, Portugal, September. Association for Computational Linguistics.

Dominic Rout, Kalina Bontcheva, Daniel Preoţiuc-Pietro, and Trevor Cohn. 2013. Where's@ wally?: a classification approach to geolocating users based on their social ties. In *Proceedings of the 24th ACM Conference on Hypertext and Social Media*, pages 11–20. ACM.

Kazufumi Watanabe, Masanao Ochi, Makoto Okabe, and Rikio Onai. 2011. Jasmine: a real-time local-event detection system based on geolocation information propagated to microblogs. In *Proceedings of the 20th ACM international conference on Information and knowledge management*, pages 2541–2544. ACM.

Kilian Weinberger, Anirban Dasgupta, John Langford, Alex Smola, and Josh Attenberg. 2009. Feature hashing for large scale multitask learning. In *Proceedings of the 26th Annual International Conference on Machine Learning*, pages 1113–1120. ACM.

Fast and Easy Short Answer Grading with High Accuracy

Md Arafat Sultan   **Cristobal Salazar**   **Tamara Sumner**
Institute of Cognitive Science
Department of Computer Science
University of Colorado, Boulder, CO
{arafat.sultan, crsa7687, sumner}@colorado.edu

Abstract

We present a fast, simple, and high-accuracy short answer grading system. Given a short-answer question and its correct answer, key measures of the correctness of a student response can be derived from its semantic similarity with the correct answer. Our supervised model (1) utilizes recent advances in the identification of short-text similarity, and (2) augments text similarity features with key grading-specific constructs. We present experimental results where our model demonstrates top performance on multiple benchmarks.

1   Introduction

Short-answer questions are a useful device for eliciting student understanding of specific concepts in a subject domain. Numerous automated graders have been proposed for short answers based on their semantic similarity with one or more expert-provided correct answers (Mohler et al., 2011; Heilman and Madnani, 2013; Ramachandran et al., 2015). From an application perspective, these systems vary considerably along a set of key dimensions: amount of human effort involved, accuracy, speed, and ease of implementation. We explore a design that seeks to optimize performance along all these dimensions.

Systems developed for the more general task of short-text semantic similarity provide a good starting point for such a design. Major progress has been made in this task in recent years, due primarily to the SemEval Semantic Textual Similarity (STS) task (Agirre et al., 2012; Agirre et al., 2013; Agirre et al., 2014; Agirre et al., 2015). However, the utility of top STS systems has remained largely unexplored in the context of short answer grading. We seek to bridge this gap by adopting the feature set of the best performing STS system at SemEval-2015 (Sultan et al., 2015). Besides high accuracy, this system also has a simple design and fast runtime.

Textual similarity alone, however, is inadequate as a measure of answer correctness. For example, while the Sultan et al. (2015) system makes the general assumption that all content words[1] contribute equally to the meaning of a sentence, domain keywords (e.g., "mutation" for biological evolution) are clearly more significant than arbitrary content words (e.g., "consideration") for academic text. As another example, *question demoting* (Mohler et al., 2011) proposes discarding words that are present in the question text as a preprocessing step for grading. We augment our generic text similarity features with such grading-specific measures.

We train supervised models with our final feature set; in two different grading tasks, these models demonstrate significant performance improvement over the state of the art. In summary, our contribution is a fast, simple, and high-performance short answer grading system which we also release as open-source software at: https://github. com/ma-sultan/short-answer-grader.

2   Related Work

A comprehensive review of automatic short answer grading can be found in (Burrows et al., 2015). Here

---

[1]meaning-bearing words (e.g., nouns and main verbs), as opposed to function words that play predominantly syntactic roles in a sentence (e.g., auxiliary verbs and prepositions).

we briefly discuss closely related work.

Early short answer grading work relied on patterns (e.g., regular expressions) manually extracted from expert-provided reference answers (Mitchell et al., 2002; Sukkarieh et al., 2004; Nielsen et al., 2009). Such patterns encode key concepts representative of good answers. Use of manually designed patterns continues to this day, e.g., in (Tandalla, 2012), the winning system at the ASAP answer scoring contest.[2] This is a step requiring human intervention that natural language processing can help to eliminate. Ramachandran et al. (2015) propose a mechanism to automate the extraction of patterns from the reference answer as well as high-scoring student answers. We adopt the simpler notion of semantic alignment to avoid explicitly generating complicated patterns altogether.

Direct semantic matching (as opposed to pattern generation) has been explored in early work like (Leacock and Chodorow, 2003). With advances in NLP techniques, this approach has gained popularity over time (Mohler et al., 2009; Mohler et al., 2011; Heilman and Madnani, 2013; Jimenez et al., 2013). Such systems typically use a large set of similarity measures as features for a supervised learning model. Features range from string similarity measures like word and character n-gram overlap to deeper semantic similarity measures based on resources like WordNet and distributional methods like latent semantic analysis (LSA). However, a large feature set contributes to higher system runtime and implementation difficulty. While following this generic framework, we seek to improve on these criteria by employing a minimal set of core similarity features adopted from (Sultan et al., 2015). Our features also yield higher accuracy by utilizing more recent measures of lexical similarity (Ganitkevitch et al., 2013; Baroni et al., 2014), which have been shown to outperform traditional resources and methods like WordNet and LSA.

Short-text semantic similarity has seen major progress in recent times, due largely to the SemEval Semantic Textual Similarity (STS) task (Agirre et al., 2012; Agirre et al., 2013; Agirre et al., 2014; Agirre et al., 2015). STS systems can serve as a source of important new features and design elements for au-tomatic short answer graders (Bär et al., 2012; Han et al., 2013; Lynum et al., 2014; Hänig et al., 2015).

Surprisingly, few existing grading systems utilize simple and computationally inexpensive grading-specific techniques like question demoting (Mohler et al., 2011) and term weighting. Our model augments the similarity features using these techniques.

3 Method

Following feature extraction, our system trains a supervised model for grading. As we discuss in Section 4, this can be a regressor or a classifier depending on the task. This section describes our features; specifics of the models are given in Section 4.

3.1 Features

3.1.1 Text Similarity

Given reference answer $R = (r_1, ..., r_n)$ and student response $S = (s_1, ..., s_m)$ (where each r and s is a word token), we compute three generic text similarity features.

Alignment. This feature measures the proportion of content words in R and S that have a semantically similar word in the other sentence. Such pairs are identified using a word aligner (Sultan et al., 2014). The semantic similarity of a word pair (r_i, s_j) is a weighted sum of their lexical and contextual similarities. A paraphrase database (PPDB, Ganitkevitch et al. (2013)) identifies lexically similar word pairs; contextual similarity is computed as average lexical similarity in (1) dependencies of r_i in R and s_j in S, and (2) content words in [-3, 3] windows around r_i in R and s_j in S. Lexical similarity scores of pairs in PPDB as well as weights of word and contextual similarities are optimized on an alignment dataset (Brockett, 2007).

To avoid penalizing long student responses that still contain the correct answer, we also employ a second version of this feature: the proportion of aligned content words only in R. We will refer to this feature as *coverage* of the reference answer's content by the student response.

Semantic Vector Similarity. This feature employs off-the-shelf word embeddings.[3] A sentence-level semantic vector is computed for each input

---

[2]https://www.kaggle.com/c/asap-sas/

[3]400-dimensional word embeddings reported by Baroni et al. (2014).

sentence as the sum of its content word embeddings (lemmatized). The cosine similarity between the R and S vectors is then used as a feature. While the alignment features distinguish only between paraphrases and non-paraphrases, this feature enables integration of finer-grained lexical similarity measures between related concepts (e.g., *cell* and *organism*).

3.1.2 Question Demoting

We recompute each of the above similarity features after removing words that appear in the question text from both the reference answer and the student response. The objective is to avoid rewarding a student response for repeating question words.

3.1.3 Term Weighting

To be able to distinguish between domain keywords and arbitrary content words, in our next set of features we assign a weight to every content word in the reference and the student answer based on a variant of *tf-idf*. While general short-text similarity models typically use only *idf* (inverse document frequency) to penalize general words, the domain-specific nature of answer grading also enables the application of a *tf* (term frequency) measure.

To fully automate the process for a question and reference answer pair, we identify all content words in the pair. The top ten Wikipedia pages related to these words are retrieved using the Google API. Each page is read along with all linked pages crawled using Scrapy (Myers and McGuffee, 2015). The in-domain term frequency (tf_d) of a word in the answer is then computed by extracting its raw count in this collection of pages. We use the same set of tools to automatically extract Wikipedia pages in 25 different domains such as Art, Mathematics, Religion, and Sport. A total of 14,125 pages are retrieved, occurrences in which are used to compute the *idf* of each word.

We augment our alignment features—both original and question-demoted—with term weights to generate new features. Each word is assigned a weight equal to its $tf_d \times idf$ score. The sum of weights is computed for (1) aligned, and (2) all content words in the reference answer (after question demoting, if applicable). The ratio of these two numbers is then used as a feature. We compute only coverage features (Section 3.1.1) to avoid comput-

ing term weights for each student response. Thus the process of crawling and reading the documents is performed once per question; all the student responses can subsequently be graded quickly.

3.1.4 Length Ratio

We use the ratio of the number of words in the student response to that in the reference answer as our final feature. The aim is to roughly capture whether or not the student response contains enough detail.

4 Experiments

We evaluate our features on two grading tasks. The first task, proposed by Mohler et al. (2011), asks to compute a real-valued score for a student response on a scale of 0 to 5. The second task, proposed at SemEval-2013 (Dzikovska et al., 2013), asks to assign a label (e.g., *correct* or *irrelevant*) to a student response that shows how appropriate it is as an answer to the question. Thus from a machine learning perspective, the first is a regression task and the second is a classification task. We use the NLTK stopwords corpus (Bird et al., 2009) to identify function words. Results are discussed below.

4.1 The Mohler et al. (2011) Task

The dataset for this task consists of 80 undergraduate Data Structures questions and 2,273 student responses graded by two human judges. These questions are spread across ten different assignments and two tests, each on a related set of topics (e.g., programming basics, sorting algorithms). A reference answer is provided for each question. Inter-annotator agreement was 58.6% (Pearson's ρ) and .659 (RMSE on a 5-point scale). Average of the two human scores is used as the final gold score for each student answer.

We train a ridge regression model (Scikit-learn (Pedregosa et al., 2011)) for each assignment and test using annotations from the rest as training examples. A *dev* assignment or test is randomly held out for model selection. Out-of-range output scores, if any, are rounded to the nearest in-range integer. Following Mohler et al. (2011), we compute a single Pearson correlation and RMSE score over all student responses from all datasets. Average results across 1000 runs of the system are shown in Table 1. Our

System	Pearson's r	RMSE
tf-idf	.327	1.022
Lesk	.450	1.050
Mohler et al. (2011)	.518	.978
Our Model	**.592**	**.887**

Table 1: Performance on the Mohler et al. (2011) dataset with out-of-domain training. Performances of simpler bag-of-words models are reported by those authors.

System	r	RMSE
Ramachandran et al. (2015)	.61	.86
Our Model	**.63**	**.85**

Table 2: Performance on the Mohler et al. (2011) dataset with in-domain training.

System	UA	UQ	UD	Wt. Mean
Lexical Overlap	.435	.402	.396	.400
Majority	.260	.239	.249	.249
ETS_1	.535	.487	.447	.460
SoftCardinality$_1$	.537	.492	.471	.480
Our Model	**.582**	**.554**	**.545**	**.550**

Table 3: F_1 scores on the SemEval-2013 datasets.

model shows a large and significant performance improvement over the state-of-the-art model of Mohler et al. (two-tailed t-test, $p < .001$). Their system employs a support vector machine that predicts scores using a set of dependency graph alignment and lexical similarity measures. Our features are similar in intent, but are based on latest advances in identification of lexical similarity and monolingual alignment.

Ramachandran et al. (2015) adopt a different setup to evaluate their model on the same dataset. For each assignment/test, they use 80% of the data for training and the rest as test. This setup thus enables in-domain model training. Their system automatically generates regexp patterns intended to capture semantic variations and syntactic structures of good answers. Features derived from match with such patterns as well as term frequencies in the student response are used to train a set of random forest regressors, whose predictions are then combined to output a single score. Results in this setup are shown in Table 2. Again, averaged over 1000 runs, our model performs better on both evaluation metrics. The differences are smaller than before but still statistically significant (two-tailed t-test, $p < .001$).

4.2 The SemEval-2013 Task

Instead of a real-valued score, this task asks to assign one of five labels to a student response: *correct*, *partially correct/incomplete*, *contradictory*, *irrelevant*, and *non-domain* (an answer that contains no domain content). We use the SCIENTSBANK corpus, containing 9,804 answers to 197 questions in 15 science domains. Of these, 3,969 are used for model training and the remaining 5,835 for evaluation. A reference answer is provided for each question.

The test set is divided into three subsets with varying degrees of similarity with the training examples. The *Unseen Answers* (UA) dataset consists of responses to questions that are present in the training set. *Unseen Questions* (UQ) contains responses to in-domain but previously unseen questions. Three of the fifteen domains were held out for a final *Unseen Domains* (UD) test set, containing completely out-of-domain question-response pairs. For this task, we train a random forest classifier with 500 trees in Scikit-learn using our feature set.

Table 3 shows the performance of our model (averaged over 100 runs) along with that of top systems[4] at SemEval-2013 (and of simpler baselines). ETS (Heilman and Madnani, 2013) employs a logistic classifier combining lexical and text similarity features. SoftCardinality (Jimenez et al., 2013) employs decision tree bagging with similarity features derived from a set cardinality measure—soft cardinality—of the question, the reference answer, and the student response. These features effectively compute text similarity from commonalities and differences in character n-grams.

Each cell on columns 2–4 of Table 3 shows a weighted F_1-score on a test set computed over the five classes, where the weight of a class is proportional to the number of question-response pairs in that class. The final column shows a similarly weighted mean of scores computed over the three test sets. On each test set, our model outperforms the top-performing models from SemEval (significant at $p < .001$). Its performance also suffers less on out-of-domain test data compared to those models.

---

[4]Systems with best overall performance on SCIENTSBANK.

Features	Pearson's r	RMSE
All	.592	.887
w/o alignment	.519	.938
w/o embedding	.586	.892
w/o question demoting	.571	.903
w/o term weighting	.590	.889
w/o length ratio	.591	.888

Table 4: Ablation results on the Mohler et al. (2011) dataset.

4.3 Runtime Test

Given parsed input and having stop words removed, the most computationally expensive step in our system is the extraction of alignment features. Each content word pair across the two input sentences is assessed in constant time, giving the feature extraction process (and the whole system) a runtime complexity of $O(n_c \cdot m_c)$, where n_c and m_c are the number of content words in the two sentences. Note that all alignment features can be extracted from a single alignment of the input sentences.

Run on the Mohler et al. dataset (unparsed; about 18 words per sentence on average), our system grades over 33 questions/min on a 2.25GHz core.

4.4 Ablation Study

Table 4 shows the performance of our regression model on the Mohler et al. dataset without different feature subsets. Performance falls with each exclusion, but by far the most without alignment-based features. Features implementing question demoting are the second most useful. Length ratio improves model performance the least.

Surprisingly, term weighting also has a rather small effect on model performance. Further inspection reveals two possible reasons for this. First, many reference answers are very short, only containing words or small phrases that are necessary to answer the question (e.g., "push", "enqueue and dequeue", "by rows"). In such cases, term weighting has little or no effect. Second, we observe that in many cases the key words in a correct answer are either not domain keywords or are unidentifiable using *tf-idf*. Consider the following:

- Question: What is a stack?
- Answer: A data structure that can store elements, which has the property that the last item

added will be the first item to be removed (or last-in-first-out).

Important answer words like "last", "added", "first", and "removed" in this example are not domain keywords and/or are too common (across different domains) for a measure like *tf-idf* to work.

5 Conclusions and Future Work

We present a fast, simple, and high-performance short answer grading system. State-of-the-art measures of text similarity are combined with grading-specific constructs to produce top results on multiple benchmarks. There is, however, immense scope for improvement. Subtle factors like differences in modality or polarity might go undetected with coarse text similarity measures. Inclusion of text-level paraphrase and entailment features can help in such cases. Additional term weighting mechanisms are needed to identify important answer words in many cases. Our system provides a simple base model that can be easily extended with new features for more accurate answer grading.

Acknowledgments

This material is based in part upon work supported by the National Science Foundation under Grants EHR/0835393 and EHR/0835381. We thank Lakshmi Ramachandran for clarification of her work.

References

Eneko Agirre, Daniel Cer, Mona Diab, and Aitor Gonzalez-Agirre. 2012. SemEval-2012 task 6: A Pilot on Semantic Textual Similarity. In *SemEval*.

Eneko Agirre, Daniel Cer, Mona Diab, Aitor Gonzalez-Agirre, and Weiwei Guo. 2013. *SEM 2013 Shared Task: Semantic Textual Similarity. In *SEM*.

Eneko Agirre, Carmen Banea, Claire Cardie, Daniel Cer, Mona Diab, Aitor Gonzalez-Agirre, Weiwei Guo, Rada Mihalcea, German Rigau, and Janyce Wiebe. 2014. SemEval-2014 Task 10: Multilingual Semantic Textual Similarity. In *SemEval*.

Eneko Agirre, Carmen Banea, Claire Cardie, Daniel Cer, Mona Diab, Aitor Gonzalez-Agirre, Weiwei Guo, Iñigo Lopez-Gazpio, Montse Maritxalar, Rada Mihalcea, German Rigau, Larraitz Uria, and Janyce Wiebe. 2015. SemEval-2015 Task 2: Semantic Textual Similarity, English, Spanish and Pilot on Interpretability. In *SemEval*.

Daniel Bär, Chris Biemann, Iryna Gurevych, and Torsten Zesch. 2012. UKP: Computing Semantic Textual Similarity by Combining Multiple Content Similarity Measures. In *SemEval*.

Marco Baroni, Georgiana Dinu, and Germán Kruszewski. 2014. Don't Count, Predict! A Systematic Comparison of Context-Counting vs. Context-Predicting Semantic Vectors. In *ACL*.

Steven Bird, Edward Loper, and Ewan Klein. 2009. Natural Language Processing with Python. O'Reilly Media Inc.

Chris Brockett. 2007. Aligning the RTE 2006 Corpus. Tech Report MSR-TR-2007-77, Microsoft Research.

Steven Burrows, Iryna Gurevych, and Benno Stein. 2015. The Eras and Trends of Automatic Short Answer Grading. *International Journal of Artificial Intelligence in Education*, 25.1.

Myroslava O. Dzikovska, Rodney Nielsen, Chris Brew,Claudia Leacock, Danilo Giampiccolo, Luisa Ben-tivogli, Peter Clark, Ido Dagan, and Hoa Trang Dang. 2013. Semeval-2013 Task 7: The Joint Student Response Analysis and 8th Recognizing Textual Entailment Challenge. In *SemEval*.

Juri Ganitkevitch, Benjamin Van Durme, and Chris Callison-Burch. 2013. PPDB: The Paraphrase Database. In *NAACL*.

Lushan Han, Abhay Kashyap, Tim Finin, James Mayfield, and Jonathan Weese. 2013. UMBC EBIQUITY-CORE: Semantic Textual Similarity Systems. In **SEM*.

Christian Hänig, Robert Remus, and Xose de la Puente. 2015. ExB Themis: Extensive Feature Extraction from Word Alignments for Semantic Textual Similarity. In *SemEval*.

Michael Heilman and Nitin Madnani. 2013. ETS: Domain Adaptation and Stacking for Short Answer Scoring. In *SemEval*.

Sergio Jimenez, Claudia Becerra, and Alexander Gelbukh. 2013. SOFTCARDINALITY: Hierarchical Text Overlap for Student Response Analysis. In *SemEval*.

Claudia Leacock and Martin Chodorow. 2003. C-rater: Automated Scoring of Short-Answer Questions. *Computers and the Humanities*, 37(04).

André Lynum, Partha Pakray, Björn Gambäck, and Sergio Jimenez. 2014. NTNU: Measuring Semantic Similarity with Sublexical Feature Representations and Soft Cardinality. In *SemEval*.

Tom Mitchell, Terry Russell, Peter Broomhead, and Nicola Aldridge. 2002. Towards Robust Computerised Marking of Free-Text Responses. In *Proceedings of the 6th International Computer Assisted Assessment (CAA) Conference*.

Michael Mohler and Rada Mihalcea. 2009. Text-to-text Semantic Similarity for Automatic Short Answer Grading. In *EACL*.

Michael Mohler, Razvan Bunescu, and Rada Mihalcea. 2011. Learning to Grade Short Answer Questions Using Semantic Similarity Measures and Dependency Graph Alignments. In *ACL*.

Daniel Myers and James W. McGuffee. 2015. Choosing Scrapy. *Computing Sciences in Colleges*, 31(1).

Rodney D. Nielsen, Wayne Ward, and James H. Martin. 2009. Recognizing Entailment in Intelligent Tutoring Systems. *Natural Language Engineering*, 15(04).

Fabian Pedregosa, Gaël Varoquaux, Alexandre Gramfort, Vincent Michel, Bertrand Thirion, Olivier Grisel, Mathieu Blondel, Peter Prettenhofer, Ron Weiss, Vincent Dubourg, Jake Vanderplas, Alexandre Passos, David Cournapeau, Matthieu Brucher, Matthieu Perrot, and Édouard Duchesnay. 2011. Scikit-learn: Machine Learning in Python. *Machine Learning Research*, vol. 12.

Lakshmi Ramachandran, Jian Cheng, and Peter Foltz. 2015. Identifying Patterns For Short Answer Scoring using Graph-based Lexico-Semantic Text Matching. In *SemEval*.

Frane Šarić, Goran Glavaš, Mladen Karan, Jan Šnajder, and Bojana Dalbelo Bašić. 2012. TakeLab: Systems for Measuring Semantic Text Similarity. In *SemEval*.

Jana Z. Sukkarieh, Stephen G. Pulman and Nicholas Raikes. 2004. Auto-Marking 2: An Update on the UCLES-Oxford University research into using Computational Linguistics to Score Short, Free Text Responses. In *Proceedings of the 30th Annual Conference of the International Association for Educational Assessment*.

Md Arafat Sultan, Steven Bethard, and Tamara Sumner. 2014. Back to Basics for Monolingual Alignment: Exploiting Word Similarity and Contextual Evidence. *Transactions of the Association for Computational Linguistics*, 2 (May).

Md Arafat Sultan, Steven Bethard, and Tamara Sumner. 2015. DLS@CU: Sentence Similarity from Word Alignment and Semantic Vector Composition. In *SemEval*.

Louis Tandalla. 2012. Scoring Short Answer Essays. https://kaggle2.blob.core.windows.net/competitions/kaggle/2959/media/TechnicalMethodsPaper.pdf.

Interlocking Phrases in Phrase-based Statistical Machine Translation

Ye Kyaw Thu, Andrew Finch and **Eiichiro Sumita**
Multilingual Translation Lab.,
Advanced Speech Translation Research and Development Promotion Center,
3-5 Hikaridai, Seika-cho, Soraku-gun, Kyoto, 619-0289, JAPAN
`{yekyawthu, andrew.finch, eiichiro.sumita}@nict.go.jp`

Abstract

This paper presents an study of the use of interlocking phrases in phrase-based statistical machine translation. We examine the effect on translation quality when the translation units used in the translation hypotheses are allowed to overlap on the source side, on the target side and on both sides. A large-scale evaluation on 380 language pairs was conducted. Our results show that overall the use of overlapping phrases improved translation quality by 0.3 BLEU points on average. Further analysis revealed that language pairs requiring a larger amount of re-ordering benefited the most from our approach. When the evaluation was restricted to such pairs, the average improvement increased to up to 0.75 BLEU points with over 97% of the pairs improving. Our approach requires only a simple modification to the decoding algorithm and we believe it should be generally applicable to improve the performance of phrase-based decoders.

1 Introduction

In this paper we examine the effect on machine translation quality of using interlocking phrases to during the decoding process in phrase-based statistical machine translation (PBSMT). The motivation for this is two-fold.

Firstly, during the phrase-pair extraction process that occurs in the training of a typical PBSMT system, all possible alternative phrase-pairs are extracted that are consistent with a set of alignment points. As a consequence, the source and target sides of these extracted phrase pairs may overlap. However, in contrast to this, the decoding process traditionally proceeds by concatenating disjoint translation units; the process relies on the language model to eliminate awkward hypotheses with repeated words produced by sequences of translation units that overlap.

Secondly, the transduction process in PBSMT is carried out by generating hypotheses that are composed of sequences of translation units. These sequences are normally generated independently, as modeling the dependencies between them is difficult due to the data sparseness issues arising from modeling with word sequences. The process of interlocking is a way of introducing a form of dependency between translation units, effectively producing larger units from pairs of compatible units.

2 Related Work

(Karimova et al., 2014) presented a method to extract overlapping phrases offline for hierarchical phrase based SMT. They used the CDEC SMT decoder (Dyer et al., 2010) that offers several learners for discriminative tuning of weights for the new phrases. Their results showed improvements of 0.3 to 0.6 BLEU points over discriminatively trained hierarchical phrase-based SMT systems on two datasets for German-to-English translation. (Tribble and et al., 2003) proposed a method to generate longer new phrases by merging existing phrase-level alignments that have overlapping words on both source and target sides. Their experiments on translating Arabic-English text from the news domain were encouraging.

Proceedings of NAACL-HLT 2016, pages 1076–1081,
San Diego, California, June 12-17, 2016. ©2016 Association for Computational Linguistics

(Roth and McCallum, 2010) proposed a conditional-random-field approach to discriminatively train phrase based machine translation in which training and decoding are both cast in a sampling framework. Different with traditional PBSMT decoding that infers both a Viterbi alignment and the target sentence, their approach produced a rich overlapping phrase alignment. Their approach leveraged arbitrary features of the entire source sentence, target sentence and alignment. (Kääriäinen, 2009) proposed a novel phrase-based conditional exponential family translation model for SMT. The model operates on a feature representation in which sentence level translations are represented by enumerating all the known phrase level translations that occur inside them. The model automatically takes into account information provided by phrase overlaps. Although both of the latter two approaches were innovative the translation performance was lower than tranditional PBSMT baselines.

Our proposed approach is most similar to that of (Tribble and et al., 2003). Our approach differs in the interlocking process is less constrained; phrase pairs can interlock independently on source and target sides, and the interlocking process performed during the decoding process itself, rather than by augmenting the phrase-table.

3 Methodology

3.1 Target Interlocking

In the decoding process for PBSMT, the target is generated from left-to-right phrase-by-phrase. The process of interlocking the phrases is illustrated in Figure 1. The s_i are the source tokens, the t_j are the target tokens, the lower target token sequence on the left represents the partial translation hypothesis, and the upper target phrase is the target side of a translation unit $(s_3s_4, t_3t_4t_5)$ being used to extend the hypothesis. An interlock of length k is can occur if the last k tokens of the partial translation match the first k tokens of the target side of the translation unit being used to extend the hypothesis. In this case the decoder may create an extended hypothesis with the target side of the translation unit interlocked with the target word sequence generated so far. In order to do this, the k interlocked words are not inserted

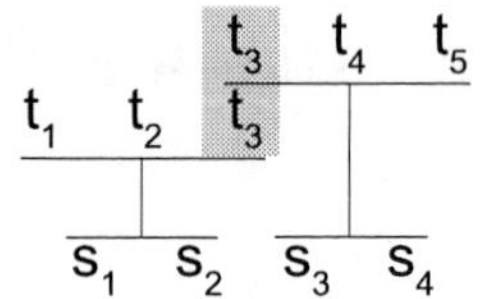

Figure 1: Interlocking target phrases.

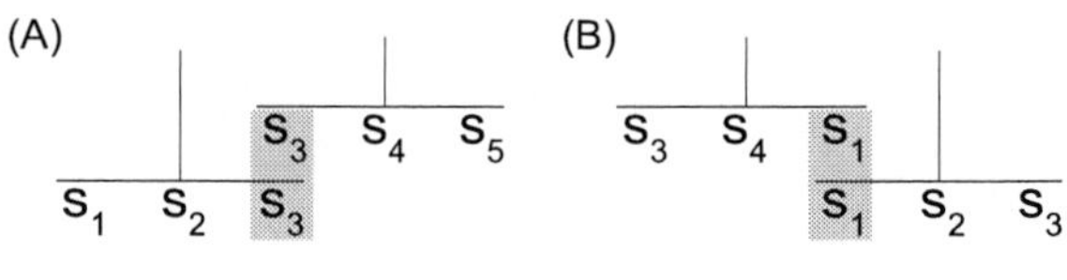

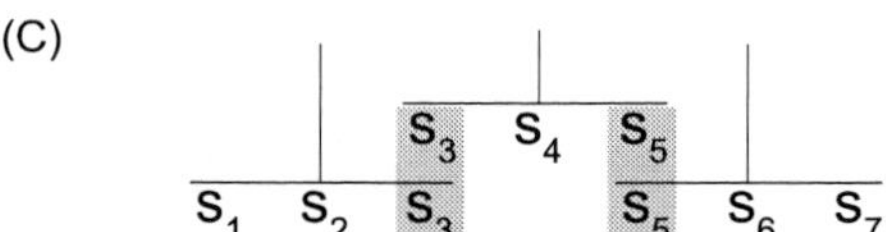

Figure 2: Interlocking source phrases.

a second time into the target token sequence and the word penalty (if pre-calculated) is adjusted to reflect this. In the example given in Figure 1, the translation resulting from extending the search with the interlocking translation unit will be $t_1t_2t_3t_4t_5$.

3.2 Source Interlocking

The interlocking of source phrases can occur in three different ways as shown in Figure 2. In Figure 2 (A), a source phrase is interlocking with source words to the left; in (B) a source phrase is interlocking with source words to the right; and in (C) a source phrase is interlocking on both sides. The interlocking process is handled before the search process begins, at the time the set of translation options used in the search is created. Additional interlocking translation options are created in which the source side phrase is permitted to overlap with the surrounding source context, however, later during the search this translation unit will only be used to translate (cover) the sequence of non-interlocking words. In this way, the decoder's search algorithm can be used without modification, when dealing with interlocking source phrases.

4 Experiments

4.1 Corpora

We used twenty languages from the multilingual Basic Travel Expressions Corpus (BTEC), which is a collection of travel-related expressions (Kikui et al., 2003). The languages were Arabic (ar), Danish (da), German (de), English (en), Spanish (es), French (fr), Italian (it), Dutch (nl), Portugese (pt), Russian (ru), Tagalog (tl), Indonesian (id), Malaysian (ms), Vietnamese (vi), Thai (th), Hindi (hi), Chinese (zh), Japanese (ja), Korean (ko) and Myanmar (my). 155,121 sentences were used for training, 5,000 sentences for development and 2,000 sentences for evaluation.

In addition, we ran experiments on two language pairs from the Europarl corpus (Koehn, 2005). The language pairs were English-German, German-English, English-Spanish and Spanish-English. The corpus statistics are given in Table 2.

4.2 Experimental Methodology

We used a modified version of our in-house phrase based SMT system which operates similarly to Moses (Koehn and Haddow, 2009). GIZA++ (Och and Ney, 2000) was used for word alignment, together with the grow-diag-final-and heuristics (Koehn et al., 2003). A lexicalized reordering model was trained with the msd-bidirectional-fe option (Tillmann, 2004). We used the SRILM toolkit to create 5-gram language models with interpolated modified Kneser-Ney discounting (Stolcke, 2002; Chen and Goodman, 1996). The weights for the log-linear models were tuned using the MERT procedure (Och, 2003). The translation performance was evaluated using the BLEU score (Papineni et al., 2001).

We ran three sets of experiments; (1) target interlocking, (2) source interlocking and (3) both source and target interlocking for all possible combinations of languages (i.e. 380 language pairs). We studied two methods for accomplishing (3). In the first, interlocking as defined in Sections 3.1 and 3.2 are permitted freely. In the second, the target is allowed to interlock if and only if the source is also interlocked. This was similar to the method proposed by (Tribble and et al., 2003).

4.3 Results

In this section, we will first present the results of the experiments on the BTEC corpora and then report the results from the experiments from the Europarl corpus.

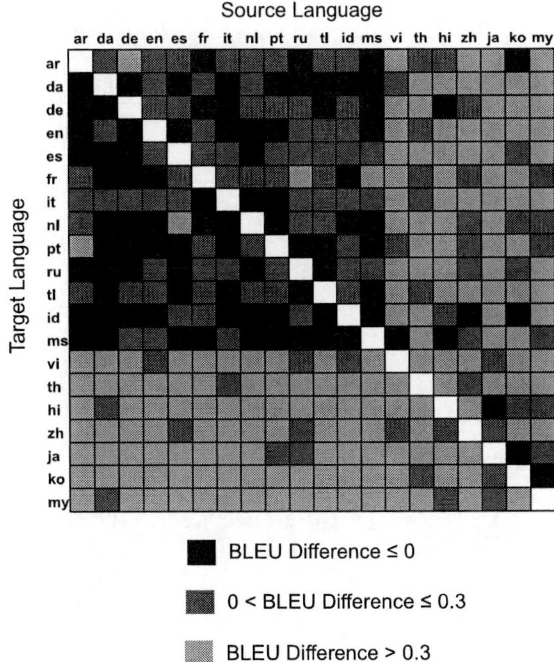

Figure 3: BLEU difference by language pair.

4.3.1 BLEU Differences

The difference in BLEU between a baseline system, a standard phrase-based SMT system without interlocking, and the proposed systems in which interlocking phrases where permitted, was calculated, and the average taken over all 380 language pairs. The results show that interlocking the phrases generally improves translation quality, and that the system gained slightly more from interlocking the target phrases, than from interlocking the source phrases. The average BLEU difference was 0.22 from interlocking target phrases, 0.14 from overlapping source phrases and 0.33 from interlocking both source and target. When the interlocking was constrained to ensure that both source and target phrases were interlocked, the average BLEU difference dropped to 0.27 BLEU. In the cases where both source and target phrases were allowed to interlock freely, 77% of the experiments showed an improvement in BLEU score.

A sequence of experiments were run on the baseline system with increasing stack size from 100, to 1000 in increments of 100. These experiments showed an increase of 0.07 BLEU points from stack

Src-Trg	Corpus Statistics (sentences)			Baseline	Interlocking		
	train	develop	test	No-interlock	Source	Target	Src & Trg
en-de	1500,000	3,000	3,000	18.70	**21.03**	18.83	18.90
de-en	1500,000	3,000	3,000	**26.08**	24.86	26.05	25.44
en-es	1500,000	3,000	3,000	33.55	**35.44**	33.68	33.89
es-en	1500,000	3,000	3,000	33.81	**36.42**	33.90	33.92

Table 2: BLEU scores for the Europarl corpora.

Kendall's Tau Distance	Avg BLEU Difference	% Expts Showing Gain
[0, 1.00]	0.33	77.3
[0, 0.95]	0.34	78.4
[0, 0.90]	0.38	80.5
[0, 0.85]	0.51	90.5
[0, 0.80]	0.58	93.5
[0, 0.75]	0.63	97.3
[0, 0.70]	0.68	97.3
[0, 0.65]	0.71	97.7
[0, 0.60]	0.72	97.2
[0, 0.55]	0.74	97.3
[0, 0.50]	0.75	100.0

Table 1: Filtering the Set of Language Pairs.

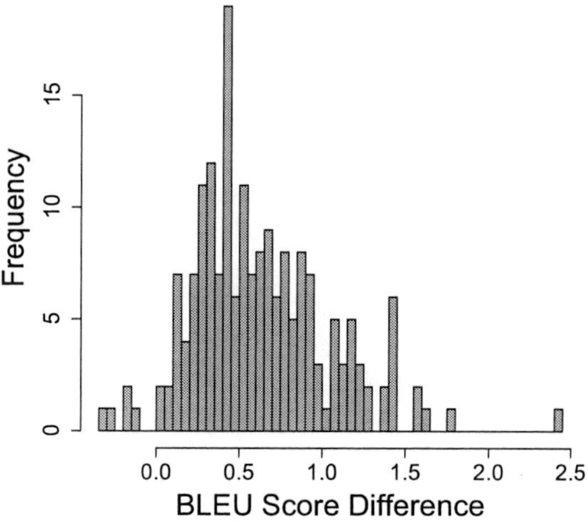

Figure 4: The Distribution of differences in BLEU score.

size 100 to stack size 200, followed by a sequence of scores that did not vary more than 0.01. Therefore, we conclude that the gains we obtained through interlocking the phrases, could not have been obtained by simply increasing the amount of searching performed by the baseline system. In other words, the interlocking method is introducing novel and useful search steps into the search space.

4.3.2 Results by Language Pair

Figure 3 shows how the gains and losses in BLEU score were distributed over the set of language pairs. Lighter cells in the figure represent gains in BLEU, the black cells represent losses. The order of the language pairs has been arranged to show the is a clear pattern. The languages on the left hand side and upper part of the figure are mostly European languages with similar word orders, whereas the remaining languages are typically Asian languages with different word orders. The language pairs that gained the most from interlocking on both source and target were: th-hi, hi-it, ko-de, ko-tl, th-ja, my-ru, my-th, my-ar, th-my, and it-ja. The languages that lost the most in BLEU score were: id-pt, ko-my, fr-id, ms-pt, id-it, da-ar, id-ko, da-es, id-ar, and de-it.

It is clear from Figure 3 that translation among the group of similar languages does not benefit from our approach, but the dissimilar languages do. This observation motivated further analysis of the data in order to develop a method for selecting language pairs

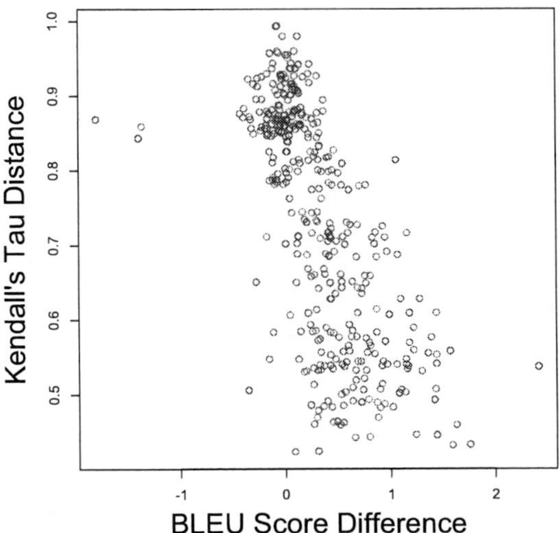

BLEU Score Difference

Figure 5: Plot of the Kendall's tau distance difference against BLEU difference.

suitable for our approach.

4.3.3 Kendall's Tau Distance

Kendall's tau distance is the minimum number of transpositions of adjacent symbols necessary to transform one permutation into another (Kendall, 1938; Birch, 2011), and is one method to gauge the amount of re-ordering that would be required during the translation process between two languages.

Figure 5 shows a scatter plot of all of the experiments, plotting BLEU difference against Kendall's tau. The points show a strong negative correlation (coefficient: -0.7). Therefore, we propose to use Kendall's tau as a means of selecting appropriate language pairs to be used with our method.

Table 1 shows the effect of filtering the set of language pairs by Kendall's tau. The effectiveness of the proposed method increases as languages with higher Kendall's tau distance are removed from the experimental set. When language pairs are selected according to Kendall's tau in the range $0 \leq \tau \leq 0.75$, the average BLEU gain of the set increases to 0.6 BLEU while still retaining approximately half of the language pairs in the set. Moreover, the proportion of experiments showing an in improvement in BLEU increases to over 97%. Figure 4 shows the distribution of BLEU differences for this subset of language pairs.

4.3.4 Europarl Corpus

The results of the previous sections were all based on experiments on the BTEC corpus. This corpus is unsual in that the sentences are short and the training data size is also small. In order to establish that our approach has more general application, we applied it to four language pairs from the much larger Europarl corpus. The results on the Europarl corpus are shown in Table 2. For three of the language pairs we observed increases in BLEU scores over the baseline for all interlocking methods with substantial gains of 1.9 to 2.6 BLEU points coming from the source interlocking technique. However, the German to English pair gave a negative result. The results from the Europarl corpus are generally very encouraging but the negative result motivates further study on more language pairs from different domain in the future.

5 Conclusion

In this paper we propose and evaluate a simple technique for improving the performance of phrase-based statistical machine translation decoders, that can be implemented with only minor modifications to the decoder. In the proposed method phrases are allowed to interlock freely on both the source and target side during decoding. The experimental results, based on a large-scale study involving 380 language pairs provide strong evidence that our approach is genuinely effective in improving the machine translation quality. The translation quality improved for 77% of the language pairs tested, and this was increased to over 97% when the set of language pairs was filtered according to Kendall's tau distance. The translation quality improved by an average of up to 0.75 BLEU points on this subset. This value represents a lower bound on what is possible with this technique and in future work we intend to study the introduction of additional features into the log-linear model to encourage or discourage the use of interlocking phrases during decoding, and investigate the effect of increasing the number of interlocked words.

References

Alexandra Birch. 2011. *Reordering Metrics for Statistical Machine Translation*. Ph.D. thesis, University of Edinburgh.

Stanley F Chen and Joshua Goodman. 1996. An empirical study of smoothing techniques for language modeling. In *Proceedings of the 34th annual meeting on Association for Computational Linguistics*, pages 310–318. Association for Computational Linguistics.

Chris Dyer, Adam Lopez, Juri Ganitkevitch, Johnathan Weese, Ferhan Ture, Phil Blunsom, Hendra Setiawan, Vladimir Eidelman, and Philip Resnik. 2010. cdec: A decoder, alignment, and learning framework for finite-state and context-free translation models. In *Proceedings of ACL*.

Matti Kääriäinen. 2009. Sinuhe – statistical machine translation using a globally trained conditional exponential family translation model. In *Proceedings of the 2009 Conference on Empirical Methods in Natural Language Processing*, pages 1027–1036, Singapore, August. Association for Computational Linguistics.

Sariya Karimova, Patrick Simianer, and Stefan Riezler. 2014. Offline extraction of overlapping phrases for hierarchical phrase-based translation. In *Proceedings of the International Workshop on Spoken Language Translation (IWSLT)*, pages 236–243.

M. G. Kendall. 1938. A new measure of rank correlation. *Biometrika*, 30(1/2):81–93.

G. Kikui, E. Sumita, T. Takezawa, and S. Yamamoto. 2003. Creating corpora for speech-to-speech translation. In *Proceedings of EUROSPEECH-03*, pages 381–384.

Philipp Koehn and Barry Haddow. 2009. Edinburgh's Submission to all Tracks of the WMT2009 Shared Task with Reordering and Speed Improvements to Moses. In *Proceedings of the Fourth Workshop on Statistical Machine Translation*, pages 160–164.

Philipp Koehn, Franz Josef Och, , and Daniel Marcu. 2003. Statistical phrase-based translation. In *In Proceedings of the Human Language Technology Conference*, Edmonton, Canada.

Philipp Koehn. 2005. Europarl: A parallel corpus for statistical machine translation. In *MT summit*, volume 5, pages 79–86.

F. J. Och and H. Ney. 2000. Improved statistical alignment models. In *ACL00*, pages 440–447, Hong Kong, China.

Franz J. Och. 2003. Minimum error rate training for statistical machine translation. In *Proceedings of the 41st Meeting of the Association for Computational Linguistics (ACL 2003)*, Sapporo, Japan.

K. Papineni, S. Roukos, T. Ward, and W.J. Zhu. 2001. *Bleu: a Method for Automatic Evaluation of Machine Translation*. IBM Research Report rc22176 (w0109022), Thomas J. Watson Research Center.

Benjamin Roth and Andrew McCallum. 2010. Machine translation using overlapping alignments and samplerank. In *Proceedings of the Ninth Conference of the Association for Machine Translation in the Americas, AMTA2010*.

Andreas Stolcke. 2002. SRILM - An Extensible Language Modeling Toolkit. In *Proceedings of the International Conference on Spoken Language Processing*, volume 2, pages 901–904, Denver.

Christoph Tillmann. 2004. A unigram orientation model for statistical machine translation. In *Proceedings of HLT-NAACL 2004: Short Papers*, HLT-NAACL-Short '04, pages 101–104, Stroudsburg, PA, USA. Association for Computational Linguistics.

Alicia Tribble and et al. 2003. Overlapping phrase-level translation rules in an smt engine.

Eyes Don't Lie:
Predicting Machine Translation Quality Using Eye Movement

Hassan Sajjad, Francisco Guzmán, Nadir Durrani, Ahmed Abdelali,
Houda Bouamor†, Irina Temnikova, Stephan Vogel
Qatar Computing Research Institute, HBKU, Qatar
†Carnegie Mellon University, Qatar

Abstract

Poorly translated text is often disfluent and difficult to read. In contrast, well-formed translations require less time to process. In this paper, we model the differences in reading patterns of Machine Translation (MT) evaluators using novel features extracted from their gaze data, and we learn to predict the quality scores given by those evaluators. We test our predictions in a pairwise ranking scenario, measuring Kendall's tau correlation with the judgments. We show that our features provide information beyond fluency, and can be combined with BLEU for better predictions. Furthermore, our results show that reading patterns can be used to build *semi*-automatic metrics that anticipate the scores given by the evaluators.

1 Introduction

Human evaluation has been the preferred method for tracking the progress of MT systems. In the past, the prevalent criterion was to judge the quality of a translation in terms of *fluency and adequacy*, on an absolute scale (White et al., 1994). However, different evaluators focused on different aspects of the translations, which increased the subjectivity of their judgments. As a result, evaluations suffered from low inter- and intra-annotator agreements (Turian et al., 2003; Snover et al., 2006). This caused a shift towards a ranking-based approach (Callison-Burch et al., 2007). Unfortunately, the disagreement between evaluators is still a challenge that cannot be easily resolved due to the non-transparent thought-process that evaluators follow to make a judgment.

The eye-mind hypothesis (Just and Carpenter, 1980; Potter, 1983) states that when completing a task, people cognitively process objects that are in front of their eyes (i.e. where they fixate their gaze).[1] Based on this assumption, it has been possible to study reading behavior and patterns (Rayner, 1998; Garrod, 2006; Hansen and Ji, 2010).

The overall difficulty of a sentence and its syntactic complexity affects reading behavior (Coco and Keller, 2015). Ill-formed sentences take longer to process, and may cause the reader to jump back while reading. Hence, by looking into how evaluators read the translations and their accompanying references, we can learn about: (*i*) the complexity of a reference sentence, and (*ii*) the quality of a translation sentence.

Using reading patterns from evaluators could be a useful tool for MT evaluation: (*i*) to shed light into the evaluation process: e.g. the general reading behavior that evaluators follow to complete their task; (*ii*) to understand which parts of a translation are more difficult for the annotator; and (*iii*) to develop *semi*-automatic evaluation systems that use reading patterns to predict translation quality.

In this paper, we make a first step towards (*iii*): using reading patterns as a method for distinguishing between good and bad translations. Our hypothesis is that bad translations are difficult to read, which may be reflected by the reading patterns of the evaluators. Motivated by the notion of reading difficulty, we extracted novel features from the evaluator's gaze data, and used them to model and predict the quality of translations as perceived by evaluators.

---

[1]Except in cases of *covert* attention.

Proceedings of NAACL-HLT 2016, pages 1082–1088,
San Diego, California, June 12-17, 2016. ©2016 Association for Computational Linguistics

2   Features and Model

A perfectly *grammatical* sentence can be difficult to read for several reasons: unfamiliar vocabulary, complex syntactic structure, syntactic or semantic ambiguity, etc. (Harley, 2013). Reading automatic translations is even more challenging due to untranslated words, incorrect word order, morphological disagreements, etc. Cognitively processing difficult sentences generally results in modified reading patterns (Garrod, 2006; Coco and Keller, 2015).

In this paper, we analyze the reading patterns of human judges in terms of the word transitions (jumps), and the time spent on each word (dwell time); and use them as features to predict the quality score of a specific translation. For the sake of simplicity, as recommended by Guzmán et al. (2015), we only consider a monolingual evaluation scenario and ignore the source text . However, our features and experimental setup can be extended to include source-side features.

2.1   Features

Jump features   While reading text, the gaze of a person does not visit every single word, but it advances in jumps called *saccades*. These jumps can go forwards (*progressions*) or backwards (*regressions*). The number of regressions correlates with the reading difficulty of a sentence (Garrod, 2006; Schotter et al., 2014; Metzner, 2015). In an evaluation scenario, a fluent reading would mean monotonic gaze movement. On the contrary, the reader may need to jump back multiple times while reading a poor translation. We classify the word-transitions according to the direction of the jump and distance between the start and end words. For subsequent words n, $n + 1$, this would mean a forward jump of distance equal to 1. All jumps with distance greater than 4 were sorted into a 5+ bucket. Additionally, we separate the features for reference and translation jumps. We also count the total number of jumps.

Total jump distance   We additionally aggregate jump distances[2] to count the total distance covered while evaluating a sentence. We have reference distance and translation distance features. Again, the

---

[2]Jump count and distance features have also shown to be useful in SMT decoders (Durrani et al., 2011).

idea is that for a well-formed sentence, gaze distance should be less, compared to a poorly-formed one.

Inter-region jumps   While reading a translation, evaluators can jump between the translation and a reference to compare them. Intuitively, more jumps of this type could signify that the translation is harder to evaluate. Here we count the number of transitions between reference and translation.

Dwell time   The amount of time a person fixates on a region is a crucial marker for processing difficulty in sentence comprehension (Clifton et al., 2007) and moderately correlates with the quality of a translation (Doherty et al., 2010). Our feature counts the time spent by the reader on each particular word. We separate reference and translation features.

Lexicalized Features   The features discussed above do not associate gaze movements with the words being read. We believe that this information can be critical to judge the overall difficulty of the reference sentence, and to evaluate which translation fragments are problematic to the reader. To compute the lexicalized features, we extract streams of reference and translation lexical sequences based on the gaze jumps, and score them using a tri-gram language model. Let $R_i = r_1, r_2, \ldots, r_m$ be a sub-sequence of gaze movement over reference and there are $R_1, R_2, \ldots, R_n$ sequences, the *lex* feature is computed as follows:

$$lex(R) = \sum_i^n \frac{\log p(R_i)}{|R_i|}$$

$$p(R_i) = \sum_j^m p(r_j | r_{j-1}, r_{j-2})$$

The normalization factor $|R_i|$ is used to make the probabilities comparable. We also use unnormalized scores as additional feature. A similar set of features $lex(T)$ is computed for the translations. All features are normalized by the length of the sentence.

2.2   Model

For predicting the quality scores given by an evaluator, we use a linear regression model with ridge regularization. The ridge coefficient $\hat{\beta}$ is the value of β that minimizes the error:

$$\sum_i (y_i - x_i^T \beta)^2 + \lambda \sum_{j=1}^{p} \beta_j^2$$

Here the parameter λ controls the amount of shrink applied to regression coefficients. A high value of λ shrinks the coefficients close to zero (Hastie et al., 2001). We used the implementation provided in the glmnet package of R (Friedman et al., 2010), which inherits a cross-validation mechanism that finds the best value of λ on the training data.

3 Experimental Setup

We used a subset of the Spanish-English portion of the WMT'12 Evaluation task. We selected 60 medium-length sentences which have been evaluated previously by at least 2 different annotators. For each sentence we selected the *best* and *worst* translations according to a human evaluation score based on the *expected wins* (Callison-Burch et al., 2012). As a result, we had 60 references with two corresponding translations each, adding up to a total of 120 evaluation tasks. Each evaluation task was performed by 6 different evaluators, resulting in 720 evaluations.

The annotators were presented with a translation-reference pair at a time. The two evaluation tasks corresponding to the same reference were presented at two different times with at least 40 other tasks in-between. This was done to prevent any possible spurious effects that may arise from remembering the content of a first translation, when evaluating the second translation of the same sentence. During each evaluation task, the evaluators were asked to assess the quality of a translation by providing a score between 0–100 (Graham et al., 2013). The observed inter-annotator agreement (Cohen's kappa) among our annotators was 0.321. This is slightly higher than the overall inter-annotator agreement of 0.284 reported in WMT'12 for the Spanish-English.[3] For reading patterns we use the EyeTribe eye-tracker at

---

[3]For a rough comparison only. Note that these two numbers are not *exactly* comparable given that they are calculated on different subsets of the same data. Still, there is a fair agreement between the our evaluators and the *expected wins* from WMT'12 (avg. pairwise kappa of 0.381)

a sampling frequency of 30Hz. Please refer to Abdelali et al. (2016) for our Eye-Tracking setup and to know about *iAppraise*, an evaluation environment that supports eye-tracking.

3.1 Evaluation

In our evaluation, we used eye-tracking features to predict the quality of a translation in a pairwise scenario in a protocol similar to the one from WMT'12. First, we obtained the predicted scores $\hat{y}_A^k$, $\hat{y}_B^k$ for translations A and B when evaluated by evaluator k. Then, we computed the agreements w.r.t. the scores y_A^k, y_B^k provided by the evaluator for the same pair of translations. That is, we considered an agreement when rankings were in order, e.g. $\hat{y}_A^k > \hat{y}_B^k \iff y_A^k > y_B^k$. Otherwise, we considered it a disagreement. Finally, we computed Kendall's tau correlation coefficient as follows: $\tau = \frac{agg-dis}{agg+dis}$. We evaluated the performance using a 10-fold cross-validation. While the folds were selected randomly, we ensured that all translations corresponding to the same sentence were included in the same fold, to prevent any overlap between train and test.

4 Results

In this section, we first analyze the results of co-herent feature sets to measure their predictive power and to validate the intuitions about the information they capture. Later, we use combination of features and assess their suitability as evaluation metrics.

4.1 Gaze as a translation quality predictor

In Table 1, we show the results for the predictive models trained on different feature sets. For simplicity, we divide the feature groups in: reference only features (I), translation only features (II), translation and reference features (III); and lexicalized features (IV). In the last group, we also add a tri-gram language model scores for comparison purposes.

Reference only features In section I of the table, we observe the prediction results for the models that only used features from the references. Unsurprisingly, most of these features lack the predictive power to determine whether translation A is better than translation B (τ from 0.06 to 0.13). One would expect that important phenomena that can be observed only on the reference (e.g. the overall difficulty of the sentence), are neutralized in a pairwise setting, because an evaluator would read both instances of the reference text similarly.[4]

However, some features like the dwell time ($\tau = 0.13$) yield better results than others. This could be explained by the need to go back to the reference, when reading a confusing translation, thus spending more time reading the reference.

Translation only features In section II, we observe the results for the translation features. At a first glance, we realize that the correlation results are much higher than for the reference features (τ from 0.17 to 0.23). This supports the hypothesis that reading patterns can help to distinguish good from bad translations. Furthermore, it also supports specific intuitions about these reading patterns. For example, the fluency of a sentence is important (forward jumps, $\tau = 0.17$), but the number of regressions are better predictors of the quality of a sentence ($\tau = 0.22$). Additionally, the time spent reading a translation (dwell time) is a good predictor of the quality ($\tau = 0.22$). All of the above validate the intuition that reading patterns capture information about the quality of a translation. In general, using translation eye-tracking features in a pairwise evaluation, can help to predict which translation is better.

Translation and reference features Reference and translation features are not independent. Inter-region jumps capture the number of times that evaluators go between translation and references before making judgment. In section III, we observe that these features can be useful to predict the quality of a translation ($\tau = 0.18$).

Lexicalized features In the last rows of the table, we show that reading patterns help to evaluate more than just the fluency of a translation. A simple language model score (B_{LM}), is a weaker quality predictor ($\tau = 0.17$) than most of the eye-tracking translation features. Using the lexicalized version of the jump features gives additional predictive power ($\tau = 0.22$). Furthermore, by adding the total num-

---

[4]Although there could be differences based on corresponding translation, which may result in different values for the reference features.

SYS	Feature Sets (total features)	τ
I. Eye-tracking: Reference		
EyeRef_{fj}	Forward jumps (5)	0.06
EyeRef_{bj}	Backward jumps (5)	0.11
EyeRef_{dist}	Total jump distance (1)	0.09
EyeRef_{visit}	Total number of jumps (1)	0.10
EyeRef_{time}	Dwell time (1)	0.13
II. Eye-tracking: Translation		
EyeTra_{fj}	Forward jumps (5)	0.17
EyeTra_{bj}	Backward jumps (5)	0.22
EyeTra_{dist}	Total jump distance (1)	0.19
EyeTra_{visit}	Total number of jumps(1)	0.23
EyeTra_{time}	Dwell time (1)	0.22
III. Eye-tracking: Inter-region		
EyeInter	Jumps b/w regions (2)	0.18
IV. Lexicalized features		
B_{LM}	Language model (6)	0.17
EyeLex_{all}	Lexicalized gaze jumps combined (6)	0.22

Table 1: Results of individual eye-tracking features based on reference region, translation region, inter-region and lexicalized information

ber of jumps and backward jumps to the LM features, we would obtain a considerable gain in correlation ($\tau = 0.30$). This suggests that the reading patterns capture information about more than just fluency.

4.2 Gaze to build an evaluation metric

So far, we've shown that the individual sets of features based on reading patterns can help to predict translation quality, and that this goes beyond simple fluency. One question that remains to be answered is whether these features could be used as a whole to evaluate the quality of a translation *semi*-automatically. That is, whether we can use the gaze information, and other lexical information to anticipate the score that an evaluator will assign to a translation. Here, we present evaluation results combining several of these gaze features, and compare them against BLEU (Papineni et al., 2002), which uses lexical information and is designed to measure not only *fluency* but also *adequacy*.

In Table 2, we present results in the following way: in (I) we present the best non-lexicalized feature combinations that improve the predictive power of the model. In (II) we re-introduce the results of lexicalized jumps feature. In (III) we present results of BLEU and the combination of eye-tracking features with it. Finally in (IV) we present the human-to-human agreement measured in average Kendall's tau and in max human-to-human Kendall's tau.

Combinations of translation jumps In section I we present several combinations of features. All of them include the backward jumps feature. This feature provides predictive power ($\tau = 0.22$), which is orthogonal to other features. This is in line with our initial hypothesis that for a bad translation, an evaluator needs to go back and forth several times to understand it. Combining the backward jumps with the total number of jumps (CTJ_1) slightly increases the correlation to $\tau = 0.25$. Adding the jump distance (CTJ_2) also increases its τ to 0.27. While this correlation is lower than BLEU ($\tau = 0.34$), it does showcase the predictive power of the reading patterns.

Combinations with BLEU When we combined BLEU with the translation jumps, we observed an increment in the τ to 0.37. Combining BLEU with the lexicalized jumps, yields the best combination ($\tau = 0.42$). Although moderate, these increments suggest that the reading patterns could be capturing additional phenomenon besides adequacy and fluency, such as structural complexity. These phenomena remain to be explored in future work.

Human performance On average, evaluators agreements with each other are fair ($\tau = 0.33$) and below the best combination (CB_3), while the maximum agreement of any two evaluators is relatively higher ($\tau = 0.53$). This tells us that on average the semi-automatic approach to evaluation that we propose here is already competitive to predictions done by another (average) human. However, there is still room for improvement with respect to the most-agreeing pair of evaluators.

5   Related Work

Eye-tracking devices have been used previously in the MT research. Stymne et al. (2012) used eye-tracking to identify and classify MT errors.

SYS	Feature Sets	τ
I. Combination of translation jumps		
$EyeTra_{bj}$	Backward jumps	0.22
CTJ_1	Backward jumps, total jumps	0.25
CTJ_2	Backward jumps, total jumps, distance	0.27
II. Eye-tracking: Best Lexicalized		
$EyeLex_{all}$	Lexicalized gaze jumps	0.22
III. Combinations with BLEU		
B_{bleu}	BLEU	0.34
CB_1	B_{bleu} + $EyeTra_{bj}$	0.38
CB_2	B_{bleu} + CTJ_2	0.39
CB_3	B_{bleu} + $EyeLex_{all}$	0.42
IV. Human performance		
Avg	Avg. human-to-human agreement	0.33
Max	Max. human-to-human agreement	0.53

Table 2: Result of combining several jump and lexicalized features with BLEU. The column *Feature Sets* shows the name of the systems whose features are combined for that particular run. We also included the average and maximum observed *tau* between any two evaluators, as a reference.

Doherty et al. (2010) conducted a study using eye-tracking for MT evaluation and showed correlation between fixations and BLEU scores. Doherty and O'Brien (2014) evaluated the quality of machine translation output in terms of its *usability* by an end user. Guzmán et al. (2015) used eye-tracking to show that having monolingual environment improves the consistency of the evaluation.

Our work is different, as we: i) proposed novel eye-tracking features and ii) model gaze movements to predict human judgment.

6   Conclusion

We have shown that the reading patterns detected through eye-tracking can be used to predict human judgments of automatic translations. To this end, we extracted novel lexicalized and non-lexicalized features from the eye-tracking data motivated by notions of reading difficulty, and used them to predict the quality of a translation. We have shown that these features capture more than just the fluency of a translation, and provide complementary information to BLEU. In combination, these features can be used to produce semi-automatic metrics with improved the correlation with human judgments.

In the future, we plan to extend our experiments to a large set of users and different language pairs. Additionally we plan to improve the feature set to take into account phenomena such as *early termination*, i.e. when an evaluator makes a judgment before finishing reading a translation. We plan to deepen our analysis to determine what kind of information is being used beyond fluency and adequacy.

References

Ahmed Abdelali, Nadir Durrani, and Francisco Guzmán. 2016. iAppraise: A Manual Machine Translation Evaluation Environment Supporting Eye-tracking. In *Proceedings of the 2016 Conference of the North American Chapter of the Association for Computational Linguistics: Human Language Technologies*, San Diego, California.

Chris Callison-Burch, Cameron Fordyce, Philipp Koehn, Christof Monz, and Josh Schroeder. 2007. (Meta-) Evaluation of Machine Translation. In *Proceedings of the Second Workshop on Statistical Machine Translation*, Prague, Czech Republic.

Chris Callison-Burch, Philipp Koehn, Christof Monz, Matt Post, Radu Soricut, and Lucia Specia. 2012. Findings of the 2012 Workshop on Statistical Machine Translation. In *Proceedings of the Seventh Workshop on Statistical Machine Translation*, pages 10–51, Montréal, Canada. Association for Computational Linguistics.

Charles Clifton, Adrian Staub, and Keith Rayner. 2007. Eye Movements in Reading Words and Sentences. *Eye Movements: A Window on Mind and Brain*, pages 341–372.

Moreno I. Coco and Frank Keller. 2015. The Interaction of Visual and Linguistic Saliency during Syntactic Ambiguity Resolution. *The Quarterly Journal of Experimental Psychology*, 68(1):46–74.

Stephen Doherty and Sharon O'Brien. 2014. Assessing the Usability of Raw Machine Translated Output: A User-Centered Study Using Eye Tracking. *International Journal of Human-Computer Interaction*, 30(1):40–51.

Stephen Doherty, Sharon O'Brien, and Michael Carl. 2010. Eye Tracking as an Automatic MT Evaluation Technique. *Machine translation*, 24(1):1–13.

Nadir Durrani, Helmut Schmid, and Alexander Fraser. 2011. A Joint Sequence Translation Model with Integrated Reordering. In *Proceedings of the Association for Computational Linguistics: Human Language Technologies (ACL-HLT'11)*, Portland, OR, USA.

Jerome Friedman, Trevor Hastie, and Rob Tibshirani. 2010. Regularization Paths for Generalized Linear Models via Coordinate Descent. *Journal of Statistical Software*, 33(1):1–22.

Simon Garrod. 2006. Psycholinguistic Research Methods. *The Encyclopedia of Language and Linguistics*, 2:251–257.

Yvette Graham, Timothy Baldwin, Alistair Moffat, and Justin Zobel. 2013. Continuous Measurement Scales in Human Evaluation of Machine Translation. In *Proceedings of the 7th Linguistic Annotation Workshop and Interoperability with Discourse*, Sofia, Bulgaria.

Francisco Guzmán, Ahmed Abdelali, Irina Temnikova, Hassan Sajjad, and Stephan Vogel. 2015. How do Humans Evaluate Machine Translation. In *Proceedings of the 10th Workshop on Statistical Machine Translation*, Lisbon, Portugal.

Dan Witzner Hansen and Qiang Ji. 2010. In the Eye of the Beholder: A Survey of Models for Eyes and Gaze. *Pattern Analysis and Machine Intelligence, IEEE Transactions on*, 32(3):478–500.

Trevor A Harley. 2013. *The Psychology of Language: From Data to Theory*. Psychology Press.

Trevor Hastie, Robert Tibshirani, and Jerome Friedman. 2001. *The Elements of Statistical Learning*. Springer Series in Statistics. Springer New York Inc., New York, NY, USA.

Marcel A. Just and Patricia A. Carpenter. 1980. A Theory of Reading: From Eye Fixations to Comprehension. *Psychological review*, 87(4):329.

Paul-Philipp Metzner. 2015. *Eye Movements and Brain Responses in Natural Reading*. Ph.D. thesis, University of Potsdam.

Kishore Papineni, Salim Roukos, Todd Ward, and Wei-Jing Zhu. 2002. BLEU: a method for automatic evaluation of machine translation. In *Proceedings of the Association for Computational Linguistics*, ACL '02, pages 311–318, Philadelphia, PA, USA.

Mary C. Potter. 1983. Representational Buffers: The Eye-Mind Hypothesis in Picture Perception, Reading, and Visual Search. *Eye Movements in Reading: Perceptual and Language Processes*, pages 423–437.

Keith Rayner. 1998. Eye Movements in Reading and Information Processing: 20 Years of Research. *Psychological bulletin*, 124(3):372.

Elizabeth R. Schotter, Randy Tran, and Keith Rayner. 2014. Dont Believe What You Read (Only Once) Comprehension Is Supported by Regressions During Reading. *Psychological science*, page 0956797614531148.

Matthew Snover, Bonnie Dorr, Richard Schwartz, Linnea Micciulla, and John Makhoul. 2006. A Study of Translation Edit Rate with Targeted Human Annotation. In *Proceedings of the 7th Biennial Conference of the Association for Machine Translation in the Americas*, Cambridge, Massachusetts, USA.

Sara Stymne, Henrik Danielsson, Sofia Bremin, Hongzhan Hu, Johanna Karlsson, Anna Prytz Lillkull, and Martin Wester. 2012. Eye Tracking as a Tool for Machine Translation Error Analysis. In *Proceedings of the International Conference on Language Resources and Evaluation*, Istanbul, Turkey.

Joseph Turian, Luke Shen, and I. Dan Melamed. 2003. Evaluation of Machine Translation and its Evaluation. In *Proceedings of Machine Translation Summit IX*, New Orleans, LA, USA.

John White, Theresa O'Connell, and Francis O'Mara. 1994. The ARPA MT Evaluation Methodologies: Evolution, Lessons, and Future Approaches. In *Proceedings of the Association for Machine Translation in the Americas Conference*, Columbia, Maryland, USA.

Making Dependency Labeling Simple, Fast and Accurate

Tianxiao Shen[1] **Tao Lei**[2] **Regina Barzilay**[2]

[1]Tsinghua University [2]MIT CSAIL

[1]shentianxiao0831@gmail.com
[2]{taolei, regina}@csail.mit.edu

Abstract

This work addresses the task of dependency labeling—assigning labels to an (unlabeled) dependency tree. We employ and extend a feature representation learning approach, optimizing it for both high speed and accuracy. We apply our labeling model on top of state-of-the-art parsers and evaluate its performance on standard benchmarks including the CoNLL-2009 and the English PTB datasets. Our model processes over 1,700 English sentences per second, which is 30 times faster than the sparse-feature method. It improves labeling accuracy over the outputs of top parsers, achieving the best LAS on 5 out of 7 datasets[1].

1 Introduction

Traditionally in dependency parsing, the tasks of finding the tree structure and labeling the dependency arcs are coupled in a joint achitecture. While it has potential to eliminate errors propogated through a separated procedure, joint decoding introduces other sources of issues that can also lead to non-optimal labeling assignments. One of the issues arises from inexact algorithms adopted in order to solve the hard joint search problem. For instance, many parsers (Nivre et al., 2007; Titov and Henderson, 2007; Zhang et al., 2013; Dyer et al., 2015; Weiss et al., 2015) adopt greedy decoding such as beam search, which may prune away the correct labeling hypothesis in an early decoding stage. Another issue is caused by the absence of rich label

---

[1]Our code is available at https://github.com/shentianxiao/RBGParser/tree/labeling.

features. Adding dependency labels to the combinatorial space significantly slows down the search procedure. As a trade-off, many parsers such as MSTParser, TurboParser and RBGParser (McDonald et al., 2005; Martins et al., 2010; Zhang et al., 2014) incorporate only single-arc label features to reduce the processing time. This restriction greatly limits the labeling accuracy.

In this work, we explore an alternative approach where the dependency labeling is applied as a separate procedure, alleviating the issues described above. The potential of this approach has been explored in early work. For instance, McDonald et al. (2006) applied a separate labeling step on top of the first-order MSTParser. The benefit of such approach is two-fold. First, finding the optimal labeling assignment (once the tree structure is produced) can be solved via an *exact* dynamic programming algorithm. Second, it becomes relatively cheap to add *rich label features* given a fixed tree, and the exact algorithm still applies when high-order label features are included. However, due to performance issues, such approach has not been adopted by the top performing parsers. In this work, we show that the labeling procedure, when optimized with recent advanced techniques in parsing, can achieve very high speed and accuracy.

Specifically, our approach employs the recent distributional representation learning technique for parsing. We apply and extend the low-rank tensor factorization method (Lei et al., 2014) to the second-order case to learn a joint scoring function over grand-head, head, modifier and their labels. Unlike the prior work which additionally requires

Proceedings of NAACL-HLT 2016, pages 1089–1094,
San Diego, California, June 12-17, 2016. ©2016 Association for Computational Linguistics

traditional sparse features to achieve state-of-the-art performance, our extention alone delivers the same level of accuracy, while being substantially faster. As a consequence, the labeling model can be applied either as a refinement (re-labeling) step on top of existing parsers with negligible cost of computation, or as a part of a decoupled procedure to simplify and speed up the dependency parsing decoding.

We evaluate on all datasets in the CoNLL-2009 shared task as well as the English Penn Treebank dataset, applying our labeling model on top of state-of-the-art dependency parsers. Our labeling model processes over 1,700 English sentences per second, which is 30 times faster than the sparse-feature method. As a refinement (re-labeling) model, it achieves the best LAS on 5 out of 7 datasets.

2 Method

2.1 Task Formulation

Given an unlabeled dependency parsing tree $\mathbf{y}$ of sentence $\mathbf{x}$, where $\mathbf{y}$ can be obtained using existing (non-labeling) parsers, we classify each head-modifier dependency arc $h \to m \in \mathbf{y}$ with a particular label $l_{h \to m}$. Let $\mathbf{l} = \bigcup_{h \to m \in \mathbf{y}} \{l_{h \to m}\}$, our goal is to find the assignment with the highest score:

$$\mathbf{l}^* = \arg\max_{\mathbf{l}} \mathrm{S}(\mathbf{x}, \mathbf{y}, \mathbf{l})$$

For simplicity, we omit $\mathbf{x}, \mathbf{y}$ in the following discussion, which remain the same during the labeling process. We assume that the score $\mathrm{S}(\mathbf{l})$ decomposes into a sum of local scores of single arcs or pairs of arcs (in the form of grand-head–head–modifier), i.e.

$$\mathrm{S}(\mathbf{l}) = \sum_{h \to m \in \mathbf{y}} \mathrm{s}_1(h \xrightarrow{q} m) + \sum_{g \to h \to m \in \mathbf{y}} \mathrm{s}_2(g \xrightarrow{p} h \xrightarrow{q} m)$$

where $p = l_{g \to h}$, $q = l_{h \to m}$.

Parameterizing the scoring function $\mathrm{s}_1(h \xrightarrow{q} m)$ and $\mathrm{s}_2(g \xrightarrow{p} h \xrightarrow{q} m)$ is a key challenge. We follow Lei et al. (2014) to learn dense representations of features, which have been shown to better generalize the scoring function.

2.2 Scoring

The representation-based approach requires little feature engineering. Concretely, let $\phi_g, \phi_h, \phi_m \in \mathbb{R}^n$ be the atomic feature vector of the grand-head, head and modifier word respectively, and

Unigram features:		
form	form-p	form-n
lemma	lemma-p	lemma-n
POS	POS-p	POS-n
morph	bias	
Bigram features:		
POS-p, POS	POS, POS-n	
form, POS	lemma, POS	
lemma, POS-p	lemma, POS-n	
Trigram features:		
POS-p, POS, POS-n		

Table 1: Word atomic features used by our model. *POS*, *form*, *lemma* and *morph* stand for the POS tag, word form, word lemma and morphology features respectively. The suffix *-p* refers to the previous token, and *-n* refers to the next.

$\phi_{g \to h,p}, \phi_{h \to m,q} \in \mathbb{R}^d$ be the atomic feature vector of the two dependency arcs respectively. It is easy to define and compute these vectors. For instance, ϕ_g (as well as ϕ_h and ϕ_m) can incorperate binary features which indicate the word and POS tag of the current token (and its local context), while $\phi_{g \to h,p}$ (and $\phi_{h \to m,q}$) can indicate the label, direction and length of the arc between the two words.

The scores of the arcs are computed by (1) projecting the atomic vectors into low-dimensional spaces; and (2) summing up the element-wise products of the resulting dense vectors:

$$\mathrm{s}_1(h \xrightarrow{q} m) = \sum_{i=1}^{r_1} [U_1 \phi_h]_i [V_1 \phi_m]_i [W_1 \phi_{h \to m,q}]_i$$

where r_1 is a hyper-parameter denoting the dimension after projection, and $U_1, V_1 \in \mathbb{R}^{r_1 \times n}$, $W_1 \in \mathbb{R}^{r_1 \times d}$ are projection matrices to be learned.

The above formulation can be shown equivalent to factorizing a huge score table $T_1(\cdot, \cdot, \cdot)$ into the product of three matrices U_1, V_1 and W_1, where T_1 is a 3-way array (tensor) storing feature weights of all possible features involving three components—the head, modifier and the arc between the two. Accordingly, the formula to calculate $\mathrm{s}_1(\cdot)$ is equivalent to summing up all feature weights (from T_1) over the structure $h \xrightarrow{q} m$.[2]

We depart from the prior work in the following aspects. First, we naturally extend the factorization approach to score second-order structures of grand-

____

[2] We refer readers to the original work (Lei et al., 2014) for the derivation and more details.

head, head and modifier,

$$s_2(g \xrightarrow{p} h \xrightarrow{q} m) = \sum_{i=1}^{r_2} [U_2\phi_g]_i [V_2\phi_h]_i [W_2\phi_m]_i$$
$$[X_2\phi_{g\to h,p}]_i [Y_2\phi_{h\to m,q}]_i$$

Here r_2 is a hyper-parameter denoting the dimension, and $U_2, V_2, W_2 \in \mathbb{R}^{r_2 \times n}$, $X_2, Y_2 \in \mathbb{R}^{r_2 \times d}$ are additional parameter matrices to be learned. Second, in order to achieve state-of-the-art parsing accuracy, prior work combines the single-arc score $s_1(h \xrightarrow{q} m)$ with an extensive set of sparse features which go beyond single-arc structures. However, we find this combination is a huge impediment to decoding speed. Since our extention already captures high-order structures, it readily delivers state-of-the-art accuracy without the combination. This change results in a speed-up of an order of magnitude (see section 2.4 for a further discussion).

2.3 Viterbi Labeling

We use a dynamic programming algorithm to find the labeling assignment with the highest score. Suppose h is any node apart from the root, and g is h's parent. Let $f(h, p)$ denote the highest score of subtree h with $l_{g\to h}$ fixed to be p. Then we can compute $f(\cdot, \cdot)$ using a bottom-up method, from leaves to the root, by transition function

$$f(h, p) = \sum_{h\to m \in \mathbf{y}} \max_q \left\{ f(m, q) + s_1(h \xrightarrow{q} m) + s_2(g \xrightarrow{p} h \xrightarrow{q} m) \right\}$$

And the highest score of the whole tree is

$$f(root) = \sum_{root \to m \in \mathbf{y}} \max_q f(m, q) + s_1(root \xrightarrow{q} m)$$

Once we get $f(\cdot, \cdot)$, we can determine the labels backward, in a top-down manner. The time complexity of our algorithm is $O(NL^2 \cdot T)$, where N is the number of words in a sentence, L is the number of total labels, and T is the time of computing features and scores.

2.4 Speed-up

In this section, we discuss two simple but effective strategies to speed up the labeling procedure.

Pruning We prune unlikely labels by simply exploiting the part-of-speech (POS) tags of the head and the modifier. Specifically, let $\mathbf{1}(\text{pos}_h, \text{pos}_m, l)$ denote whether there is an arc $h \xrightarrow{l} m$ in the training data such that h's POS tag is pos_h and m's POS tag is pos_m. In the labeling process, we only consider the possible labels that occur with the corresponding POS tags. Let K be the average number of possible labels per arc, then the time complexity is dropped to $O(NK^2 \cdot T)$ approximately. In practice, $K \approx L/4$. Hence this pruning step makes our labeler 16 times faster.

Using Representation-based Scoring Only The time to compute scores, i.e. T, consists of building the features and fetching the corresponding feature weights. For traditional methods, this requires enumerating feature templates, constructing feature ID and searching the feature weight in a look-up table. For representation-based scoring, the dense word representations (e.g. $U_1\phi_h$) can be pre-computed, and the scores are obtained by simple inner products of small vectors. We choose to use representation-based scoring only, therefore reducing the time to $O(NK^2 \cdot (r_1 + r_2) + NT')$. In practice, we find the labeling process becomes about 30 times faster.

2.5 Learning

Let $\mathbf{D} = \{(\mathbf{x}_i, \mathbf{y}_i, \mathbf{l}_i)\}_{i=1}^{M}$ be the collection of M training samples. Our goal is to learn the values of the set of parameters $\Theta = \{U_1, V_1, W_1, U_2, V_2, W_2, X_2, Y_2\}$ based on $\mathbf{D}$. Following standard practice, we optimize the parameter values in an online maximum soft-margin framework, minimizing the structural hinge loss:

$$\text{loss}(\Theta) = \max_{\hat{\mathbf{l}}} \left\{ S(\hat{\mathbf{l}}) + \|\mathbf{l}_i - \hat{\mathbf{l}}\|_1 \right\} - S(\mathbf{l}_i)$$

where $\|\mathbf{l}_i - \hat{\mathbf{l}}\|_1$ is the number of different labels between $\mathbf{l}_i$ and $\hat{\mathbf{l}}$. We adjust parameters Θ by $\Delta\Theta$ via passive-aggressive update:

$$\Delta\Theta = \max \left\{ C, \frac{\text{loss}(\Theta)}{\|\delta\Theta\|^2} \right\} \cdot \delta\Theta$$

where $\delta\Theta = \frac{\text{dloss}(\Theta)}{\text{d}\Theta}$ denotes the derivatives and C is a regularization hyper-parameter controlling the maximum step size of each update.

To counteract over-fitting, we follow the common practice of averaging parameters over all iterations.

Model	Catalan		Chinese		Czech		English		German		Japanese		Spanish	
	UAS	LAS	UAS	LAS	UAS	LAS	UAS	LAS	UAS	LAS	UAS	LAS	UAS	LAS
Best Shared Task	-	87.86	-	79.17	-	80.38	-	89.88	-	87.48	-	92.57	-	87.64
Bohnet (2010)	-	87.45	-	76.99	-	80.96	-	90.33	-	88.06	-	92.47	-	88.13
Zhang and McDonald (2014)	91.41	87.91	82.87	78.57	86.62	80.59	92.69	90.01	89.88	87.38	92.82	91.87	90.82	87.34
Alberti et al. (2015)	**92.31**	**89.17**	**83.34**	**79.50**	88.35	83.50	92.37	90.21	90.12	87.79	93.99	93.10	**91.71**	88.68
RBG	91.37	87.31	82.16	77.24	**88.88**	81.90	92.75	90.04	90.88	87.91	94.18	93.38	91.50	87.69
+ our labeling		88.29		77.12		**84.04**		**90.38**		**88.68**		**93.59**		**88.71**

Table 2: Pipelined Results on CoNLL-2009.

3 Results

Experimental Setup We test our model on the CoNLL-2009 shared task benchmark with 7 different languages as well as the English Penn Treebank dataset. Whenever available, we use the predicted POS tags, word lemmas and morphological information provided in the datasets as atomic features. Following standard practice, we use unlabeled attachment scores (UAS) and labeled attachment scores (LAS) as evaluation measure[3]. In order to compare with previous reported numbers, we exclude punctuations for PTB in the evaluation, and include punctuations for CoNLL-2009 for consistency.

We use RBGParser[4], a state-of-the-art graph-based parser for predicting dependency trees, and then apply our labeling model to obtain the dependency label assignments. To demonstrate the effectiveness of our model on other systems, we also apply it on two additional parsers – Stanford Neural Shift-reduce Parser (Chen and Manning, 2014)[5] and TurboParser (Martins et al., 2010)[6]. In all reported experiments, we use the default suggested settings to run these parsers. The hyper-parameters of our labeling model are set as follows: $r_1 = 50$, $r_2 = 30$, $C = 0.01$.

Labeling Performance To test the performance of our labeling method, we first train our model using the gold unlabeled dependency trees and evaluate the labeling accuray on CoNLL-2009. Table 3 presents the results. For comparison, we implement a combined system which adds a rich set of traditional, sparse features into the scoring function and jointly train the feature weights. As shown in the table, using our representation-based method alone is

---

[3] We use the official evaluation script from CoNLL-X: http://ilk.uvt.nl/conll/software.html
[4] https://github.com/taolei87/RBGParser
[5] http://nlp.stanford.edu/software/nndep.shtml
[6] http://www.cs.cmu.edu/~ark/TurboParser/

	Ours + Sparse Features		Ours only	
	LAS	Speed	LAS	Speed
Catalan	96.33	30	96.42	1070
Chinese	94.16	38	93.16	1304
Czech	95.54	71	95.60	2065
English	97.00	62	96.88	1751
German	96.93	113	96.89	1042
Japanese	98.92	305	98.95	2778
Spanish	96.53	43	96.68	1142

Table 3: LAS and parsing speed (sentence per second) based on unlabeled golden trees.

UAS		Labeled	Unlabeled
	RBG	93.48	93.33
LAS		Before	After
	Stanford NN	89.37	89.55
	Turbo	90.22	90.65
	RBG	91.00	91.43
Runtime		Joint	Two-step
	Stanford NN	4.4	3.3
	Turbo	182.1	119.4
	RBG	365.4	305.7

Table 4: Joint vs. Separate analysis on PTB.

super fast, being 30 times faster than the implementation with traditional feature computation and able to process over 1,700 English sentences per second. It does not affect the LAS accuracy except for Chinese.

PTB Results Table 4 shows the performance on the English PTB dataset. We use RBGParser to predict both labeled and unlabeled trees, and there is no significant difference between their UAS. This finding lays the foundation for a separate procedure, as the tree structure does not vary much comparing to the joint procedure, and we can exploit rich label features and sophisticated algorithms to improve the LAS. Our re-labeling model improves over the predictions generated by the three different parsers, ranging from 0.2% to 0.4% LAS gain. Moreover, the labeling procedure runs in only 1.5 seconds on the test set. If we use the existing parsers to only predict unlabeled trees, we also obtain speed improvement, even for the highly speed-optimzed Stanford Neural Parser.

CoNLL-2009 Results In Table 2, we compare our model with the best systems[7] of the CoNLL-2009 shared task, Bohnet (2010), Zhang and McDonald (2014) as well as the most recent neural network parser (Alberti et al., 2015). Despite the simplicity of the decoupled parsing procedure, our labeling model achieves LAS performance on par with the state-of-the-art neural network parser. Specifically, our model obtains the best LAS on 5 out of 7 languages, while the neural parser outperforms ours on Catalan and Chinese.

4   Conclusion

The most common method for dependency parsing couples the structure search and label search. We demonstrate that decoupling these two steps yields both computational gains and improvement in labeling accuracy. Specifically, we demonstrate that our labeling model can be used as a post-processing step to improve the accuracy of state-of-the-art parsers. Moreover, by employing dense feature representations and a simple pruning strategy, we can significantly speed up the labeling procedure and reduce the total decoding time of dependency parsing.

Acknowledgments

We thank Yuan Zhang for his help on the experiments, and Danqi Chen for answering questions about their parser. We also thank the MIT NLP group and the reviewers for their comments.

References

Chris Alberti, David Weiss, Greg Coppola, and Slav Petrov. 2015. Improved transition-based parsing and tagging with neural networks. In *Proceedings of the 2015 Conference on Empirical Methods in Natural Language Processing*.

Bernd Bohnet. 2009. Efficient parsing of syntactic and semantic dependency structures. In *Proceedings of the Thirteenth Conference on Computational Natural Language Learning: Shared Task*.

Bernd Bohnet. 2010. Very high accuracy and fast dependency parsing is not a contradiction. In *Proceedings of the 23rd International Conference on Computational Linguistics*.

Wanxiang Che, Zhenghua Li, Yongqiang Li, Yuhang Guo, Bing Qin, and Ting Liu. 2009. Multilingual dependency-based syntactic and semantic parsing. In *Proceedings of the Thirteenth Conference on Computational Natural Language Learning: Shared Task*.

Danqi Chen and Christopher D Manning. 2014. A fast and accurate dependency parser using neural networks. In *Proceedings of the Conference on Empirical Methods in Natural Language Processing*.

Chris Dyer, Miguel Ballesteros, Wang Ling, Austin Matthews, and Noah A Smith. 2015. Transition-based dependency parsing with stack long short-term memory. *arXiv preprint arXiv:1505.08075*.

Andrea Gesmundo, James Henderson, Paola Merlo, and Ivan Titov. 2009. A latent variable model of synchronous syntactic-semantic parsing for multiple languages. In *Proceedings of the Thirteenth Conference on Computational Natural Language Learning: Shared Task*.

Tao Lei, Yu Xin, Yuan Zhang, Regina Barzilay, and Tommi Jaakkola. 2014. Low-rank tensors for scoring dependency structures. In *Proceedings of the 52th Annual Meeting of the Association for Computational Linguistics*. Association for Computational Linguistics.

André FT Martins, Noah A Smith, Eric P Xing, Pedro MQ Aguiar, and Mário AT Figueiredo. 2010. Turbo parsers: Dependency parsing by approximate variational inference. In *Proceedings of the 2010 Conference on Empirical Methods in Natural Language Processing*. Association for Computational Linguistics.

Ryan McDonald, Fernando Pereira, Kiril Ribarov, and Jan Hajič. 2005. Non-projective dependency parsing using spanning tree algorithms. In *Proceedings of the conference on Human Language Technology and Empirical Methods in Natural Language Processing*. Association for Computational Linguistics.

Ryan McDonald, Kevin Lerman, and Fernando Pereira. 2006. Multilingual dependency analysis with a two-stage discriminative parser. In *Proceedings of the Tenth Conference on Computational Natural Language Learning*. Association for Computational Linguistics.

Joakim Nivre, Johan Hall, Jens Nilsson, Atanas Chanev, Gülsen Eryigit, Sandra Kübler, Svetoslav Marinov, and Erwin Marsi. 2007. MaltParser: A language-independent system for data-driven dependency parsing. *Natural Language Engineering*.

---

[7]Winners include Bohnet (2009), Che et al. (2009), Gesmundo et al. (2009) and Ren et al. (2009).

Han Ren, Donghong Ji, Jing Wan, and Mingyao Zhang. 2009. Parsing syntactic and semantic dependencies for multiple languages with a pipeline approach. In *Proceedings of the Thirteenth Conference on Computational Natural Language Learning: Shared Task*.

Ivan Titov and James Henderson. 2007. A latent variable model for generative dependency parsing. In *Proceedings of 10th International Conference on Parsing Technologies (IWPT)*.

David Weiss, Chris Alberti, Michael Collins, and Slav Petrov. 2015. Structured training for neural network transition-based parsing. In *Proceedings of ACL 2015*.

Hao Zhang and Ryan McDonald. 2014. Enforcing structural diversity in cube-pruned dependency parsing. In *Proceedings of the 52nd Annual Meeting of the Association for Computational Linguistics*.

Hao Zhang, Liang Zhao, Kai Huang, and Ryan McDonald. 2013. Online learning for inexact hypergraph search. In *Proceedings of EMNLP*.

Yuan Zhang, Tao Lei, Regina Barzilay, and Tommi Jaakkola. 2014. Greed is good if randomized: New inference for dependency parsing. In *Proceedings of the Conference on Empirical Methods in Natural Language Processing (EMNLP)*.

Deep Lexical Segmentation and Syntactic Parsing in the Easy-First Dependency Framework

Matthieu Constant[♠◇]   **Joseph Le Roux**[♣]   **Nadi Tomeh**[♣]

♠ Université Paris-Est, LIGM, Champs-sur-Marne, France
◇ Alpage, INRIA, Université Paris Diderot, Paris, France
♣ LIPN, Université Paris Nord, CNRS UMR 7030, Villetaneuse, France
`matthieu.constant@u-pem.fr, leroux@lipn.fr, tomeh@lipn.fr`

Abstract

We explore the consequences of representing token segmentations as hierarchical structures (trees) for the task of Multiword Expression (MWE) recognition, in isolation or in combination with dependency parsing. We propose a novel representation of token segmentation as trees on tokens, resembling dependency trees. Given this new representation, we present and evaluate two different architectures to combine MWE recognition and dependency parsing in the *easy-first* framework: a pipeline and a joint system, both taking advantage of lexical and syntactic dimensions. We experimentally validate that MWE recognition significantly helps syntactic parsing.

1 Introduction

Lexical segmentation is a crucial task for natural language understanding as it detects semantic units of texts. One of the main difficulties comes from the identification of multiword expressions [MWE] (Sag et al., 2002), which are sequences made of multiple words displaying multidimensional idiomaticity (Nunberg et al., 1994). Such expressions may exhibit syntactic freedom and varying degree of compositionality, and many studies show the advantages of combining MWE identification with syntactic parsing (Savary et al., 2015), for both tasks (Wehrli, 2014). Indeed, MWE detection may help parsing, as it reduces the number of lexical units, and in turn parsing may help detect MWEs with syntactic freedom (syntactic variations, discontinuity, etc.).

In the dependency parsing framework, some previous work incorporated MWE annotations within syntactic trees, in the form of complex subtrees either with flat structures (Nivre and Nilsson, 2004; Eryiğit et al., 2011; Seddah et al., 2013) or deeper ones (Vincze et al., 2013; Candito and Constant, 2014). However, these representations do not capture deep lexical analyses like nested MWEs. In this paper, we propose a two-dimensional representation that separates lexical and syntactic layers with two distinct dependency trees sharing the same nodes[1]. This representation facilitates the annotation of complex lexical phenomena like embedding of MWEs (e.g. *I will (take a (rain check)))*. Given this representation, we present two easy-first dependency parsing systems: one based on a pipeline architecture and another as a joint parser.

2 Deep Segmentation and Dependencies

This section describes a lexical representation able to handle nested MWEs, extended from Constant and Le Roux (2015) which was limited to shallow MWEs. Such a lexical analysis is particularly relevant to perform deep semantic analysis.

A lexical unit [LU] is a subtree of the lexical segmentation tree composed of either a single token unit or an MWE. In case of a single token unit, the subtree is limited to a single node. In case of an MWE, the subtree is rooted by its leftmost LU, from which there are arcs to every other LU of the MWE. For instance, the MWE *in spite of* made of three single token units is a subtree rooted by *in*. It comprises two arcs: *in → spite* and *in → of*. The MWE *make*

---

[1]This is related to the *Prague Dependency Treebank* (Hajič et al., 2006) which encodes MWEs in tectogrammatical trees connected to syntactic trees (Bejček and Straňák, 2010).

Proceedings of NAACL-HLT 2016, pages 1095–1101,
San Diego, California, June 12-17, 2016. ©2016 Association for Computational Linguistics

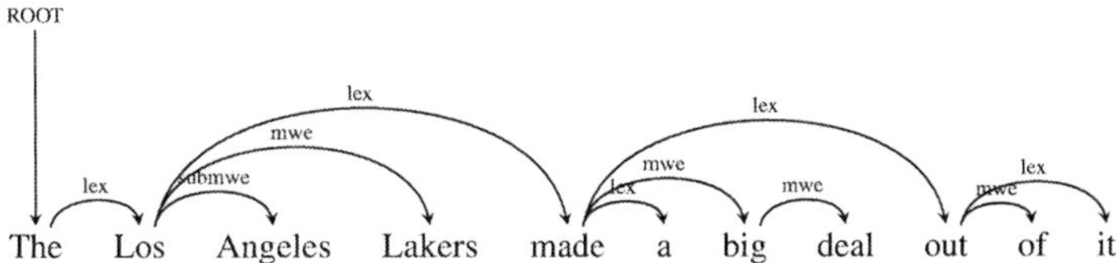

Figure 1: Deep segmentation of *Los Angeles Lakers made a big deal out of it* represented as a tree.

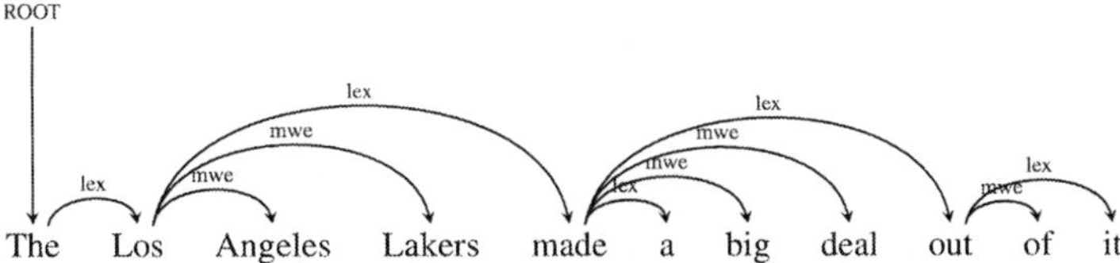

Figure 2: Shallow segmentation of *Los Angeles Lakers made a big deal out of it* represented as a tree.

big deal is more complex as it is formed of a single token unit *make* and an MWE *big deal*. It is represented as a subtree whose root is *make* connected to the root of the MWE subtree corresponding to *big deal*. The subtree associated with *big deal* is made of two single token units. It is rooted by *big* with an arc *big → deal*. Such structuring allows to find nested MWEs when the root is not an MWE itself, like for *make big deal*. It is different for the MWE *Los Angeles Lakers* comprising the MWE *Los Angeles* and the single token unit *Lakers*. In that case, the subtree has a flat structure, with two arcs from the node *Los*, structurally equivalent to *in spite of* that has no nested MWEs. Therefore, some extra information is needed in order to distinguish these two cases. We use arc labels.

Labeling requires to maintain a counter l in order to indicate the embedding level in the leftmost LU of the encompassing MWE. Labels have the form $sub^l mwe$ for $l \geq 0$. Let $U = U_1...U_n$ be a LU composed of n LUs. If $n = 1$, it is a single token unit. Otherwise, $subtree(U, 0)$, the lexical subtree[2] for U is recursively constructed by adding arcs $subtree(U_1, l+1) \xrightarrow{sub^l mwe} subtree(U_i, 0)$ for $i \neq 1$. In the case of *shallow* representation, every LUs of U are single token units.

Once built the LU subtrees (the *internal dependencies*), it is necessary to create arcs to connect them and form a complete tree : that we call *ex-*

ternal dependencies. LUs are sequentially linked together: each pair of consecutive LUs with roots (w_i, w_j), $i < j$, gives an arc $w_i \xrightarrow{lex} w_j$. Figure 1 and Figure 2 respectively display the deep and shallow lexical segmentations of the sentence *The Los Angeles Lakers made a big deal out of it*.

For readibility, we note mwe for $sub^0 mwe$ and $submwe$ for $sub^1 mwe$.

3 Multidimensional Easy-first Parsing

3.1 Easy-first parsing

Informally, easy-first proposed in Goldberg and Elhadad (2010) predicts easier dependencies before risky ones. It decides for each token whether it must be attached to the root of an adjacent subtree and how this attachment should be labeled[3]. The order in which these decisions are made is not decided in advance: highest-scoring decisions are made first and constrain the following decisions.

This framework looks appealing in order to test our assumption that segmentation and parsing are mutually informative, while leaving the exact flow of information to be learned by the system itself: we do not postulate any priority between the tasks nor that all attachment decisions must be taken jointly. On the contrary, we expect most decisions to be made independently except for some difficult cases that need both lexical and syntactic knowledge.

We now present two adaptations of this strategy to

---

[2] The second argument l corresponds to the embedding level.

[3] Labels are an extension to Goldberg and Elhadad (2010)

build both lexical and parse trees from a unique sequence of tokens[4]. The key component is to use features linking information from the two dimensions.

3.2 Pipeline Architecture

In this trivial adaptation, two parsers are run sequentially. The first one builds a structure in one dimension (i.e. for segmentation or syntax). The second one builds a structure in the other dimension, with the result of the first parser available as features.

3.3 Joint Architecture

The second adaptation is more substantial and takes the form of a joint parsing algorithm. This adaptation is provided in Algorithm 1. It uses a single classifier to predict lexical and syntactic actions. As in easy-first, each iteration predicts the most certain head attachment action given the currently predicted subtrees, but here it may belong to any dimension. This action can be mapped to an edge in the appropriate dimension via function EDGE. Function $score(a,i)$ computes the dot-product of feature weights and features at position i using surrounding subtrees in both dimensions[5].

Algorithm 1 Joint Easy-first parsing

1: **function** JOINT EASY-FIRST PARSING($w_0 \ldots w_n$)
2:     Let $\mathcal{A}$ be the set of possible actions
3:     $arcs_s, arcs_l := (\emptyset, \emptyset)$
4:     $h_s, h_l := w_0 \ldots w_n, w_0 \ldots w_n$
5:     **while** $|h_l| > 1 \vee |h_s| > 1$ **do**
6:         $\hat{a}, \hat{i} := \mathrm{argmax}_{a \in \mathcal{A}, i \in [|h_d|]} score(a,i)$
7:         $(par, lab, child, dim) := \mathrm{EDGE}((h_s, h_l), \hat{a}, \hat{i})$
8:         $arcs_{dim} := arcs_{dim} \cup (par, lab, child)$
9:         $h_{dim} := h_{dim} \setminus \{child\}$
10:    **end while**
11:    **return** $(arcs_l, arcs_s)$
12: **end function**
13: **function** EDGE($(h_s, h_l), (dir, lab, dim), i$)
14:    **if** $dir = \leftarrow$ **then**   ▷ we have a left edge
15:        **return** $(h_{dim}[i], lab, h_{dim}[i+1], dim)$
16:    **else**
17:        **return** $(h_{dim}[i+1], lab, h_{dim}[i], dim)$
18:    **end if**
19: **end function**

We can reuse the reasoning from Goldberg and Elhadad (2010) and derive a worst-case time com-

---

[4]It is straightforward to add any number of tree structures.

[5]Let us note that the algorithm builds projective trees for each dimension, but their union may contain crossing arcs.

Corpus	English EWT	French FTB	Sequoia
# words	55,590	564,798	33,829
# MWE labels	4,649	49,350	6,842
ratio	0.08	0.09	0.20
MWE rep.	shallow[+]	shallow	deep

Table 1: Datasets statistics. The first part describes the number of words in training sets with MWE label ratio. shallow[+] refers to a shallow representation with enriched MWE labels indicating the MWE strength (collocation vs. fixed).

plexity of $O(n \log n)$, provided that we restrict feature extraction at each position to a bounded vicinity.

4 Experiments

4.1 Datasets

We used data sets derived from three different reference treebanks: English Web Treebank (Linguistic Data Consortium release LDC2012T13)[EWT], French treebank (Abeillé et al., 2003) [FTB], Sequoia Treebank (Candito and Seddah, 2012) [Sequoia]. These treebanks have MWE annotations available on at least a subpart of them. For EWT, we used the STREUSLE corpus (Schneider et al., 2014b) that contains annotations of all types of MWEs, including discontiguous ones. We used the train/test split from Schneider et al. (2014a). The FTB contains annotations of contiguous MWEs. We generated the dataset from the version described in Candito and Constant (2014) and used the shallow lexical representation, in the official train/dev/test split of the SPMRL shared task (Seddah et al., 2013). The Sequoia treebank contains some limited annotations of MWEs (usually, compounds having an irregular syntax). We manually extended the coverage to all types of MWEs including discontiguous ones. We also included deep annotation of MWEs (in particular, nested ones). We used a 90%/10% train/test split in our experiments. Some statistics about the data sets are provided in table 4.1. Tokens were enriched with their predicted part-of-speech (POS) and information from MWE lexicon[6] lookup as in Candito and Constant (2014).

---

[6]We used the *Unitex* platform (`www-igm.univ-mlv.fr/~unitex/` for French and the STREUSLE corpus web site (`www.ark.cs.cmu.edu/LexSem/`) for English.

4.2 Parser and features

Parser. We implemented our systems by modifying the parser of Y. Goldberg[7] also used as a baseline. We trained all models for 20 iterations with dynamic oracle (Goldberg and Nivre, 2013) using the following exploration policy: always choose an oracle transition in the first 2 iterations ($k = 2$), then choose model prediction with probability $p = 0.9$.

Features. One-dimensional features were taken directly from the code supporting Goldberg and Nivre (2013). We added information on typographical cues (hyphenation, digits, capitalization, ...) and the existence of substrings in MWE dictionaries in order to help lexical analysis. Following Constant et al. (2012) and Schneider et al. (2014a), we used dictionary lookups to build a first naive segmentation and incorporate it as a set of features. Two-dimensional features were used in both pipeline and joint strategies. We first added syntactic path features to the lexical dimension, so syntax can guide segmentation. Conversely, we also added lexical path features to the syntactic dimension to provide information about lexical connectivity. For instance, two nodes being checked for attachment in the syntactic dimension can be associated with information describing whether one of the corresponding node is an ancestor of the other one in the lexical dimension (i.e. indicating whether the two syntactic nodes are linked via internal or external paths).

We also selected automatically generated features combining information from both dimensions. We chose a simple data-driven heuristics to select combined features. We ran one learning iteration over the FTB training corpus adding all possible combinations of syntactic and lexical features. We picked the templates of the 10 combined features whose scores had the greatest absolute values. Although this heuristics may not favor the most discriminant features, we found that the chosen features helped accuracy on the development set.

4.3 Results

For each dataset, we carried out four experiments. First we learned and ran independently two *distinct*

---

[7]We started from the version available at the time of writing at `https://bitbucket.org/yoavgo/tacl2013dynamicoracles`

baseline easy-first parsers using one-dimensional features: one producing a lexical segmentation, another one predicting a syntactic parse tree. We also trained and ran a *joint* easy-first system predicting lexical segmentations and syntactic parse trees, using two-dimensional features. We also experimented the *pipeline* system for each dimension, consisting in applying the baseline parser on one dimension and using the resulting tree as source of two-dimensional features in a standard easy first parser applied on the other dimension. Since pipeline architectures are known to be prone to error propagation, we also run an experiment where the pipeline second stage is fed with oracle first-stage trees.

Results on the test sets are provided in table 2, where LAS and UAS are computed with punctuation. Overall, we can see that the lexical information tends to help syntactic prediction while the other way around is unclear.

Model	Syntactic		Lexical		
	UAS	LAS	UAS	LAS	F1 (Pr / Rc)
FTB					
Distinct	87.44	85.09	96.69	94.75	79.47 (81.18/77.83)
Pipeline	**87.74**	**85.39**[†]	96.74	94.83	79.82 (81.56/78.15)
−*oracle trees*	88.96	86.98[†]	97.89	96.62[†]	87.27 (87.78/86.76)
Joint	87.69	85.32[†]	**96.79**	**94.89**	**80.11** (82.51/77.85)
Le Roux et al. (2014) CRF					80.49
Le Roux et al. (2014) combination					82.44
Candito and Constant (2014) graph-based parsing + CRF					
	89.24	86.97			78.60
Sequoia					
Distinct	84.88	81.74	**89.70**	**85.00**	67.60 (73.56/62.53)
Pipeline	85.91	82.84[†]	89.57	84.70	67.04 (72.24/62.53)
−*oracle trees*	85.95	83.05[†]	90.03	85.64[†]	69.36 (75.23/64.34)
Joint	**86.19**	**82.99**[†]	89.32	84.76	**68.58** (72.75/64.86)
EWT					
Distinct	87.45	83.91	93.96	90.75	**53.93** (66.42/45.39)
Pipeline	**88.45**	**84.76**[†]	**94.02**	**90.80**	53.19 (68.09/43.64)
−*oracle trees*	88.20	84.76[†]	94.23	91.09	55.05 (71.15/44.89)
Joint	87.98	84.24	93.72	90.49	51.20 (64.64/42.39)
Schneider et al. (2014a) Baseline					53.85 (60.99/48.27)
Schneider et al. (2014a) Best (oracle POS and clusters)					57.71 (58.51/57.00)

Table 2: Results on our three test sets. Statistically significant differences (p-value < 0.05) from the corresponding "distinct" setting are indicated with †. Rows *-oracle trees* are the same as pipeline but using oracle, instead of predicted, trees.

5 Discussion

The first striking observation is that the syntactic dimension does not help the predictions in the lexical dimension, contrary to what could be expected. In practice, we can observe that variations and discontinuity of MWEs are not frequent in our data sets. For instance, Schneider et al. (2014a) notice that only 15% of the MWEs in EWT are discontiguous and most of them have gaps of one token. This could explain why syntactic information is not useful for segmentation. On the other hand, the lexical dimension tends to help syntactic predictions. More precisely, while the pipeline and the joint approach reach comparable scores on the FTB and Sequoia, the joint system has disappointing results on EWT. The good scores for Sequoia could be explained by the larger MWE coverage.

In order to get a better intuition on the real impact of each of the three approaches, we broke down the syntax results by dependency labels. Some labels are particularly informative. First of all, the precision on the modifier label *mod*, which is the most frequent one, is greatly improved using the pipeline approach as compared with the baseline (around 1 point). This can be explained by the fact that many nominal MWEs have the form of a regular noun phrase, to which its internal adjectival or prepositional constituents are attached with the *mod* label. Recognizing a nominal MWE on the lexical dimension may therefore give a relevant clue on its corresponding syntactic structure. Then, the *dep_cpd* connects components of MWE with irregular syntax that cannot receive standard labels. We can observe that the pipeline (resp. the joint) approach clearly improves the precision (resp. recall) as compared with the baseline (+1.6 point). This means that the combination of a preliminary lexical segmentation and a possibly partial syntactic context helps improving the recognition of syntax-irregular MWEs. Coordination labels (*dep.coord* and *coord*) are particularly interesting as the joint system outperforms the other two on them. Coordination is known to be a very complex phenomenon: these scores would tend to show that the lexical and syntactic dimensions mutually help each other.

When comparing this work to state-of-the-art systems on data sets with shallow annotation of MWEs, we can see that we obtain MWE recognition scores comparable to systems of equivalent complexity and/or available information. This means that our novel representation which allows for the annotation of more complex lexical phenomena does not deteriorate scores for shallow annotations.

Label	gold count	distinct recall	distinct prec.	pipeline recall	pipeline prec.	joint recall	joint prec.
mod	**7782**	**80.39**	**78.18**	**80.62**	**79.13**	**80.94**	**78.68**
obj.p	6247	96.86	96.43	96.70	96.56	96.69	96.44
det	5269	97.67	97.89	97.70	97.76	97.76	97.72
ponct	4682	71.94	71.98	72.32	72.57	72.53	72.35
dep	3350	84.66	83.98	84.72	83.35	84.90	83.67
suj	2044	90.66	92.93	91.39	92.70	91.39	93.49
obj	1716	88.29	87.98	88.69	87.52	88.11	88.52
dep_cpd	**1604**	**84.66**	**87.84**	**86.28**	**87.54**	**85.10**	**89.39**
root	1235	92.23	92.23	92.79	92.79	92.96	92.96
dep.coord	**931**	**83.89**	**83.80**	**83.46**	**84.73**	**83.46**	**85.48**
coord	**832**	**58.77**	**59.27**	**60.10**	**60.39**	**59.98**	**60.71**
aux.tps	516	97.09	99.40	97.67	99.41	97.29	99.41
a_obj	398	75.13	77.06	73.37	79.56	73.62	78.98
obj.cpl	367	83.11	83.79	84.20	84.20	84.74	83.83
ats	345	79.71	83.33	79.42	82.78	79.42	83.03
mod.rel	334	70.96	76.21	70.36	73.90	68.26	73.55
de_obj	329	75.08	74.62	76.60	77.30	75.38	76.07
p_obj	268	58.58	79.70	61.19	79.61	60.45	80.60
aff	245	84.90	79.09	86.53	79.70	88.57	78.06
aux.pass	242	95.04	95.44	94.63	95.02	94.21	95.00
ato	30	33.33	83.33	40.00	85.71	43.33	86.67
arg	22	50.00	68.75	59.09	65.00	59.09	59.09
aux.caus	21	85.71	94.74	85.71	94.74	85.71	94.74
comp	11	0.00	0.00	0.00	0.00	0.00	0.00

Table 3: Results on FTB development set, broken down by dependency labels. Scores correspond to recall and precision.

6 Conclusions and Future Work

In this paper we presented a novel representation of deep lexical segmentation in the form of trees, forming a dimension distinct from syntax. We experimented strategies to predict both dimensions in the easy-first dependency parsing framework. We showed empirically that joint and pipeline processing are beneficial for syntactic parsing while hardly impacting deep lexical segmentation.

The presented combination of parsing and segmenting does not enforce any structural constraint over the two trees[8]. We plan to address this issue in future work. We will explore less redundant, more compact representations of the two dimensions since some annotations can be factorized between the two dimensions (e.g. MWEs with irregular syntax) and some can easily be induced from others (e.g. sequential linking between lexical units).

Acknowledgments

This work has been partly funded by the French *Agence Nationale pour la Recherche*, through the PARSEME-FR project (ANR-14-CERA-0001) and as part of the *Investissements d'Avenir* program (ANR-10-LABX-0083)

---

[8]for instance, aligned arc or subtrees

References

Anne Abeillé, Lionel Clément, and François Toussenel. 2003. Building a treebank for French. In Anne Abeillé, editor, *Treebanks*. Kluwer, Dordrecht.

Eduard Bejček and Pavel Straňák. 2010. Annotation of multiword expressions in the prague dependency treebank. *Language Resources and Evaluation*, 44(1-2).

Marie Candito and Matthieu Constant. 2014. Strategies for contiguous multiword expression analysis and dependency parsing. In *ACL 14-The 52nd Annual Meeting of the Association for Computational Linguistics*. ACL.

Marie Candito and Djamé Seddah. 2012. Le corpus Sequoia : annotation syntaxique et exploitation pour l'adaptation d'analyseur par pont lexical. In *TALN 2012 - 19e conférence sur le Traitement Automatique des Langues Naturelles*, Grenoble, France.

Matthieu Constant and Joseph Le Roux. 2015. Dependency representations for lexical segmentation. In *Proceedings of the international workshop on statistical parsing of morphologically-rich languages (SPMRL 2015)*.

Matthieu Constant, Anthony Sigogne, and Patrick Watrin. 2012. Discriminative strategies to integrate multiword expression recognition and parsing. In *Proceedings of the 50th Annual Meeting of the Association for Computational Linguistics (ACL'12)*, pages 204–212.

Gülşen Eryiğit, Tugay İlbay, and Ozan Arkan Can. 2011. Multiword Expressions in Statistical Dependency Parsing. In *Proceedings of the Second Workshop on Statistical Parsing of Morphologically Rich Languages*, SPMRL '11, pages 45–55, Stroudsburg, PA, USA. Association for Computational Linguistics.

Yoav Goldberg and Michael Elhadad. 2010. An efficient algorithm for easy-first non-directional dependency parsing. In *Human Language Technologies: The 2010 Annual Conference of the North American Chapter of the Association for Computational Linguistics*, pages 742–750. Association for Computational Linguistics.

Yoav Goldberg and Joakim Nivre. 2013. Training deterministic parsers with non-deterministic oracles. *Transactions of the association for Computational Linguistics*, 1:403–414.

J. Hajič, J. Panevová, E. Hajičová, P. Sgall, P. Pajas, Štěpánek, Havelka J., Mikulová J., Z. M., Žabokrtský, and M. Ševčíková Razímová. 2006. Prague dependency treebank 2.0. *Linguistic Data Consortium*.

Joseph Le Roux, Antoine Rozenknop, and Matthieu Constant. 2014. Syntactic parsing and compound recognition via dual decomposition: Application to french. In *COLING*.

Joakim Nivre and Jens Nilsson. 2004. Multiword units in syntactic parsing. *Proceedings of Methodologies and Evaluation of Multiword Units in Real-World Applications (MEMURA)*.

Geoffrey Nunberg, Ivan A. Sag, and Thomas Wasow. 1994. Idioms. *Language*, 70:491 – 538.

Ivan A. Sag, Timothy Baldwin, Francis Bond, Ann Copestake, and Dan Flickinger. 2002. Multiword expressions: A pain in the neck for nlp. In *In Proc. of the 3rd International Conference on Intelligent Text Processing and Computational Linguistics (CICLing-2002*, pages 1–15.

Agata Savary, Manfred Sailer, Yannick Parmentier, Michael Rosner, Victoria Rosén, Adam Przepiórkowski, Cvetana Krstev, Veronika Vincze, Beata Wójtowicz, Gyri Smørdal Losnegaard, Carla Parra Escartín, Jakub Waszczuk, Matthieu Constant, Petya Osenova, and Federico Sangati. 2015. PARSEME – PARSing and Multiword Expressions within a European multilingual network. In *7th Language & Technology Conference: Human Language Technologies as a Challenge for Computer Science and Linguistics (LTC 2015)*, Poznań, Poland, November.

Nathan Schneider, Emily Danchik, Chris Dyer, and Noah A Smith. 2014a. Discriminative lexical semantic segmentation with gaps: running the mwe gamut. *Transactions of the Association for Computational Linguistics*, 2:193–206.

Nathan Schneider, Spencer Onuffer, Nora Kazour, Emily Danchik, Michael T. Mordowanec, Henrietta Conrad, and Noah A. Smith. 2014b. Comprehensive annotation of multiword expressions in a social web corpus. In Nicoletta Calzolari, Khalid Choukri, Thierry Declerck, Hrafn Loftsson, Bente Maegaard, Joseph Mariani, Asuncion Moreno, Jan Odijk, and Stelios Piperidis, editors, *Proceedings of the Ninth International Conference on Language Resources and Evaluation*, pages 455–461, Reykjavík, Iceland, May. ELRA.

Djamé Seddah, Reut Tsarfaty, Sandra Kʻubler, Marie Candito, Jinho Choi, Richárd Farkas, Jennifer Foster, Iakes Goenaga, Koldo Gojenola, Yoav Goldberg, Spence Green, Nizar Habash, Marco Kuhlmann, Wolfgang Maier, Joakim Nivre, Adam Przepiorkowski, Ryan Roth, Wolfgang Seeker, Yannick Versley, Veronika Vincze, Marcin Woliński, Alina Wróblewska, and Eric Villemonte de la Clérgerie. 2013. Overview of the spmrl 2013 shared task: A cross-framework evaluation of parsing morphologically rich languages. In *Proceedings of the 4th Workshop on Statistical Parsing of Morphologically Rich Languages*, Seattle, WA.

Veronika Vincze, János Zsibrita, and Istvàn Nagy T. 2013. Dependency parsing for identifying hungarian light verb constructions. In *Proceedings of International Joint Conference on Natural Language Processing (IJCNLP 2013)*, Nagoya, Japan.

Eric Wehrli. 2014. The relevance of collocations for parsing. In *Proceedings of the 10th Workshop on Multiword Expressions (MWE)*, pages 26–32, Gothenburg, Sweden, April. Association for Computational Linguistics.

Sentiment Composition of Words with Opposing Polarities

Svetlana Kiritchenko and **Saif M. Mohammad**
National Research Council Canada
{svetlana.kiritchenko,saif.mohammad}@nrc-cnrc.gc.ca

Abstract

In this paper, we explore sentiment composition in phrases that have at least one positive and at least one negative word—phrases like *happy accident* and *best winter break*. We compiled a dataset of such opposing polarity phrases and manually annotated them with real-valued scores of sentiment association. Using this dataset, we analyze the linguistic patterns present in opposing polarity phrases. Finally, we apply several unsupervised and supervised techniques of sentiment composition to determine their efficacy on this dataset. Our best system, which incorporates information from the phrase's constituents, their parts of speech, their sentiment association scores, and their embedding vectors, obtains an accuracy of over 80% on the opposing polarity phrases.

1 Introduction

The Principle of Compositionality states that the meaning of an expression is determined by the meaning of its constituents and by its grammatical structure (Montague, 1974). By extension, sentiment composition is the determining of sentiment of a multi-word linguistic unit, such as a phrase or a sentence, based on its constituents. In this work, we study sentiment composition in phrases that include at least one positive and at least one negative word—for example, phrases such as *happy accident*, *couldn't stop smiling*, and *lazy sundays*. We refer to them as *opposing polarity phrases*. Such phrases present a particular challenge for automatic sentiment analysis systems that often rely on bag-of-word features.

Word–sentiment associations are commonly captured in *sentiment lexicons*. However, most existing manually created sentiment lexicons include only single words. Lexicons that include sentiment associations for *multi-word phrases* as well as their constituent words can be very useful in studying sentiment composition. We refer to them as *sentiment composition lexicons (SCLs)*.

We created a sentiment composition lexicon for opposing polarity phrases and their constituent words (Kiritchenko and Mohammad, 2016c).[1] Both phrases and single words were manually annotated with real-valued sentiment association scores using an annotation scheme known as Best–Worst Scaling.[2] We refer to the created resource as the *Sentiment Composition Lexicon for Opposing Polarity Phrases (SCL-OPP)*. The lexicon includes entries for 265 trigrams, 311 bigrams, and 602 unigrams.

In this paper, we use SCL-OPP to analyze regularities present in different kinds of opposing polarity phrases. We calculate the extent to which different part-of-speech combinations result in phrases of positive and negative polarity. We also show that for most phrases, knowing the parts of speech and polarities of their constituents is not enough to reliably predict the sentiment of the phrase.

We apply several unsupervised and supervised techniques of sentiment composition to determine their efficacy on predicting the sentiment of opposing polarity phrases. Our experiments indicate that

---

[1] www.saifmohammad.com/WebPages/SCL.html#OPP
[2] Best–Worst Scaling has been shown to produce reliable real-valued sentiment association scores (Kiritchenko and Mohammad, 2016a).

Proceedings of NAACL-HLT 2016, pages 1102–1108,
San Diego, California, June 12-17, 2016. ©2016 Association for Computational Linguistics

the sentiment of the last unigram or the sentiment of the most polar unigram in the phrase are not strong predictors of the overall sentiment of the phrase. Similarly, adjectives and verbs do not always dominate the sentiment in such phrases. Finally, we show that the constituent words, their parts of speech, their sentiment association scores, and their embedding vectors are all useful features—a supervised sentiment composition system that incorporates them obtains accuracies over 80% on both bigram and trigram opposing polarity phrases.

2 Related Work

A number of approaches have been proposed to address sentiment composition, which include manually derived syntactic rules (Moilanen and Pulman, 2007; Neviarouskaya et al., 2010), combination of hand-written rules and statistical learning (Choi and Cardie, 2008), and machine learning approaches (Nakagawa et al., 2010; Yessenalina and Cardie, 2011; Dong et al., 2015). Much work has been devoted to model the impact of negators and (to a lesser degree) intensifiers, words commonly referred to as contextual valence shifters, on sentiment of words they modify (Polanyi and Zaenen, 2004; Kennedy and Inkpen, 2005; Liu and Seneff, 2009; Wiegand et al., 2010; Taboada et al., 2011; Kiritchenko et al., 2014). Kiritchenko and Mohammad (2016b) created a sentiment composition lexicon for negators, modals, and adverbs (SCL-NMA) through manual annotation and analyzed the effect of these groups of modifiers on sentiment in short phrases. Recently, recursive deep model approaches have been proposed for handling sentiment of syntactic phrases through sentiment composition over parse trees (Socher et al., 2013; Zhu et al., 2014; Irsoy and Cardie, 2014; Tai et al., 2015). In this work, we apply several unsupervised and supervised techniques of sentiment composition for a specific type of phrases—opposing polarity phrases.

3 Creating a Sentiment Lexicon for Opposing Polarity Phrases

This section summarizes how we created a sentiment composition lexicon for opposing polarity phrases using the Best–Worst Scaling annotation technique. For more details we refer the reader

Term	Sentiment score
best winter break	0.844
breaking free	0.172
isn't long enough	-0.188
breaking	-0.500
heart breaking moment	-0.797

Table 1: Example entries in SCL-OPP.

to (Kiritchenko and Mohammad, 2016c). Table 1 shows a few example entries from the lexicon.

Term selection: We polled the Twitter API (from 2013 to 2015) to collect about 11 million tweets that contain emoticons: ':)' or ':('. We will refer to this corpus as the *Emoticon Tweets Corpus*. From this corpus, we selected bigrams and trigrams that had at least one positive word and at least one negative word. The polarity labels (positive or negative) of the words were determined by simple look-up in existing sentiment lexicons: Hu and Liu lexicon (Hu and Liu, 2004), NRC Emotion lexicon (Mohammad and Turney, 2010; Mohammad and Turney, 2013), MPQA lexicon (Wilson et al., 2005), and NRC's Twitter-specific lexicon (Kiritchenko et al., 2014; Mohammad et al., 2013).[3] In total, 576 opposing polarity n-grams (bigrams and trigrams) were selected. We also chose for annotation all unigrams that appeared in the selected set of bigrams and trigrams. There were 602 such unigrams. Note that even though the multi-word phrases and single-word terms were drawn from a corpus of tweets, most of the terms are used in everyday English.

Best–Worst Scaling Method of Annotation: Best–Worst Scaling (BWS), also sometimes referred to as Maximum Difference Scaling (MaxDiff), is an annotation scheme that exploits the comparative approach to annotation (Louviere and Woodworth, 1990; Louviere et al., 2015). Annotators are given four items (4-tuple) and asked which term is the Best (highest in terms of the property of interest) and which is the Worst (least in terms of the property of interest). Responses to the BWS questions can then be translated into real-valued scores through a simple counting procedure: For each term, its score is calculated as the percentage of times the term was

---

[3]If a word was marked with conflicting polarity in two lexicons, then that word was not considered as positive or negative.

SCP	Occ.	# phrases
▽adj. + △adj. → △phrase	0.76	17
▽adj. + △noun → ▽phrase	0.59	68
△adj. + ▽noun → ▽phrase	0.53	73
△adverb + ▽adj. → ▽phrase	0.89	18
△adverb + ▽verb → ▽phrase	0.91	11
▽noun + △noun → △phrase	0.60	10
△noun + ▽noun → ▽phrase	0.52	25
▽verb + det. + △noun → ▽phrase	0.65	17
▽verb + △noun → ▽phrase	0.82	17

Table 2: Sentiment composition patterns (SCPs) in SCL-OPP. △denotes a positive word or phrase, ▽denotes a negative word or phrase. 'Occ.' stands for occurrence rate of an SCP.

chosen as the Best minus the percentage of times the term was chosen as the Worst (Orme, 2009). The scores range from -1 to 1.

We employ Best–Worst Scaling for sentiment annotation by providing four (single-word or multi-word) terms at a time and asking which term is the most positive (or least negative) and which is the least positive (or most negative). Each question was answered by eight annotators through a crowdsourcing platform, CrowdFlower.[4] We refer to the resulting lexicon as the *Sentiment Composition Lexicon for Opposing Polarity Phrases (SCL-OPP)*.

Portions of the created lexicon have been used as development and evaluation sets in SemEval-2016 Task 7 'Determining Sentiment Intensity of English and Arabic Phrases' (Kiritchenko et al., 2016).[5] The objective of that task was to test different methods of automatically predicting sentiment association scores for multi-word phrases.

4 Sentiment Composition Patterns

SCL-OPP allows us to explore sentiment composition patterns in opposing polarity phrases. We define a *Sentiment Composition Pattern (SCP)* as a rule that includes on the left-hand side the parts of speech (POS) and the sentiment associations of the constituent unigrams (in the order they appear in the phrase), and on the right-hand side the sentiment association of the phrase. Table 2 shows examples. SCPs that have a positive phrase on the right-hand side will be called *positive SCPs*, whereas SCPs that

have a negative phrase on the right-hand side will be called *negative SCPs*. Below are some questions regarding SCPs and opposing polarity phrases that we explore here:

- Which SCPs are common among opposing polarity phrases?

- With the same left-hand side of an SCP, how often is the composed phrase positive and how often is the composed phrase negative? For example, when negative adjectives combine with a positive noun, how often is the combined phrase negative?

- Are some parts of speech (of constituent words) more influential in determining the sentiment of a phrase than others?

To answer these questions, each of the entries in SCL-OPP is marked with the appropriate SCP. The part-of-speech sequence of a phrase is determined by looking up the most common part-of-speech sequence for that phrase in the Emoticon Tweets Corpus.[6] Next, for every left-hand side of an SCP, we determine the ratio of 'how often occurrences of such combinations in SCL-OPP resulted in a positive phrase' to 'how often such combinations were seen in total'. We will refer to these scores as the *occurrence rates ('Occ.') of positive SCPs*. The *occurrence rates of negative SCPs* are calculated in a similar manner.

Table 2 presents all SCPs with the left-hand side combination appearing at least ten times in SCL-OPP, and whose occurrence rate is equal to or greater than 50%. For example, the second row tells us that there are 68 bigrams in SCL-OPP such that the first word is a negative adjective and the second word is a positive noun. Out of these 68 bigrams, 59% are negative, and the remaining 41% are positive, so the occurrence rate of this pattern is 0.59.

The most common SCPs in our lexicon are "△adj. + ▽noun → ▽phrase" (73) and "▽adj. + △noun → ▽phrase" (68). Observe that the occurrence rates of the patterns are spread over the entire range from 52% to 91%. Only two patterns have very high occurrence rates (around 90%): "△adverb + ▽adj. → ▽phrase" and "△adverb + ▽verb → ▽phrase".

---

[4]Let *majority answer* refer to the option most chosen for a question. 81% of the responses matched the majority answer.

[5]http://alt.qcri.org/semeval2016/task7/

[6]The corpus was automatically POS tagged using the CMU Tweet NLP tool (Gimpel et al., 2011).

Thus, for most opposing polarity phrases, their sentiment cannot be accurately determined based on the POS and sentiment of the constituents alone.

Both SCPs with high occurrence rates include adverbs that serve as intensifiers—words that increase or decrease the degree of association of the following word with positive (negative) sentiment (e.g., *incredibly slow*, *dearly missed*). Only the degree of association for the next word is changed while its polarity (positive or negative) is often preserved. Some adjectives can also play the role of an intensifier when combined with another adjective (e.g., *crazy talented*) or a noun (e.g., *epic fail*). For example, the adjective *great*, often considered highly positive, becomes an intensifier when combined with some nouns (e.g., *great loss*, *great capture*). Other adjectives determine the polarity of the entire phrase (e.g., *happy tears*, *bad luck*). Therefore, the occurrence rates of patterns like "▽adj. + △noun → ▽phrase" are low. Overall, even though adjectives and verbs are frequently the primary source of sentiment in the phrase, some nouns can override their sentiment as in *new crisis* or *leave a smile*. SCL-OPP includes phrases corresponding to many different kinds of sentiment composition patterns, and therefore, it is a useful resource for studying linguistic underpinnings of sentiment composition as well as for evaluating sentiment composition algorithms for opposing polarity phrases.

5 Automatically Predicting Sentiment

We now investigate whether accurate models of sentiment composition for opposing polarity phrases can be learned. We conduct experiments with several baseline unsupervised classifiers as well supervised techniques using features, such as unigrams, POS, sentiment scores, and word embeddings.

The problem of sentiment composition can be formulated in two different ways: a binary classification task where the system has to predict if the phrase is positive or negative; and a regression task where the system has to predict the real-valued sentiment association score of the phrase. We evaluate binary classification with simple accuracy (*acc.*) and the regression task with Pearson correlation coefficient (r). Learning and evaluation are performed separately for bigrams and trigrams.

5.1 Baseline Classifiers

The oracle 'majority label' baseline assigns to all instances the most frequent polarity label in the dataset. The 'last unigram' baseline returns the sentiment score (or the polarity label) of the last unigram in the phrase. For the regression task, we use the real-valued sentiment score of the unigram whereas for the binary classification task we use the polarity label (positive or negative). The 'most polar unigram' baseline assigns to the phrase the sentiment score (or the polarity label) of the most polar word in that phrase, i.e., the word with the highest absolute sentiment score. The 'part-of-speech (POS) rule' baseline assigns sentiment as follows:

1. If the phrase has an adjective, return the sentiment score (polarity) of the last adjective;
2. Else, if the phrase has a verb, return the sentiment score (polarity) of the last verb;
3. Else, return the sentiment score (polarity) of the most polar word.

5.2 Supervised Classifiers

We train a Support Vector Machines classifier with RBF kernel for the binary classification task and a Support Vector regression model with RBF kernel for the regression task using the LibSVM package (Chang and Lin, 2011). For both tasks, the models are trained using different combinations of the following features obtained from the target phrase: all unigrams, POS tag of each unigram, sentiment label of each unigram, sentiment score of each unigram, and the word embedding vector for each unigram. The word embeddings are obtained by running word2vec software (Mikolov et al., 2013) on the Emoticon Tweets Corpus. We use the skip-gram model with the default parameters and generate 200-dimensional vectors for each unigram present in the corpus. For each task, ten-fold cross-validation is repeated ten times, and the results are averaged.

5.3 Results

The results for all baseline and supervised methods are presented in Table 3. The 'majority label', 'last unigram', 'most polar unigram', and 'POS rule' baselines are shown in rows a to d. Observe that the sentiment association of the last unigram is not very

Features	Binary (Acc.)		Regression (Pearson r)	
	2-gr	3-gr	2-gr	3-gr
Baselines				
a. majority label	56.6	60.8	-	-
b. last unigram	57.2	59.3	0.394	0.376
c. most polar unigram	66.9	69.8	0.416	0.551
d. POS rule	65.6	63.8	0.531	0.515
Supervised classifiers				
e. POS + sent. label	65.7	64.2	-	-
f. POS + sent. score	74.9	74.8	0.662	0.578
g. row f + uni	82.0	81.3	0.764	0.711
h. row f + emb(avg) + emb(max)	78.2	79.5	0.763	0.710
i. row f + emb(conc)	80.2	76.5	0.790	0.719
j. row f + emb(conc) + uni	**82.6**	**80.9**	**0.802**	**0.753**
k. POS + emb(conc) + uni	76.3	80.2	0.735	0.744

Table 3: Performance of the automatic systems on SCL-OPP. Features used: unigrams (uni), part-of-speech of a unigram (POS), sentiment binary label of a unigram (sent. label), sentiment real-valued score of a unigram (sent. score), embeddings (emb). 'emb(conc)' is the concatenation of the embedding vectors of the constituent unigrams; 'emb(avg)' is the average vector of the unigram embeddings; 'emb(max)' is maximal vector of the unigram embeddings.

predictive of the phrase's sentiment (row b).[7] Both the 'most polar unigram' and the 'POS rule' classifiers perform markedly better than the majority baseline. Interestingly, the 'most polar unigram' classifier outperforms the slightly more sophisticated 'POS rule' approach on most tasks. Also, we found that within bigram phrases that contain adjectives or verbs, the adjective or verb constituents are the most polar words in only about half of the instances (and even less so in trigrams). This indicates that adjectives and verbs do not always dominate the sentiment in a phrase.

The results obtained using supervised techniques with various feature combinations are presented in rows e to k (Table 3). Using only POS and binary sentiment labels of the constituent unigrams, the supervised learning algorithm does not perform much better than our 'POS rule' baseline (the accuracies in row e are just slightly higher than those

---

[7]Note that the results for the 'last unigram' baseline are still better than the results of random guessing (acc = 50, $r = 0$). For the majority of n-grams in SCL-OPP, the polarity of the first unigram is opposite to the polarity of the last unigram. Thus, the results for a similar 'first unigram' baseline (not shown here) are worse than those obtained by the 'last unigram' baseline.

in row d). With access to real-valued sentiment scores of unigrams much more accurate models can be learned (row f). Furthermore, the results show that the sentiment of a phrase depends on its constituent words and not only on the sentiment of the constituents (row g shows markedly better performance than row f; all the differences are statistically significant, $p < .01$). Concatenating word embeddings was found to be more effective than averaging. (Averaging is common when creating features for sentences). Having access to both unigrams and word embedding features produces the best results. (The differences between the scores in row i and row j are statistically significant, $p < .01$.) Row k shows results of the model trained without the gold sentiment scores of the unigrams. Observe that for bigrams, there is a substantial drop in performance compared to row j (6.3-point drop in accuracy on the binary task, 6.7-point drop in Pearson correlation on the regression task) whereas for trigrams the performance is not affected as much (less than 1-point change on both tasks). Thus, having access to sentiment scores of constituents is particularly useful for determining sentiment of bigram phrases.

6   Conclusions

We created a real-valued sentiment composition lexicon for opposing polarity phrases and their constituent words, through manual annotation. We analyzed patterns of sentiment composition across phrases formed with different POS combinations. Further, we applied several unsupervised and supervised techniques of sentiment composition to determine their efficacy on opposing polarity phrases. We showed that for most phrases the sentiment of the phrase cannot be reliably predicted only from the parts of speech and sentiment association of their constituent words, and that the constituent words, their parts of speech, their sentiment scores, and their embedding vectors are all useful features in supervised sentiment prediction on this dataset.

We intend to use SCL-OPP in the following applications: (1) to automatically create a large coverage sentiment lexicon of multi-word phrases and apply it in downstream applications such as sentence-level sentiment classification, and (2) to investigate how the human brain processes sentiment composition.

References

Chih-Chung Chang and Chih-Jen Lin. 2011. LIBSVM: A Library for Support Vector Machines. *ACM Transactions on Intelligent Systems and Technology*, 2:27:1–27:27.

Yejin Choi and Claire Cardie. 2008. Learning with compositional semantics as structural inference for subsentential sentiment analysis. In *Proceedings of the Conference on Empirical Methods in Natural Language Processing (EMNLP)*, pages 793–801.

Li Dong, Furu Wei, Shujie Liu, Ming Zhou, and Ke Xu. 2015. A statistical parsing framework for sentiment classification. *Computational Linguistics*.

Kevin Gimpel, Nathan Schneider, Brendan O'Connor, Dipanjan Das, Daniel Mills, Jacob Eisenstein, Michael Heilman, Dani Yogatama, Jeffrey Flanigan, and Noah A. Smith. 2011. Part-of-speech tagging for Twitter: Annotation, features, and experiments. In *Proceedings of the Annual Meeting of the Association for Computational Linguistics (ACL)*.

Minqing Hu and Bing Liu. 2004. Mining and summarizing customer reviews. In *Proceedings of the 10th ACM SIGKDD International Conference on Knowledge Discovery and Data Mining (KDD)*, pages 168–177, New York, NY, USA.

Ozan Irsoy and Claire Cardie. 2014. Deep recursive neural networks for compositionality in language. In *Advances in Neural Information Processing Systems*, pages 2096–2104.

Alistair Kennedy and Diana Inkpen. 2005. Sentiment classification of movie and product reviews using contextual valence shifters. In *Proceedings of the Workshop on the Analysis of Informal and Formal Information Exchange during Negotiations (FINEXIN)*, Ottawa, Ontario, Canada.

Svetlana Kiritchenko and Saif M. Mohammad. 2016a. Capturing reliable fine-grained sentiment associations by crowdsourcing and best–worst scaling. In *Proceedings of The 15th Annual Conference of the North American Chapter of the Association for Computational Linguistics: Human Language Technologies (NAACL)*, San Diego, California.

Svetlana Kiritchenko and Saif M. Mohammad. 2016b. The effect of negators, modals, and degree adverbs on sentiment composition. In *Proceedings of the Workshop on Computational Approaches to Subjectivity, Sentiment and Social Media Analysis (WASSA)*.

Svetlana Kiritchenko and Saif M. Mohammad. 2016c. Happy accident: A sentiment composition lexicon for opposing polarity phrases. In *Proceedings of 10th edition of the the Language Resources and Evaluation Conference (LREC)*, Portorož, Slovenia.

Svetlana Kiritchenko, Xiaodan Zhu, and Saif M. Mohammad. 2014. Sentiment analysis of short informal texts. *Journal of Artificial Intelligence Research*, 50:723–762.

Svetlana Kiritchenko, Saif M. Mohammad, and Mohammad Salameh. 2016. SemEval-2016 Task 7: Determining sentiment intensity of English and Arabic phrases. In *Proceedings of the International Workshop on Semantic Evaluation (SemEval)*, San Diego, California, June.

Jingjing Liu and Stephanie Seneff. 2009. Review sentiment scoring via a parse-and-paraphrase paradigm. In *Proceedings of the Conference on Empirical Methods in Natural Language Processing*, pages 161–169.

Jordan J. Louviere and George G. Woodworth. 1990. Best-worst analysis. Working Paper. Department of Marketing and Economic Analysis, University of Alberta.

Jordan J. Louviere, Terry N. Flynn, and A. A. J. Marley. 2015. *Best-Worst Scaling: Theory, Methods and Applications*. Cambridge University Press.

Tomas Mikolov, Kai Chen, Greg Corrado, and Jeffrey Dean. 2013. Efficient estimation of word representations in vector space. In *Proceedings of Workshop at ICLR*.

Saif M. Mohammad and Peter D. Turney. 2010. Emotions evoked by common words and phrases: Using Mechanical Turk to create an emotion lexicon. In *Proceedings of the NAACL-HLT Workshop on Computational Approaches to Analysis and Generation of Emotion in Text*, LA, California.

Saif M. Mohammad and Peter D. Turney. 2013. Crowdsourcing a word–emotion association lexicon. *Computational Intelligence*, 29(3):436–465.

Saif M. Mohammad, Svetlana Kiritchenko, and Xiaodan Zhu. 2013. NRC-Canada: Building the state-of-the-art in sentiment analysis of tweets. In *Proceedings of the International Workshop on Semantic Evaluation*, Atlanta, Georgia.

Karo Moilanen and Stephen Pulman. 2007. Sentiment composition. In *Proceedings of Recent Advances in Natural Language Processing (RANLP)*, volume 7, pages 378–382.

Richard Montague. 1974. *Formal Philosophy; Selected papers of Richard Montague*. Yale University Press.

Tetsuji Nakagawa, Kentaro Inui, and Sadao Kurohashi. 2010. Dependency tree-based sentiment classification using CRFs with hidden variables. In *Proceedings of the Annual Conference of the North American Chapter of the Association for Computational Linguistics*, pages 786–794.

Alena Neviarouskaya, Helmut Prendinger, and Mitsuru Ishizuka. 2010. Recognition of affect, judgment, and appreciation in text. In *Proceedings of the International Conference on Computational Linguistics*, pages 806–814.

Bryan Orme. 2009. Maxdiff analysis: Simple counting, individual-level logit, and HB. Sawtooth Software, Inc.

Livia Polanyi and Annie Zaenen. 2004. Contextual valence shifters. In *Proceedings of the Exploring Attitude and Affect in Text: Theories and Applications (AAAI Spring Symposium Series)*.

Richard Socher, Alex Perelygin, Jean Y. Wu, Jason Chuang, Christopher D. Manning, Andrew Y. Ng, and Christopher Potts. 2013. Recursive deep models for semantic compositionality over a sentiment treebank. In *Proceedings of the Conference on Empirical Methods in Natural Language Processing (EMNLP)*, Seattle, USA.

Maite Taboada, Julian Brooke, Milan Tofiloski, Kimberly Voll, and Manfred Stede. 2011. Lexicon-based methods for sentiment analysis. *Computational Linguistics*, 37(2):267–307.

Kai Sheng Tai, Richard Socher, and Christopher D Manning. 2015. Improved semantic representations from tree-structured long short-term memory networks. In *Proceedings of the 53rd Annual Meeting of the Association for Computational Linguistics and the 7th International Joint Conference on Natural Language Processing*, pages 1556–1566, Beijing, China.

Michael Wiegand, Alexandra Balahur, Benjamin Roth, Dietrich Klakow, and Andrés Montoyo. 2010. A survey on the role of negation in sentiment analysis. In *Proceedings of the Workshop on Negation and Speculation in Natural Language Processing (NeSp-NLP)*, pages 60–68, Stroudsburg, PA, USA.

Theresa Wilson, Janyce Wiebe, and Paul Hoffmann. 2005. Recognizing contextual polarity in phrase-level sentiment analysis. In *Proceedings of the Joint Conference on HLT and EMNLP*, pages 347–354, Stroudsburg, PA, USA.

Ainur Yessenalina and Claire Cardie. 2011. Compositional matrix-space models for sentiment analysis. In *Proceedings of the Conference on Empirical Methods in Natural Language Processing (EMNLP)*, pages 172–182.

Xiaodan Zhu, Hongyu Guo, Saif Mohammad, and Svetlana Kiritchenko. 2014. An empirical study on the effect of negation words on sentiment. In *Proceedings of the 52nd Annual Meeting of the Association for Computational Linguistics*, pages 304–313, Baltimore, Maryland, June.

Learning to Recognize Ancillary Information for Automatic Paraphrase Identification

Simone Filice
DICII,
University of Roma, Tor Vergata
`filice@info.uniroma2.it`

Alessandro Moschitti[*]
ALT, Qatar Computing Research Institute,
HBKU
`amoschitti@qf.org.qa`

Abstract

Previous work on Automatic Paraphrase Identification (PI) is mainly based on modeling text similarity between two sentences. In contrast, we study methods for automatically detecting whether a text fragment only appearing in a sentence of the evaluated sentence pair is important or ancillary information with respect to the paraphrase identification task. Engineering features for this new task is rather difficult, thus, we approach the problem by representing text with syntactic structures and applying tree kernels on them. The results show that the accuracy of our automatic Ancillary Text Classifier (ATC) is promising, i.e., 68.6%, and its output can be used to improve the state of the art in PI.

1 Introduction

Automatic PI is the task of detecting if two texts convey the same meaning. For example, the following two sentences from the Microsoft Research Paraphrase Corpus (MSRP) (Dolan et al., 2004):

S_{1a}: *Although it's unclear whether Sobig was to blame, The New York Times also asked employees at its headquarters yesterday to shut down their computers because of "system difficulties."*

S_{1b}: *The New York Times asked employees at its headquarters to shut down their computers yesterday because of "computing system difficulties."*

are paraphrases, while these other two are not:

S_{2a}: *Dr. Anthony Fauci, director of the National Institute of Allergy and Infectious Diseases, agreed.*

S_{2b}: *"We have been somewhat lucky," said Dr. Anthony Fauci, director of the National Institute of Allergy and Infectious Diseases.*

Most previous work on automatic PI, e.g., (Madnani et al., 2012; Socher et al., 2011), is based on a direct comparison between the two texts, exploiting different similarity scores into a machine learning framework. However, these methods consider sentences as monolithic units and can thus be misled by ancillary information that does not modify the main meaning expressed in the text.

For example, the additional text fragment (ATF), *"Although it's unclear whether Sobig was to blame"*, from S_{1a} expresses ancillary information, which does not add much to the message of S_{1b}, thus the sentences are considered paraphrases. In contrast, S_{2b} contains the ATF, *"We have been somewhat lucky"*, whose meaning is not linked to any constituent of S_{1b}. Since such text expresses relevant information, the two sentences are not considered paraphrases.

In this paper, we study and design models for extracting ATFs from a sentence with respect to another one and classifying if their meaning is ancillary or important. For this purpose, we built a corpus of sentence pairs using MSRP, where at least one pair member always contains ATFs. We use SVMs with tree kernels applied to syntactic representations (Severyn and Moschitti, 2012) of ATFs for learning automatic ATCs.

The results derived on MSRP show (*i*) a promising accuracy of our ATC and (*ii*) the output of ATC

---

[*] Professor at DISI, University of Trento.

Proceedings of NAACL-HLT 2016, pages 1109–1114,
San Diego, California, June 12-17, 2016. ©2016 Association for Computational Linguistics

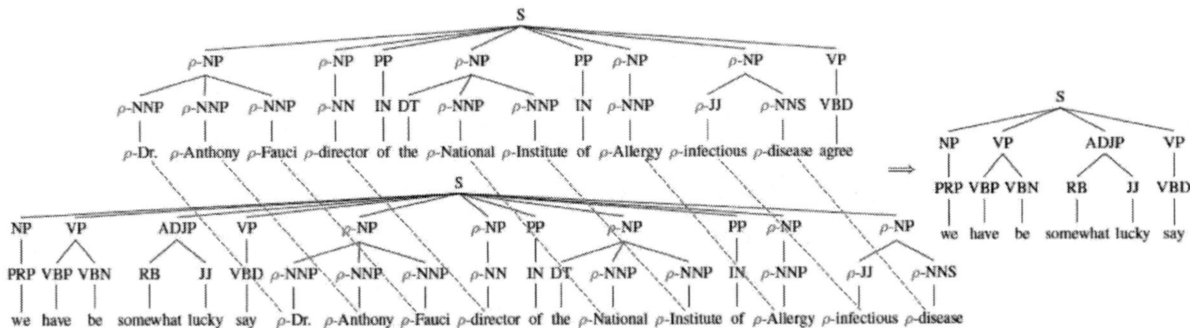

Figure 1: A pair of non-paraphrase sentences and its corresponding additional fragment.

can be used as a feature for improving the state-of-the-art PI model.

2 Ancillary clauses in PI

Our main purpose in studying computational approaches to the detection of ancillary information is its practical application to PI. Thus, given a pair of sentences (in general two texts), we define ATFs as ancillary information if their semantics:

(*i*) only appears in one of the two sentences and

(*ii*) does not change the main meaning of the sentence, i.e., either the sentences are paraphrases or, if they are not, such ATFs are not the reason for their different meaning.

The definition above along with a syntactic representation of the sentences can be applied to a paraphrase corpus to build a dataset of ancillary vs. important ATFs. For example, Fig. 1 shows the shallow tree representation[1] we proposed in (Severyn and Moschitti, 2012) of the sentences, S_{2a} and S_{2b}, reported in the introduction, where the red label ρ indicates that there is a link between the lemmas of the two sentences (also shown by the dashed edges). ρ can be propagated to the upper nodes to mark the related constituents. For example, the lemma *National* is matched by the two sentences, thus both its father node, NNP, and its grandfather constituent, NP, are marked.

Such representation makes the extraction of ATFs easier. For instance, Fig. 1 shows the text fragment

of S_{2b}, "*We have been somewhat lucky*", on the right. This is an ATF since it is not aligned with any fragments of S_{2a}. Moreover, since it expresses a central information to the sentence meaning, S_{2b} cannot be in paraphrase relation with S_{2a}. Conversely, the ATF of S_{1a}, "*Although it's unclear whether Sobig was to blame*", is ancillary to the main meaning of the sentence, indeed, the annotators marked S_{1a} and S_{1b} as a valid paraphrase.

3 Building the ATC corpus

The previous section has shown an approach to extract ATFs that can be potentially ancillary. This uses an alignment approach based on lexical similarity, which may fail to align some text constituents. However, these mistakes only affect the precision in extracting ATFs rather than the recall. In other words, we can build a corpus that considers most cases of additional information.

In particular, we design the following simple heuristic: let F_i and F_j be the largest not aligned (possibly discontinuous) word sequences appearing in the sentence pair (S_i, S_j), where $F_i \in S_i$ and $F_j \in S_j$. We define ATF as the largest text between F_i and F_j subject to $d = |size(F_i) - size(F_j)| > \tau$, where $size(F)$ is the number of words[2] appearing in F. If the condition is not satisfied no ATF is extracted.

The condition over d is important because the sentence aligner may fail to match some subsequences, creating false ATFs. However, what is missed from one sentence will be missed also in the other sen-

---

[1]The shallow trees are constituted by four levels: (*i*) word lemmas as leaves, (*ii*) POS-tags as parent of lemmas, (*iii*) phrases grouping POS-tag nodes and (*iv*) a final root S.

[2]Only verbs, nouns, adjectives, adverbs and numbers were considered, assuming all the others as "not informative words".

	Train			Test		
τ	Ancillary	Important	Total	Ancillary	Important	Total
1	971	687	1658	387	687	1074
2	426	364	790	166	151	317
3	166	169	335	62	79	141
4	59	73	132	21	36	57

Table 1: Number of additional clauses extracted from MSRP.

tence. Thus, in general, if we set a small d then F_i and F_j misalignments may generate false ATFs. In contrast, a large d would clearly prevent this problem, although small ATFs (of size $< d$) may be discarded. More precisely, smaller values of τ may cause the selection of fragments that have corresponding fragments in the other sentence, expressed with dissimilar words (i.e., the aligner failed to match those constituents). Larger values of τ make the heuristic more precise, but less effective in retrieving smaller ATFs.

The ATF corpus. We applied the heuristic above to extract an ATF (if exists) from each sentence pair of MSRP. The number of the extracted ATFs depends on τ as reported in Table 1. A manual inspection of the retrieved fragments revealed that: (*i*) small values of τ, namely, 1 and 2, cause the extraction of many fragments from one sentence corresponding to fragments expressed with different words in the other sentence: these are not ATFs. (*ii*) With $\tau = 3$, the heuristic is very precise and captures most ATFs appearing in the sentence pairs. (*iii*) Higher values of τ cause many valid fragments to be missed.

Once ATFs are generated, we need to label them as ancillary or important for PI such that this data can be used for training and testing ATC. Interestingly, the data can be automatically labeled exploiting the MSRP annotation: given a sentence pair from MSRP, we (*i*) extract the ATF from it and (*ii*) automatically annotate it as ancillary if the pair is a paraphrase and not ancillary otherwise. In other words, an ATF is considered ancillary only if it is extracted from a paraphrase pair. To verify the correctness of this approach, two experts manually labeled the obtained data extracted with $\tau = 3$ and found that only 3.3% of the data was mislabeled with respect to one annotator. The Cohen's kappa agreement between the annotators was 85%.

4 Experiments

In these experiments, we first evaluate state-of-the-art PI models to create our baseline, then we experiment with our ATC and finally, we combine them to show that ATC can improve PI.

4.1 Deriving PI baselines

Dataset. We used MSRP, which consists of 4,076 sentence pairs in the training set and 1,725 sentence pairs in test set. About 66% of the pairs are paraphrases. The pairs were extracted from topically similar Web news articles, applying some heuristics that select potential paraphrases to be annotated by human experts. We represent the sentence pairs using shallow trees generated with the Stanford parser[3].

Models. We adopted our state-of-the-art PI approach we proposed in (Filice et al., 2015). This, given two pairs of sentences, $p_a = \langle a_1, a_2 \rangle$ and $p_b = \langle b_1, b_2 \rangle$, represents instances as shown Fig. 1, and applies tree kernels to them. In particular, we used our best kernel com derived in the work above:

$$SMK(p_a, p_b) = \; sf\big(SPTK(a_1, b_1) \times SPTK(a_2, b_2),$$
$$SPTK(a_1, b_2) \times SPTK(a_2, b_1)\big),$$

where $sf(x_1, x_2) = \frac{1}{c}log(e^{cx_1} + e^{cx_2})$, and SPTK is the Smoothed Partial Tree Kernel (Croce et al., 2011). SMK considers the inherent symmetry of the PI task and evaluates the best alignment between the sentences in the input pairs. The sf is a softmax operation used in place of the max function[4], which is not a valid kernel function. SPTK uses a similarity function between words: we generated it with the word2vec tool[5] (Mikolov et al., 2013) using the

---

[3]`nlp.stanford.edu/software/corenlp.shtml`
[4]c=100 produces accurate approximation.
[5]`https://code.google.com/p/word2vec`

Model	Acc (%)	P	R	F1
LK	75.9	78.4	88.1	82.9
SMK	76.4	76.6	92.9	83.9
SMK+LK	**77.7**	79.4	8.99	**84.4**
(Socher et al., 2011)	76.8	–	–	83.6
(Madnani et al., 2012)	77.4	–	–	84.1

Table 2: Results on Paraphrase Identification.

Kernel	Acc (%)	P	R	F_1
STK	65.1 ± 6.5	65.4 ± 8.0	58.3 ± 5.6	61.5 ± 5.8
PTK	67.4 ± 8.2	69.7 ± 8.8	56.5 ± 7.7	62.4 ± 7.8
SPTK	$\mathbf{68.6} \pm 9.4$	71.0 ± 9.0	57.9 ± 9.7	63.7 ± 9.3

Table 3: Results of Ancillary Text Classifiers

skip-gram model applied to the UkWaC corpus (Baroni et al., 2009).

Results. As illustrated in Table 2, a binary Support Vector Machine equipped with SMK achieves a very high accuracy. Moreover, SMK combined with a linear kernel (LK) over similarity metrics[6] attains the state of the art in PI.

4.2 Experimental Evaluation on ATC

Dataset and models. We created an ATC dataset with $\tau = 3$ as described in Sec. 3. We make this dataset available[7]. We learned ATC with the C-SVM algorithm (Chang and Lin, 2011) inside KeLP[8]. The examples are represented using the shallow tree like the one on the right of Fig. 1. We used three different tree kernels: the Syntactic Tree Kernel (STK) by Collins and Duffy (2001), the Partial Tree Kernel (PTK) by Moschitti (2006) and SPTK using the word2vec similarity defined before.

Given the small size of such dataset (Only 8% of MSRP instances have additional fragments), we performed a 5-fold cross validation. Table 3 illustrates the Accuracy, Precision, Recall and F_1 of our models. ATC based on SPTK provides the best accuracy, i.e., 68.6%, which is a promising result for this research. The second most accurate classifier uses PTK, which is more flexible than STK.

4.3 Using ATC in PI

We carried out error analysis on PI and observed that the used classifier commits a systematic error: when two sentences share a very similar large part (identical in the extreme case) and one sentence has an ATF, it almost always classifies the sentences as paraphrases, even if the ATF contains important information that invalidates the paraphrase relation. This kind of mistakes can be corrected by ATC.

Thus, we created the following ensemble model: given a pair to be classified, we apply our heuristic for ATF extraction. If the heuristic does not find any fragment in the pair, we only rely on the prediction provided by PI. Otherwise, we combine the prediction of ATC applied to ATF with the one of the PI classifier using a stacking strategy (Wolpert, 1992), i.e., the two predictions become the input features of a third classifier that makes the final decision.

To train this meta-classifier, we need the predictions from ATC and PI computed on a validation set. Hence, we split the training set in two parts: one part is used for training ATC and PI, while the other is classified with the trained models to produce the predictions for the meta-classifier. Then, the roles of the two parts are inverted. The meta-classifier is a linear SVM (Fan et al., 2008) implemented with KeLP.

Note that: (*i*) since we use 5-fold cross-validation, for each fold, we needed to apply the process described above to each fold; and (*ii*) all the learning algorithms and kernels adopt default parameters to also facilitate the reproducibility of our results.

Results. Table 4 reports the comparison between PI and PI combined with ATC (trained with SPTK). The performance is derived only on sentence pairs with ATFs.

The first column indicates the kernel used by the PI classifier, while the second column reports '+' or '-' to indicate if PI is combined with ATC or not, respectively. We note that ATC produces a great improvement, ranging from 8 absolute percent points over LK to about 3 points over SMK+LK, i.e., the state-of-the-art model. As expected, the more accurate the baseline is, the lower the improvement is produced.

It should be noted that only a relative small subset

---

[6]These include *cosine similarities* of lemmas, POS-tags, and n-grams, *longest common substring* and *longest common subsequence* measures and Tree Kernel intra-pair similarities.

[7]http://alt.qcri.org/resources/ancillary

[8]https://github.com/SAG-KeLP

PI	ATC	Acc (%)	P	R	F_1
LK	-	62.2 ± 5.4	57.8 ± 7.0	75.1 ± 7.4	65.3 ± 6.9
LK	+	$70.4 \pm 5.5\dagger$	69.2 ± 6.8	68.2 ± 4.7	68.7 ± 5.7
SMK	-	64.7 ± 6.0	59.0 ± 6.5	84.9 ± 4.6	69.5 ± 5.9
SMK	+	$69.1 \pm 5.5\ddagger$	66.9 ± 6.4	69.7 ± 5.8	68.2 ± 5.9
SMK+LK	-	70.5 ± 4.0	66.3 ± 6.7	77.3 ± 6.1	71.2 ± 5.3
SMK+LK	+	$\mathbf{73.2} \pm 5.2\ddagger$	72.5 ± 5.4	71.3 ± 3.9	$\mathbf{71.8} \pm 3.9$

Table 4: PI classifier performance using ATC. The test set is restricted to examples having additional fragments. $\dagger$ and $\ddagger$ mark statistically significant differences in accuracy compared to the counterpart model not using ATC with confidence levels of 95% and 90%, respectively (t-test).

PI	ATC	Acc (%)	P	R	F_1
LK	-	75.5 ± 0.5	78.6 ± 0.9	87.6 ± 1.9	82.8 ± 0.4
LK	+	$76.2 \pm 1.0\dagger$	79.5 ± 0.1	87.2 ± 2.2	83.1 ± 0.8
SMK	-	75.6 ± 0.8	77.1 ± 0.4	90.7 ± 1.2	83.3 ± 0.7
SMK	+	$75.9 \pm 0.9\dagger$	77.9 ± 1.3	89.7 ± 1.2	83.4 ± 0.6
SMK+LK	-	78.1 ± 1.1	80.7 ± 0.6	88.6 ± 2.1	84.4 ± 0.9
SMK+LK	+	$\mathbf{78.3} \pm 1.1\ddagger$	81.1 ± 0.9	88.2 ± 1.8	$\mathbf{84.5} \pm 0.8$

Table 5: PI classifier performance using ATC on the testset. $\dagger$ and $\ddagger$ mark statistically significant differences in accuracy compared to the counterpart model not using ATC with confidence levels of 95% and 90%, respectively (t-test).

of MSRP contains additional fragments (about 8% when $\tau = 3$). Thus, the impact on the entire PI test-set cannot be large. Tab. 5 reports the accuracy of the previous models on the entire testset. An improvement over all models, state-of-the-art included, can be still observed, although it is less visible.

5 Conclusions

In this paper, we study and design models for learning to detect ancillary information in the context of PI. We used a heuristic rule for selecting additional fragments from paraphrase pairs, which, applied to MSRP, generates our ATF dataset. We manually annotated the latter for training and testing our ATCs.

Our experiments using several kernel models show that ATC can achieve a good accuracy (about 69%) and significantly impact the PI accuracy. Our results suggest that:

(*i*) it is possible to recognize information humans believe is ancillary; and

(*ii*) to go beyond the current results and technology for high-level semantic tasks (e.g., PI), we cannot just rely on shallow similarity features, but we rather need to build components that ana-lyze different aspects of text and then combine the output of the different modules.

In the future, it would be interesting to use methods similar to those successfully used in question answering research, e.g., matching entities in the sentence trees using linked open data (Tymoshenko et al., 2014; Tymoshenko and Moschitti, 2015) or enriching trees with semantic information automatically produced by classifiers, e.g., (Severyn et al., 2013a; Severyn et al., 2013b).

Acknowledgements

This work has been partially supported by the EC project CogNet, 671625 (H2020-ICT-2014-2, Research and Innovation action) and by an IBM Faculty Award.

References

Marco Baroni, Silvia Bernardini, Adriano Ferraresi, and Eros Zanchetta. 2009. The wacky wide web: a collection of very large linguistically processed web-crawled corpora. *Language Resources and Evaluation*, 43(3):209–226.

Chih-Chung Chang and Chih-Jen Lin. 2011. LIBSVM: A library for support vector machines. *ACM Transac-*

tions on Intelligent Systems and Technology, 2:27:1–27:27.

Michael Collins and Nigel Duffy. 2001. Convolution kernels for natural language. In *Advances in Neural Information Processing Systems 14*, pages 625–632. MIT Press.

Danilo Croce, Alessandro Moschitti, and Roberto Basili. 2011. Structured lexical similarity via convolution kernels on dependency trees. In *Proceedings EMNLP*.

Bill Dolan, Chris Quirk, and Chris Brockett. 2004. Unsupervised construction of large paraphrase corpora: Exploiting massively parallel news sources. In *Proc. of COLING '04*, Stroudsburg, PA, USA.

Rong-En Fan, Kai-Wei Chang, Cho-Jui Hsieh, Xiang-Rui Wang, and Chih-Jen Lin. 2008. Liblinear: A library for large linear classification. *J. Mach. Learn. Res.*, 9:1871–1874, June.

Simone Filice, Giovanni Da San Martino, and Alessandro Moschitti. 2015. Structural representations for learning relations between pairs of texts. In *Proceedings of the 53rd Annual Meeting of the Association for Computational Linguistics and the 7th International Joint Conference on Natural Language Processing (Volume 1: Long Papers)*, pages 1003–1013, Beijing, China, July. Association for Computational Linguistics.

Nitin Madnani, Joel Tetreault, and Martin Chodorow. 2012. Re-examining machine translation metrics for paraphrase identification. In *Proceedings of NAACL HLT '12*. ACL.

Tomas Mikolov, Kai Chen, Greg Corrado, and Jeffrey Dean. 2013. Efficient estimation of word representations in vector space. *arXiv preprint arXiv:1301.3781*.

Alessandro Moschitti. 2006. Efficient convolution kernels for dependency and constituent syntactic trees. In *Proc. of ECML'06*, pages 318–329.

Aliaksei Severyn and Alessandro Moschitti. 2012. Structural relationships for large-scale learning of answer re-ranking. In *Proceedings of the 35th international ACM SIGIR conference on Research and development in information retrieval*, pages 741–750. ACM.

Aliaksei Severyn, Massimo Nicosia, and Alessandro Moschitti. 2013a. Building structures from classifiers for passage reranking. In *CIKM*.

Aliaksei Severyn, Massimo Nicosia, and Alessandro Moschitti. 2013b. Learning adaptable patterns for passage reranking. In *CoNLL*.

Richard Socher, Eric H. Huang, Jeffrey Pennington, Andrew Y. Ng, and Christopher D. Manning. 2011. Dynamic pooling and unfolding recursive autoencoders for paraphrase detection. In *Advances in Neural Information Processing Systems 24: 25th Annual Conference on Neural Information Processing Systems 2011*.

Proceedings of a meeting held 12-14 December 2011, Granada, Spain., pages 801–809.

Kateryna Tymoshenko and Alessandro Moschitti. 2015. Assessing the impact of syntactic and semantic structures for answer passages reranking. In *CIKM*, pages 1451–1460. ACM.

Kateryna Tymoshenko, Alessandro Moschitti, and Aliaksei Severyn. 2014. Encoding semantic resources in syntactic structures for passage reranking. In *Proceedings of EACL*.

David H. Wolpert. 1992. Stacked generalization. *Neural Networks*, 5:241–259.

Learning a POS tagger for AAVE-like language[*]

Anna Jørgensen
University of Amsterdam
Science Park 107
1098 XG Amsterdam, NL
jorgensen@uva.nl

Dirk Hovy
University of Copenhagen
Njalsgade 140
2300 Copenhagen S, DK
dirk.hovy@hum.ku.dk

Anders Søgaard
University of Copenhagen
Njalsgade 140
2300 Copenhagen S, DK
soegaard@hum.ku.dk

Abstract

Part-of-speech (POS) taggers trained on newswire perform much worse on domains such as subtitles, lyrics, or tweets. In addition, these domains are also heterogeneous, e.g., with respect to registers and dialects. In this paper, we consider the problem of learning a POS tagger for subtitles, lyrics, and tweets associated with African-American Vernacular English (AAVE). We learn from a mixture of randomly sampled and manually annotated Twitter data and unlabeled data, which we automatically and partially label using mined tag dictionaries. Our POS tagger obtains a tagging accuracy of 89% on subtitles, 85% on lyrics, and 83% on tweets, with up to 55% error reductions over a state-of-the-art newswire POS tagger, and 15-25% error reductions over a state-of-the-art Twitter POS tagger.

1 Introduction

Modern part-of-speech (POS) taggers perform well on what some consider canonical language, as found in domains such as newswire, for which sufficient manually-annotated data is available. For many domains, such as subtitles, lyrics, and tweets, however, labeled data is scarce, if existing, and the performance of off-the-shelf POS taggers is prohibitive of downstream applications.

Furthermore, subtitles, lyrics and tweets are very heterogeneous. Subtitles span from Shakespeare to The Wire, and the lyrics of Elvis Costello are very different from those of Tupac Shakur. Twitter can be anything from teenagers discussing where to go tonight, to researchers discussed the implications of new findings. All three sources of data exhibit a very high degree of linguistic variation, some of which is due to the dialects of the speakers or authors.

In this paper, we use a **corpus of POS-annotated tweets** recently released by CMU,[1] consisting of semi-randomly sampled US tweets. We want to use this corpus to learn a POS tagger for **subtitles, lyrics, and tweets**, which are typically associated with **African-American Vernacular English** (AAVE). We believe our POS tagger can broaden the coverage of NLP tools, and serve as an important tool for large-scale sociolinguistic analyses of language use associated with AAVE (Jørgensen et al., 2015; Stewart, 2014), which relies on the accuracy of these NLP tools.

We combine several recent trends in domain adaptation, namely word embeddings, clusters, sampling, and the use of type constraints. Word representations learned from representative unlabeled data, such as word clusters or embeddings, have been proven useful for increasing the accuracy of NLP tools for low-resource languages and domains (Owoputi et al., 2013; Aldarmaki and Diab, 2015; Gouws and Søgaard, 2015). Since similar words receive similar labels, this can give the model support for words not in the training data. In this paper, we use word clusters and word embeddings in both our baseline and system models.

Using unlabeled data to estimate a target distribution for importance sampling, or for semi-supervised

[*]This work was supported by ERC Starting Grant No. 313695.

[1]https://github.com/brendano/ark-tweet-nlp/tree/master/data/twpos-data-v0.3

Proceedings of NAACL-HLT 2016, pages 1115–1120,
San Diego, California, June 12-17, 2016. ©2016 Association for Computational Linguistics

learning (Søgaard, 2013), as well as wide-coverage, crowd-sourced tag dictionaries to obtain more robust predictions for out-of-domain data have been succesfully used for domain adaptation (Das and Petrov, 2011; Hovy et al., 2015a; Li et al., 2012). In this paper, we use automatically-harvested tag dictionaries for the target variety(/-ies) in two different settings: for labeling the unlabeled data using a technique elaborating on previous work (Li et al., 2012; Wisniewski et al., 2014; Hovy et al., 2015a), and for imposing type constraints at test time in a semi-supervised setting (Garrette and Baldridge, 2013; Plank et al., 2014a). Our best models are obtained using partially labeled training data created using tag dictionaries.

Our contributions We present a POS tagger for AAVE-like language, mining tag dictionaries from various websites and using them to create partially labeled data. Our contributions include: (i) a POS tagger that performs significantly better than existing tools on three datasets containing AAVE markers, (ii) a new domain adaptation algorithm combining ambiguous and cost-sensitive learning, and (iii) an annotated corpus and trained POS tagger made publicly available at `https://bitbucket.org/soegaard/aave-pos16`.

2 Data

For historical reasons, most of the manually annotated corpora available today are newswire corpora. In contrast, very little data is available for domains such as subtitles, lyrics and tweets — especially for language varieties such as AAVE. Learning robust models for AAVE-like language and other language varieties is often further complicated by the absence of standard writing systems (Boujelbane et al., 2013; Bernhard and Ligozat, 2013; Duh and Kirchhoff, 2005).

In this paper, we use three manually annotated data sets, consisting of **subtitles** from the television series *The Wire*, **hip-hop lyrics** from black American artists and **tweets** posted within the southeastern corner of the United States. We do *not* use this data for training, but only for evaluation, so our experiments use unsupervised (or weakly supervised) domain adaptation.

Although the language use in the three domains vary, they have several things in common: the register is very informal, and the subtitles, lyrics and tweets contain **slang terms** such as *loc'd out, cheesing with* and *po'*, **spoken language features** such as *uh-hum, huh* and *oh*, **phonologically-motivated spelling variations** such as *dat mouf, missin'* and *niggas* and **contractions** such as *we'll* and *I'd*. These features are infrequent in or absent from most commonly used training corpora for NLP.

The data was annotated by two trained linguists with experience in analyzing AAVE, using the Universal Part-of-Speech tagset (Petrov et al., 2011). They obtained an inter-annotator agreement score of 93.6%. The test sections consist of 528 sentences (subtitles), 509 sentences (lyrics), and 374 sentences (tweets). In addition, we had 546 sentences of subtitles annotated for development data. Note that we only use one domain for development to avoid overly optimistic performance estimates.

For all experiments, we use a publicly available implementation of structured perceptron[2] and train on the 1827 tweets from the CMU Twitter Corpus (Gimpel et al., 2011). Note that despite the fact that the training data also comes from an informal domain, the distribution of POS tags in this data set is different from those of the test sets. For instance, the percentage of determiners in the CMU Twitter corpus is on average 4% lower than in our test domains, and there are 7% more pronouns in the test sets than in the CMU Twitter corpus.

We also create a large **unlabeled corpus** of data that is representative of our test sets. This corpus, consisting of 4.5M sentences, is created using subtitles from the TV series *The Wire* and *The Boondocks*, English hip-hop lyrics, and tweets from the southeastern states of the US. None of the unlabeled data overlaps with our evaluation datasets. We use this corpus for two purposes: to induce word clusters and embeddings, and to partially annotate a portion of it automatically, which we include in the training data of our ambiguous supervision model (see Section 3 below).

3 Robust learning

Word representations To learn word embeddings from our unlabeled corpus, we use the Gensim im-

---

[2]`https://github.com/coastalcph/rungsted`

plementation of the word2vec algorithm (Mikolov et al., 2013b; Mikolov et al., 2013a). We also learn Brown clusters from a large corpus of tweets[3] (Owoputi et al., 2013), and add both as additional features to our training and test sets. The word representations capture latent similarities between words, but more importantly enable our tagging model to generalize to unseen words.

Partially labeled data Model performance generally benefits from additional data and constraints during training (Hovy and Hovy, 2012; Täckström et al., 2013). We therefore also use the unlabeled data and tag dictionaries as additional, partially labeled training data. For this purpose, we extract a tag dictionary for AAVE-like language from various crowdsourced online lexicons.

Partial constraints from tag dictionaries have previously been used to filter out incorrect label sequences from projected labels from parallel corpora (Wisniewski et al., 2014; Das and Petrov, 2011; Täckström et al., 2013). We use a combination of a publicly available dump of *Wiktionary*[4] (Li et al., 2012), entries from *Hepster's glossary of musical terms*[5], a list of African-American names[6] and *Urban Dictionary*[7] (UD). We augment our tag dictionary by scraping UD for all words in our unlabeled corpus and extracting the part-of-speech information where available. See an example entry for the word *hooch* below, which has five possible parts of speech in our tag dictionary: VERB, NOUN, ADJ, PRON, ADV.

> *Hooch*: "Chewing tobacco commonly placed in the lower lip region. Hooch can be used as a verb, noun, adjective, pronoun, or an adverb."

We use the tag dictionary to label the unlabeled corpus. E.g., when we see the word *hooch*, we assign it the label VERB/NOUN/ADJ/PRON/ADV. We present two ways of using this data for learning

---

[3] http://www.cs.cmu.edu/~ark/TweetNLP/

[4] https://code.google.com/p/wikily-supervised-pos-tagger/

[5] http://www.dinosaurgardens.com/wp-content/uploads/2007/12/hepsters.html

[6] http://www.behindthename.com/submit/names/usage/african-american/3

[7] http://www.urbandictionary.com

better POS models: one where the tag dictionaries are used in an ambiguously supervised setting, and one where they are used as type constraints at prediction time in a self-training setup.

Ambiguous supervision Our algorithm is related to work in cross-lingual transfer (Wisniewski et al., 2014; Das and Petrov, 2011; Täckström et al., 2013) and domain adaptation (Hovy et al., 2015a; Plank et al., 2014a), where tag dictionaries are used to filter projected annotation. We use the tag dictionaries to obtain partial labeling of in-domain training data.

Our baseline sequence labeling algorithm is the structured perceptron (Collins, 2002). This algorithm performs additive updates passing over labeled data, comparing predicted sequences to gold standard sequences. If the predicted sequence is identical to the gold standard, no update is performed. We use a cost-sensitive structured perceptron (Plank et al., 2014b) to learn from the partially labeled data.

Each update for a sequence can be broken down into a series of transition and emission updates, passing over the sequence item-by-item from left to right. For a word like *hooch* labeled VERB/NOUN/ADJ/PRON/ADV, we perform an update proportional to the cost associated with the predicted label. If the predicted label is not in the mined label set, e.g., PRT, we update with a cost of 1.0 (multiplied by the learning rate α); if the predicted label is in the mined label set, we do not update our model. This means that the POS model is not penalized for predicting any of the five supplied labels. We did consider distributing a small cost between the candidates in the mined label sets, but this led to slightly worse performance on our development data.

In the experiments below, we also filter the partially labeled data by the amount of ambiguity observed in our labels. At one extreme, we require *all* words to have a single label, as in fully labeled data. Hovy et al. (2015b) also used a tag dictionary to obtain fully labeled data for domain adaptation. At the other end of the scale, we use all the partially labeled data, allowing up to 12 tags per words. Finally, we also experiment with using only sentences from our unlabeled data such that the tag dictionary assigns at most two (2) or three (3) labels to each word.

We also experimented with using different

Test set	Baselines			Ambiguous	Self-train	Stanford	GATE	CMU
	Baseline	+Cluster	+Clust+Emb					
Lyrics	83.9	85.0	**85.2**	**85.2**	85.0	77.7	83.0	81.5
Subtitles	87.8	88.4	**89.0**	**89.0**	88.8	83.7	87.5	85.6
Tweets	75.0	79.0	78.8	**83.0**	80.0	61.4	77.1	80.0
Average	82.2	84.1	84.3	**85.7**	84.6	74.3	82.5	82.4

Table 1: Main results

amounts of ambiguously labeled data. The best

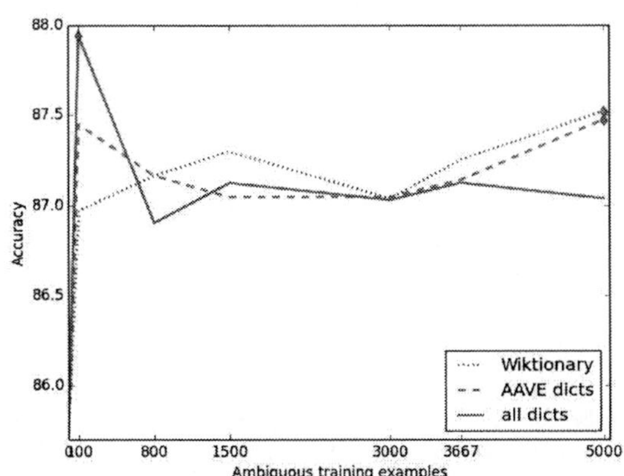

Figure 1: Learning curve ambiguous learning

performing system on development data uses both Wiktionary and the tag dictionaries associated with AAVE, only 100 ambiguously labeled data points for training, a cost of 0.0 for predicting labels in the mined label sets, no threshold on ambiguity levels (but leaving only sentences covered by our tag dictionaries), the CMU Brown clusters, and 20-dimensional word2vec embeddings with a sliding window of nine (9). The results of this system are shown in Table 1 as **Ambiguous**.

Self-training with type constraints Our second system uses the harvested tag dictionary for type constraints when making predictions on the unlabeled data for self-training. The search space of possible labels for each word is simply restricted to the tags provided for that word by the tag dictionary.

For our self-training experiments, we experiment with pool size, but heuristically set the stopping criterion to be when the development set accuracy of the tagger decreases over three consecutive iterations. we obtained the best performance on de-

velopment data using the tag dictionary without Wikipedia, using all entries for type constraints, the CMU Brown clusters, and 10-dimensional embeddings with a window size of five (5). The results of this model are listed in Table 1 as **Self-training**.

Pre-Normalization We also experimented with test-time pre-normalization of the input, using the normalization dictionary of Han et al. (2011), but this led to worse performance on development data.

4 Results and error analysis

Table 1 shows the baseline accuracies, with and without clusters and embeddings, as well as the performance of the two developed systems described above. All results for both ambiguous supervision and self-training with type constraints significantly outperform the simple baseline with $p < 0.01$ (Wilcoxon). The system using ambiguous supervision is also significantly better than the baseline with clusters and word embeddings on the Twitter data. The fact that we generally see worse performance on Twitter data than on the two other data set (even though the systems were trained on Twitter data) can be attributed to a higher type-token ratio.

We also provide the accuracies of three publicly available POS taggers in Table 1. The three POS systems are the bidirectional Stanford Log-linear POS Tagger[8] , the GATE Twitter POS tagger[9] , and the CMU POS Tagger.[10] We observe that our ambiguous learning system outperforms all three systems on all test sets.

---

[8] http://nlp.stanford.edu/software/tagger.shtml
[9] https://gate.ac.uk/wiki/twitter-postagger.html
[10] https://github.com/brendano/ark-tweet-nlp/

Test set	Lyrics	Subtitles	Tweets	Av.
Baseline	64%	78%	48%	63%
Ambiguous	**71%**	**83%**	**78%**	**77%**
Self-train	70%	82%	61%	71%

Table 2: Accuracies on unseen words

Our improvements are primarily due to better performance on unseen words. Both systems improve the accuracy on OOV items for all three test sets, with the ambiguous learning system reducing the error by an average of 14%, and the self-training system reducing it by 7.7% on average. However, we also see an average increase in performance on known words of 1% for both systems. This increase is highest for tweets (2%) and around 0.5% for the subtitles and hip-hop lyrics test sets. The main reason for the increased overall performances of our systems is therefore the improved accuracy on OOV words. Table 2 shows that the accuracy on OOVs increases on all three test sets for both developed systems over baseline.

The OOV words learned in these two test sets are mainly verbs such as *sittin'*, *gettin'* and *feelin'* (g-dropped spellings), and words that are infrequent in canonical written language such as *'em* and *ho*.

We observe that our systems improve performance on traditionally closed word classes such as pronouns, adpositions, determiners and conjunctions. These increases can be ascribed to the systems having learned from the additional information provided on spelling variations such as *'cause, fo'* and *ya* and unknown entities such as *dis, dat, sum*.

Finally, we note that increasing the number of training examples for ambiguous learning seems to come with diminishing returns. The learning curve is presented in Figure 1.

5   Conclusions

We explore several techniques to learn better POS models for AAVE-like subtitles, lyrics, and tweets from a manually annotated Twitter corpus. Our systems perform significantly better than three state-of-the-art POS taggers for English, with error reductions up to 55%. The improvements were shown to be primarily due to better handling of OOV words.

References

Hanan Aldarmaki and Mona Diab. 2015. Robust part-of-speech tagging of Arabic text. In *Proceedings of the Second Workshop on Arabic Natural Language Processing*, Beijing, China.

Delphine Bernhard and Anne-Laure Ligozat. 2013. Hassle-free pos-tagging for the Alsatian dialects. In Marcos Zampieri and Sascha Diwersy, editors, *Non-Standard Data Sources in Corpus Based-Research*, pages 85–92. ZSM Studien.

Rahma Boujelbane, Meriem Ellouze Khemekhem, and Lamia Hadrich Belguith. 2013. Mapping rules for building a Tunisian dialect lexicon and generating corpora. In *International Joint Conference on Natural Language Processing*, pages 419–428.

Michael Collins. 2002. Discriminative Training Methods for Hidden Markov Models: Theory and Experiments with Perceptron Algorithms. In *EMNLP*.

Dipanjan Das and Slav Petrov. 2011. Unsupervised part-of-speech tagging with bilingual graph-based projections. In *ACL*, pages 256–263.

Kevin Duh and Katrin Kirchhoff. 2005. Pos tagging of dialectal Arabic: A minimally supervised approach. In *Proceedings in the ACL Workshop on Computational Approaches to Semitic Languages*.

Dan Garrette and Jason Baldridge. 2013. Learning a part-of-speech tagger from two hours of annotation. In *Proceedings of NAACL-HLT*, pages 138–147.

Kevin Gimpel, Nathan Schneider, Brendan OConnor, Dipanjan Das, Daniel Mills, Jacob Eisenstein, Michael Heilman, Dani Yogatama, Jeffrey Flanigan, and Noah A. Smith. 2011. Part-of-speech tagging for twitter: Annotation, features, and experiments. In *ACL*.

Stephen Gouws and Anders Søgaard. 2015. Simple task-specific bilingual word embeddings. In *Human Language Technologies: The 2015 Annual Conference of the North American Chapter of the ACL*, pages 1386–1390.

Bo Han and Timothy Baldwin. 2011. Lexical Normalisation of Short Text Messages: Makn Sens a #twitter. In *ACL*.

Dirk Hovy and Eduard Hovy. 2012. Exploiting partial annotations with em training. In *Proceedings of the NAACL-HLT Workshop on the Induction of Linguistic Structure*, pages 31–38. Association for Computational Linguistics.

Dirk Hovy, Barbara Plank, Héctor Martínez Alonso, and Anders Søgaard. 2015a. Mining for unambiguous instances to adapt part-of-speech taggers to new domains. In *Human Language Technologies: The 2015 Annual Conference of the North American Chapter of the ACL*, pages 1256–1261.

Dirk Hovy, Barbara Plank, Héctor Martínez Alonso, and Anders Søgaard. 2015b. Mining for unambiguous instances to adapt pos taggers to new domains. In *NAACL-HLT*.

Anna Jørgensen, Dirk Hovy, and Anders Søgaard. 2015. Challenges of studying and processing dialects in social media. In *Proceedings of the ACL Workshop on Noisy User-generated Text*.

Shen Li, João V. Graça, and Ben Taskar. 2012. Wikily supervised part-of-speech tagging. In *Proceedings of the 2012 Joint Conference on Empirical Methods in Natural Language Processing and Computational Natural Language Learning*.

T. Mikolov, K. Chen, G Corrado, and J. Dean. 2013a. Efficient estimation of word representations in vector space. *ArXiv e-prints*.

T. Mikolov, W.T. Yih, and G. Zweig. 2013b. Linguistic regularities in continuous space word representations. In *Proceedings of NAACL-HLT*.

Olutobi Owoputi, Brendan O'Connor, Chris Dyer, Kevin Gimpel, Nathan Schneider, and Noah A. Smith. 2013. Improved part-of-speech tagging for online conversational text with word clusters. In *Proceedings of NAACL-HLT*.

Slav Petrov, Dipanjan Das, and Ryan McDonald. 2011. A universal part-of-speech tagset. In *Proceedings of LREC*.

Barbara Plank, Dirk Hovy, Ryan McDonald, and Anders Søgaard. 2014a. Adapting taggers to twitter with not-so-distant supervision. In *Proceedings of COLING 2014, the 25th International Conference on Computational Linguistics: Technical Papers*, pages 1783–1792.

Barbara Plank, Dirk Hovy, and Anders Søgaard. 2014b. Learning part-of-speech taggers with inter-annotator agreement loss. In *EACL*.

Anders Søgaard. 2013. *Semi-supervised learning and domain adaptation for NLP*. Morgan & Claypool.

Ian Stewart. 2014. Now We Stronger Than Ever: African-American syntax on Twitter. In *Proceedings of the Student Research Workshop to the 14th Conference of the European Chapter of the Association for Computational Linguistics*, pages 26–30, Gothenburg, Sweden, April.

Oscar Täckström, Dipanjan Das, Slav Petrov, Ryan McDonald, and Joakim Nivre, 2013. *Token and Type Constraints for Cross-Lingual Part-of-Speech Tagging*, pages 1–12. Association for Computational Linguistics.

Guillaume Wisniewski, Nicolas Pécheux, Sophir Gahbiche-Braham, and François Yvon. 2014. Cross-lingual part-of-speech tagging through ambiguous learning. In *Proceedings of the 2014 Conference on Empirical Methods in Natural Language Processing*.

PIC a Different Word: A Simple Model for Lexical Substitution in Context

Stephen Roller
Department of Computer Science
The University of Texas at Austin
roller@cs.utexas.edu

Katrin Erk
Department of Linguistics
The University of Texas at Austin
katrin.erk@mail.utexas.edu

Abstract

The Lexical Substitution task involves selecting and ranking lexical paraphrases for a target word in a given sentential context. We present *PIC*, a simple measure for estimating the appropriateness of substitutes in a given context. PIC outperforms another simple, comparable model proposed in recent work, especially when selecting substitutes from the entire vocabulary. Analysis shows that PIC improves over baselines by incorporating frequency biases into predictions.

1 Introduction

Lexical substitution (McCarthy and Navigli, 2009) is a task in which word meaning in context is described not through dictionary senses but through substitutes (paraphrases) chosen by annotators. For example, consider the following usage of the adjective *bright*: "The *bright* girl was reading a book." Valid lexical substitutions for *bright* include adjectives like *smart* and *intelligent*, but not words like *luminous* or *colorful*.

Originally introduced as a SemEval task in 2007, lexical substitution has often been used to evaluate the ability of distributional models to handle polysemy (Erk and Padó, 2008; Thater et al., 2010; Dinu and Lapata, 2010; Van de Cruys et al., 2011; Melamud et al., 2015b; Melamud et al., 2015a; Kawakami and Dyer, 2015). Recent models include a simple but high-performing method by Melamud et al. (2015b), which uses the Skip-gram model of Mikolov et al. (Mikolov et al., 2013) to compute the probability of a substitute given a sentence context,

and integrates it with the probability of the substitute given the target. The current state of the art is held by another model of Melamud (Melamud et al., 2015a), which uses a more complex architecture.

In this paper we build on the simple model of Melamud et al. (2015b), as simpler methods are easier to recreate and integrate into larger pipelines.[1] We explore a weak form of supervision that recently has proved beneficial on many NLP tasks: using a language modeling task on unannotated data. We find a strong improvement over Melamud's simple measure, particularly on the all-words ranking task. Interestingly, analysis of *PIC* shows it improves over baselines by incorporating frequency biases into predictions.

2 Prior Work

In the lexical substitution task, an annotator is given a target word in context and generates one or more substitutes. As multiple annotators label a target, the result is a weighted list of substitutes, where weights indicate how many annotators chose a particular substitute (McCarthy and Navigli, 2009).

There have been numerous approaches on the lexical substitution task of varying complexity and using various lexical resources (McCarthy and Navigli, 2007). Some approaches focus on explicitly modeling an in-context vector (Erk and Padó, 2008; Dinu and Lapata, 2010; Thater et al., 2010; Van de Cruys et al., 2011; Kremer et al., 2014; Kawakami and Dyer, 2015), while others approach it using more sophisticated pipelines, in both super-

---

[1]Code and models available at https://github.com/stephenroller/naacl2016.

Proceedings of NAACL-HLT 2016, pages 1121–1126,
San Diego, California, June 12-17, 2016. ©2016 Association for Computational Linguistics

vised (Szarvas et al., 2013) and unsupervised (Melamud et al., 2015a) settings. The latter is the current state-of-art system, and is based around generating and pruning second-order word representations using language models.

In this work, we limit our comparisons to the model of Melamud et al. (2015b), a method which performs nearly state-of-art, is extremely easy to implement, and is a good testbed for focused hypotheses. They propose a novel measure which uses dependency-based word and context embeddings derived from Skip-gram Negative Sampling algorithm (SGNS) (Mikolov et al., 2013; Levy and Goldberg, 2014a). Their measure *addCos* for estimating the appropriateness of a substitute s as a substitute for t in the context $C = \{c_1, c_2, \ldots\}$ is defined as follows:[2]

$$\text{addCos}(s|t, C) = \cos(s, t) + \sum_{c \in C} \cos(s, c).$$

They also propose a similar measure *balAddCos*, which controls for the context size:

$$\text{balAddCos}(s|t, C) = |C|\cos(s, t) + \sum_{c \in C} \cos(s, c).$$

3 Proposed Measure

We propose a new measure, called Probability-in-Context (PIC), based on SGNS context vectors to estimate the appropriateness of a lexical substitute. Similar to *balAddCos*, the measure has two equally-weighted, independent components measuring the appropriateness of the substitute for both the target and the context, each taking the form of a softmax:[3]

$$\text{PIC}(s|t, C) = P(s|t) \times P(s|C)$$

$$P(s|t) = \frac{1}{Z_t} \exp\left\{s^T t\right\}$$

$$P(s|C) = \frac{1}{Z_C} \exp\left\{\sum_{c \in C} s^T [Wc + b]\right\}$$

---

[2] We abuse notation and allow s, t and c to refer to both the lexical items and their corresponding vectors.

[3] Note that $P(s|t)$ measures paradigmatic similarity of s and t, while $P(s|C)$ is syntagmatic fit to the context. For $P(s|t)$, Mikolov et al. (2013) show that cosine similarity of SGNS embeddings predicts paradigmatic similarity. $P(s|C)$ can be interpreted as the PMI of s and C (Levy and Goldberg, 2014b).

The values Z_t and Z_C are normalizing constants to make sure each distribution sums to one. This measure has two free parameters, W and b, which act as a linear transformation over the context vectors. These parameters are estimated from the *original corpus*, and are trained to maximize the prediction of a *target* from only its syntactic contexts (c.f. Section 4.4). Given this formulation, a natural question is why not train the embeddings to optimize the softmax directly? We choose to parameterize the measure rather than the embeddings because (i) SGNS embeddings are already popular and readily available and (ii) it ensures the quality of embeddings remains constant across experimental settings.

To measure the importance of parameterization, we also compare to a non-parameterized PIC (*nPIC*), which only uses a softmax over the dot product:

$$\text{nPIC}(s|t, C) = P(s|t) \times P_n(s|C)$$

$$P_n(s|C) = \frac{1}{Z_n} \exp\left\{\sum_{c \in C} s^T c\right\}$$

4 Experimental Setup

We compare our proposed measures to three baselines: OOC, the Out-of-Context cosine similarity between the word and target ($\cos(s, t)$), and the *addCos* and *balAddCos* measures. It is important to note that existing papers on Lexical Substitution all contain subtle differences in experimental setup (vocabulary coverage, candidate pooling, etc.). We compare to our own re-implementation of the baselines, so our numbers differ slightly from those in the literature.

4.1 Data sets

We evaluate on three lexical substitution data sets.

SE07: The data set used in the original SemEval 2007 shared task (McCarthy and Navigli, 2007) consists of 201 words manually chosen to exhibit polysemy, with 10 sentences per target. For a given target in a particular context, five annotators were asked to propose up to 3 substitutes. As all our experiments are unsupervised, we always evaluate over the entire data set, rather than the original held-out test set.

Coinco: The Concepts-in-Context data set (Kremer et al., 2014) is a large lexical substitution corpus with proposed substitutes for nearly all content words in roughly 2,500 sentences from a mixture of genres (newswire, emails, and fiction). Crowdsourcing was used to obtain a minimum of 6 contextually-appropriate substitutes for over 15k tokens.

TSWI2: The Turk bootstrap Word Sense Inventory 2.0 (Biemann, 2012) is a crowdsourced lexical substitution corpus focused on about 1,000 common English nouns. The data set contains nearly 25,000 contextual uses of these nouns. Though the data set was originally constructed to induce a word-sense lexicon based on common substitution patterns, here we only use it as a lexical substitution data set.

4.2 Task Evaluation

We compare models on two variations of the lexical substitution task: candidate ranking and all-words ranking. In the *candidate ranking* task, the model is given a list of candidates and must select which are most appropriate for the given target. We follow prior work in pooling candidates from all substitutions for a given lemma and POS over all contexts, and measure performance using Generalized Average Precision (GAP). GAP is similar to Mean Average Precision, but weighted by the number of times a substitute was given by annotators. See Thater et al. (2010) for full details of the candidate ranking task.

The second task is the much more difficult task of *all-words ranking*. In this task, the model is not provided any gold list of candidates, but must select possible substitutes from the entire vocabulary.[4] We measure performance by (micro) mean Precision@1 and P@3: that is, of a system's top one/three guesses, the percentage also given by human annotators. These evaluation metrics are similar to the *best* and *oot* metrics reported in the literature, but we find P@1 and P@3 easier to interpret and analyze.

4.3 Word and Context Vectors

We use the word and context vectors released by Melamud et al. (2015b),[5] which were previously shown to perform strongly in lexical substitution tasks. These embeddings were computed from a cor-

pus of (word, relation, context) tuples extracted from ukWaC and processed using the dependency-based word2vec model of Levy and Goldberg (2014a). These embeddings contain 600d vectors for 173k words and about 1M syntactic contexts.

4.4 Training Procedure

To train the W and b parameters, we extract tokens with syntactic contexts using the same corpus (ukWaC), parser (Chen and Manning, 2014), and extraction procedure used to generate the embeddings. See (Melamud et al., 2015b) for complete details. After extracting every token with its contexts, we randomly sample 10% of the data to reduce computation time, leaving us with 190M tokens for training W and b. We use sampled softmax to reduce training time (Jean et al., 2015), sampling 15 negative candidates uniformly from the vocabulary, optimizing cross-entropy over just these 16 words per sample. We optimize W and b in one epoch of stochastic gradient descent (SGD) with a learning rate of 0.01, momentum of 0.98, and a batch size of 2048. We found all of these hyperparameters worked well initially, and did not tune them.

5 Results

Table 1 contains results for all measures across all experimental settings.

The first observation we make is that the *PIC* measure performs best in all evaluations on all data sets by a significant margin.[6] In the GAP evaluation, all measures perform substantially better than the OOC baseline, and the *nPIC* measure performs comparably to *balAddCos*. We note that context-sensitive measures give the most improvement in SE07, reflecting its greater emphasis on polysemy.

As we turn to the all-words ranking evaluations, we observe that the absolute numbers are much lower, reflecting the increased difficulty of the task. We also see the that *nPIC* and *PIC* both improve greatly over all baselines: The *nPIC* measure is a relative 30% improvement over *balAddCos* in SE07 and Coinco, and the *PIC* measure is a relative 50% improvement over *balAddCos* in 5 evaluations.

Since both measures have a clear improvement over the baselines, especially in the more difficult

---

[4] All models are also hardcoded not to predict substitutes with the same stem as the target, e.g. for the *bright girl* example, models cannot predict *brighter* or *brightest*.

[5] http://www.cs.biu.ac.il/nlp/resources/downloads/lexsub_embeddings

[6] Wilcoxon signed-rank test, $p < 0.01$

Measure	SE07	Coinco	TWSI2
Candidate Ranking (GAP)			
OOC	44.2	44.5	57.9
addCos	51.2	46.3	62.2
balAddCos	49.6	46.5	61.3
nPIC	51.3	46.4	61.8
PIC	**52.4**	**48.3**	**62.8**
All-Words Ranking (Mean Precision@1)			
OOC	11.7	10.9	9.8
addCos	12.9	10.5	7.9
balAddCos	13.4	11.8	9.8
nPIC	17.3	16.3	11.1
PIC	**19.7**	**18.2**	**13.7**
All-Words Ranking (Mean Precision@3)			
OOC	9.7	8.6	7.0
addCos	9.0	7.9	6.1
balAddCos	9.8	9.1	7.4
nPIC	13.1	12.1	7.9
PIC	**14.8**	**13.8**	**10.1**

Table 1: Lexical Substitution results for candidate ranking (GAP) and all-words ranking tasks (P@1, P@3).

all-words task, we next strive to understand why.

5.1 Analysis

We first an few cherry and lemon-picked examples to give intuitions about why our model performs better. Table 2 contains the cherry example, where our model performs better than prior work. While OOC and *balAddCos* both suggest replacements with reasonable semantics, but are all misspelled. *nPIC* and *PIC* only pick words with the correct spellings, with the exception of "realy."

Table 3 shows the lemon example, where our model performs worse. We notice that the unusual "sea-change" item is prominent in the OOC and *balAddCos* models, but has dropped from the rankings in our models. From these and other examples, we hypothesize the model is simply guessing more frequent terms.

We consider a few experiments with this hypothesis that the measures do better because they capture better *unigram* statistics than the baselines. Recent literature found that the vector norm of SGNS embeddings correlates strongly with word frequency (Wilson and Schakel, 2015). We verified this for

ourselves, computing the Spearman's rank correlation between the corpus unigram frequency and the vector length and found $rho = 0.90$, indicating the two correlate very strongly. Since the dot product is also the unnormalized cosine, it follows that *nPIC* and *PIC* should depend on unigram frequency.

To verify that the *nPIC* and *PIC* measures are indeed preferring more frequent substitutes, we compare the single best predictions (P@1) of the *balAddCos* and *nPIC* systems on all-words prediction on Coinco. Roughly 42% of the predictions made by the systems are identical, but of the remaining items, 74% of predictions made by *nPIC* have a higher corpus frequency than *balAddCos* (where chance is 50%). We find *balAddCos* and *PIC* make the same prediction 37% of the time, and *PIC* predicts a more frequent word in 83% of remaining items. The results for SE07 and TWSI2 are similar.

This indicates that the unigram bias is even higher for *PIC* than *nPIC*. To gain more insight, we manually inspect the learned parameters W and b. We find that the W matrix is nearly diagonal, with the values along the diagonal normally distributed around $\mu = 1.11$ ($\sigma = 0.02$) and the rest of the matrix normally distributed roughly around 0 (μ=2e-5, σ=0.02). This is to say, the *PIC* model is approximately learning to *exaggerate* the magnitude of the dot product, $s^T c$. This suggests one could even replace our parameter W with a single scaling parameter, though we leave this for future work.

To inspect the bias b, we compute the inner product of the b vector with the word embedding matrix, to find each word's a priori bias, and correlate it with word frequencies. We find $rho = 0.25$, indicating that b is also capturing unigram statistics.

Is it helpful in lexical substitution to prefer more frequent substitutes? To test this, we pool all annotator responses for all contexts in Coinco, and find the number of times a substitute is given correlates strongly with frequency ($rho = 0.54$).

These results emphasize the importance of incorporating unigram frequencies when attempting the lexical substitution task (as with many other tasks in NLP). Compared to cosine, the dot product in *nPIC* stresses unigram frequency, and the parameters W and b strengthen this tendency.

OOC	balAddCos	nPIC	PIC
You can sort of challenge them well, did you **really** know the time when you said yes?			
trully	proably	realy	**actually**
actually	trully	**truly**	**truly**
actaully	acutally	**actually**	already
acutally	actaully	hardly	barely
proably	probaly	**definitely**	just

Table 2: Example where the *PIC* performs better in the All-Words Ranking task. The target word and correct answers are bolded.

OOC	balAddCos	nPIC	PIC
As a general rule, point of view should not **change** during a scene.			
sea-change	**alter**	reoccur	re-occur
alter	sea-change	re-occur	appear
shift	**shift**	prevail	overstate
downshift	downshift	deviate	differ
re-configure	increase/decrease	divulged	disappear

Table 3: Example where the *PIC* performs worse the All-Words Ranking task. The target word and correct answers are bolded.

6 Conclusion

We have presented *PIC*, a simple new measure for assessing the appropriateness of a substitute in a particular context for the Lexical Substitution task. The measure assesses the fit of the substitute both to the target word and the sentence context. It significantly outperforms comparable baselines from prior work, and does not require any additional lexical resources. An analysis indicates its performance improvements derive primarily from a tendency to lean more strongly on unigram statistics than baselines. In future work, our measure could be simplified by implementing the bias as a single scaling parameter.

Acknowledgments

We would like to thank Karl Pichotta, Martin Reidl, and the anonymous reviewers for their helpful comments and suggestions. This research was supported by the NSF grant IIS 1523637 We acknowledge the Texas Advanced Computing Center for providing grid resources that contributed to these results.

References

Chris Biemann. 2012. Turk bootstrap word sense inventory 2.0: A large-scale resource for lexical substitution. In *Proceedings of the Eighth International Conference on Language Resources and Evaluation*, pages 4038–4042, Istanbul, Turkey, May. European Language Resources Association.

Danqi Chen and Christopher Manning. 2014. A fast and accurate dependency parser using neural networks. In *Proceedings of the 2014 Conference on Empirical Methods in Natural Language Processing*, pages 740–750, Doha, Qatar, October. Association for Computational Linguistics.

Georgiana Dinu and Mirella Lapata. 2010. Measuring distributional similarity in context. In *Proceedings of the 2010 Conference on Empirical Methods in Natural Language Processing*, pages 1162–1172, Cambridge, MA, October. Association for Computational Linguistics.

Katrin Erk and Sebastian Padó. 2008. A structured vector space model for word meaning in context. In *Proceedings of the 2008 Conference on Empirical Methods in Natural Language Processing*, pages 897–906, Honolulu, Hawaii, October. Association for Computational Linguistics.

Sébastien Jean, Kyunghyun Cho, Roland Memisevic, and Yoshua Bengio. 2015. On using very large target vocabulary for neural machine translation. In *Proceedings of the 53rd Annual Meeting of the Association for Computational Linguistics and the 7th International Joint Conference on Natural Language Processing*, pages 1–10, Beijing, China, July. Association for Computational Linguistics.

Kazuya Kawakami and Chris Dyer. 2015. Learning to

Represent Words in Context with Multilingual Supervision. *ArXiv e-prints*, abs/1511.04623, November.

Gerhard Kremer, Katrin Erk, Sebastian Padó, and Stefan Thater. 2014. What substitutes tell us - analysis of an "all-words" lexical substitution corpus. In *Proceedings of the 14th Conference of the European Chapter of the Association for Computational Linguistics*, pages 540–549, Gothenburg, Sweden, April. Association for Computational Linguistics.

Omer Levy and Yoav Goldberg. 2014a. Dependency-based word embeddings. In *Proceedings of the 52nd Annual Meeting of the Association for Computational Linguistics*, pages 302–308, Baltimore, Maryland, June. Association for Computational Linguistics.

Omer Levy and Yoav Goldberg. 2014b. Neural word embedding as implicit matrix factorization. In *Advances in Neural Information Processing Systems 27*, pages 2177–2185. Curran Associates, Inc.

Diana McCarthy and Roberto Navigli. 2007. Semeval-2007 task 10: English lexical substitution task. In *Proceedings of the Fourth International Workshop on Semantic Evaluations*, pages 48–53, Prague, Czech Republic, June. Association for Computational Linguistics.

Diana McCarthy and Robert Navigli. 2009. The English lexical substitution task. *Language Resources and Evaluation*, 43(2):139–159. Special Issue on Computational Semantic Analysis of Language: SemEval-2007 and Beyond.

Oren Melamud, Ido Dagan, and Jacob Goldberger. 2015a. Modeling word meaning in context with substitute vectors. In *Proceedings of the 2015 Conference of the North American Chapter of the Association for Computational Linguistics: Human Language Technologies*, pages 472–482, Denver, Colorado, May–June. Association for Computational Linguistics.

Oren Melamud, Omer Levy, and Ido Dagan. 2015b. A simple word embedding model for lexical substitution. In *Proceedings of the 1st Workshop on Vector Space Modeling for Natural Language Processing*, pages 1–7, Denver, Colorado, June. Association for Computational Linguistics.

Tomas Mikolov, Kai Chen, Greg Corrado, and Jeffrey Dean. 2013. Efficient estimation of word representations in vector space. In *Proceedings of International Conference on Learning Representations*.

György Szarvas, Chris Biemann, and Iryna Gurevych. 2013. Supervised all-words lexical substitution using delexicalized features. In *Proceedings of the 2013 Conference of the North American Chapter of the Association for Computational Linguistics: Human Language Technologies*, pages 1131–1141.

Stefan Thater, Hagen Fürstenau, and Manfred Pinkal. 2010. Contextualizing semantic representations using syntactically enriched vector models. In *Proceedings of the 48th Annual Meeting of the Association for Computational Linguistics*, pages 948–957, Uppsala, Sweden, July. Association for Computational Linguistics.

Tim Van de Cruys, Thierry Poibeau, and Anna Korhonen. 2011. Latent vector weighting for word meaning in context. In *Proceedings of the 2011 Conference on Empirical Methods in Natural Language Processing*, pages 1012–1022, Edinburgh, Scotland, UK., July. Association for Computational Linguistics.

Benjamin J. Wilson and Adriaan M. J. Schakel. 2015. Controlled experiments for word embeddings. *ArXiv e-prints*, abs/1510.02675, October.

Bootstrapping Translation Detection and Sentence Extraction
from Comparable Corpora

Kriste Krstovski[†,§] **and David A. Smith**[‡]

[†]Harvard-Smithsonian Center for Astrophysics, Cambridge, MA

[§]College of Information and Computer Sciences, University of Massachusetts Amherst, Amherst, MA

[‡]College of Computer and Information Science, Northeastern University, Boston, MA

kkrstovski@cfa.harvard.edu, dasmith@ccs.neu.edu

Abstract

Most work on extracting parallel text from comparable corpora depends on linguistic resources such as seed parallel documents or translation dictionaries. This paper presents a simple baseline approach for bootstrapping a parallel collection. It starts by observing documents published on similar dates and the co-occurrence of a small number of identical tokens across languages. It then uses fast, online inference for a latent variable model to represent multilingual documents in a shared topic space where it can do efficient nearest-neighbor search. Starting from the Gigaword collections in English and Spanish, we train a translation system that outperforms one trained on the WMT'11 parallel training set.

1 Introduction

In statistical machine translation (SMT), the quality of the translation model is highly dependent on the amount of parallel data used to build it. Parallel data has usually been generated through the process of human translation, which imposes significant costs when building systems for new languages and domains. To alleviate this problem, researchers have considered comparable corpora—a collection of multilingual documents that are only topically aligned but not necessary translations of each other (Fung and Cheung, 2004). While most previous approaches for mining comparable corpora heavily depend on initializing the learning process with some translation dictionaries or parallel text, we use multilingual topic models to detect document translation pairs and extract parallel sentences with only

minimum cross-language prior knowledge: the publication dates of articles and the tendency of some vocabulary to overlap across languages. Processing only four years of Gigaword news stories in English and Spanish, we are able to outperform the WMT'11 baseline system trained on parallel News Commentary corpus (Table 1).

2 Prior Work on Comparable Corpora

Most previous, if not all, approaches for mining comparable corpora heavily depend on bilingual resources, such as translation lexica, bitext, and/or a pretrained baseline MT system. This paper, in contrast, investigates building MT systems from comparable corpora without such resources. In a widely cited early paper, Munteanu and Marcu (2005) use a bilingual dictionary and a collection of parallel sentences to train IBM Model 1 and a maximum entropy classifier to determine whether two sentences are translations of each other. Tillmann and Xu (2009) and Smith et al. (2010) detect parallel sentences by training IBM Model 1 and maximum entropy classifiers, respectively. In later work on detecting sentence and phrase translation pairs, Cettolo et al. (2010) and Hoang et al. (2014) use SMT systems to translate candidate documents; Quirk et al. (2007) use parallel data to train a translation equivalence model; and Ture and Lin (2012) use a translation lexicon to build a scoring function for parallel documents. More recently, Ling et al. (2013) trained IBM Model 1 on bitext to detect translationally equivalent phrase pairs within single microblog posts. Abdul-Rauf and Schwenk (2009), Uszkoreit et al. (2010), and Gahbiche-Braham et al. (2011),

Proceedings of NAACL-HLT 2016, pages 1127–1132,

rather than trying to detect translated sentence pairs directly, translate the entire source language side of a comparable corpus into the target language with a baseline SMT system and then search for corresponding documents.

On the other hand, there exist approaches that mine comparable corpora without any prior translation information or parallel data. Examples of this approach are rarer, and we briefly mention two: Enright and Kondrak (2007) use singleton words (hapax legomena) to represent documents in a bilingual collection for the task of detecting document translation pairs, and Krstovski and Smith (2011) construct a vocabulary of overlapping words to represent documents in multilingual collections. The latter approach demonstrates high precision vs. recall values on various language pairs from different languages and writing systems when detecting translation pairs on a document level such as Europarl sessions. Recently proposed approaches, such as (Klementiev et al., 2012) use monolingual corpora to estimate phrase-based SMT parameters. Unlike our paper, however, they do not demonstrate an end-to-end SMT system trained without any parallel data.

Our approach differs from these and other previous approaches by not relying on any initial translation dictionary or any bitext to train a seed SMT system. Therefore, the primary experimental comparison that we perform is between no bitext at all and a system trained with some bitext.

3 Bootstrapping Approach

Our bootstrapping approach (Figure 1) is a two-stage system that used the Overlapping Cosine Distance (OCD) approach of Krstovski and Smith (2011) as its first step. OCD outputs a ranked list of candidate document pairs, which are then fed through a sentence-alignment system (Moore, 2002). A polylingual topic model (PLTM) (Mimno et al., 2009) is then trained on the aligned portions of these documents. Using the trained model, we infer topics on the whole comparable training set. Once represented as points in the topic space, documents are then compared for similarity using divergence based metrics such as Hellinger (He) distance. Results from these comparisons create a single ranked list of text translation pairs, which are on a sub document

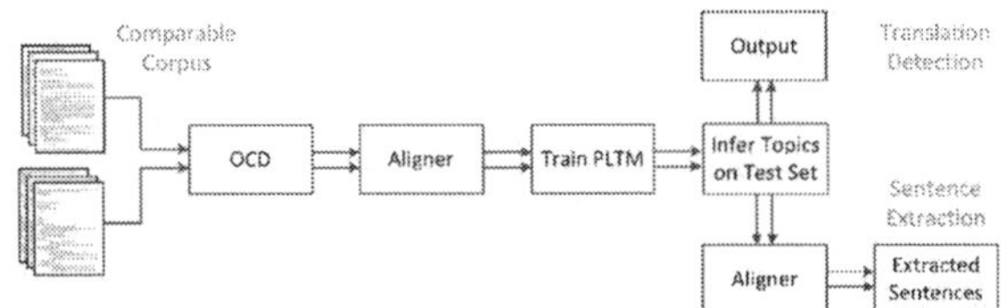

Figure 1: The bilingual collection processing pipeline.

ment length level. From this single ranked list, using thresholding, we again extract the top n candidate translation pairs that are then fed to an aligner for further refinement.

3.1 Discovering Document Translation Pairs

For a given comparable corpus, OCD assumes that there is a set of words that exist in both languages that could be used as features in order to discriminate between documents that are translations of each other, documents that carry similar content, and documents that are not related. Firstly, for each language in the collection a vocabulary is created which consists of all word types seen in the corpora of that language. Words found in both source (s) and target (t) languages are extracted and the overlapping list of words are then used as dimensions for constructing a feature vector template. Documents in both languages are then represented using the template vector whose dimensions are the tf·idf values computed on the overlapping words which we now consider as features. While the number of overlapping words is dependent on the families of the source and target languages and their orthography, Krstovski and Smith (2011) showed that this approach yields good results across language pairs from different families and writing systems such as English-Greek, English-Bulgarian and English-Arabic where, as one would expect, most shared words are numbers and named entities.

We compare these vector representations efficiently using Cosine (Cos) distance and locality sensitive hashing (Charikar, 2002). This results in a single ranked list of all document pairs. Compared to the traditional cross-language information retrieval (CLIR) task where a set of document queries is known in advance, there is no prior information on the documents in the source language that may or may not have translation documents in the target language of the collection. Due to the length invariance of Cos distance, the single ranked list may contain document pairs with high similarity value across all documents in the target language. This issue in OCD is resolved by applying length and diversity filtering. Length filtering removes translation pairs where the length of the target document t is not within $\pm 20\%$ of the source document s length, $lf : 0.8 \leq |s| / |t| \leq 1.2$. For a given source document, diversity filtering is done by allowing only the top five ranked target document pairs to be considered in the single ranked list. Limiting the number of target documents for a given source document may discard actual document translation pairs such as in a comparable corpus of news stories where documents in the target language originate from large number of news source. While it may restrict more document translation pairs to be discovered, the diversity filtering, on the other hand prevents from limiting the number of discovered similar and translation documents to be from the same topic and domain and thus introduces diversity on another, domain or topic based, level.

3.2 Representing Multilingual Collections with Topics

Latent topic models are statistical models of text that discover underlying hidden topics in a text collection. We use PLTM (Mimno et al., 2009), a multilingual variant of LDA, which assumes that document tuples in multilingual parallel and comparable corpora are drawn from the same tuple-specific multinomial distribution over topics θ. For each document in the tuple, PLTM assumes that words are generated from a language L specific topic distribution over words β_L. Using this generative model we represent documents in multiple languages in a common topic space which allows us to perform similarity comparisons across documents in different languages.

The original PLTM posterior inference is approximated using collapsed Gibbs sampling (Mimno et al., 2009). While more straightforward to implement, this inference approach requires iterating over the multilingual collection multiple times to achieve convergence. This incurs a computational cost that could be significant for large collections such as Gigaword. Moreover, detecting and retrieving document translation pairs requires all-pairs comparison

across documents in both languages with a worst case time complexity of $O(N^2)$ which is impractical for large comparable corpora. One solution to this problem is to parallelize the brute-force approach through the MapReduce framework (Ture et al., 2011; Ture and Lin, 2012) but this approach requires special programming methods.

In order to use the PLTM on large collections and avoid the bottleneck introduced by Gibbs sampling, we use the online variational Bayes (VB) approach originally developed by (Hoffman et al., 2010) for LDA model to develop a fast, online PLTM model. As in the regular VB approach, online VB approximates the hidden parameters θ, z and β using the free variational parameters: γ, ϕ and λ. Rather than going over the whole collection of documents to bring the variational parameters to a convergence point, Krstovski and Smith (2013) perform updates of the variational parameters γ and ϕ_L on document batches and update the λ_L variational parameter as a weighted average of its stochastic gradient based approximation and its value on the previous batch. The approximation is done through Expectation-Maximization (EM).

Unlike the usual metric spaces where two vectors are compared using distance metrics such as Euclidean (Eu) or Cos distance, in the probability simplex similarity is computed using information-theoretic measurements such as Kullback-Leibler, Jensen-Shannon divergence and He distance. We alleviate the $O(N^2)$ worst case time-complexity in the probability simplex by utilizing approximate nearest-neighbor (NN) search techniques proven in the metric space. More specifically, we use the formulaic similarity between He and Eu: $He(p, q) \equiv Eu(x, y)$, when $\forall i : i = 1, n$ of x_i and y_i, $x_i = \sqrt{p_i}$ and $y_i = \sqrt{q_i}$, and compute He distance using Eu based, approximate NN computation approaches such as k-d trees[1] (Bentley, 1975).

4 Experiments and Results

We demonstrate the performance of the bootstrapping approach on the task of extracting parallel sentences to train a translation system. We evaluate MT systems trained on extracted parallel sentences and

---

[1] We use k-d tree implementation in the ANN library (Mount and Arya, 2010).

compare their performance against MT systems created using clean parallel collections. MT systems were evaluated with the standard BLEU metric (Papineni et al., 2002) on two official WMT test sets that cover different domains: News (WMT'11) and Europarl (WMT'08). We trained the Moses SMT system (Koehn et al., 2007) following the WMT shared task guidelines for building a baseline system with one of two parallel training collections from WMT'11: English-Spanish News Commentary (v6) and Europarl (v6). MT systems were trained using test-domain specific language models (LM) — English News Commentary for News test and English Europarl for the Europarl test. Our comparable corpus consists of news stories from the English (LDC2011T07) and Spanish (LDC2011T12) Gigaword collections.

We perform the following processing in each step of the pipeline. We run OCD on days of news originating from multiple news agencies or more specifically on news stories originating from the same day which we consider as the "minimal supervision" in initiating the bootstrapping process. Since the OCD approach generates a single list of ranked document translation pairs, for the second stage of our pipeline we consider the top n document translation pairs. We define n to be all document translation pairs whose Cos similarity is between the range of the max (i.e. the top 1 scored document translation pair in the single ranked list) and $\frac{max}{2}$. Unlike previous thresholding based on absolute values (Ture et al., 2011), this approach allows us to utilize threshold values that are automatically adjusted to the dynamic range of the Cos distance of a particular corpus. Sentences from the top n news stories are extracted and are further aligned. The output of the aligner is then used as a training set for the PLTM model. We represent each of the news stories using the per story aligned sentences. Once trained, we use the PLTM model to infer topics back on to the news stories. We then again create a single ranked list of translation news story pairs by computing divergence based similarity using He distance (§3.2). Keeping the top n ranked news story pairs, we obtain a list of what we believe are parallel documents which we then use to extract sentence pairs. Sentences are finally processed through an aligner and then used as the training corpus to our MT system.

Training Source	Bitext	Extr.	Test Set
News Comm. (NC)	131k	0	23.75
Europarl (EP)	1,750k	0	23.91
Gigaword (GW)	0	926k	24.28*
NC+GW	131k	926k	24.92*
EP+GW	1,750k	926k	25.90*

Table 1: BLEU score values computed over the WMT'11 News test set with MT systems developed using extracted and parallel sources of training data. * denotes statistical significance level (p-value$\leq$0.001) above NC.

The Gigaword collection contains news stories generated from various agencies in different languages. On any given day, a news story in English may or may not cover the same topic as one in a different language. To perform a fair evaluation with the WMT'11 News test, we considered stories published in non-overlapping years[2]: 2010, 2009, 2005 and 2004. Table 1 shows the performance comparison, on the News test set (WMT'11), of the MT system trained on extracted parallel sentences from four years of Gigaword data (GW) with a MT system trained on two WMT'11 baseline parallel collections: Europarl (EP) and News Commentary (NC). While over 10 times bigger than NC, EP is out of domain and thus performs only slightly better. On the News test set, parallel sentences automatically extracted from only four years of Gigaword data outperform systems trained on clean NC or EP bitext.

In order to determine statistically significant differences between the results of different MT systems we ran the randomization test (Smucker et al., 2007) on the News test set with 10k iterations. In each iteration we performed permutations across the translation sentences obtained from the two MT systems whose statistical difference in performance we evaluate.

Table 2 shows the performance comparison on the Europarl test set (WMT'08) between the MT system trained on the extracted parallel sentences and the two MT baseline systems. On this test set, unsurprisingly, EP training performed very well.

Table 3 gives a summary of ablation experiments that we performed across the two stages of our bootstrapping approach. More specifically, we ex-

---

[2]We did not consider news stories from 2006-2008 due to a known issue with diacritic marks in the Spanish collection.

Training Source	Bitext	Extr.	Test Set
News Comm. (NC)	131k	0	25.43
Europarl (EP)	1,750k	0	32.06
Gigaword (GW)	0	926k	23.88
NC+GW	131k	926k	25.61
EP+GW	1,750k	926k	31.59

Table 2: BLEU score values computed over the WMT'08 Europarl test set with MT systems developed using extracted and parallel sources of training data.

Pipeline Configuration	Extr.	Test Set	
		News	Europarl
OCD	684k	$24.00^{\ddagger}$	23.84
OCD (dedup.)	469k	23.84	23.75
GW	926k	$24.28^{*,\dagger}$	23.88
GW (dedup.)	588k	$24.20^{*,\S}$	24.67

Table 3: Summary of ablation experiments: BLEU score values of MT systems trained on extracted bitext by OCD alone and with PLTM reestimation along with the deduplication (dedup.) effect. * denotes statistical significance level (p-value$\leq$0.001) above NC. ‡ denotes statistical significance level (p-value$\leq$0.05) above NC. † denotes statistical significance level (p-value$\leq$0.001) above OCD. § denotes statistical significance level (p-value$\leq$0.03) above OCD.

plored using bitext extracted by OCD alone, without PLTM reestimation, to train a MT system. Both extracted bitext sets also contained many duplicate sentence pairs. In this set of experiments we also explored the effect of deduplicating them, i.e. going over the extracted set of English-Spanish sentence pairs and removing the duplicate ones. Bitext extracted by OCD alone without PLTM reestimation performed only slightly worse on WMT'11. The OCD-only data, however, only showed 70% overlap with OCD+PLTM (GW). Deduplicating the two bitexts (dedup.) hurts OCD somewhat more than OCD+PLTM. On the Europarl test set, however, deduplicating OCD+PLTM bitext caused a significant boost from 23.88 to 24.67, while causing slight performance drop for OCD (cf. NC-trained 25.43). These interactions of test domain, redundancy, and model settings leave room for further studies of the performance of our bootstrapping approach.

5 Conclusion

We introduced a bootstrapping approach for detecting document translations and extracting parallel sentences through latent topic models that are trained with minimal prior knowledge and no lexical resources. The proposed approach is able to extract parallel sentences from comparable corpora to train MT models that outperform a baseline model trained on a parallel collection.

Acknowledgments

This work was supported in part by the Harvard-Smithsonian CfA predoctoral fellowship, in part by the Center for Intelligent Information Retrieval and in part by NSF grant #IIS-0910884. Any opinions, findings and conclusions or recommendations expressed in this material are those of the authors and do not necessarily reflect those of the sponsor.

References

Sadaf Abdul-Rauf and Holger Schwenk. 2009. On the use of comparable corpora to improve smt performance. In *EACL*, pages 16–23.

Jon Louis Bentley. 1975. Multidimensional binary search trees used for associative searching. *CACM*, 18(9):509–517.

Mauro Cettolo, Marcello Federico, and Nicola Bertoldi. 2010. Mining parallel fragments from comparable texts. In *IWSLT*, pages 227–234.

Moses S. Charikar. 2002. Similarity estimation techniques from rounding algorithms. In *STOC*, pages 308–388.

Jessica Enright and Grzegorz Kondrak. 2007. A fast method for parallel document identification. In *NAACL/HLT*, pages 29–32.

Pascale Fung and Percy Cheung. 2004. Mining very-non-parallel corpora: Parallel sentence and lexicon extraction via bootstrapping and em. In *EMNLP*, pages 57–63.

Souhir Gahbiche-Braham, Hélène Bonneau-Maynard, and François Yvon. 2011. Two ways to use a noisy parallel news corpus for improving statistical machine translation. In *the 4th Workshop on Building and Using Comparable Corpora: Comparable Corpora and the Web*, pages 44–51.

Cuong Hoang, Anh-Cuong Le, Phuong-Thai Nguyen, Son Bao Pham, and Tu Bao Ho. 2014. An efficient framework for extracting parallel sentences from non-parallel corpora. *Fundamenta Informaticae - Computing and Communication Technologies*, 130(2):179–199.

Matthew Hoffman, David Blei, and Francis Bach. 2010. Online learning for latent Dirichlet allocation. In *NIPS*, pages 856–864.

Alexandre Klementiev, Ann Irvine, Chris Callison-Burch, and David Yarowsky. 2012. Toward statistical machine translation without parallel corpora. In *EACL*, pages 130–140.

Philipp Koehn, Hieu Hoang, Alexandra Birch, Chris Callison-Burch, Marcello Federico, Nicola Bertoldi, Brooke Cowan, Wade Shen, Christine Moran, Richard Zens, Chris Dyer, Ondřej Bojar, Alexandra Constantin, and Evan Herbst. 2007. Moses: Open source toolkit for statistical machine translation. In *ACL on Interactive Poster and Demonstration Sessions*, pages 177–180.

Kriste Krstovski and David A. Smith. 2011. A minimally supervised approach for detecting and ranking document translation pairs. In *WMT*, pages 207–216.

Kriste Krstovski and David Smith. 2013. Online polylingual topic models for fast document translation detection. In *WMT*, pages 252–261.

Wang Ling, Guang Xiang, Chris Dyer, Alan Black, and Isabel Trancoso. 2013. Microblogs as parallel corpora. In *ACL*, pages 176–186.

David Mimno, Hanna Wallach, Jason Naradowsky, David A. Smith, and Andrew McCallum. 2009. Polylingual topic models. In *EMNLP*, pages 880–889.

Robert C. Moore. 2002. Fast and accurate sentence alignment of bilingual corpora. In *AMTA*, pages 135–144.

David M. Mount and Sunil Arya, 2010. *ANN: A Library for Approximate Nearest Neighbor Searching*. `http://www.cs.umd.edu/~mount/ANN`.

Dragos Stefan Munteanu and Daniel Marcu. 2005. Improving machine translation performance by exploiting non-parallel corpora. *Computational Linguistics*, 31(4):477–504.

Kishore Papineni, Salim Roukos, Todd Ward, and Wei-Jing Zhu. 2002. Bleu: A method for automatic evaluation of machine translation. In *ACL*, pages 311–318.

Chris Quirk, Raghavendra Udupa U, and Arul Menezes. 2007. Generative models of noisy translations with applications to parallel fragment extraction. In *MT Summit*, pages 321–327.

Jason R. Smith, Chris Quirk, and Kristina Toutanova. 2010. Extracting parallel sentences from comparable corpora using document level alignment. In *NAACL/HLT*, pages 403–411.

Mark D. Smucker, James Allan, and Ben Carterette. 2007. A comparison of statistical significance tests for information retrieval evaluation. In *CIKM*, pages 623–632.

Christoph Tillmann and Jian-ming Xu. 2009. A simple sentence-level extraction algorithm for comparable data. In *NAACL/HLT, Companion Volume: Short Papers*, pages 93–96.

Ferhan Ture and Jimmy Lin. 2012. Why not grab a free lunch?: mining large corpora for parallel sentences to improve translation modeling. In *NAACL/HLT*, pages 626–630.

Ferhan Ture, Tamer Elsayed, and Jimmy Lin. 2011. No free lunch: Brute force vs. locality-sensitive hashing for cross-lingual pairwise similarity. In *SIGIR*, pages 943–952.

Jakob Uszkoreit, Jay M. Ponte, Ashok C. Popat, and Moshe Dubiner. 2010. Large scale parallel document mining for machine translation. In *COLING*, pages 1101–1109.

Discriminative Reranking for Grammatical Error Correction with Statistical Machine Translation

Tomoya Mizumoto
Tohoku University
`tomoya-m@ecei.tohoku.ac.jp`

Yuji Matsumoto
Nara Institute of Science and Technology
`matsu@is.naist.jp`

Abstract

Research on grammatical error correction has received considerable attention. For dealing with all types of errors, grammatical error correction methods that employ statistical machine translation (SMT) have been proposed in recent years. An SMT system generates candidates with scores for all candidates and selects the sentence with the highest score as the correction result. However, the 1-best result of an SMT system is not always the best result. Thus, we propose a reranking approach for grammatical error correction. The reranking approach is used to re-score N-best results of the SMT and reorder the results. Our experiments show that our reranking system using parts of speech and syntactic features improves performance and achieves state-of-the-art quality, with an $F_{0.5}$ score of 40.0.

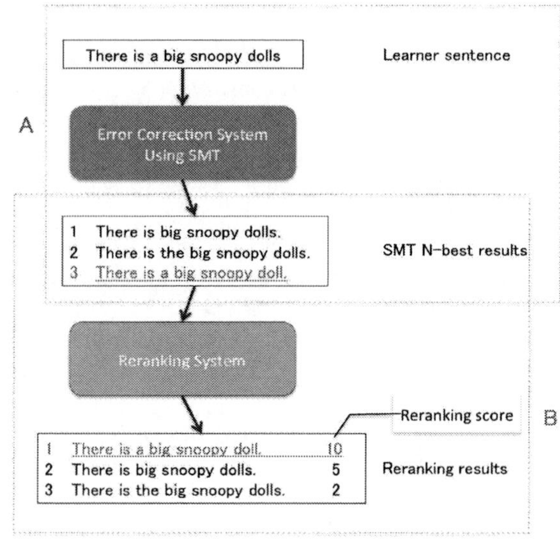

Figure 1: Flow of reranking.

1 Introduction

Research on assisting second language learners has received considerable attention, especially regarding grammatical error correction of essays written by English as a Second Language (ESL) learners. To address all types of errors, grammatical error correction methods that use statistical machine translation (SMT) have been proposed (Brockett et al., 2006; Mizumoto et al., 2012; Buys and van der Merwe, 2013; Yuan and Felice, 2013; Felice et al., 2014; Junczys-Dowmunt and Grundkiewicz, 2014). SMT-based error correction systems have achieved rankings first and third in the CoNLL2014 Shared Task (Ng et al., 2014).

SMT systems generate many candidates of translation. SMT systems generate scored candidates and select a sentence having the highest score as the translation result. However, the 1-best result of SMT system is not always the best result because the scoring is conducted only with local features. In other words, N-best (N > 1) results may be better than the 1-best result.

Reranking approaches have been devised to solve the scoring problem. Reranking is a method that re-scores N-best candidates of SMT and reorders the candidates by score. Figure 1 shows a flow of reranking. First, N-best results are obtained by a grammatical error correction system using SMT for a learner sentence (A in Figure 1). A reranking sys-

Proceedings of NAACL-HLT 2016, pages 1133–1138,
San Diego, California, June 12-17, 2016. ©2016 Association for Computational Linguistics

tem then re-scores the N-best results and reorders them (B in Figure 1).

In this study, we apply a discriminative reranking method to the task of grammatical error correction. Syntactic information is not considered in the phrase-based SMT. We show that using syntactic features in the reranking system can improve error correction performance. Although reranking using only surface features (Shen et al., 2004) is not effective for grammatical error correction, reranking using syntactic features improves the $F_{0.5}$ score.

2 Related Work for Reranking

Reranking approaches have been proposed for common SMT tasks (Shen et al., 2004; Carter and Monz, 2011; Li and Khudanpur, 2008; Och et al., 2004). Shen et al. (2004) first used a perceptron-like algorithm for reranking of common SMT tasks. However, they used only a few features.

Li and Khudanpur (2008) proposed a reranking approach that uses a large-scale discriminative N-gram language model for common SMT tasks. They extended the reranking method for automatic speech recognition (Roark et al., 2007) to SMT tasks. The approach of Carter and Monz (2011) was similar to that of Li and Khudanpur (2008), but they used additional syntactic features (e.g. part of speech (POS), parse tree) for reranking of common SMT tasks.

The reranking approach has been used in grammatical error correction based on phrase-based SMT (Felice et al., 2014). However, their method uses only language model scores. In the reranking step, the system can consider not only surface but also syntactic features such as those in the approach of Carter and Monz (2011). We use syntactic features in our reranking system.

Heafield et al. (2009) proposed a system combination method for machine translation that is similar to that of reranking. System combination is a method that merges the outputs of multiple systems to produce an output that is better than each individual system. Susanto et al. (2014) applied this system combination to grammatical error correction. They combined pipeline systems based on classification approaches and SMT systems. Classifier-based systems use syntactic features as POS and dependency for error correction. However, syntactic information

Table 1: Oracle score of grammatical error correction

N-best	Precision	Recall	$F_{0.5}$
1	43.9	24.5	37.9
10	79.1	36.7	64.3
50	89.5	43.1	73.6
100	92.3	45.3	76.4

is not considered in combining systems.

3 Why is Reranking Necessary?

Grammatical error correction using SMT has the same problem as that of common SMT task: the 1-best correction by the system is not always the best. To prove this, we conducted a grammatical error correction experiment using SMT and calculated N-best oracle scores. The oracle scores are calculated by selecting the correction candidate with the highest score from the N-best results for each sentence.

Table 1 shows oracle scores of a baseline grammatical error correction system using SMT[1]. Althogh the $F_{0.5}$ score of the 1-best output was 37.9, the $F_{0.5}$ of the 10-best oracle score was 64.3. The higher the value of N-best, the higher is the oracle score. This result reveals that the 1-best correction by a grammatical error correction system using SMT is not always the best.

Advantage of Reranking Two advantages exist for using a reranking approach for grammatical error correction. The first is that a reranking system can use POS and syntactic features unlike phrase-based SMT. With some errors, the relation between distant words must be considered (e.g., article relation between *a* and *dolls* in the phrase *a big Snoopy dolls*).

The second advantage is that POS taggers and parsers can analyze error-corrected candidates more properly than they analyze erroneous sentences, which enables more accurate features to be obtained. Thus, the fact that taggers for N-best corrected results work much better than for learner original sentences is promising.

4 Proposed Method

In this section, we explain our discriminative reranking method and features of reranking for grammati-

---

[1]See 5.1 for a baseline system

Table 2: Features for reranking. Examples show features for the sentence *I agree with this statement to a large extent*. The features excluding "Web dependency N-gram" are binary valued. "Web dependency N-gram" is unit interval [0,1] valued.

Feature name	Examples
Word 2,3-gram	I agree; I agree with; agree with; agree with this; this statement
POS 2,3,4,5-gram	PRP VBP; PRP VBP IN; PRP VBP IN DT; PRP VBP IN DT NN
POS-function word 2,3,4,5-gram	PRP VBP; PRP VBP with; PRP VBP with this; PRP VBP with this NN
Web dependency N-gram	prep-agree-with-statment; det-a-extent

cal error correction.

4.1 Discriminative Reranking Method

In this study, we use a discriminative reranking algorithm using perceptron which successfully exploits syntactic features for N-best reranking for common translation tasks (Carter and Monz, 2011). Figure 2 shows the standard perceptron algorithm for reranking. In this figure, T is the number of iterations for perceptron learning and N is the number of learner original sentences in the training corpus. In addition, $GEN(x)$ is the N-best list generated by a grammatical error correction system using SMT for an input sentence and $ORACLE(x^i)$ determines the best correction for each of the N-best lists according to the $F_{0.5}$ score. Moreover w is the weight vector for features and ϕ is the feature vector for candidate sentences. When selecting the sentence with the highest score from candidate sentences (line 5), if the selected sentence matches oracle sentence, then the algorithm proceeds to next sentence. Otherwise, the weight vector is updated.

The disadvantage of perceptron is instability when training data are not linearly separable. As a solution to this problem, an averaged perceptron algorithm was proposed (Freund and Schapire, 1999). In this algorithm, weight vector w_{avg} is defined as:

$$w_{avg} = \frac{1}{T} \sum_{t=1}^{T} \frac{1}{N} \sum_{i=1}^{N} w_t^i \quad (1)$$

To select the best correction from N-best candidates, we use the following formula:

$$S(z) = \beta \phi_0(z) + w \cdot \phi(z) \quad (2)$$

where $\phi_0(z)$ is the score calculated by the SMT system for each translation hypothesis. This score is weighted by β. Using $\phi_0(z)$ as a feature in the perceptron algorithm is possible, but this may lead to

```
1: w ← 0
2: for t = 1 to T do
3:     for i = 1 to N do
4:         yⁱ ← ORACLE(xⁱ)
5:         zⁱ ← argmax_{x∈GEN(xⁱ)} φ(z) · w
6:         if zⁱ ≠ yⁱ then
7:             w ← w + φ(yⁱ) − φ(zⁱ)
8:         end if
9:     end for
10: end for
11: return w
```

Figure 2: Perceptron algorithm for ranking.

under-training (Sutton et al., 2006). We select the value for β with the highest $F_{0.5}$ score by changing β from 0 to 100 in 0.1 increments on the development data.

4.2 Features of Discriminative Reranking for Grammatical Error Correction

In this study, we use the features used in Carter and Monz (2011) as well as our new features of POS and dependency. We use the features extracted from the following sequences: POS tag , shallow parse tag, and shallow parse tag plus POS tag sequences (Carter and Monz, 2011). From these sequences, features are extracted based on the following three definitions:

1. $(t_{i-2}t_{i-1}t_i)$, $(t_{i-1}t_i)$, (t_iw_i)

2. $(t_{i-2}t_{i-1}w_i)$

3. $(t_{i-2}w_{i-2}t_{i-1}w_{i-1}t_iw_i)$, $\quad (t_{i-2}t_{i-1}w_{i-1}t_iw_i)$, $(t_{t-1}w_{i-1}t_iw_i)$, $(t_{i-1}t_iw_i)$

Here, w_i is a word at position i and t_i is a tag (POS or shallow parse tag) at position i.

Table 2 shows our new features. For the "POS-function N-gram" feature, if words are con-

Table 3: Experimental results. TP, FN, and FP denote true positive, false negative, and false positive, respectively. Asterisks indicate that the difference between the baseline and reranking results is statistically significant (p < 0.01, bootstrap test).

		Precision	Recall	$F_{0.5}$	TP	FN	FP	GLEU
	Baseline							
1	1-best result of SMT	43.9	24.5	37.9	598	1847	764	65.7
2	Reranking by N-gram LM	39.5	**31.7**	37.6	834	1797	1280	64.7
3	CAMB (CoNLL2014)	39.7	30.1	37.3	772	1793	1172	64.5
4	CUUI (CoNLL2014)	41.8	24.9	36.8	623	1881	868	64.8
	Discriminative reranking							
5	Word 2,3-gram	43.7	24.8	37.9	606	1834	781	65.7
6	Features of Carter (2011)	44.3	26.7	39.1	669	1837	842	65.8
7	Our features (Table 2)	**45.8**	26.6	**40.0***	657	1813	778	**66.1**
8	All features (6+7)	44.4	27.1	39.4*	679	1827	851	65.8

tained in a stop word list, we use surface form, otherwise we use POS tags. "Web dependency N-gram" is feature used in Dahlmeier et al. (2012). We collect log frequency counts for dependency N-grams from a large dependency-parsed web corpus and normalize all real-valued feature values to a unit interval [0,1].

5 Experiments of Reranking

We conducted experiments on grammatical error correction to observe the effect of discriminative reranking and our syntactic features.

5.1 Experimental Settings

We used phrase-based SMT which many previous studies used for grammatical error correction for a baseline system. We used cicada 0.3.5[2] for the machine translation tool and KenLM[3] as the language modeling tool. We used ZMERT[4] as the parameter tuning tool and implemented the averaged perceptron for reranking.

The translation model was trained on the Lang-8 Learner Corpora v2.0. We extracted English essays that were written by ESL learners and cleaned noise with the method proposed in (Mizumoto et al., 2011). From the results, we obtained 1,069,127 sentence pairs. We used a 5-gram language model built on the "Associated Press Worldstream English

Service" from English Gigaword corpus and NUCLE 3.2 (Dahlmeier et al., 2013). We used these two language models as separate feature functions in the SMT system.

For training data of reranking, Lang-8 Learner Corpora was split into 10 parts and each part was corrected by a grammatical error correction system trained on the other nine parts. We selected 10 as N for N-best reranking. PukWaC corpus (Baroni et al., 2009) was used for constructing our "Web dependency N-gram" feature. We use Stanford Parser 3.2.0[5] as a dependency parser.

CoNLL-2013 test set were split into 700 sentences for parameter tuning of SMT and 681 sentences for tuning parameter beta. CoNLL-2014 test set, 1,312 sentences were used for evaluation. We used M2 Scorer as an evaluation tool (Dahlmeier and Ng, 2012). This scorer calculates precision, recall, and $F_{0.5}$ scores. We used $F_{0.5}$ as a tuning metric. In addition, we used GLEU (Napoles et al., 2015) as evaluation metrics.

5.2 Experimental Results and Discussion

Table 3 shows the experimental results. We used the 1-best result of the SMT correction system and reranking by probability of the large N-gram language model (Felice et al., 2014) as baseline systems. In addition, we compared the systems that are ranked first (CAMB) and second (CUUI) (Felice et al., 2014; Rozovskaya et al., 2014) in CoNLL2014

---

[2]http://www2.nict.go.jp/univ-com/multi_trans/cicada/

[3]https://kheafield.com/code/kenlm/

[4]http://cs.jhu.edu/~ozaidan/zmert/

[5]http://nlp.stanford.edu/software/lex-parser.shtml

Shared Task.

The discriminative reranking system with our features achieved the best $F_{0.5}$ score. The difference between the results of baseline and reranking using our features was statistically significant ($p < 0.01$). Because a large N-gram language model was adopted for reranking, recall increased considerably but precision declined. This result is extremely similar to that of the CAMB system, which is an SMT-based error correction system that reranks by using a large N-gram language model. When we compare the reranking system using our features to CUUI, our system is better in all metrics.

When we use the discriminative reranking with our features, both precision and recall increase. In the experimental results of system combination (Susanto et al., 2014), recall increases but precision declines with respect to original SMT results. In addition, precision increases but recall declines with respect to pipeline results.

The reranking that employed all features generated a lower $F_{0.5}$ score than when only our features were used. One reason for this is that the roles of features overlap. These experiments revealed that reranking is effective in grammatical error correction tasks and that POS and syntactic features are important.

6 Conclusion

We proposed a reranking approach to grammatical error correction using phrase-based SMT. Our system achieved $F_{0.5}$ score of 40.0 (an increase of 2.1 points from that of the baseline system) on the CoNLL2014 Shared Task test set. We showed that POS and dependency features are effective for the reranking of grammatical error correction.

In future work, we will use the adaptive regularization of weight vectors (AROW) algorithm (Crammer et al., 2009) instead of the averaged perceptron. In addition, we will apply the pairwise approach to ranking (Herbrich et al., 1999) used in information retrieval to rerank of grammatical error correction.

References

Marco Baroni, Silvia Bernardini, Adriano Ferraresi, and Eros Zanchetta. 2009. The WaCky Wide Web: A Collection of Very Large Linguistically Processed Web-Crawled Corpora. *Language Resources and Evaluation*, 43(3):209–226.

Chris Brockett, William B. Dolan, and Michael Gamon. 2006. Correcting ESL Errors Using Phrasal SMT Techniques. In *Proceedings of COLING-ACL*, pages 249–256.

Jan Buys and Brink van der Merwe. 2013. A Tree Transducer Model for Grammatical Error Correction. In *Proceedings of CoNLL Shared Task*, pages 43–51.

Simon Carter and Christof Monz. 2011. Syntactic Discriminative Language Model Rerankers for Statistical Machine Translation. *Machine Translation*, 25(4):317–339.

Koby Crammer, Alex Kulesza, and Mark Dredze. 2009. Adaptive Regularization of Weight Vectors. In *NIPS*, pages 414–422.

Daniel Dahlmeier and Hwee Tou Ng. 2012. Better Evaluation for Grammatical Error Correction. In *Proceedings of NAACL-HLT*, pages 568–572.

Daniel Dahlmeier, Hwee Tou Ng, and Eric Jun Feng Ng. 2012. NUS at the HOO 2012 Shared Task. In *Proceedings of BEA*, pages 216–224.

Daniel Dahlmeier, Hwee Tou Ng, and Siew Mei Wu. 2013. Building a Large Annotated Corpus of Learner English: The NUS Corpus of Learner English. In *Proceedings of BEA*, pages 22–31.

Mariano Felice, Zheng Yuan, Øistein E. Andersen, Helen Yannakoudakis, and Ekaterina Kochmar. 2014. Grammatical error correction using hybrid systems and type filtering. In *Proceedings of CoNLL Shared Task*, pages 15–24.

Yoav Freund and Robert E. Schapire. 1999. Large Margin Classification Using the Perceptron Algorithm. *Machine Learning*, 37(3):277–296.

Kenneth Heafield, Greg Hanneman, and Alon Lavie. 2009. Machine translation system combination with flexible word ordering. In *Proceedings of Workshop on SMT*, pages 56–60.

Ralf Herbrich, Thore Graepel, and Klaus Obermayer. 1999. Support Vector Learning for Ordinal Regression. In *Proceedings of ICANN*, pages 97–102.

Marcin Junczys-Dowmunt and Roman Grundkiewicz. 2014. The AMU System in the CoNLL-2014 Shared Task: Grammatical Error Correction by Data-Intensive and Feature-Rich Statistical Machine Translation. In *Proceedings of CoNLL Shared Task*, pages 25–33.

Zhifei Li and Sanjeev Khudanpur. 2008. Large-scale Discriminative n-gram Language Models for Statistical Machine Translation. In *Proceedings of AMTA*.

Tomoya Mizumoto, Mamoru Komachi, Masaaki Nagata, and Yuji Matsumoto. 2011. Mining Revision Log of

Language Learning SNS for Automated Japanese Error Correction of Second Language Learners. In *Proceedings of IJCNLP*, pages 147–155.

Tomoya Mizumoto, Yuta Hayashibe, Mamoru Komachi, Masaaki Nagata, and Yuji Matsumoto. 2012. The Effect of Learner Corpus Size in Grammatical Error Correction of ESL Writings. In *Proceedings of COLING*, pages 863–872.

Courtney Napoles, Keisuke Sakaguchi, Matt Post, and Joel Tetreault. 2015. Ground Truth for Grammatical Error Correction Metrics. In *Proceedings of ACL-IJCNLP*, pages 588–593.

Hwee Tou Ng, Siew Mei Wu, Ted Briscoe, Christian Hadiwinoto, Raymond Hendy Susanto, and Christopher Bryant. 2014. The CoNLL-2014 Shared Task on Grammatical Error Correction. In *Proceedings of CoNLL Shared Task*, pages 1–14.

Franz Josef Och, Daniel Gildea, Sanjeev Khudanpur, Anoop Sarkar, Kenji Yamada, Alex Fraser, Shankar Kumar, Libin Shen, David Smith, Katherine Eng, Viren Jain, Zhen Jin, and Dragomir Radev. 2004. A Smorgasbord of Features for Statistical Machine Translation. In *Proceedings of HLT-NAACL*, pages 161–168.

Brian Roark, Murat Saraclar, and Michael Collins. 2007. Discriminative n-gram language modeling. *Computer Speech Language*, 21(2):373–392.

Alla Rozovskaya, Kai-Wei Chang, Mark Sammons, Dan Roth, and Nizar Habash. 2014. The Illinois-Columbia System in the CoNLL-2014 Shared Task. In *Proceedings of CoNLL Shared Task*, pages 34–42.

Libin Shen, Anoop Sarkar, and Franz Josef Och. 2004. Discriminative Reranking for Machine Translation. In *Proceedings of HLT-NAACL*.

Raymond Hendy Susanto, Peter Phandi, and Hwee Tou Ng. 2014. System combination for grammatical error correction. In *Proceedings of EMNLP*, pages 951–962.

Charles Sutton, Michael Sindelar, and Andrew McCallum. 2006. Reducing Weight Undertraining in Structured Discriminative Learning. In *Proceedings of HLT-NAACL*, pages 89–95.

Zheng Yuan and Mariano Felice. 2013. Constrained Grammatical Error Correction using Statistical Machine Translation. In *Proceedings of CoNLL Shared Task*, pages 52–61.

Patterns of Wisdom: Discourse-Level Style in Multi-Sentence Quotations

Kyle Booten and **Marti A. Hearst**
UC Berkeley
Berkeley, CA 94720
kbooten@berkeley.edu, hearst@berkeley.edu

Abstract

Quotations are kernels not just of wisdom but also of beautiful and striking language. While recent studies have characterized the stylistic features of quotations, we characterize the *order* of stylistic information within quotations. Analyzing a corpus of two-sentence quotations collected from the social network Tumblr, we explore the ways that both low-level features and high-level features tend to occur in either the first or second sentence. Through analysis of examples, we interpret these tendencies as manifestations of rhetorical patterns. Results from a prediction task suggest that stylistic patterns are more prominent in quotations than in a comparison corpus.

1 Introduction

The ancient arts of rhetoric described ways of wielding language to make it particularly persuasive or memorable. Central in this endeavor—a predecessor to modern linguistics (Dolven, 2013)—was the description of rhetorical "tropes" or "figures," patterns of language from the level of the phoneme (as in the case of rhyme or alliteration) to higher-level syntactic and even logical structures (Peacham, 1954). In the figure of *epistrophe*, successive clauses end with the same words. In *pysma*, the speaker (or writer) launches a series of sharp and vehement questions; this and other rhetorical figures describe language at the level of discourse—that is, the relationship between linguistic elements across sentences.

Recent studies of quotations have described what makes certain fragments of text more memorable than others (Danescu-Niculescu-Mizil et al., 2012;

Guerini et al., 2015); this ongoing project can be seen as a contemporary, empirical investigation of the rhetorical arts. Inspired by the way that classical rhetoricians described complicated and high-level linguistic patterns, the present study takes the novel step of analyzing the way linguistic elements are sequenced within quotations. After describing a minimalistic set of stylistic features designed to capture common patterns in quotations, we demonstrate that some features tend to occur in certain positions within a quotation. We investigate whether quotes are more predictable than other genres in a "Quote Ordering Task" in which the goal is to distinguish the correct version of a quotation from one whose sentences have been reversed.

2 Related Work

2.1 Style of Memorable Language

Danescu-Niculescu-Mizil et al. (2012) used a variety of features to distinguish popular movie quotations from unmemorable lines from the same movie. By modeling word and part-of-speech sequences of quotes and non-quotes, they found that quotations tended to use less common words but that these words were placed in more common syntactic patterns. The researchers evocatively hint at some "common syntactic scaffolding" that structures quotations, and we build on this finding by characterizing these patterns. They also found that quotations tend to contain linguistic features that make them more "generalizable," such as tendency toward indefinite over definite articles.

Other researchers have attempted to analyze quotations in ways that evoke the traditional figures

Proceedings of NAACL-HLT 2016, pages 1139–1144,
San Diego, California, June 12-17, 2016. ©2016 Association for Computational Linguistics

of rhetoric. Exploring the same movie quotes corpus as well as other corpora, Guerini et al. (2015) found that memorable quotes were more euphonic, with more instances of rhyme and alliteration than their non-memorable counterparts. Kuznetsova et al. (2013) developed several methods for quantifying the creativity of word combinations like "disadvantageous peace," and found that quotes were more likely to contain creative combinations than non-quotes. In terms of classical rhetoric, such unexpected word combinations could embody figures such as *oxymoron*.

2.2 High-Level Style

To investigate quotations in a new way, we are inspired by researchers who have analyzed text quality using what may be called "high-level" features — i.e., moving beyond the specific lexical, syntactic, or phonemic properties of sentences to explore the overall structure of sentences or even the discursive relationships between them.

Feng et al. (2012) engineered features from sentences' CFG parse trees to describe their overall structure and classify them in terms of *a priori* rhetorical categories, such as *loose* vs. *periodic*. They found that these features were helpful for authorship classification, and a later study used similar features to predict the success of novels (Ashok et al., 2013). Wible and Tsao (2010) and Gianfortoni et al. (2011) designed n-gram based features to capture local lexico-syntactic sequences within sentences.

Looking at the level of discourse, Louis and Nenkova (2012) found that adjacent sentences "exhibit stable patterns of syntactic co-occurence" — i.e., certain types of sentences tend to follow certain other types of sentences. Furthermore, they demonstrated that sentences with similar communicative purposes are syntactically similar, so syntax can be taken as a proxy for communicative purpose. We build on both of these observations.

3 Data-sets

Quotations 1. We gathered a data-set of quotations from the social network Tumblr (Chang et al., 2014). Like other social networks, Tumblr has become a place where users frequently share quotations. In fact, users have the option of using a "quote" data-type, which provides separate text-entry fields for the quotation and its source. We gathered quotes via Tumblr's API. Users sometimes use the "quote" data-type to share messages that are not actually quotations, most often brief personal musings. To minimize such non-quotes in our corpus, we retained only those quotes that users themselves had described with the hashtag "#quote." Since we were interested primarily in discourse-level schemas of quotations, we retained only quotations that were exactly two sentences long. In the pre-processing of this and other corpora we removed repeats within and between corpora. We also removed quotations containing quotations (i.e. reported speech), as they were used in highly inconsistent ways in the Tumblr data. (n=4237)

Quotations 2. A test set. We repeated the same steps described above for Tumblr quotes gathered with the "#quotation" hashtag. (n=1846)

Non-Quotes 1. As a comparison corpus, we gathered two-sentence paragraphs from the Brown corpus (Francis and Kucera, 1979). After the same preprocessing steps, we were left with a collection of such paragraphs. (n=1846)

Non-Quotes 2. Again mining the Brown Corpus, we also gathered sequential pairs of sentences randomly chosen from paragraphs longer than two sentences. (n=1846)

4 Features

Take the following quotation from our data set, attributed to Philip Roth: "You cannot observe people through an ideology. Your ideology observes for you."[1] In simple terms, this quotation is a negative statement ("can*not*") followed by a positive one. Yet the opposite pattern can likewise appear in quotations, as in this one attributed to William Blake: "Great things are done when men and mountains meet. This is not done by jostling in the street." Some quotations begin with questions; others end with them. Some (like the one by Roth) begin with a generic "you," while others deploy this pronoun in the second sentence. We describe each sentence of each quotation in terms of the following features meant to capture general lexical and syntactic pat-

---

[1]This quote also exemplifies *antimetabole*, in which words in the first clause appear reversed in the second.

Feature	#S1	#S2	χ^2	NQ2?
Highest χ^2				
It	60	**175**	56.3	x
But	18	**93**	50.7	x
it	266	**436**	41.2	x
And	33	**93**	28.6	x
They	7	**44**	26.8	x
Other Unigrams				
People	**21**	2	15.7	
?	**120**	66	15.7	
simply	3	**20**	12.6	
Do	**38**	13	12.3	
Love	**19**	3	11.6	
When	**43**	22	6.8	
n't	**262**	209	6.0	
not	**212**	170	4.6	
What	**45**	28	4.0	
High-Level				
CC + NP + VP .	11	**68**	41.1	x
WHNP + SQ + S + .	**39**	9	18.7	
NP + VP + .	**883**	748	11.2	
WHADVP + SQ + .	**18**	5	7.3	
CC + PP + , + NP + VP + .	2	**12**	7.1	
CC + SBAR + , + NP + VP + .	5	**16**	5.8	
IN + NP + VP + .	2	**10**	5.3	
S + , + S + CC + S + .	**5**	0	5.0	
INTJ + , + NP + VP + .	**7**	1	4.5	
CC + NP + ADVP + VP + .	2	**9**	4.5	

Table 1: Features that preferentially occur in a sentence position, sorted by χ^2 value; dominant sentence position is in bold. *Highest χ^2* represents the top five unigrams. *Other Unigrams* represents other select examples. NQ2 is whether feature is also ordered in the same way in the comparison corpus ("x" if this is the case).

terns in quotations, regardless of what other more classical rhetorical figures they may contain.

Unigrams. As a baseline feature, we note in which sentence, 1 or 2, a unigram occurs.

High-Level Syntax. Feng et al. (2012) found that the top level of syntactic parse trees (in the case of Stanford PCFG Parser's output, which we also used (Klein and Manning, 2003), two levels beneath ROOT) provided a useful feature for authorship identification. For instance, the sentence "Forgotten is forgiven." can be represented by the construction *NP + VP + .*, a noun phrase followed by a verb phrase followed by punctuation. This feature, they argue, provides an interpretable representation of the general syntactic structure of a sentence. We directly employ this feature.

General/Abstract Words. Through qualitative analysis of our data, we noticed that many quotation make pronouncements about nouns that might be considered as generalizations or abstractions. For instance: "Peace comes from within. Do not seek it without." In this case, the abstract noun "peace" is the subject of the first sentence. To capture such nouns, we first use the Stanford Dependency Parser (Chen and Manning, 2014) to extract all words in the head position of nominal subject dependencies (excluding stopwords). Using WordNet, we check whether the word's most common synset is both within the hyponym hierarchy of the synset "abstraction.n.06" and within a minimum distance (5) of it[2]; if so, we consider this noun Abstract.[3] The most common such nouns in the Quotations 1 corpus are not necessarily concept words like "peace". For instance, the word "men" appears in this list; many quotations use the word to evoke a generalized (male) subject.[4] We consider a nominal subject to be General if it is within a minimum distance (6) of its root hypernym. As a feature, we observe which (if either) sentence contains more such Abstract or General nouns, normalized by the number of nominal subject dependencies per sentence.

5 Differences Between Sentence Positions

5.1 Feature Comparison

Using balanced subsets of Quotations 1 and Non-Quotes 1 (n=1846), we investigated which feature was more likely to occur in either one of the two sentences' positions within a two-sentence text. For each feature we used a χ^2 test (α=.05) to compare the number of times the feature occurred in first sentences with the number of times the feature occurred in second sentences. Table 1 presents features with a statistically-significant tendency to appear in one sentence or the other, limited to those features that occur at least 5 times and are among the 300 most common features of its type for that corpus. We suggest that this type of analysis can shed light on some of the overarching stylistic strategies of quotations:

Negative-to-Positive: As shown in Table 1, "n't"

---

[2]We found this number by taking the whole number above the mean of distances to the "abstraction.n.06" synset of a sample of nouns from Project Gutenberg text. For General words we did the same but averaging distances to a noun's root hypernym.

[3]Kao and Jurafsky Kao and Jurafsky (2012) investigated abstractions in poetry using a dictionary of abstract terms.

[4]"The mass of men lead lives of quiet desperation." (H.D. Thoreau)

and "not" were ore likely to occur in the first sentence position than the second sentence position. This tendency suggests that quotations that begin with a negative construction (like the earlier quote by Roth) are more common than those ending with one (like the earlier quote by Blake). Quotes that contain "not" in the first sentence often use the first sentence to make a negative claim about reality, followed by a positive claim. Such quotations tend to use repetitive structures or other types of parallelism, such as *antimetabole*:

> We are not human beings having a spiritual experience. We are spiritual beings having a human experience. (P. de Chardin)

In quotations, "Never" was also more likely to occur in the first sentence than the second sentence, as was "Do"; studying examples revealed that "Do" was very often followed by "not" or "n't." These statistical tendencies point to the ways that Negative-to-Positive constructions also take the form of a negative commandment (e.g., "Never do X") in the first sentence, followed either by a positive commandment or an explanation of the reasoning for the commandment:

> Do not worry about your difficulties in mathematics. I can assure you mine are still greater. (A. Einstein)

Cross-Sentence Conjunction: For both Quotations 1 and Non-Quotes 1, the high-level syntax feature with the highest χ^2 value was $CC + NP + VP +$ .. This feature tended to occur in the second sentence for both collections; likewise, for both sentences "But" and "And" were more likely to appear in the second sentence. This is not surprising, as coordinating conjunctions mark the "conjunction" relationship of cohesion (Halliday and Hasan, 2014) (i.e. clauses that begin with conjunctions like "But" implicitly refer back to a previous clause). However, for Quotations 1, this syntax pattern was over six times as likely to occur in the second sentence, compared to nearly two times for Non-Quotes 2, a statistically-significant difference (χ^2, $p<.01$). In the Quotations 1 corpus, other high-level features beginning with a coordinating conjunction were also more likely to occur in sentence 1 than 2, including $CC + PP +, + NP + VP +$. and $CC + SBAR +, + NP + VP +$ .. For instance:

> Where a goat can go, a man can go. And where a man can go, he can drag a gun. (William Phillips)

Similarly, the high-level syntax pattern $IN + NP + VP +$. was more likely to occur in the second sentence of quotations than the first sentence; this pattern also indicates cohesion:

> One of the most adventurous things left us is to go to bed. For no one can lay a hand on our dreams. (E.V. Lucas)

We note that either of these quotations could be rephrased as a single sentence, such as:

> One of the most adventurous things left us is to go to bed, for no one can lay a hand on our dreams.

We speculate that there is something stylistically powerful about such sentences in which the second sentence begins with a coordinating or subordinating conjunction. (Perhaps such quotations create a "dramatic" pause for the reader between the sentences.)

Questions: Table 1 shows that high-level syntax patterns that indicate questions, $WHNP + SQ +$. and $WHADVP + SQ +$. occurred more frequently in the first sentence position than the second sentence position, as did the unigram "When." Examining data with the $WHNP + SQ +$. pattern revealed that many of these quotations were actually jokes that take the form of a question/answer dyad.

Sweeping Declarations: For Quotations 1, Abstract Nouns and General Nouns as nominal subjects were more prevalent in the first than in the second sentence (χ^2, $p<.01$). For Non-Quotes 1, General Nouns were also significantly more likely to occur in the first sentence (χ^2, $p<.01$); this was not the case for General Nouns. For quotations only, however, "is" was more likely to occur in the first sentence; likewise, the $NP + VP +$. pattern was also more likely to occur in the first sentences of quotations. Remaining open to other interpretations, we suggest that these facts point to the tendency of quotations to begin with sweeping declarations about "people," "life," "truth," and other broad concepts, kernels of wisdom which the next sentence elaborates or illustrates:

> Love is a trap. When it appears, we see only its light, not its shadows. (P. Coelho)

"Simply": Certain unigrams that tend to occur in a particular sentence can also point to a very specific rhetorical pattern. For instance, the word "simply" was more likely to appear in the second sentence of a quotation than the first. Quotations that manifest this tendency often use this word to emphasize the second sentence's proposition with respect to the first sentence:

I used to dream about escaping my ordinary life, but my life was never ordinary. I had simply failed to notice how extraordinary it was. (R. Riggs)

6 Quote Order Task

We have analyzed stylistic patterns in quotations. However, are these patterns *characteristic* of quotations? To explore this question and to investigate the overall robustness of our features, we define a *Quote Ordering Task*, the goal of which is to distinguish between the original and reversed versions of a quotation. This experiment is in the tradition of tasks for evaluating models of text coherence, such as the one used by Louis and Nenkova (2012). During training, the classifier is shown either the `original` or `reversed` version of a quote. At test time, the classifier must identify each quote as either `original` or `reversed`.

We conducted two experiments. First, using Naive Bayes classifiers, we performed a 5-fold cross-validation test on balanced subsets of three of the four data-sets: Quotations 1, Non-Quotes 1, and Non-Quotes 2 (n=1846 for each). Next we trained on all of Quotations 1 (n=4237) and tested on a separate test set, Quotations 2 (n=1846). In this second test, we trained on both the `original` and `reversed` version of each quote. Table 2 reports results for both tests under various conditions.

For these tests, "high-level features" refers to high-level syntax (of the first sentence, of the second sentence, and both in a sequence), which if either sentence contains more Abstract Nouns, and which if either sentence contain more General Nouns. Combined with unigrams (including stopwords), these features offered slight but not statistically-significant benefit for Non-Quotes 1 in the cross-validation test and slight but not statistically-significant benefit in the second test (testing on Quotations 2). It remains a challenge to integrate such features for classification purposes.

In both tests, however, we were able to predict the order of quotations upwards of 60% of the time. This was not the case for the non-quotes corpora. In cross-validation, the classifier achieved a high score of 62.6% on Quotations 1, 56.0% on Non-Quotes 1, and 52.9% on Non-Quotes 2. The mean top score for Quotations 1 was higher than for the other two col-

Feature Set	Q1	NQ1	NQ2	Q2
Unigrams	**62.6**	55.6	**52.9**	63.7
All High-Level Features	57.8	54.1	52.2	58.0
All Features	**62.6**	**56.0**	52.7	**63.9**

Table 2: Performance on Quote Ordering Task for Quotations 1, Non-Quotes 1, and Non-Quotes 2 (5-fold cross-validation, baseline = 50%) and on a separate test set, Quotations 2 (baseline = 52%).

lections (two-tailed t-test, $p<.01$). This is evidence that quotations as a genre are more "formulaic" than other textual sequences, their order more easily predicted. We suggest that adherence to latent stylistic patterns is part of what makes quotations seem quotable; as rhetoricians have observed since antiquity, there is power in a pattern.

7 Conclusion

We have analyzed linguistic style not merely as the *presence* of features but also the *order* of features across sentences. In quotations, certain words as well as categories of words and syntactic patterns are more likely to appear in the first or second of two-sentence texts. While other genres may also exhibit regularities in the patterning of stylistic information, our results indicate that this stylistic patterning may be especially strong in quotations. Further research could compare a wider variety of genres. Next steps include investigating the relationship to rhetorical goals and running studies with users to determine if they are consciously aware of these stylistic elements when they post quotations. We would like to a better understanding of why people chose to share the quotations they do.

Analyzing discourse-level stylistic tendencies may prove useful for various applications. Bendersky and Smith (2012) demonstrated a method for automatically culling quotations from textual corpora, yet their method was limited to individual sentences. Taking into account the stylistic schemas of quotations could facilitate the gathering of multi-sentence quotations and assist "creative text retrieval" (Veale, 2011) more generally. In the context of social media platforms where quotes circulate, stylistic patterns could also be used to recommend users stylistically-similar quotations to read.

References

Vikas Ganjigunte Ashok, Song Feng, and Yejin Choi. 2013. Success with style: Using writing style to predict the success of novels. *Poetry*, 580(9):70.

Michael Bendersky and David A Smith. 2012. A dictionary of wisdom and wit: Learning to extract quotable phrases. In *Proceedings of the NAACL-HLT 2012 Workshop on Computational Linguistics for Literature*, pages 69–77.

Yi Chang, Lei Tang, Yoshiyuki Inagaki, and Yan Liu. 2014. What is tumblr: A statistical overview and comparison. *ACM SIGKDD Explorations Newsletter*, 16(1):21–29.

Danqi Chen and Christopher D Manning. 2014. A fast and accurate dependency parser using neural networks. In *EMNLP*, pages 740–750.

Cristian Danescu-Niculescu-Mizil, Justin Cheng, Jon Kleinberg, and Lillian Lee. 2012. You had me at hello: How phrasing affects memorability. In *Proceedings of the 50th Annual Meeting of the Association for Computational Linguistics*, pages 892–901. Association for Computational Linguistics.

Jeff Dolven. 2013. Style. In Roland Greene, editor, *The New Princeton Encyclopedia of Poetry and Poetics*, pages 1369–1370. Princeton University Press, Princeton.

Song Feng, Ritwik Banerjee, and Yejin Choi. 2012. Characterizing stylistic elements in syntactic structure. In *Proceedings of the 2012 Joint Conference on Empirical Methods in Natural Language Processing and Computational Natural Language Learning*, pages 1522–1533. Association for Computational Linguistics.

W Nelson Francis and Henry Kucera. 1979. Brown corpus manual. *Brown University*.

Philip Gianfortoni, David Adamson, and Carolyn P Rosé. 2011. Modeling of stylistic variation in social media with stretchy patterns. In *Proceedings of the First Workshop on Algorithms and Resources for Modelling of Dialects and Language Varieties*, pages 49–59. Association for Computational Linguistics.

Marco Guerini, Gözde Özbal, and Carlo Strapparava. 2015. Echoes of persuasion: The effect of euphony in persuasive communication. In *Human Language Technologies: The 2015 Annual Conference of the North American Chapter of the ACL (NAACL 2015)*, pages 1483–1493.

Michael Alexander Kirkwood Halliday and Ruqaiya Hasan. 2014. *Cohesion in english*. Routledge.

Justine Kao and Dan Jurafsky. 2012. A computational analysis of style, affect, and imagery in contemporary poetry. In *NAACL Workshop on Computational Linguistics for Literature*, pages 8–17.

Dan Klein and Christopher D Manning. 2003. Accurate unlexicalized parsing. In *Proceedings of the 41st Annual Meeting on Association for Computational Linguistics-Volume 1*, pages 423–430. Association for Computational Linguistics.

Polina Kuznetsova, Jianfu Chen, and Yejin Choi. 2013. Understanding and quantifying creativity in lexical composition. In *EMNLP*, pages 1246–1258.

Annie Louis and Ani Nenkova. 2012. A coherence model based on syntactic patterns. In *Proceedings of the 2012 Joint Conference on Empirical Methods in Natural Language Processing and Computational Natural Language Learning*, pages 1157–1168. Association for Computational Linguistics.

Henry Peacham. 1954. *The garden of eloquence (1593): a facsimile reproduction*. Scholars' Facsimiles & Reprints.

Tony Veale. 2011. Creative language retrieval: A robust hybrid of information retrieval and linguistic creativity. In *Proceedings of the 49th Annual Meeting of the Association for Computational Linguistics: Human Language Technologies-Volume 1*, pages 278–287. Association for Computational Linguistics.

David Wible and Nai-Lung Tsao. 2010. Stringnet as a computational resource for discovering and investigating linguistic constructions. In *Proceedings of the NAACL HLT workshop on extracting and using constructions in computational linguistics*, pages 25–31. Association for Computational Linguistics.

Right-truncatable Neural Word Embeddings

Jun Suzuki and **Masaaki Nagata**
NTT Communication Science Laboratories, NTT Corporation
2-4 Hikaridai, Seika-cho, Soraku-gun, Kyoto, 619-0237 Japan
{suzuki.jun, nagata.masaaki}@lab.ntt.co.jp

Abstract

This paper proposes an incremental learning strategy for neural word embedding methods, such as SkipGrams and Global Vectors. Since our method iteratively generates embedding vectors one dimension at a time, obtained vectors equip a unique property. Namely, any right-truncated vector matches the solution of the corresponding lower-dimensional embedding. Therefore, a single embedding vector can manage a wide range of dimensional requirements imposed by many different uses and applications.

1 Introduction

Word embedding vectors obtained from '*neural word embedding methods*', such as SkipGram, continuous bag-of-words (CBoW) and the family of vector log-bilinear (vLBL) models (Mnih and Kavukcuoglu, 2013; Mikolov et al., 2013a; Mikolov et al., 2013c; Mikolov et al., 2013b) have now become an important fundamental resource for tackling many natural language processing (NLP) tasks. These NLP tasks include part-of-speech tagging (Tsuboi, 2014; Ling et al., 2015), dependency parsing (Chen and Manning, 2014; Dyer et al., 2015; Alberti et al., 2015), semantic role labeling (Zhou and Xu, 2015; Woodsend and Lapata, 2015), machine translation (Sutskever et al., 2014), sentiment analysis (Kim et al., 2015), and question answering (Wang and Nyberg, 2015).

The main purpose of this paper is to further enhance the 'usability' of obtained embedding vectors in actual use. To briefly explain our motivation, we first introduce the following concept:

Definition 1 (D'-right-truncated vector[1]). *Let* $\mathbf{w}'$ *and* $\mathbf{w}''$ *be vectors, whose dimensions are* D' *and* D'', *respectively. Namely,* $\mathbf{w}' = (w'_1, \ldots, w'_{D'})$ *and* $\mathbf{w}'' = (w''_1, \ldots, w''_{D''})$. *Suppose* $\mathbf{w}$ *matches the concatenation of* $\mathbf{w}'$ *and* $\mathbf{w}''$, *that is,* $\mathbf{w} = (w'_1, \ldots, w'_{D'}, w''_1, \ldots, w''_{D''})$. *Then, we define* $\mathbf{w}'$ *as a* D'-*right-truncated vector of* $\mathbf{w}$.

This paper focuses on the fact that the appropriate dimension of embedding vectors strongly depends on applications and uses, and is basically determined based on the performance and memory space (or calculation speed) trade-off. Indeed, the actual dimensions of the previous studies listed above are diverse; often around 50, and at most 1000. It is worth noting here that each dimension of embedding vectors obtained by conventional methods has no interpretable meaning. Thus, we basically need to retrain D'-dimensional embedding vectors even if we already have a well-trained D-dimensional vector. In addition, we cannot take full advantage of freely available high-quality pre-trained embedding vectors[2] since their dimensions are already given and fixed, *i.e.*, $D\!=\!300$.

To reduce the additional computational cost of the retraining, and to improve the 'usability' of embedding vectors, we propose a framework for incrementally determining embeddings one dimension at a time from 1 to D. As a result, our method always offers the relation that '*any* D'-*right-truncated em-*

---

[1] The term 'right-truncated' is originally taken from 'right-truncatable prime'

[2] *i.e.*, 'GoogleNews-vectors-negative300' obtained from https://code.google.com/archive/p/word2vec/, and 'glove.840B.300d' obtained from http://nlp.stanford.edu/projects/glove/

Proceedings of NAACL-HLT 2016, pages 1145–1151,
San Diego, California, June 12-17, 2016. ©2016 Association for Computational Linguistics

bedding vector is the solution for D'-dimensional embeddings of our method'. Therefore, in actual use, we only need to construct a relatively higher-dimensional embedding vector 'just once', *i.e.*, $D = 1000$, and then truncate it to an appropriate dimension for the application.

2 Neural Word Embedding Methods

Let $\mathcal{U}$ and $\mathcal{V}$ be two sets of predefined vocabularies of possible inputs and outputs. Let $|\mathcal{U}|$ and $|\mathcal{V}|$ be the number of words in $\mathcal{U}$ and $\mathcal{V}$, respectively. Then, neural word embedding methods generally assign a D-dimensional vector to each word in $\mathcal{U}$ and $\mathcal{V}$. We denote $\mathbf{e}_i$ as representing the i-th input vector, and $\mathbf{o}_j$ for the j-th output vector. In the rest of this paper, for convenience the notation 'i' is always used as the index of input vectors, and 'j' as the index of output vectors, where $1 \leq i \leq |\mathcal{U}|$ and $1 \leq j \leq |\mathcal{V}|$.

We introduce $\mathbf{E}$ and $\mathbf{O}$ that represent lists of all input and output vectors, respectively. Namely, $\mathbf{E} = (\mathbf{e}_1, \cdots, \mathbf{e}_{|\mathcal{U}|})$ and $\mathbf{O} = (\mathbf{o}_1, \cdots, \mathbf{o}_{|\mathcal{V}|})$. $\mathcal{X}$ represents training data. Then, embedding vectors are obtained by solving the following form of a minimization problem defined in each neural word embedding method:

$$(\hat{\mathbf{E}}, \hat{\mathbf{O}}) = \arg\min_{\mathbf{E},\mathbf{O}} \left\{ \Psi(\mathbf{E}, \mathbf{O} \mid \mathcal{X}) \right\}, \qquad (1)$$

where Ψ represents the objective function, and $\hat{\mathbf{E}}$ and $\hat{\mathbf{O}}$ are lists of solution embedding vectors.

Hereafter, we use Ψ as an abbreviation of $\Psi(\mathbf{E}, \mathbf{O} \mid \mathcal{X})$. For example, the objective function Ψ of 'SkipGram with negative sampling (SGNS)' can be written in the following form[3] :

$$\Psi = \sum_{(i,j)} \Big(c_{i,j} L(x_{i,j}) + c'_{i,j} L(-x_{i,j}) \Big), \qquad (2)$$

where $x_{i,j} = \mathbf{e}_i \cdot \mathbf{o}_j$, and $L(x)$ represents a logistic loss function, namely, $L(x) = \log(1 + \exp(-x))$. Moreover, $c_{i,j}$ and $c'_{i,j}$ represent co-occurrences of the i-th input and j-th output words in training data and negative sampling data, respectively.

Another example, the objective function Ψ of the 'Global Vector (GloVe)' can be written in the fol-

---

Input: $\mathcal{X}$: training data, D: maximum number of dimensions (iterations)
1: $\mathbf{E}^{(0)} \leftarrow \emptyset$, $\mathbf{O}^{(0)} \leftarrow \emptyset$, and $\mathbf{B}^{(0)} \leftarrow \mathbf{0}$, $d \leftarrow 0$
2: **repeat**
3:    $d \leftarrow d + 1$
4:    $(\bar{\mathbf{q}}_d, \bar{\mathbf{r}}_d) \leftarrow \texttt{updateParams1D}(\mathcal{X}, \mathbf{B}^{(d-1)})$ // Eq. 5
5:    $\mathbf{E}^{(d)} \leftarrow \texttt{appendVec}(\mathbf{E}^{(d-1)}, \bar{\mathbf{q}}_d)$
6:    $\mathbf{O}^{(d)} \leftarrow \texttt{appendVec}(\mathbf{O}^{(d-1)}, \bar{\mathbf{r}}_d)$
7:    $\mathbf{B}^{(d)} \leftarrow \texttt{updateBias}(\mathbf{B}^{(d-1)}, \bar{\mathbf{q}}_d, \bar{\mathbf{r}}_d)$ // Eq. 4
8: **until** $d = D$
Output: $(\mathbf{E}^{(D)}, \mathbf{O}^{(D)})$

Figure 1: An algorithm for solving an iterative additional coordinate optimization formulation for obtaining embedding vectors.

---

lowing form (Pennington et al., 2014):

$$\Psi = \frac{1}{2} \sum_{(i,j)} \beta_{i,j} (x_{i,j} - m_{i,j})^2, \qquad (3)$$

where $m_{i,j}$ and $\beta_{i,j}$ represent certain co-occurrence and weighting factors of the i-th input and the j-th output words, respectively. For example, $\beta_{i,j} = \min(1, (c_{i,j}/x_{\max})^\gamma)$, and $m_{i,j} = \log(c_{i,j})$ are used in (Pennington et al., 2014), where $x_{\max}$ and γ are tunable hyper-parameters.

3 Incremental Construction of Embedding

This section explains our proposed method. The basic idea is very simple and clear: we convert the minimization problem shown in Eq. 1 to a series of minimization problems, each of whose individual problem determines one additional dimension of each embedding vector. We refer to this formulation of embedding problems as '*ITerative Additional Coordinate Optimization (ITACO)*' formulation. Fig. 1 shows our entire optimization algorithm for this formulation.

3.1 Bias terms and optimization variables

Suppose d represents a discrete time step, where $d \in \{1, \ldots, D\}$. Let $\mathbf{B}^{(d)}$ be a matrix representation of bias terms at the d-th time step, and $b_{i,j}^{(d)}$ denote the (i, j)-factor of $\mathbf{B}^{(d)}$. Then, we define that $b_{i,j}^{(d)}$ for all (i, j) and d have the following recursive relation:

$$b_{i,j}^{(d)} = \sum_{k=1}^{d} e_{i,k} o_{j,k} = b_{i,j}^{(d-1)} + e_{i,d} o_{j,d}, \qquad (4)$$

---

[3]We can obtain this form by a simple reformulation from the original objective of SGNS (Mikolov et al., 2013b).

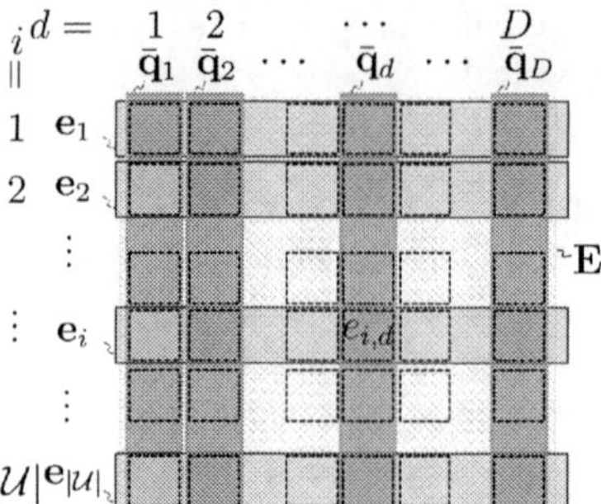

Figure 2: Relation of $\mathbf{e}_i$ and $\bar{\mathbf{q}}_d$ used to represent input vectors in this paper.

where we define $b_{i,j}^{(0)} = 0$ for all (i, j). This relation implies that the solutions of former optimizations are used as bias terms in latter optimizations.

Next, we define $\bar{\mathbf{q}}_d$ and $\bar{\mathbf{r}}_d$ as the vector representations of the concatenation of all the input and output parameters at the d-th step, respectively, that is, $\bar{\mathbf{q}}_d = (e_{1,d}, \ldots, e_{|\mathcal{U}|,d})$ and $\bar{\mathbf{r}}_d = (o_{1,d}, \ldots, o_{|\mathcal{V}|,d})$. Note that $\mathbf{e}_i$ used in the former part of this paper is a D-dimensional vector while $\bar{\mathbf{q}}_d$ and $\bar{\mathbf{r}}_d$ defined here are $|\mathcal{U}|$-dimensional and $|\mathcal{V}|$-dimensional vectors, respectively. Moreover, there are relations that $e_{i,d}$ is the d-th factor of $\mathbf{e}_i$, and, at the same time, the i-th factor of $\bar{\mathbf{q}}_d$.

Fig. 2 illustrates the relation of $\mathbf{e}_i$ and $\bar{\mathbf{q}}_d$ in this paper. We omit to explicitly show the relation of $\mathbf{o}_j$ and $\bar{\mathbf{r}}_d$, which are used to represent output vectors because of the space reason. However obviously, they also have the same relation as $\mathbf{e}_i$ and $\bar{\mathbf{q}}_d$.

3.2 Individual optimization problem

Then, we define the d-th optimization problem in our ITACO formulation as follows:

$$(\bar{\mathbf{q}}_d, \bar{\mathbf{r}}_d) = \arg\min_{\bar{\mathbf{q}}, \bar{\mathbf{r}}} \left\{ \bar{\Psi}\left(\bar{\mathbf{q}}, \bar{\mathbf{r}} \mid \mathcal{X}, \mathbf{B}^{(d-1)}\right) \right\}$$
$$\text{subject to:} \quad \frac{|\mathcal{V}|}{|\mathcal{U}|}||\bar{\mathbf{q}}||_p = ||\bar{\mathbf{r}}||_p, \tag{5}$$

where $|| \cdot ||_p$ represents the L_p-norm. We generally assume that $p = \{1, 2, \infty\}$, and often select $p = 2$. Note that $\bar{\mathbf{q}}_d$ is optimization parameters in the d-th optimization problem while $\mathbf{B}^{(d-1)}$ is the constant. Fig. 3 illustrates the relation of $\mathbf{B}^{(d-1)}$ and $\bar{\mathbf{q}}_d$.

We assume that the objective function $\bar{\Psi}$ takes an identical form as used in one of the conventional methods such as SGNS and GloVe as shown by

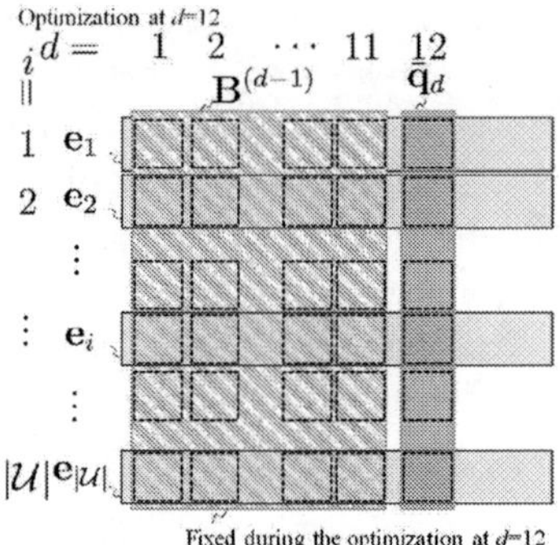

Figure 3: Relation of $\mathbf{B}^{(d-1)}$ and $\bar{\mathbf{q}}_d$, which are the constant and optimization parameters in the d-th optimization problems, respectively.

Eqs. 2 and 3. The difference appears in the variables; our ITACO formulation uses $x_{i,j} = e_i o_j + b_{i,j}$ rather than $x_{i,j} = \mathbf{e}_i \cdot \mathbf{o}_j$ as described in Sec. 2.

3.3 Improving stability of embeddings

The additional norm constraint in Eq. 5 is introduced to improve stability. The optimization problems of neural word embedding methods including SGNS and GloVe can be categorized as a *bi-convex optimization problem* (Gorski et al., 2007); they are convex with respect to the parameters $\mathbf{E}$ if the parameters $\mathbf{O}$ are assumed to be constants, and vice versa. One well-known drawback of unconstrained bi-convex optimization is that the optimization parameters can possibly diverge to $\pm\infty$ (See Example 4.3 in (Gorski et al., 2007)). This is because the objective function only cares about the inner product value of two vectors. Therefore, each parameter can easily have a much larger value, *i.e.*, $o_1 = 10^9$, if e_1 is smaller and approaches a zero value *i.e.*, $e_1 = 10^{-10}$. This is mainly caused by inconsistent scale problem. Thus, our norm constraint in Eq. 5 can eliminate this problem by maintaining the scale of $\bar{\mathbf{q}}$ and $\bar{\mathbf{r}}$ at the same level.

3.4 Optimization algorithm

To solve Eq. 5, we employ the idea of the '*Alternating Convex Optimization (ACO)*' algorithm (Gorski et al., 2007). ACO and its variants have been widely developed in the context of (non-negative) matrix factorization, *i.e.*, (Kim et al., 2014), and are empirically known to be an efficient method in practice. The main idea of ACO is that it iteratively and alternatively updates one parameter set, *i.e.*, $\bar{\mathbf{q}}$, while the other distinct parameter set is fixed, *i.e.*, $\bar{\mathbf{r}}$. In our case, ACO solves the following two optimization problems iteratively and alternately:

$$\bar{\mathbf{q}}_d = \arg\min_{\bar{\mathbf{q}}} \left\{ \bar{\Psi}(\bar{\mathbf{q}}, \bar{\mathbf{r}} \mid \mathcal{X}, \mathbf{B}^{(d-1)}) \right\} \qquad (6)$$

$$\bar{\mathbf{r}}_d = \arg\min_{\bar{\mathbf{r}}} \left\{ \bar{\Psi}(\bar{\mathbf{q}}, \bar{\mathbf{r}} \mid \mathcal{X}, \mathbf{B}^{(d-1)}) \right\}. \qquad (7)$$

There are at least two advantages of using ACO; (1) Eqs. 6 and 7 both become convex optimization problems. Therefore, the global optimum solution can be obtained when $\partial_{e_i} \bar{\Psi} = 0$ for all i and $\partial_{o_j} \bar{\Psi} = 0$ for all j, respectively. (2) ACO guarantees to converge to a stationary point (one of the local minima)[4].

For example, by a simple reformulation of $\partial_{e_i} \bar{\Psi} = 0$, we obtain the closed form solution of Eq. 6 with the GloVe objective, that is,

$$e_i = \frac{\sum_j \beta_{i,j}(m_{i,j} - b_{i,j})o_j}{\sum_j \beta_{i,j}(o_j)^2} \qquad \forall i. \qquad (8)$$

Similarly, the closed form solution of Eq. 7 is:

$$o_j = \frac{\sum_i \beta_{i,j}(m_{i,j} - b_{i,j})e_i}{\sum_i \beta_{i,j}(e_i)^2} \qquad \forall j. \qquad (9)$$

Thus, we can solve Eqs. 6 and 7 without performing iterative estimation. Next, we obtain the following equation by a simple reformulation of $\partial_{e_i} \bar{\Psi} = 0$ for the SGNS objective:

$$\sum_j c_{i,j} o_j = \sum_j (c_{i,j} + c'_{i,j})\sigma(e_i o_j + b_{i,j})o_j, \qquad (10)$$

where $\sigma(x)$ represents a sigmoid function, that is, $\sigma(x) = \frac{1}{1+\exp(-x)}$. Similarly, we also obtain the following form of the equation for Eq. 7:

$$\sum_i c_{i,j} e_i = \sum_i (c_{i,j} + c'_{i,j})\sigma(e_i o_j + b_{i,j})e_i. \qquad (11)$$

These equations are efficiently solvable by a simple binary search procedure since each equation only has a single parameter, that is, e_i or o_j,

During the optimization, there is no guarantee that the constraint $\frac{|\mathcal{V}|}{|\mathcal{U}|}||\bar{\mathbf{q}}||_p = ||\bar{\mathbf{r}}||_p$ always holds. Fortunately, the following transformations always satisfy

---

[4]We somehow prevent the divergence of optimization parameters (Gorski et al., 2007)

Input: $\mathcal{X}$: training data, $\mathbf{B}$: matrix form of bias terms, ϵ: constant for convergence check
1: $\bar{\mathbf{q}} \leftarrow \mathbf{1}$, and $\bar{\mathbf{r}} \leftarrow \mathbf{0}$
2: **repeat**
3:   $\bar{\mathbf{r}} \leftarrow$ `updateIVec1D`$(\bar{\mathbf{r}} \mid \bar{\mathbf{q}}, \mathbf{B})$ // Eq. 11 or 9
4:   $(\bar{\mathbf{q}}, \bar{\mathbf{r}}) \leftarrow$ `scaleVec`$(\bar{\mathbf{q}}, \bar{\mathbf{r}})$ // Eq. 12
5:   $\bar{\mathbf{q}} \leftarrow$ `updateOVec1D`$(\bar{\mathbf{q}} \mid \bar{\mathbf{r}}, \mathbf{B})$ // Eq. 10 or 8
6:   $(\bar{\mathbf{q}}, \bar{\mathbf{r}}) \leftarrow$ `scaleVec`$(\bar{\mathbf{q}}, \bar{\mathbf{r}})$ // Eq. 12
7: **until** `ConvergenceCheck`(ϵ)
Output: $(\bar{\mathbf{q}}, \bar{\mathbf{r}})$

Figure 4: Procedure of `updateParams1D` in Fig. 1 using the ACO-based algorithm.

this norm constraint:

$$\begin{aligned}
\tilde{e}_i &= \frac{|\mathcal{U}|}{|\mathcal{V}|} \frac{e_i}{||\bar{\mathbf{q}}||_p} \left(\frac{|\mathcal{V}|}{|\mathcal{U}|} ||\bar{\mathbf{q}}||_p ||\bar{\mathbf{r}}||_p \right)^{\frac{1}{2}} \quad \forall i \\
\tilde{o}_j &= \frac{o_j}{||\bar{\mathbf{r}}||_p} \left(\frac{|\mathcal{V}|}{|\mathcal{U}|} ||\bar{\mathbf{q}}||_p ||\bar{\mathbf{r}}||_p \right)^{\frac{1}{2}} \quad \forall j,
\end{aligned} \qquad (12)$$

which also maintain $\tilde{e}_i \tilde{o}_j = e_i o_j$, and the objective value. Thus, we can safely apply them at any time during the optimization.

Finally, Fig. 4 shows the optimization procedure when using the ACO framework.

4   Experiments

As in previously reported neural word embedding papers, our training data was taken from a Wikipedia dump (Aug. 2014). We used `hyperwords` tool[5] for our data preparation (Levy et al., 2015).

We compared our method, **ITACO**, with the widely used conventional methods, **SGNS** and **GloVe**. We used the `word2vec` implementation[6] to obtain word embeddings of SGNS, and `glove` implementation[7] for GloVe. Many tunable hyper-parameters were selected based on the recommended default values of each implementation, or suggestion explained in (Levy et al., 2015). For ITACO, we selected the Glove objective to solve Eqs. 6 and 7 since it requires a lower calculation cost than the SGNS objective.

We prepared three types of linguistic benchmark tasks, namely word similarity estimation (**Similarity**), word analogy estimation (**Analogy**), and sentence completion (**SentComp**) tasks. We gathered

---

[5]https://bitbucket.org/omerlevy/hyperwords
[6]https://code.google.com/p/word2vec/ (We made a modification to save the context vector as well as the word vector.)
[7]http://nlp.stanford.edu/projects/glove/

Methods	Analogy					
	D=10	50	100	300	500	1000
ITACO (trunc)	***2.6**	**38.0**	**51.5**	**63.5**	**65.4**	***65.6**
SGNS (trunc)	0.0	11.8	34.6	57.4	61.9	63.2
GloVe (trunc)	0.1	20.1	42.3	60.7	63.2	***65.6**
SGNS (retrain)	1.7	37.7	51.8	62.3	64.0	–
GloVe (retrain)	*2.6	*42.6	*57.0	*65.6	*66.4	–

Methods	Similarity					
	D=10	50	100	300	500	1000
ITACO (trunc)	**41.6**	**55.2**	**58.5**	**61.4**	**62.2**	62.9
SGNS (trunc)	29.0	46.1	52.5	60.7	61.8	***64.5**
GloVe (trunc)	29.3	46.2	50.6	56.8	58.5	59.9
SGNS (retrain)	*46.4	*58.2	*61.3	*63.9	*64.2	–
GloVe (retrain)	38.7	51.4	54.2	56.8	58.1	–

Methods	SentComp					
	D=10	50	100	300	500	1000
ITACO (trunc)	***29.2**	***32.3**	**32.1**	***34.3**	***35.4**	***36.6**
SGNS (trunc)	24.2	26.2	29.9	32.1	32.3	36.1
GloVe (trunc)	22.8	24.3	26.7	26.7	28.2	27.7
SGNS (retrain)	24.8	29.7	*33.0	32.7	33.9	–
GloVe (retrain)	26.3	27.3	27.1	28.1	28.1	–

Table 1: Results of right-truncated embedding vectors (trunc), and standard embedding vectors (retrain). '*' represents the best results in the corresponding column.

nine datasets for Similarity (Rubenstein and Goodenough, 1965; Miller and Charles, 1991; Agirre et al., 2009; Agirre et al., 2009; Bruni et al., 2014; Radinsky et al., 2011; Huang et al., 2012; Luong et al., 2013; Hill et al., 2014), three for Analogy (Mikolov et al., 2013a; Mikolov et al., 2013c) , and one for SentComp (Mikolov et al., 2013a).

Table 1 shows all the results of our experiments[8]. The rows labeled '(trunc)' show the performance of D-right-truncated embedding vectors, whose original vector of dimension is $D = 1000$. Thus, they were obtained from a single set of embedding vectors with $D = 1000$ for each corresponding method. Next, the rows labeled '(retrain)' show the performance provided by SGNS or GloVe that were independently constructed with using a standard setting and corresponding D. Note that the results of 'ITACO (retrain)' are identical to those of 'ITACO (trunc)'. Moreover, 'GloVe (trunc)' and 'GloVe (retrain)' in $D = 1000$ are equivalent, as are 'SGNS (trunc)' and 'SGNS (retrain)'. Thus, these results

were omitted from the table.

First, comparing '(retrain)' and '(trunc)' in SGNS and GloVe, our experimental results first explicitly revealed that SGNS and GloVe with the simple truncation approach '(trunc)' cannot provide effective lower-dimensional embedding vectors. This observation strongly supports the significance of existence of our proposed method, ITACO.

Second, in most cases ITACO successfully provided almost the same performance level as the best SGNS and GloVe (retrain) results. We emphasize that ITACO constructed embedding vectors 'just once', while SGNS and GloVe required us to retrain embedding vectors in the corresponding times. In addition, single run of ITACO for $D = 1000$ took approximately 12,000 seconds in our machine environment, which was almost equivalent to run 4 iterations of SGNS and 8 iterations of GloVe. The results of SGNS and GloVe in Table 1 were obtained by 10 iterations and 20 iterations, respectively, which are one of the standard settings to run SGNS and GloVe[9]. This fact verified that ITACO can run efficiently as in the same level as SGNS and GloVe.

5 Conclusion

This paper proposed a method for generating interesting right-truncatable word embedding vectors. Our experiments revealed that the embedding vectors obtained with our method, ITACO, in any lower dimensions work as well as those obtained by SGNS and Glove. In addition, ITACO can also be a good alternative of SGNS and GloVe in terms of the execution speed of a single run. Now, we are free from retraining different dimensions of embedding vectors by using ITACO. Our method significantly reduces the total calculation cost and storage, which improves the 'usability' of embedding vectors[10].

Acknowledgment

We thank three anonymous reviewers for their helpful comments.

---

[8]Results for SGNS and GloVe are the average performance of ten runs as suggested in (Suzuki and Nagata, 2015)

[9]The performance of 4 iterations of SGNS and 8 iterations of GloVe were much lower than those of 10 iterations and 20 iterations of SGNS and GloVe shown in Table 1, respectively.

[10]The right-truncatable embedding vectors used in our experiments will be available in author's homepage

References

Eneko Agirre, Enrique Alfonseca, Keith Hall, Jana Kravalova, Marius Paşca, and Aitor Soroa. 2009. A Study on Similarity and Relatedness Using Distributional and WordNet-based Approaches. In *Proceedings of Human Language Technologies: The 2009 Annual Conference of the North American Chapter of the Association for Computational Linguistics*, NAACL '09, pages 19–27, Stroudsburg, PA, USA. Association for Computational Linguistics.

Chris Alberti, David Weiss, Greg Coppola, and Slav Petrov. 2015. Improved Transition-Based Parsing and Tagging with Neural Networks. In *Proceedings of the 2015 Conference on Empirical Methods in Natural Language Processing*, pages 1354–1359, Lisbon, Portugal, September. Association for Computational Linguistics.

Elia Bruni, Nam Khanh Tran, and Marco Baroni. 2014. Multimodal Distributional Semantics. *J. Artif. Int. Res.*, 49(1):1–47, January.

Danqi Chen and Christopher Manning. 2014. A Fast and Accurate Dependency Parser using Neural Networks. In *Proceedings of the 2014 Conference on Empirical Methods in Natural Language Processing (EMNLP)*, pages 740–750, Doha, Qatar, October. Association for Computational Linguistics.

Chris Dyer, Miguel Ballesteros, Wang Ling, Austin Matthews, and Noah A. Smith. 2015. Transition-Based Dependency Parsing with Stack Long Short-Term Memory. In *Proceedings of the 53rd Annual Meeting of the Association for Computational Linguistics and the 7th International Joint Conference on Natural Language Processing (Volume 1: Long Papers)*, pages 334–343, Beijing, China, July. Association for Computational Linguistics.

Yoav Goldberg and Omer Levy. 2014. word2vec Explained: Deriving Mikolov et al.'s Negative-sampling Word-embedding Method. *CoRR*, abs/1402.3722.

Jochen Gorski, Frank Pfeuffer, and Kathrin Klamroth. 2007. Biconvex Sets and Optimization with Biconvex Functions: a Survey and Extensions. *Math. Meth. of OR*, 66(3):373–407.

Felix Hill, Roi Reichart, and Anna Korhonen. 2014. SimLex-999: Evaluating Semantic Models with (Genuine) Similarity Estimation. *ArXiv e-prints*, August.

Eric H. Huang, Richard Socher, Christopher D. Manning, and Andrew Y. Ng. 2012. Improving Word Representations via Global Context and Multiple Word Prototypes. In *Proceedings of the 50th Annual Meeting of the Association for Computational Linguistics: Long Papers - Volume 1*, pages 873–882. Association for Computational Linguistics.

Jingu Kim, Yunlong He, and Haesun Park. 2014. Algorithms for Nonnegative Matrix and Tensor Factorizations: a Unified View Based on Block Coordinate Descent Framework. *Journal of Global Optimization*, 58(2):285–319.

Jonghoon Kim, Francois Rousseau, and Michalis Vazirgiannis. 2015. Convolutional Sentence Kernel from Word Embeddings for Short Text Categorization. In *Proceedings of the 2015 Conference on Empirical Methods in Natural Language Processing*, pages 775–780, Lisbon, Portugal, September. Association for Computational Linguistics.

Omer Levy and Yoav Goldberg. 2014. Neural Word Embedding as Implicit Matrix Factorization. In Z. Ghahramani, M. Welling, C. Cortes, N.D. Lawrence, and K.Q. Weinberger, editors, *Advances in Neural Information Processing Systems 27*, pages 2177–2185. Curran Associates, Inc.

Omer Levy, Yoav Goldberg, and Ido Dagan. 2015. Improving Distributional Similarity with Lessons Learned from Word Embeddings. *Transactions of the Association for Computational Linguistics*, 3.

Wang Ling, Chris Dyer, Alan W Black, Isabel Trancoso, Ramon Fermandez, Silvio Amir, Luis Marujo, and Tiago Luis. 2015. Finding Function in Form: Compositional Character Models for Open Vocabulary Word Representation. In *Proceedings of the 2015 Conference on Empirical Methods in Natural Language Processing*, pages 1520–1530, Lisbon, Portugal, September. Association for Computational Linguistics.

Thang Luong, Richard Socher, and Christopher Manning. 2013. Better Word Representations with Recursive Neural Networks for Morphology. In *Proceedings of the Seventeenth Conference on Computational Natural Language Learning*, pages 104–113, Sofia, Bulgaria, August. Association for Computational Linguistics.

Tomas Mikolov, Kai Chen, Greg Corrado, and Jeffrey Dean. 2013a. Efficient Estimation of Word Representations in Vector Space. *CoRR*, abs/1301.3781.

Tomas Mikolov, Ilya Sutskever, Kai Chen, Greg S Corrado, and Jeff Dean. 2013b. Distributed Representations of Words and Phrases and their Compositionality. In C.J.C. Burges, L. Bottou, M. Welling, Z. Ghahramani, and K.Q. Weinberger, editors, *Advances in Neural Information Processing Systems 26*, pages 3111–3119. Curran Associates, Inc.

Tomas Mikolov, Wen-tau Yih, and Geoffrey Zweig. 2013c. Linguistic Regularities in Continuous Space Word Representations. In *Proceedings of the 2013 Conference of the North American Chapter of the Association for Computational Linguistics: Human Language Technologies*, pages 746–751, Atlanta, Georgia, June. Association for Computational Linguistics.

George A. Miller and Walter G. Charles. 1991. Contextual Correlates of Semantic Similarity. *Language & Cognitive Processes*, 6(1):1–28.

Andriy Mnih and Koray Kavukcuoglu. 2013. Learning Word Embeddings Efficiently With Noise-contrastive Estimation. In C.J.C. Burges, L. Bottou, M. Welling, Z. Ghahramani, and K.Q. Weinberger, editors, *Advances in Neural Information Processing Systems 26*, pages 2265–2273. Curran Associates, Inc.

Jeffrey Pennington, Richard Socher, and Christopher Manning. 2014. Glove: Global Vectors for Word Represqentation. In *Proceedings of the 2014 Conference on Empirical Methods in Natural Language Processing (EMNLP)*, pages 1532–1543, Doha, Qatar, October. Association for Computational Linguistics.

Kira Radinsky, Eugene Agichtein, Evgeniy Gabrilovich, and Shaul Markovitch. 2011. A Word at a Time: Computing Word Relatedness Using Temporal Semantic Analysis. In *Proceedings of the 20th International Conference on World Wide Web*, WWW '11, pages 337–346, New York, NY, USA. ACM.

Herbert Rubenstein and John B. Goodenough. 1965. Contextual Correlates of Synonymy. *Commun. ACM*, 8(10):627–633, October.

Ilya Sutskever, Oriol Vinyals, and Quoc V Le. 2014. Sequence to Sequence Learning with Neural Networks. In Z. Ghahramani, M. Welling, C. Cortes, N. D. Lawrence, and K. Q. Weinberger, editors, *Advances in Neural Information Processing Systems 27*, pages 3104–3112. Curran Associates, Inc.

Jun Suzuki and Masaaki Nagata. 2015. A Unified Learning Framework of Skip-Grams and Global Vectors. In *Proceedings of the 53rd Annual Meeting of the Association for Computational Linguistics and the 7th International Joint Conference on Natural Language Processing (Volume 2: Short Papers)*, pages 186–191, Beijing, China, July. Association for Computational Linguistics.

Yuta Tsuboi. 2014. Neural Networks Leverage Corpus-wide Information for Part-of-speech Tagging. In *Proceedings of the 2014 Conference on Empirical Methods in Natural Language Processing (EMNLP)*, pages 938–950, Doha, Qatar, October. Association for Computational Linguistics.

Di Wang and Eric Nyberg. 2015. A Long Short-Term Memory Model for Answer Sentence Selection in Question Answering. In *Proceedings of the 53rd Annual Meeting of the Association for Computational Linguistics and the 7th International Joint Conference on Natural Language Processing (Volume 2: Short Papers)*, pages 707–712, Beijing, China, July. Association for Computational Linguistics.

Kristian Woodsend and Mirella Lapata. 2015. Distributed Representations for Unsupervised Semantic Role Labeling. In *Proceedings of the 2015 Conference on Empirical Methods in Natural Language Processing*, pages 2482–2491, Lisbon, Portugal, September. Association for Computational Linguistics.

Jie Zhou and Wei Xu. 2015. End-to-end Learning of Semantic Role Labeling using Recurrent Neural Networks. In *Proceedings of the 53rd Annual Meeting of the Association for Computational Linguistics and the 7th International Joint Conference on Natural Language Processing (Volume 1: Long Papers)*, pages 1127–1137, Beijing, China, July. Association for Computational Linguistics.

Geoffrey Zweig and Christopher J.C. Burges. 2011. The microsoft research sentence completion challenge. Technical Report MSR-TR-2011-129, Microsoft Research, December.

MAWPS: A Math Word Problem Repository

Rik Koncel-Kedziorski*[1], Subhro Roy*[2], Aida Amini[1],
Nate Kushman[3], and Hannaneh Hajishirzi[1]
[1]University of Washington, [2]University of Illinois Urbana Champaign, [3]Microsoft Research
{kedzior, amini91, hannaneh}@uw.edu, sroy9@illinois.edu, nkushman@microsoft.com

Abstract

Recent work across several AI subdisciplines has focused on automatically solving math word problems. In this paper we introduce MAWPS, an online repository of Math Word Problems, to provide a unified testbed to evaluate different algorithms. MAWPS allows for the automatic construction of datasets with particular characteristics, providing tools for tuning the lexical and template overlap of a dataset as well as for filtering ungrammatical problems from web-sourced corpora. The online nature of this repository facilitates easy community contribution. At present, we have amassed 3,320 problems, including the full datasets used in several prominent works.

1 Introduction

Automatically solving math word problems has proved a difficult and interesting challenge for the AI research community (Feigenbaum et al., 1995). Math word problems serve as a testbed for algorithms that build a precise understanding of what is being asserted in text. Consider the following:

Rachel bought two coloring books. One had 23 pictures and the other had 32. After one week she had colored 44 of the pictures. How many pictures does she still have to color?

To solve such a problem, an algorithm must model implicit and explicit quantities in the text and their relationships through mathematical operations.

Many researchers have taken on this challenge to design data-driven approaches to solve different types of math word problems (Hosseini et al., 2014; Kushman et al., 2014; Roy and Roth, 2015; Zhou et al., 2015; Koncel-Kedziorski et al., 2015). Treatments of this task range from template-matching to narrative-building, and methods including integer linear programming, factorization, and more appear in the literature. As a result of the variety of approaches, several datasets have emerged. The variety of math word problems in these datasets is such that researchers have already begun specializing in the types of problems that their systems are able to successfully solve. Additionally, in some datasets one may find significant repetition of common words, a small set of equation templates used again and again, or problem texts which map to highly degraded grammatical structures. Therefore, designing general algorithms that can address different problem types while still being robust to the variations across datasets has remained a challenge.

In response to the burgeoning interest in this task, we present MAWPS (MAth Word ProblemS, pronounced *mops*), a framework for building an online repository of math word problems. Our framework includes a collection of varying types of math word problems, their answers, and equation templates, as well as interfaces which allow researchers to dynamically update and add more problem types. Additionally, in light of the problematic features of the current datasets cited above, our framework provides the possibility for customizing a dataset with regard to considerations such as lexical and template overlap or grammaticality, allowing researchers to choose how many of the difficulties of open domain web-sourced word problem texts they want

---

* denotes equal contribution

Proceedings of NAACL-HLT 2016, pages 1152–1157,
San Diego, California, June 12-17, 2016. ©2016 Association for Computational Linguistics

to tackle. We report the important characteristics of the current available data as well as the performance of some state-of-the-art systems on various subsets of the data. MAWPS is located at `http://lang.ee.washington.edu/MAWPS`.

2   Related Work

Recently, automatically solving math word problems has attracted several researchers. Specific topics include number word problems (Shi et al., 2015), logic puzzle problems (Mitra and Baral, 2015), arithmetic word problems (Hosseini et al., 2014; Roy and Roth, 2015), algebra word problems (Kushman et al., 2014; Zhou et al., 2015; Koncel-Kedziorski et al., 2015), and geometry word problems (Seo et al., 2015).

A few recent works, Kushman et al. (2014) and Zhou et al. (2015) focus on solving math word problems by matching quantities and variables (nouns) extracted from the problem text to templates appearing in the training data. These methods have a broad scope, but they rely heavily on overlap between templates in the training and test data. As shown in our experiments, when that overlap is reduced, the performance of the systems drops significantly.

Other work has focused on more limited domains, but aims to reduce the reliance on data overlap. Hosseini et al. (2014) solve addition and subtraction problems by learning to categorize verbs for the purpose of updating a world representation derived from the problem text. Roy and Roth (2015) treat arithmetic word problem templates as equation trees and introduce a method for learning the least governing node for two text quantities. Koncel-Kedziorski et al. (2015) focus on single equation problems and use typed semantically-rich equation trees where nodes correspond to numbers and an associated type derived from the problem text, and efficiently enumerate the space of these trees using integer linear programming.

Our work is also inspired by the recent work in introducing datasets to evaluate question answering and reading comprehension tasks that require reasoning and entailment. In contrast to Richardson et al. (2013), our work is focused on making a dataset for math word problems to evaluate robustness, scalability, and scope of algorithms in quantitative reasoning. In contrast to Weston et al. (2015), our work

has more natural text and a larger vocabulary, does not use synthetic data, and is only focused on math word problems which is an extension of the counting sub-category introduced in that work.

3   Data

We compile a dataset of arithmetic and algebra word problems of varying complexity from different websites. This data extends the published word problem datasets used in Hosseini et al. (2014), Kushman et al. (2014), Koncel-Kedziorski et al. (2015), and Roy and Roth (2015). In addition to this strong foundation, the MAWPS repository provides interfaces for adding new word problems, allowing for its extension and development.

Noting that word problem datasets have varied with regard to noisiness and repetition, we define several data characteristics to capture these properties below. We then allow a user of the repository to select a subset of the data that optimizes these characteristics. The three data characteristics that can be automatically manipulated by MAWPS are:

Lexical Overlap.   Lexical overlap describes the reuse of lexemes among problems in a dataset. For example, several problems may describe tickets being sold for a play, with only the number of adult and child tickets changed among them. These problems would have high lexical overlap. Previous work has shown that lexeme reuse in a dataset allows for spurious associations between the problem text and a correct solution (Koncel-Kedziorski et al., 2015). Researchers have sought to reduce this characteristic in their data so as to facilitate the development of more robust methods.

Template Overlap.   By *template* we mean an equation where numerical values are replaced by a consistent, ordered set of constant variables. For example, the equations $(12 * 2) + 7 = x$ and $(6 * 15) + 105 = x$ have the same template, $(a * b) + c = x$. As shown in Roy and Roth (2015) and elsewhere, the appearance of a similar template in the training data is a requirement for some systems at test time. More general math word problem solvers have been introduced that reduce or eliminate this reliance. MAWPS provides for the automatic construction of a dataset with minimized template overlap.

Grammaticality.   Many math word problems for use in AI research are drawn from user-submitted

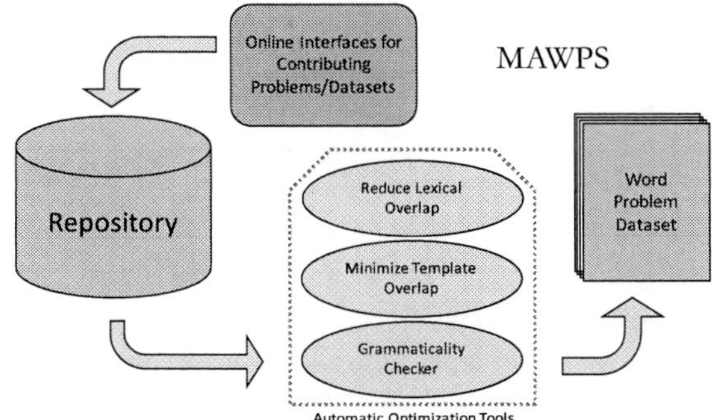

Figure 1: MAWPS System overview: Online interfaces allow for extending repository. Optimization Tools allow for real-time delivery of usable datasets with particular characteristics.

online sources. Some problems from these sources contain grammatical errors including morphological agreement failures, misspellings, and other more complicated ungrammaticalities (for example, "Joan paid \$8.77 on a cat toy, and a cage cost her \$10.97 with a \$20 bill."). While some researchers wish to develop methods robust to these kind of errors, others would focus on the subset of the data that adheres to a high-precision, expertly developed grammar of English. To facilitate both lines of research, we allow for the selection of only those problems which meet this judgment, or the full data.

4 System Overview

The goal of the MAWPS repository is to provide an extendable collection of math word problems which allows researchers to select the portion of the data that meets their needs. To facilitate the growth of the collection, our framework allows for easily adding a single word problem or a whole dataset to the repository. We design backend tools which allow researchers to select a dataset with reduced lexical overlap, minimized template overlap, or improved grammaticality characteristics even as the repository continues to grow through community contribution. Figure 1 shows an outline of the MAWPS system.

4.1 Reduce Lexical Overlap

We consider the lexical overlap of a dataset D to be the average of the pairwise lexical overlap between each pair of problems in D. First, let $W(p)$ denote the set of unique unigrams and bigrams in a problem

p. Then $PairLex(p, q) = \frac{|W(p) \cap W(q)|}{|W(p) \cup W(q)|}$ denotes the pairwise lexical overlap between problems p and q.

We formally define the lexical overlap of a dataset D as

$$\text{Lex}(D) = \frac{1}{N} \sum_{\substack{p_i, p_j \in D \\ i < j}} PairLex(p_i, p_j)$$

where $N = \binom{|D|}{2}$ is the number of problem pairs in D. Given a dataset D and a target subset size k, MAWPS automatically finds a subset D' of reduced lexical overlap by solving the following optimization problem: $\min_{D' \subseteq D, |D'|=k} \text{Lex}(D')$.

This is the remote clique problem[1], which is NP hard. As a result, we resort to a greedy strategy which gives an approximation ratio of 2 (Birnbaum and Goldman, 2007). We define $f_{\text{lex}}(p, D') = \sum_{q \in D'} PairLex(p, q)$, which describes the overlap between a problem p and dataset D'. The greedy method to generate subset D' of D is as follows: we iteratively add a problem p from $D \setminus D'$ to D' which minimizes the value of $f_{\text{lex}}(p, D')$. That is, at each step, we add a problem which has the least average pairwise lexical overlap with the problems already in D'. We repeat this process, starting with a randomly initialized singleton set, until a set of k problems is created.

4.2 Minimize Template Overlap

The template overlap of a dataset D is defined analogously to lexical overlap as the average of the pairwise template overlap between each pair of problems of D. Let $PairTempl(p, q)$ be 1 if p and q have the same template (corresponding to the gold equation), and 0 otherwise. We then define the template overlap of a dataset D as

$$\text{Tmpl}(D) = \frac{1}{N} \sum_{\substack{p_i, p_j \in D \\ i < j}} PairTempl(p_i, p_j)$$

where $N = \binom{|D|}{2}$. Given a dataset D and a target subset size k, the template overlap reduced subset of D is generated by the following: $\min_{D' \subseteq D, |D'|=k} \text{Tmpl}(D')$.

---

[1]Given a complete graph with nonnegative edge weights satisfying the triangle inequality and a positive integer p, the remote-clique problem is to find a subset of p vertices having a maximum-weight induced subgraph.

Dataset	# Probs $|D|$	# Gramm.	Lexical Overlap (Lex)			Template Overlap (Tmpl)		
			$k = |D|/2$	$k = |D|$	Reduction	$k = |D|/2$	$k = |D|$	Reduction
AddSub	395	357	6.1	7.9	22.8	33	37.2	11.3
SingleOp	562	491	6.1	7.8	21.8	24.7	25.4	2.8
MultiArith	600	526	7.8	9.4	17.0	19.7	22.1	10.9
SingleEq	508	434	5.4	6.8	20.6	11	17.9	38.5
SimulEq-S	514	437	4.7	6	21.7	2.9	12.5	76.8
SimulEq-L	1155	980	4.4	5.7	22.8	0.1	3.3	97.0

Table 1: Characteristics of datasets added to our repository. # Gramm. is no. of problems which passed our grammaticality check, the Lex column reports minimum lexical overlap for size k dataset, the Tmpl column reports minimum template overlap for size k dataset, Reduction denotes the % decrease in overlap value obtained by our system, when going from $k = |D|$ to $k = |D|/2$. We report all numbers as percentages.

Dataset	System	All $|D|$	Gramm.	Lex $(|D|/2)$	Tmpl $(|D|/2)$	Random $(|D|/2)$
SingleEq	(Koncel-Kedziorski et al., 2015)	72.2	74.2	63.6	67.0	67.2
SimulEq-S	(Kushman et al., 2014)	68.7	70.3	61.1	59.9	66.8

Table 2: Effect of lexical, template overlap and grammaticality data characteristics over various systems.

This again is an instance of remote clique problem, and we follow a similar greedy strategy. We define $f_{\text{tmpl}}(p, D') = \sum_{q \in D'} PairTempl(p, q)$, which describes the overlap between a problem p and dataset D'. The greedy method to generate subset D' of D is as follows: we iteratively add a problem p from $D \setminus D'$ to D' which minimizes the value of $f_{\text{tmpl}}(p, D')$. In other words, the algorithm iteratively chooses problem p from $D \setminus D'$ and adds it to D' such that (if possible) p adds a new template to D'. If there are no new templates to be added, then a p whose template is least frequent among those of D' is selected. This process is repeated until D' has k problems.

4.3 Template/Lexical Interaction

Given a dataset and a target subset size k, we would like a subset with the best lexical and template overlap characteristics. As an approximation, we reduce the arithmetic mean of the two overlap values. This mean can be expressed as $H(D) = \frac{1}{2}(\text{Lex}(D) + \text{Tmpl}(D))$. A similar greedy iterative approach as before generates the required dataset with the aforementioned approximation guarantee.

4.4 Grammaticality

Given a dataset, MAWPS can automatically remove ungrammatical word problems, resulting in a subset with improved grammaticality. Our system uses the broad-coverage, linguistically precise English Resource Grammar (ERG) (Flickinger, 2000;

Flickinger, 2011) for determining grammaticality. The ERG is a continually-developed implementation of the grammatical theory of Head-Driven Phrase Structure Grammar that covers an increasingly wide variety of phenomena. Moreover, the ERG makes binary decisions for sentence acceptability: if it cannot find a valid parse among its rules, it returns no parse for that sentence. This contrasts with statistical parsers whose utility for this task is limited by the difficulties of tuning a cutoff confidence threshold for acceptability. We allow for filtering problems with ungrammatical sentences.

5 Properties of Current Data

We initialize our repository by extending the publicly available datasets. We list them below in order of increasing complexity of the final equation form.

- **AddSub**: Collection of addition, subtraction problems (Hosseini et al., 2014).
- **SingleOp**: Collection of single operation arithmetic problems (Roy et al., 2015).
- **MultiArith**: Collection of multi-step arithmetic problems (Roy and Roth, 2015).
- **SingleEq**: Single equation problems from (Koncel-Kedziorski et al., 2015).
- **SimulEq-S**: Single and two equation word problems from (Kushman et al., 2014).
- **SimulEq-L**: Collection of single and multiple equation word problems, superset of **SimulEq-S**.

Table 1 shows the characteristics of the datasets under various conditions of grammaticality, lexical and template overlap. Template overlap varies greatly across datasets, and decreases sharply with increase of complexity of target equation. Lexical overlap, on the other hand, does not show much variation, with most datasets having overlap value of around 7%. Our system effectively reduces overlap, obtaining around 20% reduction in most cases (going from $k = |D|$ to $k = |D|/2$). In the case of template overlap, this reduction varies greatly based on the complexity of target equation, ranging from 2.8% for SingleOp to 97% for SimulEq-L.

As no current system can process **SimulEq-L**, we report the performance of the two most general systems (Koncel-Kedziorski et al., 2015; Kushman et al., 2014) on **SingleEq** and **SimulEq-S** under different overlap and grammaticality properties in Table 2. We use a 5-fold cross validation setup and report average accuracy across folds. We include performance on a randomly selected dataset of the same size to analyze the effect of decreased data-size on performance.

Both systems gain from the pruning of grammatically incorrect problems from the dataset. Our results support the findings of Koncel-Kedziorski et al. (2015) regarding the diminishing performance of systems when faced with reduced lexical and template overlap. We expect, as that work showed, that further reducing these characteristics would result in even lower performance. The results on a random subset of the data show that data set size does not have as strong of an effect on algorithm performance as lexical or template overlap.

6 Conclusion

In this paper, we introduced MAWPS, a repository of math word problems. MAWPS offers a large collection of data from new and published datasets, provides interfaces for adding data, and includes data optimization tools. As current results show, designing general algorithms that can address different problem types while still being robust to the template or lexical variations has remained a challenge. We hope that our framework will help facilitate comparison between results while allowing researchers to focus on targets such as all grammatical problems or all single equation problems. We also include an official 80/20 test/train split of all problems available at the time of this publication.

Acknowledgments: This research was supported by the Allen Institute for AI (66-9175), Allen Distinguished Investigator Award, NSF (IIS-1352249), DARPA (FA8750-13-2-0008) and a Google research faculty award. We thank the anonymous reviewers for their helpful comments.

References

Benjamin Birnbaum and Kenneth J. Goldman. 2007. An Improved Analysis for a Greedy Remote-Clique Algorithm Using Factor-Revealing LPs. *Algorithmica*, 55(1):42–59.

Edward A Feigenbaum, Julian Feldman, and Paul Armer. 1995. *Computers and Thought*. AAAI press.

Dan Flickinger. 2000. On building a more effcient grammar by exploiting types. *Natural Language Engineering*, 6(01):15–28.

Dan Flickinger. 2011. Accuracy vs. Robustness in Grammar Engineering. *Language from a cognitive perspective: Grammar, usage, and processing*, pages 31–50.

Mohammad Javad Hosseini, Hannaneh Hajishirzi, Oren Etzioni, and Nate Kushman. 2014. Learning to Solve Arithmetic Word Problems with Verb Categorization. In *EMNLP*, pages 523–533.

Rik Koncel-Kedziorski, Hannaneh Hajishirzi, Ashish Sabharwal, Oren Etzioni, and Siena Ang. 2015. Parsing Algebraic Word Problems into Equations. *TACL*, 3:585–597.

Nate Kushman, Yoav Artzi, Luke Zettlemoyer, and Regina Barzilay. 2014. Learning to Automatically Solve Algebra Word Problems. In *ACL*, pages 271–281.

Arindam Mitra and Chitta Baral. 2015. Learning to automatically solve logic grid puzzles. In *EMNLP*.

Matthew Richardson, Christopher JC Burges, and Erin Renshaw. 2013. MCTest: A Challenge Dataset for the Open-Domain Machine Comprehension of Text. In *EMNLP*, volume 1, page 2.

Subhro Roy and Dan Roth. 2015. Solving General Arithmetic Word Problems. In *EMNLP*.

Subhro Roy, Tim Vieira, and Dan Roth. 2015. Reasoning about Quantities in Natural Language. *TACL*.

Minjoon Seo, Hannaneh Hajishirzi, Ali Farhadi, Oren Etzioni, and Clint Malcolm. 2015. Solving Geometry Problems: Combining Text and Diagram Interpretation. In *EMNLP*.

Shuming Shi, Yuehui Wang, Chin-Yew Lin, Xiaojiang Liu, and Yong Rui. 2015. Automatically Solving Number Word Problems by Semantic Parsing and Reasoning. In *EMNLP*.

Jason Weston, Antoine Bordes, Sumit Chopra, and Tomas Mikolov. 2015. Towards AI-complete Question Answering: a set of prerequisite toy tasks. *arXiv preprint arXiv:1502.05698*.

Lipu Zhou, Shuaixiang Dai, and Liwei Chen. 2015. Learn to Solve Algebra Word Problems Using Quadratic Programming. In *EMNLP*.

Cross-genre Event Extraction with Knowledge Enrichment

Hao Li and Heng Ji

Computer Science Department

Rensselaer Polytechnic Institute

jih@rpi.edu

Abstract

The goal of Event extraction is to extract structured information of events that are of interest from unstructured documents. Existing event extractors for social media suffer from two major problems: lack of context and informal nature. In this paper, instead of conducting event extraction solely on each social media message, we incorporate cross-genre knowledge to boost the event extractor performance. Experiment results demonstrate that without any additional annotations, our proposed approach is able to provide 15% absolute F-score improvement over the state-of-the-art.

1 Introduction

The rapid development of social media and social networks since 2000s has made it an important channel of information dissemination. Because of its real-time nature, social media can be used as a sensor to gather up-to-date information about the state of the world. Effective automatic detection and extraction of events from the media will be an extremely important contribution. Recently there has been increasing interests in event extraction from social media (Yang et al., 1998; Kleinberg, 2003; He et al., 2007; Weng and Lee, 2011; Benson et al., 2011; Ritter et al., 2012).

Identifying and extracting events in social media is more challenging than traditional event extraction due to two major reasons: (1). **Lack of Context**: compared with traditional genres (e.g., new articles), social media context is usually short and incomplete (e.g., each tweet has a length limitation of 140 char-

acters). Lacking of context, a single tweet itself usually cannot provide a complete picture of the corresponding events. For example, for the tweet *"Pray for Mali - the situation is coming to light, and it isn't pretty."*, an event extraction/discovery system (e.g. (Ji and Grishman, 2008)) fails to discover that it is about the same *war* event in *Mali* as mentioned in the news article *"State military forces on Friday retook a key town in northern Mali after intense fighting that included help from French military forces, a defense ministry spokesman said."* (2). **Informal Nature**: social media messages are written in an informal style, which causes the poor performance of event extractors designed for formal genres. For example, the tweet *"#AaronSwartz, Dead @ 26, #CarmenOrtiz "pushed him to exhaustion" don't let her get away with this! #scandal."* includes an *"Die"* event with *Aaron Swartz* as the *Victim*. However, the person name "AaronSwartz" appears in the hashtag "#AaronSwartz" and "Dead at 26" is written as "Dead @ 26". Existing supervised name taggers and event extractors fail to identify the same "Die" event mentioned in the news article *"Internet activist Aaron Swartz dead at 26"*.

Based on the intuition that news articles contain more detailed and formal information than tweet messages, we apply an unsupervised knowledge enrichment algorithm to link each tweet to its most relevant news article. By incorporating the cross-genre knowledge to tweets, we are able to formulate the task of event extraction on tweets as the task of cross-genre extraction for tweets and news articles. Thus we can alleviate the previous mentioned challenges in single-genre event extraction for tweets to

Proceedings of NAACL-HLT 2016, pages 1158–1162,

San Diego, California, June 12-17, 2016. ©2016 Association for Computational Linguistics

t_1: *Crowds rally in Belfast for flag protest#thetruth*
n_1: *Protesters march in Northern Ireland: Under a gray, overcast sky, more than 1,000 protesters gathered Saturday in the Northern Ireland city of Belfast carrying large Union flags, some wrapped around their shoulders.*
te_1: *{EventPhrase = [rally, protest], EventArgument = Belfast, Time = 2013-01-14}*
ne_1: *{EventType = Conflict, EventPhrase = march, EventArgument = [protesters, Northern Ireland, Belfast]}*
e_1: *{EventType = Conflict, EventPhrase = [rally, protest, march], EventArgument = [protesters, Northern Ireland, Belfast], Time = 2013-01-14}.*

Table 1: Cross-genre Event Extraction Example

some extent. To the best of our knowledge, it is the first work to conduct cross-genre event extraction through unsupervised knowledge enrichment.

2 Problem Definition

Given a tweet t_i, our cross-genre event extraction framework first discovers its most relevant news article n_i, then identifies event tuples (event phrases and event arguments) for the tweet (te_i) and the news article (ne_i) respectively, and finally conducts merging on the event extraction outputs from both genres to produce the cross-genre event extraction result (e_i). For example in Table 1, given the following tweet t_1, n_1 is retrieved as its most relevant news article. te_1 and ne_1 are the extracted event tuples for the tweet and the news article respectively and e_1 is the final cross-genre event extraction output after merging. To evaluate the performance of an event extractor, the precision, recall and f-measure of the extracted event phrases and event arguments will be measured using the following criteria: an event phrase is correctly labeled if it matches a reference trigger; an argument is correctly labeled if it matches a reference argument.

3 Approach

3.1 Baseline Event Extraction Systems

We use two state-of-the-art event extraction systems (Ritter et al., 2012; Li et al., 2013) to extract events from tweets and news articles respectively. The tweet event extractor TwiCal-Event (Ritter et al., 2012) is able to extract open-domain significant events from Twitter. It is a supervised system that identifies event phrases and event participants with tailored part-of-speech tagging and shallow parsing for tweets. In addition, it is also able to discover event categories and classify extracted events based on latent variable models. It takes tweets as input and outputs a four-tuple representation of events which includes event participants, event phrase, calendar date, and event type. The news event extractor (Li et al., 2013) is a joint framework based on structured prediction which extracts triggers and arguments simultaneously while incorporating diverse lexical, syntactic, semantic and global features. It takes raw documents as input, distinguish events from non-events by classifying event triggers and identifying and classifying argument roles.

3.2 Knowledge Enrichment Approach

To produce the latent vector representations for the whole dataset, we follow the same procedure in (Guo et al., 2013): represent the dataset in a matrix X, where each cell stores the TF-IDF values of words. Word vectors P and tweet vectors Q are optimized by minimizing the following objective function:

$$\sum_i \sum_j W_{ij} \left(P_{\cdot,i} \cdot Q_{\cdot,j} - X_{ij}\right)^2 + \lambda ||P||_2^2 + \lambda ||Q||_2^2$$

$$+ \delta \cdot \left(\frac{Q_{\cdot,j_1} \cdot Q_{\cdot,j_2}}{|Q_{\cdot,j_1}||Q_{\cdot,j_2}|} - 1\right)^2$$

$$W_{i,j} = \begin{cases} 1, & \text{if } X_{ij} \neq 0 \\ w_m, & \text{if } X_{ij} = 0 \end{cases} \tag{1}$$

where λ is a regularization term, $Q_{\cdot,j_1}$ and $Q_{\cdot,j_2}$ are linked pairs connected by text-to-text relations, $|Q_{\cdot,j}|$ denotes the length of vector $Q_{\cdot,j}$ and the coefficient δ denotes the importance of the text-to-text links. we follow the same optimization procedure as (Steck, 2010) by alternating Least Square [ALS] is used for inference on P and Q.

After obtaining the vector representations for the whole dataset, for each tweet, we retrieve its cross-genre knowledge by finding the news article with the highest cosine similarity.

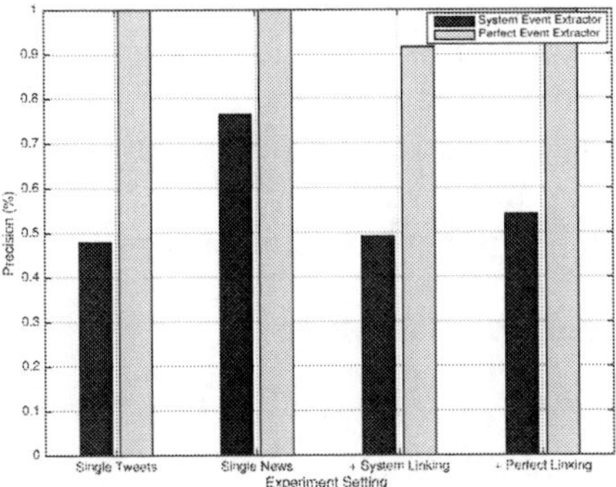

Figure 1: Event extraction precision

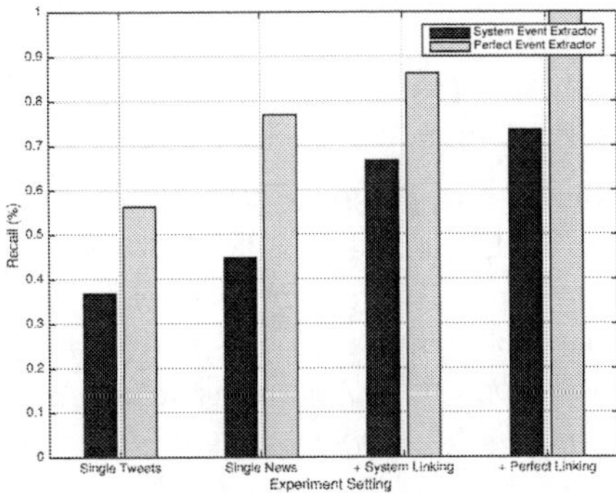

Figure 2: Event extraction recall

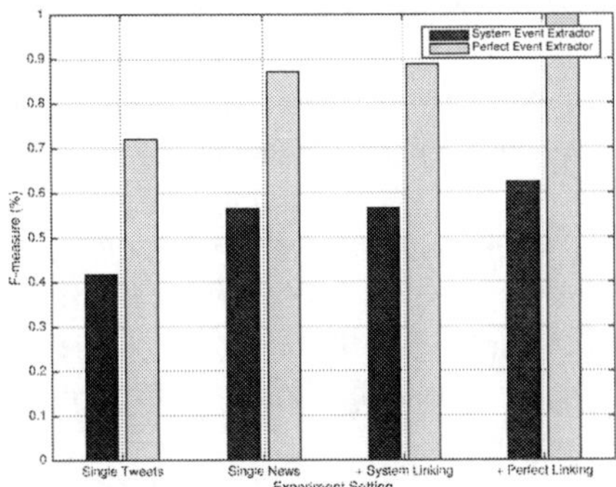

Figure 3: Event extraction f-measure

4 Experiments

4.1 Data Description

We use the same dataset as (Guo et al., 2013) which contains 34,888 tweets and 12,704 news articles. For each tweet, we consider the url-referred news article as its gold standard cross-genre knowledge – the most relevant news document. As the news event extractor is designed for a closed set of 33 event types (ace, 2005) while the tweet event extractor is for open domain, in this paper we only focus on the tweet-news pairs that the news event extraction output is not empty. We randomly selected 50 tweet-news pairs for the cross-genre event extraction annotation and evaluation.

4.2 Experiment Results

Figure 1, 2 and 3 present the Precision (P), Recall (R) and F-measure (F) of the overall event extraction performance for different settings respectively.

From these experiment results, we have the following four observations:

1. Event Extraction solely on tweet messages achieves the lowest precision, recall and f-measure. It exactly confirms our motivation of conducting knowledge enrichment for event extraction in tweet messages. Because of the informal nature of tweet messages, the event extractor misidentified 54.16% of the events thus the precision is low. Take the ill-formatted tweet in Section 1 as an example, the named entity "AaronSwartz" is in the hashtag "#AaronSwartz" and "Dead at 26" is written as "Dead @ 26". It makes the automatic event extractor extremely difficult to identify the "Die" event for the person "Aaron Swartz".

The low recall is mainly caused by the "lack of context" problem. Due to the length limitation of tweets, users tend to use recapitulate languages to describe an event. For Example, the following tweet *"Well. That sucks. 'Deepening Crisis for the Boeing 787'"* actually refers to an "emergency landing" event made by "All Nippon Airways" in "western Japan". The user only mentioned the summary "Deepening Crisis for the Boeing 787" to refer to the actual event. Therefore, the single-genre event extractor missed the event trigger "landing" and the event arguments "All Nippon Airways" and "western Japan".

2. Both single-genre event extractors can contribute to the cross-genre event extractor through the cross-genre linking process. Even with the automatic linking output, Figure 2 and Figure 3 show 29.9% recall and 14.0% f-measure improvement

over single-genre event extractor for tweets. It is because that in most cases, news articles cover more information than tweets as they are produced by professional news agencies while tweets are written by individuals with a 140-character length limitation. In the following example, although referring to the same events, the news article covers more event information than the tweet, thus the cross-genre event extractor can surpass the single-genre event extractor for tweets.

News: *Deepening Crisis for the Dreamliner The two largest Japanese airlines said they would ground their fleets of Boeing 787 aircraft after one operated by All Nippon Airways made an emergency landing in western Japan.*

Tweets: *Well. That sucks. "Deepening Crisis for the Boeing 787"*

For some certain cases, the cross-genre event extractor is also able to benefit from single-genre event extractor for tweets. For the following example, the event extractor for news articles missed the "Attack" event as "Halt an ... Advance" is an unusual phrase to describe an "Attack" event. However, in the related tweet, "Battling" is a strong indicator of an "Attack" event and the event extractor for tweets is able to catch it. As a result, we are able to extract the overall event tuples {EventPhrase=[Advance,Battling], EventPaticipant=[France,Islamist,Mali]}.

News: *French Troops Help Mali Halt an Islamist Advance France answered an urgent plea from the government of its former colony to help blunt an advance into the center of the country by Islamist extremist militants.*

Tweets: *France Battling Islamists in Mali #rebels tarnish W. African #Islam Western #intervention*

3. Either improving single-genre event extractors or achieving better cross-genre linking performance is able to boost the overall event extraction performance. From Figure 1, 2 and 3, we can observe that higher quality of single-genre event extractors will significantly enhance the precision while better linking performance will mainly contribute to a higher recall.

4. Compared with cross-genre linking accuracy, the quality of single-genre event extractors is more important. Figure 3 shows that "Gold Event Extractor + System Linking" achieved 26.3% higher F-measure score than "System Event Extractor + Gold

Linking". It is mainly because of two reasons: on one hand, the errors of single-genre event extractors will be propagated to the final event output; on the other hand, the current linking system is able to provide reasonable linking results thus the use of perfect linking will not have too much gain.

5 Remaining Challenges

Linking Errors: mistakenly linking tweets to irrelevant news articles. For example, the tweet *"The lack of investigative movement - his return and his flippant attitude is what is insulting. Not his new placement."* is about a "Movement" event that *Assemblyman* returns to *Albany* after scandal. However, the tweets express the event so implicitly that the automatic linking system is not able to discover its corresponding news article.

Extraction Errors: single-genre event extractors failed on both the tweet side and the news article side. For the following example, both single genre event extractors missed the "Threaten" event between the *vice president Hugo Chvez* and *those questioning the legitimacy of Chavez's government.*

Tweet: *#Venezuela VP warns those questioning the legitimacy of #Chavez's government: "Watch your words and your actions."*

News: *The vice president threatened action against any who question the legality of delaying the swearing-in of President Hugo Chvez, who is still in Cuba.*

6 Conclusions and Future Work

In this paper we study the bottlenecks of event extraction for tweets. We have two observations: (1). Because of the "lack of context" and "informal nature" characteristics of tweets, conducting event extraction solely on tweet messages cannot produce satisfactory results; (2) The events embedded in tweets and news articles are often complementary. Based on these observations, we proposed to link each tweet to its most relevant news article, and further incorporated this cross-genre knowledge to conduct cross-genre event extraction. Experiment results showed that without any additional annotation, our proposed cross-genre event extractor is able to outperform state-of-the-art tweet event extraction. Our future research will focus on joint modeling of cross-genre event extraction in the training stage through cross-genre knowledge enrichment.

Acknowledgment

This work was supported by the U.S. DARPA DEFT Program No.FA8750-13-2-0041, ARL NS-CTA No. W911NF-09-2-0053, NSF Award IIS-1523198, AFRL DREAM project, and a gift award from Bosch. The views and conclusions contained in this document are those of the authors and should not be interpreted as representing the official policies, either expressed or implied, of the U.S. Government. The U.S. Government is authorized to reproduce and distribute reprints for Government purposes notwithstanding any copyright notation here on.

References

2005. ACE (automatic content extraction) english annotation guidelines for events, Jan. [Online]. Available: https://www.ldc.upenn.edu/collaborations/past-projects/ace, (Date Last Accessed, Nov 4th, 2015).

Edward Benson, Aria Haghighi, and Regina Barzilay. 2011. Event discovery in social media feeds. In *ACL*, pages 389–398.

Weiwei Guo, Hao Li, Heng Ji, and Mona T. Diab. 2013. Linking tweets to news: A framework to enrich short text data in social media. In *Proc. Annu. Meeting of the Assoc. for Comput. Linguist.*, pages 239–249, Sofia, Bulgaria.

Qi He, Kuiyu Chang, and Ee-Peng Lim. 2007. Analyzing feature trajectories for event detection. In *Proc. Int. ACM SIGIR Conf.*, pages 207–214, Amsterdam, Netherland.

Heng Ji and Ralph Grishman. 2008. Refining event extraction through cross-document inference. In *Proc. Annu. Meeting of the Assoc. for Comput. Linguist.*, pages 254–262, Columbus, OH.

Jon M. Kleinberg. 2003. Bursty and hierarchical structure in streams. *Data Min. Knowl. Discov.*, 7(4):373–397.

Qi Li, Heng Ji, and Liang Huang. 2013. Joint event extraction via structured prediction with global features. In *Proc. Annu. Meeting of the Assoc. for Comput. Linguist.*, pages 73–82, Sofia, Bulgaria.

Alan Ritter, Mausam, Oren Etzioni, and Sam Clark. 2012. Open domain event extraction from twitter. In *Proc. ACM SIGKDD Conf. on Knowl. Discovery and Data Mining*, pages 1104–1112, Beijing, China.

Harald Steck. 2010. Training and testing of recommender systems on data missing not at random. In *Proc. ACM SIGKDD Conf. on Knowl. Discovery and Data Mining*, pages 713–722, Washington, DC.

Jianshu Weng and Bu-Sung Lee. 2011. Event detection in twitter. In *Proc. Int. AAAI Conf. on Web and Social Media*, pages 401–408, Barcelona, Catalonia, Spain.

Yiming Yang, Thomas Pierce, and Jaime G. Carbonell. 1998. A study of retrospective and on-line event detection. In *SIGIR*, pages 28–36.

Emergent: a novel data-set for stance classification

William Ferreira
Department of Computer Science
University College London, UK

Andreas Vlachos
Department of Computer Science
University of Sheffield, UK

Abstract

We present Emergent, a novel data-set derived from a digital journalism project for rumour debunking. The data-set contains 300 rumoured claims and 2,595 associated news articles, collected and labelled by journalists with an estimation of their veracity (*true*, *false* or *unverified*). Each associated article is summarized into a headline and labelled to indicate whether its stance is *for*, *against*, or *observing* the claim, where *observing* indicates that the article merely repeats the claim. Thus, Emergent provides a real-world data source for a variety of natural language processing tasks in the context of fact-checking. Further to presenting the dataset, we address the task of determining the article headline stance with respect to the claim. For this purpose we use a logistic regression classifier and develop features that examine the headline and its agreement with the claim. The accuracy achieved was 73% which is 26% higher than the one achieved by the Excitement Open Platform (Magnini et al., 2014).

1 Introduction

The advent of *New Media*, such as Twitter, Facebook, etc., enables news stories and rumours to be published in real-time to a global audience, bypassing the usual verification procedures used by more traditional *Old Media* news outlets. However, the line between Old and New Media is becoming blurred as news aggregators lift stories from social media and re-publish them without fact-checking.

This issue could be helped by developing methods for automated fact-checking of news stories, part of the *reporter's black box* envisioned in Cohen et al. (2011) and one of the main objectives in computational journalism. While this task is related to a variety of natural language processing tasks such as textual entailment and machine comprehension, it poses additional challenges due to its open-domain, real-world nature. Previous work by Vlachos and Riedel (2014) proposed using data from fact-checking websites such as Politifact[1], but the labelling provided by the journalists is only the degree of truthfulness of the claims, without any machine-readable verdicts to supervise the various steps in deciding it. Thus, the task defined by the dataset proposed remains too challenging for the NLP methods currently available.

In this paper we propose to use data from the Emergent Project (Silverman, 2015), a rumour debunking project carried out in collaboration with the Tow Center for Digital Journalism at Columbia Journalism School[2]. Consisting of 300 claims and 2,595 associated news articles, the Emergent project contains a rich source of labelled data that can be used in a variety of NLP tasks, created by journalists as part of their normal workflow, thus real-world and at no annotation cost.

We leverage the Emergent dataset to investigate the task of classifying the stance of a news article headline with respect to its associated claim, i.e. for each article headline we assign a stance label which is one of *for*, *against*, or *observing*, indicating whether the article is supporting, refuting, or just reporting the claim, respectively. The large number

---

[1] http://www.politifact.com/
[2] http://towcenter.org/

Proceedings of NAACL-HLT 2016, pages 1163–1168,
San Diego, California, June 12-17, 2016. ©2016 Association for Computational Linguistics

of claims in the dataset allows us to assess the generalization of the method evaluation to new claims more reliably than in previous work that either used a small number of claims (e. g. seven in Lukasik et al., 2015) or did not separate training claims from testing claims (Qazvinian et al., 2011).

We develop a stance classification approach based on multiclass logistic regression, using features extracted from the article headline and the claim, achieving an accuracy of 73% on our test data-set, also demonstrating that features relying on syntax, word alignment and paraphrasing contribute to the performance. Since the task bears similarities with textual entailment, we compare it against the Excitement Open Platform (Magnini et al., 2014) which achieved a substantially lower accuracy of 47%.

2 The Emergent data

The claims in Emergent are collected by journalists from a variety of sources such as rumour sites, e.g. snopes.com, and Twitter accounts such as @Hoaxalizer. Their subjects include topics such as world and national U.S. news and technology stories. Once a claim is identified, the journalist searches for articles that mention the claim and decides on the *stance* of each such article:

- *for*: The article states that the claim is true, without any kind of hedging.
- *against*: The article states that the claim is false, without any kind of hedging.
- *observing*: The claim is reported in the article, but without assessment of its veracity.

The journalist also summarises the article into a headline. In parallel to the article-level stance detection, a claim-level veracity judgement is reached as more articles associated with the claim are examined. The veracity of each claim is initially *unverified*, later becoming either *true* or *false* when the journalist decides that adequate evidence from the associated articles has been compiled. Finally, the source and the number of times each associated article is shared are recorded. An example of a claim verified on Emergent appears in Figure 1.

There are a number of tasks for which the Emergent data can be useful for development and evaluation. The article-level stance labels can be used to develop a stance detection system between the claim

Claim: Robert Plant ripped up an $800 million contract offer to reunite Led Zeppelin

Source: mirror.co.uk (shares: 39,140)
Headline: Led Zeppelin's Robert Plant turns down £500MILLION to reform supergroup
Stance: *for*

Source: usnews.com (shares: 850)
Headline: No, Robert Plant Didn't Rip Up an $800 Million Contract
Stance: *against*

Source: forbes.com (shares: 3,360)
Headline: Robert Plant Reportedly Tears Up $800 Million Led Zeppelin Reunion Contract
Stance: *observing*

Veracity: *False*

Figure 1: Example verification taken from `http://www.emergent.info/led-zeppelin-contract`. The full text of the articles is omitted for brevity.

and an associated article. The claim-level veracity labels would be straightforward to use for fact-checking. Finally, the article headlines can be used for focused summarization.

In this paper we focus on stance detection of an article with respect to the claim using the headline provided by the journalist. For this purpose we obtained a database dump from the developers of Emergent and extracted all claims and associated article headlines. We made no attempt to exclude a claim or article based on grammatical errors or complex syntactic structure. Our final data-set contains 300 claims, and 2,595 associated article headlines, with an average ratio of 8.65 (7.31) articles per claim; the minimum number of articles per claim is 1 and the maximum number is 50. The class distribution of article stances is 47.7% *for*, 15.2% *against* and 37.1% *observing*. This dataset was split into training and test set parts, containing 2,071 and 524 instances respectively, ensuring that each claim appeared in only one of the parts. Both the database dump and the extracted claim-article headline dataset are available from `https://github.com/willferreira/mscproject`.

3 Stance Classification

We treat stance classification as a 3-way classification task using a logistic regression classifier with

L_1 regularization (Pedregosa et al., 2011)[3] and we explore two types of features: those extracted solely from the article headline and those extracted by combining the headline and the claim. The former are aimed at capturing the cases in which the stance of headline can be determined without consulting the claim, which is often the case with *observing* cases, as they often use hedging. The latter are aimed at determining the entailment relation between them. All feature engineering was conducted using 10-fold cross-validation on the training data. Our implementation is available from `https://github.com/willferreira/mscproject`.

Headline features The features extracted from the headline are the commonly used bag of words representation (**BoW**) and whether it ends in a question mark (**Q**). In addition, we added two features representing the minimum distance from the root of the sentence to common refuting (e. g. deny) and hedging/reporting (e.g. claim, presumably) words (**RootDist**). As an example of the **RootDist** feature, consider the dependency parse in Figure 2. The minimum number of edges from the root to a hedging/refuting word ("not" in the example) is three. The dependency parses were obtained using Stanford CoreNLP (Manning et al., 2014) and the word lists were compiled using online resources.

Claim-headline features While the article headline often provides adequate features to classify its stance, we also need to take into account its entailment relation with the claim. Therefore, based on the work by Rus and Lintean (2012) we compute an alignment using the Paraphrase Database (PPDB) (Pavlick et al., 2015) and the Kuhn-Munkres algorithm (Kuhn, 1955; Munkres, 1957) as follows. For each word pairing between the claim and the headline an edge is created and assigned a score by the following scheme:

- if the stems of the words are identical, assign *maxScore*
- else, if the words are paraphrases according to PPDB, assign their maximum paraphrase score
- else, assign *minScore*

---

[3]Specifically, we used the sklearn `LogisticRegression` classifier with the default parameters, and L_1 penalization.

maxScore and *minScore* were set to +10 and -10 respectively. Running the Kuhn-Munkres algorithm on this graph finds the maximum scoring 1-to-1 word alignment and the score of this alignment, normalized by the length of the claim or headline, whichever is the shorter. An additional feature is extracted to indicate if in an aligned pair of words, one of them — either in the claim or or the article headline — is negated according to the parser. Furthermore, we extracted the subject-verb-object (SVO) triples from the claim and the article headline (typically one in each) and matched them as follows. For each component of the triples we extracted from PPDB the following labels: *equivalence*, *forwardEntailment*, *backwardEntailment*, *independence* or *noRelation*. Thus the matching of an SVO triple in the claim to one in the headline is represented by a concatenation of three labels, each corresponding to the relation between the subjects, the verbs and the objects (**SVO**). Finally, we computed the cosine similarity between the vector representations for the claim and the headline (**word2vec**). The representations were calculated by multiplying the word2vec vectors (Mikolov et al., 2013a) for each word, which we found to perform better than addition. We utilised pre-trained vectors trained on part of the Google News dataset, comprising 300-dimensional vectors for 3 million words and phrases (Mikolov et al., 2013b).

4 Results

Since none of the stance labels dominates the label distribution, we evaluate the performance primarily using accuracy, also reporting per-class Precision and Recall. A majority baseline would achieve 47%, but would always predict *for*. For a better baseline we used the lexical overlap between the claim and the article headline, which we defined as the percentage of the ratio of the number of lemmas in common between them to the number of lemmas in their union. Using the training data we calculated the average overlap for each stance and found that *for* instances exhibit higher overlap, followed by *observing* and then by *against*. Following this, we defined two overlap thresholds, *minFor* and *maxAgainst*. If the overlap of a claim-headline pair is higher than *minFor* it is labeled *for*, if lower than *maxAgainst* it

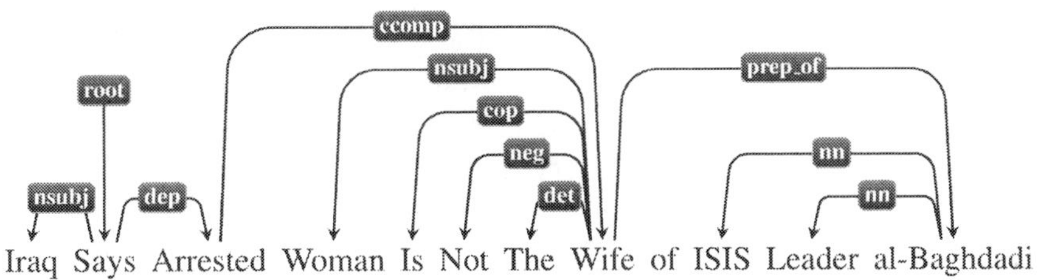

Figure 2: Dependency structure for sentence containing a refuting word.

method	acc.	*for*	*against*	*observing*
overlap	32%	50%/42%	18%/52%	32%/9%
EOP	47%	52%/77%	100%/1%	34%/29%
classifier	73%	71%/89%	82%/70%	74%/54%

Table 1: Test set accuracy and per stance precision and recall.

Feature	**10-fold cv**	**test**	chosen for stance
-BoW	1.66%	5.15%	ALL
-Q	1.85%	0.19%	*observing*
-RootDist	2.02%	2.48%	*for, observing*
-PPDB	0.47%	0.76%	*for*
-Neg	0.29%	0%	*for, against*
-SVO	0.20%	0.19%	*for, observing*
-word2vec	0.049%	-0.19%	*against*

Table 2: Ablation results: each row represents the drop in accuracy caused by removing the corresponding feature(s). The last column shows for which stance label(s) the feature(s) had non-zero weight(s).

is labeled *against*, otherwise *observing*.

The comparison between the baseline and the L_1-regularized logistic regression classifier with the features described in the previous section appears in Table 1. As it can be observed, the proposed classifier performs much better in accuracy with substantial gains in all stances. Both approaches are mostly challenged by instances of the *observing* class, since the article headlines with that stance are quite similar to the claim, which is also the case for the more populous *for* class. We also compare our classifier against the Excitement Open Platform (EOP) textual entailment classifier (Magnini et al., 2014). In particular, we used the MaxEntClassificationEDA classifier with the RTE-3 pre-trained model which we found to be the best performing one among those available achieving 33% accuracy. Finally, we trained the same classifier on the Emergent training data achieving 47%, which is 26% lower than the proposed method.

In order to assess the contribution of the features developed we conducted an ablation analysis and the results appear in Table 2. The L_1 regularization used enforces sparsity which helps highlight the features relevant for each stance. The **RootDist** feature has a substantial contribution as it helps distinguish the *observing* from the *for* class. We also evaluated a model using only **BoW**, **Q** and **word2vec** features and the performance was 3% lower than using the complete feature set, thus highlighting the contribution of the features relying on alignment, syntax and

the PPDB. Finally, the fact that **-word2vec** did not help, especially when compared to **PPDB**, can be partly attributed to the inability of methods relying solely on contexts to learn antonymy.

5 Related work

The task defined by the Emergent dataset differs from recent work in stance classification (Qazvinian et al., 2011; Lukasik et al., 2015; Zhao et al., 2015) not only in the number of claims from which the article headlines are derived, but also in that correct prediction requires considering entailment relation between the claim and the headline. It also differs from work on target-specific stance prediction in debates (Walker et al., 2012; Hasan and Ng, 2013), since the targets considered there are topic labels such as abortion, instead of event claims as in this work.

Emergent, being derived from the workflow of journalists is more realistic than data-sets designed for textual entailment such as FraCas (Cooper et al., 1996) and SICK (Marelli et al., 2014) that are constructed artificially. Compared to the crowdsourced dataset of Bowman et al. (2015), it is smaller but of a different nature, since the former assumes that all sentences are visual representations, while news tend be more varied.

Stance detection in the context of Emergent is one component in the process of fact-checking claims appearing in the news which are usually more complex than the entity-relation-entity or entity-property-number triples considered in previous work (Nakashole and Mitchell, 2014; Vlachos and Riedel, 2015). The choice of claims to fact-check is a task in its own right, as shown by Hassan et al. (2015). Finally, the only other use of data from the Emergent project is by Liu et al. (2015); however their focus was not on the NLP aspects of the task but on using Twitter data to assess the veracity of the claim, ignoring the articles and their stances curated by the journalists.

6 Conclusions - Future work

In this paper we proposed Emergent, a new real-world dataset derived from the digital journalism project Emergent which can be used for a variety of NLP tasks in the context of fact-checking. We focus on stance detection, for which the large number of claims in the dataset compared to previous work allows for more reliable assessment of the generalization capabilities of the methods evaluated. We proceed to develop a model for stance classification using multiclass logistic regression and show how features beyond the typically used bag of words can be beneficial, achieving accuracy 26% better than an RTE system trained on the same data. We make both the datasets and our code available.

Despite its advantages, the dataset collected is rather small to learn all the nuances of the task. Thus in future work we will explore ways of incorporating large amounts of raw text in training stance classification models, possibly using a neural network architecture. Finally, stance detection is one of the tasks in the fact-checking process of Emergent. In future work we will develop methods for the other tasks involved, such as classifying the stance of a whole article towards a claim and truth assessment.

Acknowledgments

Many thanks to Craig Silverman and the Tow Center for Digital Journalism at Columbia University for allowing us to use the data from the Emergent Project. The research reported in this paper was conducted while the first author was at University College London.

References

Samuel R. Bowman, Gabor Angeli, Christopher Potts, and Christopher D. Manning. 2015. A large annotated corpus for learning natural language inference. In *Proceedings of the 2015 Conference on Empirical Methods in Natural Language Processing (EMNLP)*. Association for Computational Linguistics.

Sarah Cohen, Chengkai Li, Jun Yang, and Cong Yu. 2011. Computational Journalism: a call to arms to database researchers. *Proceedings of the 5th Biennial Conference on Innovative Data Systems Research (CIDR 2011) Asilomar, California, USA.*, pages 148–151.

Robin Cooper, Dick Crouch, Jan Van Eijck, Chris Fox, Josef Van Genabith, Jan Jaspars, Hans Kamp, David Milward, Manfred Pinkal, Massimo Poesio, Steve Pulman, Ted Briscoe, Holger Maier, and Karsten Konrad. 1996. Using the framework. Technical report, The FraCas Consortium.

Kazi Saidul Hasan and Vincent Ng. 2013. Stance Classification of Ideological Debates: Data, Models, Features, and Constraints. In *IJCNLP*, pages 1348–1356. Asian Federation of Natural Language Processing / ACL.

Naeemul Hassan, Chengkai Li, and Mark Tremayne. 2015. Detecting check-worthy factual claims in presidential debates. In *Proceedings of the 24th ACM International Conference on Information and Knowledge Management*.

Harold W. Kuhn. 1955. The Hungarian Method for the assignment problem. *Naval Research Logistics Quarterly*, 2:83–97.

Xiaomo Liu, Armineh Nourbakhsh, Quanzhi Li, Rui Fang, and Sameena Shah. 2015. Real-time rumor debunking on twitter. In *Proceedings of the 24th ACM International on Conference on Information and Knowledge Management*, pages 1867–1870.

Michael Lukasik, Trevor Cohn, and Kalina Bontcheva. 2015. Classifying tweet level judgements of rumours in social media. In *Proceedings of the 2015 Conference on Empirical Methods in Natural Language Processing*, pages 2590–2595, Lisbon, Portugal, September. Association for Computational Linguistics.

Bernardo Magnini, Roberto Zanoli, Ido Dagan, Kathrin Eichler, Günter Neumann, Tae-Gil Noh, Sebastian Pado, Asher Stern, and Omer Levy. 2014. The excitement open platform for textual inferences. In *Proceedings of the ACL 2014 System Demonstrations*. ACL, 6.

Christopher D. Manning, Mihai Surdeanu, John Bauer, Jenny Finkel, Steven J. Bethard, and David McClosky. 2014. The Stanford CoreNLP natural language processing toolkit. In *Proceedings of 52nd Annual Meeting of the Association for Computational Linguistics: System Demonstrations*, pages 55–60.

Marco Marelli, Stefano Menini, Marco Baroni, Luisa Bentivogli, Raffaella Bernardi, and Roberto Zamparelli. 2014. A sick cure for the evaluation of compositional distributional semantic models. In *Proceedings of the Ninth International Conference on Language Resources and Evaluation (LREC'14)*, Reykjavik, Iceland, may. European Language Resources Association (ELRA).

Tomas Mikolov, Kai Chen, Greg Corrado, and Jeffrey Dean. 2013a. Efficient estimation of word representations in vector space. *arXiv preprint arXiv:1301.3781*.

Tomas Mikolov, Ilya Sutskever, Kai Chen, Greg S Corrado, and Jeff Dean. 2013b. Distributed representations of words and phrases and their compositionality. In C. J. C. Burges, L. Bottou, M. Welling, Z. Ghahramani, and K. Q. Weinberger, editors, *Advances in Neural Information Processing Systems 26*, pages 3111–3119. Curran Associates, Inc.

James Munkres. 1957. Algorithms for the assignment and transportation problems. *Journal of the Society for Industrial and Applied Mathematics*, 5(1):32–38.

Ndapandula Nakashole and Tom M Mitchell. 2014. Language-Aware Truth Assessment of Fact Candidates. *Acl*, pages 1009–1019.

Ellie Pavlick, Pushpendre Rastogi, Juri Ganitkevitch, Benjamin Van Durme, and Chris Callison-Burch. 2015. Ppdb 2.0: Better paraphrase ranking, fine-grained entailment relations, word embeddings, and style classification. In *Proceedings of the 53rd Annual Meeting of the Association for Computational Linguistics and the 7th International Joint Conference on Natural Language Processing (Volume 2: Short Papers)*, pages 425–430, Beijing, China, July. Association for Computational Linguistics.

F. Pedregosa, G. Varoquaux, A. Gramfort, V. Michel, B. Thirion, O. Grisel, M. Blondel, P. Prettenhofer, R. Weiss, V. Dubourg, J. Vanderplas, A. Passos, D. Cournapeau, M. Brucher, M. Perrot, and E. Duchesnay. 2011. Scikit-learn: Machine learning in Python. *Journal of Machine Learning Research*, 12:2825–2830.

Vahed Qazvinian, Emily Rosengren, Dragomir R. Radev, and Qiaozhu Mei. 2011. Rumor has it: Identifying misinformation in microblogs. In *Proceedings of the Conference on Empirical Methods in Natural Language Processing*, pages 1589–1599.

Vasile Rus and Mihai Lintean. 2012. A comparison of greedy and optimal assessment of natural language student input using word-to-word similarity metrics. In *Proceedings of the Seventh Workshop on Building Educational Applications Using NLP*, pages 157–162, Stroudsburg, PA, USA. Association for Computational Linguistics.

Craig Silverman. 2015. Lies, Damn Lies and Viral Content. `http://towcenter.org/research/lies-damn-lies-and-viral-content/`, February.

Andreas Vlachos and Sebastian Riedel. 2014. Fact Checking: Task definition and dataset construction. *Proceedings of the ACL 2014 Workshop on Language Technologies and Computational Social Science*, pages 18–22.

Andreas Vlachos and Sebastian Riedel. 2015. Identification and verification of simple claims about statistical properties. In *Proceedings of the 2015 Conference on Empirical Methods in Natural Language Processing*.

Marilyn Walker, Pranav Anand, Rob Abbott, and Ricky Grant. 2012. Stance Classification using Dialogic Properties of Persuasion. In *Proceedings of the 2012 Conference of the North American Chapter of the Association for Computational Linguistics: Human Language Technologies*, pages 592–596.

Zhe Zhao, Paul Resnick, and Qiaozhu Mei. 2015. Enquiring minds: Early detection of rumors in social media from enquiry posts. In *Proceedings of the 24th International Conference on World Wide Web*, pages 1395–1405.

BIRA: Improved Predictive Exchange Word Clustering

Jon Dehdari[1,2] and **Liling Tan**[2] and **Josef van Genabith**[1,2]

[1]DFKI, Saarbrücken, Germany
`{jon.dehdari,josef.van_genabith}@dfki.de`

[2]University of Saarland, Saarbrücken, Germany
`liling.tan@uni-saarland.de`

Abstract

Word clusters are useful for many NLP tasks including training neural network language models, but current increases in datasets are outpacing the ability of word clusterers to handle them. Little attention has been paid thus far on inducing high-quality word clusters at a large scale. The predictive exchange algorithm is quite scalable, but sometimes does not provide as good perplexity as other slower clustering algorithms.

We introduce the bidirectional, interpolated, refining, and alternating (BIRA) predictive exchange algorithm. It improves upon the predictive exchange algorithm's perplexity by up to 18%, giving it perplexities comparable to the slower two-sided exchange algorithm, and better perplexities than the slower Brown clustering algorithm. Our BIRA implementation is fast, clustering a 2.5 billion token English News Crawl corpus in 3 hours. It also reduces machine translation training time while preserving translation quality. Our implementation is portable and freely available.

1 Introduction

Words can be grouped together into equivalence classes to help reduce data sparsity and better generalize data. Word clusters are useful in many NLP applications. Within machine translation word classes are used in word alignment (Brown et al., 1993; Och and Ney, 2000), translation models (Koehn and Hoang, 2007; Wuebker et al., 2013), reordering (Cherry, 2013), preordering (Stymne, 2012), target-side inflection (Chahuneau et al., 2013), SAMT

(Zollmann and Vogel, 2011), and OSM (Durrani et al., 2014), among many others.

Word clusterings have also found utility in parsing (Koo et al., 2008; Candito and Seddah, 2010; Kong et al., 2014), chunking (Turian et al., 2010), NER (Miller et al., 2004; Liang, 2005; Ratinov and Roth, 2009; Ritter et al., 2011), structure transfer (Täckström et al., 2012), and discourse relation discovery (Rutherford and Xue, 2014).

Word clusters also speed up normalization in training neural network and MaxEnt language models, via class-based decomposition (Goodman, 2001a). This reduces the normalization time from $\mathcal{O}(|V|)$ (the vocabulary size) to $\approx \mathcal{O}(\sqrt{|V|})$. More improvements to $\mathcal{O}(\log(|V|))$ are found using hierarchical softmax (Morin and Bengio, 2005; Mnih and Hinton, 2009).

2 Word Clustering

Word clustering partitions a vocabulary V, grouping together words that function similarly. This helps generalize language and alleviate data sparsity. We discuss flat clustering in this paper. Flat, or strict partitioning clustering surjectively maps word types onto a smaller set of clusters.

The **exchange algorithm** (Kneser and Ney, 1993) is an efficient technique that exhibits a general time complexity of $\mathcal{O}(|V| \times |C| \times I)$, where $|V|$ is the number of word types, $|C|$ is the number of classes, and I is the number of training iterations, typically < 20. This omits the specific method of exchanging words, which adds further complexity. Words are exchanged from one class to another until convergence or I.

Proceedings of NAACL-HLT 2016, pages 1169–1174,
San Diego, California, June 12-17, 2016. ©2016 Association for Computational Linguistics

One of the oldest and still most popular exchange algorithm implementations is `mkcls` (Och, 1995)[1], which adds various metaheuristics to escape local optima. Botros et al. (2015) introduce their implementation of three exchange-based algorithms. Martin et al. (1998) and Müller and Schütze (2015)[2] use trigrams within the exchange algorithm. Clark (2003) adds an orthotactic bias.[3]

The previous algorithms use an unlexicalized (two-sided) language model: $P(w_i|w_{i-1}) = P(w_i|c_i)\,P(c_i|c_{i-1})$, where the class c_i of the predicted word w_i is conditioned on the class c_{i-1} of the previous word w_{i-1}. Goodman (2001b) altered this model so that c_i is conditioned directly upon w_{i-1}, hence: $P(w_i|w_{i-1}) = P(w_i|c_i)\,P(c_i|w_{i-1})$. This new model fractionates the history more, but it allows for a large speedup in hypothesizing an exchange since the history doesn't change. The resulting partially lexicalized (one-sided) class model gives the accompanying **predictive exchange algorithm** (Goodman, 2001b; Uszkoreit and Brants, 2008) a time complexity of $\mathcal{O}((B+|V|)\times|C|\times I)$ where B is the number of unique bigrams in the training set.[4] We introduce a set of improvements to this algorithm to enable high-quality large-scale word clusters.

3   BIRA Predictive Exchange

We developed a *bidirectional, interpolated, refining, and alternating* (BIRA) predictive exchange algorithm. The goal of BIRA is to produce better clusters by using multiple, changing models to escape local optima. This uses both forward and reversed bigram class models to improve cluster quality by evaluating log-likelihood on two different models. Unlike using trigrams, bidirectional bigram models only linearly increase time and memory requirements, and in fact some data structures can be shared. The two directions are interpolated to allow softer inte-

gration of these two models:

$$P(w_i|w_{i-1}, w_{i+1}) \triangleq P(w_i|c_i) \quad (1)$$
$$\cdot\,(\lambda P(c_i|w_{i-1})$$
$$+\,(1-\lambda)P(c_i|w_{i+1}))$$

The interpolation weight λ for the forward direction alternates to $1-\lambda$ every a iterations (i):

$$\lambda_i := \begin{cases} 1-\lambda_0 & \text{if } i \bmod a = 0 \\ \lambda_0 & \text{otherwise} \end{cases} \quad (2)$$

Figure 1 illustrates the benefit of this λ-inversion to help escape local minima, with lower training set perplexity by inverting λ every four iterations:

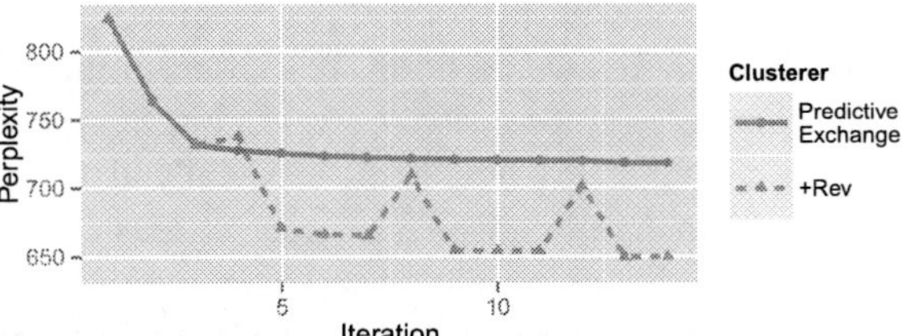

Figure 1: Training set perplexity using lambda inversion (+Rev), using 100M tokens of the Russian News Crawl (cf. §4.1). Here $a = 4$, $\lambda_0 = 1$, and $|C| = 800$.

The time complexity is $\mathcal{O}(2\times(B+|V|)\times|C|\times I)$. The original predictive exchange algorithm can be obtained by setting $\lambda = 1$ and $a = 0$.[5]

Another innovation, both in terms of cluster quality *and* speed, is *cluster refinement*. The vocabulary is initially clustered into $|G|$ sets, where $|G| \ll |C|$, typically 2–10. After a few iterations (i) of this, the full partitioning C_f is explored. Clustering G converges very quickly, typically requiring no more than 3 iterations.[6]

$$|C|_i := \begin{cases} |G| & \text{if } i \leq 3 \\ |C|_f & \text{otherwise} \end{cases} \quad (3)$$

The intuition behind this is to group words first into broad classes, like nouns, verbs, adjectives, etc. In contrast to divisive hierarchical clustering and coarse-to-fine methods (Petrov, 2009), after the initial iterations, the algorithm is still able to exchange

---

[1] https://github.com/moses-smt/mgiza

[2] http://cistern.cis.lmu.de/marlin

[3] http://bit.ly/1VJwZ7n

[4] Green et al. (2014) provide a Free implementation of the original predictive exchange algorithm within the Phrasal MT system, at http://nlp.stanford.edu/phrasal. Another implementation is in the Cicada semiring MT system.

[5] The time complexity is $\mathcal{O}((B + |V|) \times |C| \times I)$ if $\lambda = 1$.

[6] The piecewise definition could alternatively be conditioned upon a percentage threshold of moved words.

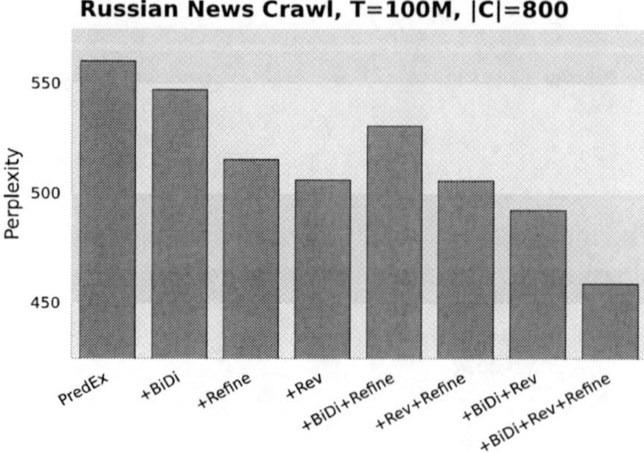

Figure 2: Development set PP of combinations of improvements to predictive exchange (cf. §3), using 100M tokens of the Russian News Crawl, with 800 word classes.

any word to any cluster—there is no hard constraint that the more refined partitions be subsets of the initial coarser partitions. This gives more flexibility in optimizing on log-likelihood, especially given the noise that naturally arises from coarser clusterings. We explored cluster refinement over more stages than just two, successively increasing the number of clusters. We observed no improvement over the two-stage method described above.

Each BIRA component can be applied to any exchange-based clusterer. The contributions of each of these are shown in Figure 2, which reports the development set perplexities (PP) of all combinations of BIRA components over the original predictive exchange algorithm. The data and configurations are discussed in more detail in Section 4. The greatest PP reduction is due to using lambda inversion (+Rev), followed by cluster refinement (+Refine), then interpolating the bidirectional models (+BiDi), with robust improvements by using all three of these—an 18% reduction in perplexity over the predictive exchange algorithm. We have found that both lambda inversion and cluster refinement prevent early convergence at local optima, while bidirectional models give immediate and consistent training set PP improvements, but this is attenuated in a unidirectional evaluation.

We observed that most of the computation for the predictive exchange algorithm is spent on the logarithm function, calculating $\delta \leftarrow \delta - N(w, c) \cdot \log N(w, c)$.[7] Since the codomain of $N(w, c)$ is

---

[7]δ is the change in log-likelihood, and $N(w, c)$ is the count

$\mathbb{N}_0$, and due to the power law distribution of the algorithm's access to these entropy terms, we can precompute $N \cdot \log N$ up to, say 10e+7, with minimal memory requirements.[8] This results in a considerable speedup of around 40%.

4 Experiments

Our experiments consist of both intrinsic and extrinsic evaluations. The intrinsic evaluation measures the perplexity (PP) of two-sided class-based models for English and Russian, and the extrinsic evaluation measures BLEU scores of phrase-based MT of Russian↔English and Japanese↔English texts.

4.1 Class-based Language Model Evaluation

In this task we used 400, 800, and 1200 classes for English, and 800 classes for Russian. The data comes from the 2011–2013 News Crawl monolingual data of the WMT task.[9] For these experiments the data was deduplicated, shuffled, tokenized, digit-conflated, and lowercased. In order to have a large test set, one line per 100 of the resulting (shuffled) corpus was separated into the test set.[10] The minimum count threshold was set to 3 occurrences in the training set. Table 1 shows information on the resulting corpus.

Corpus	Tokens	Types	Lines
English Train	1B	2M	42M
English Test	12M	197K	489K
Russian Train	550M	2.7M	31M
Russian Test	6M	284K	313K

Table 1: Monolingual training & test set sizes.

The clusterings are evaluated on the PP of an external 5-gram *unidirectional two-sided* class-based language model (LM). The *n*-gram-order interpolation weights are tuned using a distinct development set of comparable size and quality as the test set.

Table 2 and Figure 3 show perplexity results using a varying number of classes. Two-sided exchange gives the lowest perplexity across the board, although this is within a two-sided LM evaluation.

---

of a given word followed by a given class.

[8]This was independently discovered in Botros et al. (2015).

[9]http://www.statmt.org/wmt15/translation-task.html

[10]The data setup script is at http://www.dfki.de/~jode03/naacl2016.sh.

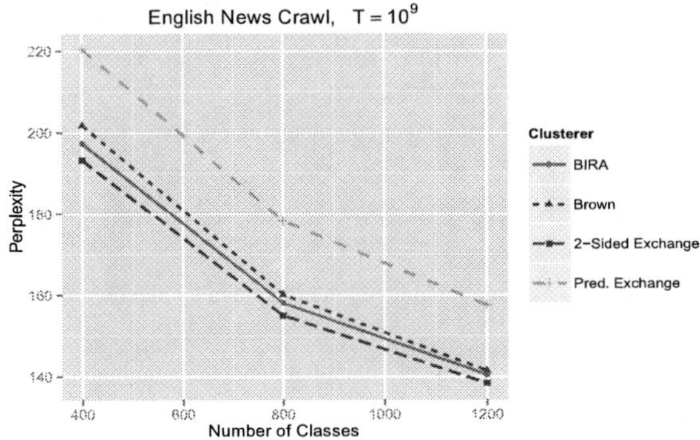

Figure 3: 5-gram two-sided class-based LM perplexities for various clusterers on English News Crawl varying the number of classes.

We also evaluated clusters derived from word2vec (Mikolov et al., 2013) using various configurations[11], and all gave poor perplexities. BIRA gives better perplexities than both the original predictive exchange algorithm and Brown clusters.[12] The Russian experiments yielded higher perplexities for all clusterings, but otherwise the same comparative results.

Training Set	2-Side Ex.	BIRA	Brown	Pred. Ex.
EN, $|C| = 400$	193.3	197.3	201.8	220.5
EN, $|C| = 800$	155.0	158.1	160.2	178.3
EN, $|C| = 1200$	138.4	140.4	141.5	157.6
RU, $|C| = 800$	322.4	340.7	350.4	389.3

Table 2: 5-gram two-sided class-based LM perplexities.

In general Brown clusters give slightly worse results relative to exchange-based clusters, since Brown clustering requires an early, permanent placement of frequent words, with further restrictions imposed on the $|C|$-most frequent words (Liang, 2005).[13] Liang-style Brown clustering is only efficient on a small number of clusters, since there is a $|C|^2$ term in its time complexity.

---

[11]Negative sampling & hierarchical softmax; CBOW & skip-gram; various window sizes; various dimensionalities.

[12]For the two-sided exchange we used mkcls; for the original pred. exchange we used Phrasal's clusterer; for Brown clustering we used Percy Liang's brown-cluster (329dc). All had min-count=3, and all but mkcls (which is not multithreaded) had threads=12, iterations=15.

[13]Recent work by Derczynski and Chester (2016) loosens some restrictions on Brown clustering.

Training Set	mkcls	BIRA	Brown	Phrasal
EN, $|C| = 400$	39.0	1.0	2.3	3.1
EN, $|C| = 800$	48.8	1.4	12.5	5.1
EN, $|C| = 1200$	68.8	1.7	25.5	6.2
RU, $|C| = 800$	75.0	1.5	14.6	5.5

Table 3: Clustering times (hours) of full training sets. Mkcls implements two-sided exchange, and Phrasal implements one-sided predictive exchange.

The original predictive exchange algorithm has a more fractionated history than the two-sided exchange algorithm. Interestingly, increasing the number of clusters causes a convergence in the word clusterings themselves, while also causing a divergence in the time complexities of these two varieties of the exchange algorithm. The metaheuristic techniques employed by the two-sided clusterer mkcls can be applied to other exchange-based clusterers—including ours—for further improvements.

Table 3 presents wall clock times using the full training set, varying the number of word classes $|C|$ (for English).[14] The predictive exchange-based clusterers (BIRA and Phrasal) exhibit slow increases in time as the number of classes increases, while the others (Brown and mkcls) are much more sensitive to $|C|$. Our BIRA-based clusterer is three times faster than Phrasal for all these sets.

We performed an additional experiment, adding more English News Crawl training data.[15] *Our implementation took 3.0 hours to cluster 2.5 billion training tokens, with $|C| = 800$ using modest hardware.*[14]

4.2 Machine Translation Evaluation

We also evaluated the BIRA predictive exchange algorithm extrinsically in machine translation. As discussed in Section 1, word clusters are employed in a variety of ways within machine translation systems, the most common of which is in word alignment where mkcls is widely used. As training sets get larger every year, mkcls struggles to keep pace, and

---

[14]All time experiments used a 2.4 GHz Opteron 8378 featuring 16 threads.

[15]Adding years 2008–2010 and 2014 to the existing training data. This training set was too large for the external class-based LM to fit into memory, so no perplexity evaluation of this clustering was possible.

is a substantial time bottleneck in MT pipelines with large datasets.

We used data from the Workshop on Machine Translation 2015 (WMT15) Russian↔English dataset and the Workshop on Asian Translation 2014 (WAT14) Japanese↔English dataset (Nakazawa et al., 2014). Both pairs used standard configurations, like truecasing, MeCab segmentation for Japanese, MGIZA alignment, grow-diag-final-and phrase extraction, phrase-based Moses, quantized KenLM 5-gram modified Kneser-Ney LMs, and MERT tuning.

$|C|$	EN-RU	RU-EN	EN-JA	JA-EN
10	20.8→20.9*	26.2→26.0	23.5→23.4	16.9→16.8
50	21.0→21.2*	25.9→25.7	24.0→23.7*	16.9→16.9
100	20.4→21.1	25.9→25.8	23.8→23.5	16.9→17.0
200	21.0→20.8	25.8→25.9	23.8→23.4	17.0→16.8
500	20.9→20.9	25.8→25.9*	24.0→23.8	16.8→17.1*
1000	20.9→21.1	25.9→26.0**	23.6→23.5	16.9→17.1

Table 4: BLEU scores (`mkcls`→BIRA) and significance across cluster sizes ($|C|$).

The BLEU score differences between using `mkcls` and our BIRA implementation are small but there are a few statistically significant changes, using bootstrap resampling (Koehn, 2004). Table 4 presents the BLEU score changes across varying cluster sizes (*: p-value < 0.05, **: p-value < 0.01). MERT tuning is quite erratic, and some of the BLEU differences could be affected by noise in the tuning process in obtaining quality weight values. Using our BIRA implementation reduces the translation model training time with 500 clusters from 20 hours using `mkcls` (of which 60% of the time is spent on clustering) to just 8 hours (of which 5% is spent on clustering).

5   Conclusion

We have presented improvements to the predictive exchange algorithm that address longstanding drawbacks of the original algorithm compared to other clustering algorithms, enabling new directions in using large scale, high cluster-size word classes in NLP.

Botros et al. (2015) found that the one-sided model of the predictive exchange algorithm produces better results for training LSTM-based language models compared to two-sided models, while two-sided models generally give better perplexity in class-based LM experiments. Our paper shows that BIRA-based predictive exchange clusters are competitive with two-sided clusters even in a two-sided evaluation. They also give better perplexity than the original predictive exchange algorithm and Brown clustering.

The software is freely available at `https://github.com/jonsafari/clustercat`.

Acknowledgements

We would like to thank Hermann Ney and Kazuki Irie, as well as the reviewers for their useful comments. This work was supported by the QT21 project (Horizon 2020 No. 645452).

References

Rami Botros, Kazuki Irie, Martin Sundermeyer, and Hermann Ney. 2015. On Efficient Training of Word Classes and their Application to Recurrent Neural Network Language Models. In *Proceedings of INTERSPEECH-2015*, pages 1443–1447, Dresden, Germany.

Peter E. Brown, Stephen A. Della Pietra, Vincent J. Della Pietra, and Robert L. Mercer. 1993. The Mathematics of Statistical Machine Translation: Parameter Estimation. *Computational Linguistics*, 19(2):263–311.

Marie Candito and Djamé Seddah. 2010. Parsing Word Clusters. In *Proceedings of the NAACL HLT 2010 First Workshop on Statistical Parsing of Morphologically-Rich Languages*, pages 76–84, Los Angeles, CA, USA.

Victor Chahuneau, Eva Schlinger, Noah A. Smith, and Chris Dyer. 2013. Translating into Morphologically Rich Languages with Synthetic Phrases. In *Proceedings of EMNLP*, pages 1677–1687, Seattle, WA, USA.

Colin Cherry. 2013. Improved Reordering for Phrase-Based Translation using Sparse Features. In *Proceedings of NAACL-HLT*, pages 22–31, Atlanta, GA, USA.

Alexander Clark. 2003. Combining Distributional and Morphological Information for Part of Speech Induction. In *Proceedings of EACL*, pages 59–66.

Leon Derczynski and Sean Chester. 2016. Generalised Brown Clustering and Roll-up Feature Generation. In *Proceedings of AAAI*, Phoenix, AZ, USA.

Nadir Durrani, Philipp Koehn, Helmut Schmid, and Alexander Fraser. 2014. Investigating the Usefulness of Generalized Word Representations in SMT. In *Proceedings of Coling*, pages 421–432, Dublin, Ireland.

Joshua Goodman. 2001a. Classes for Fast Maximum Entropy Training. In *Proceedings of ICASSP*, pages 561–564.

Joshua T. Goodman. 2001b. A Bit of Progress in Language Modeling, Extended Version. Technical Report MSR-TR-2001-72, Microsoft Research.

Spence Green, Daniel Cer, and Christopher Manning. 2014. An Empirical Comparison of Features and Tuning for Phrase-based Machine Translation. In *Proc. of WMT*, pages 466–476, Baltimore, MD, USA.

Reinhard Kneser and Hermann Ney. 1993. Improved clustering techniques for class-based statistical language modelling. In *Proceedings of EUROSPEECH'93*, pages 973–976, Berlin, Germany.

Philipp Koehn and Hieu Hoang. 2007. Factored Translation Models. In *Proceedings of EMNLP-CoNLL*, pages 868–876, Prague, Czech Republic.

Philipp Koehn. 2004. Statistical significance tests for machine translation evaluation. In *Proceedings of EMNLP*, pages 388–395.

Lingpeng Kong, Nathan Schneider, Swabha Swayamdipta, Archna Bhatia, Chris Dyer, and Noah A. Smith. 2014. A Dependency Parser for Tweets. In *Proceedings of EMNLP*, pages 1001–1012, Doha, Qatar.

Terry Koo, Xavier Carreras, and Michael Collins. 2008. Simple Semi-supervised Dependency Parsing. In *Proceedings of ACL: HLT*, pages 595–603, Columbus, OH, USA.

Percy Liang. 2005. Semi-Supervised Learning for Natural Language. Master's thesis, MIT.

Sven Martin, Jörg Liermann, and Hermann Ney. 1998. Algorithms for Bigram and Trigram Word Clustering. *Speech Communication*, 24(1):19–37.

Tomáš Mikolov, Kai Chen, Greg Corrado, and Jeffrey Dean. 2013. Efficient Estimation of Word Representations in Vector Space. In *Workshop Proceedings of the International Conference on Learning Representations (ICLR)*, Scottsdale, AZ, USA.

Scott Miller, Jethran Guinness, and Alex Zamanian. 2004. Name Tagging with Word Clusters and Discriminative Training. In Susan Dumais, Daniel Marcu, and Salim Roukos, editors, *Proceedings of HLT-NAACL*, pages 337–342, Boston, MA, USA.

Andriy Mnih and Geoffrey Hinton. 2009. A Scalable Hierarchical Distributed Language Model. In D. Koller, D. Schuurmans, Y. Bengio, and L. Bottou, editors, *Advances in NIPS-21*, volume 21, pages 1081–1088.

Frederic Morin and Yoshua Bengio. 2005. Hierarchical Probabilistic Neural Network Language Model. In *Proceedings of AISTATS*, volume 5, pages 246–252.

Thomas Müller and Hinrich Schütze. 2015. Robust Morphological Tagging with Word Representations. In *Proceedings of NAACL*, pages 526–536, Denver, CO, USA.

Toshiaki Nakazawa, Hideya Mino, Isao Goto, Sadao Kurohashi, and Eiichiro Sumita. 2014. Overview of the first Workshop on Asian Translation. In *Proceedings of the Workshop on Asian Translation (WAT)*.

Franz Josef Och and Hermann Ney. 2000. A Comparison of Alignment Models for Statistical Machine Translation. In *Proceedings of Coling*, pages 1086–1090, Saarbrücken, Germany.

Franz Josef Och. 1995. Maximum-Likelihood-Schätzung von Wortkategorien mit Verfahren der kombinatorischen Optimierung. Bachelor's thesis (Studienarbeit), Friedrich-Alexander-Universität Erlangen-Nürnburg, Germany.

Slav Petrov. 2009. *Coarse-to-Fine Natural Language Processing*. Ph.D. thesis, University of California at Berkeley, Berkeley, CA, USA.

Lev Ratinov and Dan Roth. 2009. Design Challenges and Misconceptions in Named Entity Recognition. In *Proc. of CoNLL*, pages 147–155, Boulder, CO, USA.

Alan Ritter, Sam Clark, Mausam, and Oren Etzioni. 2011. Named Entity Recognition in Tweets: An Experimental Study. In *Proceedings of EMNLP 2011*, pages 1524–1534, Edinburgh, Scotland.

Attapol Rutherford and Nianwen Xue. 2014. Discovering Implicit Discourse Relations Through Brown Cluster Pair Representation and Coreference Patterns. In *Proc. of EACL*, pages 645–654, Gothenburg, Sweden.

Sara Stymne. 2012. Clustered Word Classes for Preordering in Statistical Machine Translation. In *Proceedings of the Joint Workshop on Unsupervised and Semi-Supervised Learning in NLP*, pages 28–34, Avignon, France.

Oscar Täckström, Ryan McDonald, and Jakob Uszkoreit. 2012. Cross-lingual Word Clusters for Direct Transfer of Linguistic Structure. In *Proceedings of NAACL:HLT*, pages 477–487, Montréal, Canada.

Joseph Turian, Lev-Arie Ratinov, and Yoshua Bengio. 2010. Word Representations: A Simple and General Method for Semi-Supervised Learning. In *Proceedings of ACL*, pages 384–394, Uppsala, Sweden.

Jakob Uszkoreit and Thorsten Brants. 2008. Distributed Word Clustering for Large Scale Class-Based Language Modeling in Machine Translation. In *Proc. of ACL: HLT*, pages 755–762, Columbus, OH, USA.

Joern Wuebker, Stephan Peitz, Felix Rietig, and Hermann Ney. 2013. Improving Statistical Machine Translation with Word Class Models. In *Proceedings of EMNLP*, pages 1377–1381, Seattle, WA, USA.

Andreas Zollmann and Stephan Vogel. 2011. A Word-Class Approach to Labeling PSCFG Rules for Machine Translation. In *Proceedings of ACL-HLT*, pages 1–11, Portland, OR, USA.

Integrating Morphological Desegmentation into Phrase-based Decoding

Mohammad Salameh[†]   **Colin Cherry**[‡]   **Grzegorz Kondrak**[†]

[†]Department of Computing Science
University of Alberta
Edmonton, AB, T6G 2E8, Canada
{msalameh,gkondrak}@ualberta.ca

[‡]National Research Council Canada
1200 Montreal Road
Ottawa, ON, K1A 0R6, Canada
Colin.Cherry@nrc-cnrc.gc.ca

Abstract

When translating into a morphologically complex language, segmenting the target language can reduce data sparsity, while introducing the complication of desegmenting the system output. We present a method for decoder-integrated desegmentation, allowing features that consider the desegmented target, such as a word-level language model, to be considered throughout the entire search space. Our results on a large-scale, English to Arabic translation task show significant improvement over the 1-best desegmentation baseline.

1   Introduction

State-of-the-art systems for translating into morphologically complex languages, such as Arabic, employ morphological segmentation of the target language in order to reduce data sparsity and improve translation quality. For example, the Arabic word لدولتهم *ldwlthm* "for their country" is segmented into the prefix +ل *l+* "for", the stem دولة *dwlp* "country" and the suffix هم+ *+hm* "their." The segmentation sometimes involves performing orthographic normalizations, such as transforming the stem-final *t* to *p*. The result is not only a reduction in the number of word types, but also better token-to-token correspondence with the source language.

Morphological segmentation is typically performed as a pre-processing step before the training phase, which results in a model that translates the source language into segmented target language. *Desegmentation* is the process of transforming the segmented output into a readable word sequence, which can be performed using a table lookup combined with a small set of rules. Desegmentation is usually applied to the 1-best output of the decoder. However, this pipeline suffers from error propagation: errors made during decoding cannot be corrected, even when desegmentation results in an illegal or extremely unlikely word. Two principal types of solutions have been proposed for this problem: *rescoring* and *phrase-table desegmentation*.

The rescoring approach desegments either an n-best list (Oflazer and Durgar El-Kahlout, 2007) or lattice (Salameh et al., 2014), and then re-ranks with features that consider the desegmented word sequence of each hypothesis. Rescoring features include the score from an unsegmented target language model and contiguity indicators that flag target words that were translated from contiguous source tokens. Rescoring widens the desegmentation pipeline, allowing desegmentation features to reduce the number of translation errors. However, these features are calculated for only a subset of the search space, and the extra rescoring step complicates the training and translation processes.

Phrase-table desegmentation (Luong et al., 2010) also translates into a segmented target language, but alters training to perform word-boundary-aware phrase extraction. The extracted phrases are constrained to contain only complete target words, without any *dangling affixes*. With this restriction in place, the phrase table can be desegmented before decoding begins, allowing the decoder to track features over both the segmented and desegmented target. This ensures that desegmentation features are integrated into the complete search space, and

Proceedings of NAACL-HLT 2016, pages 1175–1180,
San Diego, California, June 12-17, 2016. ©2016 Association for Computational Linguistics

side-steps the complications of rescoring. However, Salameh et al. (2015) show experimentally that these benefits are not worth giving up phrase-pairs with dangling affixes, which are eliminated by word-boundary-aware phrase extraction.

We present a method for decoder-integrated desegmentation that combines the strengths of these two approaches. Like a rescoring approach, it places no restrictions on what morpheme sequences can appear in the target side of a phrase pair. Like phrase-table desegmentation, its desegmentation features are integrated directly into decoding and considered throughout the entire search space. We achieve this by augmenting the decoder to desegment hypotheses on the fly, allowing the inclusion of an unsegmented language model and other features. Our results on a large-scale, NIST-data English to Arabic translation task show significant improvements over the 1-best desegmentation baseline, and match the performance of the state-of-the-art lattice desegmentation approach of Salameh et al. (2014), while eliminating the complication and cost of its rescoring step. Our approach is implemented as a single stateful feature function in Moses (Koehn et al., 2007), which we will submit back to the community.

2 Method

Our approach extends the multi-stack phrase-based decoding paradigm to enable the extraction of word-level features inside morpheme-segmented models.[1] We assume that the target side of the parallel corpus has been segmented into morphemes with prefixes and suffixes marked.[2] This allows us to define a *complete word* as a maximal morpheme sequence consisting of 0 or more prefixes, followed by at most one stem, and then 0 or more suffixes.

We also assume access to a desegmentation function that takes as input a morpheme sequence matching the above definition, and returns the corresponding word as output. Depending on the complexity of the segmentation, desegmentation can be achieved through simple concatenation, a small set of rules, a statistical table (Badr et al., 2008), or a statis-

tical transducer (Salameh et al., 2013). El Kholy and Habash (2012) provide an extensive study on the influence of segmentation and desegmentation on English-to-Arabic SMT. In this work, we adopt the Table+Rules technique of El Kholy and Habash (2012) for English-Arabic SMT. The technique relies on a look-up table that stores mappings of segmented-unsegmented forms, and falls back on manually crafted rules for segmented sequences not found in the table. When a segmented form has multiple desegmentation options available in the table, we select the most frequent option.

The output of a phrase-based decoder is built from left to right, and at each step, a hypothesis is expanded with a phrasal translation of a previously uncovered source segment. We augment this process with *in-decoder desegmentation*, which monitors the target sequence of each translation hypothesis as it grows, detecting morpheme sequences that correspond to complete words and desegmenting them on the fly to generate new features. This is described in detail in Section 2.1.

The task of determining whether a word is complete is non-trivial. We are never sure if we will see another suffix as we expand the hypothesis, so we can only recognize a complete word as we begin the next word. For example, take hyp1 in Figure 1. This hypothesis ends with a stem *nšr*, which may end a complete word, as is the case when we expand to hyp2, or may represent a word that is still in progress, which occurs as we extend to hyp3. This means that the word-based scoring of the morpheme sequence *l+ nšr* must be delayed or approximated until we know what follows. A related challenge involves scoring phrase-pairs out of context, as is required for future-cost estimates. Take, for example, the target phrase *+h AfkAr* added by hyp3 in Figure 1. Without the context, we have insufficient information at the left boundary to score *+h* with word-based models, while *AfkAr* at the right boundary may or may not form a complete word. Here, there is no choice but to approximate. The quality of these approximations and the length of our delays will determine how effective our new features will be when incorporated into beam search.

---

[1]The ideas presented here could also be applied to hierarchical decoding, which would require generalizing them to account for right context as well as left.

[2]Throughout this paper, we use a token-final "+" to denote a prefix, and a token-initial "+" for a suffix.

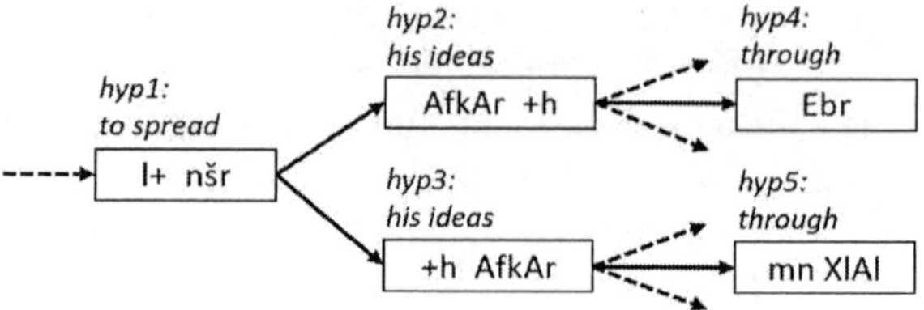

Figure 1: Decoding the Arabic translation of the phrase *"to spread his ideas through"*.

2.1 Decoder Integration

A typical phrase-based decoder represents a hypothesis with a state that contains the information to guide search and calculate features, such as the source coverage vector and the target context for the language model. Hypotheses with identical states can be recombined to improve search efficiency. We augment the state with two structures: (1) a buffer Q containing all of the morphemes that contribute to the current word in progress, represented as a queue of tokens; and (2) n-gram context C for the word-level target language model. The search's initial state begins with an empty Q and with n-1 beginning-of-sentence tokens in C.

When a state is extended with a target phrase P, we update the in-decoder desegmentation structures Q and C with Algorithm 1. Tokens are appended to Q until a token t would begin a new word, at which point the tokens from Q are desegmented and the resulting word is used to calculate features and update the target context. Following the lower decoding path in Figure 1, Q would be emptied and desegmented first during hyp3 when $t = AfkAr$, calculating features for $W = lnšrh$.

The main cost of in-decoder desegmentation comes from maintaining the context necessary to evaluate the n-gram, word-level language model. As each desegmented word in C will correspond to at least one segmented token, the system's effective language-model order in terms of segmented tokens will frequently be much larger than n. Storing larger language-model contexts make it less likely that states will be equal to one another, which reduces the amount of recombination the system can do, and increases the number of states that must be expanded during search.

Algorithm 1 Desegmentation State Update

1: Input: State variables Q, C
2: Input: Extending phrase P
3: **for** each token t in P **do**
4:     **if** t cannot continue the word in Q **then**
5:         W = Desegmentation of tokens in Q
6:         Extract word-level features for W
7:         (Word-level LM score is $p(W\,|\,C)$)
8:         Update current feature vector
9:         Update C with W
10:        Empty Q
11:     Append token t to Q

2.2 Delayed and Optimistic Scoring

In the above approach, desegmentation and feature scoring are applied only when a complete word is formed. We refer to this as **delayed scoring** because the features for a token are not applied until other tokens have been added to the hypothesis. For example, in Figure 1, the tokens l+ $nšr$ added in hyp1 are not evaluated with word-level features until hyp2 or hyp3 completes the word. This delay results in inaccurate scoring of hypotheses, as the cost from these tokens is hidden until Q is emptied. These inaccuracies can lead to poor pruning choices and search errors during beam search.

Alternatively, we can perform **optimistic scoring**, which tries to score the contents of Q as early as possible. In this case, we assume that the contents of Q form a complete word, without waiting for the next token to confirm it. With each hypothesis extension, when the last token in P is processed and added to the queue, we desegment the contents of Q and extract features, but without emptying Q. The scores of these features are cached in a variable S that does not affect recombination, as the scores are deterministic given Q, C and the model. When a later token confirms the end of the word, we subtract S from the scores derived from the actual desegmented word, to account for our earlier approximation. Note that for a Q containing only a prefix, we must still delay scoring.

2.3 Features

Three features are extracted from each desegmented form: an unsegmented language model, contiguity indicators, and a desegmented word penalty.

The unsegmented n-gram language model scores W in the context of C, as shown in Algorithm 1. This language model will heavily penalize malformed Arabic words, as they will appear as out-of-vocabulary items. Furthermore, it will evaluate well-formed Arabic words in a larger, word-level context, complementing the morpheme-level n-gram language model that is naturally included in SMT systems built over a segmented target.

We also implement the contiguity features proposed by Salameh et al. (2014). These indicators check if the desegmented form is generated from a contiguous block of source tokens, a block with 1 discontiguity, or a block with multiple discontiguities. These features enable the decoder to prefer desegmented words whose component segments were translated from contiguous or nearly contiguous source sequences. This encourages the system to select a more local, and hopefully safer, translation path when possible.

Finally, most phrase-based decoders incorporate a "word penalty" feature that counts the number of target tokens in a hypothesis. When the target language has been segmented into morphemes, this actually corresponds to a morpheme penalty. However, with in-decoder desegmentation, we now have the option to count either words or morphemes. There is reason to believe that by counting words, instead of morphemes, we will give the system greater control over the length of its output word sequence, which is particularly relevant because of BLEU's brevity penalty. We try both options in our experiments. Unfortunately, the obvious solution of including two features, a word count and a morpheme count, did not perform well during development.

2.4 Future costs

For future cost estimates, we must also provide out-of-context feature scores for each phrase-pair in our system. To do so, we ignore suffixes appearing at the beginning of a target phrase and prefixes appearing at the end. We assume that the remaining tokens form complete words, and desegment and score them to provide out-of-context scores. We also consider dangling affixes as half words, with a count of 0.5, for out-of-context scoring of the word penalty feature.

3 Experiments

We use the NIST 2012 dataset (1.49 million sentence pairs excluding UN pairs) to train an English-to-Arabic system. The system is tuned with the NIST 2004 (1353 pairs) evaluation set and tested using NIST 2005 (1056 sentences) and the newswire portion of NIST 2008 (813 pairs) and NIST 2009 (586 pairs). As there are multiple English reference translations provided for these evaluation sets, we use the first reference as our source text.

The Arabic part of the training set is morphologically segmented and tokenized by MADA 3.2 (Habash et al., 2009) using the Penn Arabic Treebank (PATB) segmentation scheme. Variants of Alif and Ya characters are uniformly normalized. We generate a desegmentation table from the Arabic side of the training data by collecting mappings of segmented forms to surface forms.

We align the parallel data with GIZA++ (Och et al., 2003), and decode with Moses (Koehn et al., 2007). The decoder's log-linear model uses a standard feature set, including four phrase table scores, six features from a lexicalized distortion model, along with a phrase penalty and a distance-based distortion penalty. KN-smoothed 5-gram language models are trained on both the segmented and unsegmented views of the target side of the parallel data. We experiment with word penalties based on either morphemes or desegmented words. The decoder uses Moses' default search parameters, except for the maximum phrase length, which is set to 8, and the translation table limit, which is set to 40. The decoder's log-linear model is tuned with MERT (Och, 2003) using unsegmented Arabic reference translations. When necessary, we desegment our 100-best-lists before MERT evaluates each hypothesis. We evaluate with BLEU (Papineni et al., 2002) measured on unsegmented Arabic, and test statistical significance with multeval (Clark et al., 2011) over 3 tuning replications.

We test four systems that differ in their desegmentation approach. The **NoSegm.** baseline involves no segmentation. The **One-best** baseline translates into segmented Arabic and desegments the decoder's 1-best output. The **Lattice** system is the lattice-desegmentation approach of Salameh et al. (2014). We implement our **in-Decoder** desegmenta-

System	WP	mt05	mt08	mt09
NoSegm.	word	33.2	18.6	25.6
One-best	morph.	33.8	19.1	26.8
Lattice	morph.	34.4	**19.7**	**27.4**
Delayed	morph.	34.1	19.4	27.0
	word	34.1	19.5	26.8
Optimistic	morph.	34.2	19.6	27.2
	word	**34.5**	**19.7**	27.2

Table 1: Evaluation of the desegmentation methods using BLEU score. Both Delayed and Optimistic refer to in-Decoder Desegmentation method used. WP shows whether Word Penalty feature is based on a complete desegmented word or a morpheme.

tion approach as a feature functions in Moses, testing scoring variants (delayed vs. optimistic), and word penalty variants (morpheme vs. word).

Table 1 shows the results on three NIST test sets, each averaged over 3 tuning replications. The lattice approach is significantly better than the 1-best system, which in turn is significantly better than the unsegmented baseline. Our **Optimistic** in-decoder approach with word penalty calculated on word tokens is significantly ($p < 0.05$) better than the 1-best approach, and effectively matches the quality of the more complex lattice approach.

All of the systems with word-level features improve over 1-best desegmentation, as their features penalize desegmentations resulting in illegal words or unlikely word sequences. We see a small, consistent benefit from optimistic scoring. Error analysis reveals that translations with many consecutive stems benefit the most from this variant, which makes sense, as our approximations would be exact in these cases. Using a word penalty calculated on word tokens appears to work slightly better on average than one calculated on morphemes.

Typically, one would hope to surpass a rescoring approach with decoder integration; however, our lattice implementation fully searches its lattice, even if composition with the word-level language model would cause the lattice to explode in size. That is, lattice desegmentation has an advantage, as it trades time-efficiency for a perfect search that ignores the complexity introduced by expanded n-gram context. A lattice beam search that dynamically calculates word-level language model scores while pruning away unlikely paths would provide a more fair, and more efficient, comparison point.

Lattice rescoring also involves many steps, requiring one to train and tune a complete segmented system with segmented references, then desegment lattices and compose them with a word LM, and then tune a lattice rescorer on unsegmented references. In contrast, our system is implemented as a single decoder feature function in Moses.[3] This one function replaces the lattice desegmentation, LM composition, and lattice rescoring steps, greatly simplifying the translation pipeline.

4   Conclusions and Future Work

We have presented a method for in-decoder desegmentation, which allows a phrase-based decoder to simultaneously consider both segmented and desegmented views of the target language. We have shown that this approach outperforms 1-best desegmentation, and matches the performance of lattice desegmentation, while eliminating the complication of its lattice transformation and rescoring steps.

We are interested in building an unsegmented, word-level language model that can provide meaningful estimates for morphological segments, which would improve scoring for out-of-context phrases and incomplete words. Also, our system currently considers only the most likely desegmentation of each segmented word. Inspired by the disambiguating desegmentation system of El Kholy and Habash (2012), we would like to extend our system to propose multiple desegmentation candidates for each word, and allow the decoder to select the correct form using its other features.

Acknowledgments

This research was supported by the Natural Sciences and Engineering Research Council of Canada (NSERC).

---

[3]This function references a desegmentation table and an unsegmented language model, which are needed to carry out Algorithm 1. Even though it is conceptually one function, it produces a vector of feature scores, producing the various features described in Section 2.3.

References

Ibrahim Badr, Rabih Zbib, and James Glass. 2008. Segmentation for English-to-Arabic statistical machine translation. In *Proceedings of ACL*, pages 153–156.

Jonathan H. Clark, Chris Dyer, Alon Lavie, and Noah A. Smith. 2011. Better hypothesis testing for statistical machine translation: Controlling for optimizer instability. In *Proceedings of ACL*, pages 176–181.

Ahmed El Kholy and Nizar Habash. 2012. Orthographic and morphological processing for English—Arabic statistical machine translation. *Machine Translation*, 26(1-2):25–45, March.

Nizar Habash, Owen Rambow, and Ryan Roth. 2009. Mada+tokan: A toolkit for Arabic tokenization, diacritization, morphological disambiguation, POS tagging, stemming and lemmatization. In Khalid Choukri and Bente Maegaard, editors, *Proceedings of the Second International Conference on Arabic Language Resources and Tools*, Cairo, Egypt, April. The MEDAR Consortium.

Philipp Koehn, Hieu Hoang, Alexandra Birch, Chris Callison-Burch, Marcello Federico, Nicola Bertoldi, Brooke Cowan, Wade Shen, Christine Moran, Richard Zens, Chris Dyer, Ondrej Bojar, Alexandra Constantin, and Evan Herbst. 2007. Moses: Open source toolkit for statistical machine translation. In *Proceedings of the 45th Annual Meeting of the Association for Computational Linguistics Companion Volume Proceedings of the Demo and Poster Sessions*, pages 177–180, Prague, Czech Republic, June.

Minh-Thang Luong, Preslav Nakov, and Min-Yen Kan. 2010. A hybrid morpheme-word representation for machine translation of morphologically rich languages. In *Proceedings of the 2010 Conference on Empirical Methods in Natural Language Processing*, pages 148–157, Cambridge, MA, October.

Franz Josef Och, Hermann Ney, Franz Josef, and Och Hermann Ney. 2003. A systematic comparison of various statistical alignment models. *Computational Linguistics*, 29.

Franz Joseph Och. 2003. Minimum error rate training for statistical machine translation. In *Proceedings of ACL*, pages 160–167.

Kemal Oflazer and Ilknur Durgar El-Kahlout. 2007. Exploring different representational units in English-to-Turkish statistical machine translation. In *Proceedings of the Second Workshop on Statistical Machine Translation*, pages 25–32, Prague, Czech Republic, June.

Kishore Papineni, Salim Roukos, Todd Ward, and Weijing Zhu. 2002. BLEU: a method for automatic evaluation of machine translation. In *Proceedings of 40th Annual Meeting of the Association for Computational Linguistics*, pages 311–318.

Mohammad Salameh, Colin Cherry, and Grzegorz Kondrak. 2013. Reversing morphological tokenization in English-to-Arabic SMT. In *Proceedings of the 2013 NAACL HLT Student Research Workshop*, pages 47–53, Atlanta, Georgia, June.

Mohammad Salameh, Colin Cherry, and Grzegorz Kondrak. 2014. Lattice desegmentation for statistical machine translation. In *Proceedings of the 52nd Annual Meeting of the Association for Computational Linguistics (Volume 1: Long Papers)*, pages 100–110.

Mohammad Salameh, Colin Cherry, and Grzegorz Kondrak. 2015. What matters most in morphologically segmented smt models? In *Proceedings of the Ninth Workshop on Syntax, Semantics and Structure in Statistical Translation*, pages 65–73, Denver, Colorado, USA, June. Association for Computational Linguistics.

The Instantiation Discourse Relation:
A Corpus Analysis of Its Properties and Improved Detection

Junyi Jessy Li and **Ani Nenkova**

University of Pennsylvania

{ljunyi,nenkova}@seas.upenn.edu

Abstract

INSTANTIATION is a fairly common discourse relation and past work has suggested that it plays special roles in local coherence, in sentiment expression and in content selection in summarization. In this paper we provide the first systematic corpus analysis of the relation and show that relation-specific features can improve considerably the detection of the relation. We show that sentences involved in INSTANTIATION are set apart from other sentences by the use of gradable (subjective) adjectives, the occurrence of rare words and by different patterns in part-of-speech usage. Words across arguments of INSTANTIATION are connected through hypernym and meronym relations significantly more often than in other sentences and that they stand out in context by being significantly less similar to each other than other adjacent sentence pairs. These factors provide substantial predictive power that improves the identification of implicit INSTANTIATION relation by more than 5% F-measure.

1 Introduction

In an INSTANTIATION relation, one text span explains in further detail the events, reasons, behaviors and attitudes mentioned in the other (Miltsakaki et al., 2008), as illustrated by the segments below:

[a] Other fundamental "reforms" of the 1986 act have been threatened as well.

[b] The House seriously considered raising the top tax rate paid by individuals with the highest incomes.

Sentence [a] mentions "other reforms" and a threat to them, but leaves unspecified what are the reforms or how they are threatened. Sentence [b] provides sufficient detail for the reader to infer more concretely what has happened.

The INSTANTIATION relation has some special properties. A study of discourse relations as indicators for content selection in single document summarization revealed that the first sentences from INSTANTIATION pairs are included in human summaries significantly more often than other sentences (Louis et al., 2010) and that being a first sentence in an INSTANTIATION relation is *the* most powerful indicator for content selection related to discourse relation sense. The sentences between which the relation holds also contain more sentiment expressions than other sentences (Trnavac and Taboada, 2013), making it a special target for sentiment analysis applications. Moreover, INSTANTIATION relations appear to play a special role in local coherence (Louis and Nenkova, 2010), as the flow between INSTANTIATION sentences is not explained by the major coherence theories (Kehler, 2004; Grosz et al., 1995). Many of the sentences in INSTANTIATION relation contain entity instantiations (complex examples of set-instance anaphora), such as "several EU countries"—"the UK", "footballers"—"Wayne Rooney" and "most cosmetic purchase"—"lipstick" (McKinlay and Markert, 2011), raising further questions about the relationship between INSTANTIATIONS and key discourse phenomena.

Detecting an INSTANTIATION, however, is hard. In the Penn Discourse Treebank (PDTB) (Prasad et al., 2008), INSTANTIATION is one of the few relations that are more often *implicit*, i.e., expressed without a discourse marker such as "for exam-

Proceedings of NAACL-HLT 2016, pages 1181–1186,
San Diego, California, June 12-17, 2016. ©2016 Association for Computational Linguistics

ple". Identifying implicit discourse relation is an acknowledged difficult task (Braud and Denis, 2015; Ji and Eisenstein, 2015; Rutherford and Xue, 2014; Biran and McKeown, 2013; Park and Cardie, 2012; Lin et al., 2009; Pitler et al., 2009), but the challenge is exacerbated due to the lack of *explicit* INSTANTIATIONS: explicit relations are shown to improve their implicit counterparts using data source expansion (Rutherford and Xue, 2015). Moreover, detecting INSTANTIATION also involves the skewed class distribution problem (Li and Nenkova, 2014a) because although it is one of the largest class of implicit relations, it constitutes less than 10% of all the implicit relations annotated in the PDTB.

In this work, we identify a rich set of factors that sets apart each sentence in an implicit INSTANTIATION and the pair as a whole. We show that these factors improve the identification of implicit INSTANTIATION by at least 5% in F-measure and 8% in balanced accuracy compared to prior systems.

2 Presence of INSTANTIATION

We use the Penn Discourse Tree Bank (PDTB) (Prasad et al., 2008) for the analysis and experiments presented in this paper. There are a total of 1,747 INSTANTIATION relations in the PDTB, of which 83% are implicit. INSTANTIATIONs make up 8.7% of all implicit relations and is the 5th largest among the 16 second-level relations in the PDTB.

3 Characteristics of INSTANTIATION

We identify significant factors[1] that characterize: *(i)* s_1 and s_2: the first and second sentence in an INSTANTIATION pair vs. all other sentences; *(ii)* s_1 vs. s_2: adjacent sentence pairs in INSTANTIATION relation vs. all other adjacent sentence pairs.

Our analysis is conducted on the PDTB except section 23, which is reserved for testing as in prior work (Lin et al., 2014; Biran and McKeown, 2015). In total, there are 1,337 INSTANTIATION sentence pairs and 43,934 non-INSTANTIATION sentences for the corpus analysis.

---

[1]$p < 0.05$ according to paired Wilcoxon signed rank test for real valued comparison between the two sentences in a relation, non-paired Wilcoxon rank sum for real valued factors in different types of sentences, and Kruskal-Wallis for binary valued features across different types of sentences.

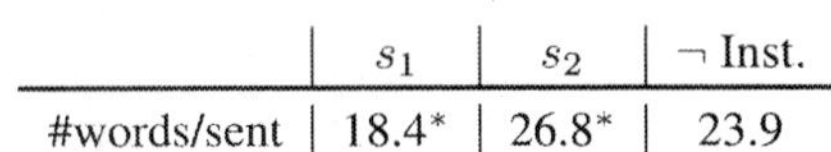

	s_1	s_2	$\neg$ Inst.
#words/sent	18.4*	26.8*	23.9

Table 1: Average # words. [*]: significant ($p < 0.05$) compared to non-instantiation sentences.

	s_1	s_2	$\neg$ Inst.
%oov/sent	0.68*	1.54	1.46

Table 2: Average % of rare words per sentence. [*]: significant ($p < 0.05$) compared to non-instantiation sentences.

Sentence length. Intuitively, longer sentences are more likely to involve details. Table 1 demonstrates that there is an average of 8.4-word difference in length between the two sentences in an INSTANTIATION relation; moreover, s_1s are significantly shorter (more than 5 words on average) than other sentences, and s_2s are significantly longer.

Rare words. For each sentence, we compute the percentage of words that are not present in the 400K vocabulary of the Glove vector representations (Pennington et al., 2014). Table 2 shows that s_1 of INSTANTIATIONs contain significantly *fewer* out-of-vocabulary words compared to either s_2 and non-INSTANTIATIONS. We also compare the difference in unigram probability[2] of content word pairs across sentence pairs, i.e., $(w_i, w_j), w_i \in s_1, w_j \in s_2$. Compared to non-INSTANTIATION, words across INSTANTIATION arguments show significantly larger average unigram log probability difference (1.24 vs. 1.22). These numbers show that the first sentences of INSTANTIATION do not involve many unfamiliar words — an indication of higher readability (Pitler and Nenkova, 2008).

Gradable adjectives. The use of gradable adjectives (Frazier et al., 2008; de Marneffe et al., 2010)—*popular, high, likely*— may require further explanation to justify the appropriateness of their use. Here we compute the average percentage of gradable adjectives in a sentence. The list of adjectives is from Hatzivassiloglou and Wiebe (2000) and the respective percentages are shown in Table 3. Compared to other sentences, s_1 of INSTANTIATION involves significantly more gradable adjectives.

---

[2]We use a unigram language model on year 2006 of the New York Times Annotated Corpus (Sandhaus, 2008).

	s_1	s_2	$\neg$ Inst.
%gradable adj	2.96*	2.22	2.22

Table 3: Average % of gradable adjectives per sentence. [*]: significant ($p < 0.05$) compared to non-instantiation sentences.

$s_1 > s_2$	CC EX JJR JJS NNS PDT RB† RBR VBG VBN VBP VBZ†
$s_1 < s_2$	NN NNP† PRP TO VBD WRB
s_1 vs $\neg$Inst.	CD$^-$ JJ$^-$ MD$^-$ NN$^-$ NNP$^-$ NNS$^+$ PRP$^-$ RB$^+$ TO$^-$ VB$^-$ VBD$^-$ VBG$^+$ VBP$^+$ VBZ$^+$ WDT$^-$
s_2 vs $\neg$Inst.	CD$^+$ DT$^+$ MD$^-$ NNP$^+$ NNS$^+$ PRP$^+$ RB$^-$ VB$^-$ VBN$^-$

Table 4: POS tags significantly different in percentage compared to non-instantiation. [$\dagger$]: significance in non-instantiation pairs in the other direction. [+/−]: used more/less often than non-instantiation.

Relation (pos)	Inst.	$\neg$ Inst.
hypernym (n)	18.01*	21.63
meronym (n)	18.66*	15.48
holonym (n)	17.14	15.07
indirect hypernym (n)	19.17	21.03
hyponym (n)	20.33	21.75
group (v)	72.5*	68.7
indirect hypernym (v)	38.5*	41.7
hypernym (v)	76.25	74.79
hyponym (v)	80.76	78.44
entailment (v)	4.94	4.18
cause (v)	17.65	17.00
similar to (adj)	3.78	2.77
also see (adj)	6.25	5.78

Table 5: Percentage of sentence pairs with Wordnet relationships. [*]: significant ($p < 0.05$) compared to non-instantiation sentence pairs.

	s_1	s_2	Δsim
Inst.	0.282*	0.275*	0.007
$\neg$ Inst.	0.390	0.358	0.042*

Table 6: Average Jaccard similarity of an adjacent sentence pair s_1, s_2 with immediate context. [*]: significant ($p < 0.05$) compared to non-instantiation sentence pairs.

Parts of speech. We study word categories that are heavily or rarely used with INSTANTIATION by inspecting the percentage of part-of-speech tags found in each sentence. In Table 4, we show POS tags whose presence is significantly different across arguments in INSTANTIATION but not so across non-INSTANTIATION, with significance in non-INSTANTIATION in the reverse direction denoted in †. Four cases of POS occurrences are inspected:

- more often in s_1 compared to s_2,
- more often in s_2 compared to s_1,
- more (+) or less (-) in s_1 compared to non-INSTANTIATION,
- more (+) or less (-) in s_2 compared to non-INSTANTIATION.

We see that s_1 of INSTANTIATION contains more characteristic POS usage than s_2. There are more comparative adjectives and adverbs as well as fewer nouns in s_1 compared to s_2 in INSTANTIATION pairs. The usage of verbs is also different between two arguments and s_1 contains more conjunctions and existential there. On the other hand, s_2 contains more nouns, numbers, determiners, personal pronouns and proper nouns, intuitively associated with the presence of detailed information.

Wordnet relations. Here we consider word-level relationships across arguments using Wordnet (Fellbaum, 1998). For each noun, verb, adjective and adverb content word pairs across arguments, we calculate the percentage of sentences with each type of Wordnet relation. Shown in Table 5, among INSTANTIATION sentence pairs there are significantly more noun-noun pairs with hypernym or meronym relationships and verbs with indirect hypernym relationship. We also observe significantly more semantically similar verbs (*group (v)*).

Lexical similarity. Finally, we inspect the similarity between sentences in each pair as well as between each sentence in a pair and their immediate prior context; specifically:

- Between s_1 and s_2;
- Between s_1 and C and between s_2 and C, where C denotes up to two sentences immediately before s_1.

We compute the Jaccard similarity between sentences using their nouns, verbs, adjectives and adverbs. INSTANTIATION arguments are significantly less similar than other adjacent sentence pairs (0.335 vs. 0.505), indicating higher difference in content.

System	P	R	F	BA
Inst. specific	0.3072	0.6986	**0.4268**	**0.7862**
Vote (L&N)	0.3052	0.6438	0.4141	0.7632
L&N	0.3028	0.4521	0.3626	0.6843
B&M	0.2542	0.2055	0.2273	0.5786
Lin et al.	0.5500	0.1507	0.2366	0.5704
Brown-concat	0.1333	0.3836	0.1979	0.5919

Table 7: Precision, recall, F-measure and balanced accuracy of identifying INSTANTIATION.

Shown in Table 6, both arguments of INSTANTIATION are less similar to the immediate context. While other sentence pairs follow the pattern that s_2 is much less similar to s_1's immediate context, this phenomenon is not significant for INSTANTIATION.

4 Experiments

In this section, we demonstrate the benefit of exploiting INSTANTIATION characteristics in the identification of the relation.

Settings. Following prior work that identifies the more detailed (second-level) relations in the PDTB (Biran and McKeown, 2015; Lin et al., 2014), we use sections 2-21 as training, section 23 as testing. The rest of the corpus is used for development. The task is to predict if an implicit INSTANTIATION relation holds between pairs of adjacent sentences in the same paragraph. Sentence pairs with INSTANTIATION relation constitute the positive class; all other non-explicit relations[3] constitute the negative class. We use Logistic Regression with class weights inversely proportional to the size of each class.

Features. The factors discussed in § 3 are adopted as the *only* features in the classifier. We use the average values of s_1 and s_2 and their difference for: the number of words, difference in number of words compared to the sentence before s_1, the percentage of OOVs, gradable adjectives, POS tags and Jaccard similarity to immediate context. We use the minimum, maximum and average differences in word-pair unigram log probability, and average Jaccard similarity across sentence pairs. For Wordnet relations, we use binary features indicating the presence of a relation.

Results. To compare with our INSTANTIATION-specific classifier (*Inst. specific*), we show results from two state-of-the-art PDTB discourse parsers that identify second-level relations: Biran and McKeown (2015) (*B&M*) and Lin et al. (2014). We also compare the results with the classifier from our prior work (Li and Nenkova, 2014b) (*L&N*). In that work we introduce syntactic production-stick features, which minimize the occurrence of zero values in instance representation. Furthermore, we re-implemented Brown-cluster features (concatenation of clusters in each sentence) that have been shown to perform well in identifying INSTANTIATION's parent class EXPANSION (Braud and Denis, 2015).[4]

Table 7 shows the precision, recall, F-measure and balanced accuracy (average of the accuracies for the positive and negative class respectively) for each system. We show balanced accuracy rather than overall accuracy due to the highly skewed class distribution. For *Inst. specific*, we use a threshold of 0.65 for positive labels[5]. We also use it along with L&N for a *soft voting* classifier where the label is assigned to the class with larger weighted posterior probability sum from each classifier[6]. Both classifiers achieved at least 5% improvement of F-measure and 8%-10% improvement of balanced accuracy compared to other systems. These improvements mostly come from a dramatic improvement in recall. The improvement achieved by the voting classifier also indicate that *Inst. specific* provide complementary signals to syntactic production rules. Note that compared to Lin et al., *Inst. specific* behaves very differently in precision and recall, indicating potential for further system combination.

Finally, we analyze the confusion matrix induced by false positives and false negatives across Lin et al., B&M, *Inst. specific* and soft vote[7]. In Table 8, we list relations contributing at least 10% to false positives for at least one system. Remarkably, INSTANTIATION is consistently confused with

---

[3]including AltLex, EntRel and NoRel

[4]The dimension of clusters are tuned on the development set. As in prior work, we use clusters in Turian et al. (2010).

[5]Tuned on development set.

[6]The weights are: 0.9 for L&N and 1.0 for *Inst. specific*, tuned on development set. We also tried voting with Brown-concat but it did not outperform combining with L&N.

[7]For other systems, we did not perform full implicit discourse parsing.

Relation	Lin et al.	B&M	Inst.	Vote
Restatement	33.3	34.1	28.7	30.8
Cause	22.2	25.0	33.9	33.6
Contrast	22.2	6.8	9.6	10.3
Conjunction	11.1	4.5	6.1	2.8
EntRel	11.1	18.2	17.4	19.6

Table 8: Relations involved in false positives, $\geq 10\%$ for least one system.

a constant set of relations: RESTATEMENT, CAUSE and EntRel. Different from other systems, the *Inst. specific* classifier demonstrates more confusion towards CAUSE than RESTATEMENT. On the false negative side, all 62 mistakes are not annotated (i.e., NoRel/EntRel) in Lin et al. For the 58 false negatives in B&M, we observe above 10%: NoRel/EntRel (56.9%), CAUSE (19.0%), RESTATEMENT (13.8%), consistent with relations relations involved in false positives.

5 Conclusion

We have characterized the implicit INSTANTIATION relation by studying significant factors that discriminate individual arguments and the sentence pairs connected by the relation. We show distinctive patterns in sentence length, word usage, semantic relationships between words as well as cross-argument and contextual similarity associated with INSTANTIATION. Using these factors as features we demonstrate significant improvement on the detection of implicit INSTANTIATION relation.

References

Or Biran and Kathleen McKeown. 2013. Aggregated word pair features for implicit discourse relation disambiguation. In *Proceedings of the 51st Annual Meeting of the Association for Computational Linguistics: Short Papers*, pages 69–73.

Or Biran and Kathleen McKeown. 2015. PDTB discourse parsing as a tagging task: The two taggers approach. In *Proceedings of the 16th Annual Meeting of the Special Interest Group on Discourse and Dialogue*, pages 96–104.

Chloé Braud and Pascal Denis. 2015. Comparing word representations for implicit discourse relation classification. In *Proceedings of the 2015 Conference on Empirical Methods in Natural Language Processing*, pages 2201–2211.

Marie-Catherine de Marneffe, Christopher D. Manning, and Christopher Potts. 2010. "Was it good? It was provocative." Learning the meaning of scalar adjectives. In *Proceedings of the 48th Annual Meeting of the Association for Computational Linguistics*, pages 167–176.

Christiane Fellbaum. 1998. *WordNet*. Wiley Online Library.

Lyn Frazier, Charles Clifton Jr., and Britta Stolterfoht. 2008. Scale structure: Processing minimum standard and maximum standard scalar adjectives. *Cognition*, 106(1):299 – 324.

Barbara J. Grosz, Scott Weinstein, and Aravind K. Joshi. 1995. Centering: A framework for modeling the local coherence of discourse. *Computational Linguistics*, 21(2).

Vasileios Hatzivassiloglou and Janyce M. Wiebe. 2000. Effects of adjective orientation and gradability on sentence subjectivity. In *Proceedings of the 18th Conference on Computational Linguistics - Volume 1*, pages 299–305.

Yangfeng Ji and Jacob Eisenstein. 2015. One vector is not enough: Entity-augmented distributed semantics for discourse relations. *Transactions of the Association for Computational Linguistics*, 3:329–344.

Andrew Kehler. 2004. Discourse coherence. *The handbook of pragmatics*, pages 241–265.

Junyi Jessy Li and Ani Nenkova. 2014a. Addressing class imbalance for improved recognition of implicit discourse relations. In *Proceedings of the 15th Annual Meeting of the Special Interest Group on Discourse and Dialogue*, pages 142–150.

Junyi Jessy Li and Ani Nenkova. 2014b. Reducing sparsity improves the recognition of implicit discourse relations. In *Proceedings of the 15th Annual Meeting of the Special Interest Group on Discourse and Dialogue*, pages 199–207.

Ziheng Lin, Min-Yen Kan, and Hwee Tou Ng. 2009. Recognizing implicit discourse relations in the Penn Discourse Treebank. In *Proceedings of the 2009 Conference on Empirical Methods in Natural Language Processing*, pages 343–351.

Ziheng Lin, Hwee Tou Ng, and Min-Yen Kan. 2014. A PDTB-styled end-to-end discourse parser. *Natural Language Engineering*, 20:151–184.

Annie Louis and Ani Nenkova. 2010. Creating local coherence: An empirical assessment. In *Human Language Technologies: The 2010 Annual Conference of the North American Chapter of the Association for Computational Linguistics*, pages 313–316.

Annie Louis, Aravind Joshi, and Ani Nenkova. 2010. Discourse indicators for content selection in summarization. In *Proceedings of the SIGDIAL 2010 Conference*, pages 147–156.

Andrew McKinlay and Katja Markert. 2011. Modelling entity instantiations. In *Proceedings of the International Conference Recent Advances in Natural Language Processing 2011*, pages 268–274.

Eleni Miltsakaki, Livio Robaldo, Alan Lee, and Aravind Joshi. 2008. Sense annotation in the Penn Discourse Treebank. In *Computational Linguistics and Intelligent Text Processing*, volume 4919 of *Lecture Notes in Computer Science*, pages 275–286. Springer Berlin Heidelberg.

Joonsuk Park and Claire Cardie. 2012. Improving implicit discourse relation recognition through feature set optimization. In *Proceedings of the 13th Annual Meeting of the Special Interest Group on Discourse and Dialogue*, pages 108–112.

Jeffrey Pennington, Richard Socher, and Christopher D Manning. 2014. Glove: Global vectors for word representation. *Proceedings of the Empirical Methods in Natural Language Processing*, 12:1532–1543.

Emily Pitler and Ani Nenkova. 2008. Revisiting readability: A unified framework for predicting text quality. In *Proceedings of the Conference on Empirical Methods in Natural Language Processing*, pages 186–195.

Emily Pitler, Annie Louis, and Ani Nenkova. 2009. Automatic sense prediction for implicit discourse relations in text. In *Proceedings of the Joint Conference of the 47th Annual Meeting of the ACL and the 4th International Joint Conference on Natural Language Processing of the AFNLP*, pages 683–691.

Rashmi Prasad, Nikhil Dinesh, Alan Lee, Eleni Miltsakaki, Livio Robaldo, Aravind Joshi, and Bonnie Webber. 2008. The Penn Discourse TreeBank 2.0. In *Proceedings of the International Conference on Language Resources and Evaluation*.

Attapol Rutherford and Nianwen Xue. 2014. Discovering implicit discourse relations through brown cluster pair representation and coreference patterns. In *Proceedings of the 14th Conference of the European Chapter of the Association for Computational Linguistics*, pages 645–654.

Attapol Rutherford and Nianwen Xue. 2015. Improving the inference of implicit discourse relations via classifying explicit discourse connectives. In *Proceedings of the 2015 Conference of the North American Chapter of the Association for Computational Linguistics: Human Language Technologies*, pages 799–808.

Evan Sandhaus. 2008. The New York Times Annotated Corpus LDC2008T19. *Linguistic Data Consortium, Philadelphia*.

Radoslava Trnavac and Maite Taboada. 2013. Discourse relations and affective content in the expression of sentiment in texts. In *11th ICGL Conference–Workshop on The semantic field of emotions: Interdisci*.

Joseph Turian, Lev-Arie Ratinov, and Yoshua Bengio. 2010. Word representations: A simple and general method for semi-supervised learning. In *Proceedings of the 48th Annual Meeting of the Association for Computational Linguistics*, pages 384–394.

Sparse Bilingual Word Representations for Cross-lingual Lexical Entailment

Yogarshi Vyas and **Marine Carpuat**
Department of Computer Science
University of Maryland
College Park, MD 20742, USA
yogarshi@cs.umd.edu, marine@cs.umd.edu

Abstract

We introduce the task of *cross-lingual lexical entailment*, which aims to detect whether the meaning of a word in one language can be inferred from the meaning of a word in another language. We construct a gold standard for this task, and propose an unsupervised solution based on distributional word representations. As commonly done in the monolingual setting, we assume a word e entails a word f if the prominent context features of e are a subset of those of f. To address the challenge of comparing contexts across languages, we propose a novel method for inducing sparse bilingual word representations from monolingual and parallel texts. Our approach yields an F-score of 70%, and significantly outperforms strong baselines based on translation and on existing word representations.

1 Introduction

Multilingual Natural Language Processing lacks techniques to automatically compare and contrast the meaning of words across languages. Machine translation (Koehn, 2010) lets us discover translation correspondences in bilingual texts, but a word and its translation often do not cover the exact same semantic space: distinct word senses might translate differently (Gale et al., 1992; Diab and Resnik, 2002, among others); semantic relations and associations do not always translate, an important issue when constructing multilingual ontologies (Fellbaum and Vossen, 2012); and words in parallel text might be translated non-literally due to lexical gaps

(Santos, 1990; Bentivogli and Pianta, 2000) or decisions of the translator, as becomes clear when comparing multiple translations of the same source text (Bhagat and Hovy, 2013).

As a result, correct word translations found in parallel corpora exhibit a variety of relations including equivalence, hypernymy, and meronymy. For instance, even after removing noisy examples (Johnson et al., 2007) from a Machine Translation bilexicon induced from parallel corpora (Koehn et al., 2007), we find that the French word "appartement" (apartment) is linked to related but not strictly equivalent English words, such as "home" or "condo".

house	|||	*foyer* (foyer)
house	|||	*maison* (house)
house	|||	*chambre* (chamber)
home	|||	*appartement*
condo	|||	*appartement*
apartment	|||	*appartement*

Table 1: Examples of translations drawn from an English-French bilexicon automatically learned on parallel text.

We aim to design models that capture these differences and similarities in word meaning across languages, beyond translation correspondences. As a first step, we introduce *cross-lingual lexical entailment*, the task of detecting whether the meaning of a word in one language can be inferred from the meaning of a word in another language. In monolingual settings, lexical entailment has received significant attention as a representation-agnostic way of modeling lexical semantics, and as a step toward textual inference (Zhitomirsky-Geffet and Dagan, 2009; Turney and Mohammad, 2015; Levy et

Proceedings of NAACL-HLT 2016, pages 1187–1197,
San Diego, California, June 12-17, 2016. ©2016 Association for Computational Linguistics

al., 2015; Pavlick et al., 2015). We hypothesize that the cross-lingual task can help do the same with multilingual texts.

Building on prior work on the monolingual task, we take an unsupervised approach, and use a directional semantic similarity metric motivated by the distributional inclusion hypothesis (Geffet and Dagan, 2005a; Kotlerman et al., 2010): we assume a word e entails a word f if the prominent context features of e are a subset of those of f. However, we face a new challenge in the cross-lingual case: how can we represent and compare word contexts across languages? Our solution leverages recent work on sparse representations for natural language processing. We develop sparse bilingual word representations that represent contexts based on interpretable dimensions that are aligned across languages.

As we will see, this approach successfully detects cross-lingual lexical entailment (with an F-score of 70%), and significantly outperforms strong baselines based (1) on machine translation, and (2) on existing dense bilingual word representations. Along the way, we construct a new dataset to evaluate cross-lingual lexical entailment, and also show the benefits of our approach in the monolingual setting.

2 A Cross-Lingual View of Lexical Entailment

Zhitomirsky-Geffet and Dagan (2009) formalize lexical entailment as a substitutional relationship. Under their definition, given a word pair (w, v), w entails v if the following two conditions are fulfilled

1. The meaning of a possible sense of w implies a possible sense of v, and

2. w can substitute for v in a sentence, such that the meaning of the modified sentence entails the meaning of the original sentence.

As a result, monolingual lexical entailment includes various semantic relations, such as synonymy, hypernymy, some meronymy relations, but also cause-effect relations (*murder* entails *death*), and other associations (*ocean* entails *water*) (Kotlerman et al., 2010).

We extend this definition to the cross-lingual case by modifying the second condition. Given a word

pair (w', v'), where w' is a word in language e and v' is a word in language f, w' entails v' if

1. The meaning of a possible sense of w' implies a possible sense of v', and

2. Given a sentence T in f containing v', w' can substitute for v' in the translation of T in e, such that the meaning of the modified sentence entails the meaning of the original sentence.

Cross-lingual lexical entailment helps us refine our understanding of semantic mappings across languages: while the French word *ouvrier* can be translated as *worker* in English, knowing that *worker* does not entail *ouvrier* could be useful in many multilingual applications, including machine translation and its evaluation, question answering or entity linking in multilingual texts.

As can be seen in Table 2, lexical entailment is not always preserved by translation: while *aspirin* entails the English word *drug*, it does not entail the French *drogue*, which only refers to the narcotic sense of *drug* and not to its medicinal sense.

English-English	English-French
affection → feeling	affection → sentiment
aspirin → drug	aspirin ↛ drogue
water → wet	water → humide
feeling ↛ nostalgia	feeling ↛ nostalgie

Table 2: Examples of monolingual and cross-lingual lexical entailment: → can be read as "entails", ↛ as "does not entail".

When evaluating lexical entailment, we use the same approach as in monolingual tasks (Baroni et al., 2012; Baroni and Lenci, 2011; Kotlerman et al., 2010; Turney and Mohammad, 2015): given a bilingual word pair, systems are asked to make a binary true/false decision on whether the first word entails the second. We describe the collection of gold standard annotations in Section 5.2.

3 Unsupervised Detection of Lexical Entailment

We choose to detect lexical entailment without supervision. As in the monolingual case, detection can be done using a scoring function which quantifies the *directional* semantic similarity of an input word pair. On monolingual tasks, despite reaching better performance, supervised systems do not really learn entailment relations for word pairs, but instead learn when a particular word in the pair is a "prototypical hypernym" (Levy et al., 2015). [1] Thus, we limit our investigation to unsupervised models. As a result, our approach only requires a small number of annotated examples to tune the scoring threshold.

We use the *balAPinc* score (Kotlerman et al., 2009), which is based on the distributional inclusion hypothesis (Geffet and Dagan, 2005b): given feature representations of the contexts of two words u and v, u is assumed to entail v if all features of u tend to appear within the features of v.

Formally, *balAPinc* is the geometric mean of a symmetric similarity score, *LIN* (Lin, 1998), and an asymmetric score, *APinc*. Given a directional entailment pair $(u \to v)$,

$$balAPinc(u \to v) = \sqrt{LIN(u,v) \cdot APinc(u \to v)}$$

Assume we are given ranked feature lists FV_u and FV_v for words u and v respectively. Let $w_u(f)$ denote the weight of a particular feature f in FV_u. *LIN* is defined by

$$LIN(u,v) = \frac{\sum\limits_{f \in FV_u \cap FV_v} [w_u(f) + w_v(f)]}{\sum\limits_{f \in FV_u} w_u(f) + \sum\limits_{f \in FV_v} w_v(f)} \quad (1)$$

APinc is a modified asymmetric version of the Average Precision metric used in Information Retrieval:

$$APinc(u \to v) = \frac{\sum\limits_{r=1}^{|FV_u|} [P(r, FV_u, FV_v) \cdot rel'(f_r)]}{|FV_u|} \quad (2)$$

where,

$$P(r, FV_u, FV_v)$$
$$= \frac{|\text{\# features of } v \text{ in top } r \text{ features of } u|}{r}$$
$$rel'(f) = \begin{cases} 1 & \text{if} f \in FV_u \\ 0 & \text{otherwise} \end{cases}$$

<hr>

[1] Given a word pair such as (dog,animal), supervised methods tend to learn that animal is very likely to be a category word i.e. one that is likely to be a hypernym, and do not take into account the relationship of animal with dog.

Thus, to use *balAPinc* for cross-lingual lexical entailment, we need a ranked list of features that capture information about the context of words in two languages. In the monolingual case, features are dimensions in a distributional semantic space. For the cross-lingual task, we need to represent words in two languages in the same space, or in spaces where a one-to-one mapping between dimensions exists.

4 Learning Sparse Bilingual Word Representations

As we will see in Section 9, there is a wealth of existing methods for learning representations that capture context of words in two different languages in the literature. However, they have been evaluated on tasks that do not require much semantic analysis, such as translation lexicon induction or document categorization. In contrast, detecting lexical entailment requires the ability to capture more subtle semantic distinctions. This requires bilingual representations to capture both the full range of word contexts observed in original language texts, as well as cross-lingual correspondences from translated texts.

We propose a new model that uses *sparse nonnegative embeddings* to represent word contexts as interpretable dimensions, and facilitate context comparisons across languages. This is an instance of sparse coding, which consists of modeling data vectors as sparse linear combinations of basis elements. In contrast with dimensionality reduction techniques such as PCA, the learned basis vectors need not be orthogonal, which gives more flexibility to represent the data (Mairal et al., 2009). These models have been introduced as word representations in monolingual settings (Murphy et al., 2012) with the goal of obtaining interpretable, cognitively-plausible representations. We review the monolingual models, before introducing our novel bilingual formulation.

4.1 Review: Learning Monolingual Sparse Representations

Previous work (Murphy et al., 2012; Faruqui et al., 2015) on obtaining sparse monolingual representations is based on a variant of the Nonnegative Matrix Factorization problem. Given a matrix $\mathbf{X}$ containing v dense word representations arranged row-wise, sparse representations for the v words can be obtained by solving the following optimization problem

$$\underset{\mathbf{A},\mathbf{D}}{\operatorname{argmin}} \ \sum_{i=1}^{v} ||\mathbf{A}_i\mathbf{D}^T - \mathbf{X}_i||_2^2 + \lambda||\mathbf{A}_i||_1$$

$$\text{subject to } \mathbf{A}_{ij} >= 0, \forall i, j \qquad (3)$$
$$\mathbf{D}_i^T\mathbf{D}_i <= 1, \forall i$$

The first term in the objective 3 aims to factorize the dense representation matrix $\mathbf{X}$ into two matrices, $\mathbf{A}$ and $\mathbf{D}$ such that the l_2 reconstruction error is minimized. The second term is an l_1 regularizer on $\mathbf{A}$ which encourages sparsity, where the level of sparsity is controlled by the λ hyperparameter. This, together with the non-negativity constraint, helps in obtaining sparsified and interpretable representations in $\mathbf{A}$ since non-negativity has been shown to correlate with interpretability. Note that the objective function on its own is degenerate since it can be trivially optimized by making the entries of $\mathbf{D}$ arbitrarily large and choosing corresponding small values as entries of $\mathbf{A}$. To avoid this, an additional constraint is imposed on $\mathbf{D}$.

4.2 Proposed Bilingual Model

Learning bilingual word representations for entailment requires two sources of information:

- Monolingual distributional representations independently learned from large amounts of text in each language. We denote them as two input matrices, $\mathbf{X_e}$ and $\mathbf{X_f}$, of respective sizes $v_e \times n_e$ and $v_f \times n_f$. Each row in $\mathbf{X_e}$ represents the representation of a particular word in the first language, e, while $\mathbf{X_f}$ represents word representations for the other language f.

- Cross-lingual correspondences that enable comparison across languages. We define a "score" matrix $\mathbf{S}$ of size $v_e \times v_f$, which captures high-confidence correspondences between the vocabularies of the two languages. There are many ways of defining $\mathbf{S}$. As a starting point, we define each row of $\mathbf{S}$ as a one-hot vector that identifies the word in f that is most frequently aligned with the e word for that row in a large parallel corpus. This reduction leads to a many-to-one mapping from e to f, which captures translation ambiguity by allowing multiple words in e to be aligned to the same word in f.

We formulate the following optimization problem to obtain sparse bilingual representations:

$$\underset{\mathbf{A_e},\mathbf{D_e},\mathbf{A_f},\mathbf{D_f}}{\operatorname{argmin}} \ \sum_{i=i}^{v_e} \frac{1}{2}||\mathbf{A}_{\mathbf{e}i}\mathbf{D_e}^{\mathrm{T}} - \mathbf{X}_{\mathbf{e}i}||_2^2 + \lambda_e||\mathbf{A}_{\mathbf{e}i}||_1$$

$$+ \sum_{j=i}^{v_f} \frac{1}{2}||\mathbf{A}_{\mathbf{f}j}\mathbf{D_f}^{\mathrm{T}} - \mathbf{X}_{\mathbf{f}j}||_2^2 + \lambda_f||\mathbf{A}_{\mathbf{f}j}||_1$$

$$+ \sum_{i=1}^{v_e}\sum_{j=1}^{v_f} \frac{1}{2}\lambda_x\mathbf{S}_{ij}||\mathbf{A}_{\mathbf{e}i} - \mathbf{A}_{\mathbf{f}j}||_2^2 \qquad (4)$$

$$\text{subject to } \mathbf{A_e} > 0 \,; \mathbf{D}_{\mathbf{e}i}^{\mathrm{T}}.\mathbf{D}_{\mathbf{e}i} \leq 1, 1 \leq i \leq v_e;$$
$$\mathbf{A_f} > 0 \,; \mathbf{D}_{\mathbf{f}j}^{\mathrm{T}}.\mathbf{D}_{\mathbf{f}j} \leq 1, 1 \leq j \leq v_f;$$

The first two rows and the constraints in Equation 4 can be understood as in Equation 3 - they encourage sparsity in word representations for each language. The third row imposes bilingual correspondence constraints, weighted by the regularizer λ_x: it encourages words in e and f that are strongly aligned according to $\mathbf{S}$ to have similar representations.

4.3 Optimization

Equations 3 and 4 define non-differentiable, non-convex optimization problems and finding the globally optimally solution is not feasible. However, various methods used to solve convex problems work well in practice. We use *Forward Backward Splitting*, a proximal gradient method for which an efficient generic solver, FASTA, is available (Goldstein et al., 2015; Goldstein et al., 2014). FASTA (Fast Adaptive Shrinkage / Thresholding Algorithm) is designed to minimize functions of the form $f(Ax) + g(x)$, where f is a differentiable function, g is a function (possibly non-differentiable) for which we can calculate the proximal operator, and A is a linear operator. For the objective function in our model, the l_1 terms form g and the l_2 terms form f.

We have now described all components of the model required to detect bilingual lexical entailment: solving objective 4 as described yields sparse representations for words in the two languages that can be compared directly using the *balAPinc* metric.

5 Constructing a Gold Standard

5.1 Existing Monolingual Test Suites

A comprehensive suite of lexical entailment test beds is available for English (Levy et al., 2015). They were constructed either by asking humans to annotate entailment relations directly (Kotlerman et al., 2010), or by deriving entailment labels from semantic relation annotations (Baroni et al., 2012; Baroni and Lenci, 2011; Turney and Mohammad, 2015). Each test set has 900 to 1300 positive examples of lexical entailment - word pairs (w, v) such that $w \rightarrow v$. All but one are balanced.

5.2 Creating a Cross-Lingual Test Set

We select French as the second language: it is a good starting point for studying cross-lingual entailment, as it is a resource-rich language with many available bilingual annotators. We will construct data sets for more distant language pairs in future work.

We aim to construct a balanced test set of positive and negative bilingual entailment examples in the spirit of the existing English test beds. While it is attractive to leverage existing English examples, we cannot translate them directly as entailment relations might be affected by translation ambiguity (as illustrated in Table 2).

We therefore obtain annotated bilingual examples using a two step process: (1) automatic translation of monolingual examples, and (2) manual annotation through crowdsourcing. For a sample of positive examples of entailment $w_e \rightarrow v_e$ in the monolingual datasets, we generate up to two French translations for v_e, v_{f1} and v_{f2}, using the top translations from BabelNet (Navigli and Ponzetto, 2012) and Google Translate. v_{f1} and v_{f2} are then paired back with w_e, thus generating two unannotated crosslingual examples. Annotation is crowdsourced on Crowdflower [2]: for each example pair (w_e, v_f), workers are asked to label it as true ($w_e \rightarrow v_f$) or false ($w_e \not\rightarrow v_f$). We select the positive examples annotated with high-agreement, and obtain the same number of negative examples by applying the same translation process to negative examples [3].

[3] Manual annotation is unnecessary for negative examples: it is unlikely that a negative example $w \not\rightarrow v$ will become positive by translating v automatically. We verified this by asking

5.3 Crowdsourcing Cross-lingual Entailment Judgments

Detecting lexical entailment for bilingual word pairs is a non-trivial annotation task, and requires a good command of both French and English. For quality control, we first ask a bilingual speaker in our group to conduct a pilot annotation task, which we use to evaluate workers' ability to perform the task. In addition, Crowdflower allows us to present this task to only workers who have a proven knowledge of French, and to georestrict the task to countries most likely to have French-English bilinguals.

N	Examples
0	(*animal,couleur*), (*animal,reptile*), (*art, serpent*)
1	(*asp, vertébré*), (*chancellor, guide*), (*psychotherapy,capacité*)
2	(*bookmark, marque*), (*postman, ouvrier*), (*endurance, force*)
3	(*cricket,insecte*), (*muse,divinité*), (*parapet, paroi*)
4	(*ape, animal*), (*reimbursement,paiement*), (*lady,adulte*)
5	(*epistle,lettre*), (*gin,boisson*), (*potato,nourriture*)

Table 3: Randomly selected examples for each level of annotator agreement: N is the number of annotators who labeled pair as true (out of five)

This approach yielded a large number of high-quality annotations quickly. 1680 cross-lingual pairs were presented to five annotators each. 24 pairs did not receive enough judgments. For the remaining 1656 pairs, four or more annotators agreed for 75% of examples (Figure 1).

This result first shows that we can indeed generate a gold standard for the challenging task of cross-lingual lexical entailment using such crowdsourcing techniques. We ensure high-quality annotations by selecting all 945 (w, v) where four or more annotators agree that $w \rightarrow v$.

In addition, the degree of agreement sheds light on how the notion of lexical entailment is interpreted by non-expert annotators. In Table 3, we present randomly selected examples for each agree-

a bilingual speaker to manually check a random sample of 100 such translated pairs, which were all found to remain negative.

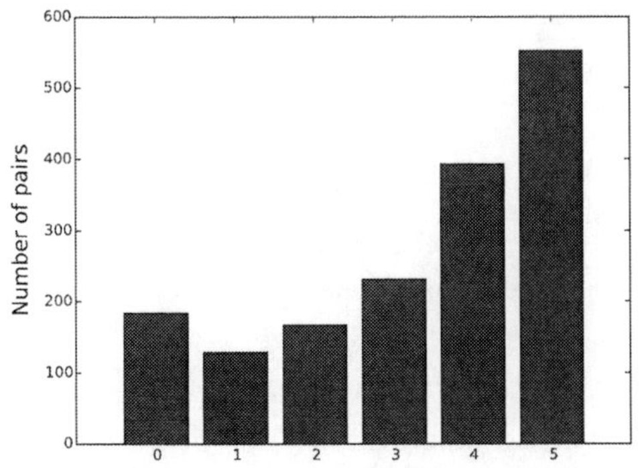

Figure 1: Agreement statistics for dataset creation. X-axis indicates number of annotators who labeled pair as true (out of five)

ment level. The bottom two rows represent clear positive examples, that are cross-lingual equivalents of hypernymy or synonymy relations: e.g., *gin* is a kind of drink (*boisson* in French). The top row represent clear negative examples, where the two words are unrelated (e.g., *art* and *serpent*, which means *snake* in English) or the directionality is wrong (e.g., *animal ← reptile*). The middle rows where one to three annotators chose to annotate the word pair as negative contain less clear-cut cases, including association relations (e.g., *endurance → force*), and examples where entailment judgments requires taking into account more subtle word sense or translation distinctions (e.g., *bookmark* can be translated as *marque* for a positive example, but the most frequent sense of *marque* translates into English as *brand*, for which the entailment relation does not hold.)

6 Experimental Conditions

We estimate the following models for evaluation on the test sets described in the previous section.

6.1 Sparse Bilingual Model

Estimating sparse, bilingual representations as described in Section 4.2 first requires learning dense monolingual representations in two languages (X_e and X_f). We can in principle use any type of dense representations. We choose to train GloVe (Pennington et al., 2014) vectors on a corpus comprised of Gigaword and Wikipedia to learn dense representations of 2000 dimensions for English and French. English vectors are trained on a corpus of 4.9B words, while

French vectors are trained on 1.2B words.

Second, we construct **S** by word-aligning large amounts of parallel corpora using a fast implementation of IBM model 2 (Dyer et al., 2013). We combine Europarl (Koehn, 2005), News Commentary [4], and Wikipedia [5] to create a large parallel corpus of 72M English tokens and 78M French tokens. All corpora are tokenized and lowercased.

We learn 100-dimensional sparse representations with hyperparameters $\lambda_e = \lambda_f = 0.5, \lambda_x = 10$.

6.2 Contrastive Models

We also learn two other sets of 100-dimensional word representations, as a basis for comparison.

First, we learn sparse monolingual English word representations, which will be used in monolingual lexical entailment experiments (Section 7.1). These are trained using the non-negative sparse method described in Section 4.1, on the same 4.9B word English corpus that was used for learning bilingual representations.

Second, we learn dense bilingual word representations using BiCVM (Hermann and Blunsom, 2014), to use as a baseline for our cross-lingual lexical entailment experiments (Section 7.2). BiCVM uses sentence aligned parallel corpora to learn representations for words in two languages, with the objective that when these representations are composed into representations for parallel sentences, the Euclidean distance between the parallel sentences should be minimized. We learn English-French vectors on the parallel corpora described in Section 6.1.

7 Results

7.1 Monolingual Tasks

We first evaluate the monolingual version of our sparse model on English test sets. While our focus is on the cross-lingual setting, the monolingual evaluation lets us compare a version of our newly proposed approach with existing lexical entailment results (Levy et al., 2015), obtained using dense word representations compared with cosine similarity. This is not a controlled comparison, as training conditions are not comparable. Nevertheless it

---

[4]http://www.statmt.org/wmt15/training-parallel-nc-v10.tgz
[5]https://sites.google.com/site/iwsltevaluation2015/data-provided

English Dataset	Levy et al.	Sparse+cosine	Sparse+*balAPinc*
Baroni et al. (2012)	.788	.745	.744
Baroni and Lenci (2011)	.197	.552	.546
Kotlerman et al. (2010)	.461	.620	.618
Turney and Mohammad (2015)	.642	.576	.587

Table 4: Evaluating sparse representations on monolingual lexical entailment (F-score): we compare previously published unsupervised results (Levy et al.) to our sparse word representations. While this is not a controlled comparison, we can see that our word representations yield roughly comparable performance to prior work.

is reassuring to see that sparse word representations are roughly on par with previously published results. This suggests that they indeed provide good features for discovering entailment relations, using both cosine and *balAPinc* as metrics[6].

Results (Table 4) show that sparse representations lead to performance comparable to previous approaches, thus providing a strong motivation for using the same for the crosslingual task.

7.2 Cross-lingual Task

Word Representations	Cosine	*balAPinc*
bilingual + dense	.528	.548
monolingual + sparse	.663	.675
bilingual + sparse	**.687**	**.703**

Table 5: F-Score on Cross-lingual Lexical Entailment Task. All results are obtained by 10-fold cross-validation. Using *balAPinc* with features from the sparse bilingual representations outperforms all other approaches.

We evaluate our proposed approach on the new English-French lexical entailment test set. We evaluate the impact of choosing a sparse representation by comparing our approach to the dense bilingual word representations obtained with the BiCVM model (Section 6.2). We also evaluate the usefulness of bilingual vs. monolingual word representations: given a bilingual example (w_e, v_f), we translate v_f into English using Google Translate, and then detect lexical entailment using English sparse representations for the English pair (w_e, v_e) as described in Section 6.2.

Results are summarized in Table 5. First, we observe that *balAPinc* outperforms cosine for all word representations, confirming that the directional metric is better suited to discovering lexical entailment. Second, all sparse models significantly outperform the model based on dense representation, which suggests that sparsity helps discover useful context features. Finally, our proposed approach (*balAPinc* with features from sparse bilingual representations) yields the best result overall, perofrming better than the second best model (cosine with features from sparse bilingual representations) by approximately 1.6 points. This difference is highly statistically significant (at $p < 0.01$) according to the McNemar's Test (Dietterich, 1998). Our model also outperforms translation followed by monolingual entailment, confirming the need for models that directly compare the meaning of words across languages, instead of using translation as a proxy.

8 Discussion

8.1 Examining bilingual dimensions learned

One motivation for using sparse representations is that they yield interpretable dimensions: one can summarize a dimension using the top scoring words in its column. Interpreting five randomly selected dimensions learned in our bilingual model (Table 6) shows that we indeed learn English and French dimensions that align well, but that are not identical - reflecting the difference in contexts observed in monolingual English vs. French corpora, as needed to detect lexical entailment.

8.2 Sparse Vectors Help Capture Distributional Inclusion

One advantage of our sparse representations over dense bilingual representations is that they can better leverage an asymmetric scoring function like

---

[6]While cosine and *balAPinc* yield comparable F-scores here, *balAPinc* is still a better metric as it captures directionality. If the test sets included examples of both entailment direction for every pair, cosine would yield incorrect predictions for as many as half of the examples, since its predictions would be the same regardless of the direction.

<table>
<tr><th>French Dimensions</th><th>English Dimensions</th></tr>
<tr><td>logiciel, fichiers, web, microsoft</td><td>files, web, microsoft, www</td></tr>
<tr><td>université, collège, lycée, conseil de administration</td><td>university, college, graduate, faculty</td></tr>
<tr><td>virus informatique, virus, infection, cellules</td><td>virus, viruses, infection, cells</td></tr>
<tr><td>doigts, genoux, jambes, muscles</td><td>bruises, fingers, toes, knees</td></tr>
<tr><td>budapest, stockholm, copenhague, buenos</td><td>lahore, dhaka, harare, karachi</td></tr>
</table>

Table 6: Top scoring words in 5 randomly selected French and English dimensions learned by our bilingual model.

balAPinc . Consider the following two pairs from our dataset - *(mesothelioma,tumeur)* and *(tumor,mésothéliome)*. The former is a positive example since *mesothelioma → tumeur*, but the latter is negative (since not all tumors are mesotheliomas.)

Cosine similarity is unable to differentiate between these two cases, assigning a high score to both these pairs, causing both of them to be labeled positive. However, *balAPinc* with sparse representations teases them apart by giving a high score to the first pair and a low score to the second.

In the bilingual sparse model, *mesothelioma* and *mésothéliome* have only one non-zero entry (in the dimension corresponding to ['virus', 'viruses', 'infection', 'cells', 'cancer']) whereas *tumeur* and *tumor* have five non-zero entries in their representations. Based on the distributional inclusion hypothesis, this difference in the number of non-zero entries is a strong basis for *mesothelioma → tumor*.

8.3 Benefits of Bilingual Modeling

Examining the results of the approach based on translation followed by monolingual entailment confirms the problems raised by sense ambiguities.

Consider the English word *drug*, which can be translated into the French *drogue* when used in the narcotics sense, and *médicament* when used in the medicinal sense. Thus the pair *(antibiotic,drogue)* that is correctly labeled as negative in the crosslingual case, gets converted to *(antibiotic,drug)* by translation and is then incorrectly labeled as positive. Similarly, the pair *(coriander, herbe)*, which is positive in the crosslingual case, gets translated to *(coriander, grass)* because the French *herbe* is primarily aligned to the English *grass* (rather than *herb*). The translated pair is labeled negative.

9 Related Work

Bilingual Word Representations Much recent work targets the problem of learning low-dimensional multilingual word representations, using matrix decomposition techniques such as Principal Component Analysis and Canonical Correlation Analysis (Gaussier et al., 2004; Jagarlamudi and Daumé III, 2012; Gardner et al., 2015), Latent Dirichlet Allocation (Mimno et al., 2009; Jagarlamudi and Daumé III, 2010), and neural distributional representations (Klementiev et al., 2012; Gouws et al., 2015; Lu et al., 2015, among others). However, these models have typically been evaluated on translation induction or document categorization, which, unlike lexical entailment, focus on capturing coarse cross-lingual correspondences.

Sparse Word Representations While cooccurrence matrices and their PPMI transformed variants are early examples of sparse representations, recent work has leveraged Nonnegative Sparse Embedding (NNSE) (Murphy et al., 2012). These models have been augmented to incorporate different types of linguistically motivated constraints, such as compositionality of words into phrases (Fyshe et al., 2015), or a hierarchical regularizer that captures knowledge of word relations (Yogatama et al., 2015).

Sparse representations have also been used for monolingual lexical entailment in the Boolean Distributional Semantic Model (Kruszewski et al., 2015), which shares our hypothesis on the usefulness of sparsity in meaning representations. However, they are meant to be used in different settings: while the boolean features can interestingly capture formal semantics, they are not as useful in our unsupervised setting, since they do not provide the feature rankings required to use the *balAPinc* metric.

Cross-Lingual Semantic Analysis To the best of our knowledge, lexical entailment has not been previously addressed in a cross-lingual setting. The long tradition of lexical semantic analysis in cross-lingual settings has mostly focused on using translations to characterize word meaning (Diab and Resnik, 2002; Carpuat and Wu, 2007; Lefever and Hoste, 2010; McCarthy et al., 2013, among others). An exception is Cross-lingual *Textual* Entailment (Mehdad et al., 2010), which aims to detect whether an English hypothesis H entails a text T written in another language. We plan to use our lexical models to address this task in the future.

10   Conclusion

In this work, we introduced the task of cross-lingual lexical entailment, which aims to detect whether the meaning of a word in one language can be inferred from the meaning of a word in another language. We constructed a dataset with gold annotations through crowdsourcing, and presented a top-performing solution based on novel sparse bilingual word representations that leverages both word co-occurrence patterns in monolingual corpora and bilingual correspondences learned in parallel text[7].

A key limitation of this work is that we address lexical entailment out of context, based on word representations that collapse multiple word senses into a single vector . These could be addressed in future work by adapting existing methods for learning sense-specific representations for dense vectors (Jauhar et al., 2015; Ettinger et al., 2016; Reisinger and Mooney, 2010; Guo et al., 2014; Huang et al., 2012; Neelakantan et al., 2015) to our sparse representations, and target cross-lingual textual entailment tasks, which focus on full sentences rather than isolated words. We also plan to study lexical entailment on more languages and example types, as well as investigate the usefulness of our bilingual representations in higher level multilingual applications such as machine translation.

Acknowledgments

The authors would like to thank Tom Goldstein, Roberto Navigli and Peter Turney for their assistance with tools and datasets, Philip Resnik and the CLIP lab at the University of Maryland for stimulating discussions, and the reviewers for their insightful feedback. This work was partially funded by an Amazon Academic Research Award.

References

Marco Baroni and Alessandro Lenci. 2011. How we blessed distributional semantic evaluation. In *Proceedings of the GEMS 2011 Workshop on GEometrical Models of Natural Language Semantics*, pages 1–10. Association for Computational Linguistics.

Marco Baroni, Raffaella Bernardi, Ngoc-Quynh Do, and Chung-chieh Shan. 2012. Entailment above the word level in distributional semantics. In *EACL 2012*, pages 23–32. Association for Computational Linguistics.

Luisa Bentivogli and Emanuelle Pianta. 2000. Looking for lexical gaps. In *Proceedings of the Ninth EURALEX International Congress, EURALEX 2000: Stuttgart, Germany, August 8th-12th, 2000*, pages 663–669.

Rahul Bhagat and Eduard Hovy. 2013. What is a paraphrase? *Computational Linguistics*.

Marine Carpuat and Dekai Wu. 2007. Improving Statistical Machine Translation using Word Sense Disambiguation. In *Proceedings of the 2007 Joint Conference on Empirical Methods in Natural Language Processing and Computational Natural Language Learning (EMNLP-CoNLL 2007)*, pages 61–72, Prague, June.

Mona Diab and Philip Resnik. 2002. An Unsupervised Method for Word Sense Tagging using Parallel Text. In *Proceedings of the 40th Annual Meeting of the Association for Computational Linguistics*, pages 255–262, Philadelphia, Pennsylvania, July.

Thomas G Dietterich. 1998. Approximate statistical tests for comparing supervised classification learning algorithms. *Neural computation*, 10(7):1895–1923.

Chris Dyer, Victor Chahuneau, and Noah A Smith. 2013. A simple, fast, and effective reparameterization of ibm model 2. Association for Computational Linguistics.

Allyson Ettinger, Philip Resnik, and Marine Carpuat. 2016. Retrofitting sense-specific word vectors using parallel text. In *Proceedings of NAACL*.

Manaal Faruqui, Yulia Tsvetkov, Dani Yogatama, Chris Dyer, and Noah A. Smith. 2015. Sparse overcomplete word vector representations. In *ACL 2015*, pages 1491–1500.

Christiane Fellbaum and Piek Vossen. 2012. Challenges for a multilingual wordnet. *Language Resources and Evaluation*, 46(2):313–326.

Alona Fyshe, Leila Wehbe, Partha P. Talukdar, Brian Murphy, and Tom M. Mitchell. 2015. A compositional and interpretable semantic space. In *Proceedings of the 2015 Conference of the North American*

---

[7]Data and code are available at http://cs.umd.edu/~yogarshi.

Chapter of the Association for Computational Linguistics: Human Language Technologies, pages 32–41, Denver, Colorado, May–June. Association for Computational Linguistics.

William A. Gale, Kenneth W. Church, and David Yarowsky. 1992. A method for disambiguating word senses in a large corpus. *Computers and the Humanities*, 26:415–439.

Matt Gardner, Kejun Huang, Evangelos Papalexakis, Xiao Fu, Partha Talukdar, Christos Faloutsos, Nicholas Sidiropoulos, and Tom Mitchell. 2015. Translation invariant word embeddings. In *EMNLP 2015*, pages 1084–1088.

E. Gaussier, J.-M. Renders, I. Matveeva, C. Goutte, and H. Déjean. 2004. A geometric view on bilingual lexicon extraction from comparable corpora. In *Proceedings of the 42Nd Annual Meeting on Association for Computational Linguistics*, ACL '04, Stroudsburg, PA, USA. Association for Computational Linguistics.

Maayan Geffet and Ido Dagan. 2005a. The distributional inclusion hypotheses and lexical entailment. In *Proceedings of the 43rd Annual Meeting on Association for Computational Linguistics*, pages 107–114. Association for Computational Linguistics.

Maayan Geffet and Ido Dagan. 2005b. The distributional inclusion hypotheses and lexical entailment. In *ACL 2005*.

Tom Goldstein, Christoph Studer, and Richard Baraniuk. 2014. A field guide to forward-backward splitting with a FASTA implementation. *arXiv eprint*, abs/1411.3406.

Tom Goldstein, Christoph Studer, and Richard Baraniuk. 2015. FASTA: A generalized implementation of forward-backward splitting, January. http://arxiv.org/abs/1501.04979.

Stephan Gouws, Yoshua Bengio, and Greg Corrado. 2015. Bilbowa: Fast bilingual distributed representations without word alignments. In *Proceedings of the 32nd International Conference on Machine Learning (ICML)*.

Jiang Guo, Wanxiang Che, Haifeng Wang, and Ting Liu. 2014. Learning sense-specific word embeddings by exploiting bilingual resources. In *Proceedings of COLING*, pages 497–507.

Karl Moritz Hermann and Phil Blunsom. 2014. Multilingual models for compositional distributed semantics. In *ACL*.

Eric H Huang, Richard Socher, Christopher D Manning, and Andrew Y Ng. 2012. Improving word representations via global context and multiple word prototypes. In *Proceedings of the 50th Annual Meeting of the Association for Computational Linguistics: Long Papers-Volume 1*, pages 873–882. Association for Computational Linguistics.

Jagadeesh Jagarlamudi and Hal Daumé III. 2010. Extracting multilingual topics from unaligned comparable corpora. In *Proceedings of the 32Nd European Conference on Advances in Information Retrieval*, ECIR'2010, pages 444–456, Berlin, Heidelberg. Springer-Verlag.

Jagadeesh Jagarlamudi and Hal Daumé III. 2012. Regularized interlingual projections: Evaluation on multilingual transliteration. In *Proceedings of the 2012 Joint Conference on Empirical Methods in Natural Language Processing and Computational Natural Language Learning*, pages 12–23, Jeju Island, Korea, July. Association for Computational Linguistics.

Sujay Kumar Jauhar, Chris Dyer, and Eduard Hovy. 2015. Ontologically grounded multi-sense representation learning for semantic vector space models. In *Proceedings of NAACL*.

John Howard Johnson, Joel Martin, George Foster, and Roland Kuhn. 2007. Improving translation quality by discarding most of the phrasetable. In *Proceedings of EMNLP 2007*, pages 967–975.

Alexandre Klementiev, Ivan Titov, and Binod Bhattarai. 2012. Inducing crosslingual distributed representations of words. In *Proceedings of COLING 2012*, pages 1459–1474, Mumbai, India, December. The COLING 2012 Organizing Committee.

Philipp Koehn, Hieu Hoang, Alexandra Birch, Chris Callison-Burch, Marcello Federico, Nicola Bertoldi, Brooke Cowan, Wade Shen, Christine Moran, Richard Zens, Chris Dyer, Ondrej Bojar, Alexandra Constantin, and Evan Herbst. 2007. Moses: Open Source Toolkit for Statistical Machine Translation. In *Annual Meeting of the Association for Computational Linguistics (ACL), demonstration session*, Prague, Czech Republic, June.

Philipp Koehn. 2005. Europarl: A parallel corpus for statistical machine translation. In *MT summit*, volume 5, pages 79–86. Citeseer.

Philipp Koehn. 2010. *Statistical Machine Translation*. Cambridge University Press.

Lili Kotlerman, Ido Dagan, Idan Szpektor, and Maayan Zhitomirsky-Geffet. 2009. Directional distributional similarity for lexical expansion. In *ACL-IJCNLP 2009*, pages 69–72. Association for Computational Linguistics.

Lili Kotlerman, Ido Dagan, Idan Szpektor, and Maayan Zhitomirsky-Geffet. 2010. Directional distributional similarity for lexical inference. *Natural Language Engineering*, 16(04):359–389.

German Kruszewski, Denis Paperno, and Marco Baroni. 2015. Deriving boolean structures from distributional vectors. *Transactions of the Association for Computational Linguistics*, 3:375–388.

Els Lefever and Véronique Hoste. 2010. Semeval-2010 task 3: Cross-lingual word sense disambiguation. In *Proceedings of the 5th International Workshop on Semantic Evaluation*, pages 15–20, Uppsala, Sweden, July.

Omer Levy, Steffen Remus, Chris Biemann, and Ido Dagan. 2015. Do supervised distributional methods really learn lexical inference relations? In *NAACL HLT 2015*, pages 970–976.

Dekang Lin. 1998. Automatic retrieval and clustering of similar words. In *Proceedings of the 36th Annual Meeting of the Association for Computational Linguistics and 17th International Conference on Computational Linguistics-Volume 2*, pages 768–774. Association for Computational Linguistics.

Ang Lu, Weiran Wang, Mohit Bansal, Kevin Gimpel, and Karen Livescu. 2015. Deep multilingual correlation for improved word embeddings. In *Proceedings of the 2015 Conference of the North American Chapter of the Association for Computational Linguistics: Human Language Technologies*, pages 250–256, Denver, Colorado, May–June. Association for Computational Linguistics.

Julien Mairal, Francis Bach, Jean Ponce, and Guillermo Sapiro. 2009. Online dictionary learning for sparse coding. In *Proceedings of the 26th Annual International Conference on Machine Learning*, pages 689–696. ACM.

Diana McCarthy, Ravi Som Sinha, and Rada Mihalcea. 2013. The cross-lingual lexical substitution task. *Language Resources and Evaluation*, 47(3):607–638.

Yashar Mehdad, Matteo Negri, and Marcello Federico. 2010. Towards cross-lingual textual entailment. In *NAACL 2010*, pages 321–324.

David Mimno, Hanna M. Wallach, Jason Naradowsky, David A. Smith, and Andrew McCallum. 2009. Polylingual topic models. In *Proceedings of the 2009 Conference on Empirical Methods in Natural Language Processing: Volume 2 - Volume 2*, EMNLP '09, pages 880–889, Stroudsburg, PA, USA. Association for Computational Linguistics.

Brian Murphy, Partha Talukdar, and Tom Mitchell. 2012. Learning effective and interpretable semantic models using non-negative sparse embedding. In *Proceedings of COLING 2012*, pages 1933–1950, Mumbai, India, December. The COLING 2012 Organizing Committee.

Roberto Navigli and Simone Paolo Ponzetto. 2012. BabelNet: The automatic construction, evaluation and application of a wide-coverage multilingual semantic network. *Artificial Intelligence*, 193:217–250.

Arvind Neelakantan, Jeevan Shankar, Alexandre Passos, and Andrew McCallum. 2015. Efficient non-parametric estimation of multiple embeddings per word in vector space. *arXiv preprint arXiv:1504.06654*.

Ellie Pavlick, Johan Bos, Malvina Nissim, Charley Beller, Benjamin Van Durme, and Chris Callison-Burch. 2015. Adding semantics to data-driven paraphrasing. In *Proceedings of the 53rd Annual Meeting of the Association for Computational Linguistics and the 7th International Joint Conference on Natural Language Processing (Volume 1: Long Papers)*, pages 1512–1522, Beijing, China, July. Association for Computational Linguistics.

Jeffrey Pennington, Richard Socher, and Christopher D. Manning. 2014. Glove: Global vectors for word representation. In *EMNLP 2014*, pages 1532–1543.

Joseph Reisinger and Raymond J Mooney. 2010. Multi-prototype vector-space models of word meaning. In *Human Language Technologies: The 2010 Annual Conference of the North American Chapter of the Association for Computational Linguistics*, pages 109–117. Association for Computational Linguistics.

Diana Santos. 1990. Lexical gaps and idioms in machine translation. In *Proceedings of the 13th conference on Computational linguistics-Volume 2*, pages 330–335.

Peter D Turney and Saif M Mohammad. 2015. Experiments with three approaches to recognizing lexical entailment. *Natural Language Engineering*, 21(03):437–476.

Dani Yogatama, Manaal Faruqui, Chris Dyer, and Noah Smith. 2015. Learning word representations with hierarchical sparse coding. In *Proceedings of the 32nd International Conference on Machine Learning*, pages 87–96.

Maayan Zhitomirsky-Geffet and Ido Dagan. 2009. Bootstrapping distributional feature vector quality. *Computational Linguistics*, 35(3):435–461.

Automatic Prediction of Linguistic Decline in Writings of Subjects with Degenerative Dementia

Weissenbacher Davy
Department of Biomedical
Informatics, ASU
Scottsdale, AZ, USA
`davy.weissen-`
`bacher@asu.edu`

Johnson A. Travis
Department of Neurology
Mayo Clinic
Scottsdale, AZ, USA

Wojtulewicz Laura
Department of Biomedical
Informatics, ASU
Scottsdale, AZ, USA

Dueck Amylou
Department of Biostatistics
Mayo Clinic
Scottsdale, AZ, USA

Locke Dona
Department of Psychiatry
and Psychology, Mayo Clinic
Scottsdale, AZ, USA

Caselli Richard
Department of Neurology
Mayo Clinic
Scottsdale, AZ, USA

Gonzalez Graciela
Department of Biomedical
Informatics, ASU
Scottsdale, AZ, USA
`Graciela.Gonza-`
`lez@asu.edu`

Abstract

Given the limited success of medication in reversing the effects of Alzheimer's and other dementias, a lot of the neuroscience research has been focused on early detection, in order to slow the progress of the disease through different interventions. We propose a Natural Language Processing approach applied to descriptive writing to attempt to discriminate decline due to normal aging from decline due to pre-dementia conditions. Within the context of a longitudinal study on Alzheimer's disease, we created a unique corpus of 201 descriptions of a control image written by subjects of the study. Our classifier, computing linguistic features, was able to discriminate normal from cognitively impaired patients to an accuracy of 86.1% using lexical and semantic irregularities found in their writing. This is a promising result towards elucidating the existence of a general pattern in linguistic deterioration caused by dementia that might be detectable from a subject's written descriptive language.

1 Introduction

Alzheimer's disease is prevalent and becoming more so as the world's population ages (Prince et al., 2014). Since no cure is known, it is hoped that early detection and intervention might slow the onset of symptomatic cognitive decline and dementia. Clinical methods to detect Alzheimer's disease are typically applied well after symptoms have progressed to a troubling degree, and may be costly. Families, however, often report earlier signs of the disease through their language interactions with their elders. This has led clinical researchers to study linguistic differences to detect the disease in conversational speech (Asp and de Villiers, 2010). One approach is to search for non-informative phrases or semantic incoherences, which was confirmed to distinguish patients with Alzheimer's disease from controls (Nicholas et al., 1985). A strong limitation for its automatic application is the need of a trained expert to annotate the incoherences and scoring by hand.

We propose in this study to use Natural Language Processing (NLP) to evaluate samples of a patient's

Proceedings of NAACL-HLT 2016, pages 1198–1207,
San Diego, California, June 12-17, 2016. ©2016 Association for Computational Linguistics

descriptive writing in order to attempt to discriminate decline due to normal aging from decline due to pre-demented conditions. The Arizona Alzheimer's Disease Center (ADC) is a longitudinal study of patients with Alzheimer's disease and normal control subjects, who receive an annual battery of clinical and neuropsychological exams, to which we added the following brief and a simple task. Participants are asked to describe, in writing, a picture typically used within the speech-based Boston battery (Nicholas and Brookshire, 1993). We collected 201 descriptions, which were transcribed (dual transcription) and analyzed. We describe here a statistical machine learning method relying on lexical, syntactical and semantical features to discriminate evidence of abnormal deterioration in the writings of the patients. Our results confirm a correlation between linguistic decline on this writing task and the cognitive decline revealed by the more time consuming neuropsychological test battery.

2 Background

Alzheimer's disease (AD) is a highly prevalent neurodegenerative dementia that increases exponentially with age. It is the most common form of dementia in the United States. AD is characterized by a severe memory deficit and at least one of the following: aphasia, apraxia, agnosia and a disturbance in the internal control of cognitive processes (such as reflection, planning, working memory, etc.) (American Psychiatric Association, 1994). Neuropathologically, it is characterized by the presence of senile plaques composed of fibrillary abeta amyloid and neurofibrillary tangles containing hyperphosphorylated tau. While clinical testing often leads to an accurate diagnosis during its middle and late stages, several signs may alert a patient's family to much earlier stages of the disease even in the absence of frank aphasia (Obler and de Santi, 2000).

Given the repeated failures of experimental therapies targeting dementia stage AD, current strategies are targeting early intervention at preclinical and early symptomatic stages thereby necessitating more accurate methods for earlier detection of AD. Mild Cognitive Impairment (MCI), is defined as abnormal cognitive decline relative to age-matched peers that does not impair normal activities of daily living (Gauthier et al., 2006). AD is a frequent but not invariant cause. Some MCI patients may even recover, but all AD patients transition through the MCI stage before developing frank dementia (Petersen et al., 2001). As a result, an increasing number of clinical studies are trying to define and predict each stage in the life of an AD patient: normal, MCI and Alzheimer (Drummond et al., 2015).

2.1 Predicting Cognitive Decline with Language

Test batteries commonly used to measure cognitive decline include exercises to evaluate the language production of patients, but they are criticized for their simplicity. For example, the Mini-Mental State Examination (MMSE), a widely used screening tool, asks to name 2 objects, to repeat a phrase, write a sentence and obey a 3-step instruction. Bucks et al., 2000, citing Sabat, 1994, assert that these structured tests break down language into artificial components that fail to represent the psychological and sociological context involved in daily conversations. As a consequence, such tests may be insensitive to early linguistic decline, when anomalies are already detectable by patients' families (Key-DeLyria, 2013).

More sophisticated exercises have been proposed to complement the existing linguistic test batteries (Asp and de Villiers, 2010). These exercises are centered around conversation and narration abilities of patients. Conversation and narration abilities are developed in the early age of children (around 2-3 years for conversation and around 4 years for narration). Since they play a fundamental role in cognitive and social development, they are intensively studied. Exercises addressing narration capabilities can probe memory, spontaneity and the quality of interactions with the interlocutor. A complex exercise is to have patients narrate a habitual task, a memorable day of their life, or an event they participated in during the last week or month through informal conversation. A simplest exercise asks patients to describe a single image representing a usual scene. In this exercise memory is not a factor, the exercise being completely controlled by the image given; topics, persons and events depicted are imposed to the patients allowing very few improvisations with no discussion with an interlocutor. An advantage of this exercise is that the examiner knows in advance what is expected. This advantage is used to derive metrics that discriminate between normal controls and AD patients. Typically, the exact utterances are not captured, but rather the examiner notes whether the expected events were mentioned. More complex variations of this exercise are to ask patients to comment on a sequence of related images or to narrate a movie previously displayed. The patients participating in our study are receiving an extensive battery of tests annually to which we added a linguistic task, so we intentionally kept it simple and brief to avoid exhausting our participants. We therefore opted for a simple exercise of image description. While the majority of the exercises testing the narration abilities are spoken, with the exception of (Hayashi et al., 2015) and (Hirst and Feng, 2012), all related studies cited in this article were working on transcribed oral corpus, we opted for a written version, a form that remains relatively unexplored (Hayashi et al., 2015).

2.2 Clinical Studies for Linguistic Decline Prediction

A seminal longitudinal study (Snowdon et al., 1996) demonstrated that writing performance in young women correlated with development of AD in old age. Since then, clinical studies of cognitive decline have been scrutinizing all linguistic levels (Reilly et al., 2011), lexical, syntactical, semantical and pragmatic (Bolshakov and Gelbukh, 2004), in order to detect elements deteriorating with normal aging, those commonly observed degraded in the MCI stage, and finally their disintegration during the continuous phases of dementia. Various properties of language are studied, *e.g.* number of words, size of sentences, number and correctness of anaphoric references, number of propositions per sentence, number of relevant facts and the structure of the narration (Hier et al., 1985; Drummond et al., 2015). These properties are most often computed manually on samples of small size (usually around 50 patients) and appropriate statistical tests are used to determine the properties which can discriminate controls, MCI and AD patients.

From these studies has emerged a general pattern of pathological language decline observed during the MCI and the early stage of dementia (Obler and de Santi, 2000). Phonology and morphology are conserved. Syntax is also mostly spared even if it tends to be simplified. Degradations are mainly found at the lexical and semantical levels (Hier et al., 1985). At the lexical level, the vocabulary is reduced with fewer words and fewer occurrences. It becomes more abstract and vague with multiple phrasal repetitions (Xuan et al., 2011). At the semantic level complex questions is reduced and, early in the dementia phase, patients have difficulty making exact and pertinent remarks (Nicholas and Brookshire, 1993). Empty words and incomplete sentences are often observed in oral exercises.

These alterations of the language seem to allow caregivers and researchers to distinguish decline due to normal aging from pathological decline but, further studies with larger patient numbers are needed to confirm these initial results. A significant limitation in clinical environment has been the need for a trained language pathologist to annotate and evaluate all linguistic productions of each patient examined. More recently, however, a practical solution has appeared in the form of automating the annotation process using NLP techniques. The next section reviews the progress made.

2.3 Automatic prediction of Linguistic Decline

A first hypothesis to detect the cognitive decline in an older person is to compare his/her youth writings with his/her older writings. In (Hirst and Feng, 2012) sophisticated stylometric measures were tested to identify the differences caused by the disease in the style of three well-known authors (2 probable ADs and 1 healthy). However, not only were results not decisive given the small number of subjects, but this approach required a large amount of writings from the same person in order to establish the shift in the style of that person, conditions rarely met with common subjects. A variant of this approach is to compute two distinct profiles by modeling separately normal subjects and aphasic subjects from their writings. The results reported in (Holmes and Singh, 1996) report 88% of subjects correctly predicted from a corpus of 100 conversations. Few features were used and the computation of some of them still required a human intervention.

Bigger set of features can be explored with the use of NLP and machine learning. A first attempt in (Thomas et al., 2005) was to combine stylometric features (Stamatatos, 2009) and language model within a classifier. Their classifier obtained reasonable performances with 70% accuracy when distinguishing cognitively impaired from normal subjects in 95 oral interviews. In (Jarrold et al., 2010), the authors evaluated 80 features from various categories computed using dictionaries and predefined rules: positive sentiments words, socially related words, use of the first person, among others. The performance reported an accuracy of 82.6% in the prediction task in 45 interviews.

The most efficient features for discrimination are semantic features which capture the abilities of a subject to understand and convey a set of pertinent information (Nicholas and Brookshire, 1993). Automatic computation of such features are still challenging for automatic systems. Therefore, several publications integrated heuristics for computing such features. A prototype to approximate the density of idea has been released by (Brown et al., 2008). Idea density can be thought of as the total number of assertions or claims whether true or false, in a proposition. The number of claims is estimated from the number of verbs, adjectives/adverbs and conjunctions given certain conditions. The integration of the idea density proved to be significant to separate AD subjects from controls in (Jarrold et al., 2010).

3 Methods

3.1 Corpus Description and Preprocessing

In the context of the ADC study we created a corpus for our experiments. At the day of writing, the total number of subjects participating in the ADC study was roughly 500 corresponding to about 200 normal controls, 100 with MCI and 200 with AD or other form of degenerative dementia. In the beginning of the year 2015, in collaboration with the five institutes participating to the ADC study, a cognitive test was added to the protocol of the study. Subjects were asked to describe an image at the end of their annual visit. This control image is the same for all subjects (Nicholas and Brookshire, 1993). The image (Figure 1) represents a family having a picnic near a lake. Subjects were asked to write (by hand) a detailed description of the scene in the picture. No time limit is imposed, and the time it takes them to write their description is noted. The test giver is asked to read the description when the subject com-

Figure 1: The picnic scene described by the ADC cohort of patients.

pletes it, asking the subjects to clarify any unreadable words and to write them in the descriptions. We collected 201 descriptions for this study, 154 from healthy subjects and 47 from subjects in decline. The collection process is still ongoing[1].

The descriptions were transcribed and linguistic elements annotated. We developed a web site to centralize the collection of the scans of the descriptions from the different institutions. The web site offers a basic interface to display the scans and to transcribe their contents. The transcription was performed by an English native speaker. The instructions given to the transcriber were to preserve, as much as possible, the original presentation of the description (*i.e.* punctuations, uppercase, indents and new lines) as well as misspellings and crossed words.

Alzheimer Patient
Jane and Joe went out to blow But the weather was windy in the Oposit Direction, so they decided To blow the joint rather place and go home and have a bond fire in Their backyard and enjoy all the cooked things they could
Normal Patient
A family outing at a lake shore showed people doing several things. Mom and Dad sat on a blanket while dad read a book. Dad was over comfortable without his shoes, while mom listened to the radio and poured herself a cup of coffee. Junior was having fun flying his kite, and the family dog was interested in what all was going on. Another of the family was spending quiet time and fisherman, and another was playing in the shallow water. Other friends waved to them as they sailed by. It was a perfect day with just enough wind to move the flag and provide lift for the kite. It must have been comfortable sitting under the shade tree.

Table 1: Example of writings AD vs Normal Patient.

The descriptions are processed through an NLP pipeline composed of several off-the-shelf NLP

---

[1] The corpus is fully de-identified and will be publicly released at the end of the study.

modules. First, a homemade tokenizer and the Stanford Lemmatizer[3] are applied. Part of Speech as well as chunks are computed thanks to Genia tagger[4]. The descriptions are split into phrases by the sentence splitter found in the ANNIE tools suites of the Gate pipeline[5]. To compute the language models we have integrated the character Ngrams module provided by LingPipe[6] as well as a specific Perl module Text::NGrams (Keselj et al., 2003) for computing character Ngram frequencies. Finally, for computing the semantic features describe below (section 3.2.3), we compute vectors of words which are semantically close to a selected subset of words occurring in our corpus that correspond to a model description. To generate these vectors we have selected the tool Word2Vec[7]. We used the vectors trained on part of Google News dataset (about 100 billion words).

Aside from the exact identities, we had access to all information acquired during the ADCC study about the subjects enrolled. This includes personal information (*e.g.* gender, sex or education), social and medical information (*e.g.* social status, smoking habit, depression) as well as subjects' results to all tests endured during the visits. For our experiments, we used the primary diagnostic made during the last visit of a subject. If the subject was diagnosed with any form of dementia, including possible or probable Alzheimer's, or with MCI, the subject was labeled as *Declined*. Otherwise we checked the score measuring the cognitive status. This score is assigned by a neuropsychologist and it summarizes the performance of the subject during the cognitive exams. If the neuropsychologist diagnosed the subject as cognitively impaired or as demented, the subject is labeled as *Declined*. Otherwise we controlled the Clinical Dementia Rating (CDR) global score (Morris et al., 1997). The CDR is a semi-structured standardized interview completed with the subject's caregiver and the subject independently. The CDR is used to help diagnose dementia, indicating: Normal, MCI, Early Dementia, Moderate Dementia, and Severe Dementia. Administrators of the CDR are trained in a standardized fashion. If the administrator indicated the subject as MCI or Dementia, then we labeled the subject as *Declined*, otherwise

the subject was *NotInDecline*. These labels were used as gold standard during our experiments.

3.2 A Classifier for Detecting Linguistic Decline

In order to automate the analysis of the descriptions of our 201 subjects we created a classifier to discriminate subjects in abnormal decline from subjects with normal aging decline. Our classifier incorporates various features proposed by us or found in the literature. The following sections details the features and the motivations for their use.

3.2.1 Lexical Features

Adjective/Noun/verb/Pronoun ratios (Thomas et al., 2005). Given an abnormal decline we expected an important impoverishment of the vocabulary. Our initial hypothesis was a sensitive diminution of the number of adjective and pronouns since they are indicative of a precise description and complex syntactic structures. These ratios were computed by taking the number of adjectives/nouns/verbs/pronouns divided by the total number of tokens contains in a description. We relied on the POS tags to determine if a word was a noun, adjective or verb. To find the pronouns we matched a list of 73 pronouns.
Type Token Ratio (Thomas et al., 2005). The use of this ratio was supported by the idea that a subject presenting an abnormal decline will see his/her vocabulary reduced and would tend to repeat general words. This ratio was computed by taking the size of the vocabulary of a description over the total number of tokens. The vocabulary was found by adding up the lemmas occurring in the description.
Documents, Sentences and Tokens length (Hirst and Feng, 2012). The length of the different components of a document are often a good indicator of the quality of the writing and the ability to produce long and complex descriptions. We expressed several statistics which describe the description. The description length is expressed in number of tokens and punctuations. The size of the longest and shortest sentences, *min-max sentence length*, were used as features as well as the average of the length of all sentences occurring in the description. The average

---

length of the tokens occurring in the description was also added as feature.

Misspelling Ratio (Proposed). For this ratio we considered only orthographic errors present in a description. Since longer descriptions are more likely to have more misspellings we normalized the metric by dividing the number of errors with the total number of tokens in the description. To discover automatically the misspellings we used the rule-based spell checker languagetool-3.0[13]. As for the previous ratios we assumed that a higher percentage of misspellings would reflect an underlying lexical problems.

3.2.2 Stylometric Features

Functional Words Ratio (Hirst and Feng, 2012). Functional words are known to be good indicators of a personal style (Stamatatos, 2009). We matched an extended dictionary of 337 entries to retrieve the functional words in our descriptions. The ratio was given by the number of functional words over the total number of tokens in a description.

Brunét's Index and Honoré's Statistic (Thomas et al., 2005). Both metrics are length insensitive versions of the *type token ratio* and often reported as useful features for discriminating abnormal decline in the literature. They were computed by the following equations:

Brunét's Index $= N^{V-0.165}$ and Honoré's Statistic $= 100 log N / 1 - \frac{V_1}{V}$ where V is the total vocabulary, N the total number of tokens and V_1 the total number of hapax.

Character NGrams and Character NGram Frequencies (Thomas et al., 2005). Ngrams of words capture lexical regularities hidden in the writing style of an author as well as its syntactic complexity. They also help to highlight syntactic errors. Since sparsity problems raise quickly when Ngrams of words are created from a small size corpus, we preferred to use Ngrams of characters. By taking the most frequent Ngrams for both profiles Normal subjects and subjects in decline, we expected to capture the set of words which are the most indicative of each profile. We set the size of the Ngrams to 5 for the character NGrams and to 10 for the Character NGram Frequencies. We limited to the 2000 most frequent Ngrams. Those parameters were set manually and can be optimized in future experiments.

3.2.3 Semantic Features

Idea Density (Brown et al., 2008) To compute the idea density detailed in section 2.3, a heuristic to estimate the quantity of information convey in the description, we integrated the software CPIDR 3.2[15]. No change has been made in the set of rules used by the software.

Word2Vec Distance (Proposed). A characteristic of subjects in abnormal decline is their inability to convey pertinent information and to digress from the initial subject. To model this characteristic we propose a new feature which takes advantage of the specificity of our corpus: all subjects, normal and subjects in decline, are describing the same image. By taking only descriptions written by normal subjects we obtained a set of words describing correctly the image. We named this set *generative words*. All functional words were removed from this set. Our hypothesis was that subjects in decline would use less words from *generative words* and add more inappropriate words (given the context of the image). Since the size of our corpus is small, not all relevant words were present in *generative words*. We extended *generative words* into a set called *Word2Vec clusters* by adding for each word of *generative words*, the corresponding vector returned by Word2Vec. These vectors are composed by words semantically close to the generative words. This includes synonyms, meronyms, hyperonyms but also correlated words. At run time, when an unknown description was submitted to the system, we created a subset of *Word2Vec clusters*, called *Filtered Word2Vec clusters*, by taking all vectors V_i in *Word2Vec clusters* related to the words W_i occurring in the unknown description. We added V_i in *Filtered Word2Vec clusters* if W_i was the generating word of V_i or if W_i was a word occurring in V_i with W_i belonging to the set *generative words*. If W_i was found in a vector $V_j \in$ *Word2Vec clusters* but V_j was generated by a word w_j not occurring in the unknown description, V_j was not added in *Filtered Word2Vec clusters*. This filtering step is crucial to guarantee good performances when using this fea-

---

[13] Available at http://wiki.languagetool.org/java-api

[15] The software and its documentation are freely available at http://ai1.ai.uga.edu/caspr/

ture. Additional tests were performed without filtering *Word2Vec clusters* and a significant drop of performances was observed due to noise or ambiguity in the vector generated by Word2Vec, for example vectors generated by *go, be* etc. The filtering step insures that the vectors of *Filtered Word2Vec clusters* contain only words semantically related with the content of the unknown description. Given the set of words in *Filtered Word2Vec clusters* the distance is the ratio of words W_i in *Filtered Word2Vec clusters* and total number of words in W_i.

3.2.4 Subject Features

All clinical information about the subjects participating in the ADC study were available during our experiments. We retained only criteria known to affect linguistic competences or known to contribute to the development of the disease. *Age* and *gender* are important factors for the Alzheimer's disease as well as the version of the *APOE* gene of a subject. The presence of an e4 allele increases significantly the risk of the disease. *Education* and *primary language* (native English speaker or not) are obvious attributes to consider to measure the linguistic abilities as well as the *social status* of the subject. A subject living alone, with relatives or spouse will not have the same opportunities to speak.

4   Results

We evaluated our classifier on the data mining platform *Weka*. This platform implements state-of-the art machine learning algorithms (Witten et al., 2011). The size of our corpus being small we opted for a leave-one-out cross validation. We chose the framework of a Bayesian Network (BN) (Koller and Friedman, 2009) to perform the evaluation of our classifier. For all following experiments we learned the structure of the network and its conditional probabilities automatically from our data. No Naive Bayes structure were *a priori* imposed during the training and the number of possible parents for a node were manually set to 20. We selected this machine learning algorithm because it learns complex decision functions, its decisions are interpretable by medical experts, it has very few global parameters to set up and it was fast to train on our problem.

Our first experiment evaluated the performances of our classifier when all features were used (Table 2). We confirmed the quality of our classifier by

comparing its performances with a baseline classifier. The baseline classifier predicted the majority class label

Classifier	Accuracy (%)	FN	FP
Baseline	76.6	47	0
Bayesian Network			
- All Features	83.1	25	9
- Selected Features	86.1	21	7

Table 2: Performances of the classifiers for decline detection. Considering Decline as the targeted class, False Positive are Normal patients labeled as patients in decline and False Negative are patients in decline labeled as Normal patients.

NotInDecline for all instances. The baseline system obtained 76.6% of accuracy (Acc). With this setting, our classifier obtained a better score with 80.6% Acc. and thus demonstrated its abilities to learn the difference between normal subjects from subjects in abnormal decline using linguistic features.

We proceeded to an ablation study to assess the benefits of each feature. We removed one at a time each feature, or complementary features such as *min-max length of sentence*, and rerun the training/testing of our classifier. The results are detailed in Table 3. For brevity we did not report in the table the features which did not change the score of our classifier once removed.

Feature removed	Accuracy (%)
None	83.1
Misspelling Ratio	85.1
Word2Vec Distance	81.9
Brunét's Index	82.1
Average Sentence Length + Min-Max Sentence Length	83.6
Ngram Frequencies	85.1
Ngrams	81.6
Patient APOE	84.1
Patient Age	82.6

Table 3: Performances of the Bayesian Network during the ablation study.

In the light of the ablation study we performed a second experiment to determine the optimal performances of our classifier. We run several feature selection/reduction algorithms implemented in the *Weka* platform. The Correlation-based Feature Selection algorithm (CFS) (Hall, 1999) found a set of features which maximized the performances of the classifier. Under this setting our classifier outperformed the baseline system with a score of 86.1 Acc. against 76.6 Acc (Table 2). Inspection of the confusion matrix shown that the classifier correctly recognized 24 patients in abnormal decline and 149 normal patients. Considering *Decline* as the targeted class, our classifier mistakenly predicted 7 False Positives (FP) and 21 False Negatives (FN). We reproduced comparable performances with other machine learning algorithms using this set of features. A multilayer perceptron got a score of 84.6% Acc., a random forest 81.1% Acc. and a bagging algorithm 83.6% Acc. Five features only were selected by the CFS algorithm: Ngrams, Honoré's Statistic, Misspelling Ratio, Age and the Word2Vec Distance. This set of features differs from the set indicated by the ablation study but obtained better performances on our task. When trained and tested using only the four features which improved the classification during the ablation study, the score of the classifier reached 85.6 Acc. with 4 FP and 25 FN.

From these experiments we can conclude that our system showed promising performances when learning to discriminate subjects in abnormal cognitive decline from their writings. The ablation study and the set of optimal features found by the CFS algorithm seem to confirm the existence of the general pattern postulated in the clinical literature where lexical and semantical capacities are damaged during the cognitive decline. The most important features were the semantic features, Ngrams and Word2Vec, with a total drop of 2.7 points when they were removed. Both features capture the tendency of the subjects in decline to describe few topics of the image, resulting in a low Word2Vec distance, and to digress from the description task by mentioning several facts or statements that could not be inferred from the image or were not plausible with its content. These digressions caused the system to compute a higher probability for the description written by a subject in decline to be generated by the profile of the abnormal subjects and a low probability for being generated by the profile of the normal subjects. The profile of abnormal subjects contained more words than the profile of normal subjects, this latter containing only words related to the image. The decline of the lexical capacities are suggested by the higher number of misspellings made by subjects in decline as well as the positive role of the

Brunét's Index or Honoré's Statistic Brunet during the classification.

4.1 Analysis of Errors

The prediction of abnormal decline is a hard learning problem. Since it is still difficult to clinically diagnose the cognitive decline and potentially the following dementia, the labels of the target class in our corpus remains uncertain. Patients labeled normal can quickly show sign of decline and MCIs can recover over time. Therefore, for our analysis, we focused more on the capacity of our classifier to detect good descriptions rather than to strictly predict the target class. Additional analysis of our errors will be carried out by pathologists specialized in aphasia.

The 7 FPs where all primary diagnosed normal during their last visit. Their ages varied from 69 to 86 year old. Our manual inspection of their writings revealed that 4 descriptions presented strong irregularities which may explain the decision of our classifier. In the first case we found short descriptions containing misspellings, repeated phrases, ungrammatical sentences and descriptions focused on small details of the image. In the second case, descriptions were longer but they all contained digressions such as *"The turtle is shuffling back to be with the water."* (no turtle is drawn in the image), or *"Mom is torn between the playtime there and being being with her friends back home"* (the woman seems perfectly relaxed). Additional analysis of such digressions on our corpus are needed to know how strongly they are correlated with the decline. The reasons the classifier tagged the last 3 descriptions as *Decline* remained unclear. The Bayesian Networks learned for these instances are currently analyzed to understand which features deceived the classifier. The BN classifiers learned are probabilistic directed acyclic graphs which represent causal relations between variables. They can be displayed in a dedicated Graphical User Interface where values for different variables observed can be manually imposed to see the changes on the likelihood of the others unseen variables.

The 21 FNs can be separated in 3 groups: 2 patients whose primary diagnosis were AD, 11 whose primary diagnosis were MCIs and 8 normal patients but whose cognitive exams results (3 patients) or global CDR (5 patients) showed signs of decline.

Our corpus contains in total 7 cases of patients diagnosed with AD, 5 cases were correctly classified by the system and 2 incorrectly, making it fairly sensitives to strong signs of decline. The majority of the classifier's errors were made on light and mild impairments. In order to understand these errors we randomly selected 10 descriptions written by these patients and proceeded to a manual examination. A clear difference with the descriptions of the FPs is the absence of digressions. Only one description mentioned some implausible facts, others strictly described the image with most of its topics commented. 6 descriptions presented anomalies like misspellings, phrases repeated, verbs/auxiliaries missing, incomplete sentences or wrong choices of pronouns and, for 2 of them, a simplified syntax with unnatural constructions (*e.g. "A coulle having a picnic, the man with a book the girl pouring a soda."*). The 4 remaining descriptions exhibit a good quality and would be difficult to discriminate with linguistic features only.

5 Conclusion and Perspectives

With the general aging of the population more attention have been given to the Alzheimer's disease. In this study we presented a NLP system to predict early signs of cognitive decline, which often precede the disease, based on the analysis of written descriptions of an image. To perform our experiments we created a corpus which is, to the best of our knowledge, unique by its nature and its size. With a final score of 86.1% Accuracy our system outperformed our baseline system and showed state-of-the-art performances with existing classifiers working on oral interviews. Our results suggest a correlation between abnormal cognitive declines and the dislocation of the language ability. Our ablation study revealed that our system discriminates patients with abnormal decline using lexical and semantical irregularities found in their writings, consolidating the hypothesis of a general pattern in the linguistic impairment already postulated in the literature. The analysis of its classification errors showed the limitation of our approach: the presence of linguistic irregularities are not always sufficient to diagnose abnormal decline and may not always be observed in writings of patients already diagnosed in abnormal decline. To overcome this limitation we are currently designing a classifier based on Conditional Random Fields. This classifier will integrate all information available about our patients (i.e. medical, cognitive, linguistic, and imaging information) and will allow the representation of the performances of the patients over the time.

References

American Psychiatric Association, 1994. Diagnostic and statistical manual of mental disorders (4th ed.).

Elissa Asp and Jessica de Villiers. 2010. When Language Breaks Down: Analysing Discourse in Clinical Contexts. Cambridge University Press.

Igor A. Bolshakov and Alexander Gelbukh, editors. 2004. Computational Linguistics: Models, Resources, Applications. Igor A. Bolshakov and Alexander Gelbukh.

C. Brown, T. Snodgrass, S.J. Kemper, R. Herman, and M.A. Covington. 2008. Automatic measurement of propositional idea density from part-of-speech tagging. Behavior Research Methods, 40(2):540–545.

R. S. Bucks, S. Singh, J. M. Cuerden, and G. K. Wilcock. 2000. Analysis of spontaneous, conversational speech in dementia of alzheimer type: Evaluation of an objective technique for analysing lexical performance. Aphasiology, 14(1):71–91.

T. Hayashi, H. Nomura, R. Mochizuki, A. Ohnuma, T. Kimpara, K. Suzuki, E. Mor. 2015. Writing Impairments in Japanese Patients with Mild Cognitive Impairment and with Mild Alzheimer's Disease. Dementia Geriatric Cognitive Disorders Extra, 5:309-319

C. Drummond, G. Coutinho, R. Paz Fonseca, N. Assuno, A. Teldeschi, R. de Oliveira-Souza, J. Moll, F. Tovar-Moll, and P. Mattos. 2015. Deficits in narrative discourse elicited by visual stimuli are already present in patients with mild cognitive impairment. Frontiers in Aging Neuroscience, 7(96).

Serge Gauthier, Barry Reisberg, Michael Zaudig, Ronald C Petersen, Karen Ritchie, Karl Broich, Sylvie Belleville, Henry Brodaty, David Bennett, Howard Chertkow, Jeffrey L Cummings, Mony de Leon, Howard Feldman, Mary Ganguli, Harald Hampel, Philip Scheltens, Mary C Tierney, Peter Whitehouse, and Bengt Winblad. 2006. Mild cognitive impairment. The Lancet, 367(9518):1262 – 1270.

Daniel B. Hier, Karen Hagenlocker, and Andrea G. Shindler. 1985. Language disintegration in dementia: Effects of etiology and severity. Brain and Language, 25(1):117–133.

Graeme Hirst and Vanessa Wei Feng. 2012. Changes in style in authors with alzheimer's disease. English Studies, 93(3):357–370.

D. Holmes and S. Singh. 1996. A stylometric analysis of conversational speech of aphasic patients. Literary and Linguistic Computing, 11:45–60.

William L. Jarrold, Bart Peintner, Eric Yeh, Ruth Krasnow, Harold S. Javitz, and Gary E. Swan. 2010. Language analytics for assessing brain health: Cognitive impairment, depression and pre-symptomatic alzheimer's disease. In Yiyu Yao, Ron Sun, Tomaso Poggio, Jiming Liu, Ning Zhong, and Jimmy Huang, editors, Brain Informatics, volume 6334 of Lecture Notes in Computer Science, pages 299–307. Springer Berlin Heidelberg.

Vlado Keselj, Fuchun Peng, Nick Cercone, and Calvin Thomas. 2003. N-gram-based author profiles for authorship attribution. In Pacific Association for Computational Linguistics.

Daphne Koller and Nir Friedman. 2009. Probabilistic Graphical Models: Principles and Techniques. MIT press.

Linda E. Nicholas and Robert H. Brookshire. 1993. A system for quantifying the informativeness and efficiency of the connected speech of adults with aphasia. Journal of Speech, Language, and Hearing Research, 36(2):338–350.

M. Nicholas, L. Obler, M. Albert, and N. HelmEstabrooks. 1985. Empty speech in alzheimer's disease and fluent aphasia. Journal of Speech and Hearing Research, 28(3):405–410.

Loraine K. Obler and Susan de Santi, 2000. Methods for Studying Language Production, chapter 20. Lise Menn and Nan Bernstein Ratner, lawrence erlbaum associates edition.

Ronald C. Petersen, Rachelle Doody, Alexander Kurz,

Richard C. Mohs, John C. Morris, Peter V. Rabins, Karen Ritchie, Martin Rossor, Leon Thal, and Bengt Winblad. 2001. Current concepts in mild cognitive impairment. Archives of Neurology, 58(12):1985–1992.

Martin Prince, Emiliano Albanese, Maelenn Guerchet,¨ and Matthew Prina. 2014. World alzheimer report 2014. Alzheimer's Disease International (ADI).

Jamie Reilly, Joshua Troche, and Murray Grossman, 2011. Language Processing in Dementia, chapter 12, pages 336–368. Wiley-Blackwell.

S. R. Sabat. 1994. Language function in alzheimer's disease: a critical review of selected literature. Language and Communication, 14:331–351.

David A. Snowdon, Susan J. Kemper, James A. Mortimer, Lydia H. Greiner, David R. Wekstein, and William R. Markesbery. 1996. Linguistic ability in early life and cognitive function and alzheimer's disease in late life: Findings from the nun study. JAMA, 275(7):528–532.

Efstathios Stamatatos. 2009. A survey of modern authorship attribution methods. JASIST, 60(3):538–556.

Calvin Thomas, Vlado Keselj, Nick Cercone, Kenneth Rockwood, and Elissa Asp. 2005. Automatic detection and rating of dementia of alzheimer type through lexical analysis of spontaneous speech. In Proceedings of the IEEE International Conference on Mechatronics and Automation.

Ian H. Witten, Eibe Frank, and Mark A. Hall. 2011. Data Mining: Practical Machine Learning Tools and Techniques. Morgan Kaufmann.

Le Xuan, Ian Lancashire, Graeme Hirst, and Regina Jokel. 2011. Longitudinal detection of dementia through lexical and syntactic changes in writing: A case study of three british novelists. Literary and Linguistic Computing, 26(4):435–461.

JC. Morris and C. Ernesto and K. Schafer and M. Coats and S. Leon and M. Sano and LJ Thal and P. Woodbury. 1997. Clinical dementia rating training and reliability in multicenter studies: the Alzheimer's Disease Cooperative Study experience. Neurology 48(6):1508-1510.

S. Key-DeLyria. 2013. What are the methods for diagnosing MCI? Neurophysiology and Neurogenic Speech and Language Disorders, 23: 14-22.

Mark A. Hall. 1999. Correlation-based Feature Selection for Machine Learning. Ph.D. thesis, University of Waikato.

Consensus Maximization Fusion of Probabilistic Information Extractors

Miguel Rodríguez and **Sean Goldberg** and **Daisy Zhe Wang**
University of Florida, Dept of Computer Science, Gainesville, FL, USA
`{mer,sean,daisyw}@cise.ufl.edu`

Abstract

Current approaches to Information Extraction
(IE) are capable of extracting large amounts
of facts with associated probabilities. Because
no current IE system is perfect, complementary and conflicting facts are obtained when
different systems are run over the same data.
Knowledge Fusion (KF) is the problem of aggregating facts from different extractors. Existing methods approach KF using supervised
learning or deep linguistic knowledge, which
either lack sufficient data or are not robust
enough. We propose a semi-supervised application of Consensus Maximization to the KF
problem, using a combination of supervised
and unsupervised models. Consensus Maximization Fusion (CM Fusion) is able to promote high quality facts and eliminate incorrect ones. We demonstrate the effectiveness
of our system on the NIST Slot Filler Validation contest, which seeks to evaluate and aggregate multiple independent information extractors. Our system achieved the highest F1
score relative to other system submissions.

1   Introduction

The abundance of unstructured text on the web such
as news, discussion forums, wiki pages, etc. has increased the interest of the research community in the
automatic extraction of information at scale. Information extractors can be used to construct or expand
Knowledge Bases (KBs) through a process known as
Knowledge Base Population (KBP) or Construction.
Facts in a KB are typically modeled as (`subject`,
`relation`, `object`) triples such as (*Facebook*,
org:city_of_headquarters, Menlo Park).

No current information extractor is perfectly
accurate and different models exhibit different
strengths and weaknesses. As a result, many state-
of-the-art KBs in academia and industry employ
multiple complementary information extractors for
KBP. NELL(Mitchell and Fredkin, 2014) employs
rules, statistically-learned pattern extractors, and
context extractors among others. YAGO (Suchanek
et al., 2007) uses heuristic extractors at text and ontological levels and Google has multiple extractors
crawling text, tables, and HTML.

Different extraction systems may also agree or
disagree on the information they extract.   Consider three systems that extract the facts (*Facebook,
org:city_of_headquarters, Menlo Park*), (*Facebook,
org:city_of_headquarters, Palo Alto*), and (*Facebook, org:city_of_headquarters, Menlo Park*) with
probabilities 0.6, 0.3, and 0.5 respectively. The *Palo
Alto* extraction is erroneous and should be removed.
The two *Menlo Park* extractions should be promoted
by agreement and have their confidences increased.

The aggregation of facts from multiple extractors
into a single probabilistic triple is known as Knowledge Fusion (KF) (Dong et al., 2014) and can be
modeled as an ensemble learning problem. Previous
ensemble approaches at the output layer divide into
unsupervised and supervised methods (Gao et al.,
2010).   Unsupervised methods establish a consensus or *majority vote* among extractors without distinguishing the merit of each, but perform poorly if all
the extractors are weak. Supervised methods such
as *stacking* achieve better performance by learning
weights for each extractor and combining them as a
weighted sum. The difficulty in obtaining training

Proceedings of NAACL-HLT 2016, pages 1208–1216,
San Diego, California, June 12-17, 2016. ©2016 Association for Computational Linguistics

data usually results in high precision, but low recall among all facts.

As a solution to the low recall problem we present a probabilistic ensemble fusion model based on Consensus Maximization (CM) (Gao et al., 2009), which is a semi-supervised learning method able to combine the strengths of both supervised and unsupervised approaches. In the knowledge fusion domain, where the number of unsupervised systems can be rather large compared to those with manually labeled data, Consensus Maximization Fusion is able to leverage both for improved performance.

We apply our CM Fusion approach to the NIST Slot Filling Validation (SFV) task, an ensemble learning problem that aims to combine multiple information extractors participating in the NIST English Slot Filling (ESF) task. Our experiments show an improved F1 score relative to the current state-of-the-art SFV systems.

We make the following overall contributions in this paper:

- Present a novel probabilistic fusion system that incorporates Consensus Maximization to solve the Knowledge Fusion problem.

- Develop an application of our system to the NIST Slot Filling Validation task.

- Outline an evaluation of our system that improves upon the previous state-of-the-art F1 score by 28%.

Though we choose to focus on the SFV task in this paper, there are clear applications beyond this and to the Knowledge Fusion problem in general. The remainder of this paper is organized as follows. In Section 2, we discuss background material on the ESF and SFV tasks as well as the Consensus Maximization algorithm. Section 3 outlines our CM Fusion system and how it maps into the knowledge fusion problem. Our experiments are detailed in Section 4 and we conclude in Section 5.

2 Background

Here we present the appropriate background knowledge on the English Slot Filling (ESF) and Slot Filling Validation (SFV) tasks that are part of the NIST Text Analysis Conference (TAC). We also introduce the Consensus Maximization framework that forms the foundation of CM Fusion.

2.1 Knowledge Base Construction: Slot Filling

A knowledge base is a repository of information about people, places, and things. The usual representation is as (`subject`, `relation`, `object`) triple. The subject and object are entities such as *Facebook* or *Menlo Park*. The relation is some property that holds between the subject and object and usually adheres to a fixed ontology such as *headquarters_in*. Knowledge Base population involves the generation of triples from unstructured text sources.

To facilitate and encourage further research into KBP, NIST has organized a series of workshops known as the Text Analysis Conference (TAC). The English Slot Filler (ESF) task involves connecting a (`subject`, `relation`, `*`) pair with a set of corresponding `object` attributes. Teams compete with each other to develop the best system for the job (Surdeanu and Ji, 2014).

Each team receives as input a set of queries in XML format and a text corpus. The queries are empty slots such (*Facebook*, *org:city_of_headquarters*, *) and the corpus is a formatted set of web pages, newswire, and discussion forums. For each query slot, the systems extract the appropriate attribute as either a single value or list of values or `NIL`. Overall evaluation is determined by final F1 score across all queries. Query evaluation occurs after submission by a team of human judges. Teams do not know their final accuracy at submission time.

2.2 Ensembling ESF: Slot Filling Validation

The massive quantity of data makes manual labeling impossible and thus system evaluation very difficult. A parallel TAC task is Slot Filling Validation (SFV), which aims to develop a meta-classifier for the purpose of validating individual systems. SFV systems receive as input the set of query results from each ESF system. Without any truth information, they must evaluate the evidence from each query and return a final slot value. The process of sorting conflicting and complementary information from different systems and aggregating into a unified KB is equivalent to the Knowledge Fusion problem.

Sys.	Slot Filler	Provenance	Prob
03_1	Menlo Park	D1:683-692	0.087
03_2	Menlo Park	D1:683-692	0.197
12_4	Menlo Park	D2:655-665	0.987
10_3	Menlo Park	D3:683-692	1.000
13_3	San Francisco	D4:974-986	1.000
07_4	San Francisco	D5:3534-3544	0.210
09_1	Chinatown	D6:3520-3529	0.200
16_1	California	D6:7250-7258	1.000
10_2	California	D7:263-267	1.000

Table 1: Slot fillers extracted by multiple systems for the query (*Facebook, org:city_of_headquarters*). The columns represent each system, their response, document provenance, and extracted probabilities.

Table 1 shows an example set of query results from different systems for the (*Facebook, org:city_of_headquarters, **) slot. Included with the slot filler are provenance information about where the filler was mentioned in the corpus and the system's confidence probability.

As stated in the introduction, previous work in SFV has used majority voting (Sammons et al., 2014) or stacking (Viswanathan et al., 2015) to combine the output of multiple ESF systems. The lack of ground truth motivated the majority voting approach of (Sammons et al., 2014), which performs decently in precision and recall. Because of the annual nature of the TAC-KBP competition, some systems repeat submissions in successive years. While current truth data is not available, for a small number of systems there is data available from previous years on a different set of queries. (Viswanathan et al., 2015) uses those systems as training data in a stacking ensemble. Viewing each triple as a binary classification problem into true or false, they extract features based on the probabilities each ESF system gave to each fact (or 0.0 if they did not extract the fact) and train an L1-regularized SVM with a linear kernel. While this gives high precision, the lack of systems participating in multiple years leads to very low recall among all extracted facts.

2.3 Consensus Maximization

Consensus Maximization (Gao et al., 2009) is an ensemble learning method that merges both supervised and unsupervised learning models into a single cohesive framework. While unsupervised models don't provide class labels, they do provide constraints that reduce the hypothesis space of the overall learning problem. Examples in the same cluster are likely to receive the same class label and may improve prediction accuracy through increased model diversity.

Like majority voting and stacking, CM operates at the output level of each individual model and aims to predict the conditional probabilities of each example belonging to each class. By providing class labels, supervised models naturally partition the example space into groups and give those groups labels. Unsupervised models do the same partitioning, but cannot label the groups. Using the supervised methods and their examples as a starting point, CM propagates labels to other unsupervised clusters containing the same examples and to other examples within those clusters.

Formally, the framework of Consensus Maximization is a constrained optimization problem over a bipartite graph. The two sets of nodes are object nodes and group nodes. Each Object node represents a single example given to each system for classification/clustering. Group nodes represent within-system partitions. There are as many partitions as there are classes. For c classes and m systems, there will be $v = cm$ total groups.

The conditional probabilities are expressed in the form of matrices $U_{n \times c}$ for objects and $Q_{v \times c}$ for groups, where rows are object or group nodes from the graph and columns are classes. Rows or columns of the matrix are denoted with the vector $\vec{u_i}$ or $\vec{q_i}$. Each element $u_{iz} \in U_{n \times c}$ represents the conditional probability of object i belonging to class z. Similarly, each element $q_{jz} \in Q_{n \times v}$ represents the conditional probability of group j belong class z as shown in the following equations:

$$u_{iz} = P(y = z | x_i) \tag{1}$$

$$q_{jz} = P(y = z | g_i) \tag{2}$$

The adjacency matrix of the bipartite graph is represented by $A_{n \times v}$ where $a_{ij} = 1$ when x_i has been assigned to group g_j by its respective model, or 0 otherwise. Initial group label assignments are provided by supervised models and encoded in the matrix $Y_{v \times c}$, where $y_{jz} = 1$ if the group g_j comes from supervised learning and belongs to class z, or 0 otherwise. The sum of the rows of Y determines if a group node belongs to a supervised or unsupervised model. Let $k_j = \sum_{z=1}^{c} y_{jz}$ binarily represent such scenario. Note that $k_j = 0$ when there is no supervised evidence for group j. The consensus among models is formulated as the following optimization problem:

$$\min_{Q,U}(\sum_{i=1}^{n} \sum_{j=1}^{v} a_{ij} \parallel \vec{u_i} - \vec{q_j} \parallel^2$$
$$+ \alpha \sum_{j=1}^{v} k_j \parallel \vec{q_j} - \vec{y_j} \parallel^2$$
$$+ \beta \sum_{i=1}^{n} h_i \parallel \vec{u_i} - \vec{f_i} \parallel^2) \qquad (3)$$
$$s.t$$
$$\vec{u_i} \geq \vec{0}, \mid \vec{u_i} \mid = 1, i = 1, \ldots, n$$
$$\vec{q_j} \geq \vec{0}, \mid \vec{q_j} \mid = 1, j = 1, \ldots, v$$

The first term finds consensus across models by minimizing the deviation between the conditional probability of object i in the vector $\vec{u_i}$, and the conditional probability of the groups, $\vec{u_j}$, where it has been originally assigned by the input models. The second term penalizes deviations of the group probability $\vec{q_j}$ from its initial assignment $\vec{y_j}$, with α being the penalization factor that has to be paid for violating supervised predictions. Consensus Maximization does not require labeled objects to estimate the probability matrices Q and U. Nevertheless, a small amount known labels can help bias the optimization and improve the model. If l objects have known labels, the matrix $F_{n \times c}$ encodes this information such that $f_{iz} = 1$ when x_i's true label is z and 0 otherwise. In this matrix, i is the index of an object node, and z a class label. The sum of rows in F determine if an object has a label assigned, $h_i = \sum_{z=1}^{c} f_{iz}$. For instance, $\vec{f_i} = \vec{0}$ represents an objects without labeled data. The third term in the objective function penalizes deviations of the conditional probability of an object $\vec{u_i}$ from its known label $\vec{f_i}$; when $h_i = 0$ this term is dismissed. Labeled variables incorporated in CM are not final. The value of β is the penalization factor for violating label constraints. For

a fuller treatment of the methodology, see (Gao et al., 2009).

3 Consensus Maximization Fusion

In this section we describe the ensemble CM Fusion system we built for combining multiple information extractors. Similar to (Viswanathan et al., 2015), we view the slot filling problem in terms of a binary classification task. The set of all extractions across all systems produce an initial knowledge base of facts. This KB is noisy and redundant and contains a lot of conflicting and complementary evidence. For each fact in the KB, we fuse decisions coming from each system into a true class and a false class.

Figure 1 shows the architecture of the system. Offline all individual extractors operate over the same corpus and produce their extractions. A preprocessing step canonicalizes strings and clusters systems producing the same extraction. The feature extraction step converts set of probabilities about each system's fact into the unsupervised feature vector. For the systems for which previous years evaluation data is available we train 6 different meta-classifiers. Their decisions on the same corpus comprise the supervised feature vector. The supervised and unsupervised data are passed into the consensus maximization component that produces a final aggregated probability for each value. As part of a final cleaning process, constraints are applied that remove certain mutually exclusive conflicting facts.

For the remainder of this section we describe each component of our Consensus Maximization Fusion system in more detail.

3.1 Preprocessing

Our system takes as input extractions produced using a number of information extractors that differ in their methodology and application. Their output is uniform and their "filled slots" correspond to a set of extracted facts. Each fact is processed by transforming all text into lower case and deleting trailing spaces. Using exact string match we map each fact onto a cluster of the multiple systems that extracted it.

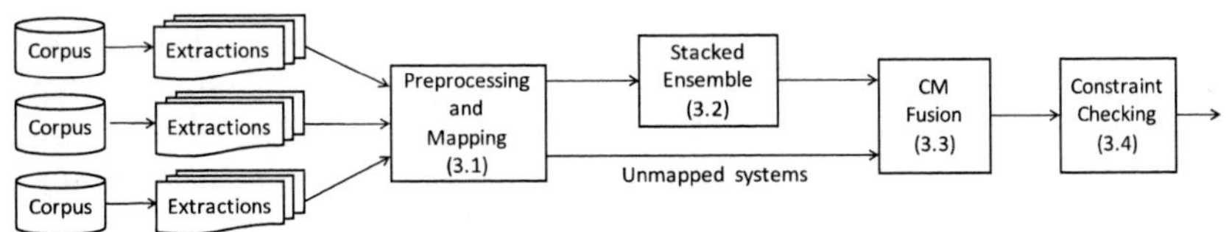

Figure 1: Consensus Maximization Fusion system components and pipeline.

3.2 Stacked Ensemble

Consensus Maximization Fusion is able to take into account supervised and unsupervised systems for knowledge fusion. The supervised portion is able to weight certain systems using previously labeled data and combine their decisions into a meta-classifier. The unsupervised portion operating over unlabeled data treats every system equally and is closer in spirit to a majority vote.

Of the extractors submitting results to ESF, about 10% had participated in previous years where labeled data was available. This idea was used in (Viswanathan et al., 2015) to generate a series meta-classifiers using stacking. A meta-classifier combines the outputs of multiple systems using learned weights. (Viswanathan et al., 2015) generate a total of 6 meta-classifiers for comparison that differ in classifier type and feature vector. The basic feature vector includes one entry for each system and with the value being that system's extraction probability. Two additional feature vectors were generated by adding relational information for each system and both relational information and provenance information. These three feature vectors were independently trained using logistic regression (LR) and SVM for a total of 6 meta-classifiers. CM Fusion runs each trained meta-classifier over the same ESF corpus and uses their output as an additional 6 systems in the ensemble combination. Though we use only 6 our method generalizes to any number of meta-classifiers.

3.3 Fusing Systems

In total there are S systems submitting runs to be ensemble by CM Fusion. N of these systems have evaluation data for the training a total of M meta-classifiers. The top half of Figure 2 shows the collection of supervised meta-classifiers and remaining unsupervised systems.

Symbol	Definition
$o_1, ..., o_k$	Unique facts extracted
$g_1, ..., g_{2m}$	Group nodes from meta-classifiers
$g_{2m+1}, ..., g_t$	Group nodes from unmapped runs
$A = [a_{ij}]$	Indicator of fact i in group j
$U = \vec{u_i}$	Conditional prob of $o_i = true$
$Q = \vec{q_i}$	Indicator of unmapped run $g_i = yes$
$Y = \vec{y_j}$	Indicator of meta-classifier $g_j = yes$
$F = \vec{f_i}$	o_i label if known a priori

Table 2: CM Fusion notations mapped to the SFV task.

Consensus Maximization operates as a bipartite graph between object nodes representing examples to classify and group nodes representing classes within each system. In the knowledge fusion domain, each object node pertains to a specific fact triple under consideration. The two classes for each system (*Yes/No*) all combined represent the set of group nodes. The translation component of CM Fusion generates the bipartite graph in Figure 2 as input to the consensus maximization component.

The overall goal of consensus maximization is to combine labeled predictions from the M supervised meta-classifiers and consensus predictions from the unsupervised systems using a constrained optimization framework. As recalled in Section 2, CM optimizes U and Q, which are conditional probabilities between object nodes (facts) and classes (*Yes/No*) and between group nodes (output classes for each system) and classes (*Yes/No*) respectively. Because we are only interested in the *Yes* class probabilities, the matrices collapse into vectors $\vec{u}$ and $\vec{q}$ as per equation 3. $\vec{u_i}$ is initialized as an uninformed prior with value 0.5 for each object node. Since unsupervised output labels are known a priori, $\vec{q_j}$ remains unchanged in the optimization process and encodes the pertinence of each group node j to a *Yes/No* class. Finally $\vec{y_j}$ includes the supervised meta-classifier output for each group. Running the

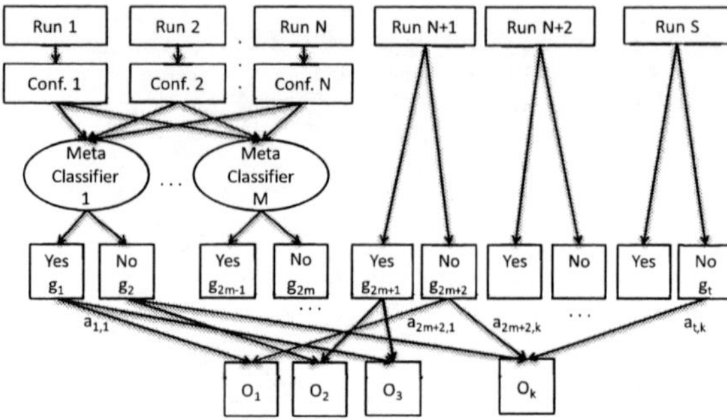

Figure 2: CM Bipartite graph for SFV. Object nodes correspond to facts. Each of S systems partition facts into *Yes* or *No* classes, which act as groups in CM translation.

optimization program generates a final $\vec{u}_i$ that gives a posterior probability for each fact. Table 2 maps all CM symbols in equation 3 to their corresponding elements in the SFV problem definition.

3.4 Enforced Constraints

After applying consensus maximization, there may be some facts that can be eliminated using functionality constraints. A slot is functional when it has only one possible value for its filler. Functional slots with different fillers may have certain facts eliminated based on mutual exclusion. As an example, consider the various slot filler responses in Table 1. An organization can only have its headquarters in one city at any given time. In this case *Menlo Park* should be chosen based on it having the maximum probability and all other facts eliminated. When the extraction probability is the same for multiple systems, one of the extractions is chosen at random. Nevertheless, this is hardly ever the case.

4 Experiments

We evaluate our system using a collection of queries supplied by TAC-KBP SFV. In this section we more fully describe the dataset and our experiment methodology. We compare to the current state-of-the-art ESF and SFV systems and show an improvement in F1 score. Finally, we provide an analysis of our results.

4.1 Datasets

Three datasets were used for training and testing spread across the three years that the English Slot

Filling task has been run. Each team in the competition submits multiple models vying for the highest score on unseen training data. Each submission is viewed as a different system in our ensemble. 2013 contains 52 systems. 2014 contains 65 and 2015 contains 69. In 2013 and 2014 we use only ESF data, but 2015 adds Cold Start Knowledge Base (CSKB) data. The total number of labeled queries in both 2013 and 2014 were 100 each. 2015 had 9340 unlabeled queries. In addition, 2015 had 164 labeled queries supplied for initial system assessment that was incorporated into the training data for 2015 submissions.

We performed two distinct experiments and compared multiple baselines for each. Table 3 shows results where we trained on 2013 only and tested on 2014 data only. Table 4 results are for training on 2013 and 2014 data and testing on 2015 data.

4.2 0-Hop and 1-Hop Queries

The 2015 ESF task introduced more complex queries into the fold. 1-hop queries use the result of a previous query to answer a new query. For example, consider a query asking for all companies headquartered in the same city as Facebook. The equivalent 1-hop query is (*Facebook*, *org:city_of_headquarters*, *?x*), (*?x*, *gpe:headquarters_in_city*, *). The second part of the query can be seen as a join to the first part using a common answer in both. The terminology exploits the idea of "hopping" from one query to another. By contrast, a regular slot filling task is a 0-hop query.

4.3 Evaluation

All systems were evaluated using the standard metrics of precision, recall, and F1 which is the harmonic mean of precision and recall. Precision is the amount of correctly extracted facts compared to the total facts extracted by the system. Recall is the amount of correct facts compared all facts in the ground truth. In review:

$$Recall(R) = \frac{Correct}{Total} \tag{4}$$

$$Precision(P) = \frac{Correct}{Extracted} \tag{5}$$

$$F1 = 2\frac{PR}{P+R} \tag{6}$$

Method	P	R	F1
LR	0.648	0.335	0.441
LR + REL	0.662	0.343	0.452
LR + PROV + REL	0.634	0.374	0.470
SVM	0.639	0.319	0.425
SVM + REL	0.720	0.299	0.422
SVM + PROV + REL	**0.729**	0.298	0.423
MV	0.467	0.447	0.457
Stanford	0.585	0.298	0.395
CM Fusion	0.549	**0.538**	**0.544**

Table 3: Result comparisons for the testing on the 2014 SFV task with training done on 2013 ESF data. The first 6 methods correspond to stacking while the others correspond to majority vote, the best performing 2014 ESF system, and CM Fusion. By increasing recall, CM Fusion has the highest F1 among all baselines.

	P	R	F1	Queries
2013 & 2014	**0.528**	0.481	0.504	
2014 only	0.477	**0.539**	**0.506**	0-Hop
BBN	0.493	0.391	0.436	
2013 & 2014	**0.393**	0.097	0.155	
2014 only	0.314	0.141	0.194	1-Hop
Stanford	0.184	**0.304**	**0.229**	
2013 & 2014	**0.503**	0.307	0.381	
2014 only	0.436	**0.358**	**0.393**	ALL
BBN	0.378	0.261	0.309	

Table 4: Summary of submissions to the SFV 2015 task for different query types. We trained the meta-classifiers on 2014 ESF data or 2013 and 2014 ESF data. Comparison is made to the highest scoring individual ESF system by F1.

The 0-hop queries are scored trivially on the correctness of the slot filler. The 1-hop queries require two verifications to undergo scoring. The 0-hop query from which it was derived must both exist and be correct. Any slot fillers that don't meet this criteria are omitted even if their 1-hop slot was ultimately correct. For example, the 1-hop extraction (*Palo Alto*, *gpe:headquarters_in_city*, *Hewlett-Packard*) will be ignored even though it is correct because the 0-hop query (*Facebook*, *gpe:city_of_headquarters*, *Palo Alto*) that derives it is incorrect (Facebook is headquarted in Menlo Park).

4.4 Results

Table 3 shows results using 2013 ESF systems as training data for the meta-classifiers and 2014 ESF systems as testing data. The first 6 rows are a combination of classifiers and feature vectors using stacking as described in (Viswanathan et al., 2015). MV refers to the majority voting described (Sammons et al., 2014). Majority voting accepts a fact if a certain number of systems above some learned threshold have extracted it. Both of these systems showcased results on the 2014 SFV task. The Stanford system (Angeli et al., 2014) was the best performing ESF system during the 2014 competition. The final row is our CM Fusion algorithm. Only 0-hop queries are used for these results.

Table 4 showcases two of the three runs we officially submitted as part of the recent 2015 SFV task for different query types. For each query, the first two rows refer to our CM Fusion system with different training data and the final row the best performing 2015 ESF system for that particular query type. 2015 results are not officially published yet for either ESF or SFV. Nevertheless, at 2015 workshop announcing the results, CM Fusion was awarded as the top ranked SFV system by F1 score.

4.5 Analysis

The main drawback between previous ensemble systems that utilize only supervised systems is high precision, but very low recall. This is evidenced in the disproportion between precision and recall in the first 6 systems of Table 3. Majority voting, while learning a threshold using supervision, does include some unsupervised consensus.

The main idea behind CM Fusion is to take into account the answers from potentially well-ranked extractors that stacking meta-classifiers omit due lack of training data. CM Fusion outperforms both approaches in terms of F1 by greatly increasing the recall while maintaining high precision. It also produces better results than the best performing 2014 ESF system. On 2015 data in Table 4, both systems outperform the best performing 2015 ESF system.

The benefit of using CM Fusion over other supervised ensemble models is the ability to use unsupervised systems that lack sufficient training data. When these systems agree on extractions, their consensus can be a source of discriminative power which CM Fusion is able to harness. For our submis-

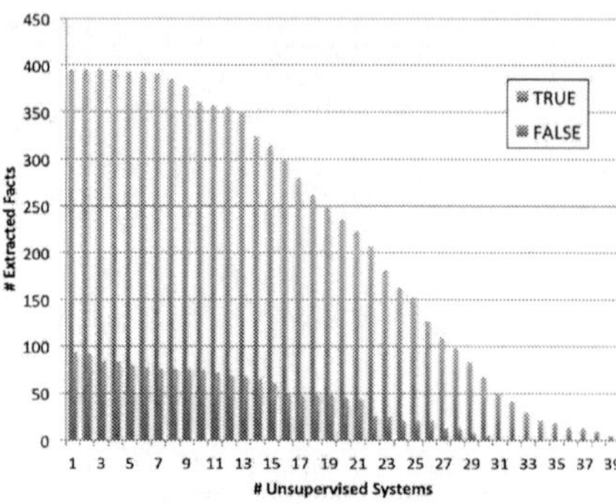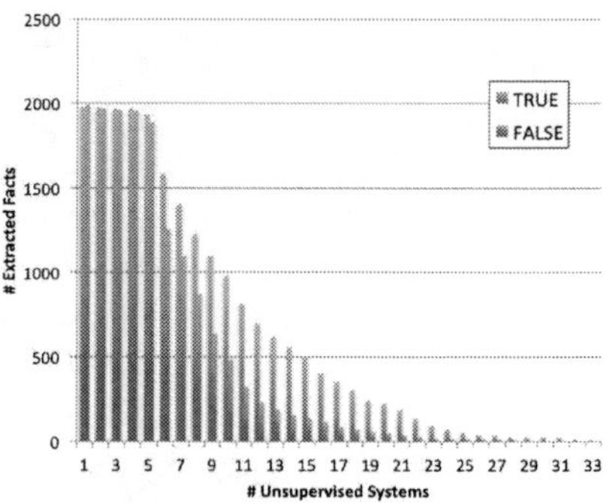

Figure 3: Extracted facts among unsupervised systems that agree with at least one supervised system using 2015 queries. The x-axis shows the minimum number of systems used for consensus.

Figure 4: Extracted facts among unsupervised systems using 2015 queries using only unsupervised consensus. The x-axis shows the minimum number of systems used for consensus. The scale is larger than Figure 3 because agreement with a supervised system is not needed.

sion trained only on 2014 ESF data, Figures 3 and 4 break down the difference between extracted facts derivable only from supervised systems and those able to be attained from unsupervised systems.

Specifically, Figure 3 measures the number of extracted facts supported by a consensus of the number of systems on the x-axis that also agree with the output of a supervised system. Blue bars represent the amount of correct extractions and red bars incorrect extractions. When only supervision is used there is good precision across the board. Figure 4 shows the number of extracted facts supported only by a consensus of systems on the x-axis without any supervision. The disparity in the scale of facts extracted supports the recall of supervised systems. When only a few systems agree on an extraction, about as many good facts are extracted as bad ones. As consensus increases, precision greatly improves. This idea of unsupervised consensus is exactly what improves CM Fusion over supervised ensemble approaches.

To understand the impact of the number of unsupervised systems fused and the quality of the fused runs in the ensemble, we applied CM Fusion in an incremental fashion by adding one unsupervised system at a time and scored the produced ensemble at each step. Techniques for ranking unsupervised systems are outside the scope of this work, for simplicity we examine the best- and worst-cases for adding systems incrementally. Ranking each unsupervised system by its final individual F1 score on

the SFV 2015 data, we ran CM Fusion adding the best performing run (CMF-BEST) and worst performing run (CMF-WORST) at each step. The results are displayed in Figure 5. For comparison, we also included the results of the best performing ESF system (BBN-F1) and the score of a supervised-only ensemble (SUP-ONLY). Fusing unsupervised systems with lower accuracy negatively affects the quality of the ensemble compared to supervised-only. When ensembleing very similar runs, such as runs submitted by the same team, the diversity of the systems is compromised and may lower the ensemble quality. On the other hand, unsupervised systems with higher accuracy can rapidly increase the quality of the ensemble above the best individual results and reach the highest ensemble score. Nevertheless, more does not necessarily mean better, as shown in the plateau of the best-case plot in Figure 5, when noisy systems are added to the ensemble the F1 score is maintained. The average case would lie somewhere in between the extremes of the best- and worst-case. As is shown, a large number of systems are extremely error-prone, but the combination using CM Fusion produces a result ultimately superior.

5 Conclusions

This paper presented our Consensus Maximization Fusion of multiple probabilistic information extractors. This approach combines supervised stacking

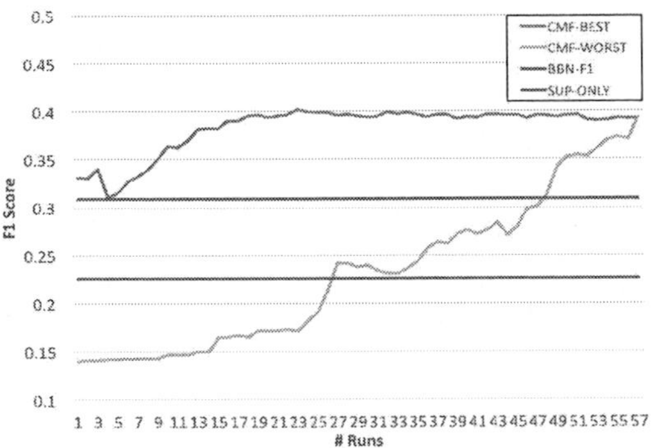

Figure 5: Incremental CM Fusion in terms of adding best-performing (blue) and worst-performing (green) systems one-by-one. Performance is ranked by F1 scores from the 2015 SFV dataset. F1 scores are in the range [0.03 − 0.309] with an average F1 of 0.140

meta-classifiers with unsupervised extraction outputs in an ensemble classifier. Our system outperformed the current state-of-the-art ensemble models submitted to the TAC-KBP Slot Filler Validation task in 2014. CM Fusion was also chosen as the leading system at the 2015 TAC-KBP Workshop. This is the first cross-model ensemble approach that fuses multiple knowledge graphs obtained from both supervised and unsupervised information extractors. Optimal performance is attained when the extractors represent different systems running over the same corpus and the shared extraction density is high.

The canonicalization of facts in CM Fusion represents a new state-of-the-art contribution to entity-centric information extraction compared to traditional document-centric approaches. While our approach has been experimentally verified using TAC-KBP data, it generalizes to overlapping ensemble of knowledge bases. Some such as NELL (Mitchell and Fredkin, 2014) have a small supervised human feedback component and others such as OpenIE (Banko et al., 2007) are entirely unsupervised. Future work concerns using CM Fusion to to align and canonicalize multiple such knowledge bases to solve the knowledge fusion problem.

Acknowledgments

This work is partially supported by NSF IIS Award #1526753, DARPA under FA8750-12-2-0348-2 (DEFT/CUBISM) and graduate fellowships from Fulbright and Sandia National Labs

References

Gabor Angeli, Julie Tibshirani, Jean Y Wu, and Christopher D Manning. 2014. Combining distant and partial supervision for relation extraction. In *Proceedings of the 2014 conference on empirical methods in natural language processing (EMNLP)*.

Michele Banko, Michael J Cafarella, Stephen Soderland, Matthew Broadhead, and Oren Etzioni. 2007. Open information extraction for the web. In *IJCAI*, volume 7, pages 2670–2676.

Xin Dong, Evgeniy Gabrilovich, Geremy Heitz, Wilko Horn, Ni Lao, Kevin Murphy, Thomas Strohmann, Shaohua Sun, and Wei Zhang. 2014. Knowledge vault: A web-scale approach to probabilistic knowledge fusion. In *Proceedings of the 20th ACM SIGKDD international conference on Knowledge discovery and data mining*, pages 601–610. ACM.

Jing Gao, Feng Liang, Wei Fan, Yizhou Sun, and Jiawei Han. 2009. Graph-based consensus maximization among multiple supervised and unsupervised models. In *Advances in Neural Information Processing Systems*, pages 585–593.

Jing Gao, Wei Fan, and Jiawei Han. 2010. On the power of ensemble: Supervised and unsupervised methods reconciled. In *Tutorial on SIAM data mining conference(SDM)*. Citeseer.

Tom Mitchell and E Fredkin. 2014. Never ending language learning. In *Big Data (Big Data), 2014 IEEE International Conference on*, pages 1–1. IEEE.

Mark Sammons, Yangqiu Song, Ruichen Wang, Gourab Kundu, Chen-Tse Tsai, Shyam Upadhyay, Siddarth Ancha, Stephen Mayhew, and Dan Roth. 2014. Overview of ui-ccg systems for event argument extraction, entity discovery and linking, and slot filler validation. *Urbana*, 51:61801.

Fabian M Suchanek, Gjergji Kasneci, and Gerhard Weikum. 2007. Yago: a core of semantic knowledge. In *Proceedings of the 16th international conference on World Wide Web*, pages 697–706. ACM.

Mihai Surdeanu and Heng Ji. 2014. Overview of the english slot filling track at the tac2014 knowledge base population evaluation. In *Proc. Text Analysis Conference (TAC2014)*.

Vidhoon Viswanathan, Nazneen Fatema Rajani, Yinon Bentor, and Raymond Mooney. 2015. Stacked ensembles of information extractors for knowledge-base population. In *Proceedings of ACL*.

Simple, Fast Noise-Contrastive Estimation for Large RNN Vocabularies

Barret Zoph*, Ashish Vaswani*, Jonathan May, and Kevin Knight
Information Sciences Institute
Department of Computer Science
University of Southern California
{zoph, avaswani, jonmay, knight}@isi.edu

Abstract

We present a simple algorithm to efficiently train language models with noise-contrastive estimation (NCE) on graphics processing units (GPUs). Our NCE-trained language models achieve significantly lower perplexity on the One Billion Word Benchmark language modeling challenge, and contain one sixth of the parameters in the best single model in Chelba et al. (2013). When incorporated into a strong Arabic-English machine translation system they give a strong boost in translation quality. We release a toolkit so that others may also train large-scale, large vocabulary LSTM language models with NCE, parallelizing computation across multiple GPUs.

1 Introduction

Language models are used to compute probabilities of sequences of words. They are crucial for good performance in tasks like machine translation, speech recognition, and spelling correction. They can be classified into two categories: count-based and continuous-space language models. The language modeling literature abounds with successful approaches for learning-count based language models: modified Kneser-Ney smoothing, Jelinek-Mercer smoothing, etc. In recent years, continuous-space language models such as feed-forward neural probabilistic language models (NPLMs) and recurrent neural network language models (RNNs)[1]

---

*Equal contribution.

[1]Henceforth we will use terms like "RNN" and "LSTM" with the understanding that we are referring to language models that use these formalisms

have outperformed their count-based counterparts (Chelba et al., 2013; Zaremba et al., 2014; Mikolov, 2012). RNNs are more powerful than n-gram language models, as they can exploit longer word contexts to predict words. Long short-term memory language models (LSTMs) are a class of RNNs that have been designed to model long histories and are easier to train than standard RNNs. LSTMs are currently the best performing language models on the Penn Treebank (PTB) dataset (Zaremba et al., 2014).

The most common method for training LSTMs, maximum likelihood estimation (MLE), is prohibitively expensive for large vocabularies, as it involves time-intensive matrix-matrix multiplications. Noise-contrastive estimation (NCE) has been a successful alternative to train continuous space language models with large vocabularies (Mnih and Teh, 2012; Vaswani et al., 2013). However, NCE in its standard form is not suitable for GPUs, as the computations are not amenable to dense matrix operations. In this paper, we present a natural modification to the NCE objective function for language modeling that allows a very efficient GPU implementation. Using our new objective, we train large multi-layer LSTMs on the One Billion Word benchmark (Chelba et al., 2013), with its full 780k word vocabulary. We achieve significantly lower perplexities with a single model, while using only a sixth of the parameters of a very strong baseline model (Chelba et al., 2013). We release our toolkit[2] to allow researchers to train large-scale, large-vocabulary LSTMs with NCE. The contributions in this paper are the following:

---

[2]www.github.com/isi-nlp/Zoph_RNN

Proceedings of NAACL-HLT 2016, pages 1217–1222,
San Diego, California, June 12-17, 2016. ©2016 Association for Computational Linguistics

- A fast and simple approach for handling large vocabularies effectively on the GPU.

- Significantly improved perplexities (43.2) on the One Billion Word benchmark over Chelba et al. (2013)

- Extrinsic machine translation improvement over a strong baseline.

- Fast decoding times because in practice there is no need to normalize.

2 Long Short Term Memory Language Models

In recent years, LSTMs (Hochreiter and Schmidhuber, 1997) have achieved state-of-the-art performance in many natural language tasks such as language modeling (Zaremba et al., 2014) and statistical machine translation (Sutskever et al., 2014; Luong et al., 2015). LSTMs were designed to have longer memories than standard RNNs, allowing them to exploit more context to make predictions. To compute word probabilities, the LSTM reads words left-to-right, updating its memory after each word and producing a hidden state h, which summarizes all of the history. For details on the architecture and computations of the LSTM, the reader can refer to (Zaremba et al., 2014). In this model the probability of word w given history $\mathbf{u}$ is

$$P(w \mid \mathbf{u}) = \frac{p(w \mid \mathbf{u})}{\mathbf{Z}(\mathbf{u})}, \qquad (1)$$

where $p(w \mid \mathbf{u}) = \exp D_w h^T + b_w$ is an unnormalized probability. D_w and b_w are the output word embedding and biases respectively, which are learned during training. The normalization constant is $\mathbf{Z}(u) = \sum_{w \in V} p(w \mid \mathbf{u})$, and V is the vocabulary.

3 Noise Contrastive Estimation For Training Neural Language Models

The standard approach for estimating neural language models is maximum liklelihood estimation (MLE), where we learn the parameters θ^* that maximize the likelihood of the training data,

$$\theta^* = arg\,max_\theta \sum_{w,\mathbf{u}} \log P(w \mid \mathbf{u}; \theta) \qquad (2)$$

However, for each training instance, gradient-based approaches for MLE require a summation over all units in the output layer, one for each word in V. This makes MLE training infeasible for large vocabularies.

Noise-contrastive estimation (NCE) (Gutmann and Hyvärinen, 2010) has been successfully adopted for training neural language models with large vocabularies (Mnih and Teh, 2012; Vaswani et al., 2013; Baltescu and Blunsom, 2014; Williams et al., 2015). NCE avoids repeated summations by training the model to correctly classify between generated noise samples and words observed in the training data. For each training pair $\mathbf{u}_i, w_i$, we generate k noise samples, $\bar{w}_{i1} \ldots, \bar{w}_{ik}$ from a noise distribution $q(w)$, which is known. We label $\mathbf{u}_i, w_i$ as true ($C = 1$), and all $\mathbf{u}_i, \bar{w}_{ik}$ as false ($C = 0$). We then train the parameters to maximize the binary classification log likelihood,

$$\mathbf{L} = \sum_i \Big(\log P(C = 1 \mid \mathbf{u}_i, w_i) + \\ \sum_k \log P(C = 0 \mid \mathbf{u}, \bar{w}_{ik}) \Big), \qquad (3)$$

where

$$P(C = 1 \mid w, \mathbf{u}) = \frac{\frac{p(w \mid \mathbf{u})}{\mathbf{Z}(\mathbf{u})}}{\frac{p(w \mid \mathbf{u})}{\mathbf{Z}(\mathbf{u})} + k \cdot q(w)}, \qquad (4)$$

and $P(C = 0 \mid w, \mathbf{u}) = 1 - P(C = 1 \mid w, \mathbf{u})$.

We learn parameters to maximize this objective with gradient ascent. In NCE, we treat $\mathbf{Z}(\mathbf{u})$ as another parameter and learn its estimate along with the rest of the parameters. Following Mnih and Teh (2012) and Vaswani et al. (2013), we freeze $\mathbf{Z}(\mathbf{u})$ to 1 and the model learns to approximately satisfy the constraint. In practice, we find that our mean for $\mathbf{Z}(\mathbf{u})$ is very close to 1 and the variance is quite small (Section 6). For each training instance, we compute gradients for the observed word and each noise word, reducing the time complexity from $\mathcal{O}(|V|)$ for MLE to $\mathcal{O}(k)$. However, unlike MLE, since we typically sample different noise samples for each training instance, our gradient computations for the NCE objective are not amenable to dense matrix operations, making it difficult to benefit from fast dense matrix arithmetic on GPUs. In this paper, we present a simple solution to this problem: sharing the noise samples across all the training instances in a minibatch. Sharing noise samples allows us to describe NCE gradients with dense matrix operations, and implement them easily on the GPU. In the next section, we describe our NCE implementation on the GPU with shared noise samples.

4   Our NCE Modification

In typical Noise-Contrastive Estimation, the objective function requires noise samples coming from some distribution (in our case, the uniform distribution). The objective function for NCE is shown above in Equation 3, where we must calculate $P(C = 1 \mid w, \mathbf{u})$ for the true word and the noise samples generated. There are three components to this calculation: $p(w \mid \mathbf{u})$, $\mathbf{Z}(\mathbf{u})$, and $k \cdot q(w)$. In NCE we fix $\mathbf{Z}(\mathbf{u})$ to be one, so we only need to calculate $p(w \mid \mathbf{u})$ and $k \cdot q(w)$. The term $k \cdot q(w)$ is simply an $O(1)$ lookup, so the only costly operation is computing $p(w \mid \mathbf{u})$ for all k noise samples and the true word. The operation to compute $p(w \mid \mathbf{u})$ for a single word w is $\exp D_w h^T + b_w$ where D_w and b_w represent the word embedding and bias corresponding to the word we are computing it for.

The main cost in calculating the NCE objective function is computing $\exp D_w h^T + b_w$, where in normal NCE a dense matrix multiplication cannot be done. The reason is that the noise samples generated per training example will be different. Therefore, when we parallelize our algorithm by running multiple training examples in parallel (a minibatch), the D_w we need are different per h^T that we are running in parallel. If a constraint is set such that the noise samples must be the same across all training examples in the minibatch, then a matrix multiplication can be done to compute $\exp D_w h^T + b_w$ for all words across that minibatch. This matrix multiplication is $D h_M^T$, where h_M^T is now a matrix of all the hidden states being used in parallel, whereas before h_T was just a vector. Additionally, D is the matrix of word embedding for the samples that are being shared across a minibatch. Before, this was not possible as the D matrix would have to be much larger, being (minibatch size) $\cdot (k + 1)$ in size, making the algorithm run much slower. An alternative is to not restrict the noise samples to be the same,

but then we must use a sparse matrix multiplication as in Williams et al. (2015), which is neither as fast nor as easy to implement. A comparison between these two approaches is shown in Figure 1. We find that sharing noise samples across the minibatch gives us significant speedups over a baseline of using different noise samples for each word in the minibatch. These timings were calculated for a single layer LSTM with 1000 hidden units, a vocabulary of $350k$, and a minibatch of 128. Not surprisingly, MLE is quite expensive, limiting it's use for large vocabularies. Additionally, the memory requirements for NCE are much lower than MLE, since we do not need to store the gradient which has the same size as the output embedding matrix. For this MLE run, we had to distribute the computation across two GPUs because of memory limitations.

5   Experiments

We conducted two series of experiments to validate the efficiency of our approach and the quality of the models we learned using it: An *intrinsic* study of language model perplexity using the standard One Billion Word benchmark (Chelba et al., 2013) and an *extrinsic* end-to-end statistical machine translation task that uses an LSTM as one of several feature functions in re-ranking. Both experiments achieve excellent results.

5.1   Language Modeling

For our language modeling experiment we use the One Billion Word benchmark proposed by Chelba et al. (2013). In this task there are roughly 0.8 billion words of training data. We use perplexity to evaluate the quality of language models we train on this data. We train an LSTM with 4 layers, where each layer has 2048 hidden units, with a target vocabulary size of 793,471. For training, we also use dropout to prevent overfitting. We follow Zaremba et al. (2014) for dropout locations, and we use a dropout rate of 0.2. The training is parallelized across 4 GPUs, such that each layer lies on its own GPU and communicates its activations to the next layer once it finishes its computation.

5.2   Statistical Machine Translation

We incorporate our LSTM as a rescoring feature on top of the output of a strong Arabic-English syntax-based string-to-tree statistical machine translation system (Galley et al., 2006; Galley et al., 2004). That system is trained on 208 million words of parallel Arabic-English data from a variety of sources, much of which is Egyptian discussion forum content. The Arabic side is morphologically segmented with MADA-ARZ (Habash et al., 2013). We use a standard set of features, including two conventional count-based language models, as well as thousands of sparsely-occurring, lexicalized syntactic features (Chiang et al., 2009). The system additionally uses a source-to-target feed-forward neural network translation model during decoding, analogous to the model of (Devlin et al., 2014). These features are tuned with MIRA (Chiang et al., 2009) on approximately 63,000 words of Arabic discussion forum text, along with three references. We evaluate this baseline on two test sets, each with approximately 34,000 words from the same genre used in tuning.

We generate n-best lists ($n = 1000$) of unique translations for each sentence in the tuning set and re-rank the translations using an approach based on MERT (Och, 2003). We collapse all features other than language models, text length, and derivation size into a single feature, formed by taking the dot product of the previously learned feature and weight vectors. We then run a single iteration of MERT on the n-best lists to determine optimal weights for the collapsed feature, the uncollapsed features, and an LSTM feature formed by taking the score of the hypothesis according to the LSTM described in Section 5.1. We use the weights to rerank hypotheses from the n-best lists of the two test sets. We repeated this experiment, substituting instead a two-layer LSTM trained on the English side of the training data.

6 Results

Our two experiments with LSTMs trained with our modification of NCE show strong results in their corresponding tasks.

Our perplexity results are shown in Table 1, where we get significantly lower perplexities than the best single model from Chelba et al. (2013), while having almost 6 times fewer parameters. We also compute the partition function values, $\log(Z(\mathbf{u}))$, for our development set and we find that the mean is 0.058 and the variance is 0.139, indicating that training has encouraged self-normalization.

Model	Parameters	Perplexity
Chelba et al. (2013)	20m	51.3
NCE (ours)	3.4m	43.2

Table 1: For the One Billion Word Benchmark, our NCE method performs significantly better than the best single model in the baseline, Chelba et al. (2013), while using many fewer parameters.

Recently, (Józefowicz et al., 2016) achieved state-of-the-art language modeling perplexities (30.0) on the billion word dataset with a single model, using importance sampling to approximate the normalization constant, $\mathbf{Z(u)}$.

Independent of our work, they also share noise samples across the minibatch. However, they use 8192 noise samples, while we achieve strong perplexities with 100 noise samples. We also show significant improvements in machine translation, exploiting self-normalization for fast decoding, in addition to releasing a efficient toolkit that practitioners can use.

Table 2 shows our re-scoring experiments. When we incorporate only the LSTM trained on the BOLT dataset we get a +1.1 BLEU improvement on Tune, +1.4 on Test 1, and +1.1 on Test 2. When we also incorporate the LSTM trained on the One Billion Word dataset as a feature, we see another +0.2 BLEU increase on Tune and Test 2. In

System	Tune	Test 1	Test 2
Baseline SMT	38.7	38.9	39.7
LSTM (BOLT)	39.8	40.3	40.8
LSTM (1b+BOLT)	40.0	40.3	41.0

Table 2: Our NCE-based language model successfully re-ranks Arabic-to-English n-best lists. The baseline is a state-of-the-art, statistical string-to-tree system. BOLT is a 208m-word, in-domain English corpus; "1b" refers to the One Billion Word benchmark corpus.

these re-scoring experiments we simply use the un-normalized numerator $p(w \mid \mathbf{u})$ as our word score, which means we never have to compute the costly partition function, $\mathbf{Z}(u)$. This is because the partition function is so close to 1 that the un-normalized

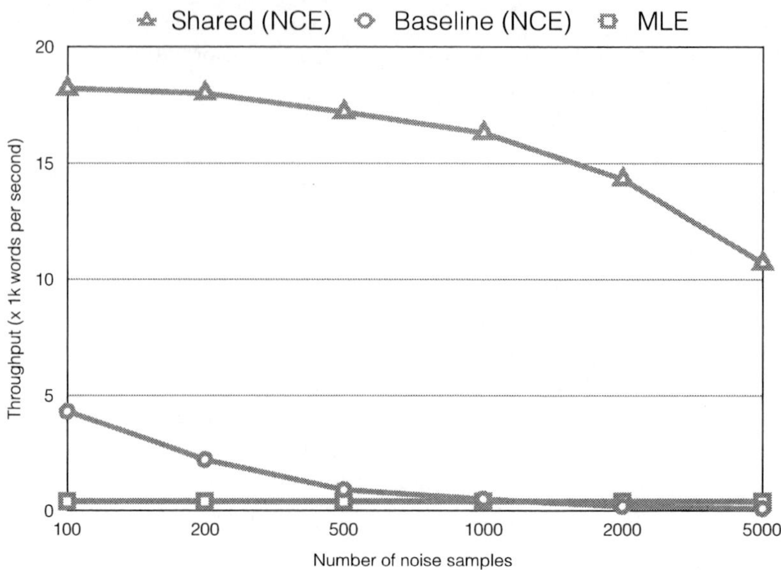

Figure 1: Sharing noise samples across the minibatch is at least 4 times faster than a baseline of not sharing them.

scores are very close to the normalized ones.

7 Conclusion

We describe a natural extension to NCE that achieves a large speedup on the GPU while also achieving good empirical results. LSTM models trained with our NCE modification achieve strong results on the One Billion Word dataset. Additionally, we get good BLEU gains when re-ranking n-best lists from a strong string-to-tree machine translation system. We also release an efficient toolkit for training LSTM language models with NCE.

8 Acknowledgments

This work was carried out with funding from DARPA (HR0011-15-C-0115) and ARL/ARO (W911NF-10-1-0533).

References

P. Baltescu and P. Blunsom. 2014. Pragmatic neural language modelling in machine translation. *arXiv preprint arXiv:1412.7119.*

C. Chelba, T. Mikolov, M. Schuster, Q. Ge, T. Brants, and P. Koehn. 2013. One billion word benchmark for measuring progress in statistical language modeling. *CoRR*, abs/1312.3005.

D. Chiang, K. Knight, and W. Wang. 2009. 11,001 new features for statistical machine translation. In *Proc. NAACL.*

J. Devlin, R. Zbib, Z. Huang, T. Lamar, R. Schwartz, and J. Makhoul. 2014. Fast and robust neural network joint models for statistical machine translation. In *Proc. ACL.*

M. Galley, M. Hopkins, K. Knight, and D. Marcu. 2004. What's in a translation rule? In *Proc. HLT-NAACL.*

M. Galley, J. Graehl, K. Knight, D. Marcu, S. DeNeefe, W. Wang, and I. Thayer. 2006. Scalable inference and training of context-rich syntactic translation models. In *Proc. ACL-COLING.*

M. Gutmann and A. Hyvärinen. 2010. Noise-contrastive estimation: A new estimation principle for unnormalized statistical models. In *Proc. AI Stats.*

N. Habash, R. Roth, O. Rambow, R. Eskander, and N. Tomeh. 2013. Morphological analysis and disambiguation for dialectal arabic. In *Proc. NAACL.*

S. Hochreiter and J. Schmidhuber. 1997. Long short-term memory. *Neural Computation*, 9(8):1735–1780.

Rafal Józefowicz, Oriol Vinyals, Mike Schuster, Noam Shazeer, and Yonghui Wu. 2016. Exploring the limits of language modeling. *CoRR*, abs/1602.02410.

M. Luong, H. Pham, and C. Manning. 2015. Effective

approaches to attention-based neural machine translation. *arXiv preprint arXiv:1508.04025*.

Tomáš Mikolov. 2012. Statistical language models based on neural networks. *Presentation at Google, Mountain View, 2nd April*.

A. Mnih and Y. W. Teh. 2012. A fast and simple algorithm for training neural probabilistic language models. *arXiv preprint arXiv:1206.6426*.

F. J. Och. 2003. Minimum error rate training in statistical machine translation. In *Proc. ACL*.

I. Sutskever, O. Vinyals, and Q. V. Le. 2014. Sequence to sequence learning with neural networks. In *Proc. NIPS*, pages 3104–3112.

A. Vaswani, Y. Zhao, V. Fossum, and D. Chiang. 2013. Decoding with large-scale neural language models improves translation. In *Proc. EMNLP*.

W. Williams, N. Prasad, D. Mrva, T. Ash, and T. Robinson. 2015. Scaling recurrent neural network language models. *CoRR*, abs/1502.00512.

W. Zaremba, I. Sutskever, and O. Vinyals. 2014. Recurrent neural network regularization. *arXiv preprint arXiv:1409.2329*.

Automatically Inferring Implicit Properties in Similes

Ashequl Qadir and **Ellen Riloff**
School of Computing
University of Utah
Salt Lake City, UT 84112, USA
{asheq, riloff}@cs.utah.edu

Marilyn A. Walker
Natural Language and Dialogue Systems Lab
University of California Santa Cruz
Santa Cruz, CA 95064, USA
mawalker@ucsc.edu

Abstract

A simile is a figure of speech comparing two fundamentally different things. Sometimes, a simile will explain the basis of a comparison by explicitly mentioning a shared property. For example, *"my room is as cold as Antarctica"* gives "cold" as the property shared by the room and Antarctica. But most similes do not give an explicit property (e.g., *"my room feels like Antarctica"*) leaving the reader to infer that the room is cold. We tackle the problem of automatically inferring implicit properties evoked by similes. Our approach involves three steps: (1) generating candidate properties from different sources, (2) evaluating properties based on the influence of multiple simile components, and (3) aggregated ranking of the properties. We also present an analysis showing that the difficulty of inferring an implicit property for a simile correlates with its *interpretive diversity*.

1 Introduction

A simile is a figure of speech comparing two essentially unlike things, typically using "like" or "as" (Paul, 1970). Comparing fundamentally different types of entities is what makes a simile figurative (Israel et al., 2004). Similes may be *closed* or *open* (Beardsley, 1981). A *closed* simile explains the basis for a comparison by explicitly mentioning a shared property. For example, the simile *"my room is as cold as Antarctica"* gives "cold" as the property shared by both the room and Antarctica. But most similes do not explicitly mention the basis for comparison, leaving people to infer what the entities have in common. An *open* simile expressing

the same comparison is *"my room feels like Antarctica"*, where the shared property of being cold is left implicit. In our study of similes in tweets, we found that 92% of similes are open similes so the property must be inferred. Our research tackles this problem of inferring the implicit property evoked by an open simile.

Inferring the basis of comparison in a simile is central to natural language understanding and metaphor interpretation. For example, *"John was like a lion in battle"* is probably a statement about John's bravery or courage, not a description of John's physical appearance. Methods to understand figurative similes could also be valuable to understand metaphor in other linguistic constructions, such as predicate nominals (e.g., *"he is a lion"*). Furthermore, identifying the implicit property of a simile could be useful for sentiment analysis, because similes are often used to express positive and negative feelings (Li et al., 2012). For example, *"John was like a lion in battle"* contains only neutral words, but inferring "bravery" as the implicit property suggests that the simile has positive polarity.

We designed a three step process to infer the implicit properties of open similes. First, we generate candidate properties for a simile by harvesting words that are associated with its verb ("event") or object of comparison ("vehicle") using a variety of methods, including syntactic patterns, dictionary definitions, and word embeddings. Each candidate property is generated from just one component of the simile. The second step of the process then evaluates each property's compatibility with the complementary component of the simile (event or vehi-

Proceedings of NAACL-HLT 2016, pages 1223–1232,
San Diego, California, June 12-17, 2016. ©2016 Association for Computational Linguistics

cle). Finally, the third step of the process aggregates all of the candidates generated by different methods and ranks them based on collective evidence from the different sources. We evaluate the performance of our approach using gold standard properties provided by seven human annotators. We also present an analysis of the similes in our data set with respect to their *interpretive diversity* (intuitively, a measure of how many plausible interpretations a simile has). We show that our method performs best on similes with low diversity, as one would expect since their implicit properties are most clear to humans.

2 Problem Description and Data

A simile typically consists of four key components: the **topic** or **tenor** (subject of the comparison), the **vehicle** (object of the comparison), the **event** (act or state), and a **comparator** (usually "as", "like", or "than") (Niculae and Danescu-Niculescu-Mizil, 2014). For the simile *"the room feels like Antarctica"*, "room" is the tenor, "feels" is the event, and "Antarctica" is the vehicle. A **property** (shared attribute) can optionally be included to explicitly state how the tenor is being compared with the vehicle, (e.g., *"the room is as **cold** as Antarctica"*).

Table 1 shows examples of open similes from our Twitter data set, along with several properties inferred by our human annotators (our data set will be described in Section 2.1). We represent each simile using just the head noun of the tenor and vehicle, and the lemma of the event. Veale and Hao (2007) observed that when a property is explicitly given, it is usually a salient property of the vehicle. Table 1 illustrates some examples of inferred properties that are strongly associated with the vehicle (e.g., "melodic" and "dulcet" are musical attributes).

We observed that implicit properties can be strongly evoked from the event as well. For example, most inferred properties for *"person buzz like fridge"* emanate from the word "buzz", such as "humming", "vibrating", "distracting", and "annoying". Similarly, the tenor can also evoke properties, as we see with the inferred property "squinty" for the simile *"eye feel like clam"* although our observation is that this is less common. The event and the tenor need to be semantically rich to evoke implicit properties. The event in many similes is a form of

"to be" or a perception verb (e.g., "feels"), which are semantically weak and contribute little. A tenor provides limited information when it is a pronoun or unknown entity (e.g., *"John drives like a snail"* is understandable without knowing who John is).

Simile	Properties Inferred by Humans
laugh be like music	melodic, pleasing, dulcet, tinkly
person sound like prophet	wise, insightful, prescient, enlightened
eye feel like clam	slimy, squinty, weary, gummy, heavy
person look like carrot	orange, thin, scrawny, slim, tall
person buzz like fridge	humming, vibrating, distracting, annoying, motorized
person fight like animal	ferociously, scratches, tenaciously
person be like shark	sneaky, primordial, dangerous, cold
time be like river	flowing, fast, winding, unending, moving
praise be like sunlight	warm, rejuvenating, energizing, cheerful

Table 1: Similes with sample properties inferred by humans.

Ultimately, an implicit property must be compatible with the vehicle, event, and the tenor in order for a simile to make sense. For example, Antarctica is strongly associated with the color "white", but it would not make sense to infer the property "white" for the simile *"my room feels like Antarctica"* because of the verb "feel". Although in this example the tenor "room" is still compatible with "white" and will not help to eliminate "white" as a property, in other similes it may (e.g., rivers can be "wide", but time can not be, so "wide" can be eliminated as an implicit property in the simile "time be like river").

A novel aspect of our work is that our architecture is designed to consider a property's compatibility with multiple components. In this research, for generating candidate properties and utilizing their influence for compatibility, we particularly focus on the vehicle and event terms. Initially, we generate candidate properties from the vehicle and the event separately. But the second step then evaluates each candidate property's compatibility with the *complementary* simile component. If a property was initially generated from the vehicle, then we evaluate its compatibility with the event; if a property was initially generated from the event, then we evaluate its compatibility with the vehicle. This approach emphasizes the need to consider multiple components of a simile when inferring implicit properties.

2.1 Collecting Similes with Implicit Properties

For our research, we created a new data set of open similes, where the property is implicit. Similes are common on Twitter, so we extracted similes from roughly 140 million English tweets collected during the time period 2/13/2013 – 4/15/2014. To identify similes, we applied a part-of-speech tagger designed for Twitter (Owoputi et al., 2013) to tweets containing the word "like" and applied rules to recognize simple noun phrases and verb phrases. We then selected tweets matching the syntactic pattern: $NP_1\ VERB\ like\ NP_2$, where NP_2 can contain only a noun and an optional indefinite article. We required similes to have a vehicle term with no premodifiers to avoid problems associated with coreference (e.g., "the man" or "that man") and to focus on vehicles that represent general concepts. We leave for future work the challenge of tackling multi-word vehicle phrases (e.g., *"my room is like stepping into a hurricane"* or *"my room is like a boots store"*).

This selection process extracted many similes, but it also extracted literal comparisons with no apparent property (e.g., *"this flower smells like a rose"*) and statements that are not comparisons (e.g., *"I called like five times"*). To focus on figurative similes with an implicit property, we further filtered the collection to only retain similes with vehicle terms that had occurred in comparisons with an explicit property. Using the same Twitter data, we extracted nouns that appeared in the following syntactic patterns, which represent comparison constructions with an adjectival property: $ADJ\ like\ [a, an]\ NOUN$ (e.g., *"red like a tomato"*) and $ADJ\ as\ [a, an]\ NOUN$ (e.g., *"red as a tomato"*). We only kept similes whose vehicle occurred in these patterns. Finally, we filtered similes that contain a pronoun (except personal pronouns in the tenor, which we generalized to a *"person"* token), common person first names[1], profanity,[2] or words not in a dictionary[3] to avoid issues with Twitter language such as misspellings, elongated words, etc.

---

[1]http://deron.meranda.us/data/census-derived-all-first.txt
[2]http://www.bannedwordlist.com/lists/swearWords.txt
[3]Using Wordnik: https://www.wordnik.com/

2.2 Gold Standard Implicit Properties

We developed a gold standard set of implicit properties for each simile using Mechanical Turk. We prequalified 7 workers, who each annotated 700 similes with frequency ≥ 3 randomly selected from our collection. Each annotator was asked to provide up to 2 properties that best captured the most likely basis for comparison between the tenor and vehicle. We also provided the annotators with the option to label a simile as Invalid if it was not a simile at all (most commonly due to parse errors, such as *"he looks like ran"*) or label a simile as having No Property (often due to literal or underspecified comparisons, such as *"she looks like my aunt"*). The annotators were asked to give adjectives, adverbs, or verbs but occasionally they provided a noun. Table 1 presents sample annotated simile properties.

Among the 700 similes, a majority of the annotators labeled 59 of them as either Invalid or No Property, so we did not use these. We set aside 183 similes (29%) as a development set and the remaining 458 similes (71%) as a test set.

3 Inferring Implicit Properties

Our research tackles the problem of inferring properties in open similes by decomposing the problem into three subtasks: (1) generating candidate properties, (2) evaluating the candidate properties with respect to multiple simile components, and (3) aggregated ranking of the properties. Figure 1 illustrates our approach.

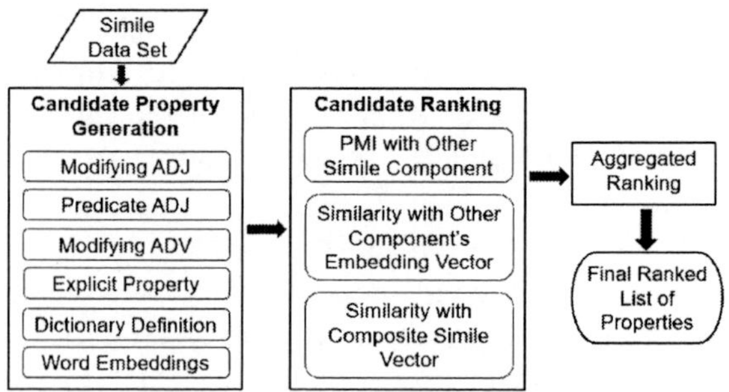

Figure 1: Framework for inferring implicit properties.

First, the vehicle and event components of a simile are used individually to generate candidate properties. We investigate a variety of candidate generation methods, including harvesting properties from syntactic structures and dictionary definitions, identifying relevant properties using statistical co-occurrence, and assessing similarity between word embedding vectors.

Second, the candidates generated by each method are evaluated based on their strength of association with the complementary component of the simile. For candidates generated from the vehicle term, we evaluate them based on their association with the event term, and vice versa. We explore three association measures: point-wise mutual information to measure statistical co-occurrence, and vector similarity using single and composite word embeddings.

Third, we produce an aggregate ranking over the entire set of properties hypothesized by *all* of the candidate generation methods. Intuitively, we view each candidate generation method as an independent source, and look at the aggregate evidence across the set of different candidate generation methods (similar to an ensemble). Each property is scored based on its average rank across the different methods, so that properties highly ranked by multiple methods are preferred.

3.1 Candidate Property Generation

We generate candidate properties from the vehicle and event words of a simile. However when the event is a form of "to be" or a perception verb (taste, smell, feel, sound, look), we do not generate candidate properties from the event because the verb is too general. Only 73 (16%) of the similes in our evaluation data have a verb other than "to be" or a perception verb. We restrict properties to be adjectives, adverbs, or verb forms that can function as nominal premodifiers (e.g., "crying baby", "wilted lettuce"). We explore a total of seven methods for generating candidate properties and generate candidates using our entire Twitter corpus.

Modifying ADJ: Given a vehicle term, we extract pre-modifying adjectives. For example, "ripe" is extracted for the vehicle "tomato" from the phrase "ripe tomato".

Predicate ADJ: Given a vehicle term, we extract adjectives in predicate adjective constructions with the vehicle. For example, "red" is extracted for the vehicle "tomato" from the phrase "tomato is red".

Modifying ADV: Given an event term (verb), we ex-tract adverbs that precede or follow the verb. For example, "immaturely" is extracted for the event "act" due to the phrase "acts immaturely".

Explicit Property: We extract properties mentioned explicitly in comparison phrases. For vehicle terms, we extract properties from phrases of the form: "ADJ/ADV like NP" (e.g., *"cold like Antarctica"*) and "ADJ/ADV as NP" (e.g., *"cold as Antarctica"*). For event terms, we extract properties from phrases of the form: "VERB ADJ/ADV like" and "VERB as ADJ/ADV as" (e.g., *"feels as cold as"*).

Dictionary Definition: Dictionary definitions often mention salient properties associated with a word. We harvest adjectives, adverbs and verbs (functioning as premodifiers) as candidate properties from the dictionary definitions of the vehicle and event terms. For the definitions, we use Wordnik[4], which contains 5 source dictionaries: Heritage Dictionary of the English Language, Wiktionary, the Collaborative International Dictionary of English, The Century Dictionary and Cyclopedia, and WordNet 3.0 (Miller, 1995).

PMI: Given a vehicle or event term, we compute point-wise mutual information (PMI) between that term and candidate properties (appearing in $\geq$ 100 tweets) in our Twitter corpus.

Word Embedding: We train a word embedding model using our tweet collection, limiting the vocabulary to nouns, verbs, adjectives and adverbs that occurred in $\geq$ 100 tweets. For training, we use word2vecf[5] (Levy and Goldberg, 2014) which allows training for arbitrary context using the skip-gram model. We use 300 dimensions for the output word and context vectors. Candidate properties are generated by selecting the words whose context vector[6] is most similar to the vehicle or event's word vector using cosine similarity. To control for noisy candidates, we require that the property occurred with the vehicle (or event) as a bigram with frequency $\geq$ 10 in the Twitter corpus.

For each generation method, we rank the candidates and select the top 20 properties. For the four methods that use syntactic patterns, we calculate

---

[4]https://www.wordnik.com/
[5]https://bitbucket.org/yoavgo/word2vecf
[6]properties are expected in the context of a component word.

P(property | vehicle) based on the number of times the property and the vehicle appear together in that syntactic construction among all times the vehicle appear in that syntactic construction. We use this probability to rank the candidates. For the dictionary definition method, we sort the properties based on how many of the 5 dictionaries mention the property in the word's definition. We break ties based on the frequency of the property in the definitions. For the word embedding-based method, we use cosine similarity scores.

3.2 Productivity of the Candidate Generation Methods

First we investigate how many candidates each method is able to generate. If a method generates too few candidates, it will not be very useful. Conversely, if a method generates a large number of candidates, then our ranking framework needs to be robust to rank the plausible properties higher than the properties that do not fit.

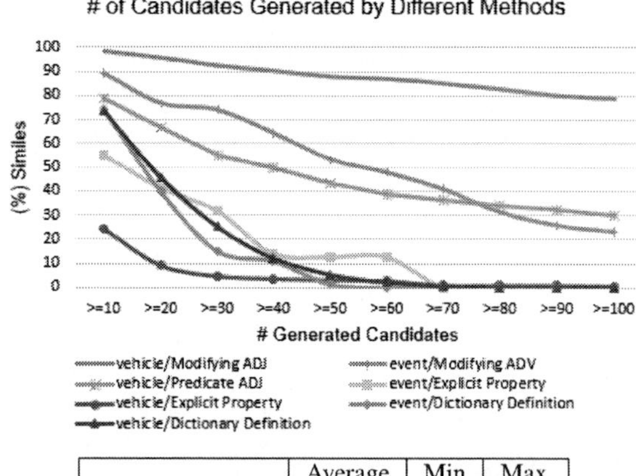

# of Candidates Generated by Different Methods

	Average	Min	Max
# of Candidates Generated from Vehicle			
Modifying ADJ	423.62	1	3177
Predicate ADJ	104.21	0	1070
Explicit Property	8.28	0	116
Dictionary Def.	20.5	0	71
# of Candidates Generated from Event			
Modifying ADV	68.67	2	223
Explicit Property	19.85	0	61
Dictionary Def.*	18.59	3	55

Figure 2: Statistics about candidates generated by different methods. Similes with a "to be" or perception verb were excluded for the methods that use the event as the source.

Figure 2 presents statistics about the candidate properties generated by different methods. The PMI and Word Embedding-based methods were excluded here as these methods evaluate all words in the corpus. The methods that used the explicit property extraction patterns and dictionary definitions generate fewer candidates than the methods that used general syntactic structures. The trend lines in Figure 2 show that these methods do not generate more than 20 candidate properties for most similes.

3.3 Coverage of the Generated Candidates

Next, we investigate the effectiveness of our candidate generation methods. The last column of Table 2 shows candidate ranking results based on Mean Reciprocal Rank (MRR) for the top 20 properties produced by each candidate generation method. MRR is calculated by:

$$MRR = \frac{1}{|S|} \sum_{s \in S} \frac{1}{(rank\ of\ 1^{st}\ acceptable\ property)}$$

where S is the set of similes. We observe that the *PMI* method (for both vehicles and events) and the *Dictionary Definition* method (for events) produced low MRR scores < 0.10. Therefore we decided not to use these candidate generation methods.[7]

One of our primary concerns is assessing the ability of our candidate generation methods to generate at least some acceptable properties. We expect them to over-generate, but they need to produce at least one acceptable property or the downstream components will be helpless. To assess this, we evaluated the coverage of each candidate generation method based on the Top 10, Top 20, and Top 30 properties that it produced. Coverage is the percentage of similes for which the method generates at least one gold standard property (from the human annotators). Table 2 shows that the *Dictionary Definitions* for vehicles was the best performing method for the Top 10 candidates, generating at least one acceptable property for 40% of the similes. The *Modifying ADJ* method performed best for the Top 30 candidates, generating an acceptable property for 63% of similes. Note that the *Explicit Property* method performs reasonably well (40% coverage for Top 30 properties generated from vehicles and 6% coverage for properties generated from events), but clearly is

---

[7]We made this decision based on similar results observed on our development data.

not sufficient on its own, showing the limitation of harvesting explicitly stated properties.

	Top10	Top20	Top30	MRR
Coverage of Candidates Generated from Vehicle				
PMI*	18%	31%	37%	.06
Modifying ADJ	39%	55%	63%	.16
Predicate ADJ	28%	39%	43%	.11
Explicit Property	37%	39%	40%	.23
Dictionary Def.	40%	47%	49%	.22
Word Embedding	35%	48%	58%	.15
ALL	76%	84%	86%	n/a
Coverage of Candidates Generated from Event				
PMI*	2%	3%	4%	.09
Modifying ADV	4%	5%	5%	.13
Explicit Property	4%	5%	6%	.16
Dictionary Def.*	3%	4%	4%	.09
Word Embedding	5%	6%	6%	.16
ALL	9%	10%	10%	n/a
All Candidates				
TOTAL	78%	86%	88%	n/a

Table 2: Coverage and MRR for the candidate generation methods. Top10, Top20, Top30 = percent of similes with a plausible property within top 10, 20, 30 ranked properties. Methods excluded in "ALL" and "TOTAL" rows are marked with (*). In the MRR calculation when the event component is source, similes with a "to be" or a perception verb were excluded.

The ALL rows show the coverage obtained by combining the property lists from all generation methods listed above in the table. The combined set of properties (Top 30) generated from vehicles yields 86% coverage, while the combined set of properties generated from events yields only 10% coverage (partly because these methods apply to only 16% of the similes), showing that vehicles are more effective for candidate generation. However, the TOTAL row shows that combining properties generated from both vehicles and events yields 88% coverage using the Top 30 candidates. The Top 20 candidates provide coverage that is nearly as good (86%) with substantially fewer properties to process downstream, so we use the Top 20 candidates for all of our experiments.[8]

3.4 Ranking the Candidate Properties Using Influence from the Second Component

Next, we investigate whether the initial ranking results in the previous step can be improved by considering the second component of the simile. Intuitively, suppose that "green", "slow", and "endangered" are generated as candidate properties from the vehicle "turtle" (e.g., for *"dad drives like a turtle"*). Taking the event verb "drive" into account can help to rank "slow" more highly than the other candidates. We explore three criteria to rank candidates generated from one simile component based on its association with the second component (unless the event is "to be" in which case we retain the original candidate ranking because the verb is too general).

PMI with second component (PMI): We calculate Pointwise Mutual Information between a candidate property and the second component of a simile.

Embedding word vector similarity with the second component (EMB_1): We use our trained word embeddings model to calculate cosine similarity between a candidate property and the second component of the simile. As before, for properties we use the context vectors.

Embedding word vector similarity with composite simile vector (EMB_2): For a given event and vehicle, we create a composite simile vector by performing element-wise addition of the vectors for the event and the vehicle, and calculate cosine similarity with the candidate properties. For example, for *"person talks like robot"*, the vectors for "talk" and "robot" are used to create a composite vector, and the similarity of the resulting vector with a candidate property's context vector is used as the ranking criteria. The intuition here is to capture what is common in the context distribution (Mikolov et al., 2013) of "robot" and "talk", and the context vector of a suitable property should have strong similarity with the resulting vector.

3.5 Results for Candidate Re-ranking

Table 3 presents MRR results after the initially generated candidates are re-ranked using the influence of the second simile component. For comparison, the MRR results from Table 2 are also presented in the first column (**Orig**).

Influence from the second simile component assessed with PMI and EMB_1 improved the MRR scores for some candidate generation methods (e.g., Predicate ADJ), but did not for others (e.g., Modifying ADV). However using the composite word embedding vector (EMB_2) to capture the common

---

Ranking Method	Orig	PMI	EMB$_1$	EMB$_2$
Candidates Generated from Vehicle				
Modifying ADJ	.16	.22	.19	**.24**
Predicate ADJ	.11	.16	.14	**.22**
Explicit Property	.23	.25	.23	**.28**
Dictionary Def.	.22	.21	.20	**.25**
Word Embedding	.15	.19	.20	**.21**
Candidates Generated from Event				
Modifying ADV	.13	.10	.13	**.19**
Explicit Property	.16	**.18**	**.18**	**.18**
Word Embedding	.16	.11	.14	**.18**

Table 3: MRR scores for candidate ranking methods.

aspects in the context distributions of the event and vehicle consistently improved MRR for all candidate generation methods. Consequently, we use the composite word embedding vector as the ranking method for each set of candidate properties.

3.6 Aggregated Ranking

Finally, we need to consider all of the properties produced by the various candidate generation methods. As we saw in Table 2, they produce complementary sets of properties and coverage is highest when we use all of them together. To produce an aggregated ranking of all candidate properties, we calculate the harmonic mean of the rank for each individual candidate generation method. This approach rewards properties that have a consistently high ranking across different methods.

For comparison, we also show results for a voting method where a candidate property is ranked based on how many different methods generated it. To break ties, we used the frequency of the candidate in our Twitter corpus.

3.7 Results for Aggregated Ranking

Our final results use two gold standard property sets: (1) Gd (Gold): uses the set of properties from the human annotators, and (2) Gd+WN expands Gold with WordNet synsets (words in the same synset of a gold property are added) and WordNet's "similar to" relation (words that are connected to a gold property by the relation are added). The reason for using *Gd+WN* is to include synonyms of a gold property that would otherwise be considered wrong (e.g., if a human annotator said "beautiful" and our system said "pretty").

The first two columns in Table 4 present MRR

	MRR		Top 1		Top 5	
	Gd	Gd + WN	Gd	Gd + WN	Gd	Gd + WN
Voted	.25	.35	14%	21%	36%	52%
Mean	**.33**	**.41**	21%	27%	46%	58%

Table 4: Aggregate ranking results.

results for our final ranking. The results show that with both *Gd* and *Gd+WN*, our aggregated ranking using harmonic mean yields much better MRR results than the individual methods and better than the Voted method, yielding our highest MRR: .33 and .41.

The last 4 columns of Table 4 present the percentage of similes for which an acceptable property was ranked #1 (Top 1) or within the Top 5. Our aggregate ranking scheme ranks an acceptable property in the Top 1 position for 27% of similes based on *Gd+WN*, and inferred an acceptable property within the Top 5 positions for 58% of all similes.

For the above evaluations, any property given by the annotators is deemed correct, and any consensus that the annotators may have had is not accounted for. To address this, we retained properties with different degrees of consensus, and subdivided the evaluation data set. Each subset of the data kept similes that have properties from a minimum number of annotators, and only those properties are used as the gold standard. WordNet synsets and "similar to" relations are also used in determining consensus.

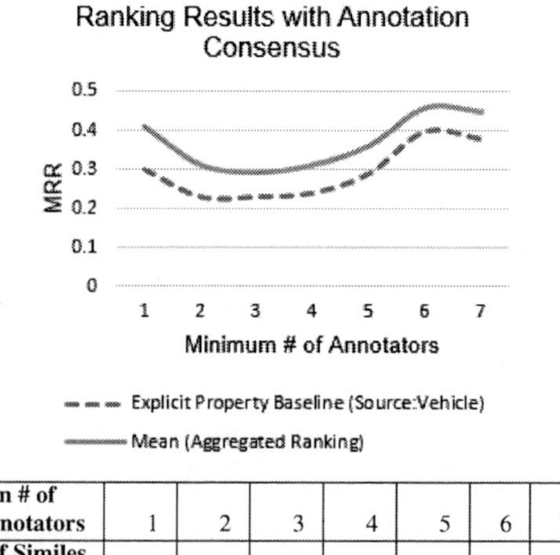

Min # of Annotators	1	2	3	4	5	6	7
# of Similes in Data Set	641	588	418	252	136	67	27

Figure 3: Ranking results tracked by annotation consensus with Gd+WN gold standard, and corresponding data set sizes.

Figure 3 shows that for all degrees of consensus, the aggregated ranking is consistently better than the method that uses the explicit property extraction patterns, which was the best individual candidate generation method. When properties given by at least 2 annotators are considered as the gold standard, MRR is lower than when properties given by any annotator are used. With higher consensus, MRR gradually increases, which is probably because the properties with high consensus have stronger association with the simile components, so are easier to infer.

4   Analysis and Discussion

Our gold standard property collection confirmed our intuition that some similes have many plausible interpretations while others do not. We hypothesized that this should contribute to the difficulty of implicit property inference. Utsumi and Kuwabara (2005) introduced "interpretive diversity" with the hypothesis that similes with more diversity in the inferred property tend to be more metaphorical, and the values of salience of the properties are more uniform. They used Shannon's entropy to measure the interpretive diversity of a simile.

To explore our hypothesis regarding difficulties associated with property inference, we first cluster our gold-standard annotated properties. When a property appears in the WordNet synset of another property, or if two properties are connected by the WordNet "similar to" relation, we group the properties to form property clusters. So each property cluster represents a set of words that are synonyms of each other. We aggregate frequency statistics of individual words in a cluster and measure interpretive diversity of a simile using Shannon's entropy (here, X is the random variable representing property clusters of a simile):

$$H(X) = - \sum_{x \in X} P(x) \log_2 P(x)$$

Figure 4 shows the entropy curve after the 641 similes are sorted by the entropy values of their property clusters. Based on changes in the slope of the curve, we then divided the data into 3 subsets, similes with high (1–100 similes), medium (101–500 similes), and low (501–641 similes) interpretive diversity. Table 5 presents examples of similes in each category. High interpretive diversity

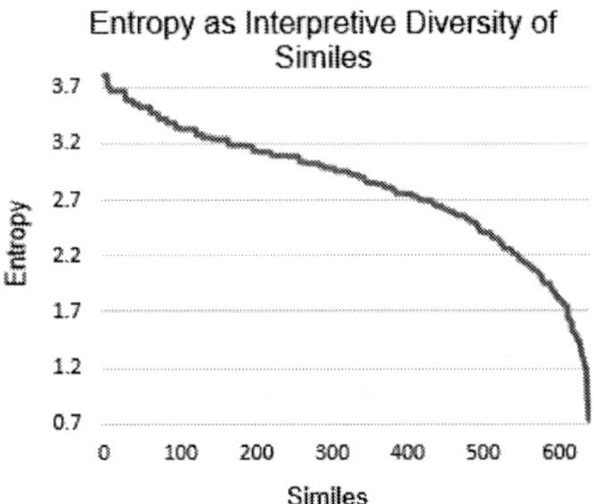

Figure 4: Entropy as interpretive diversity of similes.

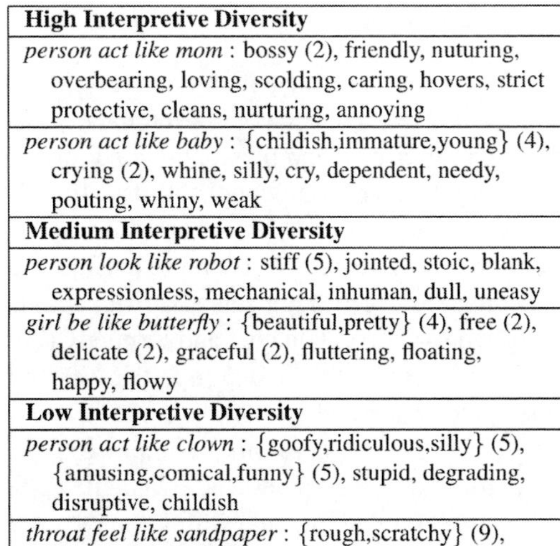

High Interpretive Diversity
person act like mom : bossy (2), friendly, nuturing, overbearing, loving, scolding, caring, hovers, strict protective, cleans, nurturing, annoying
person act like baby : {childish,immature,young} (4), crying (2), whine, silly, cry, dependent, needy, pouting, whiny, weak
Medium Interpretive Diversity
person look like robot : stiff (5), jointed, stoic, blank, expressionless, mechanical, inhuman, dull, uneasy
girl be like butterfly : {beautiful,pretty} (4), free (2), delicate (2), graceful (2), fluttering, floating, happy, flowy
Low Interpretive Diversity
person act like clown : {goofy,ridiculous,silly} (5), {amusing,comical,funny} (5), stupid, degrading, disruptive, childish
throat feel like sandpaper : {rough,scratchy} (9), coarse (2), raspy, sore, dry

Table 5: Similes with different levels of interpretive diversity. Aggregated frequencies are presented within parenthesis.

is clearly demonstrated by *"person act like mom"*, showing properties with many different characteristics attributed to mom. Note that the properties contain both positive (e.g., friendly, loving) and negative (scolding, annoying) attributes. On the other side of the spectrum are similes with low interpretive diversity, as exemplified by *"throat feel like sandpaper"* where the vocabulary of the property set is more limited.

Table 6 shows that it is much harder to infer the implicit property in similes with high interpretive diversity, demonstrated by a .19 difference in MRR score from high to low. This trend is also consistent when we see the percentage of similes for which the system ranks a plausible property at the topmost

Diversity	High	Medium	Low
MRR	.31	.40	.50
Top 1	15%	26%	37%
Top 5	47%	57%	66%

Table 6: Results for different subsets of similes divided by interpretive diversity, using Gold+WN properties.

position (Top 1) or within the Top 5. It is possible that with low interpretive diversity, when the property distribution is unimodal or bimodal, statistical associations between a property and simile components are stronger, and so more easily discovered by our candidate generation and ranking methods.

5 Related Work

Similes have been studied in linguistics and psycholinguistics to understand how humans process similes, comparisons, and metaphors, and the interplay among different components of these linguistic forms. Glucksberg et al. (1997) presented a property attribution model of metaphor comprehension where the candidate properties are selected from a vehicle and applied to a topic. Chiappe and Kennedy (2000) investigated if the number of properties varies between a metaphor and its simile form. The impacts of semantic dimensions of tenor and property salience have been compared by Gagné (2002). Fishelov (2007) experimented with affective connotation and degrees of difficulty associated with understanding a simile when a simile property is conventional or unconventional, or no property is given. Hanks (2005) manually categorized vehicle nouns of similes into semantic categories.

Automatic approaches that use computational models for similes are relatively rare. Veale and Hao (2007) extracted salient properties of vehicles from the web using "as ADJ as a/an NOUN" extraction pattern to acquire knowledge for concept categories. Veale (2012) built a knowledge-base of affective stereotypes by characterizing simile vehicles with salient properties. Li et al. (2012) used explicit property extraction patterns to determine the sentiment that properties convey toward simile vehicles. Niculae and Yaneva (2013) and Niculae (2013) used constituency and dependency parsing-based techniques to identify similes in text. Qadir et al. (2015) classified similes into positive and negative affective polarities using supervised classification, with

features derived from simile components. Niculae and Danescu-Niculescu-Mizil (2014) designed a classifier with domain specific, domain agnostic, and metaphor inspired features to determine when comparisons are figurative.

Computational approaches to work on figurative language also include figurative language identification using word sense disambiguation (Rentoumi et al., 2009), harvesting metaphors by using noun and verb clustering-based techniques (Shutova et al., 2010), interpreting metaphors by generating literal paraphrases (Shutova, 2010), etc.

Although previous research has extensively used explicit property extraction patterns for various tasks, none has explored the impact of multiple simile components for inferring properties. To our knowledge, we are the first to introduce the task of automatically inferring the implicit properties in open similes, which is fundamental to automatic understanding of similes.

6 Conclusion

In this work, we addressed the problem of inferring implicit properties in open similes. We showed that acceptable properties for most similes can be identified by harvesting properties using syntactic structures, dictionary definitions, statistical co-occurrence, and word embedding vectors. We then demonstrated that capturing the combined influence of a simile's event and vehicle terms using a composite word embedding vector improved our ability to rank candidate properties. Finally, we showed that properties harvested by different methods can be aggregated and effectively ranked using the harmonic mean of rankings from the individual methods. Our method for inferring implicit properties performed best on similes with low interpretive diversity. In future work, we plan to use the inferred properties to improve affective polarity recognition in similes.

Acknowledgments

This material is based upon work supported in part by the National Science Foundation under grants IIS-1450527 and IIS-1302668.

References

Monroe C Beardsley. 1981. *Aesthetics, problems in the philosophy of criticism*. Hackett Publishing.

Dan L Chiappe and John M Kennedy. 2000. Are metaphors elliptical similes? *Journal of Psycholinguistic Research*, 29(4):371–398.

David Fishelov. 2007. Shall i compare thee? simile understanding and semantic categories. *Journal of literary semantics*, 36(1):71–87.

Christina L Gagné. 2002. Metaphoric interpretations of comparison-based combinations. *Metaphor and Symbol*, 17(3):161–178.

Sam Glucksberg, Matthew S McGlone, and Deanna Manfredi. 1997. Property attribution in metaphor comprehension. *Journal of memory and language*, 36(1):50–67.

Patrick Hanks. 2005. Similes and sets: The english preposition like. *Languages and Linguistics: Festschrift for Fr. Cermak. Charles University, Prague*.

Michael Israel, Jennifer Riddle Harding, and Vera Tobin. 2004. On simile. *Language, culture, and mind*, 100.

Omer Levy and Yoav Goldberg. 2014. Dependency-based word embeddings. In *Proceedings of the 52nd Annual Meeting of the Association for Computational Linguistics*, volume 2, pages 302–308.

Bin Li, Haibo Kuang, Yingjie Zhang, Jiajun Chen, and Xuri Tang. 2012. Using similes to extract basic sentiments across languages. In *Web Information Systems and Mining*, pages 536–542. Springer.

Tomas Mikolov, Ilya Sutskever, Kai Chen, Greg S Corrado, and Jeff Dean. 2013. Distributed representations of words and phrases and their compositionality. In *Advances in neural information processing systems*, pages 3111–3119.

George A Miller. 1995. Wordnet: a lexical database for english. *Communications of the ACM*, 38(11):39–41.

Vlad Niculae and Cristian Danescu-Niculescu-Mizil. 2014. Brighter than gold: Figurative language in user generated comparisons. In *Proceedings of the 2014 Conference on Empirical Methods in Natural Language Processing (EMNLP)*, pages 2008–2018. Association for Computational Linguistics.

Vlad Niculae and Victoria Yaneva. 2013. Computational considerations of comparisons and similes. In *ACL (Student Research Workshop)*, pages 89–95.

Vlad Niculae. 2013. Comparison pattern matching and creative simile recognition. In *Proceedings of the Joint Symposium on Semantic Processing*.

Olutobi Owoputi, Brendan O'Connor, Chris Dyer, Kevin Gimpel, Nathan Schneider, and Noah A. Smith. 2013. Improved part-of-speech tagging for online conversational text with word clusters. In *Proceedings of the 2013 Conference of the North American Chapter of the Association for Computational Linguistics: Human Language Technologies*, pages 380–390, Atlanta, Georgia, June. Association for Computational Linguistics.

Anthony M Paul. 1970. Figurative language. *Philosophy & Rhetoric*, pages 225–248.

Ashequl Qadir, Ellen Riloff, and Marilyn Walker. 2015. Learning to recognize affective polarity in similes. In *Proceedings of the 2015 Conference on Empirical Methods in Natural Language Processing*, pages 190–200, Lisbon, Portugal, September. Association for Computational Linguistics.

Vassiliki Rentoumi, George Giannakopoulos, Vangelis Karkaletsis, and A. George Vouros. 2009. Sentiment analysis of figurative language using a word sense disambiguation approach. In *Proceedings of the International Conference RANLP-2009*, pages 370–375. Association for Computational Linguistics.

Ekaterina Shutova, Lin Sun, and Anna Korhonen. 2010. Metaphor identification using verb and noun clustering. In *Proceedings of the 23rd International Conference on Computational Linguistics*, pages 1002–1010. Association for Computational Linguistics.

Ekaterina Shutova. 2010. Automatic metaphor interpretation as a paraphrasing task. In *Human Language Technologies: The 2010 Annual Conference of the North American Chapter of the Association for Computational Linguistics*, pages 1029–1037. Association for Computational Linguistics.

Akira Utsumi and Yuu Kuwabara. 2005. Interpretive diversity as a source of metaphor-simile distinction. In *Proceedings of the 27th Annual Meeting of the Cognitive Science Society*, pages 2230–2235.

Tony Veale and Yanfen Hao. 2007. Learning to understand figurative language: from similes to metaphors to irony. In *Proceedings of CogSci*.

Tony Veale. 2012. A context-sensitive, multi-faceted model of lexico-conceptual affect. In *Proceedings of the 50th Annual Meeting of the Association for Computational Linguistics: Short Papers-Volume 2*, pages 75–79. Association for Computational Linguistics.

Visual Storytelling

Ting-Hao (Kenneth) Huang[1]*, **Francis Ferraro**[2]*, **Nasrin Mostafazadeh**[3], **Ishan Misra**[1], **Aishwarya Agrawal**[4],
Jacob Devlin[6], **Ross Girshick**[5], **Xiaodong He**[6], **Pushmeet Kohli**[6], **Dhruv Batra**[4], **C. Lawrence Zitnick**[5],
Devi Parikh[4], **Lucy Vanderwende**[6], **Michel Galley**[6], **Margaret Mitchell**[6]

Microsoft Research

1 Carnegie Mellon University, 2 Johns Hopkins University, 3 University of Rochester,

4 Virginia Tech, 5 Facebook AI Research

6 Corresponding authors: {jdevlin,lucyv,mgalley,memitc}@microsoft.com

Abstract

We introduce the first dataset for **sequential vision-to-language**, and explore how this data may be used for the task of *visual storytelling*. The first release of this dataset, SIND[1] v.1, includes 81,743 unique photos in 20,211 sequences, aligned to both descriptive (caption) and story language. We establish several strong baselines for the storytelling task, and motivate an automatic metric to benchmark progress. Modelling concrete description as well as figurative and social language, as provided in this dataset and the storytelling task, has the potential to move artificial intelligence from basic understandings of typical visual scenes towards more and more human-like understanding of grounded event structure and subjective expression.

1 Introduction

Beyond understanding simple objects and concrete scenes lies interpreting causal structure; making sense of visual input to tie disparate moments together as they give rise to a cohesive narrative of events through time. This requires moving from reasoning about single images – static moments, devoid of context – to sequences of images that depict events as they occur and change. On the vision side, progressing from single images to images in context allows us to begin to create an artificial intelligence (AI) that can reason about a visual moment given what it has already seen. On the language side, progressing from literal description to narrative helps to learn more evaluative, conversational, and abstract

---

*T.H. and F.F. contributed equally to this work.

[1]Sequential Images Narrative Dataset. This and future releases are made available on `sind.ai`.

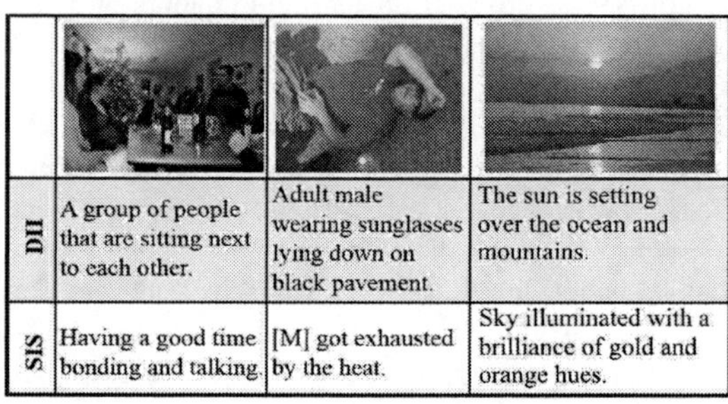

Figure 1: Example language difference between descriptions for images in isolation (DII) vs. stories for images in sequence (SIS).

language. This is the difference between, for example, "sitting next to each other" versus "having a good time", or "sun is setting" versus "sky illuminated with a brilliance..." (see Figure 1). The first descriptions capture image content that is literal and concrete; the second requires further inference about what a *good time* may look like, or what is special and worth sharing about a particular sunset.

We introduce the first dataset of sequential images with corresponding descriptions, which captures some of these subtle but important differences, and advance the task of visual storytelling. We release the data in three tiers of language for the same images: **(1) Descriptions of images-in-isolation (DII)**; **(2) Descriptions of images-in-sequence (DIS)**; and **(3) Stories for images-in-sequence (SIS)**. This tiered approach reveals the effect of temporal context and the effect of narrative language. As all the tiers are aligned to the same images, the dataset facilitates directly modeling the relationship between literal and more abstract visual concepts, including the relationship between visual

beach (684)	breaking up (350)	easter (259)
amusement park (525)	carnival (331)	church (243)
building a house (415)	visit (321)	graduation ceremony (236)
party (411)	market (311)	office (226)
birthday (399)	outdoor activity (267)	father's day (221)

Table 1: The number of albums in our tiered dataset for the 15 most frequent kinds of stories.

imagery and typical event patterns. We additionally propose an automatic evaluation metric which is best correlated with human judgments, and establish several strong baselines for the visual storytelling task.

2 Motivation and Related Work

Work in vision to language has exploded, with researchers examining image captioning (Lin et al., 2014; Karpathy and Fei-Fei, 2015; Vinyals et al., 2015; Xu et al., 2015; Chen et al., 2015; Young et al., 2014; Elliott and Keller, 2013), question answering (Antol et al., 2015; Ren et al., 2015; Gao et al., 2015; Malinowski and Fritz, 2014), visual phrases (Sadeghi and Farhadi, 2011), video understanding (Ramanathan et al., 2013), and visual concepts (Krishna et al., 2016; Fang et al., 2015).

Such work focuses on direct, literal description of image content. While this is an encouraging first step in connecting vision and language, it is far from the capabilities needed by intelligent agents for naturalistic interactions. There is a significant difference, yet unexplored, between remarking that a visual scene shows "sitting in a room" – typical of most image captioning work – and that the same visual scene shows "bonding". The latter description is grounded in the visual signal, yet it brings to bear information about social relations and emotions that can be additionally inferred in context (Figure 1). Visually-grounded stories facilitate more evaluative and figurative language than has previously been seen in vision-to-language research: If a system can recognize that colleagues look *bored*, it can remark and act on this information directly.

Storytelling itself is one of the oldest known human activities (Wiessner, 2014), providing a way to educate, preserve culture, instill morals, and share advice; focusing AI research towards this task therefore has the potential to bring about more human-like intelligence and understanding.

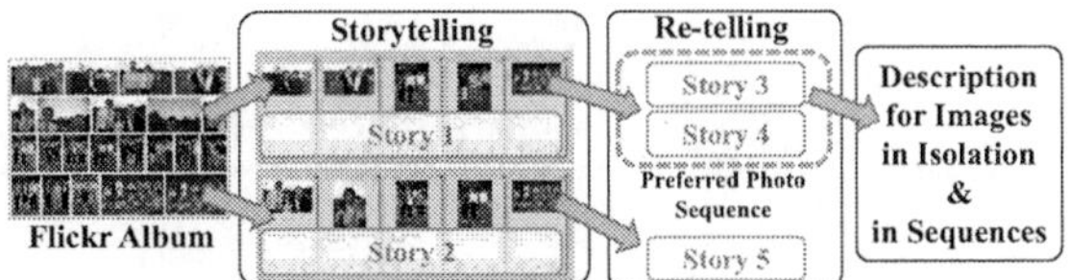

Figure 2: Dataset crowdsourcing workflow.

Figure 3: Interface for the *Storytelling* task, which contains: 1) the photo album, and 2) the storyboard.

3 Dataset Construction

Extracting Photos   We begin by generating a list of "storyable" event types. We leverage the idea that "storyable" events tend to involve some form of possession, e.g., "John's birthday party," or "Shabnam's visit." Using the Flickr data release (Thomee et al., 2015), we aggregate 5-grams of photo titles and descriptions, using Stanford CoreNLP (Manning et al., 2014) to extract possessive dependency patterns. We keep the heads of possessive phrases if they can be classified as an EVENT in WordNet3.0, relying on manual winnowing to target our collection efforts.[2] These terms are then used to collect albums using the Flickr API.[3] We only include albums with 10 to 50 photos where all album photos are taken within a 48-hour span and CC-licensed. See Table 1 for the query terms with the most albums returned.

The photos returned from this stage are then presented to crowd workers using Amazon's Mechanical Turk to collect the corresponding stories and descriptions. The crowdsourcing workflow of developing the complete dataset is shown in Figure 2.

Crowdsourcing Stories In Sequence   We develop a 2-stage crowdsourcing workflow to collect naturalistic stories with text aligned to images. The first stage is *storytelling*, where the crowd worker selects a subset of photos from a given album to form a

---

[2] We simultaneously supplemented this data-driven effort by a small hand-constructed gazetteer.

[3] https://www.flickr.com/services/api/

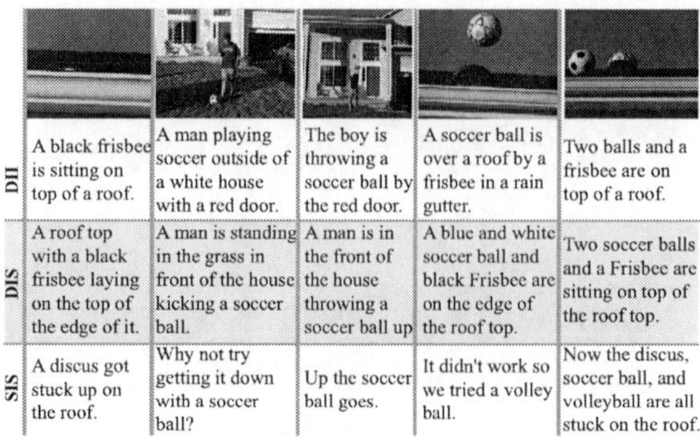

	A black frisbee is sitting on top of a roof.	A man playing soccer outside of a white house with a red door.	The boy is throwing a soccer ball by the red door.	A soccer ball is over a roof by a frisbee in a rain gutter.	Two balls and a frisbee are on top of a roof.
DII					
DIS	A roof top with a black frisbee laying on the top of the edge of it.	A man is standing in the grass in front of the house kicking a soccer ball.	A man is in the front of the house throwing a soccer ball up	A blue and white soccer ball and black Frisbee are on the edge of the roof top.	Two soccer balls and a Frisbee are sitting on top of the roof top.
SIS	A discus got stuck up on the roof.	Why not try getting it down with a soccer ball?	Up the soccer ball goes.	It didn't work so we tried a volley ball.	Now the discus, soccer ball, and volleyball are all stuck on the roof.

Figure 4: Example descriptions of images in isolation (DII); descriptions of images in sequence (DIS); and stories of images in sequence (SIS).

photo sequence and writes a story about it (see Figure 3). The second stage is *re-telling*, in which the worker writes a story based on one photo sequence generated by workers in the first stage.

In both stages, all album photos are displayed in the order of the time that the photos were taken, with a "storyboard" underneath. In *storytelling*, by clicking a photo in the album, a "story card" of the photo appears on the storyboard. The worker is instructed to pick at least five photos, arrange the order of selected photos, and then write a sentence or a phrase on each card to form a story; this appears as a full story underneath the text aligned to each image. Additionally, this interface captures the alignments between text and photos. Workers may skip an album if it does not seem storyable (e.g., a collection of coins). Albums skipped by two workers are discarded. The interface of *re-telling* is similar, but it displays the two photo sequences already created in the first stage, which the worker chooses from to write the story. For each album, 2 workers perform *storytelling* (at \$0.3/HIT), and 3 workers perform *re-telling* (at \$0.25/HIT), yielding a total of 1,907 workers. All HITs use quality controls to ensure varied text at least 15 words long.

Crowdsourcing Descriptions of Images In Isolation & Images In Sequence We also use crowdsourcing to collect descriptions of images-in-isolation (DII) and descriptions of images-in-sequence (DIS), for the photo sequences with stories from a majority of workers in the first task (as Figure 2). In both DII and DIS tasks, workers are asked to follow the instructions for image caption-

Data Set	#(Txt, Img) Pairs (k)	Vocab Size (k)	Avg. #Tok	%Abs	Frazier	Yngve	Ppl
Brown	52.1	47.7	20.8	15.2%	18.5	77.2	194.0
DII	151.8	13.8	11.0	21.3%	10.3	27.4	147.0
DIS[5]	151.8	5.0	9.8	24.8%	9.2	23.7	146.8
SIS	252.9	18.2	10.2	22.1%	10.5	27.5	116.0

Table 2: A summary of our dataset,[6] following the proposed analyses of Ferraro et al. (2015), including the Frazier and Yngve measures of syntactic complexity. The balanced Brown corpus (Marcus et al., 1999), provided for comparison, contains only text. Perplexity (Ppl) is calculated against a 5-gram language model learned on a generic 30B English words dataset scraped from the web.

Desc.-in-Iso.			Desc.-in-Seq.			Story-in-Seq.		
man	sitting	black	chatting	amount	trunk	went	[female]	see
woman	white	large	gentleman	goers	facing	got	today	saw
standing	two	front	enjoys	sofa	bench	[male]	decided	came
holding	young	group	folks	egg	enjoying	took	really	started
wearing	image		shoreline	female		great	time	

Table 3: Top words ranked by normalized PMI.

ing proposed in MS COCO (Lin et al., 2014) such as *describe all the important parts*. In DII, we use the MS COCO image captioning interface.[4] In DIS, we use the storyboard and story cards of our *storytelling* interface to display a photo sequence, with MS COCO instructions adapted for sequences. We recruit 3 workers for DII (at \$0.05/HIT) and 3 workers for DIS (at \$0.07/HIT).

Data Post-processing We tokenize all storylets and descriptions with the CoreNLP tokenizer, and replace all people names with generic MALE/FEMALE tokens,[5] and all identified named entities with their entity type (e.g., `location`). The data is released as *training*, *validation*, and *test* following an 80%/10%/10% split on the stories-in-sequence albums. Example language from each tier is shown in Figure 4.

4 Data Analysis

Our dataset includes 10,117 Flickr albums with 210,819 unique photos. Each album on average has 20.8 photos ($\sigma = 9.0$). The average time span of each album is 7.9 hours ($\sigma = 11.4$). Further details of each tier of the dataset are shown in Table 2.[7]

---

[4]https://github.com/tylin/coco-ui

[5]We use those names occurring at least 10,000 times. https://ssa.gov/oact/babynames/names.zip

[6]The DIS columns VocabSize-Ppl estimated based on 17,425 Txt,Img pairs. Full set will be updated shortly.

[7]We exclude words seen only once.

We use normalized pointwise mutual information to identify the words most closely associated with each tier (Table 3). Top words for descriptions-in-isolation reflect an impoverished disambiguating context: References to people often lack social specificity, as people are referred to as simply "man" or "woman". Single images often do not convey much information about underlying events or actions, which leads to the abundant use of posture verbs ("standing", "sitting", etc.). As we turn to descriptions-in-sequence, these relatively uninformative words are much less represented. Finally, top story-in-sequence words include more storytelling elements, such as names ([*male*]), temporal references (*today*) and words that are more dynamic and abstract (*went, decided*).

5 Automatic Evaluation Metric

Given the nature of the complex storytelling task, the best and most reliable evaluation for assessing the quality of generated stories is human judgment. However, automatic evaluation metrics are useful to quickly benchmark progress. To better understand which metric could serve as a proxy for human evaluation, we compute pairwise correlation coefficients between automatic metrics and human judgments on 3,000 stories sampled from the SIS training set.

For the human judgements, we again use crowdsourcing on MTurk, asking five judges per story to rate how strongly they agreed with the statement "If these were my photos, I would like using a story like this to share my experience with my friends".[8] We take the average of the five judgments as the final score for the story. For the automatic metrics, we use METEOR,[9] smoothed-BLEU (Lin and Och, 2004), and Skip-Thoughts (Kiros et al., 2015) to compute similarity between each story for a given sequence. Skip-thoughts provide a Sentence2Vec embedding which models the semantic space of novels.

As Table 4 shows, METEOR correlates best with human judgment according to all the correlation coefficients. This signals that a metric such as METEOR which incorporates paraphrasing correlates best with human judgement on this task. A more

---

	METEOR	BLEU	Skip-Thoughts
r	0.22 (2.8e-28)	0.08 (1.0e-06)	0.18 (5.0e-27)
ρ	0.20 (3.0e-31)	0.08 (8.9e-06)	0.16 (6.4e-22)
τ	0.14 (1.0e-33)	0.06 (8.7e-08)	0.11 (7.7e-24)

Table 4: Correlations of automatic scores against human judgements, with p-values in parentheses.

Beam=10	Greedy	-Dups	+Grounded
23.55	19.10	19.21	–

Table 6: Captions generated per-image with METEOR scores.

detailed study of automatic evaluation of stories is an area of interest for a future work.

6 Baseline Experiments

We report baseline experiments on the storytelling task in Table 7, training on the SIS tier and testing on half the SIS validation set (valtest). Example output from each system is presented in Table 5. To highlight some differences between story and caption generation, we also train on the DII tier in isolation, and produce captions per-image, rather than in sequence. These results are shown in Table 7.

To train the story generation model, we use a sequence-to-sequence recurrent neural net (RNN) approach, which naturally extends the single-image captioning technique of Devlin et al. (2015) and Vinyals et al. (2014) to multiple images. Here, we encode an image *sequence* by running an RNN over the `fc7` vectors of each image, in reverse order. This is used as the initial hidden state to the story decoder model, which learns to produce the story one word at a time using softmax loss over the training data vocabulary. We use Gated Recurrent Units (GRUs) (Cho et al., 2014) for both the image encoder and story decoder.

In the baseline system, we generate the story using a simple beam search (size=10), which has been successful in image captioning previously (Devlin et al., 2015). However, for story generation, the results of this model subjectively appear to be very poor – the system produces generic, repetitive, high-level descriptions (e.g., "This is a picture of a dog").

Beam=10	Greedy	-Dups	+Grounded
23.13	27.76	30.11	31.42

Table 7: Stories baselines with METEOR scores.

---

⁸Scale presented ranged from "Strongly disagree" to "Strongly agree", which we convert to a scale of 1 to 5.

⁹We use METEOR version 1.5 with `hter` weights.

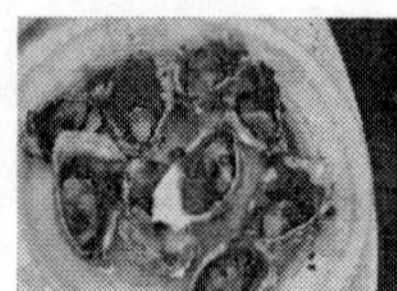

+Viterbi	This is a picture of a family. This is a picture of a cake. This is a picture of a dog. This is a picture of a beach. This is a picture of a beach.
+Greedy	The family gathered together for a meal. The food was delicious. The dog was excited to be there. The dog was enjoying the water. The dog was happy to be in the water.
-Dups	The family gathered together for a meal. The food was delicious. The dog was excited to be there. The kids were playing in the water. The boat was a little too much to drink.
+Grounded	The family got together for a cookout. They had a lot of delicious food. The dog was happy to be there. They had a great time on the beach. They even had a swim in the water.

Table 5: Example stories generated by baselines.

This is a predictable result given the label bias problem inherent in maximum likelihood training; recent work has looked at ways to address this issue directly (Li et al., 2016).

To establish a stronger baseline, we explore several decode-time heuristics to improve the quality of the generated story. The first heuristic is to lower the decoder beam size substantially. We find that using a beam size of 1 (greedy search) significantly increases the story quality, resulting in a 4.6 gain in METEOR score. However, the same effect is not seen for caption generation, with the greedy caption model obtaining worse quality than the beam search model. This highlights a key difference in generating stories versus generating captions.

Although the stories produced using a greedy search result in significant gains, they include many repeated words and phrases, e.g., "The kids had a great time. And the kids had a great time." We introduce a very simple heuristic to avoid this, where the same content word cannot be produced more than once within a given story. This improves METEOR by another 2.3 points.

An advantage of comparing captioning to storytelling side-by-side is that the captioning output may be used to help inform the storytelling output. To this end, we include an additional baseline where "visually grounded" words may only be produced if they are licensed by the caption model. We define the set of visually grounded words to be those which occurred at higher frequency in the caption training than the story training:

$$\frac{P(w|T_{caption})}{P(w|T_{story})} > 1.0 \qquad (1)$$

We train a separate model using the caption annotations, and produce an n-best list of captions for each image in the valtest set. Words seen in at least 10 sentences in the 100-best list are marked as 'licensed' by the caption model. Greedy decoding without duplication proceeds with the additional constraint that if a word is visually grounded, it can only be generated by the story model if it is licensed by the caption model for the same photo set. This results in a further 1.3 METEOR improvement.

It is interesting to note what a strong effect relatively simple heuristics have on the generated stories. We do not intend to suggest that these heuristics are the *right* way to approach story generation. Instead, the main purpose is to provide clear baselines that demonstrate that story generation has fundamentally different challenges from caption generation; and the space is wide open to explore for training and decoding methods to generate fluent stories.

7 Conclusion and Future Work

We have introduced the first dataset for **sequential vision-to-language**, which incrementally moves from images-in-isolation to stories-in-sequence. We argue that modelling the more figurative and social language captured in this dataset is essential for evolving AI towards more human-like understanding. We have established several strong baselines for the task of visual storytelling, and have motivated METEOR as an automatic metric to evaluate progress on this task moving forward.

References

Stanislaw Antol, Aishwarya Agrawal, Jiasen Lu, Margaret Mitchell, Dhruv Batra, C. Lawrence Zitnick, and Devi Parikh. 2015. Vqa: Visual question answering. In *International Conference on Computer Vision (ICCV)*.

Jianfu Chen, Polina Kuznetsova, David Warren, and Yejin Choi. 2015. Déjà image-captions: A corpus of expressive descriptions in repetition. In *Proceedings of the 2015 Conference of the North American Chapter of the Association for Computational Linguistics: Human Language Technologies*, pages 504–514, Denver, Colorado, May–June. Association for Computational Linguistics.

Kyunghyun Cho, Bart van Merrienboer, Caglar Gulcehre, Fethi Bougares, Holger Schwenk, and Yoshua Bengio. 2014. Learning phrase representations using RNN encoder-decoder for statistical machine translation. *CoRR*.

Jacob Devlin, Hao Cheng, Hao Fang, Saurabh Gupta, Li Deng, Xiaodong He, Geoffrey Zweig, and Margaret Mitchell. 2015. Language models for image captioning: The quirks and what works. In *Proceedings of the 53rd Annual Meeting of the Association for Computational Linguistics and the 7th International Joint Conference on Natural Language Processing (Volume 2: Short Papers)*, pages 100–105, Beijing, China, July. Association for Computational Linguistics.

Desmond Elliott and Frank Keller. 2013. Image description using visual dependency representations. In *Proceedings of the 2013 Conference on Empirical Methods in Natural Language Processing*, pages 1292–1302, Seattle, Washington, USA, October. Association for Computational Linguistics.

Hao Fang, Saurabh Gupta, Forrest N. Iandola, Rupesh Srivastava, Li Deng, Piotr Dollár, Jianfeng Gao, Xiaodong He, Margaret Mitchell, John C. Platt, C. Lawrence Zitnick, and Geoffrey Zweig. 2015. From captions to visual concepts and back. In *Computer Vision and Pattern Recognition (CVPR)*.

Francis Ferraro, Nasrin Mostafazadeh, Ting-Hao K. Huang, Lucy Vanderwende, Jacob Devlin, Michel Galley, and Margaret Mitchell. 2015. A survey of current datasets for vision and language research. In *Proceedings of the 2015 Conference on Empirical Methods in Natural Language Processing*, pages 207–213, Lisbon, Portugal, September. Association for Computational Linguistics.

Haoyuan Gao, Junhua Mao, Jie Zhou, Zhiheng Huang, Lei Wang, and Wei Xu. 2015. Are you talking to a machine? dataset and methods for multilingual image question. In C. Cortes, N.D. Lawrence, D.D. Lee, M. Sugiyama, R. Garnett, and R. Garnett, editors, *Advances in Neural Information Processing Systems 28*, pages 2287–2295. Curran Associates, Inc.

Andrej Karpathy and Li Fei-Fei. 2015. Deep visual-semantic alignments for generating image descriptions. In *The IEEE Conference on Computer Vision and Pattern Recognition (CVPR)*, June.

Ryan Kiros, Yukun Zhu, Ruslan R Salakhutdinov, Richard Zemel, Raquel Urtasun, Antonio Torralba, and Sanja Fidler. 2015. Skip-thought vectors. In C. Cortes, N.D. Lawrence, D.D. Lee, M. Sugiyama, R. Garnett, and R. Garnett, editors, *Advances in Neural Information Processing Systems 28*, pages 3276–3284. Curran Associates, Inc.

Ranjay Krishna, Yuke Zhu, Oliver Groth, Justin Johnson, Kenji Hata, Joshua Kravitz, Stephanie Chen, Yannis Kalanditis, Li-Jia Li, David A Shamma, Michael Bernstein, and Li Fei-Fei. 2016. Visual genome: Connecting language and vision using crowdsourced dense image annotations.

Jiwei Li, Michel Galley, Chris Brockett, Jianfeng Gao, and Bill Dolan. 2016. A diversity-promoting objective function for neural conversation models. *NAACL HLT 2016*.

Chin-Yew Lin and Franz Josef Och. 2004. Automatic evaluation of machine translation quality using longest common subsequence and skip-bigram statistics. In *Proceedings of the 42Nd Annual Meeting on Association for Computational Linguistics*, ACL '04, Stroudsburg, PA, USA. Association for Computational Linguistics.

Tsung-Yi Lin, Michael Maire, Serge Belongie, James Hays, Pietro Perona, Deva Ramanan, Piotr Dollár, and C Lawrence Zitnick. 2014. Microsoft coco: Common objects in context. In *Computer Vision–ECCV 2014*, pages 740–755. Springer.

Mateusz Malinowski and Mario Fritz. 2014. A multi-world approach to question answering about real-world scenes based on uncertain input. In Z. Ghahramani, M. Welling, C. Cortes, N.D. Lawrence, and K.Q. Weinberger, editors, *Advances in Neural Information Processing Systems 27*, pages 1682–1690. Curran Associates, Inc.

Christopher D. Manning, Mihai Surdeanu, John Bauer, Jenny Finkel, Steven J. Bethard, and David McClosky. 2014. The Stanford CoreNLP natural language processing toolkit. In *Proceedings of 52nd Annual Meeting of the Association for Computational Linguistics: System Demonstrations*, pages 55–60.

Mitchell Marcus, Beatrice Santorini, Mary Ann Marcinkiewicz, and Ann Taylor. 1999. Brown corpus, treebank-3.

Vignesh Ramanathan, Percy Liang, and Li Fei-Fei. 2013. Video event understanding using natural language descriptions. In *Computer Vision (ICCV), 2013 IEEE International Conference on*, pages 905–912. IEEE.

Mengye Ren, Ryan Kiros, and Richard Zemel. 2015. Exploring models and data for image question answering. In C. Cortes, N.D. Lawrence, D.D. Lee, M. Sugiyama, R. Garnett, and R. Garnett, editors, *Advances in Neural Information Processing Systems 28*, pages 2935–2943. Curran Associates, Inc.

Mohammad Amin Sadeghi and Ali Farhadi. 2011. Recognition using visual phrases. In *Computer Vision and Pattern Recognition (CVPR), 2011 IEEE Conference on*, pages 1745–1752. IEEE.

Bart Thomee, David A Shamma, Gerald Friedland, Benjamin Elizalde, Karl Ni, Douglas Poland, Damian Borth, and Li-Jia Li. 2015. The new data and new challenges in multimedia research. *arXiv preprint arXiv:1503.01817*.

Oriol Vinyals, Alexander Toshev, Samy Bengio, and Dumitru Erhan. 2014. Show and tell: a neural image caption generator. In *CVPR*.

Oriol Vinyals, Alexander Toshev, Samy Bengio, and Dumitru Erhan. 2015. Show and tell: A neural image caption generator. In *Computer Vision and Pattern Recognition*.

Polly W Wiessner. 2014. Embers of society: Firelight talk among the ju/hoansi bushmen. *Proceedings of the National Academy of Sciences*, 111(39):14027–14035.

Kelvin Xu, Jimmy Ba, Ryan Kiros, Kyunghyun Cho, Aaron Courville, Ruslan Salakhutdinov, Richard Zemel, and Yoshua Bengio. 2015. Show, attend and tell: Neural image caption generation with visual attention. *arXiv preprint arXiv:1502.03044*.

Peter Young, Alice Lai, Micah Hodosh, and Julia Hockenmaier. 2014. From image descriptions to visual denotations: New similarity metrics for semantic inference over event descriptions. *Transactions of the Association for Computational Linguistics*, 2:67–78.

PRIMT: A Pick-Revise Framework for Interactive Machine Translation

Shanbo Cheng, Shujian Huang, Huadong Chen, Xinyu Dai and **Jiajun Chen**
State Key Laboratory for Novel Software Technology
Nanjing University
Nanjing 210023, China
{chengsb, huangsj, chenhd, daixy, chenjj}@nlp.nju.edu.cn

Abstract

Interactive machine translation (IMT) is a method which uses human-computer interactions to improve the quality of MT. Traditional IMT methods employ a left-to-right order for the interactions, which is difficult to directly modify critical errors at the end of the sentence. In this paper, we propose an IMT framework in which the interaction is decomposed into two simple human actions: picking a critical translation error (Pick) and revising the translation (Revise). The picked phrase could be at any position of the sentence, which improves the efficiency of human computer interaction. We also propose automatic suggestion models for the two actions to further reduce the cost of human interaction. Experiment results demonstrate that by interactions through either one of the actions, the translation quality could be significantly improved. Greater gains could be achieved by iteratively performing both actions.

1 Introduction

To obtain high quality translations, human translators usually have to modify the results generated by a machine translation (MT) system (called post editing, PE). In many cases, PE needs a lot of modifications, which is time-consuming (Plitt and Masselot, 2010). To speed up the process, interactive machine translation (IMT) is proposed which instantly update the translation result after every human action (Langlais et al., 2000; Foster et al., 2002; Barrachina et al., 2009; Koehn, 2009; González-Rubio et al., 2013; Alabau et al., 2014). Because the translation quality could be improved after every update,

IMT is expected to generate high quality translations with less human actions (Sanchis-Trilles et al., 2014).

Typical IMT systems usually use a left-to-right sentence completing framework pioneered by Langlais et al (2000), in which the users process the translation from the beginning of the sentence and interact with the system at the left-most error. By assuming the translation from the beginning to the modified part (called "prefix") to be correct, the system generates new translations after the given prefix (Koehn, 2009; Barrachina et al., 2009; Ortiz, 2011; Alabau et al., 2014).

Despite the success of this left-to-right framework, one potential weakness is that it is difficult to modify critical translation errors at the end of a sentence. Critical translation errors are those errors that has large impact on the translation of other words or phrases. When a translation ambiguity occurs at the end of a sentence while it causes translation errors at the beginning, modifying this critical errors first may bring great positive effects on previous parts of the translation, which may reduce human efforts in an IMT process. Modifying from left to right will delay the modification of the ambiguity point and lowers the interaction efficiency.

Critical errors are often caused by the inherent difficulty of translating source phrases. Mohit et al. (2007) proposed a classifier to identify the difficult-to-translate phrases (DTPs), which were extracted from syntactic trees. They demonstrated that asking human to translate these DTPs can bring a significant gain to the overall translation quality compared to translating other phrases. However, to our

Proceedings of NAACL-HLT 2016, pages 1240–1249,
San Diego, California, June 12-17, 2016. ©2016 Association for Computational Linguistics

Source	南亚　　各国　　　外长　　　商讨 自由 贸易区 和 反 恐 问题
	(south asian)(countries)(foreign minister)(discuss) (free)(trade zone)(and)(anti)(terrorism)(issue)
Ref	south asian foreign ministers discuss free trade zone and anti-terrorism issues
Baseline	south asian foreign ministers to discuss the issue of free trade area and <u>the</u>
L2R	south asian foreign ministers discuss the issue of free trade area and the
PR	south asian foreign ministers **discuss free trade area and** <u>anti-terrorism</u> issues

Table 1: Examples of applying the Left-to-right (L2R) framework and the Pick-Revise framework (PR) in modifying a Chinese-English translation. Both the PR and left-to-right actions are performed only once. The first row shows the Chinese words and their translations. The following rows are the reference translations, the translation of the baseline system, the translation after a L2R interaction cycle and the translation after a PR interaction cycle, respectively. The dashed underline phrase is picked as the error to be modified by L2R. The underline phrase is picked as the error to be modified. The bold parts show the positive effects of revising the selected translation error on the translation of their contexts in a constrained decoding.

best knowledge, there is no practice in integrating these DTPs into an IMT framework.

In this paper, we propose a Pick-Revise IMT framework (PRIMT) to explicitly split the modification of a translation result into two very simple actions. Firstly, a wrongly-translated phrase is selected from the whole sentence (**Pick**); secondly, the correct translation is selected from the translation table (or manually added) to replace the original one (**Revise**). Our system then re-translates the sentence and searches for the best translation using previous modifications as constraints (Section 2). Furthermore, we propose two automatic suggestion models that could predict the wrongly-translated phrases and select the revised translation, respectively (Section 3). With the suggestion models, users only perform one of the actions (picking or revising) and let the suggestion models complete the other one. In this case, the interactions could be further simplified to be only one of the actions, which is as simple as one mouse click.

Experiment results show that by performing only one mouse click, the translation quality could be significantly improved (around +2 BLEU points in one PR cycle). Performing both two actions multiple times will bring greater gain in translation quality (+17 BLEU) with a relatively low Keystroke and Mouse-action Ratio (KSMR) (Barrachina et al., 2009) (3.3% KSMR).

2　The Pick-Revise IMT Framework

2.1　PRIMT System

We first explain the difference between Pick-Revise (PR) framework and left-to-right frame-work (Foster et al., 2002) with an example (in Table 1). For the given input source sentence, the MT system firstly generates a baseline translation. In the left-to-right framework human translator modifies the left-most error from "to discuss" to "discuss". But this modification may not bring any positive effects on the other part of the translation. So more interactions are needed to further improve the translation quality.

In our pick-revise framework, the human translator picks the phrase " 反 恐" which was considered the most critical translation error, and revise the translation from "the" to "anti-terrorism" according to phrase table. After a PR cycle, our constrained decoder re-translates the sentence. It not only generates the correct translation for the pick-revise pair (PRP), but also improves the translation around the PRP (bold parts).

Compared to left-to-right framework, our framework can modify the most critical error at first, which brings larger improvements on translation quality and improves the efficiency of human interactions.

Figure 1 shows an overview of our framework. For a source sentence $s_1...s_n$, our framework iteratively generates the translation using a constrained decoder. The constraints come from previous picking and revising processes. The picking and revising results can also be collected for model adaptation. The whole process continues until the translation is considered acceptable by the users. We explain the key components of our framework below.

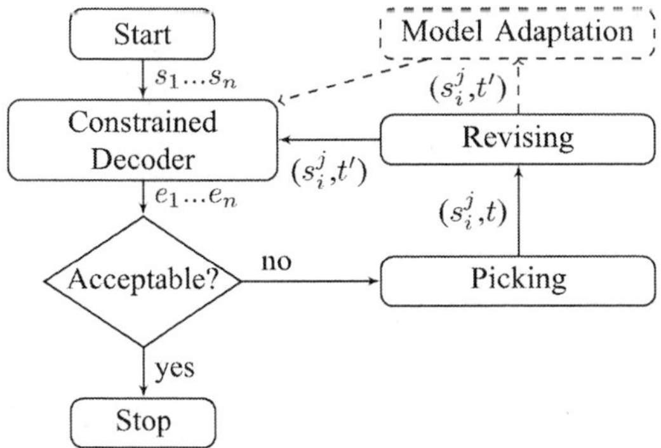

Figure 1: An overview of PRIMT framework.

2.2 Picking

In the picking step, the users pick the wrongly-translated phrase, (s_i^j, t)[1], to be revised. The picking process aims at finding critical errors in the translation, caused by errors in the translation table or inherent translation ambiguities. The more critical the error is, the larger translation quality improvement can be achieved by correcting the error (Mohit and Hwa, 2007). Critical errors might have a large influence to the translation of their context.

To make the picking step easier to be integrated into MT system, we limit the selection of translation errors to be those phrases in the previous PR-cycle output. If it's the first PR-cycle, then those errors come from phrases used to generate the baseline translation. For more convenient user interactions, in our PRIMT system, critical errors can be picked from both the source and target side by simply a mouse click on it. The correspondence/alignment between source and target phrases are visualized for easier human observation.

Green et al. (2014) demonstrated that performing post-editing, i.e. directly editing the translation errors, could get acceptable translations faster than performing left-to-right IMT. Such result also indicates that identifying critical translation errors is not a difficult task for human to perform.

2.3 Revising

In the revising step, the users revise the translation of s_i^j by selecting the correct translation t' from the translation table, or manually add one if there is no

---

[1] s_i^j is the phrase that covers the source words from index i to j, and translated into t.

correct translation in the translation table. Whether to perform selection or adding depends on the quality of the translation table. When the translation system is trained with large enough parallel data, the quality of the translation table is usually high enough to offer the correct translation.

For a picked phrase, the translation options in the phrase table could be presented to the users as a list. The users just need to click on the correct translation to complete the revising step. The users could also type a new translation through a separated input area.

2.4 Decoder and Model Adaptation

A pick-revise pair (PRP), (s_i^j, t'), is obtained after a PR cycle for a source sentence. We use a constrained decoder to search for the best translation with the previous PRPs as constraints. The constrained search algorithm is similar to the algorithm in a typical phrase-based machine translation (Koehn et al., 2003). The only exception is that it makes an extra comparison between each translation option and previous PR pairs, which ignores all the phrases that overlap with the source side of a PRP. As a result, a lot of translation options are ignored, which makes the search space much smaller than standard decoding. In this way, we could guarantee that all the PRPs are correctly translated and the whole process can be carried out in real-time.

The system could collect all PRPs and adapt the models using methods described in Germann (2014) or Marie (2015). In our current implementation, we mainly focus on the picking and revising step and leave model adaptation as future work.

3 Automatic Suggestion Models

To further reduce the human actions, we propose to use automatic suggestion models for the picking and revising step, respectively. Such models can offer suggestions to users in both picking and revising steps. Because both picking and revising actions are performing selections from multiple candidates, we use classifier-based approaches to model these two steps. In the following subsections, we will introduce how we define the picking and revising tasks as classification tasks and how we choose features to model the tasks. Note that these automatic suggestion models could be interpreted as simplified confidence measurements.

3.1 The Picking Suggestion Model (PSM)

3.1.1 PSM Training

The picking process aims at selecting critical errors which has huge impact on the translation quality of their context. The goal of PSM is to automatically recognize those phrases that might be wrongly-translated, and suggest users to pick these phrases. In real world systems, the users can either accept or refuse the suggestion.

Within all the phrases of a source sentence, we need to separate the wrongly-translated phrases and correctly-translated phrases. Because translation errors often cause low translation quality, we use the translation quality gain after the revising action as a measurement. We treat those phrases that achieve translation quality improvement after revising as wrongly-translated phrases; those lead to translation quality deterioration as correctly-translated phrases.

We select phrases that lead to a BLEU improvement/deterioration greater than a threshold as positive/negative instances. In this paper, the threshold is set as 10% of the BLEU score of the baseline sentence.

3.1.2 PSM Features

Modeling the picking process needs two aspects of information. One of them is to determine whether the phrase is difficult-to-translate; the other is to determine whether the current translation option is correct. We use features from translation models (TMs), language models (LMs), lexical reordering models (LRMs), as well as counting and lexical features in Table 2. These features cover information of the source side, target side, translation ambiguity, and context, etc.

3.2 The Revising Suggestion Model (RSM)

3.2.1 RSM Training

The revising process aims at selecting a correct translation for a given phrase under the given context. The goal of RSM is to predict the correct translation and suggest users to replace the wrong translation with the predicted one. The users can either accept it or use another translation.

Translation table has multiple translation options for one phrase. Within the translation option set of a source phrase, we need to separate the correc-

Category	Description
TM	TM scores of baseline translation
	Normalized TM scores of baseline translation
	TM entropy of all translation options
LM	LM score of baseline translation
	LM score of previous/next phrase translation
	LM score of each target word
	LM score of the bigram at the border of current and previous/next phrase
LRM	LRM scores of baseline translation
	LRM scores of previous/next phrase translation
Count	Source/target word count
	Number of translation options for current source phrase
POS	POS-tags of source words
	POS-tags of previous/next word of source phrase
Lexical	Source words
	Target words

Table 2: Features for the PSM.

t and wrong translation options. Instead of asking human translators to label these translations, we use two criteria to distinguish correct translation options from wrong translation options.

Firstly, the correct translation option should be a substring of the references, which ensures the correctness of the options itself. Secondly, the correct translation option should be consistent with pre-trained word alignment on the translated sentence pair[2]. This is to ensure that the translation option does not get credit for words that are not translations of the source side phrase. The remaining options are considered wrong translations.

With the above criteria, we select all correct translation options as positive instances for the revising step, and randomly sample the same number of wrong translation options to be negative instances. Specifically, translation options that are used by the baseline system are included as negative instances.

3.2.2 RSM Features

The features used for RSM are showed in Table 3. For translations of a given source phrase, there is no need to compare their source-side information because these translation options share the same source phrase and context. So these features mainly focus

---

[2]We trained word alignments with Giza++(Och and Ney, 2003)

on estimating the translation quality of a given translation option. As a result, features for RSM only including the scores for TM, LM and LRM, etc, which are simpler compared to PSM.

Category	Description
TM	TM scores of current translation option
LM	LM score of current translation option
	LM score of each target word
LRM	LRM scores of current translation option
count	Target word count
Lexical	Target words

Table 3: Features for the RSM

4 Experiments

4.1 Experiment Settings

4.1.1 Translation Settings

Through out the experiments, we use an in-house implementation of the phrase-based machine translation system (Koehn et al., 2003) and incorporate our PRIMT framework into the translation system. The parallel data for training the translation model includes 8.2 million sentences pairs from LDC2002E18, LDC2003E14, LDC2004E12, LDC2004T08, LDC2005T10, LDC2007T09. A 5-gram language model is trained with MKN smoothing (Chen and Goodman, 1999) on Xinhua portion of Gigaword which contains 14.6 million sentences. We use a combination of NIST02 and NIST03 to tune the MT system parameters and train the suggestion models. We test the system on NIST04 and NIST05 data. The translation results are evaluated with case insensitive 4-gram BLEU (Papineni et al., 2002). Our baseline phrase-based MT system has comparable performance with the open source toolkit Moses (Koehn et al., 2003).

4.1.2 Classification Settings

We use three classification models to model the automatic suggestion models: the maximum entropy model, the SVM model and the neural network model. We use a maximum entropy model (Zhang, 2004) with 30 iterations of L-BFGS. We use the LibSVM implementation (Chang and Lin, 2011) with RBF kernel and L2 regularization ($c = 128$, $\gamma = 0.5$). We use a feedforward neural network with the CNTK implementation (Agarwal et al., 2014). The neural network has one hidden layer of 80 nodes, with sigmoid function as the activation function.

We use one-hot representation for the source and target word features when using the maximum entropy and SVM model, and use pre-trained word embeddings (Mikolov et al., 2013) for the neural model.

4.2 Methodology

4.2.1 Simulated Human Interaction

Because real-world human interactions are expensive and time-consuming to obtain, we use simulated human interactions for picking and revising in the experiment.

Directly identifying critical errors in the translation is not an easy task without human annotation. Instead, we find critical errors by judging the influence of a given error to the translation of their context. We try picking every phrase in a baseline translation result and revising it using the simulated revising strategy (described below). The influence of the phrase is measured by the translation quality improvement after re-translation with the current phrase be revised. The phrase with the highest translation quality improvement is picked to be the simulated human picking result.

Given the phrase to be revised, the simulated revising action is straightforward. Among all the translation options that are considered correct (Sec. 3.2.1), we choose the longest one to be the simulated human revising result.

With the above simulated actions, one PR cycle takes exactly two mouse clicks and none keystroke. For fair comparison, we use the same simulated revising action for the left-to-right framework. Each cycle of left-to-right framework also takes two mouse clicks. We also compare the post editing method which selects the most critical error and edits it to be the simulated revising translation. The key-stroke count for each editing is the number of characters of the correct phrase translation.

4.3 Translation Quality Improvement in Ideal Environment

Our first experiment is to test the PRIMT performance in an ideal environment. We conduct experiments on sentences for which the reference could be generated by our current MT system using forced decoding. Forced decoding forces the decoder to gen-

Data	NIST04(forced)		NIST05(forced)	
	BLEU	KSMR	BLEU	KSMR
Baseline	44.59	0	41.48	0
PR*1	**63.21 (+18.62)**	2.2	**55.10 (+13.62)**	2.2
PR*2	**70.82 (+26.23)**	4.3	**63.03 (+21.55)**	4.4
PR*3	**73.99 (+29.50)**	6.5	**68.56 (+27.08)**	6.7
PR*4	**75.48 (+30.89)**	8.6	**72.20 (+30.72)**	8.9
PR*5	**76.59 (+32.00)**	10.8	**73.90 (+32.42)**	11.1
PR*6	**78.07 (+33.48)**	12.9	**75.22 (+33.74)**	13.3
PR*7	**79.27 (+34.68)**	15.1	**75.57 (+34.09)**	15.5
PR*8	**79.54 (+34.93)**	17.2	**76.02 (+34.54)**	17.8
L2R*1	49.32 (+4.73)	2.2	46.34 (+4.86)	2.2
PE*1	49.77 (+5.18)	8.3	46.81 (+5.33)	8.2

Table 4: Experiments on sentences that can be forced-decoded for both NIST04 and NIST05 data, with 186 and 92 sentence counts, respectively. (PR*n denotes system that repeat picking and revising for n cycles; the PE system post edits the most critical error; the L2R system modifies the left most error).

Data	NIST04		NIST05	
	BLEU	KSMR	BLEU	KSMR
Baseline	31.83	0	30.64	0
PR*1	**42.88 (+11.05)**	1.1	**41.47 (+10.83))**	1.1
PR*2	**48.21 (+16.38)**	2.2	**45.76 (+15.12)**	2.2
PR*3	**50.12 (+18.29)**	3.3	**48.33 (+17.69)**	3.3
L2R*1	35.61 (+3.78)	1.1	33.85 (+3.21)	1.1
PE*1	34.74 (+2.91)	4.3	34.18 (+2.54)	4.8

Table 5: Experiments on both NIST04 and NIST05 data. (PR*n denotes system that repeat picking and revising for n cycles; the PE system post edits the most critical error; the L2R system corrects the left most error).

ASM	Classifier	NIST04	NIST05
PSM	MaxEnt	0.70/0.62/0.66	0.69/0.60/0.64
	SVM	0.71/0.68/0.69	0.69/0.66/0.67
	Feedforward	0.71/0.73/0.72	0.68/0.70/0.69
RSM	MaxEnt	0.71/0.58/0.63	0.70/0.57/0.63
	SVM	0.70/0.61/0.0.65	0.68/0.62/0.65
	Feedforward	0.66/0.67/0.66	0.65/0.65/0.65

Table 6: Classification performance of automatic suggestion models. The three values of each cell denotes the precision, recall and F-score, respectively, calculated on positive instances of corresponding classifier.

erate translations exactly the same as the references. A reference translation could be generated by forced decoding means that it won't be necessary to input new words to generate a correct translation. Because we only simulate human revising actions as selecting the best translation option from phrase table (without adding new options), such a setting guarantees that the phrase table contains the correct translation for every phrase.

Table 4 shows that picking and revising the most critical error (PR*1) can bring +18 and +13 BLEU improvements in the two data sets, respectively. Revising the left-most error (L2R*1) only achieves an improvement around +5 BLEU. This result demonstrates that picking the critical error to be revised is critical in our PR framework. Compared to the left-to-right method, our framework has the advantage of correcting the critical errors in a high priority. By correcting such errors, the BLEU gain is much larger than left-to-right correction.

Post-editing the most critical error (PE*1) uses 8% KSMR, but only brings +5 BLEU improvement. Compared to post-editing, which just edits the critical error without affecting other parts of the translation, our PRIMT framework can re-decode for better translations with less human interactions.

In 8 PR-cycles (PR*8) (around 17% KSMR), the PRIMT achieves very high quality translation results with a BLEU score higher than 75 (around +35 BLEU to baseline). These results demonstrate the efficiency of PRIMT in multiple interactions.

4.4 Translation Quality Improvement in General Environment

We also validate the improvements of translation quality in a general environment. We perform similar experiments on all NIST04 and NIST05 data. In some of the sentences, the translation table might not contain the correct translation for source phrase, due to the limitation of the training of our current MT system.

The results are listed in Table 5. Although the BLEU score in general environment are lower than those in ideal environment, the results show basically the same trends as in the previous experiment. The third row (PR*1) in Table 5 shows that picking and revising the most critical error can bring around +11 BLEU improvements in both data sets. The improvements in L2R*1 (+3.2) and PE*1 (+2.5) are much less. Three PR-cycles (around 3.3 KSMR) can achieve +17 BLEU improvements (PR*3). Compared to left-to-right and PE methods, our framework still has a significant advantage in the general environment.

4.5 Using Automatic Suggestion Models

We validate the effectiveness of our automatic suggestion models by both classification performance and translation performance.

Table 6 shows the classification performances of the PSM and the RSM, with different models. The precision and recall are calculated on positive instances in the test set, because only those instances that are predicted as positive will be used in the IMT system. Because it is harder to automatically identify the correct translation, we keep the translation unchanged when the RSM classifies all translation options to be negative.

The performance of the three classifiers are similar. Feedforward neural network has a moderate advantage. In general, the PSM could recognize the critical translation errors with an F-score around 0.67. The RSM achieves about 0.65 F-score for recognizing the correct translation. The F-scores are all in the range between 60 and 70, which is reasonable considering the difficulty of the tasks themselves.

We also evaluate the translation improvements when automatic suggestion models are used in the PR framework (Table 7). If the picking action performs a random pick of phrase (RandomPicking), there is barely no improvement in the translation quality, even with the simulated revising action. For comparison, using PSM could achieve a significant BLEU improvement of around 2 BLEU, on both test sets. It suggests that the BLEU gain does not come from the long reference translation match in the revising step. Picking critical errors is crucial in our framework.

Choosing the most critical error and performing a random revising action (RandomRevising) brings no improvement in BLEU either. Using our RSM could still improve the translation quality by 1.5 BLEU.

In general, using one of our PSM and RSM could still achieve significant improvement in translation quality. But the uses only need to perform one type of actions, which might be more suitable to be performed by a single human translator. However, the improvement is relatively small compared to fully simulated results, suggesting that human involvement is still critical for improve the translation quality. Better modeling or training with larger data may also improvement the performance of automatic sug-

		NIST04	NIST05
	Baseline	31.83	30.64
PSM	RandomPicking	31.92 (+0.09)	30.69 (+0.05)
	MaxEnt	33.89 (+2.06)	32.57 (+1.93)
	SVM	34.01 (+2.18)	32.66 (+2.02)
	FeedForward	34.23 (+2.40)	32.81 (+2.17)
RSM	RandomRevising	31.90 (+0.07)	30.71 (+0.08)
	MaxEnt	33.62 (+1.79)	32.38 (+1.74)
	SVM	33.73 (+1.90)	32.42 (+1.78)
	FeedForward	33.77 (+1.94)	32.44 (+1.80)

Table 7: Improvements of translation quality using random selection and automatic suggestion models.

gestions.

5 Example Analysis

We further analyze the performance of our PRIMT system by examples. Table 8 shows the PRIMT procedure of improving translation quality for three different sentences.

In the first sentence, two PR cycles (4.7% KSM-R) lead to a perfect translation. In the first PR cycle (PR*1), revising the translation of " 第六" from "the" to "the 6th" improves the neighboring translation. The translation of " 证实" change from "confirms" to "confirm", which is a positive effect. In PR*2, revising the translation of " 病例" from "cases" to "case" also changes the neighborhood translation (the translation of " 禽流感 死亡 病例" changes to "death case from the bird flu"). After two PR cycles, the reference translation is obtained.

In our current settings, the reference translation could not always be obtained. The maximum achievable BLEU is around 60-70 in general environment. The next two examples shows some possible explanations.

In the second sentence in Table 8, " 需要 一定" is picked in the first PR cycle. Revising the translation from "a" to "need a certain" makes the translation of " 通常" changing from "is" to "usually". In the next PR cycle, revising the translation of " 过程" from "process" to "course" makes the neighboring translation changing from "," to ", and". Meanwhile, the position of "course" moves to the right place (in front of ","). In the last PR cycle, the translation of " 很难" is revised from "it" to "it cannot be". After three PR cycles, the translation quality improves significantly. However, the translation is still different from the

Source	世卫　　　组织　　证实　　越南　第六[1]个　禽流感　死亡　病例[2]
	(world health) (organization) (confirm) (vietnam) (6th) () (bird flu) (death) (case)
Ref	the world health organization confirms the 6th death case from the bird flu in vietnam
Baseline	the world health organization confirmed the bird flu death cases in vietnam
PR*1	the world health organization **confirms** the 6th[1] bird flu death cases in vietnam
PR*2	the world health organization confirms the 6th death case[2] **from the bird flu** in vietnam
Source	民族　　和解　　　通常　需要　一定[1] 的 过程[2] ，　很 难[3]　　一蹴而就[4]　　　。
	(national) (reconciliation) (usually) (need) (certain) () (course) (,) (cannot) (accomplish in one action) (.)
Ref	national reconciliation usually need a certain course , and it cannot be accomplished in one action .
Baseline	national reconciliation is a very difficult process takes .
PR*1	national reconciliation process **usually** need a certain[1] takes very difficult .
PR*2	national reconciliation **usually need a certain** course[2] **, and** it accomplished .
PR*3	national reconciliation usually need a certain course , and it cannnot be[3] accomplished .
Human	national reconciliation usually need a certain course , and it cannnot be accomplished in one action[4] .
Source	然而，　以色列的[2] 回答 无法[1] 充分扫除　美国　的 疑问　　。
	(however) (israel's) (reply) (fail) (full clear) (the us) () (doubt) (.)
Ref	however , israel 's reply failed to fully clear the us doubts .
Baseline	however , the israeli response to the full removal of united states .
PR*1	however , the israeli response failed to[1] **fully clear** doubts . the us
PR*2	however , israel 's[2] **reply** failed to fully clear doubts . the us

Table 8: Examples of applying PR actions multiple times in the Chinese-English translation. The superscript i of the underline phrases, P_i in source sentence denotes the underline phrase is picked in the i-th PR cycle as the critical error. The original translation of P_i is the underline phrase without superscript in PR*$(i-1)$ (Baseline is PR*0). The correct translation is the underline parts with superscript in PR*i. The bold parts shows the positive effects on other parts near the PRPs.

reference. This is because "一蹴而就" should be translated into "accomplished in one action" instead of "accomplished". But there is no suitable translation options for it in the current phrase table. So the system cannot generate a perfect translation. The problems will be less significant when real-world human translators are involved. Human translator inputs the correct translation "accomplished in one action", the system will generate the reference translation after constrained decoding (Human).

In the last sentence in Table 8, "无法" is picked as the critical error. Revising the translation from "to the" to "failed to", leads to an improvement on neighboring phrase (the translation of "充分扫除" to "fully clear"). In the second PR cycle, "以色列的" is picked. Revising the translation from "the israeli" to "israel 's", makes the translation of "回答" change from "response" to "reply", which is also a positive effect. However, after two PR cycles, all phrase translations are correct, but the translation is still different from the reference. This is because the language model and lexical reordering model prefer the wrong phrase ordering, which put "the us" at the end of the whole sentence. This problem raises from the MT system itself, which may not be solved directly in our current framework.

If more interactions are allowed, for example, performing reordering operations, the above problems could be solved. But the interactions become more complex, and may not be acceptable to human translators. Other solutions includes using better statistical models such as neural language models (Bengio et al., 2003). This is an interesting issue we will look into.

6 Conclusion

We introduced a pick-revise IMT framework, PRIMT, where the users could pick critical translation errors anywhere in the sentence and revise the translation. By correcting the critical error instead of the left most one, our framework could improve the translation quality in a quicker and more efficient way. By using automatic suggestion models, we could reduce human interaction to a single type, either picking or revising. It is also possible to let different human translators to perform different action-

s. In this case every translator will focus on a single action, which might be easier to train and may have higher efficiency.

On the other hand, the performance of current framework is still related to the underlying MT system. Further improvement could be achieved by supporting other type of interactions, such as reordering operations, or building the system with stronger statistical models. We will also conduct real-world experiments to see how this new IMT framework works when human translators are actually involved.

7   Acknowledgement

The authors would like to thank the anonymous reviewers for their valuable comments. This work is supported by the National Natural Science Foundation of China (No. 61300158, 61472183), the Jiangsu Provincial Research Foundation for Basic Research (No. BK20130580). This research is partially supported by the Collaborative Innovation Center of Novel Software Technology and Industrialization, Nanjing University. Shujian Huang is the corresponding author.

References

Amit Agarwal, Eldar Akchurin, Chris Basoglu, Guoguo Chen, Scott Cyphers, Jasha Droppo, Adam Eversole, Brian Guenter, Mark Hillebrand, Xuedong Huang, Zhiheng Huang, Vladimir Ivanov, Alexey Kamenev, Philipp Kranen, Oleksii Kuchaiev, Wolfgang Manousek, Avner May, Bhaskar Mitra, Olivier Nano, Gaizka Navarro, Alexey Orlov, Marko Padmilac, Hari Parthasarathi, Baolin Peng, Alexey Reznichenko, Frank Seide, Michael L. Seltzer, Malcolm Slaney, Andreas Stolcke, Huaming Wang, Kaisheng Yao, Dong Yu, Yu Zhang, and Geoffrey Zweig. 2014. An introduction to computational networks and the computational network toolkit. Technical Report MSR-TR-2014-112, August.

Vicent Alabau, Christian Buck, Michael Carl, Francisco Casacuberta, M García-Martínez, Ulrich Germann, Jesús González-Rubio, Robin Hill, Philipp Koehn, LA Leiva, et al. 2014. Casmacat: A computer-assisted translation workbench. In *Proceedings of the 14th Conference of the European Chapter of the Association for Computational Linguistics*, pages 25--28.

Sergio Barrachina, Oliver Bender, Francisco Casacuberta, Jorge Civera, Elsa Cubel, Shahram Khadivi, Antonio Lagarda, Hermann Ney, Jesús Tomás, Enrique Vidal, et al. 2009. Statistical approaches to computer-assisted translation. *Computational Linguistics*, 35(1):3--28.

Yoshua Bengio, Réjean Ducharme, Pascal Vincent, and Christian Janvin. 2003. A neural probabilistic language model. *The Journal of Machine Learning Research*, 3:1137--1155.

Chih-Chung Chang and Chih-Jen Lin. 2011. Libsvm: a library for support vector machines. *ACM Transactions on Intelligent Systems and Technology (TIST)*, 2(3):27.

Stanley F Chen and Joshua Goodman. 1999. An empirical study of smoothing techniques for language modeling. *Computer Speech & Language*, 13(4):359--393.

George Foster, Philippe Langlais, and Guy Lapalme. 2002. User-friendly text prediction for translators. In *Proceedings of the ACL-02 conference on Empirical methods in natural language processing-Volume 10*, pages 148--155. Association for Computational Linguistics.

Ulrich Germann. 2014. Dynamic phrase tables for machine translation in an interactive post-editing scenario. In *AMTA 2014 Workshop on Interactive and Adaptive Machine Translation, Vancouver, BC, Canada*, pages 20--31.

Jesús González-Rubio, Daniel Ortiz-Martínez, José-Miguel Benedí, and Francisco Casacuberta. 2013. Interactive machine translation using hierarchical translation models. In *Conference on Empirical Methods in Natural Language Processing*, pages 244--254.

Spence Green, Sida I Wang, Jason Chuang, Jeffrey Heer, Sebastian Schuster, and Christopher D Manning. 2014. Human effort and machine learnability in computer aided translation. In *Conference on Empirical Methods in Natural Language Processing*, pages 1225--1236.

Philipp Koehn, Franz Josef Och, and Daniel Marcu. 2003. Statistical phrase-based translation. In *Proceedings of the 2003 Conference of the North American Chapter of the Association for Computational Linguistics on Human Language Technology-Volume 1*, pages 48--54. Association for Computational Linguistics.

Philipp Koehn. 2009. A web-based interactive computer aided translation tool. In *Proceedings of the ACL-IJCNLP 2009 Software Demonstrations*, pages 17--20. Association for Computational Linguistics.

Philippe Langlais, George Foster, and Guy Lapalme. 2000. Transtype: a computer-aided translation typing system. In *Proceedings of the 2000 NAACL-ANLP Workshop on Embedded machine translation systems-Volume 5*, pages 46--51. Association for Computational Linguistics.

Benjamin Marie, Lingua et Machina, France Le Chesnay, and Aurélien Max. 2015. Touch-based pre-postediting of machine translation output. In *Conference on Empirical Methods in Natural Language Processing*.

Tomas Mikolov, Ilya Sutskever, Kai Chen, Greg S Corrado, and Jeff Dean. 2013. Distributed representations of words and phrases and their compositionality. In *Advances in neural information processing systems*, pages 3111--3119. Neural Information Processing Systems.

Behrang Mohit and Rebecca Hwa. 2007. Localization of difficult-to-translate phrases. In *Proceedings of the Second Workshop on Statistical Machine Translation*, pages 248--255. Association for Computational Linguistics.

Franz Josef Och and Hermann Ney. 2003. A systematic comparison of various statistical alignment models. *Computational Linguistics*, 29(1):19--51.

Daniel Ortiz. 2011. *Advances in fully-automatic and interactive phrase-based statistical machine translation*. Ph.D. thesis, Universitat Politècnica de València.

Kishore Papineni, Salim Roukos, Todd Ward, and Wei-Jing Zhu. 2002. Bleu: a method for automatic evaluation of machine translation. In *Proceedings of the 40th annual meeting on association for computational linguistics*, pages 311--318. Association for Computational Linguistics.

Mirko Plitt and François Masselot. 2010. A productivity test of statistical machine translation post-editing in a typical localisation context. *The Prague Bulletin of Mathematical Linguistics*, 93:7--16.

Germán Sanchis-Trilles, Vicent Alabau, Christian Buck, Michael Carl, Francisco Casacuberta, Mercedes García-Martínez, Ulrich Germann, Jesús González-Rubio, Robin L Hill, Philipp Koehn, et al. 2014. Interactive translation prediction versus conventional post-editing in practice: a study with the casmacat workbench. *Machine Translation*, 28(3-4):217--235.

Le Zhang. 2004. Maximum entropy modeling toolkit for python and c++.

Incorporating Side Information into Recurrent Neural Network Language Models

Cong Duy Vu Hoang
University of Melbourne
Melbourne, VIC, Australia
vhoang2@student.unimelb.edu.au

Gholamreza Haffari
Monash University
Clayton, VIC, Australia
gholamreza.haffari@monash.edu

Trevor Cohn
University of Melbourne
Melbourne, VIC, Australia
t.cohn@unimelb.edu.au

Abstract

Recurrent neural network language models (RNNLM) have recently demonstrated vast potential in modelling long-term dependencies for NLP problems, ranging from speech recognition to machine translation. In this work, we propose methods for conditioning RNNLMs on external side information, e.g., metadata such as keywords, description, document title or topic headline. Our experiments show consistent improvements of RNNLMs using side information over the baselines for two different datasets and genres in two languages. Interestingly, we found that side information in a foreign language can be highly beneficial in modelling texts in another language, serving as a form of cross-lingual language modelling.

1 Introduction

Neural network approaches to language modelling (LM) have made remarkable performance gains over traditional count-based $n$gram LMs (Bengio et al., 2003; Mnih and Hinton, 2007; Mikolov et al., 2011). They offer several desirable characteristics, including the capacity to generalise over large vocabularies through the use of vector space representation, and – for recurrent models (Mikolov et al., 2011) – the ability to encode long distance dependencies that are impossible to include with a limited context windows used in conventional $n$gram LMs. These early papers have spawned a cottage industry in neural LM based applications, where text generation is a key component, including conditional language models for image captioning (Kiros et al., 2014;

Vinyals et al., 2015) and neural machine translation (Kalchbrenner and Blunsom, 2013; Sutskever et al., 2014; Bahdanau et al., 2015).

Inspired by these works for conditioning LMs on complex side information, such as images and foreign text, in this paper we investigate the possibility of improving LMs in a more traditional setting, that is when applied directly to text documents. Typically corpora include rich side information, such as document titles, authorship, time stamp, keywords and so on, although this information is usually discarded when applying statistical models. However, this information can be highly informative, for instance, keywords, titles or descriptions, often include central topics which will be helpful in modelling or understanding the document text. We propose mechanisms for encoding this side information into a vector space representation, and means of incorporating it into the generating process in a RNNLM framework. Evaluating on two corpora and two different languages, we show consistently significant perplexity reductions over the state-of-the-art RNNLM models.

The contributions of this paper are as follows:

1. We propose a framework for encoding structured and unstructured side information, and its incorporation into a RNNLM.
2. We introduce a new corpus, the RIE corpus, based on the Europarl web archive, with rich annotations of several types of meta-data.
3. We provide empirical analysis showing consistent improvements from using side information across two datasets in two languages.

Proceedings of NAACL-HLT 2016, pages 1250–1255,
San Diego, California, June 12-17, 2016. ©2016 Association for Computational Linguistics

2 Problem Formulation & Model

We first review RNNLM architecture (Mikolov et al., 2011) before describing our extension in §2.2.

2.1 RNNLM Architecture

The standard RNNLM consists of 3 main layers: an input layer where each input word has its embedding via one-hot vector coding; a hidden layer consisting of recurrent units where a state is conditioned recursively on past states; and an output layer where a target word will be predicted. RNNLM has an advantage over conventional n-gram language model in modelling long distance dependencies effectively.

In general, an RNN operates from left-to-right over the input word sequence; i.e.,

$$h_t = \mathrm{RU}\left(x_t, h_{t-1}\right)$$
$$= \mathrm{f}\left(W^{(hh)}h_{t-1} + W^{(ih)}x_t + b^{(h)}\right)$$
$$x_{t+1} \sim \mathrm{softmax}\left(W^{(ho)}h_t + b^{(o)}\right);$$

where $f(.)$ is a non-linear function, e.g., tanh, applied element-wise to its vector input; h_t is the current RNN hidden state at time-step t; and matrices W and vectors b are model parameters. The model is trained using gradient-based methods to optimise a (regularised) training objective, e.g. the likelihood function. In principle, a recurrent unit (RU) can be employed using different variants of recurrent structures such as: Long Short Term Memory (LSTM) (Hochreiter and Schmidhuber, 1997), Gated Recurrent Unit (GRU) (Cho et al., 2014), or recently deeper structures, e.g. Depth Gated Long Short Term Memory (DGLSTM) – a stack of LSTMs with extra connections between memory cells in deep layers (Yao et al., 2015). It can be regarded as being a generalisation of LSTM recurrence to both time and depth. Such deep recurrent structure may capture long distance patterns at their most general. Empirically, we found that RNNLM with DGLSTM structure appears to be best performer across our datasets, and therefore is used predominantly in our experiments.

2.2 Incorporating Side Information

Nowadays, many corpora are archived with side information or contextual meta-data. In this work, we

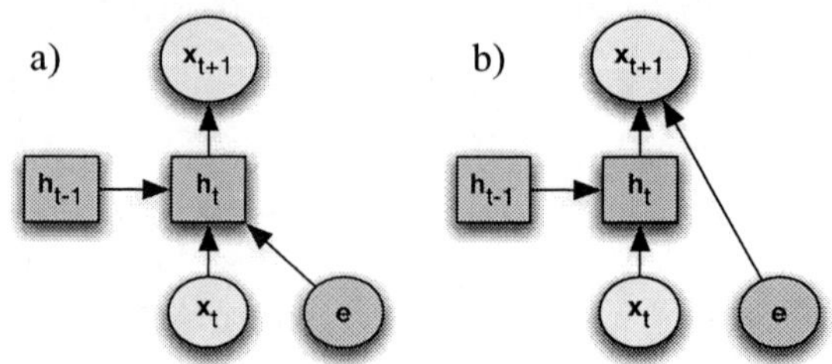

Figure 1: Integration methods for auxiliary information, e: a) as input to the RNN, or b) as part of the output softmax layer.

argue that such information can be useful for language modelling (and presumably other NLP tasks). By providing this auxiliary information directly to the RNNLM, we stand to boost language modelling performance.

The first question in using side information is how to encode these unstructured inputs, y, into a vector representation, denoted e. We discuss several methods for encoding the auxiliary vector:

BOW additive bag of words, $e = \sum_t y_t$, and

average the average embedding vector, $e = \frac{1}{T}\sum_t y_t$, both inspired by (Hermann and Blunsom, 2014a);

bigram convolution with sum-pooling, $e = \sum_t \tanh\left(y_{t-1} + y_t\right)$ (Hermann and Blunsom, 2014b); and

RNN a recurrent neural network over the word sequence (Sutskever et al., 2014), using the final hidden state(s) as e.

From the above methods, we found that BOW worked consistently well, outperforming the other approaches, and moreover lead to a simpler model with faster training. For this reason we report only results for the BOW encoding. Note that when using multiple auxiliary inputs, we use a weighted combination, $e = \sum_i W^{(ai)}e^{(i)}$.

The next step is the integration of e into the RNNLM. We consider two integration methods: as input to the hidden state (denoted **input**), and connected to the output softmax layer (**output**), as shown in Figure 1 a and b, respectively. In both cases, we compare experimentally the following integration strategies:

add adding the vectors together, e.g., using $x_t + e$ as the input to the RNN, such that

$$h_t = \mathrm{RU}\left(\boldsymbol{x}_t + \boldsymbol{e}, \boldsymbol{h}_{t-1}\right);$$

stack concatenating the vectors, e.g., using $\left[\boldsymbol{x}_t^\top \boldsymbol{e}^\top\right]^\top$ for generating the RNN hidden state, such that $\boldsymbol{h}_t = \mathrm{RU}\left(\begin{bmatrix} \boldsymbol{x}_t \\ \boldsymbol{e} \end{bmatrix}, \boldsymbol{h}_{t-1}\right)$; and

mlp feeding both vectors into an extra perceptron with single hidden layer, using a tanh non-linearity and projecting the output to the required dimensionality; i.e.,

$$\boldsymbol{h}_t' = \tanh\left(\boldsymbol{W}^{(hh')}\boldsymbol{h}_t + \boldsymbol{W}^{(he)}\boldsymbol{e} + \boldsymbol{b}^{(h')}\right)$$

$$\boldsymbol{x}_{t+1} \sim \mathrm{softmax}\left(\boldsymbol{W}^{(ho)}\boldsymbol{h}_t' + \boldsymbol{b}^{(o)}\right).$$

Note that *add* requires the vectors to be the same dimensionality, while the other two methods do not. The *stack* method can be quite costly, given that it increases the size of several matrices, either in the recurrent unit (for *input*) or the *output* mapping for word generation. This is a problem in the latter case: given the large size of the vocabulary, the matrix $\boldsymbol{W}^{(ho)}$ is already very large and making it larger (doubling the size, to become $\boldsymbol{W}^{(h'o)}$) has a size-able effect on training time (and presumably also propensity to over-fit). The *output+stack* method does however have a compelling interpretation as a jointly trained product model between a RNNLM and a unigram model conditioned on the side information, where both models are formulated as softmax classifiers. Considered as a product model (Hinton, 2002; Pascanu et al., 2013), the two components can concentrate on different aspects of the problem where the other model is not confident, and allowed each model the ability to 'veto' certain outputs, by assigning them a low probability.

3 Experiments

Datasets. We conducted our experiments on two datasets with different genres in two languages. As the first dataset, we use the IWSLT2014 MT track on TED Talks[1] due to its self-contained rich auxiliary information, including: title, description, keywords, and author related information. We chose the English-French pair for our experiments[2] . The statistics of the training set is shown in Table 1. We

---

[1] https://wit3.fbk.eu/ (IWSLT'14 MT Track)
[2] Our method can be also applied to other language pairs.

	tokens (M)	types (K)	docs	sents (K)
TED-en	4.0	18.3	1414	179
TED-fr	4.3	22.6	1414	179
RIE-en	13.7	15.0	200	460
RIE-fr	14.9	19.4	200	460

Table 1: Statistics of the training sets, showing in each cell the number of word tokens, types, documents (talks or plenaries), and sentences. Note that "types" here refers to word frequency thresholded at 5 and 15 for TED Talks and RIE datasets, respectively.

used dev2010 (7 talks/817 sentences) for early stopping of training neural network models. For evaluation, we used different testing sets over years, including tst2010 (10/1587), tst2011 (7/768), tst2012 (10/1083).

As the second dataset, we crawled the entire European Parliament[3] website, focusing on plenary sessions. Such sessions contain useful structural information, namely multilingual texts divided into speaker sessions and topics. We believe that those texts are interesting and challenging for language modelling tasks. Our dataset contains 724 plenary sessions over 12.5 years until June 2011 with multilingual texts in 22 languages[4]. We refer to this dataset by RIE[5] (**Rich Information Europarl**). We randomly select 200/5/30 plenary sessions as the training/development/test sets, respectively. We believe that the new data including side information pose another challenge for language modelling. Furthermore, the sizes of our working datasets are an order of magnitude larger than the standard Penn Treebank set which is often used for evaluating neural language models.

Set-up and Baselines. We have used cnn[6] to implement our models. We use the same configurations for all neural models: 512 input embedding and hidden layer dimensions, 2 hidden layers, and vocabulary sizes as given in Table 1. We used the same vocabulary for the auxiliary and modelled text. We trained a conventional $5-$gram language model using modified Kneser-Ney smoothing, with the KenLM toolkit (Heafield, 2011). We used the

---

[3] http://www.europarl.europa.eu/
[4] We ignored the period from June 2011 onwards, as from this date the EU stopped creating manual human translations.
[5] This dataset will be released upon publication.
[6] https://github.com/clab/cnn/

Method	test2010	test2011	test2012
5-gram LM	79.9	77.4	89.9
RNNLM	65.8	63.9	73.0
LSTM	54.1	52.2	58.4
DGLSTM	53.1	52.1	58.8
input+add+k	52.9	52.1	57.5
input+mlp+k	53.3	51.5	57.3
input+stack+k	53.7	51.9	58.1
output+mlp+k	**51.7**	**50.6**	**55.8**
output+mlp+t	**52.3**	53.5	58.3
output+mlp+d	**52.0**	49.8	**56.3**
output+mlp+k+t	**51.4**	**51.1**	**56.8**
output+mlp+k+d	**51.2**	49.7	**55.1**
output+mlp+t+d	**52.6**	51.5	**57.2**
output+mlp+k+t+d	**51.1**	**50.6**	**56.3**

Table 2: Perplexity scores based on the **English** part of TED talks dataset in IWSLT14 MT. +k, +t, +d: with keywords, title, and description as auxiliary side information respectively. **bold**: Statistically significant better than the best baseline.

Method	test2010	test2011	test2012
5-gram LM	65.1	60.3	64.8
LSTM	45.0	42.5	44.0
DGLSTM	44.0	41.9	43.0
output+mlp+t	**42.1**	**40.6**	42.5
output+mlp+d	**40.9**	**38.9**	**40.3**
output+mlp+t+d	**41.7**	**39.8**	42.8
output+mlp+k	**40.8**	**38.3**	**39.7**
output+mlp+d+k	**40.2**	**38.3**	**39.4**

Table 3: Perplexity scores based on the **French** part of TED talks dataset in IWSLT14 MT. Note that +k means with keywords in **English**.

Wilcoxon signed-rank test (Wilcoxon, 1945) to measure the statistical significance ($p < 0.05$) on differences between sentence-level perplexity scores of improved models compared to the best baseline. Throughout our experiments, punctuation, stop words and sentence markers ($\langle s \rangle$, $\langle /s \rangle$, $\langle unk \rangle$) are filtered out in all auxiliary inputs. We observed that this filtering was required for BOW to work reasonably well. For each model, the best perplexity score on development set is used for early stopping of training models, which was obtained after 2-5 and 2-3 epochs on TED Talks and RIE datasets, respectively.

Results & Analysis. The perplexity results on TED Talks dataset are presented in Table 2 and 3. RNNLM variants consistently achieve substantially better perplexities compared to the conventional 5$-$gram language model baseline.[7] Of the basic RNNLM models (middle), the DGLSTM works consistently better than both the standard RNN and the LSTM. This may be due to better interactions of memory cells in hidden layers. Since the DGLSTM outperformed others[8], we used it for all subsequent experiments. For TED Talks dataset, there are three kinds of side information, including keywords, title, description. We attempted to inject those into different RNNLM layers, resulting in model variants as shown in Table 2. First, we chose "keywords" (+k) information as an anchor to figure out which incorporation method works well. Comparing *input*+add+k, *input*+mlp+k and *input*+stack+k, the largest decrease is obtained by *output*+mlp+k consistently across all test sets (and development sets, not shown here). We further evaluated the addition of other side information (e.g., "description" (+d), "title" (+t)), finding that +d has similar effect as +k whereas +t has a mixed effect, being detrimental for one test set (test2011). We suspect that it is due to often-times short sentences of titles in that test, after our filtering step, leading to a shortage of useful information fed into neural network learning. Interestingly, the best performance is obtained when incorporating both +k and +d, showing that there is complementary information in the two auxiliary inputs. Further, we also achieved the similar results in the counterpart of English part (in French) using *output*+mlp with both +t and +d as shown in Table 3. In French data, no "keywords" information is available. For this reason, we run additional experiments by injecting English keywords as side information into neural models of French. Interestingly, we found that "keywords" side information in English effectively improves the modelling of French texts as shown in Table 3, serving as a new form of cross-lingual language modelling.

We further achieved similar results by incorporating the topic headline in the RIE dataset. The consistently-improved results (in Table 4) demonstrate the robustness of the *output*+mlp approach.

---

[7]For fair comparison, when computing the perplexity with the 5-gram LM, we exclude all test words marked as $\langle unk \rangle$ (i.e., with low counts or OOVs) from consideration.

[8]This concurs with the finding in (Yao et al., 2015), who showed that DGLSTM produced the state-of-the-art results over Penn Treebank dataset.

Method	test (en)	test (fr)
5-gram LM	55.7	38.5
LSTM	40.3	28.5
DGLSTM	36.4	25.4
output+mlp+h	**33.3**	**24.0**

Table 4: **Perplexity** scores based on the sampled RIE dataset. +h: topic headline.

4 Conclusion

We have proposed an effective approach to boost the performance of RNNLM using auxiliary side information (e.g. keywords, title, description, topic headline) of a textual utterance. We provided an empirical analysis of various ways of injecting such information into a distributed representation, which is then incorporated into either the input, hidden, or output layer of RNNLM architecture. Our experimental results reveal consistent improvements are achieved over strong baselines for different datasets and genres in two languages. Our future work will investigate the model performance on a closely-related task, i.e., neural machine translation (Sutskever et al., 2014; Bahdanau et al., 2015). Furthermore, we will explore learning methods to combine utterances with and without the auxiliary side information.

Acknowledgements

The authors would like to thank the reviewers for valuable comments and feedbacks. Cong Duy Vu Hoang was supported by research scholarships from the University of Melbourne, Australia. Dr Trevor Cohn was supported by the ARC (Future Fellowship).

References

D. Bahdanau, K. Cho, and Y. Bengio. 2015. Neural Machine Translation by Jointly Learning to Align and Translate. In *Proceedings of International Conference on Learning Representations (ICLR 2015)*, September.

Yoshua Bengio, Réjean Ducharme, Pascal Vincent, and Christian Janvin. 2003. A Neural Probabilistic Language Model. *The Journal of Machine Learning Research*, 3:1137–1155.

Kyunghyun Cho, Bart van Merrienboer, Dzmitry Bahdanau, and Yoshua Bengio. 2014. On the Properties of Neural Machine Translation: Encoder–Decoder Approaches. In *Proceedings of SSST-8, Eighth Workshop on Syntax, Semantics and Structure in Statistical Translation*, pages 103–111, Doha, Qatar, October. Association for Computational Linguistics.

Kenneth Heafield. 2011. KenLM: Faster and Smaller Language Model Queries. In *Proceedings of the EMNLP 2011 Sixth Workshop on Statistical Machine Translation*, pages 187–197, Edinburgh, Scotland, United Kingdom, July.

K. M. Hermann and P. Blunsom. 2014a. Multilingual Distributed Representations without Word Alignment. In *Proceedings of International Conference on Learning Representations (ICLR 2014)*, December.

Karl Moritz Hermann and Phil Blunsom. 2014b. Multilingual Models for Compositional Distributed Semantics. In *Proceedings of the 52nd Annual Meeting of the Association for Computational Linguistics (Volume 1: Long Papers)*, pages 58–68, Baltimore, Maryland, June. Association for Computational Linguistics.

Geoffrey E Hinton. 2002. Training Products of Experts by Minimizing Contrastive Divergence. *Neural computation*, 14(8):1771–1800.

Sepp Hochreiter and Jurgen Schmidhuber. 1997. Long Short-Term Memory. *Neural Comput.*, 9(8):1735–1780, November.

Nal Kalchbrenner and Phil Blunsom. 2013. Recurrent Continuous Translation Models. In *Proceedings of Empirical Methods in Natural Language Processing (EMNLP 2013)*.

Ryan Kiros, Ruslan Salakhutdinov, and Rich Zemel. 2014. Multimodal Neural Language Models. In *Proceedings of the 31st International Conference on Machine Learning (ICML-14)*, pages 595–603.

T. Mikolov, S. Kombrink, A. Deoras, and J. H. Burget, L.and Cernocky. 2011. RNNLM - Recurrent Neural Network Language Modeling Toolkit. In *2011 IEEE Workshop on Automatic Speech Recognition & Understanding (ASRU)*. IEEE Automatic Speech Recognition and Understanding Workshop, December.

Andriy Mnih and Geoffrey Hinton. 2007. Three New Graphical Models for Statistical Language Modelling. In *Proceedings of the 24th International Conference on Machine Learning*, pages 641–648.

R. Pascanu, C. Gulcehre, K. Cho, and Y. Bengio. 2013. How to Construct Deep Recurrent Neural Networks. *ArXiv e-prints*, December.

Ilya Sutskever, Oriol Vinyals, and Quoc V Le. 2014. Sequence to Sequence Learning with Neural Networks. In *Advances in Neural Information Processing Systems (NIPS 2014)*, pages 3104–3112.

Oriol Vinyals, Alexander Toshev, Samy Bengio, and Dumitru Erhan. 2015. Show and Tell: A Neural Image Caption Generator. In *The IEEE Conference on Computer Vision and Pattern Recognition (CVPR)*, June.

Frank Wilcoxon. 1945. Individual Comparisons by Ranking Methods. *Biometrics Bulletin*, 1 (6):80–83, Dec.

K. Yao, T. Cohn, K. Vylomova, K. Duh, and C. Dyer. 2015. Depth-Gated LSTM. *ArXiv e-prints*, August.

Capturing Semantic Similarity for Entity Linking
with Convolutional Neural Networks

Matthew Francis-Landau, Greg Durrett and **Dan Klein**
Computer Science Division
University of California, Berkeley
`{mfl,gdurrett,klein}@cs.berkeley.edu`

Abstract

A key challenge in entity linking is making effective use of contextual information to disambiguate mentions that might refer to different entities in different contexts. We present a model that uses convolutional neural networks to capture semantic correspondence between a mention's context and a proposed target entity. These convolutional networks operate at multiple granularities to exploit various kinds of topic information, and their rich parameterization gives them the capacity to learn which n-grams characterize different topics. We combine these networks with a sparse linear model to achieve state-of-the-art performance on multiple entity linking datasets, outperforming the prior systems of Durrett and Klein (2014) and Nguyen et al. (2014).[1]

1   Introduction

One of the major challenges of entity linking is resolving contextually polysemous mentions. For example, *Germany* may refer to a nation, to that nation's government, or even to a soccer team. Past approaches to such cases have often focused on collective entity linking: nearby mentions in a document might be expected to link to topically-similar entities, which can give us clues about the identity of the mention currently being resolved (Ratinov et al., 2011; Hoffart et al., 2011; He et al., 2013; Cheng and Roth, 2013; Durrett and Klein, 2014). But an even simpler approach is to use context information from just the words in the source document itself to make sure the entity is being resolved sensibly in context. In past work, these approaches have typically relied on heuristics such as tf-idf (Ratinov et

al., 2011), but such heuristics are hard to calibrate and they capture structure in a coarser way than learning-based methods.

In this work, we model semantic similarity between a mention's source document context and its potential entity targets using convolutional neural networks (CNNs). CNNs have been shown to be effective for sentence classification tasks (Kalchbrenner et al., 2014; Kim, 2014; Iyyer et al., 2015) and for capturing similarity in models for entity linking (Sun et al., 2015) and other related tasks (Dong et al., 2015; Shen et al., 2014), so we expect them to be effective at isolating the relevant topic semantics for entity linking. We show that convolutions over multiple granularities of the input document are useful for providing different notions of semantic context. Finally, we show how to integrate these networks with a preexisting entity linking system (Durrett and Klein, 2014). Through a combination of these two distinct methods into a single system that leverages their complementary strengths, we achieve state-of-the-art performance across several datasets.

2   Model

Our model focuses on two core ideas: first, that topic semantics at different granularities in a document are helpful in determining the genres of entities for entity linking, and second, that CNNs can distill a block of text into a meaningful topic vector.

Our entity linking model is a log-linear model that places distributions over target entities t given a mention x and its containing source document. For now, we take $P(t|x) \propto \exp w^\top f_C(x, t; \theta)$, where f_C produces a vector of features based on CNNs with parameters θ as discussed in Section 2.1. Section 2.2 describes how we combine this simple model with a full-fledged entity linking system. As shown in the middle of Figure 1, each feature in f_C

---

[1] Source available at
`github.com/matthewfl/nlp-entity-convnet`

Proceedings of NAACL-HLT 2016, pages 1256–1261,
San Diego, California, June 12-17, 2016. ©2016 Association for Computational Linguistics

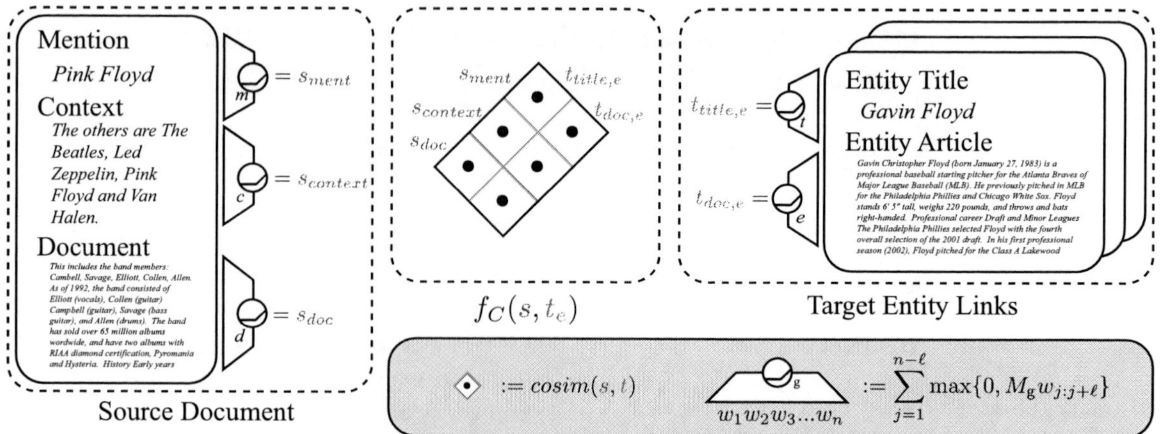

Figure 1: Extraction of convolutional vector space features $f_C(x, t_e)$. Three types of information from the input document and two types of information from the proposed title are fed through convolutional networks to produce vectors, which are systematically compared with cosine similarity to derive real-valued semantic similarity features.

is a cosine similarity between a topic vector associated with the source document and a topic vector associated with the target entity. These vectors are computed by distinct CNNs operating over different subsets of relevant text.

Figure 1 shows an example of why different kinds of context are important for entity linking. In this case, we are considering whether *Pink Floyd* might link to the article `Gavin_Floyd` on Wikipedia (imagine that *Pink Floyd* might be a person's nickname). If we look at the source document, we see that the immediate source document context around the mention *Pink Floyd* is referring to rock groups (*Led Zeppelin, Van Halen*) and the target entity's Wikipedia page is primarily about sports (*baseball starting pitcher*). Distilling these texts into succinct topic descriptors and then comparing those helps tell us that this is an improbable entity link pair. In this case, the broader source document context actually does not help very much, since it contains other generic last names like *Campbell* and *Savage* that might not necessarily indicate the document to be in the music genre. However, in general, the whole document might provide a more robust topic estimate than a small context window does.

2.1 Convolutional Semantic Similarity

Figure 1 shows our method for computing topic vectors and using those to extract features for a potential Wikipedia link. For each of three text granularities in the source document (the mention, that mention's immediate context, and the entire document) and two text granularities on the target entity side (title and Wikipedia article text), we produce vector representations with CNNs as follows. We first embed each word into a d-dimensional vector space using standard embedding techniques (discussed in Section 3.2), yielding a sequence of vectors $w_1, \ldots, w_n$. We then map those words into a fixed-size vector using a convolutional network parameterized with a filter bank $M \in \mathbb{R}^{k \times d\ell}$. We put the result through a rectified linear unit (ReLU) and combine the results with sum pooling, giving the following formulation:

$$\text{conv}_g(w_{1:n}) = \sum_{j=1}^{n-\ell} \max\{0, M_g w_{j:j+\ell}\} \quad (1)$$

where $w_{j:j+\ell}$ is a concatenation of the given word vectors and the max is element-wise.[2] Each convolution granularity (mention, context, etc.) has a distinct set of filter parameters M_g.

This process produces multiple representative topic vectors s_{ment}, $s_{context}$, and s_{doc} for the source document and t_{title} and t_{doc} for the target entity, as shown in Figure 1. All pairs of these vectors between the source and the target are then compared using cosine similarity, as shown in the middle of Figure 1. This yields the vector of features $f_C(s, t_e)$ which indicate the different types of similarity; this

---

[2] For all experiments, we set $\ell = 5$ and $k = 150$.

vector can then be combined with other sparse features and fed into a final logistic regression layer (maintaining end-to-end inference and learning of the filters). When trained with backpropagation, the convolutional networks should learn to map text into vector spaces that are informative about whether the document and entity are related or not.

2.2 Integrating with a Sparse Model

The dense model presented in Section 2.1 is effective at capturing semantic topic similarity, but it is most effective when combined with other signals for entity linking. An important cue for resolving a mention is the use of link counts from hyperlinks in Wikipedia (Cucerzan, 2007; Milne and Witten, 2008; Ji and Grishman, 2011), which tell us how often a given mention was linked to each article on Wikipedia. This information can serve as a useful prior, but only if we can leverage it effectively by targeting the most salient part of a mention. For example, we may have never observed *President Barack Obama* as a linked string on Wikipedia, even though we have seen the substring *Barack Obama* and it unambiguously indicates the correct answer.

Following Durrett and Klein (2014), we introduce a latent variable q to capture which subset of a mention (known as a *query*) we resolve. Query generation includes potentially removing stop words, plural suffixes, punctuation, and leading or tailing words. This processes generates on average 9 queries for each mention. Conveniently, this set of queries also defines the set of candidate entities that we consider linking a mention to: each query generates a set of potential entities based on link counts, whose unions are then taken to give on the possible entity targets for each mention (including the null link). In the example shown in Figure 1, the query phrases are *Pink Floyd* and *Floyd*, which generate `Pink_Floyd` and `Gavin_Floyd` as potential link targets (among other options that might be derived from the *Floyd* query).

Our final model has the form $P(t|x) = \sum_q P(t, q|x)$. We parameterize $P(t, q|x)$ in a log-linear way with three separate components:

$$P(t, q|x) \propto \exp\left(w^\top (f_Q(x, q) + f_E(x, q, t) + f_C(x, t; \theta))\right)$$

f_Q and f_E are both sparse features vectors and are taken from previous work (Durrett and Klein, 2014).

f_C is as discussed in Section 2.1. Note that f_C has its own internal parameters θ because it relies on CNNs with learned filters; however, we can compute gradients for these parameters with standard backpropagation. The whole model is trained to maximize the log likelihood of a labeled training corpus using Adadelta (Zeiler, 2012).

The indicator features f_Q and f_E are described in more detail in Durrett and Klein (2014). f_Q only impacts which query is selected and not the disambiguation to a title. It is designed to roughly capture the basic shape of a query to measure its desirability, indicating whether suffixes were removed and whether the query captures the capitalized subsequence of a mention, as well as standard lexical, POS, and named entity type features. f_E mostly captures how likely the selected query is to correspond to a given entity based on factors like anchor text counts from Wikipedia, string match with proposed Wikipedia titles, and discretized cosine similarities of tf-idf vectors (Ratinov et al., 2011). Adding tf-idf indicators is the only modification we made to the features of Durrett and Klein (2014).

3 Experimental Results

We performed experiments on 4 different entity linking datasets.

- ACE (NIST, 2005; Bentivogli et al., 2010): This corpus was used in Fahrni and Strube (2014) and Durrett and Klein (2014).

- CoNLL-YAGO (Hoffart et al., 2011): This corpus is based on the CoNLL 2003 dataset; the test set consists of 231 news articles and contains a number of rarer entities.

- WP (Heath and Bizer, 2011): This dataset consists of short snippets from Wikipedia.

- Wikipedia (Ratinov et al., 2011): This dataset consists of 10,000 randomly sampled Wikipedia articles, with the task being to resolve the links in each article.[3]

---

[3] We do not compare to Ratinov et al. (2011) on this dataset because we do not have access to the original Wikipedia dump they used for their work and as a result could not duplicate their results or conduct comparable experiments, a problem which was also noted by Nguyen et al. (2014).

	ACE	CoNLL	WP	Wiki[4]
Previous work				
DK2014	79.6	—	—	—
AIDA-LIGHT	—	84.8	—	—
This work				
Sparse features	83.6	74.9	81.1	81.5
CNN features	84.5	81.2	87.7	75.7
Full	**89.9**	**85.5**	**90.7**	**82.2**

Table 1: Performance of the system in this work (Full) compared to two baselines from prior work and two ablations. Our results outperform those of Durrett and Klein (2014) and Nguyen et al. (2014). In general, we also see that the convolutional networks by themselves can outperform the system using only sparse features, and in all cases these stack to give substantial benefit.

We use standard train-test splits for all datasets except for WP, where no standard split is available. In this case, we randomly sample a test set. For all experiments, we use word vectors computed by running word2vec (Mikolov et al., 2013) on all Wikipedia, as described in Section 3.2.

Table 1 shows results for two baselines and three variants of our system. Our main contribution is the combination of indicator features and CNN features (Full). We see that this system outperforms the results of Durrett and Klein (2014) and the AIDA-LIGHT system of Nguyen et al. (2014). We can also compare to two ablations: using just the sparse features (a system which is a direct extension of Durrett and Klein (2014)) or using just the CNN-derived features.[5] Our CNN features generally outperform the sparse features and improve even further when stacked with them. This reflects that they capture orthogonal sources of information: for example, the sparse features can capture how frequently the target document was linked to, whereas the CNNs can capture document context in a more nuanced way. These CNN features also clearly supersede the sparse features based on tf-idf (taken from (Ratinov et al., 2011)), showing that indeed that CNNs are better at learning semantic topic similarity than heuristics like tf-idf.

In the sparse feature system, the highest weighted

	ACE	CoNLL	WP
$cosim(s_{doc}, t_{doc})$	77.43	79.76	72.93
$cosim(s_{ment}, t_{title})$	80.19	80.86	70.25
All CNN pairs	84.85	86.91	82.02

Table 2: Comparison of using only topic information derived from the document and target article, only information derived from the mention itself and the target entity title, and the full set of information (six features, as shown in Figure 1). Neither the finest nor coarsest convolutional context can give the performance of the complete set. Numbers are reported on a development set.

features are typically those indicating the frequency that a page was linked to and those indicating specific lexical items in the choice of the latent query variable q. This suggests that the system of Durrett and Klein (2014) has the power to pick the right span of a mention to resolve, but then is left to generally pick the most common link target in Wikipedia, which is not always correct. By contrast, the full system has a greater ability to pick less common link targets if the topic indicators distilled from the CNNs indicate that it should do so.

3.1 Multiple Granularities of Convolution

One question we might ask is how much we gain by having multiple convolutions on the source and target side. Table 2 compares our full suite of CNN features, i.e. the six features specified in Figure 1, with two specific convolutional features in isolation. Using convolutions over just the source document (s_{doc}) and target article text (t_{doc}) gives a system[6] that performs, in aggregate, comparably to using convolutions over just the mention (s_{ment}) and the entity title (t_{title}). These represent two extremes of the system: consuming the maximum amount of context, which might give the most robust representation of topic semantics, and consuming the minimum amount of context, which gives the most focused representation of topics semantics (and which more generally might allow the system to directly memorize train-test pairs observed in training). However, neither performs as well as the combination of all CNN features, showing that the different granularities capture complementary aspects of the entity linking task.

---

destroying missiles . spy planes	has died of his wounds	him which was more depressing
and destroying missiles . spy	vittorio sacerdoti has told his	a trip and you see
by U.N. weapons inspectors .	his bail hearing , his	" i can see why
inspectors are discovering and destroying	bail hearing , his lawyer	i think so many americans
are discovering and destroying missiles	died of his wounds after	his life from the depression
an attack using chemical weapons	from scott peterson 's attorney	trip and you see him
discovering and destroying missiles .	's murder trial . she	, but dumb liberal could
attack munitions or j-dam weapons	has told his remarkable tale	i can see why he
sanctions targeting iraq civilians ,	murder trial . she asking	one passage . you cite
its nuclear weapons and missile	trial lawyers are driving doctors	think so many americans are

Table 3: Five-grams representing the maximal activations from different filters in the convolution over the source document (M_{doc}, producing s_{doc} in Figure 1). Some filters tend towards singular topics as shown in the first and second columns, which focus on weapons and trials, respectively. Others may have a mix of seemingly unrelated topics, as shown in the third column, which does not have a coherent theme. However, such filters might represent a superposition of filters for various topics which never cooccur and thus never need to be disambiguated between.

	ACE	CoNLL	WP
Google News	87.5	89.6	83.8
Wikipedia	89.5	90.6	85.5

Table 4: Results of the full model (sparse and convolutional features) comparing word vectors derived from Google News vs. Wikipedia on development sets for each corpus.

3.2 Embedding Vectors

We also explored two different sources of embedding vectors for the convolutions. Table 4 shows that word vectors trained on Wikipedia outperformed Google News word vectors trained on a larger corpus. Further investigation revealed that the Google News vectors had much higher out-of-vocabulary rates. For learning the vectors, we use the standard word2vec toolkit (Mikolov et al., 2013) with vector length set to 300, window set to 21 (larger windows produce more semantically-focused vectors (Levy and Goldberg, 2014)), 10 negative samples and 10 iterations through Wikipedia. We do not fine-tune word vectors during training of our model, as that was not found to improve performance.

3.3 Analysis of Learned Convolutions

One downside of our system compared to its purely indicator-based variant is that its operation is less interpretable. However, one way we can inspect the learned system is by examining what causes high activations of the various convolutional filters (rows of the matrices M_g from Equation 1). Table 3 shows the n-grams in the ACE dataset leading to maximal activations of three of the filters from M_{doc}. Some filters tend to learn to pick up on n-grams character-istic of a particular topic. In other cases, a single filter might be somewhat inscrutable, as with the third column of Table 3. There are a few possible explanations for this. First, the filter may generally have low activations and therefore have little impact in the final feature computation. Second, the extreme points of the filter may not be characteristic of its overall behavior, since the bulk of n-grams will lead to more moderate activations. Finally, such a filter may represent the superposition of a few topics that we are unlikely to ever need to disambiguate between; in a particular context, this filter will then play a clear role, but one which is hard to determine from the overall shape of the parameters.

4 Conclusion

In this work, we investigated using convolutional networks to capture semantic similarity between source documents and potential entity link targets. Using multiple granularities of convolutions to evaluate the compatibility of a mention in context and several potential link targets gives strong performance on its own; moreover, such features also improve a pre-existing entity linking system based on sparse indicator features, showing that these sources of information are complementary.

Acknowledgments

This work was partially supported by NSF Grant CNS-1237265 and a Google Faculty Research Award. Thanks to the anonymous reviewers for their helpful comments.

References

Luisa Bentivogli, Pamela Forner, Claudio Giuliano, Alessandro Marchetti, Emanuele Pianta, and Kateryna Tymoshenko. 2010. Extending English ACE 2005 Corpus Annotation with Ground-truth Links to Wikipedia. In *Proceedings of the Workshop on The People's Web Meets NLP: Collaboratively Constructed Semantic Resources*.

Xiao Cheng and Dan Roth. 2013. Relational Inference for Wikification. In *Proceedings of the Conference on Empirical Methods in Natural Language Processing (EMNLP)*.

Silviu Cucerzan. 2007. Large-Scale Named Entity Disambiguation Based on Wikipedia Data. In *Proceedings of the Joint Conference on Empirical Methods in Natural Language Processing and Computational Natural Language Learning (EMNLP-CoNLL)*.

Li Dong, Furu Wei, Ming Zhou, and Ke Xu. 2015. Question Answering over Freebase with Multi-Column Convolutional Neural Networks. In *Proceedings of the 53rd Annual Meeting of the Association for Computational Linguistics (ACL) and the 7th International Joint Conference on Natural Language Processing (Volume 1: Long Papers)*.

Greg Durrett and Dan Klein. 2014. A Joint Model for Entity Analysis: Coreference, Typing, and Linking. In *Transactions of the Association for Computational Linguistics (TACL)*.

Angela Fahrni and Michael Strube. 2014. A latent variable model for discourse-aware concept and entity disambiguation. In Gosse Bouma and Yannick Parmentier 0001, editors, *Proceedings of the 14th Conference of the European Chapter of the Association for Computational Linguistics, EACL 2014, April 26-30, 2014, Gothenburg, Sweden*, pages 491–500. The Association for Computer Linguistics.

Zhengyan He, Shujie Liu, Yang Song, Mu Li, Ming Zhou, and Houfeng Wang. 2013. Efficient collective entity linking with stacking. In *EMNLP*, pages 426–435. ACL.

Tom Heath and Christian Bizer. 2011. *Linked Data: Evolving the Web into a Global Data Space*. Morgan & Claypool, 1st edition.

Johannes Hoffart, Mohamed Amir Yosef, Ilaria Bordino, Hagen Fürstenau, Manfred Pinkal, Marc Spaniol, Bilyana Taneva, Stefan Thater, and Gerhard Weikum. 2011. Robust Disambiguation of Named Entities in Text. In *Proceedings of the Conference on Empirical Methods in Natural Language Processing (EMNLP)*.

Mohit Iyyer, Varun Manjunatha, Jordan Boyd-Graber, and Hal Daumé III. 2015. Deep Unordered Composition Rivals Syntactic Methods for Text Classification. In *Proceedings of the Association for Computational Linguistics (ACL)*.

Heng Ji and Ralph Grishman. 2011. Knowledge Base Population: Successful Approaches and Challenges. In *Proceedings of the Association for Computational Linguistics (ACL)*.

Nal Kalchbrenner, Edward Grefenstette, and Phil Blunsom. 2014. A convolutional neural network for modelling sentences. In *Proceedings of the 52nd Annual Meeting of the Association for Computational Linguistics (Volume 1: Long Papers)*, pages 655–665, Baltimore, Maryland, June. Association for Computational Linguistics.

Yoon Kim. 2014. Convolutional Neural Networks for Sentence Classification. In *Proceedings of the Conference on Empirical Methods in Natural Language Processing (EMNLP)*.

Omer Levy and Yoav Goldberg. 2014. Dependency-Based Word Embeddings. In *Proceedings of the 52nd Annual Meeting of the Association for Computational Linguistics (ACL)*.

Tomas Mikolov, Ilya Sutskever, Kai Chen, Greg S Corrado, and Jeff Dean. 2013. Distributed Representations of Words and Phrases and their Compositionality. In *Advances in Neural Information Processing Systems (NIPS) 26*, pages 3111–3119.

David Milne and Ian H. Witten. 2008. Learning to Link with Wikipedia. In *Proceedings of the Conference on Information and Knowledge Management (CIKM)*.

Dat Ba Nguyen, Johannes Hoffart, Martin Theobald, and Gerhard Weikum. 2014. AIDA-light: High-Throughput Named-Entity Disambiguation. In *Proceedings of the Workshop on Linked Data on the Web co-located with the 23rd International World Wide Web Conference (WWW)*.

NIST. 2005. The ACE 2005 Evaluation Plan. In *NIST*.

Lev Ratinov, Dan Roth, Doug Downey, and Mike Anderson. 2011. Local and Global Algorithms for Disambiguation to Wikipedia. In *Proceedings of the 49th Annual Meeting of the Association for Computational Linguistics (ACL)*, pages 1375–1384.

Yelong Shen, Xiaodong He, Jianfeng Gao, Li Deng, and Grégoire Mesnil. 2014. Learning Semantic Representations Using Convolutional Neural Networks for Web Search. In *Proceedings of the 23rd International Conference on World Wide Web (WWW)*.

Yaming Sun, Lei Lin, Duyu Tang, Nan Yang, Zhenzhou Ji, and Xiaolong Wang. 2015. Modeling Mention, Context and Entity with Neural Networks for Entity Disambiguation. In *Proceedings of the International Joint Conference on Artificial Intelligence (IJCAI)*, pages 1333–1339.

Matthew D. Zeiler. 2012. AdaDelta: An Adaptive Learning Rate Method. *CoRR*, abs/1212.5701.

K-Embeddings: Learning Conceptual Embeddings for Words using Context

Thuy Vu and **D. Stott Parker**
Department of Computer Science
University of California, Los Angeles
Los Angeles, CA 90095
{thuy;stott}@cs.ucla.edu

Abstract

We describe a technique for adding contextual distinctions to word embeddings by extending the usual embedding process — into two phases. The first phase resembles existing methods, but also constructs K classifications of concepts. The second phase uses these classifications in developing refined K embeddings for words, namely word K-embeddings. The technique is iterative, scalable, and can be combined with other methods (including Word2Vec) in achieving still more expressive representations.

Experimental results show consistently large performance gains on a Semantic-Syntactic Word Relationship test set for different K settings. For example, an overall gain of 20% is recorded at $K = 5$. In addition, we demonstrate that an iterative process can further tune the embeddings and gain an extra 1% ($K = 10$ in 3 iterations) on the same benchmark. The examples also show that polysemous concepts are meaningfully embedded in our K different conceptual embeddings for words.

1 Introduction

Neural-based word embeddings are vectorial representations of words in high dimensional real valued space. Success with these representations have resulted in their being considered for an increasing range of natural language processing (NLP) tasks. Recent advances in word embeddings have shown great effects that are pushing forward state-of-the-art results in NLP (Koo et al., 2008; Turian et al., 2010; Collobert et al., 2011; Yu et al., 2013; Mikolov et al., 2013a; Mikolov et al., 2013b; Mikolov et al., 2013c). Embedding learning models for words are also being adapted for tasks in other research fields (Reinanda et al., 2015; Vu and Parker, 2015). The Continuous bag of words (CBOW) and Skip-gram (Mikolov et al., 2013a) are currently considered as state-of-the-art in learning algorithms for word embeddings.

The ability of words to assume different roles (syntax) or meanings (semantics) presents a basic challenge to the notion of word embedding (Erk and Padó, 2008; Reisinger and Mooney, 2010; Huang et al., 2012; Tian et al., 2014; Neelakantan et al., 2014; Chen et al., 2015). External resources and features are introduced to address this challenge. In general, individuals with no linguistic background can generally resolve these differences without difficulty. For example, they can distinguish "bank" as referring to a riverside or a financial establishment without semantic or syntactic analysis.

Distinctions of role and meaning often follow from context. The idea of exploiting context in linguistics was introduced with a distributional hypothesis: "linguistic items with similar distributions have similar meanings" (Harris, 1954). Firth soon afterwards emphasized this in a famous quote: "a word is characterized by the company it keeps" (1957).

We propose to exploit only context information to distinguish different concepts behind words in this paper. The contribution of this paper is to note that a *two-phase word embedding* training can be helpful in adding contextual information to existing embedding methods:

- we use learned context embeddings to efficiently cluster word contexts into K classifications of concepts, independent of the word embeddings.

- this approach can complement existing sophisticated, linguistically-based features, and can be used with word embeddings to achieve gains in performance by considering contextual distinctions for words.

- two-phase word embedding may have other applications as well, conceivably permitting some 'non-linear' refinements of linear embeddings.

In the next section we present our learning strategy for word K-embeddings, outlining how the value of K affects its power in increasing syntactic and semantic distinctions. Following this, a large-scale experiment serves to validate the idea — from several different perspectives. Finally, we offer conclusions about how adding contextual distinctions to word embeddings (with our second phase of embedding) can gain power in distinguishing among different aspects of words.

2 Learning Word K-Embeddings

The use of multiple semantic representations for a word in resolving polysemy has a significant literature (Erk and Padó, 2008; Reisinger and Mooney, 2010; Huang et al., 2012; Tian et al., 2014; Neelakantan et al., 2014; Chen et al., 2015). Strategies often focus on discrimination using syntactic and semantic information.

We investigate another direction — the extension of the word embedding process into a second phase — which allows context information to be consolidated with the embedding. Rather than annotating words with features, our technique treats context as second-order in nature, suggesting an additional representation step.

Our learning strategy for word K-embeddings is therefore done, possibly iteratively, in two phases:

1. Annotating words with concepts (defined by their contextual clusters)

2. Training embeddings using the resulting annotated text.

2.1 Concept Annotation using Context Embeddings

We propose to annotate words with concepts given by learned context embeddings, which are an under-utilized output of word embedding training. Our strategy is based on the assumption that the context of a word is useful for discriminating its conceptual alternatives in polysemy. In general, our concept annotation for words is performed in two steps — clustering of context embeddings followed by annotation.

Specifically, we first employ a clustering algorithm to cluster the context embeddings. K-means is our algorithm of choice. The clustering algorithm will assign each context word to a distinct cluster. This result is then used to re-assign words in training data to their contextual cluster.

Second, we annotate words in the training data with their most common contextual cluster (of their context words). We define *context words* to mean the surrounding words of a given word. Formally, a word is annotated with a concept given by the following function:

$$\max_{c \in \mathcal{C}} \sum_{(w_i, c_i) \in W} f(c_i, c)$$

Here W is the set of context words of the current word, and $f(c_i, c_j)$ is a boolean function whose output is 1 if the input parameters are equal:

$$f(c_i, c_j) = \begin{cases} 1, & \text{if } c_i = c_j \\ 0, & \text{otherwise.} \end{cases}$$

The cluster-annotated dataset is then passed into the next training phase.

2.2 Training Word K-Embeddings

The second phase is similar to existing word embedding training systems. The number of clusters K defines the maximum number of different representations for words. Table 1 presents the statistics for different selections of K using the dataset mentioned in the **Experiments** section.

Each value K in Table 1 is shown with the total number of embeddings and vocabulary size. Words in the vocabulary can have up to K different embeddings for different annotated concepts. As K increases, the size of the vocabulary decreases —

K	total embeddings	vocabulary size	ratio
1	1,965,139	1,965,139	1.00
5	2,807,016	1,443,061	1.95
10	2,740,351	1,474,704	1.86
15	3,229,945	1,374,055	2.35
20	3,236,882	1,410,521	2.29
25	3,382,722	1,383,162	2.45
30	3,404,150	1,418,027	2.40

Table 1: Total embeddings and vocabulary size for different K for Wikipedia dataset. Words with frequency lower than 5 are filtered during pre-processing.

yet remains largely stable for different values of K greater than 1. This is explained by the count of words being scattered to different concepts, resulting in a lower word count per concept. In our setting, concept-annotated words with fewer than 5 occurrences will be discarded during training of word embeddings.

It is interesting to note that the total number of embeddings is broadly stable and less affected by K. For example, as we allow up to 10 different concepts for a word ($K = 10$), the total number of embeddings grows only slightly compared to the result for $K = 1$. The average number of embeddings for a word is 1.86 for $K = 10$. In other words, concept annotations do converge as we increase K.

2.3 Word K-Embedding Training Workflow

Figure 1 presents our proposed workflow to train context-based conceptual word K-embeddings. Our system allows each word to have at most K different embeddings, where each is a representation for a certain concept.

The input to the workflow is a large-scale text dataset. Initially, we compute context embeddings for words as presented previously. We can derive context embeddings directly from the training of almost any context-based word embeddings, where word embeddings are computed via their context words.

Subsequently, we cluster context embeddings into groups which reflect varied concepts on some semantic vector space. Each context embedding is assigned to a cluster denoting its conceptual role as a context word. Any clustering algorithm for vectors can be applied for this task.

Embeddings of annotated context words are used

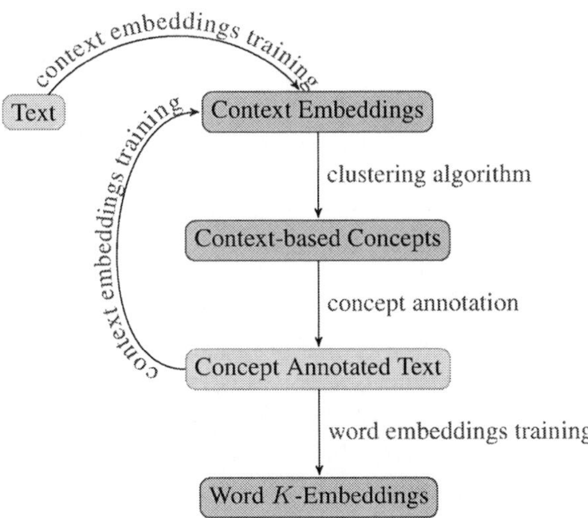

Figure 1: Training Word K-Embeddings

to compute concepts of words in a sentence. We hypothesize that the concept of a word is defined by the concept of its surrounding words. We annotate concepts for all words in the training data.

Finally, the concept-annotated training data is passed into any standard algorithm for training word embeddings for the conceptual word K-embeddings.

3 Experiments

3.1 Settings

Our training data for word embeddings is Wikipedia for English, downloaded on November 29, 2014. It consists of 4,591,457 articles, with a total of 2,015,823,886 words. The dataset is pre-processed with sentence and word tokenization. We convert text to lower-case prior to training. We consider $|W| = 5$ for the size of the context window W presented in Section 2.1.

We used the Semantic-Syntactic Word Relationship test set (Mikolov et al., 2013a) for our experimental studies. This dataset consists of 8,869 semantic and 10,675 syntactic queries. Each query is a tuple of four words (A, B, C, D) for the question "A is to B as C to what?". These queries can be either semantic or syntactic. D, to be predicted from the learned embeddings, is defined as the closest word to the vector $(A - B + C)$. We used Word2Vec for training and `scikit-learn` for clustering tasks.

We evaluate the accuracy of the prediction of D in these queries. A query is considered hit if there exists at least one correct match and all the words are in the same concept group. This is based on the assumption that if "A is to B as C is to D", either (A, B) and (C, D) OR (A, C) and (B, D) have to be in the same concept group.

3.2 Results

The embeddings learned in phases 1 and 2 can be compared, using different values for K in the K-means clustering. Word relationship performance results are shown in Table 2.

Our proposed technique in phase 2 achieves consistently high performance. For example, when $K = 5$, our absolute performance is 89% and 81% in semantic and syntactic relationship evaluations, gaining 24% and 16% from the standard CBOW model (phase 1). When $K = 25$, the performance yields the best combined result. As shown in Table 1, the total number of embeddings and vocabulary size differ by a small multiplicative factor as K increases.

In another comparison, Figure 2 plots our K-Embeddings results versus the results of a *relaxed* evaluation for CBOW, which considers the top K embeddings instead of the best. Even though our evaluation is restricted to one-best for each of the K embeddings, the overall (combined) performance for different K settings is still consistently better than the top K embeddings of CBOW. Moreover, for a specific K setting, the total number of different embeddings considered in K-Embeddings is always less than that of the top K. For example, in our peak result ($K = 25$), the total number of embeddings considered in the evaluation set is only about 76.17% of the total embeddings with the top 25 of CBOW.

In addition, we also compare the performances of K-embeddings in multiple iterations under the same K setting in Table 3. It shows that the K-embeddings are improved after certain number of iterations. Particularly, for $K = 10$, we can achieve best performance after 3 to 4 iterations, gaining roughly 1%.

Finally, it is also worth noting that the performance does not always increase linearly with the number of embeddings or vocabulary size. This suggests that as we achieve better performance in K-

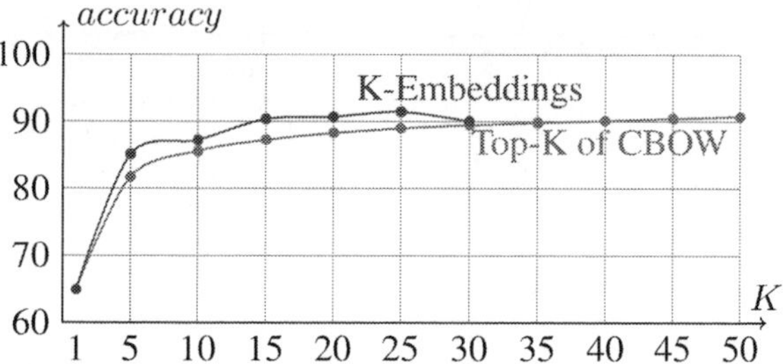

Figure 2: Word K-Embeddings and Top-K of CBOW accuracy comparison

Type	iter_1	iter_2	iter_3	iter_4	iter_5
Semantic	88.8	89.6	**90.3**	90.0	89.0
Syntactic	85.9	84.8	**86.7**	**86.7**	85.8
Combined	87.3	87.0	**88.3**	88.2	87.3

Table 3: Performance of $K = 10$ in five iterations

embeddings, we should also gain more compact conceptual embeddings.

3.3 Word Expressivity Analysis

Expressivity of word groups for "mercury" and "fan" are studied in Table 4. The first two rows shows most related words of "mercury" and "fan" without concepts annotation (baseline). The following rows present our K-embeddings result. This table illustrates the differences that arise in multiple representations of a word, and shows semantic distinctions among these representations.

For example, different representations for the word "mercury" indeed represent a spectrum of aspects for the word, ranging from related-cosmos, related chemical element, automobile, or even to music. The same can be seen for "fan" — where we find concepts related to fan as a follower/supporter, fan as in machinery, or Fan as a common Chinese surname. Indeed, we can find many different conceptual readings of these words. These not only reflect different polysemous meanings, but also their conceptual aspects in the real world. Observe that most related words are grouped into distinct concept groups, and thus yield strong semantic distinctions. The result firmly suggests that context embeddings, like word embeddings, can capture linguistic regularities efficiently.

Analogy Type	Total	CBOW	$K=5$	$K=10$	$K=15$	$K=20$	$K=25$	$K=30$
capital-common-countries	506	85.18	**100.00**	**100.00**	**100.00**	**100.00**	**100.00**	**100.00**
capital-world	4,524	78.89	96.60	97.24	99.12	99.18	**99.29**	99.27
currency	866	20.01	36.72	31.18	40.65	41.22	**42.84**	44.80
city-in-state	2,467	44.75	90.76	89.26	95.42	97.16	97.28	**97.61**
family	506	85.38	96.25	99.01	97.23	98.42	97.83	**99.21**
total semantic evaluation	8,869	64.67	89.30	88.83	92.32	92.96	93.18	**93.53**
gram1-adjective-to-adverb	992	19.76	51.41	59.98	65.73	68.95	**70.06**	61.90
gram2-opposite	812	26.72	42.12	48.52	62.81	62.19	**68.84**	56.03
gram3-comparative	1,332	87.99	97.30	97.82	**99.25**	99.17	99.02	**99.25**
gram4-superlative	1,122	52.65	71.93	74.15	**81.02**	78.88	78.70	75.22
gram5-present-participle	1,056	64.96	87.31	91.57	93.47	92.52	**96.78**	94.03
gram6-nationality-adjective	1,599	90.87	93.62	94.81	93.87	94.68	**95.37**	94.93
gram7-past-tense	1,560	65.51	66.28	94.42	94.49	95.45	**96.41**	93.72
gram8-plural	1,332	77.40	93.92	95.42	**97.90**	96.55	95.80	96.92
gram9-plural-verbs	870	66.78	83.33	94.60	94.71	95.63	**95.75**	93.22
total syntactic evaluation	10,675	65.17	81.72	85.94	88.83	88.93	**90.08**	87.21
total combined evaluation	19,544	64.94	85.16	87.25	90.42	90.76	**91.49**	90.08

Table 2: K-embeddings performance

4 Conclusion

In this paper, we have presented a technique for adding contextual distinctions to word embeddings with a second phase of embedding. This contextual information gains power in distinguishing among different aspects of words. Experimental results with embedding of the English variant of Wikipedia (over 2 billion words) shows significant improvements in both semantic- and syntactic- based word embedding performance. The result also presents a wide range of interesting concepts of words in expressivity analysis.

These results strongly support the idea of using context embeddings to exploit context information for problems in NLP. As we highlighted earlier, context embeddings are underutilized, even though word embeddings have been extensively exploited in multiple applications.

Furthermore, the contextual approach can complement existing sophisticated, linguistically-based features, and can be combined with other learning methods for embedding. These results are encouraging; they suggest that useful extensions of current methods are possible with two-phase embeddings.

#	Word	Most Similar Words
0	mercury	cadmium, barium, centaur, jupiter, venus
	fan	fans, fanbase, fan-base, supporter, fandom
1	$mercury_1$	$vanadium_1$, $iron_1$, $sulfur_1$, $polonium_1$
	$mercury_3$	$tribune_3$, $dragon_3$, $curlew_3$, $keith_3$, $stanley_3$
	$mercury_5$	$ammonia_5$, $magnesium_5$, $sulfur_5$, $mercury_9$
	$mercury_9$	$mercury_5$, $mercury_2$, $neptune_9$, $titan_9$
1	fan_1	$inlet_1$, $crinoids_1$, $sect_1$, $wedge_1$, $beach_1$
	fan_4	$supporter_4$, $likes_4$, $legend_4$, $bust_4$, $member_4$
	fan_5	fan_9, fan_0, $fans_5$, $fandom_5$, $fanbase_5$, $gamer_5$
	fan_8	$xiang_8$, $yong_8$, xin_8, $yang_8$, cui_8, guo_8
3	$mercury_1$	$polaris_1$, $mercury_3$, $mercury_6$, $cadmium_1$
	$mercury_4$	$chrysler_4$, $sheedy_4$, $mohammad_4$, $gott_4$
	$mercury_6$	$arsenic_6$, $lithium_6$, $oxygen_6$, $methane_6$, $dust_6$
	$mercury_7$	$cadmium_7$, $nickel_7$, $pollutants_7$, $impurities_7$
	$mercury_8$	$rubidium_8$, $xenon_8$, $selenium_8$, $cadmium_8$
3	fan_2	$yong_2$, ye_2, $ching_2$, hao_2, yi_2, $chang_2$, guo_2
	fan_4	$member_4$, $parody_4$, $protg_4$, $supporter_4$
	fan_6	$fanbase_6$, $buzz_6$, $fans_3$, $fandom_6$, $video_6$
	fan_7	$imprints_7$, $gnatcatchers_7$, $minuta_7$, $flat_7$
	fan_8	$impellers_8$, $inlet_8$, $spinners_8$, $springs_8$, hot_8
5	$mercury_2$	$titanium_2$, $jupiter_2$, $sapphire_2$, $saturn_2$
	$mercury_3$	$sodium_3$, $helium_3$, $oxygen_3$, $hydrogen_3$
	$mercury_6$	$blue_6$, $leopards_6$, $lotus_6$, $unilever_6$, $copper_6$
	$mercury_7$	$arsenic_7$, $sulfur_7$, $radioactivity_7$, $lithium_7$
	$mercury_9$	$chlorine_9$, $strontium_9$, $ammonia_9$, $arsenic_9$
5	fan_2	$buzz_2$, $fanbase_2$, $gamer_2$, $loudest_1$, $fans_1$
	fan_3	$blower_3$, $ducts_3$, $cooler_3$, $compressor_3$
	fan_5	$zang_5$, $huang_5$, yan_5, dun_5, $zhang_5$, kao_5
	fan_6	$youngster_6$, $participant_6$, $mobster_6$
	fan_7	$fanbase_7$, $buzz_7$, $youtube_7$, $blogging_7$
	fan_8	$supporter_8$, $fandom_8$, $enthusiast_8$, $parody_8$

Table 4: Word Expressivity Analysis

References

Tao Chen, Ruifeng Xu, Yulan He, and Xuan Wang. 2015. Improving distributed representation of word sense via wordnet gloss composition and context clustering. In *Proceedings of the 53rd Annual Meeting of the Association for Computational Linguistics and the 7th International Joint Conference on Natural Language Processing (Volume 2: Short Papers)*, pages 15–20, Beijing, China, July. Association for Computational Linguistics.

Ronan Collobert, Jason Weston, Léon Bottou, Michael Karlen, Koray Kavukcuoglu, and Pavel Kuksa. 2011. Natural language processing (almost) from scratch. *J. Mach. Learn. Res.*, 12:2493–2537, November.

Katrin Erk and Sebastian Padó. 2008. A structured vector space model for word meaning in context. In *Proceedings of the Conference on Empirical Methods in Natural Language Processing*, EMNLP '08, pages 897–906, Stroudsburg, PA, USA. Association for Computational Linguistics.

J. Firth. 1957. *A Synopsis of Linguistic Theory 1930-1955*. Studies in Linguistic Analysis, Philological. Longman.

Zellig Harris. 1954. Distributional structure. *Word*, 10(23):146–162.

Eric H. Huang, Richard Socher, Christopher D. Manning, and Andrew Y. Ng. 2012. Improving word representations via global context and multiple word prototypes. In *Proceedings of the 50th Annual Meeting of the Association for Computational Linguistics: Long Papers - Volume 1*, ACL '12, pages 873–882, Stroudsburg, PA, USA. Association for Computational Linguistics.

Terry Koo, Xavier Carreras, and Michael Collins. 2008. Simple semi-supervised dependency parsing. In *Proceedings of ACL-08: HLT*, pages 595–603. Association for Computational Linguistics.

Tomas Mikolov, Kai Chen, Greg Corrado, and Jeffrey Dean. 2013a. Efficient estimation of word representations in vector space. *CoRR*, abs/1301.3781.

Tomas Mikolov, Ilya Sutskever, Kai Chen, Greg S Corrado, and Jeff Dean. 2013b. Distributed representations of words and phrases and their compositionality. In C.J.C. Burges, L. Bottou, M. Welling, Z. Ghahramani, and K.Q. Weinberger, editors, *Advances in Neural Information Processing Systems 26*, pages 3111–3119. Curran Associates, Inc.

Tomas Mikolov, Wen tau Yih, and Geoffrey Zweig. 2013c. Linguistic regularities in continuous space word representations. In *Proceedings of the 2013 Conference of the North American Chapter of the Association for Computational Linguistics: Human Language Technologies (NAACL-HLT-2013)*. Association for Computational Linguistics, May.

Arvind Neelakantan, Jeevan Shankar, Alexandre Passos, and Andrew McCallum. 2014. Efficient nonparametric estimation of multiple embeddings per word in vector space. In *Proceedings of the 2014 Conference on Empirical Methods in Natural Language Processing (EMNLP)*, pages 1059–1069, Doha, Qatar, October. Association for Computational Linguistics.

Lin Qiu, Yong Cao, Zaiqing Nie, Yong Yu, and Yong Rui. 2014. Learning word representation considering proximity and ambiguity.

Ridho Reinanda, Edgar Meij, and Maarten de Rijke. 2015. Mining, ranking and recommending entity aspects. In *Proceedings of the 38th International ACM SIGIR Conference on Research and Development in Information Retrieval*, SIGIR '15, pages 263–272, New York, NY, USA. ACM.

Joseph Reisinger and Raymond J. Mooney. 2010. Multi-prototype vector-space models of word meaning. In *Human Language Technologies: The 2010 Annual Conference of the North American Chapter of the Association for Computational Linguistics*, HLT '10, pages 109–117, Stroudsburg, PA, USA. Association for Computational Linguistics.

Fei Tian, Hanjun Dai, Jiang Bian, Bin Gao, Rui Zhang, Enhong Chen, and Tie-Yan Liu. 2014. A probabilistic model for learning multi-prototype word embeddings. In *Proceedings of COLING 2014, the 25th International Conference on Computational Linguistics: Technical Papers*, pages 151–160, Dublin, Ireland, August. Dublin City University and Association for Computational Linguistics.

Joseph Turian, Lev-Arie Ratinov, and Yoshua Bengio. 2010. Word representations: A simple and general method for semi-supervised learning. In *Proceedings of the 48th Annual Meeting of the Association for Computational Linguistics*, pages 384–394. Association for Computational Linguistics.

Thuy Vu and D. Stott Parker. 2015. Node embeddings in social network analysis. In *Proceedings of the 2015 IEEE/ACM International Conference on Advances in Social Networks Analysis and Mining 2015*, ASONAM '15, pages 326–329, New York, NY, USA. ACM.

Mo Yu, Tiejun Zhao, Daxiang Dong, Hao Tian, and Dianhai Yu. 2013. Compound embedding features for semi-supervised learning. In *Proceedings of the 2013 Conference of the North American Chapter of the Association for Computational Linguistics: Human Language Technologies*, pages 563–568. Association for Computational Linguistics.

Convolutional Neural Networks vs. Convolution Kernels:
Feature Engineering for Answer Sentence Reranking

Kateryna Tymoshenko[†] and **Daniele Bonadiman**[†] and **Alessandro Moschitti**
[†]DISI, University of Trento, 38123 Povo (TN), Italy
Qatar Computing Research Institute, HBKU, 5825 Doha, Qatar
`{kateryna.tymoshenko, d.bonadiman}@unitn.it`
`amoschitti@qf.org.qa`

Abstract

In this paper, we study, compare and combine two state-of-the-art approaches to automatic feature engineering: Convolution Tree Kernels (CTKs) and Convolutional Neural Networks (CNNs) for learning to rank answer sentences in a Question Answering (QA) setting. When dealing with QA, the key aspect is to encode relational information between the constituents of question and answer in learning algorithms. For this purpose, we propose novel CNNs using relational information and combined them with relational CTKs. The results show that (i) both approaches achieve the state of the art on a question answering task, where CTKs produce higher accuracy and (ii) combining such methods leads to unprecedented high results.

1 Introduction

The increasing use of machine learning for the design of NLP applications pushes for fast methods for feature engineering. In contrast, the latter typically requires considerable effort especially when dealing with highly semantic tasks such as QA. For example, for an effective design of automated QA systems, the question text needs to be put in relation with the text passages retrieved from a document collection to enable an accurate extraction of the correct answers from passages. From a machine learning perspective, encoding the information above consists in manually defining expressive rules and features based on syntactic and semantic patterns.

Therefore, methods for automatizing feature engineering are remarkably important also in the light of fast prototyping of commercial applications. To the best of our knowledge, two of the most effective methods for engineering features are: (i) kernel methods, which naturally map feature vectors or directly objects in richer feature spaces; and more recently (ii) approaches based on deep learning, which have been shown to be very effective.

Regarding the former, in (Moschitti et al., 2007), we firstly used CTKs in Support Vector Machines (SVMs) to generate features from a question (Q) and their candidate answer passages (AP). CTKs enable SVMs to learn in the space of convolutional subtrees of syntactic and semantic trees used for representing Q and AP. This automatically engineers syntactic/semantic features. One important characteristic we added in (Severyn and Moschitti, 2012) is the use of relational links between Q and AP, which basically merged the two syntactic trees in a relational graph (containing relational features).

Although based on different principles, also CNNs can generate powerful features, e.g., see (Kalchbrenner et al., 2014; Kim, 2014). CNNs can effectively capture the compositional process of mapping the meaning of individual words in a sentence to a continuous representation of the sentence. This way CNNs can efficiently learn to embed input sentences into low-dimensional vector space, preserving important syntactic and semantic aspects of the input sentence. However, engineering features spanning two pieces of text such as in QA is a more complex task than classifying single sentences. Indeed, only very recently, CNNs were proposed for QA by Yu et al. (2014). Although, such network achieved high accuracy, its design is still not enough to model relational features.

Proceedings of NAACL-HLT 2016, pages 1268–1278,
San Diego, California, June 12-17, 2016. ©2016 Association for Computational Linguistics

In this paper, we aim at comparing the ability of CTKs and CNNs of generating features for QA. For this purpose, we first explore CTKs applied to shallow linguistic structures for automatically learning classification and ranking functions with SVMs.

At the same time, we assess a novel deep learning architecture for effectively modeling Q and AP pairs generating relational features we initially modeled in (Severyn and Moschitti, 2015; Severyn and Moschitti, 2016). The main building blocks of our approach are two sentence models based on CNNs. These work in parallel, mapping questions and answer sentences to fixed size vectors, which are then used to learn the semantic similarity between them. To compute question-answer similarity score we adopt the approach used by Yu et al. (2014). Our main novelty is the way we model relational information: we inject overlapping words directly into the word embeddings as additional dimensions. The augmented word representation is then passed through the layers of the convolutional feature extractors, which encode the relatedness between Q and AP pairs in a more structured manner. Moreover, the embedding dimensions encoding overlapping words are parameters of the network and are tuned during training.

We experiment with two different QA benchmarks for sentence reranking TREC13 (Wang et al., 2007) and WikiQA (Yang et al., 2015). We compare CTKs and CNNs and then we also combine them. For this purpose, we design a new kernel that sum together CTKs and different embeddings extracted from different CNN layers. Our CTK-based models achieve the state of the art on TREC 13, obtaining an MRR of 85.53 and an MAP of 75.18 largely outperforming all the previous best results. On Wik-iQA, our CNNs perform almost on par with tree kernels, i.e., an MRR of 71.07 vs. 72.51 of CTK, which again is the current state of the art on such data. The combination between CTK and CNNs produces a further boost, achieving an MRR of 75.52 and an MAP of 73.99, confirming that the research line of combining these two interesting machine learning methods is very promising.

2 Related Work

Relational learning from entire pieces of text concerns several natural language processing tasks, e.g., QA (Moschitti, 2008), Textual Entailment (Zanzotto and Moschitti, 2006) and Paraphrase Identification (Filice et al., 2015). Regarding QA, a referring work for our research is the IBM Watson system (Ferrucci et al., 2010). This is an advanced QA pipeline based on deep linguistic processing and semantic resources.

Wang et al. (2007) used quasi-synchronous grammar to model relations between a question and a candidate answer with syntactic transformations. (Heilman and Smith, 2010) applied Tree Edit Distance (TED) for learning tree transformations in a Q/AP pair. (Wang and Manning, 2010) designed a probabilistic model to learn tree-edit operations on dependency parse trees. (Yao et al., 2013) applied linear chain CRFs with features derived from TED to automatically learn associations between questions and candidate answers. Yih et al. (2013a) applied enhanced lexical semantics to build a word-alignment model, exploiting a number of large-scale external semantic resources.

Although the above approaches are very valuable, they required considerable effort to study, define and implement features that could capture relational representations. In contrast, we are interested in techniques that try to automatize the feature engineering step. In this respect, our work (Moschitti et al., 2007) is the first using CTKs applied to syntactic and semantic structural representations of the Q/AP pairs in a learning to rank algorithm based on SVMs. After this, we proposed several important improvement exploiting different type of relational links between Q and AP, i.e., (Severyn and Moschitti, 2012; Severyn et al., 2013; Severyn and Moschitti, 2013; Tymoshenko et al., 2014; Tymoshenko and Moschitti, 2015). The main difference with our previous approaches is usage of better-preprocessing algorithms and new structural representations, which highly outperform them.

Recently, deep learning approaches have been successfully applied to various sentence classification tasks, e.g., (Kalchbrenner et al., 2014; Kim, 2014), and for automatically modeling text pairs, e.g., (Lu and Li, 2013; Hu et al., 2014). Additionally, a number of deep learning models have been recently applied to question answering, e.g., Yih et al. (2014) applied CNNs to open-domain QA; Bordes et al. (2014b) propose a neural embedding model

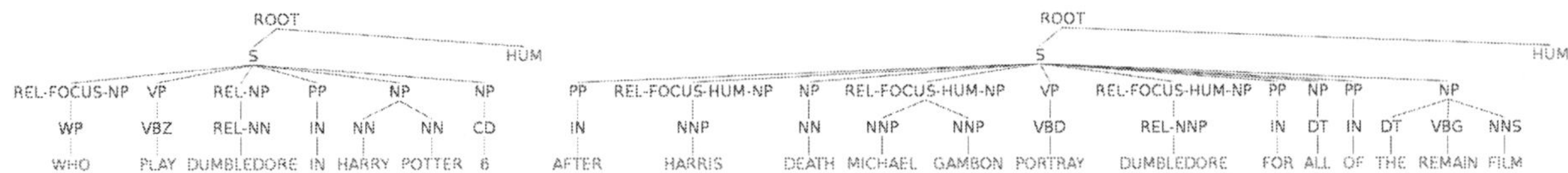

Figure 1: Shallow chunk-based tree for the Q/AP pair in the running example.

combined with the knowledge base for open-domain QA; Iyyer et al. (2014) applied recursive neural networks to factoid QA over paragraphs. (Miao et al., 2015) proposed a neural variational inference model and a Long-short Term Memory network for the same task. Recently (Yin et al., 2015) proposed a siamese convolutional network for matching sentences that employ an attentive average pooling mechanism, obtaining state-of-the-art results in various tasks and datasets. The work closest to this paper is (Yu et al., 2014) and (Severyn and Moschitti, 2015). The former presented a CNN architecture for answer sentence selection that uses a bigram convolution and average pooling, whereas in the latter we used convolution with k-max pooling. However, these models only partially captures relational information. In contrast, in this paper, we encode relational information about words that are matched betweem Q and AP.

3 Feature Engineering for QA with CTKs

Our approach to learning relations between two texts is to first convert them into a richer structural representation based on their syntactic and semantic structures, and then apply CTKs. To make our approach more effective, we further enriched structures with relational semantics by linking the related constituents with lexical and other semantic links.

3.1 Shallow Representation of Short Text Pairs

In our study, we employ a modified version of the shallow structural representation of question and answer pairs, **CH**, described in (Severyn et al., 2013; Tymoshenko and Moschitti, 2015). We represent a pair of short texts as two trees with lemmas at leaf level and their part-of-speech (POS) tags at the preterminal level. Preterminal POS-tags are grouped into chunk nodes and the chunks are further grouped into sentences. Figure 1 provides an example of this structure.

We enrich the above representation with the in-

formation about question class and question focus. Questions are classified in terms of their expected answer type. (Severyn et al., 2013) employed coarse-grained classes from (Li and Roth, 2002), namely HUM (person), ENTY (an entity), DESC (description), LOC (location), and NUM (number). In this work, we split the NUM class into three subcategories, DATE, QUANTITY, CURRENCY and train question classifiers as described in (Severyn et al., 2013). Differently from before, we add the question class node as the rightmost child of the root node both to the question and the answer structures.

We detect question focus using a focus classifier, FCLASS, trained as in (Severyn et al., 2013). However, in our previous model, we classified all words over the chunks in the question and picked the one with the highest FCLASS prediction score as a focus even if it is negative. In this work, if FCLASS assigns negative scores to all the question chunks, we consider the first question chunk, which is typically a question word, to be a focus. We mark the focus chunk by prepending the REL-FOCUS tag to its label.

In previous work, we have shown the importance of encoding information about the relatedness between Q and AP into their structural representations. Thus, we employ lexical and question class match, described hereafter.

Lexical match. Lemmas that occur both in Q and AP are marked by prepending the **REL** tag to the labels of the corresponding preterminal nodes and their parents.

Question class match. We detect named entities (NEs) in AP and mark the NEs of type compatible[1] with the question class by prepending the REL-FOCUS-QC label to the corresponding prepreterminals in the trees. The QC suffix in the labels

---

[1]Compatibility is checked using a predefined table, namely Person, Organization→HUM, ENTY; Misc→ENTY; Location→LOC; Date, Time, Number→DATE; Money, Number→CURRENCY; Percentage, Number→QUANTITY

is replaced by the question class in the given pair.

For example, in Figure 1, the *Dumbledore* lemma occurs in both Q and AP, therefore the respective POS and chunk nodes are marked with **REL**. The named entities, *Harris*, *Michael Gambon* and *Dumbledore* have the type Person compatible with the question class HUM, thus their respective chunk nodes are marked as REL-FOCUS-HUM (overriding the previously inserted REL tag for the *Dumbledore* chunk).

3.2 Reranking with Tree Kernels

We aim at learning reranker that can decide which Q/AP pair is more probably correct than others, where correct Q/AP pairs are formed by an AP containing a correct answer to Q along with a supporting justification. We adopt the following kernel for reranking: $P_K(\langle o_1, o_2 \rangle, \langle o_1', o_2' \rangle) = K(o_1, o_1') + K(o_2, o_2') - K(o_1, o_2') - K(o_2, o_1')$. In our case, $o_i = \langle Q_i, AP_i \rangle$ and $o_j' = \langle Q_j', AP_j' \rangle$, where Q and AP are the trees defined in the previous section, $K(o_i, o_j') = TK(Q_i, Q_j') + TK(AP_i, AP_j')$ and TK is a tree kernel function. Finally, we also add $(\vec{V}(o_1) - \vec{V}(o_2)) \cdot (\vec{V}(o_1') - \vec{V}(o_2'))$ to P_K, where $\vec{V}(o_i)$ is a feature vector representing Q/AP pairs.

4 Feature Engineering for QA with CNNs

The architecture of our convolutional neural network for matching Q and AP pairs is presented in Fig. 2. Its main components are: (i) sentence matrices $s_i \in \mathbb{R}^{d \times |i|}$ obtained by the concatenation of the word vectors $\mathbf{w}_j \in \mathbb{R}^d$ (with d being the size of the embeddings) of the corresponding words w_j from the input sentences (Q and AP) $\mathbf{s}_i$; (ii) a convolutional sentence model $f : \mathbb{R}^{d \times |i|} \rightarrow \mathbb{R}^m$ that maps the sentence matrix of an input sentence $\mathbf{s}_i$ to a fixed-size vector representations $\mathbf{x}_{s_i}$ of size m; (iii) a layer for computing the similarity between the obtained intermediate vector representations of the input sentences, using a similarity matrix $\mathbf{M} \in \mathbb{R}^{m \times m}$ – an intermediate vector representation $\mathbf{x}_{s_1}$ of a sentence $\mathbf{s}_1$ is projected to a $\tilde{\mathbf{x}}_{s_1} = \mathbf{x}_{s_1} \mathbf{M}$, which is then matched with $\mathbf{x}_{s_2}$ (Bordes et al., 2014a), i.e., by computing a dot-product $\tilde{\mathbf{x}}_{s_1} \mathbf{x}_{s_2}$, thus resulting in a single similarity score x_{sim}; (iv) a set of fully-connected hidden layers that model the similarity between sentences using their vector representations produced by the sentence model (also integrating the

single similarity score from the previous layer); and (v) a *sigmoid* layer that outputs probability scores reflecting how well the Q-AP pairs match with each other.

The choice of the sentence model plays a crucial role as the resulting intermediate representations of the input sentences will affect the successive step of computing their similarity. Recently, convolutional sentence models, where $f(\mathbf{s})$ is represented by a sequence of convolutional-pooling feature maps, have shown state-of-the-art results on many NLP tasks, e.g., (Kalchbrenner et al., 2014; Kim, 2014). In this paper, we opt for a convolutional operation followed by a k-max pooling layer with $k = 1$ as proposed in (Severyn and Moschitti, 2015).

Considering recent applications of deep learning models to the problem of matching sentences, our network is most similar to the models in (Hu et al., 2014) applied for computing sentence similarity and in (Yu et al., 2014) (answer sentence selection in QA) with the following difference. To compute the similarity between the vector representation of the input sentences, our network uses two methods: (i) computing the similarity score obtained using a similarity matrix $\mathbf{M}$ (explored in (Yu et al., 2014)), and (ii) directly modelling interactions between intermediate vector representations of the input sentences via fully-connected hidden layers (used by (Hu et al., 2014)). This approach, as proposed in (Severyn and Moschitti, 2015), results in a significant improvement in the task of question answer selection over the two methods used separately. Differently from the above models we do not add additional features in the join layer.

4.1 Representation Layers

It should be noted that NNs non-linearly transform the input at each layer. For instance, the output of the convolutional and pooling operation $f(s_i)$ is a fixed-size representation of the input sentence s_i. In the reminder of the paper, we will refer to these vector representations for the question and the answer passage as the question embedding (QE) and the answer embedding (AE), respectively. Similarly, the output of the penultimate layer of the network (the hidden layer whose output is fed to the final classification layer) is a compact representation of the input Question and Answer pair, which we call Joint

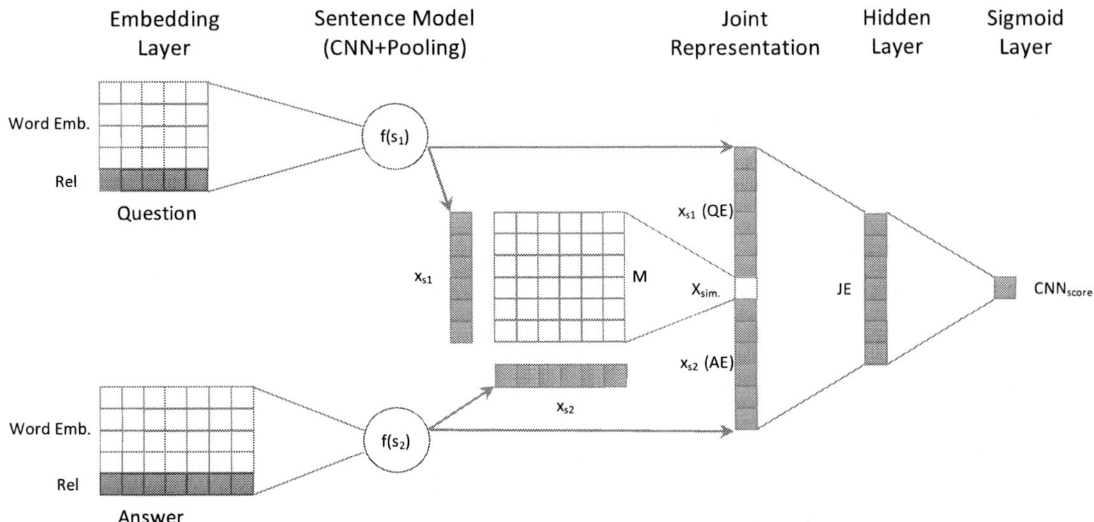

Figure 2: CNN for computing the similarity between question and answer.

Embedding (JE).

4.2 Injecting Relational Information in CNNs

Sec. 3 has shown that establishing relational links (REL nodes) between Q and A pairs is very important for solving the QA task. Yih et al. (2013b) also use latent word-alignment structure in their semantic similarity model to compute similarity between question and answer sentences. Yu et al. (2014) achieve large improvement by combining the output of their deep learning model with word count features in a logistic regression model. Differently from (Yu et al., 2014; Severyn and Moschitti, 2015) we do not add additional features such as the word count in the join layer. We allow our convolutional neural network to capture the connections between related words in a pair and we feed it with an additional binary-like input about overlapping words (Severyn and Moschitti, 2016).

In particular, in the input sentence, we associate an additional *word overlap* indicator feature $o \in \{0, 1\}$ with each word w, where 1 corresponds to words that overlap in a given pair and 0 otherwise. To decide if the words overlap, we perform string matching. Basically this small feature vector plays the role of REL tag added to the CTK structures.

Hence, we require an additional lookup table layer for the word overlap features $LT_{\mathbf{W}_o}(\cdot)$ with parameters $\mathbf{W}_o \in \mathbb{R}^{d_o \times 2}$, where $d_o \in \mathbb{N}$ is a hyper-parameter of the model, which indicates the number of dimensions used for encoding the word overlap features. Thus, we augment word embeddings with additional dimensions that encode the fact that a given word in a pair is overlapping or semantically similar and let the network learn its optimal representation. Given a word w_i, its final word embedding $\mathbf{w}_i \in \mathbb{R}^d$ (where $d = d_w + d_o$) is obtained by concatenating the output of two lookup table operations $LT_{\mathbf{W}}(w_i)$ and $LT_{\mathbf{W}_o}(w_i)$.

5 Experiments

In these experiments, we compare the impact in accuracy of two main methods for automatic feature engineering, i.e., CTKs and CNNs, for relational learning, using two different answer sentence selection datasets, WikiQA and TREC13. We propose several strategies to combine CNNs with CTKs and we show that the two approaches are complementary as their joint use significantly boosts both models.

5.1 Experimental Setup

We utilized two datasets for testing our models:
TREC13. This is the factoid open-domain TREC QA corpus prepared by (Wang et al., 2007). The training data was assembled from the 1,229 TREC8-12 questions. The answers for the training questions were automatically marked in sentences by applying regular expressions, therefore the dataset can be

noisy. The test data contains 68 questions, whose answers were manually annotated. We used 10 answer passages for each question for training our classifiers and all the answer passages available for each question for testing.

WikiQA. TREC13 is a small dataset with an even smaller test set, which makes the system evaluation rather unstable, i.e., a small difference in parameters and models can produce very different results. Moreover, as pointed by (Yih et al., 2013b), it has significant lexical overlap between questions and answer candidates, therefore simple lexical match models may likely outperform more elaborate methods if trained and tested on it. WikiQA dataset (Yang et al., 2015) is a larger dataset, created for open domain QA, which overcomes these problems. Its questions were sampled from the Bing query logs and candidate answers were extracted from the summary paragraphs of the associated Wikipedia pages. The train, test, and development sets contain 2,118, 633 and 296 questions, respectively. There is no correct answer sentence for 1,245 training, 170 development and 390 test questions. Consistently with (Yin et al., 2015), we remove the questions without answers for our evaluations.

Preprocessing. We used the Illinois chunker (Punyakanok and Roth, 2001), question class and focus classifiers trained as in (Severyn and Moschitti, 2013) and the Stanford CoreNLP (Manning et al., 2014) toolkit for the needed preprocessing.

CTKs. We used SVM-light-TK[2] to train our models. The toolkit enables the use of structural kernels (Moschitti, 2006) in SVM-light (Joachims, 2002). We applied (i) the partial tree kernel (PTK) with its default parameters to all our structures and (ii) the polynomial kernel of degree 3 on all feature vectors we generate.

Metaclassifier. We used the *scikit*[3] logistic regression classifier implementation to train the metaclassifier on the outputs of CTKs and CNNs.

CNNs. We pre-initialize the word embeddings by running the `word2vec` tool (Mikolov et al., 2013) on the English Wikipedia dump and the jacana corpus as in (Severyn and Moschitti, 2015). We opt for a skipgram model with window size 5 and filtering

---

[2] http://disi.unitn.it/moschitti/Tree-Kernel.htm

[3] http://scikit-learn.org/stable/index.html

	MRR	MAP	P@1
State of the art			
CNN_c (Yang et al., 2015)	66.52	65.20	n/a
ABCNN (Yin et al., 2015)	71.27	69.14	n/a
$LSTM_{a,c}$ (Miao et al., 2015)	70.41	68.55	n/a
$NASM_c$ (Miao et al., 2015)	70.69	68.86	n/a
Our Individual Models			
CNN_R	71.07	69.51	57.20
CH_{coarse}	71.63	70.45	56.79
CH	72.30	71.25	58.44
V_{AE+QE}	68.29	67.24	55.56
V_{JE}	67.07	65.76	52.26
Our Model Combinations			
$CH+V_{AE+QE}$	72.51	71.29	59.26
$CH+V_{JE}$	73.18	71.56	60.49
$^*CH+V_{AE+QE}$	**75.88**	**74.17**	**64.61**
$^*CH+V_{JE}$	75.52	73.99	63.79
Meta: CH, V_{JE}, CNN_R	**75.28**	**73.69**	**62.96**
Meta: CH, V_{JE}	75.08	73.64	62.55
Meta: $CH+V_{JE}$, CNN_R	73.94	72.25	61.73

Table 1: Performance on the WikiQA dataset

words with frequency less than 5. The dimensionality of the embeddings is set to 50. The input sentences are mapped to fixed-sized vectors by computing the average of their word embeddings. We use a single non-linear hidden layer (with hyperbolic tangent activation, Tanh), whose size is equal to the size of the previous layer. The network is trained using SGD with shuffled mini-batches using the Adam update rule (Kingma and Ba, 2014). The batch size is set to 100 examples. The network is trained for a fixed number of epochs (i.e., 3) for all the experiments. We decided to avoid using early stopping, in order to do not overfit the development set and have a fair comparison with the CTKs models.

QA metrics. We used common QA metrics: Precision at rank 1 (P@1), i.e., the percentage of questions with a correct answer ranked at the first position, the Mean Reciprocal Rank (MRR) and the Mean Average Precision (MAP).

5.2 Experiments on WikiQA

State of the art. Table 1 reports the results obtained on the WikiQA test set by state-of-the-art systems (lines 1-4) and our models, when removing the questions with no correct answers (this to be aligned with previous work). More in detail:

CNN_c is the Convolutional Neural Network with word count,

	TRAIN50			DEV		
	MRR	MAP	P@1	MRR	MAP	P@1
CH	69.97	68.77	55.14	67.23	65.93	51.44
V_{AE+QE}	68.70	67.18	54.32	68.14	66.46	54.73
V_{JE}	70.43	68.67	57.61	68.90	67.14	55.56
Model Combinations						
CH+V_{AE+QE}	**74.40**	**72.63**	**62.55**	**70.01**	**68.60**	57.61
CH+V_{JE}	73.53	71.69	60.49	**70.10**	**68.55**	**58.44**
Metaclassifiers:						
CH, V_{JE}, CNN$_R$	74.01	72.31	62.14	n/a	n/a	n/a
CH, V_{JE}	73.95	72.15	62.14	n/a	n/a	n/a
CH+V_{JE}, CNN$_R$	73.43	71.58	60.49	n/a	n/a	n/a

Table 2: Performance on the WikiQA using the development set or half of the training set for training

	TRAIN			TRAIN50		
	MRR	MAP	P@1	MRR	MAP	P@1
CH	74.87	74.17	63.49	71.31	70.45	57.94
V_{AE+QE}	70.32	69.75	56.35	71.06	70.33	57.14
V_{JE}	69.86	69.24	55.56	71.11	70.43	57.14
CH+V_{AE+QE}	71.29	70.79	57.94	72.62	72.18	59.52
CH+V_{JE}	71.36	70.81	57.94	71.96	71.55	59.52
*CH+V_{AE+QE}	**76.66**	**75.50**	**66.67**	**75.23**	**74.54**	**64.29**

Table 3: Performance on the WikiQA on the development set

ABCNN is the Attention-Based CNN,
LSTM$_{a,c}$ is the long short-term memory network with attention and word count, and
NASM$_c$ is the neural answer selection model with word count.

CNN$_R$ is the relational CNN described in Section 4.
CH[4] is a tree kernel-based SVM reranker trained on the shallow pos-chunk tree representations of question and answer sentences (Sec. 3.1), where the subscript $_{coarse}$ refers to the model with the coarse-grained question classes as in (Tymoshenko and Moschitti, 2015).

V is a polynomial SVM reranker, where the subscripts AE, QE, JE indicate the use of the answer, question or joint embeddings (see Sec. 4.1) as the feature vector of SVM and + means that two embeddings were concatenated into a single vector.

The results show that our CNN$_R$ model performs comparably to ABCNN (Yin et al., 2015), which is the most recent and accurate NN model and to CH$_{coarse}$. The performance drops when the embeddings AE, QE and JE are used in a polynomial

SVM reranker. In contrast, CH (using our tree structure enriched with fine-grained categories) outperforms all the models, showing the importance of syntactic relational information for the answer sentence selection task.

5.2.1 Combining CNN with CTK on WikiQA

We experiment with two ways of combining CTK with CNN$_R$: (i) at the kernel level, i.e., summing tree kernels with the polynomial kernel over different embeddings, i.e., CH+V, and (ii) using the predictions of SVM and CNN$_R$ models (computed on the development set) as features to train logistic regression meta-classifiers (again only on the development set). These are reported in the last three lines of Table 1, where the name of the classifiers participating with their outputs are illustrated as a comma-separated list. The results are very interesting as all kinds of combinations largely outperform the state of the art, e.g., by around 3 points in terms of MRR, 2 points in terms of MAP and 5 points in terms of P@1 with respect to the strongest standalone system, CH. Directly using the predictions of the CNN$_R$ as features in the meta-classifier does not impact the overall performance. It should be noted that the meta-classifier could only be trained on the

---

[4]Models marked by * use an improved version of the preference ranking framework we described in Section 3.2. It is important to show such results as they provide a referring baseline for future research in this field.

development data to avoid predictions biased by the training data.

5.2.2 Using less training data

Since we train the weights of CNN_R on the training set of WikiQA, to obtain the embeddings minimizing the loss function, we risk to have overfitted, i.e., "biased", JE, AE and QE on the questions and answers of the training set. Therefore, we conducted another set of experiments to study this case. We randomly split the training set into two equal subsets. We train CNN_R on one of them and in the other subset, (referred to as **TRAIN50**) we produce the embeddings of questions and answers.

Table 2 reports the results on the WikiQA test set which we obtained when training SVM on TRAIN50 and on the development set, **DEV**. We trained the meta-classifier on the predictions of the standalone models on DEV. Consistently with the previous results, we obtain the best performance combining the CNN_R embeddings with CTK. Even when we train on the 50% of the training data only, we still outperform the state of the art, and our best model $\text{CH}+V_{JE}$ performs only around 2 points lower in terms of MRR, MAP and P@1 than when training on the full training set.

Finally, Table 3 reports the performance of our models when tested on the development set and demonstrates that the improvement obtained when combining CTK and CNN_R embeddings also holds on it. Note, that we did not use the development set for any parameter tuning and we train all the models with the default parameters.

5.3 Experiments on TREC13 dataset

TREC13 corpus has been used for evaluation in a number of works starting from 2007. Table 4 reports our as well as some state-of-the-art system results on TREC13. It should be noted that, to be consistent with the previous work, we evaluated our models in the same setting as (Wang et al., 2007; Yih et al., 2013a), i.e., we (i) remove the questions having only correct or only incorrect answer sentence candidates and (ii) used the same evaluation script and the gold judgment file as they used. As pointed out by Footnote 7 in (Yih et al., 2014), the evaluation script always considers 4 questions to be answered incorrectly thus penalizing the overall system score.

We note that our models, i.e., CNN_R, V_{JE},

Models	MRR	MAP
State of the art		
Wang et al. (2007)	68.52	60.29
Heilman and Smith (2010)	69.17	60.91
Wang and Manning (2010)	69.51	59.51
Yao et al. (2013)	74.77	63.07
Severyn and Moschitti (2013)	73.58	67.81
Yih et al. (2013a)	77.00	70.92
Yu et al. (2014)	78.64	71.13
Wang and Ittycheriah (2015)	77.40	70.63
Tymoshenko and Moschitti (2015)	82.29	73.34
Yang et al. (2015)	76.33	69.51
Miao et al. (2015)	81.17	73.39
Individual Models		
CNN_R	77.93	71.09
V_{AE+QE}	79.32	73.37
V_{JE}	77.24	71.34
CH	**85.53**	**75.18**
Model Combinations		
$\text{CH}+V_{JE}$	79.75	74.29
$\text{CH}+V_{AE+QE}$	79.74	75.06
Meta: CH, V_{AE+QE}, CNN_R	81.67	75.77
Model Combinations using simpler CH		
CH_{smpl}	78.66	71.18
$\text{CH}_{smpl}+V_{AE+QE}$	80.19	75.01
$\text{CH}_{smpl}+V_{JE}$	80.42	74.16

Table 4: Results on the TREC13, answer selection task.

V_{AE+QE}, again align with the state of the art. In contrast, our CTK using CH largely outperforms all previous work, e.g., 7.6 points more than CNN_R in terms of MRR. Considering that the evaluation of CH with a script that does not penalize systems would show real MRR and MAP of 90.56 and 80.08, respectively, there is little room for improvement with combinations. Indeed, the table shows no improvement of model combinations over CH.

Therefore, we trained a simplified version of CH, CH_{smpl}, which employs shallow chunk-based representations without the question focus or question class information, i.e., only using the basic relational information represented by the lexical match **REL** tags. CH_{smpl} performs comparably to CNN_R, and the combination with embeddings produced by CNN_R, i.e., $\text{CH}_{smpl}+V_{AE+QE}$, outperforms both CH_{smpl} and CNN_R.

6 Discussion

The main focus and novelty of this paper is comparing and combining CTKs and CNETs. We showed that the features they generate are complementary as their combination improve both models. For the combinations, we used voting and our new method of combining network layers embedded in a polynomial kernels added to tree kernels.

We would like to stress that to the best of our knowledge we are the first to merge CNNs and CTK together. We showed that kernels based on different embedding layers learned with our CNNs, when used in SVMs, deliver the same accuracy of CNNs. This enables an effective combination between TK and CNNs at kernel level. Indeed, we experimented with different kernel combinations built on top of different CNN layers, improving the state of the art, largely outperforming all previous systems exactly using the same testing conditions. These results are important for developing future research as they provide indications on features/methods and referring baselines to compare with.

Finally, we generated modified structures and used better parsers outperforming our initial result in (Severyn and Moschitti, 2013) by more than 10 points.

6.1 Efficiency

An interesting question is the practical use of our models, which require the discussion of their efficiency. In this respect, our framework combines CTKs and CNNs by generating a global kernel. Thus, the time complexity during training is basically given by (i) training CNNs, (ii) extracting their embeddings and (iii) use these embeddings during the CTK training. The time for computing steps (i) and (ii) is linear with respect to the number of examples as the architecture and the number of optimization steps are fixed. In practice, the bottleneck of training our CNN architecture is in the number of weights.

Regarding Step (iii), since the embeddings just feed a polynomial kernel, which is slightly more efficient than CTKs, the overall complexity is dominated by the one of the CTK framework, i.e., $O(n^2)$. In practice, this is rather efficient, e.g., see the discussion in (Tymoshenko and Moschitti, 2015). The testing complexity is reduced to the number of kernel operations between the support vectors and the test examples (the worst case is $O(n^2)$), which are also parallelizable.

7 Conclusions

This paper compares two state-of-the-art feature engineering approaches, namely CTKs and CNNs, on the very complex task of answer reranking in a QA setting. In order to have a meaningful comparison, we have set the best configuration for CTK by defining and implementing innovative linguistic structures enriched with semantic information from statistical classifiers (i.e., question and focus classifiers). At the same time, we have developed powerful CNNs, which can embed relational information in their representations.

We tested our models for answer passage reranking in QA on two benchmarks, WikiQA and TREC13. Thus, they are directly comparable with many systems from previous work. The results show that our models outperform the state of the art achieved by more complex networks.

In particular, CTKs outperform our CNNs but use more information, e.g., on TREC 13, CTKs obtain an MRR and MAP of 85.53 and 75.18 vs. 77.93 and 71.09 of CNNs. On WikiQA, CNNs combined with tree kernels achieves an MRR of 75.88 and an MAP of 74.17 largely outperforming the current state of the art, i.e., MRR of 71.27 and MAP 69.14 of ABCNN by Yin et al. (2015).

It should be noted that CTK models use syntactic parsing, two statistical classifiers for focus and question classification and a named entity recognizer whereas CNNs only use words and two additional unsupervised corpora.

In the future, we would like to embed CNN similarity in CTKs. A straightforward methods for achieving this is to use the Smoothed Partial Tree Kernel by Croce et al. (2011). Our preliminary experiments using word2vec were not successful. However, CNNs may provide a more effective similarity. Finally, it would be also very interesting to exploit structural kernels in the network layers.

Acknowledgements

This work has been partially supported by the EC project CogNet, 671625 (H2020-ICT-2014-2, Research and Innovation action) and by an IBM Faculty Award. Many thanks to the anonymous reviewers for their valuable suggestions.

References

Antoine Bordes, Sumit Chopra, and Jason Weston. 2014a. Question answering with subgraph embeddings. In *EMNLP*.

Antoine Bordes, Jason Weston, and Nicolas Usunier. 2014b. Open question answering with weakly supervised embedding models. In *ECML*.

Danilo Croce, Alessandro Moschitti, and Roberto Basili. 2011. Structured lexical similarity via convolution kernels on dependency trees. In *Proceedings of EMNLP*.

David Ferrucci, Eric Brown, Jennifer Chu-Carroll, James Fan, David Gondek, Aditya Kalyanpur, Adam Lally, J. William Murdock, Eric Nyberg, John Prager, Nico Schlaefer, and Chris Welty. 2010. Building watson: An overview of the deepqa project. *AI Magazine*, 31(3).

Simone Filice, Giovanni Da San Martino, and Alessandro Moschitti. 2015. Structural representations for learning relations between pairs of texts. In *Proceedings of the 53rd Annual Meeting of the Association for Computational Linguistics and the 7th International Joint Conference on Natural Language Processing (Volume 1: Long Papers)*, pages 1003–1013, Beijing, China, July. Association for Computational Linguistics.

Michael Heilman and Noah A. Smith. 2010. Tree edit models for recognizing textual entailments, paraphrases, and answers to questions. In *NAACL*.

Baotian Hu, Zhengdong Lu, Hang Li, and Qingcai Chen. 2014. Convolutional neural network architectures for matching natural language sentences. In *NIPS*.

Mohit Iyyer, Jordan Boyd-Graber, Leonardo Claudino, Richard Socher, and Hal Daumé III. 2014. A neural network for factoid question answering over paragraphs. In *EMNLP*.

Thorsten Joachims. 2002. Optimizing search engines using clickthrough data. In *Proceedings of the Eighth ACM SIGKDD International Conference on Knowledge Discovery and Data Mining*, KDD '02, pages 133–142, New York, NY, USA. ACM.

Nal Kalchbrenner, Edward Grefenstette, and Phil Blunsom. 2014. A convolutional neural network for modelling sentences. *Proceedings of the 52nd Annual Meeting of the Association for Computational Linguistics*, June.

Yoon Kim. 2014. Convolutional neural networks for sentence classification. Doha, Qatar.

Diederik Kingma and Jimmy Ba. 2014. Adam: A method for stochastic optimization. *arXiv preprint arXiv:1412.6980*.

Xin Li and Dan Roth. 2002. Learning question classifiers. In *COLING*.

Zhengdong Lu and Hang Li. 2013. A deep architecture for matching short texts. In *NIPS*.

Christopher D. Manning, Mihai Surdeanu, John Bauer, Jenny Finkel, Steven J. Bethard, and David McClosky. 2014. The Stanford CoreNLP natural language processing toolkit. In *Proceedings of 52nd Annual Meeting of the Association for Computational Linguistics: System Demonstrations*, pages 55–60.

Yishu Miao, Lei Yu, and Phil Blunsom. 2015. Neural variational inference for text processing. *arXiv preprint arXiv:1511.06038*.

Tomas Mikolov, Ilya Sutskever, Kai Chen, Greg S Corrado, and Jeff Dean. 2013. Distributed representations of words and phrases and their compositionality. In *Advances in Neural Information Processing Systems 26*, pages 3111–3119.

Alessandro Moschitti, Silvia Quarteroni, Roberto Basili, and Suresh Manandhar. 2007. Exploiting syntactic and shallow semantic kernels for question/answer classification. In *ACL*.

Alessandro Moschitti. 2006. Efficient convolution kernels for dependency and constituent syntactic trees. In *ECML*, pages 318–329.

Alessandro Moschitti. 2008. Kernel Methods, Syntax and Semantics for Relational Text Categorization. In *Proceeding of ACM 17th Conf. on Information and Knowledge Management (CIKM'08)*, Napa Valley, CA, USA.

V. Punyakanok and D. Roth. 2001. The use of classifiers in sequential inference. In *NIPS*, pages 995–1001.

Aliaksei Severyn and Alessandro Moschitti. 2012. Structural relationships for large-scale learning of answer re-ranking. In *SIGIR*.

Aliaksei Severyn and Alessandro Moschitti. 2013. Automatic feature engineering for answer selection and extraction. In *EMNLP*.

Aliaksei Severyn and Alessandro Moschitti. 2015. Learning to rank short text pairs with convolutional deep neural networks. In *Proceedings of the 38th International ACM SIGIR Conference on Research and Development in Information Retrieval*, pages 373–382. ACM.

Aliaksei Severyn and Alessandro Moschitti. 2016. Modeling relational information in question-answer pairs with convolutional neural networks. *In Preprint arXiv:1604.01178*.

Aliaksei Severyn, Massimo Nicosia, and Alessandro Moschitti. 2013. Learning adaptable patterns for passage reranking. *CoNLL-2013*, page 75.

Kateryna Tymoshenko and Alessandro Moschitti. 2015. Assessing the impact of syntactic and semantic structures for answer passages reranking. In *Proceedings of the 24th ACM International on Conference on Information and Knowledge Management*, pages 1451–1460. ACM.

Kateryna Tymoshenko, Alessandro Moschitti, and Aliaksei Severyn. 2014. Encoding semantic resources in syntactic structures for passage reranking. In *Proceedings of the 14th Conference of the European Chapter of the Association for Computational Linguistics*, pages 664–672, Gothenburg, Sweden, April. Association for Computational Linguistics.

Zhiguo Wang and Abraham Ittycheriah. 2015. Faqbased question answering via word alignment. *arXiv preprint arXiv:1507.02628*.

Mengqiu Wang and Christopher D. Manning. 2010. Probabilistic tree-edit models with structured latent variables for textual entailment and question answering. In *ACL*.

Mengqiu Wang, Noah A Smith, and Teruko Mitamura. 2007. What is the jeopardy model? a quasi-synchronous grammar for qa. In *EMNLP-CoNLL*.

Yi Yang, Wen-tau Yih, and Christopher Meek. 2015. Wikiqa: A challenge dataset for open-domain question answering. In *Proceedings of the 2015 Conference on Empirical Methods in Natural Language Processing*, pages 2013–2018, Lisbon, Portugal, September. Association for Computational Linguistics.

Xuchen Yao, Benjamin Van Durme, Peter Clark, and Chris Callison-Burch. 2013. Answer extraction as sequence tagging with tree edit distance. In *NAACL*.

Wen-tau Yih, Ming-Wei Chang, Christopher Meek, and Andrzej Pastusiak. 2013a. Question answering using enhanced lexical semantic models. In *Proceedings of the 51st Annual Meeting of the Association for Computational Linguistics (Volume 1: Long Papers)*, pages 1744–1753, Sofia, Bulgaria, August. Association for Computational Linguistics.

Wen-Tau Yih, Ming-Wei Chang, Christopher Meek, and Andrzej Pastusiak. 2013b. Question answering using enhanced lexical semantic models. In *ACL*, August.

Wen-Tau Yih, Xiaodong He, and Christopher Meek. 2014. Semantic parsing for single-relation question answering. In *ACL*.

Wenpeng Yin, Hinrich Schütze, Bing Xiang, and Bowen Zhou. 2015. Abcnn: Attention-based convolutional neural network for modeling sentence pairs. *arXiv preprint arXiv:1512.05193*.

Lei Yu, Karl Moritz Hermann, Phil Blunsom, and Stephen Pulman. 2014. Deep Learning for Answer Sentence Selection. In *NIPS Deep Learning Workshop*, December.

F. M. Zanzotto and A. Moschitti. 2006. Automatic Learning of Textual Entailments with Cross-Pair Similarities. In *The Joint 21st International Conference on Computational Linguistics and 44th Annual Meeting of the Association for Computational Linguistics (COLING-ACL)*, Sydney, Australia. Association for Computational Linguistics.

Semi-supervised Question Retrieval with Gated Convolutions

Tao Lei   Hrishikesh Joshi   Regina Barzilay   Tommi Jaakkola
MIT CSAIL
{taolei, hjoshi, regina, tommi}@csail.mit.edu

Katerina Tymoshenko
University of Trento
tymoshenko@disi.unitn.it

Alessandro Moschitti   Lluís Màrquez
Qatar Computing Research Institute, HBKU
{amoschitti, lmarquez}@qf.org.qa

Abstract

Question answering forums are rapidly growing in size with no effective automated ability to refer to and reuse answers already available for previous posted questions. In this paper, we develop a methodology for finding semantically related questions. The task is difficult since 1) key pieces of information are often buried in extraneous details in the question body and 2) available annotations on similar questions are scarce and fragmented. We design a recurrent and convolutional model (gated convolution) to effectively map questions to their semantic representations. The models are pre-trained within an encoder-decoder framework (from body to title) on the basis of the entire raw corpus, and fine-tuned discriminatively from limited annotations. Our evaluation demonstrates that our model yields substantial gains over a standard IR baseline and various neural network architectures (including CNNs, LSTMs and GRUs).[1]

1   Introduction

Question answering (QA) forums such as Stack Exchange[2] are rapidly expanding and already contain millions of questions. The expanding scope and coverage of these forums often leads to many duplicate and interrelated questions, resulting in the same questions being answered multiple times. By identifying similar questions, we can potentially reuse

---

[1]Our code and data are available at https://github.com/taolei87/rcnn

[2]http://stackexchange.com/

Title: How can I boot Ubuntu from a USB?
Body: I bought a Compaq pc with Windows 8 a few months ago and now I want to install Ubuntu but still keep Windows 8. I tried Webi but when my pc restarts it read ERROR 0x000007b. I know that Windows 8 has a thing about not letting you have Ubuntu but I still want to have both OS without actually losing all my data ...

Title: When I want to install Ubuntu on my laptop I'll have to erase all my data. "Alonge side windows" doesnt appear
Body: I want to install Ubuntu from a Usb drive. It says I have to erase all my data but I want to install it along side Windows 8. The "Install alongside windows" option doesn't appear. What appear is, ...

Figure 1: A pair of similar questions.

existing answers, reducing response times and unnecessary repeated work. Unfortunately in most forums, the process of identifying and referring to existing similar questions is done manually by forum participants with limited, scattered success.

The task of automatically retrieving similar questions to a given user's question has recently attracted significant attention and has become a testbed for various representation learning approaches (Zhou et al., 2015; dos Santos et al., 2015). However, the task has proven to be quite challenging – for instance, dos Santos et al. (2015) report a 22.3% classification accuracy, yielding a 4 percent gain over a simple word matching baseline.

Several factors make the problem difficult. First, submitted questions are often long and contain extraneous information irrelevant to the main question being asked. For instance, the first question in Figure 1 pertains to booting Ubuntu using a USB stick. A large portion of the body contains tangential details that are idiosyncratic to this user, such as references to *Compaq pc*, *Webi* and the error message. Not surprisingly, these features are not repeated in the second question in Figure 1 about a closely related topic. The extraneous detail can easily confuse simple word-matching algorithms. Indeed, for this reason, some existing methods for question retrieval restrict attention to the question title only. While titles (when available) can succinctly summarize the intent, they also sometimes lack crucial detail available in the question body. For example, the title of the second question does not refer to installation from a USB drive. The second challenge arises from the noisy annotations. Indeed, the pairs of questions marked as similar by forum participants are largely incomplete. Our manual inspection of a sample set of questions from AskUbuntu[3] shows that only 5% of similar pairs have been annotated by the users, with a precision of around 79%.

In this paper, we design a neural network model and an associated training paradigm to address these challenges. On a high level, our model is used as an encoder to map the title, body, or the combination to a vector representation. The resulting "question vector" representation is then compared to other questions via cosine similarity. We introduce several departures from typical architectures on a finer level. In particular, we incorporate adaptive gating in non-consecutive CNNs (Lei et al., 2015) in order to focus temporal averaging in these models on key pieces of the questions. Gating plays a similar role in LSTMs (Hochreiter and Schmidhuber, 1997), though LSTMs do not reach the same level of performance in our setting. Moreover, we counter the scattered annotations available from user-driven associations by training the model largely based on the entire unannotated corpus. The encoder is coupled with a decoder and trained to reproduce the title from the noisy question body. The methodology is reminiscent of recent encoder-decoder networks in machine translation and document summarization (Kalchbrenner and Blunsom, 2013; Sutskever et al., 2014; Cho et al., 2014b; Rush et al., 2015). The resulting encoder is subsequently fine-tuned discriminatively on the basis of limited annotations yielding an additional performance boost.

We evaluate our model on the AskUbuntu corpus from Stack Exchange used in prior work (dos Santos et al., 2015). During training, we directly utilize noisy pairs readily available in the forum, but to have a realistic evaluation of the system performance, we manually annotate 8K pairs of questions. This clean data is used in two splits, one for development and hyper parameter tuning and another for testing. We evaluate our model and the baselines using standard information retrieval (IR) measures such as Mean Average Precision (MAP), Mean Reciprocal Rank (MRR) and Precision at n (P@n). Our full model achieves a MRR of 75.6% and P@1 of 62.0%, yielding 8% absolute improvement over a standard IR baseline, and 4% over standard neural network architectures (including CNNs, LSTMs and GRUs).

2 Related Work

Given the growing popularity of community QA forums, question retrieval has emerged as an important area of research (Nakov et al., 2015; Nakov et al., 2016). Previous work on question retrieval has modeled this task using machine translation, topic modeling and knowledge graph-based approaches (Jeon et al., 2005; Li and Manandhar, 2011; Duan et al., 2008; Zhou et al., 2013). More recent work relies on representation learning to go beyond word-based methods. For instance, Zhou et al. (2015) learn word embeddings using category-based metadata information for questions. They define each question as a distribution which generates each word (embedding) independently, and subsequently use a Fisher kernel to assess question similarities. Dos Santos et al. (2015) propose an approach which combines a convolutional neural network (CNN) and a bag-of-words representation for comparing questions. In contrast to (Zhou et al., 2015), our model treats each question as a word sequence as opposed to a bag of words, and we apply a recurrent convolutional model as opposed to the traditional CNN model used by dos Santos et al. (2015) to map questions into meaning representations. Further, we propose a training paradigm that utilizes the entire corpus of unannotated questions in a semi-supervised manner.

Recent work on answer selection on community QA forums, similar to our task of question retrieval, has also involved the use of neural network architectures (Severyn and Moschitti, 2015; Wang and Nyberg, 2015; Shen et al., 2015; Feng et al., 2015; Tan et al., 2015). Compared to our work, these approaches focus on improving various other aspects of the model. For instance, Feng et al. (2015) explore different similarity measures beyond cosine similarity, and Tan et al. (2015) adopt the neural attention mechanism over RNNs to generate better answer representations given the questions as context.

3 Question Retrieval Setup

We begin by introducing the basic discriminative setting for retrieving similar questions. Let q be a query question which generally consists of both a title sentence and a body section. For efficiency reasons, we do not compare q against all the other queries in the data base. Instead, we retrieve first a smaller candidate set of related questions $Q(q)$ using a standard IR engine, and then we apply the more sophisticated models only to this reduced set. Our goal is to rank the candidate questions in $Q(q)$ so that all the similar questions to q are ranked above the dissimilar ones. To do so, we define a similarity score $s(q, p; \theta)$ with parameters θ, where the similarity measures how closely candidate $p \in Q(q)$ is related to question q. The method of comparison can make use of the title and body of each question.

The scoring function $s(\cdot, \cdot; \theta)$ can be optimized on the basis of annotated data $D = \{(q_i, p_i^+, Q_i^-)\}$, where p_i^+ is a question similar to question q_i and Q_i^- is a negative set of questions deemed not similar to q_i. During training, the correct pairs of similar questions are obtained from available user-marked pairs, while the negative set Q_i^- is drawn randomly from the entire corpus with the idea that the likelihood of a positive match is small given the size of the corpus. The candidate set during training is just $Q(q_i) = \{p_i^+\} \cup Q_i^-$. During testing, the candidate sets are retrieved by an IR engine and we evaluate against explicit manual annotations.

In the purely discriminative setting, we use a max-margin framework for learning (or fine-tuning) parameters θ. Specifically, in a context of a particular training example where q_i is paired with p_i^+, we

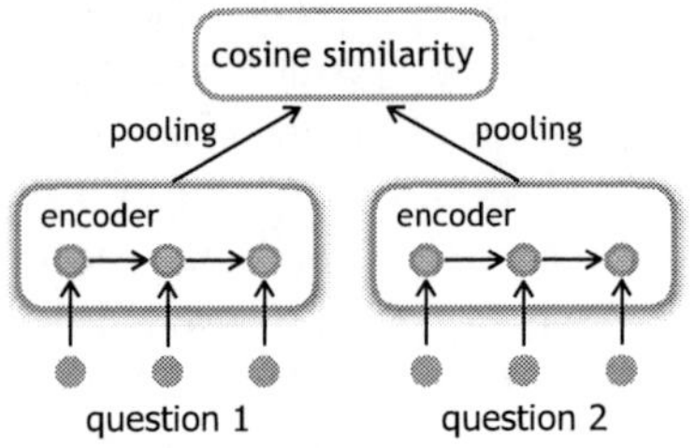
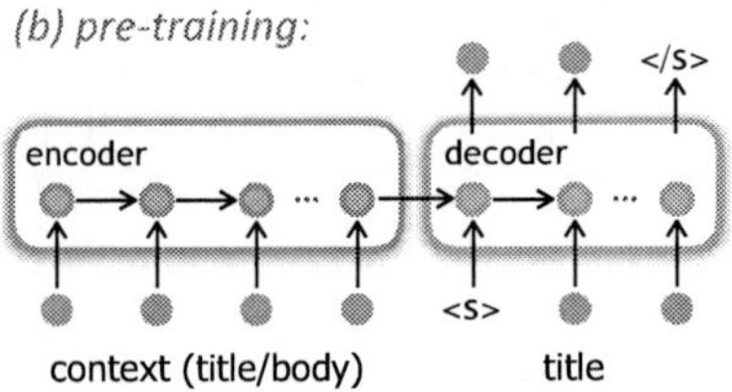

Figure 2: Illustration of our model.

minimize the max-margin loss $L(\theta)$ defined as

$$\max_{p \in Q(q_i)} \left\{ s(q_i, p; \theta) - s(q_i, p_i^+; \theta) + \delta(p, p_i^+) \right\},$$

where $\delta(\cdot, \cdot)$ denotes a non-negative margin. We set $\delta(p, p_i^+)$ to be a small constant when $p \neq p_i^+$ and 0 otherwise. The parameters θ can be optimized through sub-gradients $\partial L / \partial \theta$ aggregated over small batches of the training instances.

There are two key problems that remain. First, we have to define and parameterize the scoring function $s(q, p; \theta)$. We design a recurrent neural network model for this purpose and use it as an *encoder* to map each question into its meaning representation. The resulting similarity function $s(q, p; \theta)$ is just the cosine similarity between the corresponding representations, as shown in Figure 2 (a). The parameters θ pertain to the neural network only. Second, in order to offset the scarcity and limited coverage of the training annotations, we pre-train the parameters θ on the basis of the much larger unannotated corpus. The resulting parameters are subsequently fine-tuned using the discriminative setup described above.

4 Model

4.1 Non-consecutive Convolution

We describe here our encoder model, i.e., the method for mapping the question title and body to a vector representation. Our approach is inspired by temporal convolutional neural networks (LeCun et al., 1998) and, in particular, its recent refinement (Lei et al., 2015), tailored to capture longer-range, non-consecutive patterns in a weighted manner. Such models can be used to effectively summarize occurrences of patterns in text and aggregate them into a vector representation. However, the summary produced is not selective since all pattern occurrences are counted, weighted by how cohesive (non-consecutive) they are. In our problem, the question body tends to be very long and full of irrelevant words and fragments. Thus, we believe that interpreting the question body requires a more selective approach to pattern extraction.

Our model successively reads tokens in the question title or body, denoted as $\{\mathbf{x}_i\}_{i=1}^l$, and transforms this sequence into a sequence of states $\{\mathbf{h}_i\}_{i=1}^l$. The resulting state sequence is subsequently aggregated into a single final vector representation for each text as discussed below. Our approach builds on (Lei et al., 2015), thus we begin by briefly outlining it. Let W_1 and W_2 denote filter matrices (as parameters) for pattern size $n = 2$. Lei et al. (2015) generate a sequence of states in response to tokens according to

$$\mathbf{c}_{t',t} = \mathbf{W}_1\mathbf{x}_{t'} + \mathbf{W}_2\mathbf{x}_t$$
$$\mathbf{c}_t = \sum_{t'<t} \lambda^{t-t'-1}\mathbf{c}_{t',t}$$
$$\mathbf{h}_t = \tanh(\mathbf{c}_t + \mathbf{b})$$

where $\mathbf{c}_{t',t}$ represents a bigram pattern, $\mathbf{c}_t$ accumulates a range of patterns and $\lambda \in [0,1)$ is a constant decay factor used to down-weight patterns with longer spans. The operations can be cast in a "recurrent" manner and evaluated with dynamic programming. The problem with the approach for our purposes is, however, that the weighting factor λ is the same (constant) for all, not triggered by the state $\mathbf{h}_{t-1}$ or the observed token $\mathbf{x}_t$.

Adaptive Gated Decay We refine this model by learning context dependent weights. For example, if the current input token provides no relevant information (e.g., symbols, functional words), the model should ignore it by incorporating the token with a vanishing weight. In contrast, strong semantic content words such as "ubuntu" or "windows" should be included with much larger weights. To achieve this effect we introduce *neural gates* similar to LSTMs to specify when and how to average the observed signals. The resulting architecture integrates recurrent networks with non-consecutive convolutional models:

$$\lambda_t = \sigma(\mathbf{W}^\lambda\mathbf{x}_t + \mathbf{U}^\lambda\mathbf{h}_{t-1} + \mathbf{b}^\lambda)$$
$$\mathbf{c}_t^{(1)} = \lambda_t \odot \mathbf{c}_{t-1}^{(1)} + (1 - \lambda_t) \odot (\mathbf{W}_1\mathbf{x}_t)$$
$$\mathbf{c}_t^{(2)} = \lambda_t \odot \mathbf{c}_{t-1}^{(2)} + (1 - \lambda_t) \odot (\mathbf{c}_{t-1}^{(1)} + \mathbf{W}_2\mathbf{x}_t)$$
$$\cdots$$
$$\mathbf{c}_t^{(n)} = \lambda_t \odot \mathbf{c}_{t-1}^{(n)} + (1 - \lambda_t) \odot (\mathbf{c}_{t-1}^{(n-1)} + \mathbf{W}_n\mathbf{x}_t)$$
$$\mathbf{h}_t = \tanh(\mathbf{c}_t^{(n)} + \mathbf{b})$$

where $\sigma(\cdot)$ is the sigmoid function and $\odot$ represents the element-wise product. Here $\mathbf{c}_t^{(1)}, \cdots, \mathbf{c}_t^{(n)}$ are accumulator vectors that store weighted averages of 1-gram to n-gram features. When the gate $\lambda_t = 0$ (vector) for all t, the model represents a traditional CNN with filter width n. As $\lambda_t > 0$, however, $\mathbf{c}_t^{(n)}$ becomes the sum of an exponential number of terms, enumerating all possible n-grams within $\mathbf{x}_1, \cdots, \mathbf{x}_t$ (seen by expanding the formulas). Note that the gate $\lambda_t(\cdot)$ is parametrized and responds directly to the previous state and the token in question. We refer to this model as RCNN from here on.

Pooling In order to use the model as part of the discriminative question retrieval framework outlined earlier, we must condense the state sequence to a single vector. There are two simple alternative *pooling* strategies that we have explored – either averaging over the states[4] or simply taking the last one as the meaning representation. In addition, we apply the encoder to both the question title and body, and the final representation is computed as the average of the two resulting vectors.

Once the aggregation is specified, the parameters of the gate and the filter matrices can be learned in a purely discriminative fashion. Given that the available annotations are limited and user-guided, we instead use the discriminative training only for fine tuning an already trained model. The method of pre-training the model on the basis of the entire corpus of questions is discussed next.

---

[4]We also normalize state vectors before averaging, which empirically gets better performance.

4.2 Pre-training Using the Entire Corpus

The number of questions in the AskUbuntu corpus far exceeds user annotations of pairs of similar questions. We can make use of this larger raw corpus in two different ways. First, since models take word embeddings as input we can tailor the embeddings to the specific vocabulary and expressions in this corpus. To this end, we run word2vec (Mikolov et al., 2013) on the raw corpus in addition to the Wikipedia dump. Second, and more importantly, we use individual questions as training examples for an auto-encoder constructed by pairing the encoder model (RCNN) with an corresponding decoder (of the same type). As illustrated in Figure 2 (b), the resulting encoder-decoder architecture is akin to those used in machine translation (Kalchbrenner and Blunsom, 2013; Sutskever et al., 2014; Cho et al., 2014b) and summarization (Rush et al., 2015).

Our encoder-decoder pair represents a conditional language model $P(\text{title}|\text{context})$, where the context can be any of (a) the original title itself, (b) the question body and (c) the title/body of a similar question. All possible (title, context) pairs are used during training to optimize the likelihood of the words (and their order) in the titles. We use the question title as the target for two reasons. The question body contains more information than the title but also has many irrelevant details. As a result, we can view the title as a distilled summary of the noisy body, and the encoder-decoder model is trained to act as a denoising auto-encoder. Moreover, training a decoder for the title (rather than the body) is also much faster since titles tend to be short (around 10 words).

The encoders pre-trained in this manner are subsequently fine-tuned according to the discriminative criterion described already in Section 3.

5 Alternative models

For comparison, we also train three alternative benchmark encoders (LSTMs, GRUs and CNNs) for mapping questions to vector representations. LSTM and GRU-based encoders can be pre-trained analogously to RCNNs, and fine-tuned discriminatively. CNN encoders, on the other hand, are only trained discriminatively. While plausible, neither alternative reaches quite the same level of performance as our pre-trained RCNN.

LSTMs LSTM cells (Hochreiter and Schmidhuber, 1997) have been used to capture semantic information across a wide range of applications, including machine translation and entailment recognition (Bahdanau et al., 2015; Bowman et al., 2015; Rocktäschel et al., 2016). Their success can be attributed to neural gates that adaptively read or discard information to/from internal memory states.

Specifically, a LSTM network successively reads the input token $\mathbf{x}_t$, internal state $\mathbf{c}_{t-1}$, as well as the visible state $\mathbf{h}_{t-1}$, and generates the new states $\mathbf{c}_t, \mathbf{h}_t$:

$$\mathbf{i}_t = \sigma(\mathbf{W}^i\mathbf{x}_t + \mathbf{U}^i\mathbf{h}_{t-1} + \mathbf{b}^i)$$
$$\mathbf{f}_t = \sigma(\mathbf{W}^f\mathbf{x}_t + \mathbf{U}^f\mathbf{h}_{t-1} + \mathbf{b}^f)$$
$$\mathbf{o}_t = \sigma(\mathbf{W}^o\mathbf{x}_t + \mathbf{U}^o\mathbf{h}_{t-1} + \mathbf{b}^o)$$
$$\mathbf{z}_t = \tanh(\mathbf{W}^z\mathbf{x}_t + \mathbf{U}^z\mathbf{h}_{t-1} + \mathbf{b}^z)$$
$$\mathbf{c}_t = \mathbf{i}_t \odot \mathbf{z}_t + \mathbf{f}_t \odot \mathbf{c}_{t-1}$$
$$\mathbf{h}_t = \mathbf{o}_t \odot \tanh(\mathbf{c}_t)$$

where $\mathbf{i}$, $\mathbf{f}$ and $\mathbf{o}$ are *input*, *forget* and *output* gates, respectively. Given the visible state sequence $\{\mathbf{h}_i\}_{i=1}^l$, we can aggregate it to a single vector exactly as with RCNNs. The LSTM encoder can be pre-trained (and fine-tuned) in the similar way as our RCNN model. For instance, Dai and Le (2015) recently adopted pre-training for text classification task.

GRUs A GRU is another comparable unit for sequence modeling (Cho et al., 2014a; Chung et al., 2014). Similar to the LSTM unit, the GRU has two neural gates that control the flow of information:

$$\mathbf{i}_t = \sigma(\mathbf{W}^i\mathbf{x}_t + \mathbf{U}^i\mathbf{h}_{t-1} + \mathbf{b}^i)$$
$$\mathbf{r}_t = \sigma(\mathbf{W}^r\mathbf{x}_t + \mathbf{U}^r\mathbf{h}_{t-1} + \mathbf{b}^r)$$
$$\mathbf{c}_t = \tanh(\mathbf{W}\mathbf{x}_t + \mathbf{U}(\mathbf{r}_t \odot \mathbf{h}_{t-1}) + \mathbf{b})$$
$$\mathbf{h}_t = \mathbf{i}_t \odot \mathbf{c}_t + (1 - \mathbf{i}_t) \odot \mathbf{h}_{t-1}$$

where i and r are *input* and *reset* gate respectively. Again, the GRUs can be trained in the same way.

CNNs Convolutional neural networks (LeCun et al., 1998) have also been successfully applied to various NLP tasks (Kalchbrenner et al., 2014; Kim, 2014; Kim et al., 2015; Zhang et al., 2015; Gao et al., 2014). As models, they are different from LSTMs since the temporal convolution operation

Corpus	# of unique questions	167,765
	Avg length of title	6.7
	Avg length of body	59.7
Training	# of unique questions	12,584
	# of user-marked pairs	16,391
Dev	# of query questions	200
	# of annotated pairs	200×20
	Avg # of positive pairs per query	5.8
Test	# of query questions	200
	# of annotated pairs	200×20
	Avg # of positive pairs per query	5.5

Table 1: Various statistics from our Training, Dev, and Test sets derived from the Sept. 2014 Stack Exchange AskUbuntu dataset.

and associated filters map *local chunks* (windows) of the input into a feature representation. Concretely, if we let n denote the filter width, and $\mathbf{W}_1, \cdots, \mathbf{W}_n$ the corresponding filter matrices, then the convolution operation is applied to each window of n consecutive words as follows:

$$\mathbf{c}_t = \mathbf{W}_1 \mathbf{x}_{t-n+1} + \mathbf{W}_2 \mathbf{x}_{t-n+2} + \cdots + \mathbf{W}_n \mathbf{x}_t$$
$$\mathbf{h}_t = \tanh(\mathbf{c}_t + \mathbf{b})$$

The sets of output state vectors $\{\mathbf{h}_t\}$ produced in this case are typically referred to as feature maps. Since each vector in the feature map only pertains to local information, the last vector is not sufficient to capture the meaning of the entire sequence. Instead, we consider *max-pooling* or *average-pooling* to obtain the aggregate representation for the entire sequence.

6 Experimental Setup

Dataset We use the Stack Exchange AskUbuntu dataset used in prior work (dos Santos et al., 2015). This dataset contains 167,765 unique questions, each consisting of a title and a body[5], and a set of user-marked similar question pairs. We provide various statistics from this dataset in Table 1.

Gold Standard for Evaluation User-marked similar question pairs on QA sites are often known to be incomplete. In order to evaluate this in our dataset, we took a sample set of questions paired with 20 candidate questions retrieved by a search engine trained on the AskUbuntu data. The search engine used is the well-known BM25 model (Robert-

son and Zaragoza, 2009). Our manual evaluation of the candidates showed that only 5% of the similar questions were marked by users, with a precision of 79%. Clearly, this low recall would not lead to a realistic evaluation if we used user marks as our gold standard. Instead, we make use of expert annotations carried out on a subset of questions.

Training Set We use user-marked similar pairs as positive pairs in training since the annotations have high precision and do not require additional manual annotations. This allows us to use a much larger training set. We use random questions from the corpus paired with each query question p_i as negative pairs in training. We randomly sample 20 questions as negative examples for each p_i during each epoch.

Development and Test Sets We re-constructed the new dev and test sets consisting of the first 200 questions from the dev and test sets provided by dos Santos et al. (2015). For each of the above questions, we retrieved the top 20 similar candidates using BM25 and manually annotated the resulting 8K pairs as similar or non-similar.[6]

Baselines and Evaluation Metrics We evaluated neural network models—including **CNNs**, **LSTMs**, **GRUs** and **RCNNs**—by comparing them with the following baselines:

- **BM25**, we used the BM25 similarity measure provided by Apache Lucene.

- **TF-IDF**, we ranked questions using cosine similarity based on a vector-based word representation for each question.

- **SVM**, we trained a re-ranker using SVM-Light (Joachims, 2002) with a linear kernel incorporating several similarity measures from the DKPro similarity package (Bär et al., 2013).

We evaluated the models based on the following IR metrics: Mean Average Precision (MAP), Mean Reciprocal Rank (MRR), Precision at 1 (P@1), and Precision at 5 (P@5).

---

[5]We truncate the body section at a maximum of 100 words.

[6]The annotation task was initially carried out by two expert annotators, independently. The initial set was refined by comparing the annotations and asking a third judge to make a final decision on disagreements. After a consensus on the annotation guidelines was reached (producing a Cohen's kappa of 0.73), the overall annotation was carried out by only one expert.

Method	Pooling	Dev				Test			
		MAP	MRR	P@1	P@5	MAP	MRR	P@1	P@5
BM25	-	52.0	66.0	51.9	42.1	56.0	68.0	53.8	42.5
TF-IDF	-	54.1	68.2	55.6	45.1	53.2	67.1	53.8	39.7
SVM	-	53.5	66.1	50.8	43.8	57.7	71.3	57.0	43.3
CNNs	mean	58.5	71.1	58.4	46.4	57.6	71.4	57.6	43.2
LSTMs	mean	58.4	72.3	60.0	46.4	56.8	70.1	55.8	43.2
GRUs	mean	59.1	74.0	62.6	47.3	57.1	71.4	57.3	43.6
RCNNs	last	59.9	74.2	63.2	48.0	60.7	72.9	59.1	45.0
LSTMs + pre-train	mean	58.3	71.5	59.3	47.4	55.5	67.0	51.1	43.4
GRUs + pre-train	last	59.3	72.2	59.8	48.3	59.3	71.3	57.2	44.3
RCNNs + pre-train	last	**61.3***	**75.2**	**64.2**	**50.3***	**62.3***	**75.6***	**62.0**	**47.1***

Table 2: Comparative results of all methods on the question similarity task. Higher numbers are better. For neural network models, we show the best average performance across 5 independent runs and the corresponding pooling strategy. Statistical significance with $p < 0.05$ against other types of model is marked with $*$.

	d	$|\theta|$	n
LSTMs	240	423K	-
GRUs	280	404K	-
CNNs	667	401K	3
RCNNs	400	401K	2

Table 3: Configuration of neural models. d is the hidden dimension, $|\theta|$ is the number of parameters and n is the filter width.

Hyper-parameters We performed an extensive hyper-parameter search to identify the best model for the baselines and neural network models. For the **TF-IDF** baseline, we tried n-gram feature order $n \in \{1, 2, 3\}$ with and without stop words pruning. For the **SVM** baseline, we used the default SVM-Light parameters whereas the dev data is only used to increase the training set size when testing on the test set. We also tried to give higher weight to dev instances but this did not result in any improvement.

For all the neural network models, we used Adam (Kingma and Ba, 2015) as the optimization method with the default setting suggested by the authors. We optimized other hyper-parameters with the following range of values: learning rate $\in \{1e - 3, 3e - 4\}$, dropout (Hinton et al., 2012) probability $\in \{0.1, 0.2, 0.3\}$, CNN feature width $\in \{2, 3, 4\}$. We also tuned the pooling strategies and ensured each model has a comparable number of parameters. The default configurations of LSTMs, GRUs, CNNs and RCNNs are shown in Table 3. We used MRR to identify the best training epoch and the model configuration. For the same model configuration, we report average performance across 5 independent runs.[7]

Word Vectors We ran word2vec (Mikolov et al., 2013) to obtain 200-dimensional word embeddings using all Stack Exchange data (excluding Stack-Overflow) and a large Wikipedia corpus. The word vectors are fixed to avoid over-fitting across all experiments.

7 Results

Overall Performance Table 2 shows the performance of the baselines and the neural encoder models on the question retrieval task. The results show that our full model, RCNNs with pre-training, achieves the best performance across all metrics on both the dev and test sets. For instance, the full model gets a P@1 of 62.0% on the test set, outperforming the word matching-based method BM25 by over 8 percent points. Further, our RCNN model also outperforms the other neural encoder models and the baselines across all metrics. This superior performance indicates that the use of non-consecutive filters and a varying decay is effective in improving traditional neural network models.

Table 2 also demonstrates the performance gain from pre-training the RCNN encoder. The RCNN model when pre-trained on the entire corpus consistently gets better results across all the metrics.

---

[7]For a fair comparison, we also pre-train 5 independent models for each configuration and then fine tune these models. We use the same learning rate and dropout rate during pre-training and fine-tuning.

Method	Dev				Test			
	MAP	MRR	P@1	P@5	MAP	MRR	P@1	P@5
CNNs, max-pooling	57.8	69.9	56.6	47.7	59.6	73.1	59.6	45.4
CNNs, mean-pooling	58.5	71.1	58.4	46.4	57.6	71.4	57.6	43.2
LSTMs + pre-train, mean-pooling	58.3	71.5	59.3	47.4	55.5	67.0	51.1	43.4
LSTMs + pre-train, last state	57.6	71.0	58.1	47.3	57.6	69.8	55.2	43.7
GRUs + pre-train, mean-pooling	57.5	69.9	57.1	46.2	55.5	67.3	52.4	42.8
GRUs + pre-train, last state	59.3	72.2	59.8	48.3	59.3	71.3	57.2	44.3
RCNNs + pre-train, mean-pooling	59.3	73.6	61.7	48.6	58.9	72.3	57.3	45.3
RCNNs + pre-train, last state	**61.3**	**75.2**	**64.2**	**50.3**	**62.3**	**75.6**	**62.0**	**47.1**

Table 4: Choice of pooling strategies.

TF-IDF	MAP	MRR	P@1
title only	54.3	66.8	52.7
title + body	53.2	67.1	53.8
RCNNs, mean-pooling	**MAP**	**MRR**	**P@1**
title only	56.0	68.9	55.7
title + body	58.5	71.7	56.7
RCNNs, last state	**MAP**	**MRR**	**P@1**
title only	58.2	70.7	56.6
title + body	60.7	72.9	59.1

Table 5: Comparision between model variants on the test set when question bodies are used or not used.

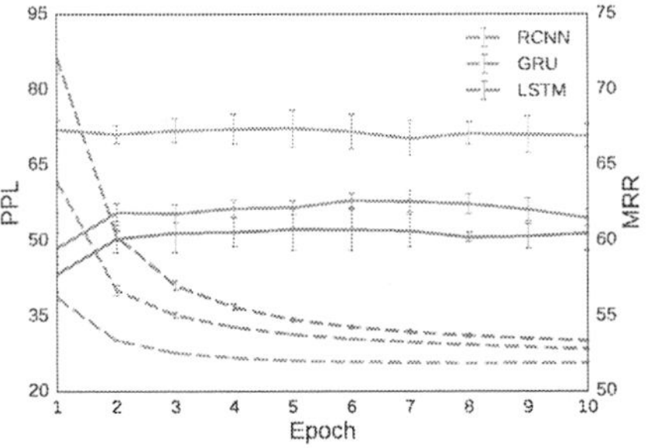

Figure 3: Perplexity (dotted lines) on a heldout portion of the corpus versus MRR on the dev set (solid lines) during pre-training. Variances across 5 runs are shown as vertical bars.

Pooling Strategy   We analyze the effect of various pooling strategies for the neural network encoders. As shown in Table 4, our RCNN model outperforms other neural models regardless of the two pooling strategies explored. We also observe that simply using the last hidden state as the final representation achieves better results for the RCNN model.

Using Question Body   Table 5 compares the performance of the TF-IDF baseline and the RCNN model when using question titles only or when using question titles along with question bodies. TF-IDF's performance changes very little when the question bodies are included (MRR and P@1 are slightly better but MAP is slightly worse). However, we find that the inclusion of the question bodies improves the performance of the RCNN model, achieving a 1% to 3% improvement with both model variations. The RCNN model's greater improvement illustrates the ability of the model to pick out components that pertain most directly to the question being asked from the long, descriptive question bodies.

Pre-training   Note that, during pre-training, the last hidden states generated by the neural encoder are used by the decoder to reproduce the question titles. It would be interesting to see how such states capture the meaning of questions. To this end, we evaluate MRR on the dev set using the last hidden states of the question titles. We also test how the encoder captures information from the question bodies to produce the distilled summary, i.e. titles. To do so, we evaluate the perplexity of the trained encoder-decoder model on a heldout set of the corpus, which contains about 2000 questions.

As shown in Figure 3, the representations generated by the RCNN encoder perform quite well, resulting in a perplexity of 25 and over 68% MRR without the subsequent fine-tuning. Interestingly, the LSTM and GRU networks obtain similar perplexity on the heldout set, but achieve much worse MRR for similar question retrieval. For instance, the GRU encoder obtains only 63% MRR, 5% worse than the RCNN model's MRR performance. As a result, the LSTM and GRU encoder do not benefit clearly from pre-training, as suggested in Table 2.

The inconsistent performance difference may be explained by two hypotheses. One is that the perplexity is not suitable for measuring the similarity of the encoded text, thus the power of the encoder is not illustrated in terms of perplexity. Another hy-

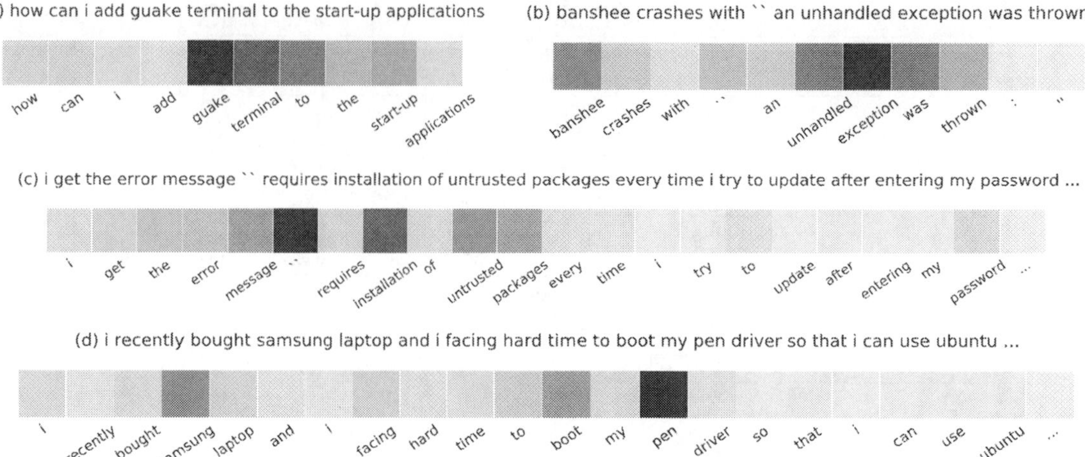

Figure 4: Visualizations of $1 - \lambda_t$ of our model on several question pieces from the data set. λ_t is set to a *scalar value* (instead of 400-dimension vector) to make the visualization simple. The corresponding model is a simplified variant, which is about 4% worse than our full model.

pothesis is that the LSTM and GRU encoder may learn non-linear representations therefore their semantic relatedness can not be directly accessed by cosine similarity.

Adaptive Decay Finally, we analyze the gated convolution of our model. Figure 5 demonstrates at each word position t how much input information is taken into the model by the adaptive weights $1 - \lambda_t$. The average of weights in the vector decreases as t increments, suggesting that the information encoded into the state vector saturates when more input are processed. On the other hand, the largest value in the weight vector remains high throughout the input, indicating that at least some information has been stored in $\mathbf{h}_t$ and $\mathbf{c}_t$.

We also conduct a case study on analyzing the neural gate. Since directly inspecting the 400-dimensional decay vector is difficult, we train a model that uses a *scalar decay* instead. As shown in Figure 4, the model learns to assign higher weights to application names and quoted error messages, which intuitively are important pieces of a question in the AskUbuntu domain.

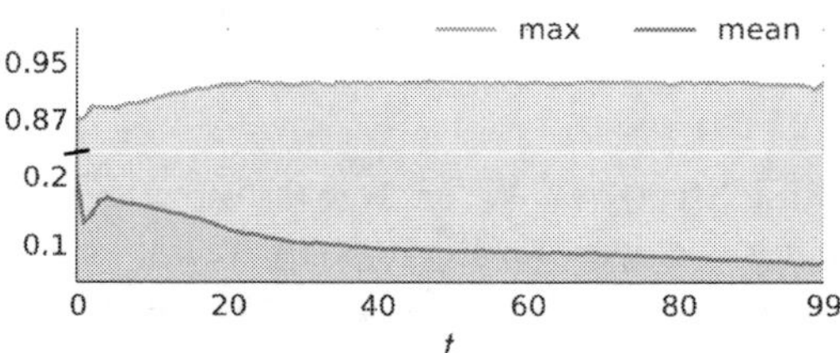

Figure 5: The maximum and mean value of the 400-dimensional weight vector $1 - \lambda_t$ at each step (word position) t. Values are averaged across all questions in the dev and test set.

8 Conclusion

In this paper, we employ gated (non-consecutive) convolutions to map questions to their semantic representations, and demonstrate their effectiveness on the task of question retrieval in community QA forums. This architecture enables the model to glean key pieces of information from lengthy, detail-riddled user questions. Pre-training within an encoder-decoder framework (from body to title) on the basis of the entire raw corpus is integral to the model's success.

Acknowledgments

We thank Yu Zhang, Yoon Kim, Danqi Chen, the MIT NLP group and the reviewers for their helpful comments. The work is developed in collaboration with the Arabic Language Technologies (ALT) group at Qatar Computing Research Institute (QCRI) within the IYAS project. Any opinions, findings, conclusions, or recommendations expressed in this paper are those of the authors, and do not necessarily reflect the views of the funding organizations.

References

Dzmitry Bahdanau, Kyunghyun Cho, and Yoshua Bengio. 2015. Neural machine translation by jointly learning to align and translate. In *International Conference on Learning Representations*.

Daniel Bär, Torsten Zesch, and Iryna Gurevych. 2013. Dkpro similarity: An open source framework for text similarity. In *Proceedings of the 51st Annual Meeting of the Association for Computational Linguistics: System Demonstrations*, pages 121–126, Sofia, Bulgaria, August. Association for Computational Linguistics.

Samuel R. Bowman, Gabor Angeli, Christopher Potts, and Christopher D. Manning. 2015. A large annotated corpus for learning natural language inference. In *Proceedings of the 2015 Conference on Empirical Methods in Natural Language Processing (EMNLP)*. Association for Computational Linguistics.

Kyunghyun Cho, Bart van Merriënboer, Dzmitry Bahdanau, and Yoshua Bengio. 2014a. On the properties of neural machine translation: Encoder-decoder approaches. *arXiv preprint arXiv:1409.1259*.

Kyunghyun Cho, Bart Van Merriënboer, Caglar Gulcehre, Dzmitry Bahdanau, Fethi Bougares, Holger Schwenk, and Yoshua Bengio. 2014b. Learning phrase representations using rnn encoder-decoder for statistical machine translation. In *Proceedings of the 2014 Conference on Empirical Methods in Natural Language Processing (EMNLP)*.

Junyoung Chung, Caglar Gulcehre, KyungHyun Cho, and Yoshua Bengio. 2014. Empirical evaluation of gated recurrent neural networks on sequence modeling. *arXiv preprint arXiv:1412.3555*.

Andrew M Dai and Quoc V Le. 2015. Semi-supervised sequence learning. In *Advances in Neural Information Processing Systems*, pages 3061–3069.

Cicero dos Santos, Luciano Barbosa, Dasha Bogdanova, and Bianca Zadrozny. 2015. Learning hybrid representations to retrieve semantically equivalent questions. In *Proceedings of the 53rd Annual Meeting of the Association for Computational Linguistics and the 7th International Joint Conference on Natural Language Processing (Volume 2: Short Papers)*, pages 694–699, Beijing, China, July. Association for Computational Linguistics.

Huizhong Duan, Yunbo Cao, Chin-Yew Lin, and Yong Yu. 2008. Searching questions by identifying question topic and question focus. In *ACL*, pages 156–164.

Minwei Feng, Bing Xiang, Michael R Glass, Lidan Wang, and Bowen Zhou. 2015. Applying deep learning to answer selection: A study and an open task. *arXiv preprint arXiv:1508.01585*.

Jianfeng Gao, Patrick Pantel, Michael Gamon, Xiaodong He, Li Deng, and Yelong Shen. 2014. Modeling interestingness with deep neural networks. In *Proceedings of the 2013 Conference on Empirical Methods in Natural Language Processing*.

Geoffrey E Hinton, Nitish Srivastava, Alex Krizhevsky, Ilya Sutskever, and Ruslan R Salakhutdinov. 2012. Improving neural networks by preventing co-adaptation of feature detectors. *arXiv preprint arXiv:1207.0580*.

Sepp Hochreiter and Jürgen Schmidhuber. 1997. Long short-term memory. *Neural computation*, 9(8):1735–1780.

Jiwoon Jeon, W Bruce Croft, and Joon Ho Lee. 2005. Finding similar questions in large question and answer archives. In *Proceedings of the 14th ACM international conference on Information and knowledge management*, pages 84–90. ACM.

T. Joachims. 2002. Optimizing search engines using clickthrough data. In *ACM SIGKDD KDD*.

Nal Kalchbrenner and Phil Blunsom. 2013. Recurrent continuous translation models. In *Proceedings of the 2013 Conference on Empirical Methods in Natural Language Processing (EMNLP 2013)*, pages 1700–1709.

Nal Kalchbrenner, Edward Grefenstette, and Phil Blunsom. 2014. A convolutional neural network for modelling sentences. In *Proceedings of the 52th Annual Meeting of the Association for Computational Linguistics*.

Yoon Kim, Yacine Jernite, David Sontag, and Alexander M Rush. 2015. Character-aware neural language models. *Twenty-Ninth AAAI Conference on Artificial Intelligence*.

Yoon Kim. 2014. Convolutional neural networks for sentence classification. In *Proceedings of the Empiricial Methods in Natural Language Processing (EMNLP 2014)*.

Diederik P Kingma and Jimmy Lei Ba. 2015. Adam: A method for stochastic optimization. In *International Conference on Learning Representation*.

Y. LeCun, L. Bottou, Y. Bengio, and P. Haffner. 1998. Gradient-based learning applied to document recognition. *Proceedings of the IEEE*, 86(11):2278–2324, November.

Tao Lei, Regina Barzilay, and Tommi Jaakkola. 2015. Molding cnns for text: non-linear, non-consecutive convolutions. In *Proceedings of the 2015 Conference on Empirical Methods in Natural Language Processing*, pages 1565–1575, Lisbon, Portugal, September. Association for Computational Linguistics.

Shuguang Li and Suresh Manandhar. 2011. Improving question recommendation by exploiting information need. In *Proceedings of the 49th Annual Meeting of the Association for Computational Linguistics: Human Language Technologies-Volume 1*, pages 1425–1434. Association for Computational Linguistics.

Tomas Mikolov, Kai Chen, Greg Corrado, and Jeffrey Dean. 2013. Efficient estimation of word representations in vector space. *CoRR*.

Preslav Nakov, Lluís Màrquez, Walid Magdy, Alessandro Moschitti, Jim Glass, and Bilal Randeree. 2015. SemEval-2015 task 3: Answer selection in community question answering. In *Proceedings of the 9th International Workshop on Semantic Evaluation*, SemEval '15.

Preslav Nakov, Lluís Màrquez, Walid Magdy, Alessandro Moschitti, Jim Glass, and Bilal Randeree. 2016. SemEval-2016 task 3: Community question answering. In *Proceedings of the 10th International Workshop on Semantic Evaluation*, SemEval '16.

Stephen Robertson and Hugo Zaragoza. 2009. *The probabilistic relevance framework: BM25 and beyond*. Now Publishers Inc.

Tim Rocktäschel, Edward Grefenstette, Karl Moritz Hermann, Tomáš Kočiský, and Phil Blunsom. 2016. Reasoning about entailment with neural attention. In *International Conference on Learning Representations*.

Alexander M Rush, Sumit Chopra, and Jason Weston. 2015. A neural attention model for abstractive sentence summarization. In *Proceedings of the 2015 Conference on Empirical Methods in Natural Language Processing*.

Aliaksei Severyn and Alessandro Moschitti. 2015. Learning to rank short text pairs with convolutional deep neural networks. In *SIGIR*.

Yikang Shen, Wenge Rong, Nan Jiang, Baolin Peng, Jie Tang, and Zhang Xiong. 2015. Word embedding based correlation model for question/answer matching. *arXiv preprint arXiv:1511.04646*.

Ilya Sutskever, Oriol Vinyals, and Quoc VV Le. 2014. Sequence to sequence learning with neural networks. In *Advances in neural information processing systems*, pages 3104–3112.

Ming Tan, Bing Xiang, and Bowen Zhou. 2015. Lstm-based deep learning models for non-factoid answer selection. *arXiv preprint arXiv:1511.04108*.

Di Wang and Eric Nyberg. 2015. A long short-term memory model for answer sentence selection in question answering. In *ACL*, July.

Xiang Zhang, Junbo Zhao, and Yann LeCun. 2015. Character-level convolutional networks for text classification. In *Advances in Neural Information Processing Systems*, pages 649–657.

Guangyou Zhou, Yang Liu, Fang Liu, Daojian Zeng, and Jun Zhao. 2013. Improving question retrieval in community question answering using world knowledge. In *Proceedings of the Twenty-Third international joint conference on Artificial Intelligence*, pages 2239–2245. AAAI Press.

Guangyou Zhou, Tingting He, Jun Zhao, and Po Hu. 2015. Learning continuous word embedding with metadata for question retrieval in community question answering. In *Proceedings of the 53rd Annual Meeting of the Association for Computational Linguistics and the 7th International Joint Conference on Natural Language Processing (Volume 1: Long Papers)*, pages 250–259, Beijing, China, July. Association for Computational Linguistics.

This is how we do it: Answer Reranking for Open-domain How Questions with Paragraph Vectors and Minimal Feature Engineering

Dasha Bogdanova and Jennifer Foster
ADAPT Centre
School of Computing, Dublin City University
Dublin, Ireland
`{dbogdanova, jfoster}@computing.dcu.ie`

Abstract

We present a simple yet powerful approach to non-factoid answer reranking whereby question-answer pairs are represented by concatenated distributed representation vectors and a multilayer perceptron is used to compute the score for an answer. Despite its simplicity, our approach achieves state-of-the-art performance on a public dataset of *How* questions, outperforming systems which employ sophisticated feature sets. We attribute this good performance to the use of paragraph instead of word vector representations and to the use of suitable data for training these representations.

1 Introduction

In contrast to factoid question answering (QA), non-factoid QA is concerned with questions whose answer is not easily expressed as an entity or list of entities and can instead be quite complex – compare, for example, the factoid question *Who is the secretary general of the UN?* with the non-factoid manner question *How is the secretary general of the UN chosen?* A significant amount of research has been carried out on factoid QA, with non-factoid questions receiving less attention. This is changing, however, with the popularity of community-based question answering (CQA) sites such as Yahoo! Answers[1], Quora[2] and the StackExchange[3] family of forums. The ability of users to vote for their favourite answer makes these sites a valuable source of training data for open-domain non-factoid QA systems.

[1] `http://answers.yahoo.com`
[2] `http://quora.com`
[3] `http://stackexchange.com/`

In this paper, we present a neural approach to open-domain non-factoid QA, focusing on the sub-task of answer reranking, i.e. given a list of candidate answers to a question, order the answers according to their relevance to the question. We test our approach on the Yahoo! Answers dataset of manner or *How* questions introduced by Jansen et al. (2014), who describe answer reranking experiments on this dataset using a diverse range of features incorporating syntax, lexical semantics and discourse. In particular, they show how discourse information (obtained either via a discourse parser or using shallow techniques based on discourse markers) can complement distributed lexical semantic information. Sharp et al. (2015) show how discourse structure can be used to generate artificial question-answer training pairs from documents, and test their approach on the same dataset. The best performance on this dataset – 33.01 P@1 and 53.96 MRR – is reported by Fried et al. (2015) who improve on the lexical semantic models of Jansen et al. (2014) by exploiting indirect associations between words using higher-order models.

In contrast, our approach is very simple and requires no feature engineering. Question-answer pairs are represented by concatenated distributed representation vectors and a multilayer perceptron is used to compute the score for an answer (the probability of an answer being the best answer to the question). Despite its simplicity, we achieve state-of-the-art performance on this dataset – 37.17 P@1 and 56.82 MRR. We attribute this improved performance to the use of paragraph vector representations (Le and Mikolov, 2014) instead of averaging over word

Proceedings of NAACL-HLT 2016, pages 1290–1295,
San Diego, California, June 12-17, 2016. ©2016 Association for Computational Linguistics

vectors, and to the use of suitable data for training these representations.

2 Approach

2.1 Learning Algorithm

We use a simple feedforward neural network, i.e. a multilayer perceptron, to predict the best answer. As shown in Figure 1, the first layer of the network is a projection layer that transforms question-answer pairs into their vector representations. The vector representation for a question-answer pair (q, a) is a concatenation of the distributed representations q and a for the question and the answer respectively. Each representation is a real-valued vector of a fixed dimensionality d, which is a parameter to be tuned. The projection layer is followed by one or more hidden layers, the number of layers and units in each of these layers are also parameters to be experimentally tuned. We use the rectified linear (ReLU) activation function. Finally, a softmax layer is used to compute the output probability p, i.e. the probabilities p_1 and p_2 of the negative (i.e. not best answer) and positive (i.e. best answer) classes respectively. For each question, all its user-generated answers are ranked according to their probability of being the best answer, as predicted by the network.

Given a question-answer pair (q, a), the possible values for the ground-truth label are 1 (best answer) and 0 (not a best answer). The network is trained by minimizing the L2-regularized cross-entropy loss function between the ground-truth labels and the network predictions on the training set. We use stochastic gradient descent to minimize the loss over the training set. The development set is used for early stopping.

2.2 Document Representations

Our approach requires question-answer pairs to be represented as a fixed-size vector. We experimentally evaluate the Paragraph Vector model (PV) proposed by Le and Mikolov (2014). The PV is an extension of the widely used continuous bag-of-words (CBOW) and skip-gram word embedding models, known as *word2vec*. However, in contrast to CBOW and skip-gram models that only learn word embeddings, the PV is able to learn representations for pieces of text of arbitrary length, e.g. sentences,

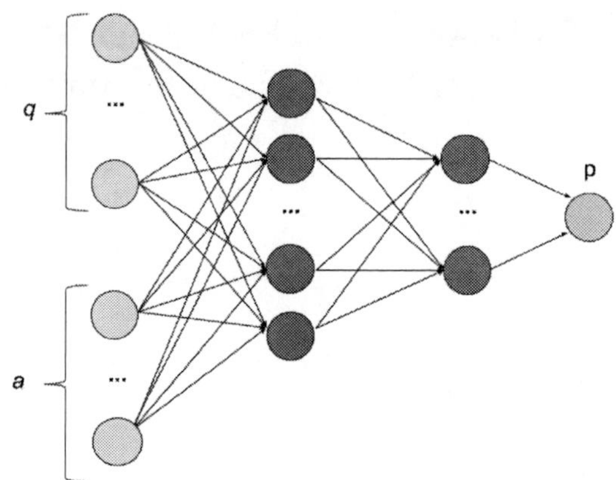

Figure 1: Neural network architecture used to predict answer ranking.

paragraphs or documents. The PV includes (1) the distributed memory (DM) model, that predicts the next word using the concatenation of the previous words and the paragraph vector, that is shared among all words in the same paragraph (or sentence); (2) the distributed bag-of-words (DBOW) model, that – similar to the skip-gram model – predicts words randomly sampled from the paragraph, given the paragraph vector. We experiment with both DM and DBOW models, as well as their combination. For comparison with recent work in answer reranking (Jansen et al., 2014; Sharp et al., 2015), we also evaluate the averaged word embedding vectors obtained with the skip-gram model (Mikolov et al., 2013) (henceforth referred to as the *SkipAvg* model).

3 Experiments

3.1 Data

In order to be able to compare our work with previous research, we use the Yahoo! Answers dataset that was first introduced by Jansen et al. (2014) and was later used by Sharp et al. (2015) and Fried et al. (2015). This dataset contains 10K *How* questions from Yahoo! Answers. Each question has at least four user-generated answers, and the average number of answers per question is nine. 50% of the dataset is used for training, 25% for development and 25% for testing. Further information about the dataset can be found in Jansen et al. (2014).

Our approach requires unlabelled data for unsupervised pre-training of the word and paragraph vectors. For these purposes we use the *L6 Yahoo! Answers Comprehensive Questions and Answers* corpus obtained via Webscope.[4] This dataset contains about 4.5M questions from Yahoo! Answers along with their user-generated answers, and was provided as training data at the recent TREC LiveQA competition (Agichtein et al., 2015), the goal of which was to answer open-domain questions coming from real users in real time.[5] The Yahoo! Answers manner question dataset prepared by Jansen et al. (2014) and described in the previous paragraph, was initially sampled from this larger dataset. We want to emphasize that the L6 dataset is only used for unsupervised pretraining – no meta-information is used in our experiments.

We also experiment with the English Gigaword corpus,[6] which contains data from several English newswire sources. Jansen et al. (2014) used this corpus to train word embeddings, which were then included as features in their answer reranker.

3.2   Experimental Setup

Following Jansen et al. (2014) and Fried et al. (2015), we implement two baselines: the baseline that selects an answer randomly and the candidate retrieval (CR) baseline. The CR baseline uses the same scoring as in Jansen et al. (2014): the questions and the candidate answers are represented using `tf-idf` (Salton, 1991) over lemmas; the candidate answers are ranked according to their cosine similarity to the respective question.

We use the *gensim*[7] implementation of the DBOW and DM paragraph vector models. The word embeddings for the SkipAvg model are obtained with *word2vec*.[8] The data was tokenized with the Stanford tokenizer[9] and then lowercased.

To evaluate our models, we use standard imple-

---

[4] `http://webscope.sandbox.yahoo.com/`
[5] `https://sites.google.com/site/trecliveqa2015/`
[6] `https://catalog.ldc.upenn.edu/LDC2003T05`
[7] `https://radimrehurek.com/gensim/models/doc2vec.html`
[8] `https://code.google.com/p/word2vec/`
[9] `http://nlp.stanford.edu/software/tokenizer.shtml`

Model	dim	P@1	MRR
Random Baseline	-	15.06	37.13
CR Baseline	-	24.83	48.82
SkipAvg Baseline	200	31.25	52.56
DBOW	100	38.95[*]	58.18[*]
DBOW	200	**39.91**[*]	**58.68**[*]
DBOW	300	39.47[*]	58.35[*]
DM	100	38.19[*]	57.01[*]
DM	200	38.35[*]	57.28[*]
DM	300	37.55[*]	56.67[*]
DBOW+DM	200	**40.55**[*#]	**59.12**[*#]
DBOW+SkipAvg	200	**40.39**[*#]	**58.91**[*#]
DBOW+DM+SkipAvg	200	**40.63**[*#]	**59.14**[*#]

Table 1: Development P@1 and MRR for different vectors representations. * indicates that improvements over the baselines are statistically significant with $p < 0.05$. # indicates that the improvement over the DBOW model with 200-dimensional vectors is not statistically significant. All significance tests are performed with one-tailed bootstrap resampling with 10,000 iterations.

mentations of the P@1 and mean reciprocal rank (MRR) evaluation metrics. To evaluate whether the difference between two models is statistically significant, statistical significance testing is performed using one-tailed bootstrap resampling with 10,000 iterations. Improvements are considered to be statistically significant at the 5% confidence level (p < 0.05).

3.3   Results

In Table 1, we report best development P@1 and MRR of the multilayer perceptron trained on Yahoo! Answers (Jansen et al., 2014) data. Early stopping is used to maximize P@1 on the development set. The distributed representations, including the SkipAvg model, beat both random and candidate retrieval baselines by a large and statistically significant margin. Likewise, the multilayer perceptron with DBOW and DM representations significantly outperform the SkipAvg representations. Both paragraph vector representations initially proposed by Le and Mikolov (2014) – DBOW and DM – provide similarly high performance, however the DBOW model performs slightly better, with the improvement over the DM model being statistically significant. Different dimensionalities of the pretrained vectors provide similar results, with

Model	P@1	MRR
Random Baseline	15.74	37.40
CR Baseline	22.63	47.17
SkipAvg	30.25	51.59
Jansen et al. (2014)	30.49	51.89
Fried et al. (2015)	33.01	53.96
DBOW	37.02^*	56.74^*
DBOW+DM	37.06^*	56.56^*
DBOW+SkipAvg	35.85^*	56.03^*
DBOW+DM+SkipAvg	$\mathbf{37.17}^*$	$\mathbf{56.82}^*$

Table 2: Test P@1 and MRR. * indicates that improvements over the baselines are statistically significant with $p < 0.05$.

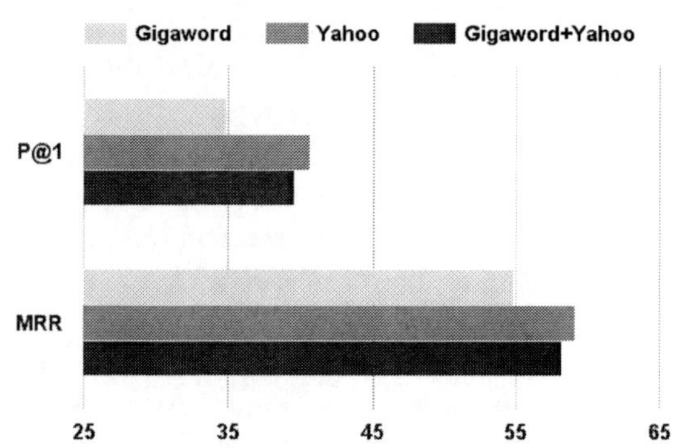

Figure 2: Development P@1 and MRR of a DBOW model pretrained on Yahoo! Answers and Gigaword corpora.

200 outperforming the rest by a small margin. The multilayer perceptron with combinations of different distributed representations reach slightly higher P@1 and MRR on the development set. However, these improvements over the 200-dimension DBOW model are not statistically significant.

Table 2 presents the results on the test set. We only evaluate the 200-dimension DBOW model and its combinations with other models, comparing these to the baselines and the previous results on the same dataset (we use the same train/dev/test split as Jansen et al. (2014)). The DBOW outperforms the baselines by a statistically significant margin. The combination of the DBOW, DM and SkipAvg models provides slightly better results, but the improvement over the DBOW is not statistically significant.

3.4 Analysis

Jansen et al. (2014) report that answer reranking benefits from lexical semantic models, and describe experiments using SkipAvg embeddings pretrained using the English Gigaword corpus. Here we compare the performance of the reranker with distributed representations pretrained on a large "out-of-domain" newswire corpus (Gigaword), versus a smaller "in-domain" non-factoid QA one (L6 Yahoo). Figure 2 shows the development P@1 and MRR of the multilayer perceptron with DBOW model on the Yahoo! Answers dataset pretrained on 30M random paragraphs from the English Gigaword corpus versus the multilayer perceptron with DBOW model pretrained on the Yahoo L6 corpus containing about 8.5M paragraphs. We also evaluate the com-

bination of the two models. The results highlight the importance of finding a suitable source of unlabelled training data since vectors pretrained on reasonably large amounts of Yahoo! Answers data are more beneficial than using a much larger Gigaword dataset.

Even our best model is still, however, far from being perfect, i.e. for about 60% of questions, the answer selected as best by the author of the question is not assigned the highest rank by our system. We believe that one of the reasons for that is that the choice of the best answer purely relies on the question's author and may be subjective (see Table 3). A possible useful direction for future research is to incorporate the user-level information into the neural reranking model. This approach has been recently found beneficial in the task of sentiment analysis (Tang et al., 2015).

Another potential source of error lies in the user-generated nature of the data. Yahoo! Answers contains a large number of spelling and grammar mistakes (e.g. *how do i thaw fozen [sic] chicken?*), non-standard spelling and punctuation (e.g. *Booorrrri-inng!!!!!*). A common way to deal with this problem is normalization (Baldwin et al., 2015). To determine whether this might be helpful, we normalized the data following the strategy described by Le Roux et al. (2012). We trained the DBOW model with 200 dimensions and applied the MLP, as described in Section 2. The best development P@1 was only 33.95, with MRR 54.23 (versus 39.91 P@1 and 58.68 MRR without normalization). Even

Question	*How should I wear my hair tomorrow?*
Best answer	*Very good question...Lets see, I think you should wear it in pigtails.....*
Other answers	*Losen it.*
	Close your eyes, grab some scissors, and GO CRAZY!
	I think you should scrunch it! It looks awesome. Just tip ur head over and put jell in ur hands and like scrunch!
	just brush it and go, it always works for me when i can't figure out what to do with it.
	pull it up in a high pony tail & small curls falling down!
	make it into braids

Table 3: Example question from the Yahoo! Answers dataset

though our preliminary experiments show that applying lexical normalization results in significantly lower performance, further study is needed. One direction is in using character-level embeddings that have been proven promising for user-generated content because of their ability to better handle spelling variation (Kim et al., 2015).

4 Conclusions

We have conducted answer reranking experiments for open-domain non-factoid QA and achieved state-of-the-art performance on the Yahoo! Answers manner question corpus using a very straightforward neural approach which involves representing question-answer pairs as paragraph vectors and training a multilayer perceptron to order candidate answers. Our experiments show that representing the question-answer pair as a paragraph vector is clearly superior to the use of averaged word vectors. We have also shown that a smaller amount of unlabelled data taken from a CQA site is more useful for training representations than a larger newswire set.

In this paper, we use general purpose distributed document representations provided by Paragraph Vector models to represent question-answer pairs. Then a machine learning algorithm is used to rank the pairs. One possible direction for future research is in learning distributed document representations and the ranking simultaneously and applying more sophisticated recurrent models such as long short-term memory (LSTM) (Hochreiter and Schmidhuber, 1997) neural networks, that have been shown to be effective in similar tasks (Wang and Nyberg, 2015; Zhou et al., 2015).

Acknowledgments

Thanks to Yvette Graham and the three anonymous reviewers for their helpful comments and suggestions. This research is supported by the Science Foundation Ireland (Grant 12/CE/I2267) as part of ADAPT centre (`www.adaptcentre.ie`) at Dublin City University. The ADAPT Centre for Digital Content Technology is funded under the SFI Research Centres Programme (Grant 13/RC/2106) and is co-funded under the European Regional Development Fund.

References

Eugene Agichtein, David Carmel, Dan Pelleg, Yuval Pinter, and Donna Harman. 2015. Overview of the TREC 2015 LiveQA Track. In *Proceedings of The Twenty-Fourth Text REtrieval Conference, TREC.*

Timothy Baldwin, Young-Bum Kim, Marie Catherine de Marneffe, Alan Ritter, Bo Han, and Wei Xu. 2015. Shared tasks of the 2015 workshop on noisy user-generated text: Twitter lexical normalization and named entity recognition. *ACL-IJCNLP 2015*, page 126.

Daniel Fried, Peter Jansen, Gustave Hahn-Powell, Mihai Surdeanu, and Peter Clark. 2015. Higher-order lexical semantic models for non-factoid answer reranking. *Transactions of the Association for Computational Linguistics*, 3:197–210.

Sepp Hochreiter and Jürgen Schmidhuber. 1997. Long short-term memory. *Neural computation*, 9(8):1735–1780.

Peter Jansen, Mihai Surdeanu, and Peter Clark. 2014. Discourse complements lexical semantics for non-factoid answer reranking. In *Proceedings of the 52nd Annual Meeting of the Association for Computational Linguistics (Volume 1: Long Papers)*, pages 977–986,

Baltimore, Maryland, June. Association for Computational Linguistics.

Yoon Kim, Yacine Jernite, David Sontag, and Alexander M Rush. 2015. Character-aware neural language models. *arXiv preprint arXiv:1508.06615, to appear at AAAI 2016.*

Quoc V. Le and Tomas Mikolov. 2014. Distributed representations of sentences and documents. In *Proceedings of the 31th International Conference on Machine Learning, ICML 2014, Beijing, China, 21-26 June 2014*, pages 1188–1196.

Joseph Le Roux, Jennifer Foster, Joachim Wagner, Rasul Samad Zadeh Kaljahi, and Anton Bryl. 2012. DCU-Paris13 systems for the SANCL 2012 shared task. *Notes of the First Workshop on Syntactic Analysis of Non-Canonical Language (SANCL).*

Tomas Mikolov, Kai Chen, Greg Corrado, and Jeffrey Dean. 2013. Efficient estimation of word representations in vector space. *ICLR Workshop.*

Gerard Salton. 1991. Developments in automatic text retrieval. *Science*, 253(5023):974–980.

Rebecca Sharp, Peter Jansen, Mihai Surdeanu, and Peter Clark. 2015. Spinning straw into gold: Using free text to train monolingual alignment models for non-factoid question answering. In *Proceedings of the 2015 Conference of the North American Chapter of the Association for Computational Linguistics: Human Language Technologies*, pages 231–237, Denver, Colorado, May–June. Association for Computational Linguistics.

Duyu Tang, Bing Qin, and Ting Liu. 2015. Learning semantic representations of users and products for document level sentiment classification. In *Proceedings of the 53rd Annual Meeting of the Association for Computational Linguistics and the 7th International Joint Conference on Natural Language Processing (Volume 1: Long Papers)*, pages 1014–1023, Beijing, China, July. Association for Computational Linguistics.

Di Wang and Eric Nyberg. 2015. A long short-term memory model for answer sentence selection in question answering. In *Proceedings of the 53rd Annual Meeting of the Association for Computational Linguistics and the 7th International Joint Conference on Natural Language Processing (Volume 2: Short Papers)*, pages 707–712, Beijing, China, July. Association for Computational Linguistics.

Xiaoqiang Zhou, Baotian Hu, Qingcai Chen, Buzhou Tang, and Xiaolong Wang. 2015. Answer sequence learning with neural networks for answer selection in community question answering. In *Proceedings of the 53rd Annual Meeting of the Association for Computational Linguistics and the 7th International Joint Conference on Natural Language Processing (Volume 2: Short Papers)*, pages 713–718, Beijing, China, July. Association for Computational Linguistics.

Multilingual Language Processing From Bytes

Dan Gillick, Cliff Brunk, Oriol Vinyals, Amarnag Subramanya
Google Research
{dgillick, cliffbrunk, vinyals, asubram}@google.com

Abstract

We describe an LSTM-based model which we call Byte-to-Span (BTS) that reads text as bytes and outputs span annotations of the form [start, length, label] where start positions, lengths, and labels are separate entries in our vocabulary. Because we operate directly on unicode bytes rather than language-specific words or characters, we can analyze text in many languages with a single model. Due to the small vocabulary size, these multilingual models are very compact, but produce results similar to or better than the state-of-the-art in Part-of-Speech tagging and Named Entity Recognition that use only the provided training datasets (no external data sources). Our models are learning "from scratch" in that they do not rely on any elements of the standard pipeline in Natural Language Processing (including tokenization), and thus can run in standalone fashion on raw text.

1 Introduction

The long-term trajectory of research in Natural Language Processing has seen the replacement of rules and specific linguistic knowledge with machine learned components. Perhaps the most standardized way that knowledge is still injected into largely statistical systems is through the processing pipeline: Some set of basic language-specific tokens are identified in a first step. Sequences of tokens are segmented into sentences in a second step. The resulting sentences are fed one at a time for syntactic analysis: Part-of-Speech (POS) tagging and parsing. Next, the predicted syntactic structure is typically used as features in semantic analysis, Named Entity Recognition (NER), Semantic Role Labeling, etc. While each step of the pipeline now relies more on data and models than on hand-curated rules, the pipeline structure itself encodes one particular understanding of how meaning attaches to raw strings.

One motivation for our work is to try removing this structural dependence. Rather than rely on the intermediate representations invented for specific subtasks (for example, Penn Treebank tokenization), we are allowing the model to learn whatever internal structure is most conducive to producing the annotations of interest. To this end, we describe a Recurrent Neural Network (RNN) model that reads raw input string *segments*, one byte at a time, and produces output *span annotations* corresponding to specific byte regions in the input[1]. This is truly language annotation from scratch (see Collobert et al. (2011) and Zhang and LeCun (2015)).

Two key innovations facilitate this approach. First, Long Short Term Memory (LSTM) models (Hochreiter and Schmidhuber, 1997) allow us to replace the traditional independence assumptions in text processing with structural constraints on memory. While we have long known that long-term dependencies are important in language, we had no mechanism other than conditional independence to keep sparsity in check. The memory in an LSTM, however, is not constrained by any explicit assumptions of independence. Rather, its ability to learn patterns is limited only by the structure of the network and the size of the memory (and of course the

---

[1] Our span annotation model can be applied to any sequence labeling task; it is not immediately applicable to predicting more complex structures like trees.

Proceedings of NAACL-HLT 2016, pages 1296–1306,
San Diego, California, June 12-17, 2016. ©2016 Association for Computational Linguistics

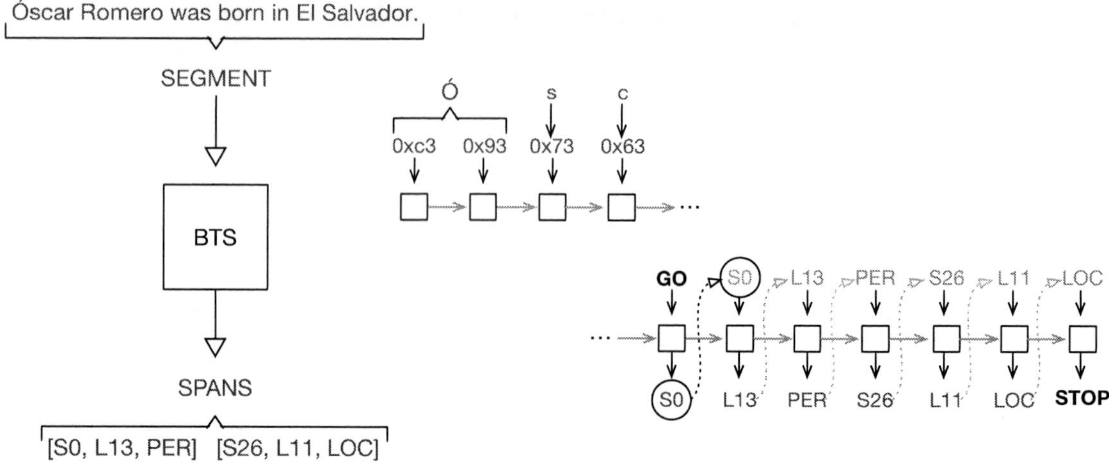

Figure 1: A diagram showing the way the Byte-to-Span (BTS) model converts an input text segment to a sequence of span annotations. The model reads the input segment one byte at a time (this can involve multibyte unicode characters), then a special Generate Output (GO) symbol, then produces the argmax output of a softmax over all possible start positions, lengths, and labels (as well as STOP, signifying no additional outputs). The prediction from the previous time step is fed as an input to the next time step.

amount of training data).

Second, sequence-to-sequence models (Sutskever et al., 2014), allow for flexible input/output dynamics. Traditional models, including feedforward neural networks, read fixed-length inputs and generate fixed-length outputs by following a fixed set of computational steps. Instead, we can now read an entire segment of text before producing an arbitrary number of outputs, allowing the model to learn a function best suited to the task.

We leverage these two ideas with a basic strategy: Decompose inputs and outputs into their component pieces, then read and predict them as sequences. Rather than read words, we are reading a sequence of unicode bytes[2]; rather than producing a label for each word, we are producing triples [start, length, label], that correspond to the spans of interest, as a sequence of three separate predictions (see Figure 1). This forces the model to learn how the components of words and labels interact so all the structure typically imposed by the NLP pipeline (as well as the rules of unicode) are left to the LSTM to model.

Decomposed inputs and outputs have a few important benefits. First, they reduce the size of the

vocabulary relative to word-level inputs, so the resulting models are extremely compact (on the order of a million parameters). Second, because unicode is essentially a universal language, we can train models to analyze many languages at once. In fact, by stacking LSTMs, we are able to learn representations that appear to generalize across languages, improving performance significantly (without using any additional parameters) over models trained on a single language. This is the first account, to our knowledge, of a multilingual model that achieves good results across many languages, thus bypassing all the language-specific engineering usually required to build models in different languages[3]. We describe results similar to or better than the state-of-the-art in Part-of-Speech tagging and Named Entity Recognition that use only the provided training datasets (no external data sources).

The rest of this paper is organized as follows. Section 2 discusses related work; Section 3 describes our model; Section 4 gives training details including a new variety of dropout (Hinton et al., 2012);

---

[2]We use the variable length UTF-8 encodings to keep the vocabulary as small as possible.

[3]These multilingual models are able to handle code-mixed text, an important practical problem that's received relatively little attention. However, we do not have any annotated data that contains code switching, so we cannot report any results.

Section 5 gives inference details; Section 6 presents results on POS tagging and NER across many languages; Finally, we summarize our contributions in section 7.

2   Related Work

One important feature of our work is the use of byte inputs. Character-level inputs have been used with some success for tasks like NER (Klein et al., 2003), parallel text alignment (Church, 1993), and authorship attribution (Peng et al., 2003) as an effective way to deal with n-gram sparsity while still capturing some aspects of word choice and morphology. Such approaches often combine character and word features and have been especially useful for handling languages with large character sets (Nakagawa, 2004). However, there is almost no work that explicitly uses bytes – one exception uses byte n-grams to identify source code authorship (Frantzeskou et al., 2006) – but there is nothing, to the best of our knowledge, that exploits bytes as a cross-lingual representation of language. Work on multilingual parsing using Neural Networks that share some subset of the parameters across languages (Duong et al., 2015) seems to benefit the low-resource languages; however, we are sharing all the parameters among all languages.

Recent work has shown that modeling the sequence of characters in each token with an LSTM can more effectively handle rare and unknown words than independent word embeddings (Ling et al., 2015; Ballesteros et al., 2015). Similarly, language modeling, especially for morphologically complex languages, benefits from a Convolutional Neural Network (CNN) over characters to generate word embeddings (Kim et al., 2015). Rather than decompose words into characters, Rohan and Denero (2015) encode rare words with Huffman codes, allowing a neural translation model to learn something about word subcomponents. In contrast to this line of research, our work has no explicit notion of tokens and operates on bytes rather than characters.

Our work is philosophically similar to Collobert et al.'s (2011) experiments with "almost from scratch" language processing. They avoid task-specific feature engineering, instead relying on a multilayer feedforward (or convolutional) Neural Network to combine word embeddings to produce features useful for each task. In the Results section, below, we compare NER performance on the same dataset they used. The "almost" in the title actually refers to the use of preprocessed (lowercased) tokens as input instead of raw sequences of letters. Our byte-level models can be seen as a realization of their comment: "A completely from scratch approach would presumably not know anything about words at all and would work from letters only." Recent work with convolutional neural networks that read character-level inputs (Zhang et al., 2015) shows some interesting results on a variety of classification tasks, but because their models need very large training sets, they do not present comparisons to established baselines on standard tasks.

Finally, recent work on Automatic Speech Recognition (ASR) uses a similar sequence-to-sequence LSTM framework to produce letter sequences directly from acoustic frame sequences (Chan et al., 2015; Bahdanau et al., 2015). Just as we are discarding the usual intermediate representations used for text processing, their models make no use of phonetic alignments, clustered triphones, or pronunciation dictionaries. This line of work – discarding intermediate representations in speech – was pioneered by Graves and Jaitly (2014) and earlier, by Eyben et al. (2009).

3   Model

Our model is based on the sequence-to-sequence model used for machine translation (Sutskever et al., 2014), an adaptation of an LSTM that encodes a variable length input as a fixed-length vector, then decodes it into a variable number of outputs[4].

Generally, the sequence-to-sequence LSTM is trained to estimate the conditional probability $P(y_1, ..., y_{T'} | x_1, ..., x_T)$ where $(x_1, ..., x_T)$ is an input sequence and $(y_1, ..., y_{T'})$ is the corresponding output sequence whose length T' may differ from T. The encoding step computes a fixed-dimensional representation v of the input $(x_1, ..., x_T)$ given by the hidden state of the LSTM

---

[4]Related translation work adds an attention mechanism (Bahdanau et al., 2014), allowing the decoder to attend directly to particularly relevant inputs. We tried adding the same mechanism to our model but saw no improvement in performance on the NER task, though training converged in fewer steps.

after reading the last input x_T. The decoding step computes the output probability $P(y_1, ..., y_{T'})$ with the standard LSTM formulation for language modeling, except that the initial hidden state is set to v:

$$P(y_1, ..., y_{T'} | x_1, ..., x_T) = \prod_{t=1}^{T'} P(y_t | v, y_1, ..., y_{t-1}) \tag{1}$$

Sutskever et al. used a separate LSTM for the encoding and decoding tasks. While this separation permits training the encoder and decoder LSTMs separately, say for multitask learning or pre-training, we found our results were no worse if we used a single set of LSTM parameters for both encoder and decoder.

3.1 Vocabulary

The primary difference between our model and the translation model is our novel choice of vocabulary. The set of inputs include all 256 possible bytes, a special Generate Output (GO) symbol, and a special DROP symbol used for regularization, which we will discuss below. The set of outputs include all possible span start positions (byte $0..k$), all possible span lengths ($0..k$), all span labels (PER, LOC, ORG, MISC for the NER task), as well as a special STOP symbol. A complete span annotation includes a start, a length, and a label, but as shown in Figure 1, the model is trained to produce this triple as three separate outputs. This keeps the vocabulary size small and in practice, gives better performance (and faster convergence) than if we use the cross-product space of the triples.

More precisely, the prediction at time t is conditioned on the full input and all previous predictions (via the chain rule). By splitting each span annotation into a sequence [start, length, label], we are making no independence assumption; instead we are relying on the model to maintain a memory state that captures the important dependencies.

Each output distribution $P(y_t | v, y_1, ..., y_{t-1})$ is given by a softmax over all possible items in the output vocabulary, so at a given time step, the model is free to predict any start, any length, or any label (including STOP). In practice, because the training data always has these complete triples in a fixed order, we seldom see malformed or incomplete spans (the

decoder simply ignores such spans). During training, the true label y_{t-1} is fed as input to the model at step t (see Figure 1), and during inference, the argmax prediction is used instead. Note also that the training procedure tries to maximize the probability in Equation 1 (summed over all the training examples). While this does not quite match our task objectives (F1 over labels, for example), it is a reasonable proxy.

3.2 Independent segments

Ideally, we would like our input segments to cover full documents so that our predictions are conditioned on as much relevant information as possible. However, this is impractical for a few reasons. From a training perspective, a Recurrent Neural Network is unrolled to resemble a deep feedforward network, with each layer corresponding to a time step. It is well-known that running backpropagation over a very deep network is hard because it becomes increasingly difficult to estimate the contribution of each layer to the gradient, and further, RNNs have trouble generalizing to different length inputs (Erhan et al., 2009).

So instead of document-sized input segments, we make a segment-independence assumption: We choose some fixed length k and train the model on segments of length k (any span annotation not completely contained in a segment is ignored). This has the added benefit of limiting the range of the start and length label components. It can also allow for more efficient batched inference since each segment is decoded independently. Finally, we can generate a large number of training segments by sliding a window of size k one byte at a time through a document. Note that the resulting training segments can begin and end mid-word, and indeed, mid-character. For both tasks described below, we set the segment size $k = 60$.

3.3 Sequence ordering

Our model differs from the translation model in one more important way. Sutskever et al. found that feeding the input words in reverse order and generating the output words in forward order gave significantly better translations, especially for long sentences. In theory, the predictions are conditioned on the entire input, but as a practical matter, the learning problem is easier when relevant information is ordered appropriately since long dependencies are harder to learn than short ones.

Because the byte order is more meaningful in the forward direction (the first byte of a multibyte character specifies the length, for example), we found somewhat better performance with forward order than reverse order (less than 1% absolute). But unlike translation, where the outputs have a complex order determined by the syntax of the language, our span annotations are more like an unordered set. We tried sorting them by end position in both forward and backward order, and found a small improvement (again, less than 1% absolute) using the backward ordering (assuming the input is given in the forward order). This result validates the translation ordering experiments: the modeling problem is easier when the sequence-to-sequence LSTM is used more like a stack than a queue.

3.4 Model shape

We experimented with a few different architectures and found no significant improvements in using more than 320 units for the embedding dimension and LSTM memory and 4 stacked LSTMs (see Table 4). This observation holds for both models trained on a single language and models trained on many languages. Because the vocabulary is so small, the total number of parameters is dominated by the size of the recurrent matrices. All the results reported below use the same architecture (unless otherwise noted) and thus have roughly 900k parameters.

4 Training

We trained our models with Stochastic Gradient Descent (SGD) on mini-batches of size 128, using an initial learning rate of 0.3. For all other hyperparameter choices, including random initialization, learning rate decay, and gradient clipping, we follow Sutskever et al. (2014). Each model is trained on a single CPU over a period of a few days, at which point, development set results have stabilized. Distributed training on GPUs would likely speed up training to just a few hours.

4.1 Dropout and byte-dropout

Neural Network models are often trained using *dropout* (Hinton et al., 2012), which tends to improve generalization by limiting correlations among hidden units. During training, dropout randomly zeroes some fraction of the elements in the embedding layer and the model state just before the softmax layer (Zaremba et al., 2014).

We were able to further improve generalization with a technique we are calling *byte-dropout*: We randomly replace some fraction of the input bytes in each segment with a special DROP symbol (without changing the corresponding span annotations). Intuitively, this results in a more robust model, perhaps by forcing it to use longer-range dependencies rather than memorizing particular local sequences.

It is worth noting that noise is often added at training time to images in image classification and speech in speech recognition where the added noise does not fundamentally alter the input, but rather blurs it. By using a byte representation of language, we are now capable of achieving something like blurring with text. Indeed, if we removed 20% of the characters in a sentence, humans would be able to infer words and meaning reasonably well.

5 Inference

We perform inference on a segment by (greedily) computing the most likely output at each time step and feeding it to the next time step. Experiments with beam search show no meaningful improvements (less than 0.2% absolute). Because we assume that each segment is independent, we need to choose how to break up the input into segments and how to stitch together the results.

The simplest approach is to divide up the input into segments with no overlapping bytes. Because the model is trained to ignore incomplete spans, this approach misses all spans that cross segment boundaries, which, depending on the choice of k, can be a significant number. We avoid the missed-span problem by choosing segments that overlap such that each span is likely to be fully contained by at least one segment.

For our experiments, we create segments with a fixed overlap ($k/2 = 30$). This means that with the exception of the first segment in a document, the model reads 60 bytes of input, but we only keep predictions about the last 30 bytes.

6 Results

Here we describe experiments on two datasets that include annotations across a variety of languages. The multilingual datasets allow us to highlight the advantages of using byte-level inputs: First, we can train a single compact model that can handle many languages at once. Second, we demonstrate some cross-lingual abstraction that improves performance of a single multilingual model over each single-language model. In the experiments, we refer to the LSTM setup described above as Byte-to-Span or BTS.

Most state-of-the-art results in POS tagging and NER leverage unlabeled data to improve a supervised baseline. For example, word clusters or word embeddings estimated from a large corpus are often used to help deal with sparsity. Because our LSTM models are reading bytes, it is not obvious how to insert information like a word cluster identity. Recent results with sequence-to-sequence auto-encoding (Dai and Le, 2015) seem promising in this regard, but here we limit our experiments to use just annotated data.

Each task specifies separate data for training, development, and testing. We used the development data for tuning the dropout and byte-dropout parameters (since these likely depend on the amount of available training data), but did not tune the remaining hyperparameters. In total, our training set for POS Tagging across 13 languages included 2.87 million tokens and our training set for NER across 4 languages included 0.88 million tokens. Recall, though, that our training examples are 60-byte segments obtained by sliding a window through the training data, shifting by 1 byte each time. This results in 25.3 million and 6.0 million training segments for the two tasks.

6.1 Part-of-Speech Tagging

Our part-of-speech tagging experiments use Version 1.1 of the Universal Dependency data[5], a collection of treebanks across many languages annotated with a universal tagset (Petrov et al., 2011). The most relevant recent work (Ling et al., 2015) uses different datasets, with different finer-grained tagsets in each language. Because we are primary interested

in multilingual models that can share language-independent parameters, the universal tagset is important, and thus our results are not immediately comparable. However, we provide baseline results (for each language separately) using a Conditional Random Field (Lafferty et al., 2001) with an extensive collection of features with performance comparable to the Stanford POS tagger (Manning, 2011). For our experiments, we chose the 13 languages that had at least 50k tokens of training data. We did not subsample the training data, though the amount of data varies widely across languages, but rather shuffled all training examples together. These languages represent a broad range of linguistic phenomena and character sets so it was not obvious at the outset that a single multilingual model would work.

Table 1 compares the baselines with (CRF+) and without (CRF) externally trained cluster features with our model trained on all languages (BTS) as well as each language separately (BTS*). The single BTS model improves on average over the CRF models trained using the same data, though clearly there is some benefit in using external resources. Note that BTS is particularly strong in Finnish, surpassing even CRF+ by nearly 1.5% (absolute), probably because the byte representation generalizes better to agglutinative languages than word-based models, a finding validated by Ling et al. (2015). In addition, the baseline CRF models, including the (compressed) cluster tables, require about 50 MB per language, while BTS is under 10 MB. BTS improves on average over BTS*, suggesting that it is learning some language-independent representation.

6.2 Named Entity Recognition

Our main motivation for showing POS tagging results was to demonstrate how effective a single BTS model can be across a wide range of languages. The NER task is a more interesting test case because, as discussed in the introduction, it usually relies on a pipeline of processing. We use the 2002 and 2003 ConLL shared task datasets[6] for multilingual NER because they contain data in 4 languages (English, German, Spanish, and Dutch) with consistent annotations of named entities (PER, LOC, ORG, and MISC). In addition, the shared task competition

---

Language	CRF+	CRF	BTS	BTS*
Bulgarian	97.97	97.00	97.84	97.02
Czech	98.38	98.00	98.50	98.44
Danish	95.93	95.06	95.52	92.45
German	93.08	91.99	92.87	92.34
Greek	97.72	97.21	97.39	96.64
English	95.11	94.51	93.87	94.00
Spanish	96.08	95.03	95.80	95.26
Farsi	96.59	96.25	96.82	96.76
Finnish	94.34	92.82	95.48	96.05
French	96.00	95.93	95.75	95.17
Indonesian	92.84	92.71	92.85	91.03
Italian	97.70	97.61	97.56	97.40
Swedish	96.81	96.15	95.57	93.17
AVERAGE	96.04	95.41	95.85	95.06

Table 1: Part-of-speech tagging accuracy for two CRF baselines and 2 versions of BTS. CRF+ uses resources external to the training data (word clusters) and CRF uses only the training data. BTS (unlike CRF+ and CRF) is a single model trained on all the languages together, while BTS* is a separate Byte-to-Span model for each language.

produced strong baseline numbers for comparison. However, most published results use extra information beyond the provided training data which makes fair comparison with our model more difficult.

The best competition results for English and German (Florian et al., 2003) used a large gazetteer and the output of two additional NER classifiers trained on richer datasets. Since 2003, better results have been reported using additional semi-supervised techniques (Ando and Zhang, 2005) and more recently, Passos et al. (2014) claimed the best English results (90.90% F1) using features derived from word-embeddings. The 1st place submission in 2002 (Carreras et al., 2002) comment that without extra resources for Spanish, their results drop by about 2% (absolute).

Perhaps the most relevant comparison is the overall 2nd place submission in 2003 (Klein et al., 2003). They use only the provided data and report results with character-based models which provide a useful comparison point to our byte-based LSTM. The performance of a character HMM alone is much worse than their best result (83.2% vs 92.3% on the English development data), which includes a variety of word and POS-tag features that describe the context

(as well as some post-processing rules). For English (assuming just ASCII strings), the character HMM uses the same inputs as BTS, but is hindered by some combination of the independence assumption and smaller capacity.

Collobert et al.'s (2011) convolutional model (discussed above) gives 81.47% F1 on the English test set when trained on only the gold data. However, by using carefully selected word-embeddings trained on external data, they are able to increase F1 to 88.67%. Huang et al. (2015) improve on Collobert's results by using a bidirectional LSTM with a CRF layer where the inputs are features describing the words in each sentence. Either by virtue of the more powerful model, or because of more expressive features, they report 84.26% F1 on the same test set and 90.10% when they add pretrained word embedding features. Dos Santos et al. (2015) represent each word by concatenating a pretrained word embedding with a character-level embedding produced by a convolutional neural network.

There is relatively little work on multilingual NER, and most research is focused on building systems that are unsupervised in the sense that they use resources like Wikipedia and Freebase rather than manually annotated data. Nothman et al. (2013) use Wikipedia anchor links and disambiguation pages joined with Freebase types to create a huge amount of somewhat noisy training data and are able to achieve good results on many languages (with some extra heuristics). These results are also included in Table 2.

While BTS does not improve on the state-of-the-art in English, its performance is better than the best previous results that use only the provided training data. BTS improves significantly on the best known results in German, Spanish, and Dutch even though these leverage external data. In addition, the BTS* models, trained separately on each language, are worse than the single BTS model (with the same number of parameters as each single-language model) trained on all languages combined, again suggesting that the model is learning some language-independent representation of the task.

One interesting shortcoming of the BTS model is that it is not obvious how to tune it to increase recall. In a standard classifier framework, we could simply increase the prediction threshold to increase

Model	en	de	es	nl
Passos	90.90	–	–	–
Ando	89.31	75.27	–	–
Florian	88.76	72.41	–	–
Carreras	–	–	81.39	77.05
dos Santos	–	–	82.21	–
Nothman	85.2	66.5	79.6	78.6
Klein	86.07	71.90	–	–
Huang	84.26	–	–	–
Collobert	81.47	–	–	–
BTS	86.50	76.22	82.95	82.84
BTS*	84.57	72.08	81.83	78.08

Table 2: A comparison of NER systems. The results are F1 scores, where a correct span annotation exactly matches a gold span annotation (start, length, and entity type must all be correct). Results of the systems described in the text are shown for English, German, Spanish, and Dutch. BTS* shows the results of the BTS model trained separately on each language while BTS is a single model trained on all 4 languages together. The top set of results leverage resources beyond the training data; the middle set do not, and thus are most comparable to our results (bottom set).

precision and decrease the prediction threshold to increase recall. However, because we only produce annotations for spans (non-spans are not annotated), we can adjust a threshold on total span probability (the product of the start, length, and label probabilities) to increase precision, but there is no clear way to increase recall. The untuned model tends to prefer precision over recall already, so some heuristic for increasing recall might improve our overall F1 results.

6.3 Dropout and Stacked LSTMs

There are many modeling options and hyperparameters that significantly impact the performance of Neural Networks. Here we show the results of a few experiments that were particularly relevant to the performance obtained above.

First, Table 3 shows how dropout and byte-dropout improve performance for both tasks. Without any kind of dropout, the training process starts to overfit (development data perplexity starts increasing) relatively quickly. For POS tagging, we set dropout and byte-dropout to 0.2, while for NER, we set both to 0.3. This significantly reduces the over-

fitting problem.

BTS Training	POS Accuracy	NER F1
Vanilla	94.78	74.75
+ Dropout	95.35	78.76
+ Byte-dropout	95.85	82.13

Table 3: BTS Part-of-speech tagging average accuracy across all 13 evaluated languages and Named Entity Recognition average F1 across all 4 evaluated languages with various modifications to the vanilla training setup. Dropout is standard in Neural Network model training because it often improves generalization; Byte-dropout randomly replaces input bytes with a special DROP marker.

Depth	Width=320	Width=640
1	76.15	77.59
2	79.40	79.73
3	81.44	81.93
4	82.13	82.18

Table 4: Macro-averaged (across 4 languages) F1 for the NER task using different model architectures.

Second, Table 4 shows how performance improves as we increase the size of the model in two ways: the number of units in the model's state (width) and the number of stacked LSTMs (depth). Increasing the width of the model improves performance less than increasing the depth, and once we use 4 stacked LSTMs, the added benefit of a much wider model has disappeared. This result suggests that rather than learning to partition the space of inputs according to the source language, the model is learning some lanuage-independent representation at the deeper levels.

To validate our claim about language-independent representation, Figure 2 shows the results of a tSNE plot of the LSTM's memory state when the output is one of PER, LOC, ORG, MISC across the four languages. While the label clusters are neatly separated, the examples of each individual label do not appear to be clustered by language. Thus rather than partitioning each (label, language) combination, the model is learning unified label representations that are independent of the language.

7 Conclusions

We have described a model that uses a sequence-to-sequence LSTM framework that reads a segment of

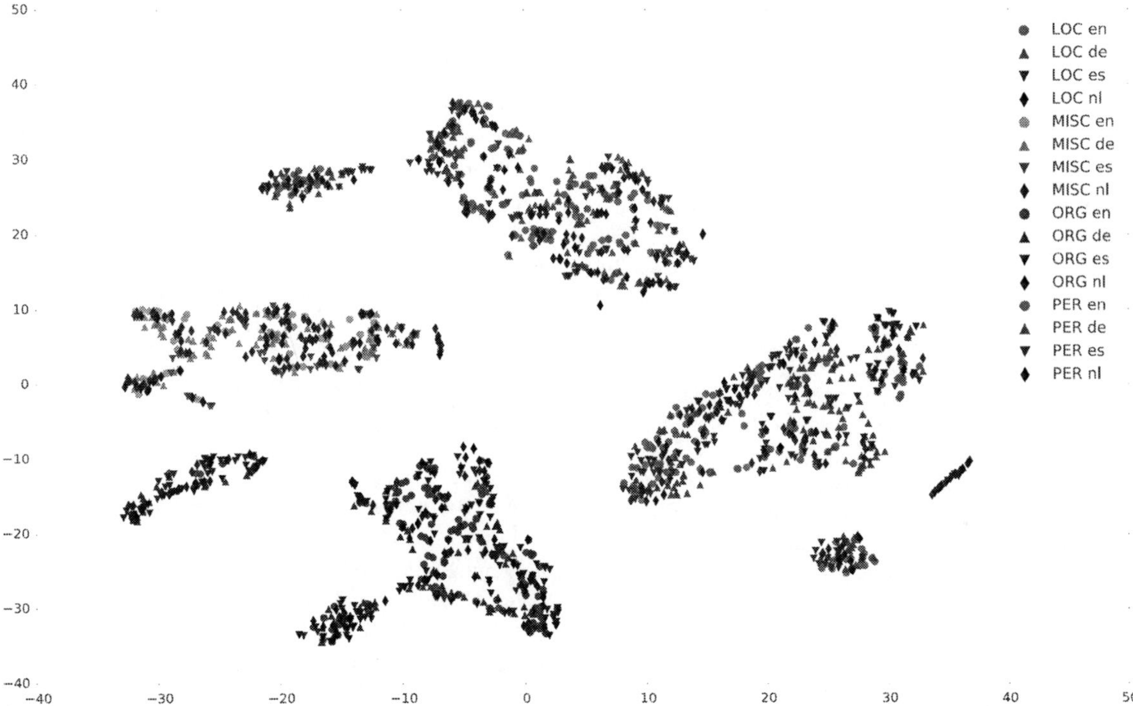

Figure 2: A tSNE plot of the BTS model's memory state just before the softmax layer produces one of the NER labels.

text one byte at a time and then produces span annotations over the inputs. This work makes a number of novel contributions:

First, we use the bytes in variable length unicode encodings as inputs. This makes the model vocabulary very small and also allows us to train a multilingual model that improves over single-language models without using additional parameters. We introduce byte-dropout, an analog to added noise in speech or blurring in images, which significantly improves generalization.

Second, the model produces span annotations, where each is a sequence of three outputs: a start position, a length, and a label. This decomposition keeps the output vocabulary small and marks a significant departure from the typical Begin-Inside-Outside (BIO) scheme used for labeling sequences.

Finally, the models are much more compact than traditional word-based systems and they are standalone – no processing pipeline is needed. In particular, we do not need a tokenizer to segment text in each of the input languages.

Acknowledgments

Many thanks to Fernando Pereira and Dan Ramage for their insights about this project from the outset. Thanks also to Cree Howard for creating Figure 1.

References

Rie Kubota Ando and Tong Zhang. 2005. A framework for learning predictive structures from multiple tasks and unlabeled data. *The Journal of Machine Learning Research*, 6:1817–1853.

Dzmitry Bahdanau, Kyunghyun Cho, and Yoshua Bengio. 2014. Neural machine translation by jointly learning to align and translate. *arXiv preprint arXiv:1409.0473*.

Dzmitry Bahdanau, Jan Chorowski, Dmitriy Serdyuk, Philemon Brakel, and Yoshua Bengio. 2015. End-to-end attention-based large vocabulary speech recognition. *arXiv preprint arXiv:1508.04395*.

Miguel Ballesteros, Chris Dyer, and Noah A Smith. 2015. Improved transition-based parsing by modeling characters instead of words with lstms. *arXiv preprint arXiv:1508.00657*.

Xavier Carreras, Lluís Màrques, and Lluís Padró. 2002.

Named entity extraction using adaboost. In *Proceedings of CoNLL-2002*, pages 167–170. Taipei, Taiwan.

William Chan, Navdeep Jaitly, Quoc V Le, and Oriol Vinyals. 2015. Listen, attend and spell. *arXiv preprint arXiv:1508.01211*.

Rohan Chitnis and John DeNero. 2015. Variable-length word encodings for neural translation models. In *Proceedings of the 2015 Conference on Empirical Methods in Natural Language Processing*, pages 2088–2093.

Kenneth Ward Church. 1993. Char_align: a program for aligning parallel texts at the character level. In *Proceedings of the 31st annual meeting on Association for Computational Linguistics*, pages 1–8. Association for Computational Linguistics.

Ronan Collobert, Jason Weston, Léon Bottou, Michael Karlen, Koray Kavukcuoglu, and Pavel Kuksa. 2011. Natural language processing (almost) from scratch. *The Journal of Machine Learning Research*, 12:2493–2537.

Andrew M Dai and Quoc V Le. 2015. Semi-supervised sequence learning. *arXiv preprint arXiv:1511.01432*.

Cıcero dos Santos, Victor Guimaraes, RJ Niterói, and Rio de Janeiro. 2015. Boosting named entity recognition with neural character embeddings. In *Proceedings of NEWS 2015 The Fifth Named Entities Workshop*, page 25.

Long Duong, Trevor Cohn, Steven Bird, and Paul Cook. 2015. Low resource dependency parsing: Cross-lingual parameter sharing in a neural network parser. In *53rd Annual Meeting of the Association for Computational Linguistics and the 7th International Joint Conference on Natural Language Processing (Volume 2: Short Papers)*, pages 845–850.

Dumitru Erhan, Pierre-Antoine Manzagol, Yoshua Bengio, Samy Bengio, and Pascal Vincent. 2009. The difficulty of training deep architectures and the effect of unsupervised pre-training. In *International Conference on artificial intelligence and statistics*, pages 153–160.

Florian Eyben, Martin Wöllmer, Björn Schuller, and Alex Graves. 2009. From speech to letters-using a novel neural network architecture for grapheme based asr. In *Automatic Speech Recognition & Understanding, 2009. ASRU 2009. IEEE Workshop on*, pages 376–380. IEEE.

Radu Florian, Abe Ittycheriah, Hongyan Jing, and Tong Zhang. 2003. Named entity recognition through classifier combination. In *Proceedings of the seventh conference on Natural language learning at HLT-NAACL 2003-Volume 4*, pages 168–171. Association for Computational Linguistics.

Georgia Frantzeskou, Efstathios Stamatatos, Stefanos Gritzalis, and Sokratis Katsikas. 2006. Effective identification of source code authors using byte-level information. In *Proceedings of the 28th international conference on Software engineering*, pages 893–896. ACM.

Alex Graves and Navdeep Jaitly. 2014. Towards end-to-end speech recognition with recurrent neural networks. In *Proceedings of the 31st International Conference on Machine Learning (ICML-14)*, pages 1764–1772.

Geoffrey E Hinton, Nitish Srivastava, Alex Krizhevsky, Ilya Sutskever, and Ruslan R Salakhutdinov. 2012. Improving neural networks by preventing co-adaptation of feature detectors. *arXiv preprint arXiv:1207.0580*.

Sepp Hochreiter and Jürgen Schmidhuber. 1997. Long short-term memory. *Neural computation*, 9(8):1735–1780.

Zhiheng Huang, Wei Xu, and Kai Yu. 2015. Bidirectional lstm-crf models for sequence tagging. *arXiv preprint arXiv:1508.01991*.

Yoon Kim, Yacine Jernite, David Sontag, and Alexander M Rush. 2015. Character-aware neural language models. *arXiv preprint arXiv:1508.06615*.

Dan Klein, Joseph Smarr, Huy Nguyen, and Christopher D Manning. 2003. Named entity recognition with character-level models. In *Proceedings of the seventh conference on Natural language learning at HLT-NAACL 2003-Volume 4*, pages 180–183. Association for Computational Linguistics.

John Lafferty, Andrew McCallum, and Fernando CN Pereira. 2001. Conditional random fields: Probabilistic models for segmenting and labeling sequence data.

Wang Ling, Tiago Luís, Luís Marujo, Ramón Fernandez Astudillo, Silvio Amir, Chris Dyer, Alan W Black, and Isabel Trancoso. 2015. Finding function in form: Compositional character models for open vocabulary word representation. *arXiv preprint arXiv:1508.02096*.

Christopher D Manning. 2011. Part-of-speech tagging from 97% to 100%: is it time for some linguistics? In *Computational Linguistics and Intelligent Text Processing*, pages 171–189. Springer.

Tetsuji Nakagawa. 2004. Chinese and japanese word segmentation using word-level and character-level information. In *Proceedings of the 20th international conference on Computational Linguistics*, page 466. Association for Computational Linguistics.

Joel Nothman, Nicky Ringland, Will Radford, Tara Murphy, and James R Curran. 2013. Learning multilingual named entity recognition from wikipedia. *Artificial Intelligence*, 194:151–175.

Alexandre Passos, Vineet Kumar, and Andrew Mc-
Callum. 2014. Lexicon infused phrase embeddings for named entity resolution. *arXiv preprint
arXiv:1404.5367.*

Fuchun Peng, Dale Schuurmans, Shaojun Wang, and
Vlado Keselj. 2003. Language independent authorship attribution using character level language models. In *Proceedings of the tenth conference on European chapter of the Association for Computational
Linguistics-Volume 1*, pages 267–274. Association for
Computational Linguistics.

Slav Petrov, Dipanjan Das, and Ryan McDonald. 2011.
A universal part-of-speech tagset. *arXiv preprint
arXiv:1104.2086.*

Ilya Sutskever, Oriol Vinyals, and Quoc V Le. 2014.
Sequence to sequence learning with neural networks.
In *Advances in neural information processing systems*,
pages 3104–3112.

Wojciech Zaremba, Ilya Sutskever, and Oriol Vinyals.
2014. Recurrent neural network regularization. *arXiv
preprint arXiv:1409.2329.*

Xiang Zhang, Junbo Zhao, and Yann LeCun. 2015.
Character-level convolutional networks for text classification. In *Advances in Neural Information Processing Systems*, pages 649–657.

Ten Pairs to Tag – Multilingual POS Tagging via Coarse Mapping between Embeddings

Yuan Zhang, David Gaddy, Regina Barzilay, and Tommi Jaakkola
Computer Science and Artificial Intelligence Laboratory
Massachusetts Institute of Technology
{yuanzh, dgaddy, regina, tommi}@csail.mit.edu

Abstract

In the absence of annotations in the target language, multilingual models typically draw on extensive parallel resources. In this paper, we demonstrate that accurate multilingual part-of-speech (POS) tagging can be done with just a few (e.g., ten) word translation pairs. We use the translation pairs to establish a coarse linear isometric (orthonormal) mapping between monolingual embeddings. This enables the supervised source model expressed in terms of embeddings to be used directly on the target language. We further refine the model in an unsupervised manner by initializing and regularizing it to be close to the direct transfer model. Averaged across six languages, our model yields a 37.5% absolute improvement over the monolingual prototype-driven method (Haghighi and Klein, 2006) when using a comparable amount of supervision. Moreover, to highlight key linguistic characteristics of the generated tags, we use them to predict typological properties of languages, obtaining a 50% error reduction relative to the prototype model.[1]

1 Introduction

After two decades of study, the best performing multilingual methods can in some cases approach their supervised monolingual analogues. To reach this level of performance, however, multilingual methods typically make use of significant parallel resources such as parallel translations or bilingual dictionaries. These resources act as substitutes for explicit annotations available in the target language for supervised methods. It is less clear what can be done without extensive parallel resources. Indeed, the motivation for our paper comes from trying to understand how little parallel data is necessary for effective multilingual transfer.

In this paper, we demonstrate that only ten word translation pairs suffice for effective multilingual transfer of part-of-speech (POS) tagging. To achieve this we make use of and integrate two sources of statistical signal. First, we enable transfer of information from the source to target languages by establishing a coarse mapping between word embeddings in two languages on the basis of the few available translation pairs. The mapping is useful because of significant structural similarity of embedding spaces across languages. Second, we leverage the potential of unsupervised monolingual models to capture language-specific syntactic properties. The two sources of signals are largely complementary. Embeddings provide a coarse alignment between languages while unsupervised methods fine tune the correspondences in service of the task at hand. While unsupervised methods are fragile and challenging to estimate in general, they can be helpful if initialized and regularized properly, which is our focus.

In order to transfer annotations, we align monolingual embeddings between languages. However, a full fine-grained alignment is not possible with only ten translation pairs due to differences between the languages and variations across raw corpora from which the embeddings are derived. Instead, we re-

---

[1]Our code and data are available at https://github.com/yuanzh/transfer_pos.

strict the initial coarse mapping to be linear and isometric (orthonormal) so as to leave lengths and angles between the word vectors invariant. One advantage is that this preserves cosine similarity between vectors, which is viewed as a proxy for syntactic/semantic similarity (Mikolov et al., 2013a; Pennington et al., 2014; Herbelot and Vecchi, 2015). The resulting coarse alignment is then used to initialize and guide an unsupervised model over the target language.

Our unsupervised model is a feature-based hidden Markov model (HMM) expressed in terms of word embeddings. By establishing a common multilingual embedding space, we can map the source HMM estimated from supervised annotations directly to the target. The resulting "direct transfer" model should be further adjusted as languages differ, and the initial alignment obtained based on embeddings is imperfect. For this reason we cast the direct transfer model as a regularizer for the target HMM, and permit the HMM to further adjust the embedding transformations and relations of embeddings to the tags both globally (overall rotation and scaling) and locally (introducing small corrections).

Our two phase approach is simple to implement, performs well, and can be adapted to other NLP tasks. We evaluate our approach on POS tagging using the multilingual universal dependency treebanks (Nivre et al., 2016). Specifically, we use English as the source language and test on three Indo-European languages (Danish, German and Spanish) and three non-Indo-European-languages (Finnish, Hungarian and Indonesian). Experimental results show that our method consistently outperforms various baselines across languages. On average, our full model achieves 8% absolute improvement over the direct transfer counterpart. We also compare against a prototype-driven tagger (Haghighi and Klein, 2006) using 14 prototypes as supervision. Our model significantly outperforms Haghighi and Klein (2006)'s model by 37.5% (67.5% vs 30%).

We also introduce a novel task-based evaluation of automatic POS taggers, where tagger predictions are used to determine typological properties of the target language. This evaluation highlights key linguistic features of the generated tags. On this task, our model achieves 80% accuracy, yielding 50% error reduction relative to the prototype model.

2   Related Work

Multilingual POS Tagging   Prior work on multilingual POS tagging has mainly focused on the *tag projection* method (Yarowsky et al., 2001; Wisniewski et al., 2014; Duong et al., 2013; Duong et al., 2014; Täckström et al., 2013; Das and Petrov, 2011; Snyder et al., 2008; Naseem et al., 2009; Chen et al., 2011). All these approaches assume access to a large amount of parallel sentences to facilitate multilingual transfer. In our work, we focus on a more challenging scenario, in which we do not assume access to parallel sentences. Instead of projecting tag information via word alignment, the transfer in our model is driven by mapping multilingual embedding spaces. Kim et al. (2015) also use latent word representations for multilingual transfer. However, similarly to prior work, this representation is learned using parallel data.

The feasibility of POS tagging transfer without parallel data has been shown by Hana et al. (2004). The transfer is performed between typologically similar languages, which enables the model to directly transfer the transition probabilities from source to the target. Moreover, emission probabilities are hand-engineered to capture language-specific morphological properties. In contrast, our method does not require any language-specific knowledge on the target side.

Multilingual Word Embeddings   There is an expansive body of research on learning multilingual word embeddings (Gouws et al., 2014; Faruqui and Dyer, 2014; Lu et al., 2015; Lauly et al., 2014; Luong et al., 2015). Previous work has shown its effectiveness across a wide range of multilingual transfer tasks including tagging (Kim et al., 2015), syntactic parsing (Xiao and Guo, 2014; Guo et al., 2015; Durrett et al., 2012), and machine translation (Zou et al., 2013; Mikolov et al., 2013b). However, these approaches commonly require parallel sentences or bilingual lexicon to learn multilingual embeddings. Vulic and Moens (2015) have alleviated the requirements by inducing multilingual word embeddings directly from a document-aligned corpus such as a set of Wikipedia pages on the same theme but in different languages. However, they still used about ten thousands aligned documents as parallel supervision. Our work demonstrates that useful multilingual embeddings can be learned with a minimal amount of parallel supervision.

3 Multilingual POS Tagger

Our method is designed to operate in the regime where there are no parallel sentences or target annotations. We assume only a few, in our case ten, word translation pairs. This small number of translation pairs together with the tags that they carry from the source to the target do not provide sufficient information to train a reasonable supervised tagger, even for very close languages where word translations would be mostly one-to-one and tags fully preserved in translation. Other cues are necessary.

The few translation pairs provide just enough information to obtain a coarse global alignment between the source and target language embeddings. We limit the initial linear transformation between embeddings to isometric (orthonormal) mappings so as to preserve norms and angles (e.g., cosine similarities) between words. Once the embeddings are aligned, any source language model expressed in terms of embeddings can be mapped to a target language model. The approach is akin to direct transfer commonly applied in parsing (McDonald et al., 2011; Zeman and Resnik, 2008) though often with more information. We use the term "direct transfer" to mean the process where no further adjustment is performed beyond the immediate mapping via (coarsely) aligned embeddings.

Direct transfer is insufficient between languages that are syntactically (even moderately) divergent. Instead, we use the directly transferred model to initialize and regularize an unsupervised tagger. Specifically, we employ a feature-based HMM (Berg-Kirkpatrick et al., 2010) tagger for both the source and target languages with two important modifications. The emission probabilities in the source language HMM are expressed solely in terms of word embeddings (cf. skip-gram models). Such distributions can be directly transferred to the target domain. Our target language HMM is, however, equipped with additional adjustable parameters that can be learned in an unsupervised manner. These include parameters for modifying the initial global linear transformation between embeddings. Beyond this linear transformation, we also add "correction terms" to each tag-word pair that are in principle sufficient to specify any HMM. Both of these additional sets of parameters are regularized towards keeping the initial direct transfer model. As a result, our strongly governed unsupervised tagger can succeed where an unguided unsupervised tagger would typically fail.

In the remainder of this section, we describe the approach more formally, starting with the coarse alignment between embeddings, followed by the supervised feature-based HMM, and the unsupervised target language HMM.

3.1 Isometric Alignment of Word Embeddings

Here we find a linear transformation from the target language embeddings to the source language embeddings using the translation pairs. The resulting transformation permits us to directly apply any source language model on the target language, i.e., it enables direct transfer. To this end, let $V_s \in \mathbb{R}^{n_s \times d}$ and $V_t \in \mathbb{R}^{n_t \times d}$ be the word embeddings estimated for the source and target languages, respectively, with vocabulary sizes n_s and n_t. All the embeddings are of dimension d. The submatrices of embeddings pertaining to k anchor words (from translation pairs) are denoted as Σ_s and Σ_t, where $\Sigma_s, \Sigma_t \in \mathbb{R}^{k \times d}$.

We find a linear transformation $P \in \mathbb{R}^{d \times d}$ that best aligns the embeddings of the translation pairs in the sense of minimizing

$$||\Sigma_t P - \Sigma_s||^2 \tag{1}$$

subject to the **isometric** (orthonormal) constraint $P^T P = I$. We use the steepest descent algorithm (Abrudan et al., 2008) to solve this optimization problem.[2] Once P is available, we can map all the target language embeddings V_t to the source language space with $V_t P$. Note that since typically in our setting $k < d$ (e.g. $k = 10$) additional constraints such as isometry are required.

Motivation behind the Isometric Constraint We impose isometry on the linear transformation so as to preserve angles and lengths of the word vectors after the transformation. A number of recent studies have explored the use of cosine similarity of word

---

[2] Our implementation is based on the toolkit available at `http://legacy.spa.aalto.fi/sig-legacy/unitary_optimization/`.

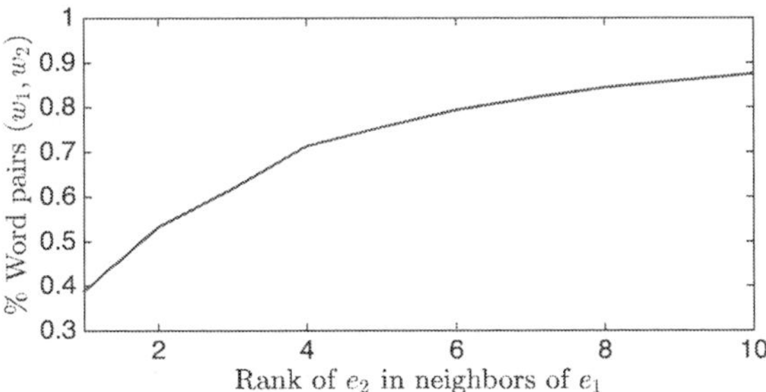

Figure 1: Cumulative fraction of word translation pairs among top 1,000 most frequent words where the nearest neighbor of a German word (vector) appears as the rth nearest neighbor after translation, measured in terms of their monolingual word embeddings.

vectors as a measure of semantic relations between words. Thus, for example, if two words have high cosine similarity in German (target), the corresponding words in English (source) should also be similar. To validate our isometric constraint further, we verify whether nearest neighbors are preserved in monolingual embeddings after translation. To this end, we take the top 1,000 most frequent words in German and their translations into English and ask whether nearest neighbors are preserved if measured in terms of their monolingual embeddings. For each word vector w_1 and its nearest neighbor w_2 in German, let e_1 and e_2 be the corresponding English vectors. We compute the rank of e_2 in the ordered list of nearest neighbors of e_1. As Figure 1 shows, in more than 50% of word pairs, e_2 is among the top-2 neighbors of e_1. In over 90% of the word pairs e_2 is among e_1's top-10 closest neighbors.

For the purposes of comparison (see Section 5), we introduce also a linear transformation without isometry. In other words, we find P that minimizes $||\Sigma_t P - \Sigma_s||^2$ via the **Moore–Penrose pseudoinverse** (Moore, 1920; Penrose, 1955). Specifically, let Σ_t^+ be the pseudoinverse of Σ_t. Then the solution takes the form $P = \Sigma_t^+ \Sigma_s$, and has the minimum Frobenius norm among all possible solutions.

3.2 Supervised Source Language HMM

Here we briefly describe how we train a supervised tagger on the source language. The resulting model, together with aligned embeddings, specifies the direct transfer model. It will also be used to initialize and guide the unsupervised tagger on the target lan-guage.

Our model has the same structure as the standard HMM but we replace the transition and emission probabilities with log-linear models (cf. feature-based HMM by Berg-Kirkpatrick et al. (2010)). The transition probabilities include all indicator features and therefore impose no additional constraints. The emission probabilities, in contrast, are expressed entirely in terms of word embeddings v_x as features. More formally, the emission probability of word x given tag y is given by

$$p_\theta(x|y) \propto \exp\{ v_x^T \mu_y \} \qquad (2)$$

Note that the parameters μ_y (one vector per tag) can be viewed as tag embeddings. This supervised tagging model is trained to maximize the joint log-likelihood with l_2-regularization over parameters. We use the L-BFGS (Liu and Nocedal, 1989) algorithm to optimize the parameters.

Once the HMM has been trained, we can specify the direct transfer model. It has the same transition probabilities but the emission probabilities are modified according to $p_\theta^{dt}(x|y) \propto \exp\{ v_x^T P \mu_y \}$ where v_x is now the monolingual target embedding, transformed into the source space via $v_x^T P$. We apply the Viterbi algorithm to predict the most likely POS tag sequence.

3.3 Unsupervised Target Language HMM

Our unsupervised HMM for the target language is strictly more expressive than the direct transfer model so as to better tailor it to the target lan-guage. Let v_x again be the monolingual target em-beddings estimated separately, prior to the HMMs. We map these vectors to the source language em-bedding space via $v_x^T P$ as discussed earlier, where P is already set and no longer considered a parame-ter. The form of the emission probabilities

$$p_\theta^t(x|y) \propto \exp\{v_x^T PM\mu_y + \theta_{x,y}\} \qquad (3)$$

includes two modifications to the direct transfer model. First, we have introduced an additional global linear transformation M to correct the initial alignment represented by P. Second, we include per-symbol parameters $\theta_{x,y}$ which, in principle, are capable of specifying any emission distribution on their own. The adjustable parameters in this model (denoted collectively θ) are M, $\{\boldsymbol{\mu}_y\}$, $\{\theta_{x,y}\}$, and the parameters pertaining to the transition probabilities. If we set $M = I$, $\theta_{x,y} = 0$ for all x and y, and borrow $\boldsymbol{\mu}_y$ and the transition parameters from the supervised HMM, then we recover the direct transfer model. Let θ_0 denote this setting of the parameters. In other words, the unsupervised HMM with initial parameters θ_0 is the direct transfer model.

Our approach include initializing $\theta = \theta_0$ and later regularizing θ to remain close to θ_0. The motivation behind this approach is two-fold. First, the initial alignment between embeddings was obtained only on the basis of the few available anchor words and may therefore need to be adjusted. Note that the linear transformation of embeddings now involves scaling and is no longer necessarily isometric. Second, the source and target languages differ and the embeddings are not strictly related to each other via any global linear transformation. We can interpret parameters $\theta_{x,y}$ as local (per word) non-linear deformations of the embedding vectors that specify the emission probabilities. We allow only small non-linear corrections by regularizing $\theta_{x,y}$ to remain close to zero, i.e., the values they have in θ_0.

Our unsupervised HMM is estimated by maximizing the regularized log-likelihood

$$L(\theta) = \sum_{i=1}^{n} \log P_\theta(\mathbf{x}_i) - \frac{\beta}{2}||\theta - \theta_0||_2^2 \quad (4)$$

where $\mathbf{x}_i$ is the ith target language sentence, $P_\theta(\mathbf{x}_i)$ is the HMM with parameters θ, and n is the number of sentences in the target text to be annotated. Since all the parameters in the model are in a log-linear form, we simply use the regularization parameter β. Once estimated, we use the Viterbi algorithm to predict the most likely POS tag sequence.

Estimation Details We maximize $L(\theta)$ using the Expectation-maximization (EM) algorithm. In the E-step, we evaluate expected counts $e_{y',y}$ for tag-tag and $e_{x,y}$ for word-tag pairs, using the forward-backward algorithm. The M-step searches for θ that maximizes

$$l(\theta) = \sum_{y',y} e_{y',y} \log p_\theta^t(y'|y) + \sum_{x,y} e_{x,y} \log p_\theta^t(x|y)$$
$$- \frac{\beta}{2}||\theta - \theta_0||_2^2 \quad (5)$$

The maximization can be be done via L-BFGS which involves computing the gradients of $\log p_\theta^t(y'|y)$ and $\log p_\theta^t(x|y)$ with respect to θ at every iteration. Because the conditional probabilities are expressed in a log-linear form, the gradients take on typical forms such as

$$\frac{dl(\theta)}{d\boldsymbol{\mu}_y} = \sum_x e_{x,y}(\boldsymbol{v}_x^T PM - \sum_{x'} p_\theta^t(x'|y)\boldsymbol{v}_{x'}^T PM)$$
$$- \beta(\boldsymbol{\mu}_y - \boldsymbol{\mu}_{0y})$$
$$\frac{dl(\theta)}{dM} = \sum_{x,y} e_{x,y}(\boldsymbol{P}^T \boldsymbol{v}_x \boldsymbol{\mu}_y^T - \sum_{x'} p_\theta^t(x'|y)\boldsymbol{P}^T \boldsymbol{v}_{x'} \boldsymbol{\mu}_y^T)$$
$$- \beta(M - I) \quad (6)$$

where $\boldsymbol{\mu}_{0y}$ are initial values for $\boldsymbol{\mu}_y$.

4   Experimental Setup

Dataset We evaluate our method on the latest Version 1.2 of the Universal Dependencies Treebanks (Nivre et al., 2016; McDonald et al., 2013). We use English as the source language and six other languages as targets. Specifically, we choose three Indo-European languages: Danish (da), German (de), Spanish (es), and three non-Indo-European languages: Finnish (fi), Hungarian (hu), Indonesian (id). All treebanks are annotated with the same universal POS tagset. In our work, we map proper nouns to nouns and map symbol marks[3] and interjections to a catch-all tag X because it is hard and unnecessary to disambiguate them in a low-resource learning scenario. After mapping, our tagset includes the following 14 tags: noun, verb, auxiliary verb, adjective, adverb, pronoun, determiner, adposition, numeral, conjunction, sentence conjunction, particle, punctuation mark, and a catch-all tag X. Note that this universal tagset contains two more tags than the traditional universal tagset proposed by Petrov et al. (2011): auxiliary verb and sentence conjunction. We follow the standard split of the treebanks for every language. For each target language, we use the sentences in the training set as unlabeled data, and evaluate on the testing set.

Word Embeddings To induce monolingual word embeddings, we use the processed Wikipedia text dumps (Al-Rfou et al., 2013) for each language.

---

[3]Examples of symbol mark include "-", "/" etc.

Language	English	Danish	German	Spanish	Finnish	Hungarian	Indonesian
Tokens (10^6)	1,888	44	687	399	66	89	41

Table 1: Number of tokens of the Wikipedia dumps used for inducing word embeddings.

While Wikipedia texts may contain parallel articles, we show in Table 1 that the amount of text varies significantly across languages. Smith et al. (2010) also demonstrated that parallel information in Wikipedia is very noisy. Therefore, direct translations are difficult to get from these texts. We use the `word2vec` tool with the skip-gram learning scheme (Mikolov et al., 2013a). In our experiments we use $d = 20$ for the dimension of word embeddings and $w = 1$ for the context window size of the skip-gram, which yields the best overall performance for our model. In our analysis, we also explore the impact of embedding dimension and window size.

Word Translation Pairs For each target language, we collect English translations for the top ten most frequent words in the training corpus. Our preliminary experiments show that this selection method performs the best. The selected words are typically from closed classes, such as punctuation marks, determiners and prepositions. We find translations using Wiktionary.[4]

Model Variants Our model varies along two dimensions. On one dimension, we use two different methods for inducing multilingual word embeddings: **Pseudoinverse** and **Isometric** alignment as described in Section 3.1. On the other dimension, we experiment with two different multilingual transfer models. We use **Direct Transfer** to denote our direct transfer model, and **Transfer+EM** for our unsupervised model trained in the target language.

Baselines We also compare against the prototype-driven method of Haghighi and Klein (2006). Specifically, we use the publicly available implementation provided by the authors.[5] Note that their model requires at least one prototype for each POS category. Therefore, we select 14 prototypes (the most frequent word from each category) for the baseline, while our method only uses ten translation pairs.

<hr>

[4]`https://www.wiktionary.org/`
[5]`http://code.google.com/p/` `prototype-sequence-toolkit/`

Evaluation Unlike other unsupervised methods, all models in our experiments can identify the label for each POS tag because of knowledge from either the source languages or prototypes. Therefore, we directly report the token-level POS accuracy for all experiments.

Other Details For all experiments, we use the following regularization weights: $\gamma = 0.001$ for supervised models learned on the source language and $\beta = 0.01$ for unsupervised models learned on the target language. During training, we also normalize the log-likelihood of labeled or unlabeled data by the total number of tokens. As a result, the magnitude of the objective value is independent of the corpus size, hence we do not need to tune the regularization weight for each target language. We run ten iterations of the EM algorithm.

5   Results

In this section, we first show the main comparison between the tagging performance of our model and the baselines. In addition, we include an experiment on typology prediction. In Section 5.2, we provide a more detailed analysis of model properties.

5.1   Main Results

Table 2 summarizes the results of the prototype baseline and different variations of our transfer model. Averaged across languages, our model significantly outperforms the prototype baseline by about 37.5% (67.5% vs 30%), demonstrating the effectiveness of multilingual transfer. Moreover, Table 2 shows that our full model (Transfer+EM with the isometric alignment mapping) consistently achieves the best performance compared to other model variations. Our model performs better on Indo-European languages than on other languages (72.9% vs. 62.1% on average), because Indo-European languages are linguistically more similar to the source language (English).

Impact of Training in the Target Language We observe that training on unlabeled data in the tar-

Method	Indo-European				Non-Indo-European			
	da	de	es	Avg.	fi	hu	id	Avg.
Prototype Model	41.3	25.5	28.7	31.8	8.2	44.5	30.1	27.6
Pseudoinverse								
Direct Transfer	56.7	49.4	68.4	58.2	54.3	60.1	57.7	57.4
Transfer+EM	64.4	65.8	74.9	68.4	57.5	**65.3**	62.7	61.8
Isometric Alignment								
Direct Transfer	59.8	55.4	67.4	60.9	54.4	61.4	57.2	57.7
Transfer+EM	**72.5**	**68.7**	**77.5**	**72.9**	**58.2**	63.4	**64.8**	**62.1**

Table 2: Token-level POS tagging accuracy (%) for different variants of our transfer model. We always use English as the source language. Target languages include Danish (da), German (de), Spanish (es), Finnish (fi), Hungarian (hu) and Indonesian (id). We average the results separately for Indo-European and non-Indo-European languages. The first row shows performance of the prototype-driven baseline (Haghighi and Klein, 2006). The rest shows results of our model when multilingual embeddings are induced with the pseudoinverse or isometric alignment method. "Direct Transfer" and "Transfer+EM" indicates our direct transfer model and our transfer model trained in the target language respectively.

get language (Transfer+EM model) consistently improves over the direct transfer counterpart. As the bottom part of Table 2 shows, running EM on unlabeled data yields an average of 12% absolute gain on Indo-European languages, while on non-Indo-European languages the gain is only 4.4%.

Impact of the Isometric Alignment Constraint As Table 2 shows, when we use Transfer+EM models, the isometric alignment method yields a 4.5% improvement over the pseudoinverse method (72.9% vs. 68.4%) on Indo-European languages. However, the improvement margin drops to 0.3% on non-Indo-European languages (62.1% vs. 61.8%). We hypothesis that this discrepancy is due to the difference in the degree of ambiguities of the anchor words across languages. For example, the anchor words of Spanish have an average of 1.5 possible translations to English, while for Indonesian the average ambiguity is 2.7. Therefore, the isometric assumption holds better and the EM algorithm finds a better local optimum for Indo-European languages than for non-Indo-European languages. We also observe a similar pattern in the direct transfer scenario.

Prediction of Linguistic Typology To assess the quality of automatically generated tags, we use them to determine typological properties of the target language. We predict values of the following five typological properties for each language: subject-

Tagging Method	Typology Accuracy
Prototype	60.0
Direct Transfer	66.7
Transfer + EM	80.0
Gold	93.3

Table 3: The accuracy (%) of typological properties prediction using the outputs from different taggers. "Gold" indicates the result using gold POS annotations.

verb, verb-object, adjective-noun, adposition-noun and demonstrative-noun. More specifically, the goal is to predict word ordering preferences such as whether an adjective comes before a noun (as in English) or after a noun (as in Spanish). We collect the true ordering preferences from "The World Atlas of Language Structure (WALS)" (Dryer et al., 2005). To make predictions, we train a multiclass support vector machine (SVM) classifier (Tsochantaridis et al., 2004) on a multilingual corpus using bigrams and trigrams of POS tags as features. The training data for SVM comes from a combination of the Universal Dependencies Treebanks, CoNLL-X, and CoNLL-07 datasets (Buchholz and Marsi, 2006; Nilsson et al., 2007), excluding all sentences in the target language. We train one classifier for each typological property, and make predictions for each of the six target languages. For evaluation, we directly report the overall accuracy on all 30 test cases (six languages combined with five typological prop-

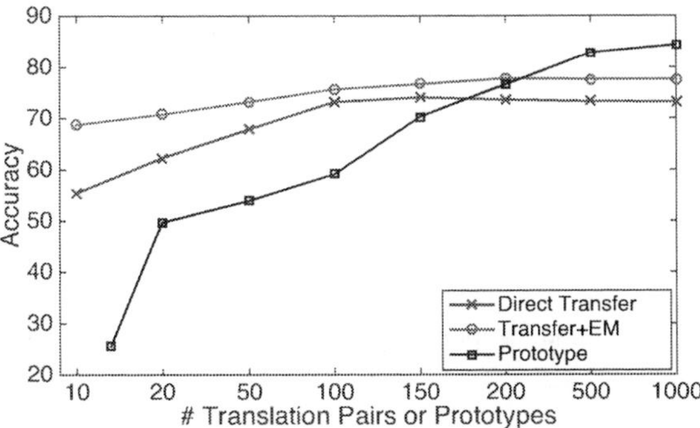

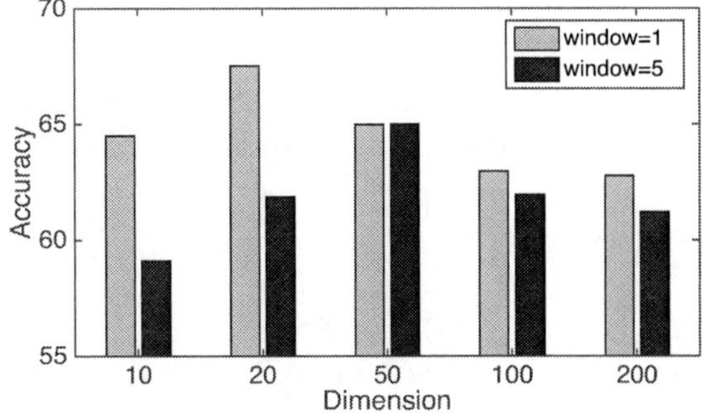

Figure 2: Accuracy of our models and the prototype baseline as a function of the amount of supervision, in German. x-axis is the number of translation pairs or prototypes used as supervision. Our models use multilingual embeddings induced with the isometric alignment method. The minimum number of prototypes used by the prototype baseline is 14.

Figure 3: The average tagging accuracy (%) with different embedding dimensions and context window sizes. The model is Transfer+EM with the isometric alignment projection method.

erties).

Table 3 shows the accuracy of predicting typological properties with different tagging models. "Gold" corresponds to the result with gold POS annotations and is an upper bound of the prediction accuracy. We observe that the typology prediction accuracy correlates with the tagging quality. With the output of our best model, we predict the correct values for 80% of the typological properties. This corresponds to a 50% error reduction relative to the prototype model.

5.2 Analyses

Impact of the Amount of Supervision Figure 2 shows the accuracy of the Direct Transfer, Transfer+EM models, and prototype baseline with different amounts of supervision in German. Specifically, the x-axis is the number of translation pairs or prototypes used as supervision. The numbers with ten pairs or prototypes are the same as that in Table 2. We automatically extract more translation pairs using the Europarl parallel corpus (Koehn, 2005) and select pairs based on the word frequency in the target language. For the prototype model, we select the most frequent words as prototypes based on annotations in the training data, and guarantee that each POS category has at least one prototype. Note that the minimum number of prototypes used by the prototype model is 14.

One particularly interesting observation is that our

model with ten pairs achieves an equivalent performance as that of the prototype-driven method with 150 prototypes. Multilingual transfer compensates for 15 times the amount of supervision. We also observe that the prototype-driven model outperforms our model when large amount of annotations are available. This can be explained by noise in the translation and the limitation from the linear embedding mapping process, which makes POS tags not preserve well across languages.

When comparing between our models, Figure 2 shows that Transfer+EM consistently improves over the Direct Transfer, while the gains are more profound in the low-supervision scenario. This is not surprising because with more translation pairs, we are able to induce higher quality multilingual embeddings, which is more beneficial to the direct transfer model.

Impact of Embedding Dimensions and Window Size Figure 3 shows the average accuracy across six target languages with different embedding dimensions and context window sizes. First, we observe that a small window size $w = 1$ consistently outperforms window size $w = 5$, demonstrating that smaller window sizes appear to produce word embeddings better for POS tagging. This observation is in line with the finding by Lin et al. (2015). Moreover, we obtain the best performance with dimension $d = 20$ when $w = 1$. On one hand, embeddings with smaller dimension (e.g. $d = 10$) have too little syntactic information for good POS tagging. On the other hand, if the embedding space has larger dimen-

Model	da	de	es	fi	hu	id	Average
All features	72.5	68.7	77.5	58.2	63.4	64.8	67.5
- Indicator features	70.8	64.8	73.9	53.7	62.9	56.8	63.8
- Transformation matrix M	60.2	65.6	73.2	58.6	59.6	70.8	64.7

Table 4: The accuracy (%) of our best Transfer+EM model with different feature sets, removing either indicator features or transformation matrix M at a time.

sion, the space will be more complex and mapping embedding spaces will be more difficult given only ten translation pairs. Therefore, we observe a performance drop with either smaller or larger dimensions.

Ablation Analysis on Features In our Transfer+EM model, we add indicator features and transformation matrix M to enhance the emission distribution (see Section 3.3). To analyze their contribution, we remove these features in turn and report the results in Table 4. Averaged over all languages, adding indicator features improves the accuracy by 3.7%, and adding a transformation matrix increases the accuracy by 2.8%.

6 Conclusions

In this paper, we demonstrate that ten translation pairs suffice for an effective multilingual transfer of POS tagging. Experimental results show that our model significantly outperforms the direct transfer method and the prototype baseline. The effectiveness of our approach suggests its potential application to a broader range of NLP tasks that require word-level multilingual transfer, such as multilingual parsing and machine translation.

Acknowledgments

The authors acknowledge the support of the U.S. Army Research Office under grant number W911NF-10-1-0533, and the support of the MIT EECS Super UROP program. We thank the MIT NLP group and the NAACL reviewers for their comments. Any opinions, findings, conclusions, or recommendations expressed in this paper are those of the authors, and do not necessarily reflect the views of the funding organizations.

References

Traian E. Abrudan, Jan Eriksson, and Visa Koivunen. 2008. Steepest descent algorithms for optimization under unitary matrix constraint. *IEEE Transaction on Signal Processing*, 56(3):1134–1147.

Rami Al-Rfou, Bryan Perozzi, and Steven Skiena. 2013. Polyglot: Distributed word representations for multilingual NLP. In *Proceedings of the Seventeenth Conference on Computational Natural Language Learning*, pages 183–192, Sofia, Bulgaria. Association for Computational Linguistics.

Taylor Berg-Kirkpatrick, Alexandre Bouchard-Côté, John DeNero, and Dan Klein. 2010. Painless unsupervised learning with features. In *Proceedings of the 2010 Annual Conference of the North American Chapter of the Association for Computational Linguistics*, pages 582–590. Association for Computational Linguistics.

Sabine Buchholz and Erwin Marsi. 2006. Conll-X shared task on multilingual dependency parsing. In *Proceedings of the Tenth Conference on Computational Natural Language Learning*, pages 149–164. Association for Computational Linguistics.

Desai Chen, Chris Dyer, Shay B Cohen, and Noah A Smith. 2011. Unsupervised bilingual POS tagging with markov random fields. In *Proceedings of the First Workshop on Unsupervised Learning in NLP*, pages 64–71. Association for Computational Linguistics.

Dipanjan Das and Slav Petrov. 2011. Unsupervised part-of-speech tagging with bilingual graph-based projections. In *Proceedings of the 49th Annual Meeting of the Association for Computational Linguistics*, pages 600–609. Association for Computational Linguistics.

Matthew S Dryer, David Gil, Bernard Comrie, Hagen Jung, Claudia Schmidt, et al. 2005. The world atlas of language structures.

Long Duong, Paul Cook, Steven Bird, and Pavel Pecina. 2013. Increasing the quality and quantity of source language data for unsupervised cross-lingual POS tagging. In *Sixth International Joint Conference on Natural Language Processing, IJCNLP 2013, Nagoya, Japan, October 14-18, 2013*, pages 1243–1249.

Long Duong, Trevor Cohn, Karin Verspoor, Steven Bird, and Paul Cook. 2014. What can we get from 1000 tokens? A case study of multilingual POS tagging for resource-poor languages. In *Proceedings of the 2014 Conference on Empirical Methods in Natural Language Processing*, pages 886–897.

Greg Durrett, Adam Pauls, and Dan Klein. 2012. Syntactic transfer using a bilingual lexicon. In *Proceedings of the 2012 Joint Conference on Empirical Methods in Natural Language Processing and Computational Natural Language Learning*, pages 1–11. Association for Computational Linguistics.

Manaal Faruqui and Chris Dyer. 2014. Improving vector space word representations using multilingual correlation. In *Proceedings of the 14th Conference of the European Chapter of the Association for Computational Linguistics*, pages 462–471.

Stephan Gouws, Yoshua Bengio, and Greg Corrado. 2014. Bilbowa: Fast bilingual distributed representations without word alignments. *arXiv preprint arXiv:1410.2455*.

Jiang Guo, Wanxiang Che, David Yarowsky, Haifeng Wang, and Ting Liu. 2015. Cross-lingual dependency parsing based on distributed representations. In *Proceedings of the 53rd Annual Meeting of the Association for Computational Linguistics*, pages 1234–1244.

Aria Haghighi and Dan Klein. 2006. Prototype-driven learning for sequence models. In *Proceedings of the 2006 Annual Conference of the North American Chapter of the Association for Computational Linguistics*, pages 320–327. Association for Computational Linguistics.

Jiri Hana, Anna Feldman, and Chris Brew. 2004. A resource-light approach to Russian morphology: Tagging Russian using Czech resources. In *EMNLP*, pages 222–229.

Aurélie Herbelot and Eva Maria Vecchi. 2015. Building a shared world: mapping distributional to model-theoretic semantic spaces. In *Proceedings of the 2015 Conference on Empirical Methods in Natural Language Processing*, pages 22–32. Association for Computational Linguistics.

Young-Bum Kim, Benjamin Snyder, and Ruhi Sarikaya. 2015. Part-of-speech taggers for low-resource languages using CCA features. In *Proceedings of the Empiricial Methods in Natural Language Processing*. Association for Computational Linguistics.

Philipp Koehn. 2005. Europarl: A parallel corpus for statistical machine translation. In *MT summit*, volume 5, pages 79–86.

Stanislas Lauly, Hugo Larochelle, Mitesh Khapra, Balaraman Ravindran, Vikas C Raykar, and Amrita Saha. 2014. An autoencoder approach to learning bilingual word representations. In *Advances in Neural Information Processing Systems*, pages 1853–1861.

Chu-Cheng Lin, Waleed Ammar, Chris Dyer, and Lori Levin. 2015. Unsupervised POS induction with word embeddings. *arXiv preprint arXiv:1503.06760*.

Dong C Liu and Jorge Nocedal. 1989. On the limited memory BFGS method for large scale optimization. *Mathematical programming*, 45(1-3):503–528.

Ang Lu, Weiran Wang, Mohit Bansal, Kevin Gimpel, and Karen Livescu. 2015. Deep multilingual correlation for improved word embeddings. In *Proceedings of the 2015 Conference of the North American Chapter of the Association for Computational Linguistics*.

Thang Luong, Hieu Pham, and Christopher D Manning. 2015. Bilingual word representations with monolingual quality in mind. In *Proceedings of the 1st Workshop on Vector Space Modeling for Natural Language Processing*, pages 151–159.

Ryan McDonald, Slav Petrov, and Keith Hall. 2011. Multi-source transfer of delexicalized dependency parsers. In *Proceedings of the Conference on Empirical Methods in Natural Language Processing*, pages 62–72. Association for Computational Linguistics.

Ryan T McDonald, Joakim Nivre, Yvonne Quirmbach-Brundage, Yoav Goldberg, Dipanjan Das, Kuzman Ganchev, Keith B Hall, Slav Petrov, Hao Zhang, Oscar Täckström, et al. 2013. Universal dependency annotation for multilingual parsing. In *Proceedings of the 51st Annual Meeting of the Association for Computational Linguistics*, pages 92–97. Association for Computational Linguistics.

Tomas Mikolov, Kai Chen, Greg Corrado, and Jeffrey Dean. 2013a. Efficient estimation of word representations in vector space. In *Proceedings of Workshop at ICLR*.

Tomas Mikolov, Quoc V Le, and Ilya Sutskever. 2013b. Exploiting similarities among languages for machine translation. *arXiv preprint arXiv:1309.4168*.

Eliakim H. Moore. 1920. On the reciprocal of the general algebraic matrix. *Bulletin of the American Mathematical Society*, 26(9):394–395.

Tahira Naseem, Benjamin Snyder, Jacob Eisenstein, and Regina Barzilay. 2009. Multilingual part-of-speech tagging: Two unsupervised approaches. *Journal of Artificial Intelligence Research*, 36:341–385.

Jens Nilsson, Sebastian Riedel, and Deniz Yuret. 2007. The CoNLL 2007 shared task on dependency parsing. In *Proceedings of the CoNLL shared task session of EMNLP-CoNLL*, pages 915–932.

Joakim Nivre, Marie-Catherine de Marneffe, Filip Ginter, Yoav Goldberg, Jan Hajič, Christopher Manning, Ryan McDonald, Slav Petrov, Sampo Pyysalo, Natalia Silveira, Reut Tsarfaty, and Daniel Zeman. 2016. Universal dependencies v1: A multilingual treebank collection. In *Proceedings of LREC*.

Jeffrey Pennington, Richard Socher, and Christopher D Manning. 2014. Glove: Global vectors for word representation. In *Proceedings of the Empiricial Methods in Natural Language Processing*, volume 12, pages 1532–1543.

Roger Penrose. 1955. A generalized inverse for matrices. In *Proceedings of the Cambridge Philosophical Society*, pages 406–413.

Slav Petrov, Dipanjan Das, and Ryan McDonald. 2011. A universal part-of-speech tagset. *arXiv preprint arXiv:1104.2086*.

Jason R Smith, Chris Quirk, and Kristina Toutanova. 2010. Extracting parallel sentences from comparable corpora using document level alignment. In *The 2010 Annual Conference of the North American Chapter of the Association for Computational Linguistics*, pages 403–411. Association for Computational Linguistics.

Benjamin Snyder, Tahira Naseem, Jacob Eisenstein, and Regina Barzilay. 2008. Unsupervised multilingual learning for POS tagging. In *Proceedings of the Conference on Empirical Methods in Natural Language Processing*, pages 1041–1050. Association for Computational Linguistics.

Oscar Täckström, Dipanjan Das, Slav Petrov, Ryan Mc-Donald, and Joakim Nivre. 2013. Token and type constraints for cross-lingual part-of-speech tagging. *Transactions of the Association for Computational Linguistics*, 1:1–12.

Ioannis Tsochantaridis, Thomas Hofmann, Thorsten Joachims, and Yasemin Altun. 2004. Support vector machine learning for interdependent and structured output spaces. In *Proceedings of the twenty-first international conference on Machine learning*, page 104. ACM.

Ivan Vulic and Marie-Francine Moens. 2015. Bilingual word embeddings from non-parallel document-aligned data applied to bilingual lexicon induction. In *Proceedings of the 53rd Annual Meeting of the Association for Computational Linguistics*. Association for Computational Linguistics.

Guillaume Wisniewski, Nicolas Pécheux, Souhir Gahbiche-Braham, and François Yvon. 2014. Cross-lingual part-of-speech tagging through ambiguous learning. In *Proceedings of the 2014 Conference on Empirical Methods in Natural Language Processing*, pages 1779–1785.

Min Xiao and Yuhong Guo. 2014. Distributed word representation learning for cross-lingual dependency parsing. *CoNLL-2014*, page 119.

David Yarowsky, Grace Ngai, and Richard Wicentowski. 2001. Inducing multilingual text analysis tools via robust projection across aligned corpora. In *Proceedings of the first international conference on Human language technology research*. Association for Computational Linguistics.

Daniel Zeman and Philip Resnik. 2008. Cross-language parser adaptation between related languages. In *IJC-NLP*, pages 35–42.

Will Y Zou, Richard Socher, Daniel M Cer, and Christopher D Manning. 2013. Bilingual word embeddings for phrase-based machine translation. In *Proceedings of the Empiricial Methods in Natural Language Processing*, pages 1393–1398.

Part-of-Speech Tagging for Historical English

Yi Yang and **Jacob Eisenstein**
School of Interactive Computing
Georgia Institute of Technology
Atlanta, GA 30308
{yiyang+jacobe}@gatech.edu

Abstract

As more historical texts are digitized, there is interest in applying natural language processing tools to these archives. However, the performance of these tools is often unsatisfactory, due to language change and genre differences. Spelling normalization heuristics are the dominant solution for dealing with historical texts, but this approach fails to account for changes in usage and vocabulary. In this empirical paper, we assess the capability of domain adaptation techniques to cope with historical texts, focusing on the classic benchmark task of part-of-speech tagging. We evaluate several domain adaptation methods on the task of tagging Early Modern English and Modern British English texts in the Penn Corpora of Historical English. We demonstrate that the Feature Embedding method for unsupervised domain adaptation outperforms word embeddings and Brown clusters, showing the importance of embedding the entire feature space, rather than just individual words. Feature Embeddings also give better performance than spelling normalization, but the combination of the two methods is better still, yielding a 5% raw improvement in tagging accuracy on Early Modern English texts.

1   Introduction

There is growing interest in applying natural language processing (NLP) techniques to historical texts (Piotrowski, 2012), with applications in information retrieval (Dougherty, 2010; Jurish, 2011), linguistics (Baron et al., 2009; Rayson et al., 2007), and the digital humanities (Hendrickx et al., 2011;

> **Original**: and drewe vnto hym all ryottours & wylde dysposed persones
> **Normalization**: and drew unto him all ryottours & wild disposed persons

Figure 1: An example sentence from Early Modern English and its VARD normalization.

Muralidharan and Hearst, 2013; Pettersson and Nivre, 2011). However, these texts differ from contemporary training corpora in a number of linguistic respects, including the lexicon (Giusti et al., 2007), morphology (Borin and Forsberg, 2008), and syntax (Eumeridou et al., 2004). This imposes significant challenges for modern NLP tools: for example, the accuracy of the CLAWS part-of-speech Tagger (Garside and Smith, 1997) drops from 97% on the British National Corpus to 82% on Early Modern English texts (Rayson et al., 2007). There are two main approaches that could improve the accuracy of NLP systems on historical texts: normalization and domain adaptation.

Normalization   Spelling normalization (also called canonicalization) involves mapping historical spellings to their canonical forms in modern languages, thus bridging the gap between contemporary training corpora and target historical texts. Figure 1 shows one historical sentence and its normalization by VARD (Baron and Rayson, 2008). Rayson et al. (2007) report an increase of about 3% accuracy on adaptation of POS tagging from Modern English texts to Early Modern English texts if the target texts were automatically normalized by the VARD system. However, normalization is not always a well-defined problem (Eisenstein,

Proceedings of NAACL-HLT 2016, pages 1318–1328,
San Diego, California, June 12-17, 2016. ©2016 Association for Computational Linguistics

2013), and it does not address the full range of linguistic changes over time, such as unknown words, morphological differences, and changes in the meanings of words (Kulkarni et al., 2015). In the example above, the word 'ryottours' is not successfully normalized to 'rioters'; the syntax is comprehensible to contemporary English speakers, but usages such as 'wild disposed' and 'drew unto' are sufficiently unusual as to pose problems for NLP systems trained on contemporary texts.

Domain adaptation A more generic machine learning approach is to apply unsupervised domain adaptation techniques, which transform the representations of the training and target texts to be more similar, typically using feature co-occurrence statistics (Blitzer et al., 2006; Ben-David et al., 2010). It is natural to think of historical texts as a distinct domain from contemporary training corpora, and Yang and Eisenstein (2014, 2015) show that the accuracy of historical Portuguese POS tagging can be significantly improved by domain adaption. However, we are unaware of prior work that empirically evaluates the efficacy of this approach on Early Modern English texts. Furthermore, historical texts are often associated with multiple metadata attributes (e.g., author, genre, and epoch), each of which may influence the text's linguistic properties. *Multi-domain adaptation* (Mansour et al., 2009) and *multi-attribute domain adaptation* (Joshi et al., 2013; Yang and Eisenstein, 2015) can potentially exploit these metadata attributes to obtain further improvements.

This paper presents the first comprehensive empirical comparison of effectiveness of these approaches for part-of-speech tagging on historical texts. We focus on the two historical treebanks of the Penn Corpora of Historical English — the Penn Parsed Corpus of Modern British English (Kroch et al., 2010, PPCMBE) and the Penn-Helsinki Parsed Corpus of Early Modern English (Kroch et al., 2004, PPCEME). These datasets enable a range of analyses, which isolate the key issues in dealing with historical corpora:

- In one set of analyses, we focus on the PPCMBE and the PPCEME corpora, training on more recent texts and testing on earlier texts.

This isolates the impact of language change on tagging performance.

- In another set of analyses, we train on the Penn Treebank (Marcus et al., 1993, PTB), and test on the historical corpora, using the tag mappings from Moon and Baldridge (2007). We apply the well-known Stanford CoreNLP tagger to this task (Manning et al., 2014), thus replicating the most typical situation for users of existing language technology.

- We show that FEMA, a domain adaptation algorithm that is specifically designed for sequence labeling problems (Yang and Eisenstein, 2015), achieves an increase of nearly 4% in tagging accuracy when adapting from the PTB to the PPCEME.

- We compare the impact of normalization with domain adaptation, and demonstrate that they are largely complementary.

- Error analysis shows that the improvements obtained by domain adaptation are largely due to better handling of out-of-vocabulary (OOV) tokens. Many of the most frequent errors on in-vocabulary (IV) tokens are caused by mismatches in the tagsets or annotation guidelines, and may be difficult to address without labeled data in the target domain.

2 Data

The Penn Corpora of Historical English consist of the Penn-Helsinki Parsed Corpus of Middle English, second edition (Kroch et al., 2010, PPCME2), the Penn-Helsinki Parsed Corpus of Early Modern English (Kroch et al., 2004, PPCEME), and the Penn Parsed Corpus of Modern British English (Kroch and Taylor, 2000, PPCMBE). The corpora are annotated with part-of-speech tags and syntactic parsing trees in an annotation style similar to that of the Penn Treebank. In this work, we focus on POS tagging the PPCMBE and the PPCEME.[1]

---

[1]Middle English is outside the scope of this paper, because it is sufficiently unintelligible to modern English speakers that texts such as Canterbury Tales are published in translation. In tagging Middle English texts, Moon and Baldridge (2007) apply bitext projection techniques from multilingual learning, rather than domain adaptation.

Period	# Sentence	# Token
1840-1914	17,770	322,255
1770-1839	23,462	427,424
1700-1769	16,083	343,024
Total	57,315	1,092,703

Table 1: Statistics of the Penn Parsed Corpus of Modern British English (PPCMBE), by time period.

Period	# Sentence	# Token
1640-1710	29,181	614,315
1570-1639	39,799	706,587
1500-1569	31,416	640,255
Total	100,396	1,961,157

Table 2: Statistics of the Penn Parsed Corpus of Early Modern English (PPCEME), by time period.

The Penn Parsed Corpus of Modern British English   The PPCMBE is a syntactically annotated corpus of text, containing roughly one million word tokens from documents written in the period 1700-1914. It is divided into three 70-year time periods according to the composition date of the works. Table 1 shows the statistics of the corpus by time period.[2] In contrast to the PTB, the PPCMBE contains text from a variety of genres, such as Bible, Drama, Fiction, and Letters.

The Penn-Helsinki Parsed Corpus of Early Modern English   The PPCEME is a collection of text samples from the Helsinki Corpus (Rissanen et al., 1993), as well as two supplements mainly consisting of text material by the same authors and from the same editions as the material in the Helsinki Corpus. The corpus contains nearly two million words from texts in the period from 1500 until 1710, and it is divided into three 70-year time periods similar to the PPCMBE corpus. The statistics of the corpus by time period is summarized in Table 2. The PPCEME consists of text from the same eighteen genres as the PPCMBE.

Penn Treebank Release 3   The Penn Treebank (Marcus et al., 1993) is the de facto standard syntactically annotated corpus for English,

---

[2]All the statistics in this section include punctuation, but exclude extra-linguistic material such as page numbers or token ID numbers.

which is used to train software such as Stanford CoreNLP (Manning et al., 2014). When using this dataset for supervised training, we follow Toutanova et al. (2003) and use WSJ sections 0-18 for training, and sections 19-21 for tuning. When applying unsupervised domain adaptation, we use all WSJ sections, together with texts from the PPCMBE and the PPCEME.

Tagsets   The Penn Corpora of Historical English (PCHE) use a tagset that differs from the Penn Treebank, mainly in the direction of greater specificity. Auxiliary verbs 'do', 'have', and 'be' all have their own tags, as do words like 'one' and 'else', due to their changing syntactic function over time. Overall, there are 83 tags in the PPCEME, and 81 in the PPCMBE, as compared with 45 in the PTB. Furthermore, the tags in the PCHE tagset are allowed to join constituent morphemes in compounds, yielding complex tags such as PRO+N (e.g., 'himself') and ADJ+NS (e.g., 'gentlemen').

To measure the tagging accuracy of PTB-trained taggers on the historical texts, we follow Moon and Baldridge (2007), who define a set of deterministic mappings from the PCHE tags to the PTB tagset. For simplicity, we first convert each complex tag to the simple form by only considering the first simple tag component (e.g., PRO+N to PRO and ADJ+NS to ADJ). This has little effect on the tagging performance, as the complex tags cover only slightly more than 1% of the tokens in the PCHE treebanks. Among the 83 tags, 74 mappings to the corresponding PTB tags are obtained from Moon and Baldridge (2007). We did our best to convert the other tags according to the tag description. The complete list of mappings is published in Appendix A.

3   Unsupervised Domain Adaptation

In typical usage scenarios, the user wants to tag some historical text but has no labeled data in the target domain (e.g., Muralidharan and Hearst, 2013). This best fits the paradigm of unsupervised domain adaptation, when labeled data from the source domain (e.g., the PTB) is combined with unlabeled data from the target domain. Representational differences between source and target domains can be a major source of errors in domain adaptation (Ben-

David et al., 2010), and so several representation learning approaches have been proposed.

The most straightforward approach is to replace lexical features with **word representations**, such as Brown clusters (Brown et al., 1992; Lin et al., 2012) or word embeddings (Turian et al., 2010), such as word2vec (Mikolov et al., 2013). Lexical features can then be replaced or augmented with the resulting word representations. This can assist in domain adaptation by linking out-of-vocabulary words to in-vocabulary words with similar distributional properties.

Word representations are suitable for adapting lexical features, but a more general solution is to adapt the entire feature representation. One such method is **Structural Correspondence Learning** (Blitzer et al., 2006, **SCL**). In SCL, we create artificial binary classification problems for thousands of cross-domain "pivot" features, and then use the weights from the resulting classifiers to project the instances into a new dense representation. We also consider a recently-published approach called **Feature Embedding** (FEMA), which achieves the state-of-the-art results on several POS tagging adaptation tasks (Yang and Eisenstein, 2015). The intuition of FEMA is similar to SCL and other prior work: it relies on co-occurrence statistics to link features across domains. Specifically, FEMA exploits the tendency of many NLP tasks to divide features into templates, and induces feature embeddings by using the features in each template to predict the active features in all other templates — just as the skipgram model learns word embeddings to predict neighboring words. The resulting embeddings can be substituted for the "one-hot" representation of each feature template, resulting in a dense, low-dimensional representation of each instance.

A further advantage of FEMA is that it can perform multi-attribute domain adaptation, enabling it to exploit the many metadata attributes (e.g., year, genre, and author) that are often associated with historical texts. This is done by accounting for the specific impact of each domain attribute on the feature predictors, and then building a domain-neutral representation from the common substructure that is shared across all domain attributes. In the experiments that follow, we use genre and epoch as domain attributes.

4 Experiments

We evaluate these unsupervised domain adaptation approaches on part-of-speech tagging for historical English (the PPCMBE and the PPCEME), in two settings: (1) temporal adaptation within each individual corpus, where we train POS taggers on the most modern data in the corpus and test on increasingly distant datasets; (2) adaptation of English POS tagging from modern news text to historical texts. The first setting focuses on temporal differences, and eliminates other factors that may impair tagging performance, such as different annotation schemes and text genres. The second setting is the standard and well-studied evaluation scenario for POS tagging, where we train on the Wall Street Journal (WSJ) text from the PTB and test on historical texts. In addition, we evaluate the effectiveness of the VARD normalization tool (Baron and Rayson, 2008) for improving POS tagging performance on the PPCEME corpus.

4.1 Experimental Settings

The datasets used in the experiments are described in § 2. All the hyperparameters are tuned on development data in the source domain. In the case where there is no specific development dataset (adaptation within the historical corpora), we randomly sample 10% sentences from the training datasets for hyperparameter tuning.

4.1.1 Baseline systems

We include two baseline systems for POS tagging: a classification-based support vector machine (SVM) tagger and a bidirectional maximum entropy Markov model (MEMM) tagger. Specifically, we use the L_2-regularized L_2-loss SVM implementation in the scikit-learn package (Pedregosa et al., 2011) and L_2-regularized bidirectional MEMM implementation provided by Stanford CoreNLP (Toutanova et al., 2003; Manning et al., 2014).

Following Yang and Eisenstein (2015), we apply the feature templates defined by Ratnaparkhi (1996) to extract the basic features for all taggers. There are three broad types of templates: five lexical feature templates, eight affix feature templates, and three orthographic feature templates.

Task	baseline		SCL	Brown	word2vec	FEMA	
	SVM	MEMM (Stanford)				single embedding	attribute embeddings (error reduction)
Modern British English (training from 1840-1914)							
→ 1770-1839	96.30	96.57	96.42	96.45	96.44	96.80	**96.84** (15%)
→ 1700-1769	94.57	94.83	95.07	95.15	94.85	95.65	**95.75** (22%)
AVERAGE	95.43	95.70	95.74	95.80	95.64	96.23	**96.30** (19%)
Early Modern English (training from 1640-1710)							
→ 1570-1639	93.62	93.98	94.23	94.36	94.18	95.01	**95.20** (25%)
→ 1500-1569	87.59	87.47	89.39	89.73	89.30	91.40	**91.63** (33%)
AVERAGE	90.61	90.73	91.81	92.05	91.74	93.20	**93.41** (30%)

Table 3: Accuracy results for temporal adaptation in the PPCMBE and the PPCEME of historical English. Percentage error reduction is shown for the best-performing method, FEMA-attribute.

4.1.2 Domain adaptation systems

We consider the unsupervised domain adaptation methods described in § 3: structural correspondence learning (SCL), Brown clustering, word2vec,[3] and FEMA, which we train in both the single embedding mode (FEMA-single), where metadata attributes are ignored, and in multi-attribute mode (FEMA-attribute), where metadata attributes are used. The domain adaptation models are trained on the union of the (unlabeled) source and target datasets. This ensures that there are no out-of-vocabulary items for the word or feature embeddings.

Following Yang and Eisenstein (2015), we do not learn feature embeddings for the three orthographic feature templates: as each orthographic feature template represents only a binary value, it is unnecessary to replace it with a much longer numerical vector. The learned representations are then concatenated with the basic surface features to form the augmented representations. For computational reasons, the domain adaptation systems are all based on the SVM tagger, as pilot studies showed that Viterbi tagging offers minimal improvements.

4.1.3 Parameter tuning

We choose the SVM regularization parameter by sweeping the range $\{0.1, 0.3, 0.5, 0.8, 1.0\}$. Following Blitzer et al. (2006), we consider pivot features that appear more than 50 times in all the domains for SCL. We empirically fix the number of singular vectors of the projection matrix K to 25,

---

[3]https://code.google.com/p/word2vec/

and also employ feature normalization and rescaling, as these settings yield best performance in prior work. The number of Brown clusters is chosen from the range $\{50, 100, 200, 400\}$. For FEMA and word2vec, we choose embedding sizes from the range $\{50, 100, 200, 300\}$ and fix the numbers of negative samples to 15. The window size for training word embeddings is set as 5. Finally, we adopt the same regularization penalty for all the attribute-specific embeddings of FEMA, which is selected from the range $\{0.01, 0.1, 1.0, 10.0\}$. All parameters were tuned on development data in the source domain. We train the Stanford MEMM tagger using the default configuration file.

4.2 Temporal Adaptation

In the temporal adaptation setting, we work within each corpus, training on the most recent section, and evaluating on the two earlier sections. For PPCMBE, the source domain is the period from 1840 to 1914; for PPCEME, the source domain is the period from 1640 to 1710. All earlier texts are treated as target domains. We transform the tags to the PTB tagset for evaluation, so that results can be compared with the next experiment, in which the PTB is used for supervision.

Settings We randomly sample 10% sentences from the training data as the development data for optimizing hyperparameters, and then retrain the models on the full training data using the best parameters. For FEMA, we consider domain attributes for 70-year temporal periods and genres, resulting in a total of 21 attributes for each corpus. The numbers of pivot features used in SCL are 4400 and 5048 for the PPCMBE and the PPCEME respectively. The best number of Brown clusters is 200, and the best embedding sizes are 200 and 100 for word2vec and FEMA.

Results As shown in Table 3, accuracies are significantly improved by domain adaptation, especially for the PPCEME. English spelling had become mostly uniform and stable since around 1700 (Baron et al., 2009), which may explain why improvements on the PPCMBE are relatively modest, especially in the 1770-1839 epoch. Among the two baseline systems, MEMM performs slightly better than SVM, showing a small benefit to structured prediction. Among the domain adaptation algorithms, FEMA clearly outperforms SCL, Brown clustering and word2vec, with an averaged increase of about 0.5% and 1.5% accuracies on the PPCMBE and the PPCEME test sets respectively. The metadata attribute information boosts performance by a small but consistent margin, 0.1-0.2% on average.

4.3 Adaptation from the Penn Treebank

Newspaper text is the primary data source for training modern NLP systems. For example, most "off-the-shelf" English POS taggers (e.g., the Stanford Tagger (Toutanova et al., 2003), SVM-Tool (Giménez and Marquez, 2004), and CRFTagger (Phan, 2006)) are trained on the WSJ portion of the Penn Treebank, which is composed of professionally-written news text from 1989. This motivates this evaluation scenario, in which we train the tagger on the Penn Treebank WSJ data and apply it to historical English texts, using all sentences of the PPCMBE and PPCEME for testing.

Settings The feature representations are trained on the union of the PTB and the PPCEME. The domain attributes for FEMA are set to include the three corpora themselves (PTB, PPCMBE, and PPCEME), and the genre attributes in the historical corpora. Note that all sentences in the Penn Treebank WSJ data belong to the same genre (news). For SCL, we use the same threshold of 50 occurrences for pivot features, and include 8089 features that pass this threshold. PTB WSJ sections 19-21 are used for

parameter tuning: we find that the best number of Brown clusters is 200, and the optimum embedding sizes are 200 and 100 for word2vec and FEMA.

Spelling normalization Spelling variants lead to a high percentage of out-of-vocabulary (OOV) tokens in historical texts, which poses problems for POS tagging. We normalize the PPCEME sentences using VARD (Baron and Rayson, 2008), a widely used spelling normalization tool that has been proven to improve performance on POS tagging (Rayson et al., 2007) and syntactic parsing (Schneider et al., 2014). VARD is designed specifically for Early Modern English spelling variation, and additional labeled data and training are required for other forms of spelling variation, which we do not consider here. Following Schneider et al. (2014), we utilize VARD's auto-normalization function with a 50% normalization threshold, achieving a balance between precision and recall. At this threshold, a total of 12% (236298/1961157) of the tokens in the PPCEME are normalized.[4]

Results As shown in Table 4, this task is considerably more difficult, with even the best systems achieving accuracies that are nearly 15% worse than in-domain training. Nonetheless, domain adaptation can help: FEMA improves performance by 1.3% on the PPCMBE data, and by 3.8% on the unnormalized PPCEME data. Spelling normalization also helps, improving the baseline systems by more than 2.5%. The combination of spelling normalization and domain adaptation gives an overall improvement in accuracy from 74.2% to 79.1%. The relative error reduction is lower than in the temporal adaptation setting: only 19% at best, versus 30% error reduction in temporal adaptation. This is because there are now at least two sources of error — language change and tagset mismatch — and unsupervised domain adaptation cannot address mismatches in the tag set.

5 Analysis

As expected, the Early Modern English dataset (PPCEME) is considerably more challenging than the Modern British English dataset (PPCMBE): the

---

[4]We only consider 1 : 1 mappings, and ignore 328 normalizations corresponding to 1 : n mappings.

Target	Normalized	baseline		SCL	Brown	word2vec	FEMA	
		SVM	MEMM (Stanford)				single embedding	attribute embeddings (error reduction)
PPCMBE	No	81.12	81.35	81.66	81.65	81.75	82.34	**82.46** (7%)
PPCEME	No	74.15	74.34	75.89	76.04	75.85	77.77	**77.92** (15%)
PPCEME	Yes	76.73	76.87	77.61	77.65	77.76	78.85	**79.05** (19%*)

Table 4: Accuracy results for adapting from the PTB to the PPCMBE and the PPCEME of historical English. *Error reduction for the normalized PPCEME is computed against the unnormalized SVM accuracy, showing total error reduction.

baseline accuracy is 7% worse on the PPCEME than the PPCMBE. However, the PPCEME is also more amenable to domain adaptation, with FEMA offering considerably larger improvements. One reason is that the PPCEME has many more out-of-vocabulary (OOV) tokens: 23%, versus 9.2% in the PPCMBE. Both domain adaptation and normalization help to address this specific issue, and they yield further improvements when used in combination. This section offers further insights on the sources of errors and possibilities for improvement on the PPCEME data.

5.1 Feature Ablation

Table 5 presents the results of feature ablation experiments for the non-adapted SVM tagger. Word context features are important for obtaining good accuracies on both IV and OOV tokens. Affix features, particularly suffix features, are crucial for the OOV tokens. The orthographic features are shown to be nearly irrelevant, as long as affix features are present. Overall, the high percentage of OOV tokens can be a major source of errors, as the tagging accuracy on OOV tokens is below 50% in our best baseline system. Note that these results are for a classification-based tagger; while the Viterbi-based MEMM tagger performs only marginally better overall ($\sim 0.2\%$ improvement), it is possible that its error distribution might be different due to the advantages of structured prediction.

5.2 Error Analysis

The accuracy on out-of-vocabulary (OOV) tokens is generally low, and spelling variation is a major source of OOV tokens. For instance, 'ye' and 'thy', the older forms of 'the' and 'your', are often incorrectly tagged as NN and JJ in the PPCEME. In general, the per-tag accuracies are roughly correlated

Feature set	IV	OOV	All
All features	81.68	48.96	74.15
− word context	79.69	38.62	70.23
− prefix	81.61	46.11	73.43
− suffix	81.36	38.13	71.40
− affix	81.22	34.40	70.44
− orthographic	81.68	48.92	74.14

Table 5: Tagging accuracies of adaptation of our baseline SVM tagger from the PTB to the PPCEME in ablation experiments.

with the percentages of OOV tokens. Some exceptions including VB, NNP and NNS, where the affix features can be very useful for tagging OOV tokens.

That said, the cross-domain accuracy on in-vocabulary (IV) tokens is also low, at roughly 80% when adapting from the PTB to the PPCEME. A major source of error here is the mismatch in annotation schemes between the two datasets, which is only partially addressed by a deterministic tag mapping. Table 6 presents the SVM accuracy per tag, and the most common error correspondingly. Most of the errors shown in the table are owing to different annotations of the same token in the two corpora.

One major cause of errors is in misalignments of punctuations and their POS tags. For example, in the PPCEME, 16.6% of commas are labeled as . (sentence-final punctuation), and 12.3% periods are labeled as , (sentence-internal punctuation); these punctuations are less ambiguous in the PTB. The historical corpora lack special tags for colons and ellipses, which are present in the PTB. In contrast to the PTB, there is no distinction between opening quotation mark and closing quotation mark in the PPCEME. Moon and Baldridge (2007) avoid these difficulties by mapping all the punctuation tokens

Tag	% of OOV	Accuracy	Most common error
IN	6.93	82.79	to/TO
NN	48.39	64.74	Lord/NNP
DT	3.45	94.62	that/IN
PRP	13.57	78.80	other/JJ
,	0.41	87.86	./.
JJ	32.20	48.60	all/DT
CC	1.98	91.29	for/IN
RB	26.22	65.74	such/JJ
.	0.56	54.43	,/,
VB	34.69	75.06	have/VBP
NNP	58.91	88.31	god/NN
NNS	59.12	73.88	Lords/NNPS
VBD	25.87	81.93	quoth/NN
VBN	37.75	63.09	said/VBD
PRP$	13.57	85.49	thy/JJ

Table 6: Accuracy (recall) rates per tag with the SVM model, for the 15 most common tags. For each gold category, the most common error word and predicted tag are shown.

to a single tag. We did not follow their setting because it would lead to a significant change of test data. However, it should be noted that these "errors" are not particularly meaningful for linguistic analysis, and could easily be addressed by heuristic post-processing.

The tagging performance is also impaired by the different annotations of many common words. For example, in the PTB, more than 99.9% of token 'to' are labeled as TO, but in the PCHE this word can also be labeled as IN, distinguishing the infinitive marker from the preposition. The words 'all', 'any' and 'every' are annotated as quantifiers in the PCHE; this tag is mapped to JJ, but these specific words are all labeled as DT in the PTB. A simple remapping from Q to DT leads to an increase of 0.78% baseline accuracy; it is possible that other changes to the tag mappings of Moon and Baldridge (2007) might yield further improvements, but a more systematic approach would be outside the bounds of *unsupervised* domain adaptation.

5.3 Improvements from Normalization

As shown above, the tagging accuracy decreases from 81.7% on IV tokens to 49.0% on OOV tokens. Spelling normalization helps to increase the accuracy by transforming OOV tokens to IV tokens. After normalization, the OOV rate for the PPCEME

System	IV	OOV	All
SVM	81.68	48.96	74.15
SCL	82.01	55.45	75.89
Brown	81.81	56.76	76.04
word2vec	81.79	56.00	75.85
FEMA-single	82.30	62.63	77.77
FEMA-attribute	82.34	63.16	77.92

Table 7: Tagging accuracies of domain adaptation models from the PTB to the PPCEME.

falls from 23.0% to 13.5%, corresponding to a reduction of 41.5% OOV tokens. Normalization is not perfectly accurate, and the tagging performance for IV tokens drops slightly to 81.2% on IV tokens. But due to the dramatic decrease in the number of OOV tokens, normalization improves the overall accuracy by more than 2.5%. We also observe performance drops on tagging OOV tokens after normalization (49.0% to 48.1%), which suggests that the remaining unnormalized OOV tokens are the tough cases for both normalization and POS tagging.

5.4 Improvements from Domain Adaptation

As presented in Table 7, the tagging accuracies are increased on both IV and OOV tokens with the domain adaptation methods. Compared against the baseline tagger, FEMA-attribute achieves an absolute improvement of 14% in accuracy on OOV tokens. SCL performs slightly better than Brown clustering and word2vec on IV tokens, but worse on OOV tokens. By incorporating metadata attributes, FEMA-attribute performs better than FEMA-single on OOV tokens, though the accuracies on IV tokens are similar. Interestingly, the venerable method of Brown clustering (slightly) outperforms both word2vec and SCL.

We further study the relationship between domain adaptation and spelling normalization by looking into the errors corrected by both approaches. Domain adaptation yields larger improvements than spelling normalization on both IV and OOV tokens, although as noted above, the approaches are somewhat complementary. The results show that among the 60,928 error tokens corrected by VARD, 60% are also corrected by FEMA-attribute, while the remaining 40% would be left uncorrected by the domain adaptation technique. Conversely, among the errors corrected by FEMA-attribute, 38% are also corrected by VARD, while the remaining 62% would be left uncorrected. The overlap of reduced errors is because both approaches exploit similar sources of information, including affixes and local word contexts.

6 Related Work

Domain adaptation Early work on domain adaptation focuses on supervised setting, in which some amount of labeled instances are available in the target domain (Jiang and Zhai, 2007; Daumé III, 2007; Finkel and Manning, 2009). Unsupervised domain adaptation is more challenging but attractive in many applications, and several representation learning methods have been proposed for addressing this problem. Structural Correspondence Learning (Blitzer et al., 2006, SCL) and marginalized denoising autoencoders (Chen et al., 2012, mDA) seek cross-domain representations that are useful to predict a subset of features in the original instances, called pivot features. Schnabel and Schütze (2014) directly induce distributional representations for POS tagging based on local left and right neighbors of the token. More recent work trains cross-domain representations with neural networks, with additional objectives such as minimizing errors in the source domain and maximizing domain confusion loss (Ganin and Lempitsky, 2015; Tzeng et al., 2015). We show the Feature Embedding model, which is specifically designed for NLP problems with feature templates (Yang and Eisenstein, 2015), achieves strong performance on historical adaptation tasks.

Historical texts Historical texts differ from modern texts in spellings, syntax and semantics, posing significant challenges for standard NLP systems, which are usually trained with modern news text. Numerous resources have been created for overcoming the difficulties, including syntactically annotated corpora (Kroch et al., 2004; Kroch et al., 2010; Galves and Faria, 2010) and spelling normalization tools (Giusti et al., 2007; Baron and Rayson, 2008). Most previous work focuses on normalization, which can significantly increase tagging accuracy on historical English (Rayson et al., 2007) and German (Scheible et al., 2011). Similar improvements have been obtained for syntactic parsing (Schneider et al., 2014). Domain adaptation offers an alternative approach which is more generic — for example, it can be applied to any corpus without requiring the design of a set of normalization rules. As shown above, when normalization is possible, it can be combined with domain adaptation to yield better performance than that obtained by either approach alone.

7 Conclusion

Syntactic analysis is a key first step towards processing historical texts, but it is confounded by changes in spelling and usage over time. We empirically evaluate several unsupervised domain adaptation approaches for POS tagging of historical English texts. We find that domain adaptation methods significantly improve the tagger performance on two historical English treebanks, with relative error reductions of 30% in the temporal adaptation setting. FEMA outperforms other domain adaptation approaches, showing the importance of adapting the entire feature vector, rather than simply using word embeddings. Normalization and domain adaptation combine to yield even better performance, with a total of 5% raw accuracy improvement over a baseline classifier in the most difficult setting. Error analysis reveals that tagset mismatch is the most common source of errors for in-vocabulary words. We hope that our work encourages further research on domain adaptation for historical texts and provides useful baselines in these efforts.

Acknowledgments This research was supported by National Science Foundation award 1349837, and by the National Institutes of Health under award number R01GM112697-01. We thank the reviewers for their helpful feedback.

References

Alistair Baron and Paul Rayson. 2008. Vard2: A tool for dealing with spelling variation in historical corpora. In *Postgraduate conference in corpus linguistics*.

Alistair Baron, Paul Rayson, and Dawn Archer. 2009. Word frequency and key word statistics in corpus linguistics. *Anglistik*, 20(1):41–67.

Shai Ben-David, John Blitzer, Koby Crammer, Alex Kulesza, Fernando Pereira, and Jennifer Wortman

Vaughan. 2010. A theory of learning from different domains. *Machine learning*, 79(1-2):151–175.

John Blitzer, Ryan McDonald, and Fernando Pereira. 2006. Domain adaptation with structural correspondence learning. In *Proceedings of Empirical Methods for Natural Language Processing (EMNLP)*, pages 120–128.

Lars Borin and Markus Forsberg. 2008. Something old, something new: A computational morphological description of old swedish. In *LREC 2008 workshop on language technology for cultural heritage data (LaTeCH 2008)*, pages 9–16.

Peter F Brown, Peter V Desouza, Robert L Mercer, Vincent J Della Pietra, and Jenifer C Lai. 1992. Class-based n-gram models of natural language. *Computational linguistics*, 18(4):467–479.

Minmin Chen, Z. Xu, Killian Weinberger, and Fei Sha. 2012. Marginalized denoising autoencoders for domain adaptation. In *Proceedings of the International Conference on Machine Learning (ICML)*.

Hal Daumé III. 2007. Frustratingly easy domain adaptation. In *Proceedings of the Association for Computational Linguistics (ACL)*, Prague.

William C Dougherty. 2010. The Google Books Project: will it make libraries obsolete? *The Journal of Academic Librarianship*, 36(1):86–89.

Jacob Eisenstein. 2013. What to do about bad language on the internet. In *Proceedings of the North American Chapter of the Association for Computational Linguistics (NAACL)*, pages 359–369, Atlanta, GA.

Eugenia Eumeridou, Blaise Nkwenti-Azeh, and John McNaught. 2004. An analysis of verb subcategorization frames in three special language corpora with a view towards automatic term recognition. *Computers and the Humanities*, 38(1):37–60.

Jenny R. Finkel and Christopher Manning. 2009. Hierarchical bayesian domain adaptation. In *Proceedings of the North American Chapter of the Association for Computational Linguistics (NAACL)*, pages 602–610, Boulder, CO.

Charlotte Galves and Pablo Faria. 2010. Tycho Brahe Parsed Corpus of Historical Portuguese. http://www.tycho.iel.unicamp.br/~tycho/corpus/en/index.html.

Yaroslav Ganin and Victor Lempitsky. 2015. Unsupervised domain adaptation by backpropagation. In *Proceedings of the International Conference on Machine Learning (ICML)*.

Roger Garside and Nicholas Smith. 1997. A hybrid grammatical tagger: Claws4. *Corpus annotation: Linguistic information from computer text corpora*, pages 102–121.

Jesús Giménez and Lluis Marquez. 2004. SVMTool: A general POS tagger generator based on support vector machines. In *Proceedings of the Language Resources and Evaluation Conference*.

Rafael Giusti, A Candido, Marcelo Muniz, Lívia Cucatto, and Sandra Aluísio. 2007. Automatic detection of spelling variation in historical corpus. In *Proceedings of the Corpus Linguistics Conference (CL)*.

Iris Hendrickx, Michel Généreux, and Rita Marquilhas. 2011. Automatic pragmatic text segmentation of historical letters. In *Language Technology for Cultural Heritage*, pages 135–153. Springer.

Jing Jiang and ChengXiang Zhai. 2007. Instance weighting for domain adaptation in nlp. In *Proceedings of the Association for Computational Linguistics (ACL)*, Prague.

Mahesh Joshi, Mark Dredze, William W. Cohen, and Carolyn P. Rosé. 2013. What's in a domain? multi-domain learning for multi-attribute data. In *Proceedings of the North American Chapter of the Association for Computational Linguistics (NAACL)*, pages 685–690, Atlanta, GA.

Bryan Jurish. 2011. *Finite-state canonicalization techniques for historical German*. Ph.D. thesis, Universitätsbibliothek.

Anthony Kroch and Ann Taylor. 2000. Penn-Helsinki Parsed Corpus of Middle English, second edition. http://www.ling.upenn.edu/hist-corpora/PPCME2-RELEASE-3/index.html.

Anthony Kroch, Beatrice Santorini, and Ariel Diertani. 2004. Penn-Helsinki Parsed Corpus of Early Modern English. http://www.ling.upenn.edu/hist-corpora/PPCEME-RELEASE-2/index.html.

Anthony Kroch, Beatrice Santorini, and Ariel Diertani. 2010. The Penn Parsed Corpus of Modern British English. http://www.ling.upenn.edu/hist-corpora/PPCMBE-RELEASE-1/index.html.

Vivek Kulkarni, Rami Al-Rfou, Bryan Perozzi, and Steven Skiena. 2015. Statistically significant detection of linguistic change. In *Proceedings of International Conference on World Wide Web (WWW)*, pages 625–635.

Yuri Lin, Jean-Baptiste Michel, Erez Lieberman Aiden, Jon Orwant, Will Brockman, and Slav Petrov. 2012. Syntactic annotations for the google books ngram corpus. In *Proceedings of the ACL 2012 system demonstrations*, pages 169–174.

Christopher D. Manning, Mihai Surdeanu, John Bauer, Jenny Finkel, Steven J. Bethard, and David McClosky.

2014. The Stanford CoreNLP natural language processing toolkit. In *Proceedings of 52nd Annual Meeting of the Association for Computational Linguistics: System Demonstrations*, pages 55–60.

Yishay Mansour, Mehryar Mohri, and Afshin Rostamizadeh. 2009. Domain adaptation with multiple sources. In *Neural Information Processing Systems (NIPS)*, pages 1041–1048.

Mitchell P. Marcus, Mary Ann Marcinkiewicz, and Beatrice Santorini. 1993. Building a large annotated corpus of English: The Penn Treebank. *Computational Linguistics*, 19(2):313–330.

Tomas Mikolov, Ilya Sutskever, Kai Chen, Greg S Corrado, and Jeff Dean. 2013. Distributed representations of words and phrases and their compositionality. In *Neural Information Processing Systems (NIPS)*, pages 3111–3119, Lake Tahoe.

Taesun Moon and Jason Baldridge. 2007. Part-of-speech tagging for middle english through alignment and projection of parallel diachronic texts. In *Proceedings of Empirical Methods for Natural Language Processing (EMNLP)*, pages 390–399.

Aditi Muralidharan and Marti A Hearst. 2013. Supporting exploratory text analysis in literature study. *Literary and linguistic computing*, 28(2):283–295.

F. Pedregosa, G. Varoquaux, A. Gramfort, V. Michel, B. Thirion, O. Grisel, M. Blondel, P. Prettenhofer, R. Weiss, V. Dubourg, J. Vanderplas, A. Passos, D. Cournapeau, M. Brucher, M. Perrot, and E. Duchesnay. 2011. Scikit-learn: Machine learning in Python. *Journal of Machine Learning Research*, 12:2825–2830.

Eva Pettersson and Joakim Nivre. 2011. Automatic verb extraction from historical swedish texts. In *Proceedings of the 5th ACL-HLT Workshop on Language Technology for Cultural Heritage, Social Sciences, and Humanities*, pages 87–95.

Xuan-Hieu Phan. 2006. CRFTagger: CRF English POS Tagger. `http://crftagger.sourceforge.net`.

Michael Piotrowski. 2012. Natural language processing for historical texts. *Synthesis Lectures on Human Language Technologies*, 5(2):1–157.

Adwait Ratnaparkhi. 1996. A maximum entropy model for part-of-speech tagging. In *Proceedings of Empirical Methods for Natural Language Processing (EMNLP)*, pages 133–142.

Paul Rayson, Dawn Archer, Alistair Baron, Jonathan Culpeper, and Nicholas Smith. 2007. Tagging the bard: Evaluating the accuracy of a modern pos tagger on early modern english corpora. In *Corpus Linguistics Conference*.

Matti Rissanen, Merja Kytö, and Minna Palander-Collin. 1993. *Early English in the computer age: Explorations through the Helsinki Corpus*. Number 11. Walter de Gruyter.

Silke Scheible, Richard J Whitt, Martin Durrell, and Paul Bennett. 2011. Evaluating an 'off-the-shelf' POS-tagger on early modern German text. In *Proceedings of the 5th ACL-HLT workshop on language technology for cultural heritage, social sciences, and humanities*, pages 19–23.

Tobias Schnabel and Hinrich Schütze. 2014. Flors: Fast and simple domain adaptation for part-of-speech tagging. *Transactions of the Association of Computational Linguistics*, 2:51–62.

Gerold Schneider, Hans Martin Lehmann, and Peter Schneider. 2014. Parsing early and late modern english corpora. *Literary and Linguistic Computing*.

Kristina Toutanova, Dan Klein, Christopher D. Manning, and Yoram Singer. 2003. Feature-rich part-of-speech tagging with a cyclic dependency network. In *Proceedings of the North American Chapter of the Association for Computational Linguistics (NAACL)*.

Joseph Turian, Lev Ratinov, and Yoshua Bengio. 2010. Word Representation: A Simple and General Method for Semi-Supervised Learning. In *Proceedings of the Association for Computational Linguistics (ACL)*, pages 384–394, Uppsala, Sweden.

Eric Tzeng, Judy Hoffman, Trevor Darrell, and Kate Saenko. 2015. Simultaneous deep transfer across domains and tasks. In *Proceedings of the IEEE International Conference on Computer Vision (ICCV)*, pages 4068–4076.

Yi Yang and Jacob Eisenstein. 2014. Fast easy unsupervised domain adaptation with marginalized structured dropout. In *Proceedings of the Association for Computational Linguistics (ACL)*, Baltimore, MD.

Yi Yang and Jacob Eisenstein. 2015. Unsupervised multi-domain adaptation with feature embeddings. In *Proceedings of the North American Chapter of the Association for Computational Linguistics (NAACL)*, Denver, CO.

Statistical Modeling of Creole Genesis

Yugo Murawaki

Graduate School of Informatics, Kyoto University

Yoshida-honmachi, Sakyo-ku, Kyoto, 606-8501, Japan

`murawaki@i.kyoto-u.ac.jp`

Abstract

Creole languages do not fit into the traditional tree model of evolutionary history because multiple languages are involved in their formation. In this paper, we present several statistical models to explore the nature of creole genesis. After reviewing quantitative studies on creole genesis, we first tackle the question of whether creoles are typologically distinct from non-creoles. By formalizing this question as a binary classification problem, we demonstrate that a linear classifier fails to separate creoles from non-creoles although the two groups have substantially different distributions in the feature space. We then model a creole language as a mixture of source languages plus a special *restructurer*. We find a pervasive influence of the restructurer in creole genesis and some statistical universals in it, paving the way for more elaborate statistical models.

1 Introduction

While most linguistic applications of computational phylogeny rely on lexical data (Gray and Atkinson, 2003; Bouckaert et al., 2012), there is a growing trend to make use of typological data (Tsunoda et al., 1995; Dunn et al., 2005; Teh et al., 2008; Longobardi and Guardiano, 2009; Murawaki, 2015). One advantage of typological features over lexical traits (cognates) is that they allow us to compare an arbitrary pair of languages even if they do not share enough cognates. For this reason, they have the potential of uncovering external relations involving language isolates and tiny language families such as Ainu, Basque, and Japanese.

However, our understanding of typological changes is far from satisfactory in at least two respects. First, typological changes are less intuitive than the birth and death of a lexical trait. Modeling word-order change with a single transition matrix (Maurits and Griffiths, 2014), for example, appears to be an oversimplification because some complex mechanisms must be hidden behind the changes (Murawaki, 2015).

The second point, the main focus of this paper, is that it is not clear whether typological data fit into the traditional tree model for a group of languages, which has long been used as the default choice to summarize evolutionary history (Schleicher, 1853). To be precise, regardless of whether typological features are involved, linguists have viewed the tree model with suspicion. A central problem of the tree model is its assumption that after a branching event, two resultant languages evolve completely independently. However, linguists have noted that horizontal contact is a constitutive part of evolutionary history. Various models for contact phenomena have been proposed to address this problem, including the wave theory (Schmidt, 1872) and the gravity model (Trudgill, 1974). As for linguistic typology, areal linguistics has worked on the diffusion of typological features across languages within a geographical area (Campbell, 2006).

In this paper, we study creole languages as an extreme case of non-tree-like evolution (Wardhaugh and Fuller, 2015). A creole is developed as a result of intense contact between multiple languages: typically one socioculturally dominant language (superstrate) and several low-prestige languages (*sub-*

Proceedings of NAACL-HLT 2016, pages 1329–1339,
San Diego, California, June 12-17, 2016. ©2016 Association for Computational Linguistics

strates). Superstrates are also known as *lexifiers* because the lexicon of a creole is largely derived from its superstrate. In spite of this, the grammar of a creole is drastically different from that of its lexifier. It is often said that creole grammars are simpler than non-creole ones although it is not easy to measure grammatical simplicity.

Creoles are not irrelevant to historical linguistics because some have speculated about the plausibility of creole status for Middle English (Bailey and Maroldt, 1977) and (pre-)Old Japanese (Kawamoto, 1974; Akiba-Reynolds, 1984; Kawamoto, 1990) while they have been criticized harshly by others.

This controversy can only be settled by fully understanding creole genesis, or the question of how creoles emerge, which also remains unresolved (Wardhaugh and Fuller, 2015). One theory called the gradualist hypothesis suggests their staged development from pidgin languages. A pidgin arises when speakers of different languages with no common language try to have a makeshift conversation, which results in a drastic simplification of grammar called *pidgin formation*. A pidgin is then acquired by children as their first language and is transformed into a fully functional language. This process of grammatical elaboration is known as *creole formation*.

We follow Bakker, Daval-Markussen and colleagues in taking data-driven approaches to this problem (Bakker et al., 2011; Daval-Markussen and Bakker, 2012; Daval-Markussen, 2013). They argue that creoles are typologically distinct from non-creoles. They compare four theories of creole genesis:

1. *Superstratist*. The lexifier plays a major role in creole genesis.

2. *Substratist*. Substrates do, instead of the lexifier.

3. *Feature pool*. Both the lexifier and substrates, but nothing else, provide a feature pool from which each feature value of a creole is selected.

4. *Universalist*. Innate ability of humans to create language is emphasized. The hypothetical linguistic universals for creole formation are called *restructuring universals*.

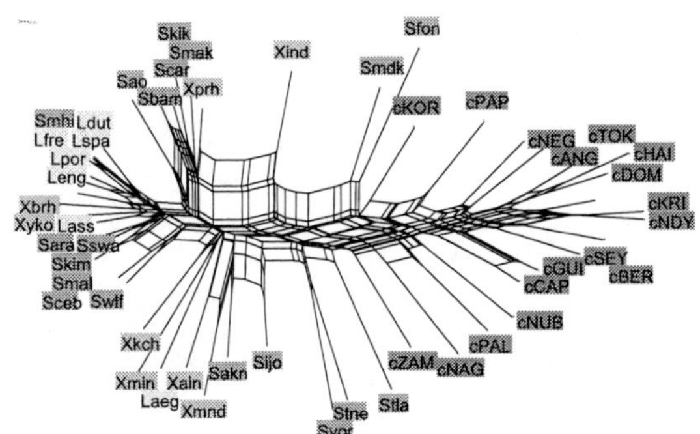

Figure 1: NeighborNet graph of creoles (c), lexifiers (L), substrates (S) and other non-creole languages (X). A language type (c/L/S/X) is followed by a three-letter language code. The bottom-up clustering (i.e., basically tree-building) method produced a cluster of creoles on the right. We reproduced Figure 5 of Daval-Markussen and Bakker (2012) using their online supplementary materials.

To test these explanations, they apply NeighborNet (Bryant and Moulton, 2004), a bottom-up, distance-based clustering method developed in the field of computational biology. By demonstrating that, as in Figure 1, creoles form a cluster distinguishable from lexifiers, substrates and other non-creole languages, they argue for the universalist position and for creole distinctiveness.

However, we find both theoretical and methodological problems in their discussion. Theoretically, the synchronic question of creole distinctiveness is confused with the diachronic question of creole genesis. If creoles are distinct from non-creoles, then something specific to creoles (e.g., restructuring universals) would play a role, but not vice versa. It is logically possible that even with restructuring universals, creoles are indistinguishable from (a subgroup of) non-creoles. Methodologically speaking, NeighborNet does not straightforwardly explain fundamentally non-tree-like evolution because it does assume tree-like evolution even though it represents conflicting signals with reticulations.

We begin by addressing the question of creole (non-)distinctiveness. Whether one is distinct from another is straightforwardly formalized as a binary classification problem. We show that an SVM classifier fails to separate creoles from non-creoles. Fol-

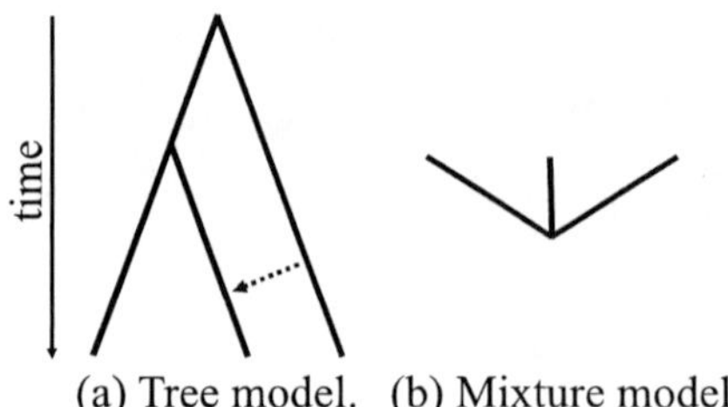

(a) Tree model.   (b) Mixture model.

Figure 2: Schematic comparison of two approaches to creole genesis.

lowing a practice in population genetics, we visualize the data using principal component analysis (PCA). The result suggests that although creoles have a substantially different distribution from non-creoles, they nevertheless overlap.

Next, we propose to model creole genesis with mixture models. In this approach, a creole is stochastically generated by mixing its lexifier, substrate(s) plus a special *restructurer*. Conceptually, this is the opposite of the tree model, as illustrated in Figure 2. Specifically, we present two Bayesian models. The first one considers one mixing proportion per creole, and the other decomposes the proportions into per-feature and per-creole factors. Our experimental results suggest that the restructurer dominates creole genesis, dismissing the superstratist, substratist and feature pool theories. We also find some statistical universals in the restructurer although we refrain from identifying them as *restructuring* universals. In this way, we represent a first step toward understanding the complex process of creole genesis through statistical models.

2   Related Work

2.1   Population Genetics

Like Bakker, Daval-Markussen and colleagues (Bakker et al., 2011; Daval-Markussen and Bakker, 2012; Daval-Markussen, 2013), we borrow ideas from computational biology. For reasons unknown to us, they chose clustering models that basically assume tree-like evolution (Saitou and Nei, 1987; Bryant and Moulton, 2004). However, creole genesis is more comparable to models that explicitly take into account genetic admixture (i.e., contact phenomena). See Jones et al. (2015), for example, to take a look at standard practices in population genetics.

Population genetic analysis of genotype data (binary sequences comparable to sets of linguistic features) can be grouped into two types: population-level and individual-level analysis. Populations, such as Sardinian, Yoruba and Japanese, are predefined sets of individuals. Population-level analysis utilizes genetic variation within a population (Patterson et al., 2012). From a modeling point of view, languages are more comparable to individuals. Although a language is spoken by a population, no linguistic data available are comparable to *a set of* individuals.

Individual-level analysis, where population labels are used only for the purpose of visualization, is often done using PCA and admixture analysis. PCA is used for dimensionality reduction: by selecting the first two principal components, high-dimensional sequences are projected onto an informative two-dimensional diagram (Patterson et al., 2006).

Admixture analysis (Pritchard et al., 2000; Alexander et al., 2009) closely resembles topic models, most notably Latent Dirichlet Allocation (LDA) (Blei et al., 2003), in NLP. It assumes that each individual is a mixture of K ancestral components (i.e., topics). One difference is that while each LDA topic is associated with a single word distribution (K distributions in total), each SNP (i.e., feature type) has its own distribution ($K \times J$ distributions in total for sequences with length J).

2.2   Linguistic Typology and Non-tree-like Evolution

Like lexical data, typological features are usually analyzed with a tree model, but Reesink et al. (2009) are a notable exception. They applied admixture analysis to Australian and Papuan languages, for which tree-building techniques had not been successful. They related inferred ancestral components to putative prehistoric dispersals and contacts.

Independently of biologically-inspired studies, Daumé III (2009) incorporated linguistic areas into a phylogenetic tree. In his Bayesian generative model, each feature of a language has a latent variable which determines whether it is derived from an areal cluster or the tree. Thus his model can be seen as a mixture model.

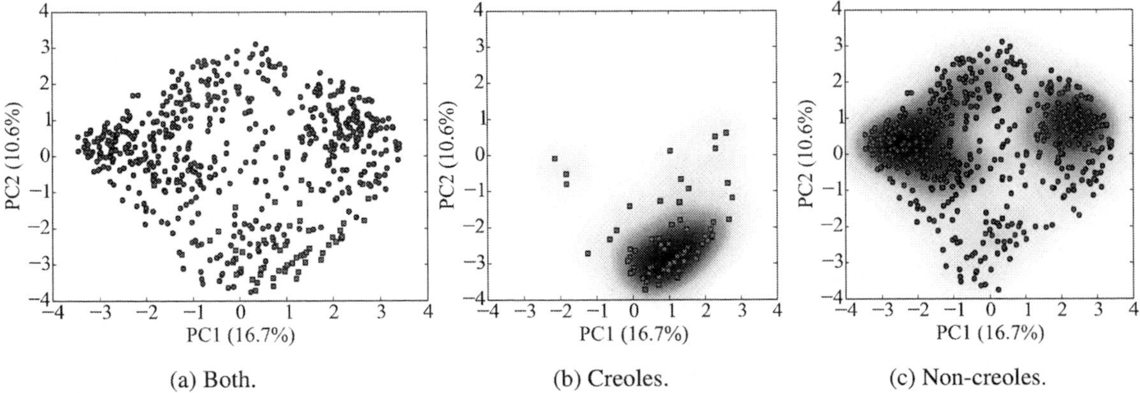

(a) Both.   (b) Creoles.   (c) Non-creoles.

Figure 3: PCA of creoles (red squares) and non-creoles (green circles) with explained variance in the labels of the axes. (a) Scatterplot of both types of languages. (b) Kernel density estimates (KDEs) of creoles. (c) KDEs of non-creoles.

3 Data and Preprocessing

We used the online edition[1] of the Atlas of Pidgin and Creole Language Structures (APiCS) (Michaelis et al., 2013), a database of pidgin and creole languages. It was larger than the datasets of Bakker et al. (2011). As of 2015, it contained 76 languages (104 varieties). It was essentially a pidgin-and-creole version of the online edition[2] of the World Atlas of Language Structures (WALS) (Haspelmath et al., 2005), but it contained sociolinguistic features, phonological inventories and example texts in addition to typological features.

As APiCS did not mark creoles, we used the sociolinguistic feature "Ongoing creolization of pidgins" as a criterion to select creoles. Specifically, we filtered out languages whose feature value was neither "Not applicable (because the language is not a pidgin)" nor "Widespread."

In APiCS, 48 out of 130 typological features were mapped to WALS features. We used these features to combine creoles from APiCS with non-creoles from WALS. Since the WALS database was sparse, we selected languages for which at least 30% of the features were present. As a result, we obtained 64 creoles and 541 non-creoles.

We imputed missing data using the R package *missMDA* (Josse et al., 2012). It handled missing values using multiple correspondence analy-

sis (MCA). Specifically, we used the `imputeMCA` function to predict missing feature values.

When investigating creole distinctiveness, we used binary representations of features. Using a one-of-K encoding scheme, we transformed 48 categorical features into 220 binary features.

Our mixture models require each creole to be associated with a lexifier and substrate(s). Unfortunately, APiCS described these languages in an obscure way (and many of them are indeed not fully resolved). We had no choice but to manually select several modern languages as *proxies* for them. For simplicity, we chose only one substrate per creole, but it is not difficult to extend our model for multiple substrates. We are aware that these are oversimplification, but we believe they would be adequate for a proof-of-concept demonstration.

4 Creole Non-distinctiveness

4.1 Binary Classification

To determine whether creoles are distinct from non-creoles, we apply a linear SVM classifier to the typological data. Here, linearity is assumed for two reasons. First, since the supposed distinctiveness is explained by restructuring universals, there is no way for creoles to have an XOR-like distribution. Second, Daval-Markussen (2013) claims that as few as three features are sufficient to distinguish creoles from non-creoles. If this is correct, it is expected that given 48 categorical features, even a simple lin-

---

[1] http://apics-online.info/
[2] http://wals.info/

		System	
		C	**NC**
Reference	**C**	54	10
	NC	7	534

Table 1: Confusion matrix of binary classification. C stands for creoles and NC for non-creoles.

ear classifier can work nearly perfectly.

The classifier is trained to classify whether a given language, represented by binarized features, is a creole ($+1$) or non-creole (-1). We use 5-fold cross validation with grid search to tune hyperparameters.

In our experiments, the accuracy, recall, precision and F1-measure were 97.2%, 88.5%, 84.4% and 86.4%, respectively. Table 1 shows the confusion matrix. We can see that the classifier failed to separate creoles from non-creoles. Although the classifier worked well, borderline cases remained.

4.2 PCA

For exploratory analysis and visualization, we applied PCA to creoles and non-creoles, again represented by binarized features. Figure 3 depicts the scatterplot of the first two principal components. We can see that creoles were characterized by quite a different distribution from that of non-creoles. The creoles were concentrated on the lower center while most non-creoles belonged to one of two clusters in the middle. However, the distribution of creoles did overlap with that of non-creoles.

Having a closer look at the diagram, we found that Negerhollands (Dutch), Cape Verdean Creole of Brava (Portuguese) and Vincentian Creole (English) were among the most "typical" creoles (lexifiers in parentheses). Tok Pisin (English) and Bislama (English) were at the periphery of the cluster. The outliers on the upper left included Korlai (Portuguese) while Kikongo-Kituba (Bantu) lay on the upper right.

On the other hand, "creole-like" non-creoles included Chontal Maya (a Mayan language of Mexico), Mussau (an Oceanic language of Papua New Guinea),[3] Catalan and other European languages. The non-creole cluster on the middle left consisted of Japanese, Kannada, Maltese and others. An-

---

[3]Interestingly, Mussau is noted for contact-induced changes (Brownie, 2012).

other non-creole cluster on the middle right included Swahili, Hawaiian and Khmer. The creoleless upper central area was occupied by Lalo (Sino-Tibetan), Maninka (Western) (Mande in West Africa), Salt-Yui (Trans-New Guinea) among others.

5 Mixture Models for Creole Genesis

5.1 Basic Idea

Forsaking the quest for synchronic distinctiveness, we take a more direct approach to the diachronic question of creole genesis. Since multiple languages are involved in creole genesis, it is reasonable to apply a mixture model. We assume that a creole is stochastically generated by mixing three sources: (1) a lexifier, (2) a substrate and (3) a global *restructurer*. Under this assumption, the main question is with what proportions these sources are mixed.

An unusual property of our model as a mixture model is that not only outcomes (creoles) but most sources (lexifiers and substrates) are observed. We only need to infer the restructurer. Thus another question is what the restructurer looks like.

Note that our model is constructed such that it does not commit to a particular theory of creole genesis. If the superstratist theory is correct, then lexifiers would dominate the inferred mixing proportions. The same is true of the substratist theory. Similarly, the feature pool theory entails that the restructurer only occupies negligible portions. Also note that even if the restructurer plays a significant role, it does not necessarily imply the universalist position. The restructurer is a set of catch-all feature distributions for those which are explained neither by the lexifier nor by the substrate (that is why we avoid calling it restructuring universals). In order for it to be linguistic universals, it must show some consistent patterns in its distributions.

5.2 MONO Model

Our idea is materialized in two Bayesian generative models. The first one, called MONO, is similar to the STRUCTURE algorithm of admixture analysis (Pritchard et al., 2000).[4]

---

[4]As seen in Section 2.1, MONO is more similar to STRUCTURE than to LDA in that each feature type has its own distributions. The difference is that while STRUCTURE infers all K global components, MONO always has one global component

Every language in the model is represented by a sequence of categorical features. The number of possible values varies among feature types. For feature j of creole i, the latent assignment variable $z_{i,j}$ determines from which source the feature is derived, a lexifier (L), a substrate (S) or the restructurer (R). Each creole i is associated a priori with a lexifier and a substrate. Let $y_{i,j,\mathrm{L}}$ and $y_{i,j,\mathrm{S}}$ be the values of feature j of creole i's lexifier and substrate, respectively. If the source is the lexifier (or substrate), the creole simply copies $y_{i,j,\mathrm{L}}$ (or $y_{i,j,\mathrm{S}}$). For the sake of uniformity, we can think of a lexifier (or substrate) as a set of feature distributions each of which concentrates all probability mass on its observed value (i.e., the δ function). The remaining source, the restructurer, is a set of categorical feature distributions each of which is drawn from a Dirichlet prior.

The assignment variable $z_{i,j}$ is generated from θ_i, which in turn is generated from a Dirichlet prior. $\theta_i = (\theta_{i,\mathrm{L}}, \theta_{i,\mathrm{S}}, \theta_{i,\mathrm{R}})$ is the parameter of a categorical distribution which specifies the mixing proportion of the three sources for creole i.[5]

More concretely, the generative story of MONO is as follows:

1. For each feature type $j \in \{1, \cdots, J\}$ of the restructurer:

   (a) draw a distribution from a symmetric Dirichlet distribution $\phi_j \sim \mathrm{Dir}(\beta_j)$

2. For each creole $i \in \{1, \cdots, N\}$:

   (a) draw a mixing proportion from a symmetric Dirichlet distribution $\theta_i \sim \mathrm{Dir}(\alpha_i)$

   (b) then for each feature type $j \in \{1, \cdots, J\}$:

       i. draw a topic assignment $z_{i,j} \sim \mathrm{Categorical}(\theta_i)$

       ii. draw a feature value

$$x_{i,j} \sim \begin{cases} \delta(y_{i,j,\mathrm{L}}) & \text{if } z_{i,j} = \mathrm{L} \\ \delta(y_{i,j,\mathrm{S}}) & \text{if } z_{i,j} = \mathrm{S} \\ \mathrm{Categorical}(\phi_j) & \text{if } z_{i,j} = \mathrm{R} \end{cases}$$

As usual, we marginalize out ϕ_j and θ_i using conjugacy of Dirichlet and categorical distributions (Griffiths and Steyvers, 2004). We use Gibbs

and two local, observed components.

[5] By letting another categorical distribution subdivide $\theta_{i,\mathrm{S}}$, we can incorporate multiple substrates into the model.

sampling to infer $z_{i,j}$, whose probability conditioned on the rest is proportional to

$$\begin{cases} \left(\alpha_i + c_{i,\mathrm{L}}^{-(i,j)}\right) \mathrm{I}(x_{i,j} = y_{i,j,\mathrm{L}}) & \text{if } z_{i,j} = \mathrm{L} \\[4pt] \left(\alpha_i + c_{i,\mathrm{S}}^{-(i,j)}\right) \mathrm{I}(x_{i,j} = y_{i,j,\mathrm{S}}) & \text{if } z_{i,j} = \mathrm{S} \\[4pt] \left(\alpha_i + c_{i,\mathrm{R}}^{-(i,j)}\right) \dfrac{\beta_j + c_{\mathrm{R},j,x_{i,j}}^{-(i,j)}}{B_j + c_{\mathrm{R},j,*}^{-(i,j)}} & \text{if } z_{i,j} = \mathrm{R} \end{cases} \quad (1)$$

where I is an indicator function, $B_j = \sum \beta_j$, $c_{i,k}^{-(i,j)}$ is the number of assignments for creole i, except $z_{i,j}$, whose values are k, and $c_{\mathrm{R},j,l}^{-(i,j)}$ is the number of observed features for feature type j, except $x_{i,j}$, that is derived from the restructurer and has l as its value. Intuitively, the first term gives priority to the source from which many other features of creole i are derived. The second term concerns how likely the source generates the feature value. For the lexifier or the substrate, it is 1 only if the source shares the same feature value with the creole; otherwise 0. To tune hyperparameters α_i and β_j, we set a vague gamma prior $\mathrm{Gamma}(1,1)$ and sample these parameters using slice sampling (Neal, 2003).

5.3 FACT Model

It is said that some features are more easily borrowed than others (Matras, 2011). For creoles, some seems to reflect substrate influence on phonology while reduced inflections might be attributed to the restructurer. Inspired by these observations, we extend the MONO model such that some feature types can have strong connections to particular sources. We call this extended model FACT.

To do this, we decomposes the mixing proportions into per-feature and per-creole factors. We apply additive operations to these factors in log-space in a way similar to the Sparse Additive Generative model (Eisenstein et al., 2011). As a result of this extension, every feature j of creole i has its own mixing proportion, $\theta_{i,j} = (\theta_{i,j,\mathrm{L}}, \theta_{i,j,\mathrm{S}}, \theta_{i,j,\mathrm{R}})$:

$$\theta_{i,j,k} = \frac{\exp(m_{j,k} + n_{i,k})}{\sum_k \exp(m_{j,k} + n_{i,k})}, \quad (2)$$

where $m_{j,k}$ is a factor specific to feature type j and $n_{i,k}$ is the one specific to creole i. To penalize extreme values, we put Laplacian priors on $m_{j,k}$ and $n_{i,k}$, with mean 0 and scale γ.

To sum up, the generative story of FACT is as follows:

Model	Sources		
	L	S	R
MONO	16.6%	9.3%	74.1%
FACT Combined	17.6%	6.0%	76.4%
FACT Per-feature	22.5%	6.8%	70.8%
FACT Per-creole	25.0%	20.4%	54.6%

Table 2: Summary of mixing proportions. The arithmetic mean of 50 samples after 5,000 iterations, with an interval of 100 iterations.

1. For each feature type $j \in \{1, \cdots, J\}$:

   (a) draw $\phi_j \sim \mathrm{Dir}(\beta_j)$
   (b) for each source $k \in \{\mathrm{L}, \mathrm{S}, \mathrm{R}\}$:
      i. draw $m_{j,k} \sim \mathrm{Laplace}(0, \gamma)$

2. For each creole $i \in \{1, \cdots, N\}$:

   (a) for each source $k \in \{\mathrm{L}, \mathrm{S}, \mathrm{R}\}$:
      i. draw $n_{i,k} \sim \mathrm{Laplace}(0, \gamma)$
   (b) then for each feature $j \in \{1, \cdots, J\}$:
      i. normalize $m_{j,k}$ and $n_{i,k}$ to obtain $\theta_{i,j}$ (Equation (2))
      ii. draw a topic assignment $z_{i,j} \sim \mathrm{Categorical}(\theta_{i,j})$
      iii. draw $x_{i,j}$ as in MONO

ϕ_j is integrated out as before, but the conjugacy no longer holds for $\theta_{i,j}$.

For inference, a modification is needed to infer $z_{i,j}$: the first term $\alpha_i + c_{i,k}^{-(i,j)}$ of Equation (1) is replaced with $\theta_{i,j,k}$. $m_{j,k}$ and $n_{i,k}$ are sampled using the Metropolis algorithm, with a Gaussian proposal distribution centered at the previous value. Hyperparameter γ is set to 10.

5.4 Results

Table 2 summarizes mixing proportions. For MONO and FACT (combined), we use a fraction of assignment variables pointing to a particular souce. Per-feature and per-creole factors are converted into probabilities as follows: per-feature proportions $\tilde{\phi}_j = (\tilde{\phi}_{j,\mathrm{L}}, \tilde{\phi}_{j,\mathrm{S}}, \tilde{\phi}_{j,\mathrm{R}})$, where $\tilde{\phi}_{j,k} = \frac{\exp(m_{j,k})}{\sum_k \exp(m_{j,k})}$. Similarly, per-creole proportions $\tilde{\theta}_i = (\tilde{\theta}_{j,\mathrm{L}}, \tilde{\theta}_{j,\mathrm{S}}, \tilde{\theta}_{j,\mathrm{R}})$, where $\tilde{\theta}_{i,k} = \frac{\exp(n_{i,k})}{\sum_k \exp(n_{i,k})}$.

We can see that the overwhelming majority of features were derived from the restructurer both in

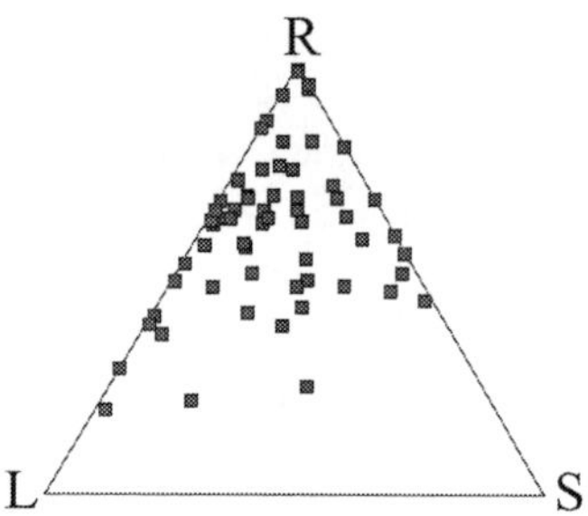

Figure 4: Mixing proportions of MONO projected onto a simplex. Each point denotes a creole. It is the parameter of the posterior predictive distribution of an assignment variable: $\tilde{\theta}_i = (\frac{\alpha_i + c_{i,\mathrm{L}}}{Z}, \frac{\alpha_i + c_{i,\mathrm{S}}}{Z}, \frac{\alpha_i + c_{i,\mathrm{R}}}{Z})$, where the normalizer $Z = \sum_k \alpha_i + c_{i,k}$. One sample after 10,000 iterations.

MONO and FACT (combined). The restructurer was followed by lexifiers, and substrates were the least influential.[6] These results can be interpreted as counter-evidence to the superstratist, substratist and feature pool theories.

MONO and FACT (combined) exhibited similar patterns. When the mixing proportions are decomposed into per-feature and per-creole factors, per-creole factors exhibited less uneven distributions than per-feature factors. This implies heterogeneous behavior of features in creole genesis. Table 3 lists top-5 feature types for each source.

Figure 4 plots creoles on a simplex of mixing proportions in MONO. Creoles scattered across the simplex but leaned toward the restructurer. This implies that a lexifier cannot be mixed with substrates without interference from the restructurer.

Compared with MONO, FACT tended to push points to the edges of the simplex. This can be confirmed in Figure 5. In particular, Figure 5(c) is directly comparable to Figure 4. It is possible that halfway points in MONO were artifacts of its limited expressive power.

Table 4 lists the top-10 feature type-value pairs that were derived from the restructurer. In other words, we stochastically removed the influence of the lexifiers and substrates from creole data. These features can be regarded as (statistical) universals

---

[6] The substrates would probably occupy a larger portion if multiple substrates are incorporated in future work.

Source	Ratio	Feature type
Lexifier	100.0%	Order of Adposition and Noun Phrase
	100.0%	Order of Relative Clause and Noun
	99.9%	Applicative Constructions
	99.5%	The Prohibitive
	98.2%	Alignment of Case Marking of Full Noun Phrases
Substrate	84.9%	Order of Genitive and Noun
	56.6%	Tone
	54.9%	Order of Subject, Object and Verb
	26.5%	Pronominal and Adnominal Demonstratives
	24.0%	Relativization on Subjects
Restructurer	100.0%	Intensifiers and Reflexive Pronouns
	100.0%	Numeral Classifiers
	100.0%	Suppletion According to Tense and Aspect
	100.0%	Expression of Pronominal Subjects
	100.0%	Polar Questions

Table 3: Top-5 feature types for each source according to per-feature factors of FACT. The arithmetic mean of 50 samples after 5,000 iterations, with an interval of 100 iterations.

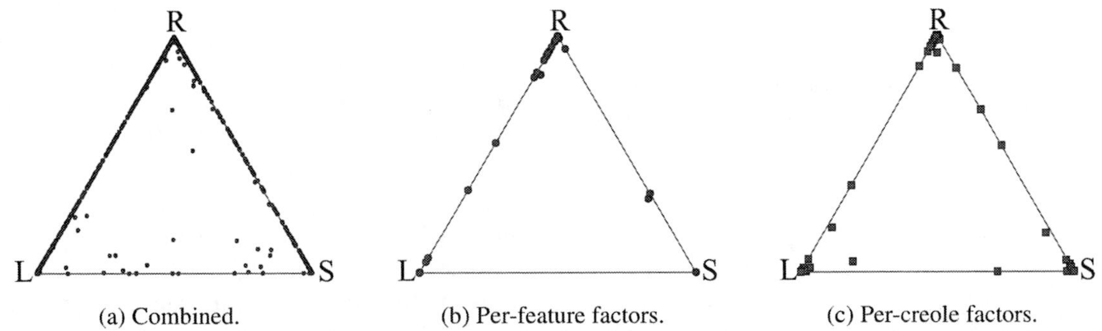

(a) Combined. (b) Per-feature factors. (c) Per-creole factors.

Figure 5: Mixing proportions of FACT projected onto a simplex. One sample after 10,000 iterations. (a) $J \times N$ points for combined mixing proportions $\theta_{i,j}$. (b) J points for per-feature factors $\tilde{\phi}_j$ as in Table 2. (c) N points for per-creole factors $\tilde{\theta}_i$.

although our model leaves the possibility that they were not *restructuring* universals. To answer this question, we need to break down the restructurer by types of linguistic universals.

Among the 10 feature type-value pairs, only four apply to Japanese (Negative Indefinite Pronouns and Predicate Negation, Intensifiers and Reflexive Pronouns, Alignment of Case Marking of Pronouns, and Order of Numeral and Noun). For reference, English has seven. Combined with the PCA analysis in Section 4.2, this suggests that Japanese is a very non-creole-like language. However, we are unsure if the possibility of creole status for (pre-)Old Japanese is completely rejected. This question might be an-swered if we figure out how long it takes to make creole-like traits disappeared.

It is often said that creoles have SVO word order. According to APiCS, the number of creoles with SVO order was 61 (exclusive) and 71 (exclusive plus shared) in the 76 language dataset. However, this feature value only gained the ratio of 67.3%. This is mainly because SVO is the word order of most lexifiers, but it can also be attributed to data representation: since WALS did not allow multi-valued features (e.g., SVO *and* SOV), some creoles with multiple word orders were mapped to a separate category "No dominant order," underestimating the influence of SVO.

Ratio	Feature type	Feature value
91.2%	Numeral Classifiers	Absent
74.3%	Gender Distinctions in Independent Personal Pronouns	No gender distinctions
72.3%	Negative Indefinite Pronouns and Predicate Negation	Predicate negation also present
70.5%	Occurrence of Nominal Plurality	All nouns, always optional
69.7%	Intensifiers and Reflexive Pronouns	Identical
68.4%	Distributive Numerals	No distributive numerals
67.2%	Expression of Pronominal Subjects	Obligatory pronouns in subject position
66.9%	Politeness Distinctions in Pronouns	No politeness distinction
66.6%	Alignment of Case Marking of Pronouns	Nominative - accusative (standard)
66.3%	Order of Numeral and Noun	Numeral-Noun

Table 4: Top-10 features derived from the restructurer in FACT. The ratio of the feature type-value pair (j, l) is defined as $|\{(i \mid x_{i,j} = l, z_{i,j} = \mathrm{R}\}| \, / \, N$. The arithmetic mean of 50 samples after 5,000 iterations, with an interval of 100 iterations.

5.5 Discussion

The main contribution of our work is the introduction of mixture models to creole studies. This is, however, only the first step toward understanding the complex process of creole genesis by means of statistical modeling. Better data are needed with respect to proxies for substrates, missing values, multi-valued features among others.

With better data, more elaborate models could uncover the detailed process of creole genesis. Our models mix several sources in one step, but we may want to model the staged development of pidgin formation and creole formation. As a result of continued influence from its superstrate, a creole might undergo *decreolization*. It is argued that pidgins themselves have several development stages, from each of which creoles can emerge (Mühlhäusler, 1997). Hopefully, these hypotheses could be tested with statistical models.

Our finding that the restructurer plays a dominant role in creole genesis has a negative implication for tree-based inference of language relationships. If most features of a language come from nowhere, we are unable to trace its origin back into the deep past. In the meanwhile, it has been argued that creole genesis only occurred in modern and early-modern, exceptional circumstances and cannot be responsible for most historical changes. Thus identifying the social conditions under which creoles arise (Tria et al., 2015) is another research direction to be explored.

6 Conclusion

In this paper, we present several statistical models of linguistic typology to answer questions concerning creole genesis. First, we formalized creole (non-)distinctiveness as a binary classification problem. Second, we propose to model creole genesis with mixture models, which makes more sense than tree-building techniques.

Recent studies on linguistic applications of computational phylogeny have been heavily influenced from computational biology. They often depend on ready-to-use software packages developed in that field. We observe that, as a result, linguistic phenomena that lack exact counterparts in biology tend to be left untouched. In this paper, we have hopefully demonstrated that computational linguists could fill the gap.

Acknowledgment

This work was partly supported by JSPS KAKENHI Grant Number 26730122.

References

Katsue Akiba-Reynolds. 1984. Internal reconstruction in pre-Japanese syntax. In Jacek Fisiak, editor, *Historical Syntax*, pages 1–23. Walter de Gruyter.

David H. Alexander, John Novembre, and Kenneth Lange. 2009. Fast model-based estimation of ancestry in unrelated individuals. *Genome Research*, 19(9):1655–1664.

Charles J. Bailey and Karl Maroldt. 1977. The French lineage of English. In Jürgen M. Meisel, editor, *Langues en contact – Pidgins – Creoles*, pages 21–53. Narr.

Peter Bakker, Aymeric Daval-Markussen, Mikael Parkvall, and Ingo Plag. 2011. Creoles are typologically distinct from non-creoles. *Journal of Pidgin and Creole Languages*, 26(1):5–42.

David M. Blei, Andrew Y. Ng, and Michael I. Jordan. 2003. Latent Dirichlet allocation. *Journal of Machine Learning Research*, 3:993–1022.

Remco Bouckaert, Philippe Lemey, Michael Dunn, Simon J. Greenhill, Alexander V. Alekseyenko, Alexei J. Drummond, Russell D. Gray, Marc A. Suchard, and Quentin D. Atkinson. 2012. Mapping the origins and expansion of the Indo-European language family. *Science*, 337(6097):957–960.

John Brownie. 2012. Multilingualism and identity on Mussau. *International Journal of the Sociology of Language*, 2012(214).

David Bryant and Vincent Moulton. 2004. Neighbor-Net: An agglomerative method for the construction of phylogenetic networks. *Molecular Biology and Evolution*, 21(2):255–265.

Lyle Campbell. 2006. Areal linguistics. In *Encyclopedia of Language and Linguistics, Second Edition*, pages 454–460. Elsevier.

Hal Daumé III. 2009. Non-parametric Bayesian areal linguistics. In *HLT-NAACL*, pages 593–601.

Aymeric Daval-Markussen and Peter Bakker. 2012. Explorations in creole research with phylogenetic tools. In *Proc. of LINGVIS & UNCLH*, pages 89–97.

Aymeric Daval-Markussen. 2013. First steps towards a typological profile of creoles. *Acta Linguistica Hafniensia*, 45(2):274–295.

Michael Dunn, Angela Terrill, Ger Reesink, Robert A. Foley, and Stephen C. Levinson. 2005. Structural phylogenetics and the reconstruction of ancient language history. *Science*, 309(5743):2072–2075.

Jacob Eisenstein, Amr Ahmed, and Eric P. Xing. 2011. Sparse additive generative models of text. In *Proc. of ICML*, pages 1041–1048.

Russell D. Gray and Quentin D. Atkinson. 2003. Language-tree divergence times support the Anatolian theory of Indo-European origin. *Nature*, 426(6965):435–439.

Thomas L. Griffiths and Mark Steyvers. 2004. Finding scientific topics. *PNAS*, 101:5228–5235.

Martin Haspelmath, Matthew Dryer, David Gil, and Bernard Comrie, editors. 2005. *The World Atlas of Language Structures*. Oxford University Press.

Eppie R. Jones, Gloria Gonzalez-Fortes, Sarah Connell, Veronika Siska, Anders Eriksson, Rui Martiniano, Russell L. McLaughlin, Marcos Gallego Llorente, Lara M. Cassidy, Cristina Gamba, Tengiz Meshveliani, Ofer Bar-Yosef, Werner Muller, Anna Belfer-Cohen, Zinovi Matskevich, Nino Jakeli, Thomas F. G. Higham, Mathias Currat, David Lordkipanidze, Michael Hofreiter, Andrea Manica, Ron Pinhasi, and Daniel G. Bradley. 2015. Upper Palaeolithic genomes reveal deep roots of modern Eurasians. *Nature Communications*, 6.

Julie Josse, Marie Chavent, Benot Liquet, and François Husson. 2012. Handling missing values with regularized iterative multiple correspondence analysis. *Journal of Classification*, 29(1):91–116.

Takao Kawamoto. 1974. Agreements and disagreements in morphology between Japanese and Austronesian (chiefly Melanesian) languages. *The Japanese Journal of Ethnology*, 39(2):113–129. (in Japanese).

Takao Kawamoto. 1990. Pijin kureōru-ka to Nihongo no keisei [Pidginization-creolization and the formation of Japanese]. In Osamu Sakiyama, editor, *Nihongo no Keisei [Formation of Japanese]*, pages 130–168. Sanseido. (in Japanese).

Giuseppe Longobardi and Cristina Guardiano. 2009. Evidence for syntax as a signal of historical relatedness. *Lingua*, 119(11):1679–1706.

Yaron Matras. 2011. Universals of structural borrowing. In Peter Siemund, editor, *Linguistic Universals and Language Variation*, pages 204–233. Walter de Gruyter.

Luke Maurits and Thomas L. Griffiths. 2014. Tracing the roots of syntax with Bayesian phylogenetics. *PNAS*, 111(37):13576–13581.

Susanne Maria Michaelis, Philippe Maurer, Martin Haspelmath, and Magnus Huber, editors. 2013. *APiCS Online*. Max Planck Institute for Evolutionary Anthropology.

Peter Mühlhäusler. 1997. *Pidgin and Creole Linguistics: Expanded and revised Edition*. University of Westminster Press.

Yugo Murawaki. 2015. Continuous space representations of linguistic typology and their application to phylogenetic inference. In *Proc. of NAACL-HLT*, pages 324–334.

Radford M. Neal. 2003. Slice sampling. *Annals of Statistics*, 31(3):705–767.

Nick Patterson, Alkes L. Price, and David Reich. 2006. Population structure and eigenanalysis. *PLoS Genetics*, 2(12):e190, 12.

Nick Patterson, Priya Moorjani, Yontao Luo, Swapan Mallick, Nadin Rohland, Yiping Zhan, Teri Genschoreck, Teresa Webster, and David Reich. 2012. Ancient admixture in human history. *Genetics*, 192(3):1065–1093.

Jonathan K. Pritchard, Matthew Stephens, and Peter Donnelly. 2000. Inference of population structure using multilocus genotype data. *Genetics*, 155(2):945–959.

Ger Reesink, Ruth Singer, and Michael Dunn. 2009. Explaining the linguistic diversity of Sahul using population models. *PLoS Biology*, 7(11).

Naruya Saitou and Masatoshi Nei. 1987. The neighbor-joining method: A new method for reconstructing phylogenetic trees. *Molecular Biology and Evolution*, 4(4):406–425.

August Schleicher. 1853. Die ersten Spaltungen des indogermanischen Urvolkes. *Allgemeine Monatsschrift für Wissenschaft und Literatur*, 3:786–787. (in German).

Johannes Schmidt. 1872. *Die Verwandtschaftsverhältnisse der indogermanischen Sprachen*. Hermann Böhlau. (in German).

Yee Whye Teh, Hal Daumé III, and Daniel Roy. 2008. Bayesian agglomerative clustering with coalescents. In *NIPS*, pages 1473–1480.

Francesca Tria, Vito D.P. Servedio, Salikoko S. Mufwene, and Vittorio Loreto. 2015. Modeling the emergence of contact languages. *PLoS ONE*, 10(4):e0120771, 04.

Peter Trudgill. 1974. Linguistic change and diffusion: Description and explanation in sociolinguistic dialect geography. *Language in Society*, 3:215–246.

Tasaku Tsunoda, Sumie Ueda, and Yoshiaki Itoh. 1995. Adpositions in word-order typology. *Linguistics*, 33(4):741–762.

Ronald Wardhaugh and Janet M. Fuller. 2015. *An Introduction to Sociolinguistics, 7th Edition*. John Wiley & Sons.

Shallow Parsing Pipeline for Hindi-English Code-Mixed Social Media Text

Arnav Sharma and **Sakshi Gupta** and **Raveesh Motlani** and **Piyush Bansal**
and **Manish Shrivastava** and **Radhika Mamidi** and **Dipti M. Sharma**
Kohli Center on Intelligent Systems (KCIS)
International Institute of Information Technology, Hyderabad (IIIT Hyderabad)
Gachibowli, Hyderabad, Telangana 500032
{arnav.s, sakshi.gupta, raveesh.motlani, piyush.bansal}@research.iiit.ac.in
{m.shrivastava, radhika, dipti}@iiit.ac.in

Abstract

In this study, the problem of shallow parsing of Hindi-English code-mixed social media text (CSMT) has been addressed. We have annotated the data, developed a language identifier, a normalizer, a part-of-speech tagger and a shallow parser. To the best of our knowledge, we are the first to attempt shallow parsing on CSMT. The pipeline developed has been made available to the research community with the goal of enabling better text analysis of Hindi English CSMT. The pipeline is accessible at [1].

1 Introduction

Multilingual speakers tend to exhibit code-mixing and code-switching in their use of language on social media platforms. Code-Mixing is the embedding of linguistic units such as phrases, words or morphemes of one language into an utterance of another language whereas code-switching refers to the co-occurrence of speech extracts belonging to two different grammatical systems (Gumperz., 1982). Here we use code-mixing to refer to both the scenarios.

Hindi-English bilingual speakers produce huge amounts of CSMT. Vyas et al. (2014) noted that the complexity in analyzing CSMT stems from non-adherence to a formal grammar, spelling variations, lack of annotated data, inherent conversational nature of the text and of course, code-mixing. Therefore, there is a need to create datasets and Natural

Language Processing (NLP) tools for CSMT as traditional tools are ill-equipped for it. Taking a step in this direction, we describe the shallow parsing pipeline built during this study.

2 Background

Bali et al. (2014) gathered data from Facebook generated by English-Hindi bilingual users which on analysis, showed a significant amount of code-mixing. Barman et al. (2014) investigated language identification at word level on Bengali-Hindi-English CSMT. They annotated a corpus with more than 180,000 tokens and achieved an accuracy of 95.76% using statistical models with monolingual dictionaries.

Solorio and Liu (2008) experimented with POS tagging for English-Spanish Code-Switched discourse by using pre-existing taggers for both languages and achieved an accuracy of 93.48%. However, the data used was manually transcribed and thus lacked the problems added by CSMT. Vyas et al. (2014) formalized the problem, reported challenges in processing Hindi-English CSMT and performed initial experiments on POS tagging. Their POS tagger accuracy fell by 14% to 65% without using gold language labels and normalization. Thus, language identification and normalization are critical for POS tagging (Vyas et al., 2014), which in turn is critical further down the pipeline for shallow parsing as evident in Table 5.

Jamatia et al. (2015) also built a POS tagger for Hindi-English CSMT using Random Forests on 2,583 utterances with gold language labels and achieved an accuracy of 79.8%. In the monolin-

---

[1] http://bit.ly/csmt-parser-api

Lang.	Sentences
English	141 (16.43%)
Hindi	111 (12.94%)
Code-mixed	606 (70.63%)
Total	858

Table 1: Data distribution at sentence level.

Lang.	All Sentences	Only CM Sentences
Hindi	6318 (57.05%)	5352 (63.34%)
English	3015 (27.22%)	1886 (22.32%)
Rest	1742 (15.73%)	1212 (14.34%)
Total	11075	8450

Table 2: Data distribution at token level.

gual social media text context, Gimpel et al. (2011) built a POS tagger for English tweets and achieved an accuracy of 89.95% on 1,827 annotated tweets. Owoputi et al. (2013) further improved this POS tagger, increasing the accuracy to 93%.

3 Data Preparation

CSMT was obtained from social media posts from the data shared for Subtask 1 of FIRE-2014 Shared Task on Transliterated Search. The existing annotation on the FIRE dataset was removed, posts were broken down into sentences and 858 of those sentences were randomly selected for manual annotation.

Table 1 and Table 2 show the distribution of the dataset at sentence and token level respectively. The language of 63.33% of the tokens in code-mixed sentences is Hindi. Based on the distribution, it is reasonable to assume that Hindi is the matrix language (Azuma, 1993; Myers-Scotton, 1997) in most of the code-mixed sentences.

3.1 Dataset examples

1. hy... try fr sm gov job jiske forms niklte h...
   Gloss: Hey... try for some government job which forms give out...
   Translation: Hey... try for some government job which gives out forms...

2. To tum divya bharti mandir marriage kendra ko donate karna
   Gloss: So you divya bharti temple marriage center to donate do

Translation: So you donate to divya bharti temple marriage center

The dataset is comprised of sentences similar to example 1 and 2. Example 1 shows code-switching as the language switches from English to Hindi whereas example 2 shows code-mixing as some English words are embedded in a Hindi utterance. Spelling variations (`sm` - some, `gov` - government), ambiguous words (`To` - So in Hindi or `To` in English) and non-adherence to a formal grammar (out of place ellipsis - `...`, no or misplaced punctuation) are some of the challenges evident in analyzing the examples above.

3.2 Annotation

Annotation was done on the following four layers:

1. **Language Identification**: Every word was given a tag out of three 'en', 'hi' and 'rest' to mark its language. Words that a bilingual speaker could identify as belonging to either Hindi or English were marked as 'hi' or 'en'. The label 'rest' was given to symbols, emoticons, punctuation, named entities, acronyms, foreign words and words with sub-lexical code-mixing like `chapattis` (Gloss: chapatti - bread) which is a Hindi word (*chapatti*) following English morphology (plural marker -*s*).

2. **Normalization**: Words with language tag 'hi' in Roman script were labeled with their standard form in the native script of Hindi, Devanagari. Similarly, words with language tag 'en' were labeled with their standard spelling. Words with language tag 'rest' were kept as they are. This acted as testing data for our Normalization module.

3. **Parts-of-Speech (POS)**: Universal POS tagset (Petrov et al., 2011) was used to label the POS of each word as this tagset is applicable to both English and Hindi words. Sub-lexical code-mixed words were annotated based on their context, since POS is a function of a word in a given context. For example, an English verb used as a noun in Hindi context is labeled as a noun.

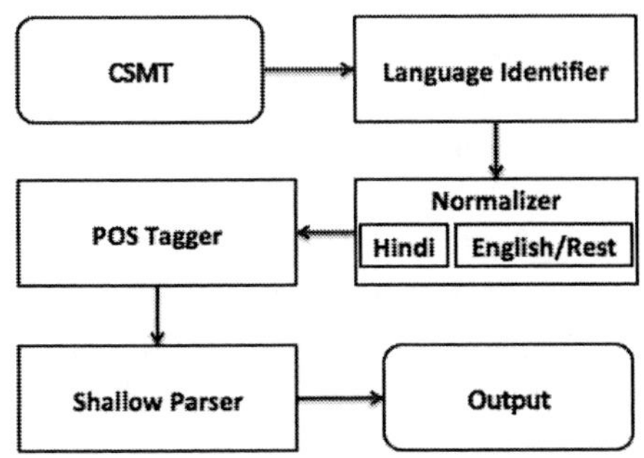

Figure 1: Schematic Diagram of the Pipeline

Features	Accuracy
BNC	61.26
+LEXNORM	71.43
+HINDI_DICT	77.50
+NGRAM	93.18
+AFFIXES	93.98

Table 3: Feature Ablation for Language Identifier

4. **Chunking**: A chunk tag comprises of chunk label and chunk boundary. The chunk label tagset is a coarser version of AnnCorra tagset (Bharati et al., 2006). Unlike AnnCorra, only one tag is used for all verb chunks in our tagset. Chunk boundary is marked using BI notation where 'B-' prefix indicates beginning of a chunk and 'I-' prefix indicates that the word is inside a chunk.

This whole dataset was annotated by eight Hindi-English bilingual speakers. Two other annotators reviewed and cleaned it. To measure inter-annotator agreement, another annotator read the guidelines and annotated 25 sentences (334 tokens) from scratch. The inter-annotator agreement calculated using Cohen's κ (Cohen, 1960) came out to be 0.97, 0.83 and 0.89 for language identification, POS tagging and shallow parsing respectively.

4 Shallow Parsing Pipeline

Shallow parsing is the task of identifying and segmenting text into syntactically correlated word groups (Abney, 1992; Harris, 1957). Shallow parsing is a viable alternative to full parsing as shown by (Li and Roth, 2001). Our shallow parsing pipeline is composed of four main modules, as shown in Figure 1. These modules, in the order of their usage, are *Language Identification, Normalization, POS Tagger* and *Shallow Parser.*

Our pipeline takes a raw utterance in Roman script as input on which each module runs sequentially. Twokenizer[2] (Owoputi et al., 2013) which

performs well on Hindi-English CSMT (Jamatia et al., 2015) was used to tokenize the utterance into words. The *Language Identification* module assigns each token a language label. Based on the language label assigned, the *Normalizer* runs the Hindi normalizer or the English/Rest normalizer. The *POS tagger* uses the output of the normalizer to assign each word a POS tag. Finally, the *Shallow Parser* assigns a chunk label with boundary.

The functionality and performance of each module is described in greater detail in the following subsections.

4.1 Language Identification

While language identification at the document level is a well-established task (McNamee, 2005), identifying language in social media posts has certain challenges associated to it. Spelling errors, phonetic typing, use of transliterated alphabets and abbreviations combined with code-mixing make this problem interesting. Similar to (Barman et al., 2014), we performed two experiments treating language identification as a three class ('hi', 'en', 'rest') classification problem. The feature set comprised of - **BNC**: normalized frequency of the word in British National Corpus (BNC)[3]. **LEXNORM**: binary feature indicating presence of the word in the lexical normalization dataset released by Han et al. (2011). **HINDI_DICT**: binary feature indicating presence of the word in a dictionary of 30,823 transliterated Hindi words as released by Gupta (2012). **NGRAM**: word n-grams. **AFFIXES**: prefixes and suffixes of the word.

Using these features and introducing a context-window of n-words, we trained a linear SVM. In another experiment we modeled language identification as a sequence labeling task, where we employed CRF into usage. The idea behind this was that

---

[2] http://www.ark.cs.cmu.edu/TweetNLP/

[3] http://www.natcorp.ox.ac.uk/

code-mixed text has some inherent structure which is largely dictated by the matrix language of the text. The latter approach using CRF had a greater accuracy, which validated our hypothesis. The results of this module are shown in Table 3.

4.2 Normalization

Once the language identification task was complete, there was a need to convert the noisy non-standard tokens (such as Hindi words inconsistently written in many ways using the Roman script) in the text into standard words. To fix this, a normalization module that performs language-specific transformations, yielding the correct spelling for a given word was built. Two language specific normalizers, one for Hindi and other for English/Rest, had two sub-normalizers each, as described below. Both sub-normalizers generated normalized candidates which were then ranked, as explained later in this subsection.

1. **Noisy Channel Framework**: A generative model was trained to produce noisy (unnormalized) tokens from a given normalized word. Using the model's confidence score and the probability of the normalized word in the background corpus, n-best normalizations were chosen. First, we obtained character alignments between noisy Hindi words in Roman script (H_r) to normalized Hindi words-format(H_w) using GIZA++ (Och and Ney, 2003) on 30,823 Hindi word pairs of the form (H_w - H_r) (Gupta et al., 2012). Next, a CRF classifier was trained over these alignments, enabling it to convert a character sequence from Roman to Devanagari using learnt letter transformations. Using this model, noisy H_r words were created for H_w words obtained from a dictionary of 1,17,789 Hindi words (Biemann et al., 2007). Finally, using the formula below, we computed the most probable H_w for a given H_r.

$$H_w = argmax_{H_{w_i}} p(H_{w_i}|H_r)$$
$$= argmax_{H_{w_i}} p(H_r|H_{w_i})p(H_{w_i})$$

where $p(H_{w_i})$ is the probability of word H_{w_i} in the background corpus.

Features	Accuracy
Baseline	69.27
+LANG	70.44
+NORM	72.61
+TPOS	73.18
+HPOS, -TPOS	73.55
+COMBINED	75.07

Table 4: Feature Ablation for POS Tagger

2. **SILPA Spell Checker**: This subnormalizer uses SILPA libindic spell-checker[4] to compute the top 10 normalized words for a given input word.

The candidates obtained from these two systems are ranked on the basis of the observed precision of the systems. The top-k candidates from each system are selected if they have a confidence score greater than an empirically observed Λ. A similar approach was used for English text normalization, using the English normalization pairs from (Han et al., 2012) and (Liu et al., 2012) for the noisy channel framework, and Aspell[5] as the spell-checker. Words with language tag 'rest' were left unprocessed. The accuracy for the Hindi Normalizer was 78.25%, and for the English Normalizer was 69.98%. The overall accuracy of this module is 74.48%; P@n (Precision@n) for n=3 is 77.51% and for n=5 is 81.76%.

4.3 Part-Of-Speech Tagging

Part-of-Speech (POS) tagging provides basic level of syntactic analysis for a given word or sentence. It was modeled as a sequence labeling task using CRF. The feature set comprised of - **Baseline**: Word based features - affixes, context and the word itself. **LANG**: Language label of the token. **NORM**: Normalized lexical features. **TPOS**: Output of Twitter POS tagger (Owoputi et al., 2013). **HPOS**: Output of IIIT's Hindi POS tagger[6]. **COMBINED**: HPOS for Hindi words and TPOS for English and Rest. The results of POS Tagger are shown in Table 4.

---

[4]https://github.com/libindic/spellchecker

[5]http://aspell.net/

[6]http://ltrc.iiit.ac.in/showfile.php?filename=downloads/shallow_parser.php

Features	L	B	C
POS Tag	88.01	78.75	76.64
+POS Context [W5]	87.92	81.36	78.09
+POS_LEX	88.18	81.46	78.58
+NORMLEX	88.25	82.17	78.73

Table 5: Feature Ablation for Shallow Parser

		P1	P2	E
LI		93.98	93.98	NA
Norm		70.32	74.48	4.16
POS		68.25	75.07	6.82
	L	75.73	88.25	12.52
SP	B	74.96	82.17	7.21
	C	61.95	78.73	16.78

Table 6: Pipeline accuracy and error propagation. LI = Language Identification, Norm = Normalizer, POS = POS Tagger, SP = Shallow Parser, L = Label, B = Boundary, C = Combined, P1 = Actual Pipeline, P2 = Gold Pipeline, E = Error Propagation

4.4 Shallow Parsing

A chunk comprises of two aspects - the chunk boundary and the chunk label. Shallow Parsing was modeled as three separate sequence labeling problems: **Label**, **Boundary** and **Combined**, for each of which a CRF model was trained. The feature set comprised of - **POS**: POS tag of the word. **POS Context**: POS tags in the context window of length 5, i.e., the two previous tags, current tag and next two tags. **POS_LEX**: A special feature made up of concatenation of POS and LEX. **NORMLEX**: The word in its normalized form. The results of this module are shown in Table 5.

5 Pipeline Results

The best performing model was selected from each module and was used in the pipeline. Table 6 tabulates the step by step accuracy of the pipeline calculated using 10 fold cross-validation.

6 Conclusion and Future Work

In this study, we have developed a system for Hindi-English CSMT data that can identify the language of the words, normalize them to their standard forms, assign them their POS tag and segment them into chunks. We have released the system.

In the future, we intend to continue creating more annotated code-mixed social media data. We would also like to improve upon the challenging problem of normalization of monolingual social Hindi sentences. Also, we would further extend our pipeline and build a full parser which has aplenty applications in NLP.

References

Steven P Abney. 1992. *Parsing by chunks*. Springer.

Shoji Azuma. 1993. The frame-content hypothesis in speech production: Evidence from intrasentential code switching. *Linguistics*, 31(6):1071–1094.

Kalika Bali, Jatin Sharma, Monojit Choudhury, and Yogarshi Vyas. 2014. i am borrowing ya mixing ? an analysis of english-hindi code mixing in facebook. In *Proceedings of the First Workshop on Computational Approaches to Code Switching*, pages 116–126, Doha, Qatar, October. Association for Computational Linguistics.

Utsab Barman, Amitava Das, Joachim Wagner, and Jennifer Foster. 2014. Code mixing: A challenge for language identification in the language of social media. *EMNLP 2014*, page 13.

Akshar Bharati, Rajeev Sangal, Dipti Misra Sharma, and Lakshmi Bai. 2006. Anncorra: Annotating corpora guidelines for pos and chunk annotation for indian languages. *LTRC-TR31*.

Chris Biemann, Gerhard Heyer, Uwe Quasthoff, and Matthias Richter. 2007. The leipzig corpora collection-monolingual corpora of standard size. *Proceedings of Corpus Linguistic*.

Jacob Cohen. 1960. A coefficient of agreement for nominal scales. *Educational and Psychological Measurement*, 134:3746.

Kevin Gimpel, Nathan Schneider, Brendan O'Connor, Dipanjan Das, Daniel Mills, Jacob Eisenstein, Michael Heilman, Dani Yogatama, Jeffrey Flanigan, and Noah A Smith. 2011. Part-of-speech tagging for twitter: Annotation, features, and experiments. In *Proceedings of the 49th Annual Meeting of the Association for Computational Linguistics: Human Language Technologies: short papers-Volume 2*, pages 42–47. Association for Computational Linguistics.

John J. Gumperz. 1982. *Discourse Strategies*. Oxford University Press.

Kanika Gupta, Monojit Choudhury, and Kalika Bali. 2012. Mining hindi-english transliteration pairs from online hindi lyrics. In *LREC*, pages 2459–2465.

Bo Han and Timothy Baldwin. 2011. Lexical normalisation of short text messages: Makn sens a# twitter. In *Proceedings of the 49th Annual Meeting of the Association for Computational Linguistics: Human Lan-*

guage Technologies-Volume 1, pages 368–378. Association for Computational Linguistics.

Bo Han, Paul Cook, and Timothy Baldwin. 2012. Automatically constructing a normalisation dictionary for microblogs. In *Proceedings of the 2012 joint conference on empirical methods in natural language processing and computational natural language learning*, pages 421–432. Association for Computational Linguistics.

Zellig S Harris. 1957. Co-occurrence and transformation in linguistic structure. *Language*, pages 283–340.

Anupam Jamatia, Björn Gambäck, and Amitava Das. 2015. Part-of-speech tagging for code-mixed english-hindi twitter and facebook chat messages. *Proceedings of Recent Advances in Natural Language Processing*, page 239.

Xin Li and Dan Roth. 2001. Exploring evidence for shallow parsing. In *Proceedings of the 2001 workshop on Computational Natural Language Learning-Volume 7*, page 6. Association for Computational Linguistics.

Fei Liu, Fuliang Weng, and Xiao Jiang. 2012. A broad-coverage normalization system for social media language. In *Proceedings of the 50th Annual Meeting of the Association for Computational Linguistics: Long Papers-Volume 1*, pages 1035–1044. Association for Computational Linguistics.

Paul McNamee. 2005. Language identification: a solved problem suitable for undergraduate instruction. *Journal of Computing Sciences in Colleges*, 20(3):94–101.

Carol Myers-Scotton. 1997. *Duelling languages: Grammatical structure in codeswitching*. Oxford University Press.

Franz Josef Och and Hermann Ney. 2003. A systematic comparison of various statistical alignment models. *Computational Linguistics*, 29(1):19–51.

Olutobi Owoputi, Brendan O'Connor, Chris Dyer, Kevin Gimpel, Nathan Schneider, and Noah A Smith. 2013. Improved part-of-speech tagging for online conversational text with word clusters. Association for Computational Linguistics.

Slav Petrov, Dipanjan Das, and Ryan McDonald. 2011. A universal part-of-speech tagset. *arXiv preprint arXiv:1104.2086*.

Thamar Solorio and Yang Liu. 2008. Part-of-speech tagging for english-spanish code-switched text. In *Proceedings of the Conference on Empirical Methods in Natural Language Processing*, pages 1051–1060. Association for Computational Linguistics.

Yogarshi Vyas, Spandana Gella, Jatin Sharma, Kalika Bali, and Monojit Choudhury. 2014. Pos tagging of english-hindi code-mixed social media content. In *Proceedings of the First Workshop on Codeswitching, EMNLP*.

Bilingual Learning of Multi-sense Embeddings with Discrete Autoencoders

Simon Šuster
University of Groningen
Netherlands
s.suster@rug.nl

Ivan Titov
University of Amsterdam
Netherlands
titov@uva.nl

Gertjan van Noord
University of Groningen
Netherlands
g.j.m.van.noord@rug.nl

Abstract

We present an approach to learning multi-sense word embeddings relying both on monolingual and bilingual information. Our model consists of an encoder, which uses monolingual and bilingual context (i.e. a parallel sentence) to choose a sense for a given word, and a decoder which predicts context words based on the chosen sense. The two components are estimated jointly. We observe that the word representations induced from bilingual data outperform the monolingual counterparts across a range of evaluation tasks, even though crosslingual information is not available at test time.

1 Introduction

Approaches to learning word embeddings (i.e. real-valued vectors) relying on word context have received much attention in recent years, and the induced representations have been shown to capture syntactic and semantic properties of words. They have been evaluated intrinsically (Mikolov et al., 2013a; Baroni et al., 2014; Levy and Goldberg, 2014) and have also been used in concrete NLP applications to deal with word sparsity and improve generalization (Turian et al., 2010; Collobert et al., 2011; Bansal et al., 2014; Passos et al., 2014). While most work to date has focused on developing embedding models which represent a word with a single vector, some researchers have attempted to capture *polysemy* explicitly and have encoded properties of each word with multiple vectors (Huang et al., 2012; Tian et al., 2014; Neelakantan et al., 2014; Chen et al., 2014; Li and Jurafsky, 2015).

In parallel to this work on multi-sense word embeddings, another line of research has investigated integrating *multilingual* data, with largely two distinct goals in mind. The first goal has been to obtain representations for several languages in the same semantic space, which then enables the transfer of a model (e.g., a syntactic parser) trained on annotated training data in one language to another language lacking this annotation (Klementiev et al., 2012; Hermann and Blunsom, 2014; Gouws et al., 2014; Chandar A P et al., 2014). Secondly, information from another language can also be leveraged to yield better first-language embeddings (Guo et al., 2014). Our paper falls in the latter, much less explored category. We adhere to the view of multilingual learning as a means of language grounding (Faruqui and Dyer, 2014b; Zou et al., 2013; Titov and Klementiev, 2012; Snyder and Barzilay, 2010; Naseem et al., 2009). Intuitively, polysemy in one language can be at least partially resolved by looking at the translation of the word and its context in another language (Kaji, 2003; Ng et al., 2003; Diab and Resnik, 2002; Ide, 2000; Dagan and Itai, 1994; Brown et al., 1991). Better sense assignment can then lead to better sense-specific word embeddings.

We propose a model that uses second-language embeddings as a supervisory signal in learning multi-sense representations in the first language. This supervision is easy to obtain for many language pairs as numerous parallel corpora exist nowadays. Our model, which can be seen as an autoencoder with a discrete hidden layer encoding word senses, leverages bilingual data in its encoding part, while the decoder predicts the surrounding words relying on the

Proceedings of NAACL-HLT 2016, pages 1346–1356,
San Diego, California, June 12-17, 2016. ©2016 Association for Computational Linguistics

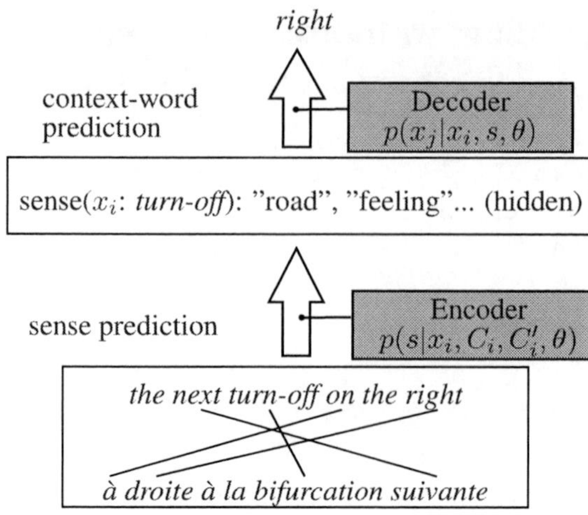

Figure 1: Model schema: the sense encoder with bilingual signal and the context-word predictor are learned jointly.

predicted senses. We strive to remain flexible as to the form of parallel data used in training and support both the use of word- and sentence-level alignments.

Our findings are:

- The second-language signal effectively improves the quality of multi-sense embeddings as seen on a variety of intrinsic tasks for English, with the results superior to that of the baseline Skip-Gram model, even though the crosslingual information is not available at test time.

- This finding is robust across several settings, such as varying dimensionality, vocabulary size and amount of data.

- In the extrinsic POS-tagging task, the second-language signal also offers improvements over monolingually-trained multi-sense embeddings, however, the standard Skip-Gram embeddings turn out to be the most robust in this task.

We make the implementation of all the models as well as the evaluation scripts available at `http://github.com/rug-compling/bimu`.

2 Word Embeddings with Discrete Autoencoders

Our method borrows its general structure from neural autoencoders (Rumelhart et al., 1986; Bengio et

al., 2013). Autoencoders are trained to reproduce their input by first mapping their input to a (lower dimensional) hidden layer and then predicting an approximation of the input relying on this hidden layer. In our case, the hidden layer is not a real-valued vector, but is a categorical variable encoding the sense of a word. Discrete-state autoencoders have been successful in several natural language processing applications, including POS tagging and word alignment (Ammar et al., 2014), semantic role induction (Titov and Khoddam, 2015) and relation discovery (Marcheggiani and Titov, 2016).

More formally, our model consists of two components: an *encoding* part which assigns a sense to a pivot word, and a *reconstruction* (decoding) part recovering context words based on the pivot word and its sense. As predictions are probabilistic ('soft'), the reconstruction step involves summation over all potential word senses. The goal is to find embedding parameters which minimize the error in recovering context words based on the pivot word and the sense assignment. Parameters of both encoding and reconstruction are jointly optimized. Intuitively, a good sense assignment should make the reconstruction step as easy as possible. The encoder uses not only words in the first-language sentence to choose the sense but also, at training time, is conditioning its decisions on the words in the second-language sentence. We hypothesize that the injection of crosslingual information will guide learning towards inducing more informative sense-specific word representations. Consequently, using this information at training time would benefit the model even though crosslingual information is not available to the encoder at test time.

We specify the encoding part as a log-linear model:

$$p(s|x_i, C_i, C'_i, \theta) \propto \exp\Big(\varphi_{i,s}^\top \big(\frac{1-\lambda}{|C_i|} \sum_{j \in C_i} \gamma_j +$$

$$\frac{\lambda}{|C'_i|} \sum_{k \in C'_i} \gamma'_k\big)\Big). \tag{1}$$

To choose the sense $s \in \mathcal{S}$ for a word x_i, we use the bag of context words C_i from the first language l, as well as the bag of context words C'_i from the second language l'.[1] The context C_i is defined as a

---

[1] We have also considered a formulation which included a sense-specific bias $b_{x_i,s} \in \mathbb{R}$ to capture relative frequency of latent senses but it did not seem to affect performance.

multiset $C_i = \{x_{i-n}, \ldots, x_{i-1}, x_{i+1}, \ldots, x_{i+n}\}$, including words around the pivot word in the window of size n to each side. We set n to 5 in all our experiments. The crosslingual context C_i' is discussed in § 3, where we either rely on word alignments or use the entire second-language sentence as the context. We distinguish between sense-specific embeddings, denoted by $\varphi \in \mathbb{R}^d$, and generic sense-agnostic ones, denoted $\{\gamma, \gamma'\} \in \mathbb{R}^d$ for first and second language, respectively. The number of sense-specific embeddings is the same for all words. We use θ to denote all these embedding parameters. They are learned jointly, with the exception of the pre-trained second-language embeddings.

The hyperparameter $\lambda \in \mathbb{R}, 0 \leq \lambda \leq 1$ weights the contribution of each language. Setting $\lambda = 0$ would drop the second-language component and use only the first language. Our formulation allows the addition of new languages easily, provided that the second-language embeddings live in the same semantic space.

The reconstruction part predicts a context word x_j given the pivot x_i and the current estimate of its s:

$$p(x_j|x_i, s, \theta) = \frac{\exp(\varphi_{i,s}^\top \gamma_j)}{\sum_{k \in |\mathcal{V}|} \exp(\varphi_{i,s}^\top \gamma_k)}, \qquad (2)$$

where $|\mathcal{V}|$ is the vocabulary size. This is effectively a Skip-Gram model (Mikolov et al., 2013a) extended to rely on senses.

2.1 Learning and regularization

As sense assignments are not observed during training, the learning objective includes marginalization over word senses and thus can be written as:

$$\sum_i \sum_{j \in C_{x_i}} \log \sum_{s \in \mathcal{S}} p(x_j|x_i, s, \theta) p(s|x_i, C_i, C_i', \theta),$$

in which index i goes over all pivot words in the first language, j over all context words to predict at each i, and s marginalizes over all possible senses of the word x_i. In practice, we avoid the costly computation of the normalization factor in the softmax computation of Eq. (2) and use negative sampling (Mikolov et al., 2013b) instead of $\log p(x_j|x_i, s, \theta)$:

$$\log \sigma(\varphi_{i,s}^\top \gamma_j) + \sum_{x \in N} \log \sigma(-\varphi_{i,s}^\top \gamma_x), \qquad (3)$$

where σ is the sigmoid non-linearity function and γ_x is a word embedding from the sample of negative (noisy) words N. Optimizing the autoencoding objective is broadly similar to the learning algorithm defined for multi-sense embedding induction in some of the previous work (Neelakantan et al., 2014; Li and Jurafsky, 2015). Note though that this previous work has considered only monolingual context.

We use a minibatch training regime and seek to optimize the objective function $L(\mathcal{B}, \theta)$ for each minibatch $\mathcal{B}$. We found that optimizing this objective directly often resulted in inducing very flat posterior distributions. We therefore use a form of posterior regularization (Ganchev et al., 2010) where we can encode our prior expectations that the posteriors should be sharp. The regularized objective for a minibatch is defined as

$$L(\mathcal{B}, \theta) + \lambda_H \sum_{i \in \mathcal{B}} H(q_i), \qquad (4)$$

where H is the entropy function and q_i are the posterior distributions from the encoder $(p(s|x_i, C_i, C_i', \theta))$. This modified objective can also be motivated from a variational approximation perspective, see Marcheggiani and Titov (2016) for details. By varying the parameter $\lambda_H \in \mathbb{R}$, it is easy to control the amount of entropy regularization. For $\lambda_H > 0$, the objective is optimized with flatter posteriors, while $\lambda_H < 0$ infers more peaky posteriors. When $\lambda_H \to -\infty$, the probability mass needs to be concentrated on a single sense, resulting in an algorithm similar to hard EM. In practice, we found that using hard-update training[2], which is closely related to the $\lambda_H \to -\infty$ setting, led to best performance.

2.2 Obtaining word representations

At test time, we construct the word representations by averaging all sense embeddings for a word x_i and weighting them with the sense expectations (Li and Jurafsky, 2015)[3]:

$$\omega_i = \sum_{s \in \mathcal{S}} p(s|x_i, C_i) \varphi_{i,s}. \qquad (5)$$

---

[2]I.e. updating only that embedding φ_{i,s^*} for which $s^* = \arg\max_s p(s|x_i, C_i, C_i', \theta)$.

[3]Although our training objective has sparsity-inducing properties, the posteriors at test time are not entirely peaked, which makes weighting beneficial.

Unlike in training, the sense prediction step here does not use the crosslingual context C'_i since it is not available in the evaluation tasks. In this work, instead of marginalizing out the unobservable crosslingual context, we simply ignore it in computation.

Sometimes, even the first-language context is missing, as is the situation in many word similarity tasks. In that case, we just use the uniform average, $1/|\mathcal{S}| \sum_{s \in \mathcal{S}} \varphi_{i,s}$.

3 Word affiliation from alignments

In defining the crosslingual signal we draw on a heuristic inspired by Devlin et al. (2014). The second-language context words are taken to be the multiset of words around and including the pivot affiliated to x_i:

$$C'_i = \{x'_{a_i-m}, ..., x'_{a_i}, ..., x'_{a_i+m}\}, \qquad (6)$$

where x'_{a_i} is the word affiliated to x_i and the parameter m regulates the context window size. By choosing $m = 0$, only the affiliated word is used as l' context, and by choosing $m = \infty$, the l' context is the entire sentence ($\approx$uniform alignment). To obtain the index a_i, we use the following:

1) If x_i aligns to exactly one second-language word, a_i is the index of the word it aligns to.
2) If x_i aligns to multiple words, a_i is the index of the aligned word in the middle (and rounding down when necessary).
3) If x_i is unaligned, C'_i is empty, therefore no l' context is used.

We use the cdec aligner (Dyer et al., 2010) to word-align the parallel corpora.

4 Parameters and Set-up

4.1 Learning parameters

We use the AdaGrad optimizer (Duchi et al., 2011) with initial learning rate set to 0.1. We set the mini-batch size to 1000, the number of negative samples to 1, the sampling factor to 0.001 and the window size parameter m to 5. All the embeddings are 50-dimensional (unless specified otherwise) and initialized by sampling from the uniform distribution between $[-0.05, 0.05]$. We include in the vocabulary all words occurring in the corpus at least 20 times. We set the number of senses per word to 3 (see further discussion in § 6.4 and § 7). All other parameters with

their default values can be examined in the source code available online.

4.2 Bilingual data

In a large body of work on multilingual word representations, Europarl (Koehn, 2005) is the preferred source of parallel data. However, the domain of Europarl is rather constrained, whereas we would like to obtain word representations of more general language, also to carry out an effective evaluation on semantic similarity datasets where domains are usually broader. We therefore use the following parallel corpora: News Commentary (Bojar et al., 2013) (NC), Yandex-1M[4] (RU-EN), CzEng 1.0 (Bojar et al., 2012) (CZ-EN) from which we exclude the EU legislation texts, and GigaFrEn (Callison-Burch et al., 2009) (FR-EN). The sizes of the corpora are reported in Table 1. The word representations trained on the NC corpora are evaluated only intrinsically due to the small sizes.

Corpus	Language	Words	Sent.
NC	Fr, Ru, Cz, De, Es	3-4 M	.1-.2 M
RU-EN	Ru	24 M	1 M
CZ-EN	Cz	126 M	10 M
FR-EN	Fr	670 M	23 M

Table 1: Parallel corpora used in this paper. The word sizes reported are based on the English part of the corpus. Each language pair in NC has a different English part, hence the varying number of sentences per target language.

5 Evaluation Tasks

We evaluate the quality of our word representations on a number of tasks, both intrinsic and extrinsic.

5.1 Word similarity

We are interested here in how well the semantic similarity ratings obtained from embedding comparisons correlate to human ratings. For this purpose, we use a variety of similarity benchmarks for English and report the Spearman ρ correlation scores between the human ratings and the cosine ratings obtained from our word representations. The **SCWS** benchmark (Huang et al., 2012) is probably the most suitable

---

[4] https://translate.yandex.ru/corpus

similarity dataset for evaluating multi-sense embeddings, since it allows us to perform the sense prediction step based on the sentential context provided for each word in the pair.

The other benchmarks we use provide the ratings for the word pairs without context. WS-353 contains 353 human-rated word pairs (Finkelstein et al., 2001), while Agirre et al. (2009) separate this benchmark for similarity (WS-SIM) and relatedness (WS-REL). The RG-65 (Rubenstein and Goodenough, 1965) and the MC-30 (Miller and Charles, 1991) benchmarks contain nouns only. The MTurk-287 (Radinsky et al., 2011) and MTurk-771 (Halawi et al., 2012) include word pairs whose similarity was crowdsourced from AMT. Similarly, MEN (Bruni et al., 2012) is an AMT-annotated dataset of 3000 word pairs. The YP-130 (Yang and Powers, 2006) and Verb-143 (Baker et al., 2014) measure verb similarity. Rare-Word (Luong et al., 2013) contains 2034 rare-word pairs. Finally, SimLex-999 (Hill et al., 2014b) is intended to measure pure similarity as opposed to relatedness. For these benchmarks, we prepare the word representations by taking a uniform average of all sense embeddings per word. The evaluation is carried out using the tool described in Faruqui and Dyer (2014a). Due to space constraints, we report the results by averaging over all benchmarks (**Similarity**), and include the individual results in the online repository.

5.2 Supersense similarity

We also evaluate on a task measuring the similarity between the embeddings—in our case uniformly averaged in the case of multi-sense embeddings—and a matrix of supersense features extracted from the English SemCor, using the **Qvec** tool (Tsvetkov et al., 2015). We choose this method because it has been shown to output scores that correlate well with extrinsic tasks, e.g. text classification and sentiment analysis. We believe that this, in combination with word similarity tasks from the previous section, can give a reliable picture of the generic quality of word embeddings studied in this work.

5.3 POS tagging

As our downstream evaluation task, we use the learned word representations to initialize the embedding layer of a neural network tagging model. We use the same convolutional architecture as Li and Juraf-
sky (2015): an input layer taking a concatenation of neighboring embeddings as input, three hidden layers with a rectified linear unit activation function and a softmax output layer. We train for 10 epochs using one sentence as a batch. Other hyperparameters can be examined in the source code. The multi-sense word embeddings are inferred from the sentential context (weighted average), as for the evaluation on the SCWS dataset. We use the standard splits of the Wall Street Journal portion of the Penn Treebank: 0–18 for training, 19–21 for development and 22–24 for testing.

6 Results

We compare three embeddings models, Skip-Gram (SG), Multi-sense (MU) and Bilingual Multi-sense (BIMU), using our own implementation for each of them. The first two can be seen as simpler variants of the BIMU model: in SG we omit the encoder entirely, and in MU we omit the second-language (l') part of the encoder in Eq. (1). We train the SG and the MU models on the English part of the parallel corpora. Those parameters common to all methods are kept fixed during experiments. The values λ and m for controlling the second-language signal in BIMU are set on the POS-tagging development set (cf. § 6.3).

The results on the **SCWS** benchmark (Table 2) show consistent improvements of the BIMU model over SG and MU across all parallel corpora, except on the small CZ-EN (NC) corpus. We have also measured the 95% confidence intervals of the difference between the correlation coefficients of BIMU and SG, following the method described in Zou (2007). According to these values, BIMU significantly outperforms SG on RU-EN, and on French, Russian and Spanish NC corpora.[5]

Next, ignoring any language-specific factors, we would expect to observe a trend according to which the larger the corpus, the higher the correlation score. However, this is not what we find. Among the largest corpora, i.e. RU-EN, CZ-EN and FR-EN, the models trained on RU-EN perform surprisingly well, practically on par with the 23-times larger FR-EN corpus. Similarly, the quality of the embeddings trained on CZ-EN is generally lower than when trained on the

---

[5]I.e. counting those results in which the CI of the difference does not include 0.

Task	Corpus	SG	MU	BIMU	BIMU-SG
SCWS	RU-EN	54.8	57.3	**59.5**	$4.7^{9.8}_{0.9}$
	CZ-EN	51.2	54.0	**55.3**	$4.1^{8.8}_{-0.6}$
	FR-EN	58.8	60.4	**60.5**	$1.7^{5.9}_{-2.6}$
	FR-EN (NC)	47.2	52.4	**54.3**	$7.1^{12.0}_{2.2}$
	RU-EN (NC)	47.3	**54.0**	**54.0**	$6.7^{12.8}_{0.6}$
	CZ-EN (NC)	47.7	**52.1**	51.9	$4.2^{10.3}_{-2.0}$
	DE-EN (NC)	48.5	52.9	**54.0**	$5.5^{11.6}_{-0.6}$
	ES-EN (NC)	47.2	53.2	**54.5**	$7.3^{13.3}_{1.1}$
Similarity	RU-EN	37.8	41.2	**46.3**	
	CZ-EN	39.5	36.9	**41.9**	
	FR-EN	**46.3**	42.0	43.5	
	FR-EN (NC)	17.9	26.0	**27.6**	
	RU-EN (NC)	19.3	27.3	**28.4**	
	CZ-EN (NC)	15.8	**26.6**	25.4	
	DE-EN (NC)	20.7	28.4	**30.8**	
	ES-EN (NC)	19.9	27.2	**31.2**	
Qvec	RU-EN	55.8	56.0	**56.5**	
	CZ-EN	**56.6**	56.5	55.9	
	FR-EN	57.5	57.1	**57.6**	
POS	RU-EN	**93.5**	93.2	93.3	
	CZ-EN	**94.0**	93.7	**94.0**	
	FR-EN	**94.1**	93.8	94.0	

Table 2: Results, per-row best in bold. SG and MU are trained on the English part of the parallel corpora. In BIMU-SG, we report the difference between BIMU and SG, together with the 95% CI of that difference. The **Similarity** scores are averaged over 12 benchmarks described in § 5.1. For POS tagging, we report the accuracy.

Model (300-dim.)	SCWS
SG	65.0
MU	66.7
BIMU	69.0
Chen et al. (2014)	68.4
Neelakantan et al. (2014)	69.3
Li and Jurafsky (2015)	69.7

Table 3: Comparison to other works (reprinted), for the vocabulary of top-6000 words. Our models are trained on RU-EN, a much smaller corpus than those used in previous work.

10 times smaller RU-EN corpus. One explanation for this might be different text composition of the corpora, with RU-EN matching the domain of the evaluation task better than the larger two corpora. Also, FR-EN is known to be noisy, containing web-crawled sentences that are not parallel or not natural language (Denkowski et al., 2012). Furthermore, language-dependent effects might be playing a role: for example, there are signs of Czech being the least helpful language among those studied. But while there is evidence for that in all intrinsic tasks, the situation in POS tagging does not confirm this speculation.

We relate our models to previously reported SCWS scores from the literature using 300-dimensional models in Table 3. Even though we train on a much smaller corpus than the previous works,[6] the BIMU model achieves a very competitive correlation score.

The results on **similarity** benchmarks and **qvec** largely confirm those on SCWS, despite the lack of sentential context which would allow to weight the contribution of different senses more accurately for the multi-sense models. Why, then, does simply averaging the MU and BIMU embeddings lead to better results than when using the SG embeddings? We hypothesize that the single-sense model tends to over-represent the dominant sense with its generic, one-vector-per-word representation, whereas the uniformly averaged embeddings yielded by the multi-sense models better encode the range of potential senses. Similar observations have been made in the context of selectional preference modeling of polysemous verbs (Greenberg et al., 2015).

In **POS** tagging, the relationship between MU and BIMU models is similar as discussed above. Overall, however, neither of the multi-sense models outperforms the SG embeddings. The neural network tagger may be able to implicitly perform disambiguation on top of single-sense SG embeddings, similarly to what has been argued in Li and Jurafsky (2015). The tagging accuracies obtained with MU on CZ-EN and FR-EN are similar to the one obtained by Li and Jurafsky with their multi-sense model (93.8), while the accuracy of SG is more competitive in our case (around 94.0 compared to 92.5), although they use a larger corpus for training the word representations.

In all tasks, the addition of the bilingual component during training increases the accuracy of the encoder for most corpora, even though the bilingual information is not available during evaluation.

6.1 The amount of (parallel) data

Fig. 2a displays how the semantic similarity as measured on SCWS evolves as a function of increasingly

---

[6] For example, Li and Jurafsky (2015) use the concatenation of Gigaword and Wikipedia with more than 5B words.

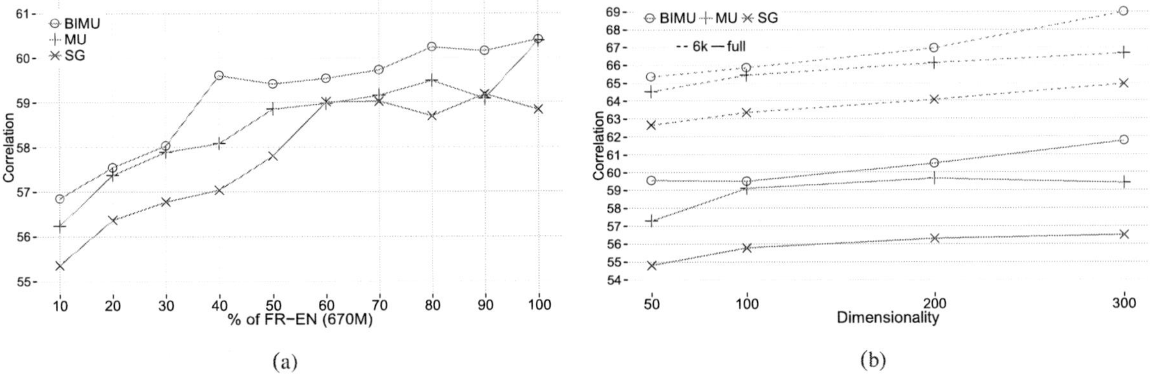

Figure 2: (a) Effect of amount of data used in learning on the SCWS correlation scores. (b) Effect of embedding dimensionality on the models trained on RU-EN and evaluated on SCWS with either full vocabulary or the top-6000 words.

larger sub-samples from FR-EN, our largest parallel corpus. The BIMU embeddings show relatively stable improvements over MU and especially over SG embeddings. The same performance as that of SG at 100% is achieved by MU and BIMU sooner, using only around 40/50% of the corpus.

6.2 The dimensionality and frequent words

It is argued in Li and Jurafsky (2015) that often just increasing the dimensionality of the SG model suffices to obtain better results than that of their multi-sense model. We look at the effect of dimensionality on semantic similarity in fig. 2b, and see that simply increasing the dimensionality of the SG model (to any of 100, 200 or 300 dimensions) is not sufficient to outperform the MU or BIMU models. When constraining the vocabulary to 6,000 most frequent words, the representations obtain higher quality. We can see that the models, especially SG, benefit slightly more from the increased dimensionality when looking at these most frequent words. This is according to expectations—frequent words need more representational capacity due to their complex semantic and syntactic behavior (Atkins and Rundell, 2008).

6.3 The role of bilingual signal

The degree of contribution of the second language l' during learning is affected by two parameters, λ for the trade-off between the importance of first and second language in the sense prediction part (encoder) and the value of m for the size of the window around the second-language word affiliated to the pivot. Fig. 3a suggests that the context from the second language

is useful in sense prediction, and that it should be weighted relatively heavily (around 0.7 and 0.8, depending on the language).

Regarding the role of the context-window size in sense disambiguation, the WSD literature has reported both smaller (more local) and larger (more topical) monolingual contexts to be useful, see e.g. Ide and Véronis (1998) for an overview. In fig. 3b we find that considering a very narrow context in the second language—the affiliated word only or a $m = 1$ window around it—performs the best, and that there is little gain in using a broader window. This is understandable since the l' representation participating in the sense selection is simply an average over all generic embeddings in the window, which means that the averaged representation probably becomes noisy for large m, i.e. more irrelevant words are included in the window. However, the negative effect on the accuracy is still relatively small, up to around -0.1 for the models using French and Russian as the second languages, and -0.25 for Czech when setting $m = \infty$. The infinite window size setting, corresponding to the sentence-only alignment, performs well also on SCWS, improving on the monolingual multi-sense baseline on all corpora (Table 4).

Model	RU-EN	CZ-EN	FR-EN
MU	63.29	59.12	64.19
BIMU, $m = \infty$	**65.61**	**62.07**	**64.36**

Table 4: Comparison of SCWS correlation scores of BIMU trained with infinite l' window to the MU baseline (vocabulary of top-6000 words).

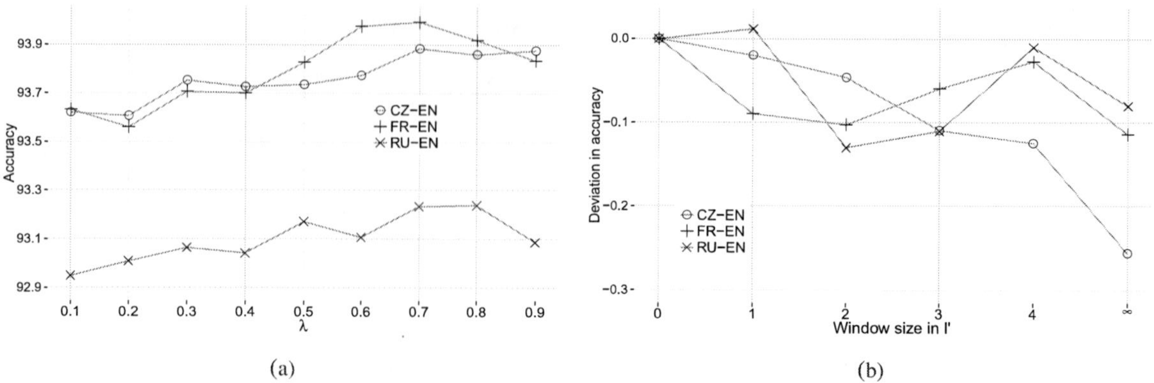

Figure 3: Controlling the bilingual signal. (a) Effect of varying the parameter λ for controlling the importance of second-language context (0.1-least important, 0.9-most important). (b) Effect of second-language window size m on the accuracy. In both (a) and (b) the reported accuracies are measured on the POS-tagging development set.

6.4 The number of senses

In our work, the number of senses k is a model parameter, which we keep fixed to 3 throughout the empirical study. We comment here briefly on other choices of $k \in \{2, 4, 5\}$. We have found $k = 2$ to be a good choice on the RU-EN and FR-EN corpora (but not on CZ-EN), with an around 0.2-point improvement over $k = 3$ on SCWS and in POS tagging. With the larger values of k, the performance tends to degrade. For example, on RU-EN, the $k = 5$ score on SCWS is about 0.6 point below our default setting.

7 Additional Related Work

Multi-sense models. One line of research has dealt with sense induction as a separate, clustering problem that is followed by an embedding learning component (Huang et al., 2012; Reisinger and Mooney, 2010). In another, the sense assignment and the embeddings are trained jointly (Neelakantan et al., 2014; Tian et al., 2014; Li and Jurafsky, 2015; Bartunov et al., 2015). Neelakantan et al. (2014) propose an extension of Skip-Gram (Mikolov et al., 2013a) by introducing sense-specific parameters together with the k-means-inspired 'centroid' vectors that keep track of the contexts in which word senses have occurred. They explore two model variants, one in which the number of senses is the same for all words, and another in which a threshold value determines the number of senses for each word. The results comparing the two variants are inconclusive, with the advantage of the dynamic variant being virtually nonexistent.

In our work, we use the static approach. Whenever there is evidence for less senses than the number of available sense vectors, this is unlikely to be a serious issue as the learning would concentrate on some of the senses, and these would then be the preferred predictions also at test time. Li and Jurafsky (2015) build upon the work of Neelakantan et al. with a more principled method for introducing new senses using the Chinese Restaurant Processes (CRP). Our experiments confirm the findings of Neelakantan et al. that multi-sense embeddings improve Skip-gram embeddings on intrinsic tasks, as well as those of Li and Jurafsky, who find that multi-sense embeddings offer little benefit to the neural network learner on extrinsic tasks. Our discrete-autoencoding method when viewed without the bilingual part in the encoder has a lot in common with their methods.

Multilingual models. The research on using multilingual information in the learning of *multi-sense* embedding models is scarce. Guo et al. (2014) perform a sense induction step based on clustering translations prior to learning word embeddings. Once the translations are clustered, they are mapped to a source corpus using WSD heuristics, after which a recurrent neural network is trained to obtain sense-specific representations. Unlike in our work, the sense induction and embedding learning components are entirely separated, without a possibility for one to influence another. In a similar vein, Bansal et al. (2012) use bilingual corpora to perform soft word clustering, extending the previous work on the monolingual case of

Lin and Wu (2009). *Single-sense* representations in the multilingual context have been studied more extensively (Lu et al., 2015; Faruqui and Dyer, 2014b; Hill et al., 2014a; Zhang et al., 2014; Faruqui and Dyer, 2013; Zou et al., 2013), with a goal of bringing the representations in the same semantic space. A related line of work concerns the crosslingual setting, where one tries to leverage training data in one language to build models for typically lower-resource languages (Hermann and Blunsom, 2014; Gouws et al., 2014; Chandar A P et al., 2014; Soyer et al., 2014; Klementiev et al., 2012; Täckström et al., 2012).

The recent works of Kawakami and Dyer (2015) and Nalisnick and Ravi (2015) are also of interest. The latter work on the infinite Skip-Gram model in which the embedding dimensionality is stochastic is relevant since it demonstrates that their embeddings exploit different dimensions to encode different word meanings. Just like us, Kawakami and Dyer (2015) use bilingual supervision, but in a more complex LSTM network that is trained to predict word translations. Although they do not represent different word senses separately, their method produces representations that depend on the context. In our work, the second-language signal is introduced only in the sense prediction component and is flexible—it can be defined in various ways and can be obtained from sentence-only alignments as a special case.

8 Conclusion

We have presented a method for learning multi-sense embeddings that performs sense estimation and context prediction jointly. Both mono- and bilingual information is used in the sense prediction during training. We have explored the model performance on a variety of tasks, showing that the bilingual signal improves the sense predictor, even though the crosslingual information is not available at test time. In this way, we are able to obtain word representations that are of better quality than the monolingually-trained multi-sense representations, and that outperform the Skip-Gram embeddings on intrinsic tasks. We have analyzed the model performance under several conditions, namely varying dimensionality, vocabulary size, amount of data, and size of the second-language context. For the latter parameter, we find that bilingual information is useful even when using the entire sentence as context, suggesting that sentence-only alignment might be sufficient in certain situations.

Acknowledgments

We would like to thank Jiwei Li for providing his tagger implementation, and Robert Grimm, Diego Marcheggiani and the anonymous reviewers for useful comments. The computational work was carried out on Peregrine HPC cluster of the University of Groningen. The second author was supported by NWO Vidi grant 016.153.327.

References

Eneko Agirre, Enrique Alfonseca, Keith Hall, Jana Kravalova, Marius Paşca, and Aitor Soroa. 2009. A study on similarity and relatedness using distributional and WordNet-based approaches. In *NAACL-HLT*.

Waleed Ammar, Chris Dyer, and Noah A. Smith. 2014. Conditional random field autoencoders for unsupervised structured prediction. In *NIPS*.

Sue B. T. Atkins and Michael Rundell. 2008. *The Oxford guide to practical lexicography*. Oxford University Press.

Simon Baker, Roi Reichart, and Anna Korhonen. 2014. An unsupervised model for instance level subcategorization acquisition. In *EMNLP*.

Mohit Bansal, John Denero, and Dekang Lin. 2012. Unsupervised translation sense clustering. In *NAACL-HLT*.

Mohit Bansal, Kevin Gimpel, and Karen Livescu. 2014. Tailoring continuous word representations for dependency parsing. In *ACL*.

Marco Baroni, Georgiana Dinu, and Germán Kruszewski. 2014. Don't count, predict! a systematic comparison of context-counting vs. context-predicting semantic vectors. In *ACL*.

Sergey Bartunov, Dmitry Kondrashkin, Anton Osokin, and Dmitry Vetrov. 2015. Breaking sticks and ambiguities with adaptive skip-gram. *arXiv preprint arXiv:1502.07257*.

Yoshua Bengio, Aaron Courville, and Pierre Vincent. 2013. Representation learning: A review and new perspectives. *IEEE Transactions on Pattern Analysis and Machine Intelligence*, 35(8):1798–1828.

Ondřej Bojar, Zdeněk Žabokrtský, Ondřej Dušek, Petra Galuščáková, Martin Majliš, David Mareček, Jiří Maršík, Michal Novák, Martin Popel, and Aleš Tamchyna. 2012. The Joy of Parallelism with CzEng 1.0. In *LREC*.

Ondřej Bojar, Christian Buck, Chris Callison-Burch, Christian Federmann, Barry Haddow, Philipp Koehn, Christof Monz, Matt Post, Radu Soricut, and Lucia

Specia. 2013. Findings of the 2013 Workshop on Statistical Machine Translation. In *WMT*.

Peter F Brown, Stephen A Della Pietra, Vincent J Della Pietra, and Robert L Mercer. 1991. Word-sense disambiguation using statistical methods. In *ACL*.

Elia Bruni, Gemma Boleda, Marco Baroni, and Nam-Khanh Tran. 2012. Distributional semantics in technicolor. In *ACL*.

Chris Callison-Burch, Philipp Koehn, Christof Monz, and Josh Schroeder. 2009. Findings of the 2009 Workshop on Statistical Machine Translation. In *WMT*.

Sarath Chandar A P, Stanislas Lauly, Hugo Larochelle, Mitesh M. Khapra, Balaraman Ravindran, Vikas C. Raykar, and Amrita Saha. 2014. An autoencoder approach to learning bilingual word representations. In *NIPS*.

Xinxiong Chen, Zhiyuan Liu, and Maosong Sun. 2014. A unified model for word sense representation and disambiguation. In *EMNLP*.

Ronan Collobert, Jason Weston, Léon Bottou, Michael Karlen, Koray Kavukcuoglu, and Pavel Kuksa. 2011. Natural language processing (almost) from scratch. *The Journal of Machine Learning Research*, 12:2493–2537.

Ido Dagan and Alon Itai. 1994. Word sense disambiguation using a second language monolingual corpus. *Computational Linguistics*, 20(4):563–596.

Michael Denkowski, Greg Hanneman, and Alon Lavie. 2012. The CMU-Avenue French-English Translation System. In *WMT*.

Jacob Devlin, Rabih Zbib, Zhongqiang Huang, Thomas Lamar, Richard Schwartz, and John Makhoul. 2014. Fast and robust neural network joint models for statistical machine translation. In *ACL*.

Mona Diab and Philip Resnik. 2002. An unsupervised method for word sense tagging using parallel corpora. In *ACL*.

John Duchi, Elad Hazan, and Yoram Singer. 2011. Adaptive subgradient methods for online learning and stochastic optimization. *The Journal of Machine Learning Research*, 12:2121–2159.

Chris Dyer, Adam Lopez, Juri Ganitkevitch, Johnathan Weese, Ferhan Ture, Phil Blunsom, Hendra Setiawan, Vladimir Eidelman, and Philip Resnik. 2010. cdec: A decoder, alignment, and learning framework for finite-state and context-free translation models. In *ACL*.

Manaal Faruqui and Chris Dyer. 2013. An information theoretic approach to bilingual word clustering. In *ACL*.

Manaal Faruqui and Chris Dyer. 2014a. Community evaluation and exchange of word vectors at wordvectors.org. In *ACL System Demonstrations*.

Manaal Faruqui and Chris Dyer. 2014b. Improving vector space word representations using multilingual correlation. In *EACL*.

Lev Finkelstein, Evgeniy Gabrilovich, Yossi Matias, Ehud Rivlin, Zach Solan, Gadi Wolfman, and Eytan Ruppin. 2001. Placing search in context: The concept revisited. In *WWW*.

Kuzman Ganchev, João Graça, Jennifer Gillenwater, and Ben Taskar. 2010. Posterior regularization for structured latent variable models. *The Journal of Machine Learning Research*, 11:2001–2049.

Stephan Gouws, Yoshua Bengio, and Greg Corrado. 2014. BilBOWA: Fast Bilingual Distributed Representations without Word Alignments. *arXiv preprint arXiv:1410.2455*.

Clayton Greenberg, Asad Sayeed, and Vera Demberg. 2015. Improving unsupervised vector-space thematic fit evaluation via role-filler prototype clustering. In *NAACL*.

Jiang Guo, Wanxiang Che, Haifeng Wang, and Ting Liu. 2014. Learning sense-specific word embeddings by exploiting bilingual resources. In *COLING*.

Guy Halawi, Gideon Dror, Evgeniy Gabrilovich, and Yehuda Koren. 2012. Large-scale learning of word relatedness with constraints. In *KDD*.

Karl Moritz Hermann and Phil Blunsom. 2014. Multilingual models for compositional distributed semantics. In *ACL*.

Felix Hill, Kyunghyun Cho, Sébastien Jean, Coline Devin, and Yoshua Bengio. 2014a. Embedding word similarity with neural machine translation. *arXiv preprint arXiv:1412.6448*.

Felix Hill, Roi Reichart, and Anna Korhonen. 2014b. Simlex-999: Evaluating semantic models with (genuine) similarity estimation. *arXiv preprint arXiv:1408.3456*.

Eric H. Huang, Richard Socher, Christopher D. Manning, and Andrew Y. Ng. 2012. Improving word representations via global context and multiple word prototypes. In *ACL*.

Nancy Ide and Jean Véronis. 1998. Introduction to the special issue on word sense disambiguation: the state of the art. *Computational linguistics*, 24(1):2–40.

Nancy Ide. 2000. Cross-lingual sense determination: Can it work? *Computers and the Humanities*, 34(1-2):223–234.

Hiroyuki Kaji. 2003. Word sense acquisition from bilingual comparable corpora. In *NAACL-HLT*.

Kazuya Kawakami and Chris Dyer. 2015. Learning to represent words in context with multilingual supervision. *arXiv preprint arXiv:1511.04623*.

Alexandre Klementiev, Ivan Titov, and Binod Bhattarai. 2012. Inducing crosslingual distributed representations of words. In *COLING*.

Philipp Koehn. 2005. Europarl: A parallel corpus for statistical machine translation. In *MT summit*, volume 5.

Omer Levy and Yoav Goldberg. 2014. Linguistic regularities in sparse and explicit word representations. *CoNLL*.

Jiwei Li and Dan Jurafsky. 2015. Do multi-sense embeddings improve natural language understanding? In *EMNLP*.

Dekang Lin and Xiaoyun Wu. 2009. Phrase clustering for discriminative learning. In *ACL-IJCNLP of AFNLP*.

Ang Lu, Weiran Wang, Mohit Bansal, Kevin Gimpel, and Karen Livescu. 2015. Deep multilingual correlation for improved word embeddings. In *NAACL*.

Minh-Thang Luong, Richard Socher, and Christopher D Manning. 2013. Better word representations with recursive neural networks for morphology. In *CoNLL*.

Diego Marcheggiani and Ivan Titov. 2016. Discrete-state variational autoencoders for joint discovery and factorization of relations. *Transactions of the Association for Computational Linguistics*, 4.

Tomas Mikolov, Kai Chen, Greg Corrado, and Jeffrey Dean. 2013a. Efficient estimation of word representations in vector space. In *ICLR Workshop Papers*.

Tomas Mikolov, Ilya Sutskever, Kai Chen, Greg Corrado, and Jeffrey Dean. 2013b. Distributed representations of words and phrases and their compositionality. In *NIPS*.

George A Miller and Walter G Charles. 1991. Contextual correlates of semantic similarity. *Language and cognitive processes*, 6(1):1–28.

Eric Nalisnick and Sachin Ravi. 2015. Infinite dimensional word embeddings. *arXiv preprint arXiv:1511.05392*.

Tahira Naseem, Benjamin Snyder, Jacob Eisenstein, and Regina Barzilay. 2009. Multilingual part-of-speech tagging: Two unsupervised approaches. *Journal of Artificial Intelligence Research*, 36:1–45.

Arvind Neelakantan, Jeevan Shankar, Alexandre Passos, and Andrew McCallum. 2014. Efficient nonparametric estimation of multiple embeddings per word in vector space. In *EMNLP*.

Hwee Tou Ng, Bin Wang, and Yee Seng Chan. 2003. Exploiting parallel texts for word sense disambiguation: An empirical study. In *ACL*.

Alexandre Passos, Vineet Kumar, and Andrew McCallum. 2014. Lexicon infused phrase embeddings for named entity resolution. In *CoNLL*.

Kira Radinsky, Eugene Agichtein, Evgeniy Gabrilovich, and Shaul Markovitch. 2011. A word at a time: computing word relatedness using temporal semantic analysis. In *WWW*.

Joseph Reisinger and J. Raymond Mooney. 2010. Multi-prototype vector-space models of word meaning. In *NAACL-HLT*.

Herbert Rubenstein and John B Goodenough. 1965. Contextual correlates of synonymy. *Communications of the ACM*, 8(10):627–633.

David E. Rumelhart, Geoffrey E. Hinton, and Ronald J. Williams. 1986. Learning internal representations by error propagation. In David E. Rumelhart, James L. McClelland, and PDP Research Group, editors, *Parallel Distributed Processing: Explorations in the Microstructure of Cognition, Vol. 1*. MIT Press.

Benjamin Snyder and Regina Barzilay. 2010. Climbing the Tower of Babel: Unsupervised Multilingual Learning. In *ICML*.

Hubert Soyer, Pontus Stenetorp, and Akiko Aizawa. 2014. Leveraging monolingual data for crosslingual compositional word representations. *CoRR*, abs/1412.6334.

Oscar Täckström, Ryan McDonald, and Jakob Uszkoreit. 2012. Cross-lingual word clusters for direct transfer of linguistic structure. In *NAACL-HLT*.

Fei Tian, Hanjun Dai, Jiang Bian, Bin Gao, Rui Zhang, Enhong Chen, and Tie-Yan Liu. 2014. A probabilistic model for learning multi-prototype word embeddings. In *COLING*.

Ivan Titov and Ehsan Khoddam. 2015. Unsupervised induction of semantic roles within a reconstruction-error minimization framework. In *NAACL*.

Ivan Titov and Alexandre Klementiev. 2012. Crosslingual induction of semantic roles. In *ACL*.

Yulia Tsvetkov, Manaal Faruqui, Wang Ling, Guillaume Lample, and Chris Dyer. 2015. Evaluation of word vector representations by subspace alignment. In *EMNLP*.

Joseph Turian, Lev Ratinov, and Yoshua Bengio. 2010. Word representations: a simple and general method for semi-supervised learning. In *ACL*.

Dongqiang Yang and David M. W. Powers. 2006. Verb similarity on the taxonomy of wordnet. In *GWC*.

Jiajun Zhang, Shujie Liu, Mu Li, Ming Zhou, and Chengqing Zong. 2014. Bilingually-constrained phrase embeddings for machine translation. In *ACL*.

Will Y. Zou, Richard Socher, Daniel Cer, and Christopher D. Manning. 2013. Bilingual word embeddings for phrase-based machine translation. In *EMNLP*.

Guang Yong Zou. 2007. Toward using confidence intervals to compare correlations. *Psychological methods*, 12(4).

Polyglot Neural Language Models:
A Case Study in Cross-Lingual Phonetic Representation Learning

Yulia Tsvetkov   Sunayana Sitaram   Manaal Faruqui   Guillaume Lample
Patrick Littell   David Mortensen   Alan W Black   Lori Levin   Chris Dyer
Language Technologies Institute
Carnegie Mellon University
Pittsburgh, PA, 15213, USA
{ytsvetko,ssitaram,mfaruqui,glample,plittell,dmortens,awb,lsl,cdyer}@cs.cmu.edu

Abstract

We introduce polyglot language models, recurrent neural network models trained to predict symbol sequences in many different languages using shared representations of symbols and conditioning on typological information about the language to be predicted. We apply these to the problem of modeling phone sequences—a domain in which universal symbol inventories and cross-linguistically shared feature representations are a natural fit. Intrinsic evaluation on held-out perplexity, qualitative analysis of the learned representations, and extrinsic evaluation in two downstream applications that make use of phonetic features show (i) that polyglot models better generalize to held-out data than comparable monolingual models and (ii) that polyglot phonetic feature representations are of higher quality than those learned monolingually.

1 Introduction

Nearly all existing language model (LM) architectures are designed to model one language at a time. This is unsurprising considering the historical importance of count-based models in which every surface form of a word is a separately modeled entity (English *cat* and Spanish *gato* would not likely benefit from sharing counts). However, recent models that use distributed representations—in particular models that share representations across languages (Hermann and Blunsom, 2014; Faruqui and Dyer, 2014; Huang et al., 2015; Lu et al., 2015, *inter alia*)—suggest universal models applicable to multiple languages are a possibility. This paper takes a

step in this direction.

We introduce **polyglot language models**: neural network language models that are trained on and applied to any number of languages. Our goals with these models are the following. First, to facilitate data and parameter sharing, providing more training resources to languages, which is especially valuable in low-resource settings. Second, models trained on diverse languages with diverse linguistic properties will better be able to learn naturalistic representations that are less likely to "overfit" to a single linguistic outlier. Finally, polyglot models offer convenience in a multilingual world: a single model replaces dozens of different models.

Exploration of polyglot language models at the sentence level—the traditional domain of language modeling—requires dealing with a massive event space (i.e., the union of words across many languages). To work in a more tractable domain, we evaluate our model on phone-based language modeling, the modeling sequences of *sounds*, rather than words. We choose this domain since a common assumption of many theories of phonology is that all spoken languages construct words from a finite inventory of phonetic symbols (represented conveniently as the elements of the the International Phonetic Alphabet; IPA) which are distinguished by language-universal features (e.g., place and manner of articulation, voicing status, etc.). Although our focus is on sound sequences, our solution can be ported to the semantic/syntactic problem as resulting from adaptation to constraints on semantic/syntactic structure.

This paper makes two primary contributions: in

Proceedings of NAACL-HLT 2016, pages 1357–1366,
San Diego, California, June 12-17, 2016. ©2016 Association for Computational Linguistics

modeling and in applications. In §2, we introduce a novel polyglot neural language model (NLM) architecture. Despite being trained on multiple languages, the multilingual model is more effective (9.5% lower perplexity) than individual models, and substantially more effective than naive baselines (over 25% lower perplexity). Our most effective polyglot architecture conditions not only on the identity of the language being predicted in each sequence, but also on a vector representation of its phono-typological properties. In addition to learning representations of phones as part of the polyglot language modeling objective, the model incorporates features about linguistic typology to improve generalization performance (§3). Our second primary contribution is to show that downstream applications are improved by using polyglot-learned phone representations. We focus on two tasks: predicting adapted word forms in models of cross-lingual lexical borrowing and speech synthesis (§4). Our experimental results (§5) show that in borrowing, we improve over the current state-of-the-art, and in speech synthesis, our features are more effective than manually-designed phonetic features. Finally, we analyze the phonological content of learned representations, finding that our polyglot models discover standard phonological categories such as length and nasalization, and that these are grouped correctly across languages with different phonetic inventories and contrastive features.

2 Model

In this section, we first describe in §2.1 the underlying framework of our model—RNNLM—a standard recurrent neural network based language model (Mikolov et al., 2010; Sundermeyer et al., 2012). Then, in §2.2, we define a Polyglot LM—a modification of RNNLM to incorporate language information, both learned and hand-crafted.

Problem definition. In the phonological LM, *phones* (sounds) are the basic units. Mapping from words to phones is defined in pronunciation dictionaries. For example, "cats" [kæts] is a sequence of four phones. Given a prefix of phones $\phi_1, \phi_2, \ldots, \phi_{t-1}$, the task of the LM is to estimate the conditional probability of the next phone $p(\phi_t \mid \phi_1, \phi_2, \ldots, \phi_{t-1})$.

2.1 RNNLM

In NLMs, a vocabulary V (here, a set of phones composing all word types in the language) is represented as a matrix of parameters $\mathbf{X} \in \mathbb{R}^{d \times |V|}$, with $|V|$ phone types represented as d-dimensional vectors. $\mathbf{X}$ is often denoted as lookup table. Phones in the input sequence are first converted to phone vectors, where ϕ_i is represented by $\mathbf{x}_i$ by multiplying the phone indicator (one-hot vector of length $|V|$) and the lookup table.

At each time step t, most recent phone prefix vector[1] $\mathbf{x}_t$ and hidden state $\mathbf{h}_{t-1}$ are transformed to compute a new hidden representation:

$$\mathbf{h}_t = f(\mathbf{x}_t, \mathbf{h}_{t-1}),$$

where f is a non-linear transformation. In the original RNNLMs (Mikolov et al., 2010), the transformation is such that:

$$\mathbf{h}_t = \tanh(\mathbf{W}_{h_x}\mathbf{x}_t + \mathbf{W}_{h_h}\mathbf{h}_{t-1} + \mathbf{b}_h).$$

To overcome the notorious problem in recurrent neural networks of vanishing gradients (Bengio et al., 1994), following Sundermeyer et al. (2012), in recurrent layer we use long short-term memory (LSTM) units (Hochreiter and Schmidhuber, 1997):[2]

$$\mathbf{h}_t = \text{LSTM}(\mathbf{x}_t, \mathbf{h}_{t-1}).$$

Given the hidden sequence $\mathbf{h}_t$, the output sequence is then computed as follows:

$$p(\phi_t = i \mid \phi_1, \ldots, \phi_{t-1}) = \text{softmax}(\mathbf{W}_{out}\mathbf{h}_t + \mathbf{b}_{out})_i,$$

where $\text{softmax}(x_i) = \frac{e^{x_i}}{\sum_j e^{x_j}}$ ensures a valid probability distribution over output phones.

---

[1] We are reading at each time step the most recent n-gram context rather than—as is more common in RNNLMs—a single phone context. Empirically, this works better for phone sequences, and we hypothesize that this lets the learner rely on direct connections for local phenomena (which are abundant in phonology) and minimally use the recurrent state to model longer-range effects.

[2] For brevity, we omit the equations describing the LSTM cells; they can be found in (Graves, 2013, eq. 7–11).

2.2 Polyglot LM

We now describe our modifications to RNNLM to account for multilinguality. The architecture is depicted in figure 1. Our task is to estimate the conditional probability of the next phone given the preceding phones and the language (ℓ): $p(\phi_t \mid \phi_1, \ldots, \phi_{t-1}, \ell)$.

In a multilingual NLM, we define a vocabulary V^* to be the union of vocabularies of all training languages, assuming that all language vocabularies are mapped to a shared representation (here, IPA). In addition, we maintain V_ℓ with a special symbol for each language (e.g., $\phi_{english}$, ϕ_{arabic}). Language symbol vectors are parameters in the new lookup table $\mathbf{X}_\ell \in \mathbb{R}^{d \times |\#langs|}$ (e.g., $\mathbf{x}_{english}$, $\mathbf{x}_{arabic}$). The inputs to the Polyglot LM are the phone vectors $\mathbf{x}_t$, the language character vector $\mathbf{x}_\ell$, and the typological feature vector constructed externally $\mathbf{t}_\ell$. The typological feature vector will be discussed in the following section.

The input layer is passed to the hidden local-context layer:

$$\mathbf{c}_t = \mathbf{W}_{c_x}\mathbf{x}_t + \mathbf{W}_{c_{lang}}\mathbf{x}_{lang} + \mathbf{b}_c.$$

The local-context vector is then passed to the hidden LSTM global-context layer, similarly to the previously described RNNLM:

$$\mathbf{g}_t = \mathrm{LSTM}(\mathbf{c}_t, \mathbf{g}_{t-1}).$$

In the next step, the global-context vector $\mathbf{g}_t$ is "factored" by the typology of the training language, to integrate manually-defined language features. To obtain this, we first project the (potentially high-dimensional) $\mathbf{t}_\ell$ into a low-dimensional vector, and apply non-linearity. Then, we multiply the $\mathbf{g}_t$ and the projected language layer, to obtain a global-context-language matrix:

$$\mathbf{f}_\ell = \tanh(\mathbf{W}_\ell \mathbf{t}_\ell + \mathbf{b}_\ell),$$
$$\mathbf{G}_t^\ell = \mathbf{g}_t \otimes \mathbf{f}_\ell^\top.$$

Finally, we vectorize the resulting matrix into a column vector and compute the output sequence as follows:

$$p(\phi_t = i \mid \phi_1, \ldots, \phi_{t-1}, \ell) =$$
$$\mathrm{softmax}(\mathbf{W}_{out}\mathrm{vec}(\mathbf{G}_t^\ell) + \mathbf{b}_{out})_i.$$

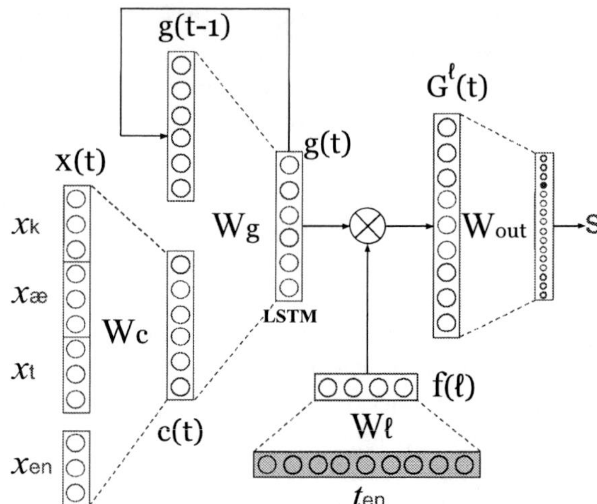

Figure 1: Architecture of the Polyglot LM.

Model training. Parameters of the models are the lookup tables $\mathbf{X}$ and $\mathbf{X}_\ell$, weight matrices $\mathbf{W}_i$, and bias vectors $\mathbf{b}_i$. Parameter optimization is performed using stochastic updates to minimize the categorical cross-entropy loss (which is equivalent to minimizing perplexity and maximizing likelihood): $H(\phi, \hat{\phi}) = -\Sigma_i \hat{\phi}_i \log \phi_i$, where ϕ is predicted and $\hat{\phi}$ is the gold label.

3 Typological features

Typological information is fed to the model via vectors of 190 binary typological features, all of which are phonological (related to sound structure) in their nature. These feature vectors are derived from data from the WALS (Dryer and Haspelmath, 2013), PHOIBLE (Moran et al., 2014), and Ethnologue (Lewis et al., 2015) typological databases via extensive post-processing and analysis.[3] The features primarily concern properties of sound inventories (i.e., the set of phones or phonemes occurring in a language) and are mostly of one of four types:

1. **Single segment represented in an inventory;**

---

[3]This data resource, which provides standardized phono-typological information for 2,273 languages, is available at `https://github.com/dmort27/uriel-phonology/tarball/0.1`. It is a subset of the URIEL database, a comprehensive database of typological features encoding syntactic and morphological (as well as phonological) properties of languages. It is available at `http://cs.cmu.edu/~dmortens/uriel.html`.

e.g., does language ℓ's sound inventory include /g/, a voiced velar stop?

2. **Class of segments represented in an inventory**; e.g., does language ℓ's sound inventory include voiced fricatives like /z/ and /v/?

3. **Minimal contrast represented in an inventory**; e.g., does language ℓ's sound inventory include two sounds that differ only in voicing, such as /t/ and /d/?

4. **Number of sounds representative of a class that are present in an inventory**; e.g., does language ℓ's sound inventory include exactly five vowels?

The motivation and criteria for coding each individual feature required extensive linguistic knowledge and analysis. Consider the case of tense vowels like /i/ and /u/ in "beet" and "boot" in contrast with lax vowels like /ɪ/ and /ʊ/ in "bit" and "book." Only through linguistic analysis does it become evident that (1) all languages have tense vowels—a feature based on the presence of tense vowels is uninformative and that (2) a significant minority of languages make a distinction between tense and lax vowels—a feature based on whether languages display a minimal difference of this kind would be more useful.

4 Applications of Phonetic Vectors

Learned continuous word representations—word vectors—are an important by-product of neural LMs, and these are used as features in numerous NLP applications, including chunking (Turian et al., 2010), part-of-speech tagging (Ling et al., 2015), dependency parsing (Lazaridou et al., 2013; Bansal et al., 2014; Dyer et al., 2015; Watanabe and Sumita, 2015), named entity recognition (Guo et al., 2014), and sentiment analysis (Socher et al., 2013; Wang et al., 2015). We evaluate phone vectors learned by Polyglot LMs in two downstream applications that rely on phonology: modeling lexical borrowing (§4.1) and speech synthesis (§4.2).

4.1 Lexical borrowing

Lexical borrowing is the adoption of words from another language, that inevitably happens when speakers of different languages communicate for a long period of time (Thomason and Kaufman, 2001). Borrowed words—also called *loan-*

words—constitute 10–70% of most language lexicons (Haspelmath, 2009); these are content words of foreign origin that are adapted in the language and are not perceived as foreign by language speakers. Computational modeling of cross-lingual transformations of loanwords is effective for inferring lexical correspondences across languages with limited parallel data, benefiting applications such as machine translation (Tsvetkov and Dyer, 2015; Tsvetkov and Dyer, 2016).

In the process of their nativization in a foreign language, loanwords undergo primarily **phonological adaptation**, namely insertion/deletion/substitution of phones to adapt to the phonotactic constraints of the recipient language. If a foreign phone is not present in the recipient language, it is usually replaced with its closest native equivalent—we thus hypothesize that cross-lingual phonological features learned by the Polyglot LM can be useful in models of borrowing to quantify cross-lingual similarities of sounds.

To test this hypothesis, we augment the hand-engineered models proposed by Tsvetkov and Dyer (2016) with features from phone vectors learned by our model. Inputs to the borrowing framework are loanwords (in Swahili, Romanian, Maltese), and outputs are their corresponding "donor" words in the donor language (Arabic, French, Italian, resp.). The framework is implemented as a cascade of finite-state transducers with insertion/deletion/substitution operations on sounds, weighted by high-level conceptual linguistic constraints that are learned in a supervised manner. Given a loanword, the system produces a candidate donor word with lower ranked violations than other candidates, using the shortest path algorithm. In the original borrowing model, insertion/deletion/substitution operations are unweighted. In this work, we integrate transition weights in the phone substitution transducers, which are cosine distances between phone vectors learned by our model. Our intuition is that similar sounds appear in similar contexts, even if they are not present in the same language (e.g., /sˤ/ in Arabic is adapted to /s/ in Swahili). Thus, if our model effectively captures cross-lingual signals, similar sounds should have smaller distances in the vector space, which can improve the shortest path results. Figure 2 illustrates our modifications to the original framework.

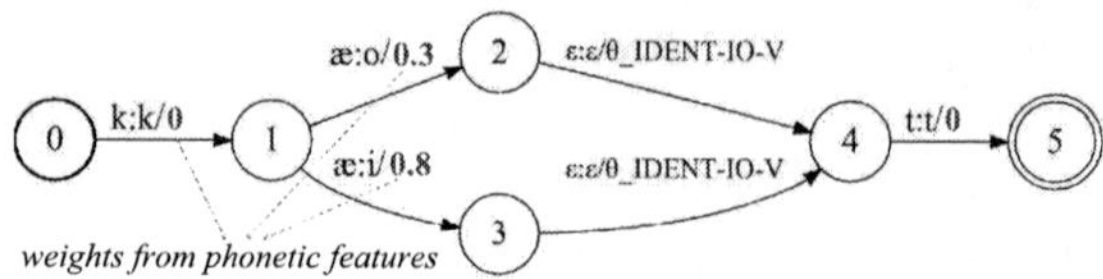

Figure 2: Distances between phone vectors learned by the Polyglot LM are integrated as substitution weights in the lexical borrowing transducers. An English word *cat* [kæt] is adapted to its Russian counterpart кот [kot]. The transducer has also an erroneous path to кит [kit] 'whale'. In the original system, both paths are weighted with the same feature IDENT-IO-V, firing on vowel substitution. Our modification allows the borrowing model to identify more plausible paths by weighting substitution operations.

4.2 Speech synthesis

Speech synthesis is the process of converting text into speech. It has various applications, such as screen readers for the visually impaired and hands-free voice based systems. Text-to-speech (TTS) systems are also used as part of speech-to-speech translation systems and spoken dialog systems, such as personal digital assistants. Natural and intelligible TTS systems exist for a number of languages in the world today. However, building TTS systems remains prohibitive for many languages due to the lack of linguistic resources and data.

The language-specific resources that are traditionally used for building TTS systems in a new language are: (1) audio recordings with transcripts; (2) pronunciation lexicon or letter to sound rules; and (3) a phone set definition. Standard TTS systems today use phone sets designed by experts. Typically, these phone sets also contain phonetic features for each phoneme, which are used as features in models of the spectrum and prosody. The phonetic features available in standard TTS systems are multidimensional vectors indicating various properties of each phoneme, such as whether it is a vowel or consonant, vowel length and height, place of articulation of a consonant, etc. Constructing these features by hand can be labor intensive, and coming up with such features automatically may be useful in low-resource scenarios.

In this work, we replace manually engineered phonetic features with phone vectors, which are then used by classification and regression trees for modeling the spectrum. Each phoneme in our phone set is assigned an automatically constructed phone vector, and each member of the phone vector is treated as a phoneme-level feature which is used in place of the manually engineered phonetic features. While prior work has explored TTS augmented with acoustic features (Watts et al., 2015), to the best of our knowledge, we are the first to replace manually engineered phonetic features in TTS systems with automatically constructed phone vectors.

5 Experiments

Our experimental evaluation of our proposed polyglot models consists of two parts: (i) an intrinsic evaluation where phone sequences are modeled with independent models and (ii) an extrinsic evaluation of the learned phonetic representations. Before discussing these results, we provide details of the data resources we used.

5.1 Resources and experimental setup

Resources. We experiment with the following languages: Arabic (AR), French (FR), Hindi (HI), Italian (IT), Maltese (MT), Romanian (RO), Swahili (SW), Tamil (TA), and Telugu (TE). In our language modeling experiments, two main sources of data are pronunciation dictionaries and typological features described in §3. The dictionaries for AR, FR, HI, TA, and TE are taken from in-house speech recognition/synthesis systems. For remaining languages, the dictionaries are automatically constructed using the Omniglot grapheme-to-IPA conversion rules.[4]

We use two types of pronunciation dictionaries: (1) AR, FR, HI, IT, MT, RO, and SW dictionaries used in experiments with lexical borrowing; and (2) EN, HI, TA, and TE dictionaries used in experiments with speech synthesis. The former are mapped to IPA, with the resulting phone vocabulary size—the number of distinct phones across IPA dictionaries—of 127 phones. The latter are encoded using the Uni-Tran universal transliteration resource (Qian et al., 2010), with a vocabulary of 79 phone types.

From the (word-type) pronunciation dictionaries, we remove 15% of the words for development, and a further 10% for testing; the rest of the data is

---

[4]http://omniglot.com/writing/

	AR	FR	HI	IT	MT	RO	SW
train	1,868/18,485	238/1,851	193/1,536	988/901	114/1,152	387/4,661	659/7,239
dev	366/3,627	47/363	38/302	19/176	22/226	76/916	130/1,422
test	208/2,057	27/207	22/173	11/100	13/128	43/524	73/806

Table 1: Train/dev/test counts for IPA pronunciation dictionaries for words (phone sequences) and phone tokens, in thousands: #thousands of sequences/# thousands of tokens.

	EN	HI	TA	TE
train	101/867	191/1,523	74/780	71/690
dev	20/169	37/300	14/152	14/135
test	11/97	21/171	8/87	8/77

Table 2: Train/dev/test statistics for UniTran pronunciation dictionaries for words (phone sequences) and phone tokens, in thousands: #thousands of sequences/# thousands of tokens.

used to train the models. In tables 1 and 2 we list—for both types of pronunciation dictionaries—train/dev/test data statistics for words (phone sequences) and phone tokens. We concatenate each phone sequence with beginning and end symbols (*<s>*, *</s>*).

Hyperparameters. We used the following network architecture: 100-dimensional phone vectors, with hidden local-context and LSTM layers of size 100, and hidden language layer of size 20. All language models were trained using the left context of 3 phones (4-gram LMs). Across all language modeling experiments, parameter optimization was performed on the dev set using the Adam algorithm (Kingma and Ba, 2014) with mini-batches of size 100 to train the models for 5 epochs.

5.2 Intrinsic perplexity evaluation

Perplexity is the standard evaluation measure for language models, which has been shown to correlate strongly with error rates in downstream applications (Klakow and Peters, 2002). We evaluated perplexities across several architectures, and several monolingual and multilingual setups. We kept the same hyper-parameters across all setups, as detailed in §5. Perplexities of LMs trained on the two types of pronunciation dictionaries were evaluated separately; table 3 summarizes perplexities of the models trained on IPA dictionaries, and table 4 summarizes perplexities of the UniTran LMs.

In columns, we compare three model architectures: *baseline* denotes the standard RNNLM archi-

tecture described in §2.1; +*lang* denotes the Polyglot LM architecture described in §2.2 with input language vector but without typological features and language layer; finally, +*typology* denotes the full Polyglot LM architecture. This setup lets us separately evaluate the contribution of modified architecture and the contribution of auxiliary set of features introduced via the language layer.

Test languages are IT in table 3, and HI in table 4. The rows correspond to different sets of training languages for the models: *monolingual* is for training and testing on the same language; +*similar* denotes training on three typologically similar languages: IT, FR, RO in table 3, and HI, TA, TE in table 4; +*dissimilar* denotes training on four languages, three similar and one typologically dissimilar language, to evaluate robustness of multilingual systems to diverse types of data. The final sets of training languages are IT, FR, RO, HI in table 3, and HI, TA, TE, EN in table 4.

training set	Perplexity ($\downarrow$)		
	baseline	+lang	+typology
monolingual	4.36	–	–
+similar	5.73	4.93	**4.24** ($\downarrow$ 26.0%)
+dissimilar	5.88	4.98	**4.41** ($\downarrow$ 25.0%)

Table 3: Perplexity experiments with IT as test language. Training languages: monolingual: IT; +similar: IT, FR, RO; +dissimilar: IT, FR, RO, HI.

training set	Perplexity ($\downarrow$)		
	baseline	+lang	+typology
monolingual	3.70	–	–
+similar	4.14	3.78	**3.35** ($\downarrow$ 19.1%)
+dissimilar	4.29	3.82	**3.42** ($\downarrow$ 20.3%)

Table 4: Perplexity experiments with HI as test language. Training languages: monolingual: HI; +similar: HI, TA, TE; +dissimilar: HI, TA, TE, EN.

We see several patterns of results. First, polyglot models require, unsurprisingly, information about what language they are predicting to obtain good modeling performance. Second, typological information is more valuable than letting the model learn representations of the language along with the characters. Finally, typology-augmented polyglot models outperform their monolingual baseline, providing evidence in support of the hypothesis that cross-lingual evidence is useful not only for learning cross-lingual representations and models, but monolingual ones as well.

5.3 Lexical borrowing experiments

We fully reproduced lexical borrowing models described in (Tsvetkov and Dyer, 2016) for three language pairs: AR–SW, FR–RO, and IT–MT. Train and test corpora are donor–loanword pairs in the language pairs. Corpora statistics are given in table 5 (note that these are extremely small data sets; thus small numbers of highly informative features a necessary for good generalization). We use the reproduced systems as the baselines, and compare these to the corresponding systems augmented with phone vectors, as described in §4.1.

	AR–SW	FR–RO	IT–MT
train	417	282	425
test	73	50	75

Table 5: Number of training and test pairs the the borrowing datasets.

Integrated vectors were obtained from a single polyglot model with typology, trained on all languages with IPA dictionaries. For comparison with the results in table 3, perplexity of the model on the IT dataset (used for evaluation is §5.2) is 4.16, even lower than in the model trained on four languages. To retrain the high-level conceptual linguistic features learned by the borrowing models, we initialized the augmented systems with feature weights learned by the baselines, and retrained. Final weights were established using cross-validation. Then, we evaluated the accuracy of the augmented borrowing systems on the held-out test data.

Accuracies are shown in table 6. We observe improvements of up to 5% in accuracies of FR–RO and IT–MT pairs. Effectiveness of the same polyglot model trained on multiple languages and integrated in different downstream systems supports our as-

sumption that the model remains stable and effective with addition of languages. Our model is less effective for the AR–SW language pair. We speculate that the results are worse, because this is a pair of (typologically) more distant languages; consequently, the phonological adaptation processes that happen in loanword assimilation are more complex than mere substitutions of similar phones that we are targeting via the integration of phone vectors.

	Accuracy (↑)		
	AR–SW	FR–RO	IT–MT
baseline	**48.4**	75.6	83.3
+multilingual	46.9	**80.6**	**87.1**

Table 6: Accuracies of the baseline models of lexical borrowing and the models augmented with phone vectors. In all the experiments, we use vectors from a single Polyglot LM model trained on AR, SW, FR, RO, IT, MT.

5.4 Speech synthesis experiments

A popular objective metric for measuring the quality of synthetic speech is the Mel Cepstral Distortion (MCD) (Hu and Loizou, 2008). The MCD metric calculates an L2 norm of the Mel Frequency Cepstral Coefficients (MFCCs) of natural speech from a held out test set, and synthetic speech generated from the same test set. Since this is a distance metric, a lower value of MCD suggests better synthesis. The MCD is a database-specific metric, but experiments by Kominek et al. (Kominek et al., 2008) have shown that a decrease in MCD of 0.08 is perceptually significant, and a decrease of 0.12 is equivalent to doubling the size of the TTS database. In our experiments, we use MCD to measure the relative improvement obtained by our techniques.

We conducted experiments on the IIIT-H Hindi voice database (Prahallad et al., 2012), a 2 hour single speaker database recorded by a professional male speaker. We used the same front end (UniTran) to build all the Hindi TTS systems, with the only difference between the systems being the presence or absence of phonetic features and our vectors. For all our voice-based experiments, we built CLUSTER-GEN Statistical Parametric Synthesis voices (Black, 2006) using the Festvox voice building tools (Black and Lenzo, 2003) and the Festival speech synthesis engine (Black and Taylor, 1997).

The baseline TTS system was built using no phonetic features. We also built a TTS system with standard hand-crafted phonetic features. Table 7 shows the MCD for the HI baseline, the standard TTS with hand-crafted features, and augmented TTS systems built using monolingual and multilingual phone vectors constructed with Polyglot LMs.

	MCD ($\downarrow$)
baseline	4.58
+monolingual	4.40
+multilingual	**4.39**
+hand-crafted	4.41

Table 7: MCD for the HI TTS systems. Polyglot LM training languages: monolingual: HI; +multilingual: HI, TA, TE, EN.

Our multilingual vectors outperform the baseline, with a significant decrease of 0.19 in MCD. Crucially, TTS systems augmented with the Polyglot LM phone vectors outperform also the standard TTS with hand-crafted features. We found that using both feature sets added no value, suggesting that learned phone vectors are capturing information that is equivalent to the hand-engineered vectors.

5.5 Qualitative analysis of vectors

Phone vectors learned by Polyglot LMs are mere sequences of real numbers. An interesting question is whether these vectors capture linguistic (phonological) qualities of phones they are encoding. To analyze to what extent our vectors capture linguistic properties of phones, we use the QVEC—a tool to quantify and interpret linguistic content of vector space models (Tsvetkov et al., 2015). The tool aligns dimensions in a matrix of learned distributed representations with dimensions of a hand-crafted linguistic matrix. Alignments are induced via correlating columns in the distributed and the linguistic matrices. To analyze the content of the distributed matrix, annotations from the linguistic matrix are projected via the maximally-correlated alignments.

We constructed a phonological matrix in which 5,059 rows are IPA phones and 21 columns are boolean indicators of universal phonological properties, e.g. *consonant, voiced, labial*.[5] We the projected annotations from the linguistic matrix and

manually examined aligned dimensions in the phone vectors from §5.3 (trained on six languages). In the maximally-correlated columns—corresponding to linguistic features *long, consonant, nasalized*—we examined phones with highest coefficients. These were: [ɐː, ʊː, iː, ɔː, ɛː] for *long*; [v, ɲ, d͡ʒ, d, f, j, t͡s, ŋ] for *consonant*; and [ɔ̃, ɛ̃, ɑ̃, œ̃] for *nasalized*. Clearly, the learned representation discover standard phonological features. Moreover, these top-ranked sounds are not grouped by a single language, e.g., /d͡ʒ/ is present in Arabic but not in French, and /ɲ, ŋ/ are present in French but not in Arabic. From this analysis, we conclude that (1) the model discovers linguistically meaningful phonetic features; (2) the model induces meaningful related groupings across languages.

6 Related Work

Multilingual language models. Interpolation of monolingual LMs is an alternative to obtain a multilingual model (Harbeck et al., 1997; Weng et al., 1997). However, interpolated models still require a trained model per language, and do not allow parameter sharing at training time. Bilingual language models trained on concatenated corpora were explored mainly in speech recognition (Ward et al., 1998; Wang et al., 2002; Fügen et al., 2003). Adaptations have been proposed to apply language models in bilingual settings in machine translation (Niehues et al., 2011) and code switching (Adel et al., 2013). These approaches, however, require adaptation to every pair of languages, and an adapted model cannot be applied to more than two languages.

Independently, Ammar et al. (2016) used a different polyglot architecture for multilingual dependency parsing. This work has also confirmed the utility of polyglot architectures in leveraging multilinguality.

Multimodal neural language models. Multimodal language modeling is integrating image/video modalities in text LMs. Our work is inspired by the neural multimodal LMs (Kiros and Salakhutdinov, 2013; Kiros et al., 2015), which defined language models conditional on visual contexts, although we use a different language model architecture (recurrent vs. log-bilinear) and a different approach to gat-

---

[5]This matrix is described in Littell et al. (2016) and is available at `https://github.com/dmort27/panphon/`.

ing modality.

7 Conclusion

We presented a novel *multilingual* language model architecture. The model obtains substantial gains in perplexity, and improves downstream text and speech applications. Although we focus on phonology, our approach is general, and can be applied in problems that integrate divergent modalities, e.g., topic modeling, and multilingual tagging and parsing.

Acknowledgments

This work was supported by the National Science Foundation through award IIS-1526745 and in part by the Defense Advanced Research Projects Agency (DARPA) Information Innovation Office (I2O). Program: Low Resource Languages for Emergent Incidents (LORELEI). Issued by DARPA/I2O under Contract No. HR0011-15-C-0114.

References

Heike Adel, Ngoc Thang Vu, and Tanja Schultz. 2013. Combination of recurrent neural networks and factored language models for code-switching language modeling. In *Proc. ACL*, pages 206–211.

Waleed Ammar, George Mulcaire, Miguel Ballesteros, Chris Dyer, and Noah A. Smith. 2016. Many languages, one parser. *CoRR*, abs/1602.01595.

Mohit Bansal, Kevin Gimpel, and Karen Livescu. 2014. Tailoring continuous word representations for dependency parsing. In *Proc. ACL*.

Yoshua Bengio, Patrice Simard, and Paolo Frasconi. 1994. Learning long-term dependencies with gradient descent is difficult. *IEEE Transactions on Neural Networks*, 5(2):157–166.

Alan W Black and Kevin A Lenzo. 2003. Building synthetic voices. http://festvox.org/bsv/.

Alan W Black and Paul Taylor. 1997. The Festival speech synthesis system: system documentation. Technical report, Human Communication Research Centre, University of Edinburgh.

Alan W Black. 2006. CLUSTERGEN: a statistical parametric synthesizer using trajectory modeling. In *Proc. Interspeech*.

Matthew S. Dryer and Martin Haspelmath, editors. 2013. *WALS Online*. Max Planck Institute for Evolutionary Anthropology. http://wals.info/.

Chris Dyer, Miguel Ballesteros, Wang Ling, Austin Matthews, and Noah A Smith. 2015. Transition-based dependency parsing with stack long short-term memory. In *Proc. ACL*.

Manaal Faruqui and Chris Dyer. 2014. Improving vector space word representations using multilingual correlation. In *Proc. EACL*.

Christian Fügen, Sebastian Stuker, Hagen Soltau, Florian Metze, and Tanja Schultz. 2003. Efficient handling of multilingual language models. In *Proc. ASRU*, pages 441–446.

Alex Graves. 2013. Generating sequences with recurrent neural networks. *CoRR*, abs/1308.0850.

Jiang Guo, Wanxiang Che, Haifeng Wang, and Ting Liu. 2014. Revisiting embedding features for simple semi-supervised learning. In *Proc. EMNLP*.

Stefan Harbeck, Elmar Nöth, and Heinrich Niemann. 1997. Multilingual speech recognition. In *Proc. 2nd SQEL Workshop on Multi-Lingual Information Retrieval Dialogs*, pages 9–15.

Martin Haspelmath. 2009. Lexical borrowing: concepts and issues. *Loanwords in the World's Languages: a comparative handbook*, pages 35–54.

Karl Moritz Hermann and Phil Blunsom. 2014. Multilingual Models for Compositional Distributional Semantics. In *Proc. ACL*.

Sepp Hochreiter and Jürgen Schmidhuber. 1997. Long short-term memory. *Neural Computation*, 9(8):1735–1780.

Yi Hu and Philipos C Loizou. 2008. Evaluation of objective quality measures for speech enhancement. *Audio, Speech, & Language Processing*, 16(1):229–238.

Kejun Huang, Matt Gardner, Evangelos Papalexakis, Christos Faloutsos, Nikos Sidiropoulos, Tom Mitchell, Partha P. Talukdar, and Xiao Fu. 2015. Translation invariant word embeddings. In *Proc. EMNLP*, pages 1084–1088.

Diederik Kingma and Jimmy Ba. 2014. Adam: A method for stochastic optimization. *CoRR*, abs/1412.6980.

Ryan Kiros and Ruslan Salakhutdinov. 2013. Multimodal neural language models. In *Proc. NIPS Deep Learning Workshop*.

Ryan Kiros, Ruslan Salakhutdinov, and Richard Zemel. 2015. Unifying visual-semantic embeddings with multimodal neural language models. *TACL*.

Dietrich Klakow and Jochen Peters. 2002. Testing the correlation of word error rate and perplexity. *Speech Communication*, 38(1):19–28.

John Kominek, Tanja Schultz, and Alan W Black. 2008. Synthesizer voice quality of new languages calibrated with mean Mel Cepstral Distortion. In *Proc. SLTU*, pages 63–68.

Angeliki Lazaridou, Eva Maria Vecchi, and Marco Baroni. 2013. Fish transporters and miracle homes: How compositional distributional semantics can help NP parsing. In *Proc. EMNLP*.

M Paul Lewis, Gary F Simons, and Charles D Fennig. 2015. *Ethnologue: Languages of the world*. Texas: SIL International. http://www.ethnologue.com.

Wang Ling, Tiago Luís, Luís Marujo, Ramón Fernandez Astudillo, Silvio Amir, Chris Dyer, Alan W Black, and Isabel Trancoso. 2015. Finding function in form: Compositional character models for open vocabulary word representation. In *Proc. NAACL*.

Patrick Littell, David Mortensen, Kartik Goyal, Chris Dyer, and Lori Levin. 2016. Bridge-language capitalization inference in Western Iranian: Sorani, Kurmanji, Zazaki, and Tajik. In *Proceedings of the Eleventh International Conference on Language Resources and Evaluation (LREC'16)*.

Ang Lu, Weiran Wang, Mohit Bansal, Kevin Gimpel, and Karen Livescu. 2015. Deep multilingual correlation for improved word embeddings. In *Proc. NAACL*.

Tomas Mikolov, Martin Karafiát, Lukas Burget, Jan Cernockỳ, and Sanjeev Khudanpur. 2010. Recurrent neural network based language model. In *Proc. Interspeech*, pages 1045–1048.

Steven Moran, Daniel McCloy, and Richard Wright, editors. 2014. *PHOIBLE Online*. Max Planck Institute for Evolutionary Anthropology. http://phoible.org/.

Jan Niehues, Teresa Herrmann, Stephan Vogel, and Alex Waibel. 2011. Wider context by using bilingual language models in machine translation. In *Proc. WMT*, pages 198–206.

Kishore Prahallad, E. Naresh Kumar, Venkatesh Keri, S. Rajendran, and Alan W Black. 2012. The IIIT-H Indic speech databases. In *Proc. Interspeech*.

Ting Qian, Kristy Hollingshead, Su-youn Yoon, Kyoungyoung Kim, Richard Sproat, and Malta LREC. 2010. A Python toolkit for universal transliteration. In *Proc. LREC*.

Richard Socher, Alex Perelygin, Jean Wu, Jason Chuang, Christopher D. Manning, Andrew Y. Ng, and Christopher Potts. 2013. Recursive deep models for semantic compositionality over a sentiment treebank. In *Proc. EMNLP*.

Martin Sundermeyer, Ralf Schlüter, and Hermann Ney. 2012. LSTM neural networks for language modeling. In *Proc. Interspeech*.

Sarah Grey Thomason and Terrence Kaufman. 2001. *Language contact*. Edinburgh University Press Edinburgh.

Yulia Tsvetkov and Chris Dyer. 2015. Lexicon stratification for translating out-of-vocabulary words. In *Proc. ACL*, pages 125–131.

Yulia Tsvetkov and Chris Dyer. 2016. Cross-lingual bridges with models of lexical borrowing. *JAIR*, 55:63–93.

Yulia Tsvetkov, Manaal Faruqui, Wang Ling, Guillaume Lample, and Chris Dyer. 2015. Evaluation of word vector representations by subspace alignment. In *Proc. EMNLP*. https://github.com/ytsvetko/qvec.

Joseph Turian, Lev Ratinov, and Yoshua Bengio. 2010. Word representations: a simple and general method for semi-supervised learning. In *Proc. ACL*.

Zhirong Wang, Umut Topkara, Tanja Schultz, and Alex Waibel. 2002. Towards universal speech recognition. In *Proc. ICMI*, page 247.

Xin Wang, Yuanchao Liu, Chengjie Sun, Baoxun Wang, and Xiaolong Wang. 2015. Predicting polarities of tweets by composing word embeddings with long short-term memory. In *Proc. ACL*, pages 1343–1353.

Todd Ward, Salim Roukos, Chalapathy Neti, Jerome Gros, Mark Epstein, and Satya Dharanipragada. 1998. Towards speech understanding across multiple languages. In *Proc. ICSLP*.

Taro Watanabe and Eiichiro Sumita. 2015. Transition-based neural constituent parsing. In *Proc. ACL*.

Oliver Watts, Zhizheng Wu, and Simon King. 2015. Sentence-level control vectors for deep neural network speech synthesis. In *Proc. Interspeech*.

Fuliang Weng, Harry Bratt, Leonardo Neumeyer, and Andreas Stolcke. 1997. A study of multilingual speech recognition. In *Proc. EUROSPEECH*, pages 359–362.

Learning Distributed Representations of Sentences from Unlabelled Data

Felix Hill
Computer Laboratory
University of Cambridge
felix.hill@cl.cam.ac.uk

Kyunghyun Cho
Courant Institute of
Mathematical Sciences
& Centre for Data Science
New York University
kyunghyun.cho@nyu.edu

Anna Korhonen
Department of Theoretical
& Applied Linguistics
University of Cambridge
alk23@cam.ac.uk

Abstract

Unsupervised methods for learning distributed representations of words are ubiquitous in today's NLP research, but far less is known about the best ways to learn distributed phrase or sentence representations from unlabelled data. This paper is a systematic comparison of models that learn such representations. We find that the optimal approach depends critically on the intended application. Deeper, more complex models are preferable for representations to be used in supervised systems, but shallow log-bilinear models work best for building representation spaces that can be decoded with simple spatial distance metrics. We also propose two new unsupervised representation-learning objectives designed to optimise the trade-off between training time, domain portability and performance.

1 Introduction

Distributed representations - dense real-valued vectors that encode the semantics of linguistic units - are ubiquitous in today's NLP research. For single-words or word-like entities, there are established ways to acquire such representations from naturally occurring (unlabelled) training data based on comparatively task-agnostic objectives (such as predicting adjacent words). These methods are well understood empirically (Baroni et al., 2014b) and theoretically (Levy and Goldberg, 2014). The best word representation spaces reflect consistently-observed aspects of human conceptual organisation (Hill et al., 2015b), and can be added as features to improve the performance of numerous language processing systems (Collobert et al., 2011).

By contrast, there is comparatively little consensus on the best ways to learn distributed representations of phrases or sentences.[1] With the advent of deeper language processing techniques, it is relatively common for models to represent phrases or sentences as continuous-valued vectors. Examples include machine translation (Sutskever et al., 2014), image captioning (Mao et al., 2015) and dialogue systems (Serban et al., 2015). While it has been observed informally that the internal sentence representations of such models can reflect semantic intuitions (Cho et al., 2014), it is not known which architectures or objectives yield the 'best' or most useful representations. Resolving this question could ultimately have a significant impact on language processing systems. Indeed, it is phrases and sentences, rather than individual words, that encode the human-like general world knowledge (or 'common sense') (Norman, 1972) that is a critical missing part of most current language understanding systems.

We address this issue with a systematic comparison of cutting-edge methods for learning distributed representations of sentences. We focus on methods that do not require labelled data gathered for the purpose of training models, since such methods are more cost-effective and applicable across languages and domains. We also propose two new phrase or sentence representation learning objectives - *Sequential Denoising Autoencoders* (SDAEs)

---

[1] See the contrasting conclusions in (Mitchell and Lapata, 2008; Clark and Pulman, 2007; Baroni et al., 2014a; Milajevs et al., 2014) among others.

Proceedings of NAACL-HLT 2016, pages 1367–1377,
San Diego, California, June 12-17, 2016. ©2016 Association for Computational Linguistics

and *FastSent*, a sentence-level log-bilinear bag-of-words model. We compare all methods on two types of task - *supervised* and *unsupervised evaluations* - reflecting different ways in which representations are ultimately to be used. In the former setting, a classifier or regression model is applied to representations and trained with task-specific labelled data, while in the latter, representation spaces are directly queried using cosine distance.

We observe notable differences in approaches depending on the nature of the evaluation metric. In particular, deeper or more complex models (which require greater time and resources to train) generally perform best in the supervised setting, whereas shallow log-bilinear models work best on unsupervised benchmarks. Specifically, SkipThought Vectors (Kiros et al., 2015) perform best on the majority of supervised evaluations, but SDAEs are the top performer on paraphrase identification. In contrast, on the (unsupervised) SICK sentence relatedness benchmark, FastSent, a simple, log-bilinear variant of the SkipThought objective, performs better than all other models. Interestingly, the method that exhibits strongest performance across both supervised and unsupervised benchmarks is a bag-of-words model trained to compose word embeddings using dictionary definitions (Hill et al., 2015a). Taken together, these findings constitute valuable guidelines for the application of phrasal or sentential representation-learning to language understanding systems.

2 Distributed Sentence Representations

To constrain the analysis, we compare neural language models that compute sentence representations from unlabelled, naturally-ocurring data, as with the predominant methods for word representations.[2] Likewise, we do not focus on 'bottom up' models where phrase or sentence representations are built from fixed mathe proposed bymatical operations on word vectors (although we do consider a canonical case - see CBOW below); these were already compared by Milajevs et al. (2014). Most space is devoted to our novel approaches, and we refer the

reader to the original papers for more details of existing models.

2.1 Existing Models Trained on Text

SkipThought Vectors For consecutive sentences S_{i-1}, S_i, S_{i+1} in some document, the **SkipThought** model (Kiros et al., 2015) is trained to predict target sentences S_{i-1} and S_{i+1} given source sentence S_i. As with all *sequence-to-sequence* models, in training the source sentence is 'encoded' by a Recurrent Neural Network (RNN) (with Gated Recurrent uUnits (Cho et al., 2014)) and then 'decoded' into the two target sentences in turn. Importantly, because RNNs employ a single set of update weights at each time-step, both the encoder and decoder are sensitive to the order of words in the source sentence.

For each position in a target sentence S_t, the decoder computes a softmax distribution over the model's vocabulary. The cost of a training example is the sum of the negative log-likelihood of each correct word in the target sentences S_{i-1} and S_{i+1}. This cost is backpropagated to train the encoder (and decoder), which, when trained, can map sequences of words to a single vector.

ParagraphVector Le and Mikolov (2014) proposed two log-bilinear models of sentence representation. The **DBOW** model learns a vector **s** for every sentence S in the training corpus which, together with word embeddings v_w, define a softmax distribution optimised to predict words $w \in S$ given S. The v_w are shared across all sentences in the corpus. In the **DM** model, k-grams of consecutive words $\{w_i \ldots w_{i+k} \in S\}$ are selected and **s** is combined with $\{v_{w_i} \ldots v_{w_{i+k}}\}$ to make a softmax prediction (parameterised by additional weights) of w_{i+k+1}.

We used the Gensim implementation,[3] treating each sentence in the training data as a 'paragraph' as suggested by the authors. During training, both DM and DBOW models store representations for every sentence (as well as word) in the training corpus. Even on large servers it was therefore only possible to train models with representation size 200, and DM models whose combination operation was averaging (rather than concatenation). Unlike other models considered in this section, for both ParagraphVector architectures an inference step is re-

---

[2]This excludes innovative supervised sentence-level architectures including (Socher et al., 2011; Kalchbrenner et al., 2014) and many others.

[3]https://radimrehurek.com/gensim/

quired after training to estimate sentence representations s for arbitrary sentences based on the v_w. This additional computation is reflected in the higher encoding time in Table 1 (TE).

Bottom-Up Methods We train **CBOW** and **Skip-Gram** word embeddings (Mikolov et al., 2013b) on the same text corpus as the SkipThought and ParagraphVector models, and compose by elementwise addition as per Mitchell and Lapata (2010).[4]

We also compare to **C-PHRASE** (Pham et al., 2015), an approach that exploits a (supervised) parser to infer distributed semantic representations based on a syntactic parse of sentences. C-PHRASE achieves state-of-the-art results for distributed representations on several evaluations used in this study.[5]

Non-Distributed Baseline We implement a **TFIDF BOW** model in which the representation of sentence S encodes the count in S of a set of feature-words weighted by their *tfidf* in C, the corpus. The feature-words are the 200,000 most common words in C.

2.2 Models Trained on Structured Resources

The following models rely on (freely-available) data that has more structure than raw text.

DictRep Hill et al. (2015a) trained neural language models to map dictionary definitions to pre-trained word embeddings of the words defined by those definitions. They experimented with **BOW** and **RNN** (with LSTM) encoding architectures and variants in which the input word embeddings were either learned or pre-trained (**+embs.**) to match the target word embeddings. We implement their models using the available code and training data.[6]

CaptionRep Using the same overall architecture, we trained (**BOW** and **RNN**) models to map captions in the COCO dataset (Chen et al., 2015) to pre-trained vector representations of images. The image representations were encoded by a deep convolutional network (Szegedy et al., 2014) trained on the

ILSVRC 2014 object recognition task (Russakovsky et al., 2014). Multi-modal distributed representations can be encoded by feeding test sentences forward through the trained model.

NMT We consider the sentence representations learned by neural MT models. These models have identical architecture to SkipThought, but are trained on sentence-aligned translated texts. We used a standard architecture (Cho et al., 2014) on all available **En-Fr** and **En-De** data from the 2015 Workshop on Statistical MT (WMT).[7]

2.3 Novel Text-Based Models

We introduce two new approaches designed to address certain limitations with the existing models.

Sequential (Denoising) Autoencoders The SkipThought objective requires training text with a coherent inter-sentence narrative, making it problematic to port to domains such as social media or artificial language generated from symbolic knowledge. To avoid this restriction, we experiment with a representation-learning objective based on *denoising autoencoders* (DAEs). In a DAE, high-dimensional input data is corrupted according to some noise function, and the model is trained to recover the original data from the corrupted version. As a result of this process, DAEs learn to represent the data in terms of features that explain its important factors of variation (Vincent et al., 2008). Transforming data into DAE representations (as a 'pre-training' or initialisation step) gives more robust (supervised) classification performance in deep feedforward networks (Vincent et al., 2010).

The original DAEs were feedforward nets applied to (image) data of fixed size. Here, we adapt the approach to variable-length sentences by means of a noise function $N(S|p_o, p_x)$, determined by free parameters $p_o, p_x \in [0, 1]$. First, for each word w in S, N deletes w with (independent) probability p_o. Then, for each non-overlapping bigram $w_i w_{i+1}$ in S, N swaps w_i and w_{i+1} with probability p_x. We then train the same LSTM-based encoder-decoder architecture as NMT, but with the denoising objective to predict (as target) the original source sentence S given a corrupted version $N(S|p_o, p_x)$ (as source).

---

[4] We also tried multiplication but this gave very poor results.

[5] Since code for C-PHRASE is not publicly-available we use the available pre-trained model (http://clic.cimec.unitn.it/composes/cphrase-vectors.html). Note this model is trained on 3× more text than others in this study.

[6] https://www.cl.cam.ac.uk/~fh295/. Definitions from the training data matching those in the WordNet STS 2014 evaluation (used in this study) were excluded.

[7] www.statmt.org/wmt15/translation-task.html

The trained model can then encode novel word sequences into distributed representations. We call this model the *Sequential Denoising Autoencoder* (**SDAE**). Note that, unlike SkipThought, SDAEs can be trained on sets of sentences in arbitrary order.

We label the case with no noise (i.e. $p_o = p_x = 0$ and $N \equiv id$) **SAE**. This setting matches the method applied to text classification tasks by Dai and Le (2015). The 'word dropout' effect when $p_o \geq 0$ has also been used as a regulariser for deep nets in supervised language tasks (Iyyer et al., 2015), and for large p_x the objective is similar to word-level 'debagging' (Sutskever et al., 2011). For the SDAE, we tuned p_o, p_x on the validation set (see Section 3.2).[8] We also tried a variant (**+embs**) in which words are represented by (fixed) pre-trained embeddings.

FastSent The performance of SkipThought vectors shows that rich sentence semantics can be inferred from the content of adjacent sentences. The model could be said to exploit a type of *sentence-level Distributional Hypothesis* (Harris, 1954; Polajnar et al., 2015). Nevertheless, like many deep neural language models, SkipThought is very slow to train (see Table 1). FastSent is a simple additive (log-bilinear) sentence model designed to exploit the same signal, but at much lower computational expense. Given a BOW representation of some sentence in context, the model simply predicts adjacent sentences (also represented as BOW) .

More formally, FastSent learns a source u_w and target v_w embedding for each word in the model vocabulary. For a training example S_{i-1}, S_i, S_{i+1} of consecutive sentences, S_i is represented as the sum of its source embeddings $\mathbf{s_i} = \sum_{w \in S_i} u_w$. The cost of the example is then simply:

$$\sum_{w \in S_{i-1} \cup S_{i+1}} \phi(\mathbf{s_i}, v_w) \tag{1}$$

where $\phi(v_1, v_2)$ is the softmax function.

We also experiment with a variant (**+AE**) in which the encoded (source) representation must predict its own words as target in addition to those of adjacent sentences. Thus in FastSent+AE, (1) becomes

$$\sum_{w \in S_{i-1} \cup S_i \cup S_{i+1}} \phi(\mathbf{s_i}, v_w). \tag{2}$$

---

[8] We searched $p_o, p_x \in \{0.1, 0.2, 0.3\}$ and observed best results with $p_o = p_x = 0.1$.

	OS	R	WO	SD	WD	TR	TE
S(D)AE			✓	2400	100	72*	640
ParagraphVec				100	100	4	1130
CBOW				500	500	2	145
SkipThought	✓		✓	4800	620	336*	890
FastSent	✓			100	100	2	140
DictRep		✓	✓	500	256	24*	470
CaptionRep		✓	✓	500	256	24*	470
NMT		✓	✓	2400	512	72*	720

Table 1: **Properties of models compared in this study** **OS:** requires training corpus of sentences in order. **R:** requires structured resource for training. **WO:** encoder sensitive to word order. **SD:** dimension of sentence representation. **WD:** dimension of word representation. **TR:** approximate training time (hours) on the dataset in this paper. * indicates trained on GPU. **TE:** approximate time (s) taken to encode 0.5m sentences.

At test time the trained model (very quickly) encodes unseen word sequences into distributed representations with $\mathbf{s} = \sum_{w \in S} u_w$.

2.4 Training and Model Selection

Unless stated above, all models were trained on the Toronto Books Corpus,[9] which has the intersentential coherence required for SkipThought and FastSent. The corpus consists of 70m ordered sentences from over 7,000 books.

Specifications of the models are shown in Table 1. The log-bilinear models (SkipGram, CBOW, ParagraphVec and FastSent) were trained for one epoch on one CPU core. The representation dimension d for these models was found after tuning $d \in \{100, 200, 300, 400, 500\}$ on the validation set.[10] All other models were trained on one GPU. The S(D)AE models were trained for one epoch ($\approx$ 8 days). The SkipThought model was trained for two weeks, covering just under one epoch.[11] For CaptionRep and DictRep, performance was monitored on held-out training data and training was stopped after 24 hours after a plateau in cost. The NMT models were trained for 72 hours.

---

[9] http://www.cs.toronto.edu/~mbweb/
[10] For ParagraphVec only $d \in \{100, 200\}$ was possible due to the high memory footprint.
[11] Downloaded from https://github.com/ryankiros/skip-thoughts

Dataset		Sentence 1	Sentence 2	/5
	News	*Mexico wishes to guarantee citizens' safety.*	*Mexico wishes to avoid more violence.*	4
	Forum	*The problem is simpler than that.*	*The problem is simple.*	3.8
STS	WordNet	*A social set or clique of friends.*	*An unofficial association of people or groups.*	3.6
2014	Twitter	*Taking Aim #Stopgunviolence #Congress #NRA*	*Obama, Gun Policy and the N.R.A.*	1.6
	Images	*A woman riding a brown horse.*	*A young girl riding a brown horse.*	4.4
	Headlines	*Iranians Vote in Presidential Election.*	*Keita Wins Mali Presidential Election.*	0.4
SICK (test+train)		*A lone biker is jumping in the air.*	*A man is jumping into a full pool.*	1.7

Table 2: Example sentence pairs and 'similarity' ratings from the unsupervised evaluations used in this study.

3 Evaluating Sentence Representations

In previous work, distributed representations of language were evaluated either by measuring the effect of adding representations as features in some classification task - *supervised evaluation* (Collobert et al., 2011; Mikolov et al., 2013a; Kiros et al., 2015) - or by comparing with human relatedness judgements - *unsupervised evaluation* (Hill et al., 2015a; Baroni et al., 2014b; Levy et al., 2015). The former setting reflects a scenario in which representations are used to inject general knowledge (sometimes considered as *pre-training*) into a supervised model. The latter pertains to applications in which the sentence representation space is used for direct comparisons, lookup or retrieval. Here, we apply and compare both evaluation paradigms.

3.1 Supervised Evaluations

Representations are applied to 6 sentence classification tasks: paraphrase identification (MSRP) (Dolan et al., 2004), movie review sentiment (MR) (Pang and Lee, 2005), product reviews (CR) (Hu and Liu, 2004), subjectivity classification (SUBJ) (Pang and Lee, 2004), opinion polarity (MPQA) (Wiebe et al., 2005) and question type classification (TREC) (Voorhees, 2002). We follow the procedure (and code) of Kiros et al. (2015): a logistic regression classifier is trained on top of sentence representations, with 10-fold cross-validation used when a train-test split is not pre-defined.

3.2 Unsupervised Evaluations

We also measure how well representation spaces reflect human intuitions of the semantic sentence relatedness, by computing the cosine distance between vectors for the two sentences in each test pair, and correlating these distances with gold-standard human judgements. The SICK dataset (Marelli et al., 2014) consists of 10,000 pairs of sentences and relatedness judgements. The STS 2014 dataset (Agirre et al., 2014) consists of 3,750 pairs and ratings from six linguistic domains. Example ratings are shown in Table 2. All available pairs are used for testing apart from the 500 SICK 'trial' pairs, which are held-out for tuning hyperparameters (representation size of log-bilinear models, and noise parameters in SDAE). The optimal settings on this task are then applied to both supervised and unsupervised evaluations.

4 Results

Performance of the models on the supervised evaluations (grouped according to the data required by their objective) is shown in Table 3. Overall, SkipThought vectors perform best on three of the six evaluations, the BOW DictRep model with pre-trained word embeddings performs best on two, and the SDAE on one. SDAEs perform notably well on the paraphrasing task, going beyond SkipThought by three percentage points and approaching state-of-the-art performance of models designed specifically for the task (Ji and Eisenstein, 2013). SDAE is also consistently better than SAE, which aligns with other findings that adding noise to AEs produces richer representations (Vincent et al., 2008).

Results on the unsupervised evaluations are shown in Table 4. The same DictRep model performs best on four of the six STS categories (and overall) and is joint-top performer on SICK. Of the models trained on raw text, simply adding CBOW word vectors works best on STS. The best performing raw text model on SICK is FastSent, which achieves almost identical performance to C-PHRASE's state-of-the-art performance for a distributed model (Pham et al., 2015). Further, it uses less than a third of the training text and does not

Data	Model	MSRP (Acc / F1)	MR	CR	SUBJ	MPQA	TREC
Unordered Sentences (Toronto Books: 70m sents, 0.9B words)	SAE	74.3 / 81.7	62.6	68.0	86.1	76.8	80.2
	SAE+embs.	70.6 / 77.9	73.2	75.3	89.8	86.2	80.4
	SDAE	**76.4 / 83.4**	67.6	74.0	89.3	81.3	77.6
	SDAE+embs.	73.7 / 80.7	**74.6**	**78.0**	**90.8**	**86.9**	78.4
	ParagraphVec DBOW	72.9 / 81.1	60.2	66.9	76.3	70.7	59.4
	ParagraphVec DM	73.6 / 81.9	61.5	68.6	76.4	78.1	55.8
	Skipgram	69.3 / 77.2	73.6	77.3	89.2	85.0	82.2
	CBOW	67.6 / 76.1	73.6	7730	89.1	85.0	82.2
	Unigram TFIDF	**73.6 / 81.7**	73.7	79.2	90.3	82.4	**85.0**
Ordered Sentences (Toronto Books)	SkipThought	**73.0 / 82.0**	**76.5**	<u>80.1</u>	<u>93.6</u>	**87.1**	<u>92.2</u>
	FastSent	72.2 / 80.3	70.8	78.4	88.7	80.6	76.8
	FastSent+AE	71.2 / 79.1	71.8	76.7	88.8	81.5	80.4
Other structured data resource	NMT En to Fr	69.1 / 77.1	64.7	70.1	84.9	81.5	**82.8**
	NMT En to De	65.2 / 73.3	61.0	67.6	78.2	72.9	81.6
	CaptionRep BOW	73.6 / 81.9	61.9	69.3	77.4	70.8	72.2
	CaptionRep RNN	72.6 / 81.1	55.0	64.9	64.9	71.0	62.4
	DictRep BOW	**73.7 / 81.6**	71.3	75.6	86.6	82.5	73.8
	DictRep BOW+embs.	68.4 / 76.8	<u>76.7</u>	**78.7**	**90.7**	<u>87.2</u>	81.0
	DictRep RNN	73.2 / 81.6	67.8	72.7	81.4	82.5	75.8
	DictRep RNN+embs.	66.8 / 76.0	72.5	73.5	85.6	85.7	72.0
2.8B words	CPHRASE	72.2 / 79.6	75.7	78.8	91.1	86.2	78.8

Table 3: Performance of sentence representation models on **supervised** evaluations (Section 3.1). Bold numbers indicate best performance in class. Underlined indicates best overall.

require access to (supervised) syntactic representations for training. Together, the results of FastSent on the unsupervised evaluations and SkipThought on the supervised benchmarks provide strong support for the sentence-level distributional hypothesis: the context in which a sentence occurs provides valuable information about its semantics.

Across both unsupervised and supervised evaluations, the BOW DictRep with pre-trained word embeddings exhibits by some margin the most consistent performance. Ths robust performance suggests that DictRep representations may be particularly valuable when the ultimate application is non-specific or unknown, and confirms that dictionary definitions (where available) can be a powerful resource for representation learning.

5 Discussion

Many additional conclusions can be drawn from the results in Tables 3 and 4.

Different objectives yield different representations It may seem obvious, but the results confirm that different learning methods are preferable for different intended applications (and this variation appears greater than for word representations). For instance, it is perhaps unsurprising that SkipThought performs best on TREC because the labels in this dataset are determined by the language immediately following the represented question (i.e. the answer) (Voorhees, 2002). Paraphrase detection, on the other hand, may be better served by a model that focused entirely on the content *within* a sentence, such as SDAEs. Similar variation can be observed in the unsupervised evaluations. For instance, the (multimodal) representations produced by the CaptionRep model do not perform particularly well apart from on the Image category of STS where they beat all other models, demonstrating a clear effect of the well-studied modality differences in representation learning (Bruni et al., 2014).

The nearest neighbours in Table 5 give a more concrete sense of the representation spaces. One notable difference is between (AE-style) models whose semantics come from within-sentence relationships (CBOW, SDAE, DictRep, ParagraphVec) and SkipThought/FastSent, which exploit the context around sentences. In the former case, nearby sentences often have a high proportion of words in common, whereas for the latter it is the general con-

| Model | STS 2014 | | | | | | | SICK |
	News	Forum	WordNet	Twitter	Images	Headlines	All	Test + Train
SAE	17/.16	.12/.12	.30/.23	.28/.22	.49/.46	.13/.11	.12/.13	.32/.31
SAE+embs.	.52/.54	.22/.23	.60/.55	.60/.60	. 64/.64	.41/.41	.42/.43	.47/.49
SDAE	.07/.04	.11/.13	.33/.24	.44/.42	.44/.38	.36/.36	.17/.15	.46/.46
SDAE+embs.	.51/.54	.29/.29	.56/.50	.57/.58	.59/.59	.43/.44	.37/.38	.46/.46
ParagraphVec DBOW	.31/.34	.32/.32	.53/.5	.43/.46	.46/.44	.39/.41	.42/.43	.42/.46
ParagraphVec DM	.42/.46	.33/.34	.51/.48	.54/.57	.32/.30	.46/.47	.44/.44	.44/.46
Skipgram	.56/.59	.42/.42	**.73/.70**	**.71**/.74	.65/.67	**.55/.58**	.62/.63	**.60/.69**
CBOW	**.57/.61**	**.43/.44**	.72/.69	**.71/.75**	.71/.73	**.55/.59**	**.64/.65**	**.60/.69**
Unigram TFIDF	.48/.48	.40/.38	.60/.59	.63/.65	**72/.74**	.49/.49	.58/.57	.52/.58
SkipThought	.44/.45	.14/.15	.39/.34	.42/.43	.55/.60	.43/.44	.27/.29	.57/.60
FastSent	**.58/.59**	**.41/.36**	**.74/.70**	.63/.66	**.74/.78**	.57/.59	**.63/.64**	**.61/.72**
FastSent+AE	.56/ **.59**	**.41/.40**	.69/.64	**.70/.74**	.63/.65	**.58/.60**	.62/.62	.60/.65
NMT En to Fr	.35/.32	.18/.18	.47/.43	.55/.53	.44/.45	.43/.43	.43/.42	.47/.49
NMT En to De	.47/.43	.26/.25	.34/.31	.49/.45	.44/.43	.38/.37	.40/.38	.46/46
CaptionRep BOW	.26/.26	.29/.22	.50/.35	.37/.31	**.78**/.81	.39/.36	.46/.42	.56/.65
CaptionRep RNN	.05/.05	.13/.09	.40/.33	.36/.30	.76/**.82**	.30/.28	.39/.36	.53/.62
DictRep BOW	.62/.67	.42/.40	.81/.81	.62/.66	.66/.68	.53/.58	.62/.65	.57/.66
DictRep BOW+embs.	**.65/.72**	**.49/.47**	**.85/.86**	**.67/.72**	.71/.74	**.57/.61**	**.67/.70**	**.61**/.70
DictRep RNN	.40/.46	.26/.23	.78/.78	.42/.42	.56/.56	.38/.40	.49/.50	.49/.56
DictRep RNN+embs.	.51/.60	.29/.27	.80/.81	.44/.47	.65/.70	.42/.46	.54/.57	.49/.59
CPHRASE	**.69**/.71	.43/.41	.76/.73	.60/.65	.75/.79	**.60/.65**	.65/.67	.60/**.72**

Table 4: Performance of sentence representation models (Spearman/Pearson correlations) on **unsupervised** (relatedness) evaluations (Section 3.2). Models are grouped according to training data as indicated in Table 3.

cepts and/or function of the sentence that is similar, and word overlap is often minimal. Indeed, this may be a more important trait of FastSent than the marginal improvement on the SICK task. Readers can compare the CBOW and FastSent spaces at `http://45.55.60.98/`.

Differences between supervised and unsupervised performance Many of the best performing models on the supervised evaluations do not perform well in the unsupervised setting. In the SkipThought, S(D)AE and NMT models, the cost is computed based on a non-linear decoding of the internal sentence representations, so, as also observed by (Almahairi et al., 2015), the informative geometry of the representation space may not be reflected in a simple cosine distance. The log-bilinear models generally perform better in this unsupervised setting.

Knowledge transfer shows some promise It is notable that, with a few exceptions, the models with pre-trained word embeddings (+embs) outperform those with learned embeddings on both supervised and unsupervised evaluations. In the case of the DictRep models, whose training data is otherwise limited to dictionary definitions, this effect can be considered as a rudimentary form of knowledge transfer. The DictRep+embs model benefits both from the dictionary data and the enhanced lexical semantics acquired from a massive text corpus to build overall higher-quality sentence representations.

Differences in resource requirements As shown in Table 1, different models require different resources to train and use. This can limit their possible applications. For instance, while it was easy to make an online demo for fast querying of near neighbours in the CBOW and FastSent spaces, it was not practical for other models owing to memory footprint, encoding time and representation dimension.

The role of word order is unclear The average scores of models that are sensitive to word order (76.3) and of those that are not (76.6) are approximately the same across supervised evalua-

Query	*If he had a weapon, he could maybe take out their last imp, and then beat up Errol and Vanessa.*	*An annoying buzz started to ring in my ears, becoming louder and louder as my vision began to swim.*
CBOW	*Then Rob and I would duke it out, and every once in a while, he would actually beat me.*	*Louder.*
Skip Thought	*If he could ram them from behind, send them saling over the far side of the levee, he had a chance of stopping them.*	*A weighty pressure landed on my lungs and my vision blurred at the edges, threatening my consciousness altogether.*
FastSent	*Isak's close enough to pick off any one of them, maybe all of them, if he had his rifle and a mind to.*	*The noise grew louder, the quaking increased as the sidewalk beneath my feet began to tremble even more.*
SDAE	*He'd even killed some of the most dangerous criminals in the galaxy, but none of those men had gotten to him like Vitktis.*	*I smile because I'm familiar with the knock, pausing to take a deep breath before dashing down the stairs.*
DictRep (FF+embs.)	*Kevin put a gun to the man's head, but even though he cried, he couldn't tell Kevin anything more.*	*Then gradually I began to hear a ringing in my ears.*
Paragraph Vector (DM)	*I take a deep breath and open the doors.*	*They listened as the motorcycle-like roar of an engine got louder and louder then stopped.*

Table 5: Sample nearest neighbour queries selected from a randomly sampled 0.5m sentences of the Toronto Books Corpus.

Supervised (combined $\alpha = 0.90$)						Unsupervised (combined $\alpha = 0.93$)							
MSRP	MR	CR	SUBJ	MPAQ	TREC	News	Forum	WordNet	Twitter	Images	Headlines	All STS	SICK
0.94 (6)	0.85 (1)	0.86 (4)	0.85 (1)	0.86 (3)	0.89 (5)	0.92 (4)	0.92 (3)	0.92 (4)	0.93 (6)	0.95 (8)	0.92 (2)	0.91 (1)	0.93 (7)

Table 6: Internal consistency (Chronbach's α) among evaluations when individual benchmarks are left out of the (supervised or unsupervised) cohorts. Consistency rank within cohort is in parentheses (1 = most consistent with other evaluations).

tions. Across the unsupervised evaluations, however, BOW models score 0.55 on average compared with 0.42 for RNN-based (order sensitive) models. This seems at odds with the widely held view that word order plays an important role in determining the meaning of English sentences. One possibility is that order-critical sentences that cannot be disambiguated by a robust conceptual semantics (that could be encoded in distributed lexical representations) are in fact relatively rare. However, it is also plausible that current available evaluations do not adequately reflect order-dependent aspects of meaning (see below). This latter conjecture is supported by the comparatively strong performance of TFIDF BOW vectors, in which the effective lexical semantics are limited to simple relative frequencies.

The evaluations have limitations The internal consistency (Chronbach's α) of all evaluations considered together is 0.81 (just above 'acceptable').[12] Table 6 shows that consistency is far higher ('excellent') when considering the supervised or unsupervised tasks as independent cohorts. This indicates that, with respect to common characteristics of sentence representations, the supervised and unsupervised benchmarks do indeed prioritise different properties. It is also interesting that, by this metric, the properties measured by MSRP and image-caption relatedness are the furthest removed from other evaluations in their respective cohorts.

While these consistency scores are a promising sign, they could also be symptomatic of a set of evaluations that are all limited in the same way. The inter-rater agreement is only reported for one of the 8 evaluations considered (MPQA, 0.72 (Wiebe et al., 2005)), and for MR, SUBJ and TREC, each item is only rated by one or two annotators to maximise coverage. Table 2 illustrates why this may be an issue for the unsupervised evaluations; the notion of sentential 'relatedness' seems very subjective. It should be emphasised, however, that the tasks considered in this study are all frequently used for evaluation, and, to our knowledge, there are no existing benchmarks that overcome these limitations.

6 Conclusion

Advances in deep learning algorithms, software and hardware mean that many architectures and objectives for learning distributed sentence representations from unlabelled data are now available to NLP researchers. We have presented the first (to our knowledge) systematic comparison of these methods. We showed notable variation in the performance of approaches across a range of evaluations. Among other conclusions, we found that the op-

---

[12] wikipedia.org/wiki/Cronbach's_alpha

timal approach depends critically on whether representations will be applied in supervised or unsupervised settings - in the latter case, fast, shallow BOW models can still achieve the best performance. Further, we proposed two new objectives, FastSent and Sequential Denoising Autoencoders, which perform particularly well on specific tasks (MSRP and SICK sentence relatedness respectively).[13] If the application is unknown, however, the best all round choice may be DictRep: learning a mapping of pre-trained word embeddings from the word-phrase signal in dictionary definitions. While we have focused on models using naturally-occurring training data, in future work we will also consider supervised architectures (including convolutional, recursive and character-level models), potentially training them on multiple supervised tasks as an alternative way to induce the 'general knowledge' needed to give language technology the elusive human touch.

Acknowledgments

This work was supported by a Google Faculty Award to AK and FH and a Google European Doctoral Fellowship to FH. Thanks also to Marek Rei, Tamara Polajnar, Laural Rimell, Jamie Ryan Kiros and Piotr Bojanowski for helpful comments.

References

Eneko Agirre, Carmen Banea, Claire Cardie, Daniel Cer, Mona Diab, Aitor Gonzalez-Agirre, Weiwei Guo, Rada Mihalcea, German Rigau, and Janyce Wiebe. 2014. Semeval-2014 task 10: Multilingual semantic textual similarity. In *Proceedings of the 8th International Workshop on Semantic Evaluation (SemEval 2014)*, pages 81–91.

Amjad Almahairi, Kyle Kastner, Kyunghyun Cho, and Aaron Courville. 2015. Learning distributed representations from reviews for collaborative filtering. In *Proceedings of the 9th ACM Conference on Recommender Systems*, pages 147–154. ACM.

Marco Baroni, Raffaela Bernardi, and Roberto Zamparelli. 2014a. Frege in space: A program of compositional distributional semantics. *Linguistic Issues in Language Technology*, 9.

Marco Baroni, Georgiana Dinu, and Germán Kruszewski. 2014b. Don't count, predict! a systematic comparison of context-counting vs. context-predicting semantic vectors. In *Proceedings of the 52nd Annual Meeting of the Association for Computational Linguistics*, volume 1, pages 238–247.

Elia Bruni, Nam-Khanh Tran, and Marco Baroni. 2014. Multimodal distributional semantics. *J. Artif. Intell. Res. (JAIR)*, 49:1–47.

Xinlei Chen, Hao Fang, Tsung-Yi Lin, Ramakrishna Vedantam, Saurabh Gupta, Piotr Dollar, and C Lawrence Zitnick. 2015. Microsoft coco captions: Data collection and evaluation server. *arXiv preprint arXiv:1504.00325*.

Kyunghyun Cho, Bart Van Merriënboer, Caglar Gulcehre, Dzmitry Bahdanau, Fethi Bougares, Holger Schwenk, and Yoshua Bengio. 2014. Learning phrase representations using rnn encoder-decoder for statistical machine translation. In *Proceedings of EMNLP*.

Stephen Clark and Stephen Pulman. 2007. Combining symbolic and distributional models of meaning. In *AAAI Spring Symposium: Quantum Interaction*, pages 52–55.

Ronan Collobert, Jason Weston, Léon Bottou, Michael Karlen, Koray Kavukcuoglu, and Pavel Kuksa. 2011. Natural language processing (almost) from scratch. *The Journal of Machine Learning Research*, 12:2493–2537.

Andrew M Dai and Quoc V Le. 2015. Semi-supervised sequence learning. In *Advances in Neural Information Processing Systems*, pages 3061–3069.

Bill Dolan, Chris Quirk, and Chris Brockett. 2004. Unsupervised construction of large paraphrase corpora: Exploiting massively parallel news sources. In *Proceedings of the 20th international conference on Computational Linguistics*, page 350. Association for Computational Linguistics.

Zellig S Harris. 1954. Distributional structure. *Word*.

Felix Hill, Kyunghyun Cho, Anna Korhonen, and Yoshua Bengio. 2015a. Learning to understand phrases by embedding the dictionary. *Transactions of the Association for Computational Linguistics*.

Felix Hill, Roi Reichart, and Anna Korhonen. 2015b. Simlex-999: Evaluating semantic models with (genuine) similarity estimation. *Computational Linguistics*.

Minqing Hu and Bing Liu. 2004. Mining and summarizing customer reviews. In *Proceedings of the tenth ACM SIGKDD international conference on Knowledge discovery and data mining*, pages 168–177. ACM.

Mohit Iyyer, Varun Manjunatha, Jordan Boyd-Graber, and Hal Daumé III. 2015. Deep unordered composition rivals syntactic methods for text classification.

---

[13]We make all code for training and evaluating these new models publicly available, together with pre-trained models and an online demo of the FastSent sentence space.

Proceedings of the 53rd Annual Meeting of the Association for Computational Linguistics.

Yangfeng Ji and Jacob Eisenstein. 2013. Discriminative improvements to distributional sentence similarity. In *EMNLP*, pages 891–896.

Nal Kalchbrenner, Edward Grefenstette, and Phil Blunsom. 2014. A convolutional neural network for modelling sentences. In *Proceedings of EMNLP*.

Ryan Kiros, Yukun Zhu, Ruslan R Salakhutdinov, Richard Zemel, Raquel Urtasun, Antonio Torralba, and Sanja Fidler. 2015. Skip-thought vectors. In *Advances in Neural Information Processing Systems*, pages 3276–3284.

Quoc V Le and Tomas Mikolov. 2014. Distributed representations of sentences and documents. In *Proceedings of ICML*.

Omer Levy and Yoav Goldberg. 2014. Neural word embedding as implicit matrix factorization. In *Advances in Neural Information Processing Systems*, pages 2177–2185.

Omer Levy, Yoav Goldberg, and Ido Dagan. 2015. Improving distributional similarity with lessons learned from word embeddings. *Transactions of the Association for Computational Linguistics*, 3:211–225.

Junhua Mao, Wei Xu, Yi Yang, Jiang Wang, and Alan Yulle. 2015. Deep captioning with multimodal recurrent neural networks (m-rnn). In *Proceedings of ICLR*.

Marco Marelli, Stefano Menini, Marco Baroni, Luisa Bentivogli, Raffaella Bernardi, and Roberto Zamparelli. 2014. A sick cure for the evaluation of compositional distributional semantic models. In *Proceedings of LREC*, pages 216–223. Citeseer.

Tomas Mikolov, Kai Chen, Greg Corrado, and Jeffrey Dean. 2013a. Efficient estimation of word representations in vector space. *arXiv preprint arXiv:1301.3781*.

Tomas Mikolov, Ilya Sutskever, Kai Chen, Greg S Corrado, and Jeff Dean. 2013b. Distributed representations of words and phrases and their compositionality. In *Advances in neural information processing systems*, pages 3111–3119.

Dmitrijs Milajevs, Dimitri Kartsaklis, Mehrnoosh Sadrzadeh, and Matthew Purver. 2014. Evaluating neural word representations in tensor-based compositional settings. In *Proceedings of EMNLP*.

Jeff Mitchell and Mirella Lapata. 2008. Vector-based models of semantic composition. In *ACL*, pages 236–244.

Jeff Mitchell and Mirella Lapata. 2010. Composition in distributional models of semantics. *Cognitive science*, 34(8):1388–1429.

Donald A Norman. 1972. Memory, knowledge, and the answering of questions.

Bo Pang and Lillian Lee. 2004. A sentimental education: Sentiment analysis using subjectivity summarization based on minimum cuts. In *Proceedings of the 42nd annual meeting on Association for Computational Linguistics*, page 271. Association for Computational Linguistics.

Bo Pang and Lillian Lee. 2005. Seeing stars: Exploiting class relationships for sentiment categorization with respect to rating scales. In *Proceedings of the 43rd Annual Meeting on Association for Computational Linguistics*, pages 115–124. Association for Computational Linguistics.

Nghia The Pham, Germán Kruszewski, Angeliki Lazaridou, and Marco Baroni. 2015. Jointly optimizing word representations for lexical and sentential tasks with the c-phrase model. In *Proceedings of ALC*.

Tamara Polajnar, Laura Rimell, and Stephen Clark. 2015. An exploration of discourse-based sentence spaces for compositional distributional semantics. In *Workshop on Linking Models of Lexical, Sentential and Discourse-level Semantics (LSDSem)*, page 1.

Olga Russakovsky, Jia Deng, Hao Su, Jonathan Krause, Sanjeev Satheesh, Sean Ma, Zhiheng Huang, Andrej Karpathy, Aditya Khosla, Michael Bernstein, et al. 2014. Imagenet large scale visual recognition challenge. *International Journal of Computer Vision*, pages 1–42.

Iulian V Serban, Alessandro Sordoni, Yoshua Bengio, Aaron Courville, and Joelle Pineau. 2015. Building end-to-end dialogue systems using generative hierarchical neural network models. *arXiv preprint arXiv:1507.04808*.

Richard Socher, Jeffrey Pennington, Eric H Huang, Andrew Y Ng, and Christopher D Manning. 2011. Semi-supervised recursive autoencoders for predicting sentiment distributions. In *Proceedings of the Conference on Empirical Methods in Natural Language Processing*, pages 151–161. Association for Computational Linguistics.

Ilya Sutskever, James Martens, and Geoffrey E Hinton. 2011. Generating text with recurrent neural networks. In *Proceedings of the 28th International Conference on Machine Learning (ICML-11)*, pages 1017–1024.

Ilya Sutskever, Oriol Vinyals, and Quoc VV Le. 2014. Sequence to sequence learning with neural networks. In *Advances in neural information processing systems*, pages 3104–3112.

Christian Szegedy, Wei Liu, Yangqing Jia, Pierre Sermanet, Scott Reed, Dragomir Anguelov, Dumitru Erhan, Vincent Vanhoucke, and Andrew Rabinovich. 2014. Going deeper with convolutions. *arXiv preprint arXiv:1409.4842*.

Pascal Vincent, Hugo Larochelle, Yoshua Bengio, and Pierre-Antoine Manzagol. 2008. Extracting and composing robust features with denoising autoencoders. In *Proceedings of the 25th international conference on Machine learning*, pages 1096–1103. ACM.

Pascal Vincent, Hugo Larochelle, Isabelle Lajoie, Yoshua Bengio, and Pierre-Antoine Manzagol. 2010. Stacked denoising autoencoders: Learning useful representations in a deep network with a local denoising criterion. *The Journal of Machine Learning Research*, 11:3371–3408.

Ellen M Voorhees. 2002. Overview of the trec 2001 question answering track. *NIST special publication*, pages 42–51.

Janyce Wiebe, Theresa Wilson, and Claire Cardie. 2005. Annotating expressions of opinions and emotions in language. *Language resources and evaluation*, 39(2-3):165–210.

Retrofitting Sense-Specific Word Vectors Using Parallel Text

Allyson Ettinger[1], Philip Resnik[1,3], Marine Carpuat[2,3]
[1]Linguistics, [2]Computer Science, [3]Institute for Advanced Computer Studies
University of Maryland, College Park, MD
{aetting, resnik}@umd.edu, marine@cs.umd.edu

Abstract

Jauhar et al. (2015) recently proposed to learn sense-specific word representations by "retrofitting" standard distributional word representations to an existing ontology. We observe that this approach does not require an ontology, and can be generalized to any graph defining word senses and relations between them. We create such a graph using translations learned from parallel corpora. On a set of lexical semantic tasks, representations learned using parallel text perform roughly as well as those derived from WordNet, and combining the two representation types significantly improves performance.

1 Introduction

Vector space models (VSMs) provide a powerful tool for representing word meanings and modeling the relations between them. While these models have demonstrated impressive success in capturing some aspects of word meaning (Landauer and Dumais, 1997; Turney et al., 2010; Mikolov et al., 2013; Baroni et al., 2014; Levy et al., 2014), they generally fail to capture the fact that single word forms often have multiple meanings. This can lead to counterintuitive results—for example, it should be possible for the nearest word to *rock* to be *stone* in everyday usage, *punk* in discussions of music, and *crack* (cocaine) in discussions about drugs.

In a recent paper, Jauhar et al. (2015) introduce a method for "retrofitting" generic word vectors to create *sense-specific* vectors using the WordNet semantic lexicon (Miller, 1995). From WordNet, they create a graph structure comprising two classes of relations: form-based relations between each word form and its respective senses, and meaning-based relations between word senses with similar meanings. This graph structure is then used to transform a traditional VSM into an enriched VSM, where each point in the space represents a word sense, rather than a word form. This approach is appealing as, unlike with prior sense-aware representations, senses are defined categories in a semantic lexicon, rather than clusters induced from raw text (Reisinger and Mooney, 2010; Huang et al., 2012; Neelakantan et al., 2015; Tian et al., 2014), and the method does not require performing word sense disambiguation (Guo et al., 2014).

In this paper, we observe that the crucial meaning relationships in the Jauhar et al. retrofitting process—the word sense graph—can be inferred based on another widely available resource: bilingual parallel text. This observation is grounded in a well-established tradition of using cross-language correspondences as a form of sense annotation (Gale et al., 1992; Diab and Resnik, 2002; Ng et al., 2003; Carpuat and Wu, 2007; Lefever and Hoste, 2010, and others). Using parallel text to define sense distinctions sidesteps the persistent difficulty of identifying a single correct sense partitioning based on human intuition, and avoids large investments in manual curation or annotation.

We use parallel text and word alignment to infer both word sense identities and inter-sense relations required for the sense graph, and apply the approach of Jauhar et al. to retrofit existing word vector representations and create a sense-based vec-

Proceedings of NAACL-HLT 2016, pages 1378–1383,
San Diego, California, June 12-17, 2016. ©2016 Association for Computational Linguistics

tor space, using bilingual correspondences to define word senses. When evaluated on semantic judgment tasks, the vector spaces derived from this graph perform comparably to and sometimes better than the WordNet-based space of Jauhar et al., indicating that parallel text is a viable alternative to WordNet for defining graph structure. Combining the output of parallel-data-based and WordNet-based retrofitted VSMs consistently improves performance, suggesting that the different sense graph methods make complementary contributions to this sense-specific retrofitting process.

2   Model

Retrofitting.   The technique introduced by Jauhar et al. (2015) is based on what we will call a *sense graph*, which we formulate as follows. Nodes in the sense graph comprise the words w_i in a vocabulary W together with the senses s_{ij} for those words. Labeled, undirected edges include word-sense edges $\langle w_i, s_{i,j} \rangle$, which connect each word to all of its possible senses, and sense-sense edges $\langle s_{ij}, s_{i'j'} \rangle$ labeled with a meaning relationship r that holds between the two senses.

Jauhar et al. use WordNet to define their sense graph. Synsets in the WordNet ontology define the sense nodes, a word-sense edge exists between any word and every synset to which it belongs, and WordNet's synset-to-synset relations of synonymy, hypernymy, and hyponymy define the sense-sense edges. Figure 1 illustrates a fragment of a WordNet-based sense graph, suppressing edge labels.

Adopting Jauhar et al.'s notation, the original vector space to be retrofitted is defined by the original word-form vectors $\hat{u}_i$ for each $w_i \in W$, and the goal is to infer a set V of sense-specific vectors v_{ij} corresponding to each sense s_{ij}. Jauhar et al. use the sense graph to define a Markov network with variables for all word vectors and sense vectors, within which each word's vector $\hat{u}_i$ is connected to all of its sense vectors v_{ij}, and the variables for sense vectors v_{ij} and $v_{i'j'}$ are connected iff the corresponding senses are connected in the sense graph.

Retrofitting then consists in optimizing the following objective, where α is a sense-agnostic weight, and β_r are relation-specific weights for types of relations between senses:

$$C(V) = \arg\min_V \sum_{i-ij} \alpha \| \hat{u}_i - v_{ij} \|^2$$
$$+ \sum_{ij-i'j'} \beta_r \| v_{ij} - v_{i'j'} \|^2 \quad (1)$$

The objective encourages similarity between a word's vector and its senses' vectors (first term), as well as similarity between the vectors for senses that are related in the sense graph (second term).

Defining a sense graph from parallel text.   Our key observation is that, although Jauhar et al. (2015) assume their sense graph to be an ontology, this graph can be based on *any* inventory of word-sense and sense-sense relationships. In particular, given a parallel corpus, we can follow the tradition of translation-as-sense-annotation: the senses of an English word type can be defined by different possible translations of that word in another language.

Operationalizing this observation is straightforward, given a word-aligned parallel corpus. If English word form e_i is aligned with Chinese word form c_j, then $e_i(c_j)$ is a sense of e_i in the sense graph, and there is a word-sense edge $\langle e_i, e_i(c_j) \rangle$. Edges signifying a meaning relation are drawn between sense nodes if those senses are defined by the same translation word. For instance, English senses *swear*(发誓) and *vow*(发誓) both arise via alignment to 发誓 (*fashi*), so a sense-sense edge will be drawn between these two sense nodes. See Figure 2 for illustration.

3   Evaluation

Tasks.   We evaluate on both the synonym selection and word similarity rating tasks used by Jauhar et al. Synonym selection nicely demonstrates the advantages afforded by sense partitioning: if we believe that *spin* means "make up a story", then we are not likely to perform well on a question in which the correct synonym is *twirl*. Word similarity rating, on the other hand, is a classic test of the extent to which vector representations simulate human intuitions of word relations in general.

For synonym selection, we follow Jauhar et al. in testing with ESL-50 (Turney, 2001), RD-300 (Jarmasz and Szpakowicz, 2004), and TOEFL-80 (Landauer and Dumais, 1997), using maxSim for multi-

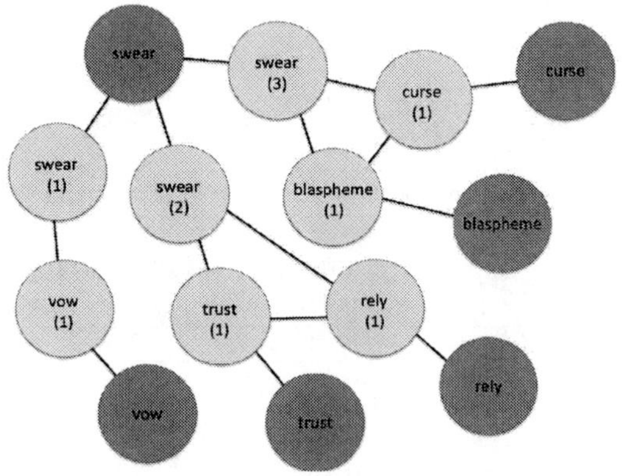

Figure 1: Illustration of WordNet-based sense graph.

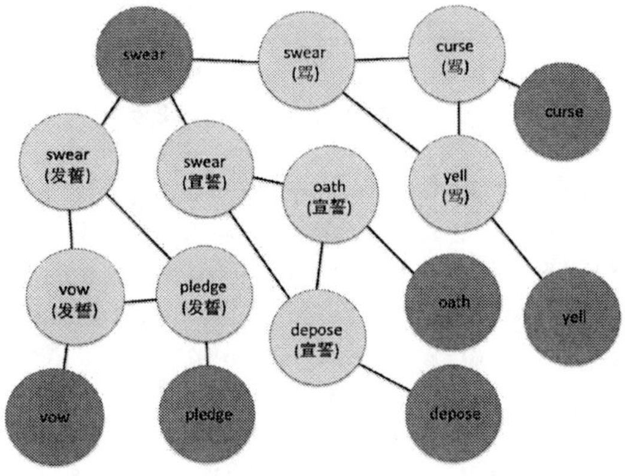

Figure 2: Illustration of parallel-text-based sense graph.

sense models (Jauhar et al., 2015, eq. 9) to select the most similar word.[1] For similarity rating, we again mirror Jauhar et al., testing with WS-353 (Finkelstein et al., 2001), RG-65 (Rubenstein and Goodenough, 1965), MC-30 (Miller and Charles, 1991), and the designated test subset (1000 items) of MEN-3k (Bruni et al., 2014), using avgSim (Jauhar et al., 2015, eq. 8) as the similarity rating, and evaluating model ratings against human similarity ratings via Spearman's rank correlation coefficient (ρ).[2]

Initial word representations. We use the word2vec (Mikolov et al., 2013) skip-gram architecture to train 80-dimensional word vectors (in keeping with Jauhar et al.), based on evidence that this model shows consistently strong performance on a wide array of tasks (Baroni et al., 2014; Levy et al., 2015). Training is on ukWaC (Ferraresi et al., 2008), a diverse 2B-word web corpus.[3]

Sense-graph construction from parallel text. To construct the sense graph per Section 2, we use

~5.8M lines of segmented Chinese-English parallel text from the DARPA BOLT project and the Broadcast Conversation subset of the segmented Chinese-English parallel data in the OntoNotes corpus (Weischedel et al., 2013).[4] We perform word alignment with the Berkeley aligner (Liang et al., 2006). We filter out noisy alignments using the G-test statistic (Dunning, 1993), with a threshold selected during tuning on a development set.

We set α (see Equation 1) to 1.0. Each sense-sense edge $\langle e_i(c_j), e_{i'}(c_j) \rangle$ has individual weight $0 < \beta_r \leq 1$, computed by obtaining the G-test statistic for the alignment of e_i with c_j and for the alignment of $e_{i'}$ with c_j, running these values through a logistic function, and averaging. Parameters for these computations, as well as the G-test statistic threshold below which we filtered out noisy alignments, were selected during tuning on the development set.

Note that we have not currently incorporated special treatment for alignments of a single word to a multi-word phrase. This does create the possibility of noisy or uninformative sense annotations (e.g., sense annotations corresponding to parts of aligned Chinese phrases) when such alignments are not filtered out by the G-test thresholding.

Experimental conditions. We evaluate the following experimental conditions: Skip-gram (SG) uses the un-retrofitted word2vec vectors, Word-

---

[1] Because it is not clear how multi-word phrases should best be treated (and this is not a question being investigated here), we filter out any questions containing multi-word phrases for any of the relevant items (probe or possible response), and any questions for which any of the relevant items is completely out of vocabulary (no vectors available) for any of the evaluated models. This leaves 48 items in ESL, 87 items in RD, and 77 items in TOEFL.

[2] The designated development set of MEN-3k (2000 items) was used for tuning.

[3] To alleviate sparsity we lemmatized the ukWaC corpus. Runs without lemmatization produced weaker results.

[4] English was lemmatized post-alignment via lookup in the XTAG morphological database (XTAG Research Group, 2001).

Net (WN) retrofits using the WordNet-based sense graph, and Parallel Data (PD) retrofits using the sense graph built from parallel text. We also combine the two retrofitting approaches (PD-WN). For synonym selection, we compute maxSim over all sense pairs for WN and PD separately, and select the sense pair with the overall maximum cosine similarity across the two. For similarity rating, we explore two PD-WN combination approaches: for each word pair, we take the avgSim from each separate model, and then we (a) take the average of the values given by the two models (avg), or (b) take the maximum value between the two models (max).

	Synonym Selection SYMM (%)		
	ESL-48	RD-87	TOEFL-77
SG	58.3	58.6	71.4
WN	66.7	74.7	81.8
PD	68.8	62.1	80.5
PD-WN	**70.8**	**79.3**	**84.4**

Table 1: Synonym selection task results: accuracy

	Word similarity: avgSim SYMM (ρ)			
	WS-353	RG-65	MC-30	MEN-1k
SG	**.708**	.729	.722	.763
WN	.610	.725	.750	.739
PD	.636	**.777**	.715	.769
PD-WN (avg)	.666	**.777**	.742	**.773**
PD-WN (max)	.630	.731	**.758**	.756

Table 2: Similarity rating task results

4 Results

Table 1 shows that combining our new method with Jauhar et al.'s WN retrofitting performs best on synonym selection across all datasets, and both retrofitted models consistently outperform the no-retrofitting model (SG). Error analysis on RD-87, the only set on which WN substantially outperforms PD, suggests that PD's errors are driven by the large number of lower frequency items that characterize this dataset. Given that WordNet is a hand-curated lexicon while the parallel data mirrors actual usage, it is not surprising that the latter suffers when it comes to low frequency items.

Error analysis also indicates that PD performs particularly well on the synonym task precisely when one would expect: when the probe and the correct answer have an alignment to the same Chinese word form, so that the corresponding sense vectors are extremely close in vector space. Occasionally, PD yields "the wrong answer for the right reason", choosing an option for which there is indeed a correct alignment that matches an alignment of the probe word. For instance, though the probe *passage* is intended to have the answer *hallway*, PD chooses *ticket* because both *passage* and *ticket* have a sense defined by alignment to the Chinese word 机票 (*jipiao*), meaning "air ticket". Though this is a less frequent sense of *passage*, it is a reasonable one.

Results on the similarity rating task (presented in Table 2) are less clearly interpretable, top performance being divided between the PD model and the combined models—with the exception of WS-353. We note that WS-353 is a test set for which human raters were explicitly told to rate relatedness, rather than similarity, while the retrofitting process is intended to encourage similarity *per se*. If we exclude this set from consideration, we can observe that SG is outperformed by at least one sense-specific model in all cases.[5]

Note that as expected, the amount of training data has an impact on the quality of the alignments and of the sense graph. Retrofitting sense-specific embeddings using only 300k sentence pairs, which represent about 5% of the total training data, does not give clear benefit over word-form embeddings.

5 Conclusions and future work

Building on Jauhar et al. (2015), we have presented an alternative means of deriving information about senses and sense relations to build sense-specific vector space representations of words, making use of parallel text rather than a manually constructed ontology. We show that this is a viable alternative, producing representations that perform on par with those retrofitted to sense graphs based on WordNet.[6]

---

[5]We also explored using maxSim for similarity ratings, on the intuition that when human annotators give similarity judgments, they are likely to judge based on senses of the given words that are biased toward the words with which they are paired. However, top performance is similarly scattered when using maxSim for similarity scores and fails to improve over the SG baseline for two of the datasets.

[6]Sample sense-specific vectors and code for generating a sense graph from parallel data can be accessed at http://ling.umd.edu/~aetting/retropd.html.

Based on these results, it would be interesting to evaluate further refinements of the sense graph: alignment-based senses could be clustered, or further filtered to reduce the impact of alignment noise; new edges could be added using other multilingual resources. Finally, it will be important to evaluate the effectiveness of the retrofitted word embeddings on extrinsic tasks that require disambiguating word meaning in context.

Acknowledgments

The authors would like to thank Sujay Kumar Jauhar for sharing software and data and for helpful discussion. Thanks also to Manaal Faruqui and Peter Turney for help in acquiring evaluation datasets, to Amittai Axelrod for his assistance with data, and to the anonymous reviewers for valuable comments and suggestions. This work was supported in part by an NSF Graduate Research Fellowship under Grant No. DGE 1322106. Any opinions, findings, and conclusions or recommendations expressed are those of the authors and do not necessarily reflect the views of the NSF.

References

Marco Baroni, Georgiana Dinu, and Germán Kruszewski. 2014. Don't count, predict! A systematic comparison of context-counting vs. context-predicting semantic vectors. In *Proceedings of the 52nd Annual Meeting of the Association for Computational Linguistics*, volume 1, pages 238–247.

Elia Bruni, Nam-Khanh Tran, and Marco Baroni. 2014. Multimodal distributional semantics. *Journal of Artificial Intelligence Research*, 49:1–47.

Marine Carpuat and Dekai Wu. 2007. Improving statistical machine translation using word sense disambiguation. In *EMNLP-CoNLL*, volume 7, pages 61–72.

Mona Diab and Philip Resnik. 2002. An unsupervised method for word sense tagging using parallel corpora. In *Proceedings of the 40th Annual Meeting on Association for Computational Linguistics*, pages 255–262.

Ted Dunning. 1993. Accurate methods for the statistics of surprise and coincidence. *Computational linguistics*, 19(1):61–74.

Adriano Ferraresi, Eros Zanchetta, Marco Baroni, and Silvia Bernardini. 2008. Introducing and evaluating ukWaC, a very large web-derived corpus of English. In *Proceedings of the 4th Web as Corpus Workshop (WAC-4) Can we beat Google*, pages 47–54.

Lev Finkelstein, Evgeniy Gabrilovich, Yossi Matias, Ehud Rivlin, Zach Solan, Gadi Wolfman, and Eytan Ruppin. 2001. Placing search in context: The concept revisited. In *Proceedings of the 10th international conference on World Wide Web*, pages 406–414.

William A Gale, Kenneth W Church, and David Yarowsky. 1992. A method for disambiguating word senses in a large corpus. *Computers and the Humanities*, 26(5-6):415–439.

Jiang Guo, Wanxiang Che, Haifeng Wang, and Ting Liu. 2014. Learning sense-specific word embeddings by exploiting bilingual resources. In *Proceedings of COLING*, pages 497–507.

Eric H Huang, Richard Socher, Christopher D Manning, and Andrew Y Ng. 2012. Improving word representations via global context and multiple word prototypes. In *Proceedings of the 50th Annual Meeting of the Association for Computational Linguistics: Long Papers-Volume 1*, pages 873–882.

Mario Jarmasz and Stan Szpakowicz. 2004. Roget's thesaurus and semantic similarity. *Recent Advances in Natural Language Processing III: Selected Papers from RANLP*, 2003:111.

Sujay Kumar Jauhar, Chris Dyer, and Eduard Hovy. 2015. Ontologically grounded multi-sense representation learning for semantic vector space models. In *Proceedings of NAACL*, pages 683–693.

Thomas K Landauer and Susan T Dumais. 1997. A solution to plato's problem: The latent semantic analysis theory of acquisition, induction, and representation of knowledge. *Psychological review*, 104(2):211.

Els Lefever and Veronique Hoste. 2010. Semeval-2010 task 3: Cross-lingual word sense disambiguation. In *Proceedings of the 5th International Workshop on Semantic Evaluation*, pages 15–20.

Omer Levy, Yoav Goldberg, and Israel Ramat-Gan. 2014. Linguistic regularities in sparse and explicit word representations. In *Proceedings of the Conference on Natural Language Learning (CoNLLL)*, pages 171–180.

Omer Levy, Yoav Goldberg, and Ido Dagan. 2015. Improving distributional similarity with lessons learned from word embeddings. *Transactions of the Association for Computational Linguistics*, 3:211–225.

Percy Liang, Ben Taskar, and Dan Klein. 2006. Alignment by agreement. In *Proceedings of the main conference on Human Language Technology Conference of the North American Chapter of the Association of Computational Linguistics*, pages 104–111.

Tomas Mikolov, Kai Chen, Greg Corrado, and Jeffrey Dean. 2013. Efficient estimation of word representations in vector space. *arXiv preprint arXiv:1301.3781*.

George A Miller and Walter G Charles. 1991. Contextual correlates of semantic similarity. *Language and Cognitive Processes*, 6(1):1–28.

George A Miller. 1995. Wordnet: a lexical database for English. *Communications of the ACM*, 38(11):39–41.

Arvind Neelakantan, Jeevan Shankar, Alexandre Passos, and Andrew McCallum. 2015. Efficient non-parametric estimation of multiple embeddings per word in vector space. *arXiv preprint arXiv:1504.06654*.

Hwee Tou Ng, Bin Wang, and Yee Seng Chan. 2003. Exploiting parallel texts for word sense disambiguation: An empirical study. In *Proceedings of the 41st Annual Meeting on Association for Computational Linguistics*, pages 455–462.

Joseph Reisinger and Raymond J Mooney. 2010. Multi-prototype vector-space models of word meaning. In *Human Language Technologies: The 2010 Annual Conference of the North American Chapter of the Association for Computational Linguistics*, pages 109–117.

Herbert Rubenstein and John B Goodenough. 1965. Contextual correlates of synonymy. *Communications of the ACM*, 8(10):627–633.

Fei Tian, Hanjun Dai, Jiang Bian, Bin Gao, Rui Zhang, Enhong Chen, and Tie-Yan Liu. 2014. A probabilistic model for learning multi-prototype word embeddings. In *Proceedings of COLING*, pages 151–160.

Peter D Turney, Patrick Pantel, et al. 2010. From frequency to meaning: Vector space models of semantics. *Journal of Artificial Intelligence Research*, 37(1):141–188.

Peter Turney. 2001. Mining the web for synonyms: PMI-IR versus LSA on TOEFL. In *Proceedings of the 12th European Conference on Machine Learning*.

Ralph Weischedel, Martha Palmer, Mitchell Marcus, Eduard Hovy, Sameer Pradhan, Lance Ramshaw, Nianwen Xue, Ann Taylor, Jeff Kaufman, Michelle Franchini, et al. 2013. Ontonotes release 5.0 ldc2013t19. *Linguistic Data Consortium, Philadelphia, PA*.

XTAG Research Group. 2001. A lexicalized tree adjoining grammar for English. Technical Report IRCS-01-03, IRCS, University of Pennsylvania.

End-to-End Argumentation Mining in Student Essays

Isaac Persing and **Vincent Ng**
Human Language Technology Research Institute
University of Texas at Dallas
Richardson, TX 75083-0688
{persingq,vince}@hlt.utdallas.edu

Abstract

Understanding the argumentative structure of a persuasive essay involves addressing two challenging tasks: identifying the components of the essay's argument and identifying the relations that occur between them. We examine the under-investigated task of *end-to-end* argument mining in persuasive student essays, where we (1) present the first results on end-to-end argument mining in student essays using a *pipeline* approach; (2) address error propagation inherent in the pipeline approach by performing *joint inference* over the outputs of the tasks in an Integer Linear Programming (ILP) framework; and (3) propose a novel objective function that enables F-score to be maximized directly by an ILP solver. We evaluate our joint-inference approach with our novel objective function on a publicly-available corpus of 90 essays, where it yields an 18.5% relative error reduction in F-score over the pipeline system.

1 Introduction

There has been a surge of interest in argumentation mining in recent years. Argumentation mining typically involves addressing two subtasks: (1) *argument component identification* (ACI), which consists of identifying the locations and types of the components that make up the arguments (i.e., Major Claims, Claims, and Premises), and (2) *relation identification* (RI), which involves identifying the type of relation that holds between two argument components (i.e., Support, Attack, None). As a first step towards mining arguments in persuasive essays,

Stab and Gurevych (S&G) annotated a corpus of 90 student essays with argument components and their relations (Stab and Gurevych, 2014a). To illustrate, consider the following excerpt from one essay:

> From this point of view, I firmly believe that (1) we should attach more importance to co-operation during primary education. First of all, (2) through cooperation, children can learn about interpersonal skills which are significant in the future life of all students. (3) What we acquired from team work is not only how to achieve the same goal with others but more importantly, how to get along with others.

In this example, premise (3) supports claim (2), which in turn supports major claim (1).

Using their annotated corpus, S&G presented initial results on *simplified* versions of the ACI and RI tasks (Stab and Gurevych, 2014b). Specifically, they applied their learned ACI classifier to classify only *gold* argument components (i.e., text spans corresponding to a Major Claim, Claim, or Premise in the gold standard) or sentences that contain no gold argument components (as *non-argumentative*). Similarly, they applied their learned RI classifier to classify only the relation between two *gold* argument components. In other words, they simplified both tasks by avoiding the challenging task of identifying the locations of argument components. Consequently, their approach cannot be applied in a realistic setting where the input is an *unannotated* essay.

Motivated by this weakness, we examine in this paper argument mining in persuasive student essays in a considerably more challenging setting than that of S&G: the *end-to-end* setting. In other words, we perform argument mining on raw, unannotated essays. Our work makes three contributions. First, we present the first results on end-to-end argument mining in student essays using a *pipeline* approach, where the ACI task is performed prior to the RI task. Second, to avoid the error propagation problem inherent in the pipeline approach, we perform *joint inference* over the outputs of the ACI and RI classifiers in an Integer Linear Programming (ILP) framework (Roth and Yih, 2004), where we design constraints to enforce global consistency. Finally, we argue that the typical objective function used extensively in ILP programs for NLP tasks is not ideal for tasks whose primary evaluation metric is F-score, and subsequently propose a novel objective function that enables F-score to be maximized directly in an ILP framework. We believe that the impact of our work goes beyond argument mining, as our F-score optimizing objective function is general enough to be applied to any ILP-based joint inference tasks.

2 Related Work

Recall that identifying argumentative discourse structures consists of (1) identifying the locations and types of the argument components, and (2) identifying how they are related to each other. Below we divide related works into five broad categories based on which of these subtasks they addressed.

Argument location identification. Works in this category aimed to classify whether a sentence contains an argument or not (Florou et al., 2013; Moens et al., 2007; Song et al., 2014; Swanson et al., 2015). The usefulness of existing works is somewhat limited by the task's coarseness: it won't tell us which portion of a potentially long sentence contains the argument, for instance, but it can serve as a potentially useful first step in argument mining.

Argument component typing. Works in this category focused on determining the *type* of an argument. The vast majority of previous works perform argument component typing at the *sentence* level. For instance, Rooney et al. (2012) classified sentences into premises, conclusions, premise-conclusions, and non-argumentative components; Teufel (1999) classified each sentence into one of seven rhetorical classes (e.g., claim, result, purpose); Burstein et al. (2003), Ong et al. (2014), and

Falakmasir et al. (2014) assigned argumentative labels (e.g., claim, thesis, conclusion) to an essay's sentences; Levy et al. (2014) detected sentences that support or attack an article's topic; Lippi and Torroni (2015; 2016) detected sentences containing claims; and Rinott et al. (2015) detected sentences containing evidence for a given claim. Sentence-level argument component typing has limitations, however. For example, it can identify sentences containing claims, but it cannot tell how many claims a sentence has or where in the sentence they are.

Argument location identification and typing. Some works focused on the more difficult task of *clause-level* argument component typing (Park and Cardie, 2014; Goudas et al., 2015; Sardianos et al., 2015), training a Conditional Random Field to jointly identify and type argument components.

Argument component typing and relation identification. Given the difficulty of clause-level argument component location identification, recent argument mining works that attempted argument component typing and relation identification are not end-to-end. Specifically, they simplified the task by assuming as input *gold* argument components (Stab and Gurevych, 2014b; Peldszus and Stede, 2015).

End-to-end argument mining. To our knowledge, only Palau and Moens (2009) addressed all the argument mining subtasks. They employed a hand-crafted context-free grammar (CFG) to generate (i.e., extract and type) argument components at the clause level and identify the relations between them. A CFG approach is less appealing in the essay domain because (1) constructing a CFG is a time- and labor-intensive task, (2) which would be more difficult in the less-rigidly structured essay domain, which contains fewer rhetorical markers indicating component types (e.g. words like "reject", or "dismiss" which indicate a legal document's conclusion); and (3) about 20% of essay arguments' structures are non-projective (i.e., when mapped to the ordered text, their argument trees have edges that cross), and thus cannot be captured by CFGs.

3 Corpus

Our corpus consists of 90 persuasive essays collected and annotated by S&G. Some relevant statistics are shown in Table 1. Each essay is an average

Essays: 90	Paragraphs: 417	Sentences: 1,673
Major Claims: 90	Claims: 429	Premises: 1,033
Support Relations: 1,312		Attack Relations: 161

Table 1: Corpus statistics.

of 4.6 paragraphs (18.6 sentences) in length and is written in response to a topic such as "should high school make music lessons compulsory?" or "competition or co-operation-which is better?".

The corpus annotations describe the essays' argument structure, including the locations and types of the components that make up the arguments, and the types of relations that hold between them. The three annotated argument component types include: **Major Claims**, which express the author's stance with respect to the essay's topic, **Claims**, which are controversial statements that should not be accepted by readers without additional support, and **Premises**, which are reasons authors give to persuade readers about the truth of another argument component statement. The two relation types include: **Support**, which indicates that one argument component supports another, and **Attack**, which indicates that one argument component attacks another.

4 Pipeline-Based Argument Mining

Next, we describe our end-to-end *pipeline* argument mining system, which will serve as our baseline. In this system, ACI is performed prior to RI.

4.1 Argument Component Identification

We employ a two-step approach to the ACI task, where we first heuristically extract *argument component candidates* (ACCs) from an essay, and then classify each ACC as either a premise, claim, major claim, or non-argumentative, as described below.

4.1.1 Extracting ACCs

We extract ACCs by constructing a set of low precision, high recall heuristics for identifying the locations in each sentence where an argument component's boundaries might occur. The majority of these rules depend primarily on a syntactic parse tree we automatically generated for all sentences in the corpus using the Stanford CoreNLP (Manning et al., 2014) system. Since argument components are a clause-level annotation and therefore a large majority of annotated argument components are substrings

(a) Potential left boundary locations

#	Rule
1	Exactly where the S node begins.
2	After an initial explicit connective, or if the connective is immediately followed by a comma, after the comma.
3	After nth comma that is an immediate child of the S node.
4	After nth comma.

(b) Potential right boundary locations

#	Rule
5	Exactly where the S node ends, or if S ends in a punctuation, immediately before the punctuation.
6	If the S node ends in a (possibly nested) SBAR node, immediately before the nth shallowest SBAR.[1]
7	If the S node ends in a (possibly nested) PP node, immediately before the nth shallowest PP.

Table 2: Rules for extracting ACC boundary locations.

of a simple declarative clause (an S node in the parse tree), we begin by identifying each S node in a sentence's tree.

Given an S clause, we collect a list of left and right boundaries where an argument component may begin or end. The rules we used to find these boundaries are summarized in Table 2. We then construct ACCs by combining each left boundary with each right boundary that occurs after it. As a result, we are able to find exact (boundaries exactly match) and approximate (over half of tokens shared) matches for 92.1% and 98.4% respectively of all ACs.

4.1.2 Training the ACI Classifier

We train a classifier for ACI using MALLET's (McCallum, 2002) implementation of maximum entropy classification. We create a training instance from each ACC extracted above. If the ACC's left and right endpoints exactly match an annotated argument component's, the corresponding training instance's class label is the same as that of the component. Otherwise, its class label is "non-

---

[1] An additional point that requires explanation is that the last two right boundary rules mention "possibly nested" nodes. In boundary rule 7, for example, this means that the S node might end in a PP node, which itself has a PP node as its last child, and so on. We generate a separate right boundary immediately before each of these PP nodes.

argumentative". Each training instance is represented using S&G's structural, lexical, syntactic, indicator, and contextual features for solving the same problem. Briefly, the structural features describe an ACC and its covering sentence's length, punctuations, and location in the essay. Lexical features describe the $1-3$ grams of the ACC and its covering sentence. Syntactic features are extracted from the ACC's covering sentence's parse tree and include things such as production rules. Indicator features describe any explicit connectives that immediately precede the ACC. Contextual features describe the contents of the sentences preceding and following the ACC primarily in ways similar to how the structural features describe the covering sentence.

4.2 Relation Identification

We consider RI between pairs of argument components to be a five class classification problem. Given a pair of ACCs A_1 and A_2 where A_1 occurs before A_2 in the essay, either they are unrelated, A_1 supports A_2, A_2 supports A_1, A_1 attacks A_2, or A_2 attacks A_1. Below we describe how we train and apply our classifier for RI.

We learn our RI classifier using MALLET's implementation of maximum entropy classification. Each training instance, which we call a training *relation candidate* (RC), consists of a pair of ACCs and one of the above five labels. By default, the instance's label is "no relation" unless each ACC has the exact boundaries of a gold standard argument component and one of the remaining four relations holds between the two gold argument components.

We create training RCs as follows. We construct RCs corresponding to true relations out of all pairs of argument components in a training essay having a gold relation. As the number of potential RCs far exceeds the number of gold relations in an essay, we undersample the "no relation" class in the following way. Given a pair of argument components A and B between which there is a gold relation, we define A_p to be the closest previous ACC in the essay as generated in Section 4.1.1 such that A_p's text doesn't overlap with A. We also define A_s as the closest succeeding ACC after A such that A_s and A do not overlap. We define B_p and B_s similarly with respect to B. From these ACCs, we generate the the four instances (A_p, B), (A_s, B), (A, B_p), and (A, B_s), all

of which have the "no relation" label, as long as the pairs' text sequences do not overlap. We believe the resulting "no relation" training instances are informative since each one is "close" to a gold relation. We represent each instance using S&G's structural, lexical, syntactic, and indicator features for solving the same problem. Briefly, RC structural features describe many of the same things about each ACC as did the ACC structural features, though they also describe the difference between the ACCs (e.g. the difference in punctuation counts). Lexical features consist primarily of the unigrams appearing in each ACC and word pairs, where each word from one ACC is paired with each word from the other. Syntactic and indicator features encode the same information about each ACC as the ACC syntactic and indicator features did.

We now apply the classifier to test essay RCs, which are created as follows. Given that this is a pipelined argument mining system, in order to ensure that the RI system's output is consistent with that of the ACI system, we generate test RCs from all possible pairs of ACCs that the ACI system predicted are real components (i.e. it labeled them something other than "non-argumentative").

5 Joint Inference for Argument Mining

5.1 Motivation

There are two major problems with the pipeline approach described in the previous section. First, many essay-level within-task constraints are not enforced. For instance, the ACI task has the constraint that each essay has exactly one major claim, and the RI task has the constraint that each claim has no more than one parent. This problem arises because our ACI and RI classifiers, like those of S&G, classify each ACI and RI test instance independently of other test instances. We propose to enforce such essay-level within-task constraints in an ILP framework, employing ILP to perform joint inference over the outputs of our ACI and RI classifiers so that the resulting classifications satisfy these constraints.[2]

---

[2] Note that while we partition *documents* into folds in our cross-validation experiments, S&G partition *instances* into folds. Hence, S&G's evaluation setting prevents them from enforcing essay-level constraints in addition to being unrealistic in practice.

The second problem with the pipeline approach is that errors made early on in the pipeline propagate. For instance, assume that a Support relation exists between two argument components in a test essay. If the pipeline system fails to (heuristically) extract one or both of these argument components, or if it successfully extracts them but misclassifies one or both of them as non-argumentative, then the pipeline system will not be able to identify the relationship between them because no test RCs will be created from them. The above problem arises because the RI classifier assumes the *most probable* output of the ACI classifier for each ACC as input. Hence, one possible solution to this problem is to make use of the *n-best* outputs of the ACI classifier for each argument component type, as this increases the robustness of the pipeline to errors made by the ACI classifier.

We obtain the n-best ACI outputs and employ them as follows. Recall that the ACI system uses a maximum entropy classifier, and therefore its output for each ACC is a list of probabilities indicating how likely it is that the ACC belongs to each of the four classes (premise, claim, major claim, or non-argumentative). This means that it is possible to rank all the ACCs in a text by these probabilities. We use this idea to identify (1) the 3 most likely premise ACCs from each sentence, (2) the 5 most likely claim ACCs from each paragraph, and (3) the 5 most likely major claim ACCs from each essay.[3] Given these most likely ACC lists, we combine pairs of ACCs into test RCs for the RI classifier in the following way. As long as the ACCs do not overlap, we pair (1) each likely premise ACC with every other likely ACC of any type occurring in the same paragraph, and (2) each likely claim ACC with each likely major claim ACC. We then present these test RCs to the RI classifier normally, making no other changes to how the pipeline system works.

Employing n-best ACI outputs, however, introduces another problem: the output of the RI classifier may no longer be *consistent* with that of the ACI classifier because the RI classifier may posit a rela-

tionship between two ACCs that the ACI classifier labeled non-argumentative. To enforce this cross-task consistency constraint, we also propose to employ ILP. The rest of this section details our ILP-based joint inference approach for argument mining, which addresses both of the aforementioned problems with the pipeline approach.

5.2 Basic ILP Approach

We perform joint inference over the outputs of the ACI and RI classifiers by designing and enforcing within-task and cross-task constraints in the ILP framework. Specifically, we create one ILP program for each test essay, as described below.

Let Xn_i, Xp_i, Xc_i, and Xm_i be binary indicator variables representing whether the ILP solver believes ACC i has type none, premise, claim, and major claim, respectively. Let Cn_i, Cp_i, Cc_i, and Cm_i be the probabilities that ACC i has type none, premise, claim, and major claim, respectively, as dictated by the ACI maximum entropy classifier's output.[4] Let a be the count of ACCs.

Let $Yn_{i,j}$, $Ys_{i,j}$, $Ya_{i,j}$, $Yrs_{i,j}$, and $Yra_{i,j}$ be binary indicator variables representing whether the ILP solver believes ACCs i and j have no relation, i is supported by j, i is attacked by j, j is supported by i, and j is attacked by i, respectively, where (i,j) appears in the set of RCs B that we presented to the RI system as modified in Section 5.1. We assume all other ACC pairs have no relation. Let $Dn_{i,j}$, $Ds_{i,j}$, $Da_{i,j}$, $Drs_{i,j}$, and $Dra_{i,j}$ be the probabilities that component candidates i and j have no relation, i is supported by j, i is attacked by j, j is supported by i, and j is attacked by i, respectively, as dictated by the modified RI classifier described in Section 5.1.[4]

Given these definitions and probabilities, our ILP program's default goal is to find an assignment of these variables X and Y in order to maximize $P(X) + P(Y)$, where:

$$P(X) = \frac{1}{a} \sum_{i=1}^{a} \log(Cn_i Xn_i + Cp_i Xp_i \qquad (1)$$
$$+ Cc_i Xc_i + Cm_i Xm_i)$$

---

[3]We select more premise than claim ACCs (3 per sentence vs 5 per paragraph) because the corpus contains over twice as many premises as claims. We select major claim ACCs only from the first and last paragraph because major claims never occur in middle paragraphs.

[4]We additionally reserve .001 probability mass to distribute evenly among Cn_i, Cp_i, Cc_i, and Cm_i (or $Dn_{i,j}$, $Da_{i,j}$, $Drs_{i,j}$, and $Dra_{i,j}$) to prevent math errors involving taking the log of 0 which might otherwise occur in the formulas below.

$$P(Y) = \frac{1}{|B|} \sum_{(i,j) \in B} \log(Dn_{i,j}Yn_{i,j} + Ds_{i,j}Ys_{i,j} \tag{2}$$
$$+Da_{i,j}Ya_{i,j} + Drs_{i,j}Yrs_{i,j} + Dra_{i,j}Yra_{i,j})$$

subject to the *integrity* constraints that: (3) an ACC is either not an argument component or it has exactly one of the real argument component types, (4) a pair of component candidates (i, j) must have exactly one of the five relation types, and (5) if there is a relation between ACCs i and j, i and j must each be real components.[5]

$$Xn_i + Xp_i + Xc_i + Xm_i = 1 \tag{3}$$

$$Yn_{i,j} + Ys_{i,j} + Ya_{i,j} + Yrs_{i,j} + Yra_{i,j} = 1 \tag{4}$$

$$(Xp_i + Xc_i + Xm_i) + (Xp_j + Xc_j + Xm_j) \tag{5}$$
$$-2(Ys_{i,j} + Ya_{i,j} + Yrs_{i,j} + Yra_{i,j}) \geq 0$$

In the objective function, a and $|B|$ serve to balance the contribution of the two tasks, preventing one from dominating the other.

5.3 Enforcing Consistency Constraints

So far we have described integrity constraints, but recall that our goal is to enforce consistency by imposing within-task and cross-task constraints, which force the ILP solutions to more closely resemble real essay argument structures. Our consistency constraints fall into four categories.

Our constraints on *major claims* are that: (6) there is exactly one major claim in each essay, (7) major claims always occur in the first or last paragraph, and (8) major claims have no parents.

$$\sum_{i=1}^{a} Xm_i = 1 \tag{6}$$

$$Xm_i = 0 \mid i \notin first\ or\ last\ paragraph \tag{7}$$

$$Ys_{i,j} + Xm_j \leq 1 \ , \ Ya_{i,j} + Xm_j \leq 1 \tag{8}$$
$$Yrs_{i,j} + Xm_i \leq 1 \ , \ Yra_{i,j} + Xm_i \leq 1$$

Our constraints on *premises* are that: (9) a premise has at least one parent, and (10) a premise is related only to components in the same paragraph.

$$\sum_{\{i|(i,j) \in B\}} (Ys_{i,j} + Ya_{i,j})$$
$$+ \sum_{\{k|(j,k) \in B\}} (Yrs_{j,k} + Yra_{j,k}) - Xp_j \geq 0 \tag{9}$$

$$for\ i < j,\ i \notin Par(j) : Xp_j - Yn_{i,j} \leq 0$$
$$for\ k > j,\ k \notin Par(j) : Xp_j - Yn_{j,k} \leq 0 \tag{10}$$

where $i < j$ and $j < k$ mean ACC i appears before j, and j appears before k, and $Par(j)$ is the set of ACCs in j's covering paragraph.

Our constraints on *claims* state that: (11) a claim has no more than one parent[6], and (12) if a claim has a parent, that parent must be a major claim.

$$\left(\Big| \{i|(i,j) \in B\} \Big| + \Big| \{k|(j,k) \in B\} \Big| \right) Xc_j$$
$$+ \sum_{\{i|(i,j) \in B\}} (Ys_{i,j} + Ya_{i,j})$$
$$+ \sum_{\{k|(j,k) \in B\}} (Yrs_{j,k} + Yra_{j,k}) \tag{11}$$
$$\leq \Big| \{i|(i,j) \in B\} \Big| + \Big| \{k|(j,k) \in B\} \Big| + 1$$

$$for\ j < k,\ Xm_k - Xc_j - Yrs_{j,k} - Yra_{j,k} \geq -1$$
$$for\ j > i,\ Xm_i - Xc_j - Ys_{i,j} - Ya_{i,j} \geq -1 \tag{12}$$

The last category, which comprises constraints that do not fit well into any other category, are: (13) the boundaries of actual components never overlap, (14) each paragraph must have at least one claim or major claim, and (15) each sentence may have at most two argument components.[7]

$$for\ i\ overlaps\ j\ ,\ Xn_i + Xn_j \geq 1 \tag{13}$$

$$\forall\ paragraphs\ P \ : \ \sum_{i \in P} Xc_i + Xm_i \geq 1 \tag{14}$$

$$\forall\ sentences\ S \ : \ \sum_{i \in S} Xp_i + Xc_i + Xm_i \leq 2 \tag{15}$$

We solve each ILP program using Gurobi.[8]

---

[5]Note that because of previous integrity constraints, the first term in constraint 5 is 1 only if we predict that i is a real component, the second term is 1 only if we predict that j is a real component, and the third term is -2 only if we predict that there is a relationship between them. Otherwise, each term is 0. Thus term 3 prevents us from predicting a relationship between i and j unless the first and second terms cancel it out through predicting that i and j are real components.

[6]The coefficient of Xc_j is equal to the number of terms in the two summations on the left hand side of the equation. The intention is that component j's claim status should have equal weight with the relations it might potentially participate in, so it is possible for j to participate as a child in a relation with all other available components unless it is a claim, in which case it can participate in at most one relation as a child.

[7]Unlike the other constraints, the last two constraints are only mostly true: 5% of paragraphs have no claims or major claims, and 1.2% of sentences have 3 or more components.

[8]http://www.gurobi.com

5.4 F-score Maximizing Objective Function

The objective function we employ in the previous subsection attempts to maximize the average probability of correct assignment of variables over the ACI and RI problems. This kind of objective function, which aims to maximize classification accuracy, was originally introduced by Roth and Yih (2004) in their seminal ILP paper, and has since then been extensively applied to NLP tasks. However, it is arguably not an ideal objective function for our task, where F-score rather than classification accuracy is used as the evaluation metric.

In this section, we introduce a novel method for constructing an ILP objective function that directly maximizes the average F-score over the two problems. Recall that F-score can be simplified to:

$$F = \frac{2TP}{2TP + FP + FN} \qquad (16)$$

where TP, FP, and FN are the counts of true positives, false positives, and false negatives respectively. Unfortunately, we cannot use this equation for F-score in an ILP objective function for two reasons. First, this equation involves division, which cannot be handled using ILP since ILP can only handle linear combinations of variables. Second, TP, FP, and FN need to be computed using gold annotations, which we don't have in a test document. We propose to instead maximize F by maximizing the following:

$$G = \alpha 2TP_e - (1 - \alpha)(FP_e + FN_e) \qquad (17)$$

where TP_e, FP_e, and FN_e, are *estimated* values for TP, FP, and FN respectively, and α attempts to balance the importance of maximizing the numerator vs minimizing the denominator.[9] We ignore the $2TP$ term in the denominator because minimizing it would directly reduce the numerator.

To maximize average F-score, we can therefore attempt to maximize the function $\frac{G_c + G_r}{2}$, where G_c and G_r are the values of G in equation 17 as calculated using the estimated values from the ACI and RI problem respectively.

The question that still remains is, how can we estimate values for TP, FP, and FN mentioned in

<hr>

[9]We tune α on the development set, allowing it to take any value from 0.7, 0.8, or 0.9, as this range tended to perform well in early experiments.

Equation 17? Our key idea is inspired by the E-step of the Expectation-Maximization algorithm (Dempster et al., 1977): while we cannot compute the actual TP, FP, and FN due to the lack of gold annotations, we can compute their *expected* values using the probabilities returned by the ACI and RI classifiers. Using the notation introduced in Section 5.2, the expected TP, FP, and FN values for the ACI task can be computed as follows:

$$TP_e = \sum_{i,g} Cg_i Xg_i \qquad (18)$$

$$FP_e = \sum_{i,g} (1 - Cg_i) Xg_i \qquad (19)$$

$$FN_e = \sum_{i,g} \left(Xg_i \sum_{h \neq g} Ch_i \right) + \sum_i Xn_i (1 - Cn_i) \qquad (20)$$

where g and h can be any argumentative class from the ACI problem (i.e. premise (p), claim (c), or major claim (m)). The formulas we use to calculate TP_e, FP_e, and FN_e for the RI problem are identical except C is replaced with D, X is replaced with Y, and g and h can be any class from the RI problem other than no-relation.

6 Evaluation

6.1 Experimental Setup

Corpus. As mentioned before, we use as our corpus the 90 essays annotated with argumentative discourse structures by S&G. All of our experiments are conducted via five-fold cross-validation on this corpus. In each fold experiment, we reserve 60% of the essays for training, 20% for development (selecting features and tuning α), and 20% for testing.

Evaluation metrics. To calculate F-score on each task using Equation 16, we need to explain what constitutes a true positive, false positive, or false negative on each task. Given that j is a true argument component and i is an ACC, the formulas for the ACI task are:

$$TP = \left| \{j \mid \exists i \,|gl(j) = pl(i) \wedge i \doteq j\} \right| \qquad (21)$$

$$FP = \left| \{i \mid pl(i) \neq n \wedge \nexists j \mid gl(j) = pl(i) \wedge i \doteq j\} \right| \qquad (22)$$

$$FN = \left| \{j \mid \nexists i \,|gl(j) = pl(i) \wedge i \doteq j\} \right| \qquad (23)$$

where $gl(j)$ is the gold standard label of j, $pl(i)$ is the predicted label of i, n is the non-argumentative class, and $i \doteq j$ means i is a *match* for j. i and j are considered an *exact match* if they have exactly

| | System | ACI | | | | | | RI | | | | | Avg |
		MC-F	C-F	P-F	P	R	F	S-F	A-F	P	R	F	F
Approx	BASE	11.1	26.9	51.9	64.0	33.6	44.0	6.1	0.8	5.7	6.2	5.8	24.9
	OUR	22.2	**42.6**	**66.0**	56.6	**57.9**	**57.2**	**21.3**	1.1	**16.8**	**28.0**	**20.4**	**38.8**
Exact	BASE	7.4	24.2	43.2	50.4	29.6	37.3	4.4	0.8	4.1	4.7	4.3	20.8
	OUR	16.9	**37.4**	**53.4**	47.5	**46.7**	**47.1**	**13.6**	0.0	12.7	15.4	**12.9**	**30.0**

Table 3: Five-fold cross-validation average percentages for argument component identification (ACI) and relation identification (RI) for OUR system and the pipeline-based BASEline system. Column abbreviations are Major Claim F-score (MC-F), Claim F-score (C-F), Premise F-score (P-F), Precision (P), Recall (R), F-score (F), Support F-score (S-F), and Attack F-score (A-F).

the same boundaries, whereas they are considered an *approximate match* if they share over half their tokens.

We perform most of our analysis on approximate match results rather than exact match results as it can be difficult even for human annotators to identify exactly the same boundaries for an argument component.[10] We use the same formulas for calculating these numbers for the RI problem except that j and i represent a true relation and an RC respectively, two relations approximately (exactly) match if both their source and target ACCs approximately (exactly) match, and n is the no-relation class.

6.2 Results and Discussion

Approximate and exact match results of the pipeline approach (BASE) and the joint approach (OUR) are shown in Table 3. As we can see, using approximate matching, OUR system achieves highly significant[11] improvements over the pipelined baseline system by a variety of measures.[12] The most important of these improvements is shown in the last column, where our system outperforms the baseline by 13.9% ab-

solute F-score (a relative error reduction of 18.5%). This is the most important result because it most directly measures our performance in pursuit of our ultimate goal, to maximize the average F-score over both the ACI and RI problems. The highly significant improvements in other measures, particularly the improvements of 13.2% and 14.6% in ACI and RI F-score respectively, follow as a consequence of this maximization. Using exact matching, the differences in scores between OUR system and BASE's are smaller and highly significant with respect to a smaller number of measures. In particular, under Exact matching OUR system's performances on the RI-P and RI-R metrics are significant ($p < 0.02$), while under Approx matching, they are highly significant ($p < 0.002$).

6.3 Ablation Results

To analyze the performance gains yielded by each improvement to our system, we show ablation results in Table 4. Each row of the table shows the results of one ablation experiment on the test set. That is, we obtain them by removing exactly one feature set or improvement type from our system.

The **B**aseline feature sets we remove include those for the **ACI** task (C_b) from Section 4.1.2 and those for the **RI** task (R_b) from Section 4.2.[13] The **ILP** improvement sets we remove are the **Default ILP** (I_d) system[14] from Section 5.2, the **Major claim** (I_m), **Premise** (I_p), **Claim** (I_c), and **Other** (I_o) constraints from Section 5.3 Equations 6−8, 9−10,

---

[10] Approximate match has been used in evaluating opinion mining systems (e.g., Choi et al. (2006), Yang and Cardie (2013)), where researchers have also reported difficulties in having human annotators identify exactly the same boundaries for an opinion expression and its sources and targets. They have adopted an even more relaxed notion of approximate match: they consider two text spans an approximate match if they share at least one overlapping token.

[11] Boldfaced results in Table 3 are highly significant ($p < 0.002$, paired t-test) compared to the baseline.

[12] All the results in Tables 3 and 4 are averaged across five folds, so it is not true that $F_{avg} = \frac{2P_{avg}R_{avg}}{P_{avg}+R_{avg}}$. Our F-score averaging method is preferable to calculating F-scores using the above formula because the formula can be exploited to give artificially inflated F-scores by alternating between high precision, low recall, and low precision, high recall labelings on different folds.

[13] When we remove a baseline feature set, we represent each instance to the corresponding classifier using no features. As a result, the classifier's predictions are based solely on the frequency of the classes seen during training.

[14] Note that removing the default ILP system (I_d) necessitates simultaneously removing all other ILP-related improvements. Thus, a system without it is equivalent to BASE, but with RCs generated as described in Section 5.1.

Mod	ACI			RI			Avg
	P	R	F	P	R	F	F
ALL	54.9	58.8	56.7	16.7	26.4	20.4	38.6
C_b	**44.0**	**38.5**	**40.9**	14.2	**14.8**	**14.4**	**27.7**
R_b	57.9	58.7	58.2	16.6	24.0	18.2	38.2
I_d	64.0	**33.6**	**44.0**	**6.6**	**21.8**	**10.1**	**27.0**
I_m	44.6	**46.7**	**45.6**	14.7	27.8	19.2	**32.4**
I_p	51.5	58.4	54.7	13.2	26.1	**17.3**	36.0
I_c	**49.0**	**51.5**	**50.2**	14.2	27.9	18.8	**34.5**
I_o	40.5	65.9	**50.1**	**7.0**	29.2	**11.2**	**30.7**
I_f	61.1	**40.4**	**48.5**	22.3	**15.7**	**18.2**	**33.4**

Table 4: Ablation results. How OUR system performs on one development set as measured by percent Precision, Recall, and F-score if each improvement or feature set is removed.

$11-12$, and $13-15$ respectively, and the **F**-score maximizing objective function from Section 5.4.

Broadly, we see from the last column that all of our improvement sets are beneficial (usually significantly[15]) to the system, as performance drops with their removal. Notice also that whenever removing an ILP improvement set harms average F-score, it also simultaneously harms ACI and RI F-scores, usually significantly. This holds true even when the improvement set deals primarily only with one task (e.g. I_o for the ACI task), suggesting that our system is benefiting from joint inference over both tasks.

6.4 Error Analysis and Future Work

Table 3 shows that OUR system has more trouble with the RI task than the ACI task. A closer inspection of OUR system's RI predictions reveals that its low precision is mostly due to predicted relationships wherein one of the participating ACCs is not a true argument component. Since false positives in the ACI task have an outsized impact on RI precision, it may be worthwhile to investigate ILP objective functions that more harshly penalize false positive ACCs.

The RI task's poor recall has two primary causes. The first is false negatives in the ACI task. It is impossible for an RI system to correctly identify a relationship between two ACs if the ACI system fails to identify either one of them as an AC. We believe ACI recall, and by extension, RI recall, can be improved by exploiting the following observations. First, we noticed that many argument components OUR system fails to identify, regardless of their type, contain words that are semantically similar to words in the essay's topic (e.g., if the topic mentions "school", argument components might mention "students"). Hence, one way to improve ACI recall, and by extension, RI recall, would be to create ACI features using a semantic similarity measure such as the Wikipedia Link-based similarity measure (Milne and Witten, 2008). Second, major claims are involved in 32% of all relationships, but OUR system did an especially poor job at identifying them due to their scarcity. Since we noticed that major claims tend to include strong stancetaking language (e.g., words like "should", "must", and "believe"), it may be possible to improve major claim identification by constructing an arguing language lexicon as in Somasundaran and Wiebe (2010), then encoding the presence of any of these arguing words as ACC features.

The second major cause of OUR system's poor RI recall is its failure to identify relationships between two correctly extracted ACs. We noticed many of the missed relationships involve ACs that mention some of the same entities. Thus, a coreference resolver could help us build features that describe whether two ACCs are talking about the same entities.

7 Conclusion

We presented the *first* results on *end-to-end* argument mining in persuasive student essays using a pipeline approach, improved this baseline approach by designing and employing global consistency constraints to perform joint inference over the outputs of the tasks in an ILP framework and proposed a novel objective function that enables F-score to be maximized directly by an ILP solver. In an evaluation on Stab and Gurevych's corpus of 90 essays, our approach yields an 18.5% relative error reduction in F-score over the pipeline system.

Acknowledgments

We thank the three anonymous reviewers for their detailed comments. This work was supported in part by NSF Grants IIS-1147644 and IIS-1219142.

---

[15]Boldfaced results are significantly lower than ALL, the system with all improvements left intact, with $p < 0.05$.

References

Jill Burstein, Daniel Marcu, and Kevin Knight. 2003. Finding the WRITE stuff: Automatic identification of discourse structure in student essays. *IEEE Intelligent Systems*, 18(1):32–39.

Yejin Choi, Eric Breck, and Claire Cardie. 2006. Joint extraction of entities and relations for opinion recognition. In *Proceedings of the 2006 Conference on Empirical Methods in Natural Language Processing*, pages 431–439.

Arthur P. Dempster, Nan M. Laird, and Donald B. Rubin. 1977. Maximum likelihood from incomplete data via the EM algorithm. *Journal of the Royal Statistical Society. Series B (Methodological)*, 39:1–38.

Mohammad Hassan Falakmasir, Kevin D. Ashley, Christian D. Schunn, and Diane J. Litman. 2014. Identifying thesis and conclusion statements in student essays to scaffold peer review. In *Intelligent Tutoring Systems*, pages 254–259. Springer International Publishing.

Eirini Florou, Stasinos Konstantopoulos, Antonis Koukourikos, and Pythagoras Karampiperis. 2013. Argument extraction for supporting public policy formulation. In *Proceedings of the 7th Workshop on Language Technology for Cultural Heritage, Social Sciences, and Humanities*, pages 49–54.

Theodosios Goudas, Christos Louizos, Georgios Petasis, and Vangelis Karkaletsis. 2015. Argument extraction from news, blogs, and the social web. *International Journal on Artificial Intelligence Tools*, 24(5).

Ran Levy, Yonatan Bilu, Daniel Hershcovich, Ehud Aharoni, and Noam Slonim. 2014. Context dependent claim detection. In *Proceedings of the 25th International Conference on Computational Linguistics*, pages 1489–1500.

Marco Lippi and Paolo Torroni. 2015. Context-independent claim detection for argument mining. In *Proceedings of the 24th International Joint Conference on Artificial Intelligence*, pages 185–191.

Marco Lippi and Paolo Torroni. 2016. Argument mining from speech: Detecting claims in political debates. In *Proceedings of the 30th AAAI Conference on Artificial Intelligence*.

Christopher D. Manning, Mihai Surdeanu, John Bauer, Jenny Finkel, Steven J. Bethard, and David McClosky. 2014. The Stanford CoreNLP natural language processing toolkit. In *Proceedings of 52nd Annual Meeting of the Association for Computational Linguistics: System Demonstrations*, pages 55–60.

Andrew Kachites McCallum. 2002. MALLET: A Machine Learning for Language Toolkit. `http://mallet.cs.umass.edu`.

David Milne and Ian Witten. 2008. An effective, low-cost measure of semantic relatedness obtained from Wikipedia links. In *Proceedings of AAAI Workshop on Wikipedia and Artificial Intelligence: an Evolving Synergy*, pages 25–30.

Marie-Francine Moens, Erik Boiy, Raquel Mochales Palau, and Chris Reed. 2007. Automatic detection of arguments in legal texts. In *Proceedings of the 11th International Conference on Artificial Intelligence and Law*, pages 225–230.

Nathan Ong, Diane Litman, and Alexandra Brusilovsky. 2014. Ontology-based argument mining and automatic essay scoring. In *Proceedings of the First Workshop on Argumentation Mining*, pages 24–28.

Raquel Mochales Palau and Marie-Francine Moens. 2009. Argumentation mining: The detection, classification and structure of arguments in text. In *Proceedings of the 12th International Conference on Artificial Intelligence and Law*, pages 98–107.

Joonsuk Park and Claire Cardie. 2014. Identifying appropriate support for propositions in online user comments. In *Proceedings of the First Workshop on Argumentation Mining*, pages 29–38.

Andreas Peldszus and Manfred Stede. 2015. Joint prediction in mst-style discourse parsing for argumentation mining. In *Proceedings of the 2015 Conference on Empirical Methods in Natural Language Processing*, pages 938–948.

Ruty Rinott, Lena Dankin, Carlos Alzate Perez, Mitesh M. Khapra, Ehud Aharoni, and Noam Slonim. 2015. Show me your evidence - an automatic method for context dependent evidence detection. In *Proceedings of the 2015 Conference on Empirical Methods in Natural Language Processing*, pages 440–450.

Niall Rooney, Hui Wang, and Fiona Browne. 2012. Applying kernel methods to argumentation mining. In *Proceedings of the 21st International Florida Artificial Intelligence Research Society Conference*.

Dan Roth and Wen-tau Yih. 2004. A linear programming formulation for global inference in natural language tasks. In *Proceedings of the Eighth Conference on Computational Natural Language Learning*, pages 1–8.

Christos Sardianos, Ioannis Manousos Katakis, Georgios Petasis, and Vangelis Karkaletsis. 2015. Argument extraction from news. In *Proceedings of the Second Workshop on Argumentation Mining*, pages 56–66.

Swapna Somasundaran and Janyce Wiebe. 2010. Recognizing stances in ideological on-line debates. In *Proceedings of the NAACL HLT 2010 Workshop on Computational Approaches to Analysis and Generation of Emotion in Text*, pages 116–124.

Yi Song, Michael Heilman, Beata Beigman Klebanov, and Paul Deane. 2014. Applying argumentation schemes for essay scoring. In *Proceedings of the First Workshop on Argumentation Mining*, pages 69–78.

Christian Stab and Iryna Gurevych. 2014a. Annotating argument components and relations in persuasive essays. In *Proceedings of the 25th International Conference on Computational Linguistics*, pages 1501–1510.

Christian Stab and Iryna Gurevych. 2014b. Identifying argumentative discourse structures in persuasive essays. In *Proceedings of the 2014 Conference on Empirical Methods in Natural Language Processing*, pages 46–56.

Reid Swanson, Brian Ecker, and Marilyn Walker. 2015. Argument mining: Extracting arguments from online dialogue. In *Proceedings of the 16th Annual Meeting of the Special Interest Group on Discourse and Dialogue*, pages 217–226.

Simone Teufel. 1999. *Argumentative Zoning: Information Extraction from Scientific Text*. Ph.D. thesis, University of Edinburgh.

Bishan Yang and Claire Cardie. 2013. Joint inference for fine-grained opinion extraction. In *Proceedings of the 51st Annual Meeting of the Association for Computational Linguistics (Volume 1: Long Papers)*, pages 1640–1649.

Cross-Domain Mining of Argumentative Text through Distant Supervision

Khalid Al-Khatib   Henning Wachsmuth   Matthias Hagen   Jonas Köhler   Benno Stein
Faculty of Media, Bauhaus-Universität Weimar, Germany
<firstname>.<lastname>@uni-weimar.de

Abstract

Argumentation mining is considered as a key technology for future search engines and automated decision making. In such applications, argumentative text segments have to be mined from large and diverse document collections. However, most existing argumentation mining approaches tackle the classification of argumentativeness only for a few manually annotated documents from narrow domains and registers. This limits their practical applicability. We hence propose a distant supervision approach that acquires argumentative text segments automatically from online debate portals. Experiments across domains and registers show that training on such a corpus improves the effectiveness and robustness of mining argumentative text. We freely provide the underlying corpus for research.

1   Introduction

Argumentation mining attracts much attention recently: it is an important building block of applications like automated decision making (Bench-Capon et al., 2009) or pro-and-con search engines (Cabrio and Villata, 2012c). In such applications, argumentation mining usually consists of solving three tasks for each document: (1) Identifying all argumentative text segments in the document, (2) classifying the type of each segment, and (3) classifying relations between the segments.

In this paper we focus on the first task taking on the retrieval perspective of a search engine: Given a large-scale collection of documents (e.g., the web) and a query on some topic, return all argumenta-

tive text segments relevant to the topic. Among others, a classifier is needed for this task that can distinguish argumentative from non-argumentative segments. Since we cannot presuppose a specific domain or register within a general retrieval scenario, the classifier needs to robustly deal with documents from diverse domains and registers. In this regard the following two key issues arise.

First, existing approaches to classifying argumentativeness usually focus on specific text domains (e.g., education) and registers (e.g., student essays). Therefore, many used features capture not only local linguistic properties of a text segment, but also global document properties (e.g., that a segment is part of the introduction). Such kinds of features tend to be effective only within a certain domain or a particular register while often failing for others.

Second, all major existing approaches follow a supervised learning scheme based on manual annotation of argumentative text segments. However, the annotation of arguments is particularly intricate and thus expensive due to the complex linguistic structure and the partly subjective interpretation of argumentativeness. Different types of argumentative and non-argumentative segments may come in any order, segment boundaries are not always unambiguous, and parts of an argument may be implicit. Studies reveal that annotators need multiple training sessions to identify and classify argumentative segments with moderate inter-annotator agreement, and crowdsourcing-based annotation does not help notably (Habernal et al., 2014). I.e., a high-quality manual annotation will not scale to large numbers of documents from diverse domains and registers.

Proceedings of NAACL-HLT 2016, pages 1395–1404,
San Diego, California, June 12-17, 2016. ©2016 Association for Computational Linguistics

We propose a solution to the outlined issues. In particular, we follow the idea of distant supervision to construct a large-scale corpus of text segments from diverse domains and registers annotated with respect to argumentativeness. Distant supervision is a well-known idea for training robust statistical classifiers. Here, we exploit online debate portals that (1) contain argumentative and non-argumentative text segments for several controversial topics, and that (2) are organized in a semi-structured form, allowing to derive annotations from it.

In several experiments we compare classifiers trained on the constructed corpus to those trained on existing corpora for argumentation mining. We classify argumentativeness using a rich set of lexical, syntax, and indicator feature types. Our results suggest that the new corpus is the most robust resource for classifying argumentative text segments across domains and registers. In addition, we observe that n-grams seem to be most domain-dependent, while syntax features turn out to be more robust.

The contribution of this paper is three-fold: First, through distant supervision we acquire a large corpus with 28,689 argumentative text segments from the online debate portal idebate.org. The corpus covers 14 separate domains with strongly varying feature distributions. It will be made freely available to other researchers.[1] Second, we obtain a robust classifier for argumentativeness, providing evidence that distant supervision does not only save money and time, but also benefits the effectiveness of cross-domain and cross-register argumentation mining. Third, we evaluate—for the first time—the robustness of several features in classifying argumentativeness across domains and registers.

Altogether, the paper serves as a starting point for bringing argumentation mining to practice. We expect that a robust identification of arguments will be a core module of future search engines, as it allows to provide rationales for retrieved documents. To this end, the search engines also need to identify the most *relevant* arguments for a given topic. The paper concludes with ideas on how to assess argument relevance with resources that are obtained through applying our proposed distant supervision technique to other datasets.

---

[1] http://www.uni-weimar.de/medien/webis/corpora

2 Related Work

Argumentation mining is still in an early stage of investigation, although several promising approaches have been proposed in the last years. Our survey of the argumentation mining literature especially covers three respects: (1) favored domains and registers, (2) techniques for annotation acquisition, and (3) the exploitation of debate portals. We combine these research lines in our approach to tackle argumentativeness classification across domains.

The existing argumentation mining approaches achieve classification accuracies ranging from 73% and 86% (Stab and Gurevych, 2014b; Levy et al., 2014; Palau and Moens, 2009) but they deal with texts from one register or one narrow domain only. For instance, Palau and Moens (2009) address the legal domain, Cabrio and Villata (2012b) as well as Boltužić and Šnajder (2014) investigate online debates and discussions, Aharoni et al. (2014) examine Wikipedia articles, Villalba and Saint-Dizier (2012) as well as Wachsmuth et al. (2014a) work on product reviews, Stab and Gurevych (2014a) focus on persuasive essays, and Peldszus (2014) on microtext. In (Wachsmuth et al., 2015), we studied the generality of sentiment-related argumentative structures across domains. In contrast, here we aim at effectiveness in cross-domain argumentation mining, which is useful for practical applications such as argument retrieval from diverse web-scale document collections.

All mining approaches above proceed as follows. Starting point is a complex and often expensive manual annotation of argumentative text segments in a collection of documents, including the segments' roles (e.g., premise or conclusion) and their relations (e.g., support or attack). Then, the classification of argumentativeness, roles, and relations is achieved via supervised machine learning using different linguistic and statistical features. Our approach avoids manual annotation. Instead, we apply distant supervision to automatically acquire annotations.

Distant supervision is a technique to automatically harvest annotations from data that has been compiled and structured intentionally by a user community on the web. Most approaches employing distant supervision so far address the problems of relation extraction (Mintz et al., 2009; Hoffmann et al., 2011) or event extraction (Reschke et al., 2014). A

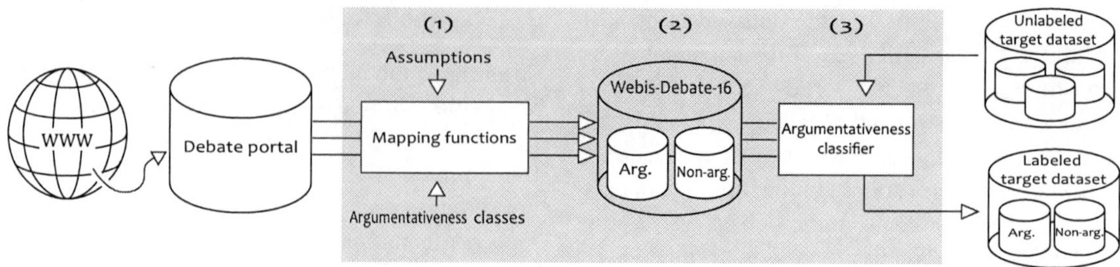

Figure 1. Overview of our distant supervision approach: The mapping functions transform the debate portal content into an annotated corpus for argumentativeness. This corpus is then used to train an argumentativeness classifier.

few others target at sentiment analysis (Marchetti-Bowick and Chambers, 2012) and emotion detection (Purver and Battersby, 2012). In case of the latter, annotations are derived from strong textual indicators like emoticons. In this paper, we exploit metadata from the debate platform idebate.org for mapping texts from the platform to argumentative and non-argumentative classes.

The idea of relying on idebate.org for argument annotation acquisition is in line with related research of Cabrio and Villata (2012c) and Gottipati et al. (2013). In these papers, however, the debate portal is used to infer text-level knowledge only (e.g., stances in debates), but not to generate a complete annotated dataset for argumentativeness.

The work that is most related to ours is the proposal of a method to exploit debate portals for semi-supervised argumentation mining by Habernal and Gurevych (2015). In particular, the authors use word embedding techniques for projecting the texts from debate portals into an annotated argument space, relying on the argument model of Toulmin (1958). On this basis they identify argumentative text segments and their roles. A clear difference to our approach is that Habernal and Gurevych (2015) consider all content of debate portals as argumentative. As a consequence, their approach concentrates mainly on exploiting the debate portals for improving the classification of segment roles, with minor impact on argumentativeness. Moreover, while being comparably effective, our approach aims for simplicity. The reason is that we apply distant supervision to derive a robust resource from the metadata of debate portals only. Thus, we allow for a rich feature space without requiring to use advanced machine learning methods. Finally, Habernal and Gurevych (2015) evaluate their approach only on one dataset from the educational domain, whereas we explicitly aim at robustness across domains. Accordingly, we conduct several experiments on different available corpora (including theirs).

3 Mining Argumentative Text through Distant Supervision

We propose an approach based on the distant supervision paradigm. Our goal is to obtain a classifier that can robustly mine argumentative texts across domains. More precisely, we focus on the task of classifying each segment of a text as being argumentative or not. We assume the text to be separated into segments already.

Our approach consists of three high-level building blocks: (1) Mapping functions that allows an automatic acquisition of argumentativeness annotations from debate portals. (2) A corpus with argumentative and non-argumentative text segments created using the functions. (3) A classifier that can distinguish the two classes of text segments. All building blocks are detailed in the following. Figure 1 depicts an overview of the approach.

3.1 Argumentativeness Mapping Functions

The basic idea of distant supervision is to generate annotations by automatically mapping unlabeled source data to a set of predefined class labels. This requires resources that are related to the given task as well as effective heuristic labeling functions. Typical resources comprise large amounts of data, often in form of user-generated content with semi-structured or structured metadata. Ideally, the resource's metadata substantially eases the mapping to the predefined labels.

In the context of argumentation mining, online debate portals serve as a rich source of argumentative

Class	Metadata	Text
–	Stance	This house believes single-sex schools are good for education.
Non-Argumentative	Introduction	Single-sex schools are schools that only admit those of one specific gender, believing that the educational environment fostered by a single gender is more conducive to learning than a co-educational school. Studies conducted have shown that boys gain more academically from studying in co-education schools, but that girls find segregated schools more conducive to achievement.
Argumentative	Points for	Boys and girls are an unwelcome distraction to each other.
Argumentative	Point	Boys and girls distract each other from their education, especially in adolescence as their sexual and emotional sides develop.
Argumentative	Counterpoint	Any negative effects of co-educational schools have been explained away by studies as the result of other factors, such as classroom size and cultural differences [1]. [1] *Bronski, M., 'Single-sex Schools'. Znet, 25 October 2002.*
Argumentative	Points against	Children need to be exposed to the opposite sex in preparation for later life.
Argumentative	Point	The formative years of children are the best time to expose them to the company of the other gender, in order that they may learn each others' behaviour.
Argumentative	Counterpoint	Children will gain exposure to the opposite sex when they reach adult life; whilst they are young, they should be around those who they feel most comfortable with.

Table 1. Excerpt of a sample discussion from idebate.org: the stance, the introduction, and some points for and against the stance. Except for parts shown in grey, all listed text segments are mapped to the listed classes.

texts on diverse topics. These portals are typically managed by user communities. Textual content can be added via a structured interface that already specifies metadata (e.g., what constitutes a topic or an argument). Thus, mapping text segments from debate portals to classes for argumentation mining is a promising instance of distant supervision.

In particular, we rely on idebate.org. This debate portal has an established community of experienced debaters and volunteers who take care of editing and monitoring semi-structured discussions on various controversial topics, subsumed under 14 high-level themes. A discussion (called "house" in the portal's terminology) starts with a one-sentence *stance* on the respective topic, followed by a more verbose introduction to the topic. Afterwards, points for and against the stance are opposed, both given as a list of arguments. Each argument in turn comes along with points (the argument itself) and counterpoints (counterarguments). Table 1 shows an example.

We downloaded all available discussions from idebate.org. For each discussion, the stance on the topic, the introduction, and the points are extracted from the URL of the web page of the respective discussion. Based on the structure exemplified in Table 1, we stipulate on the following assumptions to automatically map components from the debate portal to annotated argumentativeness instances.

[Component]: *Introduction*

- [Assumption]: The introduction explains the topic and gives important background information in a non-argumentative way.

- [Mapping]: Each sentence in the introduction is an instance of the non-argumentative class.

[Component]: *Points for & Points against*

- [Assumption]: Each point from these lists represents an argument for or against the stance on the topic of discussion.

- [Mapping]: Each point is an instance of the argumentative class.

[Component]: *Point & Counterpoint*

- [Assumption]: The main objective of a point (counterpoint) is to justify (attack) the point in the points-for or points-against list it refers to. We assume that the intention of such a point is to provide reasons for / against an argument.

- [Mapping]: Each sentence in a point / counterpoint is an instance of the argumentative class.

Domain	Documents	Argum. segments	Non-argum. segments
Politics	56	3102	635
Education	40	2057	376
Free speech	31	1435	346
International	113	6190	1324
Religion	8	336	96
Philosophy	10	545	122
Science	3	184	24
Culture	35	1765	307
Environment	11	602	128
Health	35	1985	349
Law	44	2197	440
Society	17	1031	199
Economy	23	1260	288
Sport	19	1191	175
Webis-Debate-16	445	23880	4809

Table 2. Number of documents, argumentative segments, and non-argumentative segments in each domain of our Webis-Debate-16 corpus. Domains correspond to themes from idebate.org.

To optimize the mapping quality, we manually analyzed 50 discussions and then derived three tailored cleansing rules from them: (1) We remove all literature references from the argumentative instances. (2) We delete all special brackets and symbols from the argumentative instances. (3) We delete some keywords from the non-argumentative instances that are used by the community to organize a discussion (e.g., "this house" or "this debate").

3.2 The Webis-Debate-16 Corpus

As a result of applying the defined mapping functions, we obtained a large argumentation mining corpus, called *Webis-Debate-16*. The corpus contains 28,689 text segments from the 14 themes of idebate.org (23,880 argumentative, 4809 non-argumentative). Each theme is assumed to represent one domain. Table 2 lists the distribution of documents over the domains in the corpus. Regarding the number of annotated text segments, Webis-Debate-16 is the largest dataset published so far for argumentation mining. While our review corpus from (Wachsmuth et al., 2014b) is even larger, its annotations are restricted to sentiment-related argumentation. Table 3 compares Webis-Debate-16 to other real argumentation mining corpora, namely, the Essays corpus (Stab and Gurevych, 2014a), the Web

Corpus	Documents	Argum. segments	Non-argum. segments
Essays	90	1552	327
Web discourse	340	1882	2074
ECHR	47	1067	1449
Araucaria	641	1931	1010
Webis-Debate-16	445	23880	4809

Table 3. Statistics of our Webis-Debate-16 corpus compared to four existing argumentation mining corpora. ECHR is a legal domain corpus that is not publicly available. More details on the others are given in Section 4.

discourse corpus (Habernal and Gurevych, 2015), the European Court of Human Rights (ECHR) corpus (Palau and Moens, 2009), and the Araucaria corpus (Reed and Rowe, 2004). The Webis-Debate-16 corpus will be made freely available online.[2]

3.3 A Classifier for Argumentativeness

A wide range of statistical and linguistic features has been suggested for argumentation mining and related tasks such as discourse parsing. We employ supervised machine learning to train an argumentativeness classifier based on the features employed by Stab and Gurevych (2014a), Palau and Moens (2009), and Habernal and Gurevych (2015) that cover the following:

Token n-grams: Unigrams, bigrams, and trigrams as Boolean features. In general, n-grams are the most powerful feature type in many related text classification problems (e.g., sentiment analysis).

Discourse markers: Features that represent the existence of words such as "because", which are frequently used in argumentative texts.

Syntax: This feature category contains the number of sub-clauses and production rules.

- Number of sub-clauses: Counter for the number of SBAR tags in the constituency parse tree of a text segment, referring to subordinate clauses in the Penn treebank syntactic tagset.

- Production rules: Boolean features capturing the specific production rules extracted from the constituency parse tree.

Part of speech: Features that capture information related to the parts of speech in a text segment:

[2]http://www.uni-weimar.de/medien/webis/corpora

- Verbs: A boolean feature capturing whether a segment contains a verb. Verbs such as "believe" strongly indicate of argumentative text.

- Adverbs: A boolean feature capturing whether a segment contains an adverb. Many adverbs such as "personally" can play a role in identifying argumentative text.

- Modals: A boolean feature capturing whether a segment contains a modal verb. Modal verbs such as "should" can be important for argumentativeness.

- Verb tense: Boolean features capturing whether a segment contains a past or present tense verb.

- First person pronouns: Pronouns such as "I" and "myself" can be good indicators of claims, a major component of argumentative texts.

Using these features, we train a binary statistical classifier for argumentativeness. Given a set of text segments, the classifier decides for each text segment whether it is argumentative or not.

4 Evaluation

We now report on several in-domain and cross-domain experiments with the classification of argumentativeness. The goals are (1) to demonstrate the effectiveness and robustness of training on the Webis-Debate-16 corpus for cross-domain classification, and (2) to analyze the effectiveness of the proposed features across domains and registers.

4.1 Experimental Setup

To evaluate the effect of using the Webis-Debate-16 corpus for training, appropriate argumentation corpora are needed for comparison. We consider an available corpus as appropriate if (1) the corpus is annotated in a way that allows the distinction of argumentative from non-argumentative text segments, and if (2) the corpus comes with clear annotation guidelines and reported inter-annotator agreement. In addition, we aim at corpora that differ in terms of the covered domains and registers to provide an adequate cross-domain setting. While the Araucaria corpus does not meet the second requirement (Reed and Rowe, 2004), two recently published corpora fulfill both; we refer to them as the *Essays* corpus and the *Web discourse* corpus.

Essays: The Argument Annotated Essays corpus of Stab and Gurevych (2014a) consists of 90 manually annotated persuasive student essays from the education domain. Argumentative text segments are assigned with their type (major claim, claim, or premise). Following Stab and Gurevych (2014b), we consider all sentences that do not have an annotation as being non-argumentative, and the annotated segments as argumentative.

Web discourse: The Argument Annotated User-generated Web Discourse corpus of Habernal and Gurevych (2015) consists of 340 documents from six different topics and four registers. The annotation of arguments is conducted based on the argument model of Toulmin (1958) using five types (claim, premise, backing, rebuttal, and refutation). Again, we consider all annotated text segments as being argumentative and sentences without annotation as being non-argumentative.

Only in case of the Essays corpus, the authors already provide a split into a training and a test set (72 essays for training and 18 for testing). For both the Web discourse corpus and our corpus, we randomly split the document set into 80% for training and 20% for testing. As a result, the training set of the Web discourse corpus consists of 272 documents, and its test set of 68 documents, while the training and test sets of our corpus consist of 356 and 89 documents, respectively.

We train classifiers for each of the above feature types and for the full feature set on the training set of each corpus using the default configuration of the naive Bayes implementation of Weka (Hall et al., 2009). Since all corpora are imbalanced in terms of the number of argumentative and non-argumentative text segments, we perform undersampling for all training sets—an effective technique for largely imbalanced datasets (Japkowicz and Stephen, 2002). All feature values are computed based on the output of the StanfordNLP library (Manning and Klein, 2003). For the different classifiers, we measure the resulting classification performance on all three test sets in terms of accuracy and F_1-score.

4.2 In-Domain Results

Table 4 shows the results of the in-domain experiments. For the full feature set, the achieved F_1-score

Feature type	Essays		Web discourse		Webis-Debate-16	
	Accuracy	F_1-score	Accuracy	F_1-score	Accuracy	F_1-score
N-grams	0.640	0.698	0.815	0.816	0.905	0.908
Syntax	0.599	0.664	0.874	0.874	0.855	0.664
Discourse markers	0.390	0.438	0.584	0.444	0.236	0.180
Part of speech	0.625	0.684	0.541	0.543	0.659	0.702
Full feature set	**0.668**	**0.722**	**0.877**	**0.878**	**0.918**	**0.922**

Table 4. The results of all in-domain experiments on the three corpora for each feature type and the full feature set.

of 0.922 and the accuracy of 0.918 on the Webis-Debate-16 corpus are high compared to those on the Essays and Web discourse corpus. This might be a result of guidelines suggested by the debate portal community, which make the corpus quite homogeneous in terms of style.

Using the full feature set leads to the best results on all three corpora. N-grams denote the most effective single feature type on the Essays copus and on the Webis-Debate-16 corpus, while the syntax features outperform the n-grams on the Web discourse corpus. On the Essays and on the Webis-Debate-16 corpus, the syntax features are sometimes better and sometimes worse than the part of speech features. The discourse markers are the least effective single feature type, largely failing on all test sets, especially in terms of F_1-score.

Note that a comparison to the exact values reported by Stab and Gurevych (2014b) for the Essays corpus and by Habernal and Gurevych (2015) for the Web discourse corpus is not be meaningful due to their experimental set-ups with different class sets. However, their reported results for the non-argumentative class are comparable to the performance we achieved: Stab and Gurevych (2014b) achieve an F_1-score of 0.275 with lexical features and 0.426 with syntax features on the Essays corpus, while Habernal and Gurevych (2015) obtain an F_1-score of 0.718 with lexical features and 0.671 with syntax features on the Web discourse corpus.

4.3 Cross-Domain Results

Table 5 shows the results of the cross-domain experiments. For comparison, we again show the in-domain results in grey color.

As usual, the obtained cross-domain effectiveness values are lower than the in-domain values in most cases and the full feature set usually outperforms feature subsets. One notable exception are the results for the part of speech features on the Essays corpus. The cross-domain effectiveness trained on the Webis-Debate-16 corpus is about six points higher than the in-domain effectiveness in terms of F_1-score and four points in terms of accuracy. For testing on the Web discourse corpus, training on the Webis-Debate-16 corpus using the full features gives the best cross-domain performance. For testing on the Webis-Debate-16 corpus, training on the Web discourse corpus using the n-gram feature type achieves the best cross-domain performance.

Overall, the best corpus for cross-domain classification in our evaluation is clearly the Webis-Debate-16 corpus. Training on Webis-Debate-16 leads to the best cross-domain results for the full feature set and three out of four of the single feature types (n-grams, syntax, and part of speech). Only for the discourse markers, the Web discourse corpus performs better in the cross-domain scenario.

Finally, we observe that the n-grams feature type turns out to be the most domain-dependent in our evaluation. In contrast, both the syntax and the part of speech features appear quite robust across domains. The performance of the discourse markers greatly depends on how frequent they are used in the target domain and register.

Although combining the Webis-Debate-16 corpus to the training datasets of the Essays or the Web discourse corpus increased the performance compared to training only on Webis-Debate-16, it did not outperform the in-domain performance for both corpora. For conciseness, we therefore omit to report the results of our respective experiments here.

4.4 Discussion of our Approach to Robustness

As expected, our experiments reveal the domain dependence of feature distributions in classifying argu-

Feature type	Training corpus	Test on Essays		Test on Web discourse		Test on Webis-Debate-16	
		Accuracy	F_1-score	Accuracy	F_1-score	Accuracy	F_1-score
Majority baseline	–	0.867	0.806	0.572	0.417	0.832	0.757
N-grams	Essays	0.640	0.698	0.485	0.488	0.512	0.571
	Web discourse	0.196	0.159	0.815	0.816	**0.854**	**0.867**
	Webis-Debate-16	**0.528**	**0.601**	**0.719**	**0.718**	0.902	0.908
Syntax	Essays	0.599	0.664	0.494	0.497	0.481	0.541
	Web discourse	0.163	0.095	0.874	0.874	**0.767**	**0.795**
	Webis-Debate-16	**0.573**	**0.642**	**0.719**	**0.717**	0.855	0.867
Discourse markers	Essays	0.390	0.438	**0.584**	**0.444**	0.236	0.179
	Web discourse	**0.415**	**0.468**	0.584	0.444	**0.237**	**0.181**
	Webis-Debate-16	0.387	0.434	**0.584**	**0.444**	0.236	0.180
Part of speech	Essays	0.625	0.684	0.490	0.484	**0.560**	**0.616**
	Web discourse	0.446	0.521	0.541	0.543	0.445	0.507
	Webis-Debate-16	**0.686**	**0.724**	**0.538**	**0.533**	0.659	0.702
Full feature set	Essays	0.668	0.722	0.524	0.524	0.483	0.541
	Web discourse	0.181	0.128	0.877	0.878	**0.844**	**0.859**
	Webis-Debate-16	**0.617**	**0.678**	**0.726**	**0.725**	0.918	0.922

Table 5. The results of all cross-domain experiments on the three corpora for each feature type and the full feature set.

mentativeness. This finding emphasizes the importance of explicitly dealing with domain robustness in argumentation mining whenever more than one domain (in terms of a topic, register, or similar) is of interest. To achieve robustness, we have proposed a simple but effective approach that applies distant supervision to create a corpus for classifying argumentativeness. Our results are promising: Classification clearly improves across domains when being trained on our Webis-Debate-16 corpus instead of other available argumentation mining corpora.

The obtained results suggest that our approach can be effectively leveraged to achieve domain robustness. One reason is probably the larger size and domain coverage of our Webis-Debate-16 corpus compared to the other tested corpora. This makes our corpus and the underlying distant supervision idea a valuable resource for research on argumentation. More noise reduction might even further increase the performance of training on the corpus.

In its current form, our corpus contains annotations for distinguishing argumentative from non argumentative text only. While more fine-grained annotations of argumentative texts, such as premise vs. claim, are important for argumentation mining, they cannot be obtained directly from the metadata of idebate.org. Still, the positions of segments in some parts of the debate portal (e.g, point and counterpoint) often indicate whether they are claims or premises. We plan to investigate the exploitation of such information for future versions of the corpus.

So far, we have shown how to create an annotated corpus classifying argumentativeness exploiting one specific debate portal via distant supervision. In principle, our approach is rather general and, thus, could also be applied to other argumentation resources and tasks. Indeed, idebate.org is only one of many web resources with lots of argumentative texts and argumentation-relevant metadata. Aside from debate portals, one such resource is given by Wikipedia talk pages. Very recently, Wikipedia introduced markups within these article discussions, such as *support* or *oppose*. While still being in an early stage, this metadata seems promising to derive argumentative relations from it. We plan to use our distant supervision approach for classifying argumentative relations on such resources. This can then be an important next step to enable the assessment of *argument relevance*—a core building block of an argument retrieval system.

4.5 From Argumentativeness to Relevance

As motivated in the introduction, a retrieval system for arguments not only requires the identification and classification of argumentative text segments. A successful future search engine taking argument features into account additionally needs a way of ranking arguments according to their relevance. In this regard, we propose a "PageRank for arguments" based on the link network of support and attack relations between arguments.

In particular, given robust algorithms to identify arguments and their relations across web pages (e.g., via distant supervision), we could build an *argument graph* for the web. Related research has already used the argumentation framework of Dung (1995) to find accepted arguments based on such a graph on a much smaller scale (Cabrio and Villata, 2012a). However, the size of the web would allow for recursive analysis of the graph with statistical approaches like the famous PageRank algorithm (Page et al., 1999), enabling an assessment of argument relevance. Several research questions arise from this idea (e.g., how to balance support and attack within the analysis) but argument relevance forms a very important future research direction.

5   Conclusion

Most existing approaches tackle argumentation mining in a supervised manner trained on manually annotated documents from a specific domain. Such approaches neither tend to be effective on documents from other domains, nor do they scale to applications that deal with huge document collections, such as search engines. In this paper, we investigate how to achieve robust performance for argumentation mining across domains, focusing on the classification of the argumentativeness of text segments. In particular, we approach the data side of this problem, namely, we apply distant supervision to automatically create a large annotated corpus with argumentative and non-argumentative text segments from several domains, exploiting metadata from the online debate portal idebate.org.

Based on the created corpus and on common manually annotated corpora, we conduct several in-domain and cross-domain argumentativeness experiments. Our results clearly indicate that training on the created Webis-Debate-16 corpus yield the most robust cross-domain classifier. Thereby, our approach serves as a starting point for bringing argumentation mining to practical applications like search engines. The corpus as well as an implementation of the approach will be made freely available. Besides a robust identification of argumentative segments, search engines will also need to decide which arguments are the most relevant to a given query— a very promising future research direction in the field of argumentation mining.

References

Ehud Aharoni, Anatoly Polnarov, Tamar Lavee, Daniel Hershcovich, Ran Levy, Ruty Rinott, Dan Gutfreund, and Noam Slonim. 2014. A Benchmark Dataset for Automatic Detection of Claims and Evidence in the Context of Controversial Topics. In *Proceedings of the First Workshop on Argumentation Mining*, pages 64–68.

Trevor Bench-Capon, Katie Atkinson, and Peter McBurney. 2009. Altruism and Agents: An Argumentation Based Approach to Designing Agent Decision Mechanisms. In *Proceedings of The 8th International Conference on Autonomous Agents and Multiagent Systems - Volume 2, AAMAS 2009*, pages 1073–1080.

Filip Boltužić and Jan Šnajder. 2014. Back up your Stance: Recognizing Arguments in Online Discussions. In *Proceedings of the First Workshop on Argumentation Mining*, pages 49–58.

Elena Cabrio and Serena Villata. 2012a. Combining Textual Entailment and Argumentation Theory for Supporting Online Debates Interactions. In *Proceedings of the 50th Annual Meeting of the Association for Computational Linguistics: Short Papers*, pages 208–212.

Elena Cabrio and Serena Villata. 2012b. Generating Abstract Arguments: A Natural Language Approach. In *Proceedings of the 2012 Conference on Computational Models of Argument, COMMA 2012*, pages 454–461.

Elena Cabrio and Serena Villata. 2012c. Natural Language Arguments: A Combined Approach. In *20th European Conference on Artificial Intelligence, ECAI 2012*, pages 205–210.

Phan Minh Dung. 1995. On the Acceptability of Arguments and its Fundamental Role in Nonmonotonic Reasoning, Logic Programming and n-Person Games. *Artificial Intelligence*, 77(2):321–357.

Swapna Gottipati, Minghui Qiu, Yanchuan Sim, Jing Jiang, and Noah A. Smith. 2013. Learning Topics and Positions from Debatepedia. In *Proceedings of the 2013 Conference on Empirical Methods in Natural Language Processing, EMNLP 2013*, pages 1858–1868.

Ivan Habernal and Iryna Gurevych. 2015. Exploiting Debate Portals for Semi-Supervised Argumentation

Mining in User-Generated Web Discourse. In *Proceedings of the 2015 Conference on Empirical Methods in Natural Language Processing*, pages 2127–2137.

Ivan Habernal, Judith Eckle-Kohler, and Iryna Gurevych. 2014. Argumentation Mining on the Web from Information Seeking Perspective. In *Frontiers and Connections between Argumentation Theory and Natural Language Processing*, pages 26–39.

Mark Hall, Eibe Frank, Geoffrey Holmes, Bernhard Pfahringer, Peter Reutemann, and Ian H. Witten. 2009. The WEKA Data Mining Software: An Update. *SIGKDD Explorations*, 11(1):10–18.

Raphael Hoffmann, Congle Zhang, Xiao Ling, Luke Zettlemoyer, and Daniel S. Weld. 2011. Knowledge-based Weak Supervision for Information Extraction of Overlapping Relations. In *Proceedings of the 49th Annual Meeting of the Association for Computational Linguistics: Human Language Technologies - Volume 1, HLT 2011*, pages 541–550.

Nathalie Japkowicz and Shaju Stephen. 2002. The Class Imbalance Problem: A Systematic Study. *Intell. Data Anal.*, 6(5):429–449.

Ran Levy, Yonatan Bilu, Daniel Hershcovich, Ehud Aharoni, and Noam Slonim. 2014. Context Dependent Claim Detection. In *Proceedings of the 25th International Conference on Computational Linguistics, COLING 2014*, pages 1489–1500.

Christopher Manning and Dan Klein. 2003. Optimization, Maxent Models, and Conditional Estimation Without Magic. In *Proceedings of the 2003 Conference of the North American Chapter of the Association for Computational Linguistics on Human Language Technology: Tutorials - Volume 5*, pages 8–8.

Micol Marchetti-Bowick and Nathanael Chambers. 2012. Learning for Microblogs with Distant Supervision: Political Forecasting with Twitter. In *Proceedings of the 13th Conference of the European Chapter of the Association for Computational Linguistics, EACL 2012*, pages 603–612.

Mike Mintz, Steven Bills, Rion Snow, and Dan Jurafsky. 2009. Distant Supervision for Relation Extraction Without Labeled Data. In *Proceedings of the Joint Conference of the 47th Annual Meeting of the ACL and the 4th International Joint Conference on Natural Language Processing of the AFNLP: Volume 2, ACL 2009*, pages 1003–1011.

Lawrence Page, Sergey Brin, Rajeev Motwani, and Terry Winograd. 1999. The PageRank Citation Ranking: Bringing Order to the Web. Technical Report 1999-66, Stanford InfoLab.

Raquel Mochales Palau and Marie-Francine Moens. 2009. Argumentation Mining: The Detection, Classification and Structure of Arguments in Text. In *Proceedings of the 12th International Conference on Artificial Intelligence and Law, ICAIL 2009*, pages 98–107.

Andreas Peldszus. 2014. Towards Segment-based Recognition of Argumentation Structure in Short Texts. In *Proceedings of the First Workshop on Argumentation Mining*, pages 88–97.

Matthew Purver and Stuart Battersby. 2012. Experimenting with Distant Supervision for Emotion Classification. In *Proceedings of the 13th Conference of the European Chapter of the Association for Computational Linguistics, EACL 2012*, pages 482–491.

Chris Reed and Glenn Rowe. 2004. Araucaria: Software for Argument Analysis, Diagramming and Representation. *International Journal on Artificial Intelligence Tools*, 13.

Kevin Reschke, Martin Jankowiak, Mihai Surdeanu, Christopher D. Manning, and Dan Jurafsky. 2014. Event extraction using distant supervision. In *Proceedings of the 9th edition of the Language Resources and Evaluation Conference, LREC 2014*.

Christian Stab and Iryna Gurevych. 2014a. Annotating Argument Components and Relations in Persuasive Essays. In *Proceedings of the the 25th International Conference on Computational Linguistics, COLING 2014*, pages 1501–1510.

Christian Stab and Iryna Gurevych. 2014b. Identifying Argumentative Discourse Structures in Persuasive Essays. In *Conference on Empirical Methods in Natural Language Processing, EMNLP 2014*, pages 46–56.

Stephen E. Toulmin. 1958. *The Uses of Argument*. Cambridge University Press.

Maria Paz Garcia Villalba and Patrick Saint-Dizier. 2012. Some Facets of Argument Mining for Opinion Analysis. In *Proceedings of the 2012 Conference on Computational Models of Argument, COMMA 2012*, pages 23–34.

Henning Wachsmuth, Martin Trenkmann, Benno Stein, and Gregor Engels. 2014a. Modeling Review Argumentation for Robust Sentiment Analysis. In *Proceedings of the 25th International Conference on Computational Linguistics: Technical Papers*, pages 553–564.

Henning Wachsmuth, Martin Trenkmann, Benno Stein, Gregor Engels, and Tsvetomira Palakarska. 2014b. A Review Corpus for Argumentation Analysis. In *Proceedings of the 15th International Conference on Intelligent Text Processing and Computational Linguistics*, pages 115–127.

Henning Wachsmuth, Johannes Kiesel, and Benno Stein. 2015. Sentiment Flow – A General Model of Web Review Argumentation. In *Proceedings of the 2015 Conference on Empirical Methods in Natural Language Processing*, pages 601–611, Lisbon, Portugal.

A Study of the Impact of Persuasive Argumentation in Political Debates

Amparo Elizabeth Cano-Basave and **Yulan He**
Aston University, UK
`a.cano-basave@aston.ac.uk,y.he@cantab.net`

Abstract

Persuasive communication is the process of shaping, reinforcing and changing others' responses. In political debates, speakers express their views towards the debated topics by choosing both the content of their discourse and the argumentation process. In this work we study the use of semantic frames for modelling argumentation in speakers' discourse. We investigate the impact of a speaker's argumentation style and their effect in influencing an audience in supporting their candidature. We model the influence index of each candidate based on their relative standings in the polls released prior to the debate and present a system which ranks speakers in terms of their relative influence using a combination of content and persuasive argumentation features. Our results show that although content alone is predictive of a speaker's influence rank, persuasive argumentation also affects such indices.

1 Introduction

In recent years, researchers have studied political texts detecting ideological positions (Sim et al., 2013; Hasan and Ng, 2013), predicting voting patterns (Thomas et al., 2006; Gerrish and Blei, 2011) and characterising power based on linguistic features (Prabhakaran et al., 2013). While there is a vast amount of theoretical research on the rhetoric of politicians, only recently there has been a growing interest in understanding the argumentation processes involved in political communication by means of computational linguistics (Hasan and Ng, 2013; Boltužić and Šnajder, 2014).

During a debate, a speaker tries to convince the audience of a particular point of view. This normally involves an argumentation process, where the structuring of ideas is built upon logical connections between claims and premises, and a persuasive communication style. In this paper, we study the impact of persuasive argumentation in political debates on candidates' power/influence ranking. As opposed to previous approaches, we propose to characterise political debates based on persuasive argumentation modelled through semantic frames.

Previous work (Rosenberg and Hirschberg, 2009) has analysed political speech transcripts identifying prosodic and lexical-syntactic cues which correlate with political personalities. Prabhakaran et al. (2013) proposed interactions within political debates as predictors of a candidate's relative power or influence rank in polls. More recently they also found topic-shifting to be a good indicator of candidate's relative rankings in polls (Prabhakaran et al., 2014). Argumentation in debates has been studied from the perspective of automatic argument extraction (Cabrio and Villata, 2012) and stance classification (Hasan and Ng, 2013). However, to the best of our knowledge, argumentation has not been explored as a influence rank indicator. Moreover the study of persuasion in the NLP community has been so far limited.

The novelty of our work is the proposal of a method to automatically extract persuasive argumentation features from political debates by means of the use of semantic frames as pivoting features. We have trained a rank Support Vector Machine (SVM) model based on content and persuasive ar-

Proceedings of NAACL-HLT 2016, pages 1405–1413,
San Diego, California, June 12-17, 2016. ©2016 Association for Computational Linguistics

gumentation features in order to rank debate speakers. Our experimental results on the 20 debates for the Republican primary election show that certain types of persuasive argumentation features such as *Premise* and *Support Relation* appear to be better predictors of a speaker's influence rank compared to basic content features such as unigrams. When combining with content-related features, most persuasive argumentation features give superior performance compared to the baselines.

2 Persuasive Argumentation

Argumentation has been defined as a verbal and social activity of reason which aims to increase the acceptability of a controversial standpoint by putting forward a set of connected propositions intending to justify or refute a standpoint before a rational judge (van Eemeren et al., 1996). Different argumentation theories propose various schemes for describing the underlying structure of an argument (Toulmin., 1958; Walton et al., 2008; Freemen, 2011; Peldszus and Stede, 2013). All these theories generally agree in that an argument can be structured by means of two argument components and two argumentative relations. The argument components include *claims* and *premises*. A claim is a central component of an argument and is characterised as being a controversial statement to be judged as true or false. Moreover a claim cannot be accepted by an audience without additional support. Such support is provided in the form of premises underpinning the validity of the claim. The following sentence illustrates an example[1] of an argument highlighting the claim and premises:

> **"People aren't investing in America** *because this president has made America a less attractive place for investing and hiring than other places in the world."* (Former Governor Mitt Romney)

While *argumentation* focuses on the rational support structured to justify or refute a standpoint, *persuasion* focuses on language cues aiming at shaping, reinforcing and changing a response. In persuasive communication such response ranges from perceptions, beliefs, attitudes and behaviours.

Persuasive language is characterised by the use of emotive lexicons (e.g., atrocious, dreadful, sensational, highly effective) where the speaker tries to engage with the audience's emotions (Macagno and Walton, 2014). Often words with emotive meanings can present values and assumptions as uncontroversial, acting therefore as potentially manipulative instruments of argumentation (Macagno, 2010). Other characteristics of persuasive language include the use of alliteration, which is a stylistic device characterised by the repetition of first consonants in series of words. This artistic constraint enables the speaker to sway the audience by feeling an urgency towards a rhetorical situation by intensifying any attitude being signified (Bitzer, 1968; Lanham, 1991). The use of a repeating sounds engages auditory senses leading to the evoking of emotions that engage the audience.

The following is an example of persuasive language[2]:

> "I'm convinced that part of **the *divide* that we're experiencing in the United States**, which is **un**precedented, it's **u**nnatural, and it's **un**-American, is *because we're divided economically, too few jobs, too few opportunities*" (Former Governor Huntsman).

To the best of our knowledge however, the study of the relation of persuasion and argumentation in political debates is limited. One of the main challenges is the lack of annotated corpora which include both argument annotations and persuasive messages annotations. While there has recently been released a corpus of persuasive essays (Stab and Gurevych, 2014) containing annotations for both class-level argument components and argument relations, there is yet none annotated corpora for persuasive arguments in political debates. In order to study whether persuasive cues and persuasive argumentation can be used as predictors of speakers' influence ranking on a debate, we propose to bridge between existing persuasive and political corpora through semantic frame features. The following section introduces the proposed strategy to port annotation between two corpora.

---

[1]This is extracted from our Debate corpus transcripts. Bold letters represent the argument and italics the premises.

[2]Representing emotive language in italic bold and alliteration in bold underscored.

3 Extracting Persuasive Argumentation Features from Political Debates

In order to study whether persuasive argumentation can be used as predictors of speakers' influence ranking on a debate, we propose to use the persuasive essays corpus compiled by Stab and Gurevych (2014) to study persuasive argumentation in political debates through the use of semantic frames.

3.1 Persuasive Essays (PE) Corpus

A persuasive essay is an essay written with the aim of convincing a reader on adopting a way of thinking regarding a stance taken on a topic. Unlike speech where an audience can be persuaded by means of social features or speech style, essays only rely on the written word depending therefore solely on the writer's persuasive style.

The Persuasive Essays (PE) corpus consists of 90 essays comprising 1,673 sentences. It contains annotations for both class-level argument components and argument relations. The class-level annotations include: 1) major claims; 2) claims; 3) premises and 4) the argumentative relations being either "support" or "attack". Argumentative relations are directed relations between source and target components (e.g., between premises, claims and major claims). The PE argument annotations follows the scheme described in Table 1.

Claim	Controversial Statement which is either true or false, and which should not be accepted or otherwise without additional support
Premise	Justifies the validity of a claim
ForStance	Indicates that an argument supports a claim
AgainstStance	Indicates that an argument refutes a claim
SupportRel.	Indicates which supporting premises belong to a claim
AttackRel.	Indicates which refuting premises belong to a claim

Table 1: Persuasive essays argument annotation scheme.

3.2 Presidential Political Debates (PD) Corpus

Presidential political debates enable candidates to expose and discuss their stances on policy issues contrasting them with other candidates' stances. During a debate, speakers unveil their discourse style as well as the premises supporting their claims. For our experiments, we collected the manual transcripts of debates for the Republican party presidential primary election from The American Presidency Project[3]. This political debates corpus (PD) consists of 20 debates which took place between May 2011 and February 2012. A total of 10 candidates participated in these debates with an average participation of 6.7 candidates per debate. This corpus comprises 30-40 hours of interaction time and an average of 20,466.6 words per debate.

These debates follow a common structure in which a moderator directly addresses questions to the candidates where disruptions to answers are common due to interruptions from other candidates. In this corpus, each debate transcript lists the speakers including moderator and candidates and questions asked during the debate. Each transcript also clearly delimits turns between speakers and moderators as well as mark-up occurrences of the audience's reactions such as booing and laughter.

3.3 Semantic Frames

We propose to make use of the persuasion essays corpus annotations to understand persuasive argumentation in political debates by means of the use of semantic frames. A semantic frame is a description of context in which a word sense is used. We make use of FrameNet (Baker et al., 1998), which consist of over 1000 patterns used in English (e.g., Leadership, Causality, Awareness, and Hostile encounter). In this work we extract such patterns using SEMAFOR (Das et al., 2010).

Consider the sentence in Table 2 in which two semantic frames are detected. Each parsed semantic frame consists of {Frame, SemanticRole, label} providing a higher level characterisation of a text, highlighting the semantics of the discourse used in this text. If such semantic frames appear to be some of the most prominent features for a certain persuasive argumentation annotation scheme (e.g., "Claim"), then we can extract persuasive argumentation features from the unlabelled Political Debates corpus using semantic frames as pivoting features.

In this work we propose to port annotations between the Persuasive Essays (PE) and Political Debates (PD) corpora by means of the use of semantic frames as pivoting features.

To represent the PE corpus, let $A = \{a_1, .., a_n\}$

---

[3]http://www.presidency.ucsb.edu/debates.php

Sentence:	What we need in this country is to use this issue as a national security tool.	
FRAME	SEMANTIC ROLE	LABEL
Political_locales Target		national security
Point_of_dispute Target		this issue

Table 2: Semantic frames parsed for a sentence extracted from the debates dataset.

be the set of annotation schemes described in Table 1 and let $T_a = \{t_1, .., t_n\}$ be the collection of sentences annotated with argument scheme a. To represent the PD corpus, let's $U_D = \{u_1, .., u_n\}$ be the set of speakers taking part on a debate D. Let $S_{uD} = \{s_1, .., s_n\}$ be the set of sentences generated by speaker u on debate D.

Taking the PE corpus as a reference corpus, we propose to generate a vector representation of each annotation scheme in A for each speaker in each debate of corpus PD by following the steps below: i) Based on tf-idf we extract the most representative semantic frames for each annotation scheme a in PE as the vector SF_a; ii) We compute the weighted representation of each annotation scheme a in the PD corpus as the vector $f_{d,a}^u$ for each speaker u on each debate d as follows: a) First we compute the bag of semantic frames SF_d^u from speaker u in debate d based on the speaker's content on the debate; then b) For each annotation scheme a we weight vector $f_{d,a}^u$ based on the normalised frequency of each semantic frame element in SF_d^u appearing in SF_a.

3.4 Semantic Frames and Argument Types

The statistics of the extracted semantic frames from PE for each argument type are presented in Table 3.

Arg. Type	Sentences	Semantic Frames (SF)
Claim	519	404
Premise	1,033	518
ForStance	365	369
AgainstStance	64	173
SupportRel.	1,312	535
AttackRel.	161	275

Table 3: Number of semantic frames extracted from PE.

Such semantic frames provide a vector representation characterising each persuasive argumentation scheme described in Table 1. Table 4 presents a sample of the top semantic frames representing each ar-

Arg. Type	Top 5 Semantic Frames
Claim	Reason, Stage_of_Progress, Evaluative_Comparison, Competition, Cause_to_Change
Premise	Removing, Inclusion, Killing, Cognitive_Connection, Causation
ForStance	Cause_to_Make_Progress, Collaboration, Purpose, Kinship, Expensiveness
AgainstStance	Intentionally_Act, Importance, Capability, Leadership, Usefulness
SupportRel.	Dead_or_Alive, Institutions, State_Continue, Taking_Sides, Reliance
AttackRel.	Usefulness, Likelihood, Desiring, Importance, Intentionally_Act

Table 4: Top 5 semantic frames for each argument type of PE.

gumentation type.

Using the vector representation of each annotation scheme generated from PE, we computed the persuasive argumentation features for the PD corpus. Table 5 presents a sentence sample for each argument type identified in the PD corpus along with the semantic frames characterising the sentence.

4 Influence Ranking in Political Debates

We study a speaker's influence on an audience based on his/her persuasiveness language and argumentation styles during a political debate. To measure how influential a speaker is on an audience, we make use of the *influence index* (Prabhakaran et al., 2013), which is calculated based on a speakers relative standing on poll released prior to the debate.

Poll scores describe the influence a speaker has to favourably change the electorate position towards his/her campaign. Given a debate D and the set of speakers U_D we retrieve the poll results released prior to the debate and use the percentage of electorate supporting each candidate. If for a given debate there are multiple polls then the index is computed taking the mean of poll scores. Therefore the influence index P of speaker $u \in U_D$ is:

$$P(u) = \frac{1}{|polls(D)|} \sum_{i=1}^{|polls(D)|} p_i \qquad (1)$$

where p_i is the poll percentage assign to speaker u in poll i in the reference polls.

Arg. Type	Sentence	Semantic Frames
Claim	If we can turn Syria and Lebanon away from Iran, we finally have the capacity to get Iran to pull back.	Cause_Change, Manipulation, Capability
Premise	Because they put that money in, the president gave the companies to the UAW, they were part of the reason the companies were in trouble.	Causation, Predicament, Leadership
ForStance	And the reason is because that's how our founding fathers saw this country set up.	Reason, Kinship, Perception_Experience
AgainstStance	I was concerned that if we didn't do something, there were some pretty high risks that not just Wall Street banks, but all banks would collapse.	Emotion_Directed, Intentionally_Affect, Daring
SupportRel.	I went to Washington, testifying in favor of a federal amendment to define marriage as a relationship between man and a woman.	Taking_Sides, Cognitive_Connection, Evidence
AttackRel.	But you can't stand and say you give me everything I want or I'll vote no.	Desiring, Posture, Capability

Table 5: Example sentence for each argument type and its corresponding semantic frames identified from PD. Note that there is no annotation in PD. The argument types here are assigned manually for easy reference.

4.1 Features

We characterise each speaker in each debate based on the content and emotion cues he/she generated. Specifically we analyse each candidate in three dimensions: i) what they said (content features); ii) the persuasiveness of the language they used including persuasive argumentation features and emotive language; iii) and external emotions evoked during the debates. We described each set of features below.

4.1.1 Content Features

We use a set of features which characterise content of a candidate's participation on a debate (Prabhakaran et al., 2013). These include: 1) Unigrams (UG), which represents lexical patterns by counting frequencies of word occurrences; 2) Question Deviation (QD), difference between observed percentage of questions asked to a candidate and the fair share percentage of questions in the debate; 3) Word Deviation (WD), difference between observed percentage of words spoken by a candidate and the fair share percentage of words in the debate; 4) Mention Percentage (MP), a candidate mention counts normalised based on all candidates' mentions in a debate.

4.1.2 Persuasiveness Features

We represent three types of persuativeness features as follows:

1) *Persuasive Argumentation Features.* Following the method described in the previous section, we extract the semantic frame feature vector representing each annotation scheme ($f_{d,a}^u$) for each speaker on each debate. These vectors provide information of different argumentation dimensions. We have extracted a total of 710 semantic frames in PD.

2) *Alliteration.* After removing stopwords, we computed alliteration as repetitions of part of a word or a full word within a sentence.

3) *Emotive Language.* To characterise the use of emotive language, we generated a list of emotion-related semantic frames (e.g., emotion_directed, emotions_by_stimulus, emotions_by_possibility)[4], then for each speaker u in each debate d, we generated an emotion-frame vector weighted by tf-idf.

Once the features for each speaker have been generated, we followed a supervised learning approach for ranking speakers of a debate based on their influence Index, which can be used to denote how well a speakers participation on a debate has impacted the audience endorsement of his/her campaign.

4.1.3 External Emotion Cues

Previous work (Strapparava et al., 2010) has shown that an audiences' social signal reactions to an idea, such as booing or cheering, are good pre-

---

[4]FrameNet's frame index, `http://tinyurl.com/q2ytth9`

dictors of hot-spots where persuasion attempts succeeded or at least such attempts were recognised by the audience. In this work, rather than recognising such persuasion hot-spots, we explore these audiences' reaction cues (e.g applause) as potential predictors of a candidate success on a political debate, we refer to such cues as external emotion cues. For each speaker in a debate, we computed the number of i) applauses (APL); ii) booings (BOO); iii) laughs (LAU); and iv) crosstalks (CRO) he/she received during his/her participation on a debate. These counts were normalised based on the total number of each emotion appeared on the debate.

With these features, we train a supervised learning classifier for ranking speakers of the debates based on their influence indices described in the following section.

4.2 Influence Ranking Approach

In ranking, a training set consists of an ordered data set. Let "A is preferred to B" be denoted as "$A \succ B$". Let D denote a debate with a set of speakers $U_D = \{u_1, u_2, ..u_n\}$ and influence indexes $P(u_i)$ for $1 < i < n$. We specify a training set for ranking as $R = \{(u_i, \gamma_i), .., (u_n, \gamma_n)\}$ where γ_i is the ranking of u_i based on its $P(u_i)$ so $\gamma_i < \gamma_j$ if $u_i \succ u_j$.

We want to find a ranking function F which outputs a score for each instance from which a global ordering of data is constructed. So the target function $F(u_i)$ outputs a score such that $F(u_i) > F(u_j)$ for any $u_i \succ u_j$. In this work we use the Ranking SVM (Joachims, 2006) to estimate the ranking function F.

5 Experimental Setup

For our experiments we used the Persuasive Essays (PE) and Political Debates (PD) corpora introduced in previous sections. While the PE was used as a reference corpus, all our experiments were performed on the PD corpus.

All features are computed for the aggregation of a candidate's content in a debate. For content and alliteration features, we first removed stopwords. In particular, for computing unigram features we also stemmed words using a Porter stemmer (Porter, 1997).

To compute persuasive argumentation features we used the collection of semantic frame features for the reference corpus PE.

5.1 Evaluation

In this work, the ranking task evaluation for each debate consists on comparing the generated ranked list of candidates, using the *influence ranking approach* introduced above, against a reference ranked list. Such a reference ranked list corresponds to our gold standard of ranked list of candidates generated based on the polled scores for that debate.

Following a 5-fold cross validation, we report results applying four commonly used evaluation metrics for ranking tasks, *nDCG*, *nDCG-3*, *Kendall's Tau* and *Spearman* correlations. The discounted cumulative gain metric (*nDCG*) penalises inversions happening at the top n elements[5] of a ranked list more than those inversions happening at the bottom. While the nDCG metric penalises certain elements in the list, Kendall's tau and Spearman's rank correlations penalises inversions equally across the ranked list.

6 Results and Discussion

6.1 Correlation Analysis

We performed a correlation analysis for the content and persuasive emotion numeric features[6]. We computed the Pearson's product correlation between each feature with the candidate's influence index $P(u)$ derived from the polls. The computed correlations for these features are presented in Figure 1. Darker bars indicate statistical significance correlation at $p < 0.001$; lighter dark bars at $p < 0.05$; and light bars not statistically significant.

These results show that for the content features, both question deviation (QD) and word deviation (WD) correlate moderately with the influence index; while the mention percentage (MP) feature correlates highly with the influence index ($p < 0.05$). For the emotion cues, we obtained statistically significant ($p < 0.05$) moderate correlations between the applause (APL), laugh (LAU), crosstalk (CRO) and

---

[5]*nDCG-3* therefore assigns a higher penalisation for inversions happening at the top three elements of a ranked list.

[6]Note that we can perform such correlation analysis only with the numeric features but not with vector features.

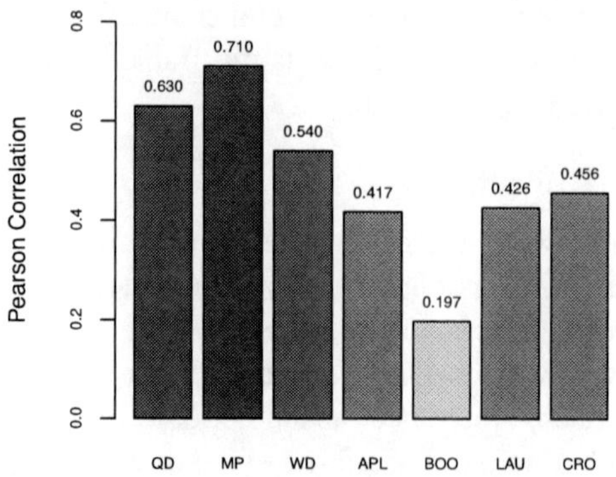

Figure 1: Pearson correlation for content and emotion cues features. Correlation windows: Negligible (0-0.19); Weak (0.2-0.39); Moderate (0.4-0.69); High (>0.69).

the influence index; while the correlation between the booing (BOO) cue and the influence index was not statistically significant. These results indicate that speakers with higher influence index spoke for longer periods of time, in line with existing empirical findings in sociological studies (Ng and Bradac, 1993; Reid and Ng., 2000; Prabhakaran et al., 2013), and were asked a higher number of questions. This analysis also indicates that speakers with higher influence index generated more crosstalk, in line with previous empirical sociological findings (Ng et al., 1995); received more applauses and made the audience laugh more often.

6.2 Influence Ranking Results

Following the results of the correlation analysis, we conducted experiments using those content and emotion cue features presenting statistically significant correlations with the influence index. Apart from these features, we also consider the persuasive argumentation features and a combination of features from both content and persuasion categories. Results for the prediction of influence ranking using these features are presented in Table 6.

For the *content features*, using the simple unigrams gives the best results. The mention percentage (MP) feature also attains competitive performance. A combination of word deviation, question deviation and mention percentage (WD+RD+MP) however degrades the performance. This is in contrast to the results reported in (Prabhakaran et al.,

2013) (denoted as [PR13] in Table 6), where the unigram feature gives much worse results and their best results were obtained using WD+RD+MP. One possible reason is that for the unigram feature used in our experiments, we have performed pre-processing by removing stop words and stemming.

For *external emotion cues*, although some emotion cues appeared to be significantly correlated with the influence index in our analysis, they did not outperform the unigram baseline. We suspect that this might be due to the fact that depending on the location of a debate, certain candidates may bring bigger crowds into the debate's venue, therefore emotion cues can be a deliberate biased way of support. Consequently emotion cues happening within the debate venue may not reflect the emotions induced to the audiences that followed the broadcast of the debate.

When analysing the *persuasion features*, alliteration and emotive language features give better results compared to external emotion cues. But they did not outperform the unigram baseline either.

We find that *persuasive argumentation* features alone provide improvement upon the unigram baseline. In particular, in terms of *nDCG* and *nDCG-3*[7], the *premise* and *support relation* types provide the best results for this feature category. In terms of *Tau* and *Spearman*[8] correlations, the *attack relation* type provides the best results. When focusing only on persuasive argumentation features, these results suggest that speakers with higher influence index tend to use well supported arguments (i.e. present more premisses supporting their claims) and/or tend to attack more other candidates by presenting premises refuting a claim.

When *combining features*, we found that the top 100 persuasive argumentation features ranked by *tfidf* together with word deviations and mention percentages significantly improve upon the baselines for particular argumentation cases including Claim, Premise, ForStance, and SupportRel.

The overall best performing features for predicting influence ranking in terms of *nDCG*, *Tau* and *Spearman* was consistently obtained with the com-

---

[7]Since *nDCG* and *nDCG-3* penalises inversions at the top of the list, good results in these metrics mean predicting accurately the top of the ranked list.

[8]These metrics provide a general evaluation of the accuracy of the full ranked list.

bined feature for the *Premise* type.

Our results improve upon those recently obtained in (Prabhakaran et al., 2014) in both *nDCG* and *Tau* where topic shift patterns have been added for influence ranking (denoted as [PR14] in Table 6).

These results suggest the relevance of "what they said", the " persuasiveness style of their arguments" and the relative importance given by others by means of mentions are good predictors of influence ranking in political debates. In particular when combining the lexical content of candidates' discourse with their persuasive argumentation style, our results indicate that candidates with higher influence ranking tend to present more premises while clearly stating their stance (i.e. supporting a claim) on a particular topic.

7   Conclusions and Future Work

In this paper, we have studied the impact of argumentation in speaker's discourse and their effect in influencing an audience on supporting their candidature. In particular, we have conducted the study in the domain of political debates. In order to extract persuasive argumentation features from political debates, we have proposed a novel method to port annotations from a persuasive essay corpus using semantic frames as pivot features.

Our experimental results on the 20 debates for the Republican primary election show that when combined with word deviations and mention percentages, most persuasive argumentation features give superior performance compared to the baselines. Particularly with the *Premise* and *SupportRel* types appear to be better predictors of a speaker's influence rank. In future work, we will aim to improve the accuracy of the extracted persuasive argumentation features by exploring other methods for identifying persuasive argumentations from text.

Acknowledgments

This work was supported by the EU-FP7 project SENSE4US (grant no. 611242)

References

C. F. Baker, C. J. Fillmore, and J. B. Lowe. 1998. The Berkeley FrameNet project. In *Proceedings of the 17th International Conference on Computational Linguistics (COLING)*, pages 86–90.

Lloyd Bitzer. 1968. *The Rhetorical Situation*. Philosophy and Rhetoric.

Filip Boltužić and Jan Šnajder. 2014. Back up your stance: Recognizing arguments in online discussions. In *Proceedings of the 1st Workshop on Argumentation Mining*, pages 49–58.

Elena Cabrio and Serena Villata. 2012. Natural language arguments: A combined approach. In *Proceedings*

Feature	nDCG	nDCG3	Tau	Spearman
Content Features				
UN	0.964	0.924	0.597	0.723
MP	0.962	0.915	0.597	0.712
WD+QD+MP	0.957	0.905	0.571	0.689
UN[PR13]	0.860	0.733	0.250	-
WD+QD+MP[PR13]	0.961	0.921	0.470	-
WD+QD+MP+TopicShift [PR14]	0.970	**0.937**	0.600	-
External Emotion Cues				
Applause	0.886	0.746	0.373	0.481
Laughter	0.870	0.721	0.335	0.423
Crosstalk	0.836	0.641	0.314	0.416
Persuasion Features				
Alliteration	0.929	0.856	0.379	0.494
Emo Language	0.928	0.846	0.478	0.588
Persuasive Argumentation				
Claim	0.957	0.902	0.559	0.691
Premise	0.968	0.927	0.600	0.731
ForStance	0.959	0.906	0.557	0.690
AgainstStance	0.951	0.897	0.512	0.643
SupportRel.	0.967	0.921	0.600	0.728
AttackRel.	0.964	0.910	0.632	0.739
Combined Features				
Persuasive Argumentation + WD + MP				
Claim	0.965	0.922	0.613	0.734
Premise	**0.973**	0.931	**0.639**	**0.766**
ForStance	0.965	0.924	0.590	0.724
AgainstStance	0.953	0.894	0.524	0.669
SupportRel.	0.971	0.929	0.619	0.753
AttackRel.	0.963	0.920	0.582	0.726

Table 6: Influence ranking results for baselines, persuasion and combined features. Statistically Significant at $p < 0.05$.

of the European Conference on Artificial Intelligence (ECAI), pages 205–210.

D. Das, N. Schneider, D. Chen, and N. A. Smith. 2010. Semafor 1.0: A probabilistic frame-semantic parser. Technical report, Carnegie Mellon University Technical Report CMU-LTI-10-001.

James B. Freemen. 2011. Argument Structure: Representation and Theory, volume 18. Springer.

Sean Gerrish and David Blei. 2011. Predicting legislative roll calls from text. In In Lise Getoor and Tobias Scheffer, editors, Proceedings of the 28th International Conference on Machine Learning (ICML), pages 489–496.

Kazi Saidul Hasan and Vincent Ng. 2013. Stance classification of ideological debates: Data, models, features, and constraints. In Proceedings of the Sixth International Joint Conference on Natural Language Processing (IJCNLP), pages 1348–1356.

T. Joachims. 2006. Training linear SMMs in linear time. In Proceedings of the ACM Conference on Knowledge Discovery and Data Mining (KDD), pages = 217–226.

Richard Lanham. 1991. A Handlist of Rhetorical Terms. Los Angeles: University of California Press.

F. Macagno and D. Walton. 2014. Emotive Language in Argumentation. Cambridge Press.

Fabrizio Macagno. 2010. The argumentative uses of emotive language. Revista Iberoamericana de Argumentacion, pages 1–33.

S. H. Ng and J. J. Bradac. 1993. Power in language: Verbal communication and social influence. Sage Publications, Inc.

S. H. Ng, M Brooke, and M. Dunne. 1995. Interruption and influence in discussion groups. Journal of Language and Social Psychology, 14(4):369–381.

Andreas Peldszus and Manfred Stede. 2013. From argument diagrams to argumentation mining in texts: A survey. International Journal of Cognitive Informatics and Natural Intelligence (IJCINI), 7(1):1–31.

M. F. Porter. 1997. Readings in information retrieval. chapter An Algorithm for Suffix Stripping, pages 313–316.

Vinodkumar Prabhakaran, Ajita John, and D. Dorée Seligmann. 2013. Who had the upper hand? ranking participants of interactions based on their relative power. In Proceedings of the 6th International Joint Conference on Natural Language Processing (IJCNLP), pages 365–373.

Vinodkumar Prabhakaran, Ashima Arora, and Owen. Rambow. 2014. Staying on topic: An indicator of power in political debates. In Proceedings of the conference on Empirical Methods for Natural Language Processing (EMNLP).

S. A. Reid and S. H. Ng. 2000. Conversation as a resource for in influence: evidence for prototypical arguments and social identification processes. European Journal of Social Psych., (30):83–100.

Andrew Rosenberg and Julia Hirschberg. 2009. Charisma perception from text and speech. Speech Communication, 51(7):640–655.

Yanchuan Sim, Brice D. L. Acree, Justin H. Gross, and Noah A. Smith. 2013. Measuring ideological proportions in political speeches. In Proceedings of the Conference on Empirical Methods in Natural Language Processing (EMNLP), pages 91–101.

Carlo Strapparava, Marco Guerini, and Oliviero Stock. 2010. Predicting persuasiveness in political discourses. In Proceedings of the 7th International Conference on Language Resources and Evaluation (LREC).

Matt Thomas, Bo Pang, and Lillian Lee. 2006. Get out the vote: Determining support or opposition from congressional floor-debate transcripts. In Proceedings of the Conference on Empirical Methods in Natural Language Processing (EMNLP), pages 327–335.

Stephen E. Toulmin. 1958. The uses of Argument. Cambridge University Press.

van Eemeren et al. 1996. Fundamentals Of Argumentation Theory: A Handbook Of Historical Backgrounds And Contemporary Developments. Hillsdale, NJ, England: Lawrence Erlbaum Associates, Inc, PsycINFO, EBSCOhost.

Douglas Walton, Chris Reed, and FabrizioMacagno. 2008. Argumentation Schemes. Cambridge University Press.

Lexical Coherence Graph Modeling Using Word Embeddings

Mohsen Mesgar and **Michael Strube**
Heidelberg Institute for Theoretical Studies gGmbH
Schloss-Wolfsbrunnenweg 35
69118 Heidelberg, Germany
(mohsen.mesgar|michael.strube)@h-its.org

Abstract

Coherence is established by semantic connections between sentences of a text which can be modeled by lexical relations. In this paper, we introduce the lexical coherence graph (LCG), a new graph-based model to represent lexical relations among sentences. The frequency of subgraphs (coherence patterns) of this graph captures the connectivity style of sentence nodes in this graph. The coherence of a text is encoded by a vector of these frequencies. We evaluate the LCG model on the readability ranking task. The results of the experiments show that the LCG model obtains higher accuracy than state-of-the-art coherence models. Using larger subgraphs yields higher accuracy, because they capture more structural information. However, larger subgraphs can be sparse. We adapt Kneser-Ney smoothing to smooth subgraphs' frequencies. Smoothing improves performance.

1 Introduction

The concept of coherence is based on cohesive semantic relations connecting elements of a text. Cohesive relations are expressed through grammar and the vocabulary of a language. The former is referred to as *grammatical coherence*, the latter as *lexical coherence* (Halliday and Hasan, 1976). Grammatical coherence encompasses coreference, substitution, ellipsis, etc. Lexical coherence comprises semantic connections among words of a text.

In this paper we measure text coherence by modeling *lexical coherence*. Lexical relations specify cohesive relations over the sentences of a text.

These lexical relations can be any kind of semantic relation: repetition, synonymy, hyperonymy, meronymy, etc. These lexical items may or may not have the same reference (Halliday and Hasan, 1976).

Why does the little boy wriggle all the time? Girls don't.

In this example the lexical items *boy* and *girls* are semantically related. Although they do not refer to the same entity, they still connect these two sentences.

There is coherence between any pair of lexical items that stand to each other in some lexico-semantic relation (Halliday and Hasan, 1976). For textual purposes it is not required to determine the type of the relation. It is only necessary to recognize semantically related lexical items, and these relations can be learned by cooccurring lexical items.

One can use world knowledge resources to determine semantic relations. This way is expensive in terms of determining the best resource, e.g. WordNet vs. Freebase. WordNet lacks broad coverage in particular with proper names, Freebase is restricted to nominal concepts and entities.

Recent improvements in embedding representations of words let us efficiently compute semantic relations among lexical items in the vector space. These models use a vector of numbers to encode the meaning of words. We use these vectors to check the existence of any kind of semantic relations between two words.

In the following example the sentences are connected because of the semantic relation between *king* and *queen* which can be induced by word em-

Proceedings of NAACL-HLT 2016, pages 1414–1423,
San Diego, California, June 12-17, 2016. ©2016 Association for Computational Linguistics

bedding models (Mikolov et al., 2013; Pennington et al., 2014).

> *... The king was in his counting-house, counting out his money,*
> *The queen was in the parlour, eating bread and honey.*

We model lexical coherence between sentences by a lexical coherence graph (LCG). We consider subgraphs of this graph coherence patterns and use their frequency as features representing the connectivity of the graph and, hence, the coherence of a text (Mesgar and Strube, 2015).

An important task for evaluating a coherence model is readability assessment. The goal of this task is to rate texts based on their readability. The more coherent a text, the faster to read and easier to understand it is. Other coherence models (Barzilay and Lapata, 2008; Guinaudeau and Strube, 2013; Mesgar and Strube, 2014) are also evaluated on this task. Pitler and Nenkova (2008) use the entity grid (Barzilay and Lapata, 2008) to capture the coherence of a text for readability assessment. Mesgar and Strube (2015) extend the entity graph (Guinaudeau and Strube, 2013) as coherence model to measure the readability of texts. They encode coherence as a vector of frequencies of subgraphs of the graph representation of a text. We build upon their method and represent the connectivity of sentences in our LCG model by a vector of frequencies of subgraphs.

Although using the frequency of subgraphs of the lexical coherence graph encodes coherence features well, the subgraph frequency method, in general, is suffering from a sparsity problem when the subgraphs get larger. Large subgraphs capture more structural information, but they occur only rarely. We resolve this sparsity issue by adapting Kneser-Ney smoothing (Heafield et al., 2013) to smooth subgraph counts (Section 3). We estimate the probability of unseen subgraphs, i.e. coherence patterns. This prediction lets us measure the coherence of a text even when its corresponding graph representation contains a subgraph which does not occur in the training data. If the unseen coherence pattern is similar to seen ones, smoothing gives it closer probability to seen coherence patterns in comparison to dissimilar unseen ones. This is due to the base probability factor in Kneser-Ney smoothing.

We evaluate our LCG model on the two readability datasets provided by Pitler and Nenkova (2008) and De Clercq et al. (2014), respectively (Section 4). The results (Section 5) indicate that the LCG model outperforms state-of-the-art systems. By applying Kneser-Ney smoothing we solve the sparsity problem. Smoothing allows us to exploit the high informativity of large subgraphs which leads to new state-of-the-art results in readability assessment.

2   Related Work

The entity grid model (Barzilay and Lapata, 2008) is based on entity transitions over sentences. It uses a two dimensional matrix to represent transitions of entities among adjacent sentences. The entity grid is applied to readability assessment by Pitler and Nenkova (2008). The entity graph (Guinaudeau and Strube, 2013) is a graph-based, mainly unsupervised interpretation of the entity grid. This model represents the distribution of entities over sentences in a text with a bipartite graph. Connections between sentences are obtained by information on entities shared by sentences. Guinaudeau and Strube (2013) perform a one-mode projection on sentence nodes and use the average out-degree of the one-mode projection graph to quantify the coherence of the given text. Mesgar and Strube (2015) represent the connectivity of the one-mode projection graph by a vector whose elements are the frequencies of subgraphs in projection graphs. This encoding works much better than the entity graph for the readability task on the *P&N* dataset and even outperforms Pitler and Nenkova (2008) by a large margin. Zhang et al. (2015) state that the entity graph model is limited, because it only captures mentions which refer to the same entity (the entity graph uses a very restricted version of coreference resolution to determine entities). Zhang et al. (2015) use world knowledge *YAGO* (Hoffart et al., 2013), *WikiPedia* (Denoyer and Gallinari, 2006) and *FreeBase* (Bollacker et al., 2008) to capture the semantic relatedness between entities even if they do not refer to the same entity. Main issues with using world knowledge are: the choice knowledge sources, selection of knowledge from the source, coverage, and language-dependence.

Word embedding approaches like *word2vec* and

GloVe (Mikolov et al., 2013; Pennington et al., 2014) show that the semantic connection between words can be captured by word vectors which are obtained by applying a neural network. The ability to train on very large data sets allows the model to learn complex relationships between words.

3 Method

We introduce a new graph representation of semantic connections over lexical items in texts. Afterwards we compute the frequency of all subgraphs, i.e. coherence patterns. The intuition is that subgraphs capture how sentence nodes are connected and, respectively, encode text coherence.

3.1 Graph Model

We model semantic relations between sentences by a graph $G = <V, E>$ where V is the set of sentence nodes and E is the set of edges between sentence nodes. Two nodes of G are adjacent if there is a semantic connection between the corresponding sentences. Two sentences are semantically connected if there is at least one strong semantic relation between the words of these sentences. We model semantic relations between words by their corresponding word embeddings (Pennington et al., 2014). Given word vectors v_a for word a of sentence A and v_b for word b of sentence B, the cosine similarity value, $cos(v_a, v_b)$, between the two word vectors is a measure of semantic connectivity of the two words. The range of $cos(v_a, v_b)$ is between $[-1, +1]$. One interpretation of cosine is the normalized correlation coefficient, which states how well the two words are semantically correlated (Manning and Schütze, 1999). The absolute value of cosine, $|cos(v_a, v_b)|$, encodes how strongly the two words are connected.

The connection between sentences is obtained from connections between their words (Figure 1). Assume sentence A precedes sentence B, each word b of sentence B is connected with word a^* of A, where

$$a^* = \operatorname*{argmax}_{a \in A} cos(b, a)$$

Then from all connections between the words of sentences A and B, the connection with the maximum weight among the words of B is selected to connect these two sentences (Figure 2).

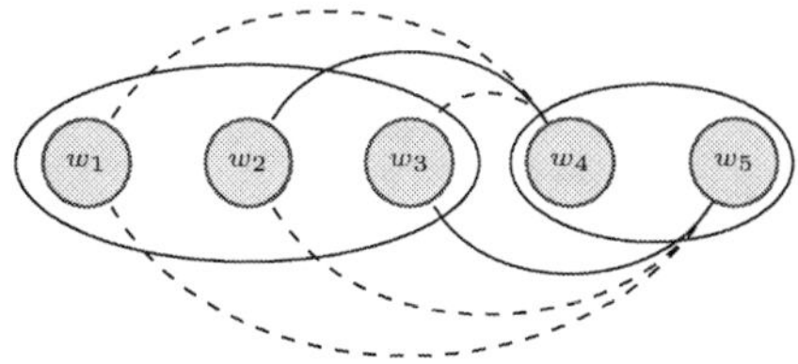

Figure 1: Sentence A with three words $\{w_1, w_2, w_3\}$ and sentence B with two words $\{w_4, w_5\}$. w_4 is highly related to w_2 and w_5 is highly related to w_3.

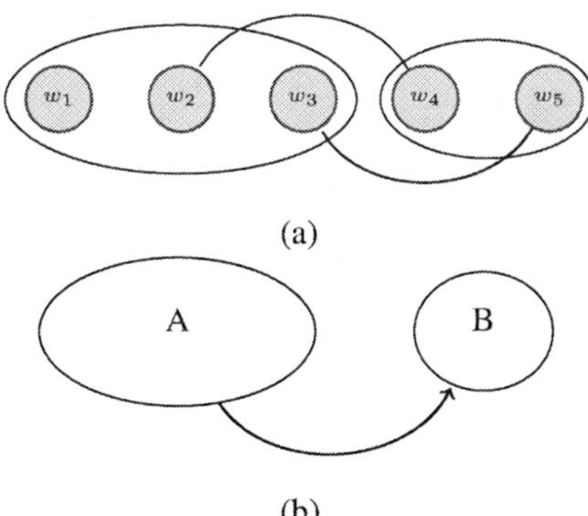

(a)

(b)

Figure 2: The word relation with the maximum weight (a) represents the connections between sentences (b).

The output of this phase is a graph whose edge weights model the strength of connections between sentences. The edges in this graph are directed to model the order of sentences.

Word embeddings relate each word in sentence A with each word in sentence B. Since the resulting graph is very dense, we filter out edges whose weights are below a threshold[1].

3.2 Coherence Features

Mesgar and Strube (2015) propose that the connection style of an entity graph can be captured by the frequency of all k-*node* subgraphs in this graph. Larger[2] subgraphs[3] can capture more information about the structure of graphs and are more informative coherence patterns than smaller ones. We experiment with $k \in \{3, 4, 5, 6\}$. Text coherence is repre-

---

[1] We set this threshold to 0.9 to connect only sentences with high confidence.

[2] The size of a subgraph is the number of its nodes.

[3] We compute *induced subgraphs* (Mesgar and Strube, 2015). However, we use the term *subgraph* for brevity.

sented by a vector whose elements are the frequency of subgraphs (coherence patterns) with k-$node$.

3.3 Smoothing

Although increasing the size k of subgraphs captures more structural information about the connections of sentence nodes, a main risk with large subgraphs is sparsity. Given a sentence graph, many large subgraph types do not occur in this graph. Small subgraph types occur frequently in most sentence graphs in the dataset, but these subgraphs do not capture enough information about the connectivity style of the graphs.

Inspired by Kneser-Ney smoothing in language models (Heafield et al., 2013), each feature vector of a sentence graph can be smoothed. Smoothing deals with the problem of zero counts in the feature vector. It also lets the model having feature values for unseen subgraphs (like OOV in language modeling) which may be seen in the testing phase.

Kneser-Ney smoothing uses a discount factor to discount the raw count of each event (subgraph) and distributes the total discount to all event (subgraph) probabilities by means of a base probability.

The estimated frequency of subgraph sg in a given sentence graph is computed as follows:

$$KN(sg) = \frac{\max\{count(sg) - \alpha, 0\}}{Z} + \frac{M \cdot \alpha}{Z} P_b(sg),$$

where α is the discount factor and M is the number of times that discount factor is applied. Z is a normalization factor to ensure that the distribution sums to one and is obtained as follows:

$$Z = \sum_{sg \in A} count(sg),$$

where A is the set of all subgraphs with k-$nodes$ and function $count(\cdot)$ computes the number of instances of subgraph sg in the given sentence graph.

$P_b(sg)$ in Kneser-Ney smoothing is the base probability of subgraph sg among all k-$node$ subgraphs (A). The base probability can be computed based on hierarchical (parent-child) relations in subgraphs. k-$node$ subgraph sg_i is a parent of $(k+1)$-$node$ subgraph sg_j, if sg_i is a subgraph of sg_j. Figure 3 shows the parent-child relation between subgraphs via a weighted tree. The root of this tree is a null

graph[4]. The weight of a parent-child relation connecting the parent subgraph sg_i and child subgraph sg_j is shown by w_{ij} and computed as follows:

$$w_{ij} = \frac{count(sg_i, sg_j)}{\sum_{sg_l \in A} count(sg_i, sg_l)},$$

where A is all subgraphs with k-$node$ and k equals the number of nodes of sg_j. Interpretation of weight w_{ij} is the normalized count of sg_i in sg_j with respect to all outgoing edges from sg_i.

The base probability of each subgraph sg_j is the inner product of the Kneser-Ney probabilities of sg_j's parents by the weights of the corresponding relations:

$$P_b(sg_j) = P \cdot W, \tag{1}$$

where P is the vector of probabilities of all parents of sg_j and W is the vector of all corresponding edge weights connecting the parents of sg_j to sg_j.

Since the root node of this tree is the null subgraph, and it is a subgraph of all possible sentence graphs, its base probability is one. Because the edge weights are in the range $[0, 1]$ the sum of the probabilities of all subgraphs with k-$node$ is always equal to one.

Proof. Assume I and J are the set of all k-$node$ and $(k+1)$-$node$ subgraphs. We also assume that I has n subgraphs and $\sum_{i=1}^{n} p(sg_i) = 1$. Considering these assumptions we prove that

$$\sum_{j=1}^{m} p(sg_j) = 1,$$

where m is the number of subgraphs in J.

We start from the left and compute the value of

$$\sum_{j=1}^{m} p(sg_j).$$

Based on the definition of base probability, the value of $p(sg_j)$ is computed based on its parents in I,

$$p(sg_j) = \sum_{i=1}^{n} w_{ij} p(sg_i),$$

where w_{ij} is the weight of the parent-child relation between sg_i and sg_j. Now we have:

---

[4]A null graph is a graph with no nodes.

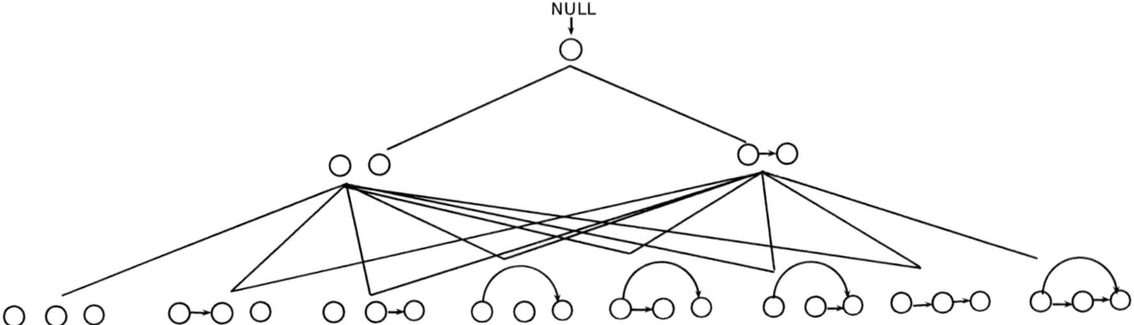

Figure 3: parent child relation.

$$\sum_{j=1}^{m} p(sg_j) = \sum_{j=1}^{m} \sum_{i=1}^{n} w_{ij} p(sg_i).$$

If we exchange the place of the sums and re-write the equation, we have:

$$\sum_{j=1}^{m} p(sg_j) = \sum_{i=1}^{n} \sum_{j=1}^{m} w_{ij} p(sg_i).$$

In this equation $p(sg_i)$ is independent of j (index of the inner sum), so it can be moved out of the inner sum:

$$\sum_{j=1}^{m} p(sg_j) = \sum_{i=1}^{n} p(sg_i) \sum_{j=1}^{m} w_{ij}$$

The inner sum equals 1.

$$\sum_{j=1}^{m} p(sg_j) = \sum_{i=1}^{n} p(sg_i).$$

Based on our assumption the right side of the equation is 1 and

$$\sum_{j=1}^{m} p(sg_j) = 1.$$

So we proved that the sum of the base probability of all k-$node$ subgraphs is 1. $\square$

This way, Kneser-Ney smoothing distributes the total discount value by considering the weights of parent-child relations among the subgraphs. The result of applying smoothing is an estimation of the frequency of each subgraph in the sentence graph.

4 Experiments

4.1 Evaluation Task

We evaluate our coherence model on the task of ranking texts by their readability. The intuition is that more coherent texts are easier to read.

Datasets. We run our experiments on two datasets annotated with readability information provided by human annotators: *P&N* (Pitler and Nenkova, 2008) and *De Clercq* (De Clercq et al., 2014).

The dataset *P&N* contains 27 articles randomly selected from the Wall Street Journal corpus[5]. The average number of sentences is about 10 words. Every article is associated with a human score between $[0.0, 5.0]$ indicating the readability score of that article. We create pairs of documents, if the difference between their readability scores is greater than 0.5. If the first document in a pair has the higher score, we label this pair with $+1$, otherwise with -1. The resulting number of text pairs in this dataset is 209.

The dataset *De Clercq* consists of 105 articles from different genres: administrative (17 articles), journalistic (43 articles), manuals (14 articles) and miscellaneous (31 articles). The average number of sentences is about 12. This dataset was annotated by De Clercq et al. (2014) by asking human judges to compare two texts based on their readability. They use five labels:

----

[5]Pitler and Nenkova (2008)'s dataset contains 30 articles. They remove one. We assume this is `wsj-0382` which does not exist in the Penn Treebank. We furthermore remove `wsj-2090` which does not exist in the final release of the Penn Discourse Treebank. We also remove `wsj-1398` which is a poem and, hence, not very informative for readability assessment.

LME: left text is much easier,

LSE: left text is somewhat easier,

ED: both texts are equally difficult,

RSE: right text is somewhat easier,

RME: right text is much easier.

We map these labels to three class labels:

+1: for text pairs where the left text is easier to read (LME or LSE),

0: for text pairs where both texts are equally difficult to read (ED),

−1: for text pairs where the right text is easier to read (RSE or RME).

Properties of this dataset are shown in Table 1.

Genre	No. of articles	No. of text pairs
Administrative	17	272
Journalistic	43	1806
Manuals	14	182
Miscellaneous	31	931

Table 1: Properties of the different genres in the *De Clercq* dataset.

4.2 Experimental Settings

Word Embeddings and Classification. In order to reduce the effect of very frequent words, stop words are filtered by using the SMART English stop word list (Salton, 1971). We use a pretrained model of GloVe for word embeddings. This model is trained on Common Crawl with 840B tokens, 2.2M vocabulary. We represent each word by a vector with length 300 (Pennington et al., 2014). For handling out-of-vocabulary words, we assign a random vector to each word and memorize it for its next occurrence (Kusner et al., 2015). The classification task is done by the SVM implementation in WEKA (SMO) with the linear kernel function. All settings are set to the default values. The evaluation is computed by 10-fold cross validation.

Graph Processing and Smoothing. In order to compare the performance of LCG with the entity graph model, we follow Mesgar and Strube (2015) and use the gSpan method (Yan and Han, 2002) to compute all common subgraphs on each dataset and their frequencies. Note that gSpan does not count all possible k-*node* subgraphs, whereas for applying Kneser-Ney smoothing it is necessary to count all possible k-*node* subgraphs, because the probability should be distributed among all possible subgraphs. This also helps to estimate the probability of unseen patterns. We use a random sampling method (Shervashidze et al., 2009) to obtain the frequency of subgraphs in a sentence graph. In this regard, we take $10,000$ samples of the given sentence graph by randomly selecting k nodes of the graph to count the occurrence of k-*node* subgraphs in this graph. We compute the base probability for at most $k = 6$. We find the best value for d in a greedy manner. First, we initialize d with 0.001. In each iteration we compute the performance. Then we multiply the discount factor by 10. We iterate as long as the discount factor is less than 1000. We report the best performance.

5 Results

In order to compare our method with related work, we run our model on the *P&N* dataset. Table 2 reports the accuracy of *LCG* with different values for k in k-*node* subgraphs. This corresponds to coherence patterns spanning different numbers of sentences.

System	Accuracy		
ZeroR	50.24%		
EGrid	83.25%		
k-*node*	EGraph	EGraph+PRN	LCG
3-node	79.43%	80.38%**	78.95%
4-node	89.00%	89.95%	89.47%
5-node	96.17%**	95.69%**	97.13%

Table 2: *P&N* dataset.

We start in Table 2 with a majority class baseline (*ZeroR*). *EGrid* is our reimplementation of Pitler and Nenkova (2008) which we use as non-trivial baseline. The column *EGraph* is the entity graph model of Mesgar and Strube (2015). In *EGraph+PRN* we extend this model by a pronoun resolution system, so that entities mentioned by pronouns also enter the graph. We apply the Stanford coreference resolution system (Lee et al., 2013). Using the full coreference resolution system, however, decreases performance, hence we only use resolved pronouns. The enriched model with resolved pronouns works slightly better for *3-node* and *4-node* subgraphs, and slightly worse for *5-node* subgraphs than the *EGraph*. The lexical coherence graph model, *LCG*, performs slightly worse than *EGraph* on *3-node* subgraphs. This could be because the graphs in *LCG* have more edges than the graphs in *EGraph*. When graphs are denser *3-node* subgraphs occur in every graph, hence their frequency is less discriminative. As shown in Table 2 larger subgraphs (*4-node* and *5-node*) capture more information and improve upon *EGraph* and for *5-node* subgraphs even upon *EGraph+PRN*. *LCG* significantly ($p\_value = 0.01$) works better than *EGraph+PRN* and *EGraph* using 5-node subgraphs. The difference between *LCG* and *EGraph+PRN* and *EGraph* using 4-node subgraphs is not significant.

Table 3 shows the performance of different models on the *De Clercq* dataset.

System	Accuracy	
ZeroR	42.312%	
k-node	EGraph+PRN	LCG
3-node	42.31%	42.31%
4-node	48.07%	49.12%**
5-node	65.77%	76.27%**

Table 3: *De Clercq* dataset.

Again, we use a majority baseline (*ZeroR*) to put our results in context. While the performance of both methods almost does not beat the baseline for *3-node* subgraphs, *4-node*-subgraphs work already better, and *5-node* subgraphs yield reasonable performance on this dataset. Although *EGraph+PRN* and *LCG* reach almost the same performance for *4-node*, the difference between them is statistically significant ($p\_value = 0.01$). With *5-node* subgraphs, *LCG* outperforms *EGraph+PRN* subgraphs by a large margin and gets a very reasonable performance on this dataset.

The general performance on the *De Clercq* dataset is lower than the performance on the the *P&N* dataset. This can have two reasons: first, the ranking task on the *De Clercq* dataset is three-label classification which is more difficult than the binary classification task on the *P&N* dataset. Second, texts in the *De Clercq* dataset are from different genres and coherence patterns may vary across genres. Hence, we take a closer look on the performance on the different genres.

5-node	EGraph+PRN	LCG
Administrative	69.49%	71.69%
Journalistic	65.01%	82.12%
Manuals	54.95%	61.54%
Misc.	70.68%	76.69%

Table 4: Accuracy of *EGraph+PRN* and *LCG* on different genres in the *De Clercq* dataset.

Table 4 shows the performance for *EGraph+PRN* and *LCG* using *5-node* subgraphs on the different genres in the *De Clercq* dataset. The performance of *LCG* is higher than *EGraph+PRN* on all genres. Unlike *EGraph+PRN*, *LCG* gets the best performance on journalistic articles. The lowest performance of both models is obtained on manuals. On administrative articles, performance of *LCG* is slightly better than *EGraph+PRN*. On miscellaneous articles *LCG* performs better than *EGraph+PRN*.

While large subgraphs are very informative for coherence modeling, extracting large subgraphs ($k > 4$) in relatively small datasets leads to a data sparsity problem, as there are very many possible subgraphs to be represented in a high dimensional vector space. Hence, many possible subgraphs have low or even zero counts. The problem for such a vector is that each graph is only similar to itself and not to any other graph. Hence, we observe a drop in performance when the model deals with large subgraphs (*6-node* subgraphs, *LCG1* for *P&N* in Table 5). We solve this problem by smoothing.

In order to apply Kneser-Ney smoothing we use a sampling method to create all possible (connected and disconnected) *k-node* subgraphs (for *LCG1* and *LCG1** we use connected and disconnected subgraphs, for *LCG* only connected ones).

Table 5 shows the performance of *LCG1* when it is applied to ever larger subgraphs. As can be seen in Table 5, the performance on the *P&N* dataset suddenly drops for *6-node* subgraphs. This is could be caused by the sparsity problem.

When we apply Kneser-Ney smoothing as described in Section 3 the results for all tested values of k are superior for *LCG1** when compared to *LCG1* (Table 5).

Kneser-Ney smoothing improves the performance of the system even with *3-node* subgraphs by a large margin. Smoothing reduces the power of fre-

	P&N		De Clercq	
k-node	LCG1	LCG1*	LCG1	LCG1*
3-node	84.52%	89.00%	42.31%	49.60%
4-node	95.69%	96.17%	65.10%	66.23%
5-node	97.61%	98.08%	79.33%	79.85%
6-node	93.26%	95.69%	76.67%	78.03%

Table 5: Applying smoothing method yields to higher accuracy for larger subgraphs.

quency and makes the frequency distribution of subgraphs more even. Smoothing reduces the values through all subgraphs by considering parent-child relations between subgraphs to relate similar subgraphs. That is the advantage of the Kneser-Ney method in comparison to the other smoothing methods like Laplace-Smoothing.

For the *P&N* dataset we achieve the best results to date. Pitler and Nenkova (2008) reported 83.25% accuracy, Mesgar and Strube (2015) 89.95%. When smoothing *5-node* subgraphs we are able to report 98.08%. This, however, indicates that this dataset may not be the best one to report performance on. Hence, we now check whether smoothing also improves the performance on the more difficult *De Clercq* dataset.

On this dataset, we basically observe the same trends. Both settings result in better performance than *LCG* (see Table 3).

Note that none of the parameters in this work is tuned on the datasets. One may get better performance by tuning the parameters. The results confirm the intuition that the lexical coherence graph *LCG* captures coherence and models lexical coherence appropriately.

Applying smoothing on graphs of *EGraph+PRN* model increases the performance of this model. But this improvement is not as high as the improvement on the *LCG* graph.

Coherence Patterns. In this part we check the Pearson correlation coefficient between *LCG1* and human judgements of a few frequent subgraphs on the *P&N* dataset. In order to be consistent with Mesgar and Strube (2015), we use the exhaustive value of subgraph frequencies, i.e. *LCG1* for our work.

For the *3-node* subgraphs only one subgraph (Figure 4) in the *LCG1* representation is significantly

(and positively) correlated (*p-value* < 0.05) with human scores. For the *4-node* subgraphs, we find six subgraphs which are significantly correlated with readability. Only one is positively correlated, while four are negatively correlated. Interestingly, both positively correlated *3-node* and *4-node* subgraphs have been determined as positively and significantly correlated by Mesgar and Strube (2015) as well. Both also capture a similar coherence pattern, indicating that our method is linguistically sound.

Pattern		ρ	p-value
3-node	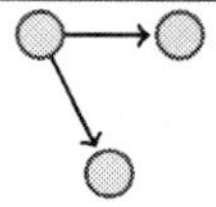	0.43	0.024
4-node	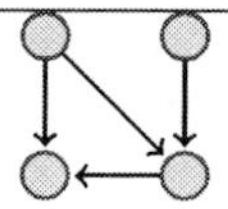	-0.45	0.018
	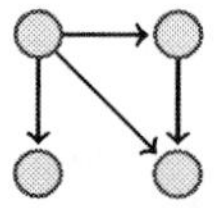	+0.39	0.047
	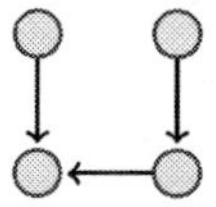	-0.43	0.024
	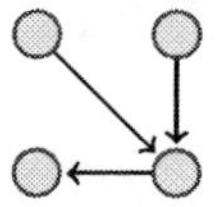	-0.59	0.001
	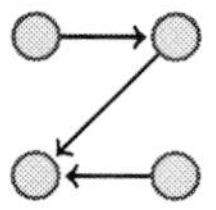	-0.55	0.003
	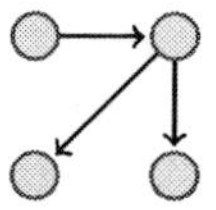	-0.55	0.003

Figure 4: Pearson correlation between *3-node* and *4-node* subgraphs and readability scores in the *P&N* dataset.

6 Conclusions and Future Work

In this paper we propose a new graph based coherence model, the lexical coherence graph, LCG. We view coherence as semantic connectedness between words which we model by word embeddings. We take only the strongest connection between sentences to create a graph with connected sentences. Then we extract large subgraphs capturing coherence patterns, which show similarity to patterns described in text linguistics (Daneš, 1974).

While the entity grid works only on sequences of up to three adjacent sentences, we are able to model relationships of up to six non-adjacent sentences. We solve the sparsity problem of large subgraphs by adapting Kneser-Ney smoothing to graphs. Smoothing prevents LCG from losing performance with large subgraphs and leads to superior performance on the Pitler and Nenkova (2008) dataset and to a first reasonable state-of-the-art on the De Clercq et al. (2014) dataset.

In future work we want to apply LCG to essay scoring as well. Also, we see that our adaption of Kneser-Ney smoothing to graphs may be useful for research in subgraph mining in general.

Acknowledgments

This work has been funded by the Klaus Tschira Foundation, Heidelberg, Germany. The first author has been supported by a HITS Ph.D. scholarship. We would like to thank Orphée De Clercq who provided the *De Clercq* dataset. We also appreciate Andreas Spitz' comments on graph processing.

References

Regina Barzilay and Mirella Lapata. 2008. Modeling local coherence: An entity-based approach. *Computational Linguistics*, 34(1):1–34.

Kurt Bollacker, Colin Evans, Praveen Paritosh, Tim Sturge, and Jamie Taylor. 2008. Freebase: A collaboratively created graph database for structuring human knowledge. In *Proceedings of the 2008 ACM SIGMOD International Conference on Management of Data*, Vancouver, B.C., Canada, 10–12 June 2008, pages 1247–1250.

František Daneš. 1974. Functional sentence perspective and the organization of the text. In F. Daneš, editor, *Papers on Functional Sentence Perspective*, pages 106–128. Prague: Academia.

Orphée De Clercq, Véronique Hoste, Bart Desmet, Philip Van Oosten, Martine De Cock, and Lieve Macken. 2014. Using the crowd for readability prediction. *Natural Language Engineering*, 20(3):293–325.

Ludovic Denoyer and Patrick Gallinari. 2006. The Wikipedia XML corpus. *ACM SIGIR Forum*, 40(1):64–69.

Camille Guinaudeau and Michael Strube. 2013. Graph-based local coherence modeling. In *Proceedings of the 51st Annual Meeting of the Association for Computational Linguistics (Volume 1: Long Papers)*, Sofia, Bulgaria, 4–9 August 2013, pages 93–103.

M. A. K. Halliday and Ruqaiya Hasan. 1976. *Cohesion in English*. London, U.K.: Longman.

Kenneth Heafield, Ivan Pouzyrevsky, Jonathan H. Clark, and Philipp Koehn. 2013. Scalable modified Kneser-Ney language model estimation. In *Proceedings of the 51st Annual Meeting of the Association for Computational Linguistics (Volume 2: Short Papers)*, Sofia, Bulgaria, 4–9 August 2013, pages 690–696.

Johannes Hoffart, Fabian M. Suchanek, Klaus Berberich, and Gerhard Weikum. 2013. YAGO2: A spatially and temporally enhanced knowledge based from Wikipedia. *Artificial Intelligence*, 194:28–61.

Matt J. Kusner, Yu Sun, Nicholas I. Kolkin, and Kilian Q. Weinberger. 2015. From word embeddings to document distances. In *Proceedings of the 32nd International Conference on Machine Learning*, Lille, France, 6–11 July 2015, pages 918–927.

Heeyoung Lee, Angel Chang, Yves Peirsman, Nathanael Chambers, Mihai Surdeanu, and Dan Jurafsky. 2013. Deterministic coreference resolution based on entity-centric, precision-ranked rules. *Computational Linguistics*, 39(4):885–916.

Christopher D. Manning and Hinrich Schütze. 1999. *Foundations of Statistical Natural Language Processing*. MIT Press, Cambridge, Mass.

Mohsen Mesgar and Michael Strube. 2014. Normalized entity graph for computing local coherence. In *Proceedings of TextGraphs-9: Graph-based Methods for Natural Language Processing, Workshop at EMNLP 2014*, Doha, Qatar, 29 October 2014, pages 1–5.

Mohsen Mesgar and Michael Strube. 2015. Graph-based coherence modeling for assessing readability. In *Proceedings of STARSEM 2015: The Fourth Joint Conference on Lexical and Computational Semantics*, Denver, Col., 4–5 June 2015, pages 309–318.

Tomas Mikolov, Ilya Sutskever, Kai Chen, Gregory S. Corrado, and Jeffrey Dean. 2013. Distributed representations of words and phrases and their compositionality. In *Proceedings of Advances in Neural Information Processing Systems 26*. Lake Tahoe, Nev., 5–8 December 2013, pages 3111–3119.

Jeffrey Pennington, Richard Socher, and Christopher D. Manning. 2014. GloVe: Global vectors for word representation. In *Proceedings of the 2014 Conference on Empirical Methods in Natural Language Processing*, Doha, Qatar, 25–29 October 2014, pages 1532–1543.

Emily Pitler and Ani Nenkova. 2008. Revisiting readability: A unified framework for predicting text quality. In *Proceedings of the 2008 Conference on Empirical Methods in Natural Language Processing*, Waikiki, Honolulu, Hawaii, 25–27 October 2008, pages 186–195.

Gerard Salton. 1971. *The SMART Retrieval System – Experiments in Automatic Document Processing*. Englewood Cliffs, N.J.: Prentice Hall.

Nino Shervashidze, Tobias Petri, Kurt Mehlhorn, Karsten M. Borgwardt, and SVN Vishwanathan. 2009. Efficient graphlet kernels for large graph comparison. In *International Conference on Artificial Intelligence and Statistics,* Clearwater Beach, Florida, 16–18 April 2009, pages 488–495.

Xifeng Yan and Jiawei Han. 2002. gSpan: Graph-based substructure pattern mining. In *Proceedings of the International Conference on Data Mining,* Maebashi City, Japan, 9–12 December 2002, pages 721–724.

Muyu Zhang, Vanessa Wei Feng, Bing Qin, Graeme Hirst, Ting Liu, and Jingwen Huang. 2015. Encoding world knowledge in the evaluation of local coherence. In *Proceedings of the 2015 Conference of the North American Chapter of the Association for Computational Linguistics: Human Language Technologies,* Denver, Col., 31 May – 5 June 2015, pages 1087–1096.

Using Context to Predict the Purpose of Argumentative Writing Revisions

Fan Zhang
Department of Computer Science
University of Pittsburgh
Pittsburgh, PA, 15260
zhangfan@cs.pitt.edu

Diane Litman
Department of Computer Science and LRDC
University of Pittsburgh
Pittsburgh, PA, 15260
litman@cs.pitt.edu

Abstract

While there is increasing interest in automatically recognizing the argumentative structure of a text, recognizing the argumentative purpose of revisions to such texts has been less explored. Furthermore, existing revision classification approaches typically ignore contextual information. We propose two approaches for utilizing contextual information when predicting argumentative revision purposes: developing contextual features for use in the classification paradigm of prior work, and transforming the classification problem to a sequence labeling task. Experimental results using two corpora of student essays demonstrate the utility of contextual information for predicting argumentative revision purposes.

1 Introduction

Incorporating natural language processing into systems that provide writing assistance beyond grammar is an area of increasing research and commercial interest (e.g., (Writelab, 2015; Roscoe et al., 2015)). As one example, the automatic recognition of the purpose of each of an author's revisions allows writing assistance systems to provide better rewriting suggestions. In this paper, we propose context-based methods to improve the automatic identification of revision purposes in student argumentative writing. Argumentation plays an important role in analyzing many types of writing such as persuasive essays (Stab et al., 2014), scientific papers (Teufel, 2000) and law documents (Palau and Moens, 2009). In student papers, identifying revision purposes with

respect to argument structure has been used to predict the grade improvement in the paper after revision (Zhang and Litman, 2015).

Existing works on the analysis of writing revisions (Adler et al., 2011; Bronner and Monz, 2012; Daxenberger and Gurevych, 2013; Zhang and Litman, 2015) typically compare two versions of a text to extract revisions, then classify the purpose of each revision in isolation. That is, while limited contextual features such as revision location have been utilized in prior work, such features are computed from the revision being classified but typically not its neighbors. In addition, ordinary classifiers rather than structured prediction models are typically used. To increase the role of context during prediction, in this paper we 1) introduce new contextual features (e.g., the impact of a revision on local text cohesion), and 2) transform revision purpose classification to a sequential labeling task to capture dependencies among revisions (as in Table 1). An experimental evaluation demonstrates the utility of our approach.

2 Related Work

There are multiple works on the classification of revisions (Adler et al., 2011; Javanmardi et al., 2011; Bronner and Monz, 2012; Daxenberger and Gurevych, 2013; Zhang and Litman, 2015). While different classification tasks were explored, similar approaches were taken by extracting features (location, text, meta-data, language) from the revised text to train a classification model (SVM, Random Forest, etc.) on the annotated data. One problem with prior works is that the contextual features used were typically shallow (location), while we cap-

Proceedings of NAACL-HLT 2016, pages 1424–1430,
San Diego, California, June 12-17, 2016. ©2016 Association for Computational Linguistics

Draft 1	Draft 2
[1] Writer Richard Louv tells us to focus more on nature through his *rhetorical questions*, parallelism, and pathos. **[2]** *Louvs rhetorical questions as us whether we value technology or nature over the other.*	**[1]** Writer Richard Louv emphasises this expanding chasm between people and nature and tries to convince people to go back to nature through his parallelism and pathos.
[First Revision: 1->1,Type: Claim, Modify], [Second Revision: 2->null,Type: Warrant, Delete]	

Table 1: Example dependency between *Claim* and *Warrant* revisions. Sentence 1 acts as the *Claim* (argument structure) of Draft 1 and sentence 2 acts as the *Warrant* for the *Claim*. Sentence 1 in Draft 1 is modified to sentence 1 (also acts as the *Claim*) of Draft 2. Sentence 2 in Draft 1 is deleted in Draft 2. The first revision is a *Claim* revision as it modifies the *Claim* of the paper by removing "rhetorical questions." This leads to the second *Warrant* revision, which deletes the *Warrant* for "rhetorical questions."

ture additional contextual information as text cohesion/coherence changes and revision dependencies.

As our task focuses on identifying the argumentative purpose of writing revisions, work in argument mining is also relevant. In fact, many features for predicting argument structure (e.g., location, discourse connectives, punctuation) (Burstein and Marcu, 2003; Moens et al., 2007; Palau and Moens, 2009; Feng and Hirst, 2011) are also used in revision classification. In addition, Lawrence et al. (2014) use changes in topic to detect argumentation, which leads us to hypothesize that different types of argumentative revisions will have different impacts on text cohesion and coherence. Guo et al. (2011) and Park et al. (2015) both utilize Conditional Random Fields (CRFs) for identifying argumentative structures. While we focus on the different task of identifying revisions to argumentation, we similarly hypothesize that dependencies exist between revisions and thus utilize CRFs in our task. While our task is similar to argument mining, a key difference is that the revisions do not always appear near each other. For example, a 5-paragraph long essay might have only two or three revisions located at different paragraphs. Thus, the types of previous revisions cannot always be used as the contextual information. Moreover, the type of the revision is not necessarily the argument type of its revised sentence. For example, a revision on the evidence argument can be just a correction of spelling mistakes.

3   Data Description

Revision purposes. To label our data, we adapt the schema defined in (Zhang and Litman, 2015) as it can be reliably annotated and is argument-

Category	# in A	# in B
Total	1267	1044
Claims/Ideas	111	76
Warrant/Reasoning/Backing	390	327
Evidence	110	34
General Content	356	216
Surface	300	391

Table 2: Distribution of revisions in Corpus A, B.

oriented. Sentences across paper drafts are aligned manually based on semantic similarity and revision purpose categories are labeled on aligned sentences. The schema includes four categories (*Claims/Ideas, Warrant/Reasoning/Backing, Rebuttal/Reservation* and *Evidence*) based on Toulmin's argumentation model (Toulmin, 2003), a *General Content* category for revisions that do not directly change the support/rebuttal of the claim (e.g. addition of introductory materials, conclusions, etc.), and three categories (*Conventions, Clarity* and *Organization*) based on the *Surface* categorizations in (Faigley and Witte, 1981). As we focus on argumentative changes, we merge all the *Surface* subcategories into one *Surface* category. As Zhang and Litman (2015) reported that both *Rebuttals* and multiple labels for a single revision were rare, we merge *Rebuttal* and *Warrant* into one *Warrant* category[1] and allow only a single (primary) label per revision.

Corpora. Our experiments use two corpora consisting of Drafts 1 and 2 of papers written by high school students taking AP-English courses; papers were revised after receiving and generating peer feedback. Corpus A was collected in our earlier pa-

---

[1]We also believe that differentiating *Warrant* and *Rebuttal* revisions requires sentiment analysis.

per (Zhang and Litman, 2015), although the original annotations were modified as described above. It contains 47 paper draft pairs about placing contemporaries in Dante's Inferno. Corpus B was collected in the same manor as A with agreement Kappa 0.69. It contains 63 paper draft pairs explaining the rhetorical strategies used by the speaker/author of a previously read lecture/essay. Both corpora were double coded and gold standard labels were created upon agreement of two annotators. Two example annotated revisions from Corpus B are shown in Table 1, while the distribution of annotated revision purposes for both corpora are shown in Table 2.

4 Utilizing Context

4.1 Adding contextual features

Our previous work (Zhang and Litman, 2015) used three types of features primarily from prior work (Adler et al., 2011; Bronner and Monz, 2012; Daxenberger and Gurevych, 2013) for argumentative revision classification. **Location** features encode the location of the sentence in the paragraph and the location of the sentence's paragraph in the essay. **Textual** features encode revision operation, sentence length, edit distance between aligned sentences and the difference in sentence length and punctuation numbers. **Language** features encode part of speech (POS) unigrams and difference in POS tag counts.

We implement this feature set as the baseline as our tasks are similar, then propose two new types of contextual features. The first type (**Ext**) extends prior work by extracting the baseline features from not only the aligned sentence pair representing the revision in question, but also for the sentence pairs before and after the revision. The second type (**Coh**) measures the cohesion and coherence changes in a 2-sentence block around the revision[2].

Utilizing the cohesion and coherence difference. Inspired by (Lee et al., 2015; Vaughan and McDonald, 1986), we hypothesize that different revisions can have different impacts on the cohesion and coherence of the essay. We propose to extract features for both impact on cohesion (lexical) and impact on coherence (semantic). Inspired by (Hearst, 1997), sequences of blocks are created for sentences

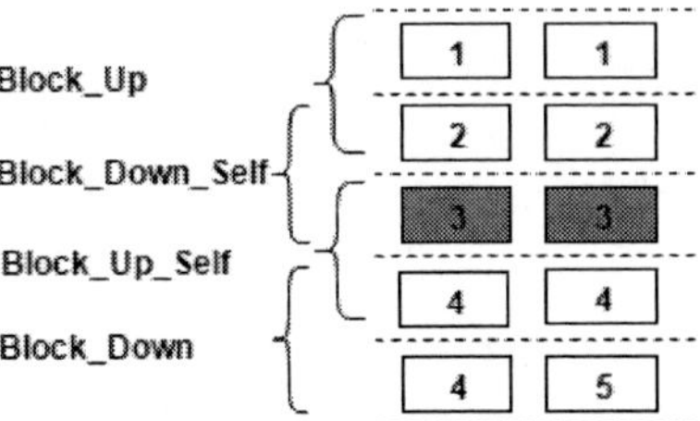

Figure 1: Example of cohesion blocks. A window of size 2 is created for both Draft 1 and Draft 2. Sequence of blocks were created by moving the window at the step of 1 (sentence).

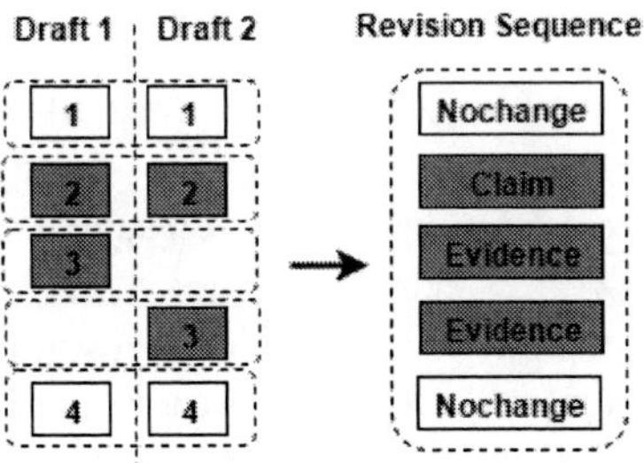

Figure 2: Example of revision sequence transformation. Each square corresponds to a sentence in the essay, the number of the square represents the index of the sentence in the essay. Dark squares are sentences that are changed. In the example, the 2nd sentence of Draft 1 is modified, the 3rd sentence is deleted and a new sentence is added in Draft 2.

in both Draft 1 and Draft 2 as demonstrated in Figure 1. Two types of features are extracted. The first type describes the cohesion and coherence between the revised sentence and its adjacent sentences. The similarity (lexical/semantic) between the revised sentence block and the sentence block before ($Sim(Block\_Up, Block\_Up\_Self)$) and after ($Sim(Block\_Down, Block\_Down\_Self)$) are calculated as the cohesion/coherence scores Coh_Up and Coh_Down. The features are extracted separately for Draft 1 and Draft 2 sentences[3]. The second type describes the impact of sentence modification on cohesion and coherence[4]. Features Change_Up and Change_Down are extracted as the division of the cohesion/coherence scores of two drafts ($\frac{Coh\_Up(Draft2)}{Coh\_Up(Draft1)}$, $\frac{Coh\_Down(Draft2)}{Coh\_Down(Draft1)}$).

A bag-of-word representation is generated for

---

[2]In this paper we consider the most adjacent sentence only.

[3]For the added and deleted sentences, features of the empty sentence in the other draft are set to 0.

[4]The feature values of sentence additions/deletions are 0.

		SVM				CRFs			
		Base(B)	B+Ext	B+Coh	All	B	B+Ext	B+Coh	All
A	**P**	0.666	0.689	0.673	0.684	0.682	**0.703**∗	0.686	0.701∗
	R	0.620	0.632	0.630	0.630	0.633	**0.642**∗	0.635	0.642∗
	F	0.615	0.630	0.619	0.626	0.632	**0.644**∗	0.633	0.643∗
B	**P**	0.530	0.543	0.559 ∗	0.553∗	0.598∗	0.615 ∗	0.639∗	**0.655**∗
	R	0.516	0.525	0.534	0.532	0.518	0.524	0.532	0.532
	F	0.502	0.510	0.524 ∗	0.520∗	0.550∗	0.559∗	0.573∗	**0.584**∗

Table 3: The average of 10-fold (student) cross-validation results on Corpora A and B. Unweighted precision (P), Unweighted recall (R) and Unweighted F-measure (F) are reported. Results of CRFs on paragraph-level segments are reported (there is no significant difference between essay level and paragraph level). ∗ indicates significantly better than the baseline, **Bold** indicates significantly better than all other results (Paired T-test, $p < 0.05$).

each sentence block after stop-word filtering and stemming. Jaccard similarity is used for the calculation of lexical similarity between sentence blocks. Word embedding vectors (Mikolov et al., 2013) are used for the calculation of semantic similarity. A vector is calculated for each sentence block by summing up the embedding vectors of words that are not stop-words[5]. Afterwards the similarity is calculated as the cosine similarity between the block vectors. This approach has been taken by multiple groups in the SemEval-2015 semantic similarity task (SemEval-2015 Task 1)(Xu et al., 2015).

4.2 Transforming to sequence labeling

To capture dependencies among predicted revisions, we transform the revisions to a consecutive sequence and label it with Conditional Random Fields (CRFs) as demonstrated in Figure 2. For both drafts, sentences are sorted according to their order of occurrence in the essay. Aligned sentences are put into the same row and each aligned pair of sentences is treated as a unit of revision. The "cross-aligned" pairs of sentences[6] (which does not often occur) are broken into deleted and added sentences (i.e, the cross-aligned sentences in Draft 1 are treated as deleted and the sentences in Draft 2 are treated as added.). After generating the sequence, each revision unit in the sequence is assigned the revision purpose label according to the annotations, with unchanged sentence pairs labeled as *Nochange*.

We conducted labeling on both essay-level and paragraph-level sequences. The essay-level treats the whole essay as a sequence segment while the paragraph-level treats each paragraph as a segment. After labeling, the label of each changed sentence pair is marked as the purpose of the revision[7].

5 Experiments and Results

Our prior work (Zhang and Litman, 2014) proposed an approach for the alignment of sentences. The approach achieves 92% accuracy on both corpora. In this paper we focus on the prediction task and assume we have gold-standard sentence alignments[8]. The first four columns of Table 3 show the performance of baseline features with and without our new contextual features using an SVM prediction model[9]. The last four columns show the performance of CRFs[10]. All experiments are conducted using 10-fold (student) cross-validation with 300 features selected using learning gain ratio[11].

For the SVM approach, we observe that the **Coh** features yield a significant improvement over the baseline features in Corpus B, and a non-significant improvement in Corpus A. This indicates that changes in text cohesion and coherence can in-

---

[5]We also tried the average of embedding vectors but observed no significant difference between the two approaches.

[6]Sentences in Draft 1 switched their positions in Draft 2, the cross-aligned sentences cannot be both in the same row and following their order of occurrence at the same time.

[7]Revisions on cross-aligned pairs are marked as *Surface*.

[8]Similar to settings in (Daxenberger and Gurevych, 2013)

[9]We compared three models used in discourse analysis and revision classification (C4.5 Decision Tree, SVM and Random Forests) (Burstein et al., 2003; Bronner and Monz, 2012; Stab and Gurevych, 2014) and SVM yielded the best performance.

[10]SVM model implemented with Weka (Hall et al., 2009) and CRF model implemented with CRFSuite (Okazaki, 2007)

[11]We tested with parameters 100, 200, 300, 500 on a development dataset disjoint from Corpora A and B and chose 300 which yielded the best performance.

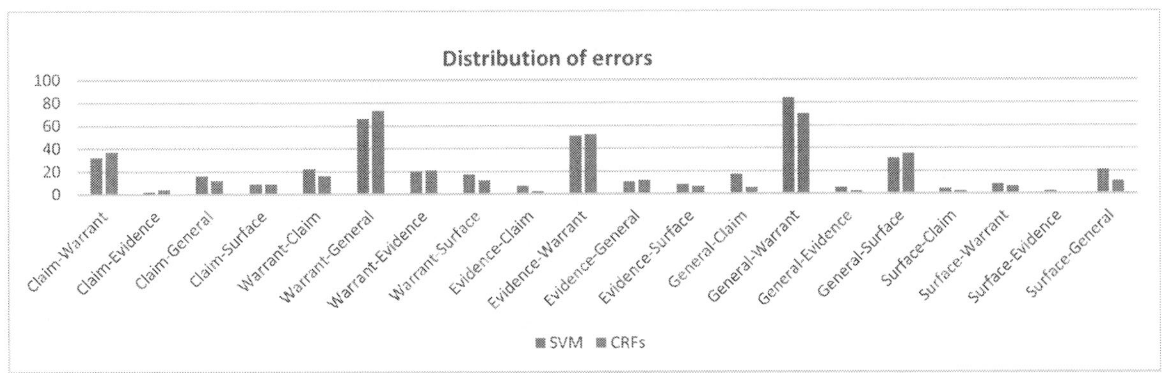

Figure 3: The number of classification errors on Corpus A, "Warrant-General" represents classifying *Warrant* as *General*.

deed improve the prediction of argumentative revision types. The **Ext** feature set - which computes features for not only the revision but also its immediately adjacent sentences - also yields a slight (although not significant) improvement. However, adding the two feature sets together does not further improve the performance using the SVM model. The CRF approach almost always yields the best results for both corpora, with all such CRF results better than all other results. This indicates that dependencies exist among argumentative revisions that cannot be identified with traditional classification approaches.

6 Error Analysis

To have a better understanding of how the sequence labeling approach improves the classification performance, we counted the errors of the cross-validation results on Corpus A (where the revisions are more evenly distributed). Figure 3 demonstrates the comparison of errors made by SVM and CRFs[12].

We notice that the CRF approach makes less errors than the SVM approach in recognizing *Claim* changes (*General-Claim, Evidence-Claim, Warrant-Claim, Surface-Claim*). This matches our intuition that there exists dependency between revisions on supporting materials and revisions on *Claim*. We also observe that same problems exist in both approaches. The biggest difficulty is the differentiation between *General* and *Warrant* revisions, which counts 37.6% of the SVM errors and 40.1% of CRFs errors. It is also common that *Claim* and *Evidence*

___
[12]Both use models with all the features.

revisions are classified as *Warrant* revisions. Approaches need to be designed for such cases to further improve the classification performance.

7 Conclusion

In this paper we proposed different methods for utilizing contextual information when predicting the argumentative purpose of revisions in student writing. Adding features that captured changes in text cohesion and coherence, as well as using sequence modeling to capture revision dependencies, both significantly improved predictive performance in an experimental evaluation.

In the future, we plan to investigate whether performance can be further improved when more sentences in the context are included. Also, we plan to investigate whether revision dependencies exist in other types of corpora such as Wikipedia revisions. While the corpora used in this study cannot be published because of the lack of required IRB, we are starting a user study project (Zhang et al., 2016) on the application of our proposed techniques and will publish the data collected from this project.

Acknowledgments

We would like to thank our annotators, especially Jiaoyang Li, who contributed significantly to the building of our corpus. We also want to thank the members of the SWoRD and ITSPOKE groups for their helpful feedback and all the anonymous reviewers for their suggestions. This research is funded by the Learning Research and Development Center of the University of Pittsburgh.

References

B. Thomas Adler, Luca De Alfaro, Santiago M. Mola-Velasco, Paolo Rosso, and Andrew G. West. 2011. Wikipedia vandalism detection: Combining natural language, metadata, and reputation features. In *Proceedings of the 12th International Conference on Computational Linguistics and Intelligent Text Processing - Volume Part II*, CICLing'11, pages 277–288, Berlin, Heidelberg. Springer-Verlag.

Amit Bronner and Christof Monz. 2012. User edits classification using document revision histories. In *Proceedings of the 13th Conference of the European Chapter of the Association for Computational Linguistics*, pages 356–366. Association for Computational Linguistics.

Jill Burstein and Daniel Marcu. 2003. A machine learning approach for identification thesis and conclusion statements in student essays. *Computers and the Humanities*, 37(4):455–467.

Jill Burstein, Daniel Marcu, and Kevin Knight. 2003. Finding the write stuff: Automatic identification of discourse structure in student essays. *Intelligent Systems, IEEE*, 18(1):32–39.

Johannes Daxenberger and Iryna Gurevych. 2013. Automatically classifying edit categories in Wikipedia revisions. In *Proceedings of the 2013 Conference on Empirical Methods in Natural Language Processing*, pages 578–589, Seattle, Washington, USA, October. Association for Computational Linguistics.

Lester Faigley and Stephen Witte. 1981. Analyzing revision. *College composition and communication*, pages 400–414.

Vanessa Wei Feng and Graeme Hirst. 2011. Classifying arguments by scheme. In *Proceedings of the 49th Annual Meeting of the Association for Computational Linguistics: Human Language Technologies-Volume 1*, pages 987–996. Association for Computational Linguistics.

Yufan Guo, Anna Korhonen, and Thierry Poibeau. 2011. A weakly-supervised approach to argumentative zoning of scientific documents. In *Proceedings of the Conference on Empirical Methods in Natural Language Processing*, pages 273–283. Association for Computational Linguistics.

Mark Hall, Eibe Frank, Geoffrey Holmes, Bernhard Pfahringer, Peter Reutemann, and Ian H Witten. 2009. The weka data mining software: an update. *ACM SIGKDD explorations newsletter*, 11(1):10–18.

Marti A Hearst. 1997. Texttiling: Segmenting text into multi-paragraph subtopic passages. *Computational linguistics*, 23(1):33–64.

Sara Javanmardi, David W McDonald, and Cristina V Lopes. 2011. Vandalism detection in wikipedia: a high-performing, feature-rich model and its reduction through lasso. In *Proceedings of the 7th International Symposium on Wikis and Open Collaboration*, pages 82–90. ACM.

John Lawrence, Chris Reed, Colin Allen, Simon McAlister, and Andrew Ravenscroft. 2014. Mining arguments from 19th century philosophical texts using topic based modelling. In *Proceedings of the First Workshop on Argumentation Mining*, pages 79–87, Baltimore, Maryland, June. Association for Computational Linguistics.

John Lee, Chak Yan Yeung, Amir Zeldes, Marc Reznicek, Anke Lüdeling, and Jonathan Webster. 2015. Cityu corpus of essay drafts of english language learners: a corpus of textual revision in second language writing. *Language Resources and Evaluation*, pages 1–25.

Tomas Mikolov, Ilya Sutskever, Kai Chen, Greg S Corrado, and Jeff Dean. 2013. Distributed representations of words and phrases and their compositionality. In *Advances in neural information processing systems*, pages 3111–3119.

Marie-Francine Moens, Erik Boiy, Raquel Mochales Palau, and Chris Reed. 2007. Automatic detection of arguments in legal texts. In *Proceedings of the 11th international conference on Artificial intelligence and law*, pages 225–230. ACM.

Naoaki Okazaki. 2007. Crfsuite: a fast implementation of conditional random fields (crfs).

Raquel Mochales Palau and Marie-Francine Moens. 2009. Argumentation mining: the detection, classification and structure of arguments in text. In *Proceedings of the 12th international conference on artificial intelligence and law*, pages 98–107. ACM.

Joonsuk Park, Arzoo Katiyar, and Bishan Yang. 2015. Conditional random fields for identifying appropriate types of support for propositions in online user comments. In *Proceedings of the 2nd Workshop on Argumentation Mining*, pages 39–44, Denver, CO, June. Association for Computational Linguistics.

Rod D Roscoe, Erica L Snow, Laura K Allen, and Danielle S McNamara. 2015. Automated detection of essay revising patterns: applications for intelligent feedback in a writing tutor. *Technology, Instruction, Cognition, and Learning*.

Christian Stab and Iryna Gurevych. 2014. Identifying argumentative discourse structures in persuasive essays. In *EMNLP*, pages 46–56.

Christian Stab, Christian Kirschner, Judith Eckle-Kohler, and Iryna Gurevych. 2014. Argumentation mining in persuasive essays and scientific articles from the discourse structure perspective. *Frontiers and Connections between Argumentation Theory and Natural Language Processing, Bertinoro, Italy*.

Simone Teufel. 2000. *Argumentative zoning: Information extraction from scientific text*. Ph.D. thesis, Citeseer.

Stephen E Toulmin. 2003. *The uses of argument*. Cambridge University Press.

Marie M Vaughan and David D McDonald. 1986. A model of revision in natural language generation. In *Proceedings of the 24th annual meeting on Association for Computational Linguistics*, pages 90–96. Association for Computational Linguistics.

Writelab. 2015. WriteLab. http://home.writelab.com. [Online; accessed 10-03-2015].

Wei Xu, Chris Callison-Burch, and William B Dolan. 2015. Semeval-2015 task 1: Paraphrase and semantic similarity in twitter (pit). In *Proceedings of the 9th International Workshop on Semantic Evaluation (SemEval)*.

Fan Zhang and Diane Litman. 2014. Sentence-level rewriting detection. In *Proceedings of the Ninth Workshop on Innovative Use of NLP for Building Educational Applications*, pages 149–154, Baltimore, Maryland, June. Association for Computational Linguistics.

Fan Zhang and Diane Litman. 2015. Annotation and classification of argumentative writing revisions. In *Proceedings of the Tenth Workshop on Innovative Use of NLP for Building Educational Applications*, pages 133–143, Denver, Colorado, June. Association for Computational Linguistics.

Fan Zhang, Rebecca Hwa, Diane Litman, and Huma Hashemi. 2016. Argrewrite: A web-based revision assistant for argumentative writings. In *Proceedings of the 2016 Conference of the North American Chapter of the Association for Computational Linguistics: Demonstrations*, San Diego, California, June. Association for Computational Linguistics.

Automatic Generation and Scoring of Positive Interpretations from Negated Statements

Eduardo Blanco and **Zahra Sarabi**
Human Intelligence and Language Technologies Lab
University of North Texas
Denton, TX, 76203
eduardo.blanco@unt.edu, zahrasarabi@my.unt.edu

Abstract

This paper presents a methodology to extract positive interpretations from negated statements. First, we automatically generate plausible interpretations using well-known grammar rules and manipulating semantic roles. Second, we score plausible alternatives according to their likelihood. Manual annotations show that the positive interpretations are intuitive to humans, and experimental results show that the scoring task can be automated.

1 Introduction

Negation is an intricate phenomenon present in all human languages (Hoeksema, 2000), and studied from a theoretical perspective since Aristotle. Acquiring and understanding negation is more challenging than language in general: children acquire negation after learning to communicate (Nordmeyer and Frank, 2013), and adults take longer to process negative sentences than positive ones (Clark and Chase, 1972). In any given language, humans communicate in positive terms most of the time, and use negation to express something unusual or an exception (Horn, 1989).

In classical logic, negation is a simple unary operator that reverses the truth value of a proposition. In natural language, negation is always marked (Horn and Wansing, 2015) and it is used to reverse polarity, i.e., turning something affirmative into negative, or something negative into affirmative. Albeit most sentences are affirmative, negation is rather ubiquitous (Morante and Sporleder, 2012): In scientific papers, 13.76% of statements contain a negation (Szarvas et al., 2008); in product reviews, 19% (Councill et al., 2010); and in a selection of Conan Doyle stories, 22.23% (Morante and Daelemans, 2012). In health records, 12.3% of concepts are tagged as negated (Elkin et al., 2005); and in OntoNotes (Hovy et al., 2006), 10.15% of statements contain a verb negated with *not, n't* or *never*.

From a theoretical perspective, it is accepted that negation conveys positive meaning (Rooth, 1992; Huddleston and Pullum, 2002). For example, when reading (1) *John doesn't eat meat*, humans intuitively understand that (1a) *John eats something other than meat*, and (1b) *Some people eat meat, but not John*. Extracting positive interpretations from negated statements automatically is not straightforward: a negated statement may convey one or more positive interpretations, and not all positive interpretations are equally likely. For example, from (2) *They didn't order the right parts*, it is very likely that (2a) *They ordered the wrong parts*, but (2b) *Somebody ordered the right parts, but not they* is unlikely.

This paper presents a methodology to automatically extract and score positive interpretations from negated statements, as intuitively done by humans when reading text. A key feature of the work presented here is that it is not tied to any existing approach to extract meaning from text—we generate positive interpretations in plain text, and these positive interpretations can be semantically represented with any existing approach. The main contributions are: (1) procedure to automatically generate plausible positive interpretations from negated statements, (2) annotations scoring plausible positive interpretations,[1] and (3) experiments detailing results with several combinations of features, as well as gold-standard and predicted linguistic information.

---

[1] Available at http://hilt.cse.unt.edu/

Proceedings of NAACL-HLT 2016, pages 1431–1441,
San Diego, California, June 12-17, 2016. ©2016 Association for Computational Linguistics

2 Background and Definitions

Negation is well-understood in grammars, the valid ways to form a negation are well-documented (Quirk et al., 2000; van der Wouden, 1997). Negation can be expressed by verbs (e.g., <u>avoid</u> doing any look-up), nouns (e.g., the <u>absence</u> of any phonic sequence), adjectives (e.g., it is <u>pointless</u> to argue with a fool), adverbs (e.g., I <u>never</u> tried Persian food before), prepositions (e.g., you can always exchange it <u>without</u> a problem), determiners (e.g., the new law has <u>no</u> direct implications to international shipping), pronouns (e.g., <u>nobody</u> will keep election promises).

Huddleston and Pullum (2002) distinguish four negation types:

- Verbal if the marker of negation is grammatically associated with a verb, e.g., *I did <u>not</u> see anything*, non-verbal if it is associated with a dependent of the verb, e.g., *I saw <u>nothing</u>*.
- Synthetic if the negation mark has a function besides marking a negation, e.g., *[<u>Nobody</u>]*_{AGENT} *liked it*, analytic otherwise, e.g., *<u>Not</u> many people liked it*.
- Clausal if the negation yields a negative clause, e.g., *The terms <u>aren't</u> negotiable*, subclausal otherwise, e.g., *The terms are <u>non</u>-negotiable*.
- Ordinary if the negation indicates that something is not the case, e.g., *That car does <u>not</u> drive smooth*, metalinguistic if it does not dispute the truth but rather reformulates a statement, e.g., *That TV is <u>not</u> small, it is tiny*.

In this paper, we target verbal, analytic, clausal and both ordinary and metalinguistic negation.

2.1 Positive Interpretations.

In philosophy and linguistics, it is generally accepted that negation conveys positive meanings (Horn, 1989). These positive meanings range from implicatures, i.e., what is suggested in an utterance even though neither expressed nor strictly implied (Blackburn, 2008), to entailments. Other terms used in the literature include implied meanings (Mitkov, 2005), implied alternatives (Rooth, 1985) and semantically similars (Agirre et al., 2013). We do not strictly fit into any of this terminology, we reveal positive interpretations as intuitively done by humans when reading text.

2.2 Scope and Focus.

From a theoretical perspective, it is accepted that negation has scope and focus, and that the focus—not just the scope—yields positive interpretations (Horn, 1989; Rooth, 1992; Taglicht, 1984). Scope is "the part of the meaning that is negated" and focus "the part of the scope that is most prominently or explicitly negated" (Huddleston and Pullum, 2002).

Consider the following statement in the context of the recent refuge crisis: (3) *Mr. Haile was <u>not</u> looking for heaven in Europe*. By definition, scope refers to "all elements whose individual falsity would make the negated statement strictly true", and focus is "the element of the scope that is intended to be interpreted as false to make the overall negative true" (Huddleston and Pullum, 2002). The falsity of any of the truth conditions below makes statement (3) true, thus the scope of the negation is (3a–3d):

3a. Somebody was looking for something somewhere. [verb *looking*]
3b. Mr. Haile was looking for something somewhere. [AGENT of looking, *Mr. Haile*]
3c. Somebody was looking for heaven somewhere. [THEME of looking, *heaven*]
3d. Somebody was looking for something in Europe. [LOCATION of looking, *in Europe*]

Determining the focus is almost always more challenging than the scope. The challenge lies on determining which of the truth conditions (3a–3d) is intended to be interpreted as false to make the negated statement true: all of them qualify, but some are more likely. A natural reading of statement (3) suggests that *Mr. Haile was looking for something (a regular life, a job, etc.) in Europe, but not heaven*. Determining that the focus is *heaven*, i.e., that everything in statement (3) is actually positive except the THEME of *looking*, is the key to reveal the intended positive interpretation. It is worth noting that other foci yield unlikely interpretations, e.g., *Somebody was looking for heaven in Europe, but not Mr. Haile* (3b, AGENT), *Mr. Haile was looking for heaven somewhere, but not in Europe* (3d, LOCATION). Note that (1) scope on its own does not yield positive interpretations, and (2) some negated statements convey several likely positive interpretations, e.g., statement (1) in Section 5, Table 3.

3 Previous Work

Within computational linguistics, approaches to process negation are shallow, or target scope and focus detection. Popular semantic representations such as semantic roles (Palmer et al., 2005; Baker et al., 1998) or AMR (Banarescu et al., 2013) do not reveal the positive interpretations we target in this paper. Shallow approaches are usually application-specific. In sentiment and opinion analysis, negation has been reduced to marking as negated all words between a negation cue and the first punctuation mark (Pang et al., 2002), or within a five-word window of a negation cue (Hu and Liu, 2004). The examples throughout this paper show that these techniques are insufficient to reveal implicit positive interpretations.

3.1 Scope Annotation and Detection

Scope of negation detection has received a lot of attention, mostly using two corpora: BioScope in the medical domain (Szarvas et al., 2008) and CD-SCO (Morante and Daelemans, 2012). BioScope annotates negation cues and linguistic scopes exclusively in biomedical texts. CD-SCO annotates negation cues, scopes, and negated events or properties in selected Conan Doyle stories.

There have been several supervised proposals to detect the scope of negation using BioScope and CD-SCO (Özgür and Radev, 2009; Øvrelid et al., 2010). Automatic approaches are mature (Abu-Jbara and Radev, 2012): F-scores are 0.96 for negation cue detection, and 0.89 for negation cue and scope detection (Velldal et al., 2012; Li et al., 2010). Outside BioScope and CD-SCO, Reitan et al. (2015) present a negation scope detector for tweets, and show that it improves sentiment analysis. As shown in Section 2, scope detection is insufficient to reveal positive interpretations from negated statements.

3.2 Focus Annotation and Detection

While focus of negation has been studied for decades in philosophy and linguistics (Section 2), corpora and automated tools are scarce. Blanco and Moldovan (2011) annotate focus of negation in the 3,993 negations marked with ARGM-NEG semantic role in PropBank (Palmer et al., 2005). Their annotations, PB-FOC, were used in the *SEM-2012 Shared Task (Morante and Blanco, 2012). Their guidelines require annotators to choose as focus the semantic role that "is most prominently negated" or the verb. If several roles may be the focus, they prioritize "the one that yields the most meaningful implicit [positive] information", but do not specify what *most meaningful* means. Consider again statement (1) *John doesn't eat meat.* Their approach would determine that the focus is the THEME of *eat*, *meat*, because it arguably yields the "most meaningful implicit [positive] information" (using our terminology, positive interpretation): *John eats something other than meat.* By design, they ignore other valid positive interpretations, e.g., *Some people eat meat, but not John.* In this paper, we improve upon their work: instead of extracting the "most meaningful" positive interpretation from a negated statement, we generate several positive interpretations and score them according to their likelihood.

Anand and Martell (2012) present a complimentary approach to annotate focus of negation. They refine PB-FOC and argue that positive interpretations arising from scalar implicatures and neg-raising predicates should be separated from those arising from focus detection. According to their annotations, 27.4% of negations with a focus annotated in PB-FOC do not actually have a focus. Blanco and Moldovan (2012) introduce the concept of fine-grained foci and refine the annotations in PB-FOC by annotating foci at the token level, and Matsuyoshi et al. (2014) annotate focus of negation in Japanese. In this paper, we are not concerned about annotating focus of negation per se, but about extracting positive interpretations from negated statements as intuitively understood by humans.

Automatic systems to detect the focus of negation (and reveal up to one positive interpretation) in English texts are trained using PB-FOC. Blanco and Moldovan (2011) obtain an accuracy of 65.5 using supervised machine learning and features derived from gold-standard linguistic information, and Blanco and Moldovan (2014) report an F-measure of 64.1. Rosenberg and Bergler (2012) report an F-measure of 58.4 using 4 linguistically sound heuristics and predicted linguistic information, and Zou et al. (2014) an F-measure of 65.62 using contextual discourse information. Unlike the work presented here, none of these systems attempts to extract and rank several positive interpretations from one negated statement.

Neg. statement		In 1995, Murdoch bought [the rest of Star TV]$_{\text{ARG}_1}$ that [he]$_{\text{ARG}_0}$ did [not]$_{\text{ARGM-NEG}}$ [own]$_{verb}$
Positive counterpart	after Step 1	In 1995, Murdoch bought the rest of Star TV that he did own
	after Step 2	In 1995, Murdoch bought the rest of Star TV that he owned
	after Step 3	In 1995, Murdoch bought the rest of Star TV that he owned (no change)
Plausible positive interpretations	from ARG$_0$	In 1995, Murdoch bought the rest of Star TV that [somebody] owned, but not *he*
	from ARG$_1$	In 1995, Murdoch bought [something] that he owned, but not *the rest of Star TV*
	from *verb*	In 1995, Murdoch bought the rest of Star TV that he [some verb], but not *owned*

Table 1: Negated statement, and automatically generated positive counterpart and plausible positive interpretations.

4   Corpus Creation

Our goal is to create a corpus of negated statements and their positive interpretations as intuitively understood by humans. We put a strong emphasis on automation. First, given a negated statement, we automatically generate plausible positive interpretations following a battery of linguistically motivated deterministic rules (Section 4.1). Second, we collect manual annotation to score the plausible positive interpretations according to their likelihood (Section 4.2). We then use these manually obtained scores to learn models that automatically score positive interpretations (Section 6).

We decided to work on top of OntoNotes (Hovy et al., 2006) instead of plain text or other corpora for several reasons. First, OntoNotes includes gold linguistic annotations such as part-of-speech tags, parse trees and semantic roles. Second, state-of-the-art role labelers trained with Propbank achieve F-measures of 0.835 (Lewis et al., 2015), and we use semantic roles to generate positive interpretations. Third, unlike BioScope, CD-SCO and PB-FOC (Section 2), OntoNotes includes sentences from several genres, e.g., newswire, broadcast news and conversations, magazines, the web.

4.1   Generating Positive Interpretations

OntoNotes[2] is a large corpus containing 63,918 sentences. Annotating all positive interpretations from all negations is outside of the scope of this paper. Instead, we target selected representative negations.
Selecting Negated Statements. We first selected all verbs negated with ARGM-NEG semantic role and obtained 6,617 verbal negations. After examining the negated verbs, it became clear that negation is not uniformly distributed across verbs in OntoNotes,

it roughly follows Zipf's law. In order to alleviate the annotation effort while accounting for all negated verbs in OntoNotes, we randomly selected up to 5 negations for each verb. The number of negated statements selected is 600.
Converting Negated Statements into Their Positive Counterparts. We apply 3 steps inspired after the grammatical rules to form negation detailed by Huddleston and Pullum (2002, Ch. 9):

1. Remove the negation mark by removing the tokens within ARGM-NEG semantic role.
2. Remove auxiliaries, expand contractions, and fix third-person singular and past tense. For example (before: after), *doesn't go: goes, didn't go: went, won't go: will go*, We use a standard list of irregular verbs,[3] and grammar rules to convert to third-person singular and past tense based on orthographic patterns.
3. Rewrite negatively-oriented polarity-sensitive items. For example (before: after), *anyone: someone, any longer: still, yet: already. at all: somewhat*. We use the correspondences between negatively-oriented and positively-oriented polarity-sensitive items by Huddleston and Pullum (2002, pp. 831).

Generating Positive Interpretations. Once the positive counterpart is obtained, we generate positive interpretations by rewriting each semantic role or the (originally negated) verb. Among others, we use the following rewriting rules: ARG$_0$–ARG$_4$: someone / some people / something, ARGM-TMP: at some point of time, ARGM-LOC: somewhere, ARGM-MNR: in some manner, ARGM-CAU: because of something and ARGM-PRP: to do something. Additionally, if the semantic role starts with a preposition, we also include it, e.g., *gave [to John]*$_{\text{ARG}_2}$:

---

[2]We use the CoNLL-2011 Shared Task distribution (Pradhan et al., 2011), http://conll.cemantix.org/2011/

[3]https://en.wikipedia.org/wiki/English_irregular_verbs

gave to someone, but not John. This methodology generated 1,888 positive interpretations from the 600 selected negations (average: 3.15).

Table 1 exemplifies the 3 steps to transform a negated statement into its positive counterpart, and the positive interpretations generated. Additional examples are provided in Table 3.

We acknowledge that some of the positive interpretations we generate automatically are not as specific or intuitive as carefully crafted, manually generated interpretations could be. For example, from $[John]_{ARG_0}$ $does[n't]_{ARGM\text{-}NEG}$ $[know]_{verb}$ $[the\ details\ about\ how\ they\ met]_{ARG_1}$, the proposed methodology would generate, among others, *John knows about something, but not about the details of how they met.* A better interpretations that we do not generate is *John knows something about how they met, but not the details.* We argue that generating interpretations automatically is the only option in order to incorporate this work into an NLP pipeline, and reserve for future work generating positive interpretations beyond rewriting semantic roles.

4.2 Ranking Positive Interpretations

Once positive interpretations were automatically generated, we asked annotators to rank them. Annotators were presented with one negated statement and one positive interpretation at a time, and were asked *Given the negated statement above, do you think the statement [positive interpretation] below is true?* They only had access to the text in the original negated statement, the positive interpretation, and the previous and next sentences as context. We did not display semantic role information for the original negated statement, its positive counterpart or the semantic role from which the positive interpretation was generated. As we shall see (Section 5.1), context often helps scoring interpretations.

Annotators were required to answer with a score from 0 to 5, were 0 means *absolutely disagree* and 5 means *absolutely agree*. We did not provide descriptions for intermediate scores or used additional categorical labels. This simple guidelines were sufficient to reliably score plausible positive interpretations automatically generated.

Sem. role	#	% sent	Mean	SD
ARG_0	392	65.17%	4.07	1.03
ARG_1	520	86.00%	4.55	0.98
ARG_2	95	15.83%	4.40	1.31
ARG_3	2	0.33%	4.50	0.50
ARG_4	5	0.83%	5.00	0.00
ARGM-ADV	101	15.67%	2.41	1.72
ARGM-CAU	13	2.17%	2.46	1.91
ARGM-DIR	11	1.83%	2.00	2.30
ARGM-EXT	12	2.00%	3.75	1.53
ARGM-LOC	21	3.33%	3.76	1.69
ARGM-MNR	37	6.00%	4.54	1.03
ARGM-PRP	7	1.16%	4.43	0.71
ARGM-TMP	81	12.50%	3.99	1.52
Verb	600	100.00%	2.17	1.41
All	1,888	100.00%	3.52	1.63

Table 2: Basic corpus analysis. For each semantic role, we show the number of positive interpretations generated (#), the percentage of sentences for which a positive interpretation is generated (% sent), and the mean and standard deviation (SD) of the annotated scores.

5 Corpus Analysis

On average, we generated 3.15 positive interpretations per negation (standard deviation: 0.82), and 74% of negations have at least one interpretation scored 4 or higher. Basic counts and statistics for the annotations are provided in Table 2. Overall, we annotated 1,888 positive interpretations generated from 600 sentences, or equivalently, from 600 verbs negated with ARGM-NEG semantic role in OntoNotes. Overall mean score is 3.52 (out of 5) and overall standard deviation, 1.63. The 25th percentile is 2.0, the 50th percentile is 4.0 and the 75th percentile is 5.0. These numbers show that most positive interpretations automatically generated are deemed likely by annotators, and over 25% are scored with a 5 (out of 5).

In general, positive interpretations generated from numbered roles (ARG_0–ARG_4) are scored higher than the ones generated from modifiers (ARGM-ADV, ARGM-CAU, ARGM-DIR, etc.). Also, positive interpretations generated from infrequent roles are generally ranked higher, e.g., ARG_4 and ARG_3 vs. ARG_0, ARGM-PRP and ARGM-MNR vs. ARGM-ADV. **Annotation Quality.** In order to ensure annotation quality, we calculated inter-annotator Pearson correlation. Kappa and other agreement measures de-

	Negated statement, context if relevant to determining scores, and all positive interpretations	Score
1	Context, previous statement: *That change will obviously impact third and fourth quarter earnings for the industry in general, he added.* Negated statement: $[He]_{ARG_0}$ *did[n't]*$_{ARGM-NEG}$ $[forecast]_{verb}$ $[Phillips'\ results]_{ARG_1}$. Context, next statement: *But security analysts say Phillips will be among the companies hard-hit by weak chemical prices and will probably post a drop in third-quarter earnings.*	
	- Interpretation 1.1 [ARG_0]: Somebody forecasted Phillips' results, but not *he*.	5
	- Interpretation 1.2 [ARG_1]: He forecasted something, but not *Phillips' results*.	5
2	Negated statement: *In 1995, Murdoch bought* $[the\ rest\ of\ Star\ TV]_{ARG_1}$ $[he]_{ARG_0}$ *did* $[not]_{ARGM-NEG}$ $[own]_{verb}$.	
	- Interpretation 2.1 (ARG_0): In 1995, Murdoch bought the rest of Star TV somebody owned, but not *he*.	5
	- Interpretation 2.2 (ARG_1): In 1995, Murdoch bought something he owned, but not *the rest of Star TV*.	0
3	Negated statement: $[You]_{ARG_0}$ $[can]_{ARGM-MOD}$$[not]_{ARGM-NEG}$ $[run]_{verb}$ $[a\ country\ with\ 23\ million\ people]_{ARG_1}$ $[with\ revenues\ of\ 16\ billion\ to\ 20\ billion\ dollars]_{ARGM-MNR}$.	
	- Interpretation 3.1 (ARG_0): Somebody can run a country with 23 million people with revenues of 16 billion to 20 billion dollars, but not *You*.	1
	- Interpretation 3.21 (ARG_1): You can run something with revenues of 16 billion to 20 billion dollars, but not *a country with 23 million people*.	5
	- Interpretation 3.3 ($ARGM-MNR$): You can run a country with 23 million people in some manner, but not with *with revenues of 16 billion to 20 billion dollars*.	5
4	Negated statement: *Do* $[not]_{ARGM-NEG}$ $[utter]_{verb}$ $[a\ word]_{ARG_1}$.	
	- Interpretation 4.1 (ARG_1): Utter something, but not *a word*.	0

Table 3: Annotation examples. We show all positive interpretations automatically generated and their scores (out of 5).

signed for categorical labels are not well-suited for our annotation task, since not all disagreements between numeric scores are the same, e.g., 4 vs. 5 should be counted as relatively high agreement, and 1 vs. 5 should be counted as high disagreement. Overall Pearson correlation is 0.761.

5.1 Annotation Examples

Table 3 presents annotation examples. We show the original negated statement including semantic role annotations from OntoNotes (square brackets), all positive interpretations automatically generated, and their scores. We also include context (previous and next sentence) if it helps determining scores.

Example (1) shows that context sometimes is vital to scoring plausible positive interpretations. Given *He didn't forecast Phillips' results* in isolation, it is uncertain if he forecasted anything at all, or whether somebody forecasted Phillips' results. However, the previous statement makes certain (5/5) the interpretation generated from ARG_1: he forecasted earnings for the industry in general. Similarly, the next statement makes very likely (5/5) the interpretation generated from ARG_0: other people (security analysts) made forecasts about Phillips. In this example, 2

positive interpretations are generated from one negation, and they are assigned the highest score (5/5).

The positive interpretations generated from example (2) can be annotated without context. Somebody other than Murdoch had to own the rest of Star TV that he bought in 1995 (score 5/5), and people cannot buy what they already own (score 0/5).

Example (3) presents a positive interpretation generated from ARG_0 that is scored low (1/5); recall that the mean score for interpretations generated from ARG_0 is 4.07 and the standard deviation 1.03 (Table 2). In this negated statement, the indefinite *you* refers to an unspecified person, thus it is not the case that *somebody can run a country with 23 million people with revenues of 16 billion to 20 billion dollars* (Interpretation 3.1, score 1/5). Interpretations 3.2 and 3.3, however, are scored high: annotators correctly understood that given the negated statement, it is the case that *You can run something with revenues of 16 billion to 20 billion dollars, but not a country with 23 million people* (you can run a country with less people with that revenue), and *You can run a country with 23 million people in some manner, but not with revenues of 16 billion to 20 billion dollar* (you could run it with more revenue).

Finally, example (4) presents a short statement from which only one positive interpretations is generated. Annotators were asked whether given *Do not utter a word*, they think *Utter something, but not a word* is true. They correctly annotated that this positive interpretations is invalid (score 0/5). Indeed, the negated statement in example (4) can only be interpreted as an order to not utter anything.

6 Learning to Score Positive Interpretations

We follow a standard supervised machine learning approach. The 1,888 positive interpretations along with their scores become instances, and we divide them into training (80%) and test splits (20%) making sure that all interpretations generated from a sentence are assigned to either the training or test splits. Note that splitting instances randomly would not be sound: training with some interpretations generated from a negated statement, and testing with the rest of interpretations generated from the same statement would be an unfair evaluation.

We trained a Support Vector Machine (SVM) for regression with RBF kernel using scikit-learn (Pedregosa et al., 2011), which in turn uses LIBSVM (Chang and Lin, 2011). The feature set and SVM parameters (C and γ) were tuned using 10-fold cross-validation with the training set, and results were calculated using the test set.

6.1 Feature Selection

We tried features derived exclusively from the negated statement from which the positive interpretation was generated, more specifically, we extract features from the negated *verb* or semantic role (*sem_role*) used to generate the positive interpretation, from both of them (*verb-sem_role*) and from the verb-argument structure of *verb* (*verbarg-struct*), i.e., all semantic roles of *verb*.

Verb features are straightforward and account for the verb word form and part-of-speech tag.

Sem_role features include the label of the semantic role from which the positive interpretation was generated (*sem_role_label*), its length (number of tokens), and the word form and part-of-speech tag of its head. Additionally, we add standard features in semantic role labeling (Gildea and Jurafsky, 2002):

the syntactic nodes (NP, PP, etc.) of the semantic role and its parent in the parse tree, as well as the left and right siblings, if any.

Verb-sem_role features are also standard in role labeling. We include a flag indicating whether the verb occurs before or after the semantic role in the negated statement (not in the positive counterpart), syntactic node of the lowest common ancestor between *verb* and *sem_role*, and the syntactic path.

Finally, *verbarg-struct* features encode characteristics of the verb-argument structure to which *verb* and *sem_role* belong to. Namely, we added flags indicating semantic role presence, and features indicating the first and last semantic roles in order of appearance in the negated statement. We also included the syntactic nodes of semantic roles and their heads.

We exemplify all features with Interpretation 3.1 generated from Statement 3 in Table 3:

- *Verb* features: verb_wf=run, verb_pos=VBP.
- *Sem_role* features: label=ARG_0, num_tokens=1, head_wf=You, head_pos=PRP, synt_node=NP, synt_node_parent=S, synt_node_left=NONE, synt_node_right=VP
- *Verb-sem_role* features: direction=after, lowest_ancestor=S, synt_path=VP+VP+S-NP
- *Verbarg-struct* features: ARG_0=1, ARGM-MOD=1, ARG_1=1, ARGM-MNR=1, first=ARG_0, last=ARGM-MNR, ARG_1_head=country, ARG_1_pos=NN, etc.

7 Experimental Results

We report results obtained with several combinations of features in Table 5. We detail results obtained with features extracted from gold-standard and predicted linguistic annotations (part-of-speech tags, parse trees, semantic roles, etc.) as annotated in the *gold* and *auto* files from the CoNLL-2011 Shared Task release of OntoNotes (Pradhan et al., 2011). All models are trained with gold-standard linguistic annotations, and tested with either gold-standard or predicted linguistic annotations.

Testing with gold-standard linguistic annotations. Using only the label of the semantic role from which the positive interpretation was generated (*sem_role_label*), yields a Pearson correlation of 0.603. Using *Verb* features is virtually useless (Pearson correlation: -0.025), this is due to the

Source	Feature description
Verb	Word form and part-of-speech tag of *verb*
sem_role	Semantic role label of sem_role, *sem_role_label*
	Number of tokens in *sem_role*
	Word form and part-of-speech tag of head of *sem_role*
	Syntactic node of *sem_role*, its parent and left and right siblings in the parse tree
verb-sem_role	Whether *verb* occurs before or after than *sem_role* in the negated statement
	Syntactic node of lowest common ancestor of *verb* and *sem_role*
	Syntactic paths from *verb* to *sem_role*
verbarg-struct	Flags indicating whether *verb* has each possible semantic role
	Semantic role labels of the first and last roles of *verb*
	Syntactic nodes and heads of each semantic role attaching to *verb*

Table 4: Features used to score positive interpretations from negated statements. Features are extracted from the negated *verb* or semantic role (*sem_role*) from which the positive interpretation was generated, from both of them (*verb-sem_role*), or from the verb-argument structure of *verb* (verbarg-struct), i.e., from all semantic roles of *verb*.

	Gold	Predicted
sem_role_label feature	0.603	0.642
verb features	-0.025	-0.022
verb + sem_role features	0.630	0.648
verb + sem_role + verb-sem_role features	0.627	0.638
verb + sem_role + verb-sem_role + verbarg-struct features	0.642	0.650

Table 5: Pearson correlations in the test set using gold-standard and predicted linguistic annotations (part-of-speech tags, parse trees and semantic roles). Results are provided using sem_role_label as only feature, and using several features incrementally. Number of test instances with gold-standard linguistic annotations is 378, and with predicted annotations, 268.

fact that our corpus includes at most 5 instances for each negated verb in OntoNotes (Section 4). Adding *sem_role* features yields a correlation of 0.630, and incorporating *verb-sem_role* features is useless (Pearson: 0.627). Considering all features, however, yields the highest correlation, 0.642.

Testing with predicted linguistic annotations. We assigned 20% of instances to the test split, totalling 378 instances (Section 6). However, some of these instances cannot be obtained using predicted role labels: a missing or incorrect semantic role will unequivocally lead to positive interpretations that are not in our corpus and thus evaluation is not straightforward. Results presented with predicted linguistic annotations are calculated using only the 268 (out of 378) positive interpretations that are generated from predicted semantic roles and are also generated (and thus annotated in our corpus) from gold-standard linguistic annotations.

Results using only *sem_role_label* feature (0.642) are better or very similar than using any combination of features (0.638–0.650) except *Verb* features alone, which perform poorly as explained earlier.

These results should be taken with a grain of salt: the number of test instances is much lower (268 vs. 378). Additionally, these 268 test instances correspond to positive interpretations generated from semantic roles that were predicted correctly automatically. Role labels are predicted better for shorter sentences without complicated syntactic structure; positive interpretations for this kind sentences are also easier to score, e.g., Statement 4 in Table 3.

8 Conclusions

Humans intuitively understand negated statements in positive terms when reading text. This paper presents an automated methodology to generate plausible positive interpretations from verbal negation, and score them based on their likelihood. We use simple grammar rules and manipulate semantic roles to generate positive interpretations. Experimental results show that these interpretations can be scored automatically using standard supervised machine learning techniques.

An annotation effort shows that most positive interpretations automatically generated are likely (scores ≥ 4), thus the amount of positive meaning revealed by the methodology presented here is substantial (on average, 3.15 interpretations are generated per negation). We believe that more annotations and a learning algorithm that scores jointly all positive interpretations generated from each negation (as opposed to individually) would yield better results.

References

Amjad Abu-Jbara and Dragomir Radev. 2012. Umichigan: A conditional random field model for resolving the scope of negation. In *Proceedings of the First Joint Conference on Lexical and Computational Semantics- Volume 1: Proceedings of the main conference and the shared task, and Volume 2: Proceedings of the Sixth International Workshop on Semantic Evaluation*, pages 328–334. Association for Computational Linguistics.

Eneko Agirre, Daniel Cer, Mona Diab, Aitor Gonzalez-Agirre, and Weiwei Guo. 2013. *sem 2013 shared task: Semantic textual similarity. In *Second Joint Conference on Lexical and Computational Semantics (*SEM), Volume 1: Proceedings of the Main Conference and the Shared Task: Semantic Textual Similarity*, pages 32–43, Atlanta, Georgia, USA, June. Association for Computational Linguistics.

Pranav Anand and Craig Martell. 2012. Annotating the focus of negation in terms of questions under discussion. In *Proceedings of the Workshop on Extra-Propositional Aspects of Meaning in Computational Linguistics*, ExProM '12, pages 65–69, Stroudsburg, PA, USA. Association for Computational Linguistics.

Collin F. Baker, Charles J. Fillmore, and John B. Lowe. 1998. The Berkeley FrameNet Project. In *Proceedings of the 17th international conference on Computational Linguistics*, Montreal, Canada.

Laura Banarescu, Claire Bonial, Shu Cai, Madalina Georgescu, Kira Griffitt, Ulf Hermjakob, Kevin Knight, Philipp Koehn, Martha Palmer, and Nathan Schneider. 2013. Abstract meaning representation for sembanking. In *Proceedings of the 7th Linguistic Annotation Workshop and Interoperability with Discourse*, pages 178–186, Sofia, Bulgaria, August. Association for Computational Linguistics.

Simon Blackburn. 2008. *The Oxford Dictionary of Philosophy*. Oxford University Press.

Eduardo Blanco and Dan Moldovan. 2011. Semantic representation of negation using focus detection. In *Proceedings of the 49th Annual Meeting of the Association for Computational Linguistics: Human Language Technologies*, pages 581–589, Portland, Oregon, USA, June. Association for Computational Linguistics.

Eduardo Blanco and Dan Moldovan. 2012. Fine-grained focus for pinpointing positive implicit meaning from negated statements. In *Proceedings of the 2012 Conference of the North American Chapter of the Association for Computational Linguistics: Human Language Technologies*, pages 456–465, Montréal, Canada, June. Association for Computational Linguistics.

Eduardo Blanco and Dan Moldovan. 2014. Retrieving implicit positive meaning from negated statements. *Natural Language Engineering*, 20:501–535, 10.

Chih-Chung Chang and Chih-Jen Lin. 2011. Libsvm: A library for support vector machines. *ACM Trans. Intell. Syst. Technol.*, 2(3):27:1–27:27, May.

H. H. Clark and W. G. Chase. 1972. On the process of comparing sentences against pictures. *Cognitive Psychology*, 3(3):472–517, July.

Isaac Councill, Ryan McDonald, and Leonid Velikovich. 2010. What's great and what's not: learning to classify the scope of negation for improved sentiment analysis. In *Proceedings of the Workshop on Negation and Speculation in Natural Language Processing*, pages 51–59, Uppsala, Sweden, July. University of Antwerp.

Peter L. Elkin, Steven H. Brown, Brent A. Bauer, Casey S. Husser, William Carruth, Larry R. Bergstrom, and Dietlind L. Wahner-Roedler. 2005. A controlled trial of automated classification of negation from clinical notes. *BMC Medical Informatics and Decision Making*, 5(13).

Daniel Gildea and Daniel Jurafsky. 2002. Automatic labeling of semantic roles. *Comput. Linguist.*, 28(3):245–288, September.

Jack Hoeksema. 2000. Negative polarity items: triggering, scope, and c-command. In L. Horn and Y. Kato, editors, *Negation and polarity*, chapter 4, pages 115–146. Oxford University Press, Oxford.

Laurence R. Horn and Heinrich Wansing. 2015. Negation. In Edward N. Zalta, editor, *The Stanford Encyclopedia of Philosophy*. Summer 2015 edition.

Laurence R. Horn. 1989. *A natural history of negation*. Chicago University Press, Chicago.

Eduard Hovy, Mitchell Marcus, Martha Palmer, Lance Ramshaw, and Ralph Weischedel. 2006. OntoNotes: the 90% Solution. In *NAACL '06: Proceedings of the Human Language Technology Conference of the NAACL, Companion Volume: Short Papers on XX*, pages 57–60, Morristown, NJ, USA. Association for Computational Linguistics.

Minqing Hu and Bing Liu. 2004. Mining and summarizing customer reviews. In *KDD '04: Proceedings of the tenth ACM SIGKDD international conference on Knowledge discovery and data mining*, pages 168–177, New York, NY, USA. ACM.

Rodney D. Huddleston and Geoffrey K. Pullum. 2002. *The Cambridge Grammar of the English Language*. Cambridge University Press, April.

Mike Lewis, Luheng He, and Luke Zettlemoyer. 2015. Joint a* ccg parsing and semantic role labelling. In *Empirical Methods in Natural Language Processing*.

Junhui Li, Guodong Zhou, Hongling Wang, and Qiaoming Zhu. 2010. Learning the Scope of Negation via Shallow Semantic Parsing. In *Proceedings of the 23rd International Conference on Computational Linguistics (Coling 2010)*, pages 671–679, Beijing, China, August. Coling 2010 Organizing Committee.

Suguru Matsuyoshi, Ryo Otsuki, and Fumiyo Fukumoto. 2014. Annotating the focus of negation in japanese text. In Nicoletta Calzolari, Khalid Choukri, Thierry Declerck, Hrafn Loftsson, Bente Maegaard, Joseph Mariani, Asuncion Moreno, Jan Odijk, and Stelios Piperidis, editors, *Proceedings of the Ninth International Conference on Language Resources and Evaluation (LREC'14)*, pages 1743–1750, Reykjavik, Iceland, May. European Language Resources Association (ELRA). ACL Anthology Identifier: L14-1606.

Ruslan Mitkov. 2005. *The Oxford handbook of computational linguistics*. Oxford University Press.

Roser Morante and Eduardo Blanco. 2012. *SEM 2012 Shared Task: Resolving the Scope and Focus of Negation. In *Proceedings of the First Joint Conference on Lexical and Computational Semantics (*SEM 2012)*, pages 265–274, Montréal, Canada, June.

Roser Morante and Walter Daelemans. 2012. Conandoyle-neg: Annotation of negation in conan doyle stories. In *Proceedings of the Eighth International Conference on Language Resources and Evaluation, Istanbul*.

Roser Morante and Caroline Sporleder. 2012. Modality and negation: An introduction to the special issue. *Comput. Linguist.*, 38(2):223–260, June.

Ann E Nordmeyer and Michael C Frank. 2013. Measuring the comprehension of negation in 2-to 4-year-old children. *Proceedings of the 35th Annual Conference of the Cognitive Science Society. Austin, TX: Cognitive Science Society*.

Lilja Øvrelid, Erik Velldal, and Stephan Oepen. 2010. Syntactic Scope Resolution in Uncertainty Analysis. In *Proceedings of the 23rd International Conference on Computational Linguistics (Coling 2010)*, pages 1379–1387, Beijing, China, August. Coling 2010 Organizing Committee.

Arzucan Özgür and Dragomir R. Radev. 2009. Detecting Speculations and their Scopes in Scientific Text. In *Proceedings of the 2009 Conference on Empirical Methods in Natural Language Processing*, pages 1398–1407, Singapore, August. Association for Computational Linguistics.

Martha Palmer, Daniel Gildea, and Paul Kingsbury. 2005. The Proposition Bank: An Annotated Corpus of Semantic Roles. *Computational Linguistics*, 31(1):71–106.

Bo Pang, Lillian Lee, and Shivakumar Vaithyanathan. 2002. Thumbs up? sentiment classification using machine learning techniques. In *Proceedings of the 2002 Conference on Empirical Methods in Natural Language Processing*, pages 79–86. Association for Computational Linguistics, July.

F. Pedregosa, G. Varoquaux, A. Gramfort, V. Michel, B. Thirion, O. Grisel, M. Blondel, P. Prettenhofer, R. Weiss, V. Dubourg, J. Vanderplas, A. Passos, D. Cournapeau, M. Brucher, M. Perrot, and E. Duchesnay. 2011. Scikit-learn: Machine learning in Python. *Journal of Machine Learning Research*, 12:2825–2830.

Sameer Pradhan, Lance Ramshaw, Mitchell Marcus, Martha Palmer, Ralph Weischedel, and Nianwen Xue. 2011. Conll-2011 shared task: Modeling unrestricted coreference in ontonotes. In *Proceedings of the Fifteenth Conference on Computational Natural Language Learning: Shared Task*, pages 1–27, Portland, Oregon, USA, June. Association for Computational Linguistics.

Randolph Quirk, Sidney Greenbaum, and Geoffrey Leech. 2000. *A comprehensive grammar of the English language*. Longman, London.

Johan Reitan, Jørgen Faret, Björn Gambäck, and Lars Bungum. 2015. Negation scope detection for twitter sentiment analysis. In *Proceedings of the 6th Workshop on Computational Approaches to Subjectivity, Sentiment and Social Media Analysis*, pages 99–108, Lisboa, Portugal, September. Association for Computational Linguistics.

Mats Rooth. 1985. *Association with focus*. Ph.D. thesis, Dept. of Linguistics, University of Massachusetts, Amherst.

Mats Rooth. 1992. A theory of focus interpretation. *Natural language semantics*, 1(1):75–116.

Sabine Rosenberg and Sabine Bergler. 2012. Uconcordia: Clac negation focus detection at *sem 2012. In *SEM 2012: The First Joint Conference on Lexical and Computational Semantics – Volume 1: Proceedings of the main conference and the shared task, and Volume 2: Proceedings of the Sixth International Workshop on Semantic Evaluation (SemEval 2012)*, pages 294–300, Montréal, Canada, 7-8 June. Association for Computational Linguistics.

György Szarvas, Veronika Vincze, Richárd Farkas, and János Csirik. 2008. The BioScope corpus: annotation for negation, uncertainty and their scopein biomedical texts. In *Proceedings of BioNLP 2008*, pages 38–45, Columbus, Ohio, USA. ACL.

Josef Taglicht. 1984. *Message and emphasis: On focus and scope in English*, volume 15. Addison-Wesley Longman Limited.

Ton van der Wouden. 1997. *Negative contexts: collocation, polarity, and multiple negation*. Routledge, London.

Erik Velldal, Lilja Ovrelid, Jonathon Read, and Stephan Oepen. 2012. Speculation and negation: Rules, rankers, and the role of syntax. *Comput. Linguist.*, 38(2):369–410, June.

Bowei Zou, Guodong Zhou, and Qiaoming Zhu. 2014. Negation focus identification with contextual discourse information. In *Proceedings of the 52nd Annual Meeting of the Association for Computational Linguistics (Volume 1: Long Papers)*, pages 522–530, Baltimore, Maryland, June. Association for Computational Linguistics.

Learning Natural Language Inference with LSTM

Shuohang Wang
School of Information Systems
Singapore Management University
shwang.2014@phdis.smu.edu.sg

Jing Jiang
School of Information Systems
Singapore Management University
jingjiang@smu.edu.sg

Abstract

Natural language inference (NLI) is a fundamentally important task in natural language processing that has many applications. The recently released Stanford Natural Language Inference (SNLI) corpus has made it possible to develop and evaluate learning-centered methods such as deep neural networks for natural language inference (NLI). In this paper, we propose a special long short-term memory (LSTM) architecture for NLI. Our model builds on top of a recently proposed neural attention model for NLI but is based on a significantly different idea. Instead of deriving sentence embeddings for the premise and the hypothesis to be used for classification, our solution uses a match-LSTM to perform word-by-word matching of the hypothesis with the premise. This LSTM is able to place more emphasis on important word-level matching results. In particular, we observe that this LSTM remembers important mismatches that are critical for predicting the contradiction or the neutral relationship label. On the SNLI corpus, our model achieves an accuracy of 86.1%, outperforming the state of the art.

1 Introduction

Natural language inference (NLI) is the problem of determining whether from a premise sentence P one can infer another hypothesis sentence H (MacCartney, 2009). NLI is a fundamentally important problem that has applications in many tasks including question answering, semantic search and automatic text summarization. There has been much interest in NLI in the past decade, especially surrounding the PASCAL Recognizing Textual Entailment (RTE) Challenge (Dagan et al., 2005). Existing solutions to NLI range from shallow approaches based on lexical similarities (Glickman et al., 2005) to advanced methods that consider syntax (Mehdad et al., 2009), perform explicit sentence alignment (MacCartney et al., 2008) or use formal logic (Clark and Harrison, 2009).

Recently, Bowman et al. (2015) released the Stanford Natural Language Inference (SNLI) corpus for the purpose of encouraging more learning-centered approaches to NLI. This corpus contains around 570K sentence pairs with three labels: *entailment*, *contradiction* and *neutral*. The size of the corpus makes it now feasible to train deep neural network models, which typically require a large amount of training data. Bowman et al. (2015) tested a straightforward architecture of deep neural networks for NLI. In their architecture, the premise and the hypothesis are each represented by a sentence embedding vector. The two vectors are then fed into a multi-layer neural network to train a classifier. Bowman et al. (2015) achieved an accuracy of 77.6% when long short-term memory (LSTM) networks were used to obtain the sentence embeddings.

A more recent work by Rocktäschel et al. (2016) improved the performance by applying a neural attention model. While their basic architecture is still based on sentence embeddings for the premise and the hypothesis, a key difference is that the embedding of the premise takes into consideration the alignment between the premise and the hypothesis. This so-called *attention-weighted* representation of the premise was shown to help push the accuracy to

Proceedings of NAACL-HLT 2016, pages 1442–1451,
San Diego, California, June 12-17, 2016. ©2016 Association for Computational Linguistics

83.5% on the SNLI corpus.

A limitation of the aforementioned two models is that they reduce both the premise and the hypothesis to a single embedding vector before matching them; i.e., in the end, they use two embedding vectors to perform sentence-level matching. However, not all word or phrase-level matching results are equally important. For example, the matching between stop words in the two sentences is not likely to contribute much to the final prediction. Also, for a hypothesis to *contradict* a premise, a single word or phrase-level mismatch (e.g., a mismatch of the subjects of the two sentences) may be sufficient and other matching results are less important, but this intuition is hard to be captured if we directly match two sentence embeddings.

In this paper, we propose a new LSTM-based architecture for learning natural language inference. Different from previous models, our prediction is not based on whole sentence embeddings of the premise and the hypothesis. Instead, we use an LSTM to perform *word-by-word* matching of the hypothesis with the premise. Our LSTM sequentially processes the hypothesis, and at each position, it tries to match the current word in the hypothesis with an attention-weighted representation of the premise. Matching results that are critical for the final prediction will be "remembered" by the LSTM while less important matching results will be "forgotten." We refer to this architecture a match-LSTM, or *m*LSTM for short.

Experiments show that our *m*LSTM model achieves an accuracy of 86.1% on the SNLI corpus, outperforming the state of the art. Furthermore, through further analyses of the learned parameters, we show that the *m*LSTM architecture can indeed pick up the more important word-level matching results that need to be remembered for the final prediction. In particular, we observe that good word-level matching results are generally "forgotten" but important mismatches, which often indicate a *contradiction* or a *neutral* relationship, tend to be "remembered."

2 Model

In this section, we first review LSTM. We then review the word-by-word attention model by Rocktäschel et al. (2016), which is their best performing model. Finally we present our *m*LSTM architecture for natural language inference.

2.1 Background

LSTM: Let us first briefly review LSTM (Hochreiter and Schmidhuber, 1997). LSTM is a special form of recurrent neural networks (RNNs), which process sequence data. LSTM uses a few gate vectors at each position to control the passing of information along the sequence and thus improves the modeling of long-range dependencies. While there are different variations of LSTMs, here we present the one adopted by Rocktäschel et al. (2016). Specifically, let us use $\mathbf{X} = (\mathbf{x}_1, \mathbf{x}_2, \ldots, \mathbf{x}_N)$ to denote an input sequence, where $\mathbf{x}_k \in \mathbb{R}^l$ ($1 \leq k \leq N$). At each position k, there is a set of internal vectors, including an input gate $\mathbf{i}_k$, a forget gate $\mathbf{f}_k$, an output gate $\mathbf{o}_k$ and a memory cell $\mathbf{c}_k$. All these vectors are used together to generate a d-dimensional hidden state $\mathbf{h}_k$ as follows:

$$
\begin{aligned}
\mathbf{i}_k &= \sigma(\mathbf{W}^i\mathbf{x}_k + \mathbf{V}^i\mathbf{h}_{k-1} + \mathbf{b}^i), \\
\mathbf{f}_k &= \sigma(\mathbf{W}^f\mathbf{x}_k + \mathbf{V}^f\mathbf{h}_{k-1} + \mathbf{b}^f), \\
\mathbf{o}_k &= \sigma(\mathbf{W}^o\mathbf{x}_k + \mathbf{V}^o\mathbf{h}_{k-1} + \mathbf{b}^o), \\
\mathbf{c}_k &= \mathbf{f}_k \odot \mathbf{c}_{k-1} + \mathbf{i}_k \odot \tanh(\mathbf{W}^c\mathbf{x}_k + \mathbf{V}^c\mathbf{h}_{k-1} + \mathbf{b}^c), \\
\mathbf{h}_k &= \mathbf{o}_k \odot \tanh(\mathbf{c}_k),
\end{aligned}
\tag{1}
$$

where σ is the sigmoid function, $\odot$ is the element-wise multiplication of two vectors, and all $\mathbf{W}^* \in \mathbb{R}^{d \times l}, \mathbf{V}^* \in \mathbb{R}^{d \times d}$ and $\mathbf{b}^* \in \mathbb{R}^d$ are weight matrices and vectors to be learned.

Neural Attention Model: For the natural language inference task, we have two sentences $\mathbf{X}^s = (\mathbf{x}_1^s, \mathbf{x}_2^s, \ldots, \mathbf{x}_M^s)$ and $\mathbf{X}^t = (\mathbf{x}_1^t, \mathbf{x}_2^t, \ldots, \mathbf{x}_N^t)$, where $\mathbf{X}^s$ is the premise and $\mathbf{X}^t$ is the hypothesis. Here each $\mathbf{x}$ is an embedding vector of the corresponding word. The goal is to predict a label y that indicates the relationship between $\mathbf{X}^s$ and $\mathbf{X}^t$. In this paper, we assume y is one of *entailment*, *contradiction* and *neutral*.

Rocktäschel et al. (2016) first used two LSTMs to process the premise and the hypothesis, respectively, but initialized the second LSTM (for the hypothesis) with the last cell state of the first LSTM (for the premise). Let us use $\mathbf{h}_j^s$ and $\mathbf{h}_k^t$ to denote the resulting hidden states corresponding to $\mathbf{x}_j^s$ and

$\mathbf{x}_k^t$, respectively. The main idea of the word-by-word attention model by Rocktäschel et al. (2016) is to introduce a series of attention-weighted combinations of the hidden states of the premise, where each combination is for a particular word in the hypothesis. Let us use $\mathbf{a}_k$ to denote such an *attention vector* for word $\mathbf{x}_k^t$ in the hypothesis. Specifically, $\mathbf{a}_k$ is defined as follows[1]:

$$\mathbf{a}_k \;=\; \sum_{j=1}^{M} \alpha_{kj} \mathbf{h}_j^s, \tag{2}$$

where α_{kj} is an attention weight that encodes the degree to which $\mathbf{x}_k^t$ in the hypothesis is aligned with $\mathbf{x}_j^s$ in the premise. The attention weight α_{kj} is generated in the following way:

$$\alpha_{kj} \;=\; \frac{\exp(e_{kj})}{\sum_{j'} \exp(e_{kj'})}, \tag{3}$$

where

$$e_{kj} = \mathbf{w}^e \cdot \tanh(\mathbf{W}^s \mathbf{h}_j^s + \mathbf{W}^t \mathbf{h}_k^t + \mathbf{W}^a \mathbf{h}_{k-1}^a). \tag{4}$$

Here $\cdot$ is the dot-product between two vectors, the vector $\mathbf{w}^e \in \mathbb{R}^d$ and all matrices $\mathbf{W}^* \in \mathbb{R}^{d \times d}$ contain weights to be learned, and $\mathbf{h}_{k-1}^a$ is another hidden state which we will explain below.

The attention-weighted premise $\mathbf{a}_k$ essentially tries to model the relevant parts in the premise with respect to $\mathbf{x}_k^t$, i.e., the kth word in the hypothesis. Rocktäschel et al. (2016) further built an RNN model over $\{\mathbf{a}_k\}_{k=1}^N$ by defining the following hidden states:

$$\mathbf{h}_k^a \;=\; \mathbf{a}_k + \tanh(\mathbf{V}^a \mathbf{h}_{k-1}^a), \tag{5}$$

where $\mathbf{V}^a \in \mathbb{R}^{d \times d}$ is a weight matrix to be learned. We can see that the last $\mathbf{h}_N^a$ aggregates all the previous $\mathbf{a}_k$ and can be seen as an attention-weighted representation of the whole premise. Rocktäschel et al. (2016) then used this $\mathbf{h}_N^a$, which represents the

whole premise, together with $\mathbf{h}_N^t$, which can be approximately regarded as an aggregated representation of the hypothesis[2], to predict the label y.

2.2 Our Model

Although the neural attention model by Rocktäschel et al. (2016) achieved better results than Bowman et al. (2015), we see two limitations. First, the model still uses a single vector representation of the premise, namely $\mathbf{h}_N^a$, to match the entire hypothesis. We speculate that if we instead use each of the attention-weighted representations of the premise for matching, i.e., use $\mathbf{a}_k$ at position k to match the hidden state $\mathbf{h}_k^t$ of the hypothesis while we go through the hypothesis, we could achieve better matching results. This can be done using an RNN which at each position takes in both $\mathbf{a}_k$ and $\mathbf{h}_k^t$ as its input and determines how well the overall matching of the two sentences is up to the current position. In the end the RNN will produce a single vector representing the matching of the two entire sentences.

The second limitation is that the model by Rocktäschel et al. (2016) does not explicitly allow us to place more emphasis on the more important matching results between the premise and the hypothesis and down-weight the less critical ones. For example, matching of stop words is presumably less important than matching of content words. Also, some matching results may be particularly critical for making the final prediction and thus should be remembered. For example, consider the premise "*A dog jumping for a Frisbee in the snow.*" and the hypothesis "*A cat washes his face and whiskers with his front paw.*" When we sequentially process the hypothesis, once we see that the subject of the hypothesis *cat* does not match the subject of the premise *dog*, we have a high probability to believe that there is a contradiction. So this mismatch should be remembered.

Based on the two observations above, we propose to use an LSTM to sequentially match the two sentences. At each position the LSTM takes in both $\mathbf{a}_k$ and $\mathbf{h}_k^t$ as its input. Figure 1 gives an overview of our model in contrast to the model by Rocktäschel

---

[1]We present the word-by-word attention model by Rocktäschel et al. (2016) in a different way but the underlying model is the same. Our $\mathbf{h}_k^a$ is their $\mathbf{r}_t$, our $\mathbf{H}^s$ (all of $\mathbf{h}_j^s$) is their $\mathbf{Y}$, our $\mathbf{h}_k^t$ is their $\mathbf{h}_t$, and our α_k is their α_t. Our presentation is close to the one by Bahdanau et al. (2015), with our attention vectors $\mathbf{a}$ corresponding to the context vectors $\mathbf{c}$ in their paper.

[2]Strictly speaking, in the model by Rocktäschel et al. (2016), $\mathbf{h}_N^t$ encodes both the premise and the hypothesis because the two sentences are chained. But $\mathbf{h}_N^t$ places a higher emphasis on the hypothesis given the nature of RNNs.

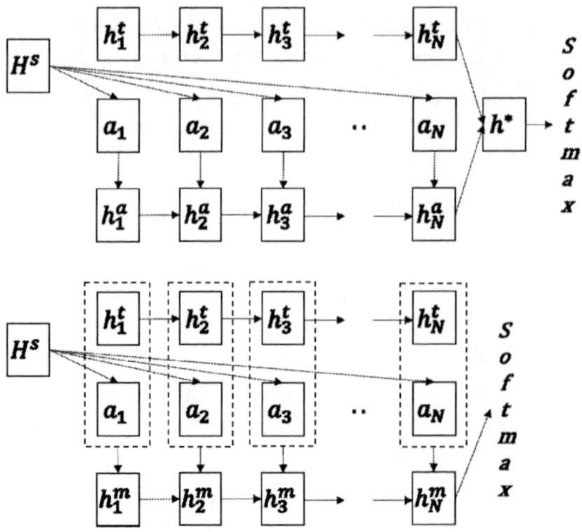

Figure 1: The top figure depicts the model by Rocktäschel et al. (2016) and the bottom figure depicts our model. Here $\mathbf{H}^s$ represents all the hidden states $\mathbf{h}_j^s$. Note that in the top model each $\mathbf{h}_k^a$ represents a weighted version of the premise only, while in our model, each $\mathbf{h}_k^m$ represents the matching between the premise and the hypothesis up to position k.

et al. (2016).

Specifically, our model works as follows. First, similar to Rocktäschel et al. (2016), we process the premise and the hypothesis using two LSTMs, but we do not feed the last cell state of the premise to the LSTM of the hypothesis. This is because we do not need the LSTM for the hypothesis to encode any knowledge about the premise but we will match the premise with the hypothesis using the hidden states of the two LSTMs. Again, we use $\mathbf{h}_j^s$ and $\mathbf{h}_k^t$ to represent these hidden states.

Next, we generate the attention vectors $\mathbf{a}_k$ similarly to Eqn (2). However, Eqn (4) will be replaced by the following equation:

$$e_{kj} = \mathbf{w}^e \cdot \tanh(\mathbf{W}^s\mathbf{h}_j^s + \mathbf{W}^t\mathbf{h}_k^t + \mathbf{W}^m\mathbf{h}_{k-1}^m). \quad (6)$$

The only difference here is that we use a hidden state $\mathbf{h}^m$ instead of $\mathbf{h}^a$, and the way we define $\mathbf{h}^m$ is very different from the definition of $\mathbf{h}^a$.

Our $\mathbf{h}_k^m$ is the hidden state at position k generated from our *mLSTM*. This LSTM models the *matching* between the premise and the hypothesis. Important matching results will be "remembered" by the LSTM while non-essential ones will be "forgot-

ten." We use the concatenation of $\mathbf{a}_k$, which is the attention-weighted version of the premise for the kth word in the hypothesis, and $\mathbf{h}_k^t$, the hidden state for the kth word itself, as input to the *mLSTM*.

Specifically, let us define

$$\mathbf{m}_k \;=\; \begin{bmatrix} \mathbf{a}_k \\ \mathbf{h}_k^t \end{bmatrix}. \quad (7)$$

We then build the *mLSTM* as follows:

$$\begin{aligned}
\mathbf{i}_k^m &= \sigma(\mathbf{W}^{mi}\mathbf{m}_k + \mathbf{V}^{mi}\mathbf{h}_{k-1}^m + \mathbf{b}^{mi}), \\
\mathbf{f}_k^m &= \sigma(\mathbf{W}^{mf}\mathbf{m}_k + \mathbf{V}^{mf}\mathbf{h}_{k-1}^m + \mathbf{b}^{mf}), \\
\mathbf{o}_k^m &= \sigma(\mathbf{W}^{mo}\mathbf{m}_k + \mathbf{V}^{mo}\mathbf{h}_{k-1}^m + \mathbf{b}^{mo}), \\
\mathbf{c}_k^m &= \mathbf{f}_k^m \odot \mathbf{c}_{k-1}^m + \mathbf{i}_k^m \odot \tanh(\mathbf{W}^{mc}\mathbf{m}_k + \mathbf{V}^{mc}\mathbf{h}_{k-1}^m \\
&\quad + \mathbf{b}^{mc}), \\
\mathbf{h}_k^m &= \mathbf{o}_k^m \odot \tanh(\mathbf{c}_k^m). \quad (8)
\end{aligned}$$

With this *mLSTM*, finally we use only $\mathbf{h}_N^m$, the last hidden state, to predict the label y.

2.3 Implementation Details

Besides the difference of the LSTM architecture, we also introduce a few other changes from the model by Rocktäschel et al. (2016). First, we insert a special word *NULL* to the premise, and we allow words in the hypothesis to be aligned with this *NULL*. This is inspired by common practice in machine translation. Specifically, we introduce a vector $\mathbf{h}_0^s$, which is fixed to be a vector of 0s of dimension d. This $\mathbf{h}_0^s$ represents *NULL* and is used with other $\mathbf{h}_j^s$ to derive the attention vectors $\{\mathbf{a}_k\}_{k=1}^N$.

Second, we use word embeddings trained from GloVe (Pennington et al., 2014) instead of word2vec vectors. The main reason is that GloVe covers more words in the SNLI corpus than word2vec[3].

Third, for words which do not have pre-trained word embeddings, we take the average of the embeddings of all the words (in GloVe) surrounding the unseen word within a window size of 9 (4 on the left and 4 on the right) as an approximation of the embedding of this unseen word. Then we do not update any word embedding when learning our model. Although this is a very crude approximation, it reduces

---

[3]The SNLI corpus contains 37K unique tokens. Around 12.1K of them cannot be found in word2vec but only around 4.1K of them cannot be found in GloVe.

the number of parameters we need to update, and as it turns out, we can still achieve better performance than Rocktäschel et al. (2016).

3 Experiments

3.1 Experiment Settings

Data: We use the SNLI corpus to test the effectiveness of our model. The original data set contains 570,152 sentence pairs, each labeled with one of the following relationships: *entailment, contradiction, neutral* and *–*, where *–* indicates a lack of consensus from the human annotators. We discard the sentence pairs labeled with *–* and keep the remaining ones for our experiments. In the end, we have 549,367 pairs for training, 9,842 pairs for development and 9,824 pairs for testing. This follows the same data partition used by Bowman et al. (2015) in their experiments. We perform three-class classification and use accuracy as our evaluation metric.

Parameters: We use the Adam method (Kingma and Ba, 2014) with hyperparameters β_1 set to 0.9 and β_2 set to 0.999 for optimization. The initial learning rate is set to be 0.001 with a decay ratio of 0.95 for each iteration. The batch size is set to be 30. We experiment with $d = 150$ and $d = 300$ where d is the dimension of all the hidden states.

Methods for comparison: We mainly want to compare our model with the word-by-word attention model by Rocktäschel et al. (2016) because this model achieved the state-of-the-art performance on the SNLI corpus. To ensure fair comparison, besides comparing with the accuracy reported by Rocktäschel et al. (2016), we also re-implemented their model and report the performance of our implementation. We also consider a few variations of our model. Specifically, the following models are implemented and tested in our experiments:

- Word-by-word attention ($d = 150$): This is our implementation of the word-by-word attention model by Rocktäschel et al. (2016), where we set the dimension of the hidden states to 150. The differences between our implementation and the original implementation by Rocktäschel et al. (2016) are the following: (1) We also add a *NULL* token to the premise for matching. (2) We do not feed the last cell state of the LSTM for the premise to the LSTM for

the hypothesis, to keep it consistent with the implementation of our model. (3) For word representation, we also use the GloVe word embeddings and we do not update the word embeddings. For unseen words, we adopt the same strategy as described in Section 2.3.

- mLSTM ($d = 150$): This is our mLSTM model with d set to 150.
- mLSTM with bi-LSTM sentence modeling ($d = 150$): This is the same as the model above except that when we derive the hidden states $\mathbf{h}_j^s$ and $\mathbf{h}_k^t$ of the two sentences, we use bi-LSTMs (Graves, 2012) instead of LSTMs. We implement this model to see whether bi-LSTMs allow us to better align the sentences.
- mLSTM ($d = 300$): This is our mLSTM model with d set to 300.
- mLSTM with word embedding ($d = 300$): This is the same as the model above except that we directly use the word embedding vectors $\mathbf{x}_j^s$ and $\mathbf{x}_k^t$ instead of the hidden states $\mathbf{h}_j^s$ and $\mathbf{h}_k^t$ in our model. In this case, each attention vector $\mathbf{a}_k$ is a weighted sum of $\{\mathbf{x}_j^s\}_{j=1}^M$. We experiment with this setting because we hypothesize that the effectiveness of our model is largely related to the mLSTM architecture rather than the use of LSTMs to process the original sentences.

3.2 Main Results

Table 1 compares the performance of the various models we tested together with some previously reported results.

We have the following observations: (1) First of all, we can see that when we set d to 300, our model achieves an accuracy of 86.1% on the test data, which to the best of our knowledge is the highest on this data set. (2) If we compare our mLSTM model with our implementation of the word-by-word attention model by Rocktäschel et al. (2016) under the same setting with $d = 150$, we can see that our performance on the test data (85.7%) is higher than that of their model (82.6%). We also tested statistical significance and found the improvement to be statistically significant at the 0.001 level. (3) The performance of mLSTM with bi-LSTM sentence modeling compared with the model with standard LSTM sentence modeling when d is set to 150 shows that using bi-LSTM to process the original sentences helps

Model	d	$|\theta|_{\text{W+M}}$	$|\theta|_{\text{M}}$	Train	Dev	Test
LSTM [Bowman et al. (2015)]	100	10M	221K	84.4	-	77.6
Classifier [Bowman et al. (2015)]	-	-	-	99.7	-	78.2
LSTM shared [Rocktäschel et al. (2016)]	159	3.9M	252K	84.4	83.0	81.4
Word-by-word attention [Rocktäschel et al. (2016)]	100	3.9M	252K	85.3	83.7	83.5
Word-by-word attention (our implementation)	150	340K	340K	85.5	83.3	82.6
mLSTM	150	544K	544K	91.0	86.2	85.7
mLSTM with bi-LSTM sentence modeling	150	1.4M	1.4M	91.3	86.6	86.0
mLSTM	300	1.9M	1.9M	92.0	**86.9**	**86.1**
mLSTM with word embedding	300	1.3M	1.3M	88.6	85.4	85.3

Table 1: Experiment results in terms of accuracy. d is the dimension of the hidden states. $|\theta|_{\text{W+M}}$ is the total number of parameters and $|\theta|_{\text{M}}$ is the number of parameters excluding the word embeddings. Note that the five models in the last section were implemented by us while the other results were taken directly from previous papers. Note also that for the five models in the last section, we do not update word embeddings so $|\theta|_{\text{W+M}}$ is the same as $|\theta|_{\text{M}}$. The three columns on the right are the accuracies of the trained models on the training data, the development data and the test data, respectively.

prediction	ground truth		
	N	E	C
N	2628	286	255
E	340	3005	159
C	250	77	2823

Table 2: The confusion matrix of the results by mLSTM with $d = 300$. N, E and C correspond to *neutral*, *entailment* and *contradiction*, respectively.

(86.0% vs. 85.7% on the test data), but the difference is small and the complexity of bi-LSTM is much higher than LSTM. Therefore when we increased d to 300 we did not experiment with bi-LSTM sentence modeling. (4) Interestingly, when we experimented with the mLSTM model using the pre-trained word embeddings instead of LSTM-generated hidden states as initial representations of the premise and the hypothesis, we were able to achieve an accuracy of 85.3% on the test data, which is still better than previously reported state of the art. This suggests that the mLSTM architecture coupled with the attention model works well, regardless of whether or not we use LSTM to process the original sentences.

Because the NLI task is a three-way classification problem, to better understand the errors, we also show the confusion matrix of the results obtained by our mLSTM model with $d = 300$ in Table 2. We can see that there is more confusion between *neutral* and *entailment* and between *neutral* and *contra-* *diction* than between *entailment* and *contradiction*. This shows that *neutral* is relatively hard to capture.

3.3 Further Analyses

To obtain a better understanding of how our proposed model actually performs the matching between a premise and a hypothesis, we further conduct the following analyses. First, we look at the learned word-by-word alignment weights α_{kj} to check whether the soft alignment makes sense. This is the same as what was done by Rocktäschel et al. (2016). We then look at the values of the various gate vectors of the mLSTM. By looking at these values, we aim to check (1) whether the model is able to differentiate between more important and less important word-level matching results, and (2) whether the model forgets certain matching results and remembers certain other ones.

To conduct the analyses, we choose three examples and display the various learned parameter values. These three sentence pairs share the same premise but have different hypotheses and different relationship labels. They are given in Table 3. The values of the alignment weights and the gate vectors are plotted in Figure 2.

Besides using the three examples, we will also give some overall statistics of the parameter values to confirm our observations with the three examples.

	ID	sentence	label
Premise		A dog jumping for a Frisbee in the snow.	
Hypothesis	Example 1	An animal is outside in the cold weather, playing with a plastic toy.	*entailment*
	Example 2	A cat washed his face and whiskers with his front paw.	*contradiction*
	Example 3	A pet is enjoying a game of fetch with his owner.	*neutral*

Table 3: Three examples of sentence pairs with different relationship labels. The second hypothesis is a contradiction because it mentions a completely different event. The third hypothesis is neutral to the premise because the phrase "with his owner" cannot be inferred from the premise.

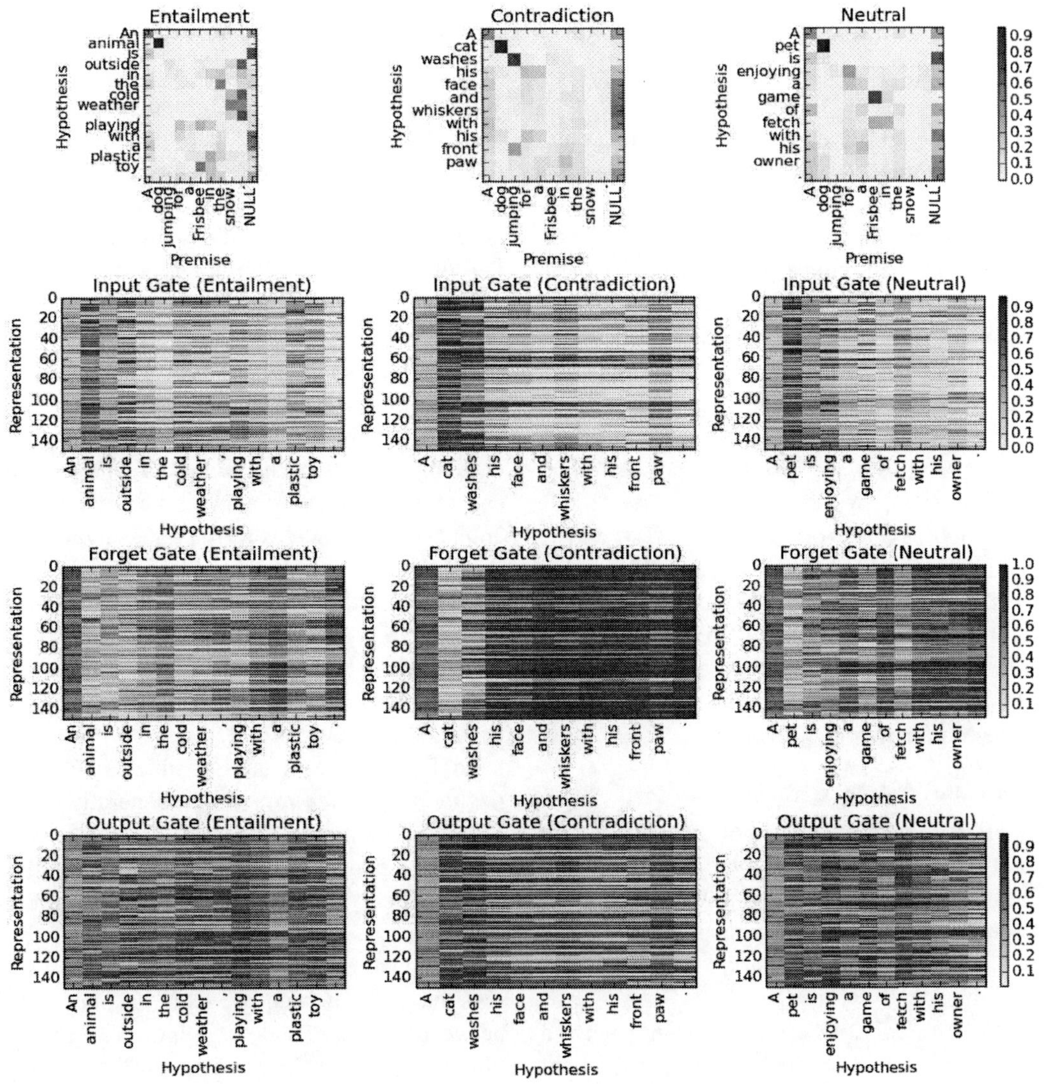

Figure 2: The alignment weights and the gate vectors of the three examples.

Word Alignment

First, let us look at the top-most plots of Figure 2. These plots show the alignment weights α_{kj} between the hypothesis and the premise, where a darker color corresponds to a larger value of α_{kj}. Recall that α_{kj} is the degree to which the kth word in the hypothesis is aligned with the jth word in the premise. Also recall that the weights α_{kj} are configured such that for the same k all the α_{kj} add up to 1. This means the weights in the same row in these plots add up to 1. From the three plots we can see that the alignment weights generally make sense. For example, in Example 1, "animal" is strongly aligned with "dog" and "toy" aligned with "Frisbee." The phrase "cold weather" is aligned with "snow." In Example 3, we also see that "pet" is strongly aligned with "dog" and "game" aligned with "Frisbee."

In Example 2, "cat" is strongly aligned with "dog" and "washes" is aligned with "jumping." It may appear that these matching results are wrong. However, "dog" is likely the best match for "cat" among all the words in the premise, and as we will show later, this match between "cat" and "dog" is actually a strong indication of a contradiction between the two sentences. The same explanation applies to the match between "washes" and "jumping."

We also observe that some words are aligned with the *NULL* token we inserted. For example, the word "is" in the hypothesis in Example 1 does not correspond to any word in the premise and is therefore aligned with *NULL*. The words "face" and "whiskers" in Example 2 and "owner" in Example 3 are also aligned with *NULL*. Intuitively, if some important content words in the hypothesis are aligned with *NULL*, it is more likely that the relationship label is either contradiction or neutral.

Values of Gate Vectors

Next, let us look at the values of the learned gate vectors of our mLSTM for the three examples. We show these values under the setting where d is set to 150. Each row of these plots corresponds to one of the 150 dimensions. Again, a darker color indicates a higher value.

An input gate controls whether the input at the current position should be used in deriving the final hidden state of the current position. From the three plots of the input gates, we can observe that generally for stop words such as prepositions and articles the input gates have lower values, suggesting that the matching of these words is less important. On the other hand, content words such as nouns and verbs tend to have higher values of the input gates, which

also makes sense because these words are generally more important for determining the final relationship label.

To further verify the observation above, we compute the average input gate values for stop words and the other content words. We find that the former has an average value of 0.287 with a standard deviation of 0.084 while the latter has an average value of 0.347 with a standard deviation of 0.116. This shows that indeed generally stop words have lower input gate values. Interestingly, we also find that some stop words may have higher input gate values if they are critical for the classification task. For example, the negation word "not" has an average input gate value of 0.444 with a standard deviation of 0.104.

Overall, the values of the input gates confirm that the mLSTM helps differentiate the more important word-level matching results from the less important ones.

Next, let us look at the forget gates. Recall that a forget gate controls the importance of the *previous* cell state in deriving the final hidden state of the current position. Higher values of a forget gate indicate that we need to remember the previous cell state and pass it on whereas lower values indicate that we should probably forget the previous cell. From the three plots of the forget gates, we can see that overall the colors are the lightest for Example 1, which is an *entailment*. This suggests that when the hypothesis is an entailment of the premise, the mLSTM tends to forget the previous matching results. On the other hand, for Example 2 and Example 3, which are *contradiction* and *neutral*, we see generally darker colors. In particular, in Example 2, we can see that the colors are consistently dark starting from the word "his" in the hypothesis until the end. We believe the explanation is that after the mLSTM processes the first three words of the hypothesis, "A cat washes," it sees that the matching between "cat" and "dog" and between "washes" and "jumping" is a strong indication of a contradiction, and therefore these matching results need to be remembered until the end of the mLSTM for the final prediction.

We have also checked the forget gates of the other sentence pairs in the test data by computing the average forget gate values and the standard deviations for *entailment*, *neutral* and *contradiction*, respectively. We find that the values are 0.446±0.123,

0.507±0.148 and 0.536±0.170, respectively. For *contradiction* and *neutral*, the forget gates start to have higher values from certain positions of the hypotheses.

Based on the observations above, we hypothesize that the way the *m*LSTM works is as follows. It remembers important mismatches, which are useful for predicting the *contradiction* or the *neutral* relationship, and forgets good matching results. At the end of the *m*LSTM, if no important mismatch is remembered, the final classifier will likely predict *entailment* by default. Otherwise, depending on the kind of mismatch remembered, the classifier will predict either *contradiction* or *neutral*.

For the output gates, we are not able to draw any important conclusion except that the output gates seem to be positively correlated with the input gates but they tend to be darker than the input gates.

4 Related Work

There has been much work on natural language inference. Shallow methods rely mostly on lexical similarities but are shown to be robust. For example, Bowman et al. (2015) experimented with a lexicalized classifier-based method, which only uses lexical information and achieves an accuracy of 78.2% on the SNLI corpus. More advanced methods use syntactic structures of the sentences to help matching them. For example, Mehdad et al. (2009) applied syntactic-semantic tree kernels for recognizing textual entailment. Because inference is essentially a logic problem, methods based on formal logic (Clark and Harrison, 2009) or natural logic (MacCartney, 2009) have also been proposed. A comprehensive review on existing work can be found in the book by Dagan et al. (2013).

The work most relevant to ours is the recently proposed neural attention model-based method by Rocktäschel et al. (2016), which we have detailed in previous sections. Neural attention models have recently been applied to some natural language processing tasks including machine translation (Bahdanau et al., 2015), abstractive summarization (Rush et al., 2015) and question answering (Hermann et al., 2015). Rocktäschel et al. (2016) showed that the neural attention model could help derive a better representation of the premise to be used to match

the hypothesis, whereas in our work we also use it to derive representations of the premise that are used to sequentially match the words in the hypothesis.

The SNLI corpus is new and so far it has only been used in a few studies. Besides the work by Bowman et al. (2015) themselves and by Rocktäschel et al. (2016), there are two other studies which used the SNLI corpus. Vendrov et al. (2015) used a *Skip-Thought* model proposed by Kiros et al. (2015) to the NLI task and reported an accuracy of 81.5% on the test data. Mou et al. (2015) used tree-based CNN encoders to obtain sentence embeddings and achieved an accuracy of 82.1%.

5 Conclusions and Future Work

In this paper, we proposed a special LSTM architecture for the task of natural language inference. Based on a recent work by Rocktäschel et al. (2016), we first used neural attention models to derive attention-weighted vector representations of the premise. We then designed a match-LSTM that processes the hypothesis word by word while trying to match the hypothesis with the premise. The last hidden state of this *m*LSTM can be used for predicting the relationship between the premise and the hypothesis. Experiments on the SNLI corpus showed that the *m*LSTM model outperformed the state-of-the-art performance reported so far on this data set. Moreover, closer analyses on the gate vectors revealed that our *m*LSTM indeed remembers and passes on important matching results, which are typically mismatches that indicate a *contradiction* or a *neutral* relationship between the premise and the hypothesis.

With the large number of parameters to learn, an inevitable limitation of our model is that a large training data set is needed to learn good model parameters. Indeed some preliminary experiments applying our *m*LSTM to the SICK corpus (Marelli et al., 2014), a smaller textual entailment benchmark data set, did not give very good results. We believe that this is because our model learns everything from scratch except using the pre-trained word embeddings. A future direction would be to incorporate other resources such as the paraphrase database (Ganitkevitch et al., 2013) into the learning process so that such prior knowledge can be utilized.

References

Dzmitry Bahdanau, HyungHyun Cho, and Yoshua Bengio. 2015. Neural machine translation by jointly learning to align and translate. In *Proceedings of the International Conference on Learning Representations*.

Samuel R Bowman, Gabor Angeli, Christopher Potts, and Christopher D Manning. 2015. A large annotated corpus for learning natural language inference. In *Proceedings of the 2015 Conference on Empirical Methods in Natural Language Processing*.

Peter Clark and Phil Harrison. 2009. An inference-based approach to recognizing entailment. In *Proceedings of the Text Analysis Conference*.

Ido Dagan, Oren Glickman, and Bernardo Magnini. 2005. The PASCAL Recognising Textual Entailment Challenge. In *Proceedings of the PASCAL Challenges Workshop on Recognizing Textual Entailment*.

Ido Dagan, Dan Roth, Mark Sammons, and Fabio Massimo Zanzotto. 2013. *Recognizing Textual Entailment: Models and Applications*. Synthesis Lectures on Human Language Technologies. Morgan & Claypool Publishers.

Juri Ganitkevitch, Benjamin Van Durme, and Chris Callison-Burch. 2013. PPDB: The paraphrase database. In *Proceedings of the 2013 Conference of the North American Chapter of the Association for Computational Linguistics*.

Oren Glickman, Ido Dagan, and Moshe Koppel. 2005. Web based probabilistic textual entailment. In *Proceedings of the PASCAL Challenges Workshop on Recognizing Textual Entailment*.

Alex Graves. 2012. *Supervised sequence labelling with recurrent neural networks*, volume 385. Springer.

Karl Moritz Hermann, Tomas Kocisky, Edward Grefenstette, Lasse Espeholt, Will Kay, Mustafa Suleyman, and Phil Blunsom. 2015. Teaching machines to read and comprehend. In *Advances in Neural Information Processing Systems*.

Sepp Hochreiter and Jürgen Schmidhuber. 1997. Long short-term memory. *Neural Computation*, 9(8):1735–1780.

Diederik Kingma and Jimmy Ba. 2014. Adam: A method for stochastic optimization. *Proceedings of the International Conference on Learning Representations*.

Ryan Kiros, Yukun Zhu, Ruslan R Salakhutdinov, Richard Zemel, Raquel Urtasun, Antonio Torralba, and Sanja Fidler. 2015. Skip-thought vectors. In *Advances in Neural Information Processing Systems*.

Bill MacCartney, Michel Galley, and Christopher D Manning. 2008. A phrase-based alignment model for natural language inference. In *Proceedings of the Conference on Empirical Methods in Natural Language Processing*.

Bill MacCartney. 2009. *Natural Language Inference*. Ph.D. thesis, Stanford University.

Marco Marelli, Stefano Menini, Marco Baroni, Luisa Bentivogli, Raffaella Bernardi, and Roberto Zamparelli. 2014. A SICK cure for the evaluation of compositional distributional semantic models. In *Proceedings of the Ninth International Conference on Language Resources and Evaluation*.

Yashar Mehdad, Alessandro Moschitti1, and Fabio Massiomo Zanzotto. 2009. SemKer: Syntactic/semantic kernels for recognizing textual entailment. In *Proceedings of the Text Analysis Conference*.

Lili Mou, Men Rui, Ge Li, Yan Xu, Lu Zhang, Rui Yan, and Zhi Jin. 2015. Recognizing entailment and contradiction by tree-based convolution. *arXiv preprint arXiv:1512.08422*.

Jeffrey Pennington, Richard Socher, and Christopher D Manning. 2014. Glove: Global vectors for word representation. *Proceedings of the Conference on Empirical Methods in Natural Language Processing*.

Tim Rocktäschel, Edward Grefenstette, Karl Moritz Hermann, Tomáš Kočiskỳ, and Phil Blunsom. 2016. Reasoning about entailment with neural attention. In *Proceedings of the International Conference on Learning Representations*.

Alexander M Rush, Sumit Chopra, and Jason Weston. 2015. A neural attention model for abstractive sentence summarization. *Proceedings of the Conference on Empirical Methods in Natural Language Processing*.

Ivan Vendrov, Ryan Kiros, Sanja Fidler, and Raquel Urtasun. 2015. Order-embeddings of images and language. *arXiv preprint arXiv:1511.06361*.

Activity Modeling in Email

Ashequl Qadir
School of Computing
University of Utah
Salt Lake City, UT 84112, USA
asheq@cs.utah.edu

Michael Gamon
Microsoft Research
One Microsoft Way
Redmond, WA 98052, USA
mgamon@microsoft.com

Patrick Pantel
Microsoft Research
One Microsoft Way
Redmond, WA 98052, USA
ppantel@microsoft.com

Ahmed Hassan Awadallah
Microsoft Research
One Microsoft Way
Redmond, WA 98052, USA
ahmed.awadallah@microsoft.com

Abstract

We introduce a latent activity model for workplace emails, positing that communication at work is purposeful and organized by activities. We pose the problem as probabilistic inference in graphical models that jointly capture the interplay between latent activities and the email contexts they govern, such as the recipients, subject and body. The model parameters are learned using maximum likelihood estimation with an expectation maximization algorithm. We present three variants of the model that incorporate the recipients, co-occurrence of the recipients, and email body and subject. We demonstrate the model's effectiveness in an email recipient recommendation task and show that it outperforms a state-of-the-art generative model. Additionally, we show that the activity model can be used to identify email senders who engage in similar activities, resulting in further improvements in recipient recommendation.

1 Introduction

Activities are a prominent characteristic of a workplace, typically governed by people's job roles and work responsibilities. Examples of workplace activities can include organizing a conference, purchasing equipment, managing candidate interviews, etc. Activities can be viewed as a collaborative work practice involving a set of people each playing a different role in the activity (Dredze et al., 2006).

Although emails are an integral part of workplace communication, current email clients offer little support for the activity oriented use of email (Khoussainov and Kushmerick, 2005). Discussions can get split across long email threads and communications about all activities can get intermixed, making activity management difficult (Balakrishnan et al., 2010).

In this work, we model activities as latent probability distributions personalized to the email sender. We present three variants of the activity model, incorporating: (1) email recipients, (2) email recipient pairs which account for co-occurrence of the email recipients, and (3) email body and subject tokens along with email recipient pairs. Additionally, we experiment with lexical (bag of words), syntactic (nouns and verb phrases), and semantic (things of interest in an email) representations of the body and subject tokens of an email. The parameters of the generative model are learned using an expectation maximization (EM) algorithm.

For evaluation, we formulate a real world task setting for email recipient recommendation, where we assume that all but the last recipient of an email has been entered by the sender, and we test the effectiveness of our activity model in recommending the last recipient. Such a system has practical applications, such as reminding an email sender about a potentially forgotten recipient or recommending the next recipient as the sender enters each recipient.

The main contributions of our research are:

- We introduce a latent activity model for emails

Proceedings of NAACL-HLT 2016, pages 1452–1462,
San Diego, California, June 12-17, 2016. ©2016 Association for Computational Linguistics

where the email contexts are governed by workplace activities;

- We present probabilistic modeling that incorporates co-occurring recipients with lexical, syntactic and semantic contexts of an email;

- We identify senders engaging in similar activities using the activity model, and show improvements in recipient recommendation.

2 Related Work

Prior research related to our work can be divided into the following three major areas presented below.

2.1 Activity in Emails

Prior research has treated emails as a communication tool for workplace activities (Moran, 2005) or a task management resource (Bellotti et al., 2003). Kushmerick and Lau (2005) formalized e-commerce activities as finite-state automata, where transitions among states represent messages sent between participants. Dredze et al. (2006) used user generated activity labels and classified emails into activities using overlapping participants and content similarity. Minkov et al. (2008) modeled user created folders and TO-DO items as activities, and created a heterogeneous graph to perform activity-centric search.

Shen et al. (2006) predicted tasks associated with an incoming email by leveraging email sender, recipients and distinct subject words. They found the body words to not provide additional prediction value. Although they used similar information as we do, they used a combination of generative and discriminative models toward task classification, and did not do recipient recommendation. Our activity model designs are closer to the model introduced by Dredze and Wallach (2008), who presented a Dirichlet process mixture model combined with author and thread information. Our designs differ as we use co-occurring recipients in the generative process, and use various linguistic representations of content.

2.2 Generative models for Emails

Latent Dirichlet Allocation (LDA) (Blei et al., 2003) is a frequently used generative topic model. Assuming a Dirichlet prior, LDA models learn probability distributions of words as latent topics in a corpus. In emails, LDA models have been used for learn-ing summary keywords (Dredze et al., 2008), analyzing how topics change over time (Wang and Mc-Callum, 2006), understanding entity relations (Balasubramanyan and Cohen, 2011), analyzing communication networks (Nguyen et al., 2013), for authorship attribution (Seroussi et al., 2012), and discovering topics associated with authors (McCallum et al., 2005).

Other generative models have also been used for analyzing email communication behavior (Navaroli et al., 2012), identifying links between an email sender and a recipient to detect potential anomalous communication (Huang and Zeng, 2006), and resolving personal names in emails (Elsayed et al., 2008). Representing workplace activities of the emails with probabilistic inference in graphical models where observed information is personalized to the email senders is what sets our work apart from previous research in computational models for emails.

2.3 Email Recipient Recommendation

For recommending email recipients, interactions among email participants and content similarity are the signals that have been explored most. Carvalho and Cohen (2007) leveraged content similarity by creating tf-idf centroid vectors and determining k-nearest neighbors of a target email. Pal et al. (2007) presented a discriminative author recipient topic model that uses transfer learning. Desai and Dash (2014) used reverse chronologically arranged implicit groups determined from sent emails. Sofershtein and Cohen (2015) created a ranking function combining temporal and textual features.

Among the generative modeling based approaches, Pal and McCallum (2006) learned probability distributions of recipients, and words in body and subject to predict recipients in email cc lists. Dredze et al. (2008) evaluated the impact of summary keywords generated using LDA, for email recipient prediction. More recently, Graus et al. (2014) predicted email recipients by estimating sender and recipient likelihood using a communication graph, email likelihood using content words, and evaluated performance on the Avocado email corpus. In our work, we use latent activity distributions, and identify senders who engage in similar activities. We compare our recipient prediction results against the generative model of Graus et al. (2014).

3 Problem Setting and Data

3.1 Activity Modeling in Emails

Our motivation for activity modeling in email stems from the assumption that in the workplace, people primarily use emails as a communication tool for their ongoing activities, and an email's recipient list, content, and other context are governed by a given activity. For example, an employee attending a conference may write emails to the conference organizers regarding registration or scheduling, or emails to a hotel for booking confirmation. The communication may span multiple emails, involving many parties, but all under the same activity.

We model the activities as a latent probabilistic variable over the email recipients and content, personalized to the email sender. Let D be the set of all emails in a corpus containing N emails, generated by $S = \{s_i \mid 1 \leq i \leq S_D\}$ senders, and sent to $R = \{r_i \mid 1 \leq i \leq R_D\}$ recipients. Let $B = \{b_i \mid 1 \leq i \leq B_D\}$, and $T = \{t_i \mid 1 \leq i \leq T_D\}$ represent the body and subject vocabulary of the emails respectively. Let K be the number of latent activities for each sender. We model the activities as probability distributions over email components S, R, B and T.

3.2 Corpus Description and Data Sets

For our experiments, we use the Avocado email corpus, available from the LDC catalog.[1] The corpus contains emails from a defunct IT company referred to as "Avocado". For learning the activity model, we extract emails from 7/1/2000 – 5/1/2001 to create a training data set, and from 5/1/2001 – 6/30/2001 for development/tuning. In this work, we did not consider threaded conversations, only retained the first email in a thread and discarded the rest.

As additional filtering steps, we only kept emails written by the Avocado employees, allowing us to confine the scope of the activities within the company. To control sparsity and noise, for each email, we enforced a a minimum of two recipients, and a maximum of ten recipients.[2] In a practical system,

Number of	Train	Train + Dev
Total emails	18,593	22,283
Unique senders	120	129
Unique recipients	3,157	3,658
Unique body words	31,386	36,005
Unique subject words	6,969	7,724
Emails per sender	154.94	172.74
Emails per recipient	5.89	6.09

Table 1: Data set statistics.

we consider it reasonable that a model only activates after some history of email is sent by a user. We therefore removed emails by the senders having fewer than 25 emails in the training data. From email bodies and subjects, we removed stopwords, and words appearing fewer than 5 times or more than 100 times.[3] When a recipient's same email alias was present multiple times, we took it only once, as well as removed a sender's email alias from the recipients list if it was present there. In this work, we focused on recipients from only the "TO" field, and did not include recipients from the "CC" or "BCC" field. Table 1 presents statistics of the data sets.

4 Activity Models

Our key assumption in modeling the activities in email is that different components of an email contain specific types of information that can help to characterize the activities that drive user behavior. In our generative process of the activity model, for an email $d \in D$, a sender $s \in S$ is first generated from a multinomial distribution with probability vector σ, then an activity a is generated from a sender personalized multinomial distribution with probability vector θ_s. Let $R_d \subseteq R$, $B_d \subseteq B$ and $T_d \subseteq T$ be the set[4] of recipients, body and subject tokens of d respectively. The generation of the email contexts (recipients and body/subject tokens) varies based on the specific design of each variant of our model. In a first simplistic model, we assume that recipient $r \in R_d$, body token $b \in B_d$ and subject token $t \in T_d$ for an email can be generated from the multinomial distributions with probability vectors $\lambda_{s,a}$, $\phi_{s,a}$, and $\tau_{s,a}$ respectively, that are conditioned s and a. Point estimates for σ can be directly

---

[1] https://catalog.ldc.upenn.edu/LDC2015T03

[2] When an email has many recipients, it is often indicative of general announcements or system generated emails, which are

less directly relevant to an employee's activities. Some emails in the Avocado dataset have more than 500 recipients.

[3] A heuristic we used to remove words that are too general.

[4] Multiset for body and subject tokens.

calculated from a training corpus, whereas θ, λ, ϕ, and τ are the unknown parameters of the model.

4.1 Model 1: Rec

In our first model Rec, we assume that the latent activities can be learned as a probability distribution over the recipients alone. The generative process is:

> **Model 1: Rec**
> For each email document $d \in D$
>   sender $s \sim$ Multinomial(σ)
>   activity $a \sim$ Multinomial(θ_s)
>   For $1 \ldots |R_d|$
>   recipient $r \sim$ Multinomial$(\lambda_{s,a})$

Figure 1 presents the plate diagram of the model. The joint probability of the Rec model is the product of the conditional distributions:

$$P(s, a, r | \sigma, \theta, \lambda) = P(s|\sigma)P(a|s,\theta) \prod_{r \in R_d} P(r|s,a,\lambda)$$

The probability of a sender s, an activity a given s, and a recipient r given s and a are defined below[5]:

$$P(s = \hat{s}) = \prod_{i=1}^{S_D} \sigma_i^{I[i=\hat{s}]}, \ s.t. \sum_i \sigma_i = 1$$

$$P(a = \hat{a} | s = \hat{s}) = \prod_{i=1}^{K} \theta_{\hat{s},i}^{I[i=\hat{a}]}, \ s.t. \ \forall_s \sum_i \theta_{s,i} = 1$$

$$P(r = \hat{r} | s = \hat{s}, a = \hat{a}) = \prod_{i=1}^{R_D} \lambda_{\hat{s},\hat{a},i}^{I[i=\hat{r}]},$$

$$s.t. \ \ \forall_{s,a} \ \sum_i \lambda_{s,a,i} = 1$$

Inference: Let d^n be the nth email, where $d^n = \{s^n, R_d^n\}$. We apply Bayes' rule to find the posterior distribution over the activities $P^n(a|d)$, which is directly proportional to the joint distribution $P^n(a, d)$. We can exactly compute this distribution by evaluating the joint distribution for every value of a and the observed document d^n.

Learning: Point estimates for σ can be directly obtained from the training corpus. We estimate the

---
[5]I is an indicator variable

parameters θ and λ by maximizing the (log) probability of observing D. We write the $\log(D)$ as:

$$\log P(D) = \sum_{n=1}^{N} \sum_a P^n(a|s, R_d) \log P^n(a, s, R_d)$$

We use the Expectation-Maximization (EM) algorithm to set the parameters. Starting with a random initialization of the parameters (with Gaussian noise), EM iterates between the E-step in which $P^n(a|s, R_d)$ is computed for each email with fixed parameter values computed in the previous M-step, and the M-step in which the parameters are updated with fixed $P^n(a|s, R_d)$ values computed in the E-step. The parameter updates are obtained by taking the derivative of $\log P(D)$ with respect to each parameter, and setting the resultant to 0, providing us with the following parameter updates:

$$\theta_{s^n,i} = \frac{\sum_{n=1}^{N} \sum_a P^n(a|d) I[i = a]}{\sum_{n=1}^{N} \sum_a P^n(a|d)}$$

$$\lambda_{s^n,a,i} = \frac{\sum_{n=1}^{N} \sum_a P^n(a|d) \sum_{r \in R} I[i = r]}{|R_d^n| \sum_{n=1}^{N} \sum_a P^n(a|d)}$$

We run EM until the change in $\log P(D)$ is less than our convergence threshold 10^{-5}.

4.2 Model 2: CoRec

Using co-occurring recipients in generative models for emails has been rarely explored in previous work. Pal and McCallum (2006) modeled co-recipient information as a probability distribution of recipients conditioned on the other recipients, and noted that this information improved their email cc prediction performance. In our $CoRec$ model, we model co-recipients as pairs of recipients generated from a probability distribution conditioned on the sender and the activity. Let $L = \{(r_i, r_j) \mid 1 \leq i \leq R_D, 1 \leq j \leq R_D\}$ having L_D pairs of recipients in the corpus. For an email d, $L_d \subseteq L$ is the set of recipient pairs in d. The $CoRec$ model first generates a sender s from the probability distribution σ, then an activity a from a distribution over latent activities θ_s personalized to s, and finally recipient pairs $r_p \in L_d$ from a distribution over recipient pairs $\omega_{s,a}$ conditioned on s and a. The generative process is summarized below:

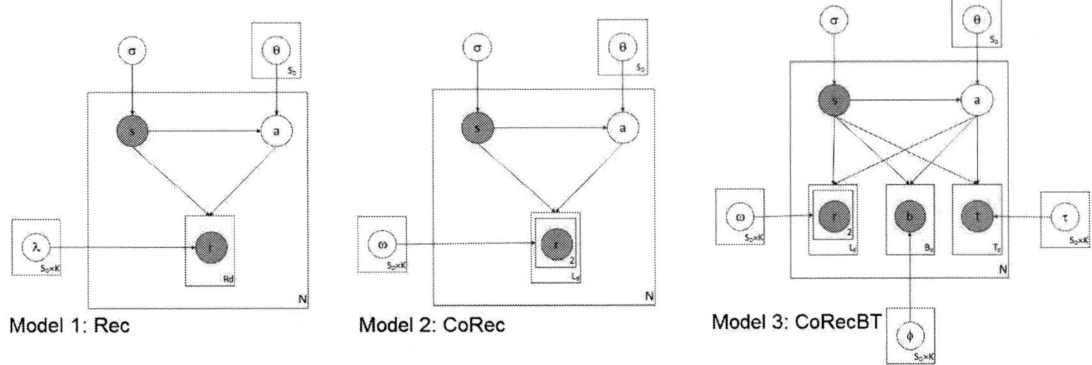

Figure 1: Activity model plate diagrams.

Model 2: CoRec
For each email document d
    sender $s \sim \text{Multinomial}(\sigma)$
    activity $a \sim \text{Multinomial}(\theta_s)$
    For $1 \dots |L_d|$
        recipient pair $r_p \sim \text{Multinomial}(\omega_{s,a})$

The joint probability of the $CoRec$ model is:

$$P(s, a, r_p | \sigma, \theta, \omega) = P(s|\sigma)P(a|s, \theta)$$
$$\prod_{r_p \in L_d} P(r_p | s, a, \omega)$$

This adds over the Rec model the probability of a recipient pair r_p given s and a, defined below:

$$P(r_p = \hat{r}_p | s = \hat{s}, a = \hat{a}) = \prod_{i=1}^{L_D} \omega_{\hat{s}, \hat{a}, i}^{I[i=\hat{r}_p]},$$

$$s.t. \quad \forall_{s,a} \quad \sum_i \omega_{s,a,i} = 1$$

The EM algorithm is applied in the same way as in the Rec model. During the M-step, update for θ remains the same. The update for ω is given below:

$$\omega_{s^n, a, i} = \frac{\sum_{n=1}^{N} \sum_a P^n(a|d) \sum_{r_p \in L} I[i = r_p]}{|L_d^n| \sum_{n=1}^{N} \sum_a P^n(a|d)}$$

4.3 Model 3: CoRecBT

Finally, in the $CoRecBT$ model, we further incorporate body and subject of emails. The generative process of the model is:

Model 3: CoRecBT
For each email document d
    sender $s \sim \text{Multinomial}(\sigma)$
    activity $a \sim \text{Multinomial}(\theta_s)$
    For $1 \dots |L_d|$
        recipient pair $r_p \sim \text{Multinomial}(\omega_{s,a})$
    For $1 \dots |B_d|$
        body token $b \sim \text{Multinomial}(\phi_{s,a})$
    For $1 \dots |T_d|$
        subject token $t \sim \text{Multinomial}(\tau_{s,a})$

The joint probability of the $CoRecBT$ model:

$$P(s, a, r_p, b, t | \sigma, \theta, \omega, \phi, \tau) = P(s|\sigma)P(a|s, \theta)$$
$$\prod_{r_p \in L_d} P(r_p | s, a, \omega) \prod_{b \in B_d} P(b | s, a, \phi)$$
$$\prod_{t \in T_d} P(t | s, a, \tau)$$

where the probability of a body token b and subject token t given s and a defined as:

$$P(b = \hat{b} | s = \hat{s}, a = \hat{a}) = \prod_{i=1}^{B} \phi_{\hat{s}, \hat{a}, i}^{I[i=\hat{b}]}$$

$$P(t = \hat{t} | s = \hat{s}, a = \hat{a}) = \prod_{i=1}^{T} \tau_{\hat{s}, \hat{a}, i}^{I[i=\hat{t}]},$$

$$s.t. \quad \forall_{s,a} \sum_i \phi_{s,a,i} = 1, \forall_{s,a} \sum_i \tau_{s,a,i} = 1$$

During the M-step of the EM algorithm, updates for θ and ω remain the same as the $CoRec$ model. The updates for ϕ and τ are given below:

$$\phi_{s^n,a,i} = \frac{\sum_{n=1}^{N} \sum_a P^n(a|d) \sum_{b \in B} I[i = b]}{|B_d^n| \sum_{n=1}^{N} \sum_a P^n(a|d)}$$

$$\tau_{s^n,a,i} = \frac{\sum_{n=1}^{N} \sum_a P^n(a|d) \sum_{t \in T} I[i = t]}{|T_d^n| \sum_{n=1}^{N} \sum_a P^n(a|d)}$$

4.4 Subject and Body Token Representations

Previous work in modeling email content mostly explored bag of words (e.g., (Graus et al., 2014)) or tf-idf vectors (e.g., (Carvalho and Cohen, 2007)) as the content representation of an email. For modeling activities in emails, we experiment with different linguistic representations of the email content. They are:

- Lexical: as the lexical representation, we use the bag of words (BOW) from email body and subject, after Penn Tree Bank (PTB) style tokenization.

- Syntactic: using heuristics on the output of a PTB constituent parser (Quirk et al., 2012), we identify Nouns (N) and Verb Phrases (VP) in email body and subject.

- Semantic: we identify phrases in emails that represent topics, concept and entities discussed in the emails. We refer to them as *Thing of Interest (TOI)*. To extract these key phrases, we use Web search queries as a source of information. Using queries as a dictionary of possible key phrases is useful but has limited coverage since many topics/concepts are discussed in emails but absent or not widely available in Web search queries. Instead of using queries directly, we use them to construct a training set of key phrases and their content and we train a discriminative model to identify the key phrases. We treat each query as a key phrase and the surrounding text from Web results as context. We use a sample of hundreds of thousands of search queries from the usage logs of a commercial Web search engine. Only queries tagged as English and from the United States locale were retained to remove geographic or linguistic variations. Queries were kept only if they have been submitted by at least 100 different users in one month. For each query, the text from the Web page that is most relevant to the query and that contains the exact query text is collected as the context for the query. Relevance is estimated by the percentage of time the page has received a long dwell time click (greater than 30 seconds) for the query. If no relevant pages exist, the query is ignored. To generate negative examples, random n-grams were extracted from web pages. We experimented with a large number of features including: first word of the phrase, last word of the phrase, n-gram features (n=1 to 3), the word right before/after the phrase, the part-of-speech tag of the first word in the phrase, the part-of-speech tag of the last word in the phrase, n-gram features (n ranges from 1 to 3) over the sequence of part-of-speech tags representing the phrase and the part-of-speech tags of the word right before/after the phrase, phrase length, how many times it appeared in the body/title, and the relative location of the first occurrence of the phrase in the body. We trained a logistic regression classifier using these features and the data described above. The trained classifier is then applied to our email data to identify the *Thing of Interest (TOI)* phrases.

4.5 Discussion

Full Bayesian Treatment: In the above models, we learn point estimates for the parameters $(\sigma, \theta, \omega, \phi, \tau)$. One can take a Bayesian approach and treat these parameters as variables (for instance, with Dirichlet prior distributions), and perform Bayesian inference. However, exact inference will become intractable and we would need to resort to methods such as variational inference or sampling. We found this extension unnecessary, as we had a sufficient amount of training data to estimate all parameters reliably. In addition, our approach enabled us to learn (and perform inference in) the model with large amounts of data with reasonable computing time.

5 Recipient Recommendation

To evaluate the effectiveness of our activity model, we formulate a recipient recommendation task.

Task Definition: For a test email document d containing the list of recipients R_d, a modified list of recipients R_d^* is created by removing the last recipient $r^* \in R_d$. Given d with R_d^*, the task objective is to recommend r^* as the next recipient for d.

5.1 Our Methods

To recommend a recipient for a test email document d written by sender s_d, we first create a candidate recipient list by combining recipients who received an email from s_d, and recipients who co-occurred with an observed recipient $r \in R_d^*$ in the training corpus. Sender s_d and any $r \in R_d^*$ are excluded from the candidate list. Next, we determine the probability distribution of the activities in d using:

$$P(a|d) = \frac{P(s,a,d|\sigma,\theta,\omega,\phi,\tau)}{\sum_a P(s,a,d|\sigma,\theta,\omega,\phi,\tau)}$$

Each candidate recipient r^* is then ranked by a score using two different methods defined below. The ranked list is used as our final recommended recipients. The two scoring methods are:

Reg Method: In the Reg method, we score using the chain rule[6]:

$$P(r^*|d) \propto \sum_a P(a|d) \prod_{r \in R_d} P(r^*,r|s,a)$$

We smooth the above function using the following linear interpolation:

$$P(r^*,r|a,s) = \alpha_1 \times P(r^*,r|a,s) + (1-\alpha_1) \times$$
$$(\alpha_2 \times P(r^*,r) + (1-\alpha_2) \times P(r_{rare}))$$

Here, $P(r_{rare})$ is the lowest probability of any recipient in the training data. We calculate α_i with a sigmoid logistic function, allowing us to determine when to rely more on the learned probabilities:

$$\alpha_i = \frac{1}{1 + e^{-k(x-x_0)}}$$

For α_1, x is the pointwise mutual information (PMI) between s and r in training data, with steepness parameter $k = 50$. For α_2, x is the frequency of r in training data, with $k = .5$. Sigmoid's midpoint

---

[6]Scoring function for the Rec model uses $P(r^*|s,a)$

x_0 is the first quartile ($Q1$) of the PMI and recipient frequency distributions respectively. The above values for k have been determined from the shape of the sigmoid curves in the training data.

Sim Method: In the Sim method, we explore the idea that the activity model can be used to identify other senders with similar activities as s_d, who we refer to as *similar senders*, S_d^*. To identify the similar senders, we evaluate senders who maximize the log likelihood of the test document d by calculating $\log P(s,d)$ for all $s \in S$, and identify the top 5 with the highest scores to add to S_d^*. The observed sender s_d is not included in S_d^*. We then calculate $P_s(r^*|d)$ for each $s \in S_d^*$ using the Reg method, along with a weight w_s:

$$w_s = \frac{\log P(s,d)}{\sum_{s \in S_d^*} \log P(s,d)}$$

The final scoring function for the Sim method is:

$$P(r^*|d) = \alpha P_{s_d}(r^*|d) + (1-\alpha) \sum_{s \in S_d^*} w_s P_s(r^*|d)$$

Here, α is determined with the frequency of s_d in training data, using the sigmoid function with $k = 0.5$ and x_0 as the $Q1$ of the frequency distribution.

5.2 Baseline Systems

As simple baseline systems to compare with our methods, we use 1) a random recipient baseline; 2) ranked recipients by $P(r = r^*)$; and 3) ranked recipients by $P(r = r^*|s = s_d)$, where the probabilities are calculated from the training data. We evaluate two additional generative baselines using 4) $P(r = r^*|R_d^*)$, and 5) $P(r = r^*|s = s_d, R_d^*)$ by applying Bayes' theorem, and assuming conditional independence among $r \in R_d^*$. For these methods, we used similar interpolation smoothing as before.

We additionally implemented the generative model presented by Graus et al. (2014) for recipient recommendation, which for test email d uses:

$$P(r^*|s_d,d) \propto P(d|r^*,s_d) \times P(s_d|r^*) \times P(r^*)$$

Graus estimated $P(d|r^*,s_d)$ by $P(b|r^*,s_d)$ where b is an observed term in the email. The evaluation task was different from ours as they predicted all recipients of an email. In our evalua-

Method	Precision@1	Precision@2	Precision@5	Precision@10	MRR
Baselines					
(1) Random	0	0	0	.10	.0025
(2) $P(r = r^*)$	2.81	4.58	7.49	17.32	.0736
(3) $P(r = r^*\|s = s_d)$	4.47	9.72	24.18	34.69	.1455
(4) $P(r = r^*\|R_d^*)$	17.26	25.59	39.42	53.93	.2857
(5) $P(r = r^*\|s = s_d, R_d^*)$	16.80	25.01	42.02	56.16	.2871
Graus Methods (Graus et al., 2014)					
(6) GrausB (BOW)	2.96	4.84	8.01	17.94	.0769
(7) GrausB (VP-TOI)	4.63	9.00	18.25	28.86	.1257
(8) GrausR	18.88	27.2	41.97	54.39	.3005
Activity Models (Reg Scoring)					
(9) Rec	12.27	19.81	30.53	44.46	.2224
(10) CoRec	21.63	29.07	41.45	52.16	.3167
(11) CoRecBT (BOW)	19.97	27.87	40.77	52.16	.3037
(12) CoRecBT (NP-VP-TOI)	20.64	28.29	40.93	51.79	.3081
(13) CoRecBT (VP-TOI)	20.59	29.17	41.39	51.95	.3104
Activity Models (Sim Scoring)					
(14) CoRecBT (NP-VP-TOI)	22.01	30.47	44.36	56.01	.3306
(15) CoRecBT (VP-TOI)	**22.26**	**33.63**	**44.57**	**57.05**	**.3336**

Table 2: Recipient recommendation results (BOW = bag-of-words, NP = noun phrase, VP= verb phrase, TOI = thing of interest). Bold indicates statistical significance over all non-shaded results using t-test (p=0.05).

tion task, we recommend the last recipient, allowing us to use the already observed recipients R_d^* for estimating $P(d|r^*, s_d)$. Consequently, we present 3 additional baselines adopting Graus' method: 6) $GrausB(BOW)$ method uses body words, 7) $GrausB(VP - TOI)$ uses the verb phrases and things of interest, and finally 8) $GrausR$ method uses R_d^* for estimating $P(d|r^*, s_d)$. $GrausR$ is equivalent to how we calculate our fifth baseline, $P(r = r^*|s = s_d, R_d^*)$, with the only difference of the smoothing function.

6 Experimental Results

6.1 Experimental Setup

To evaluate recipient recommendation, we create a test data set by extracting emails from 7/1/2001 – 8/31/2001 from the Avocado data set. First we train our activity model with the training data and determine the optimum number of activities for each method by evaluating recipient recommendation on the development data. The number of activities per model is shown in Table 3. We then combine training and tuning data to create a new training data set in order to minimize the time difference between training and test emails. From the test data, we removed emails that had a sender or recipient never appearing in the training data. Although this lim-

its the scope of the recipient recommendation evaluation task, predicting a recipient for a sender who never appeared in the training data is beyond our current modeling scope and practical settings. The final test set contains 1923 emails with 14.91 emails per sender.

Model	K
Rec	10
CoRec	3
CoRecBT (BOW)	20
CoRecBT (NP-VP-TOI)	7
CoRecBT (VP-TOI)	4

Table 3: No. of activities used for recipient recommendation.

With the ranked lists of recipients generated by each method, we calculate precision@X (X= 1, 2, 5, 10), and MRR (Mean Reciprocal Rank). Precision@X is defined as percentage of emails having the actual recipient in the top X ranked recipients.

6.2 Recipient Recommendation Results

Table 2 presents the recipient recommendation results for different methods. The first 5 rows show that the generative baselines from row (4) and (5) performed much better than the simple baselines (row (1)–(3)), yielding up to .2871 MRR. Comparatively, the GrausB(BOW) baseline in row (6) that uses body words, did not perform well, which is consistent with the finding by Shen et al. (2006) about

Figure 2: Word clouds of activity tokens.

body words not providing additional value in their task classification work. However, the GrausB(VP–TOI) in row (7) shows that using body terms more selectively has the potential for improving performance. Comparatively, the use of observed recipients (GrausR in row (8)) substantially improved recommendation results, yielding the highest MRR, precision@1, and precision@2 scores, while the generative baseline in row (5) retained the highest precision@5 and precision@10 scores.

Next, rows (9) to (13) show results for the activity models that use the Reg scoring. First, the Rec model outperformed the simple baselines from rows (1) to (3) as well as the GrausB methods from rows (6) and (7), but did not perform better than the generative baselines from rows (4) and (5) or GrausR. All the $CoRec$ models performed better at recommending a recipient at top of the ranked lists with higher precision@1 and precision@2 scores, which are more practically useful for recommendation purposes, and also resulted in higher MRR scores.

Finally, the rows (14) and (15) show the results with the Sim scoring, and we observe a substantial improvement across the board, with verb phrase and thing of interest as the body context yielding our best results. This model achieved 3.31% additional improvements in MRR, and 3.38% additional improvements in precision@1 over the best baseline results. This demonstrates that the learned activity model can be used to identify senders who are likely to engage in similar activities, improving recipient recommendation performance further.

Figure 2 shows examples of activity tokens from the emails of a sender in our training corpus, using word clouds. This is meant to serve as a case analysis, but it is not straightforward to interpret word clouds. When inspecting, we found that the names

of potential customers (Nokia, Siemens, SAP) in the first example are prominent in some of the emails of the sender in the raw data. The recipients in these emails form a small cluster of people who are mainly involved in discussions around a particular event (Mobile Business Forum) where these companies are amongst the sponsors.

The second example, from the same sender, shows a coherent set of recipients. But in this case, the model seemed to have conflated multiple topics (such as the Palm VII device and support issues). We suspect that the cause for this confusion lies in the strong and coherent cluster of recipients which forces divergent topics to coalesce. While the combined signals of co-recipients and topic words improve the overall activity model, in some of the individual cases it leads to one signal improperly dominating the other.

7 Conclusion and Future Work

We presented a latent activity model for workplace emails where the activities are modeled as probability distributions over email recipients and other contexts, personalized to the email sender. Our model incorporates co-occurring recipients as part of the generative process, and can be used to identify senders who participate in similar activities, resulting in improved performance in email recipient recommendation. Our experiments suggest that syntactic and semantic knowledge such as verb phrases and thing of interests in emails can model the activities much better than bag-of-words, as demonstrated by the recipient recommendation results. Learning topics and sub-activities under workplace activities is a promising research direction which we will explore in future work.

References

Aruna D Balakrishnan, Tara Matthews, and Thomas P Moran. 2010. Fitting an activity-centric system into an ecology of workplace tools. In *Proceedings of the SIGCHI Conference on Human Factors in Computing Systems*, pages 787–790. ACM.

Ramnath Balasubramanyan and William W Cohen. 2011. Block-lda: Jointly modeling entity-annotated text and entity-entity links. In *SDM*, volume 11, pages 450–461. SIAM.

Victoria Bellotti, Nicolas Ducheneaut, Mark Howard, and Ian Smith. 2003. Taking email to task: the design and evaluation of a task management centered email tool. In *Proceedings of the SIGCHI conference on Human factors in computing systems*, pages 345–352. ACM.

David M Blei, Andrew Y Ng, and Michael I Jordan. 2003. Latent dirichlet allocation. *the Journal of machine Learning research*, 3:993–1022.

Vitor R Carvalho and William Cohen. 2007. Recommending recipients in the enron email corpus. *Machine Learning*.

Amish Desai and Subrat Kumar Dash. 2014. Email recipient prediction using reverse chronologically arranged implicit groups. In *Contemporary Computing (IC3), 2014 Seventh International Conference on*, pages 461–466. IEEE.

Mark Dredze and Hanna Wallach. 2008. User models for email activity management. In *Proceedings of the 5th International Workshop on Ubiquitous User Modeling (UbiqUM'08)*, Gran Canaria, Spain, January. online proceedings forthcoming.

Mark Dredze, Tessa Lau, and Nicholas Kushmerick. 2006. Automatically classifying emails into activities. In *Proceedings of the 11th International Conference on Intelligent User Interfaces*, IUI '06, pages 70–77, New York, NY, USA. ACM.

Mark Dredze, Hanna M Wallach, Danny Puller, and Fernando Pereira. 2008. Generating summary keywords for emails using topics. In *Proceedings of the 13th international conference on Intelligent user interfaces*, pages 199–206. ACM.

Tamer Elsayed, Douglas W Oard, and Galileo Namata. 2008. Resolving personal names in email using context expansion. In *ACL*, pages 941–949.

David Graus, David van Dijk, Manos Tsagkias, Wouter Weerkamp, and Maarten de Rijke. 2014. Recipient recommendation in enterprises using communication graphs and email content. In *Proceedings of the 37th international ACM SIGIR conference on Research & development in information retrieval*, pages 1079–1082. ACM.

Zan Huang and Daniel Dajun Zeng. 2006. A link prediction approach to anomalous email detection. In *SMC*, pages 1131–1136.

Rinat Khoussainov and Nicholas Kushmerick. 2005. Email task management: An iterative relational learning approach. In *CEAS*.

Nicholas Kushmerick and Tessa Lau. 2005. Automated email activity management: an unsupervised learning approach. In *Proceedings of the 10th international conference on Intelligent user interfaces*, pages 67–74. ACM.

Andrew McCallum, Andres Corrada-Emmanuel, and Xuerui Wang. 2005. Topic and role discovery in social networks. *Computer Science Department Faculty Publication Series*, page 3.

Einat Minkov, Ramnath Balasubramanyan, and William W Cohen. 2008. Activity-centred search in email. In *CEAS*. Citeseer.

Thomas P Moran. 2005. Unified activity management: Explicitly representing activity in work-support systems. In *Proceedings of the European Conference on Computer-Supported Cooperative Work (ECSCW 2005), Workshop on Activity: From Theoretical to a Computational Construct*. Citeseer.

Nicholas Navaroli, Christopher DuBois, and Padhraic Smyth. 2012. Statistical models for exploring individual email communication behavior. In *ACML*, pages 317–332.

Muon Nguyen, Thanh Ho, and Phuc Do. 2013. Social networks analysis based on topic modeling. In *Computing and Communication Technologies, Research, Innovation, and Vision for the Future (RIVF), 2013 IEEE RIVF International Conference on*, pages 119–122. IEEE.

Chris Pal and Andrew McCallum. 2006. Cc prediction with graphical models. In *CEAS*.

Chris Pal, Xuerui Wang, and Andrew McCallum. 2007. Transfer learning for enhancing information flow in organizations and social networks. Technical report, DTIC Document.

Chris Quirk, Pallavi Choudhury, Jianfeng Gao, Hisami Suzuki, Kristina Toutanova, Michael Gamon, Wen-tau Yih, Lucy Vanderwende, and Colin Cherry. 2012. Msr splat, a language analysis toolkit. In *Proceedings of the 2012 Conference of the North American Chapter of the Association for Computational Linguistics: Human Language Technologies: Demonstration Session*, pages 21–24. Association for Computational Linguistics.

Yanir Seroussi, Fabian Bohnert, and Ingrid Zukerman. 2012. Authorship attribution with author-aware topic models. In *Proceedings of the 50th Annual Meeting of the Association for Computational Linguistics:*

Short Papers-Volume 2, pages 264–269. Association for Computational Linguistics.

Jianqiang Shen, Lida Li, Thomas G Dietterich, and Jonathan L Herlocker. 2006. A hybrid learning system for recognizing user tasks from desktop activities and email messages. In *Proceedings of the 11th international conference on Intelligent user interfaces*, pages 86–92. ACM.

Zvi Sofershtein and Sara Cohen. 2015. Predicting email recipients. In *Proceedings of the 2015 IEEE/ACM International Conference on Advances in Social Networks Analysis and Mining 2015*, ASONAM '15, pages 761–764, New York, NY, USA. ACM.

Xuerui Wang and Andrew McCallum. 2006. Topics over time: a non-markov continuous-time model of topical trends. In *Proceedings of the 12th ACM SIGKDD international conference on Knowledge discovery and data mining*, pages 424–433. ACM.

Clustering Paraphrases by Word Sense

Anne Cocos and Chris Callison-Burch
Computer and Information Science Department, University of Pennsylvania

Abstract

Automatically generated databases of English paraphrases have the drawback that they return a single list of paraphrases for an input word or phrase. This means that all senses of polysemous words are grouped together, unlike WordNet which partitions different senses into separate synsets. We present a new method for clustering paraphrases by word sense, and apply it to the Paraphrase Database (PPDB). We investigate the performance of hierarchical and spectral clustering algorithms, and systematically explore different ways of defining the similarity matrix that they use as input. Our method produces sense clusters that are qualitatively and quantitatively good, and that represent a substantial improvement to the PPDB resource.

1 Introduction

Many natural language processing tasks rely on the ability to identify words and phrases with equivalent meaning but different wording. These alternative ways of expressing the same information are called paraphrases. Several research efforts have produced automatically generated databases of English paraphrases, including DIRT (Lin and Pantel, 2001), the Microsoft Research Paraphrase Phrase Tables (Dolan et al., 2004), and the Paraphrase Database (Ganitkevitch et al., 2013; Pavlick et al., 2015a). A primary benefit of these automatically generated resources is their enormous scale, which provides superior coverage compared to manually compiled resources like WordNet (Miller, 1995). But automatically generated paraphrase resources currently have the drawback that they group all senses of polysemous words together, and do not partition paraphrases into groups like WordNet does

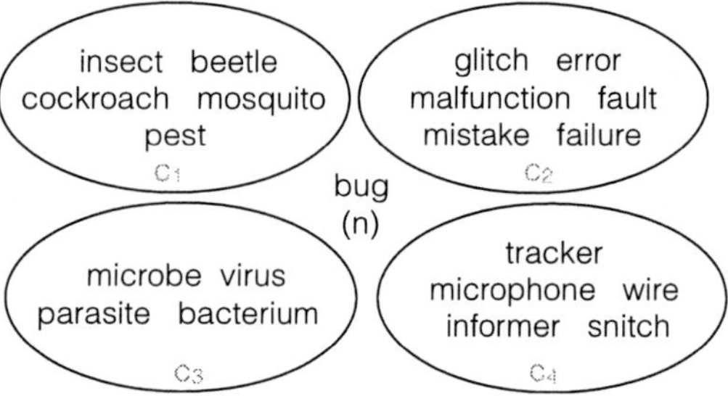

Figure 1: Our goal is to partition paraphrases of an input word like *bug* into clusters representing its distinct senses.

with its synsets. Thus a search for paraphrases of the noun *bug* would yield a single list of paraphrases that includes *insect, glitch, beetle, error, microbe, wire, cockroach, malfunction, microphone, mosquito, virus, tracker, pest, informer, snitch, parasite, bacterium, fault, mistake, failure* and many others. The goal of this work is to group these paraphrases into clusters that denote the distinct senses of the input word or phrase, as shown in Figure 1.

We develop a method for clustering the paraphrases from the Paraphrase Database (PPDB). PPDB contains over 100 million paraphrases generated using the bilingual pivoting method (Bannard and Callison-Burch, 2005), which posits that two English words are potential paraphrases of each other if they share one or more foreign translations. We apply two clustering algorithms, Hierarchical Graph Factorization Clustering (Yu et al., 2005; Sun and Korhonen, 2011) and Self-Tuning Spectral Clustering (Ng et al., 2001; Zelnik-Manor and Perona, 2004), and systematically explore different ways of defining the similarity matrix that they use as input. We exploit a variety of features from PPDB to cluster its paraphrases by sense, including its im-

Proceedings of NAACL-HLT 2016, pages 1463–1472,
San Diego, California, June 12-17, 2016. ©2016 Association for Computational Linguistics

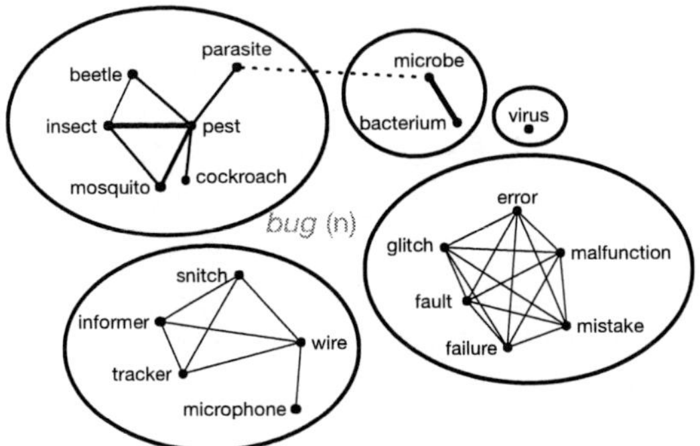

Figure 2: SEMCLUST connects all paraphrases that share foreign alignments, and cuts edges below a dynamically-tuned cutoff weight (dotted lines). The resulting connected components are its clusters.

plicit graph structure, aligned foreign words, paraphrase scores, predicted entailment relations, and monolingual distributional similarity scores.

Our goal is to determine which algorithm and features are the most effective for clustering paraphrases by sense. We address three research questions:

- Which similarity metric is best for sense clustering? We systematically compare different ways of defining matrices that specify the similarity between pairs of paraphrases.

- Are better clusters produced by comparing second-order paraphrases? We use PPDB's graph structure to decide whether *mosquito* and *pest* belong to the same sense cluster by comparing lists of paraphrases for the two words.

- Can entailment relations inform sense clustering? We exploit knowledge like *beetle* is-an *insect*, and that there is no entailment between *malfunction* and *microbe*.

Our method produces sense clusters that are qualitatively and quantitatively good, and that represent a substantial improvement to the PPDB resource.

2   Related Work

The paraphrases in PPDB are already partitioned by syntactic type, following the work of Callison-Burch (2008). He showed that applying syntactic constraints during paraphrase extraction via the pivot method improves paraphrase quality. This means that paraphrases of the noun *bug* are separated from paraphrases of the verb *bug*, which consist of verbs like *bother, trouble, annoy, disturb*, and others. However, organizing paraphrases this way still leaves the issue of mixed senses within a single part of speech. This lack of sense distinction makes it difficult to decide when a paraphrase in PPDB would be an appropriate substitute for a word in a given sentence. Some researchers resort to crowdsourcing to determine when a PPDB substitution is valid (Pavlick et al., 2015c).

Our sense clustering work is closely related to the task of word sense induction (WSI), which aims to discover all senses of a target word from large corpora. One family of common approaches to WSI aims to discover the senses of a word by clustering the monolingual contexts in which it appears (Navigli, 2009). Another uncovers a word's senses by clustering its foreign alignments from parallel corpora (Diab, 2003). A more recent family of approaches to WSI represents a word as a feature vector of its substitutable words, i.e. paraphrases (Melamud et al., 2015; Yatbaz et al., 2012). In this paper we take inspiration from each of these families of approaches, and we explore them when measuring word similarity in sense clustering.

The work most closely related to ours is that of Apidianaki et al. (2014), who used a simple graph-based approach to cluster pivot paraphrases on the basis of contextual similarity and shared foreign alignments. Their method represents paraphrases as nodes in a graph and connects each pair of words sharing one or more foreign alignments with an edge weighted by contextual similarity. Concretely, for paraphrase set P, it constructs a graph $G = (V, E)$ where vertices $V = \{p_i \in P\}$ are words in the paraphrase set and edges connect words that share foreign word alignments in a bilingual parallel corpus. The edges of the graph are weighted based on their contextual similarity (computed over a monolingual corpus). In order to partition the graph into clusters, edges in the initial graph G with contextual similarity below a threshold T' are deleted. The connected components in the resulting graph G' are taken as the sense clusters. The threshold is dynamically tuned using an iterative procedure (Apidianaki and He, 2010).

As evaluated against reference clusters derived from SEMEVAL 2007 Lexical Substitution gold data (McCarthy and Navigli, 2007), their method, which we call SEMCLUST, outperformed simple most-frequent-sense, one-sense-per-paraphrase, and random baselines. Apidianaki et al. (2014)'s work corroborated the existence of sense distinctions in the paraphrase sets, and highlighted the need for further work to organize them by sense. In this paper, we improve on their method using more advanced clustering algorithms, and by systematically exploring a wider range of similarity measures.

3   Graph Clustering Algorithms

To partition paraphrases by sense, we use two advanced graph clustering methods rather than using Apidianaki et al. (2014)'s edge deletion approach. Both of them allow us to experiment with a variety of similarity metrics.

3.1   Hierarchical Graph Factorization Clustering

The Hierarchical Graph Factorization Clustering (HGFC) method was developed by Yu et al. (2006) to probabilistically partition data into hierarchical clusters that gradually merge finer-grained clusters into coarser ones. Sun and Korhonen (2011) applied HGFC to the task of clustering verbs into Levin (1993)-style classes. Sun and Korhonen extended the basic HGFC algorithm to automatically discover the latent tree structure in their clustering solution and incorporate prior knowledge about semantic relationships between words. They showed that HGFC far outperformed agglomerative clustering methods on their verb data set. We adopt Sun and Korhonen's implementation of HGFC for our experiments.

HGFC takes as input a nonnegative, symmetric adjacency matrix $W = \{w_{ij}\}$ where rows and columns represent paraphrases $p_i \in P$, and entries w_{ij} denote the similarity between paraphrases $sim_D(p_i, p_j)$. The algorithm works by factorizing W into a bipartite graph, where the nodes on one side represent paraphrases, and nodes on the other represent senses. The output of HGFC is a set of clusterings of increasingly coarse granularity, which we can also represent with a tree structure. The algo-

rithm automatically determines the number of clusters at each level. For our task, this has the benefit that a user can choose the cluster granularity most appropriate for the downstream task (as illustrated in Figure 5). Another benefit of HGFC is that it probabilistically assigns each paraphrase to a cluster at each level of the hierarchy. If some p_i has high probability in multiple clusters, we can assign p_i to all of them (Figure 3c).

3.2   Spectral Clustering

The second clustering algorithm that we use is Self-Tuning Spectral Clustering (Zelnik-Manor and Perona, 2004). Like HGFC, spectral clustering takes an adjacency matrix W as input, but the similarities end there. Whereas HGFC produces a hierarchical clustering, spectral clustering produces a flat clustering with k clusters, with k specified at runtime. The Zelnik-Manor and Perona (2004)'s self-tuning method is based on Ng et al. (2001)'s spectral clustering algorithm, which computes a normalized Laplacian matrix L from the input W, and executes K-means on the largest k eigenvectors of L. Intuitively, the largest k eigenvectors of L should align with the k senses in our paraphrase set.

4   Similarity Measures

Each of our clustering algorithms take as input an adjacency matrix W where the entries w_{ij} correspond to some measure of similarity between words i and j. For the paraphrases in Figure 1, W is a 20x20 matrix that specifies the similarity of every pair of paraphrases like *microbe* and *bacterium* or *microbe* and *malfunction*. We systematically investigated four types of similarity scores to populate W.

4.1   Paraphrase Scores

Bannard and Callison-Burch (2005) defined a *paraphrase probability* in order to quantify the goodness of a pair of paraphrases, based on the underlying translation probabilities used by the bilingual pivoting method. More recently, (Pavlick et al., 2015a) used supervised logistic regression to combine a variety of scores so that they align with human judgements of paraphrase quality. PPDB 2.0 provides this score for each pair of words in the database. The PPDB 2.0 score is a nonnegative real number that

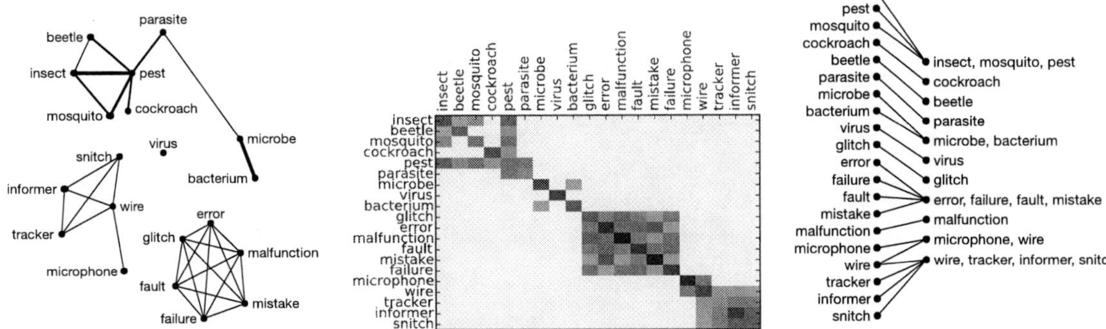

(a) Undirected graph for query word *bug*. Wider lines signify stronger similarity.

(b) The corresponding adjacency matrix W. Darker cells signify stronger similarity.

(c) The bipartite graph induced by the first iteration of HGFC. Note *wire* is assigned to two clusters.

Figure 3: The graph, corresponding adjacency matrix W, and bipartite graph created by the first iteration of HGFC for query word *bug (n)*

can be used directly as a similarity measure:

$$w_{ij} = \begin{cases} PPDB_{2.0}Score(i,j) & (i,j) \in \text{PPDB} \\ 0 & \text{otherwise} \end{cases}$$

PPDB 2.0 does not provide a score for a word with itself, so we set $PPDB_{2.0}Score(i,i)$ to be the maximum $PPDB_{2.0}Score(i,j)$ such that i and j have the same stem.

4.2 Second-Order Paraphrase Scores

Work by Rapp (2003) and Melamud et al. (2015) showed that comparing words on the basis of their *shared* paraphrases is effective for WSI. We define two novel similarity metrics that calculate the similarity of words i and j by comparing their second-order paraphrases. Instead of comparing *microbe* and *bacterium* directly with their PPDB 2.0 score, we look up all of the paraphrases of *microbe* and all of the paraphrases of *bacterium*, and compare those two lists.

Specifically, we form notional *word-paraphrase* feature vectors v_i^p and v_j^p where the features correspond to words with which each is connected in PPDB, and the value of the kth element of v_i^p equals $PPDB_{2.0}Score(i,k)$. We can then calculate the cosine similarity or Jensen-Shannon divergence between vectors:

$$sim_{PPDB.cos}(i,j) = cos(v_i^p, v_j^p)$$

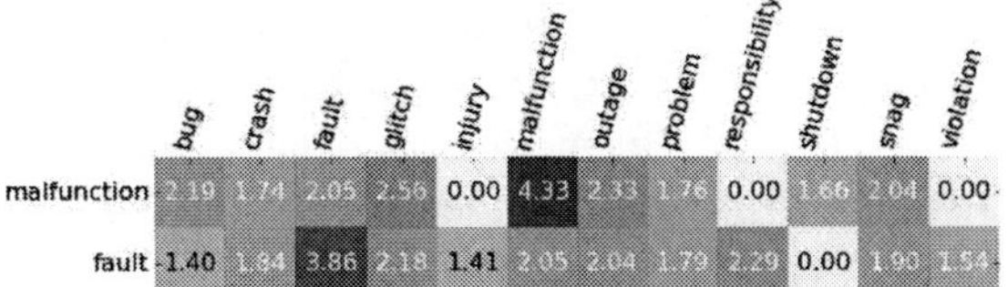

Figure 4: Comparing second-order paraphrases for *malfunction* and *fault* based on *word-paraphrase* vectors. The value of vector element v_{ij} is $PPDB_{2.0}Score(i,j)$.

$$sim_{PPDB.js}(i,j) = 1 - JS(v_i^p, v_j^p)$$

where $JS(v_i^p, v_j^p)$ is calculated assuming that the paraphrase probability distribution for word i is given by its normalized *word-paraphrase* vector v_i^p.

4.3 Similarity of Foreign Word Alignments

When an English word is aligned to several foreign words, sometimes those different translations indicate a different word sense (Yao et al., 2012). Using this intuition, Gale et al. (1992) trained an English WSD system on a bilingual corpus, using the different French translations as labels for the English word senses. For instance, given the English word *duty*, the French translation *droit* was a proxy for its *tax* sense and *devoir* for its *obligation* sense.

PPDB is derived from bilingual coropra. We recover the aligned foreign words and their associated translation probabilities that underly each PPDB entry. For each English word in our dataset, we get each foreign word that it aligns to in the Spanish and Chinese bilingual parallel corpora used by Ganitkevitch and Callison-Burch (2014). We use this to define a novel foreign word alignment similarity metric, $sim_{TRANS}(i,j)$ for two English paraphrases i and j. This is calculated as the cosine similarity of the *word-alignment* vectors v_i^a and v_j^a where each feature in v^a is a foreign word to which i or j aligns, and the value of entry v_{if}^a is the translation probability $p(f|i)$.

$$sim_{TRANS}(i,j) = cos(v_i^a, v_j^a)$$

4.4 Monolingual Distributional Similarity

Lastly, we populate the adjacency with a distributional similarity measure based on WORD2VEC (Mikolov et al., 2013). Each paraphrase i in our data set is represented as a 300-dimensional WORD2VEC embedding v_i^w trained on part of the Google News dataset. Phrasal paraphrases that did not have an entry in the WORD2VEC dataset are represented as the mean of their individual word vectors. We use the cosine similarity between WORD2VEC embeddings as our measure of distributional similarity.

$$sim_{DISTRIB}(i,j) = cos(v_i^w, v_j^w)$$

5 Determining the Number of Senses

The optimal number of clusters for a set of paraphrases will vary depending on how many senses there ought to be for an input word like *bug*. It is generally recognized that optimal sense granularity depends on the application (Palmer et al., 2001). WordNet has notoriously fine-grained senses, whereas most word sense disambiguation systems achieve better performance when using coarse-grained sense inventories (Navigli, 2009). Depending on the task, the sense clustering for query word *coach* in Figure 5b with $k = 5$ clusters may be preferable to the alternative with $k = 3$ clusters. An ideal algorithm for our task would enable clustering at varying levels of granularity to support different downstream NLP applications.

Both of our clustering algorithms can produce sense clusters at varying granularities. For HGFC this requires choosing which level of the resulting tree structure to take as a clustering solution, and for spectral clustering we must specify the number of

clusters prior to execution.[1] To determine the optimal number of clusters, we use the mean Silhouette Coefficient (Rousseeuw, 1987) which balances optimal inter-cluster tightness and intra-cluster distance. The Silhouette Coefficient is calculated for each paraphrase p_i as

$$s(p_i) = \frac{b(p_i) - a(p_i)}{max\{a(p_i), b(p_i)\}}$$

where $a(p_i)$ is p_i's average intra-cluster distance (average distance from p_i to each other p_j in the same cluster), and $b(p_i)$ is p_i's lowest average inter-cluster distance (distance from p_i to the nearest external cluster centroid). For each clustering algorithm, we choose as the 'solution' the clustering which produces the highest mean Silhouette Coefficient. The Silhouette Coefficient calculation takes as input a matrix of pairwise distances, so we simply use $1 - W$ where the adjacency matrix W is calculated using one of the similarity methods we defined.

6 Incorporating Entailment Relations

Pavlick et al. (2015b) added a set of automatically predicted semantic entailment relations for each entry in PPDB 2.0. The entailment types that they include are *Equivalent, Forward Entailment, Reverse Entailment, Exclusive*, and *Independent*. While a negative entailment relationship (*Exclusive* or *Independent*) does not preclude words from belonging to the same sense of some query word, a positive entailment relationship (*Equivalent, Forward/Reverse Entailment*) does give a strong indication that the words belong to the same sense.

We seek a straightforward way to determine whether entailment relations provide information that is useful to the final clustering algorithm. Both of our algorithms take an adjacency matrix W as input, so we add entailment information by simply

---

[1] For spectral clustering there has been significant study into methods for automatically determining the optimal number of clusters, including analysis of eigenvalues of the graph Laplacian, and finding the rotation of the Laplacian that brings it closest to block-diagonal (Zelnik-Manor and Perona, 2004). We experimented with these and other cluster analysis methods such as the Dunn Index (Dunn, 1973) in our work, but found that using the simple Silhouette Coefficient produced clusterings that were competitive with the more intensive methods, in far less time.

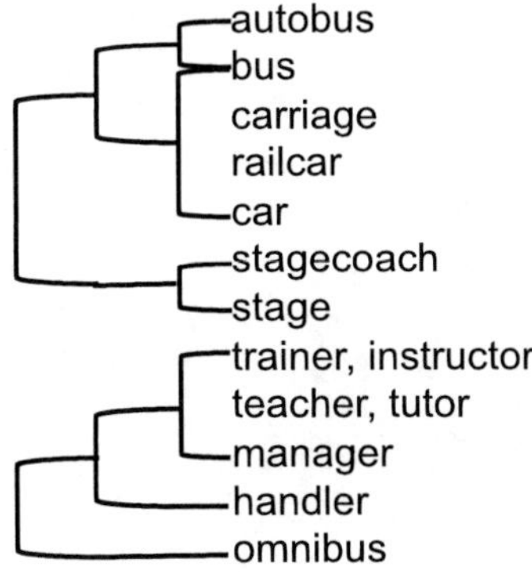

(a)   HGFC clustering result

(b)   Spectral clustering results

Figure 5: HGFC and Spectral Clustering results for *coach (n)*. Our silhouette optimization sets $k = 3$.

multiplying each pairwise entry by its entailment probability. Specifically, we set

$$
w_{ij} = \begin{cases} (1 - p_{ind}(i,j))sim_D(i,j) & (i,j) \in \text{PPDB} \\ 0 & \text{otherwise} \end{cases}
$$

where $p_{ind}(i,j)$ gives the PPDB 2.0 probability that there is an *Independent* entailment relationship between words i and j. Intuitively, this should increase the similarity of words that are very likely to be entailing like *fault* and *failure*, and decrease the similarity of non-entailing words like *cockroach* and *microphone*.

7   Experimental Setup

We follow the experimental setup of Apidianaki et al. (2014). We focus our evaluation on a set of query words drawn from the LexSub test data (McCarthy and Navigli, 2007), plus 16 additional handpicked polysemous words.

7.1   Gold Standard Clusters

One challenge in creating our clustering methodology is that there is no reliable PPDB-sized standard against which to assess our results. WordNet synsets provide a well-vetted basis for comparison, but only allow us to evaluate our method on the 38% of our PPDB dataset that overlaps it. We therefore evaluate performance on two test sets.

WordNet+   Our first test set is designed to assess how well our solution clusters align with WordNet synsets. We chose 185 polysemous words from the SEMEVAL 2007 dataset and an additional 16 handpicked polysemous words. For each we formed a paraphrase set that was the intersection of their PPDB 2.0 XXXL paraphrases with their WordNet synsets, and their immediate hyponyms and hypernyms. Each reference cluster consisted of a WordNet synset, plus the hypernyms and hyponyms of words in that synset. On average there are 7.2 reference clusters per paraphrase set.

CrowdClusters   Because the coverage of WordNet is small compared to PPDB, and because WordNet synsets are very fine-grained, we wanted to create a dataset that would test the performance of our clustering algorithm against large, noisy paraphrase sets and coarse clusters. For this purpose we randomly selected 80 query words from the SEMEVAL 2007 dataset and created paraphrase sets from their unfiltered PPDB2.0 XXL entries. We then iteratively organized each paraphrase set into reference senses with the help of crowd workers on Amazon Mechanical Turk. On average there are 4.0 reference clusters per paraphrase set. A full description of our method is included in the supplemental materials.

7.2   Evaluation Metrics

We evaluate our method using two standard metrics: the paired F-Score and V-Measure. Both were used in the 2010 SemEval Word Sense Induction Task (Manandhar et al., 2010) and by Apidianaki et al. (2014). We give our results in terms of weighted average performance on these metrics, where the score for each individual paraphrase set is weighted by the number of reference clusters for that query word.

Paired F-Score   frames the clustering problem as a classification task (Manandhar et al., 2010). It generates the set of all word pairs belonging to the same reference cluster, $F(S)$, and the set of all word pairs belonging to the same automatically-generated cluster, $F(K)$. Precision, recall, and F-score can then be calculated in the usual way, i.e. $P = \frac{F(K) \cap F(S)}{F(K)}$, $R = \frac{F(K) \cap F(S)}{F(S)}$, and $F = \frac{2 \cdot P \cdot R}{P + R}$.

V-Measure assesses the quality of a clustering solution against reference clusters in terms of clustering homogeneity and completeness (Rosenberg and Hirschberg, 2007). Homogeneity describes the extent to which each cluster is composed of paraphrases belonging to the same reference cluster, and completeness refers to the extent to which points in a reference cluster are assigned to a single cluster. Both are defined in terms of conditional entropy. V-Measure is the harmonic mean of homogeneity h and completeness c; V-Measure $= \frac{2 \cdot h \cdot c}{h + c}$.

7.3 Baselines

We evaluate the performance of HGFC on each dataset against the following baselines:

Most Frequent Sense (MFS) assigns all paraphrases $p_i \in P$ to a single cluster. By definition, the completeness of the MFS clustering is 1.

One Cluster per Paraphrase (1C1PAR) assigns each paraphrase $p_i \in P$ to its own cluster. By definition, the homogeneity of 1C1PAR clustering is 1.

Random (RAND) For each query term's paraphrase set, we generate five random clusterings of $k = 5$ clusters. We then take F-Score and V-Measure as the average of each metric calculated over the five random clusterings.

SEMCLUST We implement the SEMCLUST algorithm (Apidianaki et al., 2014) as a state-of-the-art baseline. Since PPDB contains only pairs of words that share a foreign word alignment, in our implementation we connect paraphrase words with an edge if the pair appears in PPDB. We adopt the WORD2VEC distributional similarity score $sim_{DISTRIB}$ for our edge weights.

8 Experimental Results

Figure 6 shows the performance of the two advanced clustering algorithms against the baselines. Our

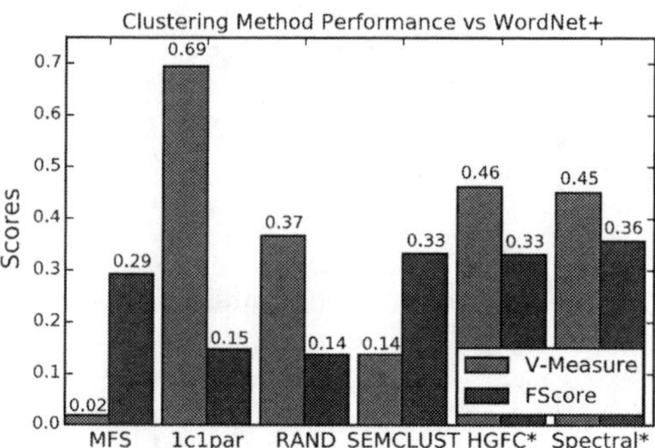

(a) Clustering method performance against WordNet+

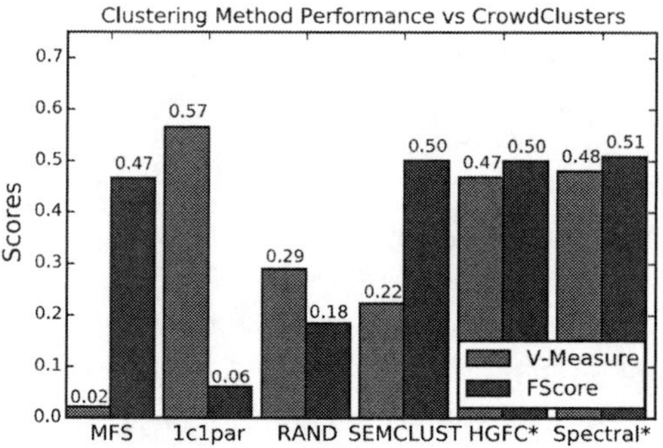

(b) Clustering method performance against CrowdClusters

Figure 6: Hierarchical Graph Factorization Clustering and Spectral Clustering both significantly outperform all baselines except 1C1PAR V-Measure.

best configurations[2] for HGFC and Spectral outperformed all baselines except 1C1PAR V-Measure, which his biased toward solutions with many small clusters (Manandhar et al., 2010), and performed only marginally better than SEMCLUST in terms of F-Score alone. The dominance of 1C1PAR V-Measure is greater for the WordNet+ dataset which has smaller reference clusters than CrowdClusters. Qualitatively, we find that methods that strike a balance between high F-Score and high V-Measure tend to produce the 'best' clusters by human judgement. If we consider the average of F-Score and V-Measure as a comprehensive performance measure, our methods outperform all baselines.

---

[2] Our top-scoring Spectral method, Spectral*, uses entailments, $PPDB_{2.0}Score$ similarities, and $sim_{DISTRIB}$ to choose k. Our best HGFC method, HGFC*, uses entailments, $sim_{DISTRIB}$ similarities, and $PPDB_{2.0}Score$ to choose k.

Method	F-Score	V-Measure	Avg # Clusters
$PPDB_{2.0}Score$	0.410	0.437	5.960
$sim_{DISTRIB}$	0.376	0.440	5.707
$sim_{PPDB.cos}$	0.389	0.428	7.204
$sim_{PPDB.JS}$	0.385	0.425	7.143
sim_{TRANS}	0.358	0.375	6.247
SEMCLUST	0.417	0.180	2.279
Reference	1.0	1.0	5.611

Table 1: Average performance and number of clusters produced by our different similarity methods.

On our dataset, the state-of-the-art SEMCLUST baseline tended to lump many senses of the query word together, and produced scores lower than in the original work. We attribute this to the fact that the original work extracted paraphrases from EuroParl, which is much smaller than PPDB, and thus created adjacency matrices W which were sparser than those produced by our method. Directly applied, SEMCLUST works well on small data sets, but does not scale well to the larger, noisier PPDB data. More advanced graph-based clustering methods produce better sense clusters for PPDB.

The first question we sought to address with this work was which similarity metric is the best for sense clustering. Table 1 reports the average F-Score and V-Measure across 40 test configurations for each similarity calculation method.[3] On average across test sets and clustering algorithms, the paraphrase similarity score ($PPDB_{2.0}Score$) performs better than monolingual distributional similarity ($sim_{DISTRIB}$) in terms of F-Score, but the results are reversed for V-Measure. This is also shown in the best HGFC and Spectral configurations, where the two similarity scores are swapped between them.

Next, we investigated whether comparing second-order paraphrases would produce better clusters than simply using $PPDB_{2.0}Score$ directly. Table 1 also compares the two methods that we had for computing the similarity of second order paraphrases – cosine similarity ($sim_{PPDB.cos}$) and Jensen-Shannon divergence ($sim_{PPDB.JS}$). On average across test sets and clustering algorithms, using the direct paraphrase score gives stronger V-Measure and F-score than the second-order methods. It also produces coarser clusters than the second-order PPDB similarity methods.

Finally, we investigated whether incorporating automatically predicted entailment relations would improve cluster quality, and we found that it did. All other things being equal, adding entailment information increases F-Score by .014 and V-Measure by .020 on average (Figure 7). Adding entailment information had the greatest improvement to HGFC methods with $sim_{DISTRIB}$ similarities, where it improved F-Score by an average of .03 and V-Measure by an average of .05.

9 Discussion and Future Work

We have presented a novel method for clustering paraphrases in PPDB by sense. When evaluated against WordNet synsets, the sense clusters produced by the Spectral Clustering algorithm give a 64% relative improvement in F-Score over the closest baseline, and those produced by the HGFC algorithm give a 50% improvement in F-Score. We systematically analyzed a variety of similarity metrics as input to HGFC and Spectral Clustering, and showed that incorporating predicted entailment relations from PPDB boosts the performance of sense clustering.

Our sense clustering provides a significant improvement to the PPDB resource that may improve its applicability to downstream NLP tasks. One possible application of sense-clustered PPDB entries is the lexical substitution task, which seeks to identify appropriate word substitutions. Given a target word in context, it would be reasonable to suggest substitutes from the target word's PPDB sense cluster most closely related to the target context. There are many possible ways to choose the best cluster for a given context, ranging from simply choosing the cluster whose members have highest average pointwise mutual information with the context, to a more complex approach based on training cluster representations using a pseudo-word approach as in Melamud et al. (2015). We leave this application for future work.

10 Software and Data Release

With publication of this paper we are releasing paraphrase clusters for all PPDB 2.0 XXL entries,

---

[3]Our Supplementary Materials file provides the full set of results for all 200 configurations that we tested.

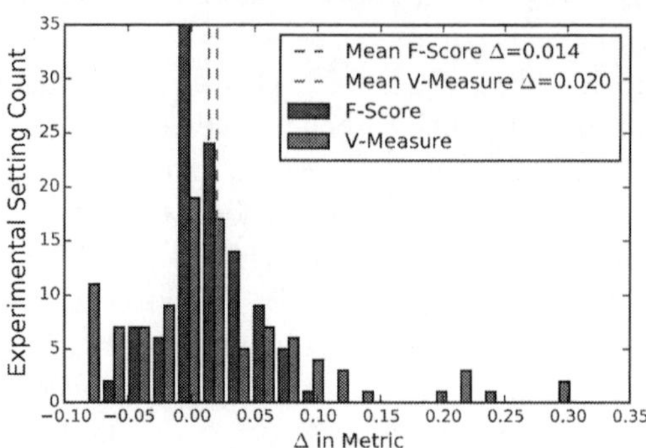

Figure 7: Histogram of metric change by adding entailment information across all experiments.

clustering code, and an interface for crowdsourcing paraphrase clusters using Amazon Mechanical Turk.

11 Supplementary Material

Our Supplementary Material provides additional detail on our similarity metric calculation, clustering algorithm implementation, and CrowdCluster reference cluster data development. We also provide full evaluation results across the entire range of our experiments, a selection of sense clusters output by our methods, and example content of our WordNet+ and CrowdCluster paraphrase sets.

Acknowledgments

This research was supported by the Allen Institute for Artificial Intelligence (AI2), the Human Language Technology Center of Excellence, and by gifts from the Alfred P. Sloan Foundation, Google, and Facebook. This material is based in part on research sponsored by the NSF grant under IIS-1249516 and DARPA under number FA8750-13-2-0017 (the DEFT program). The U.S. Government is authorized to reproduce and distribute reprints for Governmental purposes. The views and conclusions contained in this publication are those of the authors and should not be interpreted as representing official policies or endorsements of DARPA and the U.S. Government.

We would like to thank Marianna Apidianaki and Alex Harelick for sharing code used in this research, and Ellie Pavlick for her substantive input. We are grateful to our anonymous reviewers for their thoughtful and constructive comments.

References

Marianna Apidianaki and Yifan He. 2010. An algorithm for cross-lingual sense clustering tested in a MT evaluation setting. In *Proceedings of the 7th International Workshop on Spoken Language Translation (IWSLT-10)*.

Marianna Apidianaki, Emilia Verzeni, and Diana McCarthy. 2014. Semantic clustering of pivot paraphrases. In *Proceedings of the Ninth International Conference on Language Resources and Evaluation (LREC 2014)*.

Colin Bannard and Chris Callison-Burch. 2005. Paraphrasing with bilingual parallel corpora. In *Proceedings of the 43rd Annual Meeting of the Association for Computational Linguistics (ACL 05)*.

Chris Callison-Burch. 2008. Syntactic constraints on paraphrases extracted from parallel corpora. In *Proceedings of the 2008 Conference on Empirical Methods in Natural Language Processing*, pages 196–205, Honolulu, Hawaii, October. Association for Computational Linguistics.

Mona Talat Diab. 2003. *Word sense disambiguation within a multilingual framework*. Ph.D. thesis, University of Maryland.

William Dolan, Chris Quirk, and Chris Brockett. 2004. Unsupervised construction of large paraphrase corpora: Exploiting massively parallel news sources. In *Proceedings of the International Conference of Computational Linguistics (COLING 2004)*.

Joseph C Dunn. 1973. A fuzzy relative of the isodata process and its use in detecting compact well-separated clusters.

William A. Gale, Kenneth W. Church, and David Yarowsky. 1992. Using bilingual materials to develop word sense disambiguation methods. In *Proceedings of the Fourth International Conference on Theoretical and Methodological Issues in Machine Translation*.

Juri Ganitkevitch and Chris Callison-Burch. 2014. The multilingual paraphrase database. In *Proceedings of the Ninth International Conference on Language Resources and Evaluation (LREC-2014), Reykjavik, Iceland*, pages 4276–4283.

Juri Ganitkevitch, Benjamin Van Durme, and Chris Callison-Burch. 2013. PPDB: The paraphrase database. In *Proceedings of NAACL-HLT 2013*.

Beth Levin. 1993. *English verb classes and alternations: A preliminary investigation*. University of Chicago press.

Dekang Lin and Patrick Pantel. 2001. Discovery of inference rules for question answering. *Natural Language Engineering*.

Suresh Manandhar, Ioannis Klapaftis, Dmitriy Dligach, and Sameer Pradhan. 2010. SemEval-2010 Task 14: Word sense induction & disambiguation. In *Proceedings of the Fifth International Workshop on Semantic Evaluations (SemEval-2010)*.

Diana McCarthy and Roberto Navigli. 2007. Semeval-2007 task 10: English lexical substitution task. In *Proceedings of the Fourth International Workshop on Semantic Evaluations (SemEval-2007)*.

Oren Melamud, Ido Dagan, and Jacob Goldberger. 2015. Modeling word meaning in context with substitute vectors. In *Human Language Technologies: The 2015 Annual Conference of the North American Chapter of the ACL*.

Tomas Mikolov, Ilya Sutskever, Kai Chen, Greg Corrado, and Jeffrey Dean. 2013. Distributed representations of words and phrases and their compositionality. In *Proceedings of NIPS*.

George A Miller. 1995. WordNet: a lexical database for English. *Communications of the ACM*, 38(11):39–41.

Roberto Navigli. 2009. Word sense disambiguation: A survey. *ACM Computing Surveys*.

Andrew Ng, Michael Jordan, and Y. Weiss. 2001. On spectral clustering: Analysis and an algorithm. *Advances in Neural Information Processing Systems*.

Martha Palmer, Hoa Trang Dang, and Christiane Fellbaum. 2001. Making fine-grained and coarse-grained sense distinctions, both manually and automatically. *Natural Language Engineering*.

Ellie Pavlick, Johan Bos, Malvina Nissim, Charley Beller, Benjamin Van Durme, and Chris Callison-Burch. 2015a. PPDB 2.0: Better paraphrase ranking, fine-grained entailment relations, word embeddings, and style classification. In *Proceedings of the 53rd Annual Meeting of the Association for Computational Linguistics (ACL 2015)*.

Ellie Pavlick, Johannes Bos, Malvina Nissim, Charley Beller, and and Chris Callison-Burch Benjamin Van Durme. 2015b. Adding semantics to data-driven paraphrasing. In *Proceedings of the 53rd Annual Meeting of the Association for Computational Linguistics (ACL 2015)*.

Ellie Pavlick, Travis Wolfe, Pushpendre Rastogi, Chris Callison-Burch, Mark Drezde, and Benjamin Van Durme. 2015c. FrameNet+: Fast paraphrastic tripling of FrameNet. In *Proceedings of the 53rd Annual Meeting of the Association for Computational Linguistics (ACL 2015)*, Beijing, China, July. Association for Computational Linguistics.

Reinhard Rapp. 2003. Word sense discovery based on sense descriptor dissimilarity. In *Proceedings of the Ninth Machine Translation Summit*, pages 315–322.

Andrew Rosenberg and Julia Hirschberg. 2007. V-measure: A conditional entropy-based external cluster evaluation measure. In *EMNLP-CoNLL*, volume 7, pages 410–420.

Peter J Rousseeuw. 1987. Silhouettes: a graphical aid to the interpretation and validation of cluster analysis. *Journal of computational and applied mathematics*, 20:53–65.

Lin Sun and Anna Korhonen. 2011. Hierarchical verb clustering using graph factorization. In *Proceedings of the Conference on Empirical Methods in Natural Language Processing*, pages 1023–1033. Association for Computational Linguistics.

Xuchen Yao, Benjamin Van Durme, and Chris Callison-Burch. 2012. Expectations of word sense in parallel corpora. In *The 2012 Conference of the North American Chapter of the Association for Computational Linguistics*, pages 621–625, Montréal, Canada, June. Association for Computational Linguistics.

Mehmet Ali Yatbaz, Enis Sert, and Deniz Yuret. 2012. Learning syntactic categories using paradigmatic representations of word context. In *Proceedings of the 2012 Joint Conference on Empirical Methods in Natural Language Processing and Computational Natural Language Learning*, pages 940–951. Association for Computational Linguistics.

Kai Yu, Shipeng Yu, and Volker Tresp. 2005. Soft clustering on graphs. In *Advances in neural information processing systems*, pages 1553–1560.

Lihi Zelnik-Manor and Pietro Perona. 2004. Self-tuning spectral clustering. In *Advances in neural information processing systems*, pages 1601–1608.

Unsupervised Learning of Prototypical Fillers
for Implicit Semantic Role Labeling

Niko Schenk and **Christian Chiarcos**
Applied Computational Linguistics Lab
Goethe University Frankfurt am Main, Germany
`{n.schenk,chiarcos}@em.uni-frankfurt.de`

Abstract

Gold annotations for supervised implicit semantic role labeling are extremely sparse and
costly. As a lightweight alternative, this paper
describes an approach based on unsupervised
parsing which can do without iSRL-specific
training data: We induce prototypical roles
from large amounts of explicit SRL annotations paired with their distributed word representations. An evaluation shows competitive
performance with supervised methods on the
SemEval 2010 data, and our method can easily be applied to predicates (or languages) for
which no training annotations are available.

1 Introduction

Semantic role labeling (SRL) (Gildea and Jurafsky,
2002) has become a well-established and highly important NLP component which directly benefits various downstream applications, such as text summarization (Trandabăţ, 2011), recognizing textual entailment (Sammons et al., 2012) or QA systems
(Shen and Lapata, 2007; Moreda et al., 2011). Its
goal is to detect verbal or nominal predicates, together with their associated arguments and semantic
roles, either by PropBank/Nombank (Palmer et al.,
2005; Meyers et al., 2004) or FrameNet (Baker et
al., 1998) analysis. In its traditional form, however,
SRL is restricted to the *local syntactic context of the
predicate* as in the following example from Ruppenhofer et al. (2010):

[GOAL/NIIn the centre of this room] there
was an upright beam, [THEMEwhich] had been
placed [TIMEat some period] as a support for
the old worm-eaten baulk of timber which
spanned the roof.

In a FrameNet-style analysis of the sentence,
the predicate *place* evokes the PLACING frame,
with two frame elements (roles) overtly expressed
(THEME and TIME) but with one role – GOAL – beyond the embedded relative clause and thus beyond
the scope of the SRL parser. Such implicit roles, or
null instantiations (NIs) (Fillmore, 1986; Ruppenhofer, 2005) are much harder to detect automatically,
as they require to broaden the analysis to the surrounding discourse, commonly also to preceding (or
following) sentences.

State-of-the-art approaches to implicit SRL
(iSRL) are supervised and need a groundwork of
hand-annotated training data – which is costly, extremely sparse, limited to only a handful of predicates, and requires careful feature engineering (Gerber and Chai, 2012; Silberer and Frank, 2012; Li et
al., 2015). A first attempt has been made to combine
the scarce resources available (Feizabadi and Padó,
2015), but given the great diversity of predicate-
specific roles and enormous complexity of the task,
the main issues remain (Chen et al., 2010).

A promising exploratory effort recently made by
Gorinski et al. (2013) aims to overcome the annotation bottleneck by using distributional methods to
infer evidence for elements filling null instantiated
roles. The authors do not rely on gold annotations
but instead learn distributional properties of fillers
induced from a large corpus.

Our Contribution: We propose an extension of the
distributional idea for unsupervised iSRL to loosen
the need for annotated training data. Specifically, we

Proceedings of NAACL-HLT 2016, pages 1473–1479,
San Diego, California, June 12-17, 2016. ©2016 Association for Computational Linguistics

propose to induce predicate and role-specific **prototypical fillers** from large amounts of SRL annotated texts in order to resolve null instantiations as (semantically and syntactically) similar elements found in the context. Parts of our approach have been successfully applied in traditional SRL (Hermann et al., 2014), but not yet to implicit roles. Our work differs from Gorinski et al. (2013) in that we extend discrete context vectors to SRL-guided embeddings and experiment with a variety of different configurations. We intend *not* to set a new benchmark beating the current state-of-the-art for *supervised* iSRL, but rather provide a simple and alternative strategy which does not rely on manually annotated gold data. Still, we demonstrate that our method is highly competitive with supervised methods on one out of two standard evaluation sets and that it can easily be extended to other predicates for which no implicit gold annotations are available.

2 Method

2.1 Prototypical Fillers

We use large amounts of *explicit* SRL annotations to compute predicate-specific *protofillers* (prototypical fillers) for each frame element (role) individually:

$$\vec{v}^{\,protofiller} = \frac{1}{N} \sum_{i=0}^{N} E(w_i) \tag{1}$$

where N is the total number of tokens filling a particular role and $E(\cdot)$ is an embedding function which maps a word w_i to its distributed representation, i.e., a precomputed vector of d dimensions. Note that only those words contribute to the protofiller of a frame element which occur in this role.

2.2 Identifying Null Instantiations

Our approach generalizes over labeled filler instances of the frame (PLACING in the example) as found in corpus data, e.g., *placed on the middle picture, planted on the top of the church, hung over the river, laid on the table*, etc. We exploit their syntactic (here: prepositional) and semantic properties (inanimate, spacial NPs) in order to capture a composed meaning and thus to approximate the correct implicit role *in the centre of this room.* We measure similarity between a trained protofiller $\vec{v}^{\,p}$

and a candidate constituent $\vec{v}^{\,c}$ by cosine similarity $\cos(\theta) = \frac{\vec{v}^{\,p} \cdot \vec{v}^{\,c}}{\|\vec{v}^{\,p}\| \|\vec{v}^{\,c}\|}$ and predict a candidate as null instantiation which maximizes the inner product with the protofiller. As candidate constituents for an implicit argument we initially consider all terminal and non-terminal nodes in a context window of the predicate, ruling out those categories which never occur as implicit arguments, which do contain the target predicate and/or which are already overt arguments. The result set comprises mainly nouns, verbs and PPs. Candidate constituents in our evaluation data are available from their respective (manual) syntax annotation, but could easily be extracted using automated phrase-structure parsers. The candidate *vectors* for arbitrary length n-grams are derived in the same way (by means of Equation 1).

2.3 Training Resources & Tools

In accordance with domain-specific evaluation data, we chose to learn protofillers on two distinct corpora: *The Corpus of Late Modern English Texts, CLMET* (Smet, 2005) ($\approx$35M tokens, 18th–20th century novels) and a subset of the English *Gigaword corpus* (Graff and Cieri, 2003) ($\approx$500M tokens of Newswire texts). We label the first one with SEMAFOR[1] (Das et al., 2014), a FrameNet-style semantic parser. We employ MATE[2] (Björkelund et al., 2009) to obtain a PropBank/NomBank analysis for each sentence in Gigaword.

	CLMET	Gigaword
# explicit roles	21.9M	264.0M
# predicate instances	9.5M	122.5M
# roles per predicate	2.3	2.2
# predicates per sentence	7.6	4.2

Table 1: Statistics on the number of explicit fillers used for training protofillers.

Table 1 highlights general statistics on the number of predicates collected from both corpora. Two observations are worth noting: While on average the number of explicitly realized roles/frame elements per predicate/frame in both data sets is similar, we find more predicate instances in CLMET than in Gigaword. This is due to the FrameNet lexicon and its more fine-grained modeling of lexical units, as

---

[1]http://www.cs.cmu.edu/~ark/SEMAFOR/
[2]https://code.google.com/p/mate-tools/

opposed to PropBank. Also note that FrameNet currently specifies 9.7 frame elements per lexical frame[3] which – despite the fact that this number also comprises non-core arguments – is much larger than what can explicitly be labeled by the SRL systems.

Regarding the distributional component, we experimented with a variety of distributed word representations: We chose out of the box vectors; Collobert et al. (2011), dependency-based word embeddings (Levy and Goldberg, 2014) and the pre-trained Google News vectors from *word2vec*[4] (Mikolov et al., 2013). Using the same tool, we also trained custom embeddings (bag-of-words and skip-gram) with 50 dimensions on our two corpora.

3 Evaluation

In order to assess the usefulness of our approach, a quantitative evaluation has been conducted on two iSRL test sets which have become a de facto standard in this domain: a collection of fiction novels from the SemEval 2010 Shared Task with manual annotations of null instantiations (Ruppenhofer et al., 2010), and Gerber and Chai (2010)'s augmented NomBank data set. Table 2 shows some general statistics on the number of implicit roles and candidate phrases involved in our experiments. As to have a comparison with the supervised approaches referred to in this study, we also provide the size of the training data.

	SemEval	NomBank
# predicate instances		
in training set	1,370	816
in test set	1,703	437
# implicit arguments		
in training set	245	650
in test set	259	246
# of candidate phrases per predicate instance	27.6	52.2
proportion of single tokens	63.4%	47.9%
proportion of phrases	36.6%	52.1%
∅ length of candidate phrase (in tokens)	5.8	7.1

Table 2: Statistics on implicit arguments and candidate phrases from the test sections of the two evaluation sets.

---

[3] https://framenet.icsi.berkeley.edu/ fndrupal/current_status, accessed March 2016.

[4] https://code.google.com/p/word2vec/

3.1 SemEval Data

In Table 4, we report the classification scores for the (*NI-only*) null instantiation *linking* task on the SemEval data, given the parsed candidate phrases and the gold information about the missing frame element.[5] For space reasons, we only include the results of our best-performing configuration, obtained from protofillers trained on the late modern English texts and Collobert et al. (2011) embeddings (C&W) with the search space for candidate NIs limited to the current and previous sentence. As a reference, we compare our results to the two best models (M_1 and $M_{1'}$) by Silberer and Frank (2012), the vector-based resolver (VEC) by Gorinski et al. (2013) – which is most similar to ours – and, finally, their ensemble combination of four semantically informed resolvers by majority vote (4X).

	P	R	F_1
Silberer and Frank (2012) M_1	30.8	25.1	**27.7**
Silberer and Frank (2012) $M_{1'}$	**35.6**	20.1	25.7
Gorinski et al. (2013) VEC	21.0	18.0	19.0
Gorinski et al. (2013) 4X	26.0	24.0	25.0
This paper: C&W embeddings	27.2	**25.7**	26.4

Table 4: NI linking performance on the SemEval test data.

The figures in Table 4 suggest that our approach clearly outperforms the vector-based method by Gorinski et al. (2013) and is best in terms of overall recognition rate (recall) among all systems. One potential reason for that might be that, in contrast to the VEC resolver, we do not compute mere context vectors but do rely on the valuable annotations obtained from explicit SRL structures. Also, we do not restrict our analysis to *head* words only, as we have seen that syntactic information from function words is crucial for the resolution of null instantiated roles, too. Moreover, our distributional protofiller method is highly competitive with state-of-the-art performance by Silberer and Frank (2012), yet does not yield better results in terms of F_1 score. Note however that, in contrast to their approach, ours is largely unsupervised and does neither rely on gold coreference chains, nor do we need to train on im-

---

[5] This avoids error propagation from NI *detection* and allows us to directly compare our results to previous approaches on the same task. Note that Laparra and Rigau (2012) do only report their accuracies for the full pipeline.

predicates:	B F_1	Gerber & Chai			Laparra & Rigau			Proto C&W			Proto W2Vcbow		
		P	R	F_1	P	R	F_1	P	R	F_1	P	R	F_1
sale	36.2	47.2	**41.7**	**44.2**	41.2	39.4	40.3	**61.0**	29.6	39.8	60.8	26.8	37.2
price	15.4	36.0	32.6	34.2	**53.3**	**53.3**	**53.3**	14.7	25.8	18.7	21.8	36.6	27.3
investor	9.8	36.8	40.0	38.4	**43.0**	39.5	**41.2**	22.5	48.3	30.7	24.1	**57.2**	33.9
bid	32.3	23.8	19.2	21.3	**52.9**	**51.0**	**52.0**	30.4	31.5	30.9	40.0	41.5	40.7
plan	38.5	**78.6**	**55.0**	**64.7**	40.7	40.7	40.7	41.1	43.2	42.1	44.3	51.0	47.4
cost	34.8	**61.1**	**64.7**	**62.9**	56.1	50.2	53.0	32.5	19.1	24.0	49.9	29.3	36.9
loss	52.6	**83.3**	**83.3**	**83.3**	68.4	63.5	65.8	54.8	73.1	62.6	54.7	63.8	58.9
loan	18.2	**42.9**	33.3	37.5	25.0	20.0	22.2	33.9	**49.0**	**40.1**	33.2	44.2	37.9
investment	0.0	40.0	25.0	30.8	**47.6**	**35.7**	**40.8**	29.1	21.8	24.9	39.2	34.3	36.6
fund	0.0	14.3	16.7	15.4	66.7	33.3	44.4	**100.0**	**33.3**	**50.0**	75.0	25.0	37.5
Overall	26.5	44.5	40.4	42.3	**47.9**	**43.8**	**45.8**	30.2	35.2	32.5	33.5	39.2	36.1

Table 3: Classification scores for implicit argument labeling on the NomBank test section. Baseline B from Gerber & Chai (2010): uses previous occurrence of same predicate. Gerber & Chai (2010): supervised logistic regression classifier trained on implicit fillers. Laparra & Rigau (2013): algorithm based on coherence relationship between predicates and fillers. Our best-performing protofillers are obtained by Collobert et al. (2011) embeddings (**Proto C&W**) and custom trained vectors (**Proto W2Vcbow**) using Gigaword SRL annotations.

plicit semantic roles in a supervised setting. An error analysis of our method reveals that it is particularly effective for NIs encountered in the *same sentence* as the target predicate (44.4% accuracy), which seems plausible given the contextual setup in which protofillers are derived.

3.2 NomBank Data

Compared to the SemEval data, Gerber and Chai (2010)'s augmented NomBank resource covers only ten nominal predicates, which allows us to nicely visualize the distributional profile based on their prototypical fillers. For each predicate, we simply concatenate all per role computed protofillers and apply multidimensional scaling to project the so obtained vectors onto two dimensions (cf. Figure 1).

We observe that the predicate grouping is now based on the prototypical fillers that they co-occur with: In the Wall Street Journal texts, *loss*, *loan* and *investment* are similar because their proto-agents (A0 fillers) who lose, lend and invest resp. are semantically shared (i.e. companies, banks). Similarly, *bid*, *cost* and *fund* are related in that the targets or commodities (A2) are all money-financed. Finally, the predicates *sale* and *plan* are to be expected as outliers as they are less homogeneous in their prototypical argument structure.

We have empirically evaluated our protofiller

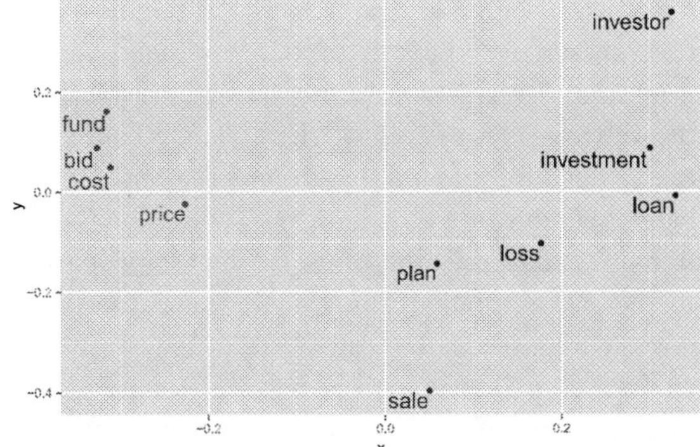

Figure 1: Clustered projection of the ten nominal predicates from Gerber and Chai (2010) in protofiller space.

method also on this data set: Table 3 reports the classification scores for implicit argument resolution compared to the state-of-the-art (Laparra and Rigau, 2013). We restrict the search for implicit arguments to certain predicate-specific parts-of-speech, since some syntactic constituents (e.g., SBAR) never occur as implicit arguments. For choosing the final implicit arguments for each individual predicate instance, we follow the same deterministic strategy as described in Gerber and Chai (2010), which informally states that, if a certain role is not overtly expressed (within a chain of mentions of the same predicate in previous sentences), it is an implicit candidate. POS lists and cosine similarity thresholds which trigger an actual prediction have been optimized on the development set. The context window for candidate NIs is optimal for the current and previous two sentences in our setting, which explains why the the number of candidate constituents is approximately twice as large for the NomBank predicates (cf. Table 2).

Our best-performing protofillers are again obtained by Collobert et al. (2011) embeddings substituting explicit SRL annotations in the Gigaword corpus, and with custom-trained embeddings using the continuous bag-of-words model. Overall, our results significantly exceed the highly informed baseline but cannot beat the state-of-the art on this test set. For some predicates, the protofillers seem to generalize better (higher recall), and in particular for the low-frequency predicates (*fund*), precision can be increased. Also, we found that the dependency-based word embeddings do perform slightly worse (not shown), compared to our optimal two configurations. This might be due to the fact that the inherent properties of dependency-based contexts mostly focus on relations between semantically valuable nouns, ignoring ("skipping") functional words and categories.[6] The same pertains to the pre-computed Google News vectors which come with a frequency cutoff excluding stop words, again a constraint which is harmful for the correct identification of implicit roles. Furthermore, skip-gram embeddings perform significantly worse than the embeddings derived by the continuous bag-of-words implementation (relative decrease in F_1 by more than 30%). Finally, we observed that inferring implicit roles for nominal predicates is much more challenging because our collected fillers exhibit a much greater variation. For example, the protoagents of *loan* can roughly be divided into two categories, institutions and countries. This in turn introduces noise and has a negative effect on the quality of the singleton protofillers which by vector average capture neither of the two groups perfectly. Promising alternatives could operate on (topic-like) protofiller **clusters** which we leave for future work.

4 Summary & Conclusion

We have described a lightweight approach for the resolution of implicit semantic roles which does not rely on manual gold annotations. For each predicate-specific role, our method generalizes over explicit SRL-guided annotations incorporating pre-trained word embeddings. This allows us to capture their idiosyncratic properties and use the so-inferred protofillers to find null instantiated roles by means of distributional similarity.

Our method has proven to be generally useful, in particular on the SemEval data, where it is competitive with supervised systems. Its greatest benefit stems from its simplicity and from that fact that it allows to induce null-instantiated roles for arbitrary predicates. As it is applicable even if no iSRL training data is available, it represents a promising technique to address iSRL data scarcity issues.

In our experiment, we employed PropBank/Nom-Bank-style (i)SRL annotations, and our general design clearly benefits from using small-scale inventories of semantic roles. It should be noted though, that our approach is not restricted to any particular SRL tagset, but can be equally applied to other role inventories with similar degrees of consistence and size. Beyond SRL annotations in a strict sense, this might even extend to syntactic dependency annotations that are occasionally taken as a substitute for semantic roles proper. In particular, we see potential in combining our experiments with on-going efforts to cross-lingual projection, adaptation and harmonization of syntax annotations along the lines of Sukhareva and Chiarcos (2014, 2016) and related approaches based on frameworks such as the Universal Dependencies (Nivre, 2015, UD).[7] If successful, an adaptation using grammatical relations rather than semantic roles represents a promising possibility to create iSRL annotation and iSRL annotation tools for other languages, as Universal Dependencies are becoming increasingly available for major and low-resourced languages and can be projected to others.

The protofillers involved in this study are available at: `http://acoli.cs.uni-frankfurt.de/resources`.

---

[6]This is also nicely illustrated in Levy and Goldberg (2014).

[7]`http://universaldependencies.github.io`

Acknowledgments

The authors would like to thank Joyce Chai and Hendrik De Smet for providing us access to their resources and corpora. We are grateful to Egoitz Laparra for sending us their evaluation script and also thank the anonymous reviewers for their valuable feedback and insightful comments.

References

Collin F. Baker, Charles J. Fillmore, and John B. Lowe. 1998. The Berkeley FrameNet Project. In *Proceedings of the 36th Annual Meeting of the Association for Computational Linguistics and 17th International Conference on Computational Linguistics (ACL-COLIG 1998)*, pages 86–90, Montreal, Quebec, Canada.

Anders Björkelund, Love Hafdell, and Pierre Nugues. 2009. Multilingual Semantic Role Labeling. In *Proceedings of the Thirteenth Conference on Computational Natural Language Learning (CoNLL-2009): Shared Task*, pages 43–48, Boulder, Colorado, June.

Desai Chen, Nathan Schneider, Dipanjan Das, and Noah A. Smith. 2010. SEMAFOR: Frame Argument Resolution with Log-linear Models. In *Proceedings of the 5th International Workshop on Semantic Evaluation (SemEval-2010)*, pages 264–267, Los Angeles.

Ronan Collobert, Jason Weston, Léon Bottou, Michael Karlen, Koray Kavukcuoglu, and Pavel Kuksa. 2011. Natural Language Processing (Almost) from Scratch. *Journal of Machine Learning Research*, 12:2493–2537.

Dipanjan Das, Desai Chen, André F. T. Martins, Nathan Schneider, and Noah A. Smith. 2014. Frame-semantic Parsing. *Computational Linguistics*, 40(1):9–56.

Parvin S. Feizabadi and Sebastian Padó. 2015. Combining Seemingly Incompatible Corpora for Implicit Semantic Role Labeling. In *Proceedings of the 4th Joint Conference on Lexical and Computational Semantics (*SEM 2015)*, pages 40–50, Denver, CO.

Charles J. Fillmore. 1986. Pragmatically Controlled Zero Anaphora. In *Proceedings of Berkeley Linguistics Society*, pages 95–107, Berkeley, CA.

Matthew Gerber and Joyce Chai. 2010. Beyond Nom-Bank: A Study of Implicit Arguments for Nominal Predicates. In *Proceedings of the 48th Annual Meeting of the Association for Computational Linguistics (ACL-2010)*, pages 1583–1592, Uppsala, Sweden.

Matthew Gerber and Joyce Chai. 2012. Semantic Role Labeling of Implicit Arguments for Nominal Predicates. *Computational Linguistics*, 38(4):755–798.

Daniel Gildea and Daniel Jurafsky. 2002. Automatic Labeling of Semantic Roles. *Computational Linguistics*, 28(3):245–288.

Philip Gorinski, Josef Ruppenhofer, and Caroline Sporleder. 2013. Towards Weakly Supervised Resolution of Null Instantiations. In *Proceedings of the 10th International Conference on Computational Semantics (IWCS 2013)*, pages 119–130, Potsdam, Germany.

David Graff and Christopher Cieri. 2003. English Gigaword. Linguistic Data Consortium, Philadelphia, LDC2003T05. Web Download.

Karl Moritz Hermann, Dipanjan Das, Jason Weston, and Kuzman Ganchev. 2014. Semantic Frame Identification with Distributed Word Representations. In *Proceedings of the 52th Annual Meeting of the Association for Computational Linguistics (ACL-2014)*, Baltimore, Maryland.

Egoitz Laparra and German Rigau. 2012. Exploiting Explicit Annotations and Semantic Types for Implicit Argument Resolution. In *Proceedings of the 6th International Conference on Semantic Computing (ICSC-2012)*, pages 75–78.

Egoitz Laparra and German Rigau. 2013. ImpAr: A Deterministic Algorithm for Implicit Semantic Role Labelling. In *Proceedings of the 51st Annual Meeting of the Association for Computational Linguistics (ACL-2013)*, pages 1180–1189, Sofia, Bulgaria.

Omer Levy and Yoav Goldberg. 2014. Dependency-Based Word Embeddings. In *Proceedings of the 52nd Annual Meeting of the Association for Computational Linguistics (ACL-2014)*, pages 302–308, Baltimore, MD.

Ru Li, Juan Wu, Zhiqiang Wang, and Qinghua Chai. 2015. Implicit Role Linking on Chinese Discourse: Exploiting Explicit Roles and Frame-to-Frame Relations. In *Proceedings of the 53rd Annual Meeting of the Association for Computational Linguistics and the 7th International Joint Conference on Natural Language Processing (ACL-IJCNLP 2015)*, pages 1263–1271, Beijing, China.

Adam Meyers, Ruth Reeves, Catherine Macleod, Rachel Szekely, Veronika Zielinska, Brian Young, and Ralph Grishman. 2004. The NomBank Project: An Interim Report. In *Proceedings of the HLT-NAACL 2004 Workshop on Frontiers in Corpus Annotation*, pages 24–31, Boston, Massachusetts.

Tomas Mikolov, Kai Chen, Greg Corrado, and Jeffrey Dean. 2013. Efficient Estimation of Word Representations in Vector Space. *CoRR*, abs/1301.3781.

Paloma Moreda, Hector Llorens, Estela Saquete, and Manuel Palomar. 2011. Combining Semantic Information in Question Answering Systems. *Journal of Information Processing and Management*, 47(6):870–885.

Joakim Nivre. 2015. Towards a Universal Grammar for Natural Language Processing. In *Proceedings of the 16th International Conference on Computational Linguistics and Intelligent Text Processing (CICLing-2015)*, pages 3–16, Cairo, Egypt. LNCS 9041, Springer.

Martha Palmer, Daniel Gildea, and Paul Kingsbury. 2005. The Proposition Bank: An Annotated Corpus of Semantic Roles. *Computational Linguistics*, 31(1):71–106.

Josef Ruppenhofer, Caroline Sporleder, Roser Morante, Collin Baker, and Martha Palmer. 2010. SemEval-2010 Task 10: Linking Events and Their Participants in Discourse. In *Proceedings of the 5th International Workshop on Semantic Evaluation (SemEval-2010)*, pages 45–50, Los Angeles, CA.

Josef Ruppenhofer. 2005. Regularities in Null Instantiation. Ms, University of Colorado.

Mark Sammons, V.G.Vinod Vydiswaran, and Dan Roth. 2012. Recognizing Textual Entailment. In Daniel M. Bikel and Imed Zitouni, editors, *Multilingual Natural Language Applications: From Theory to Practice*, chapter 6, pages 209–258. IBM Press.

Dan Shen and Mirella Lapata. 2007. Using Semantic Roles to Improve Question Answering. In *Proceedings of the 2007 Joint Conference on Empirical Methods in Natural Language Processing and Computational Natural Language Learning (EMNLP-CoNLL 2007)*, pages 12–21, Prague, Czech Republic.

Carina Silberer and Anette Frank. 2012. Casting Implicit Role Linking as an Anaphora Resolution Task. In *Proceedings of the First Joint Conference on Lexical and Computational Semantics (*SEM-2012)*, pages 1–10, Montreal, Quebec, Canada.

Hendrik De Smet. 2005. A Corpus of Late Modern English Texts. *International Computer Archive of Modern and Medieval English (ICAME)*, 29:69–82.

Maria Sukhareva and Christian Chiarcos. 2014. Diachronic Proximity vs. Data Sparsity in Cross-lingual Parser Projection. A Case Study on Germanic. In *COLING-2014 Workshop on Applying NLP Tools to Similar Languages, Varieties and Dialects (VarDial-2014)*, Dublin, Ireland.

Maria Sukhareva and Christian Chiarcos. 2016. Combining Ontologies and Neural Networks for Analyzing Historical Language Varieties. A Case Study in Middle Low German. In *Proceedings of the 10th International Conference on Language Resources and Evaluation (LREC-2016)*, Portorož, Slovenia.

Diana Trandabăţ. 2011. Using Semantic Roles to Improve Summaries. In *Proceedings of the 13th European Workshop on Natural Language Generation (ENLG-2011)*, pages 164–169, Nancy, France.

Hierarchical Attention Networks for Document Classification

Zichao Yang[1], Diyi Yang[1], Chris Dyer[1], Xiaodong He[2], Alex Smola[1], Eduard Hovy[1]
[1]Carnegie Mellon University, [2]Microsoft Research, Redmond
{zichaoy, diyiy, cdyer, hovy}@cs.cmu.edu
xiaohe@microsoft.com   alex@smola.org

Abstract

We propose a hierarchical attention network for document classification. Our model has two distinctive characteristics: (i) it has a hierarchical structure that mirrors the hierarchical structure of documents; (ii) it has two levels of attention mechanisms applied at the word- and sentence-level, enabling it to attend differentially to more and less important content when constructing the document representation. Experiments conducted on six large scale text classification tasks demonstrate that the proposed architecture outperform previous methods by a substantial margin. Visualization of the attention layers illustrates that the model selects qualitatively informative words and sentences.

1 Introduction

Text classification is one of the fundamental task in Natural Language Processing. The goal is to assign labels to text. It has broad applications including topic labeling (Wang and Manning, 2012), sentiment classification (Maas et al., 2011; Pang and Lee, 2008), and spam detection (Sahami et al., 1998). Traditional approaches of text classification represent documents with sparse lexical features, such as n-grams, and then use a linear model or kernel methods on this representation (Wang and Manning, 2012; Joachims, 1998). More recent approaches used deep learning, such as convolutional neural networks (Blunsom et al., 2014) and recurrent neural networks based on long short-term memory (LSTM) (Hochreiter and Schmidhuber, 1997) to learn text representations.

pork belly = delicious . || scallops? || I don't even like scallops, and these were a-m-a-z-i-n-g . || fun and tasty cocktails. || next time I in Phoenix, I will go back here. || Highly recommend.

Figure 1: A simple example review from Yelp 2013 that consists of five sentences, delimited by period, question mark. The first and third sentence delivers stronger meaning and inside, the word *delicious, a-m-a-z-i-n-g* contributes the most in defining sentiment of the two sentences.

Although neural-network–based approaches to text classification have been quite effective (Kim, 2014; Zhang et al., 2015; Johnson and Zhang, 2014; Tang et al., 2015), in this paper we test the hypothesis that better representations can be obtained by incorporating knowledge of document structure in the model architecture. The intuition underlying our model is that not all parts of a document are equally relevant for answering a query and that determining the relevant sections involves modeling the interactions of the words, not just their presence in isolation.

Our primary contribution is a new neural architecture (§2), the Hierarchical Attention Network (HAN) that is designed to capture two basic insights about document structure. First, since documents have a hierarchical structure (words form sentences, sentences form a document), we likewise construct a document representation by first building representations of sentences and then aggregating those into a document representation. Second, it is observed that different words and sentences in a documents are differentially informative. Moreover, the impor-

Proceedings of NAACL-HLT 2016, pages 1480–1489,
San Diego, California, June 12-17, 2016. ©2016 Association for Computational Linguistics

tance of words and sentences are highly context dependent, i.e. the same word or sentence may be differentially important in different context (§3.5). To include sensitivity to this fact, our model includes two levels of attention mechanisms (Bahdanau et al., 2014; Xu et al., 2015) — one at the word level and one at the sentence level — that let the model to pay more or less attention to individual words and sentences when constructing the representation of the document. To illustrate, consider the example in Fig. 1, which is a short Yelp review where the task is to predict the rating on a scale from 1–5. Intuitively, the first and third sentence have stronger information in assisting the prediction of the rating; within these sentences, the word delicious, a-m-a-z-i-n-g contributes more in implying the positive attitude contained in this review. Attention serves two benefits: not only does it often result in better performance, but it also provides insight into which words and sentences contribute to the classification decision which can be of value in applications and analysis (Shen et al., 2014; Gao et al., 2014).

The key difference to previous work is that our system uses *context* to discover *when* a sequence of tokens is relevant rather than simply filtering for (sequences of) tokens, taken out of context. To evaluate the performance of our model in comparison to other common classification architectures, we look at six data sets (§3). Our model outperforms previous approaches by a significant margin.

2 Hierarchical Attention Networks

The overall architecture of the Hierarchical Attention Network (HAN) is shown in Fig. 2. It consists of several parts: a word sequence encoder, a word-level attention layer, a sentence encoder and a sentence-level attention layer. We describe the details of different components in the following sections.

2.1 GRU-based sequence encoder

The GRU (Bahdanau et al., 2014) uses a gating mechanism to track the state of sequences without using separate memory cells. There are two types of gates: the reset gate r_t and the update gate z_t. They together control how information is updated to the

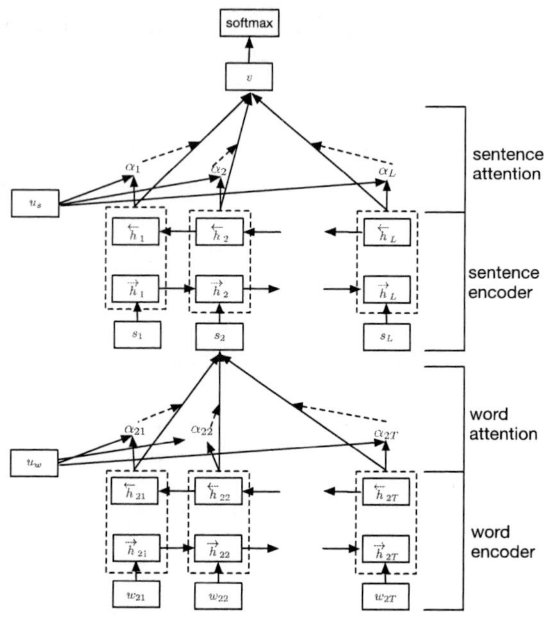

Figure 2: Hierarchical Attention Network.

state. At time t, the GRU computes the new state as

$$h_t = (1 - z_t) \odot h_{t-1} + z_t \odot \tilde{h}_t. \quad (1)$$

This is a linear interpolation between the previous state h_{t-1} and the current new state $\tilde{h}_t$ computed with new sequence information. The gate z_t decides how much past information is kept and how much new information is added. z_t is updated as:

$$z_t = \sigma(W_z x_t + U_z h_{t-1} + b_z), \quad (2)$$

where x_t is the sequence vector at time t. The candidate state $\tilde{h}_t$ is computed in a way similar to a traditional recurrent neural network (RNN):

$$\tilde{h}_t = \tanh(W_h x_t + r_t \odot (U_h h_{t-1}) + b_h), \quad (3)$$

Here r_t is the reset gate which controls how much the past state contributes to the candidate state. If r_t is zero, then it forgets the previous state. The reset gate is updated as follows:

$$r_t = \sigma(W_r x_t + U_r h_{t-1} + b_r) \quad (4)$$

2.2 Hierarchical Attention

We focus on document-level classification in this work. Assume that a document has L sentences

s_i and each sentence contains T_i words. w_{it} with $t \in [1, T]$ represents the words in the ith sentence. The proposed model projects the raw document into a vector representation, on which we build a classifier to perform document classification. In the following, we will present how we build the document level vector progressively from word vectors by using the hierarchical structure.

Word Encoder Given a sentence with words $w_{it}, t \in [0, T]$, we first embed the words to vectors through an embedding matrix W_e, $x_{ij} = W_e w_{ij}$. We use a bidirectional GRU (Bahdanau et al., 2014) to get annotations of words by summarizing information from both directions for words, and therefore incorporate the contextual information in the annotation. The bidirectional GRU contains the forward GRU $\overrightarrow{f}$ which reads the sentence s_i from w_{i1} to w_{iT} and a backward GRU $\overleftarrow{f}$ which reads from w_{iT} to w_{i1}:

$$x_{it} = W_e w_{it}, t \in [1, T],$$
$$\overrightarrow{h}_{it} = \overrightarrow{\mathrm{GRU}}(x_{it}), t \in [1, T],$$
$$\overleftarrow{h}_{it} = \overleftarrow{\mathrm{GRU}}(x_{it}), t \in [T, 1].$$

We obtain an annotation for a given word w_{it} by concatenating the forward hidden state $\overrightarrow{h}_{it}$ and backward hidden state $\overleftarrow{h}_{it}$, i.e., $h_{it} = [\overrightarrow{h}_{it}, \overleftarrow{h}_{it}]$, which summarizes the information of the whole sentence centered around w_{it}.

Note that we directly use word embeddings. For a more complete model we could use a GRU to get word vectors directly from characters, similarly to (Ling et al., 2015). We omitted this for simplicity.

Word Attention Not all words contribute equally to the representation of the sentence meaning. Hence, we introduce attention mechanism to extract such words that are important to the meaning of the sentence and aggregate the representation of those informative words to form a sentence vector. Specifically,

$$u_{it} = \tanh(W_w h_{it} + b_w) \tag{5}$$
$$\alpha_{it} = \frac{\exp(u_{it}^\top u_w)}{\sum_t \exp(u_{it}^\top u_w)} \tag{6}$$
$$s_i = \sum_t \alpha_{it} h_{it}. \tag{7}$$

That is, we first feed the word annotation h_{it} through a one-layer MLP to get u_{it} as a hidden representation of h_{it}, then we measure the importance of the word as the similarity of u_{it} with a word level context vector u_w and get a normalized importance weight α_{it} through a softmax function. After that, we compute the sentence vector s_i (we abuse the notation here) as a weighted sum of the word annotations based on the weights. The context vector u_w can be seen as a high level representation of a fixed query "what is the informative word" over the words like that used in memory networks (Sukhbaatar et al., 2015; Kumar et al., 2015). The word context vector u_w is randomly initialized and jointly learned during the training process.

Sentence Encoder Given the sentence vectors s_i, we can get a document vector in a similar way. We use a bidirectional GRU to encode the sentences:

$$\overrightarrow{h}_i = \overrightarrow{\mathrm{GRU}}(s_i), i \in [1, L],$$
$$\overleftarrow{h}_i = \overleftarrow{\mathrm{GRU}}(s_i), t \in [L, 1].$$

We concatenate $\overrightarrow{h}_i$ and $\overleftarrow{h}_j$ to get an annotation of sentence i, i.e., $h_i = [\overrightarrow{h}_i, \overleftarrow{h}_i]$. h_i summarizes the neighbor sentences around sentence i but still focus on sentence i.

Sentence Attention To reward sentences that are clues to correctly classify a document, we again use attention mechanism and introduce a sentence level context vector u_s and use the vector to measure the importance of the sentences. This yields

$$u_i = \tanh(W_s h_i + b_s), \tag{8}$$
$$\alpha_i = \frac{\exp(u_i^\top u_s)}{\sum_i \exp(u_i^\top u_s)}, \tag{9}$$
$$v = \sum_i \alpha_i h_i, \tag{10}$$

where v is the document vector that summarizes all the information of sentences in a document. Similarly, the sentence level context vector can be randomly initialized and jointly learned during the training process.

2.3 Document Classification

The document vector v is a high level representation of the document and can be used as features for document classification:

$$p = \text{softmax}(W_c v + b_c). \tag{11}$$

We use the negative log likelihood of the correct labels as training loss:

$$L = -\sum_d \log p_{dj}, \tag{12}$$

where j is the label of document d.

3 Experiments

3.1 Data sets

We evaluate the effectiveness of our model on six large scale document classification data sets. These data sets can be categorized into two types of document classification tasks: sentiment estimation and topic classification. The statistics of the data sets are summarized in Table 1. We use 80% of the data for training, 10% for validation, and the remaining 10% for test, unless stated otherwise.

Yelp reviews are obtained from the Yelp Dataset Challenge in 2013, 2014 and 2015 (Tang et al., 2015). There are five levels of ratings from 1 to 5 (higher is better).

IMDB reviews are obtained from (Diao et al., 2014). The ratings range from 1 to 10.

Yahoo answers are obtained from (Zhang et al., 2015). This is a topic classification task with 10 classes: Society & Culture, Science & Mathematics, Health, Education & Reference, Computers & Internet, Sports, Business & Finance, Entertainment & Music, Family & Relationships and Politics & Government. The document we use includes question titles, question contexts and best answers. There are 140,000 training samples and 5000 testing samples. The original data set does not provide validation samples. We randomly select 10% of the training samples as validation.

Amazon reviews are obtained from (Zhang et al., 2015). The ratings are from 1 to 5. 3,000,000 reviews are used for training and 650,000 reviews for testing. Similarly, we use 10% of the training samples as validation.

3.2 Baselines

We compare HAN with several baseline methods, including traditional approaches such as linear methods, SVMs and paragraph embeddings using neural networks, LSTMs, word-based CNN, character-based CNN, and Conv-GRNN, LSTM-GRNN. These baseline methods and results are reported in (Zhang et al., 2015; Tang et al., 2015).

3.2.1 Linear methods

Linear methods (Zhang et al., 2015) use the constructed statistics as features. A linear classifier based on multinomial logistic regression is used to classify the documents using the features.

BOW and BOW+TFIDF The 50,000 most frequent words from the training set are selected and the count of each word is used features. Bow+TFIDF, as implied by the name, uses the TFIDF of counts as features.

n-grams and n-grams+TFIDF used the most frequent 500,000 n-grams (up to 5-grams).

Bag-of-means The average word2vec embedding (Mikolov et al., 2013) is used as feature set.

3.2.2 SVMs

SVMs-based methods are reported in (Tang et al., 2015), including **SVM+Unigrams, Bigrams, Text Features, AverageSG, SSWE**. In detail, **Unigrams** and **Bigrams** uses bag-of-unigrams and bag-of-bigrams as features respectively.

Text Features are constructed according to (Kiritchenko et al., 2014), including word and character n-grams, sentiment lexicon features etc.

AverageSG constructs 200-dimensional word vectors using word2vec and the average word embeddings of each document are used.

SSWE uses sentiment specific word embeddings according to (Tang et al., 2014).

3.2.3 Neural Network methods

The neural network based methods are reported in (Tang et al., 2015) and (Zhang et al., 2015).

CNN-word Word based CNN models like that of (Kim, 2014) are used.

CNN-char Character level CNN models are reported in (Zhang et al., 2015).

Data set	classes	documents	average #s	max #s	average #w	max #w	vocabulary
Yelp 2013	5	335,018	8.9	151	151.6	1184	211,245
Yelp 2014	5	1,125,457	9.2	151	156.9	1199	476,191
Yelp 2015	5	1,569,264	9.0	151	151.9	1199	612,636
IMDB review	10	348,415	14.0	148	325.6	2802	115,831
Yahoo Answer	10	1,450,000	6.4	515	108.4	4002	1,554,607
Amazon review	5	3,650,000	4.9	99	91.9	596	1,919,336

Table 1: Data statistics: #s denotes the number of sentences (average and maximum per document), #w denotes the number of words (average and maximum per document).

LSTM takes the whole document as a single sequence and the average of the hidden states of all words is used as feature for classification.

Conv-GRNN and LSTM-GRNN were proposed by (Tang et al., 2015). They also explore the hierarchical structure: a CNN or LSTM provides a sentence vector, and then a gated recurrent neural network (GRNN) combines the sentence vectors from a document level vector representation for classification.

3.3 Model configuration and training

We split documents into sentences and tokenize each sentence using Stanford's CoreNLP (Manning et al., 2014). We only retain words appearing more than 5 times in building the vocabulary and replace the words that appear 5 times with a special UNK token. We obtain the word embedding by training an unsupervised word2vec (Mikolov et al., 2013) model on the training and validation splits and then use the word embedding to initialize W_e.

The hyper parameters of the models are tuned on the validation set. In our experiments, we set the word embedding dimension to be 200 and the GRU dimension to be 50. In this case a combination of forward and backward GRU gives us 100 dimensions for word/sentence annotation. The word/sentence context vectors also have a dimension of 100, initialized at random.

For training, we use a mini-batch size of 64 and documents of similar length (in terms of the number of sentences in the documents) are organized to be a batch. We find that length-adjustment can accelerate training by three times. We use stochastic gradient descent to train all models with momentum of 0.9. We pick the best learning rate using grid search on the validation set.

3.4 Results and analysis

The experimental results on all data sets are shown in Table 2. We refer to our models as **HN-{AVE, MAX, ATT}**. Here HN stands for Hierarchical Network, AVE indicates averaging, MAX indicates max-pooling, and ATT indicates our proposed hierarchical attention model. Results show that HN-ATT gives the best performance across all data sets.

The improvement is regardless of data sizes. For smaller data sets such as Yelp 2013 and IMDB, our model outperforms the previous best baseline methods by 3.1% and 4.1% respectively. This finding is consistent across other larger data sets. Our model outperforms previous best models by 3.2%, 3.4%, 4.6% and 6.0% on Yelp 2014, Yelp 2015, Yahoo Answers and Amazon Reviews. The improvement also occurs regardless of the type of task: sentiment classification, which includes Yelp 2013-2014, IMDB, Amazon Reviews and topic classification for Yahoo Answers.

From Table 2 we can see that neural network based methods that do *not* explore hierarchical document structure, such as LSTM, CNN-word, CNN-char have little advantage over traditional methods for large scale (in terms of document size) text classification. E.g. SVM+TextFeatures gives performance 59.8, 61.8, 62.4, 40.5 for Yelp 2013, 2014, 2015 and IMDB respectively, while CNN-word has accuracy 59.7, 61.0, 61.5, 37.6 respectively.

Exploring the hierarchical structure only, as in HN-AVE, HN-MAX, can significantly improve over LSTM, CNN-word and CNN-char. For example, our HN-AVE outperforms CNN-word by 7.3%, 8.8%, 8.5%, 10.2% than CNN-word on Yelp 2013, 2014, 2015 and IMDB respectively. Our model HN-ATT that further utilizes attention mechanism

	Methods	Yelp'13	Yelp'14	Yelp'15	IMDB	Yahoo Answer	Amazon
Zhang et al., 2015	BoW	-	-	58.0	-	68.9	54.4
	BoW TFIDF	-	-	59.9	-	71.0	55.3
	ngrams	-	-	56.3	-	68.5	54.3
	ngrams TFIDF	-	-	54.8	-	68.5	52.4
	Bag-of-means	-	-	52.5	-	60.5	44.1
Tang et al., 2015	Majority	35.6	36.1	36.9	17.9	-	-
	SVM + Unigrams	58.9	60.0	61.1	39.9	-	-
	SVM + Bigrams	57.6	61.6	62.4	40.9	-	-
	SVM + TextFeatures	59.8	61.8	62.4	40.5	-	-
	SVM + AverageSG	54.3	55.7	56.8	31.9	-	-
	SVM + SSWE	53.5	54.3	55.4	26.2	-	-
Zhang et al., 2015	LSTM	-	-	58.2	-	70.8	59.4
	CNN-char	-	-	62.0	-	71.2	59.6
	CNN-word	-	-	60.5	-	71.2	57.6
Tang et al., 2015	Paragraph Vector	57.7	59.2	60.5	34.1	-	-
	CNN-word	59.7	61.0	61.5	37.6	-	-
	Conv-GRNN	63.7	65.5	66.0	42.5	-	-
	LSTM-GRNN	65.1	67.1	67.6	45.3	-	-
This paper	HN-AVE	67.0	69.3	69.9	47.8	75.2	62.9
	HN-MAX	66.9	69.3	70.1	48.2	75.2	62.9
	HN-ATT	**68.2**	**70.5**	**71.0**	**49.4**	**75.8**	**63.6**

Table 2: Document Classification, in percentage

combined with hierarchical structure improves over previous models (LSTM-GRNN) by 3.1%, 3.4%, 3.5% and 4.1% respectively. More interestingly, in the experiments, HN-AVE is equivalent to using non-informative global word/sentence context vectors (e.g., if they are all-zero vectors, then the attention weights in Eq. 6 and 9 become uniform weights). Compared to HN-AVE, the HN-ATT model gives superior performance across the board. This clearly demonstrates the effectiveness of the proposed global word and sentence importance vectors for the HAN.

3.5 Context dependent attention weights

If words were inherently important or not important, models without attention mechanism might work well since the model could automatically assign low weights to irrelevant words and vice versa. However, the importance of words is highly context dependent. For example, the word good may appear in a review that has the lowest rating either because users are only happy with part of the product/service or because they use it in a negation, such as not

good. To verify that our model can capture context dependent word importance, we plot the distribution of the attention weights of the words good and bad from the test split of Yelp 2013 data set as shown in Figure 3(a) and Figure 4(a). We can see that the distribution has a attention weight assigned to a word from 0 to 1. This indicates that our model captures diverse context and assign context-dependent weight to the words.

For further illustration, we plot the distribution when conditioned on the ratings of the review. Subfigures 3(b)-(f) in Figure 3 and Figure 4 correspond to the rating 1-5 respectively. In particular, Figure 3(b) shows that the weight of good concentrates on the low end in the reviews with rating 1. As the rating increases, so does the weight distribution. This means that the word good plays a more important role for reviews with higher ratings. We can observe the converse trend in Figure 4 for the word bad. This confirms that our model can capture the context-dependent word importance.

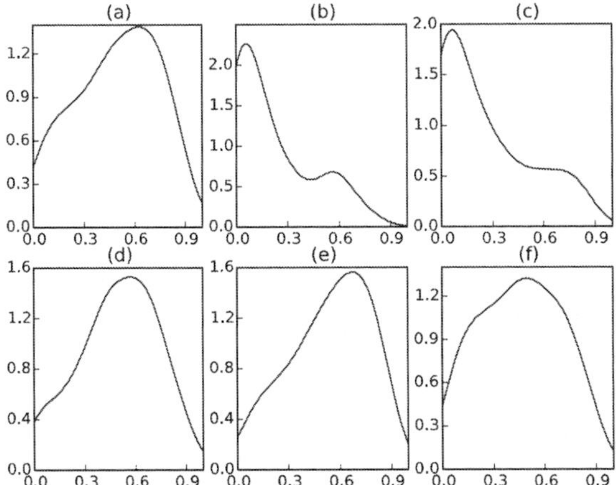

Figure 3: Attention weight distribution of good. (a) — aggregate distribution on the test split; (b)-(f) stratified for reviews with ratings 1-5 respectively. We can see that the weight distribution shifts to *higher* end as the rating goes higher.

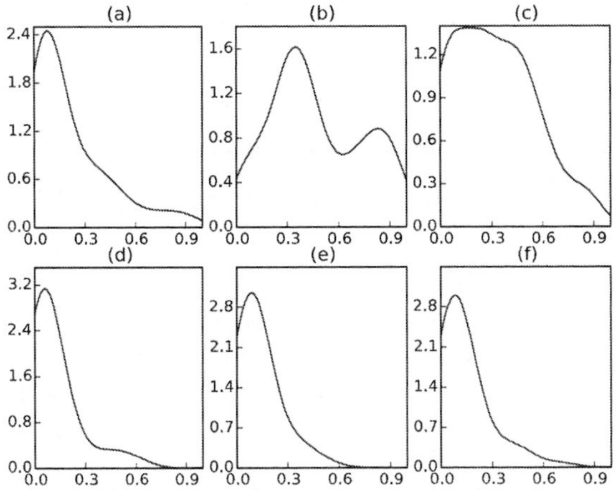

Figure 4: Attention weight distribution of the word bad. The setup is as above: (a) contains the aggregate distribution, while (b)-(f) contain stratifications to reviews with ratings 1-5 respectively. Contrary to before, the word bad is considered important for poor ratings and less so for good ones.

3.6 Visualization of attention

In order to validate that our model is able to select informative sentences and words in a document, we visualize the hierarchical attention layers in Figures 5 and 6 for several documents from the Yelp 2013 and Yahoo Answers data sets.

Every line is a sentence (sometimes sentences spill over several lines due to their length). Red denotes the sentence weight and blue denotes the word

weight. Due to the hierarchical structure, we normalize the word weight by the sentence weight to make sure that only important words in important sentences are emphasized. For visualization purposes we display $\sqrt{p_s}p_w$. The $\sqrt{p_s}$ term displays the important words in unimportant sentences to ensure that they are not totally invisible.

Figure 5 shows that our model can select the words carrying strong sentiment like delicious, amazing, terrible and their corresponding sentences. Sentences containing many words like cocktails, pasta, entree are disregarded. Note that our model can not only select words carrying strong sentiment, it can also deal with complex across-sentence context. For example, there are sentences like i don't even like scallops in the first document of Fig. 5, if looking purely at the single sentence, we may think this is negative comment. However, our model looks at the context of this sentence and figures out this is a positive review and chooses to ignore this sentence.

Our hierarchical attention mechanism also works well for topic classification in the Yahoo Answer data set. For example, for the left document in Figure 6 with label 1, which denotes Science and Mathematics, our model accurately localizes the words zebra, strips, camouflage, predator and their corresponding sentences. For the right document with label 4, which denotes Computers and Internet, our model focuses on web, searches, browsers and their corresponding sentences. Note that this happens in a *multiclass* setting, that is, detection happens before the selection of the topic!

4 Related Work

Kim (2014) use neural networks for text classification. The architecture is a direct application of CNNs, as used in computer vision (LeCun et al., 1998), albeit with NLP interpretations. Johnson and Zhang (2014) explores the case of directly using a high-dimensional one hot vector as input. They find that it performs well. Unlike word level modelings, Zhang et al. (2015) apply a character-level CNN for text classification and achieve competitive results. Socher et al. (2013) use recursive neural networks for text classification. Tai et al. (2015)

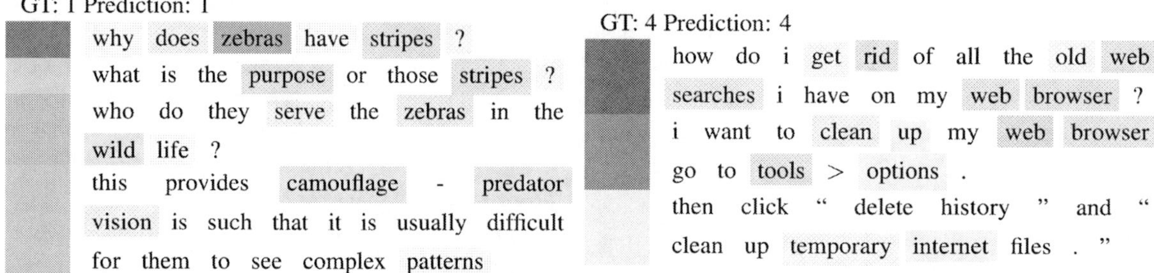

Figure 5: Documents from Yelp 2013. Label 4 means star 5, label 0 means star 1.

Figure 6: Documents from Yahoo Answers. Label 1 denotes Science and Mathematics and label 4 denotes Computers and Internet.

explore the structure of a sentence and use a tree-structured LSTMs for classification. There are also some works that combine LSTM and CNN structure to for sentence classification (Lai et al., 2015; Zhou et al., 2015). Tang et al. (2015) use hierarchical structure in sentiment classification. They first use a CNN or LSTM to get a sentence vector and then a bi-directional gated recurrent neural network to compose the sentence vectors to get a document vectors. There are some other works that use hierarchical structure in sequence generation (Li et al., 2015) and language modeling (Lin et al., 2015).

The attention mechanism was proposed by (Bahdanau et al., 2014) in machine translation. The encoder decoder framework is used and an attention mechanism is used to select the reference words in original language for words in foreign language before translation. Xu et al. (2015) uses the attention mechanism in image caption generation to select the relevant image regions when generating words in the captions. Further uses of the attention mechanism include parsing (Vinyals et al., 2014), natural language question answering (Sukhbaatar et al., 2015; Kumar et al., 2015; Hermann et al., 2015), and image question answering (Yang et al., 2015). Unlike these works, we explore a *hierarchical* attention mechanism (to the best of our knowledge this is the first such instance).

5 Conclusion

In this paper, we proposed hierarchical attention networks (HAN) for classifying documents. As a convenient side-effect we obtained better visualization using the highly informative components of a document. Our model progressively builds a document vector by aggregating important words into sentence vectors and then aggregating important sentences vectors to document vectors. Experimental results demonstrate that our model performs significantly better than previous methods. Visualization of these attention layers illustrates that our model is effective in picking out important words and sentences.

Acknowledgments This work was supported by Microsoft Research.

References

Dzmitry Bahdanau, Kyunghyun Cho, and Yoshua Bengio. 2014. Neural machine translation by jointly learning to align and translate. *arXiv preprint arXiv:1409.0473*.

Phil Blunsom, Edward Grefenstette, Nal Kalchbrenner, et al. 2014. A convolutional neural network for modelling sentences. In *Proceedings of the 52nd Annual Meeting of the Association for Computational Linguistics*. Proceedings of the 52nd Annual Meeting of the Association for Computational Linguistics.

Qiming Diao, Minghui Qiu, Chao-Yuan Wu, Alexander J Smola, Jing Jiang, and Chong Wang. 2014. Jointly modeling aspects, ratings and sentiments for movie recommendation (jmars). In *Proceedings of the 20th ACM SIGKDD international conference on Knowledge discovery and data mining*, pages 193–202. ACM.

Jianfeng Gao, Patrick Pantel, Michael Gamon, Xiaodong He, Li Deng, and Yelong Shen. 2014. Modeling interestingness with deep neural networks. In *Proceedings of the 2013 Conference on Empirical Methods in Natural Language Processing*.

Karl Moritz Hermann, Tomáš Kočiský, Edward Grefenstette, Lasse Espeholt, Will Kay, Mustafa Suleyman, and Phil Blunsom. 2015. Teaching machines to read and comprehend. *arXiv preprint arXiv:1506.03340*.

Sepp Hochreiter and Jürgen Schmidhuber. 1997. Long short-term memory. *Neural computation*, 9(8):1735–1780.

Thorsten Joachims. 1998. *Text categorization with support vector machines: Learning with many relevant features*. Springer.

Rie Johnson and Tong Zhang. 2014. Effective use of word order for text categorization with convolutional neural networks. *arXiv preprint arXiv:1412.1058*.

Yoon Kim. 2014. Convolutional neural networks for sentence classification. *arXiv preprint arXiv:1408.5882*.

Svetlana Kiritchenko, Xiaodan Zhu, and Saif M Mohammad. 2014. Sentiment analysis of short informal texts. *Journal of Artificial Intelligence Research*, pages 723–762.

Ankit Kumar, Ozan Irsoy, Jonathan Su, James Bradbury, Robert English, Brian Pierce, Peter Ondruska, Ishaan Gulrajani, and Richard Socher. 2015. Ask me anything: Dynamic memory networks for natural language processing. *arXiv preprint arXiv:1506.07285*.

Siwei Lai, Liheng Xu, Kang Liu, and Jun Zhao. 2015. Recurrent convolutional neural networks for text classification. In *Twenty-Ninth AAAI Conference on Artificial Intelligence*.

Yann LeCun, Léon Bottou, Yoshua Bengio, and Patrick Haffner. 1998. Gradient-based learning applied to document recognition. *Proceedings of the IEEE*, 86(11):2278–2324.

Jiwei Li, Minh-Thang Luong, and Dan Jurafsky. 2015. A hierarchical neural autoencoder for paragraphs and documents. *arXiv preprint arXiv:1506.01057*.

Rui Lin, Shujie Liu, Muyun Yang, Mu Li, Ming Zhou, and Sheng Li. 2015. Hierarchical recurrent neural network for document modeling. In *Proceedings of the 2015 Conference on Empirical Methods in Natural Language Processing*, pages 899–907.

Wang Ling, Tiago Luís, Luís Marujo, Ramón Fernandez Astudillo, Silvio Amir, Chris Dyer, Alan W Black, and Isabel Trancoso. 2015. Finding function in form: Compositional character models for open vocabulary word representation. *arXiv preprint arXiv:1508.02096*.

Andrew L Maas, Raymond E Daly, Peter T Pham, Dan Huang, Andrew Y Ng, and Christopher Potts. 2011. Learning word vectors for sentiment analysis. In *Proceedings of the 49th Annual Meeting of the Association for Computational Linguistics: Human Language Technologies-Volume 1*, pages 142–150. Association for Computational Linguistics.

Christopher D Manning, Mihai Surdeanu, John Bauer, Jenny Finkel, Steven J Bethard, and David McClosky. 2014. The stanford corenlp natural language processing toolkit. In *Proceedings of 52nd Annual Meeting of the Association for Computational Linguistics: System Demonstrations*, pages 55–60.

Tomas Mikolov, Ilya Sutskever, Kai Chen, Greg S Corrado, and Jeff Dean. 2013. Distributed representations of words and phrases and their compositionality. In *Advances in neural information processing systems*, pages 3111–3119.

Bo Pang and Lillian Lee. 2008. Opinion mining and sentiment analysis. *Foundations and trends in information retrieval*, 2(1-2):1–135.

Mehran Sahami, Susan Dumais, David Heckerman, and Eric Horvitz. 1998. A bayesian approach to filtering junk e-mail. In *Learning for Text Categorization: Papers from the 1998 workshop*, volume 62, pages 98–105.

Yelong Shen, Xiaodong He, Jianfeng Gao, Li Deng, and Gregoire Mesnil. 2014. A latent semantic model with convolutional-pooling structure for information retrieval. In *Proceedings of the 23rd ACM International Conference on Conference on Information and Knowledge Management*, pages 101–110. ACM.

Richard Socher, Alex Perelygin, Jean Y. Wu, Jason Chuang, Christopher D. Manning, Andrew Y. Ng, and Christopher Potts. 2013. Recursive deep models for semantic compositionality over a sentiment treebank. In *Proc. EMNLP*.

Sainbayar Sukhbaatar, Arthur Szlam, Jason Weston, and Rob Fergus. 2015. End-to-end memory networks. *arXiv preprint arXiv:1503.08895*.

Kai Sheng Tai, Richard Socher, and Christopher D. Manning. 2015. Improved semantic representations from tree-structured long short-term memory networks. In *Proc. ACL*.

Duyu Tang, Furu Wei, Nan Yang, Ming Zhou, Ting Liu, and Bing Qin. 2014. Learning sentiment-specific word embedding for twitter sentiment classification. In *Proceedings of the 52nd Annual Meeting of the Association for Computational Linguistics*, volume 1, pages 1555–1565.

Duyu Tang, Bing Qin, and Ting Liu. 2015. Document modeling with gated recurrent neural network for sentiment classification. In *Proceedings of the 2015 Conference on Empirical Methods in Natural Language Processing*, pages 1422–1432.

Oriol Vinyals, Lukasz Kaiser, Terry Koo, Slav Petrov, Ilya Sutskever, and Geoffrey Hinton. 2014. Grammar as a foreign language. *arXiv preprint arXiv:1412.7449*.

Sida Wang and Christopher D Manning. 2012. Baselines and bigrams: Simple, good sentiment and topic classification. In *Proceedings of the 50th Annual Meeting of the Association for Computational Linguistics: Short Papers-Volume 2*, pages 90–94. Association for Computational Linguistics.

Kelvin Xu, Jimmy Ba, Ryan Kiros, Aaron Courville, Ruslan Salakhutdinov, Richard Zemel, and Yoshua Bengio. 2015. Show, attend and tell: Neural image caption generation with visual attention. *arXiv preprint arXiv:1502.03044*.

Zichao Yang, Xiaodong He, Jianfeng Gao, Li Deng, and Alex Smola. 2015. Stacked attention networks for image question answering. *arXiv preprint arXiv:1511.02274*.

Xiang Zhang, Junbo Zhao, and Yann LeCun. 2015. Character-level convolutional networks for text classification. *arXiv preprint arXiv:1509.01626*.

Chunting Zhou, Chonglin Sun, Zhiyuan Liu, and Francis Lau. 2015. A c-lstm neural network for text classification. *arXiv preprint arXiv:1511.08630*.

Dependency Based Embeddings for Sentence Classification Tasks

Alexandros Komninos
Department of Computer Science
University of York
York, YO10 5GH
United Kingdom
ak1153@york.ac.uk

Suresh Manandhar
Department of Computer Science
University of York
York, YO10 5GH
United Kingdom
suresh@cs.york.ac.uk

Abstract

We compare different word embeddings from a standard window based skipgram model, a skipgram model trained using dependency context features and a novel skipgram variant that utilizes additional information from dependency graphs. We explore the effectiveness of the different types of word embeddings for word similarity and sentence classification tasks. We consider three common sentence classification tasks: question type classification on the TREC dataset, binary sentiment classification on Stanford's Sentiment Treebank and semantic relation classification on the SemEval 2010 dataset. For each task we use three different classification methods: a Support Vector Machine, a Convolutional Neural Network and a Long Short Term Memory Network. Our experiments show that dependency based embeddings outperform standard window based embeddings in most of the settings, while using dependency context embeddings as additional features improves performance in all tasks regardless of the classification method.
Our embeddings and code are available at
https://www.cs.york.ac.uk/nlp/extvec

1 Introduction

Representing words as low dimensional vectors (also known as word embeddings) has been a widely adopted technique in NLP. Word representations can be used as features for classification tasks such as named entity recognition or chunking (Turian et al.,

2010), and as a pretraining method for initializing deep neural network representations (Collobert et al., 2011; Kim, 2014). Word embeddings provide better generalization to unseen examples since they can capture general semantic and syntactic properties of words. One of the most popular methods of learning word embeddings is the skipgram model of Mikolov et al. (2013a; 2013b) where embeddings are trained by making predictions of context words appearing in a window around a target word.

The standard skipgram model ignores syntax and only partially takes into consideration the sequential structure of text, but still captures certain syntactic properties of words. A significant amount of previous research has explored methods for directly taking syntax into account for word embedding learning (Pham et al., 2015; Cheng and Kartsaklis, 2015; Hashimoto et al., 2014). One simple method is based on traditional count-based distributional semantic spaces and utilizes words with syntactic types from a dependency parse graph as context features (Padó and Lapata, 2007; Baroni and Lenci, 2010). This method has also been applied to skipgram models, where word embeddings are optimized to predict dependency context features instead of other words (Levy and Goldberg, 2014).

Syntax-based embeddings have been shown to have different properties in word similarity evaluations than their window based counterparts, better capturing the functional properties of words. However, it is not clear if they provide any advantage for NLP tasks. We show that using dependency context features can be a general method of providing syntactic information for several sentence classification

Proceedings of NAACL-HLT 2016, pages 1490–1500,
San Diego, California, June 12-17, 2016. ©2016 Association for Computational Linguistics

tasks. Furthermore, the dependency context embeddings improve performance with all classifiers we tested.

We consider the usage of word and dependency context features for three common sentence classification tasks: TREC question type classification, binary sentiment prediction on Stanford Sentiment Treebank, and SemEval 2010 relation identification. We evaluate different methods of using the dependency context embeddings as extra features besides word embeddings to inject information into sentence classifiers about the syntactic structure of a sentence. The advantage of such a method is that it can be applied to any classifier that utilizes standard word embeddings. We evaluate the usefulness of syntax-based word embeddings and dependency context embeddings with three different sentence classification methods: a Support Vector Machine (SVM), a Convolutional Neural Network (CNN) and a Long Short Term Memory network (LSTM).

In order to better utilize the structure of dependency graphs, we propose an extended version of the simple dependency based skipgram of Levy et al. (2014). This extended version considers co-occurrences in a dependency graph between pairs of words, words and dependency context features, and between different dependency context features. This scheme results in word embeddings that share properties between window based models and dependency graph based ones. More importantly, it provides additional structural information for the dependency context feature embeddings making them more effective when used in sentence classification tasks.

Our evaluation provides several insights on the role of syntax for embeddings and how they can be used for sentence classification. First, we confirm past claims about the different properties between dependency and window based skipgram embeddings in word similarity tasks. Second, we show that dependency based embeddings perform better in question classification and relation identification than window based ones. These results are robust across multiple classification methods. We show that combining dependency context feature embeddings together with word embeddings provide a simple and effective way to improve sentence classification performance. Finally, the performance gain is

higher for the extended dependency based skipgram developed in this paper.

2   Related Work

Estimating word representations from text has been the focus of a lot of research in NLP. Traditional count-based models learn representations by applying SVD in a word-word co-occurrence matrix (Turney et al., 2010). More recently, neural models have been used to learn word embeddings by optimizing for a word prediction task (Collobert et al., 2011; Mnih and Teh, 2012; Mikolov et al., 2013a). However, the most commonly used word representation techniques like word2vec's skipgram and CBoW take little consideration of syntactic structure.

Several modifications have been proposed so that word embedding learning algorithms can better utilize syntax or the sequence structure of sentences. One such model is the dependency based skipgram of Levy and Goldberg (2014) which we further extend in this paper. Evaluation of this model is limited to word similarity or lexical substitution in context (Melamud et al., 2015), and little is known about performance within other NLP tasks. Hashimoto et al. (2014) proposed a log-bilinear language model based on predicate-argument structures and report improvements on phrase similarity tasks compared to standard skipgram. In Ling et al. (2015), skipgram and CBoW models are adapted to include position specific weights for the words inside the co-occurrence window and the resulting embeddings provide slight improvements for parsing and POS tagging tasks. The C-PHRASE model (Pham et al., 2015) is another modification of the CBoW model that uses an external parser to replace windows with syntactic constituents. In Cheng and Kartsaklis (2015), a recursive neural network structured according to a sentence's parse learns word embeddings by composing into valid sentences rather than distorted ones.

Structured skipgram models (Levy and Goldberg, 2014; Ling et al., 2015) have a notable difference with other approaches of incorporating structural information into embeddings (e.g. C-PHRASE), since they also produce embeddings of the structural context features at the prediction layer. We show that in the case of dependency contexts, these structural features can provide valuable information to sentence classifiers. In our extended dependency based skipgram, we do not make a distinction between words and structural features in the training process, which results into better performing dependency context embeddings when used in sentence classification. Another difference of our skipgram model with other structured skipgram variants is that we keep the long distance word contexts used in standard window based skipgram training with the purpose of capturing both functional and topic related semantic properties of words.

Our work is also related to methods of providing explicit syntactic information to sentence classifiers. Most of the previously proposed approaches rely on tree-structured neural architectures to drive composition of word embeddings to a sentence representation (Socher et al., 2012; Tai et al., 2015; Li et al., 2015). We use a different approach where syntactic information is provided only through embeddings. Our approach is not orthogonal to using tree-structured models and the two of them could be applied together. An advantage of providing syntactic information through embeddings is that large amounts of automatically parsed textual data can be utilized in order to learn representations of dependency types.

3 Embedding Models

The skipgram model of Mikolov et al. (2013a; 2013b) optimizes vector representations of words (word embeddings) such that they can predict other context words occurring in a small window. The architecture consists of a single hidden layer feedforward network without any non-linearity applied on the hidden layer. The input to the network is the index of a target word (a one-hot vector) and the output is a vector of probabilities of appearance for context words. The network learns word embeddings by maximizing the log probability of a context word c given a target word t observed in a large corpus of textual data D. To avoid the large computational cost of applying a softmax for the whole vocabulary, a commonly used strategy is to train with negative sampling. For each target-context pair (t, c) coming from the observed data D, a small number of context words is sampled from unobserved data D'

according to a simple distribution and then used as the negative classes.

The probability of the target context pair (t, c) being observed in the data is given by:

$$P(D = 1 \mid t, c) = \sigma(v_t \cdot v_c) \qquad (1)$$

where v_t and v_c are target and context word embeddings, and σ is the sigmoid function. For a negative sampled pair (t, c), the probability of the pair not being observed in the data is given by:

$$P(D = 0 \mid t, c) = 1 - \sigma(v_t \cdot v_c) \qquad (2)$$

The objective becomes:

$$\arg\max_{v_t, v_c} \sum_{t, c \in D} \log \sigma(v_t \cdot v_c) + \sum_{t, c \in D'} \log \sigma(-v_t \cdot v_c) \qquad (3)$$

The network learns two sets of weights for each word: one for embedding words to a low dimensional representation in the hidden layer that we will refer to as the embedding layer weights, and one for assigning a probability to context words that we will refer to as the prediction layer weights. Both sets of weights assign representations to words such that words that have similar co-occurrence patterns with other words are closer in the embedding space. Typically, the embedding layer weights are used as feature representations of words for other other tasks. Due to its scalability to large corpora and the good performance of its derived word embeddings in several NLP tasks the skipgram model has become a standard solution for unsupervised learning of word representations.

While typical training of skipgarm is performed by optimizing for the prediction of other words in a window around the target word, it is possible to use other contextual features, such as contexts from dependency graphs of sentences.

We consider three variations of skipgram based on different target-context pairs:

3.1 Window-5 based skipgram (Win5)

This is a standard skipgram model that considers target-context word pairs inside a window of 5 words to the right and to the left of the target word. The window size for every target instance in the corpus is uniformly sampled from the [1,5] range, effectively providing a weighting scheme for context

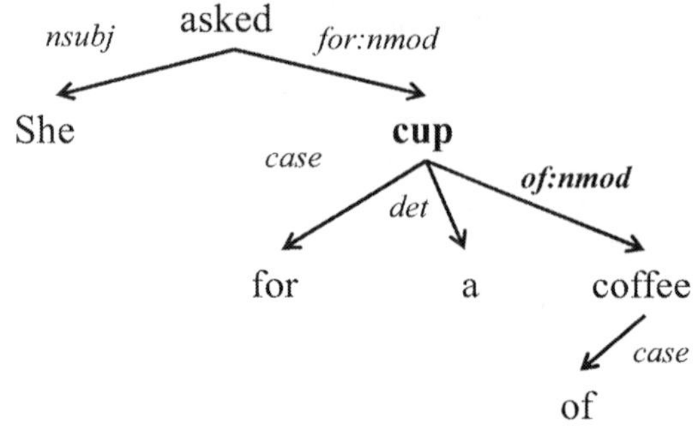

Figure 1: A sentence and its dependency parse graph. The contexts of the word "cup" are shown for each model. In addition, for the EXT model the contexts of the "of:nmod_coffee" dependency context feature are shown.

words according to their distance from the target word.

3.2 Skipgram with dependency contexts (LG)

Levy and Golberg's (2014) modification to the skipgram model replaces context words in a window by dependency contexts. A dependency context is a discrete symbol denoting a word and its syntactic role in a dependency parse graph (e.g. $nsubj\_she$, $of : nmod\_coffee$, $of : nmod^{-1}\_cup$). The directionality of dependency edges is encoded by introducing features with inverse relations. Training of this skipgram variant is similar to window based approaches, but each word is considered as a node in a dependency graph obtained by a parser, and embeddings are optimized to predict their corresponding word's immediate syntactic contexts (Figure 1). The network's weight matrices have different shapes, where representations coming from the embedding layer weights correspond to word embeddings, while representations coming from the prediction layer weights to dependency context embeddings.

3.3 Extended Dependency Skipgram (EXT)

We propose another variation of skipgram based on dependency graphs that utilizes additional co-occurrences compared to the LG variant. Each target word is taken as a node in the dependency graph and then optimize word embeddings such that they maximize the probability of other words within distance one and two in the graph. As with the Win5 model, we apply a weighting according to distance, with words having distance one from the target counted twice. This word-word prediction behaves similarly to the Win5 model, but considers the dependency parse to filter coincidental co-occurrences. The second type of predictions that embeddings are optimized for is similar to the LG model, where each word predicts its dependency contexts. We also optimize for a third type of context prediction where for each node, dependency contexts become the targets and predict the rest of dependency contexts of the same node. An example of the different target-context pairs that each skipgarm variant utilizes can be seen in Figure 1. The three types of target-context pairs for the extended dependency skipgram are interleaved during training. The weight matrices of this network are symmetric resulting in two embeddings per word and dependency context feature.

3.4 Implementation Details

We trained 300 dimensional versions of the above skipgram variants on English Wikipedia August 2015 dump of 2 billion words. Vocabularies consist of words and dependency contexts that appear more than 100 times (approximately 220k words and 1.3m dependency contexts). Training was done by applying negative sampling with 15 negative samples per target-context pair for 10 iterations over the entire corpus using stochastic gradient descent. The following commonly used methods (Mikolov et al., 2013b; Levy et al., 2015) were applied during training: drawing negative samples according to their unigram distribution raised to the power of 0.75, linear decay of learning rate with initial $\alpha = 0.25$, and subsampling of target words with probability given by $p = \frac{f-10^{-5}}{f} - \sqrt{\frac{10^{-5}}{t}}$ where f is the word's frequency. Dependency parsing for LG and EXT training was done with the Stanford Neural Network dependency parser (Chen and Manning, 2014) using Universal Dependency tags (De Marneffe et al., 2014).

4 Word Similarity Evaluation

We evaluate the effect of the different contextual features for skipgram word embeddings in two word similarity datasets: WordSim-353 (Finkelstein et al., 2001) and SimLex-999 (Hill et al., 2015). For both datasets, we compare the cosine similarity of word embeddings for a pair of words to human judgements and report Spearman's correlation in Table 1. The two datasets use a different notion of word similarity for scoring. Wordsim-353 mostly captures topical similarity (or relatedness), giving high similarity to pair of words like *clothes-closet*. SimLex-999 uses a more strict version of similarity, often called substitutional similarity, where the pair *clothes-closet* has a low similarity score and pairs like *shore-coast* have high similarity. Win5 skipgram version achieves a higher correlation for WordSim-353 compared to LG, but the results are reversed for SimLex-999. This agrees with previous research that shows that syntactic contexts correlate better with substitutional similarity judgements than using words in a window as contexts (Levy and Goldberg, 2014). As expected, the extended model represents a middle ground solution between the two. While similarity based evaluation makes obvious that different contextual features capture different properties of words, it is not clear which kind similarity notion is more useful when word representations are used as features for NLP tasks. We answer this question for sentence level classification tasks in the next section.

Embeddings	WordSim-353	SimLex-999
Win5	**0.714**	0.389
LG	0.621	**0.460**
EXT	0.678	0.414

Table 1: Spearman correlation for the 3 skipgram variants on WordSim-353 and SimLex-999 word similarity evaluation tasks.

5 Sentence Classification

We consider three common sentence classification tasks: TREC question type classification (QC), binary sentiment classification on Stanford's Sentiment Treebank (SST), and relation identification between pairs of nominals (RI) using the SemEval 2010 dataset. The experiments aim to answer two questions. First, to assess the effect of different context features for word embeddings when used in sentence classification tasks, given their different behaviour on word similarity evaluation. Second, to experiment with methods of using the dependency context embeddings themselves as a way to provide classifiers with dependency syntactic information. We carry out experiments with three different classification methods: SVMs with averaged embeddings, the Convolutional Neural Network of Kim (2014), and a Long Short Term Memory recurrent neural network (Hochreiter and Schmidhuber, 1997). These classifiers have some distinct characteristics. The SVM does not take into account the structure of the sentence, nor does it build any internal representations. On the other hand, both the CNN and LSTM networks operate on sequences of words and build internal representations before predicting the class label distribution. However, they do not have access to explicit syntactic information.

We first give a description of the classification methods and the way embeddings are used as features, followed by the description of the tasks and results.

5.1 Classification Methods

SVM with averaged embeddings We create a sentence representation by averaging embeddings of sentence features (words and dependency contexts). This can be considered the equivalent of a Bag-of-Words sentence representation in the embedding space, hence called Bag-of-Embeddings (BoE). We then train a classifier by applying a Support Vector Machine with a Gaussian kernel:

$$K(\mathbf{x}, \mathbf{x}') = \exp(-\gamma \|\mathbf{x} - \mathbf{x}'\|^2) \tag{4}$$

For hyperparameter tuning, we set parameter γ of the kernel to $1/k$, where k is the number of features (dimensionality of embeddings), and then perform cross validation for the c parameter using the standard Win5 word embeddings in the question classification task.

Convolutional Neural Network (CNN) We use the simple Convolutional Neural Network of Kim (2014) that has been shown to perform well in multiple sentence classification tasks. The network's input is a sentence matrix X formed by concatenating k-dimensional word embeddings. Then a convolutional filter $W \in \mathbb{R}^{h \times k}$ is applied to every possible sequence of length h to get a feature map:

$$c_i = tanh(W \cdot X + b) \tag{5}$$

followed by a max-over-time pooling operation to get the feature with the highest value:

$$\hat{c} = \max \mathbf{c} \tag{6}$$

The pooled features of different filters are then concatenated and passed to a fully connected softmax layer to perform the classification. The network uses multiple filters with different sequence sizes covering different size of windows in the sentence. All hyperparameters of the network are the same as used in the original paper (Kim, 2014): stochastic dropout (Srivastava et al., 2014) with $p = 0.5$ on the penultimate layer, 100 filters for each filter region with filter regions of width 2,3 and 4. Optimization is performed with Adadelta (Zeiler, 2012) on mini-batches of size 50.

Long Short Term Memory (LSTM) LSTM networks (Hochreiter and Schmidhuber, 1997) are recurrent neural networks where recurrent units consist of a memory cell c and three gates i, o and f. Given a sequence of input embeddings $\mathbf{x}$, LSTM outputs a sequence of states $\mathbf{h}$ given by the following equations:

$$\begin{pmatrix} \mathbf{i_t} \\ \mathbf{f_t} \\ \mathbf{o_t} \\ \tilde{\mathbf{c}}_\mathbf{t} \end{pmatrix} = \begin{pmatrix} \sigma \\ \sigma \\ \sigma \\ tanh \end{pmatrix} W \cdot \begin{pmatrix} \mathbf{h_{t-1}} \\ \mathbf{x_t} \end{pmatrix} \tag{7}$$

$$\mathbf{c_t} = \mathbf{f_t} \odot \mathbf{c_{t-1}} + \mathbf{i_t} \odot \tilde{\mathbf{c}}_\mathbf{t} \tag{8}$$

$$\mathbf{h_t} = \mathbf{o_t} \odot tanh(\mathbf{c_t}) \tag{9}$$

where $W \in \mathbb{R}^{4k \times 2k}$, $\tilde{\mathbf{c}}_\mathbf{t}$ is a candidate state for the memory cell and $\odot$ is element-wise vector multiplication. The distribution of labels for the whole sentence is computed by a fully connected softmax layer on top of the final hidden state after applying stochastic dropout with $p = 0.25$. We use 150 dimensions for the size of $\mathbf{h}$, Adagrad (Duchi et al., 2011) for optimization and mini-batch size of 100.

5.2 Sentence Feature Representations

We provide syntactic information to each classifier in the following manner. First we parse each sentence to get a dependency graph. Each node in the graph is associated with a word w having an embedding $\mathbf{v_w}$ and a set of dependency context features $d_1, d_2, ..., d_C$ with embeddings $\mathbf{v_{d_1}}, \mathbf{v_{d_2}}, ..., \mathbf{v_{d_C}}$ exactly like during the dependency based skipgram training process. We then create a representation $\mathbf{x}$ of that node using different combinations of its associated word and dependency context embeddings:

- *Words*: Using only word embeddings

$$\mathbf{x} = \mathbf{v_w} \tag{10}$$

- *Dep*: A node's representation becomes the average of its associated dependency context embeddings:

$$\mathbf{x} = \frac{1}{C} \sum_{c=1}^{C} \mathbf{v_{d_c}} \tag{11}$$

- *Wavg*: Combination of the word and dependency context embeddings by a weighted average scheme that assigns equal contribution to the word and dependency context part:

$$\mathbf{x} = \frac{1}{2}\mathbf{v_w} + \frac{1}{2C} \sum_{c=1}^{C} \mathbf{v_{d_c}} \tag{12}$$

- *Conc*: Similar to the Wavg, but dependency context embeddings are first averaged and then concatenated to the word embedding to form a single vector:

$$\mathbf{x} = \mathbf{v_w} \oplus \frac{1}{C} \sum_{c=1}^{C} \mathbf{v_{d_c}} \tag{13}$$

where $\oplus$ is the concatenation operator. This method keeps the word and syntactic part separate at the expense of doubling the dimensionality.

The above methods are used with the LG and EXT variants to create context specific node representations. For the EXT model, both word and dependency context embeddings used come from the embedding layer weights. The *Words* method is the only one that can be applied to the Win5 model. It is the most commonly used method to utilize word representations as features and our baseline. To make the comparison more fair for the Win5 model we include two additional variations that utilize both the embedding and prediction layer weights as an ensemble method for creating a word's representation:

- *Win5 AvgE*: Ensemble made by averaging word embeddings from the embedding and prediction layer weights of Win5 skipgram:

$$\mathbf{x} = \frac{1}{2}(\mathbf{v_w} + \mathbf{v_{w'}}) \tag{14}$$

- *Win5 ConcE*: Another ensemble made by concatenating word embeddings from the embedding and prediction layer weights of Win5 skipgram:

$$\mathbf{x} = \mathbf{v_w} \oplus \mathbf{v_{w'}} \tag{15}$$

Ensemble techniques have been reported to outperform simple word representations in some word similarity tasks (Levy et al., 2015). Since the EXT skipgram version uses symmetric weight matrices for the embedding and prediction layer, ensemble methods like the above could also be applied, but are not considered for these experiments. Note that contrary to the dependency based models, these ensemble methods do not create context specific representations.

The dependency graph's node representations are used as a sequence of embeddings respecting the order of the sentence to become the input for the CNN and LSTM. For the SVM BoE, word and dependency contexts of the whole sentence are averaged separately for the *Words* and *Dep* method, and then averaged again for the *Wavg* method or concatenated for the *Conc* method. As we are evaluating performance of embeddings, we do not perform updates during training of CNNs and LSTMs.

5.3 Datasets and Results

TREC Question Classification The TREC Question Classification dataset (Li and Roth, 2002) consists of 5452 training questions and 500 test questions. The task is to classify each question with one of six labels (e.g. location, definition, ...) depending on the answer they seek. For CNNs and LSTMs 10% of the training data were used as the dev set to pick the best model among different iterations. Classification accuracy results for each input representations and classification method can be seen in Table 2. We also report the state of the art result by the dependency convolutional neural network of Mu et al. (2015). Their model consists of a convolutional neural network that takes a dependency tree at the input layer instead of a sequence, and uses heuristics to choose the subset of nodes where pooling is applied.

Embeddings	SVM	CNN	LSTM
Win5 Words	81.4	92.8	88.4
Win5 AvgE	81.4	91.2	88.8
Win5 ConcE	82.4	92.6	90.4
LG Words	86.8	93.8	90.6
LG Dep	85.2	89.0	87.2
LG Wavg	87.2	93.4	91.2
LG Conc	84.0	94.6	92.0
EXT Words	88.4	94.2	91.8
EXT Dep	87.6	90.6	89.8
EXT Wavg	89.0	**95.0**	92.2
EXT Conc	**91.6**	93.2	**94.4**
tree CNN		96.0	

Table 2: Accuracy on 6-way TREC question classification task. Tree CNN is a CNN operating on dependency trees (Mou et al., 2015).

SST-2 The Stanford Sentiment Treebank dataset (Socher et al., 2013) has fine grained sentiment polarity scores for movie reviews on the phrasal and sentence level. The binary version of the task considers only positive and negative sentiment labels, resulting in a 6920/872/1821 split for training/dev/testing sets. All the models were trained using only the sentence level annotations. Classification accuracies for all models are reported in Table 3. The state of the art for this dataset comes from Kim (2014) using the same convolutional neural network as we do, but also utilizing the phrasal level annotations which provide about an order of magnitude larger training set. In addition, this specific configuration of the network (multichannel) uses two channels at the input layer, one updating the word embeddings during training and one that keeps them static as we do in our experiments.

Embeddings	SVM	CNN	LSTM
Win5 Words	80.1	83.5	76.1
Win5 AvgE	79.5	83.2	76.9
Win5 ConcE	80.3	82.9	77.6
LG Words	78.5	84.5	77.2
LG Dep	76.0	76.8	69.1
LG Wavg	78.9	82.0	78.6
LG Conc	79.8	82.7	79.7
EXT Words	80.5	84.1	77.6
EXT Dep	77.7	77.2	69.6
EXT Wavg	**80.6**	**84.6**	75.7
EXT Conc	**80.6**	83.5	**79.8**
CNN-multichannel		88.1	

Table 3: Accuracy on Stanford Sentiment Treebank binary classification task. CNN-multichannel is the best result reported in Kim (2014).

SemEval 2010 Relation Identification The SemEval 2010 Relation Identification task (Hendrickx et al., 2009) considers the classification of semantic relations between pairs of nominals into 19 classes. The classes are formed by 9 types of relations (e.g. cause-effect, component-whole, ...) with directionality taken into account and an extra OTHER class. We only used the shortest dependency path between the two nominals as the input to classifiers. In table 4, we report results using the official SemEval metric of macro-averaged F1-Score for (9+1)-way classifi-

cation, taking directionality into account. The best reported result for this dataset is 85.6 F1-score by Xu et al. (2015) also using a convolutional network on a sequence of word embeddings from the shortest dependency path between the pair of nominals. They also introduce negative samples during training by reversing the subject and object of the relation and WordNet features. Without using WordNet features their model achieves 84.0 F1-score.

Embeddings	SVM	CNN	LSTM
Win5 Words	72.23	81.60	77.30
Win5 AvgE	71.09	79.46	76.67
Win5 ConcE	72.74	81.33	78.09
LG Words	75.29	84.18	79.94
LG Dep	75.19	79.13	74.77
LG Wavg	77.61	83.17	79.69
LG Conc	**78.71**	83.41	78.57
EXT Words	74.93	83.69	80.24
EXT Dep	75.64	79.30	75.64
EXT Wavg	77.42	**84.31**	79.59
EXT Conc	78.53	83.93	**80.53**
CNN-NS-WN		85.6	

Table 4: F1 score for SemEval 2010 Relation Identification task. CNN-NS-WN is CNN with negative sampling and WordNet features (Xu et al., 2015).

6 Discussion

Our evaluation shows that dependency context embeddings can provide valuable syntactic information for sentence classification tasks using the three classification methods described. Out of the three tasks, Question Classification and Relation Identification showed great improvements when using dependency context embeddings compared to the baseline, while sentiment classification only showed moderate improvements. This is in agreement with previous research (Li et al., 2015), where explicit syntactic information was provided to classifiers by using tree structured networks and showed that syntax provides small improvements for binary sentiment classification in Stanford's Sentiment Treebank.

It is notable that for QC and RI, using only word embeddings that are trained with syntactic information (LG and EXT *Words* models) still outperform the baseline window based skipgram. Using the dependency context embeddings as a means to represent the dependency parse of sentences consistently outperforms the baseline method across the three tasks and for every classification method. This indicates that this additional syntactic information cannot be recovered by the CNN and LSTM even though they have access to the sequential structure of sentences, at least when trained on datasets of this size. As expected, the SVM BoE benefits the most by the addition of dependency context embeddings since these are its only source of structural information.

The dependency context embeddings from the EXT model outperform the LG model, both when used alone and when in combination with the word embeddings. This can be attributed to the additional information they are exposed to during training.

The effectiveness of the *Wavg* compared to the *Conc* method for combining word and dependency context embeddings seems to depend on the classification method. In geneatal, we observe that the CNN performs better with *Wavg*, while SVM and LSTM with *Conc*. On the other hand, the ensemble methods of the Win5 model (*AvgE* and *ConcE*) do not provide any consistent advantage over the baseline. In most cases, *AvgE* slightly hurts performance while *ConcE* slighty improves it.

Our evaluation also suggests that best performing models in word similarity tasks do not necessarily achieve the best performance in other NLP tasks. When considering only word embeddings as features for sentence classification (*Words* method), we observe that the EXT model on average performs better than the Win5 and LG models, while the opposite is true for word similarity evaluation. This indicates that providing additional contextual information for training embeddings results in less specialized embeddings for particular types of semantic similarity evaluations, but can be useful for a wide range of sentence level classification tasks.

While the purpose of our experiments is a comparison of embeddings and little hyperparameter tuning was done for the classifiers, results of the CNN using EXT Wavg representations for QC (95.0) and RI (84.31) are close to the best reported results with specifically engineered systems for these tasks: 96.0 for QC (Mou et al., 2015) and 85.6 for RI (Xu et al., 2015). As our method does not depend on a specific classification setting it would be interesting to see if those approaches can further improve using dependency based representations.

7 Conclusions

We compare a window based, a dependency based and an extended dependency based skipgram model in word similarity and sentence classification tasks of question classification, binary sentiment prediction and semantic relation identification. For the sentence classification, we use three classifiers (SVM, CNN, LSTM) and experiment with several methods of utilizing dependency context feature embeddings to create representations that capture the syntactic role of words in dependency graphs. We reaffirm that dependency based models produce word embeddings that better capture functional properties of words and that window based models better capture topical similarity. The dependency based word embeddings largely improved the performance of the three classifiers for question classification and semantic relation identification, but only marginally for sentiment prediction. Finally, using dependency context features along with the word embeddings we observed better performance for the three classifiers in each task.

Acknowledgments

Alexandros Komninos was supported by EPSRC via an Engineering Doctorate in LSCITS. Suresh Manandhar was supported by EPSRC grant EP/I037512/1, A Unified Model of Compositional & Distributional Semantics: Theory and Application.

References

[Baroni and Lenci2010] Marco Baroni and Alessandro Lenci. 2010. Distributional memory: A general framework for corpus-based semantics. *Computational Linguistics*, 36(4):673–721.

[Chen and Manning2014] Danqi Chen and Christopher D Manning. 2014. A fast and accurate dependency parser using neural networks. In *Proceedings of the 2014 Conference on Empirical Methods in Natural Language Processing (EMNLP)*, volume 1, pages 740–750.

[Cheng and Kartsaklis2015] Jianpeng Cheng and Dimitri Kartsaklis. 2015. Syntax-aware multi-sense word embeddings for deep compositional models of meaning. In *Proceedings of the 2015 Conference on Empirical Methods in Natural Language Processing*, pages 1531–1542, Lisbon, Portugal, September. Association for Computational Linguistics.

[Collobert et al.2011] Ronan Collobert, Jason Weston, Léon Bottou, Michael Karlen, Koray Kavukcuoglu, and Pavel Kuksa. 2011. Natural language processing (almost) from scratch. *The Journal of Machine Learning Research*, 12:2493–2537.

[De Marneffe et al.2014] Marie-Catherine De Marneffe, Timothy Dozat, Natalia Silveira, Katri Haverinen, Filip Ginter, Joakim Nivre, and Christopher D Manning. 2014. Universal stanford dependencies: A cross-linguistic typology. In *Proceedings of LREC*, pages 4585–4592.

[Duchi et al.2011] John Duchi, Elad Hazan, and Yoram Singer. 2011. Adaptive subgradient methods for online learning and stochastic optimization. *The Journal of Machine Learning Research*, 12:2121–2159.

[Finkelstein et al.2001] Lev Finkelstein, Evgeniy Gabrilovich, Yossi Matias, Ehud Rivlin, Zach Solan, Gadi Wolfman, and Eytan Ruppin. 2001. Placing search in context: The concept revisited. In *Proceedings of the 10th international conference on World Wide Web*, pages 406–414. ACM.

[Hashimoto et al.2014] Kazuma Hashimoto, Pontus Stenetorp, Makoto Miwa, and Yoshimasa Tsuruoka. 2014. Jointly learning word representations and composition functions using predicate-argument structures. In *Proceedings of the 2014 Conference on Empirical Methods in Natural Language Processing (EMNLP)*, pages 1544–1555.

[Hendrickx et al.2009] Iris Hendrickx, Su Nam Kim, Zornitsa Kozareva, Preslav Nakov, Diarmuid Ó Séaghdha, Sebastian Padó, Marco Pennacchiotti, Lorenza Romano, and Stan Szpakowicz. 2009. Semeval-2010 task 8: Multi-way classification of semantic relations between pairs of nominals. In *Proceedings of the Workshop on Semantic Evaluations: Recent Achievements and Future Directions*, pages 94–99. Association for Computational Linguistics.

[Hill et al.2015] Felix Hill, Roi Reichart, and Anna Korhonen. 2015. Simlex-999: Evaluating semantic models with (genuine) similarity estimation. *Computational Linguistics*.

[Hochreiter and Schmidhuber1997] Sepp Hochreiter and Jürgen Schmidhuber. 1997. Long short-term memory. *Neural computation*, 9(8):1735–1780.

[Kim2014] Yoon Kim. 2014. Convolutional neural networks for sentence classification. In *Proceedings of the 2014 Conference on Empirical Methods in Natural*

Language Processing (EMNLP), pages 1746–1751. Association for Computational Linguistics.

[Levy and Goldberg2014] Omer Levy and Yoav Goldberg. 2014. Dependencybased word embeddings. In *Proceedings of the 52nd Annual Meeting of the Association for Computational Linguistics*, volume 2, pages 302–308.

[Levy et al.2015] Omer Levy, Yoav Goldberg, and Ido Dagan. 2015. Improving distributional similarity with lessons learned from word embeddings. *Transactions of the Association for Computational Linguistics*, 3:211–225.

[Li and Roth2002] Xin Li and Dan Roth. 2002. Learning question classifiers. In *Proceedings of the 19th international conference on Computational linguistics-Volume 1*, pages 1–7. Association for Computational Linguistics.

[Li et al.2015] Jiwei Li, Thang Luong, Dan Jurafsky, and Eduard Hovy. 2015. When are tree structures necessary for deep learning of representations? In *Proceedings of the 2015 Conference on Empirical Methods in Natural Language Processing*, pages 2304–2314, Lisbon, Portugal, September. Association for Computational Linguistics.

[Ling et al.2015] Wang Ling, Chris Dyer, Alan Black, and Isabel Trancoso. 2015. Two/too simple adaptations of word2vec for syntax problems. *Proceedings of the North American Chapter of the Association for Computational Linguistics (NAACL), Denver, CO*.

[Melamud et al.2015] Oren Melamud, Omer Levy, and Ido Dagan, 2015. *Proceedings of the 1st Workshop on Vector Space Modeling for Natural Language Processing*, chapter A Simple Word Embedding Model for Lexical Substitution, pages 1–7. Association for Computational Linguistics.

[Mikolov et al.2013a] Tomas Mikolov, Kai Chen, Gregory S. Corrado, and Jeffrey Dean. 2013a. Efficient estimation of word representations in vector space. In *Proceedings of ICLR Workshop*.

[Mikolov et al.2013b] Tomas Mikolov, Ilya Sutskever, Kai Chen, Greg S Corrado, and Jeff Dean. 2013b. Distributed representations of words and phrases and their compositionality. In *Advances in neural information processing systems*, pages 3111–3119.

[Mnih and Teh2012] Andriy Mnih and Yee Whye Teh. 2012. A fast and simple algorithm for training neural probabilistic language models. In *In Proceedings of the International Conference on Machine Learning*.

[Mou et al.2015] Lili Mou, Hao Peng, Ge Li, Yan Xu, Lu Zhang, and Zhi Jin. 2015. Discriminative neural sentence modeling by tree-based convolution. In *Proceedings of the 2015 Conference on Empirical Methods in Natural Language Processing*, pages 2315–

2325, Lisbon, Portugal, September. Association for Computational Linguistics.

[Padó and Lapata2007] Sebastian Padó and Mirella Lapata. 2007. Dependency-based construction of semantic space models. *Computational Linguistics*, 33(2):161–199.

[Pham et al.2015] The Nghia Pham, Germán Kruszewski, Angeliki Lazaridou, and Marco Baroni. 2015. Jointly optimizing word representations for lexical and sentential tasks with the c-phrase model. In *Proceedings of the 53rd Annual Meeting of the Association for Computational Linguistics and the 7th International Joint Conference on Natural Language Processing (Volume 1: Long Papers)*, pages 971–981. Association for Computational Linguistics.

[Socher et al.2012] Richard Socher, Brody Huval, Christopher D Manning, and Andrew Y Ng. 2012. Semantic compositionality through recursive matrix-vector spaces. In *Proceedings of the 2012 Joint Conference on Empirical Methods in Natural Language Processing and Computational Natural Language Learning*, pages 1201–1211. Association for Computational Linguistics.

[Socher et al.2013] Richard Socher, Alex Perelygin, Jean Wu, Jason Chuang, D. Christopher Manning, Andrew Ng, and Christopher Potts. 2013. Recursive deep models for semantic compositionality over a sentiment treebank. In *Proceedings of the 2013 Conference on Empirical Methods in Natural Language Processing*, pages 1631–1642. Association for Computational Linguistics.

[Srivastava et al.2014] Nitish Srivastava, Geoffrey Hinton, Alex Krizhevsky, Ilya Sutskever, and Ruslan Salakhutdinov. 2014. Dropout: A simple way to prevent neural networks from overfitting. *The Journal of Machine Learning Research*, 15(1):1929–1958.

[Tai et al.2015] Sheng Kai Tai, Richard Socher, and D. Christopher Manning. 2015. Improved semantic representations from tree-structured long short-term memory networks. In *Proceedings of the 53rd Annual Meeting of the Association for Computational Linguistics and the 7th International Joint Conference on Natural Language Processing (Volume 1: Long Papers)*, pages 1556–1566. Association for Computational Linguistics.

[Turian et al.2010] Joseph Turian, Lev Ratinov, and Yoshua Bengio. 2010. Word representations: a simple and general method for semi-supervised learning. In *Proceedings of the 48th annual meeting of the association for computational linguistics*, pages 384–394. Association for Computational Linguistics.

[Turney et al.2010] Peter D Turney, Patrick Pantel, et al. 2010. From frequency to meaning: Vector space models of semantics. *Journal of artificial intelligence research*, 37(1):141–188.

[Xu et al.2015] Kun Xu, Yansong Feng, Songfang Huang, and Dongyan Zhao. 2015. Semantic relation classification via convolutional neural networks with simple negative sampling. In *Proceedings of the 2015 Conference on Empirical Methods in Natural Language Processing*, pages 536–540, Lisbon, Portugal, September. Association for Computational Linguistics.

[Zeiler2012] Matthew D Zeiler. 2012. Adadelta: An adaptive learning rate method. *arXiv preprint arXiv:1212.5701*.

Deep LSTM based Feature Mapping for Query Classification

Yangyang Shi and **Kaisheng Yao** and **Le Tian** and **Daxin Jiang**
Microsoft
{yangshi,kaisheng.yao,letian,djiang}@microsoft.com

Abstract

Traditional convolutional neural network (CNN) based query classification uses linear feature mapping in its convolution operation. The recurrent neural network (RNN), differs from a CNN in representing word sequence with their ordering information kept explicitly. We propose using a deep long-short-term-memory (DLSTM) based feature mapping to learn feature representation for CNN. The DLSTM, which is a stack of LSTM units, has different order of feature representations at different depth of LSTM unit. The bottom LSTM unit equipped with input and output gates, extracts the first order feature representation from current word. To extract higher order nonlinear feature representation, the LSTM unit at higher position gets input from two parts. First part is the lower LSTM unit's memory cell from previous word. Second part is the lower LSTM unit's hidden output from current word. In this way, the DLSTM captures the nonlinear nonconsecutive interaction within n-grams. Using an architecture that combines a stack of the DLSTM layers with a tradition CNN layer, we have observed new state-of-the-art query classification accuracy on benchmark data sets for query classification.

1 Introduction

Convolutional neural networks (CNNs) have achieved significant improvements for query classification. CNNs capture the correlations of spatial or temporal structures with different resolutions using their temporal convolution operators. A pooling strategy on these local correlations extracts invariant regularities.

However, CNNs use simple linear operations on n-gram vectors that are formed by concatenating word vectors. The linear operation together with the concatenation may not be sufficient to model the nonconsecutive dependency and interaction within the n-grams. For example, in the query "not a total loss", nonconsecutive dependency "not loss" is the key information that is not well addressed by the linear operation with simple concatenation.

In this paper, we propose to use deep long-short-term-memory (DLSTM) based feature mapping to capture high order nonlinear feature representations. LSTM (Hochreiter and Schmidhuber, 1997) is one type of recurrent neural networks (RNNs) that have achieved remarkable performance in natural language processing and speech recognition (Sutskever et al., 2014; Graves et al., 2013).

The DLSTM is a stack of LSTM units where different order of nonlinear feature representation is captured by LSTM units at different depth. The bottom LSTM unit extracts the first order feature representation from current word. The LSTM unit at the higher position captures the higher order feature representation relying on the outputs from LSTM units at lower position, specifically, the memory cell from lower LSTM unit at previous word position and the hidden output from lower LSTM unit at current word position. Using DLSTM, linear feature mapping in traditional CNN can be obviously extended to nonlinear feature mapping. Moreover, the memory cell together with different gates in LSTM unit are able to model the nonconsecutive feature interaction and

Proceedings of NAACL-HLT 2016, pages 1501–1511,
San Diego, California, June 12-17, 2016. ©2016 Association for Computational Linguistics

information decaying based on context. For example, in the query "not so good", the proposed DL-STM is expected to keep the information of "not" and "good" in the memory, and to decay the information about "so" via the forget gates.

Similar to CNNs where multiple convolution operations are used, we propose to stack different DLSTM feature mappings together to model multiple level nonlinear feature representations. The bottom DL-STM layer takes the original word sequence as input. The DLSTM layer at lower position fed its output to the adjacent higher DLSTM layer. In the proposed models, the concatenation of the multiple level feature representations are further reduced by the pooling operation. The prediction output is finally made based on the reduced feature representations.

We evaluated the proposed method on three benchmark data sets: Standford Sentiment Treebank dataset (Socher et al., 2013), TREC (Text Retrieval Conference) question type classification data set (Li and Roth, 2002) and ATIS (Airline Travel Information Systems) dataset (Hemphill et al., 1990). On Standford Sentiment Treebank dataset, our model obtains 51.9% accuracy on fine-grained classification and 88.7% accuracy on binary classification. The SVM based method uses a large amount of engineered features, and it outperforms LSTM and RNN based methods on TREC question type classification dataset. The DLSTM outperforms other neural network based methods without using engineered features. On ATIS data, DLSTM achieves 97.9% F1 score, which is better than the previous best F1 score of 95.6% using the same data settings.

2 Related Work

Deep neural networks (Bengio, 2009; Deng and Yu, 2014; Hinton et al., 2006) dominates natural language processing (Socher, 2012; Collobert et al., 2011; Gao et al., 2014). They have achieved cutting-edge performance in various tasks such as language modeling (Mikolov et al., 2010; Sundermeyer et al., 2012), machine translation (Bahdanau et al., 2014; Cho et al., 2014; Jean et al., 2015), slot filling (Yao et al., 2014a; Shi et al., 2015a) and syntactic parsing (Wang et al., 2015; Collobert et al., 2011). For query classifications, recurrent neural networks (RNNs) and convolutional neural networks

(CNNs) have emerged as top performing architectures (Zhang and Wallace, 2016; Kim, 2014; Kalchbrenner et al., 2014; Ravuri and Stolcke, 2015a).

Due to its superior ability to memorize long distance dependencies, LSTMs have been applied to extract the sentence-level continuous representation (Ravuri and Stolcke, 2015a; Tang et al., 2015; Tai et al., 2015). When the LSTM is applied to model a sentence, memory cell from the ending word in the sentence carries the information of the whole sentence. The LSTM hidden vector from the ending word is directly used as sentence feature representation in (Ravuri and Stolcke, 2015a). Alternatively, a sentence is represented by the average of LSTM hidden vectors from its words (Tang et al., 2015). Inspired from recursive neural networks (Socher et al., 2011a), LSTM is further combined with a tree structure to model sentence representation (Tai et al., 2015).

CNNs have been originally developed for image processing (Lecun et al., 1998). They are firstly applied by Collobert et al. (2008; 2011) for natural language processing tasks using max-over-time pooling method to aggregate convolution layer vectors. CNNs have also been applied to spoken language understanding (Shi et al., 2015b), information retrieval (Shen et al., 2014) and semantic parsing (Yih et al., 2015). Kalchbrenner et al. (2014) proposed to extend CNNs max-over-time pooling to k-max pooling for sentence modeling. Remarkable query classification performance on different benchmark datasets have been achieved by integrating CNNs with different feature mapping channels and pre-trained word vectors (Zhang and Wallace, 2015; Kim, 2014). Recently, Mou et al. (2015) proposed to model sentences by tree structured CNNs.

CNNs and LSTMs are complementary in their modeling capabilities; CNNs are good at capturing local invariant regularities and LSTMs are good at modeling temporal features. The combination of CNNs and LSTMs achieves improved performances in speech recognition (Sainath et al., 2015) and query classification (Tang et al., 2015; Zhou et al., 2015). In these models, the basic architecture is the LSTM that models sequence representation from local features captured by CNNs.

Different from the above methods, our method use LSTM units to model the nonlinear and non-consecutive local features. CNNs are placed on top of these local features for query classification. Our motivation is to use LSTM replace the linear feature mapping in convolution operation where the feature mapping is a multiplication of the word vectors with a filter matrix. So our proposed model is still CNN based model but using DLSTM as feature mapping for convolution operation.

Our work is closely related to tensor product based CNNs (Lei et al., 2015) that expand CNN feature representation capacity with non-consecutive n-grams. They improve the query modeling from two aspects. Firstly, tensor products enable the non-linear feature vector interactions between adjacent words. Secondly, an exponentially decaying weight is applied to represent non-consecutive n-gram features. Instead of using tensor products as feature mapping, we propose to apply DLSTM to address these two aspects. Nonlinear feature mapping can be achieved by the DLSTM that equipped with nonlinear activation function. The nonconsecutive feature interaction is well addressed by the memory cell and different gates in LSTM unit. In particular, the forget gate is able to decay the information according to the context rather than a fixed decaying weight in tensor product based CNNs.

3 CNN Based Query Classification Using DLSTM Feature Mapping

3.1 Linear Feature Mapping in CNN

Let k-dimensional vector $x_t \in \mathbb{R}^k$ be the continuous feature representation of the tth word in a sentence. A sentence with l words is represented by $x_{0:l-1} = [x_0; x_2; ...; x_{l-1}]$ that is a concatenation of all word vectors. The traditional CNN (Collobert et al., 2011; Kim, 2014) takes such sentence feature vector as input.

Different filters $M_j \in \mathbb{R}^{nd*h}$ are applied in convolution operation to map each n-gram feature vector $x_{t:t+n-1}, t \in (0, l-n)$ to an h-dimensional feature vector $c_{t,j}$.

$$c_{t,j} = M_j^T \cdot x_{t:t+n-1} + b_j, \tag{1}$$

where b_j is the bias in filter j.

The resulting feature vector $c_{t,j}$ are often passed through non-linear element-wise transformations (e.g. the hyperbolic tangent and rectifier linear unit)

as well as pooling operations. After aggregation or reduction by different pooling operations such as the max-over-time pooling (Collobert et al., 2011; Kim, 2014) and the average pooling (Lei et al., 2015), a constant dimensional feature vector is generated for sentences with various lengths.

In traditional CNNs, the concatenated word vectors are mapped linearly to feature coordinates as shown in Equation (1). Such linear feature mapping can be improved from the following two aspects, one is to extend linear mapping to nonlinear mapping. The other one is to improve the consecutive feature mapping to nonconsecutive feature mapping. For example, in the query "not a total loss", "not loss" is the key sentiment. By using nonconsecutive feature representation, the information about "not loss" could be addressed. Lei et al. (2015) extends the linear feature mapping to tensor based feature mapping. To model the nonconsecutive n-grams, a decaying weight is applied to control the information carryover. In this paper, we propose to replace the linear feature mapping using DLSTM that captures the nonlinear and nonconsecutive feature interaction within n-grams. Rather than setting a fixed decaying weight, the proposed architecture is able to control the information decaying according to the context information.

3.2 Feature Mapping Based on Deep Long Short Term Memory

Figure 1 gives the basic architecture of a three-order nonlinear feature mapping in DLSTM. The bottom LSTM_0 extract the first order information from word input vector x_t. It is equipped with input gate and output gate. The input gate automatically controls the information saving in memory cell that will be passed to higher order LSTM unit. The output gate modifies the information from the memory cell to represent current word.

$$i_{0,t} = sigmoid(W_i x_t + b_i) \tag{2}$$

$$\tilde{c}_{0,t} = \tanh(W_c x_t + b_c) \tag{3}$$

$$c_{0,t} = i_{0,t} * \tilde{c}_{0,t} \tag{4}$$

$$o_{0,t} = sigmoid(W_o x_t + V_o c_{0,t} + b_o) \tag{5}$$

$$h_{0,t} = o_{0,t} * \tanh(c_{0,t}) \tag{6}$$

On top of the bottom LSTM_0 unit, we analogously

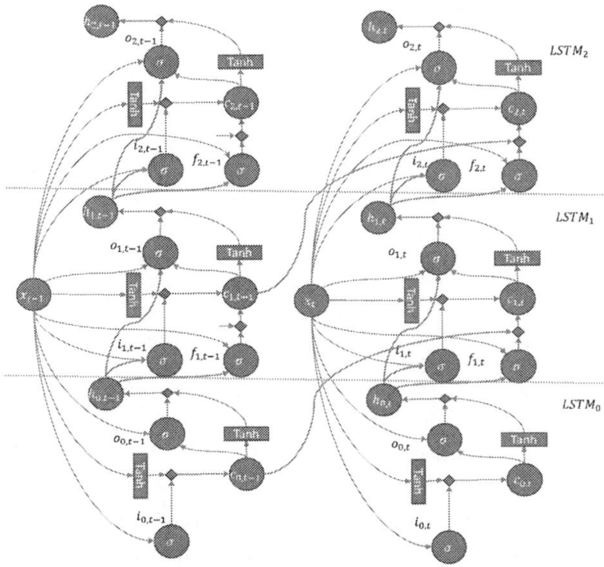

Figure 1: DLSTM based nonlinear feature mapping for bigram "$x_{t-1}x_t$". Three LSTM units are used to extract features from each word position. The bottom LSTM_0 is used for first order feature extraction from the current word. The output from the lower LSTM unit at current word position and the memory cell from lower LSTM at previous word position are fed to the higher LSTM units. Such information propagation is highlighted in the figure by bold orange lines.

stack two LSTM units LSTM_1 and LSTM_2 to extract nonlinear feature representations from bigram and trigram, respectively. The LSTM_j is formulated as follows:

$$i_{j,t} = sigmoid(W_i x_t + U_i h_{j-1,t} + b_i) \tag{7}$$

$$\tilde{c}_{j,t} = \tanh(W_c x_t + U_c h_{j-1,t} + b_c) \tag{8}$$

$$f_{j,t} = sigmoid(W_f x_t + U_f h_{j-1,t} + b_f) \tag{9}$$

$$c_{j,t} = i_{j,t} * \tilde{c}_{j,t} * c_{j-1,t-1} + f_{j,t} * c_{j-1,t} \tag{10}$$

$$o_{j,t} = sigmoid(W_o x_t + U_o h_{j-1,t} + V_o c_{j,t} + b_o) \tag{11}$$

$$h_{j,t} = o_{j,t} * \tanh(c_{j,t}) \tag{12}$$

Due to the effect from different gates that controls the information saving, expressing and decaying, LSTM_1 and LSTM_2 are able to model the non-consecutive interaction in n-grams. Take "not so good" as a example. LSTM_0 extract the nonlinear feature mapping from word "good" as $h_{0,2}$. The LSTM_1 takes $c_{0,1}$ (carries the information from word "so") and $h_{0,2}$ as input. Due to the effect of forget

gate, we expect the output $h_{1,2}$ from LSTM_1 to address more on word "good" rather than "so". By further stacking LSTM_2, information about the word "not" and "good" should be emphasized by the proposed DLSTM.

Note the sum of the resulting outputs from these LSTM units is used as the high order feature representation of a n-gram ending with word x_t. So the original sequence input $x_{0:l-1}$ is mapped to a sequence of feature vector $z_{0:l-1} = [z_0, z_1, ..., z_{l-1}]$, where $z_j = h_{0,j} + h_{1,j} + h_{2,j}$.

The proposed DLSTM architecture is characterized by the following two features:

1. Weight Sharing: LSTM_1 and LSTM_2 are identical LSTM units that share the same weights. The bottom LSTM unit LSTM_0 also shares the corresponding weights with other LSTM units such as W_i, W_c and W_o. By sharing weights among different LSTM units, we can effectively reduce the risk of model over-fitting issue. At the same time, LSTM is good at capturing temporal regularities. By sharing weights, the LSTM units can learn the temporal dependencies from being exposed to different order of n-grams during the training.

2. Memory Cell Interaction: To model the nonlinear feature interaction in n-gram vectors, traditional LSTM unit is modified by Equation (10) in which the memory cell stores the interaction of different order memory cells. In this way, the feature interaction in n-grams is characterized by the memory cell interactions.

To stack the LSTM unit deeper, the depth-gated LSTM (Yao et al., 2015) and the highway network (Srivastava et al., 2015; Zhang et al., 2015) also allow the memory cell flow across LSTM units at different depth. There are three basic differences between these architectures with the proposed DLSTM. Firstly, in their architectures, LSTM units at different depth are different LSTMs that have different weight matrices. In our model, the LSTM units in DLSTM share weight matrices with each other. Secondly, in their proposed architecture, the memory cell is carried over to higher LSTM unit for facilitating model training. Because the networking training becomes more difficult with increasing model depth. In our

DLSTM, the LSTM unit at higher position takes the memory cell from lower LSTM unit mainly for feature interaction in n-grams. Finally, an additional "depth" gate is applied in their architecture to control the information flow across different layers. In our model, the input gate in higher LSTM unit controls the interaction between the memory cells extracted from previous word and current word.

3.3 The Architecture

Figure 3 gives the whole architecture of the proposed query classification system. A DLSTM layer first maps the input sequence to a sequence of high order nonlinear feature representations z^0. Instead of being directly used for query classification, the feature representation z^0 is further processed by a stack of DLSTM layers illustrated in previous section. In such stacked DLSTM layers, the output z^i of the ith DLSTM layer, is used as the input for the $i+1$th DLSTM layer parameterized by a different set of weight matrices. As shown in Figure 3, the resulting feature representations $z^0, z^1, ..., z^d$ of all these layers are concatenated. Finally, an average pooling is applied to reduce the sentence feature representation to a fixed dimensional vector that is further fed to a softmax function to obtain the prediction output.

3.4 Learning and Regularization

In the classification layer, the prediction output is obtained by the following softmax function.

$$softmax(y)_j = \frac{\exp(y_j)}{\sum_{i=1}^{i=m} \exp(y_i)}, \tag{13}$$

where y is a m-dimensional vector. The model is trained by minimizing cross-entropy on the given training data set. To avoid overfitting during training, $L2$ regularization and dropout (Hinton et al., 2012) are used. The $L2$ regularization is applied to constrain all weight matrices using the same regularization weight. The dropout is only applied to the output of each DLSTM layer.

In the training, the model weights are updated using mini-batch stochastic gradient descent (SGD). We adapt a per-feature learning rate control method (AdaGrad) (Duchi et al., 2011) to dynamically tune the learning rate as follows:

$$\alpha_{t,i} = \frac{\alpha}{\sqrt{\sum_{j=1}^{t} g_{j,i}^2 + \varepsilon}}, \tag{14}$$

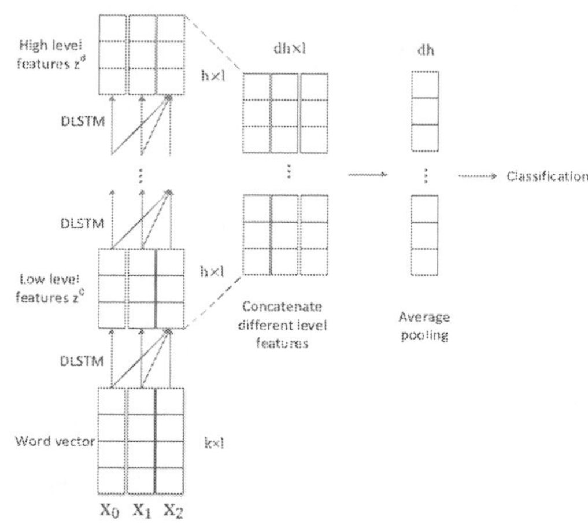

Figure 2: CNN based query classification using DLSTM feature mapping. The input sequence is represented by a $k \times l$ matrix where column t is the word vector for the tth word in the sequence. The word vectors are mapped by a stack of DLSTM layers to multi-level feature representations $z^0, ..., z^d$. As illustrated in Figure 1, each level feature representation is the sum of outputs from different LSTM units. The multi-level features are concatenated and reduced to a dh-dimensional vector where d is the number of DLSTM layers, h is the output size of each LSTM unit. A classification layer gives the prediction output.

where $\alpha_{t,i}$ is the learning rate for weight i at epoch t. $\sum_{j=1}^{t} g_{j,i}$ sums all the historical gradients of weight i. A small positive ε is applied to make the AdaGrad robust. ε is usually set to $1e-5$.

4 Experiments

4.1 Datasets

We evaluate the proposed query classification models on sentence sentiment classification, question type categorization and query intent detection tasks.

For sentence sentiment classification, the Stanford Sentiment Treebank (Socher et al., 2013) is used. In this dataset, 11855 English sentences are annotated at both sentence level and phrases level with fine-grained labels (very positive, positive, neutral, negative and very negative). We use the provided data split, which has 8544 sentences for training, 1101 sentences for developing and 2210 sentences for testing. This dataset also provides a binary classification variant that ignores the neutral sentences. The binary classification task in this dataset has 6920 sentences for training, 872 sentences for developing and 1821 sentences for testing. There are in total 17835 unique running words for fine-grained dataset and 16185 for binary version dataset.

For query intent detection, ATIS (airline travel information system) dataset (Hemphill et al., 1990; Yao et al., 2014b) is used. This dataset is mainly about the air travel domain with 26 different intents such as "flight", "$ground_service$" and "city". There are 893 utterances for testing (ATIS-III, Nov93 and Dec94), and 4978 utterances for training (rest of ATIS-III and ATIS-II). There are 899 unique running words and 22 intents in the training data.

The question type classification task is to classify a question into a specific type, which is a very important step in question answering system. In TREC (Text Retrieval Conference) data (Li and Roth, 2002), all the questions are divided into 6 categories, including "human", "entity", "location", "description", "abbreviation" and "numeric". The dataset in total has 5952 questions, 5452 of them for training, the rest for testing. The vocabulary size of TREC dataset is 9592.

Following previous work (Iyyer et al., 2015; Tai et al., 2015; Lei et al., 2015), we used word vectors pre-trained on large unannotated corpora to achieve better generalization capability. In this paper, we used a publicly available 300 dimensional GloVe word vectors that are trained using Common Crawl with 840B tokens and 2.2M vocabulary size.

4.2 Settings

We implemented our model based on Theano library (Bastien et al., 2012). All our models are trained on Nvidia Tesla K40m.

We performed extensive hyperparameter selection based on Stanford Sentiment Treebank Binary version of validation data. The selected hyperparameters were directly used for all datasets. To investigate the robustness of the proposed method, we ran each configuration 10 times using different random initialization (random seed ranges from 1 to 10).

For final models, we set the initial learning rate to 0.1, $L2$ regularization weight to $1e-5$, the dropout probability to 0.5 and mini-batch size to 64. We use hidden layer size 256 for all the models described in

model	Fine	Binary
SVM (Lei et al., 2015)	38.3	81.3
Nbow(Lei et al., 2015)	44.5	82.0
Para-vec(Le and Mikolov, 2014)	48.7	87.8
DAN(Iyyer et al., 2015)	48.2	86.8
RAE(Socher et al., 2011b)	43.2	82.4
MVRNN(Socher et al., 2012)	44.4	82.9
RNTN(Socher et al., 2013)	45.7	85.4
DRNN(Irsoy and Cardie, 2014)	49.8	86.8
RLSTM(Tai et al., 2015)	51.0	88.0
CLSTM(Zhou et al., 2015)	49.2	87.8
DCNN(Kalchbrenner et al., 2014)	48.5	86.9
CNN-MC(Kim, 2014)	47.4	88.1
CNN-nostatic(Kim, 2014)	48.0	87.2
TCNN (Lei et al., 2015)	50.6	87.0
TCNN+phrases(Lei et al., 2015)	51.2	88.6
ours	49.2	87.2
ours+phrases	**51.9**	**88.7**

Table 1: Standford Sentiment Treebank Classification accuracy results. "Fine" denotes the accuracy on the fine-grained dataset with 5 labels. "Binary" denotes binary classification results.

the experiments. The number of the DLSTM layers and the number of the LSTM units in each DLSTM are both set to 3. So basically there are 9 LSTM units are used for each word position.

For all models, we set maximum iteration number 100 to terminate the training process. For sentiment classification task, during the training, the model with the best classification accuracy on validation data was used as final model for testing. For question type classification and query intent detection, there wasn't validation data. So we simply use the model trained at the 100th iteration as the final model for testing.

4.3 Results on Stanford Sentiment Treebank

model	Acc
discriminative(Tur et al., 2010)	95.5
SVM (Shi et al., 2015b)	95.6
joint-RNN(Shi et al., 2015b)	95.2
ours	**97.9**

Table 2: ATIS intent classification accuracy comparison of different models.

Table 1 lists results for sentiment classification.

There are four blocks in the table. The bottom block gives the results from our model. The third blocks are methods related to CNNs. The second block shows the results from recursive neural network based approaches. The other baseline methods are listed in the top block.

The top block shows that the traditional methods such as SVM using ngram features and neural network using bag-of-words features (**Nbow**) perform much worse than **Para-vec** and **DAN** using word vectors that are pre-trained on large amount of unlabeled data. **Para-vec** builds a logistic regression on top of paragraph vectors. **DAN** is a deep neural network takes the average of word vectors as input.

In addition to pre-trained word vectors, syntactic compositional information can be used to improve the sentiment classification accuracy. **RAE** is a tree structured Antoencoder model based on pre-trained word vectors from Wikipedia. **MVRNN** further improves the recursive neural network by assigning each node with a matrix to learn the meaning change of neighboring words and phrases. To address large amount of different vectors and matrices involved in **MVRNN**, **RNTN** proposed to use one single tensor based function to model all nodes. By making the tree-structured recursive neural networks deeper, significant improvement has been achieved by **DRNN**. According to our knowledge, the best compositional information based model is achieved by **RLSTM** that combines LSTM unit with tree-structure.

By comparing the classification accuracy between second blocks and third blocks, we see that CNN based models in general perform better than recursive neural network based methods. Another advantage of CNN based methods is that they can be generalized to any language without dependency over compositional information. **DCNN** uses a dynamic k-max pooling operator function in CNN. To explore the task specific word vectors and the general word vectors pre-trained on large News dataset, **CNN-MC** equips CNN with two feature mapping channels. **CNN-nostatic** gives the results by only making use of general word vectors. The best published classification results are achieved by **TCNN** that is tensor based CNN.

In this paper, the proposed method is closely related to **TCNN**. Instead of using tensor products to replace linear convolution operation, our method exploits the nonlinear feature mapping through DL-STM. Rather than setting specific decaying weight to model non-consecutive n-gram features in tensor based CNN, the different gates automatically adjust the information storing, removing and outputting according to context.

Following the work of **TCNN**, to leverage the phrases level annotation in Standford Sentiment Treebank, all phrases and their corresponding labels are added to training data as additional sequences. The bottom line of Table 1 shows that our models achieved the state-of-the-art performance on sentiment classification task.

For the best settings described above, we ran each model 10 times with different random initialization. The average and standard deviation for fine-grained classification are 50.7% and 1.04%, for binary classification 88% and 0.41%. Comparing with **TCNN**, our model is more sensitive to the parameter random initialization. In the future, some efforts should be used to analyze and address this issue.

model	Acc
SVM (Silva et al., 2010)	**95.0**
Para-vec(Le and Mikolov, 2014)	91.8
AdaSent(Zhao et al., 2015)	92.4
CNN-MC(Kim, 2014)	92.2
CNN-nostatic(Kim, 2014)	93.6
DCNN(Kalchbrenner et al., 2014)	93.0
LSTM(Zhou et al., 2015)	93.2
BiLSTM(Zhou et al., 2015)	93.0
CLSTM(Zhou et al., 2015)	94.6
ours	94.8

Table 3: TREC Question type Classification accuracy comparison of different models.

4.4 Results on ATIS

ATIS dataset is widely used to test spoken language understanding system. As shown in Table 2, SVM using n-grams performs better than simple RNN and CNN based approach. **joint-RNN** is a query classification and slot filling joint training model where CNN is applied on top of slot tagging RNN for query classification. In this way, **joint-RNN** actually implicitly makes use of slot tag information for query classification. However, **joint-RNN** doesn't take ad-

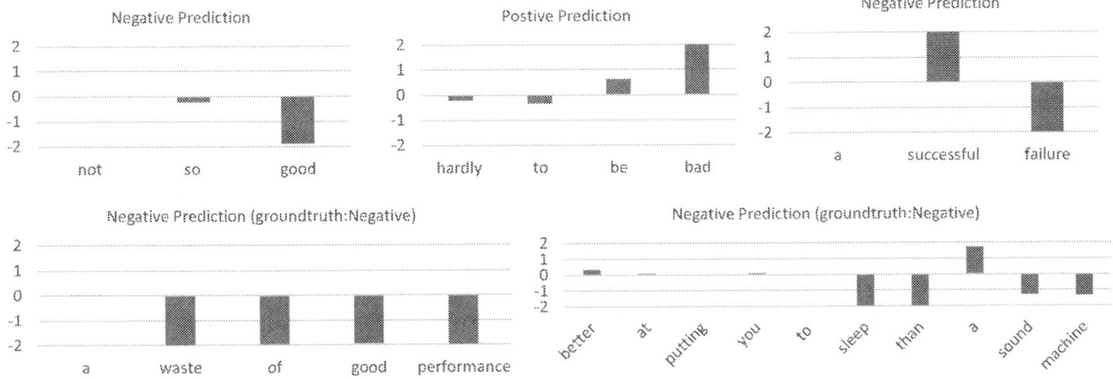

Figure 4: Example predictions given by our model trained on Stanford Sentiment Treebank fine-grained data. The expected sentiment score of each word is plotted in the figure. The score range from −2 to 2, where a score −2 means very "negative", 0 stands for "neutral" and 2 means "very positive".

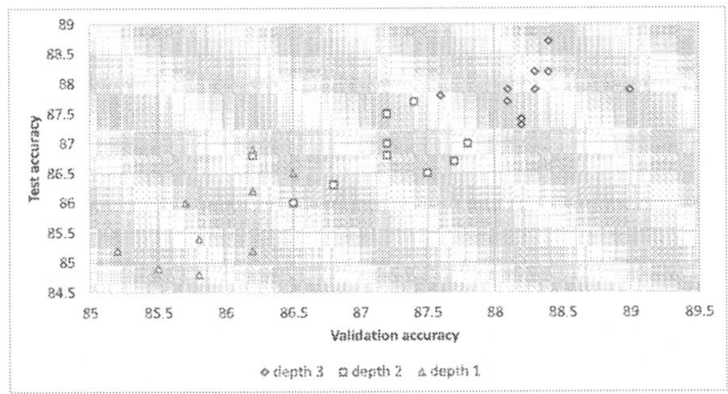

Figure 3: Stanford Sentiment Treebank Binary Classification accuracy comparison among models using the same parameter configuration except the number of DLSTM layers. For each number of DLSTM layers, 10 models are run independently using different random initialization. Horizontal axis gives the validation accuracy. Vertical axis shows the test accuracy.

vantage of word vectors trained on large amount of unlabeled data. Based on pre-trained word vectors, our models obtain more than 2% absolute classification accuracy improvement over the published best model.

In ATIS data, about 70% of queries is categorized to "flight" intent. Recent work using RNN for utterance classification (Ravuri and Stolcke, 2015b;

Ravuri and Stolcke, 2015a) simplifies it to a "flight" VS "others" binary classification task. In their paper, using word based LSTM, they achieve 97.55% classification accuracy. By using extra name entity features, word based gated RNN obtains 98.42% classification accuracy.

4.5 Results on TREC Question Type Classification

Table 3 gives the TREC question type classification accuracy of our models with other baseline models. Different from the sentiment classification task, the shallow models using diverse engineered feature performs better than CNN and LSTM based models. Previous best classification results on TREC data is achieved by **SVM** using unigrams, bigrams, wh-word, head word, POS tags, hypernyms, WordNet synsets and a bunch of hand-coded rules.

AdaSent is a self adaptive hierarchical sentence model based on gating networks with level pooling. As shown in Table 3, CNN and LSTM achieve similar performances on question type classification. Recently **CLSTM** achieves substantial improvement over previous neural network based methods. In **CLSTM**, CNN is used to extract high level phrase representation. Such local segment representation is fed into LSTM to model whole sequence representation. Different with **CLSTM** that is an LSTM based sequence model with CNN for local feature extraction, our model is CNN based model using DLSTM for non-linear feature mapping. Our model outperforms previous neural network based models without relying on task specific feature engineering.

4.6 Deep Architecture

One critical hyperparameter in the proposed method is the number of DLSTM layers. On sentiment binary classification task, we run our model 10 times by keeping all the hyperparameters the same except the number of DLSTM layers using different random initialization. As observed from Figure 3, the better performance is achieved by deeper architecture. Our model achieves the best classification result by stacking 3 DLSTM layers that actually leverages 9 different LSTM units to extract the nonlinear feature from n-grams.

4.7 Examples

Figure 4 demonstrates some examples and their sentiments predicted by our model trained on fine-grained classification data. In order to see how the nonlinear feature mapping captures the sentiment at each word position in the query, we follow the strategy used in (Lei et al., 2015) where the softmax function is directly applied on the concatenated feature mapping without passing through the average pooling layer. So the sentiment distribution p_t at tth word is computed as $p_t = W^T[z_t^0, z_t^1, ..., z_t^d]$. The expected value over the probability distribution $\sum_{s=-2}^{2} s.p_t$ is used as the sentiment score that is plotted in Figure 4. In the figure, the sentiment score ranges from -2 to 2, where -2 means very negative, 2 mean very positive and 0 means neutral.

Five examples are illustrated in the figure where the first row gives the synthetic examples to show that our model is able to model the nonconsecutive interaction within n-grams. For example, in query "hardly to be bad", even though word "hardly" is not directly modifying word "bad", our model still be able to capture such sentiment changes.

The second row of the figure shows the examples from fine-grained classification testing data. Both the example show that our model to some degree can capture sentiment of the satire. Especially the

last example, our model actually gives negative prediction, even no word in the query really means negative.

5 Conclusions

We have proposed a deep long-short-term-memory (DLSTM) nonlinear nonconsecutive feature mapping architecture to replace traditional linear mapping in the convolutional neural network based query classification. Each LSTM unit in the DLSTM is responsible for capturing different order feature representation from word segments. The bottom LSTM unit equipped with input gate and output gate, extracts the nonlinear feature from unigram. The higher LSTM unit in the DLSTM takes the outputs from lower LSTM units as input. In such way, the higher LSTM unit is able to capture nonlinear feature representation from higher order n-grams. The sum of different LSTM units is used as the output of the DLSTM layer. The DLSTM output rather than being directly used as input to convolutional neural network for query classification, is passed through a stacked DLSTM layers. The query is finally represented by the concatenation of the outputs from the stacked DLSTM layers.

We evaluated the proposed models on three benchmark datasets–Stanford Sentiment Treebank dataset, TREC dataset and ATIS dataset. On both sentiment classification dataset and ATIS dataset, our model achieved the state-of-the-art performance. On TREC question type classification, SVM based model using extra engineered features still performed better than our model. But we noticed that the proposed method outperformed all the other neural network based approaches.

References

Dzmitry Bahdanau, Kyunghyun Cho, and Yoshua Bengio. 2014. Neural machine translation by jointly learning to align and translate. *CoRR*.

Frédéric Bastien, Pascal Lamblin, Razvan Pascanu, James Bergstra, Ian J. Goodfellow, Arnaud Bergeron, Nicolas Bouchard, and Yoshua Bengio. 2012. Theano: new features and speed improvements. In *Deep Learning and Unsupervised Feature Learning NIPS 2012 Workshop*.

Yoshua Bengio. 2009. Learning deep architectures for ai. *Found. Trends Mach. Learn.*, 2:1–127.

Kyunghyun Cho, Bart van Merrienboer, Caglar Gulcehre, Fethi Bougares, Holger Schwenk, and Yoshua Bengio. 2014. Learning phrase representations using rnn encoder-decoder for statistical machine translation. In *EMNLP*.

Ronan Collobert and Jason Weston. 2008. A unified architecture for natural language processing: Deep neural networks with multitask learning. In *The Proceedings of the International Conference on Machine Learning*, pages 160–167.

Ronan Collobert, Jason Weston, Léon Bottou, Michael Karlen, Koray Kavukcuoglu, and Pavel Kuksa. 2011. Natural language processing (almost) from scratch. *Journal of Machine Learning Research*, 12:2493–2537.

Li Deng and Dong Yu. 2014. Deep learning: Methods and applications. *Found. Trends Signal Process.*, 7:197–387.

John Duchi, Elad Hazan, and Yoram Singer. 2011. Adaptive subgradient methods for online learning and stochastic optimization. *Journal of Machine Learning Research*, 12:2121–2159.

Jianfeng Gao, Xiaodong He, Wen-tau Yih, and Li Deng. 2014. Learning continuous phrase representations for translation modeling. In *Proceedings of ACL*, pages 699–709.

Alan Graves, Abdel-rahman Mohamed, and Geoffrey Hinton. 2013. Speech recognition with deep recurrent neural networks. In *The proceedings of IEEE International Conference on Acoustics, Speech and Signal Processing*, pages 6645–6649.

Charles T. Hemphill, John J. Godfrey, and George R. Doddington. 1990. The atis spoken language systems pilot corpus. In *The Proceedings of the Workshop on Speech and Natural Language*, pages 96–101.

Geoffrey E. Hinton, Simon Osindero, and Yee-Whye Teh. 2006. A fast learning algorithm for deep belief nets. *Neural Comput.*, 18(7):1527–1554.

Geoffrey E. Hinton, Nitish Srivastava, Alex Krizhevsky, Ilya Sutskever, and Ruslan R. Salakhutdinov. 2012. Improving neural networks by preventing co-adaptation of feature detectors. *CoRR*.

Sepp Hochreiter and Jürgen Schmidhuber. 1997. Long short-term memory. *Neural Comput.*, 9(8):1735–1780.

Ozan Irsoy and Claire Cardie. 2014. Deep recursive neural networks for compositionality in language. In *Proceedings of NIPS*, pages 2096–2104.

Mohit Iyyer, Varun Manjunatha, Jordan L. Boyd-Graber, and Hal Daumé III. 2015. Deep unordered composition rivals syntactic methods for text classification. In *Proceedings of ACL*, pages 1681–1691.

Sébastien Jean, Kyunghyun Cho, Roland Memisevic, and Yoshua Bengio. 2015. On using very large target vocabulary for neural machine translation. In *Proceedings of ACL*, pages 1–10.

Nal Kalchbrenner, Edward Grefenstette, and Phil Blunsom. 2014. A convolutional neural network for modelling sentences. In *Proceedings of ACL*, June.

Yoon Kim. 2014. Convolutional neural networks for sentence classification. In *Proceedings of the 2014 Conference on Empirical Methods in Natural Language Processing (EMNLP)*, pages 1746–1751, October.

Quoc V. Le and Tomas Mikolov. 2014. Distributed representations of sentences and documents. In *Proceedings of ICML*, pages 1188–1196.

Y. Lecun, L. Bottou, Y. Bengio, and P. Haffner. 1998. Gradient-based learning applied to document recognition. *Proceedings of the IEEE*, 86(11):2278–2324, Nov.

Tao Lei, Regina Barzilay, and Tommi S. Jaakkola. 2015. Molding cnns for text: non-linear, non-consecutive convolutions. In *Proceedings of the 2015 Conference on Empirical Methods in Natural Language Processing*, pages 1565–1575.

Xin Li and Dan Roth. 2002. Learning question classifiers. In *Proceedings of the 19th International Conference on Computational Linguistics*, COLING '02, pages 1–7.

Tomas Mikolov, Martin Karafiát, Lukas Burget, Jan Cernocký, and Sanjeev Khudanpur. 2010. Recurrent neural network based language model. In *The Proceedings of Interspeech*, pages 1045–1048.

Lili Mou, Hao Peng, Ge Li, Yan Xu, Lu Zhang, and Zhi Jin. 2015. Tree-based convolution: A new neural architecture for sentence modeling. *CoRR*.

Suman Ravuri and Andreas Stolcke. 2015a. A comparative study of neural network models for lexical intent classification. In *The Proceedings of IEEE Automatic Speech Recogntion and Understanding Workshop*.

Suman Ravuri and Andreas Stolcke. 2015b. Recurrent neural network and lstm models for lexical utterance classification. In *Proceedings of Interspeech*.

Tara N. Sainath, Oriol Vinyals, Andrew W. Senior, and Hasim Sak. 2015. Convolutional, long short-term memory, fully connected deep neural networks. In *Proceedings of ICASSP*, pages 4580–4584.

Yelong Shen, Xiaodong he, Jianfeng Gao, Li Deng, and Gregoire Mesnil. 2014. Learning semantic representations using convolutional neural networks for web search. In *Proceedings of WWW*. WWW 2014, April.

Yangyang Shi, Kaisheng Yao, Hu Chen, Yi-Cheng Pan, and Mei-Yuh Hwang. 2015a. Semi-supervised spoken language understanding using recurrent transductive support vector machines. In *Proceeding of ASRU*.

Yangyang Shi, Kaisheng Yao, Hu Chen, Yi-Cheng Pan, Mei-Yuh Hwang, and Baolin Peng. 2015b. Contextual spoken language understanding using recurrent neural networks. In *The Proceedings of International Conference on Acoustics, Speech and Signal Processing*.

J. Silva, L. Coheur, A. C. Mendes, and Andreas Wichert. 2010. From symbolic to sub-symbolic information in question classification. *Artificial Intelligence Review*.

Richard Socher, Cliff C. Lin, Andrew Y. Ng, and Christopher D. Manning. 2011a. Parsing Natural Scenes and Natural Language with Recursive Neural Networks. In *Proceedings of ICML*.

Richard Socher, Jeffrey Pennington, Eric H. Huang, Andrew Y. Ng, and Christopher D. Manning. 2011b. Semi-supervised recursive autoencoders for predicting sentiment distributions. In *Proceedings of EMNLP*, pages 151–161.

Richard Socher, Brody Huval, Christopher D. Manning, and Andrew Y. Ng. 2012. Semantic Compositionality Through Recursive Matrix-Vector Spaces. In *Proceedings of the Conference on Empirical Methods in Natural Language Processing*.

Richard Socher, Alex Perelygin, Jean Wu, Jason Chuang, Christopher D. Manning, Andrew Ng, and Christopher Potts. 2013. Recursive Deep Models for Semantic Compositionality Over a Sentiment Treebank. In *Proceedings of the Conference on Empirical Methods in Natural Language Processing*, pages 1631–1642.

Richard Socher. 2012. New directions in deep learning: Structured models, tasks, and datasets. *Neural Information Processing Systems (NIPS) Workshop on Deep Learning and Unsupervised Feature Learning*.

Rupesh Kumar Srivastava, Klaus Greff, and Jürgen Schmidhuber. 2015. Highway networks. *CoRR*, abs/1505.00387.

Martin Sundermeyer, Ralf Schlüter, and Hermann Ney. 2012. LSTM neural networks for language modeling. In *INTERSPEECH*, pages 194–197.

Ilya Sutskever, Oriol Vinyals, and Quoc V. Le. 2014. Sequence to sequence learning with neural networks. In *Advances in Neural Information Processing Systems*, pages 3104–3112.

Kai Sheng Tai, Richard Socher, and Christopher D. Manning. 2015. Improved semantic representations from tree-structured long short-term memory networks. In *Proceedings of ACL*, pages 1556–1566. Association for Computational Linguistics, July.

Duyu Tang, Bing Qin, and Ting Liu. 2015. Document modeling with gated recurrent neural network for sentiment classification. In *Proceedings of the 2015 Conference on Empirical Methods in Natural Language Processing*, pages 1422–1432.

G. Tur, D. Hakkani-Tur, and L. Heck. 2010. What is left to be understood in atis? In *Spoken Language Technology Workshop (SLT), 2010 IEEE*, pages 19–24.

Peilu Wang, Yao Qian, Frank K. Soong, Lei He, and Hai Zhao. 2015. A unified tagging solution: Bidirectional LSTM recurrent neural network with word embedding. *CoRR*.

Kaisheng Yao, Baolin Peng, Yu Zhang, Dong Yu, Geoffrey Zweig, and Yangyang Shi. 2014a. Spoken language understanding using long short-term memory neural networks. In *The Proceedings of IEEE workshop on Spoken Language Technology*, pages 189–194.

Kaisheng Yao, Baolin Peng, Yu Zhang, Dong Yu, Geoffrey Zweig, and Yangyang Shi. 2014b. Spoken language understanding using long short-term memory neural networks. In *The Proceedings of IEEE workshop on Spoken Language Technology*, pages 189–194.

Kaisheng Yao, Trevor Cohn, Katerina Vylomova, Kevin Duh, and Chris Dyer. 2015. Depth-gated LSTM. *CoRR*.

Wen-tau Yih, Ming-Wei Chang, Xiaodong He, and Jianfeng Gao. 2015. Semantic parsing via staged query graph generation: Question answering with knowledge base. In *Proceedings of ACL*, pages 1321–1331.

Ye Zhang and Byron Wallace. 2015. A sensitivity analysis of (and practitioners' guide to) convolutional neural networks for sentence classification. *CoRR*.

Ye Zhang and Byron Wallace. 2016. A sensitivity analysis of (and practitioners' guide to) convolutional neural networks for sentence classification. In *CoRR*.

Yu Zhang, Guoguo Chen, Dong Yu, Kaisheng Yao, Sanjeev Khudanpur, and James Glass. 2015. Highway long short-term memory rnns for distant speech recognition. *CoRR*.

Han Zhao, Zhengdong Lu, and Pascal Poupart. 2015. Self-adaptive hierarchical sentence model. *CoRR*.

Chunting Zhou, Chonglin Sun, Zhiyuan Liu, and Francis C. M. Lau. 2015. A C-LSTM neural network for text classification. *CoRR*, abs/1511.08630.

Dependency Sensitive Convolutional Neural Networks
for Modeling Sentences and Documents

Rui Zhang
Department of EECS
University of Michigan
Ann Arbor, MI, USA
ryanzh@umich.edu

Honglak Lee
Department of EECS
University of Michigan
Ann Arbor, MI, USA
honglak@eecs.umich.edu

Dragomir Radev
Department of EECS
and School of Information
University of Michigan
Ann Arbor, MI, USA
radev@umich.edu

Abstract

The goal of sentence and document modeling is to accurately represent the meaning of sentences and documents for various Natural Language Processing tasks. In this work, we present Dependency Sensitive Convolutional Neural Networks (DSCNN) as a general-purpose classification system for both sentences and documents. DSCNN hierarchically builds textual representations by processing pretrained word embeddings via Long Short-Term Memory networks and subsequently extracting features with convolution operators. Compared with existing recursive neural models with tree structures, DSCNN does not rely on parsers and expensive phrase labeling, and thus is not restricted to sentence-level tasks. Moreover, unlike other CNN-based models that analyze sentences locally by sliding windows, our system captures both the dependency information within each sentence and relationships across sentences in the same document. Experiment results demonstrate that our approach is achieving state-of-the-art performance on several tasks, including sentiment analysis, question type classification, and subjectivity classification.

1 Introduction

Sentence and document modeling systems are important for many Natural Language Processing (NLP) applications. The challenge for textual modeling is to capture features for different text units and to perform compositions over variable-length sequences (e.g., phrases, sentences, documents). As a traditional method, the bag-of-words model treats sentences and documents as unordered collections of words. In this way, however, the bag-of-words model fails to encode word orders and syntactic structures.

By contrast, order-sensitive models based on neural networks are becoming increasingly popular thanks to their ability to capture word order information. Many prevalent order-sensitive neural models can be categorized into two classes: Recursive models and Convolutional Neural Networks (CNN) models. Recursive models can be considered as generalizations of traditional sequence-modeling neural networks to tree structures. For example, (Socher et al., 2013) uses Recursive Neural Networks to build representations of phrases and sentences by combining neighboring constituents based on the parse tree. In their model, the composition is performed in a bottom-up way from leaf nodes of tokens until the root node of the parsing tree is reached. CNN based models, as the second category, utilize convolutional filters to extract local features (Kalchbrenner et al., 2014; Kim, 2014) over embedding matrices consisting of pretrained word vectors. Therefore, the model actually splits the sentence locally into n-grams by sliding windows.

However, despite their ability to account for word orders, order-sensitive models based on neural networks still suffer from several disadvantages. First, recursive models depend on well-performing parsers, which can be difficult for many languages or noisy domains (Iyyer et al., 2015; Ma et al., 2015). Besides, since tree-structured neural networks are vulnerable to the vanishing gradient problem (Iyyer et al., 2015), recursive models require heavy label-

Proceedings of NAACL-HLT 2016, pages 1512–1521,
San Diego, California, June 12-17, 2016. ©2016 Association for Computational Linguistics

ing on phrases to add supervisions on internal nodes. Furthermore, parsing is restricted to sentences and it is unclear how to model paragraphs and documents using recursive neural networks. In CNN models, convolutional operators process word vectors sequentially using small windows. Thus sentences are essentially treated as a bag of n-grams, and the long dependency information spanning sliding windows is lost.

These observations motivate us to construct a textual modeling architecture that captures long-term dependencies without relying on parsing for both sentence and document inputs. Specifically, we propose Dependency Sensitive Convolutional Neural Networks (DSCNN), an end-to-end classification system that hierarchically builds textual representations with only root-level labels.

DSCNN consists of a convolutional layer built on top of Long Short-Term Memory (LSTM) networks. DSCNN takes slightly different forms depending on its input. For a single sentence (Figure 1), the LSTM network processes the sequence of word embeddings to capture long-distance dependencies within the sentence. The hidden states of the LSTM are extracted to form the low-level representation, and a convolutional layer with variable-size filters and max-pooling operators follows to extract task-specific features for classification purposes. As for document modeling (Figure 2), DSCNN first applies independent LSTM networks to each subsentence. Then a second LSTM layer is added between the first LSTM layer and the convolutional layer to encode the dependency across different sentences.

We evaluate DSCNN on several sentence-level and document-level tasks including sentiment analysis, question type classification, and subjectivity classification. Experimental results demonstrate the effectiveness of our approach comparable with the state-of-the-art. In particular, our method achieves highest accuracies on MR sentiment analysis (Pang and Lee, 2005), TREC question classification (Li and Roth, 2002), and subjectivity classification task SUBJ (Pang and Lee, 2004) compared with several competitive baselines.

The remaining part of this paper is the following. Section 2 discusses related work. Section 3 presents the background including LSTM networks and convolution operators. We then describe our architec-

tures for sentence modeling and document modeling in Section 4, and report experimental results in Section 5.

2 Related Work

The success of deep learning architectures for NLP is first based on the progress in learning distributed word representations in semantic vector space (Bengio et al., 2003; Mikolov et al., 2013; Pennington et al., 2014), where each word is modeled with a real-valued vector called a word embedding. In this formulation, instead of using one-hot vectors by indexing words into a vocabulary, word embeddings are learned by projecting words onto a low dimensional and dense vector space that encodes both semantic and syntactic features of words.

Given word embeddings, different models have been proposed to learn the composition of words to build up phrase and sentence representations. Most methods fall into three types: unordered models, sequence models, and Convolutional Neural Networks models.

In unordered models, textual representations are independent of the word order. Specifically, ignoring the token order in the phrase and sentence, the bag-of-words model produces the representation by averaging the constituting word embeddings (Landauer and Dumais, 1997). Besides, a neural-bag-of-words model described in (Kalchbrenner et al., 2014) adds an additional hidden layer on top of the averaged word embeddings before the softmax layer for classification purposes.

In contrast, sequence models, such as standard Recurrent Neural Networks (RNN) and Long Short-Term Memory networks, construct phrase and sentence representations in an order-sensitive way. For example, thanks to its ability to capture long-distance dependencies, LSTM has re-emerged as a popular choice for many sequence-modeling tasks, including machine translation (Bahdanau et al., 2014), image caption generation (Vinyals et al., 2014), and natural language generation (Wen et al., 2015). Besides, RNN and LSTM can be both converted to tree-structured networks by using parsing information. For example, (Socher et al., 2013) applied Recursive Neural Networks as a variant of the standard RNN structured by syntactic trees to the sentiment analysis task. (Tai et al., 2015) also generalizes LSTM to Tree-LSTM where each LSTM unit combines information from its children units.

Recently, CNN-based models have demonstrated remarkable performances on sentence modeling and classification tasks. Leveraging convolution operators, these models can extract features from variable-length phrases corresponding to different filters. For example, DCNN in (Kalchbrenner et al., 2014) constructs hierarchical features of sentences by one-dimensional convolution and dynamic k-max pooling. (Yin and Schütze, 2015) further utilizes multichannel embeddings and unsupervised pretraining to improve classification results.

3 Preliminaries

In this section, we describe two building blocks for our system. We first discuss Long Short-Term Memory as a powerful network for modeling sequence data, and then formulate convolution and max-over-time pooling operators for the feature extraction over sequence inputs.

3.1 Long Short-Term Memory

Recurrent Neural Network (RNN) is a class of models to process arbitrary-length input sequences by recursively constructing hidden state vectors $\mathbf{h}_t$. At each time step t, the hidden state $\mathbf{h}_t$ is an affine function of the input vector $\mathbf{x}_t$ at time t and its previous hidden state $\mathbf{h}_{t-1}$, followed by a non-linearity such as the hyperbolic tangent function:

$$\mathbf{h}_t = \tanh(\mathbf{W}\mathbf{x}_t + \mathbf{U}\mathbf{h}_{t-1} + b) \qquad (1)$$

where $\mathbf{W}$, $\mathbf{U}$ and b are parameters of the model.

However, traditional RNN suffers from the exploding or vanishing gradient problems, where the gradient vectors can grow or decay exponentially as they propagate to earlier time steps. This problem makes it difficult to train RNN to capture long-distance dependencies in a sequence (Bengio et al., 1994; Hochreiter, 1998).

To address this problem of capturing long-term relations, Long Short-Term Memory (LSTM) networks, proposed by (Hochreiter and Schmidhuber, 1997) introduce a vector of memory cells and a set of gates to control how the information flows through the network. We thus have the input gate $\mathbf{i}_t$, the forget gate $\mathbf{f}_t$, the output gate $\mathbf{o}_t$, the memory cell $\mathbf{c}_t$,

the input at the current step t as $\mathbf{x}_t$, and the hidden state $\mathbf{h}_t$, which are all in $\mathbb{R}^d$. Denote the sigmoid function as σ, and the element-wise multiplication as $\odot$. At each time step t, the LSTM unit manipulates a collection of vectors described by the following equations:

$$\begin{aligned}
\mathbf{i}_t &= \sigma\left(\mathbf{W}^{(i)}\mathbf{x}_t + \mathbf{U}^{(i)}\mathbf{h}_{t-1} + b^{(i)}\right) \\
\mathbf{f}_t &= \sigma\left(\mathbf{W}^{(f)}\mathbf{x}_t + \mathbf{U}^{(f)}\mathbf{h}_{t-1} + b^{(f)}\right) \\
\mathbf{o}_t &= \sigma\left(\mathbf{W}^{(o)}\mathbf{x}_t + \mathbf{U}^{(o)}\mathbf{h}_{t-1} + b^{(o)}\right) \\
\mathbf{u}_t &= \tanh\left(\mathbf{W}^{(u)}\mathbf{x}_t + \mathbf{U}^{(u)}\mathbf{h}_{t-1} + b^{(u)}\right) \\
\mathbf{c}_t &= \mathbf{i}_t \odot \mathbf{u}_t + \mathbf{f}_t \odot \mathbf{c}_{t-1} \\
\mathbf{h}_t &= \mathbf{o}_t \odot \tanh(\mathbf{c}_t)
\end{aligned} \qquad (2)$$

Note that the gates $\mathbf{i}_t, \mathbf{f}_t, \mathbf{o}_t \in [0,1]^d$ and they control at time step t how the input is updated, how much the previous memory cell is forgotten, and the exposure of the memory to form the hidden state vector respectively.

3.2 Convolution and Max-over-time Pooling

Convolution operators have been extensively used in object recognition (LeCun et al., 1998), phoneme recognition (Waibel et al., 1989), sentence modeling and classification (Kalchbrenner et al., 2014; Kim, 2014), and other traditional NLP tasks (Collobert and Weston, 2008). Given an input sentence of length s: $[w_1, w_2, ..., w_s]$, convolution operators apply a number of filters to extract local features of the sentence.

In this work, we employ one-dimensional wide convolution described in (Kalchbrenner et al., 2014). Let $\mathbf{h}_t \in \mathbb{R}^d$ denote the representation of w_t, and $\mathbf{F} \in \mathbb{R}^{d \times l}$ be a filter where l is the window size. One-dimensional wide convolution computes the feature map $\mathbf{c}$ of length $(s + l - 1)$

$$\mathbf{c} = [c_1, c_2, ..., c_{s+l-1}] \qquad (3)$$

for the input sentence.

Specifically, in wide convolution, we stack $\mathbf{h}_t$ column by column, and add $(l-1)$ zero vectors to both ends of the sentence respectively. This formulates an input feature map $\mathbf{X} \in \mathbb{R}^{d \times (s+2l-2)}$. Thereafter, one-dimensional convolution applies the filter $\mathbf{F}$ to each set of consecutive l columns in $\mathbf{X}$ to produce

$(s - l - 1)$ activations. The k-th activation is produced by

$$\mathbf{c}_k = f\left(b + \sum_{i,j} (\mathbf{F} \odot \mathbf{X}_{k:k+l-1})_{i,j}\right) \quad (4)$$

where $\mathbf{X}_{k:k+l-1} \in \mathbb{R}^{d \times l}$ is the k-th sliding window in $\mathbf{X}$, and b is the bias term. $\odot$ performs element-wise multiplications and f is an nonlinear function such as Rectified Linear Units (ReLU) or the hyperbolic tangent.

Then, the max-over-time pooling selects the maximum value in the feature map

$$c_{\mathbf{F}} = \max(\mathbf{c}) \quad (5)$$

as the feature corresponding to the filter $\mathbf{F}$.

In practice, we apply many filters with different window sizes l to capture features encoded in l-length windows of the input.

4 Model Architectures

Convolutional Neural Networks have demonstrated state-of-the-art performances in sentence modeling and classification. Despite the fact that CNN is an order-sensitive model, traditional convolution operators extract local features from each possible window of words through filters with predefined sizes. Therefore, sentences are effectively processed like a bag of n-grams, and long-distance dependencies can be only captured if we have long enough filters.

To capture long-distance dependencies, much recent effort has been dedicated to building tree-structured models from the syntactic parsing information. However, we observe that these methods suffer from three problems. First, they require an external parser and are vulnerable to parsing errors (Iyyer et al., 2015). Besides, tree-structured models need heavy supervisions to overcome vanishing gradient problems. For example, in (Socher et al., 2013), input sentences are labeled for each sub-phrase, and softmax layers are applied at each internal node. Finally, tree-structured models are restricted to sentence level, and cannot be generalized to model documents.

In this work, we propose a novel architecture to address these three problems. Our model hierarchically builds text representations from input words without parsing information. Only labels at the root level are required at the top softmax layer, so there is no need for labeling subphrases in the text. The system is not restricted to sentence-level inputs: the architecture can be restructured based on the sentence tokenization for modeling documents.

4.1 Sentence Modeling

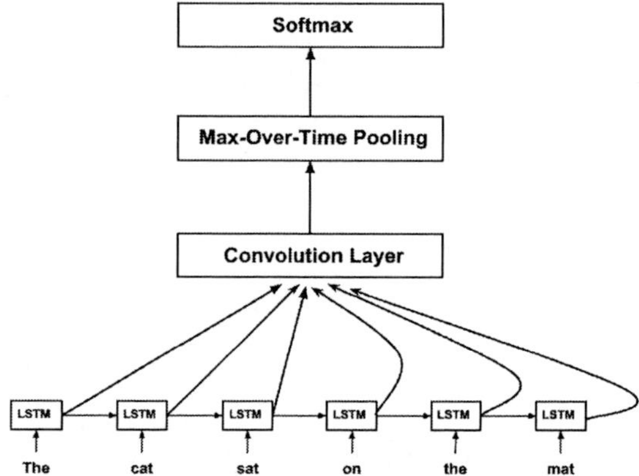

Figure 1: An example for sentence modeling. The bottom LSTM layer processes the input sentence and feed-forwards hidden state vectors at each time step. The one-dimensional wide convolution layer and the max-over-time pooling operation extract features from the LSTM output. For brevity, only one version of word embedding is illustrated in this figure.

Let the input of our model be a sentence of length s: $[w_1, w_2, ..., w_s]$, and c be the total number of word embedding versions. Different versions come from pre-trained word vectors such as word2vec (Mikolov et al., 2013) and GloVe (Pennington et al., 2014).

The first layer of our model consists of LSTM networks processing multiple versions of word embedding. For each version of word embedding, we construct an LSTM network where the input $\mathbf{x}_t \in \mathbb{R}^d$ is the d-dimensional word embedding vector for w_t. As described in the previous section, the LSTM layer will produce a hidden state representation $\mathbf{h}_t \in \mathbb{R}^d$ at each time step. We collect hidden state representations as the output of LSTM layers:

$$\mathbf{h}^{(i)} = [\mathbf{h}_1^{(i)}, \mathbf{h}_2^{(i)}, ..., \mathbf{h}_t^{(i)}, ..., \mathbf{h}_s^{(i)}] \quad (6)$$

for $i = 1, 2, ..., c$.

A convolution neural network follows as the second layer. To deal with multiple word embeddings, we use filter $\mathbf{F} \in \mathbb{R}^{c \times d \times l}$, where l is the window size. Each hidden state sequence $\mathbf{h}^{(i)}$ produced by the i-th version of word embeddings forms one channel of the feature map. These feature maps are stacked as c-channel feature maps $\mathbf{X} \in \mathbb{R}^{c \times d \times (s+2(l-1))}$.

Similar to the single channel case, activations are computed as a slight modification of equation 4:

$$\mathbf{c}_k = f\left(b + \sum_{i,j,r} (\mathbf{F} \odot \mathbf{X}_{k:k+l-1})_{i,j,r}\right) \quad (7)$$

A max-over-time pooling layer is then added on top of the convolution neural network. Finally, the pooled features are used in a softmax layer for classification. A sentence modeling example is illustrated in Figure 1.

4.2 Document Modeling

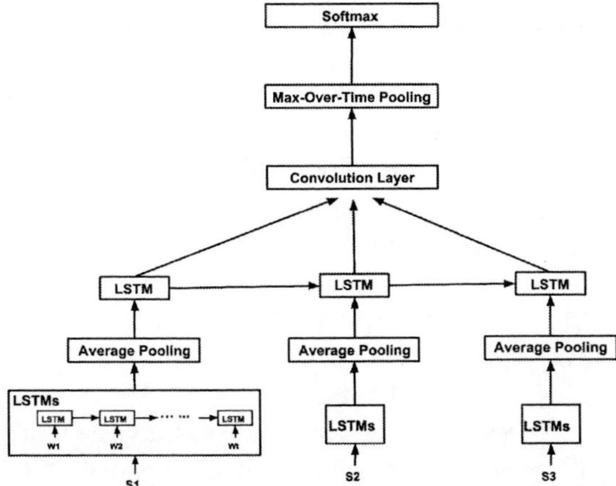

Figure 2: A schematic for document modeling hierarchy, which can be viewed as a variant of the one for sentence modeling. Independent LSTM networks process subsentences separated by punctuation. Hidden states of LSTM networks are averaged as the sentence representations, from which the high-level LSTM layer creates the joint meaning of sentences.

Our model is not restricted to sentences; it can be restructured to model documents. The intuition comes from the fact that as the composition of words builds up the semantic meaning for sentences, the composition of sentences establishes the semantic meaning for documents (Li et al., 2015).

Now suppose that the input of our model is a document consisting of n subsentences: $[s_1, s_2, ..., s_n]$. Subsentences can be obtained by splitting the document using punctuation (comma, period, question mark, and exclamation point) as delimiters.

We employ independent LSTM networks for each subsentence in the same way as the first layer of the sentence modeling architecture. For each subsentence we feed-forward the hidden states of the corresponding LSTM network to the average pooling layer. Take the first sentence of the document as an example,

$$\mathbf{h}_{s1}^{(i)} = \frac{1}{\text{len}(s1)} \sum_{j=1}^{\text{len}(s1)} \mathbf{h}_{s1,j}^{(i)} \quad (8)$$

where $\mathbf{h}_{s1,j}^{(i)}$ is the hidden state of the first sentence at time step j, and $\text{len}(s1)$ denotes the length of the first sentence. In this way, after the averaging pooling layers, we have a representation sequence consisting of averaged hidden states for subsentences,

$$\mathbf{h}^{(i)} = [\mathbf{h}_{s1}^{(i)}, \mathbf{h}_{s2}^{(i)}, ..., \mathbf{h}_{sn}^{(i)}] \quad (9)$$

for $i = 1, 2, ..., c$.

Thereafter, a high-level LSTM network comes into play to capture the joint meaning created by the sentences.

Similar as sentence modeling, a convolutional layer is placed on top of the high-level LSTM for feature extraction. Finally, a max-over-time pooling layer and a softmax layer follow to pool features and perform the classification task. Figure 2 gives the schematic for the hierarchy.

5 Experiments

5.1 Datasets

Movie Review Data (MR) proposed by (Pang and Lee, 2005) is a dataset for sentiment analysis of movie reviews. The dataset consists of 5,331 positive and 5,331 negative reviews, mostly in one sentence. We follow the practice of using 10-fold cross validation to report results.

Stanford Sentiment Treebank (SST) is another popular sentiment classification dataset introduced

Method	MR	SST-2	SST-5	TREC	SUBJ	IMDB
SVM (Socher et al., 2013)	—	79.4	40.7	—	—	—
NB (Socher et al., 2013)	—	81.8	41.0	—	—	—
NBSVM-bi (Wang and Manning, 2012)	79.4	—	—	—	93.2	91.2
SVM_S (Silva et al., 2011)	—	—	—	95.0	—	—
Standard-RNN (Socher et al., 2013)	—	82.4	43.2	—	—	—
MV-RNN (Socher et al., 2012)	79.0	82.9	44.4	—	—	—
RNTN (Socher et al., 2013)	—	85.4	45.7	—	—	—
DRNN (Irsoy and Cardie, 2014)	—	86.6	49.8	—	—	—
Standard-LSTM (Tai et al., 2015)	—	86.7	45.8	—	—	—
bi-LSTM (Tai et al., 2015)	—	86.8	49.1	—	—	—
Tree-LSTM (Tai et al., 2015)	—	88.0	51.0	—	—	—
SA-LSTM (Dai and Le, 2015)	80.7	—	—	—	—	92.8
DCNN (Kalchbrenner et al., 2014)	—	86.8	48.5	93.0	—	—
CNN-MC (Kim, 2014)	81.1	88.1	47.4	92.2	93.2	—
MVCNN (Yin and Schütze, 2015)	—	89.4	49.6	—	93.9	—
Dep-CNN (Ma et al., 2015)	81.9	—	49.5	95.4	—	—
Neural-BoW (Kalchbrenner et al., 2014)	—	80.5	42.4	88.2	—	—
DAN (Iyyer et al., 2015)	80.3	86.3	47.7	—	—	89.4
Paragraph-Vector (Le and Mikolov, 2014)	—	87.8	48.7	—	—	92.6
WRRBM+BoW(bnc) (Dahl et al., 2012)	—	—	—	—	—	89.2
Full+Unlabeled+BoW(bnc) (Maas et al., 2011)	—	—	—	—	88.2	88.9
DSCNN	81.5	89.1	49.7	95.4	93.2	90.2
DSCNN-Pretrain	82.2	88.7	50.6	95.6	93.9	90.7

Table 1: Experiment results of DSCNN compared with other models. Performance is measured in accuracy (%). Models are categorized into five classes. The first block is baseline methods including SVM and Naive Bayes and their variations. The second is the class of Recursive Neural Networks models. Constituent parsers and phrase-level supervision are needed. The third category is LSTMs. CNN models are fourth block, and the last category is a collection of other models achieving state-of-the-art results. **SVM**: Support Vector Machines with unigram features (Socher et al., 2013) **NB**: Naive Bayes with unigram features(Socher et al., 2013) **NBSVM-bi**: Naive Bayes SVM and Multinomial Naive Bayes with bigrams (Wang and Manning, 2012) $\mathbf{SVM}_S$: SVM with features including uni-bi-trigrams, POS, parser, and 60 hand-coded rules (Silva et al., 2011) **Standard-RNN**: Standard Recursive Neural Network (Socher et al., 2013) **MV-RNN**: Matrix-Vector Recursive Neural Network (Socher et al., 2012) **RNTN**:Recursive Neural Tensor Network (Socher et al., 2013) **DRNN**: Deep Recursive Neural Network (Irsoy and Cardie, 2014) **Standard-LSTM**: Standard Long Short-Term Memory Network (Tai et al., 2015) **bi-LSTM**: Bidirectional LSTM (Tai et al., 2015) **Tree-LSTM**: Tree-Structured LSTM (Tai et al., 2015) **SA-LSTM**: Sequence Autoencoder LSTM (Dai and Le, 2015). For fair comparison, we report the result on **MR** trained without unlabeled data from IMDB or Amazon reviews. **DCNN**: Dynamic Convolutional Neural Network with k-max pooling (Kalchbrenner et al., 2014) **CNN-MC**: Convolutional Neural Network with static pretrained and fine-tuned pretrained word-embeddings (Kim, 2014) **MVCNN**: Multichannel Variable-Size Convolution Neural Network (Yin and Schütze, 2015) **Dep-CNN**: Dependency-based Convolutional Neural Network (Ma et al., 2015). Dependency parser is required. The result is for the combined model ancestor+sibling+sequential. **Neural-BoW** : Neural Bag-of-Words Models (Kalchbrenner et al., 2014) **DAN**: Deep Averaging Network (Iyyer et al., 2015) **Paragraph-Vector**: Logistic Regression on Paragraph-Vector (Le and Mikolov, 2014) **WRRBM+BoW(bnc)**: word representation Restricted Boltzmann Machine combined with bag-of-words features (Dahl et al., 2012) **Full+Unlabeled+BoW(bnc)**:word vector based model capturing both semantic and sentiment, trained on unlabeled examples, and with bag-of-words features concatenated (Maas et al., 2011)

by (Socher et al., 2013). The sentences are labeled in a fine-grained way (SST-5): {very negative, negative, neutral, positive, very positive}. The dataset has been split into 8,544 training, 1,101 validation, and 2,210 testing sentences. Without neutral sentences, SST can also be used in binary mode (SST-2), where the split is 6,920 training, 872 validation, and 1,821 testing.

Furthermore, we apply DSCNN on question type classification task on TREC dataset (Li and Roth, 2002), where sentences are questions in the following 6 classes: {abbreviation, entity, description, location, numeric}. The entire dataset consists of 5,452 training examples and 500 testing examples.

We also benchmark our system on the subjectivity classification dataset (SUBJ) released by (Pang and Lee, 2004). The dataset contains 5,000 subjective sentences and 5,000 objective sentences. We report 10-fold cross validation results as the baseline does.

For document-level dataset, we use Large Movie Review (IMDB) created by (Maas et al., 2011). There are 25,000 training and 25,000 testing examples with binary sentiment polarity labels, and 50,000 unlabeled examples. Different from Stanford Sentiment Treebank and Movie Review dataset, every example in this dataset has several sentences.

5.2 Training Details and Implementation

We use two sets of 300-dimensional pre-trained embeddings, word2vec[1] and GloVe[2], forming two channels for our network. For all datasets, we use 100 convolution filters each for window sizes of 3, 4, 5. Rectified Linear Units (ReLU) is chosen as the nonlinear function in the convolutional layer.

For regularization, before the softmax layers, we employ Dropout operation (Hinton et al., 2012) with dropout rate 0.5, and we do not perform any l_2 constraints over the parameters. We use the gradient-based optimizer Adadelta (Zeiler, 2012) to minimize cross-entropy loss between the predicted and true distributions, and the training is early stopped when the accuracy on validation set starts to drop.

As for training cost, our system processes around 4000 tokens per second on a single GTX 670 GPU. As an example, this amounts to 1 minute per epoch

---

[1] https://code.google.com/p/word2vec/
[2] http://nlp.stanford.edu/projects/glove/

on the TREC dataset, converging within 50 epochs.

5.3 Pretraining of LSTM

We experiment with two variants of parameter initialization of sentence level LSTMs. The first variant (DSCNN in Table 1) initializes the weight matrices in LSTMs as random orthogonal matrices. In the second variant (DSCNN-Pretrain in Table 1), we first train sequence autoencoders (Dai and Le, 2015) which read input sentences at the encoder and reconstruct the input at the decoder. We pretrain separately on each task based on the same train/valid/test splits. The pretrained encoders are used to be the start points of LSTM layers for later supervised classification tasks.

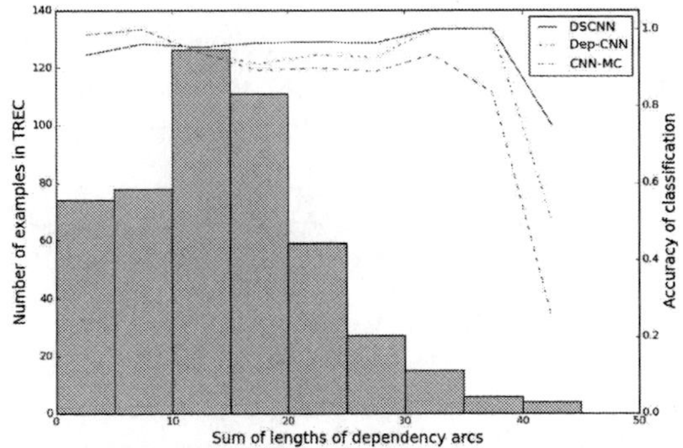

Figure 3: Number of sentences in TREC, and classification performances of DSCNN-Pretrain/Dep-CNN/CNN-MC as functions of dependency lengths. DSCNN and Dep-CNN clearly outperforms CNN-MC when the dependency length in the sentence grows.

5.4 Results and Discussions

Table 1 reports the results of DSCNN on different datasets, demonstrating its effectiveness in comparison with other state-of-the-art methods.

5.4.1 Sentence Modeling

For sentence modeling tasks, DSCNN beats all baselines on MR and TREC, and achieves the same best result on SUBJ as MVCNN. In SST-2, DSCNN only reports a slightly lower accuracy than MVCNN. In MVCNN, however, the author uses more resources including five versions of word embeddings. For SST-5, DSCNN is second only to

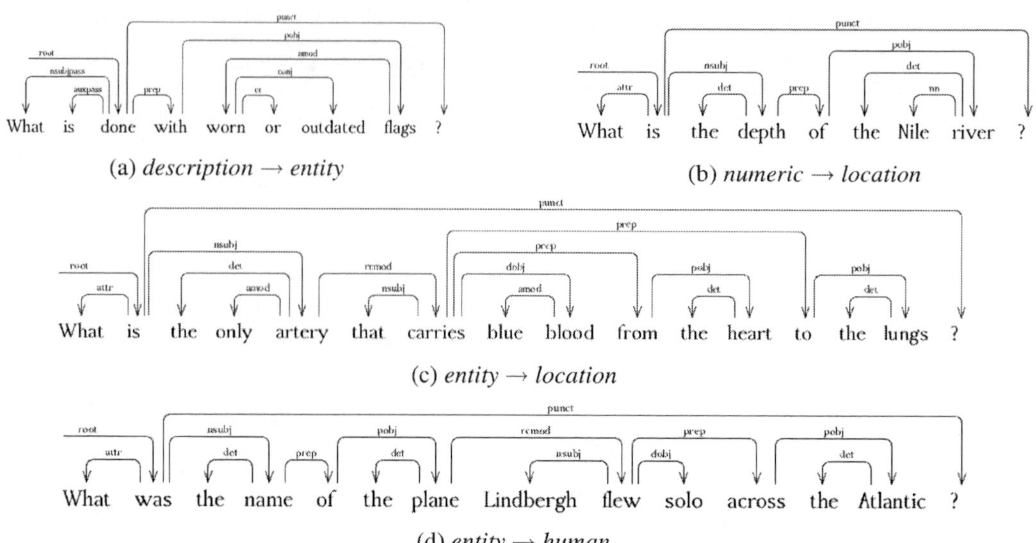

(a) *description → entity*

(b) *numeric → location*

(c) *entity → location*

(d) *entity → human*

Figure 4: TREC examples that are misclassified by CNN-MC but correctly classified by DSCNN. For example, CNN-MC labels (a) as *entity* while the ground truth is *description*. Dependency Parsing is done by ClearNLP (Choi and Palmer, 2012).

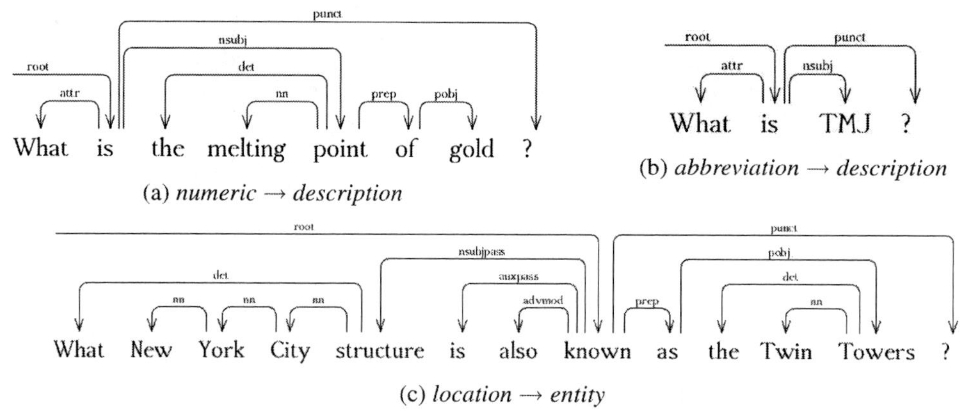

(a) *numeric → description*

(b) *abbreviation → description*

(c) *location → entity*

Figure 5: TREC examples that are misclassified by DSCNN. For example, DSCNN labels (a) as *description* while the ground truth is *numeric*. Dependency Parsing is done by ClearNLP (Choi and Palmer, 2012).

Tree-LSTM, which nonetheless relies on parsers to build tree-structured neural models.

The benefit of DSCNN is illustrated by its consistently better results over the sequential CNN models including DCNN and CNN-MC. The superiority of DSCNN is mainly attributed to its ability to maintain long-term dependencies. Figure 3 depicts the correlation between the dependency length and the classification accuracy. While CNN-MC and DSCNN are similar when the sum of dependency arc lengths is below 15, DSCNN gains obvious ad-

vantages when dependency lengths grow for long and complex sentences. Dep-CNN is also more robust than CNN-MC, but it relies on the dependency parser and predefined patterns to model longer linguistic structures.

Figure 4 gives some examples where DSCNN makes correct predictions while CNN-MC fails. In the first example, CNN-MC classifies the question as *entity* due to its focus on the noun phrase "worn or outdated flags", while DSCNN captures the long dependency between "done with" and "flags", and assigns the correct label *description*. Similarly in the second case, due to "Nile", CNN-MC labels the question as *location*, while the dependency between "depth of" and "river" is ignored. As for the third example, the question involves a complicated and long attributive clause for the subject "artery". CNN-MC gets easily confused and predicts the type as *location* due to words "from" and "to", while DSCNN keeps correct. Finally, "Lindbergh" in the last example make CNN-MC bias to *human*.

We also sample some misclassified examples of DSCNN in Figure 5. Example (a) fails because the numeric meaning of "point" is not captured by the word embedding. Similarly, in the second example, the error is due to the out-of-vocabulary word "TMJ" and it is thus apparently difficult for DSCNN to figure out that it is an abbreviation. Example (c) is likely to be an ambiguous or mistaken annotation. The finding here agrees with the discussion in Dep-CNN work (Ma et al., 2015).

5.4.2 Document Modeling

For document modeling, the result of DSCNN on IMDB against other baselines is listed on the last column of Table 1. Documents in IMDB consist of several sentences and thus very long: the average length is 241 tokens per document and the maximum length is 2526 words (Dai and Le, 2015). As a result, there is no result reported using CNN-based models due to prohibited computation time, and most previous works are unordered models including variations of bag-of-words.

DSCNN outperforms bag-of-words model (Maas et al., 2011), Deep Averaging Network (Iyyer et al., 2015), and word representation Restricted Boltzmann Machine model combined with bag-of-words features (Dahl et al., 2012). The key weakness of bag-of-words prevents those models from capturing long-term dependencies.

Besides, Paragraph Vector (Le and Mikolov, 2014) and SA-LSTM (Dai and Le, 2015) achieve better results than DSCNN. It is worth mentioning that both methods, as unsupervised learning algorithms, can gain much positive effects from unlabeled data (they are using 50,000 unlabeled examples in IMDB). For example in (Dai and Le, 2015), with additional data from Amazon reviews, the error rate of SA-LSTM on MR dataset drops by 3.6%.

6 Conclusion

In this work, we present DSCNN, Dependency Sensitive Convolutional Neural Networks for purpose of text modeling at both sentence and document levels. DSCNN captures long-term inter-sentence and intra-sentence dependencies by processing word vectors through layers of LSTM networks, and extracts features by convolutional operators for classification. Experiments show that DSCNN consistently outperforms traditional CNNs, and achieves state-of-the-art results on several sentiment analysis, question type classification and subjectivity classification datasets.

Acknowledgments

We thank anonymous reviewers for their constructive comments. This work was supported by a University of Michigan EECS department fellowship and NSF CAREER grant IIS-1453651.

References

Dzmitry Bahdanau, Kyunghyun Cho, and Yoshua Bengio. 2014. Neural machine translation by jointly learning to align and translate. *arXiv preprint arXiv:1409.0473*.

Yoshua Bengio, Patrice Simard, and Paolo Frasconi. 1994. Learning long-term dependencies with gradient descent is difficult. *IEEE Transactions on Neural Networks*, 5(2):157–166.

Yoshua Bengio, Réjean Ducharme, Pascal Vincent, and Christian Janvin. 2003. A neural probabilistic language model. *The Journal of Machine Learning Research*, 3:1137–1155.

Jinho D Choi and Martha Palmer. 2012. Guidelines for the clear style constituent to dependency conversion. Technical report, Technical Report 01-12, University of Colorado at Boulder.

Ronan Collobert and Jason Weston. 2008. A unified architecture for natural language processing: Deep neural networks with multitask learning. In *Proceedings of ICML*, pages 160–167. ACM.

George E Dahl, Ryan P Adams, and Hugo Larochelle. 2012. Training restricted boltzmann machines on word observations. *arXiv preprint arXiv:1202.5695*.

Andrew M Dai and Quoc V Le. 2015. Semi-supervised sequence learning. *arXiv preprint arXiv:1511.01432*.

Geoffrey E Hinton, Nitish Srivastava, Alex Krizhevsky, Ilya Sutskever, and Ruslan R Salakhutdinov. 2012.

Improving neural networks by preventing co-adaptation of feature detectors. *arXiv preprint arXiv:1207.0580*.

Sepp Hochreiter and Jürgen Schmidhuber. 1997. Long short-term memory. *Neural computation*, 9(8):1735–1780.

Sepp Hochreiter. 1998. The vanishing gradient problem during learning recurrent neural nets and problem solutions. *International Journal of Uncertainty, Fuzziness and Knowledge-Based Systems*, 6(02):107–116.

Ozan Irsoy and Claire Cardie. 2014. Deep recursive neural networks for compositionality in language. In *Proceedings of NIPS, 2014*, pages 2096–2104.

Mohit Iyyer, Varun Manjunatha, Jordan Boyd-Graber, and Hal Daumé III. 2015. Deep unordered composition rivals syntactic methods for text classification. In *Proceedings of ACL-IJCNLP*, volume 1, pages 1681–1691.

Nal Kalchbrenner, Edward Grefenstette, and Phil Blunsom. 2014. A convolutional neural network for modelling sentences. *arXiv preprint arXiv:1404.2188*.

Yoon Kim. 2014. Convolutional neural networks for sentence classification. In *Proceedings of EMNLP*, pages 1746–1751, Doha, Qatar, October.

Thomas K Landauer and Susan T Dumais. 1997. A solution to plato's problem: The latent semantic analysis theory of acquisition, induction, and representation of knowledge. *Psychological review*, 104(2):211.

Quoc V Le and Tomas Mikolov. 2014. Distributed representations of sentences and documents. *arXiv preprint arXiv:1405.4053*.

Yann LeCun, Léon Bottou, Yoshua Bengio, and Patrick Haffner. 1998. Gradient-based learning applied to document recognition. *Proceedings of the IEEE*, 86(11):2278–2324.

X. Li and D. Roth. 2002. Learning question classifiers. In *COLING*, pages 556–562.

Jiwei Li, Minh-Thang Luong, and Dan Jurafsky. 2015. A hierarchical neural autoencoder for paragraphs and documents. *arXiv preprint arXiv:1506.01057*.

Mingbo Ma, Liang Huang, Bing Xiang, and Bowen Zhou. 2015. Dependency-based convolutional neural networks for sentence embedding. In *Proceedings of ACL-IJCNLP*, volume 2, page 174.

Andrew L. Maas, Raymond E. Daly, Peter T. Pham, Dan Huang, Andrew Y. Ng, and Christopher Potts. 2011. Learning word vectors for sentiment analysis. In *Proceedings of ACL-HLT*, pages 142–150, Portland, Oregon, USA, June.

Tomas Mikolov, Ilya Sutskever, Kai Chen, Greg S Corrado, and Jeff Dean. 2013. Distributed representations of words and phrases and their compositionality. In *Proceedings of NIPS*, pages 3111–3119.

Bo Pang and Lillian Lee. 2004. A sentimental education: Sentiment analysis using subjectivity summarization based on minimum cuts. In *Proceedings of ACL*, page 271. Association for Computational Linguistics.

Bo Pang and Lillian Lee. 2005. Seeing stars: Exploiting class relationships for sentiment categorization with respect to rating scales. In *Proceedings of ACL*, pages 115–124. Association for Computational Linguistics.

Jeffrey Pennington, Richard Socher, and Christopher D Manning. 2014. Glove: Global vectors for word representation. *Proceedings of EMNLP*, 12:1532–1543.

Joao Silva, Luísa Coheur, Ana Cristina Mendes, and Andreas Wichert. 2011. From symbolic to sub-symbolic information in question classification. *Artificial Intelligence Review*, 35(2):137–154.

Richard Socher, Brody Huval, Christopher D Manning, and Andrew Y Ng. 2012. Semantic compositionality through recursive matrix-vector spaces. In *Proceedings of EMNLP-CoNLL*, pages 1201–1211. Association for Computational Linguistics.

Richard Socher, Alex Perelygin, Jean Y Wu, Jason Chuang, Christopher D Manning, Andrew Y Ng, and Christopher Potts. 2013. Recursive deep models for semantic compositionality over a sentiment treebank. In *Proceedings of EMNLP*, volume 1631, page 1642. Citeseer.

Kai Sheng Tai, Richard Socher, and Christopher D Manning. 2015. Improved semantic representations from tree-structured long short-term memory networks. *arXiv preprint arXiv:1503.00075*.

Oriol Vinyals, Alexander Toshev, Samy Bengio, and Dumitru Erhan. 2014. Show and tell: A neural image caption generator. *arXiv preprint arXiv:1411.4555*.

Alexander Waibel, Toshiyuki Hanazawa, Geoffrey Hinton, Kiyohiro Shikano, and Kevin J Lang. 1989. Phoneme recognition using time-delay neural networks. *Acoustics, Speech and Signal Processing, IEEE Transactions on*, 37(3):328–339.

Sida Wang and Christopher D Manning. 2012. Baselines and bigrams: Simple, good sentiment and topic classification. In *Proceedings of ACL: Short Papers-Volume 2*, pages 90–94. Association for Computational Linguistics.

Tsung-Hsien Wen, Milica Gasic, Nikola Mrksic, Pei-Hao Su, David Vandyke, and Steve Young. 2015. Semantically conditioned lstm-based natural language generation for spoken dialogue systems. *arXiv preprint arXiv:1508.01745*.

Wenpeng Yin and Hinrich Schütze. 2015. Multichannel variable-size convolution for sentence classification. In *Proceedings of CoNLL*, pages 204–214, Beijing, China, July.

Matthew D Zeiler. 2012. Adadelta: An adaptive learning rate method. *arXiv preprint arXiv:1212.5701*.

MGNC-CNN: A Simple Approach to Exploiting
Multiple Word Embeddings for Sentence Classification

Ye Zhang[1] **Stephen Roller**[1] **Byron C. Wallace**[2]

[1]Department of Computer Science
The University of Texas at Austin
{yezhang,roller}@cs.utexas.edu

[2]iSchool
The University of Texas at Austin
byron.wallace@utexas.edu

Abstract

We introduce a novel, simple convolution neural network (CNN) architecture – *multi-group norm constraint CNN (MGNC-CNN)* – that capitalizes on multiple sets of word embeddings for sentence classification. MGNC-CNN extracts features from input embedding sets independently and then joins these at the penultimate layer in the network to form a final feature vector. We then adopt a group regularization strategy that differentially penalizes weights associated with the subcomponents generated from the respective embedding sets. This model is much simpler than comparable alternative architectures and requires substantially less training time. Furthermore, it is flexible in that it does not require input word embeddings to be of the same dimensionality. We show that MGNC-CNN consistently outperforms baseline models.

1 Introduction

Neural models have recently gained popularity for Natural Language Processing (NLP) tasks (Goldberg, 2015; Collobert and Weston, 2008; Cho, 2015). For sentence classification, in particular, Convolution Neural Networks (CNN) have realized impressive performance (Kim, 2014; Zhang and Wallace, 2015). These models operate over *word embeddings*, i.e., dense, low dimensional vector representations of words that aim to capture salient semantic and syntactic properties (Collobert and Weston, 2008).

An important consideration for such models is the specification of the word embeddings. Several options exist. For example, Kalchbrenner et al. (2014) initialize word vectors to random low-dimensional vectors to be fit during training, while Johnson and Zhang (2014) use fixed, one-hot encodings for each word. By contrast, Kim (2014) initializes word vectors to those estimated via the word2vec model trained on 100 billion words of Google News (Mikolov et al., 2013); these are then updated during training. Initializing embeddings to pre-trained word vectors is intuitively appealing because it allows transfer of learned distributional semantics. This has allowed a relatively simple CNN architecture to achieve remarkably strong results.

Many pre-trained word embeddings are now readily available on the web, induced using different models, corpora, and processing steps. Different embeddings may encode different aspects of language (Padó and Lapata, 2007; Erk and Padó, 2008; Levy and Goldberg, 2014): those based on bag-of-words (BoW) statistics tend to capture associations (*doctor* and *hospital*), while embeddings based on dependency-parses encode similarity in terms of use (*doctor* and *surgeon*). It is natural to consider how these embeddings might be *combined* to improve NLP models in general and CNNs in particular.

Contributions. We propose MGNC-CNN, a novel, simple, scalable CNN architecture that can accommodate multiple off-the-shelf embeddings of variable sizes. Our model treats different word embeddings as distinct groups, and applies CNNs independently to each, thus generating corresponding feature vectors (one per embedding) which are then

Proceedings of NAACL-HLT 2016, pages 1522–1527,
San Diego, California, June 12-17, 2016. ©2016 Association for Computational Linguistics

concatenated at the classification layer. Inspired by prior work exploiting regularization to encode structure for NLP tasks (Yogatama and Smith, 2014; Wallace et al., 2015), we impose different regularization penalties on weights for features generated from the respective word embedding sets.

Our approach enjoys the following advantages compared to the only existing comparable model (Yin and Schütze, 2015): (i) It can leverage diverse, readily available word embeddings with different dimensions, thus providing flexibility. (ii) It is comparatively simple, and does not, for example, require *mutual learning* or *pre-training*. (iii) It is an order of magnitude more efficient in terms of training time.

2 Related Work

Prior work has considered combining latent representations of words that capture syntactic and semantic properties (Van de Cruys et al., 2011), and inducing multi-modal embeddings (Bruni et al., 2012) for general NLP tasks. And recently, Luo et al. (2014) proposed a framework that combines multiple word embeddings to measure text similarity, however their focus was not on classification.

More similar to our work, Yin and Schütze (2015) proposed *MVCNN* for sentence classification. This CNN-based architecture accepts multiple word embeddings as inputs. These are then treated as separate 'channels', analogous to RGB channels in images. Filters consider all channels simultaneously. MVCNN achieved state-of-the-art performance on multiple sentence classification tasks. However, this model has practical drawbacks. (i) MVCNN requires that input word embeddings have the same dimensionality. Thus to incorporate a second set of word vectors trained on a corpus (or using a model) of interest, one needs to either find embeddings that happen to have a set number of dimensions or to estimate embeddings from scratch. (ii) The model is complex, both in terms of implementation and runtime. Indeed, this model requires pre-training and mutual-learning and requires days of training time, whereas the simple architecture we propose requires on the order of an hour (and is easy to implement).

3 Model Description

We first review standard one-layer CNN (which exploits a single set of embeddings) for sentence classification (Kim, 2014), and then propose our augmentations, which exploit multiple embedding sets.

Basic CNN. In this model we first replace each word in a sentence with its vector representation, resulting in a sentence matrix $\mathbf{A} \in \mathbb{R}^{s \times d}$, where s is the (zero-padded) sentence length, and d is the dimensionality of the embeddings. We apply a convolution operation between linear filters with parameters $\mathbf{w}_1, \mathbf{w}_2, ..., \mathbf{w}_k$ and the sentence matrix. For each $\mathbf{w}_i \in \mathbb{R}^{h \times d}$, where h denotes 'height', we slide filter i across $\mathbf{A}$, considering 'local regions' of h adjacent rows at a time. At each local region, we perform element-wise multiplication and then take the element-wise sum between the filter and the (flattened) sub-matrix of $\mathbf{A}$, producing a scalar. We do this for each sub-region of $\mathbf{A}$ that the filter spans, resulting in a *feature map* vector $\mathbf{c}_i \in \mathbb{R}^{(s-h+1) \times 1}$. We can use multiple filter sizes with different heights, and for each filter size we can have multiple filters. Thus the model comprises k weight vectors $\mathbf{w}_1, \mathbf{w}_2, ...\mathbf{w}_k$, each of which is associated with an instantiation of a specific filter size. These in turn generate corresponding feature maps $\mathbf{c}_1, \mathbf{c}_2, ...\mathbf{c}_k$, with dimensions varying with filter size. A *1-max pooling* operation is applied to each feature map, extracting the largest number o_i from each feature map i. Finally, we combine all o_i together to form a feature vector $\mathbf{o} \in \mathbb{R}^k$ to be fed through a softmax function for classification. We regularize weights at this level in two ways. (1) *Dropout*, in which we randomly set elements in $\mathbf{o}$ to zero during the training phase with probability p, and multiply p with the parameters trained in $\mathbf{o}$ at test time. (2) An l2 norm penalty, for which we set a threshold λ for the l2 norm of $\mathbf{o}$ during training; if this is exceeded, we rescale the vector accordingly. For more details, see (Zhang and Wallace, 2015).

MG-CNN. Assuming we have m word embeddings with corresponding dimensions $d_1, d_2, ...d_m$, we can simply treat each word embedding independently. In this case, the input to the CNN comprises multiple sentence matrices $\mathbf{A}_1, \mathbf{A}_2, ...\mathbf{A}_m$, where each $\mathbf{A}_l \in \mathbb{R}^{s \times d_l}$ may have its own width d_l. We then apply different groups of filters $\{\mathbf{w}_1\}, \{\mathbf{w}_2\}, ...\{\mathbf{w}_m\}$ independently to each $\mathbf{A}_l$, where $\{\mathbf{w}_l\}$ denotes the set of filters for $\mathbf{A}_l$. As in basic CNN, $\{\mathbf{w}_l\}$ may have multiple filter sizes, and multiple filters of each size may be introduced. At the classification layer we then obtain a feature vector $\mathbf{o}_l$ for each embedding set, and we can simply concatenate these together to form the final feature vector $\mathbf{o}$ to feed into the softmax function, where $\mathbf{o} = \mathbf{o_1} \oplus \mathbf{o_2}... \oplus \mathbf{o_m}$. This representation contains feature vectors generated from all sets of embeddings under consideration. We call this method *multiple group CNN* (MG-CNN). Here groups refer to the features generated from different embeddings. Note that this differs from 'multi-channel' models because at the convolution layer we use different filters on each word embedding matrix independently, whereas in a standard multi-channel approach each filter would consider all channels simultaneously and generate a scalar from all channels at each local region. As above, we impose a max 12 norm constraint on the final feature vector $\mathbf{o}$ for regularization. Figure 1 illustrates this approach.

MGNC-CNN. We propose an augmentation of MG-CNN, *Multi-Group Norm Constraint CNN* (MGNC-CNN), which differs in its regularization strategy. Specifically, in this variant we impose *grouped* regularization constraints, independently regularizing subcomponents $\mathbf{o}_l$ derived from the respective embeddings, i.e., we impose separate max norm constraints λ_l for each $\mathbf{o}_l$ (where l again indexes embedding sets); these λ_l hyper-parameters are to be tuned on a validation set. Intuitively, this method aims to better capitalize on features derived from word embeddings that capture discriminative properties of text for the task at hand by penalizing larger weight estimates for features derived from less discriminative embeddings.

4 Experiments

4.1 Datasets

Stanford Sentiment Treebank Stanford Sentiment Treebank (SST) (Socher et al., 2013). This concerns predicting movie review sentiment. Two datasets are derived from this corpus: (1) **SST-1**, containing

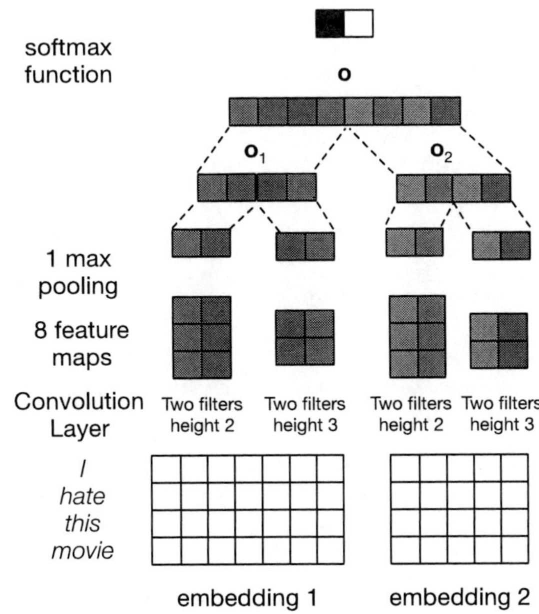

Figure 1: Illustration of MG-CNN and MGNC-CNN. The filters applied to the respective embeddings are completely independent. MG-CNN applies a max norm constraint to $\mathbf{o}$, while MGNC-CNN applies max norm constraints on $\mathbf{o}_1$ and $\mathbf{o}_2$ independently (group regularization). Note that one may easily extend the approach to handle more than two embeddings at once.

five classes: *very negative, negative, neutral, positive*, and *very positive*. (2) **SST-2**, which has only two classes: *negative* and *positive*. For both, we remove phrases of length less than 4 from the training set.[1] **Subj** (Pang and Lee, 2004). The aim here is to classify sentences as either *subjective* or *objective*. This comprises 5000 instances of each. **TREC** (Li and Roth, 2002). A question classification dataset containing six classes: *abbreviation, entity, description, human, location* and *numeric*. There are 5500 training and 500 test instances. **Irony** (Wallace et al., 2014). This dataset contains 16,006 sentences from reddit labeled as ironic (or not). The dataset is imbalanced (relatively few sentences are ironic). Thus before training, we under-sampled negative instances to make classes sizes equal. Note that for this dataset we report the Area Under Curve (AUC), rather than accuracy, because it is imbalanced.

---

[1] As in (Kim, 2014).

Model	Subj	SST-1	SST-2	TREC	Irony
CNN(w2v)	93.14 (92.92,93.39)	46.99 (46.11,48.28)	87.03 (86.16,88.08)	93.32 (92.40,94.60)	67.15 (66.53,68.11)
CNN(Glv)	93.41(93.20,93.51)	46.58 (46.11,47.06)	87.36 (87.20,87.64)	93.36 (93.30,93.60)	67.84 (67.29,68.38)
CNN(Syn)	93.24(93.01,93.45)	45.48(44.67,46.24)	86.04 (85.28,86.77)	94.68 (94.00,95.00)	67.93 (67.30,68.38)
MVCNN (Yin and Schütze, 2015)	93.9	49.6	89.4	-	-
C-CNN(w2v+Glv)	93.72 (93.68,93.76)	47.02(46.24,47.69)	87.42(86.88,87.81)	93.80 (93.40,94.20)	67.70 (66.97,68.35)
C-CNN(w2v+Syn)	93.48 (93.43,93.52)	46.91(45.97,47.81)	87.17 (86.55,87.42)	94.66 (94.00,95.20)	68.08 (67.33,68.57)
C-CNN(w2v+Syn+Glv)	93.61 (93.47,93.77)	46.52 (45.02,47.47)	87.55 (86.77,88.58)	95.20 (94.80,65.60)	68.38 (67.66,69.23)
MG-CNN(w2v+Glv)	93.84 (93.66,94.35)	48.24 (47.60,49.05)	87.90 (87.48,88.30)	94.09 (93.60,94.80)	69.40 (66.35,72.30)
MG-CNN(w2v+Syn)	93.78 (93.62,93.98)	48.48(47.78,49.19)	87.47(87.10,87.70)	94.87 (94.00,95.60)	68.28 (66.44,69.97)
MG-CNN(w2v+Syn+Glv)	**94.11 (94.04,94.17)**	48.01 (47.65,48.37)	87.63(87.04,88.36)	94.68 (93.80,95.40)	69.19(67.06,72.30)
MGNC-CNN(w2v+Glv)	93.93 (93.79,94.14)	48.53 (47.92,49.37)	**88.35(87.86,88.74)**	94.40 (94.00,94.80)	69.15 (67.25,71.70)
MGNC-CNN(w2v+Syn)	93.95 (93.75,94.21)	48.51 (47.60,49.41)	87.88(87.64,88.19)	95.12 (94.60,95.60)	69.35 (67.40,70.86)
MGNC-CNN(w2v+Syn+Glv)	94.09 (93.98,94.18)	**48.65 (46.92,49.19)**	88.30 (87.83,88.65)	**95.52 (94.60,96.60)**	**71.53 (69.74,73.06)**

Table 1: Results mean (min, max) achieved with each method. w2v:word2vec. Glv:GloVe. Syn: Syntactic embedding. Note that we experiment with using two and three sets of embeddings jointly, e.g., w2v+Syn+Glv indicates that we use all three of these.

Model	Subj	SST-1	SST-2	TREC	Irony
CNN(w2v)	9	81	81	9	243
CNN(Glv)	3	9	1	9	81
CNN(Syn)	3	81	9	81	1
C-CNN(w2v+Glv)	9	9	3	3	1
C-CNN(w2v+Syn)	3	81	9	9	1
C-CNN(w2v+Syn+Glv)	9	9	1	81	81
MG-CNN(w2v+Glv)	3	9	3	81	9
MG-CNN(w2v+Syn)	9	81	3	81	3
MG-CNN(w2v+Syn+Glv)	9	1	9	243	9
MGNC-CNN(w2v+Glv)	(9,3)	(81,9)	(1,1)	(9,81)	(243,243)
MGNC-CNN(w2v+Syn)	(3,3)	(81,81)	(81,9)	(81,81)	(81,3)
MGNC-CNN(w2v+Syn+Glv)	(81,81,81)	(81,81,1)	(9,9,9)	(1,81,81)	(243,243,3)

Table 2: Best λ^2 value on the validation set for each method w2v:word2vec. Glv:GloVe. Syn: Syntactic embedding.

4.2 Pre-trained Word Embeddings

We consider three sets of word embeddings for our experiments: (i) **word2vec**[2] is trained on 100 billion tokens of Google News dataset; (ii) **GloVe** (Pennington et al., 2014)[3] is trained on aggregated global word-word co-occurrence statistics from Common Crawl (840B tokens); and (iii) **syntactic** word embedding trained on dependency-parsed corpora. These three embedding sets happen to all be 300-dimensional, but our model could accommodate arbitrary and variable sizes.

We pre-trained our own syntactic embeddings following (Levy and Goldberg, 2014). We parsed the ukWaC corpus (Baroni et al., 2009) using the Stanford Dependency Parser v3.5.2 with Stanford Dependencies (Chen and Manning, 2014) and extracted (word, relation+context) pairs from parse trees. We "collapsed" nodes with prepositions and notated inverse relations separately, e.g., "dog barks" emits two tuples: *(barks, nsubj_dog)* and *(dog, nsubj^{-1}_barks)*. We filter words and contexts that appear fewer than 100 times, resulting in ~173k words and 1M contexts. We trained 300d vectors using word2vecf[4] with default parameters.

4.3 Setup

We compared our proposed approaches to a standard CNN that exploits a single set of word embeddings (Kim, 2014). We also compared to a baseline of simply concatenating embeddings for each word to form long vector inputs. We refer to this as Concatenation-CNN *C-CNN*. For all multiple embedding approaches (C-CNN, MG-CNN and MGNC-CNN), we explored two combined sets of embedding: word2vec+Glove, and word2vec+syntactic, and one three sets of embedding: word2vec+Glove+syntactic. For all models, we tuned the l2 norm constraint λ over the range $\{\frac{1}{3}, 1, 3, 9, 81, 243\}$ on a validation set. For instan-

[2]https://code.google.com/p/word2vec/
[3]http://nlp.stanford.edu/projects/glove/
[4]https://bitbucket.org/yoavgo/word2vecf/

tiations of MGNC-CNN in which we exploited two embeddings, we tuned both λ_1, and λ_2; where we used three embedding sets, we tuned λ_1, λ_2 and λ_3.

We used standard train/test splits for those datasets that had them. Otherwise, we performed 10-fold cross validation, creating nested development sets with which to tune hyperparameters. For all experiments we used filters sizes of 3, 4 and 5 and we created 100 feature maps for each filter size. We applied 1 max-pooling and dropout (rate: 0.5) at the classification layer. For training we used back-propagation in mini-batches and used AdaDelta as the stochastic gradient descent (SGD) update rule, and set mini-batch size as 50. In this work, we treat word embeddings as part of the parameters of the model, and update them as well during training. In all our experiments, we only tuned the max norm constraint(s), fixing all other hyperparameters.

4.4 Results and Discussion

We repeated each experiment 10 times and report the mean and ranges across these. This replication is important because training is stochastic and thus introduces variance in performance (Zhang and Wallace, 2015). Results are shown in Table 1, and the corresponding best norm constraint value is shown in Table 2. We also show results on *Subj*, *SST-1* and *SST-2* achieved by the more complex model of (Yin and Schütze, 2015) for comparison; this represents the state-of-the-art on the three datasets other than TREC.

We can see that **MGNC-CNN and MG-CNN always outperform baseline methods (including C-CNN), and MGNC-CNN is usually better than MG-CNN**. And on the *Subj* dataset, MG-CNN actually achieves slightly better results than (Yin and Schütze, 2015), with far less complexity and required training time (MGNC-CNN performs comparably, although no better, here). On the TREC dataset, the best-ever accuracy we are aware of is 96.0% (Mou et al., 2015), which falls within the range of the result of our MGNC-CNN model with three word embeddings. On the *irony* dataset, our model with three embeddings achieves 4% improvement (in terms of AUC) compared to the baseline model.

On *SST-1* and *SST-2*, our model performs slightly worse than (Yin and Schütze, 2015). However, we again note that their performance is achieved using a much more complex model which involves pre-training and mutual-learning steps. This model takes days to train, whereas our model requires on the order of an hour.

We note that the method proposed by Astudillo *et al.* (2015) is able to accommodate multiple embedding sets with different dimensions by projecting the original word embeddings into a lower-dimensional space. However, this work requires training the optimal projection matrix on laebled data first, which again incurs large overhead.

Of course, our model also has its own limitations: in MGNC-CNN, we need to tune the norm constraint hyperparameter for all the word embeddings. As the number of word embedding increases, this will increase the running time. However, this tuning procedure is embarrassingly parallel.

5 Conclusions

We have proposed MGNC-CNN: a simple, flexible CNN architecture for sentence classification that can exploit multiple, variable sized word embeddings. We demonstrated that this consistently achieves better results than a baseline architecture that exploits only a single set of word embeddings, and also a naive concatenation approach to capitalizing on multiple embeddings. Furthermore, our results are comparable to those achieved with a recently proposed model (Yin and Schütze, 2015) that is much more complex. However, our simple model is easy to implement and requires an order of magnitude less training time. Furthermore, our model is much more flexible than previous approaches, because it can accommodate variable-size word embeddings.

Acknowledgments

This work was supported in part by the Army Research Office (grant W911NF-14-1-0442) and by The Foundation for Science and Technology, Portugal (grant UTAP-EXPL/EEIESS/0031/2014). This work was also made possible by the support of the Texas Advanced Computer Center (TACC) at UT Austin.

References

Ramon F Astudillo, Silvio Amir, Wang Lin, Mário Silva, and Isabel Trancoso. 2015. Learning word representations from scarce and noisy data with embedding subspaces. In *Proceedings of Association for Computational Linguistics*, pages 1074–1084.

Marco Baroni, Silvia Bernardini, Adriano Ferraresi, and Eros Zanchetta. 2009. The wacky wide web: a collection of very large linguistically processed web-crawled corpora. *Language Resources and Evaluation*, 43(3):209–226.

Elia Bruni, Gemma Boleda, Marco Baroni, and Nam-Khanh Tran. 2012. Distributional semantics in technicolor. In *Proceedings of Association for Computational Linguistics*, pages 136–145.

Danqi Chen and Christopher Manning. 2014. A fast and accurate dependency parser using neural networks. In *Proceedings of Empirical Methods in Natural Language Processing*, pages 740–750.

Kyunghyun Cho. 2015. Natural language understanding with distributed representation. *arXiv preprint arXiv:1511.07916*.

Ronan Collobert and Jason Weston. 2008. A unified architecture for natural language processing: Deep neural networks with multitask learning. In *Proceedings of the International Conference on Machine learning*, pages 160–167.

Katrin Erk and Sebastian Padó. 2008. A structured vector space model for word meaning in context. In *Proceedings of Empirical Methods in Natural Language Processing*, pages 897–906.

Yoav Goldberg. 2015. A primer on neural network models for natural language processing. *arXiv preprint arXiv:1510.00726*.

Rie Johnson and Tong Zhang. 2014. Effective use of word order for text categorization with convolutional neural networks. *arXiv preprint arXiv:1412.1058*.

Nal Kalchbrenner, Edward Grefenstette, and Phil Blunsom. 2014. A convolutional neural network for modelling sentences. *arXiv preprint arXiv:1404.2188*.

Yoon Kim. 2014. Convolutional neural networks for sentence classification. *arXiv preprint arXiv:1408.5882*.

Omer Levy and Yoav Goldberg. 2014. Dependency-based word embeddings. In *Proceedings of Association for Computational Linguistics*, pages 302–308.

Xin Li and Dan Roth. 2002. Learning question classifiers. In *Proceedings of the International Conference on Computational Linguistics*, pages 1–7.

Yong Luo, Jian Tang, Jun Yan, Chao Xu, and Zheng Chen. 2014. Pre-trained multi-view word embedding using two-side neural network. In *Conference on Artificial Intelligence*.

Tomas Mikolov, Ilya Sutskever, Kai Chen, Greg S Corrado, and Jeff Dean. 2013. Distributed representations of words and phrases and their compositionality. In *Advances in Neural Information Processing Systems*, pages 3111–3119.

Lili Mou, Hao Peng, Ge Li, Yan Xu, Lu Zhang, and Zhi Jin. 2015. Discriminative neural sentence modeling by tree-based convolution. In *Proceedings of Empirical Methods in Natural Language Processing*, pages 2315–2325.

Sebastian Padó and Mirella Lapata. 2007. Dependency-based construction of semantic space models. *Computational Linguistics*, 33(2):161–199.

Bo Pang and Lillian Lee. 2004. A sentimental education: Sentiment analysis using subjectivity summarization based on minimum cuts. In *Proceedings of Association for Computational Linguistics*, page 271.

Jeffrey Pennington, Richard Socher, and Christopher D Manning. 2014. Glove: Global vectors for word representation. In *Proceedings of the Empirical Methods in Natural Language Processing*, pages 1532–1543.

Richard Socher, Alex Perelygin, Jean Y Wu, Jason Chuang, Christopher D Manning, Andrew Y Ng, and Christopher Potts. 2013. Recursive deep models for semantic compositionality over a sentiment treebank. In *Proceedings of Empirical Methods in Natural Language Processing*, pages 1631–1642.

Tim Van de Cruys, Thierry Poibeau, and Anna Korhonen. 2011. Latent vector weighting for word meaning in context. In *Proceedings of Empirical Methods in Natural Language Processing*, pages 1012–1022.

Byron C. Wallace, Do Kook Choe, Laura Kertz, and Eugene Charniak. 2014. Humans require context to infer ironic intent (so computers probably do, too). In *Proceedings of Association for Computational Linguistics*, pages 512–516.

Byron C. Wallace, Do Kook Choe, and Eugene Charniak. 2015. Sparse, contextually informed models for irony detection: Exploiting user communities, entities and sentiment. In *Proceedings of Association for Computational Linguistics*, pages 1035–1044.

Wenpeng Yin and Hinrich Schütze. 2015. Multichannel variable-size convolution for sentence classification. In *Proceedings of the Conference on Computational Natural Language Learning*, pages 204–214.

Dani Yogatama and Noah Smith. 2014. Making the most of bag of words: Sentence regularization with alternating direction method of multipliers. In *Proceedings of the International Conference on Machine Learning*, pages 656–664.

Ye Zhang and Byron C. Wallace. 2015. A sensitivity analysis of (and practitioners' guide to) convolutional neural networks for sentence classification. *arXiv preprint arXiv:1510.03820*.

Improving sentence compression by learning to predict gaze

Sigrid Klerke
University of Copenhagen
skl@hum.ku.dk

Yoav Goldberg
Bar-Ilan University
yoav.goldberg@gmail.com

Anders Søgaard
University of Copenhagen
soegaard@hum.ku.dk

Abstract

We show how eye-tracking corpora can be used to improve sentence compression models, presenting a novel multi-task learning algorithm based on multi-layer LSTMs. We obtain performance competitive with or better than state-of-the-art approaches.

1 Introduction

Sentence compression is a basic operation in text simplification which has the potential to improve statistical machine translation and automatic summarization (Berg-Kirkpatrick et al., 2011; Klerke et al., 2015), as well as helping poor readers in need of assistive technologies (Canning et al., 2000). This work suggests using eye-tracking recordings for improving sentence compression for text simplification systems and is motivated by two observations: (i) *Sentence compression is the task of automatically making sentences easier to process by shortening them.* (ii) *Eye-tracking measures* such as first-pass reading time and time spent on regressions, i.e., during second and later passes over the text, *are known to correlate with perceived text difficulty* (Rayner et al., 2012).

These two observations recently lead Klerke et al. (2015) to suggest using eye-tracking measures as metrics in text simplification. We go beyond this by suggesting that eye-tracking recordings can be used to induce better models for sentence compression for text simplification. Specifically, we show how to use existing eye-tracking recordings to improve the induction of Long Short-Term Memory models (LSTMs) for sentence compression.

Our proposed model *does not require* that the gaze data and the compression data come from the same source. Indeed, in this work we use gaze data from readers of the Dundee Corpus to improve sentence compression results on several datasets. While not explored here, an intriguing potential of this work is in deriving sentence simplification models that are personalized for individual users, based on their reading behavior.

Several approaches to sentence compression have been proposed, from noisy channel models (Knight and Marcu, 2002) over conditional random fields (Elming et al., 2013) to tree-to-tree machine translation models (Woodsend and Lapata, 2011). More recently, Filippova et al. (2015) successfully used LSTMs for sentence compression on a large scale parallel dataset. We do not review the literature here, and only compare to Filippova et al. (2015).

Our contributions

- We present a novel multi-task learning approach to sentence compression using labelled data for sentence compression and a disjoint eye-tracking corpus.

- Our method is fully competitive with state-of-the-art across three corpora.

- Our code is made publicly available at `https://bitbucket.org/soegaard/gaze-mtl16`.

2 Gaze during reading

Readers fixate longer at rare words, words that are semantically ambiguous, and words that are mor-

Proceedings of NAACL-HLT 2016, pages 1528–1533,
San Diego, California, June 12-17, 2016. ©2016 Association for Computational Linguistics

phologically complex (Rayner et al., 2012). These are also words that are likely to be replaced with simpler ones in sentence simplification, but it is not clear that they are words that would necessarily be removed in the context of sentence compression.

Demberg and Keller (2008) show that syntactic complexity (measured as dependency locality) is also an important predictor of reading time. Phrases that are often removed in sentence compression—like fronted phrases, parentheticals, floating quantifiers, etc.—are often associated with non-local dependencies. Also, there is evidence that people are more likely to fixate on the first word in a constituent than on its second word (Hyönä and Pollatsek, 2000). Being able to identify constituent borders is important for sentence compression, and reading fixation data may help our model learn a representation of our data that makes it easy to identify constituent boundaries.

In the experiments below, we learn models to predict the first pass duration of word fixations and the total duration of regressions to a word. These two measures constitute a perfect separation of the total reading time of each word split between the first pass and subsequent passes. Both measures are described below. They are both discretized into six bins as follows with only non-zero values contributing to the calculation of the standard deviation (SD):

0: measure = 0 or
1: measure < 1 SD below reader's average or
2: measure < .5 SD below reader's average or
3: measure < .5 above reader's average or
4: measure > .5 SD above reader's average or
5: measure > 1 SD above reader's average

First pass duration measures the total time spent reading a word first time it is fixated, including any immediately following re-fixations of the same word. This measure correlates with word length, frequency and ambiguity because long words are likely to attract several fixations in a row unless they are particularly easily predicted or recognized. This effect arises because long words are less likely to fit inside the fovea of the eye. Note that for this measure the value 0 indicates that the word was not fixated by this reader.

Words	First Pass	Regressions
Are	4	4
tourists	2	0
enticed	3	0
by	4	0
these	2	0
attractions	3	0
threatening	3	3
their	5	0
very	3	3
existence	3	5
?	3	5

Figure 1: Example sentence from the Dundee Corpus

Regression duration measures the total time spent fixating a word after the gaze has already left it once. This measure belongs to the group of late measures, i.e., measures that are sensitive to the later cognitive processing stages including interpretation and integration of already decoded words. Since the reader by definition has already had a chance to recognize the word, regressions are associated with semantic confusion and contradiction, incongruence and syntactic complexity, as famously experienced in garden path sentences. For this measure the value 0 indicates that the word was read at most once by this reader.

See Table 1 for an example of first pass duration and regression duration annotations for one reader and sentence.

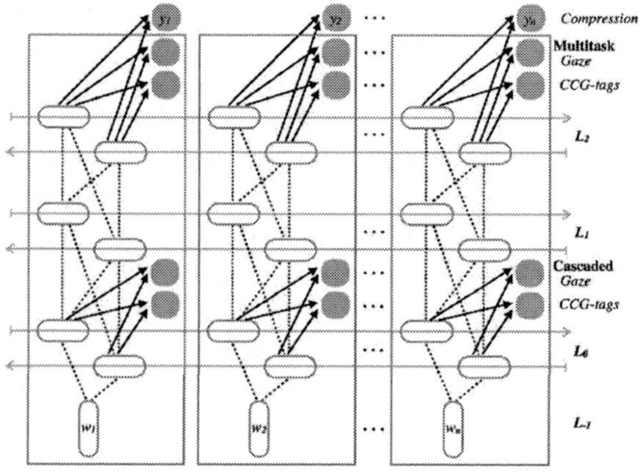

Figure 2: Multitask and cascaded bi-LSTMs for sentence compression. Layer L_{-1} contain pre-trained embeddings. Gaze prediction and CCG-tag prediction are auxiliary training tasks, and loss on all tasks are propagated back to layer L_0.

3 Sentence compression using multi-task deep bi-LSTMs

Most recent approaches to sentence compression make use of syntactic analysis, either by operating directly on trees (Riezler et al., 2003; Nomoto, 2007; Filippova and Strube, 2008; Cohn and Lapata, 2008; Cohn and Lapata, 2009) or by incorporating syntactic information in their model (McDonald, 2006; Clarke and Lapata, 2008). Recently, however, Filippova et al. (2015) presented an approach to sentence compression using LSTMs with word embeddings, but without syntactic features. We introduce a third way of using syntactic annotation by jointly learning a sequence model for predicting CCG supertags, in addition to our gaze and compression models.

Bi-directional recurrent neural networks (bi-RNNs) read in sequences in both regular and reversed order, enabling conditioning predictions on both left and right context. In the forward pass, we run the input data through an embedding layer and compute the predictions of the forward and backward states at layers $0, 1, \ldots$, until we compute the softmax predictions for word i based on a linear transformation of the concatenation of the of standard and reverse RNN outputs for location i. We then calculate the objective function derivative for the sequence using cross-entropy (logistic loss) and use backpropagation to calculate gradients and update the weights accordingly. A deep bi-RNN or k-layered bi-RNN is composed of k bi-RNNs that feed into each other such that the output of the ith RNN is the input of the $i + 1$th RNN. LSTMs (Hochreiter and Schmidhuber, 1997) replace the cells of RNNs with LSTM cells, in which multiplicative gate units learn to open and close access to the error signal.

Bi-LSTMs have already been used for fine-grained sentiment analysis (Liu et al., 2015), syntactic chunking (Huang et al., 2015), and semantic role labeling (Zhou and Xu, 2015). These and other recent applications of bi-LSTMs were constructed for solving a single task in isolation, however. We instead train deep bi-LSTMs to solve additional tasks to sentence compression, namely CCG-tagging and gaze prediction, using the additional tasks to regularize our sentence compression model.

Specifically, we use bi-LSTMs with three layers. Our baseline model is simply this three-layered model trained to predict compressions (encoded as label sequences), and we consider two extensions thereof as illustrated in Figure 2. Our first extension, MULTI-TASK-LSTM, includes the gaze prediction task during training, with a separate logistic regression classifier for this purpose; and the other, CASCADED-LSTM, predicts gaze measures from the inner layer. Our second extension, which is superior to our first, is basically a one-layer bi-LSTM for predicting reading fixations with a two-layer bi-LSTM on top for predicting sentence compressions.

At each step in the training process of MULTI-TASK-LSTMand CASCADED-LSTM, we choose a random task, followed by a random training instance of this task. We use the deep LSTM to predict a label sequence, suffer a loss with respect to the true labels, and update the model parameters. In CASCADED-LSTM, the update for an instance of CCG super tagging or gaze prediction only affects the parameters of the inner LSTM layer.

Both MULTI-TASK-LSTM and CASCADED-LSTM do multi-task learning (Caruana, 1993). In multi-task learning, the induction of a model for one task is used as a regularizer on the induction of a model for another task. Caruana (1993) did multi-task learning by doing parameter sharing across several deep networks, letting them share hidden layers; a technique also used by Collobert et al. (2011) for various NLP tasks. These models train task-specific classifiers on the output of deep networks (informed by the task-specific losses). We extend their models by moving to sequence prediction and allowing the task-specific sequence models to also be deep models.

4 Experiments

4.1 Gaze data

We use the Dundee Corpus (Kennedy et al., 2003) as our eye-tracking corpus with tokenization and measures similar to the Dundee Treebank (Barrett et al., 2015). The corpus contains eye-tracking recordings of ten native English-speaking subjects reading 20 newspaper articles from *The Independent*. We use data from nine subjects for training and one subject for development. We do not evaluate the gaze prediction because the task is only included as a way of regularizing the compression model.

S:	Regulators Friday shut down a small Florida bank, bringing to 119 the number of US bank failures this year amid mounting loan defaults.
T:	Regulators shut down a small Florida bank
S:	Intel would be building car batteries, expanding its business beyond its core strength, the company said in a statement.
T:	Intel would be building car batteries

Table 1: Example compressions from the GOOGLE dataset. S is the source sentence, and T is the target compression.

	Sents	Sent.len	Type/token	Del.rate
TRAINING				
ZIFF-DAVIS	1000	20	0.22	0.59
BROADCAST	880	20	0.21	0.27
GOOGLE	8000	24	0.17	0.87
TEST				
ZIFF-DAVIS	32	21	0.55	0.47
BROADCAST	412	19	0.27	0.29
GOOGLE	1000	25	0.42	0.87

Table 2: Dataset characteristics. Sentence length is for source sentences.

4.2 Compression data

We use three different sentence compression datasets, ZIFF-DAVIS (Knight and Marcu, 2002), BROADCAST (Clarke and Lapata, 2006), and the publically available subset of GOOGLE (Filippova et al., 2015). The first two consist of manually compressed newswire text in English, while the third is built heuristically from pairs of headlines and first sentences from newswire, resulting in the most aggressive compressions, as exemplified in Table 1. We present the dataset characteristics in Table 2. We use the datasets as released by the authors and do not apply any additional pre-processing. The CCG supertagging data comes from CCGbank,[1] and we use sections 0-18 for training and section 19 for development.

4.3 Baselines and system

Both the baseline and our systems are three-layer bi-LSTM models trained for 30 iterations with pre-trained (SENNA) embeddings. The input and hidden layers are 50 dimensions, and at the output layer we predict sequences of two labels, indicating whether to delete the labeled word or not. Our baseline (BASELINE-LSTM) is a multi-task learning

bi-LSTM predicting both CCG supertags and sentence compression (word deletion) at the outer layer. Our first extension is MULTITASK-LSTM predicting CCG supertags, sentence compression, and reading measures from the outer layer. CASCADED-LSTM, on the other hand, predicts CCG supertags and reading measures from the initial layer, and sentence compression at the outer layer.

4.4 Results and discussion

Our results are presented in Table 3. We observe that across all three datasets, including all three annotations of BROADCAST, gaze features lead to improvements over our baseline 3-layer bi-LSTM. Also, CASCADED-LSTM is consistently better than MULTITASK-LSTM. Our models are fully competitive with state-of-the-art models. For example, the best model in Elming et al. (2013) achieves 0.7207 on ZIFF-DAVIS, Clarke and Lapata (2008) achieves 0.7509 on BROADCAST,[2] and the LSTM model in Filippova et al. (2015) achieves 0.80 on GOOGLE with much more training data. The high numbers on the small subset of GOOGLE reflects that newswire headlines tend to have a fairly predictable relation to

---

[1] http://groups.inf.ed.ac.uk/ccg/

[2] On a "randomly selected" annotator; unfortunately, they do not say which. James Clarke (p.c) does not remember which annotator they used.

LSTM	Gaze	ZIFF-DAVIS	BROADCAST			GOOGLE
Baseline		0.5668	0.7386	0.7980	0.6802	0.7980
Multitask	FP	0.6416	0.7413	0.8050	0.6878	0.8028
	REGR.	0.7025	0.7368	0.7979	0.6708	0.8016
Cascaded	FP	0.6732	**0.7519**	0.8189	**0.7012**	**0.8097**
	REGR.	**0.7418**	0.7477	**0.8217**	0.6944	0.8048

Table 3: Results (F_1). For all three datasets, the inclusion of gaze measures (first pass duration (FP) and regression duration (Regr.)) leads to improvements over the baseline. All models include CCG-supertagging as an auxiliary task. Note that BROADCASTwas annotated by three annotators. The three columns are, from left to right, results on annotators 1–3.

the first sentence. With the harder datasets, the impact of the gaze information becomes stronger, consistently favouring the cascaded architecture, and with improvements using both first pass duration and regression duration, the late measure associated with interpretation of content. Our results indicate that multi-task learning can help us take advantage of inherently noisy human processing data across tasks and thereby maybe reduce the need for task-specific data collection.

Acknowledgments

Yoav Goldberg was supported by the Israeli Science Foundation Grant No. 1555/15. Anders Søgaard was supported by ERC Starting Grant No. 313695. Thanks to Joachim Bingel and Maria Barrett for preparing data and for helpful discussions, and to the anonymous reviewers for their suggestions for improving the paper.

References

Maria Barrett, Željko Agić, and Anders Søgaard. 2015. The dundee treebank. In *The 14th International Workshop on Treebanks and Linguistic Theories (TLT 14)*.

Taylor Berg-Kirkpatrick, Dan Gillick, and Dan Klein. 2011. Jointly learning to extract and compress. In *Proceedings of ACL*.

Y. Canning, J. Tait, J. Archibald, and R. Crawley. 2000. *Cohesive generation of syntactically simplified newspaper text*. Springer.

Rich Caruana. 1993. Multitask learning: a knowledge-based source of inductive bias. In *ICML*.

James Clarke and Mirella Lapata. 2006. Constraint-based sentence compression an integer programming approach. In *COLING*.

James Clarke and Mirella Lapata. 2008. Global inference for sentence compression: An integer linear programming approach. *Journal of Artificial Intelligence Research*, pages 399–429.

Trevor Cohn and Mirella Lapata. 2008. Sentence compression beyond word deletion. In *COLING*.

Trevor Cohn and Mirella Lapata. 2009. Sentence compression as tree transduction. *Journal of Artificial Intelligence Research*, pages 637–674.

Ronan Collobert, Jason Weston, Léon Bottou, Michael Karlen, Koray Kavukcuoglu, and Pavel Kuksa. 2011. Natural language processing (almost) from scratch. *The Journal of Machine Learning Research*, 12:2493–2537.

Vera Demberg and Frank Keller. 2008. Data from eye-tracking corpora as evidence for theories of syntactic processing complexity. *Cognition*, 109:193–210.

Jakob Elming, Anders Johannsen, Sigrid Klerke, Emanuele Lapponi, Héctor Martínez Alonso, and Anders Søgaard. 2013. Down-stream effects of tree-to-dependency conversions. In *NAACL*.

Katja Filippova and Michael Strube. 2008. Dependency tree based sentence compression. In *Proceedings of the Fifth International Natural Language Generation Conference*.

Katja Filippova, Enrique Alfonseca, Carlos A Colmenares, Lukasz Kaiser, and Oriol Vinyals. 2015. Sentence compression by deletion with LSTMs. In *EMNLP*.

Sepp Hochreiter and Jürgen Schmidhuber. 1997. Long short-term memory. *Neural computation*, 9(8):1735–1780.

Zhiheng Huang, Wei Xu, and Kai Yu. 2015. Bidirectional LSTM-CRF models for sequence tagging. *arXiv preprint arXiv:1508.01991*.

Jukka Hyönä and Alexander Pollatsek. 2000. Processing of finnish compound words in reading. *Reading as a perceptual process*, pages 65–87.

Alan Kennedy, Robin Hill, and Joël Pynte. 2003. The dundee corpus. In *ECEM*.

Sigrid Klerke, Sheila Castilho, Maria Barrett, and Anders
Søgaard. 2015. Reading metrics for estimating task
efficiency with mt output. In *EMNLP Workshop on
Cognitive Aspects of Computational Language Learning*.

Kevin Knight and Daniel Marcu. 2002. Summarization beyond sentence extraction: a probabilistic approach to sentence compression. *Artificial Intelligence*, 139:91–107.

Pengfei Liu, Shafiq Joty, and Helen Meng. 2015. Fine-
grained opinion mining with recurrent neural networks
and word embeddings. In *EMNLP*.

Ryan T McDonald. 2006. Discriminative sentence compression with soft syntactic evidence. In *EACL*.

Tadashi Nomoto. 2007. Discriminative sentence compression with conditional random fields. *Information
Processing and Management: an International Journal*, 43(6):1571–1587.

Keith Rayner, Alexander Pollatsek, Jane Ashby, and
Charles Clifton Jr. 2012. *Psychology of reading*. Psychology Press.

Stefan Riezler, Tracy H King, Richard Crouch, and Annie
Zaenen. 2003. Statistical sentence condensation using ambiguity packing and stochastic disambiguation
methods for lexical-functional grammar. In *NAACL*.

Kristian Woodsend and Mirella Lapata. 2011. Learning
to simplify sentences with quasi-synchronous grammar and integer programming. In *EMNLP*.

Jie Zhou and Wei Xu. 2015. End-to-end learning of semantic role labeling using recurrent neural networks.
ACL.

Feuding Families and Former Friends:
Unsupervised Learning for Dynamic Fictional Relationships

Mohit Iyyer,[1] **Anupam Guha,**[1] **Snigdha Chaturvedi,**[1] **Jordan Boyd-Graber,**[2] **Hal Daumé III**[1]
[1]University of Maryland, Department of Computer Science and UMIACS
[2]University of Colorado, Department of Computer Science
{miyyer,aguha,snigdac,hal}@umiacs.umd.edu,
Jordan.Boyd.Graber@colorado.edu

Abstract

Understanding how a fictional relationship between two characters changes over time (e.g., from best friends to sworn enemies) is a key challenge in digital humanities scholarship. We present a novel unsupervised neural network for this task that incorporates dictionary learning to generate interpretable, accurate relationship trajectories. While previous work on characterizing literary relationships relies on plot summaries annotated with predefined labels, our model jointly learns a set of global relationship descriptors as well as a trajectory over these descriptors for each relationship in a dataset of raw text from novels. We find that our model learns descriptors of events (e.g., marriage or murder) as well as interpersonal states (love, sadness). Our model outperforms topic model baselines on two crowdsourced tasks, and we also find interesting correlations to annotations in an existing dataset.

1 Describing Character Relationships

When two characters in a book break bread, is their meal just a result of biological needs or does it mean more? Cognard-Black et al. (2014) argue that this simple interaction reflects the diversity and background of the characters, while Foster (2009) suggests that the tone of a meal can portend either good or ill for the rest of the book. To support such theories, scholars use their literary expertise to draw connections between disparate books: Gabriel Conroy's dissonance from his family at a sumptuous feast in Joyce's *The Dead*, the frustration of Tyler's mother in *Dinner at the Homesick Restaurant*, and the grudging

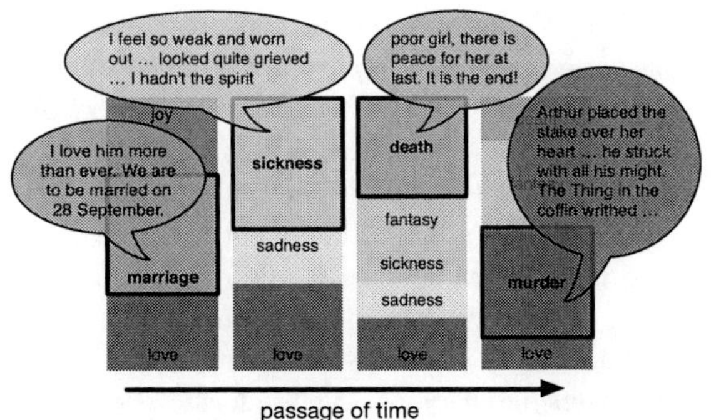

Figure 1: An example trajectory depicting the dynamic relationship between Lucy and Arthur in Bram Stoker's *Dracula*, which starts with love and ends with Arthur killing the vampiric Lucy. Each column describes the relationship state at a particular time by weights over a set of descriptors (larger weights shown as bigger boxes). Our goal is to learn—without supervision—both the descriptors and the trajectories from raw fictional texts.

respect for a blind man eating meatloaf in Carver's *Cathedral*.

However, these insights do not come cheap. It takes years of careful reading and internalization to make connections across books, which means that relationship symmetries and archetypes are likely to remain hidden in the millions of books published every year unless literary scholars are actively searching for them.

Natural language processing techniques have been increasingly used to assist in these literary investigations by discovering patterns in texts (Jockers, 2013). In Section 6 we review existing techniques that classify or cluster relationships between characters in books using a fixed set of labels (e.g., friend or en-

Proceedings of NAACL-HLT 2016, pages 1534–1544,
San Diego, California, June 12-17, 2016. ©2016 Association for Computational Linguistics

emy). However, such approaches ignore interactions between characters that lie outside of the established lexicon and cannot account for the dynamic nature of relationships that evolve through the course of a book, such as the vampiric downfall of Lucy and Arthur's engagement in *Dracula* (Figure 1) or Winston Smith's rat-induced betrayal of Julia in *1984*.

To address these issues, we propose the task of unsupervised relationship modeling, in which a model jointly learns a set of *relationship descriptors* as well as *relationship trajectories* for pairs of literary characters. Instead of assigning a single descriptor to a particular relationship, the trajectories learned by the model are sequences of descriptors as in Figure 1.

The Bayesian *hidden topic Markov model* (HTMM) of Gruber et al. (2007) emerges as a natural choice for our task because it is capable of computing relationship descriptors (in the form of topics) and has an additional temporal component. However, our experiments show that the descriptors learned by the HTMM are not coherent and focus more on events or environments (e.g., meals, outdoors) than interpersonal states like happiness and sadness.

Motivated by recent advances in deep learning, we propose the *relationship modeling network* (RMN), which is a novel variant of a deep recurrent autoencoder that incorporates dictionary learning to learn relationship descriptors. We show that the RMN achieves better descriptor coherence and trajectory accuracy than the HTMM and other topic model baselines in two crowdsourced evaluations described in Section 4. In Section 5 we show qualitative results and make connections to existing literary scholarship.

2　A Dataset of Character Interactions

Our dataset consists of 1,383 fictional works pulled from Project Gutenberg and other Internet sources. Project Gutenberg has a limited selection (outside of science fiction) of mostly classic literature, so we add more contemporary novels from various genres such as mystery, romance, and fantasy to our dataset.

To identify character mentions, we run the Book-NLP pipeline of Bamman et al. (2014), which includes character name clustering, quoted speaker identification, and coreference resolution.[1] For ev-

ery detected character mention, we define a span as beginning 100 tokens before the mention and ending 100 tokens after the mention. We do not use sentence or paragraph boundaries because they vary considerably depending on the author (e.g., William Faulkner routinely wrote single sentences longer than many of Hemingway's paragraphs). All spans in our dataset contain mentions to exactly two characters. This is a rather strict requirement that forces a reduction in data size, but spans in which more than two characters are mentioned are generally noisier.

Once we have identified usable spans in the dataset, we apply a second filtering step that removes relationships containing fewer than five spans. Without this filter, our dataset is dominated by fleeting interactions between minor characters; this is undesirable since our focus is on longer, mutable relationships. Finally, we filter our vocabulary by removing the 500 most frequently occurring words, as well as all words that occur in fewer than 100 books. The latter step helps correct for variation in time period and genre (e.g., "thou" and "thy" found in older works like the *Canterbury Tales*). Our final dataset contains 20,013 relationships and 380,408 spans, while our vocabulary contains 16,223 words.[2]

3　Relationship Modeling Networks

This section mathematically describes how we apply the RMN to relationship modeling on our dataset. Our model is similar in spirit to topic models: for an input dataset, the output of the RMN is a set of relationship descriptors (topics) and—for each relationship in the dataset—a trajectory, or a sequence of probability distributions over these descriptors (document-topic assignments). However, the RMN uses recent advances in deep learning to achieve better control over descriptor coherence and trajectory smoothness (Section 4).

3.1　Formalizing the Problem

Assume we have two characters c_1 and c_2 in book b. We define S_{c_1,c_2} as a sequence of token spans where each span $s_t \in S_{c_1,c_2}$ is itself a set of tokens

---

to character name clustering, which are further expanded upon in Vala et al. (2015), for future work.

[1]While this pipeline works reasonably well, it is unreliable for first-person narratives; we leave the necessary improvements

[2]Code and span data available at `http://github.com/miyyer/rmn`.

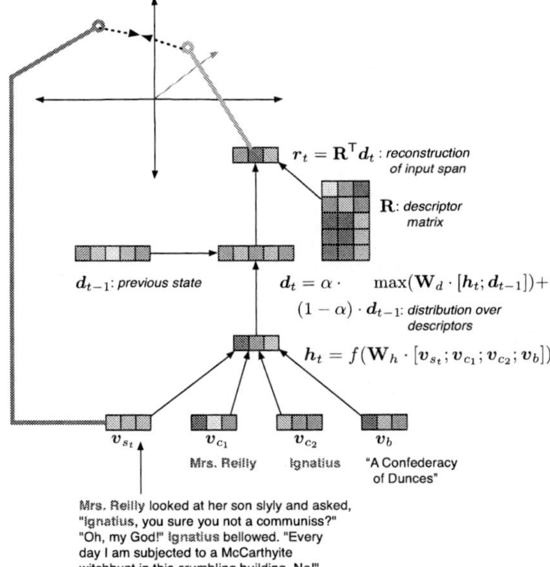

Figure 2: An example of the RMN's computations at a single time step. The model approximates the vector average of an input span (v_{s_t}) as a linear combination of descriptors from $\mathbf{R}$. The descriptor weights d_t define the relationship state at each time step and—when viewed as a sequence—form a relationship trajectory.

$\{w_1, w_2, \ldots, w_l\}$ of fixed size l that contains mentions (either directly or by coreference) to both c_1 and c_2. In other words, S_{c_1,c_2} includes the text of every scene, chronologically ordered, in which c_1 and c_2 are present together.

3.2 Model Description

As in other neural network models for natural language processing, we begin by associating each word type w in our vocabulary with a real-valued embedding $v_w \in \mathbb{R}^d$. These embeddings are rows of a $V \times d$ matrix $\mathbf{L}$, where V is the vocabulary size. Similarly, characters and books have their own embeddings in rows of matrices $\mathbf{C}$ and $\mathbf{B}$. We want $\mathbf{B}$ to capture global context information (e.g., "Moby Dick" takes place at sea) and $\mathbf{C}$ to capture immutable aspects of characters not related to their relationships (e.g., Javert is a police officer). Finally, the RMN learns embeddings for relationship descriptors, which requires a second matrix $\mathbf{R}$ of size $K \times d$ where K is the number of descriptors, analogous to the number of topics in topic models.

Each input to the RMN is a tuple that contains identifiers for a book and two characters, as well as the spans corresponding to their relationship: $(b, c_1, c_2, S_{c_1,c_2})$. Given one such input, our objective is to reconstruct S_{c_1,c_2} using a linear combination of relationship descriptors from $\mathbf{R}$ as shown in Figure 2; we now describe this process formally.

3.2.1 Modeling Spans with Vector Averages

We compute a vector representation for each span s_t in S_{c_1,c_2} by averaging the embeddings of the words in that span,

$$v_{s_t} = \frac{1}{l} \sum_{w \in s_t} v_w. \tag{1}$$

Then, we concatenate v_{s_t} with the character embeddings v_{c_1} and v_{c_2} as well as the book embedding v_b and feed the resulting vector into a standard feedforward layer to obtain a hidden state h_t,

$$h_t = f(\mathbf{W}_h \cdot [v_{s_t}; v_{c_1}; v_{c_2}; v_b]). \tag{2}$$

In all experiments, the transformation matrix W_h is $d \times 4d$, and we set f to the ReLu function, $\text{ReLu}(x) = \max(0, x)$.

3.2.2 Approximating Spans with Relationship Descriptors

Now that we can obtain representations of spans, we move on to learning descriptors using a variant of dictionary learning (Olshausen and Field, 1997; Elad and Aharon, 2006), where our descriptor matrix $\mathbf{R}$ is the dictionary and we are trying to approximate input spans as a linear combination of items from this dictionary.

Suppose we compute a hidden state for every span s_t in S_{c_1,c_2} (Equation 2). Now, given an h_t, we compute a weight vector d_t over K relationship descriptors with some composition function g, which is fully specified in the next section. Conceptually, each d_t is a *relationship state*, and a *relationship trajectory* is a sequence of chronologically-ordered relationship states as shown in Figure 1. After computing d_t, we use it to compute a reconstruction vector r_t by taking a weighted average over relationship descriptors,

$$r_t = \mathbf{R}^\top d_t. \tag{3}$$

Our goal is to make r_t similar to v_{s_t}. We use a contrastive max-margin objective function similar to previous work (Weston et al., 2011; Socher et al., 2014). We randomly sample spans from our dataset and compute the vector average v_{s_n} for each sampled span as in Equation 1. This subset of span vectors is N. The unregularized objective J is a hinge loss that minimizes the inner product between r_t and the negative samples while simultaneously maximizing the inner product between r_t and v_{s_t},

$$J(\theta) = \sum_{t=0}^{|S_{c_1,c_2}|} \sum_{n \in N} \max(0, 1 - r_t v_{s_t} + r_t v_{s_n}), \quad (4)$$

where θ represents the model parameters.

3.2.3 Computing Weights over Descriptors

What function should we choose for our composition function g to represent a relationship state at a given time step? On the face of it, this seems trivial; we can project h_t to K dimensions and then apply a softmax or some other nonlinearity that yields non-negative weights.[3] However, this method ignores the relationship states at previous time steps. To model the temporal aspect of relationships, we can add a recurrent connection,

$$d_t = \text{softmax}(\mathbf{W}_d \cdot [h_t; d_{t-1}]) \quad (5)$$

where $\mathbf{W}_d$ is of size $K \times (d + K)$ and $\text{softmax}(q) = \exp q / \sum_{j=1}^k \exp q_j$.

Our hope is that this recurrent connection will carry some of the previous relationship state over to the current time step. It should be unlikely for two characters in love at time t to fall out of love at time $t + 1$ even if s_{t+1} does not include any love-related words. However, because the objective function in Equation 4 maximizes similarity with the current time step's input, the model is not forced to learn a smooth interpolation between the previous state and the current one. A natural remedy is to have the model predict the *next* time step's input instead, but this proves hard to optimize.

We instead *force* the model to use the previous relationship state by modifying Equation 5 to include a linear interpolation between d_t and d_{t-1},

$$d_t = \alpha \cdot \text{softmax}(\mathbf{W}_d \cdot [h_t; d_{t-1}]) + \quad (6)$$
$$(1 - \alpha) \cdot d_{t-1}.$$

---

[3]We experiment with a variety of nonlinearities but find that the softmax yields the most interpretable results due to its predisposition to select a single descriptor.

Here, α is a scalar between 0 and 1. We experiment with setting α to a fixed value of 0.5 as well as allowing the model to learn α as in

$$\alpha = \sigma(v_\alpha^\mathsf{T} \cdot [h_t; d_{t-1}; v_{s_t}]), \quad (7)$$

where σ is the sigmoid function and v_α is a vector of dimensionality $2d + K$. Fixing $\alpha = 0.5$ initially and then tuning it after other parameters have converged improves training stability; for the specific hyperparameters we use see Section 4.[4]

3.2.4 Interpreting Descriptors and Enforcing Uniqueness

Recall that each descriptor is a d-dimensional row of $\mathbf{R}$. Because our objective function J forces these descriptors to be in the same vector space as that of the word embeddings $\mathbf{L}$, we can interpret them by looking at nearest neighbors in $\mathbf{L}$ using cosine distance as the similarity metric.

To discourage learning descriptors that are too similar to each other, we add another penalty term X to our objective function,

$$X(\theta) = \left\| \mathbf{R}\mathbf{R}^\mathsf{T} - \mathbf{I} \right\|, \quad (8)$$

where $\mathbf{I}$ is the identity matrix. This term comes from the component orthogonality constraint in independent component analysis (Hyvärinen and Oja, 2000).

We add J and X together to obtain our final training objective L,

$$L(\theta) = J(\theta) + \lambda X(\theta), \quad (9)$$

where λ is a hyperparameter that controls the magnitude of the uniqueness penalty.

4 Evaluating Descriptors and Trajectories

Because no previous work explores the interpretability of unsupervised relationship modeling over time, evaluating the RMN is tricky. Further compounding the problem is the subjective nature of the task; for example, is a trajectory that ignores a key event better than one that hallucinates episodes absent from source text?

---

[4]This strategy is reminiscent of alternative minimization strategies for dictionary learning (Agarwal et al., 2014), where the dictionary and weights are learned separately by keeping the other fixed.

With these issues in mind, we conduct three evaluations to show that our output is reasonable. First, we conduct a crowdsourced interpretability experiment that shows RMNs produce significantly more coherent descriptors than three topic model baselines. A second crowdsourced task indicates that our model produces trajectories that match plot summaries more accurately than topic models. Finally, we qualitatively compare the RMN's output to existing static annotations of literary relationships and find both expected and surprising results.

4.1 Topic Model Baselines

Before moving onto the evaluations, we briefly describe three baseline models, all of which are Bayesian generative models. Latent Dirichlet allocation (Blei et al., 2003, LDA) learns a single document-topic distribution per document; we can apply LDA to our dataset by concatenating all spans from a relationship into a single document. Similarly, NUBBI (Chang et al., 2009a) learns separate sets of topics for relationships and individual characters.[5]

LDA and NUBBI are incapable of taking into account the chronological ordering of the spans because they view all relationships tokens as exchangeable. While we can compare the *descriptors* learned by these models to those of the RMN, we cannot evaluate their *trajectories*. We turn instead to the hidden topic Markov model (Gruber et al., 2007, HTMM), which foregoes the bag-of-words assumption of LDA and NUBBI in favor of modeling topic segments within a document as a Markov chain. This model outputs a smooth sequence of topic assignments over a document, so we can compare the *trajectories* it learns on our dataset to those of the RMN.

4.2 Experimental Settings

In our descriptor interpretability experiments, we vary the number of descriptors (topics) for all models ($K = 10, 30, 50$). We train LDA and NUBBI for 100 iterations with a collapsed Gibbs sampler, and the HTMM uses the default setting of 100 EM iterations.

For the RMN, we initialize the word embedding matrix $\mathbf{L}$ with 300-dimensional GloVe embeddings trained on the Common Crawl (Pennington et al.,

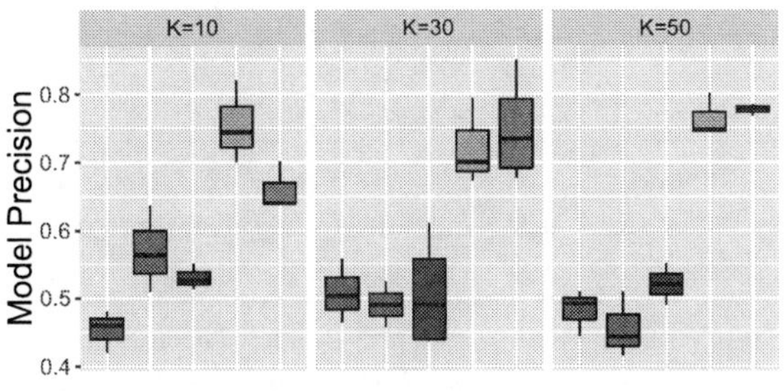

Figure 3: Model precision results from our word intrusion task. The RMN learns more interpretable descriptors than three topic model baselines.

2014). The character and book embeddings ($\mathbf{C}$ and $\mathbf{B}$) are initialized randomly. We fix α to 0.5 for the first 15 epochs of training; after the descriptor matrix $\mathbf{R}$ has converged, we fix $\mathbf{R}$ and tune α using Equation 6 for 15 more epochs.[6] Since the topic model baselines do not have access to character and book metadata, for fair comparison we also train a "generic" version of the RMN (GRMN) where the metadata embeddings are removed from Equation 2. The uniqueness penalty λ is set to 10^{-4}.

All of the RMN model parameters except $\mathbf{L}$ are optimized using Adam (Kingma and Ba, 2014) with a learning rate of 0.001 for 30 epochs; the word embeddings are not fine-tuned during training.[7] We also apply word dropout (Iyyer et al., 2015) to the input spans, removing words from the vector average computation in Equation 1 with probability 0.5.

4.3 Do Descriptors Make Sense?

The goal of our first experiment is to compare the descriptors $\mathbf{R}$ learned by the RMN to the topics learned by the topic model baselines. We conduct a word intrusion experiment (Chang et al., 2009b): workers identify an "intruder" word from a set of words that— other than the intruder—come from the same topic. For the topic models, the five most probable words are joined by a highly-probable word from a different topic as the intruder. We use the same procedure for the RMN and GRMN, except that cosine similarity to

---

[5]NUBBI requires additional spans that mention only a single character to differentiate character topics from relationship topics. None of the other models receives these extra data.

[6]Preliminary experiments show that learning α and $\mathbf{R}$ simultaneously results in less interpretable descriptors.

[7]Tuning $\mathbf{L}$ ruins descriptor interpretability; pretrained embeddings are likely already a good solution for our problem.

RMN			HTMM		
Label	**MP**	**Nearest Neighbors**	**Label**	**MP**	**Most Probable Words**
sadness	1.0	regretful rueful pity pained despondent	violence	1.0	sword shot blood shouted swung
love	1.0	love delightful happiness enjoyed	boats	1.0	ship boat captain deck crew
murder	1.0	autopsy arrested homicide murdered	food	1.0	kitchen mouth glass food bread
worship	0.1	toil pray devote yourselves gather	sci-fi	0.0	suppose earth robots computer certain
moodiness	0.3	glumly snickered quizzically guiltily	fantasy	0.0	agreed magician dragon castle talent
informal	0.4	kinda damn heck guess shitty	military	0.1	ship captain lucky hour general

Table 1: Three high-precision (top) and three low-precision (bottom) descriptors for the **RMN** and **HTMM**, along with labels from an external evaluator and model precision (MP) computed via word intrusion experiments. The **RMN** is able to learn a variety of interpersonal states (e.g., love, sadness), while the **HTMM**'s most coherent topics are about concrete objects or events.

descriptor embeddings replaces topic-word probability. To control for randomness in the training process, we train three of each model, so the final experiment consists of 1,350 tasks ($K = 10, 30, 50$ descriptors per trial, three trials per model).

We collect judgments from ten different workers for each task using the Crowdflower platform.[8] Our evaluation metric, model precision (MP), is the fraction of workers that select the correct intruder word for a descriptor k. Low model precision signals descriptors that lack cohesive themes.

On average, the **RMN**'s descriptors are much more interpretable than those of the baselines, as it achieves a mean model precision of 0.73 (Figure 3) across all values of K. There is little difference between the model precision of the three topic model baselines, which hover around 0.5. There is also little difference between the **GRMN** and **RMN**; however, visualizing the learned character and book embeddings as in Figure 6 may be insightful for literary scholars. We show example high and low precision descriptors for the **RMN** and **HTMM** in Table 1; a full list is included in the supplementary material.

4.4   Do Trajectories Make Sense?

While the previous evaluation focused only on descriptor quality, our next experiment compares the trajectories learned by the best **RMN** model from the intrusion experiment (measured by highest mean model precision) to those learned by the best **HTMM** model, which is the only baseline capable of learning relationship trajectories. Workers read a plot sum-

mary and choose which model's trajectory best represents the relationship in question. We use the $K = 30$ setting because it provides the best balance between descriptor variety and trajectory interpretability.

For this evaluation, we crawl Wikipedia, Goodreads, and SparkNotes for plot summaries associated with our 1,383 books. We then remove all relationships where each involved character is not mentioned at least five times in the summary, which results in a final evaluation set of 125 relationships.[9] We present workers with two characters, a plot summary, and a visualization of trajectories learned by the **RMN** and the **HTMM** (Figure 4). The workers then select the trajectory that best matches the relationship described by the summary.

To generate the visualizations, we first have an external annotator label each descriptor from both models with a single word as in Table 1. For fairness, the annotator is unaware of the underlying models. For the **RMN**, we visualize trajectories by displaying the label of the argmax over descriptor weights d_t at each time step t. Similarly, for the **HTMM**, we display the most probable topic at each time step.[10]

The results of this task with seven workers per comparison favor the **RMN**: for 87 out of the 125 evaluated relationships (69.6%), the workers choose the **RMN**'s trajectory over the **HTMM**'s. We compute the Fleiss κ value (Fleiss, 1971) to correct our inter-annotator agreement for chance and find that

---

[9]Without this filtering step, workers do not have enough information to compare the two models since most of the characters in our dataset are not mentioned in summaries.

[10]To reduce visual clutter, we ignore descriptors that persist for only a single time step.

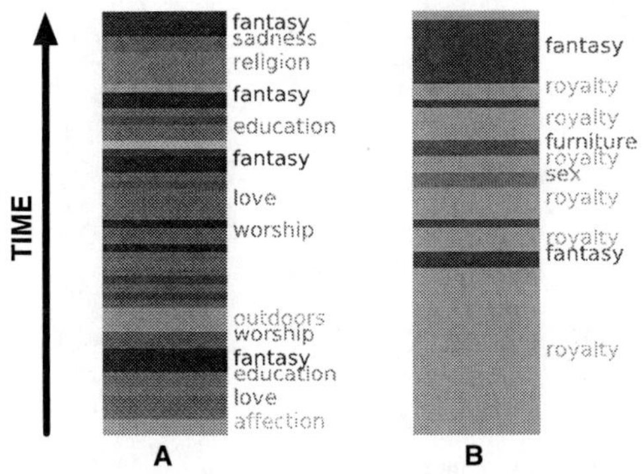

Summary: Govinda is Siddhartha's best friend and sometimes his follower. Like Siddhartha, Govinda devotes his life to the quest for understanding and enlightenment. He leaves his village with Siddhartha to join the Samanas, then leaves the Samanas to follow Gotama. He searches for enlightenment independently of Siddhartha but persists in looking for teachers who can show him the way. In the end, he is able to achieve enlightenment only because of Siddhartha's love for him.

Figure 4: An example from the Crowdflower summary matching task; workers are asked to choose the trajectory (here, "A" is generated by the **RMN** and "B" by the **HTMM**) that best matches a provided summary that describes the relationship between Siddartha and Govinda (from *Siddartha* by Hesse).

$\kappa = 0.32$, indicating fair agreement among the workers. Furthermore, thirty-four relationships had unanimous agreement among the seven workers; of these, twenty-six were unanimous in favor of the **RMN** compared to only eight for the **HTMM**.

4.5 What Makes a Relationship Positive?

While the previous two experiments show that the **RMN** is more interpretable and accurate than baseline models, we have not yet shown that its insights can aid in drawing connections across various books and genres. As a first step in this direction, we investigate what makes a relationship positive or negative by comparing trajectories from the **RMN** and **HTMM** to static affinity annotations from a recently-released dataset (Massey et al., 2015) of fictional relationships. Expected correlations (e.g., murder and sadness are strongly negative descriptors) emerge alongside surprising ones (politics is negative, religion is positive).

The affinity labeling task of Massey et al. (2015) requires workers to describe a given relationship as positive, negative, or neutral. We consider only non-neutral relationships for which two annotators agree

Model	Positive	Negative
RMN	education, love, religion, sex	politics, murder, sadness, royalty
HTMM	love, parental, business, outdoors	love, politics, violence, crime

Table 2: Descriptors most characteristic of positive and negative relationships, computed using existing annotations. Compared to the **RMN**, the **HTMM** struggles to coherently characterize negative relationships. Interestingly, both models show negative predispositions for political relationships, perhaps due to genre bias or class differences.

on the affinity label and remove all books not present in our own dataset. This filtering step results in 120 relationships, 78% of which are positive and the remaining 22% negative.

Since the annotations are static, we first aggregate our trajectories across all time steps. We compute K-dimensional "average positive" and "average negative" weight vectors $\boldsymbol{a}_p$ and $\boldsymbol{a}_n$ by averaging the relationship states $\boldsymbol{d}_t$ for the **RMN** and the document-topic distributions for the **HTMM** across all time steps for relationships labeled with a particular affinity. Then, we compute the vector difference $\boldsymbol{a}_p - \boldsymbol{a}_n$ and sort it to produce a ranked list of descriptors, where descriptors with positive differences occur more frequently in positive relationships. Table 2 shows the most positive and most negative descriptors; of particular interest is the large negative weight associated with political relationships from both models.

5 Qualitative Analysis

Our experiments show the superiority of the **RMN** over various topic model baselines in both descriptor interpretability and trajectory accuracy, but what causes the improved performance? In this section, we analyze similarities between the **RMN** and **HTMM** and look at qualitative examples where the **RMN** succeeds and fails. We also connect the findings of our affinity experiment to existing literary scholarship.

Both models are equally proficient at learning and assigning event-based descriptors (e.g., crime, violence, food). More specifically, the **RMN** and **HTMM** agree on environmental descriptions (e.g., boats, outdoors) and graphic sexual scenes (Figure 5, middle).

However, the **RMN** is more sophisticated with in-

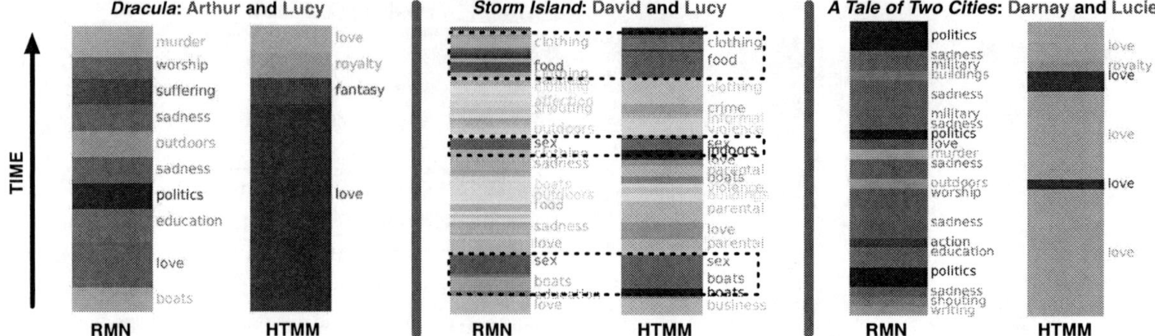

Figure 5: *Left*: the RMN is able to model Arthur and Lucy's trajectory reasonably well compared to our manually-created version in Figure 1. *Middle*: both models agree on event-based descriptors such as <u>food</u> and <u>sex</u>. *Right*: a failure case for the RMN in which it is unable to learn that Lucie Manette and Charles Darnay are in love.

terpersonal relationships. None of the topic model baselines learns negative emotional descriptors such as <u>sadness</u> or <u>suffering</u>, which explains the inaccurate HTMM trajectory of Arthur and Lucy in the left-most panel of Figure 5. All of the topic model baselines learn duplicate topics; in Table 2, one <u>love</u> descriptor is highly positive while a duplicate is strongly negative.[11] The RMN circumvents this problem with its uniqueness penalty (Equation 8).

While the increased descriptor variety is a positive, sometimes it leads the RMN astray. The model largely ignores the love between Charles Darnay and Lucie Manette in Dickens' *A Tale of Two Cities* due to book's sad tone; meanwhile, the HTMM's trajectory, while vastly simplified, does pick up on the romance (Figure 5, right). While the RMN's learnable book and character embeddings should help, the signal in a span cannot lead to the "proper" descriptor.

Both the RMN and HTMM learn that <u>politics</u> is strongly negative (Table 2). Existing scholarship supports this finding: Victorian-era authors, for example, are "obsessed with *otherness* ... of antiquated social and legal institutions, and of autocratic and/or dictatorial abusive government" (Zarifopol-Johnston, 1995), while in science fiction, "dystopia——precisely because it is so much more common (than utopia)—— bears the aspect of lived experience" (Gordin et al., 2010). Our affinity data comes primarily from Victorian novels (e.g., by Dickens and George Eliot), leading us to believe that that the models are behaving

reasonably. Finally, returning to the "extra" meaning of meals discussed in Section 1, <u>food</u> occurs *slightly* more frequently in positive relationships.

6 Related Work

There are two major areas upon which our work builds: computational literary analysis and deep neural networks for natural language processing.

Most previous work in computational literary analysis has focused either on characters or events. In the former category, graphical models and classifiers have been proposed for learning character personas from novels (Bamman et al., 2014; Flekova and Gurevych, 2015) and film summaries (Bamman et al., 2013). The NUBBI model of Chang et al. (2009a) learns topics that statically describe characters and their relationships. Because these models lack temporal components (the focus of our task), we compare instead against the HTMM of Gruber et al. (2007).

Closest to our own work is the supervised structured prediction problem of Chaturvedi et al. (2016), in which features are designed to predict dynamic sequences of positive and negative interactions between two characters in plot summaries. Other research in this area includes social network construction from novels (Elson et al., 2010; Srivastava et al., 2016) and film (Krishnan and Eisenstein, 2015), as well as attempts to summarize and generate stories (Elsner, 2012).

While some of the relationship descriptors learned by our model are character-centric, others are more events-based, depicting actions rather than feelings;

---

[11] This "duplicate love" phenomenon persists even when we reduce the number of topics.

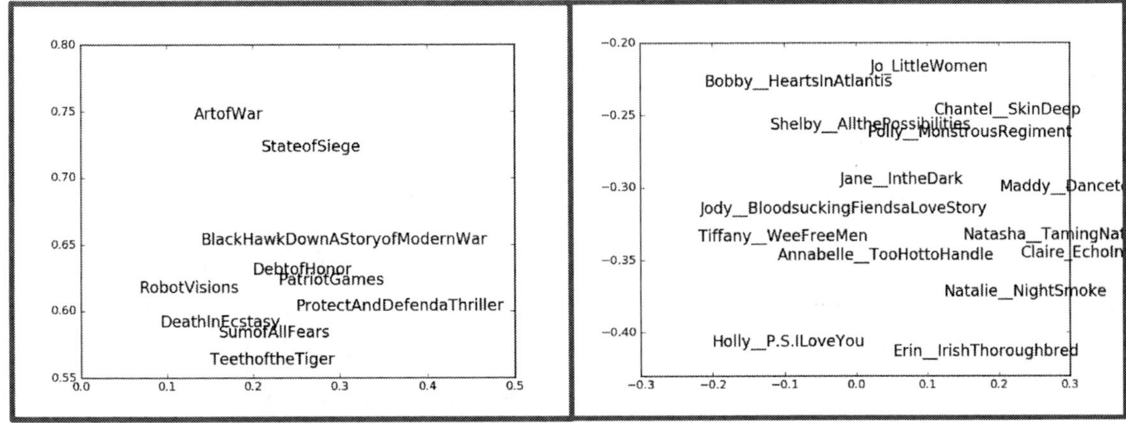

Figure 6: Clusters from PCA visualizations of the RMN's learned book (left) and character (right) embeddings. We see a cluster of books about war and violence (many of which are authored by Tom Clancy) as well as a cluster of lead female characters from primarily romance novels. These visualizations show that the RMN can recover useful static representations of characters and books in addition to the dynamic relationship trajectories.

such descriptors have been the focus of much previous work (Schank and Abelson, 1977; Chambers and Jurafsky, 2008; Chambers and Jurafsky, 2009; Orr et al., 2014). Our model is more closely related to the plot units framework (Lehnert, 1981; Goyal et al., 2013), which annotates events with emotional states.

The RMN builds on deep recurrent autoencoders such as the hierarchical LSTM autoencoder of Li et al. (2015); however, it is more efficient because of the span-level vector averaging. It is also similar to recent neural topic model architectures (Cao et al., 2015; Das et al., 2015), although these models are limited to static document representations. We hope to apply the RMN to nonfictional datasets as well; in this vein, Iyyer et al. (2014) apply a neural network to sentences from nonfiction political books for ideology prediction.

More generally, topic models and related generative models are a central tool for understanding large corpora from science (Talley et al., 2011) to politics (Nguyen et al., 2014). We show representation learning models like RMN can be just as interpretable as LDA-based models. Other applications for which researchers have prioritized interpretable vector representations include text-to-vision mappings (Lazaridou et al., 2014) and word embeddings (Fyshe et al., 2015; Faruqui et al., 2015).

7 Conclusion

We formalize the task of unsupervised relationship modeling, which involves learning a set of relationship descriptors as well as a trajectory over these descriptors for each relationship in an input dataset. We present the RMN, a novel neural network architecture for this task that generates more interpretable descriptors and trajectories than topic model baselines. Finally, we show that the output of our model can lead to interesting insights when combined with annotations in an existing dataset.

Acknowledgments

We thank Jonathan Chang and Amit Gruber for providing baseline code, Thang Nguyen for helpful discussions about our model, and the anonymous reviewers for their insightful comments. This work was supported by NSF grant IIS-1320538. Boyd-Graber is also partially supported by NSF grants CCF-1409287 and NCSE-1422492. Any opinions, findings, conclusions, or recommendations expressed here are those of the authors and do not necessarily reflect the view of the sponsor.

References

Alekh Agarwal, Animashree Anandkumar, Prateek Jain, Praneeth Netrapalli, and Rashish Tandon. 2014. Learning sparsely used overcomplete dictionaries. In *Proceedings of Conference on Learning Theory*.

David Bamman, Brendan O'Connor, and Noah A. Smith. 2013. Learning latent personas of film characters. In *Proceedings of the Association for Computational Linguistics*.

David Bamman, Ted Underwood, and Noah A. Smith. 2014. A bayesian mixed effects model of literary character. In *Proceedings of the Association for Computational Linguistics*.

David M Blei, Andrew Y Ng, and Michael I Jordan. 2003. Latent dirichlet allocation. *Journal of Machine Learning Research*, 3.

Ziqiang Cao, Sujian Li, Yang Liu, Wenjie Li, and Heng Ji. 2015. A novel neural topic model and its supervised extension. In *Association for the Advancement of Artificial Intelligence*.

Nathanael Chambers and Daniel Jurafsky. 2008. Unsupervised learning of narrative event chains. In *Proceedings of the Association for Computational Linguistics*.

Nathanael Chambers and Dan Jurafsky. 2009. Unsupervised learning of narrative schemas and their participants. In *Proceedings of the Association for Computational Linguistics*.

Jonathan Chang, Jordan Boyd-Graber, and David M Blei. 2009a. Connections between the lines: augmenting social networks with text. In *Knowledge Discovery and Data Mining*.

Jonathan Chang, Sean Gerrish, Chong Wang, Jordan L Boyd-Graber, and David M Blei. 2009b. Reading tea leaves: How humans interpret topic models. In *Proceedings of Advances in Neural Information Processing Systems*.

Snigdha Chaturvedi, Shashank Srivastava, Hal Daumé III, and Chris Dyer. 2016. Modeling dynamic relationships between characters in literary novels. In *Association for the Advancement of Artificial Intelligence*.

J. Cognard-Black, M. Goldthwaite, and M. Nestle. 2014. *Books That Cook: The Making of a Literary Meal.* NYU Press.

Rajarshi Das, Manzil Zaheer, and Chris Dyer. 2015. Gaussian lda for topic models with word embeddings. In *Proceedings of the Association for Computational Linguistics*.

Michael Elad and Michal Aharon. 2006. Image denoising via sparse and redundant representations over learned dictionaries. *IEEE Transactions on Image Processing*, 15(12).

Micha Elsner. 2012. Character-based kernels for novelistic plot structure. In *Proceedings of the European Chapter of the Association for Computational Linguistics*.

David K Elson, Nicholas Dames, and Kathleen R McKeown. 2010. Extracting social networks from literary fiction. In *Proceedings of the Association for Computational Linguistics*.

Manaal Faruqui, Yulia Tsvetkov, Dani Yogatama, Chris Dyer, and Noah Smith. 2015. Sparse overcomplete word vector representations. In *Proceedings of the Association for Computational Linguistics*.

Joseph L Fleiss. 1971. Measuring nominal scale agreement among many raters. *Psychological bulletin*, 76(5).

Lucie Flekova and Iryna Gurevych. 2015. Personality profiling of fictional characters using sense-level links between lexical resources. In *Proceedings of Empirical Methods in Natural Language Processing*.

T.C. Foster. 2009. *How to Read Literature Like a Professor*. HarperCollins.

Alona Fyshe, Leila Wehbe, Partha P Talukdar, Brian Murphy, and Tom M Mitchell. 2015. A compositional and interpretable semantic space. In *Conference of the North American Chapter of the Association for Computational Linguistics*.

Michael D Gordin, Helen Tilley, and Gyan Prakash. 2010. *Utopia/dystopia: conditions of historical possibility*. Princeton University Press.

Amit Goyal, Ellen Riloff, and Hal Daumé III. 2013. A computational model for plot units. *Computational Intelligence Journal*, 29(3).

Amit Gruber, Yair Weiss, and Michal Rosen-Zvi. 2007. Hidden topic markov models. In *Proceedings of Artificial Intelligence and Statistics*.

Aapo Hyvärinen and Erkki Oja. 2000. Independent component analysis: algorithms and applications. *Neural networks*, 13(4).

Mohit Iyyer, Peter Enns, Jordan Boyd-Graber, and Philip Resnik. 2014. Political ideology detection using recursive neural networks. In *Proceedings of the Association for Computational Linguistics*.

Mohit Iyyer, Varun Manjunatha, Jordan Boyd-Graber, and Hal Daumé III. 2015. Deep unordered composition rivals syntactic methods for text classification. In *Proceedings of the Association for Computational Linguistics*.

Matt L. Jockers. 2013. *Macroanalysis: Digital Methods and Literary History*. Topics in the Digital Humanities. University of Illinois Press.

Diederik Kingma and Jimmy Ba. 2014. Adam: A method for stochastic optimization. In *Proceedings of the International Conference on Learning Representations*.

Vinodh Krishnan and Jacob Eisenstein. 2015. "You're Mr. Lebowski, I'm The Dude": Inducing address term formality in signed social networks. In *Conference* of the North American Chapter of the Association for Computational Linguistics.

Angeliki Lazaridou, Elia Bruni, and Marco Baroni. 2014. Is this a wampimuk? cross-modal mapping between distributional semantics and the visual world. In *Proceedings of the Association for Computational Linguistics*.

Wendy G Lehnert. 1981. Plot units and narrative summarization. *Cognitive Science*, 5(4).

Jiwei Li, Minh-Thang Luong, and Dan Jurafsky. 2015. A hierarchical neural autoencoder for paragraphs and documents. In *Proceedings of the Association for Computational Linguistics*.

Philip Massey, Patrick Xia, David Bamman, and Noah A Smith. 2015. Annotating character relationships in literary texts. *arXiv:1512.00728*.

Viet-An Nguyen, Jordan Boyd-Graber, Philip Resnik, Deborah Cai, Jennifer Midberry, and Yuanxin Wang. 2014. Modeling topic control to detect influence in conversations using nonparametric topic models. *Machine Learning*, 95:381–421.

Bruno A Olshausen and David J Field. 1997. Sparse coding with an overcomplete basis set: A strategy employed by v1? *Vision research*, 37(23).

J Walker Orr, Prasad Tadepalli, Janardhan Rao Doppa, Xiaoli Fern, and Thomas G Dietterich. 2014. Learning scripts as hidden markov models. In *Association for the Advancement of Artificial Intelligence*.

Jeffrey Pennington, Richard Socher, and Christopher Manning. 2014. Glove: Global vectors for word representation. In *Proceedings of Empirical Methods in Natural Language Processing*.

Roger Schank and Robert Abelson. 1977. *Scripts, Plans, Goals and Understanding: an Inquiry into Human Knowledge Structures*. L. Erlbaum.

Richard Socher, Quoc V Le, Christopher D Manning, and Andrew Y Ng. 2014. Grounded compositional semantics for finding and describing images with sentences. *Transactions of the Association for Computational Linguistics*.

Shashank Srivastava, Snigdha Chaturvedi, and Tom Mitchell. 2016. Inferring interpersonal relations in narrative summaries. In *Proceedings of the Thirtieth AAAI Conference on Artificial Intelligence*, AAAI'16.

Edmund M. Talley, David Newman, David Mimno, Bruce W. Herr, Hanna M. Wallach, Gully A. P. C. Burns, A. G. Miriam Leenders, and Andrew McCallum. 2011. Database of NIH grants using machine-learned categories and graphical clustering. *Nature Methods*, 8(6):443–444, May.

Hardik Vala, David Jurgens, Andrew Piper, and Derek Ruths. 2015. Mr. bennet, his coachman, and the archbishop walk into a bar but only one of them gets recognized: On the difficulty of detecting characters in

literary texts. In *Proceedings of Empirical Methods in Natural Language Processing*.

Jason Weston, Samy Bengio, and Nicolas Usunier. 2011. Wsabie: Scaling up to large vocabulary image annotation. In *International Joint Conference on Artificial Intelligence*.

Ilinca Zarifopol-Johnston. 1995. *To kill a text: the dialogic fiction of Hugo, Dickens, and Zola*. University of Delaware Press.

Learning to Compose Neural Networks for Question Answering

Jacob Andreas and **Marcus Rohrbach** and **Trevor Darrell** and **Dan Klein**
Department of Electrical Engineering and Computer Sciences
University of California, Berkeley
{jda,rohrbach,trevor,klein}@eecs.berkeley.edu

Abstract

We describe a question answering model that applies to both images and structured knowledge bases. The model uses natural language strings to automatically assemble neural networks from a collection of composable modules. Parameters for these modules are learned jointly with network-assembly parameters via reinforcement learning, with only (world, question, answer) triples as supervision. Our approach, which we term a *dynamic neural module network*, achieves state-of-the-art results on benchmark datasets in both visual and structured domains.

1   Introduction

This paper presents a compositional, attentional model for answering questions about a variety of world representations, including images and structured knowledge bases. The model translates from questions to dynamically assembled neural networks, then applies these networks to world representations (images or knowledge bases) to produce answers. We take advantage of two largely independent lines of work: on one hand, an extensive literature on answering questions by mapping from strings to logical representations of meaning; on the other, a series of recent successes in deep neural models for image recognition and captioning. By constructing neural networks instead of logical forms, our model leverages the best aspects of both linguistic compositionality and continuous representations.

Our model has two components, trained jointly: first, a collection of neural "modules" that can be freely composed (Figure 1b); second, a network layout predictor that assembles modules into complete deep networks tailored to each question (Figure 1a).

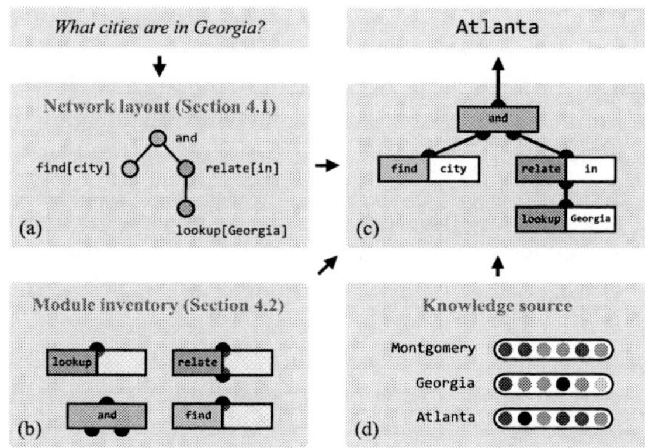

Figure 1: A learned syntactic analysis (a) is used to assemble a collection of neural modules (b) into a deep neural network (c), and applied to a world representation (d) to produce an answer.

Previous work has used manually-specified modular structures for visual learning (Andreas et al., 2016). Here we:

- *learn* a network structure predictor jointly with module parameters themselves
- *extend* visual primitives from previous work to reason over structured world representations

Training data consists of (world, question, answer) triples: our approach requires no supervision of network layouts. We achieve state-of-the-art performance on two markedly different question answering tasks: one with questions about natural images, and another with more compositional questions about United States geography.[1]

2   Deep networks as functional programs

We begin with a high-level discussion of the kinds of composed networks we would like to learn.

[1] We have released our code at http://github.com/jacobandreas/nmn2

Andreas et al. (2016) describe a heuristic approach for decomposing visual question answering tasks into sequence of modular sub-problems. For example, the question *What color is the bird?* might be answered in two steps: first, "where is the bird?" (Figure 2a), second, "what color is that part of the image?" (Figure 2c). This first step, a generic **module** called `find`, can be expressed as a fragment of a neural network that maps from image features and a lexical item (here *bird*) to a distribution over pixels. This operation is commonly referred to as the *attention mechanism*, and is a standard tool for manipulating images (Xu et al., 2015) and text representations (Hermann et al., 2015).

The first contribution of this paper is an extension and generalization of this mechanism to enable fully-differentiable reasoning about more structured semantic representations. Figure 2b shows how the same module can be used to focus on the entity *Georgia* in a non-visual grounding domain; more generally, by representing every entity in the universe of discourse as a feature vector, we can obtain a distribution over entities that corresponds roughly to a logical set-valued denotation.

Having obtained such a distribution, existing neural approaches use it to immediately compute a weighted average of image features and project back into a labeling decision—a `describe` module (Figure 2c). But the logical perspective suggests a number of novel modules that might operate on attentions: e.g. combining them (by analogy to conjunction or disjunction) or inspecting them directly without a return to feature space (by analogy to quantification, Figure 2d). These modules are discussed in detail in Section 4. Unlike their formal counterparts, they are differentiable end-to-end, facilitating their integration into learned models. Building on previous work, we learn behavior for a collection of heterogeneous modules from (world, question, answer) triples.

The second contribution of this paper is a model for learning to assemble such modules compositionally. Isolated modules are of limited use—to obtain expressive power comparable to either formal approaches or monolithic deep networks, they must be composed into larger structures. Figure 2 shows simple examples of composed structures, but for realistic question-answering tasks, even larger net-

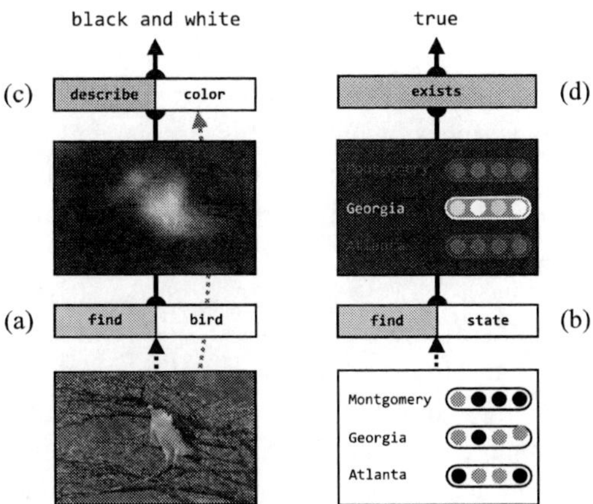

Figure 2: Simple neural module networks, corresponding to the questions *What color is the bird?* and *Are there any states?* (a) A neural `find` module for computing an attention over pixels. (b) The same operation applied to a knowledge base. (c) Using an attention produced by a lower module to identify the color of the region of the image attended to. (d) Performing quantification by evaluating an attention directly.

works are required. Thus our goal is to automatically induce variable-free, tree-structured computation descriptors. We can use a familiar functional notation from formal semantics (e.g. Liang et al., 2011) to represent these computations.[2] We write the two examples in Figure 2 as

```
(describe[color] find[bird])
```
and
```
(exists find[state])
```

respectively. These are **network layouts**: they specify a structure for arranging modules (and their lexical parameters) into a complete network. Andreas et al. (2016) use hand-written rules to deterministically transform dependency trees into layouts, and are restricted to producing simple structures like the above for non-synthetic data. For full generality, we will need to solve harder problems, like transforming *What cities are in Georgia?* (Figure 1) into

```
(and
    find[city]
    (relate[in] lookup[Georgia]))
```

In this paper, we present a model for learning to select such structures from a set of automatically generated candidates. We call this model a **dynamic neural module network**.

---

[2]But note that unlike formal semantics, the behavior of the primitive functions here is itself unknown.

3   Related work

There is an extensive literature on database question answering, in which strings are mapped to logical forms, then evaluated by a black-box execution model to produce answers. Supervision may be provided either by annotated logical forms (Wong and Mooney, 2007; Kwiatkowski et al., 2010; Andreas et al., 2013) or from (world, question, answer) triples alone (Liang et al., 2011; Pasupat and Liang, 2015). In general the set of primitive functions from which these logical forms can be assembled is fixed, but one recent line of work focuses on inducing new predicates functions automatically, either from perceptual features (Krishnamurthy and Kollar, 2013) or the underlying schema (Kwiatkowski et al., 2013). The model we describe in this paper has a unified framework for handling both the perceptual and schema cases, and differs from existing work primarily in learning a differentiable execution model with continuous evaluation results.

Neural models for question answering are also a subject of current interest. These include approaches that model the task directly as a multiclass classification problem (Iyyer et al., 2014), models that attempt to embed questions and answers in a shared vector space (Bordes et al., 2014) and attentional models that select words from documents sources (Hermann et al., 2015). Such approaches generally require that answers can be retrieved directly based on surface linguistic features, without requiring intermediate computation. A more structured approach described by Yin et al. (2015) learns a query execution model for database tables without any natural language component. Previous efforts toward unifying formal logic and representation learning include those of Grefenstette (2013) and Krishnamurthy and Mitchell (2013).

The visually-grounded component of this work relies on recent advances in convolutional networks for computer vision (Simonyan and Zisserman, 2014), and in particular the fact that late convolutional layers in networks trained for image recognition contain rich features useful for other downstream vision tasks, while preserving spatial information. These features have been used for both image captioning (Xu et al., 2015) and visual question answering (Yang et al., 2015).

Most previous approaches to visual question answering either apply a recurrent model to deep representations of both the image and the question (Ren et al., ; Malinowski et al., 2015), or use the question to compute an attention over the input image, and then answer based on both the question and the image features attended to (Yang et al., 2015; Xu and Saenko, 2015). Other approaches include the simple classification model described by Zhou et al. (2015) and the dynamic parameter prediction network described by Noh et al. (2015). All of these models assume that a fixed computation can be performed on the image and question to compute the answer, rather than adapting the structure of the computation to the question.

As noted, Andreas et al. (2016) previously considered a simple generalization of these attentional approaches in which small variations in the network structure per-question were permitted, with the structure chosen by (deterministic) syntactic processing of questions. Other approaches in this general family include the "universal parser" sketched by Bottou (2014), and the recursive neural networks of Socher et al. (2013), which use a fixed tree structure to perform further linguistic analysis without any external world representation. We are unaware of previous work that succeeds in simultaneously learning both the parameters for and structures of instance-specific neural networks.

4   Model

Recall that our goal is to map from questions and world representations to answers. This process involves the following variables:

1. w a world representation
2. x a question
3. y an answer
4. z a network layout
5. θ a collection of model parameters

Our model is built around two distributions: a **layout model** $p(z|x; \theta_\ell)$ which chooses a layout for a sentence, and a **execution model** $p_z(y|w; \theta_e)$ which applies the network specified by z to w.

For ease of presentation, we introduce these models in reverse order. We first imagine that z is always observed, and in Section 4.1 describe how to evaluate and learn modules parameterized by θ_e within fixed structures. In Section 4.2, we move to the real scenario, where z is unknown. We describe how to predict layouts from questions and learn θ_e and θ_ℓ jointly without layout supervision.

4.1 Evaluating modules

Given a layout z, we assemble the corresponding modules into a full neural network (Figure 1c), and apply it to the knowledge representation. Intermediate results flow between modules until an answer is produced at the root. We denote the output of the network with layout z on input world w as $[\![z]\!]_w$; when explicitly referencing the substructure of z, we can alternatively write $[\![m(h^1, h^2)]\!]$ for a top-level module m with submodule outputs h^1 and h^2. We then define the execution model:

$$p_z(y|w) = ([\![z]\!]_w)_y \qquad (1)$$

(This assumes that the root module of z produces a distribution over labels y.) The set of possible layouts z is restricted by module *type constraints*: some modules (like `find` above) operate directly on the input representation, while others (like `describe` above) also depend on input from specific earlier modules. Two base types are considered in this paper are <u>Attention</u> (a distribution over pixels or entities) and <u>Labels</u> (a distribution over answers).

Parameters are tied across multiple instances of the same module, so different instantiated networks may share some parameters but not others. Modules have both *parameter arguments* (shown in square brackets) and ordinary inputs (shown in parentheses). Parameter arguments, like the running `bird` example in Section 2, are provided by the layout, and are used to specialize module behavior for particular lexical items. Ordinary inputs are the result of computation lower in the network. In addition to parameter-specific weights, modules have global weights shared across all instances of the module (but not shared with other modules). We write $A, a, B, b, \ldots$ for global weights and u^i, v^i for weights associated with the parameter argument i. $\oplus$ and $\odot$ denote (possibly broadcasted) elementwise addition and multiplication respectively. The complete set of global weights and parameter-specific weights constitutes θ_e. *Every* module has access to the world representation, represented as a collection of vectors $w^1, w^2, \ldots$ (or W expressed as a matrix). The nonlinearity σ denotes a rectified linear unit.

The modules used in this paper are shown below, with names and type constraints in the first row and a description of the module's computation following.

Lookup $\qquad\qquad$ ($\rightarrow$ <u>Attention</u>)

`lookup[i]` produces an attention focused entirely at the index $f(i)$, where the relationship f between words and positions in the input map is known ahead of time (e.g. string matches on database fields).

$$[\![\texttt{lookup[i]}]\!] = e_{f(i)} \qquad (2)$$

where e_i is the basis vector that is 1 in the ith position and 0 elsewhere.

Find $\qquad\qquad$ ($\rightarrow$ <u>Attention</u>)

`find[i]` computes a distribution over indices by concatenating the parameter argument with each position of the input feature map, and passing the concatenated vector through a MLP:

$$[\![\texttt{find[i]}]\!] = \text{softmax}(a \odot \sigma(Bv^i \oplus CW \oplus d)) \quad (3)$$

Relate $\qquad\qquad$ (<u>Attention</u> $\rightarrow$ <u>Attention</u>)

`relate` directs focus from one region of the input to another. It behaves much like the `find` module, but also conditions its behavior on the current region of attention h. Let $\bar{w}(h) = \sum_k h_k w^k$, where h_k is the kth element of h. Then,

$$[\![\texttt{relate[i]}(h)]\!] = \text{softmax}(a \odot$$
$$\sigma(Bv^i \oplus CW \oplus D\bar{w}(h) \oplus e)) \qquad (4)$$

And $\qquad\qquad$ (<u>Attention</u>* $\rightarrow$ <u>Attention</u>)

`and` performs an operation analogous to set intersection for attentions. The analogy to probabilistic logic suggests multiplying probabilities:

$$[\![\texttt{and}(h^1, h^2, \ldots)]\!] = h^1 \odot h^2 \odot \cdots \qquad (5)$$

Describe $\qquad\qquad$ (<u>Attention</u> $\rightarrow$ <u>Labels</u>)

`describe[i]` computes a weighted average of w under the input attention. This average is then used to predict an answer representation. With $\bar{w}$ as above,

$$[\![\texttt{describe[i]}(h)]\!] = \text{softmax}(A\sigma(B\bar{w}(h)+v^i)) \quad (6)$$

Exists $\qquad\qquad$ (<u>Attention</u> $\rightarrow$ <u>Labels</u>)

`exists` is the existential quantifier, and inspects the incoming attention directly to produce a label, rather than an intermediate feature vector like `describe`:

$$[\![\texttt{exists]}(h)]\!] = \text{softmax}\left(\left(\max_k h_k\right)a + b\right) \qquad (7)$$

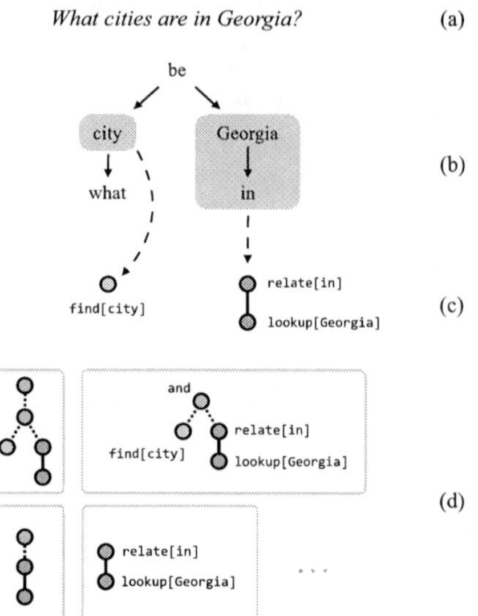

Figure 3: Generation of layout candidates. The input sentence (a) is represented as a dependency parse (b). Fragments of this dependency parse are then associated with appropriate modules (c), and these fragments are assembled into full layouts (d).

With z observed, the model we have described so far corresponds largely to that of Andreas et al. (2016), though the module inventory is different—in particular, our new `exists` and `relate` modules do not depend on the two-dimensional spatial structure of the input. This enables generalization to non-visual world representations.

Learning in this simplified setting is straightforward. Assuming the top-level module in each layout is a `describe` or `exists` module, the fully-instantiated network corresponds to a distribution over labels conditioned on layouts. To train, we maximize $\sum_{(w,y,z)} \log p_z(y|w; \theta_e)$ directly. This can be understood as a parameter-tying scheme, where the decisions about which parameters to tie are governed by the observed layouts z.

4.2   Assembling networks

Next we describe the layout model $p(z|x; \theta_\ell)$. We first use a fixed syntactic parse to generate a small set of candidate layouts, analogously to the way a semantic grammar generates candidate semantic parses in previous work (Berant and Liang, 2014).

A semantic parse differs from a syntactic parse in two primary ways. First, lexical items must be mapped onto a (possibly smaller) set of semantic primitives. Second, these semantic primitives must be combined into a structure that closely, but not exactly, parallels the structure provided by syntax. For example, *state* and *province* might need to be identified with the same field in a database schema, while *all states have a capital* might need to be identified with the correct (*in situ*) quantifier scope.

While we cannot avoid the structure selection problem, continuous representations simplify the lexical selection problem. For modules that accept a vector parameter, we associate these parameters with *words* rather than semantic tokens, and thus turn the combinatorial optimization problem associated with lexicon induction into a continuous one. Now, in order to learn that *province* and *state* have the same denotation, it is sufficient to learn that their associated parameters are close in some embedding space—a task amenable to gradient descent. (Note that this is easy only in an optimizability sense, and not an information-theoretic one—we must still learn to associate each independent lexical item with the correct vector.) The remaining combinatorial problem is to arrange the provided lexical items into the right computational structure. In this respect, layout prediction is more like syntactic parsing than ordinary semantic parsing, and we can rely on an off-the-shelf syntactic parser to get most of the way there. In this work, syntactic structure is provided by the Stanford dependency parser (De Marneffe and Manning, 2008).

The construction of layout candidates is depicted in Figure 3, and proceeds as follows:

1. Represent the input sentence as a dependency tree.
2. Collect all nouns, verbs, and prepositional phrases that are attached directly to a wh-word or copula.
3. Associate each of these with a layout fragment: Ordinary nouns and verbs are mapped to a single `find` module. Proper nouns to a single `lookup` module. Prepositional phrases are mapped to a depth-2 fragment, with a `relate` module for the preposition above a `find` module for the enclosed head noun.
4. Form subsets of this set of layout fragments. For each subset, construct a layout candidate by

joining all fragments with an `and` module, and inserting either a `measure` or `describe` module at the top (each subset thus results in two parse candidates.)

All layouts resulting from this process feature a relatively flat tree structure with at most one conjunction and one quantifier. This is a strong simplifying assumption, but appears sufficient to cover most of the examples that appear in both of our tasks. As our approach includes both categories, relations and simple quantification, the range of phenomena considered is generally broader than previous perceptually-grounded QA work (Krishnamurthy and Kollar, 2013; Matuszek et al., 2012).

Having generated a set of candidate parses, we need to score them. This is a ranking problem; as in the rest of our approach, we solve it using standard neural machinery. In particular, we produce an LSTM representation of the question, a feature-based representation of the query, and pass both representations through a multilayer perceptron (MLP). The query feature vector includes indicators on the number of modules of each type present, as well as their associated parameter arguments. While one can easily imagine a more sophisticated parse-scoring model, this simple approach works well for our tasks.

Formally, for a question x, let $h_q(x)$ be an LSTM encoding of the question (i.e. the last hidden layer of an LSTM applied word-by-word to the input question). Let $\{z_1, z_2, \ldots\}$ be the proposed layouts for x, and let $f(z_i)$ be a feature vector representing the ith layout. Then the score $s(z_i|x)$ for the layout z_i is

$$s(z_i|x) = a^\top \sigma(Bh_q(x) + Cf(z_i) + d) \quad (8)$$

i.e. the output of an MLP with inputs $h_q(x)$ and $f(z_i)$, and parameters $\theta_\ell = \{a, B, C, d\}$. Finally, we normalize these scores to obtain a distribution:

$$p(z_i|x; \theta_\ell) = e^{s(z_i|x)} \Big/ \sum_{j=1}^{n} e^{s(z_j|x)} \quad (9)$$

Having defined a layout selection module $p(z|x; \theta_\ell)$ and a network execution model $p_z(y|w; \theta_e)$, we are ready to define a model for predicting answers given only (world, question) pairs. The key constraint is that we want to minimize evaluations of $p_z(y|w; \theta_e)$ (which involves

expensive application of a deep network to a large input representation), but can tractably evaluate $p(z|x; \theta_\ell)$ for all z (which involves application of a shallow network to a relatively small set of candidates). This is the opposite of the situation usually encountered semantic parsing, where calls to the query execution model are fast but the set of candidate parses is too large to score exhaustively.

In fact, the problem more closely resembles the scenario faced by agents in the reinforcement learning setting (where it is cheap to score actions, but potentially expensive to execute them and obtain rewards). We adopt a common approach from that literature, and express our model as a stochastic policy. Under this policy, we first *sample* a layout z from a distribution $p(z|x; \theta_\ell)$, and then apply z to the knowledge source and obtain a distribution over answers $p(y|z, w; \theta_e)$.

After z is chosen, we can train the execution model directly by maximizing $\log p(y|z, w; \theta_e)$ with respect to θ_e as before (this is ordinary backpropagation). Because the hard selection of z is non-differentiable, we optimize $p(z|x; \theta_\ell)$ using a policy gradient method. The gradient of the reward surface J with respect to the parameters of the policy is

$$\nabla J(\theta_\ell) = \mathbb{E}[\nabla \log p(z|x; \theta_\ell) \cdot r] \quad (10)$$

(this is the REINFORCE rule (Williams, 1992)). Here the expectation is taken with respect to rollouts of the policy, and r is the reward. Because our goal is to select the network that makes the most accurate predictions, we take the reward to be identically the negative log-probability from the execution phase, i.e.

$$\mathbb{E}[(\nabla \log p(z|x; \theta_\ell)) \cdot \log p(y|z, w; \theta_e)] \quad (11)$$

Thus the update to the layout-scoring model at each timestep is simply the gradient of the log-probability of the chosen layout, scaled by the accuracy of that layout's predictions. At training time, we approximate the expectation with a single rollout, so at each step we update θ_ℓ in the direction $(\nabla \log p(z|x; \theta_\ell)) \cdot \log p(y|z, w; \theta_e)$ for a single $z \sim p(z|x; \theta_\ell)$. θ_e and θ_ℓ are optimized using ADADELTA (Zeiler, 2012) with $\rho = 0.95$, $\varepsilon = 1e{-}6$ and gradient clipping at a norm of 10.

Figure 4: Sample outputs for the visual question answering task. The second row shows the final attention provided as input to the top-level describe module. For the first two examples, the model produces reasonable parses, attends to the correct region of the images (the ear and the woman's clothing), and generates the correct answer. In the third image, the verb is discarded and a wrong answer is produced.

5 Experiments

The framework described in this paper is general, and we are interested in how well it performs on datasets of varying domain, size and linguistic complexity. To that end, we evaluate our model on tasks at opposite extremes of both these criteria: a large visual question answering dataset, and a small collection of more structured geography questions.

5.1 Questions about images

Our first task is the recently-introduced Visual Question Answering challenge (VQA) (Antol et al., 2015). The VQA dataset consists of more than 200,000 images paired with human-annotated questions and answers, as in Figure 4.

We use the VQA 1.0 release, employing the development set for model selection and hyperparameter tuning, and reporting final results from the evaluation server on the test-standard set. For the experiments described in this section, the input feature representations w_i are computed by the the fifth convolutional layer of a 16-layer VGGNet after pooling (Simonyan and Zisserman, 2014). Input images are scaled to 448×448 before computing their representations. We found that performance on this task was

	test-dev				test-std
	Yes/No	Number	Other	All	All
Zhou (2015)	76.6	35.0	42.6	55.7	55.9
Noh (2015)	80.7	37.2	41.7	57.2	57.4
NMN	77.7	37.2	39.3	54.8	55.1
NMN*	79.7	37.1	42.8	57.3	–
D-NMN	80.5	37.4	43.1	57.9	**58.0**

Table 1: Results on the VQA test server. NMN is the parameter-tying model from Andreas et al. (2015), while NMN* is a reimplementation using the same image processing pipeline as D-NMN. The model with dynamic network structure prediction achieves the best published results on this task.

best if the candidate layouts were relatively simple: only describe, and and find modules are used, and layouts contain at most two conjuncts.

One weakness of this basic framework is a difficulty modeling prior knowledge about answers (of the form *bears are brown*). This kinds of linguistic "prior" is essential for the VQA task, and easily incorporated. We simply introduce an extra hidden layer for recombining the final module network output with the input sentence representation $h_q(x)$ (see Equation 8), replacing Equation 1 with:

$$\log p_z(y|w,x) = (Ah_q(x) + B[\![z]\!]_w)_y \qquad (12)$$

(Now modules with output type Labels should be understood as producing an answer embedding rather than a distribution over answers.) This allows the question to influence the answer directly.

Results are shown in Table 1. The use of dynamic networks provides a small gain, most noticeably on yes/no questions. We achieve state-of-the-art results on this task, outperforming a highly effective visual bag-of-words model (Zhou et al., 2015), a model with dynamic network parameter prediction (but fixed network structure) (Noh et al., 2015), and a previous approach using neural module networks with no structure prediction (Andreas et al., 2016). For this last model, we report both the numbers from the original paper, and a reimplementation of the model that uses the same image preprocessing as the dynamic module network experiments in this paper. A more conventional attentional model has also been applied to this task (Yang et al., 2015); while we also outperform their reported performance, the evaluation uses different train/test split, so results are not directly comparable.

	Accuracy	
Model	GeoQA	GeoQA+Q
LSP-F	48	–
LSP-W	51	–
NMN	51.7	35.7
D-NMN	**54.3**	**42.9**

Table 2: Results on the GeoQA dataset, and the GeoQA dataset with quantification. Our approach outperforms both a purely logical model (LSP-F) and a model with learned perceptual predicates (LSP-W) on the original dataset, and a fixed-structure NMN under both evaluation conditions.

Some examples are shown in Figure 4. In general, the model learns to focus on the correct region of the image, and tends to consider a broad window around the region. This facilitates answering questions like *Where is the cat?*, which requires knowledge of the surroundings as well as the object in question.

5.2 Questions about geography

The next set of experiments we consider focuses on GeoQA, a geographical question-answering task first introduced by Krishnamurthy and Kollar (2013). This task was originally paired with a visual question answering task much simpler than the one just discussed, and is appealing for a number of reasons. In contrast to the VQA dataset, GeoQA is quite small, containing only 263 examples. Two baselines are available: one using a classical semantic parser backed by a database, and another which induces logical predicates using linear classifiers over both spatial and distributional features. This allows us to evaluate the quality of our model relative to other perceptually grounded logical semantics, as well as strictly logical approaches.

The GeoQA domain consists of a set of entities (e.g. states, cities, parks) which participate in various relations (e.g. north-of, capital-of). Here we take the world representation to consist of two pieces: a set of category features (used by the `find` module) and a different set of relational features (used by the `relate` module). For our experiments, we use a subset of the features originally used by Krishnamurthy et al. The original dataset includes no quantifiers, and treats the questions *What cities are in Texas?* and *Are there any cities in Texas?* identically. Because we are interested in testing the parser's ability to predict a variety of different structures, we intro-

duce a new version of the dataset, GeoQA+Q, which distinguishes these two cases, and expects a Boolean answer to questions of the second kind.

Results are shown in Table 2. As in the original work, we report the results of leave-one-environment-out cross-validation on the set of 10 environments. Our dynamic model (D-NMN) outperforms both the logical (LSP-F) and perceptual models (LSP-W) described by (Krishnamurthy and Kollar, 2013), as well as a fixed-structure neural module net (NMN). This improvement is particularly notable on the dataset with quantifiers, where dynamic structure prediction produces a 20% relative improvement over the fixed baseline. A variety of predicted layouts are shown in Figure 5.

6 Conclusion

We have introduced a new model, the *dynamic neural module network*, for answering queries about both structured and unstructured sources of information. Given only (question, world, answer) triples as training data, the model learns to assemble neural networks on the fly from an inventory of neural models, and simultaneously learns weights for these modules so that they can be composed into novel structures. Our approach achieves state-of-the-art results on two tasks. We believe that the success of this work derives from two factors:

Is Key Largo an island?

```
(exists (and lookup[key-largo] find[island]))
```

yes: correct

What national parks are in Florida?

```
(and find[park] (relate[in] lookup[florida]))
```

everglades: correct

What are some beaches in Florida?

```
(exists (and lookup[beach]
              (relate[in] lookup[florida])))
```

yes (daytona-beach): wrong parse

What beach city is there in Florida?

```
(and lookup[beach] lookup[city]
     (relate[in] lookup[florida]))
```

[none] (daytona-beach): wrong module behavior

Figure 5: Example layouts and answers selected by the model on the GeoQA dataset. For incorrect predictions, the correct answer is shown in parentheses.

Continuous representations improve the expressiveness and learnability of semantic parsers: by replacing discrete predicates with differentiable neural network fragments, we bypass the challenging combinatorial optimization problem associated with induction of a semantic lexicon. In structured world representations, neural predicate representations allow the model to invent reusable attributes and relations not expressed in the schema. Perhaps more importantly, we can extend compositional question-answering machinery to complex, continuous world representations like images.

Semantic structure prediction improves generalization in deep networks: by replacing a fixed network topology with a dynamic one, we can tailor the computation performed to each problem instance, using deeper networks for more complex questions and representing combinatorially many queries with comparatively few parameters. In practice, this results in considerable gains in speed and sample efficiency, even with very little training data.

These observations are not limited to the question answering domain, and we expect that they can be applied similarly to tasks like instruction following, game playing, and language generation.

Acknowledgments

JA is supported by a National Science Foundation Graduate Fellowship. MR is supported by a fellowship within the FIT weltweit-Program of the German Academic Exchange Service (DAAD). This work was additionally supported by DARPA, AFRL, DoD MURI award N000141110688, NSF awards IIS-1427425 and IIS-1212798, and the Berkeley Vision and Learning Center.

References

Jacob Andreas, Andreas Vlachos, and Stephen Clark. 2013. Semantic parsing as machine translation. In *Proceedings of the Annual Meeting of the Association for Computational Linguistics*, Sofia, Bulgaria.

Jacob Andreas, Marcus Rohrbach, Trevor Darrell, and Dan Klein. 2016. Neural module networks. In *Proceedings of the Conference on Computer Vision and Pattern Recognition*.

Stanislaw Antol, Aishwarya Agrawal, Jiasen Lu, Margaret Mitchell, Dhruv Batra, C Lawrence Zitnick, and Devi Parikh. 2015. VQA: Visual question answering. In *Proceedings of the International Conference on Computer Vision*.

Jonathan Berant and Percy Liang. 2014. Semantic parsing via paraphrasing. In *Proceedings of the Annual Meeting of the Association for Computational Linguistics*, volume 7, page 92.

Antoine Bordes, Sumit Chopra, and Jason Weston. 2014. Question answering with subgraph embeddings. *Proceedings of the Conference on Empirical Methods in Natural Language Processing*.

Léon Bottou. 2014. From machine learning to machine reasoning. *Machine learning*, 94(2):133–149.

Marie-Catherine De Marneffe and Christopher D Manning. 2008. The Stanford typed dependencies representation. In *Proceedings of the International Conference on Computational Linguistics*, pages 1–8.

Edward Grefenstette. 2013. Towards a formal distributional semantics: Simulating logical calculi with tensors. *Joint Conference on Lexical and Computational Semantics*.

Karl Moritz Hermann, Tomas Kocisky, Edward Grefenstette, Lasse Espeholt, Will Kay, Mustafa Suleyman, and Phil Blunsom. 2015. Teaching machines to read and comprehend. In *Advances in Neural Information Processing Systems*, pages 1684–1692.

Mohit Iyyer, Jordan Boyd-Graber, Leonardo Claudino, Richard Socher, and Hal Daumé III. 2014. A neural network for factoid question answering over paragraphs. In *Proceedings of the Conference on Empirical Methods in Natural Language Processing*.

Jayant Krishnamurthy and Thomas Kollar. 2013. Jointly learning to parse and perceive: connecting natural language to the physical world. *Transactions of the Association for Computational Linguistics*.

Jayant Krishnamurthy and Tom Mitchell. 2013. Vector space semantic parsing: A framework for compositional vector space models. In *Proceedings of the ACL Workshop on Continuous Vector Space Models and their Compositionality*.

Tom Kwiatkowski, Luke Zettlemoyer, Sharon Goldwater, and Mark Steedman. 2010. Inducing probabilistic CCG grammars from logical form with higher-order unification. In *Proceedings of the Conference on Empirical Methods in Natural Language Processing*, pages 1223–1233, Cambridge, Massachusetts.

Tom Kwiatkowski, Eunsol Choi, Yoav Artzi, and Luke Zettlemoyer. 2013. Scaling semantic parsers with on-the-fly ontology matching. In *Proceedings of the Conference on Empirical Methods in Natural Language Processing*.

Percy Liang, Michael Jordan, and Dan Klein. 2011. Learning dependency-based compositional semantics.

In *Proceedings of the Human Language Technology Conference of the Association for Computational Linguistics*, pages 590–599, Portland, Oregon.

Mateusz Malinowski, Marcus Rohrbach, and Mario Fritz. 2015. Ask your neurons: A neural-based approach to answering questions about images. In *Proceedings of the International Conference on Computer Vision*.

Cynthia Matuszek, Nicholas FitzGerald, Luke Zettlemoyer, Liefeng Bo, and Dieter Fox. 2012. A joint model of language and perception for grounded attribute learning. In *International Conference on Machine Learning*.

Hyeonwoo Noh, Paul Hongsuck Seo, and Bohyung Han. 2015. Image question answering using convolutional neural network with dynamic parameter prediction. *arXiv preprint arXiv:1511.05756*.

Panupong Pasupat and Percy Liang. 2015. Compositional semantic parsing on semi-structured tables. In *Proceedings of the Annual Meeting of the Association for Computational Linguistics*.

Mengye Ren, Ryan Kiros, and Richard Zemel. Exploring models and data for image question answering. In *Advances in Neural Information Processing Systems*.

K Simonyan and A Zisserman. 2014. Very deep convolutional networks for large-scale image recognition. *arXiv preprint arXiv:1409.1556*.

Richard Socher, John Bauer, Christopher D. Manning, and Andrew Y. Ng. 2013. Parsing with compositional vector grammars. In *Proceedings of the Annual Meeting of the Association for Computational Linguistics*.

Ronald J Williams. 1992. Simple statistical gradient-following algorithms for connectionist reinforcement learning. *Machine learning*, 8(3-4):229–256.

Yuk Wah Wong and Raymond J. Mooney. 2007. Learning synchronous grammars for semantic parsing with lambda calculus. In *Proceedings of the Annual Meeting of the Association for Computational Linguistics*, volume 45, page 960.

Huijuan Xu and Kate Saenko. 2015. Ask, attend and answer: Exploring question-guided spatial attention for visual question answering. *arXiv preprint arXiv:1511.05234*.

Kelvin Xu, Jimmy Ba, Ryan Kiros, Kyunghyun Cho, Aaron Courville, Ruslan Salakhutdinov, Richard Zemel, and Yoshua Bengio. 2015. Show, attend and tell: Neural image caption generation with visual attention. In *International Conference on Machine Learning*.

Zichao Yang, Xiaodong He, Jianfeng Gao, Li Deng, and Alex Smola. 2015. Stacked attention networks for image question answering. *arXiv preprint arXiv:1511.02274*.

Pengcheng Yin, Zhengdong Lu, Hang Li, and Ben Kao. 2015. Neural enquirer: Learning to query tables. *arXiv preprint arXiv:1512.00965*.

Matthew D Zeiler. 2012. ADADELTA: An adaptive learning rate method. *arXiv preprint arXiv:1212.5701*.

Bolei Zhou, Yuandong Tian, Sainbayar Sukhbaatar, Arthur Szlam, and Rob Fergus. 2015. Simple baseline for visual question answering. *arXiv preprint arXiv:1512.02167*.

AUTHOR INDEX

AUTHOR INDEX

Association for Computational Linguistics
209 N. Eighth Street
Stroudsburg, Pennsylvania 18360

ISBN 978-1-5108-2512-3